THE BIG BOOK OF HALLS OF FAME IN THE UNITED STATES AND CANADA

THE BIG BOOK OF HALLS OF FAME IN THE UNITED STATES AND CANADA

SPORTS

Compiled and edited by
Paul Soderberg
Helen Washington
Jaques Cattell Press

R.R. BOWKER COMPANY
New York and London 1977

Published by R. R. Bowker Co.
1180 Avenue of the Americas, New York, N.Y. 10036

Library of Congress Cataloging in Publication Data
Jaques Cattell Press.
The big book of halls of fame in the United States and Canada: sports.
1. United States—Biography. 2. Canada—Biography. 3. Biography. 4. Halls of fame—United States. 5. Halls of fame—Canada.
I. Title.
CT215.J36 973 77-82734
ISBN 0-8352-0990-3

Contents

Preface

While everyone speaks of fame, few can define it. And while there are tens of thousands of people honored by hundreds of halls of fame, few are aware of the existence of either the halls themselves or of their host of members.

The Big Book of Halls of Fame of the United State and Canada attempts to draw these two facts together by presenting the hall of fame phenomenon in its entirety. Additionally, more specific aspects of fame are presented throughout this volume, enabling the reader to view the hall of fame in context with its historical antecedents and its probable future directions.

There is a considerably larger purpose for this book, however — the presentation of the halls themselves as institutions for the preservation of the records of the famous. Criteria for inclusion were established at the outset by the nature of the subject: all members inducted into a hall of fame in North America would be eligible; and literally any hall of fame would be included, provided it has strict standards for election to membership, and it is dedicated to the preservation of records and presentation of the excellence of individuals in the field.

When preliminary research revealed the large number of halls of fame now in existence, it became necessary to divide them into three separate volumes: Volume I covers Sports; Volume II covers Arts and Entertainment, Business and Industry, North American Culture, and Science and Technology; Volume III covers Collegiate, City and State Halls of Fame (which will also include some sports halls). We plan to publish the second and third volumes late in 1978.

This volume covering Sports lists specific fields arranged alphabetically with applicable halls grouped alphabetically under each field. Each of these sections begins with an historical sketch giving the reader background on the sport — its historical antecedents, its beginning and development, the various forms it has taken, and the organizations involved in its growth and continuance. The outline for each hall presents the name, location, contact person, officers, and admission data and a listing of nearby halls for the use of the reader in the event a visit should be planned. Next appears a brief history of the creation of the hall and events leading to its present day status, material and services available, followed by a listing of the members. The format of the member entries reflect the natural variations that characterize each institution; museum-type halls include more detailed information for each member. The material given is rather limited in some instances, complete data never having been recorded. Some sportsmen and contributors have been elected to more than one hall, in which case the detailed entry is shown under the first museum-type hall appearing in the book, with cross-references under the other halls. However, each entry under their name shows to which other halls they have been elected.

The Big Book does not purport to be a detailed record book, but rather includes in the hall sketches and in biographical material for the members the information necessary to give the reader an understanding as to why this particular sports figure was considered to be worthy of inclusion in a particular hall of fame. At the conclusion of the halls listed in each category is a brief description of "halls to watch," establishments which have been or are soon to be, for which further details will not be included until they are actually a functioning hall of fame with regular inductions. While most halls sorted into the sports categories chosen by the Editors, a few covered broad fields including all sports and are therefore listed after Wrestling under a Special Fields heading.

The first section of the backmatter categorizes and indexes all the trivia and incidental information scattered through the narrative portions of each category as a further enhancement for the reader. There is also a map detailing the location of each museum-type hall where material is available for further study. And the volume concludes with a comprehensive index to the categories, the halls, their locations, and their members, including page numbers. This index is amply cross-referenced for your further convenience.

The material covering the halls and their members was primarily obtained from the personnel of the various halls. Their aid and support in supplying the data, and their patience in clarifying questionable material, were invaluable. It would be inappropriate for the Editors to select any one group for special recognition; however, their names can be found in the personnel sections of their respective halls. But it must be stated here that their dedication and generosity greatly facilitated the successful completion of this volume of *The Big Book of Halls of Fame in the United States and Canada*. The Editors must also acknowledge the assistance and collaboration offered by the Book Editorial Division of their publishers, the R. R. Bowker Company, specifically by Julia Raymunt, Managing Editor, and Doug Harris, Manager of Editorial Administration, without whose help and encouragement the completion of this volume would not have been possible.

New halls of fame are opening at the rate of approximately one every month and all halls are continually in the process of building, remodeling, or inducting additional members; therefore, some legitimate halls and some members regrettably will not appear in this volume. While the editors are confident the larger, more established halls are included without exception, they are also aware of the probability that a hundred or more new or smaller halls have escaped their attention. Such is the nature of this book — the coverage can never be complete. So we offer it to you as it stands now, trusting that you will be willing to send us your comments and suggestions, missing data, and nominations of other halls for subsequent editions or for Volumes II and III. Please address correspondence to The Editors, Jaques Cattell Press, P.O. Box 25001, Tempe, Arizona 85282.

Helen Washington, *Assistant Editor*
Paul Soderberg, *Developmental Editor*
Anne Rhodes, *Managing Editor*
Steve Nichols, *General Manager*
Jaques Cattell Press

November 1977

The Story of The Hall of Fame

A Hall of Fame is any organization which calls itself a hall of fame, which has strict standards for election to membership, and which is designed to inspire future greatness in a field by any means of preserving and presenting the excellence of great individuals in that field.

What Is Fame?

The relics of Santa Claus are preserved in the eleventh century Church of San Nicola in Bari, Italy. But because of the power and the whimsicality of fame, Santa Claus has come to be known the world over, despite his burial in a remote Italian town.

The truth of the matter is that the person we now call Santa Claus began life as a tall, thin Turk called Nicholas. He was the Bishop of Myra, an ancient city in Asia Minor. During his lifetime, he was noted for his great kindness. Until his death on December 6, A.D. 350, he customarily gave presents to people, especially children. For that and other reasons he was canonized by the Church several centuries ago, and became known as Saint Nicholas. Soon after, he was adopted as the patron saint of sailors, travelers, merchants and bakers. Eventually he became and remained the patron saint of Europe's Catholic children. Dutch settlers took him with them, so to speak, to New Amsterdam, which is now New York City. Their "Sinterklaas" in time became Santa Claus, largely because of a book written by Washington Irving in 1809. In 1822 Clement C. Moore wrote the poem, "'Twas The Night Before Christmas." Finally, the transformation was complete: the real-life Nicholas, a Turk who rode a donkey, had become famous as a Caucasian who annually drove reindeer to and from his home at the North Pole. Fame creates a splendid idealization of a person, changing him from what he actually was into what generations of people wish to *believe* he was.

There are countless definitions of fame. Socrates defined it as "the perfume of heroic deeds." Milton, in 1637, called it "That last infirmity of noble minds." Austin Bobson in 1877 mordantly described it as "a food dead men eat." The great German poet Rainer Maria Rilke cynically labeled fame as "The aggregate of all the misunderstandings that collect around a new name." There is no single definition of fame that is completely satisfactory, one that touches upon all its complexity. All, however, agree that fame is as intangible and as illusory as air. Or as W.S. Landon said in 1853: "Fame they tell you is air; but without air there is no life for any; without fame there is none for the best." That sums up both the secret of fame and its appeal: those who are "famous" are also seen as "best."

The Goddess of Fame and Her Rumor Birds

Throughout history attempts have been made to honor the achievements of individuals in one collection at one site. Nearly 600 years ago Geoffrey Chaucer dreamed that he journeyed with a mystical eagle to such a site. The "hous of Fame," he wrote in the poem relating to his dream, was situated in mid-air, "bitwixen hevene and earthe." Within this ornate structure he saw statues of all the famous poets and historians of the past and met The Goddess of Fame. As he watched, men appeared before her to establish their claims to fame. But her decisions were capricious: on some she bestowed fame; on others infamy; on most, oblivion. Meanwhile, inside the House of Rumor nearby, items of rumor in the shape of birds whirled around. Some of these flew over to the goddess, who assigned them labels and dispatched them to earth. Like carrier pigeons, the rumors were received, fed and sent on their way. A group of rumor birdwatchers developed in each generation. They proceeded to make some men powerful and to destroy others, thereby irrationally creating new claims to fame.

To protect fame from its dependence on pure chance and personal favor, and to bypass both the arbitrary goddess and the rumor-feeding public, places were built where fame could be centralized, protected and preserved. The Greeks and Romans, among many others, lined their walks with marble conqueror-gods and hero-athletes, saying in effect, "Here are our famous men — and only here!" The public were encouraged to accept their choices of men to be honored for their accomplishments and excellence.

But one key ingredient was missing from this approach to bestowing fame. Only established, impersonal authorities decided who should receive fame and who should not. The people did not nominate or elect their choices. Consequently, as a rule only men of aristocratic birth became famous. When a commoner did achieve recognition, it was invariably for some superhuman achievement. Generally, the vast majority of heroic or exceptional commoners were seen instead as merely "doing their duty." Benjamin Franklin expressed it best in his *Poor Richard's Almanack* (1734): "There have been as great souls unknown to fame as any of the most famous." The ancients did not believe in the concept that, since *every* person is valuable, even average people may become great and famous.

The credit for changing that concept, for popularizing the idea that even the humblest person was worthy of greatness, goes in great part to Horatio Alger, who died less than 80 years ago. Alger, a Harvard Divinity School graduate who became an author, told the world that a poor boy in America could make it from rags to riches, from oblivion to fame, through honesty and hard work. Alger's books for boys made The American Dream of fame and success a possibility for even the poorest person. His more than 100 books made that Dream a basic part of the American Way of Life.

A Presbyterian clergyman turned educator was the first to apply Alger's idea by creating a building to house the famous. Inspired by Statuary Hall in Washington, D.C, Westminster Abbey in London, the Pantheon in Paris and Munich's Ruhmes Halle, Henry Mitchell MacCracken of Ohio created a completely new American Institution: A Hall Of Fame For Great Americans. Built on University Heights in New York City, it was a democratic Pantheon, an expression of the nobler and non-materialistic side of the American Dream as expressed by Alger: a place to honor not only America's men of war and of peace but also its great businessmen, reformers, missionaries and teachers. Both men and women were honored for inclusion in the Hall of Fame, the first collection of notables to which the common people sent their own choices.

The Hall of Fame was dedicated on Memorial Day 1901. On that first day MacCracken told the crowd of 5000: "Our hope is that this Hall will be supported [by] . . . wise men and women who will judge and decide who are great and what is greatness to the sons and daughters of America." The words inscribed above the southern entrance arch were: "Take counsel here of Beauty, Wisdom, Power." Along the colonnade the people paraded, gazing at the 29 busts of people nominated, significantly, through a newspaper subscription.

According to Senator Depew, one of the distinguished speakers on that opening day, "The process of the elimination of reputations from current knowledge grows more destructive with each generation until cycles are marked by one survival." His words underline the hall of fame's primary function: to save its members from the ruthless, powerful urge to alter, forget or destroy reputations.

The Hall of Fame Phenomenon

Halls of fame are open-ended, on-going, never filled. Anyone achieving excellence can get into one. Hundreds do every year. Thousands of children alive today will one day enter halls of fame. Millions of people, young and old, dream of or crave being enshrined in a hall of fame. Some eventually are selected, at an average age of 66.37 years.

New halls of fame have been created in North America at the rate of about one hall every month since 1936. Though superficially they seem like highly specialized museums, they are not really museums at all. A museum contains collections of items. Some of the items will be more valuable than others. Not so in a hall of fame, where each member is valued and honored equally with all other members. There are no secondclass members in a hall of fame. Again, unlike a natural history museum which displays species, a hall of fame displays individuals. That is how, for example, the exhibit for Jim Taylor in the Pro Football Hall of Fame differs from the dodo bird exhibit in any major museum. There were many dodos before they became extinct around 1680 but in all history there has been only one Jim Taylor. His excellence is unique.

The democratic nature of the hall of fame, its permanence and the fact that many strive to be honored by being elected to one — these factors help define the institution. But there is another factor that explains its vast and ever increasing popularity. Seven miles from the city of Nara is the oldest existing temple in Japan, the Hôryûji Temple, a part of which is called the Yumendonon, or Hall of Dreams. People have gone there since A.D. 601 to stand quietly and be inspired by Shinto Gods. In North America famous men and women in halls of fame serve the same function: they inspire those who stand in their presence.

Although some halls may contain persons whose lives exemplified the Ideal American or Ideal Canadian, chances are that none contains anyone who was a *totally* accomplished person. Each of the some 50,000 "greats" in today's halls of fame excelled in one area of life. Look at Jim Thorpe and you see a great athlete who was not a philosopher; look at Benjamin Franklin and you see a great inventor who could not have run the length of a football field. However, taken en masse, halls of fame are inhabited by the outstanding men and women of our civilization. As a unified group, which is the way they are presented for the first time in this work, they are indeed, collectively, the "perfect" people of our past and present history. The single greatest message halls of fame send forth is: Be great in your personal endeavor because you thereby increase the greatness of the group; be proud of the larger group of which you are a vital and distinguished part. That message, in fact, is the criterion for induction into most halls of fame. As James L. McDowell said of the National Football Hall of Fame, it "honors men who honor the game. You have to demonstrate good citizenship, love of community, love of country. It is a question of what you give back to the game."

That fame by itself is not enough is the paradox inherent in being selected for a hall of fame: to get into one you must both rise above everyone else and yet remain one of them. Every society has its exceptional people. By the nature of their exceptional achievements, they are removed from the commonplace public of which they are part and product. By definition, those inducted into halls of fame became great without being destructive to the fabric of society. To do something exceptionally well without hurting others will result in some degree of celebrity. If the level of accomplishment is the highest yet attained, induction into a hall of fame is virtually guaranteed. But it requires effort. As long ago as 300 B.C. in China, Yang Chu stated that "The good man is not famous; if he be famous, he is not really good, since fame is nothing but falsehood." Overcoming that contradiction: becoming famous while remaining a good person is not an easy thing to do.

Thirty-five years after the establishment of the Hall of Fame for Great Americans on October 15, 1936, the first sports hall of fame was established and, as previously noted, others followed in rapid succession. These numerous halls have brought together for us thousands of men and women who would otherwise by now have been long forgotten.

The "boom" decade for halls of fame, the era when the idea finally and completely caught on, was in the 1950s. In that remarkable decade the number of halls of fame begun was 3.75 times the number that had been started during the 1940s. The average increase over a decade is 1.7 times. Many factors accounted for this phenomenon. The United States formally ended its World War II state of war with Germany in 1951. America settled down to peace and began a pursuit of excellence. The ethnic barrier that had kept minority people out of most professional sports was overcome in virtually all sports as a result of Jackie Robinson signing with the Dodgers in 1946. After 1955 the world of sports was dominated by U.S.-U.S.S.R. track and field competition. Trends were beginning that during the 1960s would challenge baseball as America's "national sport." Today pro football is the most popular sport in America, followed by college football, then baseball, then professional golf. This trend began during the boom decade for halls of fame.

In Los Angeles the Count Dracula Society Horror Hall of Fame has four members operating from an office virtually just down the street from the Citizens Savings Hall of Fame Athletic Museum with its huge facilities and over 2600 members. These are the extremes. The average hall of fame today has inducted 57.3 members, does not yet have a permanent home for them and their memorabilia, and is 12.86 years old.

Where halls of fame have appeared is as interesting and instructive as *when* they appeared. In general, they have appeared in either large cities or in very small ones. In both cases the group establishing the new hall has placed it where they themselves live and work. But some halls often appear in those small cities or towns which are historically pertinent to the theme of the hall. For example, professional football was "born" in Canton, Ohio (1975 population 110,053), which thus became the home of the Pro Football Hall of Fame. Ishpeming, Michigan (population 8245), was historically important to the sport of skiing, and so today is the site of the National Skiing Hall of Fame. One reason the International Hockey Hall of Fame was located in Kingston, Ontario (population 59,047), was that the first recorded hockey game in Canada was played there in 1849. The Country Music Hall of Fame is in Nashville, Tennessee (population 447,877), for obvious reasons. Big city halls of fame, however, have not generally followed this criterion. They have been built instead where a maximum number of people may benefit from their presence. Thus the largest cities all have clusters: Los Angeles has 41 halls of fame, New York has 29, Washington D. C, has 14, Chicago has 12, and so on. Trends investigated by the Editors during the compilation of this book indicate that, while both types will continue to be established, the small-city type will become increasingly more common, and that a major criterion for the location of future halls of fame will continue to be the historical relevance of the site.

Whether situated in a large or small city, the hall of fame does not "just happen." Long before the hall is built there must be famous persons associated with the theme of the hall. Whether it be for sled dog racing, pickle packing, lefthandedness or petroleum exploration, a hall can be founded only after a field has, so to speak, come of age. MacCracken could hardly have conceived, much less obtained the funds to build, his hall for great Americans until sufficient generations had produced some outstanding men and women. The halls therefore do not actively create fame, but passively guard it once it exists. There is, however, an important correlation between the type and size of a hall of fame and the growth rate of the field it honors. For example, pickle-packing has not grown rapidly or widely as compared to bowling, which is among the most popular sports today. Predictably, pickle-packing has but one small hall of fame in St. Charles, Illinois, while bowling has more than 30 different halls of fame (of which one is huge), located all over North America.

The physical location of a hall, the degree of public interest in the field it honors, and the concomitant availability of both financial support and tax exemption status, plus many other factors never before conclusively defined in nation-wide terms, combine to determine both the size and the growth rate of a hall of fame. This explains the fact that there are today actually three authentic types of halls of fame: the "award"-type (an award presented at regular intervals, often in a periodical); the "association"-type (plaques or mementos to or of its members housed somewhere on a temporary basis); and the "museum"-type (an association-type with a permanent home). Of these the second is by far the most common today, which reflects how recently the institution "boomed." A fourth type, the "shrine"-like hall of fame, is a museum-type that does not hold regular inductions: its membership is closed and it therefore is not an authentic hall of fame. A fifth type is represented by a single example on the North American continent, the International Sports Hall of Fame, which inducts entire sports rather than individual members. This is the "didactic"-type hall of fame, one which is pleasurably educational in its emphasis. Although no studies have been made, it probably could be shown that both the award and association types are embryonic museum-types. Given increased public and financial support they would in time obtain a permanent physical home. Such an evolutionary progression naturally need not always be followed. Some of the larger halls were quickly housed in buildings. The popularity of their fields (notably professional football) demanded a permanent hall be built as fast as possible. Similarly, numerous fields that have not yet really gotten off the ground are housed in defunct halls of fame. The American Lawn Bowls Association Hall of Fame, for example, is inactive because its director died.

The growth of the hall of fame as an institution has also been influenced by demographic and ethnic factors. The American South has more years of recorded history than any other part of the continent. Long before the Pilgrims landed at Plymouth Rock in 1620, the South had been traversed and mapped, settled and explored, mostly by Spaniards. Despite many famous Spanish figures in the history of the American South, there are no "Spanish" halls of fame.

The case of the French and their rich North American heritage is even more instructive of the "English" nature of the hall of fame. Jacques Cartier, Samuel de Champlain (the "Father of New France," or Canada) — these and scores of others attest to the early and pervasive French presence in North America. Through a series of military defeats and poor political maneuverings, France eventually lost its New World possessions. French heritage, however, remained and still remains very strong in parts of Canada and among the Creole regions of the American South. But there are no "French" halls of fame. And there are very few of any kind in the various remaining French areas of the continent. The entire province of Quebec, the largest province in Canada with 81% of its people French-Canadians, has but a single hall of fame. In marked contrast, those Southern States which have an English heritage also have more halls of fame. The District of Columbia and Virginia (where the Virginia Company of London founded Jamestown in 1607) have a total of 17. North Carolina (where Virginia Dare was born in 1587, the first English child to be born on the continent) has three substantial halls, Tennessee has five. The same is even more strikingly true in Canada: the English-speaking province of Ontario, which borders Quebec but has less than 5 percent French-Canadians in its population, has ten halls of fame, most of which are museum-types, compared to Quebec's one, which is an association-type hall of fame.

Areas with the richest non-English history did not establish their own new institutions following the two national breaks with England in 1776 and 1867. Tied to a French or some other past, they did not seize the opportunity to celebrate their own men and women of greatness in the vacuum created by the expulsion of the English. Perhaps those Canadians who still call themselves French boast that they look to the Pantheon and to the Hall of the Forty Immortals in Paris and thus do not need a Hall of Fame for Great French Canadians. Also, Canada was an English colony nearly a century longer than the United States; in the strictly legal sense, there was no such thing as a Canadian citizen until 1947. These two factors probably have much to do with the fact that the United States has approximately 35 times as many halls of fame as Canada.

Supporting these assumptions is the case of Missouri, an interesting example of a state which had strong ties to France but gave them up to become, in spirit and in fact, American. Jacques Marquette and Louis Joliet, Robert Cavelier and the founders of the city of St. Louis, Pierre Laclede Liguest and Rene Auguste Chouteau — these and many more could have been the basis of a strong French culture in the "Show Me" State. But no Missourian would call himself French today. And there are seven halls of fame in Missouri.

These factors and events suggest that the hall of fame is an English-speaking American institution which arose to meet a need created by the departure of the English from an increasingly heterogeneous population. It is significant in this connection that there is only one hall of fame in England. It is at Wimbledon, for international tennis greats. England has always had institutions serving the same function the hall of fame serves in North America — Westminster Abbey, Madame Tussaud's Wax Museum, and many others. More importantly, England has a Royal Family and a hierarchial nobility. A deserving English person receives certain centuries-old honors if he or she is an aristocrat, or if born a commoner, is made an aristocrat. American jockeys and contributors to horse racing are inducted into the appropriate halls of fame. But in England their counterparts are knighted. In other words the hall of fame is unnecessary in England; you can become a knight or be buried beside all manner of kings and poets in Westminster Abbey for exactly the same accomplishments that would get you into a hall of fame in North America. This may be another reason why Canada with its own titled aristocracy has relatively few halls of fame.

Theoretically then, the hall of fame or some similar institution might arise wherever a "new" nationalism in a heterogeneous population follows a very final or violent break with a mother country and its past. The need to recognize and honor individuals who encourage, protect, or typify the new nationalism creates the climate for the establishment of such institutions. In many of the new African states all of the above conditions hold true. Will halls of fame arise in these countries? Undeniably they or some similar institution will be created, provided that such an institution does not already exist as a holdover from the ex-mother country and that human rights are respected so that the common person can be free to rise to greatness. Athletes and artists must become as important to the national scene as soldiers and statesmen.

Will such institutions throughout the world be *called* "halls of fame"? Probably not, although the concepts and criteria will be identical to those of already established halls of fame.

Institutes and the History "Teachers" of the Future

Although the future of the hall of fame as an "American" institution seems assured, what changes it will undergo are by no means certain at this time. Because of the inevitable four-day work week, earlier retirement, increased consumer sophistication, additional leisure time and greater travel opportunities for everyone, changes in the concepts and services of a hall of fame are bound to evolve. As America changes, there are sure to be different manifestations of "The American Way of Life."

The phrase "hall of fame" has firmly entered the English language. Variations of the expression have been used in the titles of books, magazine articles, nightclubs, restaurants, manufactured items, etc. Its acceptance into idiomatic usage, interestingly, is related to a far more profound trend: the commercialization of the hall of fame. Americans traveled billions of miles last year for sightseeing and entertainment within the United States. During those travels they spent billions of dollars on entertainment and leisure time activities. Some of this money went to halls of fame. As certain types of halls become more "consumer oriented," it is reasonable to assume that each year more and more money will be spent in them. This means that many halls of fame will be able to expand and improve their facilities. It also means that their content and emphasis will change. The ultimate result will be an entirely new type of institution.

The sketches of the halls in this book indicate what will probably happen. The larger halls, specifically those established for the "major" sports, will be the first ones to evolve from "halls of fame" into something else. This evolution will be marked by their increasing use of space age displays, a proliferation of push-buttons, exhibition games and light-and-sound shows. There will be a greater emphasis on visitor/consumer participation. It will not be enough for the Past simply to "be there"; one will be involved in "things to do with the Past." Their orientation will be increasingly "Present/Future." As less reverence will be given to the past and more emphasis placed on the "now/soon" aspect of the field being honored, the hall of fame that we know today will disappear; at that point the hall of fame will have to find a new name.

To determine what these big new future-halls will probably be called, one must consider that they will be above all educational or more accurately, didactical; that is to say they will provide instruction in an entertaining manner. Teaching will be done through audio-visual aids and other sophisticated technology. The visitors will be active participants in the learning experience and will enjoy their involvement. They will have fun! The halls of fame of the future will be highly specialized schools where one will go to learn a single topic or avocation like bowling, archery or bass fishing. They will be schools where the only fee is paid at the door and where a person learns only what he wants and at the speed he chooses. But they will certainly not be traditional "schools," which after all comes from the Greek *scholē*, "having nothing to do." Though created for instruction, they will be totally different from traditional educational facilities. As organizations that promote advanced education in a specific field, and as associations of persons that collectively constitute a technical or professional authority in that field, these future-halls of fame will probably be called "institutes."

The football fan of the future may fly, for example, to Kings Mills, Ohio, for an exhilarating day at the N.F.I, the National Football Institute, which at present is still being called the National Football Hall of Fame. There he or she will find a diversity of activities and displays available, some of which may be used to earn physical education credits (for students) or degrees of proficiency (for non-students and retired persons). The fan will get to know the game of college football intimately within two to three hours, or attain in ten minutes a first-name kind of friendship with a famous college football star from the past; or, at the push of several buttons, get a video-readout showing or telling him which colleges not only offer football scholarships but also would be most appropriate for his individual wants and needs. Tickets for all the upcoming year's college games will be available there at a reduced rate. Equipment manufacturers will maintain permanent outlets within the facility. Guides will aid the visitor through this football wonderland. The following three-day weekend the same fan would return to another section of that Institute and receive additional but more detailed and sophisticated football education. If not interested after that first visit, he might fly instead to Hayward, Wisconsin, for a relaxing three-day stint of fishing education at the F.W.F.I.A, the Fresh-Water Fishing Institute of America, which for the time being is still being called the National Fresh-Water Fishing Hall of Fame. With more than 500 institutes to choose from, the fan will have a lifetime of opportunities to learn within the presence of the great and famous.

Such institutes will be designed according to new and exciting architectural principles, some of which have already been pioneered by Tom Beers, of Design and Planning, Inc, who has designed the interiors of six different halls of fame. Major sports like bowling or golf today have scores of international, national, state or provincial, city and intercity halls of fame. In the future they will have single Institutes with franchises (including computer terminals) in every village throughout the

North American continent. Hundreds of institutes and their franchises will compete for everyone's increased wealth and leisure time by offering fun *plus* education. They will in short sell a wholly new product called "*funducation.*"

If these predictions sound farfetched, consider the currently active American Mushroom Institute (A.M.I.) which supports a short course on mushroom science at Pennsylvania State University and conducts an annual international congress. The Institute of Outdoor Drama, based at the University of North Carolina, offers advisory and consultation services, sponsors conferences, and maintains extensive collections and a placement center. The Canine Behavior Institute conducts therapy sessions for owners and dogs and distributes training kits and various devices. The American Institute of Family Relations (A.I.F.R.) provides counseling services, training and guidance programs. It also holds workshops and maintains a Speakers Bureau. The Wine Institute (W.I.) conducts market surveys and a Wine Information Course, sponsors wine technology studies, and maintains collections and a library. There are scores of others. Finally and most importantly, consider the sketches of some of the larger halls of fame in this book, notably that of the International Sports Hall of Fame, for indications that the trend from traditional hall of fame to specialized institute has already begun.

What about the smaller halls of fame, particularly those which honor the greats of non-sports fields? They also will be compelled to change or evolve or risk the real danger of becoming defunct. Predictions about what they will become once they have passed through the stage of seeking to emulate or compete with the increasingly glamorous institutes are more difficult to make. This is because there are fewer visible trends to identify and because slight changes, such as from balloon to better balloon, are less apparent than quantum leaps, such as from balloon to airplane. Still, it is safe to predict that these smaller halls of fame will continue to grow within their own tradition, will remain "authentic," and will continue to be called "halls of fame." A second prediction also seems justified: their emphasis on the past not only will be reaffirmed but also will be made more entertaining. Thus, while Institutes will inspire by making the present and future exciting, halls of fame will inspire by making the past more exciting.

History as it is too often taught is a list of names, dates, wars, secessions, revolutions, depressions, etc, etc. It can be a dangerously dull subject. But history itself is neither boring nor dull. New ways to teach history can be found. It can be made more meaningful and more entertaining.

Presenting history in terms of individuals with whom people can identify, as opposed to relating it in terms of impersonal earth-shaking events, makes it more human and easier to grasp. Those halls of fame which will continue being successful will be those tailored to present history in this new, transformed way. Many are almost at that stage now. After all, more than most other institutions halls of fame celebrate the triumph of the individual — the individual whose excellence brought him or her out of the ranks of the many. Accordingly, halls of fame will become the "history teachers" of the future.

This prediction is aided and encouraged, it is hoped, by this book. Each category of halls is preceded by a sketch of the history of the category. In these sketches, pertinent historical material is presented in the "new" way that we predict future halls of fame will present and teach it. Very simply, it is history made more relevant. For instance, the Editors do not state simply that football was born in 1895; they write instead that in 1895, the year Stephen Crane wrote *The Red Badge of Courage* and Dr. John Kellogg produced the world's first flaked cereal, football was born. Such references give a much fuller flavor of the period than the presentation of facts in isolation. Bowling, to use another example, was invented in the Middle Ages and was played by Martin Luther and others. The Editors restate this information by saying that Martin Luther, a dominant religious figure in the Middle Ages, had a bowling alley built in his house so that his family and friends could play. In these historical sketches, huge events like wars and economic or political revolutions are mentioned only in passing. Such great upheavals, after all, are what traditional classrooms teach.

A key concept in the telling of history in these sketches is that of association. Two facts which are uninteresting or likely to be quickly forgotten by themselves become more interesting and likely to be remembered when associated with each other. For example, it is impressive to learn that Eddie Arcaro earned well over $30 million in a total of 31 years of riding horses. But the association of that set of facts with a similar set from history makes both sets not only more impressive but also more interesting. Thus, we also learn that Gaius Appuleus Diocles, who began racing chariots in A.D. 122, earned 36 million *sesterces* or roughly $1.7 million during his 24-year career. According to Arcaro, the best horse he ever rode was Citation who had 32 career wins. Again, that is impressive. But it becomes more interesting when compared to the fact that Diocles drove two horses to their 100th wins and one to its 200th; and that a chariot-horse named Tuscus, driven by one Fortunatus, had an incredible 386 career wins. Such a comparison makes each set of names more interesting and teaches something about ancient Rome. The same is true if you associate the fact that great horses today may be buried beneath statues of themselves, as Man o' War was, with the fact that great Roman horses were buried beneath expensive marble pyramids.

Baseball, still America's "national sport" according to many (despite the fact that pro football and college football are more popular), is interesting in itself but even more so when compared to a Navajo Indian game called *Aqejōlyedi*, Run around ball. In *Aqejōlyedi* the *jōl* was made of bark covered with two hemispherically shaped pieces of the hide of a deer, horse or other edible animal sewn together. The *bē-akăli* was made of oak and shaped like a walking cane. Holding the *bē-akăli's* curved end, the batter stood where a baseball pitcher stands. The four bases were at the four directions, East being the first place to run to, North being the place where the run is finished. After the fourth strike the batter had to run. He was out if hit by the ball, as was true through the first decades of baseball. The winning team (or individual) was the first to get an agreed-upon number of runs, which also was true of early baseball.

The sport of archery was introduced into the curriculum of Vassar in 1876. Unless you happen to be an archer or a Vassar grad, the fact is a triviality. Taken by itself it teaches little and may be uninteresting or even boring. But taken in association with other essentially uninteresting facts about 1876, it becomes meaningful, instructive and, hopefully, exciting: carpetsweepers, the gramophone and the telephone were invented that same year; the Dewey decimal system for books was devised; the Statue of Liberty was designed; *Tom Sawyer* was published; Custer died at the Little Big Horn and Robert Frost was one year old. Such facts and events, taken together, begin to reconstruct the world of 1876 in which those Vassar coeds first strung their bows. Experiments with a mechanical rabbit for dog racing were conducted in Belgium in 1740. This becomes more than an undeniable triviality when it is learned that the first true novel in the English language, *Pamela*, was published and that the "American" dialect of English was first mentioned that year.

Such smorgasbords of facts compel one to view phenomena in totally new ways. Historical facts may be grouped to allow one to glimpse what the world was like ten, a hundred, a thousand years ago. More importantly, they permit one to get the feeling for what it was like to be something so foreign as a Roman chariot driver or a Navajo Indian. A real understanding of other times and other peoples is what the study of history should be all about. And that, the Editors are convinced, is what the true halls of fame of the future will be all about.

If the concept of halls of fame as history "teachers" seems farfetched, consider this: halls of fame today are precisely such feasts of various facts, packaged in a building. Each one has a mass of trivia associated with the lives of a small group of people who were just like you or me except for their excellence in a common game or field of endeavor. That group, which almost always includes the "Father" of the game or field, teaches history in a way that de-emphasizes the great events by focusing on the great individuals of history. Facts from other cultural and social phenomena will be added that will put the hall of fame's exhibit in a larger, more meaningful context.

The future hall of fame will make increased use of educational exhibits. For example, a display of the hall's members of the 1930s might be accompanied by interesting trivia of that decade. The primary effect of such an exhibit would be: these individuals dominated this particular field in the 1930s. The secondary message would be, inferred more subtly by the accumulation of the trivia itself: This *was* the 1930s.

Additionally, the future hall of fame will include displays of the greatest names in its field from ancient history. Swimming halls of fame will have exhibits showing that Alexander the Great could not swim, that Julius Caesar could, that Augustus Caesar taught his grandchildren how to swim, and that Nero's attempt to murder his mother was foiled because she knew how to swim. The primary message would be that swimming is one of the most ancient sports in the world. The secondary message would be that to be a swimmer in North America today is to partake of a rich and illustrious heritage. The final message would be that if you become a great swimmer today, you add to the people and events that men and women centuries from now will remember about what North America was like in the twentieth century.

The flame of fame is fed by the ardor of the fan.

Muhammad Ali, Fran Tarkenton, Babe Didrikson or anyone else whose name you would recognize did not make it entirely on his or her own. The devotion and the support of the public helped them, cheered them on to greater and greater victories. Halls of fame will continue to be (to use Theodore Parker's words the way Lincoln did), "of the people, by the people and for the people." So, despite all attempts to spot trends, make predictions and use plain common sense, the people of North America will have the final say on what the hall of fame of the future will be.

The Story of Sports

Thousands of years ago Olympia, the oldest and most sacred place in Greece, was a plain in the country of Elis. On that plain stood a grove of trees dedicated to Zeus. It was called the *Altis*. Around this grove temples and public buildings were erected. Nearby was an ancient prototype of the hall of fame: an area where the bronze or marble busts or statues of many of the most famous Greeks were displayed. These temples were of secondary importance to the primary function of Olympia, the celebration of the most important of the many Greek religious festivals.

The festival was held at the *Altis* on a particular day after a full moon which occurred after 49 months, then after 50, then 49, and so on; in other words, after approximately every four years. The time intervals which separated the festivals were called Olympiads. At the close of each Olympiad, men would gather at Olympia from all over the Greek world to celebrate the festival. It began on what we could call morning but which was midday for the Greeks, who measured their days from sunset to sunset. It lasted five days, and during that time men participated in sacrifices, feasts and a foot race. Women were forbidden to participate on penalty of death. Because the first king of the country of Elis was named Aethlius, the events at the festival were called *athla* and those who participated in them were called *athlētes*.

In 884 B.C., after this festival had been held regularly for several centuries, Iphitus, then king of Elis, suggested to the rulers of neighboring Greek Kingdoms that the end of each Olympiad ought to be marked by a sacred truce. During the truce all Greek wars would cease so that all men, including soldiers, could travel to Olympia to be athletes. All the kings and rulers approved and the agreement was carved in a bronze disc, which was preserved for nearly a thousand years, but which later was lost or destroyed. That sacred truce made the festival at Olympia a truly international event of great significance and uninterrupted regularity.

This sports festival marks the first time on record that anyone sought officially to answer the perennial questions that have surrounded sports. What is the relationship between sports and war? Between sports and religion? How much emphasis on sports should there be in a person's life? Events at Olympia in 884 B.C. provided no permanent answers to these questions. But the answers they did come to at that time served well for thousands of years. Some are as valid now as they were then. Other answers did not survive into modern times. But the questions are now more pressing than ever. The history and nature of the Olympic Games are reviewed here to set the historical context for any future attempts to answer the old-new questions about the social, political and religious aspects of sports.

Aristotle was born exactly 500 years after that agreement had been carved on the bronze disc. His accomplishments in life were numerous and celebrated, but one for which he is not often remembered is his completion of the considerable task of numbering the Olympic festivals. He agreed with others who had tried to chronicle them that the one held in 776 B.C. should be considered the first. The winner of the sprint that year, a cook from Elis named Koroebus, is thus the earliest Olympic victor on record. By his own reckoning, Aristotle was born 125 Olympiads, or exactly 500 years after the establishment of the sacred truce; in other words, between the 94th and 95th Olympiads.

Throughout these many centuries people traveled from all over the world to watch a total of 23 different athletic events that ultimately were added to the original sprint. Some were held only once or twice and then removed from the program. In later centuries, the sport side of the festival was stressed more than its religious side, and both women and non-Greeks were allowed not only to attend but also to compete. The first woman victor at Olympia was Cynisca, a member of the royal house of Sparta. She won the *quadriga* (four-horse chariot) race early in the fourth century B.C. One of the last known of all winners of an Olympic chariot race was also a woman, Kasia of Elis. And the last Olympic victor on record was a non-Greek, a prince named Varazadates who won the boxing crown in A.D. 385. Later he became king of Armenia.

Everyone who was anyone in the ancient world went to the Olympic Games: Socrates went at least once, as did Plato, himself a wrestler, at the age of 70; Militiades, the greatest Greek general, who gave the helmet he had worn in the Battle of Marathon to the religious leaders at Olympia; Pythagoras, the great mathematician who believed that in an earlier life he had been killed during the Trojan War, and for whom the Pythagorean Theorem in geometry is named; Diogenes, who lived in a large ceramic pot, searched with a lantern for the "ideal" man, and told Alexander the Great to quit standing in his light; Demosthenes, who spoke with stones in his mouth to cure his stuttering, then went on to become Athens' greatest orator; Themistocles, victor of Salamis, one of the greatest sea battles ever fought; Pindar, the poet who wrote odes to the Olympic Games which were imitated by later poets like Pope and Dryden; Lucian, one of the greatest of all Sophists, who boasted of having been to Olympia seven times; Herodotus, "the father of history," anthropology and several other disciplines; Thucydides, who wrote the *History of the Peloponnesian War*. These men were only a few of the many hundreds of thousands who put aside other matters to go to the Olympics.

During later Roman times, "going to the Games" was an accepted excuse for virtually any sudden absence. To escape the resulting chaos in Rome after the murder of Julius Caesar, many important people fled to Olympia on the pretext of attending the Games, even though no Games were then being held. Nero was an Olympic fanatic. Once he even ordered the Olympics postponed so that he could compete in them. He naturally won all the events he entered: harp playing, tragic acting, trumpet blowing for distance (the winner was he whose blast could be heard from the furthest away) and chariot racing. But the results of those wrongly timed Games were erased from the records as soon as Nero died. Virtually all the other Roman emperors were also Olympic fans, though none was so fanatical. Some actively competed, some entered their own paid professionals, others are on record for having entered their friends and mistresses. Many went simply to watch; some innovated new features and a few merely tolerated the event — until A. D. 393, that is. In that year Emperor Theodosius the Great, who had been baptized a Christian thirteen years earlier, declared that the Olympic Games were unbearably pagan and must be stopped. His order ended them. The Games of the 320th Olympiad were therefore the last ones held in the ancient world.

Fifteen centuries of organized Olympic athletics ended with that Christian decree. Exactly 15 more centuries passed before the Olympic Games were revived. Those 30 centuries span virtually all of recorded human history.

Among the factors that have been present throughout that entire time are two that have had a traditional and intimate relationship: war and sports. In all 30 centuries only one year out of every 15 has been peaceful. Yet there have also been fairly constant attempts to abolish the violence. The sacred truce for the ancient Games, though narrow in scope, was one such attempt which served its purpose for a great many centuries. Those who dedicated their lives to peace respected its success. To these the great question always was: By what means may "war no more" be achieved? The answer generally took one of three forms: by religious conversion, by one last big war to end all wars, or by sports. Sports, after all, did not die in 393 — only the Olympic celebration of sports events. During the 15 centuries that followed the last Olympic Games, many old sports grew in popularity, a wealth of new ones evolved and, as a modern writer put it, many people continued to think of athletes as "excellence in the guise of men." This work on halls of fame describes the individual evolutions of many of these sports and sketches the lives of their greatest athletes. Not mentioned — because their names were never recorded — are the thousands of men and women who have tried in various ways through history to make competitive sports the permanent replacement for war. Obviously none of them succeeded. But an incredible number have tried and continue to try.

This is most vividly seen in the case of the Olympic Games, which numerous people tried to revive in spirit if not in fact. During the Middle Ages, for example, the Olympic spirit of honorable competition survived when the institution of chivalry was grafted onto the Christian code of behavior to create the ethical code of the knights. Several centuries thereafter Shakespeare was writing of the Olympian Games in *Henry VI* and of Olympian wrestling in *Troilus and Cressida*. A man named Robert Dover instituted an annual English Cotswold Olympick Games, which were markedly

Olympic-like despite the fact that one of the events was a contest for dancing girls. They were ended with Dover's death in 1641. John Milton mentioned "th' Olympian Games" a quarter of a century later in 1667 in his *Paradise Lost*. Voltaire, having watched an English athletic festival, wrote in 1721 that he was "transporté aux jeux olympiques." By 1779 people in Germany were talking about reviving the old Games. That same year Representative William Henry Drayton made reference to the Olympics in the American Congress, although for different reasons. He supported the idea of using fireworks to celebrate American independence by stating (inaccurately and irrelevantly) that the Greeks had used the Olympic Games to celebrate their birth as a nation. His fellow representative, Henry Laurens, countered the fireworks idea by pointing out (also inaccurately) that "the Olympian Games and other fooleries brought on the desolation of the Greeks." In 1790 Olympic Games were held in Paris. But they were not repeated. Eleven years later in 1801, Joseph Strutt wrote about the masterful wrestlers of Cornwall and stated that "if the Olympian games were now in fashion, [Cornish wrestlers] would come away with the victory." During the following decades numerous other ideas were proposed in Europe and North America. In 1849 an Englishman named Dr. W. P. Brookes instituted an Olympic Games in Shropshire. These were more successful than the earlier Cotswold Olympicks had been. For 40 years ladies crowned kneeling winners at Shropshire with laurel. Meanwhile, in 1852 a German archaeologist named Ernst Curtius lectured to a receptive audience in Berlin that the original Olympic Games ought to be revived.

During the 1850s Scottish immigrants who had reached Newfoundland in 1620 and New Jersey in 1683 were staging their own traditional games. The most famous and successful of these were the Caledonian Games, first held in Boston in 1853 and so-called because a Caledonian is a Scotsman (Caledonia was the Roman name for Scotland). Although the more ancient Tailteann Games that preceded these in Scotland had included such events as the stunning of three cows with a sledgehammer followed by their dismemberment and the tossing of a chariot wheel, the events at the North American Caledonian Games were remarkably Olympian. Caledonian clubs sprang up all over the continent, especially after the American Civil War. In 1867 various American and Canadian Caledonian clubs even held an international meet at Jones' Woods, New York. Three years later they federated as the North American Caledonian Association in an attempt to standardize rules, regulations and equipment for athletics. For the next 15 years that association's games were so popular and important that various countries, especially Scotland, sent their own delegations of athletes. But then baseball, bicycling and other sports began to appear, and the Caledonian Games, which after all were for Scotsmen only, declined and disappeared.

In 1859 actual Olympic Games were held in Athens. Organized and underwritten by the wealthy Evgenios Zappas and his cousin Constantine, these Olympics were repeated in 1870, 1875 and 1889. Although clearly copied from the ancient Games, these Olympics had some modern innovations. For example, three of the events included were the tug-of-war, the climbing of a greased pole and the javelin throw at a steer's head. The winner of the wrestling event in the 1859 games received not just an olive wreath but money and a milk cow as well. They were popular while they lasted, but they were for Greeks only. Like all the rest of the narrow, nationalistic attempts to revive the Olympics, they soon ended.

At that time, 1889, a Frenchman named Pierre de Coubertin was only 26 years old. A direct descendant of the man who had discovered "The Laocoon," the Greek statue that had so inspired Michelangelo, de Coubertin was in love with the Classical past. For years he had dreamed of reviving both the spirit and the glory of the Olympic Games. He was aware of the numerous previous attempts that had ended in failure and he was convinced that those failures were due in part to the narrow nationalistic approach. His basic idea was to do what no one else had done: to revive the Games on an *international* level. That approach in his view was the only way in which the ultimate expression of his dream could be realized: the revival not only of the Games but also of their sacred truce. In short, the Games were to be a tribute to universal peace and perhaps even a force *for* peace.

Pierre de Coubertin spoke everywhere about his dream. Tulane, Berkeley and Princeton were a few American institutions he visited. And he was successful. In 1893 the Olympics were officially revived. After three years of planning, the first Games of modern times began in Athens on April 5th, 1896. Thirteen countries sent 311 athletes (of which 230 were from Greece) to compete in 43 events representing nine different sports. Eighty thousand spectators attended. After fifteen hundred years of waiting, the modern world was to experience one of the greatest glories of the ancient world — The Olympic Games. The Olympic flag which was adopted in 1920 symbolizes both de Coubertin's dream and the potential of the Olympics as a moral force: the five interlocking circles represent the individual identity and linked unity of the five inhabited continents.

But de Coubertin's revived Olympics were not an immediate success. The first winner of a modern gold medal, James B. Connolly, who won the hop, step, jump event on April 6th, had been expelled from Harvard when he left to go to Athens to compete. Most of the other Americans in Athens were there, in fact, by accident. There were a few tourists and students in the stands. The Athenian newspapers referred to the loud American college cheers as "absurd shouts". The largest contingent was made up by the officers and men of the cruiser *San Francisco*, which happened to be in the harbor at the time. To virtually all other Americans, the Olympic efforts of college students in Athens were newsworthy, of course, but not more so than the news that two men had made the first transatlantic rowboat crossing, that the outboard motor, the escalator, the IQ test and the dial telephone had been invented, that a surgeon in Germany had performed heart surgery and that a duchess had actually smoked publicly in the dining room of the Savoy Hotel in London. News that the American athletes had won nine Olympic gold medals and that the Australians, with the next highest total, had won two, was rivaled in the newspapers by the dignified announcement that The Dogs' Toilet Club, the world's first poodle parlor, had opened in London. Far more significant than all of these items, however, were developments on the road. The world's first speeding conviction was handed out that year to a motorist who exceeded the 2 m.p.h. limit. The first taxi began operating in Stuttgart, Germany. The first armored car, complete with steel plating and two machine guns, was built that year and the first car theft occurred when a Pugeot was stolen in Paris. Less significant but far more exciting were developments in entertainment. Movies were shown to the public for the first time that year, the first permanent cinema opened (in New Orleans), and John Rice and May Irwin in *The Widow Jones* performed the world's first screen kiss. Nineteen years later when the first nude scene was shown (in the 1915 movie, *Daughter of the Gods*), all of this had changed. The world was no longer apathetic to the Olympics, which by then had become an international media event. But also by then the world had begun its first global war and the 1916 Olympic Games, scheduled to be held in Berlin, were canceled.

The final event of the 1896 Olympics was held to commemorate an earlier war. In 490 B.C. the Greeks under Militiades defeated the Medes and the Persians in the Battle of Marathon. A swift Athenian soldier (not Phidipides who was a creation of the poet Robert Browning) was sent to notify Athens of the victory. He ran the 24 miles and 1500 yards nonstop, entered the city, announced, "Rejoice! We have won," then fell dead from exhaustion. Nearly twenty-four hundred years later his run was commemorated when Michel Bréal, a friend of de Coubertin, suggested that a marathon race be added to the more traditional events. The Baron agreed. On hearing this, an Athenian girl named Melpomene began secretly to train. When she presented her nomination to run in the marathon, however, the Olympic Committee rejected it — not only could women not compete, but in view of historical precedent, they were fortunate even to be able to watch. Understandably upset, Melpomene rode a bicycle from Marathon to Athens in four and one-half hours to prove her ability. Newspapers applauded her. She reapplied. The Committee again refused to let her compete.

Twenty-five men began that first Olympic marathon. The gun that began it, a revolver fired by one Colonel Papadiamatopolous, was the first gun ever fired to start a race. The Australian runner, Edwin H. Flack, soon collapsed and raving, was rushed to an Athens hospital in an ambulance. Other foreigners fell down in defeat or simply gave up. Fittingly, a Greek won. He was a 25-year-old peasant named Spyros Louys, who had spent the previous evening praying in a chapel and before the race had eaten a whole chicken for strength. Before Louys reached the stadium, two Greek princes (George and his brother Constantine, the present Constantine's grandfather), vaulted down from the royal box and ran across the stadium. From there they raced with Louys to the finish line. Pandemonium broke out because a Greek had won that particularly symbolic event. The two princes had to carry the peasant to safety from the hysterically happy crowd. A woman tore a gold watch from her dress and gave it to Louys. A shoeshine boy offered him free shines for life, an Athenian tailor offered free clothes for as long as the tailor lived, a barber offered free weekly cuts and shaves, a fisherman offered daily fresh fish, a *taverna* owner offered free meals for life. He received the silver first place medal and an olive branch (second place in that event was a bronze medal and a laurel branch; no third places were recognized in any of the events). He was given a handsome silver trophy, an engraved certificate which the Americans there called a "diploma," an antique amphora that had been awarded to an Olympic victor some 2000 years before and, best of all, a wreath of wild olive branches to wear on his head. When the king of Greece asked him what else he wanted, he asked for and received a horse and a cart to transport water in and around his village. The next day he and over 300 other competitors, officials and journalists had breakfast with the king. During the meal, it was reported, the king paid Louys great attention. Among the numerous parties and receptions the hero Spyros Louys attended perhaps the most exciting was the one given by Madame Schliemann at her country villa near Athens. She was the widow of Heinrich Schliemann who had excavated Troy and Mycenae a quarter-century before. During that party an argument on the merits of baseball arose between the American athletes and several Greek princes. A fight broke out during which somebody swung a walking stick and His Royal Highness Prince George was hit with an orange.

On August 15, 1896, those first Olympic Games ended. Baron de Coubertin and others were enthusiastic about the precedent that had been set. Bearing his gifts, treasures, prizes and memories, Spyros Louys, the hero of his nation, returned to his village home on a hillside in Greece.

On the morning of August 2, 1936, almost exactly 40 years later, the airship *Hindenburg* trailed a long Olympic flag above the modern world's newest and largest stadium which already was filled with 110,000 people. More than 40,000 Storm Troopers and assorted Nazi guardsmen lined the boulevard route through Berlin down which Hitler's huge nickel-plated convertible rolled toward the opening of the magnificent and brutalized 1936 Olympic Games.

Accompanied by various dignitaries including several of Mussolini's sons, Hitler arrived at the stadium and made his way to the Marathon Gate, a wide tunnel at the western end of the mammoth stadium. His entrance from that gate was heralded by an electronically amplified fanfare of 30 trumpets. As Hitler and his entourage walked from the gate toward the Tribune of Honor, a reviewing stand, Richard Strauss, aged 72, directed a huge orchestra and a chorus of 3000 singers in several songs. These included *Deutschland über alles* and the new *Olympic Hymn* which he had written especially for the occasion. A five-year-old blonde girl in a blue dress handed Hitler a bouquet and he proceeded to the reviewing stand. A ten-foot-tall, 16½-ton bell then began to ring, summoning the 50 nations' teams of more than 5000 athletes to enter the stadium through the Marathon Gate. Though snubbed by the British contingent and the American one of 383 athletes, both of whose flag carriers refused to dip their countries' flags to him in passing, Hitler was pleased when the German contingent goose-stepped in and virtually everyone in the stadium rose to give the Heil salute. When all the athletes were in position on the field, the loudspeakers began to broadcast a phonograph record. It was the voice of Pierre de Coubertin. Ailing in Switzerland and unable to attend, he had sent a recorded message: "The important thing at the Olympic Games is not to win, but to take part, just as the most important thing about life is not to conquer, but to struggle well." A few speeches followed. Some were blatantly nationalistic, one unbashedly praised the athletic superiority of the Aryan race. Most of the 110,000 people applauded. Then Hitler, to whom conquering and winning were the most important things in life, spoke into the microphone, "I announce as opened the Games of Berlin, celebrating the eleventh Olympiad of the modern era." Everyone cheered. Hitler Youths released 20,000 doves, most of which were white. Strauss conducted the orchestra and chorus in several additional pieces. There was silence for a moment and then the first Olympic torch appeared. The idea of using a mirror to reflect sunlight to ignite a torch at Olympia, which would then be relayed to the site of the Games, was thought up by a German, Dr. Carl Diem, and had been approved in 1934. A blonde boy carried that first flame across the stadium and up to the marble platform over the Marathon Gate, where he touched it into the cauldron to light the Olympic flame. After that came the Olympic oath. To the consternation of many of the gathered athletes, the official reader intentionally grasped the tip of a swastika-emblazoned flag instead of the tip of the Olympic flag while he read the oath. Then came the "Hallelujah Chorus" from Handel's *The Messiah,* which Strauss, again, directed. Finally, a withered old man in native costume emerged from the Greek contingent of athletes. With tears running down his cheeks, he was led to the Führer, to whom he handed a sprig of wild olive brought from the sacred grove, the *Altis,* at Olympia. He said, "I present to you this olive branch as a symbol of love and peace. We hope that nations will ever meet solely in such peaceful competition." Hitler, deeply moved, shook hands with the old man, who was the peasant, Spyros Louys.

Nine months later on May 6, 1937, the magnificent *Hindenburg* crashed in flames. Four months after that the Baron Pierre de Coubertin died as he was walking in a park in Geneva. Fittingly, he was buried in two countries. His body was interred at Lausanne, Switzerland, while his heart, according to instructions in his will, was removed and taken in a small casket to Greece. A tall stone *stele* (monument) had been erected for it in the *Altis* at Olympia. Into this the Crown Prince George (a nephew of the George hit by the orange at Madame Schliemann's party) placed the casket containing the ever-optimistic Baron's heart. The *stele* was sealed up. It stands today in that grove of trees where in ancient times men had come from all over the known world to compete with each other in various sports because a sacred truce allowed and encouraged them to do so. Though the little French baron had almost singlehandedly engineered the revival of the Games, he could not singlehandedly recreate their truce. Significantly, he did not doubt that through international athletic competition, peace *could* be regained. Shortly before his death he had summed up how he felt it could be accomplished when he said simply, that "ancient solutions remain today as applicable as they ever were."

THE BIG BOOK OF HALLS OF FAME IN THE UNITED STATES AND CANADA

ANGLING

"To the best of my moderate ability to form an opinion, the finest sport is fishing with a rod, line, and hook." What makes this typical sentiment unique is that it was printed by the prioress of a famous European nunnery four years after Columbus discovered America. Evidently not much of an angler herself (as evidenced by her statement in *The Treatyse of Fysshynge wyth an Angle,* "Or he may catch nothing, but this is not a serious trouble."), Juliana Berners nevertheless has the distinction of having written the first book in English on angling. The book was for gentlemen only. But in her and Columbus' day angling was a sport for the common man as well, as it had been since pharaonic Egypt and as it has been ever since.

In 1732, the year George Washington was born, the Schuylkill Fishing Company was formed. The first angling club in North America, it is today the oldest sports body of any kind on the continent, and one of the few still in existence which may boast of having hosted President Washington at one of its functions. By 1809 (when Lincoln was born), ice fishing was flourishing in the Northern United States and throughout Canada. So popular were it and other forms of angling that supply houses for hunters and anglers were soon needed. The first to open was the Gladding Corporation, founded in 1816 (when "the Father of Modern Canada," Sir John Alexander Macdonald, was one year old) and today the oldest manufacturer of sporting goods in the United States. By the 1860s there were angling clubs in most major cities—notably the Prince of Wales Fishing Club in Montreal. Fly-casting tournaments in those days were held on grass, as there was no way of measuring casts across water. Today man's ancient, deep and strong relationship to fish is individually practiced by hundreds of millions and is jointly celebrated in North America from The Fisherman's Regatta at Pugwash, Nova Scotia (July 1), the Tommycod Ice Fishing Festival at La Perade, Quebec (Christmas Day-February 15), and the Flin Flon Trout Festival at Flin Flon, Manitoba (July 1-4), to the Maine Seafood Festival at Rockland (first weekend in August), the Freshwater Trout Derby at Livingston, Montana (August), and the Lahaina Whaling Festival on the island of Maui in Hawaii (first weekend in November). Chances are, therefore, that in any group of ten people in North America, three will be direct descendants in spirit of "Frank Forester," Captain Ahab and Zane Grey, and will also be protected by the patron saint of anglers, Izaak Walton, who wrote *The Compleat Angler* in 1653.

Homo habilis, an extinct kind of man, caught and ate African catfish. Except in those several dozen cultures where the eating of fish was and is prohibited by religious law, virtually everyone through the whole of human history has eaten fish. All sizes, shapes and kinds of saltwater and freshwater fish have been speared, netted (notably in the vast Hawaiian *hukilau* nets), trapped and caught by all the other forms and techniques listed in "Forms," below. Today, therefore, fishing and angling are two of the very few areas of human endeavor in which modern man cannot claim to have made any patentable improvement.

Fishing, of course, should not be confused with angling. The former, in which fish are harvested, has a commercial implication. Darius II awarded "a fishing contract" in 422 B.C. Angling, on the other hand, implies a form of peaceful recreation in which fish are caught singly either to be eaten or released. In fishing the emphasis is on the result, the success and the quantity of the catch; in angling it is on the process, the success and the quality of the technique. Fishing makes money on speed of completion; angling benefits in terms of inner peace or patience. Thus John James Audubon was a fisherman, not an angler: he wrote exasperatedly of having the patience to illustrate all the birds of America but not enough to stand angling for trout. Finally, fishermen seem honest men while anglers, as Rudyard Kipling described them, belong to "that fraternity who pride themselves on never deviating by one hair's breadth from the absolute and literal truth." From the other point of view, naturally, there are no such distinctions: as

Herbert Hoover said, "All men are equal before fish."

FORMS: The techniques used and the equipment needed for angling depend upon the type of angling to be done and upon the individual angler's preferences. Beyond various legal restrictions, there are no strict rules for the way to catch fish, although qualifying one's catch as a world record for its species does involve detailed witnessing and recording procedures. The basic equipment required by a serious angler includes a rod, reel, hooks or lures or natural bait, lines and leaders, sinkers and floats. Accessories may include a creel, knives, lure and tackle boxes, hand nets, scales, stringers and a pair of waders. These items are used in various combinations for the four main forms of angling: Still Fishing, Casting, Trolling and Spearfishing. An angler who remains stationary on a dock or in a boat is said to be Still Fishing. This is a widely practiced form, not nearly so popular as Casting, the major types of which are fly-, bait- and spin-casting. Trolling is done from a moving boat. Spearfishing or underwater hunting is illegal in some states and provinces. Each of these four forms is practiced in both saltwater and freshwater. There are hundreds of other ways and techniques of catching fish. Belly-tickling, for example (tickling its belly so that a fish is lulled to sleep and may be grasped) is practiced in the Rocky Mountains and elsewhere. In chumming, oily fish are cut into small pieces and scattered in the water to attract fish to the baited hook. Clubbing is also practiced, but dynamiting of rivers and streams to kill all the fish in them is strictly illegal. Gaffing or snagging is done with a large, strong hook on a pole or with a barbed spear. Gaffing with the three-pronged leister (a kind of spear), however, is usually illegal. In harling, the flow of the stream causes the bait or lure to behave like a fish while the boat is held in the current. Harpooning is a form of fishing along with "jigging" lures up and down in the water, and "jugging." Ledgering is the use of weights, usually ones made of lead. Short, baited lines are hung from a long line suspended over the water in trot-line fishing or long trotting. Netting can be either stationary, trawling and seining with large nets that have floats along the top edge and weights along the bottom, or casting. Noosing or snaring, poisoning (illegal), raking, stunning, and torchlight fishing (universally illegal) are further forms. Trapping is usually done with weirs, fence-like structures built into a stream or channel.

ORGANIZATION: Various organizations, associations, corporations, committees, societies, councils, clubs, commissions, institutes and foundations have been established to support and control the various aspects of fishing and angling. Notable among these are the American Casting Association (2500 members in 1976), the International Spin Fishing Association, the International Women's Fishing Association (450 members), the Ontario Federation of Anglers and Hunters Inc, the Association of Surf Angling Clubs (106 clubs with a minimum of 25 members each), Salmon Unlimited (2300 members), and the Sport Fishing Institute (25,000 members in 1976). In both the United States and Canada, federal, state, provincial and sometimes local agencies are actively concerned with both fish protection and utilization. (*See also* Hunting: Organization.)

Bass Fishing Hall of Fame

MEMPHIS, TENNESSEE

Mailing Address: 3568 Lamar Ave, 38138. Tel. (901) 365-9584. *Contact:* Frank Barns, Exec. Dir. *Location:* Approx. 210 mi. S.W. of Nashville, 135 mi. N.E. of Little Rock, Ark, 200 mi. N. of Jackson, Miss. *Admission:* Free 8 to 5 Monday – Saturday; closed Sunday and Christmas. *Personnel:* Frank Barns, Exec. Dir; Dale Conner, Asst. Dir; Hunter Lane, Jr, Mem. of Bd; Omar Smith, Mem. of Bd. *Nearby Halls of Fame:* Music (Nashville).

The Bass Fishing Hall of Fame will open in the winter of 1978 to commemorate the greatest bass fishermen, to preserve tackle of historical importance, and to honor contributors to the environment and ecology of bass. Unique and fascinating displays of fishing memorabilia are presently housed in the *Pro Bass Magazine* offices. A new building is being erected at the same location on Lamar Avenue containing twelve rooms on two floors with approximately 7000 square feet of exhibition area; it will also include the *Pro Bass Magazine* offices. The magazine administers and governs the Hall but financing comes from public donations and tackle manufacturers. While there is no admission charge at the present time, there will be a small entrance fee when the Hall is completed. Exhibits in the new building will include a "Species of Bass" room, the world's largest existing mounted bass, plus the world's largest tackle and lure collection. The "Ultimate Bass Boat," fully rigged, will also be displayed and given away through a drawing, with the winner's name engraved on a plaque. Bass fishing merchandise will be displayed in 50 six-foot booths. Other exhibits planned are an antique lures and equipment arrangement and a several thousand-gallon tank with live bass. Seminars will be held in conjunction with Northwestern University. A reading room containing the Hall's publication, *Pro Bass Magazine,* as well as other related magazines will be available. The second floor will have meeting rooms for clubs, groups and movies.

Members: First inductions will be in the fall of 1977 at the annual convention meeting. Nominations from tackle manufacturing companies will be voted on by sportswriters. Two individuals will be inducted yearly, preferably one professional and one amateur, in one of the two following categories: an "angler" as evidenced by exemplary skill in bass fishing tournaments and a "contributor" to the bass fishing industry, especially in the ecological balance of the environment. Emphasis will be on living anglers.

International Fishing Hall of Fame

TAMPA, FLORIDA

Mailing Address: P.O. Box 16514, Temple Terrace, 33687. Tel. (813) 988-4580. *Contact:* Lou Pease, Exec. Dir. *Location:* North Tampa Chamber of Commerce Building, 715 E. Sitka. *Admission:* Free, beginning early in 1978. *Personnel:* Louis Klewer, Pres; Ted Henson, V.Pres; Roger Cavallo, Treas; Lou Pease, Exec. Dir.

The International Fishing Hall of Fame was founded by the late Joe Godfrey in Chicago in 1928. Called the Fishing Hall of Fame, it was maintained by him for nearly 50 years. In 1976 portions of its archives and collections were moved to Tampa, Florida, and it was officially given its present name. The North Tampa Chamber of Commerce building is presently in the process of being converted to a permanent home for this Hall of Fame, which honors the greatest sportsmen of both saltwater and freshwater fishing. In addition to the display of fishing artifacts and memorabilia, the International Fishing Hall of Fame plans to hold annual fishing seminars and to publish an International Fishing Hall of Fame Annual.

Members: 600 as of 1977, of which approximately 350 are still living. List of members will be available following the opening of the facility in early 1978. Nominations must be made by an existing member, then must be investigated for usually one year by two members of the Board of Governors. Such an investigation is held to determine whether the nominee meets the four essential requirements for membership in the International Fishing Hall of Fame: he or she must be a fishing expert in some type of sports fishing; must have made some significant contribution to ecology; must have made a similar contribution to the sport of fishing; and must have worked with or for the world's youth, who according to this Hall's motto comprise "the world's greatest resource." Such investigations are carried out by serving members of the Board of Governors, on which there are now serving one member from each of the United States' 35 sectional regions plus one each from approximately 35 different foreign countries; from this total of 70 Board members, teams of two may carry out an unspecified number of nomination investigations every year. The results of their investigations are voted by a Membership Committee, which consists of four Florida members of the Hall of Fame. A unanimous decision is required for membership. Actual induction of new members is made at special ceremonies, during which three members of the Hall of Fame present the new member with the Silver Dolphin Award, "the highest honor in sports fishing."

National Fresh Water Fishing Hall of Fame

HAYWARD, WISCONSIN

Mailing Address: P.O. Box 33, 54843. Tel. (715) 634-4440. *Contact:* Bob Kutz, Founder and Secy. *Location:* Approx. 70 mi. S.E. of Duluth, Minn. *Admission:* 10 to 5 daily and weekends. Individuals 50¢, family $1.50. *Personnel:* Bob Kutz, Secy; Quentin Johnson, Pres; Bud Nelson, First V.Pres; Oscar Treland, Second V.Pres; Erv Gerlach, Treas. *Nearby Halls of Fame:* Hockey (Eveleth, Minn, 140 mi. N.), Football (Green Bay, 200 mi. S.E.).

The National Fresh Water Fishing Hall of Fame is organized under Wisconsin statutes as a nonprofit corporation. The Internal Revenue Service has granted it tax-exempt status so that all donations of monies, services, equipment, artifacts or materials are tax deductible. A Board of Trustees, consisting of business and industrial leaders from throughout the United States, will be responsible for the Hall's operation. Located on seven acres adjacent to the famous National Scenic Wild River, the Namekagon, the National Fresh Water Fishing Hall of Fame will, when completed, consist of eight structures to house artifacts and mementos of the history of fishing and of the angling achievements of the world. Plans call for a library/theatre/seminar/audiovisual center, a tournament casting pool with spectator bleachers, three museum buildings, and an aquarium complex. The most spectacular structure, however, will be the Hall of Fame Walk-Through Fish Replica, a half-block long, four and one-half story high, steel, concrete and fiberglass Muskellunge. The first museum building with more than 5000 square feet of floor space for display areas, offices and workshop was opened to the public May 1, 1976. Displays include fish mountings, an historical outboard motor collection, a photo records gallery and library for research, and a gallery of accessories. The Hall is a member of the Association of Sports Museums and Halls of Fame.

Members: The selection and induction processes have not been completed.

Angling Halls of Fame to Watch

INTERNATIONAL SALTWATER FISHING HALL OF FAME

Being Organized 1977

Now in the process of organizing and purchasing land for a permanent facility, this Hall of Fame will feature numerous displays and exhibits. Of particular interest will be displays of antique saltwater fishing equipment and boats. Fishing exhibitions are also planned. Anglers who hold world records as well as contributors to the sport of saltwater fishing will be inducted by a Hall of Fame Committee. Inquiries should be addressed to Capt. Hazen Jones, P.O. Box 927, Islamorada, FL 33036. Tel. (305) 852-9924.

WORLD SPORTFISHING HALL OF FAME

Inactive 1976

This multimillion dollar undertaking to honor noted sportsfishermen and holders of record catches throughout the world in a tropically landscaped facility, and to include various displays, a World Below Hall, an auditorium, a marina, a picnic garden and a library, has been indefinitely postponed. Letters of interest or inquiry should be addressed to Ronald E. Stroud, Pier 66, Drawer 9177, Ft. Lauderdale, FL 33310.

ARCHERY

In the 30 centuries of recorded history, only one year out of every fifteen has been peaceful. From the Egyptian Empire, which was built largely by the success of the bow over neighboring nations that still used slings and spears, to the advent of gunpowder around 1300, virtually continuous war was waged with arrows. The Buddha was an expert at archery, and Confucius was fond of it. Temmu, the fortieth emperor, instituted archery in Japan (*see* Martial Arts). The Prophet Mohammed raised it to the status of a holy religious duty. Attila, Genghis Khan and Tamerlane terrified Europe with their stout ponies and their stubby composite bows that could shoot an arrow as far as 800 yards. For their defense, Europeans had the crossbow, a murderous weapon which long before the time of William Tell was considered too cruel and inhumane for general use in war. In 1139, in fact, the Holy See prohibited, on pain of excommunication, the use of crossbows against Christians. Far more important to Europeans, however, was the bow, particularly the long bow. Edward III made archery practice compulsory on holidays and decreed that whoever played loggats, quoits, handball, football, "or other vain games of no value" would be imprisoned; moreover, that there would be a fine for shooting at targets less than 200 yards away. When the proper wood became scarce, a law was passed requiring that all merchant ships coming to England include four bowstaves per each ton of cargo. Supporting archery, Henry VIII prohibited the use of gunpowder except by special royal permission. In 1545 (two years after Copernicus said that the sun was the center of everything), Roger Ascham wrote what was the first archery book in English. Titled *Toxophilus,* it strongly supported the art and science of archery. Societies were formed and contests held to keep archery alive in England. One of these, The Scroton Arrow, competed for since 1673, is the oldest sporting trophy for which an annual open competition takes place.

The age of arrows was ending, however, and the advent of arquebusiers (an early type of portable gun, supported on a hooked staff or forked rest during firing) and guns could not be halted. Not surprisingly, Benjamin Franklin's proposal to use bows against the British was ignored. He had argued that they made no smoke or noise, were easily procured and were as accurate as muskets. The United Bowmen of Philadelphia, a club organized by four men in 1828 (the year *Webster's Dictionary* was first published) was also ignored. Archery, it appeared, had become a part of the past, or an event practiced only by primitive tribes.

It was therefore perhaps fitting that the Civil War and the postwar ban on the possession of firearms by Southerners was directly responsible for the revival of the use of the bow and, ultimately, for the development of archery into a modern sport. Two Confederate veterans, Maurice and Will Thompson, soon became proficient archers while scavenging for food in and around Okefinokee Swamp and Lake Okechobee. Maurice later wrote a little book, *The Witchery of Archery,* which produced mass archery fever and did for the sport of archery in the 1870s what *Uncle Tom's Cabin* had done for the war two decades before. That book, a series of articles on archery in *Harper's,* the introduction of archery into Vassar's curriculum in 1876, and the fact that the only other "lawn sport" of the time was croquet, brought archery as a sport to the North American continent. Today, the J. Maurice Thompson Gold Medal of the National Archery Association—which Maurice helped to found—is the highest award attainable in target archery.

Though the sport lost some of its adherents when tennis arrived, it experienced a new boom in the 1920s among gun-weary veterans of World War I. Poland instituted international archery with a tournament held in 1931. In 1970 a man performed a feat that would have amazed the Buddha, astounded Confucius, impressed even Attila, and caused Robin Hood's eyebrows to raise. On the Ivanpah Dry Lake in California the dream of all the ages was accomplished when Harry Drake shot an arrow that traveled, incredibly, more than a mile.

FORMS: Target Archery involves shooting at targets at specified distances. Field Archery simulates hunting on special courses. Bow Hunting, with from 1.5 to 4 million adherents in North America, is vastly more popular than the other forms. Bow Fishing is similarly popular among numerous archers and anglers. In flight shooting one tries only for distance; for example, Drake made his 1 mi. 101 yd. 1 ft. 8 in. shot while lying on his back, the bow virtually bolted to his feet. Crossbow Archery is also practiced. Derivatives of these forms include Popinjay Shooting, where a wooden parrot on a pole is used as a target, and Archery Darts. Archery Golf has been played for at least a century. A white cloth stretched on a frame is used as a target in Clout Shooting, while a slat 6 ft. (1.83 m.) high by 2 in. (5 cm.) wide is used as a target in Wand Shooting. Bouncing Balloons, Archery Tic-Tac-Toe and other derivative archery forms are also popular. For all of these, the basic steps are stringing the bow, attaining the proper stance, nocking the arrow (fitting the string into the nock or notch of the arrow), drawing, aiming, releasing, and following through. Equipment needed include a bow, arrows, a quiver, a finger tab, a forearm bracer and a tassel with which to clean dirtied arrows. Arrows in target archery are shot at butts, thick woven straw mats, to which the targets are attached. The target normally is 48 in. (122 cm.) in diameter and consists of five concentric circles. The gold "bull's eye" is worth 9 points, the red 7, the blue 5, the black 3, and the white 1 point. The number of arrows to be shot is called a "round." The names of the principal rounds shot in various tournament competitions are: York, Hereford, St. George, Albion, Men's Western, Men's National, National, Windsor, Columbia, American, Junior American, and Men's and Women's International Rounds. Arrows average 24 – 28 in. long, while bows average 5 ft. 6 in. in length. The two basic types of bow are the straight, derived from the English longbow, and the recurved, derived from the Turkish composite war bow. A bow of either type may be "self," which means crafted from a single piece of wood, or "backed," which means made of two or more pieces of wood, metal, fiberglass or other materials laminated together. The sculptured hand grip seen on some bows was originally devised for an archer with a weakened wrist.

ORGANIZATION: The international governing body for archery is the *Fédération Internationale de Tir à l'Arc* (FITA), while those of North America are the Federation of Canadian Archers (FCA) and the National Archery Association of the United States (NAA). In North America, target archery tournaments are held according to NAA rules, while field archery competitions are held according to the rules of the National Field Archery Association (23,412 members in 1977). There are separate organizations for professional archers (the U.S. Professional Archers Association, for example) and for amateur archers (notably the International Archery Federation, composed of the amateur archery associations of 57 different nations). All of these archers and organizations are supported by such general organizations as the Archery Lane Operators Association (based in Minnesota) and the Archery Manufacturers Organization (Illinois), as well as by the Society of Archer-Antiquaries, whose 400 members specialize in the history of archery in general and the history and development of the bow in particular from its ancient antecedents to its Space Age applications.

Archery Hall of Fame

GRAYLING, MICHIGAN

Mailing Address: Fred Bear Museum, Bear Mountain, 49738. Tel. (517) 348-9822. *Contact:* Frank Scott, Dir. *Location:* Approx. 135 mi. N.W. of Flint, 150 mi. N. of Lansing, 175 mi. N.E. of Grand Rapids. *Admission:* Free 10 to 6 daily. *Personnel:* Joe Rusniek, Pres; George Helwig, V. Pres; Dave Staples, Exec. Secy. *Nearby Halls of Fame:* Sports (Bloomfield Hills, Mich, 200 mi. S.E.).

Founded in 1972 by the American Archery Council, the Archery Hall of Fame now contains the world's largest private collection of archery artifacts. Presently housed in the Fred Bear Museum, the Hall is an independent corporation operated on contributions from the Professional Archers Association (PAA), the National Archery Association (NAA), the National Field Archery Association (NFAA), the American Lane Operators Association (ALOA) and the American Archery Council (AAC). Practice targets and free instructional advice are available for toxophiles near the Museum.

Members: 21 as of 1976. One member each from the NAA, the NFAA, the ALOA, the Professional Bowhunters Society, the American Indoor Archery Association and Robert Rhode, Historian, nominate individuals. These nominated are voted on by all living inductees from previous years. Nominees must have excelled in shooting, contributed significantly to the sport, or had an outstanding influence on archery.

1972

BEAR, Fred
Shooter

Born in Detroit, Mich; Mr. Sportsman Award 1965; now resides in Grayling, Mich.

Expert bowhunter and toxophile, Fred has tracked big game on all seven continents. His interest in bowhunting began in 1927 after he viewed a film by Art Young. Six years later Bear was making his own bows in his workshop in Detroit. This was the beginning of the Bear Archery Company. Considered by Dr. Paul Klopsteg as one of the "greatest early bowhunters," Bear promoted bowhunting by writing articles, producing motion pictures and giving lectures. For 17 years he collected trophies until a fire in 1952 destroyed the collection. When rebuilding his trophy and artifact showcase, he set aside a room at his archery manufacturing plant. The

Trophy Room, as it was eventually called, soon attracted many visitors. As the collection grew and the number of visitors increased, a better display area was planned. In September 1967 the Fred Bear Museum opened, housing not only his trophies but those of other bowhunters, sent to him for preservation. A contributor and active participant in the archery world, Fred Bear, through his unfledging promotion, is responsible for much of the present popularity of archery.

HILL, Howard
Shooter
The greatest name in modern archery, Howard is also one of the finest bowhunters. To promote bowhunting he donned Indian apparel and shot bison while riding a horse bareback. His book, *Hunting the Hard Way,* is very descriptive of all facets of the sport. Howard makes his home in Sunland, Calif.

HOOGERHYDE, Russell Buhl
Shooter
Russell became interested in archery in 1927, concentrating on indoor shooting. In the six national tournaments he won, the form and concentration developed from indoor practice carried him to victory. He won the national title in 1930, 1931, 1932, 1934, 1937 and 1940, and the Dallin Medal in 1934.

HOYT, Ann Marie Weber
Shooter
The only woman to win both the National Target and Field Championships, Ann Hoyt accomplished both in the same year, 1955. Three years later she led the U.S. women's team to first place in the World Tournament while she claimed second-place individual honors. In 1959 she placed first, and the team won the World Tournament for the second consecutive year. She also added the International Field Champion title in 1959. In addition to her international and world titles, Ann won the Eastern Target Championship 15 times and the national title in 1940, 1946, 1947, 1952 and 1953. Her overall 20-year record in world and national tournaments is eight firsts, seven seconds and three thirds.

PALMATIER, Karl E.
Contributor
Elected in 1930 as Secretary of Michigan Archery Association, Karl held the position for 30 years. In 1936 he served as president of the National Archery Association, and was director of the National Field Tournament from 1946 through 1961. Karl was one of the two men awarded both the Thompson and Compton Medals of Honor. Few individuals have done more for the organizational structure and promotion of target tournaments than Karl Palmatier.

PEARSON, Ben
Contributor
Born November 16, 1898, in Paron, Ark; moved to Pine Bluff, Ark, in 1927 and worked for local power and light company; died March 2, 1971, of a heart attack in Pine Bluff; survived by wife Mary; three children, Ben Jr, Mary Helen, Jesse Harris Jr; brother Q. A. Pearson, Lt. Col. in Navy; three grandchildren.

Store-bought bows and tackle were practically unheard of before Ben Pearson, Inc, was founded on March 19, 1938. Archery's unsung hero became interested in making archery paraphernalia after reading directions in a Boy Scout magazine. With a draw-knife, he formed his first bow from a piece of hickory, a straight bow with an 80-lb. draw, and used it in his first tournament in 1926, the Arkansas State Archery Tournament. Though he placed second to the last that year, he won it the next, and soon began making bows and arrows for friends and archery enthusiasts. He hired other craftsmen to help him in the Ben Pearson Archery Equipment Co, but his real dream was to mass produce the equipment. In the midst of the Depression, that dream was fulfilled when Oklahoma oilman, Carl Haun, financed Ben Pearson, Inc. First housed in an old brick sorghum mill, the business has since grown to 10 buildings and over 260 employees. Pearson either designed and built, or directed the development of, most of the equipment that mass produced the bows and arrows: wing trimmer, splice machine, barrel shaft sanding machine, handle wrapper, tiller machine, bow sanders, nock and point machine, knurling machine, cresting machine, feather processing machine for shaping and target machines. With these machines and the advent of fiberglass bows, another innovation by Ben Pearson, archery became a sport enjoyed by many. Pearson further popularized archery through his involvement in organizing some of the first archery associations, including the Southern Archery Association in 1928. He has also traveled throughout the United States, Mexico and Canada performing tricks and making movies of his archery hunts for public viewing. His trophies include javelina from Arizona, grizzly bear from Alaska, wild goat from Catalina and polar bear from off the Siberian coast. In 1967 Ben Pearson, Inc, was sold to The Leisure Group in Los Angeles and Pearson served as their consultant until his death. In November of 1971 the company was again sold to Consumer Division, Brunswick Corp.

THOMPSON, Maurice
Shooter
Born 1844 in Fairfield, Ind; son of Matthew Grigg Thompson, a Baptist minister, and Diantha Thompson; lived in Florida, Georgia and Kentucky.

The archery craze following the Civil War is attributed to Thompson's adventures in the Florida Everglades. Denied medical care and other aid after the war because he had been a Confederate soldier, Thompson lived by the bow in the Everglades before moving to Kentucky. Many of his experiences are chronicled in *Harper's New Monthly Magazine* and *Appleton's Journal* between 1873 and 1876. An experimenter also, he wrote the *Witchery of Archery* in 1878. After publication of this book and his other writings, hundreds of archery clubs were formed and the U.S. patent office was flooded with applications. In his honor the National Field Archery Association has designated the Maurice Thompson Medal of Honor, awarded to archers who have contributed significantly to the sport over many years.

1973

POPE, Dr. Saxton Temple
Shooter
Saxton was an outstanding archer and bowhunter. He made many memorable big-game hunting trips with Art

Young in the late 1920s and early 1930s. His book *Hunting with the Bow and Arrow* recounts those adventures and reveals the Yana secrets of making bows and arrows. Dr. Pope's research and experiments with the bow and arrow were the foundation for much of the technical development and improvement of modern bows and arrows.

POWELL, Ruben
Shooter

Between 1951 and 1958, "Rube" Powell never finished lower than third in the National Free Style Field Archery championships. He won the title in 1951, 1953, 1954, 1955 and 1956, the only archer ever to win five times. The first of the strong shooters with the use of the bowsight in field archery, "Rube" is known today as "Mr. Flight Archer." He presently resides in Chula Vista, Calif.

SHENK, Clayton B.
Outstanding Influence

Born May 13, 1908; married 1943; for fourteen years a watch-maker; three years in the Navy; presently residing in Lancaster, Pa.

Clayton Shenk has been active and influential at all levels of archery since 1932. For 39 years he was the executive secretary of the Pennsylvania State Archery Association. At the national level, he was president of the National Archery Association (NAA) in 1937 and in 1950; from 1959 to 1966 he served as the chairman of the NAA's board of directors, and, since 1966 has been its executive secretary. For the above contributions it has been said of Clayton Shenk that he, more than any other one person, is responsible for the organizational structuring of the sport of archery in North America. He has been equally significant, however, at the international level. Archery was dropped from the Olympic Games in 1922. In 1931 a world governing body for archery was formed. Called the International Archery Federation (*see* the Organization discussion in the category sketch), its primary goal was to accomplish the reinstatement of archery as an Olympic event. The NAA became a member of the IAF in 1933, from which time Clayton Shenk was concerned with that primary goal. In 1957 he organized and implemented the selection of American teams for world archery competition. In 1961 he became an administrator of the IAF, a position he still holds. Since 1969, Shenk has been qualified as an International Archery Judge. Through his and others' efforts, archery was finally, in 1972, reinstated on the Olympic Games program of regular events. That first year, the United States won both the archery gold medals, as it did at the 1976 Games. Though individual archers won them, much of the credit for those medals must go to Clayton Shenk, whose four decades of dedication to archery made them possible.

YOUNG, Art
Contributor

Died 1935.

Young was one of the best-known and most-respected sportsmen worldwide. He accompanied Saxton Pope on many big-game hunts in the late 1920s and early 1930s. He made movies promoting archery, explaining bowhunting and providing tips for tracking big game. In 1927 Fred Bear viewed one of Young's films and thereafter was an archery enthusiast. Honoring Art Young's devotion to and interest in archery, the National Field Archery Association established three awards: the Big Game Award, Art Young Prize Buck Award and Art Young Small Game Award. Any archer who earns either the big- or small-game award receives Art Young silver and gold arrows.

1974

CUMMINGS, Dorothy Smith
Shooter

Born 1903 in Newton Centre, Mass; daughter of Louis C. Smith, also in Hall (1976); married Henry S. C. Cummings; two children.

Dorothy began shooting at the city range when she was only nine years old. Within seven years she was a national champion, the youngest ever in America. The next 12 years would find Dorothy claiming the Ladies National Champion title seven times, 1919, 1921, 1922, 1924, 1925, 1926 and 1931. She won the Eastern title eleven times and the Massachusetts State Archery Association title each time she competed. She was the last champion to win the National Archery Association title and establish world records without artificial sights on the bow. For over 20 years Dorothy dominated the field of archery, retiring from competition in 1931.

DRAKE, Harry
Shooter

Born 1915; resides in Lakeside, Calif.

Since 1944 Harry has set or broken all the existing flight records in archery. He was the 1970 National Flight Champion with a record shot of 1861 yds. The following year on October 14 "Mr. Flight" set the crossbow record with a shot of 1359 yds. 29 in. at Ivanpah Dry Lake in California. One week later he established the world footbow unlimited record of 1 mi. 268 yds. In 1963 he began to manufacture a complete line of bows and has worked on all types of flight bows since then.

EASTON, James D. "Doug"
Contributor

Born 1907; married Mary Simonich in 1932; received Maurice Thompson Medal of Honor; died in 1972.

As founder of James D. Easton, Inc, Doug became a pioneer and leader in the production of aluminum arrows. He first began making custom yew wood bows and cedar arrows with special footed shafts in Watsonville, Calif, in 1922, then began working with aluminum tubing in Los Angeles in 1939. By 1941 his #1820 aluminum arrows had won the national championship, prompting Doug to develop his own aluminum tubing. In 1946 "Granny," a drawbench Doug designed and built, produced its first shafts and has been doing the same ever since. Over the years further advancements have included the thermal and work-hardened Easton 24SRT-X arrow, the high-strength aluminum XX75 in 1958 and X7 arrow in 1966. His small one-man company grew to employ over 300 people and produce ski poles, golf shafts, baseball bats and aluminum tubing items for the aircraft and aerospace industry as well. But Doug was always involved with archery, his hobby, as a member and officer of many clubs in Southern California, founder of the Professional Archery Association and an officer for the National Archery Association for 18 years. He also worked with Howard Hill to create the Marian Sparrow Archery Range (now Balboa Sports Center) in Los Angeles and worked to reinstate archery in the Olympics.

YOUNT, John
Outstanding Influence
During the late 1940s and early 1950s John Yount served as the executive secretary-treasurer of the National Field Archery Association (NFAA), which was founded primarily through his efforts. His numerous contributions to archery as a whole and to field archery in particular include the publication of a comprehensive history of the NFAA from its inception in 1934 at Redlands, Calif.

1975

CROUCH, Dr. Paul W.
Shooter
Born in LeRoy, N.Y; married; two daughters; owned property around Oxford, N.Y; lived in Boston, Mass, and Greenwich, Conn; practiced dentistry; deceased; widow lives in Boston.

A great early archer, Paul Crouch was the U.S. National Champion from 1925 to 1927. His first Single and Double American national championships established new records. A little known fact about Crouch is that he also worked very hard to obtain bowhunting areas in New York State and develop more effective laws governing conservation and hunting. He was also very active in archery associations and served as president of the Eastern Archery Association.

HOWELL, Mrs. M. C. Lydia Scott
Shooter
Between 1879 and 1920 archery was extremely popular among women in North America; thereafter, there was a decline in that popularity until the mid-1940s, when a new generation of women began to take an interest in and to excell at archery. Mrs. Howell was the leader and "Founding Mother" of that first era. Between 1883 and 1907 she won the U.S. National Archery Association championship an incredible 17 times. Her titles came in 1883, 1885, 1886, 1890-1893, 1895, 1896, 1898-1900, 1902-1905 and 1907. (*See* the biographical sketch on "Babe" Bitzenburger, below, regarding the second era of women's archery.)

LOMBARDO, Jean Lee
Shooter
Graduated from Univ. Mass. in 1947; resides in Springfield, Mass.

An injury to her right arm forced Jean Lombardo to forego archery after 1952 but not before she had rewritten all women's records in only three years. She won the U.S. National Target Championship every year from 1948 through 1951. In 1951 and 1952 she added the world title. Her extraordinary accomplishments in a few years in competition are magnified when one considers she began archery shooting in 1946 at a summer camp in Vermont.

1976

BITZENBURGER, Mrs. Henry A. "Babe"
Shooter
Born July 23, 1903; married 1929; now living in Sherwood, Oregon; a tournament-class golfer with an interest in all sports, Mrs. Bitzenburger continues to give archery demonstrations, seminars and workshops.

In the second great era of women's archery (*see* biographical sketch of Mrs. Lydia Howell, above, regarding the first era), the prime mover was Babe Bitzenburger. Her skills and achievements inspired an entire new generation of women to enter the sport and seek excellence in it. She was the most outstanding flight shooter in the late 1940s, and was National Field Archery Association champion for four consecutive years, 1946, 1947, 1948 and 1949. She also was the champion of the National Archery Association's field shoot meet in 1941, and won numerous California State archery championship titles. Beyond her leadership in the renewed interest in women's archery, her contributions to the sport have been immense. For example, she and her husband Henry Bitzenburger founded the Pasadena Roving Archery Club, which today is one of the most active archery clubs in California. Her husband invented and patented (in 1946) one of the most essential tools of an archer, the "Bitzenburger Dial-o-Fletch," which is the tool by which feathers are attached to arrow shafts.
Also in: California Archery Hall of Fame.

KLOPSTEG, Dr. Paul Ernest
Contributor
Born May 30, 1889, in Henderson, Minn; the youngest and only boy of six children; father, Julius, was a Methodist minister; mother was Magdalene Kuesthardt Klopsteg; graduate engineer; married Amanda Marie Toedt on June 11, 1914; three children, Marie, Ruth and Irmer Louise; awarded Maurice Thompson Medal of Honor in 1939.

Scholar, educator and scientist, Dr. Paul Klopsteg devoted 20 years to archery, 1930 through 1950. An expert on the intricate details of the sport, he wrote *Turkish Archery and Composite Bow* and was coauthor of *Archery the Technical Side,* considered by many as the bible for advanced knowledge in bow efficiency.

SMITH, Louis Carter
Outstanding Influence
Patent attorney for Boston, Mass; daughter Dorothy Smith Cummings is also a Hall of Famer; recipient of Thompson Medal of Honor.

Louis Smith is probably the single most important person involved with the National Archery Association (NAA). From its inception in 1879 until after W. W. I, it was just a small club. But Smith turned it into a national organization by setting up three regional associations with state associations and instigating intercollegiate championships. From 1910 to 1940 the association's headquarters were located in Boston, where Smith lived. As executive secretary and at his own expense, he mailed 264 of the official NAA *Quarterly Bulletins* to members of the Association. An archer in his early days, though not an outstanding one, Louis Smith contributed greatly to his sport.

California Archery Hall of Fame

BELL GARDENS, CALIFORNIA

Mailing Address: P.O. Box 3059, 90201. Tel. (213) 927-0926. *Contact:* Arlie Clift, Chmn. *Location:* Approx. 105 mi. N.W. of San Diego, 220 mi. S.W. of Las Vegas, Nev, 325 mi. N.W. of Phoenix, Ariz. *Personnel:* Arlie Clift, Chmn; John Slack, Co-Chmn; Kathy Clift, Secy; Lynn M. Gardner, Treas; Hugh Rich, Sr. Advisor; Douglas Walker, Historian; five mem. Nominating Comt; 10 mem. Advisory Bd. No admission. *Nearby Halls of Fame:* Citizens Savings (Los Angeles, 15 mi. S.W.), Softball (Long Beach, 12 mi. S.), Physical Fitness (Costa Mesa, 26 mi. S.E.), Auto Racing (Ontario, 31 mi. N.E.), Flight, Sports (San Diego).

Founded in April, 1976, the California Archery Hall of Fame gives permanent recognition to individuals who have contributed to the formation and growth of archery in California. Arlie Clift, who layed the foundation for the Hall of Fame, believed that many California archers had contributed greatly to the growth of the sport throughout the United States as shooters, manufacturers, inventors, environmentalists and bowhunters. With the help of Jerry Miller, he encouraged the support of many involved in archery to assist him in the founding of the Hall of Fame. John Slack has been president of the California Bowmen Hunters-State Archery Association (CBH-SAA) and is now a representative for that organization in the National Field Archery Association. Lynn Gardner is vice-president of the state archery association and publisher of the *Pacific Coast Bowhunter.* Douglas Walker was also a president of the CBH-SAA and is presently their state historian. Hugh Rich, a bower and manufacturer, has been associated with California archery for over 40 years. Sponsored by the CBH-SAA, the California Archery Hall of Fame has a temporary home in the Fresno Field Archers clubhouse, where plaques for each Hall of Fame member are displayed with 30 years of CBH-SAA history. In June through September, 1977, a fund-raising drive will help to bring about a permanent location for the Hall of Fame. Founders (giving $100 or more), Sponsors (giving $50 or more) and Donors (giving $25 or more) will have their names engraved on plaques at the Fresno Field Archers clubhouse. Memorabilia is presently being gathered—even the hat of Hall of Famer Howard Hill, who was in the original *Robin Hood* movie, will be displayed in the California Archery Hall of Fame's permanent home. A traveling Hall of Fame may also be in store, to visit the tournaments sponsored by archery clubs and associations throughout the state.

Members: 12 as of July 1977. Members may be involved in tournaments and hunting or organizational and business aspects of archery to be eligible for nomination. They must be residents of California at the time of their nomination or while achieving fame in the sport. They must also have completed their service to archery five years prior to their nomination and must be recognized in the sport as giving more than the average person. Nominations are open to anyone, but must include a resume of the nominee's achievements. During the formation of the Hall of Fame, Chairman Arlie Clift appointed a Nominating Committee to encourage nominations from around the state. The Executive Board, consisting of the Hall of Fame officers, the Nominating Committee and Advisory Board elect members to the Hall of Fame by a majority vote. Inductees are notified by mail. The first induction ceremonies were held on April 23, 1977, in conjunction with the Fresno Field Archers Safari Archery Tournament. Each new member received a personal plaque, a duplicate of which is on display at the Fresno Field Archers clubhouse. Exceptionally outstanding archers who have not been retired five years may be selected to receive a Special Achievement Award and may be considered for membership in the Hall of Fame at a later date. Olympic champion Louann Ryon was the first recipient of the award on April 23, 1977. Election of 1978 members will take place in September 1977.

1977 BITZENBURGER, Mrs. Henry "Babe." See entry in Archery Hall of Fame, 1976.

BITZENBURGER, Henry

EASTON, James D. "Doug." See entry in Archery Hall of Fame, 1974.

EASTON, Mary

HILL, Howard. See entry in Archery Hall of Fame, 1972.

HOFF, Roy

POPE, Dr. Saxton Temple. See entry in Archery Hall of Fame, 1973.

POWELL, Ruben. See entry in Archery Hall of Fame, 1973.

RICH, Hugh

SMALLEY, "Doc"

YOUNG, Art. See entry in Archery Hall of Fame, 1973.

YOUNT, John. See entry in Archery Hall of Fame, 1974.

New York State Archery Association Hall of Fame

JERICHO, NEW YORK

Mailing Address: 79 Martin Court, 11753. Tel. (516) 549-6035. *Contact:* Monroe Farber. *Location:* Approx. 25 mi. E. of New York City. *Personnel:* Phil Hoelle, Pres; Robert Elkovitch, V. Pres; Helen Renalds, Treas; Jeanette Nelson, Secy. Not open to the public. *Nearby Halls of Fame:* Heritage, Music (New York City, 25 mi. E.), Bicycle (Staten Island, 45 mi. S.W.), Harness Racing (Goshen, 60 mi. N.W.), Ice Skating (Newburgh, 60 mi. N.W.), Basketball (Springfield, Mass, 100 mi. N.W.), Heritage (Valley Forge, Pa, 115 mi. S.W.), Tennis (Newport, R.I, 120 mi. N.E.), Horse Racing (Saratoga Springs, 150 mi. N.E.), Baseball (Cooperstown, 160 mi. N.E.), Ice Skating (Boston, Mass, 160 mi. N.E.), Flight (Elmira, 190 mi. N.W.), Horseshoe Pitching (Corning, 200 mi. N.W.), Exploration and Invention (Arlington, Va, 230 mi. S.W.).

To honor those whose distinguished service or outstanding performance maintains standards of excellence in archery, the New York State Archery Association's (NYSAA) Hall of Fame was established in 1976. Its first member was elected and inducted that same year. On July 16, 1977, the two newest members of the Hall were inducted at a banquet held in conjunction with the 46th annual meeting of the New York State Archery Association in Auburn, New York.

Members: 3 as of July 1977. The Hall of Fame Committee is composed of the secretary of the NYSAA and three current members appointed by the Association with the approval of the Board of Directors. Length of service on the Committee is two years, except for the secretary who is a permanent member. Inductees are selected into the Hall of Fame in conjunction with the State Tournament Annual Awards.

1976 WILSON, Lura R. Five-time New York State champion, as a right-hander and left-hander. Current holder of the clout record for women in New York State.

1977 HICKMAN, Dr. Clarence N. Developed 93 percent efficient flat bows; studied physics of bows and arrows; wrote 47 publications on technical and historical aspects of archery; member of New Jersey Archery Association and honorary member of National Archery Association and other clubs in New York City area.

HILTON, Dr. Alice S. Three-time International archery champion; winner of New York State Archery Women's championship and Lower Lakes Archery Federation (no longer in existence) championships several times; two-time Eastern Association champion; member of New York State Archery Association for over 40 years, serving as president, secretary-treasurer, executive board member, delegate and committee member; committee member of National Archery Association and Intercollegiate chairman for three years; staff member of the World Archery Center.

AUTOMOBILE RACING

The idea was around centuries before the invention. In Homer's *Iliad* (Book XVIII) Vulcan made 20 tricycles in a single day. They rolled from place to place "self-moved, obedient to the beck of gods." Da Vinci doodled ideas for self-propelled vehicles, but went on to better or more practical inventions. Not until the year of the Great Fire of London (1666), however, was a self-propelled vehicle actually built. This was a model steam carriage, constructed by a Belgian Jesuit priest named Ferdinand Verbiest, stationed at the time in China. In 1714, the year Fahrenheit invented his thermometer, the Du Quet windmill cart with its two masts carried 28 passengers at 20 m.p.h. Then in 1769, as Napoleon was born and Captain Cook was getting ready to begin his first voyage around the world, a Frenchman named Nicholas Joseph Cugnot of Lorraine constructed a large and heavy steam-powered, four-passenger tricycle apparatus that moved at 2¼ m.p.h. and was the world's first "automobile." Four years later a man in Delaware named Oliver Evans began thinking about steam carriages. Support for his invention was lost in the interests of American independence, however, and it took him 15 years to finally obtain a patent. In 1805 he began to sell his carriages. This was the beginning of history's first automobile race—men on both sides of the Atlantic raced to perfect this marvelous new machine.

Before that race had been won, the world's first traffic signal was devised and installed in 1868 outside the British Houses of Parliament—two semaphore arms for day and two lamps for night, one red and one green. It effectively regulated traffic until the day it blew up and killed a policeman. By 1914, when the first modern traffic light was installed on Euclid Avenue in Cleveland, Ohio, not only had cars been perfected, but they had also crossed every inhabited continent—North America in 1903, Asia (Peking-Paris) in 1907, Australia between 1907 and 1908, Africa between 1907 and 1909 (the Sahara was not crossed by car until 1923), and South America (across the Andes) in 1914. Sir Ernest Shackleton even transported a car to the Antarctic in 1908.

The race to perfect the automobile spanned about a century: from a steam-driven English stagecoach (1827), to a steam bus service (1834, when the blind Frenchman, Louis Braille, invented his alphabet), to a steam airplane (patented by W. S. Henson in 1842), to the steam wagon Richard Dudgeon drove through New York City and on Long Island (in 1866).

A Stamstead, Quebec, jeweler named Henry Seth Taylor exhibited a steam buggy just two months after Dominion. It had taken seven years to build but broke down in mid-demonstration, "contretemps detracting somewhat from the interest of the occasion," the local newspaper reported. A second demonstration the following year was flawless until Taylor and Canada's first horseless carriage crashed while driving down a hill—he had not thought of brakes.

The final lap of the race to perfect the automobile began with the invention of the four-cycle, gas-fueled, internal combustion engine first devised by Alphonse Beau de Rochas in 1862. This was improved upon in 1885 by Gottlieb Daimler who used petroleum spirits (kerosene) in an engine which he applied to a bicycle—the world's first motorcycle—and then to a rowboat on the Seine—the world's first motorboat. Finally, in 1887 and 1888, Emile Lavassor won the great race by building a body around a Daimler engine, thereby becoming the actual creator of the world's first true automobile.

We hear only that the early cars panicked horses. Forgotten, or overlooked, are all the incidents that made driving a hazardous experience. Drivers were horse-whipped and excluded from stores and clubs as well as slandered in the press. Automobiles were physically attacked when not ridiculed and insulted. Rural roads were barricaded by irate farmers. A British newspaper urged laws to ban the new invention, claiming that it was responsible for political disturbances occurring in France. Although not banned, the car was strictly limited by the Locomotive Act of 1865, which stipulated that any self-propelled vehicle on a public highway be preceded by a man on foot carrying a red flag. Such vehicles could not legally exceed 2 m.p.h. in the city and 4 m.p.h. in the country. Drivers drove under these restrictions for 21 years. The day in 1896 when this ban was lifted and the limit raised to 14 m.p.h. was praised by the handful of motorists as Emancipation Day.

Detroit produced its first car that same year. Just three years later there were no less than 50 different automobile manufacturers in the United States. By 1903 some 53,000 cars were in existence—30,200 of them French-made. Three years later the first service stations appeared. The first 100 gas pumps in Germany were called "iron maidens." In 1909 the Model T appeared. It was Henry Ford's ninth model, preceded by Models A, B, C, F, K, N, R and S. Ford's better idea, the car as an affordable necessity rather than a luxurious plaything, totally transformed American life. Within a few short years the car industry had become a main economic pillar of the United States. It stimulated vast growth in the rubber, electricity, glass, paint and oil industries. City planning, highways and transportation systems, and the legal profession (auto accident cases today are by far the most common type of litigation) were also affected. Henry Ford is also famous in another way, for the first personal auto liability accident: in 1894 he rolled one of his motor cars over a young cyclist, who was severely shaken but unharmed. Immediately after Lavassor's victory in creating the first true car, the second great race began. It continues today as the endless race for more perfect automobiles.

Men making cars soon wanted to test them against other men's cars, and auto racing was born. In 1887 (the year Hollywood, California, was founded) the first auto trial was held over the 20 miles from Paris to Versailles and back. The world's first automobile race, from Paris to Rouen and back, was held June 22, 1894, between steam cars. A month later a second race was held over the 732 miles from Paris to Bordeaux and back. This race, won by Lavassor himself, confounded those skeptics who had insisted that the car would never be able to travel more than limited distances. And it was this race which inspired *The Chicago Times-Herald* to sponsor a 54.36 mile race from Chicago to Evanston and back the following year. That race—America's first—and its $2000 prize were won by J. Frank Duryea whose car averaged 7.6 m.p.h. He and his brother Charles had built the first successfully operated American automobile. Charles lived to see Sir Malcolm Campbell, a Canadian, knighted in 1931 for achieving 246.09 m.p.h. in one of his famous Bluebirds, while Frank lived to see Craig Breedlove exceed 600 m.p.h. at Bonneville.

Men from Massachusetts caused America's first auto accident and first automobile fatality. In 1873 (the year Jules Verne wrote *Around the World in Eighty Days*) a 73-year-old inventor in Cambridge raced a bicyclist with his steam tricycle and died of overexcitement. He was later found to have been suffering from a heart disease. A Massachusetts man driving in New York City on May 30, 1896, hit a cyclist in America's first automobile accident. The first true fatality involving a true car occurred on September 13, 1899, when Henry H. Bliss, a 68-year-old real estate broker in New York City, alighted from a streetcar and was run over by a car. In 1902 George F. Foss of Sherbrooke, Quebec, tried to sell a car he had built in 1897 to an amputee. The car backfired, knocked the prospective buyer down and gouged out a chunk of artificial leg in one of Canada's first automobile accidents.

The first American auto show was held in New York City in 1900 (when zeppelins were invented), but auto racing proved to be a better way to advertise cars. Races were first held on public roads but soon turned to closed-circuit tracks—especially after the Vanderbilt Cup Races of 1904 to 1908 had come to be known as the "annual Long Island blood bath." The Indianapolis Motor Speedway was built. Over 80,000 people paid a dollar each to watch the 40 cars entered in the first race. The Roaring 20s saw the establishment of a Grand Prix in virtually every country on both sides of the Atlantic, the advent of passenger cars that could roar at up to 130 m.p.h. and $40,000 handcrafted cars upholstered in matched ostrich hide with ivory buttons. In the early 1930s Hitler offered the equivalent of over $150,000 to the builder of the most successful German racing car to travel the 1934 circuits.

By 1950 one in four Americans had a car. The same was true in Canada by 1960, by which year the number of private cars in the United States exceeded the combined total of the rest of the world. By 1975 the United States was producing twice as many cars as babies. With the exception of horse racing, auto racing today is the biggest spectator sport in America. Though cars may get smaller, this sport seems destined to become ever bigger.

FORMS: By 1973 auto racing in the United States had become a major industry. It comprises all the features and events associated with professional and amateur racing at road circuits, oval tracks, dirt tracks, paved tracks, Grand Prix events, hill climbs, hill trials, slaloms, autocrosses, endurance events, rallies, rally crosses, sprints, 500-milers, vintage races, drag races, midget car races, hot rod trials, hot rod races and go-kart races. Today each of these forms of auto racing has its own racing organizations and decides its own roster of champions. Automobiles may range from production-line cars to modified stock cars to highly sophisticated racing machines. Within each of these types the cars will be further classed according to strict limits for actual or potential speed, engine size, modifications permitted and other factors. For example, in drag racing, the most popular form of auto racing, there are over 100 different classes of vehicles. A car will compete against similar cars in one of eight categories within the 100 classes (Top Fuel, Top Gas, Funny Car, Pro Stock, Competition, Modified, Super Stock and Stock). In addition to the car classification requirements, a car and its driver must meet strict official and safety standards. A car must have four wheels and a full diameter steering wheel, for example, while a driver must be licensed to race and must wear a protective helmet. An average championship car will weigh 1400 lbs. without fuel, oil or driver and will have an engine of between 500 and 600 horsepower.

A driver and his machine may race against other cars or against the clock. The track may be straight, oval (in which case the race is usually run clockwise), or meandering, and from a quarter mile to many miles in length. Officials include a clerk of the course, a secretary of the meeting, starters, stewards, timekeepers, handicappers, scrutineers and their assistants, pit and road observers, flag marshals and finishing judges. Internationally recognized flags mean the following: white—official non-racing vehicle on the course; black—car indicated must stop; red—stop race; yellow—danger; yellow with red stripes—slippery surface; motionless blue—another car following; waving blue—another car trying to pass.

ORGANIZATION: The Paris-based *Fédèration Internationale de l'Automobile* (FIA), founded in 1904, is in charge of worldwide auto racing. This is a voluntary association of the national auto clubs of some 70 countries. Only FIA-recognized races may result in world championships.

In the United States five major and scores of minor organizations sanction competitions. The major organizations are the American Automobile Association (founded 1902), the Sports Car Club of America (the main sanctioning body in U.S. racing and sponsor of the important Canadian-American Championship), the National Association for Stock Car Auto Racing, the U.S. Auto Club (sponsor of the Indianapolis 500) and the National Hot Rod Association. In Canada major organizations include the Canadian Racing Drivers Association, the Canadian Automobile Sports Club, Inc, the Canadian Auto Association, the Dominion Automobile Association, the National Automobile Association, and the Go-Kart Club of Canada. In both countries the most important races are those which count toward the winning of world championship points. Notable among these are the Canadian Grand Prix and the U.S. Grand Prix. Countless informal and unofficial races are also staged throughout the United States and Canada each year by the tens of millions of auto racing enthusiasts.

American Auto Racing Writers and Broadcasters Association Hall of Fame

ONTARIO, CALIFORNIA

Mailing Address: 922 N. Pass Ave, Burbank, 91505. Tel. (213) 842-7005. *Contact:* Mrs. Dusty Brandel, Exec. Dir. *Location:* Ontario Motor Speedway, 3901 East G St, 91764; 5 mi. E. of Pomona, 20 mi. N.W. of San Bernardino, 40 mi. E. of Los Angeles. *Admission:* Free during Speedway events. *Personnel:* Ray Marquette, Pres; Deke Houlgate, Gen. V.Pres; three regional V.Pres; Dusty Brandel, Exec. Dir. and Treas. *Nearby Halls of Fame:* Citizens Savings (Los Angeles), Softball (Long Beach, 45 mi. S.W.) and Aeronautics, Sports (San Diego, 80 mi. S.E.).

The Hall of Fame was established in 1971 by the American Auto Racing Writers and Broadcasters Association (AARWBA) as a means of recognizing and honoring individuals who have distinguished themselves throughout auto racing history, from Indianapolis to Europe and from stock cars to funny cars. In the spring of 1976, AARWBA accepted an offer from the Ontario Motor Speedway to house the Hall of Fame within the Speedway's central activities building and restaurant. The Ontario Motor Speedway was deemed appropriate because it is the only racing facility in the United States to host major events approved by each of America's major sanctioning bodies. The Hall opened in July 1976 with the aid of Ontario Motor Speedway management and financial backing from the Ogden Food Company and several racing-oriented companies and individuals. On display in the Hall of Fame are historical photographs, charcoal portraits of each member and a variety of racing memorabilia. A souvenir and gift shop are among the Speedway's facilities and plans for a motorsports library have been initiated.

Members: 29 as of 1976. The AARWBA was founded at Indianapolis in the summer of 1955 by a small group of journalists and broadcasters. It now has over 500 members from across the United States, dedicated to auto racing from a media standpoint. The Association has many functions including the Hall of Fame and the Annual Auto Racing All-American selections. Persons considered for nomination to the Hall of Fame are from all eras of auto racing as well as all aspects of motorsports, including mechanics, prominent builders, officials, drivers and members of the motorsports media. Election to the Hall of Fame is by the AARWBA membership on an annual basis.

1971

CLARK, James
Driver

Born in Fife County, Scotland; World Driving Champion 1963 – 1965; died April 1968.

Clark's career began in 1955; he was considered by many to be the greatest driver of all times. Clark was the world champion in 1963 through 1965, winning the Indianapolis 500 in 1965 and coming in second in 1964 and 1966. He was victorious in Formula I Grand Prix racing in every country. During his career he compiled 25 Grand Prix victories and was awarded the Order of the British Empire by Queen Elizabeth in 1964. Jimmy was killed in a racing accident in Hockenheim, West Germany.

FOYT, A. J.
Driver

Born January 16, 1935 in Houston, Tex; married Lucy Zarr 1955; three children, A. J, III, Jerry, Terry Lynn; National Driving Champion in 1960, 1961, 1963, 1964 and 1967; won racing's Triple Crown.

A. J. Foyt has won the Indianapolis 500 four times: in 1961, 1964, 1967 and 1977. He is second only to R. DePalma in the number of laps leading at Indianapolis, and the first man to go through an entire race at Indy without a tire change. He was the 1972 National Dirt Track Champion. In stock cars Foyt won the U.S. Auto Club title in 1968. He also won the 1964 and 1965 Daytona 400, the 1972 Daytona 500, the 1970 Riverside 500, the 1971 and 1972 Ontario 500 and the Atlanta 500. Foyt is the only driver ever to win racing's Triple Crown—the Indianapolis, Pocono and California 500s.

MAYS, Rex
Driver

National Driving Champion 1940 and 1941; died 1949.

Mays began his career in 1930 on the West Coast. Although he never won an Indy 500, he led the field at

times during 9 of the 12 races in which he participated and was awarded the pole position 4 times. He finished second at Indy in 1940 and 1941. Mays also scored many victories on the one-mile dirt tracks and was the first American to finish the 1937 International Road Race at Roosevelt Raceway. At Milwaukee in 1946 he deliberately wrecked his car to avoid hitting another driver who had been thrown onto the track. Tragically, he lost his life in a racing accident at Del Mar, Calif.
Also in: Automobile Racing Hall of Fame, Citizens Savings Hall of Fame Athletic Museum; and Indianapolis Motor Speedway Hall of Fame.

SHAW, Warren Wilbur

Driver, Promoter and Official
Born October 31, 1902 in Shelbyville, Ind; National Driving Champion 1937 and 1939; died in an airplane crash October 30, 1954 in Decatur, Ind.

Wilbur Shaw won six 100-mile championship events in 1929. He went on to win three Indianapolis 500s: in 1937 at 113.58 m.p.h.; in 1939 at 115.04 m.p.h; in 1940 at 114.28 m.p.h; he was leading in 1941 when a wheel collapsed and sent him into a wall. Shaw finished second at Indy in 1933, 1935 and 1938 and led the race at some point in 7 of the 14 Indianapolis events in which he participated. He pioneered the use of a crash helmet after a 1923 skull fracture and it was he who persuaded Tony Hulman to buy the Indianapolis Motor Speedway in 1945. Shaw served as its president and general manager until his death.
Also in: Automobile Racing Hall of Fame, Citizens Savings Hall of Fame Athletic Museum; and Indianapolis Motor Speedway Hall of Fame.

1972

FANGIO, Juan Manuel

Driver
An Argentinian of Italian descent; president of Mercedes-Benz in Argentina; World Driving Championship 1951 and 1954–1957.

Juan is the only man ever to win five world championship titles. He won the first of these at the age of 40. He was considered one of the greatest European Grand Prix drivers of the mid-1950s. By the time he retired at the age of 48 he had acquired 25 world championships, plus the 12-hour Sebring of 1956 and 1957 and the Mexican Road Race of 1953.

OLDFIELD, Berna E. "Barney"

Driver
Born January 29, 1887 in Wauseon, Ohio; began career as a professional bicycle racer; died October 4, 1946.

Barney raced bicycles until Henry Ford convinced him to drive the Ford 999. Barney had two weeks of instruction and then won the Detroit five-mile classic in 5:28. He began barnstorming the nation's tracks in such cars as the Winton Bullet, the Peerless Green Dragon, the Blitzen Benz and the front-wheel-drive Christie. Early in 1910 he averaged 131.724 m.p.h. in a Benz on the sands of Daytona Beach to surpass the world's land speed record by more than four m.p.h. In 1914 he raced his car against a daredevil pilot and the finish was so close that no one knows who won.
Also in: Automobile Racing Hall of Fame, Citizens Savings Hall of Fame Athletic Museum; and Indianapolis Motor Speedway Hall of Fame.

1973

DE PALMA, Ralph

Driver and Engineer
Born 1883 in Italy; came to the United States in 1893; National Driving Champion 1912 and 1914; uncle of race car driver Peter DePaolo; died March 31, 1956.

Regarded as one of history's all-time great drivers, Ralph DePalma began his racing career in 1903. When his career ended he had accumulated a lifetime total of 11,871 championship points, ranking him among the best in history. He scored victories on almost every major track. He drove in ten Indianapolis events, winning in 1915 with an average speed of 89.84 m.p.h. Ralph still holds the distinction of having led the Indy 500 for more laps than any other participant, 613. In 1912 DePalma was leading the Indianapolis 500 with less than a mile to go when his car died. He and his mechanic pushed the car across the finish line to be hailed as the losing heroes of the race. His other major wins were Santa Monica in 1912 and 1914, the Elgin Cup 1912 through 1914, and board track wins at Beverly Hills, Union Town, Cotati and Culver City. DePalma campaigned for, and helped design and build, the Packard V-12 that he drove to a new land speed record of 149.87 m.p.h on the measured mile at Daytona Beach in 1919.
Also in: Automobile Racing Hall of Fame, Citizens Savings Hall of Fame Athletic Museum; and Indianapolis Motor Speedway Hall of Fame.

DE PAOLO, Peter

Driver
National Driving Champion 1925 and 1927.

Peter joined his uncle, Ralph DePalma, as riding mechanic after W.W. I (1919) and made his first appearance in competition in 1922. He won the Indianapolis 500 in 1924 by averaging 101.13 m.p.h. and became the first driver to exceed 100 m.p.h. Peter won the National Driving Championship in 1925 and 1927, and placed third in 1926. He was particularly outstanding on the board tracks with victories at Fresno, Altoona, Culver City, Rockingham and Miami. He also competed in two European Grand Prix events. Although now retired, Peter DePaolo still serves racing as a goodwill ambassador.
Also in: Automobile Racing Hall of Fame, Citizens Savings Hall of Fame Athletic Museum; and Indianapolis Motor Speedway Hall of Fame.

PETTY, Richard

Driver
Born 1937; son of a well-known race car driver and golfer; as a child would help his father by keeping his cars spotless; six Grand National Titles.

Richard Petty began his driving career in 1958 and has since compiled 177 National Association of Stock Car Auto Racing Grand National racing victories in 684 starts, for a record $2,202,843. He is the only stock car competitor to top the two million mark. He has dominated the Daytona 500, winning five times. Petty attributes his success to hard work, good breaks and a crew that has been with him since his first race.

1974

BETTENHAUSEN, Melvin E. "Tony"
Driver
Born September 12, 1916 in Tinley Park, Ill; raised on a farm; quit school after eight years; two sons, Gary and Merle, both race car drivers; National Driving Champion 1951 and 1958; died 1961.

Tony began his racing career at the first races held after W.W. II. He ran on all types of tracks, dirt to pavement, scoring victories in 21 car championship events and participating in 14 Indy 500s. He placed second at Indy in 1955. Tony was one of the most enthusiastic spokesmen auto racing has ever had. He had announced his retirement on two occasions. Tony had survived so many accidents that he was considered indestructible until he was killed in a crash during a test run at the Indianapolis 500. A 10¢ bolt holding the front support fell off the car causing it to sway, and when he applied the brakes he swerved into a concrete ledge.
Also in: Automobile Racing Hall of Fame, Citizens Savings Hall of Fame Athletic Museum; and Indianapolis Motor Speedway Hall of Fame.

CHEVROLET, Louis
Driver and Engineer
Born 1878 in France; eldest of three brothers (Arthur and Gaston were also race car drivers); came to the United States in 1905; worked as mechanic for a New York importer of European cars; died 1941 at age 63.

Five years after his arrival in the United States, Louis began his racing career by driving a Fiat to victory in a three-mile race against Barney Oldfield and Walter Christie. He drove for Buick and several other manufacturers before he began building his own cars. His cars scored many notable victories including the Indianapolis 500 in 1920 (driven by his brother Gaston) and in 1921 (driven by Tom Milton). As a driver, Louis won the 395-mile 1909 Cobe Trophy Road Race and many events on the board speedways. He retired from driving in 1923.
Also in: Indianapolis Motor Speedway Hall of Fame.

COOPER, Earl
Driver and Engineer
Born 1886 in Nebraska; raised in California; worked in a San Jose garage as a mechanic; National Driving Champion 1913, 1915 and 1917; died October 22, 1965, at age 80.

Cooper's career began about 1908 on the Pacific Coast with moderate success. In 1913 he became a consistent winner for Stutz. He was particularly outstanding in road-course events during the early portion of his career. Later, he enjoyed almost equal success on the board tracks, scoring major victories as late as 1926. Earl was racing's first three-time national champion. He compiled a lifetime total of 13,530 championship points from 1912 through 1927, a total not surpassed until the 1960s. His racing career was interrupted twice by decisions to retire, but he still managed to win virtually every major race of his day including the Santa Monica and Corona road races and the Elgin Cup. He later served as an official and built Miller-powered race cars for Studebaker as well as Marmon.
Also in: Automobile Racing Hall of Fame, Citizens Savings Hall of Fame Athletic Museum; and Indianapolis Motor Speedway Hall of Fame.

DONOHUE, Mark
Driver and Engineer
Mark Donohue raced successfully in three types of motor sports, including the Indianapolis 500, sports cars and stock cars. He won the Indianapolis race in 1972 at a record-breaking speed of 163.465 m.p.h. He also took the Can-Am championship, a Trans-Am championship and the Riverside 500. A perfectionist in everything he did, he was a careful, systematic driver with great stamina. In 1975 he came out of retirement to race Formula I in Europe. It was there that he was fatally injured.

GURNEY, Dan
Driver and Engineer
Born 1931.

Dan began his racing career in the early 1950s on the West Coast. He won three championship Grand Prix races before the 1967 Belgian Grand Prix, which he won in a car designed and built by his own firm. He won seven U.S. Auto Club National Championship races on road courses. Additionally, he took five Riverside 500s, placed second in 1968 and 1969 at the Indianapolis 500 and third in 1970. He retired from driving in 1971 to concentrate on his own car design and construction firm.
Also in: Automobile Racing Hall of Fame, Citizens Savings Hall of Fame Athletic Museum.

MEYER, Louis
Driver and Engineer
National Driving Champion 1928, 1929 and 1933.

Meyer's career began in 1927. In 1928 he initiated his chain of three Indianapolis 500 victories, setting a speed record of 99.48 m.p.h. He won again in 1933 at a speed of 104.16 m.p.h. and in 1936 with a speed of 109.07 m.p.h. Meyer's record included victories on several one-mile dirt tracks. Following his retirement from driving in 1939, he joined forces with Dale Drake to build the Offenhauser engines that powered 18 consecutive winning cars at Indianapolis.
Also in: Automobile Racing Hall of Fame, Citizens Savings Hall of Fame Athletic Museum; and Indianapolis Motor Speedway Hall of Fame.

MILTON, Tommy
Driver, Engineer and Official
National Driving Champion 1920 and 1921.

Tommy Milton began his career in 1914 on the dirt tracks of the Midwest, but he was equally successful on paved and board tracks. Milton was the first person to win two Indianapolis 500s—in 1921 and 1923. He was also the first driver to win two consecutive National Driving Championships. Milton helped design and build a twin-engine Duesenberg that he drove to a new record of 156.046 m.p.h. for the measured mile at Daytona Beach in 1920. Later he served for four years as chief steward of Indianapolis.
Also in: Automobile Racing Hall of Fame, Citizens Savings Hall of Fame Athletic Museum; and Indianapolis Motor Speedway Hall of Fame.

MURPHY, James "Jimmy"
Driver
National Driving Champion 1922 and 1924; died September 15, 1924.

Murphy's racing career was a short five years, but during that time he managed to compile nearly 10,000 championship points. Overall he won 16 championship races including the Indianapolis 500 in 1922 with a record-breaking speed of 94.48 m.p.h. He was the first American to win the French Grand Prix. His other victories include three at Beverly Hills, three at Altoona, two at Fresno, two at Cotati and one at Kansas City. Jimmy lost his life in a crash at the Syracuse Speedway.
Also in: Automobile Racing Hall of Fame, Citizens Savings Hall of Fame Athletic Museum; and Indianapolis Motor Speedway Hall of Fame.

STEWART, John "Jackie"
Driver
Born 1939; from Scotland; World Championship Title 1969, 1971 and 1973.

Jackie was active from 1964 until 1973 when he retired from driving. He was always a top contender on the Formula I circuit. In his only Indianapolis 500 appearance, his car gave out near the finish line while he was leading the field to victory. During his career he won 27 Grand Prix races and held the World Title three times.

1975

HARROUN, Ray
Driver and Engineer
National Driving Champion 1910.

Ray was one of the top racers of the early days. He won important victories at Play de Rey, Calif. and several 200-mile races in Atlanta and at the Indy Motor Speedway. Harroun won the first Indy 500 in May 1911 at an average speed of 74.59 m.p.h. in a six-cylinder Marmon, which he helped pioneer. After his retirement from driving, this descendant of Arabian chieftains designed race cars for the Maxwell Company, including one to run on kerosene. Ray was the first person to use a rearview mirror.
Also in: Indianapolis Motor Speedway Hall of Fame.

HORN, Ted
Driver
Born in Glendale, Calif, as Eylard Theodore Von Horn; National Driving Champion 1946, 1947 and 1948; killed in a crash at DuQuoin Speedway October 10, 1948.

Horn's driving career began in 1930. He proved to be one of the most consistent drivers of all times, and was the first to win three consecutive National Driving Championships. Horn finished fourth or better in nine consecutive events at Indianapolis and won the pole position in 1947. He also enjoyed great success on the dirt tracks. Away from the track he was a goodwill ambassador for auto racing.
Also in: Automobile Racing Hall of Fame, Citizens Savings Hall of Fame Athletic Museum; and Indianapolis Motor Speedway Hall of Fame.

1976

ANDRETTI, Mario
Driver
Born 1940 near Trieste, Italy, on the Adriatic Sea; spent over three years in a refugee camp after W.W. II; moved to the United States in 1955; National Driving Champion 1965, 1966 and 1969.

Andretti was voted Indianapolis Rookie of the Year in 1965. He stands second in all-time championship point standings with over 26,000 achieved in 10 seasons, and is second in all-time championship wins with 32. Andretti took the Indianapolis 500 in 1969, the Sebring in 1972 and the Daytona 500 in 1973. In 1971 he won the Questor Grand Prix at Ontario, Calif, and the South African Grand Prix.

BRITT, Bloys
Motorsports Editor
Former football player; died 1974 of a heart attack.

Britt became motorsports editor for the Associated Press in 1963. He helped break the sex barrier in the National Association for Stock Car Auto Racing circle when he backed a movement to have women allowed in the pits and garage areas at the stock car events. His honesty and integrity won him thousands of friends and fans throughout the country.

BRYAN, James
Driver
From Phoenix, Ariz; fun-loving, cigar-smoking cowboy; National Driving Champion 1954, 1956 and 1957; died at age 33.

Jimmy Bryan, 6 ft, 220 lbs, is recognized as one of auto racing's greatest dirt-track drivers, but he gained additional renown through his victories on paved courses at Indianapolis and Monza. He won the National Driving Championship three times and placed second in 1955. Concrrently, he won seven consecutive dirt-track championship races. Jimmy won the Indy 500 in 1958 at an average speed of 133.79 m.p.h. with an Epperly chassis and an Offenhauser engine. In earlier attempts at Indy he finished second and third. In 1957 and 1958 he won and placed second, respectively, in the Monza 500 in Italy. Jimmy died during a race when his safety harness broke while crashing and he was thrown around inside his car.
Also in: Automobile Racing Hall of Fame, Citizens Savings Hall of Fame Athletic Museum; and Indianapolis Motor Speedway Hall of Fame.

LOCKHART, Frank
Driver and Engineer
Died 1928.

Lockhart won the Indianapolis 500 in 1926 with an average speed of 95.9 m.p.h. He led that race for 91 laps in 1927 after setting a qualifying record of 120.1 m.p.h. in a Miller Special with the help of a patented intercooler that he had developed. At Daytona Beach in 1928 Frank drove a Miller-powered Stutz Blackhawk Special with a V-16 engine that he built from two V-8 engines. He covered the measured mile in 207.552 m.p.h. in that car. His other recorded triumphs were at Altoona, Charlotte and

Rockingham, and he set world speed marks at Muroc and Atlantic City. Lockhart lost his life at Daytona Beach after a record-setting day when a tire on his car failed.
Also in: Indianapolis Motor Speedway Hall of Fame.

MULFORD, Ralph
Driver
National Driving Champion 1911.

Ralph Mulford raced from 1907 through 1925. He compiled a list of victories in all types of competition, but was especially good in long-distance events. He won the 1910 Elgin Cup races and the 1911 Vanderbilt Cup Race, and placed second in the 1911 Indianapolis 500. His victories on the board tracks include the 300-mile inaugural race at Des Moines and a new stock-car record for Hudson and Chandler. Mulford was deeply religious and held a steadfast conviction never to race on Sunday.
Also in: Automobile Racing Hall of Fame, Citizens Savings Hall of Fame Athletic Museum; and Indianapolis Motor Speedway Hall of Fame.

NUVOLARI, Tazio
Driver
Born in Italy; had a very sickly childhood.

One of Italy's all-time great drivers, Tazio achieved his greatest fame on the Grand Prix circuits of Europe. He won the 1935 Grand Prix at Nurburgring in the last of the Monopostas with 1 gal. engine. He drove successfully for the Auto Union and Mercedes teams that dominated European racing in the 1930s. During Nuvolari's brief American appearances he won the revived Vanderbilt Cup Race at Roosevelt Raceway.

Induction Year Unrecorded

RICKENBACKER, Edward Vernon "Eddie"
Driver, Promotor and Official
Born 1890 in Columbus, Ohio; forced to leave school at age 13 due to father's death; a pilot in W.W. I, shot down 22 planes; president of Eastern Airlines 1938–1959; died 1973.

Eddie Rickenbacker, known as America's "Ace of Aces," began his career in auto racing in 1910 and became one of the top competitors of the 1913–1916 era. He participated in the 1911 inaugural Indianapolis 500 as a relief driver. In 1914 he won a series of important dirt-track victories as well as triumphs on the new board speedways. During his driving career Eddie won seven major championship events, earning more than 5000 championship points. In 1927 he headed a group of investors who purchased the Indianapolis Motor Speedway. As president of the Speedway he guided it through the economic difficulties of the 1930s. He served as chairman of the American Automobile Association Contest Board for several years before selling the Speedway in 1945 to A. Hulman, Jr.
Also in: Automobile Racing Hall of Fame, Citizens Savings Hall of Fame Athletic Museum; and Indianapolis Motor Speedway Hall of Fame.

ROSE, Mauri
Driver
Born 1906 in Columbus, Ohio; National Driving Champion 1936.

Mauri Rose is one of four Indianapolis 500 winners to take that race three times: in 1941 at 115.12 m.p.h, in 1947 at 116.34 m.p.h, and in 1948 at 119.81 m.p.h. He drove at Indianapolis every year from 1937 to 1957, made the full distance without relief seven times, and placed fourth or better four times. He was the first American to finish the Vanderbilt Cup Race in 1936.
Also in: Automobile Racing Hall of Fame, Citizens Savings Hall of Fame Athletic Museum; and Indianapolis Motor Speedway Hall of Fame.

VUKOVICH, William, Sr.
Driver
Born December 13, 1918, in Calif; National Midget Champion 1951; killed in an accident May 30, 1955.

Bill Vukovich is one of four drivers to score two consecutive victories at the Indianapolis 500. He drove a total of 1690 miles in competition at Indianapolis and led during 1210 of those miles. He won the Indianapolis in 1953 and 1954. Bill died in a crash involving slower cars on the track while trying for his third straight victory at Indy.
Also in: Automobile Racing Hall of Fame, Citizens Savings Hall of Fame Athletic Museum; and Indianapolis Motor Speedway Hall of Fame.

Indianapolis Motor Speedway Hall of Fame

INDIANAPOLIS, INDIANA

Mailing Address: Box 24152, 46224. Tel. (317) 241-2501. *Contact:* Al Bloemker, V.Pres. *Location:* On W. 16 St, between the Speedway's No. 1 and No. 2 turns. *Admission:* 9 to 5 daily, closed Christmas. Adults $1.00, children under 16 free. *Personnel:* Tony Hulman, Pres; Al Bloemker, V.Pres. *Nearby Halls of Fame:* Basketball, Sports (Indianapolis), Football (Cincinnati, Ohio, 106 mi. S.E.), Business (Chicago, Ill, 181 mi. N.W.), Sports (St. Louis, Mo, 235 mi. S.W.).

The original auto racing Hall of Fame was established in 1952 by the American Automobile Association's (AAA) Contest Board in cooperation with the Edison Institute and the Ford Foundation. The purpose was to perpetuate the names and memories of outstanding racing personalities and to demonstrate racing's contribution to the development of the automobile industry. The Contest Board selected 17 members to the Hall of Fame before it disbanded in 1955. In 1956 a museum was created for automobile racing on the Indianapolis Speedway grounds. Requests for a Hall of Fame were so numerous that the old records were gathered from the Ford Foundation and action was taken to form a new Hall in the Speedway's museum. Annual election of new members to this Hall of Fame began in 1962. The Indianapolis Motor Speedway's Hall of Fame became a member of the Association of Sports Museums and Halls of Fame in 1971. The museum now holds dozens of race cars on display, including 21 of those that have won the Indy 500. Much of the Western Wing is devoted to a representative collection of classic and antique passenger cars. Trophies, race engines, helmets and goggles from early days and other items of racing memorabilia have also been assembled. The impressive Louis Chevrolet Memorial has been erected in the southwest corner of the building. Nearby is a snack bar and a souvenir and gift shop selling books about racing, racing jackets, T-shirts and photographs. The Speedway also offers a motel, dining facilities and a golf course. Bus tours of the two-and-a-half mile track are available for 50¢ when the track is not in use. This Hall of Fame is a member of the Association of Sports Museums and Halls of Fame.

Members: 46 as of 1975. The early AAA Contest Board plus press, TV and radio representatives and race historians made up the original selection committee. In 1952 they elected ten members to the Hall of Fame from persons active in racing prior to 1911. Seven more were elected in 1953 and 1954. A distinctive Hall of Fame membership medallion was created in 1962 for each of the 17 early inductees. These are displayed in the Speedway's museum. The new election committee consists of 100 qualified individuals from living Hall of Fame members, members of the Speedway Foundation's Board of Directors, press, TV and radio representatives, race historians and representatives of accessory companies associated with the sport. The requirements for candidates are: that they be drivers, mechanics or race officials from any era of racing; that they be placed on the ballot after a minimum 20-year waiting period from the date of their initial active participation in the sport; and that they receive 75% of the committee's vote.

1952

CHEVROLET, Louis
Driver and Engineer
See entry in American Auto Racing Writers and Broadcasters Association Hall of Fame, 1974.

DINGLEY, Bert
Driver
National Driving Champion 1909.

Bert earned the right to represent the United States in the second Vanderbilt Cup Race in 1905. In 1909 he was recipient of the American Automobile Association's National Driving Championship in recognition of his consistent performance in six major starts that season in which he placed second twice, third once and fourth once. His victories also include the San Francisco-to-Portland Road Race and the 202-mile Santa Monica Road Race. Bert earned national recognition as he compiled an enviable record annually until he suffered serious injuries in a 1914 racing accident at Tacoma, Wash.

FIRESTONE, Harvey Samuel
Industrialist
Born 1868; raised on a farm in Ohio; first job was a clerk and bookeeper; died 1938 at age 70.

Harvey became interested in rubber tires early in life. This interest grew while he worked for a carriage factory, and in 1900 he founded the Firestone Tire and Rubber Company. The company produced its first tires made of solid rubber in 1903, and Firestone's keen interest in technological progress caused his company to lead in technical improvements. He was quick to recognize speedway racing as an outdoor laboratory and proving ground for his products. He welcomed competition and safety improvements in order to emphasize the quality of his passenger car tires. Firestone tires won at the first Indianapolis 500. The Firestone racing division has aided greatly in the steadily growing popularity of motorsports.
Also in: Automobile Racing Hall of Fame, Citizens Savings Hall of Fame Athletic Museum.

FISHER, Carl G.
Promoter and Driver
Born 1874 in Greenburg, Ind.

In 1902 Fisher competed against other major drivers of the day in a series of exhibition events. Later he persuaded three of his business associates to join him in building the Indianapolis Motor Speedway. Fisher also urged auto manufacturers to support plans for speedways so they could prove the reliability of their products in competition. In 1923 he stepped down as president of the Motor Speedway to pursue his business interests. Fisher was the promotor for the Lincoln Highway, America's first transcontinental road, and became involved in the building up of the Miami Beach resort areas.

FORD, Henry
Driver and Car Owner
Born 1863 on a farm in Dearborn, Mich; began career as a machinist in Detroit; one of the all-time greats in the automobile industry; died 1947.

Ford began experimenting with engines about 1890, completing his first gasoline engine in 1893. He organized the Ford Motor Company in 1903. Ford was the first American to establish a land speed record when he drove his Ford 999 race car at 91.37 m.p.h. over a measured mile on the frozen surface of Lake St. Clair near Detroit, surpassing the mark set by a Frenchman several months earlier. Henry Ford considered racing an important factor in the Ford Motor Company's sales and promotion program. He always tried to be represented by a team of cars at the Indianapolis 500.
Also in: Automobile Racing Hall of Fame, Citizens Savings Hall of Fame Athletic Museum.

HARROUN, Ray
Driver and Engineer
See entry in American Auto Racing Writers and Broadcasters Association Hall of Fame, 1975.

MYERS, Theodore E. "Pop"
Promoter and Official
Born 1874 in Williamsburg, Ind; died March 14, 1954.

Pop Myers joined the staff in 1910 and devoted more than 40 years to the improvement of the Indianapolis Motor Speedway and motorsports in general. He was

general manager in 1914, treasurer in 1915 and vice president from 1927 until his death. He served as a member of the American Automobile Association Contest Board for many years and promoted the American racing fraternity throughout Europe.
Also in: Automobile Racing Hall of Fame, Citizens Savings Hall of Fame Athletic Museum.

OLDFIELD, Berna E.
Driver
See entry in the American Auto Racing Writers and Broadcasters Association Hall of Fame, 1972.
Also in: Automobile Racing Hall of Fame, Citizens Savings Hall of Fame Athletic Museum.

VANDERBILT, William Kissam
Driver and Promoter
Born December 12, 1849 in Staten Island, N.Y; son of William Henry Vanderbilt; became an officer or director of various railroads; helped found the Vanderbilt Clinic in New York City; died July 22, 1920.

Vanderbilt sponsored the famous Vanderbilt Cup Races beginning in 1904. These races provided tremendous stimulation for the automobile industry, but in 1910 they had to be discontinued because the crowds along the route became too difficult to handle. Vanderbilt earned recognition as a driver by scoring several noteworthy victories and finishing third in the 318-mile *Internationale Circuit des Ardennes* in France in 1902. He also broke Henry Ford's 999 land speed record at Daytona Beach in 1904.
Also in: Automobile Racing Hall of Fame, Citizens Savings Hall of Fame Athletic Museum.

WAGNER, Fred J.
Official
Fred Wagner's career began in 1899 and spanned more than three decades. He served as official starter for most of the championship events on all types of courses, setting the standards for other officials. Fred's showmanship contributed to the steadily growing popularity of auto racing as well as to his $1000 per day salary. His advice was sought by promoters and participants alike. Fred Wagner was as well known by fans as any prominent driver of the era.

1953 – 1954

BURMAN, Robert
Driver
Died 1916 in Calif.

As early as 1903 Bob Burman tested cars for Buick. He competed successfully in most of the major championship events on all types of race courses, including board tracks. Bob won the first feature race at the Indianapolis Motor Speedway at an average speed of 53.7 m.p.h. Five persons were killed during those first races. Plans were initiated immediately for the resurfacing of the track with brick. Burman is best known for a series of record runs, 24-hour events, match races and exhibition appearances against many of the great drivers of the day. In 1911 on the Sands at Daytona Beach, Fla, Burman shattered Barney Oldfield's land speed record by more than ten miles per hour, averaging 141.732 for a measured mile. While he was driving a Peugeot in the Corona Road Race in California, a tire blew out. The car went out of control, hitting two poles and a parked car. Bob and his mechanic were thrown from the car. Bob's wife rushed to him and he died in her arms.
Also in: Automobile Racing Hall of Fame, Citizens Savings Hall of Fame Athletic Museum.

COOPER, Earl
Driver and Engineer
See entry in American Auto Racing Writers and Broadcasters Association Hall of Fame, 1974.
Also in: Automobile Racing Hall of Fame, Citizens Savings Hall of Fame Athletic Museum.

DE PALMA, Ralph
Driver and Engineer
See entry in American Auto Racing Writers and Broadcasters Association Hall of Fame, 1973.
Also in: Automobile Racing Hall of Fame, Citizens Savings Hall of Fame Athletic Museum.

MILTON, Tommy
Driver, Engineer and Official
See entry in American Auto Racing Writers and Broadcasters Association Hall of Fame, 1974.
Also in: Automobile Racing Hall of Fame, Citizens Savings Hall of Fame Athletic Museum.

MULFORD, Ralph
Driver
See entry in American Auto Racing Writers and Broadcasters Association Hall of Fame, 1976.
Also in: Automobile Racing Hall of Fame, Citizens Savings Hall of Fame Athletic Museum.

RESTA, Dario
Driver
Born in England of Italian parents; National Driving Champion 1916; died 1924.

Resta competed successfully in European events from 1909 until 1915, when he came to the United States. His 1915 victories include the American Grand Prix, the Vanderbilt Cup, and board track events at Chicago and Sheepshead Bay. During the 1916 season he won the Vanderbilt Cup Race again, took the Indianapolis and a variety of other major events on the board speedways. During his career he earned more than 7000 championship points, ranking him third among drivers active from 1909 to 1920. Resta was killed in 1924 in a racing accident at England's Brooklands Speedway.

RICKENBACKER, Edward Vernon
Driver, Promoter and Official
See entry in American Auto Racing Writers and Broadcasters Association Hall of Fame (Induction Year Unrecorded).
Also in: Automobile Racing Hall of Fame, Citizens Savings Hall of Fame Athletic Museum.

1962

DUESENBERG, Fred
Engineer
Fred and his younger brother Augie created, designed and built championship cars for more than 20 years. The

Duesenberg entries provided the principal competition for Miller Specials during the 1920s. Duesenbergs won at Indianapolis in 1924, 1925 and 1927, finishing second or third in four of the other seven Indy events. Fred believed in proving the speed and durability of his products in competition. A Duesenberg driven by Pete DePaolo was the first Indy 500 winner to exceed 100 m.p.h. Tommy Milton drove a Duesenberg to a new land speed record of 156.046 m.p.h. in 1920 and Jimmy Murphy drove one to victory in the 1921 French Grand Prix.

1963

DE PAOLO, Peter
Driver
See entry in American Auto Racing Writers and Broadcasters Association Hall of Fame, 1973.
Also in: Automobile Racing Hall of Fame, Citizens Savings Hall of Fame Athletic Museum.

DUESENBERG, August
Engineer
Augie contributed all of his effort and ideas to the development of the early Mason race cars and the various other ingenious creations that carried the Duesenberg name to victories for more than 20 years. Augie was particularly interested in the development of smaller racing engines. Remaining in the shadow of his older brother Fred for most of his career, he designed and built the Duesenberg car in which a Cummins Diesel engine was used for the first nonstop performance in the Indianapolis 500. Ultimately, Augie assumed complete responsibility for Duesenberg's racing activities as his brother devoted his attention to corporate affairs.

HARTZ, Harry
Driver and Car Owner
Wheeler-Shebler Trophy (a permanent possession); National Driving Champion 1926.

Hartz was one of the most consistent drivers in history. He won the National Driving Championship in 1926 and scored major victories on the boards at Fresno, Culver City and Atlantic City. Hartz scored three seconds and two fourths at the Indianapolis Motor Speedway 1922–1927. He also participated in many stock car speed and endurance runs. After retiring as a driver following a near-fatal accident, Harry enjoyed success as a car owner. He prepared the Hartz-Miller cars that were driven to victory in the Indianapolis 500 in 1930 and 1932. In later years, Hartz served as a 500 official and a member of the technical committee.
Also in: Automobile Racing Hall of Fame, Citizens Savings Hall of Fame Athletic Museum.

MAYS, Rex
Driver
See entry in American Auto Racing Writers and Broadcasters Association Hall of Fame, 1971.
Also in: Automobile Racing Hall of Fame, Citizens Savings Hall of Fame Athletic Museum.

MEYER, Louis
Driver and Engineer
See entry in American Auto Racing Writers and Broadcasters Association Hall of Fame, 1974.
Also in: Automobile Racing Hall of Fame, Citizens Savings Hall of Fame Athletic Museum.

MILLER, Harry
Engineer
Harry developed the winning Miller engine and later built complete Miller-engine race cars that were to outperform all rivals on most race courses. He built rear-drive and front drive cars with equal success and later designed a rear-engine four-wheel-drive race car. His engines were developed into Offenhauser engines that later became known as Meyer-Drake Offie.

SHAW, Warren Wilbur
Driver, Promoter and Official
See entry in American Auto Racing Writers and Broadcasters Association Hall of Fame, 1971.
Also in: Automobile Racing Hall of Fame, Citizens Savings Hall of Fame Athletic Museum.

STUTZ, Harry
Engineer
In 1911 Harry designed and built the Stutz cars that competed successfully in the nation's motorsports events for a period of eight years. Harry Stutz became associated with racing by organizing the Marion team. Earl Cooper and Gil Anderson did most of the driving, winning at Elgin, Santa Monica, Corona and Point Loma. Stutz cars won the 1915 Minneapolis 500 and major events on the boards at Sheepshead Bay and Chicago, finishing well in all of the first five Indianapolis races. After selling the original company, Harry sponsored the Miller-engine car that Tommy Milton drove to victory at Indianapolis in 1923.

WILCOX, Howard "Howdy"
Driver
Howdy was among the first ten to place in four of the eleven 500-mi. races in which he participated at Indianapolis. He won the 500 in 1915 at an average speed of 88.05 m.p.h. Howdy also took the 1916 American Grand Prix at Santa Monica at a speed of 85.59 m.p.h. He was outstanding on the board tracks in the early 1920s, and served as relief driver to help Tommy Milton win the Indianapolis 500 in 1923.

1964

ALLISON, James A.
Promoter
Allison, Carl Fisher, Arthur Newby and Frank Wheeler pooled their ideas and resources to become the four founders of the Indianapolis Motor Speedway. The track's success was due in large part to Allison's sound business advice. He succeeded Carl Fisher as president shortly after W.W. I. Because of his interest in engine development, Allison formed Allison's Engineering Company, intending to stimulate the building of better race cars. This company is now the Allison Division of General Motors.

CHEVROLET, Gaston
Driver
Left France as a young man; joined his two older brothers Arthur and Louis (both race car drivers) in the United States.

Gaston began to attract attention in auto racing by finishing well in four races, including a 250-mile event on the boards at Cincinnati in 1917. He was suspended by the American Automobile Association Contest Board for the 12 months of 1918 for participating in unsanctioned events. Driving again in 1919, he placed tenth with a Chevrolet Frontenac at Indianapolis, scoring three important board track victories later that season. In 1920 he won the Indianapolis race at an average speed of 88.62 m.p.h. in a Chevrolet Monroe built by his brother Louis. At the peak of his career, he suffered fatal injuries in a crash at Beverly Hills, Calif.

HEARNE, Eddie
Driver
National Driving Champion 1923; died late 1950s.

Prior to 1911 Hearne won five out of seven free-for-all races at Indianapolis. He placed fourth in the Cobe Trophy Race in 1909, fifth in the Vanderbilt Cup Race of 1910, second in the Savannah Grand Prix in 1911 and first in a 200-mi. race at Cincinnati. After participating in the first two Indianapolis Memorial Day classics, Hearne retired from motorsports, returning to active competition after W.W. I. He finished second in the Indy event in 1919, third in 1922 and fourth in 1923. Hearne had been successful on the board speedways in 1927 when he retired after finishing seventh at Indy.
Also in: Automobile Racing Hall of Fame, Citizens Savings Hall of Fame Athletic Museum.

HORN, Ted
Driver
See entry in American Auto Racing Writers and Broadcasters Association Hall of Fame, 1975.
Also in: Automobile Racing Hall of Fame, Citizens Savings Hall of Fame Athletic Museum.

MURPHY, James
Driver
See entry in American Auto Racing Writers and Broadcasters Association Hall of Fame, 1974.
Also in: Automobile Racing Hall of Fame, Citizens Savings Hall of Fame Athletic Museum.

1967

HULMAN, Anton
Promoter
Tony Hulman purchased the Indianapolis Motor Speedway after W.W. II, restored its aging facilities and established the Speedway museum. He increased the prize money for the 500 from $96,250 to $1,015,686 in 1974. Hulman guided auto racing through its transition period from the American Automobile Association to the U.S. Automobile Club and served as racing's goodwill ambassador on his trips to Canada, Mexico, Japan and the European countries. He is still president of the Indianapolis Motor Speedway.
Also in: Automobile Racing Hall of Fame, Citizens Savings Hall of Fame Athletic Museum.

ROSE, Mauri
Driver
See entry in American Auto Racing Writers and Broadcasters Association Hall of Fame (Induction Year Unrecorded).
Also in: Automobile Racing Hall of Fame, Citizens Savings Hall of Fame Athletic Museum.

1968

BETTENHAUSEN, Melvin E. "Tony"
Driver
See entry in American Auto Racing Writers and Broadcasters Association Hall of Fame, 1974.
Also in: Automobile Racing Hall of Fame, Citizens Savings Hall of Fame Athletic Museum.

LOCKHART, Frank
Driver and Engineer
See entry in American Auto Racing Writers and Broadcasters Association Hall of Fame, 1976.

MARCENAC, Jean
Mechanic
Jean Marcenac came to the United States from Europe soon after W.W. I and enjoyed a successful 40-year career, scoring victories on most of the nation's tracks. During a six-year period beginning in 1927 his cars won four Indianapolis 500s: George Sounders in 1927, Ray Keech in 1929, Billy Arnold in 1930 and Fred Frane in 1932. Later his supercharged Novi Specials set several records at the Indianapolis Motor Speedway.

1969

HENNING, Harry "Cotton"
Mechanic and Car Owner
For more than 25 years, beginning in the early 1920s, Cotton served as crew chief for many drivers, successfully using Duesenberg, Miller, Maserati and Offenhauser engines. His winners at the Indianapolis 500 include Pete DePaolo in 1925, Bill Cummings in 1934 and Wilbur Shaw in 1939 and 1940. Ted Horn finished third and fourth at Indy in 1947 and 1948 in a car owned by Henning.

MOORE, Lou
Driver and Car Owner
Lou Moore started in nine events at Indianapolis, was on the pole once and led the field twice, finished second once and third twice. His championship victories include races at Altoona, Woodbridge and Syracuse. Lou owned the 1938 winning car at the 500, driven by Floyd Roberts. Moore built and owned the Blue Crown Spark Plug Specials in which Mauri Rose and Bill Holland dominated the 500 for three straight years.

1970

CUMMINGS, Bill
Driver
National Driving Champion 1934; died in 1938.

Wild Bill began his career on the half-mile dirt tracks. He moved up to become winner of the 1934 Indianapolis 500 with a record speed of 104.863 m.p.h. That same year he had accumulated enough points to capture the

National Driving Championship. Altogether, he was in nine races at Indy, placing third, fourth and sixth, and was awarded the pole position twice. His other wins came at Syracuse, Langhorne, Detroit and Legion Ascot. Bill placed seventh in the 1936 International Road Race at Roosevelt Raceway. He was killed in a crash when his car slid on wet pavement while homeward bound in a blinding rain storm.
Also in: Automobile Racing Hall of Fame, Citizens Savings Hall of Fame Athletic Museum.

HEPBURN, Ralph
Driver
Began career as a dirt track motorcycle racer; died May 16, 1948.

Ralph Hepburn participated in 15 Indianapolis 500s over a 20-year period and never won a race. He led the field on his rookie appearance in 1925 for several laps and again in his final Indy effort in 1946. In the 1937 race Hepburn ran the closest second in history, losing by 2.16 seconds. He took third place in 1931, fourth in 1941 and fifth in 1935, but ranks among the Indianapolis all-time mileage leaders. In 1946 he set new one-lap and four-lap records in a front drive Novi Special. Ralph died in a crash at Indy while practicing for the 1948 classic.

1972

VUKOVICH, William, Sr.
Driver
See entry in American Auto Racing Writers and Broadcasters Association Hall of Fame (Induction Year Unrecorded).
Also in: Automobile Racing Hall of Fame, Citizens Savings Hall of Fame Athletic Museum.

1973

BRYAN, James
Driver
See entry in American Auto Racing Writers and Broadcasters Association Hall of Fame, 1976.
Also in: Automobile Racing Hall of Fame, Citizens Savings Hall of Fame Athletic Museum.

1975

BIGNOTTI, George
Mechanic
George Bignotti has more U.S. Automobile Club (USAC) championship victories to his credit than any other chief mechanic. He came to the Indianapolis Motor Speedway in 1954 as a crew member and by the beginning of the 1975 season he had a total of 68 triumphs. George's cars have had wins scored at the Indianapolis Motor Speedway by A. J. Foyt in 1961 and 1964, Graham Hill in 1966, Al Unser in 1970 and 1971, and Gordon Johncock in 1973. Joe Leonard and Wally Dallenbach won for him at Ontario in 1971 and 1973, and Joe Leonard gained victory again at Pocono in 1972. Seven USAC National Driving Championships have also been won in George's cars, four by Foyt, two by Leonard and one by Unser.

1976

BERGERE, Cliff
Driver
Cliff Bergere is one of two persons who have driven in 16 Indianapolis 500s. He has completed more miles in competition at Indy than any other driver in the history of the track except A. J. Foyt, who surpassed the 6130-mile mark in 1975. Cliff led the field on three different occasions, 1941, 1946 and 1947, and was awarded the pole position in 1946. He finished third twice and eight times placed among the first ten. In 1941 Cliff was the first driver to go the full distance of the race in a conventional race car without making a pit stop.

DAWSON, Joseph
Driver
Joe was a consistent winner of outstanding events during his first year of driving (1910). His forte was truck racing, but he is remembered best for winning the 1912 Indianapolis 500 at a speed of 78.72 m.p.h. in a National. Joe finished second in the 1910 Vanderbilt Cup Race, only 26 seconds behind the winner. He retired in 1914, but was appointed to the American Automobile Association Contest Board and served there until his death shortly after W.W. II.

International Motor Contest Association Hall of Fame

OMAHA, NEBRASKA

Mailing Address: 112344 Pacific St, 68154. Tel. (712) 328-9400. *Contact:* Gaylan Brotherson, Pres. *Location:* Interstate 80; 50 mi. N.E. of Lincoln, 80 mi. S. of Sioux City, Iowa, 100 mi. S.W. of Des Moines, Iowa, 165 mi. N. of Topeka, Kans, 200 mi. N.W. of Kansas City, Mo. *Personnel:* Gaylan Brotherson, Pres; Keith Knaack, V.Pres; Lyle Klaine, Secy. Call for information. *Nearby Halls of Fame:* Agriculture (Kansas City, Mo, 200 mi. S.E, Bonner Springs, Kans, 190 mi. S.E.), Dog Racing (Abilene, Kans, 180 mi. S.W.), Roller Skating (Lincoln, 50 mi. S.W.).

The International Motor Contest Association was founded in 1911 by the American Auto Association. In 1915 the International Motor Contest Association left the American Auto Association and became a separate entity. The purpose for the Association is to design and promote stock car and sprint car racing and to create a good image of auto racing. The Hall honors those individuals who were outstanding drivers, or national top drivers, or outstanding promoters of the sport. Pictures of individuals, events and cars are housed in the Hall.

Members: 5 as of 1977. Eligibility requirements are that the individual must be an outstanding driver in his field, a national top driver, or a promoter that is outstanding. Nominations are made to the Board of Directors and then the Board votes on whom should be inducted. There is no set limit to the number of inductees at any time. Each member of the Hall is awarded a plaque, and a picture of the individual is placed in the Hall of Fame.

1971 BEAUCHAMP, Johnny. Driver.
COLLINS, Emory. Driver.
SCHRADER, Gus. Driver.
SWEENEY, Al. Promoter.
WINKLEY, Frank. Promoter.

National Stock Car Racing Hall of Fame

DARLINGTON, SOUTH CAROLINA

Mailing Address: Drawer 500, 29532. Tel. (803) 393-4041. *Contact:* Bill Kiser, Dir, Public Relations. *Location:* Approx. 10 mi. N.W. of exit 53 on I95 in S.C, at the junction of highways 34 and 151; 70 mi. N.E. of Columbia, 75 mi. S.E. of Charlotte, N.C. *Admission:* Free 9 to 5 daily. *Personnel:* Frank Vehorn, Pres; Jack Flowers, V.Pres; Pal Parker, Secy.-Treas; Bill Kiser, Dir. Public Relations; five mem. Bd. of Dirs. *Nearby Hall of Fame:* Golf (Pinehurst, N.C, 65 mi. N.E.)

The Hall of Fame is housed in the Joe Weatherly Stock Car Museum. This museum was built in 1965 as part of the Darlington International Raceway to preserve the memories of people and events involved in motorsports. Since its opening the facility has expanded to twice its original size in order to accommodate the one million annual visitors. Portraits, biographies and memorabilia of the members of the Hall of Fame are displayed in a showcase along the entire back wall of the museum. A souvenir and gift shop offer the visitor Darlington Raceway's 1968 publication on motorsports as well as mementos from the sport. The museum's special displays and activities include trophies, programs, helmets, uniforms, the world's largest collection of racing photographs, illegal car parts and a fully operative and sensory cutaway of Richard Petty's race car which can be experienced by all who visit the museum.

Members: 20 as of 1976. Members of the Hall of Fame are nominated from individuals in the motorsports world who are deceased or have been retired for five years. The nominee receiving 80% of the vote from the election committee of the National Motorsports Press Association is inducted into the Hall of Fame at the annual celebration on the Saturday and Sunday before Labor Day. It is also at this time that new officers are elected for the Press Association.

Induction Year Unrecorded

BAKER, E. G. "Cannonball"
Driver

Born May 1860; as a youth was an acrobat in vaudeville show; a devout Lutheran; neither drank nor smoked.

"Cannonball" began racing motorcycles in 1906, winning the first race at the opening of the Indianapolis Motor Speedway. During his career he established 143 cross-country records, including one in 1928 when he drove from New York to Los Angeles in 53 hours, 31 minutes, with only 30 minutes of sleep. He got his nickname after one of these cross-country trips, when a reporter from the *New York Tribune* dubbed him Cannonball after the express train. Cannonball was always breaking records in an era when roads were rutted paths. He was the first commissioner of the National Association of Stock Car Auto Racing.

BYRON, Robert "Red"
Driver

Owned a garage in Alabama near what is now Talladega Speedway; served during W.W. II as a gunner on a fighter plane; one leg smashed by shrapnel, wore a brace; Grand National Champion 1949; after retirement moved to Florida; operated a sports car shop until death from a heart attack in the late 1960s.

Red Byron won the 1949 National Association of Stock Car Auto Racing Grand National Championship at the twilight of his career. He is remembered by Joe Littlejohn for his racing on the beach at Daytona. Red was always late for the races and never appeared for time trials, and was therefore placed at the end of the competitive field to start a race. Somehow, despite his bad starting position, he would be leading by the first lap. Upon careful scrutiny, it was found that Red's secret was to drive (illegally) at the water's edge during the chaotic starts, past the congested traffic and into the forefront of the race.

COLVIN, Robert E.
Promoter

Had a hearty laugh, a good sense of humor; liked cigars; adopted Darlington, S.C, for his hometown; became active in community affairs; a member of the Lions Club, the Methodist Church, the Shriners; member of the board of Carolina Banking and Trust Co; died of a heart attack in Darlington January 1967.

Bob was president of Darlington Raceway for more than 15 years. Floyd Lane summed up Colvin when he said, "I never knew a man who gave so much of himself to his work. He was always thinking about ways to improve the raceway on a daily basis, and he always managed to maintain a sense of humor, whether times were good or bad." Colvin organized the Pure Darlington Record Club, an exclusive stock car club. He started a week of special events for the Southern 500 including parties held by participating manufacturers, the Southern 500 Beauty Pageant and the Hall of Fame Banquet. He added the Rebel 300-mile race, now 400 miles for stock car convertibles, to the raceway's events; and with his good friend Joe Weatherly, he laid the groundwork for the Weatherly Stock Car Museum at the Raceway.

FLOCK, Tim

Driver

From Atlanta, Ga; entire family involved in some form of racing; father raced bicycles; oldest brother raced motorboats; brother Fonty raced cars; had an ulcer by age 31. Grand National Champion 1952.

Tim drove a Hudson in 1952 when they were claimed to be the best cars on the road. He captured a record 18 Grand National victories in 1955 driving a Chrysler. During his career he won a total of 40 Grand National events.

FLOCK, Truman Fontella "Fonty"

Driver

From Atlanta, Ga; raced soapbox derbies as youth; Grand National Champion 1952; sells automatic car washes in Atlanta.

Fonty Flock began his career in stock cars in 1938. He captured the championship in modified cars in 1947 and 1949. During his career he saw victories at Daytona, Langhorne, Darlington, Raleigh and Detroit. Fonty captured the National Association of Stock Car Auto Racing (NASCAR), Grand National Championship in 1952 at Darlington Raceway. In 1956 he announced his retirement after 18 years of driving, but decided to return each year for as long as he could drive to run the Southern 500. In the 1957 race his car stalled in the path of Bobby Myers' car and the crash took Myers' life and sent Fonty and Paul Goldsmith to the hospital. He returned after that only to test drive cars for NASCAR's Automotive Research Bureau.

FRANCE, William H. G., Sr.

Promoter

Born in Horseshoe, Va; attended Central High School in Washington, D.C; later moved to Daytona Beach, Fla, his adopted hometown; operated a filling station.

Bill was organizer and president of the National Association for Stock Car Auto Racing from 1947 to 1972. He created the Grand National Championship in 1949 and saw the Daytona International Raceway become a reality. The Alabama International Motor Speedway, the biggest and fastest speedway yet built, was his brain child.

JARRETT, Ned

Driver

Born in Conover, N.C; son of a lumberman; father wanted him to become a bookkeeper; raced as a young man under an assumed name in the dust-bowl events; Grand National Champion 1961 and 1965.

Jarrett drove a Chevrolet in 1961 and a Ford in 1965, winning the Grand National Championship on both occasions. His biggest victories were in the Dixie 500 in 1964 and in the Southern 500 in 1965. During his career he compiled 50 victories in Grand National Stock Car racing. Jarrett contributed greatly to the promotion of auto racing by spreading the word about stock car racing everywhere he traveled. He retired from driving in 1965 but continued his involvement with the sport as general manager of the Hickory Speedway in North Carolina and as a color announcer on the Universal Racing Network.

JOHNSON, Junior

Driver and Mechanic

Born in mountains of North Carolina.

Johnson is best remembered for his association with Chevrolet and his cautionless driving. The winner of 50 races during a twenty-year career, he drove with reckless abandon to win eight Grand National events in 1963, including the Dixie 400 and the National 400. The car that left Ford Motor Company at the starting line was his famous 1963 Chevy, white with red stripes and letters. Chevy fans snickered, "Ford's spending millions of dollars chasing that one little ole Chevy." Johnson was considered one of the finest chassis tuners in stock car racing as well as the best Chevrolet engine man ever. He retired in 1966 to become the crew chief of his own racing operation.

LITTLEJOHN, Joseph

Driver and Promoter

One of the founders of the National Association for Stock Car Auto Racing, Joe was the first man to average more than 100 m.p.h. in the mile run down the Daytona Beach strip. He was also the promoter for Spartanburg fairgrounds.

McDUFFIE, Paul

Mechanic

Paul prepared the 1957 Chevrolet that Fireball Roberts drove to victory in the 1958 Southern 500, averaging better than 102 m.p.h. At the new Daytona track in 1959 one of his cars driven by Welborn set a new 100-mile record of 142 m.p.h. His capabilities were proven again in 1960 when Joe Lee Johnson moved into the winner's circle in the first running of the World 600 at Charlotte Motor Speedway. In 1960, a car went out of control coming off a turn and slammed into a pit wall killing McDuffie, Charles Sweatland, Joe Taylor, an inspector, and a crew member.

MYERS, William

Driver

Born in Clarksburg, W.Va; parents, John and Flonnie Myers; brother Bobby a race car driver; serious and business minded; attended Winston-Salem High School; began career as an electrician; married Arlene; two sons, Randy and Gary.

Billy started his career as his brother's mechanic, but soon after began driving. In 1955 alone he won 48 races throughout the nation in the National Association of Stock Car Auto Racing's Sportsman Division. After winning the National Sportsman's Championship in 1958, be became a member of the Ford Motor Company's Mercury racing team. Billy died in 1958 during a race in Winston-Salem when his car ran off the track into a clump of bushes. They found him slumped over the steering wheel. Billy's death was attributed to either cerebral hemorrhage or a heart attack. His brother Bobby was killed in a crash just one year earlier. Since their deaths, the Myers brothers have been honored in a variety of ways, including the National Motorsports Press Association's establishment of the Myers Brothers Memorial Award, given annually to the group or individual who has made the year's most outstanding contribution to stock car racing. In 1961 the Bowman Gray Stadium (the brothers' home town raceway) inaugurated the Myers Brothers Memorial Stock Car Racing Spectacular, an annual event in which Grand National modified and hobby cars compete.

OWENS, "Cotton"
Driver
Cotton was a native of South Carolina who won nine Grand Nationals during his career, eight of them in Pontiacs. He drove for Pontiac during 1961 and 1962. In 1963 he teamed up with David Pearson to create the famous Cotton Owens – David Pearson Dodge Team.

PETTY, Lee Arnold
Driver and Mechanic
Born 1914; son Richard an excellent race car driver, later turned to golf; Grand National Stock Car Champion 1954, 1958 and 1959.

Newspapermen voted Lee Petty Mechanic of the Year in 1950, while fans voted him the most popular National Association of Stock Car Auto Racing driver for three consecutive years, 1953 – 1955. Lee Petty never ended a season lower than sixth place in the National Championship point standings and was the only driver to have won three Grand National Point Championships. His best year was 1959 when he started 49 races, finished 41, won 12 and scored among the top five in 31 others. It was that year that Petty won the inaugural 500-mile race at Daytona International Speedway. In February 1961 he was involved in a car crash that put him in the hospital for several months. Petty raced very little after that.

PURCELL, James A. "Pat"
Manager and Promoter
Born December 3, 1906, in Grand Forks, N.Dak; became a cub reporter for the *Grand Forks Herald;* worked as a press agent and billboard poster for J. Alex Sloan's auto races in Western Canada; later, sports editor for the *Fargo Forum* in N.Dak. and newspapers in New York and Detroit; went into backing and promotion work in 1929; writer and editor for the *Billboard* out of Chicago in 1943; died April 4, 1966.

In 1952, Pat Purcell joined the National Association of Stock Car Auto Racing as field manager, later rising to vice president. As vice president, he was the contact man who dealt with day-to-day problems. While watching the fans filing into the stadium before a racing event, he summed up his philosophy by stating, "See those people up there? That's what this thing called racing is all about; they're the ones who make it possible. They're the ones who should get first consideration on everything."

ROBERTS, Glen
Driver
Born 1929; from Daytona Beach; studied mechanical engineering for three and a half years at the Univ. of Florida; died 1964.

During his 15-year career Glen Roberts won 32 late-model races and about $400,000 in National Association of Stock Car Auto Racing earnings. Twice he won the Southern 500 at Darlington, 1958 and 1963, taking the 1963 race in a lavender Ford named the "Purple Pontiac Eater." At the same track in 1957 and 1959 he won the 300-mile race. In 1962 Roberts was victorious at the Daytona 500 and in 1959, 1962 and 1963 he took the Daytona 400. Glen Roberts was engulfed by flames that burned 70% of his body in a three-car crash on the seventh lap of the World 600-mile race at Charlotte Motor Speedway in July 1964. Shortly thereafter, complications of pneumonia and blood infection caused his death.

TEAGUE, Marshall
Driver and Mechanic
Attended Seabreeze High School, Daytona Beach, Fla; died at age 37.

Teague began his career in a modified car at Daytona Beach in 1946. By 1949 he had won the 200-mile modified race at Daytona and two years later won the late-model event. At Darlington in 1951 he was the fastest qualifier and led the race until overheating forced him out. The following year he was victorious at Daytona as well as Gardena, Phoenix, Canfield, Grand Rapids and Jacksonville, all in the Fabulous Hudson Hornet. Teague did his best at Indianapolis in 1957 when he finished in seventh place, averaging over 100 m.p.h. Marshall dropped out of racing for a while and worked his garage just outside of Cape Canaveral. When the Daytona International Speedway opened he was there to set an unofficial U.S. record. Two days later he was killed when his front axle snapped while he was trying for an official record at Daytona International Speedway.

THOMAS, Herbert
Driver, Owner and Engineer
Retired; owner of a trucking firm in Sanford, N.C.

Herb owned and drove modified cars for a few years before entering the Grand National field in late 1949. His career stretched from 1950 to 1956, during which time he won 49 Grand National Stock Car races and never finished lower than second in the championship point standings. He started at Darlington six times, won three, finished third once, fifth once and blew an engine once. Herb won his first race there in a Hudson Hornet that helped to make him famous. He has many fond memories of the Hudsons and said, "They handled like a baby and nothing could touch them. I'd love to have one now for a family automobile."

TURNER, Curtis "Pops"
Driver
From Roanoke, Va; made money in the lumber industry; once landed his airplane in a shopping center to let a friend off; died in an airplane crash in 1970.

Known for his heavy foot and daredevil style, Pops won Grand Nationals in almost every kind of car. Turner had 17 Grand National victories before he was banned from competition for his attempt to unionize drivers in 1961. He came back after four years to take the 1965 Northern

California 500 as well as to become the first stock car driver to top 180 m.p.h. at the Daytona International Speedway, winning the pole position in 1967. During his lifetime he won more than 350 stock car races.

WEATHERLY, Joe Herbert

Driver

Grew up in the tidewater area of Va; throughout lifetime wore black-and-white saddle oxfords; Grand National Champion 1962 and 1963.

Joe was one of the most popular drivers in racing history. During his career he won 24 Grand National stock car events and was Grand National Champion two times. He twice won the Rebel 400 at Darlington and won the National 400 at Charlotte in 1961. Joe developed a warm friendship with Bob Colvin, president of the Darlington Raceway. Weatherly's sincere interest in the sport was probably his greatest gift to auto racing. His final racing car, the No. 8 Mercury, now stands in the Joe Weatherly Stock Car Museum at Darlington. Little Joe said, "I run that number (No. 8) so everybody can pick me out whether I'm running rightside up or rightside down!"

WHITE, Rex

Driver

A Northerner, moved to S.C; smallest man ever to drive stock cars; Grand National Champion 1960.

Despite his five-ft. four-in. 140 lb. stature, Rex White managed to win 26 Grand National events during his career. He captured the 1960 Grand National Championship in a Chevrolet and drove to victory in the Dixie 400 at Atlanta in 1962.

BASEBALL

Baseball is only the American tip of a vast iceberg of ball games that stretches through thirty centuries of history. Early civilizations batted balls made from two hemispherically shaped skins sewn together and filled with earth, grain, plant fibers, corn husks or pieces of metal. Egyptian pharaohs and their friends used wavy-shaped bats to hit soft leather or linen balls stuffed with cut reed or straw. Greeks and Romans held batting contests that were part of large and important religious ceremonies. Mayans batted solid rubber balls, some of great size. Seventeenth century Laplanders were seen batting balls around. Old Russia had a game called *beizbol,* the basis of their 1962 claim that they invented America's national sport. According to the *Talmud,* the ancient town of Tur-Simeon was destroyed because its people played ball on the Sabbath.

In America people did not play baseball on Sunday until the 1920s. But that was one of the few rules of the game. A bat-and-ball game with tall stakes for bases had been popular in seventeenth century England and so became popular the following century in America. This game, called "rounders," was the baseball described in *The Little Pretty Pocket-Book,* a popular children's book published in 1744, in *The Boys Own Book* (1829) and in *The Book of Sports* (1833). These and other American versions of rounders soon took names of their own, including Town Ball, the Massachusetts Game, One Old Cat, and Base Ball. A Revolutionary War soldier wrote in his diary of a game of "base" played at Valley Forge in 1778. Something called "baste ball" was played at Princeton University the year Davy Crockett was born (1786). In 1825 50 men aged 18 to 40 organized a ball club in Rochester, New York. In 1833 an Olympic Town Ball Club was established in Philadelphia. In 1839 (the year photography was invented) a West Point cadet named Abner Doubleday may have drawn a baseball diamond in the dust of Elihu Phinney's cow pasture in Cooperstown, New York. Whether he actually did so, and the evidence is against it, his fame is assured. It was Doubleday who, at Fort Sumter, fired the first Union gun in the Civil War.

By 1845 (the year Poe wrote *The Raven*), a large variety of ball games were popular in America. Players usually ran clockwise around bases, which were rocks, cleared spaces or tall stakes. Later bases were bags secured by small ropes to stakes to prevent the "base guardian" from kicking them away from the runners. Usually there were five bases—four in addition to the "striker's box"—set out in the shape of an open-sided square. Typically, the runner ran 48 ft. to first, then 60 to second, 72 to third and 72 ft. down what was called "the home stretch." Runs were called "aces," an out was "a hand out." People said, "Three hands out, all out." Any swing and miss was counted as a strike. The striker could demand a high ball or a low one and could wait for his request to be met. After nine balls, however, he walked to first. There were two bare-handed catchers, one stationed up to 50 ft. behind the batter to catch pitches on the bounce, the second even farther back to catch those balls the first catcher missed. A hit caught on the fly or on the first bounce was a hand out. A runner ran with an eye on the fielders, who attempted to "plug" him (also called "burning" or "soaking") by hitting him with the ball. From 12 to 20 men, called "scouts," played per team. Innings were unheard of. Teams agreed to play until one had a certain number of aces, sometimes as many as 65. Winning teams kept the ball. And no one played on the Sabbath.

In 1845 a young draftsman named Alexander Joy Cartwright, Jr, was appointed by his social and baseball club to standardize the game. It was a monumental task that was massively organizational rather than purely creative. One of his first rules was: "In no instance is a ball to be thrown at a player." This and most of his other rules are still in effect today. His club, the Knickerbocker Base Ball Club of New York, practiced their new game in a vacant lot that later became the site of Madison Square Garden. The first time they met in a game against another team was June 19, 1846. They lost. The contest was held at the Elysian Fields in Hoboken, New Jersey. Cartwright himself umpired. All baseball games today are the direct descendants of that first official game. Alexander Cartwright was therefore, like Washington, a young surveyor whose accomplishments would earn him "father of" status. Appropriately, he is known today as the "Father of Organized Baseball."

A number of familiar baseball features were absent from that and other early games. Chewing gum, for example, was not even invented until two years later. No one stole a base until 1865, 19 years later, or deliberately bunted until 1886, the year the Statue of Liberty was dedicated. Not until the game had been around for 25 years did anyone make a double play. Outfielders caught with their bare hands during the game's first 30 years, then began to wear gloves only at the risk of public ridicule. No whitewash marked the baseline boundaries until 1860. No newspaper featured a story about a baseball game until 1853. No president threw out the season's first ball until Taft did so in 1910. For 37 years umpires could and did ask spectators or players for advice on difficult calls. For 41 years games were stopped a maximum of five minutes to allow lost balls to be found. When Al Cumings of the Brooklyn Stars threw history's first recorded curve ball in 1864, a group of scientists declared that a ball curving en route to the plate was impossible and that Cuming's pitch, therefore, had been an optical illusion. Nobody recited the immortal "Casey at the Bat" until a Harvard graduate in San Francisco wrote it four decades after organized baseball began.

Cartwright is the father of organized ball, but a teammate of his, William Henry Wright, is the "Father of Professional Baseball." Born in England, Wright emigrated to the United States as a child and eventually became a player with the St. George Cricket Club of Staten Island. In 1846 he played for the Knickerbockers in history's first official game. Two decades later he became player-manager of the first openly all-professional team (earlier ones had consisted of both amateurs and professionals). He had a local dressmaker make his men the first knee-length uniforms. Under his management, the Cincinnati Red Stockings had the longest winning streak in the whole history of baseball: 92 wins and one tie in 93 starts. This phenomenon decisively ended what had become the farce of amateurism. The polite amateur sport became once and for all a seriously commercial amusement played by professionals and controlled by promoters. Promoters soon capitalized on baseball's growing popularity by enclosing the playing fields and charging admission—50¢ in 1858 was the first. Later developments inevitably included the first professional leagues in 1871 (the year of the great Chicago fire), turnstiles at ballparks in 1878, electric lighting of games in 1883 (the year Robert Louis Stevenson wrote *Treasure Island*), Richey's farm system of the 1920s, the Yankee dynasty of the 1920s and 1930s led by Babe Ruth, the broadcasts of games begun by radio in 1921 and by television in 1939. The color barrier was broken in 1947 with the signing of Jackie Robinson. The sex barrier was broken five years later when Eleanor Engle signed a pro playing contract (she never got to play). In 1972 Bernice Gera, the first woman umpire in pro baseball, burst into tears and resigned after her first game.

But baseball, once Cartwright had designed it and Wright had launched it, changed little compared to the massive changes America experienced in the years after 1845. John Quincy Adams, Andrew Jackson, Audubon and John "Johnny Appleseed" Chapman were still alive when Cartwright organized baseball. Lincoln was 36 years old and John Wilkes Booth was six that year. Custer was also six years old, while Crazy Horse, who later killed him, was one. Tchaikovsky was five years old. Wyatt Berry Stapp Earp, William Frederick "Buffalo Bill" Cody, and Phoebe Anne "Annie" Oakley Mozee had not yet been born. The same year baseball began, Alexandre Dumas wrote *The Count of Monte Cristo.* The great covered wagon era was just getting under way. Neither the California nor the Klondike gold rushes had yet occurred. American whaling was at its all-time high of 750 ships in 1845. Fully 1200 steamboats worked the Mississippi River that year, watched by a ten-year-old Mark Twain. Baseball was organized and active before anyone had ever heard of derby hats (invented in 1850) or stetsons (1865), safety pins (1849) or baby carriages (1848). Neither Cartwright nor any of the others who played that first game had ever seen a fountain pen (invented 1884) or a ball-point pen (1888), nor had any ever seen paper money (1861), nickel coins (1860), or any coin that read "In God We Trust" (1864). They all undoubtedly had seen passenger pigeons, which were not driven extinct until 1914; but none had seen a common sparrow, the first of which were imported from England in 1850. No one in America at the time baseball began had ever drunk an ice cream soda (invented 1874), a malted milk (1882), or had an ice cream sundae (1897); none had ever eaten Grape Nuts for breakfast (1897) or chop suey for dinner (invented in New York City in 1896). Baseball, in fact, was a relatively static part of fast-changing America long before anyone ever heard of Christmas cards (1875), toilet paper rolls (1857) or Ivory soap (1878).

With native and diffused enthusiasm, baseball grew rapidly in Canada as well. First played there around 1867, it had become so popular by the turn of the century that there were 90 different baseball clubs in Vancouver alone. One memorable game occurred in 1878, when the McGill University Saints (theology students) lost to the Sinners (medical students) 23 aces to 13. Indoor winter baseball games were held in Winnipeg and elsewhere. In those days baseball was *the* most popular sport. By 1920, however, all this had changed, as Canada had changed (*see* Hockey).

In 1860 a committee of politicians had to wait on the sidelines to tell Lincoln that he had won the presidential nomination. Abe wanted another chance to make a base hit. Certainly the Civil War and other events in America's history have had more significance. Yet a strong case could be made that baseball was one of those institutionalized forces which decisively influenced the course of American history. "Whoever wants to know the heart and mind of America," wrote the philosopher Jacques Barzun, "had better learn baseball." What would America be like today if archery, for example, or billiards had become the national sport? In a very real sense, America helped make baseball and baseball thereafter helped make America. And it can therefore be said that baseball is America.

FORMS: Baseball has been described as a game played by 18 men who don't need exercise, watched by millions who do. More accurately it is a game in which two teams of 9 men each seek to outscore each other by hitting a ball with a bat. It is played on a field which has an outfield of theoretically unlimited size and an infield, the diamond, that is 90 ft. square—not diamond-shaped—with a base at each corner. The three basemen and the shortstop on a team are called the infield, the three fielders are the outfield, and the pitcher and catcher make up the battery. The three bases, which are 1 ft. 3 in. square, are canvas bags fastened to metal pegs in the ground. Home plate and the pitcher's plate are hard in composition and flush with the ground. The pitcher must stand on the pitcher's plate when he begins his pitch of the ball, which may travel at speeds of up to 100 m.p.h. The ball is from 9 to 9½ in. in circumference and weighs from 5 to 5½ oz. Normally a ball will consist of a cork and rubber center wound with woolen yarn and encased in a cowhide cover. The introduction of this type of ball in 1911 marks the beginning of what is usually called the modern baseball era. Until 1974 ball covers were horsehide—balls are still often called "horsehides." The bat is a smooth, tapered piece of hardwood, usually ash but sometimes hackberry or hickory. It can be of any weight but not more than 2¾ in. in diameter at its thickest part and not more than 42 in. long. The most popular length bat in pro baseball is 35 in. long. Gloves, first used in 1875, are worn by all fielding players except the catcher and the first baseman, whose more heavily padded gloves are properly called "mitts." A catcher will also wear a chest protector (invented in 1885), shin guards and a padded metal mask. The first such mask was modeled after a fencing mask in 1873. Players' shoes have steel cleats for traction. Batters and runners wear protective plastic helmets. Players have worn uniforms since 1849—the first were blue and white cricket outfits with straw hats. They may not wear any polished metal or any emblem resembling a baseball. Officials include an official scorer who records the statistical details of the game, an umpire-in-chief, and umpires for each base plus two additional ones during World Series play. A game lasts nine innings, each of which has six outs, three for each team. In cases where games are forfeited by a team for any reason, the official score is 9–0 in favor of the other team. Among the many rules are proscriptions against bad manners on the field. During history's first game Umpire Cartwright fined J. W. Davis 6¢ for swearing; 109 years later Ted Williams was fined $5000 for spitting at the fans.

ORGANIZATION: Baseball today is a major sport in Italy, Japan, the Netherlands, South Africa, Taiwan and many Latin American countries. In the United States professional baseball has two major leagues, the American and the National. Each league has an Eastern Division and a Western Division comprised of six franchises, or teams, each. These 24 teams, including the Canadian one in the Eastern Division of the American League, are the most visible. Their games are covered by TV and in 1976 had a paid attendance of over 31 million. But they are merely the tip of the iceberg of the sport.

Under them more than 140 Canadian, American and Mexican teams make up the 18 minor leagues. (There have been 225 different minor leagues since baseball began—in 1949 no less than 59 were active.) Minor league teams are classified AAA (highest), AA, A or Rookie, according to the total population of all the cities in their respective league's circuit. All such teams serve in part as a training ground for players who later graduate into the majors. Many are owned by or have working arrangements with one or more particular major league teams.

The next lower level in baseball is the largest one—the highly structured world of amateur baseball which is represented by such organizations as the American Amateur Baseball Congress, the Canadian Federation of Amateur Baseball, Boys Baseball, Inc, Little League Baseball, Inc, American Legion Junior Baseball Leagues, the Babe Ruth League, the National Amateur Baseball Federation and many others. All of these organizations administer, sponsor, or otherwise support local leagues of from four to ten teams for each age group from eight years old on. For example, Little League Baseball, Inc, is an organization of teams for 9 to 18 year-olds who play a unique form of baseball that was invented in 1939 by Carl E. Sotoz (a lumber company employee in Williamsport, Pennsylvania). Each year Little League stages a Little League World Series for 9 to 12 year-olds at Williamsport, a World Series for 13 to 15 year-olds in Gary, Indiana, and a Big League World Series for 16 to 18 year-olds in Ft. Lauderdale, Florida. These and other activities are supported by the Little League Foundation, which is headquartered in Williamsport. In 1976 Little League Baseball, Inc. had over 55,000 teams in 9841 leagues in every state and in 31 foreign countries.

Finally, there are the millions of North Americans who play baseball informally with friends or relatives on weekends or holidays. The total number of people who play baseball is impossible to calculate. The far greater number of fans who watch or hear or otherwise follow all those players is impossible even to estimate. But it is accurate to say there have been more pro baseball players in the United States than pro players in all other sports combined, and that more people have paid to watch pro baseball games than have paid to see all other U.S. professional sports combined. Thus baseball is reaffirmed as America's national sport, even though 50 years ago the Supreme Court was called in to determine whether baseball was in fact a sport. Associate Justice Oliver Wendell Holmes, who was four years old when baseball was born, declared that, within the meaning of the federal antitrust laws, baseball was indeed a sport, not a business.

Amateur Baseball Hall of Fame

ST. LOUIS, MISSOURI

Mailing Address: Busch Memorial Stadium, 63166. Tel. (314) 421-6790. *Contact:* Ms. Jackie Jordan, Dir, St. Louis Sports Hall of Fame. *Location:* Near junction of Interstates 40 and 70 in western area of city. *Admission:* Free daily. *Personnel:* Don I. Gabbert, Chmn; 20-mem Bd. of Dirs. *Nearby Halls of Fame:* Sports (St. Louis), Hereford (Kansas City, 220 mi. W.) and Auto Racing (Indianapolis, 234 mi. N.E.).

The Amateur Baseball Hall of Fame was founded in 1973 when Don Gabbert and nine others decided it was time to recognize and honor the amateur baseball players, umpires and contributors of the greater St. Louis area. This nonprofit organization became a reality with the aid of baseball players, fans and media members throughout St. Louis. An award banquet each spring presents the new inductees. The new members receive a certificate and a ring, and have their names added to the roster of the Sports Hall of Fame at Busch Memorial Stadium.

Members: 77 as of 1977, 58 still living. They include amateur players, umpires and contributors to the St. Louis amateur baseball programs. The nominees are accepted and researched by a screening committee and approved by the Board for lifetime membership. More than ten and less than twenty members are inducted annually at the March Hall of Fame Banquet. There is a maximum of 20 members on the Board of Directors and vacancies are filled after a vote of the remaining members.

1974 CORCORAN, John. Player.
DAUM, William. Player.
De LONGE, Francis. Player.
EISENBATH, Bernard. Player.
ESCHENBRENNER, Harry H. Player.
FIX, Pete J. Player.
FREISE, Harry C. Player.
FULTZ, Paul L. Contributor.
KHOURY, George M. Player.
KREFT, Anthony J. Player.
KUTIS, Thomas. Contributor.
LOEHR, Edgar. Player.
MATHEWS, Martin L. Contributor.
MEYERS, Harry W. Player.
MICK, Al J. Contributor.
NEWSOM, Roy. Player.
NICOLAI, Albert A. Player.
SANDUCKY, Vernon. Player.
SCHAEFER, Melvin E. Contributor.
SCHULTEHENRICH, Gus. Player.
SCULLY, John. Player.
WEBB, Normal C. Player.

1975 BOGGIANO, Louis J, Jr. Contributor.
BRADY, Joseph. Player.
BROWN, John W. Player.
CURRIER, Warren H. Player.
DICKHERBER, George, Sr. Player.
DONOVAN, Harry. Umpire.
GROMACKI, Stanley. Umpire.
HANKINS, Leroy. Contributor.
KOEWING, Wilson C. Player.
McCONNELL, Thomas. Contributor.
McKENNA, William. Player.
MORGENTHALER, Ed. Contributor.
NETZEBAND, Roy R. Player.
SIEMER, Virgil. Player.
WATERSON, Russ G. Contributor.

1976 ARNOLD, Jake
CURDT, Harry J. Contributor.
DANNER, Raymond M, Sr. Player.
EDWARDS, Frank "Teanie." Player.
EVANS, J. Edward. Player.
GROSCH, Albert G. Contributor.
HANEBRINK, Sylvester E. Player.
HATCHARD, Lester. Umpire.
HOFER, Arthur. Player.
KELLER, Joseph D. Contributor.
KRUEGER, Robert A. Player.
LUDWIG, Fred. Player.
McCREADY, C. W. "Pat"
NOVACK, Morris L. Player.
RATHMANN, Charles "Chip." Contributor.
RINDERKNECHT, Arthur W. Player.
SANDERS, Harry "Feet." Umpire.
SCHOENBERGER, Joseph M. Contributor.
SPELLMEYER, Henry W. Player.
ZOMPHIER, Charles

1977 ANDROLEWICZ, Vincent J. Umpire.
BALLENTINE, Hubert "Dickey." Contributor.
BLESSING, Joseph W. Player.
BOEHMER, Urban J. Player.
BRACKEN, Herbert. Player.
CONNERS, Charles A. Player.
DeSALME, Gene
FRANEY, Thomas J, Jr.
HEINEMANN, Harry. Player.
HOFFMEISTER, George W. Contributor.
HUNTHAUSEN, Norvall M. Player.
JOHNSTON, Everett P. Player.
LEMMON, Robert J.
OCHTERBECK, August H. Player.
ORTMANN, William
POHLMANN, Fred H. Player.
SCHLERETH, Martin J. Player.
SEILER, Frank H. Player.
WILD, Ken, Player.
WOOD, Russell A. Umpire.

American Association of College Baseball Coaches Hall of Fame

KALAMAZOO, MICHIGAN

Mailing Address: Athletic Bldg, Western Michigan Univ, Western Michigan Ave, 49001. Tel. (413) 787-2306. *Contact:* Archie Allen, Chmn. *Location:* On the campus of Western Michigan Univ. in the N.W. section of the city. *Admission:* Free during gym hours weekdays. *Personnel:* Archie Allen, Permanent Co-Chmn; Jack Stallings, Present Co-Chmn; William Chambers, Site Dir; eight voting members from throughout the country. *Nearby Halls of Fame:* Business (Chicago, Ill, 100 mi. S.W.), Sports (Detroit 135 mi. W.) and Archery (Grayling, 175 mi. S.E.).

The Hall of Fame was founded in 1963 by the American Association of College Baseball Coaches (AACBC), with Archie Allen as its first president. The award was established to honor AACBC coaches for their service and contributions to college baseball. At present the Hall is located in one large room in the Athletic Building of Western Michigan University. This area houses the records, a growing collection of baseball memorabilia and the plaques of the members. The site was selected because it was the location of the first College World Series, between Yale and Western Michigan. Plans are now under way to move the Hall's location to Omaha, Nebr, where the College World Series is held annually. The move could occur in two to three years. This nonprofit organization is governed by the executive committee of AACBC.

Members: 74 as of 1977. Four new members are elected each year, one of whom will be deceased. Only coaches who have been a member in good standing of the AACBC for at least five years, and who have a minimum of fifteen years service as a head baseball coach in a four-year college or university, are eligible for nomination. Nominations submitted by the members of the AACBC are voted on by the association's executive committee; election is based on their contributions to the advancement and betterment of college baseball. The executive committee is made up of eight voting members, representing the eight districts in the United States, and six non-voting members. Rotation of a committee member's term of office is on a four-year basis. Two men will retire each year at the annual convention, Induction Years Unrecorded with two new members replacing them.

Induction Years Unrecorded

ALLEN, Archie. Springfield College.

ALLEN, Ethan. Yale University.

ANDERSON, J. Kyle. University of Chicago.

BAILEY, Arthur Buckner. Washington State University. See entry in College Baseball Coaches Hall of Fame, Citizens Savings Hall of Fame Athletic Museum, 1954.

BARNES, Everett "Eppy." Colgate University.

BARRY, Jack. Holy Cross College. See entry in College Baseball Coaches Hall of Fame, Citizens Savings Hall of Fame Athletic Museum, 1954.

BARRY, Justin M. "Sam." University of Southern California. See entry in College Baseball Coaches Hall of Fame, Citizens Savings Hall of Fame Athletic Museum, 1954. *Also in:* College Basketball Hall of Fame, Citizens Savings Hall of Fame Athletic Museum.

BEDENK, Joe. Pennsylvania State University.

BEIDEN, Pete. California State University, Fresno.

BISHOP, Max. United States Naval Academy. See entry in College Baseball Hall of Fame, Citizens Savings Hall of Fame Athletic Museum, 1966.

BUTLER, L. C. "Pete." University of Northern Colorado.

CARROLL, Owen. Seton Hall University.

CHRISTIAN, J. Orlean. University of Connecticut. See entry in Athletic Directors Hall of Fame, Citizens Savings Hall of Fame Athletic Museum, 1972. *Also in:* College Baseball Coaches Hall of Fame, Citizens Savings Hall of Fame Athletic Museum.

COAKLEY, Andrew J. Columbia University. See entry in College Baseball Coaches Hall of Fame, Citizens Savings Hall of Fame Athletic Museum, 1954.

COFFEY, John F. Fordham University. See entry in College Baseball Coaches Hall of Fame, Citizens Savings Hall of Fame Athletic Museum, 1954.

COLEMAN, Ralph. Oregon State University. See entry in College Baseball Coaches Hall of Fame, Citizens Savings Hall of Fame Athletic Museum, 1959.

COOMBS, John W. "Jack." Duke University. See entry in College Baseball Coaches Hall of Fame, Citizens Savings Hall of Fame Athletic Museum, 1954.

DANIELS, Norman Joseph. Wesleyan University.

DEAN, Everett. Stanford University. See entry in Indiana Basketball Hall of Fame, 1965. *Also in:* College Basketball Hall of Fame, Citizens Savings Hall of Fame Athletic Museum; and Naismith Memorial Basketball Hall of Fame.

DEDEAUX, Raoul "Rod." University of Southern California. See entry in College Baseball Coaches Hall of Fame, Citizens Savings Hall of Fame Athletic Museum, 1959.

DISCH, William J. University of Texas. See entry in College Baseball Coaches Hall of Fame,

Citizens Savings Hall of Fame Athletic Museum, 1954.

DONGES, George. Ashland College.

ECKLEY, Paul. Amherst College.

EVANS, Clinton W. University of California at Berkeley. See entry in College Baseball Coaches Hall of Fame, Citizens Savings Hall of Fame Athletic Museum, 1954.

FALK, Bibb. University of Texas. See entry in College Baseball Coaches Hall of Fame, Citizens Savings Hall of Fame Athletic Museum, 1966.

FEHRING, William "Dutch." Stanford University.

FISHER, Ray. University of Michigan.

FREEMAN, James B. Ithaca College.

FULLER, David. Florida State University.

GELBERT, Charley. Lafayette College.

GREEN, Toby. Oklahoma State University.

GREGORY, Paul. Mississippi State University.

HARRICK, Stephen. West Virginia University.

HEARN, Bunn. University of North Carolina.

HILL, Lovette Lee. University of Houston.

HODGE, Henry. Clarkson College.

HUFF, George. University of Illinois. See entry in College Baseball Coaches Hall of Fame, Citizens Savings Hall of Fame Athletic Museum, 1954.

HYAMES, Judson. Western Michigan University.

JESSE, Daniel. Trinity College (Connecticut).

JUSTICE, Joseph. Rollins College.

KARROW, Martin. Ohio State University.

KEANEY, Frank. University of Rhode Island. See entry in Naismith Memorial Basketball Hall of Fame, 1960. *Also in:* College Basketball Hall of Fame, Citizens Savings Hall of Fame Athletic Museum.

KIBLER, Thomas. Washington College.

KILLINGER, W. B. West Chester State College.

KIRSH, Donald. University of Oregon.

KLINE, Clarence "Jake." University of Notre Dame. See entry in College Baseball Coaches Hall of Fame, Citizens Savings Hall of Fame Athletic Museum, 1959.

KOBS, John. Michigan State University. See entry in College Baseball Coaches Hall of Fame, Citizens Savings Hall of Fame Athletic Museum, 1954.

LAIRD, G. F. "Red." Virginia Polytechnic Institute.

LEWANDOWSKI, A. J. University of Nebraska.

LORDEN, Earl. University of Massachusetts.

MAHER, Charles. Western Michigan University.

MANSFIELD, Arthur "Dynie." University of Wisconsin.

MARTIN, Glen "Abe." Southern Illinois University.

McCABE, William. Southern Illinois University.

McCARTHY, William. New York University. See entry in College Baseball Coaches Hall of Fame, Citizens Savings Hall of Fame Athletic Museum, 1954.

McCORMICK, Frank. University of Minnesota.

McKALE, Fritz. University of Arizona. See entry in College Athletic Directors Hall of Fame, Citizens Savings Hall of Fame Athletic Museum, 1974. *Also in:* College Baseball Coaches Hall of Fame, Citizens Savings Hall of Fame Athletic Museum.

NOBLE, Dudy. Mississippi State University. See entry in College Baseball Coaches Hall of Fame, Citizens Savings Hall of Fame Athletic Museum, 1954.

REICHLE, Arthur E. University of California at Los Angeles.

PETERSON, Hamlet. Luther College.

PITT, Malcolm U. University of Richmond. See entry in College Basketball Hall of Fame, Citizens Savings Hall of Fame Athletic Museum, 1966.

ROBINSON, Stanley. Mississippi College.

SANCET, Frank. University of Arizona.

SCHRALL, Leo "Scrapiron." Bradley University.

SCOLINOS, John. California State Polytechnic.

SEIBERT, Richard. University of Minnesota.

SIMMONS, John "Hi." University of Missouri. See entry in College Baseball Coaches Hall of Fame, Citizens Savings Hall of Fame Athletic Museum, 1966.

ST. JOHN, Gil. Ohio State University.

SWASEY, Henry. University of New Hampshire. See entry in College Baseball Coaches Hall of Fame, Citizens Savings Hall of Fame Athletic Museum, 1954.

TIMM, L. C. "Cap." Iowa State University.

TOMLINSON, J. A. "Ike." Arkansas State University.

VOGEL, Otto "Otts." University of Iowa. See entry in College Baseball Coaches Hall of Fame, Citizens Savings Hall of Fame Athletic Museum, 1954.

WHITEFORD, Mon. Northern Iowa College. See entry in College Baseball Coaches Hall of Fame, Citizens Savings Hall of Fame Athletic Museum, 1966.

YARNELL, W. W. "Rusty." Lowell Technological Institute. See entry in College Baseball Coaches Hall of Fame, Citizens Savings Hall of Fame Athletic Museum, 1959.

Association of North Dakota Amateur Baseball Leagues Hall of Fame

JAMESTOWN, NORTH DAKOTA

Mailing Address: 235 13 Ave, N.E, 58401. Tel. (701) 252-3789. *Contact:* Jack Brown, Exec. Secy. *Location:* Approx. 90 mi. W. of Fargo and 100 mi. E. of Bismarck on Interstate 94. *Admission:* Free daily. *Personnel:* Al Bergman, Pres; Abbie Peterson, V.Pres; Jack Brown, Exec. Secy; six commissioners. *Nearby Hall of Fame:* Softball (Jamestown).

The Association of North Dakota Amateur Baseball Leagues (ANDABL) was founded in 1963 to promote and sponsor amateur baseball in the state of North Dakota to unite all North Dakota leagues under the same set of rules, and to perpetuate an annual state tournament. Every team belonging to the league pays annual dues of $30. The Hall of Fame is located within the Jamestown Civic Center, where the members' names, home towns and dates of induction can be found. The first selections to the Hall were made in 1963.

Members: 37 as of 1977. Membership in the Hall of Fame is limited to those persons who participated actively in amateur baseball in North Dakota as player, umpire or officer of a league, and who have been retired for five years. Names are submitted to the Association annually for consideration by the ANDABL Commissioners. Five persons were inducted into the Hall the first year and two each succeeding year. New members are inducted at the Hall of Fame banquet held annually in a town selected by the Commission. Association officers are elected annually as well, by a majority vote of the Association's members. Qualified voters are the latest elected officers and managers of the preceding year's paid member leagues. Regional commissioners and the secretary are appointed by the Association's officers.

1963 FARLEY, Tom
SCHOONOVER, John
TOWNSEND, Earl
WOJCIK, Louis
1964 FITZGERALD, Eugene
MacLACHLAN, Jack
1965 GAUSLOW, Orris
POLING, Clarence "Chief"
1966 McMULLEN, Harvey
NESET, Oden
WOOD, Chuck
1967 MEYER, Al
REDMOND, Pete
1968 DIETRICH, Harold "Heb"
JENSEN, Clarence
1969 FORD, Joe
HEIDT, George
1970 JONES, Harold
OSWALD, Eddie
1971 BROWN, Jack
HEIM, Mel
UTKE, John
1972 BRADY, Bill
MAHAR, John
1973 BERRY, George
FAUGHT, John
FORD, Horton
HALSTEAD, Berkley
1974 KLEPPE, Tom
WOLF, Pius
1975 ERICKSON, Armond
MISKANEN, Maynard
1976 JANZ, John
KIEDEROWSKI, Dennis
NEAMEYER, Robert
1977 ORGEN, Merritt
WALLACE, Owen

High School Baseball Hall of Fame

BOSTON, MASSACHUSETTS

Mailing Address: Boston Latin High School, 78 Avenue Louis Pasteur, 02115. Tel. (617) 566-2250. *Contact:* Dave Coleman, Pres, Massachusetts State Baseball Coaches Association (MSBCA) at above address, or at 29 Brooksweld Rd, Canton, Massachusetts, 02108. *Location:* In the Boston Latin High School offices. Not open to the public. *Personnel:* Dave Coleman, Pres; Roger Tubeson, First V.Pres; Frank Carey, Second V.Pres; Tony Chinati, Secy; Fred Ebbett, Treas; Dick Berardino, Asst. Secy. *Nearby Halls of Fame:* Baseball (Cooperstown, N.Y, 205 mi. N.W.), Basketball (Springfield, 80 mi. S.W.), Harness Racing (Goshen, N.Y, 170 mi. S.W.), Heritage, Music (New York City, 206 mi. S.W.), Horse Racing (Saratoga Springs, N.Y, 150 mi. N.W.), Ice Skating (Boston; Newburgh, N.Y, 165 mi. S.W.).

This Hall was founded in 1969 to honor in perpetuity those high school baseball coaches whose careers and contributions have had a significant influence on the development of high school baseball in Massachusetts.

Members: 33 as of June 1977. An unspecified number of new members are inducted annually. Any nominee must meet three requirements: he or she must actively have coached high school baseball in Massachusetts for not less than ten years; must have been retired from coaching at least five years; and must have made a significant contribution to high school baseball. Other coaches or past players may make nominations, which are received and reviewed by the Executive Committee of the MSBCA. Final selections are decided by a vote of the Executive Committee in January of each year. The first weekend of the following February, inductions are held at a Hall of Fame Dinner, which is usually staged in conjunction with a three-day baseball clinic. The highlight of the Dinner is the induction of new members, during which the new inductees are presented their awards by those who inducted them. These awards consist of an official MSBCA certificate and a bronzed baseball mounted on a wooden base on which the member's name is inscribed.

1969 ANDRUS, Felix W.
BURNS, James J.
COGAN, Joseph W.
CONSOLATI, John
CONWAY, Joseph

1970 DANIELS, John Jack
ESPANET, Charles
FERGUSON, Howard
FITZGERALD, Charles

1971 FITZGERALD, Thomas E.
FOLEY, James "Sonny"
FOX, Arthur
GOODNOUGH, Harold

1972 IGO, Peter
JACHYM, Joseph
JONES, Lucius P. "Jeff"
LANE, Lester

1973 PENDERGAST, William J.
ROBARTS, Tremaine
SCAFATI, Orlando "Andy"
SMITH, Leo H.

1974 PERRILL, Arthur G.
STOKLOSA, Stanley

1975 URBAN, Luke
WISE, William G.

1976 ANDRUS, Felix W.
DONAHER, Francis
DRAGONE, Walter A.
SPILLANE, Clement, Sr.

1977 BENJAMIN, Stanley
HYLAND, Joseph M.
STRZELECKI, Sigmond R.
WILSON, Merrill D.

National Baseball Hall of Fame and Museum

COOPERSTOWN, NEW YORK

Mailing Address: Cooperstown, 13326. Tel. (607) 547-9988. *Contact:* Ken Smith, Dir. Public Relations. *Location:* Approx. 80 mi. N.W. of Albany, 30 mi. S.E. of Utica, and 65 mi. S.E. of Syracuse. *Admission:* 9 to 9 daily April – October, 9 to 5 daily November – March, closed Thanksgiving, Christmas and New Year's. Adults $2.50, children under 15 $1.00. *Personnel:* Paul S. Kerr, Pres; Stephen C. Clark, Jr, V.Pres; Dr. James Bordley III, V.Pres; Edward W. Stack, Secy; Howard C. Talbot, Jr, Treas; Ken Smith, Dir; Clifford Kachline, Historian; John Redding, Librarian; Peter P. Clark, Cur; Sid C. Keener, Dir. Emeritus; 15 dirs. *Nearby Halls of Fame:* Basketball (Springfield, Mass, 140 mi. S.E.), Bicycle Staten Island, 165 mi. S.E.), Flight (Elmira, 95 mi. S.W.), Harness Racing (Goshen, 85 mi. S.E.), Heritage, Music (New York City, 160 mi. S.E.), Horse Racing (Saratoga Springs, 65 mi. N.E.), Horseshoe Pitching (Corning, 100 mi. S.W.), Ice Skating (Boston, Mass, 205 mi. S.E; Newburgh, 90 mi. S.E.).

The question of the origin of baseball led researchers to Cooperstown, N.Y, where in 1839 Abner Doubleday devised a scheme for playing baseball to provide entertainment for the troops in residence. It wasn't until June 12, 1939, with the dedication of the non-profit National Baseball Hall of Fame that the dream of immortality for baseball and its participants materialized under the guidance of Stephen C. Clark. On this day 25 members were installed in the Hall, housed with the Museum in a three-story brick building. Since that time 157 players, umpires and managers have been immortalized at Cooperstown. New additions to the building were dedicated in 1950 and 1958, and the National Baseball Library opened in 1968. This research library houses the most extensive collection of baseball literature found anywhere. Films are shown daily in the library's auditorium. Offered for sale is the all-encompassing National Baseball Hall of Fame and Museum publication (c. 1976). The museum's special displays include the President's Gallery and a Babe Ruth wing where the recorded voice of Babe Ruth can be heard. Works of art by such names as Norman Rockwell and William Medcalf are displayed among the baseball trophies, mementoes and equipment that attract more than 250,000 visitors annually. New members are installed at the yearly Hall of

Fame Day followed by the Hall of Fame Game between a National League and an American League club on the nearby Doubleday Field.

Members: 163 as of 1977, 46 still living. Three separate groups are authorized to elect members to the Baseball Hall of Fame each year: The Baseball Writers' Association of America (BBWAA) select 30 candidates who have played actively in the major leagues for a period beginning 20 years before and ending five years prior to the election, and who have played in each of ten championship seasons. The Hall of Fame Committee on Baseball Veterans selects no more than two players who have been retired from the major leagues for at least 25 years and who are no longer eligible in the elections held by the BBWAA; they also select one executive, manager, or umpire who has been retired from organized baseball at least five years. The Hall of Fame Committee on Negro Leagues selects persons who played at least ten years in the Negro Baseball Leagues prior to 1946, or whose service in the Negro Baseball Leagues prior to 1946 and in the major leagues thereafter aggregates at least ten years, and who are not otherwise eligible for election. Candidates who receive 75% of the selecting group's votes are elected to membership.

1936

COBB, Tyrus Raymond
Player

Born December 18, 1889, in Narrows, Ga; son of a school teacher; made wise investments with General Motors and Coca-Cola; endowed a medical center at Royston, Ga; American League Most Valuable Player 1911; Chalmers Award 1911; died of cancer July 17, 1961, in Atlanta, Ga, at age 74.

1905 – 1926 Detroit Tigers American League, center fielder
1927 – 1928 Philadelphia Athletics American League, center fielder

Ty Cobb never hit less than .320 in 21 years of play. His lifetime average was .367 in 3034 games. Ty holds the American League stolen-base record of 96 for one season. During his major league career he stole a total of 892 bases—26 of those were home base. Cobb is regarded as the greatest hitter and baserunner in the game's history, hitting above .400 three times and leading the American League in RBI's four times. Ty played 17 games in World Series competition. To achieve greatness, Cobb practiced all aspects of the game endlessly. Every winter he walked 20 to 30 miles a day with lead in his shoes. This enabled him to run effortlessly when spring games came around.

JOHNSON, Walter Perry "Barney"
Player and Manager

Born November 6, 1887, in Humboldt, Kans; Most Valuable Player 1913, 1924. Chalmers Award 1913; did play-by-plays in Washington, D.C. after retirement; raised purebred cattle on farm in Maryland; died from a brain tumor December 10, 1946, in Washington, D.C, at 59.

1907 – 1927 Washington Senators American League, pitcher
1929 – 1932 Washington Senators American League, manager

By spending his whole career with the Senators, 6 ft. 1 in, 200 lb. Walter Johnson set an American League record for the most consecutive years with one team. His other American League records include: most games started, 666; most years led in complete games, 6; most years led in innings, 5; most years of 300 or more innings, 9; most years led in wins, 6; most years of 30 or more wins, 2; most years of 20 or more wins, 12; most consecutive wins in one season, 16; most consecutive scoreless innings, 56; lowest season ERA 1.09 in 1913; most years of 300 or more strikeouts, 2; handling 103 chances without error in 1903, a record for pitchers. Johnson is holder or coholder of the following major league records: most years led in strikeouts, 12; most consecutive years led in strikeouts, 8; most years of 100 or more strikeouts, 18; most years of 200 or more strikeouts, 7; the longest shutout, 18 innings. Walter Johnson recorded more strikeouts (3508) and shutouts (113) than any other pitcher in major league history. The "Big Train" (as he was called) was probably the fastest pitcher who ever lived. A rookie once said, "He's got a gun concealed about his person. They can't tell me he throws them balls with his arm." Walter was not as spectacular a manager as he was a pitcher; the Senators remained low in the standings while Johnson managed them.

Also in: American Indian Athletic Hall of Fame and National Association of Intercollegiate Athletics Hall of Fame.

MATHEWSON, Christopher
Player and Manager

Born August 12, 1880, in Factoryville, Pa; attended Bucknell Univ; played football, baseball and basketball in school; honor student, class president, member of the literary society and Glee Club; one son; enlisted in military with Chemical Warfare Service; died of tuberculosis at age 45 October 7, 1925, in Sarnac Lake, N.Y.

1900 – 1916 New York Giants National League, pitcher
1916 – 1918 Cincinnati Reds National League, manager

Christy Mathewson, 6 ft. 1 in, 195 lbs. developed a fadeaway pitch or reverse curve that was perfected while he was with the Giants. Matty pitched three shutouts against the Philadelphia Athletics in the 1905 World Series. During his career he pitched in 11 World Series Games. Christy set a National League record in 1913 by pitching 68 consecutive innings without issuing a walk. In 17 years of play he had 367 wins, 186 losses, for a .664 percentage; a 2.13 ERA in 634 games, with 551 starts, 434 completes, 838 walks, 2502 strikeouts and 77 shutouts. Christy served as president of the Boston Braves from 1923 until his death.

RUTH, George Herman "Babe"
Player

Born June 2, 1895 in Baltimore, Md; one of five children; father a Baltimore saloon keeper; sent to St. Mary's Industrial Home for orphans at the age of seven; American League Most Valuable Player 1923; All Star Games 1933 – 1934; died of cancer at age 53 August 16, 1948, in New York City.

1914 – 1919 Boston Red Sox American League, pitcher
1920 – 1934 New York Yankees American League, outfielder
1935 Boston Braves National League, outfielder

Babe Ruth was undoubtedly baseball's most popular, most versatile legend of all time. His teammate Harry Hooper said, "Sometimes I still can't believe what I saw: This nineteen-year-old kid, crude, poorly educated, only lightly brushed by the social veneer we call civilization, gradually transformed into the idol of American youth and the symbol of baseball the world over." Babe's pitching record for 10 years shows an ERA of 2.29. He had 17 shutouts in 163 games, with 94 wins and 46 losses, 488 strikeouts and 441 walks. As an outfielder, the 6 ft. 2-in, 215-lb. Ruth recorded 2502 games with 8399 at bats, 2873 hits for 506 doubles, 136 triples, 714 home runs, 5793 total bases, 2174 RBI, 2056 walks, 1330 strikeouts, a batting average of .342 and a slugging percentage of .690. Babe Ruth is holder or coholder of the major league's record for highest runs in a season, 177; most years leading in runs, 8; most years of 150 or more runs, 6; most years led in home runs, 12; most seasons more than 50 home runs, 4; most seasons more than 40 home runs, 11; most walks in a season, 170 (1923); and the most years led in walks, 11. Babe played in ten World Series. He had a fondness for children and would often sign autographs, visit children in hospitals and sit and chat with them in the bleachers.

WAGNER, John Peter "Honus"
Player and Coach

Born February 27, 1874, in Carnegie, Pa; son of a German immigrant; worked loading coal cars; left home at 18 to become a barber; later, operated a sporting goods store; died December 6, 1955, in Carnegie at age 81.

1897 – 1899 Louisville Colonels National League, shortstop
1900 – 1917 Pittsburgh Pirates, shortstop
1917 Pittsburgh Pirates National League, player-manager
1918 – 1951 Pittsburgh Pirates National League, coach

Honus Wagner is considered one of the greatest shortstops in history. He was a sensational base runner, a great hitter and could play any position in the field. Honus, 5 ft. 11 in, 200 lbs. is coholder of the major league records for most consecutive years leading the league in hitting, 4, and the most consecutive years leading in total bases, 4. He holds the National League record for the most career singles and the most career triples. During his 21-year career he played in 2787 games, had 10,430 at bats, with 31,415 hits—2442 singles, 252 triples, 101 home runs, 1736 runs, 1732 RBI, 722 stolen bases and a batting average of .327. He played in two World Series and after retirement he coached the Pirates until 1951.

1937

BULKELEY, Hon. Morgan G.
Contributor

Born December 26, 1837, in E. Haddam, Conn; mayor of Hartford, Conn, 1880 – 1888; Gov. of Conn. 1888 – 1893; U.S. Senator, 1905; died November 6, 1922, in Hartford.

Morgan Bulkeley was the first president of the National League in 1879. He was elected to the Hall of Fame in 1937 for his service in laying the foundation of the national game.

JOHNSON, Byron Bancroft "Ban"
Contributor

Born January 5, 1864, in Norwalk, Ohio; attended Marietta Col; played catcher in school; died March 28, 1931, in St. Louis, Mo.

Johnson was a sportswriter until his friend Charles Comiskey persuaded him to get into the managerial aspect of the game. In 1893 Johnson became president of the Western League which became the American League in 1900. Johnson changed the game from a rowdy sport into recreation appealing to the family. He insisted that the use of profanity on the field be ended, banned the sale of liquor in the parks and promoted respect for umpires. Johnson and Comiskey strengthened their league by moving to major cities and picking up big-name players. A battle for major league status was won in 1903 with the signing of the Cincinnati agreement which provided that the two leagues and the minor leagues keep their separate identities but be governed by a national commission. In later years, Ban met with conflict during the Black Sox scandal. Because of his poor health and his disillusionment he resigned in 1927.

LAJOIE, Napoleon "Larry"
Player

Born September 5, 1875, in Woonsocket, R.I; worked in the cotton mills of New England and drove hack for a livery stable; after retirement was salesman for a rubber company; died February 7, 1959, in Daytona Beach, Fla, at age 83.

1896 – 1900 Philadelphia Phillies National League, second baseman
1902 – 1902 Philadelphia Athletics American League, second baseman
1902 – 1914 Cleveland Indians American League, second baseman
1915 – 1916 Philadelphia Athletics American League, second baseman

Larry Lajoie, 6 ft. 2 in, 195 lbs. was a great hitter and the most graceful and effective second baseman of his era. He was said to be "poetry in motion." He compiled a .338 lifetime batting average in 2380 games. Nap was a member of the 3000 hit club, winning five major and minor league batting titles and leading the league six times for fielding at second base. During his career he had 82 home runs, 650 doubles, 162 triples and 1503 runs in 9589 at bats; 1599 RBI and 280 stolen bases.

McGILLICUDDY, Cornelius Alexander "Connie Mack"
Player and Manager

Born December 23, 1862, in E. Brookfield, Mass; son of an Irish immigrant; quit grade school after six years; worked in a cotton mill and shoe factory; City of Philadelphia Bok Award 1930; died February 8, 1956, in Philadelphia, Pa, at age 93.

Connie Mack, 6 ft. 1 in, 150 lbs. was a star catcher in his prime, but is better known for his managerial record. Mack had the longest managerial career in the history of baseball—53 years, 50 years with one team, the Philadelphia Athletics. His teams won 3776 games and lost 4025, won 24 and lost 19 in World Series play. They won nine American League pennants and captured five World Series. Mack twice built up a great team only to sell many

of his best players. Connie Mack was a tall slender man who always dressed in a hat and suit, and never came out on the field to argue with an umpire. His patience with his players was endless. He neither smoked, drank nor used profanity. Connie Mack was stockholder and (in later years) majority owner of the Athletics, enabling him to maintain his job during the losing years.
Also in: Noteworthy Contributors Hall of Fame, Citizens Savings Hall of Fame Athletic Museum.

McGRAW, John Joseph "Little Napoleon"
Player and Manager
Born April 7, 1873, in Truxton, N.Y; mother, sister and three brothers died of diphtheria; became a candy salesman on a train at age 16; Manager of the First National League All-Star Team 1933; died February 25, 1934, in New Rochelle, N.Y, at age 60.

1891 Baltimore American Association, third baseman
1892 – 1899 Baltimore Orioles National League, player-manager
1900 St. Louis Cardinals National League, third baseman
1901 – 1902 Baltimore Orioles American League, player-manager
1902 – 1932 New York Giants National League, manager

John McGraw was 5 ft. 7 in. tall and weighed 155 lbs. He had seven straight seasons of hitting above .300 with Baltimore. As a player he took part in 1082 games, with 1307 hits, 124 doubles, 71 triples, 12 homers and 444 stolen bases. McGraw was a scrapper. He fought with umpires, tongue-lashed players, tried to intimidate league presidents and bullied anyone who stood in the way of his winning. During games he used every trick imaginable to confuse opponents and umpires but was nevertheless voted baseball's greatest manager. Under his leadership the Giants won ten pennants and three World Series championships. His forte was the ability to judge talent. At one point he tried to get a black man into the Baltimore Club by claiming he was a full-blooded Cherokee. Ill health forced him to retire during the 1932 season.

SPEAKER, Tristram E.
Player
Born April 4, 1888, in Hubbard, Tex; American League Most Valuable Player 1912; after retirement became a sportscaster; died December 8, 1958, in Lake Whitney, Tex, at age 70.

1907 – 1915 Boston Red Sox American League, center fielder
1916 – 1926 Cleveland Indians American League, center fielder
1927 Washington Senators American League, center fielder
1928 Philadelphia Athletics American League, center fielder

The so-called "Gray Eagle" was a great defensive outfielder. He holds the major league record for most unassisted double plays by an outfielder, 4. The 5 ft. 11-in, 193-lb. Texan ranks second in putouts and total chances taken. He played the shallowest center field in major league history. No one ever covered the position so daringly, but he was always right under the ball when it fell. During his career he hit .344 in 2789 games with 3515 hits, 1881 runs, 793 doubles, 224 triples, 115 home runs and 1559 RBI.

WRIGHT, George
Player and Manager
Born January 28, 1847, in New York City; brother Harry was one of the game's founders and organizers; son later starred in the Davis Cup Tennis Championship; set up the Wright and Ditson Sporting Goods Co; died August 31, 1937, in Boston, Mass, at age 90.

1869 Cincinnati Red Stockings, shortstop
1871 – 1875 Boston National Association, shortstop
1876 – 1878 Boston Red Caps National League, shortstop
1879 Providence Grays National League, shortstop
1880 – 1881 Boston Red Caps National League, player-manager
1882 – 1883 Providence Grays National League, player-manager

Wright was an all-around athlete who starred on baseball's first professional team, the Cincinnati Red Stockings. In 1869 he hit 49 home runs in 56 games. Hitting over .330 each year, he helped Boston win four National Association flags in a row. George, at 5 ft. 9 in, 150 lbs. helped the shortstop position by introducing new methods. As manager of Providence he led that team to a pennant in 1879. During his seven years as a National League player Wright played 329 games and had a batting average of .256.

YOUNG, Denton True "Cy"
Player
Born March 29, 1867, in Gilmore, Ohio; Temple Cup 1892; died November 4, 1955, near Peolin, Ohio, at age 88.

1890 – 1898 Cleveland Spiders National League, pitcher
1899 – 1900 St. Louis Cardinals National League, pitcher
1901 – 1908 Boston Red Sox American League, pitcher
1909 – 1911 Cleveland Indians American League, pitcher
1911 Boston Pilgrims National League, pitcher

Cy Young was probably the greatest pitcher ever to play the game, setting some records that will assuredly never be broken. He is the only pitcher to win more than 200 games in each of two major leagues, 511 in all. Cy won more than 20 games 16 times and more than 30 games 5 times. During his 22-year career he pitched 906 games, 7377 innings, 77 shutouts, 313 losses, 2819 strikeouts, 7078 hits, a percentage of .620 and an ERA of 2.63. Cy played in the 1903 World Series, pitching two no-hitters and a perfect game. He had 23 consecutive hitless innings in 1904. Cy Young ranks second in games pitched on the all-time list, first in complete games, first in innings, first in wins, first in losses, third in strikeouts and fourth in shutouts. He ended his pitching career at the age of 45 and returned to farming in Ohio.

1938

ALEXANDER, Grover Cleveland "Alex"
Player
Born February 26, 1887, in Elba, Nebr; eleven brothers

and one sister; died December 4, 1950, in St. Paul, Nebr.

1911–1917 Philadelphia Phillies National League, pitcher
1918–1926 Chicago Cubs National League, pitcher
1926–1929 St. Louis Cardinals National League, pitcher
1930 Philadelphia Phillies National League, pitcher
1930 Dallas, Texas League, pitcher

Alex is famed for his easy pitching motion and control. He won 28 games for the Phillies in his first major league season. Alex holds the National League record for complete games, 437, and the all-time record for shutouts in one season, 16; he is tied with Christy Mathewson for the National League record for games won, 373. He is best known for striking out Tony Lazzeri with the bases loaded in the seventh game of the 1926 World Series. Alex liked to break training; alcohol was his main vice. It is said that he played many games suffering from hangovers. The 6 ft. 1-in, 185-lb. Nebraskan played 696 games in the major leagues for 5180 innings, 2198 strikeouts and seven World Series games. Retirement left him with only memories. He joined a flea circus and was found dead at the age of 63 in a shabby rented room in his home state of Nebraska.

CARTWRIGHT, Alexander Joy, Jr.
Founder and Contributor
Born April 17, 1820, in New York City; died July 12, 1892, in Honolulu, Hawaii.

Cartwright is known as the father of modern baseball. He drew up the first set of baseball rules and organized the first team, the Knickerbockers, in 1845. He set the standard for bases at 90 in. apart. Cartwright is said to have umpired the first game played under the new regulations. He spent the rest of his life popularizing the game. He traveled across the country to join the California Gold Rush and later established a business in Hawaii.

CHADWICK, Henry
Writer and Contributor
Born October 5, 1824, in Exeter, England; son of a prominent journalist; began career as a music teacher; became a baseball writer in the early 1850s; died April 20, 1908, in Brooklyn, N.Y, at age 83.

Chadwick is known as the father of the box score and authored the first rule book for baseball in 1858. He was chairman of the Rules Committee in the first nationwide baseball organization from 1858 to 1870. Chadwick was editor of the first weekly newspaper devoted exclusively to baseball, *Ball Players' Chronicle,* 1867–1869, and he edited the first fans' paper, *The Metropolitan,* 1882–1884. Chadwick was the author of *Art of Pitching and Fielding,* 1889, and edited *Spalding Official Baseball Guide,* 1881–1908.

1939

ANSON, Adrian Constantine "Cap"
Player and Manager
Born April 17, 1852, in Marshalltown, Ind; attended Notre Dame; died April 14, 1922, in Chicago, Ill.

1879–1897 Chicago White Stockings/Colts National League, player-manager
1898 New York Giants National League, manager

Cap Anson is identified as the first all-around baseball player and manager. As a right-handed hitter with Chicago, the 6 ft. 1-in, 227-lb. Anson played 2276 games, had 9101 at bats, with 2995 hits, 528 doubles, 124 triples, 96 home runs and 1715 RBI. In August 1884 he became the second player in history to hit three home runs in a game and in the same month of 1886 he set a National League record for the most runs in a game, 6. Anson is generally credited with inventing the hit-and-run play. He led his team to five pennants, 1880–1882, 1885 and 1886. As manager he instituted the traditional spring training season.

COLLINS, Edward Trowbridge, Sr. "Cocky"
Player and Manager
Born May 2, 1887, in Millerton, N.Y; son Eddie, Jr, played in the majors as a member of the Athletics, 1939–1942; served in the Marines during W.W. I; played football as quarterback at Columbia; played baseball under the name of Sullivan to earn extra money; died March 25, 1951, in Boston, Mass, at age 63.

1906–1914 Philadelphia Athletics American League, second baseman
1915–1926 Chicago White Sox American League, player-manager
1927–1930 Philadelphia Athletics American League, player-coach

Eddie Collins had an enviable lifetime record of 2862 games, 9949 at bats, 3311 hits (a member of the exclusive 3000 hit club), 1818 runs, 437 doubles, 186 triples, 47 home runs, 1307 RBI, 743 stolen bases for an average of .333. He played more seasons in the major league than any other twentieth-century player, 25. Eddie was with the Athletics during their pennant-winning seasons of 1910, 1911, 1913 and 1914. He had a habit of sticking a wad of chewing gum on his cap and popping it in his mouth if a pitcher got two strikes on him.

COMISKEY, Charles A.
Player, Manager and Owner
Born August 15, 1859, in Chicago, Ill; family was sole owner of the White Sox for nearly 60 years; died October 26, 1931, in Eagle River, Wis.

1882–1889 St. Louis American Association, first baseman-manager
1890 Chicago Players League, player-manager
1891 St. Louis American Association, player-manager
1892–1894 Cincinnati Reds National League, player-manager
1895–1899 St. Paul Western League, owner-manager
1900–1931 Chicago White Sox, owner

As a player, Comiskey's lifetime major league record shows 1374 games, 5780 at bats, 981 runs, 1559 hits, 199 doubles, 69 triples, 29 homers and 440 stolen bases for an average of .270. As a manager, Comiskey bought the Sioux City franchise. Under Commy's ownership the White Sox won pennants in 1901, 1906, 1917 and 1919. In 1906 and 1917 the team won the World Series. Several members of the team were barred in 1920 in the "Black Sox" scandal and the team was ruined.

CUMMINGS, William Arthur "Candy"
Player
Born October 17, 1848, in Ware, Mass; died May 16, 1924, in Toledo, Ohio, at age 75.

1867 State of Brooklyn American Association, pitcher
1872 New York Mutuals National Association, pitcher
1873 Lord Baltimores National Association, pitcher
1874 Philadelphia National Association, pitcher
1875 Hartford National Association, pitcher
1876 Hartford Blues National League, pitcher
1877 Cincinnati Reds National League, pitcher

Cummings is said to have developed the curveball in 1867. The 5 ft. 9-in, 120-lb. player was elected president of the International Association, the first minor league, in 1877.

EWING, William B. "Buck"
Player and Manager
Born October 17, 1859, in Hoaglands, Ohio; died October 20, 1906, in Cincinnati, Ohio, at age 47.

1880–1882 Troy Trojans National League, catcher
1883–1889 New York Giants National League, catcher
1890 New York Players League, catcher-manager
1891–1892 New York Giants National League, catcher-manager
1893–1894 Cleveland Spiders National League, catcher-manager
1895–1899 Cincinnati Reds National League, manager
1900 New York Giants National League, manager

During his 18 years of playing baseball, Buck Ewing, 5 ft. 10 in, 188 lbs. played all the positions on the diamond. Some say he was the greatest catcher of the nineteenth century. He had a .303 batting average for 1281 games and 5348 at bats.

GEHRIG, Henry Louis "Lou"
Player
Born June 19, 1903, in Bronx, N.Y; played football and baseball at Columbia Univ; Most Valuable Player 1927, 1931, 1934 and 1936; American League Triple Crown 1934; worked for the New York City Parole Commission from 1939 until death; died at age 37 from an incurable amyotrophic lateral sclerosis on June 2, 1941, in Riverdale, N.Y.

1923–1939 New York Yankees American League, first baseman

Lou drove in 100 runs per season for 13 consecutive years. In 1932 he hit four consecutive homers in a game. He played in 2164 games, had 8001 at bats, with 2721 hits, 535 doubles, 162 triples, 493 homers, 1991 RBI and a life-time average of .340, playing in seven World Series. Despite illness, Lou never missed a game in almost 14 years (2130 games). Six feet tall, and weighing 200 lbs, Lou established himself as the most indestructible player in history. On "Gehrig Day" July 4, 1939, in Yankee stadium, Lou told fans that he considered himself the "luckiest guy in the world" to have played for the Yankees. The Yankees retired his No. 4 uniform with him.

KEELER, William Henry
Player
Born March 3, 1872, in Brooklyn, N.Y; died January 1, 1923, in Brooklyn, at age 50.

1892–1893 New York Giants National League, third baseman
1894–1898 Baltimore Orioles National League, third baseman-right fielder
1899–1902 Brooklyn Superbas National League, right fielder
1903–1909 New York Highlanders American League, right fielder

Wee Willie Keeler used the lightest bat ever seen in the majors. The 5 ft. 4-in, 130-lb. player rarely struck out and was a very successful bunter. In 1897 he hit safely in 44 consecutive games and had the highest average for a left-handed hitter, .424 in 1897. His lifetime major league average was .345 in 2124 games, 8564 times at bat, 1720 runs, 2955 hits, 234 doubles, 155 triples, 32 home runs and 519 stolen bases.

RADBOURNE, Charles Gardner "Rad"
Player
Born December 11, 1854, in Rochester, N.Y; lost one eye in a hunting accident; operated a pool hall; died February 5, 1897, in Bloomington, Ill.

1881–1885 Providence Grays National League, pitcher
1886–1889 Boston Beaneaters National League, pitcher-right fielder
1890 Boston Players League, pitcher-right fielder
1891 Cincinnati Reds National League, pitcher-right fielder

In 1884 Radbourne won 60 games, an all-time record, while losing 12. He was 5 ft. 9 in. tall and weighed 168 lbs. When he wasn't pitching he was usually in right field. Radbourne pitched a no-hitter against Cleveland in July 1883. His lifetime record shows 517 games pitched, 4543 innings, 35 shutouts, 308 wins, 191 losses, a percentage of .617 and 1746 strikeouts. Winning the 1884 pennant for Providence, he pitched the last 27 games of the season and won 26. Radbourne won three straight games in the 1884 World Series.

SISLER, George Harold
Player
Born March 24, 1893, in Nimesiola, Ohio; two sons, Dick and Dave; graduated from Michigan Univ. in 1915; American League Most Valuable Player 1922; died March 26, 1973, in Richmond Heights, Mo, at age 80.

1915–1927 St. Louis Browns American League, first baseman-manager
1928 Washington Senators American League, first baseman
1928–1930 Boston Braves National League, first baseman

Gorgeous George was one of the great all-around players. He began his career as a pitcher, but was quickly changed to first base. George, at 5 ft. 10 in, 170 lbs, 6 times collected 200 or more hits in a season. He had a 41-game hitting streak in 1922. Leading the American League first basemen in assists for six years, George holds the major league record for most lifetime assists, 1554. George hit .340 in 2055 games, with 1284 runs, 2812 hits, 425 doubles, 165 triples, 100 home runs and 1180 RBI. A sinus condition plagued Sisler throughout his career and forced him to miss the entire 1923 season because of a related eye problem.

SPALDING, Albert Goodwill
Player and Manager

Born September 2, 1850, in Byron, Ill; formed the Spalding Sporting Goods Co. in 1876; ran, unsuccessfully, for U.S. Senate; died September 9, 1915, in Point Loma, Calif, at age 65.

1871 – 1875 Boston National League, pitcher
1876 – 1878 Chicago White Stockings National League, player-manager

While Spalding was with Boston he pitched virtually every game, collecting 207 of the team's 227 victories, becoming baseball's first 200-game winner. Al was one of the "Big Four" Boston stars lured to Chicago in 1876, managing them to a pennant that year. Al, 6 ft. 1 in, 170 lbs. organized the first worldwide baseball tour and helped draft the National League Constitution in 1876. He also founded a number of sports publications, of which *Spalding's Baseball Guide* is the best known. His sporting goods company was a great success.
Also in: Noteworthy Contributors Hall of Fame, Citizens Savings Hall of Fame Athletic Museum.

1942

HORNSBY, Rogers "Rajah"
Player and Manager

Born April 27, 1896, in Winters, Tex; married three times, divorced twice; had two sons; American League Triple Crown 1922 and 1925; Most Valuable Player 1925 and 1929; died January 5, 1963, in Chicago, Ill. at age 66.

1915 – 1926 St. Louis Cardinals National League, second baseman-manager
1927 New York Giants National League, second baseman, shortstop
1928 Boston Braves National League, player-manager
1929 – 1932 Chicago Cubs National League, second baseman-manager
1933 St. Louis Cardinals National League, manager
1933 – 1937 St. Louis Browns American League, player-manager
1952 – 1953 Cincinnati Reds National League, manager

Hornsby is regarded as the greatest right-handed hitter in the game's history. Rajah had a unique batting stance—as far away from the plate as possible, feet together. He won six batting championships in a row, 1920 to 1925, for a National League record. His lifetime batting average of .358 is the highest in National League history. In his 23 years of major league play he had a total of 2930 hits, 541 doubles, 168 triples, 302 home runs, and 1579 RBI. The 5 ft. 11-in, 175 lb. Hornsby lacked tact in dealing with people; he was as likely to tell off his boss as he was a rookie. He didn't smoke or drink, but loved ice cream. He refused to go to movies or read books because he felt it might hurt his batting eye.

1944

LANDIS, Kenesaw Mountain
Commissioner and Contributor

Born November 20, 1866, in Millville, Ohio; a U.S. District Court Judge; died November 25, 1944, in Chicago, Ill, at age 78.

Until 1921, baseball was headed by a three-man commission, but club owners became convinced that they needed one strong man to rule baseball. For 23 years Landis ruled with an iron hand. He blacklisted players, banned them for life and fined owners for wrongdoings, all to free baseball from any hint of scandal. He attacked the common practice of hiding good young players in the minor leagues and improved players' contracts. Landis was famous for his soft fedora hat and a frown. The judge requested, before his death, that there be no funeral ceremonies of any kind.

1945

BRESNAHAN, Roger Philip "Duke of Tralee"
Player and Manager

Born June 11, 1879, in Toledo, Ohio; died December 4, 1944, in Toledo.

1897 Washington Senators National League, pitcher
1900 Chicago White Stockings National League, pitcher
1901 Baltimore Orioles American League, catcher
1902 – 1908 New York Giants National League, outfielder, catcher
1909 – 1912 St. Louis Cardinals National League, catcher
1913 – 1915 Chicago Cubs National League, catcher

The 5 ft. 8-in, 180 lb. right-handed batter was skillful at getting hit by pitches for a free ride to first base. His major league record shows 1410 games played, with a .279 batting average. In his only World Series (1905), Roger hit .313. Bresnahan had excellent speed in base running and was a good clutch hitter. In 1908 he invented shinguards for catchers.

BROUTHERS, Dennis "Don"
Player

Born May 8, 1858, in Sylvan Lake, N.Y; died August 3, 1932, in East Orange, N.J, at age 74.

1879 – 1880 Troy Trojans National League, first baseman
1881 – 1885 Buffalo Bisons National League, first baseman
1886 – 1888 Detroit Wolverines National League, first baseman
1889 Boston Beaneaters National League, first baseman
1890 Boston Players League, first baseman
1891 Boston American Association, first baseman
1892 – 1893 Brooklyn Bridgegrooms National League, first baseman
1894 – 1895 Baltimore Orioles National League, first baseman
1895 Louisville Colonels National League, first baseman
1896 Philadelphia Phillies National League, first baseman
1897 – 1899 Springfield Eastern League, first baseman
1904 New York Giants National League, first baseman

Brouthers' lifetime major league batting average was .349 in 1658 games, 1507 runs, 2349 hits, 446 doubles, 212 triples, 103 homers and 263 stolen bases. When 6 ft. 2-in, 207 lb. Brouthers and the Detroit team won the pennant and the World Series in 1887, he boasted, "We slugged 'em to death." He later worked at the press gate of the Polo Grounds. Brouthers was the mightiest slugger of the era, winning five batting titles in the major leagues. He was part of the original "Big Four" at Buffalo.

CLARKE, Frederick Clifford "Cap"

Player and Manager

Born October 3, 1872, in Winterset, Iowa; brother, Josh Clarke; died August 14, 1960, in Winfield, Kans, at age 87.

1894 – 1899 Louisville Colonels National League, left fielder, manager
1900 – 1915 Pittsburgh Pirates National League, player-manager
1925 – 1926 Pittsburgh Pirates National League, coach
1926 – 1927 Pittsburgh Pirates National League, v.pres. and asst. manager

With Louisville in 1894, Clarke marked his debut with a five-for-five plate performance, a record never equaled. In 1910 he set a National League record for the most assists by an outfielder in a nine-inning game. Clarke had a major league average of .315 in 2204 games, stealing 527 bases. He was the first of the successful "Boy Managers," managing Louisville at the age of 24. Cap Clarke later won four pennants for Pittsburgh and a World Series. He served as president of the National Association of Leagues for Sandlot Clubs.

COLLINS, James Joseph

Player

Born January 16, 1870, in Niagara Falls, N.Y; died March 6, 1943, in Buffalo, N.Y, at age 73.

1895 – 1900 Boston Beaneaters National League, third baseman
1901 – 1907 Boston Red Sox American League, player-manager
1907 – 1908 Philadelphia Athletics American League, third baseman

Jimmy Collins was the first player to master the art of defense against the bunt. Some consider the 5 ft. 8-in, 160 lb. third baseman to be the greatest in history. He revolutionized third-base play by staying well away from the bag. In 1899 Collins set the National League record for the most chances accepted, exclusive of errors, for a third baseman, 601. His lifetime major league totals are 1718 games, 6792 at bats, 1057 runs, 1999 hits, 333 doubles, 117 triples, 62 homers and an average of .294. As player-manager of the Red Sox, Jimmy led them to pennants in 1903 and 1904.

DELAHANTY, Edward James

Player

Born October 3, 1867, in Cleveland, Ohio; one of five brothers, all in major leagues; died July 2, 1903, in Niagara Falls, N.Y, at age 35.

1888 – 1889 Philadelphia Phillies National League, second baseman and left fielder
1890 Cleveland Players League, outfielder
1891 – 1901 Philadelphia Phillies National League, outfielder
1902 – 1903 Washington Senators American League, outfielder

Ed Delahanty's major league career ended abruptly in 1903 when he was suspended for heavy drinking. He was found dead a week later close to Niagara Falls. It is thought that he fell off his homeward-bound train into the water and drowned. His lifetime average was .345 in 1825 games, 2593 hits, 7493 at bats, 1596 runs, 508 doubles, 182 triples, 98 homers and 478 stolen bases. At 6 ft. 1 in, 170 lbs, Big Ed was the second man to hit four homers in a game in 1896. He hit over .400 three times, is the coholder of the National League record for the most consecutive hits, ten, and is the only player ever to have two six-for-six games. He won the batting title in 1899.

DUFFY, Hugh

Player and Manager

Born November 25, 1866, in River Point, R.I; first job was in a mill in Conn; died October 19, 1954, in Allston, Mass, at age 87.

1888 – 1889 Chicago White Stockings National League, center fielder
1890 Chicago Players League, outfielder
1891 Boston American Association, outfielder
1892 – 1900 Boston Beaneaters National League, outfielder
1901 Milwaukee Brewers American League, manager
1904 – 1906 Philadelphia Phillies National League, manager
1910 – 1911 Chicago White Sox American League, manager
1921 – 1922 Boston Red Sox American League, manager
1924 – 1954 Boston Red Sox American League, scout

In 1894, Duffy's batting average of .440 was the highest ever recorded. He hit over .300 ten times. In 1894 he tied a National League record by safely reaching first base three times in one inning. Duffy's lifetime average was .330 in 1722 games, with 2307 hits and 597 stolen bases. In his later years Duffy coached at Harvard College and Boston College.

JENNINGS, Hugh Ambrose

Player and Coach

Born April 2, 1869, in Pittstone, Pa; died of spinal meningitis at age 58, February 1, 1928, in Scranton, Pa.

1891 Louisville American Association, shortstop
1892 – 1893 Louisville Colonels National League, shortstop
1893 – 1899 Baltimore Orioles National League, shortstop
1899 – 1900 Brooklyn Superbas National League, first baseman
1901 – 1902 Philadelphia Phillies National League, first baseman
1903 Brooklyn Superbas National League, first baseman
1907 – 1920 Detroit Tigers American League, manager-player
1921 – 1925 New York Giants National League, assistant manager and coach

Jennings had a .401 batting average in 1896, a major league record for shortstops. He led shortstops in fielding for five consecutive years, a National League record, and in 1896 was hit by pitched balls 49 times, also a major league record. Hughie's playing career saw 1264 games with a .314 average, 152 hits, 989 runs, 227 doubles, 88 triples and 373 stolen bases. He began his managing career with Detroit and led them to three pennants. Jennings, 5 ft. 8 in, 165 lbs, never fined his players, preferring to talk out the problem. Hughie later moved to the New York Giants with his old friend and manager John McGraw. While there he was coach and assistant manager until ill health forced his retirement.

KELLY, Michael Joseph "King"
Player and Manager
Born December 31, 1857, in Troy, N.Y; died November 8, 1894, in Boston, Mass, at age 36.

1878 – 1879 Cincinnati Reds National League, catcher, outfielder
1880 – 1886 Chicago White Stockings National League, catcher, outfielder
1887 – 1889 Boston Beaneaters National League, catcher, outfielder
1890 – 1892 Boston Players League, player-manager
1891 – 1892 Boston Beaneaters National League, outfielder
1893 New York Giants National League, outfielder

King Kelly was the Number One idol of his day. He was proclaimed by some to be the best-dressed man in the world. At 5 ft. 11 in, 180 lbs, Kelly was a versatile player and fans loved his base-running slide. His lifetime totals show 1434 games, 1853 hits, 357 doubles, 109 triples, 65 homers and 1359 runs scored. His lifetime batting average was .313 and he had 5 consecutive years when he stole 40 or more bases. During his 16 years in the majors he played on 8 pennant-winning teams.

O'ROURKE, James Henry
Player and Manager
Born August 24, 1852, in East Bridgeport, Conn; brother John played with Boston; graduated from Yale Law School; died January 8, 1919, in Bridgeport, Conn, at age 66.

1872 – 1878 Boston Red Caps National League, left fielder, catcher
1879 Providence Grays National League, left fielder
1880 Boston Red Caps National League, left fielder
1881 – 1884 Buffalo Bisons National League, player-manager
1885 – 1889 New York Giants National League, outfielder, infielder
1890 New York Players League, outfielder
1891 – 1892 New York Giants National League, outfielder
1893 Washington Senators National League, player-manager

Jim O'Rourke devoted 43 years to baseball as a player, manager, umpire and minor league president. He played until past the age of 50. Dubbed "the Orator" because of his extensive vocabulary, he was one of baseball's first missionaries. He went to England in 1874 to promote baseball there. During his career, the 5 ft. 8-in, 185 lb. New Englander played in 1750 games, got 2314 hits, 385 doubles, 139 triples, 49 homers and had a batting average of .314. His teams won six pennants during the first eight years of his pro career.

ROBINSON, Wilbert "Uncle Robbie"
Player and Manager
Born June 2, 1863, in Bolton, Mass; brother, Fred; died August 8, 1934, in Atlanta, Ga, at age 71.

1886 – 1890 Philadelphia American Association, catcher
1890 Brooklyn American Association, catcher
1890 – 1891 Baltimore American Association, catcher
1892 – 1899 Baltimore Orioles National League, catcher
1900 St. Louis Cardinals National League, catcher
1901 – 1902 Baltimore Orioles American League, player-coach
1911 New York Giants National League, coach
1914 – 1931 Brooklyn Dodgers National League, manager

Despite his long career as a player, Robinson is better known as a manager. He was the well-liked "Uncle Robbie" who preferred laughing people out of their slumps to yelling. While he was catcher for the Baltimore Orioles, they took pennants 1894 through 1896. In 17 years as a player he had 1371 games, a .273 batting average, 632 runs, 210 doubles, 54 triples, 18 homers and 219 stolen bases. Brooklyn won two pennants under his management.

1946

BURKETT, Jesse Cail "Crab"
Player
Born December 4, 1869, in Wheeling, W.Va; died May 27, 1953, in Worcester, Mass, at age 83.

1890 New York Giants National League, pitcher-left fielder
1891 – 1898 Cleveland Spiders National League, outfielder
1899 – 1901 St. Louis Cardinals National League, outfielder
1902 – 1904 St. Louis Browns American League, outfielder
1905 Boston Puritans American League, outfielder

Jesse Burkett is one of three players in history to hit over .400 two consecutive seasons. Crab specialized in line-drive singles, but was also a great bunter and base runner. The 5 ft. 8-in, 155 lb. left-handed batter had a lifetime average of .342 in 2063 games over a 16-year period. Six times Burkett batted over 200 hits; during his career he stole 392 bases. He managed a New England League team from 1906 until 1913 and coached for the New York Giants during the 1920s.
Also in: West Virginia Sports Writers Hall of Fame.

CHANCE, Frank Leroy "Husk"
Player and Manager
Born September 9, 1877, in Fresno, Calif; attended Washington Col. in Calif; died September 15, 1924, in Los Angeles at age 47.

1898 – 1912 Chicago Cubs National League, catcher, first baseman
1905 – 1913 Chicago Cubs National League, manager
1913 – 1914 New York Yankees American League, manager, first baseman
1916 – 1917 Los Angeles Pacific Coast League, owner-manager
1923 Boston Red Sox American League, manager

Frank was rated among the National League's finest hitters and first basemen of the early 1900s, but earned fame as an inspirational playing manager. As manager he built the Chicago Cubs into the greatest machine of the period, winning four pennants in five years to gain the nickname "Peerless Leader." His lifetime average was .279 in 1232 games, 796 runs and 405 stolen bases. Chance saw World Series play four times and as manager of the Cubs compiled 116 victories, unequaled in National League history.

CHESBRO, John Dwight "Jack"
Player

Born June 5, 1874, in North Adams, Mass; died November 6, 1931, in Conway, Mass, at age 57.

1899 – 1902 Pittsburgh Pirates National League, pitcher
1903 – 1909 New York Highlanders American League, pitcher
1909 Boston Red Sox American League, pitcher

In 11 years Happy Jack completed 261 out of 332 games, with 35 shutouts and 1265 strikeouts in 2897 innings. Chesbro was the only pitcher ever to lead both leagues in percentages of wins for a season. His 41 wins in 1904 is the modern National League record. Chesbro, 6 ft. 1 in, 175 lbs, also set American League records for the most starts, 51, and the most complete games, 48, that season. An early spitball ace, Jack felt that pitch ruined his arm.

EVERS, John Joseph "Crab"
Player and Coach

Born July 21, 1881, in Troy, N.Y; National League Most Valuable Player 1914; Chalmers Award; died March 28, 1947, in Albany, N.Y, at age 65.

1902 – 1912 Chicago Cubs National League, second baseman
1913 Chicago Cubs National League, player-manager
1914 – 1917 Boston Braves National League, second baseman
1917 Philadelphia Phillies National League, second baseman
1920 New York Giants National League, coach
1921 Chicago Cubs National League, manager
1922 – 1928 Chicago White Sox American League, coach-manager
1929 – 1932 Boston Braves National League, assistant manager
1933 – 1934 Boston Braves National League, scout

In 1908, besides hitting .300, Evers used his knowledge of the rules to turn the National League race around in the "Merkle boner play" at second base. He is the middleman of the famous double play combination of Tinker-to-Evers-to-Chance, popularized by a poem sent to a New York newspaper. Evers holds the National League record for the most steals home, 21. He played in four World Series during his career. Evers' overall record shows a .270 batting average in 1776 games and 6136 at bats.

GRIFFITH, Clark Calvin "Griff"
Player and Manager

Born November 20, 1869, in Clear Creek, Mo, in a log cabin; raised seven children of wife's dead brother, one of whom (Calvin) now president of Minnesota Twins; died October 27, 1955, in Washington, D.C, at age 85.

1893 – 1900 Chicago White Stockings/Colts National League, pitcher
1901 – 1902 Chicago White Sox American League, pitcher-manager
1903 – 1908 New York Highlanders American League, pitcher-manager
1909 – 1910 Cincinnati Reds National League, player-manager
1912 – 1914 Washington Senators American League, player-manager
1915 – 1920 Washington Senators American League, manager
1921 – 1955 Washington Senators American League, owner

Griff was associated with baseball for 68 years as player, playing manager, manager-executive and owner. The 5 ft. 8 in, 175 lb. player spent most of his career as a pitcher, but was a fair hitter as well. A sportswriter once remarked, "No brainier pitcher ever lived." During his 21 years as a player he had 236 wins, 145 losses and an ERA of 3.31. In 1919 the "Old Fox" got control of the Washington Senators and in 1920 became president of that club, remaining in that position until his death.

McCARTHY, Thomas Francis Michael
Player and Manager

Born July 24, 1864, in Boston, Mass; died August 5, 1922, in Boston, at age 58.

1885 Boston Beaneaters National League, right fielder
1886 – 1887 Philadelphia Phillies National League, right fielder
1888 – 1891 St. Louis American Association, player-manager
1892 – 1895 Boston Beaneaters National League, outfielder
1896 Brooklyn Bridgegrooms National League, outfielder

McCarthy, at 5 ft. 6 in, 145 lbs, was a clever, aggressive player and one of the first to develop techniques of stealing signs. With Hugh Duffy, Tommy was part of the famed "Heavenly Twins" who baffled opposing hitters in the outfield. McCarthy developed the perfect trapped ball. If an opposing player stood on base, Tommy would let the ball drop and get a force-out; if the player ran, Tommy would catch it as a fly. Another of McCarthy's tricks resulted in a rule change. The sacrifice-fly rule originally said that a runner could not leave base until the ball was held firmly in the fielder's hand, so McCarthy would juggle the ball while running to the infield. Tommy was a brilliant base runner; during his career he had 506 stolen bases. His overall major league average was .294 in 1258 games, 5055 at bats, 1485 hits, 194 doubles, 155 triples and 32 homers.

McGINNITY, Joseph Jerome "Iron Man"
Player

Born March 19, 1871, in Rock Island, Ill; worked in an iron foundry; died March 14, 1929, at age 58 from cancer.

1899 Baltimore Orioles National League, pitcher
1900 Brooklyn Superbas National League, pitcher
1901 – 1902 Baltimore Orioles American League, pitcher
1902 – 1908 New York Giants National League, pitcher

Joe used an underhand delivery that enabled him to snap a curveball with minimum arm strain. Joe holds the major league record for the most years leading in games, 8; the National League modern record for the most starts, 48; and for most innings pitched in a season, 434. He pitched two games on one day five times. While in the American League, he once became enraged by a decision made by umpire Tommy Connally, stomped on his toes, spat in his face and punched him. Joe was fined and suspended. He later apologized publicly. His major league record shows 247 wins, 145 defeats, 467 games pitched, 3455 innings and 32 shutouts. Joe was 5 ft. 11-in. tall and weighed 206 lbs.

PLANK, Edward Stewart "Eddie"
Player

Born August 31, 1875, in Gettysburg, Pa; attended Gettysburg Col; died February 24, 1926, in Gettysburg, at age 50.

1901–1914 Philadelphia Athletics American League, pitcher
1915 St. Louis Federal League, pitcher
1916–1917 St. Louis Browns American League, pitcher

Eddie ranks among the top ten winning pitchers in major league history. Plank had more complete games and more shutouts than any other left-hander in history. His 304 American League victories is a league record for left-handers. Plank, who was 5 ft. 11 in, 175 lbs, holds the American League record for the most consecutive years at 100 or more strikeouts, 13. He would agitate batters by fidgeting on the mound. Eddie helped the Athletics to six pennants and played in seven World Series games. His major league record shows 623 games played, 4503 innings, 70 shutouts, 326 wins, 192 losses, 2112 strikeouts, a .629 percentage and a 2.34 ERA.

TINKER, Joseph Bert "Joe"
Player and Manager

Born July 27, 1880, in Muscotah, Kans; operated a billiard parlor; lost one leg to diabetes; died July 27, 1948, in Orlando, Fla, at age 68.

1902–1912 Chicago Cubs National League, shortstop
1913 Cincinnati Reds National League, player-manager
1914–1915 Chicago Federal League, player-manager
1916 Chicago Cubs National League, player-manager

Joe Tinker, 5 ft. 9 in, 175 lbs, was the famed member of the Tinker-to-Evers-to-Chance double-play combination that feuded constantly. He was known for getting more hits off Christy Mathewson than anyone else. Joe led the National League in shortstop putouts in 1911 and 1912, in assists in 1908 and in fielding average in 1906, 1908, 1911 and 1913. Tinker's lifetime average was .264 in 1642 games with 1565 hits, 716 runs, 238 doubles, 106 triples, 29 home runs and 783 RBI. He was in World Series play from 1906 to 1908 and again in 1910. He was later manager and owner of a team in the Florida State League.

WADDELL, George Edward "Rube"
Player

Born October 13, 1876, in Bradford, Pa; died April 1, 1914, in San Antonio, Tex, at age 38 from tuberculosis.

1897–1899 Louisville Colonels National League, pitcher
1900–1901 Pittsburgh Pirates National League, pitcher
1901 Chicago Cubs National League, pitcher
1902–1907 Philadelphia Athletics American League, pitcher
1908–1910 St. Louis Browns American League, pitcher

The eccentric Rube Waddell withstood all attempts by his managers to keep his mind on baseball. He would often turn cartwheels from the mound to the bench. Frequently he drank before games. One time he gave up a home run and got so dizzy watching the batter circle the bases that he fell down and had to be taken out of the game. He would sneak out during a game to be found later posing as a store mannequin, wrestling alligators or chasing fire engines. Despite all his antics, this left-handed pitcher set a major league record for the most years of 200 or more strikeouts, 7, and an American League record for the most years of 300 or more strikeouts, 2. In 1902 the 6 ft. 1-in, 196 lb. Rube struck out three batters on nine pitches to tie a major league record. During his 13-year career he won 191 games and lost 141 for an ERA of 2.16 in 407 games, 2961 innings, 803 walks, 2316 strikeouts, 50 shutouts and a percentage of .574. Rube helped Philadelphia to two pennants.

WALSH, Edward Arthur "Ed"
Player

Born April 14, 1881, in Plains, Pa; died May 26, 1956, in Pompano Beach, Fla, at age 78.

1904–1916 Chicago White Sox American League, pitcher
1917 Boston Braves National League, pitcher

Big Ed Walsh, 6 ft. 1 in, 193 lbs, holds the modern major league record for the most innings played in a season, 464. He has twice tied the National League record by throwing ten or more shutouts in a season and tied an American League record for the most shutouts in a month, six. "Moose" averaged 25 victories per season over a six-year period, 1907 to 1912. The spitballer won 195 and lost 126 games with a percentage of .607. He had 1731 strikeouts and 620 walks in 2968 innings and a 1.82 ERA. Walsh had a no-hitter in 1911 and saw World Series play in 1906. He enjoyed a 27-game consecutive-win season in 1911 until his arm gave out from overwork. Walsh was later an American League umpire and coached for Notre Dame.

1947

COCHRANE, Gordon Stanley "Mickey"
Player

Born April 6, 1903, in Bridgewater, Mass; attended Boston Univ; served in navy fitness program at Great Lakes Naval Training Station during W.W. II; Most Valuable Player Award 1928; died June 28, 1962, in Lake Forest, Ill, at age 59.

1925–1933 Philadelphia Athletics American League, catcher
1934–1937 Detroit Tigers American League, player-manager

Mickey ranked as one of the game's most exciting and aggressive performers. His lifetime major league record included 1482 games, with a .320 average, 1652 hits in 5169 at bats, 1041 runs, 333 doubles, 64 triples, 119 homers, 832 RBI and 64 stolen bases. Connie Mack considered him the greatest single factor in the Athletics' winning the 1929–1930 pennants and the World Series. He led Detroit to two league championships and a World Series in 1935. In 1937, after a pitched ball struck him in the temple, he was unconscious for ten days. His skull fractured in three places, he never played again. At widely spaced intervals Mickey served as coach, scout and manager for Philadelphia, Yankees, Tigers and Detroit. At other times he worked for trucking companies and operated a dude ranch in Wyoming.

FRISCH, Frank Francis

Player and Manager

Born September 9, 1897, in New York City; son of a linen lace manufacturer; attended Fordham Univ; captain of baseball, football and basketball teams in school; on the second All-American football team in 1917; a skier, ice skater, horticulturist and lover of symphonic music and good books; Most Valuable Player Award 1931; All-Star Games 1933 and 1934.

1919–1926 New York Giants National League, second baseman
1927–1937 St. Louis Cardinals National League, player-manager
1940–1946 Pittsburgh Pirates National League, manager
1949–1951 Chicago Cubs National League, manager

Frisch went straight from college into the majors. He was an outstanding infielder, base runner and batter. In 19 seasons, the 5 ft. 10-in, 185 lb. "Fordham Flash," saw his team to eight pennants. He had 13 seasons of .300 or over and played in 8 World Series. At the end of his playing career, Frisch had played in 2311 National League games with 2880 hits, 1532 runs, 466 doubles, 138 triples, 105 homers, 1242 RBI, 419 steals and a batting average of .316. He later went into television and radio sportscasting.

GROVE, Robert Moses "Lefty"

Player

Born March 6, 1900, in Lanconing, Md; raised in the Md. coal-mining area; practiced with rocks until age 19; Most Valuable Player Award 1931; All-Star Games 1933, 1936 and 1938; with wife retired to Maryland mountains; after wife died, moved to Norwalk, Ohio; died there at age 75 on May 22, 1975.

1920–1924 Baltimore International League, pitcher
1925–1933 Philadelphia Athletics American League, pitcher
1934–1941 Boston Red Sox American League, pitcher

Lefty Grove is considered one of the greatest left-handers in American League history. He did not reach the majors until age 25, but still managed 300 victories over a 17-year span. He led the American League in strikeouts for 7 consecutive seasons and won 20 or more games for 8 seasons. During his career Lefty pitched in 616 games with 3940 innings played, allowing 3849 hits and 1339 runs. He struck out 2266 and walked 1187, earning a percentage of .682 and an ERA of 3.06. At 6 ft. 3 in, 190 lbs, Grove played in eight World Series games. He signed with the Philadelphia Athletics for $100,600 and had a great part in earning their three straight pennants, 1929 to 1931.

HUBBELL, Carl Owen "Hub"

Player

Born June 22, 1903, in Carthage, Mo; grew up on a pecan farm in Okla; Most Valuable Player 1933 and 1936; All-Star Game 1934.

1928–1943 New York Giants National League, pitcher

Hubbell was a left-handed pitcher who loved to use the screwball. The 6 ft. 2-in, 172 lb. pitcher set a National League record in 1933 by throwing 46 consecutive innings without allowing a run. He won 24 straight games in 1936 and 1937 setting another National League record. Hub led the league in total victories three times, had the best ERA in 1933, 1934 and 1936 and led the league in total innings pitched, 309. In the 1934 All-Star Game, Carl struck out Ruth, Gehrig, Foxx, Simmons and Cronin in succession. His lifetime record includes 253 wins and 154 losses for a .622 percentage, 535 games, 3591 innings, 3461 hits, 1187 earned runs, 1677 strikeouts, 725 walks and an ERA of 2.98.

1948

PENNOCK, Herbert Jeffries "Herb"

Player

Born February 10, 1894, in Kennett Square, Pa; left Wenonah Military Academy to pitch in Atlantic City at age 17; saw military service in 1918; died January 20, 1948, in New York City at age 53.

1912–1915 Philadelphia Athletics American League, pitcher
1915–1923 Boston Red Sox American League, pitcher
1923–1933 New York Yankees American League, pitcher
1934–1936 Boston Red Sox American League, pitcher
1936–1940 Boston Red Sox American League, coach

Herb Pennock was an outstanding left-handed pitcher who saw 22 major league seasons with 240 wins and 162 losses. He pitched in 5 World Series games with no losses. The record of this 6 ft, 165-lb. pitcher shows a 3.55 ERA in 617 games and 3558 innings pitched, with 1227 strikeouts and a percentage of .597. He coached the Red Sox from 1936 to 1940, was supervisor of the Red Sox farm system from 1941 to 1943 and was general manager of Philadelphia in the National League from 1944 until his death.

TRAYNOR, Harold Joseph "Pie"

Player

Born November 11, 1899, in Framingham, Mass; father a painter; played football and baseball in school; All-Star Games 1933 and 1934; died March 16, 1972, in Pittsburgh, Pa, at age 72.

1920–1937 Pittsburgh Pirates National League, third baseman
1934–1939 Pittsburgh Pirates National League, manager
1940–1972 Pittsburgh Pirates National League, scout

Pie Traynor is rated among the great third basemen of all time. He was a consistent .300 hitter whose defensive play at third base was so great it tended to overshadow his batting. His lifetime average was .320 in 1941 games with 2416 hits, 1183 runs, 371 doubles, 164 triples, 58 home runs and 1273 RBI. Pie saw World Series play in

1925 and 1927. After his managerial term he became a popular television announcer in Pittsburgh.

1949

BROWN, Mordecai Peter
Player and Manager

Born October 19, 1876, in Nyesville, Ind; died February 14, 1948, in Terre Haute, Ind, at age 71.

1903 St. Louis Cardinals National League, pitcher
1904–1912 Chicago Cubs National League, pitcher
1913 Cincinnati Reds National League, pitcher
1914 St. Louis Federal League, Brooklyn Federal League, pitcher-manager
1915 Chicago Federal League, player-manager
1916 Chicago Cubs National League, pitcher

Pete Brown was the first major leaguer to pitch four consecutive shutouts (in 1908). He posted six successive 20-victory seasons from 1906 to 1911, but his biggest year was 1908 when he was 29 to 9. The 5 ft. 10-in, 175-lb. pitcher took part in 411 major league games, had 208 wins and 111 losses. Brown was raised in a coal-mining town where he lost half of his index finger in a feed cutter during his youth. He claimed his deformity enabled him to throw the meanest curveball ever.

GEHRINGER, Charles Leonard "Mechanical Man"
Player

Born May 11, 1903, in Fowlerville, Mich; entered Navy in 1942; served in physical fitness program, ended war as a Lieutenant; supplier of items used in car interiors to auto manufacturers; Most Valuable Player 1937; played in six All-Star Games.

1924–1942 Detroit Tigers American League, second baseman

Gehringer, 5 ft. 11-in, 185 lbs, led the American League second basemen in putouts, assists and fielding average for many years. He had a major league batting average of .321 with 2323 games played, 1773 runs, 2839 hits, 574 doubles, 146 triples, 184 homers and 1427 RBI. He was persuaded to join the Tigers as manager and vice president in 1951, continuing as vice president only after 1953.

NICHOLS, Charles Augustus "Kid"
Player and Manager

Born September 14, 1869, in Madison, Wis; died April 11, 1953, in Kansas City, Mo, at age 83.

1890–1901 Boston Beaneaters National League, pitcher
1904–1905 St. Louis Cardinals National League, player-manager
1905–1906 Philadelphia Phillies National League, pitcher

Kid Nichols, who was 5 ft. 10-in, 175 lb, holds the major league record for the most seasons winning 30 or more games, 7, and the most consecutive years winning 20 or more from the beginning of his career, 10. He was one of the few pitchers to win over 300 games, 360. Nichols played in 582 games, had 530 complete games, 5067 innings, 186 strikeouts, 1245 walks and 48 shutouts, for 360 wins and 202 losses.

1951

FOXX, James Emory "Jimmy"
Player

Born October 22, 1907, in Sudlersville, Md; won honors as a sprinter and high jumper during youth; seven All-Star Games; Triple Crown 1933; Most Valuable Player twice; died July 21, 1967, in Miami, Fla, at age 66.

1925–1935 Philadelphia Athletics American League, first baseman, outfielder
1936–1942 Boston Red Sox American League, first baseman, outfielder
1942–1944 Chicago Cubs National League, first baseman, outfielder
1945 Philadelphia Phillies National League, pitcher

A large man, 6 ft, 200 lbs, Jimmy Foxx's major league totals show 534 homers in 2317 games and a .325 batting average. He played in three World Series, 1929–1931. Foxx was noted as a home-run hitter. He played a variety of positions during his career but mostly at first base.

OTT, Melvin Thomas "Mel"
Player

Born March 2, 1909, in Gretna, La; 11 times National League All-Star Team; critically injured in an auto accident November 1958, died November 21, 1958, in New Orleans, La.

1926–1948 New York Giants National League, outfielder, third baseman
1941–1948 New York Giants National League, manager

Mel was one of the few players to jump from high school into the majors. He was 16 when he reported to the Giants. Three times during his career, the 5 ft. 9-in, 170 lb. slugger scored five or more runs in one game. Mel set a major league record in 1929 with an 11-game RBI streak. He is coholder of the National League record for the most years leading in walks, six. At the time of his retirement, Mel had hit 511 home runs for a National League record. His lifetime average was .304 in 2732 games with 9456 at bats, 2876 hits, 488 doubles, 72 triples, 1708 walks, and 1860 RBI. He helped win three pennants and played in three World Series.

1952

HEILMANN, Harry Edwin "Slug"
Player and Sportscaster

Born August 3, 1894, in San Francisco, Calif; died July 9, 1951, in Detroit, Mich, of cancer at age 56.

1914–1929 Detroit Tigers American League, right fielder, first baseman
1930 Cincinnati Reds National League, right fielder, first baseman
1932 Cincinnati Reds National League, right fielder, first baseman

Heilmann, at 6 ft. 1 in, 200 lbs, was a right-handed hitter, outfielder and first baseman who won the American League batting championship four times, 1921, 1923, 1925 and 1927. Throughout his career his batting average was down in the even-numbered years and up in the odd. During his 17-year career he played 2146 games, with 7787 at bats, 1291 runs, 2660 hits, 542 doubles, 151 triples, 183 homers, 1549 RBI and an average of .342. Heilmann eventually overcame a serious liquor problem. He would tell a story of driving a small car down a flight of stairs into a basement speakeasy and right up to the bar to order a drink. Arthritis ended his playing career, but in 1940 he became a very successful sportscaster in Detroit.

WANER, Paul Glee "Big Poison"
Player

Born April 6, 1903, in Harrah, Okla; brother Lloyd *(see* 1967 inductees); Most Valuable Player 1927; All-Star Games 1927, 1933–1935; died August 29, 1965, in Sarasota, Fla, at age 62.

1926–1940 Pittsburgh Pirates National League, right fielder
1941 Brooklyn Dodgers National League, right fielder
1941–1942 Boston Braves National League, right fielder
1943–1944 Brooklyn Dodgers National League, right fielder
1944–1945 New York Yankees American League, right fielder

Paul is one of the 11 players to join the 3000-hit club. In 1926 this left-handed hitter went six-for-six. He set a modern record for the most triples by a rookie, 22, and he holds the National League record for the most years of 50 or more doubles, 3. Paul and his brother Lloyd developed their skills as youngsters swinging at corncobs with broomsticks. In spite of his fondness for alcohol, Paul had a lifetime average of .333 for 2549 games, 9459 at bats, 3152 hits, 2247 singles, 602 doubles, 190 triples, 112 homers, 1626 runs, 1309 RBI, 1091 walks and 376 strikeouts. The 5 ft. 8-in, 148 lb. player, sometimes known as "Big Poison," played in the 1927 World Series.
Also in: National Association of Intercollegiate Athletics Hall of Fame.

1953

BARROW, Edward Grant "Cousin Ed"
Manager and President

Born May 10, 1868, in Springfield, Ill; died October 15, 1953, in Port Chester, N.Y.

1903–1904 Detroit Tigers American League, manager
1918–1920 Boston Red Sox American League, manager
1921–1939 New York Yankees American League, business manager
1939–1945 New York Yankees American League, president

Cousin Ed Barrow managed the Boston Red Sox in 1918 to a pennant and the World Series. During his career as manager of the New York Yankees, the team won 14 pennants and 10 world championships. Barrow played a vital role in building up the Yankee dynasty. He was a forceful, strict disciplinarian, but a straightforward personality. His chief claims to fame are signing Honus Wagner and switching Babe Ruth from pitcher to outfielder.

BENDER, Charles Albert "Chief"
Player and Coach

Born May 5, 1884, in Brainerd, Minn; one fourth Chippewa Indian; attended Carlisle Indian School and Dickinson Col. in Pa; died May 22, 1954, in Philadelphia.

1903–1914 Philadelphia Athletics American League, pitcher
1915 Baltimore Federal League, pitcher
1916–1917 Philadelphia Phillies National League, pitcher
1925 Chicago White Sox American League, coach

As a pitcher the Chief's major league classic came in 1910 against Cleveland when only one man reached base. The 6 ft. 2-in, 185 lb. Chief has the distinction of having pitched two no-hitters during his career, one in the majors and one in the minors. He was in World Series play in 1905, 1910–1911 and 1913–1914. Connie Mack chose him to start the first game in four of his five World Series. According to Mack, if Bender was given proper rest he "did not once fail me in a dozen years." Chief Bender coached and managed from 1925 to 1953.
Also in: American Indian Athletic Hall of Fame.

CONNOLLY, Thomas Henry
Umpire

Born December 31, 1870, in Manchester, England; died April 28, 1961, in Natick, Mass, at age 90.

1898–1899 National League, umpire
1901–1953 American League, umpire

Tom umpired in the majors for 34 seasons, only 2 fewer than Bill Klem's record 36. He officiated in the first American League game in Chicago in 1901. Tom umpired in eight World Series, including the first one in 1903. He was known as the leading authority on rules and served on the Rules Committee for many years, introducing numerous changes in the game's playing code. In June 1931 he became chief of staff for the American League arbiters.

DEAN, Jay Hanna "Dizzy"
Player and Sportscaster

Born January 16, 1911, in Lucas, Ark; brother Paul in majors; son of a migrant cotton picker; no schooling beyond third grade; married Pat Walsh; National League Most Valuable Player 1934; All-Star Game 1937; died July 17, 1974, in Reno, Nev, at age 63.

1932–1937 St. Louis Cardinals National League, pitcher
1938–1941 Chicago Cubs National League, pitcher
1947 St. Louis Browns American League, pitcher

Dizzy Dean was a legend in his own time. He averaged 24 wins per season from 1932 to 1936, leading the National League in strikeouts during that time as well. Dean's major league totals show 317 games pitched, 1966 innings, 150 victories, 83 defeats for a .664 percentage. He played in five World Series games, but received an injury in the 1937 All-Star games that led to a decline in his pitching. Dean took a broadcasting job in 1941 and from there went into network sportscasting. When inducted into the Hall of Fame, Dean said: "I want to thank the good Lord for giving me a good right arm, a strong back and a weak mind."
Also in: National Sportscasters and Sportswriters Hall of Fame.

KLEM, William Joseph
Umpire

Born February 22, 1874, in Rochester, N.Y; died September 16, 1951, in Miami, Fla, at age 77.

1905–1951 National League, umpire

Bill Klem was a colorful character who knew the rules of baseball by heart. He was regarded as the game's greatest umpire, bringing dignity and respect to his profession. Klem umpired in 18 World Series and is credited with introducing arm signals indicating strikes and fair or foul balls. He was famous for drawing a line in the dirt with his shoe and telling any disputing player or coach that if he crossed that line he would be out of the game. After his retirement in 1941, Klem served as chief of the National League umpiring staff until his death.

SIMMONS, Aloysius Harry "Al"
Player and Coach
Born May 22, 1903, in Milwaukee, Wis; American League Most Valuable Player 1929; All-Star Teams 1933–1935; died May 26, 1956, in Milwaukee, at age 53 from a heart attack.

1924–1932 Philadelphia Athletics American League, outfielder
1933–1935 Chicago White Sox American League, outfielder
1936 Detroit Tigers American League, outfielder
1937–1938 Washington Senators American League, outfielder
1939 Boston Braves National League, Cincinnati Reds National League, outfielder
1940–1941 Philadelphia Athletics American League, player-coach
1943 Boston Red Sox American League, player-coach
1944 Philadelphia Athletics American League, player-coach

"Bucketfoot Al" got his name from his unusual batting style (stepping away from home plate). He tied the major league record by getting more than 200 hits for 5 consecutive seasons. During his 22-year career, 6 ft. 210-lb. Al played 2215 games, had 8761 at bats, 2827 hits, 539 doubles, 149 triples, 307 home runs, 1827 RBI and a .334 batting average. Al played in four World Series.

WALLACE, Roderick J. "Bobby" "Rhody"
Player and Manager
Born November 4, 1874, in Pittsburgh, Pa; Temple Cup Series 1896; died November 3, 1960, in Torrance, Calif, at age 85.

1894–1898 Cleveland Spiders National League, pitcher, third baseman, shortstop
1899–1901 St. Louis Cardinals National League, shortstop, third baseman
1902–1916 St. Louis Browns American League, player-manager
1917–1918 St. Louis Cardinals National League, infielder

Bobby Wallace has the distinction of having one of the longest careers in the majors, over 60 years as a pitcher, third baseman, shortstop, manager, American League umpire and scout. He set the American League record for chances, 17, in his first game as shortstop in 1902. At one time he commanded the highest salary in baseball—$6500 in 1906. During his career he had a batting average of .268 in 2369 games, with 2308 hits, 1056 runs, 395 doubles, 149 triples, 1121 RBI, 37 homers and 209 stolen bases. His pitching record was 25 wins, 18 losses, in 57 games.

WRIGHT, William Henry "Harry"
Organizer and Manager
Born January 10, 1835, in Sheffield, England; began his career as a pro cricket player; died October 30, 1895, in Atlantic City, N.J, at age 60.

1866–1871 Cincinnati Red Stockings, organizer and manager
1872–1875 Boston National Association, manager
1876–1881 Boston Red Caps National League, manager
1882–1883 Providence Grays National League, manager
1884–1893 Philadelphia Phillies National League, manager

Harry Wright is said to be the father of professional baseball. He organized and managed the first pro team, the Cincinnati Red Stockings, in 1869. Wright is responsible for more innovations in baseball than any other person. While with Boston he guided them to six pennants in seven years. Following his retirement as manager he became the National League's first chief of umpires.

1954

DICKEY, William Malcolm "Bill"
Player and Manager
Born June 6, 1907, in Bastrop, La; younger brother George ("Skeets") caught for Boston and Chicago; seven times American League All-Star Team; sells securities in Little Rock, Ark.

1928–1943 New York Yankees American League, catcher
1946 New York Yankees American League, manager
1949–1957 New York Yankees American League, coach
1959–1960 New York Yankees American League, scout, coach

Dickey played 1789 games in the majors, scored 930 runs, 6300 at bats, 1969 hits, 343 doubles, 73 triples, 202 homers, with an average of .313. He played in eight World Series. Bill caught 100 or more games for 13 consecutive seasons and hit 3 home runs in 1 game in 1939.

MARANVILLE, Walter James Vincent "Rabbit"
Player
Born November 11, 1891, in Springfield, Mass; served in Navy during both World Wars; died January 5, 1954, in New York City at age 62.

1912–1920 Boston Braves National League, shortstop
1921–1924 Pittsburgh Pirates National League, shortstop
1925 Chicago Cubs National League, manager
1926 Brooklyn Dodgers National League, shortstop
1927–1928 St. Louis Cardinals National League, shortstop
1929–1935 Boston Braves National League, shortstop

Rabbit played in more games as shortstop, 2155, than any other National League player. He was a member of the 1914 Boston Braves Miracle Team that won the pennant and went on to win the World Series from the Athletics in four games. Maranville was one of the few men who went to bat over 10,000 times, 10,078. At 5 ft. 5 in, 155 lbs, Rabbit had 2065 hits, 380 doubles, 177 triples, 28 homers, 1255 scored runs, 874 RBI, 291 stolen bases and a batting average of .258. Rabbit was a colorful humorist who made the basket catch famous. In later years he coached children in several sports.

TERRY, William Harold "Bill"
Player and Manager
Born October 30, 1898, in Atlanta, Ga; *Sporting News* Most Valuable Player 1930; All-Star Games 1933–1935.

1923–1936 New York Giants National League, first baseman

1932–1941 New York Giants National League, manager

Bill Terry was the first National League player to hit the .400 mark in 1930. He led the National League in triples in 1931 with 20, and scored 100 or more runs seven times. Terry, 6 ft. 1 in, 200 lbs, hit three successive home runs in a game in 1932. His lifetime batting average was .341 in 1721 games with 2193 hits, 1120 runs, 373 doubles, 112 triples, 154 homers and 1078 RBI. Succeeding John McGraw as New York manager, he recorded three pennants, one second- and two third-place standings.

1955

BAKER, John Franklin "Frank"
Player
Born March 13, 1886, in Trappe, Md; retired to Maryland's Eastern Shore; raised and trained hunting dogs; died June 28, 1963, in Trappe.

1908–1914 Philadelphia Athletics American League, third baseman

1916–1922 New York Yankees American League, third baseman

Frank Baker was a good all-around hitter, swinging a 52-oz. bat. He was also an excellent fielder, leading the American League third basemen in chances eight times, in putouts seven times, and in fielding average twice. The 5 ft. 11-in, 180 lb. "Home Run Baker" was American League home-run champion four years in a row, 1911 to 1914. His lifetime average was .307 with 93 homers and 1012 RBI.

DiMAGGIO, Joseph Paul
Player
Born November 25, 1914, in Martinez, Calif; father a fisherman; eighth child in a family of nine; military service 1943–1945; married Dorothy Arnold 1937 and Marilyn Monroe 1954, both marriages ended in divorce; Most Valuable Player 1939, 1941 and 1947; played on 11 American League All-Star Teams.

1932–1936 San Francisco Seals Pacific Coast League, outfielder

1936–1951 New York Yankees American League, center fielder

Joe DiMaggio is generally regarded as the game's greatest center fielder. Joltin' Joe's major league totals were 1736 games, 2214 hits, 6821 at bats, 1390 runs, 389 doubles, 131 triples, 361 homers, 1537 RBI and an average of .325. He hit safely in 56 consecutive games for a major league record in 1941. The 6 ft. 1-in, 195-lb. "Yankee Clipper" is one of the game's immortals. He helped the Yankees to ten World Series, and in 1949 became the first player to attain a $100,000 salary.
Also in: UNICO National Athletic Hall of Fame (Italian).

HARTNETT, Charles Leo "Gabby"
Player and Manager
Born December 20, 1900, in Woonsocket, R.I; eldest of 14 children; first job in a factory in Worcester, Mass; National League Most Valuable Player 1935; played in five All-Star Games; died December 20, 1972, in Park Ridge, Ill.

1922–1940 Chicago Cubs National League, catcher, manager

1941 New York Giants National League, catcher, coach

Gabby Hartnett was not only an outstanding catcher, but also a dangerous hitter, highlighting his .297 lifetime average with 236 home runs. He caught 100 or more games a season for 12 years and set the mark for consecutive chances for a catcher without error, 452 in 1933 and 1934. He had the most putouts in the National League, 7292, and the most chances accepted, 8546, both in 1990 games. During his 20-year career Gabby had 6432 at bats, 867 runs, 1912 hits, 396 doubles and 64 triples. After seven seasons in the majors something snapped in his arm during spring training and he was out for the 1929 season, but came right back the next year to have his best season. Gabby, red-faced, 6 ft. 2 in, 190 lbs, and probably one of the heartiest eaters in baseball, had an infectious smile and was Chicago's big personality. After his turn with the Giants, Gabby managed and scouted for several teams.

LYONS, Theodore Amar
Player and Manager
Born December 28, 1900, in Lake Charles, La; played basketball and second base in high school; attended Baylor Univ.

1923–1946 Chicago White Sox American League, pitcher

1946–1948 Chicago White Sox American League, manager

Ted Lyons's entire active pitching career was spent with the losing Chicago White Sox, in first division only five times during his 21-year career and never higher than third place. He won 260 games and lost 230, having a no-hitter against Boston in 1926. In 1922 Ted started and finished all 22 of the games he pitched. Lyons relied on a good curveball, a fastball, in later years a knuckleball, and control. His major league record shows 594 games, 4162 innings pitched, 1121 walks, 1073 strikeouts and ERA of 3.67. His lifetime batting average was .233 with 364 hits, 49 doubles, 9 triples, 5 homers and 149 RBI. His record as a manager was 185 wins and 245 losses.

SCHALK, Raymond William "Crocker" "Ray"
Player
Born August 12, 1892, in Harvey, Ill; operated a bowling establishment; died May 19, 1970, in Chicago, Ill, at age 77.

1912–1928 Chicago White Sox American League, catcher

1928 Chicago White Sox American League, manager
1929 New York Giants National League, catcher

Ray Schalk's speed and agility allowed him to be the first receiver to back up plays at first and third. He has the distinction of being the only catcher to have handled four no-hit games, including a perfect game in 1922. He led the American League catchers in putouts for nine years. At 5 ft. 9 in, 154 lbs, Schalk's major league record shows a batting average of .253 in 1760 games with 1345 hits, 579 runs, 199 doubles, 48 triples, 12 homers and 580 RBI. He played in the World Series in 1917 and 1919.

VANCE, Arthur Charles "Dazzy"
Player

Born March 4, 1891, in Orient, Iowa; National League Most Valuable Player 1924; operated a fishing camp in Fla; died February 16, 1961, in Homosassa Springs, Fla, at age 69.

1915 Pittsburgh Pirates National League, pitcher
1915–1918 New York Yankees American League, pitcher
1922–1932 Brooklyn Dodgers National League, pitcher
1933–1934 St. Louis Cardinals National League, pitcher
1934 Cincinnati Reds National League, pitcher
1935 Brooklyn Dodgers National League, pitcher

Dazzy didn't make the majors until he was 31 years old. Despite this tardiness, Dazzy was the greatest pitcher the Brooklyn Dodgers ever had. He was the first pitcher in the National League to lead in strikeouts for seven consecutive years. The 6 ft. 2-in, 200 lb. player became one of 11 pitchers to strike out three men in an inning with only nine pitches. He won 15 straight games in 1924 and pitched a no-hit game in 1925. During his career this fireballer threw 32 shutouts, won 197 and lost 140 in 442 games with 2045 strikeouts, 840 walks and 2967 innings for an ERA of 3.24 and a percentage of .585. Dazzy played in the 1934 World Series.

1956

CRONIN, Joseph Edward
Player and Manager

Born October 12, 1906, in San Francisco, Calif; married Mildred June Robertson; has three sons and one daughter; parents lost everything in the 1906 earthquake; played soccer, basketball and baseball in youth; won junior tennis championship of San Francisco at age 14; turned down an athletic scholarship at St. Mary's Col; American League Most Valuable Player 1930; worked in a bank; became a substitute instructor in public playgrounds.

1926–1927 Pittsburgh Pirates National League, shortstop
1928–1934 Washington Senators American League, player-manager
1935–1945 Boston Red Sox American League, player-manager

In 2124 major league games, Cronin, 5 ft. 11 in, 180 lbs, averaged .302. He had 2285 hits in 7577 at bats, with 1233 runs scored, 171 homers, 515 doubles, 117 triples and 1423 RBI. Cronin was the first player in the history of the American League to become its chief executive, president and chairman of the board.

GREENBERG, Henry Benjamin "Hank"
Player

Born January 1, 1911, in New York City; entered New York Univ. on athletic scholarship, staying only one year; Most Valuable Player 1935 and 1940; two All-Star Games; a millionaire due to wise stock-market investments.

1933–1946 Detroit Tigers American League, first baseman
1947 Pittsburgh Pirates National League, first baseman

Hank was one of baseball's greatest right-handed hitters. He set a major league record in 1938 for the most times hitting 2 or more homers in 1 game, 11 in 1 season. At one time, Hank finished a game with two broken bones in his wrist. His overall major league average was .313 in 1394 games. He had 1628 hits in 5193 at bats, scored 1051 runs, 379 doubles, 71 triples, 331 homers, and 1276 RBI. Hank played in four World Series and was the first National League player to earn $100,000. In later years he was with Cleveland as farm director and with the Indians as general manager before moving over to the White Sox.

1957

CRAWFORD, Samuel Earl "Wahoo Sam"
Player and Umpire

Born April 18, 1880, in Wahoo, Nebr; studied to be a barber; retired to work in his garden; died June 15, 1968, in Hollywood, Calif, at age 88.

1899–1902 Cincinnati Reds National League, right fielder
1903–1917 Detroit Tigers American League, right fielder
1918–1923 Los Angeles Pacific Coast League, umpire

Crawford is the only player to have led both leagues in home runs. His lifetime average was .309 for 2505 major league games, 2964 hits in 9579 times at bat. He scored 1392 runs, made 455 doubles, 312 triples (a major league record), 95 homers, and stole 367 bases. Sam is ranked among the best base stealers and was one of the first to use a wide-spread batting stance. "Wahoo Sam", at 5 ft. 11 in, 190 lbs, played in 17 World Series games.

McCARTHY, Joseph Vincent "Joe"
Manager

Born April 21, 1887, in Philadelphia, Pa; retired 1950.

1926–1930 Chicago Cubs National League, manager
1931–1946 New York Yankees American League, manager
1948–1950 Boston Red Sox American League, manager

Joe was an outstanding manager but never played ball in the major leagues. While he was with the Yankees they won eight pennants and seven World Series. He demanded that the Yankees conduct themselves with dignity on and off the field. During his 22 years of managing, his teams never finished out of the first division. Joe retired for a short time in 1946, but came back in 1948 to lead the Boston Red Sox to a runner-up position for two years.

1959

WHEAT, Zacharia Davis "Zack"
Player
Born May 23, 1888, in Hamilton, Mo; raised on a farm in Texas; operated a bowling establishment in Kansas City; operated a fishing resort in Sunrise Beach, Fla; died March 11, 1972, in Sedalia, Mo, at age 83.

1909 – 1926 Brooklyn Dodgers National League, left fielder
1927 Philadelphia Phillies American League, outfielder

Zack was a brilliant hitter and almost perfect outfielder. At 5 ft. 10 in, 180 lbs, Wheat held many Dodger records. He hit .300 or better 14 times, leading the National League in batting in 1918. That same year he hit safely in 26 consecutive games. During his career Wheat hit .317 in 2406 games with 884 hits, 1289 runs, 476 doubles, 172 triples, 132 homers and 1265 RBI. Wheat played in the World Series in 1916 and 1920.

1961

CAREY, Max George "Scoops"
Player and Manager
Born January 11, 1890, in Terre Haute, Ind; born Maximillian Carnarius; attended Concordia Col, Ft. Wayne, Ind; studied for the ministry; died May 20, 1976, in Miami Beach, Fla, at age 86.

1910 – 1926 Pittsburgh Pirates National League, center fielder
1926 – 1929 Brooklyn Dodgers National League, center fielder
1930 Pittsburgh Pirates National League, coach
1932 – 1933 Brooklyn Dodgers National League, manager
1940 Florida East Coast League, manager

Scoops Carey holds the modern National League record for the most stolen bases, 738. He held the National League record for the most games in the outfield, 2421, and repeatedly led the league in outfield putouts and assists. Carey played 2469 National League games with an average of .285. He scored 1545 runs, had 2665 hits, 419 doubles, 159 triples, 69 homers and 797 RBI. Max was brilliant in the 1925 World Series, playing the last two games with broken ribs and averaging .458.

HAMILTON, William Robert "Billy"
Player and Manager
Born February 16, 1866, in Newark, N.J; died December 15, 1940, in Worcester, Mass, at age 74.

1888 – 1889 Kansas City American Association, center fielder
1890 – 1895 Philadelphia Phillies National League, center fielder
1896 – 1901 Boston Beaneaters National League, center fielder
1902 – 1910 New England League, manager

Billy holds the National League record for stolen bases with 115 taken in the 1891 season. Although he is best remembered as a base thief, Hamilton was also a batting star. He hit better than .300 for 12 successive seasons and twice topped the 200-hit figure. He had a lifetime batting average of .344 for 1578 games, 2157 hits, 225 doubles, 94 triples and 37 homers. Billy was 5 ft. 6 in, 165 lbs.

1962

FELLER, Robert William Andrew "Bob"
Player
Born November 3, 1918, in Van Meter, Iowa, earned eight battle stars from the Navy during W.W. II; played in five All-Star games.

1936 – 1956 Cleveland Indians American League, pitcher

6 ft, 186 lb. "Rapid Robert" pitched 3 no-hit games and 12 one-hit games in the American League. He set modern strikeout records with 18 in one game and 348 for a season. Bob's lifetime record shows 266 wins, 162 losses, an ERA of 3.25 with 2581 strikeouts. He had five straight 20-victory seasons and led the American League in strikeouts seven years in a row. His fastball was rated equal to Walter Johnson's.

McKECHNIE, William Boyd "Deacon"
Player and Manager
Born August 7, 1886, in Wilkinsburg, Pa; son William Jr, president of the Pacific Coast League; *Sporting News* Major League Manager of the Year 1937 and 1940; died October 29, 1965, in Bradenton, Fla, at age 79.

1907 – 1921 Pittsburgh Pirates National League, third baseman
1922 – 1926 Pittsburgh Pirates National League, manager
1928 – 1929 St. Louis Cardinals National League, manager
1930 – 1937 Boston Browns National League, manager
1938 – 1946 Cincinnati Reds National League, manager

Deacon is the only National League manager to win pennants with three different clubs. McKechnie tied the National League record for the most teams managed, 4, and the most teams winning pennants, 3. His teams took four pennants and played in two World Series. As a player he appeared in 546 games, mostly on third base, with an average of .234 and eight homers and 127 stolen bases. Deacon Bill McKechnie was a sober, even-tempered person; brains and patience were the keys to his success.

ROBINSON, Jack Roosevelt "Jackie"
Player
Born January 31, 1919, in Cairo, Ga; on athletic scholarship at Univ. of Calif, Los Angeles; outstanding football back; *Sporting News* Rookie of the Year 1947; National League Most Valuable Player 1949; All-Star Teams 1949 – 1954; executive with New York restaurant firm; bank official; president of a land development company; worked with drug prevention programs; died October 24, 1972, in Stamford, Conn, at age 53.

1947 – 1956 Brooklyn Dodgers National League, second baseman

Jackie Robinson was the first black man in the major leagues. Branch Rickey signed him with the Dodgers in 1947. During his major league career he averaged .311 in 1382 games with 1518 hits, 947 runs, 273 doubles, 54 triples, 137 home runs and 734 RBI. He hit .300 or better six times and scored 100 or more runs five times. Robinson played in seven World Series.

ROUSH, Edd J. "Eddie"
Player
Born May 8, 1893, in Oakland City, Ind.

1913 Chicago White Sox American League, center fielder
1914 Indianapolis Federal League, center fielder
1915 Newark Federal League, center fielder
1916 New York Giants National League, center fielder
1916–1926 Cincinnati Reds National League, center fielder
1927–1929 New York Giants National League, center fielder
1931 Cincinnati Reds National League, center fielder

Roush was an instant star out of the Federal League. He spent much of his career in dispute over his pay scale, but became the highest-paid National League player of the period. Edd hit safely in 27 consecutive games in 1924 and 1927. He had eight hits in a doubleheader in 1927, led the National League in doubles in 1923 with 41 and in triples in 1924 with 21. During his major league career he hit .325 in 1748 games with 2158 hits, 1001 runs, 331 doubles, 168 triples, 63 homers and 882 RBI. Edd Roush was 5 ft. 11-in. tall and weighed 175 lbs.

1963

CLARKSON, John Gibson
Player
Born January 7, 1861, in Cambridge, Mass; a moody and sensitive man; died in a mental hospital on February 4, 1909, in Cambridge.

1882 Worcester National League, pitcher
1884–1887 Chicago White Stockings National League, pitcher
1888–1892 Boston Beaneaters National League, pitcher
1892–1894 Cleveland Spiders National League, pitcher

Clarkson was considered one of the greatest pitchers of the nineteenth century. He owned an assortment of curves and celebrated "drop" pitches. John almost single-handedly led Chicago to a National League pennant in 1885. In 12 years he had 327 wins, 177 losses, a 2.81 ERA, 4536 innings of play, 4295 hits, 1191 walks, 1978 strikeouts and 37 shutouts.

FLICK, Elmer Harrison
Player
Born January 11, 1876, in Bedford, Ohio; died January 9, 1971, in Bedford, at age 94.

1898–1902 Philadelphia Phillies National League, right fielder
1902–1910 Cleveland Indians American League, right fielder

At the turn of the century Flick, 5 ft. 9 in, 168 lbs, was ranked among the major leagues' leading hitters. He is remembered as American League batting champion with the lowest average ever, .306. Flick led the American League in triples three years in a row and in steals twice. He had a lifetime average of .315, playing 1480 games with 1764 hits, 268 doubles, 170 triples, 46 homers and 342 stolen bases.

RICE, Edgar Charles "Sam"
Player
Born February 29, 1890, in Morocco, Ind; owned a chicken farm in Maryland.

1915–1933 Washington Senators American League, right fielder
1934 Cleveland Indians American League, right fielder

Sam Rice gained success largely through his durability and consistency. The 5 ft. 9-in, 150 lb. fielder twice led the American League in putouts for outfielders with 454 in 1920 and 385 in 1922. He also led the American League in thefts in 1920 with 63. Rice's lifetime record shows 2404 games, 6269 at bats, 1515 runs, 2987 hits, 497 doubles, 184 triples, 34 homers, 1077 RBI and a batting average of .322. In the 1925 World Series Sam sailed over the center field fence to catch the ball—it was a fair catch.

RIXEY, Eppa Jephtha
Player
Born May 3, 1891, in Culpeper, Va; attended Univ of Va; owner of insurance firm in Cincinnati; died February 28, 1963.

1912–1917 Philadelphia Phillies National League, pitcher
1919–1920 Philadelphia Phillies National League, pitcher
1921–1933 Cincinnati Reds National League, pitcher

Eppa, who set a record for the most victories by a left-handed pitcher, was named all-time left-handed pitcher in Cincinnati history by fans in 1969. Eppa spent 12 of the 20 years of his career with second-division teams. His record shows 692 games, 4494 innings pitched, 39 shutouts, 266 wins, 251 losses, a percentage of .515, 1350 strikeouts for an ERA of 3.15. He was in World Series play in 1915.

1964

APPLING, Lucius Benjmin "Luke"
Player and Manager
Born April 2, 1907, in High Point, N.C; educated at Oglethorpe Col. in Atlanta, Ga; college football and baseball star; military service 1944–1945.

1930–1950 Chicago White Sox American League, shortstop
1951–1953 Memphis Southern Association, manager
1954–1955 Richmond International League, manager
1959 Memphis Southern Association, manager
1960 Detroit Tigers American League, coach
1967 Kansas City Athletics American League, manager
1968–1969 Oakland Athletics American League, scout
1971–1972 Chicago White Sox American League, coach

In 1933 Luke's batting average leveled off at above .300 and remained there for 15 years. His peak, .388 in 1936, stands as the highest mark ever attained by an American League shortstop. After leaving Chicago he accepted a variety of coaching and managerial positions throughout the country. Luke, at 5 ft. 11 in. 185 lbs, was known as "Old Aches and Pains" because of his imaginary ailments.

FABER, Urban Clarence "Red"
Player

Born September 6, 1888, in Casada, Iowa; died September 25, 1976, at age 88.

1914–1933 Chicago White Sox American League, pitcher
1946–1948 Chicago White Sox American League, coach

At 6 ft, 190 lbs, Red was a switch-hitter and the last spitballer in the American League. His lifetime ERA was 3.15. Red had 27 innings of World Series play. He returned as coach for the White Sox from 1946 to 1948.

GRIMES, Burleigh Arland "Ol' Stubblebeard"
Player

Born August 18, 1893, in Clear Lake, Wis.

1916–1917 Pittsburgh Pirates National League, pitcher
1918–1926 Brooklyn Dodgers National League, pitcher
1927 New York Giants National League, pitcher
1928–1929 Pittsburgh Pirates National League, pitcher
1930 Boston Braves National League, pitcher
1930–1931 St Louis Cardinals National League, pitcher
1932–1933 Chicago Cubs National League, pitcher

Grimes' lifetime major league record showed 615 games, 4178 innings played, 270 wins, 212 losses, for a .560 percentage with an ERA of 3.52. He won 13 games in a row for the Giants in 1927 and played in 9 World Series. The 5 ft. 10-in, 185 lb. player was the last of the legal spitballers. "Ol' Stubblebeard" gained his nickname for refusing to shave on the day he was to pitch. He managed the Brooklyn Dodgers in 1937 and 1938 and scouted for the New York Yankees from 1947 to 1952.

HUGGINS, Miller James
Player and Manager

Born March 27, 1879, in Cincinnati, Ohio; graduated from Univ. of Cincinnati Law School; died September 25, 1929, in New York City at age 50.

1904–1909 Cincinnati Reds National League, second baseman
1910–1917 St. Louis Cardinals National League, player-manager
1918–1929 New York Yankees American League, manager

During his playing days Hug hit .265 in 1573 games. He was an excellent leadoff man and a good fielder. The 5 ft. 4-in, 146 lb. infielder once drew walks in 11 consecutive games. He led the Yankees to their first series of pennants and world championships. As a manager, the "Mighty Mite" corrected Babe Ruth's disciplinary problems by imposing a $5000 fine.

KEEFE, Timothy John "Sir Timothy"
Player

Born January 1, 1856, in Cambridge, Mass; died April 23, 1933, in Cambridge, at age 77.

1880–1882 Troy Trojans National League, pitcher
1883–1884 New York American Association, pitcher
1885–1889 New York Giants National League, pitcher
1890 New York Players League, pitcher
1891 New York Giants National League, pitcher
1891–1893 Philadelphia Phillies National League, pitcher

"Sir Timothy" tied a major league record in 1883 by winning 19 consecutive games and beating every other team in the league. He saw the Giants to a pennant in 1889. Tim was one of the first pitchers to use change-of-pace pitching and he pioneered the use of the slow ball. During his major league career he pitched 5052 innings in 594 games, winning 336 and losing 224, with an ERA of 2.63. He struck out 2542, walked 1225 and had 40 shutouts. Tim played in the World Series in 1884, 1888 and 1889. He was 5 ft. 10-in. and weighed 185 lbs.

MANUSH, Henry Emmet "Heinie"
Player

Born July 20, 1901, in Tuscumbia, Ala; died May 12, 1971, in Sarasota, Fla, at age 69.

1923–1927 Detroit Tigers American League, left fielder
1928–1930 St. Louis Browns American League, left fielder
1930–1935 Washington Senators American League, left fielder
1936 Boston Red Sox American League, left fielder
1937–1938 Brooklyn Dodgers National League, left fielder
1938–1939 Pittsburgh Pirates National League, left fielder

Heinie was the first ball player ejected from a World Series game. As he argued heatedly with an umpire, Heinie grabbed the ump's bow tie, held in place by an elastic band, and let it snap back to the arbiter's neck. The Washington Senators won that game without him. Heinie led the American League in batting in 1926 with an average of .378. He hit over .300 eleven times, and four times had more than 200 hits. Manush played 2009 major league games, with 2524 hits, 1287 runs scored, 1173 RBI, 491 doubles, 160 triples and 110 homers. He played in the 1933 World Series and was later manager in the minors with Johnny Pesky as his star pupil.

WARD, John Montgomery "Monte"
Player

Born March 3, 1860, in Bellifonte, Pa; attended Columbia Law School; married actress Helen Deuvray; died of pneumonia at age 65 while on a hunting trip near Augusta, Ga, March 4, 1925.

1878–1882 Providence Grays National League, pitcher, outfielder
1883–1889 New York Gothams/Giants National League, outfielder, shortstop
1890 Brooklyn Players League, shortstop
1891–1892 Brooklyn Bridgegrooms National League, shortstop, second baseman
1893–1894 New York Giants National League, second baseman

A versatile player, Monte pitched 273 games to win 158 and lose 102 in seven years. He pitched a perfect game in 1880, and in 1882 pitched an 18-inning shutout. Monte turned to shortstop and second base after injuring his arm. He shares the major league record for the most assists by a second baseman in a nine-inning game, 12. At 5 ft. 9 in, 165 lbs, Monte led shortstops in putouts in 1885, 1887 and 1890. His lifetime average was .283 in 1810 games with 2151 hits, 1403 runs, 232 doubles, 95 triples, 29 homers and 605 stolen bases.

1965

GALVIN, James F. "Pud"
Player
Born December 25, 1855, in St. Louis, Mo; died March 7, 1902, in Pittsburgh, Pa, at age 46.

1875 St. Louis Reds National League, pitcher
1879 – 1885 Buffalo Bisons National League, pitcher
1885 – 1886 Pittsburgh American Association, pitcher
1887 – 1889 Pittsburgh Alleghenys National League, pitcher
1890 Pittsburgh Players League, pitcher
1891 – 1892 Pittsburgh Pirates National League, pitcher
1893 St. Louis Cardinals National League, pitcher

Pud Galvin totaled 685 games, 365 wins, 311 losses, struck out 1786 men and had 57 shutouts. Speed and control were the 5 ft. 8-in, 190 lb. pitcher's prime assets. Before his career ended he weighed 300 lbs.

1966

STENGEL, Charles Dillon "Casey"
Player and Manager
Born July 30, 1890, in Kansas City, Mo; died September 29, 1975, in Glendale, Calif, at age 85.

1912 – 1917 Brooklyn Dodgers National League, outfielder
1918 – 1919 Pittsburgh Pirates National League, outfielder
1920 – 1921 Philadelphia Phillies National League, outfielder
1921 – 1923 New York Giants National League, outfielder
1924 – 1925 Boston Braves National League, outfielder
1934 – 1936 Brooklyn Dodgers National League, manager
1938 – 1943 Boston Braves National League, manager
1949 – 1960 New York Yankees American League, manager
1962 – 1965 New York Mets National League, manager

Casey enjoyed a 54-year career as a player and manager in professional baseball. During his playing career he hit .284 in 1277 games with 1219 hits, 575 runs, 182 doubles, 89 triples, 60 home runs and 518 RBI. He played in 12 World Series games. As a manager the "Old Professor" guided the Yankees to ten pennants and seven World Series championships in a 12-year span. Casey, one of baseball's funniest fellows, once doffed his cap to fans and watched as a bird flew off his head.

WILLIAMS, Theodore Samuel "Ted"
Player and Manager
Born August 30, 1918, in San Diego, Calif; Triple Crown 1946 and 1949; played in 18 All-Star Games; spent five years in military as a marine pilot, both W.W. II and Korea; sports consultant for Sears, Roebuck and Co.

1939 – 1960 Boston Red Sox American League, left fielder
1969 – 1971 Washington Senators American League, manager
1972 Texas American League, manager

Ted became the second player to be fined $5000 for a spitting attack aimed at Boston fans and the pressbox. He holds the American League record for the most intentional walks in a season, 33. He had three homers in one game three times, and in 1941 became the last of the game's .400 hitters. During his 19-year career he played 2292 games with 7706 at bats, 1798 runs, 2654 hits, 525 doubles, 71 triples, 521 homers, 1839 RBI and an average of .344. Ted played in the 1946 World Series. He is the author, with John Underwood, of *My Turn at Bat: The Story of My Life,* 1968, and *The Science of Hitting,* 1972.

1967

RICKEY, Wesley Branch "Mahatma"
Player and Manager
Born December 20, 1881, in Stockdale, Ohio; law degree from Univ. of Mich; died December 9, 1965, in Columbia, Mo, of tuberculosis at age 83.

1905 – 1906 St. Louis Browns American League, catcher
1907 New York Yankees American League, catcher
1913 – 1915 St. Louis Browns American League, manager
1919 – 1925 St. Louis Cardinals National League, manager
1925 – 1942 St. Louis Cardinals National League, business manager
1942 – 1950 Brooklyn Dodgers National League, general manager
1951 – 1955 Pittsburgh Pirates National League, general manager

Branch Rickey created the farm system to let players gain experience before they came into the major leagues. As general manager of the Dodgers, Rickey continued to sign players even though everyone else had stopped because of W.W. II. When the war was over the Dodgers had plenty of young talent and during the next 11 years won 6 pennants. Rickey's greatest claim to fame came in 1947 when Jackie Robinson joined the Dodgers and broke the color barrier in baseball. In 1960 Rickey moved from the National League to become president of the Continental League. To combat this proposed third major league, the American and National Leagues expanded to include teams from some of the cities proposed for the Continental League, which consequently was abandoned.

RUFFING, Charles Herbert "Red"
Player
Born May 3, 1904, in Granville, Ill; in youth, lost four toes on left foot in a mining accident; All-Star Teams 1937 – 1939.

1924 – 1930 Boston Red Sox American League, pitcher

1930–1946 New York Yankees American League, pitcher
1947 Chicago White Sox American League, pitcher

Red's big break came when he moved to the Yankees, winning 20 or more games in each of four consecutive seasons. His pitching record shows 273 wins and 225 losses in 624 games, with 1987 strikeouts, 1541 walks, 4342 innings and 52 shutouts. Besides being a top-flight pitcher, Red, at 6 ft. 1 in, 215 lbs, was also a good hitter. His batting average was .269 with 521 hits, 98 doubles, 13 triples and 36 homers. He won seven of the nine World Series games in which he pitched.

WANER, Lloyd James "Little Poison"
Player
Born March 16, 1906, in Harrah, Okla; older brother Paul (*see* 1952 entry); All-Star Team 1938.

1927–1941 Pittsburgh Pirates National League, center fielder
1941 Boston Braves National League, center fielder
1941 Cincinnati Reds National League, center fielder
1942 Philadelphia Phillies National League, center fielder
1944 Brooklyn Dodgers National League, center fielder

"Little Poison" could hit, field, throw and steal. He batted over .300 for 10 of his first 12 seasons and as a rookie hit .355, setting a freshman record of 223 hits that still stands. Lloyd, 5 ft. 9 in, 150 lbs, holds the National League record for the most singles in a season, 198. His lifetime average was .316 in 1993 games with 2459 hits, 1201 runs, 381 doubles, 118 triples, 28 homers and 598 RBI. Waner scouted for Pittsburgh until 1949.
Also in: National Association of Intercollegiate Athletics Hall of Fame.

1968

CUYLER, Hazen Shirley "Kiki"
Player
Born August 30, 1899, in Harrisville, Mich; worked in a Buick plant in Mich; layoffs caused him to join the Bay City Team; an avid hunter, dancer (many waltz trophies); nonsmoker, nondrinker; All-Star Team 1925; died February 11, 1950, in Ann Arbor, Mich, at age 50.

1921–1927 Pittsburgh Pirates National League, center fielder
1928–1935 Chicago Cubs National League, center fielder
1935–1937 Cincinnati Reds National League, center fielder
1938 Brooklyn Dodgers National League, center fielder

Kiki's lifetime major league record showed 1879 games with an average of .321. He had 2299 hits, 1305 runs and 1065 RBI. Cuyler led the National League in stolen bases in 1926 and from 1928 to 1930. This 5 ft. 10-in, 180 lb. center fielder played in three World Series—1925, 1929 and 1932—but was kept out of the 1927 World Series because of a disagreement with Pittsburgh manager Donie Bush.

GOSLIN, Leon Allen "Goose"
Player
Born October 16, 1900, in Salem, N.J; Sally League Bat Title 1922; died May 15, 1971, in Bridgeton, N.J, at age 70.

1921–1930 Washington Senators American League, left fielder
1930–1932 St. Louis Browns American League, left fielder
1933 Washington Senators American League, left fielder
1934–1937 Detroit Tigers American League, left fielder
1938 Washington Senators American League, left fielder

Goose played in four World Series. He enjoyed 11 seasons as a .300 hitter and reached the 100 RBI mark 11 times. He hit three homers in one game three different times and retired with a .316 major league average in 2287 games. Goose recorded 500 doubles, 173 triples, 248 homers, 1483 runs and 1609 RBI.

MEDWICK, Joseph Michael "Joe"
Player
Born November 24, 1911, in Carteret, N.J; National League All-Star Teams 1934–1940, 1942 and 1944; National League Most Valuable Player 1937; Triple Crown 1937; died March 21, 1975, in St. Petersburg, Fla, at age 63.

1932–1940 St. Louis Cardinals National League, left fielder
1940–1943 Brooklyn Dodgers National League, left fielder
1943–1945 New York Giants National League, left fielder
1945 Boston Braves National League, left fielder
1946 Brooklyn Dodgers National League, left fielder
1947–1948 St. Louis Cardinals National League, left fielder

In Joe's peak year (1937) he led the league in just about every hitting department. His abrasive personality caused much friction throughout the years. In 1940 he was hit in the head by a pitched ball, resulting in a concussion. Charges and investigations were extensive. This episode left Joe a little ball shy, but he continued to hit over .300. During the 1934 World Series, Judge Landis ordered Medwick removed from the field for his own protection because Detroit fans were pelting him with fruit, vegetables and debris. Medwick played in 12 World Series games and his lifetime average was .324 in 1984 games, 2471 hits, 540 doubles, 113 triples, 205 homers, 1198 runs and 1383 RBI.

1969

CAMPANELLA, Roy "Campy"
Player
Born November 19, 1921, in Philadelphia, Pa; married three times; seven children; Most Valuable Player 1951, 1953 and 1955; lives in Hartsdale, N.Y.

1946–1948 Brooklyn Farm Teams
1948–1957 Brooklyn Dodgers National League, catcher

Campy's records include the most home runs in a season, 41, and the most runs batted in, 142. He set the National League record for chances accepted by catchers for the most consecutive years, 6. Campy tied the record for the most years in putouts, 6, and holds the record for the most consecutive years of catching 100 or more games, 9. Roy's major league average was .276 in 1215 games with 242 home runs and 856 RBI. He helped the Dodgers in five World Series, 1949, 1952, 1953, 1955 and 1956. In January 1958 his car skidded on an icy curve and turned over, leaving him partially paralyzed and ending his playing days. Campanella then began a radio sports program called "Campy's Corner." He is the author of *It's Good to be Alive,* 1959. Campy had unusual leadership qualities and was well liked and respected.

COVELSKI, Stanley Anthony
Player
Born Stanislaus Kowalewski July 13, 1890, in Shamokin, Pa; three brothers, Harry, Frank and John, all baseball players.

1912 Philadelphia Athletics American League, pitcher
1916–1924 Cleveland Indians American League, pitcher
1925–1927 Washington Senators American League, pitcher
1928 New York Yankees American League, pitcher

Stan picked up the spitball in 1915 and was one of the 17 pitchers allowed to use that pitch after it was banned in 1920. He pitched for 214 wins, 141 losses, averaging .603 with an ERA of 2.88. The 5 ft. 9-in, 175 lb. right-hander won 15 straight games in 1925. He was a steady, soft-spoken man who liked jokes and never seemed to lose his temper.
Also in: National Polish-American Sports Hall of Fame and Museum.

HOYT, Waite Charles "Schoolboy"
Player and Sportscaster
Born September 9, 1899, in Brooklyn, N.Y.

1921–1930 New York Yankees American League, pitcher
1931 Philadelphia Athletics American League, pitcher
1932 Brooklyn Dodgers, New York Giants National League, pitcher
1933–1937 Pittsburgh Pirates National League, pitcher
1937–1938 Brooklyn Dodgers National League, pitcher

Schoolboy started playing pro ball at the age of 17. He played in 12 World Series games during his career. Hoyt's major league record stands at 675 games, 3762 innings played, 237 wins, 182 losses, 4037 hits, 1780 runs, 1500 earned runs and 1206 strikeouts with an ERA of 3.59. In 1939 Hoyt, 5 ft. 11 in, 183 lbs, made the shift from playing to sportscasting. In Cincinnati he did play-by-plays for 25 years before retiring. Hoyt's keys to broadcasting success were intelligence, hard work and the ability to tell a good story.

MUSIAL, Stanley Frank
Player and Manager
Born November 21, 1920, in Donora, Pa; played basketball and baseball in high school; married Lillian Labash in 1939; one son and one daughter; National League Most Valuable Player 1943, 1946 and 1948; played in 24 All-Star Games; *Sporting News'* Player of the Decade; in Navy in 1945; operates a St. Louis restaurant.

1938–1941 St. Louis Farm Team
1941–1963 St. Louis Cardinals National League, left fielder

In 1958, when Stan got his 3000th hit, the St. Louis Cardinals presented him with a plaque that read: "To Stanley Frank Musial, an emblem of esteem from his teammates. An outstanding artist in his profession; possessor of many baseball records; gentleman in every sense of word; adored and worshipped by countless thousands; perfect answer to a manager's prayer; to this, we, the Cardinals, attest with our signatures." His lifetime average was .331 in 10,972 times at bat, 3630 hits, 725 doubles, 177 triples and 475 homers. Stan "The Man" played in four World Series with an average of .256. When his playing career ended, he managed St. Louis for one season during which the Cardinals won a pennant and a World Series championship. He resigned because of other business interests but became senior vice president of the Club.
Also in: National Polish-American Hall of Fame and Museum.

1970

BOUDREAU, Louis "Lou"
Player and Manager
Born July 17, 1917, in Harvey, Ill; attended Univ. of Ill. on a basketball scholarship to become a physical education teacher; Most Valuable Player 1948.

1940–1950 Cleveland Indians American League, shortstop, manager
1951–1954 Boston Red Sox American League, player-manager
1955–1957 Kansas City Athletics American League, manager
1960 Chicago Cubs National League, manager

Lou's father gave him a full-size infielder's glove when Lou was quite young. He still had that glove in 1941 when he was playing for Cleveland. He led the American League shortstops in fielding for eight seasons. His lifetime batting average was .295 for 1646 games. He played in one World Series and hit .355. His intelligence offset his slowness afoot to make him an excellent fielder. Lou became the youngest player-manager in American League history, leading the Cleveland Indians to a pennant in 1948.

COMBS, Earle Bryan "Kentucky Colonel"
Player and Coach
Born May 14, 1899, in Pebworth, Ky; received teaching certificate from Eastern Tenn. State Teachers Col; spent most of his time on farm after retirement; died July 21, 1976, in Richmond, Ky, at age 77.

1922–1924 Louisville American Association, outfielder
1924–1935 New York American League, outfielder
1935–1944 New York Yankees American League, coach
1947 St. Louis Browns American League, coach
1948–1952 Boston Red Sox American League, coach
1954 Philadelphia Phillies National League, coach

"Colonel" Combs was a lead-off hitter and center fielder of the Yankee champions of 1926–1928 and 1932. He holds a lifetime batting average of .325 and made 200 or more hits in three seasons, leading the American League in triples three times and in outfielders' putouts twice. In 1934, just after shifting to left field, he crashed into a wall in St. Louis and suffered a skull fracture that shortened his career. Combs was 6 ft. tall and weighed 165 lbs.

FRICK, Ford Christopher
Administrator and Contributor
Born December 19, 1894, in Wawaks, Ind; graduated from DePauw Univ. 1915; married Eleanor Cowing 1916; one son; taught English in Colo.

Frick began career with the *Colorado Springs Gazette,* then moved to radio to give news and sports. He became head of the National League Service Bureau doing publicity, and served as National League President from 1934 to 1950. From 1951 to 1965 Frick was Commissioner of Baseball. He is credited with the idea for the Baseball Hall of Fame. During his 31-year career he saw baseball through reconstruction, expansion and transition.

HAINES, Jesse Joseph "Jess"
Player
Born July 22, 1893, in Clayton, Ohio.

1920–1937 St. Louis Cardinals National League, pitcher
1938 Brooklyn Dodgers National League, coach

Jesse had a strong right arm, a burning fastball and a knuckleball. Knuckleballs were so much a part of his style that he had to be pulled in the seventh inning of the seventh game of a World Series because his knuckles were bleeding. During his career he pitched in 555 games, 3207 innings with 210 wins, 158 losses and an ERA of 3.64. He played in six World Series, but had to bow out of active play in 1937 because of arm ailments.

1971

BANCROFT, David James "Beauty"
Player and Manager
Born April 20, 1891, in Sioux City, Iowa; died October 9, 1972, in Superior, Wis.

1912–1914 Portland Pacific Coast League, shortstop
1915–1920 Philadelphia Phillies National League, shortstop
1920–1923 New York Giants National League, shortstop
1924–1927 Boston Braves National League, player-manager
1928–1929 Brooklyn Dodgers National League, player
1930 New York Giants National League, coach

Bancroft began in the minor leagues in 1909. During his major league career he averaged .279, played 1913 games, had 2004 hits with 320 doubles, 77 triples, 32 homers, 579 RBI and 145 stolen bases. He helped the Phillies to their first pennant in 1915 and later did the same for the Giants, 1921–1923. Beauty continued to coach in the minors through 1932 and then managed through 1947. He was 5 ft. 9 in. tall and weighed 140 lbs.

BECKLEY, Jacob Peter
Player
Born August 4, 1867, in Hannibal, Mo; died June 25, 1918, in Kansas City, Mo.

1888–1889 Pittsburgh Alleghenys National League, first baseman
1890 Pittsburgh Players League, first baseman
1891–1896 Pittsburgh Pirates National League, first baseman
1896 New York Giants National League, first baseman
1897–1903 Cincinnati Reds National League, first baseman
1904–1907 St. Louis Cardinals National League, first baseman

Beckley played 2368 games in the major leagues and had 23,696 putouts at first base, both major league records. Jake was one of the game's most notable performers around the turn of the century. During his career he had 2930 hits in 9476 at bats, holding a lifetime average of .309. Jake is one of the few to hit three home runs in one game (1897).

HAFEY, Charles James "Chick"
Player
Born February 12, 1903, in Berkeley, Calif; died July 2, 1973, in Calistoga, Calif, at age 70.

1924–1931 St. Louis Cardinals National League, left fielder
1932–1937 Cincinnati Reds National League, left fielder

Chick was a great outfielder who, in spite of eye and sinus problems, compiled a lifetime batting average of .317. He was the leading hitter with the National League in 1931 with .349. Chick batted .329 or better for six consecutive years. His major league totals were 1283 games, 4625 at bats, 777 runs scored, 1466 hits, 341 doubles, 67 triples, 146 homers and 833 RBI. Chick, 6 ft, 185 lbs, played in the World Series for four years with the Cardinals. In 1937 he retired to his ranch in Calif. because of illness.

HOOPER, Harry Bartholomew
Player
Born August 24, 1887, in Bell's Station, Calif; received degree in civil engineering from St. Mary's Col. 1907; postmaster of Capitola, Calif; died December 18, 1974, in Santa Cruz, Calif, at age 87.

1909–1920 Boston Red Sox American League, right fielder
1921–1925 Chicago White Sox American League, right fielder

Hooper's speed and sharp eye helped him to become the star leadoff hitter for the Red Sox. He collected 2466 hits for a career average of .281. The 5 ft. 10-in, 165 lb. outfielder had 3981 putouts, 344 assists and a lifetime fielding average of .966. Harry played in four World Series.

KELLEY, Joseph James
Player and Manager
Born December 9, 1871, in Cambridge, Mass; died August 14, 1943, in Baltimore, Md, at age 71.

1891 Boston Beaneaters National League, outfielder
1892 Pittsburgh Pirates National League, outfielder
1892–1898 Baltimore Orioles National League, left fielder, first baseman
1899–1901 Brooklyn Superbas National League, left fielder, first baseman
1902 Baltimore Orioles American League, left fielder, first baseman
1902–1906 Cincinnati Reds National League, player-manager
1908 Boston Doves National League, player-manager

Kelley hit nine-for-nine in a doubleheader in 1894. He had a lifetime batting average of .321 with 2245 hits, 353 doubles, 189 triples, 66 homers, 458 stolen bases and 1425 scored runs. He led the league with 87 stolen bases in 1896 and helped the Orioles win a pennant and/or Temple Cup for four years in a row from 1894 to 1897.

MARQUARD, Richard William "Rube"
Player

Born October 9, 1889, in Cleveland, Ohio; married a Broadway actress.

1908–1915 New York Giants National League, pitcher
1915–1920 Brooklyn Dodgers National League, pitcher
1921 Cincinnati Reds National League, pitcher
1922–1925 Boston Braves National League, pitcher

Rube Marquard received the most money ever paid to a rookie up to that time, and after his first year was dubbed the "$11,000 lemon." His game began to pick up a couple of years later and he would end his career with 536 games, 3307 innings pitched, 3233 hits, 1443 runs, 858 walks and 1593 strikeouts. Rube, 6 ft. 3 in, 175 lbs. and one of the best-dressed men in the country, is remembered for putting together a longer winning streak than any other pitcher in modern times, 19 games. Rube pitched a no-hitter in 1915 against the Dodgers and pitched in 11 World Series games during his career.

PAIGE, Leroy Robert "Satchel"
Player and Coach

Born July 7, 1906, in Mobile, Ala; sixth of eight children; married La Hona Brown, August 1942; three children; in youth, delivered ice and worked as a porter in Mobile Union Station; American League All-Star Team 1952 and 1953.

1925–1947 Negro Leagues, pitcher
1948–1949 Cleveland Indians American League, pitcher
1951–1953 St. Louis Browns American League, pitcher
1965 Kansas City Athletics American League, pitcher
1966 Atlanta Braves National League, coach

Paige had a sizzling fastball, but was famous for his hesitation pitch. After 22 years in the Negro Leagues, Satchel joined the majors. His overall record was 179 games pitched, 476 innings, 183 walks, 290 strikeouts and an ERA of 3.29. Satchel was 6 ft. 3 in, 180 lbs, and was never without his guitar. He is the coauthor of *Maybe I'll Pitch Forever*, 1962.

WEISS, George Martin
Administrator and Contributor

Born June 23, 1895, in New Haven, Conn; manager of his high school baseball club; died August 13, 1972, in Greenwich, Conn, at age 77.

1919–1932 Minor League Teams, owner–manager
1932–1947 New York Yankees Farm Team, manager
1947–1960 New York Yankees American League, general manager
1961–1966 New York Mets National League, president

George Weiss became owner of the New Haven Eastern League Club and fashioned the players into champions. In 1932 he began building up the Yankee farm system. He became general manager of the Yankees in 1947 and led them to ten pennants and seven World Series. George brought Casey Stengel to the Yankees to help with management and in 1960 they both joined the New York Mets, Weiss becoming president. George Weiss was one of baseball's greatest and most knowledgeable executives. He helped create and sustain the Yankee legend.

1972

BERRA, Lawrence Peter "Yogi"
Player and Manager

Born May 12, 1925, in St. Louis, Mo; married Carmen Short 1949; three sons; naval service during Normandy landings; played in 15 successive All-Star Games; Most Valuable Player 1951, 1954 and 1955.

1946–1963 New York Yankees American League, catcher
1964 New York Yankees American League, manager
1965–1971 New York Mets National League, player-coach
1972–1975 New York Mets National League, manager

Yogi Berra's major league average was .285 in 2120 games, 358 homers and 1430 RBI. He set the major league record for the most consecutive chances accepted by a catcher without error, 950, and for playing 148 consecutive games without error. Yogi played on more pennant winning, 14, and world championship teams, 10, than any other player in the history of baseball. He is well remembered for his brief speech to a gathering in his honor, "I want to thank all the baseball fans and everyone else who made this night necessary."
Also in: UNICO National Athletic Hall of Fame (Italian).

GIBSON, Joshua "Josh"
Player

Born December 21, 1911, in Buena Vista, Ga; grew up in Pittsburgh, Pa; Western All-Star Team 1933–1946; Negro National League Batting Champion 1936, 1938, 1942, 1945; troubled by brain tumors for four years; died of a stroke January 20, 1947, at age 35.

1930–1931 Homestead Grays, catcher
1932–1936 Pittsburgh Crawfords, catcher
1936–1939 Pittsburgh Grays, catcher
1940–1941 Vera Cruz Mexican League, catcher
1942–1946 Homestead Grays, catcher

Gibson hit nearly 800 home runs in his 17-year career. Josh, the "Black Babe Ruth," is credited with the longest home run ever hit in Yankee Stadium. Roy Campanella said of him, "Anything I could do, he could do better."

GOMEZ, Vernon Louis "Lefty"
Player
Born November 26, 1908, in Rodeo, Calif; All-Star Game, 1934.

1929 San Francisco Pacific Coast League, pitcher
1930–1942 New York Yankees American League, pitcher
1943 Washington Senators American League, pitcher

In all Lefty played 2503 innings in 368 games, had 189 victories and 102 losses giving him a .649 percentage. He struck out 1468, walked 1095 and had an ERA of 3.34. The 6 ft. 2-in, 175 lb. pitcher played in seven World Series games during his career. "El Goofy," as he was sometimes known, said in later years, "I tried to knock dirt out of my spikes the way the big hitters did, and I cracked myself in the ankle and broke a bone."

HARRIDGE, William
Administrator
Born October 16, 1881, in Chicago, Ill; died April 9, 1971, in Evanston, Ill, at age 89.

Will Harridge served almost 60 years in the employ of the American League. He began his career working for Wabash Railroad as a ticketing agent. Ban Johnson hired him as his personal secretary and when Johnson retired in 1927, E. S. Barnard, the new president of the American League, elevated Harridge to league secretary. In 1931, at the time of Barnard's death, Will was elected president. He served as major league president longer than any man in baseball history, nearly 28 years. Will served as chairman of the board of directors from 1958 until his death.

KOUFAX, Sanford
Player
Born December 30, 1935, in Brooklyn, N.Y; attended Univ. of Cincinnati on a basketball scholarship; wanted to be an architect; married Anne Heath Widmark 1969; Most Valuable Player 1963; Cy Young Award 1963, 1965 and 1966; National League All-Star Teams 1963–1966.

1955–1957 Brooklyn Dodgers National League, pitcher
1958–1966 Los Angeles Dodgers National League, pitcher

Sandy set an all-time record with four no-hitters in four years and captured the earned-run title five seasons in a row, 1962–1966. He won 25 or more games three times, had 11 shutouts in 1963 and was leader in strikeouts four times, twice striking out 18 in one game. Sandy's major league totals were 397 games, 2325 innings, 1754 hits, 713 runs, 2396 strikeouts, 817 walks, 165 games won, 87 lost, for an ERA of 2.76. The 6 ft. 2-in, 202 lb. pitcher was one of the weakest hitters in the majors, but he did hit a grand-slam homer in 1963. Sandy developed a circulatory problem in his pitching hand in 1962. This was diagnosed as traumatic arthritis of the left elbow. His pitching career ended in 1966. He signed a ten-year contract with NBC-TV, but broke it because he never felt comfortable in front of the cameras.

LEONARD, Walter Fenner "Buck"
Player
Born September 8, 1907, in Rocky Mountain, N.C; left school at age 14; after retirement from baseball, worked as an assistant probation officer; sold real estate.

1933 Brooklyn Royal Giants National Negro League, first baseman
1934–1950 Homestead Grays National Negro League, first baseman
1950–1955 Mexican League, infielder

Buck was the first baseman with the Homestead Grays when they won the Negro National League pennant nine years in a row, 1937–1945. Ranked among the leaders for home runs, he won the Negro National League batting title in 1948 with a .391 average. He usually hit above .300, but in 1947 he reached over .400. At 5 ft. 11 in, 185 lbs, Buck is one of the great black players who never played in the majors.

WYNN, Early "Gus"
Player and Manager
Born January 6, 1920, in Hartford, Ala; military service 1945–1946. All-Star Games 1955–1960; Cy Young Award 1959.

1939–1948 Washington Senators American League, pitcher
1949–1957 Cleveland Indians American League, pitcher
1958–1962 Chicago White Sox American League, pitcher
1963 Cleveland Indians American League, pitcher
1964–1966 Cleveland Indians American League, coach
1967–1969 Minnesota Twins American League, manager

Gus Wynn holds the major league record for the most years pitched in the majors, 23. This burly right-hander's brushback pitch was feared by American League hitters everywhere. The 6 ft. 220-lb. pitcher led the American League in ERA in 1950. During his career he pitched 691 games and 4566 innings, had 49 shutouts, 300 wins, 244 losses, a percentage of .551, 4291 hits, 2334 strikeouts, and an ERA of 3.54. He played in the World Series championships in 1954 and 1959.

YOUNGS, Ross Middlebrook "Pep"
Player
Born April 10, 1897, in Shiner, Tex; track and football star at Western Tex. Military Academy; died of Bright's disease at age 30 on October 22, 1927, in San Antonio.

1917–1926 New York Giants National League, right fielder

Ross Youngs led the National League outfielders in assists in 1919 and 1922. He hit .300 or better for nine of his ten years in major league play. During his career he played in 1211 games, had 4267 at bats, 812 runs, 1491 hits, 236 doubles, 93 triples, 42 home runs, 153 steals, 596 RBI and a .322 batting average. He played in the World Series 1921 through 1924.

1973

CLEMENTE, Roberto Walker

Player

Born August 18, 1934, in Carolina, Puerto Rico; National League All-Star Teams 1960 – 1971; Most Valuable Player 1966; died December 31, 1972, near San Juan, Puerto Rico, in a cargo plane crash en route to aid the victims of a Nicaraguan earthquake.

1954 Brooklyn Dodgers National League, right fielder
1955 – 1972 Pittsburgh Pirates National League, right fielder

Roberto earned batting crowns in 1961, 1964, 1965 and 1967. In August 1970 he played two successive five-hit games. Clemente sparked the Pirates to a remarkable turnabout in the 1971 World Series when he batted .414. His lifetime average was .317 in 2433 games, 240 home runs and 1300 RBI. Much of his excellence as a great hitter and brilliant right fielder can be attributed to his physical conditioning. Clemente was a member of the exclusive 3000-hit club.

EVANS, William George "Billy"

Umpire and Administrator

Born February 10, 1884, in Chicago, Ill; entered Cornell Univ. to become a lawyer; dropped out when his father died; reporter for the *Youngstown Vindicator* (Ohio); died January 23, 1956, in Miami, Fla.

1906 – 1927 American League, umpire
1927 – 1935 Cleveland Indians American League, general manager
1936 – 1940 Boston Red Sox American League, farm director
1942 – 1946 Southern Association, president
1947 – 1951 Detroit Tigers American League, general manager

Billy was an umpire, sportswriter and baseball front-office man. He continued sportswriting even as he umpired for 22 years. By 1920 over 100 newspapers were using his syndicated articles. He officiated in six World Series.

IRVIN, Monford Merrill "Monte"

Player

Born February 25, 1919, in Columbia, Ala; was a football, basketball and track star in high school in N.J; an excellent javelin thrower and good with a shotput; attended Chester Col. and Lincoln Univ; served in the Army during W.W. II.

1937 – 1948 Newark Negro National League, infielder
1949 – 1955 New York Giants National League, outfielder
1956 Chicago Cubs National League, fielder

Monte had a powerful bat and a strong arm that helped the Negro League as well as the National League. His 731 major league hits include 97 doubles, 31 triples, 99 homers, 366 runs scored and 443 RBI. He was out for the 1951 season because of a broken ankle. Monte scouted for the New York Mets in 1967 and 1968. He later joined the staff of Commissioner Bowie Kuhn doing public relations work.

KELLY, George Lange "Highpockets"

Player and Coach

Born September 10, 1895, in San Francsco, Calif; nephew of Chicago National League star Bill Lange; military service in 1918.

1915 – 1916 New York Giants National League, first baseman
1917 Pittsburgh Pirates National League, first baseman
1919 – 1926 New York Giants National League, first baseman, outfielder
1927 – 1930 Cincinnati Reds National League, infielder, outfielder
1930 Chicago Cubs National League, infielder, outfielder
1932 Brooklyn Dodgers National League, infielder, outfielder
1935 – 1937 Cincinnati Reds National League, coach
1938 – 1943 Boston Braves National League, coach
1947 – 1948 Cincinnati Reds National League, coach

George Kelly led the National League in homers in 1921 and 1923. He hit 7 home runs in six consecutive games and drove in more than 100 runs in each of four consecutive years. The 6 ft. 4-in, 190 lb. first baseman set a National League record for chances accepted, 1862, and a record for putouts by a first baseman, 1759, in 1920. During his 16-year career George Kelly played in 1622 games, made 1778 hits, 337 doubles, 76 triples, 148 homers and 65 stolen bases. He had a lifetime batting average of .297 and was in four successive World Series from 1921 to 1924.

SPAHN, Warren Edward

Player

Born April 23, 1921, in Buffalo, N.Y; father a wallpaper salesman; three years in Army; wounded in the Battle of the Bulge; All-Star Games 1947, 1949 – 1954, 1956 – 1963; Cy Young Award 1957.

1942 – 1952 Boston Braves National League, pitcher
1953 1964 Milwaukee Braves National League, pitcher
1965 New York Mets National League, pitcher
1965 San Francisco Giants National League, pitcher

Spahn was the all-time leader in victories for a left-handed pitcher with 363 out of 750 games. He threw 63 shutouts, leading the National League in 1947 and 1951, and pitched no-hitters in 1960 and 1961. The 6 ft, 185-lb. pitcher is ranked fifth for all-time wins and strikeouts. His career record shows 750 games, 5246 innings pitched, a .597 percentage, 2583 strikeouts and an ERA of 3.08. He was in World Series play in 1948, 1957 and 1958. Spahn had a cunning screwball, but he was a good hitter as well, with 35 homers and 57 doubles during his career.

WELCH, Michael Francis "Mickey"

Player

Born July 4, 1859, in Brooklyn, N.Y; died July 30, 1941, in Nashua, N.H, at age 82.

1880 – 1882 Troy Trojans National League, pitcher
1883 – 1892 New York Gothams/Giants National League, pitcher

Mickey Welch was one of 13 pitchers to win 300 or more games. He claimed that beer always helped him pitch better. He won 17 games in a row in 1885. During his 13-year career he won 308 and lost 209 in 596 games, with 1841 strikeouts, 1305 walks, 4775 innings, 41 shutouts, for a percentage of .596. Mickey struck out the first nine batters he faced in a game in August 1884. He played in the World Series in 1888 and 1889.

1974

BELL, James Thomas "Cool Papa"
Player
Born May 17, 1903, in Starkville, Miss.

1922–1932 St. Louis Stars Negro League, center fielder
1933–1937 Pittsburgh Crawfords, center fielder
1938–1942 Dominion and Mexico League, center fielder
1943–1945 Homestead Grays, center fielder
1948–1950 Kansas City Stars, player-manager

"Cool Papa" Bell was said to be the fastest man on base. He was a switch-hitting center fielder who reportedly stole 175 bases during a season of 200 games. He played ball in the Dominican Republic, Mexico, Cuba and the United States.

BOTTOMLEY, James Leroy "Sunny Jim"
Player and Manager
Born April 23, 1900, in Oglesby, Ill; served as a policeman, grocery-truck driver and blacksmith's helper; died December 11, 1959, in St. Louis, Mo, of a heart attack.

1922–1932 St. Louis Cardinals National League, first baseman
1933–1935 Cincinnati Reds National League, first baseman
1936–1937 St. Louis Browns American League, manager

After 16 years in the majors, "Sunny Jim" had played 1991 games with 7471 at bats, 2313 hits, 465 doubles, 151 triples, 219 home runs and 1422 RBI. Always smiling, Bottomley, 6 ft, 175 lbs, was the terror of the National League pitchers. He managed and scouted from 1938 to 1957.

CONLAN, John Bertrand "Jocko"
Umpire and Player
Born December 6, 1899, in Chicago, Ill.

1934–1935 Chicago White Sox American League, outfielder
1936–1938 New York–Pennsylvania League, umpire
1938–1940 American Association, umpire
1941–1965 National League, umpire

A polka-dot tie and a balloon protector became the cocky Irishman's trademarks. Conlan enjoyed the copious verbal exercise with other players and managers. He umpired many All-Star and World Series Games.

FORD, Edward Charles "Whitey"
Player
Born October 21, 1928, in New York City; married Joan Foran, April 1951; two sons and two daughters; entered Army in 1951, served two years at Ft. Monmouth, N.J, with the Signal Corps; Cy Young Award 1961; played in six All-Star Games.

1950–1967 New York Yankees American League, pitcher
1967–1968 New York Yankees American League, coach
1974–1975 New York Yankees American League, coach

Whitey Ford holds various World Series records including the most series played by a pitcher, 11, the most games pitched in the World Series, 22, most innings, 146, wins, 10, and strikeouts, 94. Whitey had 33⅔ consecutive scoreless innings. His lifetime major league record shows 498 games, 3171 innings played, 236 wins, 106 losses, for a percentage of .690. His overall ERA was 2.74. An upper arm ailment led to his retirement from playing in 1967.

MANTLE, Mickey Charles
Player
Born October 20, 1931, in Spavinaw, Okla; father a zinc and lead miner who was once a semipro pitcher; married Merlyn Louise Johnson 1951; four sons; plagued by osteomyelitis from youth; American League All-Star Teams 1952–1965, 1967 and 1968; Triple Crown 1956; Most Valuable Player 1956, 1957 and 1962; became vice president of a life insurance company in Texas.

1951–1968 New York Yankees American League, center fielder

Mickey Mantle was the most powerful switch-hitter in history. He joined the Yankees at age 19 and a year later succeeded Joe DiMaggio in center field. The Yankees won 12 pennants with Mickey in the lineup. He finished his career with a .298 average in 2401 games, with 2415 hits in 8102 times at bat, 344 doubles, 72 triples and 153 stolen bases. Mantle had ten seasons batting .300 or better, one American League batting title and four home-run titles. He led the American League in runs scored five times and led in 1956 with 130 RBI. The 6 ft, 200-lb. center fielder took part in 65 World Series games, hitting 18 homers and 40 RBI. Mickey's physical ailments were endless; he wore so much tape and bandaging he looked like a mummy. He shifted to first base in 1967. Mantle retired from active play to coaching with the Yankees.

THOMPSON, Samuel Luther "Big Sam"
Player
Born March 5, 1860, in Danville, Ind; worked as a carpenter; died November 7, 1922, in Detroit, Mich, at age 62.

1885–1888 Detroit Wolverines National League, right fielder
1889–1898 Philadelphia Phillies National League, right fielder
1906 Detroit Tigers American League, right fielder

Sam was one of the foremost sluggers of his day. He hit .336 in 1405 games with 2016 hits, 1259 runs, 326 doubles, 146 triples, 128 homers and 235 stolen bases. Big Sam, 6 ft. 2 in, 207 lbs, recorded six hits in a game in 1894. He played in the 1887 World Series. Thompson's 128 homers stood as a major league record until broken by Babe Ruth in 1922. An ailing back forced him to retire.

1975

AVERILL, Howard Earl "Rock"
Player
Born May 21, 1902, in Snohomish, Wash; son Earl catcher, 1956–1963.

1926–1928 San Francisco Seals Pacific Coast League, center fielder
1929–1939 Cleveland Indians American League, center fielder
1939–1940 Detroit Tigers American League, center fielder
1941 Boston Braves National League, center fielder
1941 Seattle Pacific Coast League, center fielder

Rock Averill was bought from San Francisco by the Cleveland Indians in 1928 for $50,000. The rookie proved his worth by hitting .331 his first season. During his career he averaged .318, playing 1669 games with 2020 hits, 1224 runs, 401 doubles, 128 triples, 238 homers and 1165 RBI. His best season average was .378 in 1936. Rock slugged three homers in the opener of a doubleheader in September 1930 and went on that evening to hit another.

HARRIS, Stanley Raymond "Bucky"
Player and Manager
Born November 8, 1896, in Port Jervis, N.Y; frail youth in Pennsylvania coal-mining town; married daughter of U.S. Senator Sutherland, 1926.

1919–1928 Washington Senators American League, second baseman–manager
1929–1933 Detroit Tigers American League, manager
1934 Boston Red Sox American League, manager
1935–1942 Washington Senators American League, manager
1943 Philadelphia Phillies National League, manager
1947–1948 New York Yankees American League, manager
1950–1954 Washington Senators American League, manager
1955–1956 Detroit Tigers American League, manager

While playing second base, Bucky was also playing pro basketball during the winters until his contract forbade it. Washington won the 1924 World Series and a 1925 pennant with Bucky as player-manager. He saw New York to a World Series victory. After his 1956 term with Detroit, he confined himself to scouting and an advisory capacity.

HERMAN, William Jennings Bryan "Billy"
Player and Manager
Born July 7, 1909, in New Albany, Ind; raised on a farm; father a minor league pitcher; at 18 pitched his Sunday school team to a championship and won a trip to Pittsburgh to see the first two games of the 1927 World Series; military service 1944–1945; played in 10 All-Star Games.

1931–1940 Chicago Cubs National League, second baseman
1941–1943 Brooklyn Dodgers National League, second baseman
1946 Brooklyn Dodgers, Boston Braves National League, second baseman
1947 Pittsburgh Pirates National League, player-manager
1948 Minneapolis American Association, player-manager
1950 Oakland Pacific Coast League, second baseman
1951 Richmond Piedmont League, manager
1952–1957 Brooklyn Dodgers National League, coach
1958–1959 Milwaukee Braves National League, coach
1960–1964 Boston Red Sox American League, coach
1965–1966 Boston Red Sox American League, manager
1967 California Angels American League, coach

Billy was said to be one of the smartest players in the National League. He was a master of hit-and-run play. Billy made 200 or more hits in a season three times and led the league in hits and doubles in 1935. He set a major league record for second basemen with five seasons of handling 900 or more chances. Billy's record of 16 putouts at second base in a doubleheader in 1933 is a major league record. His lifetime batting average was .304 for 1922 games played, 7707 at bats, 1163 runs, 2345 hits, 486 doubles, 82 triples and 47 homers.

JOHNSON, William Julius "Judy"
Player
Born October 26, 1899, at Snow Hill, Md.

1921–1930 Hilldale National Negro League, third baseman
1930 Homestead Grays, third baseman
1931 Darby Daisies, third baseman
1932–1937 Pittsburgh Crawfords, third baseman

Judy was considered the best third baseman of his day in the Negro Leagues. He was outstanding as a fielder and an excellent clutch hitter who batted over .300 for most of his career. He helped the Hilldale team win three pennants in a row, 1923–1925. Judy also played on the Pittsburgh Crawfords' 1935 championship team.

KINER, Ralph McPherran
Player
Born October 27, 1922, in Santa Rita, N.Mex.

1946–1953 Pittsburgh Pirates National League, left fielder
1953–1954 Chicago Cubs National League, left fielder
1955 Cleveland Indians American League, left fielder

Ralph was a prolific slugger, winning or sharing the National League home-run title in each of his first seven seasons. Kiner hit 369 homers during his ten-year career including 12 grand slams. He hit 2 or more homers in each of 34 games, three times had 3 homers in one game, hit 5 homers in two consecutive games twice, hit four homers in a doubleheader and 8 homers in four consecutive games. Kiner's lifetime average was .279 in 1472 games, 5205 at bats, 971 runs, 1451 hits, 216 doubles, 39 triples and 1015 RBI. Kiner retired at the age of 33 because of back ailments. He turned to sportscasting and was one of the "voices" of the New York Mets.

1976

CHARLESTON, Oscar McKinley
Player and Manager
Born October 14, 1896, in Indianapolis, Ind; played ball

during his three years of military duty in the Philippines; died October 5, 1954, in Philadelphia, Pa.

1915–1923 Indianapolis ABC's, center fielder, first baseman
1924–1929 Harrisburg Giants, player-manager
1930–1931 Hilldale and Homestead Grays, first baseman
1932–1940 Pittsburgh Crawfords, player-manager
1940–1944 Philadelphia Stars, player-manager
1945–1949 Brooklyn Brown Dodgers, manager
1950–1955 Indianapolis Clowns, manager

Charleston was a left-handed thrower and a long-ball hitter. He is rated among the all-time greats of Negro Leagues. He batted well over .300 for most of his career. Oscar was an outstanding center fielder and later first baseman.

CONNOR, Roger

Player and Manager

Born July 1, 1857, in Waterbury, Conn; brother, Joseph "Chuck" Connor; died January 4, 1931, in Waterbury, at age 73.

1880–1882 Troy Trojans National League, first baseman
1883–1889 New York Gothams/Giants National League, first baseman
1890 New York Players League, first baseman
1891 New York Giants National League, first baseman
1892 Philadelphia Phillies National League, first baseman
1893–1894 New York Giants National League, first baseman
1894–1897 St. Louis Cardinals National League, player-manager

Roger Connor was a left-handed power-hitting star of the nineteenth century. Until Babe Ruth surpassed it, his 138 home runs stood as the career high. He won the league batting championship in 1885 and made six-for-six in 1895. Connor played 1987 games with 7807 at bats and 2535 hits for an average of .325.

HUBBARD, Robert Cal

Umpire

Born October 31, 1900, in Keytesville, Mo; attended Geneva Col; All-American linesman; starred in pro football 1927–1936.

1928–1935 Piedmont League, umpire
1936–1951 American League, umpire

Cal Hubbard was one of the most efficient and authoritative umpires in the history of the game. At 6 ft. 3 in, 250 lbs, the "gentle giant" had a special knack for dealing with situations on the field. He became both feared and respected because of his size and ability. He began umpiring in 1928 in the Piedmont League. In 1936 he reached the American League. Cal worked four World Series and three All-Star Games. A shotgun pellet in his right eye ended his umpiring career in 1951. From 1959 to 1969 he served on baseball's Official Playing Rules Committee.
Also in: Green Bay Packers Hall of Fame, Louisiana State Hall of Fame; Major League Football Hall of Fame, Citizens Savings Hall of Fame Athletic Museum; National Association of Intercollegiate Athletics Hall of Fame, National Football Hall of Fame and Professional Football Hall of Fame.

LEMON, Robert Granville "Lem"

Player and Manager

Born September 22, 1920, in San Bernardino, Calif; three years in the Navy; American League All-Star Games 1948–1954; *Sporting News* Minor League Manager of the Year 1966.

1941–1942 Cleveland Indians American League, infielder, outfielder
1946–1958 Cleveland Indians American League, pitcher
1964 Hawaii Pacific Coast League, manager
1965–1966 Seattle Pacific Coast League, manager
1969 Vancouver Pacific Coast League, manager
1970–1972 Kansas City Royals American League, manager

Lem was an outstanding pitcher with the Cleveland Indians. He was the sixth pitcher in the twentieth century to post 20 or more games in each of seven seasons. He led the American League four times in total innings pitched. In 1953 he set a major league record for a pitcher by participating in 15 double plays. He helped the Indians to two pennants, in 1948 and 1954. Lem was in World Series play in 1948 and 1954, winning two and losing two. During his pitching career he played 2849 innings, had 1277 strikeouts, 1251 walks, and 3.23 ERA. As a hitter his overall average was .232, with 274 hits, 54 doubles, 9 triples and 37 homers.

LINDSTROM, Frederick Charles "Lindy"

Player

Born November 21, 1905, in Chicago, Ill.

1924–1932 New York Giants National League, third baseman, outfielder
1933–1934 Pittsburgh Pirates National League, outfielder
1935 Chicago Cubs National League, outfielder
1936 Brooklyn Dodgers National League, outfielder

Lindy entered pro ball at the age of 16 in Toledo. Two years later he was playing third base in the World Series with the Giants, the youngest player in World Series history. He had seven seasons of .300 or better and was one of three players to twice accumulate 230 or more hits a year. He tied a record by collecting nine hits in a 1928 doubleheader. Lindy's lifetime batting average was .311 in 1438 games, 5611 at bats, 1747 hits, 301 doubles, 81 triples, 103 homers and 779 RBI. Throughout his career Fred was plagued by injuries and was forced to retire at the age of 30 because of a bad back.

ROBERTS, Robin Evan

Player

Born September 30, 1926, in Springfield, Ill; *Sporting News* Pitcher of the Year 1952 and 1955; All-Star Games 1950–1956; employed by a brokerage firm in Pennsylvania.

1948–1961 Philadelphia Phillies National League, pitcher
1961 New York Yankees American League, pitcher
1962–1965 Baltimore Orioles American League, pitcher

1965 – 1966 Houston Astros National League, pitcher
1966 Chicago Cubs National League, pitcher

Robin Roberts was a highly efficient, durable right-handed pitcher with excellent control. During his career he won 286 and lost 245 in 676 games with 2357 strikeouts, 902 walks, 4689 innings pitched, with 45 shutouts. Robin holds the major league record for the most homers allowed in a season, 46. He was in World Series play in 1950.

1977

BANKS, Ernest
Player

Born January 31, 1931, in Dallas, Tex; one of 11 children; father played semi-pro baseball; played football, basketball and softball in high school; in Army in 1951 and 1952; Most Valuable Player 1958 and 1959; 13 All-Star Games; in later life had arthritis in left knee.

1948 – 1949 Amarillo Colts Negro League, infielder
1950 – 1953 Kansas City Monarchs Negro American League, infielder
1953 – 1966 Chicago Cubs National League, shortstop, first baseman
1967 – 1971 Chicago Cubs National League, player-coach
1971 Chicago Cubs National League, coach

Ernie Banks began his career as an infielder in 1948 when he was spotted playing softball in high school. He turned pro in 1953, becoming the first black member of the Chicago Cubs team. That year the rookie hit his first major league home run off Gerry Staley of the Cardinals. Continued success brought his 500th homer in 1970, putting him among the ranks of Mantle, Ruth, Mays and Aaron. During his career the wrist hitter compiled 512 home runs in 2528 games with 9421 at bats for 2583 hits, 1305 runs scored, 407 doubles and 1636 RBI. Ernie hit 12 grand slams throughout his years of play, leading the National League in homers in 1958 and 1960 and twice leading the League in shortstop fielding. After the 1971 season Banks coached for the Cubs.

DIHIGO, Martin
Player

Martin Dihigo was one of the best players of the Negro National League, playing with the Crawfords and Cuban Stars.

LLOYD, John Henry "Pop"
Player

Pop Lloyd was considered the best shortstop from the Negro Leagues, often compared to Honus Wagner. He was a powerful hitter, and one of the strongest throwers during his time. He played with the Lincoln Giants and other Negro League teams. There is a baseball field named in his honor in Atlantic City, N.J.

LOPEZ, Alfonso Ramon "Al"
Player and Manager

Born August 20, 1908, in Tampa, Fla.

1929 Atlanta Southern Association, catcher
1930 – 1935 Brooklyn Dodgers National League, catcher
1936 – 1940 Boston Braves National League, catcher
1940 – 1946 Pittsburgh Pirates National League, catcher
1947 Cleveland Indians American League, catcher
1948 – 1950 Indianapolis National League, player-manager
1951 – 1956 Cleveland Indians American League, manager
1957 – 1965 Chicago White Sox American League, manager
1968 Chicago White Sox American League, manager

Al Lopez holds the major league record for the most games caught during a career, 1918, and is coholder of the National League record for the most years catching at least 100 games, 12. He had a major league total of 1950 games, 1547 hits, 206 doubles, 42 triples, 52 homers, 613 runs, 652 RBI and an average of .261. Although a catcher in the majors for 19 years, Al was elected to the Hall of Fame for his record as a manager. He had amazing skill in handling teams. He led Cleveland to a flag and the Chicago White Sox to a pennant. His team was either first or second in the American League for 12 of the 15 seasons he managed. Bill Veeck declared, "If Al Lopez has a weakness as manager, and I said if, it is that he is too decent."

RUSIE, Amos W. "Hoosier Thunderbolt"
Player

Born May 30, 1871, in Mooresville, Ind; died December 6, 1942, in Seattle, Wash.

1889 Indianapolis Hoosiers National League, pitcher
1890 – 1898 New York Giants National League, pitcher
1901 Cincinnati Reds National League, pitcher

The "Hoosier Thunderbolt" was another of baseball's fireballing right-handers. He won two complete games in one day in 1891 and again in 1892. Amos pitched a no-hitter in 1891 and helped the Giants defeat Baltimore in the 1894 Temple Cup Series. During his ten-year career he won 253 and lost 160 in 412 games with 1953 strikeouts, 1637 walks, for a .603 percentage. Rusie was 6 ft. 1 in. tall and weighed 210 lbs.

SEWELL, Joseph W. "Joe"
Player and Coach

Born October 9, 1898, in Titus, Ala; brother Luke was catcher and manager, brother Thomas was infielder.

1920 – 1930 Cleveland Indians American League, shortstop
1931 – 1933 New York Yankees American League, shortstop
1934 – 1935 New York Yankees American League, coach

The flashy shortstop, 5 ft. 7 in, 155 lbs, played for 14 years in the majors. He led the league with only 4 strikeouts in an entire season and his total of 114 career strikeouts is the lowest of any player with 14 or more seasons of major league service. During his career his batting average was .312 in 1902 games with 2226 hits, 1141 runs, 436 doubles, 68 triples, 49 homers and 1051 RBI. He was in World Series play in 1920 and 1932. Sewell later coached at the University of Alabama for six years, and was named the Southeastern Conference Coach of the Year in 1968.
Also in: Alabama Sports Hall of Fame.

South Dakota Amateur Baseball Hall of Fame

LAKE NORDEN, SOUTH DAKOTA

Mailing Address: Lake Norden, 57248. Tel. (605) 783-3553. *Contact:* Ray Antonen, Pres. *Location:* Approx. 20 mi. S. of Watertown, 30 mi. N.W. of Brookings, 60 mi. N.E. of Huron. *Admission:* Nominal fee.

Founded in November 1957, this Hall exists to honor and preserve the past history of the South Dakota Amateur Baseball Association. Funds donated by an individual inspired plans for a $50,000 museum. The small town of Lake Norden (pop. 500) was chosen for the site of the Hall of Fame and Museum. Dedication of Salo Hall is planned for summer 1977. The Museum's special displays will include pictures and narratives of the Hall of Fame's members and a variety of memorabilia from baseball's past.

Members: 73 as of 1976, 51 still living. Persons eligible are baseball players, umpires, managers, contributors and promoters. Nominations are received from all over the state, screened by the election committee and voted on. Members are inducted at the annual Hall of Fame dinner.

1957 HALEY, D. A. "Deck." League Official.
LYKE, Howard. 1st Pres, League Official.

1958 CAIN, Joe. Player.
CHURCHILL, Barney. Player.
COLLINS, T. J. "Tommy." Umpire.
COSGROVE, F. N. "Denny." State Official.
PETRICK, Theo "Petsy." Player.
PRUNTY, William "Bill." Player.

1959 BRUFALT, Gilbert. Player.
HOLDUSEN, Frank. Player.
MEYER, Rev. P. P. State Official.
SHAW, Ray. Player.

1960 BAUHS, Victor. Player.
HALEY, Neil. State Official
McKEAGUE, B. J. Umpire and State Offical.
OAKS, Claude. Player.
PFITZER, Julius S. Player.
WAHL, Roy N. "Swede." Player.

1961 BRADLEY, Floyd. Player.
GRUENWALD, Ed. Player.
LIEM, Harry. State Official.
TERRY, John C. Player.

1962 HICKS, George. Player.
MUTSCHLER, Irvin. State Official.
PIETZ, Sam. Player.
PRED, Abe. Player.
ROBB, Harry. Player.

1964 ELKINS, Ed T. State Official.
KOSTBOTH, Bertie. Player and State Official.
NELSON, Adrian. Player.
WALTER, Joe. Player and Umpire.

1965 BEIER, George. State Official.
BUCHANAN, Leo E. Player.
BUE, Henry. Player.
BUE, Julian. Player.
FETTERLY, William "Bill." State Official.
PARDEN, George. Player.

1966 CALDWELL, Dr. G. R. Player.
CARTER, Edmund. Player.
FESER, Clayton. Player.
GILBERTSON, A. B. League Official.
LIGHT, O. B. Player.
PEARSON, Roy E. League Official.

1968 AISENBREY, Reinhold "Coops." Player.
HENNIES, Jack. Player.
IRELAND, Ken. Player and State Official.
KOSTEL, Laddie. Player.

1970 ERICKSON, Hart. Player.
GROW, Elwin "Duke." State Official.
PETERSON, Chuck. Player.

1971 DONOVAN, Jerry. Player.
MILLER, Martin "Sonny." Player.
WURING, Frank. State Official.

1972 HERTZ, Carl. Player.
JENSEN, Cy. Player.
KOSTEL, Steve. Player.
METZGER, Eddie. Player.

1973 FITZGERALD, Elmer. Player.
LUNDQUIST, Sid. Player.
MEES, Otto. Player and State Official.
STONE, Chance. Player.

1974 CUNNINGHAM, John. Player.
PAPIK, Cliff. Player.
REUER, Ed. Player.
ROEBER, Vernon. Player and State Official.

1975 COOPER, Keith. Player.
FEINER, Al. Player.
SCHLIMGEN, Leonard "Lefty." Player.

1976 BIRRENKOTT, Max. Player.
BORDEN, Arthur. Player.
DESAUTELS, Larry. Sports Writer and Organizer.
FOSSUM, R. N. "Reedy." Player.
OCHS, Casper "Cap." Player.

Baseball Halls of Fame to Watch

MINOR LEAGUE BASEBALL HALL OF FAME

Under Discussion 1977

Although various groups have shown interest in the creation of a Minor League Baseball Hall of Fame, the Society for American Baseball Research has taken active leadership by forming a Hall of Fame Committee to study the feasibility of establishing such a hall. Bob Hunter, a member of the Society and a sportswriter for the Columbus Dispatch, is heading the investigation. For further information, contact him at 1327 Carolyn Avenue, Columbus, OH 43224.

ST. PETERSBURG BASEBALL HALL OF FAME

Name Change 1976

Initially referred to as a Hall of Fame, this organization is now officially the St. Petersburg Baseball Museum, Inc. Construction on its permanent facility at Al Land Field in St. Petersburg was begun in 1976 and is now nearing completion. For further information, contact E. C. "Robbie" Robison, Chmn, (813) 895-6649.

YANKEE HALL OF FAME

Closed 1975

A Yankee Hall of Fame existed in the old Yankee Stadium in New York City. Also called The Telephonic Hall of Fame, it consisted of electronic displays at which visitors to the Stadium could listen to the recorded highlights of the greatest Yankee games. There is no such hall of fame in the new Yankee Stadium. Plans for a separate building with pictures, displays and other memorabilia have been under consideration. For further information, contact Mickey Morabito, Dir. of Public Relations, (212) 293-4300.

BASKETBALL

Basketball games were being played with solid or hollow rubber balls long before Christ was born. In the eleventh century, Omar Khayyám wrote, "You are a ball, played with by fate; a ball which God throws since the dawn of time into the catch-basket." An engraving done by de Bruys in 1603 shows a game of basketball. An *Encyclopedia of Athletics* published in 1818 describes a game played in Florida in which players attempted to throw a ball into a basket attached to the top of a pole. So throwing a ball into a basket was far from new when a gentle Canadian YMCA instructor invented modern basketball in Springfield, Massachusetts less than ninety years ago.

When Dr. James Naismith sat down to invent a game for his class of 13 Americans and 5 Canadians, he visualized one that would be good clean fun to play. An incident he had seen at a rough rugby match had led him to stress all forms of nonviolence and the benefits of clean living. He would have been appalled, therefore, to know that for nearly 2300 years people on the North American continent had played a form of basketball that must rank with gladiatorial combat as one of history's most violent games. In that game, which the Aztecs called *tlachtli,* the rubber ball bounced and rebounded at such high speeds that players hit in the stomach by it usually died. Columbus knew of the game, and one of the prize souvenirs he took back to Seville from his second voyage was one of those large rubber balls. When Cortés arrived in Mexico some 25 years later, Montezuma II was pleased to give him and his troops a demonstration game. Although amazed at the game's violence, the Spaniards were far more amazed by the ball—never had they or any other Europeans seen one solid object actually bounce off another.

The Aztec courts for the game of *tlachtli* were rectangular, with widened end zones that made them look like capital I's from the air. They were made of stone, then plastered and brightly painted and decorated with emblems of divinity. Though much narrower, they were sometimes longer than a modern professional football field. The sidelines were atop stone walls which were vertical at the bottom, then sloped outward toward the top. At the mid-point of the two long sides of the court, and eight feet above the playing surface, were two hollow stone rings. A line drawn between them and another drawn down the center of the court divided the playing area into equal quarters. These were painted red, blue, green and yellow. Each team of from two to seven men played only in set positions on its own half of the court. Games were for agreed-upon numbers of points which could be scored in various ways. Getting the ball through the opponents' ring, however, automatically won and ended the game. This rarely happened—first because the ring was only slightly larger than the ball, and second because the players could not touch the ball with their hands. A player tried to slam the ball against his opponents or against their wall by hitting the ball with his hips, buttocks or knees. A point could also be scored if the ball died in the opponents' half of the court. If the opponents themselves died, the game was forfeited. In a postgame show the captain of the losing Aztec team was killed. Supporters of the losing side gave or were forced to give the winners their cloaks.

Like Naismith's game, which only his modesty prevented from being called "Naismith-ball," *tlachtli* became by far the most important game in Aztec communities. Most towns had a court in the marketplace, sometimes in the suburbs. The annual tribute exacted by Montezuma from the lowland tribes within his empire included 16,000 balls. On the twentieth day of the festival of Panquetzaliztli in the fifteenth month of the solar calendar, a special game was held in the capital city of Tenochtitlan, which Cortés called the "Venice of the New World." A priest wearing the vestments of the god Quetzalcoatl descended the steps of the great temple. He was preceded by four captives and a bearer who carried a turquoise-covered serpent. On reaching the ball court, the captives were killed, two each in honor of the two gods of the court. Their corpses were dragged around until the entire playing surface was stained with blood.

The game could then begin. Aztec nobles retained their own professional players who wore special insignia and stiff leather padding, and toured the empire to play other nobles' champions. Each pro had his own ball which he entrusted for safekeeping between games to a special pageboy. Priests served as referees, scorekeepers and executioners.

Naismith, who specified that his new game was to be decent, likewise would have been appalled at the degree of gambling that went on at *tlachtli* matches. People wagered gold, jewelry, feather cloaks, houses and cornfields, their own wives or children, sometimes their own concubines as well. Some staked themselves on the outcome of a game and, when their team lost, were sacrificed. When a group of allies bet on one game against Montezuma II himself, the stakes were their three domesticated turkeys against his kingdom of Acolhua. An earlier emperor named Axayacatl had challenged one Xihuitlemoc, a noble, to a special match to be played between just the two of them. The emperor bet his yearly income plus several of his smaller cities against the noble's one big city and lost. To save face, or his cities, the emperor had Xihuitlemoc assassinated—although history records that he had wanted to do that in the first place.

Nearly 500 years later, it was these same elements in sports—violence, professionalism and gambling—that led James Naismith's seminary classmates to stay up entire nights praying for his soul when he decided to go into sports instead of into the ministry. And it was to avoid those elements that the 30-year-old Naismith invented modern basketball. He drew up the thirteen basic rules which are the foundation of today's game in a matter of days. They included: no running with the ball, no pushing, shoving, tripping or striking of an opponent. Naismith then asked Mr. Stebbins, the janitor, to nail two boxes to the balcony of the gym. Unable to obtain boxes, Stebbins nailed up two half-bushel peach baskets. Those baskets gave the game its initial name, basket ball. At first a ladder had to be set up to get balls back out of the baskets. Later came metal baskets with a hole in the bottom through which a pole could poke the ball out. Still later a net bag was attached to a metal hoop, and an official pulled a cord attached to the net to pop the ball out. Backboards were soon introduced to prevent spectators from leaning down and interfering with shots. The original soccer ball was replaced by laced leather balls with rubber bladders, then by laceless balls and finally by the molded balls in use today. Though in basketball's early games (as in *tlachtli)* players were confined to specific court divisions, it soon became legal for a player to move anywhere on the court. There have been numerous other minor changes and improvements. For example, a high scorer in Winnipeg in 1904 was called "a dead nut on the basket," for which "good shot" is decidedly an improvement. Within an incredibly short time, however, basketball had attained its present form. By the time the pledge of allegience to the flag was written in 1892 by Francis Bellamy for publication in a boys' magazine, basketball's growth into a major world sport was assured.

Basketball was organized and popularized more swiftly than any other sport in history. Within a year of its invention by James Naismith (not to be confused with James Nasmyth, who invented the steam hammer in 1839), women's teams were being organized. Maude Sherman, the future Mrs. Naismith, played on one of these teams. At first male spectators were banned from these basketball-in-bloomers games. This led some University of Oregon men to don dresses and veils in order to slip in and watch a game. Also within its first year of existence, colleges began to include basketball in their curriculum. Although Geneva College was the first one of these, the first actual college game was played at Cornell. Cornell also has the distinction of being the first college to ban basketball after the vibrations of its 25-man teams threatened to collapse the weak gymnasium building. By the end of that first year the game was spreading throughout Canada. Within three more years it had been played in Paris, France, and in Melbourne, Australia. Within four years serious competitions were being held, and with five, a basketball Championship of America had been staged by the YMCA. By 1898 there was a pro circuit for certain east coast teams and by 1901 an intercollegiate conference had been organized. That same year the game was featured at the Pan-American Expo in Buffalo, New York, where the players wore cleats and played on a grass court. Three years later basketball was played at the 1904 Olympic Games in St. Louis, Missouri. Incredibly, all of this growth and organization occurred before the basketball hoop was invented in 1906. By the time basketball's rules were officially decided upon in 1934, the Harlem Globetrotters were seven years old and the naming of women's All-American teams was five years old.

In 1914, as World War I was starting, Naismith wrote of basketball that "In the playground, it has found one of its most fruitful spheres." He lived to see his game played by over 20 million people (more than twice the number who died in that war), to see it brought under the control of an international body headquartered in Munich, Germany, and to see it officially included in the 1936 Olympic Games at Berlin. He died at the age of 78 in 1939, the year Canada, the country of his birth, declared war on Germany.

FORMS: Within "basketballdom," the various age and status requirements have produced what in effect are different forms of the game. For example, professional basketball has four 12-min. quarters while college basketball has two 20-min. halves. Minibasketball for boys under 13 and girls under 14 who are under 5 ft. 6 in. tall has four 6-min. quarters. Rules on all aspects of the game, including causes and values of penalties, also differ from level to level, as do courts and equipment. In handicapped basketball, for example, teams of partially blind players use large, soft, brightly colored balls, while teams of totally blind players shoot balls that have bells inside them at baskets indicated by buzzers. Officials for deaf teams use special hand signals to referee games.

Truly distinct games which may be considered forms of basketball include netball and korfball. While true international basketball has five players per team, netball has seven and korfball twelve—always six men and six women. While a basketball court is 85 by 46 ft, a netball court is slightly larger at 100 by 50 ft. A korfball court is nearly three and one-half times larger at 295 by 131 ft. The ball used in both netball and korfball is a size 5 soccer ball, which is somewhat smaller than a regulation basketball. Rules of motion, scoring and fouls for both also differ from those of basketball.

In most forms of basketball, the ball is normally made of rubber or some similar synthetic material. It may be of leather and may contain a rubber bladder. Its weight must be between 21.1 and 22.9 oz, however, and its circumference between 29.5 and 30.7 in. If dropped from a height of 6 ft. onto a solid floor, its first bounce must be between 4 and 4.7 ft. high. The ball may be passed, thrown, batted, tapped, rolled or dribbled, but may not be carried or deliberately kicked. Dribbling, which was first used in 1900, is impelling the ball by throwing, batting, rolling or bouncing it and then touching it again before any other player does. Players wear shirts and shorts with basketball boots or sneakers. The numbers on the shirts may be any number between 4 and 15 and must be of a contrasting color. Officials include an on-court referee, an umpire sitting at the table on the sidelines, a scorer, a timekeeper, and a 30-sec. operator who ensures that a team attempts a goal within 30 sec. of gaining possession of the ball.

ORGANIZATION: In Canada probably no other game has been accepted as readily as basketball. Within a few years of its invention, churches, clubs, YMCAs and schools all over the country were supporting teams. The University of Toronto had a team before more than a handful of American colleges had one, and Montreal's basketball league is the oldest in the world. The increasing need for a governing body resulted in the formation of the Canadian Basketball Association in 1922. Major governing bodies today include the Canadian Amateur Basketball Association and the Ontario Ladies Basketball Association. Although Canadian basketball predominates in the universities and schools, professional teams are experiencing monumental growth and support.

The extent of the world of basketball may be best understood, however, by its organization in the United States. There are two organizations at the top of the hierarchy, the American Basketball League (ABL) and the National Basketball Association (NBA). The ABL, founded in 1967, consists of the Eastern and Western divisions with five teams each. The NBA was founded in 1949 and is now the premier basketball league in the world. It consists of 18 teams in four divisions—the Atlantic (4 teams) and the Central (5 teams), which together form the Eastern Conference; and the Midwest (4 teams) and the Pacific (5 teams), which form the Western Conference. In addition to these two leagues, various other organizations are involved in professional basketball, including the International Association of Approved Basketball Officials which had 11,000 members in 1976, and the U.S. Basketball Writers Association with 611 members in 1976. The number of people associated annually with pro basketball is therefore immense, and the number of its fans is truly incalculable. In a single 1951 game in Berlin, for example, the Harlem Globetrotters played before 75,000 people—one of modern history's largest sports gatherings.

Far larger than pro basketball is amateur basketball, supervised by the *Fédération Internationale de Basketball Amateur* (FIBA). Headquartered in Munich, West Germany, the FIBA in 1976 had a membership of 132 national basketball federations. The annual tournament staged by the Amateur Athletic Union headquartered in Indianapolis, Indiana, draws the 16 leading amateur American teams. They may be armed forces teams, industrial teams, AAU regional winners, YMCA teams, or teams from virtually any other segment of American society.

The size and organizational structure of college, junior college and high school basketball is so vast that each might almost be considered a separate game. College basketball's first five-man team game was played in 1896. It entered its own modern, big time era in 1939 when an unexpected crowd of 16,188 fans filled Madison Square Garden for a college doubleheader. Today, over 1000 colleges and universities have teams. Generally these belong to one of some 100 college conferences, the major ones of which are the Atlantic Coast, the Big Eight, the Big Ten, the Ivy League, the Missouri Valley, the Pacific Eight, the Southeastern, the Southwest Athletic and the Western Athletic. All conference members, and some independent college teams, belong either to the National Collegiate Athletic Association (NCAA) or to the National Association of Intercollegiage Athletics (NAIA). The latter has some 500 small colleges as members. The more than 600 member schools of the NCAA belong to the University Division (Major College Division) or to the College Division (Small College Division). All of these teams, member schools and organizations are aided and supplemented by numerous related bodies such as the Eastern College Basketball Association and the National Association of Basketball Coaches of the U.S. Over 600 American junior colleges have teams. Most of these belong to the National Junior College Athletic Association (NJCAA).

High school basketball, with over 20,000 teams, is far larger than professional and college basketball combined. Most high school teams belong to conferences with nearby teams and to state high school athletic associations. These state associations in turn form the National Federation of State High School Athletic Associations. Statewide championship tournaments are held for boys in every state except California and New York and for girls in 15 states. Basketball games between high school teams draw far more spectators than games at any other level. This totals some 150 million Americans annually, which is statistically three quarters of everyone in America.

The final and still larger level of basketballdom is represented by the various minibasketball (formerly biddy basketball) leagues which sponsor teams for youngers 14 and under in every state as well as in some 20 foreign countries. This level supplements and supports the whole world of playground basketball where, each year, new millions begin to play the old "new" game.

Indiana Basketball Hall of Fame

INDIANAPOLIS, INDIANA

Mailing Address: 1241 N. Pennsylvania St, 46202. Tel. (317) 637-2543. *Contact:* Betty Stucker. *Location:* Approx. 106 mi. N.W. of Cincinnati, Ohio and 180 mi. S.E. of Chicago, Ill. *Admission:* 9:30-3 Mon. through Fri. No charge. *Personnel:* Ray Crowe, Pres; Julius Ritter and Howard Sharpe, V.Pres; Doxier Moore, Secy; Nate Kaufman, Treas; Keith Schorwaller, Chairman of the Bd; Kenneth Brown, Exec. Comm. Mem. *Nearby Halls of Fame:* Agriculture (W. Lafayette, 60 mi. N.W.), Aviation (Dayton, Ohio, 105 mi. E.), Trapshooting (Vandalia, Ohio, 110 mi. N.E.), Sports (N. Webster, 120 mi. N.E, St. Louis, 235 mi. S.W.), Business (Chicago).

The Hall was founded in 1962 by Tom Carnegie and Ranson Johnson in conjunction with the Lions' Club to honor high school basketball players and coaches in Indiana. Indianapolis was chosen as the site of the Hall because of its central location. Displays in the museum include the Champion Room which contains a history of famous basketball plays, a room for the Hall of Fame members, and the Hoosier Hoopla Room containing trophies and memorabilia.

Members: 124 as of 1977. Members are chosen annually by an anonymous committee. There is a limit of ten inductees a year, and two types of members, players and coaches. The eligibility requirements are: player—25 years after he last played high school basketball; coach—10 years after retirement from high school coaching or after 25 years of varsity experience. Inductees are honored by a dinner each spring, and awarded individual plaques and sketches identical to those placed in the Hall.

1962

FOX, William Francis, Jr.
Contributor
Grantland Rice Memorial Award; Silver Medal Award 1962; died in 1963.

William, former Sports Editor of the *Indianapolis News,* was known as "the man who pumped up the basketball Mr. Naismith invented." He had a reputation as a builder of sports beyond the confines of Indiana. No matter what the sport, he had been a familiar figure in pressboxes from coast to coast. William was dedicated to Indiana high school basketball and his widely read column, "Shootin Em and Stoppin Em," had been a must to Hoosiers for many years. He was honored, years ago, as "the man who has done more than any other for high school basketball in Indiana," by L. V. Phillips, then the Commissioner of the Indiana High School Athletic Association. Fox was the fifth winner of the Grantland Rice Memorial Award, as a sportswriter exemplifying the idealistic tradition of the late athletic authority and columnist.

LAMBERT, Ward L. "Piggy"
Coach
Born May 28, 1888, in Deadwood, S.Dak; graduated from Crawfordsville, Ind, High School, from Wabash College in 1911; Outstanding Coach 1945; NABC Metropolitan Award 1954; died Jan. 20, 1958, in Lafayette, Ind, at age 70.

1912–1916 Lebanon, Ind. High School, coach
1916–1946 Purdue University Boilermakers, coach

Trained in chemistry, Lambert played and coached basketball through all its rule changes from groups to a five-man game. He brought the Boilermakers to national prominence with eleven Big Ten titles, and a 371-152 record. He coached 9 All-American players and 19 All-Conference players, including All-American John Wooden and Charles "Stretch" Murphy. Lambert emphasized the mental factor of basketball, and was the pioneer of the fast break style of offense. He authored *Practical Basketball.* He was selected as the nation's outstanding coach in 1945, and received the National Association of Basketball Coaches Metropolitan Award in 1954.
Also in: College Basketball Hall of Fame, Citizens Savings Hall of Fame Athletic Museum; and Naismith Memorial Basketball Hall of Fame.

STONEBRAKER, Homer "Stoney"
Player
Attended Wabash College; College All-American; retired from Allisons, a division of General Motors and living in Speedway, Ind.

Stonebraker led his high school team to two state championships 1913 and 1914, and scored 18 points in the final 1914 game. There were only 12 boys in his high school, yet the team won the state championship due to his uncanny shooting. His Wabash College team beat all opposition throughout the country. He could throw the ball the length of the court and average better than .500. He played pro ball for the Fort Wayne Hoosiers and the Chicago Bruins, before retiring in 1928.

VANDIVIER, Robert P. "Fuzzy"
Player and Coach
Born December 26, 1903, in Franklin, Ind; High School All-State three times; College All-State four times and All-American three times; All Mid-West Guard 1925; one of All Time, All-Star Five of Indiana.

1919–1922 Franklin High School, guard and captain
1923–1926 Franklin College, guard and captain

One of the greatest Indiana basketball players, Vandivier was captain of the "Franklin Wonder Five." He led the high school team to the state championships 1920-1922. He and his teammates entered Franklin College and created the school's greatest basketball record. Vandivier coached at Franklin High School for 20 years, during which his teams won 5 South Central Conference championships, 20 sectionals and 10 regionals, and went to the final game once. After retiring from coach, Vandivier became the school athletic director.
Also in: Naismith Memorial Basketball Hall of Fame.

WAGNER, Ernest B. "Griz"
Coach
Born in North Vernon, Ind; graduated from Franklin High School in 1908; played basketball and baseball

three years before the state tournaments began in Indiana; attended Franklin College and lettered in two sports; deceased.

1917–1922 Franklin High School, coach
1922–1924 Franklin College, coach

His high school teams won every sectional title in the years he coached them, and he was the only coach to produce three consecutive state championship teams. He coached the "Wonder Five" from 1920 to 1922, and his college teams were state champions from 1922 to 1924.

WOODEN, John R. "India Rubber Man"
Player and Coach

Born October 14, 1910, in Martinsville, Ind; served in Navy in W.W. II; selected to All-State 1926 to 1928, All-Big Ten and Helms All-American 1930-1932; Helms All-Time All-American 1943; Grantland Rice All-Time Team 1953; Coach of the Year 1964, 1967, 1969, 1970, 1972 and 1973; retired in 1975.

1925–1928 Martinsville High School, guard
1929–1932 Purdue University, guard and captain
Indianapolis Kautskys and Hammond Caesars, guard
Kayton, Ky, High School, coach (two years)
Central of South Bend High School, coach (nine years)
1946–1948 Indiana State University, coach
1948–1975 University of California at Los Angeles (UCLA) Bruins, coach

Wooden set the conference scoring record at Purdue in 1932 and led the team to the National championships the same year. After college, he was a star in pro ball in Indianapolis, making 138 consecutive free throws in competition. His high school coaching record was 218-42 (83 percent), and at Indiana State, 47-14. In coaching for the Bruins, he made the greatest coaching record in college basketball history: 566-140 (79 percent), nine out of ten Pacific Coast titles and National Collegiate Athletic Association titles, with seven straight, from 1967 to 1973, losing only five games. In the Kareem Abdul-Jabbar era, UCLA won 88 out of 90 games (1967-1969), and 60 straight in Bill Walton's first two varsity seasons (1972-1973). Wooden coached UCLA to 75 straight wins in 1970-1973. He perfected the full-court zone press, and coached All-Americans Abdul-Jabbar, Gail Goodrich, Abdul Rahman, Curtis Rowe, Sidney Wicks, Bill Walton, Lucius Allen, and Mike Warren.
Also in: College Basketball Hall of Fame, Citizens Savings Hall of Fame; and Naismith Memorial Basketball Hall of Fame.

1963

CHADD, Archie "Little Napoleon"
Player and Coach

Born in 1905 in Bainbridge, Ind; College All-State forward 1927, 1928.

1921–1924 Bainbridge High School, forward
1925–1928 Butler University Bulldogs, forward and captain
1929 Butler Bulldogs, assistant to coach Tony Hinkle
1930–1933 Canton, Ill, High School, athletic director and basketball coach
1934–1942 Anderson High School, coach and athletic director

Chadd was captain of the freshman team at Butler in 1925, and captain of the varsity team in 1928. He was nicknamed "Little Napoleon" due to his height—5 ft. 5½ in. In 1929, as assistant coach, he helped direct the Butler Bulldogs to the national championship. He coached Canton High to a runnerup position in the state tourney; his Anderson High teams were state champions in 1935 and 1937. After retiring from coaching in 1942, he became superintendent of the Anderson city schools.

HINSHAW, Robert S.
Coach

Born December 25, 1898, in Henry County, Ind; attended Spiceland Academy; graduated from Earlham College in 1923 after lettering in football, basketball, track and baseball; deceased 1961.

1923–1946 Greenfield and Rushville High Schools, coach and athletic director
1946–1961 Indiana High Schools Athletic Association, assistant to Commissioner L. V. Phillips

Also in: Indiana Wrestling Hall of Fame.

McCRACKEN, Branch
Player and Coach

Born June 9, 1908, in Monrovia, Ind; Most Valuable Player 1925, 1926; All-Big Ten three times; Conference Most Valuable Player 1928; All-American; Balfour Award twice; Coach of the Year 1940, 1953; died June 4, 1970, in Bloomington, Ind. at age 62.

1923–1926 Monrovia High School, player
1926–1930 Indiana University Hoosiers, forward, center, guard
1930–1937 Ball State University, coach
1938–1965 Indiana University Hoosiers, coach

McCracken led his high school team to Tri-State titles in 1925 and 1926. He led Indiana in scoring for three years, setting the Big Ten scoring record his senior year. He scored 525 points in his Indiana playing career, and 32 percent of all points scored for his total playing career. He later became a great coach at Indiana (364-174), winning four conference titles and two National Collegiate Athletic Association championships in 1940 and 1953.
Also in: College Basketball Hall of Fame, Citizens Savings Hall of Fame Athletic Museum; and Naismith Memorial Basketball Hall of Fame.

MURPHY, Charles C. "Stretch"
Player

Born April 10, 1907, in Marion, Ind; High School All-State 1926; Helms All-American 1928–1930; All Time, All-American team; now Exec. Dir. of the Boys Club in Tampa, Fla.

1923–1926 Marion High School, center
1926–1930 Purdue University Boilermakers, player and captain

Murphy led his high school team to the Indiana State title. He was one of the first big men in the game, and was the Big Ten's foremost offensive threat, playing under coach Ward Lambert. Murphy, along with teammate guard John Wooden, led the team to the co-championship in 1928. He set the Big Ten scoring record in 1929 (143 pts), and the team in 1930 was undefeated, winning the conference title. He played against Michi-

gan's Bennie Oosterhaan, Wisconsin's Bud Foster and Indiana's Branch McCracken. Murphy followed his playing career by serving as coach and physical education director at Edinburg, Ind, High School for many years.
Also in: College Basketball Hall of Fame, Citizens Savings Hall of Fame Athletic Museum; and Naismith Memorial Basketball Hall of Fame.

PHILLIPS, L. V.
Contributor
IHSAA Commissioner 1944 – 1962; Silver Medal Award 1963; died in 1965.

Phillips believed that sports should develop the entire boy, not only his physique, character and competitive spirit, but also a sense of fair play. In 1944 Phillips became Commissioner of the Indiana High School Athletic Association (IHSAA). Coaching schools in football and basketball were established under his leadership. In order to improve officiating at athletic events, Phillips set up a program for testing and rating athletic officials. Phillip served for 18 years as IHSAA Commissioner devoting his service to Indiana high school basketball and high school sports in general.

SPRADLING, George C.
Player
Born 1904 in Frankfort, Ind; excelled in basketball and track at Frankfort High School; lettered in basketball, football and track at Purdue; All-Big Ten, All-Midwestern and All-Western Conference teams 1924 – 1926; died in 1973 at age 69.

1919 – 1922 Frankfort High School, player
1923 – 1926 Purdue University, player

Spradling played under Coach Ward Lambert at Purdue, and led the Big Ten scorers in 1924 and 1926, and was a runnerup in 1925. He later played industrial basketball for Firestone Tire and Rubber Co, and pro basketball with Saginaw and Detroit, Mich.

1964

CRAWLEY, Marion
Coach
Crawley lettered in sports in both high school and college. He was also one of three men ever to coach four state championship teams; he led the Lafayette Jefferson Broncos to the title in 1941, 1942, 1948 and 1964. His teams were state runnerups in 1950, 1956 and 1957, with a 503-231 record. The teams won 32 sectionals (23 in a row from 1944 to 1967), 21 regionals and 14 semi-state titles. He coached for 42 years, 32 at Lafayette Jefferson.

CURTIS, Glenn M.
Coach
Died in 1958.

1911 – 1913 Crown Center High School, player
1914 – 1917 Indiana State University, player
1918 Lebanon High School, coach
Martinsville High School, coach
1941 – 1944 Indiana State University, coach
Indianapolis Kautskys and Detroit Pistons, coach

Curtis coached the Lebanon High School Tigers to the State Championship in 1918, and the Martinsville Artesians to State 1924, 1927 and 1933. He was one of three men ever to coach four Indiana high school championship teams. He later coached pro teams, the Indiana Kautskys and the Detroit Pistons. After retiring from coaching, he returned to Martinsville and served as superintendent of schools.

GRIGGS, Haldane A. "Hal"
Player
Attended Arsenal Tech High School in Indianapolis; High School All-Sectional Forward 1920-1921 and Most Outstanding Athlete in Indiana; All-State in four sports and All-American in basketball 1924; earned 14 letters at Butler Univ; now living in Long Beach, Cal.

After college Griggs played pro basketball, football and baseball; his basketball team lost only to the Celtics.

HINKLE, Paul D. "Tony"
Coach and Contributor
Born December 19, 1899, in Losensport, Indiana; attended Calumet High School; was a three sport star in high school, and graduated in 1916; graduated from the University of Chicago in 1921; three sport star; one of only two to win three letters at Chicago; All-Conference two years; captain two years; All-American 1920; served three years in the Navy during World War II; NABC Metropolitan Award 1962; Silver Metal Award 1965; retired from Butler University on September 1, 1970.

1913 – 1916 Calumet High School, player
1917 – 1921 University of Chicago, player
1921 Butler University, assistant coach
1927 – 1942 Butler University, coach
1942 – 1944 Great Lakes Naval Training School, coach
1946 – 1950 Butler University, coach

Paul D. Hinkle arrived at Butler University in 1921, and acted as assistant to coach Pat Page. He was on the Butler staff continuously, except for three years Naval service. He later coached three sports (football, basketball, baseball), and was simultaneously Athletic Director, and eventually Dean of Indiana coaches. At one time he had 55 proteges coaching in Indiana. He led his teams to 561-393, and a National title in 1929. Tony coached Great Lakes to 98 wins, and the National Service Title in 1942 – 1943. He is the winningest coach in the Indiana Collegiate Conference with a 19-year mark of 75-29-2. In 1965 the Butler University Board of Trustees, in recognition of his many accomplishments, renamed the famous Butler fieldhouse in his honor. At his last game at Butler, the attendance was nearly 17,000 and present were Indiana Governor Whitcomb and Indianapolis Mayor Lugar; the Mayor read a telegram from President Nixon, who praised Hinkle. Hinkle was a member of the National Basketball Rules Committee 1937-1938, 1942-1948, and its chairman in 1948 – 1950. He was National American Basketball Association (NABC) president in 1954 – 1955.
Also in: College Basketball Hall of Fame and College Football Hall of Fame, Citizens Savings Hall of Fame Athletic Museum; and Naismith Memorial Basketball Hall of Fame.

MENDENHALL, Murray J.
Coach
Attended Fort Wayne Central High School and DePauw Univ; NBL Coach of the Year 1947 – 1948; died in 1972 age 74.

Mendenhall was an outstanding athlete for DePauw University. He was Fort Wayne Center High School coach for 24 years, with a record of ten sectional, eight regional, four semi-state, one state and eleven city of Fort Wayne championships. His teams won 418-152, 73.2 percent. He played semi-pro football and pro basketball, and coached the Zoellner Pistons for two years and the Anderson Packers for three years, winning the National Basketball League Championship in 1948 – 1949.

YOUNG, Jewell I.
Coach

Born January 18, 1913, in Hedrick, Ind; graduated from Lafayette Jefferson High School and Purdue University; College All-State three times; All-American 1937, 1938; Outstanding Athlete of the Year 1938; now resides in Del Ray Beach, Fla.

A 6 ft. 160 lbs, Young led the Purdue Boilermakers to the Western Conference his senior year, and was the Conference's leading scorer two years. Young was Southport High School (Marion County) head coach 17 years, retiring in 1954.

Also in: College Basketball Hall of Fame, Citizens Savings Hall of Fame Athletic Museum.

1965

DEAN, Everett S.
Coach

Born March 18, 1898, in Livonia, Ind; graduated from Salem High School and Indiana Univ; All-Conference Center, Western Conference Medal for Proficiency in Scholarship and Athletics and All-American 1921; now retired and living in Orleans, Ind.

1914 – 1917	Salem, Ind, High School, center
1919 – 1921	Indiana University, player
1922 – 1924	Carleton College, coach
1924 – 1938	Indiana University, coach
1938 – 1955	Stanford University, coach
1948	National Sports Committee, member
1949	All-American Selection Committee, member

Dean played basketball for four years in high school, and three in college. As a coach, he led Carleton to 48 out of 52 games, and then returned to Indiana University to win 163 games in 15 years, and tie for Big Ten titles 1926, 1928 and 1936. His teams won 17 Conference titles, and he led Stanford to the National Collegiate Athletic Association Crown in 1942; Dean retired in 1955 with a 374-215 record. He wrote two books about basketball.

Also in: American Association of College Baseball Coaches Hall of Fame; College Basketball Hall of Fame, Citizens Savings Hall of Fame Athletic Museum; and Naismith Memorial Basketball Hall of Fame.

HILL, Chester
Coach

Hill was one of the founders of the North Central Conference in Indiana; he also helped form the Big Four Tournament, the first high school invitational tourney in the state. He was the first school official to stage a flag-raising ceremony at high school basketball games in Indiana; he also started the "feeder" system of developing athletes in grade schools. He coached at Thorntown, Martinsville, Lebanon and Kokomo, a total high school coaching career of 15 years. His teams won 225 games. His 1915 Thornton team won the state title, and his 1925 Kokomo team was runnerup to Franklin.

ROBINSON, Guy
Player

Gimbel Award 1923; Intercollege All-Star, All-Western Conference and All-American; served as Secretary of State in Indiana; died in 1975.

1920 – 1923	Anderson High School, player
1924 – 1927	Wabash College, player and captain
1927 – 1929	Centerville High School, coach
1929	Richmond Palladiums, player

Robinson went to the state finals with his 1921 high school team, to semi-state in 1922 and again to state in 1923. He was a member of the Indiana Intercollegiate Championship team 1925 – 1926. From 1927 to 1929 he was coach at Centerville High School; then joined the Richmond Palladiums.

TRESTER, Arthur L.
Contributor

Born June 10, 1878, in Pecksburg, Indiana; graduated from Plainfield Academy (Indiana) in 1897, Earlham Col. in 1904, and Columbia Univ. in 1913; died September, 1944, in Indianapolis, Ind; Silver Medal Award 1965.

Arthur L. Trester worked for Indiana high schools, first as teacher, then coach, high school principal, and later superintendent. In 1911, he organized the Indiana High School Basketball Tournament, which was a model of its kind. He became Secretary of the struggling Indiana High School Athletic Association in 1913, and led its growth to more than 800 schools. In 1922 he became commissioner of the Association, and remained for 22 years; the organization became a model for other states.

Also in: Naismith Memorial Basketball Hall of Fame.

WELLS, W. R. Clifford "Cliff"
Coach

Born March 17, 1896, in Indianapolis, Ind; Metropolitan Award 1963; now lives in Memphis, Tenn.

1913 – 1916	Bloomington, Ind, High School, guard
1917 – 1920	Indiana University, guard
	Bloomington High School, coach (five years)
	Columbus High School, coach (one year)
	Logansport High School, coach (23 years)
1945 – 1963	Tulane University, coach
1935 – 1964	Indiana High School Coaches Association, president
	Indiana Coaching School, director
1952 – 1956	National Rules Committee, member
1959	National Association of Basketball Coaches, president
1960	National Association of Basketball Coaches, executive secretary
1962	Basketball Hall of Fame, executive director
1965	Indiana Basketball Hall of Fame, executive director

As dean of high school coaches, Wells won 617 games for 71 percent, including 50 district, regional and invitational tourneys and state championships at Bloomington in 1919 and at Logansport in 1934. He founded the Indiana High School Coaches Association. He later coached at Tulane, completing 47 years of coaching, 1303 games.

His record at Tulane was 885-418. He conducted more than 100 clinics across the nation and overseas, and has written 50 articles on basketball.
Also in: College Basketball Hall of Fame, Citizens Savings Hall of Fame Athletic Museum; and Naismith Memorial Basketball Hall of Fame.

WHITE, Donald
Coach
High School All-State 1918; All-American 1921; and one of ten All-Time All-Americans 1942.

1915 – 1918 Lebanon High School Tigers, player
1919 – 1922 Purdue University Boilermakers, player
Washington University, coach
St. Louis University, coach
University of Connecticut, coach
Rutgers University, coach
1956 U.S. State Dept, Thailand's Olympic Coach

White led the Tigers to two state championships in 1917 and 1918. The 1920 Purdue team was second in the Big Ten, the 1921 team tied for first and the 1922 team was first. He was the conference leading scorer in 1921. In 1956 he set up a basketball program in Thailand. White retired from coaching at Rutgers in 1963.

1966

CROWE, Clement
Coach
Living in Eden, N.Y.

Lafayette Jefferson High School, player
University of Notre Dame, player
St. Vincent College, coach (six years)
Xavier University, coach (12 years)
1944 University of Notre Dame, basketball coach
1945 – 1946 University of Iowa, coach

Crowe lettered in basketball, track, baseball and football in high school, and in football and basketball in college. After coaching football and basketball in college for years, he served as coach for the Buffalo Bills, Baltimore Colts, and ten years in Canadian football as coach.

GLASCOCK, David Albert "Crystal"
Coach
Graduated from Crawfordsville High School, Wabash Col, and Columbia University; now deceased.

Crawfordsville High School, player
Wabash College, player
Crawfordsville High School, coach
Indiana State University, coach ten years)

Glascock played basketball and football in high school and in college. He coached from 1909 to 1952; he coached the first high school basketball champion in the state of Indiana, the 1911 Crawfordsville High School team.

MCCULLOUGH, Harold Taylor "Mack"
Coach and Contributor

Indiana High School Athletic Association Council (ten years)
Board of Control, president
National Association of Basketball Coaches, president
Clarksburg High School, coach
Milroy High School, coach
Owensville High School, coach
Shelbyville High School, coach
Crawfordsville High School, coach

McCullough devised the first "rating of officials" system. As a coach, he led his teams to many sectional, regional championships. He served in both world wars, and is now park superintendent for the City of Crawfordsville.

NIPPER, Robert L.
Contributor
Indianapolis Tech High School All-Sectional Honors 1921 and 1922; Butler University, 12 letters in basketball, football and baseball; served in the Navy; Silver Medal Award 1966; retired in 1969.

Indianapolis Tech High School, player
Butler University, player
1931 – 1942 Shortridge High School, coach

Robert L. Nipper played basketball at Butler University, leading them to the championship in the National AAU Basketball Tournament in 1924, and winning all-tourney mention. He went back to coach at Shortridge High School, winning four city championships and tying for five others. After Navy service, he returned to Shortridge, as athletic director, and in 1948, became executive secretary of the Indiana High School Coach Association.

STAGGS, Alva Rivers
Coach
Died in 1942.

1907 – 1910 Walton High School, player
1911 – 1914 Wabash College, player
1917 Lebanon High School, coach
Anderson High School Indians, coach (ten years)
Monticello High School, coach

Staggs was a basketball and track star in high school, setting a state record in the 220 yd. dash. As a coach, he led Lebanon High School to the state championship in 1917.

VAUGHAN, Robert E. "Pete"
Coach
All-American in football at Notre Dame 1909 and All-American in football at Princeton 1911; now deceased.

1904 – 1907 Crawfordsville High School, player
1908 – 1909 University of Notre Dame, player
1910 – 1911 Princeton University, player
1912 – 1916 Purdue University, basketball coach
1919 – 1947 Wabash College, coach and athletic director
1961 – 1963 Wabash College, coach and athletic director

Vaughan lettered in four sports in high school, and played fullback for Notre Dame and Princeton Universities. His team at Notre Dame won 50 out of 52 games. As a coach, he led the 1925 Wabash team to a national championship, losing only to Wisconsin.

1967

GANT, John
Player

1919 – 1922 Franklin High School, player

1922 – 1925 Franklin College Grizzlies, player

The late John Gant played on state championship teams in high school 1920 to 1922, and was leading scorer in the state one year, hitting 40 percent in a state tournament. He led the Grizzlies to two state titles, with a 63-10 record in four years. The team won 29 games, lost 1, and then won another 48 in a row. He played pro basketball, and spent two years in Africa for Firestone.

HOOKER, Orville J. "Hook"
Player and Coach
High School All-State 1920 – 1921; All-American 1924; College All-State 1922 – 1925; deceased.

1918 – 1921 Anderson High School, player
1922 – 1925 Butler University, player and captain
Pendleton High School, coach
1932 New Castle Trojans, coach
Marion High School, coach

Hooker played at Butler under coaches Pat Page and Tony Hinkle. As a coach, he had an 83 percent win score. He led the 1932 New Castle Trojans to the state championship, and the New Castle football team to 26 straight wins. After retiring from coaching, he was a high school principal and school superintendent.

KAUFMAN, Nate
Coach and Contributor
Graduated from Shelbyville High School; Paul Cross Award for outstanding ability in the classroom and on the basketball court; Silver Medal Award 1967; trustee of Franklin College.

Nate Kaufman played semi and professional basketball for ten years. He became coach at St. Joseph High School, and the first year he led them to the National Tournament in Chicago. For over 21 years, he officiated high school basketball games and was considered one of the finest officials in Indiana. Nate worked in over 1000 games and the state tournaments from 1935 to 1941. The citizens of his home town presented him a seven-foot plaque naming him "Mr. Shelbyville" in recognition of his outstanding civic contributions. He has also been highly instrumental in raising funds for the Indiana High School Basketball Hall of Fame.

LONGFELLOW, John L.
Coach
Coach of the Year in 1950.

Napanee High School, coach and athletic director
Elkhart High School, coach
1948 – 1954 Indiana State University, coach and athletic director
U.S. Olympic team, coach

Longfellow's record shows over 500 coaching victories in high school and college. At Elkhart his record was 302 wins and 24 championships. The Sycamores won 12 titles while he coached them, and had a 122-64 record. His 1950 team won the National Association of Intercollegiate Athletics title in Kansas City. Longfellow also coached a champion U.S. Olympic team in the Pan American games.
Also in: National Association of Intercollegiate Athletics Hall of Fame.

LYBOULT, Lyman H.
Coach
Born in 1888 in Centerville, Ind; son James won the Gimble Award in 1935; died in 1964 at age 76.

1909 – 1912 Earlham College in Richmond, player
1916 – 1928 Richmond High School, coach
1929 – 1955 Richmond High School, athletic director
1955 – 1964 Richmond Recreation and Playgrounds, director

Lyboult lettered in baseball and basketball in college. He was one of the founders of the North Central Athletic Conference, and was its secretary for 25 yrs.

ROUDEBUSH, Earl David "Roudie"
Coach
Born in 1891.

1905 – 1908 Label High School, player
1909 – 1912 Indiana University, player
Monticello, coach
McCordsville High School, coach
Martinsville High School, coach
1925 Winamac High School, coach

The late Earl Roudebush helped organize and conduct the first state tournament at Bloomington in 1911. In his last eight years of coaching at Winamac, he won 70 percent of his games. Although the school had a 200 enrollment, it regularly played such teams as Elkhart, Huntington, Michigan City and Logansport. He took the 1932 team to the state finals, but they lost to New Castle 24-17.

1968

CASE, Everett "Old Gray Fox"
Coach
Born June 21, 1900, in Anderson, Ind; graduated from Univ. Wis; ACC Coach of the Year 1954, 1955, 1958; died April 30, 1966, at age 66 in Raleigh, N.C.

Columbus High School, coach
Smithfield High School, coach
Anderson High School, coach
Frankfort High School, coach
1947 – 1964 North Carolina University Wolfpack, coach

Case began his coaching career at age 18, at Indiana high schools; his prep record was 726-75 in 23 years, winning four state titles at Frankfort. He had a 376-133 record at North Carolina State, for a coaching total of 1102 wins and 208 losses. He brought prominence to North Carolina State by developing seven All-Americans and winning ten conference titles, six in the Southern and four in the Atlantic Coast (ACC). In his honor the Case Award is presented to the outstanding player in the ACC Basketball Tournament each year and the North Carolina State Athletic Center was named in his honor.
Also in: College Basketball Hall of Fame, Citizens Savings Hall of Fame.

CROWE, Ray
Coach
Born in Franklin, Ind; now director of the Indianapolis Dept. of Parks and Recreation.

Whiteland High School, player
Indiana Central College, player and captain

1950 – 1957 Indianapolis Crispus Attucks High School, coach

Crowe was the leading scorer in both high school and college his junior and senior years. He also lettered in baseball and track. As a coach, he led his 1951 team to the Final Four, and his 1957 team to be state runnerup. He had two state champions 1955 and 1956, the first undefeated team. After retiring from coaching, he began a career in business management, and, after a time in the Indiana legislature, joined the staff of the State Dept. of Public Instruction.

HUFFMAN, Vernon R.
Player
Born in 1914 in Mooreland, Ind; High School All-State Guard 1932; All-American in basketball 1935, 1936 and in football 1936.

1929 – 1932 New Castle Indiana High School, guard
1933 – 1936 Indiana University, guard
1937 – 1938 Detroit Lions, player

Huffman was on the high school state championship basketball team in 1932, and played baseball and football as well as basketball in college. He also played pro football for three years after his college days.

KELLER, Herman F.
Coach
Outstanding All-Around Athlete at Oakland City College three times and four Sports Medals.

1921 – 1924 Troy High School, player and captain
1925 – 1928 Oakland City College, player
1929 – 1930 Indiana State University, player
Plainville High School, coach (three years)
Boonville High School, coach (ten years)
Evansville Bosse High School, coach (20 years)

Keller lettered in four sports at Oakland, and majored in physical education at Indiana State, picking up an MA in 1940 at Indiana University. He coached Evansville Bosse to the state championship in 1944 and 1945. Keller also coached football, track and tennis. Keller served many years as an officer in athletic organizations, including Southern Indiana Athletic Conference, Indiana High School Athletic Association, Southern Officials Association and the National Federation of State High School Athletic Associations.

KESSLER, Robert Lewis
Player
Born in Indianapolis; All-American two years; now resides in Warren, Mich.

1929 – 1932 Anderson, Indiana, High School, player
1933 – 1936 Purdue University, player
1936 – 1939 Indianapolis Kautskys, player

Kessler played varsity basketball at Purdue for three years and pro ball with the Kautskys for three years. He also refereed many games.

MORRIS, Jim
Contributor
Graduated from Butler University; *Sports Magazine* Service Award; Silver Medal Award 1968; deceased.

A licensed physical therapist, Jim Morris never played basketball or coached a team. He has been a trainer for more than 30 years at Butler University. He not only used his skills in treating injuries, but also acted as a confidant to athletes on all levels of competition. Hall of Famer Tony Hinkle said about him, "Jim has done a world of good for coaches and athletes in Indiana. He is a man who has dedicated his talent to helping young men interested in athletics. Since graduating from Butler he has never stopped learning and has received a thorough education from books and doctors. With a fellow like Jim Morris, you know that athletes will get the best of care. He is respected not only for his ability, but also bacause of his unselfishness. The Indiana athletic scene has a great friend in Jim Morris." *Sports Magazine* presented him its Service Award, and called him more than just a trainer—he is a counselor and friend to the thousands of boys who come to him for aid. Jim is also one of the founders of the National Athletic Trainers Association.
Also in: Athletic Trainers Hall of Fame, Citizens Savings Hall of Fame Athletic Museum.

1969

FRIDDLE, Burl
Player and Coach
Born in Franklin, Ind; now retired.

1915 – 1918 Franklin High School, player
1919 – 1922 Franklin College, player and captain
Washington High School, coach
Fort Wayne South High School, coach
Toledo University, coach, athletic director

Friddle led the famous Franklin "Wonder Five" to a state championship in 1920 and captained the Franklin College national champions in 1922, when the team was undefeated. As a coach, he led Washington to the state title in 1930, Fort Wayne South, in 1938, and Toledo to the finals of the National Invitational Tournament in 1942 at Madison Square Garden. Friddle ended his career as Toledo's athletic director.

GATES, Hilliard
Contributor
Indiana Sportscaster of the Year five times; Silver Medal Award 1969.

In 1940 Hilliard Gates, a veteran broadcaster, began covering Indiana high school basketball. Then in 1954 he began television coverage of the Indiana High School Athletic Association State Finals. Hilliard is a dynamic speaker and toastmaster and has appeared before hundreds of high school groups and civic organizations, including the NBC radio originations of the Rose Bowl Games from Pasadena in 1967 and 1968, and the NBA All-Star Games. He served as president of the Indiana Sports Writers and Broadcasters Association for two terms, and is also a charter member of the National Sports Writers and Broadcasters group. Hilliard was presented an Honorary Doctorate from Tri-State College several years ago, for his long and distinguished service to broadcasting.

LYLE, Clyde
Coach
Big Ten Medal 1929.

1922 – 1925 Lawrence Central High School, player

1926–1929 Purdue University, player
Rossville High School, coach
Rochester High School, coach
Hammond High School, coach and athletic director

Lyle lettered under Ward Lambert at Purdue in basketball and baseball. He coached for 17 years, winning eight sectionals, three regionals and one semi-state championship.

O'NEILL, Leo C. "Cabby"
Coach and Contributor

Washington Catholic High School, player and captain
University of Alabama, player and captain
Epsom High School, coach
Montgomery High School, coach
Jasper High School, coach and athletic director

O'Neill captained Alabama to the Southern Conference championship. Later in his career, he wrote a booklet about modern zone defense in basketball; two years later he wrote about how to beat the zone defense. He coached the Jaspers to the state championships in 1949. O'Neill has served on the Indiana High School Athletic Association Council and board of control.

WAKEFIELD, Dr. Markham
Coach

Born in 1895 in Switz City, Ind.

Indiana University, player
Switz City High School, coach
Rochester High School, coach
Bloomington High School, coach
Evansville High School, coach
Technical of Indianapolis, coach

Wakefield lettered in basketball at Indiana, where he was a teammate of Everett Dean. While a coach, his teams won 15 sectional and 11 regional championships. They never won the state title, but were contenders seven times. He was a director of physical education at Indiana University for 22 years.

WHEELER, Harold "Babe"
Coach

High School All-State 1922; College All-Conference 1928; deceased.

1922–1924 Terre Haute Garfield High School, center
1925–1928 Purdue University, forward and captain
1928–1930 Seymour High School, coach (two years)
1930–1953 Brazil High School, coach (23 years)

At 5 ft. 10 in, he was the smallest All-State center in the history of Indiana. He led all the scoring in the 1922 tourney, scoring 13 of the team's 15 points in the loss to Franklin's "Wonder Five." He led Purdue to the Big Ten championship in 1926 and 1928. As a coach, Wheeler won 17 sectional championships, with a total score of 411-236. He was a collegiate basketball referee for eight years, and also served as Brazil High School's athletic director.

1970

ADAMS, John L.
Coach

1908–1911 Bloomington High School, player
1912–1916 Indiana University, player
Vincennes High School, coach and athletic director (39 years)

The late John Adams played on Bloomington's first basketball team, before they had a gym. As a coach, he led Vincennes to 38 straight wins, and took them to a state championship in 1923, defeating Muncie 27-18.

BARNES, Frank
Coach

Roachdale High School, player
Central Normal College, coach
Shelbyville High School, coach
Flora High School, coach (four years)
Jeffersonville High School, coach (five years)

Barnes had 28 winning seasons in 30 years of high school and college coaching. He coached the undefeated 1930 Central Normal team to the intercollegiate state championships, and Shelbyville in 1947 to the state high school championship.

CROWN, Keith A.
Coach

Born in 1892 in Iowa; deceased.

Keith Crown started in 1918 with Horace Mann School, serving as athletic director and football coach for 12 years and basketball coach for 40 years. Crown introduced and used the first white basketball shoes in the state. He pioneered in the pivot play and the technique of the jump shot. In addition to coaching, Crown organized and was president of the first High School Basketball Athletic Officials Association in Indiana, and was one of the early presidents of the Indiana State High School Coaches Association. He has officiated in more than 1000 high school basketball games. Since retiring as coach, Crown has worked with radio station WWCA of Gary as a sports commentator. He has given commentary and interviews in 452 football and basketball games in college and high school.

ESKEW, Phil N.
Contributor

Graduated from Oakland City College and Indiana University; Silver Medal Award 1970; retired.

Phil N. Eskew has been a teacher, coach, athletic official, and school administrator for many years. He has taught in the Davies County, Bloomington, Wabash, Sullivan and Huntington schools. For eight years he was superintendent of the Sullivan schools, and the Huntington schools, for three years. In 1962 he became Commissioner of the Indiana High School Athletic Association, retiring in 1976. He is also very active in many civic, health and educational organizations. Phil is a member of the United States Track and Field Federation Committee, and he is also on the Olympic committee on gymnastics.

JOLLY, Raymond "Pete"
Coach
Retired in Florida 1969.

	New Castle High School, player
	Purdue University, player
1927 – 1940	Muncie Central Bearcats, coach

Jolly was a three-sport athlete in high school, and played basketball and football at Purdue. As a coach, he led the Bearcats to state championships in 1928 and 1931.

McCREARY, Lawrence J. "Jay"
Player and Coach
High School All-State Forward 1936; All-NCAA Forward 1940.

1933 – 1936	Frankfort High School, forward and captain
1937 – 1940	Indiana University, forward
	Vincennes High School, coach
	DePauw University, head coach
	Muncie Central, coach
	Louisiana State University, coach

McCreary helped Frankfort to the state champions in 1936 and Indiana to the National Collegiate Athletic Association (NCAA) championship in 1940. As a coach, he led Muncie Central to the 1952 state championships.

PHILLIPS, Ardith Lowell "Pete"
Coach
All-Big Ten three times; now living in Muncie, Ind.

1913 – 1916	Clay Township High School, player
1916 – 1919	Indiana University, player and captain
	Angola High School, coach
	Terre Haute High School, coach
	Wiley High School, coach
	Rushville High School, coach
	Bloomington High School, coach
	Ball State University, coach

Phillips coached for 17 years in Indiana high schools and took his teams to the state finals in Indianapolis three times. He spent 10 years as varsity coach at Ball State University.

WALTER, Charles Russell "Rut"
Player
High School All-State 1925; Gimble Award 1925.

1921 – 1925	Kokomo High School, player
1925 – 1929	Northwestern University, player and captain

Charles Walter led Kokomo to the state finals against Frankfort, scoring 14 of Kokomo's 20 points in a losing battle, but was unanimous All-State selection. In his senior year at Northwestern, he captained both the basketball and track teams. After graduation, he coached track for Northwestern for 22 years before resigning to become track coach at the University of Wisconsin. He is now retired.

WARD, John Woodford
Coach
All-Western 1927.

1920 – 1923	Evansville Central High School, player
1924 – 1927	DePauw University, Player
1929 – 1945	Tipton High School, coach
1947 – 1956	Elwood High School, coach

John Ward was selected All-Western by the *Chicago Tribune* from 35 teams, before there was such a thing as an All-American team. As coach, Ward led Tipton teams to eleven sectionals, and took two teams to the Sweet 16. The 1936 team was 24-0 before losing to Kokomo in the regionals. He coached Elwood to three Central Indiana Conference titles in nine years; he was one of the founders of the Central Indiana Conference. In 1956 John Ward became Elwood's athletic director.

1971

BACON, Francis William "Bake"
Player
High School All-State 1913; College All-State 1916.

South Bend Central High School, player
Wabash College, player and captain
Em Roes of Indianapolis, player
Fort Wayne, player
Dayton, player

Francis Bacon played in the state champions his senior year in high school. Bacon was the captain of the famous Wabash Wonder Five who defeated Notre Dame, Illinois and Purdue in 1918. After college he was an aviator in W.W. I, returning to play pro ball for a time. He later was a basketball referee for 33 years in Ohio, participating in eight Ohio high school finals.

CHADWICK, Maurice "Shang"
Player
Deceased.

1919 – 1920	New Richmond Crawfordsville High School, center
1921 – 1924	Wabash College, center
	New York Celtics, center
	Fort Wayne Knights of Columbus, center (six years)
	Firestone Company Team, center

Chadwick was a member of the Wabash College Wonder Five, who were called the U.S. champions. After playing a short time with the Celtics, he played six years with the Fort Wayne Knights of Columbus team and four years with the Firestone team. He later started his own rubber company.

CROSS, Walter Mings
Coach
Gimbel Award 1919.

Walter Cross played basketball on the Thorntown High School All-State team and was awarded the Gimbel prize but a recurring knee injury kept him from playing while attending Purdue University. Cross went to Jefferson Township High in Clinton County to coach, moving to Kokomo in 1926. He took his team to the state finals in 1932. After returning as a coach, he logged much time as an official in various sports events.

CUMMINGS, Charles L.
Coach
Born in Mo; now the athletic director of Anderson High School.

Cumming's team won the North Central Conference championship in 1944, and went to the state finals. In

1946, Charlie's Anderson High School Team won the Indiana High School Athletic Association state championship. Later, he was varsity coach at Boston College, before returning to Indiana to be athletic director at Anderson High School.

DIENHART, Joseph Stanley
Coach

1919 – 1922 Lafayette Jefferson High School, guard
1923 – 1926 University of Notre Dame, guard and captain
1928 – 1938 Cathedral High School, coach
1939 – 1943 St. Joseph's College, coach
1943 Purdue University, assistant coach and assistant athletic director

Dienhart lettered in basketball and football at Lafayette Jefferson and at Notre Dame. He played against the Wonder Five seven times—three times in high school and four times at Notre Dame—and never beat them. He led Lafayette Jeff to the Indiana High School Athletic Association tourney, but they were beaten by Franklin. He coached Cathedral to the 1933 Catholic championship. At Purdue, he assisted Ward Lambert for three years and Ray Eddy for nine years, before becoming assistant athletic director.

EBERHART, Elder J. "Ebbie"
Coach
High School All-State in both football and basketball.

Evansville Central High School, player
Indiana University, player
Logansport High School, coach
Evansville High School, coach
Richmond High School, coach

Eberhart earned five letters in basketball, football and track at Indiana. As a coach, he took Richmond to the state finals in 1934 and 1935; the 1943 team won the North Central Conference title. More recently, he has been the principal and school administrator at Evansville, and the superintendent of county schools and the supervisor of health and safety for the school system.

ENGLEHARDT, Charles Harold "Shrimp"
Coach
High School All-State in 1926; retired 1970.

1923 – 1926 Marion High School, player
1927 – 1930 Wabash College, player
North Vernon High School, coach
Greenfield High School, coach
Seymour High School, coach and athletic director

Englehardt was a four-sport star in high school and lettered in both basketball and baseball in college. As a coach, he had a record of 337-173, and his teams won the Southeastern Indiana Conference title five times in seven years, seven invitational titles, ten sectional championships, three regional titles. They won the first game in the semi-state two times and were in the Sweet 16 three times.

GULLION, Blair
Coach
Born December 22, 1901; died January 30, 1959, in St. Louis, Mo. at age 58 of a fatal heart attack after 16 games of a 22-game schedule.

1917 – 1920 New Castle High School, player
1921 – 1923 Purdue University, player
1928 – 1935 Earlham College, coach
1936 – 1938 University of Tennessee, coach
1939 – 1942 Cornell University, coach
1946 – 1947 University of Connecticut, coach
1948 – 1959 Washington University, St. Louis, coach and athletic director

Gullion's career coaching record was 323-206; he stressed defense and ball handling. He was the author of three books about basketball: *Techniques and Tactics of Basketball Defense, 100 Drills for Teaching Basketball Fundamentals* and *Basketball Offense Fundamentals Analyzed.* Earlham College named their top basketball award in his honor.
Also in: College Basketball Hall of Fame, Citizens Savings Hall of Fame Athletic Museum.

NICOSON, Angus "Nick"
Contributor
Silver Medal Award 1971.

1939 – 1942 Indiana Central College, player
Franklin Central High School, coach
Indiana Central College, coach
Indiana High School All-Stars, coach

Nick played basketball with Indiana Central College, leading them to its only undefeated basketball season in 1941 – 1942. He was a member of the Central squad which racked up 30 consecutive wins over a period of three years. Nick went on to become coach at Franklin Central High School and compiled a 92-28 record. He returned to coach at Indiana Central College and had 423 victories against 231 losses, making him the ninth winningest coach in collegiate history. He remained as coach at Indiana Central College for 26 years. Nick was selected to coach the Indiana High School All-Stars in the annual summer classic against Kentucky's finest senior players. He had 19 wins and 12 losses in his 17 year ledger for this series. As of 1971, Nick had an overall record of 534 wins and 271 losses.
Also in: National Association of Intercollegiate Athletics Hall of Fame.

REIMANN, Harry, "Wally" "Dutch"
Player
Distinguished Alumni Award from Purdue for meritorious service to the university in athletics in 1953.

Reiman started playing basketball at age eleven in 1893, and devoted 26 years to the sport as a player, coach and official. He was captain of Purdue's first basketball team, and his son Bill later became a referee. Deceased.

SHARPE, Howard Lee "Sharpie"
Coach

Gary Lew Wallace High School, player
Indiana State University, player
Terre Haute Gerstmeyer High School, coach (27 years)
Terre Haute North Vigo High School, coach

Sharpe has appeared on over 1200 basketball clinics and programs. He led Terre Haute Gerstmeyer to 17 holiday tourney wins, 9 sectionals, 6 regionals and 4 semi-state championships.

1972

BARATTO, Johnnie
Coach
Coach of the Year 1960.

Indiana State Sycamores, player and team manager
Frichton, Indiana, High School, coach
East Chicago Washington Senators, coach

Baratto had a coaching record of 468-157, and coached the Senators to the state title by beating Muncie Central 75-59 in the championship game in 1960. In 1962 they were runnerups; overall, he led the Senators to 12 sectional titles, 8 regional championships, 4 semi-state titles. His coaching career spanned 26 years.

CASKEY, Jacob Lewis "Jake"
Coach

1927 – 1930 Butler University, player
1931 Indiana School for the Deaf, coach and athletic director

Caskey played basketball at Butler under coach Tony Hinkle. As a coach, he devoted his life to the handicapped, and began working at Indiana School in 1931. He joined the Indiana High School Athletic Association in 1942; prior to 1942, he coached Indiana teams to national championships for schools for the deaf on two occasions.

EDDY, Ray
Coach
All-Big Ten 1934.

1927 – 1930 Columbus, Ind, High School, player
1931 – 1934 Purdue University, Boilermakers, player
Tell City High School, coach
Madison High School Cubs, coach
1950 – 1965 Purdue, coach

Eddy lettered in basketball, baseball and track in high school. At Purdue, he played under Ward Lambert, with a 17-3 record in 1934, with two Indiana defeats to their credit. He played on three Purdue teams; two won Big Ten championships. He coached the Cubs to state, defeating Lafayette Jeff 67-44 to win the state title. Retired from coaching in 1965.

GOLDSBERRY, Alonzo E. "Goldie" "Lon"
Coach
Wife Opal; sons John and Tom; received the Gold Medal from Indianapolis alumni for outstanding athletic abilities and scholarship; died in 1966.

1917 – 1920 Wingate High School, center and captain
1921 – 1924 Wabash College, center and captain
1924 – 1931 Shortridge of Indianapolis, coach
Wabash College, coach
South Bend Adams High School, coach

Goldsberry played high school basketball for four years, and was captain of the 1920 All-Star American championship team in an interscholastic tournament. He played basketball, football and baseball at Wabash, and was captain of the team that won the national intercollegiate championship.

McANALLY, Jess
Player
Gimbel Award 1932, the only junior ever to receive that honor; died in 1936.

1931 – 1933 Greencastle High School, center
1934 – 1936 Northwestern University Wildcats, center

McAnally led Greencastle to a runnerup title at state in 1931 and 1933, losing first to Muncie and later to Martinsville. His untimely death stopped a promising college career. The auditorium-gymnasium complex at Greencastle is named in his honor.

MILLER, Dale
Contributor
Silver Medal Award 1972.

Dale Miller is known as one of the truly great basketball officials. He started officiating in 1915 and ended his career in 1937 – 1938, a total of 23 seasons. In 1919, he officiated his first sectional tourney at Logansport. In 1921 he officiated his first state final tourney, the first year the finals were played in Indianapolis. Dale officiated in 10 consecutive final tourneys. In 1926 he began to officiate in the Western Conference, and continued through the 1934 season. From 1923 through 1938 he officiated university and college games. In March of 1938 he officiated his last assignment, the DePauw-Wabash College game held at Greencastle.

REYNOLDS, Lester Mervin "Les"
Player
High School All-State 1926, 1927; All-American honorable mention in 1930; now living in Indianapolis.

1924 – 1927 Martinsville High School, captain and player
1927 – 1930 Indiana State University, player

Reynolds led the Artesians to the state finals in 1926, but the team lost to Marion, whose star was "Stretch" Murphy. He also captained the state championship Martinsville team in 1927. He placed second in the state track meet in shot put.

TOWNSEND, John Frederick "Johnnie"
Player
High School All-State; received the Dyan Medal (top athletic award in Indianapolis); All-American two times.

1931 – 1934 Arsenal Technical High School of Indianapolis, center
1935 – 1938 University of Michigan, player
Indianapolis Kautskys, player
Oshkosh All-Stars, player
Rochester Royals, player

At 6 ft. 2 in, Townsend led Arsenal to the state finals, but lost to Logansport. He was also the state champion in shot put. He played basketball for three years at Michigan and finished second in Big Ten competition in shot put and discus. After playing pro basketball, Townsend broadcast basketball games on radio WFBM for seven years.

1973

BECKNER, Arthur Joseph
Coach
Balfour Award 1928; son Joe played at Richmond for his father in the 1953 state finals; died in 1965.

1921 – 1924 Muncie Central High School Bearcats, center
1925 – 1928 Indiana University Hoosiers, center
1946 – 1951 Muncie Central High School, coach (five years)
1951 – 1956 Richmond High School Red Devils, coach (five years)

Becker led the Bearcats to state while he was a center, and they came in second. He lettered in football, baseball and basketball at Indiana and led them to a Big Ten championship in 1928. As a coach, he led the Bearcats again to a state championship in 1951; this time they won. He was the first coach ever to have the championship televised. He went to the finals again with the Red Devils in 1953.

BIRKETT, Louis
Coach
Gimbel Award 1917; wife Dolores; daughter Mary Lou; deceased.

Birkett was a basketball and baseball star in high school in Wisconsin. He played as football center for three years at Wisconsin State. He later coached Hammond Tech to the sectional championship for the first time in their history in 1940, then to the state championship. Birkett was with the Hammond School System for 32 years.

CURTIS, Claude C.
Player
Received the Gimbel Award in 1917 High School All-State.

Martinsville High School, player
DePauw University, player
University of Pennsylvania, player

Curtis played football and basketball in high school and lettered in both in college. He led his high school team to the Sweet 16 three consecutive years and later played pro basketball one year. He was the first recipient of the Gimbel Award.

KEHRT, Willard M.
Coach
Balfour Award 1935; All-Big Ten.

Shelbyville High School, player
Indiana University, player
Madison High School, coach (three years)
Terre Haute Garfield High School, coach (26 years)

Kehrt was a three-sport star in high school and lettered for three years in basketball at Indiana under coach Everett Dean. His career coaching record was 450-214, including eleven sectionals, four regionals and two semi-states. His 1947 basketball team was runnerup for state in basketball, and the teams won six Western Indiana Conference titles and four Wabash Valley championships. He retired from coaching in 1964.

McCALL, Elmer
Coach
College All-State; Coach of the Year.

Frankfort High School, player
Fresno State College, player and captain
1953 – 1957 South Bend Central High School, coach
1958 – 1973 DePauw University, coach

McCall played high school basketball under Everett Case. His coaching score in California was 113-23 and at South Bend Central, 118-34. He led South Bend to state championships in 1953 and 1957; the 1957 team was undefeated. He coached DePauw to National Collegiate Athletic Association post season events and to the Intercollegiate Conference title in 1968.

McCUTCHAN, Arad A.
Coach
Grew up in Evansville; played basketball at Bosse High School; attended Evansville College (now the University of Evansville); NCAA Coach of the Year twice; Indiana Coach of the Year ten times; Eckrich Silver Medal 1973; naval officer in pilot instruction during World War II; presently serves as director of athletics at the University of Evansville.

Evansville College, player
Bosse High School, coach
University of Evansville, head coach

Arad McCutchan started playing basketball at Bosse High School and then went on to play with Evansville College. While at Evansville College, he led the team in scoring three straight years and was team captain in 1934. Arad went on to coach high school ball in Alabama for two years. He returned to Bosse High School, where he was on the basketball staff for six years, the last two as head coach. In 1946 he returned to the University of Evansville as head coach. Arad lectures at coaches' clinics and tutors future prep stars in basketball schools throughout the state and nation, after his team finishes the season. He is always available and eager to share his vast knowledge with the awkward young prospect, the superstar, rookie coaches or veteran. As coach at Evansville, his record was a legend. His teams won 433 out of 692 games, in 26 seasons, a .640 winning percentage. He has won five National Collegiate Athletic Association college division championships and has earned or shared an even dozen Indiana Collegiate Conference titles since 1952. Arad's teams have never shied away from the so-called giants of basketball and their record includes many victories over major conference and independent teams. He was also coach of one of the United States teams taking part in the Olympic Games tryouts in 1968. In 1971 he was selected to help coach the United States team in the Pan-American Games.

SHIPP, Charles William
Player and Coach
All-League Guard nine times.

Cathedral High School, player
Oshkosh All Stars, player and coach
Fort Wayne Zoellner Pistons, player and coach
1953 – 1962 Purdue University, assistant coach
1963 – 1967 Purdue University, coordinator

Shipp led Cathedral to the state Catholic championship and in 1933 to the national Catholic championship, under Coach Joe Dienhart. He played and coached with the National Basketball League for 16 years, and led both the All Stars and the Pistons to world championships. He was assistant freshman coach at Purdue under Ward Lambert, and coordinator of intramural sports.

WOOD, Jesse A.
Player
Born in 1889.

1903 – 1906 Bedford High School, player
1907 – 1911 Indiana State Normal School, player
1912 – 1913 Wingate High School, coach

Wood played football and baseball in high school, and baseball, football and basketball in college. He led Wingate to the state tournament, and, after service in W.W. I, had a career in agriculture, from which he retired in 1956.

1974

ANDRES, Ernest
Player and Coach
Balfour Award two times; All-American 1939; and All-Big Ten Conference two times.

1932 – 1935 Jeffersonville High School, player
1936 – 1939 Indiana University, player and captain
1939 – 1944 Boston Red Sox, player (five years)
1947 Indianapolis Kautskys, coach and player (five years)
1948 – 1973 Indiana University Hoosiers, coach

Andres earned three letters in basketball and took his high school team to the state finals. He played at Indiana under Coach Everett Dean and Branch McCracken, and in 1938 set the Big Ten single game scoring record of 30 points. He played pro baseball with Boston, Minneapolis and Indianapolis, and led a pro basketball team to the world title. Ernie's career was interrupted by a stint in the U.S. Navy. He returned to one season of pro baseball and basketball, then joined the coaching staff at Indiana as head baseball coach and assistant basketball coach. At present he is alumni field secretary at Indiana University.

BAIRD, Frank A.
Coach
High School All-Sectional 1930; College All-State twice; All-American 1934; now a golf coach at Broad Ripple High School.

1927 – 1930 Arsenal Tech High School, player
1931 – 1934 Butler University, player
1938 Broad Ripple High School, coach
1938 – 1948 Indianapolis Kautskys, player

At 6 ft, Baird lettered in basketball and baseball in high school and in college, the latter under Coach Tony Hinkle. He was later assistant coach to Paul Hinkle. Frank led Broad Ripple to a 27 – 2 and a runnerup place in the state finals in 1944. As a player with the Kautskys, he set a national league scoring record in 1938 with 33 points. He also served 30 years as a high school and college basketball official.

GARRETT, William Leon
Player and Coach
All-Big Ten two times; *Look Magazine* and *Sporting News* All-American 1951; Coach of the Year 1959; deceased.

1944 – 1947 Shelbyville High School Golden Bears, player
1948 – 1951 Indiana University, player
1952 – 1955 Harlem Globetrotters, player (three years)
1955 – 1967 Crispus Attucks High School, coach and athletic director

Garrett was a three-sport letterman at Shelbyville and played basketball at Indiana under Coach Branch McCracken. He led the Golden Bears to the state championship in 1947. After his coaching years, Bill went into educational administration, first at Mallory Tech and then at Indiana University – Purdue University at Indianapolis.

NEUMAN, Paul William "Butch"
Player and Coach
Wife Marie; died in 1964.

1918 – 1921 Lafayette Jefferson High School Broncos, player
Purdue University, player
1930 – 1945 Lebanon High School Tigers, coach and athletic director

Neuman played basketball in high school, and in college under Coach Ward Lambert. He played in the Lafayette-Jeff championship games in 1919 and 1920. He coached the Tigers to 13 consecutive sectional tournaments and two times to Sweet 16 (1932 and 1934). He took the team to state in 1943. When Neuman left coaching he became principal and athletic director at Lebanon.

ODLE, Donald J. "Don"
Player and Coach
Silver Anniversary All-State team; Freedom Foundation Award.

1935 – 1938 Selma High School, player and captain
1939 – 1942 Taylor University, player
1946 Taylor University, coach

Odle was the leading scorer in 1938 at his high school and led in scoring all four years at college. He took 12 college All-Star teams to the Orient and South America. He has coached more than 400 victories, and ranks among the top ten of active U.S. coaches. Don coached the Chinese Nationalist team in the 1960 Olympics held in Rome.
Also in: National Association of Intercollegiate Athletics Hall of Fame.

PLATT, Joseph M. "Joe"
Coach
Now a teacher at Kokomo High School.

1931 – 1934 Young America High School, player
1936 – 1938 Indiana University, player and captain
Winimac High School, coach
Carleton College, coach
1950 – 1964 Kokomo High School Kats, coach

Platt played basketball for four years in high school and three years at Indiana under Coach Everett Dean. He led the Hoosiers to a Big Ten championship in 1936. After starting his coaching career at Winimac, Joe spent four years in the U.S. Navy, and coached at Carleton College in Minnesota before his return to Indiana athletics. He led the Kats to five North Central Conference championships, ten sectional crowns, nine regional championships and three Northeast semi-state titles. In 1959 Kokomo was runnerup and in 1961, state champion; they took the Indiana High School Athletic Association crown in 1961. He retired from coaching in 1964.

SCHWOMEYER, Dr. Herb
Contributor
Attended Indianapolis Manual High School; All-City in 1936; All-Sectional; graduate of Butler University; Echrich Silver Medal 1974.

Herb Schwomeyer played college basketball with Butler University, and was on their varsity for three years, playing for Coach Tony Hinkle. He was a high school game official for 11 years in both football and basketball. Herb officiated in the state basketball finals in 1955 and 1956. For four decades Herb has been a friend of Indiana high school basketball. His enthusiasm for the game and his inspiration to those young people with whom he has come in contact, have increased in proportion. Herb Schwomeyer wrote a book on Indiana basketball's history and records, called *Hoosier Hysteria.* Since 1957 Herb has assisted on telecasts of Indiana High School Athletic Association tournament games throughout the state. He is recognized as an authority on Indiana basketball records and history. Herb Schwomeyer is on the board of directors of the Indiana Baseball Hall of Fame, serving as president for four years, as board chairman one year, and now their curator.

1975

CARNEGIE, Tom
Contributor
Teacher at Butler University; founded campus radio station WAJC; president of the Indianapolis Chapter of the Fellowship of Christian Athletes 1966 and 1967; Indiana Basketball Coaches Association Coaches Medal Award 1974; Eckrich Silver Medal 1975.

When Tom Carnegie began broadcasting high school basketball, two-hand set shot was still a thing of beauty. Tom started in Fort Wayne with WOWO and WGL, and his career is still going strong. He joined the staff of WIRE, Indianapolis, in 1945 and became director of sports for WFBM (now called WRTV) eight years later. He has completed 24 years of state tournament telecasts for that station. He has been the chief track announcer for the Indianapolis Motor Speedway for 30 years, and in 1971 became track announcer for the United States Auto Club 500-mile races at Pocono, Pennsylvania, and Ontario, California. For three decades he has done on-the-scene reports of Big Ten and Notre Dame football. Tom has covered the fortune of Indiana Athletes in the Olympic Games at both Tokyo and Mexico City. He has also been a sports columnist for the *Indianapolis Star,* and has earned 10 Best Sports Story of the Year awards from the Indianapolis Press Club. Tom also served as chairman of the radio-television department at Butler University, for a period of seven years. He is one of the founders and currently vice-president of the Indiana Basketball Hall of Fame. The coaches association gives a Tom Carnegie Award annually to a person dedicated to the promotion of high school athletics.

DOERNER, Wilfred "Gus"
Player
All-American; NAIA Most Valuable Player in 1942.

1936 – 1938 Mackey High School, player
1939 – 1942 Evansville College, player
1943 – 1946 Fort Wayne Pistons, player
1946 Indianapolis Kautskys, player

Doerner was a four-year letterman at Evansville, and led the team to the National Association of Intercollegiate Athletics (NAIA) Tournament in 1942. He was the national's third highest scorer the same year. Gus was named to the first five All-American teams. He also led the Pistons to a world championship, as well as the Kautskys. He later coached in high schools.

DOWNEY, Robert M.
Coach
Downey starred in both basketball and track at Washington Catholic High School, but a serious illness prevented his competing his collegiate years. He did play pro basketball later. In 1922 he returned to Washington to coach and led the team to the state Catholic title; they came in third at the National Catholic Tournament. He stayed at Washington through 1932 when the depression closed the school. Bob returned to Washington again in 1946, and they became the first Catholic school to win a sectional in Indiana High School Athletic Association competition. Downey is now deceased.

EDWARDS, Leroy
Player
Born April 11, 1914, in Indianapolis, Ind; All-American and Player of the Year 1935; All-League center six times; died Aug. 25, 1971 of a heart attack.

1930 – 1933 Arsenal Tech High School, center
1934 – 1935 University of Kentucky, center
Oshkosh (National League), center

Edwards scored a season total of 343 points for Kentucky in 1935. He hit a high of 34 against Creighton, and scored 26 against Chicago while the entire Maroon total was 16. As center for Oshkosh, he was the league scoring champion three times and favored the right-hand hook shot.
Also in: College Basketball Hall of Fame, Citizens Savings Hall of Fame Athletic Museum.

JOHNSON, William S.
Coach
High School All-State 1935.

1932 – 1935 Jeffersonville High School, player
1937 – 1939 Indiana University, player
Jeffersonville High School, coach
Jamestown High School, coach
Angola High School, coach
Indiana University Hoosiers, coach
Wabash College, coach

Johnson played basketball for four years in high school, and three years in college under Coach Everett Dean. He led an unbeaten Jeffersonville to the state finals, and they went to the Final Four two times while he played with them. He was the tournament leading scorer. After College, Johnson coached in various high schools in Indiana, winning many titles over the years. He presently teaches at Jeffersonville.

MEYERS, James Jr.
Coach
High School All-State and Gimbel Award 1939.

1936–1939 Evansville Bosse High School, player
1940–1943 George Washington University, player
Evansville Bosse High School, coach

Meyers played high school basketball for four years, and led his team to the state tournament in 1939. He led his college team to the Southern Conference championship in 1943. After college he was a high school coach in Indiana for 28 years, winning five sectional titles, three regional championships and one semi-state. In 1962 he coached Evansville Bosse to a state championship. Jim still coaches at Bosse.

RITTER, Julius "Bud"
Player and Coach
High School All-State.

1944–1945 Evansville Bosse High School, center
1948–1949 Purdue University, center
Peru High School, coach
1955–1963 Madison High School, coach
1969– Madison High School, coach

Ritter led his high school team to two state championships in 1944 and 1945, and lettered in basketball and baseball at Purdue. He coached Peru to four sectional titles. Ritter is the only coach in Indiana to have had three consecutive undefeated seasons, starting in 1959 (at Madison). His team won 61 straight season games, also setting a record. He retired from coaching in 1963 to enter business, but returned to Madison in 1969.

SHEPHERD, William Lee "Bill"
Coach
Indiana All-Stars 1945.

1941–1944 Hope High School, player
1946–1948 Butler University, player
Mitchell High School, coach
Carmel High School, coach

Shepherd played high school basketball for four years, and college ball for three years under Tony Hinkle. He led his high school team to the sectional and regional championship in 1944. In 1945 he was named to the Indiana All-Stars. He coached Carmel to the state finals in 1970, and to 50 straight home court wins. Shepherd now serves as Carmel's athletic director.

VANCE, Walter Addington "Ag"
Player
Selected as *Indianapolis News* All-State in 1936; All-American 1940.

1934–1936 Logansport High School, guard and center
1938–1940 Northwestern University, guard and center

Vance was known as a tremendous outside shooter and defensive player. He captained the Wildcats in 1940. Ag gave up a promising pro career to join the staff of the *Crawfordsville Journal Review* in 1946, of which he is now publisher.

WEIR, Woodrow "Woody"
Coach
Born in Marion, Ind; All-Big Ten; Balfour Award 1933, 1934. Now retired.

1928–1930 Scottsburg High School, player
1932–1934 Indiana University Hoosiers, player and captain
French Lick High School, coach
Jasper High School, coach
Vincennes High School Alices, coach
1942–1943 Stanford University, assistant coach
Marion High School Giants, coach

Weir played high school basketball for three years and also college ball under Coach Everett Dean. He coached four high school teams to 12 sectionals, six regionals and two times to the Final Four.

WOOD, Marvin
Coach
Indiana All-Stars.

Morristown High School, player
Butler University Bulldogs, player
Milan High School, coach
New Castle High School, coach
North Central of Marion County, coach
Mishawaka High School, coach
Shelbyville High School, coach

Wood played three years of basketball under Coach Tony Hinkle at Butler. As a coach, he led Milan to the Indiana High School Athletic Association title in 1954. He is presently head coach at Mishawaka.

1976

CHAPMAN, Robert Charles
Player
All-State 1926; All Big-Ten; All-American.

Graduate of Marion High School; pres. of senior class; basketball team won state championship in 1926 over Martinsville, 30–23; three letters in three sports, football, track and basketball; private in U.S. Army in 1942 and active in defense of Belgium; discharged as captain in 1945; father of three children; retired in Marion after career as industrial engineer.

Chapman went to the University of Michigan where he played three years as a backguard and center. Chappie played a big part in the Michigan Wolverine co-Big Ten Championship in 1929 and was named captain of the team in his senior year. An outstanding scholar as well as an accomplished athlete, Chapman earned a scholarship for being the athlete with the highest academic standing.

CROWE, George D. "Big G"
Player
Retired; resides in New York State.

1936–1939 Franklin High School, center
1940–1943 Indiana Central, center

George Crowe became Indiana's first "Mr. Basketball" in 1939 when he led his high school team to the finals of the state championships and scored 13 of their 22 points. In college, this 6 ft. 4 in. center earned national recognition for his team, coached by Harry Good. George earned four letters in three sports at Indiana Central and went on to play seven years of both pro basketball and baseball before devoting all his time to pro baseball.

DE JERNETT, Robert David "Dave"
Player
All-State center on the *Indiana News* Honor Five 1930; died on August 4, 1964, at age 33.

1928 – 1930 Washington High School, center
1931 – 1934 Indiana Central College, center

One of the first prominent black basketball players in the State of Indiana, Dave De Jernett was outstanding in both high school and college basketball. During three seasons with Washington, De Jernett led his team to a 75 – 17 win-loss record. In 1930, after he scored 11 of 31 points, Washington won the state championship over Muncie. During a 4-year college basketball career, he scored 506 points and became one of the finest rebounders of his day. He left the Greyhounds of Indiana Central with a 57 – 13 record.

FISHER, Scott Ernest
Coach
Graduated from Clearspring High School in 1915; worked on family farm for seven years to raise money for college education; graduated from Indiana University where he was a football and wrestling star; degree from Columbia University in 1929; deceased.

As coach of the Golden Owls beginning in 1929, Scott Fisher nurtured a team that won more than 85 percent of their games, including six sectionals, two regionals and two semi-state championships. Muncie Burris was a small laboratory school set up in conjunction with Ball University. From 1939 – 1944 their basketball team surpassed the nearby, and mighty, Muncie Central Bearcats to win their six straight Muncie Sectional championships. They reached the semi-finals of the state championship in 1938 and again in 1942, to lose to Washington in the finals 24 – 18. An indication of his talent as a coach appeared in one of his players, Kenneth "Bud" Brown, Mr. Basketball of 1942, Gimbel Medal recipient and former chairman of the board for the Indiana Basketball Hall of Fame.

JERREL, Bryan Leigh "Broc"
Player
Two times All-State; Indiana All-Stars 1945; All-Southwest Conference 1948.

1943 – 1945 Evansville Bosse High School, player
1946 – 1948 Texas Christian University, player

Evansville Bosse won the state championship two years in a row, 1944 and 1945, with Broc Jerrel as their team captain. He was a varsity regular for three seasons and leading scorer in 1944. He was second in scoring and leader in assists for the 1945 season. At Texas Christian University, Jerrel was leading scorer in 1948.

POLK, Richard Frank "Dick"
Coach
Attended Gary Froebel High School; three letters in basketball, football and baseball, and two letters in track; quarterback of unbeaten 1921 football team and All-State same season; basketball captain and recipient of Sportsmanship trophy in 1922; B.S. and M.S. from University of Indiana; married with two children; retired in Gary, Ind.

In honor of Dick Polk's outstanding record as a basketball coach, a Richard Polk gymnasium was built on the Lew Wallace High School campus in Gary, Indiana. He was involved in coaching for over forty years, but is recognized mostly for his success with the high school basketball team. His men won twice as many games as they lost in the Indiana High School Athletic Association Tournament competition, 229 games, and were regional and sectional title winners as well. Following his coaching career, Polk served Lew Wallace High School as their athletic director.

SCISM, Dan
Contributor
Native of Bloomingfield, Missouri; wife and two children; attended Bloomingfield Missouri High School; team captain, had 17 straight free throws; attended Southeast Missouri Teachers College; Joe Bolin Award; Silver Medal Award 1976.

Dan Scism played at Southeast Missouri Teachers College. He has been a player, coach, promoter in basketball and all sports for 41 years. In 1926 he joined the sports staff of the *Evansville Courier,* where he began to cover high school basketball. He covered 30 state tournaments without missing a game. Dan was a football official for 10 years. In the 1920s he instituted the use of the full column box score. In addition, he founded city golf tournament, with proceeds going to college scholarships for a graduating senior. In the mid 1930s he founded a junior league baseball program for high school boys. Dan Scism also founded the *Evansville Courier* Golden Gloves Tournament, which he personally ran for 20 straight years. In 1930s he created a sports column to which fans could write and present their views. There were times when Dan received over 100 letters a day. He is a past president of the Indiana Sportswriters and Broadcasters Association. He has done his all for youths in all sports, particularly basketball.

SMITH, Alfred Dewitt
Player
Indianapolis News All-State center 1915; received degree in mechanical engineering from Purdue University; served in the military during W.W. I; following coaching began successful business career; retired in Waukegan, Ill.

Alfred Smith was a varsity player for four years and was such a great shot that his teammates had him go up to the line for all the foul shots. In fact, Smith scored 19 of 33 baskets when Thorntown won the state championship in 1915. As a sophomore at Purdue, his team was second in the Big Championship. Before entering the business world, Smith coached at Lebanon for two years and in Belvidere, Illinois, for three years.

SUDDITH, Arnold Eugene "Sally"
Player
Earned degree in physical education at Indiana University where he played basketball under Everett Dean; worked for Record Club of America for 28 yrs. before retiring in Martinsville, Ind.

1927 – 1930 Martinsville High School, starting forward

1931 – 1934 Indiana University, player

In a ten year span under Coach Glenn Curtis, Martinsville High School won the state championship three times. Their victory in 1927 was not as surprising as the fact that freshman Sally Suddith made the starting line for the championship and played starting forward for four years. Martinsville went to the championships every year Suddith played for the team, but lost in 1928, 1929 and 1930. The 1928 game was an historic event, the first game held in the new Butler Fieldhouse. Martinsville was winning 12 – 11 until a Muncie Central player took his own center jump tip and made a perfect shot from behind the center line to win the game.

VAUGHN, Ralph Lincoln "Ace"

Player

Born February 12, 1918, in Frankfort, Ind; middle name as a result of being born on Lincoln's birthday; mother wanted to name him Abe Lincoln, but father opposed the idea; Indiana All-State twice; All-American 1939, 1940; Navy lieutenant; acted in movie *Campus Cinderella;* industrial engineer for Anaconda Copper and 25 years for Kaiser Steel.

Frankfort High School, player
University of Southern California (USC), player
Chicago Bruins, player
Oshkosh All Stars, player

Ace Vaughn was declared "America's Best Basketballer" in a 1940 issue of *Life* magazine and played on America's number one team that same year, USC. In 1938 he set the conference single game record with 36 points against UCLA. His record stood for 21 years. He also led the Pacific Coast Conference in scoring in 1939. Of course, this outstanding basketball player started his career in Indiana with the Frankfort Hot Dogs. There, he led the North Central Conference in scoring for the 1935 and 1936 seasons and led his team to the Indiana High School Athletic Association title in 1936. Following his college career, Vaughn played professional ball with the Bruins and the All Stars, and was voted Most Valuable Player with the All Stars.

WILSON, John E. "Jumpin' Johnny"

Player

Mr. Basketball 1946; All-American two times; presently director of athletics, physical education and health and baseball and basketball coach at Malcolm X Community College in Chicago, Ill.

Anderson High School, player
Anderson College, player
Harlem Globetrotters, player
Wood High School, coach
Chicago City College, coach

When the Anderson Indians won the state championship in 1946, Jumpin' Johnny was the team's star performer. He set the individual scoring record for the title game, 30 points on 11 field goals and eight free throws, and broke a record that stood for 34 years. After earning All-American honors with Anderson College and playing with the Harlem Globetrotters for three seasons, Wilson began coaching, first with Wood High School in Indianapolis and later with Chicago City College.

1977

BROWN, Kenneth J. "Bud"

Player

All-Semi-State 1941; Mr. Basketball, Gimbel Award and Hoosier All-Stars 1942; Most Valuable Player at Georgetown University; Army in World War II; Dir. of Indiana Basketball Hall of Fame, Chmn. of the Bd. 1976.

Muncie Burris High School, player
Indiana University freshman team, captain
Oklahoma State University, player
Georgetown University, player

Bud Brown played basketball under Coach and Hall of Famer Scott Fisher for four years and led his team to the finals of the state championships in 1942. Taking all of the state honors that year too, Bud played on the Hoosier All-Star team that beat Kentucky. So far, he is the only player to have won both the Gimbel Award and the Mr. Basketball award. Outstanding in college basketball, especially during his three years at Georgetown University, he was drafted by the Washington Caps of the National Basketball Association, but declined the offer.

HOBBS, Larry M.

Coach

Graduated from Circleville High School; principal of Rossville High School for 19 years.

1931 – 1934 Circleville High School, coach
1935 Kempton High School, coach
1936 – 1939 Forest High School, coach
1940 – 1959 Rossville High School, coach
1947 – 1959 Sheridan High School, coach

Larry Hobbs developed many small high school basketball teams during his 28 years of coaching. In four years at his alma mater, with an enrollment of 50 students, the team had a 20 – 5 win-loss record. At Forest High, where the enrollment was 70, there was no gym, so the team played in a store building. After two years of losing seasons at Rossville, Hobbs coached the team to 17 straight winning seasons. In 1946 his team lost only once; three seasons they lost only three times. The year before he began coaching at Sheridan, the team had won only one game, but with his encouragement finished out their first season 12 – 5. They also began competing with some of the State's larger schools. After 28 years of coaching, Hobbs had a record of 460 wins and 182 losses and coached teams that won three regional titles.

HOFFMAN, Paul J. "Bear"

Player

All-State 1942, 1943; All-American at Purdue; Outstanding Player at Purdue for two years; Rookie of the Year with Baltimore Bullets 1948; father of four children; living in Glen Arm, Md; recreation director for Maryland State Dept. of Education.

1939 – 1943 Jasper High School, player
Purdue University, player
Baltimore Bullets, player
New York Knicks, player
Baltimore Bullets, general manager
Purdue University, freshman coach

Coached by Leo "Cabby" O'Neill at Jasper, Paul Hoffman earned a reputation for being a hard-nosed competitor which took him to Purdue for more basketball. There, under the coaching of Ward "Piggy" Lambert, he broke the school's all-time scoring record and received several honors. After a professional career with the Bullets and the Knicks, Hoffman returned to the Bullets to serve as their general manager for three years. He then was head coach for Purdue's baseball team while coaching the freshman basketball team as well.

JOHNSON, Ramson "Ray"
Contributor

Born and raised on a farm in Pike County; attended high school at Winslow; wife Opal; five children, two daughters and three sons; past president of the Indianapolis Downtown Lions Club; now retired; residing with wife in Cataract Lake, Owen County; Eckrich Silver Medal 1977.

Ramson Johnson brought to reality a dream with his dedication and drive. His idea was of having a place where the state's great teams, players and coaches could be recognized for their hardwood heroics, dedicated to high school basketball. In 1961 Ramson and Tom Carnegie, an Indianapolis sportscaster, proposed the Indiana Basketball Hall of Fame, and organized a committee of basketball devotees from all parts of the state. Ramson saw his dream come true in 1962, when the Indiana Basketball Hall of Fame was established, as the first permanent state shrine dedicated to high school basketball. Ramson became their committee host and chairman.

KLIER, Leo Anthony "Crystal"
Player

Born May 21, 1923, in Washington, Ind; wife Nancy; nine children; All-American two times; resides in Naperville, Ill.

1939 – 1940 Washington High School, player
University of Notre Dame, player
1947 – 1948 Indianapolis Kautskys, National League, player
1949 – 1951 Fort Wayne Pistons, player

Early in his career, Crystal Klier played basketball for Washington High School, winners of the Southern Indiana Athletic Conference championship in 1940. The team also played in the finals of the semi-state championship after winning the sectional and regional contests. At Notre Dame he established two new scoring records in 1944 and 1946 and was voted Most Valuable Player twice. As a member of the All-Star team, he played against the Fort Wayne Pistons, a team he later played with as a professional. In 1946, his last year at Notre Dame, Klier played in a second All-Star game, the East-West game at Madison Square Garden. His first year as a professional brought success as the Kautskys won the annual professional tournament in Chicago to become the world professional champions—just two years later the team became a part of the National Basketball Association as the Indianapolis Jets. Klier played a total of 213 professional games to score 672 field goals, 487 free throws and 1831 points for an 8.5 average.

MALLARD, Louis "Bo"
Coach

All-State football player in Gary, Ind; member of two-time state champions, as well as national championship track team; two years at Gary Steel Mills between college and coach career; adopted son George Taliferro football All-American; Bo now retired in Tucson, Ariz.

An all-city basketball player in Gary, Ind, Bo Mallard graduated from Western Michigan University in 1935 and two years later began a 38-year career as a basketball coach within the Gary School System. His Gary Roosevelt Panthers made it to the semi-finals of the state championship in 1965 and took the honor in 1968 after a 22 – 5 season. His center, Jim Nelson, won the Trester Award in 1968 as well.

McCONNELL, Charles A.
Coach

Outstanding football, baseball and track coach; athletic director at Richmond High School 1955 – 1966.

Francisco High School, player
Oakland City College, player
Princeton High School, coach
1933 – 1944 New Albany High School, coach
1945 – 1955 Logansport High School, coach

Before a long career as a basketball coach, Charles McConnell played four years for Francisco High School, a team unbeaten in his senior year. Taking spring and summer terms at Oakland, his team there was not quite as successful and had only one winning season. As a coach, he took Princeton to the last two Sweet 16 tournaments in Indianapolis in 1934 and 1935 and brought New Albany to first position in the State. New Albany played many top-ranked teams to reach that status, won over 65 percent of their games and were sectional champions four times, for the last time in 1940. McConnell's Logansport teams won three sectional tournaments and one regional tournament.

PRIMMER, Robert "Bob"
Coach

Attended Frankfort High School; graduated from Franklin College in 1934; presently associate professor at Ball State.

Franklin College, player
1939 – 1942 South Bend Central High School, assistant coach
1942 South Bend Adams High School, head coach
Dunkirk High School, coach
Ball State University, coach

An outstanding player, Robert Primmer started playing with Frankfort High and then with Franklin College. In 1929 Bob played on the state championship team at Frankfort, which defeated Indianapolis Tech. While at Franklin College, he was a four year member of the varsity. Robert Primmer then started his long and sparkling career as a teacher and coach. He was coach at Dunkirk, leading his team to a Jay County championship. In 1939 he became assistant coach to South Bend Central and in 1942 he was head coach at South Bend Adams. Robert was coach at North Carolina Pre-Flight, and the Naval Air Station at Atlanta, during the war. After the war he returned to South Bend, winning four straight sectional and regional titles. He took one team to the final four. Robert then became coach of the Varsity Basketball at Ball State University and later became Ball State's athletic director. A coronary demanded he retire from the coaching ranks.

RANEY, Gordon "Butch"
Coach
Attended Jeffersonville and Hanover College; led Jeffersonville in scoring as a senior guard; team captain during his four years of Varsity play; died in 1953.

Raney played college basketball for four years with Hanover College. Under Hall of Famer Frank Barnes at Salem High School, Raney spent two years learning the business of coaching. In 1945 Raney was selected to put Albany back on the winning track. Raney began a seven year coaching career taking the Bulldogs to 148 wins and 33 losses, an average of 21 victories a season. The Bulldogs won five sectionals, four regionals and two semistate titles. Raney developed great players like Paul Poff and Jim McLaughlin. He was also interested in all his players pursuing higher educations.

REICHERT, Donald Chris
Coach
Attended Fort Wayne South Side; lettered two years in basketball; graduated from Franklin College in 1941; left South Side in 1967 and became an athletic director and guidance director at Fort Wayne High School.

Franklin College, player
Covington High School, coach
Fort Wayne South High School, coach

While at Franklin College, Donald Reichert played four years of varsity ball. He was captain in both his junior and senior years, establishing a scoring record in 1941. Beginning his long and successful coaching career, he brought a state Indiana High School Athletic Association basketball championship. He spent six years as coach at Covington High, bringing them to two sectionals and one regional wins. He was coach at Fort Wayne South for 16 years and won seven sectionals, six regionals, two semistates and one state championship. In 22 years of competition, his record was 65 per cent. Two of his players became winners of the Mr. Basketball Title: Mike McCoy in 1958, and Willie Long in 1967. Donald Reichert's teams set a record which still stands, winning 34 consecutive games over other Fort Wayne teams.

STRUCK, Raymond F. "Dutch"
Coach
Attended DePauw University, 1923 – 1926; All-State in 1926; served in the Navy for two years during W. W. II; in 1946 became athletic director and chairman of the department of physical education at Hanover College; a speaker of fame throughout the United States; ambassador of Hoosier basketball; also served as football coach, baseball coach and track coach.

De Pauw University, player
Wabash High School, coach
Mishawaka High School, coach

Dutch started playing college basketball in 1923 with De Pauw University, and became a three year varsity performer. He began his 16 year coaching career with Wabash High. Remaining with Wabash High 10 years, he lead them to two regional championships in 1934 and 1937. Dutch then moved on to coach at Mishawaka, and in 1939 won the sectional title over South Bend.

Naismith Memorial Basketball Hall of Fame

SPRINGFIELD, MASSACHUSETTS

Mailing Address: Box 175, Highland Station, 01109. Tel. (413) 781-6500. *Contact:* Lee Williams, Exec. Dir. *Location:* Off I-91 on Springfield College campus; approx. 25 mi. N. of Hartford, Conn, 70 mi. N.E. of Albany, N.Y, 84 mi. S.W. of Boston. *Admission:* 9 to 6 daily July-August, 10 to 5 daily September-November, 10 to 5 Monday-Saturday, 1-5 Sunday, December-March, 10 to 5 daily April-June; closed Thanksgiving, Christmas and New Year's Day. Adults $1.50, students over 15 $1.00, students under 15 50¢, children under 6 free. *Personnel:* Lee Williams, Exec. Dir; Mrs. Ruth Silvia, Asst. Dir; Mrs. Florence Vickers, Office Mgr; 44 mem. Bd. of Trustees; staff, 13 selectors (The Honors Committee). *Nearby Halls of Fame:* Ice Skating (Newburgh, N.Y, 165 mi. S.W; Boston, 85 mi. N.E.), Harness Racing (Goshen, N.Y, 175 mi. S.W.), Horse Racing (Saratoga Springs, N.Y, 105 mi. N.W.), Tennis (Newport, R.I, 80 mi. S.E.), Baseball (Cooperstown, N.Y, 130 mi. N.W.), Bicycling (Staten Island, N.Y, 145 mi. S.W.), Music, Heritage (New York City, 150 mi. S.W.), Flight (Harris Hill, Elmira, N.Y, 215 mi. W.), Horseshoe Pitching (Corning, N.Y, 230 mi. W).

Dr. James Naismith, Canadian, invented the game of basketball in 1891 at the School of Christian Workers, now Springfield College, so it is appropriate that the Hall of Fame honoring basketball's outstanding individuals and teams should be located on this campus. The idea for the Hall was suggested by Dr. Naismith's associates after he returned from the Olympic games in 1936, when basketball was first included. W. W. II interrupted the plans for the memorial and it was not until 1968 that the Naismith Memorial Basketball Hall of Fame, a large two-story red brick building, was opened to the public. Special displays include the Honors Court in which 98 of the game's greatest heroes are enshrined. Each is honored with a portrait and information about his contribution on stained glass. Unlike the halls of fame for baseball and football, the Basketball Hall of Fame includes representatives from all levels of the game: professional, amateur, intercollegiate, military and high school. There is also a full-sized replica of the original gym, with the peach baskets Dr. Naismith attached in 1891. In the same room are exhibits that trace the original history of the game as shown by uniforms, equipment and photography. On the second floor is Hickox Library, the country's most authoritative reference source on basketball. The lower level houses basketball memorabilia and films. By 1973 the museum had been visited by 100,000 people; there were 62,000 in 1976 alone. This museum is a member of the Association of Sports Museums and Halls of Fame.

Members: 104 people and 4 teams as of 1976. Nominations from anyone on official forms with supporting articles and other information are accepted prior to July 1 for the following year's inductees; the file must be completed with at least three letters from outstanding basketball men supporting the nomination and verifying the nominee's character. Prerequisites are: player—retired five years; referee—retired five years; coach—25 years of coaching experience; contributors are eligible any time after a great contribution. Members are selected in a three-stage process: a 5-man Screening Committee votes in August, each nominee must receive at least three votes; a 13-man Honors Committee is balloted in October, each candidate must receive at least ten votes; candidates are presented to the 47-man Board of Trustees and must receive 50 percent of their vote for confirmation. Those selected are honored in April or May at an induction ceremony in Springfield. In addition to being commemorated by the stained glass window at the Hall of Fame, each inductee is given a plaque with his name engraved thereon.

1959

ALLEN, Dr. Forrest Clare "Phog"
Contributor

Born November 11, 1885, in Jamesport, Mo; grew up on a street in Independence with Harry S. Truman; graduated from Independence, Mo, High School 1905, Univ. Kans. 1909; Kans. City Col. Osteopathy 1912.

1908–1952 University of Kansas, coach and athletic director
1909 Baker University, coach
1909 Haskell Indian Institute, coach

In 1908 while still a student at Kansas, Allen took over as coach from Dr. James Naismith, the inventor of basketball. In 1909 he simultaneously coached Kansas (25–3), Baker (22–2), and Haskell (27–5) to a 74–10 record. Kansas teams were national champions 1922–1923, 1923–1924, and 1951–1952, winning a total of 591 games and losing 219. In Allen's 39 coaching seasons there, the team won 24 conference championships. Phog was a great basketball player, as well as coach; he took a degree in osteopathy to help his coaching career. His overall coaching record was 771–223; only one coach has won more games—Adolph Rupp of Kentucky, a pupil of Allen's. Allen's teams won or shared 30 titles in the Missouri Big Valley 6 and Big 7 conferences; his basketball students included Rupp, Arthur "Dutch" Lonborg, John Bunn, Forrest Cox, and Louis Menze. Phog was famous for winning records, outspoken comments on all subjects, and his sometimes bizarre training rules (e.g, pregame naps for all players and himself, and an unending war against cold feet). His teams were distinguished for their outstanding defense, and they typified the ball-control style of basketball. He was known to have said "a good big man is always better than a good little man," but he tried to minimize the effect of the big man on basketball. Allen founded the National Association of Basketball Coaches in 1926, and was its president from 1927 to 1929. He helped organize basketball in the Olympics in 1936, and the National Collegiate Athletic Association Tournament in 1939. Kansas' Allen Field House is named in his honor.

Also in: Athletic Directors Hall of Fame and College Basketball Hall of Fame, Citizens Savings Hall of Fame Athletic Museum.

CARLSON, Henry Clifford
Coach

Born July 4, 1894, in Murray City, Ohio; graduated from Bellefonte, Pa, Academy 1914, Univ. Pittsburgh 1918, medical degree, 1920; pres. National Association of Basketball Coaches 1937; head of Men's Student Health Dept. at Pitt until his death November 1, 1964.

1915–1918 Pittsburgh Panthers, player
1922–1953 Pittsburgh Panthers, coach

Carlson played both basketball and football during his college days, and was captain of the 1917 football team which was undefeated. While he was the Pitt coach, his teams won the national championship in 1928, an undefeated season, and 1930. His overall record was 370-246. He was the first coach to take an eastern team to the West Coast (in 1932) and he invented the "figure 8" offense. Carlson coached Helms All-Time All-American selection Charles Hyatt.
Also in: College Basketball Hall of Fame, Citizens Savings Hall of Fame Athletic Museum.

GULICK, Luther Halsey
Contributor

Born December 4, 1865, in Honolulu, Hawaii; graduated from Oberlin, Ohio, Prep School 1885; medical degree New York Univ. 1889; died August 13, 1918, in South Casco, Maine.

While chairman of training at Springfield College, Gulick asked James Naismith to create "an indoor game" and thus the game of basketball was born. Dr. Gulick was a leading author on physical training, and originated the "triangle" of the YMCA (mind, body and spirit), the Public School League of New York City, the Playground Association, the National Recreation Association, the Camp Fire Girls, and assisted with the Boy Scouts. He served for a time as the chairman of the AAU Basketball Committee.
Also in: Amateur Basketball Hall of Fame, Citizens Savings Hall of Fame Athletic Museum.

HICKOX, Edward J.
Contributor

Born April 10, 1878, in Cleveland, Ohio; attended Ohio Wesleyan; purple heart in W. W. I; honorary doctorate in humanities Springfield College 1961; mem. Rules Committee, Helms Hall of Fame 18 years; died January 28, 1966.

1906–1927 Eaton, Colo, High School, coach
1927–1943 Springfield College, coach
1946 American International College, coach

Hickox started playing basketball in the 1890s when peach baskets were still used. As coach, he led Eaton to victory over five colleges in 1912, including Colorado School of Mines, the Rocky Mountain Champions. In 1911 they took the three-state title over Colorado, Wyoming, and northern New Mexico. Hickox coached for 40 years, and his Springfield College record was 209–85. In one year at American International, the record was 21–3. Hickox was the first executive secretary of the Naismith Hall of Fame, president of the National Asso-

ciation of Basketball Coaches 1944 – 1946, and its historian for 20 years.
Also in: National Association of Intercollegiate Athletics Hall of Fame.

HYATT, Charles
College Player
Born February 28, 1908, in Syracuse, N.Y; graduated from Uniontown, Pa, High School 1926, Univ. Pittsburgh 1930; All-State 1925, 1926; High School All-American 1926; College All-American 1928 – 1930; nation's leading scorer 1930; AAU All-American nine seasons.

1923 – 1926 Uniontown High School, forward
1927 – 1930 University of Pittsburgh Panthers, forward
1940 Phillips 76ers, coach

In the years Hyatt played for the Panthers under coach Carlson, the team won 60 and lost 7. He led Pitt to the National championship in 1928 and 1930. Hyatt was a great shooter with a college record of 880 points. In 1930 he tallied 27 against Montana State and made a last-minute basket to win the game. He was a member of two Helms National Championship teams and is on the Helms All-Time All-American team. In 1940 he coached the Phillips 76ers to their first national title.
Also in: Amateur Basketball Hall of Fame and College Basketball Hall of Fame, Citizens Savings Hall of Fame Athletic Museum.

KENNEDY, Matthew P. "Pat"
Referee
Born January 28, 1908, in Hoboken, N.J; graduated from Hoboken Demarest High School 1926, Montclair State 1928; died June 16, 1957.

1928 – 1946 High school, college and pro basketball, official
1946 – 1950 National Basketball Association officials, supervisor
1950 – 1957 Harlem Globetrotters, official

Kennedy began as a referee at age 20 and became the nation's best-known official. He carried a heavy schedule, often as many as 10 games a week or 125 in a season. He was well known for his dramatic style.

LUISETTI, Angelo "Hank"
College Player
Born June 16, 1916, in the Telegraph Hill section of San Francisco, Calif; graduated from San Francisco Galileo High School 1934, Stanford 1938; during Naval service a nearly fatal bout with spinal meningitis; All-City three years; All-American, 1937, 1938; Helms All-Time All-American Team.

1931 – 1934 Galileo High School, player
1935 – 1938 Stanford University, forward

While at Stanford, Hank led the team to three conference titles, and was All-Time Pacific Coast selection. He was the first player to score 50 points in a regular game (1938). He scored 1596 in four years, nearly 3000 in his career. In his sophomore year, Stanford broke Long Island University's 43-game winning streak at Madison Square Garden. The 6 ft. 3 in, 184 lbs. Luisetti was one of the greatest players in Pacific Coast history, and his one-handed shot revolutionized the game of basketball. Besides being an outstanding scorer, he was an expert dribbler and feeder. Hank played and coached AAU basketball in college.
Also in: Amateur Basketball Hall of Fame and College Basketball Hall of Fame, Citizens Savings Hall of Fame Athletic Museum.

MEANWELL, Walter E. "Little Doctor"
Coach
Born January 26, 1884, in Leeds, England; graduated from Rochester, N.Y, High School, Univ. Maryland 1909; practiced medicine after retiring from coaching; died December 2, 1953.

1912 – 1917 University of Wisconsin, coach
1918 – 1920 University of Missouri, coach
1921 – 1934 University of Wisconsin, coach

The Little Doctor never played basketball, yet was a very successful coach. He won two titles while at Missouri, and his team won four Big Ten titles and had four ties when he was with Wisconsin. His collegiate record was 290 – 101. In addition to being a medical doctor and an athletic director, Meanwell was a respected author, a member of the Rules Committee and a charter member of the National Association of Basketball Coaches. He developed the valve for the laceless basketball, and the basketball shoe that bore his name. He was an early proponent of the basketball clinic.
Also in: College Basketball Hall of Fame, Citizens Savings Hall of Fame Athletic Museum.

MIKAN, George L.
College Player
Born June 18, 1924, in Joliet, Ill; graduated from Chicago Quigley Prep School 1941, DePaul Univ. 1946; *Associated Press* Top Player of the First Half Century; All-American 1944 – 1946; All-Time All-American; Player of the Year 1944 – 1945, 1945 – 1946; first commissioner American Basketball Association 1967; National Basketball Association Silver Anniversary Team 1971.

1942 – 1946 DePaul University, center
1946 – 1948 National League Chicago American Gears, center
1948 – 1956 Minneapolis Lakers, center

While in high school Mikan wanted to become a priest, and didn't play basketball until encouraged by Notre Dame coach George Keogan and DePaul coach Ray Meyer. From an awkward schoolboy, Mikan became pro ball's first superstar. At DePaul he scored 1870 points, including a high of 53 at a Madison Square Garden game against Rhode Island. Mikan led the Lakers to five titles and was All-League for nine years, with a total of 11,764 points scored, an average of 22.6 points for 520 games. Although bulky and lacking speed, Mikan, 6 ft. 10 in, 245 lbs, overpowered the opposition. He broke both legs once, as well as his wrist, nose, arch and foot. He wore thick glasses to correct nearsightedness. As a result of Mikan's playing pro ball, lanes were widened from 6 to 12 ft. It was his idea to use a red, white and blue ball.
Also in: College Basketball Hall of Fame and Major League Basketball Hall of Fame, Citizens Savings Hall of Fame Athletic Museum.

MORGAN, Ralph
Contributor
Born March 9, 1884, in Philadelphia, Pa; graduated from Germantown Friends School 1902, Univ. Pa. 1906; Pennsylvania Quakers athletic director; died January 5, 1965.

Ralph Morgan was founder of the Collegiate Rules Committee (now known as the National Basketball Rules Committee) in 1905, and a member for 26 years. He organized the Eastern Collegiate Basketball League (now the Ivy League) in 1910, and served as its secretary for many years. Morgan reviewed the Ivy League's 57 years for the *Official Collegiate Basketball Record Book.*
Also in: College Basketball Hall of Fame, Citizens Savings Hall of Fame Athletic Museum.

NAISMITH, James
Contributor
Born November 18, 1861, in Almonte, Ont; Scotch ancestry; wife Maude; 5 children, Margaret, Hellen, John, Maudann, James; graduated from McGill Univ. 1887, divinity degree from Presbyterian Col. Montreal 1890; M.D. Gross Medical School Colo. 1898; ordained Presbyterian minister 1916; chaplain First Kansas Infantry 1914–1917; YMCA work in France 1917–1919; became naturalized U.S. citizen 1925; died November 28, 1939.

Sportsman, educator, minister or physician, Dr. Naismith succeeded at whatever field he turned to. Although initially seeking a career in the ministry, he became interested in rugby football and lacrosse while at McGill, and eventually turned to physical education. In December, 1891, in response to a request from Dr. Luther H. Gulick, Dr. Naismith, then an instructor, tried to create an indoor game for the winter months, when football and baseball were out of season. The result was the game of basketball, and the first equipment consisted of a soccer ball and two peach baskets. Dr. Naismith described the game as based on three basic principles all intended to limit body contact: to eliminate tackling, don't allow the player to run with the ball; to avoid using force to score, use a high horizontal goal; penalize players guilty of excessive body contact. The game rapidly became popular in the United States, and by 1936 gained international status when it was introduced at the Olympics. The rules were translated into 30 languages by 1940, and the game was being played by 20 million people in 75 countries. In 1892 Naismith edited the *Rules for Basketball,* and wrote the *Official Guide* in 1894 with Gulick. In 1930 in response to growing public concern, Naismith made a study of the physical stresses to which a basketball player is subjected. He found that, although the game was strenuous, there was little danger of damage to the heart and kidneys. The "Father of Basketball" wrote many articles about physical education, and along with Dr. Gulick, wrote *Basketball: Its Origin and Development,* 1941. The last words of this book summarize his desires for the game: "Let us all be able to lose gracefully and to win courteously; to accept criticism as well as praise, and last of all, to appreciate the attitude of the other fellow at all times." A lesser-known fact about Dr. Naismith is that he invented the first football helmet—made of flannel and later of chamois—while he was a student at the YMCA Training School, to protect his cauliflower ear. A commemorative stamp to Dr. Naismith was issued in 1961.
Also in: Amateur Basketball Hall of Fame, College Basketball Hall of Fame and Noteworthy Contributors Hall of Fame, Citizens Savings Hall of Fame Athletic Museum; and National Association of Intercollegiate Athletics Hall of Fame.

OLSEN, Harold G.
Contributor
Born May 12, 1895, in Rice Lake, Wis; graduated from Rice Lake High School 1913, Univ. Wis. 1917; pres. National Association of Basketball Coaches (NCAA) 1933, mem. Rules Committee; died October 29, 1953, in Evanston, Ill.

1910–1913	Rice Lake High School, player
1914–1917	University of Wisconsin, player
1919	Bradley University, coach
1920–1922	Ripon College, coach
1923–1946	Ohio State University, coach
1946–1949	Chicago Stags, coach
1951–1952	Northwestern University, coach

Olsen was All-Conference for two years when he played for the Wisconsin team which was Big Ten Champion 1916 and 1917. His team at Ohio State won five titles with a record of 259–197. Olsen's overall record was 306–234. He was founder of the NCAA Tournament and its committee chairman for eight years, and a member of the 1948 Olympic Committee. He helped to adopt the 10 second rule.
Also in: College Basketball Hall of Fame, Citizens Savings Hall of Fame Athletic Museum.

SCHOMMER, John J.
College Player
Born January 29, 1884, in Chicago, Ill; graduated from Univ. Chicago 1909; also played football for Chicago; first great player of Western Conference; All-American Center four times; Helms All-Time All-American; taught at Ill. Tech. 47 years; died January 11, 1960, in Chicago.

Schommer led the Big Ten scorers 1907–1909, the first Chicago athlete to win 12 letters in four sports. During the 1908–1909 season, he held his opponents to only 4 baskets in nine games, and in one game he scored 15 goals. Chicago was named Helms National Champion in each of his three varsity seasons. The 6 ft. 1 in. center was captain of the 1909 team. Schommer was also known as a leading football and basketball official.
Also in: College Basketball Hall of Fame, Citizens Savings Hall of Fame Athletic Museum.

STAGG, Amos Alonzo
Contributor
Born August 16, 1862, in West Orange, N.J; fifth of eight children; father a shoemaker; graduated from Exeter Acad. 1884, Yale 1890, Springfield Col. 1892; studied for ministry but turned to coaching; admired for honesty and integrity; known as the "Grand Old Man of Football"; All-American End; died March 17, 1965, in Stockton, Calif.

Yale University, pitcher
University of Chicago, athletic director

Stagg was a friend and fellow instructor of Naismith's at Springfield and helped him in the early development of basketball. He played in the first public basketball game

March 3, 1892. At Chicago he coached seven basketball teams and coached football for 40 years. Stagg awarded the first varsity letter for basketball in 1908, organized the Big Ten Conference, and conducted the National High School Tournament 1917 – 1930 which did much to standardize the rules.
Also in: College Football Hall of Fame, Noteworthy Contributors Hall of Fame and Track and Field Hall of Fame, Citizens Savings Hall of Fame Athletic Museum; and National Football Hall of Fame.

THE FIRST TEAM
Team
Eighteen students from Dr. James Naismith's physical education class participated in the first basketball game in December, 1891, at Springfield Armory YMCA in Massachusetts. In 1897 the teams were changed to five players; Yale defeated Pennsylvania 32 – 10 in the first game played with five on a side on March 20, 1897. Players in the first game were: William Davis, Eugene Libby, John Thompson, George Weller, Wilbert Carey, Ernest Hildner, Lyman Archibald, T. Duncan Patton, Finley MacDonald, Raymond Kaighn, Genzaboro Ishikawa, Franklin Barnes, Edwin Ruggles, Frank Mahan, William Chase, Benjamin French, George Day and Henri Gelan.

THE ORIGINAL CELTICS
Team
Organized as the New York Celtics in 1914 by Frank McCormack, the original team represented a settlement house on the city's west side. Pete Barry and John Witty were the only members who eventually played for its namesake, which gained national and international fame. The New York Celtics broke up before W. W. I. Jim and Tom Furey reorganized the team after the war but Frank McCormack owned the rights to the name "New York Celtics" so the Furey team became known as "The Original Celtics." The Celtics barnstormed the country in addition to playing in the American Pro League. Dutch Dehnert, Nat Holman, Chris Leonard, Johnny Beckman, Horse Haggerty, Ernie Reich, Eddie Burke, Joe Trippe, Joe Lapchick, Eddie White, Benny Boregman and Dave Banks played for the team during its greatest days, and Johnny Witty coached. During the 1921 – 1929 period they recorded 120 victories and 10 losses. They won the American League title in 1926 and 1928, and then the league broke up, the team with the players going to other franchises. The team reorganized for barnstorming in the 1930s, but never attained the success of the earlier club.

TOWER, Oswald
Contributor
Born November 23, 1883, in North Adams, Mass; graduated from Drury High School 1901, Williams Col. 1907; died May 28, 1968.

Tower first played basketball at age 14, when the game was six years old, and was among the top players in the early twentieth century. An official for 35 years and a member of the Rules Committee for 49 years, Tower was the official rules interpreter from 1915 to 1959, succeeded by John W. Bunn, the noted coach. Editor of *Basketball Guide,* Tower is best known for his many contributions to the interpretation of the rules of basketball.
Also in: College Basketball Hall of Fame, Citizens Savings Hall of Fame Athletic Museum.

WOODEN, John R
College Player
Selected in 1959 as a College Player and in 1972 as a Coach; see entry in Indiana Basketball Hall of Fame, 1962.
Also in: College Basketball Hall of Fame, Citizens Savings Hall of Fame Athletic Museum.

1960

BLOOD, Ernest A. "The Prof"
Coach
Born February 5, 1872, in Manchester, N.H; died February 5, 1955.

1906 – 1915 Potsdam, N.Y, High School, coach
1915 – 1924 Passaic, N.J, High School, coach
1925 – 1949 St. Benedict's Prep School, Newark, N.J, coach
West Point Military Academy, coach
Potsdam Normal (Clarkson), coach

Blood first played basketball in 1892 and began coaching in 1897. While he coached at Potsdam, his teams never lost a game. At Passaic he compiled a 200 – 1 record, including 159 straight wins; the team was known as the "Wonder Team." The one loss was in 1919 to Union Hill in the finals of New Jersey's first state tourney. The team won 12 of its games by 100 or more points. At St. Benedict's, Blood's record was 421 – 128, including five state prep titles; he added seven state titles at Passaic. At West Point he won 56; at Clarkson, 7. Blood was himself an all-around athlete, competent in six sports, and one of the first coaches to thoroughly condition players. His overall record was 1296 – 165.

HANSON, Victor A.
College Player
Born July 30, 1903, in Watertown, N.Y; graduated from Central High School, Syracuse, 1922, Manlius Academy 1923, Syracuse Univ. 1927; Helms Player of the Year 1927; Grantland Rice All-Time All-American Player 1952; Top Amateur Athlete in N.Y. State History 1953; now retired in Minoa, N.Y.

1919 – 1922 Central High School, player
1923 – 1927 Syracuse University, player

Hanson is a great all-around athlete, outstanding and versatile. He was a four-sport high school star and led Central to the New York state title in 1921. At Syracuse Vic was a nine-letter man, a three-sport captain 1926 – 1927, and a basketball All-American 1925 – 1927. He led the 1926 team to the national title with a 19 – 1 record, and scored 25 of Syracuse's 30 points against Pennsylvania. In his last three years at Syracuse, the team won 48 and lost 7. Hanson played great pro ball with the Cleveland Rosenblums, played baseball with the New York Yankees and coached football at Syracuse from 1930 to 1936.
Also in: College Basketball Hall of Fame, Citizens Savings Hall of Fame Athletic Museum; and National Football Hall of Fame.

HEPBRON, George T.
Referee
Born August 27, 1863, in Still Pond, Md: died April 30, 1946, in Newark, N.J.

Hepbron, a friend of Naismith and Gulick, was a pioneer authority on basketball. He saw a need to curb the roughness in the game and became the first official referee in the New York City area. He organized the Brooklyn YMCA League, and refereed the first AAU Tournament at Bay Ridge Athletic Club. Hepbron helped write the first *Basketball Guide* in 1896, and was its editor 1901–1914. He was secretary of the Olympic Basketball Committee in 1903, secretary of the AAU Rules Committee (which helped codify the game) 1901–1914, and secretary of the Joint Rules Committee 1915–1936 (made life member 1936). George Hepbron conducted the first national rules questionnaire and traveled extensively to organize early basketball. In 1904 he wrote *How to Play Basketball,* the first handbook on the game.
Also in: Amateur Basketball Hall of Fame, Citizens Savings Hall of Fame Athletic Museum.

KEANEY, Frank W.
Coach
Born June 5, 1886, in Boston, Mass; graduated from Cambridge Latin High School 1906, Bates College 1911, Phi Beta Kappa; wife Winifred; died October 10, 1967.

1911–1920 Putnam, Conn, High School, coach
Woonsocket, R.I., High School, coach
Everett, Mass, High School, coach
1921–1948 University of Rhode Island, coach and athletic director

Keaney was an all-around athlete; he set two baseball records while at Bates. At Rhode Island he coached basketball and taught chemistry. He formed their physical education department with his wife Winifred, who taught sports for 13 years. Keaney often beat the opposition with better-conditioned players. He unveiled the run-shoot system in 1931, although the Rams averaged only 39.7 in 17 games. He introduced the full-court press from the opening whistle and made teams practice shooting in hoops 2 in. smaller than official baskets. His team was known for their "point a minute" play. Keaney took "Little Rhody" to the National Invitational Tournament four times. He retired from coaching in 1948 with a 401–124 record.
Also in: American Association of College Baseball Coaches Hall of Fame; and College Basketball Hall of Fame, Citizens Savings Hall of Fame Athletic Museum.

LAMBERT, Ward L. "Piggy"
Coach
See entry in Indiana Basketball Hall of Fame, 1962.
Also in: College Basketball Hall of Fame, Citizens Savings Hall of Fame Athletic Museum.

MACAULEY, Edward C.
College Player
Born March 22, 1928, in St. Louis, Mo; graduated from University High School 1945, St. Louis Univ. 1949; named to every All-American team 1946–1949; Most Valuable Player (MVP) National Invitational Tournament 1948; *Associated Press* Player of the Year 1949.

1942–1945 University High School, player
1946–1949 St. Louis University, player
St. Louis pro team, player
Boston pro team, player
St. Louis Hawks, coach

With a 6.8 point average in 81 high school games, Macauley became one of Billikin's great players. During 1946–1949 Macauley was named to every All-American team selected, led the nation with a .524 point shooting average in 1947, and helped St. Louis to a Sugar Bowl title in 1948. "Easy Ed" was All-NBA 1950–1954 and played in eight National Basketball Association (NBA) All-Star games. In nine NBA seasons, he scored 11,000 points and was the youngest man ever elected to the Naismith Hall of Fame. Macauley later coached the St. Louis Hawks to Western Division titles 1958–1960.

McCRACKEN, Branch
College Player
See entry in Indiana Basketball Hall of Fame, 1963.
Also in: College Basketball Hall of Fame, Citizens Savings Hall of Fame Athletic Museum.

MURPHY, Charles C. "Stretch"
College Player
See entry in Indiana Basketball Hall of Fame, 1963.
Also in: College Basketball Hall of Fame, Citizens Savings Hall of Fame Athletic Museum.

PORTER, Henry V.
Contributor
Born October 2, 1891; graduated from Ill. State Normal School 1918, Univ. Ill. 1925.

1913–1928 Mt. Zion, Ill, High School, coach
Keithsburg, Ill, High School, coach
Delavan, Ill, High School, coach
Athens, Ill, High School, coach

Porter coached high school basketball for several years before turning to administration. He was the executive director of the National Federation of State High School Athletic Associations, aqnd he invented the "molded" basketball, the fan shaped backboard and the 29½ in. ball. With Tower, he codified the basketball rules and started a nationwide system of rules analysis. Porter helped organize the National Basketball Commission of the United States and Canada. Porter was the first high school representative on the Rules Committee, a member for 30 years, and secretary for 18 years. He encouraged the use of films for basketball; H. V. wrote the *Basketball Handbook* and other books, which sold more than ten million copies.

1961

BORGMANN, Bernhard "Benny"
Pro Player
Born November 21, 1899, in Haledon, N.J; graduated from Clifton, N.J, High School 1917; All-Time All-Pro.

Borgmann, a brilliant 5 ft. 8 in. high school scorer, played 2500 pro games. He frequently scored a half or more of the team's total. He was a member of The Original Celtics, and a great offensive player. Benny competed in the American, National, Metropolitan, Eastern, New York State and Western Massachusetts leagues. He retired from playing basketball in 1942 to coach seven years with professional teams in Syracuse, N.Y, and Patterson, N.J, after which he coached six years at St. Michaels and Muhlenberg Colleges, compiling a 63 – 53 record at Muhlenberg. He was also a baseball scout for the St. Louis Cardinals.

BUFFALO GERMANS
Team
The team was organized in 1895 by Frederick Burkhardt, physical education director of the Buffalo German YMCA. They won the Pan-American Exposition in June, 1901, in Buffalo on a 40 by 60 ft. grass court. The players wore cleats. During the season, the Germans defeated Hobart College 134 – 0. In 1904 they won the exhibition tournament at the Olympic Games in St. Louis. Center Alfred Heerdt, William Rhode, George Redlein, Alfred Manweiler and Edward Miller were the stars. Although no official Amateur Athletic Union Tournaments were held between 1904 and 1910, the Germans were considered the best team of the period. Heerdt later became the team manager and guided the Germans until the squad disbanded in 1929.

DeBERNARDI, Forrest S. "De" "Red"
AAU Player
Born February 3, 1899, in Nevada, Mo; graduated from Kansas City North East High School 1919, Westminster Col. (Mo.) 1923; All-Tournament seven times; All-American in three positions (1921 – 1923); All-Time All-American 1938.

1915 – 1917 Iola, Kans, High School, player
1917 – 1919 Kansas City North East High School, player
1920 – 1923 Westminster College, player
1920 Kansas City Athletic Club, player
1926 – 1927 Hillyard Chemical Company, player
1928 – 1929 Cook Paint Company, player

DeBernardi was Kansas All-State, All-Kansas City, and two years All-Conference; he was one of the greatest players in the Midwest. De led the Hillyards to the Amateur Athletic Union (AAU) title in 1926 – 1927, and the Cook Painters to the same title 1928 – 1929. In 11 AAU Tournaments, he was All-Tournament seven times and All-American in three positions. DeBernardi was highly regarded for his all-around excellence.
Also in: Amateur Basketball Hall of Fame and College Basketball Hall of Fame, Citizens Savings Hall of Fame Athletic Museum; and National Association of Intercollegiate Athletics Hall of Fame.

HOYT, George H.
Referee
Born August 9, 1883, in South Boston, Mass; died November 11, 1962, in Dorchester, Mass.

Known as "Mr. Basketball," Hoyt was an early pioneer of the game, concerned with sportsmanship and fair play. He traveled through New England to introduce the principles of officiating to many referees and coaches. In 1902 he organized Boston's first basketball league, and in 1911 was admitted to the Collegiate Officials Directory. Hoyt organized the Board of Officials for Eastern Massachusetts in 1920, coached many teams, and for 34 years was associated with the Eastern Massachusetts High School Tournament as an official and honorary chief official. He was well known for his integrity, wrote numerous articles on officiating, and lectured for years to beginning officials.

KEOGAN, George E.
Coach
Born March 8, 1890, in Detroit Lakes, Minn; graduated from Detroit Lakes High School 1909, Univ. Minn; died February 17, 1943, in South Bend, Ind.

Lockport, Ill, High School, coach
Riverside, Ill, High School, coach
Superior State College, coach
St. Louis University, coach
St. Thomas College, coach
Allegheny College, coach
Valparaiso College, coach
1923 – 1943 University of Notre Dame, coach

Keogan abandoned plans for a dentistry career to coach, and his coaching career culminated in outstanding success at Notre Dame. He led the "Fighting Irish" to 327 wins in 20 years, 77 percent of the games played. During 1925 – 1928, the teams were 56 – 5, while the 1935 – 1936 and 1936 – 1937 teams won 42 and lost 5. Keogan created the "shifting man-to-man" defense, and had a disciplined set style. His overall record was 385 – 117; he coached many All-Americans. Moose Krause was Keogan's star player.
Also in: College Basketball Hall of Fame, Citizens Savings Hall of Fame Athletic Museum.

KURLAND, Robert A. "Foothills"
College Player
Born December 23, 1924, in St. Louis, Mo; graduated from Jennings, St. Louis, High School 1942, Oklahoma A&M Univ. 1946; Grantland Rice All-American; Helms All-Time All-American; retired from baseball following Helsinki Olympics; living in Atlanta.

1942 – 1946 Oklahoma A&M University, center
1947 – 1952 Phillips 66ers, player

The first dominating seven-footer, Kurland's shot-blocking methods helped put a ban on goal tending in 1944. He scored 22 points to lead Oklahoma A&M to a 49 – 45 victory over New York University for the National Collegiate Athletic Association title in 1945. He followed with 23 as the team won the championship again in 1946, and scored a career high of 58 points against St. Louis in the last college home game in 1946. Bob was elected to every All-American team and was the national scoring leader that same year. Kurland rejected pro offers to play with Phillips, and was selected All-League and All-American for six years. He scored a season high of 787 with a career total of 4092. He was the first American to play on two Olympic teams, and his one-to-one confrontations with George Mikan were the highlight of the pre-1950 era.
Also in: Amateur Basketball Hall of Fame and College Basketball Hall of Fame, Citizens Savings Hall of Fame Athletic Museum.

O'BRIEN, John J.
Contributor
Born November 4, 1888, in Brooklyn, N.Y; graduated from Commercial High School, Brooklyn, 1907, St. John's College; died December 9, 1967.

O'Brien played three sports in high school, and later pro basketball with city teams and the YMCA team. From 1920 to 1930 he was the Senior Inter-Collegiate Basketball League official. Jack refereed the first Army-Navy basketball contest in 1920. Administration was his real forte as he helped organize the Interstate Pro League in 1914 and served as president in 1915–1917. He organized the Metropolitan Basketball League in 1921, and served as its president and treasurer 1922–1928. When the American Basketball League was reorganized in 1928, he became its president; under his 25 years of leadership, new dignity and integrity were brought to owners, players, officials and the sport.

PHILLIP, Andy

College Player

Born March 7, 1922, in Granite City, Ill; graduated from Granite City High School 1940, Univ. Ill. 1947; All-Time All-American; also played college and minor league baseball; retired from basketball and now supervising probation officer in Indio, Calif.

1937–1940 Granite City High School, player
1941–1943 University of Illinois, guard
1946–1947 University of Illinois, guard
1947–1958 Chicago Stags, Philadelphia Warriors, Fort Wayne Pistons, Boston Celtics, guard

Phillip, 6 ft. 2 in, 195 lbs, was named to the first team All-State while his high school team won the coveted state title. He later became one of the nation's greatest players as a vital member of the Illini "Whiz Kids," an all-sophomore team including Gene Vance, Ken Menke, Jack Smitty and Art Mathiesen. They set Big Ten scoring records 1941–1943 as the team won two conference titles. In 1943 the two-time All-American made 111 field goals and set Western Conference records for the most points (255), most field goals (16), and the most points in a single game (40). In his sophomore year he was voted Most Valuable Player of the team and of the conference. Phillip led the team to 14 straight wins and 25 out of 27 his sophomore and junior years. He was elected captain of the 1944 team, but his collegiate career was interrupted by a three-year tour in the U.S. Marines. Upon returning to Illinois, Andy became All-American in his senior year. He was All-Western Conference 1942, 1943 and 1947; the Illinois record in 1943 was 12–0, and the conference, 17–1. Andy then embarked on a successful career in the National Basketball Association (NBA). As a pro he played 701 games for a 9.1 average, including five NBA All-Star games. Phillip led the pro league with 414 assists in 1951 and 539 in 1952. He established one-game assist records in Philadelphia (17 in 1951) and in Fort Wayne (19 in 1954).
Also in: College Basketball Hall of Fame and Major League Basketball Hall of Fame, Citizens Savings Hall of Fame Athletic Museum.

QUIGLEY, Ernest C. "Quig"

Referee

Born March 22, 1880, in New Castle, N.B; graduated from Concordia, Kans, High School 1900, Univ. Kans. 1904; won two letters in football and later coached at Mo. State Univ; died December 10, 1968, in Lawrence, Kans.

1913 National League, umpire
1914–1944 College and AAU, official
1944–1950 University of Kansas, athletic director

Quig learned basketball under Dr. Naismith, and eventually gave up the study of law to coach basketball. He broke his hand playing minor league baseball, and so began umpiring in 1910. Quig became one of the greatest year-around officials, handling all top games in football and basketball, plus 6 World Series. Before he retired as an official in 1944 to become the athletic director at Kansas, he traveled 100,000 miles a year. He refereed 5400 baseball games, 1500 basketball games and 400 football games in his career, including 3 Rose Bowls, 5 Yale-Harvard classics and 1 Cotton Bowl. He called fouls in 19 straight Amateur Athletic Union Tournaments, and the Olympic basketball finals in 1936. One of basketball's most colorful and respected officials, Quig relied on his shrill voice rather than the whistle.
Also in: National Association of Intercollegiate Athletics Hall of Fame.

ROOSMA, John S.

College Player

Born September 3, 1900, in Passaic, N.J; graduated from Passaic High School 1921, U.S. Military Acad. 1926; won coveted Army Athletic Sabre as Outstanding Athlete 1926; now living in Washington, D.C.

1918–1921 Passaic High School, player
1923–1926 U.S. Military Academy, player

Roosma was High School All-State and state tournament high scorer 1918–1921. He was a key part of the "Wonder Team" that won 41 straight games in a string of 159. Coach Blood called him Passaic's greatest. Roosma was a 10-letter winner at West Point, leading his basketball team to 73 wins and 13 losses, scoring 44 percent of the team's points, 354 in one season and 1100 overall. Roosma scored the game high of 28 points several times while starring as a defensive player, and led the Cadets to an unbeaten season in 1923. He served in the Army 1926–1956, retiring as a colonel; while in the service, he coached and played for many military teams in the United States and overseas.
Also in: College Basketball Hall of Fame, Citizens Savings Hall of Fame Athletic Museum.

SACHS, Leonard D.

Coach

Born August 7, 1897, in Chicago, Ill; graduated from Chicago's Carl Schurz High School 1914, American College of Physical Education 1923, Loyola Univ. Chicago 1935; died October 27, 1942, in Chicago.

1911–1914 Carl Schurz High School, player
Illinois Athletic Club, player
Wendell Phillips High School, coach
Marshall High School, coach
1924–1943 Loyola University, Chicago, coach

Sachs won 11 high school letters and later became the star of the Illinois Athletic Club team that won the Amateur Athletic Union title in 1918. He began coaching for the Loyola Ramblers in 1924 and his great 2-2-1 zone defense with goal tender created a new interest in the "big" man and a new rule in basketball prohibiting goal tending. In 1927–1929 Loyola teams won 32 straight, and 20 straight in 1938–1939 before losing the National Invitational Tournament to undefeated Long Island University. Sach's teams won three city titles and great recognition using meager material. He coached All-Americans Marvin Colen, Mike Novak and Wilbert

Kautz, and compiled a 224–129 record at Loyola in 19 years.
Also in: College Basketball Hall of Fame, Citizens Savings Hall of Fame Athletic Museum.

SCHABINGER, Arthur A. "Schabie"
Contributor
Born August 6, 1889, in Sabetha, Kans; graduated from Emporia, Kans, High School 1908, from Col. Emporia 1913, Springfield Col. 1915; NABC Metropolitan Award 1955; died October 13, 1972.

1905–1908 Emporia High School, player
1910–1913 College of Emporia, player
1923–1935 Ottawa University Bluejays, coach
Emporia State College, coach
Creighton University, coach

Schabie was a four-letter man in high school and college, and had an 80 percent winning mark in 20 years of coaching, with nine conference titles and a 167–67 record at Ottawa. He pioneered intersectional games, conducted clinics and helped organize the National Association of Basketball Coaches (NABC). He held many offices in that organization and was president in 1932. Schabie directed the Olympic basketball tournament in 1936, was a member of the Rules Committee, helped research the molded ball, and was founder and director of the Official Sports Film Service 1946–1956. This service was a great aid to uniform rules interpretation.
Also in: National Association of Intercollegiate Athletics Hall of Fame.

STEINMETZ, Christian
College Player
Born June 28, 1882, in Milwaukee, Wis; graduated from Milwaukee South Division High School 1902, Univ. Wis. 1905; All-Western Conference 1905; died June 11, 1963.

1899–1902 South Division High School, player
1902–1905 University of Wisconsin, player

Chris was a two-sport captain in high school and organized the first basketball team at Wisconsin. In 1905, as captain, he set three records that stood until 1951: most points scored in a game, 50, most field goals in a single game, 26, and most points in a season, 462. In the same year he had a total of 238 free throws, and averaged 25.7 points per game, also long-standing records. Chris was elected All-Western Conference as he became the first player to score over 1000 points in his college career. He gained fame as one of his state's all-time athletic greats, and for nineteen years selected the All-Western Conference teams.
Also in: College Basketball Hall of Fame, Citizens Savings Hall of Fame Athletic Museum; and Wisconsin Athletic Hall of Fame.

TOBEY, David
Referee
Born May 1, 1898, in New York City; graduated from DeWitt Clinton High School, Savage School of Physical Education 1918, New York Univ. 1935, 1940.

Tobey devoted his life to physical training and played on many early pro teams and against all the great players of his time. He enjoyed great coaching success in high schools with 367 wins, and in colleges with 348 wins, including 35 straight wins at Savage School 1924–1927. 1918–1925 Tobey refereed all the important pro games including the intersectional games at Madison Square Garden. In 1946 he was assigned the vital West Point-Syracuse game (Hanson vs. Roosma). He was the leading Eastern Intercollegiate Association official until 1946, working the most important eastern games. In 1943 he wrote *Basketball Officiating,* the first book of its kind.

TRESTER, Arthur L.
Contributor.
See entry in Indiana Basketball Hall of Fame, 1965.

WACHTER, Edward A.
Pro Player
Born June 30, 1883, in Troy, N.Y; All-Time Center 1928; civic leader and fund raiser after retiring from basketball; died March 12, 1966, in Troy.

Wachter, 6 ft. 6 in, began his playing career with the Troy YMCA team and eventually played 3000 games over a 20-year period, including nearly all the towns and leagues in the East. He was the key man on teams that carried basketball to the hinterlands where the sport was bidding for recognition. He was regularly chosen All-League, culminating when he led the Schenectady Company E team to the world's title win over the Kansas City Blue Diamonds in 1905. In 1922 Wachter was named "the greatest center in basketball." He led the scoring in every league in which he played. Wachter topped the Hudson River State League in scoring five times, and was the first pro to be sold—Haverhill, Mass, to Ware, Mass, 1902. He took part in the undefeated transcontinental tour with the Troy team, and played on twelve championship teams. He and his brother Lew were known as the "Wachter Wonders." Ed worked for common rules and conditions, and led the discussion at the first officials meeting in Boston. He was a basketball legend who played on more championship teams than anyone in his generation.

WALSH, David H.
Referee
Born October 5, 1889, in Hoboken, N.J; graduated from Hoboken High School 1907, Montclair State Col. 1911, Sargents School of Physical Education; lives in Deerfield Beach, Fla.

Walsh began teaching and coaching at Hoboken in 1911, and in 1914 he concentrated on the college game to become one of the sport's leading referees, as well as enjoying success as a coach. He was a teacher, coach or official for 45 years. From 1941 to 1956 he was associate director of the Collegiate Officials Bureau, conducting clinics, supervising, and assigning officials. Walsh was secretary-treasurer of the International Association of Approved Basketball Officials from 1948 to 1956, and he did much for rules uniformity and the improvement of officials. He is considered one of the six best eastern officials of his era.

1962

McCRACKEN, Jack
AAU Player
Born June 11, 1911, in Chickasha, Okla; graduated from Oklahoma City's Classen High School 1929, Northwest

Mo. State Col. 1933; High School All-State 1928–1929 and All-American 1929; College All-American 1931–1932; AAU All-American eight times; died January 5, 1958, in Denver, Colo.

1926–1929 Classen High School, center
1930–1933 Northwest Missouri State College, center
Phillips 66ers, Denver Pigs, Denver Nuggets, Maryville Bearcats, AAU teams, center
1943 Phillips 66ers, player and coach

McCracken was All-State in 1928–1929 and All-American 1929 when Classen finished second in a national prep tournament in Chicago. Henry Iba coached him at both high school and college, and called him one of the game's greatest players. Between 1932 and 1942 he was named All-American by the Amateur Athletic Union (AAU) eight different times. Jack played center for the legendary Maryville Bearcats who won 43 straight games, including a 31–0 season in 1930. He played for various Denver AAU teams, and was a member of three amateur championship squads.

Also in: Amateur Basketball Hall of Fame, Citizens Savings Hall of Fame Athletic Museum; and National Association of Intercollegiate Athletics Hall of Fame.

MORGENWECK, Frank "Pop" "Morgie"
Contributor

Born July 15, 1975, in Egg Harbor, N.J; died December 8, 1941.

Morgie was a great veteran of pro basketball and wielded much influence among players, coaches and owners. Starting in 1901–1902 as a manager in the National League, he was a successful leader in basketball through 1931. He introduced many young players destined for greatness, including the original Celtic stars Benny Borgmann, Johnny Beckman, and Carl and Mickey Husta. Pop led teams to various championships from 1912 to 1931. He spent 32 years managing, financing and promoting early pro games. Called the "Connie Mack of pro basketball," he handled numerous teams, primarily in the East. He coached Kingston, winner of the New York State and world pro titles in 1923; his Rochester Centrals won the American League championship in 1930.

PAGE, Harlan O. "Pat"
College Player

Born March 20, 1887, in Chicago, Ill; graduated from Lewis Institute of Chicago 1906, Univ. Chicago 1910; Helms Player of the Year 1910; died November 23, 1965, in Watervliet, Mich.

1903–1906 Lewis Institute of Chicago, player
1907–1910 University of Chicago, player
University of Chicago, coach
Butler University, coach
College of Idaho, coach
Indiana University, coach

Pat led his high school to a Midwest championship and was a great three-sport star at Chicago. A good left-handed shooter and stellar defensive player, he and John Schommer led Chicago to the Western Conference titles in 1907, 1909 and 1910, and the Amateur Athletic Union (AAU) title in 1907. The Maroons defeated the Rams for the national title in 1908 and were undefeated in 1909 with a 12–0 record; they held Minnesota to 2 points. Pat played football for Amos Stagg. He turned down 12 pro baseball offers, and assisted Stagg in football and coached basketball. He later coached the Butler Cagers to win the national AAU crown in 1924, with an overall basketball coaching record of 200–127.

ST. JOHN, Lynn W.
Contributor

Born November 18, 1876, in Union City, Pa; graduated from Monroe, Ohio, High School 1896, Ohio State Univ. 1900, Col. Wooster 1906; died September 30, 1950, in Columbus, Ohio.

1893–1896 Monroe High School, player
College of Wooster, coach
Ohio Wesleyan College, coach
1912–1919 Ohio State University, coach
1915–1947 Ohio State University, athletic director

St. John played four sports in high school, and football in college. While at Wooster, St. John coached Arthur and Karl Compton, who later became famous scientists and college presidents. He studied medicine while a coach and athletic director at Ohio Wesleyan, but gave it up to become athletic director at Ohio State. St. John was also Ohio State's baseball and basketball coach, line coach in football and athletic business manager. He had an 80–68 basketball record from 1912–1919. St. John was a member of the National Collegiate Athletic Association Rules Committee for 26 years, its chairman for 18. He chaired the Joint Committee for five years, and helped form the National Basketball Association of the United States and Canada. He was its chairman from 1933 to 1937, and a member of the Olympic Basketball Committee in 1936. A diplomatic administrative leader, St. John retired as Buckeye athletic director in 1947.

SEDRAN, Barney
Pro Player

Born January 28, 1891, in New York City; graduated from DeWitt Clinton High School 1907, City Col. New York 1911; died January 4, 1962.

1908–1911 City College of New York, guard
1912–1926 Carbondale, Fort Wayne K of C, Cleveland Rosenblums, pro player
1926–1946 Kate Smith's Celtics, New York Whirlwinds, Brooklyn Jewels, pro coach

Sedran, 5 ft. 4 in, 118 lbs, was judged too small to play for his high school team, so played independent ball before starring for City College of New York. He led in scoring for three years, and was captain in 1910. He was selected for many All-Star teams, played on 10 championship teams in 15 years, and in 1913 scored 17 goals from 25-30 feet on a court with no backboards. In the same year he scored 34 points for Utica in the New York State League. Sedran played with all the major eastern pro teams. He was with Carbondale the season they won 35 straight, 1914–1915. In his career he was teamed with such immortals as Nat Holman, John Beckman, Dutch Dehnert, Elmer Ripley and John "Honey" Russell. He and Marty Friedman were known as the "Heavenly Twins."

THOMPSON, John A. "Cat"
College Player

Born February 10, 1906, in St. George, Utah; graduated from St. George High School 1926, Mont. State Col.

1930; All-American 1928–1930; Helms Player of the Year 1929; went into business in Idaho Falls after retiring from coaching.

1923–1926 St. George (Dixie, Utah) High School, guard
1927–1930 Montana State College, player
1930–1931 Amateur Athletic Union, player
1931–1946 Idaho Falls High School, coach

Cat led his high school to the Utah state title and consolation championship at the national tournament in Chicago in 1925, where his team won six times in five days, and he scored 56 points in one game. At Montana State he led the Golden Bobcats to their greatest record—72–4 in 1928 and 1929. They were selected Helms National Champions in 1929; Thompson was captain in 1930, and selected for All-Rocky Mountain Conference teams 1927–1930, named captain of the Conference teams the last three years. In three years of play, he scored 1539 points and was selected All-American each season. Always in superb physical condition, Thompson led the team to two straight 36–2 records. Clever and quick, he got his nickname from Montana State coach G. Ott Romney, who said, "That isn't a human being—that's a tree-cat." Cat coached the Idaho Falls squad to two state titles in a row.
Also in: College Basketball Hall of Fame, Citizens Savings Hall of Fame Athletic Museum.

1963

GRUENIG, Robert F. "Ace"
AAU Player
Born December 3, 1913, in Chicago, Ill; graduated from Chicago's Crane Tech High School 1931; employed in Denver, Colo, prior to his death November 8, 1958.

1928–1931 Crane Tech High School, center
1933–1946 Rosenberg-Arvey of Chicago, Denver Nuggets, Denver Ambrose, Denver American Legion, Denver Safeways, and Murphy-Mahoney, AAU player

Ace was both All-City and All-State for three years, leading his team to a state championship. All three years he was league high scorer, with a single game high of 35 points. Gruenig, 6 ft. 8 in, 230 lbs, was an Amateur Athletic Union (AAU) immortal; he was on the first team to be All-Tournament ten times—from 1937 through 1948. In 1937 he led the Denver Safeways, and in 1942 the Denver American Legion, to AAU championships. Jack McCracken was his AAU teammate. Ace's specialty was the hook shot.
Also in: Amateur Basketball Hall of Fame, Citizens Savings Hall of Fame Athletic Museum.

NEW YORK RENS
Team
Not until Jackie Robinson broke the color line in baseball in 1946 were black athletes accepted in organized pro sports. They had their own teams and played the top teams in exhibition matches. The New York Rens were organized by Bob Douglas in 1922. They were the best basketball team in the United States from 1932 to 1936 and played two to three games a day, with a 473–49 record. They had an 88-game winning streak 1933–1934. "The Renaissance" team broke up in 1949 after a 112–15 record. Some outstanding players were Clarence Jenkins, Bill Yancey, John Holt, Pappy Ricks, Eyre Saitch, Charles "Tarzan" Cooper and Wee Willie Smith.

REID, William A.
Contributor
Born September 26, 1893, in Detroit, Mich; graduated from Adrian High School 1912, Colgate Univ. 1918; All-State Center 1912; died October 30, 1955.

1909–1912 Adrian, Mich, High School, center
1914–1917 Colgate University, player
1918–1919 American Expeditionary Force team, player
1920–1956 Colgate University, coach (10 years) and athletic director

Reid was captain and All-State center in 1912 and his team at Adrian was Michigan state champions. He led Colgate teams to a three-year, 40–12 record, and the American Expeditionary Force team to a service title in 1919. Reid coached Colgate to a 151–56 record in ten years, and later became graduate manager and athletic director for 37 years. He was the president of the Eastern Collegiate Athletic Conference 1944–1945, and vice president of the National Collegiate Athletic Association 1942–1946. In 1946 Reid received an honorary LLD at Colgate as a distinguished coach and administrator.

1964

BUNN, John W.
Contributor
Born September 26, 1898, in Wellston, Ohio; graduated from Humbolt, Kans, High School 1916, Univ. Kans. 1921, 1936; NABC Metropolitan Award 1961; now lives in Glenwood Springs, Colo.

1913–1916 Humbolt High School, player
1918–1921 University of Kansas, player
1931–1938 Stanford University, coach
1947–1956 Springfield College, coach
1957–1962 Colorado State College at Greeley, coach

Bunn was a 12-letter man in high school and became the first Kansas University athlete to win 10 letters. He assisted Phog Allen for nine years at Kansas before becoming head coach at Stanford. There his team won three Pacific Coast titles. His overall coaching record was 313–288. Bunn preceded Everett Dean at Stanford; the Indians, led by Hank Luisetti, were Helms national champions in a 25–2 season in 1937. Bunn later became the athletic director at Colorado State, Greeley. He wrote six texts on basketball and was chairman of the Basketball Hall of Fame Committee 1949–1961. He was editor of *Basketball Guide* and Official Rules Interpreter 1959–1967. Bunn was the first executive director of the Basketball Federation in 1965, and National Association of Basketball Coaches president 1949–1950.
Also in: College Basketball Hall of Fame, Citizens Savings Hall of Fame Athletic Museum.

FOSTER, Harold E. "Bud"
College Player
Born May 30, 1906, Newton, Kans; graduated from Mason City, Iowa, High School 1924, Univ. Wis. 1930; All-American 1930; NABC Metropolitan Award 1964.

1921 – 1924 Mason City High School, forward, center
1925 Mason City Junior College, player
1928 – 1930 University of Wisconsin, player
1930 – 1935 Oshkosh, Chicago, Milwaukee pro teams, player
1935 – 1959 University of Wisconsin, coach

Foster led his high school team to a third in the state tournament in 1924, and Mason City Junior College to 21 wins in 1925. Bud was a three-year star at Wisconsin; the team was Western Conference champions in 1929, losing only seven games. He was named to several All-Conference and All-Western teams in 1929 and 1930. As coach at Wisconsin, Foster's Badgers won three Big Ten titles—1935, 1941 and 1947—and were National Collegiate Athletic Association champions in 1941. The team, starring Gene Englund and John Kotz, balanced fast break with deliberate style. Foster's coaching record was 270 – 264 – 1. He was National Association of Basketball Coaches (NABC) president 1955 – 1956 and served as professor of athletics at Wisconsin since retiring from coaching.
Also in: College Basketball Hall of Fame, Citizens Savings Hall of Fame Athletic Museum.

HOLMAN, Nat
Pro Player
Born October 18, 1896, in New York City; graduated from Commerce High School 1916, Savage School of Physical Education, New York University; NABC Metropolitan Award 1941.

1913 – 1916 Commerce High School, guard
1917 – 1920 Hoboken, N.J, Bridgeport, Scranton, Germantown, New York Whirlwinds, pro player
1920 – 1928 Boston Celtics, player
1920 – 1960 City College of New York, coach

Holman, 5 ft. 11 in, played four sports in high school, and in 1916 played for Hoboken, N.J, scoring 23 of the team's 28 wins. He turned down an invitation to play with the Cincinnati Reds, and later led the Celtics as a great shooter, one of the first to average double figure scoring. "Mr. Basketball" was a fine team player and exceptional ball handler and passer. While he played for the Celtics they never lost a series. He retired from playing in 1933 and coached City College of New York to the National Invitational Tournament and National Collegiate Athletic Association titles in 1950 (a 17 – 5 year for the Beavers), a feat not previously accomplished. He was an extremely devoted coach; his City College record was 423 – 190. He was the National Association of Basketball Coaches (NABC) president 1940 – 1941 and president of the U.S. Committee for Sports for Israel.
Also in: College Basketball Hall of Fame, Citizens Savings Hall of Fame Athletic Museum.

JONES, R. William
Contributor
Born October 5, 1906, in Rome, Italy; graduated from a Rome high school 1923, Springfield Col. 1928; attended colleges in Denmark, Germany and Switzerland 1929 – 1932.

Jones introduced basketball in Switzerland in 1929. He was cofounder of the International Amateur Basketball Federation (FIBA) in 1932, and later became secretary-general of the organization, which controls all international competition including the Olympics. Due to the influence of the FIBA, basketball spread to 130 nations. Jones has supervised the competition for the Olympics each four years since 1936. He was director of UNESCO Youth Institute 1956, and was appointed secretary-general of the International Council of Sport and Physical Education in 1958. He received an honorary Doctor of Humanities in 1963 from Springfield.

LOEFFLER, Kenneth D.
Coach
Born April 14, 1902, in Beaver Falls, Pa; graduated from Beaver Falls High School 1920, Pa. State Univ. 1924, law degree from Univ. Pittsburgh; worked as a newspaper columnist in Pittsburgh while playing pro ball 1924 – 1929; now a professor at Univ. Nev.

1917 – 1920 Beaver Falls High School, player
1921 – 1924 Pennsylvania State University, player
1924 – 1929 Pro basketball, player
1929 – 1935 Geneva College, coach
1936 – 1942 Yale University, coach
1946 Denver pro team, coach
1947 – 1949 St. Louis Bombers, coach
1950 – 1955 LaSalle College Explorers, coach
1955 Eastern All-Stars, coach
1956 – 1957 Texas A&M University, coach

Loeffler starred in three sports in high school and captained his basketball team at Penn State in 1924. His coaching career spanned 25 years, 22 in colleges and three in the National Basketball Association (NBA). At LaSalle his team won the National Invitational Tournament title in 1952 and was runnerup in 1953; they also won the National Collegiate Athletic Association title in 1954 and were second in 1955. Loeffler's college record was 319 – 213; he developed All-American Tom Gola. In 1948 his St. Louis Bombers won the NBA Division Title.
Also in: College Basketball Hall of Fame, Citizens Savings Hall of Fame Athletic Museum.

RUSSELL, John D. "Honey"
Pro Player
Born May 3, 1903, in Brooklyn, N.Y; graduated from Alexander Hamilton High School 1919, Seton Hall, New York Univ. 1938; All-League 1926 – 1929; died November 15, 1973.

1916 – 1919 Alexander Hamilton High School, guard
Cleveland Rosenblums, Brooklyn-New York Jewels, Brooklyn Visitations, Chicago Bruins, Rochester Centrals, pro player (28 years)
1937 – 1943 Seton Hall, coach
1947 – 1948 Boston Celtics, coach

Russell began his pro career in high school and eventually played in every major pro league, gaining acclaim as the top defensive player of his era. He played over 3200 games leading many teams to championships, including five straight titles 1925 – 1929 for the Cleveland Rosenblums. Player-coach for 20 years, Honey was selected All-League 1926 – 1929. One of the best scoring guards in the younger days of basketball, he once held the early pro scoring record of 22 points in one game. He coached Seton Hall to a 294 – 129 record, including 44 straight wins and the National Invitational Tournament title. He was the first coach of the National Basketball Associa-

tion's Boston Celtics, developing players Walter Dukes, Richie Reagan and Bob Davies. Russell was also a baseball scout for the Montreal Expos.
Also in: College Basketball Hall of Fame, Citizens Savings Hall of Fame Athletic Museum.

1965

BROWN, Walter A.
Contributor

Born February 10, 1905, in Hopkinton, Mass; graduated from Hopkinton High School 1922, Boston Latin 1923, Exeter, N.H, Acad. 1926; NBA Championship Bowl named in his honor; died September 7, 1964.

Brown served an apprenticeship in sports promotion under his father George, who was general manager of the Boston Arena. Walter succeeded him in 1937 as president of the Boston Garden Arena Corporation, a position he held for 27 years. He made Boston the sports center of New England. He organized the Basketball Association of America in 1946, later to become the National Basketball Association, and also helped organize the Boston Celtics. Brown brought college doubleheaders and the state and New England high school tournaments to the Garden. A tireless worker for many charities and athletic projects, he was also an Olympic official and chairman of the Board of Trustees of the Basketball Hall of Fame 1961 – 1964. Brown underwrote the $5000 Naismith commemorative stamp. He was president of the Boston Celtics and the Boston Bruins, and staged the annual Boston Marathon.
Also in: Hockey Hall of Fame, International Hockey Hall of Fame and United States Hockey Hall of Fame.

HINKLE, Paul D. "Tony"
Contributor

See entry in Indiana Basketball Hall of Fame, 1964.
Also in: College Basketball Hall of Fame and College Football Hall of Fame, Citizens Savings Hall of Fame Athletic Museum.

HOBSON, Howard A. "Hobby"
Coach

Born July 4, 1903, in Portland, Ore; graduated from Portland's Franklin High School 1922; Univ. Ore. 1926, Columbia Univ. 1929, 1947; NABC president 1947 – 1948; now retired and living in Portland.

1919 – 1922	Franklin High School, player
1923 – 1926	University of Oregon, player
1926 – 1928	Kelso, Wash, and Benson, Ore, High Schools, coach
1928 – 1956	Southern Oregon College, University of Oregon, Yale University, coach

Hobby won 12 letters and was All-State in high school. At Oregon he had a brilliant two-sport record, and was captain of the basketball and baseball teams for two years. His college coaching career spanned 28 years in three sports, 1100 games, and 725 wins. His teams won 495 games at Southern Oregon, Oregon and Yale. At Oregon where he coached for 12 years with a 241 – 137 record, he won the National Collegiate Athletic Association title in 1939, along with three conference titles 1937 – 1939. His teams pioneered intersectional play; they were the first teams from the West to travel to the East for games. His Yale teams won or tied five Big Three crowns. Hobby was a member of the Olympic Committee for 12 years, the Rules Committee for four years, and contributed much to basketball through his extensive studies and writings. He conducted several basketball clinics in the United States and abroad. Before retiring, he was the vice president and sports editor of Ronald Press.
Also in: College Basketball Hall of Fame, Citizens Savings Hall of Fame Athletic Museum.

IRISH, Edward S. "Ned"
Contributor

Born May 6, 1905, in Lake George, N.Y; graduated from New York City's Erasmus Hall High School, Univ. Pa. 1928; NABC Metropolitan Award 1942.

While in high school Ned launched a newspaper career, and throughout college covered sports for three New York City and Philadelphia papers. He returned to New York City after graduation to continue newspaper work. In 1934 he became basketball director of Madison Square Garden and immediately began the college doubleheader program. Irish initiated the Madison Square Garden doubleheader after an incident at Manhattan College. He could not get into the gym to cover the game because of the crowds and, climbing through a window, ripped his best trousers. As a result, he sought a larger place for basketball. The game enjoyed instant popularity, drawing large crowds to the Garden. In 1934 the first twin bill, St. John's vs. Westminster (Pa.) and New York University vs. Notre Dame, drew 16,138. When Irish began intersectional play, basketball became truly national. He helped standardize rules and coaching, encouraged larger facilities, and assisted in the organization of the National Basketball Association (NBA). Irish also formed the New York Knickerbockers in 1946.

MOKRAY, William G.
Contributor

Born June 6, 1907, in Passaic, N.J; graduated from Passaic High School 1925, R.I. Univ. 1929; honorary life member NABC and IAABO; first chairman of Naismith Hall of Fame Honors Committee 1959 – 1964; died March 22, 1974.

Avid fan of the Passaic "Wonder Teams" 1919 – 1925, Mokray was inspired by their 159 straight wins to keep statistics on basketball. Helping Rhode Island exploit its fast-break style and "2 points a minute" led to his prolific contributions as basketball director at Boston Garden. He also worked for 13 years as publicity director for the Rams, and was later a promotion director and scout for the Boston Celtics, associated with Walter Brown. Mokray provided statistics for *Converse Yearbook* for 25 years, was editor of the *NBA Guide* and in 1957 wrote a history of the game for the Encyclopaedia Britannica. He is the author of the *Ronald Encyclopedia of Basketball* and numerous other books and articles. Mokray helped organize several basketball tournaments and was made life member of the National Association of Basketball Coaches and the International Association of Approved Basketball Officials.
Also in: College Basketball Hall of Fame, Citizens Savings Hall of Fame Athletic Museum; and National Association of Intercollegiate Athletics Hall of Fame.

1966

DEAN, Everett S.

Coach

See entry in the Indiana Basketball Hall of Fame, 1965.
Also in: American Association of College Baseball Coaches Hall of Fame; and College Basketball Hall of Fame, Citizens Savings Hall of Fame Athletic Museum.

LAPCHICK, Joe

Pro Player

Born April 12, 1900, in Yonkers, N.Y; NABC Metropolitan Award 1965; died August 10, 1970.

1917 – 1919 Western Massachusetts League and Brooklyn Visitations, Metropolitan League, center
1919 – 1923 Troy, New York State League, player
1923 – 1927 Kate Smith Celtics, player
1927 – 1930 Cleveland Rosenblums, player
1930 – 1936 Boston Celtics, player
1937 – 1947 St. John's Redmen, player
1948 – 1956 New York Knickerbockers, coach
1957 – 1965 St. John's Redmen, player

Because his immigrant parents needed support, Joe began playing at 17 without a high school education. Attracted by his agility and 6 ft. 5 in. frame, great teams sought him, and for 19 years he was the best center of his time. The Celtics, who never lost a series while Joe played for them, were finally broken up, with Joe going to the Cleveland Rosenblums. The Rosenblums won two world titles, 1927 – 1930. Lapchick reorganized the Celtics for a tour 1930 – 1936 before becoming one of America's great coaches in 20 years at St. John's. His record with the Redskins was 335 – 129 from 1937 to 1947 and 326 – 247 from 1957 to 1965. He coached the New York Knickerbockers for nine years, winning four National Invitational Tournaments, 1943, 1944, 1959 and 1965, including a memorable victory (55 – 51) over Villanova in a Madison Square Garden farewell March 21, 1965. Joe was a sports coordinator at Kutsher's Country Club before his death.
Also in: College Basketball Hall of Fame, Citizens Savings Hall of Fame Athletic Museum.

1967

BEE, Clair F. "Hillbilly"

Contributor

Born March 2, 1900, in Grafton, W.Va; graduated from Grafton High School 1917, Waynesburg Col. 1925, Rider Col, Rutgers Univ. 1932; now directs Camp All-America and Kutsher's Sports Academy and Camps, Lake Anawana, Monticello, N.Y.

1914 – 1917 Grafton High School, player
1922 – 1925 Waynesburg College, player
1929 – 1931 Rider College, coach
1932 – 1943 Long Island University Blackbirds, coach
1946 – 1951 Long Island University Blackbirds, coach
1952 – 1954 Baltimore Bullets, coach

Bee was a coach for 29 years; he lost 7 games in five years at Rider. He won 95 percent of his games at Long Island including 43 straight, the longest winning streak in college basketball history, and 139 consecutive home games. The team was undefeated 1936 and 1939, and National Invitational Tournament champions 1939 and 1941. The Blackbirds were one of seven teams involved in the 1947 – 1950 basketball scandals. As a result Long Island University deemphasized sports. Bee also coached at New York Military Academy. He had an overall coaching record of 410 – 86 with a .827 average, the best in college history. Bee coached five All-Americans. He traveled and lectured extensively abroad and was a rules innovator, including the 3-second and the 24-second rules. He invented the 1-3-1 zone defense, and wrote books and articles that remain valuable references, as well as children's books. Bee received many coaching awards around the world.
Also in: College Basketball Hall of Fame, Citizens Savings Hall of Fame Athletic Museum; and West Virginia Sports Writers Association Hall of Fame.

CANN, Howard G.

Coach

Born October 11, 1895, in Bridgeport, Conn; graduated from New York City's Commerce High School 1913, New York Univ. 1920; shotput champion at New York Univ. and tackle and fullback on the football team; Helms Player of the Year 1920; Coach of the Year 1947; East Coach 1948; New York Writers Distinguished Service Award 1967; NABC Merit Award 1967; now retired living in Irvington, N.Y.

1909 – 1913 Commerce High School, player
1917 – 1920 New York University, player
1920 Olympic track team, member
1922 – 1958 New York University, coach

Cann was a three-sport athlete in high school and college. He led the New York University Violets to the national title in 1920, in which Rutgers was defeated 49 – 24. He was considered the school's greatest all-around athlete. Cann coached basketball and football at New York University for 35 years, winning 409 – 232 for a .638 average. The Violets were named Helms National Champions following the 1935 19 – 1 season, when they outscored their opponents 740 – 489.
Also in: College Basketball Hall of Fame, Citizens Savings Hall of Fame Athletic Museum.

GILL, Amory T. "Slats"

Coach

Born May 1, 1901, in Salem, Ore; graduated from Salem High School 1920, Oregon State Univ. 1924; High School All-State 1919 – 1920; All-American and All-Conference 1924; NABC president 1957 – 1958; died April 5, 1966, in Corvallis, Ore.

1917 – 1920 Salem High School, player
1921 – 1924 Oregon State University, player
Oakland, Calif, High School, coach (2 years)
1929 – 1964 Oregon State University, coach

Gill was captain of his high school basketball team and All-State 1919 – 1920; he was All-Conference and All-American at Oregon State in 1924. Gill coached Oregon State for 36 years, winning 599 – 392, five Pacific Coast titles and eight Far West Classics. The Beavers were fourth in the National Collegiate Athletic Association Tourney in 1949 and 1963. In 1964 Gill was Olympic Trials coach and National Association of Basketball Coaches (NABC) West coach. He coached two of the

tallest college players: 7 ft. 3 in. Swede Holbrook and 7 ft. 11 in. Mel Counts.
Also in: College Basketball Hall of Fame, Citizens Savings Hall of Fame Athletic Museum.

JULIAN, Alvin F. "Doggie"

Coach

Born April 5, 1901, in Reading, Pa; graduated from Reading High School 1919; Bucknell Univ. 1923; NABC Merit Award and NABC Metropolitan Award 1967; NABC president 1966 – 1967; died July 28, 1967, in Worcester, Mass.

1916 – 1919	Reading High School, player
1920 – 1923	Bucknell University, player
1928 – 1929	Schuylkill (now Albright), coach
1937 – 1945	Muhlenberg College, coach
1946 – 1948	Holy Cross College, coach
1949 – 1950	Boston Celtics, coach
1951 – 1967	Dartmouth College, coach

Julian won 12 letters in high school and 10 in college. He was a basketball official, a catcher for the Reading International League, and a member of the Reading Key, a pro football team, before coaching three sports over a 41-year period. His basketball record was 386 – 343, with a 47 – 81 record with the Celtics. His teams were in five National Collegiate Athletic Association (NCAA) and two National Invitational Tournaments, and Holy Cross won the NCAA title in 1947. The Holy Cross Crusader champions included Bob Cousy, Joe Mullaney, George Kaftan, Frank Oftring, Bob Curran and Andy Lasky, all of whom later were college coaches. Dartmouth won three Ivy titles 1956, 1958 and 1959. A leading basketball popularizer in New England, Julian was named Coach of the Year by the Boston Writers because he brought about a renaissance in basketball in Boston and Worcester. He received the Philadelphia Writers Award in 1966, and was named coach of the National Association of Basketball Coaches (NABC) West Team in 1965.
Also in: College Basketball Hall of Fame, Citizens Savings Hall of Fame Athletic Museum.

1968

AUERBACH, Arnold J. "Red"

Born September 20, 1917, in Brooklyn, N.Y; graduated from Brooklyn Eastern District High School 1935, Seth Low Jr. Col, George Washington Univ. 1940; NBA Coach of the Year 1965.

1932 – 1935	Eastern District High School, player
1936 – 1940	Seth Low Junior College, George Washington University, player
1940 – 1943	St. Alban's Prep School and Roosevelt High School, Washington, D.C, coach
1946 – 1949	Washington Capitals, Tri-Cities, coach
1950 – 1966	Boston Celtics, coach

Auerbach was the captain of his team in both high school and college. He joined the newly formed National Basketball Association (NBA) in 1946 and led the Washington Caps and the Tri-Cities to 143 wins. Taking over the Boston Celtics in 1950, he led them to nine division championships and eight straight world titles in ten years. He coached 11 straight NBA All-Star teams, 1957 – 1967 and won 99 playoff games. Auerbach built the Boston Celtics dynasty and compiled a better win record than any other NBA coach. The Celtics took the NBA title in 1957 on the way to world professional dominance 1956 – 1966. Auerbach's overall record with the Celtics was 1037 – 548. His practice of lighting a cigar on the bench when victory was assured infuriated the opposition, but delighted Boston crowds. During a stormy career, he was assessed $17,000 in fines. He became the general manager of the Celtics in 1966, turning over the coaching duties to Bill Russell. Red was voted the Washington, D.C, Coach of the Decade. He wrote an outstanding book, traveled internationally for clinics and game promotion, and was the recipient of several civic awards. During his career, he developed many great players and led pro basketball to its greatest recognition and acclaim.

DEHNERT, Henry G. "Dutch"

Player

Born April 5, 1898, in New York City; now a clerk for the New York Racing Association.

	Eastern, Pennsylvania State, New York State, and New England Leagues, player
1920 – 1928	The Original Celtics, player
1928 – 1930	Cleveland Rosenblums, player
1930 – 1939	New York Celtics, player
	Detroit Eagles, coach
	Sheboygan Indiana, coach

Dutch, with The Original Celtics, dominated Eastern basketball for eight years, and, to make an easy game interesting, went to the foul line to receive passes from his teammates. He became famous for this "pivot play." The Celtics made a final appearance at Madison Square Garden in a ten-minute preliminary game. Dutch led the Cleveland Rosenblums to American League titles from 1927 to 1930, and the New York Celtics to 1900 wins. As coach, he led the Detroit Eagles to world titles 1940 – 1941 and the Sheboygan Indians to National League West titles 1945 – 1946. Although he discovered the pivot play by chance, he played and coached it so well that the three-second rule was adopted.

IBA, Henry P.

Coach

Born August 6, 1904, in Easton, Mo; graduated from Easton High School 1923, Westminster Col, Northwest Missouri State Col. 1929; Coach of the Year 1945 – 1946; NABC president 1968; NABC Metropolitan Award 1947.

1920 – 1923	Easton High School, player
1924 – 1929	Westminster College and Northwest Missouri State College, player
	Oklahoma City's Classen High School, coach
	Northwest Missouri State College, coach
1934	University of Colorado, coach
1935 – 1970	Oklahoma State University, coach

Iba played four years in high school and was All-Conference for two years at Westminster. Iba coached Classen High School to 51 wins in three years, then moved to Northwest Missouri State for 61 victories including 43 consecutive games won. He coached Oklahoma State to 800 wins with 14 Missouri Valley titles and the 1965 Big Eight championship. He won consecutive National Collegiate Athletic Association titles in 1945–1946 and was runnerup in 1949. His college coaching record was 767–338; he developed All-Americans Bob Kurland and Jack McCracken. The "Iron Duke" is undisputed master of slow-down, shoot-only-when-necessary basketball. He led the championship United States team in the 1964 Olympics at Tokyo and was chosen for an unprecedented second time in 1968, leading the United States to the championship at Mexico City. He lost the bid for a third gold medal in the bitterly disputed loss to Russia at Munich. Iba's son Moe played for his father at Oklahoma State and later was head coach at Memphis State. Hank was very active in the National Association of Basketball Coaches (NABC). *Also in:* Athletic Directors Hall of Fame and College Basketball Hall of Fame, Citizens Savings Hall of Fame Athletic Museum.

RUPP, Adolph F. "Baron"

Coach

Born September 2, 1901, in Halstead, Kans; graduated from Halstead High School 1919, Univ. Kans. 1923; Basketball Rules Committee member 1964–1968; NABC Metropolitan Award 1966; after retiring from the Univ. Ky. became president of ABA Memphis Rams.

1920–1923 University of Kansas, player
Marshalltown, Iowa, High School and Freeport, Ill, High School, coach
1931–1972 University of Kentucky, coach

Rupp was a member of the 1923 Kansas champions, coached by Forrest C. Allen, who won 771 games. Coach Allen saw his protege win 874–190 games to become a top-winning coach. Baron led the Kentucky Wildcats to 24 Southeastern Conference titles, four National Collegiate Athletic Association (NCAA) titles 1948, 1949, 1951 and 1958, the National Invitational Tournament title in 1946, and an NCAA runnerup in 1966. He was co-coach of the 1948 United States Olympic team in London. Rupp won every important award, including Coach of the Year four times, and the Columbus, Ohio, Touchdown Club Coach of the Century in 1967. He coached 25 All-Americans, 7 Olympic team players and 26 professional players. He has taken 11 overseas clinic trips and won many civic awards. Rupp was called the "man in the brown suit" because he always wore brown on game nights. He was stern, outspoken and controversial. Rupp was the author of *Championship Basketball.*
Also in: College Basketball Hall of Fame, Citizens Savings Hall of Fame Athletic Museum.

TAYLOR, Charles H.

Contributor

Born June 24, 1901, in Brown County, Ind; graduated from Columbus, Ind, High School 1918; died June 23, 1969, in Port Charlotte, Fla.

1914–1918 Columbus High School, player
Pro basketball, player (11 years)

Taylor played basketball for four years in high school and was All-State two years. In 1921 he developed a shoe designed for the growing game—the Converse Chuck Taylor All-Star. At North Carolina State in 1922, he gave a public demonstration of basketball—the first "basketball clinic." Taylor spent his life promoting basketball. His clinics and demonstrations took him to every major American city as well as to Puerto Rico, Canada, Mexico, South America, Africa and Europe. He began the Converse Rubber Company Yearbook in 1922, and has selected the All-American team since 1932. Taylor coached the Air Force basketball team in W. W. II and won an award for his outstanding service in conducting clinics at many bases in the United States and overseas. *Also in:* National Association of Intercollegiate Athletics Hall of Fame.

1969

CARNEVALE, Bernard L. "Ben"

Coach

Born October 30, 1915, in Raritan, N.J; graduated from Somerville High School 1934, New York Univ. 1938; NABC president 1966.

1931–1934 Somerville High School, player
1935–1938 New York University, player
1938–1940 Jersey City Reds, player
1939–1942 Cranford, N.J, High School, coach
1944–1945 North Carolina University Tarheels, coach
U.S. Naval Academy Midshipmen, coach (20 years)
New York University, director of athletics
College of William and Mary, director of athletics

Carnevale was All-District, captain, and Most Valuable Player in 1938, playing for Coach Howard Cann. He later coached the Cranford High School team to 75 wins and the Tarheels to 51–11, winning the Southern Conference for two years and the National Collegiate Athletic Association (NCAA) title in 1946. In 20 years with the Midshipmen, his record was 257–158 and his teams played in five NCAA tourneys and one national Invitational Tournament. During his Navy service he spent several days in a lifeboat after his ship was torpedoed off the coast of North Africa in 1942. He has been a member of NIT and the Eastern Collegiate Athletic Commission Holiday Festival Selection Committee since 1966. In 1968 Ben managed the 1968 Olympics in Mexico City and in 1969 was appointed chairman of the International Basketball Board.
Also in: College Basketball Hall of Fame, Citizens Savings Hall of Fame Athletic Museum.

DAVIES, Robert E.

Player

Born January 15, 1920, in Harrisburg, Pa; graduated from Harrisburg's John Harris High School 1937, Seton Hall 1942; All-American two times; NBA Silver Anniversary Team; now lives in Gettysburg, Pa.

1939–1942 Seton Hall, guard
1943 Great Lakes Training School, player
1945–1955 Rochester Royals, player
1956–1957 Gettysburg College, coach

Davies, 6 ft. 1 in, 175 lbs, had a brilliant college playing career, although he was not a high scorer (11.8 average). He was captain two years, Most Valuable Player three years, and All-American two years, leading Seton Hall to 47 straight wins. Davies was also selected Most Valuable Player in the 1942 College All-Star game in Chicago. After leading the Great Lakes Naval Training School to the service title in 1943, he joined the Rochester Royals, playing 569 games with a 13.7 average; he led the Royals in scoring three times. Davies was All-League seven years, Most Valuable Player in 1947, and led the Royals to world titles in 1946, 1947 and 1951, as well as to the National Basketball Association (NBA) championship. From 1949 to 1952 he was selected as a member of the All-Pro first team; in 1953 he was on the second team. Davies was the leading assist man for six straight years, including a record 20 in one game, and the NBA assist leader in 1949. He starred in 67 playoff games, and scored 7771 points as a pro. "Harrisburg Houdini's" original and famous behind-the-back dribble delighted the fans, and he was ranked sixth on the list of Greatest Players of the First Half Century of Basketball. Davies is considered the superstar of modern pro basketball. In 1956 – 1957 he coached Gettysburg to a 19 – 28 record.

1970

COUSY, Robert J. "Cooz"

Player

Born August 9, 1928, in New York City; graduated from Queens' Andrew Jackson High School 1946, Holy Cross Col. 1950; All-American 1948, 1949; All-NBA Silver Anniversary Team 1971.

1943 – 1946 Andrew Jackson High School, player
1947 – 1950 Holy Cross College, guard
1950 – 1963 Boston Celtics, player
1963 – 1964 Cincinnati Royals, player
1965 – 1969 Boston College, coach
1969 – 1970 Cincinnati Royals, coach
1970 Kansas City-Omaha Kings, coach

Cousy was high school All-New York City 1946, college Most Valuable Player 1949 – 1950, captain 1950, and All-American 1948 – 1949, with a 99 – 19 record. He was a freshman member of the Holy Cross National Collegiate Athletic Association champions of 1947. After graduation, he was one of three players offered in the National Basketball Association (NBA) pool to New York, Philadelphia and Boston. The Celtics wanted Max Zaslofsky or Andy Phillip, but acquired Cousy when they drew his name from a hat. He quarterbacked the Boston Celtics to six NBA titles—1957 and 1959 – 1963. As "Mr. Basketball" he helped lift the pro game to major status in his incomparable career. Cooz, 6 ft. 1 in, was All-NBA first team ten years in a row, star in all 13 All-Star games, league Most Valuable Player 1957, All-Star Most Valuable Player 1954 and 1957. He held 13 playoff records, six All-Star marks, and the NBA assist record (28) with Guy Rodgers. He had 6959 lifetime assists and scored 16,960 points in 924 games, an average of 18.4 points per game. Cooz was the most spectacular performer in the history of the game. He coached Boston College to five tournaments in 1963 – 1969 (117 – 54 record).
Also in: College Basketball Hall of Fame and Major League Basketball Hall of Fame, Citizens Savings Hall of Fame Athletic Museum.

PETTIT, Robert L.

Player

Born December 12, 1932, in Baton Rouge, La; graduated from Baton Rouge High School 1950, La. State Univ. 1954; All-American four times; NBA Rookie of the Year 1955; All-NBA 25-Year Team 1971; NBA Silver Anniversary Team; now lives in Metairie, La.

1949 – 1950 Baton Rouge High School, player
1951 – 1954 Louisiana State University, center
1955 – 1965 Milwaukee-St. Louis Hawks, forward

Although he could not make the high school team as a sophomore, Pettit, 6 ft. 9 in, 205 lbs, was All-State and All-American in 1950. He was All-Southeastern at Louisiana State in 1952 – 1954, All-American and Most Valuable Player 1952 – 1953, and Consensus All-American 1954, with a 27.4 points-per-game average for three years. Pettit was 11 years All-League; Most Valuable Player in 1956, 1958 – 1959 and 1962; was on 11 All-Star teams and the 1955 – 1964 All-Pro teams. A National Basketball Association (NBA) superstar, Pettit retired in 1965 as the highest scorer in NBA history, with 20,880 points and the fifth best scoring average—26.4 points per game. In six individual games, he topped 50 points, a record finally broken by Elgin Baylor. With 224 points, he was the second leading All-Star scorer. He had the third most rebounds in NBA history (12,851) and the third most free throws; the jump shot was his forte. Pettit led the St. Louis Hawks to the NBA title in 1958, and the runnerup in 1957 and 1959 – 1961.
Also in: College Basketball Hall of Fame and Major League Basketball Hall of Fame, Citizens Savings Hall of Fame Athletic Museum.

SAPERSTEIN, Abraham M.

Contributor

Born July 4, 1902, in London, England; graduated from Chicago's Lakeview High School 1919; died March 15, 1966, in Chicago, Ill.

1916 – 1919 Lakeview High School, player
1925 – 1965 American Legion Team, later Savoy Big Five, then Harlem Globetrotters, coach

Although barely five feet tall, Saperstein developed an enthusiasm for sports when he played baseball, track and basketball in high school. In 1925 he accepted a job coaching a black American Legion team, which he developed into the famed touring comedy team, the Harlem Globetrotters. After performing in Chicago's Savoy Ballroom, the Globetrotters played their first game in Hinckley, Ill, on January 7, 1927. Saperstein, called "Little Caesar," originally served an all-purpose role: coach, chauffeur, trainer, physician and only substitute. In the next 40 years the Globetrotters played before 5 million fans in 87 countries including 75,000 in Berlin in 1951. They won the world title in 1940 and the International Cup in 1943 – 1944, and were the only team to be the subject of two full-length movies. A tireless founder, coach and owner, and a man of great integrity, Saperstein made basketball truly international. A respected citizen of the world, he was welcomed wherever he went. His unique team created a new style of playing the game. In 1961 Saperstein formed a new pro league, the ABL (American Basketball League), which folded after 18 months. The league, however, produced the 3-point basket and the shot made from outside 25 feet.

1971

DIDDLE, Edgar A.

Coach

Born March 12, 1895, in Gradyville, Ky; graduated from Adair County High School 1915, Centre Col. 1920; died January 2, 1970.

1917–1920 Centre College, player
1921 Monticello High School, coach
1922 Greenville High School, coach
1922–1964 Western Kentucky University Hilltoppers, coach

Diddle was captain and All-Southern at Centre College in 1920. As a player, he helped Centre College achieve an 11–0 mark in 1919. John (Sherman) Cooper, later U.S. Senator, and football stars Alvin (Bo) McMillan, James (Red) Roberts and Madison Bell were among Diddle's teammates. In 1921 he coached Monticello High to the state finals, and Greenville High to regionals in 1922. One of the first coaches to use all five players on offense, he taught his Kentucky Hilltoppers to use flashy, fast-break to play in every national collegiate event. They won or shared in 32 conference titles, including 13 Kentucky Intercollegiate, 8 Southern and 11 Ohio Valley titles in the first 16 years of the conference; they participated in three National Collegiate Athletic Association and eight National Invitational Tournament Competitions. Diddle was the first coach to guide a team in 1000 games at the same college, and at the time of his election to the Hall of Fame, was the fourth-ranked college coach in victories, with a 759–302 record for .720 average. He had 18 seasons with 20 or more victories, including 10 straight years, 1934–1943. Diddle's trademark was throwing and waving a red towel. When he retired, he was presented with 759 silver dollars, one for each win. The Edgar A. Diddle Arena at Western Kentucky University was named in his honor.
Also in: College Basketball Hall of Fame, Citizens Savings Hall of Fame Athletic Museum.

DOUGLAS, Robert L.
Contributor
Born November 4, 1884, in St. Kitts, B.W.I; now lives in New York City.

Douglas came to America at age four and, in 1922, with no high school or college athletic experience, organized the Renaissance Five officially called the New York Rens. He gathered the best black players and required excellence in performance. Largely a road club, the Rens won 88 consecutive games in 1933, 128 games in 1934, and a grand total of 2318 games in 22 years. For 14 straight seasons, the Rens claimed 11 or more victories. One of the few teams to beat The Original Celtics, the Rens played the Celtics in a 12-game series and drew 25,000 fans. In 1939 they won the world's pro title in Chicago, beating the Harlem Globetrotters, en route to a record that gave Bob the highest win total of all coaches during an era when basketball needed his memorable contributions and leadership. The top players included Fats Jenkins, Bill Yancey, Pappy Ricks, Bruiser Saitch, Tarzan Cooper, and Willie Smith. Douglas was the first black to be inducted into the Naismith Memorial Basketball Hall of Fame.

ENDACOTT, Paul "Endy"
Player
Born July 13, 1902, in Lawrence, Kans; graduated from Lawrence High School 1919, Univ. Kans. 1923; Helms Player of the Year 1923; Helms All-Time All-American Team 1943; president of Phillips Petroleum Co; now retired and living in Bartlesville, Okla.

1916–1919 Lawrence High School, guard
1920–1923 University of Kansas Jayhawks, player
1924–1925 Phillips 66ers, player

Endacott was an All-State guard in 1919; Coach Phog Allen called him the "greatest player [I] ever coached." He was All-Conference second team in 1921 and on the first team in 1922–1923. The Jayhawks, led by Endacott, won the national title in 1923 and were undefeated in the conference games. Adolph Rupp was reserve on that team. In 1924 Endacott was selected All-Kansas by Dr. James Naismith, and in 1951 was selected by Dr. Allen to be a member of the National All-Time College Team. He was the recipient of the Sportsmen's World Award in 1969 as "an athlete whose championship performances have stood the test of time, and whose exemplary personal conduct has made him an outstanding inspiration for youth to emulate." Endacott is a trustee of the Naismith Memorial Basketball Hall of Fame.
Also in: College Basketball Hall of Fame, Citizens Savings Hall of Fame Athletic Museum.

FRIEDMAN, Max "Marty"
Player
Born July 12, 1889, in New York City; graduated from Hebrew Technical Institute 1908; now resides in New York City.

1906–1908 University Settlement House, guard
1909–1910 New York Roosevelts, player
1911–1922 Newburgh, Hudson, Utica, Carbondale, Philadelphia Jaspers, Albany, Easthampton pro teams, player
1923–1927 Cleveland Rosenblums, player-coach

Friedman, 5 ft. 8 in, played with the University Settlement House, the Metropolitan AAU (Amateur Athletic Union) champs 1906–1908, before turning pro with the New York Roosevelts in 1909 to begin a career playing in every pro league in the East. He was acknowledged a great defensive star and leader of each team with which he played. Friedman won championships with nearly every team, including 35 straight games with Carbondale in 1915 and the American League championships in 1926–1927. As captain of the Tours Team, American Expeditionary Force champs, he won the Inter-Allied games in 1919, followed by brilliant play with the independent New York Whirlwinds who were organized by Tex Rickard. John Murray, who became a highly regarded official, was the manager. The starting five were Friedman, Barney Sedran, Chris Leonard, Nat Holman and Harry Riconda. Marty and Barney were known as the "Heavenly Twins."

GOTTLIEB, Edward "Gotty"
Contributor
Born September 15, 1898, in Kiev, Ukraine; graduated from South Philadelphia High School 1916, Philadelphia School of Pedagogy 1918.

1916–1918 Philadelphia School of Pedagogy, player
1947–1955 Philadelphia Warriors, coach

Gottlieb was captain of his team in 1918 before organizing the team that was to represent the South Philadelphia Hebrew Association in 1918. Playing 75–80 games annually, the team peaked in the 1925–1926 season to defeat The Original Celtics and the New York Rens in a special series, before rebuilding in the 1930s to dominate the Eastern and American Leagues with 11 championships. Constantly promoting basketball, Gottlieb helped pull the pro game through difficult times. In 1946 he assisted in organizing the Basketball Association of America which later was to become the National Basketball Association (NBA). He led the Philadelphia Warriors as owner and coach to their first championship in 1946–1947, signing Joe Fulks who was destined to become a pro superstar. Later he signed Wilt Chamberlain. His coaching record with the Warriors was 263-318. Gottlieb was basketball's supersalesman, and helped organize overseas tours of the Harlem Globetrotters. He promoted pro doubleheaders, and also pro wrestling and semipro football. As chairman of the NBA Rules Committee for 25 years, he was schedule maker and a consultant to NBA Commissioner Walter Kennedy. Gottlieb is known as "the mogul" of baseball.

WELLS, W.R. Clifford
Contributor
See entry in Indiana Basketball Hall of Fame, 1965.
Also in: College Basketball Hall of Fame, Citizens Savings Hall of Fame Athletic Museum.

1972

BECKMAN, John "Becky"
Player
Born October 22, 1895, in New York City; died June 22, 1968, in Miami, Fla.

Beckman began a 27-year basketball career with St. Gabriel's and by 1922, was captain of The Original Celtics. Known as the "Babe Ruth of Basketball," Beckman was the main reason for the election of the Celtics as a team to the Hall of Fame. Swede Grimsley and Dutch Dehnert were his teammates. He annually played in more than 125 games in various leagues, and was basketball's greatest box-office attraction in the 1920s and 1930s. One of the best free-throw shooters of his era, Beckman was selected in 1935 by Nat Holman as "basketball's finest competitive athlete."

DRAKE, Bruce
Coach
Born December 5, 1905, in Gentry, Tex; graduated from Oklahoma City Central High School 1925, Univ. Okla. 1929; All-American and Player of the Year 1929; now retired and living in Norman, Okla.

1922–1925 Central High School, player
1926–1929 University of Oklahoma, player
1929–1939 University of Oklahoma, freshman coach
1939–1955 University of Oklahoma, coach

Drake was All-State at Central High School and All-Conference and All-American for Oklahoma in 1929. As coach for Oklahoma, he led the Sooners to a 200–180 record, and six Big Six and Big Seven titles. He created the "Drake Shuffle" offense, and actively supported legislation concerning goal-tending. After assisting his former Oklahoma All-American Gerald Tucker with the U.S. Olympic Team in Melbourne, Drake coached three All-American and five Olympic teams. He was Chairman of the National Basketball Association Rules Committee for four years and the National Association of Basketball Coaches president in 1951.

Also in: College Basketball Hall of Fame, Citizens Savings Hall of Fame Athletic Museum.

LONBORG, Arthur C. "Dutch"
Coach
Born March 16, 1899, in Gardner, Ill; graduated from Horton, Kans, High School 1916, Univ. Kans; law degree from Univ. Kans; also played baseball and football with Kansas; All-American 1920; NABC president 1935.

1913–1916 Horton High School, player
1917–1920 University of Kansas, player
1922–1950 McPherson College, Washburn University, Northwestern University, coach
1950–1964 University of Kansas, director of athletic events

Lonborg was captain of the basketball team at Kansas and the school's third basketball All-American. As a coach he led McPherson to 23 wins in two years, Washburn to 63 wins in four years, and Northwestern to a 237–198 record. His Washburn team, led by center Gerald Spohn, won the national Amateur Athletic Union title in Kansas City in 1925, the last time a college team won that title. In 1931 he led the Northwestern Wildcats to the Big Ten title and a Conference tie two years later. Lonborg's overall coaching record was 324–225; he coached an All-Star team to a 6–3 victory at Chicago's Exhibition Series. He chaired the National Collegiate Athletic Association Tournament Committee and the U.S. Olympic Basketball Committee, and managed the 1960 U.S. Olympic Team.
Also in: Athletic Directors Hall of Fame and College Basketball Hall of Fame, Citizens Savings Hall of Fame Athletic Museum.

RIPLEY, Elmer H. "Rip"
Contributor
Born July 21, 1891, in Staten Island, N.Y; graduated from Staten Island's Curtis High School 1909; now a resident of North Bergen, N.J.

1909–1926 The Original Celtics, Scranton, Carbondale, Troy, Cleveland Rosenblums, Washington Palace, pro player
1928–1929 Georgetown University, coach
1929–1935 Yale University, coach
1944–1945 Columbia University, coach
1946 University of Notre Dame, coach
1952–1953 U.S. Military Academy, coach
1954–1956 Harlem Globetrotters, coach
1956 Israel Olympic Team, coach
1960 Canadian Olympic Team, coach

Ripley was called "one of the ten best pros." He competed in 1914 at the San Francisco World's Fair as a member of the All-Star Team. He conducted clinics all over the world, and was honored with an "Elmer Ripley Day" in the borough of Richmond, New York, on April 29, 1967.
Also in: College Basketball Hall of Fame, Citizens Savings Hall of Fame Athletic Museum.

SCHAYES, Adolph "Dolph"
Player
Born May 19, 1928, in New York City; attended New York Univ; All-Metropolitan 1945–1946, and 1948; All-America 1948; NBA All-Star Team twelve times

1950–1961; Rookie of the Year; Silver Anniversary Team member.

1945–1948 New York University, forward
1948–1964 Syracuse Nationals, forward
1964–1966 Philadelphia 76ers, player-coach
1971 Buffalo Braves, coach
1972 Milwaukee Bucks, coach

At 6 ft. 9 in, Schayes was a skilled driver, shooter, defender and rebounder. He liked to shoot two-handed from the corners. He paced the Violets to a 22–4 mark and to the National Invitational Tournament runnerup spot in 1948. Schayes played 16 seasons for the Nationals, the most ever played by one individual; in 1059 National Basketball Association games he scored 19,249 points and made 8262 free throws. He earned 1973 points in 103 playoff games and participated in 765 consecutive games, including playoffs, from February 1952 to December 1961. Schayes had a record 3667 personal fouls and once made 50 straight free throws.

WOODEN, John R.
Coach
Selected in 1959 as a College Player and in 1972 as a Coach; see entry in Indiana Basketball Hall of Fame, 1962.
Also in: College Basketball Hall of Fame, Citizens Savings Hall of Fame Athletic Museum.

1973

FISHER, Harry A.
Contributor
Born February 6, 1882, in New York City; graduated from City College High School 1901, Columbia Univ. 1905; All-American 1905; Columbia Alumni Athletic Award 1945; died December 29, 1967, at age 85.

1902–1905 Columbia University, player
1906–1916 Columbia University, coach
1911–1917 Columbia University, graduate manager of athletics
1922–1923 U.S. Army, coach
1925 U.S. Army, coach

A team leader and scoring star from 1902 to 1905, Harry established the field goal record of 13 which stood for 48 years. The team, under coach Henry Elias, lost only two games during Harry's last two years of playing, both to the Washington Continentals from Schenectady. In 1905 Fisher was appointed to the original committee which rewrote college basketball rules. While a coach at Columbia, he led the team to a remarkable 101–39 record and three Eastern Invitational League titles, two as a result of undefeated seasons. He edited the *Collegiate Guide* until 1915. After leaving Columbia, Fisher retired from athletics, but was lured back to coaching at West Point by General Douglas MacArthur. He won 46 of 51 games to close out his career, defeating Navy all three years. He developed Hall of Famer John Roosma at Army.
Also in: College Basketball Hall of Fame, Citizens Savings Hall of Fame Athletic Museum.

PODOLOFF, Maurice
Contributor
Born August 18, 1890, in Elizabethgrad, Russia; came to America at age six; raised in New Haven, Conn; graduated from New Haven's Hillhouse High School 1909, Yale Univ. 1913, Yale Univ. Law School 1915; president of American Hockey League; retired 1963 and living in New Haven.

Appointed the first commissioner of the Basketball Association of America (BAA) June 6, 1946, Podoloff led the 11-member BAA into a merger with the National Basketball Association (NBA) in August 1949. As president he guided the NBA through the early years and secured the first television contract in 1954, which led to national recognition for the NBA. Podoloff was known for his impeccable character and his impartial attention to all 17 teams.

SCHMIDT, Ernest J.
Player
Born February 12, 1911, in Nashville, Kans; graduated from Winfield, Kans, High School 1929, Kans. State Univ. 1933; All-Arkansas Valley Conference and All-State three years; All-Conference center four years; All-American 1932; Amateur Athletic Union All-American Second Team.

1926–1929 Winfield High School, center
1930–1933 Kansas State University, center

Schmidt led his high school team to three state championships and broke the conference and tournament scoring records from 1927 to 1929. He led Kansas State to 47 straight wins and four conference titles from 1930 to 1933. Known as "One-Grand Schmidt" for scoring 1000 points, he won recognition in 1932 as the greatest college player in the Missouri Valley.
Also in: National Association of Intercollegiate Athletics Hall of Fame.

1974

BRENNAN, Joseph R. "Poison Joe"
Player
Born November 15, 1900, in Brooklyn, N.Y; graduated from St. Augustine's Academy in Brooklyn.

A varsity captain of his high school team, Brennan had a 17-year pro career, leading the Brooklyn Visitations in their rise to basketball prominence. As the league-leading scorer, he helped the Visitation Triangles to the Metropolitan League championship and the unofficial world championship in 1931. He played with the Brooklyn Jewels, Whirlwinds, Dodgers, Union City Reds and Troy, serving as captain of nearly every team. In 1950 the New York Basketball Old Timers voted him second only to Johnny Beckman as the greatest pro player of his era.

LISTON, Emil S. "Big Lis"
Contributor
Born August 21, 1890, in Stockton, Mo; attended Baker Univ; graduated from Harvard Univ. 1930; died October 26, 1949, at age 59.

As an undergraduate at Baker, Liston won 11 letters in football, basketball and baseball, and also worked for three years as coach of the Baldwin High School football team, leading them to the Kansas state title in 1912. After 1913 he coached at Fort Scott, Kans, Kemper Military, Michigan College and Wesleyan University, Connecticut, before returning to a 25-year career at

Baker University. There his football and basketball clubs won six conference titles. He organized the Kansas Coaches Association and in 1936 was the Missouri Valley Amateur Athletic Union representative. Liston originated the idea of a national small-college tournament and organized the National Association of Intercollegiate Basketball (NAIB) in 1937. The NAIB began with eight teams and has grown today to 500 members. Liston was its first executive director from 1940 to 1949.
Also in: National Association of Intercollegiate Athletics Hall of Fame.

RUSSELL, William F.
Player
Born February 12, 1934, in Monroe, La; graduated from Univ. San Francisco; Citizens Savings College Player of the Year 1956; NBA Most Valuable Player 5 times; All-Star Team 11 times; All-Pro First Team 3 times; *Sporting News* Athlete of the Decade 1970; NBA Silver Anniversary Team 1971; Citizens Savings All-Time All-American Team; All-American two times.

1953 – 1956 University of San Francisco, center
1956 – 1969 Boston Celtics, center
1972 – 1977 Seattle SuperSonics, general manager, coach

Russell led San Francisco to 55 straight victories and played in the U.S. championship games in Melbourne in 1956. The Russell-K.C. Jones combination was instrumental in San Francisco's 60-game winning streak and two National Collegiate Athletic Association titles 1955 – 1956. At the Melbourne Olympics, Russell also qualified as a high jumper but didn't participate. He joined the Celtics as the game's highest paid rookie. In defense he implemented the outstanding "team" concept that brought the Celtics 8 straight National Basketball Association (NBA) titles, 11 in 13 seasons. He accumulated 21,721 rebounds, the second highest career average, and averaged 15 points a game in his NBA career. A member of 11 All-Star teams, Russell was the league's Most Valuable Player five times. He was player-coach for three years and led the Celtics to NBA championships in 1968 and 1969. He had legendary duels with Wilt Chamberlain. In one of the game's pivotal events, the St. Louis Hawks in 1956 traded eight drafts for Russell to the Celtics for Ed McCauley and Cliff Hagan. Russell had the most minutes, 7497, the most games, 165, rebounds, 4104 and fouls, 536, as playoff records. He collected 51 rebounds in one game, 49 two times. He was the league's top rebounder four times, and made the All-Pro First Team three times. Russell retired from active competition after serving as Celtic player-coach. He gave lectures on college campuses and did the color commentary for ABC's NBA Game of the Week. Most recently he was head coach and general manager for the Seattle SuperSonics.
Also in: College Basketball Hall of Fame, Citizens Savings Hall of Fame Athletic Museum.

VANDIVIER, Robert P. "Fuzzy"
Player
See entry in Indiana Basketball Hall of Fame, 1962.

1975

GOLA, Thomas J.
Player
Born January 13, 1933, in Philadelphia, Pa; son of a policeman; graduated from LaSalle High School 1951, LaSalle Univ. 1955; NIT Most Valuable Player 1952; NCAA Most Valuable Player 1954; All-NBA 1958; *Sport Magazine* All-Time All-American 1960; All-American three times; served two terms in the Pennsylvania state legislature; lives in Philadelphia.

1948 – 1951 LaSalle High School, center, forward, guard
1951 – 1955 LaSalle University Explorers, center, forward, guard
1955 – 1966 National Basketball Association (NBA) teams, player
1968 – 1969 LaSalle University, coach

One of the finest school stars in Philadelphia history, Gola scored 2222 points in his high school career. He refused numerous out-of-city offers to play at LaSalle. He was the second four-year college All-American and one of basketball's most versatile players. Captain for two years, he averaged 21 points and 20 rebounds per game. Gola scored 2461 points and 2201 rebounds in four years. While playing for the Explorers, he was on the winning team in 101 out of 118 games, and excelled in defense. He played for the Philadelphia Warriors, the San Francisco Warriors and the New York Knickerbockers, scoring 7871 points, a leader in rebounds and assists, and an outstanding defensive player. Gola lead the teams in steals. As a 6 ft. 6 in. pro player, he played 698 games with a 11.3 average. Gola had a 37-13 record coaching at his alma mater. His last team won 23 out of 24 and ranked second nationally.
Also in: College Basketball Hall of Fame, Citizens Savings Hall of Fame Athletic Museum; and National Polish-American Sports Hall of Fame and Museum.

KRAUSE, Edward W. "Moose"
Player
Born February 2, 1913, in Chicago, Ill; graduated from Chicago's De LaSalle High School 1930, Univ. Notre Dame 1934; All-American 1932, 1933 and 1934.

1927 – 1930 De LaSalle High School, forward
1931 – 1934 University of Notre Dame, forward
1934 – 1939 St. Mary's College, Minn, coach and athletic director
1940 – 1945 Holy Cross College, coach
1946 – 1951 University of Notre Dame, coach and athletic director

In high school Krause was an all-city three-sport star. He played football in college from 1932 to 1934, as well as basketball, and was All-American three years in both sports. At 6 ft. 3 in, 215 lbs, he was the first agile, rebounding pivot man. He established the all-time college scoring records for one game, one season, and three seasons (547 points). Krause was a fine passer, and led Notre Dame to a three-year record of 54-12. Team captain in 1934 under Coach George Keogan, he later starred on Midwestern and New England pro teams.

Krause coached at Holy Cross and Notre Dame; his Notre Dame record was 92-45 with no losing seasons.
Also in: College Basketball Hall of Fame, Citizens Savings Hall of Fame Athletic Museum.

LITWACK, Harry "Chief"
Coach
Born September 20, 1907, in Glicia, Austria; graduated from South Philadelphia High School 1925, Temple Univ. 1930; New York Basketball Writers Association Coach of the Year 1958.

1922–1925 South Philadelphia High School, player
1927–1930 Temple University Owls, player
1949–1951 Philadelphia Warriors, player-coach
1953–1973 Temple University Owls, coach

A high school all-star, and college captain for two years, Litwack played for the Philadelphia SPHAs for seven years in the Eastern and American leagues. He won 15 and lost 2 coaching at Gratz High School in 1930 and 181-32 as Temple frosh coach while doubling as assistant coach of the Philadelphia Warriors under coach-owner Eddie Gottlieb. As Temple coach, he led the Owls to a 373-193 record and 13 post-season tournaments, including the National Invitational Tournament championship in 1969, and third place in the National Collegiate Athletic Association playoffs in 1956 and 1958. Coach of several all-star teams, Litwack produced four All-Americans at Temple—Guy Rodgers, Hal Lear, Bill Kennedy and John Baum.

SHARMAN, William W.
Player
Born May 25, 1926, in Abilene, Tex; graduated from University of Southern Calif. 1950; accomplished baseball player, outfielder for Brooklyn Dodgers until end of 1951 season; in basketball All-American 1949, 1950; first All-NBA team 1955–1956, 1956–1957, 1957–1958, 1958–1959; second All-NBA team 1952–1953, 1954–1955, 1959–1960; Most Valuable Player in 1954–1955 All-Star Game; NBA Silver Anniversary Team 1970–1971; earned doctorate degree; author of *Sharman on Shooting.*

1950–1951 Washington Caps, guard
1951–1961 Boston Celtics, guard
1966–1967 San Francisco Warriors, coach
1968–1971 Utah Stars, coach
1971–1972 Los Angeles Lakers, coach

One of the best players in basketball history, Bill Sharman was selected as a member of the National Basketball Association (NBA) Silver Anniversary Team in 1970–1971. With the Boston Celtics, he and Bob Cousy formed the most outstanding backcourt duo. With a polished and precise style, Sharman's best shooting took place within a 20-ft. range and made him one of the finest shooting guards of the day with a .423 percentage. He was, by far, the finest free thrower. He won the NBA title a total of seven times, in 1952–1953, 1953–1954, 1954–1955, 1955–1956, 1956–1957, 1959–1960 and 1960–1961. His lifetime average was .883 percent, 3143 successes out of 3557 chances, and he became the all-time free-thrower in the NBA in 1958–1959 with .932 percent. During this time, the Boston Celtics were outstanding, with Sharman, Cousy, Bill Russell and Ed McCauley. They won the Eastern Divisional NBA title for an entire decade, from the 1956–1957 season through the 1964–1965 season, and won the national title in 1956–1957 and 1958–1959. Even in his college days at University of Southern California, Sharman set a scoring record in 1950, then went to play a season with the Washington Caps. Following his professional career, he turned to coaching. The San Francisco Warriors won the divisional championship under his leadership in 1967. The Los Angeles Lakers, during his first season as their coach, won 69 games for an all-time National Game Average high and the NBA title after reaching the finals seven previous times.
Also in: Major League Basketball Hall of Fame, Citizens Savings Hall of Fame Athletic Museum.

1976

BAYLOR, Elgin
Player
Born September 16, 1934; graduated from Spingarn High School, Washington, D.C, 1951, Seattle Univ. 1958; High School All-American 1951; All-Star First Team 1958–1968; Co-winner of All-Star Most Valuable Player 1959, Rookie of the Year 1959; Citizens Savings Player of the Year 1959.

1947–1951 Springarn High School, forward
1954–1958 Seattle University, forward
1958–1971 Minneapolis Lakers, forward

At 6 ft. 5 in, 225 lbs, the "man of a thousand moves" is considered the greatest forward to play basketball. Baylor was All-American in high school. At Seattle he established nine school scoring and rebounding records. Known for his fluid, acrobatic style, he was Seattle All-American in 1957 and 1958 and had a 24.9 average in his rookie season. With Jerry West he formed the league's most formidable 1-2 scoring punch. Baylor suffered knee injuries in his prime, and underwent extensive surgery. In the 1958 National Collegiate Athletic Association finals he averaged 31.5 points per game, a total of 590 rebounds and scored a high 60 points in one game. In 1958 he was drafted in the first round by the Minneapolis Lakers and scored 55 points in one game, the league high. He led the Lakers in scoring, finished fourth in the National Basketball Association (NBA) scoring, was the first-team All-Star for the next ten years and played in every All-Star game during that time. Baylor was fifth on the All-time NBA regular season scoring list, with 23,149 points (27.4 average) in 846 games, second in all-time playoff scoring, with 3623 points (27 average), including a one-game figure of 61 in 1962. He was the third leading rebounder in playoff history (1725), fifth in All-Star competition (99), and seventh in career regular season totals (11,463). Laker captain for 12 years, Baylor's best scoring season was 1962 when he averaged 38.3 in 48 games. He scored single highs of 63 points in one game in 1961, 64 in 1959 and 71 in 1960, the record before Wilt Chamberlain scored 78. (Later Wilt hit 100). In the 1971 season Baylor played only two games due to a torn Achilles tendon. He retired after playing nine games of the 1972 campaign and took a job in the Lakers front office. He also does the color commentary on NBA telecasts, succeeding Bill Russell.

Also in: College Basketball Hall of Fame and Major League Basketball Hall of Fame, Citizens Savings Hall of Fame Athletic Museum.

COOPER, Charles "Tarzan"
Player

Cooper played 20 years of pro ball as a center at 6 ft. 4 in, 225 lbs. While he played with the New York Rens, the team won 1303–203, including 88 consecutive games 1932–1933. Cooper was voted Most Valuable Player and the Rens' star performer when they won the first World Professional Basketball Championship in 1939. He spent the last three years of his pro career as a player-coach and captain of the Washington Bears, leading them to the world's pro title in 1943. Cooper had also played for the Panthers and the Philadelphia Giants before playing for the "Renaissance."

GALE, Lauren "Laddie"
Player

Born April 19, 1916, in Gold Beach, Ore; graduated from Oakridge, Ore, High School and Univ. Ore; All-American 1939.

Gale was the major reason for recognition of Pacific Northwest basketball in the 1930s. He received All-State honors in 1935 in high school. As a 6 ft. 4 in. forward, he was All-Conference and All-District at Oregon 1938 and 1939 after leading his Northern Division in scoring both years. In 1939 as first-team All-American, Gale led Oregon to victory in the first National Collegiate Athletic Association Tournament. He scored 408 points in 1938 and 407 in 1939. Gale was named to the All-Time Pacific Coast North Division and made a member of Oregon's 500-point Club. He played pro ball with the Detroit Eagles and the Salt Lake City *Deseret Times.*
Also in: Oregon Sports Hall of Fame.

JOHNSON, William C. "Skinny"
Player

Born August 16, 1911, in Oklahoma City, Okla; graduated from Oklahoma City's Central High School 1929, Univ. Kans. 1933; All-Conference First Team 1933; Most Valuable Player 1933; Big Six Conference Most Valuable Player 1933; All-American First Team 1933; All-American Second Team 1934; Jim Thorpe Award as All-Time Sports Great of Oklahoma 1975.

1926–1929 Central High School, center
1930–1933 University of Kansas, center
1934–1938 South Kansas Stag Lines, player-coach

Johnson, 6 ft. 3 in, had an uncanny jumping ability. He led his high school team to All-State in 1928 and 1929, and participated in the Amos Alonzo Stagg national schoolboy tournament at the University of Chicago. In 1929 he was chosen for the All-American squad in the National Interscholastic Tournament. Under Phog Allen at Kansas, he led the Jayhawks to three straight Big Six championships from 1931 to 1933. In Amateur Athletic Union (AAU) competition in 1934, he won the Missouri Valley scoring title; his team, the South Kansas Stag Lines, took the league championship and third place nationally. During the next two years he helped the team win consecutive Missouri Valley AAU crowns. Johnson was player-coach for Cleveland's Chiropractor College in Kansas City, Mo, and concluded his playing days in the Navy at Jacksonville and Corpus Christi. Coach Hank Iba said, referring to Johnson, "There are few, if any, players during the period of 1920 and 1930 who were chosen as All-American in all of the three possible areas of high school, college, and national AAU basketball." His proteges include Frank Mulzoff (St. John's), Al McGuire (Marquette) and Lou Carnesecca (New York Mets).

McGUIRE, Frank
Coach

Born November 8, 1914, in New York City; thirteenth child of a policeman; grew up in Greenwich Village; graduated from St. Francis Xavier High School and St. John's University.

St. Francis Xavier High School, coach
St. John's University, coach
1952–1961 University of North Carolina, coach
1961–1962 Philadelphia Warriors, coach
1964– University of South Carolina Gamecocks, coach

Frank has spent 27 years as a college coach and won 500 games. He ranks second in total wins among active college coaches and is presently twelfth among college coaches for all time. The twenty-third coach to be elected to the Naismith Memorial Basketball Hall of Fame, he has won over 660 games in his overall coaching career. McGuire coached at St. Xavier for 11 years to a 126–39 record, then at St. John's for five consecutive winning seasons with a 103–35 record. As coach at North Carolina, he had eight winning seasons; the 1957 team won all 32 games and was the National Collegiate Athletic Association (NCAA) champion. Frank coached the Warriors to 49–31 and second place behind the Celtics before losing the Eastern semi-final playoffs to Boston in seven games. He led the Gamecocks to 11 consecutive winning seasons, including six straight 20-win seasons. Frank is the only college coach in history to win more than 100 games at three major basketball institutions, and the only basketball coach to capture the Atlantic Coast Conference title at two different schools, North Carolina in 1957 and South Carolina in 1971. He was the only college coach to direct two different teams to the NCAA finals, St. John's in 1952 and North Carolina in 1957. McGuire coached Wilt Chamberlain, and produced All-Americans Robert Zawoluk, Lennie Rosenbluth, Pete Brennan, York Larese, Doug Moe, Lee Schaffer, John Roche and Tom Riker. He is the author of three books on coaching.

National Wheelchair Basketball Association Hall of Fame

LEXINGTON, KENTUCKY

Mailing Address: 110 Seaton Building, University of Kentucky, 40506. *Tel:* (606) 257-1623. *Contact:* Dr. Stan Labanowich, Commissioner. *Location:* 80 mi. S. of Cincinnati, Ohio, 130 mi. N. of Knoxville, Tenn, 150 mi. S.W. of Indianapolis, Ind, 150 mi. W. of Charleston, W.Va, 150 mi. N.E. of Bowling Green, Ky, 200 mi. N.E. of Nashville, Tenn. *Personnel:* Marvin Lapicola, Pres; Norman McGee, 1st V.Pres; Ralph Smith, 2nd V.Pres; Lou Carello, Secy; George Veenstro, Treas; Stan Labanowich, Commissioner. Call for information. *Nearby Halls of Fame:* Flight (Dayton, Ohio, 125 mi. N.), Auto Racing (Indianapolis, Ind, 170 mi. N.W.), Trapshooting (Vandalia, Ohio, 150 mi. N.), Music (Nashville, Tenn, 200 mi. S.W.), Agriculture (West Lafayette, Ind, 215 mi. N.W.), Sports (North Webster, Ind, 225 mi. N.W.).

The National Wheelchair Basketball Association Hall of Fame was started in 1970 by an appointed committee with Dr. Stan Labanowich as Chairman to enshrine in the form of a permanent record those individuals who have portrayed a distinctive positive influence of unique dimension in the sport of wheelchair basketball. The Hall does not have a permanent building but plans are being made for one. This Hall of Fame is a non-profit organization supported through donations.

Members: 18 as of 1977. There are two types of memberships in this Hall. One is a person who has played wheelchair basketball and the other is a person who has an on-going interest in wheelchair basketball but is not a player. A player must meet the eligibility requirements of five years of competition in wheelchair basketball and he must have made a singular achievement in the game. The non-competitor must meet the eligibility requirements of eight years of interest in wheelchair basketball, such as a coach, administrator, official, supporter or educator. Nominations for inductees may come from any member of the National Wheelchair Basketball Association (NWBA). After nominations for inductees are in, the NWBA Committee screens the applications and a final decision on the inductees is made by a five-member Executive Committee Board. Induction is held at the annual Victory Banquet NWBA Tournament usually held the last weekend in March or the first weekend in April. The inductees become lifetime, honorary members in the Hall of Fame.

1973 GERHARDT, Jack (dec). Competitor. *Also in:* Wheelchair Sports Hall of Fame.
JOHNSON, Bill. Competitor.
MILLER, Bob. Competitor.
NUGENT, Tim. Non-competitor. *Also in:* Wheelchair Sports Hall of Fame.
WILKINS, Alonzo "Willy" (dec). Competitor. *Also in:* Wheelchair Sports Hall of Fame.

1974 CHEVES, John Carl (dec). Competitor.
CLAY, Henry (dec). Competitor.
LIPTON, Benjamin H. Non-competitor. *Also in:* Wheelchair Sports Hall of Fame.
MARKOWSKI, Chris (dec). Competitor.

1975 CASH, Carl. Competitor.
CHURCHMAN, Russ. Non-competitor.
CLEM, Billy. Competitor.
GERARD, Earle. Competitor.

1976 DeDEO, Dan. Non-competitor.
JIACAPPO, Julius. Competitor.
WELGER, Saul. Competitor.

1977 CONN, George. Competitor and Non-competitor.
SLOOTSKY, Al. Competitor.

Simpson College Basketball Hall of Fame

INDIANOLA, IOWA

Mailing Address: Cold Center, Simpson College, 50125. *Tel.* (515) 961-6251, ext. 617. *Contact:* Larry Johnson, Dir. of Athletics. *Location:* 20 mi. S. of Des Moines, 107 mi. S.W. of Cedar Rapids, 130 mi. N.E. of Omaha, Nebr. *Admission:* Free 8 to 5 daily. *Nearby Halls of Fame:* Agriculture (Kansas City, Mo, 165 mi. S.W.), Roller Skating (Lincoln, Nebr, 180 mi. S.W.).

The Hall was founded in 1977 by alumni and coaches to honor Simpson College alumni who have excelled in basketball.

Members: 12 as of 1977. Two or three members are chosen each year by the Steering Committee for the Athletic Director. Inductees are honored at a luncheon; their photos and plaques are placed in the museum.

1977 BOWLES, Glen
BOWLES, Jack
BURNS, Wayne
DEATON, Les
FREY, Burt
KERR, Chuck
KUCHAN, Chuck
McGEE, Ralph
REED, Charles Mike
SCROGGS, Richard
SJEKLOCHA, Evo
TIDGREN, Robert

Texas High School Basketball Hall of Fame

ATHENS, TEXAS

Mailing Address: First National Bank of Athens, P.O. Box 751, 75751. *Tel.* (214) 675-8511. *Contact:* Linden Lewis, Pres. *Location:* Approx. 70 mi. S.E. of Dallas, 165 mi. N.W. of Houston. *Nearby Halls of Fame:* Police Service (Waco, 85 mi. S.W.), Sports (Natchitoches, La, 175 mi. S.E.), Ethnic Groups (Anadarko, Okla, 250 mi. N.W.).

Members: 25 as of 1975. Members are chosen annually from players of the last four decades, plus a deceased star. The selection is made by a statewide committee of sportswriters, and induction is in the spring.

1971 GRAY, Jack
MARTIN, Slater
PRICE, Ed
TOMPKINS, John "Preacher"
TUCKER, Temple

1972 BACCUS, Whitey
BRANNON, Buster
IZQUIERDO, Mike
MOERS, Bobby. *Also in:* College Basketball Hall of Fame, Citizens Savings Hall of Fame Athletic Museum.
WILLIAMS, Max

1973 BLACK, Leon
BROCK, Holly. *Also in:* Volleyball Hall of Fame, Citizens Savings Hall of Fame Athletic Museum.
CARSWELL, Frank
McDOWELL, Jewell
SUMNER, Doc

1974 ALFORD, Raymond
ARNETTE, Jay
FREIBERGER, Marcus
GOMEZ, Placid
LOUDERMILK, Jan

1975 BEASLEY, John
BOND, Jim
FORTENBERRY, Joe. *Also in:* Amateur Basketball Hall of Fame, Citizens Savings Hall of Fame Athletic Museum.
SLEDGE, C. E. "Red"
WEAVER, O'Neal

Basketball Halls of Fame to Watch

ARIZONA BASKETBALL HALL OF FAME AWARD

Merged into Arizona Sports Hall of Fame

Initially presented at annual banquets, the first of which was held on February 1, 1965, this Award is no longer a separate entity, but is given with other awards by the Arizona Sports Hall of Fame.

INDIANA PACERS HALL OF FAME

Founded in 1977

This Hall was founded in 1977 to honor Indiana Pacers players, and Freddie Lewis, captain, was selected as the first member. Members must be retired from basketball and will be honored at half-time ceremonies at the first game following their retirement. For further information contact Lee Daniels, 151 N. Delaware, Lower Concourse, Indianapolis IN 46204. (317) 632-3636.

INTERNATIONAL ASSOCIATION OF APPROVED BASKETBALL OFFICIALS BASKETBALL HALL OF FAME

Discontinued Hall of Fame

Formerly a Hall of Fame at Hagerstown, Md, this organization is now officially a Past President's Gallery. For further information contact Stewart Carol Paxton, Exec. Dir. IAABO. (301) 733-4107.

NATIONAL ASSOCIATION OF BASKETBALL COACHES OF THE UNITED STATES HALL OF FAME

Discontinued Hall of Fame

This Hall at Columbus, Ohio, no longer a separate entity, is now a standing committee of the NABC, founded 1927, which aids in the governing of the Naismith Memorial Basketball Hall of Fame. For further information contact Joseph R. Vancisin, NABC Exec. Secy, 18 Orchard Ave, Branford, CT 06405. (203) 488-1232.

BICYCLING

According to *Harper's Weekly*, "It is in rapidly moving considerable bodies of infantry that the bicycle will find its highest function in time of war." That was 81 years ago. A quarter of a century before that (1870) the Italian army had begun the trend by assigning four bicycles to each of its regiments. Cycling Austrian soldiers in full gear soon were able to travel 100 miles a day, which was far better than the cavalry could do. Field Marshal Sir Henry Evelyn Wood of Crimean, Indian, Zulu and Egyptian fame called for an English corps of 20,000 cyclists. The French army adopted a bicycle with a hinged frame that allowed it to be carried on a soldier's back. The United States army rigged a Colt rapid-fire machine gun onto the handlebars of a tricycle. It was all very serious and exciting when Lieutenant Whitney of the U.S. Military Wheelmen warned, "We are told somewhere that for want of a horseshoe nail a battle was lost. In the next war, for want of a bicycle the independence of a nation may be forfeited." A few years later, Cuba won its independence from Spain and in the various battles American forces made use of their regulation bicycles. Nonmilitary types were not, however, impressed. Five years after the 1895 publication of his book, *The Time Machine*, H. G. Wells ridiculed the whole military trend by publicly suggesting that a tail be attached to each officer's cycle, with "a horse head of moulded cardboard over the handle-bars." Nevertheless, bicycles continued to be used in warfare as late as World War II. Ernest Hemingway, for example, while serving with the Italian forces in World War I, was issued a bicycle to carry messages and important communiqués.

That great war-bicycle controversy was only one in a century-long series of conflicts over the bicycle. The whole thing began the same year Washington, D.C. was founded, when the Chevalier Mede de Sivrac had a crude bicycle—the world's first—built for him. His *célérifère* (fast feet) was a child's hobbyhorse with two wooden wheels attached. It had neither steering nor brakes. He sat on it and pushed with his feet through Paris' Palais Royal Garden. He even demonstrated his skill on it to Marie Antoinette. But she was beheaded three years later, and he was ridiculed. Once the French Revolution and Napoleon had passed, however, the bicycle came back, when Joseph Nicéphore Niepce rode a similarly awkward contraption through the Luxembourg Gardens. His had a carved eagle head on its front. Perhaps ridiculed, or himself unimpressed, he went on to other things—including the invention of heliography, by which he became the "Father of Photography." The Baron Karl Drais von Sauerbronn, a German forest warden, soon after this invented a hobbyhorse that could be steered by a pivoting front wheel. Sitting on its padded saddle and pushing, he made his inspections of the forest of which he was in charge. It could attain 9 m.p.h., a dangerous speed, and so was promptly banned in the Baron's home town. It was, however, more widely accepted than all earlier models had been. His *draisine*, in fact, was used by French postmen in the 1820s; Napoleonic Era playboys made a minor fad of it; a women's model, the *draisienne*, was even produced. But most people opposed it, like poet John Keats, who called it "the nothing of the day." An English coachmaker, Denis Johnson, later began his own line of "draisines." In the same year that both *Frankenstein* and the song "Silent Night" were written (1818), he opened a training salon where people could learn to ride his 50-pound "pedestrian curricles." Then someone announced that the continuous leg motions involved caused varicose veins, and Johnson went out of business. The following year (when *Rip Van Winkle* was written), however, the first such bicycles were imported into New York City. There they were called *velocipedes* (fast walkers). Three months later the Common Council passed a law "to prevent the use of velocipedes in the public places and on the sidewalks of the city of New York." And so it went, the on-going war between the two kinds of people in the world: those who bicycled, and everyone else.

In 1839 a Scottish blacksmith named Kirkpatrick Macmillan made a monumental breakthrough for the bicycle—he invented treadle propulsion. By attaching stirrup pedals to the front wheel of a draisine, he created the world's first bicycle that could be propelled and steered without foot contact with the ground. He thereafter quickly became known as "Daft Pate" Macmillan, the 29-year-old maniac blacksmith who liked to ride his "dandy horse" steering with one hand and holding a girl on his shoulder with the other. Stopped once by the law for riding on a footpath, he escaped legal action by treating the constable to a fancy riding demonstration. But the police did prosecute him on a later occasion, and fine him five shillings, "for furious diving on the road" which resulted in his knocking a child down with his 67-pound machine. Though legal and public opposition continued, Macmillan's breakthrough had assured the bicycle's survival.

In 1868 rubber tires replaced the wood and iron ones. The year 1869 saw the introduction of wire spokes, plus 71 other different patents for bicycle design and manufacture granted by the U.S. Patent Office. New models included ones operated by hand winches and others by ropes and pulleys, ones simultaneously pedaled and cranked or rowed by hand, and others in which the rider simply sat and steered while a dog raced in an attached squirrel cage to provide the power. Unicycles ten feet in diameter appeared, as did Boneshakers, Ordinaries (called "penny-farthings" in England) and Safeties. One inventor manufactured a line of five models consecutively called Psycha, Psyche, Psychi, Psycho and Psychy.

Despite such advances, opposition to the bicycle remained stronger than the support of it. An editorial in the London *Times* stated that "The human frame is designed for higher ends than being broken upon a wheel." Cyclists everywhere were refused service by restaurant and teashop owners. The English Highway and Railway Act Amendment of 1878 required a cyclist to pull off the road and stop whenever a horse-drawn vehicle appeared on the horizon. The League of American Wheelmen fought an eight-year court battle to win the right of cyclists to ride in New York's Central Park. Colonel Albert A. Pope, the largest bike manufacturer of the 1870s and 1880s, was only one of the hundreds of "scorchers" New York's police arrested for exceeding the 12 m.p.h. speed limit for cyclists. Horsemen (and later motorists) took pleasure in running cyclists off the road. A major reason early enthusiasts formed into clubs was to protect themselves against "wanton attacks upon cyclists." Some began carrying Ki-Yi guns, which were mace-like ammonia guns for use against both dogs and attacking people. The Sears, Roebuck and Company catalog for 1898 offered a line of collapsible bicycle rifles for cyclists' self-protection.

Then suddenly the opposition was gone. In 1888 a Scottish veterinary surgeon named John Boyd Dunlop invented a successful air-filled tire for which he coined the word "pneumatic." With that, the bicycle had evolved to the point that virtually all of its later developments were mere refinements. Seemingly all at once, 400 different bicycle manufacturers in America alone were producing bicycles. These included Henry Ford, Glenn Curtiss who later invented the seaplane, Charles Duryea who built the first successful gas-powered car in America, and the Wright Brothers. The price of a bicycle went down. The bicycle craze began.

Archaeologists understand the immense pathos in the few remains of an entire civilization that flourished as if it would go on forever, then died and now is distant past. So it was with the bicycle, which for a few brief years before the big wars and before the car made the whole English-speaking world its own. Millions of bikes were produced, two million in 1897 alone. Two years later, one in every six Americans owned one. What would amount to eight million dollars today was spent by Americans in 1896 on the marvelous new toy that had hit the market. "The cycle trade is now one of the chief industries of the world," *Outing* magazine reported that year. And cycling was without doubt the chief recreational diversion of the day in Canada, England and the United States. The iron horse had not quite replaced the horse, but the new two-wheeled steel steed did. Newspapers were crammed with cycling articles contributed by Stephen Crane and countless others. Luther H. Porter's *Cycling for Health and Pleasure,* published in 1895, was just one of a mass of books that praised bicycling as the only real means of maintaining complete health. Cycling clubs and leagues were the rage. Charles E. Pratt, "Cycling's Elder Statesman," wrote *The American Bicycler* (1881) which gave the first set of road signals ever devised in North America, rules for organizing clubs, standards of cycling dress and etiquette, and even the proper pretrip menu: "either a little bread and butter, a cup of coffee and a roll, or a glass of milk." The League of American Wheelmen (LAW) sponsored chapters in virtually every American and Canadian town big enough to have a hotel. Among its 102,636 members in 1898 were Orville and Wilbur Wright and Commodore Vanderbilt; Diamond Jim Brady, also a member, made news by giving Lillian Russell a pearl-handled bicycle encrusted with rubies, diamonds and sapphires. Crowds of 15,000 or more turned out for the frequent cycling events. When the Baron de Coubertin revived the Olympic Games in 1896, cycling was one of the main events and has been on the program ever since.

The world of 1894 cheered when American Annie Londonberry began her round-the-world bicycle ride. Everybody was in love with the new freedom machine. As nothing before had done, the bicycle allowed women to emerge from their kitchens and parlors. It emancipated them from their restrictive clothing by creating rational cycling dress. At last it was socially acceptable for these "velocipedestriennes" to meet men informally on casual rides. Cycling was even credited with stopping the declining marriage rate in England in the 1890s. Nobody cared when the Women's Rescue League (which also demanded that all bachelors be forced to marry) warned that bicycling had "helped more than any other media to swell the ranks of reckless girls." Every girl was a Gibson girl in fact or at heart. Everybody pedaled through the parks humming all the new cycle songs, like "Daisy."

When people weren't talking about the latest inventions—the ferris wheel and book matches, shredded wheat and corn flakes—or about new discoveries like X-rays, radium, helium and electrons, they talked about gear ratios and punctures. Marconi's wireless and Zeppelin's airships certainly gripped the world that decade, as did the new diesel motors, elevated railways, electric submarines and turbine-propelled ships. But nothing gripped and held those years of the Gay Nineties so completely as news of new bike records, or the pictures of a new electric bicycle lamp in an 1896 issue of *Scientific American.* Books that appeared in that decade *(The Prisoner of Zenda, Quo Vadis, The Red Badge of Cour-*

age, The Jungle Book, Resurrection, Dracula) were to be read only when rain prevented cycling. Kids too young to ride at the time but anxious to do so included Hemingway, Agatha Christie, Boris Pasternak and Alfred Hitchcock. *Century Magazine* published a short story entitled "Madame Butterfly," which later was made into a play; Oscar Wilde's *Salomé,* Tchaikovsky's *Pathetic Symphony,* Guiseppe Verdi's *Falstaff* and Englebert Humperdinck's *Hänsel und Gretel* all were performed for the first time that decade. Yet in 1896 theatrical performances in the United States were way down, the watch and jewelry business fell almost to zero, piano sales were cut in half and book sales dropped—all while bicycling boomed.

Then came the Model T, the Wright brothers' airplane and countless other new toys. Abruptly the bicycle was neither new nor exciting. After all, everyone had one. As World War I neared, there were airplanes and tanks to be for or against. Soon cars were exceeding 100 m.p.h. And so the cycle set became the car set, later to become the jet set. After 600 professional American cyclists in 1895, there are none today among the over 100 million North American inheritors of that whole cycling civilization. Quite suddenly, the Golden Age was over.

Or perhaps it never really existed. In the minds of those who lived it, that decade was "now," and the present is always full of new things, some excitement, and much that should be changed. We today are the ones who called those years the "Gay Nineties." For proof we point to its remains—old newspaper articles, scattered artifacts, and the memories of those over 80. But 80-year-olds were young then. Like all young, they could not have realized how nice their world actually was. Just as we, in lionizing then, can miss much of the nice that is now's.

FORMS: A bicycle (from the Latin *bi,* "two," plus the Greek *kyklos,* "wheel" or "circle") consists of two wheels mounted one behind the other on a metal frame and propelled by the rider's feet pushing two pedals around in circles. Bicycle sizes are based on the diameter of the wheel. The main sizes in the United States are 14, 16, 20, 24, 26, and 27 inches; in metric countries the main sizes are 50, 52, 54, 56, 58, 60, and 62 centimeters. Manufacturers make three basic types of bike: lightweight—from 21–35 lbs. with 5, 10 or 15 speeds; middleweight—35–45 lbs.; and specialty—high-risers and tandems, the largest of which ever made was a 305 lb. ten-seater that was 23 ft. long. Lightweight models are normally used for the various cycling sports.

The two chief kinds of bicycle race organized by the Amateur Bicycle League of America and similar organizations are Track Races and Road Races. Track Races, the most popular kind, are staged between two individuals or between two teams on oval tracks. These tracks, which measure from 1/10 to 1/4 mi. are banked up to 55° at the curved ends. Races are run counterclockwise either for a specified distance (.25–100 mi.) or against the clock (up to one hour). Track bikes must be exceptionally light (18–20 lbs.) and therefore have neither gears nor brakes. There are six types of Track Races in world championship competition: sprint races, tandem sprints, motor-paced sprints (paced by a motorcycle, the cyclist can attain 50 m.p.h.), 1000-meter time trials, individual pursuits, and team pursuits. World records in track racing are kept for nine basic distances and times, for both indoor and outdoor tracks and, in Europe, for both amateurs and professionals—in other words, for 36 separate categories. Other nonworld championship track events include Madison racing, devil-take-the-hindmost, handicap races, point-to-point, Australian pursuits, Omnium (total points for four or five events), grass-track races, cycle speedway races, scratch races, and six-day races. The latter were especially popular in the bicycle's so-called Golden Agę, through the first few decades of this century, and again in recent years. The first six-day race was held in London in 1878. The contestants rode 1060 mi. on Ordinaries, those bicycles with the huge front wheel and the tiny rear one. The first six-day race in America was held at Madison Square Garden in 1891. William "Plugger Bill" Martin won it by riding 1466 miles and four laps in 142 hours. By 1915, six-day races were being staged in Philadelphia, Buffalo, Toronto and Chicago. They were discontinued at Madison Square Garden in 1939 but revived there in 1961.

Road Races, the second chief kind of bicycle racing, are more popular than track events in Europe, where bicycling has long been the de facto national sport of Italy, France, Spain and Belgium. They are held between unlimited numbers of contestants on any suitable surface except tracks, usually public highways. They may be for distances of from 20 to 3000 mi. and last up to 24 days. The bikes usually weigh from 22 to 24 lbs. and have as few as 24 spokes per wheel although 36 is normal. The main types of Road Race are stage races where each stage counts as an event in itself, one-day races, criteriums (circuit races through the closed streets of a town) and kermesses (shorter circuit races), motor-paced races, road records and time-trialing in which the amateur and professional classic is the Grand Prix des Nations. The best known Road Race in the world is the annual Tour de France, although the Giro d'Italia is also famous. In Canada the best-known Road Race is the annual 170 mi. Quebec–Montreal Race. In the United States the Tour of Somerville, New Jersey (50 mi.) is the best-known Road Race.

In both Track and Road Races a rider wears dark-colored racing shorts and a padded crash helmet. Shoes with metal insets laminated between the layers of the soles may also be worn. A complete contingent of officials will include a chief judge with one or more assistants, timekeepers, machine examiners, lap scorers, starters, a chief commissaire (steward) with at least one assistant commissaire, and pacing marshals.

Other cycling events are numerous. There are special track races, stationary races on sets of rollers, cyclo-crosses (in winter over the open countryside, especially around Chicago), hill climbs, time trials, and speed records (140.5 m.p.h. was attained behind a 1955 Chevy on the Bonneville Salt Flats in 1973). An American coast-to-coast record of 103½ days was set in 1884 on an Ordinary bicycle. This record was reduced in 1954 to 14 days and in 1973 to 13 days. Among the many games played on bicycles are Bicycle Polo (bikes are used in place of ponies) which is so popular that it is an event in the annual Asian Games, and Cycle Ball (an indoor game played by two teams of six bicycle riders) which is so popular that world championships are held. A form of cycling little appreciated by most Westerners is practiced by thousands of Asians, the *jinrikisha* drivers. These tricycle taxis, sometimes incorrectly called "rickshas," were first used in Japan in 1870. Curiously, this was twenty years before the dawn of the decade which we have come to call the Golden Age of Bicycling.

ORGANIZATION: The first cycling club in the world was the Pickwick Bicycle Club of London. The oldest bicycle club in North America opened in Montreal in 1878. Two opened in Boston and in Bangor, Maine earlier that same year but were later discontinued. In 1884 the Ladies Tricycle Club of New York was the "only ladies' club" in the city. Throughout their existence, these clubs and the scores of other cycling clubs and organizations have not only encouraged cycling but have also been directly responsible for considerable social improvement. The first payment ever made under law by any state for highway construction, for example, came about as a direct result of cyclists' demands for better roadways. They also encouraged the construction and refinement of early hotels. The Amateur Bicycle League of America and the *Association Cycliste Canadienne* (Canadian Cycling Federation) are the governing bodies of amateur and competetive cycling in the United States and Canada, respectively. Above them is the *Union Cycliste Internationale,* the world governing body headquartered in Geneva. Below them are the various organizations, associations, leagues and clubs that have members in virtually every village, town and city.

American Bicycle Hall of Fame

STATEN ISLAND, NEW YORK

Mailing Address: Richmondtown Restoration, 10306. Tel. (212) 351-1611. *Contact*: Ronald Geist, Secy. *Location*: Approx. 10 mi. S. of New York City. *Admission*: 2 to 5 Tuesday-Saturday, closed holidays. Donation requested. *Personnel*: Loring McMillen, Dir; Ronald Geist, Secy. *Nearby Halls of Fame*: Heritage, Music (New York City), Harness Racing (Goshen, 70 mi. N.W.), Baseball (Cooperstown, 160 mi. N.W.), Flight (Elmira, 175 mi. N.W.), Horse Racing (Saratoga Springs, 155 mi. N.), Ice Skating (Newburgh, 40 mi. N.).

Officials from the Century Road Club Association began collecting items and soliciting funds in 1958 for the American Bicycle Hall of Fame. On June 2, 1968, the dream became a reality with ceremonies at a temporary site. A permanent hall and museum are planned on the Richmondtown Restoration grounds. Loring McMillen, Director of the Staten Island Historical Society, contributed a $50,000 land grant on which a two-room structure will be built. The new Hall will continue to honor not only extraordinary cyclists, but also artists, writers, officials, and promoters who have benefited cycling as a sport and hobby. Present exhibits include the world's tallest unicycle (32 ft. high), a Gay Nineties bicycle shop complete with oil lamps and tools, and bicycles from three original wooden-wheel boneshakers dating from 1869. The late Sylvain Segal's Syls Racing Columbia of 1900 and Thomas Stevens' high-wheel Columbia, which he rode around the world in the nineteenth century, grace the museum. Copies of *Sporting Magazine, American Bicyclist,* and *Bicycle Journal* line the displays. The Old Home Day celebration occurs the third Sunday in October. A parade and exhibitions of fancy unicycling by the American Unicycling Association and high-wheel formation riding by The Wheelmen highlight the day's activities. Donations from individuals and contributions from organizations finance the Hall and Museum which are administered by the Board of Governors.

Members: 17 as of 1976. Any interested cyclist may nominate a candidate by sending that individual's record of achievement to the Director. The Board meets annually and selects one or two of the nominees.

1959

PENNELL, Joseph
Artist

Born July 4, 1857, in Philadelphia; descendant of Quakers from Nottinghamshire, England; married Elizabeth Robins June 1884; died April 23, 1926, at 69.

Joseph spent many childhood hours alone, practicing what would later be called etching. He studied for a time at the Pennsylvania Academy of Fine Arts and took evening classes at the Pennsylvania School of Industrial Art. After leaving school, Joseph immediately sold some of his drawings to *Scribner's Monthly.* He met Elizabeth when he was commissioned to do eight etchings with the text written by her. They sailed to London in July 1884 and decided to ride a tandem to Canterbury, stopping to etch and write. The product of this tour was *A Canterbury Pilgrimage* published in 1885. Later tours followed this pattern as they captured art, life and beauty. They settled permanently in Europe and Joseph continually experimented with new techniques of photo-engraving, lithography, and illustrations.

1960

MURPHY, Charles W. "Mile-a-Minute"
Cyclist

Born 1871, died February 17, 1950 in New York City at age 79; a career New York City motorcycle patrolman.

Charles "Mile-a-Minute" Murphy was the first man to pedal a bicycle one mile in less than one minute. On June 30, 1899, Murphy set a new world's record of a mile in 57 4/5 seconds behind a Long Island Railroad train. This record held until 1941. The reason for the match was to prove the value of streamlining cycles. From this experience, Murphy wrote a booklet, *A Story of the Railroad and a Bicycle.* The village of Farmingdale, N.Y, commemorated Charles Murphy in 1938 with a day-long festival.

1961

ZIMMERMAN, Authur A. "Zimmie"
Cyclist
Born July 11, 1869, in Camden, N.J; world record in the half-mile 1891; World Sprint Champion 1893; Champion of England 1893; American Amateur Sprint Champion 1893; died 1936.

A. A. Zimmerman started racing in 1880 on the high-wheel Ordinary. A natural athlete who openly flaunted all training rules, Zimmie never attempted to beat a record or win a race with more effort than was necessary. Yet he established a world record in the half-mile and won the first world championship race at the Columbian Exposition in Chicago. Sometimes referred to as the bicyclist champion, the "Flying Yankee" or "King of the Wheel," one English correspondent wrote "all eyewitnesses agree cycling has never seen and will never see his like again."

1963

POPE, Colonel Albert Augustus
Promoter
Born May 20, 1843, in Boston, Mass; son of Charles and Elizabeth Bogman Pope; married Abbey Linder; 6 children; died September 10, 1909, at age 66, in Cohasset, Mass.

Because of financial misfortunes, Albert had to work after school and during holidays and eventually withdrew from Brookline High School at the age of 15. Discharged as a colonel following the Civil War, Pope opened a manufacturing company in Hartford, producing shoes and small mechanical parts. At the Philadelphia Centennial Exposition in 1876, Pope saw his first bicycle. He went to England and studied it, returning to the United States and investing all his resources in a bicycle craze he created and captured. Enlarging his plant, Pope lobbied tirelessly for public acceptance of the bicycle, waging a vigorous campaign for equal access to parks and boulevards. Yet Pope's interest went beyond the manufacturing of bicycles into campaigns for safety races and the founding of the League of American Wheelmen and the Boston Bicycle Club. He persuaded the military to accept bicycles which, in turn, necessitated road improvement. With his financial backing and social influence, road engineering was introduced into the curriculum at M.I.T. The father of bicycle manufacturing and a pioneer for better roads, A. A. Pope made the bicycle an American institution. *Harper's Weekly* wrote, "the history of American bicycle without mention of A. A. Pope would be almost as incomplete as the Book of Genesis without reference to Adam." Pope moved into automobile manufacturing but the delay in the development of the auto forced him to reorganize his finances, hastening his death.

PRATT, Charles E.
Organizer, Promoter and Author
Born in Boston, died 1885.

Probably the most articulate spokesman in the attempt to forge public acceptance of the "birotate chariot," Charles E. Pratt was the elder statesman of cycling. Elected the first president of the League of American Wheelmen, he helped organize "The Wheel Around the Hub" tour of Boston. Despite his efforts and those of many others, public resistance to equal access to roads and parks for bicyclists continued to increase. To aid the cyclist who was often roughed up by pranksters, Pratt wrote a handbook, *The American Bicycler.* Within the handbook is the first set of road signals ever devised in America: when a driver's arm was upraised the cyclist should use caution in passing and if the arm was pumped several times the cyclist should dismount immediately for the horse had the bit in his mouth. For those organizing clubs, Pratt provided a model constitution, bylaws, and procedures for electing officials and the captain who was responsible for touring discipline. Even dress and etiquette were prescribed with a pretrip breakfast of "either a little bread and butter, a cup of coffee and a roll, or a glass of milk." Pratt was described by *The Wheelman* in October 1882: "[his] encyclopedic, accurate and scientific knowledge of all matters pertaining to the wheel has made him the highest American authority upon cycling matters."

1965

KRAMER, Frank L.
Cyclist
Born 1880; lived in East Orange, N.J; father Louis an amateur wrestler; American Amateur Sprint Champion 1898 and 1899; U.S. National Sprint Champion 1901–1916, 1918 and 1921; Grand Prix of Paris 1906; World Champion Sprinter 1912; died 1958.

Described by many writers and spectators as the greatest American bicycle racer ever, Frank L. Kramer competed for 27 continuous years, winning his last professional race in the New Jersey Velodrome at the age of 42. His terrific finishing kick enabled him to win 6 Six-Day Races. The indefatigable Kramer retired in 1922 although he later made an exhibition appearance in the New York Velodrome.

1966

GAST, Margaret
Cyclist
Born 1876 in Germany; Century Road Club of America member 1893; four world records in 1900: 500 mi. in 44: 45; 1000 mi. in 99: 55; 2000 mi. in 222: 5.5; 2600 mi. in 295: 55; died 1968 in Pawling, NY.

The champion woman cyclist of the world from 1890 to 1910, Margaret Gast immigrated to America from Germany about 1890. By profession a nurse, she spent her leisure hours in long distance training under the guidance of Centurion Sylvain Segal of the Century Road Club. After seven years of arduous training, she established four world records that still stand today. In 1906, the French female champion challenged Margaret to a match race in the velodrome at Madison Square Garden. Margaret won the race, but her bicycle was dismembered and her clothing shredded by overzealous supporters. In later years she moved into motor racing and established records in that field also. Retiring to Pawling, N.Y, Margaret Gast remained physically active and mentally acute until her death.

1967

TAYLOR, Marshall W. "Major"
Cyclist

Born November 26, 1878, in Indianapolis, Ind; son of a coachman, one of eight children, five girls and three boys; lived a strict regimen with no drinking and no smoking; wrote poetry; set three records in 1891 which still stand; tied for National Champion 1897; World Sprint Champion 1899; set records in ¼, ⅓, ½, ⅔, ¾, 1, 2-mile sprints 1899; U.S. National Champion 1900; died July 6, 1932, in Worcester, Mass.

Marshall Taylor was the first black to receive national recognition and acclaim before the color line was broken in professional sports. He began as a trick rider but switched to racing in the late 1880s. Moving from Indianapolis to Worcester in 1893, Major won consistently in Massachusetts and New Jersey. Changing sponsorship in 1898, he moved into Wisconsin winning all the Green Bay contests plus the one-mile sprint in Ashbury. Despite the foul play and handicaps forced upon him, he continued winning and in 1899 set records in every sprint distance. Major was declared national champion in 1900 after two previous championship titles were denied him by officials' conspiracy. Major Taylor is the only black to win European and American champion titles in bicycle racing. After racing in Europe from 1901 to 1904, he returned to the United States and discovered racing fading from the scene. His autobiography, *The Fastest Bicycle Rider in the World,* is distinctive for its lack of resentment toward the racial intolerance and racing chicanery directed at him.

WHITE, Dr. Paul Dudley
Promoter and Writer

Born June 6, 1886, in Roxbury, Mass; parents Herbert Warren and Elizabeth A. (Dudley); married Ina Reid; 2 children, Penelope Dudley and Alexander Warren; died October 31, 1973, in Boston at 87.

A graduate of Harvard Medical School (1911), Dr. White was a world-renowned cardiologist and cycling enthusiast. The first president of the Bicycle Hall of Fame, Dr. White urged all those who lead sedentary lives to pedal for moderate exercise. Although his initial interest in cardiovascular diseases was prompted by his sister's death from rheumatic fever, Dr. White cycled daily and realized the effects of cycling exercise on cardiovascular development. He pioneered safe-cycling campaigns, opened the first modern cycle path on Nantucket Island on June 11, 1960, and authored *Cycling in the School Fitness Program.* This evangelist for health-through-cycling commented in later years that he still clicked five or ten miles a day whenever he could.

1969

SMITH, Elizabeth Bacheler "Isabel"
Contributor

Born in New England; daughter of a minister; married Monroe W. Smith in 1924; three children, Elizabeth, Stephen and Jonathan; retired schoolteacher; resides in Orleans, Mass.

Isabel Smith's lifelong interest in nature and youth first found expression in field service with the Girl Scouts. Later with her husband, she devoted herself to the American Youth Hostel (AYH) which provides low cost accommodations for bicyclists and hikers. In 1933, while chaperoning 17 boys and girls through Europe in cooperation with the International Friendship Group of Columbia University, Isabel and Monroe learned of the youth hostel program. For the remainder of the year they studied the organization of hostels, bike trails and foot paths, and attended the International Conference in Godesburg, Germany. The following year they returned to Europe with 35 students, hosteling in Germany, Austria, Switzerland and Holland. After attending the International Conference in London, at which the American Youth Hostel was recognized as the 18th member of the International Youth Hostel Association, the Smiths opened the first AYH in Northfield, Mass, on December 27, 1934. Isabel designed the poster for AYH which is still used today. Isabel Smith described hosteling as "born of our love and work" and the results must have been gratifying. By 1937 AYH had spread to ten states with 100-plus hostels. The hostels, usually 15 miles apart, were within reach for hiker, horseback rider, canoeist, biker, skier. Isabel perceived AYH as immune from political and religious involvements, simply providing a "roomy, airy, sunny" respite for youth.

SMITH, Monroe William
Cyclist and Contributor

Born January 2, 1901, in Sunderland, Mass; married Elizabeth Bacheler in 1924; three children, Elizabeth, Stephen and Jonathan; first taught in a one-room Friends School in Germantown, Pa, then in military academies in Peekskill, N.Y. and Montclair, N.J; served as a Boy Scout executive in Rochester, N.Y. in early 1930s; national director of American Youth Hostels 1934–1949; taught in Florida public school system 1949–1971; died December 8, 1972 at DelRay Beach, Fla.

As a young boy, Monroe W. Smith traversed the Rockies with only a knapsack. This "spirit of Columbus," as his mother called it, took him to such adventures as scaling Pike's Peak and swimming in Lake Odessa; she expressed concern that he had to sleep in the open. Spurred by those maternal concerns and his hosteling in Europe in 1934, Monroe Smith set upon a lifetime goal of building a system of low-cost accommodations for youth, the American Youth Hostel (AYH). The nucleus began in December, 1934, at the Chateau annex of the Northfield Inn in Northfield, Mass. The following year a house was purchased on the main street for headquarters and staff. The barn and carriage shed served as the actual hostel. During his 15-year tenure as national director of AYH, the organization developed with field staffs and regional councils. In 1945 Smith led the first bicycle party over the Pan American highway. In 1946, at the invitation of the Ministries of Education of Holland, France and Luxembourg, he led an American group abroad to repair the war-stricken hostels. Throughout his illustrious career he symbolized fellowship and goodwill. Monroe Smith resigned as national director of AYH in 1949 and initiated another dream in Youth Argosy, a system of inexpensive transportation. Memorial to his work is found on the AYH National Campus, Delaplane, Va.

STEVENS, Thomas
Cyclist and Author
Born 1854 in England; died 1935.

When Thomas Stevens decided to cycle across America in 1884, there were no bikeways to smooth the journey; accommodations were meager and few; and the roads were unevenly marked. His high-wheel ordinary, which weighed 75 lbs, lacked maneuverability and seemed designed more for causing headers than for completing cycling tours. Undaunted, Stevens rode from Oakland to Boston in 103.5 days. Riding seems a misnomer when one considers the trickery of resentful passersby, the streams across which the high-wheeler had to be carried, and the rough and uncharted roads. Cowboys forced Stevens to ride between and around billiard tables; boatmen scorned him as their mules reared and kicked. Stevens was helpless going downhill on mountain slopes when his brake spoons heated. From Chicago to Boston Stevens was well received and feted royally. He chronicled all these incidents in *First Across America by Bicycle.* Later, the League of American Wheelmen sponsored him on a worldwide journey and, after two years of cycling, Stevens proclaimed he had "ridden everywhere there was land." His global adventures were published in a two-volume book titled *Around the World on a Bicycle;* Vol. I, *From San Francisco to Teheran*; Vol. II, *From Teheran to Yokohama.*

1970

JACOBSON, Adolph R. "Jake"
Cyclist and Official
Born 1890; died 1953.

A. R. Jacobson was one of the most influential organizers of amateur cycling. Before his founding of the Amateur Bicycle League of America (ABLA) in 1920, the National Cycling Association (NCA) governed both professional and amateur cycling. Jacobson felt the NCA ignored the needs of amateur cyclists; specifically, there was need for a nationwide organization of chapters promoting competition as well as regulating equipment and emphasizing the necessity of excellent health. The ABLA was well received. In 1920 Jacobson supervised the Olympic Road Racing trials at Long Island. He also initiated and sponsored a road-racing program for amateurs in New York City on the Old Potham Parkway. In January 1977 the ABLA became the United States Cycling Federation with more than 120 chapters nationwide.

1971

McELMURY, Audrey
Cyclist
Born January 24, 1943; married to Mike Levonas; one child, Ian; 25-Mile Scratch Champion in 1:4.44 April 1966; Women's Amateur Pursuit Champion 1966, 1969 and 1970; Women's Amateur Road Champion 1966 and 1970; Outdoor Banked Track record of 60:28.4 July 12, 1969, with the distance for one hour of 24 mi. 4098 ft. 9 in; Women's Amateur Sprint Champion 1969; World Champion Road Racer 1969; living in San Bruno, Calif, in hotel and restaurant business.

The holder of several U.S. records, Audrey McElmury is one of only two Americans ever to win a gold medal in international competition, which she captured seven seconds off the front after crashing in the rain. The successful Italian CBM team extended her an invitation following this victory, and she joined them, winning eight races while assisting in coaching. During her tenure with CBM she learned the team tactics of discipline. Now semiretired, Audrey continues to ride and divides her time between training and coaching. She and her husband write a column in *Velo-news,* a cycling magazine.

1972

SMALL, Frank
Cyclist
Born 1896; died 1971.

A prominent member of the Amateur Bicycle League of America (ABLA), Frank Small served as its president and secretary. He also edited the ABLA publication *Bicycling Magazine,* providing touring and racing information. He was a lifelong member of the Acme Wheelmen of New York. In 1920 Small qualified for the Olympic Bicycle Team, earning the comment from his coach: "He did well in the races in spite of his lack of time to familiarize himself with the Antwerp Olympic track." Later, he served on the Olympic Cycling Committee.

1974

HOWARD, John
Cyclist
Born August 6, 1947 in Springfield, Mo; married 1971; attended Southwest Missouri State Univ, majoring in sculpture; military service; National Road Champion 1968, 1972, 1973, and 1975; Pan American Road Race Gold Medalist 1971; Trans-Peninsular Tour 1975; National Time Trial Champion 1976; lives in Austin, Tex; dislikes aspirin advertising, loud salesmen, war and smog.

In the Ozark Mountains, the Mark Twain National Forest offers the avid cyclist over fifty different routes. With such a natural and ideal training facility, John Howard began his cycling career, averaging 300 to 400 miles a week. To develop and strengthen his physique, he also participated in swimming and running. Withdrawing from school to compete in the 1968 Olympics, he lost his student deferment and found himself drafted in 1970. He earned a spot on the U.S. Army Bicycle Racing Team, and was eventually described as the "finest racing cyclist" on the team. In 1971 John Howard became one of only two Americans to win a gold medal in international competition at the Pan American Games. He is America's most recognized international cyclist.

1977

YOUNG, Sheila
Cyclist
Born 1951 in Detroit; married Jim Ochowicz August 1976; Women's American Sprint Champion 1971; World

Sprint Champion 1973; Second in World Cycling Championship 1974; Women's World Sprint Champion 1976. Sheila Young was the first American woman to win a gold medal in the World Track Championships held in San Sebastian, Spain, 1973. Although nominated for the Bicycle Hall of Fame she has not been officially inducted. She has received the final approval of the board of governors.

BILLIARDS

"To play billiards well is a sign of a mis-spent youth," said the philosopher-social scientist Herbert Spencer. So seem to have thought a majority of Americans whose apathy or opposition to the sport ended its Golden Age. For some four decades from the 1890s to the 1930s billiard matches were headline news. Today professional competition in billiards is extinct almost everywhere. Yet we are indebted to billiards for an exciting sport of skill and technique: "A most genteel, cleanly and ingenious game," according to Charles Cotton who, in 1674, wrote *The Compleat Gamester,* the first book in English to describe billiards. We are also indebted to billiards for the whole plastics industry.

In 1863, the year West Virginia became the 35th state, Phelan and Collander, a major manufacturer of billiard equipment, announced a competition. The $10,000 prize would go to anyone who could develop an adequate substitute for the traditional elephant tusk ivory billiard ball. At the end of a five-year search for such a billiard ball an Albany, New York, printer named John Wesley Hyatt and his brother Isaiah invented and patented "artifical ivory," which was also called xylonite and later celluloid. This was the first artificial plastic material to receive wide commercial use. They themselves used it in the manufacture of dental plates. Their prize-winning processes both created a superior ball and began a major industry.

People were always inventing better billiard tables, too. Early ones had obstacles that gave the game a military flavor. It was even called "the fortification game" and had hoops or arches to shoot the ball through along with ivory pegs or "kings" plus pieces representing forts and batteries to be circumvented. In 1571, two years after Gerard Mercator published his famous map of the world, an artist named DeVigne designed a rectangular billiard table with pockets at each corner and one in the middle. The French king Henri III had a fine triangular table installed at his chateau in Blois around 1575. By 1800 the game was in its present form although, according to the first book in English devoted wholly to billiards (published in 1807 by E. White), the tables were not. Until the famous billiard equipment manufacturer John Thurston introduced the slate bed in 1836, table tops were felt-covered wood. While teaching math at Oxford, Charles Lutwidge Dodgston—better known by his pen name, Lewis Carroll—wrote a two-page leaflet to explain his rules for a circular billiard table he had conceived and built. Specially designed circular billiard tables today help train U.S. fighter pilots. In the wonderland of his own mind, Dodgson was also fascinated by the notion of three-dimensional billiards played weightlessly in a cube. Not until the 1850s were standarized pocketless tables being produced. At first they were made by piano manufacturers. By the 1870s tables with and without pockets like those used today had become common; after another two decades the Golden Age of the game began in the Gay Nineties.

In 1906 an 18-year-old American, Willie "Mr. Billiards" Hoppe, against incredible odds, defeated the 73-year-old master Maurice Vignaux in the first of his 51 world championship victories. On Hoppe's return home, 4000 people watched his first match. He was later invited to give a command performance on one of the most famous of all billiard tables—the one in the White House billiard room, where presidents from John Quincy Adams to Lincoln to Teddy Roosevelt had played against guests like Mark Twain.

The name of the game comes from the French word *bille* meaning stick, as does the English word billy club. Early cues were in fact heavy mallets called maces whose large ends were used to hit the ball. Later cues were reversed so that the large end was held, but the ball still had to be struck dead center. The slippery tip could not be used to give a ball "English" (spin). Still later, players roughened their cue tips by rubbing them up against whitewashed ceilings. Not until 1806 did a Frenchman, Mingaud, discover the usefulness of chalk. A second Frenchman, Mangin, invented a leather cue tip in 1823, with which the cue attained its modern form. A similar evolution occurred in the ball: from crude, irregular spheres of stone, leather or metal (an ancient Irish king's legacy included 50 brass billiard balls) to African elephant tusk ivory balls to modern balls made possible by the Hyatts' invention.

No one knows when billiards began nor how accurate are the accounts of a similar game by the sixth century B.C. traveler, Prince Anacharsis of Scythia. Nor does anyone know whether the Egyptians played billiards as Shakespeare implied in *Anthony and Cleopatra* when he wrote, "Let's to billiards: come, Charmian." It may in fact have developed out of a fifteenth-century English alley game called pall-mall for which the famous street in London is named, because it was played there. All that is definitely known is that it is ancient and that it was always a favorite game of royalty. Elizabeth I was accomplished with a cue, as is the present Queen Mother. One of the disappointments of being in prison for Mary, Queen of Scots, was that her billiard table was taken away. Louis XIV, the Sun King, was advised by his physician to play billiards each day after dinner. Both Washington and Jefferson were avid players. King Edward VII was taught the game by the great George F. Slosson, whose other pupils included President Grant, Henry Ward Beecher, Robert G. Ingersoll, Charles A. Dana, John McGraw and Mark Twain.

How it arrived in the New World is similarly unknown, though Spaniards very likely introduced it. Unlike most other sports, billiards in the United States was developed almost totally by the major manufacturers of its equipment. A merger of these companies created the Billiard Trust, which dominated the game completely by staging the championships and signing the leading players to its payroll. This led to various kinds of corruption. Nearly 20 years before the first national match held on April 12, 1859 in Detroit, Abel Pierson wrote: "There is no amusement which could be contrived, better suited to improve the shape of females, by calling into action all the muscles of the back, than the game of billiards. But this game has unfortunately come into bad repute, from being the game resorted to by profligate men of pleasure, to destroy each other's health and pick each other's pockets." Billiards became wildly popular in the United States and Canada. The first tournament for the Championship of America was held in New York City in June 1863. The first billiard championship in Canada was staged a year later in Toronto. By the time of the 1925 Chicago Tournament, billiards had reached its zenith in the United States. A Saturday evening Willie Masconi match in those days drew more spectators than a Sunday afternoon Chicago Bears football game. Masconi was the technical advisor to Paul Newman and Jackie Gleason for the movie *The Hustler.* But like many things, institutions and people, billiards never quite recovered from the Great Depression.

FORMS: In all variations of billiards, an ivory or composition ball (the cue ball) is stroked with a slender stick (the cue) so that it successively hits other balls, which in some variations drop into pockets to win points. The four main varieties on this basic theme are Pocket Billiards, also called Pool, with 15 colored, numbered balls and one white cue ball; Snooker with 15 variously colored balls, 6 red balls, and one white cue ball; English Billiards with three balls—one red, two white; and Carom, also called Cannon or French Billiards, with three balls—one red, two white. Of these four, the first three are played on tables with six pockets. The ancestor game, Carom, in which the sole object is to attain a specified number of points by causing the cue ball to strike one or both of the object balls, is played on the true pocketless table.

Though regular Pool is the most popular of these games in the United States, numerous derivative games also are played including: Balking; Straight Rail; 3-Cushion Carom; Fifteen Ball; 14.1 Pocket Billiards; Rotation or Chicago; Eight Ball; Baseball Pocket Billiards; Golf Pocket Billiards; Bottle Pocket Billiards; Russian Pool, also called Indian Pool, Slosh, or Toad-in-the-road; Cowboy; Cribbage; Forty-one; Line-up; Mr. and Mrs.; Nine Ball; One and Nine Balls; One Pocket; Pill Pool, or Kelly Pool; and Poker Pocket Billiards. Some of these derivatives themselves have derivative games. Each of these, however, has its own rules, number of players (usually two individuals or two pairs), traditions and objects of play. In practically all, the essential elements are a table with pockets, a cue, a cue ball and a number of object balls.

The table dimensions will vary according to the game, although a table will always be approximately twice as long as wide. In the United States tables are usually 5 ft. by 10 ft. and 31 in. high. The slate or synthetic surface is covered by a tight felt or feltlike material that is usually green but can be any other color. It is bounded by vulcanized rubber cushions which are 1¾ in. high and felt-covered. Into these cushions six pockets are cut, with entrances about 5 in. wide. The two side pocket entrances are slightly wider. The average cue is 57 in. long, less than half an inch wide at the narrow tip and weighs from 14 to 22 oz. The best butts are of Brazilian rosewood, the best shafts of domestic rock maple and the best tips of East Indian deer antler. Balls are 2¼ in. in diameter in Pool and 2⅜ in. in Carom. They weigh between 5½ and 6 oz. Accessories include chalk cubes, a triangle for racking the balls and long-handled mechanical bridges for awkward shots.

ORGANIZATION: The world body for amateur billiards competition is the *Union Mondiale de Billiard* headquartered in Brussels, Belgium. Its American affiliate is the Billiard Federation of the United States of America, which conducts the annual U.S. Open Pocket Billiards Championships. The Billiard Congress of America, the Professional Pool Players Association and the Billiard and Bowling Institute of America (manufacturers) are only a few of the other important organizations in the sport.

Billiard Congress of America Hall of Fame

CHICAGO, ILLINOIS

Mailing Address: 717 N. Michigan Ave, 60611. Tel. (312) 944-0246. *Contact:* Bob Goodwin, Managing Dir. *Location:* On Lake Michigan near Grant Park, the Navy Pier and Northwestern University; N.E. of junction of Interstates 90 and 94. *Personnel:* Paul Lucchesi, Pres; James Wilhem, V.Pres; Bob Goodwin, Managing Dir. Not open to the public. *Nearby Halls of Fame:* Business (Chicago), Bowling, Sports (Milwaukee, Wis, 87 mi. N.W.), Auto Racing, Basketball (Indianapolis, Ind, 181 mi. S.E.).

The Hall of Fame was founded in 1965 by the Billiard Congress of America. This nonprofit organization maintains the historical accuracy of the game's records, collects and preserves items of memorabilia, and bestows honor upon those who have achieved greatness in the game of billiards. This Hall is not open to the public, but information is available through the Association's publication *Official Rules and Record Book;* price $1.95. Members of the Hall are chosen annually and receive a plaque to honor the occasion.

Members: 15 as of 1977. Only one, Jimmy Caras, is still living. Nominees to the Hall of Fame are chosen annually by the selection committee and approved by the Board of Directors. Induction takes place during July.

1965 – 1977

CARAS, Jimmy. *Also in:* Professional Pool Players Association Hall of Fame.

COCHRAN, Welher

DeORO, Alfredo

GREENLEAF, Ralph

HOPPE, William F.

HYATT, John Wesley

LAYTON, Johnny

MASCONI, Willy

NARTZIK, Benjamin B.

PETERSON, Charles C.

RAMOW, Herman J.

SCHAEFER, Jake, Jr.

SCHAEFER, Jake, Sr.

TABERSKI, Frank

WORST, Harold

Professional Pool Players Association Hall of Fame

STATEN ISLAND, NEW YORK

Mailing Address: 86 Vanderbilt Ave, 10304. Tel. (212) 981-5943. *Contact:* Joan Margo. *Location:* In N.E. corner of Staten Island; N. of Interstate 278. *Personnel:* Bd. of Dirs: Peter Margo, Steve Mizerak, Pete Bolner, Ray Martin, Allen Hopkins and Ernie Costa. Call for information. *Nearby Halls of Fame:* Bicycles (Staten Island), Heritage, Music (New York City, 5 mi. N.), Harness Racing (Goshen, 50 mi. N.W.), Horse Racing (Saratoga Springs, 155 mi. N.), Ice Skating (Newburgh, 40 mi. N.).

The Professional Pool Players Association (PPPA) Hall of Fame was created in November 1976 by the Board of Directors of the Association. The Hall was established to honor those who have achieved greatness in pocket billiards. The first election for members was held on December 4, 1976. Three world champions were inducted into the Hall that evening at the Hall of Fame dinner. Plans are being made for future expansion into a public facility.

Members: 3 as of 1976. Nominees are elected annually to the Hall by vote of the Board of Directors of the PPPA. Member selection will be made to encompass all facets of the pool world, honoring both living and deceased.

CARAS, Jimmy. Four-time World Champion. *Also in:* Billiard Congress of America Hall of Fame.

CRANE, Irving. Seven-time World Champion.

LASSITER, Luther. Four-time World Champion.

Women's Professional Billiard Alliance Hall of Fame

BROOKLYN, NEW YORK

Mailing Address: 17 Strong Pl, 11231. *Contact:* Mrs. Billy Billing, Dir. *Location:* In S.W. Long Island; W. of J. F. Kennedy International Airport. *Personnel:* Billy Billing, Dir. Not open to the public. *Nearby Halls of Fame:* Heritage, Music (New York City), Harness Racing (Goshen, 60 mi. N.W.), Baseball (Cooperstown, 100 mi. N.W.), Horse Racing (Saratoga Springs, 120 mi. N.), Aeronautics (Elmira, 200 mi. N.W.).

The Women's Professional Billiard Alliance (WPBA) Hall of Fame was founded in 1975 specifically to honor females in the sport of billiards. The Women's Pro Billiard Alliance was formed simultaneously by Mrs. Palmer Bejird, Madelyn Whitlow and Larry Miller. Member dues and manufacturers of billiard equipment support the organization and its awards. WPBA publishes a *Newsletter* each month to keep its membership of approximately 60 informed of current events in the world of billiards.

Members: 2 as of 1977. The Hall of Fame directors selected two members for induction at the time of founding. No others have been inducted since 1975.

McGINNIS, Ruth. Player. Best female player in history. Played against men and won. Ran over 100 consecutive balls many times.

WISE, Dorothy. Player. Fought to get a women's billiard division. Won that women's division championship during its first five years of existence.

Billiard Hall of Fame to Watch

HALL OF FAME OF GREAT BILLIARD PLAYERS

Defunct 1972

Owned and operated by Georgy and Paulie (Joseph Paul or Joe) Jansco primarily to honor the great billiard players of the 1950s, particularly those who gained fame in The Hustler tournaments, this hall of fame was located in Johnston City, Illinois. It was closed in 1972.

BIRD RACING AND BREEDING

Ever since Noah's white dove, which was in fact a pigeon, returned to the Ark, the pigeon has been a universal symbol of peace. The traditional releasing of white ones at the Olympics is evidence that it still is. Under the law of Moses, squab, or nestling pigeons, were the only fowl acceptable for holy sacrifice. Throughout the ancient world and in all major religions, pigeons figured as deities, aerial vehicles of deities, and spiritual guides. They also served as couriers. Herodotus' quotation, "neither snow nor rain nor heat nor gloom of night stays these couriers from the swift completion of their appointed rounds," could well have referred to pigeons rather than to the Persian postal system of 500 B.C. During the later Crusades the Sultan of Bagdad established the world's first airmail system. Droves of well-trained homing pigeons carried messages throughout his Abbasid Empire. Though nearly every Christian knight's baggage included his own homers with which to write home, the Infidel birds proved far more effective in missions of war. The system functioned exceedingly well for a little over a century. Then it died abruptly. In 1258 the Mongols swarmed into the region, extinguished the empire, razed Baghdad and ate the birds.

For tens of centuries before this, however, pigeons' instincts and abilities had been utilized. Ramses III used them. Julius Caesar had regal war birds that had their own servants and traveled in gold and silver cages. Pigeons carried news of Colosseum wins to Roman betting booths on the outskirts of the city. Hannibal got word by homing pigeon that the pass at Mont Genevre had been left unguarded, which triggered his invasion of Italy and opened the Second Punic War. Two thousand years later, news of who had won at Waterloo was flown by pigeon to the House of Rothschild, allowing those bankers to make their fortune before anyone else received the news. Pigeons were widely used during the French Revolution, as well as in the Franco-Prussian War where many were killed by German-trained hawks. During the Spanish-American War they went ashore with Teddy Roosevelt and his Rough Riders to carry news of victory back to the Havana harbor. Baron Paul Julius de Reuter, pioneer of the speedy transmission of news, began his network with pigeons.

In W.W. I nearly 500,000 pigeons were used. The first two of the Allied birds to fly missions were a male named Gunpowder and a female named Pretty Baby. Gunpowder flew missions throughout the war and returned home to a hero's welcome. When it died it was stuffed and mounted, and now stands in a place of honor in the American Legion Hall at Aurora, Illinois. Pretty Baby was shot by an American soldier who thought it was an enemy bird. The great Cher Ami, though wounded in the breast and with its right leg blown off by sniper fire, delivered the message that saved what was left of the Lost Battalion. For this, Cher Ami was awarded the Croix de Guerre by the French government. General Pershing personally ordered the bird to be placed in the officer's cabin on a ship for the voyage home. In all, some 20,000 pigeons were killed during W.W. I. The Germans took nearly one million of them prisoner when they occupied Belgium. A monument to all pigeons who served in the war stands in Lille, France.

During W.W. II pigeons were indispensable in combat and espionage. Allied pigeons flew over 36,000 combat missions in all theaters. For their special heroism, 31 British birds and one American, G.I. Joe, received the prestigious Dickin medal, as did 18 dogs, 3 police horses, and a cat. G.I. Joe saved 1000 British troops that would have been bombed by misdirected British planes had the bird not arrived minutes before they were due to take off. One of the strongest flyers of all time was nicknamed Kaiser by the American soldiers who captured it and saw the German Imperial Crown stamped on its leg band. It was taken to the United States and lived until the age of

32 as a P.O.W. in Missouri. An unnamed homer on a 100-mile training flight back to Camp Meade, Maryland, accidentally became fouled in oil and was unable to fly. Days later this bird returned to camp. It had walked the remaining miles home.

Pigeons continue to serve as couriers today. When electronic communications are disrupted by natural disasters, Japanese news pigeons rush stories to their home offices. Chinese families send and receive dinner invitations by pigeon. Amish and Mennonite people, disregarding telephones, sometimes send their messages by this bird when urgency is called for. And everywhere in the United States deflecting a government carrier pigeon is a federal misdemeanor. In every sense the pigeon, not Mercury, is history's winged messenger.

FORMS: Worldwide, there are about 290 species of pigeon including doves, which technically are pigeons. The numerous breeds of pigeons such as pouters, runts, owls, frillbacks, jacobins, and tumblers are all descended from a single one of those species, the rock dove *(Columba livia)*. A racing pigeon, correctly called a racing homer, is one of these breeds. It is characterized by the high development of its homing instincts, and by its greater musculature and weight. It weighs about one pound, compared to the common statue pigeon's normal weight of one-quarter pound. Other varieties of homer, such as show homer and giant homer, are not raced.

Cock and hen racing homers are chosen for breeding by one or both of two main systems. In one system a study of their pedigree, past performance, conformation and type is made. In the other, a detailed study of the various features of a bird's eyes, including their color, is used. Proponents of this system claim the eye is the most accurate clue to a racer's potential.

Pigeons are monogamous and females lay two white eggs which are incubated for 19 days. When the squeakers (chicks) are hatched, they are cared for in one of two ways. The natural system allows both parents to remain with the young. In the widowhood system the hen is removed, leaving the cock to care for the young. The advantages of the latter system are two-fold: the hen then flies faster in a race to get back to its young, and the cock does the same to get back to its hen. About one-quarter billion pedigree homers are bred each year—some to be raced, others to be used strictly for breeding. Chicks receive registration rings when 7 days old and are weaned at 24 days. 4 days thereafter, training commences. On the first of January of the following year, they are declared to be one year old. At the age of two or three a bird is "old," and at its racing peak.

A race will involve owners, breeders, trainers, punters and drivers of the road transporter that carries the panniers containing up to 5000 birds to the liberation point. Convoyers who care for the birds enroute, liberators, marking officials and members of the clock committee are also usually involved in a given race. All birds start from a single point, but each ends at its own home loft. The distance flown can be up to 600 miles for old birds and 250 miles for young ones. Some races, such as the 900-mile Barcelona – England race, are longer. The winner is announced after the actual time, distance and speed of each has been calculated. A pigeon can fly 1000 miles in two days. The record speed clocked for a pigeon is 97.4 m.p.h, which may be compared to a Peregrine Falcon's 180 m.p.h. power-dive. The 24-hour record for a pigeon is 803 miles, and the greatest distance flown is about 7000 miles. The latter record was set in 1845 (the year Edgar Allan Poe wrote *The Raven*) when a British pigeon flew from West Africa to London in 55 days.

ORGANIZATION: Early in this century, Antwerp breeders frequently would send drafts of homers to England for selection by would-be purchasers with the understanding that those not wanted would be released to fly back to Belgium. Today virtually every country in the world has scores of racing and breeding clubs and practitioners, but Belgium remains the pigeon racing capitol of the world; it is the national sport there. Certain pigeon bloodlines are as jealously guarded as the bloodlines of Arabian horses. Almost every town and village has its own *Sociètè Columbophile,* and winning racers receive the adoration reserved in the United States and Canada for a champion quarterback or a brilliant hockey forward. The Belgian *Fédèration Colombophile Internationale* thus acts as an international link and adviser on the sport. Most pigeon racers in the United States and Canada belong to clubs, and adjacent clubs are sometimes joined to form a federation. Of the numerous federations, organizations and associations for the sport in the United States, the major ones are the International Federation of American Homing Pigeon Fanciers, Inc, the National Pigeon Association, the U.S. Racing Pigeon Association, the American Racing Pigeon Union, the American Pigeon Club, and the United Pigeon Fanciers of America. Fred Goldman, who founded the League of American Homing Clubs in 1891, is known as the "Father of the Racing Pigeon Sport in America."

American Racing Pigeon Union Hall of Fame

MAINEVILLE, OHIO

Mailing Address: P.O. Box 26, 45039. Tel. (513) 683-6244. *Contact:* Charles E. Herin, Secy.-Treas. *Location:* Off I-71 on Hwy. 48; 20 mi. N.E. of Cincinnati, 20 mi. S. of Dayton, 80 mi. S.W. of Columbus. *Personnel:* 5 mem. Hall of Fame "A" Comt. (Bruce Gordon, Chmn.); 5 mem. Hall of Fame "B" Comt. (Milton E. Haffner, Chmn.); Charles E. Herin, Secy.-Treas. *Nearby Halls of Fame:* Aeronautics (Dayton, Ohio, 20 mi. N.), Basketball Coaches (Columbus, Ohio, 80 mi. N.E.), Football (Canton, Ohio, 195 mi. N.E.).

The American Racing Pigeon Union Hall of Fame is divided into two Halls: Hall A for recognition of outstanding flights of racing pigeons and Hall B to honor men and women who have contributed to the sport and the Union. Conceived by Dr. E. Walter Edlund in 1929, the initial Hall of Fame A Awards were mutually sponsored by the American Racing Pigeon Union (AU) and the International Federation of American Homing Pigeons (IF). The Hall of Fame A Awards were first issued in 1931 for performances in 1930. Winners of these first awards deserving individual mention are: Cher Ami, who with one leg shot off and a wounded breast, carried a message to save the lives of the Lost Battalion in W.W. I; and Mocker, who in W.W. I, despite bullet wounds and the loss of an eye, flew a message to our artillery that successfully pinpointed silenced enemy guns. In 1932 the joint committee was dissolved, and thereafter the AU and IF established separate Halls of Fame. In 1950 the AU paid tribute to fanciers for their outstanding service by establishing the Hall of Fame B.

Members: Hall of Fame A: 86 as of 1976. Committee of five members selects two birds from each of three classes (small—under 25 lofts competing, medium—25–49 lofts, large—50 or more lofts), one of which receives the old bird Hall of Fame Award and the other honorable mention. The committee also selects in each class one bird in the young bird races of the preceding year which receives the young bird Hall of Fame Award. In each, the owners of the pigeons selected receive Hall of Fame Certificates and, in addition, the first place old bird and winning young bird receive the Hall of Fame Plaques. Hall of Fame B: 52 as of 1976. Committee of five chooses two inductees annually from nominations received for individuals living or dead who have rendered outstanding service to the sport and organization.

Hall A

1930 CHER AMI.

MISS HAVANA. Owner John Kozlowski.

MOCKER.

PRESIDENT WILSON.

1931 ZENITH. Owner Richard Wunderlich.

1932 ROLAND. Owner Morris Brothers.

WORTHY MATRON. Owner C. D. Fisher. Honorable mention certificate.

1934 TWILIGHT AND DAWN. Owner Dismer and McGann.

VINDICATION. Owner John Mahaffey.

1935 ALWAYS FAITHFUL. Owner U.S. Army Signal Corps.

1936 CENTENNIAL QUEEN. Owner P. P. Dransfield.

GENERAL ALLISON. Owner U.S. Army Signal Corps. Honorable mention certificate.

1937 LADY ANNE. Owner C. E. Ertzman.

1938 FAST TIME. Owner Edwin Lang Miller.

1940 MISS REPEATER. Owner Fred G. Thon.

OLD FAITHFUL. Owner Joe Winters. Honorable mention certificate.

TINY TOT. Owner Richard Saunders. Honorable mention certificate.

1941 NOT BAD. Owner August Ziegelmaier.

1942 JIMMIE'S PRIDE. Owner James Pryde.

SMOKEY JOE. Owner Art Nemechek. Honorable mention certificate.

1943 THE CHAMP. Owner C. W. Cozard. Honorable mention certificate.

MR. WEYMOUTH. Owner Russel C. Scammell.

1944 CONSISTENT. Owner T. C. Wright.

PATHFINDER. Owner Lt. Joseph A. Polito.

1945 DUAL KING. Owner J. W. Rindock, Jr. Honorable mention certificate.

OLD 52 GULL. Owner Paul Tutena.

ROBINETTE. Owner W. R. Pennington. Honorable mention certificate.

1946 GORDON'S. Owner Gordon and Hanson. Honorable mention certificate.

MISS AMERICA. Owner T. G. Robson.

1947 BLUE ANGEL. Owner Al Schnitzler.

MELODY. Owner B. M. Sawicki. Young bird winner.

MISS RELIABLE. Owner O. E. Roberts. Honorable mention certificate.

1948 FOLDING MONEY. Owner Klein and Mack. Honorable mention certificate.

OLD FAITHFUL. Owner Jack Malone.

1949 FREDDIE. Owner Fred DeWyse. Young bird winner.

1950 CITATION. Owner Horace Hampton.

EIGHTY-SIX. Owner Robert V. Shannon. Honorable mention certificate.

1951 BETTY LOU. Owner Louis J. Asmonga.

1952 BHAMO QUEEN. Owner J. C. Brazz.

FAST TIME. Owner Stanley P. Biesiadecki. Young bird winner.

LADY INDEPENDENCE. Owner Herman Morrison. Honorable mention certificate.

1953 DAY & NITE. Owner T. C. Wright. Honorable mention certificate.

LADY INDEPENDENCE. Owner Herman Morrison. Honorable mention certificate.

LITTLE ONE. Owner Stanley P. Biesiadecki. Young bird winner.

TOM CAT. Owner William P. Young.

1954 DARE ME. Owner Eaton Loft. Honorable mention certificate.

HAZEL. Owner Albert A. Yorio. Young bird winner.

SIS. Owner Frank J. Wimmer.

1955 DANNY BOY. Owner A. R. Zazuetta, Jr. Honorable mention certificate.

JETAWAY. Owner John L. Fierber. Young bird winner.

MOONBEAM. Owner Edward Kloss and Joe Plewniak.

1956 BRATINELLA. Owner Robert Brooks.

RONNIE. Owner Peter Boghosian. Honorable mention certificate.

1973 ANOTHER PRETTY FACE. Owner Ken Swenson (25–49 lofts).

CANADIAN KID. Owner I. R. Mitchell. Honorable mention certificate.

CONSISTENT RED. Owner Lyle Prell. Young bird winner (under 25 lofts).

ELSIE. Owner Robert Andrews. Young bird winner (50 or more lofts).

THE 581 HEN. Owner Joseph Twardzik (50 or more lofts).

LADY FORTUNE. Owner Ernie Rossi & Son. Honorable mention certificate.

SACTO QUEEN. Owner Charles Jacinth. Young bird winner (25–49 lofts).

SIR CARLISLE. Owner Charles E. Herin (under 25 lofts).

1974 BIG BROTHER. Owner Jack Wenzel. Honorable mention certificate.

BLUE BOY. Owner Earl Hopkins. Young bird winner (under 25 lofts).

BLUE RAIDER'S EZ-GO. Owner Jeana Aldridge. Honorable mention certificate.

BREAK AWAY. Owner Irene Seiger. Young bird winner (50 or more lofts).

MISS DARK EYES. Owner Ken R. Warren. Young bird winner (25–49 lofts).

OZZIE. Owner Raymond C. Hendricks. Honorable mention certificate.

PINE NEEDLE. Owner Rodney Desrosiers (25–49 lofts).

SHE'S-A-HONEY. Owner Robert G. Zawislak (50 or more lofts).

TIRELESS. Owner Edward K. Tatum (under 25 lofts).

1975 BLUE BOY, Owner Alvin M. Rubida. Honorable mention certificate.

BLUE RAIDER'S "LITTLE GOER." Owner Pam Aldridge (under 25 lofts).

JOHN'S PICK. Owner Harold W. Durkin. Young bird winner (50 or more lofts).

LITTLE SURPRISE. Owner Robert Chappell. Young bird winner (25–49 lofts).

MR. TROUBLE. Owner Kenneth Lewis. Honorable mention certificate.

OKLAHOMA FLASH. Owner Earl Hopkins. Honorable mention certificate.

TOOT-TEE-BABY. Owner Bonnie DeBortoli. Young bird winner (under 25 lofts).

TROUBLE. Owner Brian L. Neal (25–49 lofts).

TRUE GRIT. Owner Ben Fichter (50 or more lofts).

1976 ATLAS JR. Owner Ed Bert. Honorable mention certificate.

BRONCO. Owner Edward K. Tatum. Honorable mention certificate.

MISS AMERICA. Owner B. E. Morrow. Young bird winner (50 or more lofts).

MY-OH-MY. Owner Walter Pendelton (under 25 lofts).

SHORTY. Owner Joann Fair (50 or more lofts).

SUNDUST. Owner Glen Burnham (25–49 lofts).

THE MIGHTY AJAX. Owner Delk Pest Control (25–49 lofts).

WING GIRL. Owner Ted Rzodkiewicz. Young bird winner (under 25 lofts).

Hall B

1950 BUSCALL, D. C.
CARBLEY, George
CARNEY, Capt. John L.
DISMER, William
KAMINSKY, V. A.
LIEKEFET, H. W.
McMICKEN, K. B.
OPSANN, Oscar W.
SAUTER, Joseph A.
SIMON, Dr. J. C.

1951 BENNETT, O. J.
CALLIS, C. W.
ELLSWORTH, Charles
KNOBLAUCH, Dr. W. G.
KOTERSHALL, Dr. E. F.
McFADDEN, John F.
MICHALAK, J. S.
SCHMITT, Walter
TRESCH, Harold
VAN WULFEN, Ed

1953 BARRY, Peter P.
PRIEWE, Carl E.

1954 BARTELS, August
CONWAY, Dr. J. M.

1955 BARNES, Edward
DeMOOY, Ed

1956 BURKE, Harry C.
SODERBERG, William

1957 ANDERSON, Elwin
BRANCATO, Helyn

1958 FOSTER, James C. Sr.
RUZEK, James A.

1959 TOLFSON, Charles

1960 ASCHBACHER, Fred

1961 FITZGERALD, Jas. H. Sr.

1962 BRITT, William C.

1963 HOSER, Charles
STONE, Carl

1964 RUSSO, Michael J.

1965 HEIDEN, Alfred
1966 GLASER, Fred
1967 WOOD, Frank
1968 POESCHL, A. L.
1969 SEJBA, Stanley
1970 JANKOWSKI, Ed
SOUKUP, Joseph
1971 WIEMELS, John S.
1972 SELDON, Edgar
1973 BRIJA, James
1974 LEWIS, James
1975 BONWELL, Wm. A. Jr.
1976 MIEYER, Otto

Canadian Racing Pigeon Union Hall of Fame

LONDON, ONTARIO

Mailing Address: R.R. 4, N6A 4B8. Tel. (519) 681-1092. *Contact:* Dorothy Joseph, Secy. *Location:* Approx. 115 mi. S.W. of Toronto, Ont, 118 mi. N.E. of Detroit, Mich. *Personnel:* Tom Williams, Pres; Jack Hunt, V.Pres; Bill Badgerow, Awards Chmn. *Nearby Halls of Fame:* Football (Hamilton, Ont, 70 mi. N.E.), Hockey, Sports (Toronto, Ont.), Sports (Detroit, Mich.).

The Canadian Racing Pigeon Union was established in 1929 largely through the efforts of Jay Matthews, Ben Wright (who later became its first president) and other avid pigeon racers. In 1944 the Union was incorporated and later the Hall of Fame was established to award trophies for individual racing performance.

Members: Only racing pigeons are inducted into the Hall of Fame. Originally, a bird was inducted into the Hall of Fame only after winning three trophies but today that procedure is no longer used. Now 12 inductions are made per year and birds are selected according to a point system, one point per every loft won and one point for every five miles flown in a race. Four birds from each of three categories are inducted; the best young and old bird and the best young and old bird aloft are selected from A group (15 lofts or more), B group (9 to 14 lofts), and C group (8 lofts and under). Trophies are awarded annually at the October 14 convention which falls on the Canadian Thanksgiving. List of members not available.

International Federation of American Homing Pigeon Fanciers Hall of Fame

PENNINGTON, NEW JERSEY

Mailing Address: P.O. Box 368A, R.F.D. 1, 08534. Tel. (609) 737-2213. *Contact:* Nona Feuerbach, Secy.-Treas. *Location:* Approx. 7 mi. N.W. of Trenton, 25 mi. S.W. of New Brunswick, 20 mi. N.E. of Philadelphia, Pa. *Personnel:* George C. Crum, Sr, Chmn. Hall of Fame Comt; Nona Feuerbach, Secy.-Treas. *Nearby Halls of Fame:* Bicycle (Staten Island, N.Y, 40 mi. N.E.), Heritage, Music (New York, N.Y, 55 mi. S.W.) and Jockey, Lacrosse (Baltimore, Md, 130 mi. S.W.).

Organized in Philadelphia on November 8, 1881, the International Federation of American Homing Pigeon Fanciers, Inc. (popularly called IF), is the oldest organization of its kind in the United States. In 1930 and 1931 the Hall of Fame Awards were made jointly by the IF and AU (American Racing Pigeon Union) but in 1932 the IF withdrew and since then the Awards have been separate. The Federation issued its first Award in 1938 to A. Heuvelmans of Forest Hills, N.Y, for his pigeon The Spirit of '76 which had competed in races from 100 – 400 miles winning $1393. Winnings amounted to nearly $3000 when he retired in 1940.

Members: Number unknown. Two birds selected by a committee of three each year: old bird (chosen from birds of any age, flown in the first half of any year) and young bird (chosen from birds hatched the first part of the year and flown the last half). Awards are presented at the annual convention in November. Owners of the winning birds receive a silver tray and a 12 in. by 14 in. handpainted picture of their pigeon. Blank applications available only to members of the Federation upon request and completed applications should be mailed to George Crum.

1930 CHER AMI
MISS HAVANA. Owner John Kozlowski.
MOCKER
PRESIDENT WILSON
1931 ZENITH. Owner Richard Wunderlich.
1938 THE SPIRIT OF '76. Owner A. Heuvelmans.
1941 (Unnamed). Owner C.D. Marler.
1943 (Unnamed). Owner John Wryerewski.

1944 LOUISE. Owner Clarence E. Martin.
1945 DIXIE BILL. Owner George V. Chalmers.
1947 ISABEL. Owner Eugene Mannes.
1948 JOHNNY BOY. Owner John A. Roberts.
1950 ZALENSKI'S CHAMP. Owner Ben Zalenski.
1951 (Unnamed). Owner Norman Bradley & Son.
1952 461. Owner McGlynn Brothers.
1953 (Unnamed). Owner Daniel Sullivan.
1954 LADY VALIANT. Owner Harold L. Stanley.
1955 EDGEWOOD. Owner George Crum & Son.
JET BOY. Owner Fred Sykes. Young bird.
1956 SWEET SAM. Owner F. T. Schofield.

National Pigeon Association Hall of Fame

ORANGE, CALIFORNIA

Mailing Address: P.O. Box 3488, 92665. *Contact:* James Lairmore. *Location:* 4 mi. S. of Anaheim, Calif, 20 mi. N.E. of Long Beach, 50 mi. S.E. of Los Angeles. *Personnel:* Robert Johnston, Pres; Hubie Reith, V.Pres; William Rice, V.Pres; Dr. Jack Horn, Pres. of Selection Comt. *Nearby Halls of Fame:* Strength (Costa Mesa, Calif, 18 mi. S.), Softball (Long Beach), Auto Racing (Ontario, Calif, 35 mi. N.E.), Citizens Savings (Los Angeles), Aeronautics, Champions (San Diego, Calif, 75 mi. S.).

Members: Three inductions per year is the maximum set by the National Pigeon Association Hall of Fame rules. The four-member selection committee chooses which pigeon breeders to honor by reviewing applications. The criteria for selection are based on a breeder's length of time breeding and exhibiting pigeons and the merit of his contributions to pigeon fanciers. Awards are presented to the elected inductees the third weekend in January at the Grand National Show. List of members not available.

BOWLING

Stone Age cavemen and boys, it has been said, rolled large rocks at either pointed stones or sheep joints. If they did, and it seems probable, the name for their game has not survived. Neither have the names of scores of other bowling or bowlinglike games that have been played throughout history. An Egyptian game was played over 7000 years ago in which a stone ball was rolled under a three-piece marble archway at nine egg-shaped stone pins. In a game played 2000 years ago in the Italian Alps, stones were tossed underhand at one or more objects. This game was taken over by the Romans and evolved through them into the modern game of Boccie. A Greek game was played with balls bowled through rolling hoops which were often large enough for the bowler to hop through.

There are, however, as many or more bowling games whose names have survived. These include the primitive French game of *carreau* and the ancient Basque game of *quilles,* also spelled *kayless, cayles* or *keiles.* In *quilles* a wooden ball made from a tree root with a handle cut into it was pitched or rolled at nine three-foot tall pins. *Cloish, closh* or *clossygne* was also played with nine pins. There was a Scottish game of bowling on ice called curling and a game called shovelboard (*see* Shuffleboard). The ancient Polynesian game of *ula maika* was played by rolling stone balls 60 ft—the exact length of a modern bowling lane—at round, flat discs about 4 in. in diameter.

The most significant ancient game, however, seems to have been introduced by the devil. Third- and fourth-century European men, particularly Germans, carried clubs or walking sticks for sport and protection wherever they went. They called these clubs *kegles,* from which comes kegler, a modern-day term for a bowler. They would set their kegles in a corner of a church or cloister and receive from the priest a stone ball with which they would attempt to knock the kegles down. Through some quirk of Medieval reasoning, the kegles represented *Heide,* the heathen one. To knock them all down logically represented a cleansing of one's sins and a capability to slay the heathen. A good bowler was said to have "knocked the devil out of his ground." Knocking the devil down in this way was a favorite pastime at Medieval village dances and baptisms. In 1518 the city of Breslau (now Wroclaw), Poland, gave an ox to the winner of a bowling competition held at such a community affair. Martin Luther, the founder of German Protestantism and the author of "A Mighty Fortress Is Our God," was so delighted with the game or its religious implications that he had a lane built in his own home for the use of his family and friends. Before him, anywhere from 3 to 17 kegles had been used; Luther, whose contemporaries included Columbus, is credited with recommending nine as the ideal number of pins to use. Thus Ninepin Bowling was born, later modified into Tenpin Bowling, then Fivepin Bowling and all the other modern forms of the simple game cavemen might have played.

Luther and the German tradition continued to exercise a strong influence on the development of the sport. An American team played in a bowling festival at Hamburg in 1892, one of the earliest international meets. The first bowling magazine in the United States, *Gut Holz,* was printed in German. It was first issued in 1893 and the following year became the *Bowlers' Journal.* But the sport was never by any means confined to Germany.

For a time in the sixteenth century the Scots made it their national game. In England it was played in the 1100s. The Southampton Town Bowling Club—still in existence—was founded there in 1299. Englishmen called their version "bowles" and pursued it with such fervor that Edward III saw fit to outlaw it. Henry VIII declared in 1511 that "the game of bowles is an evil because the alleys are in operation in conjunction with saloons, or dissolute places, and bowling has ceased to be a sport, and rather a form of vicious gambling." His condemnation was largely ignored, however — especially after he had alleys built at Whitehall for his own use. The force of such legislation (not officially rescinded in England until 1845) was further dissipated by the various other monarchs who loved the sport. James I, for example, recommended bowling to his son in *The Book of Sports,* published in 1618. Around 1455 roofed lanes had been built in London for all-weather, year-round, round-the-clock bowling. Elizabethan Englishmen, who sometimes bowled with cannonballs, thronged to these establishments. Shakespeare mentioned the sport in several of his plays and Samuel Pepys, the diarist, wrote of meeting notable personalities at bowling alleys. In 1588 even the news of impending attack by the Spanish Armada did not dissuade Sir Francis Drake, Vice Admiral of the English fleet, from finishing and winning a game of bowling-on-the-green against Sir John Hawkins, Rear Admiral of the fleet.

The Dutch were similarly fanatical about the game and brought it with them to the New World by 1626. They used nine tall, slender pins and called the middle one the king pin, from which we get the term. To win, the Dutch bowler had to knock down a total of 31 pins and no more. William Penn, founder of Pennsylvania, called bowling one of his favorite pastimes and wrote that it furnished "a seemly and good diversion." Even those not so openly sporting could not resist the game. A Puritan wrote in 1658: "This game of bowls has bewitched me, I fear. For I played it today and for funds. . . . Woe unto me! My fellow Puritans will be shocked if they hear of this, but the more reason for my confession. I like the game, my own ability to win, and the fine folks I met on the greens. May this confession do my soul good." In 1732 the parade ground in front of Battery Fort was leased and converted into a bowling green. The area, on lower Broadway, Manhattan, is still called Bowling Green and a number of American and Canadian towns are called Bowling Green for the same historical reason. Some two years later (about 1734), officers of the garrison established a bowling green at Port Royal, Nova Scotia. Everyone of Washington Irving's day understood his analogy when he wrote in 1818 that Rip Van Winkle heard "thunder." He was alluding to deceased burghers bowling in the sky.

The Dutch, Poles, Germans, English and others traditionally bowled their balls at nine pins set up at the end of the lane in a diamond pattern. Sometime before 1803, however, a tenth pin was added in some areas. This created a triangle pattern similar to that in which pins are set today. In New York City ten pins were being used in the 1820s. Elsewhere, however, nine pins were still used. Such lack of standardization was one thing that called for the national organization of the sport in America. Another was bowling-related gambling, which became so prevalent and open in Connecticut that the state legislature was forced to ban bowling in 1841. The act stated that "ninepin alleys are prohibited whether more or less pins are used on penalty of a fine not exceeding $50.00." This act was ultimately as ineffectual as all of history's other such prohibitions.

People loved to bowl, so bowling could not be legalized out of existence. But it could be organized. A group of delegates from nine New York City bowling clubs met in 1875, the year of the first Kentucky Derby, to create the National Bowling League. It failed. This was primarily because it stressed bowling as an upper-class amusement. Certainly the upper classes enjoyed the game—the Duke of Kent, father of Queen Victoria, had a bowling green built at his estate in Bedford Basin near Halifax and the Prince of Wales (later Edward VII) enjoyed a game during his 1860 visit to Niagara Falls. But bowling was never an aristocratic sport in the way horse and greyhound racing were. The alleys, often called "pin palaces" in those days, were being built everywhere and were for everyone. In New York during the great age of whaling, the 1840s, there were bowling lanes on every block of Broadway from Fulton to Fourteenth Street. The crowds that patronized these establishments could hardly have been mistaken for the aristocrats of the day who were, after all, at the dog and horse races.

In 1890 a second attempt at national organization, the American Amateur Bowling Union, also failed. But by 1892 the sport had attained such fad proportions and continued to grow so much that by the turn of the century there were more than 100 bowling clubs in New York City alone. Some kind of controlling body was an absolute necessity. Finally in 1895 an organization was created to meet this need. The American Bowling Congress (ABC) was created at a meeting in Beethoven Hall by delegates of various clubs. This organization is "the grandfather of all bowling organizations" and the largest sports organization of any kind in the world today. It immediately gave organization and standardization to bowling, then initiated the three main trends that have occurred in bowling during the twentieth century.

The first trend was the evolution of the bowling establishment from saloon annex to family center, in which the dingy smoke-filled alleys for men were replaced with well-lit lanes to which whole families could go. The Bowling Proprietors Association was formed in 1932 for the specific purpose of raising the standards of bowling establishments. In furtherance of this trend, the Women's International Bowling Congress (WIBC), a 1916 offshoot of the ABC, banned the use of the term "alley" by its members. During W.W. II hundreds of thousands of wartime workers were introduced to bowling through their various industries. Many of these workers were women, for whom baby sitting facilities and soda fountains were soon being provided.

The second trend was the modernization of the old game of throwing balls at targets into a highly competitive and commercialized sport. It may be said to have begun in 1935 when Robert E. Kennedy, long-time ABC official, encouraged an inventor named Fred Schmidt to develop what in time became the automatic pin-spotting machine. It was approved by the ABC for official use in 1952. Early balls were constructed of *lignum vitae*, a tropical hardwood that cracked and chipped. Most early balls were red, but with the introduction of the hard rubber ball in 1905, black became the tradition. It remains so today despite the official allowance of mottled and brightly colored balls in the 1960s. The first all-synthetic pins (nonwood) were allowed in 1962. Finally, television (particularly such immensely popular shows as "Bowling For Dollars") took bowling into every home. Such innovations not only sped up the game, thereby allowing more people to play, but also modernized the sport.

The third trend may be said to have begun in the early 1900s when a group of businessmen who bowled at the Toronto Bowling Club decided to find a game that was faster and less strenuous than tenpins. Candlepins and Duckpins were tried but rejected. Then in 1909 Thomas J. Ryan developed a small, all-wood pin to be used in sets of five. The new game, Fivepin Bowling, quickly gained acceptance—so much so that a league was formed the following year. The first team champions of that league were the Senators of Toronto. In 1921 Bill Bromfield bowled 450 for the earliest known perfect game. Today one out of every three Canadians bowls, and a large percentage bowl Fivepins.

The net effect of these three trends was that bowling has become the *Jaws* of the sports world. Largely unseen compared to the more publicized and televised sports of today, bowling has everywhere met with an incredible degree of acceptance and success. This is reflected by the opening of a 116-lane bowling center in Willow Grove, Pennsylvania, and of a 504-lane center, the world's largest, in Tokyo, Japan. Until the 1950s bowling was predominately a participant sport. Since then it has largely become a spectator sport with the unique distinction that almost 100 percent of those who watch it also play it. This can hardly be said of any other sport. The dedication with which bowlers bowl is also immense if not unique in the world of sports. It is demonstrated best by the following letter received by the secretary of the ABC during a flood season in the Ohio Valley: "Dear Sec; I am writing this with pencil by candle light, in my attic. I do not think the water will get above my second floor. Have not seen my teammates for a week. Hope they're not drowned. Think I can get this letter out on the food boat in the morning. My bank is nine feet under water, but I'm enclosing my check for $75.00 entry fee in the five-men, doubles and singles for the world's championships in New York. Haven't missed my nine games in the tournament for twenty-two years and don't intend to let a flood stop me."

FORMS: Although bowling occurs in marbles when a player rolls a shot, in cricket and in many other games, bowling is properly the generic name for a variety of sports and games in which a ball, usually but not always round, is rolled or thrown down a long narrow lane (lined with gutters or not) with one of two general aims: to have the ball come to rest near a stationary ball called the "jack," as in bowls or lawn bowling, boccie or boules, green bowls, crown green bowls, curling and others; or to have the ball knock down pins. The latter aim occurs in the principal forms of bowling played in the United States, Canada, Mexico, Japan, Scandinavia, Australia, Central America and South America: Tenpins, Duckpins (primarily in the Eastern United States), Rubberband Duckpins, Barrelpins, Candlepins (played mostly in New England), Fivepins, Five Back, Skittles, Half-bowls, Ninepins and many others. Related games played in other countries are similarly too numerous to list but include the French *pétanque* or *boule*, which is derived from the older game of *jeu provençal* (similar to lawn bowls); the Irish *klootschien*, in which two players bowl or throw an iron ball along a road, the object being to cover a set distance in the fewest throws; and the Central and Eastern European bowling games of *schere, bohle* and asphalt, which is played outdoors on asphalt.

How the aim of knocking down pins is accomplished varies greatly from form to form. In Skittles, the object is to knock down the nine pins with the fewest throws of the thick flat disc. The ball is called the "cheese" because it resembles a large Edam cheese. In Half-bowls, the half sphere of wood is rolled past the 15 pins so that it will arc around and back to knock them down. In the extremely popular sport of Canadian Fivepins, two players or teams of equal numbers bowl a small, 5 in. in diameter, hard rubber ball at five pins. The ball, without fingerholes, is held between the thumb and fingers. The 12.5 in. high pins are wooden and ringed with rubber strips to deaden the blow of the ball. They are set up in an arrowhead pattern pointed at the bowler: the point pin is the number five pin, those behind it are the number three pins, the base two are the number two pins. The bowler attempts to knock all five down in the first bowl (strike), second (spare) or third. The dimensions of the lane and the scoring system of ten frames per game are identical to those of Tenpin Bowling. In Tenpins, the lane is 3 ft. 6 in. wide and 60 ft. from the foul line to the point pin, with a 15 ft. long approach area. The first 16 ft. and the last 46 in. of a lane are usually composed of thin maple, between which softer pine boards are used. Gutters on each side of a lane are normally 9 in. wide. The pins stand on spots in a 3 ft. triangle, the center of each spot being 12 in. from the center of its neighboring spots. The pins are numbered from one to ten, starting with the point pin and counting row by row from left to right. Each is 15 in. high, no more than 15 in. in circumference at its widest part, and no more than 5¼ in. in circumference at its neck; each weighs from 46 to 58 oz. but the heaviest in the set of ten may not weigh more than 4 oz. more than the lightest. Most are made of maple wood coated with plastic. The ball bowled at them is usually composed of hard rubber or plastic; metal balls are not allowed. The ball may not exceed 27 in. in circumference and is approximately 8½ in. in diameter. It usually weighs from 10 to 16 lbs. Both three- and two-finger grips are used (thumb, middle and ring finger, or thumb and middle).

From two to four individual players or teams of up to five per side take turns bowling frames. A frame is begun each time the pins are set up anew. One or two balls may be used during each frame. There are ten frames per game, several games per competition. Each pin knocked down scores a point. There are additional bonuses for strikes (all ten down with the first throw) and spares (all ten in two throws). If all frames bowled in a game are strikes, the result is a perfect 300 game. The odds against bowling such a game are 300,000 to 1, which can be compared to the 30,000 to 1 odds for hitting a hole-in-one in golf. Unless each lane is equipped with an automatic foul detecting device, the officials for a major competition will include a foul judge.

Shoes should have soft leather soles and ideally ought to have hard rubber heels. For a right-handed bowler, the right shoe should be rubber tipped. Hats are neither required nor usually worn. The famous bowler hat has nothing to do with the sport of bowling. First made in the United States in 1850 at South Norwalk, Connecticut, they were named for the Bowlers, a famous family of nineteenth-century English hatters.

Within each form of bowling there are numerous types of play, ranging from a casual game between friends to international tournament play held according to strict rules between national teams. Most bowlers, however, participate in league bowling, which is played about 30 weeks each year and conducted under relatively standard conditions at lanes throughout the continent. There are three types of league bowling: handicapped allows less-experienced bowlers to compete with more highly skilled ones; major and classic consist of increasingly greater proficiency levels of play. At the close of each season the ABC and the WIBC compile lists of the nation's high average bowlers in all three types for both men and women. In tournaments a bowler either meets one person at a time in eliminations (match game bowling), or rolls from 3 to 16 games against any number of opponents to get the highest possible score (tournament bowling).

ORGANIZATION: Discussing the organization of the sport of bowling today is like discussing planetary distances or stars—comprehending the enormous numbers is a difficult thing to do. As has been noted, by 1892 bowling had reached fad proportions in the United States. It has grown steadily ever since, so that today there are more than 140,000 lanes in over 9000 American bowling establishments. At these and similar establishments throughout the world, bowling in its various forms is played by more people than is any other sport in the world. In North America bowling's closest rivals in numbers of participants are fishing and swimming. Nearly 66 million Americans bowl annually, and one of every three Canadians bowls. A single organization, the American Bowling Congress (ABC), has enough members (4.4 million) to populate a city the size of Detroit, or a city as large as Atlanta, Phoenix and Miami combined. The Women's International Bowling Congress (WIBC) has more members—3.7 million—than San Francisco has residents and is the world's largest sports organization for women. Among the earliest of modern sports in which women competed, bowling today is by far the most popular sport among women—especially so in the Midwest. All age groups are represented in bowling, as seen in the fact that one ABC champion, Pat Romano, was 15 years old and another, E. D. "Sarge" Easter, was 67. And bowling has been adapted for the blind, the deaf, the mentally handicapped and those confined to wheelchairs. This immense popularity is certainly due to the nature of bowling, to its challenges and its rewards; but it is also very much due to bowling's highly organized, competitive league structure.

The ABC and WIBC operate jointly. Together they have 102 state groups, 5625 local groups, and 140,000 leagues. Each of these leagues in turn is composed of from 8 to 40 teams. The ABC alone sponsors more than 1,325,000 bowling teams. In addition, the ABC and WIBC each established their own intercollegiate divisions in 1966. They are affiliated with numerous other organizations, notably the American Junior Bowling Congress (AJBC) which was founded in 1935 and used to be called the American High School Bowling Congress. They also work in close association with local organizations of bowling establishment owners, with civic and fraternal organizations, with large corporations, and with scores of bowling organizations devoted to specific aspects of the sport. The latter include the Bowling Proprietors Association of America formed in 1932, the National Bowling Council (1943), the National Bowling Association (1939), the Bowlers' Victory Legion, the Bowling Writers Association of America (1927) and others.

Organized professional bowling began in 1959 with the founding of the Men's Professional Bowlers Association (PBA) and of the Professional Woman Bowlers Association (PWBA). These and other professional organizations (notably the Canadian Bowling Association, formed in 1926), together with numerous nonprofessional organizations are all either directly or indirectly under the supervision of the *Fédération Internationale des Quilleurs* (FIQ). This organization was founded in 1951 and is headquartered in Helsinki with tenpin bowling division headquarters in England. The FIQ, with a membership of some 50 national bowling organizations, is the world governing body of bowling.

Predictably, the various competitions and tournaments staged in the world of bowling are often huge affairs involving great numbers of people and vast sums of money. At the WIBC's 1973 tournament in Las Vegas, for example, over 43,000 women competed. The PBA and PWBA cosponsor tournaments in virtually every major American city, in Montreal, and in various foreign countries. The ABC tournament is the world series of bowling. The first time it was staged in 1901, 115 singles competed for $1592 in prize money. Today the ABC with the WIBC and the National Bowling Association disburses over $200,000,000 in league prize money each season for events such as the Masters Tournament, held since 1951. Among the largest individual events is the Petersen Classic, held since 1921 during ten months each year in Chicago. More than 20,000 men and women compete for a first prize of $50,000. The Bowling Proprietors Association of America has held an All-Star Championship Tournament since 1941. It was opened to women in 1949. Since 1965 the PBA has staged the $100,000 Firestone Tournament of Champions at Akron, Ohio. The first prize is $25,000. For many years the largest and most important Fivepin tournament has been conducted by the Ontario Bowling Association. The American Junior Bowling Congress (AJBC) has two annual tournaments, one of which is called the national "mailographic." In both tournaments results of local competitions are mailed to the national headquarters for comparison and decision. Still another important competition is the Tournament of the Americas, held since 1963 in Miami, Florida. The major international amateur tournament, the Olympics of Bowling, is the World Tournament sponsored irregularly since 1954 and every four years since 1963 by the FIQ. Women have competed in it only since 1963. Gold, silver and bronze medals are awarded. These, and the thousands of minor tournaments that lead up to them, help explain the claims that have been made for bowling that the supremely great bowlers like Don "Babe Ruth of Bowling" Carter, James Blouin, Henry Marino, Andy Varipapa, Marion Ladewig, Ned Day and Billy Sixty are only representatives of a host of greats, and that bowling has produced more stars than has any other sport. The latter claim is true with the exception of chariot racing (see Horse Racing and Breeding). Chariot racing died out, however. But new bowling greats are being produced all the time because every second of every minute of every day of every year somewhere in the world someone is bowling.

Arizona State Bowling Association Hall of Fame

TUCSON, ARIZONA

Mailing Address: 902 S. Erin Ave, 85711. Tel. (602) 745-0423. *Contact:* Paul Kuwahara, Exec. Secy, Ariz. State Bowling Assn. *Location:* Approx. 110 mi. S.E. of Phoenix, 230 mi. S.W. of Flagstaff.

The Hall of Fame was founded in 1967 to honor those bowlers who have contributed to the sport. The Hall is financed and administered by the Arizona State Bowling Association (ASBA).

Members: 22 as of 1977. Nominations for the Hall of Fame are made by a Committee composed of the officers and Board of Directors of the ASBA and the Hall of Fame members. Nominees must receive 75 percent of the votes cast. Inductions are held at the annual State tournament.

1967 McCLEERY, Dr. Ben. Meritorious service.
ROE, Frank B. Meritorious service.
WILSON, R. H. "Red." Bowler.

1968 PREISS, Robert. Bowler.
RAGUS, Nick. Meritorious service.
WAASON, Dale. Bowler.

1969 HAWK, William E. Bowler.
JORDAN, Thomas E. Bowler.

1970 MAJESKE, Homer "Bob." Bowler.
TRAYLOR, Vernon, Sr. Bowler.

1971 ALLEN, William A. Bowler.
BROOKSHIER, Kirk. Meritorious service.
NICHOLS, Ernest C. Meritorious service.

1972 GANO, Lynn. Bowler.
HRUBY, Stanley. Meritorious service.

1973 CHASE, Brian. Meritorious service.
MORTENSEN, M. A. Meritorious service.

1974 CHEVALIER, Albert J. Meritorious service.
MAYO, Seth L. Bowler.

1976 LARGE, Thomas. Bowler.

1977 EAST, John. Meritorious Service.
STEGMOLLER, Russell. Bowler.

Arizona Women's Bowling Association Hall of Fame

PHOENIX, ARIZONA

Mailing Address: P. O. Box 11436, 85061. Tel. (602) 973-7766. *Contact*: Mrs. Peggy Lazovich, Secy. of Ariz. Women's Bowling Assn. *Location*: Approx. 110 mi. N.W. of Tucson, 120 mi. S.W. of Flagstaff. *Personnel*: Five mem. Hall of Fame committee.

A special feature of the 1975 – 1976 bowling season for the Arizona Women's Bowling Association (AWBA) was the formation of their Hall of Fame. Created to honor and recognize Arizona women, living or deceased, who have made outstanding contributions to bowling, the Hall presently has one category of membership, Meritorious Service, but the AWBA Board of Directors may add categories from time to time. A Hall of Fame Committee appointed by the AWBA president belongs to the Board of Directors and administers the Hall of Fame.

Members: 2 as of 1977. Nominees must have been members of the AWBA for at least five years (not necessarily consecutive) and members of the Women's International Bowling Congress (WIBC) for at least 10 years (again, not necessarily consecutive). Most importantly, the nominees must have served the WIBC, the American Junior Bowling Congress, the Arizona Women's Bowling Association or a local association for a number of years. Each year no later than October 15, nomination forms prepared by the State secretary are received by the presidents and secretaries of the local bowling associations, the AWBA Board of Directors, AWBA members, life members and emeritus members requesting such forms. These forms are returned by December 1 to the Hall of Fame Committee for verification of the necessary qualifications and the addition of their own nominations. The Hall of Fame Committee must submit a list of not more than three names, with qualifications, to the AWBA Board of Directors who select one inductee at their January meeting. The Hall of Fame Committee is not required to submit any nominations to the Board of Directors, nor is the Board of Directors required to select any new members. Once a person is selected for membership in one category, they cannot be considered for membership in another category. The inductee is informed by the AWBA president of her selection and the Hall of Fame Committee handles the arrangements for publicity and photographing the new member. At the AWBA's expense, the new member is inducted at the AWBA annual meeting in a special ceremony conducted by the AWBA president and the Hall of Fame Committee. The new member receives a gold chain and pendant (which can also be worn as a pin) with a diamond or other precious stone and suitable engraving, an engraved plaque, a photograph of herself and a WIBC permanent membership. If deceased, a $200 gift is given to the member's favorite charity or the Bowlers' Victory Legion. A large plaque with the names of all Hall of Fame members and an album with photographs and histories of these members are kept in the AWBA office and are maintained by the Hall of Fame Committee.

1976 KRAFT, Millie. Meritorious Service. A bowler for 28 years, charter member of the AWBA, Tucson Women's Bowling Association (TWBA), Arizona State Junior Bowling Association and the Arizona Women Bowling Writers Association; past president of both AWBA and TWBA; currently president-elect of the Arizona Women Bowling Writers Association and still very active in junior bowling.

1977 HESTER, Lily May. Meritorious Service. A charter member of the AWBA and a past member of its board of directors; encouraged development of the official state publication *Desert Express* and was instrumental in organizing the Arizona Women Bowling Writers Association and served as its president through 1976; Also a past member of the Douglas Women's Bowling Association.

Bowling Proprietors Association of Greater Detroit Hall of Fame

SOUTHFIELD, MICHIGAN

Mailing Address: 23077 Greenfield, 48075. Tel. (313) 559-5207. *Contact:* Cass Sicilia, Exec. Dir. *Location:* Approx. 60 mi. N.E. of Toledo, Ohio, 98 mi. N.W. of Cleveland, Ohio, 125 mi. S.E. of Grand Rapids. *Personnel:* Al Winkel, Pres; Cass Sicilia, Exec. Dir. *Nearby Halls of Fame:* Sports, State (Detroit, 20 mi. N.W.), Football (Canton, Ohio, 140 mi. S.E.), Archery (Grayling, 165 mi. N.W.).

Founded in 1953 by the Bowling Proprietors Association of Greater Detroit, the Hall of Fame presents its award to bowlers who have contributed to the sport through promotion or bowling records and achievements. The Historical Museum in Detroit displays plaques in a window; there is also a special section set aside in Cobo Arena.

Members: 82 as of 1977. The Hall of Fame Committee is composed of 18 members from the media, local associations and proprietors. They are selected for their familiarity with local bowlers and serve an indefinite tenure. Bowlers from the Detroit area and members of the Committee submit credentials of bowlers for consideration. Although no stringent guidelines exist for the number inducted annually, lately two men, one woman and one posthumous bowler have been selected. The official induction ceremony is held at the annual banquet in April.

1957–1958 ALLEN, Harold J. (dec). See entry in National Bowling Hall of Fame, 1966.

BAUER, John (dec)

HILL, Emma (dec)

NORTHARD, Lloyd (dec)

SCRIBNER, Joe (dec)

KENNEDY, Robert (dec)

1958–1959 KAHL, Harold (dec)

McCULLOUGH, Howard W. (dec). See entry in National Bowling Hall of Fame, 1971.

NIEPOTH, George (dec)

NORRIS, Joseph John. See entry in National Bowling Hall of Fame, 1954.

PAULUS, John (dec)

STOCKDALE, Louise (dec). See entry in National Bowling Hall of Fame, 1953.

1959–1960 COY, Edwardina "Eddie" (dec)

CRIMMINS (Krzyminski), John "General." See entry in National Bowling Hall of Fame, 1962. *Also in:* National Polish-American Sports Hall of Fame and Museum.

DINGWELL, Al (dec)

SHILLADY, Jim (dec)

1960–1961 GARDELLA, Fred (dec)

GIES, Irv (dec)

HARTRICK, Stella. See entry in National Bowling Hall of Fame, 1972.

REPPENHAGEN, Walter (dec)

WARD, Cecil

1961–1962 BRECKLE, Fred

CLEMENTS, Fred (dec)

EKSTROM, Agnes

MERTENS, Herb (dec)

WALTER, John

ZIESSE, Ann (dec)

1962–1963 EDGAR, W. W.

GRYGIER, Cass

JACOB, Lillian C.

MITZEL, Frank G. (dec)

TOWNSEND, Les (dec)

WATTS, John D. (dec)

1963–1964 CRUCHON, Steve

DEMPSEY, Gladys

FAZIO, Basil "Buzz." See entry in National Bowling Hall of Fame, 1963. *Also in:* Professional Bowlers Association Hall of Fame.

POWERS, Connie. See entry in National Bowling Hall of Fame, 1973.

SCHEMANSKE, Frank G.

SIELAFF, Louis A. (dec). See entry in National Bowling Hall of Fame, 1968.

1964–1965 ALLEN, Clara

GAVIE, John

PAULUS, Joseph

STROH, John

1965–1966 SHABLIS, Helen. See entry in National Bowling Hall of Fame, 1977.

WOLF, Fred. See entry in National Bowling Hall of Fame, 1976.

1966–1967 AUCH, Otto (dec)

TOEPFER, Elvira. See entry in National Bowling Hall of Fame, 1976.

YOUNG, George (dec). See entry in National Bowling Hall of Fame, 1959. *Also in:* Michigan Sports Hall of Fame.

1967–1968 CANTALINE, Anita

NENNINGER, Robert, Sr. (dec)

ROBERTS, Charles J. (dec)

1968-1969 HEENAN, Ethel

JANKOWSKY, Augie (dec)

LUBANSKI, Edward Anthony. See entry in National Bowling Hall of Fame, 1971.

1969–1970 CRUCHON, Maxine

GIBSON, Therman (dec). See entry in National Bowling Hall of Fame, 1965.

LINDEMANN, Tony

WILLIAMS, Bill

1971–1972 HALEY, Thomas (dec)

SETLOCK, Ann

STRAMPE, Robert

TROPEA, James (dec)

1972–1973 BAUMAN, Phil (dec)

JOHNSON, Ruth

DOTARSKI, Charles

1973–1974 BECK, Mary V.

BUJACK, Fred (dec). See entry in National Bowling Hall of Fame, 1967.

BUNETTA, William. See entry in National Bowling Hall of Fame, 1968.

WALBY, Charles A.

1974–1975 CASE, Herb (dec)

CITO, Paul

HANNA, Ethel

1975–1976 FACH, Herb

KNECHTGES, Doris

MORRIS, Steve

RHODMAN, Bill (dec)

SCHUSTER, Gertrude "Gertie"

1976–1977 ALDRED, Dorothy

BROWALSKI, Ed

GAVIE, Hank

SCHLAFF, Cass

SMITH, Fred (dec)

Buffalo Bowling Association Hall of Fame

WILLIAMSVILLE, NEW YORK

Mailing Address: 4548 Main St, 14226. Tel. (716) 839-5050. *Contact:* Bill Marchese, Exec. Secy. *Location:* Approx. 58 mi. W. of Rochester, 58 mi. S.E. of Toronto, Ont, 120 mi. E. of London, Ont, 126 mi. W. of Syracuse, 195 mi. N. of Pittsburgh, Pa, 228 mi. N.E. of Cleveland, Ohio. *Personnel:* Edward Miller, Pres; Bill Marchese, Exec. Secy; four V.Pres. *Nearby Halls of Fame:* Football (Hamilton, Ont, 57 mi. W.), Hockey, Sports (Toronto, Ont.), Horseshoe Pitching (Corning, 99 mi. S.E.), Flight (Elmira, 115 mi. S.E.), Golf (Foxburg, Pa, 145 mi. S.W.), Hockey (Kingston, Ont, 150 mi. N.E.), Baseball (Cooperstown, 190 mi. E.), Football (Canton, Ohio, 210 mi. S.W.).

Founded in 1967 by the Buffalo Bowling Association, the Hall seeks to honor those bowlers who have contributed to the sport through their ability or service.

Members: 30 as of 1977. The Hall of Fame committee does not limit the number of annual inductees. Seven members of the media may nominate bowlers in two categories for screening by the committee. The first category, Ability, is for those in the Buffalo Bowling Association who have won a local, state or national championship or who have demonstrated excellence in competition. The second category, Meritorious Service, is for those who have improved, expanded and increased the influence and image of bowling through administrative duties. Members are elected in even-numbered years and inducted in odd-numbered years.

1967 BRANDT, Albert R. Outstanding ability. See entry in National Bowling Hall of Fame, 1960.

CARUANA, Frank J. (dec). Outstanding ability.

CARUANA, Joseph (dec). Outstanding ability.
CZERWINSKI, Steve J. Outstanding ability.
FISCHER, Fred, Sr. (dec). Outstanding ability.
KUEBLER, Irwin (dec). Meritorious service.
MILLER, Joseph (dec). Outstanding ability.
NABER, Raymond E. (dec). Meritorious service.
OBENAUER, George A. (dec). Meritorious service.
POLLACK, H. William (dec). Meritorious service.

1969 BURNS, Herbert E. Meritorious service.
LONG, Clarence A. (dec). Outstanding ability.
PRAVEL, Nelson C. Outstanding ability.
SMITH, John T. "Jake" (dec). Meritorious service.

1971 COLLIARD, Marcel C. Meritorious service.
HOLLENBECK, Bert (dec). Outstanding ability.
SIMON, William J. (dec). Meritorious service.

1973 ADAMS, Edward A. Outstanding ability.
BEHRINGER, Peter E. (dec). Meritorious service.
BRAYMILLER, Lee (dec). Outstanding ability.
DIFIGLIA, Joseph V. Outstanding ability.
FARRELL, Frank J. (dec). Meritorious service.
STUMPF, Charles (dec). Meritorious service.
WESP, Armond (dec). Veterans section.

1975 FELLER, Fred (dec). Outstanding ability.
KRUZICKI, Henry W. Veterans section.
MARCHESE, William S. Meritorious service.
TOURJIE, George F. (dec). Meritorious service.
WOJTCZAK, Frank J. Veterans section.
ZACK, Jack. Outstanding ability.

California Women's Bowling Hall of Fame

LONG BEACH, CALIFORNIA

Mailing Address: 2177 Santa Fe Ave, 90810. Tel. (213) 435-6432. *Contact:* Mrs. Mildred Peachy, Exec. Secy, California Women's Bowling Assn. *Location:* Approx. 25 mi. S.E. of Los Angeles, 100 mi. N.W. of San Diego, 390 mi. N.W. of Phoenix, Ariz. *Personnel:* Hall of Fame Comt. No admission. *Nearby Halls of Fame:* Softball (Long Beach), Citizens Savings (Los Angeles), Physical Fitness (Costa Mesa, 17 mi. S.E.), Auto Racing (Ontario, 35 mi. N.E.), Flight, Sports (San Diego).

Founded in 1964 by the California Women's Bowling Association (CWBA), the Hall of Fame honors women bowlers for meritorious service and superior bowling performance in California. The CWBA is sanctioned under the Women's International Bowling Congress and was originally established as an auxiliary to the all-male Pacific Coast Bowling Congress in 1924. Reorganized in 1930 and incorporated in 1931, the CWBA now represents 350,000 bowlers in the State. After establishing the Hall of Fame, it was dedicated to the late Philena Bohlen of Los Angeles, a pioneer in California bowling who is the Hall of Fame's first member.

Members: 16 as of July 1977. Members may be selected for their meritorious service as a result of outstanding contribution and service to bowling, locally and statewide. Members may also be selected for their superior performance as a result of career achievements and consistently high scoring averages in California leagues. A Hall of Fame Committee annually screens candidates and makes recommendations to the CWBA Board of Directors. New members are elected by a majority vote of the Board of Directors. Each year induction ceremonies are held during the weekend of the CWBA convention and state women's tournament, alternating between Northern and Southern California cities. Hall of Fame members receive gold pins and engraved serving trays.

1964 BOHLEN, Philena (dec). Meritorious service. See entry in National Bowling Hall of Fame, 1955.

1965 BERGER, Winifred. Meritorious service. See entry in National Bowling Hall of Fame, 1976.

1966 ENCK, Ethyl (dec). Meritorious service.

1967 O'MALLEY, Anna (dec). Meritorious service.

1968 STEVENS, Elva. Meritorious service.

1969 HARDY, Loveica (dec). Meritorious service. *Also in:* Southern California Bowling Hall of Fame.

1970 THRONE, Sally. Meritorious service.

1971 PEACHY, Mildred. Meritorious service. *Also in:* Southern California Bowling Hall of Fame.

1972 BECHTEL, Constance (dec). Meritorious service. *Also in:* Southern California Bowling Hall of Fame.

1973 BELLOWS, Helen. Meritorious service. *Also in:* Southern California Bowling Hall of Fame.

1974 DUVAL, Helen. Meritorious service. See entry in National Bowling Hall of Fame, 1970.

1975 DUFFY, Agnes. Meritorious service.
MATTHEWS, Merle. Superior performance. See entry in National Bowling Hall of Fame, 1974. *Also in:* Southern California Bowling Hall of Fame.

1976 JACOBSON, D. D. Superior performance. *Also in:* Southern California Bowling Hall of Fame.

NORTH, Bobbe. Superior performance. *Also in:* Southern California Bowling Hall of Fame.

NORTH, Merle. Meritorious service. *Also in:* Southern California Bowling Hall of Fame.

1977 WOODS, Esther. Superior performance. *Also in:* Southern California Bowling Hall of Fame.

Greater Cleveland Bowling Association Hall of Fame

CLEVELAND, OHIO

Mailing Address: 1375 Euclid, The Arcade, 44115. Tel. (216) 621-1522. *Contact:* Bob McCune, Secy.-Treas. *Location:* Approx. 30 mi. N. of Akron, 90 mi. S.E. of Detroit, Mich, 93 mi. S.E. of Toledo, 115 mi. N.W. of Pittsburgh, Pa, 115 mi. N.E. of Columbus, 180 mi. N.E. of Dayton, 180 mi. S.W. of Buffalo, N.Y. *Personnel:* Ed Fencsick, Pres; five V.Pres; Bob McCune, Secy-Treas. Not open to the public. *Nearby Halls of Fame:* Football (Canton, 50 mi. S.), State (Detroit, Mich.), Golf (Foxburg, Pa, 110 mi. S.E.), Football (Hamilton, Ont, 150 mi. N.E.), Hockey, Sports (Toronto, Ont, 190 mi. N.E.), Trapshooting (Vandalia, 190 mi. S.W.), Flight (Dayton), State (North Webster, Ind, 200 mi. S.W.), Horseshoe Pitching (Corning, N.Y, 240 mi. N.E.), Flight (Elmira, N.Y, 250 mi. N.E.).

The purpose of the Hall, founded in 1962, is to perpetuate the names of those persons who have displayed outstanding ability in the game of tenpins or have contributed through meritorious service to the general welfare and progress of the game in Greater Cleveland. The Board of Directors of the Greater Cleveland Bowling Association supervises and has full control of standards, methods and policies governing the Hall.

Members: 40 as of 1977. Any member of the Greater Cleveland Bowling Association may submit a bowler's resume to the Nominating and Ballot Committee. The Committee reviews the nominations and selects those candidates they deem qualified by voting, with a majority vote needed for induction. Annual inductions are limited to a maximum of two in each category: Meritorious Service and Ability. Meritorious Service requires at least 20 years of promotion or administrative activity. Ability is based on tournament wins, records established and participation in the area for 20 years. Awards are presented at the annual Awards Banquet.

1962 ACKERMAN, John. Meritorious service.

BODIS, Joseph. Ability. See entry in National Bowling Hall of Fame, 1941.

WARD, Walter G. Ability. See entry in National Bowling Hall of Fame, 1959.

1963 KOEPP, Edward. Ability.

MERCURIO, Walter "Skang." Ability. See entry in National Bowling Hall of Fame, 1967.

1964 ALBRIS, Pat. Ability.

KISSOFF, Joseph F. Ability. See entry in National Bowling Hall of Fame, 1976.

1965 FLYNN, William. Ability.

NAGY, Steve Joseph. Ability. See entry in National Bowling Hall of Fame, 1963.

RIDER, Herman. Meritorious service.

WALTER, Emory. Meritorious service.

1966 CRESANTE, Roland. Ability.

KOCH, Charles. Meritorious service.

LEONE, Dr. A. C. Meritorious service.

1967 BREIT, Joseph. Ability.

LAUSCHE, Charles. Ability.

LINSZ, Edward. Meritorious service.

REED, J. Elmer. Meritorious service.

1968 GRIEBEL, Roy. Ability

RICE, Roy. Ability.

1969 KLARES, John. Ability.

KRAUSE, Harry. Meritorious service.

NOVAK, Alex. Ability.

1970 PETRO, John. Ability.

SOSPIRATO, Frank. Ability.

1971 NIEBERDING, Howard. Ability.

STEFAN, Steve. Meritorious service.

1972 LEVINE, Sam. Meritorious service. See entry in National Bowling Hall of Fame, 1971.

MULLIN, Martin. Ability.

SIPERKE, Emil. Ability.

1973 MOSTER, Charles. Ability.

TORONSKI, Daniel. Ability.

1974 PHILLIPS, Victor. Meritorious service.

STEFANCIC, Stanley. Ability.

1975 EBOSH, Willis. Ability.

SCHULD, George. Ability.

1976 KOVACH, Ernest. Ability.

NUSSER, Peter. Ability.

WADSWORTH, Bruce. Meritorious service.

1977 STANONIK, Andrew. Ability.

Greater St. Louis Bowling Association Hall of Fame

HAZELWOOD, MISSOURI

Mailing Address: 1728 Leaf Crest Dr, 63042. Tel. (314) 664-1712. *Contact:* Cliff Leeker, Secy.-Treas. *Location:* Approx. 90 mi. S. of Springfield, Ill, 100 mi. E. of Jefferson City, 135 mi. N. of Poplar Bluff, Ark, 230 mi. S.W. of Indianapolis Ind. *Personnel:* Tom Vercellone, Pres; Cliff Leeker, Secy.-Treas; six V.Pres. *Nearby Halls of Fame:* City (St. Louis), Agriculture (West Lafayette, Ind, 220 mi. N.E.), Agriculture (Kansas City, 225 mi. W.), Basketball, Auto Racing (Indianapolis, Ind), Angling (Memphis, Tenn, 250 mi. S.)

Founded in 1962, the Greater St. Louis Bowling Association Hall of Fame honors individuals for their bowling accomplishments and outstanding service to the Association. Plaques of members are displayed in the Missouri Sports Hall of Fame. The Association publishes a yearbook containing record information, bowling news, tournament records and results, and other tournament information.

Members: 66 as of 1977. Anyone who wants to nominate a bowler may send a resume to the Greater St. Louis Bowling Association office. Nominees must be at least 40 years of age and qualify for either the Meritorious Service or Achievement category. The Hall of Fame Committee screens nominations in late fall and qualified names are placed on the ballot early the following year. Those individuals receiving the most votes are inducted at the annual Dinner Dance, usually in April.

1962 AMELING, Jerry C. Meritorious service.

CARTER, Donald James "Bosco." Achievement. See entry in National Bowling Hall of Fame, 1970. *Also in:* Professional Bowlers Association Hall of Fame.

STEIN, Otto, Jr. Achievement. See entry in National Bowling Hall of Fame, 1971.

SWEENEY, Dennis J. Meritorious service. See entry in National Bowling Hall of Fame, 1974.

1963 BURTON, Nelson, Sr. Achievement. See entry in National Bowling Hall of Fame, 1964.

GRAY, William S. Meritorious service.

HOLMES, Ray. Achievement.

JOHNSTON, Fred L. Meritorious service.

1964 HERMANN, Cornelius "Cone." Meritorious service. See entry in National Bowling Hall of Fame, 1968.

KUTIS, Thomas. Meritorious service. *Also in:* Amateur Baseball Hall of Fame.

WEBER, Richard Anthony. Achievement. See entry in National Bowling Hall of Fame, 1970. *Also in:* Professional Bowlers Association Hall of Fame.

WEINSTEIN, Mitzi. Achievement.

1965 BLUTH, Raymond Albert "Bloop." Achievement. See entry in National Bowling Hall of Fame, 1973. *Also in:* Professional Bowlers Association Hall of Fame.

HARRIS, Jerome "Whitey." Meritorious service.

McGILLIGAN, James E. Meritorious service.

SCHAEFER, Harold S. Achievement.

1966 FEUSER, Harry. Meritorious service.

GARAFOLA, Sam. Achievement.

HENNESSEY, Thomas M. Achievement. See entry in National Bowling Hall of Fame, 1976.

LUDWIG, Jerry. Meritorious service.

1967 KALEY, Clarence "Pop." Achievement.

LAUX, France J. Meritorious service.

McALLISTER, Lloyd G. Meritorious service.

PATTERSON, Claude, Jr. Achievement. See entry in National Bowling Hall of Fame, 1974.

1968 GRODZKI, Judge Frank. Meritorious service.

MUELLER, Hugo, Sr. Meritorious service.

O'DONNELL, Charles. Achievement. See entry in National Bowling Hall of Fame, 1968.

WILLEN, Fred H. Achievement.

1969 MESGER, Elvin. Achievement.

RIGONI, Joe. Meritorious service.

TAFF, Fred. Achievement.

WAIBEL, Emil. Meritorious service.

1970 DIETRICH, Louis. Meritorious service.

FRIENDLY, Otto. Meritorious service.

MATAYA, Frank. Achievement.

PALLARDY, Joseph G. Achievement.

1971 ABBEY, Henry. Meritorious service.

BADARACCO, Lee. Achievement.

HEIDEL, Frank. Meritorious service.

VRENICK, Jim. Achievement.

1972 JACKSON, Lowell. Achievement.

KELPE, Norman. Achievement.

LEEKER, Cliff. Meritorious service.

RUPPEL, Otto. Meritorious service.

STEIN, Clarence, Sr. Meritorious service.

1973 JUNG, Ray. Achievement.

SUMMERS, Henry "Hank." Achievement.

SWEENEY, Henry. Meritorious service.

ZIEGLER, Ray. Achievement.

1974 FREDERIC, Harry J. Meritorious service.

HUSLEY, Woody. Achievement.

NEWTON, Ray. Achievement.

ROHMAN, William. Meritorious service.

1975 SCHEER, Arthur D. Achievement.
SCHLECHTE, Erwin L. Achievement.
SCHROEDER, Elmer. Meritorious service.
STUPPY, Meinrad A. Meritorious service.

1976 HARTMAN, William. Meritorious service.
HOLCOMB, Harold E. Meritorious service.
REINEKE, Ted. Achievement.
SWEENEY, Edward. Meritorious service.
TONKOVIC, Chris "Buzz." Achievement.

1977 DUGGAN, William. Meritorious service.
LUCIDO, Frank. Achievement.
MEYERS, Norm. Achievement.
RUECKERT, John. Meritorious service.

Illinois Bowling Association Hall of Fame

CHICAGO, ILLINOIS

Mailing Address: 180 N. LaSalle, Room 1922, 60601. Tel. (312) 263-3151. *Contact:* Glen Higgins, Secy.-Treas. *Location:* 90 mi. S. of Milwaukee, Wis, 125 mi. S.E. of Madison, Wis, 130 mi. S.W. of Grand Rapids, Mich, 150 mi. W. of Ft. Wayne, Ind, 160 mi. E. of Dubuque, Iowa, 170 mi. N.W. of Indianapolis, Ind, 175 mi. N.E. of Springfield. *Personnel:* Glen Higgins, Secy.-Treas. *Nearby Halls of Fame:* Business (Chicago), Bowling, State (Milwaukee, Wis.), Agriculture (West Lafayette, Ind, 115 mi. S.E.), Sports (North Webster, Ind, 120 mi. S.E.), Auto Racing, Basketball (Indianapolis), Football (Green Bay, Wis, 175 mi. N.), Flight (Dayton, Ohio, 205 mi. S.E.), Trapshooting (Vandalia, Ohio, 210 mi. S.E.), State (Detroit, Mich, 240 mi. E.), Archery (Grayling, Mich, 250 mi. N.E.).

Established in 1969 under the auspices of the Illinois Bowling Association (IBA), the Hall honors achievements and service.

Members: 50 as of 1976. Bowlers whose outstanding talents, skills and records indicate unusual ability and/or bowlers who have contributed to the welfare and spirit of bowling through service are eligible for induction. Any member of the IBA or one of its affiliated local associations or members of the Hall of Fame Committee may nominate bowlers. The Committee is appointed by the president of the IBA for a three-year tenure. The secretary-treasurer and assistant secretary-treasurer of the IBA also serve on the Committee. Nominators must forward a detailed review and compilation of achievements by February 1 for the Committee to analyze. Inductees must receive at least three-fourths of the votes cast. Usually one to five members are inducted during the annual Jamboree in October. Inductees' classifications are either Bowling Achievement or Meritorious Service.

1969 BAUMGARTEN, Elmer H. See entry in National Bowling Hall of Fame, 1963.

BLOUIN, James. See entry in National Bowling Hall of Fame, 1955.

BOMAR, Herbert Booth "Buddy." See entry in National Bowling Hall of Fame, 1966.

CARLSON, Adolph Domianus "Swede." See entry in National Bowling Hall of Fame, 1941.

CHASE, LeRoy. See entry in National Bowling Hall of Fame, 1972.

COLLIER, Charles. See entry in National Bowling Hall of Fame, 1963.

FAETZ, Matt, Sr.

FITZGERALD, James

HOWARD, Judge George

HOWLEY, Peter. See entry in National Bowling Hall of Fame, 1941.

KARTHAISER, Frank Clemence "Midge." See entry in National Bowling Hall of Fame, 1967.

KRUMSKE, Paul Albert. See entry in National Bowling Hall of Fame, 1968.

LUNDAHL, Art

MARINO, Enrico "Hank." See entry in National Bowling Hall of Fame, 1941.

MOORE, Jack. *Also in:* Illinois Amateur Softball Association Hall of Fame.

PETERSON, Louis P. See entry in National Bowling Hall of Fame, 1963.

STEERS, Harry Harvey. See entry in National Bowling Hall of Fame, 1941.

WEINSTEIN, Sam. See entry in National Bowling Hall of Fame, 1970.

WILMAN, Joseph "Buck." See entry in National Bowling Hall of Fame, 1951.

WRIGHT, Frank

1970 FLIGER, Joe

HARKINS, Pat

KREMS, Edward Henry. See entry in National Bowling Hall of Fame, 1973.

SCHEUNEMAN, Leo

THOMA, Frank "Sykes." See entry in National Bowling Hall of Fame, 1971.

1971 BROSIUS, Edward J, Jr. See entry in National Bowling Hall of Fame, 1976.

FAETZ, Leo

FISCHER, Elmer

MARICICH, Eli

SVOMA, Ted

1972 FREITAG, Herb

LELLINGER, Jules

SINKE, Joe

1973 ADAMOWSKI, Judge Stephen

DAVIS, LeRoy

LIPPE, Harry

TRAUBENIK, Joe

1974 CUSHING, Charles

MARSHALL, William "Jack"

O'BRIEN, Elmer J.

SALVINO, Carmen. *Also in:* Professional Bowlers Association Hall of Fame.

1975 BUTLER, Martin

DASH, H. Russell

DENNISON, Louis

KILBOURNE, Les

ROBERTS, Jim

1976 ROGOZNICA, Andy

SEHR, Joseph G, Sr.

STEFANICH, Jim

ZIKES, Les, Jr.

Iowa Women's Bowling Association Hall of Fame

SIOUX CITY, IOWA

Mailing Address: 1615 Pierce, 51105. Tel. (712) 258-5053. *Contact:* Mrs. Lo Borschuk. *Location:* Approx. 75 mi. S. of Sioux Falls, S.Dak, 80 mi. N. of Omaha, Nebr, 120 mi. N. of Lincoln, Nebr, 150 mi. N.W. of Des Moines. *Personnel:* Mrs. Betty Meyer, Pres; Mrs. Lo Borschuk, Secy-Treas; four V.Pres; ten mem. Bd. of Dirs. Not open to the public. *Nearby Halls of Fame:* Agriculture (Bonner Springs, Kans, 250 mi. S.).

In 1963 the Iowa Women's Bowling Association initiated the Hall of Fame. The Hall recognizes those bowlers whose outstanding skills or administrative service in Iowa have contributed to the advancement and spirit of bowling.

Members: 13 as of 1976. Within the Board of Directors is the Hall of Fame Committee which screens and recommends nominees. Any bowling association in Iowa may nominate a bowler by sending that individual's records, service, achievements, etc. to the Committee. The nominees who receive a majority of votes are inducted at the annual meeting in March. There is no limit to the number that may be inducted annually.

1963 ABBOTT, Beulah

WHEELER, Phyllis

1966 ALBRECHT, Laura

1968 LINDELOF, Ethel

McWANE, Lena

1969 HARMSEN, Floy

1970 ORTNER, Beverly. See entry in National Bowling Hall of Fame, 1972.

1971 RAND, Ann

1972 MEYER, Betty

1973 SMITH, Leta

1974 CHAPMAN, Joanne

1975 SCHLENKER, Vera

1976 NICHOLSON, Nellie

Mesa Valley Women's Bowling Association Hall of Fame

MESA, ARIZONA

Mailing Address: 1833 E. Nielson Ave, 85204. Tel. (602) 962-0537. *Contact:* Oleta Rafferty, Secy, Mesa Valley Women's Bowling Assn. *Location:* Approx. 20 mi. S.E. of Phoenix, 105 mi. N.W. of Tucson, 120 mi. S.W. of Flagstaff. *Personnel:* Five mem. Hall of Fame committee.

In 1973 the Mesa Valley Women's Bowling Association (VWBA) Board of Directors formed a Hall of Fame to honor members for their service and bowling accomplishments. Research of the national Women's International Bowling Congress (WIBC) and other state Halls of Fame was compiled by Oleta Rafferty and presented to the Board of Directors for consideration. The Hall is administered by a Hall of Fame Committee consisting of two MVWBA members and three members of the MVWBA Board of Directors. A Hall of Fame plaque engraved with the names of honored members is kept by the chairman of the Committee and is displayed at all Association events and meetings.

Members: 10 as of 1977. Members are selected in one of two categories: Meritorious Service or Superior Performance. Those selected for Meritorious Service must have performed outstanding service to the WIBC on a local level for a period of ten years and must have been a member of the MVWBA for ten consecutive years (unless a break in membership was out of their control). Those selected for Superior Performance must have obtained individual success in bowling, regardless of average, and must have been a member of the MVWBA for five consecutive years (unless a break in membership was out of their control). Achievement at state and national tournaments may be taken into consideration. To nominate a person in either category, anyone may submit a name in writing with a biographical sketch and list of qualifications. New members are honored at the opening ceremony of the annual local championship tournament and receive Indian jewelry (earrings, pin, etc.) with an engraved stand. One new member from each category is elected annually.

1973 ENGLAND, Shirley. Superior Performance. Placed in city tournaments both individually and with her teams since 1963; first in Class A doubles handicap, Class A singles scratch and all-events handicap in 1972; served the MVWBA as treasurer and a board member; also a state delegate.

SCREMIN, Doris. Meritorious Service. Charter member of the MVWBA; member of the board of directors 1962 to 1968 and treasurer 1968–1971; also a state delegate from 1957 to 1972.

VanTONGEREN, Elsie. Meritorious Service. Member of the MVWBA since 1963, elected to the board of directors in 1970; state delegate three years; national delegate two years; junior coach from 1964 to 1970; member of Arizona Women's Bowling Association board of directors since 1971; is a committee member and officer of several local leagues.

1974 HOFFMAN, Virginia. Meritorious Service. Member of the MVWBA since 1959, including board of directors 1961–1962, secretary 1963–1966, president 1968–1971; served the Arizona Women's Bowling Association board of directors from 1964 to 1971; national delegate four years; was co-director of the state tournament for two years; is currently director of Mesa junior board of directors and an officer in many leagues.

JONES, Mary. Superior Performance. Bowled in MVWBA for 12 years; entered in local tournaments every year since 1963, except one; bowled a 688 series and a 289 game for a WIBC medal.

1975 RAFFERTY, Oleta. Superior Performance. A charter member of the 600 Club; received WIBA awards for three all-spare, three triplicate and a Dutch 200 game; currently secretary of the MVWBA; served as both state and national delegate.

TATE, Louine. Meritorious Service. A charter member of the MVWBA, served as secretary from 1959 to 1960, vice president in 1961, president from 1962 to 1966; currently a member of the Phoenix Women's Bowling Association; a league officer, state delegate and a state tournament committee member.

1976 GANO, Adeline. Meritorious Service. A founder, charter member and the first secretary of the MVWBA; was director of the first local tournament; served as league officer, and state and national delegate. In 1974 received the WIBC 20-year pin for participation in state tournaments.

1977 MILLER, Faye. Meritorious Service. Current president and member of the board of directors of the MVWBA; has also been active in the junior program, serving as president, vice president, secretary, and treasurer as well as junior state delegate and director. Received the service award from Arizona Women Bowling Writers in 1976; a state delegate 4 years and a national delegate 2 years; spearheaded the Association newspaper, the administrative manual, and was instrumental in achieving a joint league officers workshop with the men's association. Co-director for two junior state tournaments.

VEATER, Georgia. Superior Performance. A member of the 600 Club, all-events champion at the 600 Club Invitational in 1975. In 1975–1976 season bowled a 278 game with 9 consecutive strikes for a WIBC medal.

National Bowling Hall of Fame and Museum

MILWAUKEE, WISCONSIN

Mailing Address: 5301 S. 76th St, Greendale, 53129. Tel. (414) 421-6400 (American Bowling Congress), 421-9000 (Women's International Bowling Congress). *Contact:* Ken Hurley, ABC Exec. Secy. and Flora Mitchell, WIBC Exec. Secy. *Location:* 75 mi. E. of Madison, 80 mi. N. of Chicago, Ill. *Admission:* Free 8 to 4:30, Monday–Friday, closed weekends and holidays. *Personnel:* ABC officers: Sam Weinstein, Pres; Joe Norris, V.Pres; Ken Hurley, Exec. Secy. WIBC officers: Mrs. Alberta Crowe, Pres; Ms. Flora Mitchell, Exec. Secy. *Nearby Halls of Fame:* Bowling, State (Milwaukee), Business (Chicago, Ill.), Football (Green Bay, 100 mi. N.), Sports (North Webster, Ind, 175 mi. S.E.), Agriculture (West Lafayette, Ind, 190 mi. S.E.), Archery (Grayling, Mich, 200 mi. N.E.), Auto Racing, Basketball (Indianapolis, Ind, 250 mi. S.E.), State (Detroit, Mich, 250 mi. E.).

The National Bowling Hall of Fame and Museum is sponsored, governed and financed jointly by the American Bowling Congress (ABC) and Women's International Bowling Congress (WIBC) which joined their Halls of Fame in 1972, as a result of duplicated services, mixed bowling leagues and too-small individual facilities. Both organizations are autonomous, but remain united in their efforts to honor those bowlers "who through their competitive skills, high personal standards, and dedicated principles have enriched the general welfare, spirit, reputation and progress of the game." The museum, on the first floor of the building, houses a historical display depicting the evolution of bowling equipment (bowling balls from yesteryear, early pins, early telescore and ball returns). The Hall of Fame is on the second floor where the ABC honors its members with three dimensional photographs done in bronze and the WIBC members have oil portraits hanging. Also housed there are memorabilia, such as shoes, uniforms, scrapbooks, awards, trophies, scoresheets and photos. Both organizations contribute to a library of bowling history and bibliographic material that is unsurpassed in scope and content. Films relating to bowling are available to schools through the library. Presently located in a wing of their national headquarters, the ABC and WIBC plan a separate Hall of Fame and Museum of 50,000 square feet in the near future. This Hall is a member of the Association of Sports Museums and Halls of Fame.

Members: 146 as of 1976 (90 ABC and 56 WIBC). ABC nominees must have competed in a minimum of twenty ABC tournaments and possess an outstanding record in additional bowling events. Those nominated must receive 75 percent of the vote for induction into the Hall. Three to five members are elected annually. Equally prestigious is the Hall's Meritorious Service Award presented to an individual whose devotion, service and achievements strengthen the organization from within and advance the sport from without. Electors are writers and announcers with a minimum of ten years experience reporting major bowling events plus members from the Hall of Fame and the Hall's board and past executives. The WIBC Board of Directors, who select the inductees, announce their new members in December and officially induct them in April at the annual meeting. There are three categories of induction: Superior Performance to a bowler whose scoring record indicates extraordinary skill and achievement; Meritorious Service to an individual whose administrative ability improves bowling; and Star of Yesteryear, to a woman overlooked in the past whose accomplishments are either Superior Performance or Meritorious Service. One person from each category is inducted annually.

1941

BODIS, Joseph
Bowler
Born January 16, 1897, in Hungary; Cleveland Bowler of the Half Century 1950; died April 26, 1970.

Bodis came to national attention when he set an ABC tournament record with 8 consecutive all-events totals above 1800 in the period from 1925 to 1932. Before his bowling career ended, he added 3 more for a lifetime total of 11. He also had 4 sanctioned 300 games, and his overall average for 33 years was 193. Bodis was named Cleveland's Bowler of the Half Century in 1950.
Also in: Greater Cleveland Bowling Association Hall of Fame.

CARLSON, Adolph Domianus "Swede"
Bowler
Born June 23, 1897, in Konserum, Sweden; died January 16, 1967.

Carlson came to this country in 1912 and started bowling the following year. In 1928 he won the match game title, but lost it in 1929. He won the Illinois state all-events title in 1930, 1932 and 1933, the Chicago city all-events title in 1937, 1939 and 1943. Carlson also had four all-events above 1900 in ABC tournaments. He led the Chicago Masters Traveling League in 1957–1958 with a 201 average at the age of 61.
Also in: Illinois Bowling Association Hall of Fame.

DAW, Charley
Bowler
Born April 12, 1894, in Beloit, Wis; died January 18, 1947.

With a rocking chair motion and a great hook ball, Charley was the first man to roll two 700 series in ABC tournaments. His average for 23 years was 196. During the 1936 Olympics he was on a team that bowled special matches. During his career Charley had five sanctioned 300 games.

HOWLEY, Peter
Bowler
Born in 1882; died in 1958.

Howley was the only man to bowl in the first 46 ABC tournaments 1901–1949, averaging 178, finally retiring in ill health. He was general manager of several bowling and billiard establishments in the Chicago area, and at one time served as president of the Chicago Bowling Proprietors Association.
Also in: Illinois Bowling Association Hall of Fame.

KOSTER, John
Bowler
Born April 21, 1871, in New York City; died August 14, 1945.

The first person to win four ABC tournament titles, a record unmatched until 1954, John was on the winning team in 1902 and 1912, was first in all-events in 1902 and took first place in doubles in 1913. He carried a 188 average in 23 years of bowling.

LANGE, Herbert W.
Bowler
Born June 20, 1901; married; 7 grandchildren; retired.

Lange was the first man to roll all 200 games (nine) in one ABC tournament. He did it first in 1922 and repeated in 1934. He was also the first to have five all-events totals above 1900. Lange was president of the ABC Hall of Fame board for 12 years.

LINDSEY, Mortimer Joel
Bowler
Born December 20, 1888, in Newark, N.J; died May 16, 1959.

Lindsey was a proficient billiards and a baseball player, as well as a very good bowler. He won three ABC tournaments and his overall average in 46 years of bowling was 192.

MARINO, Enrico "Hank"
Bowler
Born November 27, 1889, in Palermo, Sicily; married; two sons; Bowler of the Half Century 1951; retired in 1965.

A bowler for many years, Hank carried an average of 185 for 57 years in a row. During his bowling days, he rolled two 700 series and had five 800 series. He also had eleven sanctioned 300 games. Hank served two terms as vice president of the Hall of Fame board and was elected Bowler of the Half Century in 1951. At one time Hank, oldtime movie comedian Harold Lloyd and Ned Day (also a Hall of Famer) operated the Llo-Da-Mar bowling center in Santa Monica, California. Hank moved to Milwaukee in 1930 where he operated a bowling establishment until his retirement.
Also in: Illinois Bowling Association Hall of Fame.

SMITH, James
Bowler
Born James Mellilo on September 19, 1882, in Brooklyn, N.Y; died April 21, 1946.

Smith embarked in 1910 on a nationwide exhibition bowling tour which lasted until 1915, and after a few months rest, continued the tour from 1916 until 1924. He earned a reputation as match game king between 1915 and 1922, and was noted for his effortless style and ability as an instructor.

STEERS, Harry Harvey
Bowler
Born October 3, 1880, in Dunlap, Iowa; died February 13, 1963.

Steers competed in 57 of the first 59 ABC tournaments; 56 were consecutive appearances. He won three ABC titles, doubles in 1902 and doubles and all-events in 1918, and the first Peterson Classic held in Chicago in 1921. He created several longevity records, including never having missed a game in 34 years with the Chicago Randolph League, which ceased operation in 1946. His average over 57 years was 181.
Also in: Illinois Bowling Association Hall of Fame.

ZUNKER, Gilbert
Bowler
Born 1899 in Milwaukee, Wis; died December 16, 1938.

In 1933 Gil was the first to roll two 700 series in an ABC tournament. His best ten year average, from 1929 to 1938, was 202 and in his 13 years of bowling, carried a 199 average.

1951

WILMAN, Joseph "Buck"
Bowler
Born December 20, 1905, in Fontanet, Ind; Billiard and Bowling Institute of America Industry Service Award 1959; died October 22, 1969.

An outstanding bowler, commentator and instructor, Wilman was the second man to win four ABC tournaments. Among his many awards and titles are a lifetime record of 13 800 series (8 in a row), three sanctioned 300 games, carried a 197 average for 36 years in a row. He was a member of Brunswick promotional staff and served the Hall of Fame board as president from 1962 to 1966. Wilman was named to the *Bowling Magazine* All-America second team in 1956 and also received the Billiard and Bowling Institute of America Industry Service Award in 1959.
Also in: Illinois Bowling Association Hall of Fame.

1952

DAY, Edward P. "Ned"
Bowler
Born November 11, 1911, in Los Angeles, Calif; died November 26, 1971.

Ned was one of bowling's most articulate spokesmen and promoters, and was one of the first to make extensive exhibition and match game tours. He won the Petersen Classic in Chicago in 1943 and was first in all-events in the ABC tournament in 1948. His best ten-year average, through 1957, was 204. Day went into semi-retirement in the late 1950s but came back to win the Championship Bowling tournament filmed in Toledo, Ohio, in 1959, shown on national television.

1953

GREENWALD, Goldie
Star of Yesteryear
Born 1891; died 1926.

Goldie's abilities crossed not only administrative and competitive boundaries, but sex boundaries as well. Bowling in a men's league in 1918, she established a 191 average and rolled a 732 series, the highest ever for a woman at that time. Two years later still competing with men, she rolled a perfect game in exhibition match play. From 1921 to 1924, Goldie served on the WIBC board of directors, including one year as first vice president. She had won more than 50 awards and medals at the time of her death.

HATCH, Grayce.
Star of Yesteryear
Of the ninety medals Grayce won during her fifty-year career, two of those awards were for winning the WIBC all-events championship in 1925 and 1927. The remainder are divided among state, city and other local association titles. During the 1936 Olympic games in Munich, Germany, she was a member of the American exhibition team. An active member of the Cleveland Women's Bowling Association, she served as president, first vice president and treasurer. Grayce also served on the WIBC board of directors for three years.

JAEGER, Emma
Star of Yesteryear
In 35 years of bowling competition, Emma amassed 125 medals and trophies. Among her many triumphs were the WIBC all-events championship in 1918, 1921, 1928 and 1929, team titles in 1919 and 1923, and three consecutive singles crowns, 1921 to 1923. Emma also won 37 local titles and nine state championships.

STOCKDALE, Louise
Star of Yesteryear
Participating in her first national tournament, Louise won the WIBC doubles in 1922 and the 1937 all-events. Her all-events included a 278 game and nine games with-

out an error. Louise bowled in Detroit's first women's league.
Also in: Bowling Proprietors Association of Greater Detroit Hall of Fame.

WARMBIER, Marie
Star of Yesteryear
Although Marie bowled only ten years before her death in 1937, she garnered seven WIBC championships. Three times she won the team title, in 1928, 1931 and 1933, captured the doubles in 1930, all-events in 1932 and 1935 and the singles in 1935. Her score of 1911 in the 1935 all-events was a WIBC record that stood until 1959. Following the 1934–1935 season, she embarked on a national exhibition tour challenging men bowlers. She rolled one perfect game, several 700 series and averaged between 190 and 200.

1954

KNOX, William
Bowler
Born April 21, 1887, in Philadelphia, Pa; died May 16, 1944.

In 1913 in Toledo, Ohio, Knox rolled the first 300 game in ABC tournament history. Ten years later he won the ABC all-events with 2018, the first total over 2000, and that record stood until 1933. After participating in 22 ABC tournaments, his average was 191.

MILLER, Dorothy
Star of Yesteryear
Quarter Century Club Bowler of the Year, 1961.

In a thirty year career, Dorothy won 10 WIBC championships: team in 1928, 1931, 1933, 1935, 1940 and 1948, doubles in 1929, 1934 and 1940, and all-events in 1938. She also had 13 state and 20 local titles for a total of 93 tournament medals and awards. Dorothy was named Quarter Century Club Bowler of the Year in 1961.

NORRIS, Joseph John
Bowler
Born February 10, 1908, in Springfield, Ill; married in 1938; retired in 1963.

Norris organized the Stroh's Beer team in 1933 and under his captaincy, the team won the 1934 ABC championship and later held the national match game championship between 1942 and 1945. He was president of the ABC Hall of Fame board from 1970 to 1973. In his 46 years of bowling, Joe held a 196 overall average.
Also in: Bowling Proprietors Association of Greater Detroit Hall of Fame.

1955

BLOUIN, James
Bowler
Born December 1, 1886, in Tres Rivieres, Que; died April 6, 1947.

Blouin won the ABC all-events title in 1909 with a 1885 total. In 1911 he captured the singles with a 681. He won the World's Open championship in 1922 and successfully defended his title until retiring in 1926. He held a 192 average over 21 years of bowling.
Also in: Illinois Bowling Association Hall of Fame.

BOHLEN, Philena
Star of Yesteryear
In 1930 Philena took her team on a cross-country exhibition tour, bowling 37 matches in 49 days against the best women's teams in 16 states. She was instrumental in organizing both the Los Angeles and the California Women's Bowling Associations. She served on the WIBC board of directors for 8 years, including four years as fifth vice president. Philena was the originator and designer of the WIBC flag.
Also in: California Women's Bowling Hall of Fame.

McMAHON, James, Jr. "Junie"
Bowler
Born January 3, 1912, in Passaic, N.J; Bowler of the Year 1950; died November 1, 1974.

James won the 1947 ABC tournament singles with a 740 and captured the all-events with a 1965. During his career, he had 8 sanctioned 300 games and carried an average of 203 for 19 years of ABC bowling. McMahon suffered a stroke in 1959 that left him partially paralyzed and unable to bowl. He was named Bowler of the Year in 1950.
Also in: New Jersey State Bowling Association Hall of Fame.

1956

McCUTCHEON, Floretta
Star of Yesteryear
Born July 22, 1888, in Ottumwa, Iowa; died February 2, 1967.

Floretta provided clinics and exhibition matches for more than a quarter million women and children. For those who could not attend her clinics, she wrote booklets covering fundamentals and tips for better bowling. For ten years she rolled exhibition matches and established herself as the dominant woman player in the 1930s. During that time she bowled more than 8000 matches with a 200-plus average. Among her many accomplishments are eleven 800 series, over one hundred 700 series, nine 299 games and ten perfect games. Floretta set the record WIBC league average of 206 in the 1938–1939 season—a record that held until 1952–1953.

1957

CHAPMAN, Emily
Star of Yesteryear
Emily organized leagues and instructed in New York City, Chicago and Poughkeepsie from 1917 until 1950. She helped organize the New York State Women's Bowling Association and served on its board. Over the years she won many local awards and titles, and in 1926 won the WIBC team championship. At the age of 71 Emily and her partner won the city doubles title.

VARIPAPA, Andrew
Bowler
Born March 31, 1891, in Carfizzi, Italy; widower with three children; Bowler of the Year 1948; hobby is golf.

Varipapa was a real trick shot bowling artist and this ability led him into starring in many bowling film shorts: his first, *Strikes and Spares,* was made in 1934. He has made more such films than any other bowler. He was also a leading instructor and exhibition bowler, one of the first to make countrywide tours. At the age of 55 he won the 1946–1947 Bowling Proprietors Association of America All-Star tournament and the very next year became the first bowler to repeat as All-Star champion. At the age of 78 Varipapa developed wrist and arm problems in his right arm, and was forced to switch to left-handed bowling. In only 18 months he was carrying an average of 180. He is a member of the Professional Bowlers Association and was elected Bowler of the Year in 1948.

1958

BENKOVIC, Frank
Bowler
Born October 7, 1904, in Racesdorf, Austria-Hungary; married in 1951; hobby is fishing.

Frank was the first to win successive doubles championships in the ABC tournament, 1932 and 1933. His 2259 pins in the 1932 Gold Coast tournament in Chicago is the nine game tournament all-events record. During World War II Benkovic gave bowling exhibitions in more than 250 camps. He was president of the Hall of Fame board from 1968 to 1970. His 44-year average is 193.

BURLING, Catherine
Star of Yesteryear
During her competition years Catherine rolled five 700 series, and carried a 190-plus average from 1936 to 1946; her highest average was 198. She is presently a bowling instructor and active in bowling center activities.

1959

MRAZ, Josephine
Star of Yesteryear
Josephine served the WIBC board of directors for seven years, three as director, three as treasurer and one as second vice president. She helped organize the national 600 Bowling Club and was a charter member of the WIBC Pioneer Club. She was also active in organizing women's bowling associations in Ohio and Pennsylvania for 45 years, having served as the secretary for the Cleveland Women's Bowling Association for 45 years.

WARD, Walter G.
Bowler
Born November 29, 1897, in Cleveland, Ohio; married in 1944; retired; hobbies are billiards, golf and gardening; lives in Scottsdale, Ariz.

During his career, Walter rolled an amazing 317 series of 700 or more pins. Among his many titles and awards, he won the Cleveland city singles in 1927, 1947 and 1959, as well as the Ohio state singles in 1938 and 1950. He has 12 sanctioned 300 games. During W. W. II, he gave exhibitions at 263 military bases.
Also in: Greater Cleveland Bowling Association Hall of Fame.

YOUNG, George
Bowler
Born October 3, 1909, in Omega, Ga; died August 30, 1959.
Young was the Georgia state champion horseshoe pitcher and didn't take up bowling until moving to Brooklyn in 1933. He operated bowling establishments in the New York area until moving to Detroit in 1944. He was a member of the ABC champion Pfeiffer Beer team three times. George was named to the Bowling Magazine All-America second team in 1956.
Also in: Bowling Proprietors Association of Greater Detroit Hall of Fame and Michigan Sports Hall of Fame.

1960

BRANDT, Albert R.
Bowler
Born December 14, 1903, in Lockport, N.Y; married; two children; self-employed.

Brandt gained his greatest fame when he put games of 297, 289 and 300 together for an 886 series on October 25, 1939. This is still the ABC sanctioned league all time high series. He is a member of the Professional Bowlers Association and served as president on the Hall of Fame board in 1975.
Also in: Buffalo Bowling Association Hall of Fame.

SIMON, Violet E. "Billy"
Star of Yesteryear
During the 1934–1935 season, Violet averaged 202 and won the 1935 WIBC doubles. In state tournament play, she won two doubles, one singles and one all-events while adding a city title in both singles and all-events. She was instrumental in organizing the Texas Women's Bowling Association, as well as other associations throughout the state and area.
Also in: San Antonio Bowling Association Hall of Fame and Texas Women's Bowling Association Hall of Fame.

1961

RUSCHMEYER, Addie
Star of Yesteryear
A bowler for over 60 years, Addie won her first bowling trophy in 1911. She was a charter member of the Greater New York City Women's Bowling Association. In 1933 she traveled with Uncle Joe Thum's bowling team to Europe and earned the women's international championship. Her highest average was 183 in 1933. Addie also competed against men bowlers in exhibitions.

SIXTY, William, Sr.
Meritorious Service
Born November 30, 1899, in Milwaukee, Wis; married; two sons; retired sportswriter.

Bill wrote for the *Milwaukee Journal* sports staff from 1914 until 1974, and was a pioneer in writing nationally syndicated bowling lessons. In 1956 he won a first prize in *Bowling Magazine* annual writers contest. He was also honored with a watch by the Bowling Writers Association of America for meritorious service. Sixty served as president of the Hall of Fame board from 1966 to 1968. His average for 47 consecutive years was 185.

WOLF, Phil
Bowler
Born November 2, 1869; died July 7, 1935.

Wolf was a member of the ABC tournament team champions in 1909 and again in 1920. In 1937 at the age of 58, he won the ABC all-events title with a 1928. His 25 year average was 198.

1962

CRIMMINS (Krzyminski), John "General"
Bowler
Born May 2, 1895, in Toledo, Ohio; Bowler of the Year 1942.

In the 1937 National Elks tournament, John shared in all four titles—team, doubles, singles and all-events—with a 2156 count in all-events that is still the record. He was elected Bowler of the Year in 1942. His average over 40 years was 195.
Also in: Bowling Proprietors Association of Greater Detroit Hall of Fame and National Polish-American Sports Hall of Fame and Museum.

RUMP, Anita
Star of Yesteryear
Anita won her first local title in 1926, the doubles crown, with her mother as her partner, In 1928 and 1930 she won the WIBC singles championships. During her competitive years she also earned 9 state all-events titles, was a member of 15 state championship teams, won 5 state doubles and 1 singles crown. She was an instructor and active in American Junior Bowlers Congress organizing. Anita was a charter member of Les Dames de 700 Club.

1963

BAUMGARTEN, Elmer H.
Meritorious Service
Born 1881; died 1961.

Baumgarten served the ABC for many years, starting as a director in 1925, third vice president in 1930, acting secretary in 1932, and finally elected secretary from 1933 to 1951. He helped guide the ABC through many trying times, especially during the Depression years and W. W. II. He believed in action and complete authority, and his rigid demands for honesty, fair play and strict adherence to the rules stamped him as "Mr. ABC" in the eyes of Congress members.
Also in: Illinois Bowling Association Hall of Fame.

COLLIER, Charles O.
Bowler and Meritorious Service
Born 1877; died 1957.

From 1912 until 1951 Collier supervised the construction and maintenance of the tournament lanes for Brunswick. He rolled 39 ABC tournaments and carried a 186 lifetime average.
Also in: Illinois Bowling Association Hall of Fame.

EASTER, Ebber Darnell "Sarge"
Bowler
Born November 20, 1882; died August 14, 1961.

Easter served 30 years in the U.S. Army and bowled his first ABC tournament in 1938, turning down reenlistment as a first sergeant in order to bowl. He went back into service as a private. He didn't begin his major competition until he was 58 years old. Easter bowled a perfect game in 1953 at the age of 70, and again in 1955 at the age of 72. His average for 16 years of bowling was 193.

FAZIO, Basil "Buzz"
Bowler
Born February 7, 1908, in Aultman, Ohio; married; two children; hobby is golf.

In the fall of 1955 Buzz won seven straight live television matches in Chicago. He rolled an 802 series in Detroit, the first live 800 ever televised. He is a member and past president of the Professional Bowlers Association. During his illustrious career he has bowled 4 sanctioned 300 games, had 17 all-events over 1800, carried a 197 average for 38 years in a row, and was named to the *Bowling Magazine* All-America second team in 1956, 1957, 1959 and the first team in 1958.
Also in: Bowling Proprietors Association of Greater Detroit Hall of Fame and Professional Bowlers Association Hall of Fame.

HAGERTY, Jack
Meritorious Service
Born in 1876; died 1955.

Hagerty spent nearly 60 years as a bowling proprietor and played a prominent role in obtaining and helping to stage five ABC tournaments in Toledo, Ohio, between 1913 and 1926. He was a charter member and president of the Bowling Proprietors Association of America, and also president of the Ohio State Bowling Association. Jack also served as an ABC director in 1912–1913. In 1947, to celebrate his 50th year as a bowling proprietor, a two-day celebration was held, including a sweepstakes tournament that 96 of the nation's outstanding teams attended.

KNEPPRATH, Jeannette
Meritorious Service
Billiard and Bowling Institute of America Industry Service Award 1961.

Jeannette Knepprath served the WIBC as president from 1924 to 1960, and during her tenure saw the WIBC membership grow from 2885 in 29 cities to nearly 2 million in over 2100 cities. She was the first woman to receive the Billiard and Bowling Institute of America Industry Service Award in 1961. Jeannette bowled in 44 WIBC championship tournaments from 1919 to 1966. She was the secretary of the Wisconsin Women's Bowling Association from 1924 until 1970. She is a WIBC life member.

LANGTRY, Abraham L.
Meritorious Service
Born August 1, 1874; died in 1941.

Langtry served the ABC as secretary for 25 years, taking office in 1907. He was responsible for moving their headquarters from Dayton, Ohio, to Milwaukee, Wisconsin. It was his vision and determination that helped the ABC build its sturdy foundation on which the game rests today.

NAGY, Steve Joseph
Bowler
Born August 10, 1913, in Shoaf, Pa; Bowler of the Year 1952, 1955; died November 10, 1966.

Nagy bowled in his first ABC tournament in 1939 and 13 years later, he and Johnny Klares bowled the all-time ABC doubles record of 1453. During his illustrious career, he bowled four sanctioned 299 games and six perfect games. Steve was elected Bowler of the Year in 1952 and again in 1955. *Bowling Magazine* named him to its All-America first team in 1956 and 1958, and the second team in 1957. His average for 24 years was 197.
Also in: Greater Cleveland Bowling Association Hall of Fame.

PETERSEN, Louis P.
Meritorious Service
Born 1883; died 1958.

Louis Petersen started his famous Petersen Classic in 1921 and that event now attracts more than 20,000 entrants. He also originated the Peterson Point system, a point for each 50 pins, a point for each game won, and it is still used today in several match game tournaments. Petersen was instrumental in forming the All-Star tournament with the *Chicago Tribune* in 1941 and was a founder of the Bowling Proprietors Association of America in 1932.
Also in: Illinois Bowling Association Hall of Fame.

RYAN, Esther
Star of Yesteryear
Esther was secretary of the Milwaukee Women's Bowling Association for 30 years. During her competitive years she won three WIBC championships: all-events in 1934, team titles in 1939 and 1947. Over the years, Esther's team won 178 individual championships, 48 of them by her.

1964

BURTON, Nelson, Sr.
Bowler
Born November 25, 1906, in New York City; married; four children; hobby is junior baseball; currently a bowling proprietor.

Burton spent most of his early years in Dallas, moving to St. Louis in 1938. In addition to his ABC tournament career, he was a fearless competitor in head match game play, often risking his own money in these matches instead of depending on sponsors. During his career he averaged 196 for 29 years. He is a member of the Professional Bowlers Association.
Also in: Greater St. Louis Bowling Association Hall of Fame.

KAY, Nora
Meritorious Service
Nora was a member of the WIBC board of directors from 1932 to 1955, including sergeant-at-arms the last 22 years, and is a life member emeritus. She served as president, vice president and director of the Wisconsin Women's Bowling Association, and was an association and league organizer in cities in New York, Wisconsin and Ohio and held local offices in nearly every city. Nora was on the runner-up team in the 1923 WIBC tournament, and also won many state and local titles.

LADEWIG, Marion Van Oosten
Superior Performance
Michigan's Woman Athlete of All-Time.

In the early 1950s Marion attained almost every possible bowling achievement, winning the 1950 WIBC all-events and team titles. She carried a 204 league average in the 1952–1953 season and in the 1955 WIBC tournament, she won the all-events and doubles title. Women's match play began in 1957, and Marion won the title, repeated the victory in 1960 and 1962 and was a runner-up in 1961. She also has eight Bowling Proprietors Association of America titles and four World's Invitational titles. She placed second in the 1962 Queens tournament. Marion was named Woman Bowler of the Year every year from 1950 to 1954, 1957 to 1959 and again in 1963. She was also named Michigan's Woman Athlete of All Time.
Also in: Grand Rapids Sports Hall of Fame and Michigan Sports Hall of Fame.

TWYFORD, Sally
Star of Yesteryear
During a career that covered 36 years Sally won 6 WIBC championships: team in 1930, all-events in 1930, 1933 and 1941, singles in 1933 and 1940. She also won 12 state and 9 local titles. Sally was a famous exhibition bowler, organizer of leagues and instructress. She starred in a bowling film for Columbia Pictures in 1943.

1965

GIBSON, Therman
Bowler
Born January 30, 1917, in Harbor Springs, Mich; died March 28, 1969.

Gibson won many titles and honors, among them three sanctioned 300 games, four sanctioned 299s and a 268 triplicate, which is the second all-time high. On January 2, 1961, Therman rolled six straight strikes on the Jackpot Bowling show and won $75,000. His average for 31 years in a row was 198.
Also in: Bowling Proprietors Association of Greater Detroit Hall of Fame.

PHALER, Emma
Meritorious Service
Emma served as Columbus Women's Bowling Association secretary in 1926 to 1927. She became executive secretary of the WIBC in 1927, serving until 1965. She initiated the WIBC Hall of Fame and is a life member of WIBC.

SCHULTE, Myrtle
Star of Yesteryear
Myrtle won the WIBC singles and all-events in 1931 and the team title in 1932. Her 1931 singles score of 650 and 1742 all-events were records for that time. She won her first city title in 1924, her first season of bowling, and later added many other championships, including the state doubles event. She organized St. Louis' first evening women's league. Myrtle also served as president and sergeant-at-arms of the St. Louis Women's Bowling Association.

1966

ALLEN, Harold J.
Bowler
Born January 6, 1897; died in 1964.

Allen became the youngest bowler ever to win an ABC championship, when at the age of 18 he and his brother Ray combined to take the doubles crown. He competed in 46 ABC tournaments, 45 of them consecutively, averaging 188. He was one of the organizers of the *Detroit Times* All-Star Classic League (now the Detroit Classic) and served as its president for the first 12 years. In 1950 Allen was president of the Bowling Proprietors Association of America, which he helped found.
Also in: Bowling Proprietors Association of Greater Detroit Hall of Fame.

BOMAR, Herbert Booth "Buddy"
Bowler and Instructor
Born September 27, 1916, in Ardmore, Okla; married; 3 children; Bowler of the Year 1945, 1947; currently stockbroker in Chicago, Ill.

Bomar was one of bowling's most articulate and prominent instructors. For many years while on the Brunswick promotion staff, he conducted nation-wide clinics on the latest teaching methods. Since becoming a stockbroker, he has retired from professional and league bowling. Buddy was elected Bowler of the Year in 1945 and 1947, and is a member of the Professional Bowlers Association.
Also in: Illinois Bowling Association Hall of Fame.

FRITZ, Deane
Star of Yesteryear
Deane won the WIBC team championships in 1919 and 1923, and all-events in 1923. Through 1969 she had bowled in 45 WIBC championship tournaments. During her bowling career she also won 21 local and state association championships. She served on the board of directors of the Toledo Women's Bowling Association.

MARTIN, Sylvia Wene
Superior Performance
Woman Bowler of the Year 1955, 1960; Pennsylvania's Sportswoman of the Year 1961; Philadelphia's Outstanding Athlete 1963.

Sylvia won the WIBC doubles in 1959, and was the only woman to bowl three perfect games, two in tournaments. She won the bowling Proprietors Association of America All-Star event in 1955 and 1960, and was named Woman Bowler of the Year those same two years. In 1961 Sylvia was named Pennsylvania's Sportswoman of the Year and Philadelphia's Outstanding Athlete in 1963.

SPECK, Berdie
Meritorious Service
Berdie was a member of the WIBC board of directors for 34 years, the last 30 years as first vice president. She bowled in 41 consecutive WIBC championship tournaments and attended 43 consecutive WIBC annual meetings. She also served the St. Louis Women's Bowling Association as secretary for 40 years and was state association president for 11 years. She is active in bowling promotion and association organizing. Berdie is a WIBC member emeritus.

1967

BUJACK, Fred
Bowler
Born January 23, 1912 in St. Joseph, Mich; died January 2, 1971.

Bujack won more ABC championships (eight) than any other bowler until fellow Hall of Famer Bill Lillard tied his mark in 1971. In 1953 he and fellow Hall of Famer Don Carter won the ABC doubles title. During his career he had two sanctioned 300 games and his 31 year average was 192.
Also in: Bowling Proprietors Association of Greater Detroit Hall of Fame.

HOCHSTADTER, Madalene
Star of Yesteryear
Madalene captained the team that won the 1927 WIBC championship. She was treasurer of the Illinois Women's Bowling Association and a director of the Chicago City Women's Bowling Association. She bowled in 46 WIBC tournaments, including 38 consecutive years, from 1930 until her death in 1970.

KARTHEISER, Frank Clemence "Midge"
Bowler
Born November 14, 1888, in Chicago, Ill, died December 19, 1968.

Frank began his bowling career at the age of 11 when he started as a pin setter. Within a few years he was a top notch bowler and joined the famous Brunswick Mineralites team where he starred for ten years. During his bowling career he had three sanctioned 300 games, and his best average came in 1926 when he carried a 212.
Also in: Illinois Bowling Association Hall of Fame.

LASHER, Iolia
Meritorious Service
Iolia was president of the New York State Women's Bowling Association from 1932 until 1958. She was a member of the WIBC board of directors from 1934 to 1963, serving as second vice president, third vice president and director. She helped organize the Albany Women's Bowling Association and served as its secretary-treasurer. Iolia is a WIBC member emeritus.
Also in: New York State Lifetime Sports Hall of Fame.

MERCURIO, Walter "Skang"
Bowler
Born July 24, 1896, in Naples, Italy; died January 25, 1972.

During his bowling career Skang won several Cleveland city and Ohio state titles, and has three sanctioned 300 games. In 25 years of ABC tournaments, he averaged 191.
Also in: Greater Cleveland Bowling Association Hall of Fame.

1968

BUNETTA, William
Bowler and Instructor
Born October 20, 1919, in Detroit, Mich; married; hobby is golf.

In addition to being a great individual performer, Bunetta is known as one of the game's finest instructors. He has worked as a commentator on several nationally televised matches. During his bowling career he rolled five sanctioned 300 games. He is a member of the Professional Bowlers Association.
Also in: Bowling Proprietors Association of Greater Detroit Hall of Fame.

CAMPI, Louis
Bowler
Born March 18, 1905, in Verona, Italy; married; three children; currently a bowling proprietor in Dumont, N.J; hobbies are baseball and bocci.

Campi won the first Professional Bowlers Association tournament, the Empire Open, in Albany, N.Y, in 1959. During his career he had six sanctioned 300 games and was named to the All-America team in 1957 by *Bowling Magazine.* He is a member of the Professional Bowlers Association.
Also in: New Jersey State Bowling Association Hall of Fame.

DOEHRMAN, William
Bowler
Born in 1888; resides in Fort Wayne, Ind.

Doehrman has bowled in 64 ABC tournaments, and is one of only two bowlers to participate in more than 60 ABC's. He has also bowled more games, 573, and knocked down more pins, 104,090, than any other bowler in the history of the ABC tournament. Doehrman has been a member of three Indiana state championship teams, as well as the co-holder of a state doubles title.

FARAGALLI, Alfred Joseph "Lindy"
Bowler
Born December 12, 1911, in Paterson, N.J; married; two children.

Faragalli is a member of the Professional Bowlers Association, and over the years has logged 3 299 games and 14 perfect games. He was first in the 1958 ABC all-events with a 2043 total. Lindy was named to the *Bowling Magazine* All-America second team in 1958.
Also in: New Jersey State Bowling Association Hall of Fame.

GERSONDE, Russell Herman
Bowler
Born September 15, 1907, in Milwaukee, Wis; widower; two children; currently a carpenter contractor; his hobby is all sports.

Gersonde won the Petersen Classic tournament in 1942 and 1944. His five Wisconsin State all-events titles in 1943, 1947, 1951, 1953 and 1961 is an all-time record. His average for 35 years is 190.

HERMANN, Cornelius "Cone"
Bowler
Born April 9, 1903, in St. Louis, Mo; Rip Van Winkle Award 1957; died in 1957.

Hermann's name is synonymous with the great Hermann Undertakers teams (named after his family funeral business) of the late 1930s and early 1940s. His team reached its peak January 27, 1937, by rolling a record league series of 3797 and a team game of 1325. Both scores have since been surpassed, but the series still ranks as the second best of all-time. Shortly before his death in 1957, Hermann received the Rip Van Winkle Award from the Bowling Writers Association of America.
Also in: Greater St. Louis Bowling Association Hall of Fame.

KAWOLICS, Edward
Bowler
Born November 15, 1907, in Scranton, Pa; married 1946; currently a business machine operator in Chicago, Ill; hobbies are golf and fishing.

Edward was the all-events winner in the Illinois State tournament in 1944 with a 1960 total. He has one sanctioned 300 game and three sanctioned 299 games. As a professional Kawolics was ineligible to compete in the fifth world tournament of the *Fédération Internationale des Quilleurs* in Mexico City in November of 1963. However, he was named coach of both the men's and women's teams, the first ever to represent the United States and ABC in world competition.

KRISTOF, Joseph Frank
Bowler
Born December 8, 1920, in Toledo, Ohio; married 1951; three children; currently a pro shop owner in Columbus, Ohio; hobbies are fishing and golf.

Kristof is a member of the Professional Bowlers Association, and during his bowling career, had two sanctioned 300 games. His ABC average for 34 years was 194.

KRUMSKE, Paul Albert
Bowler
Born July 25, 1912, in Chicago, Ill; married; Chicago's Bowler of the Half Century 1951; hobbies are golf, photography and duplicate bridge.

Krumske was secretary of the Chicago Classic league for many years. He was voted Chicago's Bowler of the Half Century in a 1951 Chicago Bowler newspaper poll. He was also selected on seven *Bowlers Journal* All-America teams. Krumske was president of the ABC Hall of Fame board from 1973 to 1975.
Also in: Illinois Bowling Association Hall of Fame.

McBRIDE, Bertha
Meritorious Service
Bertha was a member of the WIBC board of directors from 1948 to 1967, and is now a member emeritus of the WIBC. At the state and local level she served as president of the Minnesota Bowling Council, and was president for five years of both the St. Paul and the Minnesota Women's Bowling Associations.
Also in: St. Paul Bowling Association Hall of Fame.

O'DONNELL, Charles
Bowler
Born October 12, 1913, in Maryville, Mo; married in 1942; currently owns a bowling supply store in St. Louis; hobby is fishing.

During his bowling career Charles' 236.6 average for 84 games in the All-Star doubles league in 1961–1962 in St. Louis is the record in two-man competition. He rolled four sanctioned 300 games.
Also in: Greater St. Louis Bowling Association Hall of Fame.

SCHWOEGLER, Conrad Anthony
Bowler
Born January 2, 1917, in Madison, Wis; Bowler of the Year 1949; currently a bowling lanes owner; hobby is antique cars.

Schwoegler became a bowling sensation when he won the 1942 All-Star tournament at the age of 24. He repeated as champion in 1948. During his career he rolled three sanctioned 300 games. He was also elected Bowler of the Year in 1949.

SIELAFF, Louis A.
Bowler
Born December 10, 1915, in Detroit, Mich; died May 1, 1964.

Sielaff started bowling in 1927, and later captained the Pfeiffer Beer team, the only three-time ABC team and four-time team all-events champions since its organization in 1944.
Also in: Bowling Proprietors Association of Greater Detroit Hall of Fame.

SMITH, Grace
Star of Yesteryear
Grace joined the first women's league in Chicago in 1917 and was secretary for the Illinois Women's Bowling Association for 18 years. She was the local association secretary for seven years also. From 1925 to 1947 Grace instructed, organized leagues and promoted junior bowling. During her bowling career she won three WIBC team titles, including first team to win consecutive championships, 1924–1925, and two doubles titles.

SPARANDO, Tony "Ace"
Bowler
Born January 18, 1906, in Brooklyn, N.Y; married in 1942; one child; hobby is baseball.

Tony is one of the few remaining top stars who "pin" rather than spot bowl. He is a member of the Professional Bowlers Association. During his career he won the Petersen Classic in 1946 in Chicago. He has two sanctioned 300 games.

SPINELLA, Barney "Jumping Jack"
Bowler
Born February 1, 1893, in Carneto, Italy; married; one child; retired; currently lives in Miami, Fla.

Spinella was nicknamed Jumping Jack during his bowling days because of his leaping antics on the approach after delivering his ball. He was a three-time ABC tournament champion, taking the all-events title in 1922 and 1927, and the doubles with his brother Chris in 1922. His 26 year average in ABC tournaments was 192.

1969

BENSINGER, Robert F.
Meritorious Service
Born 1898.

In 1918, when Bensinger first joined the Brunswick Corporation, he was employed as a lumber wagon driver. He became vice president in 1925 and president in 1931, before becoming chairman of the board from 1931 to 1950. He served in this capacity until 1963 when he retired. Bensinger's support of bowling went far beyond the role of manufacturing firm executive. Under his guidance the company built up a large staff of star players for exhibition work and personal appearances.

HIGLEY, Margaret
Meritorious Service
Margaret is a member emeritus of WIBC having served the board of directors for 22 years, as director from 1945 to 1955 and sergeant-at-arms from 1955 to 1967. She was secretary-treasurer of the National Women Bowling Writers Association from 1956 to 1967. She was also president, vice-president and secretary of the Omaha Women's Bowling Association and president of the Nebraska Women's Bowling Association. Margaret is a director of the San Jose Women's Bowling Association and active in American Junior Bowling Congress organizations.

JOSEPH, Joseph George
Bowler
Born April 11, 1918, in Clarksburg, W.Va; married in 1940; two sons; currently a bowling proprietor; hobby is golf.

Joe Joseph is noted for one of the smoothest deliveries in the bowling game. He was an outstanding semipro football player and softball pitcher in his younger days. After turning to bowling he garnered many awards and titles. He has six sanctioned 300 games and two sanctioned 299 games. He is a member of the Professional Bowlers Association and was named to the *Bowling Magazine* second team in 1959, 1962 and 1963, as well as the first team in 1961.

LUBY, David
Meritorious Service
Born 1870; died 1925.

Luby founded the *Bowlers Journal* in 1913, and his grandson Mort, Jr, is the present editor and publisher. In 1919 he was elected an executive committeeman of the ABC, a position equivalent to today's director. He served in that capacity until his death.

MARTINO, John O.
Bowler and Meritorious Service
Born July 8, 1897, in Teano, Italy; married; one child; retired newspaper comptroller; lives in Syracuse, N.Y.

Martino made his mark in three levels of bowling. He was an outstanding bowler, holding a 190 average after 41 ABC tournaments. He was active in administrative positions, serving as president of ABC from 1947 to 1948. He was also president of the New York State and Syracuse associations. He wrote a bowling column for Syracuse newspapers and served as the first president of the Bowling Writers Association of America.

ROBINSON, Leona
Star of Yesteryear
Leona won the 1939 WIBC team championship, and during her 35 years of bowling, earned 50 medals, pins and trophies. She carried the highest averages in Kansas City for 15 years. She is responsible for organizing many leagues and during the 1930s Leona also wrote bowling columns for Kansas City newspapers.

1970

CARTER, Donald James "Bosco"
Bowler
Born July 29, 1926, in St. Louis, Mo; Bowler of the Year six times; hobbies are golf, art painting; currently lives in Miami, Fla.

Carter was the first star to score a "grand slam" of bowling's match game titles. He won the All-Star, World's Invitational, Professional Bowlers Association national championship and the 1961 ABC Masters. In 1970 Carter was voted the greatest bowler in history in a poll of veteran writers by *Bowling.* Because of periodic leg and knee troubles, he has limited his tournament play to three or four appearances a year. He is a member and was the first president of the Professional Bowlers Association. Don was named Bowler of the Year in 1953, 1954, 1957, 1958, 1960 and 1962 by the Bowling Writers Association of America. *Bowling Magazine* named him to its first All-America team every year from 1956 to 1963, and the second team in 1964. He has 13 sanctioned 300 games, and 5 sanctioned 299 games among his many awards and titles.
Also in: Greater St. Louis Bowling Association Hall of Fame and Professional Bowlers Association Hall of Fame.

DUVAL, Helen
Superior Performance
Helen won the 1969 WIBC team and all-events, the latter with a 1927 total. She has bowled in many state and local association tournaments, and carried a 210 league average in 1970–1971. She is director and second vice president of California Women's Bowling Association. Helen is also director of the Alameda County Women's Bowling Association, and active in American Junior Bowling Congress organizations.
Also in: California Women's Bowling Hall of Fame.

FELLMETH, Catherine
Star of Yesteryear
Catherine won the 1942 WIBC team title and the 1946 all-events. In 1946 she was the first woman named to the Brunswick Staff of Champions and spent the next eight years instructing bowlers and giving exhibitions in the United States and Canada.

WEBER, Richard Anthony
Bowler
Born December 23, 1929, in Indianapolis, Ind; married; 4 children, 1 grandchild; Bowler of the Year three times; currently co-owner of bowling lanes in St. Louis, Mo; hobby is golf.

Dick joined the St. Louis Budweisers in 1955, their second year. He bowled games of 258, 258 and 259 in Budweiser's record 3858 series in 1958. He has won more Professional Bowlers Association (PBA) titles, 24, than any other bowler. He is a member and past president of the PBA. During his illustrious career, Dick was named to the *Bowling Magazine* All-America first team in 1956, 1957, every year from 1960 to 1966, again in 1969 and 1971. He made their second team in 1959, 1967, 1968 and 1974. He was also named Bowler of the Year in 1961, 1963 and 1965. Weber has 17 sanctioned 300 games and 7 sanctioned 299 games to his credit.
Also in: Greater St. Louis Bowling Association Hall of Fame and Professional Bowlers Association Hall of Fame.

WEINSTEIN, Sam
Meritorious Service
Born 1914; Mort Luby Distinguished Service Award 1964; currently lives in Chicago, Ill.

Sam has been a producer and announcer of several televised bowling shows and his movie of a gag bowling routine with comedian Jerry Lewis and fellow Hall of Famer Paul Krumske raised thousands of dollars for muscular dystrophy research. In his 40 years of broadcasting on Chicago radio and television, he became known as the "Tenpin Tattler." In 1939 Weinstein established the first retail bowling pro shop. He received the Mort Luby Distinguished Service award in 1964.
Also in: Illinois Bowling Association Hall of Fame.

WOOD, Ann
Meritorious Service.
Ann has been a member of the Cincinnati Women's Bowling Association board of directors since 1930, also serving as secretary from 1938 to the present. She was a member of the Ohio Women's Bowling Association from 1943 to 1960, including second vice president. She served as a member of the WIBC board of directors from 1945 to 1968, including office of fourth vice president from 1950 to 1968; she is currently a member emeritus. Ann helped develop the format of the WIBC Queens Tournament and served as its manager through 1968.

1971

GARMS, Shirley
Superior Performance
Woman Bowler of the Year 1961, 1962; Chicago's Bowler of the Decade 1970; Queen of Chicago Bowlers five times.

Shirley captained the WIBC championship teams in 1955 and 1965, and won the doubles title in 1964. She was also runnerup in the 1964 Queens Tournament. She won the Bowling Proprietors Association of America All-Star tournament in 1962, and was named Woman Bowler of the Year in 1961 and 1962. Shirley has been named Queen of Chicago Bowlers five times and Bowler of the Decade in Chicago in 1970. During her career, she had more than 70 state, area and local tournament wins.

LEVINE, Sam
Meritorious Service
Born 1913; currently lives in Cleveland, Ohio.

Levine founded the *Cleveland Kegler* bowling newspaper in 1937 and is still its editor and publisher. He has been president of the Bowling Writers Association of America and has won first place in the editorial division of *Bowling*'s annual writing competition three times. He is secretary of the Cleveland and Ohio Bowling Proprietors Associations.
Also in: Greater Cleveland Bowling Association Hall of Fame.

LUBANSKI, Edward Anthony
Bowler
Born September 3, 1929, in Detroit, Mich; married; four children; Bowler of the Year 1959; currently a salesman; lives in Detroit.

Lubanski was a pitcher in the St. Louis Browns' farm system, but quit baseball at the age of 21 to join fellow Hall of Famer Ed Easter, then 67 years old, to become the youngest-oldest duo ever crowned national doubles champions. In 1959 Ed became the second man to win four ABC titles in one tournament—singles, all-events, team title and team all-events. He was named Bowler of the Year in 1959, and was named to *Bowling Magazine* All-America first team in 1958 and 1959, and the second team in 1960 and 1961.
Also in: Bowling Proprietors Association of Greater Detroit Hall of Fame.

McCULLOUGH, Howard W.
Meritorious Service
Born 1900; died 1974.

Howard entered the sport of bowling as a jeweler supplying high score award rings to the Detroit Bowling Association. He was active as a team sponsor, vice president of the Association for four years and president for five seasons. He was an ABC director during the 1936–1937 season. Howard was noted for his work with charity promotions, notably as chairman of the March of Dimes sports committee in the 1950s. He was instrumental in founding the Detroit Bowling Council, one of the first citywide bowling councils of its kind. He served Brunswick Corporation as an executive for 24 years before his retirement.
Also in: Bowling Proprietors Association of Greater Detroit Hall of Fame.

SMALL, Tess Morris
Star of Yesteryear
Tess won the WIBC all-events, team and doubles championships in 1940, and the team title in 1942. Her 663 team contribution was the best series in the 1942 tournament. She also won seven state team and two doubles titles in Illinois, as well as several local championships in Chicago. She is a noted bowling instructress.

STEIN, Otto, Jr.
Bowler
Born January 20, 1893, in St. Louis, Mo; died March 16, 1949.

Stein compiled an outstanding record in St. Louis as a match game bowler in the 1920s and 1930s. He was one of the first to roll three 1900 all-events totals in the ABC tournament. His average in 33 years of ABC tournament play was 192.
Also in: Greater St. Louis Bowling Association Hall of Fame.

THOMA, Frank "Sykes"
Bowler
Born January 29, 1896, in Des Plaines, Ill; retired.

Frank is the winner of several Illinois state titles. In 1916 he won the Petersen Fall Classic and also the all-events title in the ABC tournament.
Also in: Illinois Bowling Association Hall of Fame.

1972

CASSIO, Martin
Bowler
Born August 15, 1904, in Palermo, Italy; died December 20, 1972.

Cassio took up bowling in 1930 and in 1944 was one of the first to bowl a 300 game in national match game play, at a time when that type of competition didn't qualify for ABC sanction. In 1946 he starred in AMF's first bowling film, *Ten Pin Magic.* His 30-year average in ABC tournament play was 196.
Also in: New Jersey State Bowling Association Hall of Fame and Union County Bowling Association Hall of Fame.

CHASE, LeRoy
Meritorious Service
Born 1908; died 1971.

Chase spent 40 years writing about the game as a member of the *Peoria Journal-Star* sports staff. He served in such executive capacities as president of the Illinois Bowling Association, and the Bowling Writers Association of America. LeRoy was elected to the ABC board of directors in 1959, and became a vice-president in 1965. He was third vice president at the time of his death.
Also in: Illinois Bowling Association Hall of Fame.

HARTRICK, Stella
Star of Yesteryear
Stella earned a special award for high series, 620, in the 1941 WIBC tournament, and in 1942 won the doubles championship. She was a member of seven state championship teams, won two state singles and two all-events, as well as many local titles. At the age of 74 Stella rolled a three-game series of 578.
Also in: Bowling Proprietors Association of Greater Detroit Hall of Fame.

LILLARD, William Terrell
Bowler
Born October 13, 1927, in Ft. Worth, Tex; married; two sons; Bowler of the Year 1956; currently lives in Houston; co-owner of a bowling center.

In 1956 Lillard was the first man to win four titles in one ABC tournament, bowling with the team and team all-events champion Falstaffs, partnering with Stan Gifford for the doubles and capturing the individual all-events. In 1951 he won the Texas state and Dallas city all-events titles and in 1952, the Houston city all-events. He was named Bowler of the Year in 1956 and named to the *Bowling Magazine* All-America first team in 1956 and 1957 and the second team in 1958 and 1966. During his career he has rolled four sanctioned 300 games. He is a member of the Professional Bowlers Association.
Also in: Texas Sports Hall of Fame.

ORTNER, Beverly
Superior Performance
Beverly has the distinction of being the first woman to bowl an 800 three-game series (267-264-287=818) and the first to bowl a four-game series over 1000 (1005). She averaged 206 during 1967–1968 and 205 in two leagues in 1968–1969. She has one perfect game and 22 three-game series over the 700 mark. Beverly was a member of the 1969 WIBC team champions. She has also won many state and local titles in Sioux City, Iowa.
Also in: Iowa Women's Bowling Association Hall of Fame.

RAYMER, Milton
Meritorious Service
Born 1906.
In 1946 Raymer founded the American Junior Bowling Congress and served 15 years as its executive secretary. From a membership of 8767 in 1946, he watched it grow to 410,000 boys and girls of high school age and under. The program is now sponsored by the ABC and WIBC and has more than 750,000 members. Raymer spent much of his time traveling nationwide to encourage youngsters to bowl, and taught adults how to instruct young bowlers and organize leagues.

RISHLING, Gertrude
Meritorious Service
Gertrude is a member emeritus of the WIBC and served on its board of directors from 1954 to 1971. She was the WIBC representative on the National Bowling Council for one and a half years. She is the president of the Omaha Women's Bowling Association and first vice president of the Nebraska Women's Bowling Association. She originated the 600 Club in Omaha and served on the Omaha Junior Bowling Association board. Gertrude has been president of every league she ever bowled in for 42 years.

1973

BLUTH, Raymond Albert "Bloop"
Bowler
Born December 31, 1927, in St. Louis, Mo; married; 4 children; currently a bowling lanes owner in St. Louis; hobby is collecting antique player-piano music rolls.

Intense concentration and an almost perfect delivery made Ray Bluth a consistent winner. He rolled the first 300 game in ABC Masters finals play in 1962. His 806 series for the first three games of that set is a Masters record. He is a member and past president of the Professional Bowlers Association. Among his many titles and awards are 12 sanctioned 300 games and 4 sanctioned 299 games. He was named to *Bowling Magazine* All-America second team in 1956, 1957, 1958, 1964 and 1965, and the first team every year from 1959 to 1963.
Also in: Greater St. Louis Bowling Association Hall of Fame and Professional Bowlers Association Hall of Fame.

DITZEN, Walt
Meritorious Service
Born 1914; Rip Van Winkle Award; Billiard and Bowling Institute of America Distinguished Service Award; died in Phoenix, Ariz, in 1973.

Ditzen created the popular "Fan Fare" three panel cartoon strip covering all sports, but two of its best known characters were "Gutter Gus" and "Gutter Gussie." His always humorous but sometimes irreverent remarks about bowling gave Ditzen a wide following. He was honored with the Distinguished Service Award of the Billiard and Bowling Institute of America and received the Rip Van Winkle Award from the Bowling Writers Association of America.

KREMS, Edward Henry
Bowler
Born February 2, 1893, in Chicago, Ill; married; retired; lives in Chicago.

Krems was possibly the best all-around bowler in Chicago in the 1920s, starring in team, doubles and individual competition. He bowled a 779 three-game series in a 1922 tournament which was a record. His highest average was 211 while bowling in the old Randolph League in Chicago.
Also in: Illinois Bowling Association Hall of Fame.

POWERS, Connie
Star of Yesteryear
Connie bowled in 35 consecutive WIBC championship tournaments. She won the doubles in 1939 and was on the winning team in 1957 and 1959. Connie bowled a 987 series across eight lanes in four games in the 1951 All-Star competition, a record for men and women that stood for ten years. In state competition she claimed one team, one doubles and three all-events as well as numerous local championships.
Also in: Bowling Proprietors Association of Greater Detroit Hall of Fame.

SWITZER, Pearl
Meritorious Service
Pearl is a member emeritus of the WIBC and dedicated 32 consecutive years of service to the board of directors from 1934 to 1966. She was president of the South Bend-Mishawaka Women's Bowling Association for 11 years and secretary for 23 years. She was active in American Junior Bowling Congress work. Pearl bowled in 34 consecutive tournaments from 1933 to 1969.

1974

HOLM, Joan
Superior Performance
Joan set the Illinois Women's Bowling Association all-events record in 1964 with a 1920 total. In 1965–1966

she led the nation's women with a 207 average, the first 200 plus average by a Chicago woman. She also recorded a 300 game. Her 198 average was third among all women bowling in WIBC tournaments from 1969 to 1973. She is the holder of ten Illinois and eight Chicago Women's Bowling Associations crowns. Joan captained the U.S. women to two team titles in the 1971 *Féderation Internationale des Quilleurs* (FIQ) Tournament and was a member of the Sixth FIQ American Zone Tournament.

HOOVER, Richard Lee

Bowler

Born December 15, 1929, in Roseville, Ohio; married; three children; currently lives in Akron; a bowling proprietor; hobbies are water skiing and boating.

In 1946 Hoover rolled the highest series, 847, ever compiled in league play by a teenager. He is also the youngest to win the All-Star tournament, winning the 1950–1951 event one day after his 21st birthday. He was named to *Bowling Magazine* All-America first team in 1956, 1957 and 1962, and the second team in 1958. His average for 28 years of ABC tournament bowling is 199. He is currently a member of the Professional Bowlers Association.

LUBY, Mort, Sr.

Meritorious Service

Born 1897; died 1956.

Luby served as publisher of the *National Bowlers Journal* from 1925 until his death in 1956, having taken over upon the death of his father, Hall of Famer Dave Luby. The Lubys are the only father-son Hall combination. Mort covered the ABC tournament for 35 years for the wire services and dozens of newspapers in addition to his own magazine. He was a founding father of the Bowling Writers Association of America (BWAA) and the BWAA Distinguished Service Award is named for him. Luby named the first All-America team in 1937 and founded the Bowlers Journal Championships.

MATTHEWS, Merle

Star of Yesteryear

Merle captained the Linbrook Bowl team to back-to-back WIBC team titles in 1962 and 1963. The team score of 3061 in 1962 set a WIBC tournament record. She won the 1958 Bowling Proprietors Association of America All-Star tournament. Merle won 8 California and 18 Los Angeles Women's Bowling Associations titles. She was instrumental in organizing the Professional Women Bowlers Association, serving as the second president. She also helped organize the Western Women Bowlers Association. During her career Merle has recorded eight 700 plus series and a 290 game.

Also in: California Women's Bowling Hall of Fame and Southern California Bowling Hall of Fame.

PATTERSON, Claude, Jr. "Pat"

Bowler

Born October 30, 1925, in St. Louis, Mo; died May 9, 1972.

Patterson was a member of the Budweiser Club when it was organized and succeeded Whitey Harris as captain. He remained as captain of the group when it later became the Don Carter Gloves Team and he helped the club to the 1962 Classic team title. He was low man with 736 when the Buds bowled the record 3858 series in 1958. During his career he rolled 11 sanctioned 300 games and 5 sanctioned 299 games.

Also in: Greater St. Louis Bowling Association Hall of Fame.

SWEENEY, Dennis J.

Meritorious Service

Born 1864; Rip Van Winkle Award; died 1965.

Sweeney founded the WIBC and was one of the first to campaign the cause of women in the field of bowling. He was a charter member of the Bowling Proprietors Association of America. At one time he published his own Sunday newspaper besides covering bowling for the five St. Louis dailies in existence at that time. He received the Rip Van Winkle Award from the Bowling Writers Association of America.

Also in: Greater St. Louis Bowling Association Hall of Fame.

VEATCH, Georgia E.

Meritorious Service

Georgia is a member emeritus of the WIBC, after having served on the board of directors from 1948 to 1974. She served 12 years as first vice president; chairman of many committees, including the WIBC building committee in the planning of the ABC/WIBC joint headquarters; editor of *The Woman Bowler* for 12 years. Georgia was also president of Chicago Women's Bowling Association for 26 years and helped originate its publication. She founded the Professional Women Bowlers Association in 1959 and was executive director for 9 years. For 16 years Georgia edited the *Prep Pin Patter,* then the official American Junior Bowling Congress publication.

1975

BAKER, Frank K.

Meritorious Service

Born June 14, 1907, in Coffeyville, Kans; retired in 1972; lives in Milwaukee, Wis.

Baker became secretary of ABC in 1951; and as membership in ABC grew, so did its service program under his guidance. He became active in the international world of tenpins and was soon elevated to an officer's position in the *Féderation Internationale des Quilleurs.* Although retired, Baker has remained active in his role of secretary emeritus, principally working with the NBC promotion committee and on the international scene.

FALCARO, Joseph Lawrence "Chesty"

Bowler

Born in 1896 in New York City; died September 6, 1951.

Falcaro gained early fame as a trick bowler, especially in the East where he gave many benefit exhibitions under the sponsorship of the Coca-Cola Company. In 1925 he won the Illlinois State all-events title and the New York State all-events in 1929.

MARTORELLA, Mildred

Superior Performance

Woman Bowler of the Year 1967; Alberta E. Crowe Star of Tomorrow Award 1967.

Mildred has won eight WIBC titles: Queens Tournament in 1967, 1970 and 1971, team in 1970 and 1972, all-events in 1972 and doubles in 1971 and 1973. She is the only woman to roll a perfect game in the Professional Women Bowlers Association tournament play. She also set the WIBC record for the highest one-season average of 219 in 1967–1968. She won the 1973 U.S. Women's Open. Mildred has 45 sanctioned three-game 700 plus series. She was named Woman Bowler of the Year in 1967, and received the Alberta E. Crowe Star of Tomorrow Award that same year.

WELU, William Joseph
Bowler
Born July 30, 1932, in Houston, Tex; died May 16, 1974.

Welu became captain of the St. Louis Falstaffs and led them to national honors in ABC and BPAA team action. He is past president of the Professional Bowlers Association (PBA) and was the "color" commentator on the PBA tour telecasts along with broadcaster Chris Schenkel. Billy won many honors, titles and awards during his career; among them are five sanctioned 300 games. He was named to the *Bowling Magazine* All-America first team in 1959, 1961, 1963 and 1964, and the second team in 1958, 1960, 1962 and 1965.
Also in: Professional Bowlers Association Hall of Fame.

WHITE, Mildred
Meritorious Service
Mildred served the WIBC board of directors from 1944 to 1972, serving as director, fifth vice president and second vice president. With the exception of finance and budgeting, she served on every committee, including WIBC's American Junior Bowling Congress committee. She was chairman of the Illinois Junior Bowling Association for 28 years, and helped organize the Rockford Junior Bowling Association. As president of the Illinois Women's Bowling Association, she was the recipient of the first meritorious service award in 1968. She is a WIBC member emeritus since 1972.

WHITNEY, Vern Eli
Meritorious Service
Born September 18, 1893, in Jones County, Iowa; died in 1956.
Whitney founded the ABC Hall of Fame in 1941, a year after he joined the Congress staff as its first public relations manager. Among his innovations for the Congress were the ABC *News Letter*, the bowling writing competition sponsored by *Bowling*, the official monthly publication for which he served as executive editor and the Rip Van Winkle Award of the Bowling Writers Association of America, which he helped organize in 1934. Whitney worked on the *Des Moines Register, Chicago Herald-American* and *Wisconsin Evening News*. He founded the *Chicago Bowler* newspaper in 1934 and was one of the first to adapt high speed sequence photography to bowling action.

WINANDY, Cecilia
Star of Yesteryear
Cecilia won the all-events in the 1949 WIBC tournament with a nine-game 1840 series. She also won seven Chicago Women's Bowling Association titles. She earned 13 Illinois Women's Bowling Association titles, including consecutive all-events victories in 1940, 1941 and 1942. Cecilia was a member of the Budweiser Girls exhibition teams of the 1930s that finished in second place in WIBC tournaments in four consecutive years, 1936 to 1939.

1976

BERGER, Winifred
Meritorious Service
Winifred was elected to the WIBC board of directors in 1946, serving as a director until 1970. She began bowling in 1928 and held every league office during the ensuing 47 years. She was either president or treasurer of the San Francisco Women's Bowling Association for 13 consecutive years and held every office in the California Women's Bowling Association, with the exception of treasurer. She won seven local and one state doubles title. During W. W. II, Winifred as active in "Wings of Mercy," the Bowlers Victory Legion Fund and Red Cross work. She received a WIBC certificate in 1945 commemorating her war service.
Also in: California Women's Bowling Hall of Fame.

BROSIUS, Edward J, Jr.
Bowler
Born May 30, 1920, in Chicago, Ill.

Brosius won the 1952 doubles national title with another Hall of Famer, Junie McMahon.
Also in: Illinois Bowling Association Hall of Fame.

CASTELLANO, Grazio
Bowler
Born July 2, 1917, in Brooklyn, N.Y; lives in New York City.

Castellano was the first to to bowl a 300 game on live television (1953). Few rivaled his six major match titles of 79 to 124 games in length. He bowled on the Faber Cement Block team.

COBURN, Doris
Superior Performance
Doris started bowling in 1939, but didn't start participating in competitive leagues until 1950. She turned professional in 1963. Since 1973 her record has been outstanding, as she won the richest women's tournament and also rolled her first perfect game in 1975. During 1974 she bowled the women's second best three-game series, 813. She was captain of the 1970 and 1972 WIBC tournament team titlists and she also won 6 state and 13 local association awards. In the prestigious Queens Tournament, Coburn ranks ninth on the overall list of money winners since 1963. Aside from her bowling honors, Doris was named Erie County Mother of the Year and was one of seven persons named as Outstanding Citizens for 1975 in Buffalo.

GLOOR, Olga
Star of Yesteryear
Olga began bowling in 1946. She was a member of the 1954 WIBC championship team. In 1959 she won the World's Invitational and helped to organize the Professional Women Bowlers Association (PWBA). She later won two PWBA titles. Over the years Olga earned seven

state titles, four in Illinois and three in California. She was twice named Queen of the Chicago Bowlers, and her 1902 all-events total in the 1963 Chicago Women's Bowling Association is still a local record. She was a member of the United States team in the American Zone Championships of the *Fédération Internationale des Quilleurs* (FIQ) in November, 1974, winning, at age 54, the women's all-events title; and was a member of the winning five-woman team. She also was part of the United States team at the FIQ World Bowling Championships in October, 1975.

HENNESSEY, Thomas M.
Bowler
Born May 11, 1925 in St. Louis, Mo; lives in St. Louis.

As a member of the renowned St. Louis Budweisers, Hennessey captured four ABC Classic titles and three Southern Match titles and also won the 1958 Masters.
Also in: Greater St. Louis Bowling Association Hall of Fame.

KISSOFF, Joseph F.
Bowler
Born March 21, 1901, in Hungary; lives in Cleveland, Ohio.

Kissoff's ability to make the "kiss" shot in billiards prompted him to change his name from Zelinsky. He won the 1953 ABC doubles and won the Elks National all-events. He also has two Ohio State all-events titles.
Also in: Greater Cleveland Bowling Association Hall of Fame.

LAUMAN, Henry "Hank"
Bowler
Born January 23, 1919, in St. Louis, Mo; lives in Los Angeles, Calif.

Bowling with the famous Hermann Undertakers Team out of St. Louis, Lauman rolled three 800 series and four perfect games. He is said to be the first bowler to receive a yearly salary.
Also in: Southern California Bowling Hall of Fame.

SOUTAR, Judy
Superior Performance
Alberta E. Crowe Star of Tomorrow 1963; Woman Bowler of the Year 1973, 1975.

Judy Soutar is the second youngest woman bowler ever inducted into the Hall of Fame. She began bowling at a very early age, turning professional at the age of 16. She was runnerup in the World's Invitational tournament at the age of 18. In 1974 Judy won three WIBC titles, all-events, team, and the prestigious Queens Tournament. With Gloria Bouvia she won the 1969 and 1970 doubles titles, the 1969 win with a record 1315 total. At local and state levels, she has four championships. Judy bowled a 300 game in a pro tournament in October, 1974, her best three-game series was 754, and she carried the top league average of 202. She led all women professionals in 1973 and 1975 in money winnings and tour averages. She was named Alberta E. Crowe Star of Tomorrow in 1963 and Woman Bowler of the Year in 1973 and again in 1975.

TOEPFER, Elvira
Star of Yesteryear
Queen of Detroit Bowlers eight times.

Elvira is noted for a combination of title winning, instructing and exhibition talents. During the 1950s and 1960s, she traveled extensively giving exhibitions and conducting clinics. In 1956 she and her teammate Anita Cantaline won the Women's National doubles championships; they placed second in 1959. Elvira was on WIBC champion teams in 1957 and 1959, and in 1958 was second in the World's Invitational. She has also earned 12 state titles, including 4 individual match games and 15 titles in Detroit Women's Bowling Association events. Elvira was a member of Detroit's All-City Team five times and was named Queen of Detroit Bowlers eight times. She still averages 189 in two Detroit major leagues and works as a bowling instructress.
Also in: Bowling Proprietors Association of Greater Detroit Hall of Fame.

WOLF, Fred
Bowler and Meritorious Service
Born May 26, 1911, in Poughkeepsie, N.Y; lives in Detroit, Mich.

Fred was a member of the Stroh's Beer team for seven years, before his career was prematurely shortened by an injury. Moving from the hardwood lanes to a commentator's role, he achieved new heights with his radio and television announcing.
Also in: Bowling Proprietors Association of Greater Detroit Hall of Fame.

1977

BAETZ, Helen
Meritorious Service
When Helen's team won the class B title in the local association tournament in 1943, she began to really get involved by joining several leagues, and eventually held every league office several times. She has been captain of her Porter Loring Team for more than 23 years. Helen served the San Antonio Women's Bowling Association from 1944 to 1969 in many positions, including secretary, vice president and director. She was elected state secretary of the Texas Women's Bowling Association in 1945, and served until 1966. She was first elected to the WIBC board of directors as a director in 1952 and began 24 years of national service. She was appointed fifth vice president in 1962 and in 1974, was named third vice president. She retired from the board in 1977 and was named member emeritus. She was secretary-treasurer of the National Women Bowling Writers Association from 1967 to 1976 and received the NWBWA award for distinguished service to the game in 1967. She was instrumental in inaugurating the American Junior Bowling Congress programs across the state. She was president of the San Antonio Bowling Council for three years and secretary of the state's Twenty Year Club for eight years.
Also in: San Antonio Bowling Hall of Fame and Texas Women's Bowling Association Hall of Fame.

BURNS, Nina Van Camp
Star of Yesteryear
A self-taught bowler, Nina took up the sport in 1937. She was on the Logan Square Buicks Team that won the 1942 WIBC team title. The team's 2815 total was the

second best ever at the time. Nina anchored the team with a 655, then added 637 in doubles and 596 in singles to win the WIBC all-events medal with 1888, also a second best in WIBC tournament records in 1942. At the height of her bowling career, Nina was competing in five leagues each week and carried a 191 average. She rolled two sanctioned 700 series. She was named "the most popular bowler in Chicagoland" in 1948. Nina quit bowling competitively in 1952 because of an arthritic condition in her right hand, but she did continue to bowl off and on for about eight more years.

CARTER, LaVerne

Superior Performance

Born in Brentwood, Mo; two children; currently operates a bowling center in Las Vegas, Nev.

LaVerne started bowling in a junior league in 1939 in Tucson, Ariz, but moved to California in 1945. By 1947 she had established herself as a great bowler and originated a program called "Bowl with LaVerne," which soon became a traveling roadshow. She toured the country offering a combination of instruction clinics and challenging local favorites in match games. LaVerne's first title came in the team event of the 1948 California state tournament, the first of many wins in state and local affairs in Los Angeles and California, as well as in St. Louis and Missouri. She won her first WIBC tournament in 1951, the all-events crown with a 1788, and placed second in singles play that year. In Queens Tournament play, she finished second in 1965, third in 1970 and fifth in 1962. She is one of only four women to have competed in all 16 Queens Tournaments. In 1974 LaVerne contributed a 279 game and 716 series total as her Kalicak International Construction Team won the WIBC title. Her 716 is the second-best ever in WIBC tournament play and best in the team event. She teamed with long-time friend Marion Ladewig to win the 1958 and 1959 National Women's doubles, sponsored by the Bowling Proprietors Association of America. She also earned the Rupert-Brunswick title in 1959. LaVerne is a charter member of both the Professional Women Bowlers Association (PWBA) and the Ladies Professional Bowlers Association (LPBA). She served as PWBA vice president for six years and won two PWBA titles, one in 1964 and a second in 1970. Her sanctioned bests are: 197 league average in 1957–1958, high among all WIBC members that season; a 741 series in 1963–1964; and a 298 game in 1965–1966. She has had three unsanctioned 300 games, one coming while she was touring in Japan in 1970 in an exhibition match.

HAAS, Dorothy Taylor

Meritorious Service

Dorothy joined her first league in 1944 and was averaging 130 by the end of the season. She became interested in the administrative side of bowling and wanted to know "what made things tick." She attended league meetings and soon became involved as a league officer, first serving as treasurer, then as president and secretary. She was elected vice president and later president of the Central Jersey Women's Bowling Association (CJWBA) and was also sergeant-at-arms and president of the New Jersey Women's Bowling Association (NJWBA). She is currently a director of the New Jersey Junior Bowling Association and a member of the New Jersey Bowling Council and the National Women Bowling Writers Association. Dot became involved on a national scale when she was appointed to the WIBC board of directors in 1962. In 1967 she was elected sergeant-at-arms and was responsible for supervising the setting up of facilities for each WIBC annual meeting. Another favorite assignment was working with the WIBC Hall of Fame Committee, which she chaired for four years. She retired from the WIBC board in 1976, and was named member emeritus. She received the Distinguished Service Award from the Metropolitan Bowling Writers Association of the New York City area. She also originated the *Garden State Maples,* the official publication of the NJWBA and served as their official photographer. She is a life member of both the NJWBA and CJWBA.

SHABLIS, Helen

Star of Yesteryear

Helen started bowling in 1936 and for 12 years taught bowling at the Merri-Bowl Lanes in Livonia, Michigan. She supervised the local Parks and Recreation Department's bowling program for school children, as well as instructing on a volunteer basis for the nearby hospital for the mentally and physically handicapped. In 1963 Helen capped several near-triumphs in the WIBC championship tournaments, with a winning 1849 total, thereby earning a spot on the first U.S. team to compete officially in an international tenpin event. She joined a squad of five women sponsored by WIBC and nine men sponsored by ABC at the fifth World Bowling Championships of the *Fédération Internationale des Quilleurs* (FIQ) in Mexico. That competition was the first FIQ event to include women. As captain of the women's team, she led them to the team title, and paired with Dottie Wilkinson of Phoenix, Ariz, claimed the doubles medal, and went on to win the women's all-events with a 4535 for 24 games. She also had the women's high game of 237. As a result of her WIBC and world triumphs, Helen was signed to the Brunswick Advisory Staff, one of the few nonprofessionals to achieve that status. Over the years, Helen participated in 22 WIBC national events, all of them from 1947 through 1969. In 1957 she was second in WIBC all-events and singles. At her peak, Helen bowled in five leagues a week. Her best performances were a 195 average in 1954–1955 and a 285 game and 703 series.

Also in: Bowling Proprietors Association of Greater Detroit Hall of Fame.

New Jersey State Bowling Association Hall of Fame

NUTLEY, NEW JERSEY

Mailing Address: 317 Chestnut St, 07110. Tel. (201) 667-1670. *Contact:* Victor Hesse, Secy.-Treas. *Location:* Approx. 6 mi. N. of Newark. *Personnel:* Henry Chomicki, Pres; six V.Pres; Victor Hesse, Secy.-Treas. *Nearby Halls of Fame:* Bicycling (Staten Island, N.Y, 18 mi. S.E.), Education, Heritage, Music (New York City, 18 mi. S.E.), Harness Racing (Goshen, N.Y, 35 mi. N.), Ice Skating (Newburgh, N.Y, 40 mi. N.), Baseball (Cooperstown, N.Y, 140 mi. N.W.), Horse Racing (Saratoga Springs, N.Y, 145 mi. N.), Flight (Elmira, N.Y, 150 mi. N.W.), Horseshoe Pitching (Corning, N.Y, 175 mi. N.W.).

The original idea for the Hall came in September, 1967, from Edward J. Woods who was secretary of the Union County Bowling Association and eventually the first chairman of the Hall of Fame Committee. The Hall honors those demonstrating outstanding bowling ability and/or those who have contributed, through meritorious service, to the general welfare and progress of the tenpins game in New Jersey.

Members: 28 as of 1977. A chairman and six additional members are appointed each summer to the Hall of Fame Committee. The electors are officers of the state association, delegates from local associations and active past presidents. All nominations must be received by the Committee in December; voting is in March. Those inducted must receive a two-thirds majority vote. A maximum of four a year may be inducted, two in the Ability category and two in the Meritorious Service category. Those in Ability must have 15 years of active participation within the New Jersey State Bowling Association (NJSBA) and those in Meritorious Service must have made outstanding contributions through administration or organizational work.

1969 McMAHON, James, Jr. "Junie." Ability. See entry in National Bowling Hall of Fame, 1955.

1970 CAMPI, Louis. Ability. See entry in National Bowling Hall of Fame, 1968.

FARAGALLI, Alfred Joseph "Lindy." Ability. See entry in National Bowling Hall of Fame, 1968.

McMANUS, John J. Meritorious service. *Also in:* Union County Bowling Association Hall of Fame.

1971 BANCROFT, George A. Meritorious service.

CASSIO, Martin. Ability. See entry in National Bowling Hall of Fame, 1972. *Also in:* Union County Bowling Association Hall of Fame.

GRINSTED, Harvey A. Meritorious service.

1972 KELLER, William J. Meritorious service.

NIEMIEC, Stanley. Ability.

SEMIZ, Teata. Ability.

1973 BROWN, Joseph. Ability. *Also in:* Union County Bowling Association Hall of Fame.

ENGAN, Ralph. Ability.

1974 BOGLE, H. Wesley. Meritorious service.

BOTTEN, Edward. Ability.

COLETTI, Gordon. Ability. *Also in:* Union County Bowling Association Hall of Fame.

KOLLMAR, Carl E. Meritorious service.

LUETHY, Bernhard. Meritorious service.

SLOAN, Warren. Meritorious service.

1975 FOXIE, Louis. Ability.

HESSE, Victor. Meritorious service. *Also in:* Union County Bowling Association Hall of Fame.

LUCCI, Vince, Sr. Ability.

1976 BAHR, Edward J, Sr. Meritorious service.

DAYON, John. Ability. *Also in:* Union County Bowling Association Hall of Fame.

HART, Cecil A. Ability.

THORNTON, William R. Meritorious service.

1977 LENING, H. Fred. Ability.

ROBERTS, Donald M. Meritorious service.

WOODS, Edward J. Meritorious service. *Also in:* Union County Bowling Association Hall of Fame.

North Dakota Bowling Hall of Fame

JAMESTOWN, NORTH DAKOTA

Mailing Address: 212 Third Ave, N.E, 58401. Tel. (701) 252-3168. *Contact:* Jim Lusk, Exec. Secy. *Location:* 75 mi. W. of Bismarck, 80 mi. W. of Fargo, 100 mi. E. of Aberdeen, S. Dak. *Nearby Halls of Fame:* Softball (Harvey, 80 mi. N.W.).

Founded in 1972, the Hall honors bowlers of extraordinary ability and administrative skill. It is governed by the North Dakota State Bowling Association, Inc.

Members: 10 as of 1976. The state bowling associations nominate candidates for membership and the Council of Delegates (18 officials), select from the list. Two bowlers are inducted annually at the Bowling Jamboree in September.

1972 CADY, Roger

SCHNEIDER, Dan

SEIBEL, Fred (dec.)

SOULIS, John N.

1973 ZAHN, Joe

1974 GIMBLE, Bill

STRAEK, Louis

1975 FLYNN, Leonard

KELSVEN, L. O.

1976 WHITE, Don

Professional Bowlers Association Hall of Fame

AKRON, OHIO

Mailing Address: 1720 Merriman Rd, 44313. Tel. (216) 836-5568. *Contact:* Jerry Levine, Secy. *Location:* 25 mi. S. of Cleveland, 45 mi. W. of Youngstown, 125 mi. N.E. of Columbus, 125 mi. E. of Toledo, 220 mi. N.E. of Cincinnati. *Personnel:* Joseph Antenore, Exec. Dir; Jerry Levine, Secy. *Nearby Halls of Fame:* Football (Canton, 30 mi. S.), Golf (Foxburg, Pa, 80 mi. E.), Trapshooting (Vandalia, 190 mi. S.W.), Flight (Dayton, 215 mi. S.W.), Horseshoe Pitching (Corning, N.Y, 230 mi. N.E.), Flight (Elmira, N.Y, 235 mi. N.E.).

Founded in 1975 and governed by the Professional Bowlers Association (PBA), the Hall annually honors individuals with outstanding achievements in bowling in one of two categories: Records and Achievements or Meritorious Service. Electors are committees of the PBA.

Members: 11 as of 1976. Voting by the committees is done annually, with induction in April at the Firestone Country Club in Akron.

1974 BLUTH, Raymond Albert "Bloop." See entry in National Bowling Hall of Fame, 1973. *Also in:* Greater St. Louis Bowling Association Hall of Fame.

CARTER, Donald James "Bosco." See entry in National Bowling Hall of Fame, 1970. *Also in:* Greater St. Louis Bowling Association Hall of Fame.

ESPOSITO, Frank. Meritorious Service.

PEZZANO, Chuck. Meritorious Service.

SALVINO, Carmen. *Also in:* Illinois Bowling Association Hall of Fame.

SMITH, Harry

WEBER, Richard Anthony. See entry in National Bowling Hall of Fame, 1970. *Also in:* Greater St. Louis Bowling Association Hall of Fame.

WELU, William Joseph. See entry in National Bowling Hall of Fame, 1975.

1975 ELIAS, Eddie

FAZIO, Basil "Buzz." See entry in National Bowling Hall of Fame, 1963. *Also in:* Bowling Proprietors Association of Greater Detroit Hall of Fame.

SCHENKEL, Chris. Meritorious Service.

St. Paul Bowling Hall of Fame

ST. PAUL, MINNESOTA

Mailing Address: 1022 Arkwright St, 55101. Tel. (612) 699-0272. *Contact:* Loren S. Olson, Secy.-Treas. *Location:* Approx. 10 mi. E. of Minneapolis, Minn, 205 mi. N.E. of Sioux Falls, S.Dak, 240 mi. N.E. of Des Moines, Iowa. *Personnel:* Emery Engelbretson, Pres; Arlene Eck, V.Pres; Loren Olson, Secy.-Treas; 12 mem. Hall of Fame Comt. *Nearby Halls of Fame:* Hockey (Eveleth, 170 mi. N.), Football (Green Bay, Wis, 250 mi. S.E.).

The Hall of Fame was established in 1962 by the Greater St. Paul Bowling Association and the St. Paul Women's Bowling Association, to honor past and present bowling personalities for outstanding achievements in the tenpin game. The budget committee of the Men's and Women's Bowling Associations finance and administer the Hall.

Members: 42 as of July 1977. There are three categories for induction into the Hall of Fame: Superior Performance, Meritorious Service and Pioneer of Yesterday. Superior performance is for those bowlers with outstanding accomplishments in any American Bowling Congress or Women's International Bowling Congress sanctioned leagues and/or tournaments. Meritorious Service covers exceptional accomplishments of an officer of the men's or women's bowling associations, member of their board of directors or a sponsor of bowling teams over a long period, and/or character, accomplishments or activities of a bowling personality worthy of consideration. Pioneer of Yesterday covers those bowlers, living or dead, who became active in bowling prior to 35 years ago and who have accomplishments worthy of Superior Performance and/or Meritorious Service.

Open nominations must be postmarked by August 1 and should include the qualifications of each individual. After August 10, the Hall of Fame Committee, five members each from the Men's and Women's Bowling Associations plus one man and one woman from the Hall, screens the nominations and prepares a ballot which is mailed to the voters by September 1. Hold over nominees from the previous year are also considered. Those who elect the new members are the officers, past officers, Board of Directors and honorary life members of the Men's and Women's Bowling Associations and their living Hall of Fame members. Returned ballots must be postmarked by September 15. Election requires a majority of the votes cast. If no one receives a majority, then plurality rules and the candidate who receives the most votes is elected. If there is a tie, both candidates are elected. Up to ten members can be elected in each category. After September 15 the Hall of Fame Committee reviews the ballots and announces the new members. On the first Saturday of November a Bowler's Recognition Dinner is held to honor the new Hall of Fame members as well as the All-City men's and women's teams, the King and Queen of the Men's and Women's Bowling Associations and other awardees. Hall of Famers receive plaques, and pictures of them are displayed in the foyer of the St. Paul Auditorium.

1963 HARKINS, Tom. (dec). Well-known bowling proprietor who brought bowling to the fore in St. Paul; was a member of the Hamm's team; belonged to 800 Club; installed the first automatics in the city.

MARTIN, Henry, Sr. (dec). He bowled a 300 game in his seventies.

MATAK, Emil. (dec). He was considered the greatest left-handed bowler in St. Paul history; won numerous titles, including the state doubles.

MITCHELL, Jimmy. (dec). He was noted for his control of a slight backup ball; rolled 18 300 games.

NOONAN, Jerry. (dec). Once won the City all-events title; was secretary of Greater St. Paul Bowling Association for 17 years.

RAGOGNA, Ossie "Rags." He rolled three 800 series as a member of the famous Hamm's team; is still a member of the St. Paul City League.

ROUNDS, Hon. John L. (dec). Former judge; well-known bowling enthusiast who became president of the American Bowling Congress (ABC) and who helped get the 1941 ABC tournament awarded to St. Paul.

1964 GIBBONS, Tom. (dec). See entry in Boxing Hall of Fame, Citizens Savings Hall of Fame Athletic Museum.

MATAK, Rudy. (dec). Rudy tied for the 1907 ABC singles title, but lost in the rolloff; well-known member of Schmidt's City League teams.

McBRIDE, Bertha. (dec). See entry in National Bowling Hall of Fame, 1968.

METCALF, Bill. (dec). Was leadoff man of the famous Hamm's team; won several tournaments in Minnesota.

O'BRIEN, Rose Schneider.

SWANSON, Charles.

1965 BACHRODT, Emma. Bowled one unsanctioned 300 game; now in her 33rd consecutive year in the same league; has attended 22 national tournaments.

BERMAN, Harry. (dec). Was a sporting goods dealer, a long time bowler himself and sponsored teams for 50 years.

COOK, Archie. (dec). Started bowling in 1907; won numerous tournaments; carried a 175 average in his seventies; had 9 perfect games.

GODBOUT, Charles. (dec). He made Ripley's "Believe It or Not" column with scores of 225, 226 and 227 for a 678 total; highest game was 299; has St. Paul's highest triplicate game of 223; sponsored many teams from 1921 until his death.

MADY, Ed. Has won numerous tournaments; was the only two-time winner of the Tribune Classic; has a 25 year national tournament average of 191.

WITWICKE, Marcella. Won State all-events title in 1955, City all-events four times, City singles once and shared City doubles twice; many years service to local association and board as either president or secretary; bowled a 712 series in 1959.

1966 CASSIDY, Lucille. (dec). Was instrumental in helping to secure the WIBC tournament for St. Paul in 1950; was a member of the City League since 1939, serving as president and sergeant-at-arms; bowled in 20 national tournaments while serving as a delegate for 15 years.

DODOR, George. (dec). Was treasurer of the Men's City Association for 19 years and on the executive committee for 25 years, until his death in 1965; won numerous titles and awards; carried a composite average of 197 for 29 years.

MUGGLEY, Harry. (dec). Was a well-known proprietor and sponsor; was a member of the first team to record a 3000 total in ABC tournament play with the Flor De Knispel team rolling a 3006 in 1913, and with the Aquilas team in 1918 when they rolled a 3022 for the third 3000 in ABC history. He rolled an unheard of 700 in that series and both of these 3000 plus totals were ABC championships in their respective years.

VOGES, Harold. (dec). Was a member of the famed Hamm's team of the 1930s; had many titles to his credit; had numerous 700 series, one 300 game and average around the 200 mark for many years.

1967 MEYERS, Herman S. Past president of Greater St. Paul Bowling Association and served executive committee many years; member of the board of governors of the St. Paul Classic and Minneapolis Tribune Classic; averaged between 195 and 200 for over 15 years.

1968 EVANS, Harry "Bob." (dec). Was a member of the famed Hamm's team in the 1930s; had two sanctioned 300 games, one in 1929 and one in 1934; rolled numerous 700 totals.

1969 ECK, Arlene. Holds numerous awards and titles at state and national level; named Queen of the St. Paul Woman Bowlers four times; served the St. Paul Women's Bowling Association's executive board for over ten years, presently as sergeant-at-arms; averaged in high 180s for many years.

1970 LANGE, Leslie. Former member of the executive committee of the Greater St. Paul Bowling Association; for many years was St. Paul leader in Bowlers Victory Legion; currently on the Tribune Classic board of governors.

MAEHREN, Edward.

1971 STAHL, Edward. (dec). One of the organizers of the St. Paul All-Star League; member of the St. Paul 700 Club; two sanctioned 300 games; averaged 214 in 1944; an outstanding sponsor and proprietor.

1972 DALSEN, Margo. Member of St. Paul 600 Club with a high of 669; only St. Paul bowler to become a finalist in Women's International Bowling Congress' (WIBC) Queens Tournament; member of many city, state and national championship teams; president of the St. Paul Women's Bowling Association in 1949; chairman of ways and means committee for the 1950 WIBC tournament bid.

1973 WEIDELL, Bernice "Bunny."

1974 ABRAMS, Norm. Has two santioned 300 games and high series of 791; captured the St. Paul 700 Club title in 1958; bowled for 21 years, with many city, state, and national awards and titles to his credit.

BEYER, Elmer. Meritorious Service. Has served Greater St. Paul Bowling Association board of directors for 27 years and secretary for 15 years and is past president of the Association; member of the Minnesota State Bowling Association for 15 years and current secretary of the State Bowling Council, his third term; member of the St. Paul 700 Club; was instrumental in St. Paul's hosting the 1965 ABC tournament.

BIES, Ted, Sr. "Lefty." Pioneer of Yesterday. Sponsored bowling teams for more than 40 years; member of St. Paul 700 Club; has 25 series over 700; has two 1800 series in ABC tournament competition; has bowled in the Petersen Classic tournament 34 of the past 35 years; still an active bowler after 50 years, with a lifetime average of 190 plus.

MANN, Leo. A league bowler for past 26 years; named King of Bowlers four times; has many titles at city, state, national and international levels; has over 90 series of 700 or over.

MORRISSETTE, Fran. Superior Performance. Has three sanctioned 300 games, two of which came in a space of 28 days; high series is 788; named King of Bowlers in 1957; has many city, state and national titles and awards to his credit; won the St. Paul 700 Club tournament in 1956 with a 920 series.

1975 BARTHOL, Paul. (dec). Pioneer of Yesterday. Began bowling in 1918 and was still active at age 74, covering 55 years; has four 700 totals to his credit, two of which were rolled at age 70; at that same age, held the high average in two leagues of 199; participated in four leagues in the 1973–1974 season with a composite average of 179.

POUSETTE, Howard. Superior Performance. Has many titles to his credit, including wins in Minnesota and Iowa; a league bowler for 45 years with a lifetime average of 198; has been a Petersen Classic sponsor for 23 years; member of the St. Paul 700 Club with a high of 772.

SCHABERT, Bob. Meritorious Service. One of the originators of the St. Paul Bowling Hall of Fame, he served as its first president; one of the originators of the Bowler's Recognition Dinner; served on board of directors of both St. Paul Men's and Minnesota State Bowling Associations for over 25 years; past president and former secretary of the Bowling Writers Association of America, as well as the Minnesota Bowling Council; has been an ABC delegate 10 times and competed in 17 ABC tournaments; is executive secretary of the St. Paul Bowling Proprietors Association.

1976 BOVITZ, Vince. Meritorious Service. Was president of the ABC, 1975–1976, vice president 1967; member of ABC legal committee for five years and served on collegiate division, foreign competition, tournament prize high score and awards review, and industry relations committees; on board of directors of Greater St. Paul Bowling Association since early 1950s and was president during 1959–1960; currently president of Minnesota State Men's Bowling Association and on board of directors since 1962; past president of the Minnesota State Bowling Council.

OHLANDER, Oscar. Pioneer of Yesterday.

SACEVICH, Martin "Mike." Superior Performance. Noted for his outstanding ABC Tournament record; in one five-year span, he held the highest ABC average of 206; in 1962 rolled a 1934 all-events total; has eight 1800 totals to his credit and a lifetime ABC average of 191; has a 48 game average of 191 in World's Invitational; has one sanctioned 300 game; has numerous city and state titles also.

San Antonio Bowling Hall of Fame

SAN ANTONIO, TEXAS

Mailing Address: 442 E. Vestal, 78221. Tel. (512) 922-7625. *Contact:* Madelyn Spreng, Secy, San Antonio Bowling Council. *Location:* Approx. 75 mi. S. of Austin, 186 mi. W. of Houston, 175 mi. S.E. of San Angelo. *Nearby Halls of Fame:* Police Service (Waco, 170 mi. N.E.).

The Hall was founded in 1970 by the San Antonio Bowling Council (SABC) to honor men and women who have contributed to the sport of bowling through ability and leadership. The SABC governs, finances, and administers the award with inductees receiving plaques.

Members: 21 as of 1977. Open nominating forms are placed in public bowling lanes in May. The names submitted to the Hall of Fame committee for screening must be received by July 31st. The Board of Directors of the SABC votes on the nominees with the official induction in the fall. The number inducted annually varies. Those inducted receive plaques for their contributions in leadership and/or ability.

1970 SIMON, Violet "Billy." Leadership and ability. See entry in National Bowling Hall of Fame, 1960. *Also in:* Texas Women's Bowling Association Hall of Fame.

TREUTER, Charlie. Ability.

1971 SCHEWITZ, Harold. Leadership.

1972 BAETZ, Helen. Leadership. See entry in National Bowling Hall of Fame, 1977. *Also in:* Texas Woman's Bowling Association Hall of Fame.

HARRIS, Bob. Ability.

1973 BASKIN, Grace. Ability.

GRANIERI, Willie. Ability.

PFEIFFER, Gus. Leadership.

1974 BUCKNER, H. L. Leadership and ability.

CANFIELD, Lil. Leadership and ability.

DEFILY, Myrtle. Ability.

GRASSO, Clara. Leadership. *Also in:* Texas Women's Bowling Association Hall of Fame.

HAUFLER, Erna. Leadership. *Also in:* Texas Women's Bowling Association Hall of Fame.

NOVAK, Jo. Leadership.

PENHORN, Norbie. Ability.

WELTENS, Bert. Ability.

1975 HAYES, Gayle. Leadership.

ILTIS, Alice. Ability.

1976 LEVINSON, Lew. Leadership.

MERCK, Jerry, Sr. Ability.

WISE, Betty. Leadership and ability.

Southern California Bowling Hall of Fame

LOS ANGELES, CALIFORNIA

Mailing Address: P. O. Box 45333, 90045. Tel. (213) 625-2345. *Contact*: Don Snyder (for Women's Division) and Bill Franklin (213) 678-7739 (for Men's Division). *Location*: Approx. 102 mi. N. of San Diego. *Personnel*: Don Snyder, Pres; James P. Morris, Secy; Robert C. Weaver, Treas. *Nearby Halls of Fame*: Citizens Savings (Los Angeles), Softball (Long Beach, 35 mi. S.), Auto Racing (Ontario, 45 mi. S.E.), Physical Fitness (Costa Mesa, 45 mi. S.), Flight, Sports (San Diego).

The Men's Division was founded in 1963 by the Alliance of Southern California Bowling Associations. In 1969 a Women's Division was created by a committee of veteran women bowlers and in 1971, turned over for perpetuation to the Southern California Bowling Writers Association. Both have the purpose of honoring the greatest bowlers and bowling leaders of all time in Southern California, where bowling has long been a major recreational and competitive sport.

Members: 60 as of 1976. From one to six individuals may be selected annually by the Hall of Fame Committee. The Men's Hall elects only on bowling performance on the lanes while the Women's Hall elects on both bowling performance and meritorious service. Those nominated must receive two-thirds majority vote of the ballots to be elected. Inductions are held at the annual Southern California Bowling Awards Banquet.

1963 GREGG, Ona
HOPPING, Harry
McCORD, Joe
MEEKS, Dad
SHAFER, Tim
SHAY, Ernie
1964 GOJUN, George
McKENZIE, J. B.
MONTEVERDE, Tony
1965 DEPAOLI, Joe
1966 DELOUX, Don
SMITH, Ralph
SOEST, Ernie
1967 ROSNICK, Walt
1968 BADE, Roy
LUND, Wallace
1969 CROUCH, Dottie
HOLMES, Howard
HOPPING, Mildred
MATTHEWS, Merle. See entry in National Bowling Hall of Fame, 1974. *Also in*: California Women's Bowling Hall of Fame.
TASHIMA, Chiyo
1970 DUNIVAN, Paul
EASTWOOD, Fred
HARDY, Loveica. *Also in*: California Women's Bowling Hall of Fame.
RUDELL, Doris
1971 ANDERSON, Wilma
ETTIEN, Jo
GARDENS, Max
MRAK, Alyce
PORTER, Doris
1972 RICCILLI, Fred
RICCILLI, Hope
SHEPPARD, Alice
1973 BELLOWS, Helen. *Also in*: California Women's Bowling Hall of Fame.
KIKUTA, Judy
LAUMAN, Henry "Hank." See entry in National Bowling Hall of Fame, 1976.
LEE, Kay Rupp
NORTH, Bobbe. *Also in*: California Women's Bowling Hall of Fame.
OLSON, Nadine
WOODS, Esther. *Also in*: California Women's Bowling Hall of Fame.
1974 BECHTEL, Constance. *Also in*: California Women's Bowling Hall of Fame.
BURKETT, Phyllis Vogel
FARLEY, Peggy
MOKLER, Mary
MYERS, Billy
RAMIREZ, Bob
RICH, Juanita
1975 HARTNETT, Ed
HELLER, Pearlie
HOLMES, Dottie
NORTH, Merle. *Also in*: California Women's Bowling Hall of Fame.
PHILLIPS, Betty
WARE, Lucille
1976 BELCHER, Foy
DAVID, Roger
FREY, Robbie
HARMAN, Janet
JACOBSON, D. D. *Also in*: California Women's Bowling Hall of Fame.
MIVALEZ, Betty
PEACHY, Mildred. *Also in*: California Women's Bowling Hall of Fame.

Texas Women's Bowling Association Hall of Fame

FORT WORTH, TEXAS

Mailing Address: 117 Melbourne, 76117. Tel. (817) 589-0791. *Contact*: Lil Poole, Secy. *Location*; Approx. 30 mi. W. of Dallas, 80 mi. N. of Waco, 185 mi. S. of Oklahoma City, Okla. *Personnel*: Dorothy Cornelison, Pres; Doris Coffman, Treas; Lil Poole, Secy. *Nearby Halls of Fame*: Police Service (Waco), Ethnic (Anadarko, Okla, 175 mi. N.W.), Western Heritage, Softball (Oklahoma City, Okla.), Wrestling (Stillwater, Okla, 175 mi. N.W.).

Founded in 1965 by the Texas Women's Bowling Association (TWBA) Board of Directors, the Hall honors those individuals who contribute to bowling in an administrative capacity. TWBA emphasis is placed on those who laid the foundation for today's organization and its 113 local associations.

Members: 15 as of 1977. The Hall of Fame Committee is

composed of three members of the Board of Directors plus the president and secretary of the TWBA. Nominations are received from local associations for review with inductions at the annual meeting in May. Inductions are limited to one person per year.

1962 BAETZ, Helen. See entry in National Bowling Hall of Fame, 1977. *Also in*: San Antonio Bowling Hall of Fame.

1963 GRASSO, Clara. *Also in*: San Antonio Bowling Hall of Fame.

1964 SIMON, Violet "Billy" "Tut." See entry in National Bowling Hall of Fame, 1960. *Also in*: San Antonio Bowling Hall of Fame.

1965 HAYS, Ann

1966 WAGNER, Ruby

1967 HENDERSON, Geraldine

1968 VOLLMER, Ethel

1969 FISK, Rae

1970 JENKINS, Willie Ray

1971 STARR, Jule

1972 McCRORY, Estha

1973 BISHOP, Mary

1974 WENDLANDT, Ford

1975 GANTENBEIN, Shirley

1976 HAUFLER, Erna. *Also in*: San Antonio Bowling Hall of Fame.

Union County Bowling Association Hall of Fame

ROSELLE PARK, NEW JERSEY

Mailing Address: 23 W. Westfield Ave, 07204. Tel. (201) 241-5533. *Contact*: Len Spanjerberg, Secy. *Location*: Approx. 8 mi. S.W. of Newark. *Personnel*: Harold Kinney, Pres; five V.Pres; Len Spanjerberg, Secy; George Strenge, Treas. *Nearby Halls of Fame*: Bicycle (Staten Island, N.Y, 10 mi. S.E.), Heritage, Music (New York City, 18 mi. S.E.), Harness Racing (Goshen, N.Y, 43 mi. N.), Ice Skating (Newburgh, N.Y, 48 mi. N.), Baseball (Cooperstown, N.Y, 140 mi. N.W.), Horse Racing (Saratoga Springs, N.Y, 145 mi. N.), Flight (Elmira, N.Y, 150 mi. N.W.) Horseshoe Pitching (Corning, N.Y, 175 mi. N.W.).

Founded in 1958 by the Union County Bowling Association (UCBA), the Hall honors individuals who contribute to bowling through ability, meritorious service or are of veteran's status. UCBA administers and governs the award in conjunction with the New Jersey State Bowling Association.

Members: 89 as of 1976. Any member of UCBA may submit a name along with qualifications to the Hall of Fame Committee. The Committee is composed of officers of UCBA, three past presidents, one proprietor, one sportswriter and two members of the Hall. A maximum of five names may be placed on the ballot with 75 percent of the votes cast needed for election. The categories for induction are: Bowling Achievement, must have participated in organized bowling for 15 years or more with 10 years or more in Union County in league performance, city and state tournaments, ABC Tournaments and/or other county tournaments; Meritorious Service, distinguished service in the promotion of bowling; and Veterans Bowling Achievement, those individuals 65 years of age and older. The official induction takes place in October at the annual Hall of Fame Dinner.

1958 CASSIO, Martin. Achievement. See entry in National Bowling Hall of Fame, 1972. *Also in*: New Jersey State Bowling Association Hall of Fame.

1959 GELHAUSEN, Felix. Achievement.

1960 LAMPERTI, Charles. Achievement.

1961 POTTS, Joe. Achievement.

1962 DAYON, John. Achievement. *Also in*: New Jersey State Bowling Association Hall of Fame.

SEASON, Frank. Achievement.

1963 BARR, Dave. Meritorious service.

MILLER, William, Sr. Achievement.

MUNN, Whitey. Achievement.

SEERY, Joe. Meritorious service.

1964 DUCKAT, Lipman. Meritorious service.

McMANUS, John J. Meritorious service. *Also in*: New Jersey State Bowling Association Hall of Fame.

SAUER, Leonard. Achievement.

SLOMENSKI, Stanley. Achievement.

1965 HURLEY, Mal. Meritorious service.

SCHMIDT, William. Meritorious service.

STRANICH, Albert. Achievement.

WEBER, Al. Achievement.

1966 CESTONE, Tom. Meritorious service.

FIGUARELLI, Frank. Achievement.

GARDNER, George. Meritorious service.

GRIPPE, Frank. Achievement.

SOBON, August. Meritorious service.

1967 COLETTI, Gordon. Achievement. *Also in*: New Jersey State Bowling Association Hall of Fame.

DOWNEY, Clarence. Meritorious service.

HAYS, George. Meritorious service.

KRAUSS, William. Achievement.

PRIMIANO, Nicholas. Meritorious service.

1968 BORINSKY, Rueben. Meritorious service.

FINIZIO, Armando. Meritorious service.

MARKS, Louis. Meritorious service.

MILLER, William. Achievement.
MURZINSKI, Michael. Achievement.
1969 McELHONE, Frank. Achievement.
MUELLER, Carl. Meritorious service.
SEARRY, Fred. Achievement.
WOODS, Edward J. Meritorious service. *Also in*: New Jersey State Bowling Association Hall of Fame.
1970 DROZDO, Steve. Veterans.
GIVENS, John. Meritorious service.
HANSEN, Alfred. Achievement.
KNAPP, Richard. Achievement.
SAWICKI, Al. Meritorious service.
TARLOWE, Sam. Meritorious service.
1971 ARGESTA, James. Achievement.
HESSE, Victor. Meritorious service. *Also in*: New Jersey State Bowling Association Hall of Fame.
LOESER, Edward. Meritorious service.
McGIHLEY, Charles. Veterans.
REINFURT, George. Achievement.
REITEMEYER, Harold. Achievement.
STURCKE, Harry. Meritorious service.
1972 BROWN, Joseph. Achievement. *Also in*: New Jersey State Bowling Association Hall of Fame.
FATIGATI, John. Meritorious service.
FORSTER, Jacob. Veterans.
HAVANKI, Charles. Meritorious service.
LUSARDI, Raymond. Veterans.
REITHEL, William. Meritorious service.
TOWNLEY, William. Achievement.
TROWBRIDGE, Robert, Sr. Achievement.
VISCO, Phil. Achievement.
1973 ARTZ, Blacky. Veterans.
DeFRANCESCO, Rocky. Achievement.
LANCE, Theodore. Veterans.
REYNOLDS, Vince. Meritorious service.
ROCKFORD, Dick. Meritorious service.
ROSS, Randall. Meritorious service.
SIANA, Tom. Veterans.
TIETZ, Edward. Achievement.
1974 CARUSO, Frank. Achievement.
COSGREN, Gil. Veterans.
MacQUESTION, Bill. Veterans.
METZ, Albert. Achievement.
O'DELL, Jack. Achievement.
SHOLTIS, Robert. Achievement.
ZUSI, Chris. Meritorious service.
1975 DELLARAGIONE, Frank. Meritorious service.
DEPARRE, Sam. Achievement.
GROPPE, Vic. Veterans.
HAMPSON, Gene. Meritorious service.
HENNINGER, Fred. Achievement.
O'DONNELL, Jerry. Achievement.
OGIER, Roman J. Veterans.
SCHAFFER, Michael. Achievement.
SCHUTT, Herbert. Meritorious service.
1976 BUCHHOLZ, Howard. Meritorious service.
FARB, Milt. Meritorious service.
GRIFFIN, Warren. Achievement.
KIELBASA, Stan. Veterans.
NATKIE, Walter. Veterans.
TILLOU, Dave. Achievement.

Bowling Halls of Fame to Watch

AMERICAN LAWN BOWLS ASSOCIATION HALL OF FAME

Incorporated into an Existing Museum 1972

A hall of fame and biographical archives were maintained by the American Lawn Bowls Association (founded 1915) in Sun City, Ariz, until 1972 at which time these materials were donated to the Citizens Savings Athletic Foundation and Hall of Fame; the ALBA Hall of Fame ceased to exist as a separate entity. *See* appropriate entries under Citizens Savings Hall of Fame Athletic Museum.

CLEVELAND WOMEN'S BOWLING ASSOCIATION HALL OF FAME

Internal Development 1977

By 1977 this hall of fame had inducted 21 members, the photographs of whom are displayed on a Hall of Fame Plaque in the Association's offices. Names of the members are not available. For more information contact Zee Fabri, Secy, or Bernice Yanuzzi, Pres. of the Association, 1900 Euclid Avenue, Room 212, Cleveland, OH 44115. (216) 771-0232.

DENVER BOWLING ASSOCIATION HALL OF FAME

Internal Development 1977

By 1977 this hall of fame had inducted approximately 30 members, a list of whom is not available. For additional information contact Joseph M. Maher, 5512 W. First Ave, Denver, CO 80219, or call Wayne Johnson, Chairman of the Hall of Fame Comt, (303) 922-8163.

FIVEPIN BOWLERS HALL OF FAME

Internal Reorganization 1970

The Ontario Bowlers Congress (OBC), a major governing body in Canadian bowling, has plans to reorganize this hall of fame, which was founded in 1970 to honor the greatest of the 1 to 3 million Canadians who bowl fivepins every week. Ten members were inducted in 1970: Dick Brett, Mens Division; Charles Demelis, Mens Division; Edward Hawkes, Mens Division; Tom Mallon, Mens Division; Mabel McDowell, Ladies Division; Ollie Miller, Mens Division; Thomas Ryan (the man who invented fivepin bowling in 1909), Builders Division; John "Jake" Smith, Mens Division (*also in*: Buffalo Bowling Association Hall of Fame); Vera Ward, Ladies Division; and Robert "Bob" Woods, Builders Division. No elections or inductions have been held since 1970. Criteria for nomination are being reconsidered and may include the requirement of 25 years as an active participant in the game. Under discussion is the inclusion of the Fivepin Bowlers Hall of Fame in a planned amateur sports hall of fame at Brayside, near Scarborough. For further information, contact Bert Garside, Exec. Secy. of the OBC, 147 Nantucket Blvd, Unit 1, Scarborough, ON M1P 2N5. (416) 752-1327.

OMAHA BOWLING ASSOCIATION HALL OF FAME

Internal Development 1977

By 1977 this hall of fame had inducted 127 members, a list of whom is not available. Inquiries should be addressed to Jack Williams, Chairman of the Hall of Fame Committee, 3167 Leavenworth, Omaha, NE 68105. (402) 571-1000, Exten. 647, or 342-0517.

BOXING

From the greatest to "the greatest"—Theagenes to Muhammad Ali—the art of fighting with gloved fists, of delivering without receiving blows, has survived over 30 centuries of attempts to regulate, control or utterly ban it. Theagenes, a Greek, was indisputably the greatest pugilist who ever lived. The son of Timosthenes, a priest of Hercules, he gained the title of boxing champion by killing the reigning one, then held the title by killing his next 1425 challengers. His fame was so great that his townsmen raised a statue to him. A rival boxer tried to topple it one night. The statue fell on top of him and killed him, so that Theagenes may be said to have had 1427 career wins. He fought under the Theseus Rules of 900 B.C, by which two men or boys sitting with noses almost touching began belting each other with bare knuckles, leather-thonged fists, or metal-studded or steel-spiked cestuses. The loser was the first to give up or the first to die. Some say the Romans, who fought in circular rings, invented standing up to fight. There were, of course, both Greeks and Romans who frowned upon boxing or attempted to ban it. But it was too popular (*see* Martial Arts, Track and Field). Greece and Rome both fell; boxing has survived over 3000 years. Though not as popular as it has been in the past, it is today one of the world's major sports.

During the nineteenth century, the Classics were idolized and Greek and Roman institutions were widely copied. Thus the Olympic Games were revived, and halls of fame themselves were invented (*see* main introduction). Boxing, however, was one of the few Classic institutions which was not copied. In fact, it was largely illegal. Even the invention of mufflers (boxing gloves) by Jack Broughton, the "Father of Boxing" (now buried in Westminster Abbey), did not lessen the resistance to boxing. Newspapers ignored it, women's groups condemned it. When the American champion John Heenan met the reigning British champion in London in 1860, their 42-round match was illegal. Despite that, numerous notables including William Thackeray and Charles Dickens were there to see the two hour and twenty minute fight end in a draw.

In North America, too, the same fight was waged for decades between the popularity of it and the laws against it. A bill debated and passed in February 1881 forbade prizefighting in Canada, and it was forbidden in the United States until a New York law legalized it in 1896 (the year heart surgery was pioneered in Frankfurt, Germany). After four years boxing again became illegal, to remain that way for 20 more years until the Walker Law.

That law, the immense popularity of John L(awrence) Sullivan, the use of boxing as training during W.W. I and the institution of the annual Golden Gloves Tournament by the *Chicago Tribune* in 1927 ushered in the Golden Age of Boxing. This age saw the greatest names of the game (except Theagenes), the first million-dollar gate, and the largest amount of money ever paid at the gate for a single fight—$2,658,660.

Sullivan (1858–1918) was the main force in the popularization of boxing in North America. The first American World Heavyweight Champion, he spanned the bare knuckle era and the era of gloves. With keen showman instincts, he played Simon Legree in a stage production of *Uncle Tom's Cabin.* That part fit, since he had strong racial prejudices. He disliked training. "I'd have rather fought 12 dozen times," he said, "than train once." He was a man everyone watched and either loved or hated. His habits of lifting kegs of nails over his head for exercise, and of hardening his hands and face by washing them in his own secret mixture that included rock salt and white wine, were as famous as his knockout wins. Though in his day boxing was largely illegal, he was the first fighter whose career earnings topped the $1 million mark. All of these factors made John L. Sullivan, the Victorian Ali, our first great sports myth. He more than anyone else before or since changed the definition of boxing from disgraceful, lewd, and grotesque to manly, invigorating, and a test of courage and fitness.

The Golden Age of Boxing is gone now and in its place are multimillion dollar purses, televised boxing, and the carefully nurtured memories of the great might-have-been fights between Dempsey and Willis, Sullivan and Jackson, Johnson and Marciano, Wilkinson and Hyfield. The latter could have been a great fight had the police not prevented it. Elizabeth Wilkinson, through a newspaper ad in June 1722, had challenged Hannah Hyfield to a boxing match in which each would hold a coin. The winner was to receive $15, the loser was to be the one who first dropped her coin.

FORMS: There are styles for virtually every country, notably Chinese or shadow boxing, Thai boxing, Burmese boxing and *Boxe Français*. *Boxe Français* is derived from the deadly *savaté* as well as from *savaté's* more sophisticated form, *chausson* (*see* Martial Arts).

Two individuals seek to hit each other without being hit, the object being to win on points or by a knockout. Points are awarded for each round according to various point systems. Points are usually awarded by five ringside judges for scoring blows on the target (the front or sides above the belt) or for out-classing the opponent. A technical knockout (TKO) occurs when one boxer is unable or unwilling to continue, but has not been counted out by the referee. A count of ten for a total of ten seconds is a knockout. Equipment needed for each boxer includes a pair of gloves (6 – 8 oz. for pros, 8 – 12 oz. for amateurs), shorts, shoes with soft elk leather soles, a rubber gum shield, and a groin and/or breast protector. The elevated ring is padded and canvas covered, from 14 ft. to 24 ft. square and is bordered vertically by three 1 in. ropes. A referee supervises the fight, which is scheduled for from 3 to 15 rounds (3 min. each for pros, 2 min. each for amateurs). Rounds are separated by 1-minute rest periods. Opponents are matched according to various factors, especially their relative weights. There are at least 12 amateur and pro divisions—from flyweight at 112 lbs. through bantam, feather, light, welter, and middleweight to heavyweight at 175 lbs. or more in pros, 178 lbs. or more in amateurs.

ORGANIZATION: The governing body closest to an international authority is the World Boxing Council. In the United States the World Boxing Association and the New York State Athletic Commission operate independently of each other, each announcing its own world champions in the various weight divisions. The Amateur International Boxing Association controls amateur boxing, including the Olympic Games events. The chief regulatory organization in Canada is the Canadian Boxing Federation.

Boxing Hall of Fame

NEW ROCHELLE, NEW YORK

Mailing Address: 35 Brady Avenue, 10805. Tel. (914) 235-0955. *Contact:* Scoop Gallello, Pres. *Location:* 20 mi. N.E. of New York City, 110 mi. S. of Albany. *Nearby Halls of Fame:* Heritage, Music (New York City), Bicycle (Staten Island, 30 mi. S.E.), Harness Racing (Goshen, 50 mi. N.W.), Baseball (Cooperstown, 140 mi. N.E.), Horse Racing (Saratoga Springs, 150 mi. N.).

The Boxing Hall of Fame Award honors those great pugilists who have fought in Westchester County, N.Y. Ring Thirty of the International Veterans Boxing Association founded this award in 1969 under the guidance of Mr. Scoop Gallello. The Association governs, administers, and finances the award. The Hall of Fame Plaque hangs in New Rochelle City Hall. Eventually a separate room within City Hall will house collections of memorabilia for the public to view.

Members: 15 as of 1977. The eight-member Hall of Fame Committee nominates individuals on the basis of their achievements in and contributions to boxing. The inductees must receive at least 65% of the vote; one or two are chosen annually. Selection is made in January and announced at the annual dinner in June.

1969 ANTONACCELI, Al "Sparks"
FLOWERS, Bruce

1970 COYLE, George
DEL GENIO, Leonard

1971 BURNSTEIN, Jack
RUFFALO, Patsy

1972 GRIPO, Al
ROCCO, John

1973 DERUZZA, Pete
HYNSE, Nel "Pickles"

1974 MERCURIAL, Jim
STURIONO, Joe "Iron Horse"

1975 FERRARO, Tony

1976 BERLENBACH, Paul "Astoria Assassin." See entry in the Boxing Hall of Fame, Citizens Savings Hall of Fame Athletic Museum. *Also in: Ring Magazine* Boxing Hall of Fame.

1977 LAPERA, Frankie

Boxing Hall of Fame Award

INDIANAPOLIS, INDIANA

Mailing Address: 3400 W. 86 St, 46268. Tel. (317) 297-2900. *Contact:* Col. Don Hull, U.S. Army Ret. (201) 567-1339. *Location:* 106 mi. S.W. of Cincinnati, Ohio, 101 mi. N.E. of Louisville, Ky, 181 mi. S.E. of Chicago, Ill, 235 mi. N.E. of St. Louis, Mo. *Nearby Halls of Fame:* Auto Racing, Basketball (Indianapolis), Poultry (West Lafayette, 60 mi. N.W.), Business (Chicago, Ill.) and Sports (St. Louis, Mo.).

The award was established in 1967 to honor outstanding service to boxing. It is given under the direction of the Amateur Athletic Union's National Boxing Committee and financed by the *San Francisco Examiner*.

Members: 11 as of 1977. A national committee of 75 members votes on nominees selected by a subcommittee of 9 from the national committee. Usually one person is selected each year at the national convention, and the inductee is presented with a plaque at the All-Sports Luncheon held each fall.

1967 SANDELL, Al
SHEEHAN, John J. "Tan"
1968 DUFFY, F. X. "Pat"
1969 STAFF, Pat
1970 BECKER, Dr. Ben
1971 SALAKIN, Leo
1972 SCHWARTZ, Roland
1973 DOWNEY, Bill
1975 KUISENBERRY, Clyde
SURKEIN, Robert J.
1976 WOODWARD, Verne

Canadian Boxing Hall of Fame

TORONTO, ONTARIO

Mailing Address: Ste. 4, 43 Victoria St, M5C 2A2. Tel. (410) 869-1933. *Contact:* Tony Unitas, Pres. & Exec. Dir. *Location:* Approx. 90 mi. N.W. of Rochester, N.Y, 100 mi. N.W. of Buffalo, N.Y, 226 mi. N.E. of Detroit, Mich. *Personnel:* Tony Unitas, Pres. & Exec. Dir; Vic Bagnato, V.Pres; Harvey Dubs, Secy; 6 mem. Election Comt. Call for further information. *Nearby Halls of Fame:* Sports, Ice Hockey (Toronto), Football (Hamilton, 40 mi. S.), Ice Hockey (Kingston, 150 mi. N.E.) and Sports (Detroit, Mich.).

Inititated and directed by Tony Unitas, the Canadian Boxing Hall of Fame attempts to unite "amateur and professional boxing in the task of promoting their highest standards, interests, and those of humanity by developing and elevating the mental and moral character of all those involved." Membership is international in scope, admitting any boxer who displays sportsmanship and courage, and who upholds the highest standards of achievement in competition. The Hall also recognizes the broadest principles of humanity as it sponsors assistance to the widows, orphans, ill and poor. The Hall is financed by Mr. Unitas' personal funds, advertising and subscriptions to its publications *Official Olympic Boxing Magazine* and *Tony Unitas Weekly Boxing News*.

Members: 408 as of October 1976, 158 of whom have been officially inducted. The electors, selected by Mr. Unitas to serve a five-year term, induct six or seven new members annually. Each is presented the Max Award (named for Emperor Maximus, 455–457, the world's first boxing fan) at a banquet the last Friday in October.

Induction Years Unrecorded

ANDERSON, Gordon
ARMSTRONG, Spider
BAGNATO, Joey
BAGNATO, Vic
BAGNATO, Vince
BAKER, Charles
BASS, Bobby
BATTAGLIA, Frankie
BEATTIE, Eddy
BEAUDRY, Nan
BEAUDRY, Nels
BLAND, Georgie
BLAND, Tommy
BOLTON, Bill
BONNER, Gene
BOWMILE, Morris
BRACE, Ellis "Jackie"
BRANDINO, Patsy
BRANDINO, Tony
BRASSEAU, Eugene
BRENNAN, Doug
BROWN, Joe
BURGESS, Joe
BURKE, Jackie
CALLURA, Angelo
CALLURA, Jackie. See entry in Canada's Sports Hall of Fame.
CARROLL, Eddy
CASTANZA, Domenic
CASTILLOU, Dave
CHARD, Howard "Baldy"
CHRETIEN, Fernand
CHUVALO, George
CORDINO, Corky Frank
CRAIK, Tarzan
CROWE, Art
CURRAN, John
DALTON, Tommy
DAVIS, Harry
DAY, Delmore Buddy
DEVISON, Johnny
DEXTRASE, General J. A.
DiFLORIO, Rudy
DOIRON, Jerry, Sr.
DONNELLY, Jim
DOWNEY, Dave

DOYLE, Mickey
DUBS, Harvey
DUGGAN, Jackie
DUNN, Henry
DUNNELL, Milt
DUPUIS, Adam
FALCIONI, George
FALLETTA, Dr. Joseph
FIFIELD, Billy
FIFIELD, Georgie
FIELDING, Carman
FIELDING, Cecil
FRASER, Colin
GAGNON, Omer
GAINES, Larry
GALLIVAN, Earl
GARLASH, Mike
GENOVESE, Frank
GLADMAN, Gerry
GLIONNA, Mel
GRAY, Clyde
GREGERSON, Rev. Greggy
GWYNNE, Horace "Lefty." See entry in Canada's Sports Hall of Fame.
HEADLEY, Eric
HEADLEY, Ron
HENRY, Walter
HILTON, Davey
JENKINS, William
KENNY, Clayton
KERNAGHN, Jimmy
KERWIN, Gale
KING, Lil' Arthur
KLIMITS, John
LAFFERTY, Louis "Kid"
LAFFRIDI, Johnny
LANDRY, Bill
LANTZ, Russell "Kid"
LAPADULA, John
LARIVEE, Roger
LASCELLE, Harvey
LASCELLE, Ronnie
LATHAM, George
LEVIN, Dr. Herman
LEWIS, Doug
LIGHTHEART, Phil
LINEHAM, Richard "The Lion"
LUFTSPRING, Sammy
MacDONALD, Alex
MacDONALD, Grant
McCARTHY, Russ
McCLUSKEY, Tom
McFATER, Allan
McGEE, Bill "Kid McCoy"
McGRORY, Tim
McKINNON, Sailor Don
McLARNIN, Jimmy. See entry in Canada's Sports Hall of Fame. *Also in:* Boxing Hall of Fame, Citizens Savings Hall of Fame Athletic Museum; and *Ring Magazine* Boxing Hall of Fame.
McLEAN, John-Joe
McWHIRTER, Cliff
MARMONO, Jimmy
MITCHELL, Pinky
MORRISSEY, Willey
NEMIS, Johnny
NORTHUP, Tommy
OSBORNE, Tommy
PAGE, Johnny
PAUL, Davey Peters
PERCIVAL, Lloyd
PHILLIPS, Clarke
PIETRAS, Leo
POULTON, Harry "Kid"
POWELL, Bill
PRYOR, Bill
RANDELL, Benny "Red"
REECE, Reggie "Roughie"
RICHARDSON, Blair
ROBERT, Hec
ROBERTSON, Dr. Robbie
ROBINSON, Kenny
ROSKO, Mike
ROSS, Don
ROSS, "Rock-a-bye"
SANDULO, Joey
SAUNDERS, Mark "Killer"
SAUVE, Wilf
SCARVARELLI, Nels
SENOS, Eddy
SEQUIN, Lou
SHEARS, Jerry
SHERMAN, Sam
SHIPTON, Arnold
SHROTT, Sammy
SILVERS, Jackie
SMITH, Don
SOWERY, Cliff
SPENCER, Tommy-Gun
STEVENSON, Vern
SUTTON, Lloyd "Cochise"
SWALLOW, Angus

SWARTMEN, Mel
TEALE, Johnny
THOMAS, Ralph
TUNNEY, Frank
UNGERMAN, Irv
UNITAS, Tony
WADSWORTH, Lenny
WALTON, Rocky
WARRINGTON, Tiger
WEBB, Danny
WILLIAMS, Chuck
YACK, Norman "Baby"
ZADUK, Peter

Pennsylvania Boxing Hall of Fame

PHILADELPHIA, PENNSYLVANIA

Mailing Address: 1410 Tasker St, 19145. Tel. (215) 336-4058. *Contact:* Tony Morgano. *Location:* Approx. 30 mi. N.E. of Wilmington, Del, 100 mi. N.E. of Baltimore, Md, 100 mi. S.W. of New York City, 110 mi. E. of Harrisburg, 122 mi. S.E. of Scranton, 133 mi. N.E. of Washington, D.C, 240 mi. N. of Richmond, Va. *Personnel:* Tony Morgano, Pres; Joe Carto, Secy; Tony Georgette, Treas; 14 mem. Hall of Fame Comt. (Frank Cincinnati, Chmn.). Not open to the public. *Nearby Halls of Fame:* Heritage (Valley Forge, 25 mi. W.), Heritage, Music (New York City), Jockeys (Baltimore), Technology (Arlington, Va, 140 mi. S.W.), Harness Racing (Goshen, N.Y, 175 mi. N.), Aeronautics (Elmira, N.Y, 240 mi. N.E.).

The Veterans Boxing Association founded the Pennsylvania Boxing Hall of Fame as a nonprofit corporation in March 1967. Under the direction and governance of the Hall of Fame Committee, the Boxing Hall of Fame seeks to "promote and foster character, integrity, good citizenship and the spirit of good sportsmanship among persons engaged in the profession of boxing, to elect to membership those boxers worthy of admission and to maintain a plaque honoring meritorious boxers." Located in the Museum are 20,000 photographs depicting pugilists, the history of boxing and memorable moments from great fights, dating from the turn of the century. There are gloves, souvenirs and other personal memorabilia on display. The Museum is now open only to members of the Veterans Boxing Association. The Hall of Fame, Inc, has however applied to the city of Philadelphia for "historical site" status for the Boxing Museum. If this is granted, the Museum will be open to the public. In addition to honoring pugilists and maintaining the Museum, the Hall of Fame, Inc, sponsors social service activities in the community.

Members: 40 as of 1977. The Hall of Fame Committee screens applications submitted by groups or individuals. The applications must be in the Committee files no later than the third week in March for the April 1 vote. A majority of the 14 votes from the Committee is required for induction. There are two categories for nominees: Boxers and Non-Boxers. Boxers must be retired at least five years, have been a resident of Pennsylvania or campaigned during their career in the State and have brought credit to the sport. Non-Boxers, a category including referees, timekeepers, writers, etc, are judged on their devotion to the sport and their contribution to its advancement as a more ideal form of athletic competition. There is no retirement requirement for Non-Boxers. Members are inducted on Mother's Day at a banquet and their names are inscribed on a plaque which is displayed in Convention Hall. Each year three individuals are elected. There is also a Mother of the Year Award presented at the Mother's Day banquet to honor a boxer's wife or sister.

1977 BLACKBURN, Jack
DUNDEE, Angelo
WOLFE, Henry "Kid"

Induction Year Unrecorded

ANGOTT, Sammy. *Also in: Ring Magazine* Boxing Hall of Fame.
BARRETT, Bobby
BASS, Benny
BRADLEY, Bob
BRADLEY, Pat
BROWN, Harry "Kid"
BURNS, Johnny
CARIS, Frankie
CASTELLANI, Rocky
CERVINO, Joe
CONN, Billy. See entry in Boxing Hall of Fame, Citizens Savings Hall of Fame Athletic Museum. *Also in: Ring Magazine* Boxing Hall of Fame.
COOL, Eddie
DeMARCO, Cuddy
DORAZIO, Gus
ERNE, Yi Yi
EVANS, Mike
GREB, Harry. See entry in Boxing Hall of Fame, Citizens Savings Hall of Fame Athletic Museum. *Also in: Ring Magazine* Boxing Hall of Fame.
HOUCK, Leo. *Also in: Ring Magazine* Boxing Hall of Fame.
JADICK, Johnny
JAFFE, Lou
JOHNSON, Harold
KAUFFMAN, Benny
KELLY, Freddy

KLAUS, Frank. See entry in Boxing Hall of Fame, Citizens Savings Hall of Fame Athletic Museum. *Also in: Ring Magazine* Boxing Hall of Fame.

LATZO, Pete

LEMISCH, Bernard

LEVINSKY, Battling. See entry in Boxing Hall of Fame, Citizens Savings Hall of Fame Athletic Museum. *Also in: Ring Magazine* Boxing Hall of Fame.

LEWIS, Harry

LOUGHRAN, Tommy. See entry in Boxing Hall of Fame, Citizens Savings Hall of Fame Athletic Museum. *Also in: Ring Magazine* Boxing Hall of Fame.

LOUGHREY, Young

MAHER, Billy

MASSEY, Lew

McCARRON, Jack

McCURLEY, Lanse

McGUIGAN, Jack

MEALEY, Johnny

MENDO, Jimmy

MONTGOMERY, Bob

MOORE, Pal

MORGANO, Tony

O'BRIEN, Jack "Philadelphia Jack." See entry in Boxing Hall of Fame, Citizens Savings Hall of Fame Athletic Museum. *Also in: Ring Magazine* Boxing Hall of Fame.

O'TOOLE, Tommy

PALUMBO, Frank

ROCAP, Billy

SMITH, Sammy "Young Sammy"

SOOSE, Billy

SPEARY, Billy

TAYLOR, Herman

TENDLER, Lew. See entry in Boxing Hall of Fame, Citizens Savings Hall of Fame Athletic Museum. *Also in: Ring Magazine* Boxing Hall of Fame.

TOMASCO, Pete

TOPPI, Jimmy

TURNER, Gil

WEINER, Frank

WOLGAST, Bobby

WOLGAST, Midget. See entry in Boxing Hall of Fame, Citizens Savings Hall of Fame Athletic Museum. *Also in: Ring Magazine* Boxing Hall of Fame.

ZIVIC, Fritzie. *Also in: Ring Magazine* Boxing Hall of Fame.

Ring Magazine Boxing Hall of Fame

NEW YORK, NEW YORK

Mailing Address: 120 W. 31 St, 10001. Tel. (212) 564-0354. *Contact:* Nat Loubey, Pres. *Location:* 135 mi. N.E. of Philadelphia, Pa, 135 mi. N.W. of Scranton, Pa, 154 mi. S. of Albany, 206 mi. S.W. of Boston, Mass, 233 mi. N.E. of Washington, D.C. *Personnel:* Nat Loubey, Pres; Dan Daniel, Secy. Call for information. *Nearby Halls of Fame:* Heritage, Music (New York City), Bicycle (Staten Island, 5 mi. S.W.), Ice Skating (Newburgh, 45 mi. N.W.), Harness Racing (Goshen, 75 mi. N.E.), Heritage (Valley Forge, Pa, 105 mi. N.E.), Baseball (Cooperstown, 135 mi. N.W.), Horse Racing (Saratoga Springs, 150 mi. N.E.), Flight (Elmira, 170 mi. N.W.), Horseshoe Pitching (Corning, 185 mi. N.W), Jockey (Baltimore, Md, 196 mi. S.W.), Ice Skating (Boston).

Nat Fleischer founded *Ring Magazine* in 1922. As publisher and editor, he strove to rid boxing of disreputable characters while providing the sport with a medium to improve the image of qualified pugilists and display their skills. In 1954 he initiated *Ring Magazine* Boxing Hall of Fame award to honor noteworthy boxers and promoters who advance the welfare of boxing. The award is sponsored, governed, financed and administrated by *Ring Magazine.*

Members: 134 as of 1976. There are no restrictions on annual inductions into the three categories. Members in the first category, Pioneers, are elected by the Board of Directors of *Ring Magazine*. The inductees may or may not have boxed professionally, but they all must have promoted the positive facets of boxing. Those in the second category, Old-Timers, are elected by 20 boxing experts; 15 votes are needed for induction. The Old-Timers are classified as those active 35 or more years ago. Members in the third category, Moderns, are elected by sportswriters and announcers and others familiar with boxing. Requirements demand retirement for two or more years and active participation within the past 35 years. Nominees must receive 75% of the total vote to be inducted.

1954 ARMSTRONG, Henry Jackson, Jr. Modern. See entry in the Boxing Hall of Fame, Citizens Savings Hall of Fame Athletic Museum (Induction Year Unrecorded). *Also in:* Black Athletes Hall of Fame.

BARROW, Joseph Louis "Joe Louis." Modern. See entry in the Boxing Hall of Fame, Citizens Savings Hall of Fame Athletic Museum (Induction Year Unrecorded). *Also in:* Michigan Sports Hall of Fame.

BROUGHTON, Jack. Pioneer. "Father of Boxing."

CHAMBERS, Arthur. Pioneer.

CORBETT, James John. Old-Timer. Known as Gentleman Jim. See entry in the Boxing Hall of Fame, Citizens Savings Hall of Fame Athletic Museum (Induction Year Unrecorded).

CRIBB, Tom. Pioneer.

DEMPSEY, William Harrison "Jack." Modern. See entry in the Boxing Hall of Fame, Citizens Savings Hall of Fame Athletic Museum (Induction Year Unrecorded).

DEMPSEY, Jack. Old-Timer. Known as "The Nonpareil."

FIGG, James. Pioneer.

FITZSIMMONS, Robert L. Old-Timer. See entry in the Boxing Hall of Fame, Citizens Savings Hall of Fame Athletic Museum (Induction Year Unrecorded).

GANS, Joe. Old-Timer. Known as "The Old Master." See entry in the Boxing Hall of Fame, Citizens Savings Hall of Fame Athletic Museum (Induction Year Unrecorded).

GRIFFITH, Alfred. Pioneer.

HEENAN, John C. Pioneer. Known as "The Benecia Boy."

HYER, Tom. Pioneer.

JACKSON, John. Pioneer.

JEFFRIES, James Jackson. Old-Timer. Known as "The Boilermaker." See entry in the Boxing Hall of Fame, Citizens Savings Hall of Fame Athletic Museum (Induction Year Unrecorded).

JOHNSON, John Arthur "Jack." Old-Timer. See entry in the Boxing Hall of Fame, Citizens Savings Hall of Fame Athletic Museum (Induction Year Unrecorded).

KETCHEL, Stanley. Old-Timer. See entry in the Boxing Hall of Fame, Citizens Savings Hall of Fame Athletic Museum (Induction Year Unrecorded). *Also in:* Grand Rapids Sports Hall of Fame and Michigan Sports Hall of Fame.

MACE, Jem. Pioneer.

McAULIFFE, Jack. Pioneer.

MENDOZA, Daniel. Pioneer.

MORRISSEY, John. Pioneer.

SAYERS, Tom. Pioneer. Known as the "Napoleon of the Prize Ring."

SULLIVAN, John Lawrence. Pioneer. See entry in the Boxing Hall of Fame, Citizens Savings Hall of Fame Athletic Museum (Induction Year Unrecorded).

1955 ATTELL, Abraham W. "Abe." Old-Timer. See entry in the Boxing Hall of Fame, Citizens Savings Hall of Fame Athletic Museum (Induction Year Unrecorded).

GREB, Harry. Modern. See entry in the Boxing Hall of Fame, Citizens Savings Hall of Fame Athletic Museum (Induction Year Unrecord). *Also in:* Pennsylvania Boxing Hall of Fame.

LANGFORD, Sam. Old-Timer. See entry in Canada's Sports Hall of Fame. *Also in:* Boxing Hall of Fame, Citizens Savings Hall of Fame Athletic Museum.

LEONARD, Benjamin. Modern. See entry in the Boxing Hall of Fame, Citizens Savings Hall of Fame Athletic Museum (Induction Year Unrecorded).

McGOVERN, John Terrence "Terry." Old-Timer. See entry in the Boxing Hall of Fame, Citizens Savings Hall of Fame Athletic Museum (Induction Year Unrecorded).

RICHMOND, William. Pioneer.

THOMPSON, William "Bendigo." Pioneer.

TUNNEY, James Joseph "Gene." Modern. See entry in the Boxing Hall of Fame, Citizens Savings Hall of Fame Athletic Museum (Induction Year Unrecorded).

WALCOTT, Joe. Old-Timer. See entry in the Boxing Hall of Fame, Citizens Savings Hall of Fame Athletic Museum (Induction Year Unrecorded).

WALKER, Edward Patrick "Mickey." Modern. See entry in the Boxing Hall of Fame, Citizens Savings Hall of Fame Athletic Museum (Induction Year Unrecorded).

1956 CANZONERI, Tony. Modern. See entry in the Boxing Hall of Fame, Citizens Savings Hall of Fame Athletic Museum (Induction Year Unrecorded).

DIXON, George. Old-Timer. See entry in Canada's Sports Hall of Fame. *Also in:* Boxing Hall of Fame, Citizens Savings Hall of Fame Athletic Museum.

DRISCOLL, Jem. Old-Timer.

JACKSON, Peter. Pioneer.

LOUGHRAN, Tommy. Modern. See entry in the Boxing Hall of Fame, Citizens Savings Hall of Fame Athletic Museum (Induction Year Unrecorded). *Also in:* Pennsylvania Boxing Hall of Fame.

McLARNIN, Jimmy "Baby Face." Modern. See entry in Canada's Sports Hall of Fame. *Also in:* Boxing Hall of Fame, Citizens Savings Hall of Fame Athletic Museum; and Canadian Boxing Hall of Fame.

RICHMOND, Bill. Pioneer.

ROSS, Barney. Modern. See entry in the Boxing Hall of Fame, Citizens Savings Hall of Fame Athletic Museum (Induction Year Unrecorded).

1957 CARRORA, Joseph. Modern. Fought as Johnny Dundee. See entry in the Boxing Hall of Fame, Citizens Savings Hall of Fame Athletic Museum (Induction Year Unrecorded).

DARCY, James Leslie "Les." Old-Timer.

McCOY, Charles "Kid." Old-Timer. See entry in the Boxing Hall of Fame, Citizens Savings Hall of Fame Athletic Museum (Induction Year Unrecorded).

McFARLAND, Packey. Old-Timer.

MITCHELL, Charley. Pioneer.

NELSON, Batling. Old-Timer. See entry in the Boxing Hall of Fame, Citizens Savings Hall of Fame Athletic Museum (Induction Year Unrecorded).

1958 GIBBONS, Mike. Old-Timer. See entry in the Boxing Hall of Fame, Citizens Savings Hall of Fame Athletic Museum (Induction Year Unrecorded).

MOLINEAUX, Tom. Pioneer.

RYAN, Tommy. Old-Timer. See entry in the Boxing Hall of Fame, Citizens Savings Hall of Fame Athletic Museum (Induction Year Unrecorded).

WOLGAST, Adolph "Midget" "Ad." Old-Timer. *Also in:* Pennsylvania Boxing Hall of Fame.

ZALE, Tony. Modern

1959 GULLY, John. Pioneer.

HERMAN, Pete. Old-Timer. See entry in the Boxing Hall of Fame, Citizens Savings Hall of Fame Athletic Museum (Induction Year Unrecorded).

LAVIGNE, George "Kid." Old-Timer. See entry in Boxing Hall of Fame, Citizens Savings Hall of Fame Athletic Museum (Induction Year Unrecorded). *Also in:* Michigan Sports Hall of Fame.

MARCIANO, Rocky. Modern. See entry in the Boxing Hall of Fame, Citizens Savings Hall of Fame Athletic Museum (Induction Year Unrecorded). *Also in:* UNICO National Athletic Hall of Fame.

PRICE, Ernest Cutler. Old-Timer. Fought as Jack Dillon. See entry in the Boxing Hall of Fame, Citizens Savings Hall of Fame Athletic Museum (Induction Year Unrecorded).

SARDINIAS, Eligio "Chocolate Kid." Modern. See entry in the Boxing Hall of Fame, Citizens Savings Hall of Fame Athletic Museum (Induction Year Unrecorded).

SHARKEY, Thomas J. Old-Timer. See entry in the Boxing Hall of Fame, Citizens Savings Hall of Fame Athletic Museum (Induction Year Unrecorded).

WILDE, Jimmy. Old-Timer.

1960 BRESLIN, William J. Modern. Fought as Jack Britton. See entry in the Boxing Hall of Fame, Citizens Savings Hall of Fame Athletic Museum (Induction Year Unrecorded).

BURNS, Tommy. Old-Timer. See entry in Canada's Sports Hall of Fame.

CHOYNSKI, Joe. Old-Timer.

DONNELLY, Don. Pioneer.

KILBANE, John Patrick "Johnny." Old-Timer. See entry in the Boxing Hall of Fame, Citizens Savings Hall of Fame Athletic Museum (Induction Year Unrecorded).

THOMAS, Frederick Hall. Old-Timer. Known as "The Welsh Wizard."

1961 ROOT, Jack. Old-Timer. See entry in the Boxing Hall of Fame, Citizens Savings Hall of Fame Athletic Museum (Induction Year Unrecorded).

SPRING, Tom. Pioneer.

TENDLER, Lew. Modern. See entry in the Boxing Hall of Fame, Citizens Savings Hall of Fame Athletic Museum (Induction Year Unrecorded). *Also in:* Pennsylvania Boxing Hall of Fame.

VILLA, Pancho. Old-Timer. Real name Francisco Guilledo.

1962 BEL-ABBES, Sidi. Modern. Known as the "Casablanca Clouter."

PETROLLE, Billy. Modern.

PRICE, Ned. Pioneer.

RICHIE, Willie. Old-Timer. See entry in the Boxing Hall of Fame, Citizens Savings Hall of Fame Athletic Museum (Induction Year Unrecorded).

1963 GIBBONS, Tommy. Old-Timer. See entry in the Boxing Hall of Fame, Citizens Savings Hall of Fame Athletic Museum (Induction Year Unrecorded).

PEP, Willie. Modern. See entry in the Boxing Hall of Fame, Citizens Savings Hall of Fame Athletic Museum (Induction Year Unrecorded).

WARD, Jem. Pioneer.

1964 AMBERS, Louis. Modern. See entry in the Boxing Hall of Fame, Citizens Savings Hall of Fame Athletic Museum (Induction Year Unrecorded).

BRADDOCK, James J. "Jim." Modern.

CARPENTER, Georges. Old-Timer. Known as "The Orchid Man."

COLLYER, Sam. Pioneer.

LEWIS, Ted "Kid." Old-Timer. See entry in the Boxing Hall of Fame Athletic Museum (Induction Year Unrecorded).

1965 CONN, Billy. Modern. See entry in the Boxing Hall of Fame, Citizens Savings Hall of Fame Athletic Museum (Induction Year Unrecorded). *Also in:* Pennsylvania Boxing Hall of Fame.

CORBETT, Young II. Old-Timer.

COULON, Johnny. Old-Timer. See entry in Canada's Sports Hall of Fame. *Also in:* Boxing Hall of Fame, Citizens Savings Hall of Fame Athletic Museum.

KILRAIN, Jake. Pioneer.

MORAN, Owen. Old-Timer.

1966 BURKE, James "Deaf." Pioneer.

GAVILAN, Kid. Modern.

LEVINSKY, Battling. Old-Timer. See entry in the Boxing Hall of Fame, Citizens Savings Hall of Fame Athletic Museum (Induction Year Unrecorded). *Also in:* Pennsylvania Boxing Hall of Fame.

MOORE, Archibald Lee "Archie." Modern. See entry in the Boxing Hall of Fame, Citizens

Savings Hall of Fame Athletic Museum (Induction Year Unrecorded).

1967 AARON, Barney "Young." Pioneer.

JEANNETTE, Joe. Old-Timer.

ROBINSON, Sugar Ray. Modern. See entry in the Boxing Hall of Fame, Citizens Savings Hall of Fame Athletic Museum (Induction Year Unrecorded).

1968 BAER, Max. Modern.

HYER, Jacob. Pioneer.

O'BRIEN, Jack "Philadelphia Jack." Old-Timer. See entry in the Boxing Hall of Fame, Citizens Savings Hall of Fame Athletic Museum (Induction Year Unrecorded). *Also in:* Pennsylvania Boxing Hall of Fame.

1969 BASILIO, Carmen. Modern.

CREAM, Arnold Raymond. Modern.

GOSS, Joe. Pioneer.

HOUCK, Leo. Old-Timer. *Also in:* Pennsylvania Boxing Hall of Fame.

JEFFORDS, Jerome. Old-Timer.

1970 CHARLES, Ezzard. Modern.

DONOVAN, Mike "Professor Mike." Pioneer.

GUTENKO, John "Kid Williams." Old-Timer. See entry in the Boxing Hall of Fame, Citizens Savings Hall of Fame Athletic Museum (Induction Year Unrecorded).

SCHMELING, Maximilian "Max." Old-Timer. See entry in the Boxing Hall of Fame, Citizens Savings Hall of Fame Athletic Museum (Induction Year Unrecorded).

WILLS, Harry. Old-Timer.

1971 BERLENBACH, Paul "Astoria Assassin." Old-Timer. See entry in the Boxing Hall of Fame, Citizens Savings Hall of Fame Athletic Museum (Induction Year Unrecorded). *Also in:* Boxing Hall of Fame.

CLARK, Nobby. Pioneer.

FLOWERS, Tiger. Old-Timer.

GRAZIANO, Rocky. Modern.

SADDLER, Joseph "Sandy." Modern. See entry in the Boxing Hall of Fame, Citizens Savings Hall of Fame Athletic Museum (Induction Year Unrecorded).

1972 CHANDLER, Tom. Pioneer.

JACK, Beau. Modern.

LaBARBA, Fidel. Old-Timer. See entry in the Boxing Hall of Fame, Citizens Savings Hall of Fame Athletic Museum (Induction Year Unrecorded).

PAPKE, Billy. Old-Timer. See entry in the Boxing Hall of Fame, Citizens Savings Hall of Fame Athletic Museum (Induction Year Unrecorded).

ROSENBLOOM, Maxie. Modern. See entry in the Boxing Hall of Fame, Citizens Savings Hall of Fame Athletic Museum (Induction Year Unrecorded).

ZIVIC, Fritzie. Modern. *Also in:* Pennsylvania Boxing Hall of Fame.

1973 ANGOTT, Sammy. Modern. *Also in:* Pennsylvania Boxing Hall of Fame.

DELANEY, Jack. Old-Timer. See entry in Canada's Sports Hall of Fame. *Also in:* Boxing Hall of Fame, Citizens Savings Hall of Fame Athletic Museum (Induction Year Unrecorded).

DiGENNARA, Frank. Old-Timer. Fought as Genaro. See entry in the Boxing Hall of Fame, Citizens Savings Hall of Fame Athletic Museum (Induction Year Unrecorded).

LESNEVICH, Gus. Modern.

RYAN, Paddy. Pioneer.

1974 CHANEY, George "K. O." Old-Timer.

CURTIS, Dick. Pioneer.

KLAUS, Frank. Old-Timer. See entry in the Boxing Hall of Fame, Citizens Savings Hall of Fame Athletic Museum (Induction Year Unrecorded). *Also in:* Pennsylvania Boxing Hall of Fame.

IHETU, Dick. Modern.

TUNNEY, Gene. Modern.

1975 BERARDINELLI, Guiseppe Antonio. Modern. See entry in the Boxing Hall of Fame, Citizens Savings Hall of Fame Athletic Museum (Induction Year Unrecorded).

BERGMAN, Judah "The Whitechapel Whirlwind." Modern. Also fought as Jackie "Kid" Berg.

BROWN, Aaron L. "The Dixie Kid." Old-Timer. See entry in the Boxing Hall of Fame, Citizens Savings Hall of Fame Athletic Museum (Induction Year Unrecorded).

ELIAS, Samuel. Pioneer.

ESCOBAR, Sixto. Modern.

FLEISCHER, Nat. Pioneer. See entry in Canada's Sports Hall of Fame. *Also in:* Boxing Hall of Fame, Citizens Savings Hall of Fame Athletic Museum (Induction Year Unrecorded).

Boxing Hall of Fame to Watch

MADISON SQUARE GARDEN HALL OF FAME
Name Change 1972
An exhibit of photographs and trophies of the world of professional boxing, this hall of fame existed in a facility at the Garden which became a private club in 1972. The exhibit remained in the facility as a special feature of the club. Persons purchasing box seat tickets at the Garden obtain automatic membership in this club, which is called The Hall of Fame Club. For information call (212) 563-8156 or 564-4400.

DOGS AND DOG RACING

In some cultures dogs are despised for religious reasons. But in virtually all cultures today and ever since their domestication some 10,000 years ago, dogs above all other creatures have received "man's best friend" status. In these cultures they have been used for transport, haulage, companionship, protection, magic, medicine and war. All over the world they were and are pitted against each other. In Spain dogs were pitted against bulls until the Church forbade it. The breeding and fighting of dogs is a major sport in Afghanistan today. Mastiffs bred as shock troops for war fought along with their Celtic masters to repel Roman legions. The Knights of Rhodes trained their dogs to sniff out Turks. The conquests of Mexico and Peru would not have been so swift had not the Conquistadores been aided by their fearsome Spanish bloodhounds. Aristotle speculated upon the possibilities of mating mastiffs to Indian tigers. Socrates' pupil, Xenophon, if not a great philosopher was at least a great dog breeder. Down through the ages, whenever a human need arose, a dog was bred to meet it: bulldogs to kill Christians in the Colosseum and later to bait bulls in sixteenth-century England; Egyptian salukis, the world's oldest breed, to bring down desert gazelle; dachshunds to chase game through tight burrows where long-legged dogs could not go. There were draft dogs in Britain until 1885, and in Belgium until 1939. That year their haulage earned $9 million. They are still eaten by Thais, Chinese, Micronesians and others. They figure as ancestors, jokers, or spiritual helpers in the legends of most of the 300-some North American Indian tribes. They were even worshipped once in Egypt as the dog or jackal gods Wepwawet, Khenti-amentiu, and Anubis. A town there was called Cynopolis, city of the dog. In myth and legend they are recognized as Cerberus, guard of the gates to Greek hell; Sirius, the brightest star and the larger of Orion's two dogs; Lelaps, the mythological greyhound; Argos, Ulysses' hunting dog, who alone recognized the hero dressed as a beggar when Ulysses returned from his 20-year absence. Not worshipped, but certainly venerated, were later dogs: Aibe, the twelfth century super-wolfhound; Barry, the nineteenth century dog that rescued 40 people from alpine deaths and made its kennel at the monastery of St. Bernard famous (a statue of Barry stands in Paris); Greyfriars Bobby, a Skye terrier, that lived beside its master's grave ten years until its own death in 1868 at the age of 14; Caesar, Edward VII's pet terrier, that led the procession of kings and princes at its master's royal funeral in 1910; Igloo, Byrd's fox terrier, the first dog to fly over both poles; Fala, F.D.R.'s Scottish terrier; and last but certainly not least, everyone's favorite childhood dog. It was perhaps fitting, therefore, that after such a long and illustrious heritage with man on earth, a dog, the Russian Laika, should precede the first man into space.

FORMS: At one time the earth was roamed by dogs the size of Kodiak bears with awesome teeth and jaws but small brains. Like the dinosaurs these soon died out. Today the dog family consists of 3 subfamilies, 14 genera and 38 species, the more familiar of which include the dog, wolf, coyote, jackal, fox, zorro, dingo and dhole. As a rule, all have 42 teeth, five toes per forepaw and four toes per hindpaw. Only one of those 38 species is a true dog. That species, *Canis familiaris,* has been manipulated genetically into hundreds of different breeds, of which about 120 are still in existence. Most of the tens of millions of dogs in the United States and Canada today are random mixtures of these various breeds, although the purity of many breeds is carefully maintained. The most popular breed in the United States is the poodle. In 1971 the American Kennel Club registered 256,491 poodles, as compared to 111,355 of the next largest breed, the German shepherd. Of the numerous sports involving dogs, three have halls of fame: Field Trials, Greyhound Racing and Sled-Dog Racing.

ORGANIZATION: Each breed has local and national clubs and associations concerned particularly with its maintenance and development. Governing all of North American dogdom, however, are the American Kennel Club (AKC) founded in 1884 and the Canadian Kennel Club (CKC) founded in 1888. The CKC, founded by Canadian members of the AKC, is today the only kennel club in the world run by volunteer officers and governed by the individual membership. Both these major kennel clubs are associations of numerous clubs. Both serve to maintain stud books and to recognize the establishment of new breeds. Both sponsor major dog shows and, with slight variation, recognize all breeds as belonging to one of six classes: sporting (hunting), hound (including the greyhound), working (including sled dogs), terrier, toy and nonsporting. Similarly, their respective dog shows decide champions according to slightly different systems of awarding points.

FIELD TRIALS

When the advent of agriculture had allowed subsistence activities like hunting to become pastimes, people began in earnest to develop breeds of dogs specific to different types of game. This very gradual trend was accelerated by one of the most famous hunting books of all time, *Livre du Chasse,* written in 1387 by a French nobleman named Gaston de Foix who kept as many as 1000 hunting dogs in his own kennels. The beagle, for example (from the French *beigle,* small, because they were tiny enough to ride around in Elizabethan saddlebags), was at first and still is a specialist on rabbits. Staghounds, wolfhounds, and mastiffs were bred to be uniquely suited to hunting wild boar.

The most popular breed, certainly in England, was the foxhound. It was first used exclusively to hunt foxes in 1698, the year after *The Tales of Mother Goose* was written. Two hundred years before the Declaration of Independence, foxhounds were roaming what would become America. Some, no doubt, were descendants of hounds that had escaped in 1541 from Hernando De Soto who had used them to hunt Indians. Lord Baltimore, founder of Maryland, required that each new family settling in the New World bring at least one good dog. Thus his friend, Robert Brooke, "Father of American Fox Hunting," arrived in 1650 with his wife, ten children, assorted servants and supplies, and his hounds. There were many famous early fox hunters. Washington was a foxhound fanatic and was displeased with the seven prize staghounds the Marquis de Lafayette gave him as a present. Jefferson, Marshall, and Hamilton were also foxhunters. Dr. Thomas Walker was a rambunctious and enthusiastic sportsman and fox hunter to whom we owe the expression, "the Devil and Tom Walker". Manhattan Island was a favorite locale among foxhunting club members, but the Gloucester Fox Hunting Club, organized in a Philadelphia coffee house in 1776, was one of the earliest clubs.

Other breeds were developed through the years as new needs in hunting were perceived. Jonathan Plott's German boar hounds are today among the most popular of all hunting breeds.

In view of these events, it was only natural that contests be held to decide champions. One between pointers and setters held near Stafford, England in 1886 was the first on record. Eight years later the first American Field Trials were held near Memphis by the Tennessee State Sportsmen Association. Eleven years later, in 1885, the first Canadian Field Trials were held near Winnipeg, Manitoba by the Northwestern Field Trial Club. Today two things may be said of the increasingly popular sport of Field Trials: it is one of the relatively few sports without a legitimate record of antiquity; and the spiritual and ecological values of hunting with a dog are poorly understood, if at all, by virtually all except the actual practitioners of it.

FORMS: Field Trials are either professional or amateur land and/or water competitions for hunting dogs, also called sporting dogs or gun dogs in Britain. They are held under natural or simulated hunting conditions, usually on about five acres of land. Dogs are judged on such traits as speed, range, hunting intelligence, game and gun manners, style and intensity, scenting, pointing, flushing, and retrieving. The game used is usually quail, pheasant, prairie chicken, ruffled grouse, woodcock, chukar, or Hungarian partridge. Two to three judges declare winners according to various systems. In the point system a number of points are awarded for each piece of good work by the dog. In the heat system a dog is judged against its bracemate, the winner rebraced, and so on. In the spotting system a dog is in competition against all other dogs at the Trial. Beyond the declaration of champions, however, Field Trials have the secondary but important purpose of disseminating knowledge about breed improvements and of promoting game conservation.

The main groups of hunting dogs used are each composed of a number of specific breeds. Setters, pointers, spaniels (from *Hispania,* the Roman word for Spain), retrievers, and hounds are used. Of all breeds concerned, only the Chesapeake Bay retriever and the American water spaniel are distinctively American breeds. All others are imports, chiefly from Europe. The breed chosen will depend upon the type of Trial, the hunter's preferences, and the type of game used. As is the case in all sports involving dogs, the individual dog's instincts must be directed through training. A show setter, for example, would be useless in a Field Trial, as would a Trial dog in a best-of-breed show.

Field Trial stakes include: puppy (not over 18 months old—20 min. heats), derby (not over 30 months old—30 min. heats), all-age (30 – 60 min. heats), shooting dog, championship (1 – 3 hour heats), novice, and limited.

ORGANIZATION: Separate Field Trials are held for each breed. All recognized pointer trials, for example, are held under the auspices of the American Field Trial Club and Amateur Field Trial Club of America. All recognized beagle trials and clubs operate under the supervision of the Federation of Beagle Clubs. All spaniel trials are held under the English Springer Spaniel Club of America and the American Spaniel Club (including the National Springer Championships, staged since 1947). All recognized retriever trials are staged according to the specifications laid down by the National Retriever Club. The same holds true for each of the many other breeds involved. Over 850 such Trials are held in the United States annually, of which the main ones are the American Field Futurities, the National Championships, the National Free-for-All Quail Championships, the Continental Quail Championships, the Prairie Chicken Championships, the Grand National Grouse Championships, and the National Amateur Championships. About 300 individual sportsmen's clubs sponsor recognized pointing dog trials.

GREYHOUND RACING

Dog racing strictly means greyhound racing. Greyhound racing technically began in 1909 when an Arkansas engineer, Owen P. Smith, tested his ideas for a mechanical rabbit at Tucson, Arizona. Similar ideas had been used in Belgium in 1740, and in London in 1876, where a railed hare was operated by a windlass. Nevertheless, Smith invented the device that turned the ancient sport of coursing (two or more greyhounds released to run down live game, usually rabbits) into what today has been called "America's fastest growing spectator sport." For this he is known as the "Father of Modern Greyhound Racing." In England Brigadier-General Alfred Cecil Critchley (a Canadian) became known as the "Father of Greyhound Racing in Britain" for his additional developments. The accomplishments of these two men, plus that of the Frenchman Oller who in 1872 invented a totalisator betting system that he called "pari-mutuel," are responsible for the modern sport of greyhound racing. But beyond them modernity ends.

No one even knows the origin of "greyhound." All anyone seems certain of is that it definitely did not come from the color grey. It may have come from *Graius* (Grečian, Greek), or from the ancient British word for dog, *grech* or *greg.* Perhaps it came from *gazehound,* since a greyhound hunts by sight instead of scent, or its derivation could be from the Icelandic *greyhundr* (*grey* meaning dog). Neither is it known how the breed arrived in England—with the Gallic tribes, with the Phoenicians, or with the Cretans. Greyhounds raced in Mesopotamia 4000 years before Nebuchadnezzar the Great, and were a favorite of Cleopatra. St. Patrick, escaping from slavery in England, hid in a boat whose main cargo was greyhounds being exported for use in Roman arenas. All that is certain is that the Sport of Queens is an ancient one, and that the breed itself is one of the oldest in existence today. In fact, coursing, the ancestor of all dog sports, may well be the oldest of all sports. From it we name races at a track—for example, the Flagler Course and the Southland Course.

But whatever their history, greyhounds have always been prized. In the eleventh and twelfth centuries in Britain the price of a good greyhound-hawk hunting team was equal to that of a man. A stiff fine during the reign of King John required the payment of ten leashes of greyhounds. The Forest Laws of 1014–1377 largely restricted greyhounds to royalty and the nobility. The elaborately carved gates at the foot of magnificent English stairways were to keep the greyhounds downstairs. Serfs and villeins were expressly prohibited from ownership on pain of death. Freemen might keep them but only at a distance from any royal forest. Number 31 of the Laws of Canute (enacted 1010) specified that if a freeman would keep greyhounds within ten miles of such preserves the dogs must be lamed ("knees be cut") to prevent their use in poaching. Such ownership rules were observed well into the sixteenth century.

When the Earl Marshall of Elizabeth I, Thomas, Duke of Norfolk, codified the different rules and practices of coursing into his *Laws of the Leash,* the pastime became an organized sport. Two hundred years later Lord Orford, the "Father of Modern Coursing," founded the first coursing club, the Swaffham Club (1776). In the continental United States the sport was first practiced in Kansas and continues to be popular predominately in the Prairie States. Then came Smith, with a stuffed rabbit and the idea of applying electricity to the sport.

The entire history of greyhound racing can be summarized by a few of its more significant enthusiasts. A Roman aristocrat wrote *Cynegeticus,* the first book on greyhounds in A.D. 150. A famous English nun in 1486 wrote the first hunting book in English, in which is the best description of a greyhound to date: "A greyhound should be heeded lyke a Snake and neckyd lyke a Drake, footed lyke a Catte, taylled lyke a Ratte." Sioux Indians killed two of America's most colorful greyhound enthusiasts: Gen. George Armstrong Custer and his orderly, Maj. James "Hound Dog" Kelly.

FORMS: The greyhound family includes the English greyhound, the Egyptian saluki, the Russian borzoi, the Indian rampur, the Afghan hound, the Spanish balearic, the Thai phy-quac and the Cretean ibiza. There are also Arabian, Highland, Irish, Italian, Persian, Scotch and Turkish greyhounds. Further, greyhounds are classed as black, white, blue, brindle, fawn, red or tickled (light or dark specks). The ancestry of practically all registered greyhounds today, however, whether English, Australian, American, African or Indian, can be traced back over 135 years to an English champion named King Cob whose dam (mother) was one-eighth bulldog.

Any greyhound to be raced is reported to the National Coursing Association within ten days of whelping, and registered and tattooed in each ear within 60 days. Every dog must obtain a Bertillon identification card to compete at American Greyhound Track Operators Association (AGTOA) and other approved tracks. All owners, moreover, must have an owner's license.

In competition the dogs race against each other chasing a speed-controlled artificial hare around a dirt or sand oval. The dogs are usually greyhounds, but Scottish deerhounds, borzois, salukis and other breeds that hunt by sight are also raced; although rarely, Afghans are sometimes raced at Westbury, New York, kennel shows. The hare begins 12 yds. ahead of the starting traps which trigger a timer on opening; the dogs race across a photo finish beam which, when cut, stops the timer. The hare disappears behind a screen or curtain, and the dogs are retrieved by their trainers or handlers.

Greyhounds race in classes or grades given by the racing secretary. These reflect their past record of victories or losses: A or AA (best), B, C, D, E and M (maiden, nonwinners). Dogs usually race from 16 months until about 6 years of age. The fastest time on record is 41.72 m.p.h. While seven, eight or nine dogs may compete in a single race, eight is the usual number in the United States.

The tracks measure from 400 to 500 yds. by an average 22 ft. wide. Races are the sprint at 230 yds. and the marathon at 1200 yds. Each can be run over a flat track or over hurdles.

Types of races are open (between licensed trainers), kennel (between certain kennels), inter-racecourse (between track's teams), private, invitation (specified dogs only), and produce (between dogs of a single litter). Each dog must wear a safety muzzle while racing and a numbered jacket of a particular color; each color refers to a certain starting trap. Dogs may be disqualified for fighting and expelled for fighting continuously. A person may be disqualified for any corrupt or fraudulent practice in any way associated with the sport, including cruelty to a dog. Personnel at any approved race include a racing manager or secretary, stewards, a weighing clerk, a starter, a timekeeper, a hare operator, a security officer, a veterinary surgeon, and a racecourse trainer. As with horse racing, pari-mutuel betting is a major attraction.

ORGANIZATION: Each country, including Mexico, France, South Africa, China, Macao, Indonesia, New

Zealand, Holland and Sweden, has its own governing body, all of which are subject to the authority of the World Greyhound Racing Federation, founded by Britain, Ireland, Australia and the United States and headquartered in the Limerick offices of the governing body in Ireland, the *Bord na gCon.* The 38 racing tracks in the United States are controlled by the American Greyhound Track Operators Association (AGTOA) which is headquartered in Miami, Florida and by individual state racing commissions. Greyhound racing is presently legal in Alabama, Arizona, Arkansas, Colorado, South Dakota, Florida, Massachusetts, New Hampshire and Oregon. The world's oldest track in continuous existence is in St. Petersburg, Florida.

SLED-DOG RACING

Dogs were always an integral part of Arctic life. Eskimos used them to hunt seal and polar bear. To the Lillooet of British Columbia a good hunting dog was worth a large dressed elk hide. The Gilyaks of the Amur River region in Siberia believed that the soul of a hunter passed into his favorite dog, which accordingly was lavished with food and attention before being sacrificed upon its master's grave. Like snowshoes and canoes, dogs were used for hunting and transportation long before 1577 when Richard Hakluyt wrote in his book, *Voyage,* that the natives of the Labrador coast "keepe certaine dogs not much unlike wolves, which they yoke to a sled." Vitus Bering the Dane (1680–1741), discoverer of Alaska, used them in his Siberian travels. A year before he was murdered in Hawaii, Captain Cook sent dog sled dispatches 6000 miles across Russia from Okhutsk to the British ambassador in St. Petersburg. In the Gold Rush Days made famous by Jack London, dogs were bartered, bought or stolen. From the signing of the Northwest Mounted Police Act in 1873 to just a decade or so ago, the Mounties used dog teams as their basic mode of transportation across the Arctic and the Laurentian Shield. In 1915 the French government was seeking to establish an alpine corps and sent a lieutenant the 10,000 miles to Nome to select the dogs that were needed. And years before O. P. Smith invented dog racing with his mechanical hare, sled dogs were racing in derbies at Nome (1908) and at La Pas, Manitoba (March 1915). The winner of the 408-mile race at Nome clocked 119 hrs. and 15 mins.

Three things imbued the Arctic sport with the romance and fame it holds for many today: the Gold Rush and Jack London, Leonard Seppala's mercy mission, and the Seppala-St. Godard races. Seppala had rushed diptheria serum 650 miles through a blizzard to Nome. One of his lead dogs on that mission was Balto, who is honored by a bronze statue in New York's Central Park. The series of Seppala-St. Godard races were held from 1925 to the mid-1930s in Manitoba, Alaska, Minnesota and New Hampshire. The race held at the 1932 Winter Olympics in Lake Placid, New York, was the last one in the series. When St. Godard won, Seppala (aged 54) declared him the greatest. At its peak, the St. Godard team raced 1500 miles per season and was led by Toby, a half-huskie, half-greyhound. St. Godard's kindness to his dogs is legendary. Once ice crystals caused their feet to bleed, so he stopped—within sight of the finish line. And when Toby no longer was up to the grind, St. Godard himself retired. For these traits, as well as for his records and wins, Emile St. Godard stands as the only musher in the Canada's Sports Hall of Fame.

FORMS: Sled-dog teams are usually composed of wolf-spitz breeds with short prick ears, very heavy fur and a tail curving up over the back. Notable among these breeds is the Alaskan malamute, which is named after the Malamute Indians, an Innuit tribe, and is the only purebred registered native Alaskan breed. Two others are the samoyed, the oldest of these breeds, and the Siberian husky, or chuchi, which was first imported to Alaska for racing in 1909. The nonregisterable Mackenzie River husky and the Eskimo dog of Greenland and Labrador are also of the wolf-spitz group. Other purebred cart and sled dogs include the Bernese Mountain dog (Switzerland), the Great Pyrenees dog (Spain) and the Newfoundland dog (Newfoundland).

The sport today consists of racing a lightweight sled over special trails in the snow to obtain the shortest elapsed time. The sled must have sufficient space to carry an injured dog in the required canvas sled bag. The musher (driver), sometimes aided by a dog handler, runs behind, pushing or riding on the sled's runners. The sled is usually crafted of wood, 6 to 13 ft. long by 12 to 24 in. wide. The dogs are attached to the sled by neck lines, harnesses and collars. The number of dogs in a team varies with the race and the terrain. In general, and for world championship races, the minimum number of dogs is seven: a lead dog, followed by two point dogs, then two swing dogs, and finally two wheel dogs. Any breed may be raced and Field Trial winners have been used successfully in sled teams. Dogs of the wolf-spitz group normally make up the teams, however. Although teams may attain 33 m.p.h., championship teams average about 15 m.p.h. When comparing this with the more than 40 m.p.h. of a Thoroughbred with a jockey and the 38 m.p.h. for a greyhound, it should be remembered that sled-dog teams race over long distances. Remarkable, too, is these dogs' strength: in 1954 a 93-lb. malamute pulled a load of nearly 2200 lbs. The team is controlled by voice commands. "All right," "let's go," or "mush" are used to start a team, although some breeds will respond only to "put-put!" "Gee" commands a turn to the right and "haw" a turn to the left. Though standard racing equipment includes a whip, a musher may receive a foul for using a whip for any purpose other than cracking. From the holding area and the starting line the trail is marked to the finish line with red markers for turns and green markers for straight ahead. A team may be disqualified for leaving the trail, or if the musher administers drugs of any kind to the dogs. If a dog is injured, it must be carried to the finish line. Failure to do this results in automatic disqualification. Officials include a chief judge, assistant judges and a course manager. Hazards to dogs include pregnancy, injury and disease—especially diarrhea or pneumonia. Wolves and chill factor temperatures of minus 120 degrees are additional dangers of sled dog racing which occur in no other sport.

ORGANIZATION: Sled dogs are raced virtually wherever there is snow—all over Canada, in the northeastern United States, Alaska, California (Soda Springs), Arizona, Washington and Oregon. In the United States, governing bodies include the International Sled Dog Racing Association, the Lakes Region Sled Dog Club and the New England Sled Dog Club, Inc. (organized 1924) which stages the Laconia World Championship Sled Dog Derby, the largest race outside Alaska. Anchorage also stages a world championship, the Fur Rendezvous. Fairbanks runs the annual North American Race and Whitehorse holds the Sourdough Rendezvous. In Canada the chief eastern race is the Quebec International Dog Derby at Quebec City. Numerous races are held in Ontario, notably at Ottawa and Yellowknife. Manitoba's outstanding annual event is the World Championship Dog Derby held as part of the Trapper's Festival at La Pas each February. The McMurray – Ft. Chipewyan Race is staged in nothern Alberta. The most spectacular event in the sport, however, is the Iditarod Trail Race from Anchorage to Nome—a 1150-mile marathon which annually attracts the best mushers from all over the world.

Canine Hall of Fame for Lead Dogs

KNIK, ALASKA

Mailing Address: P.O. Box 202, Wasilla 99687. Tel. (907) 376-5631. *Contact:* Mrs. Dorothy G. Page, V.Pres, Wasilla-Knik-Willow Creek Historical Society. *Location:* Knik Hall; approx. 20 mi. S.W. of Wasilla, 30 mi. S.E. of Willow, 50 mi. N. of Anchorage. *Admission:* Free 10 to 5 daily, Memorial Day through Labor Day; appointment needed for group tours or tours at other times of the year—contact Vi Redington, (907) 376-5562. *Personnel:* Volunteer staff and members of Wasilla-Knik Centennial Commission and Wasilla-Knik-Willow Creek Historical Society.

One of Alaska's most unusual visitor attractions, the Canine Hall of Fame for Lead Dogs was founded in 1967 as a project of the Wasilla-Knik Centennial Commission for the 100th anniversary of the purchase of Alaska from Russia. The settlement of Alaska would not have been possible without the loyal and reliable lead dogs to guide mushers through the snow and ice to deliver mail, mining equipment and medical supplies to the most desolate parts of Alaska. In the gold rush days, Knik was the main stopping point on the Iditarod Trail between Anchorage and Nome. With two grants from the Alaska State Museum, and a building and one acre of land donated by Mrs. Lois Bjorn Birdsell of Knik, the historical site of Knik Hall was restored for the Hall of Fame. The Canine Hall of Fame for Lead Dogs is located on the upper floor with the Dog Mushers' Hall of Fame. As soon as enough photographs are collected and paintings of the dogs are completed, they will be displayed with memorabilia such as mushing equipment, sleds and the pawprint of Hall of Famer, Baldy.

Members: Exact number of members unavailable as of June 1977. Nomination sheets are sent out to dog mushing clubs throughout Alaska and are published in the *Iditarod Trail Annual.* There is no limit to the number of nominations that can be made by any one person. Usually lead dogs are nominated with their musher, as the musher would be nothing without his dog. Members of the Wasilla-Knik-Willow Creek Historical Society elect the new member from the nominations they receive. Paintings will eventually be done of each lead dog by Knik artist Evaline Rowsey.

Dog Mushers' Hall of Fame

KNIK, ALASKA

Mailing Address: P.O. Box 202, Wasilla 99687. Tel. (907) 376-5631. *Contact:* Mrs. Dorothy G. Page, V.Pres, Wasilla-Knik-Willow Creek Historical Society. *Location:* Knik Hall; approx. 20 mi. S.W. of Wasilla, 30 mi. S.E. of Willow, 50 mi. N. of Anchorage. *Admission:* Free 10 to 5 daily, Memorial Day through Labor Day; appointment needed for group tours or tours at other times of the year—contact Vi Redington, (907) 376-5562. *Personnel:* Volunteer staff and members of Wasilla-Knik Centennial Commission and Wasilla-Knik-Willow Creek Historical Society.

The Dog Mushers' Hall of Fame, like the Canine Hall of Fame for Lead Dogs, was founded in 1967 as a project of the Wasilla-Knik Centennial Commission. Since sled dog teams played such a big part in the settlement of Alaska during those first 100 years, it was fitting to honor the mushers, some of them doctors, lawyers and gold miners, on such a special occasion. Knik, a word from the Eskimo meaning fire, was selected for the Hall of Fame because it was a main stop-off on the famous Iditarod Trail to gold mine camps between Anchorage and Nome. Today Knik is listed in the National Register of Historic Places and consists of a log cabin, a city cemetery, two Indian cemeteries and poolroom saloon roadhouse. With two grants from the Alaska State Museum and the generosity of Mrs. Lois Bjorn Birdsell of Knik, the roadhouse, now Knik Hall, became the home of the museum on the first floor and the Dog Mushers' Hall of Fame on the second floor. Exhibited in the Hall are oil portraits of each member painted by Evaline Rowsey of Knik, and other sled dog memorabilia.

Members: 21 as of January 1977. Ten sled dog mushers and contributors to the sport were inducted when the Dog Mushers' Hall of Fame was founded and one member has been added each year since. Dog mushing clubs throughout Alaska receive nomination sheets—which are also printed in the *Iditarod Trail Annual*—and can submit an unlimited number of nominations. Members of the Wasilla-Knik-Willow Creek Historical Society elect one of the nominees as a member of the Hall of Fame. Each new member receives a certificate and is honored at the annual Iditarod Trail Banquet in Knik, usually in March before the Iditarod Trail Race. A portrait of each is painted by Evaline Rowsey for display in the Hall.

1967

ALLAN, Allan Alexander "Scotty"
Racer
Enlisted in the service of France with team of dogs and carried mail in the Alps during W.W. I.

Before the days of Leonhard Seppala (Allan's well-known student), Scotty Allan was the greatest musher who ever lived. Sponsored by Esther Birdsall Darling, his partner in their Nome racing kennels, he raced with a lead dog, Blady, who was already a hero of the North. In eight All-Alaska Sweepstakes this famous team won three times, in 1909, 1911 and 1912, came in second three times and third two times. The prize for his win in 1909 alone netted him $8000. Scotty Allan was also recognized for his knowledge of sled dogs and was asked by the great explorer Stefansson to select the dogs for his Canadian-Arctic Expedition. On behalf of the French government, Lt. Rene Haas went to Allan to obtain sled dogs for service in the Vosque Mountains. Since then they have become an "indispensable addition to the Alpine Corps in the matter of transportation where the use of horses and mules is impossible."

DOWNING, Ben
Driver
Ben Downing was a sled dog driver who laid the first mail trails from Dawson in the Yukon Territory to Alaska. As a mail carrier, he was noted for dependable service, especially in harsh weather conditions.

McLAIN, Carrie
Historian and Contributer
Pioneer Nome resident, settled there in 1905; school teacher, bank teller and city clerk; Nome's all-time historian; helped to start the Nome Museum; author of *Gold Rush Nome* and *Pioneer Teacher;* lived in Palmer Pioneers Home before her death.

In the early days of the Dog Mushers' Hall of Fame, Carrie McLain was indispensable as a source of information to the Wasilla-Knik Centennial Commission. Since she had witnessed the growth of sled dog racing and knew many of the Nome mushers personally, she was able to give addresses and biographical data for those who are in the Hall of Fame. She was a strong supporter of the Iditarod Trail Race. After visiting the Dog Mushers' Hall of Fame in 1967, she nominated many outstanding sled dog racing mushers, racers and non-racers, for election to the Hall of Fame.

MITCHELL, Gen. William "Billy"
Contributor
Born 1879 in Nice, France, to American parents; Father of U.S. Air Force; died in 1936.

Billy Mitchell became a dog sled racing enthusiast while stationed in Alaska to build a telegraph line across the Territory. Stationed at Eagle, Alaska, as a lieutenant in the U.S. Signal Corps from 1901–1903, he used sled dog teams to run lines from Eagle across Thompson Pass to Valdez. In 1927 the corps initiated the Signal Corps Derby with a trophy donated by the Washington–Alaska Military Cable and Telegraph System. A 58-mile race, it started in Fairbanks at a 430-ft. elevation, climbed to a 2240-ft. elevation at Summit, then looped back to Fairbanks. The trophy was retired in 1935 to the first three-time winner of the Signal Corps Derby.

RAMSAY, Maule "Fox"
Racer
Born in Scotland; second son of Earl of Dalhousie; graduate of Oxford Univ.; came to Nome in 1908 with uncles Col. Charles Ramsay and Col. Weatherly Stuart; family had money invested in Nome gold fields; left Nome in 1912 to spend a year traveling by boat, dog and reindeer team across Siberia; visited Nome briefly in 1913; rumored that he returned to Scotland and succeeded brother as Earl of Dalhousie.

While racing in the 1909 All-Alaska Sweepstakes with mixed-blood malamutes, Fox Ramsay observed and was impressed by the steady work, gentle nature and perseverance of the Siberian huskies. He then took a trip to Siberia and purchased 70 dogs, at a cost of $2500, hired two men who knew how to handle them and returned to Nome. The next year, to the dismay of many spectators, he entered three teams of these new dogs in the All-Alaska Sweepstakes Race. The dogs were much smaller than those on other teams, but they came in first in record time, 74:14.37 for 408 miles. Also in 1910 Ramsay introduced these dogs to the Nome Race where they came in second. Following these races, he kept one team and gave the other two to the mushers and, according to records, did not continue to race. Some say that his dogs were not actually Siberians, but *Anadyr* dogs of the same general type. In any case, their breeding improved the temperament and racing ability of the sled dog in Alaska.

ROMIG, Dr. Joseph Herman
Contributor
Dr. Joseph Romig was one of the brave doctors who ministered to the adventurous residents of isolated towns in the Bethel area of Alaska. Without his medical care and supplies many of them would surely have died. *Dog Team Doctor* is his story about his journeys on dog sled to many of the developing towns in Alaska.

SEPPALA, Leonhard
Racer
Born in Norway; first arrived in Nome 1900 seeking gold, but had no luck; moved to Fairbanks 1928, associated with Fairbanks Exploration and Mining Co; moved to Seattle, Wash, 1947; met wife Constance in Nome; died 1967 in Seattle, Wash, at age 89; wife sprinkled his ashes along the Iditarod Trail; 1967 Trail Race in memory of Seppala; in drawing for starting positions, wife drew number one and it was permanently retired in honor of Seppala.

It was 30 degrees below zero in 1925 when Leonhard Seppala reached Shaktoolik to pick up the serum for the diptheria epidemic in Nome. He traveled 268 miles over the frozen Norton Sound to Golovin, the longest distance and the most perilous part of the serum relay race, with his lead dog, Togo. The event brought international fame to this accomplished musher who, in 45 years of racing, won 43 silver trophy cups and bowls and 8 gold medals. It was not the only time, though, that Seppala raced to save the lives of men: he once mushed 102 miles in one day, from Dime Creek to Candle, his dogs pulling him and two other men, one of them severely injured. A pupil of Hall of Famer Scotty Allan, Seppala was asked to train a team of Siberian huskies for the explorer Roald Amundsen. When the expedition was abandoned Seppala was allowed to keep the huskies and over the years demonstrated extreme pride in the accomplishments of these dogs, their speed, stamina and temperament. His earliest race was the All-Alaska Sweepstakes in Nome which he won three consecutive times—1915, 1916 and 1917. In 1916 he also won the Ruby Derby, a 58-mile race from Ruby to Long City. Traveling 675 miles in three days in 1920, he became the fastest dog musher in Alaska and the United States, then went to New England and Eastern Canada to further demonstrate his speed. The news of the serum race had prompted the interest of New England residents in sled dog racing. News of Arthur Walden, who created the Chinook Kennels in Wonalancet, Mass, and won many races, enticed Seppala to travel East and challenge Walden. To cover the expenses of his trip, Seppala and Togo exhibited their talents across the country and finally arrived at Madison Square Garden several months later. Seppala was 50 years old at this time. In 1927 at Poland Springs, Seppala and Walden met for their challenge. Though Seppala first went over a stone wall and through a woman's cabin, when his dogs smelled her dinner, he won the 25-mi. race, run in two heats, by seven minutes. Competition he met with in Canada and New England included Hall of Famer Émile St. Godard. In New England he also met Roland Lombard to whom he gave two Siberian huskies. While in the East, Seppala and Mrs. Peg Nansen formed a kennel for Siberian huskies and bred the first pure-bred huskies, descendants of Togo, to be registered by the American Kennel Club. Says one of the founders of the Alaska Dog Mushers Association about Seppala's breeding: "With the importation of Siberian dogs from across the Bering Sea to Nome, Seppala decided to breed this strain exclusively. In 42 years of breeding, he developed a dog of uniform gait, color and disposition, with which he set and still holds today more racing records than any other man." Leonhard Seppala will always be the number one racer in the Iditarod Trail Race and in the memory of those who know of his great accomplishments.

THOMPSON, Raymond L.
Contributor

Raymond Thompson has contributed to sled dog racing in many ways from writing to editing to innovating and promoting. As early as 1914 he was using sled dogs on traplines and in the fur trade in northwest Canada. Between 1926 and 1938 he moved fur trade headquarters to Edmonton, Alberta, where sled dogs are still being used in the fur trade today. While living in the Seattle area from 1958 to 1968, Thompson established the Martha Lake Siberian Husky Kennels and provided teams for local and regional races. For many years he has edited the column "Sled Dog Trails" in the *Alaska Sportsman* magazine and has written numerous articles himself on the subject. He authored one of the most complete guides on sled dogs, the *Sled Dog Encyclopedia,* and with Louise Foley wrote *The Siberian Husky.* Thompson is also the former publisher of *Northern Dog News* and *Siberian Husky News* and owns Raymond Thompson Co. in Lynnwood, Wash. As an innovator, Thompson has developed superior snow hooks, sleds and harnesses to make the life of a musher a little easier.

WICKERSHAM, Judge James
Contributor

City Attorney in Tacoma, Wash; elected to Washington legislature in 1898; appointed U.S. District Judge of Third Judicial Div. of Territory of Alaska, approx. 1500 people, from 1900–1908; resided in Eagle City where he built his own log cabin; established civil government in Tanana; 1901 assisted judge in Nome, Second Judicial Div, when number of miners was growing rapidly; 1903 attempted to climb Mt. McKinley on a two-month expedition and blazed trail to northern base; 1908 elected Representative in Congress, held office for 12 years; author of *Old Yukon-Tales-Trails-Trials* and *A Bibliography of Alaskan Literature;* editor of seven-volume *Alaska Law Reports.*

When James Wickersham arrived in Alaska in 1900 to serve as U.S. District Judge, the only way to travel in the winter was by dog sled. So from his residence in Eagle City he traveled more than 1000 miles each winter with his team of native dogs, blankets, food and the court's files and documents to hold court in Nome, Rampart, Fairbanks, Circle and Valdez. The 500-mile trip to Rampart was often in weather 40 and 50 degrees below zero and left Wickersham with swollen ankles and blistered heels and his dogs with sore feet. Along the way, they met mail carriers on sleds, slept in roadhouses and stayed with friends and relatives. On all his journeys Wickersham kept a diary of events on the Alaskan trails. "Every dog in our team was quivering with excitement and plunging in the collar anxious to be gone. With a highly developed dog-team sense they knew that another journey over snowy trails was to be taken and they were ready to start. Whether it was a trip to another mountain hunting camp or to some distant settlement in pursuit of a fleeing criminal, they did not know, and probably did not care, for any journey is better than confinement at the end of a short dog chain fastened to a cold kennel in the back yard. On the trail there is change and exercise, long and exciting races with other teams along the icy surface of the river trails, bells jingling sweet music in the clear and frosty air, warm rations of rice and bacon deliciously boiled over the evening campfire, with every canine eye on the cook and the steaming kettle. Mouths water while waiting for the savory supper served hot in separate pans at the evening and only meal of the day. Then, too, there are friendly meetings with strange teams and sometimes jolly good fighting at the overnight road houses, and more often with passing teams crowding in narrow snow trails. Dogs and boys, be they young or old, love Alaskan winter snow trails and the joy of their travel."

WILLIAMS, Clyde C. "Slim"
Contributor

Arrived in Valdez, Alaska, at age 18 in early 1900s; immediately interested in sled dogs; began crossing them with wolves for stamina; developed one of the best teams in Alaska; met his wife Gladys at the Chicago World's Fair—she came to admire his dogs.

For nine months and seven days, from November 21, 1932, until September 16, 1933, Slim Williams traveled by dog sled team from Copper Center, Alaska to the Chicago World's Fair—4700 miles—to promote an international highway from the United States to Alaska. Traveling with a McKenzie River husky, Rembrandt or "Brant" for short, the first two months of his trip were on partial trails or remains of trails. Each day ended with breaking a new trail for the next day and traveling back to camp. For 68 days he lived on game he had trapped and shot with only ten shells. For the distance between Hazelton, B.C, and the World's Fair, Williams remodeled an old Ford chassis for wheels under his sled. Since the dogs had to travel on paved roads, the women of British Columbia made special booties for their feet. The booties had to be replaced every ten miles. Once at the Fair, Slim put up a tent right outside the Alaskan exhibit where he also cooked his meals over a campfire and watched over his dogs. He first started lecturing on the international highway and the wonders of Alaska at the Fair, but then traveled another 900 miles to Washington, D.C, to speak with President Roosevelt and many other government officials. Studies and surveys were made and opposition to the international highway continued, but Slim went on lecturing for his cause. He returned to the Fair first, then made another trip over a similar route in 1939, this time by motorcycle. It was only after the United States entered W.W. II and feared enemy attack from Alaska that his highway became a reality. Completed in October 1942, it was not over the route Slim had proposed, but he and his wife traveled the highway and offered youngsters an Alaskan Highway tour beginning in Chicago and ending in Alaska. After his death, the route Slim originally traveled by dog sled, between the British Columbia coastal range and the Rockies, did become a highway. At the Hall of Fame is a faded banner he carried on his dog sled for that first trip from Alaska, and on it are the signatures of many of the people he met on his 5600-mile trek.

1973

MARSTON, Col. Marvin R. "Muktuk"

Contributor

Single-handedly, Muktuk Marston traveled 1000 miles by dog team across the Seward Peninsula to enlist Eskimos in the Alaska Territorial Guard in defense of Alaska during W.W. II. In this way, he was responsible for establishing the National Guard in Alaska. In 1973 he donated to the Iditarod Trail Race $10,000 in prize money, representing the number of miles he had traveled by dog team.

1976

NORRIS, Earl

Racer

Resident of Willow, Alaska; wife Natalie musher and Hall of Fame member.

Earl Norris is recognized as the founder of the Fur Rendezvous Races in Anchorage and was himself an early winner of the "Rondy" in 1947 and 1948. The Fur Rendezvous, when it first started in 1936, consisted of displays of furs and pelts for auction throughout downtown Anchorage, numerous sports events including hockey, skiing, skating, boxing and Eskimo games, and festivities such as torchlight parades, fireworks and concerts. Shortly after W.W. II, sled dog racing was incorporated in the Fur Rendezvous, but it was not until 1949 that a 25-mile race became an established part of the festivities. In 1951 the purse for the race had grown to $6000 and broadcasting of the event had nurtured its growth. It became so popular that in 1953, when all the snow melted, the street department trucks hauled in tons of snow at the cost of $10,000 so the race could be held. Norris has been mushing since the early days of the Fur Rendezvous Races and placed 24th in the first Iditarod Trail Race in 1967.

NORRIS, Natalie

Racer

Wife of Hall of Famer Earl Norris; resident of Willow, Alaska.

Natalie Norris entered and won the Women's Championship Race of the Fur Rendezvous winter carnival in 1954.

Induction Year Unrecorded

ATTLA, George, Jr.

Racer

A former village chief in Huslia, George Attla, Jr, shares the name of "Huslia Hustler" with other famous dog drivers like Jimmy Huntington, Cue Bifelt, Warner Vent, Alfred Attla and Bergman Sam. But George Attla had to overcome a physical handicap to keep on with his racing and was therefore a more popular musher. In 1958, 1962 and 1968 he won the Fur Rendezvous Races and received the Al Fox Memorial Trophy in each of those years. In 1973 he won $1250 when he came in fourth. In the first Iditarod Trail Race in 1967 Attla placed fifth and won $1500, but won the race in 1969. In 1973 he actually had the fastest running time for the 1049-mile race, but had bad luck when a blizzard hit and his dogs came down with the flu.

BLATCHFORD, Percy

Racer and Contributor

Born in England; moved to Nome in early 1900s to start liquor business with brother and A. G. Oliver; after racing career began delivering mail; married native wife; four sons; wife and three sons died in flu epidemic 1918; later remarried, moved to Shishmaref, operated a store and raised a second family; returned to Nome in W.W. II, then moved to Seward; widow now lives in Palmer.

Percy Blatchford was a three-time entrant in the All-Alaska Sweepstakes. In the first race (1908) he placed third behind Hall of Famers John Hegness and Scotty Allan. He came in second behind Scotty Allan in 1909 and raced again in 1910 but did not place. Though well-known for his racing, Blatchford was more famous for his dependable mail runs in the isolated Nome area. In an often dangerous job, he brought news of civilization to remote parts of Alaska by dog sled. These mail carriers were brave men, with teams of eight to ten dogs and specially built sleds, often weighing 800 to 1000 lbs. They traveled from station to station, covering a distance of 25 to 30 miles each day, and had the right-of-way over all other vehicles according to United States law. Carriers were always given the best seat at the table and were the first to be served at roadhouses along the way. They were the most respected men of the Alaska trails.

DELZENE, Faye

Racer

Most active in the All-Alaska Sweepstakes, Faye Delzene entered his first race in 1911, but did not place. He skipped the race of 1912 and won the Sweepstakes in 1913 in 75:42.27, only 1:28 behind the 1910 record of John "Iron Man" Johnson. Missing the 1914 and 1915 races, he came back for his last Sweepstakes in 1916, a close second behind Leonhard Seppala. Delzene also entered the Solomon Derby Race in 1916, a 65-mile contest from Nome to Solomon and back, and though he was not one of the mushers who broke the standing record, his dogs ran a good race.

HEGNESS, John

Racer

John Hegness was a dog musher in Nome and was the first winner of the All-Alaska Sweepstakes Race, initiated in 1908. This race, organized and sponsored by the Nome Kennel Club, was 408 miles long, from Nome to Candle and back to Nome. Bad weather conditions made for an especially long run, 119:15 for Hegness. The All-Alaska Sweepstakes Race proved to be very important in the development of sled dog racing as a winter sport and in proving to skeptics that the dogs, if properly fed and trained, enjoyed the sport as much as the mushers.

LOMBARD, Dr. Roland

Racer

Originally from Weyland, Mass, Lombard came to Alaska to compete in the first World Championship Race in 1960, in which he won one heat. Entering the race numerous times, he won in 1963, 1964, 1965 and 1967, but lost to Joee Redington, Jr, in 1966. With a famous lead dog, Nellie, purchased from Hall of Famer George Attla, he entered the 1968 race, won the first heat, but lost the championship to George Attla and placed fourth. He was a popular entrant in the Fur Rendezvous Races and was the winning musher in 1963, 1964 and 1965, the same years he won the Al Fox Memorial Trophy. Having won three times as of 1965, he was given his own trophy to retire. In 1973, when he placed third, he won $1900. Lombard also entered the first Iditarod Trail Race in 1967, finished 11th and won $450 in prize money.

PAUL, Raymond

Racer

From Galena, Raymond Paul was the first native musher who excelled in sled dog racing. He was 21 when he first entered dog racing circles in 1950, and a year later won the Anchorage Fur Rendezvous Races. He repeated that win in 1954 and 1955, thus retiring the Al Fox Memorial Trophy after three wins. He later contended for the North American Championship in Fairbanks, but had to quit when his dogs became temperamental. Paul was nominated to the Hall of Fame by George Attla, Jr, who considers Paul to have been a great musher. Unfortunately his racing days ended prematurely when he drowned in a boating accident on the Yukon River in 1956.

SEELEY, Eva B.

Racer and Contributor

Author of *My Fifty Years with Sled Dogs,* and *Chinook and His Family;* co-author of *The Complete Alaskan Malamute;* resides Chinook Kennels in Wonalancet, N.H.

Eva Seeley was the only woman to race in the 1932 Winter Olympics in Lake Placid, N.Y, and, in fact, raced sled dogs for 15 years. But her involvement in dog training and breeding and the promotion of dog racing is recognized throughout the country. She and her husband Milton raised and trained sled dogs for the Byrd Antarctic Expedition, as well as for U.S. Army, Navy and Air Force Expeditions, including search and rescue missions. When Arthur T. Walden, founder of the New England Sled Dog Club and trainer of dogs for the Byrd Expedition, accompanied Admiral Byrd, he left his kennels in Wonalancet in the care of the Seeleys. In 1928 Eva was a prime mover in continuing the New England Sled Dog Races which, at the time, were faced with financial difficulty and almost disbanded. She donated money to cover the expenses of races held at Wonalancet, Chocura and Tamworth, N.H. It was Eva Seeley also who established the Siberian Husky and Alaskan Malamute Breed Clubs of the American Kennel Society and in 1955 assembled and trained 60 sled dogs and directed the drivers-training school as chief advisor for the Antarctic "Operation Deepfreeze." For this she was awarded a scroll from the United States government. Today Mrs. Seeley still lives at Chinook Kennels and has been very active in promoting junior sled dog racing; and today New Hampshire holds more races and has more sled dog kennels than any other New England state.

ST. GODARD, Émile

Racer

When Leonhard Seppala reached New England, his stiffest competition came from Emil St. Goddard, a Canadian well known in his country and New England as a champion musher. Though his dogs came from crossbred strains, which Seppala considered inferior and in most cases were inferior to his Siberian huskies, they were lean and hardened from running the tough 150-mile race at La Pas, Manitoba, and performed well for St. Goddard. St. Goddard and Seppala first met in Quebec, but it was in Laconia, N.H, that their competition encouraged the growth in membership of the New England Sled Dog Club. St. Goddard, the only musher in Canada's Sports Hall of Fame, once held the world's record for nonstop dog races and defeated Seppala in the sled dog races at the 1932 Winter Olympics.

Field Trial Hall of Fame

CHICAGO, ILLINOIS

Mailing Address: c/o American Field Publishing Co, 222 W. Adams St, 60606. Tel. (312) 372-1383. *Contact:* William F. Brown, Pres. *Location:* Approx. 90 mi. S.E. of Milwaukee, Wis, 184 mi. N.W. of Indianapolis, Ind, 220 mi. S.E. of Green Bay, Wis. *Personnel:* William F. Brown, Pres; Dr. H. A. Gray, Exec. V.Pres; George M. Rogers, James M. Bryan, Dr. D. E. Hawthorne, Curtis W. Miles, Regional V.Pres; William F. Brown, Jr, Secy.-Treas; seven mem. Exec. Comt. (Delmar Smith, Exec. Dir.). *Nearby Halls of Fame:* Business (Chicago), Bowling, Sports (Milwaukee), Football (Green Bay).

On September 17, 1954, 24 well-known field trialers adopted by-laws and elected officers for the Field Trial Hall of Fame, Inc, a nonprofit corporation supported by public gifts and donations. The purposes they established were to build a Hall of Fame and Museum, to promote research and knowledge of upland game birds used in the sport, to protect and conserve their natural habitats, and to acquire areas for field trials. Plans are still in the making for a Hall of Fame and Museum in Oklahoma City, near the National Cowboy Hall of Fame and Western Heritage Center and the National Softball Hall of Fame.

Members: 63 Bird Dogs and 63 Contributors as of January 1977. Bird Dogs (deceased) who exhibited outstanding talent in field trials and/or had a "record of producing winning progeny" and people who have made contributions and have been of continued service to the sport are nominated by those involved in field trial. The ten of each who receive the largest number of nominations are considered by electors for the Hall of Fame. At least 15 electors are selected yearly from presidents of field trial clubs or associations, judges of championships and/or editors of sporting dog publications. Two bird dogs and two people are selected every year as permanent members of the Field Trial Hall of Fame.

1954 AMES, Hobart. Contributor.
DUFFIELD, Carl E. Contributor.
FISHEL'S FRANK. Pointer.
HOCHWALT, Albert F. Contributor.
JOHN PROCTOR. Pointer.
PROCTOR, Cecil S. Contributor.
LUMINARY. Pointer.
MARY MONTROSE. Pointer.
MUSCLE SHOALS' JAKE. Pointer.
SAGE, A. G. C. Contributor.

1955 COUNT GLADSTONE IV. Setter.
KING, Dr. T. Benton. Contributor.
MORTON, Clyde. Contributor.
SPORT'S PEERLESS. Setter.

1956 AIR PILOT'S SAM. Pointer.
AVENT, James M. Contributor.
FARRIOR, Edward. Contributor.
THE TEXAS RANGER. Pointer.

1957 ARIEL. Pointer.
SCOTT, Reuben H. Contributor.
SHELLEY, E. M. Contributor.
SIOUX. Setter.

1958 EUGENE M. Setter.
HARRIS, Chesley H. Contributor.
McCALL, Bethea. Contributor.
TYSON. Pointer.

1959 ALFORD'S JOHN. Pointer.
BISHOP, Jake. Contributor.
COUNT NOBLE. Setter.
DOCTOR BLUE WILLING. Pointer.
PALADIN. Pointer.
ROWE, Dr. Nicholas. Contributor.
TITUS, W. W. Contributor.
WHITE, W. Lee. Contributor.

1960 BECKY BROOM HILL. Pointer.
COUNT WHITESTONE. Setter.
GATES, John S. Contributor.
HOAGLAND, Raymond. Contributor.
LESTER'S ENJOY'S WAHOO. Pointer.
MERRIMAN, Col. Arthur. Contributor.
RIP RAP. Pointer.
ROSE, David E. Contributor.

1961 CAHOON, Herbert H. Contributor.
DEXTER, Edward. Contributor.
GLADSTONE. Setter.
KIRKOVER, Harry D. Contributor.
LYTLE, J. Horace. Contributor.
MANITOBA RAP. Pointer.
MISSISSIPPI ZEV. Setter.
WARHOOP JAKE. Pointer.

1962 COMANCHE FRANK. Pointer.
FISHEL, U. R. Contributor.
MOHAWK II. Setter.
PHELPS, Claudia L. Contributor.
SEAVIEW REX. Pointer.
SMITH, Ray. Contributor.
SPORT'S PEERLESS PRIDE. Setter.
YOUNG, Frank W. Contributor.

1963 BOBBITT, Louis M. Contributor.
BRUETTE, Dr. William A. Contributor.
BUCKINGHAM, Nash. Contributor.
EUGENE'S GHOST. Setter.
FAST DELIVERY. Pointer.
HARD CASH. Pointer.
LADY FERRIS. Pointer.

WALPOLE, Stewart J. Contributor.

1964 ANTONIO. Setter.
BUCKLE, C. E. Contributor.
DAVIS, Henry P. Contributor.
JINGO. Pointer.
REILY, Frank. Contributor.
SATILLA WAHOO PETE. Pointer.
SEMINATORE, Michael. Contributor.
SPUNKY CREEK BOY. Pointer.

1965 BABCOCK, Charles H. Contributor.
BETTEN, Henry L. Contributor.
CRANGLE, George M. Contributor.
GENEVA. Setter.
LADY'S COUNT GLADSTONE. Setter.
LIVINGSTONE, Mrs. G. M. Contributor.
PALAMONIUM. Pointer.
VILLAGE BOY. Pointer.

1966 LEWIS, Guy H. Jr. Contributor.
LULLABY. Pointer.
OEHLER, Dr. George E. Contributor.
WAYRIEL ALLEGHENY SPORT. Pointer.

1967 COMMANDER'S HIGHTONE BEAU. Setter.
MAYTAG, Lewis B. Contributor.
SOPH, Edward. Contributor.
THE GABERDASHER. Pointer.

1968 ASH, Frank C. Contributor.
HOME AGAIN MIKE. Pointer.
LIGHT, Sam R. Contributor.
PALADIN'S ROYAL HEIR. Pointer.

1969 GLENCREST DOCTOR. Setter.
GREER, Rowan A. Contributor.
SAFARI. Pointer.
WALKER, Paul S. Contributor.

1970 FEAGIN'S MOHAWK PAL. Setter.
GUNSMOKE. Pointer.
HOLMES, H. N. Contributor.
SMITH, Luther. Contributor.

1971 CURTIS, Arthur S. Contributor.
SHORE'S BROWNIE DOONE. Pointer.
SMITH, Herman. Contributor.
TURNTO. Setter.

1972 ASKEW'S CAROLINA LADY. Irish Setter.
HARPER, Jack P. Contributor.
RAMBLING REBEL DAN. Pointer.
WIMMER, Walter H. Contributor.

1973 AMES, Julia C. Contributor.
HARDEN, George L. Jr. Contributor.
RED WATER REX. Pointer.
THE ARKANSAS RANGER. Pointer.

1974 BISSELL, Lebbeus F. Contributor.
LONE SURVIVOR. Pointer.
TINY WAHOO. Pointer.
WEHLE, Robert G. Contributor.

1975 RIGGINS WHITE KNIGHT. Pointer.
HINTON, Jimmy. Contributor.
OLIVER, Mary C. Contributor.
WONSOVER. Setter.

1976 BEROL, Henry. Contributor.
MR. THOR. Setter.
OKLAHOMA FLUSH. Pointer.
O'NEALL, John S. Sr. Contributor.

Greyhound Hall of Fame

ABILENE, KANSAS

Mailing Address: 407 S. Buckeye, 67410. Tel. (913) 263-3000. *Contact:* Ed Scheele, Dir. *Location:* 1 mi. S. of I-70; approx. 87 mi. W. of Topeka, 150 mi. W. of Kansas City, Mo. *Admission:* Free (donations accepted) 9 to 5 Apr. – Oct, 9 to 5 weekends Nov. – Mar. Tours available throughout the year by advance request. *Personnel:* Ed Scheele, Dir; eight mem. Board of Trustees, four from National Greyhound Association (NGA) and four from American Greyhound Track Operators Association (AGTOA). *Nearby Halls of Fame:* Agriculture (Bonner Springs, 150 mi. E, Kansas City, Mo.).

In 1963 the NGA and the AGTOA combined their efforts to establish a Hall of Fame that would preserve the history of and educate people about greyhounds and greyhound racing. On April 21, 1963, the Greyhound Hall of Fame was dedicated, three pylons depicting the breeding, coursing and track racing of greyhounds were laid at the National Greyhound Association and the first three greyhounds were enshrined in the Hall of Fame. Abilene is an appropriate location for the Hall of Fame since it is the birthplace and capital of greyhound racing. Racing started in Kansas in 1886 and each spring and fall the NGA conducts races in Abilene. Headquarters for the NGA and the registry for all racing greyhounds in the United States are located in Kansas. Construction of a building across the street from Eisenhower Center began in 1972 and is now visited by 28,000 people annually. The Hall of Fame consists of displays on outstanding greyhounds and individuals enshrined in the Hall of Fame, including an international section honoring greyhounds from other countries, a theatre where racing films are shown periodically during the day, a bookstore in the lobby area, and a museum with greyhound history from 5000 B.C. to modern times. Also in the museum is a

160-sq. ft. model of a greyhound race track with a multiple screen projection to illustrate the various aspects of track operation. On a tour one can see the growth, feeding, training and development of greyhound puppies into sleek racing dogs. Funds from the Hall of Fame are used to advance and improve the sport through research and scholarship (in veterinary medicine, for example), and plans are being made to develop a reference library. The Hall is a nonprofit organization supported by donations from the NGA, the AGTOA and racing enthusiasts, and is a member of the Association of Sports Museums and Halls of Fame.

Members: 24 as of January 1977. Members may be greyhounds or individuals. Greyhounds must have outstanding accomplishments as competitors, sires or dams and must have been deceased for at least five years before being nominated to the Hall of Fame. They must have raced in states having legalized pari-mutuel greyhound racing on commercial tracks licensed by the racing commission, or in coursing meets under the supervision of the National Coursing Association. Individuals are recognized for outstanding service or contribution to any area of greyhound racing. Open nominations are received by the Executive Secretary along with records and documents supporting the nominees' qualifications. Eight Trustees, elected to serve two-year terms, review nominations and elect any number of qualified nominees by their unanimous vote. Members are inducted in ceremonies held at the Greyhound Hall of Fame. Plaques are given to the individuals and the greyhound owners.

1963

FLASHY SIR "Mr Greyhound" "Seabiscuit"
Competitor
Whelped 1943 out of Lucky Sir and Flashy Harmony; grandson of Lucky Roll (Greyhound Hall of Fame); brindled male bred and owned by Ohlinger and Blair Kennel, Jewell, Kans.

Experts regard Flashy Sir as the greatest track dog in racing history. Between 1944 and 1947 he set records at Flagler, Taunton, Raynham, Biscayne, Wonderland and St. Petersburg tracks. In 80 starts, he finished his career 60 – 10 – 4, with 18 consecutive wins and earnings of $50,000 in one year. He was one of the original three dogs enshrined in the Greyhound Hall of Fame.

REAL HUNTSMAN
Competitor
Whelped 1948 out of Never Roll (Greyhound Hall of Fame) and Medora; brindled male racer owned by Gene Randle.

Real Huntsman was one of the original three greyhounds to be enshrined in the Hall of Fame. His record was 67 – 9 – 12 in 105 starts and his total earnings were $62,493. During his racing years he competed in nine two-day match races and won all of them and, between June 1950 and April 1951, accumulated a record of 27 consecutive wins at U.S. tracks.

RURAL RUBE "Man o' War"
Competitor
Whelped 1938 in Kansas out of My Laddie (Greyhound Hall of Fame) and Lady Gangdrew; sister Fern Nature (Greyhound Hall of Fame); male racer owned by R. B. Carroll.

Some say that Rural Rube had very human qualities on and off the track, but as a racing greyhound he had 51 victories in 80 starts.

1964

GANGSTER
Courser
Imported; whelped 1930 out of Non Pareil and Dusty Louise; male courser owned by wrestling champion John Pesek.

Gangster was the first greyhound to be inducted into the Hall of Fame as a result of his accomplishments in coursing. During his lifetime he won three straight National Derby Cups and one Waterloo Cup.

INDY ANN "Caliente Queen"
Competitor and Dam
Whelped 1953 out of Pageant and Praying Darkie; female racer and dam owned by Ed Williard, San Ysidro, Calif.

Indy Ann, the first female to be enshrined in the Hall of Fame, has won more races than any other greyhound in American history. She had a record of 137 – 37 – 18 between 1954 and 1957, and was only unplaced 31 times. She also recorded the greatest number of wins in one year: 61 in 1956. As a dam, she whelped four litters, 34 pups total, that were outstanding in Mexico—Preston Adams had an 82-race win and Stylish Daisy had a 77-race win.

LUCKY PILOT
Competitor and Sire
Whelped 1944 out of Never Roll (Greyhound Hall of Fame) and Dixie By; grandson of Lucky Roll (Greyhound Hall of Fame); male racer and sire, bred and owned by Ray E. Holmes.

With a record of 61 – 13 – 7 in 91 starts, Lucky Pilot once held four world records at a time. At his death he was the leading sire in the United States.

TRAFFIC OFFICER
Competitor and Sire
Whelped 1925 out of Meadows and Vixen; male racer and sire bred by Art Wilson; sold in 1926 to George Oswald for $3300.

Traffic Officer was one of the best all-around greyhounds in America, in coursing, track racing and breeding. In 1930 he won first at the $5000 match race in Agua Caliente, Mexico.

1965

FERN NATURE
Competitor
Whelped 1939 out of My Laddie (Greyhound Hall of Fame) and Lady Gandrew; brother Rural Rube (Greyhound Hall of Fame); female racer owned by R. B. Carroll.

Many say that Fern Nature was the best female racer in track history. During her career she won three Flagler

Derbies in a row, one Biscayne Derby, the Flagler Futurity and two Miami inaugurals.

GOLDEN SAHARA
Courser
Whelped 1929 out of Jovial Judge and Jeletz; male courser; sired great coursers Sonny Sahara, Sahara Son and Rhu; owned by Arch DeGeer, a pioneer in racing.

Golden Sahara was the second racer enshrined in the Hall of Fame based on his coursing record. He won the Derby and Waterloo Cups in 1931.

LUCKY ROLL
Competitor and Sire
Whelped 1931 out of Just Andrews, Imported (Greyhound Hall of Fame) and Mustard Roll (Irish dam sired by Mutton Cutlet); male sire bred by George Hackett, Anaconda, Mont; owned by J. A. Austin.

Known as the greatest of modern sires, Lucky Roll can claim most American runners as his descendants. He also was the first greyhound to win 60 times during the parimutuel era of racing.

MY LADDIE
Competitor and Sire
Whelped out of Traffic Officer (Greyhound Hall of Fame) and Kitty Darling; owned by Frank W. Jones, Miami, Fla; sired Rural Rube (Greyhound Hall of Fame).

Well-known as a sire, My Laddie was also a racer who won the 1932 $10,000 Gold Collar Sweepstakes match race and set a world record for the 5⁄16 mi.

1966

BEACH COMBER "King of the Greyhounds" "Shorty"
Competitor
Whelped 1945 out of More Taxes and Soapy Hands; brindled male with short legs; owned by Paul Sutherland.

Between 1947 and 1950, Beach Comber accumulated a record of 99–51–18 in 218 starts and was popular among crowds for his famous victory roll at the end of his winning races. Tracks in the United States still hold Beach Comber Nights and run races in his honor.

KITTY DUNN
Competitor
Whelped 1928 out of Flint Rock, Imported and Lee's Lady, Imported; a popular female racer owned by Ralph McMinimy.

Kitty Dunn is well-known for her racing ability, especially in bad weather conditions: in a racing season of 93 days at the West Flagler track, it rained 63 days, yet Kitty Dunn raced and won. In 1930 she won the stake race at the Flagler track.

UPSIDEDOWN
Courser and Sire
Imported; whelped out of Mutton Cutlet (Greyhound Hall of Fame) and Wealthy Widow; male courser and sire owned by Vernie Mikels.

As a sire, Upsidedown produced coursers that dominated the fields in the 1930s. As a courser himself, he won the 1934 Waterloo Cup.

1967

SUNNY CONCERN "Queen of Greyhounds"
Courser
Whelped 1923 out of Unconcern, Imported and Sunkist; female courser owned by Frank Lawman.

Art Wilson, greyhound owner, said that Sunny Concern was the best greyhound that coursed in a futurity year, but she ran only fast enough to win on the track.

1968

NEVER ROLL
Competitor
Whelped 1939 out of Lucky Roll (Greyhound Hall of Fame) and Never Fail; male racer; sons Lucky Pilot and Real Huntsman also in the Greyhound Hall of Fame; owned by H. A. Alderson.

As a breaker and finisher, Never Roll won the Wonderland Derby and broke four consecutive world records in 1942.

1970

MIXED HARMONY
Competitor and Sire
Whelped 1944 out of Larry of Waterhall, Imported and Thrilling Sport; male racer and sire owned by J. R. Hodges.

Mixed Harmony was the national sire champion in 1954 and 1955 and had pups that won more than 7000 races. He was also a well known racer in Florida and at the Raynham and Caliente tracks.

1971

ROCKER MAC
Sire
Imported; whelped 1951 out of Chief Havoc (Greyhound Hall of Fame) and Mystery Rocca; male sire owned by R. H. Stevenson.

As America's top-rated sire, Rocker Mac produced, over a seven-year period, pups who won a record 22,000 races.

1973

CALLAGHAN, Dennis "Mr. NCA"
Contributor
Born in Ireland, Callaghan is one of two men to be enshrined in the Greyhound Hall of Fame. He has served greyhound racing for twenty years as a committeeman, secretary, vice-president and president of the National Greyhound Association. He provided the "wisdom, guidance, and inspiration vitally needed by the owners' and breeders' organization."

SMITH, Owen Patrick

Engineer by profession; lived in Hot Springs, S. Dak; died 1940.

In 1904 Smith brought a greyhound coursing meet to Hot Springs, S. Dak, to stimulate business in the town. He liked the sport so much he began promoting commercial coursing meets, but received opposition because the dogs chased live rabbits. Smith organized an Intermountain Coursing Association meeting in Salt Lake City in 1907. He raised money to build a small circular track in the city and experimented with a successful mechanical lure, a stuffed rabbit skin run around the track on a motorcycle. In his efforts to popularize greyhound track racing he received over 50 patents for mechanical lures and opened tracks in Emeryville, Calif, East St. Louis and Chicago, Ill, Erlanger, Ky, and Hialeah, Fla. (all later shut down). In 1920 he formed the International Greyhound Racing Association in Tulsa, Okla, and his partner introduced betting, through bookmakers, despite Smith's protests. In 1925 Smith built a track in St. Petersburg, Fla, later called Derby Lane, which is now the oldest continuously operating greyhound racing track in the world. Greyhound racing was internationally recognized in 1926 and Smith travelled with businessman Charles Munn to introduce the sport in England. Owen Patrick Smith is known as the "Father of Greyhound Racing."

1974

FELDCREST

Racer

Sired by No Refund and brother to Beach Comber (Greyhound Hall of Fame); male racer owned by Orville Moses.

Feldcrest was an outstanding track racer who won 73 times and over $51,000. He twice lowered the world record for the 5/16 mi. and in 1958 won the American Derby by a surprising eight lengths. Feldcrest was Greyhound of the Year in 1958 with 40 victories.

1975

CHIEF HAVOC "Patches"

Competitor and Sire

Whelped 1944 out of Trion and Thelma's Mate; sire of Rocker Mac, Imported (Greyhound Hall of Fame); white male racer with fawn patches owned by Jack Millered.

Chief Havoc is one of two members in the international section of the Greyhound Hall of Fame and is Australia's most legendary greyhound. As a racer he broke or equaled 19 track records in 36 career starts; in a solo performance before 17,000, he broke five new records and tied another. As a sire he can claim as his descendants nearly all Australian greyhounds and half of all American greyhounds.

JUST ANDREWS

Sire

Imported; male racer purchased in Australia by wrestling champion John Pesek in 1933.

Just Andrews is best known as a sire, claiming no less than ten of the Greyhound Hall of Fame members as his offspring, including the first three members, Rural Rube, Flashy Sir and Real Huntsman. 90% of the racing greyhounds in the United States are his descendants as well.

MUTTON CUTLET

Sire

Whelped 1921; bred in Ireland by Brig. Gen. R. McCalmount; later purchased and placed at public stud by T. A. Morris, Keeper of the Irish Stud Book.

Mutton Cutlet represents England and Ireland in the international section of the Greyhound Hall of Fame and is the greatest name in greyhound breeding. Not only is it probable that all registered greyhounds in England and Ireland are his descendants, but probably 75% of all modern greyhounds are as well. His descendants were known to adapt well to the electric track.

FOOTBALL

Of the many sports and games that developed in one way or another out of warfare (archery, certain track and field events and chess, to name only a few), none has so consistently retained its martial flavor as football. We speak of the long bomb, the offense and defense, the sustained attack, tactics, strategies, squad, rifle arm, and so on. And players wear helmets—the wife of Dr. James Naismith, the inventor of basketball, made the first helmet out of chamois skin to protect her husband's ears when he played football. But these linguistic hints to the game's past are only minor ones compared to the hints given by the nature of the game. In 1974, for example, 86 percent of all high school players received at least one injury, and 28 were reported to have died from football injuries. Beginning prior to 1890 and until the appearance of helmets, college players let their hair grow from June first so that they would have a protective mass of hair by autumn. Some backs sewed or riveted leather handles to the shoulders of their jackets and to the hips of their canvas trousers so their teammates could pull them ahead should they be gang-tackled or injured but still able to clutch the ball. Jim Thorpe, the sport's first glamorous drawing card, armed himself with shoulder pads that were reinforced with sheet metal. Of himself he said, "When old Jim hits them, they rattle." From 1827 until 1860 when it was banned, Harvard had an annual freshman initiation ritual (called Bloody Monday) that involved a football-like game.

Violence has not always been confined to the playing field in the history of football. The custom of cheering at games dates from the years after the Civil War when spectators gave either the Rebel yell or some Northern regiment's battle cry in support of their team. The custom developed after it was found that players did not have enough wind to both fight for the ball and yell. The courthouse steeple in Latrobe, Pennsylvania, had to be straightened on its base after one spirited mob finished celebrating a hometown victory. Police dogs have been used to keep order at Grey Cup All-Canada Championship games which have been described as a "savouring of civil war." Phillip Stubbes, a Puritan pamphlet writer, wrote in his sixteenth-century *Anatomie of Abuses* that with a hundred "murthering devices" the football of the day caused "fighting, brawling, contortion, quarrel kicking, homicide, and great effusion of blood, as experience dayly teacheth."

Those words would aptly describe the state of football in 1905. During that year's football season 159 players were injured and 18 died. One of those injured that year was Bob Maxwell, Swarthmore's 250-pound linesman. A newspaper photograph showed Maxwell, battered and bleeding, being led off the field. President Theodore Roosevelt was so enraged by that photograph that he issued an ultimatum to representatives of Yale, Harvard and Princeton that they should "Clean up your game or I'll see that it's abolished." As a result of that threat, a rules committee banned the flying wedge and legalized the forward pass in 1906. But even T.R.'s "big stick" tactics could not take the excitement out of violence, or the violence out of the game. Thus the statement made by Sir Thomas Elyot in the year 1531 (three years before Mercator published his map of the world), "Foote balle, wherin is nothinge but beastly Furie and exstreme violence whereof procedeth hurt," was rephrased by Frank Gifford in 1960: "Pro football is like nuclear warfare. There are no winners, only survivors."

That theme—football as warfare over a bag of air—has been the single most significant factor in the development of what today has replaced baseball as America's national game in the minds of millions as well in fact. It is also the key to understanding both that curious malaise called "football fever," and that religious devotion to the game which has led Canadian evangelists to encourage all to "follow the Great Coach down the Gridiron of Life."

So it is unexpected to read that Augustus, who was Caesar during the life of Christ, banned the Roman form of football because it was too gentle a game for men of war. And it is illuminating to discover that the "Father of American Football," Walter Camp, grew faint at the sight of blood. Camp, who lived from 1859 to 1925, altered the game significantly by emphasizing tactics and strategy over brute strength and by inventing the scrimmage line. He is representative of the other side of the sport, the side Roosevelt wanted to encourage. Football is not just four quarters of fifteen minutes of violence. Just as military genius has always been more significant in battle than numbers of troops, so too have skill and intelligence long been far more significant than raw power in football. For that reason, General Douglas MacArthur, while superintendent of West Point, said that the two games he wanted the cadets to learn were football and chess. In fact, football has been defined as "a game which embraces the elements of chess, geometry, and warfare," and more graphically as a "lightning-fast chess game with pawns weighing 250 pounds."

There are almost as many games in the history of football as there are penalties in modern professional play—fully 60 different ones. All of them, particularly the forms played in North America, are mere twentieth century versions of the ancient application of foot to ball. Some 2500 years ago people in parts of China played *tsu chu,* a team game invented in 1697 B.C. by the emperor Huang-Ti. *Tsu* came from "to kick the ball with feet" and *chu* from "ball made of leather, and stuffed," normally with cork and hair. By 600 B.C. the Japanese were playing their own version of this game which they called *kemari.* From the many centuries that *tsu chu* was played, no player has been better remembered than the emperor Chen-Ti. He lived from 32 B.C. to A.D. 16. Courtiers attempted to dissuade him from "showing so much enthusiasm, because such behavior [is] inconsistent with Imperial Dignity." Similarly, the ancient Egyptians stuffed leather balls which they could have kicked or thrown, and Berber peoples of 600 B.C. had a ball game called *koura* which was associated with a fertility rite.

Ancient Greeks had numerous team and individual games involving feet, hands and balls. In *episkuros,* for example, two teams of equal numbers stood on opposite sides of a *skuros,* a line of stone chips. Each team tried to force the other back over a goal line by throwing a ball that had to be caught—there was no footwork in this game. In this and the other Greek ball games, the emphasis was on the grace, skill and agility of the players rather than on their accumulation of points and victories. As with everything else, the Greeks had a word for it. *Harpastum,* the name of one game, was derived from *harpazein,* to pass forward. *Hufarpasai* was intercepting and the word for our expression "call for it!" was *keleuson.* The term *phaininda* was used when a player showed the ball to one man but then threw it to another. Plato was the first to use the metaphor "keeping the ball in the air" to describe one who participates skillfully in conversation. In certain Greek games, a player who dropped a catch was called donkey or ass, while a player who never dropped catches was called the King. These Greek games employed at least five different types of ball: the *pila* (a compactly stuffed, very hard ball), the *follis* (A flabby, soft feather-filled ball), the *paganica* (also filled with feathers), the *trigonalis,* and the *harpastum* (in colloquial Greek, the word meant snatch). Some of these were made from a pig's bladder tightly stuffed with hair, others were large air-filled bladders. Some had differently colored leather panels called leaves sewn together to form a cover for the bladder.

All of these games were greatly popularized by Alexander the Great, who took up ball after quitting athletics. A fine runner, he tired of racing because his competitors always let him win. His interest in ball games began a trend. Within a generation of his death, all "acceptable" Greek homes had a *sphairisterion,* a special court for playing ball.

Most of these games were far from modern-day football except in spirit. They were primarily gymnastic exercises to be played between friends during free time or as entertainments after banquets. Not serious competitions, they were never included in the Olympic Games' program. They were, however, included in the aspects of Greek culture adopted by the Romans. Except for Horace who disapproved of ball games, and Augustus who banned them as being too gentle, these football games were popular all over Roman Italy. Ovid—writer of *Ars Amatoria,* The Art of Love—warned that ball games should not be played by women. A second century A.D. engraved pillar from Sinj, Dalmatia (on the Dalmatian coast of modern Yugoslavia), shows a young man holding a ball made of hexagonal leather sections. Whenever the Romans went on conquest, they took their own ball games and found new ones. Residents of the English town of Derby are said to have defeated a visiting team of Roman legionnaires at the Greco-Roman game of *harpastum* in A.D. 276. Julius Caesar found Teutonic tribes playing a kicking game with a ball that turned out to be a human head. This was not an uncommon game throughout history and in particular throughout Asian history. Tamerlane customarily played polo or some other game with the head of each enemy he defeated. Between 1016 and 1049 English workmen excavating an old battlefield dug up a hated Dane's skull and began kicking it. Soon a popular game called kicking the Dane's head had developed. At any rate, Roman ball games lasted longer than Rome did. One game carried over through the Middle Ages in Tuscany and Florence was called *calcio.*

Other forms were adapted and preserved by the Church. The Latin regulations of the Monastery of Auxerre dated April 18, 1397 (three years before Geoffrey Chaucer died), contain a special *Ordinatio de pila facienda* requiring newly admitted clerics to bring footballs with them. These balls, about the size of a soccer ball, were used for recreation and in certain ceremonies like the Easter ball game played around 1400: "Then the dean seizes the ball with his left hand and paces solemnly in time to the music. The others join hands and dance around the master. While they are dancing, the dean throws the ball to the individual dancers in turn, and they throw it back ... When song and dance are ended, the company goes to lunch." Even outside the Church the old ball games were being played as part of religious ceremonies. "Play ball" was being played in London and at Chester on Shrove Tuesday, the day before Ash Wednesday, every year as early as 1175. Teams of students and trade apprentices played each other.

But the nonreligious versions had long been more popular. Just three years after the Norman invasion of England in 1066, "futballe" had been organized and was being played. The name seems to have been applied to the game to distinguish it from various ball games that were played on horseback. At any rate, futballe soon became an extremely rugged and popular sport in which whole towns played or battled each other for possession of an inflated bladder. In these games kicking, holding and throwing the ball were all allowed, and the offsides penalty was a kick in the shins.

Violence and popularity of such a sport ultimately led Henry II, whose followers murdered St. Thomas à Becket, to order imprisonment for any "futballe" player who would not "cease playe." Other rulers such as Richard II, Henry IV, Henry VIII and Elizabeth I similarly banned the game. Among other grievances they had against it, it was distracting their subjects from compulsory archery practice. But Edward II banned it in 1314 as a public nuisance: "For as much as there is great noise in the city caused by hustling over large balls . . . we command and forbid on behalf of the King, on pain of imprisonment, such game to be used in the city in the future." Edward III followed this with a more sweeping ban against playing "skittles, quoits, fives, football or other foolish games which are of no use." In that 1349 ban, "football" appears in the English language for the first time. But all such bans and laws could not stop the growth of the game. Although the threat of fine or imprisonment may have dampened enthusiasm for some to join in what a sixteenth century writer called "the thronging of a rude multitude, with bursting of shinnes and breaking of legges," football remained insistently popular. Stubborn Irishmen in Dublin even went so far in ignoring the English bans as to develop their own unique version of the game. Gaelic football is today one of the world's most violent sports.

Eventually, after four centuries, the bans were lifted and football was allowed to develop. Until the nineteenth century, however, the various forms of football were all kicking games. The players' hands were used only on each other. Then a student changed everything. A monument to him that may be seen today at Rugby School in England records the event: "This stone commemorates the exploit of William Webb Ellis who with a fine disregard for the rules of football, as played in his time, first took the ball in his arms and ran with it, thus originating the distinctive feature of the rugby game A.D. 1823." Although running with the ball was not legalized until 1846, the two most significant games of the world today developed within several decades. The traditional, primarily kicking game became "association football," abbreviated "assoc," from which we get the word "soccer," today the world's biggest sport (*see* Soccer). The new game inspired by Ellis' disregard for the rules became "English Rugby," "Union Football" or "rugger," which led directly to the development of the different forms of modern North American ball-carrying football. History reversed itself 166 years after Ellis when a Rhodes Scholar at Oxford, Pete Dawkins of West Point, revolutionized modern rugby with his long (legal) downfield passes.

Football in North America dates from both B.E. (Before Ellis) and A.E. Prior to 1823 numerous football-like games had been played both by indigenous peoples and by newcomers. Numerous tribes had various ball-kicking or throwing games, colonial New Englanders kicked inflated pig bladders, and British troops in Canada played the football games they had learned at home. Not until the decade of the Civil War, however, was the modern organization of these games attempted.

The first football club in the United States, the Oneida Football Club of Boston, was organized by 17-year-old Gerritt Miller in 1862, the year Julia Ward Howe wrote "The Battle Hymn of the Republic." The first formal football club in Canada, the Montreal Football Club, was organized in 1868. Both clubs, and the numerous others that began to appear, played according to English rugby rules.

The first American intercollegiate football game was played under a modified set of the London Football Association rules, which meant that the game was more soccer than football. It was played between Princeton (then called Nassau Hall) and Rutgers on November 6, 1869. The two schools had long had a rivalry over the possession of a rusty Revolutionary War cannon. Rutgers had ended the rivalry by putting the cannon in cement. They played a game of football in which there were up to 25 players per side on a 120 yd. by 75 yd. field. Neither running with nor throwing the ball was allowed, and the first side to score six goals won. The game was frequently stopped so that the round rubber ball could be repaired. Rutgers won, but did not defeat Princeton again for 69 years. The school was cheered on by the Rutgers supporters among the crowd of 300 who gave the battle cry of New York's Seventh Regiment in one of college football's first cheers. The major papers didn't mention that first game at all. They carried instead the pro and con arguments in a debate over whether to move the nation's capital to the middle of the continent. And gave whole columns to advertisements such as "Ladies dressing the hair elaborately will find that BURNETT'S COCOAINE will keep it in perfect shape and beauty."

Encouraged by the adoption of formal rules in 1871 and 1873, students at eastern schools continued to play both rugby and soccer until 1874. In that year, when "Humpty Dumpty" was playing at the Broadway Theatre in New York, Harvard played McGill University of Montreal in two games at Cambridge, Massachusetts. This set the stage for the unique evolution of American football. A group of Harvard students had asked President Elliot in the spring of 1871 for permission to play the new Boston Game in which the round rubber ball could be picked up. A year later on December 3, 1872, the Harvard Foot Ball Club was organized. So when Harvard met McGill on May 14, 1874, and won 3 – 0, the game was something significantly different from the ones other schools were playing. Still the papers ignored that game. Minor news from distant North Dakota was considered more interesting to readers than football. The *New York Times* carried the note that "Christopher Weaver, owner of a wood-yard between Forts Stephenson and Berthold, was murdered by Sioux Indians last Monday. . . Preparations are being made at Fort Abraham Lincoln, near Bismark, to follow the Indians, if necessary. Gen. Custer's command is preparing to take the war-path." The fact that American football was born that day was not mentioned.

Between 1874 and 1895 football evolved in the United States and Canada in subtle, slow ways. An Intercollegiate Football Association was formed in 1876 that directed the American hybrid game away from soccer and allowed it to evolve even further out of rugby. In 1878 players discarded their tights in favor of canvas pants and jackets. In 1879 the first midwestern game was played (Michigan v. Racine) and the October 31 Toronto *Daily Globe* carried the announcement that "There are six young ladies in the city of Ottawa at present all unknown to fame, who are desirous of acquiring a reputation as athletes, and one of them has written to us to say that they are willing to challenge any six young ladies in this town to a game of football, for a silver cup." The year 1880 saw the invention of the quarterback position, the introduction of the custom of the center passing the ball back to the quarterback (which meant rugby's scrum was replaced with football's scrimmage line), the reduction of teams from 15 players to 11, and the reduction of the 140 by 70 yd. field to 110 by 53. Signals were first used in 1882 and in that year it was ruled in the American game that a team must move the ball a certain distance in a fixed number of downs, a practice duplicated in the Canadian game in 1907. Walter Camp, the "Father of American Football," invented the concept of four downs. As late as 1884 a football safety counted as one point, a touchdown as two (not worth six points until 1912), a point-after-touchdown was four, and a field goal was worth five points. But the evolution of the scoring system was also slowly changing. In 1889 Caspar Whitney of *The Week's Sports* began the practice of annually selecting an All-American team. Numerous modifications in the game remained to be made, of course, as indicated by the fact that in 1893, after a Chicago-Purdue game, the Tippecanoe County district attorney threatened to indict every player for assault and battery. The following year, McGill University formed an Athletic Association, one of whose responsibilities was to ensure that any student who took part in football or "other violent athletic games" got a thorough medical examination.

By 1895 football was distinctly football—never again to be confused with rugby or soccer. That was the year Stephen Crane wrote *The Red Badge of Courage;* Dr. John Kellogg produced his Granose Flakes, the world's first flaked breakfast cereal; and a North Carolina fullback made the first forward pass in an official game. And it was in that year, specifically in an August 31 game at Latrobe, Pennsylvania, between Latrobe and Jeanette, that American professional football was born. Sixteen-year-old John Brallier, who later became a dentist, received $10 plus expenses to quarterback for Latrobe, which won 12–0. Even that significant game was ignored by the newspapers, who that day reported instead (*New York Times,* p. 3) that "Charles Amery of South Rutherford, N.J, has been making preparations for the past week for a trial of his flying machine. He located on the highest point here, on the edge of a cliff. He started at 3 o'clock to fly to Jersey City Heights. The machine is a contrivance of bamboo rods and spring steel covered with canvas.... The man and the machine fell down the hillside, turning several somersaults. Amery will make another attempt Saturday."

Other innovations followed through the following years. They were for the most part unknown to all but Douglas MacArthur (a high school quarterback in 1898) and a handful of other Americans. The first Rose Bowl game was held in 1902 (Michigan v. Stanford). The Rose Bowl has been held annually only since 1916, and from then until 1923 was called the Tournament of Roses Association Game. The National Collegiate Athletic Association (NCAA), later to have a profound impact on college football, was formed in 1905, though it was not called by that name until 1910. Passing was legalized in 1906. Numbers on players, although not a general practice until the 1920s, were first used in 1908. In 1909 football began to attract attention in Canada with the donation of the Grey Cup, today the symbol of Canadian football supremacy. In 1911 the touchdown was increased in value to five points, and in 1912 (the year the Titanic sank) to six. In 1912 too, the number of downs was officially made four and Frank "Shag" Shaughnessy, ex-president of a baseball team and a former Notre Dame football captain, became the first professional football coach in Canada. The first black player, Henry McDonald, born in 1890 in Haiti, played with the Oxford Pros in 1911 and with the Rochester Jeffersons in 1912. Also in 1912 there was a young player so promising that he had been dubbed "The Kansas Cyclone." His name was Dwight D. Eisenhower, and he might have become great had not a knee injury that year ended his football career. He subsequently distinguished himself in real war. So did John F. Kennedy, who played end for Harvard until injured, and who said, "I'm like a good many other Americans who never quite made it but love it." Football gained considerably in popularity through the enthusiasm of such players, and particularly after a 1913 Army-Notre Dame game in which Knute Rockne masterfully pioneered the use of brains over brawn, thereby establishing Notre Dame as a significant football school.

The first admittedly professional team played in 1914—nineteen years after Brallier got his $10. On September 17, 1920, professional football became organized with the formation of the American Professional Football Association. That organization occured during a meeting at an automobile shop, Hay's Hupmobile showroom, in Canton, Ohio. Jim Thorpe was elected its president. In 1921 and 1922 the Association's name was changed to National Football League (NFL). Franchises in those days cost from $50 to $100—today, $10 million might buy an inexpensive one.

In 1921 Canadian teams were reduced to 12 men—the size they are today, the side-scrum was dropped, and the center began to put the ball into play with a direct pass to the quarterback. The year 1921 also saw the invention of the Rorschach test, the burial of the first Unknown Soldier, and the first outdoor use of the huddle by Bob Zuppke, the Illinois coach. In 1924 *Rhapsody in Blue* was written and the first rating system was devised by Frank G. Dickinson. Five years later the first training camp opened. By the 1930s the football had attained its modern form, having come a long way from the early plump, pumpkin-shaped one that was thrown shot-put fashion. In 1931 Canadian football formally adopted the forward pass. It had long been in use in the United States, but not until the masterful passing of Sammy Baugh during the decade of the 1930s was the air attack an integral part of football. Incidentally, the same decade saw the evolution of the air attack in real warfare. Nineteen thirty-four saw not only the invention of six-man football but also Richard M. Nixon playing left end and tackle for Whittier College and missing the first college draft which was held in 1936.

The Football Writers Association of America became a working organization on December 5, 1941—two days before the attack on Pearl Harbor. During the war years some 350 colleges were forced to drop football, as college players joined the 638 NFL players who served in the Armed Forces. The death of Jim Thorpe in 1953 ended the era of early football; and after the 1952 Grey Cup game, 10,000 Eskimo pies were distributed on the streets of Toronto. The latter, not highly significant in itself, does show that by the time newspapers, magazines and television finally took note of the game (on which today TV and radio advertisers spend over $100 million), football had become a major sport with old traditions, long rivalries, and a vast, strong base of public support.

Not everyone, of course, loves the gridiron. Many, perhaps especially the football widows, would echo Shakespeare's line from *King Lear*: "You base foot-ball player!" But, as has been shown, strong opposition to its existence has always been a part of the gridiron war. No one really knows when it was first called a gridiron, but it is known that some early football fields were marked in squares or grids by white lines of lime. To an unknown sportswriter, they resembled a cooking utensil then in common use, a grate for broiling food called a gridiron. Today the gridiron has moved into the living room, people play the modern version of what a 1716 English poet described as "the furies of the foot-ball war." A lady named Miriam Chapin in 1959 gave what is perhaps the best clue to the utter unreality which distinguishes this modern version from both real war and all its ancient ancestor ball games. Describing twentieth century football fever in Canada, she commented simply that, "all these heroes are hired men."

FORMS: Of the numerous forms of football played today, the most significant ones include Australian Rules football, Gaelic football, Harrow football, Winchester College football, various other special school games, Rugby and Soccer, American secondary school or "Pop Warner" football, college football, American professional football, and Canadian football; in addition to all of these there are the fully developed sports of touch football, flag football, and six-man football. The latter game was invented in 1934, had become popular in Canada by 1938, and was being played by about 30,000 teams in 1976. Teams consist of two lines of three players each and play is on fields which measure 240 by 120 ft.

College football differs from American professional football in few respects. For example, in college football a conversion counts one or two points, while in the pro game only one; in college the goal posts are 23 ft. 4 in. apart, while in pro they are 18 ft. 6 in. apart. In most other basic respects the two games are identical. The field is a level or slightly beveled grass or synthetic surface which is 360 ft. long including 60 ft. of end zone, by 160 ft. wide, with 21 white horizontal or latitudinal lines, including the two goal lines, marking off 5-yard intervals. To retain possession of the ball, a team must move it at least 10 yds. in four tries or downs. To accomplish this to gain points, offensive teams will employ a succession of plays. Although the number of plays is virtually infinite, ones often used include the buck, the counter, the dive, the dropback, the off-tackle, the option, the rollout, the screen, the sneak, the sweep, and the trap. Points are awarded for a touchdown (6), a field goal (3), a safety which is downing a player inside his own goal area (2), and a conversion (1 or 2). Teams consist of eleven players, each of whom will play one of the following specific offensive or defensive positions: center, guard, tackle, end, offensive back, linebacker, or quarterback (there are more specific names for the variations of these positions). A college game, officiated by a number of referees, umpires, field judges, back judges, linesmen, clock operators, marker-movers and waterboys, lasts for four 15-minute quarters. Quarters are separated by three invervals in the following order: 1 minute, 15 minutes (halftime), and 1 minute. A pro game's 60 minutes of actual playing time are divided similarly, but by intervals of 2, 15, and 2 minutes. Penalties exist for over 60 different infringements of the rules and include loss of a down, loss of various amounts of yardage and expulsion from the game.

The ball is an inflated spheroid that weighs 14 – 15 oz. when inflated 12.5 – 13.5 lbs per sq. in. pressure. It measures 11 – 11.25 in. long and 7 in. maximum diameter (i.e, 21.25 – 21.5 in. middle circumference and 28 – 28.5 in. long circumference). The first patent for a football cover, issued in 1867, was for a canvas layer to go over the traditional rubber rugby bladder. Because the best balls were later made of pigskin, the ball is often called a pigskin, although cowhide, rubber or various plastics make the best balls today. Regardless of what is used, a football is made of four pieces of material sewn together with tight, inside seams. Other equipment includes those items worn by each player: helmet, face mask, jersey and pants which may not be colored similar to the color of the ball, chest and shoulder pads, rib and kidney pads, below-the-belt pads, thigh and shin pads, and lightweight shoes. Each player's jersey must carry an assigned number in figures at least 8 in. high on the chest and at least 10 in. high on the back. Players playing the various end positions are assigned numbers from 80 – 89, tackles from 70 – 79, guards from 60 – 69, the center from 50 – 59, and backs from 10 – 49.

Although Canadian football is a distinct game in every respect—it is the only successful professional team sport played solely in Canada today—its basic features are largely identical to those of American professional football. Those features which are uniquely its own include: a 12 man team instead of eleven—a flying wing man is added; the size of a field, 110 by 65 yds, which is much larger than the American; the size of the end zones, 25 yds. each as opposed to 10 yds. each in the American game; the absence of the fair catch; three instead of four downs for retaining possession of the ball; the motions rules which allow all offensive backs to be in motion before the ball is put into play, whereas in American football only one back may be in motion; the line-up distance where a defensive player may not be nearer than 1 yd. to the ball, whereas American players virtually touch each other in the line-up at scrimmage. The scoring system is identical to the American game's except for the existence of: the "rouge," a single point scored if the receiving team is unable to return the ball out of its own end zone; the conversion distance from the 10 yd. line instead of from the 2; the absence of time outs, which can be called in the American game; and the intervals of time dividing the four quarters—in Canadian football the halftime is 20 minutes instead of 15. These unique features of the Canadian game make it faster moving and more open and exciting than the American game which evolved out of Rugby.

ORGANIZATION: The world of organized football in North America may be said to begin with the tiny tots. That is, within the Pop Warner Junior League Football organization, founded in 1929, are over 6000 teams that play under safety-first rules. These teams are composed of hundreds of thousands of youngsters aged 8 to 15 and are classified by age and weight into seven groupings: Tiny Tot, Junior Peewee, Peewee, Junior Midget, Midget, Junior Bantam and Bantam. Significantly, the founder of Pop Warner football, Joe Tomlin, declared that one of the objectives of the organization was "to keep the welfare of participants free of any adult ambition or personal glory."

Above this level is the far larger level of high school or American secondary school football. The 1977 membership of a single organization, the National Federation of State High School Associations (NFSHSA), demonstrates the truly vast size of the world of high school athletics in general and of football in particular. The organization is a federation of 50 State high school athletic associations, 9 Canadian ones and 1 Philippine affiliate, which together have a total membership of over 20,100 high schools. Most of the latter have football teams. For all of them (through its 60 member associations), the NFSHSA supervises and coordinates activities, maintains a national press service and an official sports film service, and annually publishes rules and officials' training materials for football and other sports. The same services are performed at the next level, junior college football, by the National Junior Collegiate Athletic Association (NJCAA), which in 1977 had 869 member schools in 22 regional groups.

The highest nonprofessional level in the football world, however, is college football. It is also the largest of those levels—far larger in attendance and public interest than all the lower levels combined. In 1967 college football was rated as the Number Two sport in the nation, exceeded only by pro football. Baseball was number three. Among the numerous four-year college teams, over 800 are associated with the National Collegiate Athletic Association (NCAA). The football teams of these colleges compete with each other within seven NCAA regions: East (10 conferences), South (12 conferences), Midwest (13 conferences), Missouri Valley (11 conferences), Rocky Mountain (5 conferences), Southwest (5 conferences), and Pacific Coast (7 conferences). Since 1933 that huge selection of college teams has served as a de facto pro football farm system, through which over 7000 college players have become professional players. In Canada amateur football including college football (not yet largely developed) is aided by the various provincial amateur football associations which have been organized in Alberta, British Columbia, Manitoba, New Brunswick, Ontario (2), Nova Scotia, Quebec, and Saskatchewan.

As of 1975 American professional football, the highest level in the world of football, is governed by the NFL, which has two conferences, the National, formed from the NFL, and the American, formed from the AFL, each of which has three divisions (Eastern, Central and Western). These divisions in turn are comprised of 28 professional teams. Each of these teams competes with others in its own division and division champions play each other at the end of each season. This results in one team representing each of the two conferences in the Super Bowl which was first staged in 1967 and is usually held on the first Sunday after Christmas. The Super Bowl winner is the National Pro Football Champion for that year. Similarly, Canadian football is governed by the Canadian Football League, founded in 1960, which in 1975 had two conferences, the Eastern and Western with four and five teams, respectively. Conference champions meet each other in the Grey Cup All-Canada Championship held on the last Sunday of each November. The winner is the Canadian National Champion for that year. In order to limit American influence on the Canadian game, each Canadian team may have only 14 American citizens on its roster of 32 active players.

In addition to the organizations directly concerned with professional football in both the United States and Canada are those organizations which largely serve to support and control related aspects of the game: the American Football Coaches Association (1921), the Football Writers Association of America (1941), the National Football League Alumni Association, the Professional Football Writers of America, the Canadian Football League Players Association, the National Football League Players Association and many others. The new wave of the future at this highest level of football may be represented by the various professional football teams for women, which exist in Los Angeles, Toledo, Dallas and Detroit, and which are planned for Cleveland, New York and Buffalo. The existence of these should not be surprising—women in war is a strong tradition that stretches back through history to the Amazons, who amputated their right breasts so that they could shoot their bows and arrows better (*a* "without" plus *mazos* "breast").

Canadian Football Hall of Fame

HAMILTON, ONTARIO

Mailing Address: 58 Jackson St, W. Tel. (416) 525-7011. *Contact:* Denis Lee, Operations Mgr. *Location:* Approx. 35 mi. S.W. of Toronto, 60 mi. N.W. of Buffalo, N.Y, 110 mi. N.E. of Cleveland, Ohio. *Admission:* 9 to 5 weekdays and Saturdays, 12 to 5 Sundays, closed Christmas Day, New Year's Day and Easter Sunday. Adults $1.00, students 50¢, children 14 and under 25¢, family $2.00. *Personnel:* Larry Smith, Dir; seven mem. Bd. of Dir. (J. G. Gaudaur, Chmn.); 13 mem. Mgt. Comt. (Alderman Wheeler, Chmn; Alderman Valeriano, V.Chmn; J. R. Jones, Treas; W. V. Cockman, Gen. Mgr.); 10 mem. Selection Comt. (J. M. Breen, Chmn.); 17 mem. Induction Dinner Comt. (Alderman Wheeler, Chmn; Ernie Seager, Coordr.). *Nearby Halls of Fame:* Hockey, Sports (Toronto), Horseshoe Pitching (Corning, N.Y, 160 mi. S.W.), Flight (Elmira, N.Y, 175 mi. S.W.), State (Detroit, Mich, 175 mi. S.W.), Hockey (Kingston, 185 mi. N.E.).

To the citizens of Hamilton, the Canadian Football Hall of Fame is more than just a monument to the mighty men of the gridiron. Organized on February 16, 1962, to honor founders, developers and stars, the Hall had its original home in an old residence made available by the Parks Board. In 1965 the Board of Education forced the move of the Hall's treasures elsewhere as the old building was razed. Seven long years followed in which Hamilton football faithfuls devoted much time and effort in an attempt to raise funds for a new hall. In November 1972 their dream was fulfilled and the Canadian Football Hall of Fame (building and contents valued at over one million dollars) was officially opened. Operated by the City of Hamilton and Hamilton District Visitors and Conventions Bureau, it is aided by provincial and federal grants and an annual grant from the Canadian Football League. Members were selected yearly beginning in 1963 but none were officially inducted until the Hall opened. The first grand induction ceremony took place in mid-September 1973, when 73 members were honored, 24 as builders and 49 as players. Beautifully constructed of marble and glass, the Hall has special displays including an audiovisual presentation of a century of football, life-size steel-moulded busts of the celebrated inductees, and a highly computerized reference library of Canada's football heritage. This Hall of Fame is a member of the Association of Sports Museums and Halls of Fame.

Members: 91 as of November 1976. An unspecified number are inducted, usually 4 to 6 per year in two categories: Players—chosen on qualities of character, sportsmanship, playing ability and contribution to team or football in general, retired at least 3 years; and Builders—defined as those whose service, other than as an active player, was responsible for an exceptional and unquestioned contribution to Canadian Football, including both team and league executives, coaches, and game officials, not necessarily retired. Awards are given each year for the Most Outstanding Player, Canadian Player of the Year and Lineman of the Year.

1973

BACK, Leonard P.

Builder

Born July 21, 1900, in Hamilton, Ont; played for the Hamilton Tiger Juniors in 1918 and 1919; skull fracture ended his playing.

1920 Hamilton Tiger Juniors, manager
1921 – 1925 Hamilton Intermediates, manager
1926 – 1927 Hamilton Tiger Seniors Ontario Rugby Football Union, manager
1928 – 1940 Hamilton Tigers Interprovincial League, manager
1941 – 1943 Hamilton Wildcats, manager
1945 – 1949 Hamilton Tigers, manager
1950 – Hamilton Tiger-Cats, manager

Possessed of a special ability in dealing with players and a great knowledge of and devotion to football, Len Back began his career as general manager with the Hamilton Tigers in 1920. After managing the Hamilton Intermediates and the Hamilton Tiger Seniors, Back joined the Tigers of the Interprovincial League until the club suspended operations in 1940 because of the war. Then he and Hall of Famer Brian Timmis organized the Hamilton Wildcats, which Back managed and led to a Grey Cup victory in 1943. After W.W. II he returned to managing the Hamilton Tigers until they combined with the Wildcats. Since 1950 Back has been team manager and director of the Hamilton Tiger-Cats, and over the years he has been involved with player relations, program advertising and public relations on behalf of the Hamilton Club and football in general.

BAILEY, R. Harold

Builder

1927 – 1955 Ontario Rugby Football Union, secretary-treasurer
1931 – 1950 Canadian Rugby Union Rules Committee, member
1941 Canadian Rugby Union, president

Serving football for almost a lifetime, Harold Bailey was secretary-treasurer of the Ontario Rugby Football Union (ORFU) for nearly thirty years. As president of the Canadian Rugby Union in 1941 and long-time member of the rules committee, he was influential in the establishment of interscholastic football throughout all Ontario and promoted friendly relations between Eastern and Western football, making playoffs between the two sections possible. He headed the ORFU during the war years and was honored in 1955 by a Grey Cup Dinner for his contributions to the game.

BATSTONE, Harry L.

Player

Enrolled as medical student at Queen's University in 1922 at age 23; later served as faculty member of Queen's.

1920 – 1921 Toronto Argonauts, halfback and captain
1922 – 1928 Queen's University, halfback
1929 – 1931 Queen's University, coach

Harry Batstone was running and kicking halfback and captain of the Toronto Argonauts when they won the Interprovincial Football championship in 1920 and 1921. Though he was of medium height and weighed only 155 lbs, he could run, kick and plunge over players twice his size. Along with Hall of Famer Lionel Conacher, he ran in the Argos backfield in a 23 – 0 victory over Edmonton in the first East-West Grey Cup final in 1921. Playing for Queen's University, he and Hall of Famer "Peps" Leadlay led the Tricolour to four consecutive Intercollegiate championships, three straight Grey Cup triumphs and 26 consecutive victories. After his playing days, he coached the Queen's team to two Intercollegiate titles and later served as a member of the Canadian Intercollegiate Athletic Union Football Rules Committee and was an Intercollegiate representative on the Canadian Rugby Union rules committee.
Also in: Canada's Sports Hall of Fame.

BEACH, Ormond

Player

All-American; All-League; All-Canadian; killed in a Sarnia explosion; is honored with a memorial at Univ. Kans. as player deemed most valuable by his teammates; Ormond Beach Trophy to the Outstanding Football Player in Sarnia; and Ormond Beach Memorial Stadium, a 20,000-seat park in his original Pawhuska High School.

1929 – 1933 University of Kansas, offensive fullback, defensive linebacker
1934 – 1937 Sarnia Imperials, offensive fullback, defensive linebacker

As an All-American at Kansas, Ormond Beach helped lead the Jayhawkers to a scoreless tie against the Fighting Irish of Notre Dame and their first Big Six title. He then lead the Sarnia Imperials to four senior Ontario Rugby Football Union championships and two Grey Cup finals. He was named All-League and All-Canadian in each of his playing years, and overwhelmed Eastern and Western teams with his powerful running. Easily the most popular player ever adopted by Sarnia, Ormond Beach was adjudged to be an outstanding anatomical example of the "Perfect Man" by Dr. James Naismith, Professor of Physical Education and inventor of the game of basketball.

BOX, Albert "Ab"
Player
Jeff Russel Memorial Trophy 1934.

1926 – 1927 Malvern Collegiate, kicking and running back
1928 – 1929 Malvern Grads, kicking and running back
1930 – 1931 Balmy Beach, kicking and running back
1932 – 1934 Toronto Argonauts, kicking and running back
1935 – 1938 Balmy Beach, kicking and running back

Sixty-yard punts were not uncommon for Ab Box, star of the Malvern Collegiate and Malvern Grads. A protégé of Hall of Famer Teddy Reeve, he played with Reeve for the Balmy Beach who, powered by Ab's kicking, took the Grey Cup in 1930, beating Regina 11 – 6. Box joined Toronto to help them win the Grey Cup, then returned to Balmy Beach for four more years. He is considered one of the all-time great halfbacks for his combination of kicking and running ability.
Also in: Canada's Sports Hall of Fame.

BREEN, Joseph M.
Player
All-around athlete in baseball, track and field; attended Univ. of Toronto 1914 – 1916 and 1919 – 1920; joined Canadian Engineers for overseas service 1916; two years with Toronto Harbour Commission 1921 – 1922; joined Canada Cement Company 1922; presently chairman of the board, with headquarters in Montreal.

1914 – 1916 University of Toronto, backfielder
1919 – 1920 University of Toronto, captain
1921 – 1923 Parkdale Canoe Club, captain
1924 Toronto Argonauts, captain
1925 Oarsmen, backfielder
1929 – 1934 University of Western Ontario, coach
1935 – 1941 Interprovincial Union, referee

As player, coach and referee, Joe Breen earned football honors with the University of Toronto, Parkdale Canoe Club and Toronto Argonauts before serving as coach of the University of Western Ontario. During his Varsity years, interrupted by overseas duty during the war, he twice captained the Toronto team. In 1920 he led the Blues to a victory over the Argonauts in the Grey Cup final, 16 – 3. After an outstanding career with Parkdale and the Argonauts, he took over the head coaching position at Western Ontario, where he compiled an enviable record and led the team to its first major athletic triumph, the Intercollegiate Football championship in 1931.
Also in: Canada's Sports Hall of Fame.

BRIGHT, John
Player
All-American 1951; Eddie James Memorial Trophy four times; Schenley Award 1959; WIFO All-Star seven times; all-around athlete; holds over 20 sports records at Drake Univ. in football, pole vaulting and high jump; graduated from Drake 1951; degree in education 1958; played professional basketball with Harlem Globetrotters; pitched a no-hit game in World Professional Fastball Tournament.

1948 – 1951 Drake University, fullback
1952 – 1953 Calgary, fullback
1954 – 1964 Edmonton Eskimos, fullback

An All-American at Drake University in 1951, and a first-round draft choice of the Philadelphia Eagles, Johnny Bright was part of the most dynamic backfield in Canadian football in the mid-fifties. At Drake, he played 25 games with 40 touchdowns, 240 points and a 9.6 average points per game and accumulated numerous records. With 1950 yds. in 1949 and 2400 yds. in 1950, Bright was major college total-offense leader. Season records included: passing yards per attempt, 9.3 yds; rushing yards per carry, 6.7 yds; and pass completion percentage, .591. During his football career at Drake he was first in total-offense yards, 5903 yds, and total-offense yards per play with 7.16; he was second in rushing yards, 3134 yds, and in rushing yards per carry, 6.1 yds. In 1952 he won the league rushing title with Calgary, then teamed up with Hall of Famers Normie Kwong and Jackie Parker to guide the Eskimos to three consecutive Grey Cups. Bright carried for 1679 yds. in 1957 while Kwong carried for 1050 yds, and the two of them set a backfield rushing record unmatched by any pair of runners in any league. Bright set a new rushing record in 1958, carrying the ball 296 times for a monumental 1722 yds. As a fullback for most of his 13 seasons, he gained 10,909 yds, second highest career mark in the Canadian Football League history.

BROWN, D. "Wes"
Builder
Admired and respected by colleagues from coast to coast in Canada, Wes Brown devoted his entire life to the development of football. He served as director, treasurer and secretary of the Ottawa Football Club and as secretary of the Interprovincial Union. In 1948 he became a permanent secretary of the Eastern Division of the Canadian Football League, a position he held until his death in 1962. He offered football exceptional service in many capacities for more than 40 years and was specially honored with a Grey Cup Dinner plaque, reserved for the most unselfish contributors to Canadian football.

CASEY, Thomas "Citation"
Player
Born July 30, 1924, in Wellsville, Ohio; football at Westinghouse Memorial High School in Wilmerding, Pa, 1939 – 1942, entered Hampton Institute on academic scholarship 1942, degree and highest honors 1948; served with U.S. Navy as hospital corpsman 1944 – 1946; College All-American, All-Conference, and Most Valuable Player; Eddie James Memorial Trophy 1950; All-Canadian four times; All-Western six times; honor student in medicine at Univ. Man; after one year of graduate work at Winnipeg General Hospital went to England to study neurology; later established practice in Cleveland, Ohio.

1942 – 1943 Hampton Institute, halfback
1946 – 1947 Hampton Institute, halfback
1948 – 1949 New York Yankees, All-American Football Conference, back
1949 Hamilton Wildcats, halfback
1950 – 1955 Winnipeg Blue Bombers, back

As a college player, Tom Casey was named to the All-Conference team for four years and was a Black All-American and Most Valuable Player in his last two years at Hampton Institute. Casey joined the Yankees to set a conference record for the longest punt return, but was cut from the team near the end of 1949 and joined the Hamilton Tigers. As a Blue Bomber for six seasons, Casey was named All-Western six times, All-Canadian four times and was the Western Conference rushing leader in 1950. After earning a degree in medicine at the University of Manitoba, he retired at the end of the 1955 season. One of the finest halfbacks of his time, and tremendously popular with players and fans alike, Casey was later to earn high acclaim in the field of medicine.

CHIPMAN, Arthur U.
Builder

1936 – 1948 Winnipeg Football Club, committee chairmen, vice president and president
1949 Western Interprovincial Rugby Union, president
1952 Canadian Rugby Union, president

Arthur Chipman joined the executive branch of the Winnipeg Football Club in 1936 to serve as chairman of various committees, vice-president and eventually president in 1945. Through his efforts, the club reached a position of stability and security and was operated on a businesslike basis, very unusual for an athletic group. As president of the Western Interprovincial Rugby Union and the Canadian Rugby Union, he was largely responsible for bringing East and West football together and for keeping football in operation during the war years. With each organization Chipman left a legacy of financial security and development.

CONACHER, Lionel Pretoria
Player

Born May 24, 1901, in Toronto, Ont; grew up in tough Davenport Road area in Toronto; father a teamster with ten children; brother Charlie member of Hockey and International Hockey Halls of Fame; other family members outstanding in softball and track; attended Ketchum Public Schools; dropped out after eighth grade to work; at 16 won Ontario 125-lbs. wrestling championship; at 20 entered and won his first competitive bout, Canadian light-heavyweight championship; several rounds in exhibition match against Jack Dempsey; lacrosse with Toronto Maitlands, winning Ontario Amateur Lacrosse League championship 1922; offered place on Canada's 1924 Olympic discus team; played on Toronto Maple Leafs baseball team, winning Triple A championship 1926; hockey with Pittsburgh Pirates, New York Americans, Montreal Maroons and Chicago Black Hawks; on Stanley Cup-winning team with Chicago in 1934 and Montreal in 1935; at one time played professionally in five different sports; Canadian Press Poll Greatest All-Around Athlete 1900 – 1950; member of Parliament for Trinity riding in Toronto 1937; elected to House of Commons 1949; promoted government aid for community parks in poorer sections of the city; son Lionel, Jr, fullback star for Western Univ; son Brian winger for Father Bauer's national team and author of *Hockey in Canada: The Way It Is*; died 1954 of a heart attack during a softball game between members of Parliament and parliamentary press gallery.

1920 Torontos, Ontario Rugby Football Union
1921 – 1922 Toronto Argonauts, fullback
1923 Bellefonte Academy

Called the "Big Train" after Hall of Famer Smirle Lawson, Lionel Conacher was named Canada's greatest all-around athlete and football player of the 1900 – 1950 era by a Canadian Press poll. Conacher began playing football at the age of 12 in the Toronto City Rugby League and was middle wing for the Toronto Central Y when they won the Ontario championship in 1918. In 1920 he was on the senior team in the Ontario championship semifinals against the Argos, which he joined the next year. He led them to an undefeated season, scoring 15 points in the Grey Cup final win over Edmonton, an individual record unmatched until 1938 when Red Storey tied it. In the days before the forward pass, the emphasis was on kicking, running the ends and evading tacklers. Conacher was a good kicker and fast runner, gaining 120 yds. against Ottawa in three downs and 227 yds. against Montreal in 1922. One of the foremost coaches in America, Carl Snavely of Cornell, said of Conacher: "He was probably the greatest athlete that I have ever coached in football or in any other form of athletics. . . . I don't believe I have ever had a fullback who was a better runner in an open field, or who was a better punter, or who so fully possessed all of the qualities of speed, skill, dexterity, aggressiveness and self-control. . . ."
Also in: Canada's Sports Hall of Fame and Canadian Lacrosse Hall of Fame.

COX, Ernest
Player

Jeff Russel Memorial Trophy 1928; League and Canadian All-Star many times.

1919 Hamilton Rowing Club
1920 – 1935 Hamilton Tigers, center

Ernest Cox learned to play football on the sandlots of Hamilton, served in W.W. I until 1919, then launched a career that spanned 16 seasons, one with Hamilton Rowing Club, the rest with the Tigers. Many times selected league and All-Canadian All-Star, Cox was acknowledged as the greatest center in Canadian football in the late twenties. He was a member of the Tigers' Grey Cup champions 1928 – 1930, and played on the Hamilton Eastern finalist teams against Balmy Beach in 1927 and 1930. Under coach and Hall of Famer Mike Rodden, Cox was responsible for the introduction of the cross-field direct snap to halfbacks, two of which led to touchdowns in Grey Cup games. Upon retirement, Cox wistfully concluded, "the way football was now being conducted, it seemed like you needed roller skates to play the game."
Also in: Canada's Sports Hall of Fame.

CRAIG, Ross Brown "Husky"
Player

Born July 1, 1884, in Peterborough, Ont; three years of service in W.W. I.

1906 – 1909 Dundas Intermediates, lineman
1909 – 1910 Hamilton Rowing Club, lineman
1911 – 1912 Hamilton Alerts, lineman
1913 – 1920 Hamilton Tigers, lineman

Between 1906 and 1920, Husky Craig became the greatest line-plunging ball-carrier of his day. He began his football career in Peterborough and played with Dundas Intermediates, Hamilton Rowing Club, Hamilton Alerts and the Hamilton Tigers. A leader on the Ontario Rugby Football Union championship teams, Craig was also a Grey Cup figure with the Alerts in 1912 and the Tigers in 1913. Particularly memorable was the 1913 Grey Cup

final in which Craig scored 15 points on three touchdowns, a single-game record that stood for over 40 years; it was later tied in 1921 by Hall of Famer Lionel Conacher and in 1938 by "Red" Storey, and beaten by Hall of Famer Jackie Parker in 1956 and Jim Van Pelt in 1958. In the days when play offered a minimum amount of running room, Craig's fast starts from one or two steps made him a consistent scorer for his teams.
Also in: Canada's Sports Hall of Fame.

CRONIN, Carl

Player

Born in Chicago, Ill; graduated from Univ. Notre Dame 1932; resides in Chicago.

1932-1933 Winnipeg, linebacker, coach
1935-1940 Calgary Bronks (Stampeders), coach

After an outstanding high school career as quarterback, and despite his small size, 5 ft. 9 in, 170 lbs, Carl Cronin made Knute Rockne's Notre Dame team. He played on two national championship teams as a defensive back, reserve quarterback behind Frank Carideo and field-goal specialist. He was one of the last dropkickers of major college football. After graduating from Notre Dame, Cronin became the first American import brought into Winnipeg to help win the Grey Cup and sell football as a major sport. As a playing coach with Hall of Famers Gred Kabat and Russ Rebholz, Cronin was a leader both on and off the field. He molded nondescript rookies into a formidable football club through drilling in fundamentals, his forte. As a player he was a fine field general, a superb passer and a vicious linebacker. Winnipeg proved the West to be formidable competition for Hall of Famer Lew Hayman's Argonauts in the Grey Cup of 1933. Through a mix-up Cronin lost the job as Hamilton's Coach in 1934, but accepted the head coaching job with the Calgary Bronks (now the Stampeders) in the spring of 1935. In five years he established Calgary as a major force in football, playing the kind of tough game he himself was noted for.

CUTLER, Wesley

Player

Born February 17, 1911, in Toronto, Ont; graduated from Univ. Toronto 1932, placing first in class honors; Canadian Press All-Star team 1933-1938; Jeff Russel Memorial Trophy 1938; died June 10, 1956; survived by wife Katharine.

1927-1928 Oakwood Collegiate Institute
1929-1932 University of Toronto
1933-1938 Toronto Argonauts, end

A native of Toronto, Wes Cutler played his first football with Oakwood Collegiate Institute, then entered the University of Toronto in 1929 where he helped the Varsity team to the Intercollegiate Union championship in 1932 and graduated with the varsity bronze "T," the highest athletic award in the university. In 1931, as a member of the Varsity Ontario Rugby Football Union, Toronto came close to upsetting the Hamilton Tigers in a memorable Eastern final. As a fine blocker, deadly tackler and an exceptional pass receiver, Cutler helped the Argos to Grey Cup victories in 1933, 1937 and 1938 and captained the team in 1936. Without a doubt, Wes Cutler was one of the finest players in the years just preceding the modern era.
Also in: Canada's Sports Hall of Fame.

DAVIES, Dr. Andrew P.

Builder

Native of Ottawa, Ont; graduated from McGill Univ; died 1956.

1915-1948 Ottawa Football Club, player, officer, physician
1928 Ottawa Football Club, president
1937 Big Four Union, president
1940 Canadian Rugby Union, president

Andy Davies played college football at McGill, then returned to his hometown to serve as an outstanding player for the Rough Riders. From 1915 until 1948 he made many contributions to the Ottawa club as a player, officer of the club and club physician. Following his playing career, he became an executive member of the Ottawa club, and coached the Riders in the Big Four in the late twenties. He was president of the Ottawa club in 1928 and in 1937 was named president of the Big Four Union. In 1940 he served as president of the Canadian Rugby Union. In recognition of his enviable record of service to the game Dr. Davies was honored by the Grey Cup Dinner.

DeGRUCHY, John

Builder

Since before the turn of the century, amateur sports promoter John DeGruchy has been connected with football in various capacities, first with the old Toronto Athletic Club and later with the Toronto Rugby and Athletic Association. He was president of the Ontario Rugby Football Union in 1925, 1930 and 1935, and was again in office as vice president when he died in 1940. He not only instituted the Toronto city title series among the Argonauts, Varsity and Balmy Beach, but also donated the Reg DeGruchy Memorial Trophy for the series. This trophy was in memory of his son Reg, who with another son, Hal, served as outstanding referees after long and brilliant playing service. Largely responsible for the development of six-man football in Ontario schools, he also promoted the annual Thanksgiving Day classic between Sarnia and Balmy Beach.
Also in: Canada's Sports Hall of Fame.

DuMOULIN, Septimus Stuart "Seppi"

Builder

Alderman, controller and a candidate for the mayoralty in Hamilton, Ont; awarded Coronation Medal by King George VI 1937.

"My warmest memories are of football and my associations in the great game; my friendships with teammates and opposing players alike—great and thrilling moments with fine athletes and outstanding sportsmen." Probably one of the earliest players in the Hall of Fame, Seppi DuMoulin was devoted to the game for almost seventy years. From Trinity College Schools, Port Hope, to the Hamilton Tigers as an exceptional kicking backfielder 1894-1906, DuMoulin's playing career included a record of having played for no fewer than six Canadian championship teams. The 1904 Tiger team scored a staggering 349 points in eight games and had only 47 points scored against them. As captain in 1906 DuMoulin led the team to the Dominion Championship. As a Builder he held the unique distinction of being the only man in Canadian football to hold chief offices in the Interprovincial Union (also chairman of the board of governors), the Ontario

Rugby Union and the Western Rugby Union. He was president of the Hamilton Tiger Football Club, honorary coach of the Hamilton Tigers and of the Winnipeg Football Club. When he moved west, DuMoulin became a prime mover in the formation of the Saskatchewan Football League and the Western Interprovincial Union and was responsible for pioneering numerous beneficial rule changes and operational procedures in the Canadian game. DuMoulin was honored in 1954 at the Grey Cup Dinner as one of Canada's most outstanding players.

ELIOWITZ, Abe
Player
Jeff Russel Memorial Trophy 1935; All-Star 1934–1937.

1933–1935 Ottawa Rough Riders, flying wing, halfback
1936–1937 Montreal, flying wing, halfback

Abe Eliowitz, a former Michigan State star, joined the Ottawa Rough Riders in 1933 and immediately established himself as an outstanding left-handed passer and kicker. In 1934 and 1935 he made the All-Star team as a flying wing and a halfback, and was leading scorer in 1935 with 62 points. He then moved on to Montreal where he again was an All-Star in 1936 and 1937 as flying wing and halfback. Eliowitz left Canadian football at his peak to accept a high school coaching berth in Detroit, but his name is firmly impressed upon Canadian fans and in the interprovincial records.

EMERSON, E. K. "Eddie"
Player
Born March 11, 1892, in Cordile, Ga; presently on the Ottawa Club executive.

1912 Ottawa College, center
1913–1915 Ottawa Rough Riders, fullback, linebacker
1919–1937 Ottawa Rough Riders, fullback, linebacker

The distinction of having served one club as a player for 26 seasons belongs to the "Iron Man" of football, Ottawa's Eddie Emerson. A native of Georgia, he moved to Ottawa in 1909 and began playing for the Rough Riders three years later as a center. In 1913 when Ottawa College and the Ottawa Rough Riders joined forces, Eddie moved to the flying wing position (fullback in the early football days) and doubled as a linebacker which was sometimes necessary in the days of 18-man football. Emerson helped Ottawa to two Grey Cup titles along the way, and was twice nominated for the Jeff Russel Memorial Trophy. He became president of the Rough Riders in 1930–1931 and again from 1947–1951; he has been a member of the Ottawa Club executive for more than 40 years. In addition, he was a member of the Interprovincial Union executive for more than 25 years, and served also as secretary and as president 1948–1949. For his extended service to Canadian football, Emerson was honored with a Grey Cup Dinner award by the citizens of Ottawa.
Also in: Canada's Sports Hall of Fame.

ETCHEVERRY, Sam
Player
Born in Carlsbad, N. Mex; graduated from Univ. Denver; Schenley Award 1954; Jeff Russel Memorial Trophy 1954 and 1958.

1952–1960 Montreal Alouettes, quarterback
1965 Montreal Alouettes, assistant coach, head coach

Sam Etcheverry played at the University of Denver before being brought to Montreal in 1952 by "Peahead" Walker. He was the star of the Alouette powerhouse of the fifties and led his team to Eastern championships 1954–1956. Leaving Montreal in 1961 to play for the St. Louis Cardinals of the National Football League, he later returned to the Alouettes in the mid-sixties as an assistant to coach Jim Trimble. As head coach in 1970, he led Montreal to the Grey Cup title in just six months. As "The Rifle," he is still second on the all-time passing lists, in spite of the fact that passing records were not kept until the beginning of his third season. In seven years of recorded statistics he passed for 25,582 yds, completing 1630 out of 2530 passes thrown for a .567 average and 174 touchdowns. The Rifle will live on as a legend in Canadian professional football.

FEAR, A. H. "Cap"
Player
Born June 11, 1901, in Gloucestershire, England; arrived in Canada 1911; runner-up welterweight boxing champion of Canada; stroked for Toronto Argonaut 150-lb. crew in Henley Regatta; played hockey with Hall of Famer Lionel Conacher; Eastern Canadian All-Star team six times.

1919–1926 Toronto Argonauts, outside wing
1927 Montreal Amateur Athletic Association, outside wing
1928–1932 Hamilton Tigers, outside wing

Cap Fear first played football with Toronto Central YMCA's junior team and moved up to the Toronto Argonauts, playing his first game against Hamilton in 1919. Starring with the Argos, he helped them win three Big Four championships and one Grey Cup. Fear moved to Montreal in 1927 and played two games for the old Montreal Amateur Athletic Association club, then transferred to Hamilton. There he played with the Tigers who won three Big Four championships and two Grey Cups.
Also in: Canada's Sports Hall of Fame.

FERRARO, John F.
Player
Born in Buffalo, N.Y; sandlot football, baseball and basketball; at Masten Park High 1924–1928, captain of his senior football team, captain all-high football; letters in football, basketball, baseball; Cook Academy, Montour Falls, N.Y. 1929–1930, letters in football (undefeated team), basketball, baseball; Cornell University 1930–1934, freshman basketball, football, varsity football 1931–1934; captain in 1933; honorable mention as All-American 1931–1933; Best Forward Passer Award 1933; Ormond Beach Trophy and Imperial Oil Trophy as Most Outstanding Player 1938; All-League and All-Canada seven years.

1934 Hamilton Tigers, player-coach
1935 Hamilton Tigers, player
1936–1937 Montreal Football Club, player-coach
1938 Montreal Nationals, Ontario Rugby Football Union, player
1939–1940 Montreal Football Club, player

One of the finest players of any time, John Ferraro came from a brilliant career at Cornell to star in Canada as a player and coach for seven years. He was All-League and All-Canada every one of those years, and was selected to Lew Hayman's Ten-Year All-Canadian Team for the thirties. He was outstanding in every aspect of play as quarterback, fullback, punter, placekicker and coach, and was almost unequaled in his defensive ability and his ability to bring out the best in his teammates.

FOULDS, William C.
Player-Builder

1909–1910 University of Toronto, quarterback
1911 Toronto Argonauts, coach
1914 Toronto Argonauts, coach
1921–1954 Canadian Rugby Union, president, referee, committee chairman

A quarterback with the Grey Cup champions of 1909 with Hall of Famers Hugh Gall and Smirle Lawson, Billy Foulds later coached the Grey Cup-bound Toronto Argonauts in 1911 and 1914. He became one of the best-known football figures in Canada, mainly through his executive talents and his service on rules committees. As president of the Canadian Rugby Union he put up his own $4000 to establish the East-West final for the Dominion Championship. For more than 30 years, until his death in 1954, Foulds served the Canadian Rugby Union as president, referee-in-chief and as the original chairman of the rules committee.

GEORGE, Albert Henry
Builder

Born 1851; fourth Earl Grey; largely responsible for success of Quebec tercentenary celebrations 1908; suggested battlefield of the Plains of Abraham be presented as national park.

After serving two years as Administrator of Rhodesia, 1896–1897, Lord Grey was appointed Governor General of Canada on December 10, 1904. Throughout his career he worked diligently for imperial unity. In 1909 he donated the Lord Earl Grey Cup as a trophy for the amateur rugby football championship of Canada. Not until 1921, when the West began to compete for the Dominion Championship, did the significance of this trophy prove to be one of imperial unity. Vast distances divided the West and the Eastern Maritimes, Ontario and Quebec. Differences in rules made interleague play difficult and a short season only complicated matters. But all these hurdles were overcome when East and West clashed on the gridiron for football supremacy. Despite the wishes of its donor, the Grey Cup was never to be a trophy for amateur sports; Lord Grey was an immensely popular man, but he abhorred professionalism. Over the years, his $48 trophy has brought a sense of national unity to a country of cultural and geographic differences, and carries a more lasting significance than its donor could ever realize.

GALL, Hugh
Player

1908–1912 Univ. of Toronto, kicking halfback

With Hall of Famers Smirle Lawson and Billy Foulds, Hugh Gall and the University of Toronto became the first champions of the Grey Cup in 1909 in a game against Parkdale. Noted for his outstanding play under the most severe and adverse circumstances, he reportedly could punt 70 yds. with either foot, even though he weighed only 160 lbs. When the University of Toronto was victorious over Hamilton in the 1910 Grey Cup, the game was so popular that ticket scalpers could have sold tickets for as much as $100 apiece. Gall played halfback for Toronto 1908–1912, then went on to coaching and served as president and referee for the Canadian Rugby Union. As a referee Gall made an unfortunate error in the semifinal game between the Ontario Rugby Football Union Torontos and the Big Four Argonauts in 1920 with the result that the second half of their game had to be replayed the following week.
Also in: Canada's Sports Hall of Fame.

GOLAB, Tony
Player

Attended Port Huron College 1938; Big Four All-Star team 1939–1941; Jeff Russel Memorial Trophy 1941; served overseas in W.W. II with Royal Canadian Air Force as fighter pilot; shot down over Cassino, Italy, January 1944; suffered serious shrapnel wounds in arms and legs.

1938 Sarnia Imperials, halfback
1939–1941 Ottawa Rough Riders, halfback
1945–1951 Ottawa Rough Riders, halfback

Following an all-star career at Kennedy Collegiate, Tony Golab began playing for the great Sarnia Imperials. Joining the Ottawa Rough Riders in 1939, the tall, handsome, blond halfback became known as the "Golden Boy" of Canadian football and played a key role in the Riders' Eastern championships of 1939 and 1941 and the Grey Cup victory of 1940. Following injuries in the war, it appeared that Golab's gridiron career was at an end, but, to the amazement of most people, he returned to the field to star with the Rough Riders until 1951.
Also in: Canada's Sports Hall of Fame.

GRIFFING, Dean
Player

Graduate of Kansas State Univ; All-Canadian Center three times.

1936–1947 Regina Rough Riders, center, playing coach
1954–1956 Regina Rough Riders, manager

After a college career at Kansas State and a stint with the Chicago Cardinals, Dean Griffing joined the Regina Rough Riders in 1936 and helped them to a Western championship that same year. Unfortunately, several "imports" from the United States who were on the team were ruled ineligible by the Canadian Rugby Union, so club managers Al Ritchie and "Piffles" Taylor decided to forfeit their chance at the Grey Cup rather than play without Griffing and the other men. Griffing was a three-time All-Canadian center, a team leader for the Rough Riders and a rugged, hard-hitting player who excelled at intimidating and antagonizing his opponents. After an outstanding playing career, he retired in 1947 to help reorganize football in Calgary. When he returned to Regina in 1954 he managed the Rough Riders, then joined the Denver Broncos of the American Football League as a manager for a short time. During his years in the Canadian game, he spearheaded many outstanding teams, played exciting and daring football and served as one of the most valuable contributors to the game in Western Canada.

GRIFFITH, Dr. Harry Crawford

Builder

Attended Ridley College and Trinity College Schools.

1899 – 1907 Ridley College, coach
1908 – 1910 University of Toronto, coach
1911 – 1949 Ridley College, coach

An exceptional contributor to Canadian football for over 50 years, Harry Griffith was the coach of the first official Grey Cup champions, the University of Toronto. Hall of Famers Smirle Lawson, Hugh Gall and Billy Foulds were a part of that victory. Griffith was a significant Builder in the formative years of Canadian football, coaching Ridley College and later the Toronto Varsity, who won the Canadian championship twice. He possessed a special ability to impart his knowledge of football to his young players and get them to work together as a team. Noted for his development of 60-minute teams, he also stressed conditioning to prevent injuries on the field. He was innovative in rule changes and new coaching techniques, although he opposed Frank Shaughnessy's Americanization of Canadian football, involving tactics and trick plays. One of Canada's most gifted educators, Dr. Griffith served with distinction in the Canadian Rugby Union as president and as a member of the rules committee.
Also in: Canada's Sports Hall of Fame.

HALTER, G. Sydney

Builder

Born April 18, 1905, in Winnipeg, Man; graduated from Manitoba Law School as a Gold Medalist 1924; admitted to Manitoba Bar 1927; appointed to King's Council 1947; served in W.W. II as senior judicial officer in Royal Canadian Air Force, earning rank of squadron leader.

1934 – 1953 Winnipeg Blue Bombers, executive member
1935 Winnipeg Blue Bombers, treasurer
1942 Winnipeg Blue Bombers, president
1952 Winnipeg Interprovincial Football Union, deputy commissioner
1953 Winnipeg Interprovincial Football Union, commissioner
1957 – 1966 Canada's National Football Commissioner

Sydney Halter first became involved in Winnipeg sports when he helped Joe Ryan and Frank Hannibal reorganize the Blue Bombers in 1934. As commissioner of the Winnipeg Interprovincial Football Union, he was instrumental in the negotiations that led in 1956 to the merging of the Winnipeg Interprovincial Football Union into the Canadian Football Council with two conferences, the Eastern and Western. As registrar of the council, it was Halter's responsibility to maintain a negotiation list so that the conferences would not bid against each other for American players. The first step in the formation of the present Canadian Football League, the only national professional sports organization in Canada, was taken in 1957 when Halter became the National Football Commissioner. Since that time, Canadian football has grown and matured under his leadership.
Also in: Canada's Sports Hall of Fame and Canadian Amateur Athletic Hall of Fame.

HANNIBAL, Frank J.

Builder

Born in Bristol, England; moved to Canada at age nine; served overseas rising to rank of Major during W.W. I.

Frank Hannibal was completely dedicated to football. His tremendous zeal, unceasing effort and inspired leadership contributed considerably to the building of Western football's present eminent state. Arriving in Winnipeg in 1934, he lifted the status of football almost instantly upon being elected vice president of the Winnipeg Rugby Football Club. He recruited an executive and fired it with determination to build a Grey Cup contender and, in one year, his efforts were rewarded when he saw the Bombers defeat Hamilton Tigers, in Hamilton, for the first Grey Cup championship ever taken by a Western club. Hannibal was president of the Winnipeg Club four times and president of the Western Interprovincial Football Union. For a period of nearly 30 years he held many offices, standing as one of the great Builders of Western Canada Football.

HANSON, Fritz

Player

Hanson was one of the American imports who turned Winnipeg into a powerhouse in the mid-thirties. His speed more than compensated for his small size, and he was a dangerous broken-field runner. He led the 1935 Bombers to an upset Grey Cup victory, the first ever for a Western team, over Hamilton, piling up over 300 yds. on 7 punt returns on a muddy field. His 78-yd. touchdown run late in the game gave Winnipeg the margin of victory as they won 18 – 12. Said a weary and dejected Hamilton player after the game, "Sure, Winnipeg won the Grey Cup. But they had to send a greyhound to fetch it!" Hanson played with the Blue Bombers 1935 – 1945 and his presence lent new excitement to football in Western Canada and helped to bring Eastern dominance to an end.

ISBISTER, Robert, Sr.

Player

A native Hamiltonian; relived his football days in the careers of four sons: Bob, Jr, of Toronto Varsity and Hamilton Tigers' fame, Allan, Phillip and Donald, all outstanding high school stars.

Robert Isbister is considered one of the greats of Hamilton. He came out of the Hamilton City League in 1905 to begin a long career with the famous Hamilton Tigers. Earning fame for his all-round ability, his great defensive qualities, and his sportsmanship, he served with the Tigers from 1906 to 1919 as flying wing (fullback) and lineman. After retirement he went back to help his team in the difficult 1919 season, then took up refereeing in the Interprovincial and Intercollegiate Unions. Bob was president of the Big Four in 1920 and in 1933 a member of the board of governors of the Hamilton Club.
Also in: Canada's Sports Hall of Fame.

JACKSON, Russ

Player

Born July 28, 1936, in Hamilton, Ont; attended McMaster Univ, won all conference honours in both football and basketball; declined nomination for Rhodes Scholarship in graduating year; Schenley Award Outstanding Canadian 1959, 1963, 1966 and 1969; Jeff Russel Memorial Trophy 1959 and 1969; Schenley Award Most Outstanding Player 1963, 1966 and 1969; Ontario's Outstanding Athlete; Canada's Outstanding Male Athlete; Leading Passer in the East; All-Canadian All-Star at Quarterback; second leading passer in CFL history.

Russ Jackson was drafted by Ottawa Rough Riders in 1958. He played exclusively for Ottawa Rough Riders from 1958 through 1969. In 1959, his second year in the pro ranks, he won the first-string quarterback job. An exceptional quarterback, he led the Riders into the playoffs every year he played, winning the Grey Cup championship three times. Playing 12 years with the Riders, never missing a game, he rushed for 5045 yds. averaging 6.8 yds. per carry; passed for 24,593 yds. with a completion average of .524, scoring 185 touchdowns. Russ Jackson was described by Eddie MacCabe as perhaps the last of a vanishing breed — the Canadian Quarterback.
Also in: Canada's Sports Hall of Fame.

JACOBS, Jack "Indian Jack"
Player
Born 1921 in Holdenville, Okla; moved to Winnipeg 1950; Jeff Nicklin Memorial Trophy and most Valuable Player 1952; All-American Team 1950; also excelled in baseball and basketball; amateur golf champion of Manitoba; died January 12, 1974.

A native of Holdenville, Okla, Jacobs played service football and played for a short time with Cleveland, Washington and Green Bay Packers of the NFL before coming to Winnipeg in 1950, where he was an overnight sensation. He led the Bombers to an impressive 10–4 record in his first year. In 1953 he led the Bombers to the Grey Cup final, where they bowed to Hamilton 12–6 in spite of Jacobs' 28 for 46 passing performance for 326 yds. During a decade of outstanding leadership at Winnipeg, he rewrote the passing records for Western Canada, completing 700 passes on 1330 attempts for 11,094 yds. and 104 touchdowns, while kicking 57 singles. Later Jacobs went on to coach the London Lords and was assistant coach with Hamilton, Montreal and Edmonton. Jack Jacobs remained involved with football for a period of 22 years. A brilliant passer, he lifted Western football into new prestige, created more interest in the game and won practically every individual honor open to a player.

JAMES, Eddie "Dynamite"
Player
One of the great veterans of Western Canadian Football, Eddie James starred with Winnipeg, the Regina Pats, Winnipeg St. Johns and the Regina Rough Riders through the 1920s and the early 1930s. He was a great plunging back and a devastating force as a sixty-minute man who was equally at home on either defense or offense. Eddie played a big part in building a firm foundation for Western football in the difficult early times. Dynamite Eddie was regarded as one of the hard rocks of the game when football brought hard knocks but little glory. With records lacking, contemporaries recall him as a great all-round player with outstanding scoring ability and the faculty of making friends with players and fans alike. Eddie was the father of Winnipeg's famous Gerry James who became an outstanding fullback with the Winnipeg Blue Bombers.
Also in: Canada's Sports Hall of Fame.

KABAT, Greg
Player
Attended Univ. Wis.

1933–1940 Winnipeg Blue Bombers, player-coach
1933–1940 St. Paul's High School, coach
1941 Vancouver Grizzlies, coach

One of the first imports into Canadian football and a key figure on the great Winnipeg teams of the thirties, Kabat joined the Bombers in 1933 out of the University of Wisconsin. He immediately became a player-coach, serving 5 positions, quarterback, fullback, wing, guard and placekicker, when necessary. A fierce competitor and outstanding blocker, Kabat was also the heart of the Winnipeg defense. In the 1938 Grey Cup final, made memorable by the great work of Argos' "Red" Storey, Kabat played the entire game with a broken toe. The collapse of the Bombers' defense in the second half was probably due to Coach Threlfall's being unaware that his field leader was injured. After retirement Kabat coached the Vancouver Grizzlies in 1941 and served in many capacities with that club during its brief life. During his stay in Winnipeg, he coached St. Paul's High School through eight outstanding seasons. Kabat later returned to the United States where he went back to teaching and coaching high school football in the Los Angeles area.

KROL, Joe "King"
Player
Canada's Outstanding Athlete 1946 and 1947; Jeff Russel Memorial Trophy 1946; Lou Marsh Trophy 1948.

1939–1942 University of Western Ontario, quarterback
1943–1944 Hamilton Wildcats, quarterback
1945–1953 Toronto Argonauts, quarterback

Krol played on championship teams at Kennedy Collegiate in Windsor and at Western Ontario before joining the Hamilton Wildcats, helping them to the Canadian final in 1943. Joining Teddy Morris' Toronto Argonauts in 1945, Joe led them to a string of three straight Grey Cup victories. He would become one of Argos' best-loved stars and play in five Grey Cup championships before retiring. Perhaps his greatest clutch performance came in the 1947 Grey Cup when he threw a touchdown pass and kicked four singles to lead the Argos to lead the Argos to a come-from-behind 10–9 victory over Winnipeg. He holds the Grey Cup record of 30 points scored in career Grey Cup play 1952; Krol also quarterbacked Toronto to the Dominion Championship in 1950 and 1952.
Also in: Canada's Sports Hall of Fame.

KWONG, Norm
Player
Rushing Titles two times; All-Star Team five times; Schenley Award for Outstanding Canadian 1955 and 1956; Canada's Athlete of the Year 1955.

In fourteen seasons with Calgary and Edmonton, the "China Clipper" established himself as one of the greatest running backs in Canadian football history. The powerful Edmonton backfield of Kwong and Johhny Bright led the Eskimos to three straight Grey Cup victories, 1954, 1955 and 1956. In eleven years of recorded statistics, Kwong gained 9022 yds. on 1735 carries for a phenominal 5.2 yds. per carry. He ranks third on the all-time rushing lists. Kwong has regaled crowds as an outstanding after-dinner speaker of fluency and pungent wit in his post-playing days.
Also in: Canada's Sports Hall of Fame.

LAWSON, Smirle
Player
Graduate of Univ. Toronto; service during W.W. I; Ontario's chief coroner 1937–1951.

Dr. Smirle Lawson, the original "Big Train," rose to lasting stardom with the University of Toronto's great prewar teams. In 1909 and 1910 Lawson, along with teammates Al Ritchie, Jack Newton, Hughie Gall and Billy Foulds and coached by Harry Griffith, led the Varsity Blues to the Canadian championship. Varsity was the first team to oficially win the Grey Cup in 1909. After graduation the great plunging halfback went on to captain the Big Four Argonauts to some of their finest seasons before breaking off his football career to serve overseas. Smirle Lawson was honored in 1959 at the Annual Sports Celebrities Dinner in Toronto, where he was cheered as one of the truly all-time greats in Canadian football.
Also in: Canada's Sports Hall of Fame.

LEADLAY, Frank "Pep"
Player
Graduated from Hamilton Central Collegiate 1914; served overseas in W.W. I 1916–1918; attended Queen's Univ. four years.

1919–1920 Hamilton Tigers, back
1921–1925 Queen's University, back, captain
1926–1930 Hamilton Tigers, back, captain

Frank Leadlay played with the Hamilton Tigers Intermediate, Canadian champions of 1915, before going overseas. He entered Queen's University in 1921 with a wealth of football experience, having played with the Hamilton Tigers in the Interprovincial Union in 1919 and 1920. He helped Queen's win five Intercollegiate championships and three successive Grey Cups. Leadlay starred in Queen's 54–0 Grey Cup triumph over Regina in 1923, when the larger and tougher Regina team members put dollars bills in their hats for the first man to draw blood and the lineman planted his fist in the face of the man over him on the last play of the game. The 1924 Grey Cup was the last for university football. Leadlay then rejoined the Hamilton Tigers in 1926 and remained with them until 1930, leading them to four Interprovincial titles and two more Grey Cups. Pep kicked 9 points in a single Grey Cup Game and had a total of 23 scoring points in six Grey Cups with 12 converts and 11 singles on punts. A leader in captaining both the Tigers and Queen's, he later became a member of the Canadian Intercollegiate Union rules commission and the Canadian Rugby Union rules committee.
Also in: Canada's Sports Hall of Fame.

LEWIS, Leo
Player
Born in Des Moines, Iowa; went to high school in St. Paul, Minn; furthered his education at Lincoln College in Mo; All-Star six times; All-Time Kickoff Return Record (5444 yds. on 187 returns); following retirement from football, went back to school for training as veterinarian; served as head coach at Lincoln Univ.

Leo Lewis was discovered by a Winnipeg sportswriter who heard talk about a halfback who was burning up the league for Lincoln University. The sportswriter, Hal Sigurdson, advised Bill Biovin, then manager of the Bombers', who called Lewis. Leo Lewis joined the Bombers in 1955. The record-breaking, six-time all-star stayed to spend 11 seasons with the Blue Bombers, scoring 450 points, and ran for 48 touchdowns, catching passes for 26 of those. Still number four in the all-time book, "The Lincoln Locomotive" rushed for 8861 yds. averaging 6.6 yds. per carry. He made the 1000-yd. club twice and in pass receiving caught the ball 234 times averaging 18.2 yds. Leo was honored by Winnipeg fans at a "night" when he retired, and went back to school for more training.

LIEBERMAN, Moe
Builder
Born June 16, 1891, in Toronto, Ont; attended high school in Kingston, Ont, playing football, hockey and baseball for his school teams; attended Univ. of Alberta; CFL Award for Outstanding Contributions to Football.

1919–1921 Edmonton Eskimos, quarterback
1922 Edmonton Eskimos, manager
1949–1957 Edmonton Eskimos, member board of directors
1955–1956 Edmonton Eskimos, president

Active in football for almost 60 years as player, manager, official and executive, Moe Lieberman came West in 1912 and played quarterback for the University of Alberta in 1915 earning a Block A Award. He joined the Edmonton Eskimos as a player in 1919 and continued as quarterback until injuries forced him to retire his playing career in 1921. As a result of his efforts, sufficient money was raised to finance the first Western challenge for the Grey Cup between Toronto and Edmonton. Moe became manager of the Eskimos in 1922 and continued his interest in football for many years, acting as an official in Western Canada. He also took part in the organizational aspect of the game as a president of the Western Canada Rugby Football Union and vice president of the Edmonton Eskimos Organization. From 1949 to 1957 he served as a member of the board of directors for the Edmonton organization and was president of the club when the Eskimos won the Grey Cup in 1955 and 1956. A member of the board of governors and active in the formation of the Edmonton Alumni Club since his retirement, Moe has also taken part in many community affairs and in the affairs of his profession.

McCAFFREY, Jimmy P.
Builder
Ottawa Rough Riders, general manager
1940 Big Four, president
1955 Canadian Rugby Union, president
1956 Big Four, president

The former manager of the St. Brigid's Football Club of the Ottawa City League, Jimmy McCaffrey was hired as general manager of the Rough Riders in 1923. He immediately effected a merger with St. Brigid's and brought on a number of outstanding players, saving the Riders from disbandment and starting them on the road to success. Staying on as manager, except during the war years, he took the Rough Riders to the Grey Cup finals seven times, four of which they won. He also found time to be Big Four president in 1940 and 1956, and president of the Canadian Rugby Union in 1955. When the Big Four suspended operations during the war, he helped form the

Eastern Football League to keep things moving. For 12 years McCaffrey acted as a member of the Big Four's executive in various capacities. In 1955 he served as one of the Scheney Award trustees. During his long service in Canadian football, McCaffrey earned a reputation as one of the most respected general managers in the league.

McCANN, Dave
Builder
Dave McCann was one of Canada's outstanding players. He is highly regarded as a coach and one of the country's foremost authorities on Canadian football. Both quarterback and halfback for the Ottawa Rough Riders from 1907 to the war years, he took up coaching after the war and led the Riders to Grey Cup championships in 1925 and 1926. Successful as a player, coach and league official, he chaired the Canadian Rugby Union rules committee for many years and was instrumental in effecting many significant rule changes.

McGILL, Frank
Player
Born 1893; Sir Vincent Meredith Trophy—Best All-Around Athlete of MAAA 1913; graduated from McGill Univ. School of Commerce 1914; joined Royal Naval Air Service and flew as pilot 1915, earning high rank of Air Vice-Marshall during W. W. II; aide-de-camp to Viscount Alexander during the latter's term of office as Governor General of Canada; also participated as swimmer and water polo player on five MAAA championship teams; played hockey for Emeralds, MAAA Juniors, Knox Church and Montreal High School and starred for McGill; first Canadian Swimming champion, coached by George Hudgson; Canadian Olympic Champion; received eight more medals for national titles and records; Dominion Champion for mile in track; waterpolo captain for three of the five MAAA championships; organized No. 115 Auxiliary Squadron for the Royal Canadian Air Force in 1934.

An all-round athlete particularly noted for his feats in football and aquatic sports, Frank McGill's career was fostered by McGill University and Montreal Amateur Athletic Association (MAAA), though he had already shown himself to be an outstanding athlete at Montreal High School. The summit of his football career came when he captained and quarterbacked the MAAA to the Big Four title in 1919. McGill thought the Tigers had broken signal code (no huddles, so quarterback called out set numbers), so he called out French signals and no one on the Tigers team had French. His team was unable to compete for the Grey Cup because the Canadian championship finals were cancelled owing to the late season. Frank McGill made a contribution to Canadian sports as an executive and administrator and at various times he was a member of the athletic board of McGill, on the advisory committee of the Canadian Olympics Committee, a director and vice president of the MAAA, president of the Big Four and a member of the Canadian Rugby Union rules committee.
Also in: Canada's Sports Hall of Fame.

MOLSON, Capt. Percival M.C.
Player
Son of Percival Molson, Sr, of the brewing Molsons; graduated from McGill Univ. 1913; excelled in track, hockey, racquets, golf, tennis, cricket, billiards and aquatic sports; became captain and received M.C; killed in action in W.W. I 1917.

Percy Molson was a versatile athlete who, at Montreal High and McGill University, excelled in many different sports. He played football both at Montreal High and McGill University before moving to the Montreal Amateur Athletic Association where he captained and starred as back 1903 – 1904. Molson was noted for his sure hands, great running ability and exceptional kicking. In 1913 Molson and George D. McDonald set up a graduates' stadium committee to construct a stadium and fieldhouse at McGill, but Molson was killed in combat before he could see it completed. Molson Stadium at McGill University was named after him, a home of senior football in Montreal until 1968 and again for a year in 1972.
Also in: Canada's Sports Hall of Fame.

MONTGOMERY, Kenneth G.
Builder
Born January 5, 1907, in Wetaskiwin, Alta; resident of Edmonton since 1924.

1934 – 1940	Edmonton Athletic Club, president, executive officer
1938 – 1939	Edmonton Eskimo Football Club, secretary
1952 – 1954	Edmonton Eskimos, president
1956	Canadian Rugby Union, president
1957	Western Interprovincial Football Union, president

Ken Montgomery was associated with championship junior hockey teams in Alberta both as player and as a coach, and was an executive of the Edmonton Athletic Club in the late thirties. He was one of the founders of the original Edmonton Eskimo Club in 1938 – 1939 and president of the Eskimos from 1952 – 1954, winning Edmonton's first Grey Cup in 1954. He also served as president of the Canadian Rugby Union in 1956 and president of the Western Interprovincial Football Union in 1957. Montgomery is one of the founders of the Canadian Football League. He was also instrumental in initiating the East-West professional Shrine charity games in 1954. Over the years he served in many different executive capacities with the Edmonton club, as well as acting as trustee of the Canadian Shenley Awards, 1958 – 1963, and as vice chairman of the Alberta Saskatchewan Thoroughbred Racing Society (racing commission). Over a period of more than 30 years, Montgomery made innumerable contributions to sports in Western Canada in general, and to football in particular.

MORRIS, Alan B. "Teddy"
Player – Builder
Born 1910 in Toronto, Ont; Jeff Russel Memorial Trophy 1937.

1931 – 1939	Toronto Argonauts
1940 – 1941	Toronto Argonauts, assistant coach
1942 – 1944	H.M.C.S. York Navy Team, coach
1945 – 1949	Toronto Argonauts, coach

After serving an apprenticeship with Toronto playground teams, the Native Sons (juniors in Winnipeg) and a place in the Canadian junior championship final, Morris launched a spectacular career with the Toronto Argonauts in 1931. He starred with Toronto for nine

years, helping the Argos to three Canadian championships. Teddy was an assistant coach with the Argonauts in 1940 and 1941, and coached H.M.C.S. York navy teams in 1942, 1943 and 1944, winning the service championship in 1944, after which he returned to Toronto in 1945. In his five years as head coach with the Argos, he led them to three Grey Cup championships—1945, 1946 and 1947—and four Eastern titles. Morris put his heart and soul into coaching; he lived and died with each play on the field. Not a glamorous or flamboyant coach, he nevertheless commanded great respect from his players.
Also in: Canada's Sports Hall of Fame.

NEWTON, Jack

Player – Builder

Born 1887 in Limehouse, Ont; Intercollegiate All-Stars 1909.

1902 – 1905 Sarnia Collegiate Institute Juniors, player
1907 – 1909 University of Toronto, player
1912 – 1914 Toronto Argonauts, coach
1919 – 1920 Sarnia Collegiate, coach
1921 – 1928 Sarnia Intermediates, coach
1929 Sarnia Imperials, coach

A highly respected and knowledgeable figure in football at all levels, Jack Newton for more than 50 years was a steadfast contributor to Canadian football. Newton saw active service with Sarnia Collegiate Institute and Sarnia Juniors from 1902 through 1905. He played with the University of Toronto 1907 – 1909 and made the Intercollegiate All-Stars in 1909. Newton helped win the intercollegiate championship in 1908 and 1909, and went on to the Grey Cup with Varsity in 1909. He was head coach of Toronto Argonauts 1912 – 1914, and served as head coach of Sarnia Collegiate, Sarnia Intermediates and in 1929 was also head coach of the Sarnia Imperials. During his career he coached Argos to two Big Four titles and one Grey Cup victory, 1914. With Sarnia Collegiate he won one Ontario championship and led the Sarnia Intermediates to many provincial and Canadian titles; he captured the senior Ontario Rugby Football Union title with the Senior Imperials. He was undoubtedly one of the greatest contributors to the game in all of Canada.

PARKER, Jackie

Player

Attended Mississippi State Univ; All-American; moved to Edmonton 1954; All-Star eight times; Schenley Award three years; Jeff Nicklin Trophy seven years.

1954 – 1962 Edmonton Eskimos, halfback
1963 – 1965 Toronto Argonauts
1968 – 1970 British Columbia Lions, assistant coach, coach, manager

An All-American at Mississippi State and the leading scorer in the Southeast Conference, Parker came to Edmonton in 1954. He starred for the Eskimos for the next nine years, leading them to three Grey Cup victories, making eight straight All-Star teams and scoring 750 points. His 84-yd. fumble return in the final minutes of the 1954 Grey Cup game gave the Eskimos a 26 – 25 victory over Montreal. In spite of bad knees, Parker played three more years with Toronto after retiring from the Eskimos. In 1968 he joined the British Columbia Lions as a playing assistant coach. He served as head coach briefly during the 1969 season before taking over as general manager in 1970. Now an Edmonton businessman, he is still remembered for his spectacular plays, scrambling ability and ball-handling magic.

PATTERSON, Hal

Player

Jeff Russel Memorial Trophy 1956; Schenley Award, Canada's Most Outstanding Player 1956.

1953 – 1960 Montreal Alouettes, receiver
1961 – 1965 Hamilton Tiger Cats, receiver

Possessing a magnetic charisma, "Prince Hal" filled football stadiums with fans attracted solely by his presence in a truly remarkable football career spanning 13 seasons. A statistician's nightmare, he rewrote the record books scoring 75 touchdowns, 64 on pass receptions, 3 on kickoff returns. His longest kickoff return was 105 yds. and his longest gain on a pass reception was 109 yds. In 1956 Patterson set another record, still standing today, gaining 338 yds. on pass receptions in a single game. Most of his career was spent with the Montreal Alouettes but he was traded to the diminishing Hamilton Tiger Cats in 1961. Making his presence known, Hal led the Ti-Cats to five consecutive Grey Cup championships. A fine gentleman on and off the field, Hal Patterson will be remembered by hundreds of thousands of enraptured fans who thrilled to his outstanding catches and spectacular runs on the Canadian gridiron.

PERRY, Gordon

Player

Jeff Russel Memorial Trophy 1931.

One of the few great football players to come out of Quebec City, Perry was the captain of the 1931 Montreal Amateur Athletic Association Winged Wheelers, a team that went undefeated and won the Grey Cup 22 – 0 over Regina. Perry was not an elusive runner, relying mainly on his speed when carrying the ball. He moved inside as well as outside and was hard to catch or tackle in the open field. An outstanding all-round athlete, Perry was a fine baseball player and hockey player as well, an equestrian enthusiast and later president of the Winter Fair.
Also in: Canada's Sports Hall of Fame.

PERRY, Norman

Player

Most Valuable Player 1934; Senior All-Star six times; Eastern Canada All-Stars twice.

An outstanding running halfback, Perry combined with Ormond Beach and Alex Hayes to form the great backfield that made the Sarnia Imperials a football power in the thirties. He played junior and intermediate football for eight years, then spent eight years with the Imperials in the Senior Ontario Rugby Football Union winning the league championship seven times and the Grey Cup once. Incomparable as a broken field runner, he made the ORFU senior all-star team six times, was twice on the Eastern Canada All-Stars, and captain of the Sarnia Grey Cup champions in 1934. Distinguished as a player and a gentleman, Norm Perry was honored when Sarnia's Athletic Park was renamed the Norman Perry Memorial Stadium. The Norm Perry Trophy annually rewards the most valuble high school player in Sarnia. A prominent citizen, Perry served as alderman in Sarnia

1936–1938 and in 1939 became mayor of the city. He also served as president of the Canadian Rugby Union in 1953.
Also in: Canada's Sports Hall of Fame.

QUILTY, Sylvester Patrick "Silver"
Player
Born February 8, 1891, near Renfrew, Ont; graduate of high school in Renfrew; began playing football in a high school football league that included Pembroke and Arnprior; attended Ottawa Univ. 1907–1912; enrolled in medicine at McGill Univ. 1914.

1907–1912	Ottawa University, back
1913	Ottawa Rough Riders, back
1914	McGill University, back

An outstanding football performer, Quilty began his career at Ottawa University. As a freshman, age 16, he made the senior intercollegiate team at the outside wing position playing that year against McGill, Queen's and University of Toronto. In 1907 Ottawa won the championship, but there were no further play-offs. Continuing with Ottawa from 1908–1912, Quilty was the prime ball-carrier during these years and handled the kicking duties 1908–1909. He played for the Ottawa Rough Riders in 1913, and then enrolled in medicine at McGill where he ended his playing career in 1914. Following his retirement, Quilty became a referee in the intercollegiate union for two years and then spent three years in the interprovincial. He was also a member of the rules committee of the intercollegiate and interprovincial unions and coached various teams in the 1920s. Quilty excelled in other sports also, and served at length in various administrative positions adding to his prominence as an exceptional figure in all sports.
Also in: Canada's Sports Hall of Fame.

REBHOLZ, Russ
Player
Attended Univ. of Wisconsin.

1932–1934	Winnipeg St. John's, back
1935–1938	Winnipeg Blue Bombers, back

Russ Rebholz is one of the first two imports to play football in Winnipeg. He was recruited from the University of Wisconsin to play for Winnipeg St. John's Club in 1932. Serving Winnipeg Clubs with distinction for seven years, he brought three Western championships to Winnipeg and one Grey Cup. In the Bombers' great win over the Hamilton Tigers in 1935, "The Wisconsin Wrath" threw two touchdown passes to Joe Perpich and Bud Marquardt bringing the Cup West for the first time. A superbly versatile all-round backfielder, Rebholz contributed largely to the development of modern football in Western Canada, giving leadership both on and off the field.

REEVE, Edward H. "Teddy"
Player
Born 1902 in Toronto, Ont; raised in the Beaches district where as youth worked at bookstore run by his mother; there had first contact with great literature; .300-plus hitter in topflight softball; high scoring in basketball; a fine hockey player; as lacrosse player won three Mann Cups, 1926, 1928 and 1930, playing four years for Brampton Excelsiors and Oshawa; in 1928 started writing a daily column "Sporting Extras" in *Toronto Telegram*, his style of writing developed from reading everything even *Encyclopaedia Britannica*; also has annual Christmas Eve story in his column; married Alvern Florence Donaldson; during W.W. II was a major in Conn Smythe's 30th Battery Unit, served as gunner in Europe for three years; fractured elbow during fighting around Caen and in 1944 was invalided home; greeted by mobs on return from Europe; resumed column after war; presently continuing as sports columnist for the *Toronto Telegram*.

1923	Toronto Argonauts
1924–1930	Toronto Balmy Beach, player-coach
1924–1931	Toronto Malvern Collegiate, coach
1931	Montreal Royals, coach
	Queen's University, coach
1945–1946	Toronto Beaches, coach
1948	Beaches-Indians, coach

Reeve, 6 ft, 200 lbs, toiled for Toronto Argonauts and Balmy Beach. He was outstanding on defense, specializing in blocking kicks and stopping plungers as they tore through the line. He is best remembered for playing an entire 1930 semifinal game against Hamilton with a broken shoulder, then coming off the bench against Regina in the final minutes to lead defense in 10–6 victory, despite adding a cracked collar bone to the shoulder injury. He led Balmy Beach to Grey Cup victories in 1927 and 1930. Reeve retired from active participation in 1930. He started coaching, and coached the Malvern Collegiate to three Canadian junior finals between 1929 and 1932. He also coached Queen's University, leading the Tricolour to five college play-offs and three championships. Reeve has been the personal cement binding sportswriter, athlete, coach and manager together in a long fellowship. During his career as an active player he received two skull fractures, a broken leg, broken nose and broken fingers, and saw his arthritis condition gradually worsen. As a coach, Reeve believed, "One bad regulation was if you substituted, the guy you took out of the game couldn't come back until the next quarter. Naturally there were no platoons and we think the game was better that way. But it was certainly rough on the substitutes. You tried to get a kid in the game for reward or experience and if he went bad, you couldn't get the regular back in. Every now and then some rookie would perform beyond his dreams so we guess that evened up also."
Also in: Canadian Lacrosse Hall of Fame.

RITCHIE, Alvin "Silver Fox"
Builder
Born December 12, 1890, in Cobden, Ont; father a school teacher; interest in sports came from father who was a fine baseball player; played baseball and rugby football in Midland, Ont; moved with his family to Regina 1911; joined local football team and was coached by Fred Ritter, Princeton football player; served in W.W. I in Europe; in 1919 was instrumental in organizing an amateur hockey league with teams from Regina, Saskatoon and Moose Jaw, bringing the Regina Pats (hockey) to Memorial Cups in 1925 and 1930; full-time employee of customs office; before his death was scout for New York Rangers hockey club; died 1966.

In 1919 Al Ritchie moved into the Regina Football Club. He was instrumental in forming the constitution for the Saskatchewan Football League. He also played an impor-

tant part in sending the Regina team into 56 consecutive victories and nine championships. In 1921 his team, Regina Rough Riders, was defeated by Edmonton, the first Western team to challenge for the Grey Cup. In 1925 he organized the Regina Patricias, who won the Western title but lost the Canadian play-offs to Montreal Amateur Athletic Association. Ritchie took over the senior Rough Riders with Howie Milne in 1928, and still coached the Pats. In 1928 the Patricias won the junior championship and the Rough Riders went to the Grey Cup with 17 – 0 victories on the line, but lost to undefeated Hamilton 30 – 0. The pattern continued with the Regina club winning Western championships 1927 – 1932, but losing in the Grey Cup each time. Still Ritchie encouraged the interest in the Grey Cup nationally. He was credited with many rule changes and beneficial developments over the years. In 1920 the Western Canadian Union adopted the reduction of the number of players from 14 to 10, three-yard interference instead of one, ten-yard blocking instead of five; in 1929 Ritchie introduced the forward pass (two years before the East) and imported United States players to improve the game (not acceptable to Canadian Rugby Union until after W.W. II). Ritchie is the only man in Canadian sports history to coach national champions in both hockey and football. He died before the Regina Rough Riders would bring the cup West in 1966.
Also in: Canada's Sports Hall of Fame.

RODDEN, Michael J.
Player – Builder
Born 1891 in Mattawa, Ont; attended Univ. Ottawa 1906 – 1909; graduated from Queen's Univ. 1913; All-Star four times, at a different position each time; won 15 letters in various sports, a record never equaled; avid sportswriter, sports editor and columnist; wrote for *Toronto Globe* and *Kingston Whig Standard* until 1973; now residing in Kingston, Ont.

1910 – 1913 Queen's University, player
1914 McGill University
1916 Queen's University, coach
1919 Toronto Argonauts, middle wing
1920 Toronto Argonauts, coach
1921 – 1922 Parkdale Canoe Club, coach
1924 Balmy Beach, coach
1926 Toronto Argonauts, coach
1927 – 1930 Hamilton Tigers, coach
1937 Hamilton Tigers, coach

Michael J. Rodden began his football career at Queen's University and played four seasons with them, and for a brief time became their coach. After Queen's University he played one season with the Argonauts, then coached the Argonauts to the Grey Cup final the following year. He coached Parkdale Canoe Club to two Ontario Rugby Football Union titles, 1921 and 1922, and guided Balmy Beach to the Dominion final in 1924 before losing 11 – 3 to Queen's. Taking over the head coaching position at Hamilton, Rodden led the Tigers to a 1928 Grey Cup victory over an undefeated Regina team and a repeat performance in 1929. An innovative football coach, he also earned honors in hockey, soccer and lacrosse, and became one of the country's most noted hockey referees. Rodden coached for 42 seasons, won 27 league championships and two interscholastic titles, in addition to making five Grey Cup appearances and winning twice. He is known also for his knowledge of the history of sportswriting.
Also in: Hockey Hall of Fame; International Hockey Hall of Fame.

ROWE, Paul
Player
Born in Victoria, B.C; graduated from Univ. Ore; Dave Dryburgh Memorial Trophy 1939 and 1940; Greatest Plunging Fullback in Canadian Football 1948; All-Star 1939, 1940, 1946 and 1947; Western All-Stars four times; served in W.W. II 1941 – 1945; retired 1950.

1938 – 1940 Calgary Bronks, fullback
1945 – 1950 Calgary, fullback

After attending the University of Oregon, Rowe joined the Calgary Bronks in 1938. He stayed three years in Calgary, then left for four years in the service, returning in 1945. Rowe played for six more years before injuries ended his career in 1950. One of the greatest plunging fullbacks in Canadian football, Rowe was selected to the Western All-Stars four times and led the Western League in scoring in 1939 and 1948. In 1948 he led the Stampeders into the Grey Cup final where they defeated Toronto 12 – 7. After his enforced retirement, Rowe continued in the game as coach and adviser in minor football.
Also in: Canada's Sports Hall of Fame.

RUSSEL, Jeff
Player
Died tragically in 1926 trying to repair a power line in a raging storm.

1917 – 1920 Royal Military College, halfback
1920 – 1921 McGill University, halfback
1922 – 1925 MAAA Winged Wheelers, halfback

One of the all-time great competitors and sportsman of the Canadian game, Russel was ranked one of the greatest backfielders in the Big Four. He starred with Lucas School in Montreal, Lower Canada College, Royal Military College, McGill University and Montreal Amateur Athletic Association (MAAA) Winged Wheelers. It was natural, perhaps, after his accidental death in 1926, that friends brought into play the famous Jeff Russel Memorial Trophy, awarded annually to the player in the Big Four adjudged the most useful to his team, with courage, clean play and sportsmanship requisites.
Also in: Canada's Sports Hall of Fame.

RYAN, Joseph B. "Rufus"
Builder
Born April 11, 1902, in Starbuck, Manitoba; educated in Winnipeg; Canadian Rugby Union Plaque for Outstanding Service to Canadian Football 1945.

1930 – 1942 New Winnipegs (Blue Bombers), manager
1960 – 1963 Edmonton Eskimos, manager

Joe Ryan became associated with Canadian football in 1930, when he was appointed manager of the New Winnipegs (later changed to the Blue Bombers, 1936). The following year he was responsible for the amalgamation of the Winnipeg Rugby Club and St. John's, a move that changed two weak clubs into one strong one. In 1933 he brought in Carl Cronin from Notre Dame to take over as head coach, and one year later the Bombers won the Western title. Along with Frank Hannibal, G. S. Halter

and others, Ryan helped strengthen the club by scouting the Dakotas for players in 1934. Revitalized by the addition of several American players, the Bombers upset Hamilton in the 1935 Grey Cup final. Between 1931 and 1937, Ryan's Winnipeg teams won a remarkable six Western and three Dominion titles. In 1942 Ryan went East where, with Lew Hayman and Leo Dandurand, he helped to revive football in Montreal. In 1960 he joined the Edmonton Eskimos as general manager, guiding them to a Grey Cup that same year, remaining with the Edmonton club in various executive capacities since that time. As a 14-year member of the Canadian Rugby Union rules committee, Ryan was responsible for much of the modernization of Canadian football that took place in the forties. His many contributions to football in Winnipeg were acknowledged when he was made a life member of the Winnipeg Football Club in 1941, and when he became the first life member of the Blue Bomber Alumni Association in 1958.
Also in: Canada's Sports Hall of Fame.

SHAUGHNESSY, Francis "Shag"
Builder
Graduated from Notre Dame in pharmacy and law 1901; served with Royal Canadian Artillery as captain during W.W. I; eight sons and one daughter; proficient in many sports; coached Ottawa National Hockey League team to a championship; in baseball achieved fame as player, manager, owner; 24 years as president of the International Baseball League and president of all minor leagues.

After graduation from Notre Dame, Shaughnessy spent a brief period in a brokerage business, played and coached baseball at all levels up to major league, and spent 20 years, with brief interruptions, as football coach at McGill University. He was the first professional coach to enter Canada from the United States and was largely responsible for the forward pass, 12-man teams and the direct snap from center. He introduced the Canadian lateral series to United States college football, and, on retiring from McGill, introduced forward passer Warren Stevens to the Montreal Amateur Athletic Association to further revolutionize Canadian football. His football coaching also included spells at Clemson College and Washington and Lee Universities. He is probably the best-known American immigrant to Canada before 1914. When he left Canadian football in 1932, he had breathed life into the game, opened it up and changed it beyond recognition.

SIMPSON, Benjamin L.
Player
Born in Peterborough, Ont; taught school there at age 17; graduated from Queen's Univ; taught in Central Collegiate, Hamilton; presently retired from Westdale Secondary School where he was a principal.

An outstanding kicker, Simpson played with Hamilton Tigers from 1904 to 1910, aiding them to win the Big Four championship in 1908 and the Grey Cup final in 1910. His ability to repeatedly kick into touch, thus preventing the runback, was a constant source of frustration for Hamilton's foes. He served as president of both the Tiger Football Club and the Big Four, later director of the Interprovincial Union. He was considered the master of the onside kick.
Also in: Canada's Sports Hall of Fame.

SPRAGUE, David S.
Player
All-Eastern and All-Canadian almost every year.

1930 – 1932 Hamilton Tigers, backfielder
1933 – 1944 Ottawa Rough Riders, captain

Sprague began his football career at Delta Collegiate, where he and Huck Welch brought their team the Dominion Championship. Joining the Hamilton Tigers in 1930, he helped the Tigers to two Interprovincial and one Grey Cup championships. A hard-driving power runner, Sprague with Brian Timmis gave Hamilton the strongest backfield in Canada during his tenure with the Tigers. Moving to Ottawa in 1933, he sparked the Riders to three Big Four championships and a Grey Cup in 1940. Twice captain of the Ottawa club, he earned All-Eastern and All-Canadian ratings in almost every year of his career. His reckless enthusiasm for the game and his disregard for his own safety are reflected in his medical history: a broken back, torn Achilles tendon, broken nose six times, cartilage problems, shoulder separation and 167 assorted stitches. His skill and courage have earned him a place among Canada's football greats.
Also in: Canada's Sports Hall of Fame.

STEVENSON, Art
Player
All-Star four times; League Scoring Title 1941; earned medical degree from Univ. of Man; served with Royal Canadian Army Medical Corps 1941 – 1945.

A Little All-American at Hastings College in Nebraska, Stevenson was called one of the first all-round backfielders in college football. In 1937 he joined the Winnipeg Blue Bombers, enrolling at the same time in the University of Manitoba School of Medicine. An accomplished runner, passer and kicker, he quarterbacked the Bombers in both the 1938 and 1939 Grey Cups, losing the first to Toronto, but winning the second 8 – 7 over Ottawa as he kicked the deciding point. In 1940 Stevenson tied for the league scoring title, and won it outright the following year, although a knee injury kept him out of Winnipeg's Grey Cup victory in 1941. An All-Star every year he played, either as a halfback or quarterback, Stevenson retired after the 1941 season to join the Royal Canadian Army Medical Corps. He was a superb student both on and off the field and an outstanding player, and made a lasting impression on Canadian football.

STIRLING, Hugh "Bummer"
Player
Born 1910 in St. Thomas, Ont; ORFU Most Valuable Player 1936 and All-Star 1932 – 1937; Eastern All-Star 1934 – 1936.

An outstanding high school football player, Stirling starred for the 1930 Dominion junior champions. Moving to Sarnia Imperials of the senior Ontario Rugby Football Union (ORFU), he earned a reputation as one of the best triple-threat backfielders in the game, and one of the greatest kickers in the history of Canadian football. He was a long and accurate punter and an exceptional running halfback. Stirling served exclusively with the Imperials from 1931 through 1937, and was a senior ORFU All-Star six times and Eastern All-Star three years. His combination of natural football talent and competitive spirit made him an outstanding sixty-minute

player who established himself as an Ontario football legend.
Also in: Canada's Sports Hall of Fame.

TAYLOR, N. J. "Piffles"
Builder
Attended Univ. of Toronto; prisoner of war, released 1918; died 1946.

Taylor was instrumental in the development of football in Western Canada, rising through the ranks to become president of the Regina Rough Riders, of the Western Interprovincial Football Union (four times) and of the Canadian Rugby Union. Playing his early football with Regina teams, the westerner from Collingwood, Ont, quarterbacked the Rough Riders to their fifth western championship defeating Calgary 13 – 1. He also quarterbacked the Regina Boat Club in 1922. In 1934 he became president of the club and held various executive positions. Western Canada's general football development may be attributed to a great degree to the vision and energetic management of this remarkable gentleman.

TIMMIS, Brian M.
Player

1924 – 1938 Hamilton Tigers, player
1943 Hamilton Flying Wildcats, coach
1945 Hamilton Tigers, coach
1947 Toronto Indians, coach

One of the greatest players Canada ever produced, Brian was noted for his boundless energy, enthusiasm and a reckless disregard for his own safety. Timmis was the finest plunging back of his day. Helmetless, he helped the Hamilton Tigers smash their way to three Grey Cups, 1928, 1929 and 1932. In 1937 at the age of 38 he came out of retirement to assist the Tigers in a play-off against Ottawa. In spite of infected tonsils, and neuritis in his shoulder that made him unable to use his left arm, he played 58 minutes, earning a thundering standing ovation that stopped the game in the final minutes.
Also in: Canada's Sports Hall of Fame.

TUBMAN, Joe
Player
Born August 18, 1897, in New Edinburgh, Ottawa; enlisted in Canadian Army where he played football and hockey 1916; retired after fifty years service with Grand Trunk and Canadian National Railway.

Joe Tubman played football in Ottawa with a junior city league prior to 1916, then joined the Canadian Army where he played football and hockey during W. W. I. In 1919 he joined the Ottawa Senior City League and after one game jumped to Ottawa Rough Riders as a kicking halfback, staying with them until 1931, a total of 13 seasons, and leading them to two Grey Cup victories, 1925 and 1926. He also served as captain. Tubman then became an official of the Interprovincial and Ontario Rugby Football Union (ORFU), as referee and umpire. He refereed in Big Four and ORFU until 1944, when he retired at the advice of his physician. A star in all sports, Tubman was known as one of Canada's greatest canoeists, winning numerous championships with Ottawa crews.
Also in: Canada's Sports Hall of Fame.

WARNER, Clair J.
Builder
Born March 30, 1903, in Pierre, S. Dak; arrived in Canada 1917, settling in Regina 1919; Canadian Rugby Union Plaque, Grey Cup Dinner 1956.

1925 – 1933 Regina Rough Riders, halfback, outside wing, end
1934 – 1941 Regina Rough Riders, manager
1941 Regina Rough Riders, president
1948 Western Interprovincial Union, president

Arriving in Canada in 1917, Clair Warner played junior football from 1920 – 1924, moving to the Regina senior club in 1925 for a stay that lasted through the 1933 season. He played eight out of nine seasons with the Rough Riders, participating in four Grey Cup finals. After a brief spell as coach of Regina juniors, Warner graduated into the executive end, serving the Western Interprovincial Union executive for six years, as president in 1948. He served also as a member of the Canadian Rugby Union rules committee for five years. In 1934 he became a member of the Rough Riders executive, served the Rough Riders as manager for twelve seasons and was president in 1941. He also served on the management committee for fifteen years.

WARWICK, A. H. "Bert"
Builder
Born 1902 in Ft. Chipewyn; attended St. John's College; was representative of Canadian Football League Commissioner in Edmonton at the time of his death in 1963.

Bert Warwick was a player, coach and executve. He graduated from football at St. John's College in Winnipeg to officiating and coaching. After leading YMHA juniors in Winnipeg, he became assistant coach of Winnipeg Blue Bombers, and as head coach led the Bombers to the Western Canada crown in 1945. A life member and executive with the Winnipeg Club, he rendered great service to St. Paul's College and was president of Winnipeg Junior Bombers. Warwick was chairman of the rules committee of the Canadian Football League and the Canadian Rugby Union for eight years. He was responsible for rule changes that accelerated the advance of football in Western Canada, and was generally credited with being one of the most knowledgeable of all football executives.

WELCH, Hawley "Huck"
Player
Born 1907 in Toronto, Ont; attended Delta Collegiate; Big Four All-Star twice; All-Canadian three times; Jeff Russel Memorial Trophy 1933; served overseas with rank of major in Royal Hamilton Light Infantry in W. W. II.

1928 – 1929 Hamilton Tigers, kicking halfback
1930 – 1934 MAAA Winged Wheelers, kicking halfback
1935 – 1937 Hamilton Tigers, kicking halfback
1938 Delta Collegiate, coach
1948 – 1950 Kelvin Collegiate, coach

One of the great kicking halfbacks in Canadian football history, Welch's football career began at Delta Collegiate in Hamilton where he was twice league scoring champion and helped to win three Canadian interscholastic championships. Welch joined the Tigers in 1928, leading them to two interprovincial and two Grey Cup titles. In 1931 he played with the undefeated Grey Cup champion Winged Wheelers where he was twice selected as a Big Four All-Star, and twice named All-Canadian. Returning to the Hamilton Tigers in 1935, he was, that same year, All-Canadian, twice interprovincial scoring champion

and twice runner-up. Welch boasted an all-time record of 102 single points kicking. After retirement, he coached Delta seniors and Eastwood juniors in Hamilton. He served overseas, where he took part in a wartime championship in England in 1944. In 1946 he became the first postwar president of the Hamilton Tigers. He coached Kelvin Collegiate in Winnipeg from 1948 through 1950, Regina juniors in 1953, and served on the executive of the Regina Football Club. In 1959 he became Hamilton representative of the Canadian Football League Commissioner.
Also in: Canada's Sports Hall of Fame.

1974

CURRIE, Andrew
Builder
Born 1911; presently living in Winnipeg.

1925 – 1933	St. John's College, University of Manitoba, Regina Pats, Regina Rough Riders and Winnipeg Blue Bombers, player
1934 – 1950	Winnipeg High School, coach
1949	Manitoba Football Official's Association, organizer
1951 – 1957	Physical Education and Athletics in Winnipeg Schools, director
1954	British Columbia Football Officials' Association, organizer
1957	Western Conference, commissioner's officiating supervisor
1965	Canadian Football League Rules Commission, chairman

Currie has distinguished himself in various areas of football. In 1928, at the age of 17, he played 30 minutes for Regina Rough Riders against Hamilton in the Grey Cup Final. Currie was permitted to retain his junior eligibility by special permission received from the Canadian Rugby Union and he played for the Regina Pats the following week in the Dominion Junior Championship against St. Thomas. After eight years of playing on the gridiron, which included four East-West finals, Currie turned to coaching high school football. From 1947 through 1950 his high school team won consecutive Winnipeg championships. Currie subsequently became the Director of Physical Education and Athletics for Winnipeg schools. He was responsible for the recruiting, training and appointment of football officials in Winnipeg and prepared the first rules examination for all officials. Currie has served as a member of the Canadian Football League rules committee continually since its inception and was the chairman of the committee when he revised and rewrote the new rule book.

DIXON, George
Player
Born in Bridgeport, Conn; retired from football 1965; Jeff Russel Memorial Trophy 1962; Schenley Award, Canada's Most Outstanding Player 1962.

A product of Bridgeport, Conn, Dixon came to the Montreal Alouettes in 1959, demonstrating in five full seasons and parts of two others that he was one of the league's most productive and exciting ball carriers. "Let George do it," was the Alouette's theme during the early sixties and in 1962 he just about did, as it was the only year in the past decade that the Alouettes reached the Eastern Conference finals. Dixon set an Eastern Conference rushing record (which still stands) of 1520 that season scoring 15 touchdowns, 11 running and 4 on pass receptions, to lead the league. He was unanimously chosen as All-Canadian and a runaway choice for the Calvert as the most popular Alouette with the fans. George had that instinctive knack of cutting through the smallest hole behind the flimsiest of blocks that placed him a niche above others. Suffering a series of injuries in his last two years of pro ball, George retired in 1965.

FALONEY, Bernie
Player
Graduated from Maryland Univ. 1953; All-American; served with U.S. Air Force 1955 – 1956; Schenley Award, Canada's Most Outstanding Player 1961; Jeff Russel Memorial Trophy 1965; one of Top Five All-Time Passers; married; presently living in Hamilton, Ont; part owner of a machinery company.

1953	San Francisco 49ers, defense
1954	Edmonton Eskimos, quarterback
1955 – 1956	USAF Bolling team, captain
1957 – 1964	Hamilton Tiger Cats, quarterback
1965 – 1967	Montreal Alouettes, player
1967	British Columbia Lions, player

An All-American at Maryland University, Bernie Faloney was drafted in 1953 by the San Francisco 49ers to play defense. He and Jackie Parker led the Eskimos to a Grey Cup victory over Montreal in 1954. Back in the United States for two years with the U.S. Air Force, he played and captained the Bolling Air Force Base team to two undefeated seasons. Faloney joined the Hamilton Tiger Cats in 1957, leading the team into six Grey Cup finals 1957 – 1964. Signed by Montreal in 1965, he played two years, finishing his career with the British Columbia Lions in 1967. Bernie is listed in the record books as one of the Top Five All-Time Passers with a .519 percentage of completions, total yds. of 24,264 and an average of 16.3 yds. per pass. His ability to punt, especially the quick, and his success in running the option, placed him in the triple-threat category. Jim Trimble stated that there may be more accomplished quarterbacks but none had more intensity to win than Faloney.

HUGHES, Wilfred Perry 'Billy"
Builder
Graduated from McGill Univ. 1912.

1919	Montreal Winged Wheelers, coach
1922 – 1926	Queen's University, coach
1932 – 1933	Hamilton Tigers, coach
1935 – 1936	Ottawa Rough Riders, coach
1940 – 1944	RCAF Manning Pool, coach

Upon graduating from McGill University, where he was a regular playing member of intercollegiate champion football and hockey teams, Billy Hughes started coaching while teaching at Westmount High School. In 1919 he coached Montreal Winged Wheelers to the Big Four championship and in the fall of 1922 was called to Kingston to finish out the season as coach of Queen's University, winners of the Intercollegiate title that same year. Hughes remained with Queen's through the 1926 season accumulating a record never equaled by leading his team to three consecutive Grey Cup championships and winning 26 league and exhibition games in succession. As coach of the Ottawa Rough Riders, he guided them to the Big Four title in 1936. During W. W. II he coached the RCAF Manning Pool to the league championship in 1942–1943. Highly reputed as a coach, Hughes later was called upon to "sell" football in the Maritimes.

LEAR, Les
Player

Les Lear began his gridiron career in 1938 with the Winnipeg Blue Bombers. He subsequently played for three teams that won the Grey Cup, Winnipeg in 1939, Winnipeg in 1941, and Calgary in 1948. Lear was selected on the All-Canadian team by *MacLeans Magazine* for 1939–1942. He was also selected on Lionel Conacher's All-Canadian team three times. Les Lear was the first Canadian-developed player ever to go to the National Football League. He played first-string guard with the Cleveland Rams, the Los Angeles Rams and the Detroit Lions. In 1948 Lear returned to Canada to coach the Calgary Stampeders to their first Grey Cup victory. When the Stampeders won the Grey Cup in 1948, they played a total of 15 league and playoff games without losing one single game. Lear was the last coach in Canada to coach a team that completed an entire season without suffering a defeat. Currently living in Florida, he is now associated with horse racing.

RUBY, Martin
Player

Born 1922 in Waco, Tex; Southwest Intercollegiate Conference 1941; graduated from Texas A&M 1942; All-Star seven times; presently in the British Columbia interior.

1946–1948 Brooklyn Dodgers, lineman
1949–1950 New York Yankees, lineman
1951–1957 Saskatchewan Rough Riders, lineman

One of the last great two-way linemen in Canadian football, Martin Ruby started his pro career with the Brooklyn Dodgers in 1946. After three years he switched to the New York Yankees, and two years later, in 1951, signed with the Saskatchewan Rough Riders. Playing seven years with the Riders, Ruby was conference All-Star seven times including three years when he was saluted both offensively and defensively. A man who rarely left the field, Martin Ruby was described as a quiet personality off the field, and a leader and inspirational force on it, respected and appreciated by teammates and opponents alike.

STUKUS, Annis "Stuke"
Builder

Currently involved in promoting professional hockey in Winnipeg.

1935–1941 Toronto Argonauts, quarterback, end, center, fullback, tackle, flying wing
1942 Oakwood Indians, quarterback, backfield coach
1943 Balmy Beach, quarterback
1944 Navy York Bulldogs, player
1945–1946 Toronto Indians, charter member
1949–1951 Edmonton Eskimos, coach, manager
1953–1955 British Columbia Lions, promoter

Starting his football career with the Toronto Argonauts in 1935, Stukus played with distinction through 1941 with the Argos, playing six positions (quarterback, end, center, fullback, tackle and flying wing) in 1936. He was quarterback and backfield coach for the Oakwood Indians in 1942 and Balmy Beach in 1943. He joined the Navy in 1944 and played for the York Bulldogs. A charter member of the Toronto Indians in 1945 and 1946, he hoped for eventual amalgamation of the Indians and Balmy Beach to form a second team in Toronto, plans that never materialized. In 1947 Stukus retired as an active player and went into newspaper work, but responded to a call from the newly franchised Eskimos in 1949 to serve as coach, general manager, water boy, etc. Finishing that season with a payroll of $45,000, he bought players like Gene Kiniski and Peter Lougheed, now premier of Alberta. In one memorable game in which there was no place-kicker available, Stuke volunteered and kicked bareheaded and wearing a wristwatch, infuriating opponents. Returning to newspaper work briefly, he answered the call of a group forming the British Columbia Lions in 1953, realizing a profit of $37,000 on the first year's operation. Stukus, after a distinguished playing career, was the master promoter who put Edmonton and the British Columbia Lions franchises on the map. He retired after the 1955 season.

1975

BAILEY, Byron L.
Player

Born in Omaha, Nebr; graduated from Washington State Univ; presently a member of the British Columbia Lions directorate.

A native of Omaha, Nebr, Bailey was with Detroit and Green Bay briefly, then recruited for the Lions by another Hall of Famer, Annis Stukus. Bailey had the honor of scoring B.C.'s first touchdown in Canadian Football League (CFL) competition as they both made their CFL debuts in the same year, 1954. Not only did he score the Lions' first touchdown, he also scored the only touchdown on the historic night when they won their first game, 9–4, against Calgary in 1954. As a fullback, Bailey rushed 783 times for 3643 yds, and 26 touchdowns. He also caught 101 passes for 1161 yds. In his spare time, he ran back 128 kickoffs for 3114 yds. He also returned punts, but they didn't save his totals for posterity, except for 1956 when he led the West with 680 yds. Another 1956 feat: Bailey led the league for most yardage on kickoff returns, one game (147) and longest runback (96 against Winnipeg). Considered a gentleman both on and off the field, By Bailey is putting something back into the game now as a Lions' director.

BROOK, T. L. "Tom"
Builder

Moved to Toronto from New York 1935; then to Calgary 1941; took out Canadian citizenship papers 1961; presently president of a small oil company and Schenley Awards trustee.

A man of action, United States–born Tom Brook came to Calgary in 1941, where he made an amazing impact on Canadian football. In 1948, when Calgary football was at a low ebb, he rounded up Les Lear to recruit some good players for the Stampeders. Guaranteeing the salaries on his own personal overdraft, Brook was duly rewarded when the Stampeders came through with an undefeated season, climaxed with Calgary's first Grey Cup victory, 12 – 7 over Ottawa. The team that Brook built set a record never equaled. Counting a tie and two wins in 1948 playoffs, the Calgary team went 25 games without a loss. But Tom's major contribution came in 1949 at a Canadian Rugby Union (CRU) meeting in Winnipeg. A faction in the CRU was trying to promote a two-game Grey Cup series, instead of the conventional one-game. Tom delivered a logical oratory that saved the day for Canada's finest single sports spectacle. After serving four years as president of the Stampeders, setting them in the right direction, Tom drifted from the scene, but returned briefly as director when the club again appeared to be in trouble.

HAYMAN, Lew

Builder

Born 1908; attended Syracuse Univ; All-American and an outstanding basketball, baseball and football player; came to Toronto from New York 1932; presently serving as president of the Toronto Argonauts.

1932 – 1941 Toronto Argonauts, coach
1942 – 1945 RCAF Toronto Hurricanes, coach
1946 – 1955 Montreal Alouettes, part owner, coach
1956 Toronto Argonauts, manager
1969 Canadian Football League, president

Lew Hayman came to Toronto in 1932 as coach of the University of Toronto basketball "Seconds." Helping Buck McKenna coach the Argos in 1932, Lew took over as coach when Buck became ill midway through the season. In 1933, as a 25-year-old head coach, he won the Grey Cup—his first of five; he never lost a Grey Cup game. Lew continued as coach for the Argos through the 1941 season and by 1942 was in the RCAF coaching the Toronto Hurricanes to victory. Perhaps the most important contribution Hayman made to Canadian football was in 1946 when he took over a staggering Montreal franchise, renamed the team Alouettes, assembled a strong, colorful aggregation and worked at getting French-Canadian sports fans interested in football. Returning to the Argonauts in 1956 as general manager, Lew is now president of the Argos, and is considered by many the most respected legislator in the league. One qualified observer said of league meetings, "Lew doesn't speak too often, but when he does, everybody listens." In 1969 he was Canadian Football League president.

PLOEN, Ken

Player

Attended Univ. Iowa; Rose Bowl Player of the Game 1957; All-Western Conference Quarterback 1957, 1959 and 1965; All-Canadian 1965; Record Longest Touchdown Pass Play in Canadian Football League 109 yds. 1965; Sixth on All-Time List of Canadian Football League Passers; a permanent resident of Winnipeg; presently working on the Blue Bomber executive.

1957 University of Iowa, player
1957 – 1967 Winnipeg Blue Bombers, quarterback, halfback

Starting his pro football career by completing an unusual double, Ken Ploen played in a Rose Bowl Game and a Grey Cup Game the same year, 1957. He starred with University of Iowa as they demolished Oregon State 35 – 19 in the Rose Bowl, but was a victim of defeat as his Winnipeg Blue Bombers lost out to Hamilton Tiger Cats 32 – 7 late that year. Playing for Winnipeg eleven seasons, Ploen made it to six Grey Cup finals and was on the winning side of four of them. He quarterbacked Winnipeg in all of them except one in which he played safety and offensive halfback. Hero of the 1961 Grey Cup victory over Hamilton, the only one ever to go into overtime, he was also the winning quarterback in the 1962 season, when he had a record low yield of only four interceptions from 208 passes and the same season set a high average completion record of .658 that held for 10 years. He retired after the 1967 season when he became a permanent resident of Winnipeg, representing many charitable causes and serving on the Blue Bomber executive.

SHATTO, Dick

Player

Born in Springfield, Ohio; attended Univ. Ky. but dropped out as junior; All-Canadian 1963 and 1964; All-Eastern 1956 – 1959, 1961 – 1964; wife Lynn; five children, Randy, Becky, Cindy, Jay and Kathy; Cindy has represented Canada all over the world in diving and won two gold medals in the Commonwealth Games; very active member of his community, has served with numerous charity organizations.

Retiring from competitive football in 1965, after 12 seasons with Toronto Argonauts, Dick Shatto had scored more touchdowns, caught more passes and accounted for more offensive yardage, rushing and receiving, than any player in the history of Canadian football. He still holds 13 Argonaut club records. His 91 touchdowns were exceeded only by George Reed, his 13,642 rushing-receiving yardage topped only by Reed and he was only the third Canadian Football League player ever to reach the 500-point level in scoring, finishing with 542 points. As a citizen, Dick served as campaign chairman for the Ontario Red Cross, received an award of merit for acting as spokesman for the Arthritis Society, and has made a number of speeches on behalf of the United Appeal, Easter Seals, Brotherhood Week and the Big Brothers organization. He is also an Honorary Director of the Canadian College Bowl. In *Profile of a Pro,* Russ Jackson states, "Of all the Toronto teams I have played against, Dick Shatto has to be the All-Toronto Argonaut. But he would rate on any all-pro, all-star team as an offensive back. He had everything. He ran pass patterns from a halfback position as well as anybody I have ever seen in Canadian football."

TRAWICK, Herb

Player

All-Eastern Conference 1946 – 1950; All-Star Guard seven times; permanent resident of Montreal and outstanding citizen; well known for work for numerous charitable organizations.

One of the first imports selected to build the powerful Montreal team, Trawick played magnificently for 12 years, from 1946 to 1957, for the Alouettes. Noted for his incredible speed, despite having quite a large build, Herb was named to the All-Eastern Conference for his first five years in Canadian football. Later he was named to the All-Star team as a guard. The 1955 selection gave him the distinction of being the first player to make the All-Star team seven times. Trawick was probably the only lineman to score two touchdowns in Grey Cup games, one in 1949 and the other in 1954, the latter nullified, unfortunately, by a quick whistle. Montreal lost that game to Edmonton 26 – 25.

1976

BARROW, John

Player

Born October 31, 1935, in Delray Beach, Fla; graduated from Georgia Military Academy; attended Univ. of Florida, advertising major in School of Journalism; Lineman of Year Southeastern Conference; Schenley Award, Outstanding Lineman Eastern Conference five times; Schenley Award, Outstanding Lineman in Canada 1962; Outstanding Lineman in History of Canadian Football 1967; married Vangie; three children, Gregg, Elaine and Kyle; owner of Hamilton's "Huddle" Restaurant which is managed by Vangie; keeps fit by frequent visits to the Y.

1956 University of Florida, lineman, captain
1957 – 1970 Hamilton Tiger Cats, lineman

John Barrow was named to more All-Star teams than any other player in the history of Canadian football. Despite being a third-round draft choice of the Detroit Lions, the All-American from University of Florida signed with Hamilton in 1957 and was voted All-Canadian 11 years in a row, 1957 – 1967. He was voted All-Star 16 times; in four consecutive years (1957 – 1960) he was an all-star tackle on both offense and defense. He missed all-star selection in only one of his 14 seasons in Canadian football. An outstanding contributor to the Tiger Cats, John aided them into nine Grey Cup games, helping to win four of them. Barrow was practically an automatic selection to Hamilton's All-Star Team of the modern era—1950 – 1957. Barrow is a firm believer in native Canadian football talent, and spent four years as managing director of the Toronto Argonauts, striving to build up this area in particular. After taking out his citizenship papers, he played as a Canadian during his latest years as a Ti-Cat.
Also in: Florida Sports Hall of Fame.

HARRIS, Carrol Wayne

Player

Born May 4, 1938, in Hampton, Ark; attended Univ. Ark. 1957 – 1960; Most Popular Player Award 1965 and 1966; Schenley Award, Outstanding Lineman 1965, 1966, 1970 and 1971; Calgary Athlete of the Year 1967; Demarco-Becket Trophy; Calgary Stampeder President Award 1967 and 1970; wife Anne; three children, Wayne Jr, Heather and Andrew; employed by Can-Tex Drilling and Exploration Ltd. since August 1962; hobbies include skiing, woodwork, hunting and fishing

1959 – 1960 University of Arkansas, lineman
1961 – 1972 Calgary Stampeders, lineman

After 12 years with the Calgary Stampeders, Wayne Harris retired and was honored by his fans with a special Appreciation Day. The club retired his sweater number 55 as a tribute to his great contributions to the team. Rated by many as the greatest middle linebacker ever to play Canadian football, he was selected to the Western Conference All-Star Team for 11 consecutive seasons. Known as "The Thumper" at Arkansas because of his robust tackling, Harris not only dominated All-Star selection but was voted All-Canadian for 8 of his 11 full seasons of play. During his 12 years with the Stampeders, Wayne helped his team into 3 Grey Cup games. When they finally won the title in 1971, for the first time in 23 years, he was selected as the outstanding player of the game for his superlative performance, which included recovery of an opponent's fumble. Harris planted his roots in Calgary as soon as he arrived there and has been a member of the community ever since.

McCANCE, Chester

Player

A born athlete; excelled in football, basketball, curling, soccer and lacrosse; worked to assist youth as member of St. Andrew's Church in Winnipeg; son William; coached high school and college football.

1937 – 1941 Winnipeg Blue Bombers
1942 – 1943 Winnipeg RCAF Bombers
1945 Winnipeg Blue Bombers
1946 – 1950 Montreal Alouettes

Twice during his career, McCance's accurate kicking lifted him to second place in the Eastern Conference scoring race and in the Grey Cup game of 1941 he kicked two field goals, including the winning score, and two converts as Winnipeg defeated Ottawa 18 – 16. McCance graduated from junior football in Winnipeg, where he was a two-way end, and joined the Blue Bombers in 1937. Following W. W. II, when the Montreal Alouettes club was formed, he joined the team as player and assistant coach and in 1949 contributed seven points to a 28 – 15 Grey Cup victory over Calgary. He scored 17 points in Grey Cup games. McCance was known for his spirit receiving ample reward from the sheer joy of competition and his unstinting effort in every game.

SIMPSON, Robert

Player

Born April 20, 1930, in Windsor, Ont; played basketball 1950 – 1952 with Tillsonburg Livingstons, was with the team as Canada's Olympic representatives at Helsinki, Finland, 1952; Schenley Award three times; Hiram Walker Trophy; Ottawa's Most Valuable Player; Gord Strutridge Trophy; married Mary Frances, former singer on Country Hoedown; five children, Robert John, Gary Lee, Lynn Patricia, Mark Stanley and Mary Leigh; presently executive director of the National Capital Region Amateur Sports Council.

1948 Paterson Collegiate, player
1949 Windsor Rockets Seniors, player
1950 – 1962 Ottawa Rough Riders, offensive and defensive back, offensive end, captain

An outstanding athlete who came out of Windsor scholastic circle to become tremendously successful in Canadian football, Simpson owned the record from 1962 to 1975 of having caught more touchdown passes than any other Canadian Football League performer. He scored 65 of his 70 career touchdowns on pass receptions, exceeded only by Terry Evanshen in 1975. His value as a two-way performer and versatility in different positions made him an All-Star selection eight times, and Bob made it not only as an offensive end but also as an offensive and defensive back. His leadership qualities led him to captain the Rough Riders from 1956 to 1962, his last seven years with the team. He was known for being deceptively swift as a runner and an intelligent, thinking performer. Simpson inspired Ottawa to a playoff victory over Toronto Argonauts in 1960 by engineering a "sleeper" play with quarterback Ron Lancaster. The play worked for an 80-yd. gain and set up the decisive touchdown two plays later. It also put him into his second Grey Cup game, and again he was a member of the winning team. His sweater number 70 was retired in 1960.

SPRING, Harry C. F.
Builder
Born in Moose Jaw, Sask; moved with family to B. C. at age 16; worked for brief time in office of Canadian Pacific Steamships at Vancouver and in the Orient; graduated from Univ. B. C. 1940; served in Royal Canadian Artillery 1940–1945, commencing with rank of lieutenant and leaving with rank of major; wife Constance; two children, Robert and Elaine; presently senior partner of Vancouver Law Firm Macrae, Montgomery, Spring and Cunningham.

1951 Western Conference, Canadian Football League, chairman
1955–1956 British Columbia Lions, treasurer
1957 British Columbia Lions, vice president
1958 British Columbia Lions, president
1961–1977 Commissioner's Representative in Vancouver

An outstanding contributor in the building of Canadian football, Harry Spring served as chairman of the group that laid the groundwork for a Vancouver franchise in the Western Conference of the Canadian Football League. A life member and original director of the British Columbia Lions, Harry served as treasurer, vice president and president between 1955 and 1959, the important years in the growth and development of the British Columbia team. Playing high school football in Moose Jaw and later becoming an active member of the Saskatchewan Rough Riders, Spring came to Vancouver with some football expertise. He quarterbacked Vancouver Meralomas to the British Columbia senior football title, then became active at the executive level with the junior Meralomas. He has served as the Commissioner's representative in Vancouver for 16 years, since he was first appointed in 1961. Harry was honored in 1967 at the Grey Cup Dinner, when he was presented with a plaque for "Outstanding Service to Football."

Green Bay Packer Hall of Fame

GREEN BAY, WISCONSIN

Mailing Address: P.O. Box 3776, 54303. Tel. (414) 499-4281. *Contact:* Jim Van Matre, Mgr. *Location:* 1901 S. Onieda St; approx. 85 mi. S.E. of Wausau, 100 mi. N. of Milwaukee, 120 mi. N.E. of Madison. *Admission:* 9 to 5 daily and weekends, closed Christmas Day. Adults $2.35, children $1.00, family $6.00. *Personnel:* Tom Hutchinson, Pres; Peter Allerup, V.Pres; Bill Brault, Secy; Harold Pfotenhauer, Treas. *Nearby Halls of Fame:* Bowling, State (Milwaukee).

Established in 1968 as a small hallway exhibit in Brown County Veterans Memorial Arena, the Green Bay Packer Hall of Fame has grown into an 11,000-sq. ft. shrine to the Packer legend. Sparked by public demand and funded by public subscription, the building was dedicated on April 3, 1976, when President Ford presided over the unveiling ceremony. At that time work on the interior and the exhibits had just begun. Three months and $350,000 later, the unusual Hall was opened to the public. Twelve major exhibits immerse the visitor in the rich tradition of the Packer story. The initial experience is the Packer Locker Room extravaganza—a 20-minute multimedia film that graphically depicts the Packers' history through the use of nine 35mm. projectors and a 16mm. projector on an automated turntable. Then, moving through the corridor, visitors arrive at the Packer Playing Field. In an almost totally dark exhibit floor, individually lighted displays offer a close-up look at the players, their families, the coaches, the disappointments and victories. For the "weekend football widow," there are recorded interviews with sympathetic Packer wives. Life-sized figures of famous Packers such as Curly Lambeau, Bart Starr and Vince Lombardi invite visitors to see and hear their individual life stories. At the Field Goal Kicker participant exhibit, the football fan can test his skills; a huge photo of an on-rushing lineman provides the game-like atmosphere for the fan as he tries to kick a regulation National Football League football through the uprights. The Blooper Theatre features an amusing collection of comic football disasters, and the Players' Lounge contains a gift shop with one of the biggest collections of Packer souvenirs. This Hall is a member of the Association of Sports Museums and Halls of Fame.

Members: 60 as of 1977. Persons eligible are Green Bay Packer players who have been retired or deceased for at least five years and who have shown outstanding performance as Packer players. For each player enshrined, there is a sponsoring member of the Hall of Fame Association who donates $250 to finance a plaque in the player's honor. In addition, contributors (directors, officers, coaches, staff members or fans) are eligible to become members provided the contributor has shown outstanding dedication to the well-being of the Green Bay Packers. Up to five players and not more than one contributor are inducted each year. A nominating committee of at least three members selected by the Green Bay Packers Hall of Fame Executive Committee nominates 24 players and 6 contributors. This list of nominees is initially submitted to the Green Bay Packers Alumni Association who then select one inductee from the first half of the years from 1919 through the current year and one inductee from the second half. This selection is held during the annual Alumni Weekend in Green Bay. The remaining 22 nominees are submitted to a committee of at least 15 total votes consisting of ballots cast by Wisconsin Sportswriters and Sportscasters, two ballots from the Green Bay Packer Alumni Association, and one ballot from the Green Bay Packer Public Relations Department. The Committee votes for one player from the first half of years and two players from the second half of years and one contributor. The Hall of Fame Executive Committee tabulates the final ballots. New members are inducted at the annual Hall of Fame Banquet, held the fourth Saturday of January.

1970

DARLING, Bernard "Boob"
Player
Attended Beloit College; past president of the Packer Alumni Association; active for nearly 40 years as a leader in Green Bay's business, civic and sports life; died 1968.

Playing five seasons 1927 – 1931 as center with the Packers, Darling helped them to their first triple title, 1929, 1930 and 1931. Remembered by Mike Michalske for his positive effect on the team's morale, Boob was consistently eager and willing to add humor and wit that was a real boost for the club.

DILWEG, Laverne "Lavvie"
Player
Attended Marquette Univ; All-American; All-Pro four years.

1926 Milwaukee Badgers, end
1927 – 1934 Green Bay Packers, end

An All-American in football at Marquette, Dilweg had the honor of being named to the first All-Pro team ever selected (1931). He continued as an All-Pro selection for a total of four years as an outstanding pass receiver as well as a deadly tackler. He had 14 career touchdowns and 2 extra points for a total of 86 career points.
Also in: Wisconsin Athletic Hall of Fame.

EARPE, Francis "Jug"
Player
Attended Monmouth College.

1921 Rock Island Independents, guard
1922 – 1932 Green Bay Packers, guard

An experienced guard, Jug made his presence known during his collegiate days at Monmouth, and later in the pros was referred to by sportswriters as "the man-mountain of professional ball." Francis Earpe began his pro career with the Rock Island Independents. After a one-year stint with the Independents, he joined the Green Bay Packers where he played guard 1922 – 1932.

HUBBARD, Robert C. "Cal"
Player
Born October 11, 1900; All-American at both Geneva College and Centenary College; All-NFL 1928 – 1933; NFL All-Time Offensive Tackle 1969; played pro baseball for New York Giants and Pittsburgh Pirates 1936; American League baseball umpire 1936 – 1952; supervisor of umpires 1952 – 1970; retired and lives in old hometown.

1927 – 1928 New York Giants, end
1929 – 1935 Green Bay Packers, tackle

After college football Hubbard, 6 ft. 5 in, 260 lbs, was the rookie star of the Giants' great 1927 defensive team. He went on to become the most feared lineman of his day. Later he anchored the line for the Packers' 1929 – 1931 title teams. Extremely fast and strong, he excelled as a blocker on offense and as a linebacker on defense; he was All-NFL six years. College coach Bo McMillin said, "Hubbard was the greatest football player of all times, college or professional."
Also in: Major League Baseball Hall of Fame and Major League Football Hall of Fame, Citizens Savings Hall of Fame Athletic Museum; Louisiana Sports Hall of Fame, National Association of Intercollegiate Athletics Hall of Fame, National Baseball Hall of Fame, National Football Hall of Fame and Professional Football Hall of Fame.

LAMBEAU, Earl "Curly"
Founder and Coach
Born April 9, 1898, in Green Bay, Wis; played one season at Notre Dame; died June 1, 1965, at age 67.

1919 – 1949 Green Bay Packers, coach and halfback
1950 – 1951 Chicago Cardinals, coach
1952 – 1953 Washington Redskins, coach

In 1919 Lambeau pursuaded his boss at the Indian Packing Company in Green Bay to sponsor a local football team—this was the genesis of the Packers. The team joined the National Football League in 1921 with Curly as their player-coach. He played halfback 1919 – 1927 with 12 touchdowns, 19 extra points and 6 field goals in his playing career for a total of 109 points. His 29-year coaching career with Green Bay is the longest uninterrupted tenure in pro history. He was the first coach to make the forward pass an integral part of the offense. During his career, he won seven divisional and six NFL titles with a record of 231 – 133 – 23. He resigned from the Packers when he was no longer able to maintain one-man rule over the club.
Also in: Major League Football Hall of Fame, Citizens Savings Hall of Fame Athletic Museum; Professional Football Hall of Fame and Wisconsin Athletic Hall of Fame.

LEWELLEN, Verne
Player
Attended Nebraska Univ; currently living in Green Bay.

1924 – 1932 Green Bay Packers, back
1954 – 1959 Green Bay Packers, general manager
1959 – 1966 Green Bay Packers, business manager

Scoring 50 touchdowns and 1 extra point, Lewellen compiled a career total of 301 points. After his playing career, he served as the Packers' general manager and business manager. Verne now serves the club on various committees.
Also in: Wisconsin Athletic Hall of Fame.

McNALLY, John "Johnny Blood"
Player
Born November 27, 1904, in New Richmond, Wis; won letters in four sports at St. John's Univ. (Minn); attended Notre Dame turning down football position when coach tried converting him to tackle; All-Pro Squad in 1930s; adopted nickname "Johnny Blood" from the movie *Blood and Sand;* maintained a swinging life-style once engaging in a Shakespeare-quoting contest with John Barrymore in a Pittsburgh bar; occupied various

positions including bartender, stenotyper, air force sergeant and cryptographer in China; presently living in St. Paul, Minn, involved in the operation of two employment agencies.

1925 – 1927 Milwaukee Badgers, running back
1926 – 1927 Duluth Eskimos, running back
1928 Pottsville Maroons, running back
1928 – 1936 Green Bay Packers, running back
1937 – 1938 Pittsburgh Pirates, running back
1939 Pittsburgh Steelers, running back, coach

Joining the Packers in 1928 after brief stints with the Milwaukee Badgers, Duluth Eskimos and Pottsville Maroons, Johnny played a major role in the Packers' drive to their first three championships 1929 – 1931. An excellent pass receiver and elusive runner, he also helped the Packers win a fourth world title in 1936. Johnny scored 37 touchdowns and 2 extra points with the Packers totaling 224 career points.
Also in: Major League Football Hall of Fame, Citizens Savings Hall of Fame Athletic Museum; Professional Football Hall of Fame and Wisconsin Athletic Hall of Fame.

MICHALSKE, August "Mike" "Iron Mike"

Player

Born April 24, 1903, in Cleveland,Ohio; attended Penn State Univ; All-American 1925; All-Pro 1931, 1935; great stamina and endurance earned him nickname "Iron Mike"; presently living in De Pere, Wis; vice president of Green Bay Packers Alumni Association.

1926 – 1928 New York Yankees, guard
1929 – 1935 Green Bay Packers, guard
1937 Green Bay Packers, guard
1942 – 1947 Iowa State University, head coach

An All-American at Penn State in 1925, Michalske was rated as one of the game's greatest guards during pro football's "two-way" era. Extremely fast, Mike was equally effective on both offense and defense. Signing with the Packers in 1929, Michalske was a member of the Packers' world championship teams his first three seasons. He is remembered for playing almost 60 minutes of every game. After his playing career, Mike went on to become head coach at Iowa State and at various times assistant coach at Lafayette, St. Norbert, Baylor, Texas A&M, Texas and Baltimore Colts.
Also in: Professional Football Hall of Fame.

1972

BRUDER, Hank

Player

A native of Perkin, Ill; attended Northwestern Univ; All-American; nicknamed "Hard Luck Hank" due to a series of injuries that plagued him throughout his school days.

Gaining All-American status at Northwestern University as a college back, Hank came directly to the Packers in 1931. He remained with the Packers through the 1939 season distinguishing himself as one of the hardest blockers and toughest tacklers in the business.

GANTENBEIN, Milt

Player

Attended Wisconsin Univ; now residing in Carmichael, Calif.

A great two-way performer, playing end both offensively and defensively, Milt was regarded by his teammates as "the best blocking end in football." Scoring 9 touchdowns for Green Bay, Milt compiled a career total of 54 points 1931 – 1940. Later in his career he became the defensive captain of the team.

GOLDENBERG, Charles "Buckets"

Player

Attended Wisconsin Univ; named to Best in 1930s Team; currently a member of the Green Bay Packers board of directors; residing in Milwaukee, Wis.

An all-round athlete, Goldenberg played fullback, blockingback and guard 1933 – 1944 with Green Bay. Before being switched to guard, Buckets scored 60 points on 10 touchdowns. He played right guard on offense and middle guard on defense. Charles was named to the Best in the 1930s Team by pro sportswriters who were selecting the first 50-year team.

HERBER, Arnold "Flash"

Player

Born April 2, 1910, in Green Bay, Wis; attended Wisconsin Univ. as freshman, then transferred to Regis Col. in Denver; All-Pro 1932; died October 14, 1969, in Green Bay.

1931 – 1941 Green Bay Packers, quarterback
1944 – 1945 New York Giants, quarterback

Herber signed with his hometown team in 1931, remaining with them until 1941. Teaming up with Don Hutson, they formed the feared Herber-to-Hutson pass combination during the mid-thirties. Leading the league in passing in 1932, 1934 and 1936 (his best year), Arnold threw for 1239 yds. and 13 touchdowns. He won three National Football League passing titles and was an All-Pro selection in 1932. Arnold accumulated a career total of 481 completions for 8033 yds. He made 7 touchdowns and 2 extra points for a total of 44 career points. The Flash was also an accomplished punter.
Also in: Major League Football Hall of Fame, Citizens Savings Hall of Fame Athletic Museum; and Professional Football Hall of Fame.

HINKLE, William Clarke

Player

Born April 10, 1912, in Toronto, Ont; attended Bucknell Col; All-NFL four times; All-Pro 1936 – 1938, 1941; presently living in Steubenville, Ohio.

1929 – 1931 Bucknell College, player
1932 – 1941 Green Bay Packers, back, linebacker, kicker

A star at Bucknell before joining the Packers, Hinkle led the 1931 Bucknell team to an undefeated season with his powerful running. An outstanding back on offense and linebacker on defense, he also kicked for Green Bay, leading the league in field goals in 1940 and 1941. Hinkle was the National Football League's (NFL) scoring leader in 1938 with 58 points. His career totals show 3877 yds. gained on 1180 carries and 43 touchdowns. Hinkle, 5 ft. 11 in, 196 lbs, was excellent as a fullback. Green Bay coach Curly Lambeau said of him: "Hinkle runs the middle, runs wide, and blocks and tackles viciously. He punts and placekicks with the best. He can do a job as a pass receiver. And in defense against aerial attack, Hinkle has no superior in professional football."

Also in: Major League Football Hall of Fame, Citizens Savings Hall of Fame Athletic Museum; National Football Hall of Fame, Professional Football Hall of Fame and Wisconsin Athletic Hall of Fame.

HUTSON, Donald M.
Player
Born January 31, 1913, in Pine Bluff, Ark; attended Univ. Ala; All-Pro nine times; All-Century Team 1934; Modern All-Time All-American Team; currently serving on board of directors of Green Bay Packers residing in Racine, Wis.

1932 – 1935 University of Alabama Crimson Tide, end
1935 – 1945 Green Bay Packers, end

A sure-handed receiver with incredible speed and athletic ability, the "Alabama Antelope" played 118 games with the Packers catching 489 passes for 8010 yds. and 100 touchdown passes. Inventor of many plays, he was half of the famed Herber-to-Hutson duo. Averaging six to eight receptions per game, Don set a league record by catching 17 touchdown passes in one season. Hutson, 6 ft. 1 in, 175 lbs, was the National Football League (NFL) receiving leader in 1936, 1937, 1939, 1941 – 1945 and NFL scoring leader 1940 – 1944, setting a record in 1942 (138 points) that stood until 1960. On October 7, 1945, in the second quarter, he scored 29 points against the Detroit Lions. When he retired he held records for points (825) and touchdowns (105).
Also in: College Football Hall of Fame and Major League Football Hall of Fame, Citizens Savings Hall of Fame Athletic Museum; National Football Hall of Fame and Professional Football Hall of Fame.

ISBELL, Cecil
Player
Attended Univ. Purdue; All-Star Trophy for Outstanding College Player 1938; All-League 1941, 1942; presently residing in Calumet, Ill.

1935 – 1937 University of Purdue, quarterback
1938 – 1942 Green Bay Packers, quarterback

Isbell's best season with the Boilermakers was 1936, when he led Purdue to a 6 – 2 record; overall, the team won 13, lost 9 and tied 2 during his varsity career. As a junior he figured in 15 of 23 Purdue touchdowns, and did the bulk of the punting. Cecil Isbell was the Number One draft choice of the Packers in 1938. He scored 10 touchdowns and 3 extra points in five seasons totaling 63 points. His rushing record was 1522 yds. averaging 3.6 yds. per carry. Completing 419 passes in five seasons, he quarterbacked the Packers to one world title. In 1943 he returned to Purdue as backfield coach, and in 1944 was named head coach. Cecil rounded out his coaching career with the Baltimore Colts, Chicago Cardinals and Louisiana State University.
Also in: National Football Hall of Fame.

LAWS, Joe "Tiger"
Player
Attended Univ. Iowa; currently living in Green Bay, Wis.

1934 – 1945 Green Bay Packers, back

Voted the Most Valuable Player in the Big Ten in his collegiate days, Tiger was as good on defense as he was on offense. An aggressive player, Joe had three interceptions in a game against the New York Giants. Laws was a left-handed passer, known for his intelligent play calling. He scored 133 points on 22 touchdowns in his career with the Packers.

LETLOW, Russ
Player
Attended Univ. San Francisco; All-Pro 1938; presently living in Delano, Calif.

1936 – 1942 Green Bay Packers, guard
1946 Green Bay Packers, guard

Considered one of the best guards of the National League, Russ Letlow spent eight years with the Packers. In 1938 he made the All-Pro team after being placed on the second honor team the previous year. He also received honorable mention in 1939 and 1940.

SVENDSEN, George
Player
Currently living in Minneapolis, Minn.

A duo performer, Svendsen played center on offense and linebacker on defense 1935-1941 with Green Bay. A big, strong, durable lineman, George was known for his constant accuracy in snapping the ball. He was a good runner and an athlete whose devotion and desire to play football enabled him to make it in the pros.

1973

BROCK, Charlie
Player
Attended Nebraska Univ; All-Decade team; presently residing in Green Bay, Wis.

1939 – 1947 Green Bay Packers, center

A two-way performer, Brock played center on offense and linebacker on defense. Most famous for stealing the ball from his opponents, Charlie was also an indestructible blocker. He was a member of the All-Decade team and a past president of the Packer Alumni Association.

CANADEO, Anthony
Player
Born 1919; attended Gonzaga Univ. 1938 – 1940; called the Grey Ghost of Gonzaga for his elusive running abilities; All-Pro 1943 and 1949; All-Pro Squad of the 1940s; lives with his family in Green Bay; presently serving as a member of the Green Bay Packers' executive committee.

1941 – 1943 Green Bay Packers, back
1946 – 1952 Green Bay Packers, back

A versatile athlete, Tony played the positions of running back, quarterback, punter and kick returner. He is the second all-time leading Packer rusher. In 1025 attempts, he rushed for 4197 yds., an average of 4.1 yds. per carry, with 54 yds. his longest run. Scoring 31 touchdowns for 186 points, Tony is the Packers' sixteenth all-time scorer and eighteenth all-time receiver with 69 for 579 yds. In 1949 he attained 1052 yds. which earned him a membership in the 1000-yd. club. Tony is 5 ft. 11 in. tall and weighs 195 lbs.
Also in: Major League Football Hall of Fame, Citizens Savings Hall of Fame Athletic Museum; National Association of Intercollegiate Athletics Hall of Fame and Professional Football Hall of Fame.

CRAIG, Larry
Player
Attended Univ. of South Carolina; All-Decade Team; lives in Ninety-Six, S.C.

A tough, durable back, Craig scored six points in his career with the Packers 1939-1949. He was a two-way performer, a blocking back on offense and both tackle and end on defense.
Also in: University of South Carolina Sports Hall of Fame.

FORTE, Bob
Player
Attended Univ. Ark; lives in Greendale, Wis.

Forte was an offensive blocking back for the Packers 1946-1953. He sometimes alternated with Don Hutson as a defensive back. Scoring four touchdowns, Bob's career points total 24. In 1952 he gained 50 yds. on four interceptions. Bob also held the position of Packer team captain.

FRITSCH, Ted
Player
Attended Univ. Wis, Stevens Point; also active in pro basketball and pro baseball; currently living and working in Green Bay, Wis.

An outstanding fullback and kicker for Green Bay, 1942-1950, Fritsch was the National Football League's scoring champion in 1946. In his eight-year tenure with the Packers, Ted had a total of 31 touchdowns, 62 extra points and 36 field goals for 392 career points. In one memorable game against the New York Yanks, Fritsch kicked a 52-yd. field goal.

MONNETT, Bobby
Player
Attended Michigan State Univ; All-Decade Team; now residing in Galion, Ohio.

Monnett played at left halfback on offense during his years with the Packers 1933–1938. He compiled a career total of 97 points on nine touchdowns, 28 extra points and five field goals.

RAY, Buford "Baby"
Player
Attended Vanderbilt Univ; All-Decade Team; currently serving as area scout for Green Bay Packers; lives in Nashville, Tenn.

Ray played the position of left tackle with the Green Bay Packers 1938–1948. He was a four-time all-league tackle.

URAM, Andy
Player
Attended Univ. of Minn; settled in Green Bay, Wis, with his family.

Uram was one of the greatest running backs in Packers' history. He gained 1065 yds. on 238 attempts during his career with Green Bay 1938–1943. Appearing often in record manuals for "longest" performances, his 90-yd. punt return against Brooklyn in 1941 is the second best in Packers' records. In a game against the Cardinals in 1939, Andy's 97-yd. run from scrimmage was the longest run in Packers' history. Uram scored 95 career points on 16 touchdowns and 2 extra points.

WILDUNG, Richard K.
Player
Born 1921 in St. Paul, Minn; played football at Laverne High School in Minn; attended Univ. Minn; Navy Lt. in W.W. II; All-Decade Team; presently living in Minneapolis.

1940–1942 University of Minnesota, tackle
1946–1951 Green Bay Packers, tackle
1953 Green Bay Packers, tackle

An exceptionally strong tackle, Richard starred at the University of Minnesota where he was consensus All-American twice, 1941 and 1942. After serving in the Navy, he joined the Green Bay Packers in 1946 playing through the 1951 season and again in 1953. An outstanding pass rusher, he was chosen to play in the 1952 Pro Bowl game.
Also in: College Football Hall of Fame, Citizens Savings Hall of Fame Athletic Museum; and National Football Hall of Fame.

WOODIN, "Whitey"
Player
Attended Marquette Univ.

Known for his tough blocking, Whitey was considered an early-day "Fuzzy" Thurston. He was a fierce competitor and a great team player. Woodin had 10 career points on 1 touchdown and 4 extra points in his nine years with the Packers, 1922–1930.

1974

CARMICHAEL, Albert R. "Hoagy"
Player
Born November 10, 1929, in Boston, Mass; graduated from Univ. Southern Calif; presently living in San Clemente, Calif.

1953–1958 Green Bay Packers, back
1960–1961 Denver Broncos, back

A first-round draft choice of the Packers in 1953, Carmichael, 6 ft. 1 in, 200 lbs, was an immediate starter at right halfback. In 1953 and again in 1957 Albert was Number Two in the National Football League in punt returns. He was the league kickoff-return leader with 14 for 418 yds, averaging 29.9 in 1955. Hoagy set a record in 1956 in a game against the Chicago Bears by returning a kickoff 106 yds. Scoring 6 touchdowns, his total career points amounted to 36. Carmichael ended his career third in kickoff returns (lifetime) with 191, and yards returned on kickoffs (lifetime) with 4798.

CONE, Fred
Player
Attended Clemson Univ.

A number three draft choice in 1951, Fred led the team in scoring four out of his first five years with the Green Bay Packers. With a career total of 455 points, Cone is the fourth all-time Green Bay scorer. He had 16 touchdowns, 200 extra points and 53 field goals. The amazing 200 points-after-touchdowns is a Packer all-time record. Fred's longest run was 41 yds. and he had a rushing total of 1156 yds. Cone played with Green Bay 1951–1957.

DILLON, Robert
Player
Born February 23, 1930, in Pendleton, Tex; attended Univ. Texas; All-Pro four times; currently living in Temple, Tex.

1949 – 1951 University of Texas, back
1952 – 1959 Green Bay Packers, defensive back

A smart back, Bobby Dillon, who was blind in one eye, ended his collegiate career as one of the country's leading punt returners. Dillon gained 830 yds. on 47 returns, an average of 17.7. He joined the Green Bay Packers in 1952 as a third-round draft choice. In his eight-year tenure with the Packers, Bobby intercepted 52 passes for 976 yds. placing him at the top of the list as the all-time Packers' interception leader. Dillon, 6 ft. 1 in, 185 lbs, was chosen an All-Pro safety four times and played in four Pro Bowl games.

FERGUSON, Howie
Player
Lives in Lake Charles, La.

A hustling fullback, Howie signed with the Packers as a free agent in 1953 after trying out with the Los Angeles Rams. In 1954 he became a starter. He scored 7 touchdowns totaling 42 career points in his six years with Green Bay 1953 – 1958. Howie is the eighth all-time Packers' rusher with 2120 yds. He is the tenth all-time Packers' receiver catching 127 passes for 1079 yds. The 6 ft. 2-in, 210-lb. fullback played in the 1956 Pro Bowl.

FORESTER, Bill
Player
Attended Southern Methodist Univ; All-Pro 1960 – 1963.

Forrester was a third-draft choice of Green Bay in 1953. Starting out as a defensive guard and tackle, he was moved to the position of linebacker in 1954. Bill became a defensive captain in his eleven years with the Packers 1953 – 1963. He played in the Pro Bowl 1960 – 1963.

HANNER, Dave
Player
Attended Univ. Ark; All-Pro 1954, 1955; retired from playing 1965; currently serving as member of Packer coaching staff heading up the defensive unit.

Dave Hanner, 6 ft. 2 in, was a fifth-round draft choice for the Packers in 1952. Becoming an immediate starter with the club, he continued a starter all 13 years of his playing career 1952 – 1964. He was a perfect selection for the position of defensive tackle. Dave was a jubilant, bald-headed man who utilized his powerful strength on the field in every possible way. He was named defensive line coach with the Packers upon his retirement in 1965 and became defensive coordinator in 1972.

HOWTON, William
Player
Born July 3, 1930, in Littlefield, Tex; attended Rice Univ; All-American playing end 1951; All-Pro 1956-1957.

1949 – 1951 Rice University, end
1952 – 1958 Green Bay Packers, end
1959 Cleveland Browns, end
1960 – 1963 Dallas Cowboys, end

After starring three years at Rice University, Howton was drafted on the first round of the Green Bay Packers in 1952. Leading the Packers in receiving his entire six years with the club, he had his best year in 1956 when he caught 55 passes for 1188 yds. and 12 touchdowns. With a total of 303 catches for 5581 yds. and 43 touchdowns, he is the fourth all-time Packers' receiving leader. The trio of Howton, Parilli and Rote gave the Packers the top passing attack in the National Football League in 1952. Howton set a Packers' single-game reception record of 257 yds. in seven catches in 1956. Later, in 1963 while playing for the Dallas Cowboys, he exceeded Don Hutson's career record on pass receptions with 8000 yds.

MARTINKOVIC, John
Player
Attended Xavier Univ; chosen Little All-American; also earned letters in basketball and baseball along with football; All-Pro 1954, 1955; currently living in Green Bay Wis.

1951 Washington Redskins, end
1951 – 1956 Green Bay Packers, defensive end
1957 New York Giants, end

John was traded to the Green Bay Packers from the Washington Redskins in 1951. He was considered one of the best defensive ends in the National Football League, and was selected for two Pro Bowl games, 1954 and 1955.

RINGO, James
Player
Born November 21, 1932, in Orange, N.J; attended Phillipsburg, N.J, High School and Syracuse Univ; played center and linebacker in college and played in 1953 Orange Bowl; All-Pro 1957, 1959, 1960 – 1963; currently head coach of the Buffalo Bills; lives in Orchard Park, N.Y.

1953 – 1963 Green Bay Packers, center
1964 – 1967 Philadelphia Eagles, center
1969 – 1971 Chicago Bears, coach
1972 – 1973 Buffalo Bills, offensive line coach

Jim was drafted on the seventh round by the Green Bay Packers in 1953. He set a National Football League record with the Packers and the Eagles, playing 182 consecutive games, that stood until 1971. Jim was the Packers' captain for eight of his eleven years with the team. He was named to ten Pro Bowls, seven with the Green Bay Packers and three with the Eagles. He played in three National Football League championship games. *Also in:* Major League Football Hall of Fame, Citizens Savings Hall of Fame Athletic Museum.

ROTE, Tobin C.
Player
Born in San Antonio, Tex; attended Rice Univ. 1946 – 1949, playing for them in 1947 Orange Bowl game and 1950 Cotton Bowl; presently living in Southfield, Mich.

1947 – 1950 Rice University, quarterback
1950 – 1956 Green Bay Packers, quarterback
1957 – 1959 Detroit Lions, quarterback
1960 – 1962 Toronto Argonauts, quarterback
1963 – 1964 San Diego Chargers, quarterback
1966 Denver Broncos, quarterback

Rote was the second-draft choice for the Green Bay Packers in 1950. He led the Packers in passing the entire seven years he played with the team. Completing 826 of

1854 passing attempts, he gained 11,535 yds. and 80 touchdowns. Tobin ranks seventh on the all-time Packers' rushing list with 419 carries for 2202 yds. Some of his other Packers' feats include: most completed passes in a season—184 in 1954, most passes attempted in a season—382 in 1954, and the longest pass completion—96 yds. Tobin played in one Pro Bowl game while with the Packers. He is the first and only quarterback to lead championship teams in both the National Football League (NFL) and the American Football League (AFL). In 1957 he directed the NFL title win by 59 – 14 over the Cleveland Browns and in 1963, at quarterback for San Diego, won the AFL title over the Boston Patriots by a 51 – 10 score.
Also in: Major League Football Hall of Fame, Citizens Savings Hall of Fame Athletic Museum.

1975

CHANDLER, Donald G. "Babe"
Player

Born September 9, 1934, in Council Bluffs, Iowa; attended Univ. Fl; gained recognition as National Collegiate Athletic Association punting champion 1955; retired 1968; resides in Tulsa, Okla.

1953 – 1955 University of Florida, punter, kicker
1956 – 1964 New York Giants, end, kicker
1965 – 1967 Green Bay Packers, end, kicker

Don Chandler, 6 ft. 2 in, 215 lbs, played nine years with the New York Giants before being purchased by the Green Bay Packers in 1965. Coming to the Packers with a wealth of football experience and successful kicking ability, he made 48 field goals in 80 attempts and his punts averaged 41.9 yds. on 135 kicks in his career with the Packers. In 1965, in a game with the San Francisco 49ers, Don set a National Football League (NFL) record on a 90-yd. punt. In a tight-scoring game in 1965, he scored the winning field goal, 25 yds, in overtime against the Baltimore Colts. Don played in nine NFL championship games tying Lou Groza for most championship games played. In Super Bowl II against Oakland, Don completed 4 out of 4 creating a new and still existing record of 15 points on 4 field goals and 3 extra points. Tenth on the list of Packers' all-time scorers, Don compiled 261 points with the Packers and 429 career points in the NFL.

DAVIS, William
Player

Born July 24, 1934, in Lisbon, La; raised in Texarkana, Ark; attended Booker T. Washington High School; played varsity football as both defensive tackle and offensive end; earned scholarship to Grambling Univ, making captain junior and senior years; graduated with B.S. 1956; U.S. Army, 1957, selected on both All-Army and All-Service teams; M.B.A. Univ. Chicago 1968; Pro Bowl 1963 – 1967; All-NFL 1964 – 1967; Byron Award for Citizenship and Athletic Excellence 1967; All-Pro five times; retired 1970; presently residing in Los Angeles, Calif.

1956 Cleveland Browns, defensive end
1959 – 1968 Green Bay Packers, defensive end

Willie Davis was drafted on the fifteenth round of the Cleveland Browns in 1956. In 1959 he was traded to Green Bay Packers for A. D. Williams. In his career with the Packers, Willie was selected All-Pro five times and was chosen to play in five Pro Bowl games. A smart man with a huge build, 6 ft. 3 in, 245 lbs, he was a perfect choice as captain of the Packers defensive unit. Davis recovered 21 opponents' fumbles in his career tying him for second highest in National Football League (NFL) history. Excluding six NFL title games and two Super Bowls, Willie participated in 148 consecutive games.
Also in: National Association of Intercollegiate Athletics Hall of Fame.

HORNUNG, Paul
Player

Born December 23, 1935, in Louisville, Ky; Notre Dame All-Star 1954 – 1956; Heisman Trophy in 1956; Most Valuable Player 1961; called into Army 1961 but released same year ten days before NFL title game; retired 1967 after being picked by New Orleans Saints in expansion draft.

1954 – 1956 University of Notre Dame, halfback
1957 – 1962 Green Bay Packers, halfback, kicker
1964 – 1966 Green Bay Packers, halfback, kicker

Earning recognition as an excellent all-round football player at Notre Dame, Hornung was chosen as Green Bay Packers' bonus number-one draft pick in 1957. Paul ranks second in all-time Packers' scoring records with 62 touchdowns, 196 extra points and 66 field goals for a career total of 760 points. He was the National Football League's (NFL) leading scorer in 1959 with 94 points, and scored a record 176 in 1960 and 146 in 1961. He also holds a Packers' record for the most consecutive extra points ever kicked, 96, and is the Packers' fourth all-time career rusher. He totaled 3712 yds. on 893 carries for a 4.1 yd. average and 50 touchdowns. "Golden Boy" Hornung holds the still-existing NFL title game record by scoring 19 points on 1 touchdown, 4 extra points, and 3 field goals against the Giants in 1961.

JORDAN, Henry W.
Player

Born January 26, 1935, in Emporia, Va; attended Univ. Va; participated in wrestling in high school, winning Amateur Athletic Union title at 16; continued in college and won Athletic Coast Conference title, becoming runner up for National Collegiate Athletic Association Wrestling Championship in senior year; selected in the College All-Star Football Game in 1957; All-NFL 1960 – 1964; Pro Bowl Lineman 1962; Most Valuable Player 1964.

1954 – 1956 University of Virginia, tackle
1957 – 1958 Cleveland Browns, tackle
1959 – 1969 Green Bay Packers, defensive tackle

An exceptional defensive tackle, Hank was drafted on the fifth round in 1957 by the Cleveland Browns. He played two seasons with the Browns before being traded to the Green Bay Packers for a fourth-draft choice in 1959. Jordan, 6 ft. 3 in, 250 lbs, stayed through the 1969 season with the Packers playing in seven National Football League (NFL) championship games, 1957, 1960 – 1962, 1965 – 1967, Pro Bowls 1961, 1962, 1964 and 1967, and two Super Bowls in 1967 and 1968. Jordan was credited with four quarterback sacks during the 1967 Western Division playoff win over Los Angeles.

KRAMER, Gerald L.
Player

Born January 23, 1936, in Jordan, Mo; attended Univ. Idaho; All-NFL 1960, 1962, 1966, 1967; author of *Instant Replay* and *The Green Bay Packer Diary of Jerry Kramer*; edited *Lombardi: Winning Is the Only Thing;* retired after 1968 season; currently living in Parma, Idaho.

A fourth-round draft choice of the Packers in 1958, Kramer spent his entire career with the team. He became known as part of the best guard tandem in football history. Six ft. 3 in, 245 lbs, Kramer compiled an 11-year pro record of 136 games, scoring 177 points on 90 out of 94 extra points and 29 of 54 field goals. In the National Football League (NFL) championship game of 1963 against New York, Jerry successfully completed three out of five field goals. He played in five NFL championship games and two Super Bowls.

KRAMER, Ronald
Player

Born June 24, 1935, in Girard, Kans; played end for Univ. Mich. 1954 – 1956; also participated in basketball and high jump and threw shot put and discus; All-NFL 1962; presently residing in Detroit, Mich.

1957 Green Bay Packers, tight end
1959 – 1964 Green Bay Packers, tight end
1965 – 1967 Detroit Lions, end

Ron was a unanimous All-American at Michigan before joining the Packers in 1957. At 6 ft. 3 in, 235 lbs, he became the perfect example of the big, power-blocking, pass-receiving tight end. In his career in the National Football League (NFL), Ron scored 14 touchdowns and two conversions totaling 90 points. He ranks seventh on the all-time Packers' receiving list with 170 receptions gaining 2594 yds, a 15.2 average.

LOMBARDI, Vincent T.
Coach

Born June 11, 1913, in Brooklyn, N.Y; played football at guard while attending Fordham Univ; Coach of the Year 1961; street on which Packers' offices are located and trophy given to Super Bowl champions named after him; died September 3, 1970, in Washington, D.C.

1939 – 1946 St. Cecilia's High School, coach
1947 Fordham University, freshman coach
1948 Fordham University, varsity assistant coach
1949 – 1953 U.S. Army, coach
1954 – 1958 New York Giants, assistant coach
1959 – 1968 Green Bay Packers, head coach, general manager
1969 Washington Redskins, coach

After 20 years of various coaching jobs, Vince Lombardi was named head coach of the Green Bay Packers in 1959. He stayed with the team nine years serving as both head coach and general manager. In that period, the Packers never finished lower than third and became known as a standard against which all other teams, past and present, are judged. A football legend in his own time, Lombardi guided his team to six Western Division titles, five National Football League (NFL) titles and two Super Bowls. The Packers became the first NFL team to capture three straight NFL championships. In 12 post-season games, the Packers finished with 10 victories, an .833 winning percentage. His NFL record for eleven years was 141 – 39 – 4. In 1969 Vince coached the Washington Redskins to their first winning season in 14 years. Vince was a vital force behind the merger of the NFL and the AFL.

Also in: Major League Football Hall of Fame, Citizen Savings Hall of Fame Athletic Museum; and Professional Football Hall of Fame.

McGEE, William M. "Max"
Player

Born July 16, 1932, in Saxton City, Nev; attended Tulane College, played halfback; one of four brothers all of whom play football; interrupted career in 1956 – 1957 to serve in Air Force as pilot and flight instructor; currently living in Elm Grove, Wis.

1954 Green Bay Packers, end
1957 – 1967 Green Bay Packers, end

Max McGee, 6 ft. 3 in, 205 lbs, spent his entire National Football League (NFL) career with the Green Bay Packers. He led the team in receiving in 1958, 1960, 1961 and 1962. He was first in the nation in kickoff returns with a 21.8 yd. average. Max played on five NFL championship teams and in two Super Bowls. In Super Bowl I, versus Kansas City, Max set a record for number of touchdowns in a game, 2, and for total yards gained, 138, on seven catches. His career totals amount to 345 receptions for 6289 yds, an 18.2 average with 82 yds. being the longest. He also scored 51 touchdowns. Max played in the Pro Bowl games in 1962 and 1963.

TAYLOR, James
Player

Born September 20, 1935, in Baton Rouge, La; delivered newspapers in grammar school and later worked on the rigs for oil companies; in high school was better at basketball than football; attended Louisiana State Univ. 1956 – 1957, played fullback; a devotee of weightlifting; All-American 1957; 1000 Yd. Club 1960 – 1964; All-NFL and All-Pro 1962; NFL Most Valuable Player 1965; presently a New Orleans businessman residing in suburban Metairie.

1958 – 1966 Green Bay Packers, fullback
1966 – 1967 New Orleans Saints

Jim was Green Bay Packers' second-round choice in 1958. He never made it past special teams as a rookie, but went on to become All-Pro, to play in four Pro Bowls, 1962 – 1965, to play in four National Football League championships, 1961, 1962, 1965 and 1966 and the Super Bowl in 1967. Characterized by rugged and sometimes ferocious play, and by determination, the 6-ft, 215-lb. fullback recovered from infectious hepatitis one season to run for 1018 yds. on 248 carries. He holds the single-season record of 19 rushing touchdowns (1962), and had a record five straight years of 1000 yds. He gained 8579 yds. rushing, making him football's third leading lifetime rusher. He averaged 4.4 yds. on 1941 carries, caught 225 passes, gained 10,538 yds. combined and scored 558 points (83 touchdowns). "Football," he said, "is really a game of inches .... When it comes to getting those inches, it's between me and the defense. The best man wins. And no one is going to hit me harder than I hit them." After the 1962 title game, Sam Huff, a Giants linebacker, said, "No human could have stood the

punishment he got today." Norm Van Brocklin commented, "Jimmy is tougher than Japanese arithmetic."
Also in: Professional Football Hall of Fame.

THURSTON, Frederick C. "Fuzzy"
Player
Born November 29, 1933, in Altoona, Wis; attended Valparaiso Univ. with intention of playing basketball; developed into All-Indiana Collegiate offensive guard instead; All-Pro 1961, 1962; now owner of a restaurant in Neenah, Wis.

1958 Baltimore Colts, guard
1959 – 1967 Green Bay Packers, guard

An outstanding guard, Thurston tried out with the Philadelphia Eagles before joining the Baltimore Colts. After one season with the Colts, he came to the Packers for Marv Mutazak in 1959. A major support in the club's offensive line for nine seasons, Fuzzy played in five National Football League championship games. In one of his finest games as half of the most famous guard tandem in football history, he helped the Packers defeat the Kansas City Chiefs of the American Football League in Super Bowl I. The 6 ft. 1-in, 250-lb. guard was voted All-Pro twice, accumulating more All-Pro votes than any other player in the 1962 selections.

1976

DUNN, Joseph "Red"
Player
Attended Marquette Univ.

1924 – 1925 Milwaukee Badgers, back
1925 – 1926 Chicago Cardinals, back
1927 – 1931 Green Bay Packers, back

Serving the Green Bay Packers from 1927 through 1931, Joe led the team to their first world championship in 1929. The Packers won three consecutive National Football League titles, 1929 – 1931, with Red acting as field supervisor. He scored 58 total points on one touchdown, 46 extra points and two field goals, while a member of the "Pack."
Also in: Wisconsin Athletic Hall of Fame.

GREMMINGER, Hank
Player
Attended Baylor Univ; presently living and working in Dallas, Tex.

Hank was drafted in the seventh round of the Green Bay Packers in 1956 and stayed with them through the 1965 season. Drafted as an offensive end, he played instead the positions of left cornerback and safety. He ranks fifth on the Packers' all-time interception list with 28 for a total of 421 yds.

JORGENSEN, Carl "Bud" "Jurgy"
Trainer
Graduated from West High School in Green Bay, Wis; attended St. Mary's College, Calif; currently serving as trainer for the Univ. of Wisconsin at Green Bay.

1924 – 1939 Green Bay Packers, tackle, equipment manager, assistant trainer
1940 – 1970 Green Bay Packers, head trainer

Devoting nearly 50 years of dutiful service to the Green Bay Packers, Bud was duly honored by being inducted into the Green Bay Packer Hall of Fame in 1976. Acting as equipment manager and assistant trainer for 16 years, he rose to the position of head trainer in 1940 and worked in that capacity until 1970. Bud was considered by the Packers a vital force in ten world championship Packer teams.

KNAFELC, Gary
Player
Attended college in Colorado; a successful businessman, presently living with his family in Green Bay, Wis.

1954 Chicago Cardinals, receiver
1954 – 1962 Green Bay Packers, receiver, end
1963 San Francisco 49ers, receiver

Recognized as a star performer at both wide receiver and tight end, Knafelc was a second-round draft choice by the Chicago Cardinals in 1954. The 6 ft. 4-in player accepted a position with the Packers in late 1954 and went on to become the eighth all-time Packers' receiver catching 136 passes for 1939 yds. and 21 touchdowns. Gary played on the Packers' Divisional title team in 1960 and on the world championship clubs of 1961 and 1962.

SKORONSKI, Robert F.
Player
Born in Chicago, Ill; attended Ind. Univ; served in armed forces 1957 and 1958; currently president of Valley School Supply in Appleton, Wis.

1953 – 1955 Indiana University Hoosiers, tackle, captain
1956 Green Bay Packers, offensive tackle
1959 – 1968 Green Bay Packers, offensive tackle

Bob was a fifth-round draft choice of Green Bay in 1956. He played one season with the Packers before spending two years in the armed forces. He was a natural for the position of tackle and immediately started at left tackle upon his return to the Packers in 1959. Captain of the offensive unit for four years, he led them to three straight National Football League championships, 1965 – 1967. Bob played in the Pro Bowl in 1968.

WHITTENTON, Urshell "Jesse"
Player
Born May 9, 1934, in Big Spring, Tex; attended college at Texas Western Univ, now Univ. Texas at El Paso; interrupted football career 1957 and 1958 to serve in armed forces; All-Pro 1961; involved in restaurant business throughout his playing career; presently golf pro in El Paso.

1956 – 1957 Los Angeles Rams, defensive back
1958 Chicago Bears, defensive back
1958 – 1964 Green Bay Packers, cornerback

A powerful runner, Jesse had the ability to run with any receiver or halfback in the league. He played two seasons with the Los Angeles Rams, having been their sixth-round draft choice in 1956. He signed with the Packers in 1958 as a free agent, remaining there for seven years. Whittenton accumulated 20 interceptions and one touchdown in his career with the Packers. He was chosen for three Pro Bowl teams 1962 – 1964. In the 1961 Western Conference championship Jesse stole the ball from Alex Webster of the New York Giants resulting in the winning touchdown.

1977

BUCK, Howard "Cub"
Player
Now deceased, Cub Buck was the first professional player for the Green Bay Packers, earning $75 for each game. He stayed with the "Pack" from 1921 through the 1925 season as a tackle. In 1915 Buck was an All-American tackle for the University of Wisconsin.
Also in: Wisconsin Athletic Hall of Fame.

GREGG, Forrest A.
Player
Born October 18, 1933, in Birthright, Tex; attended Southern Methodist Univ; briefly interrupted playing career in 1957 to serve in military; All-NFL 1960–1967.

1956	Green Bay Packers, tackle
1958–1970	Green Bay Packers, tackle, coach
1971	Dallas Cowboys, tackle
1972	San Diego Chargers, offensive line coach

A second-round draft choice of Green Bay in 1956, Gregg played a total of 14 years with the Packers. He was the mainstay of the powerful Green Bay offensive line. During last two years he acted as player-coach for the team. Gregg set a National Football League record playing a total of 188 consecutive games in his playing career. He played in the Pro Bowl 1962–1967 and 1971, and in three Super Bowls, 1967, 1968 and 1972.
Also in: Major League Football Hall of Fame, Citizens Savings Hall of Fame Athletic Museum; and Professional Football Hall of Fame.

MATHYS, Charlie
Player
Charlie Mathys was first a football player at Green Bay West High School. He then played for Indiana University and professional football for Hammond, Indiana. As a Green Bay Packer quarterback 1922–1926, he totaled 32 points with five touchdowns and two field goals. Since 1926, Mathys has been a member of the Green Bay Packers Board of Directors.

STARR, Bryan B. "Bart"
Player
Born January 9, 1934, in Montgomery, Ala; attended high school at Sidney Lanier in Montgomery; attended Univ. of Alabama, played in Orange Bowl 1953 and Cotton Bowl 1954; Jim Thorpe Trophy, Player of the Year 1966; Super Bowl Most Valuable Player 1967 and 1968; wife Cherry; two sons, Bart Jr. and Bret; presently living in Green Bay, Wis; car dealer and pro analyst for CBS-TV.

1956–1971	Green Bay Packers, quarterback
1972	Green Bay Packers, assistant coach

A seventeenth-round draft choice of the Green Bay Packers in 1956, Bart spent his entire pro career with the Packers. He evolved into one of the greatest quarterbacks in the history of football. Recognized for his leadership and ability to motivate fellow teammates, he directed the Packers to five league championships and two Super Bowl victories. He led the National Football League (NFL) in passing in 1962, 1964 and 1966 and set NFL records for highest career passing percentage, 57.5, in 1964. In 1965 he set an NFL record for successfully completing 294 consecutive passes. His NFL passing totals amount to 1808 completions on 3149 attempts, an average of 57.4 percent for 24,718 yds. He also completed 1952 touchdown passes and had 138 interceptions, a 7.85-yd. average. Bart played in the Pro Bowl 1961–1963 and 1967.
Also in: Major League Football Hall of Fame, Citizens Savings Hall of Fame Athletic Museum; and Professional Football Hall of Fame.

TURNBULL, Andrew B.
Contributor
As owner of the *Green Bay Press Gazette,* Andrew Turnball organized the support of local businessmen and passed the hat at the Green Bay Packers' football games to organize the Green Bay Packers Football Corporation in 1923. He served as the first president of the corporation until 1927.

WOOD, Willie
Player
Born December 23, 1936, in Washington, D.C; attended Armstrong High School, Coalinga Junior College and Univ. Southern Calif; All-NFL 1964–1968; All-National Football Conference 1970.

1960–1971	Green Bay Packers, back
1972–	San Diego Chargers, defensive back coach

Following his quarterback days at the University of Southern California, Wood signed as a free agent with the Green Bay Packers and soon became one of pro football's most feared defensive backs. In 12 seasons with the Packers, he intercepted 48 passes and returned 187 punts for 1391 yds. In 1961 he led the National Football League (NFL) with his 16.1 yds. per return. Wood played in two Super Bowls, eight Pro Bowls and six NFL championship games. He is the holder of the Super Bowl punt return record. In 1972 Wood accepted the position of defensive back coach with the San Diego Chargers.

National Football Hall of Fame

KINGS MILLS, OHIO

Mailing Address: P.O. Box 300, 45034. Tel. (513) 241-5410 or 398-5336. *Contact:* Jack Wyant, Gen. Mgr. *Location:* 6300 Kings Island Dr, approx. 106 mi. S.E. of Indianapolis, Ind, 108 mi. S.W. of Columbus, 244 mi. S.W. of Cleveland. *Personnel:* Richard W. Kazmaier, Pres; Robert Whitelaw, Secy; Stanley T. Crossland, Treas; James L. McDowell, Jr, Exec. Dir; Vincent dePaul Draddy, Chmn. of the Bd. Offices not open to the public.

Nearby Halls of Fame: Flight (Dayton, 50 mi. N.E.), Football (Canton, 55 mi. N.E.), Trapshooting (Vandalia, 55 mi. N.E.), Auto Racing, Basketball (Indianapolis, Ind), Agriculture (W. Lafayette, Ind, 150 mi. N.W.), Sports (N. Webster, Ind, 165 mi. N.W.).

Founded by the National Football Foundation (with offices in New York City) in 1947, the National Football Hall of Fame honors outstanding amateur and college football players and coaches, and educates people about the history and principles of football. Originally located in New York City, the Hall of Fame is awaiting the official opening of its 10-acre site at Kings Island, Ohio, 25 mi. north of Cincinnati, in the spring of 1978. The state has long been known for football, with its 34 colleges and universities. The University of Cincinnati and Miami University of Ohio have one of the oldest football rivalries; and Miami is considered to be the cradle of coaches. The new $7.5 million Hall of Fame will be located in the Kings Island Family Entertainment Center with the Jack Nicklaus Professional Golfers' Association Golf Center, a large theme park, Lion Country Safari wildlife preserve, an inn and a campground. Some of the special features of the Hall include a Time Tunnel through which visitors can walk to see and hear the history of football from its beginnings to the present. There will be two theatres, one that will offer live shows and another that will continuously feature a variety of football topics. A computer information center will answer visitors' questions regarding players, coaches and team records. There will be research and historical libraries for use by the public with the assistance of a resident research librarian. These libraries will contain over 1200 volumes and 173,000 feet of film dating back to the 1920s. Rare memorabilia will also await football fans, including books, programs, equipment, autographed balls and trophies dating back to the 1800s. Hall of Fame members will be honored in a special room with their names cut into panels of glass. Outside the room, visitors will view pictures and listen to recorded interviews about the honored players and coaches. In addition to sponsoring the National Football Hall of Fame, the National Football Foundation sponsors numerous scholarship and awards. The MacArthur Bowl is given to the nation's top major college football team and trophies are presented to both the National Collegiate Athletic Association and the National Association of Intercollegiate Athletics college divisional championship teams. The Gold Medal is given to national leaders formerly associated with football who have excelled in their profession. Five presidents have received this award. The Distinguished American Award is given to outstanding leaders who have shown special devotion to the game. This Hall of Fame is a member of the Association of Sports Museums and Halls of Fame.

Members: Nearly 400 college football players and over 70 football coaches as of July 1977. Each of the 82 chapters of the National Football Foundation sends the names of five nominees to their District Screening Committee. There are eight districts within the National Football Foundation, each with a Screening Committee of six members: a chairman from the district's largest chapter, a football coach, a member of the College Sports Information Directors of America, a sportscaster, a football writer and an athletic director or National Collegiate Athletics Association member. After reviewing the nominations from each chapter in the district, the District Screening Committees submit the names of five nominees to the secretary of the Honors Court of the National Football Foundation. In October each year, the Honors Court sends to each dues-paying member of the National Football Foundation a ballot containing approximately 40 names, including holdover nominees from the previous year. Each year beginning with 1976, one coach and 11 players will be inducted into the Hall of Fame at a December banquet held at the Waldorf Astoria in New York City. Players must be graduated from college or retired from their professional football careers at least ten years prior to their elections. Coaches must be retired at least three years before election to the Hall of Fame if they served as head coach a minimum of ten years. Since the Hall's inception, over two million players and coaches have been nominated for membership.

1951 ALEXANDER, William A. Coach. See entry in Athletic Directors Hall of Fame, Citizens Savings Hall of Fame Athletic Museum, 1971. *Also in:* College Football Hall of Fame, Citizens Savings Hall of Fame Athletic Museum.

BAUGH, Samuel A. "Slingin' Sammy." Player. See entry in Professional Football Hall of Fame, 1963. *Also in:* College Football Hall of Fame and Major League Football Hall of Fame, Citizens Savings Hall of Fame Athletic Museum.

BIBLE, Dana X. Coach. See entry in College Football Hall of Fame, Citizens Savings Hall of Fame Athletic Museum.

BROWN, John H, Jr. "Babe." Player. See entry in College Football Hall of Fame, Citizens Savings Hall of Fame Athletic Museum.

CAMP, Walter. Coach. See entry in College Football Hall of Fame, Citizens Savings Hall of Fame Athletic Museum. *Also in:* Noteworthy Contributors Hall of Fame, Citizens Savings Hall of Fame Athletic Museum.

CLARK, Earl H. "Dutch." Player. See entry in Professional Football Hall of Fame, 1963. *Also in:* Athletic Trainers Hall of Fame, College Football Hall of Fame and Major League Football Hall of Fame, Citizens Savings Hall of Fame Athletic Museum.

COWAN, Hector W. Player. See entry in College Football Hall of Fame, Citizens Savings Hall of Fame Athletic Museum.

COY, Edward H. "Ted." Player. See entry in College Football Hall of Fame, Citizens Savings Hall of Fame Athletic Museum.

DALY, Charles D. Player. See entry in College Football Hall of Fame, Citizens Savings Hall of Fame Athletic Museum.

DOBIE, Gilmour "Gloomy Gil." Coach. See entry in College Football Hall of Fame, Citizens Savings Hall of Fame Athletic Museum.

DONAHUE, Michael J. Coach. See entry in College Football Hall of Fame, Citizens Savings Hall of Fame Athletic Museum.

ECKERSALL, Walter H. Player. See entry in College Football Hall of Fame, Citizens Savings Hall of Fame Athletic Museum.

FRIEDMAN, Benjamin "Benny." Player. See entry in College Football Hall of Fame, Citizens Savings Hall of Fame Athletic Museum.

GIPP, George "Gipper." Player. See entry in College Football Hall of Fame, Citizens Savings Hall of Fame Athletic Museum.

GRANGE, Harold "Red." Player. See entry in Professional Football Hall of Fame, 1963. *Also in:* College Football Hall of Fame and Major League Football Hall of Fame, Citizens Savings Hall of Fame Athletic Museum.

HALL, Edward K. Coach. Illinois 1892–1893.

HARE, Truxton. Player. See entry in College Football Hall of Fame, Citizens Savings Hall of Fame Athletic Museum.

HARLEY, Charles W. "Chick." Player. See entry in College Football Hall of Fame, Citizens Savings Hall of Fame Athletic Museum.

HAUGHTON, Percy D. Coach. See entry in College Football Hall of Fame, Citizens Savings Hall of Fame Athletic Museum.

HAZEL, Homer H. "Pop." Player. See entry in College Football Hall of Fame, Citizens Savings Hall of Fame Athletic Museum.

HEFFELFINGER, William W. "Pudge." Player. See entry in College Football Hall of Fame, Citizens Savings Hall of Fame Athletic Museum.

HENRY, Wilbur F. "Fats." Player. See entry in Professional Football Hall of Fame, 1963. *Also in:* College Football Hall of Fame and Major League Football Hall of Fame, Citizens Savings Hall of Fame Athletic Museum; and National Association of Intercollegiate Athletics Hall of Fame.

HINKEY, Frank A. "Silent Frank." Player. See entry in College Football Hall of Fame, Citizens Savings Hall of Fame Athletic Museum.

HOLLENBACK, William M. "Big Bill." Player. See entry in College Football Hall of Fame, Citizens Savings Hall of Fame Athletic Museum.

HUTSON, Donald M. "Alabama Antelope." Player. See entry in Green Bay Packer Hall of Fame, 1972. *Also in:* College Football Hall of Fame and Major League Football Hall of Fame, Citizens Savings Hall of Fame Athletic Museum; and Professional Football Hall of Fame.

JONES, Howard H. Coach. See entry in College Football Hall of Fame, Citizens Savings Hall of Fame Athletic Museum.

KERR, Andrew. Coach. See entry in College Football Hall of Fame, Citizens Savings Hall of Fame Athletic Museum.

KINARD, Frank M. "Bruiser." Player. See entry in Professional Football Hall of Fame, 1971. *Also in:* College Football Hall of Fame, Citizens Savings Hall of Fame Athletic Museum.

KINNICK, Nile Clark, Jr. Player. See entry in College Football Hall of Fame, Citizens Savings Hall of Fame Athletic Museum.

LAYDEN, Elmer F. Player. See entry in College Football Hall of Fame, Citizens Savings Hall of Fame Athletic Museum.

MAHAN, Edward W. "Natick Eddie." Player. See entry in College Football Hall of Fame, Citizens Savings Hall of Fame Athletic Museum.

McGUGIN, Daniel E. "Dan." Coach. See entry in College Football Hall of Fame, Citizens Savings Hall of Fame Athletic Museum.

McMILLIN, Alvin N. "Bo." Player. See entry in College Football Hall of Famc, Citizens Savings Hall of Fame Athletic Museum.

MULLER, Harold P. "Brick." Player. See entry in College Football Hall of Fame, Citizens Savings Hall of Fame Athletic Museum.

NAGURSKI, Bronislaw "Bronko." Player. See entry in Professional Football Hall of Fame, 1963. *Also in:* College Football Hall of Fame and Major League Football Hall of Fame, Citizens Savings Hall of Fame Athletic Museum.

NEVERS, Ernest A. Player. See entry in Professional Football Hall of Fame, 1963. *Also in:* College Football Hall of Fame and Major League Football Hall of Fame, Citizens Savings Hall of Fame Athletic Museum.

O'NEILL, Frank J. "Buck." Coach. Colgate 1904–1905; Syracuse 1906–1907, 1913–1919; Columbia 1920–1922.

OWEN, Benjamin G. Coach. See entry in College Football Hall of Fame, Citizens Savings Hall of Fame Athletic Museum.

ROCKNE, Knute K. Coach. See entry in College Football Hall of Fame, Citizens Savings Hall of Fame Athletic Museum. *Also in:* Noteworthy Contributors Hall of Fame, Citizens Savings Hall of Fame Athletic Museum.

ROPER, William W. Coach. See entry in College Football Hall of Fame, Citizens Savings Hall of Fame Athletic Museum.

SCHULZ, Adolph "Germany." Player. See entry in College Football Hall of Fame, Citizens Savings Hall of Fame Athletic Museum.

SLATER, Frederick F. "Duke." Player. See entry in College Football Hall of Fame, Citizens Savings Hall of Fame Athletic Museum.

SMITH, Andrew L. Coach. See entry in College Football Hall of Fame, Citizens Savings Hall of Fame Athletic Museum.

STAGG, Amos Alonzo. Player and Coach. See entry in College Football Hall of Fame, Citizens Savings Hall of Fame Athletic Museum; and Naismith Memorial Basketball Hall of Fame, 1959. *Also in:* Noteworthy Contributors Hall of Fame and Track and Field Hall of Fame, Citizens Savings Hall of Fame Athletic Museum.

SUTHERLAND, John B. "Jocko." Coach. See entry in College Football Hall of Fame, Citizens Savings Hall of Fame Athletic Museum.

THOMAS, Frank W. Coach. See entry in College Football Hall of Fame, Citizens Savings Hall of Fame Athletic Museum.

THORPE, James F. Player. See entry in Professional Football Hall of Fame, 1963. *Also in:* American Indian Athletic Hall of Fame; College Football Hall of Fame and Major League Football Hall of Fame, Citizens Savings Hall of Fame Athletic Museum; National Track and Field Hall of Fame and United States Track and Field Hall of Fame.

WARNER, Glenn S. "Pop." Coach. See entry in College Football Hall of Fame, Citizens Savings Hall of Fame Athletic Museum.

WEIR, Ed S. Player. See entry in College Football Hall of Fame, Citizens Savings Hall of Fame Athletic Museum.

WILLIAMS, Henry L. "Doc." Coach. See entry in College Football Hall of Fame, Citizens Savings Hall of Fame Athletic Museum.

WILSON, George. Player. See entry in College Football Hall of Fame, Citizens Savings Hall of Fame Athletic Museum.

YOST, Fielding H. "Hurry Up." Coach. See entry in College Football Hall of Fame, Citizens Savings Hall of Fame Athletic Museum.

ZUPPKE, Robert C. "Zupp." Coach. See entry in College Football Hall of Fame, Citizens Savings Hall of Fame Athletic Museum.

1954 ALEXANDER, Joseph A. Player. See entry in College Football Hall of Fame, Citizens Savings Hall of Fame Athletic Museum.

BARNES, Stanley N. Player. See entry in College Football Hall of Fame, Citizens Savings Hall of Fame Athletic Museum.

BASTON, Albert P. "Bert." Player. See entry in College Football Hall of Fame, Citizens Savings Hall of Fame Athletic Museum.

BAUSCH, James. Player. Halfback for Kansas 1929–1930.

BERWANGER, John Jacob "Jay." Player. See entry in College Football Hall of Fame, Citizens Savings Hall of Fame Athletic Museum.

BEZDEK, Hugo F. Coach. See entry in College Football Hall of Fame, Citizens Savings Hall of Fame Athletic Museum.

BROWN, Gordon F. "Skim." Player. Guard for Yale 1887–1900.

CAGLE, Christian K. "Red." Player. See entry in College Football Hall of Fame, Citizens Savings Hall of Fame Athletic Museum; and Louisiana Sports Hall of Fame.

CARIDEO, Frank F. Player. See entry in College Football Hall of Fame, Citizens Savings Hall of Fame Athletic Museum.

CAVANAUGH, Francis W. "Cav, " "Iron Major." Coach. See entry in College Football Hall of Fame, Citizens Savings Hall of Fame Athletic Museum.

CRISLER, Herbert Orin "Fritz." Coach. See entry in Athletic Directors Hall of Fame, Citizens Savings Hall of Fame Athletic Museum, 1970. *Also in:* College Football Hall of Fame, Citizens Savings Hall of Fame Athletic Museum.

DALRYMPLE, Gerald. Player. See entry in College Football Hall of Fame, Citizens Savings Hall of Fame Athletic Museum.

DeWITT, John R. Player. See entry in College Football Hall of Fame, Citizens Savings Hall of Fame Athletic Museum.

DORAIS, Charles E. "Gus." Coach. See entry in College Football Hall of Fame, Citizens Savings Hall of Fame Athletic Museum.

DRURY, Morley E. Player. See entry in College Football Hall of Fame, Citizens Savings Hall of Fame Athletic Museum.

FESLER, Wesley E. Player. See entry in College Football Hall of Fame, Citizens Savings Hall of Fame Athletic Museum.

FISH, Hamilton, Jr. Player. See entry in College Football Hall of Fame, Citizens Savings Hall of Fame Athletic Museum.

GARBISCH, Edgar W. Player. See entry in College Football Hall of Fame, Citizens Savings Hall of Fame Athletic Museum.

HARDWICK, Huntington R. "Tack." Player. See entry in College Football Hall of Fame, Citizens Savings Hall of Fame Athletic Museum.

HARLOW, Richard C. Coach. See entry in College Football Hall of Fame, Citizens Savings Hall of Fame Athletic Museum.

HARMON, Thomas D. "Old 98." Player. See entry in College Football Hall of Fame, Citizens Savings Hall of Fame Athletic Museum.

HART, Edward J. "E. J." Player. See entry in College Football Hall of Fame, Citizens Savings Hall of Fame Athletic Museum.

HEIN, Melvin J. Player. See entry in Professional Football Hall of Fame, 1963. *Also in:* College Football Hall of Fame and Major League Football Hall of Fame, Citizens Savings Hall of Fame Athletic Museum.

HEISMAN, John W. Coach. See entry in College Football Hall of Fame, Citizens Savings Hall of Fame Athletic Museum.

HESTON, William M. Player. See entry in College Football Hall of Fame, Citizens Savings Hall of Fame Athletic Museum.

HIGGINS, Robert A. Coach. See entry in College Football Hall of Fame, Citizens Savings Hall of Fame Athletic Museum.

HITCHCOCK, James F. Player. See entry in College Football Hall of Fame, Citizens Savings Hall of Fame Athletic Museum.

HOGAN, James J. "Yale." Player. See entry in College Football Hall of Fame, Citizens Savings Hall of Fame Athletic Museum.

JOESTING, Herbert W. Player. See entry in College Football Hall of Fame, Citizens Savings Hall of Fame Athletic Museum.

JONES, Lawrence M. "Biff." Coach. See entry in College Football Hall of Fame, Citizens Savings Hall of Fame Athletic Museum.

KAW, Edgar L. Player. See entry in College Football Hall of Fame, Citizens Savings Hall of Fame Athletic Museum.

KIMBROUCH, John "Jarrin' Jawn." Player. See entry in College Football Hall of Fame, Citizens Savings Hall of Fame Athletic Museum.

McCORMICK, James B. Player. Fullback for Princeton 1905–1907.

McEVER, Eugene T. "Wild Bull." Player. Halfback for Tennessee 1928–1931.

McWHORTER, Robert L. Player. See entry in College Football Hall of Fame, Citizens Savings Hall of Fame Athletic Museum.

MOORE, Bernice H. Coach. Mercer 1925–1927; Louisiana State 1935–1947.

MORRISON, J. Ray. Coach. See entry in College Football Hall of Fame, Citizens Savings Hall of Fame Athletic Museum.

OBERLANDER, Andrew J. "Swede." Player. See entry in College Football Hall of Fame, Citizens Savings Hall of Fame Athletic Museum.

OOSTERBAAN, Benjamin G. Player. See entry in College Football Hall of Fame, Citizens Savings Hall of Fame Athletic Museum.

PECK, Robert D. Player. See entry in College Football Hall of Fame, Citizens Savings Hall of Fame Athletic Museum.

PENNOCK, Stanley B. Player. See entry in College Football Hall of Fame, Citizens Savings Hall of Fame Athletic Museum.

POLLARD, Frederick D. "Fritz." Player. See entry in College Football Hall of Fame, Citizens Savings Hall of Fame Athletic Museum. *Also in:* Providence Gridiron Hall of Fame.

ROMNEY, Ernest L. "Dick." Coach. See entry in Athletic Directors Hall of Fame, Citizens Savings Hall of Fame Athletic Museum, 1972. *Also in:* College Football Hall of Fame, Citizens Savings Hall of Fame Athletic Museum.

SAUER, George H. Jr. Coach. New Hampshire 1938–1942; Kansas 1946–1947; Navy 1948–1949; Baylor 1950–1956.

SHEVLIN, Thomas L. Player. See entry in College Football Hall of Fame, Citizens Savings Hall of Fame Athletic Museum.

SINKWICH, Frank "Fireball Frankie." Player. See entry in College Football Hall of Fame, Citizens Savings Hall of Fame Athletic Museum.

TICKNOR, Benjamin. Player. See entry in College Football Hall of Fame, Citizens Savings Hall of Fame Athletic Museum.

WEEKES, Benjamin Harold. Player. See entry in College Football Hall of Fame, Citizens Savings Hall of Fame Athletic Museum.

WEST, D. Belford "Belf." Player. See entry in College Football Hall of Fame, Citizens Savings Hall of Fame Athletic Museum.

WHITE, Byron R. "Whizzer." Player. See entry in College Football Hall of Fame, Citizens Savings Hall of Fame Athletic Museum.

WIDSETH, Edwin. Player. See entry in College Football Hall of Fame, Citizens Savings Hall of Fame Athletic Museum.

WILCE, John W. Coach. See entry in College Football Hall of Fame, Citizens Savings Hall of Fame Athletic Museum.

1955 BATTLES, Clifford. Player. See entry in Professional Football Hall of Fame, 1968. *Also in:* Major League Football Hall of Fame, Citizens Savings Hall of Fame Athletic Museum; National Association of Intercollegiate Athletics Hall of Fame and West Virginia Sports Writers Hall of Fame.

BELL, Madison "Moanin' Matty." Coach. See entry in Athletic Directors Hall of Fame, Citizens Savings Hall of Fame Athletic Museum, 1970. *Also in:* College Football Hall of Fame, Citizens Savings Hall of Fame Athletic Museum.

BIERMAN, Bernard W. "Bernie." Coach. See entry in College Football Hall of Fame, Citizens Savings Hall of Fame Athletic Museum.

DES JARDIEN, Paul R. "Shorty." Player. See entry in College Football Hall of Fame, Citizens Savings Hall of Fame Athletic Museum.

FEATHERS, William Beattle "Big Chief." Player. See entry in College Football Hall of Fame, Citizens Savings Hall of Fame Athletic Museum.

FLOWERS, Allen R. "Buck." Player. Halfback for Georgia Tech 1918–1920.

FRANK, Clinton E. Player. See entry in College Football Hall of Fame, Citizens Savings Hall of Fame Athletic Museum.

GRAYSON, Robert H. Player. See entry in College Football Hall of Fame, Citizens Savings Hall of Fame Athletic Museum.

KILPATRICK, Gen. John Reed. Player. See entry in Hockey Hall of Fame, 1960. *Also in:* International Hockey Hall of Fame.

LITTLE, George E. Coach. See entry in Athletic Directors Hall of Fame, Citizens Savings Hall of Fame Athletic Museum, 1976.

MERCER, E. LeRoy. Player. See entry in College Football Hall of Fame, Citizens Savings Hall of Fame Athletic Museum.

O'BRIEN, Robert D. "Davey." Player. Halfback for Texas Christian 1936–1938.

OLIPHANT, Elmer Q. "Ollie." Player. See entry in College Football Hall of Fame, Citizens Savings Hall of Fame Athletic Museum.

PARKER, Clarence "Ace." Player. See entry in Professional Football Hall of Fame, 1972. *Also in:* College Football Hall of Fame, Citizens Savings Hall of Fame Athletic Museum.

ROBINSON, Edward N. "Robbie." Coach. See entry in College Football Hall of Fame, Citizens Savings Hall of Fame Athletic Museum.

SCHREINER, David N. Player. End for Wisconsin 1940 – 1942.

SINGTON, Frederick W. Player. See entry in College Football Hall of Fame, Citizens Savings Hall of Fame Athletic Museum.

SMITH, Harry E. "Blackjack." Player. See entry in College Football Hall of Fame, Citizens Savings Hall of Fame Athletic Museum.

SPEARS, Clarence W. "Doc," "Fat," "Cupid." Player. Guard for Dartmouth 1914 – 1915. *Also in:* West Virginia Sports Writers Hall of Fame.

WADE, Wallace. Coach. See entry in College Football Hall of Fame, Citizens Savings Hall of Fame Athletic Museum.

WOJCIECHOWICZ, Alexander "Wojie," "Alex." Player. See entry in Professional Football Hall of Fame, 1968. *Also in:* College Football Hall of Fame and Major League Football Hall of Fame, Citizens Savings Hall of Fame Athletic Museum; and National Polish-American Sports Hall of Fame and Museum.

1956 AGASE, Alexander. Player. Guard for Purdue 1943; Guard for Illinois 1942, 1946.

ALBERT, Frank C. Player. See entry in College Football Hall of Fame, Citizens Savings Hall of Fame Athletic Museum. *Also in:* Major League Football Hall of Fame, Citizens Savings Hall of Fame Athletic Museum.

BOMAR, R. Lynn. Player. See entry in College Football Hall of Fame, Citizens Savings Hall of Fame Athletic Museum.

CHRISTMAN, Paul C. "Pitchin' Paul." Player. See entry in College Football Hall of Fame, Citizens Savings Hall of Fame Athletic Museum.

DUDLEY, William M. "Bullet Bill." Player. See entry in Professional Football Hall of Fame, 1966. *Also in:* College Football Hall of Fame and Major League Football Hall of Fame, Citizens Savings Hall of Fame Athletic Museum.

GILBERT, Walter. Player. Center for Auburn 1934 – 1936.

GRAHAM, Otto Everett, Jr. "Automatic Otto." Player. See entry in Professional Football Hall of Fame, 1965. *Also in:* College Football Hall of Fame and Major League Football Hall of Fame, Citizens Savings Hall of Fame Athletic Museum.

HARPSTER, Howard. Player. See entry in College Football Hall of Fame, Citizens Savings Hall of Fame Athletic Museum.

LEECH, James C. Player. See entry in College Football Hall of Fame, Citizens Savings Hall of Fame Athletic Museum.

MEYER, Leo R. "Dutch," "Saturday Fox," "Old Iron Pants." Coach. See entry in Athletic Directors Hall of Fame, Citizens Savings Hall of Fame Athletic Museum, 1971. *Also in:* College Football Hall of Fame, Citizens Savings Hall of Fame Athletic Museum.

NEYLAND, Robert R. Coach. See entry in Athletic Directors Hall of Fame, Citizens Savings Hall of Fame Athletic Museum, 1971. *Also in:* College Football Hall of Fame, Citizens Savings Hall of Fame Athletic Museum.

TINSLEY, Gaynell C. "Gus." Player. See entry in College Football Hall of Fame, Citizens Savings Hall of Fame Athletic Museum; and Lousiana Sports Hall of Fame.

WASHINGTON, Kenneth S. Player. See entry in College Football Hall of Fame, Citizens Savings Hall of Fame Athletic Museum.

WHITMIRE, Donald B, Player. See entry in College Football Hall of Fame, Citizens Savings Hall of Fame Athletic Museum.

WIEMAN, E. E. "Tad." Coach. See entry in Athletic Directors Hall of Fame, Citizens Savings Hall of Fame Athletic Museum, 1973.

1957 ARMSTRONG, Ike J. Coach. See entry in College Football Hall of Fame, Citizens Savings Hall of Fame Athletic Museum.

BROWN, John Mack. Player. See entry in College Football Hall of Fame, Citizens Savings Hall of Fame Athletic Museum.

CARPENTER, C. Hunter. Player. See entry in College Football Hall of Fame, Citizens Savings Hall of Fame Athletic Museum; and Virginia Hall of Fame.

CORBUS, William. Player. See entry in College Football Hall of Fame, Citizens Savings Hall of Fame Athletic Museum.

MAUTHE, J. L. "Pete." Player. Halfback for Penn State 1910 – 1912.

NEWELL, Marshall "Ma." Player. See entry in College Football Hall of Fame, Citizens Savings Hall of Fame Athletic Museum.

PFANN, George R. Player. See entry in College Football Hall of Fame, Citizens Savings Hall of Fame Athletic Museum.

PINCKERT, Ernie. Player. See entry in College Football Hall of Fame, Citizens Savings Hall of Fame Athletic Museum.

RODGERS, Ira E. "Rat." Player. Fullback for West Virginia 1917 – 1919.

STRONG, Kenneth E. Player. See entry in Professional Football Hall of Fame, 1967. *Also in:* College Football Hall of Fame and Major League Football Hall of Fame, Citizens Savings Hall of Fame Athletic Museum.

WELLER, John A. C. "Jac." Player. Guard for Princeton 1933 – 1935.

WILDUNG, Richard K. Player. See entry in Green Bay Packers Hall of Fame, 1973. *Also in:* College Football Hall of Fame, Citizens Savings Hall of Fame Athletic Museum.

1958 BARRETT, Charles. Player. Quarterback for Cornell 1913 – 1915.

CAMPBELL, David C. Player. See entry in College Football Hall of Fame, Citizens Savings Hall of Fame Athletic Museum.

GOLDBERG, Marshall "Biggie." Player. See entry in College Football Hall of Fame, Citizens Savings Hall of Fame Athletic Museum.

JONES, Thomas A. D. "Tad." Coach. Syracuse 1909 – 1910; Yale 1920 – 1927.

KIPKE, Harry G. Player. See entry in College Football Hall of Fame, Citizens Savings Hall of Fame Athletic Museum.

LUND, Francis L. "Pug." Player. Halfback for Minnesota 1932 – 1934.

SCHWAB, Frank J. "Dutch." Player. See entry in College Football Hall of Fame, Citizens Savings Hall of Fame Athletic Museum.

STUHLDREHER, Harry. Player. See entry in College Football Hall of Fame, Citizens Savings Hall of Fame Athletic Museum.

YOUNG, H. K. Player. Halfback for Washington and Lee 1913 – 1916.

1959 BLANCHARD, Felix A, Jr. "Doc" "Mr. Inside." Player. See entry in College Football Hall of Fame, Citizens Savings Hall of Fame Athletic Museum.

DODD, Robert L. Player. See entry in College Football Hall of Fame, Citizens Savings Hall of Fame Athletic Museum.

HICKMAN, Herman M, Jr. Player. See entry in College Football Hall of Fame, Citizens Savings Hall of Fame Athletic Museum.

HINKLE, Clark C, Jr. Player. Center for Vanderbilt 1935 – 1937.

KECK, J. Stanton "Stan." Player. Tackle for Yale 1902 – 1904.

McFADDEN, James Banks. Player. See entry in College Football Hall of Fame, Citizens Savings Hall of Fame Athletic Museum.

MUNN, Clarence L. "Biggie." Coach. Albright 1935 – 1936; Syracuse 1946; Michigan State 1947 – 1953.

PHILLIPS, Henry D. Player. Guard for University of the South 1901 – 1904.

TRIPPI, Charles L. Player. See entry in Professional Football Hall of Fame, 1966. *Also in:* College Football Hall of Fame and Major League Football Hall of Fame, Citizens Savings Hall of Fame Athletic Museum.

WALKER, Ewell Doak, Jr. "Doaker." Player. See entry in College Football Hall of Fame, Citizens Savings Hall of Fame Athletic Museum. *Also in:* Major League Football Hall of Fame, Citizens Savings Hall of Fame Athletic Museum; and Texas High School Football Hall of Fame.

1960 ALDRICH, Charles C. "Ki." Player. See entry in College Football Hall of Fame, Citizens Savings Hall of Fame Athletic Museum.

BORRIES, Fred, Jr. "Buzz." Player. Halfback for Navy 1932 – 1934.

GELBERT, Charles S. Player. End for Pennsylvania 1894 – 1896.

LITTLE, Lawrence B. "Lou." Coach. See entry in College Football Hall of Fame, Citizens Savings Hall of Fame Athletic Museum.

LOCKE, Gordon C. Player. See entry in College Football Hall of Fame, Citizens Savings Hall of Fame Athletic Museum.

LUCKMAN, Sidney. Player. See entry in Professional Football Hall of Fame, 1965. *Also in:* College Football Hall of Fame and Major League Football Hall of Fame, Citizens Savings Hall of Fame Athletic Museum.

LUJACK, John. Player. See entry in College Football Hall of Fame, Citizens Savings Hall of Fame Athletic Museum.

SNOW, Neil Worthington. Player. See entry in College Football Hall of Fame, Citizens Savings Hall of Fame Athletic Museum.

TURNER, Clyde. Player. See entry in Professional Football Hall of Fame, 1966. *Also in:* Major League Football Hall of Fame, Citizens Savings Hall of Fame Athletic Museum.

1961 CALDWELL, Charles, Jr. Coach. See entry in College Football Hall of Fame, Citizens Savings Hall of Fame Athletic Museum.

DAVIS, Glenn W. "Mr. Outside." Player. See entry in College Football Hall of Fame, Citizens Savings Hall of Fame Athletic Museum.

FAUROT, Donald B. Coach. See entry in College Athletic Directors Hall of Fame, Citizens Savings Hall of Fame Athletic Museum, 1970. *Also in:* College Football Hall of Fame, Citizens Savings Hall of Fame Athletic Museum; Missouri Sports Hall of Fame.

HUMBLE, Weldon G. Player. Guard for Rice 1941 – 1942.

JUSTICE, Charles "Choo Choo." Player. See entry in College Football Hall of Fame, Citizens Savings Hall of Fame Athletic Museum.

McAFFEE, George A. "One Play." Player. See entry in Professional Football Hall of Fame, 1966. *Also in:* Major League Football Hall of Fame, Citizens Savings Hall of Fame Athletic Museum.

PAZZETTI, Vincent J. "Pat." Player. Quarterback for Wesleyan 1908 – 1909.

REEDS, Claude. Player. Fullback for Oklahoma 1910 – 1913.

REYNOLDS, Robert Odell "Horse." Player. See entry in College Football Hall of Fame, Citizens Savings Hall of Fame Athletic Museum.

SUFFRIDGE, Robert L. Player. Guard for Tennessee 1938 – 1940.

1962 BOYNTON, Benny Lee. Player. Quarterback for Williams 1917 – 1920.

CHAMBERLIN, B. Guy. Player. See entry in Professional Football Hall of Fame, 1965. *Also in:* College Football Hall of Fame, Citizens Savings Hall of Fame Athletic Museum.

HILL, Dan W. "Tiger." Player. Center for Duke 1936 – 1938.

HUBBARD, Robert C. "Cal." Player. See entry in Green Bay Packer Hall of Fame, 1970 and National Baseball Hall of Fame, 1976. *Also in:* Major League Baseball Hall of Fame and Major League Football Hall of Fame, Citizens Savings Hall of Fame Athletic Museum; Louisiana Sports Hall of Fame, National Association of Intercollegiate Athletics Hall of Fame and Professional Football Hall of Fame.

KING, Philip. Player. Quarterback for Princeton 1890 – 1893.

McEWAN, John J. "Cap." Player. Center for Army 1914 – 1916.

McLAUGHRY, DeOrmand C. "Tuss." Coach. See entry in College Football Hall of Fame, Citizens Savings Hall of Fame Athletic Museum. *Also in*: Providence Gridiron Club Hall of Fame.

MINDS, John H. "Jack." Player. Fullback for Pennsylvania 1894 – 1897.

O'DEA, Patrick J. "Human Kangaroo," "Patrick." Player. See entry in College Football Hall of Fame, Citizens Savings Hall of Fame Athletic Museum.

ROUTT, Joseph E. Player. Guard for Texas A&M 1935 – 1937.

SPEARS, William D. Player. Quarterback for Vanderbilt 1925 – 1927.

WYANT, Andrew R. E. Player. Center for Bucknell 1888 – 1891; Guard for Chicago 1892 – 1894.

1963 CONNOR, George. Player. See entry in Professional Football Hall of Fame, 1975. *Also in:* College Football Hall of Fame, Citizens Savings Hall of Fame Athletic Museum.

HALE, Edwin. Player. Halfback for Mississippi College 1915 – 1916, 1920 – 1921.

KAVANAUGH, Kenneth W. "Ken." Player. See entry in College Football Hall of Fame, Citizens Savings Hall of Fame Athletic Museum. *Also in:* Arkansas Hall of Fame and Louisiana Sports Hall of Fame.

McCLUNG, Thomas L. "Bum." Player. Halfback for Yale 1889 – 1891.

MONTGOMERY, Clifford. Player. Quarterback for Columbia 1931 – 1933.

PUND, Henry R. "Peter the Great." Player. Center for Georgia Tech. 1926 – 1928.

TRYON, J. Edward. Player. See entry in College Football Hall of Fame, Citizens Savings Hall of Fame Athletic Museum.

WHARTON, Charles M. "Buck." Player. Guard for Pennsylvania 1893 – 1896.

WOODRUFF, George W. Coach. Pennsylvania 1892 – 1901; Illinois 1903; Carlisle 1905.

1964 BLAIK, Earl H. "Red." Coach. See entry in College Football Hall of Fame, Citizens Savings Hall of Fame Athletic Museum.

CARROLL, Charles O. Player. See entry in College Football Hall of Fame, Citizens Savings Hall of Fame Athletic Museum.

EVANS, Raymond. Player. Halfback for Kansas 1941 – 1942, 1946 – 1947. See entry in College Basketball Hall of Fame, Citizens Savings Hall of Fame Athletic Museum.

HERWIG, Robert J. Player. Center for California 1935 – 1937.

HUBERT, Allison T. S. "Pooley." Player. Fullback for Alabama 1922 – 1925.

LEA, Langdon "Biffy." Player. See entry in College Football Hall of Fame, Citizens Savings Hall of Fame Athletic Museum.

MALLORY, William N. "Memphis Bill." Player. Fullback for Yale 1921 – 1923.

RINEHART, Charles. Player. Guard for Lafayette 1894 – 1897.

ROTE, Kyle W. Player. See entry in Major League Football Hall of Fame, Citizens Savings Hall of Fame Athletic Museum. *Also in:* Texas High School Football Hall of Fame.

SPRACKLING, William E. "Sprack." Player. Quarterback for Brown 1908 – 1911.

1965 CANNON, John J. Player. Guard for Notre Dame 1927 – 1929.

GULICK, Merle A. "Hobart Hurricane." Player. Quarterback for Toledo 1925; Quarterback for Hobart 1927 – 1929.

HAMILTON, Thomas J. Player. Halfback for Navy 1924 – 1926. See entry in Athletic Directors Hall of Fame, Citizens Savings Hall of Fame Athletic Museum.

HOLLAND, Jerome H. "Brud." Player. See entry in College Football Hall of Fame, Citizens Savings Hall of Fame Athletic Museum.

McLAREN, George W. "Tank." Player. Fullback for Pittsburgh 1915 – 1918.

SNAVELY, Carl G. "King Carl." Coach. See entry in College Football Hall of Fame, Citizens Savings Hall of Fame Athletic Museum.

TIPTON, Eric G. "The Red." Player. Back for Duke 1936 – 1938.

WILLIAMS, James "Froggy." Player. End for Rice 1947 – 1949. *Also in:* Texas High School Football Hall of Fame.

1966 BACON, Clarence Everett. Player. Quarterback for Wesleyan 1909 – 1912.

BOOTH, Albert J. "Albie." Player. Halfback for Yale 1929 – 1931.

CARNEY, Charles R. Player. End for Illinois 1918 – 1921. See entry in College Basketball

Hall of Fame, Citizens Savings Hall of Fame Athletic Museum.

CONERLY, Charles A. Player. Tailback for Mississippi 1947 – 1948.

CROWLEY, James H. "Sleepy Jim." Player. Halfback for Notre Dame 1922 – 1924.

HUBBARD, John. Player. Halfback for Amherst 1903 – 1906.

JUHAN, Frank A. Player. Center for University of the South 1908 – 1910.

KAZMAIER, Richard W, Jr. "Kaz." Player. See entry in College Football Hall of Fame, Citizens Savings Hall of Fame Athletic Museum.

McGOVERN, John F. Player. Quarterback for Minnesota 1908 – 1910.

MILLER, Edgar E. "Rip." Player. Tackle for Notre Dame 1922 – 1924.

PIHOS, Peter L. "Big Dog." Player. See entry in Professional Football Hall of Fame, 1970. *Also in:* Major League Football Hall of Fame, Citizens Savings Hall of Fame Athletic Museum.

ROSENBERG, Aaron. Player. Guard for Southern California 1931 – 1933.

VAN BROCKLIN, Norman. "Dutchman." Player. See entry in Professional Football Hall of Fame, 1971. *Also in:* Major League Football Hall of Fame, Citizens Savings Hall of Fame Athletic Museum.

WALDORF, Lynn O. "Pappy." Coach. See entry in College Football Hall of Fame, Citizens Savings Hall of Fame Athletic Museum.

1967 CUTTER, Slade D. Player. Tackle for Navy 1932 – 1934.

DOUGHERTY, Nathan W. "Big One." Player. Guard for Tennessee 1907 – 1909.

HUNT, O. Joel. Player. Halfback for Texas A&M 1925.

ISBELL, Cecil F. "Cece." Player. See entry in Green Bay Packer Hall of Fame, 1972.

MICKAL, Abe. Player. Halfback for Louisiana State 1933 – 1935.

NEALE, Earle "Greasy." Coach. See entry in Professional Football Hall of Fame, 1969. *Also in:* Major League Football Hall of Fame, Citizens Savings Hall of Fame Athletic Museum; and West Virginia Sports Writers Hall of Fame.

SCHOONOVER, Wear K. Player. End for Arkansas 1927 – 1929.

SCHWEGLER, Paul "Schweg." Player. See entry in College Football Hall of Fame, Citizens Savings Hall of Fame Athletic Museum.

STEIN, Herbert Q. Player. Center for Pittsburgh 1918 – 1921.

WISTERT, Francis M. "Whitey." Player. Tackle for Michigan 1931 – 1933.

1968 CASEY, Edward L. "Natick Eddie." Player. Halfback for Harvard 1916, 1919.

CLEVENGER, Zora "Clev." Player. Halfback for Indiana 1900 – 1903.

INGRAM, Jonas. Player. Fullback for Navy 1904 – 1906.

KETCHAM, Henry M. Player. Center for Yale 1911 – 1913.

LAYNE, Robert. Player. See entry in Professional Football Hall of Fame, 1967. *Also in:* Major League Football Hall of Fame, Citizens Savings Hall of Fame Athletic Museum; and Texas High School Football Hall of Fame.

PINGEL, John. Player. Halfback for Michigan State 1936 – 1938.

ROGERS, Edward L. Player. End for Carlisle 1896 – 1900; End for Minnesota 1901 – 1903. *Also in:* American Indian Athletic Hall of Fame.

SHAUGHNESSY, Clark D. Coach. See entry in College Football Hall of Fame, Citizens Savings Hall of Fame Athletic Museum.

SIMONS, Claude, Jr. "Big Monk." Player. See entry in Athletic Trainers Hall of Fame, Citizens Savings Hall of Fame Athletic Museum.

STEVENSON, Vincent M. "Steve." Player. Quarterback for Pennsylvania 1903 – 1905.

WALSH, Adam J. Player. See entry in College Football Hall of Fame, Citizens Savings Hall of Fame Athletic Museum.

WISTERT, Albert A. "Ox." Player. See entry in College Football Hall of Fame, Citizens Savings Hall of Fame Athletic Museum.

YOUNG, Claude H. "Buddy." Player. See entry in College Football Hall of Fame, Citizens Savings Hall of Fame Athletic Museum.

1969 AMES, Knowlton L. "Snake." Player. Fullback for Princeton 1886 – 1889.

BEDNARIK, Charles. Player. See entry in Professional Footlball Hall of Fame, 1967. *Also in:* Major League Football Hall of Fame, Citizens Savings Hall of Fame Athletic Museum.

BROOKE, George H. Player. Halfback for Pennsylvania 1894 – 1895.

BUNKER, Paul D. Player. Tackle and Back for Army 1901 – 1902.

CAFEGO, George "Bad News." Player. Halfback for Tennessee 1937 – 1939.

CORBIN, William H. "Pa." Player. Center for Yale 1886 – 1888.

HORRELL, Edwin C. "Babe." Player. See entry in College Football Hall of Fame, Citizens Savings Hall of Fame Athletic Museum.

HORVATH, Leslie. Player. See entry in College Football Hall of Fame, Citizens Savings Hall of Fame Athletic Museum.

JOHNSON, James E. Player. Quarterback for Carlisle 1899 – 1903. *Also in:* American Indian Athletic Hall of Fame.

KELLEY, Lawrence M. Player. End for Yale 1934 – 1936.

KELLY, William "Wild Bill." Player. Quarterback for Montana 1924 – 1926.

KITZMILLER, John. Player. Halfback for Oregon 1927–1929.

MANN, Gerald. Player. Quarterback for Southern Methodist University 1925–1927.

POE, Arthur. Player. End for Princeton 1898–1899.

STEFFEN, Walter P. Player. Quarterback for Chicago 1907–1908.

WHEELER, Arthur L. "Beef." Player. Guard for Princeton 1892–1894.

WILKINSON, Charles B. "Bud." Coach. See entry in Athletic Directors Hall of Fame, Citizens Savings Hall of Fame Athletic Museum. *Also in:* College Football Hall of Fame, Citizens Savings Hall of Fame Athletic Museum.

1970 BOCK, Edward. Player. Guard for Iowa State 1936–1938.

CODY, Josh C. Player. See entry in College Football Hall of Fame, Citizens Savings Hall of Fame Athletic Museum.

DALTON, John P. Player. Halfback for Navy 1911.

DAVIES, Thomas Joseph "Tom." Player. See entry in College Football Hall of Fame, Citizens Savings Hall of Fame Athletic Museum.

EXENDINE, Albert A. Player. End for Carlisle 1906–1907. *Also in:* American Indian Athletic Hall of Fame.

HERSCHBERGER, Clarence. Player. Fullback for Chicago 1898.

HILLEBRAND, A. R. T. "Doc." Player. Tackle for Princeton 1898–1899.

HOWELL, Millard Fillmore "Dixie." Player. See entry in College Football Hall of Fame, Citizens Savings Hall of Fame Athletic Museum.

LANE, Myles J. Player. Halfback for Dartmouth 1925–1927. See entry in United States Hockey Hall of Fame, 1973.

LEAHY, Frank. Coach. See entry in College Football Hall of Fame, Citizens Savings Hall of Fame Athletic Museum.

MILLER, Donald. Player. Back for Notre Dame 1922–1924.

OSGOOD, Winchester D. "Win." Player. Back for Cornell 1891–1892.

REID, William T. Player. Fullback for Harvard 1898–1899.

SCARLETT, Hunter. Player. End for Pennsylvania 1898.

SMITH, Ernest F. Player. See entry in College Football Hall of Fame, Citizens Savings Hall of Fame Athletic Museum.

SPRAGUE, Mortimer E. "Bud." Player. See entry in College Football Hall of Fame, Citizens Savings Hall of Fame Athletic Museum.

THORNE, Samuel B. "Brinck." Player. Back for Yale 1895.

TIGERT, John J, Jr. Player. Back for Vanderbilt 1902–1903.

WICKHORST, Frank H. Player. Tackle for Navy 1924–1926.

WYCKOFF, Clinton. Player. Quarterback for Cornell 1895–1896.

1971 ANDERSON, Edward N. Coach. See entry in College Football Hall of Fame, Citizens Savings Hall of Fame Athletic Museum.

BENBROOK, Albert. Player. Guard for Michigan 1908–1910.

BREWER, Charles. Player. Halfback for Harvard 1892–1894.

COCHRAN, Garret B. "Gary." Player. End for Princeton 1896–1898.

EDWARDS, William H. "Big Bill." Player. Tackle for Princeton 1898–1899.

FALASCHI, Nello D. "Flash." Player. Back for Santa Clara 1934–1936.

FENTON, G. E. "Doc." Player. Quarterback for Louisiana State 1907–1908.

GUYON, Joseph N. "Indian Joe," "Joc." Player. See entry in Professional Football Hall of Fame, 1966. *Also in:* American Indian Athletic Hall of Fame.

HARPER, Jesse C. Coach. See entry in College Football Hall of Fame, Citizens Savings Hall of Fame Athletic Museum.

HICKOK, William O. "Wild Bill." Player. Guard for Yale 1892–1894.

HINKLE, William Clarke. Player. See entry in Green Bay Packer Hall of Fame, 1972. *Also in:* Major League Football Hall of Fame, Citizens Savings Hall of Fame Athletic Museum; Professional Football Hall of Fame and Wisconsin Athletic Hall of Fame.

KILLINGER, W. Glenn. Player. Back for Pennsylvania State 1918–1921.

MARSHALL, Bobby. Player. End for Minnesota 1905–1906.

MATTHEWS, Raymond "Rags." Player. End for Texas Christian 1925–1927.

McMILLAN, Dan. Player. Tackle for Southern California 1916–1917; Tackle for California 1919–1922.

MOFFAT, Alexander. Player. Halfback for Princeton 1881–1883.

MORLEY, William R. Player. Halfback for Columbia 1900–1902.

NEELY, Jess Claiborne. Coach. See entry in College Football Hall of Fame, Citizens Savings Hall of Fame Athletic Museum.

NORTON, Homer H. Coach. See entry in College Football Hall of Fame, Citizens Savings Hall of Fame Athletic Museum.

SALMON, Louis "Red." Player. Fullback for Notre Dame 1900–1903.

SANFORD, George F. "Sandy." Coach. Columbia 1899–1901; Rutgers 1913–1924.

SCHMIDT, Francis A. Coach. See entry in College Football Hall of Fame, Citizens Savings Hall of Fame Athletic Museum.

SCOTT, Clyde "Smackover." Player. Halfback for Navy 1945; Halfback for Arkansas 1946–1948.

STEUBER, Robert J. Player. Halfback for Missouri 1940–1942; End for DePauw 1943.

THOMPSON, Joseph. Player. Back for Geneva 1900–1904; Back for Pittsburgh 1904–1906.

TORREY, Robert G. Player. Center for Pennsylvania 1902–1905.

WARNER, William J. Player. Guard for Cornell 1900–1904.

WILLIS, William. Player. See entry in Professional Football Hall of Fame, 1977.

1972 ALDRICH, Malcolm. Player. Halfback for Yale 1919–1921.

BECKETT, John. Player. Tackle for Oregon 1916.

BERTELLI, Angelo B. "Accurate Angelo." Player. See entry in College Football Hall of Fame, Citizens Savings Hall of Fame Athletic Museum.

BOMEISLER, Douglas "Bo." Player. Guard for Yale 1912.

BUTLER, Robert P. "Butts." Player. End for Wisconsin.

EICHENLAUB, Ray. Player. Back for Notre Dame 1913.

FENIMORE, Robert "Blonde Blizzard." Player. See entry in College Football Hall of Fame, Citizens Savings Hall of Fame Athletic Museum.

GODFREY, Ernest R. Coach. Wittenberg 1916–1928; Ohio State 1929–1961.

HAMILTON, Robert A. "Bones." Player. Halfback for Stanford 1933–1935.

HUNTINGTON, Ellery C, Jr. Player. Quarterback for Colgate 1912–1914.

KAER, Morton A. "Devil May." Player. See entry in College Football Hall of Fame, Citizens Savings Hall of Fame Athletic Museum.

MACOMBER, Bart. Player. Back for Illinois 1913–1915.

MORTON, William H. "Air Mail." Player. Quarterback for Dartmouth 1929–1931.

O'HEARN, Jack. Player. End for Cornell 1913–1915.

O'ROURKE, Charles C. "Chuckin' Charley." Player. Tailback for Boston College 1937–1940.

SHAW, Lawrence T. "Buck," "Silver Fox." Coach. See entry in Major League Football Hall of Fame, Citizens Savings Hall of Fame Athletic Museum.

SMITH, Bruce P. "Boo." Player. See entry in College Football Hall of Fame, Citizens Savings Hall of Fame Athletic Museum.

STRUPPER, Everett. Player. See entry in College Football Hall of Fame, Citizens Savings Hall of Fame Athletic Museum.

STYDAHAR, Joseph L. "Jumbo Joe." Player. See entry in Professional Football Hall of Fame, 1967. *Also in:* Major League Football Hall of Fame, Citizens Savings Hall of Fame Athletic Museum; and West Virginia Sports Writers Hall of Fame.

VAN SURDAM, Henderson "Dutch." Player. Quarterback for Wesleyan 1903–1905.

WENDELL, Percy L. "Bullet." Player. End for Harvard 1910–1912.

WYATT, Bowden. Player. End for Tennessee 1936–1938.

1973 ABELL, Earll C. "Toughey." Player. Tackle for Colgate 1912–1915.

BALLIN, Harold R. Player. Tackle for Princeton 1912–1914.

BETTENCOURT, Lawrence. Player. Center for St. Mary's 1924–1927.

CAIN, John L. "Sugar." Player. Fullback for Alabama 1930–1932.

CRAWFORD, Fred E. Player. Tackle for Duke 1931–1932.

DEVINE, Aubrey A. Player. Quarterback for Iowa 1919–1921.

ENGLE, Charles A. "Rip." Coach. See entry in College Football Hall of Fame, Citizens Savings Hall of Fame Athletic Museum. *Also in:* Providence Gridiron Hall of Fame.

FISHER, Robert. Player. Guard for Harvard 1909–1911.

GEYER, Forest P. "Spot." Player. Fullback for Oklahoma 1913–1915.

HANSON, Victor A. Player. End for Syracuse 1924–1926. See entry in Naismith Memorial Basketball Hall of Fame, 1960. *Also in:* College Basketball Hall of Fame, Citizens Savings Hall of Fame Athletic Museum.

HART, Leon J. Player. See entry in College Football Hall of Fame, Citizens Savings Hall of Fame Athletic Museum.

HOWE, Arthur. Player. Quarterback for Yale 1911.

INGRAM, William A. Coach. William and Mary 1922; Indiana 1923–1925; Navy 1926–1930; California 1931–1934.

JENNINGS, Morley. Coach. See entry in College Football Hall of Fame, Citizens Savings Hall of Fame Athletic Museum.

MAULBETSCH, John F. Player. Halfback for Michigan 1912–1914.

McCOLL, William. Player. See entry in College Football Hall of Fame, Citizens Savings Hall of Fame Athletic Museum.

McCRACKEN, G. Herbert "Herb." Coach. Allegheny 1921–1923; Lafayette 1924–1935.

MOOMAW, Donn D. Player. See entry in College Football Hall of Fame, Citizens Savings Hall of Fame Athletic Museum.

OSMANSKI, William T. Player. Fullback for Holy Cross 1936–1938. *Also in:* Providence Gridiron Hall of Fame.

PEABODY, Endicott "Chub." Player. Guard for Harvard 1939–1941.

PHELAN, James M. "Jimmy." Coach. See entry in College Football Hall of Fame, Citizens Savings Hall of Fame Athletic Museum.

SEIBELS, Henry G. Player. Back for Swanee 1898–1899.

SHELTON, Murray N. Player. End for Cornell 1913–1915.

STINCHCOMB, Gaylord R. "Pete." Player. Halfback for Ohio State 1918–1920.

SWANSON, Clarence E. Player. End for Nebraska 1919–1921.

WAGNER, Hube. Player. End for Pittsburgh 1910–1913.

WILSON, Harry E. "Lighthorse Harry." Player. Halfback for Pennsylvania State 1921–1923.

WILSON, Robert E. Player. Halfback for Southern Methodist University 1933–1935. *Also in:* Texas High School Football Hall of Fame.

1974 AGANNIS, Harry "Golden Greek." Player. Quarterback for Boston University 1949–1952.

ANDERSON, Heartley "Hunk." Player. Guard for Notre Dame 1918–1921.

DRISCOLL, John L. "Paddy." Player. See entry in Professional Football Hall of Fame, 1965. *Also in:* Major League Football Hall of Fame, Citizens Savings Hall of Fame Athletic Museum.

FERRARO, John. Player. See entry in College Football Hall of Fame, Citizens Savings Hall of Fame Athletic Museum.

FINCHER, William E. "Bill." Player. See entry in College Football Hall of Fame, Citizens Savings Hall of Fame Athletic Museum.

HEALEY, Edward "Ed." Player. See entry in Professional Football Hall of Fame, 1964.

HIRSCH, Elroy L. "Crazylegs." Player. See entry in Professional Football Hall of Fame, 1968. *Also in:* Major League Football Hall of Fame, Citizens Savings Hall of Fame Athletic Museum.

KOCH, Barton "Botchey." Player. Guard for Baylor 1929–1931.

KUTNER, Malcolm J. Player. End for Texas 1939–1941.

LOURIE, Donald B. Player. Quarterback for Princeton 1919–1921.

MADIGAN, Edward P. "Slip." Coach. See entry in College Football Hall of Fame, Citizens Savings Hall of Fame Athletic Museum.

MAXWELL, Robert W. "Tiny." Player. Guard for Chicago 1904; Guard for Swarthmore 1906.

MILLER, Eugene "Shorty." Player. Quarterback for Pennsylvania State 1910–1913.

MURRAY, William D. Coach. See entry in Athletic Directors Hall of Fame, Citizens Savings Hall of Fame Athletic Museum, 1974. *Also in:* College Football Hall of Fame, Citizens Savings Hall of Fame Athletic Museum.

MYLIN, Edward E. "Hooks." Coach. See entry in College Football Hall of Fame, Citizens Savings Hall of Fame Athletic Museum.

PARKER, James. Player. See entry in Professional Football Hall of Fame, 1973. *Also in:* College Football Hall of Fame, Citizens Savings Hall of Fame Athletic Museum.

POOLE, George Barney. Player. See entry in College Football Hall of Fame, Citizens Savings Hall of Fame Athletic Museum.

SCHWARTZ, Marchmont "Marchy." Player. Halfback for Notre Dame 1930–1931.

STEVENS, Marvin A. "Mal." Player. Back for Washburn 1918–1920; Back for Yale 1923.

TRAVIS, Ed. Player. Tackle for Tarkio 1916; Tackle for Missouri 1917–1920.

UTAY, Joe. Player. Halfback for Texas A&M 1905–1907.

VESSELS, Billy W. "Curly." Player. Halfback for Oklahoma 1930–1931.

WEYAND, Alexander M. "Babe." Player. Tackle for Army 1911–1915.

1975 AMECHE, Alan D. "The Horse." Player. See entry in College Football Hall of Fame, Citizens Savings Hall of Fame Athletic Museum.

BAKER, Hobart Amery Hare "Hobey." Player. Back for Princeton 1911–1913. See entry in Hockey Hall of Fame, 1945. *Also in:* International Hockey Hall of Fame and U. S. Hockey Hall of Fame.

COLEMAN, Don. Player. Tackle for Michigan State 1949–1951.

DANIELL, Averell. Player. Tackle for Pittsburgh 1934–1936.

DAWKINS, Peter M. Player. Halfback for Army 1956–1958.

EDWARDS, Albert Glen "Turk." Player. See entry in Professional Football Hall of Fame, 1969. *Also in:* College Football Hall of Fame and Major League Football Hall of Fame, Citizens Savings Hall of Fame Athletic Museum.

GAITHER, Alonzo S. "Jake." Coach. See entry in Athletic Directors Hall of Fame, Citizens Savings Hall of Fame Athletic Museum, 1976.

GIEL, Paul R. Player. Back for Minnesota 1951–1953.

GIFFORD, Francis. Player. See entry in Professional Football Hall of Fame, 1977. *Also in:*

Major League Football Hall of Fame, Citizens Savings Hall of Fame Athletic Museum.

GLADCHUK, Chester. Player. Center for Boston College 1938 – 1940.

GORDON, Walter. Player. Tackle for California 1916 – 1918.

LAUTENSCHLAEGER, Lester. Player. Back for Tulane 1922 – 1925.

McDOWALL, Jack. Player. Back for North Carolina State 1925 – 1927.

NEWMAN, Harry L. Player. Back for Michigan 1929 – 1932.

SKLADANY, Joseph "Muggsy." Player. End for Pittsburgh 1931 – 1933.

SMITH, John "Clipper." Player. Guard for Notre Dame 1925 – 1927.

STAFFORD, Harrison "Harry." Player. Back for Texas 1930 – 1932.

VAN SICKEL, Dale. Player.

WARBURTON, Irvine E. "Cotton." Player. Back for Southern California 1932 – 1934.

WELCH, Gus. Player. Back for Carlisle 1910 – 1914. *Also in:* American Indian Athletic Hall of Fame.

ZARNAS, Gust. Player. Guard for Ohio State 1935 – 1937.

1976 CAMERON, Edmund McCullough. Player. See entry in Athletic Directors Hall of Fame, Citizens Savings Hall of Fame Athletic Museum.

CROW, John David. Player. Halfback for Texas A&M 1955 – 1957.

DERY, Dexter W. Player. End for Pennsylvania State University 1909 – 1912.

FEARS, Thomas. Player. See entry in Professional Football Hall of Fame, 1970. *Also in:* Major League Football Hall of Fame, Citizens Savings Hall of Fame Athletic Museum.

JANOWICZ, Victor. Player. Halfback for Ohio State University 1949 – 1951.

JENKINS, Darold. Player. Center for University of Missouri at Columbia 1940 – 1941.

MARKOV, Victor. Player. Tackle for University of Washington 1935 – 1936.

MATSON, Oliver G. Player. See entry in Professional Football Hall of Fame, 1972. *Also in:* Major League Football Hall of Fame, Citizens Savings Hall of Fame Athletic Museum.

MILLER, Creighton. Player. Halfback for University of Notre Dame 1941 – 1943.

MUNGER, George A. Coach. University of Pennsylvania 1938 – 1953.

PARKER, Jack D. Player. See entry in Canadian Football Hall of Fame, 1973.

SWIACKI, William (dec). Player. End for Holy Cross 1941 – 1942; End for Columbia University 1946 – 1947.

1977 BAGNELL, Francis "Reds." Player. Running back for Pennsylvania 1948 – 1950.

BANKER, Bill. Player. Back for Tulane 1927 – 1929.

BELLINO, Joe. Player. Back for Navy 1965 – 1967.

CASANOVA, Leonard. Coach. See entry in Athletic Directors Hall of Fame, Citizens Savings Hall of Fame Athletic Museum, 1975. *Also in:* College Football Hall of Fame, Citizens Savings Hall of Fame Athletic Museum.

CZAROBSKI, Ziggie. Player. Tackle for University of Notre Dame 1942 – 1943, 1946 – 1947.

DANIELL, Jim. Player. Tackle for Ohio State 1939 – 1941.

FRANCIS, Harrison "Sam." Player. Back for Nebraska 1934 – 1936.

FRANZ, Rod. Player. See entry in College Football Hall of Fame, Citizens Savings Hall of Fame Athletic Museum.

MacLEOD, Bob. Player. Back for Dartmouth 1936 – 1938.

MILSTEAD, Century (dec). Player. Tackle for Wabash 1920 – 1921.

NOMELLINI, Leo. Player. See entry in Professional Football Hall of Fame, 1969. *Also in:* College Football Hall of Fame and Major League Football Hall of Fame, Citizens Savings Hall of Fame Athletic Museum.

SAYERS, Gale E. Player. See entry in Professional Football Hall of Fame, 1977. *Also in:* College Football Hall of Fame, Citizens Savings Hall of Fame Athletic Museum.

Professional Football Hall of Fame

CANTON, OHIO

Mailing Address: 2121 Harrison Ave, N.W, 44708. Tel. (216) 456-8207. *Contact*: Donald R. Smith, Dir. Public Relations. *Location*: off I-77 and U.S. Hwys. 30 and 62; approx. 20 mi. S.E. of Akron, 50 mi. S.E. of Cleveland, 75 mi. N.W. of Pittsburgh, Pa, 145 mi. S.E. of Detroit, Mich, 165 mi. N.E. of Dayton. *Admission*: 9 to 8 daily and weekends, Memorial Day through Labor Day; 9 to 5 daily Labor Day to Memorial Day; closed Christmas Day. Adults $2.00, children under 14 50¢, family $4.50, group rates available. *Personnel*: Dick Gallagher, Dir; 14 mem. Bd. of Dir. including 9 mem. from Canton and/or Stark County; 10 mem. Enshrinee's Comt; 13 mem. Festival Comt; 29 mem. Bd. of Selectors; staff of 28. *Nearby Halls of Fame*: Golf (Foxburg, Pa, 120 mi. N.E.), State (Detroit, Mich.), Flight (Dayton).

Canton was the ideal location for a pro football hall of fame for two reasons: it was the home of the Canton Bulldogs, the team starring Jim Thorpe in the 1920s, and it was there that the American Pro Football Association (forerunner of the National Football League) was organized on September 17, 1920. A civic campaign from 1959 to 1963, approved by the National Football League, culminated in a magnificent structure, towered by a 52-foot football-shaped dome, being constructed on a wooded park donated by the city of Canton. The building was first opened to the public September 7, 1963; an expansion project completed in May, 1971, almost doubled the interior space, which has become the historical showplace and repository for pro football, "the sport's treasure chest," and the hallowed honoring spot for its greats. There are three large exhibition areas, two enshrinement areas, a 250-seat theater in which a different movie is shown every hour, offices, a large gift shop, a research library and special displays including the Pottsville Maroon Controversy, the Modern Era, Pro Football Today, Evolution of the Uniform, the Top Twenty, and the Maturing Years. Also of special interest are the Enshrinees Memento Room and the Hall of Heroes. Over a quarter of a million people visit these facilities annually to view those special exhibits, to see the seven-foot bronze of Jim Thorpe, to hear taped voices of the sport's past greats, and to use the rearview projectors and the two selectro-slide machines. Thousands more participate in activities sponsored by the Hall: the Hall of Fame Festival Queen's Pageant held in June, and in late July or early August the Tenth Anniversary Class Reunion and Football's Greatest Weekend, which involves a breakfast, fashion show and luncheon, a banquet, a parade, the enshrinement ceremonies and the annual AFC-NFC Hall of Fame pre-season football game, held in adjacent Fawcett Stadium.

Members: 93 as of January 17, 1977. The 29-member Board of Selectors is made up of sportswriters—one each from cities having pro teams, two from New York City which has two teams—and a 29th member who is the highest officer of the Pro Football Writers Association who is not already a member. The overall membership includes five veteran members who form a Senior Committee to name each year one enshrinee from the pre-1952 era. The Selection Committee meets each year on the day before the Super Bowl to elect a new class of enshrinees. The Board has previously screened all nominees by mail ballot and will have before them a list of approximately 15 final candidates and a detailed biography of each. To be elected, a nominee must obtain approximately 80 percent of the vote of those selectors in attendance. Present rules call for the election of between three and six new enshrinees each year. Any fan may nominate any contributor or player by writing to the Pro Football Hall of Fame; the only limitation is that a player must have been retired at least five years and a coach must be retired. Other contributors (owners, administrators, etc.) may be nominated and elected while they are still active. Each new member will receive a ring engraved with his own name and with the Hall of Fame's insignia at the enshrinement ceremonies.

1963

BAUGH, Samuel A.
Player

Born March 17, 1914, in Temple, Tex; College All-American twice; All-NFL six times; retired 1952 to a Texas ranch.

1937–1952 Washington Redskins, quarterback
1960–1961 New York Titans, coach
1964 Houston Oilers, coach

Twice an All-American at Texas Christian, Baugh was the first-draft choice of the Redskins in 1937. Considered by many to have been the most accurate passer of all time, he led the National Football League (NFL) in passing for six years (an NFL record), and was named All-NFL six times. In 1943 "Slingin' Sammy" led the league in passing, punting and interceptions; in addition to his offensive talents, he was a superb defensive back with a share of the single-game interception record (4), and was the greatest punter in NFL history. He led the league four years and holds NFL records for career and season punting averages. He passed for 21,886 yds, completed 186 touchdowns; had 28 lifetime interceptions and held a lifetime punting average of 45.1 yds. His 70.3 completion average in 1945 is also an all-time record. Baugh came out of retirement to coach the Titans and the Oilers. Bones Taylor, a Redskin receiver, said, "In football you have throwers, and you have passers . . . and then you have Sammy Baugh."

Also in: College Football Hall of Fame and Major League Football Hall of Fame, Citizens Savings Hall of Fame Athletic Museum; and National Football Hall of Fame.

BELL, DeBenneville "Bert"
Coach and Owner

Born February 25, 1895, in Philadelphia, Pa; son of former state attorney general John C. Bell; a star of Ziegfeld Follies; attended Univ. Pa; wife Frances Upton; three children, Jamie, Bert Jr. and Upton; grandson a congressman and brother a state governor; died October 11, 1959, at age 64 of a heart attack in Franklin Field during the last two minutes of a game between the Philadelphia Eagles and the Pittsburgh Steelers.

University of Pennsylvania, Coach
Temple University, coach
1933–1940 Philadelphia Eagles, owner
1941–1946 Pittsburgh Steelers, coach and co-owner
1946–1959 National Football League, commissioner

A star quarterback at Pennsylvania before and after a stint in the Army in W. W. I, Bell went on to coach at Pennsylvania and Temple in the 1920s. Having lost a fortune in the stock market crash, he scraped together $2500 to buy a share of the Frankford Yellowjackets (later renamed the Philadelphia Eagles) in 1933. Soon he was able to buy out his partners. Elected National Football League (NFL) Commissioner in 1946, he led the league during its war with the rival All-American Football Conference. He built the NFL's image to unprecedented heights by setting up far-sighted television policies, establishing strong antigambling controls, recognizing the NFL Players Association, and proposing the adoption of the college draft. The NFL pension plan instituted in 1962 is named for him.

Also in: Major League Football Hall of Fame, Citizens Savings Hall of Fame Athletic Museum.

CARR, Joseph F.
Administrator

Born October 22, 1880, in Columbus, Ohio; died May 20, 1939, at the age of 58.

Sportswriter Joe Carr was the promoter, founder and first owner of the Columbus Panhandles team in 1904. Co-organizer of the National Football League (NFL) in 1920, he became president in 1921, succeeding the first president, Jim Thorpe, and held that position until 1939. Serving the NFL with distinction for 19 years, Joe's contributions are numerous. He gave the NFL stability and integrity with rigid enforcement of rules, introduced the standard players contract, banned the use of collegians in NFL play, and worked endlessly to interest financially capable new owners.
Also in: Major League Football Hall of Fame, Citizens Savings Hall of Fame Athletic Museum.

CLARK, Earl H. "Dutch"
Player

Born October 11, 1906, in Fowler, Colo; attended Colo. Col; won 12 letters in four sports, baseball, basketball, football and track; College All-American; All-NFL 1931, 1932, 1934–1937; currently an executive in sales for a Detroit tool and die company.

1931–1932 Portsmouth Spartans, quarterback
1934–1938 Detroit Lions, quarterback, coach
1939–1942 Cleveland Rams, coach

Having gained recognition as an All-American at Colorado College, Clark began his pro career with the Portsmouth Spartans in 1931. Playing with the Spartans through the 1932 season, he led the National Football League (NFL) in scoring and field goals that same year. In 1934 he moved with the Spartans to Detroit, where they changed their name to the Lions, and remained with the team until 1938. An intelligent, quick-thinking team leader, in 1935 he directed the Lions to the NFL championship. He was again the NFL's scoring champ in 1935 and 1936. During his last two years with the Lions Dutch acted as player-coach before taking on a coaching position with the Cleveland Rams in 1939. In his playing career Clark scored 368 points on 42 touchdowns, 71 extra points and 15 field goals.
Also in: Athletic Trainers Hall of Fame, College Football Hall of Fame and Major League Football Hall of Fame, Citizens Savings Hall of Fame Athletic Museum; and National Football Hall of Fame.

GRANGE, Harold "Red"
Player

Born June 13, 1903, in Forksville, Pa; suffered leg injury at age 15 and was told he would never again play football; went on to win 16 letters in four years in high school baseball, basketball, football and track; also known as "Galloping Ghost", "Wheaton Ice Man" and "Old 77"; attended Univ. Ill; All-American 1923-1925; Citizens Savings Player of the Year 1924; Silver Football 1924; All-Pro 1931; Modern All-Time All-American Team; Parke Davis' All-Time All-American Team; after football career went into insurance business; became Chicago Bears' radio and television announcer; presently retired in Florida; plays golf; enjoys fishing and boating.

1925 Chicago Bears, halfback
1926 New York Yankees (AFL), halfback
1927 New York Yankees (NFL), halfback
1929–1934 Chicago Bears, halfback

In his first collegiate game played against Nebraska in 1923, Grange scored three touchdowns; and by the end of the season he had scored 12 touchdowns and gained 1296 yds. In 1924 in a game against Michigan, Red scored 4 touchdowns in the first 12 minutes, later scored another and finished with 402 total yds. Signed in 1925 to play for the Chicago Bears, Grange packed the stadiums and earned over $100,000 that year. After a money dispute, Grange and his manager, "Cash and Carry" Pyle, started their own league with the New York Yankees. The idea was a disaster and the league folded after one year. New York was then given a National Football League (NFL) franchise, and Red played for the team for one year before sustaining a knee injury. He did not play in 1928. He returned to the Bears but suffered another knee accident in 1935 and never played again. From high school to pros, Grange played in 247 games, carried the ball 4013 times for 33,820 yds.
Also in: College Football Hall of Fame and Major League Football Hall of Fame, Citizens Savings Hall of Fame Athletic Museum; and National Football Hall of Fame.

HALAS, George Stanley "Papa Bear"
Coach

Born February 2, 1895, in Chicago, Ill; played college football at Univ. Ill; also played baseball and captained basketball team; suffered a broken jaw in college; entered Navy during W. W. I and led Great Lakes Naval Training Station football team to Rose Bowl; in 1919 played outfield for New York Yankees (baseball) participating in six games and then suffered leg injury sliding; Citizens Savings Rose Bowl Player of the Game 1919; reentered Navy during W. W. II, 1943; retired from coaching 1968; now president of Halas and Keefe, Inc., based in Chicago.

1920–1921 Decatur Staleys, player-coach
1922–1929 Chicago Bears, player-coach
1933–1942 Chicago Bears, owner, coach
1946–1955 Chicago Bears, owner, coach
1958–1967 Chicago Bears, owner, coach

Halas was the founder and coach of the Decatur Staleys (later the Chicago Bears). He played end for the Bears for eleven seasons. His 98-yd. run with a recovered fumble established a National Football League (NFL) record that stood for nearly 50 years. He was a cofounder of the NFL and the only person associated with the NFL through its entire first 50 years. Halas recorded many "firsts" in pro coaching and administration and pioneered in many aspects of the game. He coached the Bears for 40 seasons and won a record five NFL championships. He holds records for the most years as head coach and for the most championship games won, seven. His 325 career coaching wins is also a record. He retired as player and "fired" himself as coach in 1929. In 1932 he borrowed money to buy out partner Dutch Sternaman, becoming sole owner of Bears, and returned to coaching in 1933. His success with T-formation, man-in-motion attack in the 1940 title game set the style for modern football. He developed the use of two receivers rather than one, and flanker as receiver rather than decoy. Halas was the first coach to hold daily practices, utilize films of opponents, barnstorm team, have games broadcast on radio and use tarpaulin on field for weather

protection. He also campaigned for dual Rookie of the Year Awards, for both offense and defense. Halas is the only man still in game to have started from pro football's inception in 1920.
Also in: Major League Football Hall of Fame, Citizens Savings Hall of Fame Athletic Museum.

HEIN, Melvin J.
Player
Born August 22, 1909, in Redding, Calif; All-American for Wash. State Univ. Rose Bowl team 1930; All-Pro 1933–1940; Most Valuable Player 1938; Modern All-Time All-American Team; now supervisor of officials, American Football Conference; resides in New York.

An All-American at Washington State in 1930, Hein wrote to three National Football League (NFL) clubs offering his services. The Giants bid highest at $150 per game. A flawless ball-snapper, powerful blocker and superior pass defender, Hein was a 60-minute regular 1931–1945. He was injured only once and never missed a game. He played in seven NFL championship games and was voted All-Pro from 1933 to 1940. Grantland Rice said, "Some sort of Oscar ought to go to Hein for stamina."
Also in: College Football Hall of Fame and Major League Football Hall of Fame, Citizens Savings Hall of Fame Athletic Museum; and National Football Hall of Fame.

HENRY, Wilbur F. "Pete" "Fats"
Player
Born October 31, 1897, in Mansfield, Ohio; attended Washington and Jefferson Univ; lettered in four sports; Citizens Savings Player of the Year 1917; Earlyday All-Time All-American Team; died February 7, 1952, at age 54.

1920–1923	Canton Bulldogs, tackle
1925	Akron Pros, tackle
1925–1926	Canton Bulldogs, co-coach
1927	New York Giants, tackle
1927–1928	Pottsville Maroons, coach
1930	Staten Island Stapletons, tackle

Henry was a three-time All-American at Washington and Jefferson University. Among the largest players of his time at 5 ft. 10 in, 230 lbs, he had extraordinary quickness and agility and was the bulwark of Canton's 1922–1923 championship line. A 60-minute performer, he excelled as a placekicker and as a punter. He made 49 straight dropkicks, and shares the record for the longest dropkick fieldgoal, 50 yds. His 94-yd. punt set a record that stood for 45 years. Following his retirement and until his death he served as the athletic director at his alma mater. Walter Camp said, "I rate him one of the most remarkable performers ever seen on a gridiron." Grantland Rice called him "the best tackle I ever saw."
Also in: College Football Hall of Fame and Major League Football Hall of Fame, Citizens Savings Hall of Fame Athletic Museum; National Association of Intercollegiate Athletics Hall of Fame and National Football Hall of Fame.

HUBBARD, Robert "Cal"
Player
See entry in Green Bay Packer Hall of Fame, 1970.
Also in: Major League Baseball Hall of Fame and Major League Football Hall of Fame, Citizens Savings Hall of Fame Athletic Museum; Louisiana Sports Hall of Fame, National Association of Intercollegiate Athletics Hall of Fame, National Baseball Hall of Fame and National Football Hall of Fame.

HUTSON, Don
Player
See entry in Green Bay Packer Hall of Fame, 1972.
Also in: College Football Hall of Fame and Major League Football Hall of Fame, Citizens Savings Hall of Fame Athletic Museum; and National Football Hall of Fame.

LAMBEAU, Earl "Curly"
Founder, Player and Coach
See entry in Green Bay Packer Hall of Fame, 1970.
Also in: Major League Football Hall of Fame, Citizens Savings Hall of Fame Athletic Museum; and Wisconsin Athletic Hall of Fame.

MARA, Timothy J.
Owner
Born July 29, 1889, in New York City; quit school at 13 to support himself and widowed mother; sold newspapers, worked as theater usher and runner for bookmakers; became a full-time bookie, died February 16, 1959, in New York City.

In 1925 Mara bought the New York Giants franchise for $500. Although he lacked technical knowledge regarding football, he molded the Giants into a solid organization under his family enterprise. Following his leadership his sons Jack and Wellington ran the club. Wellington, in fact, is still president and Mara's grandson Timothy J. is now vice president and treasurer. Mara was known as a man who kept his word; he retained coach Steve Owen for 22 years on nothing more than a verbal agreement and a handshake. Under Mara's guidance, the Giants grew to a National Football League (NFL) powerhouse, winning three NFL championships and eight divisional titles.
Also in: Major League Football Hall of Fame, Citizens Savings Hall of Fame Athletic Museum.

MARSHALL, George Preston
Owner
Born October 11, 1896, in Grafton W.Va; attended Randolph-Macon Col; made fortune in laundry business; died August 9, 1969, in Washington, D.C.

1932	Boston Braves, owner
1933–1936	Boston Redskins, owner
1937–1969	Washington Redskins, owner

In 1932 Marshall acquired the Boston franchise and moved the team five years later to Washington where they assumed the name of Redskins. Marshall was a flamboyant, controversial, innovative master showman who pioneered gala halftime activities. He organized the first team band, sponsored progressive rule changes and the splitting of the National Football League (NFL) into two halves with title playoffs. During his reign, the Redskins won six divisional and two NFL titles.
Also in: Major League Football Hall of Fame, Citizens Savings Hall of Fame Athletic Museum.

McNALLY, John
Player
See entry in Green Bay Packer Hall of Fame, 1970.
Also in: Major League Football Hall of Fame, Citizens

Savings Hall of Fame Athletic Museum; and Wisconsin Athletic Hall of Fame.

NAGURSKI, Bronislaw "Bronko"
Player
Born November 30, 1908, in Rainy River, Ont; attended Univ. Minn, played tackle and fullback; All-Pro 1932 – 1934; Tackle on Modern All-Time All-American Team; son Bronko Jr. played for Notre Dame and then Canadian Football League.

1930 – 1937 Chicago Bears, running back
1943 Chicago Bears, running back

Nagurski joined the Chicago Bears after completing a legendary college career at Minnesota, where he was consensus All-American. With the Bears he became professional football's symbol of power, ruggedness and determination. He was both a bulldozing runner on offense and a bone-crushing linebacker on defense. Led by Nagurski, the Bears won the National Football League title in 1932, 1933 and 1943. His two touchdown passes clinched the Bears' 1933 victory. As an example of Nagurski's power, when two members of the Pittsburgh Pirates tried to stop him from reaching the end zone, one suffered a broken shoulder and the other was knocked cold. George Halas once said of Nagurski, "He's the only man I've ever seen who runs his own interference."
Also in: College Football Hall of Fame and Major League Football Hall of Fame, Citizens Savings Hall of Fame Athletic Museum; and National Football Hall of Fame.

NEVERS, Ernest
Player
Born June 11, 1903, in Willow Grove, Minn; attended Stanford Univ; eleven-letter man; consensus All-American; Modern All-Time All-American Team; Citizens Savings Rose Bowl Player of the Game 1925; played professional baseball and basketball; pitched 45 games for St. Louis Browns 1925-1927; died May 3, 1976.

1926 – 1927 Duluth Eskimos, running back
1929 – 1931 Chicago Cardinals, running back

Nevers's career at Stanford was remarkable. Primarily a running back, he also passed, punted and played defense. His Stanford coach, the famous Pop Warner, said he was superior even to Jim Thorpe, whom he also coached at Carlisle. After college, Nevers played professional football with the Duluth Eskimos, professional baseball with the St. Louis Browns and professional basketball. Later, 1929 – 1931, he signed with the Chicago Cardinals where he missed only 27 minutes of a 29-game schedule. In a game against the Bears in 1929, he broke the National Football League scoring record with 40 points, six touchdowns and four points after touchdown.
Also in: College Football Hall of Fame and Major League Football Hall of Fame, Citizens Savings Hall of Fame Athletic Museum; and National Football Hall of Fame.

THORPE, James F.
Player
Born May 28, 1888, in Prague, Okla; of American Indian descent; great-grandfather was Black Hawk, Sac and Fox war chief; twin brother Charles died in boyhood; by doing farm work and hunting, acquired strength, stamina and speed; attended Carlisle 1908 – 1912; All-American 1911 and 1912; also competed in high jump, finishing fourth and seventh, respectively; set world record in decathlon, winning high jump, hurdles, shotput and 1500-m. race; winner of both pentathlon and decathlon in Stockholm Olympic Games 1912; presented trophies by King Gustavos of Sweden that were later forfeited because it was discovered he played minor league baseball 1909 – 1910; sixty years later, in 1973, trophies and medals were restored; Earlyday All-Time All-American Team; played pro baseball 1913 – 1919 with New York Giants, Cincinnati Reds and Boston Braves; movie of his life, starring Burt Lancaster as Thorpe, made 1951; died March 28, 1953, at age 64.

1915 – 1917 Canton Bulldogs (pre-NFL), halfback
1919 Canton Bulldogs (pre-NFL), halfback
1920 Canton Bulldogs, (pre-NFL), halfback
1921 Cleveland Indians, (pre-NFL), halfback
1922 – 1923 Oorang Indians, (pre-NFL), halfback
1923 Toledo Maroons, (pre-NFL), halfback
1924 Rock Island Independents, (pre-NFL), halfback
1925 New York Giants, (pre-NFL), halfback
1926 Canton Bulldogs, (pre-NFL), halfback
1928 Chicago Cardinals, (pre-NFL), halfback

Jim Thorpe was an All-Star at Carlisle where he scored 25 touchdowns and 198 points in 1912. Against Harvard he kicked four long field goals and scored a touchdown for a startling 18 – 15 Carlisle victory in 1911. Jim Thorpe was the first big-name athlete to play pro football. After he graduated from Carlisle, he signed with the Canton Bulldogs in 1915. He is considered by many as the greatest all-around athlete of all time. He was elected president of the Professional Football Association in 1920. In a 1969 poll, sports editors throughout the United States voted Thorpe Number One among all football backfield stars of the first 50 years. He was also voted greatest football player and male athlete of first half century in Associated Press poll 1950.
Also in: American Indian Athletic Hall of Fame; College Football Hall of Fame and Major League Football Hall of Fame, Citizens Savings Hall of Fame Athletic Museum; National Football Hall of Fame, National Track and Field Hall of Fame and United States Track and Field Hall of Fame.

1964

CONZELMAN, James G.
Player, Coach and Owner
Born March 6, 1898, in St. Louis, Mo; attended Washington Univ, St. Louis; All – Most Valuable Coach 1919; Most Valuable Player 1928; extremely versatile—also a newspaper publisher, board of directors with St. Louis Cardinals, song writer, radio commentator, writer, middleweight boxing champion, and advertising executive; died July 31, 1970.

1920 Decatur Staleys, quarterback
1921 – 1922 Rock Island Independents, quarterback
1923 – 1924 Milwaukee Badgers, quarterback
1925 – 1926 Detroit Panthers, quarterback, coach, owner
1927 – 1930 Providence Steamrollers, quarterback and coach
1940 – 1942 Chicago Cardinals, coach
1946 – 1948 Chicago Cardinals

All-Most Valuable Coach in 1919 for Washington University in St. Louis, Conzelman went on to win the National Football League (NFL) title in 1928 with Providence. A knee injury ended his 10-year playing career and he subsequently coached the Cardinals to 1947 NFL and 1948 division crowns. A pro head coach at age 24, he guaranteed the Card's owner Charles Bidwill the title if Bidwill could secure the "dream backfield" of Christman, Harder, Trippi and Goldberg. Bidwill died before Conzelman could make good on his promise. A 34-31-3 record with the Cardinals gave Jimmy an overall pro coaching record of 82-69-14.
Also in: Major League Football Hall of Fame, Citizens Savings Hall of Fame Athletic Museum.

HEALEY, Edward
Player
Born December 28, 1894, in Indian Orchard, Mass; attended Dartmouth College 1918-1920, where he was an excellent end.

1920-1922 Rock Island Independents, tackle
1922-1927 Chicago Bears, tackle

A rugged two-way star, Healey was was perennial All-Pro. He was sold to the Bears in 1922 for $100, the first player sale in the history of the National Football League. According to George Halas, Healey was "the most versatile tackle ever."
Also in: National Football Hall of Fame.

HINKLE, William Clarke
Player
See entry in Green Bay Packer Hall of Fame, 1972.
Also in: Major League Football Hall of Fame, Citizens Savings Hall of Fame Athletic Museum; National Football Hall of Fame and Wisconsin Athletic Hall of Fame.

LYMAN, William Roy "Link"
Player
Born 1898 in Table Rock, Nebr; played no sports in high school, since only seven boys attended; first athletics were at Univ. Nebr; quickly overcame lack of experience; owner of insurance agency in San Marino, Calif. until death in 1972.

1922-1923 Canton Bulldogs, tackle
1924 Cleveland Bulldogs, tackle
1925 Canton Bulldogs, tackle
1925 Frankford Yellowjackets, tackle
1926-1928 Chicago Bears, tackle
1930-1934 Chiago Bears, tackle

Lyman starred for the powerful Nebraska team of 1921, which lost only to Notre Dame in eight games and outscored its opposition 283-27. In 1933 Lyman was instrumental in helping the Bears win the National Football League championship. As a tackle, Lyman was exceptionally agile and was outstanding at diagnosing plays. He was one of the first linemen to shift positions at the snap of the ball. After retiring from active competition, he returned to his alma mater as a line coach.
Also in: Major League Football Hall of Fame, Citizens Savings Hall of Fame Athletic Museum.

MICHALSKE, August "Mike" "Iron Mike"
Player and Coach
See entry in Green Bay Packers Hall of Fame, 1970.

ROONEY, Arthur J.
Founder, Administrator and Owner
Born January 27, 1901, in Coulterville, Pa; attended Georgetown Univ. and Duquesne Univ; all-round athlete; boxed professionally, played semipro football and minor league baseball, batted .372 and stole 55 bases for Wheeling, W. Va, of Middle Atlantic League 1925; five sons, David, Arthur, Timothy, Patrick and John; with sons controls 10 different corporations; now president of the Pittsburgh Steelers; resides in Pittsburgh; also director of Pompano Raceway; prize-fight promoter and horse breeder.

1933-1937 Pittsburgh Pirates, owner
1938 Pittsburgh Steelers, owner

Known as the "Grand Old Man" of pro football, Rooney is one of the most revered of all sports personalities. He organized and operated the western Pennsylvania semipro grid teams before 1933 when he bought the new Pittsburgh Pirates franchise for $2500. He renamed them the Steelers in 1938. In that year he started the National Football League with the $15,000 signing if Whizzer White. His faith in pro football was a guiding light during the dark Depression years—a faith finally rewarded when the Steelers won back-to-back titles in 1974-1975.

TRAFTON, George
Player
Born December 6, 1896, in Chicago, Ill; offered many scholarships; selected Notre Dame; expelled by Knute Rockne for playing semipro football on the side; pursued boxing career for brief period, ended when he was kayoed by Primo Carnera, 54 sec. into first round; All-Pro Squad of 1920s; died September 5, 1971, at age 74.

1920 Decatur Staleys, center
1921 Chicago Staleys, center
1922-1932 Chicago Bears, center

Trafton was one of the finest centers in the Bear's history. Known as "The Brute," he was once described by teammate Red Grange as "the toughest, meanest, most ornery critter alive." He once knocked out four opponents in a stretch of 12 plays. After 13 years at center, Trafton turned to coaching and was the assistant coach for the world champion Green Bay Packers in 1944. In 1945 he was a coach on the Cleveland Rams.
Also in: Major League Football Hall of Fame, Citizens Savings Hall of Fame Athletic Museum.

1965

CHAMBERLIN, B. Guy
Player
Born January 16, 1894, in Blue Springs, Nebr; played college football for Univ. Nebr. and was All-American 1915; Missouri Valley Conference Most Valuable Player 1914, 1915; died April 4, 1967, at age 73.

1919 Canton Bulldogs (pre-NFL), end
1920 Decatur Staleys, end, running back
1921 Chicago Staley, end, running back
1922-1923 Canton Bulldogs, player-coach
1924 Cleveland Bulldogs, player-coach
1925-1926 Frankford Yellowjackets, player-coach
1927-1928 Chicago Cardinals, coach

Chamberlin was a legendary grid hero of Nebraska, considered to be the premier end of the National Football League (NFL) in the 1920s. According to George Halas, Chamberlin "was the greatest two-way end of all time." An extremely durable two-way performer, he didn't play in a single losing game from his high school days through the first four pro seasons of his career. Chamberlin was the player-coach of four NFL championship teams and his six-year coaching record of 56–14–5 gave him a remarkable .780 percentage.
Also in: College Football Hall of Fame, Citizens Savings Hall of Fame Athletic Museum; and National Football Hall of Fame.

DRISCOLL, John "Paddy"
Player
Born January 11, 1896, in Evanston, Ill; graduated from Northwestern Univ; played pro baseball for Chicago Cubs; entered military service 1918; All-Pro Squad of 1920s; All-NFL six times; died June 29, 1968, at age 72.

1919 Hammond Pros (pre-NFL), quarterback
1920 Decatur Staleys, running back
1920–1925 Chicago Cardinals, player-coach
1926–1929 Chicago Bears, assistant coach, head coach

Driscoll was a triple-threat on attack and flawless as a defense man. During his career, he dropkicked a record four field-goals in one game and a total record of 49 field-goals and 377 points. He was sold by the Cardinals to the Bears of the National Football League (NFL) in 1926 to thwart signing with the rival American Football League. In spite of it all, he sparked the Bears for four years and made All-NFL six times.
Also in: Major League Football Hall of Fame, Citizens Savings Hall of Fame Athletic Museum; and National Football Hall of Fame.

FORTMANN, Daniel J.
Player
Born April 11, 1916, at Pearl River, N. Y; attended Colgate Univ; Phi Beta Kappa scholar; All-NFL 1938–1943; earned medical degree while playing in the National Football League; now one of nation's top orthopedic surgeons on staff at St. Joseph's Hospital in Burbank, Calif.

At 19, Fortmann was the youngest starter in the National Football League. A 60-minute line leader, he was excellent at diagnosing enemy plays. He was All-NFL for six straight years from 1938 through 1943. According to his Chicago coach, George Halas, Fortmann was one of the all-time great guards. In 1957 Fortmann was team physician for the Los Angeles Rams.
Also in: Major League Football Hall of Fame, Citizens Savings Hall of Fame Athletic Museum.

GRAHAM, Otto Everett, Jr.
Player
Born December 6, 1921, in Waukegan, Ill; one of four musical brothers; played piano, cornet, violin and French horn; as Illinois prep made all-state team in basketball and football; also played baseball, ran in track meets and was a good swimmer; offered basketball scholarships by several colleges; chose Northwestern Univ. 1941–1943; won eight letters, three in basketball, three in football and two in baseball; after graduation entered V-12 program for Navy pilots, sent to Colgate where he played basketball and became All-American for second time; after W. W. II played basketball for Rochester Royals; first on NFL All-Time passing list; All-NFL 1951–1955, 1957; athletic director at United States Coast Guard Academy in New London, Conn.

1946–1949 Cleveland Browns (AAFC), quarterback
1950–1955 Cleveland Browns (NFL), quarterback
1966–1968 Washington Redskins, coach

Graham joined the Cleveland Browns at the start of their first season. A tailback in college, he switched to T-quarterback in the pros, where he topped All-American Football Conference (AAFC) passers for four years and National Football League (NFL) passers for two years. "Automatic Otto" was all-league nine years out of ten, and led the Browns to ten out of ten division or league crowns. In their 1950 NFL title win Graham had three touchdowns running, and in the 1954 NFL title game had three touchdowns passing. He passed for 23,584 yds, 174 touchdowns and scored 276 points on 46 touchdowns. Paul Brown said, "The test of a quarterback is where his team finishes. So Otto Graham, by that standard, was the best of all time." Graham was the youngest member elected to the Professional Football Hall of Fame.
Also in: College Football Hall of Fame and Major League Football Hall of Fame, Citizens Savings Hall of Fame Athletic Museum; and National Football Hall of Fame.

LUCKMAN, Sidney
Player
Born November 21, 1916, in Brooklyn, N.Y; attended Erasmus High School in New York City; offered many scholarships, but accepted a bid from Columbia Univ; All-American 1938; All-Pro 1941–1944, 1947; Bears voted him share of playoff money in 1956; after retirement was executive with a Chicago cellophane company and tutored many Bear quarterbacks.

Prior to his brilliant professional career, Luckman was well known as an outstanding college tailback. As a three-year regular under coach Lou Little, he became one of the best triple-threats in the country. In 1937 he made an 82-yd. kickoff return against Army, a 72-yd. punt against Syracuse and a 60-yd. pass against Pennsylvania. He also connected on a 65-yd. pass against Brown in 1938. His college passing record was 180 completions, 376 attempts for 2413 yds. or a percentage of 47.9. Following college he was drafted by the Pittsburgh Steelers, but was traded to the Chicago Bears where he was introduced to the T-formation by George Halas. He soon became a symbol of excellence as a T-quarterback. While Luckman quarterbacked, the Bears won five Western Conference titles and four National Football League championships, 1940, 1941, 1943 and 1946. During his professional career he completed 904 of 1744 passes, 51.8 percent, for 14,683 yds, 139 touchdowns, reaching an average gain of 8.42 and consistently startling Chicago fans for 11 seasons with his unforgettable performances.
Also in: College Football Hall of Fame and Major League Football Hall of Fame, Citizens Savings Hall of Fame Athletic Museum; and National Football Hall of Fame.

VAN BUREN, Steve W.
Player
Born December 28, 1920, in La Ceiba, Honduras; parents died when young; grew up with grandparents in New

Orleans; attended Louisiana State Univ; All-Pro Squad of 1940s; All-Pro 1945 and 1947 – 1949.

Van Buren, who is primarily remembered for his brilliant professional career, also was a dynamic and powerful running back in college. In the 1944 Orange Bowl game, his three touchdowns were the only scores as his Louisiana State University squad was victorious over Texas A&M. In the same year, Van Buren is credited with amassing 847 yds. and scoring 14 touchdowns (still the Louisiana State record for a single season). With the Philadelphia Eagles Van Buren, the number-one draft pick of 1944, made All-NFL four of the first five years with the team. He won the National Football League (NFL) rushing title four times, won the 1944 punt return and 1945 kickoff return first-place position. In 1948 and 1949 Van Buren led the Eagles to two NFL championships, despite a snowstorm in the first and a torrential rain in the second. Philadelphia Coach Greasy Neale called Van Buren "the best offensive halfback who ever lived." When Van Buren retired in 1952, he retired as pro football's greatest rusher with 5860 yds. on 1320 carries for a 4.1-yd. average. During his pro career, Van Buren scored an amazing 71 touchdowns.
Also in: Major League Football Hall of Fame, Citizens Savings Hall of Fame Athletic Museum; Louisiana Sports Hall of Fame.

WATERFIELD, Robert S. "Rifle"
Player
Born July 26, 1920, in Elmira, N.Y; attended Univ. of California at Los Angeles; Most Valuable Player and Rookie of the Year 1945; All-Pro 1945 and 1946; formerly married to Jane Russell (actress); three children, Thomas, Tracy and Robert.

1945	Cleveland Rams, quarterback
1946 – 1952	Los Angeles Rams, quarterback

Waterfield was drafted by the Rams on the third round as a future in 1944. He led the Rams to the National Football League (NFL) championship, throwing two touchdown passes in the title game of 1945, despite three broken ribs. Waterfield played defense the first four years with the Rams, intercepting 20 passes and was named NFL passing champion twice. In 1946 he averaged 44.7 yds. as a punter, and twice recorded 88-yd. punts during his career. Waterfield completed 46 passes for 672 yds. in four title games. He played in two NFL championships, 1945 and 1952. Waterfield developed the "bomb," or long touchdown pass, that became one of football's most powerful weapons. Rams' end Bob Boyd recalled, "The thing I remember about Bob Waterfield was his leadership. He had an inner strength. Everybody on the ball club respected the guy." His career marks include 11,849 yds, 98 touchdown passes; 573 points on 13 touchdowns, 315 points-after-touchdown, 60 field-goals and a 42.4-yd. punting average. George Wilson, former Chicago player and Detroit coach, said "He was the greatest athlete I've ever seen." After retiring as a player, Waterfield went on to coach the Rams from 1960 to 1962.

Also in: Major League Football Hall of Fame, Citizens Savings Hall of Fame Athletic Museum.

1966

DUDLEY, William M. "Bullet Bill"
Player
Born December 24, 1921, in Bluefield, Va; called too small to play football; attended Univ. Va. 1938 – 1942; Consensus All-American 1941; Maxwell Award 1941; All – National Football League 1942 and 1946; Sammy Award, 1964; served in Army Air Corps; only man ever to win Most Valuable Player awards in college, service and pro football.

1942	Pittsburgh Steelers, halfback
1945 – 1946	Pittsburgh Steelers, halfback
1947 – 1949	Detroit Lions
1950 – 1951	Washington Redskins
1953	Washington Redskins

Dudley, Virginia's first All-American, was the Steeler's number-one draft choice. He was a small and slow player with an unorthodox but extremely efficient style. One of football's last 60-minute players, he was the National Football League's (NFL) rushing leader in 1942 and 1946, and NFL interception leader in 1946. He gained 8147 combined net yds, scored 484 points and had 23 interceptions in his career. In 1946 he played for $20,000—highest salary in those days.
Also in: College Football Hall of Fame and Major League Football Hall of Fame, Citizens Savings Hall of Fame Athletic Museum; and National Football Hall of Fame.

GUYON, Joseph "Indian Joe" "Joc"
Player
Born November 26, 1892, on White Earth Indian Reservation in Minnesota; backfield star for Georgia Tech under John Heisman; Consensus All-American 1918; blocked for Jim Thorpe; Heisman considered him one of the three or four greatest players of all time; died November 27, 1971, at age 79.

1919	Canton Bulldogs (pre-NFL), halfback
1920	Canton Bulldogs, halfback
1921	Cleveland Indians, halfback
1922 – 1923	Oorang Indians, halfback
1924	Rock Island Independents, halfback
1924 – 1925	Kansas City Cowboys, halfback
1927	New York Giants

A triple-threat halfback in the pros, Guyon was big, fast, an exceptional blocker and ball-carrier and could handle punting. He played with Jim Thorpe on four National Football League teams before a pro baseball injury ended his football career. On November 14, 1920, Guyon punted 95 yds, a pro record that stood for 50 years until the 98-yd. punt by Steve O'Neal (New York Jets).
Also in: American Indian Athletic Hall of Fame and National Football Hall of Fame.

HERBER, Arnold
Player
See entry in Green Bay Packer Hall of Fame, 1972.
Also in: Major League Football Hall of Fame, Citizens Savings Hall of Fame Athletic Museum.

KIESLING, Walter
Player and Coach
Born May 27, 1903, in St. Paul, Minn; attended St. Thomas Col; All-Pro 1932; died March 2, 1962, at age 58.

1926–1927	Duluth Eskimos, guard
1928	Pottsville Maroons, guard
1929	Boston Braves, guard
1929–1933	Chicago Cardinals, guard
1934	Chicago Bears, guard
1935–1936	Green Bay Packers, guard
1937–1938	Pittsburgh Steelers, guard
1939–1942	Pittsburgh Steelers, coach
1943	Philadelphia Eagles-Pittsburgh Steelers, co-coach
1944	Chicago Cardinals-Pittsburgh Steelers, co-coach
1954–1956	Pittsburgh Steelers, coach

Kiesling's career spanned 34 years as he served as pro player, assistant coach and head coach. A rugged two-way lineman with six National Football League teams, he starred on the Bears unbeaten juggernaut in 1934. As coach, he led the Steelers in 1942 to their first winning season.
Also in: Major League Football Hall of Fame, Citizens Savings Hall of Fame Athletic Museum; and National Association of Intercollegiate Athletics Hall of Fame.

McAFEE, George A. "One Play"
Player
Born March 13, 1918, in Ironton, Ohio; attended Duke Univ. 1937–1939; teammate of Tommy Prothro; All-American 1939; All-Pro 1941; retired due to injured bone in heel; later coached Univ. Calif. Los Angeles and the Los Angeles Rams.

1940–1941	Chicago Bears, halfback
1945–1950	Chicago Bears, halfback

As a running back for Duke University, McAfee teamed with fullback Eric Tipton for an outstanding combination that sparked the team's 24–5 record and 17 shutouts. In 1938 his Duke squad was 9–0 until losing to University of Southern California in the Rose Bowl. With the Chicago Bears for nine years, McAfee proved to be a phenomenal two-way star and was a long-distance scoring threat on any play. In 1948 he was the National Football League's punt-return champion. This versatile star, who also passed left-handed, kicked and pioneered the low-cut shoe, was one of the fastest players of his day running the 100-yd. dash in 9.8. With the Bears he scored 234 points, gained 5022 yds, intercepted 21 passes and broke the punt-return average with 12.78 yds.
Also in: Major League Football Hall of Fame, Citizens Savings Hall of Fame Athletic Museum; and National Football Hall of Fame.

OWEN, Steve
Player and Coach
Born April 21, 1898, in Cleo Springs, Okla; attended Phillips Univ; died May 17, 1964.

1924–1925	Kansas City Cowboys, tackle
1926–1930	New York Giants, player-captain
1931–1955	New York Giants, coach

Owen was one of the great defensive stars of the 1920s. He captained the Giants 1927 title team that held its opponents to a record low 20 points. As a Giants coach for 23 years, he built a 150–100–17 record with eight divisional and two National Football League title teams. Owen was always recognized as an innovator; some of his well-known introductions were the A-formation offense, the umbrella defense and the two-platoon system.
Also in: Major League Football Hall of Fame, Citizens Savings Hall of Fame Athletic Museum.

RAY, Hugh "Shorty"
Official
Born September 21, 1884, in Highland Park, Ill; attended Univ. of Illinois; basketball captain; devoted to sports safety; died September 16, 1956.

1938–1952	National Football League, supervisor of officials

Ray was universally recognized as the absolute authority on rules in football. As a supervisor of officials, he visited pro training camps annually to explain rules and rule changes to players and coaches. He gave officials stringent tests to insure their responsibleness on the field. Throughout his career he worked tirelessly to improve the quality of officiating and streamlined the rules to increase safety.

TRIPPI, Charles L.
Player
Born December 14, 1922, in Pittston, Pa; attended Univ. Ga. 1942, 1945–1946; All-American; All-Time Rose Bowl Team; Citizens Savings Rose Bowl Player of the Game 1943; All–National Football League 1948; called "Scintillating Sicilian" and "Triple-threat Trippi"; presently in private business in Atlanta, Ga.

Trippi was an All-American from Georgia who, as a substitute for the injured Frankie Sinkwick, gained 115 yds. rushing and 88 yds. passing in the 1943 Rose Bowl game in which Georgia beat University of California at Los Angeles 9–0. Before graduating, Trippi collected the Maxwell Award and was Hiesman Trophy runner-up. In his first year out of Georgia, Trippi signed a four-year contract with the Chicago Cardinals for $100,000 and spent the rest of his professional career with them (1947–1955). In his years with the Cardinals, Trippi proved extremely versatile, playing halfback for five years, quarterback for two years and defense two years. He formed the fourth link in the Cardinals' "dream backfield" that led the Cardinals to the 1947 National Football League championship. Trippi finished his pro career with 3506 yds. on 687 carries for a 5.4 yd. average. He also scored 22 touchdowns. At retirement, Trippi held almost all team rushing, punting and punt-return records.
Also in: College Football Hall of Fame and Major League Football Hall of Fame, Citizens Savings Hall of Fame Athletic Museum; and National Football Hall of Fame.

TURNER, Clyde "Bulldog"
Player
Born November 10, 1919, in Sweetwater, Tex; attended Hardin-Simmons Univ; All-NFL six times; wife Gladys; now breeds quarter horses on his ranch near Gatesville, Tex.

Turner was the Bears' number-one draft choice in 1940. He was a rookie starter at the age of 20. Turner was a terrific blocker, superb pass defender, flawless ball-snapper and had halfback speed. He led the National Football League (NFL) with eight pass interceptions in 1942. He stole 16 passes in his career, including four in five NFL championship games. Bears' quarterback Sid

Luckman, said, "When Bulldog walked on the field, he was all class. He was motivated. He played both ways and he was a vicious football player. He looked out for all of us. If there was trouble, Bulldog was there." Turner anchored four NFL championship teams.
Also in: Major League Football Hall of Fame, Citizens Savings Hall of Fame Athletic Museum; and National Football Hall of Fame.

1967

BEDNARIK, Charles
Player
Born May 1, 1925, in Bethlehem, Pa; son of immigrant steel worker from Czechoslovakia; as a boy, helped family financially by chopping trees while father worked in steel mill during the Depression; played football with a stocking stuffed with rags; as a B-24 aerial gunner, flew 30 combat missions over Germany in W. W. II and won Air Medal with five Oak Leaf Clusters and five Battle Stars; attended Univ. Pa. 1945–1948; made All-State 2nd team in basketball; was a baseball catcher; played on varsity as freshman; All-American twice; Maxwell Trophy for the Nation's Outstanding College Player 1948; Consensus All-American 1947–1948; Modern All-Time All-American second team; Citizens Savings Player of the Year 1948; named to 33 All-American Teams; Rookie of the Year 1949; Most Valuable Player 1954; John Wanamaker Award 1960; National Football League's All-Time Center 1969; retired from pros 1962.

Bednarik was the first player chosen in the 1949 draft. A rugged, durable, bulldozing blocker and bone-jarring tackler, he missed only 3 games in the 14 years he played with the Philadelphia Eagles (1949–1962). The last two-way player in the National Football League (NFL) he played 58 minutes and made the game-saving tackle in the 1960 league title game. Eight times named All-NFL he played in eight Pro Bowls. George Munger, Bednarik's coach at Penn, said, "He would have been an All-American at any position."
Also in: Major League Football Hall of Fame, Citizens Savings Hall of Fame Athletic Museum; and National Football Hall of Fame.

BIDWILL, Charles W, Sr.
Owner
Born September 16, 1895, in Chicago, Ill; attended Loyola Univ. of Chicago; close friend of George Halas, owner of rival Chicago Bears; died April 19, 1947.

In 1933 Bidwill purchased the Chicago Cardinal franchise, displaying staunch faith in the National Football League (NFL) during the troublesome Depression years. He dealt the All–American Football Conference its most stunning blow with the $100,000 signing of Charley Trippi in 1947. He then assembled the "dream backfield" of Trippi, Christman, Goldberg and Harder that won the NFL title—the first for the Cardinals. Unfortunately, Bidwill died before he could see his dream played out.
Also in: Major League Football Hall of Fame, Citizens Savings Hall of Fame Athletic Museum.

BROWN, Paul
Coach
Born September 7, 1908, in Norwalk, Ohio; graduated from Miami Univ. (of Ohio) 1930; played college football; coached Miami, Ohio State and Great Lakes Naval Training Station; coached Massillon, Ohio, High School 1932–1940; appointed head coach of Ohio State 1941; received degree from Ohio State.

1946–1949	Cleveland Browns (AAFC), coach
1950–1962	Cleveland Browns (NFL), coach
1968–1969	Cincinnati Bengals (AFL), coach
1970–1975	Cincinnati Bengals (NFL), coach

Exceptionally successful at all levels of coaching, Brown was a revolutionary innovator with many coaching "firsts" to his credit. He made football into an exact science. In 1946 he organized the Cleveland Browns in the All-American Football Conference (AAFC) and built a great Cleveland dynasty with a record of 158–48–8. His team won four AAFC titles, six consecutive Eastern Conference National Football League (NFL) championships and three world championships. In 17 years Brown lost only one season. Ironically, the early Browns were so strong that they helped hasten the demise of the AAFC because they so completely dominated that league. A second-rate team when they joined the NFL, the Browns quickly affirmed their excellence and won the league title in their first year in the new league. Brown was elected to the Professional Football Hall of Fame before coming out of retirement to coach the expansion Cincinnati Bengals of the American Football League (AFL). By 1973 he had made them a championship contender and guided them to American Football Conference Central Division titles in 1970 and 1973. After the 1975 season, Brown retired as head coach to devote full time to his duties as the general manager of the Bengals. He ranks third in wins among pro coaches with a 195–94–9 record.
Also in: Major League Football Hall of Fame, Citizens Savings Hall of Fame Athletic Museum.

LAYNE, Robert
Player
Born December 19, 1926, in Santa Anna, Tex; attended Highland Park High School; attended Univ. Texas 1944–1947; first T-formation quarterback in the Southwest; College All-American in 1947; All-Pro 1952 and 1956; wife Carol Krueger; currently business consultant in Lubbock, Tex.

1948	Chicago Bears, quarterback
1949	New York Bulldogs, quarterback
1950–1958	Detroit Lions, quarterback
1958–1962	Pittsburgh Steelers, quarterback

As a quarterback for the University of Texas, Layne set numerous records including: 25 touchdown passes, 410 attempted passes, 200 completions, 3145 yds. passing, 3990 yds. total offense, 6.2-yd. average per play, 9 touchdown passes in a single season, three touchdown passes in a single game, an 80-yd. longest pass completion and four touchdowns. In 1946 he led the National Collegiate Athletic Association in pass completions with 77 for 144 attempts, a percentage of .55. In 14 years as a professional, Layne was considered the most productive quarterback in the pros. He threw 3700 passes, completing 1814, and achieved a remarkable 49.0 percentage. In his career he threw for 196 touchdown passes and 26,768 yds. One of his most impressive seasons was 1956 when he made five touchdowns, 33 points after touchdown and 12 field goals for 99 points. In 1957 he led the Lions to a National Football League championship.

Also in: Major League Football Hall of Fame, Citizens Savings Hall of Fame Athletic Museum; National Football Hall of Fame and Texas High School Football Hall of Fame.

REEVES, Daniel F.
Owner
Born June 30, 1912, in New York City; heir to grocery store chain fortune; graduated from Georgetown Univ; stubborn personality; tried unsuccessfully to buy Pittsburgh Steelers and Philadelphia Eagles; suffered from Hodgkins's disease; died April 15, 1971, in Los Angeles, Calif.

1941 – 1945 Cleveland Rams, owner
1946 – 1971 Los Angeles Rams, owner

Reeves was one of football's great innovators and is credited with opening up the West Coast to football and other professional sports by moving his Rams from Cleveland to Los Angeles. His experiments with television paved the way for modern National Football League policies. He also was the first postwar owner to sign a black player (Kenny Washington) and the first to employ a full-time scouting staff.
Also in: Major League Football Hall of Fame, Citizens Savings Hall of Fame Athletic Museum.

STRONG, Kenneth E.
Player
Born August 6, 1906, in West Haven, Conn; All-State twice at West Haven High School; attended New York Univ. 1926 – 1928; promising professional career in baseball halted due to wrist injury in minors; hit 450-ft. homer and batted .342 for one minor season; All-NFL 1934.

1929 – 1932 Staten Island Stapletons, running back
1933 – 1935 New York Giants, running back
1936 – 1937 New York Yankees, running back
1939 New York Giants, assistant coach
1944 – 1947 New York Giants, kicking specialist

As an All-American at New York University, Strong excelled in every phase of the game—blocking, running, passing and placekicking. During his senior year he led the nation with 160 points and gained 2100 yds. Strong began his professional career with the Staten Island Stapletons, but after several years joined the Giants, where he established his meritorious record. In his 14 years of Giant competition, Strong scored 479 points and led the National Football League in 1933 with 64 points. In 1944 he led the league again, this time in field-goal points. When he retired from the Giants his record read 147 extra points, 67 consecutive extra points and 72 single-season points. He is also credited with kicking a famous 47-yd. field goal that took the club record. In the famous "Sneakers Game" of 1934, the icy field forced the Giant players to don tennis shoes at intermission, and decided the 1934 NFL championship at the expense of the Chicago Bears. Strong retired in 1939 but was lured back to serve the Giants as a kicking specialist.
Also in: College Football Hall of Fame and Major League Football Hall of Fame, Citizens Savings Hall of Fame Athletic Museum; and National Football Hall of Fame.

STYDAHAR, Joseph "Jumbo Joe"
Player
Born March 17, 1912, in Kaylor, Pa; lived most of his early life in Shinnston, W. Va; recruited by Pittsburgh but left school after one month due to homesickness; enrolled at West Virginia Univ; All-Pro Squad of 1930s; All-NFL 1937 – 1940; *Sports Illustrated* Silver Anniversary All-American Team 1960; currently president of Big Bear Container Corp. in Chicago.

1936 – 1942 Chicago Bears, tackle
1945 – 1946 Chicago Bears,

At West Virginia, Stydahar was an outstanding football and basketball player and twice was named to the All-Eastern Conference in the latter. In 1936 he was the number-one draft choice in the National Football League (NFL) and was selected by the Bears. Stydahar was always a 60-minute performer who bulwarked the Bears' line in the famous "Monsters of the Midway" era. He played on five divisional and three NFL championship teams. After retiring as a player, Stydahar coached the Los Angeles Rams from 1950 to 1952 and led them to an NFL title. He also coached the Chicago Cardinals from 1953 to 1954.
Also in: Major League Football Hall of Fame, Citizens Savings Hall of Fame Athletic Museum; National Football Hall of Fame and West Virginia Sports Writers Hall of Fame.

TUNNELL, Emlen
Player
Born March 29, 1925, in Bryn Mawr, Pa; graduated from Radnar, Pa, High School; attended Univ. Toledo; suffered broken neck in his one football season; also played basketball; Coast Guard service interrupted collegiate career; resumed studies at Univ. Iowa; NFL All-Time Safety 1969; All-NFL four times; died July 22, 1975, at age 50.

1948 – 1958 New York Giants, defensive back
1959 – 1961 Green Bay Packers, defensive back

Tunnell, signed by the Giants as a free agent in 1948, keyed their famed "umbrella defense" of the fifties and was known as the Giants' "offense on defense." In 1952 he gained more yds. (923) on interceptions and kick returns than the National Football League's (NFL) rushing leader. Tunnell played in 167 NFL games, 158 consecutively; both were records at one time. He played in nine Pro Bowls. He set and still holds pro marks for interceptions, 79; interception yardage, 1282; punt returns, 258; and punt-return yardage, 2209. He was the first black player to sign with the Giants. After retirement, he served as scout and defensive coach for Giants. He is also the first black coach in the NFL and the first black elected to the Hall of Fame.
Also in: Major League Football Hall of Fame, Citizens Savings Hall of Fame Athletic Museum.

1968

BATTLES, Clifford
Player
Born May 1, 1910, in Akron, Ohio; attended W. Va. Wesleyan Univ. 1921 – 1931; played football; Phi Beta Kappa Scholar and Rhodes Scholar; All-American halfback 1931; All-NFL 1933, 1936, and 1937; currently working for General Electric in Washington, D.C., and serving as president of the Washington Touchdown Club.

1932 Boston Braves, halfback
1932 – 1936 Boston Redskins, halfback

1937 Washington Redskins, halfback
1938–1956 Columbia University, assistant to Lou Little

Battles was the first (1933) to gain over 200 yds. in one game. He was the league-leading rusher that same year with 737 yds. and also in 1937 with a total of 874 yds. He played two divisional championship games, 1936 and 1937, and subsequently retired when his salary was frozen at $3,000.
Also in: Major League Football Hall of Fame, Citizens Savings Hall of Fame Athletic Museum; National Association of Intercollegiate Athletics Hall of Fame, National Football Hall of Fame and West Virginia Sports Writers Hall of Fame.

DONOVAN, Arthur Jr.
Player
Born June 5, 1925, in Bronx, N.Y; son of a famous boxing referee; educated at Boston College; All-Pro 1954–1957; grandfather Mike middleweight champion and gave lessons to Teddy Roosevelt; currently owns private country club.

1950 Baltimore Colts, defensive tackle
1951 New York Yanks, defensive tackle
1952 Dallas Texans, defensive tackle
1953–1961 Baltimore Colts, defensive tackle

Donovan joined the Colts as a 26-year-old rookie and became a vital part of Baltimore's rise to power in the 1950s. He was a fierce tackler, very strong and remarkably quick for his size. A great morale builder for the team, he played in five Pro Bowls and was the first Colt to enter the Professional Football Hall of Fame. Alex Darras once said, "Artie Donovan is the best defensive tackle I've seen."
Also in: Major League Football Hall of Fame, Citizens Savings Hall of Fame Athletic Museum.

HIRSCH, Elroy L. "Crazylegs"
Player
Born June 17, 1923, in Wausau, Wis; attended Wausau High School and Univ. Wis; holds letters in basketball, baseball and track; enlisted in Marines and went through V-12 officer candidate program; involved in two movies, *Crazylegs* (1953), and *Unchained* (1954); All-Time NFL Flanker 1969; brought a suit against Crazylegs panty hose in 1973, claiming he owned the right to that name; presently director of athletics at University of Wisconsin at Madison.

1946–1948 Chicago Rockets, halfback, end
1949–1957 Los Angeles Rams, end
1960 Los Angeles Rams, general manager

Hirsch played college football at Wisconsin and Michigan, and led the College All-Stars in their 1946 upset of the Rams. Playing with the Rockets, he suffered numerous injuries including a fractured skull in October 1948. He combined a sprinter's speed with a halfback's elusiveness, and in 1949 became a key part of the Ram's revolutionary "three-end" offense. He led the National Football League in receiving and scoring in 1951. Ten of his 17 touchdown catches that year were long-distance "bombs." Hirsch caught a total of 387 passes for 7209 yds, made 60 touchdowns and scored a grand total of 405 points. He caught touchdown passes in a record eleven consecutive games (1950–1951), and his 17 touchdown catches in 1951 tied Don Hutson's single-season record.
Also in: Major League Football Hall of Fame, Citizens Savings Hall of Fame Athletic Museum; and National Football Hall of Fame.

MILLNER, Wayne
Player and Coach
Born January 13, 1913, in Roxbury, Mass; attended Univ. Notre Dame; All-American twice; served in the U.S. Navy 1942–1944; presently a public relations director for an auto dealer and part-time scout for the Redskins.

1936 Boston Redskins, end
1937–1941 Washington Redskins, end
1945 Washington Redskins, end

Millner was a two-time All-American from Notre Dame and is often remembered for his famous last-minute touchdown against Ohio State in 1935 that saved the game 18–13. Millner, always a fierce competitor and at his best in crucial games, starred on four Redskins divisional title teams. During his professional years he caught 124 passes, including 55-yd. and 77-yd. touchdown passes in the 1937 National Football League championship game against the Chicago Bears. Retiring from active competition in 1946, Millner began a coaching career, first as assistant coach to the Redskins and later as assistant coach for Catholic University, the Baltimore Colts and the Philadelphia Eagles. In 1951 Millner served as head coach for the Eagles.
Also in: College Football Hall of Fame, Citizens Savings Hall of Fame Athletic Museum.

MOTLEY, Marion
Player
Born June 5, 1920, in Leesburg, Ga; attended McKinley High School in Canton, Ohio; high school team lost only three games in three years; attended Great Lakes Naval Training Station and Univ. Nev; All-Pro Fullback 1950.

1946–1949 Cleveland Browns (AAFC), running back, fullback
1950–1953 Cleveland Browns (NFL), fullback
1955 Pittsburgh Steelers, fullback

Under Coach Paul Brown, Motley led the Cleveland Browns to four All-American Football Conference (AAFC) and two National Football League (NFL) titles as the starring fullback. Motley is the record holder for the AAFC with an impressive 3024 yds. on 489 carries for 31 touchdowns. He was also the leading rusher in the NFL in 1950. Motley was recognized as a deadly pass blocker and was a peerless runner with a lineman's strength and a sprinter's speed. The "Motley Trap" became one of the Browns' most effective plays, running Motley on the inside.
Also in: Major League Football Hall of Fame, Citizens Savings Hall of Fame Athletic Museum.

WOJCIECHOWICZ, Alexander "Wojie"
Player
Born August 8, 1915, in South River, N.J; attended Fordham Univ. 1935–1937; played alongside teammate Vince Lombardi; All-American twice; All-Pro Squad of 1940s; presently affiliated with New Jersey Real Estate Dept.

1938–1946 Detroit Lions, center, linebacker
1946–1950 Philadelphia Eagles, defensive back

Wojciechowicz was a two-time All-American from Fordham University and played on the famous "Seven Blocks of Granite" team that led the school to a 18–2–5 record. In 1938 he was the Lions' number-one draft choice and played four games his first week as a pro. During eight and one-half years with the Lions, Wojie played both offense and defense and proved to be a devastating blocker as well as tackler. He was known for his exceptionally wide center stance. With the Eagles, Wojie played only as a defensive specialist and is credited with 16 interceptions.
Also in: College Football Hall of Fame and Major League Football Hall of Fame, Citizens Savings Hall of Fame Athletic Museum; National Football Hall of Fame and National Polish-American Sports Hall of Fame and Museum.

1969

EDWARDS, Albert Glen "Turk"

Player

Born September 28, 1907, in Mold, Wash; Rose Bowl star and All-American at Washington State Univ. 1930; All-Pro Tackle 1932, 1933, 1936 and 1937; after retirement in 1948, operated a sporting goods store in Seattle; also held political office; died January 12, 1973, at age 65 in Seattle, Wash.

1932 Boston Braves, tackle
1933–1936 Boston Redskins, tackle
1937–1949 Washington Redskins, assistant coach, head coach

Edwards joined the newly formed Boston Braves for $150 a game in 1932. Turk was a giant of his era—an immovable, indestructible 60-minute workhorse. In one season of 15 games, he played all but ten minutes. He was a steamrolling blocker and a smothering tackler. A bizarre knee injury suffered just after a pregame coin toss ended his playing career in 1940. He then coached the Redskins until retirement. During his career he was an iron man considered by many to be the National Football League's all-time lineman.
Also in: College Football Hall of Fame and Major League Football Hall of Fame, Citizens Savings Hall of Fame Athletic Museum; and National Football Hall of Fame.

NEALE, Earle "Greasy"

Player and Coach

Born November 5, 1891, in Parkersburg, W. Va; acquired the name Greasy from boyhood friend who caught him eating bread with butter oozing over his face; attended W. Va. Wesleyan Univ. 1912–1914; played three sports; liked games of all kinds; worthy competitor in football, basketball, baseball, golf and bridge; played outfield seven years for Cincinnati Reds, batted .357 in famous 1919 World Series; died November 2, 1973, in Lake Worth, Fla.

Neale's extensive college coaching career, following a remarkable college career and a later professional career with the Cincinnati Reds in baseball and the Irontown Lions in football, included directing such schools as Virginia, West Virginia, Washington and Jefferson, Yale and Marietta. His Washington and Jefferson team was referred to as the "Wonder Team" in 1922 and tied powerful California 0–0. In 1941 Neale took over as head coach of the Philadelphia Eagles and during his tenure won the Eastern Division title in 1947 and two world championships, 1948 and 1949. Neale was always an innovative coach and developed the five-man defensive line, man-to-man pass defense and the fake and triple reverse. He tutored two superstar backs, Clint Frank at Yale and Steve Van Buren of the Eagles.
Also in: Major League Football Hall of Fame, Citizens Savings Hall of Fame Athletic Museum; National Football Hall of Fame and West Virginia Sports Writers Hall of Fame.

NOMELLINI, Leo

Player

Born June 19, 1924, in Lucca, Italy; grew up in Chicago; attended Univ. Minn; Consensus All-American 1948 and 1949; All-Pro 1951–1954, 1957 and 1959; All-Pro Squad for 1950s; participated in invasion of Okinawa as a marine in W.W. II; professional wrestler during off-season; named heavyweight wrestling champ for Big Ten; presently vice president for customer relations for Northwestern Title and a radio sportscaster in the San Francisco Bay area.

1950–1963 San Francisco 49ers, tackle

As a college player at Minnesota, Nomellini was Consensus All-American in 1948 and 1949. In his 13 years with the 49ers, Nomellini was a ferocious and intimidating defensive tackle who was never injured and held the record for participating in the most consecutive season games. He appeared in 10 Pro Bowls and was named one of 16 all-time great pros. Playing both ways, Nomelleni was an excellent pass rusher on defense and an outstanding offensive blocker.
Also in: College Football Hall of Fame and Major League Football Hall of Fame, Citizens Savings Hall of Fame Athletic Museum; and National Football Hall of Fame.

PERRY, Fletcher "Joe"

Player

Born January 27, 1927, in Stevens, Ark; prep track star at Jordan High School in Los Angeles; attended Compton Junior College and scored 22 touchdowns in one season; All-Pro fullback 1953-1954.

1948–1949 San Francisco 49ers (AAFC) fullback
1950–1960 San Francisco 49ers (NFL) fullback
1961–1962 Baltimore Colts, fullback
1963 San Francisco 49ers, fullback

While playing for the Alameda Naval Air Station Perry impressed the 49ers and they signed him up in 1948. In 1949 he led the All-American Football Conference (AAFC) in rushing and by 1953 led the National Football League (NFL) in total yards in a season. His 1018 yds. in 1953 made him the fourth professional player to pass the 1000-yd. figure. During his career, Perry rushed for 9723 yds, maintained a 5.0-yd. average and scored 71 touchdowns. He retired with more yardage than any back in NFL history, an amazing 10,346 yds.
Also in: Major League Football Hall of Fame, Citizens Savings Hall of Fame Athletic Museum.

STAUTNER, Ernest

Player

Born April 20, 1925, in Calm, Bavaria; served in Marine Corps; attended Boston College; All-Pro Squad of 1950s; All-Pro 1958.

After graduating from Boston College in 1950 Stautner was drafted by the Steelers where he had an outstanding career as a tackle, recovering 21 fumbles, scoring three safeties and achieving a reputation as a tackle with excellent mobility, burning desire, extreme ruggedness and unusual durability. Also assuming the offensive guard position occasionally, Stautner played in nine Pro Bowls. Following retirement from the Steelers in 1963, Stautner became defensive coordinator of the Dallas Cowboys from 1966 to 1973 and developed the famous "doomsday defense."
Also in: Major League Football Hall of Fame, Citizens Savings Hall of Fame Athletic Museum.

1970

CHRISTIANSEN, Jack L. "Chris"
Player
Born December 20, 1928, in Sublette, Kans; attended Colorado State Univ. 1948–1950; All-Pro 1952-1957; currently head football coach at Stanford Univ.

1951–1958 Detroit Lions, defensive halfback
1963–1967 San Francisco 49ers, head coach

The leader of the "Chris Crew," Christiansen was the National Football League's interception leader for two years and holds the record for the most touchdowns returning punts. The opposing teams tried to follow two standard rules—don't pass or punt anywhere near Christiansen. He owns a lifetime average of 12.75 yds. on punt returns, a career record of 85 punt returns for a total of 1584 yds, and a record eight touchdowns. His interception record stands at 46 for 717 yds.

FEARS, Tom
Player
Born December 3, 1923, in Los Angeles, Calif; attended Univ. Calif. at Los Angeles; All-American 1947; All-NFL 1950; appeared in movie *No. 1* about a football player; currently living in Viejo, Calif.

A spectacular pass receiver, Fears caught a record 18 passes in one game and ended with a career mark of 400 catches for 5397 yds. He led the National Football League's (NFL) receivers for his first three seasons setting an NFL record. Fears had three touchdown interceptions in a 1950 division title game and caught a 73-yd. pass to win the 1951 NFL title. He was a precise pattern-runner and specialized in the button-hook route. Fears appeared in NFL championship games four times. After playing with the Los Angeles Rams 1948–1956, Fears coached under Lombardi and was the first head coach for the New Orleans Saints with a record of 14–40–2.
Also in: Major League Football Hall of Fame, Citizens Savings Hall of Fame Athletic Museum; and National Football Hall of Fame.

McELHENNY, Hugh "King"
Player
Born December 31, 1928, in Los Angeles, Calif; attended George Washington High School and Compton Junior College; Rookie of the Year 1952; All-Pro Halfback 1952, 1953; suffered numerous football injuries.

1952–1960 San Francisco 49ers, halfback
1961–1962 Minnesota Vikings, halfback
1963 New York Giants, halfback
1964 Detroit Lions, halfback

As Washington University's All-American college back, McElhenny was the 49ers first draft pick in 1952. On his first play as a professional, he scored a 40-yd. touchdown and went on to complete a phenomenal season, winning all National Football League honors. He played in six Pro Bowls, gained 11,375 yds. and completed 264 pass receptions for 360 points.
Also in: Major League Football Hall of Fame, Citizens Savings Hall of Fame Athletic Museum.

PIHOS, Peter L. "Big Dog"
Player
Born October 22, 1923, in Orlando, Ill; attended Indiana Univ; college career interrupted by Army service; All-Pro 1947, 1948, 1953–1955; now in insurance business in Fort Wayne, Ind.

While at Indiana, Pihos broke all career records for pass receiving, total points and touchdowns, and led the Hoosiers to the conference title in 1945. Drafted by the Philadelphia Eagles in 1945, Pihos played nine years for them as a two-way end. He led the league with 373 receptions for 6519 yds. and 61 touchdowns.
Also in: Major League Football Hall of Fame, Citizens Savings Hall of Fame Athletic Museum; and National Football Hall of Fame.

1971

BROWN, James
Player
Born February 17, 1936, on St. Simons Island, Ga; outstanding career in high school football; offered scholarships by 45 colleges; attended Syracuse Univ, in senior year scored 43 points for a major college record on six touchdowns and seven points-after-touchdown; All-American in lacrosse and football; starred in collegiate basketball; placed fifth in national decathlon championships; Jim Thorpe Trophy 1958, 1963 and 1965; NFL Most Valuable Player 1958 and 1965; Pro Bowl Most Valuable Player 1962, 1963; presently a film actor and businessman.

Jim Brown was the first-draft choice of the Cleveland Browns in 1957. He is the most feted fullback in football. He was declared All-NFL eight of his nine years in football and played in nine straight Pro Bowls. Brown is considered the most awesome runner in the history of the sport. He holds the National Football League (NFL) career records for the most rushing yardage and the most touchdowns scored. He gained 12,312 yds. rushing; had 262 catches, 15,459 combined net yds. and 756 points scored on 126 touchdowns, setting new records in almost every category. He led the NFL rushers eight times for another NFL record. He averaged 5.2 yds. per carry over a nine-year career to set an additional NFL record.
Also in: Major League Football Hall of Fame, Citizens Savings Hall of Fame Athletic Museum.

HEWITT, William
Player
Born October 8, 1908, in Bay City, Mich; attended Univ. Mich; All-Pro 1933, 1934, 1936, 1937; All-NFL; killed in an auto accident at age 38 on January 14, 1947.

1932 – 1936 Chicago Bears, end
1937 – 1939 Philadelphia Eagles, end
1943 Philadelphia Eagles-Pittsburgh Steelers, end

Hewitt was famous for his super-quick defensive charges. He was fast, elusive and innovative on offense. He invented many trick plays such as the forward-lateral that gave the Bears the 1933 National Football League (NFL) title. Hewitt was an anti-rules man—he played without a helmet. He was the first player to be named All-NFL with two teams.
Also in: Major League Football Hall of Fame, Citizens Savings Hall of Fame Athletic Museum.

KINARD, Frank, M. "Bruiser"
Player
Born October 23, 1914, at Pelahatchie, Miss; one of four brothers to play football at Ole Miss; also played baseball and track; All-Pro 1940 – 1944; Modern All-Time All-American Team.

1938 – 1944 Brooklyn Dodgers, tackle
1946 – 1947 New York Yankees, tackle

Kinard was a two-time University of Mississippi All-American, too small for the tackle position, but tough, aggressive, fast and durable. He was a 60-minute man who went out with injuries only once. Kinard was an outstanding blocker and a smothering tackler. He was the first man to earn both All-NFL and All-AAFC honors for five years consecutively. In 1948 joined Ole Miss staff as line coach.
Also in: College Football Hall of Fame, Citizens Savings Hall of Fame Athletic Museum; and National Football Hall of Fame.

LOMBARDI, Vincent T.
Coach
See entry in Green Bay Packer Hall of Fame, 1975.
Also in: Major League Football Hall of Fame, Citizens Savings Hall of Fame Athletic Museum.

ROBUSTELLI, Andy
Player
Born December 6, 1930, in Stamford, Conn; played with tiny Arnold College (now part of Bridgeport Univ.); wife Jean; All-Pro 1953, 1954, 1956 – 1960; presently director of operations for New York Giants.

1951 – 1955 Los Angeles Rams, end
1956 – 1964 New York Giants, end

As the Rams' 19th-draft choice, Robustelli went on to become All-Pro twice with the Rams. Due to a disagreement with the Rams' management, Robustelli was traded to the Giants in 1956, a move the Rams often regretted as he was named All-Pro for five years with the Giants and made seven Pro Bowl appearances.
Also in: Major League Football Hall of Fame, Citizens Savings Hall of Fame Athletic Museum; and National Association of Intercollegiate Athletics Hall of Fame.

TITTLE, Yelberton A. "Y.A."
Player
Born October 24, 1926, in Marshall, Tex; attended Louisiana State Univ; wife Minette Risch; three children, Diane, Mike and Pat; AAFC Rookie of the Year 1948; All-NFL 1957, 1962 and 1963; NFL Most Valuable Player 1961; now owns an insurance business in Palo Alto, Calif.

1948 – 1949 Baltimore Colts (AAFC), quarterback
1950 Baltimore Colts (NFL), quarterback
1951 – 1960 San Francisco 49ers, quarterback
1961 – 1964 New York Giants, quarterback

Tittle joined the Baltimore Colts in 1948, but in 1951 when the Colts disbanded he went to the San Francisco 49ers. He led the 49ers to ten successful seasons. In 1961 he was traded to the Giants for lineman Lou Cordileone. Tittle led the Giants to division titles 1961 – 1963. In 1962 he threw 33 touchdown passes and the following year threw 36—a National Football League (NFL) record. He played in six Pro-Bowls and shares the NFL single-game record for touchdown passes. Giants' teammate Kyle Tote said, "Y.A. Tittle could throw the ball as well as anyone in the history of football. And he had the enthusiasm of a little kid." His career record includes: 2427 completions, 33,070 yds, 242 touchdowns and 13 games over 300 yds. passing, third all-time in total yardage and fourth in touchdown passes.
Also in: Major League Football Hall of Fame, Citizens Savings Hall of Fame Athletic Museum.

VAN BROCKLIN, Norman "Dutchman"
Player
Born March 15, 1926, in Eagle Butte, S. Dak; watchmaker's son; eighth of nine children; started athletic life at Acalanes High School, Walnut Creek, Calif; attended Univ. Ore; All-American 1948; Most Valuable Player 1960; All-NFL 1960.

1949 – 1957 Los Angeles Rams, quarterback
1958 – 1960 Philadelphia Eagles, quarterback

Van Brocklin was the Rams' fourth-round draft pick in 1949. He was the greatest long-ball thrower of his time, and equally famous for his leadership and hot temper. Van Brocklin led the National Football League (NFL) in passing three times and punting twice. In 1951 his 73-yd. touchdown pass gave the Rams the title. Also that year, he threw for 554 yds, a one-game passing record that still stands. Van Brocklin joined the Eagles in 1958, leading them to the 1960 NFL crown. He played in nine Pro Bowls, and also played in NFL championship games in 1949 – 1951, 1955 and 1960. He retired after the 1960 season to coach the new Minnesota team and later coached the Atlanta Falcons. Don Burroughs, a Van Brocklin teammate with the Los Angeles Rams and Philadelphia Eagles, said, "With him, there is no substitute for winning." He had 1553 career completions for 23,611 yds. and 173 touchdowns.
Also in: Major League Football Hall of Fame, Citizens Savings Hall of Fame Athletic Museum; and National Football Hall of Fame.

1972

HUNT, Lamar
Owner
Born August 2, 1932, in El Dorado, Ariz; attended Southern Methodist Univ; currently president of Kansas City Chiefs and American Football Conference; resides in Dallas, Tex.

1960 – 1962 Dallas Texans, owner
1963 Kansas City Chiefs, owner

Hunt was continually frustrated in his efforts to gain a National Football League (NFL) franchise. As an alternative, he developed the idea of a rival American Football League (AFL) and was the driving force behind its organization in 1959. He founded the Dallas Texans in 1960, and subsequently moved the team to Kansas City in 1963 where the ball club became a solid enterprise. Because of the strength of the Chiefs, the AFL possessed enough stability to survive the AFL-NFL war. In 1966 Hunt was responsible for spearheading merger negotiations with the rival NFL.

MARCHETTI, Gino
Player

Born January 2, 1927, in Antioch, Calif; son of Italian immigrant tavern owner; at 14 was sent with parents to detention farm in California due to war; enlisted in Army at 18; after discharge and parents' release, worked in father's tavern; invited to play football at Univ. San Francisco, after which he enrolled; All-Pro Squad of 1950s; All-League 1956, 1957, 1959–1964; voted Best Defensive End in History of NFL; currently owner of a chain of hamburger stands on the East Coast.

1952 Dallas Texans, tackle
1953–1964 Baltimore Colts, tackle, end
1966 Baltimore Colts, end

Following a successful college career in San Francisco, Marchetti was the second-round draft choice of the New York Yankees football squad in 1952. The team moved to Dallas in the same year and to Baltimore the following year where they assumed their present name, the Colts. He first played defensive tackle without much success, then moved to offensive tackle. In 1954 head coach Weeb Ewbank moved Marchetti to defensive end. In the 1958 title game, Marchetti stopped New York from scoring a needed first down, allowing the Colts to regain the ball and score the tying field goal. Marchetti was recognized as an all-round great defender and was well known for his ferocious pass rushing. Bobby Lane once said of Marchetti. "Did you ever run into a tree in the dark? Well, it's like a pillow compared to Marchetti." In 12 seasons with the Colts, he played prominent roles in two National Football League championships and three Western Conference titles.
Also in: Major League Football Hall of Fame, Citizens Savings Hall of Fame Athletic Museum.

MATSON, Oliver G.
Player

Born May 1, 1930, in Trinity, Tex; attended Univ. San Francisco; All-American 1951; won gold medal in 1952 Olympics; All-Pro 1954-1957; Pro Bowl Player of the Game 1955; presently resides in Los Angeles, Calif.

1952 Chicago Cardinals, halfback
1954–1958 Chicago Cardinals, halfback
1959–1962 Los Angeles Rams, halfback
1963 Detroit Lions, halfback
1964–1966 Philadelphia Eagles, halfback

At the University of San Francisco, Matson was named the National Collegiate Athletic Association rushing champion gaining 1566 yds. on 245 rushes in nine games. He was All-American in 1951 and leading scorer with 126 points. Against Fordham he tied the record for touchdown kickoff returns when he ran for two during the game. He finished his college career with a rushing record of 3166 yds. on 547 plays in 30 games. He averaged a remarkable 105.5 yds. per game and scored 35 touchdowns. Before starting his professional career, Matson participated in the Helsinki Olympics and brought home a gold medal in the 1600-m. (494-ft.) and a bronze medal in the 400-m. (122-ft.). In 1952 Matson was the first-round draft choice of the Chicago Cardinals. Three years later he led the league in punt returns with an average of 18.8 yds. Against the Redskins in 1956, Matson returned a kickoff 105 yds. In 1959 he was traded to the Rams for nine players and later traded to the Lions and Eagles. In 1964, after 14 years of professional participation, Matson retired holding the second best record in combined yardage with 12,844 yds.
Also in: Major League Football Hall of Fame, Citizens Savings Hall of Fame Athletic Museum; and National Football Hall of Fame.

PARKER, Clarence "Ace"
Player

Born May 17, 1913, in Portsmouth, Va; attended Duke Univ; All-American; played college baseball as well as football; All-Pro 1938 and 1940; League Most Valuable Player 1940; All-Pro Quarterback 1940; currently a scout for National Football League; residing in Portsmouth, Va.

1937–1941 Brooklyn Dodgers, quarterback
1945 Boston Yankees, quarterback
1946 New York Yankees (AAFC), quarterback

Parker was an All-American at Duke University and was both a passer and runner. He was the number-one draftee of the Brooklyn Dodgers (football) in 1937, but he signed a contract with the Philadelphia Athletics to play professional baseball. By 1938, however, Parker returned to football and was named All-Pro. Parker was recognized as a triple-threat two-way back who led the Dodgers to their greatest seasons in 1940 and 1941. With the Yankees in 1946, he helped the team clinch the All-American Football Conference (AAFC) Eastern title. Following his career as a professional athlete, Parker coached Duke baseball and football for many years.
Also in: College Football Hall of Fame, Citizens Savings Hall of Fame Athletic Museum; and National Football Hall of Fame.

1973

BERRY, Raymond
Player

Born February 27, 1933, in Corpus Christi, Tex; NFL receiving leader 1958–1960; All-NFL three years; currently coach for Detroit Lions.

1955–1967 Baltimore Colts, end
1968–1969 Dallas Cowboys, assistant coach
1970–1972 Arkansas, assistant coach

Berry was an excellent receiver and holds many records in spite of various physical problems. He had one leg shorter than the other, suffered from poor eyesight and had to use a canvas support strap for a back ailment. He formed an exceptional pass-catch team with Johnny Unitas and set the National Football League (NFL) title game mark with 12 catches for 178 yds. in 1958 during

an overtime game. Berry fumbled only once in his 13-year career. In 1964 he reached his career peak of 506 receptions, breaking the existing all-time NFL record of 503. He eventually retired with 631 receptions, 9275 yds. and 68 touchdowns.
Also in: Major League Football Hall of Fame, Citizens Savings Hall of Fame Athletic Museum.

PARKER, Jim
Player
Born April 3, 1934, in Macon, Ga; from poor family with six children; moved to Toledo while in high school; attended Ohio State Univ; potential recognized by Woody Hayes; All-Pro 1958–1964; Modern All-Time All-American Team; All-Pro Squad of 1950s; retired 1967 and presently living in Baltimore.

At Ohio State, Parker was named Consensus All-American and played guard on offense and linebacker on defense. His Buckeye squad won 23 of 28 games and defeated Southern California in the Rose Bowl in Parker's sophomore year. One of his biggest moments defensively was against Northwestern when he grabbed a fumble and ran 42 yds. for a touchdown. Starting with the Baltimore Colts in 1957, he concentrated on offense and his pass protection for Johnny Unitas was unsurpassed. He turned in remarkable performances in the 1958–1959 and 1964 National Football League championship games.
Also in: College Football Hall of Fame, Citizens Savings Hall of Fame Athletic Museum; and National Football Hall of Fame.

SCHMIDT, Joseph
Player and Coach
Born January 18, 1932, in Pittsburgh, Pa; at 14 played against grown men; attended Univ. Pittsburgh; All-American 1952; All-Pro Squad of 1950s.

1953–1965 Detroit Lions, linebacker
1966 Detroit Lions, linebacker coach
1967–1972 Detroit Lions, head coach

In 1952 Schmidt was named to the All-American squad as a representative from Pittsburgh. Following his senior year he was drafted by the Detroit Lions and moved to middle linebacker. According to Vince Lombardi, Schmidt was "a great diagnostician, a great tackler and a strong defensive leader." As team captain for the Lions for nine years, Schmidt had 24 interceptions and proved a superb field leader making the All-Pro team nine times and playing in ten Pro Bowls. After retiring from active competition, Schmidt served as linebacker coach in 1966 and as head coach from 1967–1972. Following the 1972 season, Schmidt quit in order to spend more time with his family.
Also in: Major League Football Hall of Fame, Citizens Savings Hall of Fame Athletic Museum.

1974

CANADEO, Anthony
Player
See entry in Green Bay Packers Hall of Fame, 1973.
Also in: Major League Football Hall of Fame, Citizens Savings Hall of Fame Athletic Museum; and National Association of Intercollegiate Athletics Hall of Fame.

GEORGE, William J.
Player
Born October 27, 1930, at Waynesburg, Pa; attended Wake Forest College.

1952–1965 Chicago Bears, linebacker
1966 Los Angeles Rams, linebacker

George was one of the first great middle linebackers. An astute strategist, he called the Bears defensive signals for eight years. He was the defensive leader of the 1963 championship team that allowed only 144 points in 14 games. George was All-NFL eight times and played in eight straight Pro Bowls from 1955 through 1962. He intercepted 18 passes and recovered 16 fumbles in his career. His 14 years with the Bears were the longest in service of any player. George Halas said of George, "Bill was certainly an excellent choice for the Pro Hall of Fame. He was a great linebacker, a great team man. He was, and still is, a man of character."

GROZA, Louis
Player
Born January 25, 1924, in Martins Ferry, Ohio; attended Ohio State Univ, played only freshman football; entered the U. S. Army, served with 96th Infantry in Far East 1943–1945; brother Alex Kentucky All-American basketball player; All-Pro 1951–1955 and 1957; Sporting News Player of the Year 1954; NFL Player of the Year 1954; currently an insurance executive and part-owner of a dry cleaning company and boys camp.

1946–1949 Cleveland Browns (AAFC), offensive tackle, kicker
1950–1959 Cleveland Browns (NFL), offensive tackle, kicker
1961–1967 Cleveland Browns, kicker

Groza suffered a back injury in 1961 and subsequently served primarily as a kicker, earning his name "The Toe." He played in four All-American Football Conference (AAFC) title games and nine National Football League (NFL) title games. Groza holds the NFL single-season field goal percentage record and had the longest field goal in a title game, 52 yds. in 1951. In his NFL career, he scored 641 points-after-touchdown, including a streak of 138. He also booted 234 straight field goals. He was All-NFL tackle for six years and played in nine Pro Bowls.
Also in: Major League Football Hall of Fame, Citizens Savings Hall of Fame Athletic Museum.

LANE, Dick "Night Train"
Player
Born April 16, 1928, in Austin, Tex; football star at Anderson High School; played end for Scottsbluff Junior College; served three years in Army and played ball at Fort Ord; discharged 1952; walked into office of Los Angeles Rams and got a contract; All-Pro 1956, 1960–1963; retired after 1964 season and worked in Detroit Lions' front office.

1952–1953 Los Angeles Rams, defensive back
1954–1959 Chicago Cardinals, defensive back
1960–1965 Detroit Lions, defensive back

In his rookie year, Lane led the National Football League in interceptions with a record-setting 14, amassed 298 yds. and returned one interception for 80 yds. In 1954 he was traded to the Chicago Cardinals and

again topped the league in interceptions with ten for 181 yds. with his longest at 64 yds. In 1955 Lane caught a remarkable 98-yd. touchdown pass from Ogden Compton. He was traded in 1960 to the Detroit Lions where Vince Lombardi called him the best cornerback he had ever seen. Opposing coaches usually ordered their quarterbacks never to throw passes near his area. In 1962 he played in the Pro Bowl with great stomach pains (he was operated on two days later for appendicitis) and still intercepted a pass and ran 42 yds. for the West's first score.
Also in: Black Athletes Hall of Fame.

1975

BROWN, Roosevelt "Rosie"
Player
Born October 20, 1932, in Charlottesville, Va; attended Morgan State Univ; Black All-American 1951 and 1952, NFL Lineman of the Year 1956, All-NFL 1956-1963.

Brown was the Giants' 27th pick in the 1953 draft. He started his career as a green 20-year-old and quickly won a starting role. He held that role for 13 seasons as an excellent downfield blocker, a classic pass protector and a fast mover. He was All-NFL for eight straight years and played in nine Pro Bowls.
Also in: National Association of Intercollegiate Athletics Hall of Fame.

CONNOR, George
Player
Born January 21, 1925, in Chicago, Ill; All-American at Notre Dame 1946–1947; Outland Trophy 1946; All-NFL five times.

Connor was drafted first by the Boston Tanks in 1946 and then traded to the Bears. Throughout his career, he was a two-way performer and was able to play three different positions. Connor was big and fast, agile enough to break up an opposing power play, and was exceptional at diagnosing the opponents' plays. He played in the first four Pro Bowls and was a five-time All-NFL player. He ended his playing career in 1955.
Also in: College Football Hall of Fame, Citizens Savings Hall of Fame Athletic Museum; and National Football Hall of Fame.

LAVELLI, Dante
Player
Born February 23, 1923, in Hudson, Ohio; left Notre Dame to play under Paul Brown at Ohio State Univ; played only one varsity season with Ohio and was often injured; following season the Army ruled its officer trainees ineligible for college sports; participated in Battle of the Bulge; after war signed under Paul Brown with Cleveland Browns; All-Pro 1951 and 1953; presently owns furniture and appliance store in Cleveland.

1946–1949 Cleveland Browns (AAFC), end
1950–1956 Cleveland Browns (NFL), end

Lavelli, in his early years with the Browns, formed a tremendous pass-catch tandem with Mac Speedie. In the four-year history of the All-American Football Conference (AAFC), Lavelli caught 142 passes for 2580 yds. and scored 29 touchdowns. His 142 receptions rank fourth on the all-time AAFC list. Combining his AAFC and later National Football League (NFL) accomplishments, his record reads: 386 receptions for 6488 yds. and 62 touchdowns. Lavelli set a championship game record with 24 catches for 340 yds. Paul Brown commented regarding "Glue Fingers" Lavelli, "Lavelli had one of the strongest pair of hands I've ever seen. Nobody could take it away from him once he had it in his hands."

MOORE, Leonard
Player
Born November 11, 1933, in Reading, Pa; graduate of Pa. State Univ; All-NFL 1958–1961 and 1964; winner of Jim Thorpe Trophy.

As a running back for Penn State, Moore led the National Collegiate Athletic Association in average yds. gained per rush with 8.0 in 1954. In 18 college games he rushed for 2380 yds, an average of 6.2 yds. per carry. Upon graduation in 1956, Moore was drafted by the Colts and became an immediate star. In 1961 he suffered a head injury, in 1962 a broken kneecap and in 1963 damaged ribs. Following an emergency appendectomy in 1963 that kept him from the last five games, he was almost traded; however, in 1964 he was switched from flanker to halfback and made a remarkable comeback. In the 1964 season, Moore set the National Football League (NFL) record of 20 touchdowns and led the league with 120 points. He carried the ball 157 times and gained 584 yds. in addition to catching 21 passes for another 472 yds. Moore holds many Colts' records, including 120 points in single season, four touchdowns in one game and 20 touchdowns in a season. He played in the Pro Bowl 1959-1962 and 1964.

1976

FLAHERTY, Ray
Coach
Born September 1, 1904, in Spokane, Wash; played college football at Gonzaga Univ; All-NFL 1928, 1932; now retired and living in Hayden Lake, Ind.

1936 Boston Redskins, coach
1937–1942 Washington Redskins, coach
1946–1948 New York Yankees (AAFC), coach
1949 Chicago Hornets (AAFC), coach

Flaherty played end with the Los Angeles Wildcats (first American Football League), the New York Yankees and the New York Giants before he started his coaching career. He compiled an 80–37–5 coaching record and won two National Football League (NFL) titles with the Redskins and the same number of divisional crowns with the All-American Football Conference (AAFC) Yankees. He was an innovative coach who introduced the behind-the-line screen pass during a 1937 title game. Another Flaherty first was the two-platoon system with one unit rushing and one unit passing.
Also in: Major League Football Hall of Fame, Citizens Savings Hall of Fame Athletic Museum.

FORD, Leonard Guy
Player
Born February 18, 1926, in Washington, D.C; played college ball at Morgan State Univ. and Univ. Mich; All-

NFL 1951-1955; died March 14, 1972, at age forty of a heart attack.

1948 – 1949 Los Angeles Dons (AAFC), end
1950 – 1957 Cleveland Browns, end
1958 Green Bay Packers, end

An offensive star in college and with Los Angeles, Ford caught 67 passes as a two-way end with the Dons. After the All-American Football Conference (AAFC) folded, the Browns converted him to a full-time defensive end and altered the defense team to take advantage of Ford's exceptional pass-rushing ability. He recovered 20 of his opponents' fumbles during his career and overcame serious injuries in 1950 in order to play ball for eight more years. Ford played in four Pro Bowls. Coach Paul Brown said, "Len was the finest defensive end I have ever seen." Ford's teammate, Paul Wiggin, said simply, "He was a man among boys."

TAYLOR, James
Player
See entry in Green Bay Packer Hall of Fame, 1975.

1977

GIFFORD, Francis
Player
Born August 16, 1930, in Bakersfield, Calif; attended Bakersfield High School 1945 – 1947; attended Bakersfield Junior College one year, then transferred to Univ. Southern Calif; All-American 1951; All-AFL 1955 – 1957, 1959; Jim Thorpe Trophy, Most Valuable Player 1956; handsome, modest, articulate, was football glamour boy; retired after 1964 season to do color on Giant telecasts and other work for CBS sports; brief Hollywood career, including a movie with Tony Curtis called *All American;* presently ABC television sportscaster; play-by-play man on Monday Night Football.

1952 – 1960 New York Giants, halfback
1962 – 1965 New York Giants, flanker

Gifford started playing football while attending Bakersfield High School, where he played end and tailback. He was defensive safety, tailback and placekicker for Southern California. In 1950 against Washington State he made a 69-yd. touchdown run, gaining 155 yds. rushing. Gifford was drafted by the New York Giants in 1952, and remained with them from 1952 – 1960 and 1962 – 1965. He was used as a two-way man in 1953 and 1954, becoming the Giants' regular halfback. Gifford gained 819 yds. running that season and caught 51 passes for an additional 603 yds. leading the Giants to the championship. In 1960 he suffered a severe brain concussion playing against the Philadelphia Eagles, and as a result was out of the game all of 1961. Returning in 1962, Gifford was shifted to flanker. Retiring after the 1964 season, he had scored more points than any other Giant, 484; caught more passes, 387; gained more yards with catches, 5434; scored more touchdowns, 78; kicked 10 points-after-touchdown and 2 field goals, and caught 3 touchdown passes in championship games, giving him a career total of 840 rushing attempts, with a gain of 3609 yds, an average of 4.3. Gifford played in the Pro Bowls 1954, 1956 and 1960 – 1964.

Also in: Major League Football Hall of Fame, Citizens Savings Hall of Fame Athletic Museum; and National Football Hall of Fame.

GREGG, Forrest A.
Player
See entry in Green Bay Packer Hall of Fame, 1977.
Also in: Major League Football Hall of Fame, Citizens Savings Hall of Fame Athletic Museum.

SAYERS, Gale E.
Player
Born May 30, 1943, in Wichita, Kans; grew up on farm near Speed, Kans; moved to Omaha and attended Central High School; attended Univ. Kans; Rookie of the Year 1965; All-NFL 1965 – 1969; All-Pro Back 1966; Offensive Player of the Game 1967; George Halas Award (Most Courageous Player of the Year) 1970; Modern Era All-Star 1977; autobiography *I Am Third*—"Lords are first, my friends are second and I am third"—inspired the story *Brian's Song;* wife Linda; retired 1971; assistant athletic director at Univ. Kans.

Sayers, an outstanding halfback, complemented 9.5 speed with tremendous running instinct. While at the University of Kansas, Sayers rushed for 2675 yds. in 1962 – 1964, and in three seasons rushed for a 6.5-yd. average. He was drafted by the Chicago Bears in 1965 and set a National Football League (NFL) record by scoring 22 touchdowns in his rookie season. On December 17, 1965, against the San Francisco 49ers, he scored six touchdowns. In 1966 he won the league rushing title with 1231 yds. Following a 1968 knee injury, he won his second rushing title in 1969, picking up 1032 yds. Sayers injured his other knee in 1970 and, when surgery failed to correct the problem, spent the next two years mainly on the Chicago bench, playing briefly in only four games. Sayers played in the Pro Bowl 1966 – 1968 and 1970. His total career record shows he rushed for 4956 yds. on 991 carries, scored 39 touchdowns, and as kickoff returner had a 30.6 yd. average (still unsurpassed). Sayers held an overall NFL record 8 times and 15 Chicago records. In 1970 the Pro Football Writers Association, in giving him the George Halas Award, named Sayers "Most Courageous Player of the Year." When he accepted the award, he paid tribute to his friend and teammate, Brian Piccolo, who was dying of cancer: "I tell you here and now I accept this award for Brian Piccolo, a man of courage who should receive it. It is mine tonight but Brian Piccolo will have it tomorrow . . . When you hit your knees tonight, please ask God to let him live." Sayers, at 33 years of age, is the youngest player in the Hall of Fame.
Also in: College Football Hall of Fame, Citizens Savings Hall of Fame Athletic Museum; and National Football Hall of Fame.

STARR, Byron B. "Bart"
Player
See entry in Green Bay Packer Hall of Fame, 1977.
Also in: Major League Football Hall of Fame, Citizens Savings Hall of Fame Athletic Museum.

WILLIS, William
Player
Born in Columbus, Ohio; attended East High School in Columbus, Ohio State Univ; All-American 1944; All-

AAFC and All-NFL seven times; devoted much of his life to working with troubled youngsters; presently serving as deputy director of Ohio State Youth Commission in Columbus.

Willis, 6 ft. 4 in, 205 lbs, began playing football while attending East High School. At Ohio State he played tackle for Paul Brown in 1942 and 1943 and for Carroll Widdoes in 1944, playing with the wartime team composed of freshmen, deferred students and 4-F's that went undefeated and untied. The team finished second to Army in national rankings. Willis joined the Cleveland Browns in 1946, converting to guard and remaining with the team for eight years, 1946-1953. He was the first black signed to play pro football after W. W. II, and was outstanding on line play, extremely powerful and fast. His speed was his greatest asset.
Also in: National Football Hall of Fame.

Providence Gridiron Club Hall of Fame

KINGSTON, RHODE ISLAND

Mailing Address: University of Rhode Island, 02881. Tel. (401) 792-2409. *Contact:* James Norman, Sports Information Dir. *Location:* Approx. 25 mi. S.W. of Providence, 65 mi. S.E. of Hartford, Conn, 75 mi. S.E. of Springfield, Mass. *Nearby Halls of Fame:* Tennis (Newport, R.I, 15 mi. E.), Ice Skating (Boston Mass, 70 mi. N.E.), Basketball (Springfield, Mass.).

The Providence Gridiron Club has been in existence for 30 years meeting six times each fall for dinner with a prominent guest speaker. In 1973 the Club decided to create its own Hall of Fame. Its purpose is to honor those people prominent in football and/or athletics in general who have contributed their time and effort over the years to the Club. The Hall has not established any type of physical structure and has no display or collection.

Members: 42 as of 1976. Initial inductions took place in 1974 when 32 members were selected and assigned years in order to honor a large number of people. Five new members were added to the list in each of the following years. The criteria, method and frequency of selection are decided at a once-a-year committee meeting during which members to be inducted are discussed and voted upon.

1971 CRONIN, Jack

ENGLE, Charles "Rip." See entry in College Football Hall of Fame, Citizens Savings Hall of Fame Athletic Museum. *Also in:* National Football Hall of Fame.

GILBANE, Tom

HALLORAN, Bill

HART, Jimmy

KEANEY, Frank

MARTIN, Jack

McGEE, Joe, Sr.

McLAUGHRY, De Ormond C. "Tuss." See entry in College Football Hall of Fame, Citizens Savings Hall of Fame Athletic Museum. *Also in:* National Football Hall of Fame.

MERRITT, Carl

ODEN, Curly

PEARCE, Pard

POLLARD, Frederick D. "Fritz." See entry in College Football Hall of Fame, Citizens Savings Hall of Fame Athletic Museum. *Also in:* National Football Hall of Fame.

SAVARIA, Gus

SAVASTANO, A. A. "Savy"

STEBBINS, Ed

1972 BEGLEY, Aloysius O. P.

BUONANNO, Joseph

BURKE, John

HAUGHEY, J. Patrick

PARISEAU, Anthony "Gig"

ZABILSKI, Joseph

1973 ABBRUZZI, Louis "Duke"

DELANEY, Joseph

GILBANE, William

JOHNSON, Pearce

OSMANSKI, William. *Also in:* National Football Hall of Fame.

1974 BRIDE, Thomas

LANNING, Frank

MAZNICKI, Frank

MULLANEY, Raymond

SOAR, Henry

1975 GILMARTIN, Edmund

MATHEWS, William "Dixie"

McHENRY, Joseph

MELLO, James

SHERMAN, Robert

1976 ABBRUZZI, Pasquale

GOFF, Kenneth

LAUDATI, Peter A, Sr.

MELLAKAS, John

ZABILSKI, Edward

Simpson College Football Hall of Fame

INDIANOLA, IOWA

Mailing Address: Cold Center, 50125. Tel. (515) 961-6251 ext. 617. *Contact:* Larry Johnson, Athletic Dir. *Location:* 20 mi. S. of Des Moines, 125 mi. N.E. of Omaha, Nebr. *Admission:* Free 8 to 5 daily; closed weekends. *Nearby Halls of Fame:* Rollerskating (Lincoln, Nebr, 180 mi. W.), Agriculture (Kansas City, Mo. 195 mi. S.W.), Agriculture (Bonner Springs, Kans. 210 mi. S.W.).

The Simpson College Football Hall of Fame was founded in 1969 to honor and preserve the past history of the Simpson College football players. Simpson alumni and the athletic department coaches were responsible for the inception of the college-funded Hall of Fame.

Members: 47 as of May 1977. Nominees must have been graduated from Simpson College at least ten years prior to their selection. They are not required to have attended Simpson College for a full four years prior to graduation, but must have been football players who have exhibited professional success and service to and good standing in their communities. Not more than five new members are inducted each year from a time period beginning with the founding of the Iowa Conference, about 1920.

1969 ANDERSON, Thomas M. Class of 1931.
FARNHAM, Dr. John B. Class of 1943.
HULEN, Bill L. Class of 1959.
KLISARES, Robert L. Class of 1956.
McCOY, Charles D. Class of 1928.
McCOY, Walter E.
MEEK, Joseph T. (dec). Class of 1924.
MERCER, Kenneth "Moco" (dec). Class of 1928. *Also in:* National Association of Intercollegiate Athletics Hall of Fame.
RICHARDS, Elvin C. "Kink." Class of 1932.
WEEKS, Edward L. Class of 1953.
WRIGHT, James G. Class of 1950.

1970 BERLIN, Brig. Gen. Frank W. Class of 1940.
CARLSON, John R. Class of 1935.
CLARK, Herman. Class of 1930.
FAWCETT, Harold T. Class of 1924.
HIDLEBAUGH, Dr. Everett J. Class of 1956.
KARR, Kenneth L. Class of 1925.
MATHEW, James M. Class of 1952.
MILLER, Robert L. Class of 1951.
REED, John A. Class of 1948.
WELLS, Claude G. Class of 1935.

1971 MILLS, John P. Class of 1950.
SHARPLES, Thomas. Class of 1937.
TANNATT, Kenneth R. Class of 1942.

1972 NORRIS, Dudley D. Class of 1957.
RUBLE, Olan G. Class of 1928.

1973 DYER, Rollin. Class of 1948.
HOGENDORN, Paul. Class of 1929.
LIGGETT, Max. Class of 1948.
TANNATT, Kermit. Class of 1948

1974 BINKERD, Gerald A. Class of 1934.
BURNETT, Charles M. Class of 1947.
NORRIS, R. G. "Bob." Class of 1951.

1975 BOUGHTON, Merlyn "Red." Class of 1946.
PARR, Larry. Class of 1951.
SHULTZ, John G. Class of 1924.

1976 ANDERSON, Ray
LOVE, Malcom
MOORE, Bob
SPENCER, Tony

Texas High School Football Hall of Fame

BRECKENRIDGE, TEXAS

Mailing Address: Swemson Museum of Stephens County, Old First National Bank Bldg, 76024. Tel. (817) 559-3700. *Contact:* Bill Creagh, Dir. *Location:* 70 mi. E. of Abilene, 90 mi. W. of Ft. Worth. *Admission:* Free 9 to 5 daily. *Personnel:* 13 mem. Bd. of Dir. *Nearby Halls of Fame:* Western Heritage, Softball (Oklahoma City, Okla. 240 mi. N.E.).

The first induction ceremony took place in 1968 to recognize the achievements of high school football players throughout the state of Texas. Financial support is provided through association membership fees and there are plans for a fund-raising drive in order to build a permanent hall.

Members: 30 as of 1977. Every August a committee of sportswriters from around the state meets to select five new members. Four are selected from the football eras 1920 – 1929, 1930 – 1939, 1940 – 1949 and 1950 – 1959, and a fifth is either deceased or from one of the four eras. Players are eligible ten years after playing for a Texas high school football team. Inductees are honored at a banquet held on the first Monday of December.

1968 BALDWIN, Leo. Scored every touchdown made by Wichita Falls in 1923.

JOHNSON, John Drew "Boody" (dec). A standout on the 1922 Waco High School state championship team; scored 231 points, gained 1907 yds, 300 of those in a single game.

MAGNESS, Boyce "Boone" (dec). Known by many as the greatest of the Buckaroos. Led Breckenridge to the 1929 state co-championship.

MILLS, Buster. Mr. Great at Ranger High School in 1926. Considered the greatest punter in Texas Interscholastic League.

SMITH, Clarence "Blue." Led Cleburne High to ten straight victories and the state championship game in 1921.

1969 DANIEL, Chal (dec). Spearheaded Longview's state championship team in 1937 and was called the finest lineman in schoolboy history.

GREGORY, Glynn. Great runner, blocker, kicker and defensive star for Abilene in the mid-1950s. A star player for Southern Methodist University, later played for the Dallas Cowboys.

IRVIN, Cecil P. "Honk." Fabulous tackle and fullback at Cisco in the 1920s. Played professional football with the New York Giants of the National Football League.

ROTE, Kyle W. A great star with San Antonio Jefferson, almost leading his team to a state championship in 1946. Starred as a college player at Southern Methodist University from 1948 to 1950 and played professional ball with the New York Giants. See entry in Major League Football Hall of Fame, Citizens Savings Hall of Fame Athletic Museum. *Also in:* National Football Hall of Fame.

WILSON, Robert E. Corsicana's mighty halfback of 1929–1931. Played at Southern Methodist University making All–Southwest Conference and All-American in his last year, and sparking his team to the Rose Bowl in 1935. *Also in:* National Football Hall of Fame.

1970 COULTER, DeWitt. The biggest man to play for Masonic Home of Ft. Worth. All-American at West Point in 1945 and played professional football with the New York Giants.

HARRISON, Bob. Stamford's stand-out center 1952–1954, making All-State in his final season. All-American for Oklahoma in 1958 and played professional football for San Francisco and Pittsburgh as a 220-lb. linebacker.

LUMPKIN, Roy "Father." A star at Oak Cliff 1923–1925 in the early days of Texas high school football. Still regarded as one of the best all-time players.

MARSHALL, Bert. Played at Greenville 1933–1935. Quarterbacked the team as a sophomore to the state championship when he weighed only 125 lbs. and was only 14 years old. All-American at Vanderbilt.

MAULDIN, Stan (dec.). Outstanding player at Amarillo High School in 1938. All–Southwest Conference tackle in 1942. Played professional football with the Chicago Cardinals.

1971 HILLIARD, Bohn. Captained the Orange High School team in 1926 and was named All-State in 1927. Earned All-American recognition at the University of Texas from 1932 to 1934.

MILSTEAD, Karl Don. Most sought-after lineman in Texas high school history when he graduated from Athens High in 1957. Starred for the University of Oklahoma.

TODD, Dick. Scored 664 points in four years at Crowell High School. All-Conference and All-American honors at Texas A&M, and then professional football with the Washington Redskins for ten years.

TUBBS, Jerry. Earned All-State and All-American honors as a senior at Breckenridge High School. Became a unanimous All-American during his senior year at University of Oklahoma. Went on to star in professional ball and is now a Dallas Cowboy coach.

WILLIAMS, James "Froggy." Standout on the 1943–1945 Waco High School teams and was All-District end for three years. Made All-State twice. Lettered for four years at Rice and was All-American in 1949. *Also in:* National Football Hall of Fame.

1972 APPLETON, Scott. Two-time All-State tackle for Brady High School 1958–1959. Three times won All-District honors. At the University of Texas made All-Conference twice and All-American. Played professional football for Houston and San Diego.

BUFKIN, Burl. Ranked as one of the greatest of Amarillo High School football players and named on Harold Ratliff's All-Time Texas High School team. As a senior scored 163 points on offense and was rated the best linebacker in the state in 1930.

HAAS, Charlie. A great punter, an outstanding defensive halfback, and a sensational runner and passer. Led the Corpus Christi High School team to the finals in 1934. Twice named to All-State teams and went on to star in football and baseball at the University of Texas.

JACKSON, Leete. Played at Lubbock High School and made All-District four times and All-State twice. His team went to the state finals in 1938 and won the state crown in 1939. Starred at Texas Tech, playing on two championship teams that went to the Sun Bowl.

SMITH, Herb (dec.). Outstanding performer at San Angelo High School in the mid-1930s when he started every game and was named to the All-State team two years. Went on to star for Texas A&M and earned All-Southwest Conference and All-American honors in 1939.

1973 FOUTS, Jerry. Named 1949's most outstanding Texas high school football player. As All-State end caught a touchdown pass and kicked two extra points to lead Wichita Falls to a 14 – 13 win in the State finals.

LAYNE, Robert. Broke records in high school, college and professional football. From Highland Park High School, played for the University of Texas. Fifteen years of professional football for Chicago, New York, Detroit and Pittsburgh. See entry in Professional Football Hall of Fame, 1967. *Also in:* Major League Football Hall of Fame, Citizens Savings Hall of Fame Athletic Museum; and National Football Hall of Fame.

STAMPS, Billy. Played for Corsicana High School where chosen outstanding schoolboy lineman in the Southwest and selected by state sportswriters as the greatest guard in Texas Interscholastic League history. Went on to play on the Southern Methodist University team that went to the Rose Bowl in 1936.

WALKER, Ewell Doak, Jr. "Doaker." From Dallas Highland Park High School; generally acknowledged to be the greatest all-around football player in Texas history. Three-year All-American at Southern Methodist University where he is given credit as "The man who built the Cotton Bowl." After college played with the Detroit Lions. See entry in College Football Hall of Fame, Citizens Savings Hall of Fame Athletic Museum. *Also in:* Major League Football Hall of Fame, Citizens Savings Hall of Fame Athletic Museum; and National Football Hall of Fame.

WELCH, W. R. "Pest." Won just about every honor a high school player could get and earned a scholarship to Purdue where he made All-American in 1929. Later head coach at Washington University, taking them to the Rose Bowl in 1944.

Football Halls of Fame to Watch

AMERICAN FOOTBALL COACHES ASSOCIATION HALL OF FAME

Merger 1976

The American Football Coaches Association, founded in 1921, maintained its own Hall until 1976, when its archives and memorabilia were incorporated into the National Football Foundation and Hall of Fame.

ARIZONA FOOTBALL HALL OF FAME

Proposed 1969

Proposed for establishment under the leadership of Judson High School, Paradise Valley, Arizona, this Hall has yet to be realized.

ARIZONA FOOTBALL HALL OF FAME

Merger 1970

Established on August 27, 1970, as a Chapter of the National Football Foundation and Hall of Fame, not presently active as a separate entity.

DALLAS COWBOY HALL OF FAME

Name change 1976

Originally a Hall of Fame in 1975, now officially The Ring of Honor, consisting of the names of three members, which have been placed in a position of prominence at the Texas Stadium in Dallas.

ORANGE BOWL HALL OF FAME

Name change 1976

Originated during the 1970 – 1971 football season with the announcement of four inductees as the Orange Bowl Committee honored the charter members at the kickoff luncheon of the Orange Bowl Festival in Miami on December 29, 1970, it then became inactive. The Hall was revived in 1976 as the Orange Bowl Football Classic Hall of Honor, the area at the Orange Bowl Stadium was refurbished, and three new members were added to the roster. Regular inductions are planned as a primary event during the annual Orange Bowl festivities. For more information contact Dan McNamara, Exec. Dir, or Gil Sloan, Publicity Dir. of the Orange Bowl Committee, P.O. Box 748, Miami, FL 33135. (305) 642-1515.

ROSEBOWL HALL OF FAME

Discontinued in 1960s

Formerly housed at the Rose Bowl Stadium but no longer in existence, the Rose Bowl Hall of Fame was founded in 1945, financed by Paul Helms, who now finances the ongoing Citizens Savings Hall of Fame Athletic Museum. In the 1960s the Hall of Fame was dismantled and photographs and memorabilia were moved to the Rose Bowl Room at the Wrigley Mansion in Pasadena. Located at 391 S. Orange Grove Blvd, 91105, this exhibit is open to the public free of charge every Wednesday afternoon. Call (213) 449-4100 for more information. A display of the Players of the Rose Bowl Game, one selected each year since 1902, can be seen at the Citizens Savings Hall of Fame Athletic Museum, 9800 S. Sepulveda Blvd, Los Angeles, 90045, free of charge from Monday through Thursday 9 to 5, Friday 9 to 6, and Saturday 9 to 3. For more information call (213) 670-7550.

UNIVERSITY OF TENNESSEE FOOTBALL HALL OF FAME ROOM

Not technically a Hall of Fame

This room at the University of Tennessee's Stokely Athletic Center performs the function of honoring outstanding University of Tennessee football players and coaches who have been inducted into the National Football Hall of Fame of the National Football Foundation, of which Eastern Tennessee was the largest chapter in 1976. The room has biographical material for each player and coach recorded on tapes for the interest of visitors, as well as a video-tape for viewing outstanding moments of sports at the University of Tennessee. The room is open to visitors daily from 8 to 5 (closed Sundays). For more information contact the Athletic Department, Knoxville, TN 37916. (615) 974-3373.

GOLF

It was at first a "forbidden, disgraceful recreation," and therefore a highly popular one. King James "Fiery Face" II in 1457, James III in 1471, and James IV around 1491 all officially ordered that ". . .Golfe be utterly cryed downe and not be used." People who played it during divine services were fined 40 shillings. Clergymen who played it when they ought to have been preaching were deposed from their offices. In 1657 the sheriff of Fort Orange (later Albany, New York) filed a complaint against three men to the effect that they, as players of *het kolven,* a similar Dutch game, were endangering the good citizens with their practices, as well as playing it on the ice on Sundays. James Reston called golf "a plague invented by the Calvinistic Scots as a punishment for man's sins," and Max Beerbohm defined it as "The most . . . perfect expression of national stupidity." In the late 1880s a Doctor Lockhart was arrested in New York's Central Park for hitting golf balls in a sheep pasture. In 1895 socialite Mrs. Charles B. Brown was startled to learn that she had won a game and was thus the first United States national women's champion. She preferred to treat the whole affair as a lucky joke. Even Mark Twain was not truly appreciative of golf when he described it as "A good walk spoiled." Yet in the single decade from 1890 to 1900 fully 1000 golf courses came into existence in the United States. The total today is closer to 12,000, on which some 12 million Americans hit the little white balls for which they spend some $50 million per year.

In a very real sense, the history of golf is in the balls that have been used. Romans disliked participant sports but nevertheless had three types of balls: the *paganica* (from the word *paganus,* countryman) which was 4 to 7 in. in diameter and stuffed with feathers, the *pila trigonalis* and the *harpastum.* The latter two were smaller and filled with hair. All three types were either tossed or batted around with bent sticks. Though the Romans played them primarily to work up sweats, perhaps these games were the ancestors of golf. And perhaps Hadrian's Wall and the Antonine Wall did not prevent these Roman games from slipping north to Scotland. The walls were built across northern England between A.D. 120 and 140 and were a total of 110 mi. long. At any rate, Scottish and English golfers who may have started out on their own using balls of boxwood soon were using what they called "featheries." For each feathery a tophat-full of steamed or boiled goose feathers was stuffed into a small softball-like leather bag sewn together with waxed thread. These balls, hardened and painted, worked very well but wore out quickly. Early wooden clubs, though made by the best bowyers into long and graceful tools, were still sledgehammer-sized mallets, and the iron ones were forged by blacksmiths. Hit by either of these when wet, a feathery usually would explode.

In 1843 the Reverend Doctor Robert Adams Paterson received a black marble statue of Vishnu from his son in India. It was crated for shipping in a resinous rubber stuff called *gutta-percha.* With it he made the world's first gutty, a more durable and better performing ball that made the feathery obsolete by 1845. Not a golfer himself, the Reverend later emigrated to America where he founded the American Bible College at Binghamton, New York, the first school of its kind for the training of women missionaries.

The gutty was hand-hammered and later machine-marked to give it a longer, more accurate flight, then aged or cured. In other words, a golfer not only had to pick choice clubs, but also had to select balls that were ripe. The gutty, along with better clubs of harder hickory from Russia and Tennessee and a new device called a golf bag, ruled golfdom until this century.

Then in 1902, the year *The Hound of the Baskervilles* was published, a Cleveland dentist named Coburn Haskell and a friend of his who worked for B. F. Goodrich in Akron invented the modern ball. They did this by discovering a process by which rubber from the Amazon River Basin could be drawn out into a fine thread, which then could be wound around a rubber core filled with liquid. The whole, encased in a cover made of *balata,* a substance similar to *gutta-percha,* was the direct ancestor of all golf balls in use today. Other innovations quickly followed its appearance on the market. A dental surgeon named William Lowell invented the first marketable all-wood tee to replace for all time the traditional mound—early courses had a box or bucket of sand on every tee-off area from which the golfer pinched enough to make a little mound to set his ball upon. Increasingly, balls and equipment became more highly advanced as they were tooled with greater and greater precision. Diehards remained. Golf, said Woodrow Wilson, is "a game in which one endeavors to control a ball with implements ill adapted for the purpose."

Perhaps uniquely, golf was always a game of the people, one in which nobles and commoners, kings and cobblers could tee off together. Even today it is by far the most participant oriented of all sports. Once the royal bans on it had been lifted, most monarchs became avid players—one of the charges against Mary, Queen of Scots was that she had been seen playing golf within days of the murder of Darnley, her husband. She was also famous for having first used the French word *cadet,* from which we get "caddie." When Charles I learned of the Irish Rebellion, he was playing golf near Edinburgh with friends. During his later confinement before his beheading in 1649, he played it by himself. In its imperial expansion, England took golf all over the world. In 1829, the year London's police were first called bobbies and just eight years after the death of Napoleon, Englishmen were playing golf in India at the Royal Calcutta Golf Course. Soon there were as many courses in India as there were in England.

Even earlier, golf had arrived in Canada, carried there either by ships' officers on shore leave or by fur traders employed by the Hudson's Bay Company. In 1854 a Glasgow sailor "carried his clubs to the heights of Abraham and there entertained himself in solitary contentment." The first golf club on the continent, the Royal Montreal Golf Club, was formed in 1873. Though much ceremony attended the matches in those days—players were required to wear red coats, white flannel trousers and sometimes white gloves—golf had remained what it always had been, the "Royal and Ancient Sport" of the people.

In the United States golf was played in New York, Georgia, South Carolina, West Virginia and Virginia as early as 1779. The first club was founded by Joseph Mickle Fox of Philadelphia in 1887, the year contact lenses were first made.

The following year the far more influential St. Andrews Golf Club of Yonkers was founded by John "Jock" Reid, the "Father of American Golf." Its first course consisted of three holes in a cow pasture that was Reid's back yard in Yonkers. Later Reid and members of that club played six holes in Henry Tallmadge's larger pasture. Still later in 1892, they moved to an apple orchard on Palisades Avenue. There they became known as the Apple Tree Gang—perhaps for recommending that apple trees be made a regulation part of every golf course. After a fourth move to a nine-hole course, they moved to their present home, the eighteen-hole course at Mt. Hope, New York. Now the oldest permanent American golf club, St. Andrews of Yonkers helped bring about a virtual explosion in golf popularity.

It was a 20-year-old Boston caddie, however, whose amazing success began the trend that would turn the sport into what it is today. Francis D. Ouimet (1893 – 1967) beat two of Britain's greatest players, Harry Vardon and Edward Rey, in the 1913 U.S. Open. The man who held the flag markers for that match was Bernard Darwin, a grandson of Charles Darwin. Within a few years of Ouimet's victory the United States was the leading golf nation in the world. Symbolically and true to the spirit of the sport, a complete unknown, a commoner outside the country club set, had made golf a major American sport.

FORMS: Games similar and perhaps historically related to golf included *paganica* (Rome), *cambuca* (England), *chole* (Belgium), *kolfspel* or *kolven* (Holland), *jeu de mal* (France), shinty or hurly (Ireland) and the North England game of knur and spell, also called "poor man's golf," in which the object is to strike the knur (ball) as far as possible. The word "golf" probably comes from the Dutch word *kolf,* which is related to the German word *kolbe* and the Danish word *holbe* for club. The word tee comes from the Dutch word *tuitje,* pronounced "toytee", for the mound of sand from which the Dutch golfer hit his ball. The word putt is from *put,* the hole the Dutchman directed his ball toward. Today golf is decidedly one game, in fact, one of the more carefully and completely defined sports. In practical terms it may be defined as hitting a small white ball with a specialized stick, the object being to force the ball into a series of sunken cups with a series of shots in as few strokes as possible.

In the United States and Canada the ball must have a minimum diameter of 1.68 in. English and international team competition prescribe a smaller ball. The maximum weight is 1.62 oz. It is composed of a liquid-filled rubber core around which elastic thread is wound tightly, all of which is encased in a dimpled plastic cover. The dimples, which improve accuracy and distance of flight, are .013 in. deep.

The clubs used to strike the ball at speeds of up to 250 m.p.h. are of three types: woods for long drives, irons for shorter shots, and putters for shots of zero trajectory along the ground. Clubs are numbered in order of increasing loft—the more steeply angled the face of the club (from 13 to 47°) the more sharply lifting the flight and the higher the number. A player or team may carry a maximum of 14 clubs. Prior to 1938 professionals would carry up to 30 clubs as paid endorsements for various manufacturers.

A standard course will contain up to 7000 yds. laid out over about 150 acres and will consist of 18 holes, each from 100 to 600 yds. long. Each hole consists of a tee-off area where play for that hole begins, a fairway of mowed grass along which the player aims, the rough which flanks each side of the fairway, hazards such as bunkers (sand traps) and areas of water, and a putting green in which the hole, 4 in. deep by 4¼ in. in diameter, is located. There are generally three types of courses: traditional with elevated tees, greens or fairways, and bunkers; sculptured where earth-moving equipment is used to manipulate the landscape; and naturalistic where the natural contours and features of the land are changed as little as possible. In most games (tennis, football, and basketball to name a few) the playing area is exactly uniform everywhere. In golf, however, each course's characteristics and dimensions differ as widely from every other's as possible—a golf course may be laid out virtually anywhere. A golf links, strictly speaking, refers only to a golf course laid out next to a stretch of seashore or a large body of water.

Par is the theoretical number of strokes needed to complete a hole perfectly. It is usually from three to six, though in 1912 a Pennsylvania woman took 166 strokes on a single hole. After teeing off, hitting the ball from a small wooden or plastic rest called a tee, the player cries "Fore!" This comes from the early British expression, "Look out before!" A ball holed in one stroke less than par is called a birdie, in two under par an eagle, in one more than par a bogey. This last term, first used in 1891, came from a line in an American song, "Hush, hush, hush, here comes the Bogey man!" The odds of hitting a hole-in-one are 30,000 to one. Compare this with the ten times greater odds for a perfect 300 score in bowling of 300,000 to one.

Golf is usually played between two to four people. There are different systems of handicapping and course-rating. Some of these are: best-ball, foursomes or Scotch foursomes, four ball, Bogey competition, Greesome, Stableford, Eclectic, and Bisque. In either professional or amateur competition a golf game will be either matchplay or strokeplay. In matchplay the side winning the majority of 18 or 36 holes wins the match, and in strokeplay, sometimes incorrectly called medal play, the player who finishes 72 holes with the fewest number of strokes wins. Strokeplay predominates in the United States.

Accessories include a golf bag and sometimes a golf cart. A player is allowed one caddie whose duties historically included finding balls, shooing away rabbits, carrying the clubs in the crook of one arm, warning strolling or picnicking people to stay out of the way and requesting cavalry regiments to drill elsewhere.

ORGANIZATION: In 1975 more than 15 million Americans and Canadians played golf on some 15,000 courses. Many players belong to clubs, many of which are affiliated with larger organizations. The more significant of these are the United States Golf Association (USGA) established in 1894 for amateurs, the Professional Golfers' Association of America (1916), the Ladies Professional Golf Association (1946), the World Amateur Golf Council, the Canadian Professional Golf Association and the Canadian Ladies Golf Union. The Royal and Ancient Golf Club of St. Andrews, Scotland, has ultimate *de jure* authority over all of these as well as over all the other national golfing organizations in virtually every country in the world. The world's oldest club in continuous existence, it became golf's ultimate authority in 1919 and today is the Mecca of golfdom. Its 13 original rules have evolved over the years into 41 main laws, numerous subclauses, a written book of etiquette, 35 definitions, and a vast body of case-law. Representatives of the Royal and Ancient Golf Club meet every four years with members of the USGA to agree upon revisions to existing rules or laws. The primary differences between the regulations of these two organizations are the size of the ball and the specifications governing the classification of an amateur. Unlike many sports, golf is essentially the same game no matter where it is played.

American Golf Hall of Fame

FOXBURG, PENNSYLVANIA

Mailing Address: P.O. Box 100, 16036. *Tel.* (412) 287-5459. *Contact:* Kenneth A. Christy, Exec. Secy. *Location:* 4 mi. off I-80 at Exits 5 or 6; 55 mi. N.E. of Pittsburgh, 80 mi. S.E. of Erie, 130 mi. S. of Buffalo, N.Y. *Admission:* Free 10 to 6 daily and weekends April–November. *Personnel:* John W. Brand, Pres; Robert S. Swanson, Jr, V.Pres; Edward C. Kruck, Jr, V.Pres. Promotion; Kenneth A. Christy, Exec. Secy; James D. Berry III, Treas. and Chmn. Bd. of Dirs; 20-40 mem. Bd. of Dirs: Lowell Thomas, Chmn. Selection Comt. *Nearby Halls of Fame:* Heritage (Valley Forge, 225 mi. S.E.), Football (Canton, Ohio, 95 mi. S.W.), Horseshoe Pitchers (Corning, N.Y, 145 mi. N.E.), Flight (Elmira, N.Y, 160 mi. N.E.), Track & Field (Charleston, W.Va, 200 mi. S.).

Golf has been a part of Foxburg, home of the American Golf Hall of Fame, as long as the game has been played in the United States. Following golf's introduction to this country by Joseph Mickle Fox who had learned the fundamentals of the game from Tom Morris, Sr, in Scotland, land was provided by the Fox family for the newly formed Foxburg Country Club. Golf has been played here at the oldest golf club in the United States every year since 1887. The American Golf Hall of Fame and Museum are housed in the log clubhouse at this historical site. With a charter procured on June 28, 1954, the Hall of Fame actively promotes the advancement of golf, selects and inducts golfing greats and outstanding contributors, and equips and maintains a museum and library to reflect the history of the game of golf. The museum, located on the second floor of the three-story clubhouse, was officially dedicated on May 15, 1965, by Laurie Auchterlonie, Honorary Professional to the Royal and Ancient Golf Club of St. Andrews, Scotland. Displayed in 20 large glass-enclosed cases is one of the most complete collections of golfing artifacts. Many of the artifacts were obtained by Kenneth A. Christy, past president of the American Golf Hall of Fame Association, on five trips to Scotland. Feather balls used from 1400 to 1850, *gutta percha* golf balls dating from 1850 to 1902 and two 1898 American Haskel golf balls are part of the collection. The museum also displays antique clubs from 1695, outlawed clubs, water, sand and grass clubs, dead-stop clubs and even the entire collection of trick clubs used by Joe Kirkwood, which were willed to the museum in 1970. Adjacent to the Foxburg Country Club, a new and larger American Golf Hall of Fame Museum is under construction and will be completed and open to the public in late 1977. This year the Hall of Fame will sponsor the 13th Annual Pro-Am Golf Tournament at the Foxburg Country Club. Golfers from throughout the country will pay a $200 entry fee for a chance at $1000 prizes and the thrill of playing on the historic nine-hole course.

Members: 49 as of 1977. The first Hall of Fame awards were made on August 20, 1965, by Lowell Thomas, well-known radio announcer, Robert Trent Jones, distinguished golf-course architect, and Joe Kirkwood, golf's trick-shot artist. Since then, three or four members, at least 40 years old and winners of at least two major tournaments, have been inducted each year. New members are still elected by the original selection committee of 1965: Lowell Thomas; Robert Trent Jones; Laurie Auchterlonie; former *Golfdom Magazine* editor Herb Graffis; past president of the Professional Golfers' Association of America (PGA), George Ferrier; secretary-treasurer of the United States Golf Association, Fred Brand, Jr; and member of the Royal and Ancient Golf Club, John P. Sawyer. Ten nominations, made by members of the American Golf Hall of Fame Association, are mailed to each member of the selection committee. The members of the committee rank the nominees from one to ten; the top three or four are elected. Induction ceremonies are held at the Allegheny Club, Three Rivers Stadium in Pittsburgh, at the convenience of the inductees, in order that they all be present. Bobby Locke of South Africa has traveled the longest distance to receive his Hall of Fame scroll. Either he or Lowell Thomas speaks at the special induction ceremony and banquet.

1965

ARMOUR, Thomas Dickson
Golfer

Born September 24, 1896, in Edinburgh, Scotland; while serving with Black Watch regiment in W.W. I, received a head wound that resulted in six months of blindness; after recovering, with use of one eye, immigrated to the United States; loss of eye said to have affected putting; died September 11, 1968, in the United States.

As an amateur in Britain, the "Silver Scot" played against the United States, but as a professional in the United States beginning in 1924, he played against Britain. He won many tournaments during his golfing career: French Open 1920; Walker Cup (British) 1922; Ryder Cup (U.S.) 1926; Canadian Open 1927, 1930 and 1934; U.S. Open and National Open 1927; U.S. PGA Championship 1930; British Open 1931. He was an excellent driver and is credited with the longest measured drive, 430 yds, aided by a strong following wind. His putting required much concentration, calculation and "a great many sidelong glances at the hole and as many waggles with his club." Armour had very strong hands, a graceful style and a personality that stories were told about. He had a very high regard for the rules of golf: once when he saw a player tee-up a ball in the rough, he ground the ball into the dirt and told the man to "play it from there." Armour is well known in golf for his abilities as a teacher and author; after his retirement from tournament play, he taught at Boca Raton, Fla, and Winged Foot Club, N.Y, and is the author of *How to Play Your Best Golf All the Time* and *A Round of Golf with Tommy Armour.*

Also in: Golf Hall of Fame, Citizens Savings Hall of Fame Athletic Museum; Professional Golfers' Association of America Hall of Fame and World Golf Hall of Fame.

BRAID, James
Golfer

Born 1870 in Earlsferry, Fife, England; left school at 13 to become an apprentice joiner while playing amateur golf; father was an Elie ploughman who did not understand son's golf; known as an "immensely painstaking man of few words, a warm and true friend"; died 1950 in London, England, at age 80.

James is probably best remembered as one of the Triumvirate, along with Harry Vardon and John Taylor, all from England. After he turned professional in 1893, he went to England as an apprentice club maker and played golf Sundays and evenings. He developed quite a swing, hitting with "a divine fury," as Horace Hutchinson claimed. As a professional, he won the British Open 1901, 1905, 1906, 1908 and 1910; the British Professional Matchplay (the first winner of the matchplay) in 1903, 1905, 1907 and 1911; and the French Open 1910. Braid was the first man to win the British Open five times. He served as the golf "pro" at Walton Health Golf Club in England 1904–1950. He was one of the first professionals to be named an honorary member of the Royal and Ancient Golf Club of St. Andrews, Scotland. Braid became known as a fine golf-course architect and did much to raise the standards of golf professionals. Being too young to fight in W.W. I, Braid, with Vardon and Taylor, offered his services to war charities.
Also in: World Golf Hall of Fame.

COTTON, Thomas Henry
Golfer

Born January 26, 1907, in London, England; attended Alleyn's School in Dulwich; first professional job in golf at Langley Park in Kent, then at Royal Waterloo Club in Belgium and in Ashridge, Hertfordshire, England; at one time operated a golf school in Monte Carlo; military service during W.W. II raising funds for Red Cross and for a time with Royal Air Force; awarded the Order of the British Empire; numerous visits to Cannes in South France; eventually settled in Algarve district of Portugal, where he designed a golf course from an old rice field; designed other courses in several European countries; Vardon Trophy winner 1938.

Henry Cotton had a great influence on the game of golf not only as a player, but as a teacher, writer of several books and inventor. His relaxed manner around people and fastidious way of living brought a new style and dignity to golf. Through intense, hard practice as a young man, which often left his hands sore and blistered, he developed a smooth, powerful swing. This led him to a most impressive victory at the 1934 British Open when he broke the record of ten straight American wins. He was victorious again in 1937 and 1948 and won the British Professional Golfers' Association tournament three times as well. Also impressive are the many Open championships he won throughout Europe: the Belgian 1930, 1934 and 1938, Italian 1936, Czechoslovak 1937–1939 and the French Open 1946 and 1947. Cotton was a team member for the Ryder Cup 1929 and 1937, captain 1947 and nonplaying captain 1953. And in 1932,

1940 and 1946 he participated in British Professional Matchplay. This long record of distinguished achievement was recognized when he was one of the first three professional golfers, with Walter Hagen and Bobby Locke, to be made an honorary member of the Royal and Ancient Golf Club.

EVANS, Charles, Jr. "Chick"
Golfer

Born 1890 in Indianapolis, Ind; from childhood, mother encouraged him to remain an amateur.

Evans' more than 50 years of golf championships began at the age of 17 when he won his first of six Chicago City Amateur championships. He played in 50 consecutive U.S. Amateur championships, seven of them before he won in 1916. Chick also won in 1920, and was runnerup in 1912, 1922 and 1927. He played an excellent game of golf and, despite his insecure putting, won many other championships—Western Amateur 1909, 1912, 1914–1915 and 1920–1923; Western Open 1910, French Amateur Open and North and South Amateur 1911, U.S. Open 1916—and competed on five Walker Cup teams. Until Bobby Jones, Evans was the only man to have won both the U.S. Amateur and Open in the same year (1916). Before he retired, he established the Evans Scholarship Foundation at Northwestern University, administered by the Western Golf Association, to give caddies "a chance in life they would not otherwise have had."
Also in: Golf Hall of Fame, Citizens Savings Hall of Fame Athletic Museum; Professional Golfers' Association of America Hall of Fame and World Golf Hall of Fame.

HAGEN, Walter Charles
Golfer

Born December 21, 1892, in Rochester, N.Y; died October 6, 1969, at age 77.

Hagen was the first full-time tournament professional, beginning in 1919. With his flamboyant personality and excellent golfing record, "The Haig" made the professionals aware of what was possible in the world of golf. He had the perfect temperament for golf: he could break his concentration to chat with spectators and project his personality so easily during matches that he put opponents at a disadvantage. Through his influence, he improved the standing of professional golfers; when he won the British Open in 1928, he did not attend the presentation in the clubhouse to protest the fact that none of the professionals were allowed near there during the tournament. With a supreme putting ability (and not so supreme ability in wooden-club play), Hagen won many tournaments: U.S. Open 1914, 1919; Western Open 1916, 1921, 1926, 1927, and 1932; French Open 1920; British Open 1922, 1924, 1928 and 1929; North and South Open 1923 and 1924; Belgian Open 1924; and Canadian Open 1931. He was the first American to hold both the French and British titles the same year (1922). Hagen won five U.S. PGA Championships, four in a row (1924–1927). He was U.S. Ryder Cup team captain 1927–1937. The height of Hagen's career was in the 1920s but he continued to compete in the 1930s.
Also in: Golf Hall of Fame, Citizens Savings Hall of Fame Athletic Museum; Professional Golfers' Association of America Hall of Fame and World Golf Hall of Fame.

HOGAN, William Benjamin
Golfer

Born August 13, 1912, in Dublin, Tex; turned professional at 19; married in his early 20s; had a serious automobile accident in 1949; out of golf until 1950; Vardon Trophy 1940, 1941, 1948; PGA Player of the Year 1948, 1950, 1951 and 1953; following participation in tournament play retired to his home in Fort Worth, Tex.

Ben Hogan is known as the finest stroke player golf has ever known and has a consistently good golf record to prove it: he is one of four players (others are Gene Sarazen, Gary Player and Jack Nicklaus) to have won all four major world titles, winning the U.S. and British Opens in the same summer, 1953—and that was after recovering from his near-fatal automobile accident. In 14 consecutive U.S. Opens 1947–1960 and 14 consecutive U.S. Masters tournaments 1943–1956 he was always in the top 10, and 18 times in the top 4. With Willie Anderson and Bobby Jones, "Bantam Ben" won the U.S. Open a record number of four times, 1948, 1950, 1951 and 1953. He won the U.S. Masters twice, 1951 and 1953, as well as the U.S. PGA Championship 1946 and 1948, and was a member of four Ryder Cup teams 1941, captain in 1947–1948 and 1951. During his golf career he won 63 tournaments on the American professional tour.
Also in: Golf Hall of Fame, Citizens Savings Hall of Fame Athletic Museum; Professional Golfers' Association of America Hall of Fame and World Golf Hall of Fame.

JONES, Robert Tyre, Jr.
Golfer

Born March 17, 1902, in Atlanta, Ga; obtained degrees in engineering, literature and law, graduating from Atlanta School of Technology and Harvard Univ; fought in W.W. II and rose to rank of Lt. Col; died December 17, 1971.

Bobby Jones, variously known as "Emperor Jones," "Grand Slammer" and "The Boy Wonder," began his well-known amateur career at an early age; he was 9 years old when he won his first championship at Atlanta Athletic Club, 14 when he won his first Georgia State Amateur championship and 15 when he won the Southern Amateur championship. Following the style of professional Scots he watched at East Lake Club, he went on to win the U.S. Open 1923, 1926, 1929 and 1930, U.S. Men's Amateur 1924, 1925, 1927, 1928 and 1930, British Open 1926, 1927 and 1930, British Men's Amateur 1930, and was a member of six Walker Cup teams 1922–1924, 1926, 1928 and 1930—captain. In a span of eight years as an amateur, 1923–1930, he was the winner of 13 major championships, and was the first man to finish the Grand Slam by winning all four of the world's major titles 1930. Following his retirement at the young age of 28, he continued to play in public for a "good cause," made instructional films, wrote articles and, most importantly, with Cliff Roberts established and popularized the Masters Tournament in Augusta, Ga. In 1950 Jones developed a muscular disease that eventually crippled him, but he continued his involvement in the Masters Tournament even after he was unable to watch it. In 1958 he inaugurated the first World Amateur Team

Championship for the Eisenhower Trophy and received the "freedom of the Burgh of St. Andrews." Following his death, a service was held in St. Andrews to commemorate his life. Some say that Jones was the greatest golfer ever.
Also in: Golf Hall of Fame, Citizens Savings Hall of Fame Athletic Museum; Professional Golfers' Association of America Hall of Fame, World Golf Hall of Fame and National Association of Left-Handed Golfers' Hall of Fame.

NELSON, John Byron, Jr.

Golfer

Born February 4, 1912, in Fort Worth, Tex; barred from W.W. II because he was a bleeder; worked as a caddie and turned professional in 1933; Bob Jones Award for Outstanding Contribution to the game 1974.

The height of Nelson's golfing career occurred during World War II. His long periods of low scoring in 1944 and 1945 have never been equalled and, if all major championships except the U.S. PGA had not ended during the war, he would have won more than five championships. Over 6 ft. tall, with large hands, the "Gold Dust Twin" was an excellent player of long irons and pin-point driving; he was not an outstanding putter but had a smooth swing and a deep understanding of the game. His record of championships (he was prize money winner in 113 consecutive tournaments) includes the U.S. Open 1939, U.S. Masters 1937 and 1942, U.S. PGA 1940 and 1945, Canadian Open 1945 and French Open 1955. Nelson holds the record of tournament wins in one season, 19 out of 31 in 1942.
Also in: Golf Hall of Fame, Citizens Savings Hall of Fame Athletic Museum; Professional Golfers' Association of America Hall of Fame and World Golf Hall of Fame.

OUIMET, Francis D.

Golfer

Born May 8, 1893, in Brookline, Mass; died October 2, 1967, in Newton, Mass, at age 74.

As a 20-year-old amateur, Ouimet surprised the world of golf by winning the 1913 U.S. Open, ahead of Harry Vardon and Ted Ray, and gave American golf an impetus it had never known. He began his amateur career as a caddie in Boston and went on to win the U.S. Amateur 1914, 1920 and 1931, Western Open 1917, North and South Amateur 1920 and played on many Walker Cup teams 1922, 1923–1924, 1926, 1928, 1930, 1932, 1934 and was nonplaying captain 1936, 1938, 1947 and 1949. His golf style was the interlocking grip and upright swing from a narrow stance; his personal style was friendly and modest.
Also in: Golf Hall of Fame, Citizens Savings Hall of Fame Athletic Museum; Professional Golfers' Association of America Hall of Fame and World Golf Hall of Fame.

SARAZEN, Gene

Golfer

Born February 27, 1902, in Harrison, N.Y; original name Eugene Saraceni; father studied to be a priest in Italy but money ran out and turned to carpentry; mother outstanding Italian cook; one older sister; did odd jobs—sold *Saturday Evening Post,* collected metal, picked fruit, lighted gas lamps; started to caddie at eight; played golf during recess at school; quit school at 15 to work for father until pneumonia forced him to take it easy; built barracks during part of war which strengthened wrists; married Mary Henry June 10, 1924; two children, Gene Jr, and Mary Ann; honorary member of Royal and Ancient Golf Club.

With a natural talent for swinging a club and Walter Hagen as his hero and rival, Sarazen has had the longest career in the history of golf (over 50 years from Vardon to Jacklin), which included the famous double-eagle in his 1935 U.S. Masters win and a hole-in-one in the 1973 British Open at the age of 71. He was also the first of four (others are Hogan, Nicklaus and Player) to win the four major world tournaments, one of three to win the British and U.S. Opens in the same year (1932), and one of two (also Hogan) to win the U.S. Open and U.S. PGA in the same year (1922). He was the youngest to win the U.S. Open—20 years old in 1922—and the first winner of the four Grand Slam tournaments. Sarazen's other wins include the U.S. PGA 1923 and 1933, U.S. Masters 1935 and even the PGA Seniors 1954 and 1958 when he was 56 years old. After 1923 his game slowed down, but after practicing and improving on his simple, sturdy, straightforward swing, he came back into prominence. Following his active career in golf, Sarazen became an adviser in the design of golf courses and worked on the film series *Wonderful World of Golf;* with Herbert Warren Wind, he wrote the best-seller *Thirty Years of Championship Golf* as well as *Better Golf After 50* and *The Golf Clinic.*
Also in: Golf Hall of Fame, Citizens Savings Hall of Fame Athletic Museum; Connecticut Golf Hall of Fame, Professional Golfers' Association of America Hall of Fame and World Golf Hall of Fame.

SNEAD, Samuel Jackson

Golfer

Born May 27, 1912, in Hot Springs, Va; caddied barefoot in snow (shoes were for school and church); learned to play golf very young by hitting ball with crooked stick and watching his brother Homer; won driving contests as a sophomore and junior at Valley High School in Hot Springs; was so unknown when he began tournament play that no one could spell his name; said to be extremely thrifty—Fred Corcoran commented in *Unplayable Lies* that Snead wanted a bargain on shoe polish, but did not think twice about investing $50,000 in fishing tackle company in Florida; Hat is legendary—very rare to see Slammin' Sam without hat, although Corcoran claimed he took it off for showers, church, dinner and bed; known for his Southern drawl and hillbilly stories; Vardon Trophy 1938, 1949, 1950 and 1955; PGA Player of the Year 1949.

Known as the "Slammer" because of his long accurate drives, Snead probably has the best swing in the world. The "fluency, rhythm and classic proportions" as well as the perfect timing of his swings all came naturally and led him to win many championships. He turned professional in 1933 and in four years had won five major tournaments. His entire career includes the Canadian Open 1938, 1940 and 1941, U.S. PGA 1942, 1949 and 1951, British Open 1946 and U.S. Masters 1949, 1952 and 1954. However, Snead never won the U.S. Open though runnerup in 1937, 1947 and 1953, and joint runnerup in 1949. He has had a long career in golf; Snead

won over 84 PGA tournaments since 1937, more than anyone else. He has won the PGA Senior championship six times, 1964–1967, 1970, 1972 and 1973; the World Senior championship five times, 1964, 1965, 1970, 1972 and 1973; and holds the low score for 18 holes in PGA tournaments (60), the low score for 18 holes in non-PGA tournaments (59) and the low score for 36 holes. Snead was on the Ryder Cup team 1937, 1939, 1941, 1947, 1949, 1951 (captain) and 1969 (non-playing captain). He also played on the U.S.-Canada Cup team 1956, 1960 and 1961. Snead has written many books: *The Driver Book, Education of a Golfer, How to Hit a Golf Ball from Any Sort of Lie, How to Play Golf, Professional Tips on Improving your Score, Rules of the Game of Golf, Natural Golf, Sam Snead on Golf* and *Sam Snead's Quick Way to Better Golf.*
Also in: Golf Hall of Fame, Citizens Savings Hall of Fame Athletic Museum; Professional Golfers' Association of America Hall of Fame, West Virginia Sports Writers Hall of Fame and World Golf Hall of Fame.

TAYLOR, John Henry
Golfer
Born March 19, 1871, in Northam, North Devon, England; left school at 11 and became a caddie at Westward Ho!, bootboy in the home of Horace Hutchinson's father, gardener's boy and mason's laborer; became a member of the greenskeeping staff at Westward Ho! at 17; Army and Navy turned him down because of poor eyesight; wrote regularly and authored *Golf, My Life's Work* and *Taylor on Golf: Impressions, Comments and Hints,* and read Dickens and Boswell; honorary member Royal and Ancient Golf Club of St. Andrews 1950; president of Royal North Devon Club 1957; died February 10, 1963, in Devonshire, England, at age 92.

Taylor was the first outstanding British professional and one of the famous British Triumvirate with James Braid and Harry Vardon. At 19 he turned professional and became a greenskeeper at Burnham in Somerset; later he took up a post at Winchester, Wimbledon and Royal Mid-Surrey, where he stayed for over 40 years. Every game was like a battle for Taylor, who was a very high-strung, emotional golfer. He won a record of five British Opens 1894, 1895, 1900, 1903 and 1913, the French Open 1908 and 1909, German Open 1912, British PGA 1904 and 1908. Taylor represented England ten times in international play and recorded 10 holes-in-one during his golf career. He was also the founder and chairman of the first professional golfers' association in 1901, the forerunner of the British PGA.
Also in: World Golf Hall of Fame.

VARDON, Harry
Golfer
Born May 9, 1870, in Grouville, Isle of Jersey, Eng; author of *The Complete Golfer, Progressive Golf, How to Play Golf, Success at Golf* and *My Golfing Life;* died March 20, 1937, in London.

Vardon learned to play golf when he was seven years old as a caddie at Grouville and with the advice of his brother, assistant professional to St. Anne's, later took up a post at Ripon, Yorkshire, in 1890. During his golf career, he popularized the overlapping grip which bears his name, developed the open stance and his own graceful, rhythmic upright swing. He used lighter clubs than most golfers—when he borrowed clubs it was usually from a woman's set—and was well known for his play of full-wood shots. Whatever the weather, Vardon wore knickerbockers and jacket to play golf. In the prime of his career at the turn of the century, he won a record of six British Opens 1896, 1898, 1899, 1903, 1911 and 1914, the U.S. Open 1900, the German Open 1911 and the British PGA 1912, representing England 18 times in 12 years in international competition. Vardon is probably best remembered as one of Britain's Triumvirate (others are James Braid and John Taylor) which raised the standards of golf. Vardon's own tour of the United States in 1900 helped greatly to promote the sport in this country. The Vardon Trophy, given annually to the golfer with the lowest score for 18 holes in one year of PGA tournaments, is named after Harry Vardon.
Also in: World Golf Hall of Fame.

WETHERED, Joyce (Lady Heathcoat Amory)
Golfer
Born November 17, 1901, in Great Britain; brother Roger Henry Wethered was a well-known British amateur golfer in the 1920s; author of *The Game of Golf, Golfing Memories and Methods,* and *Golf from Two Sides* (with brother, Roger).

Though her golf career lasted only nine years, Lady Amory's ability was supreme. She was the best woman golfer, better than most men, and is often compared to Bobby Jones who thought she was the best golfer he had ever seen. She had intense concentration (but a sense of humor as well) to match her perfectly balanced swing. As an unknown 19-year-old, she won her first British Ladies' Open and went on to win five in a row 1920–1924. She also won the French Ladies' Open 1921, the Women's British Championship four times 1922, 1924, 1925 and 1929, and the Worplesdon Foursomes eight times with seven different partners 1922, 1923, 1927, 1928, 1931–1933 and 1936. In 1929 whe son the Women's British Amateur against Glenna Collett Vare, an outstanding U.S. golfer, and in 1935, during two exhibition matches in a tour of the United States, Joyce Wethered even outscored Babe Zaharias, top U.S. woman golfer.
Also in: Ladies Professional Golfers' Association Hall of Fame and World Golf Hall of Fame.

ZAHARIAS, Mildred Didrikson "Babe"
Golfer
Born June 26, 1914, in Port Arthur Tex; one of seven athletic children; parents were originally from Norway where father was a sailor and mother had been ice skater and skier; father became furniture refinisher in Texas, encouraged children in sports by reading sports pages in the newspaper and building a gym in their backyard; as a child, played sports with neighborhood boys; so good at hitting home runs in baseball, called Babe after Babe Ruth, a hero at time; played harmonica, worked in a fig-packing plant and a potato gunnysack factory; wanted to be greatest athlete that ever lived; had a keen sense of competition and was always active in sports: junior high and high school basketball, All-American basketball player, a record-breaking 1932 Olympic track star who placed first in three events (high jump, javelin, low hurdles) and won two gold medals (disqualified in high jump), and a tennis player; met George Zaharias, an out-

standing wrestler, at Los Angeles Open in 1938; engaged July 1938, and married December 23, 1938; in April, 1953, had colostomy for cancer—George claims she played golf in sleep during recovery; went on to win U.S. Open in 1954 despite serious operation; Vare Trophy 1954; Associated Press Woman Athlete of the Year 1932, 1945–1947, 1950 and 1954; Associated Press Greatest Woman of the Half Century 1900–1950; very active in fight against cancer; opened 1954 Annual Cancer Crusade with President and Mrs. Eisenhower; opened Babe Didrikson Zaharias Chapter of the American Cancer Society in Seattle; did numerous radio spots and made television appearances for American Cancer Society and Damon Runyon Foundation; cancer developed again in 1955; died October 27, 1956, in Galveston, Tex, at age 41.

Babe's first game of golf was during the 1932 Olympics; at the time she thought "how silly it was for people to hit a little white ball and then chase it," and did not even know about teeing up the ball for a drive. Having succeeded in basketball and track, and having discovered that a thrown-out shoulder from javelin-throwing hampered her tennis game, Babe concentrated her attention on golf. She took lessons from Stan Kertes, George Aulbach and Jack Burke and practiced so much for her first tournament, the Texas State Women's Golf championship (1935), that her hands bled. She went on to win over Peggy Chandler, a veteran of the tournament who had reached the finals four times in a row and won the championship one of those times. The United States Golf Association declared her ineligible for women's amateur golf in 1935 but reinstated her in 1943. Babe had great power as a golfer and could out-drive many men. Her talent brought championships in the U.S. Amateur and Trans-Mississippi Amateur 1946, North and South Amateur 1947, British Ladies' 1947 (the first American to win), U.S. Women's Open 1948, 1950 and 1954 and Western Open 1940, 1944, 1945 and 1950. Despite her serious operation in April, 1953, she played in the Tam o' Shanter. All-American and World Championship three and one-half months later and was sixth in the women's money winners in 1953. Together with her outstanding ability in sports, her recovery from cancer and return to professional golf was probably her greatest achievement. She is the author of two books, *Championship Golf* and *This Life I've Led,* an autobiography as told to Harry Paxton.

Also in: Colorado Golf Hall of Fame, Ladies Professional Golfers' Association Hall of Fame, Professional Golfers' Association of America Hall of Fame, World Golf Hall of Fame; Golf Hall of Fame, Track and Field Hall of Fame and Women's Basketball Hall of Fame, Citizens Savings Hall of Fame Athletic Museum; National Track and Field Hall of Fame and United States Track and Field Hall of Fame.

1966

BALL, John

Golfer

Born December 24, 1861, in Hoylake, Cheshire, England; father owned Royal Hotel at Hoylake, first headquarters for the Royal Liverpool Golf Club; served with the Cheshire Yeomanry in Boer War; after retirement from golf, settled in Holywell, North Wales; died there December 2, 1940.

Rated as one of the finest amateurs, Ball had remarkable dominance in golf at a time when competition was not as intense as it is today. At 15 he competed and placed sixth in the British Open and became the first amateur to win the championship in 1890. With a beautiful swing, he won a record number of British Amateur titles 1888, 1890, 1892, 1894, 1899, 1907, 1910 and 1912. His 1912 win was at the age of 51. Ball was captain of the English team against Scotland 1902–1911 and was a competitor in golf until the age of 60. Despite his great success, he was a golfer of moods and was known to sometimes play the Hoylake links backward or left-handed to add interest to his game.

HILTON, Harold Horsfall

Golfer

Born January 12, 1869, in West Kirby, Cheshire, England; authored several books on golf, including *My Golf Reminiscences;* editor of *Golf Illustrated* for a time; died March 5, 1942, in Westcote, England.

A great amateur in the prewar period, Hilton was the first of three men to hold the British and U.S. Amateur titles at the same time. Though Bobby Jones and Lawson Little were to repeat this feat, in 1911 he was the only English player to win the U.S. Amateur. He made a good showing in the British Amateur as well: he won a total of four times, 1900, 1901, 1911 and 1913, and placed second three times, 1890, 1891 and 1896. Hilton won the British Open in 1892 and again in 1897 by beating one of the Triumvirate, James Braid. He added the St. George's Cup in 1893 and 1894 and 1897 brought him the first of four victories in the Irish Open, which he also won 1900–1902. These victories probably came as a result of his scientific approach to the game and deep knowledge of technique. He had an explosively fast swing, jumping up on his toes just before he began it, but he also had great control and good touch with a putter as well as a mastery of the backswing.

MORRIS, Thomas Sr, "Old Tom"

Golfer

Born 1821 in St. Andrews, Scotland; father a letter carrier; intended to be a carpenter, but apprentice and journeyman (five years each) to a club and ball maker, Allan Robertson, who later became golfing partner; greenskeeper for Prestwick Club 1851–1865; honorary greenskeeper for St. Andrews 1904–1908; died 1908 in St. Andrews at age 87.

Tom Morris, Sr, was one of the pioneering Scots of professional golf and was probably the greatest matchplayer of all time. He won the British Open four times, 1861, 1862, 1864 and 1867, and participated in every Open through 1896 when he was 75 years old. Old Tom was the reigning champion when his son Tom, Jr, won the British Open in 1868 (the youngest to win the British Open, at 18). Said Old Tom of his son, "I could cope wi' Allan mysel' but never wi' Tommy." Recognized by a full grey beard, Old Tom's portrait hangs in the Royal and Ancient Golf Club.

Also in: World Golf Hall of Fame.

PARK, Willie, Sr.

Golfer

Born around 1844; brother Mungo won British Open 1874; son Willie, Jr, won British Open 1887 and 1889.

Willie Park, Sr, made history when he won the first British Open in 1860 and repeated his victory in 1863, 1866 and 1875. He continued a long line of family association with golf and was followed by his brother and son. Willie, Sr, was a fine shotmaker, player and putter and was constantly challenging or challenged by Tom Morris, Sr, for supremacy in golf. As a boy he learned his golf at the Musselburgh course by practicing over the "baker's holes" where local bakers engaged in putting matches while selling pies to golfers.

VARE, Glenna Collett
Golfer

Born June 20, 1903, in New Haven, Conn; author of *Golf for Young Players.*

The Vare Trophy, awarded annually to the holder of the lowest stroke average of the Ladies Professional Golfers' Association tour in one season, is named after this fine woman golfer. Vare began to study and practice golf when she became interested in the sport at 15. As the most outstanding woman golfer of her time, she won the U.S. Women's Amateur a record six times, 1922, 1925, 1928–1930 and 1935, the Canadian Ladies' Open 1923 and 1924, French Ladies' Open 1925, British Ladies' Open 1929 and 1930, and the North and South Women's Championship 1922–1924, 1927, 1929 and 1930. In 1929–1931 Vare won 19 consecutive matches for a United States Golf Association record; she won 49 amateur championships in her 18-year career. Unfortunately, her career coincided with that of Joyce Wethered, who prevented her from winning the memorable 1929 Women's British Amateur at St. Andrews. She returned to England several times as a member of the Curtis Cup team (captain 1934, 1936 and 1948, non-playing captain 1950) and was popular among her British audiences.
Also in: Golf Hall of Fame, Citizens Savings Hall of Fame Athletic Museum; Ladies Professional Golfers' Association Hall of Fame and World Golf Hall of Fame.

1967

LEITCH, Charlotte Cecilia Pitcairn "Cecil"
Golfer

Born April 13, 1891, in Silloth, Cumberland, England.

In her first serious competition, Cecil Leitch reached the semifinals of the British Ladies' championship in 1908 and, though her career was interrupted for a time by W.W. I, it did not hinder her ability to win a succession of French Ladies' Opens 1912, 1914, 1920, 1921 and 1924, and British Ladies' championships 1914, 1920, 1921 and 1926. In fact, she has won more British Ladies' championships than any other woman golfer, even Joyce Wethered, and has the unique distinction of being victorious in each of the four home countries of the tournament. She also played in the Home Internationals, 1910–1928, winning 29 (halving one) of 33 matches, and became Canadian Ladies' Open champion in 1921. Cecil's greatest opposition was Joyce Wethered. Their competition drove women's golf to the front page of the newspapers for the first time and improved the general quality of play. They first met in 1920 when Joyce Wethered won the English championship. With an outstanding use of woods and irons, Leitch won the playoffs against Wethered in the 1921 British Ladies' and French Ladies' Open, but Wethered won when they met again at the 1922, 1924 and 1925 British Ladies'. Despite Wethered's dominance of these tournaments, it is a credit to Leitch that she was such close competition to one of the greatest woman golfers ever.

MORRIS, Thomas, Jr.
Golfer

Born in Fife, Scotland; father Thomas Morris, Sr, Scotch professional golfer; married for a year when his wife and newborn baby died; Tom, Jr, never recovered from the shock and died of a "broken heart" December 25, 1875, at age 24; memorial marks his resting place in St. Andrews Cathedral.

Tom, Jr, was the youngest as well as four-time winner of the British Open 1868, 1869, 1870 and 1872. As a result of winning the Open three times in a row (no Open in 1871), he was given permanent possession of the champion belt which now rests in the Royal and Ancient clubhouse. He had great power and the promise of being a great golfer.
Also in: World Golf Hall of Fame.

SWEETSER, Jess W.
Golfer

Born April 18, 1902, in Cobb, Ky; quarter-miler and graduate of Yale.

Always an amateur, Jess played golf in college and won the 1920 National Collegiate championship. Two years later he won the U.S. Amateur title, beating Chick Evans in the finals with the best golfing of his career. In 1926 he won the British Amateur with the flu, an injured knee and sprained wrist, and became the first American champion since Walter Travis in 1904. With these two victories in 1922 and 1926, Sweetser gained the rare distinction of winning both the U.S. and British Amateur titles. A member of many U.S. Walker Cup teams, 1922–1924, 1926, 1928, 1932 and nonplaying captain in 1967 and 1973, he has another distinction of being the only player ever to lose at extra holes. In 1922, after a tie with C. V. L. Hooman on 36 holes, he and Hooman were told to continue playing. Thereafter it was decided to halve ties after 36 holes. Despite this loss, he won an overwhelming victory at Muirfield and impressed many with his powerful "grooved" swing.
Also in: Golf Hall of Fame, Citizens Savings Hall of Fame Athletic Museum.

1968

ANDERSON, James
Golfer

Born 1842 in St. Andrews, Fife, Scotland; father David "Old Daw" Anderson; brother David also professional golfer; caddie at St. Andrews and later a fine club maker at Ardeer and Perth; died 1912.

Known for his accurate playing and quick games, Anderson was often compared with Willie Park, Sr, the first British Open champion (1860). Like most young people in St. Andrews, he began golfing at an early age. He went on to win three consecutive British Opens 1877–1879; only Tom Morris, Jr, had won four. Following championship competition he continued playing golf in foursome matches, often with Bob Ferguson, another three-in-a-row winner of the British Open.

ANDERSON, Willie
Golfer
Born May 1879 in North Brunswick, Scotland; died 1910 at 32 from arteriosclerosis, though appeared to be in good health to the very end; played three 36-hole matches the week before he died.

Two years after immigrating to the United States from Scotland, Willie Anderson was runnerup in the U.S. Open 1897 at the age of 17. His finest accomplishment was to be the first man to win the U.S. Open four times, and the only man to win it three times in a row, 1901, 1903–1905. He also was in the top five of eleven U.S. Opens and won the Western Open four times, 1902, 1904, 1908 and 1909. During his lifetime he held professional posts at ten clubs including the Pittsburgh Country Club and clubs in Apawamis, N.Y, and Onwentsia, Ill. It is hard to say how he would compare with modern-day golfers, considering the differences in clubs and balls, but he had a full, smooth swing and was a good putter; his favorite club was the mashie.
Also in: Golf Hall of Fame, Citizens Savings Hall of Fame Athletic Museum; Professional Golfers' Association of America Hall of Fame and World Golf Hall of Fame.

KIRKWOOD, Joseph H.
Golfer
Born March 22, 1897, in Sydney, Australia; came to the United States 1921; spent the last five yers of his life as pro at Stowe Country Club, Vt; died October 29, 1970, in Burlington, Vt.

Joe Kirkwood played on over 6470 different golf courses and could tee a ball on the face of a watch and drive it 250 yds. He could also hit balls suspended by strings, or hit balls and run forward to catch them, and could slice and hook on command. As the leading trick-shot artist who learned his trade while entertaining soldiers during W.W. I, he went on tours around the world with both Gene Sarazen and Walter Hagen. He also was a fine stroke player, winning his first championships, both the Australian and New Zealand Opens, in 1920 at age 23. Despite the fact that his jerky swing and light grip would not carry him through moments of extreme pressure in tournaments, he won the California, Houston and Illinois Opens in 1923, the Canadian Open in 1933 and was a regular contender in the British Open for years, placing or tying for fourth three times.

1969

FERGUSON, Bob
Golfer
Born 1848 in Musselburgh, Scotland; died 1915.

Ferguson grew up with golf, starting as a caddie at the Musselburgh links when he was eight years old. At 18 he beat all the great pros of the day in the Leith tournament with a bag of borrowed clubs and went on to become an outstanding British golfer. He was backed in many matches, including those of 1868 and 1869, against Tom Morris, Sr, whom he beat six times. Ferguson won the British Open three consecutive times, 1880–1882, a record equaled only by Peter Thomson and Jamie Anderson and bettered by Tom Morris, Jr, who won four.

HURD, Dorothy Iona Campbell
Golfer
Born May 6, 1883, in Edinburgh, Scotland; moved to the United States in 1909; later to Canada; killed while changing trains in Yemassee, N.C, March 20, 1945.

Dorothy Hurd became the outstanding woman golfer in Scotland when she won the Scottish Ladies' championship in 1905, 1906 and 1908 and represented her country in Home International matches. She traveled to Birkdale in 1909 and nearly lost the British Ladies' title by disqualification when, after defeating her third-round opponent on the 11th green, she forgot to report the result of the match to the officials. While they discussed possible disqualification, she practiced lofting stymies and, when the game resumed, won the fourth-round match on the last green with a brilliantly lofted stymie. With her next win at the 1909 U.S. Women's Amateur she became the first British-born woman to win the championship and the first woman to win both the British and U.S. amateur titles in one year. She repeated her victory at the British Ladies' in 1911 and at the U.S. Women's Amateur in 1910 and 1924. With a win at the 1910 Canadian Open as well, she again managed a double title in one year. In all, Dorothy Hurd won 11 major championships, ten between 1905 and 1912, and even won the 1938 U.S. Women's Senior tournament at the age of 55.
Also in: Golf Hall of Fame, Citizens Savings Hall of Fame Athletic Museum; Ladies Professional Golfers' Association Hall of Fame.

PALMER, Arnold Daniel
Golfer
Born September 10, 1929, in Latrobe, Pa; father Milfred worked at Pennsylvania steel mill before becoming professional at Latrobe Country Club; given cut-down clubs at age three; father taught him importance of good grip and ability to play any shot; Vardon Trophy 1961, 1962 and 1967; Bob Jones Award for Distinguished Sportsmanship 1971.

Any golfer who thinks of the 1950s and 1960s thinks of Arnold Palmer, one of the "Big Three" (others are Nicklaus and Player). He had a magnetic personality that attracted sports fans, admirers and organizers who wanted him for their clinics, exhibitions and advertisements. His participation in the British Open restored the tournament to its position as a leading world championship by drawing other Americans to the Open. During his career he captured the U.S. Amateur 1954, U.S. Masters 1958, 1960, 1962 and 1964, U.S. Open 1960, and the British Open 1961 and 1962. He was the first four-time winner of the U.S. Masters and the first pro golfer to exceed $1 million in prize money. Arnie was also the first golfer to fly his own plane to tournaments.
Also in: World Golf Hall of Fame.

1970

LITTLE, William Lawson, Jr.
Golfer
Born June 23, 1910, in Newport, R.I; father a colonel in the Army Medical Corps; Little spent early years at bases all over the United States and China; died February 1, 1968, in Pebble Beach, Calif.

The thick, curly, black hair and solid 5 ft. 9¾-in. frame of Lawson Little were a familiar sight on golf courses in the 1930s and early 1940s. He was a powerful hitter and an accurate putter with intense determination. As an amateur, he completed a "Little Slam" by winning both the British and U.S. Amateurs in 1934 and 1935. This double victory, involving 31 consecutive matches against the best golfers in both nations, remains a unique accomplishment in golf. In the 1934 British Amateur he won by 14 and 13, another record. Perhaps his best golf, he played 12 of 23 holes in three strokes. As a great matchplayer, he paired up with Johnny Goodman on the 1934 U.S. Walker Cup team and won the foursome against Roger Wethered and Cyril Tolley. Little turned professional and won the Canadian Open in 1936. In 1940 he capped his career with a U.S. Open victory by defeating Gene Sarazen in the playoffs. Little later won the Los Angeles Open in 1940 and the Texas Open in 1941.
Also in: Golf Hall of Fame, Citizens Savings Hall of Fame Athletic Museum; California Golf Hall of Fame and Professional Golfers' Association of America Hall of Fame.

PARK, Willie, Jr.
Golfer
Born 1864 in Musselburgh, Scotland; father Willie Park, Sr, first winner of the British Open; at 16 began four years as the professional and greenskeeper at Ryton, then returned to Musselburgh to start a business as a club and ball maker; died 1925 of a nervous complaint in Edinburgh.

Coming from a family associated with golf in Scotland for over 400 years, Willie, Jr, was almost destined to become a great golfer. He won his first tournament at Alnmouth when he was 17 and the British Open in 1887 and 1889. His 1887 victory involved a tie with Andrew Kirkaldy. Not an urgent matter in those days, the playoff was held three days later with Willie, Jr, the winner by five strokes. A lover of challenge matches, he played a four-green match against Kirkaldy a few months after the Open. His opponent came out on top, 8 and 7, but this was not a large margin over 144 holes and the match produced some wonderful golf. In 1896 he won over J. H. Taylor, British Open champion in 1894 and 1895; however, in 1899, he lost to Harry Vardon. Willie, Jr, once said, "a man who can putt is a match for anyone," but he could not beat Vardon's long drives. "Old Pawsky" was his famous putter and with it he practiced his deadly shots up to eight hours a day. Following his famous matches, Park became a writer as well as the first in a long line of distinguished golf architects. He designed the famous Sunningdale Old, West Hill and Huntercombe courses in addition to others in the United States and Canada.

THOMSON, Peter William
Golfer
Born August 23, 1929, in Melbourne, Australia; lived near a golf course as a child; traveled to Britain 1951; active supporter of a true world tour, largely responsible for the development of the Far East tour; services to the game merited award of Order of the British Empire; well known in Australia for his newspaper column and television commentaries; often reports on tournaments he competes in; administrator of Australian Professional Golfers' Association; golf-course architect; coauthor of *This Wonderful World of Golf.*

An international golfer, Peter Thomson has won tournaments all over the world. Beginning south of the equator, he won a long succession of nine New Zealand Opens 1950, 1951, 1953, 1955, 1959–1961, 1965 and 1971; he also won three Australian Opens 1951, 1967 and 1972. He ventured to Britain in 1951 and began preparing for his outstanding record at the British Open. After a sixth place in 1951 and a second in 1952, Thomson won the Open a total of five times, 1954–1956, 1958 and 1965, topped only by Harry Vardon's six and equaled by J. H. Taylor and James Braid. In the late 1950s Thomson went to the United States to play golf. He was not quite as successful there as in Britain, and did not find the courses as challenging; he did win the Texas Open in 1956. In other parts of the world Peter has won three Hong Kong Opens, a German, Philippine, Spanish, Italian and two Indian Opens. Thomson also excelled in matchplay: he participated in the 1954, 1961, 1966 and 1967 British Professional Matchplay and won the Canada Cup for Australia with Ken Nagel in 1954 and 1959.

1971

BOROS, Julius Nicholas
Golfer
Born March 3, 1920, in Fairfield, Conn; very interested in fishing.

As the easy-going "Old Man River," Boros has had a long and profitable career in golf. At 43 he was the second oldest winner of the U.S. Open (Ted Ray was 26 days older when he won it in 1920) and the oldest winner, at 48, of the 1968 Professional Golfers' Association of America (PGA) tournament. Beginning in 1950, he won $900,000 in 25 years on the PGA tour, $400,000 after he was 40. He was the leading money winner in 1952 and 1955. His long success is attributed to a calm temperament and relaxed attitude toward the game, very obvious in his swing. Tony Lema, winner of the 1964 British Open, says it was "all hands and wrists, like a man dusting the furniture," but his swing won him numerous tournaments. In addition to his PGA and 1963 U.S. Open wins, he won the U.S. Open in 1952, breaking up Ben Hogan's long record of wins, and was nine times in the first ten. He was on the U.S. Ryder Cup team in 1959, 1963, 1965 and 1967, losing only three matches out of 16, and won the World Championship of 1952 and 1955. "Old Man River" continued to play as a senior golfer and won the PGA Senior title in 1971.
Also in: Golf Hall of Fame, Citizens Savings Hall of Fame Athletic Museum; Connecticut Golf Hall of Fame and Professional Golfers' Association of America Hall of Fame.

HUTCHISON, Jock
Golfer
Born June 6, 1884, in St. Andrews, Fife, Scotland; came to the United States in the early 1900s and settled in Pittsburgh area; during W. W. I moved to Chicago and became a member of the Glen View Country Club; gave golf exhibitions for charities during W. W. I.

Jock was one of many golfing Scotsmen who settled in the United Stats at the beginning of the century. He was

a nervous, talkative player with a rhythmic but three-parted swing. With so much excess energy, he bounded forward after each shot; between shots he talked, laughed, twiddled his thumbs and even waved his hands to let the perspiration dry. He was small, only 140 lbs, but ranked with Walter Hagen and Jim Barnes as one of America's finest. In 1916 he was runnerup to Jim Barnes in the first Professional Golfers' Association of America (PGA) championship and runnerup to Chick Evans in the U.S. Open; he and Chick were the first to break 290 in the U.S. Open with a 288 and 286, respectively. In 1920 Hutchison came back to win the PGA Championship and the Western Open as well (also in 1923). In 1921 he was victorious at the North and South Open and became the first American to win the British Open. He left the United States some time before the tournament, practiced the St. Andrews course dozens of times and eventually won the playoff against Roger Wethered for an historic victory. Even as Jock got older, he continued playing golf. In the first eight years of the PGA Seniors tournament, he was never lower than third; he won in 1937 and 1947 and was even runnerup at 67 years of age in 1951. He could shoot a 66 at 66 and was still playing in his 80s. He and fellow octogenarian Freddie McLeod were the lead-off pair at the Masters tournament for many years.
Also in: Golf Hall of Fame, Citizens Savings Hall of Fame Athletic Museum; Professional Golfers' Association of America Hall of Fame.

MIDDLECOFF, Dr. Cary "Doc"
Golfer
Born January 6, 1921, in Halls, Tenn; followed father and two uncles into dentistry; served in U.S. Army beginning in 1943; author of *Advanced Golf*; chairman of PGA Tournament Committee 1954–1955; Vardon Trophy 1956.

After playing golf in Tennessee, Cary Middlecoff was the first amateur to win the North and South Open in 1945. He was invited to play on the first Walker Cup team, but declined and turned professional in 1947. In 1949 at the Motor City Open, he and Lloyd Mangrum played the longest sudden-death playoff in Professional Golfers' Association of America (PGA) history—11 extra holes before they were halted by darkness—and became co-champions, splitting the $5000 first prize. He also won the U.S. Open that year and, between 1950 and 1957, won at least one tournament a year and was also one of the top ten money winners. He was known to be a slow player, especially in calculating his putts, but was a fine driver and theoretician of the game. In 1953, 1955 and 1959 Middlecoff was part of the U.S. Ryder Cup team. In 1955 he won six tournaments, including the Western Open and the U.S. Masters with an 82-ft. putt on the 13th green for an eagle in the final round. He finished the year with $39,567. After a victory in the 1956 U.S. Open, his 79 lost to Dick Myers's 72 in the 1957 playoffs. He won the 1961 Memphis Open, but began having back problems due to his 6 ft. 2-in. height. Middlecoff finished his career with wins in 35 PGA events, a low competitive round of 62 and a low four-round total of 264.
Also in: Golf Hall of Fame, Citizens Savings Hall of Fame Athletic Museum; Professional Golfers' Association of America Hall of Fame.

TRAVIS, Walter J.
Golfer
Born January 10, 1862, in Malden, Victoria, Australia; founder and editor of *American Golfer* magazine in 1905; golf course architect; one of the builders of the Garden City Golf Club course where the 1924 Walker Cup matches and 1936 U.S. Amateur tournament were played; credited with helping to develop Bobby Jones into a fine putter; died July 31, 1927, in Denver, Colo.

Walter Travis was known as "The Old Man" because he did not begin golfing until he was in his thirties. What he lacked in power, he made up for with an aggressive, competitive nature, accuracy and an excellent short game. He won the U.S. Amateur three out of four years, 1900, 1901 and 1903, an accomplishment approached only by Bobby Jones who won five out of seven years. And Travis's first win was at 38 years of age. In 1904 he was the first foreigner to win the British Amateur to Britain's apparent displeasure; he was treated coldly during and after the tournament. Later they outlawed his famous Schenectady putter, a center-shafted club with a mallet head, very similar to many in common use today. Travis returned to the United States, never to return to Britain, and was still competing in his fifties, with a win at the Metropolitan Amateur in 1915. His tournament play ended when the U.S. Golf Association ruled his editorship and golf-course architecture illegal for amateurs. He began playing for invitationals and sectionals and continued in such play even after the decision was rescinded. Travis will be remembered as the small, bearded man smoking a black cigar who even improved the game of President Taft with his Schenectady putter.
Also in: Golf Hall of Fame, Citizens Savings Hall of Fame Athletic Museum; Professional Golfers' Association of America Hall of Fame.

1972

BERG, Patricia J.
Golfer
Born February 13, 1918, in Minneapolis, Minn; father, mother and brother low handicappers in golf; as youngster loved skating and at 15 won girl's junior division of Minnesota State Speed championship, later competed in national finals; a tomboy, playing tackle football with neighborhood boys, one was Bud Wilkinson later to become football coach for Univ. Okla; auto accident while doing exhibitions for British War Relief in 1941, disabled 18 months by compound fracture of the knee; enlisted in Marine Corps Women's Reserve 1943–1945; made occasional war bond exhibitions; Sports Writers of America outstanding Woman Athlete of the Year 1938 and 1943; Vare Trophy 1953, 1956; 12-year Ladies' PGA Competitive Record for 18 holes 1952; charter member and first president of Ladies PGA; Ladies' PGA leading money winner 1954, 1955 and 1957.

Patty Berg, called "The Red-Headed Tomboy" and "The Minneapolis Tomboy," began her bright career at 14 and at 16 became the medalist in the 1935 Palm Beach (Fla.) Winter Invitational. At 17 she was runnerup in the U.S. Amateur and at 19 won the championship (1938). After turning pro in 1940, and following her re-

covery from a serious automobile accident, she went on to win more than 80 events in her golfing career, including the U.S. Women's Open 1946, World Chmpionship 1953 – 1955 and 1957. Patty was a member of two Curtis Cup teams 1936 and 1938. She made her first hole-in-one during championship play in 1959. Patty has conducted thousands of instructional clinics throughout the world and has written a book, *Golf Illustrated.*
Also in: Golf Hall of Fame, Citizens Savings Hall of Fame Athletic Museum; Ladies Professional Golfers' Association Hall of Fame and World Golf Hall of Fame.

CASPER, William Earl, Jr.
Golfer
Born 1931 in San Diego, Calif; served with U.S. Navy; briefly attended Notre Dame before becoming a professional golfer; plagued by allergies, even to insecticides on golf courses; went on a well-publicized antiallergy diet that consisted of such exotic foods as elephant and whale meat; visited troops in Vietnam; also visited Morocco numerous times to give golf lessons to the king; an elder in the Mormon church; Vardon Trophy 1960, 1963, 1965, 1966 and 1968; Player of the Year 1966, 1968 and 1970; Alcan Golfer of the Year 1967.

With competitors like the great Palmer, Player and Nicklaus, Billy Casper won 52 tournaments during his golf career, a total second only to Ben Hogan's. Casper turned professional in 1954, began the Professional Golfers' Association of America tour in 1955 and became one of its most consistent golfers—he consistently won. His first tournament victory was the U.S. Open in 1959. He won the Open again in 1966 in a playoff against Arnold Palmer and was leading money winner that year, as well as in 1968. He also won the Canadian Open in 1967, the U.S. Masters in 1970 and was a member of eight U.S. Ryder Cup teams, every one between 1961 and 1975. He has the record of winning the most singles, 11, in Ryder Cup Trophy competition. Casper was not an extroverted player like Palmer, Player and Nicklaus and did not catch the eye of the public, but he was a leading putter and a fast player with a superb swing. He is third among the all-time money winners, with over $1,600,000 in prize money, and has been recognized many times for his golfing abilities.
Also in: California Golf Hall of Fame.

GULDAHL, Ralph
Golfer
Born November 22, 1911, in Dallas, Tex; at one time an automobile salesman.

When Ralph Guldahl was at his best he could withstand the pressure of a tournament from tee to green, but he was a golfer with ups and downs. In the early 1930s he was on his way to following the sucess of Bobby Jones but, after placing second in the 1933 U.S. Open, his form collapsed and he almost quit the American tour in 1935. After some persuasion and practice, Guldahl came back to win ten tournaments in the next five years. He won the Western Open three straight times, 1936, 1937 and 1938. In 1938 he became one of four golfers to successfully defend a U.S. Open title and broke the tournament record with a 281. Just before he stepped up to his last and winning putt, he stopped to comb his hair. He played with the U.S. Ryder Cup team in 1937 and was selected for the 1939 team, when the match was not held. Suddenly, after winning the 1939 U.S. Masters (runner-up in 1938), Guldahl lost his touch. Despite all efforts to make a comeback, he never won another tournament.
Also in: Golf Hall of Fame, Citizens Savings Hall of Fame Athletic Museum; Professional Golfers' Association of America Hall of Fame.

LOCKE, Arthur d'Arcy "Bobby"
Golfer
Born November 20, 1917, in Germiston, Transvaal, South Africa; son of Irish immigrants; joined South African Air Force in W. W. II and served in Middle East as bomber pilot; involved in road accident in 1960 that kept him in the hospital and impaired his sight; Vardon Trophy 1946, 1950 and 1954.

Like Gary Player, Locke came from South Africa where he won his first tournament at 14, the Transvaal Junior Championship. By 20 Bobby had won most everything worth winning in South Africa, so he began traveling all over the world picking up victories as he went: the Irish and New Zealand Opens in 1938, the Canadian Open in 1947, the British Open an amazing four times, 1949, 1950, 1952 and 1957; he also won the 1950 Tam O'Shanter All-American tournament, the 1952 and 1953 French Open, the 1954 Dunlop Masters, and the Egyptian and Swiss Opens. If it had not been for all this traveling, Locke probably would have won more than the nine South African Opens he did (1935, 1937 – 1940, 1946, 1950, 1951 and 1955). Locke came to the United States for the first time in 1947 at Sam Snead's invitation; in 1946 he and Snead had played 16 matches together in South Africa and Snead was impressed with Bobby's 12 wins. Locke's first tournament in the United States was the 1947 Masters and, although he placed 15th in it, he was never lower than seventh in the other 12 stroke-play tournaments he entered and ended the year as the second leading money winner with $24,000. In 1948 he entered 25 tournaments, placed in the top ten in all but three and was the fourth leading money winner for the year. Most notable about Bobby Locke was his putting, rated with that of Hagen, Jones and Palmer. With complete composure he followed a detailed methodical preparation for each putt and never allowed himself to be rushed. He had such a passion for golf that he could be seen in his familiar white cap playing at least nine holes a day.

1973

BARNES, James "Long Jim"
Golfer
A naturalized American born 1887 in Lelant, Cornwall, England; emigrated to United States at 19 but always proud of English birth; known for lock of unruly hair over forehead and a sprig of clover or grass continuously sucked on during a golf game; author of *Picture Analysis of Golf Strokes* (1919), a first in the field; died May 24, 1966, in East Orange, N.J.

Before coming to the United States, this courteous and reserved golfer was assistant to the Lelant Golf Club professional in Cornwall for four years. There on the Cornish coast he developed his methodical style and

windproof long straight drives. His first win was the 1916 Professional Golfers' Association of America (PGA) tournament. He again won the PGA tournament in 1919, along with the North and South, the Western, the Shawnee and the Southern Opens. Long Jim, 6 ft. 3 in, placed fourth in his second appearance at the U.S. Open, when Francis Ouimet beat Harry Vardon and Ted Ray, and competed three times before he won in 1921. He was the only winner of the Open to receive the trophy from a U.S. President, Warren G. Harding. After placing 24th in the U.S. Championship of 1925, he surprisingly won the British Open, another major victory for Jim Barnes.
Also in: Golf Hall of Fame, Citizens Savings Hall of Fame Athletic Museum; Professional Golfers' Association of America Hall of Fame.

DEMARET, James Newton
Golfer
Born May 10, 1910, in Houston, Tex; completed two years at Houston's North Side High School before starting his golf career; worked in Jack Burke, Sr.'s golf shop in Houston; also a nightclub singer; red-haired wife Idella; enjoys colorful clothes, flashy golf outfits and caps; in 1954 owned 43 "lids" including a Scotch-plaid fedora and "the wildest tam you ever did see"; owns and operates the Champions Golf Club with Jack Burke in Houston, Tex; wrote *My Partner Ben Hogan* about his long-time friend and fellow golf enthusiast; Vardon Trophy 1947.

Jimmy Demaret was 12 when he won his first tournament, a Houston caddy championship in 1923. After 20 years in golf, he had won over 40 tournaments and was leading money winner in 1947 with $27,936. Demaret was the first golfer to win the U.S. Masters three times. In 1940, after five straight tournament wins, he captured his first Masters with four strokes up on Lloyd Mangrum and a record of 30 on the back nine. (This was equaled by Gene Littler in 1966 and Ben Hogan in 1967.) He beat Byron Nelson by two strokes in 1947 and came out ahead of Jim Ferrier to win his third Masters in 1950. He has also won the Argentine, Los Angeles, St. Paul and Miami Opens. Demaret and the legendary Ben Hogan have been friends and golf partners for over 22 years; it was Demaret who talked Hogan into making his historic trip to Scotland to win the British Open and complete his Grand Slam. Together they won four Miami Internationals, four Inverness Round Robin Four-Ball events, and played on Bobby Jones' and Gene Sarazen's American challenge teams against the Ryder Cup aggregations of 1940 and 1941 (and won). As members of the U.S. Ryder Cup team in 1947 and 1951, Demaret and Hogan were undefeated. With another undefeated victory on the 1949 Ryder Cup team, Demaret is the only golfer to win every match three times. His most memorable wins are the 1940 Masters, especially his 30 on the back nine with six birdies and three pars, and the 1938 San Francisco Matchplay championship, when he beat Sam Snead.
Also in: Golf Hall of Fame, Citizens Savings Hall of Fame Athletic Museum; Professional Golfers' Association of America Hall of Fame.

WRIGHT, Mary Kathryn "Mickey"
Golfer
Born February 14, 1935, in San Diego, Calif; attorney father wanted boy named Michael, hence nickname; in 1952 entered Stanford Univ. to study psychology and play golf, returned to college in mid-1960s, Southern Methodist Univ; Vare Trophy 1960–1964; Associated Press Woman Athlete of the Year 1963, 1964; author of *Play Golf the Wright Way*; president of Ladies PGA 1964.

Mickey Wright is an outstanding woman golfer, especially in iron play, who has broken numerous records during her career. She won the U.S. Junior Girls' in 1952 and turned professional in 1954. She holds the record (with Elizabeth Earle-Raws) of four wins in the U.S. Open 1958, 1959, 1961 and 1964, and has won the Ladies PGA Championship four times 1958, 1960, 1961 and 1963. She holds the world's record for longest recorded drive by a woman (272 yds.) and has the lowest recorded score on 18-hole course for a woman (1964). She also has a record of 13 tournaments won in a single year, 1963. Though Mickey announced her retirement in the 1960s, she continued to compete in golf tournaments.
Also in: Ladies Professional Golfers' Association Hall of Fame and World Golf Hall of Fame.

1974

de VICENZO, Robert
Golfer
A champion of over 130 tournaments all over the world, de Vicenzo turned professional in 1938 at the age of 15 and joined the U.S. tour in 1947. He won nine tournaments, but experienced a great disappointment at the 1968 U.S. Masters. The Argentinean would have been eligible for a playoff with Bob Goalby had his partner recorded a correct 3, rather than 4, on his playing card and had de Vicenzo checked the card more carefully before he signed it. The Masters committee ruled that there would be no playoff and declared Goalby the winner. But de Vicenzo had his notable 1967 British Open win to fall back on. He not only beat Jack Nicklaus by two strokes, but at the age of 44 became the oldest winner of the Open since Tom Morris, Sr, in 1867.

LITTLER, Eugene Alec
Golfer
Born July 21, 1930, in San Diego, Calif; wife Shirley: two children; enjoys working on vintage cars, particularly Rolls-Royces; underwent operation for cancer of the lymph glands spring of 1973, but made a complete recovery and was back on the golf tour in the fall; Golf Writers' Award 1973; Ben Hogan Award from U.S. Golf Association 1973; resides in La Jolla, Calif.

Often called "Gene the Machine," Littler came to the world of golf with a natural, perfectly rhythmic swing like Sam Snead; he was hailed as a likely successor to Hogan after he won his first tournament, the U.S. Amateur, in 1953. He did not disappoint anyone as he won the Walker Cup in 1953 and the San Diego Open in 1953; he participated on every U.S. Ryder Cup team from 1961 to 1971. Gene continued to win, with victories in the U.S. Open 1961, the Canadian Open 1965, and the World Series in 1966. Though he lost the 1970 U.S. Masters to Billy Casper, his boyhood rival from San Diego, he shares the record of 30 for the back nine with Jimmy Demaret and Ben Hogan. And Littler would have won more tournaments with his natural talent if he had had some of the fierce determination that got other golfers to

the top. However he seems satisfied to maintain his position among the leading players, make himself a substantial income and return to his home in La Jolla. Despite his relaxed attitude toward golf, he is one of the leading money makers with over $800,000 in prize money.
Also in: California Golf Hall of Fame.

TRAVERS, Jerome Dunstan
Golfer
Born May 19, 1887, in New York City, to a wealthy family; unsuccessful as a professional golfer; became an inspector for Pratt and Whitney Aircraft.

Travers was a brilliant amateur golfer who played when so inclined; in fact, he missed entering an amateur tournament for which he was the title holder. He played in his first U.S. Amateur when he was only 15 years old. Known as a great matchplayer, an excellent putter (he used Walter Travis' putter, the Schenectady), but only a passable driver, he had an even temperament and independent nature. As a man who had the ability to pull off recovery shots when in trouble, Travers won many tournaments: Nassau Invitational 1904, Metropolitan 1906, 1907, 1911 and 1913, U.S. Amateur 1907, 1908, 1912 and 1913, and a surprise victory at the U.S. Open 1915 at the end of his career.
Also in: Golf Hall of Fame, Citizens Savings Hall of Fame Athletic Museum; Professional Golfers' Association of America Hall of Fame and World Golf Hall of Fame.

1975

RUNYAN, Paul Scott
Golfer
Born July 12, 1908, in Hot Springs, Ark.

Only 5 ft. 7½ in, Paul Runyan was known as "Little Poison"; he won over 50 PGA tournaments in his career. Though he turned professional in 1922 and was leading money winner in 1933, he did not receive national attention until he won the 1934 PGA tournament against his old teacher, Craig Wood. In one of the three longest finals of the tournament, Runyan finally beat Wood at the 38th hole. One of the best putters in golf, he had an unconventional swing with a decided sway but still won seven tournaments in 1933 and 1934 and was leading money winner both years. He was also selected for the 1933 and 1935 Ryder Cup teams. With the biggest margin in the history of the PGA, Runyan beat Sam Snead 8 and 7 in 1938 and then won the Argentine Open. In later years he became an outstanding teacher of golf and won the U.S. Professional and the World Senior Professional in 1961 and 1962.
Also in: Golf Hall of Fame, Citizens Savings Hall of Fame Athletic Museum; and Professional Golfers' Association of America Hall of Fame.

SHUTE, Herman Densmore "Denny"
Golfer
Born October 25, 1904, in Cleveland, Ohio; picked up golf at age 3; professional at Portage Country Club in Akron, Ohio, from 1948 until retirement in 1971; died in Akron on May 13, 1974.

Denny Shute's favorite shot was a 3 wood off the 18th fairway at Pinehurst in the finals of the 1936 PGA Championship when his shot stopped 4 ft. from the pin to give him an eagle and a win. This was the first of two consecutive wins in the PGA Championship making Shute the last golfer to win two in a row—1936 and 1937. Three years earlier in 1933 he beat Johnny Goodman, the reigning U.S. champion, in a challenge match and won the British Open at St. Andrews after a playoff with Craig Wood. In 1937 he won another challenge match against the U.S. Open champion, this time Ralph Guldahl, but lost in the U.S. Open that year to Henry Cotton, 6 and 5. He was third in the Open of 1939 and runnerup in 1941. Shute, who turned professional in 1929, participated on the Ryder Cup teams of 1931, 1933 and 1937, and was still playing golf in 1955 when he tied for second in the PGA Seniors Championship.
Also in: Golf Hall of Fame, Citizens Savings Hall of Fame Athletic Museum; and Professional Golfers' Association of America Hall of Fame.

1976

WORSHAM, Lewis Elmer
Golfer
Born October 5, 1917, in Alta Vista, Va; divides time between Oakmont Country Club in Pennsylvania and Fort Lauderdale, Fla, as golf professional.

As the first television golfing champion, Lew Worsham made an exciting game of the 1947 U.S. Open. In the playoff against Sam Snead, both of the last putts were less than a yard from the hole, but Snead missed his shot by 30 in. Worsham again appeared before a television audience for the 1953 Tam O'Shanter World Championship. He needed a birdie 3 to tie Chandler Harper for the title. With a 110 yd. approach he used his wedge to hole an eagle for $25,000. Worsham began golfing as a caddie and turned professional in 1935 when 18 years old, and won seven PGA tournaments. He was top money winner in 1935 and was selected for the Ryder Cup team in 1947 when he and Ed Oliver won, 10 and 9, against Henry Cotton and Arthur Lees.
Also in: Golf Hall of Fame, Citizens Savings Hall of Fame Athletic Museum.

Arizona Golf Hall of Fame

PHOENIX, ARIZONA

Mailing Address: 3225 N. Central Avenue, 85012. *Tel:* (602) 264-7607. *Contact:* Don Fuller, Pres, Ariz. Golf Assn. *Location:* 100 mi. N.W. of Tucson, 110 mi. S. of Flagstaff, 325 mi. S.E. of Los Angeles, Calif, 250 mi. S.E. of Las Vegas, Nev. *Personnel:* Don Fuller, Pres; Ed Updegraff, V.Pres; Bob Laubach. V.Pres; William J. Orr,

Secy; Clarence Eickenburger, Treas; John Riggle, Exec. Dir. Not open to the public.

In 1968 when John Riggle, past president of the Arizona Golf Association, was researching the history of golf in Arizona, he decided to initiate a Hall of Fame to honor "outstanding contributions to golf in the state of Arizona." Soon thereafter, the first inductees were honored at a Hall of Fame dinner and received commemorative plaques.

Members: 24 as of 1976. Until 1975 a committee of three, John Riggle, Robert Goldwater and Bert Cavanaugh, selected members for the Hall of Fame. Beginning in 1975 members have been selected by the Arizona Golf Association Board of Directors. There is no limit on the number of selections made each year, but each member must be at least 60 years old "in order that years of service might merit the honor." Inductees are recognized at the State Seniors' Tournament held at Camelback Country Club in Phoenix.

1968 ALLEN, V. O. "Red." Professional golfer.
ALLISON, Bob. Sportswriter.
ARMSTRONG, Vic. Amateur golfer.
BANNISTER, Kim. Amateur golfer.
BOWERS, Herbert L. Professional golfer.
CORBETT, Hi. Amateur golfer.
GOLDWATER, Robert. Amateur golfer.
GRILL, Larry. Sportswriter.
LOW, Willie. Professional golfer.
TOVREA, Harold. Amateur golfer.
URICH, Doll, Professional golfer.

1969 ASKINS, Herbert. Amateur golfer.
BOUTELL, Bill. Amateur golfer.
BULLA, John. Professional golfer.
COGGINS, Milt. Professional golfer.
CURRY, Lewis. Amateur golfer.
MADISON, Gray. Amateur golfer.
RIGGLE, John. Amateur golfer.
UPDEGRAFF, Dr. Ed. Amateur golfer.
WARREN, Bob. Amateur golfer.

1970 McARTHUR, Charles H. Amateur golfer.
WANSA, Willie. Professional golfer.

1975 FARKAS, Bill. Professional golfer.
SNYDER, Art. Amateur golfer.

California Golf Hall of Fame

PEBBLE BEACH, CALIFORNIA

Mailing Address: Founders Lane, 93953. Tel. (408) 624-8241. *Contact:* Robert Hanna, Exec. Dir, Northern Calif. Golf Assn. *Location:* Spy Glass Hill Golf Course on Monterey Peninsula; approx. 90 mi. S. E. of San Francisco, 170 mi. S.W. of Sacramento, 250 mi. S.W. of Lake Tahoe. *Personnel:* Administration of Hall of Fame by Northern Calif. Golf Assn. under auspices of the Calif. Golf Writers Assn. Not open to the public.

In 1956 the California Golf Writers Association (CGWA) founded the California Golf Hall of Fame to honor outstanding contributors to the sport in California and outstanding golfers, either native Californians or those who had established outstanding golf records in the State. With members of the CGWA spread all over the State, the administration of the Hall of Fame was difficult, so the Northern California Golf Association (NCGA) supports the Hall of Fame. In the next five years the NCGA plans to purchase land on the Monterey Peninsula for a new golf course and new headquarters where the Hall of Fame will be permanently housed for public display. Photographs and playing records of each member as well as golf memorabilia are presently being collected for a permanent exhibit.

Members: 30 as of June 1977. (No elections were held in 1974 and 1975.) The Hall of Fame annually solicits nominations from the CGWA membership. These nominations are then handed over to the CGWA officers for election of one or two new members. Each member receives a special Hall of Fame plaque. Induction ceremonies have been held in conjunction with an awards dinner and golf tournament in the spring for several years, but hopefully in the future they will take place each January with the Bing Crosby National Pro-Amateur tournament. Two members of the Hall of Fame, Art Bell and Bing Crosby, are recipients of another award given annually by the CGWA, the Golden State Award, for outstanding contribution to the sport in California.

1960 DUTRA, Olin. See entry in Golf Hall of Fame, Citizens Savings Hall of Fame Athletic Museum. *Also in:* Professional Golfers' Association of America Hall of Fame.

FERRARI, Charles

LITTLE, William Lawson, Jr. See entry in American Golf Hall of Fame, 1970. *Also in:* Golf Hall of Fame, Citizens Savings Hall of Fame Athletic Museum; and Professional Golfers' Association of America Hall of Fame.

MANGRUM, Lloyd Eugene. See entry in Golf Hall of Fame, Citizens Savings Hall of Fame Athletic Museum. *Also in:* Professional Golfers' Association of America Hall of Fame.

WARD, Marvin Harvey. See entry in Golf Hall of Fame, Citizens Savings Hall of Fame Athletic Museum.

1961 HUNTER, Willie

NEVILLE, Jack

SMITH, Macdonald "Mac." See entry in Golf Hall of Fame, Citizens Savings Hall of Fame Athletic Museum. *Also in:* Professional Golfers' Association of America Hall of Fame.

1962 GRANT, Douglas

WARD, Edward Harvie. See entry in Golf Hall of Fame, Citizens Savings Hall of Fame Athletic Museum. *Also in:* North Carolina Sports Hall of Fame.

1963 BLACK, John

HARRISON, E. J. "Dutch." *Also in:* Professional Golfers' Association of America Hall of Fame.

1966 FRY, Mark

1967 LoPRESTI, Tom

1968 CASPER, William Earl, Jr. See entry in American Golf Hall of Fame, 1972.

1969 LEMA, Tony

SEAVER, Charles

1970 CALLISON, Verne

TAYLOR, Dr. Frank

1971 BELL, Art

ROSBURG, Bob

1972 CROSBY, Bing

LITTLER, Eugene Alec. See entry in American Golf Hall of Fame, 1974.

1973 GOGGINS, Willie

HAY, Peter

1976 HINES, Jimmy

Colorado Golf Hall of Fame

DENVER, COLORADO

Mailing Address: c/o Joan Birkland, 615 Bellaire, 80220. *Tel:* (303) 333-4197. *Contact:* Harry Farrar. *Location:* Approx. 30 mi. S.E. of Boulder, 60 mi. N. of Colorado Springs, 100 mi. S. of Cheyenne, Wyo, 200 mi. E. of Grand Junction. *Personnel:* Robert Rolander, Pres; 14 mem. Exec. Comt. *Nearby Hall of Fame:* Ski (Vail, 70 mi. W.).

The Colorado Golf Hall of Fame, a nonprofit organization governed by Colorado Golf Hall of Fame, Inc, was founded by Noble Chalfant in 1973 to honor those who have contributed to golf in Colorado. This year the Hall of Fame will open a display area at Park Hill Country Club in Denver.

Members: 17 as of 1977. Outstanding contributors to golf in Colorado are nominated and elected by a Selection Committee appointed by the Executive Committee; there is no limit to the number elected each year. New members are inducted into the Hall of Fame at an annual banquet in September at the Park Hill Golf Club, Denver, and receive portraits of themselves.

1973 HILL, Dave. Winner of many pro tour events, former Ryder Cup team member and Vardon Trophy winner, representing lowest round average among top pros during a year.

LIND, Charles "Babe." One of Colorado's greatest amateur golfers.

ZAHARIAS, Mildred "Babe" (dec). Greatest woman golfer of her time. See entry in American Golf Hall of Fame, 1965. *Also in:* Ladies Professional Golfers' Association Hall of Fame, National Track and Field Hall of Fame, Professional Golfers' Association of America Hall of Fame; Golf Hall of Fame, Track and Field Hall of Fame and Women's Basketball Hall of Fame, Citizens Savings Hall of Fame Athletic Museum; United States Track and Field Hall of Fame and World Golf Hall of Fame.

1974 IRWIN, Hale. Former U.S. Open champion and one of the top money winners of all time.

McINTIRE, Barbara. Winner of every amateur women's tournament in the United States and Great Britain.

MORRIS, N. C. "Tub." For many years Colorado's Mr. Golf; director of hundreds of local and state tournaments.

WRIGHT, Claude. Winner of every men's amateur golf tournament in Colorado.

1975 CLARK, Bob, Sr. Outstanding Colorado amateur golfer for many years.

FLENIKEN, Carol. One of Colorado's outstanding women golfers and winner of many amateur tournaments.

ROGERS, John. Outstanding as a longtime club pro and one of Colorado's finest professional players.

TUTT, William Thayer. As boss of Broadmoor Hotel, he brought many national golf tournaments to the hotel's courses. *Also in:* United States Hockey Hall of Fame.

1976 BELL, Judy. One of Colorado's best women golfers and member of important national golf committees.

CHALFANT, Noble. Outstanding club pro and player.

DUDLEY, Ed. Outstanding club pro and player.

HAINES, Jim. Renowned in Colorado and nationally as a pioneer golf course superintendent and originator of acclaimed turf management systems.

ROOT, Gene. Outstanding club pro and player.

ZESCH, Oscar. Longtime contributor to all phases of Colorado golf through donations of his time and money to tournaments.

Connecticut Golf Hall of Fame

HARTFORD, CONNECTICUT

Mailing Address: 11 Asylum Street, 06103. *Tel:* (203) 522-4171. *Contact:* Gerald A. Stewart, Dir. *Location:* Approx. 90 mi. S.W. of Boston, Mass, 105 mi. N.E. of New York City. *Personnel:* Gerald A. Stewart, Dir; volunteers from Greater Hartford Junior Chamber of Commerce. *Nearby Halls of Fame:* Baseball (Cooperstown, N.Y, 130 mi. N.W.), Basketball (Springfield, Mass, 25 mi. N.), Bicycle (Staten Island, N.Y, 135 mi. S.W.), Flight (Elmira, N.Y, 205 mi. N.W.), Football (Kingston, R.I, 65 mi. S.E.), Harness Racing (Goshen, N.Y, 85 mi. S.W.), Heritage (New York City, 105 mi. S.W.), Horseshoe Pitchers (Corning, N.Y, 220 mi. N.W.), Horse Racing (Saratoga Springs, N.Y, 110 mi. N.W.), Ice Skating (Boston, Mass, 90 mi. N.E, Newburgh, N.Y, 75 mi. S.W.), Music (New York City, 105 mi. S.W.), Tennis (Newport, R.I, 100 mi. S.E.).

The Connecticut Golf Hall of Fame honors Connecticut golfers who have made outstanding contributions to the game. Founded in 1955, the idea was originated by Stuart "Skip" Henderson of the *Hartford Times.* Robert P. Nichols, Gerald A. Stewart and Gene F. Bruyette worked to implement the idea of a Hall of Fame.

Members: 22 as of 1977. One golfer or promoter of golf who has made outstanding contributions to golf in Connecticut is inducted each year. A committee of four or five interested and knowledgeable people (in the past, newspaper editors William Lee, *Hartford Courent,* and Fred Post, *Middletown Post;* golfing amateur and first member of the Connecticut Golf Hall of Fame, Bob Grant) is coordinated with Gerald Stewart to select the names of four or five outstanding Connecticut golfers. The Connecticut Sports Writers' Alliance, consisting of approximately 250 members, vote by mail to elect one person from the list of names. At the annual spring Connecticut Professional Golfers' Association meeting, the new member receives a replica of the Hall of Fames' permanent trophy, which is kept at Weathersfield Country Club.

1955 GRANT, Bobby
CLARE, Charlie

1957 SHERMAN, Mike

1958 ROSS, Frank

1959 BISHOP, Georgiana

1960 MANDLY, Holly

1961 BOROS, Julius Nicholas. See entry in American Golf Hall of Fame, 1971. *Also in:* Golf Hall of Fame, Citizens Savings Hall of Fame Athletic Museum; Professional Golfers' Association of America Hall of Fame.

1962 SARAZEN, Eugene. See entry in American Golf Hall of Fame, 1965. *Also in:* Golf Hall of Fame, Citizens Savings Hall of Fame Athletic Museum; Professional Golfers' Association of America Hall of Fame and World Golf Hall of Fame.

1963 BURKE, Billy. See entry in Golf Hall of Fame, Citizens Savings Hall of Fame Athletic Museum. *Also in:* Professional Golfers' Association of America Hall of Fame.

1964 MANERO, Tony

1965 TORZA, Felice

1966 REARDON, Dr. John

1967 O'SULLIVAN, Pat

1968 LENCZYK, Dr. Ted

1969 CRONIN, Grace Lenczyk

1970 NEALE, W. H. "Widdy"

1971 BURKE, Eddie

1972 FORD, Doug. See entry in Golf Hall of Fame, Citizens Savings Hall of Fame Athletic Museum. *Also in:* Professional Golfers' Association of America Hall of Fame.

1973 NETTLEBLADT, Harry

1974 SIDEROWF, Dick

1975 COURVILLE, Gerry

1976 DOLAN, Marcia

Ladies Professional Golfers' Association Hall of Fame

AUGUSTA, GEORGIA

Mailing Address: 919 Third Avenue, New York, N.Y, 10003. *Tel:* (212) 751-8181. *Contact:* Jeff Adams, Publicity Chmn. *Location:* August Golf and Country Club; 65 mi. S.W. of Columbia, S.C, 110 mi. S.W. of Savannah, 110 mi. N.W. of Charleston, S.C, 130 mi. S.W. of Charlotte, N.C, 135 mi. E. of Atlanta. *Admission:* Free, 8 a.m. to midnight, Tuesday-Sunday. *Nearby Halls of Fame:* Auto Racing (Darlington, S.C, 140 mi. N.E.), Golf (Pinehurst, N.C, 180 mi. N.E.).

In 1950 a group of six men, probably members of the press, formed a committee and elected seven outstanding women golfers into a Ladies Golf Hall of Fame. In 1967 these seven women became the first members of the Ladies Professional Golfers' Association (Ladies PGA) Hall of Fame established at an annual meeting in Corpus Christi, Texas. At the Augusta (Georgia) Golf and Country Club, an alcove for the Ladies Professional Golf Association Hall of Fame was set up by Fred Corcoran, founder of the Ladies PGA. Many pictures and trophies, including those of Mildred "Babe" Zaharias, are displayed there to honor the achievements of women in golf.

Members: 14 as of 1977. Eligible women golfers must have ten consecutive years of membership in the Ladies PGA and must have participated in: 1) 30 official tour events, with two major championships, 2) 35 official tour events, with one major championship, or 3) 40 official tour events, with no major championships. It is more or less an unwritten law that Hall of Fame members be retired from active participation on the tour. Until 1976 an executive board of five or six members, selected by Ladies PGA members, elected eligible women golfers to the Hall of Fame. Since 1976 this responsibility has been that of the Player Council, five members each representing an age group of players on the Ladies PGA tour. Any number of eligible women could be elected in one year and were inducted either at the annual meeting of the Association or its golf championship. Presently Association officials are reviewing their selection procedures and changes may occur in the near future.

1950 CURTIS, Margaret. See entry in Golf Hall of Fame, Citizens Savings Hall of Fame Athletic Museum.

FRASER, Alexa Stirling. See entry in Golf Hall of Fame, Citizens Savings Hall of Fame Athletic Museum.

HOYT, Beatrix. See entry in Golf Hall of Fame, Citizens Savings Athletic Museum Hall of Fame.

HURD, Dorothy Campbell. See entry in American Golf Hall of Fame, 1969. *Also in:* Golf Hall of Fame, Citizens Savings Hall of Fame Athletic Museum.

VAN WIE, Virginia. See entry in Golf Hall of Fame, Citizens Savings Hall of Fame Athletic Museum.

VARE, Glenna Collett. See entry in American Golf Hall of Fame, 1966. *Also in:* Golf Hall of Fame, Citizens Savings Hall of Fame Athletic Museum; and World Golf Hall of Fame.

WETHERED, Joyce (Lady Heathcoat Amory). See entry in American Golf Hall of Fame, 1965. *Also in:* World Golf Hall of Fame.

1951 BERG, Patricia. See entry in American Golf Hall of Fame, 1972. *Also in:* Golf Hall of Fame, Citizens Savings Hall of Fame Athletic Museum; and World Golf Hall of Fame.

JAMESON, Elizabcth. Scc cntry in Golf Hall of Fame, Citizens Savings Hall of Fame Athletic Museum.

SUGGS, Louise. See entry in Golf Hall of Fame, Citizens Savings Hall of Fame Athletic Museum.

ZAHARIAS, Mildred Didrikson "Babe" (dec). See entry in American Golf Hall of Fame, 1965. *Also in:* Colorado Golf Hall of Fame, National Track and Field Hall of Fame, Professional Golfers' Association Hall of Fame; Golf Hall of Fame, Track and Field Hall of Fame and Women's Basketball Hall of Fame, Citizens Savings Hall of Fame Athletic Museum; United States Track and Field Hall of Fame and World Golf Hall of Fame.

1960 RAWLS, Elizabeth Earle "Betsy." See entry in Golf Hall of Fame, Citizens Savings Hall of Fame Athletic Museum.

1964 WRIGHT, Mary Kathryn "Mickey." See entry in American Golf Hall of Fame, 1973. *Also in:* World Golf Hall of Fame.

1974 WHITWORTH, Kathrynne Ann

National Association of Left-Handed Golfers Hall of Fame

CAMDEN, SOUTH CAROLINA

Mailing Address: P.O. Box 489, 29020. *Tel:* (803) 432-4244. *Contact:* Frank Elder, Exec. Secy.-Treas. *Location:* Approx 20 mi. E. of Columbia, 100 mi. N. of Charleston, 65 mi. S. of Charlotte, N.C, 90 mi. N.E. of Augusta, Ga. *Personnel:* Dick Bily, Pres; Tom Braddock, V.Pres; Frank L. Elder, Exec. Secy.-Treas. *Nearby Halls of Fame:* Automobile Racing (Darlington, 50 mi. E.), Flight (Manteo, N.C, 240 mi. N.E.), Golf (Pinehurst, N.C, 60 mi. N.).

At a board meeting of the National Association of Left-Handed Golfers (NALG) on July 27, 1961, at Sedgefield Inn, Greensboro, N.C, a motion was passed to establish a Hall of Fame of left-handed golfers, to honor five living and five deceased left-handed golfers in 1961, and elect one living and one deceased member each consecutive year. The Hall is a non-profit organization governed by the National Association of Left-Handed Golfers.

Members: 23 as of 1976. Living and deceased golfers are nominated by an Executive Committee of the Board of Governors and one of each is elected by the Board of Governors of the NALG. There have been years in which no one was elected. Selection is based on consistency of playing record in national events, participation in state and regional activities, contribution to the NALG and overall character and reputation. Interesting to note is that all five honorary life members are right-handed golfers. Each member of the Hall of Fame is presented with a special NALG crest at an annual dinner held during the week of the National Left-Handed Amateur Tournament.

1961 CHISOLM, Scott (dec.)
DOUGLAS, Al
EVERETT, Alvin (dec.)
FREEDMAN, Michael
GAMMON, Nancy
HARLOW, Lillian
JAMES, Norman S. "Pinkie"
JONES, Robert T. See entry in American Golf Hall of Fame, 1965. *Also in*: Golf Hall of Fame, Citizens Savings Hall of Fame Athletic Museum; Professional Golfers Association of America Hall of Fame and World Golf Hall of Fame.
LILLARD, Ross (dec.)
RICHTER, Ben (dec.)
ROMBERGER, Robert (dec.)
SHOEMAKER, Harry
WALTERS, Jack
WOODS, Len

1962 CHARLES, Robert

1966 GARRARD, Ralph
PORRITT, Sam (dec.)

1967 ELDERKIN, C. C. "Pete"

1968 BARBOUR, Jess (dec.)
WILDER, Robert E.

1969 REGISTER, J. Willard "Bob"

1974 SHARP, W. W, Jr. (dec.)
TURNER, Joe (dec.)

North Dakota Golf Hall of Fame

FARGO, NORTH DAKOTA

Mailing Address: P.O. Box 2231, 58102. *Tel:* (701) 235-6418. *Contact:* Kou Miller, Secy.-Treas, N.D. State Golf Assn. *Location:* 180 mi. E. of Bismarck, 200 mi. S.E. of Minot, 190 mi. S. of Winnipeg, Man, 210 mi. N.W. of Minneapolis, Minn, 220 mi. N. of Sioux Falls, S.Dak. *Personnel:* Seven mem. Bd. of Regents; four mem. Bd. of Governors. *Nearby Halls of Fame:* Water Sports (Winnipeg, Man.) Hockey (Eveleth, Minn, 200 mi. N.E.), Softball (Jamestown, N.Dak, 90 mi. W.).

A committee of the North Dakota State Golf Association met on December 1, 1966, to discuss the feasibility of a Hall of Fame and to decide on recommendations for presentation to the Association's Board of Directors in the spring of 1967. Research was conducted by Committee members to establish rules and regulations for the Hall of Fame. Board members Ed Agnew, Reece Dickey, Ernie Hauser and Camy Mills were involved in founding the North Dakota Golf Hall of Fame in 1968. Formed to honor outstanding North Dakota golfers and contributors to golf, the Hall of Fame sponsors an annual Senior Golf tournament, held during the first week of August. The tournament moves to a different town each year; in 1976 it was held in Minot and in 1977 it will be held at the Oxbow Country Club in Fargo. About 200 golfers pay a $2.00 entry fee (senior golfers pay an additional $5.00), which helps support the Hall of Fame and a $300 Junior Golf scholarship. Started in 1967 – 1968 the scholarship goes to the annual winner of the Junior Golf tournament and is sent to the college of his/her choice to help with school expenses.

Members: 20 as of 1976. Members are selected on the basis of outstanding contribution to golf in North Dakota, either as players or as supporters. Five members were elected when the Hall was founded and one or two have been elected each year since. The members of the Board of Regents representing the populous areas of the state nominate people from their areas. The Board of Governors elect members by a majority vote. Those on the Board of Regents and the Board of Governors serve three to four years. During the Senior Golf tournament, a Hall of Fame banquet and program are held; special guests may include the governor or state senators, Lawrence Welk and other celebrities, as well as high school and college choirs. New members receive a special plaque; the permanent Hall of Fame plaque with the names of the members is displayed in the clubhouse sponsoring the Senior Golf tournament.

1969 COOK, Paul
HULL, Thomas
KOSTELECKY, Bill
O'LEARY, Paul
REUTER, John, Jr.

1970 HAUSER, Ernie
HINTGEN, Jack
WINTER, W. V. "Doc"

1971 BEYER, Charles
GARRANEY, James E.

1972 BARRETT, James
CRAM, George, Jr.

1973 DAHL, Herman
HILBER, Jack

1974 AGNEW, Robert

1975 McCOY, G. W.
PETERSON, George
WESTLIE, Gordon

1976 BRIDSTON, J. B.
SCHUMACHER, Ralph

Professional Golfers' Association of America Hall of Fame

LAKE PARK, FLORIDA

Mailing Address: P.O. Box 12458, 33403. Tel. (305) 848-3481. *Contact:* Earl Collings, Dir. of Communications, Professional Golfers' Assn. of America (PGA). *Location:* Approx. 55 mi. N. of Ft. Lauderdale, 80 mi. N. of Miami, 150 mi. S.E. of Orlando, 170 mi. S.E. of Tampa. *Nearby Halls of Fame:* Swimming (Ft. Lauderdale), Stars (Orlando).

The suggestion for a Professional Golfers' Association of America (PGA) Hall of Fame came originally from Grantland Rice, one of the world's best-known sports writers, in a syndicated newspaper column. In 1940 a joint panel of golf writers and PGA representatives founded the Hall of Fame to "preserve and present the excellence of the greats" of golf and selected the first 12 members. Construction of a permanent shrine at the new PGA headquarter complex in Palm Beach, Fla, will begin in 1977 and the Hall of Fame should be open to the public within the next few years.

Members: 45 as of January 1977. Methods for selecting members have changed several times since 1940 when the first 12 were elected. There were no additions to the membership until 1953 when the Golf Writers' Association of America selected three more members. From 1954 to 1958 a new format allowed only one new member each year, nominated by local PGA sections and elected by PGA members and people on the PGA press list. In 1959 PGA members were authorized to elect more than one member, but election was again limited to one each year in 1965. Between 1960 and 1965 electors changed from PGA and Hall of Fame members to just Hall of Fame members. Presently, each member is nominated and elected by a Selection Committee made up of PGA Hall of Fame members, PGA officers, Executive Committee and past presidents, the commissioner of golf, editors of the six leading golf publications, the executive directors of the major golf associations, and the officers and executive committee of the Golf Writers' Association of America. Each Selection Committee member receives one vote/nominee and each nominee receiving more than one-third of the total votes is elected to the Hall of Fame. Each member, a golfer retired from active competition, receives a plaque at an official PGA banquet held each year at the Seniors' championship. Mildred "Babe" Zaharias became the first female member when her husband accepted her posthumous award at the Seniors' championship on January 28, 1977.

1940 ANDERSON, Willie (dec.). See entry in American Golf Hall of Fame, 1968. *Also in:* Golf Hall of Fame, Citizens Savings Hall of Fame Athletic Museum; and World Golf Hall of Fame.

ARMOUR, Thomas Dickson (dec.). See entry in American Golf Hall of Fame, 1965. *Also in:* Golf Hall of Fame, Citizens Savings Hall of Fame Athletic Museum; and World Golf Hall of Fame.

BARNES, James M. (dec.). See entry in American Golf Hall of Fame, 1973. *Also in:* Golf Hall of Fame, Citizens Savings Hall of Fame Athletic Museum.

EVANS, Charles Jr. "Chick." Amateur golfer. See entry in American Golf Hall of Fame, 1965. *Also in:* Golf Hall of Fame, Citizens Savings Hall of Fame Athletic Museum; and World Golf Hall of Fame.

HAGEN, Walter (dec.). See entry in American Golf Hall of Fame, 1965. *Also in:* Golf Hall of Fame, Citizens Savings Hall of Fame Athletic Museum; and World Golf Hall of Fame.

JONES, Robert Tyre, Jr. Amateur golfer (dec.). See entry in American Golf Hall of Fame, 1965. *Also in:* Golf Hall of Fame, Citizens Savings Hall of Fame Athletic Museum; National Association of Left-Handed Golfers Hall of Fame and World Golf Hall of Fame.

McDERMOTT, John J. See entry in Golf Hall of Fame, Citizens Savings Hall of Fame Athletic Museum (Induction Year Unrecorded).

OUIMET, Francis D. Amateur golfer (dec.). See entry in American Golf Hall of Fame, 1965. *Also in:* Golf Hall of Fame, Citizens Savings Hall of Fame Athletic Museum; and World Golf Hall of Fame.

SARAZEN, Eugene. See entry in American Golf Hall of Fame, 1965. *Also in:* Golf Hall of Fame, Citizens Savings Hall of Fame Athletic Museum; Connecticut Golf Hall of Fame and World Golf Hall of Fame.

SMITH, Alex (dec.). See entry in Golf Hall of Fame, Citizens Savings Hall of Fame Athletic Museum (Induction Year Unrecorded).

TRAVERS, Jerome Dunstan (dec.). Amateur golfer. See entry in American Golf Hall of Fame, 1974. *Also in:* Golf Hall of Fame, Citizens Savings Hall of Fame Athletic Museum; and World Golf Hall of Fame.

TRAVIS, Walter J. (dec.). See entry in American Golf Hall of Fame, 1971. *Also in:* Golf Hall of Fame, Citizens Savings Hall of Fame Athletic Museum.

1953 HOGAN, William Benjamin. See entry in American Golf Hall of Fame, 1965. *Also in:* Golf Hall of Fame, Citizens Savings Hall of Fame Athletic Museum; and World Golf Hall of Fame.

NELSON, John Byron, Jr. See entry in American Golf Hall of Fame, 1965. *Also in:* Golf Hall of Fame, Citizens Savings Hall of Fame Athletic Museum; and World Golf Hall of Fame.

SNEAD, Samuel Jackson. See entry in American Golf Hall of Fame, 1965. *Also in:* Golf Hall of Fame, Citizens Savings Hall of Fame Athletic Museum; and World Golf Hall of Fame.

1954 SMITH, Macdonald (dec.). See entry in Golf Hall of Fame, Citizens Savings Hall of Fame Athletic Museum (Induction Year Unrecorded). *Also in:* California Golf Hall of Fame.

1955 DIEGEL, Leo (dec.). See entry in Golf Hall of Fame, Citizens Savings Hall of Fame Athletic Museum (Induction Year Unrecorded).

1956 WOOD, Craig Ralph (dec.). See entry in Golf Hall of Fame, Citizens Savings Hall of Fame Athletic Museum (Induction Year Unrecorded).

1957 SHUTE, Herman Densmore "Denny." See entry in Golf Hall of Fame, Citizens Savings Hall of Fame Athletic Museum (Induction Year Unrecorded).

1958 SMITH, Horton (dec.). See entry in Golf Hall of Fame, Citizens Savings Hall of Fame Athletic Museum (Induction Year Unrecorded).

1959 COOPER, Harry. See entry in Golf Hall of Fame, Citizens Savings Hall of Fame Athletic Museum (Induction Year Unrecorded).

HUTCHISON, Jock, Sr. See entry in American Golf Hall of Fame, 1971. *Also in:* Golf Hall of Fame, Citizens Savings Hall of Fame Athletic Museum.

RUNYAN, Paul Scott. See entry in Golf Hall of Fame, Citizens Savings Hall of Fame Athletic Museum (Induction Year Unrecorded).

1960 BRADY, Michael Joseph (dec.)

DEMARET, James Newton. See entry in American Golf Hall of Fame, 1973. *Also in:* Golf Hall of Fame, Citizens Savings Hall of Fame Athletic Museum.

McLEOD, Frederick Robertson (dec.)

1961 FARRELL, Johnny. See entry in Golf Hall of Fame, Citizens Savings Hall of Fame Athletic Museum.

LITTLE, William Lawson, Jr. (dec.). See entry in American Golf Hall of Fame, 1970. *Also in:* California Golf Hall of Fame; and Golf Hall of Fame, Citizens Savings Hall of Fame Athletic Museum.

PICARD, Henry C. See entry in Golf Hall of Fame, Citizens Savings Hall of Fame Athletic Museum.

1962 DUTRA, Olin. See entry in Golf Hall of Fame, Citizens Savings Hall of Fame Athletic Museum (Induction Year Unrecorded). *Also in:* California Golf Hall of Fame.

HARRISON, E. J. "Dutch." *Also in:* California Golf Hall of Fame.

1963 GULDAHL, Ralph. See entry in American Golf Hall of Fame, 1972. *Also in:* Golf Hall of Fame, Citizens Savings Hall of Fame Athletic Museum.

REVOLTA, John. See entry in Golf Hall of Fame, Citizens Savings Hall of Fame Athletic Museum.

1964 DUDLEY, Edward Bishop (dec.)

MANGRUM, Lloyd Eugene (dec.). See entry in Golf Hall of Fame, Citizens Savings Hall of Fame Athletic Museum (Induction Year Unrecorded). *Also in:* California Golf Hall of Fame.

1965 GHEZZI, Victor. See entry in Golf Hall of Fame, Citizens Savings Hall of Fame Athletic Museum.

1966 BURKE, William "Billy" (dec.). See entry in Golf Hall of Fame, Citizens Savings Hall of Fame Athletic Museum. *Also in:* Connecticut Golf Hall of Fame.

1967 CRUICKSHANK, Robert Allan (dec.)

1968 HARBERT, Melvin R. "Chick"

1969 HARPER, Chandler

1974 BOROS, Julis Nicholas. See entry in American Golf Hall of Fame, 1971. *Also in:* Golf Hall of Fame, Citizens Savings Hall of Fame Athletic Museum; and Connecticut Golf Hall of Fame.

MIDDLECOFF, Dr. Cary "Doc." See entry in American Golf Hall of Fame, 1971. *Also in:* Golf Hall of Fame, Citizens Savings Hall of Fame Athletic Museum.

1975 BURKE, Jack, Jr. See entry in Golf Hall of Fame, Citizens Savings Hall of Fame Athletic Museum (Induction Year Unrecorded).

FORD, Doug. See entry in Golf Hall of Fame, Citizens Savings Hall of Fame Athletic Museum (Induction Year Unrecorded). *Also in:* Connecticut Golf Hall of Fame.

1976 ZAHARIAS, Mildred Didrikson "Babe" (dec.). See entry in American Golf Hall of Fame, 1965. *Also in:* Colorado Golf Hall of Fame, Ladies Professional Golfers' Association Hall of Fame, World Golf Hall of Fame, United States Track and Field Hall of Fame, National Track and Field Hall of Fame; Golf Hall of Fame, Track and Field Hall of Fame and Women's Basketball Hall of Fame, Citizens Savings Hall of Fame Athletic Museum.

World Golf Hall of Fame

PINEHURST, NORTH CAROLINA

Mailing Address: World Golf Hall of Fame, 28374. *Contact:* Norma M. Smith, Cur. *Location:* 30 mi. N.W. of Fayetteville, 60 mi. S.W. of Raleigh, 70 mi. E. of Charlotte, 110 mi. N.E. of Columbia. *Admission:* 9 to 5 daily. Adults $2.00, children 50¢, family $4.50. *Personnel:* Donald C. Collett, Pres; Mrs. Norma M. Smith, Cur. *Nearby Halls of Fame:* Auto Racing (Darlington, S.C, 60 mi. N.), Flight (Manteo, 210 mi. N.E.).

The World Golf Hall of Fame was founded by Diamondhead Carp and Donald C. Collett and was opened on September 11, 1974, dedicated by President Gerald R. Ford. It is a nonprofit organization supported through public donations. The 500-year history of golf is depicted on a 90-foot display, the Golf History Wall, and various memorabilia are displayed in the exhibition hall. In the shrine are plaques for each person elected to the World Golf Hall of Fame. The buildings cover nearly 30,000 square feet and are adjacent to Pinehurst Country Club's much heralded Number Two Course, designed by the late Donald Ross. Each year the World Golf Hall of Fame holds a Hall of Fame Day, during which golfers try to match the scores of Arnold Palmer and Gary Player, and the Hall of Fame Celebrity Pro-Am, during Pinehurst's Grand Week of Golf. The Hall of Fame "Golfmobile" tours approximately 30 Professional Golfers Association of America tournaments throughout the country every year to display mementos and pictures of great golfers. Junior, patron and executive sponsorships are encouraged by the "Put Your Name in the Hall of Fame" program that prints sponsors' names on computerized listing kept in the Hall of Fame. Sponsors also receive the quarterly *Hall of Fame Happenings.* The World Golf Hall of Fame is a member of the Association of Sports Museums and Halls of Fame.

Members: 26 as of 1976. Members may be elected by the Golf Writers' Association of America from three categories: Modern Era (since 1939), Pre-Modern Era and Distinguished Service. They must receive at least 75 percent of all possible votes and they must have made great achievements or contributions to golf. Induction ceremonies take place every year in September at the World Golf Hall of Fame as part of the Pinehurst's Grand Week of Golf.

1974

BERG, Patricia Jane
Modern Era
See entry in American Golf Hall of Fame, 1972.
Also in: Golf Hall of Fame, Citizens Savings Hall of Fame Athletic Museum; and Ladies Professional Golfers' Association Hall of Fame.

HAGEN, Walter Charles
Pre-Modern Era
See entry in American Golf Hall of Fame, 1965.
Also in: Golf Hall of Fame, Citizens Savings Hall of Fame Athletic Museum; and Professional Golfers' Association of America Hall of Fame.

HOGAN, William Benjamin
Modern Era
See entry in American Golf Hall of Fame, 1965.
Also in: Golf Hall of Fame, Citizens Savings Hall of Fame Athletic Museum; and Professional Golfers' Association of America Hall of Fame.

JONES, Robert Tyre, Jr.
Pre-Modern Era
See entry in American Golf Hall of Fame, 1965.
Also in: Golf Hall of Fame, Citizens Savings Hall of Fame Athletic Museum; Professional Golfers' Association of America Hall of Fame and National Association of Left-Handed Golfers Hall of Fame.

NELSON, John Byron, Jr.
Modern era
See entry in American Golf Hall of Fame, 1965.
Also in: Golf Hall of Fame, Citizens Savings Hall of Fame Athletic Museum; and Professional Golfers' Association of America Hall of Fame.

NICKLAUS, Jack William
Modern Era
Born January 21, 1940, in Columbus, Ohio; son of pharmacist; earned letters in basketball and baseball in high school; left Ohio State Univ. two semesters before finishing a degree in business administration; married; five children; in insurance while playing as amateur golfer; enjoys business and fishing; wrote *My 55 Ways to Lower Your Golf Score;* designed a golf course in Toronto, Ont, which opened late 1976.

Jack Nicklaus probably has more records in golf than any other participant in the sport, including that of being the largest money winner in golf with $2,250,245, from the time he turned professional in 1962 until December, 1974. He is a man of great power and deep concentration; he uses the interlocking grip and is very deliberate in his shots and is considered a slow player. Nicklaus has won numerous championships; U.S. Amateur 1959 and 1961, U.S. Open 1962, 1967 and 1972, U.S. Masters 1963, 1965, 1966 and 1972, U.S. PGA 1963, 1971 and 1973, British Open 1966 and 1970, Australian Open 1964, 1968 and 1971, and the Hawaiian Open 1974. He is the only golfer to have won the British and U.S. Opens, U.S. PGA, U.S. Amateur and U.S. Masters twice each; he completed the Grand Slam of golf by winning the 1963 British Open. He had the lowest scoring round in the British Open (65 in 1973) and the low score for the U.S. Masters (271 in 1965). He also holds the record for the lowest round in golf (64 in 1965) and the lowest 72-hole aggregate (275 at the U.S. Open in 1967). Even as an amateur, Nicklaus was the youngest golfer to win the U.S. National Amateur in 50 years (19 in 1959) and won the Walker Cup, the Royal St. George's Gold Challenge Cup and the World Amateur Team championship. He played on the World (Canada) Cup Team 1963, 1964, 1966, 1967, 1971 and 1973, and on the Ryder Cup team 1969, 1971 and 1973.

OUIMET, Francis D.
Pre-Modern Era
See entry in American Golf Hall of Fame, 1965.
Also in: Golf Hall of Fame, Citizens Savings Hall of Fame Athletic Museum; and Professional Golfers' Association of America Hall of Fame.

PALMER, Arnold Daniel
Modern Era
See entry in American Golf Hall of Fame, 1969.

PLAYER, Gary
Modern Era
Born November 1, 1935, in Johannesburg, Transvaal, South Africa; small stature; retreats to farm in South Africa between tournaments; believes in staying healthy by jogging, lifting weights, exercising and eating natural foods; outspoken; usually dresses in black on golf course; has written *Grand Slam Golf, Play Golf with Player, 124 Golf Lessons* and *Positive Golf;* Richardson Award from Golf Writers' Association of America 1975.

As an author, Gary Player really has a story to tell about the world of golf. He has an outstanding career, beginning at age 15 and including tournament wins in the South Africa Open 1956, 1960, 1965–1969 and 1972, Australian Open 1958, 1962, 1963, 1965, 1969 and 1970, Australian Masters and PGA, and the U.S. Masters 1961 and 1974, U.S. PGA 1962 and 1972, U.S. Open 1965, British Open 1959, 1968 and 1974, Brazilian Open, Australian Dunlop International, Piccadilly Match Play five times, World Series 1965, 1968 and 1972. Player also won individual championships at the Canada Cup 1965 and in 1974 won nine championships following surgery in 1973. Player was the first non-American to win the U.S. Masters, the first South African to win the U.S. Open, and the only golfer to win so many major events throughout the world. He turned professional in 1952, became one of four to win the four major titles of the world, was part of the Big Three (others are Nicklaus and Palmer) and earned over $1 million in his 21-year career. He holds the record for low score in non-PGA tournaments (59 in the Brazilian Open in 1974).

SARAZEN, Gene
Pre-Modern Era
See entry in American Golf Hall of Fame, 1965. *Also in:* Golf Hall of Fame, Citizens Savings Hall of Fame Athletic Museum; Connecticut Golf Hall of Fame and Professional Golfers' Association of America Hall of Fame.

SNEAD, Samuel Jackson
Pre-Modern Era
See entry in American Golf Hall of Fame, 1965. *Also in:* Golf Hall of Fame. Citizens Savings Hall of Fame Athletic Museum; Professional Golfers' Association of America Hall of Fame and West Virginia Sports Writers Hall of Fame.

VARDON, Harry
Pre-Modern Era
See entry in American Golf Hall of Fame, 1965.

ZAHARIAS, Mildred Didrikson "Babe"
Modern Era
See entry in American Golf Hall of Fame, 1965.
Also in: Colorado Golf Hall of Fame, Ladies Professional Golfers' Association Hall of Fame, Professional Golfers' Association of America Hall of Fame, National Track and Field Hall of Fame, United States Track and Field Hall of Fame; Golf Hall of Fame, Track and Field Hall of Fame and Women's Basketball Hall of Fame, Citizens Savings Hall of Fame Athletic Museum.

1975

ANDERSON, Willie
Pre-Modern Era
See entry in American Golf Hall of Fame, 1968.
Also in: Golf Hall of Fame, Citizens Savings Hall of Fame Athletic Museum; and Professional Golfers' Association of America Hall of Fame.

CORCORAN, Fred
Distinguished Service
Born April 4, 1905, in Cambridge, Mass; known as a "genial companion, with a quixotic humour and a fund of stories ..."; Richardson Award; Walter Hagen Award 1968.

Fred Corcoran began his involvement with golf in 1916 as a caddie in Belmont, Mass, then as a caddie master and club secretary. As a promoter, he gave to American golf what no other man has given. He was cofounder of the Professional Golfers' Association of America (PGA) and the Ladies Professional Golfers' Association (Ladies PGA) Halls of Fame, and was involved with the founding of the Golf Writers' Association. While Corcoran was the PGA tournament director, the American tour grew into an organized rotation of events; and through his involvement, the earnings possible in professional golf increased greatly and the sport was raised to "major league" status. Additionally, Corcoran was the vice president and tournament director for the International Golf Association, served as Massachusetts State Golf Handicapper 1927 1936, PGA tournament director 1936–1943 and its executive director 1936-1947. He also served as the tournament director of the Ladies PGA 1949–1961 and managed four Ryder Cup teams 1937, 1939, 1941 and 1953.

DEY, Joseph C, Jr.
Distinguished Service
Born November 17, 1907, in Norfolk, Va; attended Univ. Pa; had intended to study for ministry; was sportswriter for *Philadelphia Public Ledger* and *Philadelphia Evening Bulletin.*

Joseph Dey, Jr, is well known as a dedicated administrator of golf. While he served as executive director of the United States Golf Association (USGA) 1933–1968, five new championships and two international contests were started. He also helped to codify the rules of the USGA demonstrating a high regard for justice and fairness. Dey helped establish the Golf House, then in New York. He served as commissioner of tournament players division of the Professional Golfers' Association of America (PGA) from 1968 through 1974. As a commissioner with the PGA, he eased the tension within the association and developed it into an $8,000,000 program in 1937.

EVANS, Charles, Jr. "Chick"
Pre-Modern Era
See entry in American Golf Hall of Fame, 1965.
Also in: Golf Hall of Fame, Citizens Savings Hall of Fame Athletic Museum; and Professional Golfers' Association of America Hall of Fame.

MORRIS, Thomas, Jr.
Pre-Modern Era
See entry in American Golf Hall of Fame, 1967.

TAYLOR, John Henry
Pre-Modern Era
See entry in American Golf Hall of Fame, 1965.

VARE, Glenna Collett
Pre-Modern Era
See entry in American Golf Hall of Fame, 1966.
Also in: Golf Hall of Fame, Citizens Savings Hall of Fame Athletic Museum; and Ladies Professional Golfers' Association Hall of Fame.

WETHERED, Joyce (Lady Heathcoat Amory)
Pre-Modern Era
See entry in American Golf Hall of Fame, 1965.
Also in: Ladies Professional Golfers' Association Hall of Fame.

1976

ARMOUR, Thomas Dickson
Pre-Modern Era
See entry in American Golf Hall of Fame, 1965.
Also in: Golf Hall of Fame, Citizens Savings Hall of Fame Athletic Museum; and Professional Golfers' Association of America Hall of Fame.

BRAID, James
Pre-Modern Era
See entry in American Golf Hall of Fame, 1965.

MORRIS, Thomas, Sr. "Old Tom"
Pre-Modern Era
See entry in American Golf Hall of Fame, 1966.

TRAVERS, Jerome Dunstan
Pre-Modern Era
See entry in American Golf Hall of Fame, 1974.
Also in: Golf Hall of Fame, Citizens Savings Hall of Fame Athletic Museum; and Professional Golfers' Association of America Hall of Fame.

WRIGHT, Mary Kathryn "Mickey"
Modern Era
See entry in American Golf Hall of Fame, 1973.
Also in: Ladies Professional Golfers' Association Hall of Fame.

Golf Hall Of Fame To Watch

TEXAS NATIONAL GOLF HALL OF FAME
Conceived in 1977
The Texas National Golf Hall of Fame, sponsored by Texas National Golf and Development, Inc, was conceived in 1977 by golf course designer, Jack Miller, and will celebrate its official beginning with a golf tournament in the fall of 1977 or in early 1978. This historic event will take place between Willis and Conroe at the Texas National Golf Course, one of three golf subdivisions in the area designed by Miller. At the clubhouse plans are being made for a Hall of Fame Room where plaques for the members will be displayed. Before the tournament the Selection Committee, consisting of Texas sports writers, will elect the first four members from public nominations. Announcement of the members will be made at the opening tournament and members will receive Hall of Fame plaques. Each year four additional members will be elected, one from each of the following categories: touring professional, past great man, past great woman and amateur. For further information, contact Russell Wiggins, Pres, P.O. Box 585, Willis, TX 77378. (713) 756-8876 or 756-1512.

HOCKEY

The origin of the word "hockey" has caused almost as many off-the-ice fights as the question of who played the first game. The word itself was in use by 1527, the year Machiavelli died, and probably derives from the Old French *hoquet,* a shepherd's crook or curved staff. On the other hand, there are those who would derive it from the Iroquoian Indian phrase *ho-gee,* it hurts. Then there is the intriguing statement from the year 1785 which reads that "they call it Hockey and it consists in dashing each other with mud, and the windows also."

There is no disagreement over what hockey is. Canadian novelist Hugh McLennan lovingly called it "sheer insanity." Another Canadian author, Scott Young, said the same thing, but more poetically, when he described hockey as "the combination of blood, sweat and beauty." That combination, on ice at high speeds, ranks hockey with the world's lustiest sports and its fans with the world's most dedicated. It and jai-alai (pelota) are, respectively, the world's fastest team and individual sports. Though a greyhound can attain 40.9 m.p.h, a girl shot from a cannon 45 m.p.h, a riderless Thoroughbred 50.9 m.p.h, a cheetah 70 m.p.h. (it can accelerate from 0 to 45 m.p.h. in two seconds), the fastest human sprinter can only reach a top speed of 27.9 m.p.h, which is said to be lightning fast. But Bobby Hull has been clocked on the ice at 29 m.p.h, and his slap-shot pucks have been measured at 118.3 m.p.h. Although the fastest team sport, hockey is by no means the world's most violent. In contact *karate* the infliction of blows that would be lethal if delivered at full force is the goal of every match. This is not true in hockey, where the scoring of points is the technical goal of the game. Injuries, maimings and unintentional accidents do occur frequently and sixty-eight percent of National Hockey League players lose at least one tooth during their professional careers. Few other sports have a specific penalty for molesting an official. But far more players are hurt every year in football and more referees are hurt in soccer every year than in hockey. The national sport of Afghanistan, *buzkashi,* in which a decapitated calf is fought over by sometimes hundreds of horsemen, is totally devoid of rules and makes hockey look like a very tame team game indeed. In over a century of hockey, only a few players have died as a result of the game. Bud McCourt died in 1907 of head wounds received in a hockey game brawl. Howarth Morenz, the "Babe Ruth of Hockey," died in 1937 of a heart embolism while he was hospitalized with a leg broken in four places during a game eleven days earlier. And Bill Masterton died in 1968 of massive brain damage received in a game. But more people are killed each year by bee stings, or after slipping in their bathtubs, than have been killed during the entire history of professional hockey. Still, though it is not statistically the most violent sport, hockey is preeminently considered North America's violent game in the minds of millions. Major Constantine "Conn" Smythe, the great general manager of the Toronto Maple Leafs, has said that "hockey guys play if they can breathe." Though technically untrue, that statement accurately sums up what is expected or believed of the players by their fans. What is emphatically true is that it is a sport in which the potential for violent disruption is always present. Those players who accept or transcend that fact, and can still excel at playing, provide the beauty of the sport and are thereby its heroes.

Included among these players are some truly fascinating men, the all-time greatest of whom are sketched in the pages that follow. One was the spat-wearing, ukulele-playing Morenz, who changed his suits two or three times a day. Another was the cowboy boot and stetson-wearing Bobby Hull, the "Golden Jet," who once paid $5000 for a hair transplant. Sprague "King" Cleghorn wore a derby hat and yellow chamois gloves. He boasted of having been in 50 stretcher-case fights. While recovering from a broken leg in 1918, he was arrested and charged with having hit his wife with his crutch. Johnny "Black Cat" Gagnon put five lbs. of stones in his pockets so that he would weigh enough to be accepted at a professional training camp. Georges Vezina, the "Chicoutimi Cucumber," had 22 children, never learned English and died of tuberculosis at the age of 37. His nickname resulted from his consistently cool manner. Frank Boucher, who had previously been a Royal Canadian Mounted Policeman, hired the owner of Mama Leone's restaurant to mix a magic elixir, consisting mostly of clam juice, that would make his team win. Jacques Plante, who introduced the goalie's mask in 1959, overcame asthma to enter the pros. He claimed that he was allergic to his underwear and that the air in Toronto was poisonous to him. Lester Patrick, the "Silver Fox," although a coach, would play on the ice for his own injured goalies. Edouard "Newsy" LaLonde was so nicknamed because of his earlier job as a Linotype operator. Glenn Hall, who had a nervous stomach, vomited before every game. Mervyn "Red" Dutton nearly lost both legs in W.W. I but rehabilitated himself and returned to star in the rinks. Cooper Smeaton, a referee, was given a gift by Ottawa fans "because they liked the way [he] handled their abuse." Then there was the incomparable Eddie Shore, who wore a five-gallon hat off the ice and, sometimes, a toreador's cape on the ice. Kyle Crichton wrote of him in *Colliers* magazine that "what makes him [the greatest drawing card in hockey] is the hope, entertained by spectators in all cities but Boston, that he will some night be severely killed."

For the most part, these and the rest of hockey's heroes have been totally uninvolved in the biggest hockey fight of them all, the one that has been waged for decades over the question of where the first game was played. No one will ever know any more than that ancestral forms of it were played in Egypt before 2000 B.C, in Ireland before 1272 B.C, in Iran before 600 B.C, and in Greece before 478 B.C, as well as all over North, Central and South America throughout ancient times. There were countless forms. In Argentina the Araucaños played one called *cheuca,* the twisted one (with reference to the Araucanian game's stick). The only reasonably certain fact is that hockey is the forerunner of all of today's stick-and-ball games—that baseball, softball, cricket, polo, lacrosse and other such related games are all younger, historically speaking, than hockey.

When and where it was first played on ice is an altogether simpler question. The answer is in Canada. Other games were played on ice, the Dutch *kolven* or *het kolven,* for example, but none with a puck. As early as 1783, English troops stationed at Fort Frontenac in Cataraqui (the Indian name for Kingston) played field hockey in the summer and field hockey on ice during the winter months. In 1837, the year Canada's first railroad began using steam locomotives, hockey was played on ice in Montreal between teams that called themselves the Dorchesters and the Uptowns. Games of hockey-on-the-ice were played in Kingston in 1843, the year the town of Victoria was settled by the Hudson's Bay Company, and in 1845 (the year F. X. Garneau's *Histoire du Canada,* still considered by French-Canadians to be their standard history, was published). The same year the Canadian geologist Abraham Gresner distilled the first kerosene oil (1852), hockey or shinty on skates was played in both Ottawa and Halifax. Men of the Royal Canadian Rifles, an Imperial Unit just back from the Crimean War, played hockey at Halifax and Kingston in 1855. Twenty years later, a McGill and Dalhousie student from Halifax named James George Aylwin Creighton led a group of students in organizing a game between nine-man teams at Montreal's Victoria Rink. The issue of the *Gazette* on the day they played their first game announced: "Some fears have been expressed . . . that accidents were likely to occur through the ball flying about in too lively a manner, to the imminent danger of lookers-on, but we understand that the game will be played with a flat, circular piece of wood, thus preventing all danger of its leaving the surface of the ice." Creighton and other members of the Victoria Rink later played a game against the Montreal Football Club, who wore their red and black rugby football uniforms on the ice. The following year, 1877 (when Schiaparelli discovered the "canals" on Mars), saw hockey legitimately organized. Several regular clubs were formed and Creighton himself captained the earliest one, the Metropolitans. More importantly, a full set of rules was adopted and printed. The appearance of those clubs and rules in Montreal was the birth of ice hockey. Its gestation took place throughout Canada and lasted nearly a century.

The game grew quickly into its present form and has changed relatively little during the years since. Matches were played at winter ice carnivals in Montreal in 1882. Teams were reduced to seven men in 1884, the year Greenwich Mean Time was established. In 1885, when the Canadian Pacific Railroad succeeded in spanning the continent, the first league was formed in Kingston out of four local clubs. In 1893, by which time there were leagues throughout Canada and over 100 teams or clubs in Montreal alone, hockey was introduced into the United States at Yale College and Johns Hopkins University. That was also the year Lord Stanley donated a silver cup to encourage hockey championship competition.

The first formal league in the United States, the Amateur Hockey League, was organized in New York City in 1896. McGill University played Queens University on artificial ice in New York in 1897, the year the Klondike Gold Rush began. Hockey nets were first used in 1899 and officially adopted the following year. The idea was introduced by Francis Nelson who had seen fishing nets used in lacrosse games in Australia. In 1900 the modern face-off was introduced by Fred Waghorne, a referee. Within a few years women's leagues were organized. In 1903 the first openly professional team appeared—the Portage Lakes, owned by a dentist named J. L. Gibson, who imported Canadian players to Houghton, Michigan. Through the efforts of Magnus, a Frenchman, a world governing body was formed in 1908. The National Hockey Association, predecessor of the National Hockey League, was established in 1909, the year of the first airplane flight in Canada (J. A. D. McCurdy flew over Baddock Bay, Nova Scotia). The first European championships were held in the Swiss Alps the next year. Artificial ice was in widespread use in Canada by 1912. By the time the National Hockey League was formed in 1917, the sport was for all practical purposes the sport it is today.

One characteristic of hockey has not changed much at all. Rules have changed, innovations have been made, teams have come and gone, but hockey today is as powerful and exciting as ever. It is also as Canadian now as it was a century ago when, for all of Canada, Montreal gave the world in organized form one of its lustiest sports.

FORMS: Hockey (correctly Ice Hockey) is extremely popular in Canada, where it was invented, as well as in the United States and Bulgaria, Czechoslovakia, Germany, Great Britain, Italy, Japan, Poland, Sweden and the U.S.S.R. It is only one of a large number of stick-and-ball games in which each player has a stick as opposed to a similarly large number of stick-and-ball games in which all players use the same stick (softball, baseball, rounders, cricket and others). Some of these are historically related to hockey, some are not. They include field hockey and all its own related games—the English cambuca, the French *jeu de mail,* the Dutch *het kolven,* and from other parts of the world, *paille maille, palamaglio, pele-mele, chicane* and hawkie. Underwater hockey was invented in the 1960s in South Africa and is called octopush in England. Skinny is a variety of field hockey, called shanty or *camanachd* in Scotland, where the stick is called a *caman.* Hurling is an Irish combination of field hockey and lacrosse in which each player uses his broad-bladed hurley to catch and balance the ball while running. Bandy is especially popular in Sweden, where there are over 1265 bandy clubs, but is also popular in Finland, Norway, the U.S.S.R, Mongolia and elsewhere. Bandy is very similar to ice hockey but is played on a much larger rink. Roller hockey—hockey on roller skates—lacrosse, box lacrosse and many others also utilize a stick and ball.

In official ice hockey teams are composed of six players each—one goaltender (or minder or keeper), two defense men, and three forwards called center, right wing and left wing. Each team may have up to 15 players and a spare goaltender in uniform at the start of a game, however. Each team selects its captain and up to two alternate captains, who then wear the letter "C" or "A" on their sweaters. Ice hockey is the only major sport that allows substitutions during play. In play the teams skate on a rink which measures a maximum of 100 by 200 ft. and is surrounded by a wooden barrier called the boards which is from 40 to 48 in. high. The surface of the rink is marked off by a red center line and blue center circle, two blue zone marking lines, four red face-off circles, two red goal lines and two red goal creases. The crease is the area in front of the goal which may not be entered by attacking players except under certain conditions. In games played according to International Ice Hockey Federation (IIHF) rules, the crease is a semicircular area, while in National Hockey League (NHL) games it is a rectangular area. At each end of the rink are the goal judges' boxes. The team benches with seating for nine and the penalty bench with seating for eight players are on opposite sides of the rink. Each goal net is 4 ft. high and 6 ft. wide and is shaped like two half-circles joined side by side and opening toward the rink. Their frame posts and crossbar must be red. A game normally consists of three 20-min. playing periods during which the clock may be stopped, as in football. They are separated by two 10-min. breaks. The ice is usually flooded and thereby resurfaced between periods.

Officials normally include a scorer, a game timekeeper, a penalty timekeeper, two goal judges, and either two referees, one for each half of the rink (IIHF rules), or one referee and two linesmen (NHL rules). Referees wear small red armbands and regulate the game. This includes calling icings (the puck is iced if it is passed in certain illegal ways), off sides, interference, penalties and fouls. Fouls are called for abusive language, board checking (violently throwing someone against the boards), butt-ending (spearing someone with the butt of a stick), charging (into someone), clipping (falling and sliding into the puck-carrier's path), cross-checking (checking someone's progress with a blow across the body), elbowing, excessive roughness, falling on the puck, fighting (in which a distinction is made between starting a fight, fighting back, and continuing to fight back), handling the puck (in the hand), high-sticking (carrying the stick shoulder high or higher with destructive intent), holding (onto another player), hooking (with the stick), kicking or deliberately injuring, kneeing, misconduct (toward officials), slashing (swinging the stick to impede or intimidate someone) and spearing (with the blade of the stick). Stick-checking may also be called a foul and consists of three different illegal uses of the stick—poke-checking, hook-checking and sweep-checking. Throwing the stick and tripping are also fouls. For these and other fouls, penalties are frequently imposed. These may be minor penalties of 2 min. off the ice; bench minor penalties of 2 min. served by a designated team member when the actual offender is not known; and major penalties of 5 min. for the first offense, 15 for a second major penalty and expulsion from the game for the third. For example, wearing illegal equipment constitutes a minor penalty, while a major gross misconduct penalty is imposed on any player who intentionally molests an official, particularly when it is difficult to compel him to cease doing so. Of the many greats who have spent large portions of their professional careers in the penalty box, none is better remembered than the Toronto Maple Leaf's Jim Dorey, who once spent 48 min. of a 1968 game's 60 min. in his team's box.

Play is commenced by a face-off in which the puck is dropped by the referee between the sticks of the two centers. A goal is scored whenever a stick hits the puck fairly so that it passes entirely over the goal line between the goal posts. Goals count one point each. A team which scores while preventing the opposing team from scoring is said to have made a shut-out win. A hat-trick occurs when a player scores three goals in a single game. Of history's thousands of players, the one who scored the greatest number of goals was the Montreal Canadiens' Joseph Henri Maurice Richard—a career total of 626. In 1952 he presented his 325th scoring puck to Queen Elizabeth II.

The puck is a round, black, vulcanized rubber disc 3 in. in diameter and 1 in. thick. It weighs between 5.5 and 6 oz. Before use in a game, it is frozen to reduce its resilience. Up to 20 pucks may be kept in a freezer for use in a single game. When hit expertly, the puck may travel at speeds in excess of 115 m.p.h. (118.3 m.p.h. is the record as has been mentioned). A hockey stick, though largely handmade to player specifications, is numbered, as a golf club is, according to its lie—the angle between the shaft and the blade. The numbers range from 1 for a very obtuse angle to 10 for a near right angle. The most popular lies are 5, 6 and 7. The dimensions of a stick are standardized at a maximum of 4 ft. 5 in. length for the shaft and a maximum 1 ft. 2½ in. length and 3 in. width for the blade. Goaltenders' sticks are 3½ in. wide and consequently heavier. Wood used in the construction of a hockey stick (normally northern white ash or rock elm) is first air-dried for six months. Some teams go through as many as 4000 sticks a season.

In addition to a stick, each player will have a sweater numbered on the sleeves and the back (9 has been the most popular number among pro players, 13 the least popular), special shorts, long stockings, and gauntletlike gloves. Helmets are optional. Other protective articles worn underneath the clothing include elbow and knee pads, kidney pads, ankle and shoulder guards and instep shields. Each goaltender has the same outfit except his protective equipment is larger and stronger and he also has a chest protector, a face mask and leg guards for additional protection. For more than 40 years the best goal pads have been those hand tailored by members of the Kenesky family of Hamilton, Ontario. The most important part of a player's outfit, however, is his skates. These must be of an approved design, which differs from that of skates used in either speed or figure skating, making hockey skates considerably more expensive. The skate blade is straight and 1/16 in. wide. It is attached by two uprights, the stanchions, to a plate screwed to the boot. The boot, usually made of calf or "nubuck," is ideally half a size smaller than the wearer's street-shoe size. The blades normally require sharpening after every 13 hours of play.

ORGANIZATION: The world governing body for hockey is the International Ice Hockey Federation *(Ligue Internationale de Hockey sur Glace),* located in London. The IIHF was formed in 1908 by Belgium, Bohemia, France, Great Britain and Switzerland. It was instrumental in the acceptance of ice hockey as a regular event on the Winter Olympic Games program when it was first played in the 1920 Games at Antwerp, Belgium; Canada won the gold medal. Its membership today includes 30 countries' national ice hockey federations. The two in North America are the Canadian Amateur Hockey Association *(Association canadienne de hockey amateur)* and the Amateur Hockey Association of the United States (AHAUS). Each of these organizations is very large. The AHAUS, for example, in 1976 had 200,000 nonprofessional members representing 10,298 teams in various leagues from pee-wee, midget, junior on up. Both serve the important function of conducting national championships in various classifications. Working with these two national organizations for the benefit and control of the sport in North America are numerous smaller organizations. Notable are the Ontario Hockey Association, the British Columbia Amateur Hockey Association, the Eastern College Hockey Association (United States) and the American Hockey Coaches Association (for university, college and secondary school ice hockey coaches) which sponsors the annual All America Squads and the Coach of the Year Awards. Many of these (as well as all American schools where hockey is played) are affiliated with or play by the rules of the National Collegiate Athletic Association. Canadian teams and several American leagues, on the other hand, play according to NHL rules.

Although there are numerous other leagues—such as the American Hockey League with 12 teams, the International Hockey League with 8, the Western Hockey League with 6 teams, the Central Hockey League and the World Hockey League, as well as hundreds of other nonleague teams—the NHL stands alone as the major league in North America. It is composed of two conferences within which are divisions named after hockey greats: the Prince of Wales, which consists of the 5 teams in the James Norris Division and the 4 teams in the Charles F. Adams Division; and the Clarence Campbell, which consists of the 4 Lester Patrick Division teams and the 5 Conn Smythe Division teams. Ninety-eight percent of the men on all of these 18 NHL teams are Canadian. Members of these and other leagues' teams are selected through an annual and elaborate drafting procedure which includes the intraleague, interleague, amateur and reverse drafts of new players. During the NHL season, from mid-October to April, a team may play up to 78 games and the winner of the NHL playoffs each year receives hockey's highest team award, the prestigious Stanley Cup. This cup was donated by Lord Stanley of Preston, Governor-General of Canada, in 1893. The winning playoff team also receives $63,000 for distribution among the team members. Two NHL awards are given automatically on the basis of performance. The Ross Trophy is awarded to the individual scoring champion and the Vezina Trophy is awarded to the best goaltender. Other trophies are awarded by a consensus vote of hockey writers, broadcasters and telecasters in each league city polled. They include the Conn Smythe Trophy for outstanding performance in the Stanley Cup playoffs, the Lester Patrick Trophy for outstanding service to hockey in the United States, the Hart Trophy for most valuable player, the Calder Memorial Trophy for rookie of the year, the Lady Byng Memorial Trophy for sportsmanship and gentlemanly conduct, and the James Norris Memorial Trophy for the best defense man. Closely associated with the NHL is the National Hockey League Player's Association which was founded in 1967 in Toronto and had 400 members in 1976. It annually presents the Lester B. Pearson Award to the season's outstanding NHL player. Other leagues conduct division and league championships, for which similarly prestigious awards are given at the end of each season. The winning team of the finals in the World Hockey League, for example, receives the AVCO World Trophy. Nonprofessional ice hockey teams in Canada compete for numerous amateur trophies, of which one representing senior amateur hockey supremacy is the prestigious Allan Cup. The latter was first won by the Ottawa Cliffsides in 1908. That, co-incidentally, was the year paper cups were first introduced by the Public Cup Vendor Company of New York.

Hockey Hall of Fame

TORONTO, ONTARIO

Mailing Address; Exhibition Pl, M6K 3C3. Tel. (416) 366-7551, local 251 or 532-0393. *Contact:* M. H. "Lefty" Reid, Cur. *Location:* Center of Exhibition Place on the Lakeshore near downtown Toronto, directly E. of Queen Elizabeth Bldg; approx. 40 mi. N.E. of Hamilton, 50 mi. N.W. of Niagara Falls, N.Y, 75 mi. N.W. of Buffalo, N.Y, 225 mi. N.E. of Detroit, Mich. *Admission:* Free, 10:30 to 4:30 daily; 10:30 to 8:30 Tuesday – Sunday, May 15 – Labor Day; closed Christmas Day, New Year's Day, and one day prior to annual opening of Canadian National Exhibit; hockey films shown to groups of 30 or more by special arrangement, except in July and August. *Personnel:* 12-Mem. Selection Comt. (Frank J. Selke, Chmn.); 12-mem. Governing Comt. (Clarence S. Campbell, M.B.E, Chmn.); M. H. "Lefty" Reid, Cur. *Nearby Halls of Fame:* Sports (Toronto), Football (Hamilton), Hockey (Kingston, 150 mi. N.E.), Horseshoe Pitching (Corning N.Y, 155 mi. S.E.), Flight (Harris Hill, Elmira, N.Y, 165 mi. S.E.), Baseball (Cooperstown, 230 mi. S.E.).

The Hockey Hall of Fame originated in Kingston, Ontario as the International Hockey Hall of Fame founded by Capt. James T. Sutherland (*see* International Hockey Hall of Fame sketch). After Sutherland's death in 1955 the project in Kingston ran into difficulty and the new Hockey Hall of Fame took up temporary location in Stanley Barracks and the Press Building in Toronto. In 1958 National Hockey League (NHL) President Clarence S. Campbell and Frank Selke were appointed by the NHL to confer with Harry I. Price of the Canadian National Exhibit (CNE) in Toronto about combining the Hockey Hall of Fame with the Sports Hall of Fame (established at the CNE two years before). One large room was then set aside for hockey and received so much support that the governors of the NHL began plans for the construction of a new building. In August 1959 the new Hockey Hall of Fame Selection Committee met at the CNE grounds and all of the first Hall of Fame members, except three, attended a special luncheon in their honor. In 1960 the dignitaries from the CNE Board, the city of Toronto and the NHL (with the Canadian Amateur Hockey Association) agreed that the city of Toronto would begin construction of the new building. The six clubs of the NHL pledged to give their financial support to the project. The new home of the Hockey Hall of Fame was completed on May 1, 1961, and an official opening by Prime Minister John F. Diefenbaker and U.S. Ambassador Livingston T. Merchant took place on August 26, 1961. On special occasions 14 aluminum flagpoles along the front of the building are dressed with the flags of the NHL Canadian Amateur Hockey Association and the U.S. Amateur Hockey Association to denote the active sponsorship of their clubs which led to the successful completion of the building. Set off by a fountain, planting beds and patios, the Hockey Hall of Fame "though exhibition in character, is a museum in function." A large entrance concourse leads to the main exhibition hall on the ground floor. Displayed here are all major trophies of the NHL, skates, hockey sticks and pucks of famous events, sweaters of defunct teams and a special display highlighting the Hall of Fame inductees. The Stanley Cup is exhibited most of the year, except for official presentation or for the addition of names. The mezzanine level contains a gallery overlooking the main hall, a library with manuscripts and documents about hockey and a theatre that seats 100 people for special showings of hockey movies. A basement area provides space for storage, workshops and mechanical equipment. In 1967 Canada's Sports Hall of Fame constructed an additional wing to the building and now shares the main entrance and other facilities in the building with the Hockey Hall of Fame. As a special souvenir for visitors the Hall of Fame publishes *Hockey's Heritage,* a 90-page booklet containing pictures and brief biographies of each honored member in the Hall of Fame, as well as an explanation and list of winners for all major NHL trophies. This Hall is a member of the Association of Sports Museums and Halls of Fame.

Members: 211 as of January 1977. Members are elected in two categories: Builders (which includes officials) and Players. They are selected on the basis of "playing ability, integrity, character and their contribution to their team and the game of hockey in general." Players must have completed active participation three years prior to their election, though exceptions can be made by the Governing Committee, and Builders may still be active in the sport. A Selection Committee, made up of former players or newspapermen "knowledgeable in the history, tradition and skills of the game," nominates and elects the Players. A Governing Committee, comprised of representatives from founding organizations and the Canadian Amateur Hockey Association, nominates and elects the Builders. Although the number of Players elected each year is limited to three, the number of Builders elected is left to the discretion of the Governing Committee. Honored members receive a cloth crest of membership and a ring or cufflinks with the insignia of the Hockey Hall of Fame. A special induction dinner is held in their honor during the Canadian National Exhibition, usually on the last Thursday in August.

1945

ALLAN, Sir Montagu
Builder

Born October 13, 1860, in Montreal, Que; sportsman and financier; died September 26, 1951, in Montreal, at age 91.

Sir Montagu Allan donated the Allan Cup to symbolize amateur hockey supremacy in 1908. Valued between $300 and $500 then, the Cup was governed by a Board of Trustees who monitored bona fide challenges for the Cup. Queen's University defeated the Ottawa Cliffsides to become the first champions. In 1928 the Cup was given outright to the Canadian Amateur Hockey Association. A symbol for amateur supremacy was necessitated by the Stanley Cup becoming the professional cup.
Also in: International Hockey Hall of Fame.

BAIN, Donald H. "Dan"
Player

Born 1874 at Belleville, Ont; moved with family at age 6 to Winnipeg; died August 15, 1962, in Winnipeg, at age 88.

A great all-around athlete, Bain's talents were equaled only by his achievements. As an amateur hockey player with the Winnipeg Victorias, he was on two Stanley Cup teams, 1895–1896 and 1900–1901. Excelling in other sports, Bain was champion gymnast of Winnipeg at the age of 17, won the Manitoba 3-mi. roller skating title and was three–time winner of the 1-mi. bicycle race, 1894, 1895 and 1896. Retiring in 1903, he began trapshooting and won the Canadian title shortly thereafter. In his mid-50s, he was still winning championships in speed-skating, figure skating, roller skating, snowshoeing, lacrosse and golf.
Also in: Canada's Sports Hall of Fame and International Hockey Hall of Fame.

BAKER, Hobart Amery Hare
Player

Born January 15, 1892, in Wissahickon, Pa; attended St. Paul's School in Concord, N.H; military service with U.S. unit of Lafayette Esquadrille during W.W. I in France; died while testing a new plane in Toul, France, December 21, 1918.

In the days of seven-man hockey, Baker was the rover. Known for his endurance, speed, agility, stick handling and effortless grace, the Princeton team was called Baker and the Six Other Players. After playing four years at Princeton (1910–1914), the last two as captain, he played one year for the St. Nicholas Club. While at Princeton he participated in golf, track, swimming, gymnastics and football. His senior year he was football captain. His 43-yd. dropkicked field goal tied Yale. The Princeton hockey arena is named after him and St. Paul's School competes for the coveted Hobey Stick.
Also in: International Hockey Hall of Fame, National Football Hall of Fame and U.S. Hockey Hall of Fame.

BOWIE, Russell "Dubbie"
Player

Born August 24, 1880, in Montreal, Que; died April 8, 1959 in Montreal, at age 79.

Turning aside all offers for professional hockey, including a grand piano, Dubbie scored a career total of 234 goals as a ten-year amateur. He played as rover and center for the Montreal Victorias 1898–1908. He began at the age of 17, weighing only 112 lbs, finding his career prematurely ended by a broken collarbone in 1908. He was then scoring an average of three goals a game. One of the few players to score 10 goals in one game, in his final year he had 37 goals in ten games. After retirement he became a referee.
Also in: International Hockey Hall of Fame.

GARDINER, Charles Robert
Player

Born December 31, 1904, in Edinburgh, Scotland; emigrated to Canada with his parents in 1911; won the Vezina Trophy 1932, 1934; made the league's first All-Star team 1932, 1934; voted to the second team 1933; died June 13, 1934, of a brain tumor at age 30 at his home in Winnipeg.

Charlie was a goaltender from the start and advanced rapidly through the various minor leagues in his adopted city, turning pro in 1926. After only one season with the Winnipeg Maroons of the old Western League, Chuck was signed by the Chicago Black Hawks in 1927. In his seven years with the Hawks as goalie he played 315 games, allowed 673 goals (average of 2.13 goals against) and registered 42 shutouts; also played in 21 Stanley Cups, scoring 5 shutouts and 35 goals (1.66 goals against average.)
Also in: International Hockey Hall of Fame.

GERARD, Edward George
Player

Born February 22, 1890, in Ottawa, Ont; a star participant in football, paddling, cricket, tennis, lacrosse and hockey; retired as a player in 1924 because of asthma; died in Ottawa August 7, 1937, of a throat ailment at age 47.

1913–1923 Ottawa Senators, defenseman, later captain.
1924–1930 Montreal Maroons, coach
1930–1932 New York Americans, manager
1934–1935 St. Louis Eagles, player-coach

Eddie turned professional with the Ottawa Senators in the 1913–1914 season, becoming captain in 1920–1921. He was on four Stanley Cup winners during the ten years he was with the Ottawa Senators. In 1919–1920, he had his first Stanley Cup victory, with a triumph over the Seattle Metropolitans. His other victories were over Vancouver Millionaires in 1920–1921, both Vancouver and Edmonton Eskimos in 1922–1923 and in 1921–1922 he was loaned to Toronto St. Pats, to replace the injured Harry Cameron, defeating Vancouver Millionaires. Eddie was credited with being the deciding factor in this game. In 1924 he became the Montreal Maroons' coach and led them to a Stanley Cup victory in 1925–1926. He remained with the Montreal Maroons until 1930 and then left to become manager of the New York Americans. In 1934–1935 he joined the St. Louis Eagles, but was forced to quit halfway through the season. He was considered a gentleman on and off the ice.
Also in: Canada's Sports Hall of Fame, Greater Ottawa Sports Hall of Fame and International Hockey Hall of Fame.

McGEE, Francis
Player

Born in the 1880s; sighted in only one eye; died September 16, 1916, in Courcelette, France, during W.W. I.

During his brief professional career as center with the Ottawa Silver Seven 1903-1906, Frank tallied 71 goals in 23 games, scoring 5 goals in a game 7 times. In 22 playoff games he added 63 goals. The Silver Seven won three consecutive Stanley Cups with Frank, as he recorded 14 goals on January 16, 1905, against Dawson City, Yukon. Ottawa won the game 23–2. Frank also holds the three-goal and four-goal outputs by an individual, with three in 90 secs. and the fourth goal 50 secs. later. In the same game he totaled eight goals in 8 min. and 20 secs.
Also in: Greater Ottawa Sports Hall of Fame and International Hockey Hall of Fame.

MORENZ, Howarth William "Stratford Streak"
Player

Born September 21, 1902, in Mitchell, Ont; at 14 his family moved to Stratford; called by French-speaking Quebec fans "L'homme-eclair"; sang and played the ukelele; changed clothes two or three times daily; Hart Trophy 1928, 1931, 1932; NHL All-Star first team twice; All-Star second team once; died March 8, 1937 from an embolism incurred when four leg bones were broken in a game.

1923–1934 Montreal Canadiens, forward
1934–1935 Chicago Black Hawks, forward
1935–1936 Chicago Black Hawks, New York Rangers, forward
1936–1937 Montreal Canadiens, forward

The Stratford Streak attracted the attention of the Canadiens when he scored nine goals in an amateur game in Montreal in 1922. Signing a $1000 bonus in 1923, his reckless headlong rushes, adept speed and uncanny balance earned him the admiration of millions of fans. After eleven seasons with the Canadiens, Howie was traded to

the Chicago Black Hawks where he spent one season and then in 1935 he was on to New York in midseason. The man who scored 40 goals in 44 games in 1929 and 30 goals in 30 games in 1925 returned to Montreal in 1936. On January 28, 1937, he broke four bones in his left leg and ankle in a game against the Black Hawks. After five weeks in the hospital he died of an embolism. Funeral services were held at center ice in the Forum where literally thousands wept for "Le Grande Morenz."
Also in: Canada's Sports Hall of Fame and International Hockey Hall of Fame.

PHILLIPS, Thomas Neil "Nibs"
Player
Born May 22, 1880, in Kenora, Ont; died in Toronto, 1923, after removal of an infected tooth.

Nibs played college hockey for McGill University and later with the Montreal AAA in 1902–1903. He helped the Toronto Marlboros of the Ontario Hockey Association win the senior championship while he was attending the University of Toronto. Signing with his hometown Thistles in 1905, he captained the team to two Stanley Cup challenges, losing to Ottawa the first time but winning the rematch in 1907. The following season Ottawa obtained his skills for right wing and Nibs responded with 26 goals in ten games.
Also in: International Hockey Hall of Fame.

PULFORD, Harvey
Player
Born 1875 in Toronto, Ont, but grew up in Ottawa; died October 31, 1940, in Ottawa.

Pulford was an all-around athlete and a fine hockey player of his day. As a defenseman, he was a star of the Ottawa Silver Seven from 1893 until 1908. The team was one of the first winners of the Stanley Cup, taking the trophy three years in a row, 1903, 1904 and 1905. Pulford was one of the most effective body checkers of his era and had a reputation for being a clean player. His accomplishments in other sports rivaled his talent in hockey, especially in oaring in which he was recognized on national and international levels. In 1898 he took the Eastern Canadian double- and single-blade championship in paddling. He was an Ottawa Rough Rider when the team won the Canadian football title in 1898, 1899, 1900 and 1902. Pulford was also light-heavy and heavyweight boxing champion of Eastern Canada from 1896 to 1898 and a member of the Ottawa Rough Riders squash team when they were title winners in 1924.
Also in: Greater Ottawa Sports Hall of Fame and International Hockey Hall of Fame.

ROSS, Arthur Howie
Player
Born January 13, 1886, in Naughton, Ont; died August 5, 1964 in Boston, Mass.

Art was the man who established professional hockey in Boston. First as coach and later manager of the Boston Bruins, he acquired the stars that brought three Stanley Cups to the Hub in 1929, 1939 and 1941. As a player, he tallied 85 goals in 167 games with 6 goals in 16 playoff games. He began in the Canadian Amateur Hockey Association in 1905 with Kenora, which won the Stanley Cup in 1907. He then played with the Wanderers in 1908, on to Haileyburg, Ottawa, and then the Wanderers as a defenseman 1917–1918. He was also a referee, noted for using a bell instead of a whistle. The Art Ross Trophy has been awarded to the league's leading scorer since 1947.
Also in: Canada's Sports Hall of Fame and International Hockey Hall of Fame.

STANLEY, Frederick Arthur G. C. B.
Builder
Born January 15, 1841, in England; died June 14, 1908, in England.

The Governor-General of Canada from 1888 to 1893, Lord Stanley of Preston donated a trophy, the Stanley Cup, in 1893 to be awarded to the championship hockey club in Canada. Initially, only amateur teams competed for the Cup until 1906. In 1910 the Cup was coveted by professional teams, traveling east and west in Canada. With the demise of the Western Canada League in 1926, the National Hockey League has preempted sovereign rights for the Cup that symbolizes hockey supremacy. Costing only 10 guineas, or $50, in 1893, the oldest trophy in North America stands nearly 3 ft. high.
Also in: International Hockey Hall of Fame.

STUART, William Hodgson
Player
Born 1880 in Ottawa, Ont; brother Bruce inducted into the Hall in 1961; died June 23, 1907 in Belleville, Ont, from a tragic diving accident.

1898–1899 Ottawa Senators
1900–1901 Quebec Bulldogs
1906–1907 Montreal Wanderers

Hodg played with his brother Bruce on the Ottawa Senators and the Quebec Bulldogs. He followed his brother into the International Professional Hockey League not only as a player but as captain and manager for Calumet in 1902. He played for the Montreal Wanderers in 1906–1907 when they deafeted the Kenora Thistles to regain the Stanley Cup only two months after losing it to the Thistles. That was his final season as he became embroiled in a dispute concerning the referee for a game in Sault Ste. Marie, Mich.
Also in: Greater Ottawa Sports Hall of Fame and International Hockey Hall of Fame.

VEZINA, Georges
Player
Born January, 1888, in Chicoutimi, Que; father of 22 children; played on 5 Stanley Cup teams, winning in 1916 and 1924; died of tuberculosis March 26, 1926, at age 39.

Georges signed with the Montreal Canadiens in 1910 for an illustrious career highlighted by 328 consecutive league games and 39 playoffs. As a stand-up goalie, he allowed only 1267 goals against, for an over-all average of 3.45. Masks were not standard equipment even when the sport prohibited goalies from playing on their knees (a rule that was changed in 1922). Georges had never missed a game until his final season in 1925–1926, when chest pains felled him in the game against Pittsburgh on November 28. Tuberculosis was diagnosed and he died four months later. The following season Montreal owners Leo Dandurand, Louis Letourneau and Joe Cattarinich presented the Vezina Trophy to the National Hockey League to be awarded annually to the goalie having

played a minimum of 25 games with the fewest goals scored against his team.
Also in: International Hockey Hall of Fame.

1947

CALDER, Frank
Builder
Born 1887 in Scotland; died February 4, 1943.

Calder was first president of the newly formed National Hockey League (NHL) from 1917–1943, also secretary for the old National Hockey Association. Firm but judicious in his dealings with the players, management and rule changes during the early days of the fledgling organization, he soon commanded the respect of everyone near him. In memory of his 26 years of service in planting the granite foundation for the NHL as it exists today, the Calder Trophy is presented annually to the rookie of the year.
Also in: International Hockey Hall of Fame.

CLAPPER, Aubrey Victor "Dit"
Player
Born 1907 in Newmarket, Ont; topflight lacrosse player as a teenager; All-Star first team 1939, 1940, 1941; All-Star second team three times; survived heart attack in 1964; resides in Peterborough, Ont.

The first 20-year player in the National Hockey League (NHL), Dit was also the first active player to be inducted into the Hall of Fame. In his second full season the Bruins won the NHL championship and Stanley Cup. He served as defenseman, forward and coach for the Boston Bruins 1927–1947. During his career, the Bruins won 6 championships, 4 while he was defenseman. Dit also coached the Bruins in 1945–1946 and 1948–1949. His high single season was 41 goals and 20 assists in a 44-game schedule, 1929–1930; his career totals are 228 goals, 246 assists as well as 12 goals and 23 assists in playoffs. Clapper officially retired and his number 5 jersey was permanently retired in a ceremony at center ice in Boston Garden on February 12, 1947.
Also in: Canada's Sports Hall of Fame and International Hockey Hall of Fame.

HEWITT, William Archibald
Builder
Born May 15, 1875, in Cobourg, Ont; son Foster is Hall of Famer; newspaper business for 41 years; served Big Four football league in 1907; president and secretary of Canadian Rugby Union; patrol judge at Woodbind Racetrack; presiding steward at Ontario tracks for 14 seasons; died September 8, 1961, at age 86.

W. A. Hewitt was a man of sports through and through, and shared his enthusiasm with others as sports editor of the *Toronto Star* for 31 years. Involved in hockey for over 60 years, he served 39 of those as registrar and treasurer of the Canadian Amateur Hockey Association as well as secretary of the Ontario Hockey Association from 1903–1961. He was also manager of three champion Canadian teams and became the first attractions manager of the Maple Leaf Gardens when it opened in 1931. When he got tired of disputes over whether or not a puck had gone between the goalposts, he decided to drape them with a fishnet to catch the shots; thus, the net in hockey was originated.
Also in: International Hockey Hall of Fame.

JOLIAT, Aurel Emile "Little Giant" "Mighty Atom"
Player
Born August 29, 1901, in Ottawa, Ont; star fullback with the Ottawa Rough Riders; broke leg and turned to hockey; Hart Trophy 1934; All-Star first team once; All-Star second team three times; resides in Ottawa.

After brief stops in New Edinburgh, Iroquois Falls and Saskatoon, he signed with the Canadiens and served as forward 1922–1938. Although benched his first season in Montreal, he eventually teamed with Howie Morenz for an all-time high of 270 goals, plus three Stanley Cup championships 1924, 1930, 1931. The Little Giant could stop any opponent despite his 135 lbs. After retiring from hockey he joined the Canadian National Railway.
Also in: Canada's Sports Hall of Fame, Greater Ottawa Sports Hall of Fame and International Hockey Hall of Fame.

NELSON, Francis
Builder
Died April, 1932.

The sports editor for the *Toronto Glove,* he was also vice-president of the Ontario Hockey Association (OHA) 1903 to 1905. The following year he was named the OHA Governor to the Amateur Athletic Union and later became a life member. Well-versed in all sports, Francis is best known for his interests in thoroughbreds.
Also in: International Hockey Hall of Fame.

NIGHBOR, Frank
Player
Born 1893 in Pembroke, Ont; Hart Trophy 1923–1924; Lady Byng Trophy 1925, 1926; died of cancer, April 13, 1966, in Pembroke.

1913–1914 Toronto Maple Leafs, player
1914–1915 Vancouver Millionaires, player
1915–1929 Ottawa Senators, player

Frank turned professional with Toronto in 1913. He played on five Stanley Cup champions, the first one in 1915 and the last four with Ottawa in 1920, 1921, 1923 and 1927. He spent the last half of the 1928–1929 season with Toronto.
Also in: Greater Ottawa Sports Hall of Fame and International Hockey Hall of Fame.

NORTHEY, William M.
Builder
Born April 29, 1872 in Leeds, Que; died April 9, 1963.

As president of the Montreal Amateur Athletic Association and life member of the Canadian Amateur Hockey Association, William solicited the Allan Cup, emblematic of amateur supremacy, from Sir Allan himself. Northey was the first trustee for the Cup. He also directed the building of the original Montreal Forum, serving many years as the managing director for the structure.
Also in: Canadian Amateur Athletic Hall of Fame and International Hockey Hall of Fame.

PATRICK, Lester "Silver Fox"
Player, manager, coach
Born December 31, 1883, in Drummondville, Que; his father Joseph Frank was in lumber business; mother's name was Grace; one of eight children; died June 1, 1960, in Victoria, B.C.

1905–1906 Montreal Wanderers, player
1912–1913 Victoria Aristocrats, captain and manager
1926–1946 New York Rangers, goalie and manager

Before playing with the Renfrew Millionaires in the new National Hockey Association, Lester was a member of two Stanley Cup champions with the Montreal Wanderers, 1905 and 1906. Lester and his brother Frank initiated the Pacific Coast Hockey League in 1911, which they sold in 1926. He was the captain and manager of the Victoria Aristocrats 1912–1913 when they defeated Quebec for the world title. One of hockey's first rushing defensemen, he retired from active playing in the NHL after one game as goalie for the New York Rangers during the 1927–1928 playoffs. He masterminded the Rangers dynasty that would win three Stanley Cups 1928, 1933 and 1940. A brilliant administrator and strategist, Lester developed the first farm system and collaborated with his brother on the playoff system and other rule changes. Recognizing his contributions to hockey growth in the eastern United States, the Rangers in 1966 inaugurated the Lester Patrick Trophy for outstanding service to hockey in the U.S.
Also in: British Columbia Sports Hall of Fame, Canada's Sports Hall of Fame and International Hockey Hall of Fame.

ROBERTSON, John Ross
Builder
Born 1850; died May 31, 1918.

The manager of the *Toronto Telegram,* and founder of the Hospital for Sick Children, he was president of the Ontario Hockey Association (OHA) 1898–1904. In his first speech to the OHA John said, "A manly nation is always fond of manly sports. We want our boys to be strong, vigorous and self-reliant and must encourage athletics. Sport should be pursued for its own sake." The year of his selection as president, 1898, he donated three trophies for annual competition to be awarded to the champions of senior, intermediate and junior divisions. A member of Canadian Parliament, he was offered knighthood but refused it.
Also in: International Hockey Hall of Fame.

ROBINSON, Claude C.
Builder
Born December 17, 1881, in Harriston, Ont.

A player with the Winnipeg Victorias, the team won both the Allan Cup and Stanley Cup. He was the first executive secretary of the Canadian Amateur Hockey Association in 1914 and suggested the formation of a national association to compete for amateur hockey championships. He managed the Canadian team in the 1932 Olympics.
Also in: Canadian Amateur Athletic Hall of Fame and International Hockey Hall of Fame.

SHORE, Edward William
Player
Born November 25, 1902, in Ft. Qu'Appelle, Sask; amateur hockey with Melville Millionaires from 1923–1924; professional with Regina Caps, Western Canada League in 1924; with Edmonton in 1925, where he became known as the Edmonton Express; Hart Trophy 1933, 1935, 1936 and 1938; on All-Star first team seven times; All-Star second team once.
1926–1939 Boston Bruins, defenseman
1939–1940 Boston Bruins, New York Americans, defenseman

Bostonians became such loyal hockey fans while Eddie Shore played for the Bruins that the Boston Garden was built to house them all. With a fighting temper, Shore was a crowd-pleaser, involved in many brawls and fistfights, and his fans knew that when he was in control of the puck "he would either end up bashing somebody, get into a fight or score a goal." In his 13 years with the Bruins Shore brought the team from last to second place in the National Hockey League American Division, played on two Stanley Cup winning teams and, in the process, received 978 stitches, broke his nose 14 times, shattered his jaw 5 times and lost most of his teeth. His most celebrated fight took place on December 12, 1933, in Toronto. After Hall of Famer Red Horner shoved Shore into the boards, the Edmonton Express went after the culprit, but mistakenly checked Ace Bailey. Bailey fractured his skull when he hit the ice and, after requiring delicate brain surgery, was never able to play hockey again. Shore was suspended for a month. In the 1939–1940 season Shore became the owner and manager of the minor league team, the Springfield Indians, and his new duties demanded so much time that he was available only for the Bruins' home games. The team did not take well to that and sold him to the New York Americans where he finished his last season of professional hockey and ended his career with 105 goals and 179 assists. He continued to manage the Indians until he sold the team in 1967.
Also in: Canada's Sports Hall of Fame, Ice Skating Hall of Fame and International Hockey Hall of Fame.

SUTHERLAND, Capt. James T.
Builder
Born 1870 in Kingston, Ont; played amateur hockey as a center prior to military duty in W.W. I; died September 30, 1955.

Often referred to as the "Father of Hockey," Captain Sutherland persuaded the Canadian Amateur Hockey Association (CAHA) and the National Hockey Association to support the International Hockey Hall of Fame concept. A life member of the Ontario Hockey Association, he climbed the administrative ladder from district representative to the presidency in 1915. After a two-year stint as president, he assumed identical duties with the CAHA in 1919 and used it as a base for the Hall of Fame campaign. He lived his entire life in Kingston, playing amateur hockey, then coaching the Frontenac Juniors to several championships, briefly as a referee, finally in managerial positions ardently promoting the sport. He died before the Hall was built in Kingston, but will long be remembered for bringing together two associations to advance the sport by memorializing the achievements of the participants.
Also in: International Hockey Hall of Fame.

TAYLOR, Fred O.B.E. "Cyclone"
Player
Born June 23, 1883, in Tara, Ont; decorated with the Order of the British Empire by King George VI for his services with the Canadian Immigration Service in W.W. II; nicknamed Cyclone for his great speed in hockey; Vancouver Citizen of the Year 1966; residence in Van-

couver, B.C; member of the Hall of Fame Selection Committee.

A legend from the early days of organized hockey, Cyclone Taylor boasted that he once scored a goal in the National Hockey Association by skating backward through the whole Ottawa team. He first played as a forward in Listowel and Thessalon in Ontario and Portage La Prairie, Manitoba. He turned professional with the Houghton, Mich. team in 1906 and played for Ottawa in 1907 – 1909, winning the Stanley Cup in his last season with the team. Renfrew was his team in 1909 – 1911, but he played out the rest of his career with Vancouver from 1912 – 1921. The team won the Stanley Cup in 1914 – 1915 and Taylor won the Pacific Coast Hockey League scoring championship with 32 goals. At the end of his career he had accumulated the legendary 194 goals in 186 games.
Also in: British Columbia Sports Hall of Fame, Canada's Sports Hall of Fame, Greater Ottawa Sports Hall of Fame and International Hockey Hall of Fame.

1950

DAVIDSON, Allan M. "Scotty"

Player

Born in the 1890s in Kingston, Ont; served with the First Canadian Contingent in Belgium during W.W. I; died June 6, 1915.

1909 – 1911 Kingston Frontenac Juniors, right wing
1911 – 1914 Toronto Arenas, right wing

During the 1910 – 1911 championship series in the Ontario Hockey Association, Scotty scored a hat trick in the last minute of the final championship game to give the Kingston Juniors their second consecutive crown. A popular player with an overpowering shot, he was coached by the "Father of Hockey," James T. Sutherland. He played on his third championship team during the 1913 – 1914 season with Jack Marshall's Toronto club.
Also in: International Hockey Hall of Fame.

DRINKWATER, Charles Graham

Player

Born February 22, 1875, in Montreal, Que; member of championship football and hockey teams in 1894 at McGill University; died September 26, 1946, in Montreal.

1892 – 1894 Montreal AAA, player
1894 – 1899 Montreal Victorias, player

A career amateur player, Charles played on four Stanley Cup champions. Winning his first Cup with the Victorias in 1895, the club lost it the following season to Winnipeg before claiming three consecutive titles, 1897 to 1899.
Also in: International Hockey Hall of Fame.

DUDLEY, George S.

Builder

Born April 19, 1894, in Midland, Ont; died May 8, 1960.

Active in promoting amateur hockey internationally for over a half-century, George arranged for the initial visits of Russian teams to Canada. Often referred to as "the best man amateur hockey ever had," at the time of his death his multiple responsibilities included treasurer of the Ontario Hockey Association, president of the International Ice Hockey Federation and chairman of the hockey committee for the 1960 Olympics. His initial duties began in 1925 with the Canadian Amateur Hockey Association, later serving as president and secretary.
Also in: Internation Hockey Hall of Fame.

GRANT, Michael

Player

Born in the 1870s; outstanding speed skater; at age 11 won titles in three classifications, under 12, under 14 and under 16; died in 1961.

Mike was asked to try out for the Crystal Junior Hockey Club. He made the team and became team captain, and led them to the junior championship. He then became the captain of the intermediate club and led them to two championships. In 1894 he joined the Montreal Victorias and soon after became captain, leading them to a Stanley Cup that same year. Mike played with three Montreal teams, Crystals, Shamrocks and Victorias and was captain of each. He had been captain of three Stanley Cup winners. After playing the sport, he refereed games in the same league. After his retirement, he became one of the first hockey ambassadors by demonstrating and organizing exhibition hockey in the United States.
Also in: International Hockey Hall of Fame.

GRIFFIS, Silas Seth "Sox"

Player

Born in the 1880s; weighed 195 lbs; outstanding in other sports; won many events as an oarsman; in 1905 successfully stroked the Junior Four at the Canadian Henley at St. Catharines; champion left-handed golfer; great 10-pin bowler; died July, 1950, at age 67.

Griffis started as a rover in the seven-man game, but later moved back to play cover point (defense). He started playing with Kenora, Ont, team winning the Stanley Cup in 1906 – 1907. He was captain of the Vancouver Millionaires that won the Stanley Cup in 1914 – 1915, but didn't play because of a broken leg sustained in the last game of the regular season. He was given a purse of gold and was offered a house in Kenora by the citizens, but moved to Vancouver. Griffis retired from hockey until 1911, when the Patricks started the Pacific Coast League. He remained with them until 1918, when he retired for good.
Also in: International Hockey Hall of Fame.

LALONDE, Edouard "Newsy"

Player

Born October 31, 1887, in Cornwall, Ont; worked in newsprint plant as Linotype operator from which his nickname came; outstanding in lacrosse; selected Canada's outstanding lacrosse player of the half-century in 1950; died in Montreal, Que, November 21, 1970.

1917 – 1922 Montreal Canadiens, defenseman, forward
1932 – 1935 Montreal Canadiens, coach

Newsy Lalonde began his professional career in 1905 on the Cornwall team, then played on teams in Toronto, Woodstock, Sault Ste. Marie and Renfrew in Ontario, and Vancouver and Saskatoon in western Canada. Before his five seasons with the Montreal Canadiens, he played with the New York Americans. Known as one of the roughest players of his time, he and Hall of Famer Joe

Hall of the Quebec Bulldogs had many feuds in the Montreal Westmount Arena. Lalonde was also a brilliant scorer. He scored 441 goals in 365 games and was scoring champion five times in the National Association Pacific Coast League and the National Hockey League (NHL). In the NHL alone he was fourth-highest scorer during the 1917 – 1918 season with 23 goals, second with 42 in 1919 – 1920 and leading scorer in 1918 – 1919 and 1920 – 1921 with 32 and 41, respectively. Once Lalonde scored 38 goals in an 11-game schedule and later scored 27 goals in 15 games with Vancouver. After retirement he was one of several professional players to begin coaching NHL teams. He and Hall of Famer Leo Dandurand coached the Canadiens during the 1934 – 1935 season.
Also in: Canada's Sports Hall of Fame, Canadian Lacrosse Hall of Fame and International Hockey Hall of Fame.

MALONE, Maurice Joseph
Player
Born February 28, 1890, in Quebec City, Que, died May 15, 1969.

1910 – 1917 Quebec Bulldogs, forward
1917 – 1919 Montreal Canadiens, forward
1919 – 1921 Hamilton, forward, coach, mgr.

Joe led the National Hockey League (NHL) in scoring 1912 – 1913, tied with Frank Nighbor, 1916 – 1917, and topped the league with 44 goals in 20 games in 1918. Between 1909 and 1924 he tallied 379 goals and during his 8 most productive seasons, 5 with Quebec, 2 with Hamilton and 1 with Montreal, he totaled 280 goals in 172 games. Against the Sydney Millionaires in the 1913 Stanley Cup playoff game, Joe skated for 9 goals. Other feats include 8 against Montreal in 1917 and 7 against Toronto in 1921, which is the modern-day record.
Also in: Canada's Sports Hall of Fame and International Hockey Hall of Fame.

PICKARD, Allan W.
Builder
Died April 7, 1975, in Exeter, Ont.
Administrator and organizer par excellence for over three decades, Al served as coach and president of the Regina Aces in the Regina YMCA League during the 1920s. A stalwart personality in the development of the Saskatchewan Amateur Hockey Association, he served the Association as executive member, president and president of the Saskatchewan Senior League in 1941. From 1947 to 1950 Al was president of the Canadian Amateur Hockey Association. He had also been the president of the Western Canada Senior League, governor of the Saskatchewan Junior League and of the Western Canada Junior League.
Also in: International Hockey Hall of Fame.

RAYMOND, Sen. Donat
Builder
Born January 30, 1880 in St. Stanislas de Kostka, Que; died June 5, 1963, at age 83.

Donat Raymond regularly attended hockey games at the Westmount Arena until it burned down in 1918. Seeing a need for a place where professional hockey could be played in Montreal, he became president of the company that built the Montreal Forum and organized the Maroons to play in the National Hockey League. When the Canadiens moved from the Mount Royal Arena to the Forum in 1925, a great rivalry between the Canadiens and the Maroons packed the arena with fans and professional hockey took root in Montreal. During difficult times in the 1930s, the Maroons folded and, had it not been for the faith and financial support of Donat Raymond, the Canadiens would have also. Raymond remained president of the company until 1955 when he became chairman of the board, a position he held until his death in 1963.
Also in: International Hockey Hall of Fame.

RICHARDSON, George
Player
Born in the 1880s in Kingston, Ont; commanding officer of No. 2 Company with the Canadian Expeditionary Force, Second Battalion, during W.W. I; killed in France February 9, 1916.

Always an amateur player, George was a member of the Queen's University team that won the Canadian Amateur Hockey Association senior championship in 1909. Two years previously he had played with the 14th Regiment of Kingston, losing the Ontario Hockey Association final series in 1907 and winning the series a year later. George Richardson Stadium at Queen's University was erected in his honor.
Also in: International Hockey Hall of Fame.

TRIHEY, Henry Judah "Harry"
Player
Born December 25, 1877; outstanding in lacrosse and football; organized 55th Regiment out of which emerged the 199th Battalion, Duchess of Connaught's own Irish Canadian Rangers; Lt. Col. and Commanding Officer of battalion; died in Montreal, Que, December 9, 1942.

Harry's involvement with hockey was varied, but all began when he was star of the McGill University hockey team as an excellent stickhandler, good shot and clever skater. Later, as captain, coach and rover of the Montreal Shamrocks, he led the team to Stanley Cup wins for two consecutive years, 1898 – 1899 and 1899 – 1900. He was the first to use a three-man line with a fourth man (a rover) to roam free, and encouraged defensemen to carry the puck. After his retirement from the team in 1901 he became secretary-treasurer and later president of the Canadian Amateur Hockey League, leading the league through many disputes with the Federal League in 1904 – 1905. Trihey also advised the Wanderers for several years and refereed many league and Stanley Cup games.
Also in: International Hockey Hall of Fame.

1952

BOON, Richard R.
Player
Born February 14, 1874, in Belleville, Ont; died May 3, 1961, in Outremont, Que, at age 83.

1901 – 1902 Montreal AAA, defenseman
1903 – 1918 Montreal Wanderers, defenseman, manager

Boon began playing in 1897 with the Montreal Monarch Hockey Club. Graduating from the junior to senior level, he was on the Montreal AAA's that won the Stanley Cup in 1902 over the Winnipeg Victorias. One of the first players to use the poke-check for stealing the puck from

the opposing player, he was instrumental in the three Stanley Cup wins by the Wanderers. In 1904 he was appointed director and coach of the club.
Also in: International Hockey Hall of Fame.

COOK, William Osser
Player

Born October 6, 1896, in Brantford, Ont; his brother Bun Cook also played for the New York Rangers; served overseas with Canadian field artillery outfit in 1917; saw action at Ypres, Vimy Ridge, the Somme and Flanders; joined a group of Canadians attached to the Royal Russian Army and fought Bolsheviks near the Arctic Circle in 1919; returning to Canada, tried farming in Saskatchewan on his veteran's land allotment, but found farming too dull; on All-Star first team, 1930, 1931, 1932; All-Star second team four times.

1926 – 1937 New York Rangers, forward
1951 – 1953 New York Rangers, coach

The adjacent forward to his brother Bun along with playmaking center Frank Boucher, Bill starred with the Rangers during their Stanley Cup years of 1927 – 1928 and 1932 – 1933. He was the National Hockey League's leading scorer in 1926 with 33 goals in 44 games, repeated in 1932 – 1933 with 28 goals and tied Charlie Conacher in 1932 with 34 goals. He led the Western Canada League in scoring three times when he played for the Saskatoon Sheiks in 1922. Aggressive play trademarked Cook's career; he often used the stick as a weapon. The most memorable brouhaha occurred during the 1935 Stanley Cup finals against the Montreal Maroons. Nels Crutchfield received eight stitches and was knocked unconscious by the butt end of Cook's stick. In Cook's opinion, Crutchfield had interfered and the referee failed to call it so the butt end of the stick became the arbitrator. After retiring in 1937 he coached in Cleveland one season. His leatherneck philosophy carried into coaching. When one of his players was felled by an opponent's rough style, Bill borrowed a uniform and skates and retaliated, placing the ruffian in the hospital. Eventually Cook's aggressive retaliatory raiding style of hockey was his undoing. Lasting less than two full seasons as coach with the Rangers, the players simply could not understand his fighting philosophy and failed to respond.
Also in: Canada's Sports Hall of Fame and International Hockey Hall of Fame.

GOHEEN, Francis Xavier "Moose"
Player

Born February 9, 1894, in White Bear Lake, Minn; outstanding in football and baseball; overseas in U.S. Army during W.W. I.

As a member of one of the strongest amateur hockey clubs in the early 1900s, Moose Goheen played his first season of hockey in 1915 – 1916 with the St. Paul Athletic Club. He was a high-scoring defenseman who led the team to a McNaughton Trophy win in 1916 – 1917 and again in 1917 – 1918, when the trophy became the Art Ross Cup. By winning the Cup from Lacime, Quebec, the St. Paul Athletic Club became the top amateur American hockey team. After W.W. I, Goheen returned to the Club when they again won the Art Ross Cup in 1920. Though drafted by the Boston Bruins, he refused to report and leave his good position with the Northern States Power. Later offered a contract by Toronto, he refused that also. Moose remained with the St. Paul Athletic Club until 1932, even after it became the professional team of the St. Paul Saints in 1925 – 1926. Goheen originated the wearing of helmets or headgear, not so much to ward off injury but to protect the players from sustained injuries.
Also in: International Hockey Hall of Fame and U.S. Hockey Hall of Fame.

JOHNSON, Ernest "Moose"
Player

Born 1886 in Montreal, Que; died March 25, 1963, in White Rock, B.C.

1905 – 1911 Montreal Wanderers, defenseman
1912 – 1916 New Westminster Royals, defenseman

The man with the longest reach in hockey history, 99 in, Moose played on four Stanley Cup winners with the Wanderers in 1906, 1907, 1908 and 1910. At the beginning of W.W. I, he moved to Portland, Ore, and played with the New Westminster Royals in the Pacific Coast League. The Royals won the league title in 1916. Johnson retired in 1931 after stints with the Victoria Maroons, Los Angeles and other teams in the Western Hockey League.
Also in: International Hockey Hall of Fame.

MacKAY, Duncan McMillan "Mickey"
Player

Born May 21, 1894, in Chesley, Ont; suffered heart attack while driving a car, involved in an accident and died in Nelson, B.C, May 21, 1940.

1926 – 1928 Chicago Black Hawks, forward
1928 – 1929 Pittsburgh Pirates, forward
1929 – 1930 Boston Bruins, forward

Manager Frank Patrick says of Mickey, "MacKay was a crowd-pleaser, clean, splendidly courageous, a happy player with a stylish way of going. He was sensational in quick breakaways, a sure shot in alone with a goalie and could stickhandle. He was outstanding in every way." This mild-mannered man first played hockey with the Chesley Colts and then with a senior team in British Columbia before joining the Vancouver Millionaires of the Pacific Coast League in 1914. In his rookie year he scored 33 goals, one point short of the scoring title, but did later capture the scoring title three times with the Millionaires. Also in his rookie season, his team won the Stanley Cup. In the only year of the Stanley Cup playoffs where a decision was not reached, 1918 – 1919, a celebrated fight took place between Seattle's Cully Wilson and MacKay. With a cross-check, Wilson broke MacKay's jaw, then was fined $50, received a match penalty and was eventually suspended from the Pacific Coast League. MacKay was the team's leading scorer when he played a season with the National Hockey League Chicago Black Hawks. After half a season with the Pirates, he played with Boston to win the Stanley Cup, then retired at the beginning of 1929 – 1930 and finished the season as the team's business manager.
Also in: International Hockey Hall of Fame.

1958

BOUCHER, Frank "Raffles"

Player

Born October 7, 1901, in Ottawa, Ont; as a member of a hockey-playing family, his brother George played with Ottawa, Billy and Bob with the Canadiens, and Frank with Vancouver; he joined North West Mounted Police as a 17-year-old but bought himself out with $50, which took him a full year to repay; Lady Byng Trophy 1928–1931, 1933–1935; All-Star first team 3 times; All-Star second team 4 times; resides in Regina, Sask.

1921–1922 Ottawa Senators, forward
1922–1926 Vancouver Maroons, forward
1926–1944 New York Rangers, forward

Boucher joined Ottawa for $1200 in 1921 and played with fellow Hall of Famers Frank Nighbor, Clint Benedict, Eddie Gerard, Cy Denneny, Punch Broadbent and his brother George. After a four-year stint in the Pacific Coast League (until its demise), Frank signed with the Boston Bruins who traded him to the New York Rangers before he played a single game. Frank played his career with the Rangers, leading them to two Stanley Cup wins. He scored 161 goals and 262 assists in 557 games and 18 goals and 18 assists in 67 playoffs. Retiring as a player in 1938, he won a 3rd Stanley Cup as coach in 1940.
Also in: Canada's Sports Hall of Fame, Greater Ottawa Sports Hall of Fame and International Hockey Hall of Fame.

CLANCY, Francis Michael "King"

Player

Born February 25, 1903, in Ottawa, Ont; inherited nickname from his equally famous father; All-Star first team twice; All-Star second team twice.

1921–1930 Ottawa Senators, defenseman
1930–1937 Toronto Maple Leafs, defenseman
1950–1953 Toronto Maple Leafs, coach

Clancy began professional play at the age of 18 with the Ottawa Senators, and with Eddie Gerard's retirement, established himself as an outstanding regular. The key figure in a 1930 trade, Conn Smythe paid a record $35,000 plus two players to obtain King. Smythe described it as "the best deal in hockey" and King proved it when he led the Leafs to their first Stanley Cup in 1931. Although small in stature and weight (150 lbs.) for a defenseman, his great speed and agility powered the team to two more National Hockey League championships before his retirement in 1937. Returning to coach the Leafs 1950 to 1953, he was later named assistant to general manager Punch Imlach. Many fine athletes have come from Ottawa, but King rates as one of the most refreshing and dynamic of the Irish breed. His career record reads 136 goals and 145 assists in 16 seasons; also 9 goals, 8 assists in 13 playoffs.
Also in: Canada's Sports Hall of Fame, Greater Ottawa Sports Hall of Fame and International Hockey Hall of Fame.

CLEGHORN, Sprague

Player

Born 1890 in Montreal, Que; died July 11, 1956.

1909–1910 New York Crescents, defenseman
1912–1918 Montreal Wanderers, defenseman
1918–1921 Ottawa Senators, defenseman
1921–1925 Montreal Canadiens, defenseman
1925–1928 Boston Bruins, defenseman

Sprague Cleghorn was one of the greatest, but roughest, defense players the game of hockey has ever known. In 17 seasons—he missed 1918 because of a broken leg—Cleghorn scored 163 goals. He also played with two Stanley Cup championship teams, the Ottawa club of 1920 and the Canadiens of 1924. His National Hockey League record is 84 goals, 29 assists in 10 seasons, 5 goals and 7 assists in 8 playoffs. Cleghorn retired in 1928.
Also in: International Hockey Hall of Fame.

CONNELL, Alex

Player

Born 1901 in Ottawa, Ont; secretary of the Ottawa Fire Department; played lacrosse with Ottawa's Eastern Canada champions; baseball catcher in the Interprovincial League; served in Army at Kingston during W.W. I, talked into playing goalie at this time; died after a lengthy illness, May 10, 1958, in Ottawa.

1924–1931 Ottawa Senators, goalie
1931–1932 Detroit Falcons, goalie
1932–1933 Ottawa Senators, goalie
1934–1935 Montreal Maroons, goalie
1936–1937 Montreal Maroons, goalie

Signing with the Ottawa Senators in 1924, his goaltending skill was instrumental in their Stanley Cup victory 1926–1927. The following year he established a record that held for over 40 years—6 consecutive shutouts, not scored upon for 446 min. and 9 secs. He sat out the 1933–1934 season, returned with the Montreal Maroons for a year, resting again in 1935–1936, played one more year and retired. His National Hockey League record is 827 goals in 415 games for a 1.99 average and 82 shutouts. His playoff average was 1.24.
Also in: Greater Ottawa Sports Hall of Fame and International Hockey Hall of Fame.

DUTTON, Mervyn "Red"

Player

Born July 23, 1898, in Russell, Man; mem. Hall of Fame Selection Comt; has business interests in Calgary, Alta.

1926–1930 Montreal Maroons, defenseman
1931–1936 New York Americans, defenseman
1936–1942 New York Americans, coach and manager

During W.W. I, Red was hit by a shrapnel blast at Wimy and almost lost his leg but recovered and practiced seven hours a day to strengthen it. From 1921 to 1925 Red played with Calgary, a team from the Pacific Coast Hockey League. In 1926 he began playing with the Montreal Maroons until 1930, when the Patricks sold the Western Canada League. From defenseman of the New York Americans, he became coach and manager of the team until the club ceased to operate in 1942. Red was one of the most penalized players in hockey. Although he had a mean reputation as a rough player, he was a model of decorum while president of the National Hockey League, 1943–1945.
Also in: International Hockey Hall of Fame.

FOYSTON, Frank C.
Player

Born February 2, 1891, in Minesing, Ont, 60 mi. N. of Toronto; died January 24, 1966 in Seattle, Wash.

1915–1920 Seattle Pacific Coast Hockey League (PCHL), forward
1924–1926 Victoria (PCHL), forward
1926–1928 Detroit Cougars, forward

Frank started playing hockey in a small, covered rink in his hometown. At 17 years of age he moved to organized hockey with the Barrie Dyment Colts. At 20 years of age he stepped into senior hockey with the Eatons of Toronto, and they won the Ontario Hockey Association title. Frank turned professional with Toronto of the National Hockey Association and was playing center for that team when they won the Stanley Cup in 1913–1914. Later, with the Seattle team, he was another Stanley Cup winner, the first U.S.-based team to win this historic trophy. He stayed with Seattle for nine years; moving on to play with Victoria for two seasons, and again capturing the Stanley Cup in 1924–1925. Detroit then purchased the team, and Frank went east and stayed two years in the Motor City, retiring as a player in the 1927–1928 season. Frank accumulated 186 goals in 11 seasons.
Also in: International Hockey Hall of Fame.

FREDRICKSON, Frank
Player

Born in Winnipeg, Man; returned from overseas duty in W.W. I with Canadian forces in 1919; served in the Royal Canadian Air Force in W.W. II; resides in Vancouver, B.C.

1924–1926 Victoria (Pacific Coast Hockey League), forward
1928–1930 Pittsburgh Pirates, center, coach and manager
1930–1931 Detroit Falcons, forward

Frank played his first senior hockey with the Winnipeg Falcons in 1913–1914, and in 1915 was captain of the University of Manitoba Club. In 1919 Frank joined the Winnipeg Falcons and captained them to an Allan Cup triumph and the 1920 Olympic crown at Antwerp. In 1920 he signed with Lester Patrick's Victoria Aristocrats (later changed to Cougars) and remained with them until the Western Coast League sold out. In 1925 they were Stanley Cup winners, but lost in finals the following year to Montreal Maroons. He played in Detroit for half a season, then Boston, and then went to play with Pittsburgh. There he played center and was both coach and manager, until a leg injury virtually ended his playing days. The following season he played with Detroit and retired. Frank scored 142 goals and led both the Pacific Coast League and the Western Coast League in 1920 and 1923. He continued coaching Winnipeg and Princeton University after his retirement.
Also in: International Hockey Hall of Fame.

GARDINER, Herbert Martin
Player

Born May 8, 1891, in Winnipeg, Man; on survey party for the Canadian Pacific Railway during 1910 to 1914; the next four years were spent in the Canadian Army; served overseas from 1915 to 1918, and won commission in the field; did surveying in the summer; Hart Trophy 1926–1927; died January 11, 1972, after a lengthy illness.

1920–1925 Calgary Tigers (Pacific Coast Hockey League), defenseman
1926–1929 Montreal Canadiens, defenseman

Herb didn't arrive in the National Hockey League until he was 35 years old. His true potential will never really be known. Herb started his hockey career in 1908 with the Winnipeg Victorias. Then in 1909–1910 he played with the Northern Crown Banks in the Bankers League, but was out of hockey for the next eight years. He returned to play in 1919 for the Calgary Rotarians. During 1920 to 1925 he played with the Calgary Tigers of the Western Canada League. In 1924 his team challenged the Montreal Canadiens for the Stanley Cup, and was unsuccessful, but Herb joined his opponents for the 1926–1927 season. In 1929 he was loaned to Chicago, where he acted as manager of the team. He went back to Montreal for the playoffs, but was later sold to Boston, and they in turn sold him to the Philadelphia Arrows. With the Philadelphia Arrows he became manager and coach, and remained with them until 1949. Later, Herb coached the Ramblers and Falcons.
Also in: International Hockey Hall of Fame.

HAY, George William
Player

Born January, 1898, in Listowel, Ont; weighed 156 lbs; uncle of Bill Hay, who played eight seasons with Chicago; All-Star team 1927–1928; died July 13, 1975, at Stratford.

1926–1927 Chicago Black Hawks, forward
1927–1930 Detroit Cougars, forward
1930–1933 Detroit Falcons, forward

George started playing with Winnipeg in his early days. He became an excellent stickhandler with the Winnipeg Monarchs Juniors of 1915 and 1916. During the 1920–1921 seasons, George played with the Regina Vics. He turned professional with the Regina Caps, and in the four years that he played with that team, he scored 87 goals and had 57 assists. He then moved on to play with the Portland Rosebuds where he scored 18 goals. The team was sold to Chicago and he moved into the National Hockey League. He didn't do well that season with Chicago, playing much of it with torn ligaments in his left shoulder, and was dealt to Detroit prior to the 1927–1928 season. While with the Cougars (later called the Red Wings) he led the club with 22 goals and 13 assists. He moved on to play three seasons with the Detroit Falcons. In his five National League seasons he accumulated 73 goals and collected 54 assists.
Also in: International Hockey Hall of Fame.

IRVIN, James Dickenson
Player

Born July 19, 1892, in Limestone Ridge, Ont; family moved to Winnipeg in 1899; served with the Canadian Army during W.W. I; died May 16, 1957, in Montreal.

1915–1916 Portland Rosebuds, forward
1921–1925 Regina Capitals, forward
1926–1930 Chicago Black Hawks, forward
1930–1931 Toronto Maple Leafs, forward
1940–1955 Montreal Canadiens, coach

James began playing in church and junior leagues around Winnipeg. In 1912, as an emergency replacement for the senior league Monarchs, he scored 6 goals in 2 games in the Allan Cup final, yet the team still lost to the visiting Winnipeg Victorias. In a 1914 exhibition series against the Toronto Rugby and Athletic Association, he scored 9 goals in one game. The Monarchs won the Allan Cup that same year. His professional career was interrupted with military service, returning in 1921 with the Regina Capitals after beginning with the Portland Rosebuds. As the first captain of the Chicago Hawks, he scored 18 goals with 18 assists in 1926–1927 for the second highest score in the league. A fractured skull in the twelfth game of the 1927–1928 season ended his career. He did return in 1931 for a Stanley Cup season with the Toronto team before retiring permanently. He added three more Stanley Cup winners while coaching the Canadiens.
Also in: Canada's Sports Hall of Fame and International Hockey Hall of Fame.

JOHNSON, Ivan Wilfrid "Ching"
Player
Born December 7, 1897, in Winnipeg, Man; incurred shrapnel wounds at Pass Chandaelle, France, during W.W. I; All-Star first team three times; All-Star second team twice.

1926–1937 New York Rangers, defenseman
1937–1938 New York Americans, defenseman

Ching was purchased by the New York Rangers in 1926 after spending three years with the Eveleth Miners and three years with the Minneapolis Millers. During his 11 seasons with the Rangers, Ching suffered broken leg, collar bone and jaw, plus an infection resulting from a sunlamp burn in 1936. At the age of 41 he retired from the National Hockey League with 463 games and 969 penalty minutes, 38 goals and 48 assists, plus two Stanley Cup championships. He played hockey for five additional years after retirement in Minneapolis, Marquette, Mich, Washington, D.C, and Hollywood, Calif.
Also in: International Hockey Hall of Fame.

KEATS, Gordon Blanchard "Duke"
Player
Born March 1, 1895, in Montreal, Que; moved to North Bay, Ont, when he was young; Canadian Army during W.W. I; died January 16, 1972, in Edmonton, Alta.

1926–1927 Boston Bruins, Detroit, forward
1927–1928 Detroit, Chicago Black Hawks, forward
1928–1929 Chicago, forward

At the age of 14 Duke was playing hockey in a Cobalt area for $75 a month. Following the war, he turned professional in 1919, with the Edmonton club in the Western Canada League, and led the league in scoring in 1923. After the Patricks sold the League in 1926, Duke joined Boston and then Detroit. He probably played for more teams and more leagues during his career than any other player. Following his trade to Chicago in the 1927–1928 season, he engaged the owner, Major McLaughlin, in a dispute that caused Duke's transfer to the American Association's Tulsa team for $5000. Although his National Hockey League career lasted only two seasons, and 30 goals, he played in various associations across western Canada for many years.
Also in: International Hockey Hall of Fame.

LEHMAN, Frederick Hugh
Player
Born October 27, 1885, in Pembroke, Ont; died April 8, 1961, in Toronto.

1926–1928 Chicago Black Hawks, goalie
1927–1928 Chicago Black Hawks, coach

Hughie Lehman was a goalie for 23 years, starting out in the Pembroke club which won the Citizens Shield in 1905–1906. After a season of hockey with the International Professional League in Sault Ste. Marie, Ont, he returned to Pembroke for semiprofessional hockey, but found himself playing three seasons with Berlin (now Kitchener) in the Ontario Professional Hockey League. Moving west in 1911–1912, Lehman played three seasons with the New Westminster Royals of the Pacific Coast League. He moved to the Vancouver Millionaires for the 1914–1915 season and stayed with the team until it was sold by the Patricks after the 1925–1926 season. His career with the National Hockey League began then, and he played 48 games with 136 goals against and six shut-outs. In his last year with the Black Hawks, Lehman was co-coach with Barney Stanley. In his years as goalie, he played on eight Stanley Cup challenges and had success with the Vancouver Millionaires in 1914–1915. He holds the record, with Percy Le Sueur, of playing for two different challenging teams within two months, Galt against Ottawa and Berlin against the Wanderers in 1909–1910.
Also in: International Hockey Hall of Fame.

MORAN, Patrick Joseph "Paddy"
Player
Born March 11, 1877, in Quebec City, Que; died January 14, 1966, in Quebec City.

Paddy began playing organized hockey at age 15 with the Sarsfield city juvenile team. After two seasons with the Quebec Dominion juniors, he moved into intermediate play with the Crescent team, winning the Canadian intermediate championship in 1901. His final 15 seasons (1901–1916) were spent with the Quebec Bulldogs as goalie where he allowed 5.4 goals in 201 games while winning the Stanley Cup in 1912 and 1913.
Also in: International Hockey Hall of Fame.

McNAMARA, George
Player
Born August 26, 1886, in Penetang, Ont; moved to Sault Ste. Marie when very young; served with the 228th Sportsman's Battalion during W.W. I; died March 10, 1952.

1908–1909 Montreal Shamrocks
1909–1912 Halifax Crescents
1912–1913 Toronto Tecumsehs
1913–1914 Toronto Ontarians

George began playing hockey around Sault Ste. Marie. His big-time debut came with the Michigan Soo team in 1907. The following year he joined the Shamrocks of the Eastern Canada League. After three seasons in the Maritime League with Halifax, he ended his career with the Ontarians in 1914. Until departing for overseas, he played for the Canadian Sportsman's Battalion. Returning in 1921, he coached the Sault Ste. Marie Greyhounds to the Allan Cup in 1924.
Also in: International Hockey Hall of Fame.

NORRIS, James

Builder

Born December 10, 1879, in St. Catharines, Ont; died December 4, 1952.

Making a fortune in grain commodities, James bought the Chicago Shamrocks of the American Hockey League in 1930. Three years later, he and his son purchased Olympia Stadium and the National Hockey League (NHL) franchise Detroit Falcons. They changed the name to Red Wings and built them into three-time Stanley Cup champions, 1936, 1937 and 1943. With only six NHL teams, the Norris family owned interests in three of them, Chicago, Detroit and the New York Rangers.
Also in: International Hockey Hall of Fame.

PATRICK, Frank A.

Builder

Born December 23, 1885, in Ottawa, Ont; his father Joseph Patrick was in the lumber business; mother's name was Grace; one of eight children; played hockey for McGill University; died of a heart attack on June 29, 1960.

A star player in college and with the Renfrew Millionaires of the fledging National Hockey Association, Frank refereed the Montreal Senior League at age 20. In 1911 Frank and his brother Lester originated the Pacific Coast League. They constructed the first artificial ice arena in Vancouver costing $350,000 and seating 10,000. This was the largest building in Canada at the time. Frank was the manager and captain of the Vancouver Millionaires, winning the Stanley Cup in 1915 and reaching the finals two other times. One of the largest and most influential decisions in hockey history occurred in 1926 when the Patricks sold their six teams and players to eastern interests, forming the National Hockey League. An innovator and doer, Frank was an integral part of the new league, serving as manager and director of the National Hockey League and as coach for the Boston Bruins and Montreal Canadiens. He is the originator of the blue line, only one of 22 pieces of legislation he introduced into the new league.
Also in: British Columbia Sports Hall of Fame, Canada's Sports Hall of Fame and International Hockey Hall of Fame.

SMYTHE, Constantine Falkland Cary M.C.

Builder

Born February 1, 1895 in Toronto, Ont; Irish father, English mother; father Albert Ernest Stafford Smythe was a newspaperman; mother died when he was 7; father wanted him to be a lawyer, so he was surrounded by Tennyson and Dickens; attended University of Toronto before and after the war, completing courses in civil engineering; artillery man overseas in W.W. I; commissioned in battle and won Military Cross in 1916; transferred to Royal Flying Corps as reconnaissance pilot; worked for Toronto's public works department; fought army policy to fight in W.W. II; just before discharge precipitated national crisis by risking a court-martial to denounce army's recruiting methods; conflict led to the resignation of the minister of national defense; owned horse-racing stable and won Queen's Plate in 1953 and 1967; also owned a sand and gravel business; closely associated with the Ontario Society for Crippled Children.

Conn Smythe was a tough man, and in his 50 years, he contributed greatly to the growth and respectability of hockey. His first involvement in the sport was as captain of the varsity team that won the Ontario Championship in 1915. He later coached the varsity seniors to a 1927 Allan Cup victory and the varsity grads to the 1928 Olympic title. His early prominence in hockey brought him to the New York Rangers in 1927 – 1928, where he assembled the Stanley Cup winning team. After being fired from the Rangers, he spent years waiting to get his revenge. He soon bought the Toronto St. Pats (eventually the Maple Leafs) and even built the team a stadium, the Toronto Maple Leaf Garden, which was unveiled on November 12, 1931, with a crowd of 13,542 to watch Chicago beat Toronto, 3 – 1. Smythe would accept nothing but the best of his team. In 1930 – 1931, he decided that he needed King Clancy, and Ottawa agreed to trade him for two players and $35,000. During the depression, this was a tremendous financial burden for everyone but Conn Smythe. After borrowing money from a few friends, he bet it on a long-shot horse, his own Rare Jewel, and got the money for King Clancy. When player Turk Broda was overweight, he called the goalie into his office and told him that he was not playing any hockey until he lost ten pounds. Broda knew Smythe meant business, went on a crash diet, attended gym where he was boiled and pounded, lost ten pounds and only one game. In 1931 – 1932 with Charlie Conacher, Harvey Jackson and Joe Primeau, Smythe finally got his revenge against the New York Rangers by winning 3 straight games, 6 goals in each, and the Stanley Cup. The team won the Cup six more times while Smythe was in charge—1941 – 1942, 1944 – 1945, 1946 – 1947, 1947 – 1948, 1948 – 1949 and 1950 – 1951. They also finished first 5 times in the league and, by Smythe's doing, broadcast their Saturday night games from coast to coast. Smythe was probably one of the most publicized hockey figures because he knew feuds with rival teams made good copy. After serving the Maple Leafs as coach, general manager, managing director and chairman of the board, he finally resigned in 1961—from Florida—when his successors staged a heavyweight fight in the Garden. Even with the pride he took in supervising the construction of the Hockey Hall of Fame, he resigned from the Hall of Fame Committee when he opposed the induction of Busher Jackson in 1971. In honor of this great hockey man, the Maple Leaf Gardens, since 1964, has awarded the Conn Smythe Trophy annually to the most valuable player in the Stanley Cup playoffs.
Also in: Canada's Sports Hall of Fame, Canadian Horse Racing Hall of Fame and International Hockey Hall of Fame.

TURNER, Lloyd

Builder

Born 1884 in Elmvale, Ont; lived in Sault Ste. Marie and Fort William before arriving in Calgary in 1909; played with famous McNamaras at the Soo; coached, played and managed team in Fort William.

Perhaps the most rewarding accomplishment of Lloyd Turner, often called "Mr. Hockey," was the organization of Alberta's Indian tribes into teams for tournament competition. He liked to involve everyone in hockey. When he arrived in Calgary he organized both a team (which eventually became the Calgary Tigers) and a

hockey league. He even installed ice in an old roller skating rink when his team had a bid for the Stanley Cup in 1924 and reorganized the Western Canada League in 1931 when he returned from Minneapolis and Seattle. Another of his many accomplishments, Turner played a part in the resurgence of the Allan Cup competitions in the early 1930s.
Also in: International Hockey Hall of Fame.

1959

ADAMS, John James "Jack"
Player
Born June 14, 1895, in Fort William, Ont; at 16 he played in the Northern Amateur League with Peterboro and Sarnia; died May 1, 1968, at age 72, of a heart attack.

1917 – 1919 Toronto Arenas, forward
1919 – 1922 Vancouver Maroons, forward
1922 – 1926 Toronto St. Pats, forward
1926 – 1927 Ottawa Senators, player
1927 – 1947 Detroit Red Wings, coach, manager
1947 – 1962 Chicago Black Hawks, general manager

Jack Adams dominated the hockey scene, on and off the ice, in Detroit for 35 years. Beginning in 1927 as coach, he produced 12 regular season championships (7 of those were consecutive) nd 7 Stanley Cups. His innovative farm system developed the incomparable Gordie Howe. As a National Hockey League player, Adams' career statistics read 82 goals and 29 assists in 7 seasons. He was a member of two Stanley Cup winners as a player, first with the Toronto Arenas and then with King Clancy at Ottawa. Before joining Ottawa for the 1926 – 1927 season, Jack had won the Pacific Coast League scoring title with Vancouver, recording 24 goals and 18 assists in 24 games. Following his 35-year affliation with the Red Wings, Jack joined the Chicago Black Hawks as general manager. He served the Central Professional League as president from 1962 to 1968.
Also in: Canada's Sports Hall of Fame and International Hockey Hall of Fame.

DENNENY, Cyril Joseph
Player
Born December 23, 1891, in Farran's Point, Ont; moved to Cornwall in 1897; died September 1970.

1912 – 1913 Russell, left wing
1913 – 1914 O'Brien Mine, left wing
1914 – 1916 Toronto Shamrocks, left wing
1916 – 1928 Ottawa Senators, left wing
1928 – 1929 Boston Bruins, left wing

With a 14-year professional career, Cy played on 5 Stanley Cup winners, 4 with Ottawa and one with Boston. During his 1917 – 1918 season, he tallied 36 goals in 22 games, his best single season. Moving to the Bruins for his final season as a player, he was largely responsible for coaching and assisting the general manager. His last coaching position was with Ottawa in the 1933 – 1934 season. Cy also refereed in the National Hockey League, 1929 – 1930.
Also in: Greater Ottawa Sports Hall of Fame and International Hockey Hall of Fame.

THOMPSON, Cecil "Tiny"
Player
Born May 31, 1905, in Sandon, B.C; Vezina Trophy 1929 – 1930, 1932 – 1933, 1935 – 1936, 1937 – 1938; All-Star first team twice; All-Star second team twice; one of the chief scouts for the Chicago Black Hawks.

1928 – 1938 Boston Bruins, goalie
1938 – 1939 Boston Bruins, Detroit Red Wings, goalie
1939 – 1940 Detroit Red Wings, goalie

His first experience with hockey was in Sandon before he played amateur hockey with the Calgary Monarch Juniors, the Pacific Grain Seniors, Bellvue Bulldogs and Duluth, in the Minor Central League. Thompson joined Minnesota for two seasons in 1924 and turned professional when they did and then was purchased by Boston. In his first season with the Bruins, he took over the goalie position from Hal Winkler and went with Boston for their first Stanley Cup victory. After ten seasons with the Bruins, he then finished out his professional career in Detroit with a 2.27 average in league games and a 2.0 average in playoff games. His most memorable game was in 1933 against Toronto, which lasted 104.46 before Toronto finally won, 1 – 0.
Also in: International Hockey Hall of Fame.

1960

ADAMS, Charles Francis
Builder
Born October 18, 1876, in Newport, Vt; started as chore boy in a small grocery and made a fortune as head of grocery chain; his son Weston W, Sr, also in Hockey Hall of Fame; died in 1947 at age 71.

After forming the Boston Bruins in 1924 with Art Ross, Adams bought the entire Western Canada League from the Patrick brothers for $300,000. The influx of new players from the Western League transformed the National Hockey League into the paramount professional league. Players like Eddie Shore, Harry Oliver and Duke Keats joined the Bruins and helped bring the Stanley Cup to the Hub in 1929. Adams built the Boston Garden by guaranteeing $500,000 over a five-year span for the 24 home games. With the completion of the Garden in 1927, Adams saw his Bruins win three Stanley Cups before his death in 1947.
Also in: Canada's Sports Hall of Fame and International Hockey Hall of Fame.

BOUCHER, George "Buck"
Player
Born 1896, Ottawa, Ont; member of the celebrated Boucher hockey family; brother Frank in the Hall of Fame, Billy and Bob played with Canadiens, Frank with Vancouver, George with Ottawa; played football for three years with Ottawa Rough Riders as halfback; died October 17, 1960, from throat cancer.

1917 – 1928 Ottawa Senators, defenseman
1928 – 1931 Montreal Maroons, defenseman
1931 – 1932 Chicago Black Hawks, defenseman

As a member of the Ottawa Senators, the team won four Stanley Cup titles between 1920 and 1927. Toward the end of his career, he played for Montreal and Chicago,

achieving a career total of 122 goals for a defenseman. Retiring in 1934, he turned to coaching. His Ottawa amateur club won the Allan Cup in 1949. He helped select and train the Ottawa RCAF that won the 1948 Olympics for Canada. Other teams he directed were Boston, St. Louis, and Chicago.
Also in: Greater Ottawa Sports Hall of Fame and International Hockey Hall of Fame.

KILPATRICK, Gen. John Reed
Builder
Born June 15, 1889; outstanding athlete in many sports; at Yale University, captain of track team in 1911 and captain of football team which was unscored on in 1910; twice voted All-American end and credited with throwing the first overhand pass, against Princeton in 1907; died May 7, 1960, at age 71.

Kilpatrick liked to boast that he was New York's Number One hockey fan and admitted that the National Hockey League (NHL) provided his favorite spectator sport. He was first elected NHL governor in 1936 and became the original director of the NHL Player's Pension Society when it was established in 1946. He served the Society until his death in 1960. Kilpatrick was also president of Madison Square Garden and president of the New York Rangers for 22 years, during which time he watched the team win two Stanley Cups.
Also in: International Hockey Hall of Fame and National Football Hall of Fame.

MANTHA, Sylvio
Player
Born April 14, 1903 in Montreal, Que; All-Star second team 1931 – 1932; died August 7, 1974, in Montreal.

1923 – 1936 Montreal Canadiens, defenseman, coach
1936 – 1937 Boston Bruins, defenseman

Sylvio began hockey in the junior league in 1918. He was a forward with the Notre Dame de Grace club. Moving through junior and senior ranks, he signed with the Canadiens and switched to defense in 1923. Instrumental in the two Stanley Cups 1930 and 1931, he later turned to coaching the Canadiens before his trade to Boston. After retirement he became a linesman in the National Hockey League. Tiring of travel, he returned to Montreal and coached junior and senior teams for many years.
Also in: International Hockey Hall of Fame.

SELKE, Frank J.
Builder
Born May 7, 1893, in Kitchener, Ont; began work at 13 in a furniture factory; later an electrician and union executive; resides near Montreal.

As an adolescent, Frank spent all his spare time involved with sports, becoming manager of the Iroquois Bantams at the age of 14. In 1918 Selke began a lasting friendship with Hall of Famer Conn Smythe and a close association with the Toronto Maple Leafs, which won the Stanley Cup three times while he was their assistant general manager. In 1946 he replaced Tommy Gorman as managing director of the Montreal Canadiens. In the 18 years he managed the team, the won the Stanley Cup 6 times, 5 times consecutively. Maurice "The Rocket" Richard dominated hockey on the Canadiens team in Selke's time, and it was Selke who gave Hall of Famer Red Horner his break into professional hockey, not so much for his skating ability but for his sheer determination. In almost 60 years as coach, manager and front office executive, Selke was involved with the construction of Maple Leaf Gardens, Cincinnati Gardens, Rochester War Memorial and numerous other arenas. One of his most satisfying accomplishments was his involvement with the formation of the Hockey Hall of Fame, where he is currently a member of the Governing Committee and chairman of the Selection Committee.
Also in: Canada's Sports Hall of Fame and International Hockey Hall of Fame.

WALKER, John Phillip "Jack"
Player
Born November 28, 1888, in Silver Mountain, Ont; named most valuable player with Seattle 1920 and 1930; most valuable player with Detroit 1927 and 1928; died in Seattle February 16, 1950.

1912 – 1913 Moncton Maritime League
1913 – 1915 Toronto Arenas
1916 – 1917 Seattle Metropolitans
1924 – 1925 Victoria Cougars
1926 – 1928 Detroit Cougars
1928 – 1929 Edmonton Eskimos
1931 – 1932 Hollywood Stars

Jack Walker, as the originator of the hook-check, played mostly on western teams. He learned the game in Port Arthur and beginning in 1906, played on four consecutive city championship teams. He was on 3 Stanley Cup teams—Toronto Arenas 1913 – 1914, Seattle Metropolitans 1916 – 1917 and the Victoria Cougars 1924 – 1925—before going into the National Hockey League with the Detroit Cougars. During his National Hockey League career, he had 5 goals and 8 assists in two seasons. Retiring from active play in 1934, Jack continued to manage, coach and referee in the Pacific Coast League.
Also in: International Hockey Hall of Fame.

1961

APPS, Joseph Sylvanus
Player
Born January 18, 1915, in Paris, Ont; attended McMaster University, excelling in hockey, football and track; won the British Empire pole-vaulting championship in 1934, the Canadian championship in 1934 and 1935; finished sixth in pole-vault in 1936 Olympics; Calder Trophy 1936; All-Star first team twice; All-Star second team 3 times; Lady Byng Trophy 1942; served in Canadian Armed Forces 1943 – 1945; currently a member of Parliament; resides in Kingston, Ont.

Spending his entire career with the Maple Leafs 1936 – 1948, Apps was the first rookie to win the Calder Trophy. Returning from military duty for the 1945 – 1946 season, he played 3 years and scored 24, 25 and 26 goals for a career total of 201, plus 231 assists. In his 69 playoff games, he scored 25 goals and 28 assists. During his career, Apps averaged 20 goals a season for 10 years. He retired in 1948.
Also in: Canada's Sports Hall of Fame, Canadian Amateur Athletic Hall of Fame and International Hockey Hall of Fame.

BROWN, George V.
Builder
Born October 21, 1880, in Boston, Mass; founder of the famed Boston Marathon; died October 17, 1937.

With the completion of the Boston Arena in 1910, Brown initiated the Boston Athletic Association (BAA) hockey team. His club competed against colleges and top amateur clubs in eastern U.S. and Canada. In 1918 the Arena was decimated by fire and Brown headed a corporation for the Boston Garden while still directing the BAA. When the Bruins moved into the Garden, he started the Canadian-American League, forerunner of the American Hockey League. During the 1924 Olympics, 7 of the 10 players of the BAA played in the Olympics, finishing second to the Canadian squad. He served as general manager of the Boston Garden until his death.
Also in: International Hockey Hall of Fame and U.S. Hockey Hall of Fame.

CONACHER, Charles William, Sr.
Player
Born December 10, 1909, in Toronto, Ont; brothers Ray and Lionel played in the National Hockey League (NHL); All-Star first team 3 times; All-Star second team twice; died of cancer December 30, 1967, in Toronto.

1929–1938 Toronto Maple Leafs, forward
1938–1939 Detroit Red Wings, forward
1939–1941 New York Americans, forward

Jumping directly from junior hockey to the NHL, Charlie played 13 seasons, winning the top-scorer title in 1934 and 1935, and shared that same honor with Bill Cook in 1932 and Bill Thoms in 1936. Charlie retired in 1941 and turned to coaching junior hockey, but returned to the professional ranks in 1947 as coach of the Chicago Black Hawks until 1950 when he again retired, this time to the business world. His NHL career totals include 225 goals, 173 assists in 13 seasons, along with 17 goals, 18 assists in 9 playoffs.
Also in: Canada's Sports Hall of Fame and International Hockey Hall of Fame.

DAY, Clarence Henry "Happy"
Player
Born June 14, 1901, in Owen Sound, Ont; studied pharmacy at the University of Toronto; presently involved with the manufacturing of construction tools in St. Thomas, Ont.

1924–1926 Toronto St. Patricks, defenseman
1926–1937 Toronto Maple Leafs, defenseman
1937–1938 New York Americans, defenseman
1950–1957 Toronto Maple Leafs, coach, general manager

A player, coach, referee and general manager for 33 years, Happy was captain of the first Toronto Maple Leafs team ever to win the Stanley Cup, in 1931–1932, scoring 3 goals in that series. During his playing career, he scored a total of 86 goals, 116 assists in 14 seasons, as well as 4 goals, 7 assists in 9 playoff series. Happy played his final seasons in 1937–1938 with the New York Americans. He refereed 2 seasons, then returned to the Maple Leafs as coach from 1940 to 1950, winning 5 Stanley Cups (3 in a row). He became general manager in 1950 until retirement in 1957, when he entered business life. He also coached the West Toronto Nationals to a Memorial Cup in 1936.
Also in: International Hockey Hall of Fame.

ELLIOTT, Edwin S. "Chaucer"
Referee
Born in 1879 in Kingston, Ont; died of cancer on March 13, 1913, at age 34.

Chaucer was a natural athlete who recorded great achievements in many sports, particularly hockey, baseball and football. He played point on the Queen's University hockey team which he captained, and also captained the Granite football team which won the Canadian championship in 1899. In 1903 he joined the Toronto baseball team in the Eastern League and 3 years later (in 1906) coached the Toronto Argonauts football team, as well as the Hamilton Tigers, who won the Canadian championship. Later he joined the Montreal AAA as football coach and ultimately became adviser of the entire organization. Chaucer became a hockey referee in 1903 for the Ontario Hockey Association, serving in that capacity for 10 years.
Also in: International Hockey Hall of Fame.

HAINSWORTH, George
Player
Born June 26, 1895, in Toronto, Ont; Vezina Trophy 1927–1929; died October 9, 1950, in an auto accident.

1923–1926 Saskatoon
1926–1933 Montreal Canadiens, goalie
1933–1936 Toronto Maple Leafs, goalie

Hainsworth moved as a youth to Kitchener, Ont, and made his debut in hockey. His composure under fire and an unquestionable skill brought him to the attention of Kitchener Juniors in 1912 and from there he quickly moved into the senior ranks. George played with championship teams all the way, including an Allan Cup winner in 1918. He turned professional in 1923 with Saskatoon, shifting to the Montreal Canadiens where he was an immediate sensation. In the 1928–1929 season, Hainsworth performed the incredible feat of 22 shutouts in 44 games. He allowed only 43 goals that year, an average of less than one per game. His National Hockey League record shows that he allowed 938 goals in 465 games for 2.02 average, 91 shutouts; gave up 112 goals in 52 playoffs for 2.15 average, 8 shutouts. He retired in 1937.
Also in: International Hockey Hall of Fame.

HALL, Joseph Henry
Player
Born May 3, 1882, in Staffordshire, England; family moved to Winnipeg when he was 2 years old, moved to Brandon, Man, in 1900; died April 5, 1919, of influenza.

1910–1916 Quebec Bulldogs, defenseman
1917–1919 Montreal Canadiens, defenseman

Joe started playing hockey in 1897 and turned professional in 1905 with Kenora. He was playing with Brandon in 1907, but went with Kenora for the Cup series, although he did not play. During the years with the Bulldogs, he played on two Stanley Cup teams, 1911–1912 and 1912–1913. Joe finished his career with the Canadiens, who won the National Hockey League title in 1918–1919 and went west to play for the Stanley

Cup in Seattle. The series progressed through 5 games with each team winning 2 games and tying 1 when the local Department of Health called the series off because of an influenza epidemic. Joe was the most seriously stricken of the players who contracted the disease and died of it.
Also in: International Hockey Hall of Fame.

ION, Fred J. "Mickey"
Referee
Born February 25, 1886, in Paris Ont; excelled in baseball and lacrosse, played professionally with the Toronto Tecumsehs, Vancouver Salmonbellies and New Westminster; died October 26, 1964.

Mickey began refereeing in 1913 in amateur leagues around British Columbia. Frank Patrick, founder and promoter of the Pacific Coast League (PCL), admired Mickey's ability to control the game and signed him into the professional ranks. With the demise of the PCL Mickey transferred into the National Hockey League (NHL). He refereed the Howie Morenz Memorial Game in the Montreal Forum, November 2, 1937, and continued as an NHL official until his retirement in 1941.
Also in: International Hockey Hall of Fame.

LeSUEUR, Percy
Player
Born November 18, 1881 in Quebec City, Que; not only a hockey player, but also manager, referee, arena manager, broadcaster, columnist and inventor; developed the gauntlet-type gloves for goalies and the net used by the National Association and the National Hockey League (NHL) 1912–1925; joined 48th Highlanders for W.W. I in 1916; original member of radio's Hot Stove League; died in Hamilton, Ont, January 27, 1962.

First an intermediate hockey player in Quebec City, Percy switched from right wing to goalie while playing senior hockey in Smith Falls, Ont. In 1906 he joined the Ottawa Senators and played in his first Stanley Cup playoffs. The Kenora Thistles won that year, but the Senators were victorious in 1908–1909 and 1910–1911. LeSueur was captain for three seasons and coached-managed for part of 1913–1914, after which he joined Toronto for a season. Following the war, he refereed and then coached the Hamilton team of the NHL. He was also the first manager of the Detroit Olympia team.
Also in: Greater Ottawa Sports Hall of Fame and International Hockey Hall of Fame.

LOICQ, Paul
Builder
Born in Brussels, Belgium in 1890; graduated from university as a lawyer; served with distinction as a Colonel in the Belgian Army during W.W. I, being cited for bravery; date of death unknown; posthumously elected to the Hall of Fame in 1960 and official crest was presented to his widow December 4, 1961, by the president of the Belgian Olympic Committee.

Paul started skating in 1906 and 3 years later was selected as a member of Belgium's national hockey team, playing continuously for his country until retirement after the 1924 Olympic Games at Chamonix, France. Loicq was elected president of the International Ice Hockey Federation in 1927 and served with honor and distinction for 20 years, not only as an executive, but as a referee of international stature. Hockey men generally agree that it was Loicq's influence which brought about acceptance of hockey as an official part of the Winter Olympic Games.
Also in: International Hockey Hall of Fame.

RANKIN, Frank
Player
Born April 1, 1889, in Stratford, Ont.

1906–1909 Stratford Juniors
1910–1912 Eaton Athletic Association
1912–1915 Toronto St. Michaels

Frank was a rover in the era of 7-man hockey, first playing as a member of the Stratford Juniors. His team won the Ontario Hockey Association (OHA) title 3 consecutive seasons, 1906–1907, 1907–1908 and 1908–1909. With the formation of the Eaton Athletic Association in Toronto, Rankin became its first captain and rover and led them to the Ontario title in 1910–1911 and 1911–1912. Each year Eaton played in the Allan Cup finals and each time lost to the Winnipeg Victorias. As a member of Toronto St. Michaels, he played in the OHA finals, losing to Toronto. Trying for a third OHA title, his team was defeated by the Toronto Victorias. He later went on to become a successful coach and in 1924, directed the Toronto Granites to an Olympic championship, winning the world amateur title at Chamonix, France.
Also in: International Hockey Hall of Fame.

RICHARD, Maurice "The Rocket"
Player
Born August 4, 1921, in Montreal, Que; second of seven children; All-Star first team 8 times and second team 6 times; resides in Montreal with several business interests, including fishing equipment sales.

After a brief stint with the Verdun juniors and the Canadiens senior team, Maurice was brought into the parent club in 1942. He played with the Canadiens as a forward 1942–1960. Scoring 5 goals in his first 16 games, he then broke an ankle and remained sidelined for the remainder of the year. Although he was to miss only 12 games in the next 6 seasons, injuries plagued The Rocket to the end of his playing days. He became the first man to score 50 goals in a 50-game season. He holds records for winning goals (83) and tying goals (28). During his career, the ambidextrous Rocket tallied 544 goals and 421 assists in 978 league games as well as 82 goals and 44 assists in 133 playoffs. A slashed Achilles tendon abruptly ended his career in 1960. The five-year retirement requirement was waived and Maurice was elected into the Hall only 9 months after leaving the game. He coached briefly in the World Hockey Association for Quebec but resigned in 1972 because of a nervous condition.
Also in: Canada's Sports Hall of Fame and International Hockey Hall of Fame.

SCHMIDT, Milton Conrad
Player
Born March 5, 1918, in Kitchener, Ont; joined Royal Canadian Air Force during W.W. II; Hart Trophy 1952; All-Star first team 3 times and second team once; presently general manager of the Boston Bruins.

Milt first played hockey in the Kitchener area, before turning professional with Providence and moving to the Boston Bruins, where he played his entire National Hockey League (NHL) career (1936–1966). There he became the center of the well-known "Kraut Line" with Kitchener schoolmates Bobby Bauer and Woody Dumart. He was a determined player but received numerous injuries during his career. In one Stanley Cup playoff game, Schmidt's knees became so swollen that he could not bend them. He had his legs taped from ankle to thigh and was lifted off the table and into his skates to finish the game. The Bruins won four straight NHL championships, beginning in 1938, and 2 Stanley Cup victories in 1939 and 1941. Schmidt captured the League's scoring title in 1939–1940 and accumulated 229 goals and 346 assists in his 16 seasons; 24 goals and 25 assists in 86 playoffs. Milt gave up playing midway through the 1954–1955 season to to become the Bruins coach, for 7 seasons, before moving into the general manager's spot.
Also in: Canada's Sports Hall of Fame and International Hockey Hall of Fame.

SEIBERT, Oliver Levi
Player
Born March 18, 1881, in Berlin, Ont; son Earl was elected to Hall of Fame in 1963; once raced against a trotter horse on the ice of the Grand River and won after one mile; died of a stroke on May 15, 1944.

In his early hockey days, Seibert played on a team comprised entirely of his own well-known family. Though other players followed, Oliver was the first Berlin player to turn professional. Starting with the Houghton, Michigan team, he later played with London and Guelph in the Ontario Professional League and the Northwestern Michigan League. He joined the Berlin Rangers, starting as a goalie but switching to a forward position and was with this team when they won the Western Ontario Hockey Association championship 6 consecutive years, 1900–1906. Seibert was also one of the first Canadians to play on artificial ice.
Also in: International Hockey Hall of Fame.

SMEATON, J. Cooper
Referee
Born in 1890 in Carleton Place, Ont; moved to Montreal as a child; moved back to Montreal for family reasons; married in 1913; overseas in W.W. I and received the Military Medal; currently a branch manager of the Sun Life Insurance Company.

J. Cooper Smeaton played baseball, football, basketball and hockey for the Westmount Amateur Athletic Association in his earlier years. Although he had many offers to become a professional hockey player, he rejected them all, becoming instead, an outstanding official, working in that capacity for more than 25 years. He was refereeing amateur hockey games before his appointment to the staff of the National Hockey Association where he handled many playoff games of both the Allan and Stanley Cup series. Smeaton managed the Philadelphia Quakers of the National Hockey League (NHL) in the 1930–1931 season, but returned to refereeing the next year when Philadelphia withdrew from the league. Smeaton was appointed referee-in-chief of the NHL and continued until 1937 when he retired to devote his time to business. He was appointed a trustee of the Stanley Cup in 1946, a position he still holds.
Also in: International Hockey Hall of Fame.

STUART, Bruce
Player
Born 1882 in Ottawa Valley, Ont; died October 28, 1961.

1898–1900 Ottawa Senators
1900–1901 Quebec Bulldogs
1901–1902 Ottawa Senators
1907–1908 Montreal Wanderers
1908–1911 Ottawa Senators

Bruce developed into an all-around forward, capable of playing any of the positions, although he excelled as a rover. In 45 scheduled games during his career, Stuart scored 63 goals and once scored six goals in a single game. During his major league career, he played on three Stanley Cup champion teams—Montreal in 1908 and Ottawa in 1909 and 1911.
Also in: Greater Ottawa Sports Hall of Fame and International Hockey Hall of Fame.

WAGHORNE, Fred C.
Builder
Born in 1866 in Tunbridge Wells, England; died in 1956 at age 90.

In 50 years of officiating more than 2000 hockey games and 1500 lacrosse games, Fred Waghorne became quite an innovator in the sport. It was he who initiated the system of dropping the puck between the stickhandlers, rather than placing it between the players, stick blades in a faceoff. Waghorne was also the first referee to use a whistle for stopping play, rather than the bell, which was sometimes heavy and cumbersome. He was one of the pioneers of the Toronto Hockey League, formed in 1911.
Also in: Canadian Lacrosse Hall of Fame and International Hockey Hall of Fame.

1962

AHEARN, T. Franklin
Builder
Born May 10, 1886, Ottawa, Ont; died November 17, 1962, at age 86.

After purchasing the Ottawa Senators from Tommy Gorman in 1924, Frank Ahearn assembled one of the most formidable teams ever with such Hall of Famers as Alex Connell, Hooley Smith, Frank Nighbor and Syd Howe. His team won the Stanley Cup in 1926–1927. With the approaching 1930s and the depression, Ahearn was forced to sell and trade his stars in a series of shrewd deals. Eventually, he sold his rink and lost an estimated $200,000 in hockey, a loss he never regretted.
Also in: International Hockey Hall of Fame.

BROADBENT, Harry L. "Punch"
Player
Born 1892 in Ottawa, Ont; awarded Canadian Military Medal for W.W. I service; died March 6, 1971.

1918–1924 Ottawa Senators, forward
1924–1927 Montreal Maroons, forward
1927–1928 Ottawa Senators, forward
1928–1929 New York Americans, forward

A member of four Stanley Cup winners, three with Ottawa and one with Montreal, Punch recorded 118 goals in his ten seasons. During the 1921–1922 season he led the National Hockey League in scoring and penalties. "I had a hard time controlling those elbows of mine." Playing one season with the New York Americans, he quit hockey after the stock market crash and joined the Royal Canadian Air Force.
Also in: Greater Ottawa Sports Hall of Fame and International Hockey Hall of Fame.

BROWN, Walter A.
Builder
Born February 10, 1905, in Boston, Mass; father George is also in Hall of Fame; died September 7, 1964, in Boston.

Walter followed in the footsteps of his father George, as a strong promoter of hockey in schools and colleges. He succeeded his father as general manager of Boston Garden in 1937. He coached the Boston Olympics between 1930 and 1940 when this team won 5 U.S. national amateur championships and one world title. At the time of his death, he was chairman of the Basketball Hall of Fame Corporation, member of the Hockey Hall of Fame governing committee and past president of the International Olympic Ice Hockey Federation. He was also coowner and president of the Boston Bruins, as well as coowner and president of the Boston Celtics basketball team.
Also in: International Hockey Hall of Fame, Naismith Memorial Basketball Hall of Fame and U.S. Hockey Hall of Fame.

CAMERON, Harold Hugh "Harry"
Player
Born February 6, 1890, in Pembroke, Ont; died October 20, 1953, in Vancouver, B.C.

1917–1918	Toronto Maple Leafs, defenseman
1918–1919	Toronto Arenas, Ottawa Senators, defenseman
1919–1920	Toronto St. Pats, Montreal Canadiens, defenseman
1920–1923	Toronto St. Pats, defenseman

An outstanding scoring record for a defenseman, 171 goals in 312 games, Cameron played on three Stanley Cup winners—Toronto, 1914, 1918 and 1922. One of the first to curve a shot without treating his stick, he always topped defensemen in scoring while competing against the likes of Newsy Lalonde, Joe Malone, Frank Nighbor, Cy Denneny, Babe Dye and Punch Broadbent. In 1923 he was traded to Saskatoon, later played for Minneapolis and St. Louis, but returned as coach for Saskatoon in 1932.
Also in: International Hockey Hall of Fame.

CRAWFORD, Samuel Russell "Rusty"
Player
Born November 7, 1884, in Cardinal Ont; died December 19, 1971.

1912–1917	Quebec Bulldogs, forward
1917–1919	Ottawa, Toronto Arenas, forward
1919–1921	Saskatoon, forward
1921–1925	Calgary, forward
1925–1929	Vancouver, forward

After several seasons of amateur hockey with the Verdun team in the Western Canada League, Rusty turned professional and joined the Stanley-Cup-winning Quebec squad in 1912. He remained with Quebec for five seasons, was traded to Ottawa before the beginning of the 1917–1918 season and only played four games with the Senators before being traded to Toronto. Rusty's adept skating skill and left-handed slapshot contributed to the Arenas capturing the 1918 Stanley Cup. His final season was 1928–1929.
Also in: International Hockey Hall of Fame.

DARRAGH, John Proctor "Jack"
Player
Born December 4, 1890, in Cornwall, Ont; died June 25, 1924, in Ottawa.

Jack started playing hockey in a church league, with a team called Stewartons, moved up to the famed Cliffsides and turned professional in 1911, immediately joining a Stanley Cup championship team. He went on to play for 3 more Stanley Cup teams in 1920, 1921 and 1923. At his peak, he was a member of a unit called the "Super Six." He played for the Ottawa Senators as forward 1917–1924. A left-handed forward who usually played right wing, Jack totaled 195 goals in his career, 24 goals in a 22 game schedule during the 1919–1920 season.
Also in: Greater Ottawa Sports Hall of Fame and International Hockey Hall of Fame.

GARDENER, James Henry
Player
Born May 21, 1881, in Montreal, Que; died November 7, 1940, in Montreal.

Jimmy learned to play hockey on the sidewalks with another great player, Dickie Boon. He was on two Stanley Cup winning teams: Montreal Hockey Club's "Little Men of Iron" (1901–1902) and the Montreal Wanderers (1909–1910.) He played one season with each team. Then in 1907 he moved to Pittsburgh and after one season, he moved back to Montreal and played one season with the Shamrocks. He joined the Wanderers again for a Stanley Cup victory. In 1911, he joined New Westminster of the Pacific Coast League, but only played two seasons and returned to Montreal. Next he played two seasons for the Canadiens coaching that team for two more seasons. In the 1917–1918 season, Jimmy shifted to officiating, refereeing in the minors and then the Western Canada League in 1923–1924. In 1924–1925 he coached the Hamilton Tigers, but the team withdrew from the league in a celebrated salary dispute.
Also in: International Hockey Hall of Fame.

GILMOUR, Hamilton Livingstone "Billy"
Player
Born March 21, 1885, in Ottawa, Ont; died March 13, 1959, at age 73, in Mount Royal, Que.

In 1902–1903 Billy joined the Ottawa Silver Seven and was with the club for three Stanley Cup victories. They lost the Cup in 1905–1906 after which Billy retired for a year. His best season was 1902–1903, when he collected 10 goals in 7 games and scored 5 goals in 4 games in the playoffs. In 1907–1908 Billy returned to hockey with the Montreal Victorias of the Eastern Canada Amateur

Hockey Association. In 1908–1909 he played right wing for the Ottawa Senators, and won the Stanley Cup the same year. He finished the season with 11 goals in 11 games. Billy returned to play with the Ottawa Senators, but only for two seasons, after which he retired officially as a player.
Also in: Greater Ottawa Sports Hall of Fame and International Hockey Hall of Fame.

GREEN, Wilfred Thomas "Shorty"
Player
Born July 17, 1896, in Sudbury, Ont; in 1916 he enlisted in the Canadian Army. He was gassed at Passchendale in 1917, and returned home the following year; died of cancer, April 19, 1960.

1923–1925 Hamilton Tigers, forward, later captain
1925–1927 New York Americans, forward

Shorty showed such good early form that he never played junior hockey. In 1914–1915 he played with the Sudbury Seniors, who won the Northern Ontario Hockey Association title. Prior to this he had played two seasons with Sudbury Intermediates. He also played with the Sudbury Wolves until early 1916, when he joined the Canadian Army. In 1919 he joined the Hamilton Tigers and helped them win the Allan Cup that same year. Shorty then returned to Sudbury and remained until the autumn of 1923, when he turned professional with the Hamilton Tigers, winning league honors in 1925. As captain of the Hamilton Tigers, he acted as spokesman for the players, who refused to be in playoffs unless each player received $200 compensation. The owners refused to give in, so Toronto and the Canadiens played a series to decide the title. On December 19, 1925, Shorty scored the first goal in Madison Square Garden as the Americans bowed 3–1 to the Canadiens. Shorty remained with the New York Americans until 1927 when a serious injury sidelined him as a player, but he continued to coach until retiring in 1933. Shorty staged the first player strike in the National Hockey League history, as captain of the Hamilton Tigers.
Also in: International Hockey Hall of Fame.

HERN, William Milton "Riley"
Player
Born December 5, 1880, in St. Mary's, Ont; was twice champion of Rosemere Golf Club; president of the St. Rose Boating Club; a member of several other sports organizations and also served on the board of many business organizations; died in Montreal, June 24, 1929.

Riley started playing hockey with the local Ontario Hockey Association junior team as a goaltender. He moved through intermediate and senior ranks, playing for awhile with a team in London, Ont, as a forward. In 1904 he played goaltender for the Portage Lake team. In 1906, Hern was signed up as a goalie by the Montreal Wanderers, and made this city his permanent home. He made the Stanley Cup the same year and was one of the outstanding players in the team. The Montreal Wanderers won the Stanley Cup again in 1907–1908 and in 1909–1910, with Riley as an outstanding drawing card. In 1910–1911, the pressure of business finally forced him out of athletics, but he stayed in constant touch with the game as a referee and goal judge. Riley had a record of playing on seven championship teams in his first nine years in hockey.
Also in: International Hockey Hall of Fame.

HOOPER, Charles Thomas
Player
Born November 24, 1883, in Rat Portage (later Kenora), Ont.

Tom played his first organized hockey on the high school team, defeating Kenora's senior squad in an exhibition match. After graduation he earned a spot on the senior team helping the squad to the Manitoba and Northwestern League championship. After two unsuccessful attempts to win the Stanley Cup from Ottawa in 1903 and 1905, the Thistles gained the Cup for two months in 1907 before losing it to the Montreal Wanderers. He later played for the Wanderers before retiring in 1908.
Also in: International Hockey Hall of Fame.

HUME, Fred John
Builder
Born May 2, 1892, in New Westminster, B.C; died February 17, 1967.

During his lifetime Fred was active in sports and politics. He was elected mayor of New Westminster at the age of 38 and later served as mayor of Vancouver. On the sports scene, he played with, and later became president of, the New Westminster Salmonbellies lacrosse team. He was also president of the New Westminster Royals soccer squad which won three Canadian titles. At one time, Hume owned the Vancouver hockey club and in 1955 brought professional baseball to Vancouver.
Also in: Canadian Lacrosse Hall of Fame and International Hockey Hall of Fame.

HUTTON, John Bower "Bouse"
Player
Born 1877 in Ottawa, Ont; goalie in lacrosse and fullback in football; died in 1962.

Bouse was a member of the Ottawa amateur champions in 1898–1899. He played six seasons with the Silver Sevens, allowing 28 goals in 12 Stanley Cup games. He is the only man to play on three championship teams in one year, 1907, beginning with the Ottawa Rough Riders in football, the Canadian lacrosse winner and the Stanley Cup. After retiring he still coached junior and senior Ottawa teams for several seasons.
Also in: International Hockey Hall of Fame.

HYLAND, Harry
Player
Born January 2, 1889, in Montreal, Que; died August 8, 1969, in Montreal.

1908–1909 Toronto Shamrocks, right wing
1909–1911 Montreal Wanderers, right wing
1912–1913 New Westminster, right wing
1913–1918 Montreal Wanderers, right wing

Harry played on two national championship teams in the same year, 1910, with the Stanley-Cup-winning Wanderers and the Toronto Shamrocks in lacrosse. Switching to the Pacific Coast League in 1912, Harry led the New Westminster squad to the league championship with 16 goals in 12 games. After returning to Montreal, Harry

scored an unbelievable eight goals in one game against Quebec in 1913.
Also in: International Hockey Hall of Fame.

LAVIOLETTE, Jean Baptiste "Jack"
Player
Born July 27, 1879 in Belleville, Ont; a lacrosse player in Canada Sports Hall of Fame; died in Montreal, January 10, 1960.

Moving to Valleyfield, Que, at a young age, Jack Laviolette played hockey with the Overlands and Canadian Pacific Telegraphs, then joined a team at Sault Ste. Marie, Mich, where he was selected as an International League All-Star. In 1909, while the Canadian Hockey Association and the National Hockey Association battled for supremacy, Laviolette formed Les Canadiens of Montreal (now the Montreal Canadiens). In 1915–1916 the team won the Stanley Cup and reached the playoffs in 1918–1919 when the series was canceled because of the flu epidemic. He first played defense, but moved to the team's line with Hall of Famers Didier Pitre and Newsy Lalonde. Laviolette retired at the end of the 1918–1919 season, playing 18 games with the Canadiens after they joined the National Hockey League. Even after losing a foot in a 1918 accident, Laviolette returned to hockey to do some refereeing.
Also in: Canada's Sports Hall of Fame and International Hockey Hall of Fame.

McGIMSIE, William George
Player
Born June 7, 1880, in Woodsville, Ont; family moved to Kenora the next year; died October 28, 1968 in Calgary.

Billy spent his ten-year career with the Kenora Thistles, the team remembered for being the smallest town ever to win the Stanley Cup, January 1907, but losing it a few months later to the Montreal Wanderers. Billy challenged for the Cup four times, losing the first two times to Ottawa in 1903 and 1905. Other Thistle players were Eddie Giroux, Art Ross, Si Griffis, Tom Hooper, Tom Phillips and Roxy Beaudro. Billy's career ended when he injured his shoulder in an exhibition match against Ottawa.
Also in: International Hockey Hall of Fame.

MAXWELL, Fred G. "Steamer"
Player
Born May 19, 1890, in Winnipeg, Man.

1914–1918 Winnipeg Monarchs, player, coach
1918–1925 Winnipeg Falcons, coach
1925–1926 Winnipeg Rangers, coach
1926–1928 Winnipeg Maroons, coach

Steamer, so called because of his tremendous skating ability, joined the Winnipeg Monarchs in 1914–1915 and the team went on to win the Allan Cup that year. He skated with them one more season, becoming a full time coach in 1917. He coached the Falcons in 1918–1919 and took that team to an Allan Cup triumph, adding both the Olympic and World hockey championships the following year. In 1925–1926 the Rangers won the Manitoba championship and he moved on to the Maroons, until the league terminated in 1928. Returning to coaching amateur teams, he obtained yet another victory with the Elmwood Millionaires in 1929–1930 when they won both junior and senior Manitoba championships. Another world champion to his credit occurred in 1934–1935 when the Winnipeg Monarchs won the title at Davos, Switzerland. Maxwell also officiated many pro and amateur games between 1910 and 1940.
Also in: International Hockey Hall of Fame.

NOBLE, Edward Reginald
Player
Born June 23, 1895, in Collingwood, Ont; died January 19, 1962, in Alliston, Ont.

1917–1919 Toronto Arenas, left wing
1919–1925 Toronto St. Patricks, left wing
1925–1927 Montreal Maroons, left wing
1927–1930 Detroit Cougars, defenseman
1930–1932 Detroit Falcons, defenseman
1932–1933 Montreal Maroons, left wing

Reg began his career with the Collingwood Business College which won the Ontario Hockey Association (OHA) group title in 1914–1915. The following season he played for the OHA senior title with the Toronto Riversides. When the Arenas disbanded in mid-1917 he spent the remainder of the season with Montreal but returned to Toronto in the newly formed National Hockey League (NHL). The Toronto club won the Stanley Cup in his initial season, as Reg contributed 28 goals in 22 games. The second Stanley Cup came in 1922 against Vancouver as the club was now called St. Pats. He won his last Stanley Cup with the Maroons in 1925 before spending five seasons as a defenseman in Detroit. After his NHL career, he spent one season in the International League with Cleveland and two seasons as a referee.
Also in: International Hockey Hall of Fame.

NORRIS, James D.
Builder
Born November 6, 1906, in Chicago, Ill; died of a coronary ailment on February 25, 1966.

James D. Norris entered the sports ownership business with his father James Sr, in 1933 when the family purchased the Detroit Falcons. In 1946 he also became a coowner (with Willard Wirtz) of the Chicago Black Hawks. The perennial dormant Hawks were stocked through their farm system and James' shrewd trading into Stanley Cup winners in 1961. Norris had other sporting interests, such as promoting championship boxing matches in his role as president of the International Boxing Club for nine years, plus his avocation in Thoroughbred horse racing.
Also in: International Hockey Hall of Fame.

O'BRIEN, John Ambrose
Builder
Born May 7, 1885, in Renfrew, Ont; played hockey for the University of Toronto and Renfrew; died April 25, 1968, in Ottawa.

When the application for an Eastern Canada Association hockey club for Renfrew was denied, John enlisted his father's financing and organized the rival National Hockey Association (NHA) in 1909. The O'Brien plan was a Stanley Cup for Renfrew, so he stocked his Millionaires (one of four teams in the new league), with such stars as Lester and Frank Patrick, Fred Whitcroft and Fred "Cyclone" Taylor. The league grew with such teams as Colbalt, Haileybury, Montreal Shamrocks and Ottawa. The most famous and successful team to survive

this organization and flourish is the Montreal Canadiens. It was decided the O'Brien Cup, a silver trophy given by his father, Sen. Michael J. O'Brien, would be the championship emblem of the NHA. This trophy was later adopted by the National Hockey League for league championships. It is now out of competition and rests in the Hockey Hall of Fame.
Also in: International Hockey Hall of Fame.

PITRE, Didier
Player
Born in 1884 in Sault Ste. Marie, Ont; died July 29, 1934.

Pitre was the first player signed to Jack Laviolette's Les Canadiens team in 1909. He played with them until his retirement in 1923. At right wing he utilized his speed and cannonball shots to 30 goals in 1915, one-half the team total. The Canadiens won the Stanley Cup that season with Pitre, Laviolette and Newsy Lalonde on the line. He played a career of 19 seasons with 240 goals in 282 games. In playoffs he scored 14 goals in 27 games.
Also in: International Hockey Hall of Fame.

RODDEN, Michael J.
Referee
Born April 24, 1891, in Mattawa, Ont; played football, lacrosse, baseball and hockey as a youth; played football for the University of Ottawa; appointed assistant sports editor of the *Toronto Globe* in 1918, sports editor in 1928 and remained with the paper until 1936; in 1944 became sports editor of the *Kingston Whig Standard* until retiring in 1959; as a football coach, was involved in 27 championship games, including five in Inter-Provincial Union, two in Ontario Royal Football Union and two Grey Cup winners; resides in Kingston.

Mike was a player, coach and sportswriter for hockey, as well as a referee. He played hockey for Queen's University and also Toronto St. Patricks. He coached Toronto De LaSalle College, Toronto St. Mary's, St. Pat's and the University of Toronto. He refereed 2864 hockey games, 1187 games in the National Hockey League.
Also in: Canadian Football Hall of Fame and International Hockey Hall of Fame.

RUTTAN, J. D. "Jack"
Player
Born April 5, 1889, in Winnipeg, Man; died January 7, 1973, in Charleswood, Man.

During his first four seasons of organized hockey competition, Jack was a member of a championship team. Beginning in 1905–1906, when Armstrong's Point won the juvenile title of Winnipeg, he then went over to the Rustler club in 1906–1907 to another juvenile title. In 1907–1908 with St. John's College team, he won the Manitoba University Hockey League title. The following year he joined the Manitoba Varsity team which won the Winnipeg Senior Hockey League championship. In 1912 Jack played for the Winnipeg Hockey Club, a team that won everything in sight—the Winnipeg League for a start and the Allan Cup for a finish. He also officiated in the Winnipeg Senior League for 2 seasons before assuming head coaching duties at the University of Manitoba in 1923.
Also in: International Hockey Hall of Fame.

SCHRINER, David "Sweeney"
Player
Born November 30, 1911 in Calgary, Alta; amateur hockey at public school and with North Hill midgets; then with the Tigers juvenile team, the Canadian junior club and senior status with the Bronks, coached by Rosie Helmer; Calder Trophy 1935; All-Star first team once and All-Star second team once; now lives in Calgary.

1934–1939 New York Americans, forward
1939–1943 Toronto Maple Leafs, forward
1944–1946 Toronto Maple Leafs, forward

After one season of professional hockey with Syracuse in 1933–1934, Sweeney moved to New York and became the league's outstanding rookie with 18 goals. During his stay with the Americans, he was league scoring champion in 1935–1936 with 45 points and 19 goals, and in 1936–1937 with 46 points and 21 goals. After being traded to the Toronto Maple Leafs, he stayed with the team for six seasons to play on two Stanley Cup championship teams. In the 1941–1942 playoffs, Sweeney scored 6 goals and in the 1944–1945 playoffs scored 3. In 11 seasons with the National Hockey League, he scored 201 goals and made 204 assists as a leftwinger, also 18 goals, 11 assists in 57 playoffs.
Also in: International Hockey Hall of Fame.

SIMPSON, Harold Joseph "Bullet Joe"
Player
Born in Selkirk, Man; served with Canadian Armed Forces in W.W. I, first with Winnipeg 61st Battalion, then with 43rd Cameron Highlanders, rose to rank of Lt, wounded two times in battle at Somme and Amiens; won the Military Medal; died in December, 1973.

1925–1931 New York Americans, defenseman
1932–1935 New York Americans, general manager

Harold Simpson was well known for his quickness on a pair of skates and was named Bullet Joe for that reason. In 1914–1915 he first played amateur hockey with the Winnipeg Victorias and during his service with the 61st Battalion played on a team that won the Allan Cup. After one season with the Selkirk Fishermen, 1919–1920, he led the Edmonton Eskimos to the Canadian Hockey League championship twice in four seasons. Simpson received offers from the Vancouver Maroons and the Ottawa Senators before joining the New York Americans for six seasons as player and manager. He later managed the New Haven and Minneapolis teams before permanently retiring from the game.
Also in: Canada's Sports Hall of Fame and International Hockey Hall of Fame.

SMITH, Alfred E.
Player
Born June 3, 1873, in Ottawa, Ont; oldest of seven brothers, most of whom had tried out with the Ottawa Silver Seven in the 1890s; only three were able to stay with first-class hockey; brother Tommy a member of the Hall of Fame; first played hockey with the Ottawa Electrics, then for the Capitals and Pittsburgh; died August 21, 1953 in Ottawa.

Smith's greatest achievement in hockey was coaching the Ottawa Silver Seven to three consecutive Stanley Cup victories in 1902–1903, 1903–1904 and 1904–1905, and playing with the team as rightwing with Hall of Famer

Frank McGee at center. He also led the Silver Seven to the league championships in the last two seasons and had played with the team previously, for three seasons beginning in 1895. In 1907 he joined the Kenora Thistles, who, in March of that year, lost the Stanley Cup they won just 2 months earlier, to the Montreal Wanderers. After returning to Ottawa for one season, 1907–1908, Smith played his final season of hockey in Pittsburgh with a professional City League and coached the Ottawa Cliffsides to an Allan Cup win in 1909. After retiring as a player, he continued to coach in Renfrew and North Bay, Ont, Moncton, N.B. and for the New York Americans.
Also in: Greater Ottawa Sports Hall of Fame and International Hockey Hall of Fame.

SMITH, Frank D.
Builder
Born June 1, 1894; died June 11, 1964.

The Beaches Hockey League was founded in Toronto on December 29, 1911, by a small group of men, one of whom was Frank D. Smith, the league's new secretary. He served as secretary for 50 years (resigning in 1962) and guided the growth of the league into the largest organization of minor amateur leagues in the world, the Metropolitan Toronto Hockey League. It was obvious to many that Frank was a fine organizer and contributor to the sport of hockey. He was later made a life member of the Metropolitan Toronto Hockey League, received the Gold Stick Award from the Ontario Hockey Association in 1947 and the top award from the Canadian Amateur Hockey Association, and the City of Toronto Award of Merit.
Also in: International Hockey Hall of Fame.

STANLEY, Russell "Barney"
Player
Born June 1, 1893, in Paisley, Ont; died June 16, 1971, in Edmonton, Alta.

1915–1919 Vancouver Millionaires, forward
1919–1920 Edmonton Eskimos, forward, coach
1920–1922 Calgary Rigers, forward, coach
1922–1924 Regina Capitals, forward, coach
1924–1926 Edmonton, defense
1926–1927 Winnipeg Maroons, defense, coach
1927–1928 Chicago Black Hawks, coach, manager
1928–1929 Minneapolis Millers, defense
1929–1932 Edmonton Pooler, coach

In a 15-year career, Barney played every position except goalie, often doubling as coach. Turning professional with Vancouver, Barney would win one Stanley Cup with the club before meandering through the league with many teams. Of 144 career goals, on two occasions he scored 5 in one game. He played all three forward positions before switching to defense midway through his career.
Also in: International Hockey Hall of Fame.

STEWART, Nelson Robert "Old Poison"
Player
Born December 29, 1900, in Montreal, Que; family moved to Toronto when he was young; Hart Trophy 1926 and 1930; died August 21, 1957, at his summer home near Toronto.

1925–1932 Montreal Maroons, forward
1932–1935 Boston Bruins, forward
1935–1936 New York Americans, forward
1936–1937 Boston, New York, forward
1937–1940 New York Americans, forward

Nels learned to play hockey in Toronto with childhood friend Hooley Smith in the Balmy Beach district. A member of the "S-line" along with Babe Siebert and Hooley Smith, Nels played center and was the marksman of the trio. His deadly accurate shots earned him the nickname Old Poison from goalies around the National Hockey League (NHL). He scored 134 goals and added 56 assists over the 5 years the line played together as a unit. As a rookie with the Maroons, he scored 34 goals and was a member of the team which won the Stanley Cup in 1925–1926. He was the first to score more than 300 goals in the NHL, a record that stood for many seasons.
Also in: Canada's Sports Hall of Fame and International Hockey Hall of Fame.

WALSH, Martin
Player
Born in 1883 in Kingston, Ont; died in a sanatorium in Gravenhurst, Ont, in 1915.

Walsh first attracted the attention of the Ottawa Silver Seven when he played against them on the Queen's University team of the Ontario Hockey Association. Even though his team lost, Ottawa tried to recruit Walsh when their own center retired. But Marty played for the International Professional League, where he broke his leg, before he joined the Silver Seven. In 5 seasons with Ottawa (1908–1913), he scored 135 goals and was on 2 Stanley Cup teams, in 1908–1909 and 1910–1911. He also had 26 goals in 8 playoffs. He was leading scorer in the National Hockey Association for three seasons.
Also in: International Hockey Hall of Fame.

WATSON, Harry E. "Moose"
Player
Born July 14, 1898, in St. John's, Nfld; traveled extensively; attended school in England; moved with family to Winnipeg 1908; moved to Toronto 1915; served in Canadian Army during W.W. I; nicknamed Moose because of his large size; died in Toronto, September 11, 1957.

1919–1920 Toronto Dentals, forward
1920–1925 Toronto Granites, forward

Considered the best amateur center at the time, Moose was offered a professional contract with the Toronto St. Patricks and also a $30,000 contract with the Montreal Maroons, but he turned them both down. In Toronto, he had played for St. Andrew's College, the Aura Lee juniors and another senior hockey team before W.W. I. Returning from duty, Watson played one season with the Toronto Dentals, then joined the Granites, who won the Allan Cup in 1921–1922 and 1922–1923. He was on the team representing Canada which won the 1924 Winter Olympics (Watson scored 13 goals against Czechoslovakia). He retired as a player in 1925, but returned in 1931 as a player and coach with the Toronto National Sea Fleas and this team later won the Allan Cup in 1932.
Also in: International Hockey Hall of Fame.

WESTWICK, Harry "Rat"
Player
Born April 23, 1876, in Ottawa, Ont; played lacrosse and starred with the Ottawa Capitals for several seasons;

nicknamed Rat because of his small size; died in Ottawa on April 3, 1957.

Harry started playing hockey as a goaltender, but switched his position with the Ottawa Seconds to become one of the best rovers of his time. After playing with the Aberdeens of the Ottawa City League, Westwick joined the Ottawa Senators, who won the Stanley Cup three consecutive times beginning in 1902 – 1903. His best year was 1904 – 1905 when the Silver Seven won their third Stanley Cup and Westwick scored 24 goals in 13 games. Although he retired in 1907, he retained close ties with the game and became a referee for a short time for the National Hockey Association.
Also in: International Hockey Hall of Fame.

WHITCROFT, Frederick
Player
Born in the 1880s in Fort Perry, Ont; moved to Vancouver, B.C, after retirement and traveled all over the world; died in Vancouver in 1931.

Fred Whitcroft first played hockey for the Peterboro Colts in 1901 when they won the Ontario Hockey Association's junior championship. He joined the Midland, Ont, team for the 1905 – 1906 season, but returned to Peterboro to captain the intermediate club, which won the Ontario Hockey Association championship in 1906 – 1907. He helped the Kenora Thistles to a Stanley Cup victory in early 1907 and moved to Edmonton later in the season to become captain of their senior hockey club and scored 49 goals in 1908. Edmonton challenged Ottawa for the Stanley Cup in 1908 – 1909, but lost in two straight games. In 1909 – 1910 Whitcroft completed his career with the Renfrew Millionaires.
Also in: Vancouver, British Columbia Hall of Fame and International Hockey Hall of Fame.

WILSON, Gordon Allan "Phat"
Player
Born December 29, 1895 in Port Arthur, Ont; standout baseball player in northern Ontario as youth; retired from Port Arthur Public Utilities commission at age 65 and resided in that city until his death in August, 1970.

Gordon Wilson was a star defenseman for the Bearcats team in Port Arthur between 1923 and 1933. His team won three Allan Cups, in 1925, 1926 and 1929, toured western Canada in 1926 and 1928 and won the Western Canada title in 1930. Wilson first began playing hockey in 1918 with a senior team, the Port Arthur War Veterans. He remained with that team until playing one season in Iroquois Falls for the Northern Ontario Hockey Association league champions, 1921 – 1922. Retiring from active competition in 1933 at the age of 37, Wilson continued as coach of the Bearcats in 1933 – 1934, 1938 – 1939 and 1940 – 1941.
Also in: International Hockey Hall of Fame.

1963

DANDURAND, Joseph Viateur "Leo"
Builder
Born July 9, 1889, in Bourbonnais, Ill; died June 26, 1964.

Leo became associated with Joseph Cattarinich and later with Louis Letourneau to become known as the "Three Musketeers of Sport." This trio bought the Montreal Canadiens in 1921 for $11,000 and built the club into the "Flying Frenchmen" with such stars as Howie Morenz, Newsy Lalonde, Georges Vezina, Joe Malone and Aurel Joliat, to name but a few. The club was sold in 1937 for $165,000. Dandurand was interested in other sports as well, and was a key figure in the rejuvenation of professional football, was active in horse racing and directed the Montreal Royals baseball team. Earlier, Leo had been a referee in the National Hockey Association as well as a delegate to the organizational meeting of the Canadian Amateur Hockey Association in 1914.
Also in: International Hockey Hall of Fame.

GOODFELLOW, Ebenezer R. "Ebbie"
Player
Born April 9, 1907, in Ottawa, Ont; All-Star second team 1935 – 1936, All-Star first team 1936 – 1937 and 1939 – 1940; Hart Trophy 1940; now retired in Florida and currently a member of Hockey Hall of Fame selection committee.

1929 – 1930 Detroit Cougars, forward
1930 – 1933 Detroit Falcons, forward
1933 – 1943 Detroit Red Wings, defenseman, captain

Ebbie started playing amateur hockey with the Montagnards and in 1927 – 1928, he was an All-Star center and the leading scorer as the team won the city championship. In 1928 – 1929 Detroit assigned him to the Olympics of the International League, where he again achieved All-Star status and led the League in scoring. In 1929 – 1930 he moved into the National Hockey League club and scored 17 goals. Ebbie led the American division of the League with 25 goals in 1930 – 1931, and after 5 seasons as captain, he retired in 1942, and Sid Abel became captain of the team. Goodfellow scored 134 goals and 190 assists, as well as 8 goals and 8 assists in 8 playoff series.
Also in: Greater Ottawa Sports Hall of Fame and International Hockey Hall of Fame.

GORMAN, Thomas Patrick
Builder
Born June 9, 1886, in Ottawa, Ont; was associated with lacrosse, horse racing, baseball and figure skating; was sports editor of the *Ottawa Citizen;* also played on the Canadian Olympic lacrosse team in 1908; died May 15, 1961.

Tommy was surrounded by sports activity all his life. He was owner or coach of seven Stanley Cup teams. Tommy was one of the founders of the National Hockey League in 1917. He held the National Hockey Association together when he picked up the Ottawa franchise during W.W. I. Tommy was manager of the Ottawa Senators, winning the Stanley Cup in 1921, 1922 and 1923. In 1934 he was coaching the Chicago Black Hawks when they won the Stanley Cup. He coached the Montreal Maroons to the Stanley Cup in 1935, and was general manager of the Montreal Canadiens when they won the Stanley Cup in 1944 and 1946.
Also in: Canadian Horse Racing Hall of Fame, Greater Ottawa Sports Hall of Fame and International Hockey Hall of Fame.

HEWITSON, Robert W.
Referee
Born January 23, 1892, in Toronto, Ont; retired in 1967; died of a heart attack January 9, 1969.

Although small in stature, Bobby achieved outstanding success in both lacrosse and football, and later became a highly respected hockey official. He was a member of the Maitlands lacrosse club which won the Ontario junior championship in 1913 and quarterback for the Capitals which won the Canadian junior football title that same year. About the same time, Bobby started a career in sportswriting, working for the *Toronto Globe* and later for the *Toronto Telegram,* retiring as sports editor in 1957. Hewitson was refereeing prior to 1920, not only hockey, but lacrosse and football as well. He officiated in the National Hockey League for ten years until 1934. Bobby was active in other areas of sport, serving as secretary of the Canadian Rugby Union for nearly 25 years, and was closely associated with horse racing. He was also one of the original members of the Hot Stove League broadcasting hockey. Later, Bobby became the first curator of both the Hockey Hall of Fame and Canada's Sports Hall of Fame.
Also in: Canada's Sports Hall of Fame and International Hockey Hall of Fame.

McLAUGHLIN, Major Frederic
Builder
Born June 27, 1887, in Chicago, Ill; father a wealthy coffee importer; graduated from Harvard in 1901; married Irene Castle, widow of Vernon Castle, in 1932; died December 17, 1944, in Chicago at age 57.

The irascible Major pioneered professional hockey in Chicago as owner and first president of the Chicago Black Hawks in 1926. When the Patrick brothers decided to disband and sell the six Western Canada League teams, Major was involved in the negotiations. He named the team Black Hawks after the regiment he commanded in W.W. I. During his reign as owner and president, the club won two Stanley Cup championships, 1934 and 1938.
Also in: International Hockey Hall of Fame.

PRIMEAU, A. Joseph
Player
Born January 29, 1906, in Lindsay, Ont; Lady Byng Trophy 1931–1932; All Star second team 1933–1934; retired from hockey to go into business, and now represents cement block manufacturer in Toronto and Islington, Ont.

1928–1936 Toronto Maple Leafs, forward
1950–1953 Toronto Maple Leafs, coach

Joe Primeau was the center for the "Kid Line" of the Maple Leafs, with Hall of Famers Charlie Conacher and Harvey Jackson as wings. They were a threat to many teams in the National Hockey League, but especially to the New York Rangers line, with Bill and Bun Cook and Frank Boucher in the 1933–1934 season when they were both vying for the top scoring line. Primeau coordinated moves for scoring as a very persistent checker and was second in league scoring in 1931–1932 and 1933–1934 and fifth in 1929–1930. He was a strong penalty killer as well. Primeau did not put on a pair of skates until the age of 12. Conn Smyth first saw him when he was center for St. Michael's College junior team and turned him professional with the Toronto Maple Leafs in 1927. But Primeau played with the Ravinas to win the scoring title in the Canadian Pro League. He started with the Leafs in 1928, but finished with London and did not stay with the Leafs until the 1929–1930 season. After retirement Primeau began a 23-year coaching career, and by 1970 was the only man to coach teams to the Memorial Cup, the Allan Cup and the Stanley Cup, which the Maple Leafs won in the 1950–1951 season.
Also in: Canada's Sports Hall of Fame and International Hockey Hall of Fame.

SEIBERT, Earl Walter
Player
Born December 7, 1911, in Kitchener, Ont; father Hall of Famer Oliver Seibert; won annual skating carnival in Kitchener a number of times; All-Star first team 10 times; resides in Agawam, Mass.

1931–1935 New York Rangers, defenseman
1935–1936 New York Rangers, Chicago Black Hawks, defenseman
1936–1944 Chicago Black Hawks, defenseman
1944–1945 Chicago Black Hawks, Detroit Red Wings, defenseman
1945–1946 Detroit Red Wings, defenseman

Earl Seibert exhibited great rushing ability during his 15½ years with the National Hockey League. He was a standout in defense and was always willing to drop down to the ice to block a puck before it reached the goalie. After playing junior hockey, Seibert turned professional with the Springfield Indians, a farm club for the New York Rangers, and then finished his career with 89 goals and 276 points in scheduled league games and 11 goals and 8 assists in playoffs. Under Hall of Famer Lester Patrick's guidance, the 1932–1933 Rangers team won the Stanley Cup. After Seibert moved to the Black Hawks, they won the Stanley Cup in 1937–1938.
Also in: International Hockey Hall of Fame.

1964

BENTLEY, Douglas Warner
Player
Born September 13, 1916, in Delisle, Sask; All-Star first team 1942–1943, 1943–1944 and 1946–1947; Half-Century Award as Chicago's best player 1950; died from cancer on November 24, 1972, in Saskatoon, Sask.

1939–1952 Chicago Black Hawks, forward
1953–1954 New York Rangers, forward

A member of the "Pony Line" with his brother Max and Bill Mosienko, each player scored more than 200 goals in their National Hockey League careers. Bentley possessed all the qualities of a superb athlete—speed, power, stamina, showmanship. During his 12-year NHL career, he never played with a Stanley Cup winner. Retiring as a player in 1954, he remained active as a coach and scout.
Also in: International Hockey Hall of Fame.

CAMPBELL, Angus Daniel
Builder
Born March 19, 1884, in Stayner, Ont; B.A. in mine engineering from the University of Toronto in 1911; resides in Toronto.

Campbell played hockey and lacrosse while studying at the University of Toronto. Later, as a student mine engineer, he continued his hockey in Cobalt, Ont, helping to establish the Ontario Hockey Association. When the Northern Ontario Hockey Association formed in 1919, Campbell was elected its first president.
Also in: International Hockey Hall of Fame.

CHADWICK, William L.
Referee
Born October 10, 1915, New York City; analyst on New York Rangers broadcasts and television.

1939 – 1955 National Hockey League, referee

Chadwick began refereeing by accident, literally. Playing for the New York Rovers, he was sidelined by a leg injury. When the designated referee did not arrive, Chadwick was asked to substitute. Thus, the beginning of over 1200 regular season and 125 playoff games. During his 16-year career, he earned the respect of players by chatting with them off the ice. "My secret was to be consistent but not over-officious." The only American to achieve senior official status in the NHL, Chadwick developed the hand signals (similar to those used in football) for designating penalties. He refereed the 1952 Stanley Cup finals, and retired in 1955.
Also in: International Hockey Hall of Fame and U.S. Hockey Hall of Fame.

DILIO, Francis Paul
Builder
Born April 12, 1912, in Montreal, Que; Canadian Amateur Hockey Association Meritorious Award, 1963; retired and lives in Montreal.

Frank devoted 25 years of service in administrative capacities to amateur hockey. He was secretary and later president of the Junior Amateur Hockey Association from 1939 until 1943. Moving to the Quebec Amateur Hockey Association, he doubled as registrar and secretary until retiring in the early 1960s.
Also in: International Hockey Hall of Fame.

DURNAN, William Ronald
Player
Born January 22, 1915, in Toronto, Ont; Vezina Trophy 1944 – 1947, 1949 and 1950; All-Star first team six times; worked in public relations for a brewery until his death in Toronto on October 31, 1972.

Bill Durnan was playing for the Sudbury juniors in the 1933 – 1934 Ontario Hockey Association finals when he was first recognized as an outstanding player. He then played three seasons with teams in the Northern Ontario Hockey Association before playing goalie for the Kirkland Lake Blue Devils, who won the Allan Cup in 1939 – 1940. Durnan joined the Montreal Canadiens after a short time with the Montreal Royals and won the Vezina Trophy in his first season with the National Hockey League (NHL). During his seven seasons with the Canadiens, he became the first goalie to win the trophy four consecutive years. In the 1948 – 1949 season he captured the record for shutouts (4), with 309.21 shutout time. He played 34 shutouts in NHL action and played 383 scheduled games, allowing 901 goals for a 2.36 goals-against average. After playing on 4 league championship teams and 2 Stanley Cup winners for the Canadiens, he quit the club during the 1950 Stanley Cup playoffs due to frayed nerves.
Also in: International Hockey Hall of Fame.

SIEBERT, Albert C. "Babe"
Player
Born January 14, 1904, in Plattsville, Ont; All-Star first team 1935 – 1936, 1936 – 1937 and 1937 – 1938; Hart Trophy 1937; drowned at St. Joseph, Ont, August 25, 1939.

1925 – 1932 Montreal Maroons, forward
1932 – 1933 New York Rangers, defenseman
1933 – 1934 New York Rangers, Boston Bruins, defenseman
1934 – 1936 Boston Bruins, defenseman
1936 – 1939 Montreal Canadiens, defenseman

Babe first played minor hockey in Zurich, Ont, and later played with Kitchener of the Ontario Hockey Association junior league in 1922 – 1923 and the Niagara Falls seniors in 1924 – 1925. When he turned professional and joined the Maroons, he became one of the players in the "S-line," with Hall of Famers Hooley Smith and Nels Stewart, for five seasons. Siebert was traded to the Rangers, then the Bruins and finally the Canadiens. By then his speed was gone, but he was a great defenseman, using his weight, strength and good sense of balance to block opponents. In his first seasons with both the Maroons and the Rangers, his teams won the Stanley Cup playoffs, and in 1931 – 1932 he was eighth in League scoring. He finished his career with 140 goals and 156 assists, as well as 8 goals and 7 assists in 54 playoffs.
Also in: International Hockey Hall of Fame.

STEWART, John Sherratt "Black Jack"
Player
Born May 6, 1917, in Pilot Mound, Man; father was wheat farmer; W.W. II duty; Detroit's Most Valuable Player 1942 – 1943; All-Star first team 1942 – 1943; 1947 – 1948 and 1948 – 1949; All-Star second team 1945 – 1946 and 1946 – 1947; lives in Detroit where he is connected with horse racing.

1938 – 1950 Detroit Red Wings, defense
1950 – 1952 Chicago Black Hawks, defense

Early in Black Jack's junior hockey career, he earned a reputation for his blunt checks coupled with frequent fights. Coaches appreciated his skating ability and fans filled the arenas to witness his strong, hard-hitting style of play. After two seasons with Portage La Prairie, he signed professionally with Detroit, who immediately sent him to their farm team in Pittsburgh. He was recalled for 33 games and quickly established himself as a great defenseman. During his years with the Red Wings, he played on 2 Stanley Cup Winners (1943 and 1950). Shortly after joining the Black Hawks, he was sidelined with a slipped disc in his back. Surgery followed and many thought his playing days were over. John made a come-back the following season, but suffered a fractured skull in a collision with teammate Clare Martin and New York Rangers Edgar Laprade, retiring midway through the 1951 – 1952 season. After leaving the professional ranks, Stewart coached and managed the Chatham Maroons of the Ontario Hockey Association senior league. He later coached teams in Windsor and Kitchener, Ont, and Pittsburgh of the American Hockey League. He fi-

nally retired from hockey in 1963. His National Hockey League career reads: 324 goals, 191 assists in 15 seasons; 15 goals and 11 assists in 12 playoffs.
Also in: International Hockey Hall of Fame.

1965

BARRY, Martin A.
Player
Born December 8, 1904, in St. Gabriel, Que; Lady Byng Trophy 1936 – 1937; All-Star first team 1936 – 1937; died August 20, 1969, in Halifax, N.S, of a heart attack.

1927 – 1928 New York Americans, forward
1928 – 1929 New Haven Eagles, forward
1929 – 1936 Boston Bruins, forward
1936 – 1938 Detroit Red Wings, forward
1939 – 1940 Montreal Canadiens, forward

Marty began his amateur career with Gurney Foundry in the Mt. Royal Intermediate League. After one season with St. Michael's and two with St. Anthony, Newsy Lalonde signed him for the New York Americans. Playing only 7 games with the Americans, he spent the remainder of the 1927 – 1928 season with the Philadelphia Arrows. He won the league scoring title with the New Haven Eagles the following year before joining the Bruins. He was a member of the Stanley Cup champion Detroit Red Wings in 1936 and 1938. Retiring in 1940, he later was a coach.
Also in: International Hockey Hall of Fame.

BENEDICT, Clinton "Benny"
Player
Born 1894 in Ottawa, Ont; currently lives in Ottawa.

1917 – 1924 Ottawa Senators, goalie
1924 – 1930 Montreal Maroons, goalie

Benny began playing hockey at the age of 6, and by 15 was playing senior hockey. At the age of 34, he was forced into retirement after stopping two rifle-like shots off the stick of Howie Morenz. The first shot shattered his nose and the second (in a later game) injured his larynx. The first accident affected his vision and prompted Benny to become the first goalie to try wearing a face mask. The specially designed mask obscured his vision on low shots so he gave it up. He was on four Stanley Cup champion teams, three with Ottawa and one with Montreal. During his career, Benny allowed 874 goals in 364 games for a 2.37 average, 57 shutouts; gave up 87 goals in 49 playoffs for 1.76 goals-against average with 16 shutouts.
Also in: International Hockey Hall of Fame.

FARRELL, Arthur F.
Player
Arthur began playing with the Montreal Shamrocks in 1897 and ended in 1901, following playoffs against the Winnipeg Victorias. He played four years with the team (missed the 1898 season) and scored a total of 29 goals in 26 games, plus 13 goals in 8 playoff games. In 1899 the Shamrocks captured their first Stanley Cup and finished in first place in the league. In 1900 Arthur had his best playoff, scoring 10 goals in 5 games. The best game of his career was on March 2, 1901, where he scored 5 goals against the Quebec Bulldogs. The Montreal Shamrocks finished third and Arthur retired at the end of the season. He is known as one of the men responsible for revolutionizing the game from the idea of individual play to complete team effort. He played on two first-place teams in the Canadian Amateur Hockey League as well as two Stanley Cup champions.
Also in: International Hockey Hall of Fame.

HEWITT, Foster William
Builder
Born November 21, 1902, in Toronto, Ont; son of William A. Hewitt; intercollegiate boxing champion while attending the University of Toronto; successful in business world as owner of radio station in Toronto.

The voice of Foster Hewitt on radio is known the world around. Back in March, 1923, he aired one of the first hockey radio broadcasts from the Mutual Street Arena in Toronto and greatly influenced the growth and development of hockey around the world in the years that followed. With more years of service than any other sportscaster, Hewitt broadcast thousands of hockey games, including national, world and Olympic championships in Canada, the United States and Europe, and brought contests in almost every major sport to faithful fans everywhere.
Also in: Canada's Sports Hall of Fame and International Hockey Hall of Fame.

HORNER, George Reginald "Red"
Player
Born May 28, 1909, in Lynden, Ont; retired; has a home in Portugal, a summer house in Toronto and a farm near Owen Sound, Ont.

Red was team captain during the 1937 – 1938 season, an honor he considers the highest of his playing career. During his 12 seasons in the National Hockey League with the Maple Leafs, this defenseman tallied 42 goals and 110 assists, also 7 goals and 10 assists in 11 playoff games. Not a particularly graceful skater, he could break as fast as anyone, except King Clancy and Howie Morenz. He was also a fine playmaker. Red led the league in penalties for 8 successive seasons (1932 – 1940). He also set a league record for penalties in a single season, spending 167 minutes in the box in 43 games of the 1935 – 1936 season, a record that was to stand for 20 years.
Also in: International Hockey Hall of Fame.

HOWE, Sydney Harris
Player
Born September 28, 1911, in Ottawa, Ont.

1930 – 1931 Ottawa Senators, forward
1931 – 1932 Philadelphia Quakers, Toronto Maple Leafs, forward
1932 – 1935 Ottawa Senators, forward
1935 – 1936 St. Louis, forward
1936 – 1946 Detroit Red Wings, forward

Syd began skating on double runners at the age of three and two years later graduated to a single blade. He starred in both public and high school levels in Ottawa and was a member of the first Ottawa team to play in the Memorial Cup finals, losing to Regina in 1928. Turning professional in 1930, he signed with Ottawa, later moving in and out of other National Hockey League franchises. On February 3, 1944, Howe was the first to

score 6 goals in one game. The late Jim Norris credits Howe with being the man who started the upsurge in attendance at Detroit. In his 16 seasons he totaled 237 goals and 291 assists, as well as 17 goals and 27 assists in 9 playoffs.
Also in: Greater Ottawa Sports Hall of Fame and International Hockey Hall of Fame.

LOCKHART, Thomas F.
Builder
Born March 21, 1892, in New York City; resides in New York; active as an official in the Amateur Athletic Union.

Tommy is closely associated with amateur hockey in the United States, mainly in organizational and promotional capacities. In 1934 he organized the Eastern American Hockey League and in 1935 became its president. Two years later he organized the American Hockey Association of the United States and served as first president. Between 1932 and 1952 Lockhart supervised the Metropolitan American League and, at intervals during these years, coached and managed the New York Rovers; from 1946 until 1952 he was the business manager of the New York Rangers. In hockey Tommy has been a member of both the U.S. Olympic committee and the International Ice Hockey Federation council. Other activities include serving as vice president of the Metropolitan Association of the Amateur Athletic Association, as well as eight years as member or vice chairman of its boxing committee.
Also in: International Hockey Hall of Fame and U.S. Hockey Hall of Fame.

MARSHALL, John C.
Player
Born March 14, 1877, in St. Vallier, Que; played in the 1897 football championship for Britannica Club; played soccer for Point St. Charles, which won the Caledonia Cup championship three times in the 1890s; died August 7, 1965 in Montreal.

1900–1901 Winnipeg Victorias, center
1901–1903 Montreal AAA, center
1903–1905 Montreal Wanderers, center
1906–1907 Montreal Montagnards, center
1907–1908 Montreal Wanderers, center
1908–1910 Montreal Shamrocks, center
1910–1912 Montreal Wanderers, defenseman
1913–1915 Toronto, defenseman
1915–1917 Montreal Wanderers, defenseman

Jack was a member of the Stanley-Cup-winning Winnipeg Victorias in 1901. This was the first of five Cups during his 17-year hockey career. He switched to defense in 1910. After moving to the Toronto club, he doubled as player and coach in 1913, leading them to the Stanley Cup. His career record reads 99 goals in 132 league games with 13 goals in 18 playoff games.
Also in: International Hockey Hall of Fame.

MOSIENKO, William
Player
Born November 2, 1921, in Winnipeg, Man; Lady Byng Trophy 1945; All-Star second team 1945 and 1946; lives in Winnipeg.

1939–1941 Providence-Kansas City, right wing
1941–1955 Chicago Black Hawks, right wing
1955–1960 Winnipeg Warriors, right wing, coach

In the 1940s Bill was a member of the "Pony Line" along with the Bentley brothers, Max and Doug. His association with the Black Hawk organization lasted 14 years through 711 games and 538 points. He holds the record for the fastest three goals in one game (21 secs.) against the New York Rangers on March 23, 1952. In over two decades of professional hockey, Bill incurred only 129 penalty minutes in 1030 games. Following retirement from the National Hockey League, he launched professional hockey in Winnipeg with Alf Pike in 1955. The hometown Warriors won the Edinburgh Trophy the first season, 1955–1956. Bill was a player with them four seasons and coached one year, 1959–1960.
Also in: International Hockey Hall of Fame.

RUSSELL, Blair
Player
Born September 17, 1880, in Montreal, Que; died December 7, 1961, in Montreal.

Equally skilled as scorer or checker, Blair played his entire amateur career with the Montreal Victorias, scoring 110 goals in 67 games. He once tallied seven goals in a game against the Shamrocks and also had games of six and five. Playing with the incomparable Russell Bowie, Blair drew few raves of recognition until Bowie turned professional and Blair moved to right wing. When the Eastern Canada Amateur Hockey Association became a professional league in 1909, Blair retired into a highly successful business career.
Also in: International Hockey Hall of Fame.

RUSSELL, Ernest
Player
Born October 21, 1883, in Montreal, Que; captain of the Montreal Amateur Athletic Association football team that won the Canadian junior title in 1903; died February 23, 1963.

Ernie first played senior hockey with the Winged Wheelers in 1905, but the remainder of his playing career (1905–1912) was spent with the Montreal Wanderers. He was a proficient scorer, and scored 3 goals per game in 5 consecutive games. He also scored in 10 consecutive games during the 1911–1912 season and led the league with 42 goals in 1906–1907. Ernie played on Stanley Cup winning teams in 1906–1908 and 1910. In 98 league games he tallied 180 goals.
Also in: International Hockey Hall of Fame.

SCANLAN, Frederick
Player
Born c. 1880; retired 1903.

1897–1901 Montreal Shamrocks, forward
1901–1903 Winnipeg Victorias, forward

One of the greatest forward lines in the early days of hockey belonged to the Shamrocks, winners of the Stanley Cup in 1899 and 1900. Fred Scanlan, along with Hall of Famers Harry Trihey and Arthur Farrell, originated combination passing plays in the days when only lateral passing was allowed. In 31 regular games, Fred scored 16 goals and in 17 playoffs, scored 6.
Also in: International Hockey Hall of Fame.

1966

BENTLEY, Maxwell Herbert Lloyd

Player

Born March 1, 1920, in Delisle, Sask; one of 13 children, including 7 sisters; brother Doug also in Hall of Fame; served 2 years in the military; Lady Byng Trophy 1943; Art Ross Trophy 1945 and 1946; Hart Trophy 1946; All-Star first team 1945 – 1946; now lives in Delisle where he coaches amateur teams.

1940 – 1948 Chicago Black Hawks, forward
1948 – 1953 Toronto Maple Leafs, forward
1953 – 1954 New York Rangers, forward

Max Bentley was such a frail-looking person, he was turned down by the Boston Bruins, and the Montreal Canadiens team doctor told him he had a heart condition and shouldn't even play hockey. Chicago took a good long look at him and finally signed him. Max, his brother Doug and Bill Mosienko became the famous "Pony Line" with the Hawks. Max developed into an all-time great playmaker and was so good, that midway through the 1947 – 1948 season, he was traded to Toronto for six other players. While plaing with the Maple Leafs, Max played on three Stanley Cup winners. He retired in 1954, but his career totals include 245 goals and 299 assists in 646 games, also 18 goals in 44 playoffs.
Also in: International Hockey Hall of Fame.

BLAKE, Hector "Toe"

Player

Born August 21, 1912, in Victoria Mines, Ont; Hart Trophy 1939; Lady Byng Trophy 1946; All-Star first team 3 times; All-Star second team twice; resides in Montreal.

Blake played his first organized hockey in the Sudbury-Nickel Belt League in 1929-1930. In the latter part of 1931 – 1932, he was a member of the team that won the Memorial Cup. He played for the Hamilton Tigers, a senior team, for most of the next three seasons, joining the Montreal Maroons in 1934. He came over to the Canadiens in February of 1935 when the Maroons traded him and Bill Miller for goalie Lorne Chabot. Along with Elmer Lach and Maurice "The Rocket" Richard, Blake became part of the famous "Punch Line". While on the team, the Canadiens won two Stanley Cups. He broke a leg and retired as a player in 1948, and went into coaching in minors, but returned to the Canadiens as a coach in 1955, where he guided the club to eight more Stanley Cups. He retired following the 1967 – 1968 season.
Also in: Canada's Sports Hall of Fame and International Hockey Hall of Fame.

BOUCHARD, Emile Joseph "Butch"

Player

Born September 11, 1919 in Montreal, Que; All-Star first team 1947, 1948, 1950; All-Star second team 1951, 1952; resides in Montreal.

He rode his bicycle 50 mi. to training camp, earning a spot on the team. He used his great size and bulk not for intimidation but as a playmaking defenseman, helping the Montreal Canadiens to become one of the truly dominant clubs during his tenure. After playing 1941 – 1956, he retired and became coach and president of junior teams.
Also in: International Hockey Hall of Fame.

BRIMSEK, Frances Charles "Mr. Zero"

Player

Born September 26, 1915, in Eveleth, Minn; Coast Guard duty from 1943 to 1945; played on Coast Guard hockey team in Eastern Amateur League; Calder Trophy 1938; Vezina Trophy 1938, 1942; All-Star first team twice; All-Star second team six times; settled in Virginia, Minn.

1938 – 1949 Boston Bruins, goalie
1949 – 1950 Chicago Black Hawks, goalie

Coached by Cliff Thompson at Eveleth High School and later a player at what is now St. Cloud State, Frankie replaced Tiny Thompson in the net in 1938. Six of his first eight games were shutouts, achieving scoreless three-game stretches of 231 min. and 220.24 min. In his rookie year his goals-against average was 1.60 for 43 games; his ten season regular and playoff goals against average was 2.74 with 42 shutouts. During his first three years with Boston, they won the Stanley Cup twice. An intensive player, he did not like his teammates to score against him in practice. After returning from W. W. II military duty, he played four more years with Bruins even though "my legs and nerves were shot."
Also in: International Hockey Hall of Fame and U.S. Hockey Hall of Fame.

CAMPBELL, Clarence S, M.B.E.

Builder

Born July 9, 1905, in Fleming, Sask; graduated from University of Alberta; Rhodes Scholar at Oxford; lawyer; commanded 4th Canadian Armored Division headquarters in W. W. II; joined Canadian War Crimes Unit after war; refereed hockey and lacrosse; resides in Toronto.

Formerly a referee, he succeeded Mervyn "Red" Dutton as president of the National Hockey League (NHL) in 1946 and is still president today. His two most outstanding administrative achievements have been the establishment of the NHL Pension Society in 1946 and the expansion of the league from six to twelve teams.
Also in: Canada's Sports Hall of Fame and International Hockey Hall of Fame.

KENNEDY, Theodore S.

Player

Born December 12, 1925, in Humberstone, Ont; Hart Trophy 1954-1955; lives in Ontario.

At 16 Ted Kennedy went to the Montreal Canadien training camp, but became so homesick that he packed his bags and returned home. Two years later, the Toronto Maple Leafs traded their rights for Frank Eddolls and brought Kennedy into the National Hockey League where he played 14 seasons (1942 – 1956) as a forward, playing 696 league games and scoring 231 goals and 329 assists. He possessed a great competitive spirit which carried the team to five Stanley Cup victories, 1944 – 1945, 1946 – 1947, 1947 – 1948, 1948 – 1949 and 1950 – 1951. He followed Hall of Famer Syl Apps as team captain in 1948. Retiring after the 1955 – 1956 season, Kennedy returned to assist the injury-riddled Canadiens in January 1957, but permanently retired at the end of the season. He will be remembered as one of the greatest face-off men in the history of hockey.
Also in: International Hockey Hall of Fame.

LACH, Elmer James
Player

Born January 22, 1918, in Nokomis, Sask; Hart Trophy 1944–1945; Art Ross Trophy 1944–1945 and 1947–1948; All-Star first team 3 times; All-Star second team twice; now lives in Montreal; public relations director for transport firm.

Elmer Lach began as an amateur playing junior hockey with the Regina Abbots and a senior with the Weyburn Beavers and the Moose Jaw Millers. After turning professional, he was the center for the famous Canadiens' "Punch Line" with Hall of Famers Maurice "The Rocket" Richard and Hector "Toe" Blake (1940–1954). He was leading scorer in the league in the 1944–1945 season with 28 goals and 54 assists, and in his last year on the line (1947–1948) also led the league in scoring. Lach was center when Richard scored his record of 50 goals in 50 games in the 1944–1945 season, and on November 8, 1952, the same night that Richard scored his record 325 goals, Lach scored his 200th goal. Over the years, he played on 3 Stanley Cup winning teams, 1944, 1946 and 1953. Upon retirement, he had played 646 scheduled games for 215 goals and 408 assists, adding 19 goals and 45 assists in playoff games.
Also in: International Hockey Hall of Fame.

LINDSAY, Robert Blake Theodore
Player

Born July 29, 1925, in Renfrew, Ont; during career, went into partnership with another Detroit player, Marty Pavelich in a plastics firm; All-Star first team eight times; All-Star second team once; resides in Detroit; offered job of general manager for Detroit Red Wings in April, 1977.

1944–1957 Detroit Red Wings, forward
1957–1960 Chicago Black Hawks, forward
1964–1965 Detroit Red Wings, forward

Ted Lindsay started in junior hockey in Kirkland Lake, Ont, where his father operated an ice rink, going on to Toronto St. Michael's and later, a member of the Oshawa junior team that won the Memorial Cup in 1944. Turning professional at the age of 19, he very quickly became a member of the famous "Production Line" (along with Sid Abel and Gordie Howe) and brought the Red Wings to seven straight league titles and four Stanley Cup victories between 1948 and 1955. Lindsay was one of the highest scoring left wings in the National Hockey League (NHL), ending his playing career with 379 goals and 458 assists in 17 seasons. But he also had the reputation as one of the most penalized forwards in the game and still holds the record for the most penalty minutes in the NHL with 1808 minutes. In 1957 Lindsay was traded to the Black Hawks, where he played until his retirement after the 1959–1960 season. He involved himself in his highly successful business but in 1964 made a brief come-back with the Detroit team. That year the Red Wings won their first league championship in eight years and Lindsay was an inspiration in their also winning the Prince of Wales Trophy.
Also in: International Hockey Hall of Fame.

PRATT, Walter "Babe"
Player

Born January 7, 1916 in Stoney Mountain, Man; Hart Trophy 1944; played once on the All-Star first and second teams.

1935–1942 New York Rangers, defenseman
1942–1943 New York, Toronto Maple Leafs, defenseman
1943–1946 Toronto, defenseman
1946–1947 Boston Bruins, defenseman

Babe played on the first Winnipeg playground championship team in 1932, the Elmwood Maple Leafs, that won the Manitoba midget title. The following year the Leafs won the juvenile crown, the second of five championships for Babe in one year before joining the Rangers' farm team in 1935. During his seven years with the Rangers, they won one Stanley Cup (1940) and one league championship (1942). Traded to Toronto in November 1942, he returned to the United States with the Bruins for the 1946–1947 season. After retiring from the National Hockey League in 1947, Babe played with Hershey, New Westminster, B.C, and Tacoma.
Also in: International Hockey Hall of Fame.

REARDON, Kenneth
Player

Born April 1, 1921, in Winnipeg, Man; parents died when he was a child; lived with guardian uncle in British Columbia; served in Canadian Army during W.W. II; played on the Ottawa Commandos army team, who won the Allan Cup in 1943; also played in Great Britain and Belgium; received Field Marshall Montgomery's Certificate of Merit for service in Europe; All-Star first team 1947, 1950; All-Star second team 1946, 1948 and 1949; resides in Westmount, Que.

Reardon played hockey with the Edmonton juniors before being signed with the Montreal Canadiens in 1940. After his military stint, he rejoined the Montreal club and for the next five seasons, was named to the All-Star teams of the National Hockey Leauge. He also played on a Stanley Cup winning team in 1945 –1946. He retired as a player in 1950 to become vice-president of the Canadiens, retiring in May, 1964.
Also in: International Hockey Hall of Fame.

1967

BRODA, Walter "Turk"
Player

Born May 15, 1914, in Brandon, Man; Canadian Armed Forces during W.W. II; Vezina Trophy 1940–1941, 1947–1948, co-winner with Al Rollins in 1950–1951; All-Star first team four times; died of a heart attack on October 17, 1972, in Toronto, Ont.

Broda starred in amateur hockey with Brandon juvenile and junior teams, playing his last junior year with Winnipeg Monarchs in 1933–1934. He played for the International League champion Detroit Olympics in 1934–1935 and shortly after was sold to Toronto Maple Leafs, where he played his entire professional career (1936–1952). During his 16 seasons with Toronto, Turk played in 101 Stanley Cup games and allowed only 211 goals for an average of 2.08 — both records. Retiring as a player in 1952, he turned to coaching.
Also in: International Hockey Hall of Fame.

COLVILLE, Neil MacNeil
Player
Born August 4, 1914, in Edmonton, Alta; navigator with Royal Canadian Air Force 1942 – 1945; captain of the Ottawa Commandos team that won the Allan Cup, 1942 – 1943; All-Star second team 1938 – 1939, 1939 – 1940 and 1947 – 1948.

Neil played three seaons of junior hockey in and around Edmonton before joining the Rangers in 1936, where he played his entire career (1935 – 1949). Neil, his brother Mac and Alex Shibicky played on the famous "Bread Line" for six years, during which time the Rangers won the Stanley Cup in 1940 and the National Hockey League championship in 1942. He was also captain of the team for six seasons. He retired in 1949.
Also in: International Hockey Hall of Fame.

OLIVER, Harold
Player
Born October 26, 1898, in Selkirk, Man.

1920 – 1926 Calgary, forward
1926 – 1934 Boston Bruins, forward
1934 – 1937 New York Americans, forward

During his 11 seasons in the National Hockey League, Oliver never carried more than 24 penalty minutes in any one season. Known for his style and smooth gliding on ice, Harold scored 218 goals and 144 assists in his career. His deportment on and off the ice was a tribute to the sport. He played on a Stanley Cup winner in 1928 – 1929, and retired in 1937.
Also in: International Hockey Hall of Fame.

STOREY, Roy Alvin "Red"
Referee
Born in 1918 in Barrie, Ont; resides in Montreal, Que.

Storey was among the most colorful officials ever employed by the National Hockey League. He served them for nine years, from 1951 until April, 1959, when he resigned. Before coming into the hockey scene, Red's first claim to fame came in 1938 as a Toronto Argonaut football player. He scored three touchdowns in the final 13 min. of the Grey Cup game (one of them on a 102-yd. run), scoring a victory over the Winnipeg Blue Bombers. A knee injury in 1940 prematurely ended his football career, but he continued as an official from 1946 until 1957 and also officiated lacrosse for ten years. As a lacrosse player, he once scored 12 goals for Ville St. Pierre, a mark that still stands as a Quebec record. Red was also a proficient baseball player. Overall, Storey refereed more than 2000 hockey games. He is currently vice-president of the Montreal Old Times hockey team which plays charity benefits, and he is the referee-in-charge of all their games.
Also in: International Hockey Hall of Fame.

1968

COWLEY, William Mailes
Player
Born June 12, 1912, in Bristol, Que; moved to Ottawa in 1920; Hart Trophy 1941, 1943; All-Star first team four times; All-Star second team once; operates hotels at Smiths Falls, Ont.

1934 – 1935 St. Louis Eagles, center
1935 – 1947 Boston Bruins, center

Bill spent 13 seasons in the National Hockey League and played on two Stanley Cup winners, both with Boston. He also played on Boston championship teams in 1939 – 1941. During the 1943 – 1944 season, he almost captured the scoring title, with 72 points in 36 games, but an injury forced him to the sidelines for six weeks. His lifetime statistics read 195 goals and 353 assists plus 12 goals and 34 assists in playoff competition.
Also in: Greater Ottawa Sports Hall of Fame and International Hockey Hall of Fame.

DUNN, James A.
Builder
Born March 24, 1898; served in W.W. I and received the Military Medal for bravery; currently resides in Winnipeg, Man.

When Jimmie Dunn was inducted into the Hall of Fame in 1968, he had already served hockey for 50 years. Immediately after W.W. I, Jimmie was a league secretary, then convener and timekeeper when the Manitoba Amateur Hockey Association (MAHA) took over his leagues in 1927. He was vice-president of the MAHA 1942 – 1945 and president, 1945 – 1951. He later served as vice-president and president of the Canadian Amateur Hockey Association. He retained interest in Manitoba hockey affairs, acting as convenor of World Hockey tournaments in 1967 and 1968 and secretary-treasurer of the Manitoba Hockey Players Foundation. Jimmie has also held office in a variety of other sports: baseball, lacrosse, football, boxing and track and field, to name a few.
Also in: International Hockey Hall of Fame.

HENDY, James Cecil Vladamar
Builder
Born May 6, 1905, in Barbados, B.W.I; emigrated to Vancouver, B.C. at age 6; as a youth, worked as a rancher, sailor, telegrapher and sports and fiction writer; died in Cleveland, Ohio, January 14, 1961.

Jim was the real founder of hockey statistics, which are the lifeblood of the game's publicity and yardstick of player evaluation today. He first learned about hockey as a rink rat in the arena built by the Patrick brothers. Jim had other interests, but at all times maintained his hockey interest as he compiled player's performances and personal statistics. He published *The Hockey Guide* continually from 1933 to 1951, when pressure of other work forced him to give it up. He turned over his records and rights to the National Hockey League, asking only that they continue his work.
Also in: International Hockey Hall of Fame.

1969

ABEL, Sidney Gerald
Player
Born February 22, 1918, in Melville, Sask; U.S. Army during W.W. II; Hart Trophy 1948 – 1949; All-Star first team 1949; All-Star second team 1951; resides in Farmington, Mich.

1938 – 1951 Detroit Red Wings, center, forward
1952 – 1954 Chicago Black Hawks, player, coach

1955 – 1971 Detroit Red Wings, coach, general manager
1971 St. Louis Blues, coach, general manager

Sid Abel was a member of the famed "Production Line" with Gordie Howe and Ted Lindsay. A player for 14 seasons, Sid accumulated 189 goals and 283 assists in 610 games, including 28 goals and 30 assists in 97 playoffs. As a player/coach with Chicago, Abel led the Black Hawks to a third place tie with Boston for Chicago's first playoff berth in seven years. Sid spent the major part of his professional career with the Red Wings organization, but resigned as general manager in mid-1971 over managerial policy. He then signed with the St. Louis Blues as coach, becoming general manager before the season was over.
Also in: International Hockey Hall of Fame.

HEXTALL, Bryan Aldwyn
Player
Born July 31, 1913, in Grenbell, Sask; two sons hockey players; All-Star first team three times; All-Star second team twice; now a businessman in Poplar Point, Man.

1934 – 1935 Vancouver Lions, forward
1935 – 1936 Philadelphia, forward
1936 – 1948 New York Rangers, forward

Bryan tallied 20 or more goals in 7 of his 12 National Hockey League seasons. In 449 league games, his totals are 187 goals and 175 assists, leading the league during the 1941 – 1942 season with 56 points (24 goals and 32 assists). Although retired, he still assists in coaching minor league players. He played on one Stanley Cup champion team, scoring the winning overtime goal against Toronto in 1940.
Also in: International Hockey Hall of Fame.

KELLY, Leonard Patrick "Red"
Player
Born July 19, 1927, in Simcoe, Ont; married to former U.S. Olympic ice skater Andrea McLaughlin; Lady Byng Trophy 1951, 1953, 1954 and 1961; James Norris Memorial Trophy 1954; All-Star first team six times; All-Star second team twice; member of Canadian Parliament, 1962 – 1965; Coach of the Year 1970.

1947 – 1960 Detroit Red Wings, defenseman
1960 – 1967 Toronto Maple Leafs, defenseman

Red Kelly played with the Toronto St. Michael's Majors before joining the National Hockey League at age 19. Kelly became the fifth highest scorer in the Red Wings history and was the first recipient of the Norris Trophy. His team won four Stanley Cups and received the Prince of Wales Trophy eight times. In the middle of the 1959 – 1960 season he became a member of the Toronto Maple Leafs defense and later played center in the 1966 – 1967 season. The Leafs won four Stanley Cups and the Prince of Wales Trophy once. At his retirement, after the 1966 – 1967 season, he was runner up to Gordie Howe for the most games played (1316) in a regular season. He competed in 19 Stanley Cup playoffs (a record) for 164 playoff games (also a record). In 1967 he coached the Los Angeles Kings, who went to the playoffs in the next two seasons, went to the Pittsburgh Penguins in 1969 as coach for three and a half seasons, then on to Toronto in 1973.
Also in: Canada's Sports Hall of Fame and International Hockey Hall of Fame.

LEADER, George Alfred
Builder
Born December 4, 1903 in Barnsley, Man; naturalized U.S. citizen in 1933; Patrick Trophy 1976; resides in Seattle, Wash.

Al Leader was involved with hockey from the time he played as a 16-year-old around Watson, Sask, until he retired as president of the Western Hockey League after 25 continuous years of service. His activity in the administration of hockey began in 1933 when he started as secretary of the Seattle City League, where he also played, coached, managed and officiated. In 1940 he formed a Defense Hockey League through which he established contact with professional hockey. In 1944 he was elected secretary-manager of the Pacific Coast League.
Also in: International Hockey Hall of Fame.

NORRIS, Bruce A.
Builder
Born February 19, 1924, in Chicago, Ill; graduated from Yale; father James Norris, Sr, president of Norris Grain Co; Patrick Trophy 1976; resides in Liberty, Ill.

One of the bulwark families in sports, the Norris' are legendary figures in Detroit hockey history. Succeeding his sister, Mrs. Marguerite Norris Riker, as president of the Red Wings in 1955, Bruce remodeled Olympia Stadium at a cost of $2.5 million. The family has owned the Detroit club since 1933.
Also in: International Hockey Hall of Fame.

WORTERS, Roy
Player
Born October 19, 1900, in Toronto, Ont; Hart Trophy 1928 – 1929; Vezina Trophy 1930 – 1931; All-Star second team twice; died of throat cancer in Toronto on November 7, 1957.

1925 – 1928 Pittsburgh Pirates, goalie
1928 – 1929 New York Americans, goalie
1929 – 1930 New York Americans, Montreal Canadiens, goalie
1930 – 1937 New York Americans, goalie

Although one of the smallest goalies ever to play in the National Hockey League (NHL), Roy Worters was the first goalie to win the Hart Trophy. He was only 5 ft. 2 in. and seldom weighed more than 130 lbs, but he starred in the NHL for 12 seasons. During his career he allowed 1154 goals in 484 games for a 2.38 average, 66 shutouts; gave up 24 goals in 11 playoff games for a 2.18 average, 3 shutouts. After retiring in 1937, Roy was quite active in the NHL Oldtimers Association and he also worked on behalf of crippled children.
Also in: International Hockey Hall of Fame.

1970

DYE, Cecil Henry "Babe"
Player
Born May 13, 1895, in Hamilton, Ont; moved to Toronto with his parents before he was one year old; star halfback with the Toronto Argonauts; refused $25,000 to

play baseball for Connie Mack's Philadelphia team; foreman with a Chicago paving contract firm; died January 3, 1962.

1920 – 1926 Toronto St. Pats, forward
1926 – 1927 Chicago Black Hawks, forward
1928 – 1929 New York Americans, forward

Babe's hockey career began with the Toronto Aura Lee, Ontario Junior Champs, in 1917. He joined the Toronto St. Pats in 1919 – 1920, had difficulty breaking into the starting lineup, but scored 11 goals in 21 games. Babe played for six seasons with the Toronto St. Pats, and had 163 goals in 143 games. He was leading scorer four times in the league; scored two times in 11 consecutive games and twice scored five goals in a game. He left the Toronto St. Pats team in 1925 – 1926 and joined the Chicago Black Hawks, but broke his leg while in training camp and missed the season. He then joined the New York Americans, but only scored one time in 41 games. In 1921 – 1922, he was a Stanley Cup winner with the Toronto St. Pats. Following his retirement, he coached the Chicago Shamrocks in the American Association and refereed for five years. Babe accumulated a total of 200 goals in 255 games.
Also in: International Hockey Hall of Fame.

GADSBY, William Alexander
Player
Born August 8, 1927, in Calgary, Alta; left-handed player; when 12 years old, he and his mother were aboard the Athenia, returning from England at the outbreak of W.W. II; ship torpedoed; spent five hours in Atlantic before being rescued; survived polio in 1952; All-Star first team three times; All-Star second team four times; resides in Detroit, Mich.

1946 – 1954 Chicago Black Hawks, defenseman
1955 – 1961 New York Rangers, defenseman
1961 – 1966 Detroit Red Wings, defenseman

Bill played his first junior hockey with Edmonton. He then signed to play with the Chicago Black Hawks and was sent to Kansas City for seasoning. In 1952 he became team captain, then was struck by polio, but "beat the rap." He got 12 stitches in his first game with the Black Hawks, and almost 600 before retiring. In 1954 he was traded to the New York Rangers. He was traded again in 1961, to the Red Wings and played his last 5 seasons with them. He coached the Red Wings for the 1968 – 1969 season and two games of 1969 – 1970. Bill became one of the few players to last 20 seasons with the National Hockey League.
Also in: International Hockey Hall of Fame.

JOHNSON, Thomas Christian
Player
Born February 18, 1928, in Baldur, Man; Norris Trophy 1958 – 1959.

1947 – 1963 Montreal Canadiens, defenseman
1963 – 1965 Boston Bruins, defenseman

In a professional career spanning 15 seasons, Tom played on six Stanley Cup champions, skated in 978 games and tallied 51 goals and 213 assists. A team leader, especially when shorthanded, he frequently played center when the team needed a goal late in the game. Plagued by injuries, he had two eye impairments inflicted by his teammates, the second one cut facial tissue and eye muscles threatening his sight. A severed leg nerve forced his retirement in 1965.
Also in: International Hockey Hall of Fame.

LeBEL, Robert
Builder
Born September 21, 1905, in Quebec City; former mayor of Chambly, Que, where he now resides.

As a youngster Bob came up through the minor ranks to play in the Cote de Beaupre Junior League, then in the Quebec City senior league and later in New York State. In 1944 Bob founded the Interprovinicial Senior League and became its first president serving until 1947. Thus began what was to be a full time career at the organizational and administrative level of the game. He served as president of the Quebec Amateur Hockey Association (QAHA) from 1955 to 1957, president of the Canadian Amateur Hockey Association (CAHA), from 1957 – 1959 and as president of the International Ice Hockey Federation from 1960 – 1962, the first French-Canadian to hold the latter two offices. He is currently president of the Quebec Junior "A" League and is a trustee for both the George T. Richardson Memorial Trophy (Eastern Canada junior championship) and the W. G. Hardy Trophy (Canadian intermediate championship). LeBel has also been named a life member of both the QAHA and the CAHA.
Also in: International Hockey Hall of Fame.

1971

JACKSON, Harvey "Busher"
Player
Born January 19, 1911, in Toronto, Ont; All-Star first team 1932, 1934, 1935, 1937; All-Star second team 1933; died June 25, 1966, in Toronto.

1929 – 1939 Toronto Maple Leafs, left wing
1939 – 1941 New York Americans, left wing
1941 – 1944 Boston Bruins, left wing

Along with Charlie Conacher and Joe Primeau, Busher gained fame as a member of the famous "Kid Line" with the Maple Leafs. He was on the team that three times won the league championship and also won the Stanley Cup in 1931 – 1932. When Conacher suffered injuries and Primeau retired in 1936, Busher played on a unit with his brother Art and Pep Kelly. He injured his shoulder in the 1938 – 1939 season and that was his last appearance with Toronto. He was traded (along with three other players) to New York and in 1942, to the Bruins where he closed out his career in 1943 – 1944.
Also in: Canada's Sports Hall of Fame and International Hockey Hall of Fame.

ROBERTS, Gordon
Player
Born September 5, 1891; graduated from McGill University with an M.D. in 1916; died September 2, 1966.

1910 – 1911 Ottawa Silver Seven, forward
1911 – 1916 Montreal Wanderers, forward
1916 – 1917 Vancouver Millionaires, forward

While studying medicine at McGill, Roberts played for the Wanderers and then moved to the Pacific Coast

Hockey Association where he set an all-time scoring record with 43 goals in 23 games in 1917. Hospital duties took him to Seattle where he played for the Metropolitans before returning to Vancouver in 1920 and finishing his career with Jack Adams and Fred Taylor.
Also in: International Hockey Hall of Fame.

SAWCHUK, Terrance Gordon
Player
Born December 28, 1929, in Winnipeg, Man; married; 3 children; Vezina Trophy 1952, 1953, 1955, co-winner with John Bower 1965; All-Star first team 1951–1953; All-Star second team four times; died May 31, 1970, in New York City.

1949–1955 Detroit Red Wings, goalie
1955–1957 Boston Bruins, goalie
1957–1964 Detroit Red Wings, goalie
1964–1967 Toronto Maple Leafs, goalie
1967–1968 Los Angeles Kings, goalie
1968–1969 Detroit Red Wings, goalie
1969–1970 New York Rangers, goalie

Terry was the first player to win the rookie award in three professional leagues—the old U.S. Hockey League in 1947–1948, the American Hockey League in 1948–1949 and the National Hockey League in 1950–1951. During his 20 years in the game, he appeared in 106 Stanley Cup games, had 267 goals-against for a 2.64 average and earned 12 shutouts. A career highlight was the 1952 Stanley Cup playoffs when he led Detroit to the Cup in a minimum 8 games, collecting 4 shutouts and allowing only 5 goals. In regular-season action, he played 953 complete games and had 2401 goals-against for an average of 2.52, registering 103 shutouts. Sawchuk was one of the greatest goaltenders in hockey—he played more seasons, more games and recorded more shutouts than any other goalie in the history of the National Hockey League.
Also in: Canada's Sports Hall of Fame and International Hockey Hall of Fame.

WEILAND, Ralph "Cooney"
Player
Born November 5, 1904 in Seaforth, Ont; acquired nickname in childhood; retired 1971.

1928–1932 Boston Bruins, forward
1932–1933 Ottawa Senators, forward
1933–1934 Ottawa Senators, Detroit Red Wings, forward
1934–1935 Detroit Red Wings, forward
1935–1939 Boston Bruins, forward
1939–1941 Boston Bruins, coach

Cooney played his minor hockey at Seaforth, but went to Owen Sound, Ont, to play junior hockey in 1923. The next season Owen Sound won the Memorial Cup (junior championship of Canada). From 1925 to 1928, he played at Minneapolis. When Weiland joined the Boston Bruins, he teamed up with "Dutch" Gainor and Hall of Famer "Dit" Clapper to form the "Dynamite Line"; the team won the Stanley Cup their first season together. In 1929–1930 when a new ruling allowed passing in all three zones, Weiland was leading point maker with 73, including 43 goals. His team was the highest scoring team and the American Division champions with a record of 14 straight wins. In 1932–1933 Weiland was sold to Ottawa, but in mid-season joined the Detroit Red Wings. After retiring as a player from the Bruins, he coached the team to a Stanley Cup victory in 1940–1941 and later coached at Hershey and New Haven for the American Hockey League and at Harvard University until his retirement in 1971.
Also in: International Hockey Hall of Fame.

WIRTZ, Arthur M.
Builder
Born January 23, 1901, in Chicago, Ill; son William Hall of Fame member.

Hockey needed a man like Arthur Wirtz to contribute to its growth and ultimate survival. In 1931 he went into partnership with Hall of Famers James Norris, Sr, and James D. Norris to purchase the Detroit Red Wings and the Olympic Stadium. In 1933 the three Hall of Famers acquired control of the Chicago Stadium Corporation and later Madison Square Garden, St. Louis Arena and others in which they developed farm systems for the Detroit team. In 1954, two years after the death of James Norris, Sr, James D. Norris and Wirtz gave up their interests in Detroit to buy the Chicago Black Hawks, losing $2.5 million in three years to rebuild the team. From an all-time low attendance, the two built the Black Hawks into one of the most successful National Hockey League teams. Wirtz is also credited with persuading the National Hockey League to give a franchise to St. Louis in 1966, and is a founder of the Hockey Hall of Fame.
Also in: International Hockey Hall of Fame.

1972

ADAMS, Weston W, Sr.
Builder
Born April 9, 1904, in Springfield, Mass; father Charles also in Hall of Fame; Harvard graduate; Commander in U.S. Navy during W.W. II; died March 19, 1973, at age 69.

From 1924 when his father, the late Charles F. Adams, was awarded a National Hockey League franchise until his death in 1973, Weston Adams was continuously and closely associated with the Boston Bruins. He succeeded his father as the Bruins' president in 1936, but military service intervened. Later, when the Bruins fortunes flagged, he personally scouted all over North America. He became chairman of the board in 1956 and by 1964 was president again, remaining there until 1969 when he retired in favor of his son. He was president during two Stanley Cup victories, 1939 and 1941 and he assembled the executive associates and coaching staff which produced two more, in 1970 and 1972.
Also in: International Hockey Hall of Fame.

BELIVEAU, Jean A. "Le Gros Bill"
Player
Born August 31, 1931, in Trois Rivieres, Ont; Art Ross Trophy 1955–1956; Hart Trophy 1955–1956, 1963–1964; Conn Smythe Trophy 1964–1965; All-Star first team six times; All-Star second team four times; presently vice president in charge of corporate relations for the Montreal Canadiens.

Beliveau first came to the attention of the Montreal club while playing for the Quebec Aces in the Quebec Senior

League. They had attempted to obtain his services earlier, and in the end, were forced to purchase the entire League. He was given a five-year, $100,000 contract (practically unheard of at that time) and a $20,000 bonus. From the beginning he was a team leader, although he didn't officially become team captain until 1961. He scored 507 goals during his 18 full seasons (1953 – 1971) in the National Hockey League (NHL), an all-time record for a center. He still holds the record for most consecutive years in Stanley Cup playoffs (16) and he played 17 in all. Jean's highest single goal-scoring season was 1955 – 1956 with 47 goals and 41 assists. Including playoffs, Jean played a total of 1287 games in NHL action. In his final season, 1970 – 1971, Jean collected 16 playoff assists, another record. He was honored with a Jean Beliveau Night on March 24. 1971, in Montreal Forum.
Also in: Canada's Sports Hall of Fame and International Hockey Hall of Fame.

GEOFFRION, Bernard "Boomer"
Player
Born February 16, 1931, in Montreal, Que; Calder Trophy 1952; All-Star second team 1954 – 1955, 1959 – 1960; Art Ross Trophy 1955 and 1961; All-Star first team 1960 – 1961; Hart Trophy 1961; married daughter of Hall of Famer Howie Morenz; 3 children.

1950 – 1964 Montreal Canadiens, forward
1966 – 1968 New York Rangers, forward, coach

Geoffrion never played minor league hockey, making the big jump from the junior ranks to the Canadiens in 1951. Boomer scored 8 goals in 18 games of his first season and won the National Hockey League (NHL) Rookie of the Year Award. He was the second player to reach the 50-goal plateau in one season (1960 – 1961), the same year he achieved a personal high of 95 points. Another highlight of his career was a 5-goal game against New York Rangers in 1955. Geoffrion retired as a player after the 1963 – 1964 season, but came back after missing two seasons to score 17 goals with the Rangers. Physical infirmities cut his career short in 1967 – 1968. He took a brief coaching job with the Rangers, and scouted for them until offered the new challenge in Atlanta. Boomer's NHL career record reads: 393 goals, 429 assists in 883 games; 58 goals and 60 assists in 132 playoffs.
Also in: International Hockey Hall of Fame.

HOLMES, Harold "Hap"
Player
Born April 15, 1889, in Aurora, Ont; after retiring, operated a papaya farm in Florida; died June 27, 1941.

1917 – 1918 Toronto Arenas, goalie
1918 – 1920 Seattle, goalie
1920 – 1921 Vancouver, goalie
1924 – 1926 Victoria, goalie
1926 – 1928 Detroit, goalie

Harry starred in five professional hockey leagues: the National Hockey Association, Pacific Coast Hockey Association, Western Canada Hockey League, Western Hockey League and the National Hockey League. His career goals-against average is 2.9 for 405 league games with 41 league shutouts and 6 playoff shutouts. He played on seven championship teams and four Stanley Cup winners, plus a fifth Cup series that was never completed because of the flu epidemic in Seattle. Following a brilliant career, he toured Australia extensively attempting to promote hockey. The memory of this great goalie is perpetuated in the Harry Holmes Memorial Trophy, awarded annually since 1941 to the leading goalie of the American Hockey League.
Also in: International Hockey Hall of Fame.

HOWE, Gordon "Gordie"
Player
Born March 31, 1928, in Floral, Sask; Art Ross Trophy 1951 – 1954, 1957, 1963; Hart Trophy 1952, 1953, 1957, 1958, 1960, 1963; All-Star first team twelve times; All-Star second team nine times; Canada's Outstanding Male Athlete 1963; Medal of Service from the Order of Canada 1971.

1946 – 1971 Detroit Red Wings, forward
1973 – 1977 Houston Aeros, forward

Considered by many as "Mr. Hockey," Gordie has contributed more records and goodwill to hockey than any other player in history. Spending his entire National Hockey League career with the Red Wings, his effortless skating style yet domineering presence on the ice totaled 786 goals in 25 seasons. Although not a bully on the ice, Gordie tangled with opponents when needed, such as the 1950 fight with Lou Tontinato of the New York Rangers which left Lou with a broken nose. The same year during the Stanley Cup playoff against Toronto, Gordie collided head-on with Ted Kennedy and suffered serious brain injury. Hours of surgery relieved the pressure on the brain, leaving Gordie with only an uncontrollable blink. Retiring from the Detroit club in 1971 because of an arthritic left wrist, he came out of retirement in 1973 and joined his sons, Mark and Marty, on the World Hockey Association Houston Aeros.
Also in: Canada's Sports Hall of Fame and International Hockey Hall of Fame.

SMITH, Reginald Joseph "Hooley"
Player
Born January 7, 1903, in Toronto, Ont; nicknamed by father after the Happy Hooligan cartoon character; outstanding oarsman, rugby player and amateur boxer; amateur hockey in Montreal as standout member of Granite team that won the Olympic championship for Canada in 1924; All-Star first team once; All-Star second team once; died in Montreal August 24, 1963.

1924 – 1927 Ottawa Senators, forward
1927 – 1936 Montreal Maroons, forward
1936 – 1937 Boston Bruins, forward
1937 – 1941 New York Americans, defenseman

Hooley Smith was a fierce player who, in his first season with the Ottawa Senators, developed a sweeping hookcheck making him a formidable player. In the finals of the 1926 – 1927 Stanley Cup playoffs, Smith attacked Harry Oliver of the Bruins and was suspended for one month at the beginning of the next season by league president Frank Calder. At the end of the 1926 – 1927 season he was traded to the Montreal Maroons for $22,000 along with Nels Stewart and Babe Siebert. The three of them formed the "S Line," known for its great scoring power and aggressive play. Smith was the captain of this team when they won the Stanley Cup in 1934 – 1935 and continued in that capacity until joining

the Bruins. In 1932–1933 he was fourth in league scoring with 20 goals and sixth in 1935–1936 with 19 goals. With the New York Americans he scored the 200th goal of his career and retired at the end of the 1940–1941 season.
Also in: International Hockey Hall of Fame.

1973

HARVEY, Douglas Norman
Player
Born December 19, 1924, in Montreal, Que; rejected offers in both professional football and baseball; once while demonstrating football plays on a blackboard, Harvey pushed the chalk so hard that he broke the chalk and fractured his knuckle; played one season of professional baseball in Ottawa in 1949; Norris Trophy seven times between 1954–1955 and 1961–1962; All-Star first team ten times; All-Star second team once.

1949–1961 Montreal Canadiens, defenseman
1961–1964 New York Rangers, defenseman, coach
1966–1967 Detroit Red Wings, defenseman
1968–1970 St. Louis Blues, defenseman, assistant coach
1970–1973 Los Angeles Kings, assistant coach
1973 Houston Aeros, World Hockey League, assistant coach

After playing senior hockey with the Royals, Harvey began his 21 seasons in professional hockey with the Montreal Canadiens, who won five straight Stanley Cup championships beginning in 1955–1956. Between playing for the New York Rangers and the Detroit Red Wings, Harvey coached the Quebec Aces of the American League in 1964 and played minor hockey with Quebec, Baltimore, Pittsburgh and Kansas City. Not until he joined the St. Louis Blues did he play on another Stanley Cup team, but they lost to the Canadiens. In all, Harvey played 1113 games with the National Hockey League and scored 88 goals. His 43 assists in 1954–1955 and 45 in 1945 were both records for a defenseman.
Also in: Canada's Sports Hall of Fame and International Hockey Hall of Fame.

MOLSON, Hartland de Montarville, O.B.E.
Builder
Born May 29, 1907, in Montreal, Que; father Col. Herbert Molson, founder of the Canadian Arena Co; served with R.C.A.F. in W.W. II, shot down during the Battle of Britain, 1940; received the Order of the British Empire 1945; appointed to the Senate 1955; resides in Montreal.

Molson was one of six club owners who agreed to finance the Hockey Hall of Fame. He also played an active role in strengthening owner-player relations while on the National Hockey League finance committee. He was president of the Canadian Arena Company and the Les Canadiens Hockey Club from 1957 to 1968. He also rejuvenated the Forum to provide excellent vision from any angle. Long noted for his charitability and philanthropic contributions, the Molson Foundation grants three prizes annually to Canadian citizens.
Also in: International Hockey Hall of Fame.

RAYNER, Claude Earl "Chuck"
Player
Born August 11, 1920, in Sutherland, Sask; one of six children; father a butcher; served with Royal Canadian Navy, 1943–1945; Hart Trophy 1949–1950; All-Star second team three times; resides in Kenora, Ont.

1940–1941 New York Americans, goalie
1941–1942 Brooklyn Americans, goalie
1945–1953 New York Rangers, goalie

Chuck Rayner played hockey in Sutherland from 1935–1936, but at 15 played junior hockey in Saskatoon with the Wesleys team that went to the Western Canada finals. He then joined the Kenora Thistles for three seasons, reaching the Memorial Cup finals in 1938–1939, but losing to the Oshawa Generals. Rayner played a few games of the 1939–1940 season with the Springfield Indians before being sold to the New York Americans. He played 36 games with them before joining the Royal Canadian Navy, then finished out his National Hockey League career with the New York Rangers. In 425 league games he had 1295 goals against for a 3.50 average, a respectable figure considering the team only made the playoffs twice. He also registered 25 shutouts in regular league play. In 18 playoff games Rayner had a 2.56 goals against average, but in three All-Star games had an excellent average of .67.
Also in: International Hockey Hall of Fame.

SMITH, Thomas J.
Player
Born September 27, 1885, in Ottawa; one of 13 children; eight boys in the family of which five were adept hockey players; brother Alf was inducted into the Hall of Fame in 1962; died August 1, 1966.

1912–1913 Moncton, forward
1913–1917 Quebec, forward
1917–1918 Montreal Canadiens, forward
1919–1920 Quebec, forward

Tommy began playing organized hockey in 1906 with the Federal Amateur Hockey League, leading the league in scoring his initial season. The following season he moved to the International League and led his Pittsburgh teammates in scoring with 23 goals in 22 games. Playing rover for Brantford in the Ontario Professional Hockey League, for the second time in his brief career he led his league in scoring. A total of five times in his career he either led a team or league in scoring. In 1906 he had scored 8 goals in one game, in 1909 and 1914 he totaled 9 goals in a game, four times he recorded 5 and once he scored in 14 consecutive games. Twice he challenged for the Stanley Cup and twice he lost, with Galt in 1911 and Moncton in 1912. The third time, playing along with Joe Malone and Jack Marks, Tommy earned the coveted Cup with Quebec in 1913. He retired at the age of 35 during the 1919–1920 season. He had played 10 games with Quebec and was scoreless. Discounting records for the 1912–1913 season, which are not available, Tommy played in 171 league games with 239 goals, and 15 goals in 15 playoffs.
Also in: International Hockey Hall of Fame.

UDVARI, Frank
Referee

Born 1924 in Yugoslavia; parents moved to Canada 1931; grew up in Kitchener, Ont; active with community youth programs in Kitchener-Waterloo area; now a successful businessman.

Frank was brought into the National Hockey League (NHL) by Carl Voss, the referee-in-chief at the time. A referee in the American Hockey League, Western League, Eastern League and Central League, Frank earned the respect of his peers with a no-nonsense approach that controlled the game. The same philosophy dominated his 15 years (1951–1966) in the NHL and moved Voss to comment that he had never met another man with higher standards for oneself. Acknowledged as the best on the roster for many years, Frank missed only two assignments because of coincidental family illnesses. After 788 games—718 regular season and 70 playoffs—Frank was appointed supervisor in 1966. Enlarging upon the duties of his new position, he started hockey schools in Canada and the United States with two in Germany for the Canadian Army. Many students and juniors in these schools have progressed into the NHL, another measure of Frank's influence in the sport.
Also in: International Hockey Hall of Fame.

1974

BURCH, William
Player

Born November 29, 1900, Yonkers, N.Y; Hart Trophy 1925; Lady Byng Trophy 1927; died in December, 1950.

1923–1926 Hamilton Tigers, defenseman, forward
1926–1933 New York Americans, defenseman
1933–1934 Boston Bruins, Chicago Black Hawks, defenseman

An excellent playmaker and stickhandler, he was the leading scorer on his team in 1924–1927 and 1929. He centered the line with the Green brothers at Hamilton, winning first place in the National Hockey League in 1925. After the team was transferred to New York, he was made captain. During the 1933–1934 season he broke a leg and decided to retire. His best chance for a Stanley Cup came in 1925 but a dispute with management on payment for the series dropped the team from the playoffs.
Also in: International Hockey Hall of Fame.

COULTER, Arthur Edmund
Player

Born May 31, 1909, in Winnipeg, Man; served in military during W.W. II; All-Star second team 1935 and 1938–1940; lives in Florida.

1931–1935 Chicago Black Hawks, defenseman
1936–1942 New York Rangers, defenseman

Art started his hockey career with the Pilgrim Athletic Club in 1924 and turned professional in 1929 with Philadelphia. He teamed up with Taffy Abel as a strong defense unit when Chicago won the Stanley Cup in 1933–1934. Coulter succeeded Bill Cook as the Rangers' captain in 1935–1936. He played on one more Stanley Cup winner with the Rangers in 1940 and after two more seasons, entered the military service, ending his professional career. During his eleven National Hockey League seasons, Art had a record of 30 goals and 83 assists, with 4 goals and 5 assists in 49 playoffs. He was named as the first president of the NHL Players Association.
Also in: International Hockey Hall of Fame.

DUNDERDALE, Thomas
Player

Born May 6, 1887, in Benella, Australia; moved to England, then Canada, settling in Ottawa in 1904; died in 1960 in Winnipeg.

1910–1911 Toronto Shamrocks, forward
1911–1912 Quebec Bulldogs, forward
1912–1924 Victoria, forward

The only Australian-born hockey player in the Hall of Fame, Thomas was an excellent stickhandler with explosive speed. During the existence of the Pacific Coast Hockey Association (PCHA), Thomas scored more goals than any other player in the league. In 1914 he recorded a goal in all 15 games and was named the PCHA All-Star center. His career totals read 225 goals in 290 games with 6 goals in 12 playoff games. After retiring, he turned to coaching teams in Los Angeles, Edmonton and Winnipeg.
Also in: International Hockey Hall of Fame.

HAY, Charles
Builder

Born in 1902 in Kingston, Ont; moved to Saskatoon, Sask, in 1913; attended the University of Saskatchewan; son William (Red) Hay played in the National Hockey League with Chicago; died October 24, 1973.

Charles Hay will be remembered in sports history as the man who finally brought the best teams of Canada and the Soviet Union together in the first "world series" of hockey. In 1968 he helped organize and became the first president of an organization known as Hockey Canada, a group set up to operate a national hockey team to represent Canada in international competition. He was a prime co-ordinator of talks which culminated in the Team Canada-Soviet Nationals hockey series in September, 1972. Many consider this first series the greatest sports event in Canadian history.
Also in: International Hockey Hall of Fame.

IVAN, Thomas Nathaniel
Builder

Born January 31, 1911, in Toronto, Ont; lives in a Chicago suburb.

Tommy was an outstanding amateur player in the Canadian Amateur Hockey Association before an injury cut short his career. He started as a scout with the Detroit Red Wings, then as a coach at Omaha and Indianapolis, before moving into the National Hockey League with the Red Wings as coach in 1947. Tommy coached six consecutive championship teams and three Stanley Cup winners before leaving Detroit in 1955. He then joined the Chicago Black Hawks as general manager, combining coaching as well for a year and a half. He is credited with much of the success in moulding the Hawks from league doormats (both on the ice and at the gate) into one of the most successful organizations in the league. He helped rebuild a fine farm system and under his tenure as general manager, the Black Hawks won their first

Stanley Cup in 23 years, in 1960 – 1961, and their first East Division title in 1966 – 1967, another in 1970 and the West crown in 1971.
Also in: International Hockey Hall of Fame.

MOORE, Richard Winston
Player

Born January 6, 1931, in Montreal, Que; one of ten children; All-Star first team 1957 – 1958, 1958 – 1959; All-Star second team 1960 – 1961; operates several businesses; lives in Montreal.

1951 – 1963 Montreal Canadiens, forward
1964 – 1965 Toronto Maple Leafs, forward
1967 – 1968 St. Louis Blues, forward

Moore played with Montreal Junior Royals and Junior Canadiens, both Memorial Cup winners, before turning professional in 1951 – 1952. He was called up to the Montreal senior club that same year, where he remained for 12 seasons. Although plagued with injuries throughout his career, he twice led the National Hockey League in scoring. His first title in 1957 – 1958 was achieved despite a broken left wrist with three months left of the season. He never missed a game, playing with a cast on his wrist which enabled him to grip the stick and he topped the league with 36 goals and 48 assists. The following season he scored 96 points, breaking the existing record of 95 set by Gordie Howe. He retired at the end of the 1962 – 1963 season, but returned twice to play 38 games for Toronto in 1964 – 1965 and 27 games with St. Louis Blues in 1967 – 1968, when he retired for good. His National Hockey League career record reads: 261 goals and 347 assists in 719 games and 46 goals with 64 assists in 135 playoffs.
Also in: International Hockey Hall of Fame.

TARASOV, Anatoli Vladimirovitch
Builder

Anatoli Tarasov is generally recognized as the architect of the Soviet Union hockey power. In the late 1940s and early 1950s, he played on the Soviet team when it emerged from obscurity to challenge the Canadians for the first time. He coached his nation's National team to nine straight world amateur championships and three consecutive Olympic titles before he was retired after winning the Olympic title at Sapporo, Japan in 1972. He has written many books on hockey and also supervised the Soviet Golden Puck tournament for boys, in which he claimed he had one million youngsters registered.
Also in: International Hockey Hall of Fame.

VOSS, Carl Potter
Builder

Born January 6, 1907, in Chelsea, Mass; lives in Florida.

Voss was a member of the Kingston Frontenacs in 1926, when they were in the Memorial Cup finals and had already played on two Grey Cup winning teams as a halfback with Queen's University football team. He played hockey with seven different clubs in his six years as a player in the National Hockey League (NHL). He later became president of the U.S. Hockey League and in 1950 was named the first referee-in-chief of the NHL. As hockey developed, he also became referee-in-chief of other senior minor leagues which used officials provided by the NHL. Voss conducted hundreds of officiating schools and clinics.
Also in: International Hockey Hall of Fame.

1975

ARMSTRONG, George Edward "Chief"
Player

Born July 6, 1930, in Skead, Ont; winner of the Charlie Conacher Citizens Citizenship Award in 1969 for work with retarded children.

George was a standout junior at Stratford and with the Toronto Marlboros, then played for Marlboro seniors when they won the Allan Cup in 1950. While at the national senior finals in Alberta, an Indian tribe officially dubbed him "Big Chief Shoot-the-Puck" and he was "Chief" thereafter. He joined the Toronto club in the 1949 – 1950 season and was team captain for 13 of his 21 years with them. During his tenure as captain, the Leafs won the Stanley Cup in 1962 – 1964 and 1967. Retiring as an active player in October, 1972, George retained a post in the Toronto front office with some scouting duties. His career totals read: 296 goals, 417 assists in 1187 games, also 26 goals and 32 assists in 110 playoff games.
Also in: International Hockey Hall of Fame.

BAILEY, Irvin Wallace "Ace"
Player

Born July 3, 1903, in Bracebridge, Ont; presently in the insurance business in Willowdale, Ont.

Ace Bailey played junior hockey in his hometown and senior hockey at Peterborough. He joined the Toronto Maple Leafs in 1926, and led the National Hockey League in scoring in 1928 – 1929 with 32 points, 22 of them goals. His career was relatively short—a collision with Eddie Shore resulted in a fractured skull, requiring delicate brain surgery—Bailey stopped playing in 1933. The Leafs retired his No. 6, but Bailey requested that it be given to Ron Ellis. He later coached, then joined the staff of minor officials at Maple Leaf Gardens where he is still active. His career totals read: 111 goals and 82 assists, also 3 goals and 4 assists in 4 playoffs.
Also in: International Hockey Hall of Fame.

BUCKLAND, Frank
Builder

Born 1901 in Gravenhurst, Ont; graduated from University of Toronto; Canadian Amateur Hockey Association Meritorious Award 1965; Golden Stick Award 1965; life mem. Ontario Hockey Association 1973; Sports Achievement Award 1974.

Frank's interest in hockey began while attending the University of Toronto. He was coach for an amateur hockey club, later becoming the manager, then president. Following graduation from the University, he coached junior and senior teams in Peterborough, Ont, 1932 – 1940. Frank served as president of the Ontario Hockey Association from 1955 to 1957 and as treasurer since 1961.
Also in: International Hockey Hall of Fame.

DRILLON, Gordon Arthur
Player

Born October 23, 1914, in Moncton, N.B; Lady Byng

Trophy 1937 – 1938; All-Star first team 1937 – 1938 and 1938 – 1939; All-Star second team 1941 – 1942.

1936 – 1942 Toronto Maple Leafs, forward
1942 – 1943 Montreal Canadiens, forward

Drillon joined the Maple Leafs lineup in 1936 – 1937 as a temporary replacement for ailing Charlie Conacher. He was a standout in the next two seasons, when he, Syl Apps and Bob Davidson sparked the team to the league championship in 1937 – 1938. In 1940 – 1941 he led the team in scoring for the third straight season and in his final season with Toronto, was on the Stanley Cup winning team. He played with Montreal for one more season, ending his career with a 50 point effort. His overall National Hockey League record reads 155 goals and 139 assists and 26 goals and 15 assists in 7 playoffs.
Also in: International Hockey Hall of Fame.

HALL, Glenn Henry
Player
Born October 3, 1931, in Humboldt, Sask; learned to tend goal in Humboldt on outdoor rinks; Vezina Trophy 1963, 1967 and 1969; Conn Smythe Trophy 1968; All-Star first team seven times; All-Star second team four times; resides in Edmonton, Alta.

1952 – 1953 Detroit Red Wings, goalie
1954 – 1957 Detroit Red Wings, goalie
1957 – 1967 Chicago Black Hawks, goalie
1967 – 1968 St. Louis Blues, goalie

Hall holds a number of records for a goalie in the National Hockey League. Beginning in his first full season with Detroit, he played a string of 502 games, the most consecutive games played by a goalie in the National Hockey League, and until the last half-season of his career, played without a mask. Appearing in a total of 906 games, Hall also had the record for shutouts in six seasons, including his rookie year. In Stanley Cup playoffs, he played the most games for a goalie, 113, and the most minutes, 6899. The St. Louis Blues paid a record $45,000 to have Hall in the first National Hockey League expansion draft. As one of the league's most consistently outstanding goalies, he ended his career with 2239 goals-against, 84 shutouts and a 2.51 average.
Also in: International Hockey Hall of Fame.

JENNINGS, William Mitchell
Builder
Born December 14, 1928; Lester Patrick Award 1971; resides in New York City.

Jennings began his association with hockey in 1959 when he was counsel for the Graham-Paige Corporation when it acquired controlling interest in Madison Square Garden Corporation, which in turn owned the New York Rangers club. He became president of the Rangers and its governor in 1962, holding both offices today. In 1966 he was the originator of the Lester Patrick Award and Dinner for persons who have rendered outstanding service to hockey in the United States. For his own distinguished services, Jennings was himself the recipient of this award in 1971. He was also instrumental in the founding and successful operation of the Metropolitan Junior Hockey Association in the New York area, starting in 1966.
Also in: International Hockey Hall of Fame.

PILOTE, Pierre Paul
Player
Born December 11, 1931, in Kenogami, Ont; family moved to Lake Erie, Ont, when he was 14; Norris Memorial Trophy 1963 – 1965; All-Star second team 1960 – 1962; All-Star first team 1963 – 1967; presently coaching amateur teams in Toronto.

1955 – 1968 Chicago Black Hawks, defenseman
1968 – 1969 Toronto Maple Leafs, defenseman

Rated as one of the most outstanding defensemen of his era, few defensemen rivaled Pierre's scoring ability of 80 goals and 418 assists. During his 13-year affiliation with the Hawks, he never missed a game during his first five seasons; a shoulder operation in 1962 broke his performance record. The Hawks won the 1961 Stanley Cup. Pierre was chosen captain of the team for six consecutive seasons beginning in 1963. He was traded to Toronto in 1968 where he completed his 976 career games, 559 points and 1353 penalty minutes.
Also in: International Hockey Hall of Fame.

1976

BOWER, John William
Player
Born November 8, 1924, in Prince Albert, Sask; only boy in a family of nine; four years in Canadian Army, two overseas during W. W. II; Les Cunningham Trophy three times; Harry Holmes Trophy three times; All-Star first team 1961; Vezina Trophy co-winner with Terry Sawchuk 1965; currently handles eastern Canada scouting duties for Toronto Maple Leafs.

1953 – 1957 New York Rangers, goalie
1958 – 1970 Toronto Maple Leafs, goalie

Bower did not reach the National Hockey League until age 29 when he joined the Rangers after spending 14 years in the minors. After three seasons in New York, he went to Toronto and played on four Stanley Cup winners during his 11 year stint. His career regular-season shutouts total 37, plus 5 in 71 playoff games. His goals-against average is 2.52 for 533 games.
Also in: International Hockey Hall of Fame.

GIBSON, John L. "Jack"
Builder
Born September 10, 1880, in Berlin, Ont; graduated from Detroit Medical School and set up a dental practice at Houghton; died October 7, 1955, in Calgary.

Jack Gibson was instrumental in organizing the Portage Lake team in 1902 – 1903 and soon became captain as well as leading scorer. The 1903 – 1904 team played 26 games (winning 24) and scored 273 goals, and had only 48 against. Opponents included teams from Pittsburgh, St. Paul, St. Louis and the famous Montreal Wanderers, whom they defeated twice. Portage Lake, in 1905, challenged Ottawa's famous Silver Seven to a championship series and in 1906, a similar challenge was issued to Montreal, but both were refused. About that time, Canadian clubs were luring away the great Portage Lake

players and Gibson returned to Canada, eventually setting up practice in Calgary, where he resided until his death.
Also in: International Hockey Hall of Fame and U.S. Hockey Hall of Fame.

QUACKENBUSH, Hubert George "Bill"
Player
Born March 2, 1922 in Toronto, Ont; Lady Byng Trophy 1949; All-Star first team five times; All-Star second team twice.

1942 – 1949 Detroit Red Wings, defenseman
1949 – 1956 Boston Bruins, defenseman

First a junior hockey player at Brantford under Tommy Ivan who later coached him with the Detroit Red Wings, Bill joined the National Hockey League (NHL) in 1942. After seasoning in Indianapolis, he played only ten games before he broke his wrist and missed playing in the Stanley Cup championship. That break later reduced his shooting power, but he became quite a puck-control artist. He played 13 full seasons with the NHL, joining Hall of Famers Jack Stewart and Red Kelly to form the defense for the Detroit Red Wings and later teaming with the Boston Bruins. He ended his NHL career with 62 goals and 222 assists.
Also in: International Hockey Hall of Fame.

ROSS, Philip Dansken
Builder
Born in Montreal, Que; died July 1949.

A participant in many sports while attending McGill University, Philip was the football captain in 1876 when the team beat Harvard. He was also a member of Canadian championship rowing crews, a lacrosse player, and founded several golf clubs. He was a trustee of the Minto Cup (Canadian lacrosse championship) and turned down trusteeship of the Grey Cup (Canadian football championship). He was the first trustee of the Stanley Cup, a position he held for 56 years. Before his death in 1949, he donated full authority of the Cup to the National Hockey League.
Also in: International Hockey Hall of Fame.

WIRTZ, William Wadsworth
Builder
Born October 5, 1929; father Arthur Hockey Hall of Fame member.

Bill Wirtz was highly respected for his efforts to make expansion of the National Hockey League a success and thus, after many years of involvement with hockey, he was elected chairman of the board of governors twice for two year terms in the early 1970s. His "patience, tenacity and especially his personal credibility" brought about a collective bargaining agreement with the National Hockey Players' Association and smoothed many of the rough edges during a troubled time for the league. Bill Wirtz's whole life was hockey: when he was only two years old, his father and the Norrises purchased the Detroit Red Wings and turned them into a powerful component of the National Hockey League. When his father acquired the Black Hawks in 1954, Bill joined the organization and soon became vice president. The team began to strengthen and won the Stanley Cup in 1960 – 1961 and the Eastern Division championship in 1970. Wirtz was club president beginning in 1966 and once the Black Hawks had transferred to the Western Division they won three consecutive Campbell Bowl victories.
Also in: International Hockey Hall of Fame.

International Hockey Hall of Fame

KINGSTON, ONTARIO

Mailing Address: P.O. Box 62, K7L 4V6. Tel. (613) 544-2355. *Contact:* J. A. Leo La Fleur, Cur. *Location:* Corner of Alfred & York Sts. at Memorial Centre; approx. 90 mi. S.W. of Ottawa, 85 mi. N. of Syracuse, N.Y, 150 mi. N.E. of Toronto. *Admission:* 2 to 5 and 7 to 9 daily and weekends, July – Aug; 2 to 5 weekends, Sept. – June. Adults 50¢, children 12 – 15 25¢, children under 12 free, family $1.00; special tours by request to Mus. Cur. *Personnel:* John Kelly, Pres; William Fitsell, First V.Pres; Pete Radley, Second V.Pres; Josh Nichols, Third V.Pres; Steve Mulkerns, Secy; Paul Bourque, Treas; J. A. Leo La Fleur, Cur. and Bd. of Dirs. *Nearby Halls of Fame:* Horseshoe Pitching (Corning, N.Y, 115 mi. S.W.), Baseball (Cooperstown, N.Y, 130 mi. S.E.), Horse Racing (Saratoga Springs, N.Y, 145 mi. S.E.), Flight (Harris Hill, N.Y, 150 mi. S.W.), Hockey (Toronto), Football (Hamilton, 180 mi. S.W.).

Closely associated with the Hockey Hall of Fame in Toronto, the International Hockey Hall of Fame was founded in 1946 by Capt. James T. Sutherland to present the history of the game of hockey and to honor the people who have been a part of its national and international development. In 1943, Kingston was selected by the National Hockey League (NHL) and the Canadian Amateur Hockey Association (CAHA) as the proper location for a permanent exhibit; early British troops had played shinny (hockey-on-the-ice) to liven up their winters while stationed in Kingston, and the Royal Military College cadets had introduced the game of hockey in 1886 when they played against Queen's College in Kingston. An International Hockey Hall of Fame Committee was appointed and constitution and officers were approved in 1944; the first nine members were named in 1945. Both the NHL and the CAHA donated money for construction. Architects began plans for a building in 1951. In 1958 Clarence Campbell, president of the NHL, announced that they were transferring allegiance to Toronto where, in 1959, the Canadian National Exhibition provided them with a site for a Hall of Fame; this became the Hockey Hall of Fame (*See* Hockey Hall of

Fame sketch for further details). The Kingston committee continued efforts for an International Hockey Hall of Fame and was granted a site for a shrine on the Memorial Centre grounds in Kingston. The building was completed in 1965. A public auditorium is located on the first floor, while the Hall of Fame is housed on the second floor. A special gallery contains pictures and accounts of the top amateur and professional hockey stars who are members of the Hall of Fame. Displays within the museum include the world's oldest puck (1886), the second oldest hockey stick (1888) with a history of the development of the hockey stick, the evolution of ice skates over the past 100 years, original hockey cards from the four-team National Hockey Association and the Tommy Gorman collection of pictures of Ottawa teams showing uniforms and protective equipment. A special corner is reserved for "Hockeyana" Capt. James T. Sutherland, founder of the International Hockey Hall of Fame. In an international display is the bronze urn presented to the Battleford (Saskatchewan) Millers in 1934 as the first team to tour Japan, a hockey stick from Russia, a pennant from Norway, and pictures of the first professional hockey team in the world (Portage Lakers). Women's team are also featured in the museum. Future plans for the Hall of Fame include the addition of a display covering the evolution of the game of hockey and more international artifacts.

Members: 212 as of December 1976. Members may be players, referees or builders. Players must be retired from active playing for at least three years, though exceptions can be made. Selection is based on playing ability, integrity, sportsmanship, character and contribution to the team and hockey in general. There is no limit to the number of members elected each year, though the annual number elected is usually around five. Those selected for membership are elected by committees of the Hockey Hall of Fame in Toronto (*see* Hockey Hall of Fame sketch) and are then approved for the International Hockey Hall of Fame by a committee appointed by the Board of Directors; the committee has the right to delete or add people to the membership list from the Hockey Hall of Fame. At present the membership of the two halls of fame differs by only one person, Fred "Bun" Cook, who is enshrined in the International Hockey Hall of Fame. As hockey grows, selection methods will change. New members are honored by both the Hockey and International Hockey Halls of Fame simultaneously. Plaques and certificates are presented at a special banquet held each year around August 28 during the Canadian National Exhibit in Toronto.

1966

COOK, Frederick Joseph "Bun"
Player

Born September 18, 1903 in Kingston, Ont, home of the International Hockey Hall of Fame; All-Star second team 1930 – 1931; brother William "Bill" Cook is also a member of the International Hall of Fame; presently runs a parking lot in Kingston.

1926 – 1936 New York Rangers, forward
1936 – 1937 Boston Bruins, forward

When Madison Square Garden obtained its franchise for the New York Rangers in 1926 – 1927, Bun Cook, his brother Bill and Frank Boucher were signed up for the line of that first team, organized by Hall of Famer Conn Smythe. Under the guidance of Lester Patrick, another Hall of Famer, the Rangers' line dominated hockey in the American Division for nearly ten years, and scored over 1000 goals. Though Bill Cook and Frank Boucher outscored Bun, he was seventh in National Hockey League scoring for 1927 – 1928 with 14 goals and 14 assists, tenth in 1930 – 1931 with 18 goals and 17 assists and eighth in 1932 – 1933 with 22 goals and 15 assists. The Rangers line ended when Bun was sold to the Boston Bruins, but in 11 seasons in the National Hockey League he scored 158 goals and 144 assists.

United States Hockey Hall of Fame

EVELETH, MINNESOTA

Mailing Address: P.O. Box 657, 55734. Tel. (218) 749-5167. *Contact:* Roger A. Godin, Exec. Dir. *Location:* Off Hwy. 53 on Hat Trick Ave; approx. 60 mi. N.W. of Duluth, 180 mi. N.E. of Minneapolis-St. Paul. *Admission:* summer (June 15 – Labor Day) 9 to 8 Monday – Saturday, 10 to 8 Sunday; Winter, 9 to 5 Monday – Saturday, 12 to 5 Sunday. Family (two adults and up to four children under 18) $4.00, adults $2.00, juniors (13-17) $1.00, children (6 – 12) 50¢, five years and under free; group rates available on request. *Personnel:* Donald M. Clark, Pres; J. Lawrence Cain, V.Pres; D. Kelly Campbell, Secy; Larry E. Doyle, Treas; 8-mem. Selection Comt; 21-mem. Bd. of Dirs. (Honorable Thomas F. Lockhart, Chmn.); Roger A. Godin, Exec. Dir. *Nearby Halls of Fame:* Fishing (Hayward, Wis, 115 mi. S.E.).

Located in the middle of winter sports country is a small town called Eveleth, Minn. Over the years many fine hockey players came from that town and had a great impact on hockey in the United States. In fact, 11 of their fine players rose to fame in the National Hockey League (NHL) and many more made a name for this small town on teams in the minor professional, college and senior amateur leagues. Even Eveleth High School hockey team members brought attention to their hometown by winning 5 Minnesota state championships and making 13 appearances in 30 tournaments. Is it surprising that Eveleth is known as the "amateur hockey capital of the USA?" In 1967 D. Kelly Campbell, a local mining executive, conceived the idea of a U.S. Hockey Hall of Fame in Eveleth. It caught on quickly and he was soon appointed chairman of the Project H Committee to study the feasibility of a Hall of Fame. In 1968 the American Hockey Association of the United States (AHAUS) endorsed the concept and in 1969 U.S. Steel donated the site. A federal grant in 1971, a $100,000 three-year grant from the NHL in August, 1972, a $666,400 grant from the Economic Development Administration in 1973 and fund-raising projects throughout the State made a permanent Hall of Fame reality. Governor Wendell Anderson, Mayor Joe Bergich and NHL star Gordie Howe, among others, were part of the ground-breaking ceremonies on February 16, 1972. Construction began that April and dedication ceremonies and the official opening took place on June 21, 1973. Inside, on the first floor, a Great Hall honors the members of the Hall of Fame with specially designed (by Tom Beers, who also designed the interiors of the Pro Football, Texas Sports, World Golf and American Golf Halls of Fame) pylons displaying pictures and biographies of those enshrined. A 91-seat theater shows 30-min. hockey movies four times daily and televises hockey games during building hours. A souvenir shop, miscellaneous displays and the executive director's office are also located on the first floor. The mezzanine has a library that can hold up to 60 people for meetings, a lounge with a television for broadcasting hockey games, a current events board (with results of professional, college, high school and amateur games), additional offices and a receiving room. Major displays for high school, amateur, collegiate, professional and international hockey are located on the second floor. The Evolution of Hockey Time Tunnel, a circular walk-through exhibit, takes visitors into hockey's past through sight and sound. Slides and audio presentations tell about amateur hockey, and lifesize cutouts represent its seven classes from Squirt (9 to 10 years old) to Senior (over 19 years old). Other displays show the evolution of the hockey stick and skates. Telephones in the information gallery tell about the spectators, players, coaches, managers and sportscasters, as well as rinks and facilities for hockey. Displays on players, leagues and the Stanley Cup of professional hockey, and an international area symbolized by a line map of the world imprinted on a hockey puck, complete the collection. Between 6000 to 7000 people visit the U.S. Hockey Hall of Fame each month in the summer and 500 to 600 visit during each winter month. This Hall is a member of the Association of Sports Museums and Halls of Fame.

Members: 42 as of October 1976. On September 16, 1972, a nine-member Selection Committee, headed by North Star Pres. Walter L. Bush, Jr. selected the first 25 members and made a formal announcement of the new inductees in New York City, January 1973, at a luncheon honoring retiring AHAUS president and Hall of Famer to-be, Tom Lockhart. The first enshrinement ceremony and dedication of the Hall of Fame took place on June 21, 1973, with Walter L. Bush, Jr. as the keynote speaker. The 27th Annual American Hockey Association convention was held in conjunction with the dedication ceremonies. In 1974 the first Enshrinement Hockey Game, a new addition to Enshrinement Day, was held at the Eveleth Hippodrome. The University of Minnesota, NCAA champions played the University of Minnesota-Duluth, NIT champions. Since the first enshrinement ceremony, a special day in October is set aside for a festival of hockey, beginning with the special enshrinement ceremonies in the Hall's theater, a social hour followed by a banquet at the Holiday Inn, the Enshrinement Game at the Eveleth Hippodrome, and post-social activities at the Eveleth Elks Club and VFW Post. Admission to the Hall of Fame is free all day. Enshrinement Day, 1977, was on October 22. Annual selection of members takes place alternately between New England and Minnesota; the 1977 inductees were selected on June 23 in Boston. Three deserving players, coaches, referees, administrators or support personnel (no one has yet been selected from this category), from high school coaches to NHL players, are enshrined each year and receive special plaques from the U.S. Hockey Hall of Fame.

1973

ABEL, Clarence John "Taffy"
Player
Born May 28, 1900 in Sault Ste. Marie, Mich; died August 1, 1964.

1926 – 1929 New York Rangers, defenseman
1929 – 1934 Chicago Black Hawks, defenseman

Taffy played as an amateur with Fields Nationals, who won the McNaughton Cup in 1919. He joined St. Paul as an amateur, enabling him to represent the United States in the 1924 Olympics in Chamonix, France, where he carried the flag when he took the Olympic oath for the hockey players. Abel returned in 1925 – 1926 to play with "Ching" Johnson on the Minneapolis Millers, joining the Rangers the following season. The Rangers won the division title that year, and the Stanley Cup the next year against the Montreal Maroons. During his career, he scored 18 goals and 18 assists in 8 seasons with one goal and one assist in 38 playoff games.

BAKER, Hobart Amery Hare
Player
See entry in Hockey Hall of Fame, 1945.
Also in: International Hockey Hall of Fame and National Football Hall of Fame.

BRIMSEK, Francis Charles "Mr. Zero"
Player
See entry in Hockey Hall of Fame, 1966.
Also in: International Hockey Hall of Fame.

BROWN, George V.
Administrator
See entry in Hockey Hall of Fame, 1961.
Also in: International Hockey Hall of Fame.

BROWN, Walter A.
Administrator
See entry in Hockey Hall of Fame, 1962.
Also in: International Hockey Hall of Fame and Naismith Memorial Basketball Hall of Fame.

CHASE, John P.
Player
Born June 12, 1906, in Milton, Mass; played baseball at Harvard University and later with amateur teams; graduated from Harvard in 1928.

After playing hockey at Milton Academy in 1922–1923 and Exeter Academy in 1923–1924, Chase began his outstanding amateur hockey career at Harvard University. In his freshman year, he was a regular at center ice, and in the next three years he was first line center. He was selected varsity team captain in his senior year. After graduation Chase began a business career and declined offers to turn professional. He did continue to play hockey, first with the Boston Athletic Association and then with the Boston University Club and Brac Burn Hockey Club. In 1932, he captained the U.S. Olympic team, which won the Silver Medal at Lake Placid, N.Y. He became Harvard University varsity hockey coach from 1942 to 1950.

DAHLSTROM, Carl S. "Cully"
Player

Born July 3, 1913, in Minneapolis, Minn; played high school hockey in Minneapolis; amateur hockey with Pillsbury House before turning professional in 1933; Rookie of the Year 1937; Calder Trophy 1937–1938.

In his first year (1937) with the Black Hawks, Dahlstrom was a key man in the team's victory against Toronto for the Stanley Cup. 1943–1944 was Dahlstrom's most outstanding year. In a full 50-game season, he scored 20 goals and 22 assists. Before retiring after the 1944–1945 season, he had scored 92 goals and 126 assists. He was offered a job by the Kansas City coach but turned it down to devote his interests to business.

GARRISON, John B.
Player

Born February 13, 1909, in West Newton, Mass; unparalleled record of six years on the hockey team at Country Day School in West Newton.

John Garrison was one of the finest hockey players in the 1930s, adept at both forward and defense positions. He played for Harvard University 1928–1932, first as a regular on the freshman team and then three years on the varsity team at center ice. Though he chose a career in business rather than one as a professional hockey player, he led many amateur teams to the U.S. National title. In 1932 he was on the U.S. Olympic Silver Medal team. In 1933 he was on the U.S. world championship team and scored the unassisted overtime goal against Canada to give the United States a win at Prague, Czechoslovakia. He was captain of the 1936 U.S. Olympic Bronze Medal team and coach of the 1948 U.S. Olympic hockey team.

GIBSON, John L. "Jack"
Administrator

See entry in Hockey Hall of Fame, 1976.
Also in: International Hockey Hall of Fame.

GOHEEN, Francis Xavier "Moose"
Player

See entry in Hockey Hall of Fame, 1952.
Also in: International Hockey Hall of Fame.

GORDON, Malcom K.
Coach

Born January 10, 1868, in Baltimore, Md; served in W.W. I; worked in real estate until 1927; founded Malcom K. Gordon School at Garrison, N.Y. and was headmaster until his retirement in 1952; taught school until shortly before his death on November 13, 1964, in Garrison N.Y, at age 96.

While Gordon was the head of the history department at St. Paul's School in Concord, N.H, as well as football and cricket coach, he became involved with hockey. In 1885 he wrote the first set of rules for hockey in the United States and became St. Paul's hockey coach in 1887; he served the intramural team in that capacity until 1917. During that time, Gordon developed fine hockey players for the Eastern colleges, including Hobey Baker, who became Princeton University hockey team captain for two years. St. Paul's School still competes for a "Hobey Stick" in honor of this hockey player who was so well trained by Malcom Gordon.

JEREMIAH, Edward J.
Coach

Born November 4, 1905, in Wooster, Mass; high school at Somerville, Mass, and prep school at Hebron Academy, Maine; earned nine letters at Somerville, three each in football, baseball and basketball; two football, three hockey and two baseball letters at Dartmouth; served in W.W. II; died in Hanover, N.H, June 7, 1967.

Jeremiah began his three-league career in 1930–1931 with the New Haven hockey team of the Canadian-American League. In 1931–1932 he played for both the New York Americans and the Boston Bruins of the National Hockey League and played eight games total. He returned to the Canadian-American League in the 1932–1933 season to play for the Boston Cubs and New Haven team and moved to the International League with Cleveland in 1934–1935. After retiring from an active career, Jeremiah coached the Boston Athletic hockey team and led them to the National Amateur Athletic Union championship in 1935–1936. He returned to Dartmouth, where he played college hockey, and except for military service, coached the team continuously from 1936 to 1967.

KARAKAS, Michael G.
Player

Born December 12, 1911 in Aurora, Minn, but raised in Eveleth; began playing hockey in a lot near Spruce Mine with other sons of Oliver Iron Mining Co. employees; played three years for the Eveleth High School team, coached by Hall of Famer Cliff Thompson; while attending Eveleth Junior College, played for an amateur team, the Rangers; Calder Trophy 1935–1936; All-Star second team 1944–1945.

1935–1940 Chicago Black Hawks, goalie
1943–1946 Chicago Black Hawks, goalie

Karakas was spotted for the pros when the Rangers won the Minnesota state championship in 1931. A scout for the American Hockey Association (AHA) was attracted by Karakas' work and brought him to the Chicago Shamrocks where he played backup goalie one season and regular the next, and received the AHA Cup for most valuable goalie in the league. After two years with the AHA's St. Louis and Tulsa teams, he joined the National Hockey League's (NHL) Chicago Black Hawks. His first season in the NHL proved to be a fine one. With a 1.92 goals against average and 9 shutouts in the 48-game season, Karakas was voted NHL Rookie of the Year. In the team's 1937 – 1938 Stanley Cup victory, he registered 2 shutouts during the 8-game playoff. Karakas left the Black Hawks to play out the end of the 1939 – 1940 season with the Montreal Canadiens, then played three seasons with the Providence Reds of the AHA. He returned to the Black Hawks in 1943 – 1944 and played in the Stanley Cup finals against the Montreal Canadiens and shared the league leadership in shutouts in 1944 – 1945. After the 1945 – 1946 season, Karakas finished his career with the Providence Reds.

LANE, Myles J.

Player

Born October 2, 1903, in Melrose, Mass; graduated from Dartmouth College in 1928 where he played three seasons of football as a halfback and was part of the 1925 team declared National champion; three letters and All-American in football; one letter in baseball; became one of the nation's most successful trial lawyers and a foe of organized crime.

1928 – 1929 New York Rangers, defenseman
1928 – 1930 Boston Bruins, defenseman
1933 – 1934 Boston Bruins, defenseman

Lane was an all-around athlete at Dartmouth College, but was especially outstanding as a defenseman and captain of the hockey team. He not only earned three letters in hockey but also set Dartmouth records for the most goals in one game by a defenseman (5), most goals in one season by a defenseman (20), and the most career goals by a defenseman (50). In 1927 – 1928, as captain, Lane led his team to a 6 – 4 record. With an outstanding college career, he became the first American collegian to successfully enter the professional ranks. He began with the New York Rangers in 1928 – 1929, but was sold mid season to the Boston Bruins, who won the Stanley Cup that year over the Montreal Canadiens. He continued with the Bruins for part of the 1929 – 1930 season and returned with them for the 1933 – 1934 season.
Also in: National Football Hall of Fame.

LOCKHART, Thomas F.

Administrator

See entry in Hockey Hall of Fame, 1965.
Also in: International Hockey Hall of Fame.

LoPRESTI, Samuel L.

Player

Born January 30, 1917, in Elcor, Minn, but raised in Eveleth; entered U.S. Navy in 1942, aboard a merchant ship that was torpedoed in February 1943 and spent 42 days in a lifeboat before being rescued.

One of the 11 native sons of Eveleth to make it to the National Hockey League (NHL), LoPresti is only one of two American Hockey League players to have their names in the NHL record book. In a game against the Boston Bruins on March 4, 1941, LoPresti registered 27 saves the first period, 31 in the second and 22 in the last. (His team, the Chicago Black Hawks, won 3 – 2). He started goaltending in his second year of high school. At Eveleth Junior College in 1936, he was coached by Hall of Famer Cliff Thompson. After a year at St. Cloud Teacher's College he returned for another year at Eveleth Junior College. It did not take long for the NHL to notice LoPresti while he played with the St. Paul Saints of the American Hockey Association in 1939. He started with the Black Hawks in their 1940 – 1941 season and finished his hockey career with 236 goals-against and 4 shutouts in 74 regular games and 17 goals-against with one shutout in 8 playoff games.

MARIUCCI, John P.

Player

Born May 8 1916, in Eveleth, Minn; graduate of the University of Minnesota where he played outstanding football; joined the Coast Guard during W.W. II; played on Coast Guard hockey team in the Eastern Amateur League; in 1967 became special assistant to Wren Blair, general manager for the Minnesota North Stars; performs coaching duties as well as college scouting, road secretarial work and dinner speaking; lives in Bloomington, Minn.

1940 – 1942 Chicago Black Hawks, defenseman
1945 – 1948 Chicago Black Hawks, defenseman

Mariucci was coached by Hall of Famer Cliff Thompson before playing with the University of Minnesota hockey team and starring on their 1939 – 1940 undefeated team. He turned professional in 1940 for a brief start with the Providence team of the American Hockey League, then joined the Chicago Black Hawks to finish out the season. While a Black Hawk, he played 223 games with 11 goals and 34 assists, also 3 assists in 8 playoff games. Not known to back away from a fight, he was second in penalty minutes with 110 in the 1946 – 1947 season. After retirement from playing, Mariucci returned to the University of Minnesota and coached the varsity team from 1953 to 1965. He believed that the Americans could be as good as the Canadians if given the chance and recruited mostly Americans for that reason. His 1953 – 1954 team went all the way to the National Collegiate Athletic Association finals before losing to Rensselaer Polytechnic Institute.

OWEN, George, Jr

Player

Born December 2, 1901, in Hamilton, Ont, grew up in Boston and learned to play hockey there; graduated from Harvard University where he played football and was baseball team captain during his senior year; entered the brokerage business following graduation.

In five seasons with the Boston Bruins (1928 – 1933), Owen scored well for a defenseman—of the 44-game schedule, 46 goals and 38 assists. The Bruins won the Stanley Cup in his first season of play and again in 1931, a win credited to his goal against the Montreal Canadiens. He often played beside Lionel Hitchman and Eddie Shore, a Hockey Hall of Famer. Owen came to the Bruins from the Boston University Club and Harvard University. Starting at Harvard on the freshman team in 1919, he then served two terms as varsity captain, a rare feat at the Ivy League school. He was equally comfortable playing defense or center. Unfortunately, business obligations prevented him from participating on the U.S. Olympic hockey team in 1924.

PALMER, Winthrop H. "Ding"

Player

Born December 5, 1906, in Warehouse Point, Conn; died in Madison, Conn, February 4, 1970.

Ding Palmer was a most outstanding amateur hockey player, especially during his years at Yale University, 1925–1930. In the 1927–1928 season, he scored an astounding 41 goals and netted 7 in one game against New Hampshire. In his senior year he played both defensive and offensive positions and led the nation in scoring with 27 goals and 9 assists. Individually, Palmer became the all-time leading scorer in the history of Yale University with a total of 87 and ranked fourth among Yale's best hockey players with 96 points. The team broke records as well. In three years they only lost six games and were hailed as the greatest amateur hockey team in history with a 17–1–1 record in 1929–1930. After leaving Yale, Palmer was a member of the U.S. Olympic team that won a Silver Medal at Lake Placid in 1932. In 1933 he was a member of the National team that won the world championships at Prague, Czechoslovakia, for the first in the two times the United States has won the championships since 1920.

ROMNES, Edwin N. "Doc"

Player

Born January 1, 1907, in White Bear Lake, Minn; moved to Togo, Minn, while young; father became mayor, justice of the peace and general municipal official in the city; Doc played high school hockey in White Bear Lake and St. Paul, Minn; nicknamed Doc because he studied premed at St. Thomas (Minn.) College; played a year of hockey at St. Thomas, then three seasons with the St. Paul Saints, 1927–1930; Lady Byng Trophy, 1935–1936.

1930–1938 Chicago Black Hawks, forward
1938–1939 Toronto Maple Leafs, forward
1939–1940 New York Americans, forward

As the only U.S. Hockey Hall of Fame member to receive the Lady Byng Trophy, Romnes exhibited outstanding sportsmanship and playing ability throughout his career. In 403 regular and playoff games he accumulated only 46 penalty minutes. His National Hockey League record stands at 68 goals and 136 assists in 10 seasons of regular play, with 7 goals and 18 assists in 7 playoff series. 10 seasons of NHL play took him to 5 Stanley Cup finals: 1930–1931, 1933–1934 and 1937–1938 with the Chicago Black Hawks and in 1938–1939 with the Toronto Maple Leafs. He was on the winning Stanley Cup team in 1933–1934 with Hall of Famer Taffy Abel and in 1937–1938 with Hall of Famers Cully Dahlstrom and Mike Karakas. After retiring in 1940, Romnes coached the Michigan Tech hockey team until 1945, then led the Kansas City Pla Mors to the U.S. Hockey League championship and the playoff title in 1945–1946. In 1947–1952 he was varsity coach for the University of Minnesota hockey team.

THOMPSON, Clifford R.

Coach

Born September 10, 1893 in Minneapolis, Minn; died June 5, 1974.

As Eveleth High School coach from 1926 to 1958, Cliff's team won 536, lost 26 and tied 9 games. His career was highlighted in 1948–1951 when they accumulated 78 successive victories and the Minnesota state championship four times in a row. He simultaneously coached the Eveleth Junior College team, gathering 171 wins and 28 losses. Thompson had deep concern for all his players. He got them the best equipment and even took it upon himself to find them good skates during the depression. In 1951 at the Sportsman's Show in Minneapolis, he was presented with a trophy and honored for his coaching record and efforts to train players in athletics and good citizenship. In 1957 he was made an honorary member of the American Hockey Coaches Association, one of only 36 men honored in this way.

TUTT, William Thayer

Administrator

Born March 2, 1902, in Coronado, Calif; president of El Pomar Foundation and the Broadmoor Hotel, Inc, with its related companies; active on U.S. Olympic Committee, the National Cowboy Hall of Fame, golf and figure skating; presently resides in Colorado Springs.

During the 1947–1948 college season, a group of coaches, including Hall of Famer Vic Heyliger, approached Tutt about sponsoring a National Collegiate Athletic Association (NCAA) hockey tournament. With his support, the tournament was held for the first time at the Broadmoor Hotel in 1948. This was the beginning of college hockey as a national sport. From 1949 to 1957 the NCAA tournament was held at the Broadmoor Hotel, began moving annually from college to college in 1958, with a return visit to the hotel in 1969. Since 1959 the "Father of the NCAA Hockey Tournament" has been involved with the world spectrum of the sport as a member and president of the International Ice Hockey Federation. During this time hockey gained prominence, and finally worldwide attention in September 1972 with the Russia-Team Canada series. Tutt continued his involvement with hockey by succeeding Hall of Famer Tom Lockhart, founder of the Amateur Hockey Association of the United States, as president. He is presently the North American vice president of the International Ice Hockey Federation.

WINSOR, Alfred "Ralph"

Coach

Born in 1881 in Brookline, Mass; graduated from Harvard University in 1902; deceased.

Ralph Winsor was the dominating figure during the first 20 years of hockey at Harvard University. In 1901 he played, and in 1902 captained the team. Then he became coach from 1902 to 1917, and led his teams through 124 wins and 29 losses. He also recorded 23 wins and 5 losses against their arch rival, Yale. The teams of 1903–1906, 1909 and 1919, when he was assistant coach, were undefeated. Winsor was an innovator who took part in the development of the modern hockey stick and shoe skates. He also computed and adopted the official radii for the blades, known for years as the "Harvard Radius". He also developed new tactics such as back checking, and the shift of defensemen from point and coverpoint to the present pairing of positions. It is reported that in all those years, Winsor never took any money for his coaching duties and his modesty kept him from appearing in any team pictures. He aided young schoolboys and other colleges in developing their hockey programs. In 1932 he coached the U.S. Olympic hockey team to a Silver Medal victory at Lake Placid, N.Y. U.S. Hall of Famers John Chase, John Garrison and Ding Palmer were members of that team.

WINTERS, Frank J. "Coddy"
Player
Born 1884 in Duluth, Minn; played ice polo and developed good speed as a skater; following retirement from hockey, worked in Cleveland, Ohio, in the sporting goods business; died in Cleveland, November 17, 1944.

Coddy Winters is often compared to Hobey Baker as one of the greatest native American hockey players. He used the great speed he developed in ice polo to play with the Duluth Northern Hardware team through 1908. That season Duluth played a series of games with the Cleveland All-Stars. He liked their city so much he decided to move there and play out his hockey career with various amateur teams in the area. In 1909–1911 he played rover and switched to defense in 1912. Despite many offers to turn professional, Winters remained an amateur in Cleveland for 17 years during which time he played on three championship teams, 1911–1912, 1913–1914 and 1921–1922. He also coached. While playing for the Cleveland Winters, he coached the Case Tech team and made many trips to Philadelphia to work with the University of Pennsylvania team.

WRIGHT, Lyle Z.
Administrator
Born September 28, 1898 in Winnipeg, Man; served with the Canadian artillery in W.W. I; moved to Minneapolis, Minn. in 1919; involved in figure skating, the Ice Follies and the Minneapolis Aquatennial; died May 24, 1963, in Minneapolis.

Lyle Wright was involved with organized hockey since it found its way to Minneapolis. After playing four years of hockey there he became involved with the Minneapolis Millers and served as their manager from 1928 to 1931. In 1931 he moved to Chicago as business manager of the Black Hawks, but returned to Minneapolis in the early 1930s to finish what he had started. He served the Minneapolis Arena from 1934 to 1963 in many positions, including president, and not only maintained his interest in the Millers but was influential in establishing hockey as a major high school sport. It was also at the Minneapolis Arena that the University of Minnesota hockey team got its start and grew to need its own hockey arena on campus. Wright believed that Minneapolis could be a major league hockey town and was instrumental in bringing such greats as Tiny Thompson, Stew Adams and U.S. Hall of Famer Taffy Abel to his city.

1974

CHADWICK, William L. "The Big Whistle"
Referee
See entry in Hockey Hall of Fame, 1963.
Also in: International Hockey Hall of Fame.

CHAISSON, Raymond C.
Player
Born June 23, 1918 in Cambridge, Mass; graduate of Boston College; served in U.S. Navy during W.W. II; following retirement from hockey in 1947, began work with Ginn and Co.

Boston College was left with some unforgettable hockey memories when Ray Chaisson graduated. When the Eagles played out the 1939–1940 season with a 12–5–1 record and the 1940–1941 season with 13–1–0, forward Chaisson led the East in points, 67 and 59, and scoring. In a win over Cornell in 1939, he made 5 goals in one game and finished up the season with 36 in only 18 games. In 14 games of the 1940–1941 season, he became Boston College's all-time leader in average goals per game with 2.07. By the end of his college years he was one of the top point leaders for the Eagles with a 126 total after 32 games in two seasons. His eight goals in one game is still a school record. It is no wonder that his coach, U.S. Hall of Famer John "Snooks" Kelley, remembers him as one of the finest players during his 36 years of college coaching. Following his service in W.W. II, Chaisson played senior amateur hockey with the Los Angeles Monarchs of the Pacific Coast Hockey League. He continued his outstanding performance by leading the league in scoring with 101 points in the 1945–1946 season.

DES JARDINS, Victor A.
Player
Born July 4, 1900, in Sault Ste. Marie.

1930–1931 Chicago Black Hawks, forward
1931–1932 New York Rangers, forward

Vic played a key role in the early days of Eveleth hockey when the town was represented in the United States Amateur Hockey Association (USAHA). At that time, there was no professional hockey in the United States and the USAHA represented the highest level of the game in the nation. He went into professional hockey with St. Paul of the American Hockey Association (AHA). In 1927–1928 he captured the league scoring title with 20 goals and 8 assists, and in the very next season, took second place in the race with 25 goals and 10 assists. Des Jardins' scoring abilities led him to the National Hockey League, where he played with the Black Hawks, going all the way to the Stanley Cup finals before losing to the Montreal Canadiens. With the Rangers the following year, he was again in the Stanley Cup finals against the winning Toronto Maple Leafs. He closed out his professional career with six more years in the AHA with Tulsa and Kansas City. The highlight of these later years was a second place finish in the 1933–1934 scoring race with 18 goals and 15 assists with Tulsa.

EVERETT, Douglas
Player
Born April 3, 1905, in Cambridge, Mass; following graduation from Dartmouth College, entered insurance business with Morrill and Everett, Inc, in Concord, N.H, and is still chairman of the board.

Doug played on his first hockey team at Colby Academy and was team captain in 1921–1922. While on the Dartmouth team from 1922 to 1926, he was named to the All-College team by the *Boston Transcript* in his sophomore and junior years and was on one of the earliest All-Star teams selected by the *New York Herald Tribune*. After graduation, professional offers came from the Boston Bruins, New York Rangers and the Toronto Maple Leafs, but he declined them all to play with the University Club of Boston and to pursue a career in insurance. As a teammate of U.S. Hall of Famer George Owen, he played one of his greatest games against Princeton, scoring six goals. In 1932, with U.S. Hall of Famers John Chase, John Garrison and Ding Palmer, he played on the U.S. Olympic Silver Medal team and scored two of the three American goals against Canada in that series.

HEYLIGER, Victor
Coach
Born September 26, 1915, in Concord, Mass; graduated from the University of Michigan in 1937.

1937 – 1938 Chicago Black Hawks, forward
1943 – 1944 Chicago Black Hawks, forward

Vic played high school hockey at Concord and prep school hockey at Lawrence Academy in Groton, Conn. As a player with the University of Michigan, he starred from 1935 to 1937 and set a university record with 116 goals. As a coach, he provided outstanding leadership for teams at his alma mater, the U.S. Air Force Academy and the University of Illinois from 1938 to 1943. Heyliger's greatest years were at the University of Michigan, starting with the first National Collegiate Athletic Association championships ever staged (in 1948 at Colorado Springs) when his Wolverines captured the national title and followed this victory with five more 1951 – 1953, 1955 and 1956. After a period of retirement, Heyliger became coach at the U.S. Air Force Academy guiding that relatively new hockey program through its early years before retiring at the close of the 1973 – 1974 season.

JOHNSON, Virgil
Player
Born March 14, 1912, in Minneapolis, Minn; graduated from Minneapolis South High School where he was quarterback of the football team.

1937 – 1938 Chicago Black Hawks, defenseman
1943 – 1945 Chicago Black Hawks, defenseman

Johnson spent a large part of his career with the St. Paul Saints of the American Hockey Association after playing amateur hockey in the Twin Cities area. He was with the Black Hawks for their 1937 – 1938 season and played in all seven of the Stanley Cup games, where the Hawks emerged victorious over the Toronto Maple Leafs. He didn't return to the National Hockey League until the 1943 – 1944 season when he played the entire schedule as well as nine Stanley Cup games as the Hawks lost to Montreal in four straight games in the finals. After the 1946 – 1947 season with Minneapolis of the U.S. Hockey League, Johnson retired from professional hockey.

KELLEY, John "Snooks"
Coach
Born July 11, 1907, in Cambridge, Mass; graduated from Boston College in 1930; taught at Cambridge Latin and Dean Academy; U.S. Navy 1942 – 1946; Spencer Penrose Award 1959 and 1972.

Snooks Kelley gave up playing with the Boston Hockey Club in 1933 in order to coach the Boston College team. Under his guidance, they developed into one of the finest teams in the nation and in 1949 were invited to the National Collegiate Athletic Association championships and became the first Eastern champions. Boston College was invited to the western-dominated championships nine times—more than any other eastern team. Victory was common for this team: they captured eight New England championships, made nine appearances in Eastern College Athletic Conference (ECAC) Division One post-season playoffs, captured one ECAC playoff crown and eight Beanpot Tournament titles. Kelley had a record of 501 victories, 242 losses and 15 ties. As a coach, he felt strongly about recruiting and developing American players, rather than Canadians. As a result, 16 of his players were All-Americans and some played for the U.S. Olympic-National Teams.

MOE, William Carl
Player
Born October 2, 1916, in Danvers, Mass; grew up in Minneapolis, Minn.

First attracted to amateur hockey in Minneapolis, Bill later played with the Eastern League Baltimore Orioles before turning professional. He played on the Philadelphia Rockets and the Hershey Bears, both of the American Hockey League, and gained laurels as the most valuable player in the American League for the 1943 – 1944 season. He attracted the attention of Lester Patrick, manager of the New York Rangers, who gave up four players to obtain his services (1944 – 1949). Moe played at a time when there were only two other Americans—Frank Brimsek and John Mariucci—in the National Hockey League. A fractured vertebra limited his Stanley Cup playoff apearances to one game.

PURPUR, Clifford Joseph "Fido"
Player
Born September 26, 1914, in Grand Forks, N.Dak; resides in Grand Forks; raising six hockey-playing sons.

1934 – 1935 St. Louis Eagles, forward
1941 – 1944 Chicago Black Hawks, forward
1944 – 1945 Chicago Black Hawks, Detroit Red Wings, forward

Fido Purpur became the first native son of North Dakota to play in the National Hockey League when he joined the St. Louis Eagles in 1934. The next season the Eagles folded and he signed with the St. Louis Flyers of the American Hockey Association. There, he was idolized by the fans for his "gutsy" play, great speed and small stature, and his friendliness and willingness to sign autographs. His best season with the Flyers was in 1938 – 1939 when he scored 35 goals and 43 assists in regular play and 3 goals and 3 assists in playoffs. The team won the Harry F. Sinclair Trophy for the league championship that year. In 1941 the Chicago Black Hawks bought Purpur and in the 1942 – 1943 season he played in all 50 games with 13 goals and 16 assists. The Black Hawks went to the Stanley Cup finals in 1943 – 1944 but lost to Montreal. Purpur left the Black Hawks mid-way through the 1944 – 1945 season and went to his second Stanley Cup finals with the Detroit Red Wings, this time against Toronto. He ended his professional career in 1947, returned to his home state and coached the University of North Dakota hockey team from 1949 to 1956.

1975

CONROY, Anthony

Player

Born October 19, 1895, in St. Paul, Minn; served in W.W. I.

While still in high school, Conroy took to hockey and played with the old Phoenix septet (teams were made up of 7 players then). From 1911 to 1914 he played every position, but finally settled as rover and wing. Joining the St. Paul Athletic Club, he helped the team win the McNaughton Trophy in 1916–1917. The team then played Lachine, Quebec, for the Ross Cup International Championship and won, despite having to play 6-man hockey for the first time. He was one of the Club's four members to make the 1920 U.S. Olympic team, where they finished second to Canada. Conroy had a strong Olympics and scored 10 goals in a 29–0 rout of Switzerland. The Club took Western division honors in 1921–1922 and 1922–1923, but in the National finals, lost both times to Boston. The St. Paul Athletic Club turned professional as the St. Paul Saints of the American Hockey Association; despite offers from the National Hockey League, Conroy remained with them until his retirement after the 1928–1929 season.

HARDING, Austie

Player

Born September 26, 1917, in Boston, Mass; four years of varsity hockey in prep school; military service in W.W. II; All-American 1938–1939; John Tudor Memorial Cup 1938–1939.

Austie Harding was considered the best college center in the United States while he played hockey for Harvard University. He started out as captain of the freshman team in 1935–1936, played three years varsity and was team captain in his senior year. Harvard won the Ivy League title for the 1936–1937 season, and was a strong contender for the title the next two years. In his last game with Harvard he played 58 min. of the 60-min. game and scored 4 goals and 3 assists to bring his team to a 7–4 victory. As leading scorer for three years, Harding attracted numerous scouts from professional teams. Unfortunately, W.W. II came and dispersed any hopes of a professional career for Harvard's talented center. Following the war Harding returned to hockey with the Boston Athletic Association. As testimony of his outstanding ability as a player, hockey historian S. Kip Farrington named Harding center of the 1921–1945 Harvard era team.

IGLEHART, Stewart

Player

Born February 22, 1910 in Valparaiso, Chile; an outstanding polo player, he represented the United States in the 1933 International Match, the 1936 and 1939 winning Westchester Cup teams, and against Mexico in 1946; he was on the winning side five times in U.S. championships, playing for Templeton and Old Westbury; handicap 10; one of only a few to earn a ten-goal rating in polo.

"I have played many sports, some better than others, but hockey was always number one. I felt it gave me wings, an extra dimension and when I dream dreams of past accomplishments, let me dream in hockey." That is quite a statement for a champion of polo to make about his love for hockey. But Stewart Iglehart was at least equally as talented in hockey as he was in polo. As a boy, he learned many secrets about playing hockey from C. C. Pell, former Harvard great, at the well-known hockey breeding ground, St. Paul School. From 1929 to 1932 Iglehart played on the varsity team at Yale and became one of the most outstanding defensemen in college circles. He was part of the 1930–1931 championship team that recorded only one loss the entire season. Unable to play on the Olympic teams of 1932 and 1936, due to conflicting responsibilities, he played defense, right wing and center on the 1933 World Championship team. Following that game, Iglehart joined the Crescent Athletic Club, later to become the New York Rovers. He was among such talent as Colville, Shebicky and Patrick and could easily have moved up to the New York Rangers, but decided to pursue a business career. He did remain active with hockey as a member of the legendary St. Nicholas Club of New York City during his career in business.

LINDER, Joe

Player

Born August 12, 1886, in Hancock, Mich; captain of football, baseball and hockey teams every year he attended Hancock High School; after retirement from hockey entered grocery business in Superior, Wis; died June 28, 1948 in Superior.

Joe Linder was considered the first great American-born hockey player by many of his contemporaries as well as modern hockey historians. His adeptness at skating and playmaking first caught the eye of Hall of Famer Doc Gibson who recruited him for league and championship play with the immortal Portage Lakers. Not long with the professionals, he returned to amateur play in 1905–1911 in the Copper Country, upper peninsula of Michigan, and then joined the American Amateur Hockey Association out of Duluth in 1912–1920. On March 7, 1914, his team experienced a rare victory: they became the first American team to defeat the Winnipeg Victorias. In a 1941 review of American and Canadian hockey in *Esquire,* an author claimed that "any list of thirty best hockey players the whole world has had would have to include the American-born Linder." When he retired from active play he did not lose his interest in hockey, but became coach, manager and sponsor of hockey teams in the Superior-Duluth area and from 1920 until his death, was involved in some way with the Hancock, Shamrock and Duluth hockey clubs.

MOSLEY, Fred

Player

Born July 13, 1913, in Brookline, Mass; played football and baseball in college; All-American 1933–1934; graduated from Harvard University in 1936.

Laden with honors, Mosley will be remembered by Harvard hockey fans as one of their most outstanding forwards. After playing four years of varsity hockey at Noble and Greenough prep schools, he followed Hall of Famers Ralph Winsor, John Garrison and George Owen to the Ivy League school in 1932–1936. When his year as a regular on the freshman team was over, there was no question about who the man on center ice would be next

season—only two seasons earlier John Garrison had been on center ice. In 1935 – 1936 when he was captain, Harvard finished with a 14 – 4 – 2 record and won the Ivy League title, 5 – 1. One of many honors was bestowed on Mosley in 1932 – 1933 when he received the John Tudor Memorial Cup as the most valuable member of the Harvard hockey team, displaying ability, sportsmanship, leadership and team cooperation. The award had been established by members of the Porcellian Club who had been classmates with John Tudor, 1929 graduate and 1928 – 1929 hockey team captain. Later, hockey historian S. Kip Farrington named Mosley to the All-Harvard era team of 1921 – 1945 with Hall of Famer Austie Harding. Following his college career, Mosley devoted his time to the St. Nicholas Club and Beaver Dam of the Winter Club League.
Also in: Varsity Club (Harvard) Hall of Fame.

1976

CLEARY, William

Player

Born August 19, 1934, in Cambridge, Mass; played hockey at Belmont Hill prep school; John Tudor Award, 1954 – 1955; All-Ivy, All-East, All-American and Most Valuable Player in the East 1954 – 1955.

In 1960, the United States became the third country to beat Canada and win a Gold Medal in Hockey at the Olympics. Only Great Britain and Russia had done it before in the 9 times hockey competition was held since 1920. The outstanding player on that team was Bill Cleary. His 12 points on 6 goals and 6 assists made him the top player, and his early goal against Russia made the United States a Gold Medal team. Cleary came to the Olympics after an outstanding hockey career at Harvard from 1952 – 1956. As a forward there, he broke such school records as most goals in a season (42), most points in a season (89, also a National Collegiate Athletic Association (NCAA) record), most goals in a game (6, shared with two other players) and most assists in a game (8). In his most outstanding season, 1954 – 1955, Cleary led his team to victory with a third in NCAA competition, and a Beanpot and Ivy League championship, with a 17 – 3 – 1 record for the season. At the 1955 NCAA consolation game the next year, Cleary's three goals led the Crimsons to a victory of 6 – 3 over St. Lawrence and the mythical championship of the East. Not to stop after a flaming Crimson career, Cleary played on four Olympic-National teams, including the Gold Medal win, between 1956 – 1960. In 1968 he changed his role from player to coach and returned to Harvard with the freshman team. When Cooney Weiland retired in March 1971, Cleary became coach of Harvard's varsity hockey team. Hockey historian S. Kip Farrington has named Cleary center of the All-Harvard era team, 1946 – 1970.

MAYASICH, John

Player

Born May 22, 1933 in Eveleth, Minn; All-American 1952 – 1953, 1953 – 1954 and 1954 – 1955; presently works for KSTP Radio-TV in Minneapolis-St. Paul, Minn.

John had three great years of hockey while attending the University of Minnesota. In 1953 – 1954, with a 29 – 49 – 78 scoring log, and in 1954 – 1955, with 41 – 39 – 80, he captured the Western Collegiate Hockey Association scoring title. In 1954, when his team played a close overtime game in the National Collegiate Athletic Association tournament against Rensselaer Polytechnic Institute, Mayasich scored four goals and five assists in both tournament games and was named to the first team. He was selected All-American three consecutive years and was recently named to the All-Minnesota team on defense by hockey historian S. Kip Farrington. Between 1956 and 1969 Mayasich played on eight U.S. Olympic-National teams, two of which were the 1956 Silver Medal and the 1960 Gold Medal Olympic teams. In 1960 it was his slap shot converted into a goal that determined the U.S. victory over Canada and their final game with Russia. Mayasich declined many professional offers in order to play amateur hockey with the Green Bay Bobcats.

RIDDER, Robert Blair

Administrator

Born July 21, 1919 in New York City; graduate of Harvard University; presently director of U.S. Hockey Hall of Fame.

Bob Ridder began his involvement with hockey in the 1940s with the Duluth Heralds, a senior amateur team. One of his greatest achievements came in October 1947 when he, Don Clark (president of the U.S. Hockey Hall of Fame) and Everett "Buck" Riley of International Falls founded the Minnesota Amateur Hockey Association. Started because Ridder saw a need for a state organization to represent all levels of hockey, the association has become one of the largest of its kind in North America, behind only Ontario and Quebec in the number of registered players. In 1952, with Connie Pleban of Eveleth, Minn, Ridder managed the U.S. Olympic team. Under his leadership, the team was properly organized and financed—and they came home with a Silver Medal. Another Silver Medal was in store for the U.S. Olympic hockey team of 1956 which Ridder managed. To continue a long involvement with hockey, Ridder became one of nine owners of the North Stars in 1966 when professional hockey came to Minnesota.

Hockey Hall of Fame to Watch

UNITED STATES FIELD HOCKEY ASSOCIATION HALL OF FAME

Under Discussion 1977

Archives and memorabilia have been collected and a list of honorary members of the United States Field Hockey Association (USFHA) has been prepared. Those interested in the eventual establishment of a hall of fame that would incorporate these materials, as well as those concerned with the furtherance either of the USFHA or of the sport of field hockey, should contact Ruth Tergesen, Executive Secretary, P.O. Box 4016, Lynchburg, VA 24502. (804) 237-3502.

HORSE RACING AND BREEDING

Two things have almost totally preoccupied this world's recorded history—war and art, while four things have largely dominated male conversation—God, money, women and horses. The necessity of God, money and women is understood. But horses rank with art and war as things mankind doesn't really need but has never really been able to get along without. Why this should have been so is a mystery. The horse, like all mysteries, is surrounded by an incredible body of literature and myth, folklore and superstition.

The Irish say that because the horse was in the stable when Jesus was born it was given magical power. But it had that long before the time of Christ. Moses forbade his people to keep or breed horses, the symbol of Pharaonic power, and directed them to kill any captured ones. People in India, Greece and Rome conceived of the black horses of the underworld and of the sun as a chariot of fire pulled by seven white horses. People everywhere have believed in fairy horses, heavenly horses ridden by angels, ghost horses, headless phantom horses and demon horses. Our word "hobgoblin" is from the Old English word "hob," small horse, and originally meant demon horse. "Hobby," as in stamp collecting, has the same derivation.

In Europe any piebald horse was considered curative—a hair of a piebald, or even the smell of its stable, was believed to cure numerous diseases. Genghis Khan worshiped horse skulls. He also died from spinal injuries suffered when his horse threw him while he was out with his men hunting wild ponies for sport. At his funeral 40 girls and 40 white horses were sacrificed to accompany him into death. This custom is symbolically duplicated in American state or military funerals today, notably by the riderless black horse with reversed boots that followed President Kennedy's body to Arlington. To many peoples the horse was the corn spirit. The Huzul people of the Carpathian Mountains fastened horses' heads to poles in their gardens to protect their cabbages from caterpillars. One of the most potent and important Roman rites was the Fifteenth of October festival held on the Field of Mars in Rome. It involved staging a chariot race, after which the right-hand horse of the winning team was speared and beheaded. The head was adorned with a string of loaves of bread and the tail was rushed to the king's palace to drip blood on the hearth. Meanwhile, the blood from the body was collected and kept by the vestal virgins until April 21, at which time it was distributed to shepherds for the fertilization of their flocks. Tamerlane's Tartars sealed all alliances with foreign nations in a ceremony that included the sacrifice of a white horse. The Chinese emperor Wu Ti dispatched two separate expeditions to Ferghana to obtain certain heavenly, blood-sweating horses—the horses suffered from a rare parasite that caused skin hemorrhages. The first expedition was unsuccessful. The second returned in 101 B.C. with several of the breed, as well as with the Ferghana ruler's head. Horseshoes have been a magical sign of good luck for thousands of years (see Horseshoe Pitching). Admiral Lord Nelson, a firm believer in their power, nailed one to the mast of his flagship Victory. This did not prevent him from being killed aboard in 1805 however. In Old Russia oaths were taken on the blacksmith's anvil rather than on the Bible. The last execution for witchcraft in Scotland in 1722 was of a woman accused of having transformed her daughter into a pony and having the Devil shoe it. In 1589 an English juggler and his famous dancing horse Marocco (mentioned by Shakespeare) were found guilty of magic when on tour in Rome. No horse could do the things Marocco could do, the ruling said, so both of them were burned to death. History's most magical horse was Pegasus. When Perseus beheaded the gorgon Medusa, the mere sight of whom turned people to stone, she was pregnant by Poseidon, god of the sea and god of horses. From her decapitated body sprang the warrior Chrysaor and the winged horse Pegasus. Later tamed with a golden bridle, Pegasus was ridden by Bellerophon in his conquest of the Amazons who, led by the horse-lady, Hippolyta, hunted and fought on horseback with their sometimes husbands, the Sarmatians. In three places where Pegasus stamped his hoof, a spring gushed forth. The water of those three springs was said to inspire poetry, so that sometimes today when a poet is beginning to write he is said to "mount his Pegasus."

Pegasus inspired poetry, horses inspired literature from the country of the Houyhnhnms in *Gulliver's Travels* to Washington Irving's headless horseman to Longfellow's *Paul Revere's Ride* to Steinback's *The Red Pony.* They have had a greater impact on the English language than has any other animal. We have horsefly, horse mackerel, and horsefoot crab, as well as horseradish, horsemint, horsebriar, horse chestnut and horse mushroom. We have the horseback, a geological formation in Maine, and the horse latitudes, just above and below the two Tropics. Also called the doldrums, these are the regions where many horses died of thirst on ships becalmed between New England and the West Indies. The invention of the horsecollar in the Middle Ages allowed horses to replace oxen in feudal farming. It also gave us our customary unit of work, the horsepower, which is equal to 550 foot-pounds per second. In politics we have "dark horses," an expression first used in the modern sense by Prime Minister Benjamin Disraeli in his novel, *The Young Duke.* We still have a "horse of another color," an expression popular in Shakespeare's time. We have horse sense, horseplay, and horse laugh, beating a dead horse, holding one's horses, and the inability to make a horse drink. We have translated *Equi donati dentes non inspiciuntur* from the Latin as "Don't look a gift horse in the mouth." "Straight from the horse's mouth" has been a stamp of truth ever since Achilles' horse Xanthus predicted his master's death in grammatically correct Greek.

Pervasive in the English language, deified and demonized, pampered and feared, horses have contributed much on the mundane side of history. They were responsible for the invention of trousers by Scythian nomads who found riding in robes impractical. They have served in the cause of human progress in shoes, gloves, aviators' clothing, luggage, baseball covers, razor strops and belts, glue and pet food. In France, cavemen ate Stone Age horses, whose tails they took as trophies. A traditional dish at the Harvard University Faculty Club used to be called Fillet of Filly. Today it is called Horse Steak—Traveller's Delight ($2.25 on the luncheon menu). Mongols drank mare's milk, or fermented it into a drink called *koumiss,* the distillate of which was called *skhou,* or further fermented it into a highly potent brew called *arak.* On long campaigns in winter they would open a horse's neck vein, drink the blood, close the cut, remount and ride on.

With the possible exception of the sail, the horse was man's first attempt to employ nonhuman power for locomotion. As a beast of burden, the horse has never been excelled for versatility and speed, a fact recognized by the American Pony Express and by the twelfth century postal system of the Mongols. The latter employed 300,000 horses stationed at 10,000 posts throughout the huge Mongol empire. Bells attached to these horses announced their approach in what was perhaps the world's first siren system.

Stirrups were invented in India in the second century B.C.—these were rope ones into which the rider fitted only his big toes. When they appeared in Europe during the Middle Ages, they caused a revolution in the whole concept of warfare. For the first time a warrior could hold onto his spear and hit his target with the vastly greater force of his moving horse.

To horses we owe the main remedy for snakebite. Horse blood, used in the development of snake-venom serum, has also been used to fight diphtheria and tetanus. The idea of fishing line very likely also came from horses. Tail hairs of white stallions were considered the best lines and leaders in Columbus' time and for a long while thereafter. And the derby hat was named for the famous Derby horse race in England. In 1850 James Knapp of Connecticut manufactured his first consignment of Americanized English bowler hats, which a race-loving clerk of his suggested be called "derbies."

Our word circus comes from the kind of round arena in which Romans staged their equestrian entertainments, as does our word stadium, discussed below. These examples indicate yet another ancient association, that of horses with structures, buildings, and entire cities. The Great Wall of China, for example, was built in the years 219 – 204 B.C. along the route a mysterious white horse wandered. The city badge of the royal and ancient Balkh, which Marco Polo called "the Mother of Cities," was the galloping horse, the symbol of commercial traffic. To horses we owe Mexico's Spanish heritage; the conquistadores themselves wrote that their Conquest would have been impossible without horses and, of course God, on their side. In 1535 twelve horses escaped on the east coast of South America. Spaniards returning to that region forty-seven years later discovered that those initial dozen had multiplied into a huge herd of horses. This proved to them that the region was extremely favorable and led them in that year, 1582, to found a city there, Buenos Aires. If there is any truth in myth—and there often is—Rome also owes its existence to the horse. Roman mythology relates how Romulus told his men to grab the Sabine women who had come to watch a horse race. The resulting families built the city, though not in a day. Athens nearly was named for them. Zeus proclaimed a contest to select a name for the city, the winner to be that god or goddess who created the most useful object for the service of the human race. Poseidon, god of the sea, created the horse, and would have had the city named after him had not Athene, goddess of war, weaving and a number of other useful things, beat him by creating the olive tree.

Horses also gave us the Olympic Games, if another Greek myth relates real history. King Oenomanus, ruler of Olympia in Elis in Southwestern Greece, loved chariot racing and was an over-protective father. He announced that his daughter Hippodamia, whose name means horse-tamer, would wed whoever could escape with her in a chariot. Thirteen suitors tried, but each time the king caught up with and speared the man to death. Finally Pelops bribed the royal charioteer to sabotage the royal axle, which broke the next day when the king was nearly within spearing distance. The king's neck was broken, Pelops won the girl, and to celebrate both these triumphs he staged a series of games there on the plains at Olympia. It was an idea that caught on, or so the myth would have us believe. Not mythical at all is the historical fact that the whole avocation of sports reporting owes its existence to the horse. Nearly 2800 years ago Homer in his *Iliad* reported on the chariot races held at Troy. In these races the first prize was a lady, who had the added distinction of being skilled in domestic duties, and the second prize was a mare in foal.

While greyhound racing is the sport of queens or the queen of sports, horse racing is the sport of kings or the king of sports. This is due in part to horse racing's long association with royalty and with the upper classes of various societies in which a man who rode instead of walked was by definition a gentleman, and the man with the most or best horses usually was king. As Cervantes wrote in *Don Quixote*, "The seat of a horse makes gentlemen of some and grooms of others." It is no coincidence that the word chivalry originally meant "a horseman," as did *cavalier* and *caballero*. Thus, despite Ben Jonson's remark that a horse "will throw a Prince as soon as his groom," the history of kingship and royalty is also a history of the horse.

In early Greece the bridling of a wild horse intended for a sacrificial horse feast was a coronation rite, and each king at the end of his prescribed reign was literally torn to pieces by naked women wearing horse-masks and palomino manes, then eaten. In later Hellenic times, the cannibalistic horse cult was replaced by an end-of-reign rite in which the king was killed in an organized chariot crash, then dragged around behind his chariot. A similar rite was observed during Babylonian New Year festivities. The insignia of Roman royalty were the purple robe, the armed palace guard, the diadem or crown and the white horse. The first royal Roman racing fanatic was Caligula. He ordered that no one beneath the senatorial rank could race chariots, and that the track be covered with a layer of bright red or green powder before each race. Julius Caesar attended races regularly but was criticized for attending to state documents and correspondence during the races. Other later racing fanatics included the emperors Vespasian who began the construction of the Colosseum, Titus who finished it, and Domitian who not only introduced the use of female gladiators in the Colosseum but also held 100 chariot races a day in the Circus Maximus. In A.D. 385 the emperor Theodosius issued an edict that limited the weight of a saddle to 60 lbs. Today an excessively heavy Western-style saddle weighs 45 lbs. The later Byzantine emperor Constantine, the first Christian king, introduced a new idea, the *kathisma*, or royal box, from which royalty have watched the races while the masses have watched the royalty ever since. In ancient India an extremely elaborate ritual requiring about two years to complete was used by kings to expand their domains. Called the *ashvameda* or horse sacrifice, it involved freeing a consecrated white stallion. For the span of a year, any territory through which the horse wandered was claimed by the king as his own. Contested claims resulted in battles. At the end of the year the horse was returned to the capital, where it was annointed and adorned with pearls, coins and perfume before being strangled to death by the king and his chief queen. Then the queen performed certain acts of bestiality with the cadaver beneath a white sheet after which the horse was dissected, cooked and eaten. This rite was last performed in 1750, when George Washington was 18 years old and women were still being killed as witches in England. Hammurabi used horse-drawn chariots in the 1700s B.C. David was the first Israelite king to break the Mosaic ban on keeping horses. His son, King Solomon, even went so far as to import horses from the old enemy, Egypt. Nearly 500 years earlier (about 1350 B.C.), Kikkulus, royal master of the horse for King Suppliuliumas of Mitanni, dictated a comprehensive treatise on horse training on clay tablets. A similar office today is that of the Master of the Horse, a member of the royal household of Great Britain.

From the time of William the Conqueror, whose conquest of England was made possible largely by better-armed men and a stronger breed of horse, horse racing and breeding have been popular with England's royalty. Henry I in A.D. 1110 bought an Arabian stallion to mate with native English mares. During the reign of Richard the Lion Hearted, (1189 – 1199), horse racing became a favorite pastime of knights. His brother King John (1199 – 1216), who was the target of the Magna Carta, imported numerous horses and founded a royal stud farm at Eltham. Charles II won a race at Newmarket on October 14, 1671, riding his own horse, Old Rowley. Queen Anne introduced the first sweepstake in 1714. Her horse Star won. A favorite trainer of her's, Tregonwell Frampton (1641 – 1727), the "Father of the English Turf," had been appointed Keeper of the Running Horses of His Sacred Majesty under William III. He held the same office under Georges I and II, and ranks as modern history's first professional horse trainer. After the War of the Roses there was a shortage of horses in England.

Henry VII in 1496 forbade any export of them. His son and successor, Henry VIII, began a large-scale program to import horses. In 1515 Ferdinand V of Spain, who had aided Columbus and organized the Inquisition, sent as gifts to Henry VIII two Spanish horses valued at 100,000 ducats (between \$110,000 and \$232,000). His contemporaries thought him insane to have parted with those two particular horses. They ascribed his insanity to an aphrodisiac dinner given him two years earlier by his new young wife, Germaine de Fois, from which (or whom) he had not yet recovered. He died in 1516 of "hunting and matrimony." In 1859 Henry VIII's descendant, Queen Victoria, donated a prize, the Queen's Plate, to the Toronto Jockey Club, which thereby became the oldest annually staged stakes race in North America. Although lacking royalty, the United States never lacked for horse-loving presidents. Andrew "Old Hickory" Jackson was one of the founding fathers of the Nashville racecourse. During the War of 1812 he had time to run his best horses against those of Charles Dickinson, who won, and whom Jackson later killed in a duel. While president, Jackson was conscientious enough to race under a pseudonym.

But perhaps the clearest examples of the ancient association of horse racing and royalty came from the Russian revolution. At the start of the revolution the Bolsheviks arrested a famous race horse, a son of the great Suntar. As it had won a prize cup offered by the tsar, the horse was court-martialed for "having had dealings with the old regime," sentenced to death, then shot. Later, in 1919, a similar fate befell the great Russian trotter, Krepysh, whose career winnings had totalled nearly $100,000. Krepysh was shot by the Bolshevik Liberation Committee for being "a bourgeois horse."

As consistent and strong as the association of royalty with horses has been the association through the centuries of individual men and women with individual horses. George Washington and Magnolia (whose sire was rescued from a shipwreck), the Duke of Wellington and Copenhagen, Napoleon and Marengo, Robert E. Lee and Traveler, Ulysses S. Grant and Cincinnati, Cortés and Morzillo (later deified by the Indians, who had never seen a horse before), Buddha and Kanthaka, Roy Rogers and Trigger, the Lone Ranger and Silver are just a few of the pairs.

There are numerous other examples in history. Nearly as famous as the emperor Caligula—and possibly more sane—was his horse Incitatus, whose private villa included a marble stable, an ivory manger, a whole retinue of servants and furniture for those special guests invited by the emperor to dine with his horse. Caligula was unpopular for many reasons. For one thing, he murdered numerous people including one of his sisters. For another, he claimed to be divine. Other emperors had done this and been accepted. But Caligula claimed to be all the gods at once. He was assassinated not only because he tried to have Incitatus made a consul of Rome, although that was one of the reasons given at the time. Another tyrant, Diomedes, king of Thrace, owned four mares that he valued so highly he fed them human flesh. Strangers to Thrace were the usual diet, but the mares were not particular. During a battle Diomedes was dislodged from his chariot, whereupon the mares ate him. Both Glaucus, father of Bellerophon (who tamed Pegasus), and King Lycurgus were torn apart and eaten by horses. Such fates gave rise to a Roman expression, *Praeda caballorum,* to be eaten up by horses, which today is used with reference to the expense involved in keeping a horse. Interestingly, Arabian horses today are fed dried fish, horses in Afghanistan eat raw eggs by the score, horses in India used to be fed boiled meat, and among the famous racehorses in seventeenth century England was one named Kill-'em-and-Eat-'em.

There were only two survivors of the Union forces in the Battle of the Little Big Horn June 25, 1876. Custer, his horse Vic, all his men and all but two of their horses were killed that day. One, a paint belonging to an Indian scout named Little Soldier, wandered into an Arikara Indian village several days after the battle. The other was Comanche. Comanche had been foaled in 1863 during the Civil War, and had belonged to Captain Myles W. Keogh who died with Custer. For nearly a year after the battle, Comanche was in a body sling recovering from severe wounds. Treated as an army hero and decorated, the horse was later ridden at the Battle of Wounded Knee December 29, 1890. There it lost its second master. The great horse died at the age of 28 November 6, 1891—some say of heartbreak. Its body was stuffed, displayed at both the Chicago and the St. Louis World's Fairs, and is now in a temperature-controlled glass case on the fifth floor of the Natural History Museum at the University of Kansas at Manhattan. Similarly, the skeleton of Marengo, Napoleon Bonaparte's favorite horse and the charger he rode at the Battle of Waterloo, is on permanent display in a glass case in the Victoria and Albert Museum in London.

A deep affection developed between M. W. Savage of Minneapolis and his horse Dan Patch who, fabled in story and song, is one of the all-time great American horses. Dan Patch died on July 11, 1916; Savage died the following day. Man o' War died in 1947 less than a month after the death of his groom, Will Harbut, who had called Man o' War "de mostest hoss." Several of the famous jockeys who had ridden the legendary stallion were buried beside it in Kentucky. All have since been exhumed and currently are in Lexington warehouse awaiting burial in a multi million dollar horse museum. Man o' War's ancestor, the Godolphin Arabian (foaled in Yemen in 1724 and discussed below), had as a stablemate a cat named Grimalkin. They were inseparable. After Grimalkin died, the horse tried to kill any cat he saw.

Everyone in the world named Philip or Phillip loves horses—at least that's how the name translates from the Greek: *philos-hippos,* meaning "lover of horses." King Philip II of Macedon, during the course of a single day in 356 B.C, received the following news items: his troops had defeated the Illyrians and taken the important city of Potidaea, his team of horses had won the prestigious chariot racing event at the Olympic Games, and his wife had given birth to a son. That son, Alexander, later called "the Great," is one of history's famous horse lovers. His love of horses and his brilliant use of them in battle were legendary even during his short life. When his favorite warhorse Bucephalus (the name meant bullheaded or ox-headed) died of old age and exhaustion after the Battle of the Hydaspes, Alexander ordered a city built at the burial site. That city, Bucephala, is still standing today in West Pakistan. Now called Jhelum, it is certainly the greatest monument ever erected to an animal.

Perhaps that is what the mystery of the horse has always been. Behind the myriad of myths and superstitions, behind all the bizarre rituals and exotic beliefs, perhaps there has always been the significant fact that a powerful kind of magic exists when a particular person loves a particular horse and vice versa.

FORMS: The number of sports, games and activities involving horses is immense. They range from polo (from the Persian *pulu,* the willow root from which the balls have been made since 600 B.C.) to the ancient Persian game of *tchigan* (virtually tennis on horseback) to *buzkashi,* the national sport of Afghanistan. In *buzkashi,* up to 1000 riders compete for possession of a decapitated calf, which has replaced the original decapitated prisoner of war played with by the Mongol originators of the game. By the year Washington, D.C, became the capital of the United States (1800), feral horses—those whose domesticated ancestors escaped—were a pest in California. Games people played there at that time included *juego de gallo,* in which galloping riders attempted to grab a live chicken that was buried in sand up to its head. Horse-fighting was popular in sixteenth century Europe, as were other blood sports like bear-baiting, cock-fighting, and dog-fighting. Some of history's horse games were tried once but not repeated. For example, the city of Sybaris was the horse center of the ancient world. Among the things they taught their horses to do, the Sybarites (from whom we get our word for one who is a voluptuary or sensualist, a sybarite) trained their horses to dance, Lippanzaner-like, to a certain flute tune at lavish banquets. Spies from the enemy city of Crotona attended one such banquet and learned the tune. Later in 510 B.C, they attacked Sybaris, whereupon the Sybarites rode out to repel them. At that point the Crotonians played the tune. The Sybarite horses reared up to dance. Their riders, thrown off, were trampled to death—Sybaris was destroyed through a horse game that failed. Interestingly, Thurri, the city built upon the ruins of Sybaris, produced the horses and the man that taught the Romans how to race chariots.

All equestrian events evidently originated as exercises for both horse and rider approximately 3000 years ago. They were of little value according to Plato. But they have always been popular. Various events survived and were taught at Mills College in 1864. Except for walking which was offered at Mt. Holyoke in 1837, horseback riding was the first sport in which instruction was given in American institutions of higher learning. Other equestrian exercises evolved into the various events which make up the widely popular international competitions today. These events include dressage (the French word for schooling, the training of horses), show jumping, and three-day events (also called horse trials or *militaire*), each of which has numerous forms, features and organizations. Still others evolved into the endless varieties of races: those for individual breeds, steeplechasing (races with obstacles, so named because the first in 1752 in Ireland was between two churches and their steeples), point-to-point races and endurance races. In the history of endurance races, one of the most incredible participants was Frank T. Hopkins. In the late 1800s he won more than 400 endurance races. These included an 1800-mile race from Galveston, Texas, to Rutland, Vermont, in 31 days; and a 1000-mile race from Kansas City, Missouri, to Chicago, Illinois, in 12 days and 6 hours. In 1889 he rode his mustang Hidalgo in the 1000-year-old Arabian Desert Endurance Race from Aden across the great desert to Syria and, astoundingly, won over a field of native Arabian horses.

Horse shows have been frequent and consistently popular for centuries. The first in the United States, and the oldest still being held, was at Upperville, Virginia, in 1853. That same year, incidently, the first bronze equestrian statue in the United States, of General Andrew Jackson, was unveiled at Lafayette Park in Washington, D.C. Canada's biggest horse breeder and most famous shower of horses in the late 1890s and early 1900s was Joseph Seagram, the whiskey distiller.

The one horse-related game of activity that did not evolve out of ancient equestrian exercises was bookmaking which began in Philadelphia in 1866, the year the American Society for the Prevention of Cruelty to Animals was founded and the year Congress first issued the nickle coin.

ORGANIZATION: There are more American and Canadian federal and state or provincial clubs, guilds, museums, councils, federations, societies, services, registries and associations for the various aspects of horse breeding and racing than there are for any other sport or group of sports: at least 108 in 1976. This total could be compared to the 20 major ones for football and the 30 for baseball. The active memberships of these 108 in the same year was close to one million. Add to that the far larger number of members in city, intercity, district and private organizations and you have evidence for the two claims that have been made about horse racing: it is the most popular of North American sports, and it is the most completely controlled sport in the United States—no other major sport is so highly organized, commercialized and taxed. Although America's love affair with the automobile largely ended her far longer love affair with the horse (in the early 1970s American farmers owned 8 million horses compared to 20 million in 1910), horses today are being bred and raced with as much passion and with more sophistication than ever. If anything, the various sports of horses have become "more pure" as wars and economics have abandoned the horse. Winston Churchill rode in history's last major cavalry charge at the Battle of Omdurman September 2, 1898. The U.S. Army gave up cavalry horses for tanks during World War II. But interest in horses and their sports is booming today. As Fletcher Knebel of the *Register and Tribune Syndicate* said, "Never give up. For 50 years they said the horse was through. Now look at him—a status symbol."

HORSE BREEDING

Horses are Perissodactyls, odd-toed hoofed mammals, as are rhinoceroses and the South American tapirs. Neither the sole nor the heel of a Perissodactyl's foot touch the ground when the animal stands or is in motion. The feet are so constructed that the animal's weight is supported on its middle toes, which in the case of the horse are hooves. Unlike the even-toed mammals (cows, deers, pigs, etc.), horses and other Perissodactyl's have simple stomachs, two mammae in the female, and lie down by bending their forelegs first (whereas the reverse is true of cows); they have neither gallbladders nor collar bones. Males have canine teeth, females generally do not; male horses have 40 teeth, females have 36 (humans have 32). A horse drinks from 12 to 20 gallons of water a day but may go three days without water. Normally it eats three times a day. Its stomach holds about 18 quarts of food compared to the 1 quart a human stomach holds. Like dogs and cats, horses shed their body hair and have summer and winter coats. Tail and mane hair, however, is never shed, which explains why Maud, a California horse at the turn of the century (1905), had a mane 18 ft. long. The heartbeat of a horse is the same as that of an elephant, 25–40 beats per minute, which is lower than that of a squid (40–80), a man (72), or a rat (300–500). This low heartbeat contributes to horses living for 20 to 30 years and up to 62 years in exceptional cases. The only animals with longer recorded lifespans are the macaw, a parrot with a record of 64 years, and certain types of tortoise with a record of 177 years. A horse's normal body temperature of 101 degrees F. is slightly higher than a man's. Horses are not color-blind, but most are near-sighted. The pupils of its eyes are structured like a cat's—they become narrow, black horizontal slits in bright light, and open very wide so they see well in dim light or at night. The positioning of the eyes allows a horse a full 180-degree sweep of vision on each side of its head; the muscles of the eyes allow them to be moved independently of each other, chameleonlike, so that a horse may look straight forward and straight backward simultaneously. The horse's eyes are about one and a half times the size of a man's and are larger than those of any other land animal except the ostrich.

Horses alter their gait by varying the way they move their legs. Their three natural gaits are the walk (4 m.p.h.), the trot (2-beat, 9 m.p.h.), and the canter (3-beat, 12 m.p.h. or more). Originally the canter was used to describe the pace at which people made pilgrimages to

Canterbury, the *Canterbury Tales.* "To go at the Canterbury pace" later became "to canter." A fast canter is called a gallop during which the stride of a horse like Secretariat is 25 ft, and the speed is up to 45 m.p.h. At one point in each galloping stride all the horse's feet are off the ground at the same time. This has not always been known. In the early 1870s at a racetrack in Sacramento, Leland Stanford, founder of Stanford University, bet some friends that galloping horses were airborne for an instant in each stride. To decide the question, they hired a scientist, Eadweard Muybridge, to take a series of photographs. These several thousand photographs were later taken to Thomas Edison, and led to his invention of motion pictures. Consequently, the horse's gallop not only won Stanford a lot of money, but was also the preliminary to the entire motion picture industry. Unnatural, learned gaits include the rack or single-foot, the slow gait or running walk and the pace. These are discussed in more detail below.

At five years old, a horse is considered to have attained its full height and weight. Height is measured from the withers (shoulders) to the ground in hands (1 hand equals 4 in.). The world's smallest breed, the Shetland Pony, stands 8½ hands (34 in.) while some of the largest breeds stand 20 hands (6½ ft.) at the shoulder. Any full-grown horse whose height is 14.2 hands or less is called a pony—the term has nothing to do with the animal's age. Colors of horses range from black to white, gray to blue, yellow to pinkish or red. Normally, a gray horse is born black and a white horse (such as the Lippanzan) is born gray. The palomino color type (there is no such thing as a palomino breed) is found in almost every breed except the Thoroughbred. Paint horses, those of two or more colors, include piebalds, skewbalds, calicos and pintos.

Horses, zebras, guaggas, asses, onagers, kiangs, burros, jackasses, tarpans, mbidais, mbwetes, ezels (from which comes our word easel, as in painting), pferdes, akhdas and many more are members of *Equidae*, the horse family. All true horses, regardless of size, shape or color, comprise one species, *Equus caballus*. Among other things, this means that any two horses of opposite sex may produce offspring. In one intriguing experiment demonstrating this, male and female Shetland Ponies, the world's smallest breed, were bred with female and male Shires, the world's largest breed. In both cases the resulting offspring grew to be normal size horses. Horses may also be bred to zebras and other members of the family. (For instance, the offspring of a male ass and a female horse is a mule; that of a female ass and a male horse is a hinny.) This explains the wide variety of horse breeds. Whenever Man had a certain need, a horse was bred to meet it. The Roman poet Oppian recommended that horses with bluish eyes be bred for hunting bears, ones with yellowish eyes for leopards, fiery and flaming eyes for boars, and horses with gleaming gray eyes for hunting lions. The Welsh Pony was originally bred specifically for use in the confined spaces of coal mines. By the tenth century, as European weapons of great penetrational power were developed, increasingly heavy armor was needed. To carry this added weight a new breed of horse was produced, the European Great Horse, also called the Charger of the *Destrier*. Standing up to 18 hands at the shoulder, these giants were capable of carrying a knight, his armor and complete set of horse armor. This load weighed up to 450 pounds—four and a half times the weight of jockey and equipment a modern Thoroughbred carries. Because their endurance was minimal, these Great Horses were led to battle, then mounted. After the fighting, the knight dismounted, removed his armor, and rode a regular horse home—from which practice we have the expression "to get off your high horse." An English act of 1535 levied strict penalties against allowing a mare to be bred to any stallion "under fourteen handfuls"; Edward VI prohibited the importation of any horse under 14 hands; and Henry VIII proclaimed that any man whose wife wore a velvet hat must keep at least one horse of 14 hands or suffer a stiff fine, and that all horses of shorter stature should be destroyed as useless. Gunpowder and other innovations soon made the Great Horse obsolete. Today their descendants—the Clydesdales, Percherons, Shires and others—perform in circuses and pull beer wagons. Another famous breed ridden by aristocrats from the Middle Ages to the seventeenth century, when it became extinct, was the Limousin, named for a region of central France, from which we also get the word for any luxurious sedan, the limousine.

Virtually every country today has a breed of which it is especially proud: The Achal-Teke in the U.S.S.R, the Achean in Greece, the Alter in Portugal, the Andalusian in Spain, the Holstein in Germany, the Brumby in Austria, the Basuto Pony in South Africa, the Batak in Sumatra, etc. Of the world's best-known breeds, 16 were created in Great Britain (including the Clydesdale bred near the Clyde River in Scotland), and 7 were created in the United States: the Morgan, the quarter horse, the mustang, the Tennessee walking horse, the American saddle horse, the Standardbred, and the Hambletonian. Some older breeds were only recently officially recognized: the Tennessee walking horse in 1935, for example, and the Appaloosa in 1950. Some that were created and then became extinct through neglect or misfortune were later re-created, notably the European Forest Horse.

Brazil in 1971 was the world's leading horse-raising country with 9,050,000 horses. The United States, with 7,800,000 horse, ranked second. In the United States that same year, the leading horse-raising state was Texas, with 625,000 horses.

FORMS AND ORGANIZATION: Most breeds of horses at all common in North America are represented and controlled by various societies, associations and registries. Members and their horses are eligible for numerous activities, the most important of which are international horse shows. Of the latter, most in the United States follow the rules of the American Horse Shows Association. Founded in 1917, this association had 15,200 members in 80 regional and state groups in 1976, all of whom participated in the promotion of interest in fully 1250 different horse shows. A similarly large and active organization is the Canadian Horse Shows' Association, which establishes and enforces rules governing hundreds of other shows. The National Horse Show, held annually at Madison Square Garden in New York City since 1883, ranks as the largest annual horse event of any kind in the United States. Smaller events are the many hundreds of horse shows held by American and Canadian horsemen's clubs, societies and associations.

While the list of individual breeds and types of horse is almost endless—Albino, Buckskin, Connemara, Gotland, Hackney, American Indian Horse, Morgan, Mustang, Paint, Part-Blooded, Quarter, Shetland Pony,

Shire, Suffolk, Percheron, Walking, Appaloosa, Belgian Draft, Chickasaw, Cleveland Bay, Clydesdale, Morocco Spotted, Cutting Horse, Palomino, Welsh Pony, etc.—the two functions of the organizations which represent them are closely similar: to maintain the purity or survival of the breed or type, and to stimulate interest in it. The former function is accomplished through breed or type registries. For example, the Arabian Horse Registry of America, headquartered in Colorado, had 120,000 registrations as of 1976, while the Thoroughbred Half-Bred Registry in California maintains records and card files of horses and owners registered since 1918. The stimulation of interest and public support is accomplished through some of the above-mentioned shows, through sales of horses and related paraphernalia, through meetings and seminars, and through the publication of various annual, monthly, bimonthly or quarterly newsletters and magazines. For example, these functions are performed for the Mustang (from the Spanish *mesteño* meaning strays from the *mesta*, horse breeders) by the American Mustang Association in California, the International Society for the Protection of Mustangs and Burros in Nevada, the Wild Horse Organized Assistance in Nevada, the National Mustang Association in Utah, and the Spanish Mustang Registry in Texas. These organizations had a total of three newsletters, two magazines, numerous pamphlets, booklets and leaflets, one rule book, a stud book, 38,450 members and numerous meetings in 1976. Similar totals could be made for organizations of the other breeds and types. All these organizations have related or supportive groups such as the American Association of Sheriff Posses and Riding Clubs, the Horsemen's Benevolent and Protective Association, the Horse Book Readers Service, the Horsemen's Book Society and the American Horse Publications (whose members are executives of horse-related magazines and newspapers).

HARNESS RACING

Chariot racing today is nothing compared to what it once was. The Chuck Waggon races of the Canadian rodeo circuit and the end-of-March races in Pocatello, Idaho, staged by the World Championship Cutter and Chariot Racing Association are about all that is left of a sport that ruled supreme in the Western World for over a thousand years. However, a direct descendant of chariot racing is one of the most popular sports today. It is the more civilized sport of harness racing; 20 million North American fans annually pay to watch 20,000 horses run hundreds of trotting and pacing races. Those races, horses and fans are the inheritors and protectors of the very ancient tradition of horses pulling men in swift, two-wheeled vehicles. As long ago as 1350 B.C, horses were trained for "the speed of the trot" for King Suppilulimas of the Kingdom of Mitani. A racing chariot of a similar age was found in a tomb at the Necropolis of Thebes. Ever since, the driving of horses has been an art or a skill, a serious business, or a sport.

Warriors in those ancient days never rode on horseback. Instead, they were carried to the site of the battle by their two-horse chariots, where they stepped down and fought while their charioteers stood by. The same custom was followed in ancient India where horses were at first considered too valuable to risk in actual combat. Later, they were used extensively, and were made to drink wine before each battle so they would be more ferocious. The Persians bred horses specifically to be war chargers, chariot horses, polo ponies, or pace horses. In Greece horse races with riders were not added to the Olympic Games program until 648 B.C.—22 years after chariot racing had become a regular event. By 400 B.C, however, the Games included regular events for two-horse chariots, four-horse chariots, four-wheel carts and mule carts; in addition, there were mares-only races, races for colts of the same age, and races for boy riders who were perhaps the world's first jockeys. An interesting Olympic event, the *kalpé* or trotting race, was added for the 496 B.C. Games. This was a race for mares with a twist: for the last lap the riders jumped off and grasping bridles, ran to the finish line beside their mounts. Later, stallions were allowed. The Romans had a similar event, the last part of which was the *pedibus ad quadrigam,* on foot with the chariot.

Of course the Romans had everything when it came to chariot racing. Roman racing promoters formed companies or factions (syndicates), each with its own stables and professional drivers who were free to jump to rival factions for a higher salary. Although the wealthy sometimes entered their own teams in various events, those factions controlled the world of racing with an iron fist. There were six of them, each with a distinctive color worn by its drivers: Red, White, Gold, Purple, Blue and Green. The Gold and Purple factions were never widely supported, the Blues later absorbed the Reds, and the Whites merged with the Greens, so that for over twice as long as the United States has been in existence the real battles of the Roman Empire were fought between men whose main allegiance was to Blue or to Green.

Though races with single drivers were by far the most popular, team races of two, three or four drivers per team were held. Similarly, the number of horses per chariot varied from one to six, although four was considered the ideal number. Nero, an insanely dedicated supporter of Green, tried to personally introduce ten-horse chariot racing. He was thrown out of the chariot, whereupon the rival drivers reined in, allowing him to remount his vehicle and win the race. Most races were in circuses, immense outdoor stadiums. Nero constructed one of these on the slopes of Vatican Hill and adorned its *spina*, the barrier down the center to separate the up and down lanes, with an obelisk specially brought from Egypt. The track is now buried beneath buildings, but the obelisk stands today in front of St. Peter's Basilica. His race days at the far more popular Circus Maximus opened with a huge statue of his grandmother Livia—one of the few blood relatives he didn't murder—drawn around the *spina,* and were enlivened by animal fights held on the track after every fifth race.

These and other races of chariot racing's 1000-year history, along with theater presentations and arena gladiator fights, were the three main sources of Roman entertainment. Of the three, racing was the most important—as the poet Juvenal said, "all that was needed to keep the populace happy was *Panem et Circenses*" (bread and chariot races). At the various circuses, the populace stayed happy consulting their *tabella* (race programmes) and betting with each other on each race. Interestingly, there was never any major Roman attempt to organize and control betting. The emperor and his entourage sat in the royal box. In Constantine's day it was called the *kathisma,* to which our word cathedral is related. Supporters of the Blues sat to the emperor's right (west), those of the Greens on his left (east). Roman senators and knights, wealthy businessmen called *equites* or horsemen, sat in special seats beneath awnings in air made more acceptable by perfumed spray. The people, citizens and foreigners, sat everywhere else in differently priced seats or, if they arrived early enough, in a section called the *gratuita loca* (free seats). Compared to the racing crowd of today, the Roman racing crowd was somewhat less dignified. At one meet two senators and others were crushed to death. People arriving early one morning to get the *gratuita loca* at the Circus Maximus caused so much noise that the Emperor Caligula ordered the area cleared. In the ensuing riot a large number of people were killed, including 20 women and 20 knights. That was nothing. In January, A.D. 512, a riot broke out between Blue and Green fans in Constantinople. It lasted several days. When it ended, not less than 30,000 were dead—nearly half the total number of Confederate soldiers killed during the entire American Civil War.

As a boy, Nero Claudius Drusus Germanicus played with toy, ivory *quadrigae*, four-horse chariots. Later in his short life (he committed suicide at the age of 31), he played with the real thing. Whenever he entered a racing contest, he ordered that the statues of all its previous winners be torn down, thrown into the sewers and replaced by statues of himself. One of these, set up in the great baths in the Campus Martius, was soon after struck by lightning and reduced to a great shapeless lump of bronze. Nero traveled all over his empire to demonstrate his abilities and to win prizes (including the crowns for harp playing and tragic acting at the 211th Olympics). He regularly drank powdered wild boar dung in his wine. This was the standard medicine for charioteers who had received sprains, blows, severe bruises or fractures, or had been dragged behind their chariots. It could also be taken dried or boiled in vinegar, either swallowed or applied externally. Pliny the Elder wrote that "in an emergency it can be used fresh," and that "if you cannot get wild boar's dung, the next best is that of the domestic pig." The reddish-blond, extremely nearsighted Nero, the last blood relative of the Caesars, liked to associate himself with the sportsmen he loved best, the charioteers. One of history's first true sports freaks, he never missed a horse race when in Rome, which during his time meant up to 50 every day. When his second wife, Poppaea, scolded him for getting home so late from the races, he kicked her to death.

The one who had started it all for the Romans was King Tarquinius Priscus, who began construction on the Circus Maximus. Seating 260,000 people, this mammoth structure was the largest sports arena ever built. In comparison, the largest stadium in the United States today, the Rose Bowl in Pasadena, seats a mere 101,025 including temporary seating; and the largest in the world today, the Maracaña Stadium in Rio de Janeiro, seats only 205,000. Square at one end, round at the other, the Circus Maximus was one *stadium* wide and three *stadia* long. *Stadium* originally meant about 630 ft, from the Greek *stadion*, the distance between the end pillars of the foot-race area at Olympia. At the square end were the 12 prison stalls where the chariot teams started. (In earlier Greek races, which were run over the open landscape, there were from 50 to 60 starters.) Positions in the 12 stalls were decided by a drawing of lots from an urn. At the drop of a napkin (a practice begun by Nero) or the sound of a trumpet blast, the hinged starting gates swung open simultaneously. The latter were introduced in 429 B.C. and not radically improved until 1945, when today's auto-mounted starting gate was perfected by Steve Phillips. The course was left-handed (counter clockwise). Races were for seven laps, which involved 13 tight turns. Especially brilliant wins resulted in a *revocatus*, a revocation, in which the driver was recalled onto the track for additional laps and applause.

In each team of two, four or six, the horses were harnessed in a line abreast of each other. Those in the middle of the line, on either side of the tongue or pole, were in what is called the yoke-horse position, while those on the outside of these two were in what is called the trace-horse position. Among the Romans, the best or most experienced horse of the four was regarded as the captain and was harnessed in the right-hand yoke-horse position. The Greeks, to the contrary, put the best horse of a team in the right trace-horse position. Whereas the Greeks considered mares to be superior for chariots, Romans raced stallions. The horses ran with bandage-protected legs; their drivers wore leather leggings, rib-cage reinforcements, crash helmets, and special daggers to cut themselves free should they be thrown to the hard baked clay track and dragged—a real concern since they tied the reins around their waists to take up the slack and to achieve greater leverage on the turns. Regular races were supervised by numerous officials, the titles of some of which were *dominus*, *conditor*, *hortator*, *medicus*, *doctor* and *sellarius*. With other duties, they had the authority to decide a *facinus* (foul), or when a driver had committed a *fraudatus* (had cheated). Crashes, which were frequent, were called *occidis*. Roman drivers were accused of many vices, but hardly ever of accepting bribes. It simply was not done. Anything and everything else was. This explains in part why 40 drivers were killed in one race in 466 B.C.—mid-race murder was an accepted, useful and, after all, thrilling racing tactic. So was sorcery—so much so that chariot drivers were considered the experts in the field. Vast sums of money were spent on rituals invoking the powers of darkness and designed to kill, maim, or otherwise injure key rivals and their horses. Written curses were the most potent and sometimes ran to nearly 100 lines. Whoever completed the seven laps first won the race.

Most drivers were sons of slaves who worked in the racing stables. A successful driver might eventually buy his freedom and go on to accumulate a large fortune by selling his services to the highest bidders, sometimes several times during a single day. Three of the greatest drivers were Scorpus who had 2048 wins and died before he was 27 years old, Musclosus with 3599 victories, and Gaius Appuleius Diocles from Lusitania in the province of Spain. Diocles' career spanned 24 years during which he raced *quadrigae* (four-horse chariots) in 4257 starts and placed 2900 times. Of the latter, 1462 were wins, 861 were seconds, 576 were thirds and one was a fourth-place finish. Of the 1462 wins, 1064 were in singles, 347 were with teams of two chariots, and 51 were with teams of three (three men, 12 horses). His total career winnings were 35,863,120 sesterces—which today would be nearly $2 million. Other statistics available are the tactics Diocles used in each of his wins, the number of times he beat each rival faction, and the records he broke together with the names of their previous holders. Additionally, there are lists of his horses' names, breeds, colors and sires, and it is recorded that he drove nine of his horses to their 100th victory, and one to its 200th. These items illustrate that Roman harness racing was as statistic conscious as any sport today. The Romans prized and praised the best drivers far above the best horses. When the great Felix died all of Rome grieved. At his cremation, which was mobbed with mourners, one of his anguished fans threw himself onto the pyre and was burned to death.

FORMS: The two basic forms of harness racing today are trotting and pacing. Each has its own rules, traditions, governing bodies and special features; each has its own triple crown and its own variations. One variation of the trotting form was ice trotting; regular winter meets were held on the river at Ottawa in the early 1880s.

While ridden races employ the Thoroughbred breed (to be discussed below), harness races employ the Standardbred breed. The breeding goal that resulted in the latter was a horse that could pace or trot a mile in standard time, which today has shrunk to two min. 20 sec. or less for a two-year-old horse. This is akin to par in golf. Compared to a Thoroughbred, a Standardbred has a longer body, a shorter stature (averaging 15½ to 16 hands), heavier legs, and more stamina. Its average speed is only from 25 to 35 m.p.h. due to the fact that the gallop is illegal in both forms of harness racing.

Within the Standardbred breed are two main strains, the trotter and the pacer. The trotter is high-stepping, wears a checkrein to hold its head high (which helps it maintain both stride and balance), has a left-to-right head-nodding movement, and races free legged. The pacer (generally a fraction of a second faster than the trotter) also wears a check rein, but in addition wears hopples, leather or plastic straps connecting its front and rear legs on the same side. The reason for these is that the pacer moves its legs on the same side in unison (contrary to the trotter whose diagonal legs move in unison. This results in a characteristic easy, side-to-side swaying motion. The two strains' feet and shoes also differ: the trotter's front toe or hoof is slightly longer, with a more acute angle of front and sole of hoof (46° – 48°), and its shoe is heavier (8 oz.). The pacer's front toe is shorter, with a less acute angle (48° – 50°), and its shoe is lighter (5 oz.). In both strains a flat shoe is worn on the front hooves and a creased swedge-type shoe on the hind ones to provide more traction. In addition, the harness horse will wear pads (boots) because it is likely to knock or rub its legs against each other while running: elbow boots high on the front legs, knee boots on the knee joints, quarter boots on the heels, and bell boots just above the hoof to protect the pastern area.

By the time a two-year-old horse is ready to race, it will have been driven a total of some 350 miles in training. Approximately half of these miles are completed clockwise around tracks and half counterclockwise. Since all races are run counterclockwise around the track, the horse is worked out clockwise and trained to run whenever it faces the other direction. Usually a horse will continue to race if it is at all successful, but all harness horses have a mandatory retirement age of 15. During its career it will be valued at approximately its total earnings during the preceding year—from $2500 to $3000 is the average value.

Today fully 90 percent of all male Standardbreds of both strains racing on American tracks are direct descendants of a horse whose name was Rysdyk's Hambletonian. Foaled in Orange County, New York, in 1849 (the year Edgar Allan Poe died), Hambletonian was bought by William Rysdyk for $125. Largely for having sired 1331 foals, Hambletonian today is known as the "Father of American Trotting," or the "Father of the Breed." The "Great Sire" of the breed, however, was a gray named Messenger, who was foaled in England in 1780, imported to America in 1788, and buried with military honors in 1808. Messenger appears three times in Hambletonian's pedigree, as well as once in Man o' War's. The blood of both these great horses also dominates in all countries where harness racing is practiced, except the Soviet Union and France. In the case of the pacer strain, all blood lines can also be traced in various degrees to the Narragansett, a breed of pacer, now extinct, which worked and raced in Rhode Island and was favored by George Washington.

Around 1840 two-wheeled carts called sulkies began to replace the four-wheeled ones that had been popular. They were high wheeled so the driver could see over the horse's back. Not until 1892 was the low-wheeled sulky introduced. This type used bicycle wheels as does today's. A sulky today with two bicycle wheels on a strengthened aluminum frame weighs an average of 39 lbs. Most models include a long head pole which serves to prevent the horse's head from turning to the right.

In harness racing there are five classes of races, most of which begin in motion behind a gate which gradually increases speed to 35 m.p.h. These classes are: conditioned races where horses are grouped by gait, age, sex, winnings, or by some other condition; claiming races where horses are grouped by value; stakes and futurities, the latter being those races between horses which were nominated to race prior to their birth; early and late closing events where horses are entered either more or less than six weeks before the race; and open races in which any horse may race. Betting is popular at most of these classes of race; at many a handicapper weighs up to 500 pieces of individual information on each horse before deciding its odds. At most meets public favorites win from 35 to 38 percent of the time.

ORGANIZATION: Goshen, New York, one of the places Paul Revere stopped on his famous ride, was at one time the nation's capital for the breeding and racing of harness horses. The sport quickly spread all over the continent so that a national organization was needed. Attempts to meet that need were made in 1825 when the New York Trotting Club was founded, the first organization of its kind in the United States. In 1870 (when Dexter, whom General U.S. Grant had driven, did the mile in 2 min. 14¼ sec.) a larger attempt was made by the formation of the National Trotting Association, the first real national governing body. By the 1930s, two other national bodies had been formed, and in 1938 the three combined to form the U.S. Trotting Association. The latter, headquartered in Columbus, Ohio (Ohio is the leading producer of Standardbreds), is today the governing body for all North American harness racing. It divides the United States into ten districts, with the Maritime Provinces of Canada (New Brunswick, Nova

Scotia, and Prince Edward Island) making an eleventh district. Each of these has from three to five district directors who are elected by the local members of the Association. Supporting and supplementing the Association's efforts are numerous other organizations such as the Harness Tracks of America, the U.S. Harness Writers' Association, Inc, the Standardbred Owners' Association, the Canadian Trotting Association. All of these organizations seek to encourage interest and support of the sport in the several dozen states and provinces where pari-mutuel harness racing is allowed. The grass roots or life blood of the sport is the fair circuit, which consists of over 400 small fair meetings, run on more than 500 tracks, sponsored by county fair boards in virtually every state. The Grand Circuit, the "Major League of Harness Racing" sometimes called the Ragin' Grand, is an organization of tracks founded in 1873 that plans an annual itinerary and awards over $4 million in purses at its races. The chief ones of these comprise harness racing's two triple crowns. Pacing's Triple Crown consists of the Little Brown Jug Classic in Ohio, the William H. Crane Futurity in New York, and the Messenger Stake in New York. Trotting's Triple Crown consists of the Hambletonian in Du Quoin, Illinois, the Kentucky Futurity, and the Yonkers Futurity.

HORSE RACING

Some experts say that horses were first domesticated around 2700 B.C. by people in the Ukraine who quickly thereafter became pastoral nomads. No one knows for sure. What is certain—and incredible—is how quickly the breeding, use and racing of horses became an integral part of life throughout Europe and Asia. By 2300 B.C. bridles and bits had been invented and records of sires were being kept. By 2000 B.C. famous purebreds were being bred in North Africa, and by 1600 B.C. the Hittites had written instructions for the crossbreeding of horses. The primitive step pyramids in Egypt were built by the even more primitive Hyksos Shepherd Kings, nomadic people whose horses gave them a vast advantage in their invasion of Egypt around 1500 B.C. By 1400 B.C. the jointed snaffle bit had been invented; a thousand years after that, in the fourth century B.C, the curb bit was invented; in the 23 centuries since then, there has been no basic new idea in bits. In fact, there have been few innovations in riding and racing since men first rode horses, the first actual account of which is on clay tablets from the twelfth century B.C. reign of Nebuchadnezzar I (whose successor some five hundred years later, Nebuchadnezzar II, threw Daniel to the lions).

The greatest horsemen who ever lived were the Parthians, whose other main achievement was the defeat of Mark Antony in 36 B.C. The later Huns were less superb on horseback and less successful against Roman generals, but did cause a revolution of their own in horseback riding. Attila's Huns, crouching down over their horses American Indian-style, were regarded by shocked, upright-riding Europeans as cripples who could not walk but had to be secured in their saddles. (Attila, a nickname meaning roughly little daddy, was appropriate, as Attila was a congenital dwarf.) The marvelous invention that allowed them to ride that way was the stirrup, not seen in Europe until that time. As mentioned above, it had been invented 600 years before in India for barefoot riders. Centuries after the Huns during the Age of Chivalry (which originally meant the Age of Horsemen), European knights were still riding straight-legged with long stirrups and deep saddles. The Moors introduced bent legs. But the stirrup had vastly increased the horses' potential. By the time of Columbus, the horse was an integral part of European warfare.

Columbus took no horses with him in 1492. On his second voyage in 1495, he took 20 stallions and a number of brood mares. Just five years later a royal stud farm had been established on Hispaniola, an island near Cuba. It was from that stud farm, and other later ones in Cuba, that horses were obtained for the conquest of Mexico. In this they were invaluable. Cortés launched the Conquest with a mere eleven stallions and five mares. One of his men, Narváez, singlehandedly routed an entire Aztec army simply by charging them on his bell-bedecked horse. Though the Mexican peoples later stole, rode, ate, wore and deified horses, the animal's initial effect upon them was one of utter devastation, due largely to their logical assumption that horse and rider were one creature which, whenever a Spaniard dismounted, was able to split itself in two.

A number of Cortés' horses remained on the continent. In 1539 De Soto took some 300 horses to Florida. He was followed a quarter of a century later by Menéndez with 100 horses. Descendants of all of these horses were bought and raced by English colonists in Virginia. And so the horse returned to North America—Ice Age horses lived on every continent except Australia and Antarctica. Some escaped to begin generations of feral horses. (Wild is the wrong word—the only true wild horses in the world are the Przhwalski's Horse and the European Forest Horse which became extinct in the 1880s but was re-created through selective breeding.) These feral horses which were called mustangs were captured by Indian tribes, whose cultures were totally revolutionized by them in the 1600s. Chief among these were the Cheyenne, the Arapaho, the Sioux and the Commanche, who were particularly fond of both racing and betting. These tribes were all farming village-dwellers until the horse made them nomadic hunters. When Jamestown was founded in 1607, the settlers had no horses. In 1610 the colonists purchased from the Indians six mares and a stallion, all of which they were then forced to eat because of a hard winter. Later, they purchased a number of Chickasaws from the nearby Choctaw, Seminole, Cherokee and Creek tribes who had by then become horse breeders. Though these were successfuly kept and bred, there were still only 200 horses in Virginia by 1650, the year tea was first imported into England. The importation of horses continued: the first ones arrived in the Massachusetts Bay Colony in 1629, the same year the Swedes brought horses to Delaware; Flemish settlers brought others to New York in 1660; French immigrants brought horses to Canada five years after that. By 1668 the situation in Virginia had so improved that horses were being exported to other colonies.

While they were scarce, horses were extremely valuable in the New World. In Cortés' time a single horse was worth 100 slaves. Even when they were far more common, their value was immense. The various horse tribes, for example, counted coups (the more a warrior made, the greater his status) which included killing an enemy, capturing an eagle or stealing a horse. Those who owned one or more horses had high status similar to that of the *hippeis* in the time of Solon (639–559 B.C.)—an upper class of citizens who owned at least one horse each. Later, cowboys of the American West had a strict horse etiquette by which horse stealing was frowned upon, as headstones in Tombstone, Arizona's Boot Hill Cemetery, attest. The same had been true among the Mongols, where a horse thief was required to repay nine horses for every one stolen, or give up his own children, or die in one of a number of unpleasant ways.

As horses in the New World multiplied, new sports for them were found and new laws established. In 1674 (the year protozoa were discovered) a Puritan decree forbade horse racing in the streets of Plymouth: "whatsoeuer p'son shall run a race with any horse in any street or Common road shall forfeite fiue shillings in Mony forth with to be leuied by the Constable or set in the stockes one houre if it be not payed." That same year in Virginia, James Bullocke, a tailor, was fined 100 pounds of "tobacco and caske" for racing his mare, "... it being contrary to Law for a Labourer to make a race, being a sport only for gentlemen ..." The man Bullocke raced, Matthew Slader, was ordered put in the stocks for one hour for rigging the race. Twenty-four years later in 1698, a legal action claimed nonpayment of a 5 pound wager on a horse race—the horse backed by the plaintiff was owned by Thomas Jefferson, grandfather of the future president. In the early 1800s Thoroughbred racing was outlawed in New York, New England, and most of the other northern states because of the "rowdies, racketeers and scalawags" that were being attracted to it in increasing numbers. In the years since, scores of other laws and regulations were passed and enforced for better or for worse. Most of these attempted to regulate what men did with horses; recent ones have been concerned more with what men do to horses. In 1971 a law was passed by Congress to protect America's feral horses.

As North American horse racing evolved out of its aristocratic heritage into a democratically popular sport, and as sire lines imported from England improved native breeds, race courses began to be built and regular races held. Soon after Sir Richard Nicholls received the surrender of New Amsterdam in 1665 and became the first royal governor of New York, he laid out America's first full-sized course at Hempstead Plains, Long Island. It was named Newmarket after the Newmarket Town Plate instituted by Charles II in 1664. Its prize was called the Governor's Cup. The first races in North America run on a regular basis were held there. Other race courses were soon being built in New York and elsewhere, including one at Greenwich Village on Manhattan Island. Before the Revolutionary War there were 20 in Virginia alone. In 1789, the year of the mutiny aboard the *Bounty*, Quebec organized its Turf Club. Montreal had a Jockey Club by 1828, the year after Beethoven died, and by 1839 the state of Tennessee had ten different Jockey Clubs. Kentucky had not less than 17 race courses by 1840. At least eight different courses from those days are buried beneath the modern city of San Francisco. Neither wars nor times of crisis or deprivation have hampered the growth of the racing of horses in North America. Andrew Jackson himself raced during the War of 1812. The first American Derby was run at Paterson, New Jersey, in 1864 when the end of the Civil War was still more than a year away. Racing enthusiasts at Lexington, Kentucky, missed only one season during the entire war, and then only because an army was camped on their race course.

Horse racing today is deeply rooted in North America, where it is a relatively new sport. Only yesterday in the history of horse racing a secretary wrote, the "jockeys, inspired with thoughts of applause, and in the hope of victory, clap spurs to the willing horses, brandish their whips, and cheer them with their cries." The writer was the personal secretary to Saint Thomas à Becket, Archbishop of Canterbury, who was murdered on the steps of his cathedral in 1170.

Not everyone in history has liked horses and horse racing, of course. "I am the more astonished that so many thousands of grown men should be possessed again and again with a childish passion to look at galloping horses, and men standing upright in their chariots." So wrote Pliny the Younger in the second century A.D. Plato, more objective about all things, commented simply that spectators at battles ought to have fast horses handy nearby.

FORMS: Three hundred and fifty years ago most jockeys were midgets. Sometimes weighing only 42 lbs, they were fed gin in their youth to stunt their growth. Jockey is a diminutive form of Jack, or of the Scotch form of John. At one time all horse traders and breeders were addressed as Jack or Jock. The cap worn by modern jockeys is an almost exact duplicate of the Roman chariot driver's leather cap; their brightly colored silks recall Rome's racing factions that wore red, white, blue, green, purple or gold. Although there are amateur riders in numerous horse events today, most jockeys (among the world's highest paid sportsmen) are professionals. The first race for a monetary prize was held between knights for a purse of 40 pounds in "ready gold." The first racing trophy was a wooden ball adorned with flowers presented in 1512 (the year Michelangelo finished painting the Sistine Chapel). This later was replaced by a silver ball, still later by a golden one. The custom of giving three prizes dates from 1609 (the year Shakespeare wrote his *Sonnets*), when the sheriff of Chester asked the local silversmith to make a silver ball to be presented at the annual race. Twice the smith's work was unacceptable, so the sheriff ended up with three prizes to give instead of one. Horse races today decide champion horses, but this was not always the case. In Byzantine times the winner of a chariot race would challenge his defeated opponent to exchange teams and rerun the race so as to prove that the driver's skill, not the horses' had won. Today, there are as many people who can name the greatest jockeys as there are people who know great horses' names.

A horse's racing career, it may be said, begins long before the horse is foaled or even conceived. Desiring particular features in a horse such as speed or endurance, the breeder selects a sire and a dam who have exhibited those features outstandingly. Pedigrees are extensively consulted through numerous sources, particularly through the *Stud Book*, first published in 1791. In Pliny's day, A.D. 23 – 79, it was believed that "In Lusitania the mares turn to the west wind; they become impregnated by it, and the foals so conceived are amazing for speed." From 10 to 14 months after conception, the horse is foaled. Twins are generally aborted; a mare usually has 5 or 6 foals in her lifetime but may have as many as 19. Regardless of when it is born, a racehorse's official birthday is January 1—a horse born December 31 is officially one year old the next day. Once foaled, the horse receives an identification number, which in a relatively painless procedure is tattooed on the inside of its upper lip. It is also given a name which must be approved by the Jockey Club and must not exceed three pronounceable words with a maximum of 18 letters—a marked improvement over Roman times when up to 30 adjectives were sometimes used to describe the color of a horse. From birth the horse receives extra special care and attention. Such attention was specified as long ago as 1500, when Wynkynde Worde wrote *Properties and Medeycines for an Horfs*, one of the first books ever printed in England. Today the science is very highly developed, so that a horse receives medicines and vaccinations against lethal diseases like Venezuelan equine encephalomyelitis (VEE). The horse begins training at an early age, so that within two to three years it will be ready to run for roses, daisies and carnations in the American Triple Crown. If phenomenally successful, the horse becomes a hero and is retired to stud to continue the breeding of champions.

Virtually all horses of the Thoroughbred breed in the world today are descendants of one of only three who survived out of nearly 200 Arabian, Turkish and Barbary horses imported into England in the seventeenth and eighteenth centuries. The stirps (lines of descent) of those three read like an endless biblical string of begats. The first, a war charger named the Byerly Turk was captured in 1688 by Capt. Robert Byerly at Buda (across the Danube from Pest); its greatest descendant was Herod. The second was foaled in Yemen in 1724 and was called the Godolphin Arabian. Its grandson was the great Matchem who was the direct ancestor of My Man o' War (the auctioneer who sold history's greatest racehorse for $5000 in 1917 dropped the "My" from the name). The third was foaled in Syria in 1700 and was named the Darley Arabian. Its line is by far the strongest of the three. One of its sons, Bulle Rock, was the first Thoroughbred to go to America in 1730; another, The Flying Childers, was the world's first widely famous Thoroughbred racehorse; a third son, named Bleeding Childers because it broke blood vessels during training, was not famous in its own right but did gain a kind of immortality through a son it sired by a mare named Snake. That son, foaled on All Fool's Day (April 1st) in 1764, the year of the great solar eclipse, was named Eclipse. This was the most famous of five horses of that name. Toward the end of its two-year racing career, during which it was never beaten and only once was seriously challenged, Eclipse was being handicapped at an incredible 168 lbs. Retired to stud at the age of six, Eclipse in the next 19 years insured the survival and proliferation of its breed: about 90 percent of all Thoroughbreds today are its direct descendants, for which reason Eclipse has been called "the most influential breeding animal that ever lived."

ORGANIZATION: In A.D. 210 Roman soldiers stationed at Netherby in Yorkshire organized a race between Arabians taken to England by Emperor Septimus Severus. Although there undoubtedly had been earlier races (Caesar met highly trained charioteers using native horses when he invaded Britain in 55 B.C.), that race at Netherby stands as the first recorded horse race in England. The Brehon Laws of A.D. 800 required that every man of every rank be taught to drive horses. They also ruled that no penalty or compensation was payable for damage caused by flying horseshoes. By the twelfth century, horse races in England were being held at town fairs every Friday. The first recorded one dates from 1174 (eight years before St. Francis of Assisi was born). By this time European battles were sometimes interrupted by truces arranged so that horse races could be held on the no-man's-land between the respective armies. In those centuries Ireland was one of the world centers of horse racing. The Irish rode bareback, used bits and bridles but mounted on the right side of the horse, the wrong side. They were forbidden by law to do so after the Anglo-Norman invasion. Irish town fairs, called *Aenach* and held August 1 through August 6 every three years, included a full day of horse racing and driving events. The pagan Irish heaven, in fact, promised unlimited horse racing. For tens of millions of people today heaven (or more often its alternate) is the race track. Certain horses are avenging angels, and saintliness is measured in milliseconds and in furlongs (220 yds. or 1/8 mi. equals one furlong).

The principal tracks in the United States today include: Arlington Park in Illinois; Belmont Park and Saratoga Springs, both in New York; Hialeah Park in Florida where the photo finish was introduced in 1936; Churchill Downs in Kentucky; Laurel Park in Washington; and Pimlico in Maryland. Since 1842 the center of Canadian racing has been Toronto. Most tracks are dirt or "skinned," meaning covered with closely cut grass; this places emphasis on speed instead of stamina. All tracks have their own special features and receive considerable care and attention. This was true as early as 1764 when the July 5 edition of *La Gazette de Quebec* warned that any dogs found on the race grounds "will be put to death by the Parties concerned."

On today's many hundreds of American and Canadian tracks, various types of races are run, usually between horses classed according to their speed and handicapped by adding or removing weight to make competition keener. The most common type is the claiming race in which horses of similar cash value compete and then may be claimed, or purchased. Another type is the sweepstakes or stake race, in which horses are handicapped according to their previous win–lose records. Maiden races are those run between horses who have never won a race. Many races are named; for example, the Santa Anita Derby, the Hollywood Derby, the Hollywood Gold Cup, the Charles H. Strub Stakes, the California Stakes, the Canadian Derby at Edmonton, the Canadian Oaks, the British Columbia Derby, the Coronation Futurity, and so on. The most important of named races are those included in various nations' Triple Crowns. The three races which comprise Great Britain's Triple Crown are the 2000 Guineas, the Derby and the St. Leger. The Canadian Triple Crown consists of the Queen's Plate founded in 1861 and run at Toronto in June, the Prince of Wales Stakes and the Breeders Stakes. The American Triple Crown consists of the Kentucky Derby run since 1875 at Lexington in early May, the Preakness Stakes run since 1873 at Pimlico in May, and the Belmont Stakes run since 1867 at Belmont Park, New York, in early June.

At any race the highest authority is the race steward. Other officials may include a racing secretary (clerk of the course), a weighing officer (clerk of the scales), a handicapper, a judge who declares the results—win, place (second), and show (third)—usually after consulting photographs, a starter and a camera crew or patrol. Many famous men have officiated at horse races; one is

George Washington who served as a race official both before and after the Revolutionary War.

In 1823 (the year Charles Macintosh invented his waterproof raincoat) some 60,000 people—the first really large crowd ever gathered for an American sporting function—watched a much-publicized race between the North's American Eclipse and the South's Sir Henry. The North's horse won. Six years later, crowds flocked to see the first race betwen American and British Thoroughbreds. The American, Rattler, won. Such publicity and popularity inevitably attracted gangsters, gamblers and other undesirable elements, from all of whom protection was soon needed. Thus America's oldest organized sport is today also among the most highly organized and controlled of all sports in the world. The same year Dostoevsky wrote *Crime and Punishment* (1866), the American Jockey Club was formed as a national governing body. It was partially modeled after the much older Jockey Club in England which, like Lloyd's of London, was begun in a coffee shop (the Star and Garter) in 1750. Ever since 1773 the Jockey Club has published the *English Racing Calendar* to announce matches and sweepstakes in Britain and Ireland. Since 1791, the *Stud Book* has been published, and is today controlled by the Jockey Club. The American Jockey Club, re-formed in 1894 and now headquartered in New York, publishes the *American Stud Book* and issues its own *Racing Calendar*. Other aspects of the racing world are organized and controlled by numerous popular and influential groups such as the American Trainers Association, the Canadian Thoroughbred Horse Society, the Jockey's Guild, the National Equestrian Federation of Canada, the National Turf Writers Association, the Thoroughbred Club of America, the Thoroughbred Racing Protective Bureau. In each state where horse races take place, the governor appoints three racing commissioners, who are perhaps at the peak of the immense organizational iceberg that promotes and controls for the benefit of millions the ancient and exciting world of the games people play with the Thoroughbred horse.

American Association of Owners and Breeders of Peruvian Paso Horses Hall of Fame

CALIFORNIA CITY, CALIFORNIA

Mailing Address: P.O. Box 2035, 93505. Tel. (714) 373-4722. *Contact*: Verne R. Albright, Exec. Dir. *Location*: N. of Edwards Air Force Base; 60 mi. E. of Bakersfield; 70 mi. N. of Pasadena. *Personnel*: Verne R. Albright, Exec. Dir. *Nearby Halls of Fame*: Auto Racing (Ontario, 70 mi. S.), Citizens Savings (Los Angeles, 80 mi. S.), Physical Fitness (Costa Mesa, 95 mi. S.), Flight, Sports (San Diego, 170 mi. S.).

The American Association of Owners and Breeders of Peruvian Paso Horses (AAOBPPH) Hall of Fame Award was created in 1975 as an award for exceptional merit. The award, a ten-pound cast bronze, full-size replica of a 150-year-old Peruvian Stirrup, is given when a horse has accumulated 2000 points in competition. The recipients will also be entitled to use symbols after their names indicating they have received this high honor. As of 1977 no horse has qualified for the Hall of Fame award, eliminating the necessity at present for a physical site for the Hall. The AAOBPPH also gives a Harry Bennett Award to horses in eight categories for the highest number of points accumulated in a single year of competition.

Members: None as of 1977. The Hall of Fame Award will be presented for 2000 points accumulated by a single horse in one division at AAOBPPH approved shows. Any horse to be judged U.S. National Champion of Champions three times will automatically receive the award. The three divisions in which a horse may be entered are Breeding, Luxury Gelding, and Pleasure. Awards will be presented in a major approved show during a special ceremony held in an arena before spectators.

American Shetland Pony Club Hall of Fame

FOWLER, INDIANA

Mailing Address: P.O. Box 435, 47944. Tel. (317) 884-1242. *Contact*: Art Cooke, Exec. Secy. *Location*: On Rte. 52, 30 mi. N.W. of Lafayette. *Admission*: Free 8 to 4:30 weekdays. *Personnel*: T. R. Huston, Pres; Dennis Lang, V.Pres; Art Cooke, Exec. Secy. *Nearby Halls of Fame*: Agriculture (West Lafayette, 45 mi. S.E.), Auto Racing, Basketball (Indianapolis, 75 mi. S.E.), Business (Chicago, Ill, 145 mi. N.W.).

The American Shetland Pony Club Hall of Fame was founded in 1967 by the American Shetland Pony Club to perpetuate the memories of those Shetland ponies that have achieved the same high standards and awards in showing. The three types of members are Roadsters, those shown hooked to a two-wheel cart; Harness, those shown hooked to a four-wheel cart called a Viceroy; and Halter, those ponies shown wearing only a halter. The newly enshrined ponies have their names engraved on an 18-by-24-in. plaque on display in the Club's main office. The Hall of Fame is governed and supported by the American Shetland Pony Club.

Members: 86 as of December 1976. A pony in any or all of the three categories (Halter, Harness and Roadster) is inducted into the Hall of Fame automatically upon completing the eligibility requirements. Those requirements are that the show ponies must have 100 points and have won five consecutive Grand Championship titles. It is at this time that the pony's name is added to the roster of superlative competitors.

1967 PONY-VISTA'S MAGIC MYSTERY D.M.R. 46897. Harness. Owner Joey Dorignac, New Orleans, La.

1968 APPIN SCANDAL 117535. Halter. Owner David Coots, LeRoy, N.Y.

BAR-G'S UNKLE SAM 103741. Harness. Owner Gerald Barga, Versailles, Ohio.

BLACK LARGIO'S SPORTSMAN 95400. Harness. Owner Dennis Lang, West Seneca, N.Y.

BO-JAN'S TOP LADY 118308. Halter. Owner T. R. Huston, Hanna City, Ill.

CEDARGROVE'S FASCINATION RED 195012. Roadster. Owner Elbert Runnels, Tyler, Tex.

DEFENDER'S RAMBLER 77860. Roadster. Owner Merle Butts, Terre Haute, Ind.

FERNWOOD FRISCO LEE 69724. Roadster. Owner Fernwood Farm, Barrington, Ill.

FERNWOOD STORMY RHYTHM 89542. Roadster. Owner Ed McCarthy, Syracuse, N.Y.

HI HOOF'S PRIDE OF PRINCESS CODY 66059. Harness. Owner L. H. McNett, Wakarusa, Kans.

MELODY'S SON 70786. Harness. Owner Charles Wheeler, Rankin, Ill.

MELODY'S SON 70786. Halter. Owner Charles Wheeler, Rankin, Ill.

OHIO JUBILEE 93713. Roadster. Owner Robert Fies, Lewisburg, Ohio.

PRAIRIE HILL'S CURTAIN CALL 101703. Halter. Owner Mabel Peabody, Olean, N.Y.

WAIT AND SEE STAR LITE 95431. Harness. Owner Joey Dorignac, New Orleans, La.

1969 CRESCENT'S COPPER MISTY 101112. Roadster. Owner Ben Hinkle, Portland, Ore.

FERNWOOD LARGIO FLASH 55401. Harness. Owner L. Archie Carson, Saugus, Calif.

GREEN PASTURE'S PETER PAN 110735. Roadster. Owner Jim Mastelotto, Bakersfield, Calif.

H. V. RED CRESCENT KING'S TOP FLIGHT 72109. Roadster. Owner W. W. Wetenkamp, Lincoln, Nebr.

JONES' EXTRA! EXTRA! 99121. Harness. Owner G. A. Schoeny and J. P. Sprinkle, Evansville, Ind.

ORLENA'S TOPPER'S CHOICE 59202. Halter. Owner Melvin Richins, Grindley, Calif.

PIERRE CODY'S BLACK CRYSTAL 99597. Halter. Owner Paul Kitch, Wichita, Kans.

RANGEMORE'S TOP BRASS 111979. Halter. Owner Lewis Reblitz, Fond du Lac, Wis.

ROXIE'S TOPPER 66502. Roadster. Owner Joey Dorignac, New Orleans, La.

SHAGBARK'S STEP ASIDE 106685. Halter. Owner Judy Peterson, Lafayette, Ind.

SPRING FANCY 121858. Halter. Owner Mabel Peabody, Olean, N.Y.

1970 ARISTOCRAT'S DAINTY MISS 124354. Halter. Owner R. L. Hartman, Rockville, Ind.

BAR-G'S MARY-ANN 101856. Roadster. Owner Martin Smith, Elmira, N.Y.

BAR-G'S VICTORENE 119610. Halter. Owner Thomas and Merle Michael, Camden, Ohio.

B'S SHOW MAN 106778. Halter. Owner Gerald Barga, Versailles, Ohio.

FAY CODY 93967. Halter. Owner Durward Ruoff, Addison, Mich.

FERNWOOD FRISCO BANDIT 112721. Harness. Owner Ray Houston, Richmond, Mich.

FERNWOOD FRISCO VICKIE 119610. Halter. Owner Ray Houston, Richmond, Mich.

LA MOYNE'S STAR OF PATTON 53600. Roadster. Owner J. W. Murphy, Sunny Valley, Ore.

LARIGO'S TORCHLITE 90518. Halter. Owner William Vullings, Mosinee, Wis.

PRAIRIE HILL'S CURTAIN CALL 101703. Harness. Owner Mabel Peabody, Olean, N.Y.

SILVER MANE'S FRISCO CODY 101346. Harness. Owner Ed Windemuller, Byron Center, Mich.

SQUIRE'S BIG CHANCE 116661. Halter. Owner R. H. Bielenbert, Sr, Elgin, Ill.

1971 DEFENDER'S HOLIDAY RAMBLER 116287. Roadster. Owner Robert Roudebush, Thorntown, Ind.

HOLY HILL'S FIRECRACKER 114844. Roadster. Owner Gerald Barga, Versailles, Ohio.

LARIGO'S LU-ELLEN 80057. Roadster. Owner William Rooks, Holland, Mich.

LARIGO'S TORCHLITE 90518. Harness. Owner William Vullings, Mosinee, Wis.

MIGHTY SWEET DUCHESS 96675. Roadster. Owner Gene Adams, Riverside, Calif.

OVERLOOK DELIGHT 115352. Halter. Owner Bertha A. Ainsworth, Swartz Creek, Mich.

RIVER VIEW'S PISTOL PETE 124169. Roadster. Owner R. K. Richards and Family, Janesville, Wis.

SILVER MANE'S FRISCO CODY 101346. Halter. Owner Ed Windemuller, Byron Center, Mich.

1972 BAR-G'S LITTLE FELLER 117459. Harness. Owner Gerald Barga, Versailles, Ohio.

HALBROOK BLAZE OF GLORY 115449. Roadster. Owner Wayne and David Showers, Beloit, Wis.

MICHIGAN'S KING OF THE TAYLORS 124856. Halter. S. F. Taylor, Hudson, Mich.

MICHIGAN'S MARIA 124857. Halter. Owner S. F. Taylor, Hudson, Mich.

MICHIGAN'S MONEY MAKER 123784. Halter. Owner S. F. Taylor, Hudson, Mich.

RUOFF'S PROTESTOR 126175. Halter. Owner Durward Ruoff, Addison, Mich.

SON'S FIRST EDITION 126007. Halter. Owner Charles Wheeler, Rankin, Ill.

TERRY JEAN'S CAPTAIN PICK 110362. Roadster. Owner Gale Bennett, Lexington, Mo.

WILSON'S RED COUPON 113386. Harness. Owner Lloyd T. Wilson, Hammondsville, Ohio.

1973 B.F.S. SUDDEN BEAUTY 125023. Halter. Owner Dale Baxter, Walnut, Ill.

CAROLYN'S SURPRISE 125264. Halter. Owner Jay A. Robb, Midhurst, Ont, Can.

DEFENDER'S SILVER FOX 112465. Roadster. Owner Robert Roudebush, Eugene Sheets, Lafayette, Ind.

FAIRVIEW'S TOMMY WALKER 06331. Roadster. Owner Duane Rolando, Orland Park, Ill.

HI HOOF'S BRIGHT SPOT 121688. Halter. Owner Al Richardson, Walnut Creek, Calif.

HOLY HILL'S BRIGHT FLAME 118069, Harness. Owner R. L. Husban, Scottsdale, Ariz.

MICHIGAN'S WEE WILLY 120485. Halter. Owner Walter Farwell, Port Byron, Ill.

SUNNY ACRES BILLY JACK 107562. Harness. Owner Roy Strawhaker, Ottumwa, Iowa.

TAMERLANE'S GOLDEN ROSE 71623. Roadster. Owner Tom Wells, White Rock, B.C., Can.

1974 BAR-G'S ROCKEY 124899. Halter. Owner J. B. Everline, Zion, Ill.

GRANDEE DONA'S MACK 113144. Halter. Owner Donald Gilmore, Frankfort, Ind.

LARIGO'S DRUM-MAJOR 90524. Roadster. Owner William Vullings, Mosinee, Wis.

MISTER BAY BOY 120457. Halter. Owner Richard Jenkins, Gurnee, Ill.

MISTER BAY BOY 120457. Harness. Owner Richard Jenkins, Gurnee, Ill.

MR. QUO-VADIS 128334. Halter. Owner William Vullings, Mosinee, Wis.

SUNNY ACRES AIR BORNE'S ROCKET 105533. Harness. Owner John Yeary, Cleburne, Tex.

1975 DUN-HAVEN GLAMOURINE 107089. Harness. Owner Richard L. Stocton, Colfax, Iowa.

HI HOOF'S BRIGHT SPORT 121688. Roadster. Owner Al Richardson, Walnut Creek, Calif.

HI HOOF'S SOMETHING SPECIAL 122095. Halter. Owner Al Richardson, Walnut Creek, Calif.

MY MARK'S PRIM MISS 127329. Roadster. Owner Adrian Slager, Holland, Mich.

RAMBLE RIDGE RUSTLER 108137. Harness. Owner Maurice Tinnes, Davenport, Iowa.

RANGEMORE'S ROYAL REBEL 124005. Roadster. Owner Norman R. Masters, Nebraska City, Nebr.

RIDGELIEU'S DAINTY DUTCHESS 128944. Halter. Owner Fred Pimentel, Smith Parish, Bermuda.

1976 DEFENDER'S FROST 117380. Roadster. Owner Gregory Gilmore, Frankfort, Ind.

DUN-HAVEN ROYAL AIRE 116762. Harness. Owner Edward Smith, South Lyon, Mich.

HIGH HOOF'S CODY COLORIFIC 121681. Roadster. Owner Al Richardson, Walnut Creek Calif.

PONY-LEA'S SENSATION 126895. Roadster. Owner Sheets and Roudebush, Thorntown, Ind.

RAMBLE RIDGE REPORTER 118646. Harness. Owner John Baraks, Milan, Ill.

STANDING OVATION 129197. Harness. Owner Bill Tompkins, Meadville, Mo.

WINDWOOD'S BANDIDO 125308. Roadster. Owner Vern Houston, Richmond, Mich.

WINDWOOD'S DEPUTY 128297. Halter. Owner Jack Snyder, Bloomington, Ill.

Arizona Horse Racing Hall of Fame

PHOENIX, ARIZONA

Mailing Address: P.O. Box 9165, 85023. Tel. (602) 265-4614. *Contact*: Bob Tryon, Cur. *Location*: On 19th Ave. and Bell Rd, in Phoenix take Black Canyon Freeway N. past the airport to 19th Ave. and Bell Rd. 95 mi. N. of Tucson, 115 mi. S. of Flagstaff. *Admission*: Free during racing events. *Personnel*: Robert E. Tryon, Cur.

The Arizona Horse Racing Hall of Fame was founded c. 1960 by Bob Tryon in order to pay due respect to those persons who have been outstanding members of the Arizona horse racing community. These persons are from all phases of horse racing including inventors, commissioners, media members, owners, trainers and jockeys. The Hall of Fame is located in the main lobby of the Turf Paradise racetrack; on display are plaques of the members. Turf Paradise was chosen as the home of Arizona's Horse Racing Hall of Fame as it is Arizona's largest track and the site of two major meetings. The track also holds the only $100,000 race in Arizona, the Phoenix Futurity, run annually in April. Turf Paradise and Arizona Downs offer the Hall financial support.

Members: 19 as of January 1977. Members are elected to the Hall of Fame from the many facets of Arizona horse racing. Jockeys are nominated from those who have won eight consecutive times on Arizona tracks and from those Arizonans who have gone on to become famous. No specific number of candidates is inducted annually. Nominations are made by a selection committee strictly on the basis of merit. The selection committee is comprised of people with a background in Arizona horse racing; membership is rotated at irregular intervals.

Induction Year Unrecorded

ARTERBURN, Jack. Jockey.

BURNS, Eddie. Jockey.

COLCORD, Frank. Horse owner and trainer.

ELLSWORTH, Rex. Horse owner and trainer.

ERB, Dave. Kentucky-Derby-winning jockey.

GUINUP, Charles. Jockey. Died on a track in Tucson.

HAZELTON, Richard. Trainer.

HERBUVEAUX, James, Sr. Track President.

LAMBERT, Jerry. Jockey.

LEE, Dick. Racing writer.

LUMM, Roy. Jockey.

McDANIEL, O. L. Racing commissioner.

PARDEE, C. W. Race horse owner and breeder.

PIERCE, Don. Jockey.

PUETT, Clay. Starting gate inventor.

ROEBUCK, Lee. Track superintendent.

SANDE, Earl. Jockey. See entry in National Jockeys Hall of Fame, 1959. *Also in*: Racing Hall of Fame.

SHOEMAKER, William. Jockey. See entry in National Jockeys Hall of Fame, 1955. *Also in*: Racing Hall of Fame.

YEAGER, Bob. Jockey.

Canadian Horse Racing Hall of Fame

REXDALE, ONTARIO

Mailing Address: 48 Belfield, M9W 1G1. *Tel*: (416) 247-6247. *Contact*: Dave Gorman, Exec. V.Pres. *Location*: Suburb of Toronto, off Highway 27, N. of Toronto International Airport, 80 mi. S.W. of Peterborough, 95 mi. N.E. of London, 200 mi. N.E. of Detroit, Mich. *Personnel*: Morris Taylor, Pres; Dave Gorman, V.Pres; 35 mem. Bd. of Dirs. Call for information. *Nearby Halls of Fame*: Hockey, Sports (Toronto), Football (Hamilton, 30 mi. S.), Hockey (Kingston, 170 mi. N.E.), Sports (Detroit, Mich, 230 mi. S.W.), Archery (Grayling, Mich, 240 mi. W.), Golf (Foxburg, Pa, 250 mi. S.).

The Canadian Horse Racing Hall of Fame was founded in 1975 when the National Association of Canadian Racetracks decided to form a hall of fame. Although the Hall of Fame has no permanent building now, it is projected that in one to two years there will be a permanent building in Toronto to house their Hall. The Canadian Horse Racing Hall of Fame was conceived to honor outstanding jockeys, riders and horses (Thoroughbred and Standardbred) and to provide a history of the sport of horse racing.

Members: 70 as of 1977. There are three categories of members: Driver or Jockey; Thoroughbred or Standardbred horse; and a Builder. The eligibility requirements are that the jockey or rider must have made a significant contribution to Canadian Horseracing and that they must bring honor to their field of sport. An inducted horse may be either Thoroughbred or Standardbred. There is no limit to the number of inductees per year. As of now, there is no special ceremony for inductees into the Hall of Fame. Each inductee is given a plaque commemorating his entrance into the Hall of Fame; the inductee is an honorary, lifetime member in the Hall.

1976 ARMBRO FLIGHT. Standardbred.

ARMSTRONG, J. Elgin. Builder.

BUNTY LAWLESS. Thoroughbred.

CHILCOTT. Standardbred.

DOMINION GRATTEN. Standardbred.

DOTTIE'S PICK. Standardbred.

DR. STANTON. Standardbred.

DUCHESS OF YORK. Thoroughbred.

FILION, Herve. Driver. See entry in Hall of Fame of the Trotter, 1975. *Also in:* Canada's Sports Hall of Fame.

FLEMING, Vic. Driver.

FRESH YANKEE. Standardbred.

GEORGE ROYAL. Thoroughbred.

GRATTEN BARS. Standardbred.

HAROMETER. Thoroughbred.

HENDRIE, William. Builder.

INFERNO. Thoroughbred.

INVINCIBLE SHADOW. Standardbred.

JOEY. Thoroughbred.

KING ARVIE. Thoroughbred.

LA PREVOYANTE. Thoroughbred.

LEVESQUE, Jean-Louis. Builder.

LONGDEN, John. Jockey. See entry in National Jockeys Hall of Fame, 1956. *Also in*: Canada's Sports Hall of Fame and Racing Hall of Fame.

MacKINNON, Colonel Dan. Builder. See entry in Canada's Sports Hall of Fame.

MICHAUD, Maurice. Builder.

NIJINSKY II. Thoroughbred.

NORTHERN DANCER. Thoroughbred. See entry in Racing Hall of Fame. *Also in:* Canada's Sports Hall of Fame.

O'BRIEN, Joseph C. Driver. See entry in Hall of Fame of the Trotter, 1970. *Also in:* Canada's Sports Hall of Fame.

PATTERSON, T. C. Builder.

ROSS, Commander J. K. L. Builder.

ROWE, W. Earl. Builder.

SAUNDERS, William. Jockey.

SEAGRAM, Joseph E. Builder.

SHEPPERTON. Thoroughbred.

SILENT MAJORITY. Standardbred.

SIR BARTON. Thoroughbred. See entry in Racing Hall of Fame, 1957.

SPEERS, Robert James. Builder. See entry in Canada's Sports Hall of Fame.

STRIKE OUT. Standardbred.

TAYLOR, Austen C. Builder.

TAYLOR, E. P. Builder. See entry in Canada's Sports Hall of Fame.

TIE SILK. Standardbred.

VICTORIA PARK. Thoroughbred.

WHITE, Roger. Driver.

WINNIPEG. Standardbred.

WOOLF, George "Iceman." Jockey. See entry in National Jockeys Hall of Fame, 1955. *Also in:* Canada's Sports Hall of Fame and Racing Hall of Fame.

1977 ARMBRO NESBITT. Standardbred.

AVERY, Earle. Driver.

BALDWIN, Ralph. Driver. See entry in Hall of Fame of the Trotter, 1971.

BELL, Max. Builder.

BULL PAGE. Thoroughbred.

CHOP CHOP. Thoroughbred.

DAVIES, Lou. Builder.

DIAMOND, Jack. Builder.

GALLANT KITTY. Thoroughbred.

GOMEZ, Avelino. Jockey.

GORMAN, T. P. Builder. See entry in Hockey Hall of Fame. *Also in:* Greater Ottawa Sports Hall of Fame and International Hockey Hall of Fame.

HENDRIE, George. Builder.

HERBERT, Bill. Builder.

HODGINS, Clint. Driver. See entry in Hall of Fame of the Trotter, 1972.

LANGILL, Sydney. Builder.

McLAUGHLIN, R. S. Builder. See entry in Canada's Sports Hall of Fame.

MIRON, Adrien. Builder.

MISS VERA BARS. Standardbred.

NEARTICE. Thoroughbred.

PERLMAN, J. Samuel. Builder.

ROGERS, Chris. Jockey.

SCHILLINGS, George. Builder.

SMYTHE, Conn. Builder. See entry in Hockey Hall of Fame. *Also in:* Canada's Sports Hall of Fame and International Hockey Hall of Fame.

VEILLEUX, Jerard. Builder.

WHITE, Ben. Builder.

YOUVILLE. Thoroughbred.

Hall of Fame of the Trotter (Living Hall of Fame)

GOSHEN, NEW YORK

Mailing Address: 240 Main St, 10924. Tel. (914) 294-6330. *Contact*: Phil Pines, Dir. *Location:* 90 min. from midtown Manhattan, just above the New Jersey border, 20 mi. W. of the Hudson River. *Admission:* Free 10 to 5 daily; 1:30 to 5 weekends; closed Thanksgiving, Christmas and New Year's. *Personnel:* Philip A. Pines, Dir; Jean Musgrove, Registrar; E. Roland Harriman, Pres; Delvin G. Miller, Secy. *Nearby Halls of Fame:* Ice Skating (Newburgh, 15 mi. N.E.), Heritage, Music (New York City, 45 mi. S.E.), Bicycle (Staten Island, 50 mi. S.E.), Baseball (Cooperstown, 95 mi. N.W.), Horse Racing (Saratoga Springs, 120 mi. N.E.), Flight (Elmira, 130 mi. N.W.), Horseshoe Pitching (Corning, 135 mi. N.W.).

The Hall of Fame of the Trotter was founded in 1949 by the Trotting Horse Club of America. It was not many years later that the Trotting Horse Club of America dissolved and turned the Hall of Fame over to self-government. The Hall of Fame feels its duties are to collect, classify and preserve archives, records, relics and other personal property and items of interest, and to establish memorials in connection with the origin and development of the Standardbred horse. The Hall is a member of the Association of Sports Museums and Halls of Fame. The Trotting Horse Museum is housed in the former Good Time Stable with two additional wings built to accommodate the ever-expanding exhibits. Inside the Museum is the first mobile starting gate, skullies that were once hitched to famed trotting and pacing champions, prints, wood carvings, bronzes, dioramas and paintings, including a collection of Currier and Ives. Housed in a separate room within the Hall of Fame of the Trotter is the U.S. Harness Writers Association's Living Hall of Fame. This hall honors the sport's great personalities with 14-in. high lifelike statuettes portraying the men in a manner representing their position in harness racing. These statuettes were designed by the Connecticut artist Beverly Lopez. The 24 personalities in this hall have been elected since 1961, honoring trainer-drivers, administrators, innovators, owners and breeders. Special arrangements can be made for group or class tours. The tour through the Museum and around the historic track is augmented with films and minilectures. The Hall of Fame also sponsors free matinee racing programs on Saturdays in late May. This nonprofit organization is sustained by its membership and publishes a bimonthly newsletter, *News.* The Standardbred library contains 9000 volumes and is the most complete anywhere. Souvenirs, such as horseshoes, jewelry and books, can be bought at the Weathervane shop in the Museum.

Members: 24 as of December 1975. The personalities in the Living Hall of Fame have been elected since 1961 by the U.S. Harness Writers Association in national balloting. Each person is enshrined at special ceremonies and is at that time presented with a Hall of Fame ring as a personal reminder of his accomplishments.

1961

HARRIMAN, E. Roland
Administrator
Father E. H. Harriman; brother Averill Harriman, politician; B.A. from Yale in 1917; Lt. in W. W. II; married Gladys C. C. Fries of New York City in 1917; two children, Elizabeth H. "Betty" Dixon and Phyllis Connery; Episcopalian; banker since 1922; chmn. bd. Union Pacific Railroad; dir. of Delaware and Hudson Railroad, *Newsweek,* American Bank Note Company and Anaconda Copper Mining Company.

E. R. Harriman was the founder of the Arden Homestead Stables, under blue and orange colors. He helped rescue the sport of harness racing from extinction in the 1920s and 1930s when he went to the aid of the *Register* and kept the book of breeding records functional. Harriman was instrumental in the founding of the Trotting Horse Club of America and the U.S. Trotting Association. He is president of the Hall of Fame of the Trotter, chairman of the board of the Hambletonian Society and president of the Grand Circuit.

PHILLIPS, Stephen G.
Innovator
Stephen Phillips was the developer of the modern-day mobile starting gate first seen at Xenia, Ohio, in 1937. Roosevelt Raceway and Yonkers Raceway were the first tracks to use it sucessfully in 1946.

1966

LEVY, George Morton
Innovator
George Levy earned his title as the "Father of Modern Harness Racing" with the development of racing under lights at Roosevelt Raceway in 1940. He also worked with Steve Phillips on the mobile starting gate at Roosevelt Raceway in 1946.

1967

BLAKE, Octave
Owner, Breeder and Trainer
Born 1895 in New York City; father Isreal Octave Blake; mother Jeannette Bugbee Blake; wife Esther Houghton; married January 15, 1936, New York City; graduated from Princeton University in 1918; played varsity football; U.S. Naval Air Force Lieutenant; owner Curtiss Aeroplane and Motor Corporation; pres. Pine Hill Crystal Spring Water Company and Cornell Electric Manufacturing Company.

Octave Blake founded the Newport Stock Farm and built a successful breeding establishment with Island Wilkes and Island Wilkes, Jr. The top horses under his blue and gold colors were Jeritza, Atlantic McElwyn, Brittanic, Voltaire, Newport Dream, Newport Star and Forbes Chief. Blake served as president of the Grand Circuit for more than 20 years.

SHEPPARD, Lawrence B.
Owner and Administrator
Lawrence Sheppard has participated in harness racing for over 40 years. He was the founder of Hanover Shoe Farm, president of the U.S. Trotting Association and honorary lifetime president of that Association, first chairman of the Pennsylvania Racing Commission and one of the founders and vice president of the Hall of Fame of the Trotter.

SHIVELY, Bion
Trainer and Driver
Bion Shively trained and drove Hambletonian winner Sharp Note in 1952. He was also in the sulky behind the champion Rodney in the 1940s.

1968

ERVIN, Frank
Trainer and Driver
Frank Ervin drove his first 2-min. mile in 1951 in Delaware, Ohio. Since that time he has accumulated 108 2-min. drives. His victories include the Hambletonian, the Kentucky Futurity and pacing's Triple Crown. Ervin's champion horses include Yankee Hanover, Good Time and Bret Hanover.

HAUGHTON, William
Driver and Trainer
Born November 2, 1923, in Gloversville, N.Y; family dairy business in upstate New York; high school basketball letter; attended New York State Institute for Agriculture 1943–1944; married Dorothy Bischoff 1951; five children, William, Peter, Tommy, Robert and Holly Ann.

William Haughton got his start helping Billy Muckle at fairground tracks in upstate New York. He came into his own around 1949 and since then has ranked in the top 25 dash winners each season. His earnings have ranked him in the top ten for the past 25 years. Haughton has won more purse money than any other harness race driver, over $2 million. In 1971 he represented the United States in the second annual Harness Tracks of America World Driving Championship. He finished the cross-country marathon in second place. Bill received the special Grand Circuit Centennial Gold Medallion for his outstanding service to the sport of harness racing. Some of the horses driven in his 4000-victory career are Romulus Hanover, Laverne Hanover, Duke Rodney, Handle with Care, Christopher T, Rising Wind, Spartan Hanover, Pammy Lobell and Rum Customer, the first North American-bred millionaire pacer.

MICHAEL, Walter J.
Owner and Administrator
Walter Michael began harness racing in 1937 when he bought his first Standardbred. He developed Pickwick Farm and owns a racing stable. Michael is president of Grandview and Northfield parks, chairman of the board of Painesville Raceway and past president of the U.S. Trotting Association.

MILLER, Delvin
Trainer and Driver
Delvin Miller marked 57 horses with their first 2-min. miles during his career of over 1700 races all over the world, winning nearly $7 million. Miller owns and operates Meadow Lands Farm and is a former president of the Grand Circuit.

1969

DANCER, Stanley
Trainer and Driver
Born July 25, 1927, in Edinburg, N.J; underwent cervical disc surgery in 1973; was back to the tracks in 1974; now resides in New Egypt, N.J.

Stanley Dancer's career began in 1946 at Harrington, Del. Dancer became the first horseman to sweep both trotting's Big Five (1968) and pacing's Big Five (1971). Stan has won the Hambletonian twice and the Little Brown Jug three times. His Triple Crown wins number three. In 1972 he was national UDRS champion with a .448 average. During his career, Dancer was victorious 2954 times, with earnings of $16,667,701. He has driven 165 2-min. miles and had seven consecutive seasons of million-dollar earnings. Some of the winning horses he has driven include Nevele Pride, Superbowl, Su Mac Lad, Albatross, Most Happy Fella, Cardigan Bay and Noble Victory. Dancer trained and rode three Horses of the Year and handled two of pacing's three millionaires.

SMART, Wayne "Curly"
Trainer and Driver
Curly Smart has been in the sport of harness racing for 50 years. He was a private trainer for Castleton Farms and ran his own stable. Smart has had 45 2-min. drives during his career with champions like Poplar Byrd, Leander Labell and Ensign Hanover. Smart is director of the U.S. Trotting Association.

1970

O'BRIEN, Joseph C.
Trainer and Driver
Born in Alberton, P.E.I, Can; seriously injured in 1972 five-horse accident; hospitalized for a month; now resides in California.

Joe O'Brien has trained and raced two Horse of the Year winners, Scott Frost (1955 and 1956) and Fresh Yankee (1970). He drove Steady Star to the world's fastest mile 1:52 in 1971. During his 3000 wins he drove Fresh Yankee, Steady Star, Armbro Nesbit, Scott Frost, Melvin's Woe, Flower Child and Sunbell.
Also in: Canada's Sports Hall of Fame and Canadian Horse Racing Hall of Fame.

POWNALL, Harry
Trainer and Driver
Harry Pownall was the head trainer with Arden Homestead Stables for over 30 years. He drove Titan Hanover to the first 2-min. mile ever raced by a two-year-old of either gait in 1944. His victories include the Hambletonian, the Dexton Cup and the Kentucky Futurity. Harry Pownall's outstanding performers include Star's Pride, Florican, Tassell Hanover, Matastar and Titan Hanover.

RUSSELL, Sanders
Owner and Trainer
Sanders Russell owns and operates a public stable that has been in his family for over 70 years. He is best known for his work with A.C.'s Viking, the 1962 Hambletonian winner. He bought Fresh Yankee for $900 and drove her during her two to four-year-old campaigns.

1971

BALDWIN, Ralph
Trainer and Driver
Ralph Baldwin was a trainer with Castleton Farms and later the head trainer for Arden Homestead Stables. He won over $5 million in purses during his career. Some of his victories include the Hambletonian, the Kentucky Futurity and the Colonial. Ralph developed Speedy Scott and Dartmouth.
Also in: Canadian Horse Racing Hall of Fame.

SIMPSON, John
Driver and Administrator
John Simpson has accumulated lifetime earnings of almost $3 million by winning all six races of both Triple Crown series, scoring two Hambletonian victories and three Little Brown Jug triumphs. He has also set 15 major world records and driven 90 2-min. miles. Simpson serves as president and general manager of the Hanover Shoe Farm.

1972

HODGINS, Clint
Trainer and Driver
Clint has had 2000 wins and earned nearly $6 million in purses since the U.S. Trotting Association began keeping records in 1939. He has had 42 2-min. miles during his career. Some of the horses he drove are Proximity, Adios Butler, Bye Bye Byrd and Sing Away Herbert.
Also in: Canadian Horse Racing Hall of Fame.

1974

BEISSINGER, Howard
Trainer and Driver
Howard Beissinger drove Lindy's Pride to win the Yonkers Futurity, Kentucky Futurity, Hambletonian, Dexter

Cup and the Colonial, taking trotting's Big Five in 1969. He developed Speedy Crown and Tarport Lib, and drove Entrepreneur to the two-year-old record time of 1:56.4.

CAMERON, Adelbert
Trainer and Driver
Adelbert Cameron recorded over 1200 wins, including the Hambletonian three times and the Little Brown Jug. He earned over $4 million in purses and drove 49 2-min. miles.

DUNNIGAN, James
Administrator
James Dunnigan has helped found three race tracks and is currently chairman of the board at Los Alamitos, carrying on a harnass racing tradition started by his father.

VAN LENNEP, Frederick
Owner and Administrator
Frederick Van Lennep owns Castleton Farms. He is director of the U.S. Trotting Association, president of the Harness Tracks of America, director of the Hambletonian Society, president of Wolverine and Pampano Park raceways, vice president of the Grand Circuit, chairman of the board of American Horse Council and a trustee of the Hall of Fame of the Trotter.

1975

FILION, Herve
Owner, Trainer and Driver
Born February 1, 1940, in Angers, Que, Can; raised in a farming community; one of ten children; raced for the first time at age 9, won for the first time at age 12; wife Barbara Ann; three children; bought his own helicopter to get to races; owner of Capital Hill Farm.

During his career, Filion has won over 5000 races and nearly $16 million in purses. One day he completed 20 races, afternoon and evening. Some of his well-known horses include Southhampton V, Otaro Hanover, Isle of Wight, Keystone Pebble and Nancy Isle. Filion received the U.S. Harness Writers 1973 Proximity Award and the HTA's Driver of the Year Award from 1969 through 1972. He has also received the Medal of Honor from the Canadian Prime Minister and the Lou Marsh Trophy.
Also in: Canada's Sports Hall of Fame and Canadian Horse Racing Hall of Fame.

GERRY, Elbridge Thomas "Ebby"
Administrator
Born November 22, 1908 in New York City; father Robert Livingston Gerry in real estate; mother Cornelia Harriman Gerry; B.A. from Harvard University 1931; wife Majorie Y. Kane of Long Island, married May 21, 1932; three children, Elbridge, Jr, Peter G. and Marjorie K; banker.

Ebby Gerry has been active in harness racing for 40 years. He was New York State's first harness racing commissioner in 1940. Positions held include treasurer of the U.S. Trotting Association, president and director of the Standardbred Owners Association, director of the Hambletonian Society, vice president and director of the Orange County Driving Park Association and a founder and treasurer of the Hall of Fame of the Trotters. Gerry is also a partner in the Arden Homestead Stables, which have produced many great champions.

National Cutting Horse Association Hall of Fame

FORT WORTH, TEXAS

Mailing Address: P.O. Box 12155, 76116. Tel. (817) 244-6188. *Contact:* Zack T. Wood, Jr, Secy.-Treas. *Location:* 4704 Benbrook Hwy. (Hwy. 377), 20 mi. E. of Dallas, S. of Corswell Air Force Base, in S.W. area of city. *Admission:* Free 8:30 to 4:30 daily, closed weekends and holidays. *Personnel:* James Reno, Pres; Samuel Wilson, V. Pres; Zack T. Wood, Jr, Secy.-Treas; 15-mem. exec. comt. *Nearby Halls of Fame:* Texas Rangers (Waco, 70 mi. S.), Heritage, Softball (Oklahoma City, Okla, 145 mi. N.), Wrestling (Stillwater, Okla, 220 mi. N.E.).

An idea presented to the Executive Committee of the National Cutting Horse Association (NCHA) blossomed in 1962 when the first members were inducted into the Hall of Fame. The Hall honors cutting horses and nonprofessional riders who have earned over $35,000 in association-approved events. A cutting horse is valued for his ability to enter a herd of cattle, cut an animal from the herd and prevent that animal's return to the herd, whether it be for medical attention, relocation to another pasture or transportation to market. The Association's objective is the development of a standard method under which all cutting horse contests could be conducted in an equitable manner. Encouragement of fair play among contestants and the performance of well-trained horses are of top priority to the NCHA. The Hall of Fame is located in the conference room of the Association's home office. On display are plaques and pictures of the award's recipients. In addition, each horse and person annually inducted in the Hall is publicly recognized in December of the year in which they reach this plateau and further remembered in a résumé of their achievements in the Association's magazine. This non-profit organization receives its financial backing from member dues.

Members: 38 as of January 1, 1977. Horses and persons are inducted automatically upon reaching the $35,000 mark in nonprofessional cutting horse competition that has been approved by the Association. A 15-member executive committee and its officers oversees the Hall of Fame.

1962 BOOGER RED. Owner Manuel Kulwin, Chicago, Ill.

MARION'S GIRL. Owner Marion Flynt, Midland, Tex.

MISS NANCY BAILEY. Owner Bob Burton, Arlington, Tex.

POCO LENA. Owner Skipper Cattle Co, Longview, Tex.

POCO MONA. Owner Orange Rice Milling Co, Orange, Tex.

POCO STAMPEDE. Owner Mrs. G. F. Rhodes, Abilene, Tex.

SANDHILL CHARLIE. Owner Slim Trent, Fallon, Nev.

SLATS DAWSON. Owner George J. Pardi, Uvalde, Tex.

SNIPPER W. Owner Primo Stables, Victoria, Tex.

1963 LITTLE TOM W. Owner Don Strain, White River, S. Dak.

MISS ELITE. Owner Gabe McCall, Aurora, Colo.

1965 HOLLYWOOD CAT. Owner Louis Dorfman, Dallas, Tex.

HOPPEN. Owner Del Jay Associates, Ohio and Wichita Falls, Tex.

1966 DOLLY BRIAN. Owner R. L. "Sonny" Chance, Houston, Tex.

HOLLYWOOD LIN. Owner Dave and Jane Gage, Wichita Falls, Tex.

VEGAS BOY. Owner Walt Gardner, Las Vegas, Nev.

1967 SENOR GEORGE. Owner Senor George Enterprises, Mt. Clemens, Mich.

1968 HEART 109. Owner Sonny Braman, Shaker Heights, Ohio.

SNAPPY DUN. Owner Edgar R. Brown, Fort Pierce, Fla.

STARDUST DESIRE. Owner Douglas Lake Cattle Co, Douglas Lake, B.C, Can.

1969 ALICE STAR. Owner, Houston Clinton, Burnett, Tex.

PATTY CONGER. Owner, E. H. Mooers, Richmond, Va.

SWEN MISS 16. Owner, L. N. White, Chiefland, Fla.

1970 CHICKASHA DAN. Owner, Casey Cantrell, Nara Visa, N. Mex.

JOSE UNO. Owner, John Bradford, Gadsden, Ala.

ROYAL CHESS. Owner, Clyde Bauer, Victoria, Tex.

1971 FIZZABAR. Owner, Don Dodge, Marysville, Calif.

GANDY'S TIME. Owner, Jim Lee, Iowa Park, Tex.

PEPPY SAN. Owner, Douglas Lake Cattle Co, Douglas Lake, B.C, Can.

1972 MR. HOLEY SOX. Owner, J. T. Fisher, Bridgeport, Tex.

1973 SUGAR VAQUERO. Owner, Sandy Currie and Glendon Johnson's Brazos Bend Ranch, Houston, Tex.

1974 MR. SAN PEPPY. Owner, Agnew & Welch, Leese-King Ranch, Kingsville, Tex.

1975 CHICO GANN. Owner, Andy Nored, Bowie, Tex.

1976 GAGE, David. Rider.

KINGSTREAM. Owner David Gage, Wichita Falls, Tex.

MARBO McCUE. Owner Jimmy Orrell, Monticello, Ark.

MILNER, Jim. Rider.

ROSE, Carol. Rider.

National Jockeys Hall of Fame

BALTIMORE, MARYLAND

Mailing Address: Pimlico Race Course, 21215. Tel. (301) 542-9400. *Contact:* Sam Siciliano, Public Relations Dir. *Location:* Off Northern Pkwy. in the city of Baltimore, W. of Fall Expwy, (I83), E. of Reisterstown Rd, N.W. of the Druid Hill Zoo; 37 mi. N.E. of Washington, D.C. *Admission:* Track admission fees; open during racing events for 60 days prior to May 30. *Personnel:* Samuel P. Siciliano, Public Relations Dir. *Nearby Halls of Fame:* Lacrosse (Baltimore), Golf (Valley Forge, Pa, 100 mi. N.E.), Heritage, Music (New York, N.Y, 193 mi. N.E.).

The National Jockeys Hall of Fame was founded in 1955 by the Maryland Jockey Club and is permanently quartered at Pimlico Race Course in the Clubhouse Dining Room. The Hall was established to honor the nation's leading jockeys for their expertise in horse handling. Elections to the National Jockeys Hall of Fame began in 1955 and continued until the Hall was destroyed by fire in 1966. It was not until 1975 that the Hall of Fame again began selecting members to fill its ranks. The collection of portraits, one of each member, has been repainted by the original artist, Henry Cooper of Baltimore. Pimlico Race Course is the home of the Preakness Stakes, "the middle Jewel in the coveted Triple Crown." On Preakness day the magnificent Woodlawn Vase, symbol of Preakness victory, is on display in the clubhouse. The priceless 115-year-old ornate silver vase is 34 in. tall and weighs nearly 30 lbs. A gift shop is open to the public during racing events, offering racing mementos, jewelry, publications and Preakness souvenirs.

Members: 24 as of 1977. Membership in the Hall of Fame is limited to jockeys. The criterion for selection is simple: he must be the best all-around jockey in the nation. Each year the Maryland Jockey Club selects five top jockeys as nominees. A selection committee made up of racing's leaders (i.e, presidents and chairpersons of racing associations) vote to enshrine one of the five nominees in the Hall of Fame.

1955

ARCARO, Eddie

Jockey

Born 1916 in Cincinnati, Ohio; lived most of his early life in Newport, Ky; Triple Crown 1941 and 1948; retired in 1961; now a businessman.

In 1938 Eddie Arcaro, Calumet Farm jockey, won his first Kentucky Derby on Lawrin. He went on to win four more, on Whirlaway in 1941, Citation in 1948, Hill Gail in 1952 and Hoap Jr. in 1945. Arcaro also took the Belmont and the Preakness, six times each. He won the Triple Crown twice, in 1941 on Whirlaway and in 1948 on Citation. His other mounts include Kelso, Bold Ruler and Assault. At the time of his retirement, Arcaro had won 4779 races, finished second 3807 times and third 3302 times in his 24,092 rides, earning $30,039,543 in purses. Arcaro believes that Citation was the best horse he ever rode.
Also in: Racing Hall of Fame, and UNICO National Athletic Hall of Fame (Italian).

SANDE, Earl

Jockey

Born 1898; Triple Crown 1930; died 1968.

Earl Sande stands out as the only jockey ever to have a poem written about him. Sande won three Kentucky Derbys, one Preakness and five Belmonts. Earl Sande is one of seven others to have won a Triple Crown. He was national money-winning champion in 1921, 1923 and 1927. His mounts included Gallant Fox, Zev and Flying Ebony.
Also in: Racing Hall of Fame, and Arizona Horse Racing Hall of Fame.

WOOLF, George "Iceman"

Jockey

Died January 3, 1946, at age 31.

Woolf was racing's first free-lance stakes riding specialist. For three straight years George Woolf was aboard the winner of the Belmont Futurity: Occupation in 1942, Occupy in 1943 and Pavot in 1944. He won the first three runnings of the Hollywood Gold Cup on Seabiscuit in 1938, Kayak II in 1939 and Challedon in 1940; also took three consecutive victories in the Havre de Grace Handicap, 1938–1940. The Kentucky Derby was the only one of America's major stakes in which he could not take a first. During his 18-year career, Woolf compiled 721 victories from 3784 mounts, earning $2,856,125 in purses. At the Santa Anita of 1946, Woolf was fatally injured when his head struck the inner railing of the track as he fell from the stumbling Please Me.
Also in: Canada's Sports Hall of Fame, Canadian Horse Racing Hall of Fame and Racing Hall of Fame.

1956

LONGDEN, John

Jockey

Born 1907 in Wakefield, England; father a miner in Calgary, Alta; during youth rode horses in the county fair doing stunts; Triple Crown Winner 1943.

John Longden was the "winningest" jockey in the world until Bill Shoemaker supplanted his 6032 top mark for winners. His career was highlighted by his Triple Crown victory in 1943 astride Count Fleet. During his career Longden finished second in 4914 races and was third in 4373 runs. His total number of mounts reached 32,406 and his earnings reached $24,665,800. As a trainer Longden saddled Majestic Prince to win the Kentucky Derby and Preakness of 1969, only to see him finish second in the Belmont. In 1973 Longden's homebred Money Lender won the California Breeder's Champion Stakes.
Also in: Canada's Sports Hall of Fame, Canadian Horse Racing Hall of Fame and Racing Hall of Fame.

MURPHY, Isaac

Jockey

Born 1861 on David Tanner Farm in Fayette County, Ky; father James Burns a freeman; educated by a black trainer; later took his grandfather's name, Murphy; well respected for his honesty, kindness and race record; weakened by years of strict, unsupervised diet, died February 12, 1896 in Lexington at age 36.

Isaac Murphy rode his first winner in 1876 in Lexington, Ky. He went on to become the first rider to win the Kentucky Derby three times. He holds a career record of 628 wins in 1412 races, for a lifetime average of 44 percent. In the late 1960s his grave was moved to a site near Man o' War's statue, to honor the man who said, "Just be honest and you'll have no trouble and plenty of money.
Also in: Racing Hall of Fame.

SLOAN, Tod

Jockey

Born 1874 in Kikomo, Ind; named James Forman but nicknamed "toad," then Tod by father; orphaned at five; adopted by Mrs. D. G. Bouser; at age 17 traveled with carnival balloonist; after racing career ended, tried the movies; died penniless in 1933 in California.

Tod Sloan began riding in the Midwest, then rode for James R. Keene and William C. Whitney. He is credited with creating the short stirrup leathers style of riding, with the jockey crouched over the withers of the horse. This style was first called "monkey-on-a-stick." In 1897 Sloan rode 137 winners in 369 mounts and in 1898 he had 166 winners in 362 mounts. At the peak of his career he moved to England to become even more famous as a rider, changed his name to J. Todhunter Sloan, and became a big spender and fancy dresser.
Also in: Racing Hall of Fame.

1957

ATKINSON, Ted

Jockey

Born 1916 in Toronto, Ont; neat and well-dressed at all times; a gentleman on and off the track; rode Handicap Triple Crown winner.

Ted Atkinson was jockey for Wheatley and Greentree Stables. He was the nation's leading race rider in 1944 with 286 winners and again in 1946 with 233 victories. In 1949 Ted was twice fined for hand-slapping his two-year-old horses. The highlight of "Teddy Boy's" career was riding Tom Fool for Greentree Stable. Tom Fool became the second horse in history to win the Handicap Triple Crown: the Brooklyn, Metropolitan and Suburban. Other winners he rode include Nashua, Bold Ruler, War Relic, Hall of Fame, Snow Goose, My Request, Olympia, One Hitter, Devil Diver and Coaltown. During his career he scored 3795 victories, 3300 seconds and 2970 thirds. His mounts earned $17,449,360. After his retirement from riding, Ted became an official.
Also in: Racing Hall of Fame.

MILLER, Walter
Jockey
Born 1890 on the East Side of New York City; father a cobbler; real name Goldstein.

When Walter Miller first hit the track in 1903 he attracted the attention of Sunny Jim Fitzsimmons. They went to California where Walter gained experience with Sunny Jim as his agent. In 1906 he won 388 races, a record for that time. His most impressive scores were in the Brooklyn Handicap, Dwyer, Alabama, Preakness, Toboggan, Belmont, Futurity, Saratoga Cup and the Travers. When excess weight caught up with him, he transferred his activities to Europe and Australia, though with little success. During his short career Miller rode more than 1000 mounts.
Also in: Racing Hall of Fame.

WORKMAN, Raymond "Sonny"
Jockey
Born 1909 in Hoboken, N.J; raised in Washington, D.C; in later years businessman in real estate in D.C; died 1966 after long illness at age 57.

Sonny was jockey for Harry Payne Whitney, Cornelius Vanderbilt Whitney and Alfred G. Vanderbilt. Workman's ride on Equipoise in the 1930 Futurity has been billed as the "most spectacular race in decades." C. V. Whitney's Top Flight was guided to championship recognition in 1931 and 1932 as best filly by Workman. He was also aboard Whichone and Now What during their top years. He won the 1928 Preakness on Victorian. During his 15-year career, Workman compiled 1169 victories, 870 seconds and 785 thirds for total earnings of $2,862,667. He retired at age 31 to become a successful businessman.
Also in: Racing Hall of Fame.

1958

FATOR, Laverne
Jockey
Born 1900 in Idaho; rode cow ponies as a youth; in 1936, in delirium plunged to death from hospital window.

Laverne Fator rode for Rancocas Stable. He was third in the national standings his first year of riding, 1919. He was America's leading money-winning jockey in 1925 and 1926, when he rode 143 winners from 511 horses. Fator won back-to-back Futurities at Belmont Park in 1925 with Pompey and in 1926 with Scapa Flow. During his 13-year career he rode over 1000 winners and earned in excess of $2.5 million.
Also in: Racing Hall of Fame.

GARRISON, Edward R.
Jockey
Born 1868 in New Haven, Conn; blacksmith's apprentice at age 12; worked as stable hand three years under Father Bill Daly; died 1930 at age 64.

Edward Garrison first rode at the age of 14 for Father Bill Daly, later for August Belmont. He became famous for his come-from-behind finishes. "Snapper Jack" dominated horse racing for 15 years. Garrison won the 1891 Belmont Stakes with Foxford. In 1893 he managed to delay the American Derby for 90 mins, until everyone was tired, and then brought Boundless home for a win of $50,000. During his career he won nearly 700 races and over $2 million in purses.
Also in: Racing Hall of Fame.

McLAUGHLIN, James
Jockey
Born 1861 in Conn; a quiet youth; grew a handlebar mustache; started in racing by walking horses; died 1927.

In 1878 Jimmy McLaughlin won on three mounts at Nashville. In 1885 he won on five mounts at Monmouth. It was during the 1880s that Jimmy started his rise to fame, winning 67 stakes races. He was six-time winner of the Belmont Stakes on horses owned by the Dwyer Brothers. McLaughlin also won the Kentucky Derby on Hindoo in 1881 and the Preakness on Tecumseh in 1885. Other well-known stakes events won by McLaughlin include the Alabama, the Brookdale Handicap, the Carlton, Champagne, Clark, Dwyer Stakes, Flash, the Futurity, Hudson, Ladies Handicap and the Lawrence Realization.
Also in: Racing Hall of Fame.

1959

GARNER, Mack
Jockey
Born in Centerville, Iowa; died of a heart attack October 28, 1936.

Garner won the Belmont twice on Blue Larkspur in 1929 and on Hurry-off in 1933. He won the 1934 Kentucky Derby with Cavalcade, and was the nation's leading jockey in purses and winners in 1915. During his career he scored 1346 victories; his mounts earned $2,419,647 in purses.
Also in: Racing Hall of Fame.

SHILLING, Carroll "Cal"
Jockey
Born on a ranch in Texas; died in 1950 at age 64; his body was found under a horse van at Belmont Park.

Sam Hildreth said of Cal Shilling in his book *The Spell of the Turf,* "I have never seen a better jockey than this boy. He had an almost uncanny ability to break a two year old away from the post; his judgment of the pace made you think he must have a stopwatch ticking before

his very eyes, a seat so light that he was like a feather on a horse's back and a knack for getting every ounce out of his mount." Cal rode for E. R. Thomas, Sam Hildreth and J. K. L. Ross. Shilling was denied his license in 1912 for rough riding, so he turned to developing the stable of J. K. L. Ross. Guy Bedwell, Ross and other prominent horsemen continued to fight for Cal's reinstatement, until Bedwell lost his license. Shilling, sour on the world, took to drinking.
Also in: Racing Hall of Fame.

SHOEMAKER, William Lee "The Shoe"
Jockey
Born August 19, 1931, in Fabens, Tex; National Jockey Champion, 1950, 1953, 1954, 1958 and 1959.

Willie Shoemaker was five times national jockey champion in the United States. He led the nation's jockeys in terms of money won ten times and in a single season topped the $2 million mark in 1957 and every year thereafter. In 1953 he rode a record 485 winners and won more than 80 races worth over $100,000 each. In 1970 he broke Longden's record of 6032 wins. Shoemaker became one of the best-known jockeys in the history of racing. At 4 ft. 11 in. and 100 lbs, he is an ambassador for thoroughbred racing.
Also in: Arizona Horse Racing Hall of Fame and Racing Hall of Fame.

1960

LOFTUS, John
Jockey
Johnny Loftus was the rider of the very first Triple Crown winner (1919), Sir Barton, owned by Commander J. K. L. Ross. Loftus was also the primary jockey for Man o' War, riding the great horse to stakes wins in the Keene Memorial, Youthful, Hudson, Tremont, United States Hotel, Grand Union, Hopeful and the Futurity. Loftus was riding Man o' War for the great upset at the Sanford. Some blame Loftus, while others maintain that it was simply bad luck.
Also in: Racing Hall of Fame.

1961

McATEE, Linus
Jockey
Born in Secaucus, N.J; moved to Baltimore, Md. as a child; called "Pony" by the press; retired in 1932 to the golf links.

Linus McAtee rode for Captain William Presgrave, J. K. L. Ross, R. L. Gerry, Harry Payne Whitney and George D. Widener. For Ross he won his first major stakes, the Preakness in 1916 with Damrosch. His first of two Kentucky Derby victories was aboard Whiskery in 1927 and the second was in 1929 on Clyde Van Dusen, the diminutive son of Man o' War. For Widener he won three Futurities and Champagnes, as well as three Flash Stakes, four Astaritas and three Saratoga Specials. His mounts included Twenty Grand, Exterminator, James Town, Bateau and Mother Goose. McAtee rode his first winner in 1914 and was the leading rider by 1928 with $301,295 in purses. Even though rated as the best jockey in the country in 1932, McAtee retired.
Also in: Racing Hall of Fame.

NOTTER, Joseph A.
Jockey
Born 1890 in Brooklyn, N.Y; rode his first winner at age 13 in Morris Park; Handicap Triple Crown 1913; died April 10, 1973 in Brentwood, N.Y. at age 83.

Joe Notter was the first person to ride and train winners of the Belmont Futurity, including Maskette, Thunderer and Kerry Patch. Notter rode Whisk Broom II when he won the Handicap Triple Crown in 1913, as well as Regret when she became the only filly ever to win the Kentucky Derby. Riding for James R. Keene, he saddled Colin, Peter Pan, Sweep and Pennant. In all, Notter was credited with riding the winners of 56 major stakes, including Fair Play, Celt, Helmet, and Borrow. He retired to training in 1918 and retired from racing completely in 1938.
Also in: Racing Hall of Fame.

1962

BROOKS, Steve
Jockey
During his career Brooks rode 4447 winners and his horses earned $18,214,947 in purses. His rides include such top horses as Round Table, Citation, Ponder, Princequillo, Wistful, Stymie and Armed. He won the Kentucky Derby with Ponder in 1949 and was ranked with the top jockeys of that time. Brooks rode Citation to a win in the Hollywood Gold Cup in 1951, making Citation the first million-dollar winner.
Also in: Racing Hall of Fame.

1963

HARTACK, William John
Jockey
Born 1932 in Johnstown, Pa.

Hartack equaled the all-time record of five Kentucky Derby victories. He was the first rider to win $3 million in a year (1957) as he recorded 43 stakes victories. At the age of 40 he became the fifth jockey in history to win more than 4000 races. Because of his unwillingness to compromise owners and trainers, he felt that "Nobody gives me a mount unless they think they have to."
Also in: Racing Hall of Fame.

1964

ADAMS, John
Jockey
Born 1915 in Carlisle, Ark; son J. R. Adams rider; grandson J. K. Adams rider on California fair circuit; mother refused to grant permission for him to become jockey; lied about age so no signature was required.

Marble Girl was John's first winner at Riverside Park in 1934. In 1939 he won the Santa Anita Handicap on C. S. Howard's Kayak II. As first-call jockey for Hasty House Farm, Adams rode Hasty Road, winner of the 1954 Preakness, Sea O'Erin, Stan, Platan and Rhue. Adams' 24-year riding career ended in 1958 with a record of 3270 firsts, 2704 seconds and 2635 thirds on 20,159 mounts for winnings of $9,743,109.
Also in: Racing Hall of Fame.

1965

WESTROPE, Jackie
Jockey
Born 1918, Jackie Westrope died at the age of 40 after having won 2467 races during his career. His mounts earned more than $8 million.

1975

PINCAY, Laffit, Jr.
Jockey
Laffit Pincay raced mainly in California. He was the nation's leading money-winning jockey in 1970 through 1974. The U.S. champion rode 1627 mounts as of 1971 with 380 victories, 288 seconds and 214 thirds. Pincay received the coveted Eclipse Award three times.
Also in: Racing Hall of Fame.

1976

BAEZA, Braulio
Jockey
Braulio Baeza was the nation's leading money-winning jockey from 1965 through 1968 and again in 1975. He was the recipient of the Eclipse Award in 1972 and 1975.
Also in: Racing Hall of Fame.

Racing Hall of Fame

SARATOGA SPRINGS, NEW YORK

Mailing Address: Union Ave, 12866. Tel. (518) 584-0400. *Contact*: Elaine E. Mann, Dir. *Location*: From New York City take the New York State Thruway to exit 24 at Albany-Northway (No. 87) to Union Ave. exit 14. Approx. 30 mi. N. of Albany and 25 mi. N.E. of Amsterdam. *Admission*: Free 9:30 to 5 daily; 12 to 5 weekends; August, 9:30 to 7 daily. *Personnel*: John W. Hanes, Chmn; Charles E. Mather II, Pres; four V.Pres; Paul R. Rouillard, Secy.-Treas; Elaine E. Mann, Dir; 43-mem. Bd of Trustees. *Nearby Halls of Fame*: Baseball (Cooperstown, 70 mi. S.W.), Harness Racing (Goshen, 115 mi. S.W.), Heritage, Music (New York City, 160 mi. S.W.), Flight (Elmira, 165 mi. S.W.), Horseshoe Pitching (Corning, 175 mi. S.W.).

The National Museum of Racing was founded in 1950 and formally dedicated in August of 1955 along with the Hall of Fame. It is located directly across from Saratoga Racetrack in a handsome Georgian-colonial design brick structure. The Museum is the country's oldest thoroughbred racing center and is recognized as the capital of horse racing in America. This privately supported Museum was established to collect and preserve all materials and articles associated with the origin, history and development of horse racing and the breeding of the Thoroughbred horse. The first president of the Museum was Cornelius Vanderbilt Whitney, who served from 1950 to 1953. He was succeeded by Walter M. Jeffords from 1953 to 1960. It was during this time that the Walter M. Jeffords Memorial wing was added (1960) and that the patrons of the Turf Gallery built an addition to the Museum to house portraits of distinguished figures in the sport. Approximately 250 oil paintings are on exhibit. These include paintings of Man o' War, Citation, War Admiral, Domino, American Eclipse, Kelso and many more. The artists represented include Ben Marshall, Franklin B. Voss, Rembrandt Peale, Sir Alfred J. Mummings, Henry Stull and Richard Stone Reeves, as well as an entire gallery devoted to paintings by Edward Troye. On display are 200 sets of famous racing colors, bronze statuary and gold and silver trophies won by famous horses. The visitor will also find the saddle and boots worn by Johnny Loftus on Man o' War, the auctioneer's gavel used when Man o' War was sold, jockey scales and a variety of other memorabilia of the sport's earliest days. Special exhibits and films relating to horse racing are shown during August, the racing season. A small souvenir and gift shop specializing in "horsey" articles, jewelry, prints and books on horses and horse racing is open to those visiting the Museum.

Members: 166 as of 1976. Selections for the Hall of Fame are made by a nominating committee of three or more persons appointed by the Executive Committee of the National Museum of Racing, Inc. The voting committee is made up of approximately 100 members who are sportswriters or radio and television announcers. They are from all sections of the country. Candidates are selected from three categories: Horses retired from racing; a possible total of five can be elected each year from the categories of old time and modern, male and female flat horses and one steeplechase horse. Trainers who have either retired or have served over 20 years in U.S. racing; one modern and one old-timer may be chosen. One jockey who has retired or served for over 20 years in the United States. The new members are installed in August of each year at the National Museum of Racing in Saratoga Springs, N.Y.

1955

BEN BRUSH
Horse
Born 1893; bay colt; sire Bramble; dam Roseville; bred by Catesby Woodford and Ezekiel F. Clay; owned by Ed

Brown and H. Eugene Leigh, and Michael F. Dwyer; trained by Ed Brown and Hardy Campbell; sired Broomstick, Sweep, Delhi, Pebbles, Theodore Cook and Vandergift; died 1918.

1895	16 starts,	13 wins,	$21,398 earnings
1896	8 starts,	4 wins,	26,755 earnings
1897	16 starts,	7 wins,	17,055 earnings
	40 starts,	24 wins,	$65,208 earnings

Ben Brush won his first five races as a two-year-old, then lost three and finally picked the Holly Handicap. After that race he was sold to Michael Dwyer for more than ten times what he was bought for as a yearling. Ben Brush continued victorious in the Prospect Handicap and the Nursery, Albany and Champagne Stakes. He began his three-year-old season by capturing the Kentucky Derby in a close finish. Next he took the Shutte Stakes in a runoff. He also won the Buckeye Stakes and the Latonia Derby. As a four-year-old Ben Brush had seven victories including the Suburban Handicap, the Omnium Handicap, the Brighton Handicap and the Citizen's Handicap. During his racing career Ben Brush finished out of the money only six times in 40 starts. After his racing career he was established as one of the leading sires of the early twentieth century.

BOSTON "Old White Nose"

Horse

Born 1833; chestnut colt; sire Timoleon; dam Daughter of Alderman; bred by John Wickham; owned by Nathaniel Rives, Col. W. R. Johnson and James Long; trained by John Belcher and Arthur Taylor; sired Lexington and Lecomte; fiery and evil-tempered; some recommended castration or death, neither was carried out; blind and arthritic during final years; died 1850.

1836	3 starts,	2 wins,	$ 700 earnings
1837	4 starts,	4 wins,	2,000 earnings
1838	11 starts,	11 wins,	8,900 earnings
1839	9 starts,	8 wins,	19,300 earnings
1840	7 starts,	7 wins,	14,700 earnings
1841	5 starts,	4 wins,	2,900 earnings
1842	5 starts,	3 wins,	2,400 earnings
1843	1 start,	1 win,	800 earnings
	45 starts,	40 wins,	$51,700 earnings

Boston's first race as a three-year-old was a success until he stopped dead and refused to move. Another of his favorite tricks was to roll over and knock off his rider. Many long battles with trainers ensued. Boston won his last two races of his first season and went on to have an outstanding career of 45 starts and 40 wins. Boston proved to be an excellent stud, but was given the opportunity only during his last few years.

BURCH, William P.

Trainer

Born 1846 in Cheraw, S.C; as a teenager, in the Confederate cavalry; sons Preston and Selby horsemen; grandson Elliot horseman; died at Saratoga 1926 at age 80.

In 1878 William P. Burch offered an opportunity on the track to a postal clerk who was to become one of the greatest horsemen in history, Andrew Jackson Joyner. Burch also helped Gwyn Tompkins, eventually a great trainer, and George M. Odom, the only man to ride and train Belmont winners. William Burch distinguished himself as one of the South's foremost horsemen and one of the nation's most celebrated trainers. Among the horses he developed were Biggonet, Grey Friar, Telie Doe, General Mart Geary, Burch, Wade Hampton and My Own.

DOMINO

Horse

Born 1891; brown colt; sire Himyar; dam Mannie Gray; bred by Maj. Barak G. Thomas; owned by James R. Keene, Foxhall P. Keene; trained by Billy Lakeland; sired only 19 foals, including Commando; died from overfeeding in 1897.

1893	9 starts,	9 wins,	$170,790 earnings
1894	8 starts,	6 wins,	19,150 earnings
1895	8 starts,	4 wins,	3,610 earnings
	25 starts,	19 wins,	$193,550 earnings

Domino won all nine of his two-year-old races, including the Great American Stakes, the Great Eclipse and the Great Trial Stakes. At three he won his first race, the Withers Stakes, and was then declared lame and rested for two months. He came back to win the Flying Stakes, the Ocean Handicap and the Culver Stakes. At four Domino won four of his eight races, including the Coney Island Handicap and the Sheepshead Bay Handicap. He retired with earnings of $193,550.

FATOR, Laverne

Jockey

See entry in National Jockeys Hall of Fame, 1958.

GARRISON, Edward R.

Jockey

See entry in National Jockeys Hall of Fame, 1958.

HANOVER

Horse

Born 1884; chestnut colt; sire Hindoo; dam Bourbon Belle; bred by Catesby Woodford, Ezekiel F. Clay; owned by Philip J. Dwyer, Michael F. Dwyer; trained by Frank McCabe; sired Hamburg, Halma, Yankee and Half Time; led sire list in 1895 through 1898; died 1899.

1886	3 starts,	3 wins,	$ 14,335 earnings
1887	27 starts,	20 wins,	87,632 earnings
1888	3 starts,	0 wins,	1,450 earnings
1889	17 starts,	9 wins,	15,470 earnings
	50 starts,	32 wins,	$118,887 earnings

The Dwyer Brothers bought Hanover for $1,350 at an 1885 auction, but let him stand by while they raced their hopeful, Tremont. Tremont broke down and Hanover, at three, brought home 20 victories for 27 starts. He won the Carlton Stakes, the Brooklyn Handicap, the Withers, the Belmont Stakes, the Brooklyn Derby, the Swift Stakes, the Tidal Stakes, the Coney Island Derby, the Emporium, the Spindrift, Lorillard, Stockton, Barnegat and Stevens Stakes. At four he went lame in his right forehoof and the Dwyers had the nerve cut. He came back at five and won 9 of 17 races. At six Hanover was sold to Col. Milton Young for stud duty at McGrathiana Stud.

HEALEY, Thomas Jefferson

Trainer

Born 1866; deeply religious; none but the most essential tasks was done on Sunday; everyone was sent to church; died in 1944 at age 78.

Thomas Healey was one of the great trainers during racing's rebuilding era. He trained Olambala, a stakes winner; Campfire, leading money winner of 1916; and Pillory, Preakness winner in 1922 for owner Richard T. Wilson. Under the pink and blue colors of Walter J. Salmon, Healey won with the evil-tempered Display, Vigil, Dr. Freeland, Careful and Step Lightly. Over the years Healey monopolized the Preakness, winning five renewals from 1901 to 1929. After 1931 he took a division of the Whitney Stable and developed Top Flight, which won seven stakes as a two-year-old. He also trained Equipoise and Chocolate Soldier. In 1939 he became an official in the New York tracks and continued to serve as such until his death.

HILDRETH, Samuel

Trainer

Born 1866; earned reputation for being a hard-nose; displayed no traces of sentiment; horses were business, died 1929.

Sam Hildreth was a master of judging both men and horses. He trained five horses that won over $100,000 each: Zev, Mad Hatter, Grey Lag, Mad Play and King James. He was leading money-winning trainer for nine seasons, as well as America's leading owner for three consecutive seasons. Hildreth dominated the handicapping scene, winning the Suburban five times, the Brooklyn seven times, the Saratoga three times, the Metropolitan five times and the Empire City and Mad Hatter each twice. In addition, he won the Belmont Stakes more often than any trainer in history except James Rowe.

HINDOO

Horse

Born April 1878; bay colt; sire Virgil; dam Florence; bred by Daniel Swigert; owned by Daniel Swigert, Philip J. Dwyer, Michael F. Dwyer; trained by Lee Paul, Ed Brown, James G. Rowe, Sr; sired Hanover, Sallie McClelland, Buddhist, Hindoocraft and Merry Monarch; died 1899.

1880	9 starts,	7 wins,	$ 9,800	earnings
1881	20 starts,	18 wins,	49,100	earnings
1882	6 starts,	5 wins,	12,975	earnings
	35 starts,	30 wins,	$71,875	earnings

Hindoo won his first race and continued on to win seven consecutive races. The Dwyer Brothers bought Hindoo for $15,000. As a three-year-old Hindoo scored 18 consecutive triumphs. At four years old he won five of six races before a tendon problem forced him out of training. The Dwyers traded the stallion to Col. E. F. Clay for $9,000 and a filly named Miss Woodford. Hindoo was a succesful stud and Miss Woodford became the first $100,000 winner in America.

JOYNER, Andrew Jackson

Trainer

Born 1860 in a small town in North Carolina; worked in the post office in Weldon, N.C, in 1879; died September 1, 1943.

It is said that William P. Burch gave Joyner his start in racing. Burch noticed Joyner's racing prints hung in the post office, took him over to a nearby track and got him started. In 1905 Joyner signed with Haggin and Paget. That year he took Cairngorm to Preakness victory, as well as 184 other wins from his stable. Shortly thereafter Joyner went to England for Harry Payne Whitney, with the yearling Wisk Broom II. This horse took the 1913 Suburban Handicap of one and a quarter miles in 2 min. flat. When Joyner returned to the States, he trained and managed for George Widener's Erdenheim Farm. While there he developed Eight Thirty, and captured the Travers, Whitney, Saratoga, Suburban, Metropolitan and Massachusetts Handicaps.

KINGSTON

Horse

Born 1884; brown colt; sire Spendthrift; dam Kapariga; bred by James R. Keene; owned by E. E. Snedeker, J. F. Cushman, Dwyer Brothers, Michael F. Dwyer; trained by E. V. Snedeker, Frank McCabe, Hardy Campbell; sired Ballyhoo Bey, Novelty, Admiration, The Lady, Federal Vulcain, Della Gorra, Ildrim and King's Courier; America's leading sire twice; died 1912.

1886	6 starts,	2 wins,	$ 11,350	earnings
1887	18 starts,	13 wins,	17,850	earnings
1888	14 starts,	10 wins,	17,045	earnings
1889	15 starts,	14 wins,	22,520	earnings
1890	10 starts,	9 wins,	16,890	earnings
1891	21 starts,	15 wins,	26,815	earnings
1892	20 starts,	13 wins,	17,390	earnings
1893	25 starts,	9 wins,	7,660	earnings
1894	9 starts,	4 wins,	2,675	earnings
	138 starts,	89 wins,	$140,195	earnings

Kingston won the Camden and the Select Stakes and finished second four times as a two-year-old. The Dwyers bought him for $12,500 to keep him from perhaps upsetting Hanover's 17-race winning streak. He went on to win 13 of 16 for Dwyers at three, including the Oriole Stakes in which he set an American time record. Kingston won two of his first six races at four and then scored eight consecutive victories. At five Kingston won his first start, lost his second, and then won his remaining 13 starts, setting an American record in the First Special. As a six-year-old he won nine in a row, including his third First Special. Kingston continued to win stakes at seven and eight. When he was retired to stud in 1894, he had surpassed Hanover as America's greatest money earner with $140,195. He was unplaced in only four races during his entire career.

LEXINGTON

Horse

Born 1850; bay colt; sire Boston; dam Alice Carneal; bred by Dr. Elisha Warfield; owned by Richard Ten Broeck; trained by Burbridge's Harry, J. B. Pryor; sired Norfolk, Asteroid, Kentucky, General Duke, Vauxhall, Harry Basset, Tom Bowling, Acrobat, Duke of Magenta, Idlewild, and Sultana; America's leading sire from 1861 until 1875 and two years posthumously; died 1875.

1852	0 starts,	0 wins,	0
1853	5 starts,	4 wins,	$30,600
1854	2 starts,	2 wins,	26,000
	7 starts,	6 wins,	$56,600

Lexington's breeder, Dr. Warfield, thought that the colt at birth looked like John Sartorius' painting of foundation sire Darley Arabian, and decided to name him Darlymey. Darlymey's name changed when he was sold to Richard Ten Broeck to represent Kentucky in the Great State Post Stakes in New Orleans. Lexington won the $20,000 Great State Post Stakes in straight 4-mile heats, defeating Lecomte. After his fourth year, Lexington was retired to stud and was later sold for $15,000 to R. A. Alexander at Woodburn Stud.

LUKE BLACKBURN
Horse
Born 1877; bay colt; sire Bonnie Scotland; dam Mevada; bred by James Franklin, A. C. Franklin; named for Kentucky's governor, Luke Blackburn; owned by S. L. Wartzfeld, Capt. Jim Williams, Dwyer Brothers; trained by Capt. Williams, James G. Rowe, Sr; sired only three stakes winners, the best Proctor Knott; died 1904.

1879	13 starts,	2 wins,	$ 1,985 earnings
1880	24 starts,	22 wins,	46,975 earnings
1881	2 starts,	1 win,	500 earnings
	39 starts,	25 wins,	$49,460 earnings

After placing nine times as a two-year-old, Luke Blackburn was sold to the Dwyers for $2500. He was turned over to trainer Rowe and as a three-year-old, he reeled off seven consecutive victories. In his next race at Gravesend, Luke Blackburn crossed his legs and fell. He came back to go undefeated for the rest of his three-year-old season. That year Luke Blackburn won 22 of 24 races, setting two American records and earning $46,975. Luke Blackburn broke down in his second race of his four-year-old season. The Dwyers sold him to Gen. W. M. Jackson for stud.

MAHER, Daniel
Jockey
Born October 29, 1881, in Hartford, Conn; began riding in Providence, R.I.; moved to England in 1900 and became naturalized citizen; married an English actress; died November 9, 1919, in England.

Danny Maher was champion jockey of the United States in 1898 with 167 winners. In 1900 he won the Metropolitan aboard Ethelbert, as well as the Ladies Handicap with Oneck Queen. In 1899 Maher was aboard the favored Banastar in the Suburban. His loss of that race caused his honor to be questioned. Although he was eventually cleared of all charges, he valued his reputation so highly that he left the United States for England. From 1900 to 1913 he rode 1421 winners from 5624 mounts in England and was hailed as one of the greatest jockeys ever to ride in that country. Some of his horses included Paiute, Bad News, Circero, Rock Sand and Spearmint. The latter three were Epsom Derby winners.

McLAUGHLIN, James
Jockey
See entry in National Jockeys Hall of Fame, 1958.

MILLER, Walter
Jockey
See entry in National Jockeys Hall of Fame, 1957.

MURPHY, Isaac
Jockey
See entry in National Jockeys Hall of Fame, 1956.

ODOM, George M.
Jockey and Trainer
Born 1882; quiet, unassuming man; wore a straw hat; smoked cigars; his brother Bob and son George, Jr, trainers.

Odom is best remebered for being the only person to win the Belmont Stakes as both a rider and a trainer. As a rider he compiled an impressive record of stakes victories in the years from 1899 to 1904 on such runners as Delhi, Banastar and Broomstick. As a trainer his greatest achievement came in 1935 when he saddled Marshall Field's Tintagal to win the Futurity worth $66,450. He also trained for Mrs. W. P. Stewart, Robert L. Gerry, Louis B. Mayer and others. He believed in giving a horse plenty of time between races. Odom's forte was having his horse in top form on a given race day. Because of his expertise in judging horseflesh, he was often called upon to officiate horse shows.

ROGERS, John W.
Trainer
Born 1844; died 1908.

John Rogers is best remembered for his Futurity victory with Artful over the previously unbeaten Sysonby at Sheepshead Bay in 1904; following that loss by five lengths, Sysonby never lost another race. John Rogers launched the Whitney family into racing with Tanya, winner of the 1905 Belmont, and Burgomaster, winner of the Belmont in 1906. Rogers would never let one of his horses carry a single pound of overweight. He would even ride an outside jockey if it would save a few pounds.

ROWE, James, Sr.
Trainer
Born 1857 in Fredericksburg, Va; at age 10 worked a newsstand in a hotel in Richmond, Va; for his first winning ride received a peppermint stick of candy; died 1929 at age 72.

Col. David McDaniel hired Rowe as an apprentice rider at the age of 10. Before he was 15 he had won his first of three consecutive national riding titles. He rode Joe Daniels and Springbok to consecutive Belmont victories. Rowe became a successful trainer for the Dwyer Brothers with horses like Bramble, Runnymede, Luke Blackburn, Hindoo, Miss Woodford, and George Kinney and Panique, both winners of the Belmont. Training for James R. Keene, Rowe had six Belmont winners, including unbeaten Colin, Commando Delhi, Peter Pan, Sweep and Prince Eugene. He also trained for August Belmont and Harry Payne Whitney. Hindoo took the Kentucky Derby and Broomspun the Preakness. At the end of his career Rowe had only one request for his epitaph: "He trained Colin."

SALVATOR
Horse
Born 1886; chestnut colt; sire Prince Charlie; dam Salina; bred by Daniel Swigert; owned by James Ben Ali Haggin; trained By Matthew Byrnes; died 1909.

1888	6 starts,	4 wins,	$ 17,590 earnings
1889	8 starts,	7 wins,	70,450 earnings
1890	5 starts,	5 wins,	25,200 earnings
	19 starts,	16 wins,	$113,240 earnings

As a two-year-old, once Proctor Knott had retired for the season, Salvator won the Flatbush, Maple, Tackahoe and the Titan Stakes. At three he won the Tidal Stakes and the Lawrence Realization. After his third-place finish in the Omnibus Stakes, Salvator never lost another race. As a four-year-old he became a national hero. After winning the Suburban Handicap over Tenny, the two owners arranged a match with each horse carrying 120 lbs. At the wire Salvator won by a nose in new American record time. Later Salvator and Tenny raced again in separate events, against the clock. Salvator again topped Tenny with a record time that stood for 28 years.

SANDE, Earl
Jockey
See entry in National Jockeys Hall of Fame, 1955. *Also in:* Arizona Horse Racing Hall of Fame.

SIR ARCHY
Horse
Born 1805; chestnut colt; sire Diomed; dam Castianira; bred by Col. John Taylor III, Capt. Archibald Randolph; owned by Ralph Wormeley VI, Col. W. R. Johnson; trainers, Thomas Larkin, Arthur Taylor; sired over 50 exceptional foals; died in 1933.

Sir Archy was an average runner until his training was taken over by Arthur Taylor. At four he was a different horse. Sir Archy won four of five races at four. All were 4-mile races. Following the matches, he was purchased for $5000 by General William R. Davie, a Revolutionary War hero and governor of North Carolina. Sir Archy was sent to stud and was an unqualified success. Nearly every good Thoroughbred was closely inbred to this stallion.

SLOAN, Tod
Jockey
See entry in National Jockeys Hall of Fame, 1956.

TARAL, Fred "Dutch Demon"
Jockey
Born 1867; inseparable companion John L. Sullivan, the duo known as Big and Little Casino by the press; rode in Europe until W. W. I, retiring to the United States; died 1925.

Fred Taral commanded top money riding for Walcott, Campbell and Keene. Taral's nickname of Dutch Demon was apparently well deserved. It was the whipping of Domino's flanks that caused the colt to hate the sight of Taral. The horse had to be hooded before Taral could mount him safely. In 1894 Taral swept the Handicap Triple, winning the Metropolitan and Suburban with Ramapoo and took the Brooklyn with Dr. Rice. He also won the Preakness that season on Assignee and took it again in 1895 with Belmar. In 1899 Taral won the Derby on Manuel. He also accounted for most of the major stakes of the time.

TURNER, Nash
Jockey
Born 1881; died 1937.

Nash Turner is best remembered for his riding of the darling of the Gay Nineties, Imp. In 1899 Turner and the black filly won the Suburban Handicap. During his career Nash won many other stakes, including the inaugural of the Debutante Stakes in 1895, two Great Americans, two Saratoga Specials, the Alabama, the Clark, the Flash, the Jerome, the Matron, the National Stallion, the Swift and the Withers. Turner also took the 1900 Belmont Stakes on Eugene Leigh's Ildrim.

WOOLF, George
Jockey
See entry in National Jockeys Hall of Fame, 1955. *Also in:* Canada's Sports Hall of Fame and Canadian Horse Racing Hall of Fame.

1956

ARTFUL
Horse
Born, 1902; brown filly; sire Hamburg; dam Martha II; bred by W. C. Whitney; owned by H. P. Whitney; trained by J. W. Rogers; produced only four foals; died 1927.

1904	5 starts,	3 wins,	$57,805 earnings
1905	3 starts,	3 wins,	23,320 earnings
	8 starts,	6 wins,	81,125 earnings

In the Futurity at Sheepshead Bay, Artful faced the strongest competition ever assembled for the race. Nine of the 15 starters were stakes winners. Artful, carrying 114 lbs, passed front-running Sysonby to take the race by five lengths. Four days later, Artful easily won the Great Filly Stakes as a 1 – 15 favorite. Six weeks later, she won the White Plains Handicap at Morris Park with an additional 16 lbs, setting a world record time of 1:08, not broken until 1954. Shortly thereafter, Artful was bought at auction by Harry Payne Whitney for $10,000. At three years, Artful took three races, one of them the one-and-a-quarter-mile Brighton Handicap. Taking the lead on the first turn, Artful leisurely won her final race. She was sent to Brookdale Stud in New Jersey and later shipped to England.

BELDAME
Horse
Born 1901; chestnut filly; sire Octagon; dam Bella Donna; bred and owned by August Belmont II; leased to Newton Bennington; trained by John J. Hyland and Fred Burlew; Horse of the Year, 1904; Champion Three-Year-Old Filly, 1904; Handicap Mare of the Year, 1905; died 1923.

1903	7 starts,	3 wins,	$ 21,185 earnings
1904	14 starts,	13 wins,	54,100 earnings
1905	10 starts,	2 wins,	26,850 earnings
	31 starts,	17 wins,	$102,135 earnings

In her 1903 debut Beldame finished second, but went on to win the Vernal Stakes three weeks later. She was leased to Newton Bennington and took her first race for him. In 1904 Beldame was nothing short of spectacular. She won the Alabama Stakes and 12 other races. At four years Beldame won the $20,000 added Suburban. Beldame retired as the third filly in racing's history to earn over $100,000.

BROOMSTICK
Horse
Born 1901; bay colt; sire Ben Brush; dam Elf; bred by Col. Milton Young; owned by Capt. Samuel S. Brown; trained by Peter Wimmer and Robert Tucker; sired Wisk Broom II, Meridian, Sweeper, Regret Cudgel, Wildair, Spot Cash, Transmute, Halcyon, Bostonian, Tippety Witchet and Dr. Clark; died 1931.

1903	9 starts,	3 wins,	$25,400 earnings
1904	15 starts,	6 wins,	37,970 earnings

1905 15 starts, 5 wins, 11,360 earnings
39 starts, 14 wins, $74,730 earnings

Broomstick was not known for his track record, but for his record as a stallion. He was leading sire for three years and ranked among the top ten sires through seven consecutive years. Of the 280 foals Broomstick sired, 68 were stakes winners, 24.3%. In 1903 Broomstick won his first three races, the Juvenile, Expectation and Great American Stakes. The 1903 Brighton Handicap was Broomstick's finest race. His winning time of 2:02 was an American record that lasted until 1913. At four Broomstick was retired to Capt. Brown's Senorita Stud. He was sold to Harry Payne Whitney in 1908.

COLIN

Horse

Born 1905; brown colt; sire Commando; dam Pastorella; bred and owned by James R. Keene; trained by James G. Rowe, Sr; sired 81 foals for 11 stakes winners; born with an enlarged hock, did not affect his racing; died 1932.

1907 12 starts, 12 wins, $129,205 earnings
1908 3 starts, 3 wins, 48,905 earnings
15 starts, 15 wins, $178,110 earnings

Colin won his first race setting a track record at Belmont Park and winning the National Stallion Stakes. He won the Eclipse Stakes and remained unchallenged to win the Great Trial, Brighton Junior, Saratoga Special, Grand Union Hotel, Futurity, Flatbush, Produce, Matron, Champagne Stakes, setting many records along the way. As a three-year-old, Colin came out of the rain and fog to just barely beat Fair Play in the Belmont. Colin was shipped to England for racing in 1909, but was injured after a trial and was retired to stud.

COMMANDO

Horse

Born 1898; bay colt; sire Domino; dam Ema C; bred and owned by James R. Keene; trained by James G. Rowe, Sr; sired Kuroki, Peter Pan, Colin and Celt among his 24 stakes winners; picked up a stone in hoof, contracted tetanus and died March 1905 at Castleton Farm.

1900 6 starts, 5 wins, $41,084 earnings
1901 3 starts, 2 wins, 17,112 earnings
9 starts, 7 wins, $58,196 earnings

Commando was slow to develop, but easily won his debut, the 1900 Zephyr Stakes. That year he won the Great Trial, the Montauk Stakes, the Brighton Junior Stakes and the Junior Champion Stakes. Commando won his three-year-old debut, the Belmont Stakes. After winning seven out of nine races he was retired to stud at four. His trainer Rowe commented, "As a race horse, we never knew how good he was, as nothing could extend him."

DUKE, William

Trainer

Duke first achieved success as a trainer in Passy, France. In 1925 he returned to the United States to train for Gifford A. Cochran, who had purchased two colts, Coventry and Flying Ebony. Coventry was placed in the Preakness and won by four lengths. Eight days later Duke entered Flying Ebony in the Kentucky Derby and watched her win by a length and a half. Duke had offers to return to Europe, but he remained in Cochran's employ.

FAIR PLAY

Horse

Born 1905; chestnut colt; sire Hastings; dam Fairy Gold; bred and owned by August Belmont II; trained by A. J. Joyner; sired 49 stakes winners, including Man o' War, Mad Hatter, My Play, Chance Shot, Chance Play, and Mad Play; was the country's leading sire in 1920, 1924 and 1927; in England he developed an aversion to turf and had to be led to a road to be exercised; died 1929.

1907 10 starts, 3 wins, $16,735 earnings
1908 16 starts, 7 wins, 70,215 earnings
1909 6 starts, 0 wins, 0 earnings
32 starts, 10 wins, $86,950 earnings

Fair Play had a bumpy career until Colin and Celt were retired, when Fair Play was a three-year-old. At two years old he won the Nomtauk and Flash Stakes. At three he finished first and second in 15 of his 16 races. When betting on a horse race became a crime in New York, Fair Play, along with many other horses, was sent to England. He went unplaced in six races and was retired to stud.

GOOD AND PLENTY

Horse

Born 1900; bay gelding; sire Rossington; dam Famine; bred by F. B. Harper; owned by Thomas Hitchcock, Jr; trained by Charles Kiernan; was destroyed at age seven in 1907 because of greatly deformed navicular bone causing chronic problems.

1904 10 starts, 8 wins, $17,140 earnings
1905 2 starts, 2 wins, 11,570 earnings
1906 4 starts, 3 wins, 14,455 earnings
1907 5 starts, 1 win, 2,650 earnings
21 starts, 14 wins, $45,815 earnings

Good and Plenty is regarded as the best steeplechaser America has produced. He did not make his first start until he was four years old, at which point he won seven consecutive steeplechases. At five he raced only twice, taking the New York Steeplechase Handicap and the Whitney Memorial. At six Good and Plenty won the Grand National with a burden of 170 lbs.

GRIFFIN, Henry "Harry"

Jockey

Grew up in an orphanage on Staten Island, N.Y; he and his brother became indentured servants to James Shields; sent the largest portion of his earnings to his two sisters in Connecticut, his brother John, also a jockey, and his aunt, a nun, in Montreal.

Harry Griffin got his first mount, Little Jim, and finished second at Guttenberg. By his third year of racing he was riding for the most prominent owners. In his best years, 1894 – 1897, Griffin rode Henry of Navarre to the Withers, Manhattan and the Suburban Handicaps; Hastings to the Belmont and Toboggan; Don de Ore to the Tremont and Eclipse; and Margrave to the Preakness, Hempstead and Boulevard Stakes. One of Griffin's major triumphs came in 1895 when he rode Gideon and Requital to victory in the Futurity at Belmont for his fourth victory of the day.

HYLAND, John J.

Trainer

During 1900s clergy called for abolishment of horse racing; Hyland returned a wallet to its owner, a minister;

the minister wrote letters to *New York Times* proclaiming that not all horsemen were bad; died in Germany in 1910 from a stomach disorder.

John Hyland's horses, Hastings, Henry of Navarre and Masterman, all captured the Belmont Stakes. Hastings was the grandsire of Man o' War. Louis Feustel, an apprentice rider under Hyland, became Man o' War's trainer. Hyland conditioned the first filly ever to win the Futurity, Butterflies.

McATEE, Linus
Jockey
See entry in National Jockeys Hall of Fame, 1961.

McDANIEL, Henry
Trainer
Born in New Jersey; father Col. David McDaniel, owner and trainer; died in Coral Gables, Fla, January 24, 1948, at age 81.

McDaniel saw his first victory as a trainer at the age of 18 at the St. Louis fairgrounds. Willis Sharpe Kilmer commissioned McDaniel to purchase Exterminator, which as a three-year-old won the Kentucky Derby at 30-to-1 odds. Exterminator went on to win a total of 50 races during his eight-year career. McDaniel trained Sir Barton for Commander J.K.L. Ross to the first Triple Crown championship. He also trained J. E. Widener's Hurry Off to the Belmont Stakes victory in 1933. Henry McDaniel sent out winners for 62 years until he retired at the age of 80.

O'CONNOR, Winnie
Jockey
Born in Brooklyn, N.Y; ran away from home at the age of 10; married twice, both times to actresses; was an accomplished boxer and held a bicycle speed record.

In 1901 Winnie O'Connor was America's leading rider with 235 winners, 221 seconds and 192 thirds, out of 1047 mounts. Belmont sent him to Europe in 1902, where he had to turn to steeplechasing because of weight problems. In Europe he wore the silks of such personages as Baron Alphonse de Rothchild, Kaiser Welhelm, King Alphonse and G. H. de Mumm. King Alfonso of Spain presented him with a diamond stick pin that became his trademark in European circles. O'Connor squandered away his fortune. Winnie published a book of his reminiscences called *Jockeys, Crooks and Kings* as told to Earl Chapin.

O'NEILL, Frank
Jockey
Frank O'Neill is remembered for his association with Beldame. In 1904 he rode this filly to victory in the Alabama, Cater, Gazelle, and Saratoga Cup. He rode her again the following year when she won the Suburban. His other stakes victories include renewals of the Brooklyn, Adirondack, Great American, Aqueduct, Astoria, Juvenile, Lawrence Realization, Matron, National Stallion Saranac, Spinaway, Swift and Travers. In 1911 he moved to Europe where he successfully rode Novelty and Hampton Court. O'Neill established himself as a trainer at Maison Lafitte until W.W. II.

PETER PAN
Horse
Born 1904; bay colt; sire Commando; dam Cinderella; bred and owned by James R. Keene; trained by James G. Rowe, Sr; sired 48 stakes winners, including Pennant, Black Toney, Tryster, Prudery, Vexatious, Brainstorm, Arcady, Exodus and Vermajo; died 1933.

1906	8 starts,	4 wins,	$ 29,660 earnings
1907	9 starts,	6 wins,	85,790 earnings
	17 starts,	10 wins,	$115,450 earnings

As a two-year-old Peter Pan won the Surf Stakes, the Flash Stakes and the Hopeful Stakes by two lengths under 130 lbs. The richest victory of his career was the Belmont Stakes as a three-year-old. He went on to take the Standard Stakes, the Brooklyn Derby, the Tidal Stakes, the Advance Stakes and the Brighton Handicap by a nose. Shortly thereafter he bowed a tendon and was retired to Castleton Stud as America's seventh leading money earner.

REIFF, John
Jockey
Born 1885 in Middeltown, Mo; father a hardware merchant; one of seven children; attended school in Wichita, Kans; older brother Lester a jockey in England; died 1974 at age 89.

John Reiff stood less than 5 ft. in height and weighed approximately 65 lbs. His first winning mount was the filly Mary Black in 1898. John and his older brother Lester rode together in Chicago and San Francisco in 1898, where Johnny proved a great success. In April 1899 he rode three winners at the Oakland track and finished twice on a six-race program. In June 1899 John accompanied his brother to England. He had 27 winners abroad that season. In 1907 he rode Orby to victory at the Epsom Derby and in 1912 he took the Blue Riband on Tagalie. John was as popular in England as he had been in the United States. He also rode extensively in France, capturing the French Derby in 1902.

ROSEBEN "The Big Train"
Horse
Born 1901; bay gelding; sire Ben Strome; dam Rose Leaf; bred by Mrs. Thomas J. Carson; owned by John A. Drake, Davy C. Johnson, Lucien O. Appleby; trained by Enoch Wishard, Charles Oxx, Frank D. Weir; later given to New York Congressman James Wadsworth's daughter as a pleasure horse; died 1918.

1903	1 start,	0 win,	0 earnings
1904	9 starts,	3 wins,	$ 2,405 earnings
1905	29 starts,	19 wins,	22,085 earnings
1906	22 starts,	11 wins,	27,870 earnings
1907	14 starts,	7 wins,	13,995 earnings
1908	26 starts,	9 wins,	6,340 earnings
1909	10 starts,	3 wins,	2,415 earnings
	111 starts,	52 wins,	$75,110 earnings

In 1905 the four-year-old Roseben raced to a sound victory in the Toboggan Handicap. He continued on to win the Claremont Handicap and the Manhattan Handicap. Roseben won half of his 22 starts as a five-year-old. He was a classic sprinter. Roseben established records for six and seven furlongs with extreme weight concessions. He was assigned 130 lbs. 59 times and gave weight to all of his rivals in 86 races. He was retired after his eighth year.

SYSONBY
Horse
Born 1902; bay colt; sire Melton; dam Optime; bred and owned by James R. Keene; trained by James G. Rowe, Sr; so small as a yearling that Keene wanted to sell him; trainer feigned illness to keep the colt from being sent abroad; died June 1906 from a liver disease and blood problem known as variola; 4000 persons attended burial in front of Keene stables; later body was exhumed; skeleton on display in the American Museum of Natural History in New York City.

1904	6 starts,	5 wins,	$ 40,058 earnings
1905	9 starts,	9 wins,	144,380 earnings
	15 starts,	14 wins,	$184,438 earnings

Sysonby won his first four races by margins of no less than four lengths, but he never found his stride in that year's Futurity, coming in third. One of his grooms later confessed, after having been found with a bank roll, that he tranquilized the colt before the race. Sysonby came back three weeks later to win the Junior Champion Stakes by three lengths. At three the little bay won the Tidal Stakes, the Commonwealth Handicap, the Lawrence Realization, the Iroquois Stakes, the Brighton Derby, the Great Republic Stakes, the Century Stakes and the Annual Champion Stakes. At the close of his career he had won 14 of 15 starts, and had been drugged to his only defeat.

WORKMAN, Raymond "Sonny"
Jockey
See entry in National Jockeys Hall of Fame, 1957.

1957

ATKINSON, Ted
Jockey
See entry in National Jockeys Hall of Fame, 1957.

BLUE LARKSPUR
Horse
Born 1926; bay colt; sire Black Servant; dam Blossom Time; bred and owned by Col. E. R. Bradley's Idle Hour Stock Farm; trained by H. J. Thompson; Horse of the Year 1929; Three-Year-Old Colt Champion 1929; sired Revoked, Blue Swords, Myrtlewood, Blue Delight, Bloodroot, Elpis, Bee Ann Mac and Blue Grass; died 1947.

1928	7 starts,	4 wins,	$ 66,970 earnings
1929	6 starts,	4 wins,	153,450 earnings
1930	3 starts,	2 wins,	51,650 earnings
	16 starts,	10 wins,	$272,070 earnings

As a two-year-old Blue Larkspur won the National Stallion Stakes and the Saratoga Special. He was favored for the 1929 Kentucky Derby, but his trainer was ill and his stable assistant forgot to shoe the colt with mud caulks for the rainy Derby. He slid all over the track and finished fourth. Blue Larkspur came back after the Derby to win the Withers Stakes at Belmont Park and the one-and-a-half-mile race there as well. He won his last race of the year, beating Rose of Sharon in the Arlington Classic. He was retired for the rest of the year with a bowed tendon and $153,450 in earned winnings. He returned to the track in 1930 to win the Stars and Stripes Handicap and the Arlington Cup, but bowed a tendon again and was retired permanently to stud at Idle Hour.

EQUIPOISE "the Chocolate Soldier"
Horse
Born 1928; chestnut colt; sire Pennant; dam Swinging; bred by Harry Payne Whitney; owned by C. V. Whitney; trained by Fred Hopkins, T. J. Healey; Horse of the Year and Champion Handicapper 1932; Horse of the Year and Champion Handicapper 1933; Champion Handicap Horse 1934; sired nine stakes winners, including Shut Out; was plagued by shelly feet and a chronic quarter crack; died 1938.

1930	16 starts,	8 wins,	$156,835 earnings
1931	3 starts,	1 win,	3,000 earnings
1932	14 starts,	10 wins,	107,375 earnings
1933	9 starts,	7 wins,	55,760 earnings
1934	6 starts,	3 wins,	15,490 earnings
1935	3 starts,	0 wins,	150 earnings
	51 starts,	29 wins,	$338,610 earnings

As a two-year-old Equipoise won 8 times in 16 starts, including the Kentucky Jockey Club Stakes. A short time later H. P. Whitney died and his son C. V. Whitney took control of the interests. Equipoise was the first horse C. V. Whitney raced in his own colors. In that race, the Pimlico Futurity, he edged out Mate and Twenty Grand in the final strides. As a four-year-old, Equipoise won 10 of 14 races, establishing himself as the top handicapper and Horse of the Year. The following year he won seven of nine races and was again Horse of the Year and Champion Handicapper. As a six-year-old, Equipoise won six big races, the Philadelphia and the Dixie Handicaps and the Whitney Gold Trophy. He was named Champion Handicap Horse for the third consecutive year. At seven he was retired to stud.

EXTERMINATOR "Old Bones"
Horse
Born 1915; chestnut gelding; sire McGee; dam Fair Empress; bred by F. D. Dixie Knight; owned by J. Cal Milam, Willis Sharp Kilmer; trained by J. Cal Milam, Henry McDaniel, J. Simon Healy, Will McDaniel, F. Curtis, Bill Knapp, Eugene Wayland, Will Shields and John I. Smith; died at the age of 30 in New York.

1917	4 starts,	2 wins,	$ 1,350 earnings
1918	15 starts,	7 wins,	36,147 earnings
1919	21 starts,	9 wins,	26,402 earnings
1920	17 starts,	10 wins,	52,805 earnings
1921	16 starts,	8 wins,	56,827 earnings
1922	17 starts,	10 wins,	71,075 earnings
1923	3 starts,	1 win,	4,250 earnings
1924	7 starts,	3 wins,	4,140 earnings
	100 starts,	50 wins,	$252,996 earnings

Willis Sharpe Kilmer bought Exterminator as a work horse for Sun Briar. On Derby day Sun Briar did not run, Exterminator did, winning by a length at odds of 30 to 1. He later won the Carrollton, Ellicott City and Pimlico Autumn Handicaps. His winning races at four included the Galt House Handicap, by five lengths. At five he set an American time record in the Saratoga Cup and Autumn Gold Cup. At six he took the Toronto Autumn Cup and won a second Autumn Gold Cup. Exterminator had his best year at seven, winning 10 of 17 and earning $71,075. The gelding was retired from racing in 1924. During this eight seasons of racing, Exterminator met 100 challenges and won 50 of them.

GALLANT FOX

Horse

Born 1927; bay colt; sire Sir Gallahad III; dam Marguerite; bred and raced by William Woodward, Sr.'s Belair Stud in Maryland; trained by James Fitzsimmons; Triple Crown 1930; sired 20 stakes winners from 320 foals, including Omaha and Granville; died 1954.

1929	7 starts,	2 wins,	$ 19,890 earnings
1930	10 starts,	9 wins,	308,275 earnings
	17 starts,	11 wins,	$328,165 earnings

At two, Gallant Fox was given to crowd-gazing and was slow from the gate. In 1930 Earl Sande was persuaded to come out of retirement to ride Gallant Fox. Sande guided him to a four-length victory at the Wood Memorial, took the Preakness and the Kentucky Derby and went on to win the Belmont Stakes by three lengths. Gallant Fox became America's second Triple Crown winner. His three-year-old earnings amounted to $308,-275, a single season record that stood for 17 years. He retired to stud with total earnings of $328,165, a world record, for that time.

GREY LAG

Horse

Born 1918; chestnut colt; sire Star Shoot; dam Miss Minnie; bred by John E. Madden; owned by Max Hirsh, Harry F. Sinclair; trained by Max Hirsh, Sam Hildreth; sired 19 foals, only one stakes winner; died 1942.

1920	13 starts,	4 wins,	$17,202 earnings
1921	13 starts,	9 wins,	62,596 earnings
1922	6 starts,	5 wins,	26,937 earnings
1923	5 starts,	4 wins,	26,990 earnings
1927	2 starts,	2 wins,	1,400 earnings
1928	4 starts,	1 win,	1,500 earnings

Max paid $10,000 for Grey Lag as a yearling and then sold him to Harry F. Sinclair for $60,000. As a three-year-old Grey Lag took a series of eight victories, including the Brooklyn Handicap, the Dwyer Stakes and the Devonshire International. He was generally considered the best of his age. At four Grey Lag suffered his only defeat of the season at the hoofs of Exterminator. He won four of five races at five, and was then retired to stud at Rancocas Farm, N.J. He was returned to racing at 9, winning twice, and again at 13, earning $40. Sinclair repurchased Grey Lag and he was returned to Rancocas Farm as a pensioner.

MAN O' WAR

Horse

Born 1917; chestnut colt; sire Fair Play; dam Mahubah; bred by August Belmont II; owned by Samuel D. Riddle; trained by Louis Feustel; sired 64 stakes winners, including War Admiral, Crusader, Bateau, American Flag, Edith Cavell and Battleship; America's leading sire in 1926 commanded America's highest stud fee; died 1947.

1919	10 starts,	9 wins,	$ 83,325 earnings
1920	11 starts,	11 wins,	166,140 earnings
	21 starts,	20 wins,	$249,465 earnings

At two Man o' War won nine of his ten races; he was defeated by a horse named Upset, although Man o' War beat him soundly in six other meetings. At three he won the Preakness and set records in the Withers, Belmont Stakes, the Dwyer, Lawrence Realization, the Jockey Club Stakes and the Kenilworth Park Gold Cup. Unbeaten in 11 races at three, Man o' War was retired to stud.

REGRET

Horse

Born 1912; chestnut filly; sire Broomstick; dam Jersey Lightning; bred and owned by Harry Payne Whitney; trained by James G. Rowe, Sr; produced only minor stakes winners; died 1934.

1914	3 starts,	3 wins,	$17,390 earnings
1915	2 starts,	2 wins,	12,500 earnings
1916	2 starts,	1 win,	560 earnings
1917	4 starts,	3 wins,	4,643 earnings
	11 starts,	9 wins,	$35,093 earnings

Regret made her first start in the Saratoga Special; she won by a length. She won twice more and retired for the year. At three she was sent out and won the Kentucky Derby. Her only other race at three was the Saranac Handicap, which she won. As a five-year-old, Regret won the Belmont with an eight-length allowance.

SARAZEN

Horse

Born 1921; chestnut gelding; sire High Time; dam Rush Box; bred by Dr. Marius E. Johnston; owned by Col. Phil T. Chinn, Mrs. W. K. Vanderbilt III's Fair Stable; trained by Col. Chin, Max Hirsch; acquired a reputation as a sulker; died December 12, 1940.

1923	10 starts,	10 wins,	$ 37,880 earnings
1924	12 starts,	8 wins,	95,640 earnings
1925	10 starts,	5 wins,	48,160 earnings
1926	14 starts,	4 wins,	42,970 earnings
1927	4 starts,	0 wins,	100 earnings
1928	5 starts,	0 wins,	250 earnings
	55 starts,	27 wins,	$225,000 earnings

Sarazen finished his juvenile year undefeated in ten outings. As a three-year-old he won the Carter Handicap, the Fleeting Handicap, Saranac, Huron Stakes, Manhattan and the third International Special. At four he won half of his ten races, including the Dixie, Fleetwing, Arverne Handicaps and the Bryon Memorial. At five Sarazen was recognized as the best handicapper in training. In 1927 he no longer wanted to win; after he failed to win in nine outings he was retired to Brookdale Farm.

SIR BARTON

Horse

Born 1916; chestnut colt; sire Star Shoot; dam Lady Sterling; bred by John E. Madden, Vivian A. Gooch; owned by John E. Madden, Comdr. J. K. L. Ross; trained by W. S. Walker, H. Guy Bedwell; Triple Crown, 1919; sired six stakes winners, including Easter Stockings; had shelly feet and was apt to throw a shoe, once lost all four during a race; took no interest in other horses and completely ignored and despised all human beings; died 1937.

1918	6 starts,	0 wins,	$ 4,113 earnings
1919	13 starts,	8 wins,	88,250 earnings

1920	12 starts,	5 wins,	24,494 earnings
	31 starts,	13 wins,	$116,857 earnings

After finishing no better than fifth in his first four races as a juvenile, Sir Barton was sold for $10,000 to J. K. L. Ross. As a three-year-old Sir Barton won the Kentucky Derby by five lengths. He then took the Preakness, the Withers Stakes and the Belmont Stakes, setting a record and winning the Triple Crown. As a four-year-old, Sir Barton won 5 of his 12 starts. He lost by seven lengths to three-year-old champion Man o' War in the Kenilworth Gold Cup. He was soon thereafter retired to stud.
Also in: Canadian Horse Racing Hall of Fame.

TWENTY GRAND
Horse

Born 1929; bay colt; sire St. Germans; dam Bonus; bred and owned by Mrs. Payne Whitney's Greentree Stable; trained by Thomas W. Murphy, James G. Rowe, Jr, William Brennan, Cecil Boyd-Rochfort; died March 2, 1948.

1930	8 starts,	4 wins,	$ 41,380 earnings
1931	10 starts,	8 wins,	218,545 earnings
1932	2 starts,	1 win,	915 earnings
1935	5 starts,	1 win,	950 earnings
	25 starts,	14 wins,	$261,790 earnings

Twenty Grand won his first start, took the Kentucky Jockey Club Stakes and placed in his final two races, retiring as one of the leading prospects for the following year. At three he won eight of ten races, including the Kentucky Derby, Belmont Stakes, Saratoga Cup, Travers Stakes and the Jockey Club Gold Cup. He was acclaimed the best horse in training in 1931. Twenty Grand was injured in the Gold Cup race and only ran twice at four before he was retired to stud. He proved sterile and was returned to training. He was unsuccessful in his attempts both here and in England and was pensioned at Greentree Stud until his death.

1958

ARCARO, Eddie
Jockey

See entry in National Jockeys Hall of Fame, 1955.
Also in: UNICO National Athletic Hall of Fame (Italian).

FITZSIMMONS, James E. "Sunny Jim," "Mr. Fitz"
Trainer

Born 1874; died 1966.

Sunny Jim's problems with weight ultimately drove him from jockey to trainer. Although he trained for many owners during his 78-year career, he was most closely associated with the Woodward and Phipps families. During his career he had 148 stakes winners, including Diavolo, Dark Secret, Granville, Seabiscuit, Vagrancy, Gallant Fox, Bold Ruler and Nashua. He won two Triple Crowns with Gallant Fox and Omaha, a Preakness with Bold Ruler and both a Preakness and a Belmont with Nashua. Mr. Fitz had 2266 winning races that brought in purses of $13,001,500. His refreshing good nature and even disposition earned him the nickname of Sunny Jim.

JACOBS, Hirsch
Trainer

Born 1905; Stymie Manor, Md, owner, trainer, breeder; died 1970.

Jacobs began his career racing pigeons in New York. By 1933 he was the leading horse trainer in America, a position that he occupied for 11 years. Jacobs dealt in volume and ran his horses often. Jacobs' favorite horse, Stymie, had won 35 races in 131 starts. By the end of his career Stymie was the world's leading money winner. With the $918,485 that Stymie won, Jacobs and his partner, Isidor Bieber, bought a farm near Monkton, Md. Between 1946 and 1969 Jacobs bred horses that won 3513 races, among them Hail to Reason, Affectionately, Straight Deal and Regal Gleam.

JONES, Ben Allyn
Trainer

Born 1883 in Parnell, Mo; father Horace Jones, banker; of Welsh ancestry; attended agricultural college in Colorado; son Jimmy Jones trainer.

After years of the Western fair circuit, Jones was hired to train for Woolford Farm in 1932. His horse Lawrin won the Kentucky Derby. In 1939 he moved to Calumet Farm and scored six victories at the Kentucky Derby, a record. He led the nation in earnings 11 times. Jones trained Whirlaway to the Triple Crown in 1941 and aided in the training of Citation, which swept the Triple Crown in 1948. Four times his horses were named horse of the year. His other winners were Pensive, Twilight Tear, Armed, Coaltown, Fervent, Faultless, Bewitch, Wistful and Pot o' Luck.

LONGDEN, John
Jockey

See entry in National Jockeys Hall of Fame, 1956.
Also in: Canada's Sports Hall of Fame and Canadian Horse Racing Hall of Fame.

SEABISCUIT
Horse

Born 1933; bay colt; sire Hard Tack; dam Swing On; bred by Wheatley Stable (Mrs. H. C. Phipps and Ogden Mills); owned by Wheatley Stable, Charles S. Howard; trained by Jim Fitzsimmons, Tom Smith; Horse of the Year 1938; died 1947.

1935	35 starts,	5 wins,	$ 12,510 earnings
1936	23 starts,	9 wins,	28,995 earnings
1937	15 starts,	11 wins,	168,580 earnings
1938	11 starts,	6 wins,	130,395 earnings
1939	1 start,	0 wins,	400 earnings
1940	4 starts,	2 wins,	96,850 earnings
	89 starts,	33 wins,	$437,730 earnings

Three-year-old Seabiscuit was sold for $7500 to Charles S. Howard, automobile industry tycoon. At four Seabiscuit won 11 of 15 races, emerging as the year's leading money winner. He set track records at San Juan Capistrano, Yonkers, Massachusetts and Riggs Handicap. Seabiscuit's five-year-old campaign was highlighted by two races. The first was against Bing Crosby's Ligaroti in a $25,000, winner-take-all match. Seabiscuit won by a nose, setting a time 4 secs. faster than the track record. The next match was against War Admiral for $15,000, winner-take-all. All were shocked to see Seabiscuit pull away from the Triple Crown winner to a victory by three lengths, in track record time. Seabiscuit was 1938's horse of the year. He went lame at six but came back at seven to become the first horse to earn more than $400,000.

SHOEMAKER, William Lee
Jockey
See entry in National Jockeys Hall of Fame, 1959.
Also in: Arizona Horse Racing Hall of Fame.

WAR ADMIRAL
Horse
Born 1943; brown colt; sire Man o' War; dam Brushup; bred and owned by Samuel D. Riddle's Glen Riddle Farm; trained by George Conway; Triple Crown 1937; Horse of the Year 1937; sired 40 stakes winners; leading sire in America in 1945; died 1959.

1936	6 starts,	3 wins,	$ 14,800 earnings
1937	8 starts,	8 wins,	166,500 earnings
1938	11 starts,	9 wins,	90,840 earnings
1939	1 start,	1 win,	1,100 earnings
	26 starts,	21 wins,	$273,240 earnings

War Admiral won his first two races at two. He began his three-year-old campaign by winning the Havre de Grace and the Chesapeake Stakes. War Admiral won the Kentucky Derby by one-and-three-fourths lengths, the Preakness and the Belmont for a Triple Crown sweep. He had injured a hoof in the Belmont and rested for the remainder of the year. He still managed to pick up the 1937 horse of the year award. At four War Admiral won nine of his eleven starts. He was beaten by Seabiscuit in the Pimlico Special. At five he suffered a wrenched ankle and was retired to stud.

1959

CITATION
Horse
Born 1945; bay colt; sire Bill Lea; dam Hydroplane II; bred and owned by Warren Wright, Sr.'s Calumet Farm; trained by B. A. Jones and Jimmy Jones; Champion Juvenile Colt 1947; Triple Crown 1948; Horse of the Year and Champion Three-Year-Old Colt 1948; sired Silver Spoon and Fabius; died 1970.

1947	9 starts,	8 wins,	$ 155,680 earnings
1948	20 starts,	19 wins,	709,470 earnings
1949	0 starts,	0 wins,	0 earnings
1950	9 starts,	2 wins,	73,480 earnings
1951	7 starts,	3 wins,	147,130 earnings
	45 starts,	32 wins,	$1,085,760 earnings

Citation made his first appearance in 1947, winning eight of nine races that year. At three years Citation lost only one race to Saggy, but easily took the Triple Crown under the Calumet colors. That year he earned $709,470 and was also named horse of the year and champion three-year-old colt for 1948. Citation was plagued by an osselet at four and was never able to regain his form. He was retired to stud in 1952.

HARTACK, William John
Jockey
See entry in National Jockeys Hall of Fame, 1963.

HIRSCH, Max
Trainer
Born 1880 in Fredericksburg, Tex; parents German immigrants; at age 11 worked quarter horses on Morris ranch; at age 12 stowed away in shipment of race horses bound for Baltimore; at age 14 became a jockey; three children: Buddy Hirsch succeeded him at King Ranch; Mrs. Mary McLennan first woman to be licensed as a trainer on major tracks; and Mrs. Catherine Reynolds; died 1969 at age 88.

Max Hirsch began training at the age of 20 and continued for 68 years. He had his first winner at New Orleans in 1902. Training predominantly for the King Ranch, Hirsch ran three Kentucky Derby winners: Bold Venture, 1936, Assault, 1946, and Middleground, 1950. He won the Preakness with Bold Venture, the Belmont with Vito (1928), Middleground (1950) and High Gun (1954). Assault swept the Triple Crown in 1946. Hirsch won 123 races before becoming overweight.

JONES, Horace Allyn "Jimmy"
Trainer
Born 1908 in Parnell, Mo; father Ben Jones a trainer; elected mayor of Parnell.

Jimmy Jones trained eight of Calumet Farm's 16 champion horses: A Glitter, Armed, Barbizon, Bewitch, Citation, Coaltown, Tim Tam and Two Lea. His Kentucky Derby winners were Citation in 1948, Iron Liege in 1957 and Tim Tam in 1958. His outstanding achievement, Citation, won the Triple Crown and became racing's first millionaire. Jimmy Jones gave up his position as trainer at Calumet Farms after 25 years (in 1964) to become director of racing at Monmouth Park.

LOFTUS, John
Jockey
See entry in National Jockeys Hall of Fame, 1960.

WHIRLAWAY "Mr. Longtail"
Horse
Born 1938; chestnut colt; sire Blenheim II; dam Dustwhirl; bred and owned by Warren Wright, Sr.'s Calumet Farm; trained by Ben A. Jones; had a tendency to run wide in the stretch until Jones fashioned special blinders; Triple Crown and Horse of the Year 1941; Horse of the Year 1942; sired 17 stakes winners, including Scottered, Rock Drill and Lady Pitt; died 1953.

1940	16 starts,	7 wins,	$ 77,275 earnings
1941	20 starts,	13 wins,	272,386 earnings
1942	22 starts,	12 wins,	211,250 earnings
1943	2 starts,	0 wins,	250 earnings
	60 starts,	32 wins,	$561,161 earnings

At two Whirlaway was somewhat erratic, winning 7 of 16 races, which included the Saratoga Special, the Hopeful Stakes and the Breeder's Futurity. At three, with Eddie Arcaro aboard, Whirlaway won the Derby in record time. He easily won the Preakness and the Belmont for a sweep of the Triple Crown. He was voted Horse of the Year for 1941. At four Whirlaway won 12 races and became the first horse to earn over $500,000. He was again voted Horse of the Year. At five after two starts, he was retired to stud at Calumet Farm. He was later leased to Marcel Boussac in France, where he died.

1960

MOLTER, William
Trainer
Born 1910 in Fredericksburg, Tex; at age 12 rode in Quarter Horse races; died in 1960 from a heart attack.

Bill Molter saw his first win as a trainer in 1935 at Mexico's Caliente track. In the decade between 1946 and 1955, Molter's horses won 1392 races and earned over $7 million. His prize horse was Round Table. As a three-year-old, Round Table was the season's leading money winner. In 1958, as a four-year-old, he was Horse of the Year and by the time Round Table retired at five, he had won 43 of 66 starts and earned $1,749,869. Molter also transformed Bobby Brocato from a sprinter to a longer course champion. Bobby Brocato won the Santa Anita Handicap and the San Juan Capistrano one-and-three-quarter-mile races. At the time of his death, Molter had had 2158 winners and earnings of $11,983,035.

NEVES, Ralph
Jockey
Today a restaurateur in Pasadena, Calif.

In May 1936 Ralph Neves was pronounced dead after he slammed head first into a fence and was pounded by four horses. His body was taken to the hospital for transport to the morgue. Ten minutes after he was alone in the room, Neves awoke. He yelled for help and then stumbled out of the hospital wearing only a sheet. He hailed a cab and was at the track the next day to win the race. During the next 30 years he became a legend in California. He won 536 races and 31 major stakes at Santa Anita. He won 173 stakes and almost $14 million in purses. At the time he retired he was ranked sixth among American jockeys, with 3771 victories.

TOM FOOL
Horse
Born 1949; bay colt; sire Menow; dam Gaga; bred by Duval Headley; owned by Mrs. C. S. Paysen, John H. Whitney's Greentree Stable; trainer, John M. Gaver; Handicap Triple Crown 1952; Horse of the Year and Champion Handicapper 1952; sired 34 stakes winners, including Tim Tam, Buckpasser, Weatherwise, Jester and Tompion; bothered by cracked heels during early part of career.

1951	7 starts,	5 wins,	$155,960 earnings
1952	13 starts,	6 wins,	157,850 earnings
1953	10 starts,	10 wins,	256,355 earnings
	30 starts,	21 wins,	$570,165 earnings

Tom Fool won five of his seven races as a two-year-old. The following year he missed the Triple Crown events due to a fever and cough. He was slow to come back after the illness for his third year, but at four he was perfect, winning ten of ten. Tom Fool won the Metropolitan by a half a length, took the Suburban and easily won the Brooklyn for the first victory of the Handicap Triple Crown since 1913. That year he was voted Horse of the Year and Champion Handicapper. He was retired to Greentree Stud at the end of his four-year-old campaign.

1962

COUNT FLEET
Horse
Born 1940; brown colt; sire Reigh Count; dam Quickly; bred and owned by Mrs. John D. Hertz; trained by G. D. Cameron; Juvenile Champion 1942; Triple Crown 1943; sired 38 stakes winners, including Counterpoint, One Count, Kiss Me Kate and Count Turf; died 1973.

1942	15 starts,	10 wins,	$ 76,245 earnings
1943	6 starts,	6 wins,	174,055 earnings
	21 starts,	16 wins,	$250,000 earnings

Count Fleet won 10 of 15 races at two. He finished third in the Belmont Futurity and thereafter never lost a race. He was undisputed juvenile champion. At three Count Fleet went unbeaten and unchallenged. He won the Wood Memorial, swept the Kentucky Derby by three and the Preakness by eight, completing the Triple Crown. A rapped front ankle in the Belmont resulted in Count Fleet's retirement from racing. He ranked among the top 20 leading sires a total of seven times. He was insured for $550,000, believed the largest policy ever written on a horse.

ENSOR, Buddy
Jockey
Born 1896 in Baltimore, Md; died from exposure near the Jamaica track in Brooklyn, N.Y, November 1947.

Buddy Ensor's first race was in 1917 at Hot Springs, Ariz, when he won eight of eleven races. Though his career extended from 1917 to the 1940s, his peak years were in 1919 and 1920. He rode Exterminator, Hannibal, Cirrus and Grey Lag. In 1919 he rode 33 winners in 11 days and then he began to fade out. His attempts at comebacks were unsuccessful.

1963

ARMED
Horse
Born 1941; brown gelding; sire Bull Lea; dam Armful; bred and owned by Warren Wright, Sr.'s Calumet Farm; trained by B. A. Jones and Jimmy Jones; Handicap Horse of the Year, 1945; Horse of the Year, 1947; died May 5, 1964.

1944	7 starts,	3 wins,	$ 4,850 earnings
1945	15 starts,	10 wins,	91,600 earnings
1946	18 starts,	11 wins,	288,725 earnings
1947	17 starts,	11 wins,	376,325 earnings
1948	6 starts,	1 win,	12,200 earnings
1949	12 starts,	3 wins,	36,250 earnings
1950	6 starts,	2 wins,	7,525 earnings
	81 starts,	41 wins,	$817,475 earnings

Armed came into his own in 1945. Prior to that he had been overshadowed by greater stars. In 1945 he won ten races, ran second in four others and earned $90,000. The next year he won seven handicaps and was voted best handicap horse of the year. His best year was in 1947 when he won eight added-money races and defeated the ailing Assault by eight lengths in a special $100,000 winner-take-all match at Pimlico. That year he was a nearly unanimous choice as Horse of the Year. Midway through 1947 Armed won the Sysonby Mile Handicap and for a short while he claimed the record as top money-winning Thoroughbred. Armed retired to Calumet Farm in 1950.

BROOKS, Steve
Jockey
See entry in National Jockeys Hall of Fame, 1962.

BURCH, Preston M.

Trainer

Born 1844 in Augusta, Ga; father William P. Burch a horseman; one of three children; grew up in Washington, D.C; left school in 1902 for the races; son Elliot a trainer.

Pres Burch trained for many. He advised Sanford to buy George Smith and watched as the colt took the 1916 Kentucky Derby. It was at Mrs. Dodge Sloane's Brookmeade Stable that Burch enjoyed his greatest success. There he developed Atlanta, Bold, Capeador, Closed Door, Dart By, Flower Bowl, Grandharva, Going Away, Grand Canyon, More Sun, Picador, Sailor, Sunny Dale and Tritium. Pres Burch was a breeder, owner, stable agent and bloodstock adviser during his career. "People keep asking me why, with the increased foal production, we don't produce more Man o' Wars. I tell 'em, 'Well, we've been having more and more people in this country, but not too many more George Washingtons.' " He also wrote *Training Thoroughbred Horses,* a reference book for professionals and fans alike.

GALLORETTE

Horse

Born 1942; chestnut filly; sire Challenger II; dam Gallette; bred by Preston M. Burch; owned by William L. Brann; Brann and Burch made a deal to breed their horses Challenger II and Gallette, each man owning the foals alternately; Gallorette, the first foal, went to Brann; trained by Edward A. Christmas; among seven foals were stakes winners Lovely Gale and Courbette; Champion Handicap Mare 1946; died 1959.

1944	8 starts,	3 wins,	$ 7,950 earnings
1945	13 starts,	5 wins,	94,300 earnings
1946	18 starts,	6 wins,	159,160 earnings
1947	18 starts,	3 wins,	90,275 earnings
1948	15 starts,	4 wins,	93,850 earnings
	72 starts,	21 wins,	$445,535 earnings

At three Gallorette defeated Hoop Jr, that year's Kentucky Derby winner, and took consecutive victories in the Acorn Stakes, the Pimlico and the Delaware Oaks. At four competition slackened and she emerged as the best older mare in training. At five she placed in 14 of her 18 starts and became the leading money-winning mare of all time, with earnings of $351,685. Gallorette took four more races at six and was then retired. She was bought for a reported $150,000 by Mrs. Mary A. Moore of High Hope Farm, Va.

NATIVE DANCER

Horse

Born 1950; gray colt; sire Polynesian; dam Geisha; bred and owned by Alfred G. Vanderbilt; trained by W. C. Winfrey; Juvenile Colt Champion and Coholder of Horse of the Year 1952; Horse of the Year 1954; sired 45 stakes winners, including Kauai King, Hula Dancer and Dancer's Image; died after undergoing surgery for an intestinal blockage in November 1967 at Sagamore Farm.

1952	9 starts,	9 wins,	$230,495 earnings
1953	10 starts,	9 wins,	513,425 earnings
1954	3 starts,	3 wins,	41,320 earnings
	22 starts,	21 wins,	$785,240 earnings

Native Dancer won his first race at Jamaica in 1952 and went on to take the Youthful Stakes and the Futurity. He charged to victory in the Widener Chute in world record time and easily scored in the East View Stakes. He was the unanimous choice as Juvenile Colt Champion and was coholder of the Horse of the Year honors with One Count. At three Native Dancer won the Gotham Stakes and the Wood Memorial, but was defeated by Dark Star in the Kentucky Derby. It was the only loss of his career. Following the Derby, Native Dancer won the Preakness, the Belmont, the Dwyer, the Travers and the American Derby. He won three for three as a four-year-old, raising his total earnings to $785,240. He was voted the 1954 Horse of the Year and retired to stud at Vanderbilt's Sagamore Farm.

NOTTER, Joseph A.

Jockey

See entry in National Jockeys Hall of Fame, 1961.

TWILIGHT TEAR "Suzie"

Horse

Born 1941; bay filly; sire Bill Lea; dam Lady Lark; bred and owned by Warren Wright, Sr.'s Calumet Farm; trained by Ben A Jones; Horse of the Year 1944; produced Coiner, A Gleam, and Bardstown; died 1954.

1943	6 starts,	4 wins,	$ 34,610 earnings
1944	17 starts,	14 wins,	167,555 earnings
1945	1 start,	0 wins,	0 earnings
	24 starts,	18 wins,	$202,165 earnings

At two the filly won the rich Arlington Classic. At three she took 14 of her 17 races and was voted 1944 Horse of the Year. She won the Acorn Stakes, the Coaching Club American Oaks, the Princess Doreen, the Skokie Handicap over Pensive (Derby and Preakness winner) in track record time and the Arlington Classic, which was her eleventh consecutive victory. After one race as a four-year-old she was retired.

1964

ASSAULT

Horse

Born 1943; chestnut colt; sire Bold Venture; dam Igual; bred and owned by Robert J. Kelberg, Jr.'s King Ranch; trainer, Max Hirsch; as a colt stepped on a nail that came through the front wall of the right forefoot; gait was awkward at walk and trot, but no effect on gallop; Triple Crown 1946; Horse of the Year 1946; Champion Three-Year-Old 1946; died 1971.

1945	9 starts,	2 wins,	$ 17,250 earnings
1946	15 starts,	8 wins,	424,195 earnings
1947	7 starts,	5 wins,	181,925 earnings
1948	2 starts,	1 win,	3,250 earnings
1949	6 starts,	1 win,	45,900 earnings
1950	3 starts,	1 win,	2,950 earnings
	42 starts,	18 wins,	$675,470 earnings

Assault won the 1945 Flash Stakes. In 1946 he was unbeatable. He placed fourth in the Derby Trial. Starting in the Kentucky Derby he was fourth choice to win, but after a mile Assault rallied to win by eight lengths. No horse has ever won by a greater margin. His next race was the Preakness, which he took by a narrow margin. At the one-and-a-half-mile Belmont Stakes, he came from behind to win by three lengths. Following this Triple Crown victory he lost five straight, but came back to win two. He was retired to stud in 1948, but proved sterile and was put back in training in 1949. He won that year's Brooklyn Handicap and was retired permanently in 1950 to King Ranch.

BUSHER

Horse

Born 1942; chestnut filly; sire War Admiral; dam Baby League; bred by Col. E. R. Bradley's Idle Hour Stock Farm; owned by Col. E. R. Bradley, L. B. Mayer; trained by J. W. Smith, George Odom; Horse of the Year, Champion Three-Year-Old and Champion Female Handicapper 1945; her only foals were Jet Action and Popularity; died 1955.

1944	7 starts,	5 wins,	$ 60,300 earnings
1945	13 starts,	10 wins,	273,735 earnings
1946	0 starts,	0 wins,	0 earnings
1947	1 start,	0 wins,	0 earnings
	21 starts,	15 wins,	$334,035 earnings

Busher won her first race by a half-length in 1944. She went on to take the Adirondack handicap and a divisional championship in the Selima Stakes. Col. Bradley sold her to L. B. Mayer in 1945 for $50,000. Soon after she won three straight at Santa Anita, took the Santa Susana Stakes and the San Vicente Handicap. Busher easily handled older fillies in the Santa Margarita Handicap, as well as her own age group in the Cleopatra Handicap. She met Armed in the Washington Park Handicap and won by one and a half lengths, breaking a track record. In two seasons she had earned $334,035, then a record for a filly. At five she retired and was sold to Mrs. Elizabeth N. Graham, owner of Maine Chance Farm.

FEUSTEL, Louis

Trainer

Louis Feustel for Glen Riddle Farm trained Man o' War to win 20 of his 21 races. Man o' War earned $186,087 for 11 wins in 1920, to make his trainer the leading money winner of that season. Under Feustel's training program, Man o' War set records at the Withers, Belmont, Dwyer, Lawrence Realization and the Jockey Club Stakes. Louis Feustel gave Man o' War the nickname of "Big Red."

1965

ADAMS, John

Jockey

See entry in National Jockeys Hall of Fame, 1964.

IMP "My Coal Black Lady"

Horse

Born 1894; black filly; sire Wagner; dam Fondling; bred and owned by Daniel R. Harness; trained by Charles E. Brossman, Peter Wimmer; received her nickname from the popular song of that title; everytime she won a race the band struck up that song; died 1909.

1896	11 starts,	3 wins,	$ 1,310 earnings
1897	50 starts,	14 wins,	4,934 earnings
1898	35 starts,	21 wins,	12,340 earnings
1899	31 starts,	13 wins,	30,735 earnings
1900	31 starts,	8 wins,	18,185 earnings
1901	13 starts,	3 wins,	2,565 earnings
	171 starts,	62 wins,	$70,069 earnings

Imp began to blossom as a three-year-old, when she won 14 of her 50 starts. At four she took 21 out of 35. As a five-year-old she brought home her best-remembered victory, The Suburban. Carrying 114 lbs, Imp won the one-and-a-quarter mile Suburban by two lengths in 2.05, becoming the first mare to do so. At six she took the lead in the Advance Stakes to win by an estimated 30 lengths, breaking the 19-year-old track record. During her six-year career on the track, Imp went to the post 171 times and returned to the top-three finishers on 126 occasions. She won 62 races, beating some of the best colts of her day.

JOLLY ROGER

Horse

Born 1922; chestnut gelding; sire Pennant; dam Lethe; bred by Harry Payne Whitney; owned by Mrs. Payne Whitney's Greentree Stable; trained by Vincent Powers; died July 3, 1948 at the age of 26.

1924	7 starts,	1 win,	$ 850 earnings
1925	4 starts,	2 wins,	3,880 earnings
1926	11 starts,	4 wins,	13,110 earnings
1927	8 starts,	6 wins,	63,075 earnings
1928	7 starts,	3 wins,	45,950 earnings
1929	4 starts,	0 wins,	4,050 earnings
1930	8 starts,	2 wins,	12,325 earnings
	49 starts,	18 wins,	$143,240 earnings

Jolly Roger was trained over fences to his first win as a three-year-old at Belmont Park. At four he won his first four starts, but in 1927 when five years old he had his best year. He won six of his eight starts, all of which were stakes races. In his seven starts in 1928, Jolly Roger was never out of the money, winning the Grand National for the second time and the Corinthian Steeplechase Handicap. At seven he finished in second and third places due to handicappers. As an eight-year-old Jolly Roger won the North American and the Glendale Steeplechase Handicaps prior to bowing a tendon and ending his jumping career. During his career Jolly Roger's earnings amounted to $143,240, a world record for steeplechasers that remained unbroken until July 1948 when Elkridge surpassed it. Jolly Roger was retired to Greentree Stud in Kentucky.

NASHUA

Horse

Born 1952; brown colt; sire Nasrullah; dam Sequla; bred by William Woodward, Sr.'s Belair Stud; owned by William Woodward, Jr, Leslie Combs II; trained by James Fitzsimmons; Horse of the Year 1955; ranked in the top 2 percent as a stallion.

1954	8 starts,	6 wins,	$ 192,865 earnings
1955	12 starts,	10 wins,	752,550 earnings
1956	10 starts,	6 wins,	343,150 earnings
	30 starts,	22 wins,	$1,288,565 earnings

As a two-year-old, Nashua won the Juvenile, Grand Union Hotel, Hopeful and Futurity Stakes, and was voted Champion Juvenile. At three Nashua won the Flamingo Stakes and the Florida Derby. In New York he took the Wood Memorial in the final ten yards. Nashua lost the Kentucky Derby to Swaps, but set a record in the Preakness and scored by nine lengths in the Belmont Stakes. The most famous race of Nashua's career was the $100,000 winner-take-all match at Chicago's Washington

Park against Swaps. Nashua took the lead, turned Swaps back three times and won by six and a quarter lengths. He continued on that year to take the Jockey Club Gold Cup and the nomination for Horse of the Year. Owner Woodward died and Nashua was purchased by Leslie Combs II through sealed bids for $1,251,200, making him the first million-dollar horse. His six victories at four included the Widener Handicap, Camden Handicap, and the Jockey Club Gold Cup, in which he set an American time record.

OMAHA

Horse

Born 1932; chestnut colt; sire Gallant Fox; dam Flambino; bred and owned by William Woodward, Sr.'s Belair Stud; trained by James Fitzsimmons, Cecil Boyd-Rochfort; Triple Crown 1935; sired only seven stakes winners; died in 1959; was buried at the grandstand entrance to Ak-Sar-Ben Racetrack.

1934	9 starts,	1 win,	$ 3,850 earnings
1935	9 starts,	6 wins,	142,255 earnings
1936	4 starts,	2 wins,	8,650 earnings
	22 starts,	9 wins,	$154,755 earnings

As a two-year-old, Omaha won only once in nine outings. At three he placed third in the Wood Memorial, but went on to win the Kentucky Derby by one and a half lengths. The following week he took the Preakness by six lengths and then lost the Withers, but thundered home in the Belmont Stakes to Triple Crown honors. Omaha developed signs of lameness and was raced no more at the age of three. The four-year-old colt was shipped to England and won the Victor Wild Stakes and Queen's Plate, losing the Ascot Gold Cup by a nose to the English filly Quashed. He was returned to the States for stud.

1966

ELKRIDGE

Horse

Born 1938; bay gelding; sire Mate; dam Best Test; bred by Joseph F. Flanagan; owned and trained by Thomas Hitchcock, Jr, Kent Miller; had a fondness for jelly doughnuts; would take sugar lumps from his trainer's teeth and put his head on his trainer's lap; Champion American Steeplechaser 1942 and 1946.

1941	1 start,	1 win,	$ 1,000 earnings
1942	20 starts,	7 wins,	28,130 earnings
1943	18 starts,	2 wins,	8,455 earnings
1944	8 starts,	4 wins,	17,235 earnings
1945	15 starts,	3 wins,	27,575 earnings
1946	9 starts,	3 wins,	35,285 earnings
1947	9 starts,	2 wins,	19,275 earnings
1948	15 starts,	3 wins,	31,225 earnings
1949	11 starts,	3 wins,	26,950 earnings
1950	7 starts,	3 wins,	29,925 earnings
1951	10 starts,	0 wins,	5,625 earnings
	123 starts,	31 wins,	$230,680 earnings

Elkridge was sent out for the first time at three and won by seven lengths. A four-year-old steeplechaser, Elkridge won the Broad Hollow, North American, Indian River, Battleship, Governor Ogle and Manly Steeplechase Handicaps. Voted Champion American Steeplechaser as a four-year-old in 1942 and again as an eight-year-old, Elkridge raced on through the age of 13. He fell only once in his 123 races, winning 31 times and earning $230,680.

GAVER, John M.

Trainer

Graduate of Princeton in 1924; taught languages; worked as a bank clerk.

John Gaver began his career as a friend and assistant to Jim Rowe, learning the ways of racing and the operation of a racing stable. When the Whitneys were searching for a man to take charge of the Greentree breeding farm at Lexington, Ky, Gaver was there. Gaver was the leading money-winning trainer in America in 1942 and 1951. He developed many outstanding winners, including Shut Out, Devil Diver, Third Degree, Capot, Tangler, Quillatine, Stage Door Johnny and Tom Fool, the two-year-old champion of 1951 and four-year-old handicap champion in 1953.

NEJI

Horse

Born 1950; chestnut gelding; sire Hunters Moon IV; dam Accra; bred by Mrs. Marion duPont Scott; owned by Rigan McKinney, Mrs. Ogden Phipps; trained by Rigan McKinney, G. H. Bostwick, D. M. Smithwick, Dan Moore; Champion Steeplechaser of the Year 1955, 1957 and 1958.

1953	2 starts,	0 wins,	$ 200 earnings
1954	18 starts,	5 wins,	41,005 earnings
1955	8 starts,	5 wins,	92,630 earnings
1956	6 starts,	2 wins,	26,820 earnings
1957	4 starts,	3 wins,	75,975 earnings
1958	5 starts,	2 wins,	34,246 earnings
1959	3 starts,	0 wins,	141 earnings
1960	3 starts,	0 wins,	3,010 earnings
	49 starts,	17 wins,	$274,047 earnings

At four, after a relatively unnoticed juvenile career, Neji won the three divisions of the National Maiden Hurdles at Aqueduct, Monmouth, and Saratoga. At five he won the Grand National, the Temple Gwathmey, the Brooke and the International Steeplechase and was voted Steeplechaser of the Year. As a six-year-old Neji won the Meadow Brook and the Indian River Steeplechase Handicap before suffering a fractured splint bone. At seven he won the Grand National carrying 168 lbs, the Temple Gwathmey and the Harbor Hill as well as Champion Steeplechase honors. Neji won the Grand National again the following year carrying 176 lbs. and was again voted Champion Steeplechaser of the Year. At nine he was sent to Ireland, but returned with a rapped tendon. He was used as a hunter and show jumper by Cynthia Phipps until he retired to S. H. R. Fred's farm as a pensioner at the age of 18.

SWAPS

Horse

Born 1952; chestnut colt; sire Khaled; dam Iron Reward; bred and owned by Rex C. Ellsworth; trained by Meshach Tenney; Horse of the Year 1956; died 1972.

1954	6 starts,	3 wins,	$ 20,950 earnings
1955	9 starts,	8 wins,	418,550 earnings
1956	10 starts,	8 wins,	409,400 earnings
	25 starts,	19 wins,	$848,900 earnings

Swaps was the winner of three California races as a two-year-old. That year he was ridden in the Kentucky Derby by Bill Shoemaker to victory by one and a half lengths. He returned to California after the Derby and won the Will Rogers Stakes, the Western Stakes and the California Stakes. A match race between Swaps and Nashua was arranged. Swaps made several bold challenges, but Nashua led throughout, winning by six and a half lenghts. At four Swaps won eight of his ten races, setting four world records, tieing one other and taking the honor of Horse of the Year. He fractured a cannon bone during a workout and was sent to stud at Darby Dan Farm. He later moved to Spendthrift Farm.

TOP FLIGHT

Horse

Born 1929; dark brown filly; sire Dis Donc; dam Flyatit; bred by Harry Payne Whitney; owned by C. Vanderbilt Whitney; trained by T. J. Healey; produced five stakes winners, including Flight Commander; thought awkward and unpromising as a yearling; once on the track, became graceful, possessing effortless speed; died 1949.

1931	7 starts,	7 wins,	$219,000	earnings
1932	9 starts,	5 wins,	56,900	earnings
	16 starts,	12 wins,	$275,900	earnings

At two she had seven wins in seven starts. Top Flight beat members of both sexes in her age group in the Clover Stakes by five lengths, the Spinaway Stakes, the Saratoga Special, the Futurity at Belmont and the Pimlico Futurity. At three Top Flight was able to maintain her dominance over fillies, but lost all four of her tries against colts of her age group. She won the Acorn Stakes, the Coaching Club American Oaks, the Arlington Oaks, Alabama Stakes and the Ladies Handicap. Top Flight was retired to stud after having set a new earning record during her 1931 season.

1967

BUSHRANGER

Horsc

Born 1930; chestnut gelding; sire Stefan the Great; dam War Path; bred and owned by Joseph E. Widener; trained by J. Howard Lewis; Steeplechase Horse of the Year 1936; died 1937.

1932	5 starts,	0 wins,	$ 250	earnings
1933	0 starts,	0 wins,	0	earnings
1934	7 starts,	4 wins,	3,050	earnings
1935	4 starts,	3 wins,	5,730	earnings
1936	5 starts,	4 wins,	11,605	earnings
	21 starts,	11 wins,	$20,635	earnings

At the age of three with little prior success, Bushranger was placed in the hands of J. Howard Lewis, America's leading trainer of steeplechasers. At four Bushranger made his debut over fences, starting seven times, winning four and finishing second once. At five, he won three of four starts, including the Broad Hollow and the Charles L. Appleton Memorial Cup. At six, wearing Widener's colors, Bushranger had four wins in four starts, including the Grand National. His life ended when he fractured a leg schooling over fences in 1937.

BYERS, J. Dallet "Dolly"

Trainer

Died in December 1966 at his home in Aiken, S.C. Dolly Byers was a three-time National Steeplechase Riding Champion. Once he rode five consecutive winners at the Manley Steeplechase in Maryland. On another occasion he had four wins in a row at Temple Gwathmey Steeplechase. After his riding career, Byers turned his attention to training. The best known of those he conditioned over the years was Mrs. Ambrose Clark's Tea-Maker. As a nine-year-old Tea-Maker won four stakes events and earned recognition as the year's Sprint Champion. During his career as a trainer Dolly had 28 victories in 114 starts.

CICADA

Horse

Born 1959; bay filly; sire Bryan; dam Satsuma; bred and owned by Christopher T. Chenery; trained by J. H. "Casey" Hayes; Champion Two-Year-Old Filly 1961; Champion Three-Year-Old Filly 1962; Champion Handicap Filly 1963; first foal was Cicada's Pride.

1961	16 starts,	11 wins,	$384,676	earnings
1962	17 starts,	8 wins,	298,167	earnings
1963	8 starts,	4 wins,	100,481	earnings
1964	1 start,	0 wins,	350	earnings
	42 starts,	23 wins,	$783,674	earnings

Cicada came to the races first as a two-year-old. She won five of her ten races, including the National Stallion and Blue Hen Stakes, and then finished the season with six consecutive wins. She closed her two-year-old season with record earnings. As a three-year-old, Cicada won the first two parts of the filly Triple Crown. After several losses and a five-week rest, Cicada came back to win the Beldame Stakes in record time. At four she won her seasonal debut, the Columbian Handicap, and went on to take the Pocosaba Sheepshead Bay Handicap and the Delaware Handicap. Cicada became the first filly ever to be named champion at two, three and four years old. At five she retired at that time the leading money-earning race mare of history.

KELSO

Horse

Born 1957; dark bay gelding; sire Your Host; dam Maid of Flight; bred and owned by Mrs. Richard C. duPont's Bohemia Stable; trained by Dr. John Lee, Carl H. Hanford; Horse of the Year 1960–1964.

1959	3 starts,	1 win,	$ 3,380	earnings
1960	9 starts,	8 wins,	293,310	earnings
1961	9 starts,	7 wins,	425,565	earnings
1962	12 starts,	6 wins,	289,685	earnings
1963	12 starts,	9 wins,	569,762	earnings
1964	11 starts,	5 wins,	311,660	earnings
1965	6 starts,	3 wins,	84,034	earnings
1966	1 start,	0 wins,	500	earnings
	63 starts,	39 wins,	$1,977,896	earnings

Kelso's training was taken over by Carl Hanford at three. He began late in the season that year, but won seven of nine races, and was voted top three-year-old and Horse of the Year. That year he began his string of five successive victories in the Jockey Club Gold Cup. At four Kelso won seven of nine, including the Metropolitan Handicap in which the gelding carried 130 lbs. to victory by a neck. That same year Kelso began his series of tries on the turf at Laurel Race Course, Md, finally winning in record time in 1964. Following his retirement, Kelso was foxhunted until arthritis led to his pensioning.

KURTSINGER, Charles F. "Chicken"
Jockey
Born 1907 in Shepherdsville, Ky; called Chicken because he loved to eat the bird; could never gain over 109 lbs. even though he ate constantly; died of pneumonia and complications at age 39 in Louisville, Ky.

Charlie Kurtsinger rode Twenty Grand to win the Kentucky Derby in 1931. He won the Preakness with Head Play in 1933 and in 1937 with Sam Riddle's War Admiral became the fourth rider in history to win the Triple Crown. His other outstanding Thoroughbreds were Captain Hal, Menow and Dark Secret. After his loss on Twenty Grand in 1938 to Seabiscuit, at Pimlico, his career seemed to fade away.

MISS WOODFORD
Horse
Born 1880; brown filly; sire Billet; dam Fancy Jane; bred by George W. Bowen; owned by G. W. Bowen, Catesby Woodford, Ezekiel F. Clay, Dwyer Brothers; trained by J. Hannigan, James G. Rowe, Sr, Frank McCabe; the sale of Fancy Jane for a barrel of whiskey to Col. E. F. Clay and Col. Catesby Woodford was not reported and consequently George W. Bowen is listed as the breeder; died 1899.

1882	8 starts,	5 wins,	$ 6,600 earnings
1883	12 starts,	10 wins,	51,230 earnings
1884	9 starts,	9 wins,	21,070 earnings
1885	12 starts,	7 wins,	19,370 earnings
1886	7 starts,	6 wins,	20,000 earnings
	48 starts,	37 wins,	$118,270 earnings

Miss Woodford won her first start at three, the Lady's Stakes, and went on to take the Mermaid, Monmouth Oaks, and the Alabama. Shortly thereafter Miss Woodford had a string of 16 consecutive victories over three seasons, including the Pimlico Stakes. At four Miss Woodford established an American record that still stands in the Long Island Stakes. Her most memorable race was at six when she became the first horse in America to earn over $100,000 in the Eclipse Stakes. It was at this race that Miss Woodford, literally, brought the house down. Spectators were crowded into the press box to get a better view and the structure collapsed.

MULHOLLAND, Bert
Trainer
Died at age 84.

Bert Mulholland worked as an assistant to Andrew Jackson Joyner in Widener's Stable. He succeeded Joyner as trainer and for the following 35 years sent out winners of more than 800 races and exceeded earnings of $6.5 million. Mulholland regarded Eight Thirty and Lucky Draw as the best horses he ever trained. His other winners included Battlefield, Jaipur, Jamestown, High Fleet, Bold Hour, Crewman, Evening Out, Platter, Ring Twice, Rare Treat, Seven Thirty, Stefanito and Steeple Jill. Mulholland was still training actively when he suffered a heart attack at the age of 83. He died one year later.

1968

BOSTWICK, George H.
Jockey
Uncle was owner F. Ambrose Clark; was trained by Maj. Tom McCreary; also a polo player, fox hunter and trainer.

George Bostwick is best known as a steeplechaser and flat racer. He first rode for Howe Stable. He was noticed by Thomas Hitchcock and took Hitchcock's horses Bangle and Darkness to victories at Corinthian in 1929 and 1930. He won the Meadow Brook three years in a row, 1929 through 1931, with Canterbury, Chenango and Darkness. He also rode in the Grand National at Aintree three times. In 1932 Bostwick registered his own colors. Among the horses to carry them were Burglar, Uncovered, Road Agent, Blind Bowboy, Pompeius and Uncanny. His best jumper was Cottesmore, who won the Meadow Brook, North American, Beverwyck, Grand National and Temple Gwathmey. Bostwick's favorite was Nellie Bly, which won the Beldame under his tutelage. In 1973 Bostwick turned the training over to J. J. Weipert.

CHILDS, Frank E.
Trainer
Born December 27, 1887; his grandfather arrived in Oregon in a covered wagon, raced Standardbreds; father trainer Lewis A. Childs; as a child Frank rubbed down horse for his father; died 1973 at age 85.

Frank Childs had one Kentucky Derby winner, Tommy Lee in 1959, but he trained dozens of other good horses, including Sir Ribot, Occupy, Bolero, Berseem, Weldy and Carpenter's Rule. At one point Frank induced owner Fred Turner, Jr, to put Weldy in the Futurity. Weldy won $62,390. The tall, straight Frank Childs continued to train horses until the time of his death.

McKINNEY, Rigan
Jockey
Born January 2, 1908, in Wickliffe, Ohio; father respected horseman Price McKinney; won first race at 14 on Miss Elizabeth in Painesville, Ohio, fair; was a wizard in the show ring; proficient in polo; accomplished trainer; commercial breeder.

Rigan McKinney's talent was bringing out the best in the jumper. His first major conquest came in 1930 at the Harbor Hill Steeplechase aboard Cree. McKinney was the 1931 leading money-winning steeplechase rider. That same year in the Grand National he set a record on Green Cheese that lasted a quarter of a century. Some of his other horses were Rioter, Chenango, Beacon Hill, Annibal, Ammagansett and Ossabaw. He was the leader in both races won and purses earned in 1933, 1936 and 1938. Once his mount, Alligator, fell at the first fence but McKinney still managed to win the race by 20 lengths.

OLD ROSEBUD
Horse
Born 1911; bay gelding; sire Uncle; dam Ivory Bells; bred by John E. Madden; owned by Col. Hamilton C. Applegate, Frank D. Weir; trained by F. D. Weir; suffered chronic ankle problems throughout career; destroyed 1922.

1913	14 starts,	12 wins,	$19,057 earnings
1914	3 starts,	2 wins,	9,575 earnings
1917	21 starts,	15 wins,	31,720 earnings
1919	30 starts,	9 wins,	12,182 earnings
1920	8 starts,	1 win,	1,295 earnings
1921	2 starts,	1 win,	700 earnings
1922	2 starts,	0 wins,	200 earnings
	80 starts,	40 wins,	$74,729 earnings

At two Old Rosebud started 14 times and won 12, including the Yucatan Stakes, Louisville and Saratoga. He pulled up lame in the last race of the season. Old Rosebud recovered sufficiently to win the 1914 Kentucky Derby in record time. His record stood for 16 years. In his next race he bowed a tendon and retired for the season. The gelding spent his four- and five-year-old seasons recovering from injuries. At six he won 15 of 21 races, breaking down again that year. He returned as an eight-year-old and won 11 of 42 starts over the next four years. Old Rosebud was destroyed at the age of 11, when he stepped in a hole at the Jamaica track.

STOUT, James
Jockey
In 935 Scout won 111 races for Bill Dwyer. Sunny Jim Fitzsimmons bought his contract and put him on Granville for the Kentucky Derby. At the start Bold Venture ran into Granville, Jimmy became unbalanced and hit the ground about 50 yds. later. Stout and Granville came back to take the Belmont. Riding Johnstown, Stout took the 1939 Derby by ten lengths. Stout on Bousset was a member of racing's first triple dead heat in a major stakes, the Carter Handicap. Stout's other victories included the Jockey Club Gold Cup with Count Arthur in 1936 and Fenelon in 1940, the Brooklyn Handicap with Isolater in 1940 and Fenelon in 1941. During his career Stout rode 2056 winners in 25 years, for earnings of nearly $7 million.

1969

BATTLESHIP
Horse
Born in 1927; chestnut colt; sire Man o' War; dam Quarantaine; bred and owned by W. J. Salmon, Sr. and later owned by Mrs. Marion DePont Scott; trained by Jack Pryce, S. L. Burch and Reginal Hobbs; sired 57 foals with a 21 percent stakes winners; Aintree Grand National Steeplechase 1938; foals include Shipboard, War Battle, Floating Isle, Tide Rips, Navigate, Westport Point, Navy Gun, Eolus, Sea Legs, Cap-A-Pie and Mighty Mo; died 1958.

1933	4 starts,	3 wins,	$ 2,150 earnings
1934	6 starts,	4 wins,	8,600 earnings
1936	5 starts,	1 win,	808 earnings
1937	13 starts,	5 wins,	4,553 earnings
1938	5 starts,	1 win,	37,150 earnings
	33 starts,	14 wins,	$53,361 earnings

At the age of four, Battleship won the one-and-a-sixteenth-mile Great Lakes Handicap at Hawthorne and was third in the Bay View Claiming Stakes, ending his career on the flat with 10 wins out of 22 starts. Bought in 1931 by Mrs. Scott, Battleship began his steeplechase career at the age of six. He won the Billy Barton Steeplechase at Pimlico and the National Hunt Club Handicap at Brookline that year. In 1934 Battleship won the Grand National Steeplechase at Belmont Park. He was shipped to England and won five during 1936 and 1937. In 1938 the smallish Battleship became the first American-owned horse to take the Aintree Grand National Steeplechase. He was in the lead halfway through the event, but was challenged by Ireland's Royal Danieli. Battleship was victorious by a nose.

DISCOVERY
Horse
Born 1931; chestnut colt; sire Display; dam Ariadne; bred by Walter J. Salmon, Sr; owned by Adolphe Pans, Alfred G. Vanderbilt; trained by John R. Pryce, J. H. Scotler; Horse of the Year and Champion Handicap Horse 1935; Champion Handicap Horse 1936; sired 26 stakes winners, including Find, Conniver and Loser Weeper; died 1958.

1933	14 starts,	2 wins,	$ 8,397 earnings
1934	16 starts,	8 wins,	49,555 earnings
1935	19 starts,	11 wins,	102,545 earnings
1936	14 starts,	6 wins,	34,790 earnings
	63 starts,	27 wins,	$195,287 earnings

Discovery won twice as a two-year-old and attracted the attention of Alfred Vanderbilt, who purchased him for $25,000. Because Cavalcade was dominating the three-year-olds, Discovery was sent to start against older horses. He won the Brooklyn Handicap and seven other races that year, setting a world record at the Rhode Island Handicap. Discovery had his best year as a four-year-old when he won 11 races in 19 starts, carrying an average of 130 lbs. At five he won 6 of 14 races. Discovery was retired to stud in Maryland in 1936.

GARNER, Mack
Jockey
See entry in National Jockeys Hall of Fame, 1959.

KNAPP, Willie
Jockey
Willie Knapp participated in some major surprises during his career. In 1917 he won the Brooklyn Handicap with a nine-year-old horse named Borrow, beating out two Kentucky Derby winners. Normally, he was the regular jockey for Sun Briar owned by Willis Sharpe Kilmer. The two-year-old champion had won five of nine starts and was being prepared for the Kentucky Derby when he went lame. Knapp was instead carried by Exterminator, a 30–1 shot. He won by a length. The 1919 Sanford Stakes brought Willie's greatest coup. His mount, Upset, took the lead and managed to hold off Man o' War just long enough to win the race. In 1920 Knapp turned to training.

LEWIS, John Howard
Trainer
Father one of founders of Rose Tree Hunt Club, Pa; attended Swarthmore College; great amateur steeplechase rider; died at age 85.

Lewis' career included everything from riding to breeding to training. In a limited stud operation at Highwood Farm in Pennsylvania, Lewis bred Swarthmore in 1884. He went on to train steeplechasers for Joseph Widener and over the years he had 150 stakes winners. His stable won the Manly Memorial eight times, the Temple Gwathmey six times, the Charles L. Appleton five times and the Grand National five times. Duettiste was his best horse, winning the International Steeplechase in 1924.

THOMPSON, Herbert John "Derby Dick"
Trainer
Born September 21, 1881, in Detroit, Mich; began his career in harness racing.

Derby Dick Thompson went to work for Col. E. R. Bradley as an aide to trainer Cliff Hammond in 1909. He took over as trainer in 1918 and recorded four Kentucky Derby winners in less than 20 years. Derby Dick's winners included Behave Yourself in 1921, Bubbling Over in 1926, Burgoo King in 1932 and Broken Tip in 1933. Thompson's record shows 373 winners and $1,296,761 in purses as a trainer.

1970

ADAMS, Frank David "Dooley"

Jockey

Born in Port Chester, N.Y; father managed Greenwich Polo Club; rode in first race at age 14; acquired trainer's license at age 16.

Dooley Adams rode three winners in 1944 in New York. In 1946 he had 28 winners and the following year he rode 23 to victory. From 1949 through 1955 Dooley was undisputedly Number One of the jumping jockeys. Over the years he had won most of the major steeplechase stakes at least once. His favorite horses were Neji, Elkridge and Refugio, which he trained himself. After retiring from riding, Dooley bought a training quarters, Refugio Farm in North Carolina.

AMERICAN ECLIPSE

Horse

Born, 1814; chestnut colt; sire Duroc; dam Miller's Damsel; bred and owned by Gen. Nathaniel Coles and W. Van Ranst; sired Medoc, Mingo, Ariel and Black Maria; died 1847.

1818	1 start,	1 win,	$ 300 earnings
1819	2 starts,	2 wins,	1,000 earnings
1820	0 starts,	0 wins,	0 earnings
1821	1 start,	1 win,	500 earnings
1822	3 starts,	3 wins,	3,200 earnings
1823	1 start,	1 win ,	20,000 earnings
	8 starts,	8 wins,	$25,000 earnings

In the early nineteenth century American Eclipse brought northern racetracks back to life. He started racing as a four-year-old in 1818 and won a 3-mile heat in New York for $300. Sold in 1819 for $3000 to Van Ranst, American Eclipse won two $500 4-mile heats that year and was then retired to stud. He was brought back into competition after two seasons at stud. The seven-year-old defeated Lady Lightfoot in two consecutive heats for $500. As an eight-year-old he was challenged to a match with the famous Sir Charles, but James J. Harrison, his owner, forfeited the match when Sir Charles injured a tendon. In 1823 a match was arranged between American Eclipse and Sir Henry for $20,000. Sir Henry won the first match, but American Eclipse won the second and third heats to take the purse. With a record of eight for eight, American Eclipse was permanently retired to stud.

BUCKPASSER

Horse

Born 1963; bay colt; sire Tom Fool; dam Busanda; bred and owned by Ogden Phipps; trained by W. C. Winfrey, Eddie A. Neloy; Champion Juvenile Colt 1965; Horse of the Year 1966; sired La Prevoyante and Numbered Account.

1965	11 starts,	9 wins,	$ 568,096 earnings
1966	14 starts,	13 wins,	669,078 earnings
1967	6 starts,	3 wins,	224,840 earnings
	31 starts,	25 wins,	$1,462,014 earnings

At two Buckpasser won nine of eleven races, taking the Champagne Stakes and the Arlington-Washington Futurity. At three Buckpasser was unbeatable for 16 months, but missed all of the Triple Crown events due to a quarter crack. He came back to take the Arlington Classic, the American Derby, the Travers Stakes, the Lawrence Realization and the Jockey Club Gold Cup. After his fourth year he was retired to Clairborne Farm in Kentucky.

COLTILETTI, Frank

Jockey

Born in the Bronx, N.Y; was 5 ft. 8 in, usually weighed about 105 lbs.

Coltiletti won many of the country's great stakes, including the Travers, Chesapeake, Dixie Handicap, Hopeful, Futurity, Preakness and Coaching Club American Oaks, but in seven tries he never won the Kentucky Derby. His service was in great demand because the horses "just seemed to run for him." Particularly alert, Frankie was usually able to gain two lengths at the post.

PATRICK, Gilbert "Gilpatrick"

Jockey

Gilpatrick raced in the era of 4-mile heats, but his talent was in his ability to switch from 4-mile heats to 1-mile races, more like those of today. Gilpatrick began racing around 1936. Probably the most renowned of his mounts was Boston, though a mare named Charmer who was never beaten was his favorite. In 1855, on Lexington, Gilpatrick set a record of 7:19 in a 4-mile exhibition. He is considered by many the best jockey of the nineteenth century.

PURDY, Samuel

Jockey

Samuel Purdy gained fame as a jockey in the early nineteenth century, but his true glory came at New York's Union Course on May 1823, when he was called from the spectators to ride American Eclipse in the final heats of the Northern horse versus the Southern horse, Henry. He was 38 years old and retired, but had anticipated the North's problems and came to the course wearing colors, covered by a long coat. Purdy won two heats and was eulogized on the floor of Congress by John Randolph of Roanoke as "the most skillful of jockeys."

SHILLING, Carroll "Cal"

Jockey

See entry in National Jockeys Hall of Fame, 1959.

VAN BERG, Marion Harold "Mr Van"

Trainer

Born in Columbus, Nebr; most of life a livestock dealer and farmer; died shortly after a heart attack in Omaha, Nebr, on May 3, 1971.

Mr. Van made his official debut as an owner at the age of 41. At first he relied on C. A. Tanner to train his horses, but in 1945 he became his own trainer. He raced mostly in the Midwest, leading owners in numbers of victories in 1952, 1955, 1956 and from 1960 to 1970. As his stable expanded he called on his son Jack, R. L. Irwin and K. D. Kelper to help him out with various aspects. In 1963 Irwin handled 27 wins at Hazel Park to take the lead among trainers. Mr. Van then came on to produce 47 winners to beat out Irwin for the championship. His yellow silks with a purple V raced nearly 2000 horses with 4691 wins and $13,936,965 in purses.

WALDEN, R. W.

Trainer

Died April 28, 1905.

R. W. Walden holds a record for having won the Preakness seven times. His first was in 1875 with Tom Ochiltree. In 1878 Duke of Magenta began a streak of five consecutive Preakness wins as well as four Belmont victories for owner George Lorillard. Following Lorillard's death in 1880, Walden remained active in the sport with horses bred on his own Bowling Brook Stud in Middleburg, Md. His winners included Galore, Compute, Filigrante and the Friar. Walden's sound training techniques earned him more than a million dollars.

1971

BEDWELL, Harvey Guy "Hard Guy"

Trainer

Born 1876 in Roseboro, Ore; at age 13 was a cowboy on the Oregon range; county clerk in Grand Junction, Colo; operated a livery stable; died in 1950.

By the age of 33 Guy had established himself as the leading trainer in the nation, with 122 winners. He purchased Sir Barton for $10,000. Sir Barton became the first Triple Crown winner in 1919. Guy Bedwell trained for Commander J. K. L. Ross, Harold Hecht, Capt. Ral Par and Maine Chance Farm. Guy was persistent, patient and a perfectionist.

DR. FAGER

Horse

Born 1964; bay colt; sire Rough 'N Tumble; dam Aspidistra; bred and owned by Tartan Farms; trained by John A. Nerud; 16.5 hands high; named for Dr. Charles Fager, Boston brain surgeon who saved the trainer's life after a fall from a pony in 1965; Horse of the Year 1968.

1966	5 starts,	4 wins,	$ 112,338 earnings
1967	9 starts,	7 wins,	484,194 earnings
1968	8 starts,	7 wins,	406,110 earnings
	22 starts,	18 wins,	$1,002,642 earnings

At two Dr. Fager won his first four starts, including the World's Playground and Cowdin Stakes. At three he won the Withers by six lengths, took the Jersey Derby, the Arlington Classic and set a track record in the Rockingham Special. He closed out that season by winning the Hawthorne Gold Cup and Vosburgh handicap. At four Dr. Fager won the Roseben, the Californian, the Suburban, the Whitney by eight lengths, the Washington Park Handicap by ten lengths and the United Nations. Dr. Fager was voted Champion Sprinter, Champion Grass Horse, Champion Handicapper and Horse of the Year in 1968. His career earnings were over $1 million.

JAY TRUMP

Horse

Born 1957; dark bay gelding; sire Tonga Prince; dam Be Trump; bred by Jay Frank Sensenich; owned by J. F. Sensenich, Mrs. Mary C. Stephenson; trained by F. Sensenich, H. Robertson Fenwick, Fred Winter; Hunters Triple Crown 1964; Grand National Steeplechase at Aintree 1965; was a terror on the track; many jockeys refused to ride him; retired at age nine.

1959	4 starts,	0 wins,	0 earnings
1960	4 starts,	0 wins,	$ 220 earnings
1961	0 starts,	0 wins,	0 earnings
1962	2 starts,	2 wins,	650 earnings
1963	2 starts,	1 win,	trophy earnings
1964	6 starts,	3 wins,	1,840 earnings
1965	5 starts,	5 wins,	61,715 earnings
1966	3 starts,	2 wins,	trophy earnings
	26 starts,	12 wins,	$64,425 earnings

Tommy Smith was attracted by Jay Trump's size and conformity. He was purchased by Smith as a hunter for his godmother. Jay Trump was sent to Maryland for training and was used in the hunt during his four-year-old season. He was returned to competition in 1962, winning two official jumping races. The next year he won the Maryland Hunt Cup. In 1964 Smith and Jay Trump swept the Triple Crown of the hunters: Butler Grand National, My Lady's Manor and Maryland Hunt Cup. Jay Trump was shipped to England for the 1965 Grand National Steeplechase at Aintree. He was neck and neck over the last jump, but he fought off the challenger to win by a length. Jay Trump was retired the following year after again taking the My Lady's Manor and the Maryland Hunt Cup.

JOHNSON, Albert

Jockey

Albert Johnson's victories include two triumphs in the Kentucky Derby, one in 1922 with Morvich and one in 1926 with Bubbling Over; and the Belmont Stakes in 1925 and 1926 with American Flag and Crusader, respectively. He also won the Black Eyed Susan at Pimlico twice, the Brooklyn handicap with Exterminator, the Champagne on Bubbling Over, the Belmont Futurity, the Pimlico Futurity, Dwyer, Coaching Club Oaks and Fashion. In 1922 Johnson was the country's leading money winner with $345,054.

LONGFELLOW "King of the Turf"

Horse

Born 1867; brown colt; sire Leamington; dam Nantura; bred, owned and trained by John Harper; sired The Bard, Freeland, Lonstreet, Thora, Leonatus and Riley; America's leading sire in 1891; called Longfellow because of the length of his legs (17 hands high); died 1893.

1870	5 starts,	4 wins,	$ 3,100 earnings
1871	6 starts,	5 wins,	4,450 earnings
1872	5 starts,	4 wins,	3,650 earnings
	16 starts,	13 wins,	$11,200 earnings

Because of his extreme growth, no attempt was made to race Longfellow as a two-year-old. At three he scored consecutive victories in the Produce and Ohio Stakes and later took the Post Stakes. As a four-year-old he was considered the best and had trouble finding competition. At five a meeting of Longfellow and the eastern star, Harry Bassett, was arranged. Longfellow won with such ease as to throw suspicion on the fairness of the contest. He met Harry Bassett again but twisted the shoe on his left forefoot at the start, losing by only a length. His foot had been so mutilated from the effort that he was retired to stud. Walter S. Vosburgh claimed, "No horse of his day was a greater object of public notice. His entire career was sensational; people seemed to regard him as a superhorse."

SMITHWICK, D. Michael "Mikey"
Trainer

Brother A. Patrick Smithwick steeplechase jockey; rode amateur as teenager for six wins at Maryland Hunt Club.

Mikey and his brother Paddy achieved unparalleled fame in steeplechasing with Paddy riding the horses Mikey trained. Mikey was the nation's leading steeplechase money winner, 13 times during a 14-year period from 1957 to 1970. In 1970 one of Mikey's horses, Top Bid, took the first Colonial Cup offered by Mrs. Marion duPont Scott. The following year another of his horses, Inkslinger, captured the second running of the Colonial Cup.

WINFREY, William C.
Trainer

Stepfather Carey Winfrey; rode at age 6; 16-year-old jockey; quit after six months because of weight problems.

Winfrey's first stakes winner was Postage Due, at Jamaica in 1938. He trained for Alfred G. Vanderbilt from 1949 to 1958, producing horses like Native Dancer, Social Outcast, Bed o' Roses and Next Move. From 1963 to 1965 he was with the Phipps' runners Buckpasser, Bold Lad and Queen Empress. The highlight of his career was his 1964 title of leading money-winning trainer with earnings of over $1 million in one season.

1972

BASSETT, Carroll K.
Jockey

Born in Summit, N.J; began career as a fox hunter and a high-goal polo player; also a sculptor, specializing in horses; died 1972.

Bassett's best-known mount was Mrs. Marion duPont Scott's Battleship, which he rode in all of his American races. Battleship became the first American-bred and owned horse to win the Grand National at Aintree. He also took two wins in the Maryland International Grand National and Belmont Parks Grand National. Another of his horses was Annapolis, which won the Master of Foxhounds Steeplechase at Pimlico. Bassett led all steeplechasers in the number of races won from 1932 through 1935. His other well-known mounts were Sable Muff, Wild Son, Brattinious and Passive.

GUERIN, Eric
Jockey

Born 1924; began his career at the age of 16.

Guerin won the 1947 Kentucky Derby on Jet Pilot. In 1951 he was riding Your Host when the colt tripped and fell, fracturing his foreleg in four places. He was saved for stud and eventually sired Kelso. The following year, riding Native Dancer, Guerin scored victories in all nine of his starts, but lost the Derby. Someone commented that "he took that colt (Native Dancer) everywhere on the track except to the ladies' room." Guerin came back to take the Belmont Stakes with High Gun. His lifetime record shows that with over 20,000 mounts, Guerin finished first with 2700 and in the money with almost 5000. He won over $17 million in purses.

KUMMER, Clarence
Jockey

Kummer is best remembered as Man o' War's regular rider. Due to a broken collar bone he was fortunately not aboard Big Red in the famous Sanford Stakes upset. Later in his career Kummer rode Vito to win the Belmont Stakes and a horse named Coventry to win the Preakness. His career was cut short by an untimely death in 1930.

NERUD, John
Trainer

Born February 9, 1913 in Nebraska; rode in match races and rodeos during teens; served in Navy in W.W. II; rubbed horses and mucked stalls; a jockey agent.

John Nerud became a licensed trainer at the age of 18. He did not gain national prominence until 1956, when he won the Palm Beach and McLennon Handicaps with Switch On. In 1957 Gallant Man missed the Derby by a nose, but went on to take the Belmont in record time. At Tartan Farms in Florida Nerud's purchase of Intentionally guaranteed him breeding success. Dr. Fager was to be his greatest success. Nerud named the horse after a Boston surgeon who saved the trainer's life after he suffered a head injury in a fall. Dr. Fager won 18 of 22 starts and earned $1,002,642 in 1968, the season in which he was Horse of the Year.

PAN ZARETA
Horse

Born 1910; chestnut filly; sire Abe Frank; dam Caddie Griffith; bred by J. F. Newman; owned by J. F. and H. S. Newman, E. T. Colton and Joe Marrone; trained by H. S. Newman, E. "Doc" Foucon, E. T. Colton and J. C. Kirkpatrick; died of pneumonia December 25, 1918, in New Orleans; was buried in the infield of the track.

1912	19 starts,	13 wins,	$ 3,512 earnings
1913	33 starts,	15 wins,	8,895 earnings
1914	28 starts,	13 wins,	7,085 earnings
1915	26 starts,	15 wins,	7,540 earnings
1916	11 starts,	7 wins,	3,085 earnings
1917	34 starts,	13 wins,	8,965 earnings
	151 starts,	76 wins,	$39,082 earnings

Pan Zareta raced at minor tracks during her first five seasons, campaigning in Mexico, Idaho, Montana, Kentucky, Canada, Texas, Louisiana and Arkansas. No mare ever carried such weight. She carried 130 lbs. 38 times and in seven races carried 140 lbs. or more. In 1916, E. T. Colton bought Pan Zareta for $10,000 and the next season she arrived in New York. She won at Aqueduct and Empire City with weights of 137 and 140 lbs. She was retired for breeding in 1918, but failed to get in foal and was returned to training in New Orleans.

ROUND TABLE
Horse

Born 1954; bay colt; sire Princequello; dam Knight's Daughter; bred by A. B. Hancock, Jr.'s Claiborne Farm;

owned by A. B. Hancock, Jr, Travis M. Kerr; trained by Moody Jolley, William Molter; Horse of the Year 1957; Turf Champion 1957, 1958 and 1959; topped America's sire list in 1972.

1956	10 starts, 5 wins,	$ 73,326	earnings
1957	22 starts, 15 wins,	600,383	earnings
1958	20 starts, 14 wins,	662,780	earnings
1959	14 starts, 9 wins,	413,380	earnings
	66 starts, 43 wins,	$1,749,869	earnings

As a two-year-old Round Table won half of his ten races, including the Breeder's Futurity and the Lafayette Stakes. He was purchased by Travis Kerr for $145,000 and 20 percent in the horse's breeding qualities. Round Table won his first races in Kerr colors. He was shipped to the East Coast for the Derby, placing third behind Iron Liege and Gallant Man. At four Round Table surpassed the $1 million mark in earnings. He was hampered by a quarter crack at five, but continued to win and increased his earnings to $1,749,869, a record surpassed only by Kelso. He was named Turf Champion for the third consecutive year and retired to stud at Claiborne Farm.

1973

BOLD RULER
Horse

Born April 1954; dark bay colt; sire Nasrullah; dam Miss Disco; bred and owned by Mrs. Henry Carnegie Phipps' Wheatley Stables; trained by James E. Fitzsimmons; Horse of the Year 1957; Three-Year-Old Champion 1957; sired 75 stakes winners including Secretariat, Lamb Chop, Gamely, American's Bold Lad, England's Bold Lad, Successor, Bold Bidder, Vitriolic, Queen of the Stage and Queen Empress; born with a hernia; hampered by a rheumatic condition; suffered a tongue injury as a yearling; pulled a back muscle and sustained a hock injury at two; died of cancer 1971.

1956	10 starts, 7 wins,	$139,050	earnings
1957	16 starts, 11 wins,	415,160	earnings
1958	7 starts, 5 wins,	209,994	earnings
	33 starts, 23 wins,	$764,204	earnings

Despite the physical problems, Bold Ruler began his career at two with five wins and the third fastest time recorded for the Futurity. At three years he took the Wood Memorial, was fourth in the Kentucky Derby, won the Preakness and lost the Belmont Stakes after tiring in the last quarter of a mile. Bold Ruler climaxed the year by beating the Belmont winner in the Trenton Handicap. Bold Ruler won five of seven starts at four years old, but lameness caused his retirement to stud.

BOULMETIS, Sam
Jockey

Born 1928 in Baltimore, Md; his son Sam, Jr, also a jockey.

Sam Boulmetis rode his first horse in 1948. He was the leading rider at Hialeah in the winter of 1950. He signed to ride for Glen Riddle Farm, until Riddle died. After that he was associated with Greentree Stable for a couple of years, until 1961. During his 19-year career as a jockey, Sam won 2783 races for earnings of $15,425,935. He considers Tosmah the best horse he ever rode, with Vertex, Errand King and Helioscope following her. Upon his retirement from riding, Boulmetis became a racing official and in the mid-1970s was appointed state steward on the New Jersey circuit.

BURLEW, Fred
Trainer

A stable hand at age 11; a jockey for a short time; died of a brain tumor in 1927 at age 56.

Fred Burlew began his training career at age 18 in 1889. In 1903 he began training Beldame, while she was leased to Newton Bennington. Beldame was one of the best fillies ever to race. Burlew went abroad just before W. W. I. When the hostilities began he rescued many horses from the war. One of those was Inchcape, winner of the Tremont Stakes in 1920. Sam Hildreth paid the highest price ever paid for a two-year-old at that time for Inchcape. Morvich was Burlew's greatest challenge. The weak sprinter looked as though he would break down at the gate, but as a two-year-old in 1921 he won 11 races. The following year he took the Kentucky Derby. During his career that spanned 37 years as a trainer, Burlew saddled 977 winners and won 124 stakes races with 75 of them.

CRAWFORD, Robert H. "Specs"
Jockey

Called Specs because of his freckles; tall, had trouble keeping his weight down; retired to Scottsdale, Ariz.

Specs Crawford's peak riding years were from 1918 to 1928, when his winning percentage was about 40. He began his rise to fame by winning the 1918 Beverwyck, Glendale and Shillelah on The Brook. Crawford won the Grand National on Lytle in 1922 and took the same race on Erne II in 1926. In 1928, Jolly Roger carried Crawford to victory at the Grand National and the Brook Steeplechase, earning $143,240 in purses. His other stakes winners included Barklie, Not Much, Hibler, Rabel, Bullseye, Mirata, Caribinier and Thorndale. Crawford trained jumpers for several years before retiring.

HITCHCOCK, Thomas, Sr.
Trainer

Born 1861; a well-known polo player; captain of America's first international polo team; wife died from a fall in the hunt in 1934; son Thomas, Jr, the greatest polo player in U. S. history, killed in an Air Force plane crash in England in 1944; died in 1941 at age 80.

Thomas Hitchcock's interest gradually shifted from polo to steeplechase. He won the 1906 American Grand National with Good and Plenty. He won the same ride again in 1938 with Annibel. His other stars included Bangle, Amagansett, Yenasee, Salitta, Ossabaw and Cottesmore. Hitchcock began a horse colony in Aiken, S.C, in the early 1900s. He was a member of the Jockey Club and one of the founders of Belmont Park in 1905.

HUGHES, Hollie
Trainer

Born near Amsterdam, N.Y.

At the age of 15 he became a trainer's helper at Hurricana Farm near his home. Later, when Will Hayword became trainer for the Sanford Family, Hughes became assistant trainer. In 1913 Hughes was named head trainer. In 1916 he won the Kentucky Derby with George

Smith and two years later the one-and-a-half mile Bowie Handicap with the same horse. Hughes is probably best known for his training of steeplechasers, winning the Grand National at Belmont Park six times. A jumper named Sergeant Murphy won the Grand National at Aintree in 1920.

SMITHWICK, Alfred Patrick "Paddy"
Jockey
Brother Mikey a trainer of steeplechasers; National Steeplechase Champion Jockey 1956 – 1958 and 1962; died of cancer in November, 1973, at age 46.

Paddy Smithwick won the title of Champion Jockey of the National Steeplechase and Hunt Association four times, 1956 through 1958 and 1962. In all Paddy had 400 winners over the obstacles. During his career he rode two National Champions, Neji (1955, 1957 and 1958) and Bon Nouvel (1958). His victories included four runnings of the Temple Gwathmey and six each in the Georgetown and Meadowbrook. Paddy and his brother Mikey were steeplechasing's best for more than a decade. Paddy's riding career ended when he fractured his neck in a spill at Monmouth Park.

TUCKERMAN, Bayard, Jr.
Jockey
Born 1889; at 11 years old had saved enough money to buy a Thoroughbred mare; died 1974 in South Westport, Mass.

In his earlier years Tuckerman was one of the few amateurs who would compete against professionals. He became one of the world's leading steeplechase riders, riding alongside some of the world's most famous people. He was the riding champion of Edward, Duke of Windsor. After purchasing the 200-acre Little Sunswick Farm, he became interested in breeding Thoroughbreds. He once said that his greatest pleasure came from breeding a good horse and seeing him win. Among his top horses were Steel Viking, Lavender Hill, Orco and the Crack. In 1935 Tuckerman was elected president of the Suffolk Downs and to the Jockey Club in 1953. The Suffolk Downs stages the annual Bayard Tuckerman, Jr, Handicap to honor him for his contribution to New England racing and breeding.

1974

DAMASCUS
Horse
Born 1964; bay colt; sire Sword Dancer; dam Kerala; bred and owned by Mrs. Thomas M. Bancroft; trained by Frank Y. Whiteley, Jr; Horse of the Year 1967.

1966	4 starts,	3 wins, $	25,865 earnings
1967	16 starts,	12 wins,	817,941 earnings
1968	12 starts,	6 wins,	332,975 earnings
	32 starts,	21 wins,	$1,176,781 earnings

Damascus had a light two-year-old campaign of only four races. At three Damascus secured his bid for Horse of the Year by beating his two closest contenders in the Woodward Stakes by ten lengths. He then won nine of his next ten races, including the Preakness Stakes, Belmont Stakes, American Derby, Dwyer, Travers and Aqueduct, and then added the two-mile Jockey Club Gold Cup, setting a one-year earnings record of $817,941. As a four-year-old, Damascus and Dr. Fager rivaled for back and forth wins. Damascus was later retired after he came out of the Jockey Club Gold Cup with a bowed tendon.

DARK MIRAGE
Horse
Born 1965; dark bay filly; sire Persian Road II; dam Home By Dark; bred by Duval A. Headley; owned by Lloyd I. Miller; trained by E. W. King; at four years old, dislocated sesamoid developed complications; Filly Triple Crown 1968; died summer 1969.

1967	15 starts,	2 wins, $	19,906 earnings
1968	10 starts,	9 wins,	322,433 earnings
1969	2 starts,	1 win,	20,450 earnings
	27 starts,	12 wins,	$362,789 earnings

Dark Mirage was the first to win the Filly Triple Crown and gained recognition as one of America's best fillies. She had nine straight wins as a three-year-old. Dark Mirage raced very little as a four-year-old. Tragedy brought her destruction that summer.

McCREARY, Conn "Convertible Conn"
Jockey
Born 1921 in St. Louis, Mo; at age 16 was apprenticed to Steve Judge.

Conn McCreary's greatest success came at the low point of his career in 1951. Against all advice he rode Conn Turf in the Kentucky Derby. McCreary won the race by four lengths for earnings of $98,050. During the height of his career, McCreary rode Calumet Farm's Pensive to an upset victory in the 1944 Kentucky Derby as well as the Preakness and finished second in the Belmont Stakes. McCreary won a number of stakes after 1951, including the 1952 Preakness on Blue Man.

SECRETARIAT
Horse
Born 1970; chestnut colt; sire Bold Ruler; dam Somethingroyal; bred by Meadow Stud; owned by Meadow Stable; trained by Lucien Laurin; Horse of the Year 1972; Horse of the Year and Triple Crown 1973.

1972	9 starts,	7 wins, $	456,404 earnings
1973	12 starts,	9 wins,	860,404 earnings
	21 starts,	16 wins,	$1,316,808 earnings

At two Secretariat won seven of his nine starts, including the Hopeful, the Futurity and the Garden State Stakes. Before his three-year-old campaign, Secretariat became the highest priced horse in history ($5,080,000). With Ron Turcotte aboard, Secretariat won the Kentucky Derby in record time, took the Preakness and dazzled everyone with a 31-length triumph in the Belmont Stakes. He was the first Triple Crown winner since Citation. Many place Secretariat above Man o' War as the all-time great horse.

WHITTINGHAM, Charlie "Bold Eagle"
Trainer
Born April 13, 1913 in San Diego, Calif; parents ranch farmers in Chula Vista; older brother Joe trained horses; went to work as stable hand during teens; delivered newspapers on horseback; served four years in Pacific during W. W. II as Marine; lost his hair from tropical disease.

Charlie Whittingham got his trainer's license in 1931 and signed on with Horatio Luro as assistant trainer. In the mid-1950s he went out on his own, taking over some horses for the Llangolen Farm and opening a public stable. During his 50 years on the track, Whittingham trained about 200 stakes winners with more than 35 of them winning over $100,000. He is one of the few trainers to top $1 million in earnings during a season for five seasons straight. Many times his charges would come in one, two, three. Some of Charlie's better known winners are Potterhouse, Mister Gus, Nashville and Black Sheep.

1975

CARRY BACK
Horse
Born 1958; sire Saggy; bred by J. A. Price; Champion Three-Year-Old 1961.

Carry Back won the 1960 Garden State Stakes. In 1961 he won the Kentucky Derby and the Preakness with J. Sellars aboard but lost the Belmont. That same year Carry Back took the Flamingo Stakes. In 1962 he took the Metropolitan Handicap. With 61 starts, 21 wins, 11 seconds, 11 thirds, Carry Back's earnings were $1,241,165.

JERKENS, A. H. "Allen"
Trainer
Allen Jerkens was a trainer for Habeau Farm. He trained Onion which beat Secretariat in the Whitney at Saratoga in August 1973. As a trainer Jerkens saw 368 of his horses start for 73 wins, 58 seconds, 53 thirds and $606,089 in purses. Cordero recalls that "the man was absolutely amazing. Take Step Nicely, sired by Watch Your Step and out of Beau Gar. If you put that colt in a yearling sale he wouldn't bring the first bid, but that's the kind Jerkens makes into stakes winners."

PINCAY, Laffit, Jr.
Jockey
See entry in National Jockeys Hall of Fame, 1975.

RUTHLESS
Horse
Ruthless won the first running of the Belmont Stakes with J. Gilpatrick aboard in 1867. That same year he also won the Travers Stakes.

SHUVEE
Horse
Born 1966; filly; sire Nashua; bred by Whitney Stone; Champion Handicap Filly 1970 and 1971.

Shuvee won the 1968 Selima Stakes at Laurel Race Course and the Frizette Stakes at Belmont for a total earnings of $199,246 in 1968, making her the leading stakes and feature race winner in only two races that season. In 1969 she took the Alabama Stakes and the Coach Club American Oaks. In 1970 Shuvee ran to victory in the Beldame Handicap and won the Jockey Club Gold Cup in 1970 and 1971. From 1968 through 1971 Shuvee had 44 starts, 16 wins, 10 seconds, 6 thirds for a total earnings of $890,445.

STYMIE
Horse
Born 1941; colt; sire Equestrian; bred by Max Hirsh; Champion Handicap Horse of the Year 1945.

Stymie won the 1945 Brooklyn Handicap, the Grey Lag Handicap and was voted Champion Handicap Horse of the Year. He again won the Grey Lag Handicap in 1946 and went on to win the 1947 Massachusetts Handicap and the 1947 and 1948 Metropolitan Handicaps. Stymie's total earnings for the years 1943 through 1948 amounted to $918,485, with 131 starts, 35 wins, 33 seconds, and 28 thirds.

WINFREY, C. "Carey"
Trainer-Owner
As an owner Carey Winfrey saw 51 starts, 5 firsts, 4 seconds, 9 thirds and earnings of $27,140. As a trainer his mounts started 83 times, for 7 wins, 3 seconds, 8 thirds and earnings of $37,225.

1976

ALSAB
Horse
Born 1939; colt; sire Good Goods; bred by Thomas Piatt; Champion Two-Year-Old 1941; Champion Three-Year-Old 1942.

Alsab won the Champagne Stakes in 1941. In 1942 he won the American Derby, the Lawrence Realization, the Withers Stakes and the Preakness with B. James aboard. For the two years Alsab had 25 wins, 11 seconds, 5 thirds and $350,015 earnings.

BAEZA, Braulio
Jockey
See entry in National Jockeys Hall of Fame, 1967.

BED O' ROSES
Horse
Born 1947; filly; sire Rosemont; bred by A. G. Vanderbilt; Champion Two-Year-Old Filly 1949; Champion Handicap Filly 1951.

Bed O' Roses won the 1949 Matron Stakes and the Selima Stakes. In 1950 she took the Lawrence Realization. She had 18 wins, 8 seconds, 6 thirds and $383,925 total earnings 1949 – 1951.

BON NOUVEL
Horse
Born 1960; mahogany bay colt; sire Duc De Fur; dam Good News; bred by Dr. A. C. Randolph of Virginia; owned by Mrs. Theodora A. Randolph; over 16 hands high; Champion Steeplechase Horse of the Year 1964, 1965 and 1968.

Bon Nouvel was not raced as a two-year-old. He failed on the flat at three with one win and one place. Bon Nouvel was introduced to hurdle racing late in his three-year-old year. After being in the money three times, he won his final start in 1963. In 1964 he carried 156 lbs. in the Grand National Steeplechase and won that race easily. He also won the Harbor Hill, Broad Hollow and the Brook under handicap conditions. Bon Nouvel was only twice out of the money in 13 starts in 1964. On one occasion Bon Nouvel was involved in a seven-horse mishap in the Aqueduct Spring Steeplechase. He was still racing at the age of eight. Bon Nouvel had $62,805 lifetime earnings.

NORTHERN DANCER
Horse
Born 1961; colt; sire Nearctic; dam Natalma; bred and owned by Mr. and Mrs. E. P. Taylor of Canada; Champion Three-Year-Old Colt 1964; leading sire 1971.

As a two-year-old, Northern Dancer had an impressive record of seven wins in nine starts and two seconds for earnings of $90,635. At three he won the Flamingo, the Florida Derby, Keeneland's Blue Grass, the Kentucky Derby, the Preakness and the Canadian Queen's Plate. His 1963-1964 record was 14 wins, 2 seconds, 2 thirds for total earnings of $580,806. Northern Dancer was being readied for his Saratoga campaign when he pulled up lame with a tendon injury. He was retired to stud at Windfield Farm in 1965.
Also in: Canada's Sports Hall of Fame and Canadian Racing Hall of Fame.

RUFFIAN
Horse
Ruffian was expected to be the next Secretariat. The filly accepted a special challenge match held in the summer of 1975 at Churchill Downs. Just after taking off from the starting gate, she tripped and broke her leg. The three-year-old filly had to be destroyed.

SMITH, Robert A. "Whistling Bob"
Trainer
Born in Newburgh, N.Y; ran away from home; sold newspapers in the Bowery before working at the track for August Belmont I in 1881; successful in boxing as manager of lightweight champion Frank Erne; died in 1943 at age 73.

Even at an early age, good-natured Bob Smith demonstrated a special talent for developing calm, gentle horses and sensing champion yearling Thoroughbreds. After becoming an exercise rider for David Pulsifer in 1887, Whistling Bob bought a yearling at a public auction for $210—Tenny became one of Pulsifer's best horses. Bob also worked for Walter M. Jeffords, Sr, Audley Farm, Adm. Cary T. Grayson, Phil T. Chinn and others, but his greatest success came as trainer for Mrs. Isabel Dodge Sloane's Brookmeade Stable. He produced horses like Good Goods, Psychic Bid and Inlander. Cavalcade, a horse he bought as a yearling for $1500, won the 1934 Kentucky Derby the same year High Quest, a $3500 yearling, won the Preakness for two-thirds of a Triple Crown. A $700 yearling, Time Clock, later won the Florida Derby. For his efforts, Whistling Bob was the country's leading trainer in 1933 and 1934, and was leading money-winner the latter year with $249,938.

STEPHENS, W. C. "Woody"
Trainer
During his career as a trainer, Woody Stephens watched his mounts start 263 times for 43 wins, 41 seconds, 28 thirds and purses of $289,524.

SUSAN'S GIRL
Horse
Born 1969; mare; sire Quadrangle; dam Quaze; bred in Florida and owned by F. W. Hooper; trained by J. L. Newman.

Susan's Girl won the Eclipse Award at three and four years old, but missed the competition at five years old due to a fractured sesamoid in training in California during the spring of 1974. Following a successful operation and conditioning in Florida, this horse returned to racing in November and won an allowance event at Churchill Downs and won the Falls City Handicap. Following three starts at the Santa Anita track, two seconds and a third place, Susan's Girl's first win of 1975 was the Apple Blossom Handicap at Oakland Park on March 1. She went on to win the Long Beach Handicap at Hollywood Park, the Matchmaker Stakes at Atlantic City, the Delaware and Maskette Handicaps and the Beldame and Spinster Stakes. With 17 starts and 7 wins, Susan's Girl won a total of $361,951 for the year.

Horse Racing & Breeding Halls of Fame to Watch

CALGARY BREWERY HORSEMAN'S HALL OF FAME
Closed 1975
The Calgary Brewery Horseman's Hall of Fame in Calgary, Alberta, was permanently closed in 1975, when its internationally famous collection of memorabilia and records was presented to the Glenbow Alberta Institute to complement the existing Glenbow collection. The materials may be seen there today, although the separate identity of the Hall of Fame is completely lost. The Glenbow Alberta Institute (founded 1955) and the Glenbow Foundation are at Glenbow Centre, 9th Ave. & First St. S.E, Calgary. (403) 264-8300.

DAILY RACING FORM TWENTIETH CENTURY HALL OF FAME
Discontinued 1969
For a number of years during the 1960s, Triangle Publications, Inc., published an official and authoritative compilation of horse racing facts and statistics. A major regular feature of these annual publications was a section

HALL OF FAME FOR ARIZONA COW HORSES

Proposed 1957

A Hall of Fame for Arizona Cow Horses was proposed in Phoenix, Ariz, in May, 1957. It has not as yet been eventualized. Cow horse is the common term for any breed of horse which is highly trained for use on a ranch in connection with cow driving and roping. Persons interested in cow horses should contact Bob Benson or Duwayne Martin, Exec. Mgr, Rodeo Cowboy Association, 2929 W. 19th Ave, Denver CO 80204. (303) 629-0657.

called the Daily Racing Form Twentieth Century Hall of Fame, into which many of history's greatest Thoroughbreds were inducted. In 1969 these included (with year foaled): Citation (1945), Colin (1905), Count Fleet (1940), Equipose (1928), Exterminator (1915), Kelso (1957), Man o' War (1917), Nashua (1952), Native Dancer (1950), Swaps (1952), Sysonby (1902), and Tom Fool (1949). This Hall of Fame was discontinued following the reorganization of Triangle Publications, Inc.

HORSESHOE PITCHING

There was a time when pitching iron horseshoes would have been considered an absurdly stupid thing to do. For one thing, those peoples whose only iron came from meteorites, including the Mayas, the Incas and the Aztecs, considered iron to be more precious than gold. For another, those peoples who knew the process of smelting ores into iron held the latter to be very central in certain important social rites. For example, in Scandinavia and north Germany it was and still is the custom to shoe a horse as part of the rite of initiation into secret societies and the rite by which a groom entered the society of married men. Such widespread customs stemmed from the universal notion that the whole earth was sexualized. This notion is still reflected among jewelers who distinguish diamonds according to their brilliance as either male or female. Specifically, according to that ancient notion, ores grew like embryos in the belly of mother earth, miners were obstetricians who delivered those ores, and smiths were powerful magicians who gave ores their final form by turning them into metal. That is why smiths were so important and their products so potent virtually all over the ancient world. In most places the smiths, who had mastery over both fire and metal, were ranked in communal importance second only to the shamans or religious leaders. Sometimes they were black or evil magicians. In more numerous cases, however, smiths used their powers for good. In Siberian, Central Asian and European folklore, the role of blacksmith is played by Jesus Christ or certain saints. Good or bad, their products, including horseshoes, were powerful. And the idea of pitching them at pegs in the ground would have been considered reckless, blasphemous, sacrilegious and downright dangerous.

In some parts of the world that idea would still be seen that way, but for a somewhat different reason. For centuries the horseshoe's shape has been seen as a symbol of *mano cornuta,* or horns believed to be capable of warding off the potent influences of the evil eye. In Italy the characteristic gesture made by a fist with the index and little fingers extended is a symbol of those horns. The use of horns, the crescent moon and other items of that shape as protective symbols predates even ancient Egypt's cow-goddesses, Isis and Hathor, who were depicted wearing cow horns. The Virgin Mary is sometimes represented as a crescent moon conjoined with a cross. When viewed from the air, the Vatican is horn-shaped. From England to India, cow and other horns were nailed to the sides of houses and stables. When horn-shaped horseshoes were invented, they too were nailed up. In Scotland butter refusing to form would be blamed on the evil eye, whereupon the housewife would drop a horseshoe into the churn. All over Europe, more significant disasters like the loss of crops, the wasting of cattle, the rotting of pork, the molding of food and the souring of wine as well as maladies like disease, sterility, abortion and mental disorder were blamed on the evil eye. The horseshoe offered security and good luck against them all. The point is simply that to many people in the world throwing your horseshoes away from you is not a particularly wise thing to do.

Seen as more precious than gold and, in the shape of a pair of horns, as more powerful than a cross, iron understandably was not at first used to cover horses' feet. The Greeks, who didn't shoe their horses with iron, did keep in their stables wagonloads of oval stones to be used for filing down excess hoof. Under adverse conditions or on awkward terrain, they improvised: hipposandals (*hippos,* horse), boots or sackcloth covers were used to protect the toes of Grecian horses from sand and snow. In Japan, where iron horseshoes were not used until the middle of the nineteenth century, horse sandals were made of rice straw or cotton. Those for the horses of the very rich, however, were made of layers of silk. The Romans could not resist the utilitarian value of iron on horses hooves, particularly after witnessing its effectiveness on the horses of their major enemy, the Parthians. Leather horse boots with metal plates on the bottom soon were replaced by iron shoes nailed directly onto the horse's hooves. Nero tried to improve upon this by shoeing his imperial mules with silver and those of his second wife, Poppaea, with gold.

From the Roman *ferrarius,* of iron, came a common English name for blacksmiths, farrier. Farriers, like masons and other Medieval artisans, belonged to guilds. Such guilds existed all over the world, were usually secret, and sometimes required strange initiations. Such guilds in time became professions, which by 1265 were producing hundreds of horseshoes and thousands of nails every year. By 1465, when Englishmen were ordered to adopt and use surnames, the blacksmith profession was an ancient and traditional one. Thus Edward IV proclaimed, "They shall take unto them a surname, either of some Towne or some Colour as Blacke or Brown, or some Arte or Science, as Smyth or Carpenter, or some office as Cooke or Butler." Many who were not themselves blacksmiths chose to take that surname, Smith, for its powerful or magically protective connotations. So many did so that Smith today is the most connom surname in the English language. The same name, from other words for blacksmith, is also one of the most common surnames in many European countries: *Schmidt* in Germany, *Lefevre* in France, *Kuznyetzvo* in the Soviet Union, and *Ferraro* in Italy (as well as derivative forms of it, such as *Ferrari,* the name of a great car).

By the time Henry Burden of Troy, New York, patented the first horseshoe manufacturing machine in 1835, there was a tremendous need for horseshoes. A few years later, about the time Longfellow wrote "Under the spreading chestnut tree the village smithy stands . . ." the Burden Ironworks was producing 51 million shoes annually. With such mass production came excess, with excess came waste and devaluation, after which it was the most natural thing in the world to throw horseshoes at pegs stuck in the ground.

Interestingly, the game was around long before the horseshoe. Throwing an object like a shotput or discus is very ancient. Archilles' men in Homer's *Iliad* threw both. Out of discus throwing, a game developed in which the discus was reduced to a flattened, hollow ring called a quoit. Late Greeks and early Romans of around A.D. 150 tried to throw these quoits over stakes in the ground long before horseshoes became common.

Though military men quickly became partial to horseshoe pitching, civilians and gentlemen pitched quoits at pins in the ground. In England these pins were called hobs, the old English word for horse. Later Atlantic sailors adapted the game into deck quoits which used rings made of rope. In North America quoits was played longer and with more fervor in Canada than in the United States. Semiformal competitions were held in 1876 and sporadically thereafter until about 1900 when the beginning of the automobile age put horseshoes out of work. Though still popular in British Columbia and in some of Canada's prairie provinces, quoits has been superseded or replaced by horseshoe pitching. The latter now ranks as one of North America's popular and least publicized sports.

FORMS: The sport of horseshoe pitching is a series of paradoxes: a casual, recreational pastime, it requires sophisticated skill and technique; a game for picnicking families, it is intensely competitive; easy to play without rules of any kind—the object being simply to toss the shoe so that it encircles the stake—it has hundreds of rules, regulations and stipulations. In National Horseshoe Pitchers Association (NHPA) sanctioned competitions, there is also a basic division between the men's game and the women's, each of which has its own age groups—seniors, intermediates and juniors. In men's horseshoe pitching, the two pegs or stakes are set 40 ft. apart, while in women's they are 30 ft. apart. The shoe normally weights 2½ lbs. At its heel, the opening between the caulks (projections once welded to the ends of the shoe) is 3½ in. wide. In pitching a shoe, the player executes a turn, which is as essential as the swing is to golf—a one-and-one-quarter turn, a one-and-three-quarter turn, a flip turn, and so on. Scoring by the all-count method requires that the individual shoe be within at least 6 in. of the stake. A ringer counts three points, the nonringer closest to the stake and within 6 in. of it counts one point. Far more complex scoring methods are used at some competition levels, such as the cancellation scoring method. Handicap systems are used in some competitions. As in other sports, statistics are valued in horseshoe pitching, particularly the ringer percentage—the number of shoes pitched divided by the number of ringers. In 1968, for example, Elmer Hohl, 13-time Canadian champion and 4-time world champion, pitched an all-time tournament high of 88.5 ringer percentage. Horseshoe pitching may be played singles (the walking game) or doubles in which team members pitch their shoes back and forth to each other. In both, a player throws 2 shoes per turn for 25 innings—a total of 50 shoes pitched. Additional equipment required of championship-level competitors include files, rules, calipers, straight edges and shop cloths.

ORGANIZATION: As the automobile tire pushed the horseshoe off American roads, the increasingly larger number of people who liked to play horseshoes began to form clubs. In 1894 one was formed at Meadville, Pennsylvania, and another at East Liverpool, Ohio. Six years later, in 1900, 600 people formed a similar club at Long Beach, California. The real evolution of the sport, however, occurred in the Midwest. In Kansas and Missouri numerous clubs have been active and have staged tournaments since the final years of the last century.

The first major tournament held anywhere was staged in Manhattan, Kansas, in 1905, and was won by the now-legendary pitcher Frank Jackson of Idaho. Four years later Jackson won a world championship at Bronson, Kansas. In addition to the prize money, he received a Championship Belt studded with miniature horseshoes. There were so many clubs and members by 1914 that the first American national organization was formed. Called the Grand League of the American Horseshoe Pitchers Association, it standardized rules, established point values (5 for a ringer and 3 for a leaner), raised the pegs to a standard 8 in. and set them a standard 38½ ft. apart. The following year, on October 23 in Kellerton, Kansas, the Association held the first National Championship, and Jackson won again. A second world championship was staged in 1919 by the Sunshine Pleasure Club of St. Petersburg, Fla. That title was won by Fred Brust of Ohio, the first man to ignore horses completely by manufacturing shoes specifically for the game. By 1921 there were so many clubs, associations, leagues, rules, and champions in existence that a national organization was needed. The National Horseshoe Pitchers Association of America (NHPA) was formed in 1915; it absorbed the Grand League of American Horseshoe Pitchers and merged with the National Association of Horseshoe and Quoit Pitchers to become the single national body. Today the NHPA is also the world governing body for the sport of horseshoe pitching. It sanctions most international and all American national, state and regional championships, and is represented by 53 state and provincial chapter affiliates throughout the United States and Canada. These chapters work in close cooperation with the scores of local leagues and clubs that exist everywhere on the continent. In Canada, where additional organization is provided by provincial associations, the prominent governing body is the Ontario Horseshoe Players' Association, which is located on Kingston Road in Toronto.

Eastern Pennsylvania Horseshoe Pitchers Hall of Fame

NEW CUMBERLAND, PENNSYLVANIA

Mailing Address: R.D. 1, 17070. Tel. (717) 938-2945. *Contact:* Daniel Beshore, Secy.-Treas. *Location:* 2 mi. S. of Harrisburg and 95 mi. S.W. of Philadelphia. *Nearby Halls of Fame:* Heritage (Valley Forge, 80 mi. S.E.), Exploration and Invention (Arlington, Va, 90 mi. S.), Flight (Elmira, N.Y, 130 mi. N.W.), Horseshoe Pitching (Corning, N.Y, 130 mi. N.W.), Bicycling (Staten Island, N.Y, 140 mi. N.E.), Heritage, Music (New York City, 140 mi. N.E.), Golf (Foxburg, 150 mi. N.W.), Harness Racing (Goshen, N.Y, 160 mi. N.E.), Ice Skating (Newburgh, N.Y, 176 mi. N.E.), Baseball (Cooperstown, N.Y, 195 mi. N.E.), Horse Racing (Saratoga Springs, N.Y, 250 mi. N.E.).

The Eastern Pennsylvania Horseshoe Pitchers Hall of Fame was founded in 1976.

Members: 1 as of 1977.

1976 FULTON, John E. Farmer who began pitching horseshoes in 1931; winner of ten state championships between 1935 and 1960, more than any other man; first man to break 70 percent barrier in a state tournament; also contender for Eastern National championship and competitor in four world championships; uses indoor pit for year-round activity.

Florida Horseshoe Pitchers Association Hall of Fame

CLEARWATER, FLORIDA

Mailing Address: 1908 Nugget Dr, 33515. Tel. (873) 443-2892. *Contact:* Norman Gaseau, Secy.-Treas. *Location:* 20 mi. N.W. of St. Petersburg and 21 mi. W. of Tampa. *Personnel:* Kenneth Reeb, Pres; Oscar Gaudette, V.Pres. Call for information. *Nearby Halls of Fame:* Shuffleboard (St. Petersburg), Entertainment (Sarasota, 52 mi. S.E.), Movies (Orlando, 100 mi. N.E.), Swimming (Ft. Lauderdale, 215 mi. S.E.).

The Hall was founded in 1975 by the Florida State Horseshoe Pitchers Association to honor contributions to the game by supporters, organizers and players.

Members: 9 as of 1977. Members are chosen either as players or organizers, each of whom must have been a resident of Florida for five years. There is a limit of two inductees per year. The Hall of Fame Committee considers nominations and sends recommendations to the state association. New members are honored at the annual state meeting in April and their names are inscribed on the Hall of Fame plaque.

1975 BEACH, Dr. E. C.

ERNAPINGER, H. L.

RISK, Jimmy. *Also in:* National Horseshoe Pitchers Association of America Hall of Fame.

SEAS, W. J.

STEVENS, Charles

1976 CLINGAN, John

RADEMACHER, John

1977 DAVIS, Lee

PORTER, Harold

Iowa Hawkeye Horseshoe Pitchers Association Hall of Fame

DES MOINES, IOWA

Mailing Address: 1220 S.W. Evans, 50315. Tel. (515) 285-0131. *Contact:* Danny Sease. *Location:* 195 mi. N. of Kansas City, Mo. and 132 mi. S.E. of Omaha, Nebr. *Personnel:* Glen Henton, Chmn; John Packston, Rev. David Schaeffer, Earl Wigis and Art Reed, Comt. Call for information. *Nearby Halls of Fame:* Agriculture (Kansas City, Mo.), Agriculture (Bonner Springs, 210 mi. S.W.).

The Hall was founded in 1976 to recognize contributions to horseshoe pitching.

Members: 7 as of 1977. One player and one promoter may be selected annually based on their performance and contributions to the sport. Inductees are honored at a special ceremony, during which they are given a plaque.

1976 DIXON, Dale. *Also in:* National Horseshoe Pitchers Association of America Hall of Fame.

HOPKINS, Lucille

JACKSON, Frank. *Also in:* National Horseshoe Pitchers Association of America Hall of Fame.

LUNDEEN, Frank

MORTENSEN, Leland "Lee". *Also in:* National Horseshoe Pitchers Association of America Hall of Fame.

MOSSMAN, Putt. *Also in:* National Horseshoe Pitchers Association of America Hall of Fame.

ZIMMERTON, Guy. *Also in:* National Horseshoe Pitchers Association of America Hall of Fame.

Massachusetts Horseshoe Pitching Hall of Fame

NORTHHAMPTON, MASSACHUSETTS

Mailing Address: 17 Fort Street, 01060. Tel. (617) 924-8068. *Contact:* Bernard Herfuth, Chmn. *Location:* 15 mi. N. of Springfield, Mass. and 75 mi. W. of Boston. *Personnel:* Amos Whitaker, Al Hamel, Bill McMahon and Russel Sweeney, Comt. Call for information. *Nearby Halls of Fame:* Basketball (Springfield), Ice skating (Boston), Horse Racing (Saratoga Springs, N.Y, 90 mi. N.W.), Tennis (Newport, R.I, 105 mi. S.E.), Baseball (Cooperstown, N.Y, 120 mi. N.W.).

The Hall was founded in 1974 to honor Massachusetts pitchers and organizers.

Members: 9 as of 1977. A pitcher must have played five years in the A class to be eligible for membership. Inductees receive a plaque upon selection and induction.

1974 COMEAU, Joseph. *Also in:* New England Horseshoe Association Pitchers Hall of Fame.

FORSSTROM, Ralph. *Also in:* National Horseshoe Pitchers Association of America Hall of Fame and New England Horseshoe Pitchers Association Hall of Fame.

HERFUTH, Bernard. *Also in:* New England Horseshoe Pitchers Association Hall of Fame.

LANDRY, Edgar. *Also in:* New England Horseshoe Pitchers Association Hall of Fame.

O'SHEA, James. *Also in:* New England Horseshoe Pitchers Association Hall of Fame.

1975 MERRIPT, Melvin

SWEENNEY, Russell

1976 HOWE, Kersey

KADDY, Donald

Minnesota State Horseshoe Hall of Fame

ST. JAMES, MINNESOTA

Mailing Address: 317 N. Third St, 56081. Tel. (507) 375-3404. *Contact:* Nancy Gjerstad, Secy. *Location:* 100 mi. S.W. of Minneapolis and 100 mi. N.E. of Sioux Falls, S.Dak. *Personnel:* Arnold Erickson, Chmn; Lunnie Rapaulski and Glen Werk, Comt. Call for information.

The Hall was founded in 1969 by Joe Anzaldi to recognize excellence in horseshoe pitching.

Members: 17 as of 1977. Members are chosen in categories of either pitcher or promoter. A pitcher must have been affiliated with horseshoe pitching for ten years and preferably be a state champion. There is a limit of three inductees each year. New members are honored on Labor Day weekend by inclusion in the Hall of Fame Scrapbook.

1969 CHERRIER, Ron

STINSON, Frank. *Also in:* National Horseshoe Pitchers Association of America Hall of Fame.

TAGLARINI, Andy

1970 ANDERSON, Archie

KNUTSON, Herb

1971 HUBER, Ken

PETERSON, Nils

1972 ANDERSON, George "Hots"

MAGNUSON, Gus

1973 ANDREWS, Si

CUMMING, Art

1974 ERICKSON, Arnold

HOLTER, Art

1975 GANZ, Howie

HENDRICKSON, Al

1976 ANZALDI, Joe

WORSECH, Doc

National Horseshoe Pitchers Association of America Hall of Fame

LUCASVILLE, OHIO

Mailing Address: Rte. 5, 45648. Tel. (714) 639-8804. *Contact:* Wally Shipley, Pres. *Location:* Approx. 75 mi. S. of Columbus and 85 mi. S.E. of Cincinnati. *Personnel:* Bernard Hersuth, Chmn; Cletus Chapelle, Co-Chmn. Call for information. *Nearby Halls of Fame:* Flight (Dayton, 87 mi. N.W.), Football (Canton, 150 mi. N.E.).

The Hall was founded in 1965 by Bob Pence, secretary of the National Horseshoe Pitchers Association of America (NHPA), to honor players and organizers.

Members: 39 as of 1977. Members are selected by an NHPA committee of 14. Those elected may either be players over 65 years of age or promoters, organizers and NHPA officials. Since 1975, one "Old Timer" has also been inducted in either of the same two categories (player or organizer). Four new members may be selected each year. Each is given a plaque at a special ceremony during the convention held in conjunction with the annual World Tournament.

1966 ALLEN, Ted

COTTRELL, David. See entry in New York State Horseshoe Pitchers Hall of Fame.

GREGSON, Archie

HOWARD, R.

ISIAS, Fernando

JACKSON, Frank. *Also in:* Iowa Hawkeye Horseshoe Pitchers Association Hall of Fame.

STOKES, Arch

1967 BELLER, Elmer

MOSSMAN, Putt. *Also in:* Iowa Hawkeye Horseshoe Pitchers Association Hall of Fame.

ZIMMERMAN, Guy. *Also in:* Iowa Hawkeye Horseshoe Pitchers Association Hall of Fame.

1968 DAVIS, Charlie

JONES, Casey

WOODFIELD, Harry "Pop"

1969 DAY, Curt

HOHL, Elmer

PENCE, Bob

1970 COBB, Ellis

NUNAMAKER, Blair

WINSTON, Vicki

1971 GORDON, John

LANHAM, Mrs. C.

MORTENSEN, Leland. "Lee." *Also in:* Iowa Hawkeye Horseshoe Pitchers Association Hall of Fame.

RISK, Jimmy. *Also in:* Florida Horseshoe Pitchers Association Hall of Fame.

1972 FORSSTROM, Ralph. *Also in:* Massachusetts Horseshoe Pitching Hall of Fame and New England Horseshoe Pitchers Association Hall of Fame.

MAY, George

STEINFELDT, Carl. See entry in New York State Horseshoe Pitchers Hall of Fame.

1973 DIXON, Dale. *Also in:* Iowa Hawkeye Horseshoe Pitchers Association Hall of Fame.

DYKES, Ralph

STINSON, Frank. *Also in:* Minnesota State Horseshoe Hall of Fame.

1974 McGRATH, Leo

McLAUGHLIN, Dean

RENO, Harold

1975 FOCHT, Paul

FRANKE, Henry

GREGSON, Katie

HANGEN, Ruth

1976 CARSON, Dale

KUCHCINSKI, Sue and Danny

SNART, Bert

New England Horseshoe Pitchers Association Hall of Fame

HAMPDEN, MASSACHUSETTS

Mailing Address: Wilburham Rd, 01036. Tel. (413) 566-3283. *Contact:* Ralph Forsstrom, Chmn. *Location:* 12 mi. N. of Springfield, Mass. and 40 mi. W. of Worcester, Mass. *Personnel:* John Renfro, Mass; Frank Wagner, Conn; Thomas Robinson, R.I; Richard Bilbo, N.H; Robert Griffin, Maine; Merle Baillargeon, Vt; Comt. Call for information. *Nearby Halls of Fame:* Basketball (Springfield), Horse Racing (Saratoga Springs, N.Y, 85 mi. N.W.), Ice Skating (Boston, 85 mi. N.E.), Tennis (Newport, R.I, 90 mi. S.E.), Ice Skating (Newburgh, N.Y, 95 mi. S.W.), Baseball (Cooperstown, N.Y, 120 mi. N.W.), Harness Racing (Goshen, N.Y, 120 mi. S.W.), Bicycle (Staten Island, N.Y, 160 mi. S.W.), Heritage, Music (New York City, 160 mi. S.W.), Flight (Elmira, N.Y, 215 mi. S.W.), Heritage (Valley Forge, Pa, 215 mi. S.W.), Horseshoe Pitching (Corning, N.Y, 220 mi. S.W.), Hockey (Kingston, Ont, 225 mi. N.W.).

The Hall was founded in 1968 by Roger Bolduk.

Members: 14 as of 1977. Members are chosen by a committee and are honored with plaques at the New England championship. There is a limit of two inductees a year and they are elected in the category of either player or organizer. An active player must have pitched in Class A for 15 years; if inactive, he must have pitched for 5 years. An active organizer must have assisted with the game for 15 years; if inactive, he must have helped for 5 years.

1968 FORSSTROM, Ralph. *Also in*: Massachusetts Horseshoe Pitching Hall of Fame and National Horseshoe Pitchers Association of America Hall of Fame.

1969 WAGNER, Frank

1970 GEORGINA, Lester

O'SHEA, James. *Also in*: Massachusetts Horseshoe Pitching Hall of Fame.

1971 LANDRY, Edgar. *Also in*: Massachusetts Horseshoe Pitching Hall of Fame.

1972 CLARK, Porter

1973 BOVUK, Roger

HERFUTH, Bernard. *Also in*: Massachusetts Horseshoe Pitching Hall of Fame.

1974 COMEAU, Joseph. *Also in*: Massachusetts Horseshoe Pitching Hall of Fame.

WHITE, Howard

1975 MERRITT, Melvin

VECUSITTO, Mickey

1976 BRINKMAN, Gilbert

HEROUX, Peter

New York State Horseshoe Pitchers Hall of Fame

CORNING, NEW YORK

Mailing Address: Cinderella Softball League Headquarters, Box 1977, 10017. Tel. (212) 836-0149. *Contact*: Louis J. Gancos, Marge Ouellette. *Location*: 10 mi. N.W. of Elmira, N.Y. and 90 mi. S.W. of Rochester, N.Y. *Admission*: Free 9 to 5 Monday–Friday. *Personnel*: Carl Steinfelt, Ruth Hangen, Lorraine Thomas, Tony Sauro, George LaRose, Steve Fenicchia, Anthony Ginger Matele, David T. Leonard, Comt. *Nearby Halls of Fame*: Flight (Elmira), Baseball (Cooperstown, 115 mi. N.E.), Harness Racing (Goshen, 140 mi. S.E.), Golf (Foxburg, Pa, 160 mi. S.W.), Hockey (Kingston, Ont, 160 mi. N.E.), Ice Skating (Newburgh, 160 mi. S.E.), Football (Hamilton, Ont, 165 mi. N.W.), Hockey, Sports (Toronto, Ont, 170 mi. N.W.), Heritage (Valley Forge, Pa, 175 mi. S.E.), Horse Racing (Saratoga Springs, 175 mi. N.E.), Heritage, Music (New York City, 185 mi. S.E.), Bicycle (Staten Island, 185 mi. S.E.), Exploration and Invention (Arlington, Va, 250 mi. S.E.).

The Hall was founded in 1974 by Judge Wilbert B. Hyland, the Hornley Town Justice. Displays include historical horseshoes and quoits.

Members: 22 as of 1977. Persons may be nominated for membership as either a pitcher or a promoter. Members are inducted annually at the New York State Tournament.

1974

BROWN, Robert
Pitcher

Born in Rochester, N.Y; a track star at Alfred University.

Brown was New York State Champion three times, 1931, 1932 and 1935, and was one of the first pitchers to break the 50 percent barrier. He was the first pitcher to average more than 70 percent ringers in 1935, and gave exhibitions of trick pitching in New York City.

COTTRELL, David
Promoter

Born in North Cohocton, N.Y; partner in Moore-Cottrell Publishing Clearing House; died 1937.

Cottrell was the secretary for the National Horseshoe Pitchers Association from 1925 to 1933. He designed the official score sheets used in local, state and national competition, and wrote a history of the game in 1927.
Also in: National Horseshoe Pitchers Association of America Hall of Fame.

FELICCIA, Vito
Pitcher
Born in New York City; worked for Pfizer Chemical Co. until his retirement.

Feliccia pitched between 100 and 125 tournaments in 1928, the first year he was pitching. In 1936 he took the state title, with the highest ringer percentage to date: 75 percent. In 1949, he was pitching 73.8 percent, and was active in the game until 1968. He gave exhibitions of trick shots throughout his career.

FENNICHIA, Steve
Pitcher
Born in Rochester, N.Y; now a caretaker at Cennacle Convent in Rochester

Fennichia pitches from 70 to 80 percent, and in 1963, with 69.9 percent, won the State Title Falconer. He was the top contender in national eastern open and western tournaments. In exhibition games, he starts with a one and one-fourth and switches to a flopover shoe in the middle of the game.

HANZEN, Ruth
Pitcher
Born in Buffalo, N.Y; now living in Getzville, N.Y.

Hanzen has had worldwide fame since the 1960s; from 1970 to 1973 and in 1976 she took first place in the women's world tournament. She began competing in 1965, and took sixth place in the World Championship. In 1967 and 1968 she took third place; in 1969 she was runner-up. From 1968 to 1963, she was the champion of the Greenville, Ohio, Ringer Classic, and from 1967 to 1971 took the Midwest Ringer Tournament. At the women's regulation distance of 30 ft, she can toss 75 to 80 percent ringers. She has been the president of Lockport Women's Horseshoe Association. On the Mike Douglas television show, she pitched against Bobby Riggs. She has recently been working with the Erie County Recreation Department teaching horseshoe pitching and conducting matches for senior citizens, paraplegics and others confined to wheelchairs.

HOELZLE, Ruth Allen
Pitcher
Born in Lindenhurst, N.Y; husband John; three children.

Hoelzle took second place in the Long Island open tournament in 1937 with 58 percent, and in 1938 took third in Long Island and became the first woman in the official New York State Tournament. Since there was no women's division, she pitched with men at 40 ft. In 1938 she won her third Nassau County championship and the Syracuse State Farm agricultural tournament. She also won an international pitching exhibition between New York City and Toronto at Canada, averaging 58 percent ringers.

JASKULEK, Byron "Jake"
Promoter
Jaskulek edited and published *Horseshoe Pitcher* (similar to the current *Horseshoe Pitcher Digest*), a nonprofit magazine in 1948.

LEONARD, David T.
Pitcher
Leonard was the first recognized New York State champion, winning the honor in 1921.

NATALE, Anthony "Ginger"
Pitcher
Born in Rochester, N.Y; three children; works for Delco Products of Rochester.

Natale took two New York State titles, the first in 1969 with a 70.9 percent average and the second in 1971 with a 78.7 percent average. He was a Class A pitcher.

NIVEN, Frank "Hands"
Promoter
Born in Rochester, N.Y.

Niven was the 1929 New York State champion, and spent the next seven years promoting horseshoe pitching. He was a member of the Tutt Mossman Horseshoe Co. of Rochester, which developed the first "hooked" shoe.

ROUNELL, Tom
Pitcher
Born in Amsterdam, N.Y.

Rounell averages 75 to 80 percent, and has been the New York State champion six times.

STEINFELDT, Carl
Pitcher
Born in Rochester, N.Y; worked for the Rochester Product's Co; wife Beatrice; two children, Carl, Jr, and Betty.

Steinfeldt had many state and world-level victories, and took the New York State title 18 times. He was the national eastern champion six times and was two times runnerup in the World Championship in 1964 and 1974. In 1964 he entered his first state tournament and placed thirteenth. He is capable today of maintaining a 90 percent average. Carl was the world champion in 1976.
Also in: National Horseshoe Pitchers Association of America Hall of Fame.

THOMAS, Lorraine
Pitcher
Like Ruth Hanzen, Lorraine throws one flip shoe from 30 ft. and has thrown as high as 36 double ringers in 100 shoes. She pitched a record 92 percent for a single game in the New York State Tournament. She won the World Championship in 1968 and 1974, and the New York State title 1963–1966, 1970, 1972–1974. She was the eastern national champion from 1967 to 1968 and 1972 to 1973 and the Greenville, Ohio, Ringer Classic champion in 1974.

VONDERLANCKEN, Carl
Promoter
Lives in Panama City, Fla.

VonderLancken was chairman of the Hall of Fame Committee until 1976 when he moved to Florida. From 1925 to 1937 he organized the Chalistauqua Horseshoe Club, and in 1936 he gave the first exhibition of horseshoe pitching in England, France and Spain. From 1926 to 1937 he was president of the Tulsa, Okla, Horseshoe Club, and was the first champion of the Washington, D.C. Indoor League. In 1938 he assisted in promoting the Knickerbocker Horseshoe League in New York City, which became the largest horseshoe league in the Metropolitan area. He later became the New York City parks champion. From 1950 to 1953 he introduced the sport to Brazil. He was the president of the New York State Association and helped to form the Hall of Fame.

ZICHELLA, Joseph
Pitcher
Born in the Bronx, N.Y.

Zichella began playing at age 19 and won his first horseshoe tournament at the New York City Department of Parks Championship in 1943. In 1955 he won the Pennsylvania Open at New Freedom, the Rhinegold International at Newark, N.J, and the Massachusetts Open. He had a record of 25 straight ringers, and as a Class A pitcher, took between second and fifth place in all the New York State tournaments that he entered.

1975

POLLOCK, Joseph
Promoter
Born in Binghamton, N.Y; works for La Torrain Coffee Co.

Pollock has been secretary of the State Association longer than any other person, and he promoted tournaments from league level to the county and state levels. He is known as the "spark plug" of the Binghamton League, which has been in existence from the early 1930s.

PROUDMAN, Lawrence
Promoter
Born in Rochester, N.Y.

Proudman promoted horseshoes in the Falconer-Jamestown area, and was the New York State Association president.

SAURO, Anthony
Pitcher
Born in Syracuse, N.Y.

Sauro was the city champion 12 times, had a record of 17 county titles in Onondaga County, and was a runnerup in the New York State Farm Bureau tournament three times. He finished in the top four of the New York State competition five times, and took second in 1959. At Keene, N.H, in 1974, he finished fourth in Class A. He is a member of the Hall of Fame Committee.

1976

LA ROSE, George
Pitcher

LaRose was city champion 17 times, and several times champion of the county. In 1935 he averaged 60.1 percent at the State tournament, and in 1938 pitched his best game, with 93 ringers out of 100 (93 percent). He was Farm Bureau champion in 1949, and in the same year pitched 79 percent against Vito Feluccia.

1977

HYLLAN, Wilbert
Pitcher
Born in Corning, N.Y; won the national high and prep school cross-country championship at Newark, N.J.

Hyllan was the tournament director of El-Co League for six years and of the Crystal City Open tournament for eight years. In 1968 he placed third in Class D at the western tournament and third in the intermediate in 1971. He was the president of the New York State Association 1959 – 1960.

MICHALEK, Frank
Pitcher
Born in Binghamton, N.Y.

Michalek was county champion and city champion several times; he was Number One in the Binghamton area.

THOMAS, Paul
Promoter
Born in Lockport, N.Y; wife Lorraine; works for Harrison Radiators.

Thomas began pitching in 1958, and later established a women's league in the Lockport area, which is now the largest league in the country. He was president of the men's league, and in 1966 was elected president of the New York State Association. He set up the handicap system, which has proven to be popular in the city tournaments.

Texas Horseshoe Pitchers Association Hall of Fame

DENTON, TEXAS

Mailing Address: 2319 Fowler, 76201. Tel. (713) 729-9528. *Contact:* Bob Graham. *Location:* 35 mi. N.W. of Dallas and 35 mi. N.E. of Fort Worth. *Personnel:* Archie Roach, Chmn. Not open to the public. Call for information. *Nearby Halls of Fame:* Police Service (Waco, 115 mi. S.), Ethnic (Anadarko, Okla, 145 mi. N.W.), Softball,

Western Heritage (Oklahoma City, Okla, 160 mi. N.), Wrestling (Stillwater, Okla, 200 mi. N.E.), Ethnic (Tahlequah, Okla, 225 mi. N.E.).

The Hall was founded in 1972 to recognize contributions to and outstanding achievement in the field of horseshoe pitching in Texas.

Members: 7 as of 1977. Members are chosen for the category of either pitcher or promoter, with a limit on one in each category per year. They are selected by a five member Hall of Fame Committee and are inducted during the state tournament in July. Inductees are honored with an engraved plaque.

1972 BOWERS, Matt
BURGESS, Marvin
McFARLAND, Ed
SIPPLE, Berlin
1974 WOODSON, Jim
1975 GRAHAM, Bob
ROACH, Archie

Washington State Horseshoe Pitchers Hall of Fame

BREMERTON, WASHINGTON

Mailing Address: 11018 Kitsap Way, 98310. Tel. (206) 478-5041. *Contact:* Art Sperber, Secy.-Treas. *Location:* Approx. 15 mi W of Seattle and 130 mi. N. of Portland, Ore. *Personnel:* Bill Owens, Pres; Al Simon, V.Pres; Ellis West and Irv Okson, Exec. Secy; Henry Knuff, Edward Fishell, James Patrick and Don Tysper, Comt. Call for information. *Neaby Halls of Fame;* State and Province (Vancourver, B.C, 115 mi. N.).

The Hall was founded in 1972.

Members: 9 as of 1977. Members are chosen on the basis of participation in the Washington State Association, promotion of activities, sportsmanship and pitching ability. Inductees are honored with a plaque at the annual tournament. There is no limit on the number of inductions per year.

Washington State Horseshoe Pitchers Hall of Fame Members:

1974 ALLONS, Berdy
LIES, Art
ONOSITH, John
SAYRE, Floyd
WINETROT, Francis

1975 ETHLL, Louis
FISHEL, Edward
LEOTIO, Al

1976 KAUFF, Henry

HUNTING

Kings of ancient Persia washed their heads only once a year, and then only with great care and much ceremony. Roman women washed theirs annually only on August 13th, the day of Diana, goddess of the hunt. Intense heat or fire was said to have issued from the top of the Buddha's head during his times of meditation. Dozens of tribes around the world, most notably the Jivaro of Brazil and the Dyak of Borneo, took, cured and kept what they considered to be the most spiritually powerful part of men and other animals, the head. Samson's power deserted him after a simple haircut. Frankish kings, from childhood, never cut their hair. If a Maori chieftain in New Zealand accidently touched his own head, he would immediately place his fingers to his nose and snuff back up the sanctity that they had acquired by their touch, thereby restoring it to its rightful place atop his head. If anyone else touched a Maori chieftain's head, the penalty was summary execution. The belief underlying all of these examples manifested itself centrally in hunting as well. It was the belief that the head (or hair or organs) of a being contained great psychic or spiritual power which could be transferred to whoever took and preserved the being's head. In a very real sense, therefore, men never really hunted merely for food. And hunters who keep trophy heads today are simply abiding by a very ancient and once very central tradition that used to be worldwide in its distribution.

There is a second tradition that has been held by peoples all over the world and throughout the ages. It is the concept that men and animals are not really that different—that animals have their own tribes, chiefs, customs and languages. This belief was the basis for the high ritualization of relations between the Eskimo and the polar bear, the Australian aborigine and the kangaroo, the Andaman Islander and the sea turtle, the California Indian and the salmon. It was also the basis of the grizzly hunting rituals of the Thompson Indians of British Columbia. Those rituals consisted intially of praying to the grizzly tribe that they not be angry and that they deliver one of their number up without much of a fight. The Thompson practice of placing the killed bear's head high in a pine tree out of respect for the individual bear and to avoid the vengeance of its entire tribe was part of the same ritualization. Similarly, Bering Strait Eskimos believed that polar bears and seals could not only understand human speech but could also hear it from a very great distance. In hunting them, the Eskimo would talk of bears and seals with the greatest respect and would pretend out loud that he was in fact hunting some other kind of game. In other parts of the world, identical beliefs were held regarding jaguars, elephants, cobras and tigers. In most parts of Africa it was believed that the lion could understand all human languages, and that to speak its name out loud would cause it to appear. Thus the lion was and is referred to in normal conversation as the "owner of the land," "boy with the beard," "great beast," "king of beasts," or simply as "sir."

Those two beliefs—that a living thing's body parts contain spiritual or psychic power; and that all beings, though essentially alike, are different enough to allow the killing of those not of one's own tribe—form the intellectual framework upon which the world's infinite number of hunting customs and practices have been based, and within which the following examples have made sense to the peoples involved. When the Washo and Paviotso Indians of western Nevada hunted rabbits, they would elect the most competent among them to be the "rabbit boss," the one who best understood the rabbit tribe. In other parts of western North America Carrier Indian marten hunters slept with small sticks pressed against their necks in the deep, religious conviction that to do this would cause the fall-sticks of their traps to drop on martens' necks. In Malaysia a crocodile trapper would traditionally swallow three lumps of curried rice in quick succession to ensure that the baits would slide down the crocodiles' throats smoothly. Eskimo women refused to lift the family bedding while their men were out whale hunting. To do so, they believed, would cause the ice to crack and drift and the men to be lost. A typical Moxos Indian of Bolivia firmly believed that if his wife were unfaithful to him while he was away hunting, he would be bitten by a snake or mauled by a jaguar. If he were in fact then bitten or mauled while hunting, she would be punished severely or killed. In Sierra Leone on the west coast of Africa were, and perhaps still are, highly secret groups of men called Leopard Societies. Among other activities the members of these groups dressed up as leopards and prowled around at night growling and coughing loudly the way leopards do. Their goal was always to hunt a human being, which leopards rarely do. The victim would be disembowled with iron claws, after which the leopard men would make paw and claw marks around the site with specially carved wooden shoes to make it appear as if a real leopard had killed.

These leopard men, and the hundreds of other groups of New Guinea, Brazil and elsewhere who practiced cannibalism or took human trophy heads, were not hunters, although that same intellectual framework explains their customs. Instead they were culturally sanctioned killers. Although they hunted and killed just as hunters do, they did so as priests, for religious reasons, in the same way that Aztec priests ripped hearts from living victims—on certain days at the rate of one every 15 seconds—for use as offerings to the sun. They were not hunters in the same way that beef-butchers are not hunters—the ritual of killing and the uses of the victim were what was important to them. In true hunting, quite to the contrary, the killing never has been and is not the most important thing. To any true hunter, the thing that is preeminently important is a set of beliefs which for several centuries now has been known as "the Sportsman's Code."

This code, embodying both rights and obligations, is the hunter's value system, according to which the greatest sin is the commercial or wasteful killing of anything (animal or plant) and by which the second greatest sin is the destruction or disruption of habitat. These values are meaningless to anyone who regards animals as competitors, as sources of profit or as sources of fun. But they are unquestioned by those whose contact with nature leads them to involve themselves personally in the biological rhythms of nature, the primary ones of which are living and dying. Such personal involvement demands more than the mere technical skills of tracking and killing. It requires the utilization and development of courage, caution, strength, perseverance, activity, thoughtfulness and kindness toward all living things including target animals. A true hunter is a gentleman. One who is rude or cruel to people could probably never be a true hunter of animals. It is no coincidence that venery, an English synonym for hunting, is related to the word venerate.

Long before the fourteenth century invention of firearms, there were rules for hunting and for wildlife management which expressed the Sportsman's Code. The Maori of New Zealand tabooed hunting in both the forest and the sea during certain seasons. The Ojibwa of Canada kept a careful census of animals in their territories so that game would not be depleted. Kublai Khan, with whom Marco Polo lived for 17 years (1275–1292), established one of the first official closed seasons by prohibiting the killing of certain species during their March-to-October breeding season. Since the signing of the Magna Carta in 1215, the English Crown has had property rights to all wild game in the realm and by the Forest Charter of that same document, has had the right either to grant or to withhold hunting freedoms. One of the earliest and most famous books on hunting, *Livra de La Chasse,* was written by Count Gaston de Foix in 1387. It was translated into English 26 years later by Edward, Second Duke of York, while imprisoned. He added chapters of his own on game management.

The first New World colony to pass laws designed to protect wildlife was Rhode Island, in which a closed season on deer was enacted in 1646. Around 1680, the year the dodo was clubbed into extinction, the Plains Indians delegated supreme dictatorial powers to a buffalo police force, whose duty was to ensure that no one hunted buffalo prematurely in the season or in ways that were not allowed. Punishments ranged from whipping and confiscation of all ill-gotten game to destruction of the offender's lodge. In 1698 Massachusetts enacted a law to protect deer. It was repealed two years later, then reenacted in 1715 with the added proviso that each town might appoint a deer-reeve to enforce it. Canada's first protective act was passed by Nova Scotia in 1794 to preserve grouse and duck. Ontario adopted its first game law in 1821, the year Dostoievsky was born. Four years later Maine enacted its first closed season on deer and one of the first closed seasons on moose. The great New Brunswick forest fire of that same year (1825) burned 6000 square miles of forest and 15,000 settlers' homes. It also wiped out the wildlife of the entire region, which focused attention on the problems of game management and depletion.

Meanwhile, various hunters' clubs and organizations were being formed. The New York Sporting Club was established in 1844 and later became the New York State Game Protective Association. Members of this pioneer club—themselves hunters—pressed for tighter game laws and organized vigilante groups to deal with violators of existing hunting laws. The violation of these laws, particularly by professional hunters who killed in quantity for money, resulted in the extinction of many species. Several of the world's 120 extinct mammals and 150 extinct birds—out of totals of 4000 and 8500 respectively—and many of the 900 species endangered today would be thriving had it not been for those who made money through mass-killing. Such men have always been despised by those who have lived by the Sportsman's Code, and who themselves cannot be blamed for the extinction of a single species of animal. Quite to the contrary, these true hunters are the ones largely responsible for the fact that there are more deer in North America today than there were when Europeans first set foot on the continent. The first attempt to establish systematic forestry in the United States was made by the Blooming Grove Park Association, established in Pennsylvania in 1871 by such true hunters. The U.S. Fish and Wildlife Service was established by C. Hart Merriam, the National Audubon Society by William Dutcher, and the Boy Scout movement was started by Ernest Thompson Seton, Lord Baden-Powell and Daniel Carter Beard, all of whom were hunters. Hunters were also instrumental in the founding of the Camp Fire Club of America, Ducks Unlimited, the American Game Protective and Propogation Association and the American Ornithologists' Union. A group of hunters formed the Boone and Crockett Club, which in turn helped establish both the Bronx Zoo and the American Committee for International Wildlife Protection. Hunters have contributed greatly to specimen collections which have made the

American Museum of Natural History in New York, the Field Museum of Chicago and the National Museum in Washington, D.C. among the most significant museums in the world today. And of the 500 national and provincial or state parks, wilderness areas and reserves in North America today, many were established directly or indirectly because of the efforts of true hunters. Among them are: Yellowstone, the first American national park, established in 1872; Banff, the first Canadian one, established in 1887; Yosemite in 1890; Glacier in 1910; Lassen Volcanic in 1916; Mt. McKinley in 1917; Grand Canyon in 1919; Great Smoky Mountains in 1930; Isle Royle in 1940; and Everglades in 1947. The growth of wildlife management as a science, due largely to the efforts of the hunter-professor Aldo Leopold the "Father of Ecology," and the enactment of modern laws, most notably the Pittman-Robertson Federal Aid in Wildlife Restoration Act of 1937, were aided and applauded by all North American hunters who accepted the Sportsman's Code. This is only the beginning of the vast list of acts, institutions and contributions North American hunters have made virtually since Columbus' time. We owe our appreciation to those hunters that parts of the continent are still a paradise—a word which comes from an ancient Persian word that meant "hunting preserve."

FORMS: Everyone "hunts" for things like buried treasure or Easter eggs. Hunting for game to kill is similarly done by vast numbers, a handful of whom are true sportsmen, the rest being weekend animal killers, commercial hunters, poachers and perverts. Hunting for animals to kill is defined in Great Britain and in parts of Canada as the taking of wild animals with the aid of hounds that hunt by nose rather than by sight (*see* Dogs and Dog Racing). In those places it is called "the chase" rather than hunting. In most of North America hunting refers to the sport of taking large or small game in one of three main ways: with hand-held implements (firearms, bows and arrows, crossbows, boomerangs, slings, bolas, clubs, poisoned arrows or darts shot from blowguns, spears with or without spear throwers, harpoons, and many others); with self-operating implements (traps, snares, lures, water nets, air nets, land nets, pitfalls, decoys, bird lime and others); and with trained animals (coursing with greyhounds or salukis, field trials with hounds, falconry, and similar forms which have developed into whole sports in their own right). Associated with these three branches of hunting are a seemingly endless variety of techniques, such as stalking, tracking, sitting up (in a tree), still hunting or posting, calling, hunting with disguises, driving, pass shooting, jump shooting, and hundreds more. To a large extent, the mode of hunting and its associated techniques is determined by local custom, individual preference and type of game to be hunted. The four major groups of game in North America are: upland game, waterfowl, big game and medium and small game (varmints and predators). Upland game species include dove, grouse, pheasant, rabbit and squirrel which are usually hunted with a 22 rifle or with a 12-, 16- or 20-gauge shotgun. Waterfowl species include duck, goose, swan and related birds. They are normally hunted with a standard 12-, a 12 magnum, or a 10-gauge shotgun and often with the use of decoys. In both upland game and waterfowl hunting, dogs are also used. Big game species include antelope, mountain sheep, bear, deer and buffalo, all of which are usually hunted with extensive stalking and posting and with a fast-loading, high-powered weapon. Medium and small game species include gopher, racoon, wolf, coyote and mountain lion which are hunted like big game but do not require powerful weapons.

Within all these modes and associated techniques of hunting are various proficiency systems akin to those symbolized by karate's differently colored belts. Such systems, though they are largely unknown and unrecognized except among hunters themselves, exist or have existed everywhere in the world where hunting has been practiced. By far the most difficult and prestigious system was that institutionalized by the Black Lahu, a hill tribe of Southeast Asia. The highest level was called Supreme Hunter. To attain this level a man could use any weapon of his choosing in order to earn or accumulate ten points during his lifetime. Of these, the first four were awarded for the taking of 40 heads each of four different species. These 160 kills could be of either sex but had to be obtained during the proper season. In the days before poachers, commercial hunters and industrial developers decimated many Southeast Asian species, the earning of those four points was not unduly difficult though it might take several decades. But earning the remaining six points was a somewhat larger undertaking. Killing one each of the big six—tiger, leopard, bear, boar, elephant and gaur, a wild buffalo often over six ft. high at the shoulder—counted for those six points. The individual animals had to meet two qualifications: each had to be a male animal and each had to be a killer. To be a killer, the animal had to have killed at least one human being, or it had to demonstrate a willingness and intent to do so. The latter meant that the animal had to be killed head-on during its charge. One who chose instead to flee the hunter did not qualify. Many hunters were killed before they could accumulate all ten points. One Black Lahu tribesman who did earn his ten is now a legend for having done so with a crossbow, which is so difficult to reload that he had only one shot each time. Only one non-Lahu ever became a Supreme Hunter, the legendary Gordon Young, a member of the Explorers Club in New York, whose dedication to conservation and wildlife management was as famous as his 30.06 rifle.

ORGANIZATION: While out hunting one evening John Quincy Adams wondered about the difficulties of achieving wildlife conservation in a democratic society. Those difficulties were not overcome in the United States for nearly a century. Not until the 1870s did hunters respond to various socioeconomic post-Civil War factors in order to overcome them. Their response was to form themselves into wildlife conservation clubs and associations. Nearly 100 such associations were organized in a single year, 1875; in addition, 1 national and 11 state organizations were formed. By 1878 there were 308 associations dedicated to both hunting and to the establishment, observance and enforcement of game laws. These associations were aided in their programs and goals by the various magazines their members initiated during that decade: *American Sportsman* (1871), *Forest and Stream* (1873), and *Field and Stream* (1874), to name a few. The modern descendants of those early North American hunting organizations number in the thousands. Many are concerned with related aspects of sport hunting such as trap and target shooting, animal breeding, equipment standards and manufacturing, recreational guiding and legal aid. They include the Western Guides and Outfitters Association (Canada), the

National Rifle Association of America, the National Shooting Sports Foundation (United States), and the North American Game Breeders and Shooting Preserve Association (United States). Many others are concerned with regional aspects of sports hunting, like the Alberta Fish and Game Association, the Toronto Anglers and Hunters Association, the Cranbrook District Rod and Gun Club (Canada), the Western Association of State Game and Fish Commissioners (United States), the Association of Midwest Fish and Wildlife Commissioners (United States and Canada), and the Association of American Rod and Gun Clubs, Europe (for American military forces in Europe, North Africa and the Near East). Still others, like the St. Hubert Society of America and the New England Board for Fish and Game Problems, are concerned with conservation and the general preservation of game for future hunters. Finally, many of today's organizations are concerned with the hunting and conservation of specific groups or species of game. Upland game species are the concern of the Ruffled Grouse Society of North America, the Society of *Tympanuchus cupido pinnatus* (the Prairie Chicken), the United States National Wild Turkey Federation, and others. Waterfowl are the concern of such major organizations as Ducks Unlimited and the Atlantic Waterfowl Council. Big game species are the major concern of numerous organizations, the most prestigious of which is the Boone and Crockett Club, while the American Coon Hunters Association, the United States Naitonal Fox Hunters Association and many others are concerned with the hunting and conservation of medium and small game. Not all members of these organizations are true hunters, although 22 million Americans and a similar number of Canadians buy hunting licenses every year. True hunters differ from all other kinds in their observance of the Sportsman's Code, a strict morality in which all living things are viewed in a uniquely natural and respectful way.

Hunting Hall of Fame Foundation

RANCHO SANTA FE, CALIFORNIA

Mailing Address: P.O. Box 1493, 92067. Tel. (714) 756-1758. *Contact*: Dr. Kenneth W. Vaughn, Chmn.

The Hunting Hall of Fame Foundation, the world's first and only hunting hall of fame, was founded by Dr. Vaughn and others in 1972 to honor in perpetuity those individuals and groups of individuals who have made significant contributions to the history and development of American hunting. These individuals and groups, it may be said, preeminently embody the hunter's value system known as "the Sportsman's Code" (*see* p. 404).

Members: 25 Honored Hunters and 242 Life Members of the Foundation as of June 1977. An unspecified number of distinguished Americans, usually from two to six, are inducted annually as Honored Hunters in three classes of honors, each of which is symbolized by a special award: The Highest Distinction Award honors individual accomplishment in four distinct segments of the field of hunting: I. Exploration, Exploitation and Settlement; II. Responsibility and Control; III. Management, Conservation, Education and Recreation; and IV. International Influences. The Distinguished Service Award honors special service rendered to American hunting. The Distinguished Merit Award honors those who have had an outstanding educational influence on American hunting in any medium. A fourth class of honor, planned but not yet awarded, will be the Distinguished Award, which will honor classes of hunters or of people whose influence on American hunting was significant. For example, the American, as exemplified by Hiawatha and others, will be inducted to honor the numerous contributions of the Indian to American hunting; nineteenth century Gunmakers will be inducted as a group under this class of membership for their significant contributions. Nominations for all four of these classes of honors are received by a distinguished Selection Committee. Those duly selected for honors are formally inducted at annual ceremonies held in various cities throughout the country.

AUDUBON, John James, Highest Distinction Award I.

BEAR, Fred. Highest Distinction Award III.

BOONE, Daniel. Highest Distinction Award I.

BROOKS, Barry D. Highest Distinction Award III.

BUCKINGHAM, Nash. Highest Distinction Award III.

CLARK, James L. Highest Distinction Award III.

CLARK, William. Highest Distinction Award I.

DUCKS UNLIMITED. Distinguished Service Award.

EDMOND-BLANC, F. Highest Distinction Award IV.

FOSS, Joseph J. Highest Distinction Award III.

GUTERMUTH, C. R. Highest Distinction Award III.

HIS IMPERIAL HIGHNESS PRINCE ABDOR-REZA OF IRAN. Highest Distinction Award IV.

HORNADAY, William T. Highest Distinction Award II.

LAGARDE, John. Highest Distinction Award III.

LEWIS, Meriwether. Highest Distinction Award I.

MACHRIS, Maurice. Distinguished Merit Award.

O'CONNER, Jack. Highest Distinction Award III.

OLIN, John M. Highest Distinction Award III.

PAGE, Warren K. Highest Distinction Award III.

ROOSEVELT, Theodore. Highest Distinction Award II.

SELOUS, Frederic. Highest Distinction Award IV.

THE ARK OF THE TWENTY-FIRST CENTURY. Distunguished Merit Award. This movie chronicling the fight for survival of the Arabian Oryx, and producer Maurice Machris, were honored jointly.

THE BOONE AND CROCKETT CLUB. Distinguished Service Award.

THE LEWIS AND CLARK EXPEDITION. Distinguished Service Award.

THE STATE GAME, FISH AND CONSERVATION DEPARTMENTS OF THE 50 STATES. Distinguished Service Award.

ICE SKATING

At 32°F. or 0°C. the molecules that make up water slow in their vibratory motion so much that the water crystallizes. Such slow water is said to be frozen. Because that process causes a volume of liquid water to expand by 1/11—so that, for example, eleven cubic inches of liquid water become 12 cubic inches of frozen water—such crystallized water floats. It will do this regardless of size—from the smallest cube to the world's largest berg. The latter, sighted in the South Pacific in 1956, had a surface area of approximately 12,000 square miles—ten times larger than Yosemite National Park, or roughly as large as Vermont and Delaware combined. Usually white, frozen water is sometimes green or even black, as when ancient vegetable matter has been frozen within glaciers.

What water is called in that frozen, floating state depends upon who you are and what you wish to do with it. Most people in the world call it *bing*, since Chinese is spoken by more people in the world, over 600 million, than any other language. The next largest group, the 400 million English-speakers, call it ice. In Persian it's *yakh* (while snow is *barf*), in Russian it's *lyed* and in Polish *lod*. Turks call it *buz*, Spaniards *hielo*, Italians *ghiaccio*, Germans *das Eis*, Greeks *ó phágos*, Dutch people *ijs*, Danes and Norwegians *is* and Indonesians *ès*. Speakers of various Eskimo languages have numerous words for it: *sermeq*, ice on solid objects, *sermerpa*, the cold water that covers something with ice, *sermerpoq*, that which is covered with ice, *sermerňarpoq*, the water that freezes to ice on one's clothes or on the boat, *sermerssuaq*, inland ice, *nilak*, a piece of freshwater ice, *iluliaq*, ice floe or hunk of floating ice, *nilakarpoq*, glazed frost, *dikuletciaq*, new ice, *sikuliaq*, young ice and several dozen others. Ice can vary greatly in age, from seasonal ice formed each winter to one- to two-year-old ice in polar ice packs to icebergs and their parent glaciers, which are thousands of years old.

Regardless of what you call it, there are numerous things you can do with this super-slow water. Millions fish through it, fall through it, or "harvest" it for commercial purposes (in the same agricultural vein, the natural process by which ice bergs separate from their parent glaciers is called "calving"). Hundreds of millions of people drink it in iced tea, for example, which was invented in St. Louis in 1904, or chill things with it as Explorers Club members did in 1951 after air-lifting a block of the Mendenhall Glacier in Alaska to their annual gala banquet in New York City. And tens of millions of people young and old skate on it which, in the words of Johann Wolfgang von Goethe, himself a skater, is to create "poetry in motion."

Many of the latter group skate on artificial ice—a misleading term because only its production is artificial. This was done as early as 1842, when a "miniature pine lake," a skating rink with a salts-of-soda surface, was opened on Baker Street in London—years before Sherlock Holmes lived on that street. In 1876 English scientists mixed glycerine with water, chilled it with ether, then circulated it through water-covered copper pipes to produce artificial ice as it is known today. Before the end of that year the Glaciarium opened in London. The world's first skating rink, it was indoors with walls that had been decorated with Swiss alpine scenes painted by Durand of Paris. Later experiments in New York in 1897 used a brine solution as a refrigerant. The same solution is used today. At the Maple Leaf Gardens in Toronto, for example, 30,000 gallons of brine are circulated through ten miles of pipes one inch beneath the arena floor, which is then flooded to produce an ice surface.

For some skaters (like Janet Lynn, the "Richest Sportswoman in the World," who earned $750,000 in 1974) skating involves numerous stunts—counters, axels, mohawks, mazurkas, spirals and spread eagles. For one Doctor Barrin, skating included cutting one of his initials in the ice with one foot while cutting the other initial simultaneously with the other foot. For the fabulous Frenchman, J. Garcin, skating involved the combination of "horror," "sweetness," and other emotions with his stunts. It was Garcin who introduced the *pas de huit* or eight-step as well as more than 30 other movements—including the comic "post boy stuck in the mud" which involved running straight backward, then making large steps as though to go forward while remaining stationary. To a post-Civil War ballet master from Chicago, Jackson Haines, skating meant gliding, spiraling, twisting and waltzing while costumed as a polar bear, a lady, a Russian or a fairy prince. He died in Finland at the age of 39 and his tombstone in the town of GamlaKarleby is inscribed: The American Skating King. To these and millions of other people throughout the world and throughout the centuries, skating has also meant countless other things. In Holland there was ice touring—racing 124 miles and 483 yards between eleven cities in the shortest possible time. In England there was fen running—speed skating on frozen, shallow marshy areas called fens. At Stamford, Connecticut, there was a 100-mile skating race in 1893, the year Engelbert Humperdinck wrote *Hansel und Gretel.* At Montreal's Victoria Rink in the last century there was barrel racing—racing to each of a series of barrels and crawling through them. At the Palais de Glace in Paris there was the ice-skating waltz, first performed there in 1894. In Chicago there were ice cabarets, notably at the Sherman Hotel, where in 1914 a miniature rink was built in the dining room.

All such events and stunts were made possible by the invention of the skate. Over seventeen centuries ago the first ones were made out of animal bones strapped onto the feet. The word itself probably came from the German *schake*, a shank or leg bone (*schaats* in Dutch, *scatch* in early English). In Holland today the word *schenkel*, shank, is used to name a skate's iron blade. Next came wooden skates. These were unsatisfactory, however. Once damp, they would abruptly stick to the ice, causing the skater to tumble. Such a fall in A.D. 1396 broke a 16-year-old Dutch girl's rib. The remainder of that girl's 53-year life was so exemplary that she was canonized in 1891; as St. Siedwi (or Liedwi or Lydwina), she became the patron saint of skaters everywhere. Despite her protective influence, Dutch mothers bound padded cushions within a framework of whalebone and ribbons onto the heads of their very young children to prevent head injuries. In 1697, the year Charles Perrault wrote "The Tales of Mother Goose," Peter the Great of Russia ordered the world's first skating boots—skates permanently fastened onto a pair of boots—from Zaandam, the Netherlands. It was seen as just another of his numerous excesses. It was in Philadelphia, long the skating capital of the United States, that E. Bushnell caused a skating revolution in 1848. That was the year Charles Dickens' newspaper, the *Daily News*, published the world's first weather reports as well as the year Bushnell invented the first all-iron skate. Costing the then phenomenal price of $30, his new skates allowed twists, turns, leaps, and far more versatility than had been possible with all earlier versions. Some years later, in 1866, an all-metal screw clamp-skate was patented. The Norwegian Axel Paulsen, whose fabulous outside forward three jump with one and a half revolutions is now known as the axel, caused a second major trend in skating design by his construction of a racing skate. It had two thin metal tubes attached to a blade only 1/16 in. wide and was the precursor of the modern ice hockey skate, which has a 1/32 in.-wide blade. (For additional information on both ice and ice skates *see* Hockey.)

While the evolution of the skate encouraged development and specialization in skating, clubs and associations increased the sport's popularity. The first of these was founded in 1742. George Washington was ten years old at the time. Called the Edinburgh Skating Club, it required its members to pass two proficiency tests: skating a complete circle on each foot in turn, and jumping over one, two, then three hats placed on the ice. Four notable skaters of that era were: Marie Antoinette, an expert on blades; the poet William Wordsworth, who liked to skate out his name in the ice; Benjamin West, the great painter; and Napoleon Bonaparte who, as a 22-year-old student at a military school, skated on the moat of the fort at Auxerre, France, and at least once narrowly escaped drowning. In 1813, a year before the White House was burned, British skaters began to publish *Frostiana*, a skating journal. That periodical, plus the Skating Club of London, founded in 1830, greatly popularized the sport in general and certain stunts in particular. One of these involved nine members skating around an orange placed on the ice to produce a "changing flower" effect. The first such club in the United States, called the Philadelphia Skating Club and Humane Society, was formed in 1849. Members were required to carry rope with them whenever they went skating, and to rescue anyone who fell through the ice. In 1869 alone, they made 259 such rescues and collected a $12 reward for each. By that year skating was becoming more and more popular in North America, largely because of two things that had happened four years before in 1865. The first was the publication of *Hans Brinker or, The Silver Skates.* This is a story by Mary Elizabeth Mapes Dodge, who was born in New York City, about two poor Dutch children—Gretel, who wins a pair of silver skates, and her brother Hans. The second was the formation that year of the Amateur Skaters Association of Canada by Louis Rubenstein, Canadian Champion from 1878 to 1889 and American Champion of 1888. Additional publicity was given to the sport in 1896, the year of the first modern Olympics, when the International Skating Union sanctioned a world figure-skating competition.

Far greater attention was given to ice in 1912, however: a massive berg sank the *Titanic* that year, and in Berlin the world's first ice show opened. Called "Flirting at St. Moritz," that show later played for 300 days at the Hippodrome in New York City and inspired the first film about ice skating, *The Frozen Warning* (1916). In 1912, too, Sonja Henie was born. To her, perhaps more than to any other single person, ice skating's present world-wide popularity is due. Her life and career were an inspiration to many of today's great skaters, who in turn are an inspiration to millions of skaters. A Norwegian, she was nicknamed the "Queen of the Ice," the "Girl in White" and the "Norwegian Doll." In 1924, when twelve years old, she introduced the miniskirt. She left amateur competition at the age of 23 with three Olympic gold medals, six European championship titles and ten consecutive world championship titles. She later starred in nine movies, the first and most famous of which was *One in a Million.* She not only toured the world with lavish ice revues, but also produced several of her own. The Sonja Henie Ice Revue and The Hollywood Ice Review were two of these. Her total earnings eventually exceeded $25 million. Two Minnesota ice show clowns were so inspired by her success that they organized their own ice carnival. They were Eddie Shipstead and Oscar Johnson and their carnival, the Ice Follies, has played to over 60 million people since it began in 1936. Other similar shows, like those staged by the Ice Capades, quickly became popular and successful. The ice skating shows staged by the Holiday on Ice Productions, Inc, seen annually by over 20 million people in 75 countries, are the world's costliest live entertainment. All such extravaganzas have done on a grand scale what the greatest skaters have done as individuals: inspired millions to enter the remarkable sport that consists of creating poetry in motion on crystallized, super-slow water.

FORMS: The three main forms of ice skating are ice figure skating, ice speed skating and ice dancing. The most recent of these, ice dancing, was initiated by the International Skating Union in 1950. Competitions in it are divided into two halves—compulsory, with three specific forms, and freestyle. Each half is worth 50 percent of a couple's total score as assessed by a panel of up to nine judges. That assessment is made on the basis of each couple's artistic impression and technical merit. Lifts are not allowed as they are in pair skating; in other words, each dancer must have one skate on the ice at all times. The figures actually skated are selected from a total of about 70, which are divided among the nine proficiency levels. The skate normally used in ice dancing, as well as in figure skating, is typically black for men and white for women. It has a toe rake at the front of the blade that allows spinning, and is hollow ground along the edge of the blade—that is, a concave groove down the length of the blade creates two edges.

Figure skating competitions are held for men, women and pairs. Like ice dancing they are divided into two halves: compulsory and freestyle. The compulsory half requires that each skater trace up to six specific figures on the ice. The freestyle half allows 4 min. for women and 5 min. for men and pairs for the performance of individually selected figures. The class or level of a skater's competition in any of these events is determined by past attainment of various proficiency levels. These are designated by certificates and medals, the highest of which is Eighth Level, represented by a gold medal. In single and paired figure skating as well as in ice dancing, the official rink is a rectangle not more than 66 by 33 yds.

In the third major form of skating, ice speed skating, a longer skate of from 12 to 18 in. is used. Like track sprinters and racers, speed skaters race various distances. Unlike them, however, a speed skater must excel in all of four races (500 m, 1500 m, 5000 m, 10,000 m.) in order to be judged an international individual champion. Such champions are the world's fastest self-propelled human beings, attaining 30 m.p.h. Normally in these races, two skaters race in a counterclockwise direction around an ice track. The one in the outer lane will wear a red arm band, the one in the inner lane a white arm band. There often are, additionally, relay races and pursuit races over identical distances. Such races have been a part of the Olympics since 1924 for men and since 1960 for women. On the other hand, the first women's speed skating competition was organized at Leeuwarden, the Netherlands, long before most men had even heard of skating competitions. It was held in 1805—a year before carbon paper was invented, three years before the first practical typewriter was invented, and seventy years before the first women office workers were hired.

ORGANIZATION: In 1892, representatives of Austria, Germany, Great Britain, Holland, Hungary and Sweden held a skating congress and formed the International Skating Union (ISU). The ISU now includes the North American governing bodies—the United States Figure Skating Association (USFSA) and the Canadian Figure Skating Association (CFSA)—as well as those of numerous other countries. The ISU establishes standards for the World Championships, which have been held annually since 1896, the year Utah became the forty-fifth state. In conjunction with the International Olympic Committee, the ISU also dictates competitive skating procedures for the various Winter Olympic Games skating events. The USFSA, founded in 1921, governs competitions in the United States on regional, sectional and national levels, determines amateur status and appoints officials. There are 340 amateur ice skating clubs within the USFSA, with a total of more than 35,000 members. Notable among these clubs are the International Figure Skating Club of Philadelphia, the Chicago Figure Skating Club and the Sun Valley Figure Skating Club. Members from all such clubs compete in nine regional contests, each of which qualifies three skaters for the Eastern, Midwestern or Pacific Coast sectional contests. The three top sectional winners are then qualified to test for world and Olympic competition. In Canada the CFSA performs similar functions through various provincial governing bodies, and sets up biennial North American championship competitions. The specific sport of speed skating is organized and governed in Canada by two groups, the Canadian and Ontario Amateur Speed Skating Associations, and in the United States by the United States International Skating Association. A third organization, the Ice Skating Institute of America, was founded in 1960 to certify skating instructors and to increase public interest in the sport. Formed of 550 member rink operators in nine regional groups, this organization conducts recreational tests and registration programs and seeks improvement of ice rinks throughout the continent. In addition, every November it sponsors National Ice Skating Month.

Hall of Fame of the Amateur Skating Union of the United States (National Speedskaters Hall of Fame)

NEWBURGH, NEW YORK

Mailing Address: 375 Washington St, 12550. Tel. (914) 561-3232. *Contact*: Ed Gordon. *Location*: Adjacent to Delano Recreation Park; approx. 55 mi. N. of New York City, 80 mi. S. of Albany, 95 mi. S.W. of Springfield, Mass, 145 mi. S.W. of Newport, R.I, 150 mi. S.W. of Boston, Mass. *Admission*: Free 8 to 5 daily; after hours or on weekends, call Eldred P. Carhart, Jr, Cur, (914) 561-0214. *Personnel*: Five mem. Hall of Fame Comt. (of the Amateur Skating Union, Dr. Milan Novak, Chmn.); Eldred P. Carhart, Jr, Cur. *Nearby Halls of Fame*: Harness Racing (Goshen, 12 mi. S.W.), Heritage, Music (New York City), Bicycle (Staten Island, 60 mi. S.), Baseball (Cooperstown, 90 mi. N.W.), Basketball (Springfield, Mass.), Heritage (Valley Forge, Pa, 105 mi. S.W.), Horse Racing (Saratoga Springs, 110 mi. N.E.), Flight (Elmira, 140 mi. N.W.), Tennis (Newport, R.I.), Ice Skating (Boston, Mass.) and Horseshoe Pitching (Corning, 155 mi. N.W.).

The Lions Club of Newburgh, which sponsors the Hall of Fame of the Amateur Skating Union of the United States, has long been involved with skating in their town. One of the charter members, Harry Cohen, had already started skating races for school age children when this oldest Lions Club in New York State was founded in 1923. They began sponsoring the Outdoor Racing Championships for speed skating in 1924, and since 1926 the races have been held in Newburgh. Over the years, the Lions Club has built a shelter house for skaters at the Recreation Park, sent skaters to national speed skating races and has donated many dollars from the annual Outdoor races to the Newburgh Skating Club and other good causes. Newburgh's close proximity to the Hudson River has produced two world champion speed skaters as well, Charles F. June and Hall of Famer Joseph Donoghue. Thus, in 1960, after the Amateur Skating Union of the United States had created a Hall of Fame in 1959 and established a permanent committee of five members, Joseph P. Monihan, past president and charter member of the Newburgh Lions Club, traveled to the annual meeting of the Amateur Skating Union in Colorado Springs, Colo, to convince the members that the Hall of Fame should be located in Newburgh. The suggestion was approved and Monihan was selected to locate the Hall of Fame and establish exhibits. Before his death in 1972, Monihan put together the largest collection of skates in the world (600 pairs), now on exhibit with trophies, photostat copies of newspaper reports on early speed skating races, uniforms, photographs and winter skating scenes. The Hall of Fame was first located in the Crawford House, a Newburgh colonial landmark, moved to the Columbus Trust Building for six years, and then to its own building, dedicated on March 31, 1974. A bronze sculpture of three speed skaters distinguishes the Hall of Fame, and just inside the entrance is a special plaque with the names of each Hall of Fame member. The Lions Club now has plans for an Olympic Village in Newburgh, to include, among other features, a two-lane European-style speed skating rink.

Members: 50 as of April, 1977. Members are elected by the Hall of Fame Committee at the annual meeting of the Amateur Skating Union each May, from nominations submitted by skating clubs all over the country. Each member must have completed a competitive career at least five years prior to election, must have competed at least five years in the Senior Class and must have competed one of the following: won two National championships in Senior Class, set two National speed skating records or won a medal in the Olympics or World meets. Special consideration is given to those who meet the above criteria and have also promoted the sport during or after their competitive careers.

1960

DONOGHUE, Joseph
Skater

Born February 11, 1871, in Newburgh, N.Y; died 1921.

The first member of the Hall of Fame, Joe was the first American to win the World speed skating title in Europe, beginning a slow but steady growth of American participation in international competition. This early champion trained by skating 18 mi. on the frozen Hudson River to Poughkeepsie and sometimes 90 mi. to Albany. The results of his training were the National, North American and International Men's Outdoor championships in 1891 and 1892.

JOHNSON, John S.
Skater

For three consecutive years, from 1893 through 1895, John was National, North American and International Men's Outdoor champion.

1961

LAMY, Edmund
Skater

Born January 18, 1891; died September 8, 1962.

In 1908, 1909 and 1910 Lamy was not only the National Men's Indoor champion speed skater but the North American and International champion as well. On January 27, 1910, he set the U.S. Amateur Indoor record for the 1.5-mile race in Cleveland, Ohio, with a time of 4:25.0.

McWHIRTER, Roy
Skater

Born August 2, 1895.

In 1920 and 1922, Roy won both the National and North American Men's Outdoor championships.

STAFF, Arthur
Skater

Born February 4, 1897.

Art was the National and North American Men's Indoor and Outdoor champion of 1917 and a World champion speed skater.

1962

McGOWAN, Everett
Skater and Contributor
Born 1901.

Everett was an ice skater in many forms, but first the International Men's Outdoor champion in 1920. He then became a professional speed skater, show skater, figure skater and ice hockey player, ice rink operator and skating instructor, and still a producer of ice shows and a builder of ice rinks.
Also in: Ice Skating Hall of Fame.

SHEA, John A. "Jack"
Skater
Born September 10, 1910.

It was a spectacular year for the Americans when Jack Shea and Hall of Famer Irving Jaffee took their skates to the 1932 Winter Olympics. While Jaffee won gold medals in the 5000- and 10,000-m. races, Shea won gold medals in the 500- and 1500-m. races. Earlier in his career, Shea had won the 1929 North American Men's Outdoor championship and the 1930 National Men's Outdoor championship.
Also in: Winter Sports Hall of Fame, Citizens Savings Hall of Fame Athletic Museum.

WOOD, Morris
Skater
Born January 28, 1882.

For seven consecutive years, Morris was the National, North American and International Men's Outdoor champion, 1901 through 1907. And in 1906 and 1907 he became the National, North American and International Men's Indoor champion as well.

1963

BIALAS, Valentine
Skater
Born January 10, 1903; Bialas reached his peak in speed skating in 1928.

JEWTRAW, Charles
Skater
Born May 5, 1900.

The earliest American Olympic speed skater, Charles won a gold medal in the 500-m. race of the 1924 Olympics with a time of 44 secs. That was a highlight of his career that began as the National and North American Men's Outdoor champion of 1921 and the International Men's Outdoor champion of 1923.
Also in: Winter Sports Hall of Fame, Citizens Savings Hall of Fame Athletic Museum.

O'SICKEY, Ben
Skater
Born August 19, 1894.

During the peak of his speed skating career, Ben set the U.S. Amateur Indoor record for 880 yd. in Pittsburgh, Pa, on March 1, 1916. His time was 1:15.6.

1964

McLEAN, Bobby
Skater
Born 1895.

Dominating speed skating competition, Bobby, a World champion, won the National North American and International Men's Indoor and Outdoor championships from 1911 through 1914.

MOORE, Joseph
Skater

Joe won the 1921 International Men's Outdoor championship, but won the International Men's Indoor championship for four consecutive years, from 1921 to 1924. Moore set the record for U.S. Amateur Indoor 4-mi. race in 13:41.8 February 27, 1927, in Brooklyn, N.Y.

OUTLAND, Kit Klein
Skater
Born 1910.

A consistently outstanding speed skater of the 1930s, Kit won major races from 1932 through 1935. She won the North American Women's Indoor championship in 1932 and the National, North American and International Women's Outdoor championships in 1933. In 1934 she captured the North American Women's Outdoor title for a second time, and in 1935 won the National Women's Outdoor championship for the second time.
Also in: Winter Sports Hall of Fame, Citizens Savings Hall of Fame Athletic Museum.

1965

BAPTIE, Norval
Skater and Contributor
Born 1885.

A World Outdoor champion, Baptie reached his peak in 1907. He later became a teacher of skating and a performer, producer and director of ice skating shows.
Also in: Canada's Sports Hall of Fame and Ice Skating Hall of Fame.

DAVIDSON, Harley
Skater
Born 1880.

Harley was the U.S. Outdoor champion in 1910.

NILSSEN, John
Skater
Born July 8, 1877.

For two years, 1896 and 1897, John won the National, North American and International Men's Outdoor championships.

1966

FLATH, Al
Contributor
Born 1874.

An early promoter of speed skating, Al proposed and

adapted cycling rules for the mass starts in speed skating. He was an official timer for the sport for 70 years.

HORN, Madeline
Skater
Born June 10, 1911.

On February 11, 1939, in Saranac, N.Y, Maddy broke the record for 220 yd. in U.S. Amateur Senior Women's Outdoor racing. Her time of 0:20.2 still holds as a record today. She was also an outstanding racer in National and North American competition. In 1933 she won the North American Indoor championship, and in 1937 and 1938 won the National Indoor championships. In 1937, 1939 and 1940 Maddy captured the National Outdoor title, and in 1939 and 1940 captured the North American Outdoor title.

KAAD, Harry
Skater
Born 1888.

Harry was both the Western and Illinois State champion. Nominated by the Amateur Skating Association of Illinois and Dr. Milan Novak, he reached his peak in speed skating in 1914.

KEMPER, Henry
Contributor
Born June 8, 1888.

A speed skating promoter and official, Kemper founded the St. Louis Silver Skates. He served skating largely during the 1930s.

LANGKOP, Dorothy Franey
Skater
Born 1915.

A rare accomplishment, Dorothy broke two U.S. Amateur Senior Women's Indoor records. The first, on February 25, 1933, at St. Louis, Mo, was the 1/6 mile in a time of 0:31.0. The second record was set on February 15, 1936, in St. Paul, Minn, for the 220-yd. race, in a time of 0:21.6. In competition, Dorothy won the National Women's Outdoor championship in 1934 and 1936 and the North American Women's championship in 1936 and 1937.

1967

FISHER, Charles T.
Skater
Born 1886.

Charles was 12 times Wisconsin State champion and a Western Indoor and Outdoor champion. He reached the peak of his speed skating career in 1910.

HALL, Kenneth
Contributor
Born 1886.

Kenneth originated the Detroit Gold and Silver Skates Derby. With 50 years experience as a National official, he also edited the *Amateur Skating Union Official Handbook.*

JAFFEE, Irving
Skater, Coach and Instructor
Born 1906.

Jaffee came to prominence in speed skating in 1928 when he set the world record for the mile and won a gold medal in the Olympics 10,000-m. race. He then won gold medals in the 5000- and 10,000-m. races at the 1932 Olympics. His special ability as a speed skater led to a coaching position with the Delano-Hitch Speed Skating Club and a position in 1946-1947 with the Recreation Park in Newburgh, N.Y, to teach youngsters speed skating.
Also in: Winter Sports Hall of Fame, Citizens Savings Hall of Fame Athletic Museum.

NOAH, Harry
Contributor
Born 1881.

Harry was involved in the organizational aspects of speed skating as a promoter, officer, editor, referee and organizer. Through his work, the conduct of speed skating meets was improved.

POTTS, Allan
Skater
Born 1904.

Early in his career, Allan won the National Men's Indoor championship and the National Men's Outdoor championship in 1928 and 1929, respectively. A member of more than one U.S. Olympic speed skating team, Potts set the world's record for 500 m. in 1936.

1968

BARTHOLOMEW, Kenneth
Skater and Contributor
Born February 10, 1920.

Bartholomew won the National Outdoor championship 14 times, in 1939, 1941, 1942, 1947 and 1950–1956 and tied in 1957, 1959 and 1960. He won the North American championship in 1941, 1942 and 1956 and was an Olympic medalist in 1948. A devoted speed skater, Bartholomew also promoted youth programs in the sport.
Also in: Ice Skating Hall of Fame.

FREISINGER, Leo
Skater and Coach
Born February 7, 1916.

After winning an Olympic medal in speed skating in 1936, Freisinger won the National Men's Indoor championship of 1937 and 1938. He coached the U.S. Olympic team in 1964.

McLAVE, Elsie Muller
Skater
Born November 25, 1895.

In 1928 Elsie won four championships: the National, North American and International Women's Outdoor and the National Women's Indoor.

NEITZEL, Loretta
Skater
Born February 11, 1908.

In 1929 Loretta was not only National Women's Outdoor champion but North American and International Women's Outdoor champion as well. In 1930 and 1931 she captured the National Women's Indoor championship.

SCHROEDER, Edward
Skater and Coach
Born 1911.

First a World champion in the 10,000-m. race of 1933, Edward won the North American Men's Outdoor championship in 1933. In 1960 he was coach for the Olympic speed skating team at Squaw Valley.

1969

BERNARD, Carmelita Landry
Skater
Born July 1, 1917.

Carmelita was a National and North American Outdoor champion who reached the peak of her speed skating career in 1942.

BLUM, Ray
Skater
Born April 11, 1919.

The National Men's Outdoor champion in 1949, Ray went on to win the North American Men's Outdoor championship in 1950 and tie for the championship with Terry Browne and Hall of Famer Art Longsjo in 1952. He was North American Men's Indoor champion in 1952 also.

LAMB, Delbert
Skater and Contributor
Born October 22, 1914.

An Olympic speed skater, Delbert made the fastest time in the World championships since 1893 when he turned in a time of 0:42.6 in 1936. On February 19, 1948, he broke the record in the U.S. Amateur Outdoor 1-mile race on a 400-m. track in Oslo, Norway, with a time of 2:29.7. Delbert later served speed skating as a National referee and coach of the 1956 U.S. Olympic speed skating team.

MARSHALL, Patricia Gibson
Skater
Born January 2, 1935.

Sixteen years after Hall of Famer Maddy Horn set the U.S. Amateur Outdoor record for 220 yd, five-time National Outdoor champion Patricia Marshall matched her time of 0:20.2. The history-making event took place on January 30, 1955, in St. Paul, Minn.

WERKET, John
Skater and Coach
Born 1924.

John is the only American to have won World gold and silver medals four times each. The gold medals came in 1948, 1949 and 1950 for the 1500-m. race and in 1950 for the 500-m. race. With that experience, it was natural for him to coach the World team for 1967.

1970

BERZ, Harry
Contributor
Born March 21, 1891.

As a national official, Harry helped to develop the standards and procedures for speed skating over a 50-year period. He also introduced the use of heat cards.

HENRY, Kenneth
Skater
Born January 7, 1929.

When Kenneth won the 500-m. race in the 1949 Men's World championships, he became one of the few American men to accomplish such a feat. But even more amazing, he won it again in 1952, cutting his time to 0:43.4, 2.9 secs. less than in 1949, along with a gold medal in the Olympic 500-m. race. To honor his outstanding achievements, Henry carried the torch for the United States in the 1960 Winter Olympics in Squaw Valley.
Also in: Winter Sports Hall of Fame, Citizens Savings Hall of Fame Athletic Museum.

LONGSJO, Arthur Mathew
Skater
Born October 23, 1931; Olympic competitor in cycling 1956.

In 1952 Arthur tied with Terry Browne and Hall of Famer Ray Blum for the North American Men's Outdoor championship. In 1954 he not only captured that title in his own right but also won the North American Men's Indoor championship as well. In 1956 he took both his bicycle and his speed skates to the Olympics in Italy.

OTTSEN, Lamar
Skater and Contributor
Born September 10, 1912.

Since 1930 Lamar has served both pack style and Olympic speed skating in many ways. First as an outstanding indoor skater, he has also been an officer, National official and a World and Olympic team coach.

SANDVIG, Gene
Skater and Contributor
Born February 8, 1931.

Gene was both a two-time competitor in the Winter Olympics and winner of the 1958 and 1959 National Men's Outdoor championships. He was also a National official and active promoter for speed skating.

DISNEY, William D.
Skater and Contributor
Born April 3, 1932; brother Jack was North American Men's Indoor champion in 1957 and National Men's Indoor champion in 1958.

William is one of the few Americans to have won an Olympic medal in a sport that is dominated by the Scandinavians and Russians. A silver medal was his at Squaw Valley in 1960. He was previously North American and National (tied with Jay Hasbrouck) Men's Indoor champion in 1955 and later a National official, promoter and team coach.

FARRELL, J. O'Neil
Skater and Coach
Born August 28, 1906.

A member of two Olympic teams, Farrell won a bronze

medal in 1928 and later coached the 1936 Olympic speed skating team. 1926 was the year he captured the International Men's Outdoor championship.

SHEFFIELD, James
Contributor
Born November 12, 1909.

Since 1930 Sheffield has served speed skating as a National official, Amateur Skating Union president and an international board member.

1972

DAME, Edgar J, Jr.
Skater
Born December 10, 1927.

The North American Men's Indoor champion in 1949, 1950 and 1953, Edgar set seven National indoor records during his speed skating career.

SAND, Mary Novak
Skater, Coach and Contributor
Born February 17, 1938.

Reaching the peak of her career in 1960, Mary was the first speed skater to win the National Outdoor championships in all classes. In 1958 she won the National Women's Indoor championship, which she again won in 1960 and 1961 along with titles in the North American and International Women's Indoor championships. In the 1960 Women's Outdoor championships, Mary cleaned the slates with victories in National, North American and International races. She continued her involvement in speed skating after her competitive years as an organizer and coach of several new skating clubs and co-author of promotional literature for the sport.

SCHWARZ, Herbert F.
Contributor
Born 1898.

A National official and officer, Herbert promoted and organized the National Outdoor championships in St. Paul, Minn. He also managed the 1956 U.S. Olympic speed skating team.

KRUMM, Philip O.
Contributor
Born October 9, 1906.

Nominated for election into the Hall of Fame by the Wisconsin Skating Association, Philip encouraged recognition in the United States of achievements in Olympic style skating. He also served as president of the U.S. Olympic Committee.

FITZGERALD, Robert
Skater
Born October 3, 1923.

A National and North American Outdoor champion, Bob set three National Outdoor records during his speed skating career. The highlight of his racing came in 1948 when he tied for the silver medal in the Olympic 500-m. race. He participated on two Olympic speed skating teams.

Ice Skating Hall of Fame

WILMETTE, ILLINOIS

Mailing Address: 1000 Skokie Blvd, 60091. Tel. (312) 256 5060. *Contact*: Thomas E. Hall, Exec. Dir. *Location*: 15 mi. N.W. of Chicago, 70 mi. S.E. of Milwaukee, Wis, 150 mi. S.W. of Grand Rapids, Mich, 195 mi. N.W. of Indianapolis, Ind. *Admission*: Free 8:30 to 4:30 Monday to Friday. *Personnel*: Thomas E. Hall, Exec. Dir; 5 mem. Awards and Citation Comt. *Nearby Halls of Fame*: Business (Chicago), Bowling, Sports (Milwaukee), Agriculture (West Lafayette, Ind, 210 mi. S.E.), Sports (North Webster, Ind, 115 mi. S.E.), Auto Racing, Basketball (Indianapolis) and State (Detroit, Mich, 230 mi. N.E.).

Charter members of the Ice Skating Institute of America began meeting in 1959, but it was not until 1963, when the Institute was recognized as a nonprofit organization, that the Ice Skating Hall of Fame was formed. Certificates and photographs of outstanding contributors to the sport and recreation of ice skating are displayed in the Wilmette headquarters as well as in rinks across the country through the Ice Skating Hall of Fame Gallery. This is a fairly recent promotional tool established by the Institute to increase interest in ice skating, to bring to skating enthusiasts the tradition of skating established by Hall of Famer Jackson Haines, the color of skating demonstrated by Sonja Henie and the information that Zamboni is more that just a machine.

Members: 22 as of January 1977. Nomination forms are sent to the membership of the Ice Skating Institute of America once a year and are then screened by a five-member Awards and Citation Committee, selected by the Institute president with approval from the Board of Directors. After screening, ballots are sent to the membership who are given at least three weeks to vote for one person. The one person who receives the greatest number of votes is elected to the Hall of Fame. He or she must have made a contribution of national significance not later than three years before being nominated for membership. Contribution may be in the following categories: participation as a skater, teacher or judge of competition, advancement of skating through the publication of books, presentation of skating programs or other activity that increases public awareness of ice skating, or the development and improvement of ice skating facilities. Only one person is elected each year, unless two or more persons have been jointly responsible for the same contribution. Results are announced at the annual convention of the Institute, and members are inducted at the Awards and Citation Banquet held during that time. Members receive Hall of Fame scrolls, while their certificates and photographs are sent to skating rinks throughout the country for display in the Ice Skating Hall of Fame Gallery.

1963 BAPTIE, Norval. Performer, producer and director of ice skating shows, and a teacher. See entry in Hall of Fame of the Amateur Skating Union of the United States, 1965. *Also in:* Canada's Sports Hall of Fame.

HENIE, Sonja. See entry in United States Figure Skating Association Hall of Fame, 1976.

1964 BARTHOLOMEW, Kenneth. See entry in Hall of Fame of the Amateur Skating Union of the United States, 1968.

GOODFELLOW, Arthur R. Historian of ice skating achievements and ice rink development; organizer of ice rink industry.

OWEN, Maribel Vinson. See entry in United States Figure Skating Association Hall of Fame, 1976.

1965 BUTTON, Richard Totten. See entry in United States Figure Skating Association Hall of Fame, 1976. *Also in*: Winter Sports Hall of Fame, Citizens Savings Hall of Fame Athletic Museum.

JOHNSON, Oscar. See entry in United States Figure Skating Association Hall of Fame, 1976.

SHIPSTAD, Eddie. See entry in United States Figure Skating Association Hall of Fame, 1976.

SHIPSTAD, Roy. Member of Shipstad and Johnson Ice Follies; pioneer in organizing traveling ice skating shows.

ZAMBONI, Frank J. Inventor of machines for smoothing ice skating rink surfaces.

1966 HARRIS, John H. Twenty-five years producer and director of the Ice Capades.

1967 HAINES, Jackson. See entry in United States Figure Skating Association Hall of Fame, 1976.

1968 KIRBY, Michael. Amateur and professional skater, teacher and author of ice skating textbooks.

1969 CHALFEN, Morris. Sender of numerous ice skating groups to all parts of the world.

1970 SHORE, Eddie. Pioneer in hockey; active with ice skating for over 45 years; ice rink management. See entry in Hockey Hall of Fame, 1947. *Also in*: Canada's Sports Hall of Fame and International Hockey Hall of Fame.

1971 MARKHUS, Orrin and THOMAS, Irma. Ice skating partners for 25 years in an act known as "The Old Smoothies."

1972 McGOWAN, Everett. Amateur and professional speed skater, show skater, figure skater and ice hockey player; ice rink operator; instructor; producer of ice shows and builder of ice rinks. See entry in Hall of Fame of the Amateur Skating Union of the United States, 1962.

1973 HEISS, Carole E. (Jenkins). See entry in United States Figure Skating Association Hall of Fame, 1976. *Also in*: Winter Sports Hall of Fame, Citizens Savings Hall of Fame Athletic Museum.

1974 ALBRIGHT, Tenley. See entry in United States Figure Skating Association Hall of Fame, 1976. *Also in*: Winter Sports Hall of Fame, Citizens Savings Hall of Fame Athletic Museum.

1975 FLEMING, Peggy Gale (Jenkins). See entry in United States Figure Skating Hall of Fame, 1976. *Also in*: Colorado Sports Hall of Fame and Winter Sports Hall of Fame, Citizens Savings Hall of Fame Athletic Museum.

1976 PERRY, Russell. Executive director of the Ice Skating Institute.

United States Figure Skating Association Hall of Fame

BOSTON, MASSACHUSETTS

Mailing Address: Sears Crescent, Suite 500, City Hall Plaza, 02108. Tel. (617) 723-2290. *Contact*: Mrs. Jean Winder, Museum Comt. mem. *Location*: In the heart of historic Freedom Trail, exit from Central Artery at Haymarket Sq; approx. 40 mi. N.E. of Providence, R.I, 65 mi. N.E. of Newport, R.I, 80 mi. N.E. of Springfield, 206 mi. N.E. of New York City. *Admission*. Free 8:30 to 4:30, Monday-Friday. *Personnel*: Theodore G. Clark, Chmn; five mem. Museum Comt. (Benjamin T. Wright, Chmn.). *Nearby Halls of Fame*: Tennis (Newport), Basketball (Springfield), Horse Racing (Saratoga Springs, N.Y, 140 mi. N.W.), Baseball (Cooperstown, N.Y, 200 mi. W.), Heritage, Music (New York City, 206 mi. S.E.), Bicycle (Staten Island, N.Y, 206 mi. S.E.), Harness Racing (Goshen, N.Y, 250 mi. S.W.).

Prior to the founding of the United States Figure Skating Association (USFSA) Hall of Fame, a museum of figure skating was housed at The Skating Club of Boston, as the city had long been the center of activity for the sport. In 1975, the USFSA central offices moved from another part of Boston to the Sears Crescent Building, a red brick structure erected in 1841, typical of the architecture of that era. Though a satellite collection remains at The Skating Club of Boston, the museum also moved to the Sears Crescent Building at that time. Prominent in the collection are medals, trophies and skating pins from around the world representing many eras in the history of figure skating. Works of art, paintings, prints and porcelains demonstrate the immense influence skating has had on the artistic world. Some cases in the Museum proper contain skates with the various changes in boot and blade designs occurring in the evolution of skating, and others contain commemorative and Winter Olympic medals collected by a devoted contributor to the Hall of Fame, Benjamin T. Wright. After the Hall of Fame was founded, a special display was set

up in the Museum with pictures and biographies of each member. Pictures and biographies of all USFSA presidents are displayed in the President's Corner. There is also a collection of badges of three-time Olympic champion and Hall of Famer Gillis Grafström, donated to the museum by his widow, Mrs. Cecile Grafström. The USFSA Museum also consists of a library containing a most unusual collection of rare books and artifacts; all are specially catalogued. Original manuscripts and correspondence of Hall of Famers Sonja Henie, Maribel Vison Owen and Ulrich Salchow are kept here along with the complete works of T. D. Richardson, covering a span of over 50 years of figure skating history. In his work as an international correspondent on winter sports for London-based periodicals and newspapers, he collected many photographs of internationally known skaters and Hall of Fame members. In 1961 a USFSA Memorial Fund was established in memory of the U.S. World Team killed in a plane crash on their way to the World Figure Skating championships in Prague, Czechoslovakia. Letters, newspaper articles, telegrams and photographs document the incident and memorialize the team members. Albums, scrapbooks and greeting and postal cards with skaters and skating scenes also bring the history of figure skating alive. By special arrangement, visitors can view the library's film collection with clips of national and world champions, many of whom are in the Hall of Fame. This Hall is a member of the Association of Sports Museums and Halls of Fame.
Members: 28 as of January 1977. Members from around the world are elected in one of three categories: (A) amateur skaters retired from competition at least five years, with outstanding competitive records, or contributions to style or technique; (B) nonskating contributors, inactive at least one year, who have served the USFSA, or other amateur figure skating associations; and (C) professionals in skating who have made noteworthy contributions to figure skating as professionals. Nomination forms with space for ten names are printed in the November and December issues of *Skating* and are available from the USFSA central office. A person can submit up to ten nominations (on one form) each year without regard to category. After the annual January 31 deadline, the Museum Committee classifies nominations by category and may even submit their own nominations. Twenty-seven electors, three from each USFSA region, are appointed by the president according to recommendations submitted annually by the vice president. The Museum Committee provides the electors with necessary biographical information about each nominee. In 1976, the first year for the Hall of Fame, electors voted for 20 candidates in Category A and 10 each in Categories B and C. Nominees who received at least 18 votes in their categories were elected. If no person was elected in a category on the first ballot, an additional ballot was taken in that category and the number of required votes was reduced to 15. Presently, electors are limited to 10 votes each in Category A and five each in Categories B and C. Each member of the USFSA Hall of Fame receives an inscribed award (the award is given to the family of a deceased member). A similar award and a picture of the member become part of the USFSA Museum's permanent collection and the person's picture and biography are published in *Skating*. Hall of Fame members are inducted annually in May at the USFSA governing council meeting.

1976

ALBRIGHT, Tenley E.
Amateur
Following the 1956 Olympics, received doctorate in medicine from Harvard Univ. Medical School; today a practicing surgeon with her father and brother Nile; married with three daughters.

Known as a skater with an exceptional combination of grace, artistry and skill, Tenley was a silver medalist in the 1952 Olympic Games and a gold medalist in 1956. She was also World champion in 1953 and 1955, North American champion, 1953 to 1955, and United States champion for five consecutive years, 1952 to 1956. She is a director of the U.S. Olympic Committee and is a recognized authority in the field of sports medicine.
Also in: Winter Sports Hall of Fame, Citizens Savings Hall of Fame Athletic Museum; and Ice Skating Hall of Fame.

BADGER, Sherwin C.
Amateur
Graduate of Harvard University; married with 4 children; died in 1972.

Representing the Skating Club of Boston, Badger gained prominence as a five-time United States champion, 1920 to 1924, and became the first North American champion in 1923. A member of the 1928 U.S. Olympic team, he was able to show the world his outstanding free skating and dynamic style at St. Moritz, Switzerland. The next time he participated in the Olympics was in 1932 as a pairs skater with Beatrix Loughran where they won the World championships in 1930. Representing the Skating Club of New York, they returned with an Olympic silver medal and remained World champions through 1932. Badger was first vice president of the United States Figure Skating Association in 1928, president, 1930 – 1932 and 1934 – 1935; he also served as chairman of the eastern, sanctions and judges committees and was a member of the executive committee for 22 years.

BLANCHARD, Theresa Weld
Contributor
Theresa Blanchard influenced skating for over 60 years, first as a competitive skater and then as an active member of the USFSA. Representing the Skating Club of Boston, she won the first United States championship and repeated the victory from 1920 to 1924. In 1920 Theresa became the first United States woman to win an Olympic skating medal, a bronze, and in 1923 won the first North American Ladies championship. She and her partner, Nathaniel W. Niles, won the United States Pairs in 1918, again from 1920 to 1927 and were the only United States representatives at the 1920 Olympics. In 1925 they became the North American champions. She was also on the 1924 and 1928 Olympics teams, won the U.S. Dance championship in 1931 and was a member of the winning U.S. Champion Four in 1934. As a member of the USFSA, she served on numerous committees: publicity and publications committee 1923 – 1944, executive committee 1925 – 1938, publications committee 1944 – 1957, publications advisory committee 1957 – 1963, central office 1950 – 1953 and professionals 1937 – 1943 and 1945 – 1947. She was also a team official for the 1932 and 1936 Olympics and a World judge. In 1923 she co-founded *Skating* and was editor from 1924 to 1963, when

she became emeritus editor and was elected honorary member of the USFSA.

BROKAW, Irving
Amateur

After winning the Champion of America competition in 1906 and becoming the first United States international competitor in the 1908 Olympics, Irving traveled through Europe to study ice skating. When he returned to the United States, he began lecturing on the form of figure skating and wrote a textbook explaining all the movements of the European style. The international style was thus introduced to this country and spread quickly. Through his efforts the first national fancy (or figure) skating tournament in the United States was held in New Haven, Conn, in 1914. In 1915, at Brokaw's suggestion, the German skating ballets came to the Hippodrome in New York, along with amateur and professional exhibitions. Booklets illustrating the methods of the international style were distributed to the audiences. Brokaw was honorary president of the USFSA in 1923.

BRUNET, Pierre
Contributor

Engineer by profession; married to competitive skater Andrée Joly.

Following competition as a singles skater in the 1924 and 1928 Olympics, and later as a pairs skater with his wife, Pierre became a highly respected teacher. He and his wife joined the Skating Club of New York after moving to the United States before W. W. II. There he applied the principles of his profession to an innovative training program which produced many fine skaters such as Carol, Nancy and Bruce Heiss and Gordon McKellen, Jr. Some students even came from France to study under Brunet. He also helped with the establishment of successful summer skating sessions in St. Paul, Minn, and in Michigan, Illinois and New York as well.

BUTTON, Richard Totten
Contributor

Born July 18, 1929; James E. Sullivan trophy 1949; honors student at Harvard Univ, degree in 1952, graduate of Harvard Law School in 1956; married with 2 children; producer and sports commentator for television; covered 1976 Winter Olympics at Innsbruck, Austria as commentator; author of *Dick Button Skates* in 1955 and *Instant Skating* in 1964.

Dick began seriously studying ice skating at the age of 12, and at 15, won the U.S. Junior championship and was only 16 when he won the U.S. Senior championship, the youngest ever to hold this title. During his entire career, he emphasized the athletic content of figure skating: Button's double axel, three consecutive double loop jumps, triple loop jump and the "Button Camel" stunned the figure skating world. As a pupil of Gustave Lussi (Hall of Famer and father of the American school of figure skating), Button was U.S. Champion from 1946 to 1952, North American champion in 1947, 1949 and 1951 and Olympic gold medalist in 1948 and 1952, the first United States man to win the Olympic championship in figure skating. He also won the World championship from 1948 to 1952. Dick was the first and last American to win the European championship in 1948, the event promptly being closed to North American entrants thereafter. He was also the only winter sports athlete to receive the James E. Sullivan Trophy, given by the United States Amateur Athletic Union to the nation's outstanding athlete of the year, in 1949.

Also in: Winter Sports Hall of Fame, Citizens Savings Hall of Fame Athletic Museum; and Ice Skating Hall of Fame.

FLEMING, Peggy Gale
Professional

Born July 27, 1948, in San Jose, Calif; graduate of Hollywood Professional School; married to Dr. Gregory L. Jenkins; one child; ABC-TV Sports Award 1967; Associated Press Female Athlete of the Year 1968; Reader's Digest Woman of the Year 1969; lives in San Francisco, Calif. area.

Peggy won her first national title as the youngest Senior Ladies champion in 1964, a title she held until 1968. Later she won the World championship (1966 to 1968), the North American championship (1967), and the Olympic gold medal for women's singles in figure skating, 1968. Since retiring from amateur competition, Peggy has been a featured performer in the Ice Capades since 1968 and has had her own television specials.

Also in: Colorado Sports Hall of Fame, Winter Sports Hall of Fame, Citizens Savings Hall of Fame Athletic Museum; and Ice Skating Hall of Fame.

GERSCHWILER, Jacques
Contributor

Native of Switzerland; entered Open Professional championship of Great Britain in 1933 and 1934, winning second and third, respectively.

Gerschwiler was the founder of the British school of figure skating. He believed in a scientific approach and was an excellent teacher of compulsory figures. Concentrating on technique first, his school provided figure skating with a solid foundation for a more creative and graceful development, but one that also included a very high degree of skill. The talent of Cecilia Colledge of Great Britain was a result of Gerschwiler's training. She reigned as European champion for three years from 1937 to 1939, was World champion in 1937 and won the silver medal at the 1936 Winter Olympics. Other skaters trained by Gerschwiler include Jeannette Altwegg of England, European, Olympic and World champion in 1951, and Karin Iten of Switzerland, European and World champion in 1974. He has recently written a book on figure skating in German, which hopefully will be translated into English soon.

GRAFSTRÖM, Gillis
Amateur

Born June 7, 1893, in Sweden; architect by profession; following his death, his widow, Mrs. Cecile Grafström, donated his collection of badges to the Hall of Fame.

Gillis Grafström brought about a new freedom of execution and interpretation in figure skating. He began his outstanding competitive career in the early 1900s and won the Swedish championship from 1917 to 1919. He won his first Olympic gold medal in 1920, followed by two more, in 1924 and 1928. He was a World champion in 1922, 1924 and 1929. In 1932 he was an Olympic silver medalist. In addition to being a fine skater, Grafström also originated the flying sit spin and developed combinations of jumps and spins.

HAINES, Jackson
Contributor
Born in 1840; birthplace unknown; went to Europe in 1864; died in Finland in 1879; his gravestone is inscribed American Skating King.

The world of figure skating experienced many major changes as a result of Jackson Haines. With considerable background in dancing and skating, even Champion of America in 1863–1864, he went to Europe and started the Viennese school. He watched the grace and smoothness of waltzers and decided to incorporate their movements and music in skating. (A common occurrence today, figure skating to music had never been done before.) The idea quickly spread throughout Europe, then Canada and the United States through exhibitions and schools established by Haines. Greater control was made possible when Haines developed a new skate that served as a model for the next 70 years: the blade was forged onto toe and heel plates and then screwed onto the sole of the shoes. In skating eights and turning threes to a center, Haines for the first time used arms and legs to execute movements and developed a theatrical flair. Even the use of eye-catching costumes is credited to Haines. He also originated the sit spin, later developed into the flying sit spin by Hall of Famer Gillis Grafström. Figure skating has never been the same since Jackson Haines founded the international style.
Also in: Ice Skating Hall of Fame.

HEISS, Carol E.
Amateur
Married Hall of Famer Hayes Alan Jenkins in 1960; three children; resides in Akron, Ohio; doing promotional and advertising work.

In her time Carol compiled the best competitive record in international competition for ladies of anyone from North America. At 13 she was fourth in the World championships of 1953 and in 1955 was runnerup, going on to win in 1956. She retained this championship 5 times from 1956 to 1960. She also won the North American championship in 1957 and 1959 and the United States championship from 1957 to 1960. Carol won the Olympic championship for ladies in Squaw Valley, Calif, in 1960. After retiring from the competitive ranks, she did some show skating and appeared in a movie.
Also in: Winter Sports Hall of Fame, Citizens Savings Hall of Fame Athletic Museum; and Ice Skating Hall of Fame.

HENIE, Sonja
Professional
Born in 1912 in Norway; studied ballet and started skating at age 7; died of leukemia in 1969.

As the 11-year-old Norwegian champion in 1924, Sonja placed last out of eight women in the 1924 Olympic women's figure skating, but came back to win a gold medal in 1928, 1932 and 1936, a record in ice skating competition. She was Norwegian champion again in 1925 and 1929; World champion ten consecutive times from 1927 to 1936; and won the European championship eight consecutive times from 1929–1936. In her routines she demonstrated great athletic ability and a wide repertoire of spins and jumps. In order to perform such athletics, Sonja introduced the short skirt and revolutionized the wearing apparel worn by female skaters today. During the first 15 years of her professional career, Sonja entertained between 15 and 20 million people and spread the popularity of skating through her charm and talent. She appeared in a total of ten Hollywood films, including *One in a Million,* a full-length skating film released in 1936. In 1976 the president of the Norwegian Skating Union took Sonja's Hall of Fame plaque to Oslo for placement with her other championship trophies.
Also in: Ice Skating Hall of Fame.

JENKINS, David W.
Amateur
Honors graduate of Colorado Col; later graduated from Western Reserve Univ. Medical School; now a physician in Tulsa, Okla; married with 3 children.

David became North American champion in 1957 and won his first World title that same year in Colorado Springs. Successfully defending his World title in 1958 and 1959, he went on to win the Olympic championship at Squaw Valley, Calif, in 1960. He was also United States champion four times from 1957 to 1960.
Also in: Winter Sports Hall of Fame, Citizens Savings Hall of Fame Athletic Museum.

JENKINS, Hayes Alan
Amateur
Graduated Phi Beta Kappa from Colorado Col, Harvard Univ. Law School; wife Carol Heiss; 3 children; currently an international lawyer for Goodyear Tire and Rubber Co. in Akron, Ohio.

Winning the Olympic championship in 1956, Jenkins was also World champion four times, 1953 to 1956, twice North American champion, 1953 and 1955, and four times United States champion, 1953 to 1956.

JOHNSON, Oscar
Contributor
Starting in St. Paul, Minn, Oscar Johnson and his partner Eddie Shipstad became popular as exhibition skaters, especially with their "Bicycle Built for Two" routine. They were asked to perform throughout the country, eventually with a 16-week engagement at the College Inn of the Sherman Hotel in Chicago, one of the first hotel shows in the country. In 1936 they began the first touring show, Shipstad and Johnson Ice Follies, with 28 performers; Eddie and Oscar were the coproducers and comedy team, while Roy Shipstad (Eddie's brother), Bess Ehrhardt, Lois Dworshak, Everett McGowan and Ruth Mack were the featured stars. Their first opening was in Tulsa, Okla, and within a short time they were established as a wholesome form of entertainment for audiences in the United States and Canada, putting skating first and spectacle second. Richard Dwyer, successor to Roy Shipstad, 16-year-old U.S. Junior Champion in 1949, has been with the well known Ice Follies for more than 25 years.
Also in: Ice Skating Hall of Fame.

JOLY, Andrée
Contributor
Originally from France; came to the United States before W. W. II; son Jeanne-Pierre won the U.S. Pairs championship in 1945 and 1946, but was killed in an automobile

accident in 1948; trophy in son's memory presented in 1950 by Oscar A. Morgan of the Skating Club of New York as a permanent award for the U.S. Novice championship for men.

Andrée Joly enjoyed an outstanding career as a singles skater before teaming with her husband Pierre Brunet to make their greatest mark in figure skating as pairs champions. They developed shadow skating to a fine art and were one of the first pairs to do lifts during routines, beginning in 1924. As silver medalists of the 1925 World championships, Brunet and Joly returned to win four more times, 1926, 1928, 1930 and 1932. In 1928 and 1932 they won gold medals in pairs skating at the Olympics and also in 1932 won a silver medal in the European Pairs championship. Turning professional after the 1932 Olympics, they exhibited their unusual talent in carnivals in the United States and abroad and placed second in the Open Professional Pairs championship of Great Britain in 1937.

LUSSI, Gustave
Contributor
Native of Switzerland; lives in Lake Placid, N.Y.

Gustave Lussi could accurately be called the father of the American figure skating schools, as he developed specialized methods of instruction, incorporated athletics and brought the science and technology of multiple revolution jumps and jump-spin combinations to figure skating. Lussi began teaching at Lake Placid and developed his first pupil, Egbert S. Cary, Jr, into the United States Junior champion of 1924. After moving to Toronto, Ont, he trained Hall of Famer Bud Wilson and his sister, Constance, who became Canadian and North American pairs champions and dominated competition in the late 1920s and early 1930s. Lussi passed the Canadian Gold Medal Test in 1931, only the sixth person to do so, and the first teaching professional ever to pass this highest figure test of the United States or Canada. Another of his Canadian students was Barbara Ann Scott, who later became the 1948 World and Olympic champion. After W. W. II, Lussi returned to Philadelphia, Pa, and continued to develop future champion skaters, such as Dick Button and the Jenkins brothers. He helped to establish the first regular summer skating sessions in North America at Lake Placid.

NICHOLSON, Howard
Contributor
Originally from St. Paul, Minn, Howard first learned to skate as a speed skater and hockey player. Taking up figure skating as early as 1910, he began his professional career as a show skater, appearing at the Hippodrome in New York and later the College Inn in Chicago. Traveling to Europe in 1923, Nicholson taught for 16 years in England and Switzerland, at the same time actively exhibiting and competing. He earned the International Skating Union First Class (Gold) Test in 1926 and was the first Open Professional champion of Great Britain 1931–1933. Nicholson currently lives in Lake Placid, N.Y, where he is continuing his outstanding teaching career.

OWEN, Maribel Vinson
Professional
Born in 1912 in Winchester, Mass; died in 1961.

Maribel was a fine singles and pairs skater as well as a teacher. She was nine times United States Singles champion (from 1928 to 1933 and 1935 to 1937), North American Singles champion in 1937 and a member of three Olympic teams, placing fifth, third and second. She also won silver and bronze medals in the World Championship of 1934. In 1928–1929, 1933 and 1935–1937, she won the National Pairs championship and the North American Pairs title in 1935. She turned professional in 1937 and toured the country with her own show, but continued her involvement in skating as a teacher. Maribel was the first woman sportswriter for the *New York Times* following her retirement from active competition, and authored two books, *Primer of Figure Skating* and *The Fun of Figure Skating.* Maribel and both her daughters were members of the 1961 World Team, all of whom died in a plane crash near Brussels, Belgium.
Also in: Ice Skating Hall of Fame.

PAULSEN, Axel
Amateur
A world record holder in speed skating in 1885, 1886 and 1888, Axel Paulsen incorporated speed into figure skating and invented the jump. He was the originator of the axel, which begins from the outside forward edge of one skate, then one and a half turns in the air, followed by a landing on the back outside edge of the other skate. A double axel, which Paulsen made famous, consists of two and one half revolutions in the air. Not only did he revolutionize figure skating, but he and another skater constructed a new racing skate with two thin metal tubes and a blade 1/16 in. wide. The skate was more secure and much lighter than previous designs and was later used as a model for hockey skates. Paulsen's influence also eventually brought about international competition for speed skating. The president of the Norwegian Skating Union accepted the Hall of Fame plaque for Axel and returned it to Oslo to go on display with Paulsen's other trophies.

RICHARDSON, T. D.
Contributor
As an international correspondent on winter sports for several London-based periodicals and newspapers, T. D. Richardson kept a close eye on figure skating for over 50 years. His interest in the sport began when he and his wife were pairs skaters and helped to popularize the modern-day shadow skating, skating side by side and moving close together. Richardson, a National Skating Association gold medalist, and his wife competed in the 1924 Olympic Games. Richardson was also chairman of the National Skating Association ice figure committee, a world referee and founder of the Commonwealth Winter Games. Following his death, his widow, Mrs. Mildred Richardson, donated the complete collection of his works, including photographs and correspondence of Hall of Famers Sonja Henie, Karl Schafer and Gillis Grafström, to the United States Figure Skating Association Museum and Hall of Fame. These have been compiled in albums and are available for viewing in the library.

SALCHOW, Ulrich
Amateur
Born 1877 in Sweden; date of death unknown.

Ulrich Salchow was one of the pioneers in figure skating.

Through practice and training, he performed his figures almost to perfection and exhibited the well-spaced movements of the Swedish school in his free skating programs. Salchow was Swedish champion 1895–1897, European champion 1898–1900, 1904, 1906, 1907, 1909 and 1910. He gained the World championship in 1909 and repeated the victory nine times, 1902-1905 and 1907-1911. He was the first man to win an Olympic gold medal for figure skating in 1908. He ended his career with a total of 38 gold medals. He was the originator of the salchow (a skating movement named after him) which requires a skater to take off from the back inside edge of one skate, rotate in midair, then land on the back outside edge of the opposite skate.

SCHÄFER, Karl

Professional

Born in Austria; competed on Austrian Olympic swimming team; wife Christine Engelmenn, daughter of his figure skating trainer; author of instructional skating book with illustrations on flip pages, *Living Pictures of My Figure Skating* (1937); died in 1976 at age 67.

Coming from the home of the waltz, Karl Schäfer exemplified throughout his career the fluidity of motion and grace like that of dancing and carried on the tradition that Hall of Famer Jackson Haines began. First training under the famous Engelmenn family, founders of the rink and club that truly preserved the legacy of Haines in Austria, he demonstrated his potential in 1927 by finishing second in the Austrian championship and third in the European and World championships. In 1928 he placed second in the European and World championships and fourth in the Olympics. From 1929 to 1934 he was Austrian champion, from 1929 to 1936 European champion and from 1930 to 1936 he was World champion. He also won Olympic gold medals in 1932 and 1936. In 1930, 1932 and 1934 Schäfer made trips to North America and appeared in major club carnivals to demonstrate and popularize figure skating. After turning professional in 1936, he became the featured star in many carnivals in the United States and toured with Guy Owen and Hall of Famer Maribel Vinson in their show, the "Gay Blades," forerunner to the Ice Capades. Since then, Schäfer has taught figure skating in North America and assisted the Austrian World Team.

SCHOLDAN, Edi

Amateur

Born in Vienna, Austria; came to the United States in 1938 by invitation of Walter Brown, sports promoter (*See* Hockey Hall of Fame); wife Roberta Jenks, nationally ranked competitor; daughter Ruthie and son Jimmy killed with him in plane crash in Brussels, Belgium, en route to 1961 World Figure Skating championships.

Edi Scholdan had established himself as a skater in Europe before coming to the United States. In 1933 he placed sixth in the World championships as a former Junior champion of Austria. Turning professional shortly thereafter, he was fourth in the Open Professional championship of Great Britain in 1934 and seventh in 1935. Having already passed his National Skating Association First Class (Gold) Test, he then became an initial member of the instructional staff at the Sports Stadium in Brighton, England, in 1935. He continued his teaching in the United States at the Commonwealth Figure Skating Club at the old Arena in Boston and, following W. W. II, moved to Colorado. There he was instrumental in establishing the successful summer school at the Broadmoor. He became known worldwide as a teacher.

SHIPSTAD, Eddie

Contributor

Starting in St. Paul, Minn, Eddie Shipstad and partner Oscar Johnson became popular as exhibition skaters, especially with their "Bicycle Built for Two" routine. They were asked to perform throughout the country, eventually with a 16-week engagement at the College Inn of the Sherman Hotel in Chicago, one of the first hotel shows in the country. In 1936 they began the first touring show, Shipstad and Johnson Ice Follies, with 28 performers; Eddie and Oscar were the coproducers and comedy team, while Roy Shipstad (Eddie's brother), Bess Ehrhardt, Lois Dworshak, Everett McGowan and Ruth Mack were the featured stars. Their first opening was in Tulsa, Okla, and within a short time they were established as a wholesome form of entertainment for audiences in the United States and Canada, putting skating first and spectacle second. As a successor to Roy Shipstad, Richard Dwyer, 16-year-old U.S. Junior Champion in 1949, has been with the well-known Ice Follies for more than 25 years.

Also in: Ice Skating Hall of Fame.

WELD, A. Winsor

Contributor

Born in 1869; graduated from Harvard Univ. 1891; with American Red Cross in Greece during W. W. I; 4 children; died in 1956 at age 87.

After W. W. I Weld saw the need for a central organization to represent skating. He founded the United States Figure Skating Association in 1921 and served as the president until 1925, when he was elected honorary president for life. Weld quickly obtained membership in the International Skating Union for the Association, which also received recognition from the American Olympic Committee (now the U.S. Olympic Committee) as sole governing body for figure skating. Rules defining tests, competition and amateur status were established and an agreement with the Canadian Figure Skating Association was negotiated for co-sponsorship of the North American championships. This agreement led to the mutual growth and cooperation in the sport for the two countries.

WILKIE, Reginald J.

Contributor

Married; 2 children; died in 1962.

Ice dancing became an accepted event in the Winter Olympics of 1976 as a direct result of years of work by Reginald Wilkie. He first became involved in skating at Hammersmith, near London, in 1930 and joined the National Skating Association of Great Britain in 1931. Interested in ice dancing, he founded the Ice Dance Committee, under the skating association, and served as its chairman from 1933 to 1962. During that time he prepared and introduced the original schedule of National Skating Association Dance Tests and was an active competitor in ice dancing. In 1937 he and partner Daphne Wallis became the first British Dance champions and in 1939 they won the first official championships in Great Britain. In the same years, Wilkie and Wallis were silver medalists in the Pairs championships of Great Britain. After his retirement from competition, Wilkie worked to gain acceptance for ice dancing as an international competitive event by first standardizing its form, a monumental task. An ad hoc committee, with Wilkie as a member, was authorized at the 1947 Congress of the International Skating Union to develop and present the foundation and rules for ice dancing. After demonstrations of ice dancing at the 1948 Olympics, a week-long conference in London and lots of hard work, the rules were adopted at the 1949 Congress and the International Skating Union Technical Committee was formally established, with Wilkie as chairman from 1953 to 1962. He was instrumental in arranging the first international ice dancing competition in London in 1950. It was held in conjunction with the World championships that year, but did not become a formal part of the competition until 1952. Through Wilkie's influence, ice dancing was incorporated into the European championships in 1954; as a result of numerous articles he wrote for *Skating World*, the standardization of ice dancing was made possible.

WILSON, Montgomery S. "Bud"
Contributor

Born c. 1910; served in W. W. II in field artillery, gained rank of major and earned Bronze Star; married; 3 children; died in 1964.

Bud first entered the Canadian Championships in 1924, placing second. He also placed second in the British championship in 1928. He won his first senior men's singles title in 1929, going on to take that title nine more times from 1929 to 1935 and 1938 to 1939. He also won his first men's title in the biennial North American championships in 1929. Bud earned the bronze medal in the 1932 Olympics and was runnerup in the World championships in Montreal that same year. Bud was also a fine pair skater; he and his sister Constance were North American Pair champions in 1929, 1931 and 1933, and Canadian Pair champions from 1929–1930 and again from 1932 to 1934.

LACROSSE

Bear, Deer, and Terrapin challenged Eagle, Hawk, and the great bird Tlániwă to a game of lacrosse. While the birds preened and went through their other ritualistic preparations, two tiny creatures approached them. As they were obviously rodents, the birds told them to play on the side of the animals. But the animals had ridiculed and rejected them, the small ones said. So the birds, taking pity, cut a pair of leather wings from their drum. These they attached to the first little creature who thereby became Bat. Having no more leather, they took the second creature between their beaks and stretched it into Flying Squirrel. Then the game began, and with the aid of Bat and Flying Squirrel, who could keep the ball in the air, the birds won easily. And that is why the Cherokee, who told the legend, attached small pieces of bat wings wrapped in buckskin to their lacrosse sticks and wove bat whiskers into the sticks' netting.

The Cherokee lived and farmed in Tennessee and the Carolinas after having been driven away from the Great Lakes by the Iroquois and the Delaware. Subsequently they were driven by the whites along the Trail of Tears to Oklahoma. One of the so-called Five Civilized Tribes, the Cherokee are famous for many reasons today. Will Rogers was part Cherokee. One of their early chiefs, Sequoya, for whom the trees were named, devised the first written Indian language. This led to the publication of the first Indian newspaper. Called *The Cherokee Phoenix,* it was first issued in 1828, the year the first *Webster's Dictionary* was published. While they lived in the Carolinas and Tennessee, however, the Cherokee were most famous for their lacrosse. As with many of the more than 50 tribes who played it, the Cherokee's basic tactic in the game was to disable first, score later. They called their version *anetsa,* the "little brother of war."

The tribe was a confederation of red (war) and white (peace) towns of from 30 to 60 houses each. These towns would challenge each other to lacrosse games to be played in summer during any of the full phases of the moon. Interestingly enough, the ancient Olympics in Greece were held only in summer and only during the full phases of the moon. Once a date had been set, the 9 to 12 players of each Cherokee town began their ritual preparations. These usually required seven days for completion, although special matches required 28 days of ritual preparation. A central part of those preparations was the strict diet, in which no timid, sluggish, young or brittle-boned animals or fish could be eaten. This included frogs, which were a normal Cherokee staple. Neither could any brittle-stalked plant be eaten, nor could salt or hot food be consumed. If a man's wife was pregnant, he could not play. If a man touched an infant or a woman during those seven or 28 days his strength would be drained and he could not play. If a woman touched a lacrosse stick on the eve of the game, the stick was rendered useless and she was killed. Meanwhile, the town's shamans would attempt to foretell the outcome of the game and to kill, disable, or otherwise wreak havoc on the opposing team. Countermeasures were also taken by them, it being understood that the opponents' shamans were working similar magic. During the pregame dancing, a man referred to as *talala,* the woodpecker, ran up and down the line of dancers uttering sharp, loud woodpeckerish shouts of a single word that meant, "They are already beaten!" Others had the job of secretly smearing a soup made of the hamstrings of rabbits (timid, easily confused creatures) along the opponents' trails. On the day of the game the principal shaman gave his team a pep talk in the rapid, jerky tones auctioneers use today. Each player was then scratched some 224 times with turkey bone splinters. Herbs were rubbed into these bleeding wounds before the player dressed. His outfit, a breechclout, was attached loosely so that if it were grasped it would fall off and he could escape. Eagle feathers for keen eyesight, deer tails for speed, and the rattles of snakes to instill fear were then attached as hair ornaments. Finally the player's body was rubbed with grease, or chewed bark of either the slippery elm or the sassafras, so that he would be as slippery as an eel. White or red paint might be daubed on but never blue, the color of defeat.

To start the game the two teams had a face off in which the players were matched. Anyone without an opponent had to drop out of the game. Play lasted until one team had scored 12 goals. Officials included each team's "drivers" whose job it was to run onto the field to retrieve discarded playing sticks and to break up unnecessary fights with long, stout switches. Throughout the game a team's head shaman stayed some distance away, usually beside a river, making incantations and chants. He had an assistant who relayed reports to him on the progress of the game brought by seven "counselors," at least one of whom was always on the sidelines. Exhausted players were allowed to drink only a sour mixture concocted of green grapes and wild crabapples. After the game was over the defeated team asked for a rematch before leaving the field. The victors returned to their town where they staged a feast and performed rituals designed to avert the defeated town's certain attempts to get magical revenge. Then everyone set about replacing his stick's lost bat whiskers and wings, eating frogs, and touching women and children.

Throughout North America similar versions of lacrosse were played for centuries. Algonquin tribes in the valley of the St. Lawrence River invented it long before 1492, and the various Indian trade routes and migrations introduced it virtually everywhere. As a rule, the northern and eastern tribes played with a single stick or crosse per player, the southern and western tribes with two. The ball might be made of pine wood, buckskin stuffed with grass or hair, or baked clay covered with buckskin. It might be stitched like a baseball or formed by a knotted drawstring. The Ojibway, called Chippewa by the English, played with a three-inch red ball that had a hole in it to emit a whistling noise as it sped through the air. In the Passamaquoddy (Maine) version, initial possession of the ball was determined by the flip of a chip: a man in the center of the field spat on a wood chip, then flipped it up, the team captains called "dry" or "wet." Playing fields were usually large, especially those of the Mohawk, and were usually on an east–west axis. Some tribes played with two goals, others with one. Some games lasted through the entire daylight hours of three days. The Menominee of Wisconsin divided their game into quarters, and the host of the game gave presents to the winners of each quarter. The Miamis of Michigan and Ontario sometimes fielded 2000 players, the Missisauga of Ontario and the Shawnee of Ohio allowed women to play with the men. The Santee Dakota (Sioux) of Minnesota played their version in winter on the ice. Among many tribes the shaman kept score by cutting notches in a tally stick—required because games of more than 100 goals scored might be played. Most spectacular perhaps was the version played in Mississippi and Louisiana, and later in Oklahoma, by the Choctaw, in which up to 1000 players per team tied brightly dyed horsehair manes around their necks and attached flowing white horse tails to the back of their beaded belts. The Cheyenne, the Chickasaw and the Chinook, the Sauk and the Fox, the Penobscot, Nipissing, Caughnawaga and Huron, the Onondaga and the Seneca, the Gualala, Pomo, Yokuts and Miwok, the Muskogee and the Seminole, the Skokomish and the Winnebago—from British Columbia to California and from Florida to Ontario, people played lacrosse. As the Civil War loomed, everyone who knew anyone was talking about the great Choctaw champion Tullock-chish-ko, "He who drinks the juice of the stone." In 1860, after watching a Chippewa (Wisconsin) game, J. G. Kohl wrote, "Nowhere in the world, excepting, perhaps, among the English and some of the Italian races, is the graceful and manly game of ball played so passionately and on so large a scale."

Jean de Brebeuf, a Jesuit missionary, saw Hurons playing their version near Thunder Bay, Ontario, now Georgian Bay. To him the stick they used resembled *la crosse,* French for a bishop's crozier. And so he gave the whole game its present name. That was in 1636, the year Harvard was founded. Not until two centuries later, however, in 1834 did Europeans pay much attention to the game. Any initial enthusiasm they may have had for it was dampened by a game staged in 1763, the year Charles Mason and Jeremiah Dixon fixed the Mason-Dixon line. The Ottawas under the great chief Pontiac and the Ojibways under their chief Minavavana offered to treat the British garrison at Fort Michillimackinac to an exhibition game in honor of King George III's birthday, June 4. They played for several hours until soldiers wishing to get a closer view opened the fort gates. The Indians stormed in and massacred all but three men, who escaped in what was probably history's only sports event in which the teams massacred the spectators.

Eighteen thirty-four was the last year suicides in Britain were buried at crossroads transfixed through the heart by a wooden stake. In Montreal that year, a group of whites arranged for a group of Indians to stage a friendly game. Interest in lacrosse was thereby kindled, although it was not until a decade later that whites actually participated in a game against the aborigines, as Indians were called. Sporadic play occurred in and around Montreal, the "cradle of modern lacrosse," until 1856. With the founding of the La Crosse Club of Montreal that year, an incredible transformation occurred. It seemed that clubs began everywhere. The Hochelaga Club was begun in 1858—"Hochelaga" was the Iroquois name for Montreal. The Beaver Club was begun in 1859. On August 27, 1860, the Prince of Wales attended a match between whites and Indians. The 19-year-old prince approved of the game, but stopped it before the Indians could win. The Boston Fusiliers' band then played "God Save the Queen" and "Yankee Doodle" which was often played on formal occasions because the U.S. Congress had not yet adopted a national anthem. The prince went on to become King Edward VII of England, and the game to which he had given his royal nod went on to become the king of Canadian sports. Then came one of the more amazing years in history—1867.

In 1867 dynamite, the typewriter, barbed wire, reinforced concrete, the automatic vending machine and the refrigerator were invented. School meals and regular cartoons in newspapers were introduced. Emperor Maximilian of Mexico was shot and Garibaldi marched on Rome. Alaska was bought from Russia and Nebraska became the thirty-seventh state. All Canadian provinces were united under one government when the British North American Act established the Dominion of Canada. Karl Marx wrote Part I of his *Das Kapital,* Strauss wrote his *Blue Danube* waltz. And lacrosse literally exploded from an aboriginal game into Canada's national sport. Seventy-five new clubs were added to the handful of existing Canadian lacrosse clubs that year. Fifty-two delegates representing 29 established clubs founded the Canadian National Lacrosse Association and adopted a championship banner with the slogan Our Country and Our Game. The Mohawk Lacrosse Club, the first lacrosse club in the United States, was established that year. In the first college game ever played, the University of Toronto beat Upper Canada College that year by a score of 3 – 1. Before the year was over a team of Caughnawaga Indians had been sent as missionaries for lacrosse on a European tour. They played demonstration games at the World's Fair in Paris and at the Crystal Palace in London. Everybody in Canada, it seemed, was playing it—or dancing to the lively dance tune written by J. Holt of Toronto that year called "The Lacrosse Gallop."

One man, virtually singlehandedly, did all of that for lacrosse. He was a Montreal dentist-poet-songwriter who bore a striking physical resemblance to the mystic General Charles "Chinese" Gordon of Khartoum fame. His name was William George Beers. Born in 1843, Beers was the white's goalkeeper in that 1860 game watched by the future king of England. Although he was Canada's first prolific sports journalist, the founder and editor of its first dental journal, and the dean of the first school of dentistry in Canada (in Quebec), he is best remembered as the "Father of Lacrosse." The supreme achievement which earned him this epithet was his drafting of the first official rules for the game. But he is also remembered for writing the world's first book on lacrosse published in 1868, for replacing the hair-stuffed ball with the India-rubber sponge one, for helping to organize both the first national championship game, won by the St. Regis Indian team, and the first Canadian-American match won by Canada, as well as for his efforts to gain acceptance for lacrosse overseas. Everywhere he went he promoted it, pointing out that in lacrosse there was "no beastly snobbishness." In 1876 he organized a tour for two Canadian teams, one white, one Indian, through Belfast, Dublin, Glasgow, Edinburgh, Newcastle, Manchester, Sheffield, Birmingham, Bristol and London. In London at Windsor Castle after tea, they played a command performance for Queen Victoria, who considered it "very pretty to watch" and gave each player an autographed picture of herself. That tour, and a second one Beers conducted in 1883, were directly responsible for the formation of numerous teams and lacrosse unions in England.

The game was introduced into Australia in 1874, into New Zealand four years after that, and into Tasmania in 1895. It remained popular on that island until W. W. I. When New York University played Manhattan College in Central Park in 1877, it was already a major American sport.

Due to many factors, not the least of which was George Beers, lacrosse continued to boom in Canada. For the upper classes it became a "society game," while the North-West Mounted Police organized lacrosse games to "keep people off the streets." New teams such as the New Westminster Salmon Bellies, new leagues and associations, and an Indian World Championship appeared. Attempts were made to play lacrosse indoors on ice. In what may have been modern history's first night game in any sport (the Greeks in Plato's time had a number of night games, including torch races on horseback), an innovative team played "fire ball" lacrosse in 1868. The ball, saturated with turpentine, ignited and fell apart; the netting of the crosses it had touched caught fire. Canada won a gold medal in lacrosse at the Olympic Games of 1904 and 1908. To stimulate amateur play, the Earl of Minto, Governor General of Canada, donated the silver Minto Cup and Sir Donald Mann donated a $2500 gold cup later named for him. Increasingly, newspapers and magazines praised lacrosse as the "gayest, liveliest, and manliest of games." It all seemed so immortal. But then as suddenly as it had begun, Canadian lacrosse began to die.

For the 64 years between 1867 and 1931, Canada dominated the world of lacrosse. This began to end, however, with the coming of W. W. I. Many factors could be blamed. Perhaps it was the excessive professionalism and gambling, along with the injuries and the violence, which the newspapers began to refer to as "savagery." The failure of most colleges and universities to adopt it and the growth of alternative sports—especially baseball and hockey—could also be blamed. Poor leadership in the national organizations, the desertion of patrons and fans as well as the transfer of the symbolic Mann Cup to the new sport of boxla were undoubtedly contributing reasons. The removal of Indians to special reserves, the increase of national homogeneity and the decrease in importance of the religious and racial partisanships that had lent early lacrosse its fanaticism also might have led to lacrosse's demise in Canada. And perhaps the fact that so much had been done by a single man counted as a factor when that one man, Beers, died in 1900. A newspaper article prophesied it: "Died in New Westminster on Saturday, October 4, 1913, professional lacrosse, for many years a resident of the Royal City . . ." Though Britishers of the Sixth Manchester Regiment valiantly played lacrosse in Egypt during W. W. I, though in the 1920s crowds of 8000 still turned out for Saturday afternoon games in Toronto, and though lacrosse has continued to be played in parts of Canada, the golden age was over by 1931. Exactly one hundred years after that incredible 1867, Canada was beaten by both the United States and Australia at the first International Centennial Lacrosse Tournament. No one was really surprised. From the 1930s on, other nations had reigned supreme in what was, after all, an aborigine game.

To some, of course, Canadian lacrosse's golden age, if it ever existed, was but a chapter in a far larger story. To the old Iroquois, thunderheads are still the place where the seven thunder gods play lacrosse with lightning balls. And to the old Cherokee, the full moon is still the lacrosse ball that was shot there by the gods.

FORMS: Games similar to lacrosse but historically unrelated were played by the ancient Greeks and Phoenicians. In the days of Darius the Persians played a version on horseback. Ninth century Viking settlers in Iceland likewise played a similar game which they called *knattleikr.* In France an ancient form of football called *la soule* was played with a curved stick, after which it was called *la jeu de la crosse.* Cricket, historically played with a crooked stick, is still called *la crosse* in certain mountainous parts of France. In North America French settlers and voyagers translated both "racket," as in tennis, and "snowshoe" to the word *raquette.* French Creoles in the American South still sometimes refer to lacrosse today as raquette. Rather than use the Indian names for the game (lacrosse in Iroquois, for example, was *tehontshik-s-aheks),* English colonists followed the French by calling lacrosse "racket." Interestingly, the Indians as a rule named the game for the ball, while Europeans named it for the stick. Lacrosse has been called a "gentleman's game," the "fastest game on foot," and "snowshoeing's summer face." An 1873 article in the

Montreal *Gazette* called it a "Scientifically beautiful recreation, combining gentlemanly contest with just as much *vim* and *abandon* in which civilized players ought to indulge." On the other hand, a 1935 article in *Collier's* called it "Murder on the Lawn." Somewhat cryptically, Walter Camp of football fame called it "a well deserved sport." Lacrosse, or La Crosse, is today the name of a United States surface-to-surface missile, a river, a city, a county in Wisconsin, and cities in Arkansas, Florida, Indiana, Kansas, Virginia and Washington.

Four major forms of lacrosse are played today: the twelve-a-side game for women, the ten-a-side game for men, seven-a-side lacrosse, and box lacrosse or boxla. The first two of these are played internationally and are over a hundred years old; the latter two are played only in North America, boxla only in Canada, and are less than fifty years old. In all four, the ball is caught, thrown, and carried by crosses fitted with nets. The object is to score points by throwing, rolling or kicking the ball into the goal net. Play behind the goal is allowed. The tactics employed are similar to those of football and especially of hockey: get the ball as quickly as possible into a position from which a shot at the goal can be attempted. When one team is in possession of the ball, that whole team is on the attack, while the entire opposing team is on the defensive. In theory, the game is played in the air, although in practice the ball often touches the ground. Fast, accurate passing and shooting are required; stick- and body-checking of an opponent are allowed except in the women's game but must not be excessive. The other rules are few and simple. Lacrosse may be played at any time of the year, although normally it is not played during the summer. The major countries playing it are the United States, Australia, England, and Canada. Its popularity, however, is growing in Hong Kong, Japan, Holland and elsewhere. In Canada it is played predominately on the West Coast. The main American center for lacrosse is Maryland (whose official sport, however, is jousting), particularly in and around Baltimore.

Women's lacrosse was first played in 1866 by girls at a school in northern England. The promotional trips of Doctor Beers in 1876 and 1883 increased its popularity throughout that country. In 1890 women invaded golf's holiest of holies, the Royal and Ancient Golf Club of St. Andrews, Scotland, for a lacrosse game. The first women's lacrosse club, the Southern England Ladies Lacrosse Club, was established in 1905, and in 1912 the Ladies Lacrosse Association was formed. This association introduced women's lacrosse into the United States prior to 1920 through immigrating English schools teachers. In the United States today the game is most widely played in the Eastern States, although it is spreading rapidly to the South and the Midwest. Since no bodily contact is allowed, there is no need for the equipment worn in the men's game—helmets, face masks, shoulder harnesses, padding, gauntlets. For the same reason, the women's game is preeminently one of speed, skill, elegance and finesse. The 12 players per team compete on a field which has no unnatural boundaries except for creases which are areas marked off by lines in front of the goal cages. The field measures 100 yards between the two goals. The men's field is smaller. While the men's game has 15-min. quarters with two 2-min. breaks, women's games have 25-min. halves. Both forms have a 10-min. halftime. Men's games which end in a tie go into overtime; women's do not. The officials for both forms may include a field umpire in charge of the game, two referees on the field in women's lacrosse or two crease umpires for men's games, a timekeeper, and a scorer who records goals and fouls. While the women's crosse may be of any length, the men's must be at least 3 ft. long—most men's, in fact, are 6 ft. long and 10 in. wide at the net end. Defensive players generally use heavier and longer crosses than do offensive players. The ball used by both forms is almost exactly the size and weight of a regulation baseball, although a slightly larger and heavier one is used in Canada. It is made of solid rubber. For women it may be black, white or yellow, while for men it is orange or white in the United States and Australia, orange in Canada and yellow in England—as opposed to the Cherokee red and white colors. A proper lacrosse ball will bounce from 47 to 50 in. when dropped from a height of 100 in. onto concrete. Men's games begin and restart after goals and some stoppages of play with two men kneeling or crouching on opposite sides of the ball. This is called a "face," or "face-off." In the women's game, the ball is put back into play by a "draw," in which two women stand facing each other holding the ball between their crosses. A goal is scored when the ball passes completely over the goal line and into the goal net. The goal crease is a circle 18 ft. in diameter. The goal net is inside the circle and attached to a six foot square open frame.

The two strictly North American forms of lacrosse are also the most recent ones. Box lacrosse dates from 1930, seven-a-side lacrosse from the late 1960s. The latter form uses men's lacrosse techniques but is played on a smaller field. With its reduced-bounce ball, it may be played in gymnasia or on handball courts. Seven-a-side games are started differently, however, and have different types of goals. There are no goalkeepers, and there are two umpires instead of three.

Box lacrosse, or boxla, appeared phoenixlike from the ashes of Canadian field lacrosse. Initial enthusiasm for it was so great that the Canadian Lacrosse Association adopted it as its official game in 1931. That same year a professional boxla league was formed for the Toronto Maple Leafs, the Cornwalls Colts, the Montreal Maroons and the Montreal Canadiens. Because it could be played in a covered area as a confined spectacle, and because it was heavily sponsored, boxla completely dominated the traditional field game from the time it was first played. Despite attempts to introduce it into the United States with an exhibition game at Madison Square Garden, boxla today is almost exclusively a Canadian sport. It is played in spring or autumn in gyms or arenas, often on ice hockey rinks covered with green matting. It is also played outdoors on smaller fields enclosed by wooden or net walls. Teams consist of seven players, but ten substitutions are allowed. The officials are a referee, a timekeeper, and two goal judges.

ORGANIZATION: Numerous organizations have been established for the control and promotion of the four forms of lacrosse. An international governing body was formed in 1928, the International Federation of Amateur Lacrosse (IFAL). Its members today are Australia, Canada, England and the United States. By tradition, its secretary is the secretary of the English Lacrosse Union. The women's game has its own governing body, the International Federation of Women's Lacrosse Associations which was formed at Williamsburg, Virginia, in 1973. This federation is composed of various national organizations. One of these, the All-England Women's Lacrosse Association formed in 1912 had affiliations with a total of 232 clubs, schools and colleges in 1973. Another member, the U.S. Women's Lacrosse Association (1931), is affiliated with more than 100 colleges and schools. Boxla is organized on a regional league basis. The leading clubs in each region play each other for the national championships. The major trophy in boxla is the Mann Cup, although junior teams compete for the Minto Cup.

In Canada the Canadian Lacrosse Association is the primary governing body for lacrosse in general. Numerous other organizations exist, however. For example, in Ontario alone there are the Ontario Lacrosse Association, the Ontario Lacrosse Referees' Association and the Ontario Minor Lacrosse Association. The latter, created in 1957, sponsors lacrosse in five age categories: novice (under 10 years old), pee wee (under 12), bantam (under 14), midget (under 16), and juvenile (under 21). Governing bodies for the sport in the United States include the U.S. Intercollegiate Lacrosse Association, founded in 1883, and the U.S. Lacrosse Coaches' Association. Various state and regional organizations also exist, notably in Maryland. There the Maryland Lacrosse Association annually awards a Men's Trophy. The most prestigious trophy in America, however, is the Wilson Wingate Trophy, awarded since 1936 to the year's best college team. All-American lacrosse teams have been named since the 1920s.

Lacrosse games were played at the Olympic Games of 1904, 1908, 1928, 1932 and 1948. At the 1932 Games in Los Angeles, a crowd of over 150,000 watched three games. Lacrosse is not, however, an Olympic event today.

A truly unique organization produces the game's crosses. Metal may not be used in the construction of a crosse. It must be shaped so that it cannot be used to hook either an opponent or his crosse, and its net must be strung so that the ball will not become lodged in it. Women form the nets of vertical hide thongs interwoven with catgut. Men generally complete the rest of the process which involves cutting the hickory, seasoning it, then steaming and shaping it. It takes a full year to make a single crosse. Ninety-seven percent of the world's supply comes from the small Chisholm factory on Cornwall Island, Ontario, where about 20,000 are made annually. At that factory only Mohawk Indians from nearby St. Regis Indian Reserve are employed.

Canadian Lacrosse Hall of Fame

NEW WESTMINSTER, BRITISH COLUMBIA

Mailing Address: 65 E. Sixth Ave, V3L 4G6. Tel. (604) 521-8087. *Contact*: Jack Fulton, Chmn. of the Bd. *Location*: Sixth Ave. at Cumberland at Centennial Community Centre; approx. 12 mi. E. of Vancouver and 147 mi. N. of Seattle. *Admission*: Free 9 to 9 daily and 9 to 6 weekends, closed holidays. *Personnel*: W. H. Armstrong, V.Chmn, Secy; 17-mem. Bd. of Govs. *Nearby Halls of Fame*: State and Province (Vancouver), Ski (Rossland, 250 mi. S.W.).

In 1964 the Canadian Lacrosse Association awarded the Canadian Lacrosse Hall of Fame to New Westminster due to the historical significance of the sport in that town. New Westminster's lacrosse heritage and current participation made it the prime site for this Hall of Fame. The Hall, founded to honor box and field lacrosse players, teams and contributors, is financed largely by New Westminster and an annual Board of Governors' Old-Timers Benefit Game. Private donations and federal grants supplement the Hall's city funds. The hall is located in the Centennial Community Centre whose facilities include a gym, pool and curling rink. The Museum itself consists of a 35-by-70-ft. room displaying the solid gold Mann Cup, various medals, trophies, mementos and pictures and bronze plaques inscribed with the names of the Hall's members.

Members: 183 as of 1976. 48 charter members were elected at the founding, but current selection rules provide that both the Eastern and Western Selection Committees elect three Players and two Builders each for a total of ten inductees per year. In recent years this limit has occasionally been exceeded but 1977 induction will abide by these rules. All inducted Players must be retired for five years, whereas Builders may still be active. Members are officially inducted at an annual ceremony and banquet in October.

1964 – 1965 ANTHONY, Bill. Box player.

BAKER, Henry. Box player. *Also in*: Lacrosse Hall of Fame and Museum.

BEERS, Dr. W. G. Builder.

CLARKE, Bun. Field player.

CONACHER, Lionel Pretoria. Field player. See entry in Canadian Football Hall of Fame, 1973. *Also in:* Canada's Sports Hall of Fame.

CROOKALL, John "Dot." Field player.

DAFOE, Dr. W. A. Builder.

DAVY, Alfred. Box player.

DICKINSON, Bill. Box player.

DOPP, E. J. Gene. Builder.

DOUGLAS, Jim. Box player.

FITZGERALD, William J. Field player. *Also in:* Canada's Sports Hall of Fame.

GIBBONS, David. Field player.

GIFFORD, Jim. Field player.

GRAUER, Rudy. Builder.

HARSHAW, Norman. Field player.

HOOBIN, Henry. Field player.

HUME, Fred. Builder. See entry in Hockey Hall of Fame, 1962. *Also in*: International Hockey Hall of Fame.

ISAACS, Bill. Box player.

JONES, Con. Builder.

KALLS, George. Field player.

KELLY, M. E. F. "Mike." Builder.

LALLY, Joe. Builder. *Also in:* Canada's Sports Hall of Fame.

LALONDE, Edouard "Newsy." Field player. See entry in Hockey Hall of Fame, 1960. *Also in*: Canada's Sports Hall of Fame and International Hockey Hall of Fame.

LONGFELLOW, Edward. Field player.

MADSEN, Carl "Gus." Box player.

MAITLAND, Pat. Builder.

MATHESON, George. Field player.

McARTHUR, William. Field player.

McCONAGHY, Jim. Builder.

McDONALD, Jack. Builder.

McKENZIE, Dan. Builder.

MORPHETT, Bill. Field player.

MURPHY, Jim. Builder.

MURRAY, Ernie. Field player.

PEELE, Clarence "Biscuits." Field player.

PICKERING, Harry. Field player.

QUERRIE, Charles. Field player.

REEVE, Edward "Ted." Field player. *Also in*: Canadian Football Hall of Fame, 1973.

RENNIE, George. Field player.

SPRING, Clifford "Doughy." Field player.

SPROULE, George. Field player.

TURNBULL, Alex "Dad." Field player.

WAGHORNE, Fred C. Builder. See entry in Hockey Hall of Fame, 1961. *Also in*: International Hockey Hall of Fame.

WHITE, Eric "Rusty." Box player.

WILKES, Bill. Box player.

WILSON, Bill. Box player.

WOOTTON, Lloyd. Box player.

1966 ALLEN, "Bones." Field player.

BAYLEY, Ed. Builder.

BRENNAN, "Paddy." Field player.

CAVALLIN, John. Box player.

DIXON, Archie. Box player.

DOWNEY, Ed. Box player.

FAVELL, Doug. Box player.

FEENEY, Patrick. Field player.

GAIR, Norm. Builder.

GIFFORD, Tom "Sharkey." Field player.

LEE, Bob. Box player.

McDERMOTT, Ed. Builder.

McKENZIE, Merv. Builder.

McMAHON, Wandy. Box player.

MURTON, "Sport." Field player.

PAUL, Andy. Builder.

ROWAN, Charles. Builder.

SPRING, Gordon "Grumpy." Builder.

THOM, Gord. Field player.

1967 BAKER, Ray. Box player.

BARNES, Erwin E. Builder.

BARNETT, Pete. Field player.

BEATTY, Stewart. Field player.

BROWN, Albert "Ab." Builder.

CHEEVERS, Joe. Box player.

COULTER, Bill. Field player.

DALE, John. Box player.

DAVIDSON, Charles. Box player.

JACOBS, Fred. Builder.

KELLY, Russell T. Builder.

LARGE, Bert. Field player.

LEE, Walt. Box player.

MARSHALL, David "Buck." Field player.

NICHOLSON, Leo. Builder.

POWERS, Edward, Sr. Field player.

SMITH, Leonard. Builder.

STODDART, Haddie. Field player.

WHITTAKER, Bill. Box player.

WOOD, Jack. Field player.

1968 BAIN, Frank "Piper." Field player.

BLACK, Clayton. Box player.

DAMIEN, Brother. Builder.

DAVIS, Ivan "Turk." Builder.

DeGRAY, Kelley. Field player.

FLETCHER, Doug. Builder.

MATHESON, Don. Box player.

McDONALD, Angie. Field player.

MORTON, Roy. Box player.

SWANSON, Oscar. Builder.

1969 BISHOP, Jim. Builder.

BLAIR, Ed. Builder.

FEENEY, George. Field player.

FERGUSON, Arnold. Box player.

GAIR, Gordon. Box player.

GIFFORD, Hugh. Field player.

GILMORE, Les. Builder.

GORDON, Tom. Builder.

KENDALL, Jerry. Field player.

POWLESS, Ross. Box player.

1970 CAVALLIN, Roy "Fritzie." Box player.

DAVIS, Grenville "Dutch." Field player.

FERGUSON, Mervin E. Builder.

FITZGERALD, W. K. Box player.
GODFREY, Harry. Field player.
GRAUER, Carl L. Builder.
McDONALD, Blain. Box player.
McLEOD, J. C. "Jim." Builder.
PEART, Max. Builder.
SEVERSON, Fred "Whitey." Box player.

1971 BROWN, Blyth. Field player.
BROWNING, Archie. Box player.
CALDER, Bill. Builder.
CARTER, Harry. Box player.
CONRADI, Fred K. Builder.
DICKINSON, Les. Builder.
McDONALD, Wilfred. Box player.
STIMERS, Rex. Builder.
STORME, Thure. Field player.
SULLIVAN, Ed. Field player.
THOMPSON, George. Field player.
TURNBULL, Leonard. Field player.
VERNON, John D. Field player.
WIPPER, Harry R. Box player.

1972 BRADBURY, Ted. Box player.
CHISHOLM, Colin. Builder.
FELKER, Neil. Field player.
FRIEND, George. Builder.
GUNN, James. Field player.
HILDEBRAND, Ike. Box player.
LANDON, Edwin. Builder.
MULLIS, Bill. Box player.
NORTHRUP, Jack. Box player.
PERRETT, Dr. T. S. Builder.

1973 ANDERSON, Chick. Builder.
BRYANT, Bert. Box player.
EWING, Will Buck. Field player.
FITZGERALD, Jerry. Box player.
GATECLIFF, Jack. Builder.
GIMPLE, Gordon. Box player.
MacPHAIL, Don. Box player.
MILLER, Douglas. Builder.
PHILLIPS, R. Pop. Builder.
SEPKA, Cliff. Box player.

1974 ALLAN, Bob. Box player.
ASHBEE, Don. Box player.
BLANCHARD, Bernard "CoCo." Builder.
BIONDA, Jack. Box player.
CHISHOLM, Bill. Box player.
DELMONICO, Henry. Builder.
GORE, Roy. Field player.
HOPE, Bill. Builder.
PITTENDRIGH, George. Builder.
WORTHY, Jack. Field player.

1975 ARMSTRONG, E. Herbert. Builder.
BRADFORD, Bo. Box player.
BYFORD, Jack. Box player.
CAMPBELL, Charles D. Box player.
CONNELL, Charles. Field player.
DOUGLAS, John. Box player.
MORO, Lou. Builder.
MURPHY, Walter Joe. Box player.
ROCHE, Val. Builder.
WAGHORNE, Fred, Jr. Builder.

1976 BUCHANAN, Harry. Box player.
DAOUST, Arthur. Builder.
DIXON, Ken. Box player.
JOHNSON, Alex "Buck." Field player.
JOSEPH, Stan. Box player.
MADGETT, Carl. Builder.
OLIVER, Robert. Builder.
PATCHELL, Willis. Field player.
PROCTOR, Jake. Box player.
ROWLAND, Douglas. Builder.
SCOTT, Tommy. Box player.
STARLING, Fred. Field player.

Lacrosse Hall of Fame and Museum

BALTIMORE, MARYLAND

Mailing Address: Newton H. White, Jr, Athletic Center, 21218. Tel. (301) 235-6882. *Contact*: Jay H. Elliot, Exec. Dir. *Location*: Approx. 37 mi. N.E. of Washington, D.C, 55 mi. S.W. of Wilmington, Del, 196 mi. S.W. of New York City. *Admission*: Free, 9 to 5 daily, mid-September-early June. *Personnel*: George M. Chandlee, Jr, Pres; Benjamin R. Goertemiller, V.Pres; Fred H. Eisenbrandt, Secy; William S. Keigler, Treas; Jay H. Elliot, Exec. Dir. *Nearby Halls of Fame:* Jockeys (Baltimore), Exploration and Invention (Arlington, Va, 45 mi. S.W.), Heritage (Valley Forge, Pa, 75 mi. N.E.), Harness Racing (Goshen, N.Y, 180 mi. N.E.), Ice Skating (Newburgh, N.Y, 185 mi. N.E.), Bicycle (Staten Island, N.Y, 190 mi. N.E.), Heritage, Music (New York City), Flight (Elmira, N.Y, 205 mi. N.E.), Horseshoe Pitching (Corning, N.Y, 225 mi. N.E.).

The Lacrosse Hall of Fame and Museum may be said to have been initiated in 1954 when the United States Intercollegiate Association appointed a Hall of Fame Committee with Francis Morris Touchstone as chairman. Temporary headquarters were established at Rutgers University where the Committee began the task of formulating plans and collecting material for the archives. In 1959 a nonprofit corporation, the Lacrosse Hall of Fame, Inc, was chartered for the purpose of maintaining the Hall of Fame. The Hall's purpose is to honor those individuals who are outstanding in performance by playing, coaching or officiating, or who have rendered outstanding service to the game and actively promote lacrosse in every way possible. Much preliminary work was done between 1954 and 1966, and finally in June, 1966, actual physical facilities were made available for the Hall of Fame and Museum. Today on display at the Hall are all kinds of pictures, lithographs, paintings, plaques and busts of the celebrated lacrosse "greats." Also on display in cabinets are artifacts and equipment used in the game. The Hall maintains a library with a multitude of books, records, magazine articles, a file of lacrosse guides and miscellaneous documents of historical interest. One of the most significant honors awarded by the Hall, granted to the attack player of the year, is the Jack Turnbull Memorial Award, named in memory of a former Johns Hopkins University All-American who lost his life in action during W. W. II. Publications by the organization include a *Lacrosse Newsletter* released eight times per year and the *Lacrosse Guide* and *Lacrosse In*, both printed annually. The corporation also publishes books, some of which are sold along with souvenirs in the archives. A list of names and addresses of some 8000 former players, arranged according to geographical location, is available to those desiring assistance in furthering the growth of the sport in any particular area. Interested schools and clubs can receive supplies and assistance for starting new teams through the extension kit plan operated by the Lacrosse Hall of Fame, Inc. This Hall is a member of the Association of Sports Museums and Halls of Fame.

Members: 123 as of November, 1976. Eligible candidates are players, coaches and officials or any contributor who has rendered outstanding service to the game of lacrosse. The only qualification is that 15 years must have elapsed since the candidate graduated from college. A committee is appointed by the president and approved by the board at the first board meeting held in each calendar year. The committee reviews questionnaires of approximately 30 of the apparently best qualified candidates, of which 15 will be selected for nomination. These 15 are then presented to the Board of Directors at the November board meeting, at which time the board votes upon and actually elects the individuals to be honored.

1957

COX, Laurie D.

Coach and Contributor

Born August 18, 1883, in Londonderry, Nova Scotia; graduated from Acadia Univ. 1903, Harvard Univ. 1908; married; three children; played intramural basketball and ice hockey; taught landscape engineering and headed dept. Syracuse Univ. 1915–1947; president of New England Col. 1947–1950 and 1952–1956; deceased.

While at Harvard Laurie Cox played varsity lacrosse 1906–1908, playing goal, point, second defense and second attack, and was known a a great stick handler. Lacrosse was introduced to Syracuse by Laurie, coaching an informal team in 1916–1917; in 1918 it was made a major sport and Laurie continued as head coach until 1931. His team compiled a record of 141 wins, 44 losses and 4 ties winning the national championship in 1922–1924 and 1925, one of three undefeated teams in 1926. Laurie also coached the All-American teams in our International Series 1930, 1935 and 1937. Introducing lacrosse to New England College in 1948, he coached their teams 1948–1950 and 1954–1957. Cox's overall coaching record is 189 wins, 65 losses, and 5 ties. In the early days he officiated many games, and was a member of the first rules committee 1922–1929 and chairman of the international committee 1922, 1926 and 1930. He selected the All-American team in 1922, and continued to serve until the first official committee was set up in 1933, on which he served as chairman for many years.

MARSTERS, Charles E.

Player and Contributor

Born June 9, 1883, in Brooklyn, N.Y; graduated from Harvard Univ. 1907; served in the Navy in W. W. I; USILA Award (for person who did the most for lacrosse) 1951; deceased.

Charles Marsters played freshman lacrosse at Harvard and was on the varsity team three years. He moved to New England in 1913 and with the assistance of Paul Gustafson, organized the Boston Lacrosse Club for the purpose of acquainting the area with the game. He served as manager of the team and played for 16 years in the defense position, point and crosspoint. In 1915 he encouraged Yale to add lacrosse to their physical education program and over the years worked with student groups and athletic directors to get their institutions to field teams, including Brown, Massachusetts Institute of Technology, Tufts and New Hampshire. With Tom Dent, Charlie formed the New England Lacrosse League which comprises fourteen members, and served his lifetime as a member of the executive board. He selected the All-New England College team and the All-Prep School team for many years, and served as an officer and committee member for the U.S. Intercollegiate Lacrosse Association (USILA) for over 40 years. Marsters served ten years on the All-American committee and was a member of the international committee that took the 1930 All-American team to Toronto to play club world champions.

MILLER, Cyrus Chace

Player and Contributor

Born November 2, 1866; graduated from New York Univ. 1888, Columbia Univ. 1891; law practice and public service; trustee of New York Univ; died January 12, 1956.

Cy Miller played with the New York University team, serving as its captain. After graduation, he joined the Staten Island Athletic Club lacrosse team where he was captain when they won the national championship in 1890. Cy later played for the Crescent Athletic Club 1895-1912. He held the office of president of the Professional Lacrosse Association, and served many years as a member of the U.S. Intercollegiate Lacrosse Association executive committee.

SCHMEISSER, William C.

Coach and Contributor

Born August 4, 1880, in Baltimore, Md; graduated from Baltimore City Col. 1889, Johns Hopkins Univ. 1902, Univ. Md. Law School 1907; successful law practice; wife Isabel Wooldridge; two children; died in 1941.

Bill Schmeisser played on the lacrosse team at Johns Hopkins 1900–1902, and 1905 (while doing graduate work), captaining the national collegiate championship team in 1902. After he graduated from law school, because of his intense interest in lacrosse, he served without pay as the coach of the Johns Hopkins team. He also was instrumental in the organization of the Mt. Washington Club team. He worked with the Hopkins varsity all his days, and never received any financial remuneration for his work. He was with their team of 1928 which represented the United States in the Amsterdam Olympics, and acompanied an all-star team to England in 1937. In 1904 "Father Bill" wrote a book on the coaching of lacrosse which was the standard textbook for coaches for over fifty years. He was active in the U.S. Intercollegiate Lacrosse Association and served several times on the rules committee, as chief referee, and as president.

TAYLOR, Roy

Player, Official and Contributor

Born October 17, 1887, in Brooklyn, N.Y; graduated from Cornell Univ. 1910; married; one son; served in W. W. I, reaching rank of Major in Engineers before discharge; deceased.

Roy Taylor played lacrosse all four years at Cornell 1907–1910; in 1910 they tied for the championship. Roy played for the Crescent Athletic Club 1910 through 1925, serving as captain during 1920 and 1921 when the Crescents won the Mythical National Championships. He played both midfield and close attack. During those years the Crescents were named best team in the country several different years. Roy helped start the sport at the Montclair Athletic Club and was instrumental in setting up the teams at Yale University and West Point. He started officiating lacrosse when Bill Schmeisser first appointed officials; he was named chief referee in 1925, a position he held for twenty years until Andy Kirkpatrick took over in 1955. Roy also served on committees and as an officer with the U.S. Intercollegiate Lacrosse Association for over 30 years, and was a member of the American Olympic committee in 1932. Roy gave lectures on lacrosse at Wingate Memorial during the late 1920s; these lectures were later published in *Talks by Great Coaches* which included all sports.

1958

ABERCROMBIE, Ronald Taylor

Player and Contributor

Born January 19, 1879, in Baltimore, Md; graduated from Johns Hopkins Univ. 1901, medical degree 1905; married Jennie Scott Waters November 21, 1906; three children; professor at Johns Hopkins many years; deceased.

Abercrombie's first game of lacrosse was in 1896 between the Maryland Athletic Club and the Crescent Athletic Club. He played as a freshman on the Johns Hopkins team in 1898, and was captain of the 1899 and 1900 championship teams. He also played on the 1902 championship team coached by Bill Schmeisser. Ron played center and was especially noted for his wonderful face-off ability. It has been said he "never lost a draw in his playing career." His last years at Hopkins, he both coached and played. He organized the first Mt. Washington team in 1904, the same year he had published the first illustrated article on how to play lacrosse. He also edited Bill Schmeisser's book on playing lacrosse, and was instrumental in bringing the game to the U.S. Naval Academy. He introduced the lacrosse net and also the shorter net and shorter handled sticks used by attack men in 1898. Dr. Abercrombie served lacrosse as an officer and chairman, and was responsible for the revision of the rules published in 1901. He also officiated at many games before the association organized officials, and acted as a voluntary coach at both Mt. Washington and Johns Hopkins over a period of years.

BRISOTTI, Albert A.

Player, Coach, Contributor and Official

Born December 21, 1888, in New York City; graduated from New York Univ. 1911; married in 1913 to Frances McClory; three children; longtime editor of *Lacrosse Guide*; deceased.

Al Brisotti began playing lacrosse with football and ran on the track team in high school. In college he also played football and lacrosse and participated in track meets. Later Al played on different club teams in the New York area, continuing until the 1942 season. He also coached at Stevens Institute 1918–1920, Rutgers University 1921–1925, New York University 1926–1933, Hofstra 1949 and Post 1959. Al officiated from 1926 through 1951, and was very active in coaching different boys' clubs in the box lacrosse leagues the fifteen years he was out of college coaching. He was one of the founders of the Long Island Lacrosse Association and its president from 1935 to 1953. A founder and past president of the Metropolitan Sunday Lacrosse League, he served on numerous committees to promote interest in the game. He wrote and lectured on lacrosse throughout his adult life, editing the *Guide* from 1938 until his death.

COLLINS, Carlton Palmer

Player and Contributor

Born September 27, 1893, in Cheswold, Del; graduated from Cornell Univ. 1916; married; author of *The Great Lacrosse Revolution*; deceased.

"Collie" played football and lacrosse during his high school days, and won letters in both lacrosse and football at Cornell. He was on the team that were champions of the Northern champion division in 1914, and captain of the 1916 team that also won the Northern champion division. Collie played lacrosse for Crescent Athletic Club from 1920 through 1929. He organized, financed and coached a lacrosse team at Stamford High School in 1932, and officiated at games from 1922 through 1942. He was president of the U.S. Intercollegiate Lacrosse Association in 1925 when it became an association instead of a league. He also served them as officer and committee member for many years. During his chairmanship of the rules committee, the field of play was shortened from 100 yds. between goals to 80 yds, a fixed boundary was instituted and the number of players on each team was cut to 10 instead of 12, sanction to wear face mask and football shoes was granted, and the periods were ended by pistol instead of horn.

KIRKPATRICK, Andrew Maxwell, Jr.
Player, Coach and Official
Born November 14, 1901, in Granite, Md; graduated from Baltimore City Col. 1919, St. John's Col. 1923, law degree, Univ. Baltimore 1932, married October 21, 1925, to Catherine Kerr; newspaper reporter and editor; died June 13, 1955.

Andy played lacrosse in City College and St. John's, and was an All-American at St. John's. He played for the Mt. Washington Club 1924, 1925 and 1928, and the L'Hirondelle Club in 1926 and 1927, captaining their team in 1926. He coached lacrosse at Baltimore City College 1925 – 1928 and at Donaldson School in 1929. Andy was one of the leading officials in lacrosse and football from 1927 through 1939; he was chief referee for the Maryland-Virginia district in 1948 and 1949, and again in 1950 – 1953. In 1954 he was appointed commissioner of the Southern Officials Association. He served on the All-American selection committee and was an official on the Baltimore Lacrosse League. The alumni association of Baltimore City College has established a memorial trophy in his name.

1959

BARNARD, Norris Clements
Player and Official
Born January 21, 1897, in Westfield, N.J; graduated from Swarthmore Col. 1919; military service W. W. I; married Elizabeth Jones on October 29, 1921; two children; lives in Medford, N.J.

Barnard played lacrosse in high school and at Swarthmore 1916 – 1919. He then played seven years with the Crescent Athletic Club, captain of the team for at least three of those years. Norris moved to Philadelphia and played on the Philadelphia Lacrosse Club team in 1927 and 1928, then the Penn Athletic Club for six years through 1934, being captain of the 1930 and 1931 teams. The next three years, 1935 – 1937, he played with the Montclair Athletic Club in New Jersey. From 1921 through 1928, Norris was a leading official and refereed many games in eastern colleges. He is an honorary life member of the U.S. Lacrosse Coaches' Association and has served on the executive committee of the U.S. Intercollegiate Lacrosse Association. Norris organized two different teams to play against the Crescent Athletic Club.

BROWER, Cyril De Cordova "Darb"
Player, Official and Contributor
Born November 20, 1898, at Woodmere, N.Y; graduated from Hobart Col. 1921; married Doris Searle on June 12, 1923; one daughter; died October 16, 1954, in Englewood, N.J.

Darb received letters in lacrosse at Hobart, and also was a member of the football team, basketball team, and captain of the track team. He was an outstanding player with the Crescent Athletic Club 1922 – 1929. He officiated in the metropolitan area both in lacrosse and football, and became a member of the rules committee of the U.S. Intercollegiate Lacrosse Association for many years; he also served as president and on its executive board.

DAVIS, William
Player
Born 1862; All-American in lacrosse 1884; played lacrosse in the late 1880s for the Crescent Athletic Club; worked for the U.S. Employment Service, was a sports writer and real estate agent; deceased.

FRIED, Waldemar H. "Pat"
Player and Official
Born March 29, 1889, in Brooklyn, N.Y; graduated from Cornell Univ. 1906; married Marion White in 1923; two daughters; married Elizabeth Abbott in 1957; lives in Providence, R.I.

Pat played lacrosse all four years at Cornell, captaining the 1911 team. After college he played lacrosse with the Crescent Athletic Club, serving as their captain in 1919. In the early 1920s he began refereeing, and continued for many years, at one time being chief referee with the association. Pat coached lacrosse at the University of Pennsylvania 1924 – 1927, and helped out at Brown University when he was 71. Pat Fried will be remembered as one of the officials at the first Army-Navy lacrosse game.

HUDGINS, William Harkinson
Player and Coach
Born in 1886 in Baltimore, Md; graduated from Johns Hopkins Univ. 1905, law degree Univ. Md. 1908; 1st Lt. in W. W. I; wife Laura Woods; died in 1956.

Bill Hudgins played lacrosse at Johns Hopkins in 1904 and 1905, and was a member of their championship team in 1906. He was a very outstanding attack man, going on to play with the Mt. Washington Club 1907 – 1909, where he captained the team in 1908 and 1909. Bill helped start lacrosse at the Naval Academy and helped coach their team in the early days. He worked officiating lacrosse in the Maryland area and devoted much time and energy trying to develop the game.

KNIPP, John Christian
Player and Coach
Born December 7, 1895, in Baltimore, Md; graduated from Baltimore City Col. 1912, Johns Hopkins Univ. 1917; married Marian Guthrie in April, 1918; three children; All-Time Hopkins Lacrosse Team; deceased.

John Knipp played lacrosse with Baltimore City College when the 1911 and 1912 teams won the championship. He played with Johns Hopkins 1913 through 1917 and captained the 1917 team. He played with the Mt. Washington Club in 1920, 1925 and 1926, having captained the 1920 team. In 1915 Johnny played with the championship University of Toronto team. After his playing days, he coached lacrosse at Mt. Washington and Johns Hopkins. He was an honorary member of the U.S. Lacrosse Coaches' Association, and on the board of directors of the Lacrosse Hall of Fame Foundation.

STARZENSKI, Victor
Player, Coach, Official and Contributor
Born July 20, 1886, in Clayton, Kans; graduated from Stevens Institute of Technology 1907; 1st Lt. in W. W. I;

married Frieda Schoeffler in 1924; one son; USILA Award for man who had done most for lacrosse in 1947; deceased.

While at Stevens, Vic played lacrosse 1903 – 1907, doing an outstanding job, especially considering he weighed only 123 lbs. and was 6 ft. 3 in. tall. He coached at Union College from 1922 through 1928, then at R.P.I. in 1944 and 1945, at the University of New Mexico in 1946, returning to Union during the seasons from 1948 through 1950. Vic started the lacrosse teams at all three of these schools. He officiated from 1923 to 1950 and spent a term on the rules committee of the U.S. Intercollegiate Lacrosse Association (USILA).

STROBHAR, Thomas
Player and Coach
Born September 25, 1883, in Savannah, Ga; graduated from Johns Hopkins Univ. 1904; married Frances Eagan on October 25, 1909; four daughters; married Florence H. on May 6, 1949; served as Lieutenant in Coast Guard in W. W. I; deceased.

Tom played on the Johns Hopkins lacrosse team 1902 – 1905; the 1904 and 1905 teams were intercollegiate champions. He later played for the Mt. Washington Club 1905 – 1908, during which they won three championships. He moved to the Philadelphia Lacrosse Club 1909 – 1913 and played for the Philadelphia Comets 1929 – 1931 and the Seagulls in 1932 and 1933. These last two were both box lacrosse teams and he was one of the best goalies around. Tom helped coach at Navy in 1905 and 1906, Lehigh University in 1907 and 1908, University of Pennsylvania 1909 – 1911, the Penn Athletic Club 1925 – 1928, and Swarthmore College 1927 – 1930. From 1922 through 1936 he officiated lacrosse games, mainly in the Philadelphia area.

TRUITT, Reginald Van Trump
Coach and Official
Born August 12, 1891, in Snowhill, Md; graduated from Univ. Md. 1914, American Univ. 1921 and 1929; married Mary Harrington in 1930; two daughters; service in W. W. I and II; Special M Club Award 1950; Gold Lacrosse Pendant for coaching the National Champion Team in the 1920s; lives in Stevensville, Md.

At the University of Maryland, Truitt won a letter in both lacrosse and track, 1911 – 1914, and was student coach of his team. He was the first official coach at the University from 1919 to 1927. He was very active in officiating in the 1920s and 1930s, and wrote many articles for the daily and Sunday papers on lacrosse. At one point Dr. Truitt helped in bringing two teams from Oxford-Cambridge to play a series of American colleges. From 1919 through the next decade he held many offices in the U.S. Intercollegiate Lacrosse Association.

WYLIE, William Caspari
Player, Official and Contributor
Born January 13, 1893, in Baltimore, Md; graduated from Baltimore City College 1911, Univ. Md. 1914; Captain in U.S. Army in W. W. I; married Janet Wood on November 27, 1923; Evening Sun Medal for outstanding record as a player; died August 16, 1949, in Baltimore.

Wylie played lacrosse three years at City College, captaining the championship team in his senior year. He organized, played for and captained the Walbrook Athletic Club team 1912 – 1914 before transferring to the Mt. Washington Club team where he played 1915, 1916 and 1920 – 1927. Casper was one of the original group that organized the lacrosse team at the University of Maryland. He officiated from 1922 through 1936, and was considered one of the best officials of the game. He arranged for the lacrosse teams participation in the 1928 Olympics at Amsterdam and served as vice president of the International Federation of Amateur Lacrosse that year. His offices at the U.S. Intercollegiate Lacrosse Association included vice president in 1925, president in 1926 and 1927, executive board 1926 – 1929, member of the ranking committee 1928 – 1930, of the Olympic committee in 1930, and on the play-off committee for the Olympics in 1932.

1960

KENNEDY, J. Sarsfeld
Player and Official
Born in Canada; came to the United States at the turn of the century to play lacrosse; member of the Crescent Athletic Club lacrosse team in Brooklyn; architect by profession; did some officiating at lacrosse games around 1910; deceased.

LYDECKER, Irving Brown
Player and Coach
Born December 12, 1893, in Nyack, N.Y; graduated with law degree from Syracuse Univ. 1922; All-American 1922; served in W. W. I in the Air Force; married Jean Page on March 24, 1934; two children; deceased.

Irv played basketball, football and baseball during his senior year of high school, and at Syracuse played lacrosse 1920 – 1922, captaining the 1922 team which won the intercollegiate championship, and was named All-American. In 1923 Irv went to Europe with the team that won the International Lacrosse Cup. He played with the Crescent Club 1923 – 1934. In 1925 and 1926 he coached the Harvard lacrosse team and refereed many intercollegiate games 1927 – 1933. Irv also coached the White Plains High School team 1935 – 1939. He served on many different committees for the U.S. Intercollegiate Lacrosse Association, and was president in 1932.

MALLONEE, C. Gardner
Player, Coach and Contributor
Born October 8, 1903, in Baltimore, Md; graduated from Baltimore Polytechnic Institute 1922, Johns Hopkins Univ. 1928; married Esther Felter on November 24, 1932; six children; All-Maryland and All-American honorable mention for football 1926 and 1927; All-American for lacrosse 1928; played pro basketball 1931 – 1934; presently lives in Baltimore.

Gardner played football, lacrosse and basketball at Baltimore Poly, and football and lacrosse at Johns Hopkins, on the university lacrosse team 1926 – 1928. He played on the U.S. Olympic lacrosse team in 1928, on the Crescent Athletic Club team 1929 and on the Johns Hopkins Olympic Club team in 1930 – 1932. From 1929 through 1935 he was assistant football and lacrosse coach at Johns Hopkins, and then moved into the directorship of athletics. He left Hopkins in 1949 to become a teacher and coach at Forest Park High School. Mal served as an officer, vice president and president of the U.S. Intercollegiate Lacrosse Association, was group chairman of the North-South game for many years, and wrote several outstanding articles on lacrosse for the *Lacrosse Guide.*

MILLER, Leon A.
Player, Coach, Official and Contributor
Born July 15, 1895, in Cherokee, N.C; attended Cherokee Indian School 1905–1909, graduated from Carlisle Indian School 1916; married Margaret in 1938; taught at City College of New York; deceased.

While at Carlisle, Leon played lacrosse 1912–1915, was a member of the varsity track squad 1911–1914, and a varsity football player 1911–1913. He became head coach of lacrosse at City College of New York in 1932 and continued until the 1960 season. He officiated for ten years from 1919 to 1929 and played lacrosse for the New York Lacrosse Club. He wrote many articles on lacrosse for the New York papers and several syndicated features.

PAIGE, John Hewitt
Player and Contributor
Born December 18, 1908, in Ogdensburg, N.Y; graduated from Colgate Univ. 1930; All-American Lacrosse Team 1930; married Lois Ferguson in December, 1935; five children; worked many years for the telephone industry; lives in Elm Grove, Wis.

At Colgate John played basketball as well as football, but his real love was lacrosse, playing on the varsity team 1927 through 1930; he was field captain of the All-American team that played a series of games in 1930 with the Canadian champions in Toronto. John continued to play lacrosse at the Crescent Athletic Club, captaining their 1938 team. He also played in the Olympic Trial games in the 1932 and 1936 seasons. John was very active in all phases of lacrosse; he held all of the offices in the U.S. Intercollegiate Lacrosse Association and was a member of the executive committee for many years until he moved away in 1948. John played a big part in starting the North-South All-Star Game just before W. W. II.

SCOTT, Herbert Thompson
Player, Coach and Official
Born April 8, 1895, in Toronto, Ont; attended Jarvis Collegiate Institute, Toronto; served in W. W. I; married; two sons; insurance business; lives in New Rochelle, N.Y.

During his youth in Canada, Herb played hockey as well as lacrosse. He played lacrosse with Riverdale and St. Simon's Lacrosse Club of Toronto. These teams won provincial and eastern Canada honors in various years from 1912 to 1922, where Herb played in the goals. He joined the Crescent Athletic Club in 1922 where he was an outstanding player 1922–1932. Herb also coached the Crescent Athletic Club 1928–1932, when they had some very outstanding teams. He played in England with the Canadian Army team during the war. From 1924 through 1940, Herb officiated intercollegiate lacrosse.

STUART, Edward M.
Player and Contributor
Born April 16, 1896, in Baltimore, Md; graduated from Baltimore City Col. 1913, Johns Hopkins Univ. 1917; Captain in W. W. I; wife Dorothy Townsend; two children; *Baltimore Evening Sun* Athletic Medal 1925; lives in Golden Beach, Fla.

Eddie played lacrosse and football at City College and Johns Hopkins, and was active in track. He played lacrosse all the years at both schools, and then for the Mt. Washington Club 1919–1925. He played for the Crescent Athletic Club in 1926 and 1927. He assisted in coaching lacrosse both at Harvard University and Massachusetts Institute of Technology while living in the Boston area. He served as officers and on committees for the U.S. Intercollegiate Lacrosse Association, and helped to promote lacrosse in the New England area.

TOUCHSTONE, Francis Morris
Coach and Contributor
Born October 2, 1897, in Baltimore, Md; graduated from Baltimore City Col. 1918, George Williams Col. 1923, attended Univ. Chicago; married Lillian Stanform on March 20, 1926; two children; Lacrosse Award for man who had done most for game 1957; Coach of the Year 1958; military service in Army 1941–1946; died November 7, 1957, at West Point, N.Y.

Morris played several years at the Mt. Washington Athletic Club under Bill Schmeisser. He coached varsity lacrosse, soccer and freshman gymnastics at Yale University 1924–1928, then moved to the U.S. Military Academy at West Point, where he coached lacrosse until his death. Morris had an outstanding record as coach, winning 214 games, losing 73 and tying 8. He served as assistant to the graduate manager of athletics from 1937 through 1957; three of his West Point teams won or shared the intercollegiate championships, winning in 1944, and co-champions in 1945 and 1951. Morris served in important positions both for the U.S. Intercollegiate Lacrosse Association and the Lacrosse Coaches Association; he was one of the originators of the Hall of Fame.

1961

BLAKE, Avery F.
Player, Coach and Contributor
Born April 8, 1907, in Buffalo, N.Y; graduated from Baltimore Polytechnic Institute 1925, Swarthmore College 1928; married Mabel Nield on April 14, 1928; two children; son Avery, Jr, three-time All-American; deceased.

Avery played basketball, football, and four years of lacrosse at Polytech, and one year of football and lacrosse at Swarthmore. He coached at Baltimore Polytech 1927–1930 while playing with Mt. Washington Club and the pro box team of Baltimore. He also played for the Swarthmore Box Lacrosse Team 1931–1955. He coached lacrosse and assisted in football at Swarthmore College from 1931 until he joined the staff at the University of Pennsylvania in 1960. At Poly Avery's record was three championship scholastic teams and at Swarthmore, he won the Penn-Delaware Championship for 13 years; in 1953 he won the USILA "B" Championship. He also coached the All-American team that went to England in 1937, and three North-South squads during his years at Swarthmore. At the University of Pennsylvania his teams won many divisional championships. Avery served actively with the U.S. Intercollegiate Lacrosse Association (USILA) and was founder and president of the

Penn Lacrosse Coaches Association. He helped to organize, played with and refereed for the old Sunday Lacrosse League in Baltimore. Ave promoted three clinics at Swarthmore and coached at the Florida Forum for one year.

FITCH, Frederic A.
Player, Coach and Contributor
Born September 15, 1900, at Fishers Island, N.Y; graduated from Syracuse Univ. School of Forestry 1924; All-American Defense Honors 1924; married Dorothy Dean on September 22, 1935; one daughter; private school teacher and government work for the state; lives in Niantic, Conn.

Fred played on the lacrosse team at Syracuse 1921 – 1924, the 1922 and 1924 teams being national champions. In 1923 he played on a touring Syracuse team in England; Fred played with the Syracuse Crescents, the Brooklyn Crescents, and the Montclair Athletic Club. He organized teams to play the Onondaga Indians for several years in Cortland, N.Y. Fred Fitch had a coaching career dating from 1926 to 1950 during which he developed many fine teams at Rutgers University. Not only were these teams known for hard play but their sportsmanship was outstanding. He coached two All-Star North Teams in the annual North-South games. Fred served on All-American and U.S. Intercollegiate Lacrosse Association committees, and has a commendable record of his contributions to the sport of lacrosse.

HARKNESS, William John
Player and Coach
Born June 23, 1888, in Belfast, North Ireland; moved to Canada late 1800s; married Anna MacDonald in June, 1915; two sons; deceased.

Bill played lacrosse and hockey. He played on outstanding lacrosse teams: Ottawa Stars Junior Champions 1908, Ottawa Shamrocks City League Champions 1909 and 1910, Ottawa Nationals 1911, and the Ottawa Capitals Professional-National Lacrosse Union 1912 – 1918. Bill coached lacrosse and hockey at Union College 1929 – 1940; from 1945 to 1948 he coached the R.P.I. lacrosse team which played in London in 1948 and was undefeated. He coached the Yale freshman lacrosse team 11 years. Bill has officiated in both amateur clubs and college games from 1932 through 1940, and has written several articles on coaching and playing hints. While living in Florida in the late 1940s and early 1950s he did a lot of work to get lacrosse started there. He helped run the North-South game in Troy and also the R.P.I. and Yale tours of England and Scotland.

MADDREN, William
Player
Graduated from Booklyn Col. 1896, Johns Hopkins Univ. 1901; was a lacrosse player for Hopkins all four of his college years; named to All-Time Hopkins Lacrosse Team; prominent physician and surgeon; died in 1955.

MOORE, William H, III "Dinty"
Coach and Contributor
Born July 11, 1900, in Baltimore, Md; graduated from Baltimore Polytechnic Institute 1919, Johns Hopkins Univ. 1923, honorary degree Curry Col. 1940; first president Lacrosse Hall of Fame Foundation; married Mabelle Symington in 1931; two children; lives in Baltimore.

Dinty played lacrosse at college until injured in 1922, but later played for the L'Hirondelle Lacrosse Club 1924 – 1928 and captained the championship team in 1928. He also played in the Sunday Lacrosse League in 1929 and 1930. Dinty coached for 32 years: St. John's College 1927 – 1935 and U.S. Naval Academy 1935 – 1958, during which time his teams won 232 games and lost only 57. He had eight undefeated teams, 1929, 1931, 1935, 1938, 1945, 1946, 1949 and 1954, and two additional national championship teams in 1930 and 1943. He holds the record for the greatest number of championships won by one single coach. He coached St. John's to a series win over Canada in 1931, representing the United States. He also coached an All-American team in 1936 which toured Western Canada, and coached the South All-Star team to a tie in 1945 and a win in 1949. Dinty has written many articles promoting lacrosse and founded the *Lacrosse Newsletter* and published it for three years. He served in many capacities with the U.S. Lacrosse Coaches Association and the U.S. Intercollegiate Lacrosse Association (USILA). The Moore Trophy is awarded to the winner of one of the divisions of the USILA in his honor.

SUTHERLAND, Conrad James "Suds"
Player, Official and Contributor
Born April 7, 1901, in Brooklyn, N.Y; attended Rutgers Univ. 1920 – 1921, graduated from Princeton Univ. 1924, law degree, St. Lawrence Univ. 1927; married Lavinia Peters on January 29, 1930; two sons; All-American 1924; USLCA Award for loyal service to the game of lacrosse 1955; USILA Award for the person who has done the most for lacrosse 1948; deceased.

Suds started playing lacrosse on the 1921 team at Rutgers, then played on the Princeton varsity on the 1922, 1923 and 1924 teams; the 1924 team was the Big Three champion and it was in that year that he was named All-American. He played on the Crescent Athletic Club team 1925 – 1932, during which time they won several open championships. Suds was one of the leading officials from 1932 through 1954. He wrote several articles on lacrosse which were published in the *Lacrosse Guide*. He served in many offices of the U.S. Intercollegiate Lacrosse Association (USILA) and was chairman of the North-South game committee three or four different times. He was a member of the U.S. Lacrosse Coaches Association (USLCA), and contributed much to their organization.

1962

BILLING, Fred C.
Player
Attended Erasmus Hall 1914 – 1918, Princeton Univ. 1919 – 1921, graduated from U.S. Naval Academy 1925; Thompson Cup for athletic ability 1925; served in W. W. II; deceased.

At the Naval Academy Fred Billing played football, hockey and tennis. Freddie had the unusual distinction of having been picked first team All-American at close attack for three straight years 1923 – 1925. Navy's opponents knew he was the man who had to be stopped but he never was. He was one of the greatest dodgers of all time, and a fine stick handler in the days when stick work hadn't the universal perfection it has now. After his Academy years he played for the Crescent Athletic Club and Montclair Athletic Club. He participated as a player for 21 years, then coached for 2 years and officiated for 5. Freddie took time to promote lacrosse among the prep schools in New Jersey.

FORD, Henry Crawford

Player and Coach

Born March 4, 1904, in Buffalo, N.Y; graduated from Swarthmore Col. 1927, Temple Univ; married Christine in 1931; two children; spent his life working with children as a teacher and counselor; lives in Swarthmore, Pa.

Hank played his first lacrosse at Swarthmore, becoming an outstanding midfielder on some of their best teams. After graduation, he played for the Penn Athletic Club; as a member of the box lacrosse team in Swarthmore, he was an outstanding center for many years. He started to coach at Swarthmore College under Tom Strobhar, then went to the University of Pennsylvania as freshman coach until 1934. He returned to Swarthmore in 1935 and assisted Blake until the 1943 season. He returned again to Swarthmore in 1959 as assistant coach and went on in 1960 to the University of Pennsylvania as freshman coach. In 1946 Hank started lacrosse at Lower Merion High School where he was head coach through the 1958 season, and produced many fine teams and players. Hank started, coached, and equipped a boys' lacrosse club in Chester, Pa, that continued to play through 1945. At that time he also started and coached a boys' lacrosse club in Bala Cynwyd, Pa, and in 1958 organized and coached a girls' team.

MEISTRELL, Harland W. "Tots"

Coach and Contributor

Born July 2, 1900, in Brooklyn, N.Y; attended Rutgers Univ. 1920 – 1921, Princeton Univ. 1921 – 1922; law degree, St. John's Univ; wife Lois Valieant; two lacrosse playing brothers and two lacrosse playing nephews; died February 20, 1962.

Tots attended the Erasmus Hall High School in 1916 where he helped organize their first lacrosse team, and went on to captain the 1919 team. At Rutgers he had the opportunity to reorganize lacrosse which had not been played since 1883. In 1921 he transferred to Princeton and organized, assisted in coaching and arranged a schedule of games. In 1958 the Tots Meistrell Bowl was awarded to the winner of the annual Rutgers-Princeton lacrosse game for the first time; it is a perpetual award. Tots played for the Crescent Athletic Club and helped organize and coach at the Peekskill Military Academy, organized and coached the Squadron "C" Cavalry team, and played in many club games including the Olympic Trials in 1932. He was one of the original founders of the Metropolitan Lacrosse Association and was its first president. Hank refereed for ten years, coached for eight and was an active player over a period of 19 years.

MORRILL, William Kelso

Player, Coach, Official and Contributor

Born December 15, 1903, in Baltimore, Md; graduated from Baltimore City Col. 1921, Johns Hopkins Univ. 1925, masters degree 1927, doctorate 1929; married Mary Kirk in 1934; two children; Trophy for man who has done most for lacrosse 1953; Kelly Post Award for Baltimore Citizen who has contributed much to lacrosse over the years; deceased.

Kelso won four letters in lacrosse at Johns Hopkins; the 1925 team won the Silver Medal and the 1926 and 1927 teams were both national champions. He played with the Mt. Washington Club and the Baltimore Olympic Club, and started his coaching at the old Marstons School. Kelso also coached at Park School and Towson High School before joining the coaching staff at Johns Hopkins. During his coaching career, the Hopkins teams were national champions 1932 – 1934, 1941 and 1950. Kelso was a very active member of the U.S. Intercollegiate Lacrosse Association. He coached for 25 years, officiated for 10 years, and served as president of the Southern Lacrosse Officials Association. He coached several all-star prep school teams and served as head coach of the North-South game. He directed two educational films, *How to Play Lacrosse* and *Fouls of Lacrosse* and participated in making *File 7,* a TV picture on Hopkins lacrosse. He authored a book called *Lacrosse* published in 1951.

NORRIS, Walter Oster "Kid"

Player and Coach

Born July 17, 1904, in Baltimore, Md; attended Friends School in Baltimore, St. John's College; married Katherine Corning in October, 1927, a lacrosse player; died November 9, 1958.

After the Kid left St. John's he played at the Mt. Washington Club, on the football, baseball, tennis and lacrosse teams. He became one of the finest mid-fielders in the history of lacrosse. He played and coached lacrosse at Mt. Washington for 30 years. For the 15 years he played, Mt. Washington won 110 games out of 119 played; after he started coaching in 1938, Mt. Washington won the open championship eight times. In 1937 he was a member of the All-Star team that toured England and was undefeated. Kid was also active in badminton, field hockey, duck shooting and was an accomplished yachtsman during the summers. He was a very strong leader and influenced the lives of a great many of the young men with whom he played and also coached.

ROSS, Victor K. D.

Player and Official

Born November 13, 1900, in Hungary; graduated from Syracuse Univ. Col. of Engineering 1922, law degree 1924; All-American three years; married August 12, 1929; one daughter; deceased.

Vic played both soccer and lacrosse at Syracuse, and was awarded All-American honors 1922 – 1924; after graduation he played with the New Rochelle lacrosse team and the Brooklyn Lacrosse Club. He officiated for over 26 years, and coached for two years at Syracuse and Brooklyn; Vic helped introduce the game to Union, Williams and Springfield. He helped organize the Box Lacrosse League. Vic went to England with the 1923 Syracuse team which won the International Lacrosse Trophy. During the twenty years he played lacrosse, he was an outstanding attack man.

TURNBULL, Douglas C, Jr.
Player
Born July 23, 1904, in Baltimore, Md; graduated from Johns Hopkins Univ. 1924; All-American 1923–1925; married Virginia Steuart in 1927; five children; lives at Cockeysville, Md.

Doug attended Baltimore Polytechnic, captain of their lacrosse team in 1921. He was a big football star at Hopkins as well as a four-time All-American selection for lacrosse; he served as captain of the 1924 and 1925 teams. In 1923 and 1924 Hopkins was champion of the Southern Division of the Intercollegiate Lacrosse Association and in 1924 Doug made Schmeisser's Honor Roll of Hopkins Lacrosse Tradition. He played against Oxford-Cambridge, Onondaga Indians, Mt. Washington and the top colleges. Doug played 20 consecutive years of lacrosse, 3 for Poly, 4 for Hopkins, and 13 for the Mt. Washington Club. He played every position on the team with distinction, except goalie. While he was with the Mt. Washington Club, they were open champion 1927–1935. He captained the 1930 team, and managed the ice hockey team in 1932 and 1933. In 1934 Doug coached lacrosse at Gilman School.

1963

ALEXANDER, Fred Cammeyer
Player
Born July 24, 1888, in Brooklyn, N.Y; graduated from Harvard Col. 1910; married; active in all sports; military service during W. W. I; deceased.

Fred played lacrosse and ice hockey in high school, and also played baseball and was a member of the rifle team. At Harvard he played lacrosse all four years, serving as captain on the 1910 team. The 1908 team won the intercollegiate championship, and the 1909 team tied. The 1910 team went on to win the Northern intercollegiate championship. Fred normally played center, but played every position including goalie. At Harvard he helped coach and also helped coach the Rindge Tech High School team in 1909. Fred wrote several articles on lacrosse and was a real strength in the New England area in all phases of the development of the game.

BIDDISON, Thomas N, Sr.
Player
Born July 4, 1908, in Baltimore, Md; graduated from Johns Hopkins Univ. 1928, law degree, Univ. Md. 1931; wife Robin Smith; three children; both sons lacrosse players at Johns Hopkins; died August 7, 1958.

In high school Tom won letters in football and lacrosse, and was a four year letterman in lacrosse at Hopkins, playing on three national championship teams 1926–1928. An All-American for three years, he is the only player to make the All-American team at both close defense and then close attack. He was a member of the All-Time Hopkins Lacrosse Team and the 1928 Olympic team. He coached for three years at Baltimore Friends School after leaving Johns Hopkins.

FABER, John Edgar
Coach
Born January 13, 1908, in Harrisburg, Pa; graduated from Univ. Md. 1926, masters degree 1927, doctorate 1937; All-American 1927; Coach of the Year 1959; married Olyure Hammack on December 24, 1929; military service in W. W. II; lives in College Park, Md.

Jack lettered in three sports at Maryland, football, basketball and lacrosse. He was captain of the lacrosse team in 1925 and All-American in 1927. His coaching career started in 1926 and ended in 1963, with the exception of four years in the army during W. W. II. He coached not only lacrosse but had success in football and basketball as well. His overall lacrosse coaching record shows 255 wins, 59 losses, and 2 ties, all at the University of Maryland. Jack's teams won national championships in 1936, 1939, 1940, 1955 and 1956, and were co-champions in 1937 and 1959. He coached the All-Star teams in 1940, 1946, and 1956.

HARTDEGEN, Carl
Player
Born December 5, 1889, in Newark, N.J; graduated from Lehigh Univ. 1914; married in 1915; two children; 1st Lt. in W. W. I; died May 3, 1963.

At Lehigh Carl played basketball as well as lacrosse. He was one of Lehigh's all time great lacrosse players and captained the 1914 team. Lehigh had one of the top teams in the country and in 1914 tied for the national championship. Carl played for many years with the Crescent Club and was one of the greatest defensemen in his time.

POOL, Robert B.
Player and Contributor
Born October 12, 1908, in Baltimore, Md; graduated from Baltimore Polytechnic Institute 1927, St. John's Col. 1931; married Dorothy in 1931; two children; owned a sporting goods store in Baltimore; lives in Willingboro, N.J.

Bob started with the Mt. Washington Juniors 1921–1923, then at Poly his lacrosse teams were champions 1924–1927 and he was the outstanding player in the school ranks. While at St. John's, Bob won All-American mention three years, and was captain and best bet All-American in 1931; he also was the leading scorer that year. The 1929 St. John's team was national open champion and the 1930 and 1931 teams were intercollegiate champions; Bob captained the 1931 team. He played professional box lacrosse in Canada in 1931 and 1932, and coached at Harvard for several years, with an outstanding record, winning the New England League in 1935. Bob also played box lacrosse in the Swarthmore Chester League, organized and played box lacrosse for TV in 1950 and 1951. He coached the Maryland Lacrosse Club. Bob developed new style lacrosse equipment including sticks, helmets, etc, which was a great contribution to the game.

STRANAHAN, Jason G.
Coach and Contributor
Born October 31, 1906, in Oneonta, N.Y; graduated from Union Univ. 1930, masters degree, New York Univ. 1937; married Erma Bethel on May 26, 1933; one son, an All-American lacrosse player at Hofstra in 1956; served in the infantry in W. W. II; lives in Manhasset, N.Y.

Jay played football and participated in track events at Union as well as playing lacrosse. He was an outstanding mid-fielder at Union 1929–1930, and the 1929 team were intercollegiate champions. Jay started coaching and directing athletic teams at Manhasset High School where his record is outstanding in all sports. He also coached the Manhasset Lacrosse Club for 20 years 1935–1955. Jay played club football and lacrosse in the New York area for many years and played a short time in professional box league lacrosse for both the New York Yankees and Toronto. He has written articles over the years for the local papers on lacrosse and was editor of the Metropolitan and Long Island Scholastic Lacrosse Association annual report for a time. He served twelve years as a member of the U.S. Intercollegiate Lacrosse Association development committee.

THOMSEN, Ferris

Player, Coach, Official and Contributor

Born December 25, 1907, in Baltimore, Md; graduated from Baltimore Friends School 1926; attended Swarthmore Col. two years; graduated from St. John's Col; married Helen Walter in October, 1929; two sons, both lacrosse players in school; resides at Holderness, N.H.

Ferris played on the national championship team in 1928 at St. John's. While playing at Swarthmore, he scored fourteen goals in one game which is still the unofficial record in college lacrosse. Ferris played four years with the Mt. Washington Club after college before taking up coaching as a career. He coached McDonogh School 1930–1934, Gilman School 1934–1945, University of Pennsylvania 1945–1950, and moved to Princeton University to coach until he retired. Ferris coached football as well as lacrosse at all these schools, and also held administrative positions in the athletic department. After his playing days, he officiated for 16 years, serving five or six years as the chief referee for the Maryland district. He has served in various positions with the U.S. Intercollegiate Lacrosse Association and the U.S. Lacrosse Coaches Association. Very dedicated to lacrosse, Ferris has spent his life striving to improve the game and organizing lacrosse teams for schools all over the East.

WILSON, Harry E.

Player

Born in Mingo Junction, Ohio; attended Pa. State Col. 1920–1924, graduated from U.S. Military Academy 1928; military service W. W. II, retired 1956 with rank of Col; married Helen P. in 1932; three daughters; resides in New Smyrna Beach, Fla.

At Penn State "Lighthorse Harry" played on championship lacrosse teams in 1922 and 1923, along with football and basketball. At West Point, he played four years on their lacrosse team, being named All-American 1928, when Army lost to Hopkins in the Olympic playoff game. Harry was also All-American in football and basketball, and went on to a brilliant career in coaching in these two sports.

1964

BAKER, Henry Fenimore, Jr.

Player and Official

Born February 13, 1897, in Bound Brook, N.J; graduated from Baltimore Friends School 1915, Swarthmore Col. 1917; married Helen Graham on June 1, 1921; three children; 1st Lt. in W. W. I, service in W. W. II; married Ethel Minor on February 9, 1963; resides in Baltimore, Md.

Fenny played lacrosse for the Mt. Washington Club teams from 1905 through 1929, participating with the Midget, Junior and Senior teams; he was also a team captain in 1921. He played lacrosse at Swarthmore in 1916, and had played lacrosse and football at the Friends School. He also played football, basketball and baseball at Swarthmore, being captain of each team. In 1915 he was elected to the Sunpapers Scholastic Hall of Fame. Fenny officiated in the Southern College Division in lacrosse from 1917 through 1935. He was chief referee for the district for a five-year period.

Also in: Canadian Lacrosse Hall of Fame.

BREYER, Frank Gottlob

Player and Coach

Born December 21, 1886, in Baltimore, Md; graduated from Baltimore City Col, Johns Hopkins Univ. 1908; married Marjorie Baker in December, 1909; four daughters; deceased.

Frank played lacrosse three years at City College and on four intercollegiate lacrosse champion teams at Johns Hopkins. He was also a cross country champion at Hopkins. Later he coached lacrosse at the Naval Academy and Lehigh University. Frank officiated some games at Lehigh and Swarthmore during his coaching days.

COLLINS, Walter Thomas

Player and Coach

Born June 11, 1898, in Stanford, Conn; graduated from Yale Col. 1923; military service in Army W. W. I, Col. in Marines in W. W. II, retired 1958; married Virginia Lind on November 23, 1934; one daughter; lives at Lighthouse Point, Fla.

Collie played on the Yale Varsity team in 1921, 1922 and 1923, being selected as captain in 1923. He was honorable mention that year for All-American and played in 1925 and 1926 on the Crescent Athletic Club team. Collie helped coach the Yale freshmen in 1923 and from 1923 to 1933 was an official high school and freshman referee in New Haven, Stanford and White Plains. He provided adequate newspaper coverage for the Yale lacrosse games throughout his career. In 1955 he was donor of the Collins Bowl for the outstanding player of the year on the Yale lacrosse team.

KRAUS, Francis Lucas "Babe"

Player, Coach and Contributor

Born September 2, 1899, in Fulton, N.Y; attended Colgate Univ. 1920–1921, graduated from Hobart Col. 1924; All-American lacrosse 1924; married Margaret Brosemer in 1924; four children; deceased.

Although he played football, basketball and baseball in high school and a private academy, he did not play lacrosse until he reached Hobart College, but was a two year letterman in lacrosse at Hobart, and named All-American in lacrosse. Babe coached freshman football, varsity and freshman basketball, varsity and freshman lacrosse and varsity baseball at Hobart. He was on the North coaching staff for the lacrosse North-South game 1942, 1947 and 1954. He served many years in committees with the U.S. Intercollegiate Lacrosse Association, and was director of athletics at Hobart 1932–1963.

MOORE, Miller

Player, Coach, Official and Contributor

Born July 26, 1905, in Kansas City, Mo; graduated from Erasmus Hall High School 1924, Univ. Pa. 1928; banking business; married Catherine Law on January 6, 1933; three daughters; resides in Del Ray Beach, Fla.

Miller played four years of lacrosse in high school, captain of the team in 1924 and first team all-scholastic New York City 1923 and 1924. He was captain of the freshman lacrosse team at University of Pennsylvania and played three years on the varsity team, team captain in 1928 and made the All-American team in 1928 as the leading scorer. He also played football for Erasmus and Pennsylvania. He was an assistant playing coach at the Crescent Club for six years. Miller worked as an official for many high school, college and club games 1928–1939, being head referee for six annual Army-Navy games. He served on various committees for the U.S. Intercollegiate Lacrosse Association (USILA) and was treasurer, vice president and president 1930–1936. During those years the number of players was changed from 12 to 10 and the field reduced from 120 to 100 yards. Miller also organized and played in the first North-South tournament in June, 1934, in Brooklyn. While president of USILA, he took an All-American team for an eight-game tour of Canada including the last Lally trophy matches in 1935.

O'CONNOR, Claxton J. "Okie"

Player, Coach and Contributor

Born December 14, 1907, in Baltimore, Md; attended Baltimore Polytechnic Institute 1922–1926, Loyola Col. 1926–1927; graduated from St. John's Col. 1930; married Laura Ellis in August, 1932; lives in Glen Burnie, Md.

At Baltimore Poly he played on MSA lacrosse championship teams in 1925 and 1926, and won a varsity lacrosse letter in 1928 and 1930 at St. John's when they won the national championship. He did not letter in 1929 because he had broken his ankle. He played football and participated in varsity track at all three schools. Okie taught math and was football, basketball and lacrosse coach at Boys Latin School in Baltimore from 1930 to 1960. In 1961 he moved to the Glen Burnie High School as a math teacher and lacrosse coach. He served on many U.S. Intercollegiate Lacrosse Association committees and was an officer for a number of years of the U.S. Lacrosse Coaches Association. He served also as a director of the Lacrosse Hall of Fame.

POWELL, Edwin Emerson

Player and Coach

Born July 6, 1889, in Baltimore, Md; attended Baltimore City Col; graduated from Univ. Md. 1913; 1st Lt. in W. W. I; married Frances Hagen in June, 1924; two children; resides in Baltimore, Md.

Powell played for the Mt. Washington Juniors 1904–1907 and the Seniors 1911–1912. He lettered in lacrosse at Maryland 1910–1913 where he also played tennis. He organized and coached the first lacrosse team at Maryland in 1910. The University of Maryland gives an annual award known as the Powell Lacrosse Award to the outstanding player for meritorious service in the advancement of lacrosse in Maryland.

SIMMONS, Roy D.

Player, Coach and Contributor

Born September 27, 1901, in Philadelphia, Pa; graduated from Syracuse Univ. 1925; married Thelma Rees in June 1926; two children; military service in W. W. I and II; owner and director of a day camp for boys in Cazenovia, N.Y.

At Syracuse Roy played football, organized a boxing team, and played varsity lacrosse in 1924 and 1925, playing every minute of all games, Syracuse was national champion both years. He was appointed backfield football coach at Syracuse as well as varsity boxing coach, and was appointed varsity lacrosse coach in 1932 where he spent the rest of his career. Roy helped coach the North for the annual North-South games 1946, 1952, 1954 and 1963, being head coach in 1954 and 1963. He has been a member of the National Collegiate Athletic Association rules committee twice.

1965

DECKMAN, Joseph H.

Player, Coach and Contributor

Born July 29, 1908, in Bel Air, Md; graduated from Univ. Md. 1927; ill health delayed his athletic career the latter part of high school; All-American honorable mention for lacrosse 1930; point position on All-America Lacrosse Team 1931; Defense Captain of Baltimore American Newspaper All-America Team 1931; Best Bet on Sunpapers All-Maryland Team 1931; member of All-Star Maryland University Lacrosse Team; Charles Linhart Athletic Achievement Ring 1931; Honorary Captain of Lacrosse 1931; married Florine Greene in 1938; two sons; deceased.

Joe assisted as a volunteer coach of defense in lacrosse at the University of Maryland 1932 and in 1933 coached the undefeated Maryland freshman team. From 1933 through 1956 Joe scouted off and on for the lacrosse team. In 1936 he managed, coached and played for the Maryland team in the Baltimore Sports Arena Box Lacrosse League, and played defense for the Tri City team in the Mt. Washington Box Lacrosse League that same year. He played first defense for the Baltimore Athletic Club team in 1937, and this team won the national open. In 1939 he helped organize the Washington Athletic Association (WAA) and from 1939 through 1941 he coached, managed and played a close attack position on the WAA lacrosse team. In 1958 Joe became co-donor of the Deckman-Silber Lacrosse Award given to the most improved defense man on the Maryland lacrosse squad each year. He was active in the Lacrosse Hall of Fame Foundation after 1959.

FRANK, Henry Samuel

Player

Born February 17, 1887; graduated from Baltimore City College 1905, Johns Hopkins Univ. 1908, studied law 1909; became active in settlement work and Jewish charities; deceased.

Henry was a member of the Hopkins varsity lacrosse team 1906–1909, captain of the team in 1909, in which year they won the national championship. When in college it was said "he was a lacrosse player by vocation and a student by avocation."

HEAGY, Albert B.

Player and Coach

Born December 3, 1906, in Rockville, Md; graduated from Univ. Md. 1930; married Elizabeth on August 8, 1940; two children; lives in College Park, Md.

In addition to lacrosse, Al played football and basketball at Maryland, lettering in all three. He was captain of the 1930 lacrosse team, a member of the All-Star All-Maryland University lacrosse team 1930, and was selected on the All-American team that year. He played on the All-Star South. After graduation he started as an assistant coach and coached continually until he retired after the 1965 season. He was co-coach with Jack Faber for 25 years or more and became head coach after the 1963 season. While Al was coaching at Maryland, the lacrosse team won the championship 1936, 1937, 1939, 1940, 1955, 1956 and 1959. He held many offices in the lacrosse association, was a member of the State of Maryland Athletic Hall of Fame, and served the university and community in many capacities over the years.

JULIEN, Joseph J. "Frenchy"

Player, Official and Contributor

Born November 19, 1907, in Parry Sound, Can; graduated from Rutgers Univ. 1932, masters degree from Columbia Univ. 1948; married Claire Gelinas on August 23, 1953; one son; served in Army 1943–1945; lives in Roslyn Heights, Long Island, N.Y.

In high school Frenchy made four letters in lacrosse as well as four in soccer, two in basketball and four in swimming. At Rutgers he won letters in all four sports his freshman year but dropped swimming and won three letters as a senior in basketball, football and lacrosse, was captain of the lacrosse team and in 1931 was the nation's highest scorer. Frenchy played mid-field on the 12-man teams and switched to attack after the teams were cut to 10 men. After Rutgers he played four years with the Crescent Club, and started officiating almost immediately, helped organize and start lacrosse in the high schools on Long Island, as well as starting and coaching a team at St. Francis College in 1934. Frenchy became district chief referee in 1956 for the New York area and in 1958 took over the chief referee position with the U.S. Intercollegiate Lacrosse Association. He undoubtedly refereed longer than any man and did an outstanding job organizing officials' associations and upgrading the officiating throughout the country. He worked more Army-Navy games and North-South games than all the other officials put together. Frenchy ran the publication of *Lacrosse News* for five years.

LAMB, Philip E.

Player and Contributor

Born December 1, 1884, in Baltimore County; graduated from Swarthmore Col. and Univ. Md. Law School; married Marjory Matthews on September 23, 1916; two daughters; served in the YMCA Ambulance Corps in W. W. I; deceased.

Phil played four years of lacrosse at Swarthmore when they and Johns Hopkins were the perennial national champs. He was the star for the national championship teams of 1904 and 1905. In 1905 he starred as center for the new Mt. Washington Club team by commuting from Philadelphia to Baltimore. He was named as one of the greatest lacrosse centers of all time and one of the five men most responsible for the success of instituting lacrosse at Mt. Washington; he was chosen on the first list of those selected for the Mt. Washington Lacrosse Honor Roll. Phil Lamb was an ardent supporter of youth athletics and did much work in this area in his lifetime. The Towson YMCA has named one of their playing fields in his honor.

THIEL, Glenn Nicholas

Player, Coach and Contributor

Born November 23, 1909, in Syracuse, N.Y; graduated from Syracuse Central High School 1928, Syracuse Univ. 1934; married Veronica Kinnally in August, 1937; four children; directed the physical training program for ASTP-AAF and the V-12 program during 1942 through 1945 at Penn State; professor in Penn State athletic department for his entire career.

Nick first played lacrosse in the eighth grade, playing on sandlot and junior high school teams, and playing with and against many Indians from the Onondaga Reservation. He played with the Syracuse Crescent Lacrosse Club while still in junior high. In high school he played four years, the last two of which the team was undefeated and he captained it in 1929. He also played basketball and football in high school. At Syracuse Nick played freshman lacrosse under Roy Simmons and went on to three years varsity under Laurie Cox. He played in 1932 against Rutgers in the Olympic playoff series, and captained the Syracuse team in 1933. He played in the first intercollegiate box lacrosse game, in which Cornell beat Syracuse 12 to 7 in the Rochester Armory before 6000 spectators. After college, Nick assisted Roy Simmons at Syracuse and developed, manufactured, and sold early types of face masks. Nick was assigned head lacrosse coach at Pennsylvania State University 1935–1956. In his 22 years of coaching he had 11 winning seasons. Nick served in many capacities for the U.S. Intercollegiate Lacrosse Association and the U.S. Lacrosse Coaches Association. He served two years as assistant coach of the North All-Star team in 1941 and 1943, and was head coach in 1942, 1946 and 1949. He originated and edited the *Lacrosse Newsletter* from 1946 through 1951. Nick was awarded a trophy for the person who had done the most for lacrosse in 1945 and 1947.

TURNBULL, John Iglehart

Player

Graduated from Baltimore Polytechnic Institute and Johns Hopkins Univ; All-American three times; selected on All-Maryland football teams; All-American lacrosse teams and Schmeisser's Honor Roll of Lacrosse Tradition; served as a Lt. Col. in the Air Force in W. W. II, losing his life on October 18, 1944, when his plane was shot down over Belgium.

Called the "Babe Ruth" of lacrosse, Jack gave the game everything he had. Jack normally played close attack, but occasionally shifted to center to get the ball on a face-off or to out-play the opponent and hold down the score; sometimes he played at close defense to tie up the attack of the opposition. He was admired and looked up to by his teammates, and his leadership and accomplishment developed an espirit de corps seldom attained by others. Jack played football, basketball and lacrosse at Poly, participated in football and lacrosse at Hopkins, and helped found an ice hockey team. His first team lacrosse at Mt. Washington began in 1928 and 1929 and continued for eight years after graduation from Hopkins. He served as assistant lacrosse coach at Gilman School in 1934. The U.S. All-Star lacrosse team for which he was selected toured England in 1937 and won seven straight games. He also played top-flight badminton in the 1930s, and joined the Thunderbirds Flying Club.

1966

ERLANGER, Milton S.

Player and Official

Born February 28, 1888, in Baltimore, Md; graduated from Johns Hopkins Univ. 1907; married Alene Stern on June 1, 1914; three children; deceased.

Milton Erlanger entered Johns Hopkins when he was 15 years old; he played on the varsity lacrosse team three years and after graduation commuted from New York to play on the graduate team composed of recently-graduated Hopkins stars. The 1906 and 1907 Hopkins varsity teams had the best record in the United States and were champions of the Southern division. Milton was chosen for the All-Time Hopkins Lacrosse Team picked by Bill Schmeisser in 1915. He also served on the board of governors of the U.S. Intercollegiate Lacrosse League in 1915 and was elected president in 1916 and 1917. Milton officiated at lacrosse games for the League and for many years after graduating from Hopkins. He established in his brother's memory a memorial fund used to give an award to an outstanding Hopkins lacrosse player.

EVANS, William Wilbur "Moon"

Player

Born in October, 1907, in Chevy Chase, Md; graduated from Univ. Md. 1930; law degree, George Washington Univ. 1934; Capt. in Marines in W. W. II; All-Maryland, All-Southern, All-American in football 1929; All-American attack player in lacrosse 1928–1930; Best Bet selection 1929 and 1930; deceased.

Moon won freshman numerals in football, basketball and lacrosse, and won varsity letters in all three sports. He served as captain of the basketball team in the 1929–1930 season. Moon was called the "best all-around lacrosse player in the country, and in some cases, called the best player in the decade and of all-time." He led the country in scoring in both his junior and senior years. Moon played with the U.S. All-Star lacrosse team against Canada, led the scoring in this series, and was voted most valuable player. He played with Baltimore in the Box Lacrosse League in 1932, the team being undefeated and winning the championship. Again, Moon was the high scorer in the league.

FLIPPIN, Royce Norwood

Player, Official and Contributor

Born June 16, 1902, in Lawrenceburg, Ky; graduated from Somerset High School 1920; two years at Center Col; graduated from U.S. Naval Academy 1926; All-American 1926; married Elizabeth in 1933; five children; served in the Navy 1926–1928 and 1942–1945; resides in Upper Montclair, N.J.

Royce was involved in athletics through high school, college and his Naval Academy years. At the Academy he played four years of football, basketball and lacrosse, and at graduation was awarded the Naval Academy Athletic Sword for general excellence in athletics, the highest award the Navy gives an athlete. His lacrosse team at the Academy had two undefeated years 1925 and 1926 and were national champions in 1925. Royce had only three goals scored against him in his three years of varsity play, all occurring in his first year of varsity competition. After leaving the Navy, in 1929 and 1930, he played for the Montclair Athletic Club and coached their basketball team for five years. From 1930 to 1939 he was an active lacrosse official for the Intercollegiate Lacrosse Association. In 1966 Royce helped coach the Montclair High School team, and helped in developing high school lacrosse in New Jersey. He served on the rules committee, as president, and on the board of directors of the U.S. Intercollegiate Lacrosse Association.

GOULD, Avery H. "Red"

Player

Born November 10, 1907, in Amityville, N.Y; graduated from Manual Training High School, Brooklyn and Pawling School 1926, Dartmouth Col. 1930; All-American 1929–1930; married Julie in June, 1942; served in Air Force in W. W. II; resides in Bradenton, Fla.

Red Gould played four years with the lacrosse team at Manual Training High School, the 1923 team being champions of their league, and Red captained the 1925 team. He also played lacrosse four years at Dartmouth, was captain of the team his senior year. Red played with the Crescent Athletic Club 1930–1943; the 1930 team was national open champion. Red returned to the Crescent Club as player coach in 1946 and 1947. He also played with the Box Lacrosse League in 1947, and was chosen as a member of the All-Time Intercollegiate Lacrosse Team 1920–1938. After leaving Dartmouth Red officiated at the high school level for a few years.

KELLY, Donaldson N.

Player and Coach

Born September 25, 1912, in Baltimore, Md; graduated from Baltimore Friends School 1930, Johns Hopkins Univ. 1934; All-Maryland in basketball and lacrosse; All-American Lacrosse Team four times; married Gay DuBois on July 11, 1942; five daughters; resides in Chestertown, Md.

At Friends School Don captained football, basketball and lacrosse. He was chosen All-Maryland in both basketball and lacrosse, and his Friends School lacrosse team was scholastic champion in 1928 and 1929. He won eleven letters at Hopkins, three in football and four each in basketball and lacrosse, and his lacrosse team was national champions 1932–1934. He again won All-Maryland honors in both basketball and lacrosse, and was chosen on the All-American Lacrosse Team four straight years—third team 1931, second team 1932, and first team 1933 and 1934. Don was chosen for the 1932 Olympic lacrosse team and in 1937 played on the American Flannery Cup team. After his college days, Don helped form the Baltimore Athletic Club lacrosse team and played for them 1935–1941; then won the open championship in 1937. He coached the lacrosse team at the Friends School from 1936 through 1938, and they won the Maryland scholastic championship the first two years. While running his car agency in Chestertown, Don coached the Washington College lacrosse teams after 1957; he has also served on the National Collegiate Athletic Association rules committee and was chosen by his peers as Coach of the Year in Lacrosse.

LOTZ, Edwin Leroy
Player
Born August 27, 1910, in Ellicott City, Md; graduated from St. John's Col. 1931, Johns Hopkins 1934, 1938; All-Maryland Tackle 1930; Best Bet 1930; two children; lives in Banner Elk, N.C.

St. John's won the national championship 1929-1931, the international championship 1931, winning the Lally Cup Series, while Ed Lotz was playing with their lacrosse team. He won All-American first team honors in 1930 and 1931, and in one season his team on a 12-game schedule scored 150 points to the opponents' 6. Ed was considered one of the greatest defensive men of all time. Ed continued to play lacrosse after college with the Baltimore Athletic Club (BAC) Lacrosse team and helped organize and played on the Montclair Athletic Club team after leaving the BAC.

MacINTYRE, Malcolm A.
Player
Born January 28, 1908, in Boston, Mass; graduated from Yale Univ. 1929; Rhodes Scholar to Oxford Univ. 1930-1932; law degrees from Oxford Univ. and Yale Law School; law practice in New York; married Clara Bishop in December, 1933; three children; Col. in Air Force in W. W. II; lives in Scarsdale, N.Y.

Mac won four letters at Yale, being the captain of their 1929 team and was elected to the first All-American team in his senior year. He played lacrosse at Oxford, lettering three years, and captaining the 1932 team. Their 1931 team was the champion in England, and Mac organized the combined Oxford-Cambridge team that toured the United States in 1931, playing fifteen games and losing only to St. John's. He was picked three times on the All-Star English team. When he attended law school at Yale in 1933, he coached the Yale championship lacrosse team. During the 1930s he served on several rules and legal committees devoted to lacrosse.

1967

BOUCHER, John W.
Player and Coach
Born March 29, 1907, at Grantsville, Md; graduated from St. John's Col. 1929; married Louise Kean in April, 1938; two sons; served in the Navy in W. W. II, retiring with the rank of Commander in 1946; worked in the soft drink industry in Birmingham, Ala.

John had not seen a game of football or lacrosse before going to college, yet he won letters in football 1926–1928, and played in every minute of every game of lacrosse after playing in the first game he had ever seen. He was named to the lacrosse first team All-American 1929, the first St. John's player to receive this honor; he played on their first national championship team also in 1929. John started coaching as a freshman coach of football, basketball and varsity lacrosse at Randolph-Macon College for the season of 1929–1930. In 1930 he returned to Baltimore to coach football and lacrosse and teach history at Woodbrook School. In 1931–1933 he coached swimming and lacrosse and assisted in football at Tome School, Port Deposit, Md, after which he left coaching and teaching for private industry. John played some lacrosse with the Penn Athletic Club in Philadelphia in the spring and summer of 1930, and in 1931 played for Mt. Washington Lacrosse Club. The summer of 1931 he played defense for the Cornwall Colts of the Canadian Professional Box Lacrosse League. In 1931 he played for the Baltimore Rough Riders in a newly formed pro league. John also played some pro and semi-pro football during this period. He is the inventor of the Long John Flip, a means of flipping a dodging attackman over his knee without violating the holding rule.

GUILD, Lorne Randolf
Player
Born March 7, 1911, in San Antonio, Tex; graduated from Baltimore City Col. 1928, Johns Hopkins Univ. 1932; married Marjorie Downs on June 12, 1942; one daughter; lives in Baltimore, Md.

Lorne won a varsity letter at Baltimore City College and four varsity letters at Johns Hopkins. He was selected for the All-American lacrosse team in 1931 and 1932. A member of the 1932 national championship team, he also played on the 1932 Olympic team that represented the United States at the Games in California. This team defeated the Canadians for the championship. Lorne played lacrosse with Mt. Washington for nine years and was a member of the 1937 All-Star team that went undefeated when they toured England. He has been selected as a member of the All-Time Hopkins team as well as the All-Time Mt. Washington Team.

HAWKINS, Russell S, Sr.
Player
Born February 18, 1904, in Brooklyn, N.Y; attended Boys High School, Brooklyn, Brown Univ. 1922-1924, New York Univ. 1924-1927; married Elizabeth Rogers in 1932; three sons and one daughter; lives in Halsite, Long Island, N.Y.

During high school Russell was captain of the lacrosse team and was selected as center on the New York All-Scholastic Team 1922. At New York University he played varsity basketball three years and varsity lacrosse two years. In 1925 he was interim lacrosse coach at New York University; in 1927 he was captain of the lacrosse team. Russell played for the Crescent Athletic Club 1927–1936, captaining the team of 1932 and was coach of the 1935 team. He also served on the New York Metropolitan Committee to develop lacrosse teams in New York colleges. Russell was said to be one of the best center mid-fielders of his day; he possessed blazing speed, great endurance and was an accurate shot, as well as being an inspirational leader.

JENKINS, Victor J.
Player
Born June 10, 1901, in Gas City, Ind; graduated from Syracuse Univ. N.Y. State Col. Forestry 1925; All-American lacrosse 1924 and 1925; married Vera McComb in 1931; two daughters; resides in Rocks Beach, Fla.

Vic played four years of varsity lacrosse at Syracuse and was a member of the undefeated USILA championship team of 1924. He received All-American recognition at the position of out home in 1924 and 1925, and received the Syracuse "Block S" the same years. Vic played for the Crescent Athletic Club lacrosse team 1926–1934, captaining the 1930 team. In 1925 he helped coach at North High School, Syracuse and officiated a few college games in New York City in 1932. He is one of the great attackmen of the game of lacrosse.

LINKOUS, Fred Cecil
Player
Born in September, 1905, in Tazewell County, Va; graduated from Univ. Md. 1928; died of a throat infection on March 27, 1930.

Fred won his freshman numerals in football, basketball and lacrosse at the University of Maryland, winning three varsity letters in each. In 1928 at the conclusion of his senior year, this outstanding attackman was voted the best senior athlete of the University of Maryland and a member of the "M" Club's All-Star football team, as well as guard on the All-Star Southern Conference basketball team. Fred coached football and taught at Severn School in Maryland until his untimely death.

PEARRE, Sifford
Player
Born July 14, 1884, in Baltimore, Md; graduated from Johns Hopkins Univ. 1905; married Angelica Yonge on September 9, 1930; two children; interested in individual sports—shooting, fishing, sailing, polo, tennis and was involved in fox-hunting; deceased.

Sifford played varsity lacrosse at Johns Hopkins and was a defenseman on the 1904 team that attracted much attention. For eight years he played lacrosse with the Mt. Washington team. He was selected as a member of the Schmeisser All-Time team at Hopkins and also of the Mt. Washington All-Time team. He was captain of the Hopkins football team in 1905.

TWITCHELL, Albert Wheeler
Player and Coach
Born in Dedham, Mass; graduated from Rutgers Univ. 1935; wife Eileen; three children; lives in Pompano Beach, Fla.

At Rutgers he was selected as defense to the All-American lacrosse team, received honorable mention All-American as a football player, and was the recipient of the Donald Coursen Outstanding Athletic Award. In 1935 he taught and coached at North Plainfield High School in New Jersey, moving in 1937 to Sewanhaka High School on Long Island, then to Hofstra College for three years as assistant football coach and director of intramural athletics. While serving as lacrosse coach at Sewanhaka High, two of his teams won the Metropolitan Interscholastic Lacrosse Championship. He was appointed freshman lacrosse coach in 1947 at Rutgers when he returned for graduate study. In the spring of 1950 he became head lacrosse coach. During his seasons, his lacrosse teams won 90 games, lost only 39, and tied 1. Several of his players were All-American and All-Star standouts. His 1955 team was co-champion of the Laurie Cox Division. Rutgers maintained a high ranking in the Lacrosse League during his tenure.
Also in: Collegiate Athletic Directors Hall of Fame, Citizens Savings Hall of Fame Athletic Museum.

1968

AUER, Gaylord R. "Peck"
Contributor
The first person elected to the Hall of Fame as a non-player; USILA Man of the Year Award 1961; USLCA honorary life member; wife Virginia; one daughter; lives in Baltimore, Md.

Some forty years ago, Peck entered the lacrosse world via the sporting goods business. He developed a lacrosse factory on Cornwall Island in the St. Lawrence River with the cooperation of the Canadian teacher, Colin Chisolm and the Indians. Peck was made an honorary Indian, Chief Tioneka, because of the industry he helped to develop on their reservation. He has constantly worked to keep the cost of equipment down, and to help spread the game of lacrosse to all parts of the United States. He was instrumental in organizing and supervising a loan pool and then supported the loan kit program which replaced the pool, and which was sponsored by the U.S. Intercollegiate Lacrosse Association (USILA) and the U.S. Lacrosse Coaches Association (USLCA). Peck served on the committee which originated the North-South lacrosse game, and was on the original committee that established the Morris Touchstone Memorial Trophy. In 1963 he became curator of the Hall of Fame Museum, and has served in many capacities in the lacrosse organizations. Wooster College has a Peck Auer Most Valuable Player Award, and has given him a bronze plaque in recognition of his work in helping to establish lacrosse at this college.

GILMORE, Morris D.
Player and Contributor
Born November 19, 1889, in Pennsylvania; graduated from the U.S. Naval Academy in 1911; served in W. W. I and II; married; two daughters; one son who was a lacrosse player and who lost his life in W. W. II; active in civic affairs after retirement; died October 2, 1960.

Gilmore played on the first lacrosse team at the Academy and was an outstanding defenseman for three years. He served on the executive committee of the U.S. Intercollegiate Lacrosse Association for a number of years, and was elected second vice president 1944, first vice president 1946, and president 1948–1950. He also served on a number of their committees and was active in the establishment of the Hall of Fame.

IGLEHART, James Davidson
Player and Contributor
Born in 1850 in Anne Arundel County, Md; graduated from St. John's Col. 1872; active in athletics in school; distinguished medical career; married Monterey Watson in 1889; one daughter; died in July, 1934.

James Inglehart was one of the pioneers of lacrosse in Baltimore, and captain and goalie of the early Baltimore Athletic Club team. He helped to organize their team and played in its first game on November 23, 1878. He played with them for the following three years, playing club teams from all around the East. Dr. Inglehart was referee in some of the contests away from Baltimore. He was first vice president of the U.S. National Lacrosse Association in its second year, 1880, and became president in 1881. The interest sparked by these teams and by the early enthusiasts, including Dr. Inglehart, ensured Baltimore becoming the center of lacrosse in the United States.

LOTZ, Philip Lee

Player and Official

Born in Ellicott City, Md; graduated from St. John's Col. 1932; law degree, Univ. Md. 1935; married Josephine Gibbs; one son; served in Counter Intelligence in W. W. II; lives and practices law in Staunton, Va.

Phil played on the college team that was intercollegiate champion in 1931 and which defeated Canada in the Lally Cup Series that same year. Playing along side his equally famous brother to form the backbone of a defense which allowed a total of seven goals over a ten game schedule, he was selected for All-American in 1931 and 1932, and after the 1932 season was selected as captain of the All-Time American Lacrosse Team. Phil played for Baltimore in the Box Lacrosse League and in the summer of 1933 played for Cornwall in the Canadian League. In 1934 he was a member of the Baltimore Athletic Club lacrosse team which won the open championship. Phil officiated in lacrosse in Virginia for a few years and was helpful in starting the program at Washington and Lee University.

PUGH, Gordon Scott "Willie"

Player and Coach

Born July 11, 1909, in East Carondelet, Ill; graduated from Baltimore Polytechnic Institute 1928; attended Butler Univ; graduated from Univ. Md. 1933; graduate work at Univ. Md. and Columbia Univ; wife Emily Wright; two daughters; served in the Dental Corps in the Army in W. W. II; died in January 1969.

During high school Willie earned eleven major letters, outstanding in football, track and lacrosse. He was captain of the 1927 lacrosse team. At the University of Maryland he earned first team All-American honors for three straight years. He was a high scorer and never permitted an opponent to score against him until his final college game. He had amazing stamina, ability and versatility. One of the greatest face-off players in lacrosse, he played with the Mt. Washington Club for two years and was the first lacrosse coach at St. Paul's School.

SMITH, Winthrop A. "Pinky"

Player, Coach and Contributor

Born December 8, 1907, in Milford, Conn; graduated from Yale Univ. 1931; active in football, basketball, baseball and track in high school; served as intelligence officer in W. W. II; married Louise Moulton in 1935; three sons; always a resident of Milford.

As star center on the Yale lacrosse team for three years, Pinky was selected on the All-American team in 1930 and 1931. In 1930 he played on the All-Star team that represented the United States in the Canadian Lally Cup Series. He played on the Yale freshman team which was Big Three champion in 1928 and on the varsity Big Three champion team in 1929 and 1931; he was captain of this 1931 team. Pinky began as junior varsity lacrosse coach at Yale in 1932, and took over as freshman coach the next year, then two years was varsity coach. He returned to Yale after the war as varsity coach for the 1947 season, and accompanied the Yale lacrosse team to England in 1950. He stayed active in the Yale lacrosse program in an advisory capacity and encouraged Choate School and Milford Academy to form lacrosse teams. In 1961 Pinky helped to bring the Oxford-Cambridge lacrosse team to the United States.

1969

ARMSTRONG, A. Gordon

Player and Official

Born March 17, 1886, in Baltimore, Md; graduated from Baltimore City Col. 1903, Johns Hopkins Univ. 1908; Mt. Washington Club Honor Roll; wife Clarisse; died August 10, 1967, in Wellesley, Mass.

Gordon played lacrosse at Baltimore City College in 1903; he played for Johns Hopkins only one year but was selected for their All-Time team. He was a member of the Hopkins intercollegiate championship team of 1908 and was selected for the Olympics but could not go. He played with the Hopkins University graduate team for one year and then played with the Mt. Washington Club lacrosse team 1909 – 1916. He was a familiar figure in the Mt. Washington attack and was one of the leaders responsible for the great success of his team. He captained the team in 1915. Gordon was known for his effective face dodge. He helped start lacrosse at the U.S. Naval Academy. He worked with and encouraged the Mt. Washington Junior team 1910 – 1913. He was active for many years as a lacrosse official.

Also in: State of Maryland Athletic Hall of Fame.

ELLINGER, Charles F, Sr.

Player and Official

Born March 2, 1914, in Baltimore, Md; graduated from Baltimore City Col. 1933, Univ. Md. 1937; All-American Out Home 1935 – 1937; served in the Navy in W. W. II; married June Werner in 1936; two sons and two daughters; deceased.

Charlie played lacrosse with the Hopkins Bulldogs and then Baltimore City College High School. He was a member of their Maryland Scholastic Association championship team in 1933. He played on the national collegiate championship teams of 1935 – 1937 at University of Maryland, and was selected an All-American Out Home all three years. He also was a member of the U.S. teams that played in Vancouver in 1935 and 1936. After college he played for three years with the Baltimore Athletic Club. He also played football in his playing years. Charlie was an official for twenty years, serving with the Maryland Lacrosse Officials and Southern Lacrosse Officials Associations, and was district chief referee for each. He served as an official for the U.S. Lacrosse Coaches Association and other academic and community organizations.

KELLY, Caleb Redgrave, Jr.

Player, Coach and Official

Born January 6, 1911, in Baltimore, Md; graduated from Baltimore Friends School 1929, Johns Hopkins Univ. 1933; brother Donaldson a lacrosse player also in the Hall of Fame; married; two sons; lives in Cockeysville, Md.

Caleb did not play lacrosse until his junior year at Friends School, but in that year he was the creaseman on the only unbeaten high school team in Maryland. He won varsity letters in football, basketball and lacrosse and again was part of a championship lacrosse team his senior year. He did not play lacrosse regularly at Johns Hopkins until his junior year, and then as a mid-fielder he played on the undefeated team that represented the United States in the 1932 Olympic Games. This team won two out of three games played against Canada in Los Angeles, the first game played before 100,000 people. In his senior year he again played mid-fielder on a championship Hopkins lacrosse team and won six varsity letters in 1933. Caleb helped organize the Baltimore Athletic Club lacrosse team in 1935, and played mid-field and attack, and also helped coach the team which won the open championship in 1936. After W. W. II, Caleb officiated in the Baltimore area for 16 years. As chairman of the Officials Association for seven years, in 1959 he completely recodified the lacrosse rules under the sponsorship of the U.S. Intercollegiate Lacrosse Association. In 1948 the University of Baltimore organized a lacrosse team which Caleb coached. In 1952 he helped in running the Palm Beach Lacrosse Forum and the exhibition game. He was also active in the formation of the Lacrosse Hall of Fame.

KELLY, John F, Jr.

Player, Coach and Contributor

Jack played lacrosse at the Boys' Latin School in Baltimore where he was a member of the 1932 Maryland Scholastic Association champions. He was an All-Maryland Prep selection as goalie. Kelly played three years with the University of Maryland team which was undefeated in collegiate competition in 1936 – 1937 and won the W. Wilson Wingate Trophy in 1936, and shared it with Princeton in 1937. Jack was an All-American goalie first team selection in 1936 and 1937; the team only lost one collegiate game during the three years he was guarding the Maryland goal. In 1938 Kelly was named head coach of lacrosse at Loyola College when they resumed a program after ten years absence. He coached until the end of 1941, his Greyhounds never having a losing season, winning 65 percent of all their games. After W. W. II, he was named editor of the Lacrosse Coaches Association *Newsletter* and continued to edit and publish it for many years. He promotes lacrosse wherever he goes, and is responsible for many high school students being able to go on to college to play lacrosse. His assistance to the University of Notre Dame resulted in their setting up the John F. Kelly Trophy, to be awarded to the winner of the Notre Dame Invitational Lacrosse Tournament.

LaMOTTE, F. Gibbs

Player and Coach

Born May 10, 1889, in Carroll County, Md; wife Hilda; two sons; insurance business; deceased.

Gibbs' family moved to Baltimore when he was very young, then moved to Mt. Washington in 1901. About 1905 the families of the community created the Mt. Washington Club. Baseball and football teams were organized and a few years later, lacrosse was added. After graduating from Baltimore Polytechnic Institute in 1909, Gibbs went into business with his father. Gibbs played on the team the first year he started a lacrosse career at Mt. Washington. He specialized in defense and played full time at point in every game during the 16 years between 1909 – 1925. All but 6 years of this time he also coached. In 1925 his handling of his players helped to make them the championship lacrosse club of the nation. In those days, Mt. Washington won 98 percent of their games.

LOGAN, William F.

Player and Coach

Born October 25, 1905, in Texas, Md; graduated from Johns Hopkins Univ. 1927; All-Time Johns Hopkins Lacrosse Team 1928; married; two daughters; lives in Rockledge, Fla.

With neither basketball or baseball being played at Johns Hopkins the year Bill transferred there from Mount St. Mary's College, he decided to try lacrosse. After he learned the fundamentals of stick handling, he was placed on the first team a week before opening game of the 1927 season, to replace an injured player. Teaming with Norman Robinson in his first intercollegiate game, Bill fired nine goals and went on to become one of the top scorers in the country. He was selected All-American In Home 1927. Bill graduated in 1927 and under Hopkins existing rules returned as a graduate student to play another season. That year they won the national playoffs and represented the United States in the 1928 Olympics in Amsterdam. In 1929 Bill began coaching the high school varsity at Baltimore City College, and moved to Princeton in the fall of 1930 to coach the freshmen in soccer and lacrosse. He continued as head coach of lacrosse through the spring of 1944, coaching soccer and basketball intermittently during those years. While Bill was their coach, the Princeton lacrosse teams ranked among the top four teams in the country every year. They ranked jointly with the University of Maryland in 1937 and in 1942 were declared intercollegiate champions. He helped coach the North team in the North-South games several years. Bill returned to Johns Hopkins in 1945 as director of admissions and assisted in the coaching of the freshman and varsity lacrosse teams. He also served on committees and as an officer in the foremost lacrosse organizations during his active years.

WYATT, Frederic A.

Player, Coach and Official

Born October 13, 1910; graduated from Union Col. 1932; served with the Navy in W. W. II; married Barbara Powers in 1956; two daughters and two sons; lives in North Hollywood, Calif.

Fred played lacrosse at Union for four years, being selected All-American at third attack his senior year. That same year he was a member of the team selected to play exhibition games en route to the Olympic Games. Fred was freshman lacrosse coach, assistant varsity coach and for ten years varsity lacrosse coach at Union following his graduation. In 1932 he helped organize the Mohawk Lacrosse Club in Schenectady and played with the club for ten years, also being its coach, captain and playing manager. Fred was a member for many years of the New England and Middle Atlantic Officials Association. In 1956 Fred moved to North Hollywood and continued his involvement with lacrosse, joining the Southern California Lacrosse Association and actively promoting the game. He has conducted lacrosse demonstrations between the halves of Rams games at the Los Angeles Coliseum.

1970

MARTY, Ivan M.

Player and Coach

Born July 13, 1900, in Kansas City, Mo; graduated from Baltimore City College 1919, St. John's College 1924; married Elizabeth Tabb in August, 1924; two sons; died August 29, 1966.

Ivan attended high school at City, leaving to serve in W. W. I. He returned to school to finish his senior year and that same year captained the lacrosse team and made the Maryland All-Scholastic lacrosse team. He was player-coach and captain of the lacrosse team his freshman year at St. John's. Marty attended the University of Maryland the next four years and won three varsity lacrosse letters and in 1923 and 1924 was first team All-American at close defense. In 1924 he was captain of the Maryland team which defeated Hopkins and gave Navy its first defeat in eight years. He was selected for an All-Maryland player and the University of Maryland All-Star team. After graduation he played with the L'Hirondelle Club lacrosse team for one year and was defense coach at the University of Maryland for the years 1928 – 1932.

STUDE, Fritz R.

Player and Official

Born August 6, 1910, in Baltimore, Md; married Darline Hixson; four sons; served in the Air Force in W. W. II; lives in Baltimore.

Fritz did not atttend a high school that had lacrosse, and played basketball his freshman year at Johns Hopkins, then played varsity basketball and lacrosse for two years. In 1932 he was the goalie on the Hopkins national championship team which, after an eight-team playoff in the Baltimore Stadium, represented the United States at the tenth Olympic Games in Los Angeles, the team being declared world champions. Fritz played in the goal for the Mt. Washington Club team 1930 – 1940; the team won seven national championships during this period. He was a member of the All-American team which toured England in 1937, and received a Knights of Columbus Gold Lacrosse Stick as a "Lacrosse Standout." Fritz is a member of the All-Time Great Teams for Johns Hopkins and Mt. Washington. He was active as a lacrosse official 1945 – 1961, and served a term as president of the Southern Lacrosse Officials. For sixteen years he coached youngsters of the Mt. Washington Warriors and saw five of his former players become college All-Americans in one year.

TRUXTUN, Thomas

Player

Born January 21, 1914, in Washington, D.C.; graduated from U.S. Military Academy 1937; All-American first string center three years; married Peggy Cruikshank in 1939; two daughters; killed in action June 6, 1945, in the Philippine Islands.

Tom followed a family tradition and entered the U.S. Naval Academy, playing lacrosse on the plebe team. Then he entered West Point in July, 1933, and played plebe lacrosse and three years of varsity soccer and lacrosse. After he graduated he was stationed at Ft. Bragg where he played polo, tennis and rode in horse shows. When selected for All-American, Laurie Cox, chairman of the selection committee, described Tom as the "greatest lacrosse player in the country."

1971

FERRIS, Carlton J.

Player and Official

Born June 23, 1915, in Ellisburg, N.Y; graduated from Hobart Col. 1937; married Adele Dobbin in 1940; four children; lives in Palm Bay, Fla.

At Hobart College Carlton helped his team win the Laurie Cox Division title in 1936 and 1937. He held an unofficial scoring record by amassing an incredible 9 goals against Syracuse in 1937, and was chosen Most Valuable Player on the team in 1936 and 1937. Carlton was selected for the first All-American lacrosse team 1936 and 1937, and played with the All-American teams against Canada in 1936 and against England in 1937. He also participated in the North-South games in those years. After college he officiated in the Eastern Pennsylvania Lacrosse Officials Association for eight years.

HEWITT, Frederic M. "Rip"

Player and Coach

Born September 16, 1916, in Baltimore, Md; graduated from Baltimore Polytechnic Institute 1936, University of Maryland 1939; served in the Corps of Engineers in W. W. II; married Sallie Ellis in November, 1948; three daughters; resides in Towson, Md.

Rip won letters in football, ice hockey and lacrosse at Polytech, and was All-Maryland in 1934. He played football and lacrosse at University of Maryland; on the 1937 and 1938 lacrosse teams, Rip was first team center moving to close attack in his senior year. Because of his outstanding ability to gain the center draw he performed this function for the team even when he played close attack. He was All-Maryland at both center and close attack in 1937 through 1939, and All-American close attack his senior year. He played for the Mt. Washington Club 1940 – 1949 as center, except in 1949 when he moved to the feeder position on the close attack by Oster Norris, then coach. He captained the 1946 Wolfpack team and was selected as mid-fielder on the All-Time Mt. Washington team. Rip coached the freshman lacrosse team at University of Maryland in 1940 and 1941, losing one game in two years. Served as assistant coach 1950 – 1954 at Mt. Washington, Rip moved to head coach in 1955 – 1956. The team won the open championship in 1955 and club championship both years. Rip enjoyed other sports and was selected for the 1948 U.S. Olympic field hockey team and played with them in England.

MYERS, Howard, Jr.

Coach

Born August 23, 1910, in Bel Air, Md; graduated from Boys Latin School, Univ. Va. 1932; lives in Hampden-Sydney, Va.

Howdy was involved in lacrosse as a head coach for 39 years, 14 in high school and 25 in college, during which time he attained a fantastic record with 17 championships. He coached one year at Donaldson School with a 15 – 1 record, then moved to Friends School for two years with a 23 – 5 – 1 record. His next coaching job was at St. Paul's School where he ran up a record of 137 – 18 – 2. During his eleven years at St. Paul's his teams won seven straight championships through 1946. His last four teams at St. Paul's were undefeated and compiled a record of 61 wins and no losses. Going to John's Hopkins in 1947 his teams did not lose a collegiate game in his three years there, and were national champions 1947 – 1949; lacrosse in the decade of the 1940s was dominated by this man and his teams—10 straight championships at St. Paul's and Hopkins and a record of 122 wins and no losses. His record at Hopkins was 24 wins, 2 losses, and 0 ties. Next Howdy went to Hofstra University as director of athletics, head football and lacrosse coach. During his 22 years there his teams achieved a record of 180 wins, 115 losses and 3 ties, winning seven divisional championships. As of 1971 Howdy's lifetime record was 379 wins, 141 losses and 6 ties; he also has a record in football of 208 wins with 291 in basketball for a total of 878 in career wins.

SPRING, Arthur F.
Player
Born December 25, 1908, in Laconia, N.H; graduated from U.S. Naval Academy 1930; selected a career in the naval service; married Clare Murphy of San Francisco; one son; both he and wife killed in plane crash in the Philippines on November 14, 1960.

Art was a star football player at the Naval Academy. In his sophomore year he acquired national prominence as Navy's starting halfback, scoring the first Navy touchdown ever scored against Notre Dame. In the spring of 1928 he first played lacrosse. In his first year he was selected as first team All-American defense and led Navy to the national championship. The following year he again was selected All-American as Navy's leading scorer in its undefeated season in which Navy outscored its opponents 90 – 17.

YEARLEY, Church
Player
Born January 2, 1913, in Baltimore, Md; graduated from Baltimore City Col. 1930, Johns Hopkins Univ. 1934; served four years in the Navy during W. W. II; resides in Atlanta, Ga.

Church started his lacrosse career at the age of thirteen when he was awarded a stick as a Sunday School prize. He played two years with the Hopkins Midgets, an organized team of pre-high school boys. At City College he earned letters in 1928 – 1930 and was elected captain of the 1930 team. He was named to the All-Maryland Scholastic team that year. Church earned a minor letter his freshman year at Hopkins and played varsity in 1932 – 1934. In 1932 he played on the Olympic team. He was named to the All-American teams in 1933 and 1934 and was selected to play on the All-Star team both years. Church played with the Crescent Club of Brooklyn, but in 1936 moved to the Mt. Washington Club, commuting to Baltimore each weekend for the games. He served from 1936 until 1953 on the executive board of the U.S. Intercollegiate Lacrosse Association.

1972

DOBBIN, William H.
Player, Coach and Official
Graduated from Hobart College 1940; served five years in the Marines in W. W. II; wife Rita; four children; resides in Geneva, N.Y.

Bill played inside attack for Hobart, winning All-American honorable mention in 1939, and in 1940 named to the second team. As a senior he was chosen to play in the first All-Star classic, and the North-South game scoring the tying goal for the North—North went on to win 6 – 5 in the game. Dobbin won four letters in college in lacrosse and basketball. Bill spent 20 years officiating as a member of the Central New York Officials Association and was chief referee for ten years. He also served as a director on the Hall of Fame Foundation and was twice general chairman of the North-South game. The U.S. Intercollegiate Lacrosse Association named him Lacrosse Man of the Year in 1956 for his chairmanship of the North-South game that year. Dobbin helped start high school teams in Geneva, Waterloo and Seneca Falls in the late 1950s, and donated goals at each school. He was head coach of the Geneva Lacrosse Club in 1968 and 1969.

LATIMER, George Alvah
Player
Born May 16, 1909 in Cortland, N.Y; graduated from Cortland High School 1927, Rutgers Univ. 1932; married Hazel Stillwell; two sons; resides in Cortland, N.Y.

George Latimer starred in lacrosse and football at high school and earned letters in football and lacrosse four years at Rutgers. He was chosen for the first All-American lacrosse team 1930 – 1932, and was the outstanding player of a selected All-American team that played Canadian teams in 1930. In 1932 George was awarded the Donald L. Coursen Trophy at Rutgers. He played in the tryouts for the Olympics in 1932 and because of his role, the Rutgers lacrosse team reached the semi-final round.

RITCH, William N, Sr.
Player and Coach
Graduated from Peekskill Military Academy and Syracuse Univ; All-American 1938 and 1940; served with the Navy in W. W. II; Governor's Trophy for 25 years service to lacrosse 1970; Nassau County Coach of the Year 1972; Dartmouth Alumni Trophy; USLCA Secondary School Area Coach of the Year; married; three sons; lives in Huntington, N.Y.

Bill began as a player at Peekskill and continued through four years at Syracuse, team captain in high school and college. He was a member of the All-American squad in 1938 and 1940, and played for the North in the North-South game in 1940. Bill has been head coach of the Sewanhaka lacrosse teams except for two years when he coached the freshman team at Hofstra University. He played three years after college with the Crescent Athletic Club before going to Sewanhaka High School as coach. The teams under his tutelage have a record of 262 – 54 – 1. They went undefeated for eight consecutive seasons, 1948 – 1957. They were Long Island champs from 1949 to 1959 and broke the national high school record by winning 91 consecutive games. In 1970 and 1971 he coached the Long Island Athletic Club to the United States lacrosse club championship, with a cumulative record of 25 wins and 3 losses. Bill Ritch's teams have won 297 games, lost 65 and tied once. Bill has been active in all lacrosse organizations as well as community affairs.

SOTHERON, Norwood S.
Player and Coach
Born September 9, 1911, in Charlotte Hall, Md; graduated from Univ. Md. 1934; served in W. W. II, reaching rank of Col; Commandant at Charlotte Hall Military Academy; married; four children; resides in Lexington Park, Md.

Norwood won letters in four sports at Maryland, football, baseball, basketball and lacrosse. Selected for the first team All-American in lacrosse 1933 and 1934, he was also selected for honors in football. He received the senior award for the best athlete in his class. After spending five years in the Army, he spent almost 23 years as coach of the lacrosse team at the Charlotte Hall Military Academy.

TOLSON, John C.
Player
Born June 22, 1918, in Baltimore, Md; graduated from Baltimore City Col. 1937, Johns Hopkins Univ. 1941; served four years in the Navy in W. W. II; married Mary Grace Devine in 1948; three children; lives in Baltimore.

At City College John earned three varsity letters in lacrosse, the team winning the 1936 Maryland Scholastic Championship. He was chosen All-Maryland Scholastic first team at point, and was chosen again in 1937 when his team repeated the record. In his freshman year at Johns Hopkins he won a varsity letter and was selected on the third team All-American first defense in 1938. John never played another losing game after the 1938 season. In his sophomore year he was selected to the first team All-American 1939 and again in 1940, also playing that year on the South team in the North-South game. In 1941 John was captain of the undefeated Hopkins national championship team and was named to the first team defense position on the All-American first team for the third consecutive year. He was also selected for the Schmeisser All-Time Hopkins Team. After the war John played with the Mt. Washington Club in 1946 and 1947. In 1971 he was chosen for the Lacrosse Honor Roll of the Mt. Washington Club.

1973

BEGGS, Harry G.
Player
Graduated from Yale University in 1932; All-American 1930 – 1932; was asked to play on lacrosse team against Canada in 1930; played three years with the varsity team at Yale; management consultant; lives in Weston, Conn.

BILDERBACK, Willis P.
Coach
Graduated from Rutgers Univ. 1930; began coaching high school lacrosse teams in 1930 with Neptune High School; moved to Irvington High School 1935 – 1942; joined the Navy in 1942 and assigned to U.S. Naval Academy; six unbeaten seasons as plebe coach at the Academy 1947 – 1958; varsity coach 1959 – 1972 with a 123-22 win-loss record; one of his teams was the first to win four national championships. Resides in Annapolis, Md.

CAMPBELL, Tyler
Player
Graduated from Gillman High School where he was captain of the hockey and lacrosse teams; All-American at Princeton Univ. in lacrosse 1941 and 1942; left school in 1942 to join Army; killed in action in France in 1944.

LANG, John D.
Player
Graduated from Baltimore Polytechnic School 1926, Johns Hopkins Univ. 1930; played lacrosse, football, basketball, soccer and member of swimming team at prep school; also played these sports at college; member of championship lacrosse team 1927 and 1928; captain of team 1928; selected first team All-American 1927 – 1928; member of Olympic team of 1928 at Amsterdam; member of the All-Time Hopkins Lacrosse Team; lives in Port Charlotte, Fla.

SMITH, Everett W, Jr.
Player
Graduated from St. John's Col. 1937; All-American lacrosse player in high school 1932 and 1933; captain of both lacrosse and football teams in high school; lettered four times on the varsity lacrosse team at St. John's; scored the most goals in the nation in 1934 and 1935; All-American three times; 1934 – 1940 played lacrosse for the Montclair Athletic Club; served as Lt. in W. W. II; resides in Westfield, N.J.

1974

CHRISTHILF, John F.
Graduated from Baltimore Friends School, Univ. Md. 1936; at Friends School was interscholastic All-Star lacrosse player in 1931 and 1932; was leading scorer on the Maryland team; team was national intercollegiate champions in 1936; named All-American 1934 – 1936; played lacrosse for the Baltimore Athletic Club 1937 – 1941; selected for the United States team that played in the Lally Cup series against Canada in 1936; resides in Baltimore, Md.

DONOHUE, John C.
Player and Coach
Graduated from St. John's Col. 1935; All-State football and basketball at St. John's; All-American lacrosse 1933 – 1935; football and lacrosse coach at St. John's 1935 – 1939; assistant coach at U.S. Naval Academy 1948 – 1952; officiated both football and lacrosse; member of Southern College Officials Association; resides in Baltimore, Md.
Also in: State of Maryland Athletic Hall of Fame.

KAESTNER, Benjamin H, Jr.
Player
Graduated from Baltimore Friends School 1939; Johns Hopkins Univ. 1943; married; ten children; played four years lacrosse at Friends School; All-State All-Star in

football and basketball 1938 and 1939; four years varsity lacrosse at Hopkins; All-American 1941 – 1943; played in the North-South game 1941 – 1943; All-Time Hopkins Lacrosse Team; played lacrosse nine years at Mt. Washington Club; Mt. Washington All-Time Lacrosse Team; lives in Baltimore, Md.

McANALLY, Charles G.
Player, Coach, Official and Contributor
Graduated from Univ. Pa. 1922; began playing lacrosse as a sophomore at Pennsylvania; captained Southern divisional championship team as senior and selected for the first team All-American; played for the Philadelphia Lacrosse Club 1923 – 1925; officiated for the U.S. Intercollegiate Lacrosse League 1925 – 1928; also coached the freshman lacrosse team at University of Pennsylvania and promoted lacrosse in the Philadelphia area.

ROBBINS, Louis A.
Player, Coach and Official
Graduated from Erasmus Hall High School, Syracuse Univ. 1935; was on the New York All Scholastic lacrosse team in junior and senior years at high school; All-American 1934 and 1935 at Syracuse, captain of the 1935 team; member of the United States team in the Lally Cup Series in 1935 against Canada; assistant coach of the Erasmus Hall lacrosse team; member of the New York Lacrosse Club; high school lacrosse official; service in W. W. II, retired as a Lt. Col; lives in Cape Coral, Fla.

1975

ADAMS, James Frederic "Ace"
Player and Coach
Born April 10, 1928, in Baltimore, Md; graduated from St. Paul's School 1946, Johns Hopkins Univ. 1950; married to Betty Jane Sparks; five daughters; resides in Swarthmore, Pa.

Ace Adams earned nine varsity letters in football, basketball and lacrosse in high school. He earned varsity letters four years at Hopkins, where the team was national collegiate champion all four years. He was named to the first team All-American 1949 as a mid-fielder; Penniman Award in 1949 was given to Adams for outstanding lacrosse playing. In 1950 he won the Turnbull-Reynolds Award for leadership and sportsmanship. In all his four years in high school and four years in college, his teams in lacrosse won the state and national championships respectively. Ace coached his former high school team, St. Paul's to state championships 1951 – 1953. In his 22 years as head coach, he won national championships for the Mt. Washington Club in 1957 and for the U.S. Military Academy 1958, 1959, 1961 and 1969. In 1969 Adams moved to head coach and assistant athletic director at the University of Pennsylvania. A former president of the U.S. Lacrosse Coaches Association, he has served on virtually every committee of the U.S. Intercollegiate Lacrosse Association and helped with the Lacrosse Hall of Fame Foundation.

BUNTING, Lloyd M, Jr.
Player and Contributor
Graduated from Forest Park High School, Baltimore, 1944, Johns Hopkins Univ. 1950; served in Air Force 1945 – 1946; married to Claire Gough; two sons and two daughters; resides in Wilmette, Ill.

Lloyd was first team All-Maryland defenseman his senior year in high school. He was also selected as first team All-Maryland in ice hockey that same year, having been selected first team All-Maryland as a football player in previous years. He was varsity letterman for the Blue Jays four years, being nominated as an honorable mention All-American once and a first team All-American three times. In 1948 and 1949 he was named to the little All-American football team and in 1950 became captain of the Hopkins team. Lloyd played one year (1952) for the Mt. Washington Lacrosse Club. In 1953 he founded the Richmond Lacrosse Club where he played for two years. Lloyd moved to Illinois in 1965 where he helped start the Chicago Lacrosse Club and played until 1967.

CHAMBERS, J. H. Lee, Jr.
Player and Contributor
Attended Johns Hopkins one year, transferred to U. S. Naval Academy, graduated 1949; Turnbull Trophy 1949; U.S. Naval Academy Athletic Association Award for outstanding athlete in the class of 1949; married to Kathryn Tyson; three sons; resides in Baltimore, Md.

Lee did not play lacrosse in high school, but won a varsity letter his first year at the Naval Academy and was selected to first team All-American. In his sophomore year he was selected second team All-American, but first team All-American again his junior and senior years. After graduation he served one year as assistant coach at the Academy before entering the Marine Corps for three years. Returning home, he entered the field of interior design. Lee Chambers is responsible for the interior design of the Lacrosse Hall of Fame.

HARTINGER, Lt. Gen. James V.
Player
Graduated from U.S. Military Academy 1949; first team All-American 1947 – 1949; married to Susan Allensworth; two sons; resides in Sumter, S.C.

General Hartinger was drafted into the infantry in 1943 after graduating from high school. Following W. W. II he entered the U.S. Military Academy and obtained varsity letters as a midfielder in 1947, 1948 and 1949, and was selected to All-American all three years. After leaving West Point, he resumed his military career.

HOOPER, William Upshur, Jr.
Player and Contributor
Graduated from St. Paul's School 1946, Univ. Va. 1951; married; resides in Owings Mills, Md.

Billy was a four-year letter man at St. Paul's. In all four years he was a first team All-American attack man and in each year his team were state champions. In 1947 he played for the Mt. Washington Lacrosse Club, then went on to the University of Virginia where he was a first team letterman four years. He was selected in 1948 to the third team All-American, 1949 to the second team, and selected to the first team in 1950 and 1951. After graduation he returned to play attack at Mt. Washington, where he concluded his career after the 1958 season. He organized lacrosse at Towson State and fielded their first official team in 1959. In 1960 he assisted as a coach at the University of Baltimore.

1976

BUDNITZ, Emil A, Jr. "Buzzy"

Player, Coach and Contributor

Graduated from Baltimore City College and Johns Hopkins University; Turnbull Trophy; first team All-American soccer 1952; married; three children; lives in Baltimore, Md.

Buzzy was first team All-Maryland attack man in 1949 at City College. At Johns Hopkins he was named to the honorable mention All-American team his first varsity year, and named to first team All-American in 1952 and 1953. He was awarded the Turnbull Trophy in 1953, naming him the outstanding attack player in the country. After fulfilling his military obligation, Buzzy played ten years with the Mt. Washington Wolfpack, twice honored as the outstanding player by the U.S. Club Lacrosse Association (USCLA) 1962 and 1965. He donated his services as coach to Loyola High School in 1956 and 1957, to Gilman School 1961 – 1966, and to Johns Hopkins University 1966 – 1974. He currently presides as the Commissioner of the USCLA.

KAPPLER, James Raymond

Player

Graduated from Baltimore Polytechnic Institute 1952, Univ. Md. 1957; C. Markland Kelley Award for outstanding goalie in the nation three times; Charles P. McCormick Award 1957; Cone Award 1957; Maryland Ring 1957; resides in Towson, Md.

In 1955 Jimmy was selected to the second team All-American in his first varsity year, and selected to the first team the next two years. He was a member of the 1957 South All-Star team and was picked every year to the Club All-Star team from 1960 through 1967. He was an outstanding player at the Mt. Washington Club for ten years and was placed on their Club Honor Roll.

LINDSAY, Stewart, Jr.

Player and Coach

Graduated from Phillips Exeter and Syracuse University; Most Valuable Player, Phillips Exeter, 1952; Most Valuable Player, Syracuse Univ, 1956; Club All-Star 1968 and 1972; married Mary Desborough in June, 1956; five daughters; served in the Navy.

As a varsity letterman in all three years of his lacrosse playing at Phillips Exeter, Stew scored a high school career high of 100 goals in 29 games; four times during his prep school days he scored 8 goals in a single game with a season high of 49 goals in one year. At Syracuse University he played one year as a freshman and three as varsity. He has the career scoring record at Syracuse with 119 goals in 32 games and once equaled his high school record of 8 goals in a single game. Elected as honorable mention All-American in his sophomore year, he was third team All-American his junior year and first team All-American his senior year. He played for the Connecticut Valley Lacrosse Club after graduation, scoring a career high of 290 goals in 119 games. He coached Chesire Academy for seven years and Kingswood school for another seven; Stew then went on to coach his former club team for a period of five years.

SCOTT, Robert Harvey

Player and Coach

Graduated from Johns Hopkins 1952; married; two daughters; lives in Towson, Md; retired in 1974 to become athletic director of Johns Hopkins University.

Scotty lettered on the Hopkins 1950 national championship team. In 1952 he was picked as honorable mention All-American mid-fielder. He played on the 1952 South All-Star team before going to fulfill his military obligation. After returning from the Army he was named head coach of Johns Hopkins varsity lacrosse team, a career that would span two decades. Scotty coached seven national championship teams 1957, 1959, 1967 – 1969, 1970 and 1974. Scott was named National Coach of the Year in 1965, 1968 and 1972, and Heros Inc. College Coach of the Year in 1970 and 1971. He has served lacrosse as committee member for the U.S. Intercollegiate Lacrosse Association and the U.S. Lacrosse Coaches Association.

TUNSTALL, W. Brooke

Player

Attended Baltimore Polytechnic Institute, Union Col, Cornell Univ, and Johns Hopkins Univ; Turnbull Trophy 1947 and 1948 for outstanding attack player in the country; Turnbull-Reynolds Trophy 1932 for the Olympic lacrosse team; married; three daughters.

Brooke was first team All-Maryland in all three of his varsity years at Polytech. At Union College he was nominated as an honorable mention All-American 1942; during that same year he lettered on the varsity football team also. With the advent of W. W. II, he accepted a commission in the Marine Corps. In 1944 while in the military, he spent a year at Cornell University where he was a first team All-American for both lacrosse and ice hockey. Brooke entered Johns Hopkins in 1946 and lettered on their 1947 and 1948 national collegiate championship lacrosse teams. He was named first team All-American those two years. He also captained those champion teams. Brooke was named to the All-Time Hopkins Lacrosse Team. He is believed to be the only player to have competed on both the North and South All-Star teams, due to his being affiliated with more than one school during the war. In 1942 he represented Union College as a member of the North and appeared as a South All-Star on behalf of Johns Hopkins. Brooke earned a place on Mt. Washington's Lacrosse Honor Roll with his play on their team 1946, 1949, 1950 and 1952.

MARTIAL ARTS

Mars was the Roman god of war. His name was not only the origin of our name for the month of March, but also of the word *martialis,* from which came our word martial, of or belonging to Mars. The martial arts, in other words, are war arts. As such they are not to be confused with javelin-throwing, archery, football, lacrosse, and the various other war sports—activities which were once combat-related but are no longer. The key word is art. It comes from the Latin word *ars,* as seen in the title of the Medieval guidebook for souls, *Ars Moriendi,* "The Craft of Dying." In that usage, an art is anything in which skill or power is attained through study and practice and then is displayed. *Kung fu* has the same meaning in Chinese—any training or labor that results in a desired end. So, strictly speaking, there is no single martial art called *kung fu.* In that same sense of arts as crafts, we speak of the art of navigation or, broadly, of the art of war.

Once a skill or power is attained and displayed by someone, that person is said to have mastered the art and to be a master in it. One who has mastered certain Japanese forms of *karate,* for example, is called *sheehan,* honorable professor. The same is true in most professions. In the Sanskrit language in India before the time of Christ there were over 330 synonyms for the word prostitute. Of these, *devadasi,* god's slave, referred to the most sacred type. Another type was the one who had mastered the "Sixty-Four Arts." These included reading, writing, singing, poetry, stained-glass work, irrigation, cooking, miming, philosophy, geology, mineralogy, ornithology, gardening, linguistics, alchemy, clay sculpture, flower arrangement, sports, sword play, staff fighting, military tactics and strategy, and archery. A woman who had mastered all 64 was not called an artist, however; she was called *ganika,* master, which was one of the most prestigious terms of the more than 330.

A warrior in feudal Japan was called a *bushi.* His trade or profession, officially begun exactly 100 years before Columbus discovered America, was known as *bugei,* martial arts. To become a *bushi,* a later type of which was called *samurai,* a man studied and practiced under various masters. His goal was to attain perfection, mastery, in over 50 arts or techniques *(jutsu).* These included *jujutsu* (fighting without weapons—often misspelled *jujitsu), kyujutsu* (archery), *bajutsu* (horsemanship), *kenjutsu* (offensive swordsmanship), *iaijutsu* (defensive swordsmanship), *hojojutsu* (binding an enemy), *suieijutsu* (swimming and fighting in water while clad in armor) and *noroshijutsu* (sending signal fires). To become a *bushi* a man additionally had to acquire mastery of the arts of flower arrangement, the tea ceremony, poetry, calligraphy and painting. Once he had attained mastery of all these skills, a *bushi* displayed his proficiency in them according to the *bushi-do,* the way of the warrior. This, an ethical code or way of life, included numerous privileges, one of which was *kirisute gomen,* killing and going away, the right to kill a disrespectful commoner on the spot. But it also demanded restraint, excellence and etiquette at all times. In other words, the *bugei* (martial arts) were only one part of the all-encompassing *bushi-do,* which was a complete way of life. They were never a way of life in themselves. This point is perhaps most strikingly made in the case of Jigoro Kano, the modern-day *bushi* who invented *judo,* yet made his living working for the Japanese Ministry of Education.

The fact that they permeate their practitioner's whole life is what distinguishes the true martial arts from all sports that are played in a rink or arena, in a park or on a field. To say that such arts are violent is to miss their point completely. In some of them, in fact, there are no offensive movements at all. Initially, there were none in *aikido.* Its name means way to union with God and it is one of the most graceful of all martial arts as well as one of the most potent. When it was decided that competitions in it should be held, a system of offensive moves had to be invented. Thus, today, in some competitions each *aikidoka* in turn attempts to score points by swiftly touching the other with a knife. But that is not true *aikido.* The latter, in fact, is an art, an exercise and a metaphysical religion—as are all true martial arts.

If one man could be said to have had the most profound influence on the martial arts, that man would be Siddhartha. An Indian prince of Mongolian stock who spoke a language called Magadhi, Siddhartha became better known as Sakyamuni, the Buddha. In 483 B.C, three years after the Battle of Thermopylae in Greece, he died after eating bad mushrooms and pork. He was about 85 years old. Immediately thereafter, his disciples and followers began to develop the sermons he had delivered into various doctrines. They recorded these both in Magadhi and in Pali, the official language of Buddhism. These doctrines profoundly influenced all Asian life, including all its arts and sports, from then on.

It has been said that his most significant sermon was "The Sermon of the Lotus," in which he spoke no words at all. He merely sat before his followers holding a gold-colored lotus in his hand. Only one of those present, a disciple named Kashyapa, realized the sermon's meaning—that in what is visible the ineffable and indescribable is also visible to those who have insight. The Buddha, therefore, named Kashyapa as the first Great Patriarch. Over the following centuries there were 27 other patriarchs. The last or 28th Great Patriarch was Tamo, who is better known as Bodidharma. It was Bodidharma who first laid down the principles, initially expressed by Kashyapa, of the *Dhyana* or Meditation sect. In A.D. 480 he left South India riding a water buffalo to carry that sect to China, where it became known as *Ch'an.* Later, taken to Japan, it would become known as *Zen* Buddhism. In China Bodidharma taught that the way to sudden, as opposed to gradual, enlightenment consisted of "facing the wall", turning one's face away from all desire and disturbance, and of meditation by direct intuitive method. The method was to center one's mind on "the point where the unmanifest becomes manifest," which was what the Buddha's lotus had been meant to illustrate. After teaching these principles for some time, Bodidharma retired to a cave north of Canton, where he sat contemplating a wall of the cave for nine years. At one point he pulled out his eyelids, which he could not keep from drooping. And so he is always pictured, especially on Japanese *kakemono* (hanging scrolls) and on samurai sword mountings as a gnarled, bearded man with strangely staring eyes. Sprouts of a strange plant grew where he tossed his two eyelids. His disciples cultivated these until aromatic leaves were produced. From them they made a beverage, thereby inventing tea, the drinking of which enabled them, too, to stay awake.

Various martial arts had been in existence long before these events are recorded to have transpired. *Vajramushti,* for example, a system of weaponless fighting for warriors, had been practiced in India 4500 years before the Buddha was born. In China in 2674 B.C, Huang Ti, the "Yellow Emperor," trained his soldiers in *go-ti,* a primitive form of combat in which two men wearing horns attempted to gore each other. *Go-ti* later evolved into *sumo* wrestling. By 770 B.C, the approximate date of the beginning of the Jewish captivity in Babylon, countless forms of such weaponless fighting arts had long been highly developed in China. But all of these were mere killing techniques until they were given their strongest component, a spiritual-ethical core. That core—an understanding of how a man should act in life—came largely from Lao-Tzu's *Tao-te ching,* Classic of the Way and Its Virtue. This was a small book of about 5250 words that, in stating Taoism, utterly affected all Chinese life and history. Its principal doctrine was *wu-wei,* nonaction, meaning "the taking of no action that is contrary to the *Tao,*" that is, to the way of Nature. In 518 B.C, Lao Tzu was visited by K'ung Fu-tzu, who was about 20 years his junior. K'ung was his family name, Ch'iu his private name, *Fu-tzu* a title meaning, roughly, Grand Master. In Buddhist terminology, *k'ung* means empty of specific characteristics, and *fu* means man. All of this was Latinized much later into Confucius. Confucius died at the age of 73, five years after the Buddha died, and was the first man in Chinese history to devote his entire life to teaching. His teachings, like the Buddha's, also had an utterly profound impact upon all later Chinese life. All Chinese moral institutions, in fact, were founded by him.

When Bodidharma arrived in China nearly 600 years later, therefore, both the tradition of unarmed combat and a spiritual code based upon complete resignation to the *Tao,* or Way, were there, ready to be merged. His own unique contribution of the *Dhyana-Ch'an-Zen* sect or doctrine stimulated that merger because of the place where he taught it. It was in Honan province, on the northern side of Shaoshih Mountain, south of Sung Shan Mountain, one of the Five Sacred Mountains of China, at the famous Shaolin Monastery. In that monastery —which today is familiar to television viewers because of the *Kung Fu* series—Bodidharma taught the monks and novices exercises designed to cultivate the *ch'i* force within each body. These exercises were a form of moving meditation. Called *ch'uan fa* then and now incorrectly called *kung fu,* they were extended to the use of that *ch'i* force outside the body—that is, to combat in "Shaolin boxing and weapons training." Although there were over 400 other kinds of Chinese boxing, the Shaolin style reigned as the supreme martial art in China for a thousand years. Its wide acceptance and vast popularity was based on two simple and demonstrable facts: mastery in it led to external power and internal peace. During that millenium the Shaolin style of exercising and fighting spread throughout eastern Asia, evolving and ultimately developing wherever it went into entirely new martial arts.

All of these were called *wu-su* or, in modern Western usage, *kung fu.* Two distinct trends or schools soon developed, however. The first, introduced about the time Columbus was born (1446) by a Taoist monk named Chang San-fung, became known as the "soft fist" or Internal School. The four distinct arts in it all stressed four things: the centrality of *i,* the will; the cultivation of the *ch'i,* the vital force or soul (note that carbonated water in Chinese is *ch'i suei*); nonaction or effortlessness; and potentially devastating physical activity or spontaneity. Combined, these four things resulted in a complete choreography of mind and body that could be described accurately as yoga with a dynamite punch. The most wide-spread art of this School was *t'ai-chi,* developed prior to 1736 (the year Charles Lynch, the American military leader from whom we get the word "lynching," was born). Primarily a hygienic mode of exercise *t'ai-chi* had a devastating combat side in which a master's arm was said to be "like iron wrapped with cotton." *T'ai chi chuan,* in fact, means "grand ultimate fist." An earlier

Internal School art was *hsing-i,* mind-fist, developed about the time Harvard College was founded as a seminary (1636). In the *hsing-i* art were five basic forms—splitting, crushing, drilling, pounding and crossing. There were also 12 styles built from the characteristics of animals and named for them: dragon, tiger, monkey, horse, lizard, cock, hawk, snake, eagle, bear, swallow, and mythical bird. Nearly two centuries later, just prior to the world's first parachute jump in 1797, the third main art developed. Called *pa-kua,* it stressed circular movements whereas *hsing-i* stressed linear ones. Its main styles were named snake, stork, lion, dragon, monkey, hawk and bear. Fairly quickly, by the early 1800s, *hsing-i* and *pa-kua* were merged. They have usually been taught together ever since. The fourth of the main Internal School arts was *noi cun,* divine technique. *Noi cun* exercises were designed to result after at least 15 years of practice in the ability to generate massive internal power. Such power, which might be visualized as a controlled nuclear reaction of the *ch'i* directed in a laserlike beam from the palm of the hand, could be used by a *noi cun* master to unbalance, cripple or kill an attacker at a distance, without ever touching him. A related art was that of *tien-hsueh,* spotting, which is called *atemi* in its Japanese form, *keupso chirigi* in its Korean and *rahasia* in its Malaysian form. An extension of acupuncture, in which there are 708 "holes" or "switches" in the human body, *tien-hsueh* involved the application of various degrees of force to more than 240 body pressure points in order to cause immediate or future illness, internal damage or death. The amount of force almost surgically applied or spotted by the mere touch of a *tien-hsueh* master, for example, could cause instantaneous death, death after a few hours, or sudden death after several weeks or months. Not surprisingly, *noi cun* and *tien-hsueh* are among the numerous martial arts which twentieth century science has been unable to fathom.

The second of the two major trends were those martial arts that became known as the "hard fist" or External School. It stressed the same four values as the Internal School—the will, the vital energy, effortlessness and spontaneity. These far more numerous arts differed in the importance they placed upon technique, speed and extreme physical, as opposed to inner, strength. While the four Internal School arts were devised solely as means of self-protection, the External School arts, of which there are 360 documented kinds and probably an equal number of unrecorded or secret ones, were all devised for offensive attacking as well as for defensive blocking. Interestingly, virtually any of them can be mastered in less than ten years—about half the time it takes to master any one of the Internal ones. Similarly interesting is the fact that all the hard fist arts began to evolve more than a century later than the four soft ones. In the forty-four years before Shakespeare was born (1564), a monk named Chueh Yuan revised all the previous styles of Shaolin Temple combat into 72 deadly styles. Thereafter, with a sage named Pai Yu-feng, he divided those 72 into 170 specific actions, which in turn were subdivided into five forms: dragon, tiger, leopard, snake and crane. These five were the basis for the myriad distinct External arts that later evolved. Of these, three were *an ch'i, ch'in kung* and *wing chun. An ch'i,* hidden weapons, is the art of perfection at throwing coins, chopsticks, paper or any other handy object. *Ch'in kung,* light technique, is the art of overcoming seemingly impossible obstacles, such as completely smooth, vertical walls. And *wing chun* is the hardest of all the "hard" arts because of its complete reliance on technique. This art was invented by a woman, Yim Wing Chun, after inspiration received from a Buddhist nun.

Bodidharma's *ch'uan fa* exercises, in their diffusion out from the Shaolin monastery, were taken to the Ryukyu Islands prior to A.D. 618. The Ryukyus (the same root-word, *kyu,* means student in *karate* terminology) stretch in a 600-mile-long arc between Taiwan and Japan. In Okinawa, the main island, martial arts and weapons techniques developed through a thousands years of feudal history. In the year that Rembrandt died and phosphorus was discovered (1669), Japanese forces then in control of the 60-some Ryukyus prohibited the native import, production, use or possession of weapons. The Okinawans, therefore, developed their own bodies into highly effective weapons. Especially potent in these relatively new arts was the hand, *te.* Each town's style was therefore called by the town's name plus the word for hand—*Shuri-te, Naha-te, Tomari-te.* It was one of these that Basil Hall, an English traveler, saw around 1810. Later, at an interview in Paris, he told Napoleon Bonaparte that Okinawans fought without weapons. Napoleon is reported to have sneered. At any rate, in 1869, exactly two hundred years after the ban against weapons, two people whose lives would have a profound impact upon human history were born: Ghandi in India, Gichin Funakoshi on Okinawa. From the age of eleven, Funakoshi studied the various Okinawan *te* forms, especially *Shuri-te* and *Naha-te.* Not long after he had mastered some of them, it was officially decided in Okinawa to replace the name *te,* an Okinawan word, with the name *Kara-te,* a Japanese word with the Okinawan suffix. Kara was one of the old provinces of China and, during the reign of the so-called Kara Kingdom, that name had come to mean China as a whole. Fairly quickly, the Japanese word *jutsu* ("art") was added, to produce *karate-jutsu,* the "China hand art." That name is still used for one form of *karate.* In Japan, however, it was soon subtly altered in meaning: the word *kara* came to mean empty, which thus obfuscated the debt to China. This was never meant as "without weapons," which it has come to mean in English—rather, *kara* meant "empty" in the sense that a mirror is empty though it contains everything a viewer sees in it; in other words, empty of all emotions or disturbances while capable of the perfect reflection of such emotions or disturbances. Funakoshi took the new martial art of *karate* to Japan in 1922. During and after W. W. II, North Americans came into contact with it there, mastered it and took it home. The first *karate* school in North America was opened in 1946 in Phoenix, Arizona, by Robert A. Trias. Thus, while Mahatma Ghandi popularized non-violence, Gichin Funakoshi popularized the world's most famous form of self-defense.

Meanwhile, other arts or ways *(do)* had evolved from the old forms or arts *(jutsu).* Of the numerous forms of Shaolin Temple *ch'uan fa* taken to Japan, several were learned by one Chan Yuan-bin, who studied them at the Bushiu Temple in Tokyo (*bushi,* warrior). Around 1682, two years before Sir Isaac Newton established his Law of Gravity, Chan invented his own form. He called it *jujutsu,* the soft, yielding art. Exactly two hundred years later, in 1882 (when pineapples were first introduced into Hawaii), a *jujutsu* master named Jigoro Kano invented the soft, yielding way. He did this by borrowing from those two centuries' several hundred *jujutsu* forms and deleting all killing elements. His new martial art, *judo,* was immediately popular, as were his two slogans: "Maximum Efficiency with Minimum Effort" and "Mutual Welfare and Benefit." It was quickly adopted by the Japanese school system, in part because Kano worked for the Ministry of Education. It was later introduced into Great Britain in 1899 as a music-hall act by one Yukio Tani. A year later, the first *judo* school in England opened. Five years after that, in 1905, the first *judo* for women was taught by the English Mrs. Roger Watts, at the Prince's Club. At about the same time, *judo* was introduced into North America. Among its first practitioners was President Theodore Roosevelt, who eventually earned a brown belt. The popularity of *judo* spread and grew, an international federation for it was created in 1951, and in 1964 it was officially added to the Olympic Games.

A second master of *jujutsu,* Morihei Uyeshiba, also became famous for his synthesis of about 200 old martial arts into an entirely new one. He called his form *aiki-jutsu,* the art of union with the *ki* force, despite the fact that that name had already been in use for several centuries. Having invented and named it, he was dissatisfied with it. So he went back to studying, observing and meditating. Twelve years later, in 1942, he came up with what he had wanted—a balletlike martial art completely devoid of offensive tactics yet of immense spiritual power. He called his revised form *aiki-do,* or *aikido,* the way to union with the *ki.* In 1951, the year of the first nationwide telecast in the United States, *aikido* reached France. Two years later, it reached San José, California, to which a master had been invited by a martial arts group. From there, it spread throughout North America.

The saddest story, of course, is what happened to the Shaolin Temple itself. From the death of Bodidharma in A.D. 557 to the beginning of the Sung Dynasty in 960, the various forms of Shaolin combat became widely known and highly respected all over China. Those 403 years, in fact, might be called "the Age of the Fighting Monks." Several centuries passed in which the monks' arts lay dormant, so to speak; they continued to evolve or develop but not spectacularly so. This was especially true during the Ming Dynasty, from 1368-1648. Then the Manchurians invaded from the north, ousted the Mings, and set up their Manchu dynasty. Everybody hated them. The Shaolin Monastery quickly became the logical headquarters for the Ming resistance movement. As a result, Manchu forces destroyed the monastery and killed all but five of the fighting Shaolin monks. Those five escaped and in time built a second Shaolin Temple. The Manchus eventually found and destroyed it as well. Thereafter, the surviving monks went underground for good. For more than two centuries, they continued to harass the Manchus whenever they could. To do so more effectively, and because they could have no central headquarters, they formed themselves into countless secret societies. Members of some of these later went to the United States to work on the railroads and thereafter were responsible for the infamous Tong Wars in San Francisco. Members of some others took part in the famous Boxer Rebellion, China's attempt to throw out both the Europeans and the Manchus in 1900. It was called the Boxer Rebellion because that was the only word the Americans there had to describe the *ch'uan fa* techniques the rebel soldiers used. The Rebellion failed—largely because the Manchu Empress Dowager succeeded in identifying and executing its leaders and closing down all the known halls where members of the secret societies had trained. One secret Shaolin group whose leaders escaped her wrath was called "the Triads." One of these leaders, who had attended an Anglican college in Honolulu from 1879 to 1882, fled to Hong Kong after the Boxer Rebellion failed. His name was Dr. Sun Yat-sen. After founding the *T'ung Meng Hui* ("Revolutionary Alliance") in 1905, he led the revolt that ultimately toppled the Manchus in 1911. He then became the provisionary president of China's first and only democracy, a job he held for exactly two months. Edged out by undemocratic rivals in 1912, he again fled. From then until his death in 1925, he sought to restore himself to power so that his democratic ideals could be instituted. To do this he reorganized his Revolutionary Alliance into a political party called the Kuomintang, in which he was aided by, among others, Chiang Kai-shek. During this time, a 24 year-old revolutionary published his first article. Entitled "A Study of Physical Culture," it appeared in a 1917 issue of the *Hsin Ch'ing Nien* or New Youth periodical and called for a revitalization of the old martial arts. The author, Mao Tse-tung, then went on to state that "The principal aim of physical education is military heroism."

FORMS: It has been said that "One technique mastered is worth one thousand sampled." Many masters would agree that this is true. It has also been said that there are as many martial arts as there are human languages. That is not true. There have been, in fact, far fewer languages. Amazing as this may seem, the martial arts that have existed through history and do exist today number in the tens of thousands, while the total number of history's languages is only between eight to ten thousand. For example, among the peoples who speak the various Chinese, Japanese and Korean languages, there are over 100 forms of *karate* and over 360 forms of External School *ch'uan fa (kung fu)*, each qualifying as a distinct art. Moreover, in Japan alone there are 725 officially documented forms of *jujutsu.* The official motto of Indonesia, Unity in Diversity, aptly describes the group of Indonesian martial arts. The main one, *pentjak-silat*, the art of fending off, has 157 officially recorded forms. There are hundreds of distinct martial arts in the Philippines, and each of the major ethnic groups in Burma has its own unique *thaing*, self-defense form. And there are countless more literally everywhere else in the world. In England there is the art of nutting, in which a master can deliver lethal blows with his head (nut is Liverpool slang for head). In India hundreds of descendants of the ancient art of *vajramushti*, fierce wrestling, are practiced. France has dozens of forms of the deadly kicking art of *savaté*, and even more of *la boxe française*. Brazil has *panmo*, combat-wrestling, Mexico has highly sophisticated razor fighting arts, and Macedonia has the art of the buttock attack in which a master's buttocks can fracture the pelvis of an attacker. In the Soviet Union *sambo*, Russian judo, is practiced, as are the Soviet slapping arts that induce facial neuralgia, reputedly the most intense pain a human being can experience. And so it goes all around the globe. All these arts, however, are only the ones still extant; many thousands of others have been lost, died out with their inventors, or evolved into whole new forms during the past millennia, in which wars have been fought, statistically speaking, fourteen years out of every fifteen.

There are two broad classes of martial art: those in which one fights an opponent and those in which one fights an enemy. The latter are the more ancient or classical ones which were devised for battlefield use. In Japanese, they were called the *bugei*, martial arts. The more modern ones, those against opponents, were devised for physical education or for use in sport; they are called the *budo*, martial ways. Often, the suffix on the name of a form will distinguish which of these two classes the art belongs to: the *bugei*, classical arts against an enemy, have the suffix *-jutsu*, meaning technique, while the *budo*, modern arts against an opponent, have the suffix *-do*, meaning way. No *do* form exists without a *jutsu* form from which it sprang. *Jujutsu* is a classical combat technique; *judo*, its derivative, is a modern sport. Similarly, first came *karatejutsu* (from the Chinese *kara*, empty, plus the Okinawan *te*, hand, plus the Japanese *jutsu*, technique), from which came *karatedo*. The hundreds of distinct styles of these two practiced today are, however, called simply *karate*.

The same endings exist in—and tell much about the history of—numerous other martial arts of Japan. *Bajutsu*, for example, is the ancient art of horsemanship, *shurikenjutsu* is the art of throwing small, bladed weapons, *sojutsu* is the art of spear-throwing, *suieijutsu* is the art of swimming and fighting in water while wearing armor, and *sodegaramijutsu* is the art of ensnaring victims with a barbed pole. Similarly, *aikido* is the way to union with the *ki*, *jodo* is the way of small-stick fighting (a similar word, *jodo*, means land of purity and is a Buddhist term for paradise or heaven), *judo* is the flexibility way or way of flexibility, *kendo* is the way of the sword, *taekwondo*, often written *tae kwon do*, is the kicking-punching way. Unfortunately, there are numerous exceptions to that two-suffix rule in the Japanese martial arts: *uchi-ne*, the art of throwing arrows by hand, *fuki-bari*, the art of blowing needles out of the mouth, *sumo*, formerly called *sumai*, the art of unclad wrestling, *kumi-uchi*, the art of grappling in armor.

Another exception to the rule that *jutsu* forms gave birth to *do* forms was *ninjutsu*, the art of stealing in, the way of the *ninja*. *Ninjutsu* began in Japan prior to A.D. 628—in other words, during the lifetime of the prophet Mohammad. The *ninja* were a class of ultrasecret, highly feared and often despised feudal agents. Their profession was espionage and assassination. To practice it they employed a great variety of techniques, including seven standard disguises: actor, entertainer, wandering priest, Buddhist priest, mountain priest, farmer and merchant. They also used eleven distinct ways of walking, several of which enabled them to walk across snow without leaving any marks. They were able to run 125 miles nonstop. There were five escaping techniques including the use of poison smoke screens, standing like a scarecrow, and using breathing tubes to remain motionless underwater. Numerous acrobatic maneuvers included walking on their hands in a dark house to avoid tripping over anything. There were also several flying techniques. They used crude gliders, or were flown into an enemy camp on huge black kites. Certain drugs, insect repellents and medicines were also used by *ninja*. Their *kito-gan* pills delayed thirst for five days. Women *ninja*, in addition, were highly trained in dancing and seduction techniques. Men, through muscular control training, were able to retract their testes into the body cavity to prevent them from being struck during combat. This was a widespread technique, also practiced by *sumo* wrestlers and in India. All *ninja* used a fantastic variety of weapons, including swords, daggers, bows and arrows, blowguns, sickles, chains, *shuriken* (small metal objects of various designs which could be thrown with extreme accuracy up to 35 feet), grenades *(nage teppo)*, land mines *(uzume bi)*, and weasels that had been starved for a week. There are no known traditional *ninja* today. The last one was the late Fujita Seiko. In other words, no *do* form evolved out of the classical *ninjutsu* form, though the latter lasted over 13 centuries.

Most of the major martial arts today became major ones because they became sports. An examination of two of them, *karate* and *judo*, reveals this. In *karate* there are *kata-shiai*, traditional movements tournaments, and *kumiti-shiai*, sparring tournaments. In the latter, two contestants are paired as opponents by weight and past proficiency. They compete on a 26 ft. square mat for 2 to 7 min, watched by one referee and four judges who award points or half-points for certain kicks and blows, each of which is delivered within from 2/5 to 4/5 of a second, most of which are "pulled" the instant before contact. In the United States, however, such *kumiti-shiai* are sometimes expressly contact matches. These, at which blood is expected, are rapidly gaining in popularity. The same five officials then serve as judges of the *kata-shiai*, awarding from one to ten points for an individual contestant's performance of each series of traditional movements. There are over 50 such series. For all practical purposes, the more one wins, the more one is promoted within the belt-color ranking system. The most traditional system is: White (lowest), Yellow, Green, Purple, *Ikkyu* Brown (first degree; the suffix *-kyu* means student), *Nikyu* Brown (second), *Sankyu* Brown (third), *Shodan* Black (first level; *-dan* means graduate), *Nidan* Black (second), *Sandan* Black (third), *Yondan* Black (fourth), *Godan* Black (fifth), *Rokudan* Black (sixth), *Shichidan* Black (seventh), *Hachidan* Black (eighth), *Kyudan* Black (ninth), and *Judan* Black (tenth—highest—to date never attained by anyone). *Judoka*, *judo* practitioners, use the same basic terminology. They progress from White to Yellow to Orange to Green to Blue to Brown to Black, which has five different *dan*, to Red and White, with three *dan*, to Red, also with three *dan*, to White, with one *dan*. This last *dan*, the twelfth, has also never been attained. The underlying symbolism is that the highest master, having completed the cycle, once again becomes a student. In *judo* tournaments of 2 to 10 min. matches one referee and two judges watch two contestants attempt to score points. Points are obtained by making a clean throw, by pinning for 30 seconds, or by applying a submission hold which cuts off the flow of blood—not of air—to cause temporary unconsciousness. Defeat may be signified by tapping the mat or the opponent twice. In neither *karate* nor *judo* official competition does an individual's spiritual maturity matter anymore. Having become highly popular world sports with mass spectator appeal, they have in fact become all *do* and no *jutsu*. If Bodidharma could see them today, he would probably wish he had not torn out his eyelids.

ORGANIZATION: All martial arts in existence today are practiced in schools. These range in size from a master's personal courtyard or training hall (*dojo*) to the eight-story *kodokan* in Tokyo, which has eating, sleeping and training facilities for hundreds of *judo* students and teachers. Each art's system of schools and its larger organizational structure in turn is largely determined by the size of its following—anywhere from a handful to well over a million men and women, boys and girls. By 1951 there were so many *judo* schools and practitioners that a world governing body was formed. That body, the International Judo Federation, today consists of 96 national *judo* organizations. These include the Canadian Kodokan Black Belt Association and the United States Judo Federation. The United States organization was founded in 1952 and today has over 25,000 members in 32 regional groups and 550 local groups. Although not as large a participant sport, *kendo* (sword way) also has a world governing body, the International Kendo Federation (IKF). It is composed of the national organizations that represent numerous groups, clubs and members. The IKF stages world championships every three years. Its first was in Tokyo in 1970. In Los Angeles and San Francisco in 1973, Canada placed second after Japan in the team title. The same year the IKF was founded, the World Union of Karate-do Organizations (WUKO) was established in Japan. Today it is composed of over 70 national organizations, such as the National Karate Association of Canada. Every other year the WUKO stages a world championship tournament. In the United States national championships are staged by the Amateur Athletic Union which sponsors the United States Karate Championship, and by the United States Karate Association (USKA) which sponsors the Grand Nationals. The USKA also sponsored the first World Karate Tournament, held in Chicago in 1963. Competitors at these two annual events represent hundreds of smaller organizations, schools and clubs. Most of these belong to the United Karate Federation, which has a membership of 10,000 recognized karate schools and institutions in the United States alone. In addition to all of these competitive organizations are many which represent a trend back to *karatejutsu,* traditional *karate.* Most of these were founded in the 1970s, of which the Feminist Karate Union and the Women's Martial Arts Union are perhaps the best known. These organizations stress *karate* as a means of insuring health, which includes self-defense, and as a way toward the realization of Self. In those goals they are the most direct descendants in spirit of those Okinawan schools of *te* founded over 300 years ago to throw off the Japanese overlords.

Black Belt Hall of Fame

BURBANK, CALIFORNIA

Mailing Address: 1845 W. Empire Ave, 91504. Tel. (213) 843-4444. *Contact:* Rick Zimerman, *Black Belt* Editor. *Location:* 35 mi. N.W. of Anaheim, 125 mi. N.W. of San Diego, 390 mi. N.W. of Phoenix, Ariz. *Personnel:* Rainbow Publications' Staff; Patrick Conner, Advertising Coordinator. Not open to the public. *Nearby Halls of Fame:* Citizens Savings (Los Angeles, 20 mi. S.W.), Softball (Long Beach, 30 mi. S.E.), Auto Racing (Ontario, 40 mi. S.E.), Physical Fitness (Costa Mesa, 45 mi. S.E.), Flight, Sports (San Diego).

The Black Belt Hall of Fame, the leading award bestowed upon martial artists, was started in 1968 by Mito Uyehara, the president of Rainbow Publications, and Han Kim, Rainbow's publisher. At present the inductees' names are engraved on an attractive totem pole in the Rainbow offices, but the Hall hopes to eventually have their own building. Tournaments, programs and seminars are given throughout the year by individual Hall of Famers who remain active in the sport.

Members: 55 as of 1977. There are five or six inductees annually, suggested by past Hall of Famers; the final section is made by a board of martial arts experts. Inductees receive bronze plaques with their names engraved thereon, and their names are added to the totem pole register on view in the Rainbow offices.

1968 FULLERTON, Frank. Martial Artist of the Year.
MIKAMI, Shuji. Kendo.
NAGANO, Kiro. Judo instructor.
NISHIOKA, Hayward. Judo player. Judo instructor 1977.
NORRIS, Chuck. Karate player. Karate instructor 1975. Martial Artist of the Year 1977.
OHSHIMA, Tsutomu. Karate instructor.
TOHEI, Koechi. Aikido Instructor of the Year.

1969 ALLRED, Sam. Martial Artist of the Year.
CAMPBELL, Ben. Judo player.
DEMURA, Fumio. Karate instructor. Martial Artist of the Year 1975.
JAY, Wally. Jujutsu.
LaPUPPET, Thomas. Karate player.
TANURA, Masato. Judo instructor.
YAMAMOTO, Yukiso. Aikido Instructor of the Year.

1970 COAGE, Allen. Judo player. Judo player 1977.
KIM, Ki Whang. Karate instructor.
KOIWAI, Eichi K. Martial Artist of the Year.
MARCHINI, Ronald. Karate player.
SUZUKI, Shihichi. Aikido Instructor of the Year.
WILSON, George. Judo instructor.
WONG, Ark Y. Kung fu.

1971 CHO, S. Henry. Martial Artist of the Year.
HARRIS, George. Judo instructor.
MARUYAMA, Paul. Judo player.
MIYAHARA, Maki. Kendo.
STONE, Mike. Karate player.
YAMADA, Yoshimitsu. Aikido Instructor of the Year.
YARNALL, Robert. Karate instructor.

1972 GRAHAM, Doug. Judo player.
HAYES, Joseph. Karate player.
IVAN, Dan. Martial Artist of the Year.
LEE, Bruce (dec.). Jeet kune do. Martial Artist of the Year 1974.
SONE, Traizo. Judo instructor.
YAMAGUCHI, Gosei. Karate instructor.

1973 ASHIDA, Sachio. Judo instructor.
BREGMAN, Jim. Judo player.
HO'O, Marshall. T'ai chi chuan.
KIM, Richard. Karate instructor.
LIEB, Ernest. Martial Artist of the Year.
WALLACE, Bill. Karate player. Karate player 1977.

1974 ALEXANDER, Gary. Karate instructor.
BURRIS, Pat. Judo instructor. Judo player 1976.
GEIS, Karl. Judo player.
JACKSON, Howard. Karate player.
KONG, Bucksam. Kung fu.

1975 CAHILL, Willie. Judo instructor.
LEWIS, Joe. Karate player.
MARTIN, Tommy. Judo Player.

1976 OKADA, Shag. Judo instructor.
PARKER, Ed. Martial Artist of the Year.
SMITH, Jeff. Karate player.
WILL, Jay T. Karate instructor.

1977 DACASCOS, Al. Kung fu.
INOSANTO, Dan. Jeet kune do.
KENNY, Glenn. Karate instructor.

Martial Arts Halls of Fame to Watch

SALLE PALASZ AND TRI-WEAPON CLUB HALL OF FAME

Restricted Membership 1977

Salle Palasz members are adults, Tri-Weapon Club members are boys, all of whom are instructed in the ancient art of fencing at this school, the acronym of which is SP,TWC. Within the facility is a picture gallery "Hall of Fame" of past fencing students and teams coached by the famous Fencing Master, Richard F. Oles. Included in this hall of fame are those students who distinguished themselves in fencing and who contributed to the school or its programs. The latter include the teaching of fencing as an art and a sport, the staging of demonstrations, tournaments and exhibitions, the organization of teaching and officiating seminars and the compilation of statistics. For further information contact the SP,TWC at 30 Alco Place, Baltimore MD 21227. (301) 242-3430 or 945-5359.

ROLLER SKATING

The origin of roller skating is probably more colorful and at the same time more inauspicious than that of any other sport. In 1760, just five years after Samuel Johnson's *Dictionary of the English Language* appeared, a musical instrument maker named Joseph Merlin emigrated from his home in Huy, Belgium, to London, England. An accomplished violinist, he was also an inventor. Among the first things he invented in London was "a pair of skaites." Later in that first year in England he was invited to a masquerade ball at the elegant Carlisle House, home of the celebrated Mrs. Cornelly, in what is now London's Soho district. After the festivities had begun, Merlin, strapped into his new invention, came gliding into the ballroom playing his priceless antique violin. All present watched as, unable either to stop or to slow down, he rolled the length of the large room toward a great gilded mirror valued at over 500 pounds. Besides shattering the mirror, which severely wounded him, he also smashed his priceless violin. Understandably, Merlin the inventor does not appear again in history; it was nearly 30 years before anyone else tried to skate on dry land.

Beginning around 1790 when there were only 3.9 million people in the United States, roller skating's evolution was accelerated by events in Europe. A French model of the roller skate named the *patin-à-terre* and a German one called the *Erdschlittischuh* both appeared about then. Both names translate as ground skate or shoe, as distinct from one to be used on ice. In 1823, the year raincoats were invented, Robert John Tyers, a Piccadilly fruit seller, demonstrated his "volitos." These, with five small wheels arranged in single file on each boot, were patented "for the purpose of travelling or pleasure." Another ingenious though unseccessful model was patented about the same time—it had only one wheel per shoe.

The year stagecoach service began on the Santa Fe Trail (1849) was the biggest year in the history of the roller skate since Merlin cracked the mirror. That year both an opera, Giancomo Meyerbeer's *The Prophet,* opened in Paris and a ballet, Paul Taglioni's *Winter Pastimes; or, The Skaters,* opened in Berlin. Each had a scene in which "ice skaters" rolled around on the stage on roller skates. Both shows were successful, primarily because people flocked to them just to see the skating scenes. A fad began. New attempts were made to invent a more versatile skate, which amounted to one that would allow its wearer to remain upright.

Such a skate was invented and patented in America in 1863. Despite the fact that the Civil War was going on, the first great roller skating craze swept the United States and Western Europe. The remarkable skate which caused it all was invented by James L. Plimpton of Boston. It had four rubber-cushioned wheels made of Turkish boxwood and was the prototype of the modern skate. With them it was suddenly possible not only to maintain one's balance but also to execute intricate stunts. That skate's craze was amplified the following year (1864) when Horace Greeley said to Josiah Grinnell, "Go West, young man," as well as when Jackson Haines, the "American Ice Skating King," took up roller skating. Soon Haines had become a master, inspiring people wherever he skated with his roller skating ballet. Two years later, in the same year that the James-Younger gang staged their first robbery, roller skating was so popular that Plimpton opened the world's first roller skating rink. It was located in Newport, Rhode Island, in the Atlantic House, which later became an Elk's Home. Like any craze, that first one passed. The second lasted from 1870 to 1875. It was prompted by the introduction of a new and better roller skate and ended with the dawning of the bicycle age. Thirty-three years later, other innovations and commonplace faddishness prompted another craze that lasted from 1908 to 1912. Thirty-six years after that, another roller skating boom occurred from 1948 to 1954. Roller Derbies were among the first widely televised sports and accounted for much of roller skating's popularity at that time.

During all those years, numerous advances and innovations were made in the sport and in the skate itself.

Roller hockey, called rink polo at the time, was invented in the 1870s. Rinks were established throughout Canada during that same decade. In 1879 a 75-hour "roller skating walk" was staged at one in Toronto. The ball bearing wheel was invented in 1884, the year the Ringling Brothers began their circus in Baraboo, Wisconsin. Six-day roller skating races were introduced at Madison Square Garden, where the winner of the first one skated 1091 mi. (*see* Bicycling). History's largest roller skating rink was opened in 1893. Dubbed the Grand Hall, it had a skating area of 68,000 sq. ft. It covered about as great an area as an American football field plus three regulation-size basketball courts. Control of the sport was assumed in 1893 by the National Skating Association of Great Britain, which had been formed 14 years earlier for ice skating. A world governing body for roller skating was established in 1924, the year Gershwin wrote "Rhapsody in Blue." World figure- and dance-skating competitions were introduced in Washington, D. C, in 1947.

All of these and numerous other advances and innovations were critical to the evolution of the sport. But roller skating's popularity—its craze potential—was due far more to its unusual applications. The most recent of these was Clint Shaw's 3100 mi. New York-Santa Monica roller marathon in 1974. Earlier, in 1967, he had skated 4900 mi. across Canada from Victoria, British Columbia, to St. John's, Newfoundland. Before that, there was skateboarding, which was adapted from both surfing and roller skating. It was a national mania in 1965 and remains wildly popular. And before skateboarding, there was the Roller Derby, a copyrighted name like Kleenex, Xerox and Ping Pong. Interestingly, the Roller Derby is the only major non-derivative sport invented by an American. James Naismith, the inventor of basketball, was Canadian; softball, invented by an American in Chicago, was a direct derivation of baseball; lacrosse was invented by Algonquin Indians long before there was such a thing as "an American." The Roller Derby was invented in Chicago in 1935, near the end of the dance marathon craze, by Leo A. "Bromo" Seltzer. Four years earlier, Seltzer had staged the first commercially successful Walkathon. His first Derby was held on August 13 in the Chicago Coliseum. Fifty contestants in teams of two skated a total of 57,000 laps, or about 4000 miles. The 20,000 spectators were impressed, but not nearly so much as they were three years later when a fight broke out among some Derby skaters. So impressed were they, in fact, that the rules were amended, fighting was promptly added to the Roller Derby the next day, and the modern form of the sport was born. Its popularity, aided by another new invention, television, was soon immense. New millions of young and old throughout North America were suddenly roller skating themselves or watching others. New patents were filed. New models appeared. The spirit of Merlin rolled on.

FORMS: The main forms of roller skating are identical to those of ice skating, from which they were developed: speed skating and artistic skating (*see* Ice Skating: Forms). Roller skating, however, has a unique combat-entertainment form, best exemplified by the Roller Derby and its professional competitor in roller-rink skating, Roller Games, another copyrighted name. These events, which have lovingly been described as "madness on skates," are strictly professional—there are neither Roller Derby facilities for amateurs nor any places for public instruction in it. An additional form is skateboarding. Finally, there is roller hockey. Although a fully developed game in its own right, it is in fact hockey on roller skates played with a ball instead of a puck.

In speed skating and the Derby, contestants or teams skate counterclockwise on an oval track. In Derbies, the track measures 310 ft. in circumference. In other words, it would fit into a 50 ft. by 90 ft. rectangle. It is composed of hardwood coated with a thin veneer of plastic. In speed skating, the track's width ranges from 8 to 20 ft. to accomodate from 2 to 6 contestants. The distances raced in world championship events differ among races for men at 1094, 5468, 10,936 and 21,872 yds; relay races, most of which are run the same distances; and races for women at 547, 3281 and 5468 yds. The winner of any of these races is the first to cross the finish line with either skate. Titles are awarded for individual events, unlike ice speed skating where skaters compete in all events for best over-all performances. Both of these forms are unique among sports in that more women compete in them than men—slightly more than 50 percent in Roller Derbies, far more in speed skating. They differ from each other, however, in that no body contact or impeding of other skaters is allowed in speed skating, while in Roller Derbies body contact has been developed to a high art. In fact, the act of falling down has been given a name of its own. "To brodie" means to fall and is named after Steve Brodie, who either jumped or fell off the Brooklyn Bridge. Penalties in Roller Derbies consist of being taken out of the race for 1 or 2 min, as determined by the referee. In speed skating the penalty for infractions, such as passing anyone on the inside of the track, is often disqualification. Speed skating officials include three judges, a starter, a lap scorer, a recorder, two track stewards and a competitors' steward.

In marked contrast to the above is artistic roller skating. There are four main classes of competition: men's figure skating, women's figure skating, pairs' figure skating, and roller dancing. In these, which are often performed to music, grace and style are judged on a point scale of 1 to 6. They are of equal value to proficiency and technique. In all four classes, competition is divided between compulsory and freestyle figures. Pair figure skaters, unlike roller dancers, may separate from each other for the execution of dissimilar but complementary movements. Ideally, pair skaters create an impression of perfect union. Unnecessarily spectacular movements by roller dancing pairs are counted against them. All four classes of artistic skating are performed on rectangular rinks surfaced with asphalt, asbestos, cement or hardwood, the best of which is American sugar maple.

There are two basic types of skate—those worn in roller-rink skating, and those worn in all the other forms. In the type worn in speed skating and in all four classes of artistic skating, a mount of four ball-bearing wheels is clamped and screwed onto a separately bought shoe and secured with a strap around the ankle. Skates used in artistic skating have a higher boot and larger wheels than the speed skater's skate, which is light with a long, low wheelbase. In addition, the artistic skate has a rubber toe-stop, which is used in the execution of spins and other difficult stunts. A drop of thin oil in both sides of each wheel is required once a month as maintenance for this type of skate. The second type is the shoe skate in which the shoe and the skate are bought already attached. This skate has rubber-cushioned wooden, fiberglass or plastic wheels. The fastest roller skater at 25.78 m.p.h. is only slightly slower than the fastest ice skater at 29.3 m.p.h. The mile record for roller skating on a rink is 2 min. 25.1 sec, set by Gianni Ferretti of Italy. The one-hour roller skating records for men and women are 22 mi. 465 yds. and 20 mi. 1355 yds, respectively. For comparative speeds, *see* pages 291 and 614; for additional information on skates (all types), consult the appropriate listings in the Trivia Index.

ORGANIZATION: One of the reasons Leo Seltzer invented the Roller Derby in 1935 was that he had read in a magazine that roller skating was America's largest participant sport. While this is no longer true, it is still one of the truly big sports. Across the North American continent today approximately 20 million people roller skate in over 6000 rollerdomes and in another 6000 church, school or community facilities. West Point and Purdue University, to name only two institutions of higher learning, offer instruction in the sport. Girl Scouts, Cub Scouts and Camp Fire Girls may all earn merit badges in roller skating.

In 1949 the sport was so popular all over the world that an international governing body was formed. That body, the *Fédération Internationale de Patinage à Roulettes* (FIPR), International Roller Skating Federation, is today headquartered in Barcelona, Spain, where it was founded. It sponsors world championship competition among its members, the national roller skating organizations of numerous countries. In the United States this affiliate is the United States of America Confederation (USAC), headquartered in Lincoln, Nebraska. Formed in 1942 and re-formed in 1971, the USAC today has a membership of over 25,000 active roller skaters. Its annual championships are recognized by the FIPR as America's National Championships. The Roller Skating Rink Operators Association of America (RSROA), founded in 1937, is an organization of 1200 independent roller-skating rink operators in 24 state groups. It is the parent body for the Society of Roller Skating Teachers of America which has 600 teachers and 150 apprentice teachers. Besides leadership in the roller-skating rink industry, the RSROA stages its own annual National Championships. Other major organizations include the *Fédération Internationale de Roller Skating* and the Roller Skating Foundation of America, whose membership in 1976 consisted of 5432 rink owners, operators and manufacturers.

The world of professional roller skating competition, which is an entertainment as well as a sport, has an organization uniquely its own. It consists almost entirely of the International Roller Derby League (IRDL), which operates the Roller Derby, all teams of which are owned by the Seltzer family; and of the National Skating Derby (NSD), which operates the Roller Games. Annual Roller Derby awards include Most Valuable Player, National Champion Team, Roller Derby Queen, Roller Derby King, Rookie of the Year, and the Fred Cohen Memorial Cup, awarded for special contribution to the Derby. Roller hockey, in turn, is governed largely by the National Roller Hockey Association, formed in 1905, the year of the first Coca-Cola advertisement. Its name at the time was the Amateur Rink Hockey Association.

Significantly, all of these numerous organizations are completely independent of the once parental but now separate sport of ice skating.

Roller Skating Hall of Fame

LINCOLN, NEBRASKA

Mailing Address: P.O. Box 81846, 68510. Tel. (402) 489-8811. *Contact:* Patti Wood assoc. ed. *Location:* Approx. 57 mi. S.W. of Omaha, 126 mi. E. of Kearney, 180 mi. S.W. of Des Moines, Iowa. *Admission:* Free, 8 to 5 daily. *Personnel:* Gary Castro, pres; George Pickard, exec. dir; R. W. Brown, treas; 11-mem bd. of dir. (Gary Castro, chmn.). *Nearby Halls of Fame:* Agriculture (Bonner Springs, Kan, 165 mi. S.E.), Agriculture (Kansas City, Mo.).

The Roller Skating Rink Operators Association (RSROA) Hall of Fame was founded by the RSROA board of control at their annual convention in 1955. It was created to honor those who made a valuable contribution to the development of roller skating both on a competitive sporting basis as well as on a trade industry basis. From 1937 to 1972, the United States Amateur Confederation of Roller Skating (USACRS) and the RSROA were one, resulting in the combined Hall of Fame. But in 1972, the two associations separated, with the RSROA assuming control of the Hall of Fame. The USACRS does not have a hall of fame. Located in the Board of Directors Room in the National Roller Skating headquarters office, each Hall of Famer is perpetuated with a plaque recording upon it his picture, city and state, year of birth and death and major contribution to roller skating.

Members: 25 as of November 1976. Any person who has given outstanding service to roller skating is eligible. Nominations are made by the Honors Committee as early as May of each year, and are then voted on by the Board of Directors at their November board meeting. There is no limit to the number of members inducted per year. The new inductees are honored at the Presidents Dinner at the RSROA convention held annually in May.

1955 WARE, Ralph. Founder of the Chicago Roller Skate Co, innovators of the 45-degree action rink roller skate in 1920.

1957 MARTIN, Fred A. (dec). Introduced first waltz on skates; first grand pipe organ music introduced in rink he was managing (White City Rink, Chicago) in the late 1920s; secretary-treasurer of RSROA, 1937–1951; and president, 1951; held top speed record for skating 309 miles in Madison Square Garden.

RAWSON, Perry. (dec). A Wall Street broker who became a millionaire in his early thirties;

constructed two rink studios, one on his estate in Deal, N.J, and the other at his summer home in New Hampshire; converted both into "skate laboratories" to research skating techniques; responsible for advancement of dancing on roller skates; author of many RSROA dance textbooks.

BROWN, Victor J. "Buddy" (dec). President of RSROA, 1937 – 1938, and 1940; a prime figure in the move to organize the RSROA; instigator of the Skating March of Dimes, acting as its chairman for a number of years; well versed in the sports world, he was at various times a jockey riding in the Kentucky Derby, Preakness, Suburban and Brooklyn Handicaps; a baseball player with the Bronx Giants; boxer at the New Polo Amateur Association; a swimming promoter at Starlight Park in New York; more recently promoted boxing at Dreamland Park in New Jersey until his death in 1968.

1959 FREEMAN, Fred H. Originator of the Freeman Class System, an instructional technique devised to teach roller skating to the masses; taught artistic dance and introduced and systemized dress standards for roller rinks; president of RSROA, 1941 – 1943.

1963 BROWN, William T. "Pop." President of RSROA, 1944 – 1947; Roller Skating World Congress president, 1947 – 1965; devoted much of his time to the ideal of international recognition of the RSROA; held posts with the advisory and finance committees, served as chairman of the nominating committee, national master of ceremonies at board meetings; acted as chaplain at all association official affairs.

KISH, Alfred W. A veteran speed skater, Al was one of the original 17 rink operators present at the 1937 meeting during which the RSROA was originally founded; served on numerous executive committees and was a member of the board of directors.

CIONI, Roland (dec). One of the greatest professional speed skaters of all time, he was world professional speed skating champion at age of 15; held world title from 1914 until he retired still undefeated in 1951; became rink instructor in 1936 where he and his wife, Margaret, taught dance, figures, pairs and speed, turning out national champions by the dozens.

McMILLAN, William (dec). Innovator, teacher, and coach, Bill was a recognized leader among his contemporaries, active in the formation of the Society of Roller Skating Teachers of America (SRSTA); considered the top pairs coach of the decade (1940s); served on various committees, including the professional figure skating committee of the SRSTA.

SEIFERT, Joseph P. (dec). A 20-year member of the RSROA; provided continuous leadership on the board of the RSROA in its formative years; honored with a life membership in 1955.

1964 LAVENTURE, Edward H. (dec). President of RSROA, 1948 – 1949; a tireless worker in the quest for better skating; served on the advisory committee and was a member of the board of directors; was made an RSROA life member in 1955.

1966 HYDE, Max (dec). President of the Hyde Athletic Shoe Co; recognized for his outstanding work on perfecting the skating boot and for his unlimited contributions to the growth and development of roller skating as a sport and recreation.

1967 BOYDSTON, Thomas. Began skating at age 16 as a trick skater in exhibitions; vice president of RSROA, 1944, 1946 – 1948, president, 1955 – 1956, on board of control, 1949, 1952 and 1958, board of directors, 1949 – 1961, chairman and member of numerous committees, responsible for inception of the advisory board.

MARTIN, Robert D. (dec). Secretary-treasurer of RSROA, 1951 – 1958; author of the first roller skating textbook; one of the first instructors in history; cited for his contributions in the development of artistic and figure skating.

1968 SHATTUCK, Meredith M. "Red." An artistic sculptor prior to the depression; entered the skating profession at age of 29; rose through the ranks to serve in many capacities as a leader in the association; noted for his outstanding work in the promotion of roller skating at the internatonal level; American representative for roller skating in the Pan-American Sports Organization; served as the United States hockey commissioner; president of RSROA, 1957 – 1959.

PARKER, Roy W. (dec). President of RSROA, 1966 – 1967, board of directors, 1959 – 1966; recognized as a respected rink operator who contributed stability and integrity in the forward progress of the association.

1969 KEMPF, Edward J. "Uncle Ed" (dec). Known as Uncle Ed throughout the roller skating world, acting as parent, confidant and chaperone to champion skaters; devoted more than 30 years service as chief clerk of the American and National championships; received Roller Skating Service Award, 1959, Amateur of the Year, 1962.

1972 WINTZ, John (dec). Founder of the Sure-Grip Skate Co; contributed the John Wintz Memorial Award presented to the home club of each United States roller skating champion; unselfishly devoted his time and resources to the development and recognition of roller skating in business, sport and recreation.

1974 SNYDER, Charles. A tool maker for Frigidaire in the 1940s, he made his first pair of skates for his daughter who went on to win the US senior women's title on them in 1943 and 1944; quit his job in 1943 and established the Snyder

Roller Skate Co, making his skates available throughout the world; a firm supporter of the RSROA and all its programs from the early 1940s.

BERGIN, Fred J. (dec). RSROA president, 1950–1951; first and only dean of the Society of Roller Skating Teachers of America; wrote the first looseleaf dance manual in 1940, and judged the first gold medals in dance; coach of national champions and designer of teaching programs for tests and competitions, Fred conducted many seminars for teachers that resulted in the first full-scale conference held in Denver in 1945.

GILES, Perry. A former rink operator, devoted 30 years to the research and development of plastic floor coatings that have added traction to the roller rink floor.

FOWLKES, George Vernon (dec). Introduced the modern toe stop at the 1948 national convention; originator of the first plastic roller skating wheel; founder of Fo-Mac Enterprises, manufacturer of wheels, toe stops and various other skating products; participated in RSROA trade shows, conventions, seminars and chapter meetings.

1975 RIEDELL, Paul F. Founder of Riedell Shoe Co, manufacturers of high quality skating boots; staunch supporter of the RSROA, he remains one of its leading and most respected spokesmen.

TILLINGHAST, Oliver Louis "Tilli." Began working in skating rinks at the age of 14; introduced the nationally famous "Tilli Originals"—skating tights and boot covers—in 1957; became noted as planner, builder and flooring expert in the United States with installations of portable rinks and floors in 45 states.

1976 APDALE, George F. Master of ceremonies who typically does the awarding to new Hall of Fame inductees; dedicated more than 35 years to amateur roller skating; largely responsible for development of international style of roller skating.

Roller Skating Hall of Fame to Watch

ROLLER DERBY HALL OF FAME

Postponed 1977

The owners of the Roller World Training Center for Bay Promotions, Inc, San Francisco, are in the process of establishing a hall of fame to honor those who have participated in roller skating as a competitive sport. However, the opening of this Hall has been indefinitely postponed. For further information contact the Center, 631 Buena Vista Ave, Alameda, CA 94501. (415) 521-5700.

SHUFFLEBOARD

At one time the best English homes or mansions had shuffleboard tables in their respective Great Halls. These tables were of various shapes and sizes but usually measured 3½ ft. wide and 40 ft. long. They were exquisitely constructed of up to 300 pieces of fine wood glued smoothly together. Flat metal weights were slid along the table's smooth surface toward scoring diagrams marked at the far end. There was considerable variation, however, in what a game consisted of, how it should be played, and even what it should be called. Thus while Henry VIII played and lost large wagers at *shovilla bourde,* other Englishmen played shovelboard, shoveboard, shove groat, slide groat, slide thrift, slyp groat, and horse billiards. In the pub version of these games, still widely played in English pubs today, much smaller tables were used and shillings or halfpennies were slid. In Shakespeare's *King Henry IV* Falstaff cries, "Quoit him down, Bardolph, like a shove-groat shilling!"

Where all these games came from is anyone's guess, although it is known that similar games were played in ancient Persia and in North America. Dakota Sioux and Assiniboin women played a winter game on ice in which flat stones were shoved with sticks toward scoring areas.

Various English forms eventually crossed the Atlantic to New England. There, however, in 1845, the peak year of the Great Age of Whaling, it was banned as a "gambler's pastime." Two decades later, though, the game began to be accepted on board ships. One of the 60 passengers aboard the *Quaker City* when it set sail from New York in 1867 bound for the Mediterranean was Mark Twain. Besides not getting seasick, of which he later boasted in *The Innocents Abroad,* and seeing a miniature of Olivia, whom he later married, Twain played shuffleboard in its horse billiards form. He described it as "a fine game . . . a mixture of hop-scotch and shuffleboard played with a crutch." It was played, he continued, "with some broad wooden disks [which] you send forward with a vigorous thrust of the crutch" toward a scoring diagram marked in chalk on the deck. Games of horse billiards ended when one of the individuals or teams of two had accumulated 100 points.

By 1873, the year barbed wire was invented and Jules Verne wrote *Around the World in 80 Days,* ships of the Peninsula and Orient Line sailing between England and Australia featured shuffleboard as a major entertainment or pastime for their passengers. Decades later in 1912 the *Titanic* of the White Star Line featured shuffleboard courts in addition to gymnasiums, squash rackets courts, swimming pools and a miniature golf course.

Acceptance of the game on land did not occur in North America until the 1890s, when it began to be tolerated as a children's game. Then Mr. and Mrs. Robert Ball, owners of the Lyndhurst Hotel in Daytona Beach, Florida, began the shuffleboard boom. They accomplished this in 1913, the year the crossword puzzle was invented, by painting courts on the sidewalk in front of their hotel and developing standard rules. Guests who stayed there during the winter months returned to homes all over the continent to set up their own courts and games. So rapid was this process of diffusion that national rules and regulations were established at a conference in St. Petersburg, Florida, in 1924—two years before the Swiss-born Ernst Bloch composed the song "America." These national rules replaced all the English, shipboard and neighborhood rules. Shuffleboard had become so popular that a national organization was also needed. To meet that need, the National Shuffleboard Association was established in 1931, the year American George Simon composed "Of Thee I Sing". Since then the "boom" has gone on—millions play it today on sidewalks, in playgrounds and on regulation courts. It is played as a pastime, as a hobby, or in highly competitive tournaments like the annual Masters. Additionally, thousands of people still play it on the decks of ships.

FORMS: Shuffleboard games may be singles consisting of two persons or doubles consisting of two teams of two. Each person attempts in turn to propel a disc by means of a cue onto a scoring diagram at the opposite end of the court. The court is preferably a concrete surface but may be terrazzo and is 6 ft. by 52 ft. Before a game begins, one end of the court is designated as the Head and the other as the Foot. Games begin at the

Head of the court. At either end is a scoring area, a 10½ ft. long triangular diagram which is divided into six parts of 10, 8, 7, or minus 10 point values. An alternate form of target area is oval shaped with three columns of three sections each centered between the 10 and the minus 10 parts. Each column adds up to 15—8, 3 and 4; 1, 5 and 9; 6, 7 and 2.

Players use cues, each of which is a maximum of 6 ft. 3 in. long with a half-moon shaped base at the playing end. With the cue a player pushes the disc or, to use Twain's expression, vigorously thrusts it. In tournament play the disc often travels at speeds up to 60 m.p.h. There are eight such discs to a set—four red and four black. Each is from ¾ to 1 in. thick, 6 in. in diameter, and weighs between 11½ and 15 oz. A red disc is always shot first to start a game. It is shot from the right side of the Head of the court and from the left side of the Foot of the court.

Players or teams attempt to win a game by accumulating 50, 75 or 100 points. During a game penalties are applied for a variety of errors and infractions. For example, ten points are taken from a player's score for balking, not following through with a shot, or for talking to coach a partner; five points are taken away for talking to disconcert an opponent or for intentional stalling. The application of such penalties is made by a court referee stationed at the Head of the court, who is assisted by a court umpire stationed at the Foot and who may consult with a divisional referee. Both the court referee and the umpire call out scores after each half round, which are recorded by a court scorer. These four officials are under the authority of a tournament manager who has complete charge of play, including the determination and awarding of penalties.

In England and elsewhere, various derivative forms of shuffleboard are played, especially in clubs and pubs. These are called shove-penny, shove-ha'penny, Justice, Jervis, or Jarvis. All involve pushing coins along polished boards so that they stop between closely ruled lines.

ORGANIZATION: The governing body of world shuffleboard is the National Shuffleboard Association (NSA) which has been based in Miami, Florida, since 1931. It is a federation of 12 state shuffleboard associations. Besides assisting those associations, the NSA establishes official rules and promotes the game through its regular publications which include *National Rules* and an annual *Review*. It also supervises tournaments, the most prestigious of which is the U.S. National Championship. In addition, it promotes the game all over the continent and in foreign countries. Currently NSA courts exist in 39 states, 2 provinces (British Columbia and Ontario) and Mexico.

In 1939, just a quarter of a century after the game was introduced in its present regulation form, there were over 200,000 players throughout the country, of which 25,000 were playing in Florida. Twelve years later in 1951, there were 5000 public courts in 455 different cities, on which approximately 5 million people played regularly. In 1973 there were 300 shuffleboard clubs with more than 55,000 members playing on 2913 courts in Florida alone; and every year since, the game has grown more and more popular.

The world's largest shuffleboard club is that of St. Petersburg, Florida, where the Masters has been held annually since 1960. Whereas all the main winter tournaments are held in that state, annual summer national championships are staged in Michigan, New Hampshire, North Carolina and Ohio.

National Shuffleboard Hall of Fame

ST. PETERSBURG, FLORIDA

Mailing Address: Shuffleboard Club, Mirror Lake Dr, 33701. Tel. (305) 922-7219. *Contact:* George Merz, Cur. *Location:* Approx. 20 mi. S.W. of Tampa, 35 mi. N. of Sarasota, 100 mi. S.W. of Orlando. *Admission:* During tournaments and by appointment. *Personnel:* William Johnstone, Pres; Omero Catan, First V.Pres; Art Davis, Second V.Pres; Larry Booth, Third V.Pres; George Merz, Treas; Dorothy Hahn, Secy. *Nearby Halls of Fame:* Entertainment (Sarasota), Movies (Orlando), Swimming (Ft. Lauderdale, 200 mi. S.E.).

In the discussion stages since the 1950s, the National Shuffleboard Hall of Fame did not have a physical structure until 1970. The president of the National Shuffleboard Association (NSA) entered into an agreement with builders of a new community development in West Palm Beach with rooms to be set aside in the clubhouse. With the accumulation of records, trophies and memorabilia, a new building was secured in St. Petersburg in 1972. Land was provided by the St. Petersburg Club, and through private donations and support from the NSA, the new structure evolved into private ownership. The Hall seeks to honor those individuals who promote shuffleboard through distinguished service or excel in competition and demonstrate true sportsmanship. Within the building are displays explaining the organizational history of the NSA and origins of land shuffleboard play, which took place in 1913 in Daytona Beach. The center area displays trophies, while dedication plaques, pictures and the Honor Roll—a posting of contributors—grace the walls. There is a historical exhibit of vintage and modern discs and cues. Manuals of shuffleboard playing and techniques and reading shelves of historical records are available for perusal.

Members: 45 as of 1976. The nominating committee submits a list of eligible inductees to the Board of Officers and Delegates. The candidate must receive a majority of the votes cast. To be eligible for induction as an Executive, one must spend at least ten years in shuffleboard as player, executive officer, tournament director or other distinguished contribution to the game. To be eligible for induction as a Player, one must win numerous national and/or state championships and have proven to be a sportsman of the game. The maximum number inducted annually is three, usually one in the

Executive category and two Players. Official induction takes place at the annual NSA Banquet with the inductees receiving diamond-studded Hall of Fame lapel buttons and a certificate in Old English. Their names are placed on two black walnut tablets in the hall.

1961 GAHAN, Pierce V. Executive.
SCALISE, Mary. Player.
SMITH, Webster H. Player.
1962 CLOSE, Amy. Player.
SLATER, U. Michael. Executive.
SPILLMAN, Carl. Player.
1963 BADUM, Henry. Player.
DEWART, Don. Executive.
SMITH, Janet. Player.
1964 MERZ, George. Executive.
TOUTMAN, Marie. Player.
WILCOX, Carrie. Player.
1965 FOLBERTH, William. Player.
HALL, Mae. Player.
STREETER, Lee P. Executive.
1966 GLAWSON, Ernest. Executive.
HENDERSON, Bess. Player.
HILL, Pat. Player.
1967 BRUNER, Farrell. Player.
JAMISON, T. S. Executive.
MATHEWS, Ted. Player.
1968 BALDWIN, Arthur T. Executive.
HAWKINS, Elsie. Player.
HOLMES, Lucille. Player.
1969 BRASHARES, Mark G. Player.
GAUSTAD, Josephine. Player.
SAUNDERS, Fairfax G. Executive.
1970 HARRISON, Frank F. Executive.
RICHARDS, J. Arthur. Player.
WAGERS, Mel A. Player.
1971 BLACKMAN, Ralph. Player.
HAWKINS, Howard. Player.
SMOCK, Herbert K. Executive.
1972 CASS, Lyle. Player.
CHANDLER, Earl. Executive.
GLADNEY, Jack. Player.
1973 JOHNSTONE, William R. Executive.
SNODDY, Jay. Player.
1974 BRYANT, Fred E. Executive.
HALEY, Audrey. Player.
KINSELLA, Esther. Player.
1975 GLENN, Ernest M. Player.
SUTTON, Austin. Executive.
SUTTON, Marie. Player.
1976 BOWEN, Willard L. Player.

SKIING

In A.D. 986, about halfway through the three centuries in which Norsemen in their dragon-ships completely terrorized Europe, a Norseman named Bjarni Herjulfsson sighted North America. He did not go ashore, though. Instead he returned to his base in Greenland where, fourteen years later, a Norwegian named Leif "the Lucky" Ericsson bought his ship from him. In it, Leif went from Iceland to North America twice, first in A.D. 1000 with 35 men, again in 1007 with enough additional ships to carry 160 men and women. A colony was settled. It could have been in Labrador, Newfoundland, Nova Scotia or Maine—no one yet knows its precise location. One of the most significant events that occurred at the settlement is known, however: the birth of a boy in 1007 to Thorfinn Karlsefni and Gudrid, the widow of Thorstein Ericsson, Leif's brother. That boy, named Snorro, was the first Caucasian child born on the North American continent. When the settlement failed, he returned to Iceland with his parents and the remaining settlers who had not been killed by Indians. There he grew up, was active in politics, and eventually died. During Snorro's lifetime two things were new and two things were already very old. The new ones were North America and the concept of *viking*, an Old Norse verb loosely meaning "to go on a trade-or-plunder voyage." The old ones were the Norse gods and skiing. About A.D. 1100 the so-called Viking Age ended almost as swiftly as it had begun. North America was not resettled, and for all practical purposes was forgotten until Columbus rediscovered it. But the gods lived on, and so did skiing.

Odin was the greatest *Ass* of them all. With Thor, Thor's wife Frigg and Tiw, who were the other major gods or *Aesir* (the plural of *Ass*), he lived in a kind of Viking Mount Olympus called *Asgard*. The latter was located in an eastern land the Norse referred to as *Asaland*, from which the word Asia is derived. These gods' names in turn gave us our names for four of the days of the week: Odin added to *daeg*, the Old English word for day, gave us Wednesday, Thor resulted in Thursday and his wife Frigg became Friday, Tiw plus *daeg* became Tuesday. Beneath these major gods were the *Vanir*, a group of lesser gods who dwelt in a special place of their own called *Vanaheim*. They included Njord, god of the sea, and his two illegitimate twin children. One of the twins was Frey, whose name translates as Lord, and the other was Freyja, whose name meant Lady. Freyja was the Norse goddess of love and the "possessor of the slain-in-battle." Frey characteristically rode a magical boar that had golden bristles and was called Hildisvini, the Battle Swine. Norsemen out *viking*, or trading, sealed their business oaths with the phrase, "So help me Frey and Njord and almighty Thor." Among the many other Norse gods, giants, monsters and dwarfs were a giant stepson of Thor named Ullr, the god of winter, and Njord's giant wife, whose name was Skadi. Her title was *Öndurdis*, Ski Lady (*dis* in any Old Norse name meant "woman of high rank"). She and Ullr were the Norsemen's goddess and god of skiing.

Each is always pictured wearing skis. The giant Ullr is always pictured with skis the size of dragon-ships strapped to his feet. Skadi is similarly pictured wearing huge skis, as well as jewelry made out of icicles. Of the two, Ullr was more important to Norse skiers. Many wore or carried images of him. But both were very significant divinities because the Norsemen were utterly terrified of frost and of the power of ice—*Ragnarök*, the end of the world, would be a mighty winter, they believed. They also feared the *Jólasveinar*, malicious spirits who lived in the snow and were particularly active during the winter solstice, December 22 when the sun is farthest south of the equator. They called this one most-dangerous day *jól*, avoided skiing as well as virtually everything else the entire day, and made *jól* the last of a 12-day feast that served a protective function for them. They also believed that during that same time of year, Norsemen who had drowned held a feast of their own in the hall of Ran, the sea goddess, where they dined on lobster and drank ale. The two major events in each *jól* feast were the lighting of a large bonfire and the selection of an appropriate boar to represent Hildisvini,

Frey's Battle Swine. Once selected, the boar was designated as the *sónargöltr*, the atonement boar, and as such was believed to take everybody's sins on itself. It was then sacrificed and cooked with a lemon, the Norse symbol of plenty, wedged into its mouth. The *sónargöltr* was carried into the great hall, where everyone in turn placed a hand on its now-holy bristles and either took an oath or swore a vow. A boar or its head is still eaten in parts of England at certain Oxford colleges, for example. In December Swedish mothers bake Christmas cakes that are boar-shaped. The Norsemen's twelve-day feast became the twelve days of Christmas, the dangerous day called *jól* became our happy Christian day of yule. In Norway today Christmas Day is called *Juledag*. The Norse bonfire and *jól*-day feast became our yule log and Christmas dinner.

Besides all of that, the Norsemen gave us skiing. In the eastern Alps today skiers often carry bronze coins embossed with an image of Ullr. How skiing developed among the Norsemen is anyone's guess. Even the derivation of the word is open to doubt. It probably came from *skid,* the Old Norse word for a ski, as do the English words skid and skip. Skis from 2500 B.C, the time of the early pharaohs, have been found intact in Sweden and Siberia. Others from Sweden and Finland seem to have been made later, some 2000 years before Christ. It is thus startling to realize that skiing did not become a sport until 1767, a year after Christie's auction shop opened in London. In all of those centuries skis were used for transportation only, particularly in winter war.

In 1184, when St. Francis of Assisi was a two-year-old, Sverre was crowned king of Norway. A civil war between the Baglars, an aristocratic and clerical party, and the Birkebeiners, the birch-legs—a party of common people who supported Sverre, had been going on for seven years. It did not stop when Sverre was crowned. It was waged, in fact, for many years. In 1200 Sverre sent ski-scouts to reconnoiter the enemy camp before the Battle of Oslo. Chronicles of that event are the earliest factual account of the use of skis. Two years later, Sverre died. And two years after that in 1204, the son who had succeeded him died. That son, however, posthumously had a son who was named Haakon Haakonsson and who as King Haakon IV was destined to become Norway's greatest king. But there were many who doubted his paternity, and thus his rights to the throne. For that reason, and because of the political instability of the time, he was raised in secrecy by the Birkebeiners. One of the best-known events in all of Norwegian history occurred when two Birkebeiner loyalists saved the infant prince from enemy Baglars by skiing him across the Dovre Mountains in the dead of winter. At the age of 13 he was made king by the Birkebeiner party. A year later his mother went through "the ordeal by hot irons" to prove his paternity to those who had doubted it. Then everyone was happy. During his 46-year reign Norway's Golden Age began (1217-1319). Among the many artists and poets who lived at his court was Snorri Sturluson, the man who first recorded the Norse myths and legends. Without his two *Eddas*, we would know very little today about Odin and the other *Aesir*, Njord, Frey and the gods of skiing, the Battle Swine and atonement boars. The rescue of the infant Haakon by the Birkebeiners has been commemorated in Norway since 1932 by an annual race called the *Birkebeinerlauf (lauf* means a run, or race). It is run over the supposed same route, Lillehammer to Rena, a distance of some 35 miles.

A race held annually in Sweden since 1922—the 53-mile *Vasaloppet* from Sälen to Mora—commemorates a similar episode in which skis were critical to a nation's greatest king. Gustavus Eriksson was born in 1496, one year before Leonardo da Vinci finished painting *The Last Supper*. He hated the Danes; they had imprisoned him and killed his father; additionally, Denmark had ruled both Sweden and Norway with an iron fist for over a century. So in 1520 (the year Cortés killed Montezuma) Gustavus tried to get the people of Dalarna (today called Kopparberg) to revolt. They refused. So he began to flee toward Norway. Just 15 miles from the border at Sälen, Dalarnian skiers caught up with him to tell him that the people had changed their minds. He returned with them to Mora, raised an army, and after three years of fighting threw out the Danes. During one battle against them in 1521, Gustavus' troops stretched animal skins between pairs of skis to remove their dead and wounded from the battlefield—thus inventing the stretcher. Finally the Danes were out. For leading the Swedes to independence, Gustavus was elected king as Gustavus I, or Gustavus Vasa—all because those skiers reached him before he crossed the border. The annual *Vasaloppet* today commemorates all these events. Incidentally, it has the largest number of participants of any competitive sporting event in the world. In 1975, for example, there were 9051 starters, of whom 8812 finished. A final note about Gustavus Vasa: during his reign in 1530, Norway's first skiing postman began making his mail route.

Because of the ski's long association with warfare, it was perhaps fitting that military men should be the ones to introduce skiing as a sport. In 1716 the Norwegian army had organized a skiing company. In 1733 a captain of that company had written and published the first skiing manual. In 1767 (as mentioned above in connection with Christie's) soldiers of that company stationed in and around Kristiania (now called Oslo) competed in rapid-fire rifle contests and in downhill ski races for money prizes. The races featured a slalomlike event in which the soldiers were required to ski "between bushes without falling or breaking their skis." Breaking skis was common in those days. One reason was their primitive construction. Typically, there was an 8 to 12 ft. *langski* on one foot and a 4 to 6 ft. *ondurr* ski on the other foot. The skier glided on the *langski* and kicked with the *ondurr* ski. Additionally, there was no effective way of turning sharply, jumping or even stopping.

The man who solved both these problems was a farmer's son from Morgedal in Telemark province. His name was Sondre Nordheim. He was born in 1825, the same year the *Restaurationen* (Restoration) sailed from Stavanger harbor with the first 53 Norwegians to immigrate to America. Symbolically enough, it set sail on July 4. Nordheim, who was two years old when Beethoven died, began to ski as a very young child. At the age of 15 he was adept enough to make history's first officially recorded ski jump. Thereafter, he went on to invent a better binding for skis that enabled both jumping and turning. More importantly, his bindings and technique enabled controlled stopping from speeds of up to 11 m.p.h. That method of stopping, which revolutionized skiing and greatly increased its popularity, soon became known as "the Telemark turn." Nordheim's other achievements include winning the world's first real ski-jumping competition in 1866. Another of his contributions to the sport was his basic ski design which has never been improved upon. Nordheim is remembered today as the "Father of Skiing" in general and, in particular, as the "Father of Ski Jumping and Slalom," and is thus one of the extremely elite class of individuals who have been designated as the "Father of" more than one thing—another was Hambletonian *(see* p. 351).

More important than his innovations themselves, however, was the fact that he taught others how to use them. Two of his best pupils were the brothers Mikkel and Torjus Hemmestveit, from Kristiania (Oslo), who went on to innovate on their own. Besides opening the world's first ski school in 1879, they invented their own style of turning-stopping. This was soon known as the "Kristiania turn" or Christiania. Today it is often referred to as the christie.

During Nordheim's lifetime the trend begun by the *Restaurationen* was accelerated. The first great wave of Norwegian immigration to America lasted from 1866 to 1873. During the second great wave from 1879 to 1893, both Nordheim and the Hemmestveit brothers went to America. Relative to their nation's population, more people immigrated to the United States from Norway than from any other country except Ireland. Today there are more than half as many Norwegian-Americans as there are Norwegians. The effect on the sport of skiing by the immigration of Nordheim and the Hemmestveits is incalculable. The brothers introduced ski jumping to America at Red Wing, Minnesota, and helped form the first ski team in the United States. They eventually returned to Norway. Nordheim, like most of his countrymen, remained.

Like many in that day, Nordheim went west in search of additional freedom and greater wealth. He never found them. He died in North Dakota the year the Klondike Gold Rush began—in December, 1897, around the "dangerous" time, the winter solstice his ancient Norse ancestors had so feared. It was a severe winter. His body was laid out in his house until the ground could be dug the following spring, then was buried in the Norway Lutheran Church cemetery.

Another Norwegian who came to America was two years younger than Nordheim but is far more famous today: Jon Thoresen Rue. Born in 1827, the same year as the Swiss Johanna Spyri who later wrote *Heidi,* he immigrated to America in 1838, the year John Wilkes Booth was born. There he changed his name to John Albert Thompson. In 1855, the year *Haiwatha* was written, he was the only applicant for the $200-a-month job of carrying the mail over the Sierra Nevadas. It involved skiing 90 miles in three days with up to 120 lbs. of mail from Placerville, California, to Genoa, Nevada. It is one of the roughest winter regions in the country, evidenced by the fact that a four-day record 108 in. snow fell there in January, 1952. His success at that difficult job quickly earned him the nickname "Snowshoe Thompson," skis in those days being called "snowshoes." When he started the job, the Pony Express was still four years away. The Pony Express lasted only one year from 1860 to 1861, but Thompson skiied back and forth with the mail for nearly 20 years. His endurance is commemorated by the Snowshoe Thompson Cross-Country Ski Race, run annually since 1945. Thompson died in poverty in 1876, the year the two richest gold mines ever discovered in the Western Hemisphere, the Deadwood and the Lead, both in South Dakota, were opened.

In 1960 a ski historian named Jakob Vaag and the Norwegian skiers who were to compete at the Squaw Valley Olympics placed a commemorative plaque on Snowshoe Thompson's ski-crested grave. The grave and the plaque may be seen there today at Lake Tahoe, just outside Genoa (population 115), which is the oldest town in Nevada and was the end of his ski run. The Olympic torch for those same 1960 Winter Games at Squaw Valley was ignited on the hearth of the cottage in Norway where Sondre Nordheim had lived. Six years later—exactly a century after the "Father of Skiing" won history's first ski-jump competition—the same Jakob Vaag placed a commemorative plaque on Nordheim's grave. It may be seen there today in the cemetery of the Norway Lutheran Church, which is near Denbigh (population 20), about 35 miles east of Minot on U.S. Highway 2 in North Dakota.

Gold has always been a major goal in skiing—natural gold at one time, Olympic gold now. Scandinavians participated in America's first gold rush at Dahlonega, Georgia. Discovery of gold in California in 1848, and in eastern Australia two years later, stimulated the migration to those places of numerous Scandinavians. These men skied, staged informal races, and banded themselves into various Norwegian snowshoe clubs. Real clubs, however, were not organized until later during the 30-year period that started with the gold rush to New Zealand and ended with Robert Womack's great gold strike at Cripple Creek, Colorado, 1861-1891. The first club in the world was the *Trysil Skytter og Skiloberforening* (Trysil Skate and Ski Club), founded in Norway in 1861. The first one in Australia was the Kiandra Ski Club, founded in the Australian Alps in 1871. Interestingly, this was 31 years before formal skiing reached Switzerland. The Kiandra Club was followed a year later in 1872 by the founding of the Berlin Ski Club in Berlin, New Hampshire—the first official one in the United States. The first in Canada was the Revelstoke Ski Club, established in British Columbia in 1891, the end of the 30-year period. That year is also marked by the consolidation of eleven Michigan ski clubs into what was called the Central Organization which, though ultimately unsuccessful, was the forerunner of modern skiing's tremendous organizational structure.

That same three-decade period is also marked by two events which in time had an immense impact upon skiing: the birth of the Norwegian Fridtjof Nansen in 1861, and the publication in English and German of his *Across Greenland on Ski,* in 1891. In that book, which stresses that skiing develops not only the body but also the soul, Nansen wrote that "this sport is perhaps of far greater importance than is generally known." Through him and his book, it quickly became more widely known. Three acquaintances of his who read that book and later went on to their own inspirational journeys were Admiral Robert Edwin Peary, Roald Amundsen and Captain Robert Falcon Scott. Peary, an American, in 1909 was the first man to reach the North Pole. In 1911 Roald Amundsen, a Norwegian, was the first to reach the South Pole. Captain Scott, an Englishman, died in a blizzard after reaching the South Pole only a month after Amundsen had been there. All of these widely publicized events stimulated additional interest in snow and snow sports, particularly in skiing. Though Nansen himself continued to ski up until virtually the day he died, he did go on to other careers. For example, in 1894 he published a paper titled "On the Development and Structure of the Whale: Part I," and in 1911 another titled "Norsemen in America." He became a university professor and was for a time a museum curator. In 1922 he was made the League of Nations High Commissioner for Prisoners of War. In this capacity he toured the United States and Canada on speaking tours. For his humanitarian achievements he was awarded the Nobel Peace Prize—the only skier and the only athlete to be so honored. In 1930, well-off but far from rich, he died and was buried on May 17, Norway's Constitution Day.

It has been said of Nansen that in his skiing adventures he never lost a single life, and by his later repatriation work saved hundreds of thousands. It may equally be said of him, of Nordheim and of Thompson that they invigorated millions of lives through their gift of the sport of skiing. There probably never was an Odin, a Thor, a Tiw or a Frey, nor a Njord, a Skadi or an Ullr. But, among many others, there were those three Norwegians who did turn skiing into a modern sport. They died in relative poverty, but as in the title of that great Norwegian novel by Ole Rölvaag, they are now "giants in the earth."

FORMS: Skiing, which is basically the art of gliding on skis, is probably the only sport in the world with geographical forms. That is, in the mountains or wherever there is snow, its form is snow skiing, the subject of this sketch. In fresh or salt water its form is water skiing. On land in summer, there is sand skiing—for example, on the dunes of Lake Erie near Port Stanley, Ontario. There is grass skiing on close-cut grassy slopes in Germany, Austria, Switzerland and France. Ice skiing is yet another form—practiced during the summer months at the Columbia Icefield between Banff and Jasper in Alberta, for example. Related to the winter-snow form are numerous sports which borrow much from skiing but are not strictly forms of it. There is ski mountaineering which is mountain climbing using both climbing and skiing techniques. *Skijoring*, literally "ski-doing," involves being towed on skis by a horse, a car or a plane—in the case of the latter, at speeds up to 110 m.p.h. In ski parachuting one skis out into space—off a high cliff, for instance—wearing a parachute. Ski-bobbing is the riding of a "bicycle with ski-runners" at up to 104 m.p.h. The Ski-Bob was invented and patented in Hartford, Connecticut, in 1892. Snowmobiling, a more recent innovation, involves speeds up to 128 m.p.h. For comparative speeds, *see* pages 291, 463, and 614.

Within the sport of winter-snow skiing itself are two basic divisions, recreational skiing and competitive skiing. There are various groupings of different forms of skiing in each. The latter, in turn, each demand numerous special techniques, for which sometimes highly specific styles and equipment are required. In general, the basic divisions are causally related. Virtually all competitive forms of skiing were once recreational forms; wide acceptance resulted in competition, thereby making them modern competitive forms. Perhaps the best example of this process is freestyle or Hot Dog skiing, which is dangerous and difficult stunt skiing. Until 1971, adept skiers only occasionally performed such stunts. In that year, however, so many skiers started stunting that official national competition in it was begun in the United States. Today it is a highly popular part of many major skiing events. Skiing itself reflects that same causal relationship between the same two basic divisions. Once purely recreational and utilitarian, it evolved into such a highly sophisticated sport that competitions in some of its events are electronically timed to the thousandth of a second.

Within the competitive division today are two major groupings of events—Nordic or Classical, and Alpine or Downhill. Each is comprised of specific competitive forms. In Nordic skiing, those forms are ski jumping, ski flying, and individual and relay cross-country skiing. In Alpine skiing, the forms are downhill or straight racing, the slalom and the giant slalom, from the Norwegian *slalaam*—*sla*, smooth hill plus *laam*, drag marks or track. In international competition a combination of the results of the downhill, the slalom and sometimes the giant slalom events is called the Alpine Combined. Similarly, the jumping and the 15-km. cross-country events together are called the Nordic Combined. The competitive combination of cross-country and rifle shooting is called the Biathlon.

The major difference between ski jumping and ski flying is the distance involved. In jumping, the distance is 99 yds. from the lip of the ramp to the point at which the hill's slope begins to level off. In flying the distance is 132 yds. The actual distance flown, however, can exceed 192.5 yds, nearly the length of two football fields placed end-to-end. Cross-country skiing events may be over courses of 9.4, 15.7, or 31.3 mi, although one, the *Vasaloppet*, is 53 mi. Interestingly, a cross-country racer's peak years are from 20 to 35, as compared to an Alpine racer's 20 to 28. Downhill or straight racing is, literally, racing straight downhill at up to 120 m.p.h. Yuichiro Miura, who skied 1.6 mi. down Mt. Everest in 1970, reached 93.6 m.p.h. The difference between it and the two slaloms is that the latter are raced through from 55 to 75 "gates," which are pairs of flagpoles. The giant slalom differs from the slalom in that its gates are set farther apart, its course is longer, and the speeds attained are faster, though not as fast as those possible in downhill racing. In all of these Nordic, Alpine and Combined forms, there are rules and regulations and specific distances for men's events, women's events, team events, and others.

Of all sports, the diveristy of skiing events—their demands, training methods and styles—is exceeded only by the diversity of events in track and field. In probably no other sport, however, is there as great a variety and diversity of equipment as there is in skiing. Although all a skier really needs is a pair of skis, two ski boots, two ski bindings which secure the boots to the skis, and two ski poles, there is incredible diversity and sophistication in each of these items. More than 200 varieties of skis exist. They are constructed of wood, synthetic materials or metal, of different lengths and for specific events. A slalom ski, for example, is constructed so that it is more flexible in the middle than a downhill ski which needs to be more flexible at its front. There is a comparable variety of boots, bindings and poles. Then there are all the accessories. These include sunglasses or goggles to prevent snow blindness—snow is the world's best natural reflector of the sun's ultraviolet rays. Creams or lotions are used to reduce sunburn and windburn. An incredibly large selection of special ski clothing has become available since the invention of stretch material in 1955. There are specific varieties of ski waxes for very dry, dry, moist, mushy or wet snow types of skiing.

In view of such diversity, the frequent statement that no one appreciates the snow more than the Eskimos is obviously untrue. They do, indeed, have a whole snow language—*qanik*, snow flake, *qanit*, snow in the air, *qangnerpoq*, snowing, *nivtailoq*, air thick with rain or snow, *nivtaitdlat*, regular snow flakes, *mikissut*, fine snow flakes, *aput*, snow on the ground, *aperdlaut*, newly fallen snow, *apusineq*, snow drift. But Eskimos do not ski at all. To any one who skis, an intimate knowledge of and appreciation for snow is the most important item of equipment.

ORGANIZATION: The organizational structure of the sport of skiing was set during the 30-year period of 1861 to 1891. The actual structure that did develop and which is in existence today, however, began during a 21-day period in 1924 that saw the inauguration of the Winter Olympics on January 25, the formation of a world governing body for competitive skiing on February 2, and the founding in Switzerland on February 13 of the Kandahar Ski Club. The prestigious organization stages the Arlberg-Kandahar (A-K) race. The world body, founded by representatives of 26 countries, was the *Fédération Internationale de Ski* (FIS). Its membership today consists of the national skiing associations of 48 different countries. Headquartered in Stockholm, Sweden, it decides specifications and rules including the rules of eligibility. It also sanctions and organizes international competitions of which the major ones are the Olympic skiing contests and the World Championship. That the FIS has excelled in these functions is both a reason for and a reflection of the amazing growth of the sport of skiing during the last 50 years. For example, at the 1924 Olympics there were 300 competitors of whom 102 were skiers, while at the 1968 Winter Olympics there were 1293 competitors including 612 skiers. For every skier active in the 1920s, in fact, there are more than 1000 active skiers today.

Most of the national members of the FIS are composed of smaller organizations. There are two in North America. The United States Ski Association (USSA) was organized in 1904 and consists today of over 500 ski clubs in nine regional groups, with a total 1976 membership in excess of 109,000. The Canadian Ski Association (CSA, also widely known as *Association Canadienne de ski*) was founded in 1920. The CSA, headquartered in Ottawa, Ontario, has regional, provincial and interprovincial divisions and zones to support a total of some 375 ski clubs whose total membership in 1977 was approximately 80,000. Both the USSA and the CSA, though active in all aspects of skiing including its recreational side, are primarily concerned with competitive skiing. This combination of goals and emphases is shared by numerous other organizations like the Ski East Association in Canada and the Pacific Northwest Ski Association, a division of the USSA with 8500 members in Idaho, Oregon and Washington. The Eastern Ski Association is also an autonomous division of the USSA with 35,000 members in 792 local groups which are themselves organized into 17 regional groups. On a higher level, those same goals are held by the National Ski Council in Canada and, in the United States, by the National Ski Study Group. Formed in 1963, the seven members of this National Ski Study Group are the U.S. Forest Service, the USSA, the National Ski Areas Association, the National Ski Patrol System, the Professional Ski Instructors of America, the Ski Industries America and the United States Ski Writers Association.

This incredible number and variety of organizations is indicative of what is perhaps most remarkable about this sport. Despite its diversity of forms, its worldwide distribution and its relatively recent emergence as a sport, it is among the most specifically organized sports in the world. Every aspect of skiing has at least one organization. In addition to the numerous organizations, associations and clubs dedicated to the individual events such as the International Ski Racers Association and the Ski Touring Council, there are organizations for its areas and resorts such as the U.S. National Ski Areas Association, the Canadian Ski Operators Association, the Canadian National Ski Resorts Association and the Ontario Ski Resorts Association. In the Unites States alone more than 800 skiing areas have ski-lifts. Equipment manufacturers are organized through the Canadian National Ski Industries Association, the U.S. Ski Area Suppliers Association, the U.S. Ski Retailers International, the U.S. Ski Retailers Council, the Ski Industries of America, and others. Teachers have formed the Canadian Coaches Federation, the American Ski Teachers Association of Natur Teknik, the Canadian Ski Instructors' Alliance, the U.S. Ski Educational Foundation and the Professional Ski Instructors of America. Writers belong to the U.S. Ski Writers Association and the U.S. International Ski Writers Association. Skiing's proselytization activities are also organized. The 44,000-member Student Ski Association, for example, arranges discounts for ski trips, lift rides, lessons and rentals. Skiing's community service activities are best exemplified by the Canadian Ski Patrol System and by the U.S. National Ski Patrol System, which has 24,000 emergency-trained members in ten regional groups. All of these larger and smaller organizations fulfill their functions through numerous seminars and meetings, a vast array of publications, and the staging of events. During the 1976-1977 season in Canada, the CSA alone sanctioned over 600 skiing competitions. The first major skiing competitions in North America were held at Red Wing, Minnesota in 1887 and Red Mountain near Rossland, British Columbia in 1896. In the United States such competitions today are held at more than 1200 ski areas in at least forty states—including the fiftieth. Between February and March there is snow on the island of Hawaii's Mauna Loa, which from its base on the ocean floor to its peak is 31,784 ft, which makes it the tallest mountain on the Earth.

Despite such extensive and intensive organization, the act of skiing is still a uniquely individual one. That individualism, Nordheim's basic ski design, and snow itself, are perhaps the only three things in skiing that have not changed since "Snowshoe Thompson" said of his competitive ski jumping, "When my shoes stop running, my back shall be turned toward the outcome and my face up hill." By this he meant that he always felt a greater urge to gaze back at the hill he had just jumped than to know the outcome of his jump as determined by the judges. Twelve years after Thompson's death, Fridtjof Nansen expressed an equally strong emotion unique to skiing when he described it as that sport in which "the whole burden of civilization is suddenly washed from your mind."

British Columbia Ski Hall of Fame

ROSSLAND, BRITISH COLUMBIA

Mailing Address: P.O. Box 26, VOG 1YO. Tel. (604) 364-7200. *Contact:* J. D. McDonald, Pres. *Location:* Rossland Historical Museum, at hwy. junction entering Rossland; approx. 250 mi. E. of Vancouver. *Admission:* 9 to 5 daily, weekends and holidays, October through May, except by appointment. Adults 50¢, children 25¢. *Personnel:* J. D. McDonald, Pres; Jim Heidt, V.Pres; Ernie Pierpoint, Cur; Rossland Historical Museum Assn. *Nearby Halls of Fame:* State and Province (Vancouver).

After Canadian champion Nancy Greene won her second World Cup in 1968, her hometown of Rossland decided to honor her accomplishments with the addition of a Nancy Greene Wing at the Rossland Historical Museum. The British Columbia legislature approved the plan and the provincial government funded the project with $2.00 for every $1.00 the Rossland Historical Museum Association received as a donation. The Museum itself was built in 1967 as a Canadian Confederation Centennial Project and contains artifacts related to the area as a mining center and even includes an underground mine tour. In 1970 the Nancy Greene Wing was officially opened by the skiing champion herself and became the home of the British Columbia Ski Hall of Fame. The special wing contains the equipment and trophies of Rossland's heroine, as well as memorabilia of the first dominion champion, Olaus Jeldness.

Members: 2 as of January 1977. The Rossland Historical Museum Association offered to provide an appropriate place for Nancy Green's skiing equipment and trophies if she would keep them in Rossland. Since Nancy preferred to have them displayed in her hometown, despite offers from the National Ski Museum in Ottawa and the British Columbia Sports Hall of Fame in Vancouver, the Nancy Greene Wing was constructed and she became a natural part of the Hall of Fame. The wing also contained some memorabilia of Olaus Jeldness when it was first built, but the collection grew when the Eastern Washington State Museum sent its collection to Rossland where it was felt it could be displayed more appropriately. Champion skiers like Nancy Greene and Olaus Jeldness are few and far between and it may be many years before other skiers are selected as members of the British Columbia Ski Hall of Fame. When such an occasion arises, it will most likely be at the discretion of the Rossland Historical Museum Association.

JELDNESS, Olaus

Skier

Born in Stangvik, Norway; emigrated to the United States and claimed land in Spitzbergen for the Arctic Coal Co; worked in silver mines of Colorado at age 22; entered mining ventures in booming gold mining town of Rossland; retired to Spokane, Wash; deceased; ashes were dispersed on the top of Red Mountain, his favorite ski hill, in Rossland.

After moving to Rossland in the late 1800s, it was the Norwegian Olaus Jeldness who first introduced skiing to the area in 1896. He began organizing annual ski races and ski jumping competitions, which eventually led to the Dominion Championships of 1900 at the Rossland Winter Carnival. Above all in the Championship, Jeldness won the gold medal for ski running and ski jumping. He also won the McIntosh Cup three times, which entitled him to keep the Cup. A big jovial man, he later instigated the Jeldness Tea Party. Unsuspecting guests were lured into climbing the nearby Red Mountain later to be wined and dined in front of a big open fire. He then sent them down the hill on skis and had an ambulance waiting to rescue those who would not reach the end of their ride standing up. After his 1900 championship, Jeldness donated a cup for future winners of the Dominion Championship. The Jeldness Cup is displayed in the British Columbia Ski Hall of Fame and is inscribed: "Play not for gain—but sport, Leap not for gold—but glee, O! Youth play well thy part, Whatever life's gain may be."

RAINE, Nancy Greene

Skier

Born May 11, 1943 in Ottawa, Ont; raised in Rossland, B.C; British Columbia Athlete of the First Century; Sally Deaver Award 1965; following retirement from competitive skiing in 1968, married Al Raine, former Canadian ski team coach and head Alpine coach of the Canadian Amateur Ski Assn; twin sons; now lives in Burnaby, B.C; Nancy Greene Recreational Area in Rossland named to honor her accomplishments.

From Rossland and the Red Mountain ski area came Nancy Greene, Canada's "Tiger of the Slopes." On her first pair of skis at the age of 3, she later showed promise as a young member of the Red Mountain Ski Club and competitor on junior teams at the age of 14. Three years later she went to the Olympics as an alternate on the Canadian ski team, of which her sister was already a member, but returned to the 1964 Olympics in Innsbruck as a competitor. In the first year of the World Cup events, in 1967 at Jackson Hole, Wyo, Greene became the first person to win the World Cup in the women's division. But she was yet to become the female counterpart of Jean-Claude Killy at the 1968 Winter Olympics in Grenoble, France. Against competition like Marielle Goitschel, Annie Famose and Isabelle Mir of France and Olga Pall of Austria, Nancy Greene won a gold medal in the giant slalom and a silver in the slalom. And later that year she won the World Cup for a second time.

Also in: British Columbia Sports Hall of Fame, Canada's Sports Hall of Fame, Canadian Amateur Athletic Hall of Fame and National Ski Hall of Fame.

Colorado Ski Museum-Colorado Ski Hall of Fame

VAIL, COLORADO

Mailing Address: Box 1976, 81657. Tel. (303) 476-1876. *Contact:* Margaret Randall, Admin. Asst. *Location:* 15 Vail Road, near center of Vail Village, across from the Bank of Vail; approx. 70 mi. W. of Denver, 110 mi. N.W. of Colorado Springs, 135 mi. S.W. of Cheyenne, Wyo. *Admission:* 12 to 6 daily, except Monday. Adults $1.00, children under 12 and school groups free by arrangement. *Personnel:* Don Simonton, Exec. Dir; Margaret Randall, Admin. Asst; 20 mem. Bd. of Dirs. (J. Dudley Abbott, Pres.).

Just opened on February 20, 1977, the Colorado Ski Museum-Colorado Ski Hall of Fame has found an appropriate home in the snow country of the Rocky Mountains. Conceived by several men in Vail during the Centennial/Bicentennial program—Colorado became the 38th State on August 1, 1876—the idea received support from the U.S. Forest Service, the U.S. Dept. of Agriculture and the Town of Vail. Assistance has come from local, State and federal government interests, private citizens, businesses and regional and national corporations. The Museum contains equipment, artifacts and memorabilia for viewing by the public and the Hall of Fame honors outstanding contributors to skiing in Colorado. A two-story structure, the first floor is divided into several areas of interest: 19th century skiing in Colorado, skiing presidents of the United States, historic ski jumpers of Colorado, the evolution of ski equipment, military skiing, ski area development in Colorado, the role of the U.S. Forest Service in Colorado skiing, ski fashions and clothing. The final area is the Hall of Fame in the entrance lobby to the museum building. In the center of this area is a round brass centerpiece which will display bronze plaques, photographs and biographies of the most recent inductees of the Hall of Fame. As the Hall grows, the preceding year's inductees will be displayed along the walls of the lobby area. The first floor also contains a library and a shop with souvenir T-shirts and books on skiing. Not yet completed, the second floor of the museum building will serve as an area for lectures and film programs, to be sponsored monthly by the Hall. Until completed, the lectures and film presentations will be held in facilities in Vail. The Hall of Fame also sponsors a membership program and is planning publication of a periodic newsletter to include facts about Colorado skiing and announce activities for the Hall.

Members: 10 as of February, 1977. For the first elections in 1977 the Board of Directors were called upon to select new members from open nominations from interested people, skiers and visitors to the museum. In keeping with the nearly 150 year history of skiing in Colorado, the first ten members were all chosen posthumously. An independent committee will review and select additional individuals. Presently, there is no limitation on the number of members elected each year, but this may change as the Hall of Fame grows. The first induction ceremonies took place on July 22, 1977, in conjunction with official dedication ceremonies for the Museum-Hall of Fame building. New members were honored at a banquet at The Mark in Vail where official Colorado Hall of Fame plaques were given to their families.

1977

ASHLEY, Frank M.
Skier

Born 1906; resident of Denver, Colo; died in 1976.

From 1934 to 1940 Frank Ashley was considered to be Colorado's finest downhill racer. In 1936 he was the winner of the Estes Park Slalom Race and in 1939 was the winner of the Berthoud Pass (ski area developed by Hall of Famer Thor Groswold) and Sun Valley Downhill Races. Serving the Southern Rocky Mountain Ski Association as president 1939–1942, Ashley directed his efforts toward the development of winter sports clubs. For part of 1946-1947 he was general manager for the Aspen Ski Corporation.

CRANMER, George E.
Contributor

Born 1884 in Denver, Colo; died 1975.

George Cranmer contributed greatly to the growth of the ski industry in Colorado. From 1935 to 1947 he was manager of improvements and parks for the City and County of Denver and was instrumental in developing the ski facilities at Winter Park Winter Sports Area.

DOLE, Charles Minot "Minnie"
Contributor

Born in 1899; amateur New England sportsman; skiing lessons at Lake Placid in 1927 from Erling Strom, champion Norwegian skier who competed in Colo; died in 1976.

Minnie Dole had an idea. It began developing in 1938 when he set up a system for patrolling the national downhill race in Mt. Mansfield, Vt, and grew as he was appointed to study accidents in and the safety of skiing by the president of the Amateur Ski Club of New York, Ronald Palmedo. A final report concluded that there was a great need for trained people to deal with the safety and accidents of skiers; his idea culminated in the establishment in 1938 of the National Ski Patrol System. Dole was named chairman of the national committee. Another idea was formulated as W. W. II developed. After much difficulty, Dole was allowed to approach some U.S. Army officers at Governor's Island about mobilizing American skiers as a well-trained winter striking force, with the National Ski Patrol System as its nucleus. After further discussing the plans with Gen. George C. Marshall in Washington, the First Battalion, 87th Infantry, was activated November 15, 1941, and the National Ski Patrol System was hired by the War Department as the first civilian agency given full military recruiting powers. It was Minnie's job to recruit 25,000 men in 60 days for the Tenth Mountain Division, permanently based at Camp Hale, Colo. This division was activated in 1942 and arrived in Naples for combat in 1945. Upon their return to the United States, members of this famous division were to take part in almost every facet of American skiing.

Over the years, the National Ski Patrol System has spread throughout the country and Europe and Dole has become known as the "Father of the National Ski Patrol System" and is sometimes called "Father of the Tenth Mountain Division."
Also in: National Ski Hall of Fame; and Winter Sports Hall of Fame, Citizens Savings Hall of Fame Athletic Museum.

DYER, Father John Lewis
Contributor
Born 1812; died 1901.

Father John moved from Minnesota to Denver in 1861 to become one of the first Methodist ministers to tour the mining camps in Colorado's high country. He was 50 years old when he received orders to take over the Blue Ridge Mission in Summit County in 1861, and a year older when he received orders for Bark City (Alma), Fairplay and Leadville. To make his treks between the mining camps, Father John made himself a pair of 11-ft. long Norwegian snowshoes (skies) from split logs with turned up tips. Often in 20-in. drifts, he made trips over the 13,188 ft. Mosquito Range, spreading goodwill, the word of God and delivering the mail from camp to camp. He was often called "The Snowshoe Itinerant," and gained the title of Father through his concern for people in the mining communities.

GROSWOLD, Thor C, Sr.
Skier and Contributor
Born in Kongsberg, Norway, on October 28, 1895; immigrated to United States in 1923 after competitive skiing in Norway; friend of many in the ski troops of the Tenth Mountain Division; founder of Zipfelberger Ski Club; member of Arlberg Ski Club; long-time resident of Denver, Colo; died in 1973.

Thor Groswold became a pioneer ski manufacturer when he began his Groswold Ski Company in 1934. Known for the finest skis in America, he provided equipment for ski enthusiasts, especially for Olympic competitors, and for many of the soldiers in the Tenth Mountain Division, based at Camp Hale, Colo. With ski instructor Otto Schneibs, he designed his own downhill skis. This was a new area of involvement for Groswold, who moved to Colorado after emigrating to the United States, and shortly thereafter joined the Denver-Rocky Mountain Ski Club. He was first a competitor, winning the 1924 Interstate Ski Jumping Championship and the Colorado Ski Association Jumping Championship in 1925 and 1926. While he served the Denver Ski Club as president in 1927, he placed third in the Class B division of the National Championships. In 1928 he won the U.S. Western Amateur Ski Association's (USWASA) Class A Jumping Championship and in 1933 won the first divisional Alpine Championships held in the United States; he also won honors in the downhill, slalom and combined events of the USWASA. Groswold also found time to become a top ski jumping judge, experiment with ski equipment and encourage the development of Berthoud Pass, and co-found the Arapahoe Basin area, all the while saying, "You put back into skiing more than you take out."
Also in: National Ski Hall of Fame.

HOWELSEN, Carl
Skier and Contributor
Born in Oslo, Norway, in 1877; emigrated to United States when 28 years old; returned to Norway after National Ski Assn. (NSA) championship in 1922 to visit parents; married and settled in native country; continued to ski; died in 1955.

Through the influence of this Norwegian skiing champion, Steamboat Springs, Colo, has become "Ski Town USA," a competitive-recreational complex that has possibly developed more Olympic champions than any other area in North America. In 1895, back in Norway, Howelsen began competing in the Holmenkollen's ski jumping and cross-country events with the hope of winning a combined victory. In 1902 he won the 50-km. (31 mi.) cross-country and the next year completed his combined victory in the greatest Nordic tournament in the world. He also won the Crown Prince Silver Cup and the King's Silver Cup along with the Holmenkollen Gold Medal. When he came to the United States, Howelsen was a ski performer in the Ringling Brothers Circus and helped to organize the Norge Ski Club in Chicago. He moved to Colorado around 1910. Through his encouragement, the residents of Hot Sulpher Springs hosted their first annual winter carnival with Howelsen as a competitor in the ski jumping tournament. In Steamboat Springs two years later, he instructed the townspeople in skiing and ski jumping, built the ski jump takeoff for the town's first annual winter carnival in 1914 and, with a distance of 108 ft, won the ski jumping competition. Settling in Strawberry Park, this Norwegian champion lived only a few miles from the snow-covered slope now called Howelsen Hill, in honor of his great contribution to skiing in Colorado.
Also in: National Ski Hall of Fame.

ISELIN, Fred
Skier and Contributor
Born in Glarus, Switz, in 1914; father Christof Iselin officer in Swiss Army and founder of Swiss Alpine Troops; attended world famous Rosay School for Boys in Zuoz; good sense of humor; Lt. in Swiss Army; died of embolism in 1971 at age 57.

Starting in Aspen, Fred Iselin influenced the development of skiing in Colorado as a ski instructor and ski school director. At the age of four he began skiing on his way to school and back home. Later he became a teacher and tour guide for ski parties in Switzerland and Austria. As a racer in Europe he won at Brevant-Chamonix, Grand Prix de Chamonix and Lognian, but his most impressive win of all was the Grand Prix de Aiguille du Midi, a race which was discontinued because it was too dangerous. Fred arrived in the United States in 1939 to coach at Sun Valley and represent that club in the *Fédération Internationale de Ski* (FIS) competition. His American victories included the 1939 FIS International Championships and a second place in the downhill tournament at the Auburn Ski Club. In 1947 he moved to Aspen, Colo, as a ski teacher and director of ski schools at Aspen, Buttermilk Mountain and then at his own school in Aspen Highlands. His knowledge of skiing, and his wit, came to life in his best-selling book *Invitation to Skiing,* revised twice as *The New Invitation to Skiing* and *Invitation to Modern Skiing.*
Also in: National Ski Hall of Fame.

JOHNSON, Albert A.
Contributor
"Today he is still that legend—in man's eyes, he still can be seen, in a racer's tuck, the fifty pound mail sack on his back, his eyes squinting against the bright sun, and his scarf waving in the breeze as he rockets down the narrow trail in Crystal Canyon at speeds of sixty miles an hour on the last leg of his homeward journey carrying the 'Snowshoe Express.' " Originally from Canada, Al Johnson, the "Snowshoe Expressman," settled in Crystal, Colorado in 1880 to prospect for silver. But he became a living legend as the town's first postmaster, a post he held for 20 years. He carried the weekly mail and mining supplies between Crystal and Crested Butte on 11-ft. skis, passing through the 27 percent grade of Crystal Canyon, Devil's Punchbowl and the 10,700-ft. Schofield Pass of Gunnison Country. When Crystal became a ghost town at the turn of the century, Johnson mysteriously disappeared, but his legend has lived on.

WEGEMAN, Alvin A.
Instructor and Coach
Born 1900; died 1950.

Al Wegeman was the first ski instructor and coach to be hired by a Colorado high school and elementary school system to teach jumping and ski racing. In Steamboat Springs from 1943–1949 Wegeman developed youth ski programs on Howelsen Hill. Many of the students became members of Colorado's Junior National ski team and some even became Olympic skiers—Hall of Famer Wallace "Buddy" Werner, Loris and Skeeter Werner, Keith and Paul Wegeman, Katy Rudolph, Jon and Jere Elliot and Marion Crawford.

WERNER, Wallace "Buddy"
Born 1936 in Steamboat Springs, Colo; Beck International Trophy 1956, 1957 and 1958; Ski Athlete of the Year 1959; killed by an avalanche on the alpine slopes of Samedan, Seitz, with top West German racer, Barbara Maria Henneberger, April 12, 1964.

In 1960 Buddy Werner was by all standards the unofficial number one racer in the world. He came up through the ranks as National Junior Boy's champion in 1952 to gain international prominence with a victory at the Holmenkollen in Norway at 17. From then on he gathered victories in the United States and around the world: two Harriman Cups, two Roch Cups, a Silver Belt Trophy at Mt. Lincoln, a Lauberhorn Combined and the Grand Prix de Chamonix Downhill. He also became the first American man to win a major European downhill race with a Hahnenkamm Downhill victory. Unfortunately, he did not have much success at the Olympics. A team member in 1956, Werner came back in 1960 as America's hope for a stunning victory only to break a leg in pregame training. In 1964 he placed eighth, but was there to give teammates Jimmy Heuga and Billy Kidd inspiration for victory. In his first *Fédèration Internationale de Ski* World Championships of 1958, Werner placed fourth in slalom, fifth in giant slalom but lost a bid for the combined medal by falling a few feet from the finish in the downhill. In 1962 he lost his way and "spun out in a blinding blizzard." His best year was in 1959 when he won the North American, National and Vermont slalom and combined events and placed second in the North American Giant Slalom. In 1961 and 1963, as part of the University of Colorado ski team, he was the National Collegiate Athletic Association Alpine combined champion. The rest of the world really had to fight to keep their place in skiing while Bud Werner was racing. First recipient of a Wallace "Bud" Werner Award was William "Billy" Kidd for outstanding contribution to international good will and ski ability.
Also in: National Ski Hall of Fame; and Winter Sports Hall of Fame, Citizens Savings Hall of Fame Athletic Museum.

National Ski Hall of Fame

ISHPEMING, MICHIGAN

Mailing Address: P.O. Box 191, 49849. Tel. (906) 486-9281. *Contact:* Ray Leverton, Cur. *Location:* Off Hwy. 41; approx. 15 mi. W. of Marquette, 145 mi. N. of Green Bay, Wis, 220 mi. E. of Duluth, Minn. *Admission:* Free, 10 to 4 daily, mid-June through Labor Day; 1 to 4, Wed.–Sun. remainder of the year. *Personnel:* J. H. "Red" Carruthers, Nat. Chmn; Ray Leverton, Cur.-Mgr; Dr. Russell Magnaghi, Nat. Historian; Marquette Co. Advisory Bd. (Burton Boyum, Chmn.); Marie Hult, Secy; assistants from Neighborhood Youth Corps and Senior Citizens' Council of Ishpeming and work aid project at Northern Michigan University. *Nearby Halls of Fame:* Hockey (Eueleth, Minn, 130 mi. S.E.), Football (Green Bay, Wis.), Archery (Grayling, 195 mi. S.E.).

Just down from Suicide Hill in "Skisport" country is the National Ski Hall of Fame in Ishpeming, the birthplace of organized skiing in the United States. It was appropriate that the Hall of Fame be dedicated there during the golden anniversary of the National Ski Association of America (NSA), now the United States Ski Association (USSA), on February 21, 1954. Plans for the Hall of Fame actually had their start in 1928–1929 by the suggestion of NSA president Harold Grinden. The idea was revived during the 40th anniversary of the NSA by Arthur J. Barth, Harold Grinden, John Hostvedt and Roger Langley when a committee of the Ishpeming Ski Club was organized. At the central convention in 1947 this committee's plans were adopted and, at the national convention in Chicago, November, 1948, a national committee was appointed to study the matter further. After its report was approved by the Sun Valley national convention in 1950 and a fund drive was established by the Ishpeming committee, construction was approved by the national convention in 1953. Now skiing has a place to perpetuate its history and honor its great enthusiasts in a two-story Winter-Land structure. The upper floor features the Honor-of-Greatness display first dedicated on July 14, 1971, consisting of photobiographic composites of each member of the Hall of Fame. Skis, poles, ski clothing, posters, photographs and other memorabilia of great skiers in North America are also displayed there with the world's oldest ski and pole. In the downstairs area are all national trophies of the USSA as well as records, photographs and artifacts related to skiing, some of which are 100 years old. A very complete library on skiing would be of interest to researchers and writers. A recommendation made two years ago was adopted in June, 1976, at the Boston national convention to set up regional museums in support of the National Ski Hall of Fame. The first such museum has been set up at Boreal Ridge, Calif, by the Auburn Ski Club. The National Ski Hall of Fame also produces a monthly newsletter and is beginning publication of monographs on skiing. With a $5000 grant from the Mather Foundation, the first of a series of monographs will be prepared on skis and bindings with a later monograph on the history of the USSA, hopefully to be ready for the 75th anniversary of the Association in 1979. The Association is hopeful that the 1979 national convention will be held in Ishpeming, with an open house of the Hall of Fame and the National Ski Jumping tournament. Since the Hall of Fame operates on a small budget from the USSA and mostly from voluntary donations, the Marquette County Advisory Board has issued a Ski Hall of Fame Commemorative Medallion, designed by Roger Junak. Made of bronze or sterling silver, it has a picture of Hall of Famer Snowshoe Thompson with three other skiers on one side and a picture of the National Ski Hall of Fame on the other side. The Marquette County Advisory Board, consisting of 24 members (probably to become the Society of the National Ski Hall of Fame), is responsible for managing the displays at the Hall of Fame and preparing traveling displays including those used at the USSA national conventions. This Hall is a member of the Association of Sports Museums and Halls of Fame.

Members: 186 as of January 1977. Members may belong to any of four categories: Athlete, Athlete-of-the-Year, Skisport Builder or Foreign Member. Athletes must be at least 40 years old, though this ruling can be waived for preeminence and skill. Athletes who win gold, silver or bronze medals at the Olympics are automatically inducted into the Hall of Fame, and a rule allowing for automatic induction of *Fédèration Internationale de Ski* medal winners will probably be adopted at the June 1977 national convention. Skisport Builders must have made significant contributions at divisional, national and international levels or combined contribution with a competitive career. Foreign Members must have made major contributions to skiing in North America. Each of the nine divisions of the USSA makes two or three nominations a year which are then reviewed and screened by a panel of national and divisional officers and members of the National Historical Committee. Biographical material is prepared for each nominee. Ballots are given to members of the National Historical Committee who elect two or three new members to the Hall of Fame. Induction usually takes place on the Saturday closest to February 21, the founding day for the NSA, beginning with a breakfast meeting at which the new members are first recognized. Later in the morning the photobiographical plaques for each member are unveiled at the Hall of Fame, and in the evening members receive their own special plaques at a banquet in their honor.

1956

BARTH, Arthur J. "Red"
Skisport Builder

National Ski Patrol System Trophy; Julius Blegen Trophy for Distinguished Service, 1947; died January 27, 1956; memorial fund set up in his honor for the National Ski Hall of Fame; Donor's Plaque in Hall of Fame lists fund drive sponsors who provided financing for displays in the Hall of Fame.

Red Barth served skiing for over 25 years on local, divisional, national and international levels. As a founder of the Central United States Ski Association, he was active with the association in some way continuously from 1928, as well as serving as secretary and president. He also served the National Ski Association as secretary, president and honorary director and was a founder of the National Ski Hall of Fame. As a great supporter and fan of ski jumping, he became the first American Olympic ski jumping judge in Europe and organized Olympic and *Fédèration Internationale de Ski* squads. Barth also promoted recreational skiing, junior skiing programs and the National Ski Patrol System.

HOLTER, Aksel
Skisport Builder

Born February 10, 1873, in Oslo, Norway; emigrated to St. Paul, Minn, then moved to Ishpeming, Mich, and later Ashland, Wis; died August 30, 1951 at age 77.

Aksel Holter served skiing in the United States to such an extent that he was even recognized by the Norwegian National Ski Association for his work. As one of the founders of the National Ski Association, he was its first secretary for 15 years, 1904–1919, and editor of the early *American Ski Annual.* He also promoted programs for officiating and instruction.

TAYLOR, Edward F.
Skisport Builder

Co-captain of the Colorado School of Mines ski team; organized the first Rocky Mountain Intercollegiate Ski Association; member of Colorado Mountain Club, Zipfelberger (president, 1952) and Arlberg Ski Clubs (board member, 1954); specialist in U.S. Army Air Corps in search and rescue operations; construction engineer in W. W. II with Air Corps Technical Training Command; member of Gen. Mark Clark's advisory committee on mountain and winter warfare in U.S. Army field forces after W. W. II; NSPS Award 1943; Outstanding Zipfelberger 1943; Halstead Trophy 1950; died November 9, 1957 in New York City at age 56.

Though active in many facets of skiing, Edward Taylor was especially involved with the National Ski Patrol System (NSPS). First a volunteer member in 1937 at Berthoud Pass in Colorado, he became a senior patrolman in 1938 and later a divisional chairman in 1946. As the national director of the NSPS 1950–1955, he helped to persuade the War Department to organize ski trooper training programs just before W. W. II. His involvement did not stop there. He wrote the first editions of the NSPS manual, expanded the patrol to Alaska and Europe and integrated it with the National Ski Association. In other facets of skiing, Taylor served on two Winter Olympics committees and was president of the Rocky

Mountain Ski Association and president of the National Ski Association for two years.

TELLEFSEN, Carl

Skisport Builder

Born September 29, 1854, in Trondheim, Norway; emigrated to the United States in 1887; jumping competitor in the early days of competition in Michigan; worked at Ishpeming National Bank; died 1908.

Often called the "Father of American Organized Skiing," Carl Tellefsen was the first president of the National Ski Association from its inception in 1904 until his death. In his home country of Norway he had been an organizer of the *Trondhjem Skilber Forening* and the organizer and first president of the Trondhjem Ski Club formed in 1884. Once in the United States, Tellefsen joined the Norden Ski Club in Ishpeming. Through a love of skiing, he pioneered many ski tournaments and became a leader in the formation of a national organization of skiing, still a rather new sport in the United States. His outstanding contribution to skiing has merited him the honor of being the first member of the National Ski Hall of Fame.

1957

HARRIS, Fred

Skisport Builder

Born September 8, 1887, in Brattleboro, Vt; deceased.

In 1910 (a year before the first U.S. ski factory opened in St. Paul, Minn.) while a junior at the college, Fred Harris founded the Dartmouth Outing Club to which many ski champions have since belonged. Later, he built the first ski jump at Hanover, N.H, for his club members. In 1922 he was a co-founder of the Eastern Ski Association and the founder of the Brattleboro Outing Club. Quickly, through his devoted work for skiing, other towns began to understand why his home section of the country called him "Father of Skiing." His contributions of the Winged Ski Trophies are highly recognized in skiing circles. He served as an officer in the National Ski Association and also as chief measurer in the 1932 Winter Olympic Games. Twenty years after founding the Dartmouth Outing Club, Harris represented the National Ski Association at the *Fédération Internationale de Ski* in Oslo, Norway. The next year his home club named its ski jumping hill after him, and in 1952 he designed and financed a 130-ft. jump for beginners and high school competitors. Not limiting his scope to the National Ski Association or the U.S. Eastern Amateur Ski Association (USEASA), Harris also contributed materially to skiing as a member of the USEASA Ski Judges Association.

McNEIL, Fred H.

Skisport Builder

Born 1893; a newsman for *The Oregon Journal* in Portland; died 1958; so devoted to skiing that he had his ashes scattered over Mt. Hood; at the 6,000 ft. outcropping of Mt. Hood's west side, a plaque appears in his honor.

Fred McNeil began working with skiing in Oregon where he spearheaded the formation of the Pacific Northwest Ski Association in 1930 and served as the association's first president 1930–1935. From there, he became a divisional delegate, committee chairman and officer. With the National Ski Association (NSA) McNeil was concerned with the recreational use of mountains as chairman of the public lands committee. He worked well on resolutions and legislative action and devoted a great deal of time to ski concerns related to the U.S. Forest Service and the National Park Service. He also served the NSA as vice president for five years under Hall of Famer Roger Langley.

1958

DOLE, Charles Minot "Minnie"

Skisport Builder

See entry in the Colorado Ski Museum-Colorado Ski Hall of Fame, 1977.

Also in: Winter Sports Hall of Fame, Citizens Savings Hall of Fame Athletic Museum.

DURRANCE, Richard

Athlete and Skisport Builder

American Ski Trophy 1939; helped direct the *Fédération Internationale de Ski* Alpine Championships of 1950 in Aspen, Colo; a top filmmaker of ski movies.

Dick Durrance will long be remembered as one of America's top Alpine competitors of the late 1930s. First representing the Dartmouth Outing Club and then the Sun Valley Ski Club, he left record after record for the books of Dartmouth College and the National Ski Association. In 1936 Durrance competed in the Winter Olympics and was selected as a team member for the 1940 Olympics that were canceled. He was on the Dartmouth team that won the first East-West college meet held at Sun Valley over Christmas in 1937 and was the first winner of the Harriman Cup, personally presented to him by Averell Harriman (Hall of Fame member) in 1937. 1937 also brought him victories in the National Downhill, National Slaloms and Alpine Combined. The Downhill and Combined honors he repeated in 1939 and 1940 and the Slalom victory he repeated in 1939, 1940 and 1941. Following active competition, Durrance became a National Ski Association official, and left future skiing champions with quite an example to follow.

Also in: Winter Sports Hall of Fame, Citizens Savings Hall of Fame Athletic Museum.

GRINDEN, Harold A.

Skisport Builder

Lifetime Historian of the National Ski Association; Central U.S. Ski Association Division Medal for Outstanding Service 1952; Julius Blegen Award 1954.

While president of the National Ski Association 1928–1929, Harold Grinden first proposed a special building for American skiing in the tradition of the Skidmuseet in Stockholm and at the Holmenkollen in Oslo. He served on the National Ski Association Hall of Fame Committee from 1934. In all, Grinden served skiing for over 30 years, from creating the Flash Card System of open scoring for ski jumping competitions to developing junior skiing programs on local, divisional and national levels. A member of the Duluth Ski Club, he was president and chairman six times, as well as secretary and a member of the board of directors. Not only was he president of the National Ski Association and secretary for six years but he was a six-term president and two-term vice president of the Central U.S. Ski Association. A ski official and four-events judge, Grinden also volunteered his services as a ski jumping competition announcer for over 30 years.

LANGLEY, Roger
Skisport Builder
Born 1901 in Natick, Mass; graduated from Natick High School and later earned B.Ed. and M.Ed. degrees; married; three children; director of athletics at Englebrook School, Deerfield, Mass, where he started the first full-time junior ski program in a private school; principal of Rice School in Holden, Mass, and High Plains School; NSPS Trophy 1946; Julius Blegen Trophy 1947; honorary director and honorary member of USEASA 1949; American Ski Trophy 1953.

Roger Langley became interested in skiing as athletic director at Englebrook School. In 1925 he joined the U.S. Eastern Amateur Ski Association (USEASA) and attended every annual convention, except one, from then until 1955. He also served the USEASA as vice president and director and organized and directed the first Eastern Junior Championship during the winter of 1930. Langley was also on the 1936, 1948, 1952 and 1956 Olympic Ski Games committee. While president of the National Ski Association (NSA) 1936–1948, he directed the organization of the National Ski Patrol System (NSPS) with Hall of Famer Minnie Dole; Langley holds NSPS Number 1. Roger was vice president of the *Féderation Internationale de Ski* 1946–1951 and editor of the *American Ski Annual* 1941–1954. He continued to serve the NSA until retiring from active work in the organization in 1955.

LAWRENCE, Andrea Mead "Andy"
Athlete
Born in Rutland, Vt; began skiing at age 3; entered junior races while very young; serious competition at 10–11 years, beginning with the Kate Smith Trophy Race; White Stag Trophy as winner of Ladies Combined Downhill Slalom 1949, 1952 and 1955.

A great victory for the United States in women's Olympic skiing came in 1952 when Andrea Mead Lawrence won two gold medals at Oslo, one in slalom and one in giant slalom. U.S. women captured their first Olympic gold medal four years earlier when Hall of Famer Gretchen Fraser won the slalom, but two gold medals was a first in 1952. Since her senior racing career began in 1942, Andy had been preparing for an accomplishment such as this. In 1948 she was on the U.S. Olympic team with Gretchen Fraser and placed third in the Arlberg-Kandahar Race in Chamonix, France. The National Women's Downhill and Slalom titles were hers in 1949 and in 1950 she was part of the U.S. *Féderation Internationale de Ski* squad. In 1951 Andy Lawrence won firsts in Kitzbühel, Austria, the Hannes Schneider Pokal Slalom in St. Anton, Austria, and the International Week in Chamonix, France. In her memorable Olympic year she also captured the National Women's Alpine Combined. Not to stop after two gold medals, Lawrence was first in the North American Downhill and Slalom events, first in The National Women's Giant Slalom and winner of the combined in the Harriman Cup tournament in 1953. Major victories in 1955 were a first in the National Women's Alpine Combined and in three events at the Internationals in Stowe, Vt. The last major event of her fine career was the 1956 Olympic giant slalom in which she placed fourth. These many championships represent the accomplishments of an outstanding woman skier.
Also in: Winter Sports Hall of Fame, Citizens Savings Hall of Fame Athletic Museum.

SCHNEIDER, Hannes
Skisport Builder
Born 1890 in Steuben, Austria; began skiing at age 8; one of the first to adapt Norwegian cross-country skiing to the Austrian Alps; father wanted him to be a cheesemaker, but in December, 1907, set up a ski school in St. Anton with Hall of Famer Luggi Foeger on his staff; in W. W. I served in Russia and Italy training troops to ski; died April 26, 1955.

The versatility and control of high-speed skiing was made possible when Hannes Schneider, the "Father of Modern Skiing," developed the Arlberg, or Schneider, technique. Almost single-handedly he changed the character of skiing "from a gingerly used tool of the winter mountaineer to a sport in its own right." At his now internationally known school in St. Anton, his students progressed through "slow turns on gentle slopes to high speed control." They eventually mastered the snowplow, snowplow turn, the stem turn, stem Christiania and parallel swing, all part of the Arlberg technique of rotating the body in the direction of turns. Between 1920 and 1924, Schneider formalized his instructional system as the first truly Alpine technique and in 1925 the German Ski Association adopted the system and taught it throughout the Austrian Tyrol. Because he was an opponent of Hitler, the Nazis seized Schneider's school and imprisoned him on March 12, 1938, during the Austrian invasion. A year later he was released and the late Harvey D. Gibson, a New York banker, brought him to the United States to reestablish his school at the new Cranmore mountain ski area. With his son Herbert, Schneider took part in the slope and trail development of the Cranmore ski area and assisted with that of Lake Placid, Banff, Sun Valley and Squaw Valley.

STRAND, Marthinius A. "Mark"
Skisport Builder
Born October 5, 1887, in Dramen, Norway; received education in gunmaking and electrical engineering; moved to the United States in 1910; honorary life director of National Ski Association; president of the North American Athletic Assn; president of the Utah Soccer League, manager of the Viking Soccer Club, president of the Norwegian Athletic Club and president of the Male Chorus Norge; during and after W. W. II, chairman of the Utah Norwegian War Relief Committee until disbanded in 1946; died October 26, 1965, at age 78.

A ski jump competitor as a youngster, Mark Strand maintained an interest in skiing throughout his life. In 1916 he organized the Utah Ski Club, one of the first ski jumping clubs in the United States, and served as president for many years. When the Western Amateur Ski Association was first formed, Strand was elected president for four years, and later helped to organize the Rocky Mountain Amateur Ski Association, which he also served as president. He was founder and first president of the Intermountain Ski Association 1938–1944. As a member of the Utah defense committee, Strand was appointed to a civilian ski and mountain patrol post by the Utah governor. Continuing in such activities, he was an adviser to the Secretary of the Interior and reviewed potentially suitable ski development sites in national parks and national forests of the Intermountain country. Also involved in the National Ski Association, Strand was vice president, director and a registered ski jumping judge for 35 years.

WREN, Gordon

Athlete and Skisport Builder

Born in Steamboat Springs, Colo; Paul Nash Layman, Jr, Trophy as winner of National Nordic Combined Competition 1949; Halstead Trophy for service to Colorado skiing 1949; honorable mention for American Ski Trophy Award 1949; Russell Wilder Award for furthering junior skiing 1959; Ashby Award.

Gordon Wren was an outstanding competitor as well as a coach and promoter of ski programs. A participant in all four skiing events, he was the first American ever to qualify for all four events in the Winter Olympics. His best performances, however, were in ski jumping. Competing on three U.S. Olympic teams, Wren received a fifth-place medal in 1948 in the Special Jumping event. He was also part of the 1950 *Féderation Internationale de Ski* jumping team. His ski jumping records were numerous: the longest jump at Roch Run in Aspen, Colo, the official record for the ski hill at Arosa, Switz, and the unofficial mark on the jumping hill at St. Moritz. To top it off, Wren was the first American to break the 300-ft. mark previously set by the Europeans. Following his active skiing career, Wren became involved in coaching and developing skiers in numerous programs. In 1950–1954 he was an instructor with the Steamboat Springs Winter Sports Club and from 1955 to 1959 he was recreational director in Reno, Nev, for the largest ski training program in the United States, 1400 youngsters. Wren became head of the Loveland Basin ski program of Georgetown, Colo, in 1959. As a result of his efforts, he produced many fine skiers and juniors who won over 20 divisional championships and eight National titles.

1959

BRIGHT, Alexander

Athlete and Skisport Builder

Born 1897 in Cambridge, Mass; baseball and hockey in college; graduated from Harvard Univ; Major with 91st Bombing Group in W. W. II; member of Ski Club Hochgebirge and Woodstock Ski Runners Club; married to Hall of Famer Clarita Heath; Silver Ski Trophy from Old Carriage Road Runners "for advancing skiing along sane and sensible lines" 1937.

It is not at all unusual for an outstanding skier to become involved in the organizational matters of skiing following competition. Such was the case for Alexander Bright. Champion of the 1935 Eastern Downhill and member of the 1936 U.S. Olympic downhill squad, Bright served the National Ski Association (NSA) and the U.S. Eastern Amateur Ski Association from the 1930s until 1952, except for the war years, 1942–1945. A vice president of the NSA, he was also on the Olympic selection committee in 1939, 1948 and 1951. And while serving as chairman of the NSA finance committee, Bright instituted Nickel-a-Night, a financial program to raise funds for ski associations. Bright also helped to make progressive changes in the rules and regulations pertaining to competitors and ski competitions.

ELMER, Dr. Raymond S. "Doc"

Skisport Builder

High school football coach in 1911; interested many boys in skiing; active in Bellows Falls Outing Club in early 1920s; special award from NSA for service as administrator and official 1946; died May 16, 1947.

Doc Elmer was a great official in skiing "who stood for a sense of fairness and a spirit of sportsmanship that builds great traditions in skiing." A national and international ski official in ski jumping, he served at many competitions, including the 1932 Nationals in Lake Tahoe, Calif. He was also a member of the Olympic and International competitions committees. In 1922 he was one of a small group that organized the U.S. Eastern Amateur Ski Association at Saranac Lake, N.Y, and served as their president 1928–1946. He was later one of the founders of the Ski Union of the Americas. While president of the National Ski Association (NSA) 1930–1932, he helped develop plans for the 1932 Olympic Games held at Lake Placid, N.Y.

ENGEN, Alf

Athlete and Skisport Builder

Born May 15, 1909, in Nijondalem, Norway; came to the United States around 1914, first lived with relatives, then moved to Chicago; joined soccer team and learned English from fellow Norwegians; won over 500 trophies in soccer, skiing, hockey and ice skating in the United States and Europe; brothers Corey and Sverre are in Hall of Fame; Skier of the Century 1950; Utah Ski Cup 1966.

A native of the Skisport country of Norway, Alf Engen came to the United States and influenced not only competition but the organization of skiing as a whole. In 1931 he won his first of five national professional jumping championships, after winning several regional titles. He continued to win a long series of professional and amateur titles in jumping and Alpine events. Returning to amateur ranks in 1937, Engen captured the 1940 and 1946 (open) National Men's Jumping Championship, the 1941 National Nordic Combined Championship and the 1942 (open) National Men's Alpine Combined Championship. For the 1940 Winter Olympics, which were never held, he qualified for the jumping, downhill and slalom events. After his retirement from competition, Engen helped to organize and direct the Alta Ski School at Alta, Utah, for the Salt Lake Winter Sports Association. In 1948 he went to the Olympics as a ski coach, and in 1949 qualified as a master ski instructor. During and after his competitive years, Engen worked for the U.S. Forest Service as a technical adviser, helping with the development of winter sports areas in national forests in Utah, Idaho, Nevada and Wyoming. He also assisted in the development of the ski center in Sun Valley, Idaho, as sports adviser and supervisor. In all, over 27 ski areas in the Intermountain region bear the mark of Alf Engen.
Also in: Winter Sports Hall of Fame, Citizens Savings Hall of Fame Athletic Museum.

McLEAN, Robert L. "Barney"
Athlete
Born December 23, 1917, in Lander, Wyo; member of Zipfelberger Ski Club; hobbies of water skiing, photography, baseball and mountain climbing; American Ski Trophy 1947; in 1959 foreman at Groswold Ski Co.

Barney McLean began skiing at age 6 and worked his way up to several national championships. As a junior skier he won the Western Junior Jumping Championship in 1930 and the National Class B Jumping event in 1935. As a senior skier he won the Southern Rocky Mountain Ski Association Slalom Championship five consecutive years, 1938–1942, and in that last year he won the Eastern Downhill and Combined events. National victories include the Men's Slalom in 1942 and the Alpine Combined in 1946. McLean's last major win was in the highly respected Harriman Cup Slalom of 1947.

PROCTOR, Charles N.
Skisport Builder
Author of *The Art of Skiing;* member of Yosemite Winter Club, life member of Kandahar Ski Club of Great Britain and Swiss Academic Ski Club; honorary certified instructor of the U.S. Eastern Amateur Ski Association.

Charles Proctor has been involved in skiing in almost every possible way. First as a competitor, he won the Canadian Nordic Combined title, the Intercollegiate Jumping and Slalom Championships as captain of the Dartmouth ski team and the first Mt. Moosilauke downhill race in 1927. In the 1928 Winter Olympics he competed in the cross-country and Nordic combined events. Later he took part in skiing demonstrations in Boston and Madison Square Gardens and coached the Harvard ski team. He was director of ski operations at Badger Pass 1938–1958. As co-designer of the D.O.C. ski binding and designer of many trails cut in New England, he added another dimension to his involvement in skiing. And still another dimension was his membership on the National Ski Association certification committee and certification as a Far West Ski Association ski official.

TOKLE, Torger
Athlete
Born in Norway; moved to the United States in 1939; Franklin D. Roosevelt Trophy 1939, 1941, 1942; joined the U.S. Army on October 1, 1942; first served in the infantry, then transferred to the "Ski Troops"—the 86th Mountain Regiment; killed in action March 3, 1945, while fighting German detachment in mountains of Italy; Torger Tokle Memorial awarded for the first time in 1948 by the Norway Club of New York to the United States Ski Association Ski Jumping Champion; kept at the National Ski Hall of Fame.

Often referred to as the Babe Ruth of skiing, Torger Tokle was a dominant figure in skiing from the time he arrived in the United States. Only hours after he stepped onto American soil, he was inducted into the Norway Ski Club of Brooklyn and rushed to Bear Mountain where he won, on borrowed skis, his first of many championships. In the next six years Tokle won 42 of 48 ski jumping competitions and set 24 hill records. He broke the American record in 1941 at Leavenworth with a jump of 273 ft, then jumped 288 ft. at Hyak, Wash, and 289 ft. at Iron Mountain, Mich, in 1942. 1941 brought him victories in the National Men's Jumping Championship in Seattle, as well as the U.S. Eastern Amateur Ski Association and Central U.S. Ski Association titles. Early in 1942 he retired the famed Winged Trophy at Brattleboro. Unfortunately, his career ended too quickly, but his name will be perpetuated on the Torger Tokle Memorial Trophy.

1960

FRASER, Gretchen
Athlete
NSA Beck International Trophy for outstanding international performance 1948.

Originally from Vancouver, Wash, Gretchen Fraser was the first American to bring home a gold medal in skiing from the Winter Olympics. In 1948 she won the gold in slalom and a silver in the Alpine combined event and received flowers, gifts and telegrams from proud people all over the United States. In 1940 a Silver Belt Trophy was revived by San Francisco lawyer Sherman Chickering and Hall of Famer Hannes Schroll to be held on Mt. Lincoln at the Sugar Bowl in the Sierras of California. The event was a part of the regular racing schedule until 1971, and Gretchen Fraser was the first recipient of the coveted Silver Belt. At Sun Valley, Hall of Famer Averell Harriman's dream-come-true, there was a weekly running of the Diamond Races. A fixed course was set up on Mt. Baldy and any competitor who finished within a certain period of time was awarded a silver, gold or diamond pin. Skiers from all over came to win a pin, but Gretchen Fraser was the first woman ever to be awarded a diamond pin. She also took honors in national events: the 1941 (open) National Women's Alpine Combined and the 1942 (open and closed) National Women's Slalom. Following competition, Fraser became an officer and committee member of the National Ski Association (NSA) and a promoter of skiing competitions in the Pacific Northwest Ski Association division.
Also in: Winter Sports Hall of Fame, Citizens Savings Hall of Fame Athletic Museum.

1963

DEVLIN, Arthur
Athlete
Paul Bietila Trophy for the American-born competitor placing highest in the National Ski Jumping Championships 1942, 1946, 1949, 1950 and 1951; Hall of Fame Award for "Devoted Service to the Sport of Skiing" 1963; completed military service as a fighter pilot with the Army Air Force in 1946; owns Olympic Motel in Lake Placid; internationally famous television sportscaster.

Arthur Devlin has been called more eagle than man for his record as a ski jumper. Only a boy, he was almost ready for the Olympics when they came to his home in Lake Placid. Art had a natural style and a special longing for spectacular, soaring jumps. In 1944, a member of the Sno Birds of Lake Placid, he was a four-way competitor on the All-American ski team, and in 1946 became national jumping champion. He nearly killed himself at the 1948 Winter Olympics, but returned in 1952 for 11th place and in 1956 to tie 9th place, the top American in each case. The eagle in him came out in 1950 when he made a 307-ft. jump at Steamboat Springs for a North American distance record. He would have been the *Fédération Internationale de Ski* (FIS) champion too with the longest jump by 24 ft, but with a few lost points on style he still made an impressive showing with a fourth place. At the 1954 FIS competitions he was the highest placing American in tenth place. Slowing down in the late 1950s, Devlin missed the Squaw Peak Olympic team by one point and then retired.

HAUGEN, Anders

Athlete and Skisport Builder

Presently resides in Yucaipa, Calif; member of Lake Tahoe Ski Club; brother Lars a Hall of Famer; honorary member of United States Ski Association and Far West Ski Association.

In 1974, at the age of 86, Anders Haugen finally received his bronze medal for a ski jump he made in the 1924 Winter Olympics. Back in Chamonix, France, Thorleif Haug of Norway, who won a gold medal in the 18- and 50-km. (60- 96.3-ft.) cross-country and Nordic combined events in 1924, was also declared the bronze medal winner by a miscalculation of scores. Recalculations in the early 1970s showed that Haugen had actually won by 1.75. One of five living members of the 1924 team, Anders Haugen traveled to Oslo, Norway, in 1974 and received his medal in a special ceremony. In addition to that landmark achievement, Haugen was also a four-time National Ski Association jumping champion, the winner of the 1910 and 1920 professional class ski jumping titles, the 1923 and 1926 amateur ski jumping titles and a member of the 1928 U.S. Olympic ski team. Later, he coached at the Lake Tahoe Ski Club and developed many Nordic and Alpine champions. Even at 75, Haugen was directing a junior Alpine program for youngsters in California; his ability surpassed that of many of his students.

HAUGEN, Lars

Skisport Builder

Brother Anders Olympic bronze medal winner and Hall of Famer; member of Lake Tahoe Ski Club; died in Minneapolis, Minn, March 15, 1963.

Lars is credited with bringing ski jumping to the Sierras. He went west with good qualifications as professional jumping champion of 1912, 1915, 1918 and 1922 and amateur jumping champion of 1924, 1927 and 1928. By request of ski manufacturer C. A. Lund, Lars and his brother used a dragline and horse to build what they hoped would be the largest ski hill in the world. Located near Granlibakken, the result was Olympic Hill, officially opened in 1930 with a jump by Lars Haugen. Later, the 1931 divisional jumping trials and the 1932 national championships were held here. The 1932 Olympic Games did not take place in the Sierras as was hoped, but Hall of Famer and ski historian Bill Berry feels that the work of Lars (and brother Anders) indirectly led to the 1960 Olympic Games in Squaw Valley. Lars remained in the area for nearly seven years to coach such Sierra skiers as Bechdolt, Poulsen, Henry and Henrikson.

OIMOEN, Casper

Athlete

1930 was a climactic year for ski jumper Casper Oimoen of Canton, S. Dak. He not only won the eastern, central and national championships but placed eight firsts for a national record. As America's most outstanding skier, he was voted captain of the mythical All-American Sectional Ski Team (once more in 1931) by Hall of Famer Harold Grinden, then secretary of the National Ski Association. In 1929 he had won the central championship for the first time. Oimoen repeated this victory in 1931 when he also won the national championship for a second time. In 1930–1931 he set six new hill records, was selected most graceful rider six times as well and won two state championships. With such a record behind him, it was not surprising that he placed fifth at the 1932 Olympics against the world's greatest jumpers.

SATRE, Magnus

Athlete

From Salisbury, Conn; member of Salisbury Outing Club; brother Johan won National Cross-Country Championship 1927, brother Ottar, in 1935; Gale Cotton Burton Memorial Trophy as winner of National Cross-Country 1928, 1929, 1930 and 1933; Paul Nash Layman, Jr, Trophy as winner of National Nordic Combined 1933.

To carry on in the family tradition, Magnus Satre won the National Cross-Country Championship four times. He was a crowd-pleasing Nordic performer who was known as "the iron man." In 1933 he won the National Nordic Combined and was a part of the 1936 U.S. Olympic team.

1964

MIKKELSEN, Roy Johan

Athlete and Skisport Builder

Born September 15, 1907 in Kongsberg, Norway; winner of many junior tournaments in Norway after 1918; emigrated to the United States in 1924; worked on uncle's farm in Black Duck, Minn, three years, then moved to Madison, Wis, with brother Halvor and later to Chicago; eventually moved to Auburn; married Esther Gilkey, a member of Auburn Ski Club, on April 24, 1937; enlisted in U.S. Army in 1942 and became a part of the Tenth Mountain Division and 99th Norwegian-American Battalion that fought under Gen. George Patton from Normandy to Norway; discharged as Captain in 1945; Silver Medal Award from Kongsberg Ski Club and Norwegian Ski Association for contribution to skiing in the United States; California Ski Association Award 1942; died October, 1967, in Auburn, Calif.

A skiing career that had its start in Norway was to continue after Roy Mikkelsen joined the Norge Ski Club in 1928 in Chicago. After winning the Eastern Championship in 1931, Mikkelsen was selected as a member of the 1932 Olympic team; he became an American citizen that year. At the Olympics he met Wendell Robie, founder of the Auburn Ski Club and leading official of the California Ski Association, who attracted him to Auburn and its ski club, which Mikkelsen joined in 1932. A long string of championships was to follow in the next few years. In 1933 and 1935 he won the National Ski Jumping Championship. Also in 1933 he won the first slalom sanctioned in California. In 1934 and 1955 Mikkelsen won the Divisional Class A Jumping Championship; he won slalom championships in 1937 and 1938 and a downhill championship in 1939. A team member in the 1936 Olympics, Mikkelsen also competed in the 1939 *Fédération Internationale de Ski.* He was on the winning California Jeffers Cup team at Sun Valley in 1939, 1941 and 1942. In 1946, and for many years afterward, Mikkelsen was a ski jumping judge for events all over the United States in addition to his involvement in junior skiing and other programs. When he served on California's Olympic commission, $16,000 was raised to finance Squaw Valley's bid for the 1960 Winter Olympics. As a tribute to a man who gave so much to skiing, the Roy J. Mikkelsen Memorial Ski Jumping Hill was dedicated on March 8, 1970. Maintained at Boreal Ridge by the Auburn Ski Club, the hill honors Mikkelsen for supporting competitive programs of high schools and universities and those of the Far West Ski Association and the U.S. Ski Association.

MONSEN, Rolf
Athlete
Born January 8, 1899, in Norway; emigrated to United States in 1921 and became a U.S. citizen in 1927; member of Sugar Bowl Ski Club and affiliate of Far West Ski Association.

Rolf Monsen was the first American skier to participate on three U.S. Olympic teams, registering the best performances of any American two out of three times. In 1928 Monsen was sixth in the Special Jump event and in 1932 he was ninth in the Nordic combined event. Injured before the 1936 Olympic Games, Monsen was the U.S. flag bearer. Previous to his Olympic career, Monsen won the Canadian Combined in 1922 and 1923, the Quebec Jumping Championship and the U.S. Eastern Combined in 1923 and the Quebec Combined in 1924 and 1925. In 1927 he won every competition he entered, including the jumping, cross-country and combined events at the Vermont State Championships and the Lake Placid Invitational. Monsen turned to judging when he received national and international certification for judging ski jumping in 1938. In 1940 he was hired by the U.S. War Department to train U.S. Army ski troops.

ROBIE, Wendell T.
Skisport Builder
Very active in the organization of skiing, Robie founded the Auburn Ski Club and served as its first president. He later founded the California Ski Association, now known as the Far West Ski Association. At the 1932 Olympics at Lake Placid he met Roy Mikkelsen and was influential in Mikkelsen's move to California. As a leader of the Auburn Ski Club, he was also influential in persuading legislators to approve funds for removing snow to open the roads leading into the Sierras, increasing its popularity as a ski area. With Roy Mikkelsen, Robie was also a promoter of the 1960 Squaw Valley Olympics.

WERNER, Wallace "Buddy"
Athlete
See entry in Colorado Ski Museum-Colorado Ski Hall of Fame, 1977.
Also in: Winter Sports Hall of Fame, Citizens Savings Hall of Fame Athletic Museum.

1965

BIETILA, Walter
Athlete and Skisport Builder
Born February 12, 1916 in Ishpeming, Mich; one of the well-known Flying Bietila brothers (Paul and Ralph also Hall of Famers); graduated from Ishpeming High School, two years at Univ. Mich, two years at Univ. Wis; Lt. Sr. Grade, Naval Air Force, W. W. II; Paul Bietila Trophy 1941 and 1948.

From the home of the National Ski Hall of Fame, Walter Bietila began ski jumping at the age of 10. He progressed from junior class champion at 13 to a second, behind Hall of Famer Roy Mikkelsen, in the National Jumping Championships in 1935. After competing in the 1936 Winter Olympics at Garmisch-Partenkirchen, Germany, Bietila returned to Europe in 1938 to compete in the Obertsdorf and Holmenkollen races. In 1948 he traveled to St. Moritz, Switz, as captain of the U.S. Olympic team. In Class A competition beginning in 1938 he placed sixth, fourth in 1942 and second in 1948. Representative of his talent as a jumper, Walter Bietila won his brother's memorial trophy in 1941 and 1948 as the American-born skier scoring highest in the National Ski Jumping Championships, a span of seven years. A second part of Bietila's involvement in skiing began with Central U.S. Ski Association where he served as treasurer for 4 years, vice president for 4 years, director for 15 years, and many times as central delegate to the national convention. In 1960 the Olympics gained a devoted worker when he served on the Olympic committee, chairman of the ski jumping selection committee, Olympic team coach and manager and chief of the takeoff at the Olympic ski jump at Squaw Valley. Also in 1960 Bietila served as a member of the international competitions committee for the National Ski Association. Not to stop there, he went to Zakipane, Poland, to coach the *Fédération Internationale de Ski* (FIS) jumping team in 1962 and to Norway in 1966 as one of two U.S. judges for the FIS World Championships.

BOYUM, Burton
Skisport Builder
Originally from Timigami, Ont; resides in Ishpeming, Mich.

Burt Boyum was the first curator of the National Ski Hall of Fame and was one of the leaders responsible for the Hall's existence. As a ski sports administrator, he was on the national committee that presented plans for the Hall to the national convention in 1950. Boyum served as curator for ten years.

LITTLE, Dr. Amos R, Jr.
Skisport Builder
Born November 7, 1916, in Lincoln, Mass; began skiing in winter of 1931–1932; first competition was novice race at Gunstock Mountain in 1934; member of Vermont Academy ski team 1935 and Dartmouth College ski team 1936–1939; Western Maryland downhill champion in 1941; Air Rescue Service and mountain and ski rescue activities in 1943–1946; Bass Award and American Ski Trophy in 1960; Julius Blegen Award 1960; resides in Helena, Mont.

With first-hand experience in the sport, Amos Little had a special concern for the needs of skiing. He was not only active in his own ski club but also represented the concerns of his division at National Ski Association conventions as a delegate of the Northern Rocky Mountain Ski Association from 1948 to 1963. Through the years he took on considerable responsibility with the Olympic Games. He was a member of the Olympic ski games committee in 1952, 1963 and 1964, the manager of the U.S. Olympic Alpine ski team in 1960, member of the Olympic Alpine subcommittee in 1956, 1963 and 1964 (chairman in 1963–1964), and a referee for the slalom event in the 1964 Winter Olympics. With the *Fédèration Internationale de Ski* (FIS), he was a member of the Alpine committee in 1950, 1961–1963 (chairman in 1950) and manager of the U.S. ski team at the FIS World Championships in 1962. Dr. Little participated in the activities of many skiing organizations through his active years.

PETERSEN, Eugene
Skisport Builder
Born April 12, 1885, Oslo, Norway; came to the United States in October 1904.

Eugene Petersen joined the Norge Ski Club when he settled in Chicago in 1913. An active member for 41 years, he first served as vice president, then president for 2 years and secretary for 15 years. During those years he also edited at least 75 percent of the club's souvenirs and ski programs and their 25th and 50th anniversary books. He was secretary of the National Ski Association (NSA) 1918–1921. In the Central U.S. Ski Association (CUSSA) Petersen was president for five terms as well as a prominent figure at CUSSA and NSA conventions. Petersen also served skiing as a jumping and competition official.

1966

AUTIO, Asario
Athlete
In the days when skiing was very young, Asario Autio was billed as a former world champion from Finland. In the same year that Hall of Famer Hannes Schneider began his ski school at St. Anton, Austria, the United States held its first national cross-country ski race in Ashland, Wis. As the winner of this race in 1907, Asario Autio received the Gale Cotton Burton Memorial Award.

HEISTAD, Erling
Skisport Builder
Born 1897 in Tonsberg, Norway; settled in Lebanon, N.H, after arrival in United States in 1912; as mechanical engineer designed and supervised building of 13 ski jumps, 7 in Lebanon; also designed steel structure erected in 1954 by Lebanon Improvement Society and dedicated to him; died in Hanover, N.H, May 15, 1967.

Small, slender Erling came to be called the "Father of Lebanon Skiing" as coach of the Lebanon High School ski team for 25 years. Erling Heistad firmly believed in training his men in all four events from the first sign of snow in the fall to the last snow before spring. It was said that his high school team could match any varsity college team, and indeed many of his men became college champions and record breakers. Heistad was proud to claim nine straight years as the Triple Crown winners in eastern school circles and not one broken bone in 25 years. In addition to his coaching responsibilities, Erling was active on the eastern committee to run a school for amateur ski instructors, and served on the national, eastern and New Hampshire State junior committees. As a national and eastern jumping judge, he also officiated at the 1960 Winter Olympics.

LAWRENCE, David
Athlete
Dave Lawrence was the first national men's giant slalom champion. He won this historic victory in 1949 at Slide Mountain, Nev.

MAURIN, Lawrence B.
Skisport Builder
Skied to school as boy in Upper Michigan; military service in W. W. II with 87th Mountain Division; competed for 21 years in Nordic and Alpine events.

As a promoter of skiing, Lawrence Maurin has talked about it on television and radio and has written regular columns in sports and ski publications for over 30 years. For over 40 years he has been a very active club member and has served the Central Division and U.S. Ski Association as a committee member and administrator. As a Nordic official for 16 years, Maurin visited nearly every jumping hill in the United States. For the 1960 Winter Olympics he was the start and finish referee for the cross-country events, and in 1964 he was the jumping style judge at Innsbruck. Maurin was specially honored when he was the first American invited to judge ski flying in Oberstdorf, Germany.

McCRILLIS, John W.
Skisport Builder
Born 1897 in Newport, N.H; member of Mt. Sunapee Area Ski Club of New Hampshire.

John McCrillis influenced the world of skiing as co-author of the first American book on skiing, *Modern Ski Technique,* and producer of the first American ski instructional movies. His first experience with skiing dates back to 1910 when he practiced in his backyard and later became a member of the Dartmouth College ski team in 1918. McCrillis was one of the first to recognize the growth of skiing into downhill and slalom racing and, as a delegate to the Eastern Amateur Ski Association national convention, he helped convince its members to sanction Alpine events. In 1933 he was a referee for the first National Downhill Championships on Mt. Moosilauke.

McKNIGHT, Grace Carter Lindley
Athlete
From Wayzata, Minn, McKnight grew up in the middle of Skisport country. The same year she gained national prominence, Hall of Famer Charles "Minnie" Dole was named chairman of the National Ski Patrol System, the first certification of ski instructors was held at Woodstock and the Canadian Ski Instructors Alliance was formed. 1938 was also the first year of the National Women's Slalom Championships in Stowe, Vt. McKnight was the winner. She also won the National Women's Downhill Championships of 1940.

PROCTOR, Charles Albert
Skisport Builder
Resided in Hanover, N.H; professor at Dartmouth College when active with skiing.

Charles A. Proctor was active in skiing when it was still a very young sport, especially on the intercollegiate level. As a faculty adviser and chairman of the board of directors, he helped organize skiing in the eastern United States and Canada, beginning with a relay race between Dartmouth College and McGill University. Since then, many of the Dartmouth alumni have become very active in the organization and operation of skiing. Through his association with Hall of Famer Sir Arnold Lund of Great Britain, slalom skiing came to North America. Proctor set up the first American slalom course in 1923 and the event was part of the National Championships for the first time in 1935, sponsored by the Dartmouth Outing Club. The Club also sponsored the first National Downhill Championships in 1933. Charles Proctor was involved with skiing in other areas as well. He and Lund supported the U.S. Olympic ski team of 1924 and 1928, and Proctor was an organizer and official for the 1932 Olympic Games in Lake Placid. His research of ski jump flight dynamics influenced the design and competition of ski jumping for the *Fédération Internationale de Ski.* Throughout his involvement with skiing he emphasized accuracy and fairness in rules and scoring techniques.

SCHROLL, Hannes
Athlete
A member of the Sugar Bowl Ski Club residing in San Francisco, Hannes Schroll cleaned the boards at the 1935 National Championships near Seattle, Wash. He not only won the downhill event but the slalom and Alpine combined events as well.

THOMAS, Lowell Jackson "Tommy"
Skisport Builder
Lecturer, famous voice of radio, newsreel celebrity, world traveler; born April 6, 1892, in Woodington, Ohio, near Annie Oakley's birthplace in Greenville; author of 51 books, many best-sellers; resides in Hammersley Hill, Pawling, N.Y, on a 500-acre farm complete with a 12-hole golf course, ski run, baseball diamond and radio station.

Lowell Thomas did his first skiing when he was assigned to the Italian Ski Troops of W. W. I to compile a history of the conflict for Woodrow Wilson. But it was not until the 1932 Winter Olympics at Lake Placid that skiing became an obsession for him. There he was inspired by the talents of Birger and Sigmund Ruud (National Ski Hall of Fame, 1970) to sign up for lessons with Erling Strom (National Ski Hall of Fame, 1972) for members and guests of the Lake Placid Club. He has been skiing ever since, becoming one of the most famous recreational skiers in the history of the sport. At Franconia, N.H, Thomas was one of the first to welcome Hannes Schneider (National Ski Hall of Fame, 1958) and learn the Arlberg technique. He has been known to travel 5000 miles for a week of skiing and claims to have a dozen pair of skis, even a pair of "goonies" for "clowning." It was because of this interest in skiing that his famous radio broadcasts began coming from ski areas like Lake Placid, Sun Valley, Aspen, Donner Pass, Camp Hale, Mount Hood, Alaska, and even from Mont Tremblant where a temporary studio had been set up in the ladies' room of a tiny railroad station. Through his broadcasts, Thomas sold the excitement of skiing to people all over the country and increased the number of ski enthusiasts by jumps and leaps. Not only did he sell the sport, he was very involved with the development of numerous ski areas in the United States and Canada. He helped Roland Palmedo (National Ski Hall of Fame, 1968) and others to finance New England's first chairlift on Mt. Mansfield in Stowe, Vt, and encouraged the building of ski slopes in New Hampsire, Maine, Colorado and Mont Tremblant in Canada. Additionally, he founded the Sahuaro Club in the Santa Catalina Mountains of Tucson, Ariz. Nothing has slowed down Thomas' activity in skiing; he continued skiing even after nearly ending his life with a broken hip in Tibet. For his fiftieth birthday, he skied the 1000-ft. Headwall at Tuckerman's Ravine, N.H, and was still seen on the slopes at 75.

THOMPSON, Conrad
Athlete
The year was 1904 when the National Ski Association was founded and the first Canadian jumping meet took place. It was also the first year of the National Ski Jumping Championships in Ishpeming, Mich. The winner of that historical race was Hall of Famer Conrad Thompson.

WEGEMAN, Kathy Rudolph Wyatt "Katy"
Athlete
After the 1952 Winter Olympics in Norway, her name was romantically linked to giant slalom gold medalist Stein Eriksen; U.S. Olympic team member Paul Wegeman revealed their secret marriage and was discharged from the Naval Aviation Cadet program; White Stag Trophy as winner of the Ladies Combined Downhill Slalom 1951 and 1953.

Originally from Las Vegas, Nev, Katy Wyatt won the first National Women's Giant Slalom Championship held at Slide Mountain, Nev, in 1949. A string of victories followed. In 1951 she accomplished the amazing feat of winning the downhill, slalom and Alpine combined events in the National Championships. She almost repeated the three-event victory in 1953 when she won the downhill and slalom events.

WIGGLESWORTH, Margaret McKean "Marian"
Athlete
Marian Wigglesworth was one of the top female skiers of the late 1930s. Under the managership of Hall of Famer Alice Kiaer, she was stiff competition for the Europeans and usually placed in the top ten. At the World Championships of 1938 she was sixth in the downhill and eighth in the combined events. Back in the United States, Marian Wigglesworth won the downhill and combined events in the first National Women's Championships in Stowe, Vt.

WOODS, Henry S.
Athlete and Skisport Builder
The Dartmouth Outing Club, founded in 1909, was well known for the champion skiers it produced. It was not surprising then that when the club sponsored the first National Downhill Championships in 1933 with the organizational skill of their faculty adviser, Hall of Famer

Charles A. Proctor, a member of the Dartmouth Outing Club won it. Henry Woods has since then served skiing as a national jumping judge and as a member of the U.S. Eastern Amateur Ski Association Judge Association. In 1966 he was still competing in veteran Alpine events.

1967

BLOOD, Edward J.

Athlete and Skisport Builder

Born August 15, 1908, in Bradford, Vt; lived in Hanover, N.H, from 1919 to 1927; skated and snowshoed in prep school and college.

After learning to ski at the tender age of two, Blood entered championships in all four events and the combined during his prep school and college days. His adeptness took him to the 1932 Olympics to place 14th in the Nordic combined; in 1936 he returned to place 36th. While ski coach at the University of New Hampshire 1937–1967, Blood worked on the cross-country courses for the 1960 Winter Olympics and had charge of the start to finish areas during the games in Squaw Valley.

HALL, Henry Christian

Athlete

Originally from Ishpeming, Mich; one of five brothers to ski; Paul Nash Layman, Jr, Trophy 1932; with wife in Farmington, Mich, on two-and-one-half acre farm complete with scaffold hill for jumping 70 ft, skating pond, toboggan run, bobsled track and downhill slope; still teaching Alpine skiing at 70.

Proud Americans stuck a flag into Henry Hall's hand and carried him back to his hotel when he became the first American to establish a world ski jumping record. March 3, 1917, was the historic day Hall jumped 203 ft. at Steamboat Springs, Colo. Four years later, he established another record at Revelstoke, B.C, 229 ft. That was quite an accomplishment for the 1916 winner of the National Ski Jumping Championships.

HVAM, Hjalmar

Athlete and Skisport Builder

Born 1902 in Kongsberg, Norway; moved to Canada at age 19; later moved to the United States and joined the Cascade Ski Club, Portland, Ore; following competitive career, inventor of first release toe iron, first heel-release cableless bindings, with finger-lift latchspring for fit and adjustment rings for different sizes.

In five years Hjalmar Hvam accumulated over 150 ski trophies as a most outstanding four-way competitor. In 1932 alone he won three gold medals in the National Championships: National Class A Cross-Country Race, the National Class B Special Jumping and the National Class C Combined Championship. In Pacific Northwest Ski Association division championships, he won the cross-country, downhill, slalom and combined Alpine events at least once each between 1932 and 1937. In 1936–1937 he won 12 consecutive downhill races, including the "Silver Skis" race at Mt. Ranier, and would have competed in the 1936 Olympics if he had been a U.S. citizen. In 1937 he won 400 points in a four-way international meet at Mt. Baker with a first in downhill, cross-country, slalom and ski jumping. In 1935 at Beaver Lake Hill, Hvam also gained the distinction of being the first man to make a jump in the Northwest in excess of 200 ft.

KINMONT, Beverly Jill

Athlete

Born February 16, 1936, in Los Angeles, Calif; graduated from Bishop High School 1953; brother Bob Kinmont skiier winning 1954 Boy's Slalom; book and movie *The Other Side of the Mountain* life story; married John Booth in November, 1976; resides in Bishop, Calif, where movie sequel is being made.

Kinmont began skiing in 1948, when her family moved to Bishop, Calif. In 1951 she began racing, both downhill and slalom, with Bishop High School team. Since her coach judged her ability as only average, she trained especially hard, and vowed to win a gold medal when in 1952, Andrea Mead Lawrence won a gold in the Olympics. In 1953 she was voted the Sportsmanship Trophy by the American Legion Juniors in Sun Valley, and in the 1954 Junior Nationals, she took first in the slalom and second in the downhill. In the 1954 Nationals in Aspen, she took first in the amateur and open slalom, second in the combined, and third in the downhill. While participating in the 1955 Snow Cup Giant Slalom in Alta, Utah, she broke her neck, which made her a quadriplegic, with no feeling or motor control below her shoulders. Despite her disability, she graduated from the University of California, Los Angeles in 1961 with a degree in education.

MATT, Anton Josef "Toni"

Born in St. Anton am Arlberg, Austria; came to the United States to train with Hall of Famer Hannes Schneider in North Conway, N.H; competed for the Eastern Slope Ski Club; served in W. W. II with Tenth Mountain Infantry Division; lives in Quaker Hill, Pawling, N.Y.

When Toni Matt began his career in the United States in the 1938–1939 season, he was one of the fastest men on a pair of skis. He could cut 5 and 10 secs. off American course records with little trouble, and sometimes even finished 30 secs. ahead of the record time. A little-known fact is that Toni Matt holds the largest winning margin in the history of modern American skiing. In 1939 at the Inferno Race on Mt. Washington, Matt sped down the 6000-ft. slope at 85 m.p.h. to finish in 6 min. and 29.4 secs, one whole minute ahead of second-place Hall of Famer Dick Durrance. In 1939 Matt won the National Men's Downhill Championship, and repeated the victory in 1941, with firsts in the slalom and Alpine combined events as well. In 1950 he was captain of the U.S. team for the *Féderation Internationale de Ski* World Championships in Aspen, Colo. A broken leg in the 1953 Harriman Cup races almost crippled him for life. He had hoped to win again in order to retain his trophy permanently, having won twice before. He served as president of the Northern Rocky Mountain Ski Association 1954–1956.

McCOY, David

Athlete and Skisport Builder

Born August 24, 1915, in Los Angeles, Calif; member of

Mammoth Mountain Ski Club; member of Far Western Ski Association for over 30 years.

Dave McCoy began a racing career in 1936 and three years later won the slalom title at Yosemite, Calif, and competed on the U.S. team attending the *Fédération Internationale de Ski* (FIS) meets. Following his win at the 1940 California State Slalom Championship, McCoy seriously injured his leg in a ski race at Sugar Bowl, Calif. It took four years for his leg to mend and consequently his racing career came to an early end. But McCoy continued his involvement in skiing as a coach for women ski racers and a supporter of junior ski teams. During W. W. II he set up a rope tow at Mammoth Mountain, Calif, and later worked to develop it as a ski area where youngsters could have fun as well as develop their ski racing abilities. During his over 30 years of service to skiing, he also helped many skiers who became members of Olympic and FIS teams—Linda Meyers, Joan Hannah, Jean Saubert, Ken Lloyd, Bev Anderson, Margo Walters and more.

OMTVEDT, Ragnar

Athlete

Born in Oslo, Norway; member of Norge Ski Club and club in Steamboat Springs, Colo; residing in Cary, Ill, at his election to the Hall of Fame.

Ragnar Omtvedt came to the United States in 1912 to compete for the Norge Ski Club Championships that year and stayed to show skiers of the day what ski jumping really was. In 1913 and 1914 he won the National Men's Ski Jumping Championship with a world distance record of 169 ft. in 1913. In 1916 he increased his record distance to 192 ft. 9 in. at Steamboat Springs. He won the National Championship again in 1917. Omtvedt traveled to Canada in 1922 to win their ski jumping championship. At another competition in Ottawa, before the Governor General and a crowd of thousands, he took off from a hill he thought to be 200 ft, only to find out too late it was short by 50 ft. He flew an amazing 203 ft. in flawless style beyond the outrun and crashed on the flats of the river beyond, breaking both ankles. As a member of the 1924 Olympic team in Chamonix, France, he fell, broke his leg and became partially paralyzed. But Ragnar Omtvedt continued to enjoy the outdoors as a cross-country skier. He is responsible for developing one of the world's greatest ski jumping hills at Revelstoke, B.C, where Hall of Famer Henry Hall set a world record with a 229-ft. jump in 1921.

SCHNEIBS, Otto

Skisport Builder

Born 1894 in Germany; learned to ski at age 3; managed own ski school in Bavaria; hauled machine guns in Carpathian Mountains during W. W. I; arrived in the United States to escape the stupidity of war and set up business as a watchmaker; daughter Elvira was a student at St. Lawrence Univ. when father returned to coaching; first Safety Trophy from the U.S. Eastern Amateur Ski Association; New England Council Silver Bowl 1963 for stimulating more interest in skiing than any other person in country.

For Otto Schniebs skiing was more than just a sport, it was a way of life. During his years of involvement with the sport he shared its exhilarations and thrills with thousands of people. He was quite a salesman, starting out a presentation at Smith College in all innocence, "I am here tonight to tell you how to do it and how not to do it . . . on skis." And from there he had the audience enraptured with his lessons on skiing. A desire to teach carried through his entire career in skiing. In the winter of 1927–1928 he held his Alpine Ski School, one of the earliest in the United States, in West Newton and Boston. Lessons were 50¢ for two hours. At Dartmouth College 1930–1936, Schneibs not only coached the varsity and B ski teams but also the speed skating, figure skating and snowshoeing teams as well. Under his guidance, Jack Shea from Dartmouth won two gold medals in the 1932 Olympics. In 1931 he authored his first of many instructional books. Claiming that most books were too technical, he stated, "A beginner, unless he is a mathematician, can't understand them." Retiring to Lake Placid in 1936, he returned to coaching at St. Lawrence University (1941–1956) after his daughter, the director of athletics and the dean of the university convinced him that his coaching services were needed. Otto Schneibs was a much admired man. He has received letters from fans all over the country, including Lowell Thomas, Roland Palmedo, Dick Durrance, Sel Hannah and others. The 1957 Dartmouth Carnival program was dedicated to him. And just a few yards from where he earlier predicted there would be a great ski center is a monument dedicated to him—Schneibs Pass, Aspen, Colo.

TEICHNER, Hans H. "Peppi"

Skisport Builder

Born 1908; Alpine competitor on German National Team eight years; top ski professional at Sun Valley; Diamond Sun Award; Tenth Mountain Infantry Division, W. W. II; died in 1957.

Due to the interest of Hans Teichner in developing skiing, from junior programs to adult education classes, the sport grew tremendously in Lower Michigan during the 1940s. Coming to Michigan in 1946, he managed the Sugar Loaf Winter Sports project in Leeland. He was responsible for overall supervision and development of the project as well as supervision of the ski school, promotion of skiing, organization of races, coaching publicity, tow construction and layout of the ski area. A boom in skiing resulted when he went to Traverse City to direct junior ski programs and coach the Leelanau Schools Ski Team. Through his work on the Michigan Department of Education athletic committee, skiing became a sanctioned sport in Michigan high schools. In addition to his promotion of skiing programs, Teichner also developed the first certification rules, standards and procedures for ski instructors. After they were approved at the 1955 Central U.S. Ski Association (CUSSA) convention, he became one of the examiners and instructors of candidates for certification, and was himself one of the first certified ski instructors. He was one of the developers of Aspen as a ski center.

1968

BLEGEN, Julius P. "Uncle Yoolus"

Skisport Builder

Born in Norway; attended school in Oslo; 1940 NSA head for Camp Little Norway in Toronto, Ont, where refugee Norwegian skiers trained to become Air Force fighters in W.W. II; also in charge of securing funds for refugees; formed a Camp Little Norway with seven others in Minneapolis, Minn; first recipient of the NSA gold medal; Frihetskors Award from Norway for efforts in Camp Little Norway.

In his earlier days, Julius Blegen was a proficient cross-country skier and ski jumper in Norway, where he competed at the Holmenkollen, and then in the United States, where he became national cross-country champion in 1911 and 1912 and was named to the 1924 Olympic team. Later Blegen became indispensable as an administrator in skiing. In 1928 he founded and became the first president of the Central United States Ski Association (CUSSA). In 1932 he went to Lake Placid as the head coach for the U.S. Olympic ski team and served on the selection committee for the Olympics; he served on the committee again in 1936. He has served skiing in other ways too: as a ski jumping judge and National Ski Association (NSA) ski official, on the board of ski jumping for the International Ski Federation and as a member of the National Ski Patrol. In 1946 a Julius Blegen Memorial Plaque and Medal were established by the CUSSA to be given annually to a member of the United States Ski Association who has been of outstanding service to skiing. Blegen's trophies and medals are now on display at the Kilby Idraettslag Chalet in Norway which is managed by his brother, Martinus Gran.

BRIGHT, Clarita Heath

Athlete and Skisport Builder

Born August 27, 1916, in Pasadena, Calif; married to Hall of Famer Alexander Bright; resides in Brookline, Mass; member of Arrowhead Ski Club, Southern Skis (Calif.), Alteburger (Boston), Sun Valley Ski Club and Hochebirgers of U.S. Eastern Amateur Ski Association.

While traveling in Europe in 1935, Clarita Heath Bright went to Kitzbühel and learned to ski. She began winning races, was recommended to the National Ski Association officials as a qualified competitor and went to the Olympics on the first women's team in 1936. 1937 was probably her peak year when she placed higher than any other U.S. woman in international competition. At the *Féderation Internationale de Ski* World Championships, Bright was fourth in downhill, fourth in slalom and fourth in combined. She could be counted on to finish in the top ten of any European race she entered. In 1939 she won the slalom championship of the Far West Kandahar, in 1941 received the Silver Belt at the Sugar Bowl and in 1942 won the slalom and combined events of the Harriman Cup Races. 1942 also brought her the National Women's Alpine Combined Championship. She won the Silver Dollar Derby in 1948 and is one of only seven women to have won the Diamond Sun Award at Sun Valley. In other areas of skiing, Clarita Bright became a certified ski instructor in Austria in 1937, a charter member of the California Ski Instructors Association in 1939 and received professional certification with the Far West Ski Instructors' Association in 1956.

CARLETON, John P.

Athlete

Born September 13, 1899, in Hanover, N.H; graduated from Dartmouth College 1922; Rhodes scholar to Oxford Univ; resides in Manchester, N.H.

John Carleton competed in both Nordic and Alpine events in the early days of competitive skiing in the United States. He first entered the Dartmouth Winter Carnival as a schoolboy in 1910. As a student at Phillips Andover Academy, he participated in skiing and was later captain of both the Dartmouth and Oxford ski teams. In 1924 Carleton was a ski jumper on the U.S. Olympic team. Known for his somersaults from ski jump trajectories, he took the first ski run down the head wall of Tuckman's Ravine with Hall of Famer Charles N. Proctor in 1931 and competed in the first downhill champion race of the U.S. Eastern Amateur Ski Association in 1932. He was also a very active member of the Dartmouth Outing Club.

DOUGLAS, Henry Percy

Skisport Builder

Born August 18, 1873, in Tarrytown, N.Y; moved to Canada in 1898 to work for Otis Elevator Co; later became insurance company executive; author of *My Skiing Years* (1951); died 1956.

Competitive skiing was booming when Henry Douglas skied for Cornell University using 8-ft. skis and steel-spiked bamboo poles. When he moved to Canada and joined the Montreal Ski Club, he became involved in the movement toward sponsorship of organized skiing at the intercollegiate and club levels. His club sponsored Nordic events for clubs and colleges from eastern Canada and the United States, and in 1913 McGill University and Dartmouth College began competing together in Hanover, N.H. This great spurt in the interest in skiing required some sort of central organization, which Douglas founded as the Canadian Amateur Ski Association in 1921. Douglas served as its first president for ten years. The early competitions between McGill University and Dartmouth College led to the organization of the Intercollegiate Winter Sports Union in 1923–1924.

ELVRUM, John

Skisport Builder

Born in Norway, John Elvrum came to the United States to set up residence in Portland, Ore, and become the first champion of the Pacific Northwest Ski Association competitions. He became nationally known when he set a new United States distance record in 1934, 240 ft, at Big Pines, Calif. As a recreational ski area developer, Elvrum began a ski school for California youngsters that led to the development of Snow Valley, officially opened in 1941.

HALVORSON, Alf

Skisport Builder

A native of Berlin Mills, N.H, Alf Halvorson became interested in skiing as a ski jumper and cross-country runner. A member of two of the earliest ski clubs, the Nansen and Berlin Mills Ski Clubs, he was one of five men to organize the U.S. Eastern Amateur Ski Association in 1922. Subsequently, many other ski clubs were organized within the division by Halvorson. In 1923 he assisted Henry Percy Douglas, Hall of Fame member, in organizing the Canadian Amateur Ski Association. In 1932 he was assistant coach for the U.S. Olympic team.

HANNAH, Seldon J.

Athlete

Born November 8, 1913; wife Polly Hannah; daughter Joan Olympic skier, third in giant slalom of 1962 *Fédération Internationale de Ski* World Championships.

Seldon Hannah was already skiing at age 4, and has since skied down over 250 mountains in North America. He has been a part of skiing, from instructing paratroops in Alta, Utah, in 1942 to involving himself with the design and construction of snow sports facilities. As a competitor, Hannah won one of his first races in 1926, his divisional Class C jumping competitions. In 1932–1935 he represented Darmouth College as a four-way competitor and was team captain in his senior year. In 1936 he represented McGill University, winning the Ski Union cross-country and the Nordic Combined Championship of Montreal and the Dominion of Canada. Before coaching at Dartmouth in 1945, Hannah won the Eastern Downhill Championship in 1941 and the Franconia Cross-Country Championship in 1948. Still skiing in the 1950s, he won the Senior National Slalom Championship in 1954, placed second in the Combined and third in the Downhill, and was third in the Eastern Amateur Veterans' Class Four. A "skier's skier," Seldon Hannah won 85 ski trophies in his competitive days. As an administrator, he has been president of the Franconia Ski Club and director of the Eastern Amateur Ski Association.

KOTLAREK, George

Athlete

A native of Denver, Colo; has two sons in junior ski program; presently vice president of the Duluth Ski Club.

George started his skiing on a local level in his home club. In 1927 he won the small boy's National Ski Association title Class D at Denver, Colo. He is a member of the Duluth Ski Club. George has won the Duluth city title 12 times, in a period of more than 25 years, and has a long record of wins in divisional and out of division ski jumping competitions. He has won national titles in Class D, Class C and Class A. In 1932, he won the Central U.S. Ski Association Class B title and was then elected to Class A. In 1947 he entered the Veterans Division. In 1947, 1952 and 1954 he won the CUSSA Veterans title. In 1947, 1948, 1950 and 1954 he won the NSA Veterans title. George has served his local club well as an officer and director.

LUNN, Sir Arnold

Foreign Member

Born 1888 in India; father was a medical missionary who later saw possibility of winter sports for a large public and founded the travel agency known as Sir Henry Lunn, Ltd; skied for the first time in 1898; a mountaineering fall in Wales made one leg shorter than the other by 2 in. but he continued to ski; author of more than 50 books on philosophy, mountaineering and skiing; wrote *History of Skiing* (1927) and *Story of Skiing* (1953); edited the *British Ski Year-Book* for more than 50 years; knighted by Queen Elizabeth in 1952 for "services to British skiing and Anglo-Swiss relations"; died 1974.

Sir Arnold Lunn was an innovator in skiing who set up both the first downhill ski race and slalom courses. In 1908 he founded the Alpine Ski Club, then began to organize a downhill race for January 7, 1911. Named after Lord Roberts of Kandahar who donated the Challenge Cup, the race has been compared to that of the Olympics and the *Fédération Internationale de Ski* (FIS) World Championships. The first modern slalom course was set up by Lunn in Murren in 1922, after which he founded the Kandahar Ski Club in Murren. By invitation of Hannes Schneider, Lunn set the first slalom course in Austria for a 1972 schoolboy race in St. Anton. This prompted the first Arlberg-Kandahar downhill slalom race held on March 3 and 4, 1928, and the establishment of many Kandahars throughout the world such as the Scotland, Quebec, Far West, Yosemite and New England Kandahars. Seeing a need for uniform competition, he also drafted the first downhill-slalom racing rules accepted at the 1930 FIS convention. Slalom spread quickly, but Lunn was to become critical of its development away from the more natural zigzagging among the trees. Lunn made vital contributions to the development of the U.S. Women's ski team and was generous in releasing Hall of Famer Helen McAlpin from the British team to become the first U.S. woman to participate in international competition. With the popularity of slalom and downhill competition, the events became part of the Winter Olympics in 1935, with Lunn as a referee for the men's slalom.

MANGSETH, Ole R.

Athlete and Skisport Builder

Born in Elverum, Norway; two sons, Ronald and Rolf, who are past national boy's champions; died 1953 in Cokeraine, Minn.

Ole placed second during the national tourneys of 1905 and 1906. He established a national distance record of 114 ft. in 1907. In the national tourneys of 1909 and 1910, he placed fourth. He was considered among the top-flight ski jumpers in the pioneering days of the National Ski Association (NSA). Ole was very much involved in the development of junior skiers and served the NSA and the United States Ski Association for 48 years.

McALPIN, Helen Bendelari Goughton-Leigh

Athlete

Born in Cleveland, Ohio; married to Malcolm McAlpin, member of the championship U.S. Olympic hockey team in 1936.

Primarily a slalom competitor, Helen McAlpin was the first American woman to take part in international competition. She first competed for Britain, qualifying for the Kandahar Ski Club in 1928 and passing the first class test for the Ski Club of Great Britain in 1929. Throughout 1928–1934 she won many Kandahar races, finally the Kandahar Diamond K for downhill and slalom, and was a slalom winner in St. Anton in the Arlberg Jubilee in 1932. She was also on Britain's teams in the 1932, 1933 and 1934 *Fédération Internationale de Ski* (FIS) meets. With a release from Sir Arnold Lunn of Britain, McAlpin returned to the United States to captain the U.S. FIS team in 1935 and finish seventh in the combined race. In 1936 she was team captain and competitor of the U.S. Olympic team, but retired from racing in 1937 to help organize the Snow Chasers' Club in Morristown, N.J.

PALMEDO, Roland

Skisport Builder

Graduated from Williams College, and started the Williams Outing Club in 1915.

Palmedo was one of the main organizers of the National Ski Association's (NSA) first international ski teams in 1934. He helped to organize a women's team in 1935 with Alice Kiaer, as well as the 1936 Olympic women's team. In 1937 he was the head of the NSA International competition committee, a member of the Congress of the Ski Union of the Americas, founder and president of the Ski Club of New York and honorary member of the Ski Club of Great Britain, the Kandahar Ski Club, Ski Club Chile, Club Andine Boliviano and Mt. Mansfield Ski Club. In 1949 he established the Mad River Glen in Vermont. He was a U.S. Ski Association official and author of *Skiing, the International Sport.*

PEDERSON, Ernest O.

Athlete

Born April 3, 1907 in Berlin, N.H; attended Univ. of N.H; Rifle Company Commander, 87th Mountain Infantry, regimental director of ski school and then executive officer of the Mountain Welfare Training Center at Camp Hale in Colorado; retired from military service 1967; resides at Springfield, Mass; teaches mathematics at Springfield Trade School.

Ernest began his ski career in 1925, winning the Boy's Jumping Championship of the United States Eastern Amateur Ski Association at Brattleboro, Vt. He was a nationally famous ski star at the University of New Hampshire. Ernest competed and won in the Intercollegiate Winter Sports Union, an international competition involving Americans and Canadians. In 1927, 1928 and 1930 Ernest was the all-around champion, as well as capturing numerous honors in jumping, cross-country, downhill and slalom. Ernest represented the United States Eastern Amateur Ski Association in divisional and national tourneys. In 1928 he was among the 15 men named eligible for the U.S. Olympic team, but did not compete because of financial problems. He is considered among the earliest truly great native-born four-way competitors in jumping, cross-country, downhill and slalom.

1969

BATSON, LeMoine

Athlete

Born 1898 in Eau Claire, Wis, LeMoine Batson became the first American youth named to the U.S. Olympic team in 1924. Selected as an alternate for the team in 1932, Batson entered ski competitions from 1917 to 1939. On an administrative level, he served as chairman of the Central Ski Association meeting in 1925 and was president of the Association in 1939–1940 when it incorporated slalom and downhill clubs in its membership.

BOWER, John

Athlete

Paul Nash Layman, Jr, Trophy as winner of National Nordic Combined Competition 1963, 1966–1968.

John Bower has proven to be the best Nordic champion in American skiing as well as an accomplished four-way skier. He won the National Nordic Championship in 1963 and then repeated the victory three consecutive times, 1966–1968. The United States will never forget when he became the first, and so far the only, American to win the Homenkollen Cross-Country and Combined in 1968, the world's most coveted ski honor. As a result, an age waiver was approved for this 28-year-old in 1969 for induction into the Hall of Fame.

BRADLEY, Dr. Harold C. "Doc"

Skisport Builder

Born in 1879; moved to Wisconsin at age 28 to become chemistry professor at Univ. Wis. Medical School; seven sons: Charles a jumper and Tenth Mountain Trooper; Harold, Jr, ski jumping dropout turned mountain climber; David national four-way competitor and manager of 1960 U.S. Olympic team; Steve four-event skier, now manager of Colorado Winter Park; Joseph devoted ski fan; Richard four-way skier and skiiing mountaineer; William all-around skier and Tenth Mountain Trooper; also one daughter.

After a move from California to Wisconsin, Harold Bradley became interested in skiing too late to be a competitor, but greatly influenced the growth of skiiing in the United States. When his daughter, Mary Cornelia, died at age 7, the Bradleys set up a memorial trophy to complement Averell Harriman's Bradley Plate as a four-event individual championship at Sun Valley. The first winners were Kathleen Harriman and Steve Bradley. It was also Dr. and Mrs. Bradley who established the Paul Bietila Trophy for the National Ski Association in 1940, as they had sponsored the "Flying Bietila" at the University of Wisconsin. As secretary of the Central Ski Association, he encouraged an interest in skiing that eventually led to the founding of the University of Wisconsin's Hoofer's Club. He and his wife, with faculty and students from the University of Wisconsin, started a winter vacation trend that encouraged the development of Michigan's Upper Peninsula, Sun Valley and ski areas in Colorado. Bradley enjoyed exploring the Sierras and in 1920 followed the trail of Snow-Shoe Thompson from Placerville to Truckee. In 1925 with the Sierra Ski Club, he skied Donnor Summit and in 1935, with son Charles, crossed the Tioga Pass from Lee Vining to Yosemite National Park. In 1947 he went into the High Sierras with Lee Vining for six weeks. He was still skiing at the age of 85.

GILLIS, Rhona Wurtele

Athlete

Originally from Montreal, Que, Rhona Gillis came to the United States to win four national championships: the National Slalom in 1946, the Giant Slalom in 1952 and the National Combined in 1946 and 1947. Early fame came for both her and her twin sister Rhoda, as members of the Penguin Ski Club in Montreal, followed by international recognition in the Kate Smith Trophy competition of 1943 in Lake Placid, N.Y. The competition was set up for Canadian and American women's downhill and slalom racers to forge a link of goodwill between the two nations; Rhona and her sister, along with two Americans, Paula Kann and Rebecca Fraser, took the top honors. During her career Rhona represented both the Canadian Amateur Ski Association and the National Ski Association.

HARRIMAN, William Averell
Skisport Builder
Born November 11, 1891; graduated from Yale Univ. 1913; married Kitty Lanier Lawrence in 1915 (divorced in 1930); two daughters, Mary and Kathleen; second to Mrs. Marie Norton Whitney in 1930 (died in 1970); third to Pamela Digby Churchill Hayward in 1971; became special representative to Great Britain and U.S. ambassador to the U.S.S.R. under President Franklin Roosevelt; ambassador to Great Britain and secretary of commerce under President Truman; governor of New York in 1955 – 1958, U.S. ambassador-at-large in 1961 and 1965 – 1969 and U.S. representative at Vietnam peace talks in Paris in 1968 – 1969; author; resides in Washington, D.C.

The Sun Valley ski area was the inspiration of Averell Harriman, as chairman of the board for the Union Pacific Railroad Co, to encourage people to travel west on the company's new streamlined passenger trains. In 1936 Harriman sent Count Felix Schaffgotsch to locate an area for a ski resort. The Austrian Alpine expert spent six weeks traveling through Washington, Oregon, Colorado, California and Utah until he arrived at Ketchum, Idaho, where the slopes were more impressive than anywhere else in the United States. The railroad bought 43,000 acres at $3 million—during the depression. Architects began plans, engineers from the railroad designed the first chairlifts in the world and up went the first resort in the United States designed primarily for winter sports. Since the establishment of Sun Valley, Harriman has given his backing to competitive college skiing by holding a four-way intercollegiate tournament at Christmas in Sun Valley for many years. He also founded the Harriman Cup Ski Tournament and personally awarded the Cup to Dick Durrance, international skier, in 1937 and 1940, and made the presentation in Sun Valley as often as his duties abroad would permit.

HICKS, Harry Wade
Skisport Builder
Born in 1872; died in 1960.

A builder of skiiing in every sense, Harry Hicks was secretary of the Lake Placid Club when it placed the sport on an organized basis beginning in 1904, the same year the National Ski Association was founded in Ishpeming. In 1932 he was director of the Olympic Winter Games at Lake Placid and later was chairman of the New York State committee on skiing, helping to make the Whiteface ski area a reality at Lake Placid. He also worked with the National Park Service to develop recreation areas throughout the country and with the National Ski Association in Nordic, Alpine and Intercollegiate skiing. At the request of the National Ski Association in 1939, Hicks prepared and published a survey, *Cross-Country Skiing,* from communications with ski leaders across the country and predicted the direction cross-country skiing would take in the future. He also published *Community Organization for Winter Sports* (1936), which emphasized the importance of outdoor activity during winter months as well as at other times of the year. His most notable accomplishment was the founding of the U.S. Eastern Amateur Ski Association in 1926; he served as its president 1926 – 1927.

HOSTVEDT, John
Skisport Builder
Born April 18, 1904 in Grand Rapids (now Wisconsin Rapids), Wis; banker by profession; Julius Blegen Award 1949; Central Division Silver Anniversary Award for "outstanding promotion of the sport by serving the local, divisional and national organization" 1952.

A native of skisport country, John Hostvedt, together with Hall of Famers Harold Grinden, Arthur J. Barth and Roger Langley, created the National Ski Hall of Fame in 1954. Hostvedt was treasurer of the National Ski Association at the time (1943 – 1954) and had already served skiing in many ways. He had previously been treasurer of the Central Ski Association 1933 – 1949. He was an organizer of the Tri-Norse Ski Club in Wisconsin Springs as well as the Central Ski Officials Association. On a national and international level he represented the National Ski Association in 1935 at the *Fédération Internationale de Ski* congress in Germany. He served as an official at the 1936 Winter Olympics and the World Championships at Lake Placid in 1950. In the latter years of his service, his objectives were aimed toward the establishment of a Hall of Fame to preserve the history of skiing.

HOWELSEN, Carl
Athlete
See entry in Colorado Ski Museum-Colorado Ski Hall of Fame, 1977.

KIAER, Alice Damrosch Wolfe
Skisport Builder
Born in 1893; learned to ski in 1930 on a mountain expedition in Switzerland; won Parsenn Derby at Davos, Switz, 1931; died 1967.

Alice Kiaer was involved with women's affairs in the National Ski Association (NSA) for over 30 years, and was largely responsible for gathering together a women's ski team that could finally compete with the Europeans. With Roland Palmedo she assembled women skiers and was manager for the 1935 *Fédération Internationale de Ski* (FIS) World Championships, in which Hall of Famer Helen McAlpin raced, and was manager for the women's team in the 1936 Winter Olympics. She hired Walter Haensli to coach the 1948 U.S. Olympic women's ski team and went as a chaperon to witness Gretchen Fraser's gold medal victory in the slalom. For the NSA she served on the Women's subcommittee and was the first woman to represent the NSA at the FIS congress in 1938, going again as a representative in 1949, 1951 and 1953. In 1952 she was chairman of the Olympic selection committee for women. For the 1950 FIS World Championships in Lake Placid, N.Y, and Aspen, Colo, Kiaer worked with the New York City reception committee, opening up her house and providing sight-seeing tours for the visiting team members. As members of the Olympic Ski Games committee, she and Mrs. Stanley Mortimer outfitted the women's team for the Olympics, and in close association with the World Game committee, was chaperon, manager and adviser for teams traveling to Europe in 1954. In 1960 Kiaer was involved with the reception committees for the Olympics in Squaw Valley.
Also in: Winter Sports Hall of Fame, Citizens Savings Hall of Fame Athletic Museum.

LEACH, Col. George Emerson
Skisport Builder
Born 1876; Minneapolis mayor four terms during the time it was known as the "Ski Capital of America"; fought in W. W. I; decorated with medals, including Order of the Knight of St. Olaf; died in 1955.

Europeans did not think much of the growth of skiing in the United States when Col. Leach was selected to represent the National Ski Association (NSA) at the International Ski Congress in 1924. Only recently have some of the U.S. ski team members been reinstated to amateur status and the NSA's professional class outlawed. Through Leach's able leadership, the NSA became a member of the Congress and the United States has become very much a part of international competition. Leach also managed the first U.S. Olympic team in 1924, consisting of Hall of Famers Sigurd Overby, Ragnar Omtvedt, Harry Lien, Lemone Batson, John Carleton and Anders Haugen. And it has recently been discovered that Anders Haugen placed third, rather than fourth, in the special ski jumping competition for a bronze medal, an impressive accomplishment for the first U.S. Olympic team.

LIEN, Harry
Athlete
Born 1895 in Norway; served in U.S. Army in W. W. I; emigrated to the United States in 1921; carpenter by profession.

After a competitive career in Norway prior to W. W. I, Harry Lien was a member of the first U.S. Olympic team in 1924. He had become a member of the Norge Ski Club in 1922 and won tournaments and awards for the longest standing and most graceful ski jumps and placed well in many tournaments in the United States and Canada. He was also involved with the development of skiing through the Sons of Norway.

McCULLOCH, Ernie
Athlete
Born 1926 in Three Rivers, Que; learned to ski at age 4; ski jumping ace in eastern Canada at 14; member of Sun Valley and Mont Tremblant Ski Clubs; resides in Mont Tremblant, Que.

Voted the Skier of the Half Century by a board of well-known sportswriters, Ernie McCulloch had a phenomenal career between 1950 and 1953. World press called him the "Grand Slam Champion" when he won the National Giant Slalom (Alta, Utah), the North American Championship (Aspen, Colo.), the National Downhill Championship (Whitefish, Mont.), and the Harriman Cup (Sun Valley, Idaho). In 1949 McCulloch went to Sun Valley to enter the Harriman Cup Races and stayed to teach and compete in the open class. In 1950 he tied with Jack Reddish for the National Men's Slalom Championship and won the National Men's Alpine Combined in both 1950 and 1951. He repeated a victory in the Harriman and won the National Downhill Championship again in 1952. Additionally, McCulloch won many Canadian championships, coached American and Canadian national team members and the Canadian demonstration team at the World Ski Congress in 1964, and was one of four coaches at the summer ski racing school at Oregon's Mt. Hood. McCulloch has also written instructional booklets and has served as chief examiner of the Canadian Ski Instructors' Alliance.

PABST, Fred
Skisport Builder
Born April 12, 1899, in Milwaukee, Wis; learned business administration at Harvard and worked in family brewery for a time; resides in Manchester, N.H.

Throughout the 1920s and 1930s, Fred Pabst busily promoted the growth of skisport in the eastern United States. His first venture was organizing the Badger Ski Club and encouraging the construction of a jumping scaffold at the University of Wisconsin. In 1925 his interests spread to developing a junior ski program that would educate 400 youngsters in the art of ski jumping at Milwaukee Ski Club. Touring Europe in 1926–1927, Pabst became a member of the Ski Club of Great Britain, participating in its downhill and slalom tests, enrolled in Hall of Famer Hannes Schneider's ski school at St. Anton and taught youngsters ski jumping at Zermatt. Upon his return to the United States, Pabst began developing ski areas at Ste. Sauver, Que, where he set up several rope tows and encouraged snow trains to bring people from Montreal. He also set up rope tows at Stowe, Vt, Lake Placid and Ticonderoga, N.Y, Houghton and Iron Mountain, Mich, and Minneapolis, Minn. When business commitments limited his time, Pabst concentrated his efforts on lecturing, advertising and promoting his ski resort at Big Bromley. It opened in 1941 and became the East's first major snow-making operation in 1965.

RAINE, Nancy Greene
Athlete
See entry in British Columbia Ski Hall of Fame. *Also in:* British Columbia Sports Hall of Fame, Canada's Sports Hall of Fame and Canadian Amateur Athletic Hall of Fame.

REDDISH, Jack
Athlete
Resides in Beverly Hills, Calif, with wife Paula; three children; movie director.

Jack Reddish won almost every Intermountain and American award offered and several European awards in a competitive career that began in 1939. Representing the Alta Ski Club in 1942, he became the youngest competitor, at 14, to jump Ecker Hill and win the Class B Championship. After winning the Alta Cup in 1945 and the Bradley Four-Way Championship in 1947, Reddish experienced the most successful year of his career in 1948. At the Nationals he won the downhill, slalom and combined events, then went to Europe to place seventh in the Olympic slalom and win the Kandahar race, a feat never duplicated by another American. He again won the National Slalom and Combined Championships in 1950 and 1952.

SMITH-JOHANNSEN, Herman "Jack Rabbit"
Skisport Builder
Born June 15, 1875, in Herten, Norway; trained in Norwegian army; emigrated to Canada via Cleveland, Ohio; married to Alice Robinson; degree in civil engineering; engineer for Panama Canal project.

An engineer by profession, when Smith-Johannsen arrived in Canada, he developed many ski trails: Maple Leaf Trail in the Laurentians, the Canadian West and Canada's eastern townships. He even developed trails in Stowe, Vt, and Sun Valley, Idaho. Saying that slalom developed from cross-country runners avoiding natural obstacles, he he set the first slalom run at St. Sauver in 1927. A skier himself, Smith-Johannsen had a cabinet full of trophies and was still beating racers many years his junior at the age of 60. The Canadian Schoolboy Ski Championships are now named in his honor.

STEINWALL, Siegfried

Athlete and Skisport Builder

Born 1893 in Sweden; enjoyed gymnastics and always in top physical condition; gave up skiing in 1965 due to heel injury; lifetime member of the Swedish Ski Club, New York.

Sig has been part of skiing in three countries, Sweden, the United States and Canada, in a span of over 60 years. In Sweden he was honored with the Fiskartorp-spokalen Cup, the highest distinction for a Swedish jumper, as a four-time entrant in the Holmenkollen. First in the Boys' Class in 1913, his home team of 1914 outscored the Norwegians and the Finns; he then entered as a Class B in 1915 and Class A in 1917. In the United States Sig founded the Swedish Ski Club of New York and was invited to Chicago in 1918 by the Norge Ski Club to become the top-rated amateur jumper in the United States. He visited the world's largest jumping hill in Revelstoke, B.C, then traveled to Banff and Calgary in Alberta and Dillon and Steamboat Springs in Colorado. Sig was ski director and coach at Dartmouth 1927 – 1928. As part of exhibition skiing for 33 years, visitors to the Century of Progress Fair in Chicago in 1934 saw him perform, as well as visitors to the New York's Fair in 1839 – 1940, where he made 1000 leaps and was one of 14 foreign-born American athletes honored on the Wall of Fame of Sports. In 1931 Sig returned to Sweden as an American representative from the United States Eastern Amateur Ski Association. In 1932 he went to the Winter Olympics as an attache for the Swedish team, an especially valuable part of the team after learning the organizational aspects of skiing in the United States. Perhaps his greatest honor came in 1968 when he represented the United States Ski Association at the Swedish Ski Association's 60th anniversary celebration in Stockholm.

WATSON, George H.

Skisport Builder

Born 1882; miner, prospector, and stockbroker in Salt Lake City; died in 1952.

In Wasatch National Forest, in Cottonwood Canyon near Alta, when winter came George Watson used skis to get around. In reading sports magazines Watson realized how much like a ski resort area his home looked. He sent 200 letters of inquiry to areas in the United States and Canada and declared himself "mayor" of Alta, which in 1934 was nothing more than a ghost town. Hall of Famer Alf Engen, with Bud Keyser, Mike O'Neill and others, came out to scout the area and found it more than suitable for skiing. Within a year things were happening in the town. Watson owned most of the mining area around Alta, but donated the surface rights of 1800 acres in the Alta Basin to the federal government, and then spent thousands of his own dollars to clear title so that the lands could be accepted by the federal government for national forest purposes to further the Alta project. His own cabin, "The Mayor's Cabin," became suites of rooms where famous skiers from all over the world have stayed, and where Watson himself stayed on his visits to the area. And Alta has become one of the largest ski resort areas in North America.

WOOLSEY, Betty

Athlete and Skisport Builder

One of the earliest female international skiers, Betty Woolsey went with Hall of Famers Alice Kiaer and Helen McAlpin as a member of the first U.S. Women's Ski team to the *Fédération Internationale de Ski* World Championships in 1935. In 1936 she was on the first U.S. women's Olympic ski team and placed seventh in the slalom and fourteenth in the downhill, a good showing for such a young team. In her second World Championships in 1936 she was tenth, and added to that an eighth in the Alberg-Kandahar. She won the National Downhill and Combined Championships in 1939 and was to compete in the 1940 Olympics, which were canceled. After her competitive career ended, Betty continued to support skiing as the editor of *Ski Illustrated* and author of many articles for the *American Ski Annual.*

WURTELE, Rhoda

Athlete

Coming from Montreal, Que, Rhoda and her sister, Rhona Wurtele Gillis, won numerous tournaments in both the United States and Canada. She first represented the Canadian Amateur Ski Association and then the National Ski Association, but reached an early fame as a member of the Penguin Ski Club in Montreal. In 1943 Rhoda participated in the Kate Smith Trophy competition in Lake Placid, N.Y, and received her first international recognition, taking top honors with her sister and two other skiers. In 1947 she won the National Downhill and in 1949 won the North American Downhill. *Also in:* Canadian Amateur Athletic Hall of Fame.

1970

BIETILA, Paul

Athlete

Born February 28, 1918, in Ishpeming, Mich; graduate of Ishpeming High School with honors; played basketball and football; studied physical education at Univ. Wis; member of jumping team; one of seven brothers who performed as the "Flying Bietilas," Ralph and Walter also Hall of Fame members; died from skiing accident February 26, 1939.

Such a great jumper was Paul Bietila, that at age 12 he is believed to have set the boy's world record at 186 ft. and captured eight Central U.S. Ski Association and National Ski Association Class C titles in his last year as a boy competitor. He competed in one Class B tournament before being elevated to Class A. In 1938 he was third in the National Championships, only behind the Norwegian wonders, the Ruud brothers, and first in the International Intercollegiate Ski Meet at Brattleboro, Vt. After breaking nine individual hill records and being declared the best ski jumper in the United States, Bietila hit an iron restraining post on a practice jump before the national tournament at St. Paul, Minn, in 1939. He left a record that would be very hard for any ski jumper to match. In 1940 Hall of Famer Dr. Harold Bradley and his wife established a Paul Bietila Trophy to be awarded annually to the American-born skier scoring highest in the National Ski Jumping Championships.

BRUUN, Fred
Skisport Builder
First a competitor and later a leader in the development of American ski judges associations, Fred Bruun has been involved with skiing for over 50 years. As a professional and later Class A competitor from 1913 to 1928, he represented the Norge Ski Club, starring at Howelsen Hill (named after Hall of Famer Carl Howelsen) in 1915, behind Hall of Famer Ragnar Omtvedt and ahead of Carl Howelsen. He also won two races on Norge Hill in Chicago and captured second prize in a 1922 race in Minneapolis, Minn, against all the best skiers. After a first place in Oconomowoc, Wis, in 1926, Bruun turned to organizational matters, beginning with judging the Nationals at Red Wing, Minn. Very active in the Central U.S. Ski Association (CUSSA), he was the founder and first president (for ten years) of the first ski judges association, the CUSSA Ski Officials Association. This opened the doors for improved skiing and made it possible for the first time for U.S. judges to be approved for service in international meets. Judges associations began in other ski divisions, and Bruun set up a system of testing prospective members of these associations. On the board of directors for the CUSSA, he was a delegate to its conventions approximately 25 times. In the Norge Ski Club, Bruun was corresponding secretary, financial secretary and hill captain before serving as club president for seven years, 1925, 1932 – 1934, 1937 – 1939—a record in 1970.

CLAIR, John, Jr.
Skisport Builder
Born in 1908; two sons and one daughter; director of New York State Winter Sports Council 1952 – 1968, its secretary in 1966 – 1967 and president in 1967 – 1968; deceased.

Would you believe that "Mr. Ski" learned the sport by sliding down the hills of the Jamaica, Long Island, golf course? That was many years before John Clair, Jr, founded the Long Island Ski Club in 1938, but was sufficient to serve as inspiration for his many years of service to skisport. After founding his Long Island Ski Club he represented the club at the New York Council for 30 years, served as its treasurer in 1949 and chairman in 1948 – 1949. He was also active in the National Ski Patrol System (NSPS) as Ski Patrolman #1158 and founding member of the Long Island Ski Patrol. On the board of trustees for the NSPS in 1952, he later served as chairman of the finance committee in 1968. His interest in skiing brought involvement as a U.S. delegate to the *Fédération Internationale de Ski* Congress at Igls, Austria, in 1953 and at Falun, Sweden, in 1954. For the Olympics, he represented the U.S. Eastern Amateur Ski Association at the 1953 and 1957 quadrennial meeting of the U.S. Olympic Association, was chairman of the games committee in 1956, a member of the finance committee in 1960 – 1964 and the transportation committee in 1964. He was also on the executive committee of the New York committee for the U.S. Ski Team Fund, and served other ski organizations in various capacities.

DEWEY, Godfrey
Skisport Builder
Born in 1888; graduated from Harvard Univ. 1909; carried American flag as manager of U.S. Olympic team in 1928; author, businessman, educator; president of Emerson Col. 1949 – 1950; received Freedom Foundation Award 1950; resides at Lake Placid, N.Y.

Back in 1904 – 1905 the father of this Hall of Famer established the Lake Placid Club's winter program, which included the "sport of skiing, only recently imported from the Scandinavian countries." Thus, commercialized skiing was born and Melvil, Godfrey's father, provided customers with hickory skis with simple toestrap bindings from Norway and poles to be used as rudders. Godfrey, on the other hand, was responsible for the design and construction of all the facilities, such as ski hills, skating and hockey rinks and toboggan slides, between 1908 and 1920. The 1932 Winter Olympics held at Lake Placid were made possible as a result of Godfrey's efforts as chairman of the Olympic organizing committee. He traveled through Europe to study the problems of staging the Olympics, came back to the United States to secure the bid for Lake Placid, and was responsible for the location, design and construction of its facilities. He even personally designed the ski jump, and continued to design jumps at Middlebury College, St. Lawrence University, three more at Lake Placid, and was consulted by many people on others. Godfrey was a pioneer skisport developer for more than 45 years.

ELDRED, William T.
Skisport Builder
Born 1913; died 1965.
Through his own devotion to skiing, William Eldred encouraged the growth of skiing and the interest of other enthusiasts. He was publisher of the national *Ski* magazine and other publications and, as such, urged accurate reporting of the sport and increased concern toward ski safety. A knowledgeable man, he often spoke out about what he felt was not in the best interests of skiing.

GROSWOLD, Thor C, Sr.
Athlete and Skisport Builder
See entry in Colorado Ski Museum-Colorado Ski Hall of Fame, 1977.

HEGGE, Ole
Athlete
Born 1889 in Norway; learned to ski at age 6; emigrated to the United States in 1929 and became American citizen; very reserved individual.

Ole Hegge won over 50 tournaments in his career in both the United States and Norway. He won five Norwegian national titles in cross-country and combined competition, three times runnerup in the Holmenkollen, two King's Cups from the late King Haakon VII for his supremacy in the combined, a gold medal from Sweden's Crown Prince and a first in the combined event of the Nordiska Spelan (held every four years and comparable to the Olympics). In 1928 he won the Olympic silver medal in the 17-mile cross-country and finished fifth in the 31-mile race despite the fact that his skis broke 9.5 miles from the end. His ability did not diminish after coming to the United States. First, at Everett, Wash, he won second place in a jumping contest in 1929, had an easy victory at Greenfield, Mass, in 1930, placed second in the National Cross-Country and Combined Championships at Salisbury, won four U.S. Eastern Championships and captured the titles for the 31-mile, 11.3 mile, and the combined races in several tournaments in the East. Not yet a U.S. citizen, Hegge competed on the Norwegian Olympic team and placed fourth in the 31-mile race. Though he retired from competition in 1936, Ole became an international judge, has taught skiing at Vassar College, Millbrook School for Boys and in 1970 was the resident manager of the YMCA Camp Sloane at Lakeville, Conn.

HILL, Cortlandt T.

Skisport Builder

Born in St. Paul, Minn; education at St. Paul Academy, Phillips Exeter, Yale Univ; competed in the Nationals in 1940; won two Harriman Cups; won FWSA races 1940 – 1953; two silver belts in California's Sugar Bowl; NSPS Award 1942; Bass Trophy 1952; two awards from U.S. Olympic Committee; Class A racer; published *Skiers Handbook* in 1947.

A very devoted skisport builder, Corty Hill has been associated with the National Ski Patrol System (NSPS), the Far West Ski Association and the National Ski Association (NSA), and has represented both the *Fédération Internationale de Ski* and the Olympics. Early in his career he organized the first slalom race on the eastern slope of the High Sierra at McGee Creek, and the divisional Alpine championships he supported in 1945 – 1946 led to a boom in skiing following W. W. II. In California he was a member of both the winter sports committee and the statewide travel and recreation committee of the Chamber of Commerce from 1948 to 1953. In 1948 he was also the manager for the U.S. Olympic team and witnessed Hall of Famer Gretchen Fraser win the first U.S. gold medal in skiing. In 1950 Corty was general chairman of the NSA team committee for the first FIS congress held in the United States in Aspen, Colo. While a member of the international downhill-slalom committee for the FIS in 1951 – 1953, 1955 and 1957, Corty was chairman of the international competition committee in 1951. He was both chairman of the NSA committee for the certification of ski instructors and chairman of the U.S. Olympic ski games committee in 1952, the year Andrea Mead Lawrence won two gold medals at the Olympics. He also served both the NSA and the NSPS as director and executive committee member. Additionally, with Hall of Famers Luggi Foeger and Hannes Schneider, he financed surveys for the possible development of ski areas from San Gorgonio in Southern California to Mt. Bachelor in Oregon, with the cooperation of the U.S. Forest Service.
Also in: Winter Sports Hall of Fame, Citizens Savings Hall of Fame Athletic Museum.

JOHNSON, Jannette Burr

Athlete

Father a ski maker; grew up in the shadow of Mt. Ranier and Mt. Baker; attended the Univ. Wash, degree in physical education; North American Champion 1950; Swiss National Champion 1952; FIS Bronze Medal 1954; Olympic Games U.S. Team Alternate 1956; resides in Sun Valley, Idaho.

Jannette Burr did not begin skiing until 1945. Her incredible balance and competitive spirit moved her to the top of the ski world in a short period of time. She proved herself an outstanding slalom and downhill racer and was competing against European women by 1950. During the two years prior to the 1952 Olympic Games in Norway, Jannette won the Swiss National, placed second in the downhill at the Ladies International, was awarded the Silver Belt from the *Fédération Internationale de Ski* (FIS), and overall won five first places in European competition. She was placed on the 1952 Olympic team, but her efforts brought no medals. Jannette took a third place bronze medal for the giant slalom at the 1954 FIS, which was the only award won by an American skier at that event. Other highlights of her career include the Pacific Northwest Ski Association Combined, the Daffodil Cup, the Golden Poles, the Northwest Intercollegiate Giant Slalom, the Penguin Giant Slalom, the Sir Arnold Lunn Race, the Sun Valley Ski Club Championship, the Golden Rose Race and the Heather Cup twice.

MacNAB, L. B. "Barney"

Skisport Builder

Born in 1902; attended Notre Dame where a broken back prevented a possible football career; a shuffled walk remained with him; founded successful insurance office in Portland; died in 1968.

It was Barney McNab with other Mt. Hooders in Oregon who joined together and founded the first ski patrol in a major area with the help of the U.S. Forest Service in 1937 – 1938. Volunteer climbers, hikers and first-aiders called themselves the Mt. Hood Ski Patrol and Barney MacNab was their first president and number one patrolman. The success of this unit prompted the National Ski Association to ask MacNab for advice when it formed the National Ski Patrol System (NSPS), and he served as director of the Northwest Region of the NSPS and patrolman #17. Members of the Mt. Hood Ski Patrol demonstrated their competence when nearly all of the 25 became charter members of the NSPS.

MOVITZ, Richard

Athlete

Attended Univ. Utah, member of the championship ski team; private first class in Air Force during W.W. II; attended Arctic Training School in Northwest Canada; National Slalom Champion 1946; FIS World Champion, 1950; resides in Salt Lake City, Utah.

Early in his career Dick Movitz was racing for Little Kandahar Ski Club and the Utah Ski Club. At the age of 19 and on a special 60-day leave from the Air Force, Dick won the National Slalom Championship. As his career continued he won the Silver Dollar Derby Downhill, Slalom and Combined Championship, the California Ski Association Downhill, Slalom and Combined, and the Alta Cup Races for a second in the combined, a first in the giant slalom and a fourth in the slalom. While enrolled at the University of Utah, Movitz won the National Collegiate Athletic Association Slalom Championship in 1947 and was a member of that year's championship team. The same year he placed second in the Slalom Nationals and went on to participate in the 1948 Olympic Games, though he did not take a medal. Dick holds the 1950 *Fédération Internationale de Ski* (FIS) World Championship raced at Aspen, Colo. A few years later, from 1956 to 1958, Dick was the youngest Alpine official to serve on the international competition committee. He also served on the 1960 Olympic committee.

NEWETT, George A.
Skisport Builder
Born October 6, 1856, in Janesville, Wis; editor and publisher of Ishpeming *Iron Ore;* died in 1928.

George Newett was one of ten persons present at the founders meeting of the National Ski Association of America. This nonskiing newspaper man was the only American-born member of the ten. Newett's contribution to the sport was through its promotion and development, accomplishing this via his newspaper columns. Most considered him the "man who Americanized the sport of skiing." In his later years Newett took the time to write a history of skiing of the Ishpeming Ski Club. He was a qualified historian because "he was there." This colorful account of the ski world is now housed with the National Ski Association's records.

RUUD, Birger
Athlete
Born in 1911; toured the United States with ski jumping brother Sigmund in 1937 – 1938.

Before the 1932 Winter Olympics at Lake Placid, Birger Ruud had won the Holmenkollen and other European tournaments as well as the ski jumping event at the 1931 *Fédération Internationale de Ski* (FIS) World Championships. Come 1932, he won the gold medal for ski jumping and, along with his brother, did more to encourage the growth of skiing in the United States than any other skier; even Hall of Famer Lowell Thomas was inspired to take up skiing after witnessing Birger's performance at the Olympics. Returning to the Olympics in 1936, he won a gold medal in the downhill and special ski jumping events. He coached the Norwegian Olympic team in 1948, but at the last minute was needed as a substitute in the ski jumping event and, with an amazing comeback, won a silver medal behind another Norwegian, Petter Hugsted. In 1934 he established a new world distance mark of 102 yds, won the FIS ski jumping championship in 1935 and 1937 and won the 1938 National Open Championship in men's ski jumping. No wonder Americans were awed by this skier, Birger Ruud.

RUUD, Sigmund
Athlete
Sigmund Ruud was 1928 Olympic silver medalist and 1929 *Fédération Internationale de Ski* (FIS) World Championship ski jumper. With his brother Birger, he is credited with doing more to influence the growth of skiing in the United States than any other person. Before touring the United States in 1937 – 1938, with his brother Sigmund set the world distance record four times: 90.5 yds. in 1931, 93.3 yds. in 1933, 95.5 yds. in 1934, and 97.2 yds. in 1937 and then won the National Men's Ski Jumping Championship in 1937. Sigmund also chaired the FIS jumping committee for more than 15 years.

SEVERUD, Lloyd "Snoball"
Athlete and Skisport Builder
Born in 1918 near Chetek, Wis; attended high school in Chetak, Wis; nicknamed Snoball by high school basketball coach because a towhead; four years in Marines during W.W. II.

Lloyd Severud began competing in skiing at age 9 for clubs in the Wisconsin snowbelt. He joined the Eau Claire Ski Club in 1946 and was still with them in 1970 as an unofficial coach. Snoball took the National Veterans Jumping Championship in 1953 and from 1956 to 1959. It was during this time that he completely dominated tournaments across the nation. After coaching during the late 1950s, Severud accepted the position of head coach of the 1960 U.S. Olympic team for the Games in California. Snoball has spent many years studying the art of ski jumping, always trying to improve the caliber of the skiers. He was instrumental in getting action films into daily training routines. During the mid-1960s, he was head coach of the Canadian Amateur Ski Association's jumping program, taking that country's team to the 1968 Olympic Games in France.

THOMPSON, John Albret "Snow-Shoe"
Skisport Builder
Born April 3, 1827, in Telemarken, Norway; emigrated to the United States in 1837; died May 15, 1876, at his Diamond Valley Ranch in Alpine, Calif.

For 20 years, from 1856 to 1876, Snow-Shoe Thompson (it has also been spelled Thomson and Thomsen) provided the only winter land communication between the East and California. Using 7½- to 8-ft. grooveless, but cambered, skis he carried as much as 120 lbs. of mail at $2 per letter over 30- to 50-ft. deep snow. He wrote about skiing in the area during the gold and silver rushes, describing ski contests much like modern-day downhill and slalom races. The slalom consisted of "stakes to be stuck in a straight line every hundred ft. through the track, and I will leave the first one to the right, the next one to the left, and so on until I get through." After 13 years of dependable mail service, Thompson filed a claim for $6000 that he felt Congress owed him. He received a thank-you letter, but no check, and some say that he never recovered from the rebuff from Congress. In 1960 Jakob Vaage, Norwegian ski historian, came to the United States for the Olympics at Squaw Valley. During that time, he and the Norwegian ski team made a pilgrimage to the grave of Snow-Shoe Thompson and left a plaque which says, "As a tribute to a great compatriot from Telemark, this plaque was presented by the Norwegian Olympic Ski Team competing at Squaw Valley in February 1960." Visitors to the Western American Skisport Museum at the Auburn Ski Club in Boreal Ridge, Calif, can see Snow-Shoe's skis and mailbag and the Norwegian Ski Federation's Snow-Shoe Thompson Commemorative Holmenkollen Cup. The Museum is also headquarters for the Snow-Shoe Thompson Cross-Country Ski Race, begun in 1945.

TOKLE, Arthur
Athlete
Born in Norway; immigrated to the United States in 1947 at age 25; brother Torger a great American ski jumper in the 1940s, married Oddfried Larsen 1948; two children, Vivian and Arthur, Jr; National Champion 1951 and 1953; three-time winner of Winged Trophy.

Art Tokle made his first appearance in the American ski world shortly after his arrival from Norway. He earned the National Ski Jumping Championship in 1951 and 1953 as well as a spot on the 1952 Olympic team. This exciting figure took his place on the 1950, 1954 and 1958 *Fédération Internationale de Ski* teams for the United States. At the age of 38, Art again took a spot on the 1960 Olympic team. Along with his brother and Art Devlin he was a three-time winner of the Winged Trophy of the Brattleboro Outing Club. In 1962 at the age of 40, Art won 12 out of 13 engagements. From 1960 to 1963 Tokle was the U.S. Ski Association's coach, serving on the U.S. Olympic staff as jump coach in 1964 and 1968.

VALAR, Paula Kann
Athlete
Kate Smith Trophy 1943 and 1944; husband Paul U.S. Eastern Amateur Ski Assn. certified professional ski teacher; resident of Franconia, N.H.

Paula Kann dominated the eastern amateur ski racing scene during and following W.W. II. In 1943 Paula was a member of the downhill championship team at the Kate Smith International Team Trophy Races. At that same race in 1944 she took the slalom championship. Paula had an across-the-board third-place sweep at the 1947 National and Olympic trials in Utah and went on to place 11th in the Olympic Games slalom event in Switzerland. Other highlights of her career include a fourth place in the National Giant Slalom in 1949, a fourth place in the Combined, National Downhill and Slalom the same year, as well as sixth place in the North American Championships Combined competition. Ms. Valar was a member of the *Fédération Internationale de Ski* U.S. team in 1950 and is now a U.S. Eastern Amateur Ski Association certified professional ski teacher working at the Mittersill Ski Area in New Hampshire.

WICTORIN, John "Mr. Swix"
Skisport Builder
Born 1907 in Ludvika, Sweden; champion competitor in Nordic events in Sweden; wife Lillian; two skiing daughters; won New York State Cross-Country Championship shortly after arriving in the United States; resided in Ridgefield, N.J; died suddenly on first return to Stockholm, Sweden, June 26, 1969.

A rebirth of cross-country skiing took place in the United States as a result of John Wictorin's support of the Ski Touring Council organized in 1962. From developing simple ski touring techniques to holding clinics to discuss waxing and the use of touring equipment, he won over ski touring enthusiasts. He even laid out trails in the Palisades and Harriman State Park and Ward-Poundridge Reservation and introduced the sport in Bear Mountain and sponsored the first *Ski Touring Bulletin.* Wictorin was also a tournament official and adviser to many competitors, divulging his methods for a proper jump or for winning the cross-country events. As founder and president of the Swedish Ski Club of New York City, one of the oldest clubs in the U.S. Eastern Amateur Ski Association, he was of utmost assistance in planning two National Ski Association conventions, one in the early 1940s and the other in 1954. Internationally acclaimed as a ski waxing expert, he will be remembered as the man weighed down with his ski waxes who explained the mysteries of the process.

1971

ANDERSON, Reidar
Foreign Member
Anderson was a sort of worldwide commuter on skis. Twice he came to the United States and Canada across the globe from his hometown of Oslo, Norway. In 1932 the first tour was necessitated by the location of the third Winter Olympics at Lake Placid, N.Y. But in 1936 he was back in Europe for the Games at Garmisch-Partenkirchen, Germany, in which he placed third. He won the hotly competitive Holmenkollen three times in the jumping event, and in 1935 set the world distance record at 331.5 ft. It was 1939 when Anderson returned to North America, scattering victories in his tour's wake, a grand total of 18 tournament firsts. Among these were the National Championships at St. Paul, Minn, the Canadian Tourney at Fort William, Ont, and the International Championship Tourney at Treasure Island of the San Francisco World's Fair.

CHIVERS, Warren "Winger"
Athlete
Born in Saxtons River, Vt; member of all-ski family of Hanover, N.H; attended Dartmouth Col. in mid-1930s; coach and teacher at Vermont Academy.

When it came to choosing the category of race he'd run, perhaps Warren relied on "winging" it, as he was diversified enough to excel in any style or type of skiing. In his career he has performed equally well in ski jumping, cross-country racing, downhill and slalom racing, and the combinations of Nordic and Alpine. 1937 was the second year that the National Cross-Country Championship was won by an American-born contestant, specifically Chivers of New Hampshire. He was selected for the Olympics in 1936 and 1940 and in 1937 traveled to Chile as the U.S. representative in the Pan-American Alpine Championships. That year he also won the National Nordic Combined, another feather in his outstanding collegiate skiing career cap.

ENGEN, Sverre
Athlete
Born 1911 in Nijondalem, Norway; came to America at age 18 to join brother Al, also Hall of Famer; served in Norwegian Battalion of the 10th Mountain Troops in W. W. II; established Snow Valley resort in Southern California; taught ski instructors under auspices of G.I. Bill; resides in Salt Lake City, Utah.

Sverre was just age 6 when he won his first ski trophy, which was not exactly a great achievement as skiing was the Norwegian way of life. Once settled in America, the yen for the slopes persisted and Sverre helped celebrate the birth of jumping competitions in the United States. In fact, the immigrant barely got settled when the skier in him took hold. During his first winter in the United States, Sverre won two championships, the Class B central contest and the Norge tournament in Chicago, placing third in a national jumping contest staged in North Dakota. Then seven years in a row, Engen joined with 13 other Scandinavian immigrant champs who spread the good word about the new ski sport all across U.S. snow country. In 1937 Engen earned his most prized trophy, a one-shot honor, that of the Norge Ski Club Medal, which was awarded him for placing first in Class A competition.

ENGL, Sigi
Athlete and Skisport Builder
Born in Austria; came to the United States in 1936; was in 10th Mountain Division during W. W. II; head of Sun Valley Ski School, Idaho.

Engl came to the United States in answer to a request by management at Yosemite, where he taught the basics of skiing for two years. In the 1930s leading up to this global leap, he made a name for himself on the European racing circuit. In 1931 he won the International Italian Downhill and Slalom, then the German slalom title at Garmisch-Partenkirchen in 1932. Two times he took the Austrian Downhill and Slalom and was chosen for membership on the Austrian *Fédération Internationale de Ski* Alpine team, then world champions. In America the stint at Yosemite sent him in search of a resort site in the eastern Sierras, but another invitation to teach nipped plans in the bud. Engl went to Sun Valley in 1939, winning the Harriman Cup Downhill a year later, then the National Open Slalom at Yosemite and the Diamond Sun races in 1941. After the war, Sigi went back to Sun Valley where he devoted his time to innovative teaching, using the short skis and videotape in analyzing beginners' difficulties. Due to his impetus, the Sun Valley Ski School flourished and attracted other instructors to its successful program. It presently operates with 150 instructors under the direction of Sigi Engl.

GOODRICH, Nathaniel
Skisport Builder
Goodrich's contribution to skiing was not of a physical nature but one of mental selection. As Dartmouth librarian he chose the material to be included in the *American Ski Annuals* of the 1930s and 1940s. Not only did Goodrich's editorial talent show perceptive regard for literature but also a respect for quality in writing. The late Goodrich was affiliated with the Eastern Amateur Ski Association at its inception and became associated with Sir Arnold Lunn and Professor Charles A. Proctor, both in the Hall of Fame. All three were essential in the introduction and development of Alpine competition in America.

GRIFFITH, James
Athlete
Born 1929 in Ketchum, Idaho; military service in the U.S. Air Force; member of 1952 Olympic team; died December 6, 1951, in Salt Lake City, Utah.

Although he was a member of the 1952 Olympic team, Griffith never made it to the shining slopes of Oslo. While training for the Games at Alta, he negotiated a sharp turn that sent him flying head-on into a tree. He died four days later, 22 years old and barely launched on a championship career. At the time of death he was considered a formidable contender in Olympic downhill and slalom, having won the National Downhill Championship of 1950 as representative of the Sun Valley Ski Club. He was also a member of the U.S. *Fédération Internationale de Ski* team. Griffith had the Argentine-Chile Kandahar title to his credit, and, in proof of his skiing commitment, had acted as amateur coach and manager of the U.S. of Colorado Ski Team.

HENDRICKSON, James R.
Athlete
Born 1913 in Eau Claire, Wis, member of the 1936 Olympic team; died January 18, 1948, in Chicago, Ill.

Jimmy began reaping honors early, winning the National Class B Championship some years before trekking off to Garmisch-Partenkirchen, thereby receiving acknowledgment as the best ski jumper of the United States. His success could have been predicted when at age 16 he outdid all jumpers in competition at a national meet in St. Paul, Minn. And in his early twenties he won the Central and West Coast titles. Up to age 35, Hendrickson kept active in contests of all sorts. At the Norge tournament at Fox River Grove, Ill, Jimmy sustained fatal injuries during competition.

HUDSON, Sally Neidlinger
Athlete
Born in Hanover, N.H, with twin Susan; attended Univ. of Colo; pursued career as ski equipment outfitter and buyer for 13 years; actively officiates and coaches novice skiers including son; resides in Olympic Valley, Calif.

The Neidlinger twins started skiing in earnest when rope tows showed up on the slopes at Woodstock, Vt. But Sally soon left her sister behind and entered her first races as a representative of the Dartmouth Outing Club. Stints with several ski clubs ensued, including Buffalo, Arapahoe and Denver. At the National Downhill in 1946, Sally placed third but went on to set downhill records at the Kate Smith Trophy Race and the Fiske Trophy Race in 1947. That year at the Nationals in Utah, she finished fourth in downhill, sixteenth in slalom and ninth in combined. At Sun Valley a year later, Sally entered the Harriman Cup competition and won slalom honors, then placed ninth in combined at the 1949 Nationals. As a result of such a fine showing, she was chosen as a member of the *Fédération Internationale de Ski* team. The 1951 season saw Sally active in many racing events which got her a berth on the 1952 Olympic team. At the Olympic tryouts she nabbed a clean sweep of firsts in downhill, slalom and combined, then went on to win three more titles: the Roch Cup, the Silver Belt in Sugar Bowl, and North American Women's Slalom. She expanded to take the National Combined Championship in 1953, meanwhile winning a second Roch Cup and a second Harriman Cup. In the next year Sally was awarded the distinguished "Gold Harriman," having placed in that contest for a third time. From then on Mrs. Hudson channeled efforts in an administrative and leisurely rather than competitive vein, acting as president of the Squaw Valley Ski Club, overseeing junior races, and heading for the wide open spaces on cross-country skis.

IGAYA, Chiharu "Chick"
Athlete

Born in 1935 in Japan; attended Dartmouth Col; came to be regarded as international goodwill skiing ambassador for 20 years; representated Japan at two Olympic Games; now an agent for business firms based in Japan; resides in New York City.

Albeit a Japanese, Chick Igaya was a North American phenomenon, constantly at the top of ski champ rosters throughout the early and mid-1950s. While at Dartmouth he served as captain of the famed Big Green ski team and boosted its overall performance by taking six National Collegiate Athletic Association (NCAA) championships all by himself. From 1955 through 1957 he aced all contenders in NCAA slalom, additionally taking downhill honors the first year, plus Alpine combined titles in 1955 and 1956. As for National Ski Association Alpine Championships, five belonged to Chick—the slalom and combined in 1954, the downhill and combined in 1955, and the giant slalom in 1960. At Cortina d'Ampezzo, Italy, site of the 1956 Winter Olympics, Igaya did his home Japan team proud by taking the silver medal in slalom. It was a rough go at first, as he had to scramble for a recovery upon catching a ski tip six gates out. Another medal fell into his hands after taking third at the *Fédération Internationale de Ski* championships in 1958. Rounding out the list of kudos to Igaya are two White Stag Trophies awarded him in 1954 and 1955 for top performance in Men's Alpine Combined.

MACKENZIE, Ron
Athlete

MacKenzie's view of skiing is usually from above, as planner, organizer, supervisor and promoter. For over 50 years he has gone to bat for skiing's betterment on a national scale. As charter member of the New York State Winter Sports Council, Ron fought tooth and nail for 20 years to secure state-owned lands for transformation into a ski development. Then in 1937 he directed the organization of the Lake Placid Ski Patrol plus other patrols in the vicinity. Twice he has taken on responsibilities with the *Fédération Internationale de Ski* (FIS) as coach and manager of the U.S. Nordic team in 1954 FIS World Championships in Sweden, and as director of competition for the 1950 FIS World Nordic Championships. Keeping to the continent, MacKenzie acted as race chairman for the 1961 North American Alpine Championships and assumed added duties as a jack-of-all-trades, by judging ski jumping, tracking down technicalities, and officiating at races. A pet plan was to bring the Olympics back to New York, and Ron has been a strong voice of the Lake Placid Winter Olympic organizing committee, submitting bids for the Games since before 1960. And since 1963 his first time as delegate to the FIS Congress held that year in Greece, Ron has energetically represented his community of Lake Placid at every world congress, pushing for development and fresh ideas regarding the skiing industry and sport.

NELSEN, Nels
Athlete

In the course of his life (1894–1943) Nels Nelsen was a dominant ski personality in western Canada and the states of Washington and Oregon. His center of influence was at Revelstoke, B.C, where he established a 240-ft. distance record in 1925. This prompted townsfolk to name the jumping hill of Mt. Revelstoke National Park in Nelsen's memory. During the early 1920s he took active part in the Canadian Amateur Ski Association and competed in national tourneys all across North America, from Denver, Colo, to Brattleboro, Vt. Some of his ski jumping adversaries are also Hall of Famers—Sig Steinwall, Ragnar Omtvedt, and Harry Lien—who helped to further the popularity of ski jumping and influenced the Canadians' construction of the singularly famous jumping run at Revelstoke.

PAULSEN, Guttorm
Athlete and Skisport Builder

Born October 20, 1906, in Oslo, Norway; came to the United States in 1928 and settled in Chicago; deceased.

Soon after arriving in the United States, Guttorm caught the ski jumping bug, joined the Norge Ski Club headquartered in Chicago, and stayed a member for life. For 11 years he tried for trophies, and in 1929 won his first as New York State Champion, then snatched 10 out of 11 in Class B competition that same year, culminating with the National Ski Association (NSA) Class B title. Paulsen took the U.S. Eastern Amateur Ski Association Championship in 1930, which he hung onto through the year following, adding the Central U.S. Ski Association title for Class A Championship in 1932. Then his jumping activity took a turn toward officiating and administrating, especially in assessing quality of competitors' style. At the Olympics and at *Fédération Internationale de Ski* competitions, Paulsen served as style official, in addition to various NSA National Championships. On the home level, he was the Norge Ski Club president for two years and recording secretary for four.

PERRAULT, Paul Joseph "Jumping Joe"
Athlete

Jumping Joe started a revolution in ski competition that for years had consistently favored the Europeans and Scandinavians over the Americans. On the historic day, February 26, 1949, within a span of two hours Perrault beat two big world champions and shattered the North American distance record not once but twice. He was up against the Olympic champions of the moment, Petter Hugstead of Norway, and Matti Pietikainen of Finland, who won the next year's *Fédération Internationale de Ski* World Championship. But such illustrious competition didn't faze the young American who tackled Pine Mountain slide at Iron Mountain, Mich, with fervor. The day made him famous and an inspiration to upcoming North American contenders. In 1950 Perrault was given the American Ski Trophy in recognition of his tradition-breaking victory. Two years later he went to Oslo as a member of the U.S. Olympic team. And in 1970 Jumping Joe was given a special award on behalf of the Iron Mountain ski establishment. The unique trophy acknowledged his spectacular feat as the most outstanding individual performance to have taken place in 30 years since the inception of the famous Pine Mountain Ski Hill. It may have been predicted by his having been awarded in 1947 the Paul Bietila Trophy which annually honors the American-born skier who scores highest in national ski jumping contests.

SATRE, Ottar

Athlete

Born in Norway; immigrated to Salisbury, Conn, with pioneer ski family; chosen for Norwegian Olympic team of 1932 but had to refuse as U.S. citizen; represented the United States on 1936 Olympic team; retired in 1950, opting for active organization of junior programs.

Ottar began skiing competitively through the years 1930–1942 in several styles, cross-country, jumping and combined, winning his first big national title for cross-country in 1935 at Canton, S.Dak. Later that year in contests held at his hometown, Ottar took third in cross-country and finished as runner-up in both combined and jumping. But he hung on to take the eastern Class A titles in jumping two times, the Class B jumping title once and Class A and B honors in combined three times altogether. Finally in 1936 he got the chance for an Olympiad that was much anticipated after the 1932 decision not to accept the berth on Norway's team. And Satre chose to do double allegiance to the United States by entering the Holmenkollen, the oldest and most venerated ski competition in the world, and in which he placed thirty-sixth in 1936. Ottar chalked up over 30 firsts in tournaments throughout his skiing career, including several New York State championships. Even before quitting the competitive scene in 1950, he won seven meet titles in a row as a jumper of the veteran class. Many times Satre has been acclaimed as a forerunner of stylish skiers.

SIGAL, Albert E.

Skisport Builder

Educated in electrical engineering at New Mexico A&M; retired from business after attaining corporation executive status with Safeway Stores; has devoted nearly 20 years service to ski organizations.

Albert Sigal has functioned in many capacities as a driving force behind constant organization and ongoing improvement in the sport of skiing. He has devised work programs and provided financial support in ways that have nurtured wintertime enjoyment and safety throughout North America. On an international level, he took part in the Olympic Games ski committee as president from 1947 through 1948 and served four years on the executive committee of the U.S. Olympic Association from 1953 through 1956. He was executive committee member and vice president of the National Ski Association (NSA) 1942–1947 and president 1954–1956. He served actively in several capacities in the National Ski Patrol System (NSPS) and the Far West Ski Association. In 1953 Sigal was awarded the Julius Blegen Award for outstanding contributions to the NSA, one decade after he had been given the NSPS Award.

1972

BAKKE, Hermod

Skisport Builder

Born June 2, 1902, in Hurum, Norway; came to America in 1928 soon after brother Magnus; both settled in Leavenworth, Wash; together engineered jumping hills in Washington. Hermod supervised hill construction for 1960 Olympics; became involved in coaching and devising junior ski jumping programs.

Upon arriving in the United States with a Class B competition ranking, Hermod concentrated on moving upward to Class A. Finally in 1935 he hit a high point when asked to represent the Pacific Northwest Ski Association in the Olympic trials at Salt Lake City. But a fall during a jump prevented his qualifying for the 1936 team. In 1939 at the San Francisco World's Fair International Championships at Treasure Island, a ski jump exhibition was staged, with Hermod Bakke as one of the performers. Although Hermod was also a top cross-country skier, his most remarkable contributions to skiing were with hills and kids. In 1933 he and his brother redesigned what came to be known as the 90-Meter Leavenworth Ski Jumping Hill, alias "Bakke Hill." In commemoration of their years of coaching and countless hours spent in making the 1946 Winter Sports Club Carnival a huge success, it seemed appropriate to name the jump for its dynamic builders. In 1950 Hermod on his own created a 300-ft. jump that made new records possible and more exciting tournaments a rule. He became known as the "Chief of Jumping Hills" especially after the Olympic committee officially placed him in charge of hill maintenance for the 1960 Squaw Valley Olympics. Eventually a collection of hills around Leavenworth was called "Bakke Hills" and even a "Bakke Hills Trophy" was awarded the brothers, kept as a permanent possession of the town's Winter Sports Club. Each year a replica of the 54-in. trophy is awarded to the Junior Expert class champion in remembrance of years and years spent coaching schoolboys.

BAKKE, Magnus

Skisport Builder

Born June 15, 1899, in Lyngdal, Norway; came to America in 1923; lived in North Dakota, then Wenatchee and Leavenworth, Wash; worked 33 years for the U.S. Forest Service; aided brother Hermod in construction of ski jumping hill at Leavenworth; certified as cross-country judge and official since 1938.

As a child in Norway, Magnus developed talents in ski jumping, cross-country racing and biathlon, all of which affected the direction of his adult life. A larger life influence came after he'd established a new life in Washington State and had joined the Forest Service. He became conscious of the layout and maintenance of forest service trails and roads, which qualified him to assist his brother in the development of "Bakke Hills." But of the two, Magnus became more directly involved with coaching and officiating, in which he took active part for 39 years. At meets throughout the United States and Canada, Magnus has judged jumping, cross-country and biathlon competitions. In 1960 he assessed all three sport categories at the Squaw Valley Olympics. And at National Junior Championships, from Bozeman, Mont, to Yakima, Wash, Magnus has officiated at Nordic events. Following his retirement from the U.S. Forest Service, Magnus worked at the Mission Ridge Ski Area in Wenatchee, Wash, as a trail and slope engineer. He has designed jumping hills of 59 ft. and 98 ft. for suitable use by junior ski jumpers.

COOKE, Nancy Reynolds

Skisport Builder

Graduated from Bennington Col. 1937; serves as trustee of college and president of alumni association; husband

J. Negley Cooke (Cookie) developed Mt. Mansfield chair lift with comrade; two sons, both accomplished skiers; Cookes resides in Armonk, N.Y, and Stowe, Vt, conduct fund-raising New York Ski Ball annually.

Nancy Cooke has been an extraordinary sportswoman since the day she infiltrated the ranks of Dartmouth men at the annual Carnival in Hanover, N.H. When she went back to Bennington, it was with a plan for a ski day in her head. After graduating, she became an alternate member of the American Women's Team in Europe for the 1938 *Fédération Internationale de Ski* (FIS) competition and a year later was named to the U.S. Olympic team, although W. W. II prevented its occurrence. All through 1940 her performance had been particularly impressive as she won the National Women's Closed and Open Slalom Championship at Sun Valley, the Alpine Combined at an FIS-sanctioned meet in Utah, the combined title of the Far West Kandahar at Mt. Hood, Wash, the Silver Skis Downhill at Mt. Rainier, and second place in the first annual Silver Belt in California's Sugar Bowl. She was internationally rated a Class A competitor as a result of the fine showing. In 1941 she took the closed downhill and combined championship at Aspen, Colo. For seven years, from 1944 through 1950, Mrs. Cooke arranged junior ski lessons and swap equipment programs at Brattleboro, Vt. Then with her husband, Cookie, she located a new ski area at Mad River, where the two of them had climbed on an outing. Now a financial supporter of skisport, Mrs. Cooke constantly keeps shoulder to the wheel in instigating money-raising schemes under the auspices of the New York ski committee.

FRASER, Donald

Skisport Builder

Born 1914 in Seattle, Wash; became known for his gray whipcord downhill racer pants; selected for 1936 Olympic team; married Hall of Famer Gretchen Kunigk, first American to win Olympic gold medal; resides in Vancouver, Wash.

Donald Fraser believed in control and manipulation of his skis and became one of the first to popularize and develop slalom technique. The northwest corner of the United States was his as far as competition dominance was concerned. In 1933 he won the first slalom ever held by the Pacific Northwest Ski Association (PNSA), and a year later took the title for the mass-start Silver Skis Downhill, which singled him out as first among 67 contenders. After a PNSA Combined Championship win in 1935, attention was drawn to the young spitfire. He was selected for the 1936 Olympic team but was injured shortly before departure for Garmisch-Partenkirchen, yet he was able to compete in and finish twelfth in the *Fédération Internationale de Ski* slalom at Innsbruck, Austria, later that year. 1937 was Fraser's greatest year, and fans applauded his capture of the Northwest Alpine Combined for the third time. At the Pan-American Games in Chile he took the slalom honors while finishing fifth in downhill and second in combined in the midst of ruthless competition. A second victory at the wild Silver Skis race was his again in 1938. He was chosen for the 1940 Olympic team but didn't go since W.W. II prevented it. But his continuing devotion beyond years of competition in terms of officiating and promoting have made him a chief proponent of skiing as a rugged enjoyable sport.

ISELIN, Fred

Athlete and Skisport Builder

See entry in Colorado Ski Museum-Colorado Ski Hall of Fame, 1977.

LAMING, Sigrid Stromstad

Athlete

Born in 1897 in Baerum, near Oslo, Norway; one of five children, all prize-winning skiers; Sigrid came to America and settled in California; died in 1971.

While her two brothers and younger twin sisters skied to their hearts' content in the Scandinavian countries, Sigrid managed to get the ball rolling with a powerful nudge in the United States. In 1932 she became the first woman champion of the National Ski Association, having won the first event ever to sanction women contestants. The California Ski Association, now Far West Ski Association, sponsored the championships held at Lake Tahoe, which featured a variety of races but only one of which allowed women, the women's cross-country. Sigrid, a Californian, won the race as a representative of the Auburn Ski Club. Although competition was limited to cross-country, Sigrid was also a proficient ski jumper, known to have hit the 105-ft. mark. But even before the historic first honor, Sigrid was involved in many aspects of skiing. In 1931 she performed duties as an official at the Olympic ski team tryouts.

LITTLE, Earle B.

Skisport Builder

As a member of the Leavenworth Ski Club, Earle began his activity promoting ski jumping in 1929. Earle was then elected vice president and director of the club in 1934. He was in charge of publicity and transportation. By 1940 he had been elected president and served in that capacity until 1948. He had set the pattern to run a successful jumping tournament, and that pattern is still in effect today. He set all the rules and regulations. He became a judge for the Pacific Northwest Ski Association in 1940. Then in 1948, Earle became a national judge for the United States Ski Association. By 1953 he was certified as a federal international ski judge. He compiled and had printed charts which made the ski jumpers' points for distance immediately available upon completion of a jump. This was actually done in the mid-1940s, and the chart was accepted by the National Ski Association (NSA) and is still used today. He rewrote and published examinations for jumping judges, also adopted by the NSA. He assisted in arranging for college scholarships for foreign students who were attending colleges in Washington, Oregon, Idaho and Montana, those who were interested in ski jumping. He was selected to be the lone U.S. judge at the World Championships at Falun, Sweden. In 1956 he was named to judge at the Winter Olympics in Cortina, Italy. He served as director of competition at the North American Championships at Squaw Valley, Calif, in 1959. Then in 1960 he was secretary of competition at the Olympics at Squaw Valley. Before his death he was known throughout the world for his knowledge and authority of ski jumping.

MORGAN, John E. P.

Skisport Builder

Born August 9, 1895, in Lenox, Mass; attended Middlesex School 1907–1913, and Harvard Col. 1913–1917, where he first became associated with athletics; played ice hockey and football; wife Anita is also a skier; granddaughter member of National Junior Ski Championship Team of the ISA and competed in the 1971 championships that were held at Boreal Ridge near Soda Springs, where John had skied 34 years earlier; service in Navy in W.W. I; died August 24, 1971, in St. Paul, Minn; National Ski Patrol System Gold Merit Award.

John first started skiing in eastern Canada and the Adirondacks, and in the late 1920s joined the Amateur Ski Club of New York. He was appointed by Roland Palmedo, then president of the Amateur Ski Club of New York, to study and make a report on skiing accidents and safety in skiing. The report showed the need for special training in the handling of ski accidents and emphasized the great lack of knowledge of this growing problem. The National Ski Patrol System (NSPS) was born after the death of a young man at a ski race near Pittsfield. It was decided that the growing sport needed help and then they organized the NSPS, making Minnie Dole chairman with John Morgan as treasurer. For over 19 years John was chairman of the finance committee of the National Ski Association (NSA). He raised $60,000 for the 1952 Olympics. John Morgan was employed by Averell Harriman as assistant to the chairman of the board of the Union Pacific Railroad to work on the development of Sun Valley during 1934–1936. John and Charles Proctor laid out the first trails and runs. He helped design and construct the first chair lift in the world and also designed the first hot-water circular pools for Sun Valley. In March, 1937, John secured the Nationals and helped organize them with the Pacific Northwest Ski Association. He also organized the Sun Valley Ski Club and got Al Lindley to be its first president. He was involved with the Tenth Mountain Division along with Minnie Dole. He went to Washington and worked out arrangements with the War Department and the NSA in 1940. He drew a most unusual contract between the War Department and the NSA which laid the groundwork for the postwar growth of skiing. In 1952 after the Olympics, he resigned as treasurer of the NSPS and chairman of the finance committee of the NSA.

NEBEL, Dorothy Hoyt

Athlete

Born in 1905 in the United States; attended Schenectady High School; married to Charles Nebel in 1942; schoolteacher first in Schenectady, then to Seattle, and back to Schenectady where she became head of the mathematics department; now the couple lives in New Jersey.

Dorothy Hoyt Nebel was 15 years old when she first took up skiing. She knew no skiers, but nevertheless was fascinated by ski jumping hills and cross-country touring trails. Dot wished to participate so her father purchased a pair of skis and together they made bindings to keep them on her feet. There were Norwegians who had a jump in a nearby public park and Dot waited until the boys had finished practice and took the slide. This was supposed to be a manly Nordic art and she was better at it than many of the participants. In the late 1920s Dot helped form the Schenectady Winter Sports Club, and around 1930 the Club ran snow trains to North Creek, N.Y. Along with other members, she mounted her own steel edges on skis—strips of steel from the General Electric Co, which were drilled and countersunk. She received her first Alpine ski pointers from Otto Schniebs, coach at Dartmouth College, when he came to talk to the Club. Dot was already racing against men, there being no female competitors in those days in the north woods. Dot was teaching in the Schenectady school system, but took a leave and went to Europe to improve her skiing in 1936. Roland Palmedo of the ski team committee observed her skiing and recommended her for the U.S. ski team. In 1938 she participated in the *Fédèration Internationale de Ski* Championships. She took third in downhill, ninth in slalom and placed third in the combined in the National Women's Championships held at Stowe, Vt. Dot switched from the Eastern amateur slopes to those of the Pacific Northwest during 1938–1939, a move made possible by an exchange program operating between Mont Pleasant High School in Schenectady and Garfield High School in Seattle, Wash. Here she taught math, coached a girls' team and raced as a member of the Washington Ski Club, winning the Christmas Race at Sun Valley, Idaho, the Arnold Lunn Trophy at Mt. Hood, the Silver Skis at Mt. Ranier and the Pacific Northwest Ski Association Slalom Championship. Following high placings in the National Alpine Championships at Mt. Hood, she was named to the 1940 U.S. Olympic ski team. But because of W.W. II, the Olympic Winter Games were canceled. She returned to Schenectady for the 1939–1940 season. She was head of the mathematics department, coached the high school ski team and the Union College ski team. Dot organized high school races of local teams, but also found time to compete in divisional events. Dot swept the Eastern Amateur Women's Combined Downhill and Slalom Championships at Pico Peak, setting a record down Sunset Schuss and having no trouble whatsoever in the slalom. In 1941 she sprang another repeat performance when the Eastern Women's Championships were decided at Waterville Valley, N.H. She married in 1942 and moved to New Jersey, where she started teaching at Pico Peak at the request of Janet Mead, the owner. She coached Andrea Mead (winner of two gold medals) and managed the U.S. Girls' Team for the Canadian-American competitions. By request of Otto Schniebs, she taught at Gore Mountain, North Creek, N.Y, and after a year she was managing the ski school. She helped form the New York State Professional Ski Instructors' Association. This was the first professional organization of ski teachers in the United States, but later disbanded when the U.S. Eastern Amateur Ski Association organized to certify teachers. In 1950 she headed the ski school at Belleayre. Dot was involved in ski trail and ski area design and construction, and did work for the state of New York at Gore Mountain in the southern Adirondacks and at Belleayre in the central Catskills.

OLSON, Willis S. "Billy the Kid"

Athlete

Born 1930 in Eau Claire, Wis; married; two children; often referred to as Billy "The Kid" Olson.

In 1950 Willis S. Olson, a ski jumper from Eau Claire, Wis, outclassed an international field at Iron Mountain, Mich, and stole the show by leaping 297 ft. to equal the then current North American distance record. This was to be the beginning of his career, and during the next 20 years he compiled one of the most consistent ski jumping records in the American history of sports. There is probably no other ski jumper in the United States who has won so many championships in so many different areas of the sport. Olson has been the only American ski jumper to have won national championships in the four current classes. He won the National Class C title in 1948, the Class B title in 1949 and the coveted Class A championship in 1958. In 1965, when he reached the 32-year-old bracket, he competed in the Veterans Class. He went through 12 straight tournaments without being defeated and won his first Veterans title. Olson repeated as champion in 1966, and in 1968 won his third Veterans title. He also skied in the Olympic Games of 1952 and 1954, as a mem¢ber of the U.S. Olympic teams. He was also a member of the United States *Fédèration Internationale de Ski* teams in 1950 and 1954. The longest jump he ever achieved was 393 ft. at Obertsdorf, Germany. He has also won three straight National Collegiate Athletic Association Jumping Championships as a member of the University of Denver ski team. Olson went through three seasons of collegiate ski jumping without being beaten.

STROM, Erling
Skisport Builder

Born August 26, 1897, in the mountains of Norway; spent the first eight years of life above timberline in Norway, where winter lasted for seven or eight months; father an engineer who put in big installations and tunnels; received first pair of skis at age 2; in 1907 when 10, began winning prizes as jumper in small-boy competition in hills above Oslo.

Erling became involved in major competition when he was 19 and continued for four years with a number of firsts in top competition. He represented Norway in the Stockholm Nordiskaspelen which was the forerunner of the Winter Olympics. He took part in the Holmenkollen on a much more difficult jumping hill than used today. He was among the ski experts who coached the Crown Prince, now King Olav, and served in the King's Guard in 1918. In March, 1919, he came to America and during his early years rode the range and herded cattle as a cowboy in Arizona. His hay fever caused him to give up range life and go to visit a friend who was an engineer. He discovered Colorado, in those days the ski jumpers' mecca. He borrowed skis to enter a meet, won first prize the first day he put them on, and soon became Colorado State Champion in jumping. He also won the title in cross-country the following year. Erling was U.S. Western Champion in 1927, in the combined, winning the prize offered by the *Denver Post* for running up the highest point score in Colorado's five major ski meets in both jumping and cross-country. On a dare that same year, Erling with several other Vikings made the first, and so far as we know, the only ski ascent of Long's Peak. Later he and Lars Haugen, when told it was impossible, crossed the range on skis, making the trip from Estes Park to Steamboat Springs and back. "Quite a trip," says Erling Strom, "when you have to break trail in deep snow all the way." In 1927 he was asked to come to the Adirondacks to the Lake Placid Club, where he spent 11 winters instructing people in recreational skiing. One of his first students was C. Minot "Minnie" Dole, father of the American Ski Patrol System, and often referred to as the father of the Tenth Mountain Division. Erling became associated at Lake Placid with The Marquis D'Albizzi, a Russian-Italian soldier-of-fortune and former officer in the Czar's cavalry as well as an officer in the Italian Mountain Troops in W.W. I. They began spring ski trips in the Canadian Rockies to Mt. Assiniboine. He had his own ski areas including ski schools in the Canadian Rockies and at Stowe, Vt. In 1931 Erling led a 250-mile expedition across the Canadian Rockies for a winter ascent of the Columbia icefields, accompanied by Alfred Lindley of Minneapolis, later head of the Sun Valley Ski Club and prominent in the American ski world. In 1932 he carried out an even more notable feat accompanied by his friend Al Lindley and two Alaskans, Grant Pearson, later first superintendent of Mt. McKinley National Park, and Harry Leek. He led the way on skis up North America's highest mountain, which was the first skiing conquest of Mt. McKinley. He has been regarded as a raconteur and nonprofessional entertainer, and over the years he appeared before scores of audiences from coast to coast lecturing and urging Americans to go out and enjoy the thrills of skiing.

TORRISSEN, Birger
Skisport Builder

Birger was born in 1901 in Bardu, Norway, north of the Arctic Circle. He started his successful jumping and cross-country career at age 8 and at 13 won the Northern Norway Championship in class under 16, and at 22 won three major tournaments in the Nordic Combined in Norway. He was considered a quiet, modest, hard-working individual who often preferred to stay in the background while his accomplishments bore fruit. Birger has earned his place in the ski world. He specialized in the 18-, 30- and 50-km. cross-country competition; he was also among the top performers in ski jumping and combined during the 1930s and early 1940s. Birger came to America in 1929. While in this country, Birger was named by National Historian Harold Grinden to the All-American Cross Country Ski Team in 1931. His career included many firsts at Bear Mountain Park, Norsemen Hill and Rumford, Maine, including the New York State crown and second in both the 18-km. and 50-km. cross-country Eastern championships. In the late 1930s he helped build the two jumps at Norfolk, Conn, scene of international competition on crushed ice. He was on All-American Cross-Country team in 1931. Birger was a member of Uncle Sam's Olympic team in 1936 at Garmisch-Partenkirchen. He developed the junior program at Lake Placid at the behest of Ski Hall of Famer Harry Wade Hicks, and assisted in the development of other skiers who ranked among the best jumpers this country has ever had. Birger was a ski instructor in the ski troops at Fort Lewis, Wash. He designed and tested cold weather equipment and vehicles while with the Mountain and Winter Warfare Board at Camp Hale, Colo, and organized the first military ski race in the United States, a 30-km. championship for the 10th Mountain Division; he then became a civilian instructor with the Mountain and Cold Weather Training Command at Fort Carson, Colo, simplifying methods of teaching for thousands of troops each season. In 1950 he coached the U.S. cross-country team for the *Fédèration Internationale de Ski* at Lake Placid. Birger was one of two men called by the

Air Force during the big snowstorm of Christmas, 1951, to come to the rescue of the 26-man crew of a freight train stuck in the southern Rocky Mountains. He also trained an American team to compete in the international military races in Switzerland in 1953, and had four members of his Armed Forces team make the 1956 Olympic team that competed in Cortina, Italy. Birger was also with the Strategic Air Command Survival School. In preparation for the 1960 Winter Olympics at Squaw Valley, Calif, Birger served as a 1958 delegate to the Swedish national biathlon races and the world biathlon championships, and was in charge of the Olympic jumping hills in 1959 – 1960. He designed and helped construct the biathlon course and served as director of the Olympic biathlon competition. Birger was technical delegate to the National Biathlon Championships at Rosendale, N.Y, 1965, and Lake Placid, 1966. He received his jumping judge's card in Norway in 1926, and has held judges' cards in the Eastern and Rocky Mountain Associations. Birger presently is a certified U.S. Ski Association Nordic official.

1973

CARTER, Hannah Locke

Athlete

Born May 13, 1914, in Morristown, N.J; grew up in Philadelphia; family spent many winter weekends at the Lake Placid Club in New York's Adirondacks; enjoyed winter sports—tobagganing and skating; married to Edward Carter, president of Broadway-Hale, a regent of the University of California at Los Angeles and a founder of the Los Angeles Art Museum.

Hannah joined skiers who climbed Mt. Marcy in 1935. Her figure skating received her best attention and she had hopes of becoming an Olymic skater. She was recruited prior to the 1936 Olympics by Ronald Palmedo of the Amateur Ski Club of New York to make up the women's ski team. With no previous ski record she became a member of the 1936 training squad, an alternate with the Olympic team in Europe, and her first race was during the 1936 *Fédèration Internationale de Ski* (FIS) World Championships. She continued to compete with the U.S. team in all of the major races that season. She was tenth in the 1937 Kandahar race, very much a part of the growth and development of American competition with Europe. Hannah was one of the first women to be recognized as a certified ski teacher. She trained at Sun Valley for the 1940 Olympics in Finland and the FIS scheduled for Norway, with major competitions at the National Alpine Tourney and Olympic tryouts at Tom, Dick and Harry Ski Bowl of Mt. Hood in Washington and the climactic Harriman Cup Races at Sun Valley's Mt. Baldy. In the Olympic tryouts Hannah placed second in combined scoring, her points garnered by placing second in slalom and fourth in downhill of the amateur division of the open-class cometition. Overall she was sixth and eighth, respectively. Named to the 1940 Olympic team, she placed fifth in combined scoring against other Olympians and international competitors. Hannah Carter was considered the third-best American behind Miss McKean and Miss Heath.

CHIVERS, Howard "Amos"

Athlete

Originally from Lyme, N.H; attended Hanover High from 1930 to 1934, attended Deerfield Academy in 1935, then Dartmouth Col. 1937 – 1939; married; three brothers, Warren, Roland and John; Warren 1971 Ski Hall of Famer; three years in the U.S. Navy; parents also very involved in skiing.

A star skier during his high school years (1930 – 34) at Hanover, topped the prep school field while at Deerfield Academy in 1935, winning the downhill, slalom and cross-country races in the Cushing (Mass.) Academy Carnival. At Dartmouth he established one of the finest records in Nordic and classic combined in college history. As a freshman he won the abbreviated Inferno Downhill from the lip of the famous Tuckerman Ravine down to the Appalachian Mt. Club camp. Howard was a Canadian Dominion cross-country champion at Banff, tops in the langlauf and combined in Dartmouth's famous carnival, second in the U.S. Eastern Amateur Ski Association (USEASA) slalom and a member of the U.S. team to Chile for the Pan-American Championships in 1937. In 1938 he was first in the first National College Championship between Dartmouth and the University of Washington at Sun Valley. He was the best in cross-country and the combined at Dartmouth Carnival, combined champion and runnerup in the Intercollegiate Ski Union title meet, Eastern Class B jump ruler, tops in the Olympic combined tryouts at Berlin, N.H, and first in cross-country, second in the jump, fourth in slalom and first in the Nordic combined at Lac Beauport, Que. In 1939 Howard again topped the Dartmouth Carnival cross-country and combined field, placed runnerup in the cross-country and combined at the *Fédèration Internationale de Ski* meet at Lake Placid, captured the intercollegiate crown in cross-country and Nordic combined, the USEASA title games and set a winning pace at the Cannon Mountain cross-country even. Howard was a member of Uncle Sam's Olympic team, cross-country and combined in 1940, and coached the ski team and organized the first Outing Club at New Hampton (N.H.) School. He was fourth in the Class A big jump at Rumford, Maine. In 1942 Howard won the National Nordic Combined Championship at Brattleboro, Vt, also the Eastern's divisional title. Howard was numbered among those few Americans and Canadians to capture ski titles on both sides of the border; he parlayed the Canadian Cross-Country Championship of 1939 at Banff, Alta, into a top honor of the National Ski Association of America. He became teacher-coach at Gould Academy in Bethel, Maine, and his acumen as a coach came to the fore quickly as his charges won the Maine State and New England interscholastic crowns. His Gould team became tops in the Eastern schoolboy circles, his students being especially outstanding in the classic events. He then served as teacher and coach for the U.S. Military Academy at West Point in 1947. He returned to his home in Hanover, N.H, to manage the famous Hanover Inn Ski School and headed the Ford Sayre Memorial Junior Ski Council, one of the largest junior programs in the world with more than 800 youngsters in five local towns. Howard managed the Dartmouth Skiway, planning the trail layout, lift-line installation and designing its expansion in trail and lift facilities.

ENGEN, Corey

Athlete and Skisport Builder

Born March 30, 1916 in Norway; migrated to America in 1933 at the age 17; married; children; two brothers, Alf and Sverre, both Hall of Famers; started a skisport career in Salt Lake City, Utah, which brought fame as top-ranked competitor and sports builder throughout the United States; Russell Wilder Memorial Award 1963 for contributions to junior skiing.

Corey has compiled an impressive record as an athlete and builder of the sport in many ways. He has won over 200 trophies in Alpine and Nordic events, including national championships, and twice has been an Olympian. Corey began his American competitive career as a ski jumper representing the Utah Ski Club and then moved to McCall, Idaho, in 1937 to become a local ski leader and active competitor. He was selected for the U.S. ski jumping team for the 1940 Olympics, canceled because of W.W. II. He captained the U.S. Olympic Nordic team for the 1948 competitions at St. Moritz, Switz. He was the top placing American, 3rd in the combined jumping and 26th in cross-country. Corey moved to Ogden, Utah, where he was ski school director at Snow Basin in 1945 – 1951 and also served as coach of the Intermountain Ski Association Junior Team. In 1951 Corey returned to McCall to direct junior ski programs and produced 11 national champions. Among these champions was his own son, David and some youngsters who went on to U.S. Olympic teams and intercollegiate championship teams. During his competitive years, Corey accomplished what few skiers have—a record of 200 trophies and awards in all events of Alpine and Nordic competitions. He won the famous Alta Snow Cup race three times, 1945, 1956 and also the Veterans Class in 1958; he won the National Nordic Championships in 1952; Corey also won the National Veterans Alpine Combined Championships in 1959, 1962 and 1969. Corey handled national junior teams for the Pacific Northwest Ski Association (PNSA), also active on competition committees and an official in PNSA races. He has been a part of setting Alpine and Nordic courses for national tournaments and officiated during national and international events: 1960 Winter Olympics in Squaw Valley, Calif, the Senior Alpine Nationals in 1965 at Crystal Mountain, Wash, and was national delegate at Bogus, Idaho, in 1969. Corey planned, built and developed Brundage Mountain near McCall, and managed it for nine years. He is now directing the area's ski school, and continues to devote much of his time to developing junior skiers; he remains active as a coach and race official within the PNSA. He was also a member of the Pacific Northwest Ski Area Operators' Association for nine years, serving on various committees.

FOEGER Luggi

Skisport Builder

Luggi Foeger was born 1908 in Austria's Tyrol. He is known throughout North America as a beloved top international competitor turned ski teacher, mountain trooper, photographer, motion picture director, area developer and a homespun landscape architect whose ski slope development techniques have been applauded by conservationist-minded experts. His ski racing career was mainly in Austria: he raced for the Ski Club Arlberg during the 1926 – 1932 era. In six Parsen Derbies, he placed second, third and fourth; in the Arlberg-Kandahar he always placed within the top ten and as high as fourth; he won the Schwarzwald Race and also held a second place. Luggi won a Voralberg championship at Bodelle, a downhill, in 1929; he also captured the downhill at Tschagguns in 1928 and about that time was selected to the Austria *Fèdèration Internationale de Ski* team. His racing career in America was brief, including a top placing in the prestigious Far West Kandahar at Yosemite in 1939. This event was one that he subsequently directed on several occasions, including its last time out in the Far West Division several years ago. Luggi was in the Tenth Mountain Division, stationed in Camp Hale in Colorado. While in the military, Luggi made many important contributions to the research and development of the original system of military skiing that was adopted and has been used by the U.S. Army with few modifications ever since. He contributed to the publication of the first *United States Army Field Manual* on military skiing. In 1938 Luggi was given 24 hours grace to depart his homeland by Hitler's Nazis who were invading the country. He came to California at the request of Dr. Don Tressider of Yosemite to head the ski school at Badger Pass. With Hannes Schneider he surveyed areas in California and Nevada, with reports for U.S. Forest Service to develop ski areas. Later Luggi became associated with Sugar Bowl in Tahoe National Forest and then was a part of the development of Alpine Meadows, using his natural abilities in landscape architecture. He also started skiing instructions there.

FREDHEIM, Sverre

Athlete

Born 1907 in Gran, Hadeland, Norway; migrated to the United States 1927; settled first in North Dakota, then moved to St. Paul Minn, 1930; first job at Mounds Park Hospital 1930; joined St. Paul Ski Club and entered city championships; married; two daughters, Sonja and Diane; enjoys skating, horseshoes, soccer, golf and bowling; still does some occasional downhill skiing; resides in New Brighton, Minn; employed as carpenter.

Sverre won his first ski meet at age 8. He also did a great deal of speed skating and when 12 won a district junior title in Norway. In 1930 he joined the St. Paul Ski Club and won the city title, and started a jumping career that may never be equaled. Sverre's first "out of town" meet was at the old Glenwood slide in Minneapolis. He competed in Class B, won the title and had the longest standing jump setting a new hill record of 147 ft. In 1931 he competed in the Central U.S. Ski Jumping Championships at Canton, S.Dak, won the Class B title and was elevated into Class A. He then attended a special long-standing event after the meet and won that, leaping 192 ft. not only surpassing the hill record but outjumping all Class A competitors. In 1934 he won the Class A Central U.S. Ski Association (CUSSA) title at Devils Lake, N.Dak, and was second in the Nationals at Fox River Grove, Ill. In winning the Central title he defeated the national champion. Since he was not an American citizen, he was ineligible to try out for the Olympic team; in 1935 Sverre became a citizen. He placed second in the Nationals at Canton, S.Dak. He defeated the national titleholder that same year when he won the Olympic tryouts at Ecker Hill in Salt Lake City, Utah. Harold Grinden, historian for the CUSSA, listed Fredheim as the Number Two jumper on a listing of the All-American ski jumpers. Because of bad weather, the Central Championships were not held in 1935. In 1936 Sverre represented the United States in the Olympics at Garmisch-Partenkirchen, Germany. Sverre placed highest of all American skiers and was 11th in the finals. He won first place in eight meets in the Central in 1937. He set the Central hill record of 212 ft. at Devil's Lake, N.Dak. Other meets won by Sverre were Bush Lake, Minn, Canton, S.Dak, Duluth Minn, Cameron, New London and Eau Claire, Wis. and St. Paul, Minn. Sverre won the Class A Central title at Soldier's Field in Chicago as well as having the longest jumps and defeating the national titleholder. Centrals were again held in Soldier's Field, Chicago, in 1938. Although he did not repeat as a winner, he did have the longest leap, 162 ft. He placed third in the Nationals at Brattleboro, Vt, in 1938. Sverre placed fourth in the Nationals held in St. Paul, Minn, in 1939. He was third-time winner of the Central U.S. Class A title at New London, Wis, and received the Governor Heil Trophy. Sverre won the Olympic tryouts at Berlin, N.H, and was selected to represent the United States in the 1940 Olympics in Finland. The Olympics were canceled because of the war. Sverre tied the hill record in St. Paul of 197 ft. in 1940. He won the Class A Championships in 1942. In 1947 after the war, he again tried out for the Olympic team in Seattle, Wash. He placed fifth on Saturday's meet and first on Sunday's, with leaps of 260 and 262 ft. The 1948 Olympics were held at St. Mortiz, Switz. and he was second highest of the American skiers. Sverre competed in several meets in Europe and placed second at Davos and third at LaRosa, both in Switzerland. In 1951 he placed ninth in the Olympic tryouts at Iron Mountain, Mich. In 1955 he moved into the Veteran Class, after competing and winning in Class A since 1931. He won silver and bronze medals in national and central championships in Veteran Class even while past the age of 50. Sverre competed until 1968.

HOLMSTROM, Carl

Athlete

Born June 12, 1910, in Boras, Sweden; immigrated to United States in 1914 to settle with parents at Duluth, Minn; became citizen when father was naturalized in 1920; attended Duluth High School; resides in Duluth, Minn; also interested in ice hockey, high jumping and running.

Carl's interest in skiing started at a very early age. At age 7 he was using one ski (his parents could not afford two) and was sliding down the hills of Duluth. In 1922 Carl first entered organized skiing and ski jumping in Duluth. He competed in boys' classes, winning numerous first places and establishing several hill records, up to and including 1927, which included Northwest Boys' Jumping Championships of 1924 at Minneapolis, Minn, and a hill record; the same year he won the Duluth City Championships. Carl set a hill record in 1925 and won the boys' class at Ely, Minn, and as a junior rode hills at Coleraine, Virginia and Chisholm, all in Minnesota; they were all affiliated with the old Arrowhead Division of the National Ski Association. He was advanced to Class B competition in 1928, and captured the divisional championships at Duluth. Carl went on to win the 1929 championships, as Class A rider of the Arrowhead Division during the annual tourney at Duluth. He also entered the National Intercollegiate Jumping Championships of 1929 at Brattleboro, Vt, and placed second. Carl left Duluth and became associated with the Bear Mountain Sports Association during the summer of 1929. While at Bear Mountain, N.Y, he represented the club as a Class A rider and continued through the winter. He was named to the 1932 Olympic jumping team where he participated as an alternate at Lake Placid. Because of an alternate entry, his rides at Placid's Intervales Olympic Jump were scored as "exhibitions." His second ride was good for 62½ m. and among 16 flights that day which exceeded the old hill record of 61 m. The American Olympic report quotes Coach Julius Blegen: "Carl Holmstrom, first alternate, delivered two exhibition jumps which are well worth mentioning—60½ and 62½ meters." In 1935 he tried out for the 1936 Olympic team, but due to financial conditions he was unable to make the trip to Europe. Carl's competitive record was outstanding during his 17 years as a Bear Mountain entrant, even including entry in such pioneering Alpine events as the 1933 National Downhill at Warren, N.H, and the first downhill in 1939 at Whiteface at Lake Placid. Other records include: hill record of 173 ft. in 1934 at Norfolk, Conn; the Middle Atlantic jumping championship at Fishkill, N.Y, in 1935; first place at Bear Mountain 1930–1935; placing third in 1937 behind world-famous Norwegians Sigmund Ruud and Sverre Kolterud during the Eastern divisional championships at Laconia, N.H; winning two Class A special events at Lake Placid in 1933 and 1936; instituting the triple jump in the Eastern division at Bear Mountain in 1934, and successfully completing it on the 70-m. hill in 1936 at Lake Placid along with Kenneth Kempe and Hans Strand. Carl was twice a runnerup in National Ski Jumping Championships, placing fourth in 1933 at Chicago and repeating at Salisbury, Conn, in 1934. Carl has been active in officiating in both ski jumping and the classic combined competitions during the past 25 years. He was elected president of the Central Ski Officials' Association in 1960 and served two years. He was elected secretary-treasurer of the Central Officials' Association in 1962 and has since been reelected four times. Carl has officiated at many Olympic ski team tryouts, national championships and international events, including the first *Fédération Internationale de Ski*-sanctioned ski flying competition at Ironwood, Mich, in 1969. Carl has devoted 14 years of service to the Duluth junior ski program, which is considered to be among the best, and has developed more national junior jumping champions than any other. He has officiated as many as 10 to 15 junior competitions each season and expects to do so for many years to come. Since 1933 he has been an honorary life member of the Duluth Club. Carl has completed 50 consecutive years of participation in affairs of the United States Ski Association, 25 years in competition and 25 years of service. The Duluth Ski Club saluted Carl Holmstrom on that milestone during the 1971–1972 Winter Sports Season.

KNUDSEN, Arthur G.

Skisport Builder

Born May 8, 1912, in Racine, Wis; married, wife's name Helen; adult life devoted to promotion of skisport, first as competitor, next as club and divisional officer and as volunteer ski-team-pins-sales fund raiser; U.S. Ski Association Award of Merit 1971.

Arthur G. Knudsen's ski jumping career began in Racine at 14 years of age with rides on a hill good for 50 m. Then two years later the ski club constructed a 70-m. trajectory. In 1934 he joined the Racine Ski Club at 22 years of age. He continued his jumping career through the 1948 season, which included a third place in the annual tourney at Racine. He next took up recreational skiing, with one unsuccessful fling at downhill racing, and then moved to "work for the sport of skiing." Art is an honorary lifetime member of the Racine Ski Club whose work in support of the nation's ski teams has been recognized divisionally, nationally and internationally. Art also holds lifetime memberships in the Snowflake Ski Club of Westby, Wis. the Kiwanis Ski Club of Iron Mountain, Mich, the Norge Ski Club of Chicago, the Snomads of Racine, and the Ski Club of Eau Claire, Wis. During his 41 years of membership of the Racine Ski Club, Art has held the presidency on 22 occasions. He holds a perfect attendance record at conventions, as an officer of the Central Division for 39 years. In 1970 he was elected director emeritus, the first such honor bestowed, after being divisional director for 14 years. Art served in the 1959 North American championships during tryouts of Olympic facilities and again in 1960 for the real thing. In 1970 as a volunteer, he attended the *Féderation Internationale de Ski* World Championships ski jumping. He has used professional painting skills to create three-color ski team sales booths proclaiming "support your ski teams," which he erects at ski shows, ski tourneys and ski conclaves throughout the country, traveling almost at his own expense. Art decorates ski jump outruns and ski race finish lines with flags. He has averaged $4000 in his ski team pin sales a season.

MACOMBER, George "The Cat"

Athlete

Born in 1927; graduated from Mass. Inst. Technology, 1948; married, wife's name Andy; three children; now living in Concord, Mass.

George Macomber raced in interscholastic competitions between 1935 and 1944. At the age of 15 he placed fifth in the 1942 AMC Wildcat downhill competition. With slalom being his strong suit, he was generally in the first three positions in collegiate competition in 1945. In 1946, with a year off, he trained at Alta and placed first in the downhill, third in the giant slalom and eighth in the slalom, for a fourth in the combined of the Alta Cup. He placed fourth in California's Sugar Bowl Silver Belt giant slalom that same year. In 1947 he placed third in the slalom in the SRMSA championships at Aspen, a slalom third and third in the combined at the IASA championships at Jackson Hole, and a third in downhill and combined at Sun Valley Olympic tryouts. He was selected for the 1948 Olympic team. In 1948, after placing second in New York's giant slalom at Davos, Switz, George was injured in training and missed the Olympic Games. He came back later in the year to win the Silver Belt giant slalom in Sugar Bowl. In 1949 he tied for first in the Gibson Trophy Race, placed second in the Sun Valley Ski Club Championships and scored first across the board at the Nationals at Whitefish, Mont. Despite injury, George came back for a sixth in the slalom and an eighth in the combined at the Harriman Cup, Sun Valley, and a tie for third in the national giant slalom at Reno's Slide Mountain. He was injured at Aspen while training, as a member of the U.S. team at the *Féderation Internationale de Ski* World Championships in 1950. Nevertheless, he scored 15th in the slalom and 22nd in downhill and 42nd in giant slalom in those championship events. In the Eccles Cup giant slalom at Ogden that year, he placed fourth, and fifth in slalom and sixth in the combined North American at Banff. He scored ninth in the downhill and ninth in the combined at Sun Valley's Harriman Cup. He won the downhill, scored fifth in slalom, and fourth in the combined in the Eastern Championships at Stowe. George won the Webber Cup downhill on the ever dangerous Wildcat. George was injured in the slalom of Lauberhorn in 1951, but earned a 21st in the downhill Lauberhorn Trophy in Wengen beforehand. George placed a third in the Webber Cup downhill in 1954; and between 1954 and 1962 many other first and high placements. He was a dominant figure in Veteran competition in the East and at the Nationals. He swept the Group 3 (age 40–47) National Veterans Championships in 1967.

McLANE, Malcolm

Athlete and Skisport Builder

Born October 3, 1924, in Manchester, N.H; graduated from Dartmouth, Col; attended Oxford Univ. as Rhodes Scholar; Harvard Law School; married, wife's name Susan Neidlinger; five children; military service 1942–1944, 1st Lt. in Army Air Force, flew 73 fighter missions, shot down in December, 1944, prisoner of war until released in May, 1945; earned Distinguished Flying Cross, Air Medal with 13 clusters and Purple Heart; partner in law firm; now living in Concord; Blegen Memorial Plaque 1959.

Malcolm McLane began skiing as a boy by sliding down local hills on toe-strap slats. In the mid-1930s, Malcolm was skiing for St. Paul's School in Concord, N.H, and for the Dartmouth College ski team. He was a member of the Dartmouth College team from 1946 to 1948, and was honored as its captain in 1948. That same year Malcolm participated in the European Student Ski Championships at Sestriere, Italy, where he placed second in downhill. Following were the ski racing at Lenzerheide, Switz, and the Arlberg-Kandahar at Murren. In 1949 he competed at Sestriere, Italy, in the Oxford-Cambridge University Championships. Malcolm then followed ski trails previously tracked by another Dartmouth Outing Club member, Hall of Famer John Carleton. This ski trail led Malcolm from the Uncanoonics of Goffstown, N.H, Oak Hill at Hanover and Suicide Six of Woodstock, Vt, past the now long-forgotten Huckins Hill of Plymouth, N.H, to Gunstock, Mt. Mooselauke, Spyglass Farm, Cannon, Wildcat and Tuckerman's to the white heights of Europe. In 1952 he competed in the Mt. Washington Inferno after which he would compete in Veteran racing. Malcolm served from gatekeeper at beginner events to technical delegate for international *Féderation Internationale de Ski* (FIS) calendar events, being a certified divisional, national and FIS official. He founded the Wildcats Ski Corp, of which he has served as president. In 1950 he became a member of the Ski Club Hochebirge and later a member of the Wildcat Mountain Ski Club, and has held these memberships ever since. In 1953 he began a series of duties that marked him as one of the great builders of the sport of skiing. The same year he was elected a director of the United States Eastern Amateur Ski Association, and held this post for over ten years. Malcolm began a tour of duty as a director of the National Ski Association in 1958, a post held through the 1962 name change to United States Ski Association. In 1964, as director of the U.S. Olympic committee, he began a nine-year tour of duty, which terminated in 1972 at his resignation. Malcolm oversaw four Winter Olympics, 1960, 1964, 1968 and 1972, while chairman of the U.S. Olympic committee between 1957 and 1972.

MULLIN, J. Stanley
Skisport Builder

Stanley Mullin became an officer in the Lake Arrowhead Ski Club in 1936, and founder of the Southern Ski Club in 1939. He is a member of the Sun Valley Ski Club, the Ski Club of Great Britain, Ski Club of Davos and Ski Club Arlberg. Stanley served as secretary of the California Ski Association (now Far West Ski Association) for two years following W.W. II and then vice president of the National Ski Association (NSA), due to his early club memberships. Stanley revised the constitution and bylaws of the California Ski Association as well as those of the NSA, both of which were finally adopted. He prepared the plan for classification (point system) for the NSA. He served on the eligibility committee, which led him to similiar activity on behalf of the *Féderation Internationale de Ski* (FIS), where he serves as a member of a three-man committee on eligibility. He attended the 1948 and 1956 Olympic Games and the 1950 FIS championships in a semiofficial capacity. As U.S. delegate he attended the 1951 and 1955 Congress of the FIS. He is a member of the 1960 Olympic Games organizing committee. Stanley is one of the incorporators of the National Ski Patrol System and he is a past trustee and section chief. He has contributed materially to the progress of the sport of skiing on local, divisional, national and international levels. He has served on numerous committees. He is recognized as the outstanding American on the international level.

SORENSEN, Harald "Pop"
Athlete and Skisport Builder

Born 1905 in Vollen, Asker, Norway; emigrated to the United States in 1929; U.S. Army 1941; Halstad Memorial Award; Russell Wilder Memorial Award 1971; resides at Winter Park, Colo.

Harald's skiing started when he could just about walk, so he could get to school in Vollen in Asker. His first competition was at the age of 13, triumphs at Hyttli Hill, outside Oslo; he won many junior meets, then advanced to Class A, placing second in tryouts for the world-famous Holmenkollen; he was one-tenth of a point behind the fabulous Sigmund Ruud, 1970 Hall of Famer; he placed third in the Holmenkollen, third in the Norwegian Nationals, third in the Swedish Nationals and combined victories in Finland, Norway and Sweden before coming to this country. Harald was a member of the National Ski Associations' All-American jumping team twice. He has captured the Eastern, New York State, New England, Northwest and a host of other crowns; cracked hill records at Norsemen, Bear Mountain, State Island, Brattleboro, Norway Ski Club and Rumford slides; has finished runner-up in Class A Nationals twice; was picked for the 1936 U.S. Olympic team but could not compete in Garmisch-Partenkirchen, Germany, because he was not a citizen. In 1941, while in the U.S. Army, he taught the Eastern experimental ski patrol at Old Forge, N.Y, instructed the 87th Regiment, the Second Division; one of 20 American instructors attached to the British School, teaching skiing to the Allied Forces in Italy; continues with the army as technical adviser to the Mountain-Ski Committee, fifth U.S. Army Recondo Center at Fort Carson, Colo. In 1937 Pop became a national jumper judge, and still participates actively in officiating; coached the U.S. ski team in the World Nordic Championships at Lake Placid in 1950; in 1952 was Olympic jump coach for this country at Oslo, Norway; has been a certified ski instructor since 1946, and still teaches hundreds of children the art of ski jumping, while serving as a civilian instructor to the Army. Today he is still teaching at the Denver Post-Winter Park Ski School, free to kids from 4 to 18. Pop's ski school for jumpers takes place on an amazing complex of nine hills, each higher, until a 60-m. slide provides the finishing touches for the more expert.

1974

BUEK, Richard
Athlete

Born November 4, 1929, in Oakland, Calif; father operated ski shop along with mother and sister; family group combined into a fearsome ski racing team, often entered top Alpine competitions of the Far West Ski Association, each won divisional snowflake pins during 1950s and early 1960s; motorcyclist, high diver, airplane pilot, parachutist; motorcycle accident in May, 1953, almost ended ski career; in 1955 suffered broken back on ski practice run at Stowe, Vt; second broken back while employed as power company lineman; died November 3, 1957, in Donner Lake day before 28th birthday, in airplane crash with fellow skier Dick Robarts.

Dick Buek first entered competition in 1947, as a member of the Sugar Bowl Ski Club in the inaugural of Sacramento Bee Silver Ski Team Trophy competition on Mt. Disney, and registered the fastest time of the day. He had a setback in the 1948 Inferno Race, the first-time-ever straight schuss from the top to flat run out of Mt. Lassen, which saw the next and only other competitor to accept the challenge, Yasi Teramoto of Donner Ski Ranch, clipping Richard's time by a split second. In 1949 Richard joined the newly organized Donner Summit Ski Racing Club. He won the Silver Dollar Derby and Far West Ski Association Downhill Championships at Reno's Slide Mountain and Mt. Rose Bowl. He later joined the Sun Valley Ski Club and was selected as alternate for the 1950 *Féderation Internationale de Ski* (FIS) ski team. In 1951 he became a top downhill contender, going on to win the 1952 National Championships at Stowe, Vt; this followed his return from the Olympic Winter Games in Norway, where he placed 12th in downhill despite a fall. After his motorcycle accident in 1953, right knee and left shoulder wired and pinned together, he went on to win the 1954 National Downhill at Aspen, Colo; he was bypassed when the 1954 FIS team was picked. The following summer after injury to his back, his record included national downhill seconds twice, third once and fourth once. His spectacular ski career gained him the title of "The Madman of Donner Summitt." In times when downhill was known as "the straight race," he always went full bore because he had no fear; it was his favorite event.

ELKINS, Frank

Skisport Builder

Born in the United States in 1910; married, wife's name Flora; son Howard, Jr, a ski competitor; ski editor of the *Long Island Press* for 18 years; earlier had spent 28 years on the sports staff of the *New York Times;* a contributor to official ski publications throughout the United States, Canada and Europe; a Frank Elkins Memorial Scholarship has been created; Medal of St. Olav 1946, awarded by King Haakon VII, for foreigners who have been helpful to Norway; honors from National Ski Association, United States Ski Association and National Ski Areas Association; died September 6, 1973.

Frank began his journalistic career when he joined the *New York Times* in 1928. His 45-year newspaper career produced an unprecedented flow of ski reporting, snowsports historical research and ski columnizing. Frank was a contributor to official ski publications throughout the United States, Canada and Europe. Other than articles and columns in the *Long Island Press* and the *New York Times,* there were magazine articles and two major books, *The Complete Ski Guide* and *The World Ski Book and Encyclopedia.* These books were compiled by Frank in cooperation with historian Harold Grinden and historian Bill Berry, and contained many valuable American and Canadian skisport records. The only gathering that he ever missed during his writing career was the 51st annual convention of the Eastern Ski Association; he was ill. He was honored in a national broadcast in which his role in the formation of the National Ski Patrol System was discussed by his long-time friend and skiing crony, Lowell Thomas. He maintained archives in his home, which were invaluable to the establishment of the National Hall of Fame. He was also very active in academic and public relations circles. The Ski Hall of Fame as it exists today in Ishpeming would not have been possible without Frank Elkins' help.

ERICKSON, E. O. "Buck"

Skisport Builder

Resides at Iron Mountain, Mich; retired after 38 years in newspaper work due to physical disability; still able to write and plans to continue promoting ski jumping.

Buck Erickson is a former editor and sports editor of *The News* at Iron Mountain. In 1974 he completed 35 years as publicity director for the Pine Mountain ski jumping classics. He began when he was publicity director for the dedication tournament of the $125,000 WPA project hill in 1939. He produced the annual popular ski section in *The News.* This section was acclaimed nationwide and his largest issue, eight pages, was reproduced in photographs in the *American Ski Annual.* His ski releases were and are still being sent to 75 news media throughout the Midwest and across the nation. Erickson was responsible for bringing the first foreign jumpers to Pine Mountain tournaments from Switzerland, Norway, Finland, Italy and Canada. Erickson served on the public relations committee of the United States Ski Association and is currently public relations director as a member of the ten-man National Ski Hall of Fame committee. He is considered to have the longest ski jumping and promotion career in the United States. Buck has been honored for his contributions to skisport by the Ishpeming Ski Club, the Central Ski Association, the United States Ski Association and the Ski Associations of Finland, Norway and Switzerland. He owns plaques from the Italian Ski Association, the Kiwanis Ski Club and the Iron Mountain-Kingsford Winter Sports Association.

FLAA, James E.

Skisport Builder

Born September 17, 1894, in Ishpeming, Mich; father came from Trondheim, Norway, married his Norwegian sweetheart in America and settled in Ishpeming; fifth of six children; outstanding athlete in school, football and basketball star, played with semipro teams; U.S. Navy; honored with a specially struck gold medallion in recognition of his services to Central and to the skiing sport by Central Ski Association at 25th Anniversary Celebration.

In 1921 Jim Flaa became a member of the Ishpeming Ski Club. Because of his influence as a member, he was named secretary. Jim held this post for 17 years. The Ski Club grew and the town became a mecca for skiers in the Midwest. The Flying Bietilas went out from Ishpeming under the direction of Jim Flaa. He was involved with the formation of the National Ski Association with Harold Grinder. Jim was responsible for the resurgence of the Central Ski Association and served as its vice president. He was also responsible for the development of junior skiing in Ishpeming, which continued to grow around the country. In 1945 he was named first chairman of a committee to establish a ski hall of fame, and then National Ski Association president. Jim remains an active member of the Ishpeming Ski Club and he still enjoys skiing.

HILL, Clarence "Coy"

Athlete and Skisport Builder

Clarence Hill began his competitive career before age 10, and was consistently the long jumper in most tournaments, as well as being an outstanding stylist. As time went on, Coy worked his way up through the junior ranks to become a member of the senior club at Ishpeming, Mich. He developed into one of this country's outstanding ski jumpers and competed in many tournaments throughout the Central Division and other areas of the United States. Among his most notable victories and accomplishments were: first in U.S. National Class A Championships 1952, Salisbury, Conn, new hill record, 203 ft; several times placed second and third in National Class A Championships; Central United States Ski Association champion 1952, Oconomowoc, Wis; and South Rocky Mountain Ski Association Champion 1952, Steamboat Springs, Colo. He was overall champion of a two-week competition held at Los Angeles, Calif; winner of champion's trophy each week, and had the longest jump of the competitors against seven Olympic jumpers and Olympic alternates. In 1955 he was Wisconsin Open champion at Westby, Wis. In 1956 he won Michigan Open Championships at Ishpeming. Coy was alternate in the 1956 Olympic jumping team. He was National Veterans champion in 1965 at Ishpeming, and co-national Veteran champion in 1970 at Eau Claire, Wis. He also competed internationally and made a significant mark overseas as well, including a member of a three-man team to Austria in 1952 as guests of the Austrian Ski Association; he placed 13th (9th and 16th) in a two-day meet at Kulm's Ski Flying Hill, jumped 325 ft; placed 8th at Seefeld, Austria, with the two longest jumps; placed 5th at Obersdorf, Germany, where he had the second longest jump. Coy worked on Suicide Hill, as skisport builder, lending his own talents and jumping and skiing abilities. He was a vast knowledge of the jumping sport and is interested in the progress and development of young jumpers.

KOZIOL, Felix C.
Skisport Builder
Felix C. Koziol has served 42 years with the U.S. Forest Service, 21 years as supervisor of the Wasatch National Forest in Utah. He first became interested in skiing in 1936 and has since been an ardent booster and hard working supporter of the sport. As recreational staff officer in the Ogden Regional Forest Service in 1938, he had an opportunity to start promoting skiing by helping to survey and plan many ski areas in Utah, Wyoming and Idaho, which are now considered some of the best in the world. As supervisor of the Teton National Forest in Jackson, Wyo, in 1942, he played an important part in the development and promotion of skiing in that area. He was president of the Jackson Hole Ski Club and had been president of the Ogden Ski Club while residing in Ogden. Felix was transferred to the Wasatch National Forest in Utah in 1943, where the opportunity for developing skiing really grew. He helped get the avalanche program under way. Felix hired and trained the first snow rangers who carried on a scientific research program. He secured artillery to be used in avalanche control in 1952, a major step in dealing with this problem. In 1947, recognizing the need, he co-authored the first official publication on avalanches, which was entitled *Alta Avalanche Studies.* Then in 1954 he authored the first government handbook on avalanches, followed in 1961 by *Snow Avalanches,* a handbook in forecasting and control measures that has become the bible for snow rangers everywhere. Felix helped institute highway and traffic safety programs for the canyons while working with the state road commission of Utah. He always found time to serve in all phases of skiing, even though he had a busy schedule with the Forest Service. He was an active judge and timer of ski competitions for many years. He was secretary for the Intermountain Ski Association for ten years, as well as Intermountain editor for the *American Ski Annual.* During this time Felix was also a delegate to many national ski association meetings. He helped promote the first program for certification of ski instructors and their official professional organization. In 1952 he received the Julius P. Blegen Memorial Emblem Citation, presented by the National Ski Association of America for outstanding service to the sport of skiing, and received a Citation from the U.S. Olympic committee for dedication and support of the U.S. ski team in the 1952 Olympics in Oslo, Norway. In 1966 Felix received a citation from Utah State University for outstanding contributions to Utah sports; as a member of Governor Rampton's committee to study and apply for the 1972 Olympic Games in Utah, he went to Rome to help present the application to the International Olympic committee. The same year he received the Governor's Annual "Ski Utah" Cup Award.

KRAUS, Dr. Hans
Skisport Builder
One of the world's foremost figures in promoting physical fitness and therapeutic rehabilitation exercises; member of the President's council on physical fitness and youth fitness; married to former Madi Springer-Miller, former U.S. women's Olympian; Viennese orthopedist; served several times as physician for Austrian Olympic teams; at one time professor of rehabilitation and physical medicine at New York University; interest in skiing, hiking, mountain climbing (with many first ascents), judo, boxing, acrobatics and fencing; continues to lecture, advise and help recreational and competitive skiers by constant exhortations and articles emphasizing the need to be physically fit and the importance of practicing therapeutic exercises for skiing; continues to be a rabid skier and mountain climber.

Dr. Kraus entered the correspondent's office at the *New York Times* in 1938, with an introduction from Hannes Schneider, and the following week he served as medical adviser for the National Alpine Championships. He served as the medical adviser for these all-important games and was on hand when Roger Langley, president of the National Ski Association, was so impressed with the work of the improvised patrol, headed by Minnie Dole, that he established the National Ski Patrol Committee. There are now some 27,000 members of the National Ski Patrol System, a volunteer, nonprofit organization, who patrol the hundreds of ski areas of this country. He has written extensive syndicated newspaper articles, a variety of periodicals, several books and many medical papers emphasizing the need of keeping physically fit and in good condition and good health, and stressing the prevention of accidents and the need for reconditioning and rehabilitation for post-injuries. Dr. Kraus, along with another outstanding skiing colleague, Bonnie Prudden, shocked the world with the results of a survey that showed "most of the people of this country, oddly enough, are not really well physically; we are hardly fit for ordinary living, let alone for the strenuous activity of skiing." It also showed "that our children by the lowest set standards are woefully unfit—in spite of generally superior medical care and nutrition." It was these valuable studies that inspired President Eisenhower to organize the President's Council on Youth Fitness, of which Dr. Krauss was an important part. Dr. Krauss also treated the late President Kennedy for his back injury and was a member of his Physical Fitness Committee. In a book published in 1940, *A Complete Ski Guide,* Dr. Kraus' article emphasizing the importance of physical fitness for skiers through preseason exercising, conditioning, etc., created nationwide publicity. Having earned his badge in 1944, Dr. Kraus continues to be very active in the National Ski Patrol System. He has been the national medical adviser for the Eastern Ski Patrol System, Belleayre Ski Patrol and has memberships on the advisory board of the joint legislative committee on sports and physical fitness in New York, the President's Council on juvenile delinquency and the New York Committee of the U.S. Ski Team Fund. Dr. Kraus, through his established and innovative orthopedic and therapeutic exercises, has brought back many outstanding competitive skiers, as well as recreational skiers, to their former physical ability after suffering serious injuries. Some of these distinguished ski figures include

Buddy Werner, Toni Matt, Lowell Thomas and Billy Kidd.

MERRILL, C. Allison "Al"
Skisport Builder

Born 1924; originally from Andover, Maine; a 1947 graduate of Univ. N.H; married; two children; presently director of outdoor affairs for Dartmouth Col, in charge of over 30,000 acres of college's wilderness lands, incorporating use of these lands into the academic curriculum through Environmental Studies programs, as well as overseeing Dartmouth's extracurricular outdoor programs, including activities of world-famous Outing Club; Julius Blegen Award 1967.

Al's career as a coach began in 1952 at Lebanon (N.H.) High School; then in 1957 he went on to become head ski coach at Dartmouth College, Hanover, where he remained until 1972. His teams never finished lower than fifth in the National Collegiate Championships. They were first once, second three times, third several times, and only once lower than fourth. He designed and created a national program to develop the top U.S. athletes into international competitors, and also developed many athletes from a local program into national caliber athletes. Over ten men from Al's high school or college program went on to become Olympic skiers. In the late 1950s and 1960s he was involved in the United States Nordic skiing. He coached the 1954 *Fédèration Internationale de Ski* (FIS) Nordic Combined team and the 1956 Olympic team. From 1962 to 1968 Al was head Nordic coach for the U.S. ski team, and was the U.S. Ski Association's first Nordic program director from 1968 to 1970. He was team leader and head coach for the 1964 and 1968 Olympic Nordic teams and the 1966 FIS World Championship team. Al was also the 1973 U.S. Nordic combined team coach. During this time, great strides were taken by the U.S. Nordic program. National training camps were first held; national coaches were hired and national teams and training squads for a given year, as opposed to specific events, were also introduced. These innovations helped elevate the United States to at least respectability and credibility in international Nordic competition. Al was chief of course (cross-country) for the 1960 Winter Olympics at Squaw Valley, Calif, and FIS technical delegate for cross-country at the 1972 Winter Olympic Games in Sapporo, Japan. Al has been a long-standing member of the FIS cross-country committee. He served as a member of the board of directors of the U.S. Eastern Amateur Ski Association, now the Eastern Ski Association, and as its president in 1964–1965.

MIKKELSEN, Strand H.
Athlete

Born November 3, 1904, in Kongsberg, Norway; emigrated to Canada in 1924; he was a veteran of W.W. II, serving in the U.S. Army; he came from a famous Norwegian skiing family; three brothers, all top competitors; died February 6, 1964.

Strand H. Mikkelsen won his first ski trophy at age 8. At 17 he finished second in an open jumping competition in a national meet on Gusta Ski Hill, Gaitus, Norway, with a jump of 46 m, 9 m. off the world's record at that time. Strand won many prizes in European tournaments before moving to Canada. In 1926 and 1927 he won the Canadian Western Championships. In 1929 he won the U.S. National title at Brattleboro, Vt, and the Swedish Ski Club tournament at Bear Mountain, N.Y; placed second in the U.S. Eastern Amateur Ski Association Championships at Rumford, Maine; won the U.S. National jump title and set a hill record in International Ski Championships at Lake Placid, N.Y. Later in 1929 he moved to Greenfield, Mass, where he operated a ski shop and became a ski instructor at Greenfield's Weldon Hotel. Strand broke a ski at the end of a jump and on one ski broke the 179-ft. record during the Olympic trials of 1932 at Greenfield. In 1934 he became a professional and was the founder of the Eastern Professional Ski Association. As president, his association sponsored indoor meets in Boston and in New York City's Madison Square Garden. In 1934 at Ecker Hill, Salt Lake City, Utah, he made the longest jump of 257 ft. At this time he was considered the leading ski jumper in the United States. In 1951 Strand moved to Worcester, Mass, and operated a ski shop at Mt. Wachusett, Princetown, Mass. He became a member of the Scandinavian Ski Club of Worcester.

NORHEIM, Sondre
Skisport Builder

Born 1825 in Morgedal, Telemark, Norway; father a farmer; died in North Dakota in December, 1897, but because of severe winter held in house until spring 1898 and was buried in graveyard at Norway Lutheran Church near Denbigh; one hundred years after the first real ski jumping competition in the world in 1866 in Telemark, a stone with a plaque was set up on grave, dedicated through the joint effort of the North Dakota Historical Society and Norway's *Foreningen Ski-Idrettens Premme* (Society for the Promotion of Skiing), the plaque reads as follows: "In memory of Sondre Norheim. He introduced ski bindings and the Telemark and Christiania turns and developed slalom and ski jumping. Born in 1825 in Morgedal, Telemark, Norway. Died in the United States 1897." His grave is flanked by the Norwegian and American flags.

Sondre saw skis as more than a practical means of transportation, and in 1850 in Norway, developed bindings with shoots of birch roots, soaked them in hot water to make them flexible and twisted them together to fit around the heel and hold it in place. Only a toe strap had been used for 4000 years. And now Sondre had skis that could be mastered. He made some changes in the shape of the skis, which allowed him to jump, twist and turn. People were fascinated by this man who "flew through the air like a bird." Although Morgedal was isolated and had poor communication, in 1861 the Central Association for Sport and Shooting was organized and the popularity of sports, including skiing, rapidly grew. In fact, it grew to be Norway's national sport, resulting from military ski races with marksmanship competitions begun in 1867 and regional contests staged throughout Norway. Skiing competitions in Norway began in 1862, the first of which was downhill racing with small jumps in the track. The first cross-country competition was held in Tromso in the north of Norway in 1843, and ski jumping events in 1866. Sondre won the first ski jumping competition in Telemark in 1866 at Hoydalsmo and was awarded a clock. He won the third ski competition sponsored by Central Sports Association in Christiania (capital city at the time) in 1868. People were astonished to observe how he was able to turn and handle his skis. His sudden stop on skis became known as the "Telemark" and he also displayed a parallel turn, the "Christiania." His skis had curved sides and were of shorter lengths. He never discovered prosperity on the steep hillsides of Norway; instead he came to America, the flat country of North Dakota, and didn't do very much skiing. He is known as the "Father of Modern Skiing" for his contributions to the sport. In the 1960 Squaw Valley Olympics, Hall of Famer Andrea Mead Lawrence carried the Olympic Torch fired from the hearth of a Norwegian cottage where Sondre Norheim had lived.

SCHAEFFLER, Willy
Skisport Builder

Born 1916 in Kaufbeuren, Germany; Penal Battalion in Hitler's army; after applying for visa to get out of Germany, injured, tortured on Russian front, joined German underground; presently director of U.S. Ski Team National Training Center; immigrated to the United States in 1948; graduated from Univ. Denver.

Willy Schaeffler was a ski coach at the University of Denver from 1948 to 1970. His team won 14 of 16 National Collegiate Athletic Association Championships from 1954 to 1969. Willy was coach of the 1966, 1968, and 1970 *Féderation Internationale de Ski* (FIS) teams. He was director of ski events for the 1960 Olympics, and a long-standing member of the FIS course approval committee. In 1968 he was president of the Eighth International Congress of Ski Instructors in Aspen. He officiated as FIS technical delegate at Olympic, World Championships, and World Cup Events. He was also team leader of the 1972 U.S. Olympic Alpine team in Sapporo. During 1971 – 1973, he was U.S. Alpine program director. In the 1974 FIS Championships at St. Moritz, he was referee of the men's downhill. Willy is the founder of the Professional Ski Instructors Association. He is a four-way Austrian junior champion. Willy was among those who helped build Arapahoe Basin, and he directed the ski school there. Willy is responsible for gaining skiing recognition as an NCAA sport in 1945. He was a ski instructor at Garmisch-Partenkirchen after the war, and also coached the U.S. Army team.

1975

BIETILA, Ralph G.
Athlete

Born July 8, 1924, in Ishpeming, Mich; five brothers, Anselm, Walter, Leonard, Roy and Paul; quickly introduced to the winter sport by members of his family, who came to be known as the "Flying Bietilas" among ski jumping aficionados; family received Bass Award 1946 for contributions to skiing.

Ralph started skiing at age 6 using hand-me-down skis, and competed in his first ski tournament when he was age 9. In 1940 he gained his first major skiing award, placing third in Class C competition in Berlin, N.H. At 16 he won his first tournament title by capturing the National Junior Class Championship crown in an Iron Mountain, Mich, tournament. He set a hill record of 262 ft. and a national distance record that withstood all challenges for a number of years. In 1941 he finished with a title at a national tournament in Hyak, Wash, and continued winning three championships in Oconomowoc, Wis, Iron Mountain and Beloit, Wis. In 1945 Ralph took a Class B title in Iron Mountain. In 1947 he placed first in Class A competition held by the Rocky Mountain Ski Association. In 1948, at the age of 23, he gained a spot on the U.S. Olympic team that traveled to Davos, Switz, but a broken arm kept him from competing in the international ski jumping games. Ralph was named to the U.S. ski jumping squad that competed in the *Féderation Internationale de Ski* World Championships at Lake Placid, N.Y. In 1952 he was again asked to be a member of the U.S. Olympic contingent to the Winter Games in Oslo, Norway, but a foot injury kept him out of the competition. In 1953 he took Class A in the Paul Bietila Memorial Tournament held in Ishpeming, Mich. He finished third in a tournament at Steamboat Springs, Colo. In 1954 he took second in Westby, Wis. In 1955 he took a third and a second in Steamboat Springs and Westby, respectively. He represented the United States in international competition in Sweden and Finland. In 1963 he won the National Veterans Class Championship at the age of 39. At the Steamboat Springs, Colo. hill, his jump of 261 ft. set a distance record for Veterans Class jumpers that has not been broken. In 1974 at the age of 49, he donned a pair of skis and competed in a pair of ski jumping tournaments on his hometown's Suicide Hill.

ELLINGSON, Jimmy
Skisport Builder

Born May 2, 1906, in Eau Claire, Wis; son of Norwegian immigrant; builder of champions; married, wife's name Helen; after W.W. II, took employment at Wausau, Wis; one of the trails on the nearby Rib Mountain ski area today bears name; died July 2, 1971; Eau Claire Distinguished Service Award 1939.

Jimmy was working as a janitor at the Fourth Ward Grade School and was the man behind the "Flying Eagles," started in January 1933 by seven boys to become an influential factor in ski jumping throughout the world. During its existence more than 1000 boys and girls have been a part of the junior club, which is still active today and claims to be the country's oldest junior organization in terms of consecutive years. With his guidance, 17 of the original 100 Flying Eagles became state champions and Midwest champions. They almost always swept honors and were known for their outstanding riding and style. Ocar Severson was the club's outstanding rider in the Midwest in that time, a flawless stylist who jumped the big as well as the small hills and was rarely beaten. He went on to become a top-notch senior rider in the late 1940s, holding the North American Class B distance record at one time. Billy Olson was the Flying Eagles' most famous product. He joined the club when he was age 5, went on to ski in two Olympics and became the only American to win National Championships in four classes. Unfortunately, many club members who had great potential were killed in W.W. II and others found themselves too long away from the sport to return. The club's hill was located on the grounds of the school and accommodated jumps of 15 to 60 ft. The hill was erected as a WPA project in 1936, and under Ellingson's influence kids would ski before and after school, at noon, during recess and even at night once the lights were added. On February 28, 1937, he gained nationwide attention when the first night ski jumping tournament was held. Ellingson, a fine ski jumper himself, gave it up to serve youth and American skisport. He was named Central junior ski jumping chairman in 1939 and was granted the city's Distinguished Service Award for his service to youth. In 1970 a testimonial was held in his honor at Eau Claire in conjunction with the national tournament. Nearly 100 of his Eagles returned to pay tribute to him. Included were judges, lawyers, school administrators, doctors and many other successful business people who had been guided by his influence. Ellingson was more than an outstanding ski coach—he was a leader, counselor, minister, teacher and disciplinarian all rolled into one, and he stressed sportsmanship, honesty and politeness. He was especially proud that none of his skiers ever got into serious trouble with the law.

HAUK, A. Andrew "Andy"
Skisport Builder
Born 1912; resides in Los Angeles, Calif.

Andrew Hauk is more than a skier. He has established a career of involvement. He has been a ski club member and Olympic Games organizer. He has also done numerous voluntary roles in organized skisport: area development advocate, racing competitor, author and speaker.

JOHANSON, Sven S.
Athlete and Skisport Builder
Born November 25, 1924, in Neder-Kaliz, Sweden; seven brothers and three sisters; father former ski competitor; lived on farm and hard work produced the physique and competitive spirit that gained national records in walking, speed skating, bicycling, track and Nordic skiing; won regional and district championships in bicycling and speed walking; in 1946 won the 10,000-m. track championship, and the national 50-km. speed walking championship; in 1947 with three brothers won the Swedish National Speed Walking Championship; moved to Stockholm to continue education; served in Swedish Army from 1943 to 1948; in 1950 emigrated to Astoria, Ore. Astoria was not for him and in July, 1951, he moved to Anchorage, Alaska; from 1954 through 1959 won the Seward, Alaska, Mountain Running Marathon; in 1968 won national 200-m. prone large-bore rifle championship; first Alaskan to win a National Cross-Country Ski Championship, and first Alaskan to win place on U.S. Olympic team.

Sven won his first regional cross-country ski race at age 8 in Sweden, after which his successes progressed through local, district and regional championships. At 17 he won the Swedish National Junior Cross-Country Championship. He moved to Stockholm to further his education. While in the Swedish Army, Sven won the Swedish Army Cross-Country Ski Championships in 1944 and 1945, the Biathlon championships in 1945–1947 and a near second-place finish in 1946. In 1948 he was a member of the third-place Military Ski Patrol at the *Conseil Internationale du Sport Militaire* ski games at Andermatt, Switz. In 1950 he moved to Astoria, Ore, and then in 1951 he moved to Anchorage, Alaska. He joined the Anchorage Ski Club, the Alyeska Ski Club, and finally the Anchorage Nordic Club. Sven dominated Alaskan skiing in the early 1950s, winning the Alaskan Championships 1951–1956 and the Pacific Northwest Championships 1951–1954. He also won the John Craig Memorial Race 1952–1954. He won the Donner Memorial Race 1953–1955. He won the North American Championships in St. Paul, Minn, in 1955. He won a spot on the U.S. Olympic cross-country team, but because of an administrative error in obtaining his citizen's papers, he was unable to compete. He won the National championship in Lyndonville, Vt, in 1957. Sven won a spot on the U.S. *Fédèration Internationale de Ski* team in 1958, and in 1960 he became a member of the U.S. Olympic cross-country team. He also won championships in Eastern, New York, New Hampshire, Maine and Vermont competitions. Sven was selected as coach for the U.S. Modern Winter Biathlon Training Center at Fort Richardon, and remained at this post from 1961 to September, 1973, when the center was disbanded. He trained every U.S. biathlon team to compete in 1964, 1968 and 1972 Winter Olympics, which maintained a higher relative placement than any other Nordic team during this period. In 1962–1963, 1965–1967 and 1967–1971, he served as ski coach for the U.S. World Championship Biathlon teams. He was the ski coach for all U.S. military ski teams that attended *Conseil Internationale du Sport Militaire* Ski Weeks from 1962 to 1973. Many of his biathletes have gone on to coaching. He was a member of the American College of Sports Medicine for several years, and wrote *Handbook of Biathlon Training,* a comprehensive study of training methods, rules and regulations, mostly pertaining to biathlon, but applicable as well to all phases of skiing. Sven and a few other Alaskan Nordic skiers work with young skiers and help develop a strong Nordic program. *Also in:* Swedish Sports Hall of Fame.

KNOWLTON, Steve P.
Athlete and Skisport Builder
Born August 3, 1922, in Pittsburgh, Pa; attended Holderness School, Plymouth, N.H, and the Univ. N.H; served with Tenth Mountain Division in the Aleutian Islands and Italy during W.W. II; avid golfer, shoots par; in 1948 manufacturer's representative selling ski equipment to sporting goods stores in 11 western states; during winter taught skiing and operated ski shop in Aspen; initiated and became manager of the Broadmoor Ski Area; served as executive director of the 1962 World Hockey Tournament, held at the Broadmoor and in Denver.

Steve's competitive career dates back to 1938, as a member of the Holderness ski team. He was a member of the University of New Hampshire ski team 1941–1942. In the 1942 Dartmouth Winter Carnival, he placed first in downhill, third in slalom and first in combined. He took third in combined at the Alta Cup, Utah, 1944. In 1945 he took third in the Grossglockner (Austria) and first in the Tenth Mountain Division Race (Italy). In 1946 he placed second in giant slalom at the Silver Belt Race, Sugar Bowl, Calif, and placed first in the U.S. National Downhill Championships at Franconia, N.H, where he skied for the Aspen Ski Club, and took fourth in slalom. He was the 1946 men's slalom Class A champion, and placed first in men's open slalom, second in men's downhill Class A and second in men's downhill open event; he placed second in men's combined A and Open Classes at the Southern Rocky Mountain Ski Association (SRMSA, now Rocky Mountain Division). Again in 1947 he was the SRMSA champion for men's downhill Class A event and placed second for men's downhill Open event. Steve took a fifteenth place in slalom at St. Moritz as a member of the 1948 U.S. Olympic team. In SRMSA in 1949, he placed third in men's slalom and combined events. He was a *Fédération Internationale de Ski* team member in 1950. Steve placed second in Class A slalom in SRMSA in 1951, and in 1952 recaptured first place in men's slalom Open competition; he placed third in men's downhill Open and men's combined Open. He placed first in the men's slalom Open championships and first in the men's slalom at Aspen in 1954. Steve raced as a Senior in the Silver Belt Race in 1955 and took third place. He took first in the 1957 National Veterans race in slalom and combined events. The same year he took second at the Silver Belt Seniors Race at Sugar Bowl, Calif. In the United States Ski Association (previously National Ski Association) Championships in 1958, he took first place in Veterans I Slalom and Veterans Combined, as well as first in Veterans I Downhill National Championships. Steve is a certified national race official and he is rated a top official with a full competitive record. He has worked with the junior program in skiing. He has earned coveted awards as an outstanding athlete and builder of the sport. In the summer of 1963 he was asked to be the managing director of a new, nonprofit organization designed to promote Colorado skiing. He had two television shows and a daily radio program devoted to the sport of skiing and the promotion of Colorado skiing in general. He participated as a fund raiser for the Denver Winter Olympics in 1968 and was the Announcer for the Eighth Interski at Aspen that year.

QUINNEY, S. Joseph
Skisport Builder
Born 1894 in Utah; graduate of Utah State Agricultural Col. and Harvard Law School; senior partner in Salt Lake City law firm; at age 81 was still active skier and year-round participant in Utah's ski activities.

Joseph S. Quinney, while never having been active as a competitor, made great contributions to the Nordic portion of the sport. Joseph organized, conducted, officiated and judged at many national regional jumping contests at Ecker Hill and at Alta. For many years he helped organize and direct activities of the Utah Ski Club. His greatest contribution to skiing comes perhaps from his role in making skiing possible at Alta for millions of persons, and then remining at the helm of the operation, which has always been regarded as one of the finest ski areas in the world. George was among the pioneers who invested money, time and talent to help form the Salt Lake Winter Sports Association, parent of Alta Ski Lifts. George served first as secretary-treasurer of the company and then for about 20 years as company president. When most major ski areas began increasing the cost of lift passes, he was instrumental in keeping lift passes at a reasonable cost to allow more people to ski, and emphasized the importance of high-quality and well-maintained equipment as opposed to expenditures on housing and real estate.

REID, Robert H.
Athlete
Born May 27, 1898, in Berlin, N.H; graduated from Berlin High in 1916; contemporary of Hall of Famer Alf Halvorson; noted in his racing heydey for remarkable endurance, gained from trudging around in the North Country woods as a surveyor.

After apprenticeship in Nordic skiing, Robert began serious competition with an entry in the Canadian Championships at Montreal in 1921, placing ninth in the 11-mile cross-country. Robert placed second in 10- and 8-mile races at Gorham, N.H. In 1923 he placed third in the 20-mile Mt. Washington race, despite a dislocated shoulder. In 1924 with the Weeks Trophy up for grabs in the Mt. Washington event, he won and set a new record. The same year he won the National Cross-Country Championship at Brattleboro, Vt; he placed second in the Canadian National championship at Shawbridge, and won the Nansen Ski Club Championship at Berlin, N.H. In 1925 he took second place in the Vermont Championships, but ruptured himself and was out of competition for the remainder of the year. In 1926 he won the 100-mile Portland, Maine, to Berlin, N.H, race, and placed second in the Mt. Washington race; Robert's record of 2 hrs. and 55 min. still stands. In 1927 he placed second in the National Cross-Country race at Steamboat Springs, Colo; placed first in the Ontario Championships at Ottawa; placed second at the Berlin 11-mile Cross-Country Championships; and second in the 50-km. Olympic tryouts at Lake Placid. He won the 1927 Canadian Cross-Country Championships. Robert was 34 years old when he made the 1932 Olympic ski team. He was one of the first American-born to break Scandinavian supremacy in Nordic ski competition in America.

STILES, Dr. Merritt Henry
Skisport Builder
Born September 10, 1899, in Stiles, N.Dak; attended Univ. Washington, graduated in medicine from Univ. Pa; practiced in Philadelphia until 1942; in 1937 married Tana, a registered nurse; two sons, and two daughters by previous marriage; served in Italy in the U.S. Army Ambulance Service during W.W. I; enlisted as major in U.S. Army Medical Corps in 1942 and served in a number of Army hospitals all over the country; discharged Lt. Col. in 1946; U.S. Ski Association Blegen Award 1965; honorary member National Ski Patrol System; U.S. Ski Writers Association Golden Quill Award 1965; U.S. Olympic Association Torch Award for outstanding leadership 1969.

Dr. Stiles, known nationally as an internist and heart specialist, first put on a pair of skis at age 55, to watch his son race on nearby Mt. Spokane. He and his wife went down to Squaw Valley and took some lessons. It took him 2 hrs. and 40 min. to come down the old Number One chairlift, but he returned right after the 1960 Olympics and made it in 4 min. His enthusiasm made up for his late start in skiing, turning him into a creditable advanced intermediate capable of handling most any hill he cared to tackle. Before he started skiing he weighed 196 lbs. and he had trouble leaning over to tie his shoes without running out of breath; thus he started an exercise program of jogging and running and then skiing. He became involved with Dr. Robert D. O'Malley of Holyoke, Mass, in writing *Ski at Any Age,* published in 1971, dedicated to proving that people over 50 years of age can become healthier by skiing. Dr. Stiles has been a nonstop prophet for the sport's health benefits, but also stresses the benefits of regular exercises of all kinds. He has been heavily involved in organized skiing locally, regionally, nationally and internationally since 1958. His greatest accomplishment was the backing and inspiration he gave Dr. Bud Little and Bob Beattie to get things started in moving the U.S. ski competition program from a part-time activity toward its present full-time status.

STRAND, Hans

Athlete

Born 1905 in Melbu, Norway; emigrated to the United States in 1925; married, wife's name Mary; two children, Debora and Hans, Jr; from 1928 to 1933 he held various jobs until he finally settled at working in the inn at Bear Mountain State Park in New York, where he remained until his retirement in 1973.

Hans won his first tournament at age 10 in Norway. In 1925 when he came to the United States, he joined the Norwegian-American Ski Club of Rockford, Ill. In 1928 as a Class B jumper, he beat all Class A competitors at a meet held at Racine, Wis, and established a hill record. He joined the Bear Mountain Sports Association, during which time he jumped at Racine, Oconomowoc and Westby in Wisconsin; Ogden Dunes in Indiana; Fox River Grove in Illinois; Canton in South Dakota; Ogden, Utah; Red Wing, Duluth and Minneapolis in Minnesota; and in the early 1940s at Lake Placid, N.Y; Berlin, N.H; Brattleboro, Vt; Salisbury Mills, Rosendale, and Bear Mountain, N.Y. Hans has a room filled with trophies, medals and countless photos of that era. His greatest day was perhaps that day in 1942 when he won the senior men's jumping championship at Berlin, N.H. Then in 1943 he captured the Eastern Veterans championship and also the New York State Veterans championship. In the early 1950s, he was the one who helped sell the idea of buying chipped ice for the hill at Bear Mountain, and even now its jumping schedule goes off, snow or no. During W.W. II he was among those who pleaded for the State Park to keep ski jumps open despite the gas rationing and lack of finances to keep them open. Hans, along with Carl Holmstrom and Nick Nylund, got crowds talking about their triple jump from a 50-m. hill. He qualified for the tryouts in the 1932 Olympics, but was knocked out by an injury.

TOWNSEND, Ralph J.

Skisport Builder

Born December 28, 1921, in Lebanon, N.H; attended Lebanon High School, graduated from Univ. N.H. 1949; three brothers, Richard, Harold and Paul, who also performed in skiing on the Lebanon High School team; during W.W. II, with the Tenth Mounted Division; recipient of Purple Heart; resides at Williamstown, Mass.

Ralph is a product of two Hall of Famers, the late Erling Heistad, who coached him at Lebanon High School, and Edward J. Blood, who was his mentor at the University of New Hampshire. He was a member of the Wildcats ski team during his college years, and became Eastern cross-country champion in 1941, Nordic combined in 1941 and 1946 and Eastern slalom and Alpine combined in 1947, national Nordic combined champion in both 1947 and 1949, he represented the United States in its 1946 Nordic ski team duel with Canada, was a member of the 1948 U.S. Olympic ski team and the 1951 U.S. *Fédération Internationale de Ski* ski team. Ralph also gathered numerous honors along the way. He was also very involved with other phases of skiing as well. In 1950 he was head coach of the Williams College ski team until his retirement in 1972; served on the rules committee for the formation of the Eastern Intercollegiate Ski Association (EISA) in 1950, and served as its president in 1958, 1959 and 1960; he was on the EISA executive committee in 1956–1972, as well as other committees; he served as secretary of the National Collegiate Athletic Association (NCAA) in 1962–1964 and 1969–1973; also served on the NCAA skiing rules committee in 1960–1964 and 1969–1973; director of the United States Eastern Amateur Ski Association (now Eastern Ski Association, ESA) in 1951–1952, and a member of its cross-country committee for many years and its chairman in 1959–1960; an Alpine and Nordic official; in 1960 was coach of the ESA National Junior Nordic team. Ralph has given countless hours and service to the United States Ski Association: Olympic Ski Games, 1960–1964; International competition, 1960–1964; Intercollegiate, 1961–1965; Coaches System, 1965–1968; Nordic competitions, 1959–1960, and cross-country. Ralph has been a member of the National Ski Patrol System and a Ski Patrol Leader. He is a certified professional ski instructor. He was an entertaining toastmaster at major ski functions as well.

1976

BERRY, William Banks

Skisport Builder

Native of Potsdam, N.Y; now resides in Reno, Nev; newspaperman for many years, was on staff of *Ottawa Journal;* attended some of the earliest events of the Canadian Amateur Ski Association in 1921.

Beginning his skisport career in Canada, Bill Berry returned to the United States in 1923 and became a member of the Auburn Ski Club, Calif. Now historian emeritus for the U.S. Ski Association, no one can begin to estimate the number of hours he spent researching the members of the Hall of Fame so that they might have complete biographies in Ishpeming. Through his research, he found that Hall of Famer Anders Haugen had actually won the bronze medal in ski jumping at the 1924 Winter Olympics and, funded by grants from the Auburn Ski Club, represented the United States in a special ceremony for Haugen in Oslo, Norway, in 1974.

COCHRAN, Barbara Ann

Athlete

Born January 4, 1951, in Claremont, N.H; first coached by father Mickey, who later became head coach of the U.S. Alpine Team in 1973; coached Vermont Women's Ski Team during the 1974–75 season; Billy Kidd Award 1972; Coronet Skier of the Year Award 1972; Vermont Athlete of the Year Award 1972; Beck International Trophy 1972; works for a ski company, a ski binding company and ski clothing manufacturer.

Barbara Ann first started skiing at age 4. Her first race was at age 6 in the Lollipop Slalom at Mt. Ascutney in Vermont. She won her first championship at the age of 15 in the giant slalom of the 1966 Junior Nationals at Winter Park, Colo. She finished fifth overall in the World Cup with a second in slalom and third in giant

slalom in 1970. She was also a silver medalist in slalom at the 1970 *Fédération Internationale de Ski* (FIS) World Championships. She won the slalom and giant slalom in the World Cup races in 1971 at California's Heavenly Valley. In 1972 she won a gold medal in women's slalom in the Winter Olympics at Sapporo, Japan, beating Daniele Debernard from France by a mere .02 sec.—1:31.24 to 1:31.26. In 1974 she became a member of the FIS team.
Also in: Winter Sports Hall of Fame, Citizens Savings Hall of Fame Athletic Museum.

COUCH, Edmund, Jr.
Skisport Builder
Born July 5, 1906, in Philadelphia, Pa; went West with parents when father became forest ranger in Pike National Forest; brother Sam; attended Univ. Denver, graduated from Univ. Wis, 1934; civil engineer; completed active military service in 1947.

Edmund first put on a pair of skis in Colorado, after father fashioned some skis to get around the grounds and then made little skis for Ed and his brother Sam. He found out that it was fun and skied in the yard the rest of the winter. Then the family moved to Dillon for the winter of 1915–1916, where Ed found out that skisport was already an established way of life. Ed and Sam constructed small jumps and learned to ski through the trees and make turns. Skisport boomed in Dillon during the winter of 1918–1919. From that time on Ed was hooked on ski jumping and would build ski jumps of one sort or another. By the winter of 1920–1921 the Couch brothers were deeply enmeshed in a junior jumping program sponsored by Pete Pestrud. They both won prizes that winter. In 1923 Ed joined the Denver Ski Club, moving from Class C to Class B and won the divisional championships of 1927. With George Steele, and representing the University of Denver, won the 1929 Ski Team Trophy. At the University of Wisconsin he was greatly influenced by Hall of Famer Dr. Harvard Bradley and competed in intercollegiate and divisional tournaments of the Central Division. In 1934 he joined the local ski club in Whitehall, Wis. At age 31 his competitive career ended when he broke his right leg. He then became very active as a ski jumping judge and ski designer. He was involved in organizing the Ski Hill Engineering Committee, which interpreted standards in the 1936 *Fédération Internationale de Ski Rule Book* and gave guidance and advice in engineering problems connected with the construction of properly designed ski jumps. His first engineering work was for a new jump at Whitehall. After W.W. II, engineering committees were organized in other divisions under the newly activated national committee, which Ed chaired from 1947 to 1971. Ed had done the original design and analysis in 1941 of the large ski jump at Steamboat Springs, and in 1949 updated it. This most famous of Colorado's numerous ski jumps was named in honor of Carl Howelsen, and it was here that the first leaps of over 300 ft. were made in North America. In 1946 Ed carried forward the original investigations for ski flying at Ironwood, Mich. He designed and constructed North America's only ski flying hill. He also designed jumps in Wisconsin, Minnesota, Colorado and many more locations. He became a certified ski judge in the Central Division, the Eastern Amateur Division and retains National card No. 9. He was chief ski jump designer for the Denver Olympic committee. In 1958 he designed and directed the construction of the first "man-made-snow" ski area below the Mason-Dixon Line at Shawneelan, Va. In 1957 he worked on the original reconnaisance for Squaw Valley and in 1958 directed the final review of the planning. Also a member of the Ski Club of Washington, D.C, since 1947, he served as president for two terms and was elected an honorary member in 1957 for work in developing skiing for those in the capital area. He was designated as an FIS judge in 1938.

HEGGTVEIT, Dorothy Anne (Hamilton)
Athlete
Born January 11, 1939, in Ottawa, Ont; married to Ross Hamilton; major goal was to become an Olympic gold medalist; watched Canada's Barbara Ann Scott return to Ottawa as the Olympic figure skating gold medalist of 1948, greatest influence on ski career; first non-European to win the FIS gold medal for Alpine combined as well as the Arlberg-Kandahar; first Canadian to win an Olympic gold medal in skiing; Lou Marsh Trophy as Canada's Outstanding Athlete of the Year 1960; appointed to the prestigious Order of Canada; retired from skiing October 1, 1960.

Dorothy Anne won her first race when she was age 7, a ladies' senior and combined event at Wakefield, Que. She placed second in the Central Canadian Championships at age 9. At 10 she won the Ontario Slalom and Combined; at 13 she had won all local senior ladies' events. In 1953, at 14 years of age, she was selected a member of the Canadian team to be sent to Europe for training. Anne won the Holmenkollen giant slalom in Norway, competing against the world's top skiers, just two weeks after her 15th birthday. She placed ninth in the World Downhill at Aare, Sweden, and was seventh in the slalom the same season. She was fifth in slalom a week later at the Arlberg-Kandahar. She was in a cast for six months following a leg fracture while practicing slalom at Mt. Tremblant on January 31, 1955. In 1956, still handicapped by her injury, she placed fifteenth in the combined at the Cortina Olympics and placed ninth in the Arlberg-Kandahar at Sestriere, Italy. While remaining in North America for the 1957 season, Anne won every race she entered in Canada and the United States. She sprained an ankle at Aspen, Colo, while training for the United States Nationals and was out for the balance of the season. In the 1958 *Fédération Internationale de Ski* World Championships, she placed sixth in combined, and then went on to take third in the Holmenkollen. In 1959 Anne won the Moritz White Ribbon Tournament and the Arlberg-Kandahar. In Canada, she won all three events of the Quebec-Kandahar and the Canadian Alpine Championships. In 1960 she suffered a severe cut by a shovel wielded by a workman while practicing at Grindenwald. A week later she went west and won the United States National Slalom and Giant Slalom Championships at Alta, Utah. Anne also swept three events of the Roch Cup at Aspen, Colo. At Squaw Valley she won the Olympic and FIS gold medals for slalom and the FIS gold medal for Alpine combined. She was ranked top Alpine skier of 1960.
Also in: Canada's Sports Hall of Fame, Canadian Amateur Athletic Hall of Fame and Greater Ottawa Sports Hall of Fame.

HEUGA, James
Athlete
Born September 22, 1943, in Tahoe City, Calif; graduated from Univ. Colo. 1968; began suffering from incurable multiple sclerosis; sales representative for Beconta Ski and liaison between ski manufacturer and organized skisport; headquarters in San Francisco and New York; National Ski Hall of Fame Athlete of the Year Award 1964; Beck International Trophy 1967; Wallace "Bud" Werner Award 1967.

The skiing career of Jimmy Heuga has been one of continuous victory, beginning in 1958 when he won his first giant slalom championship at Yosemite Winter Park. He then won the slalom championship for the U.S. National Junior and National Senior competitions in 1960, the junior combined of the Sel-am-See and the Alpine combined at the Harriman Cup races in 1961 and the Lauberhorn and Wengen Medals and the Emile Allais Silver Disk in 1962. He took the Aurora Cup, third in the Nationals at Alyeska, Alaska, and the National Collegiate Athletic Bronze Medal in 1963. In 1964 Heuga won the Harriman Cup Gold Bowl for first in the downhill, the Arlberg Kandahar Gold Cup for first in the combined race and the Bronze Snowflake in the *Fédération Internationale de Ski* World Championships. In 1964 Heuga followed Hall of Famer Billy Kidd by .24 sec. in the men's slalom at the Winter Olympics and won himself a bronze medal; he and Billy Kidd became the first American men to win medals in Olympic skiing. He was welcomed home by a giant parade of people along the highways who presented him with the Chamber of Commerce Man of the Year Award. Not finished then, Heuga won the Alpine Holiday Classic Gold in slalom in 1965, the Slalom Gold First at Bariloche, Argentina, and the Vail Trophy Silver Bowl for a first in slalom and combined in 1966. He also won the first place Colorado Cup in 1966 and 1967 and the Werner Cup, Roch Cup and the Australian Thredbo Cup for first in the combined, slalom and giant slalom in 1967. Following participation in the 1968 Olympics, Heuga retired, but his bronze medal remains a major attraction at the U.S. Ski Team display in the Western America Skisport Museum at Boreal Ridge, Calif, along with many other trophies Heuga won in his outstanding career.

KIDD, William Winston
Athlete
Born April 13, 1943, in Burlington, Vt; graduated from Univ. Colo. 1969; resides at Steamboat Springs, Colo; participated in the pro racing circuit for two years and represented a ski manufacturer and the Steamboat ski area in promotional tours; commentator on World Olympic competition and hosting syndicated television program "The American Ski Scene"; member of the President's Council on physical fitness and sports; coaches at the Red Lodge Summer Racing Camp; acts as adviser and part-time coach to the U.S. ski team.

Billy started his racing career at age 12 in Stowe. He was sponsored by the Mt. Mansfield Ski Club and was racing around North America through high school. In 1961 Billy won the Harriman Cup slalom. In 1962 he placed eighth in slalom and twelfth in giant slalom at the *Fédération Internationale de Ski* (FIS) World Championships in Chamonix, France. In 1963 he sprained an ankle in an early season race at Lake Placid, N.Y, and was out for the season. Billy captured a silver medal during the 1964 Olympic Winter Games at Innsbruck, Austria (split seconds behind first). Billy also won the FIS bronze medal in combined. In 1965 he won eight consecutive races in the United States. In 1966 he traded wins with Jean-Claude Killy during January; in April he had surgery for ankle injury; and during the World Championships in Chile he broke the other leg and was out for the 1967 season. In 1968 he sprained both ankles in practice, which kept him out of competition at Grenoble, France. Then in 1969, he won the World Cup slalom at Squaw Valley. In 1970 Billy netted his world championship title and the first U.S. gold medal, at the FIS World Championships in Val Gardena, Italy, placing first in combined scoring. Billy turned professional and two weeks later won the 1970 World Professional Championships in Verbier, Switz, placing first in giant slalom and first in the combined. Billy was named director of skiing for the Steamboat ski area, director of racing at Hart Ski Co. and racing editor for *Ski Magazine.*

KOCH, William
Athlete
Born June 7, 1955; residing in Guilford, Vt.

William Koch won a silver medal in the 12th Winter Olympic Games at Innsbruck, Austria, in 1976 for the 30-km. cross-country. He has established himself as a top-rated international competitor and an inspiration for the rapidly expanding Nordic ski programs of the United States Ski Association. Bill Koch is a product of the Eastern Ski Association.

KREINER, Kathy
Athlete
Kathy Kreiner is 19 years old, and resides in Timmins, Ont. She won the giant slalom in the 12th Winter Olympic Games at Innsbruck, Austria, in 1976. Her gold medal triumph was acclaimed by all North Americans.
Also in: Canadian Athletic Hall of Fame and Canada's Sports Hall of Fame.

NELSON, Cindy
Athlete
Cindy Nelson is 21 years old, and resides in Lutsen, Minn. She won a bronze medal in the 12th Winter Olympic Games at Innsbruck, Austria, in 1976, when she placed third in downhill. She is rated the United States Ski Association's best-ever downhill. She was the United States flag bearer for the Olympic opening ceremonies.

NISHKIAN, Byron F.
Skisport Builder
Born January 28, 1916, in San Francisco, Calif; graduated from Univ. Calif; while attending university played ice hockey and competed in state figure skating events; while growing up in San Francisco couldn't participate in Boy Scout summer trips into the Sierra because of violent susceptibility to poison oak, so went on winter ski trips to Donner Summit instead; married; three children; business firm has done lift and other design work for such areas as Badger Pass, Alpine Meadows, Squaw Valley, Mt. Lassen, Rocky Mountain National Park, Homewood, Sugar Bowl, Donner Ski Ranch, Harding Ice Field and the Sikkim Life Line and Chair Lift on the Tibetan border; Julius Blegen Award 1975.

Byron was involved in officiating at ski meets. He joined the Yosemite Winter Club and was on his way to a fruitful ski career. In 1956 he became president of the Yosemite Winter Club. He established the Century Club, and sparked the charter flight program while serving as a board member of the Far West Ski Association (FWSA). Byron became president of the FWSA in 1958, serving for three terms, and was also on the U.S. Ski Association (USSA) board of directors. Within the division, he formulated successful membership programs and directed the appointment of the division's first full-time executive director. He was made a member of the organizing committee for the 1960 Squaw Valley Olympics, contributing his administrative abilities and engineering skills to the Winter Games' planning. Byron was also involved in the women's cross-country program, encouraging the USSA executive office and the Nordic competition personnel to organize a ladies' cross-country program. Because of his involvement and contributions to organized skiing at the national level, he was elected USSA president in 1965 at the Spokane convention and held this post for three terms. Among his contributions in the USSA top office are his efforts of membership development. He supported the funding of the National Ski Hall of Fame at Ishpeming, Mich. Byron was also involved in the *Féderation Internationale de Ski* (FIS) eligibility and citation committees. In 1975 he arranged and hosted the first FIS Congress in California, which drew some 350 delegates for a week-long program of business and social events. He spent six months setting up plans, which resulted in one of the most successful FIS conclaves ever held.

OVERBYE, Sigurd
Athlete

Sigurd Overbye was a noted Nordic combined competitor, strongest at cross-country and winner of national championships in 1916, 1923 and 1926. He was a member of the 1924 U.S. Olympic team. Now all members of the 1924 Olympic ski team are members of the National Ski Hall of Fame.

PEABODY, Roger A.
Skisport Builder

Born September 10, 1920, in Littleton, N.H; graduated from Dow Academy in Franconia in 1938, attended the Univ. N.H. from 1938 to 1942; father Roland Peabody was manager of the Cannon Mountain ski complex; married, wife's name Louise; six children, Jere, Jon, Joel, Jånet, Jay and Jennifer, all ski for fun, Jere and Joel both professional ski patrolmen. Roger has been active in other sports as well as skiing. He has played basketball and baseball and has been an official as well as a player. He served as an official for 11 years and is past president of the National Basketball Officials.

POLLARD, Harry G, Jr.
Skisport Builder

Born June 29, 1907, in Lowell, Mass; served in the Navy from 1942 to 1948.

Pollard began jumping and cross-country skiing in Middlesex School in Concord, Mass, in 1925. In 1926 to 1927 he skied in New Haven, Conn, which surprised the local populace, who had never seen skis. He gave up skiing from 1927 to 1934 because he couldn't find anyone with whom to ski; he started skiing again in 1935 and made skis in a local woodworking shop. In 1972 he helped to organize the American Ski Federation and was the first vice president. Harry wrote articles on ski safety and education, and is currently a member of the U.S. Ski Touring Council. He devoted 52 years to skiing.

REILLY, Betsy Snite
Athlete

From Norwich, Vt; attended high school in Hanover; married Bill Reilly of the Mount Mansfield Corporation in Stowe, Vt.

Betsy first joined the Carcarjan Ski Club, but her competitive career was actually sponsored by the Dartmouth Outing Club. To prepare herself for the games, Betsy, among Americans, skied in Europe during the 1959 season. At Grindenwald, Switzerland, Betsy placed second in downhill and won the giant slalom and earned the combined titles. Betsy also took a fifth in downhill at St. Moritz. She was a member of the training squad. She gained valuable experience from top racing schedules in the United States. It was a well-balanced group, and the squad had depth. She was among those selected for the 1960 Winter Olympic Games.

SAUBERT, Jean

Originally from Cascadia, Ore; father Jack Saubert; graduated from Ore. State Univ, graduate studies at Univ. Utah; involved in a teaching career ever since racing days, first at Vail Country Day School in Colorado and now at Brigham Young Univ, Provo, Utah; coaches ski racers, especially children, attends summer racing camps; resides at Orem, Utah; director of the Intermountain Ski Division and serves on several committees of the United States Ski Association.

Jean started her racing career when her father was a Forest Service district ranger, in charge of Forest Service administration of Hoodoo Ski Bowl. Then she skied at Warner Valley when the family moved to Lakeview, Ore. She had been racing all along, winning National Junior Championships and was on the road to Senior titles and Olympic and *Féderation Internationale de Ski* (FIS) World Championship competitions. Her big step forward came when Dave McCoy, area owner and himself a long-time competitor, invited her to train at Mammoth. When she reached Mammoth, there were a string of National Junior Championships. She had won the 1957 National slalom and National combined titles at Slide Mountain, Nev, while competing out of the Pacific Northwest Ski Association. In 1959 she again picked up the same titles at White Pass, Wash, by the time she began training at Mammoth Mountain with Dave McCoy. Jean soon proved a skier for Mammoth Mountain; her triumphs included the 1962 FIS World Championships at Chamonix, France, placing sixth in giant slalom, seventeenth in slalom, ninth in downhill and ninth in Alpine combined; and won the 1963 National downhill at Alyeska, Alaska. The U.S. Olympic ski team trained at Mammoth ahead of the 1964 Winter Games. She had another sparking performance, which included a clean sweep of the National downhill, slalom, giant slalom and Alpine combined championships at Colorado's Winter Park. She also won several European events. The Associated Press tabbed her "best woman of the year" going into the Winter Games. During the 1964 Olympic Winter Games at Innsbruck, Austria, she won a silver medal in a second-place tie in giant slalom and a gold medal, placing third in slalom. In 1965 Jean competed in American International Team Races at Vail, Colo, and tied with Marielle Goitschel to win the slalom and had a fifth in downhill. Even though Jean had won a place on the 1966 FIS team, she elected not to race in the 1966 FIS Championships and remained to continue graduate studies. But she did enter the World University Winter Games in Sestriere, Italy, and took a silver medal in downhill and a bronze in the slalom. She then entered the summertime FIS Championships held in Chile and was fourth in slalom and eleventh in downhill; this was the end of her competitive career.

Also in: Winter Sports Hall of Fame, Citizens Savings Hall of Fame Athletic Museum.

VAAGE, Jakob

Foreign Member and Skisport Builder

Born February 9, 1905, in Oslo, Norway; winner of Norwegian Junior Ski Jumping Championship; 1925, became certified ski jumping judge; 1935, coach of Norwegian jumpers for *Fédération Internationale de Ski* World Championships and chairman of Norwegian slalom committee; 1936, manager of Olympic slalom team; 1939, first chairman of ski instructors' committee; several years chairman of the Norwegian ski judges; ten years member of the *Fédération Internationale de Ski* judges' committee; accomplished student of languages; he and wife Berit retired educators; currently resides in Bekkestua, a suburb of Oslo close to the Norwegian Ski Museum.

A walking history book of skiing, Jakob Vaage has been researching and writing about skiing since 1939 when he wrote *On Steel Edges,* about slalom racing, and followed that with *The Holmenkollen Hill, Sports Books of Norway,* listing 1500 books written in the last 200 years, and *Norwegian Skis Conquer the World* in 1952. He has also written numerous sports reports, articles and historical materials for ski publications, newspapers and periodicals in the United States and Norway, has written 30 years for the Norwegian yearbook *Sno og Ski* and has given over 1000 lectures on skisport. Putting this vast amount of knowledge to use, Vaage has been the curator of the Norwegian Ski Museum in Holmenkollen since 1947. He had obtained skis like those used by Hall of Famer Snow-Shoe Thompson to carry the mail in the Sierras, skis and bindings as developed by Sondre Norheim and the skis used to introduce ski jumping to Red Wing, Minn, in 1891 by Norwegians Mikkel and Torjus Hemmestveit. Since 1947 Vaage has visited the United States three times, first in 1954 to present 20 pairs of historic skis at the dedication ceremonies for the National Ski Hall of Fame. He returned again in 1960 for the Olympics in Squaw Peak and, with the Norwegian Olympic ski team, placed a plaque on the grave of Snow-Shoe Thompson. In 1967 he memorialized Sondre Norheim with a plaque on his grave in Denbigh, N.Dak.

VAUGHN, Lucile Wheeler

Athlete

Born January 14, 1935, in Montreal, Que; ski racing career was encouraged by parents; hobbies include riding, golf, swimming, tennis and fishing; also musical and has flair for writing; opened the modern era of ski racing for Canada when she won the first Olympic medal ever won by a Canadian; still active as leader in development of young racers in Quebec's eastern townships; Order of Canada.

Lucile Wheeler first learned to ski at age 2, carrying messages from her home in St. Jovite over the three-quarter-mile snow route to a resort operated by her father. At age 10, she entered her first competition, a downhill race at Mt. Tremblant in which she placed second among 21 Senior ladies. Lucile was promoted to Class B two years later, and became the junior downhill and combined champion of Canada. She was named to the ladies' team for the International Meet at Lake Placid, N.Y, an annual series from which emerged a format for the current Can-Am racing circuit. Lucile continued her winning ways in local races the following year: placing first in the Ste. Agathe slalom, first in the Taschereau among seniors and juniors, first junior in the Canadian National downhill and second in the Quebec Kandahar. At 15, Lucile was named to the Canadian ski team for the *Fédération Internationale de Ski* World Championships in Aspen, Col, in 1950. In 1952 she participated in her first Olympic Winter Games in Norway, and raced the balance of the season in Europe. In 1953 she remained in North America, competing in the Quebec Kandahar, the Canadian National Championships, the Harriman Cup at Sun Valley, the United States National and the North American Championships. In 1954 she returned to Europe and gained valuable experience. Lucile placed second in the Ryan Cup, won the Alpine combined of the Canadian National and again took part in the Harriman Cup in 1955, and other competitions in the United States. She placed second at Kitzbühel, Austria, just two weeks prior to the 1956 Olympics. With a spectacular run, Lucile captured the bronze medal of the Olympic Winter Games at Cortina, Italy. In 1957 she placed first in the Hahnenkammen Kitzbühel, Austria, and competed in other international competitions. Lucile was named by the FIS as one of the three top women skiers in the world. She won two gold medals—the downhill and the giant slalom—and was runner-up in the Alpine combined in the 1938 World Championships at Badgastein, Austria. In 1958–1960 Lucile and teammate Anne Heggtveit combined to dominate women's skiing by winning four out of the eight available gold medals in the FIS championships.

ZIMMERMAN, Penelope Pitou

Athlete

Born 1938 in Bayside, N.Y; moved to New Hampshire with her parents when 3; divorced from Egon Zimmerman; mother Christian and Kim; tennis champion, ski fashion consultant, motion picture actress and television personality; during the winter of 1975 coached Laconia High School girls' ski team; became the first American to win an Olympic medal in the downhill; amateur ski racing career climaxed in 1961 when name was entered in the National Ski Hall of Fame records as "best Alpine skier of the year"; traded in her tight racing uniforms for the more comfortable ski school parkas of a professional ski teaching career and established successful ski schools in New Hampshire and Massachusetts.

Penny first put on skis at age 4, and before long she was skiing better than the other girls. At age 8 she was racing boys and defeating them. In 1955 she won the downhill, slalom and Alpine combined championships of the Junior Nationals at Whitefish, Mont. Penny was named to the U.S. ski team for the Winter Olympics in Italy at the age of 17, but her placings were low (31st in slalom, 34th in giant slalom and 34th in downhill). Penny returned to Europe for the *Féderation Internationale de Ski* World Championships of 1958; she gained reputation and new skills at Badgastein, Austria, and decided to remain overseas to gain further experience for the big events ahead. She polished her German and French and soon was fluent in both languages. She climbed the Matterhorn, without a guide, and skied, practiced and trained with the boys, who were masters at skiing. In 1958 she placed second in slalom in the Arlberg-Kandahar, placed first in downhill and combined in the Coppa Foemina at Abeton, Italy and placed second in giant slalom and second in combined in the Grand Prix at Zakopane, Poland. In 1959 she placed first in downhill and first in combined in the Internationals at Grindelwald, Switz, placed second in downhill and second in combined at Hahnenkammen, Austria, and placed first in downhill and combined in the Grand Prix at St. Gervals, France. Penny was a participant in ski shows, ski promotions and sports events, aiding overall expansion of skisport and ski industry throughout North America. In the 1960 Olympic Winter Games at Squaw Valley, Calif, she captured a silver medal in the downhill (1 sec. behind the winner) and another silver medal in the giant slalom (1/10 sec. behind first place).

Also in: Winter Sports Hall of Fame, Citizens Saving Hall of Fame Athletic Museum.

ZOBERSKI, Susan Corrock

Athlete

Born November 31, 1951; originally from Seattle; skiing was always considered a family recreation; married to Skeeter Zoberski; retired from the United States ski team in March, 1973; currently residing in Salt Lake City.

Susan first started skiing at age 5, and was racing at 10. Her junior racing career began as a member of the Fat City Ski Club. In 1968 Susan was second in the downhill and fourth in giant slalom of the Junior National at Bozeman, Mont. She finished third behind Gertrude Gable and Marilyn Cochran in the 1968 Silver Belt in Sugar Bowl in California. During 1969, she raced throughout the United States. The family moved to Ketchum, Idaho, and joined the Sun Valley Ski Club. During her first tour of Europe, Susan placed eighth in two World Cup slaloms. In 1970 she won the United States Senior Giant Slalom Championship and placed second in combined. Susan placed sixth in the World Cup downhill at Sugar Loaf, Maine; tenth in the Tall Timber Classic; placed second in slalom and second in giant slalom and first in combined of the Far West Kandahar; winner of the French National junior championships—all in 1971. In 1972 she placed fifth in the World Cup downhill at Crystal Mountain, Wash, and scored seventh place in World Cup downhill standings. Susan won a bronze medal in the women's downhill of the Olympic Winter Games of 1972 in Japan. For Susan it was the best run of her ski career and she said: "I didn't make any mistakes." After retiring from the United States ski team in March, 1973, she went on to compete in the Senior Nationals in April. She won the National Senior Combined crown with a second in downhill, fourth in slalom and tenth in giant slalom. Susan turned professional in 1974, and took part in the Hang Ten Cup events of the Women's Professional Ski Racing circuit, and was crowned National women's combined professional champion of 1975.

Skiing Hall of Fame to Watch

U.S. SKIBOB FEDERATION HALL OF FAME

Under Consideration

The U.S. Skibob Federation was founded in 1967 by dealers, distributors, manufacturers and enthusiasts interested in developing the sport of skibobbing in the United States. The skibob resembles a small low bicycle with a four-foot rear ski and a 30-inch front ski in place of wheels. Handlebars are used to maneuver the front ski, and short 18-inch outrigger skis are used to help in braking and stopping the skibob. The Federation is interested in sanctioning competitions in the United States, and organizing and training a team for international competition, with the idea of developing skibobbing as an Olympic event sometime in the future. Also in the future planning will be a Hall of Fame to commemorate those who have contributed to the sport, and to collect memorabilia, photographs, equipment and literature in a permanent location for the use of those interested in skibobbing. For further information, contact Leland MacDonald, Dir. of the Federation, P.O. Box 102, Littleton, CO 80120. (303) 979-5722.

SOCCER

Modern soccer was born the same year Alfred Nobel invented dynamite, 1863. Representatives of ten informal soccer clubs met at the Freemason's Tavern in London on October 26 of that year (Lincoln was still alive, the battles of Gettysburg and Vicksburg were just three months past) to set up new rules. The meeting lasted more than a month. Besides setting up rules for the game, those present decided to officially call it association football, as distinct from rugby football. They might be said to have instigated the modern American and Canadian forms of football. At that formative meeting those who wanted football without hands and without hacking (kicking an opponent's legs, also called "shinning") formalized the association game. From those who wanted hacking and the use of hands in their game came rugby, which was itself formalized eight years later with the formation of the Rugby Union. From rugby North American football soon developed (*see* Football for the latter evolution, as well as for the more ancient Chinese, Greek, Roman and early English history of soccer). On December 5th, a few days after the meeting ended, the supporters of the association game published their rules in a magazine called *Bell's Life.* Apparently a Latin-speaking student or don, noting that association comes from the Latin *socius,* companion, and adding *er* according to the English laws of student slang (by which breakfast becomes brekker), coined the word soccer. Mothers were doubtlessly happy with the game, its rules and its name, particularly those who had demanded a tamer game which involved "less tumbling on the ground, [and was] less dirtying and damaging to the clothes." So throughout British Empire schools, where "muscular Christianity" was taught, the new, clean game of foot-skill spread. And soccer was born.

Almost everywhere in the world today, however—in Afghanistan, Indonesia, in Thailand and even among the scientists who live in Antarctica—it is called football. By whatever name it is called (it was once a "refined and fashionable spectacle"), and despite the opposition of some (the poet Oscar Wilde, for example, himself fond of dominoes, once remarked that "Football may be all right for rough girls. But it's hardly the game for delicate boys"), it is unquestionably today the most popular sport in the world.

It is also one of the most paradoxical of the world's many sports. Played by teams, it stresses the mastery and inventiveness of the individual player far more than team tactics or strategy. A highly sophisticated sport in practice, in theory it is among the world's simplest of games. A nonviolent sport compared to many, it has the unique distinction of being the only sport ever used as an excuse for the invasion of one country by another. Rioting after a three-game World Cup playoff in 1969 was followed by the military invasion of Honduras by 12,000 El Salvador troops. No other sport has resulted in the destruction of an entire town. Bari, Italy, suffered such a fate in a conflict over the results of a 1955 game. Nor has any sport been capable of producing such enthusiastic fans in recent times. After a 1964 game in Lima, Peru, for example, 309 people were killed, more than 1000 were injured. (For ancient violence, *see* p. 350.)

Its modern evolution into such a paradoxical sport is fascinating. It all began in a very literary year, 1841, when *Punch* magazine and the *New York Herald Tribune* were first issued and the first paperback books were published. It was the year that Dickens's *Old Curiosity Shop* and Dana's *Two Years Before the Mast* were first published. In that same year the first soccer club was formed. It was at Cambridge University, where students were playing essentially the same game that would be called association football after the 1863 meeting. Through the 1840s other clubs sprang up in England, and the game played by Cambridge's club continued to be played. In 1846 (a year before Captain Hanson Gregory invented the doughnut hole—an event still annually celebrated in Maine) J. C. Thring attempted to unify the various clubs' games into a single official game which he dubbed "The Simplest Game." The ten rules he ended up with were essentially those adopted at the 1863 meeting in London. Perhaps the most interesting is rule number 3, which states that "Kicks must be aimed only at the ball." While discussion of whether to adopt Thring's rules went on, the game continued to develop. Eighteen fifty-two was a momentous year in many ways. It was the year *Uncle Tom's Cabin* and *Roget's Thesaurus* were first published. It was the year "Old Boys" clubs and interschool rivalries in soccer began, the latter with the playing of Harrow, Winston Churchill's school, against Westminster. It was also the year the first successful public lavatories were opened, constructed in London by Sir Samuel Morton Peto, who earlier had erected Nelson's Column in Trafalgar Square, along with his friend Sir Henry Cole, the inventor of the Christmas card, who was famous for his campaign against the use of nude models by artists. The following year, in 1853, the potato chip was invented and the first hotel waitresses were hired, both at hotels in New York State; and championship soccer games began to be played. Two years later, in 1855, the Sheffield Football Club of England was founded. Today it is the oldest surviving soccer club in the world. In 1859 Jules Leotard, for whom the body-stocking was named, performed the first flying trapeze circus act. This had little or no effect on the evolution of soccer, but inspired the song "That Daring Young Man on the Flying Trapeze," and coincided with the arrival of the English game in North America. And four years later those English clubs met in London for that month-long meeting out of which soccer was officially born.

It has experienced many stages, events and innovations in the century since. The first soccer club in Canada, the Montreal Football Club, was founded in 1868. A rule making it legal for goalies to touch the ball with their hands was adopted in 1871, the year microfilm, circus safety nets and margarine were invented. The first international game was staged between England and Scotland in 1872. The first floodlit match was staged and the rule making it illegal to charge an opponent by leaping at him was adopted in 1878. This was the same year that the typewriter shift-key was invented and the first American detective novel, *The Leavenworth Case,* was published. The official to be known as the referee was incorporated in 1880. Before this, it had been assumed that gentlemen did not need to be umpired. The size of the ball was standardized in 1882 and the first league of clubs outside England, the American Soccer Association, was formed in 1884. Professional soccer was legalized in 1885, a year before Dr. John Pemberton of Atlanta invented his "Esteemed Brain Tonic and Intellectual Beverage," now called Coca-Cola. The St. Louis Kingstons and numerous other Northern American clubs were formed in 1890. Goal nets and the penalty kick were introduced in 1891, the same year that the telephoto lens, the traveler's check and the baby incubator were invented. National clubs, leagues, and associations were founded throughout Europe and South America. In 1894, the year the striptease and the sports film were introduced, gardeners employed by the Baron Rothschild formed the First Vienna Club, played their first game, and contributed to the establishment of the Austrian Football Union. Referees, linesmen and players were prohibited from betting in 1902, the same year a cartoon showing Teddy Roosevelt refusing to shoot a bear cub inspired the invention of the Teddy Bear. (The inventor, Morris Mitchom of Brooklyn, received a letter from the President which said in part, "I don't think my name is worth much to the toy bear business, but you are welcome to use it.") An international governing body was established in 1904 and the U.S. Soccer Football Association was established in 1913, the year the crossword puzzle was invented. The numbering of players was introduced in 1928 and the Jules Rimet Cup was suggested. It was first played for in 1930 and today is called the "World Cup." Pelé was born October 23, 1940, and scored his 1000th goal in 1969. He was only 10 when a total of 205,000 fans watched a 1950 game in Rio de Janeiro and set an attendance record.

These innovations and events, plus fan fervor, have produced the paradoxical soccer of today. Vastly popular throughout the world, it has until recently been unappreciated in North America. A team sport, its stress is on the individual. Highly sophisticated, it has been called the simplest of games since Thring's day. A nonviolent game, it can stimulate unbelievable excesses of enthusiasm in its fans. Soccer is all of these things today, as more and more North Americans are discovering. When played masterfully, it is also beauty—a blend of ballet and blitzkrieg. The words muttered by the French general while watching the charge of the Light Brigade on October 25, 1854, are an apt description of soccer: "C'est magnifique, mais ce n'est pas la guerre!" Though it isn't really war, it is magnificent.

FORMS: Association football, soccer, is only one of a large family of foot-and-ball games, some of which also allow the use of hands. This family of games includes American football and Canadian football, which have been described in a section of their own. It also includes Australian rules football which is played in the Australia-New Guinea region and involves 18 players per team who seek 6-point goals or 1-point behinds with an oval ball. Speedball is played widely in the United States and consists of 11 players per team who seek to score goals of 1, 2 or 3 points with a round ball. Gaelic football, among the world's most violent sports, is played especially in Ireland, but also in Canada and across the United States. It requires 15 players per team who seek to score 3-point goals with a round ball. Team handball is one of the world's fastest sports but also has one of the lowest injury rates. Played in over 50 countries, it involves 5, 7, or 11 players per team who seek to score 1-point goals with a round ball. Harrow football, played only at Harrow School in England, calls for 11 players per team who seek to score 1-point bases with a flattened spheroid ball. Winchester College football is played only at Winchester College in England. Six or 15 players per team seek to score 3-point goals by kicking a round ball across one of the two goal lines, called worms. Rugby League football is played all over the world, but especially in Australia, England, France and New Zealand. In this game 13 players per team seek to score 3-point tries with an oval ball. Rugby Union football, played far more widely than the rugby league game, entails 15 players per team who seek to score 2-point conversions and 3-point tries with an oval ball. All these games are played on rectangular fields except Australian rules football, which is played on a large oval field. Virtually all are historically related. Of them all, only team handball and soccer are regular Olympic sports.

Soccer itself is among the simplest of all sports. Through a combination of individual skills and group tactics the eleven players, consisting of one goalkeeper plus backs, forwards, lefts, wings and rights, attempt to propel the ball into the opposing team's goal net. Propelling the ball means, preeminently, kicking it; but the ball may also be hit with the head, chest or thigh. Only the goalkeeper may touch the ball with his hands. Among the many skills employed is the tackle, which in soccer means an attempt to take the ball away from an opponent's feet. There are nine major fouls (most for unnecessary roughness), for any one of which the opposing team receives a direct free kick. Minor infractions result in indirect free kicks, in which the ball must be passed to a teammate before a goal may be attempted. Two teams do all of this for one 45-min. half, rest 5 min, then do it again for a second 45-min. half. Substitutions, prohibited until 1965, are severely limited. Soccer is one of the world's most demanding games in terms of required endurance. Eleven players with that endurance, uniforms, a ball, two goals and a level field are virtually all that is really required for a regulation soccer game.

A uniform consists of a numbered jersey or shirt, for which every country has its own national colors, along with shorts, socks, and shoes. Shoes are studded with six leather, rubber, aluminum or plastic studs, each up to 3/4 in. long. The wearing of shin pads by players is optional, as is the wearing of gloves by goalkeepers. Regulation balls are usually made of leather, but sometimes of plastic. They measure from 27 to 28 in. in circumference, and are filled to a pressure of 15 lbs. per sq. in. so that they weigh from 14 to 16 oz. Each goal consists of a hemp, jute or nylon net supported by two white uprights and a crossbar, which create an open area that measures 24 ft. wide and 8 ft. tall. The field measures from 50 to 100 yds. wide by 100 to 130 yds. long depending on the rules used, and is marked off by lines indicating the various goal areas and penalty areas. A center or Touch line bisecting a center circle in which play begins divides the field in half.

Officiating all regulation games are a referee and two linesmen whose job it is to assist the referee. The soccer referee is probably the most powerful official in the entire world of sports. He not only makes all decisions on major or minor fouls, but also has the authority to eject players from the game. He is also the sole official timekeeper which means that no one else knows exactly when the game will end. Because of this power, the referee's job is also probably the most dangerous in the world of sports. That fact was recognized during the construction of the Maracaña Stadium in Rio de Janeiro. It is the world's largest, and has a seating capacity of 205,000. A huge water-filled moat surrounds the playing field. Many people would assume it is there for its beauty, but its primary purpose is to dissuade attacking spectators from reaching the referee. Numerous soccer referees have been injured or killed on fields that lacked such protective measures. One who made an unpopular decision at a soccer game in an African nation disappeared after the game. He is reported to have been eaten.

ORGANIZATION: Soccer is the biggest game in the world in terms of spectators and in terms of participants. It has the largest, though by no means the most complex, organizational structure of any sport. At the summit of that structure is the world governing body, the *Fédération Internationale de Football Associations* (FIFA), founded by delegates of seven European nations in 1904 and now headquartered in Zurich, Switzerland. Among its numerous functions are the control of the international rules of the game through its publication of such items as the annual *FIFA News* and the periodic *Referees' Instructors Handbook,* as well as through a semiautonomous suborganization called the International Football Association Board.

Since 1930 a second major function of the FIFA has been the organization of quadrennial World Cup competitions, more accurately called the Jules Rimet Cup. This is only one of the several thousand soccer championships staged annually at national, regional, state, city and interclub levels in virtually every country on earth, but it is the supreme soccer championship. Eight hundred million people watched the 1970 World Cup playoffs on television, more than watched Neil Armstrong step onto the moon.

The FIFA's third major function is the promotion of soccer throughout the world. It fulfills this through its membership of the national soccer organizations. As of 1976, there were 142 countries represented. They are administratively grouped into six regional confederations. The African Football Confederation has 38 member nations. The *Confederación Norte-Centroamericana y del Caribe de Fútbol* (CONCACAF) includes the United States and Canada along with 20 other nations. The *Confederación Sudamericana de Fútbol* (CONMEBOL) includes 10 nations. The Asian Football Confederation has 34 member nations as does the Union of European Football Associations (UEFA). The Oceania Football Confederation (OFC) has four member nations, including Australia. It is somewhat mind-boggling to try to contemplate the numbers of clubs, teams, players and officials represented by those six confederations: 17,840,288 registered professional and amateur players in 827,544 different teams and affiliated clubs, all the soccer games of which are officiated by 292,025 registered referees. One way to visualize 17,840,288 registered soccer players would be to say that, if recorded human history were to have begun 30 centuries ago, then today there would be over 1.5 soccer players for every single day of recorded human history. And that would be a low estimate—the 17.8 million figure does not include the millions of unregistered soccer players around the world today. Equally amazing, perhaps, are the figures for the United States and Canada: a combined total of 133,557 registered players in 5722 clubs and teams, the games of which are officiated by 1491 registered referees. That would be 44.5 North American soccer players for each year of recorded human history.

The national governing bodies in North America are the Canadian Soccer Association and the United States Soccer Federation. The latter consists of 42 state soccer associations. The two national organizations serve not only to promote the sport at all levels but also to select and organize their respective countries' national and Olympic teams. Both are aided and supported in these goals by such organizations as The Ontario Soccer Association Inc. and the German-American Football Association. The specific youth, high school, college, amateur and professional levels of the game are in turn supported, assisted or controlled by organizations of their own. High school soccer in the United States is played according to rules published by the National Federation of State High School Associations, while college soccer is played according to National Collegiate

Athletic Association rules. Additionally, college soccer is promoted and supported by the Intercollegiate Soccer Association of America, which consisted of 342 member junior colleges, colleges, and universities in 1976. There are also several other organizations whose primary function is the training and support of soccer officials—the Eastern College Soccer Association, the National Soccer Coaches Association of America, and the National Intercollegiate Soccer Officials Association, for example.

In contrast to the case in virtually all other countries where pro soccer is played according to FIFA rules, professional soccer in North America plays according to its own rules. It is governed by such organizations as the National Professional Soccer League and the North American Soccer League (NASL), which in 1977 consisted of 20 different teams. These organizations are themselves assisted and supplemented by additional ones such as the Ontario Soccer Referees' Association which publishes *Can-So-Ref!*, a quarterly. Nonassociation publications also exist for the benefit of the game at all levels. Notable among these are *Soccer America* based in Berkeley, California, *Soccer Monthly* of New York City, and *Soccer World* of Mountain View, Calif.

Though most pro players in North American soccer are foreign-born—the first draft of college players did not occur until 1972—NASL rules state that each team must have at least six American or Canadian citizens on its team roster of sixteen. They may be naturalized citizens, however. One of the foreigners on one of the NASL teams, the New York Cosmos, is Pelé, the Brazilian superstar. He has been said to represent "soccer in its purest form," and is the world's highest-paid athlete. In 1975 he signed a three-year, $4.5 million contract with the Cosmos. His mere presence on a North American team has already sparked a new national interest in soccer and, in the near future, is likely to exert a profound influence upon soccer's organizational structure in both the United States and Canada.

United States Soccer Federation Hall of Fame

NEW YORK, NEW YORK

Mailing Address: 350 Fifth Ave, Suite 4010, 10001. Tel. (212) 736-0915. *Contact:* Julius G. Alonso. *Location:* Empire State Building; approx. 210 mi. S.W. of Boston, Mass. *Personnel:* Harry Fairfield, George Fishwick, J. Eugene Ringsdorf, Erwin Single, Hall of Fame Comt. (Thomas E. Sager, Chmn.); Veteran's Comt; S. T. N. Foulds, Historian. Not open to the public. *Nearby Halls of Fame:* Heritage, Music (New York City), Bicycle (Staten Island, 5 mi. S.W.), Ice Skating (Newburgh, 45 mi. N.W.), Harness Racing (Goshen, 75 mi. N.E.), Heritage (Valley Forge, Pa, 104 mi. N.E.), Basketball (Springfield, Mass, 120 mi. N.E.), Baseball (Cooperstown, 135 mi. N.W.), Tennis (Newport, R.I, 140 mi. N.E.), Horse Racing (Saratoga Springs, 150 mi. N.E.), Flight (Elmira, 170 mi. N.W.), Horseshoe Pitching (Corning, 185 mi. N.W.), Jockeys (Baltimore, Md, 196 mi. S.W.), Ice Skating (Boston, Mass, 206 mi. N.E.), Exploration and Invention (Arlington, Va, 210 mi. S.W.).

In 1947 nearly 133 men who played soccer for the Merchant Shipyard in Harrison, Pennsylvania, during the 1920s had their first reunion as the Philadelphia Old Timers' Association. News of the get-together spread and by 1949 the membership of the Association had grown to 800. The members were determined to return the city to its soccer glories of the past and in doing so founded their Philadelphia Hall of Fame in 1949 from recommendations by the state soccer associations. On February 18, 1950, the first 15 members were inducted at the annual reunion of the Philadelphia Old Timers' Association. In 1953 the Hall of Fame was officially recognized nationally and became the United States Soccer Football Association Hall of Fame. In 1974 when the United States Soccer Football Association (USSFA) became the United States Soccer Federation (USSF), the Hall of Fame changed its name again.

Members: 133 as of July 1977 (including 16 recipients of the Meritorious Award, one 13-man team induction in 1976, and 104 full members). Members are either recognized for their administrative achievements with a meritorious award or for their playing achievements. Meritorious award recipients must be players who have completed successful soccer careers and have remained active on a national, state, league, or club level as a coach, soccer journalist, etc. They also can be considered for membership in the Hall of Fame as players. Players must have participated in top grade soccer for at least seven years and represented the United States in international competition or have had outstanding success on the club level in challenge, amateur, league or cup finals. Nominations are solicited from associations affiliated with the USSF and must include documentary proof of the nominees' achievements. In 1977 a Veteran's Committee was established to submit names of people who may have been overlooked by the associations. Nominations are due 60 days prior to the annual meeting and are reviewed by the Hall of Fame Committee. No more than two from each category are elected every year. Those elected are invited to attend the annual meeting of the USSF where they are awarded with a certificate and a lifetime pass to soccer games.

1950 BROCK, Dr. John J. Captain and coach of first soccer team at Springfield Col. 1906; became varsity coach 1929; led team to two national and four New England Intercollegiate championships; retired during war years but returned 1946 and 1947 for two undefeated seasons, after which teams for those seasons were designated as national champions by Soccer Coaches Association.

BROWN, Andrew M. Born 1870 in Paisley, Scotland; immigrated to the United States at age

20; died 1948; president of American Association, credited with convincing the organization to become present-day United States Soccer Federation (USSF); secretary and president of USSF; delegate at numerous foreign and domestic soccer conventions. *Also in:* New Jersey Old Timers' Soccer Association Hall of Fame.

CAHILL, Thomas W. Played major role in formation of USSFA as secretary of American Amateur Association; manager of several United States teams that toured Europe; executive secretary of USSFA 1913–1921, 1923–1924 and 1928; contact with Thomas R. Dewar in London resulted in donation of National Challenge Cup in 1912.

FERGUSON, John "Jock." Scottish and English pro player before immigrating to the United States; played with Bethlehem Steel team for nine consecutive seasons before playing with Pawtucket, after which returned to Bethlehem; played for the United States against Canada 1925.

GONSALVES, Bill "Mr. Soccer." Born 1908 in Fall River, Mass; phenomenal career spanned more than 25 years; holds record number 8 National Challenge Cup medals in 11 finals; played for United States teams in Italy, Germany, Mexico, Haiti and throughout North America; later coached various teams in Newark, South Carolina; never censured by a referee for rough play or for ungentlemanly conduct on the field. *Also in:* New Jersey Old Timers' Soccer Association Hall of Fame.

GOVIER, Sheldon. With Pullman Football Club of Chicago for over 25 years; center halfback for Chicago All-Stars when they became the only team to defeat the leading amateur club of England, Pilgrims Football Club.

KEMPTON, George "Barney." Played soccer in Belfast, Ireland, six years in Los Angeles and San Francisco, then in Seattle, Vancouver, Prince Rupert Island, and throughout Washington State; served as junior commissioner of Washington State Soccer Association; organizer of 20-team Parochial League as commissioner of Associated Boys' Club.

LANG, Millard. Several times All-Maryland Scholastic team member; top scorer of Cantons in American League; also played in Cleveland, Chicago, Baltimore and elsewhere; player-coach of Baltimore Soccer Club and later president of Maryland and D.C. State Associations; president of Baltimore Major League; served many years as writer for *Soccer News*.

LEWIS, Horace Edgar. Born 1896 in Wales; immigrated to the United States at age 14; vice president of Bethlehem Steel Co, in which capacity organized one of greatest teams in United States soccer history; donated Lewis Cup.

MANNING, Dr. G. Randolph. Born in London, England; died 1953; president of American Amateur Association; first president of USSFA; president of New York State Association 1928–1948; first American council member of International Federation; represented USSFA at almost all international congresses; first to resign from American Olympic committee as protest against games in Japan while Japan was at war with China.

MILLAR, Robert. Born in England; immigrated to the United States in 1911; played soccer in Scotland and the United States; coached 1930 U.S. World Cup team; played for United States against Canada 1925; set record in 1915 with 54 goals scored in 33 games.

RATICAN, Harry. Played with Christian Brothers Col, St. Louis Univ, the Ben Millers, Bethlehem Steel Co, Robins Drydock and Todd Shipyards; coached West Point varsity team while playing with Fall River; holder of two National Open medals won with Bethlehem and Robins; toured Sweden with St. Louis team; coached St. Louis All-Star teams and vice chairman of Missouri Soccer Commission.

STARK, Archie. Born 1900 in Scotland; immigrated to the United States 1912; one of the greatest scoring center forwards of time; toured Europe with several teams; played for the United States against Canada 1925 and 1926; won National Open championship medal with Bethlehem Steel team in 1926. *Also in:* New Jersey Old Timers' Soccer Association Hall of Fame.

STEWART, Douglas. Organized and became secretary of Football Association of Pennsylvania 1903; did same in 1904 with Referees' Association; head coach at Univ. Pa. 1910–1942; helped to form USSFA 1913; president of Football Association of Pennsylvania 1913–1926; vice president of USSFA 1921 and 1922; many times chairman of rules and revisions and appeals committee.

WILSON, Peter. Born in Scotland; immigrated to the United States in 1898; before arriving in United States played right fullback with St. Johnstone of the Scottish League in 1896 and 1897 as pro; settled in New Jersey and played for Scottish Americans, Paterson Rangers and Pawtucket; in Pennsylvania played for Hibernians of Philadelphia; active player for 25 years.

1951 BRITTAN, Harold. Played for English League after W.W. I; later played for Bethlehem Steel Co. and Fall River teams; one of the outstanding players of the time, both on and off field.

BROWN, Dave. Born in New Jersey; set record of 53 goals during 1926–1927 season; in three successive games netted 13 markers and later netted 5 against Providence; played for Ford, West Hudson, Paterson, Erle, Newark and New York Giants; coached Brooklyn Soccer Club for three years; played for the United States against Canada 1925 and 1926; toured

Sweden 1919 with Bethlehem Steel Co. and 1920 with St. Louis team at request of Swedish Association. *Also in:* New Jersey Old Timers' Soccer Association Hall of Fame.

COLLINS, George M. "Old Stonewall." Born in Scotland; immigrated to the United States in 1908; played with Boston Rovers and Charlestown as wing forward and halfback; organized Massachusetts State Soccer Association and served as secretary for nine years; president of Boston League, Williamson and Brieve Cup competitions; served as delegate to USSFA, and assisted in creation of National Amateur Cup tournament; manager of 1924 U.S. Olympic team; manager of Brotherhood Football of Worcester, which played throughout New England and England; third vice president of USSFA 1916–1917; soccer editor of Boston *Globe* 1914–1950.

DONAGHY, Edward J. Born in Scotland; immigrated to the United States in 1911; played for Tacony, Philadelphia Hibernians, Bethlehem, Braddock, Homestead and Castle Shannon; holder of seven league and cup championship medals; refereed in West Pennsylvania, officiated in two National Open and two Eastern Amateur Cup finals; refereed three World Cup elimination games in Mexico City 1934; past president of New York National and New York Referees committee; served as member of arbitration board of Eastern District League 1949.

EPPERLEIN, Ruddy. Born in Germany; immigrated to the United States; gained fame playing in native land, later promoted sport in and around Buffalo; did much to encourage present growth in popularity of soccer.

FERNLEY, John A. Died 1934; delegate from southern New England District on formation of the USSFA; became first vice president of USSFA 1914, then served as president 1915–1917.

FRYER, William. Born in England; played for Newcastle and Barnsley in English major league; played for Tebo, Todd Shipyard, Paterson and New York Giants in the United States; sold to Fall River team for a record $1500, later sold to Brooklyn Wanderers, Brooklyn, Newark and Clan Gordon; won two National Cup medals; received more than 20 other league medals and cup championship medals. *Also in:* New Jersey Old Timers' Soccer Association Hall of Fame.

HEALEY, George. Died 1960; played soccer as a schoolboy in England, later played in Detroit; organized Michigan State Association and served as president 1913–1919; active as USSFA officer, including president 1919–1923.

IGLEHART, Alfredda "Missa." During teaching career of more than 30 years, coached more than 1200 boys in fundamentals of soccer, of whom many later went on to become championship players; played in eight sectional tournaments and one national game in Boston.

JEFFREY, Bill. Played semi-pro in Scotland before immigrating to the United States in 1920; highly successful college coach, setting records of 13 unbeaten seasons, 9 consecutive unbeaten teams and winning streak of 65 games; 1950 winner of National Coaches Honor Award; coached 1950 U.S. World Cup team that defeated England in Brazil—*see* 1976 entry below.

McGUIRE, James P. Born in Scotland; died 1974; coached numerous successful teams; became president of American League 1946; active as an official of USSFA, including term as president.

McGUIRE, John. Played pro soccer in England before immigrating to Canada 1919; played for Toronto Ulster United, including participation in several all-star games; moved to the United States in 1922; won two National Cup medals; played for the United States against Canada in 1926.

McSKIMMING, Dent. Born in St. Louis, Mo; lived in Buenos Aires, Havana, Mexico City, Montevideo and elsewhere; active as early newspaper reporter of major soccer games throughout Americas.

MORRISON, Robert. Played for Scotland against England before immigrating to the United States in 1910; as member of great Bethlehem team of 1913, won numerous medals in championship play.

PEEL, Peter J. Born in Dublin, Ireland; following visit to Chicago World's Fair in 1893, remained in the United States; died 1969; elected president of Illinois State Soccer Association; in 1909 donated Peel Cup, today the oldest soccer trophy in the United States, to the Illinois State Soccer Association; past president USSFA.

RENZULLI, Peter. Born in the United States; won three National Challenge Cup medals and runnerup for four others; besides starring on field, exceptionally active in the promotion and organization of soccer, serving as official in Public Schools Athletic League for 25 years; a founder of National Junior Cup.

SCHROEDER, Elmer. Died 1953; manager of 1930 National Challenge Cup champion Philadelphia Americans team; managed same team to National Amateur Cup wins 1933 and 1934, as well as American league pennants 1935, 1942, 1944, 1947 and 1948 and to Lewis Cup wins 1941 and 1942; served as USSFA president 1933–1934; managed U.S. World Cup team in Italy 1934, Olympic team in Berlin 1936 and national team in Mexico City 1937, co-managed 1936 U.S. Olympic team in Berlin (*see* James Armstrong, 1952 below).

SMITH, Alfred A. Played on Springfield Col. varsity team 1911 and 1912, became coach

1913; after founding Private and Interacademic leagues, teams won championship 15 times; served as member of Philadelphia's Coaches Association and as editor of *National Collegiate Soccer Guide.*

SPALDING, Dick. Considered probably the greatest-ever American-born fullback; named to All-American team which played Norway and Sweden 1916; a substantial fund raised in Philadelphia for the erection of a memorial.

SWORDS, Thomas. Born in Fall River, Mass; played on numerous New England teams; captained All-American team that defeated Sweden 3–2 in Stockholm and tied Norway 1–1 in Oslo in 1916.

TRINER, Joseph. Died 1969; active in organization and administration of sport at all levels, president of numerous teams, associations and commissions, managed the United States team that toured Czechoslovakia for 12 games in 1926, and served as chairman of Illinois State Athletic Board; past president, USSF.

1952 ARMSTRONG, James. Born in Carlisle, England; parochial school teacher before immigrating to Milwaukee, Wis; later active as soccer official in Brooklyn, N.Y, including secretary of New York State Soccer Association; wrote history of soccer which was regarded as a standard work; managed U.S. Olympic team in Berlin 1936 with Elmer Schroeder, 1951 Inductee (see above); died 1952.

BOOTH, Joseph. Born in Bradford, England; immigrated to the United States in 1910, lived in Bridgeport, Conn, until death in 1947; famous for administrative ability; secretary of Connecticut State Soccer League; in 1914 organized Connecticut State Soccer Association and served as secretary for 25 years; for many years chairman and secretary of National Soccer Football Writers Association, and member of USSFA National Challenge Cup commission.

FAIRFIELD, Harry. Born in England; while spectators and 21 other players at 1910 game in England stood transfixed by appearance of Halley's Comet, ignored it to score winning goal; immigrated to the United States where, in one game, flipped the ball over head into own net; active in West Pennsylvania Soccer Association and in USSFA, including term as president from 1945 to 1948; helped organize North American Confederation of the United States, Canada and Mexico; from 1923 was sports reporter for the Pittsburgh Press; currently member of USSF Hall of Fame committee.

GIESLER, Walter. Born 1910 in St. Louis, Mo; died 1976; five years as referee; gained national fame as capable organizer; active on various teams, associations and commissions; chairman of 1952 USSFA Olympic commission and manager of United States team that went to Helsinki; coached 1948 U.S. Olympic team that played in London; manager of 1950 U.S. World Cup team (*see* 1976 entry below); past president USSF.

JOHNSTON, Jack. Born 1877 in Glasgow, Scotland; immigrated to the United States in 1904; died 1951; in addition to 30 years active service to game of soccer, including 20 years as referee, professional bicycle rider and golf pro; shot near heart in 1947 in non-game-related accident, made spectacular recovery.

PALMER, William. Born in Yorkshire, England; immigrated to the United States in 1908; served as team manager, league vice president, and later league delegate to Football Association of Eastern Pennsylvania; in latter organization, served more than 25 years; secretary of Allied Amateur Cup; William Palmer Memorial Cup in his honor, for which Philadelphia teams have competed annually for many years.

SCHWARCZ, Erno. Born Budapest, Hungary; began playing at age 17; following 12-game tour in 1926, remained in the United States; player and player-manager of various teams, including own, the New York Americans, until broken leg ended playing career in 1937; continued as active officer of numerous soccer organizations, including the American Soccer League and USSFA.

TINTLE, George. Born 1894 in Harrison, N.J; played on numerous teams, including various ones which toured Sweden, Norway, Denmark and other Scandinavian countries; after retirement, served as captain of Harrison Fire Department. *Also in:* New Jersey Old Timers' Soccer Association Hall of Fame.

WOOD, John W. Born in Nottingham, England; after immigrating to the United States, active in teams in Connecticut, Pennsylvania, and Illinois; became president of Illinois Referees Association; served many years as chairman of National Junior Cup; named as coach to 1952 U.S. Olympic team that played in Helsinki.

1953 BARRISKILL, Joseph J. Born in Northern Ireland; player-manager of Crescent Club of Brooklyn, later New York state delegate to USSFA, served as president 1934–1936; chairman of National Challenge Cup committees 1928–1940; served without pay as honorary executive secretary of USSFA from 1944; executive secretary of North American Federation of United States, Canada, Cuba and Mexico, from 1949; USSF Life Member and Secretary Emeritus.

CUMMINGS, Wilfred R. Born in Chicago; secretary-treasurer of Illinois State Soccer Association and Peel Challenge Cup for more than 30 years; managed 1930 U.S. World Cup team that defeated Belgium and Paraguay in Uruguay.

FOULDS, Proveso A. L. "Pal." Oldest active soccer official in New England at the time of death, actively associated with soccer in both

United States and Canada for nearly 60 years; son Samuel T. N. Foulds also in present Hall of Fame (*see* 1969).

GOULD, David L. Born in Ayhshire, Scotland; immigrated to the United States in 1891 at age 18; died 1939 at age 68; was exceptional player on various New England and Pennsylvania teams before turn of century and after; in 1911 became assistant coach at Univ. Pa, a position held for 28 years; coached 1934 U.S. World Cup team in Italy; served as president of Referees' Examining Board and of Referees Association; honored by David Gould Memorial Trophy, annually awarded to Most Valuable Varsity Player at Univ. Pa.

JAPP, Johnny. Born in Bellshill, Scotland; played on various United States and United Kingdom teams, including great Bethlehem Steel Co. team; as coach did much to encourage junior teams and thus to stimulate growth of soccer as a major sport in the United States.

KLEIN, Paul. Born Alexandria, Egypt, of German parents, returned to Germany 1914; immigrated to the United States in 1923; coached and managed numerous winning teams, won National Amateur Cup 1949, German-American League pennant 1947, 1948 and 1949, and New Jersey State Challenge Cup 1949; for 30 years service to soccer in New Jersey, elected to New Jersey Old Timers' Soccer Association Hall of Fame in 1952.

MacEWEN, John J. Born in Egmodville, Ontario; began playing soccer in Cleveland, Ohio; became president of Cleveland Soccer League and later of Ohio State Soccer Association; served as commissioner for all National Cups in Michigan for eleven years; was columnist for *National Soccer News;* 1953 awarded a plaque by USSFA for lifetime of unselfish service to soccer.

MARRE, John. After playing with various turn-of-the-century teams, organizer and manager of own team, the Marres and the Tablers; active in keeping soccer alive in St. Louis area during Great Depression; served more than ten years on Missouri Soccer Commission; served on National Challenge Cup committee.

1954 DONELLI, Aldo T. "Buff." Famous as exceptional player for numerous Pennsylvania teams; played on 1934 World Cup games in Rome; after coaching professional football teams (Pittsburgh Steelers, Cleveland Rams), became director of athletics and head coach at Boston Univ.

DOUGLAS, James E. Born in East Newark, N.J; began playing soccer 1907 and for next 14 years played as amateur; turned pro 1922; named to 1924 U.S. Olympic team that played in Paris, Ireland and Poland; goalie in 1930 World Cup competition at Montevideo; retired 1932. *Also in:* New Jersey Old Timers' Soccer Association Hall of Fame.

MILLS, James. Born in Scotland; immigrated to the United States in 1922; played for various Philadelphia teams; retired as player 1935 but continued to manage winning teams, including ones which won American League pennant in 1949, 1950, 1951 and 1953, Lewis Cup in 1949, 1951 and 1952, and numerous other titles.

1955 DUGGAN, Tommy. Born in Liverpool, England; immigrated to the United States in 1911, in addition to playing on and against various United States teams, including stint with National Open champion team, the Paterson Football Club, played against visiting teams from Scotland, Spain, Czechoslovakia, Austria and Uruguay; retired from active play 1934.

POMEROY, Edgar. Born 1867 in England, just four years after London meeting at which soccer was officially born; immigrated to California in 1888, the following year organized various YMCA classes in addition to two soccer teams; organized Oakland Hornets, whose major games were against visiting British merchant seamen; formed first San Francisco Bay area league, the first game of which was played 1902; continued active in organization, promotion and administration of soccer until 1942; elected honory president of Northern California Football Association 1942.

1956 ANDERSEN, William

WESTON, Vic

1957 RAMSDEN, Arnold

REESE, Vernon R.

1958 FERRO, Charles

NETTO, Fred. Died 1969; past president of USSF.

RYAN, John

YOUNG, John

1959 CARRAFI, Ralph

CRADDOCK, Robert

1960 KOZMA, Oscar

SCHILLINGER, Emil

1961 BOXER, Matthew J. Born in Siberia; first played soccer with juvenile team in China; member of 1923 championship French team in Shanghai; immigrated to the United States; active as coach in San Francisco area; extremely active in league affairs, secured City Council support for construction of $150,000 stadium; fielded Boxer's T.V. Juniors and organized all-black Booker T. Washington Juniors; named junior soccer commissioner for USSFA 1958; active in promotion of soccer throughout California, the United States and the world; current third vice president, USSF, member of budget committee, and member of USSF Hall of Fame committee.

HEMMINGS, William P. Born 1907 in Nottingham, England; immigrated to the United States in 1931; after active and successful play on various teams, including German-American

Soccer Club and Schwaben Soccer Club in Chicago, served as vice president and later president of National League for 15 years.

1963 KRAUS, Harry A. Born 1908 in Vienna, Austria; immigrated to the United States in 1922; elected New York State Soccer Association secretary 1932; also active in numerous other associations, leagues and organizations, notably German-American League; became youngest-ever vice president of USSFA 1937; became president of German-American League, served until retirement 1952; voted honorary president of German-American League; engineered USSFA 50th anniversary convention in New York City.

KUNTNER, Rudy

NIOTIS, Dr. Dimitrios J. Born in Greece; played for Athens and Constantinople teams; immigrated to the United States in 1923; active in numerous organizations, including Illinois State Soccer Commission and Pan-American Committee; author of *Sand Lot Soccer;* life member of Chicago National League.

ZAMPINI, Daniel

1964 FLAMHAFT, Jack. Lawyer, active in representation of USSF in various significant cases of litigation; also served elective offices, including two years as president; currently serving as member of USSF appeals committee; honorary member for life of USSF rules and revisions committee.

GARCIA, Prudencio "Peter." Born in Spain; immigrated to St. Louis Mo, in 1907; played on numerous teams; promoted games through active membership in Spanish Society; as member of Soccer Coaches Association, promoted clinics in local schools; member of St. Louis Referees' staff until 1957; founded Missouri Referees' Association; refereed 1949 World Cup qualifying rounds in North American Section; named 1950 World Cup final referee.

1965 BEARDSWORTH, Fred. Born in England; immigrated to the United States in 1914, settled in New England; played on various New England League teams; retired from major league competition 1921; devoted many years to establishment and management of New Bedford Textile School team; received National Association of Intercollegiate Athletic Award for Merit 1964.

GLOVER, Teddy. Born in England; immigrated to the United States in 1928; played on various New England and New York teams; League championship medal 1930; transferred to German-American League 1941.

1966 CHESNEY, Stanley R. Born 1910 in Bayonne, N.J; began playing at age 17; goalie on winning team of N.J. State Amateur Cup 1930–1931; played many years as pro, including service on teams that won 1935 American League Duffy Cup, 1937 National Open Challenge Cup and 1937 West Hudson Charity Cup; played against teams from Mexico, England, Scotland, Israel, Brazil, Czechoslovakia, Italy and Canada.

HUDSON, Maurice J. Born in England; immigrated to Monterey Co, Calif, 1907; played for Barbarian Club 1910–1926; played on U.S. team in the Inter-Allied Tournament in Paris 1919; elected secretary-treasurer of the University and Club League, served 1919–1935; served as both secretary of California Football Association and the San Francisco League 1935–1950, later became first vice president of San Francisco Soccer League.

1967 COMMANDER, Colin. Known as the "Father of Ohio Soccer"; born 1906 in England; immigrated to Cleveland, Ohio, 1921; played soccer 1922–1939, until knee injury forced retirement; in 1940s when popularity of soccer diminished in Ohio, kept sport alive through organizational and leadership skills; received first "Mr. Soccer Award" given in State of Ohio 1958.

FLEMMING, Harry G. Born in Scotland; immigrated to Kensington district of Philadelphia 1927; played on various teams until retirement 1936; served as owner-manager of Fairhill Club 1931–1939, during which time also served as officer of Allied and Pennsylvania Leagues; present hall of fame begun with two others as function of Philadelphia Old-Timers Association, later incorporated into the USSFA.

MORRISSETTE, William. Played with various junior teams 1916–1918; returned to soccer as league official 1945, helped organize Massachusetts Inter-State Soccer League; later helped organize New England Soccer League during 1962–1963 season; extremely influential in stimulating recent rise in popularity of soccer.

PETERS, Wally (Walter Paricciuoli). Born 1917 in Gallantin, Pa; played on numerous amateur and pro teams until 1954; managed Paterson Dovers from 1952 and New Jersey All-Star teams of 1950, 1951, 1952, 1954, 1955 and 1967; extremely active and influential in various leagues, associations and organizations in and around New Jersey.

1968 DRESMICH, John. Born in Lithuania; at early age immigrated to panhandle area near Pittsburgh; died 1968; played on various Pennsylvania teams; active in various organizational roles, including reorganization of West Pennsylvania Referee Association and West Pennsylvania State Soccer Commissioner.

OLIVER, Arnold. Born in New Bedford, Mass; tied with Andy Stevens, Archie Stark and Dave Brown for most goals scored during 1928 season; member of first U.S. World Cup team, which participated in competition at Montevideo, Uruguay 1930, affiliated with National Soccer Coaches Association of America, National Association of Intercollegiate Athletics

Coaches, and member of New Bedford, Mass, soccer scholarship committee; highly successful term as soccer coach.

SAGER, Thomas E. Past president USSF; current chairman of finance committee and chairman of USSF Hall of Fame committee.

SHIELDS, F. (Zibikowski)

1969 CRAGGS, Edmund G. Born 1897 in Columbo, Ceylon, of English parents; moved to England at age five; began playing soccer at age eleven; moved to Canada 1914 at age 17; played on numerous Canadian teams in British Columbia, Ontario and Quebec; moved to Seattle, Wash, 1947; became secretary-treasurer of Washington State Soccer Association; for years of coaching soccer in various Catholic youth organizations, became the first non-Catholic to receive high honor *Pro Deo et Juventute*.

FOULDS, Samuel T. N. Born in Sherbrooke, Que; moved to Boston, Mass, at age four; played on various New England teams; organized and served as president of Bay State League 1924–1936; served as president of numerous other organizations 1923–1970, including Eastern Massachusetts League, Inter-City League, Boston and District League, Massachusetts League and New England League; coached soccer at Revere High School and Brandeis Univ; awarded Certificate of Merit by National Soccer Coaches Association 1964; frequent contributor to *Soccer World* magazine; currently serving as historian of USSF; father P. A. L. Foulds also in present Hall of Fame (*see* 1953).

STEUER, August. Born 1902 in Grossheubach, Germany; immigrated to the United States in 1923; died in New York 1969; in addition to playing on various teams, instrumental in numerous administrative capacities, particularly in German-American Football Association, served as president for several years; active in promoting international good will through sports; served as advisor on immigration matters to President Lyndon B. Johnson; decorated by both United States and West German governments.

1970 FOWLER, Daniel W. Born in the United States; played on various high school and other teams until retirement from active playing 1948; from 1947 was exceptionally active in various administrative capacities in numerous soccer organizations, including Northwestern Inter-City League and New York State Soccer Association, served as president 1951–1961 and registrar from 1951; also served as National Cup commissioner of all cups; Northwestern State Association Junior Cup called the Dan Fowler Cup in his honor.

MAHER, Jack. Immigrated to the United States near turn of century; extremely active in growth of soccer in Illinois; after organizing, managing and officiating many games, became referee, in which capacity known as "the fairest and most dedicated"; later served as president of Illinois Referee Unit.

1971 PATENAUDE, Bertrand A. Born in Fall River, Mass, of French-Canadian descent; at age 21 member of first U.S. World Cup team, which played in Uruguay 1930; at age 28 called by journalist "one of the greatest center forwards in American soccer"; played for numerous championship teams; compiled exceptional scoring record.

OLAFF, Gene. Born 1920 in Bayonne, N.J; began playing soccer at age 12; playing career spanned over 20 years; considered Number One goal keeper in American soccer; teams played visiting teams from Scotland, Italy, Sweden, Israel, Ireland, Mexico, Germany and England; in addition to devotion to soccer, exceptionally active in community affairs in and around Bayonne, N.J.

1972 ALONSO, Julius G. "Mr. American Soccer League." Born 1905 in Luanco, Asturias, Spain; began playing soccer in West Virginia in 1911; later played on numerous teams, including Marino Football Club, Madrid Football Club, Blick's Arcadians and Juventud Gallega; formed with brother Canton (Ohio) Sporting Football Club and later Donora (Pennsylvania) Spanish Football Club and Benevolent Association still in existence; extremely active and influential in various organizations as referee, coach, manager and official; in American Soccer League devoted 32 years of service prior to semi-retirement 1968, as secretary, various vice presidential posts, business manager, on numerous committees, and first executive secretary; received citation from Henry L. Stimson, U.S. Secretary of War, for meritorious service during W.W. II on Manhattan Project; currently active in USSF affairs (*see* sketch of USSF Hall of Fame above).

DUFF, Duncan. Recipient of Meritorious Award.

1973 DeLACH, Joseph. Recipient of Meritorious Award.

GRYZIK, Joseph

1974 DiORIO, Nick. Recipient of Meritorious Award.

DUNN, James. Recipient of Meritorious Award.

FISKWICK, George E. Past president USSF, currently member of USSF Hall of Fame committee (*see* sketch of USSF Hall of Fame above).

MIETH, Werner

1975 CORDERY, Ted. Recipient of Meritorious Award.

WEIR, Alexander

1976 On July 27, 1950, at Belo Horizonte, Brazil, the United States World Cup team scored a sensational upset victory 1–0 over the favored English team, for which achievement the entire team was inducted as a group.

BAHR, Walter

BORGHI, Frank
COLOMBO, Charles
GAETJENS, Joseph
GIESLER, Walter. *See* 1952 entry above.
JEFFREY, William. *See* 1951 entry above.
KEOUGH, Harry
MACA, Joseph
McILVENEY, Edward
PARIANI, Cino "Bill"
SOUZA, Edward
SOUZA, John
WALLACE, Frank

1977 HYNES, John "Jacky"
McLAUGHLIN, Bernard "Benny"
WASHAUER, Adolph. Recipient of Meritorious Award.

Induction Year Unrecorded
ABRONZINO, Umberto. Recipient of Meritorious Award.
ARDIZZONE, John. Recipient of Meritorious Award.
McCLAY, Allan. Recipient of Meritorious Award.
MEROVICH, Peter. Recipient of Meritorious Award.
MILLER, Milt. Recipient of Meritorious Award.
MOORE, James. Recipient of Meritorious Award.
ROTTENBERG, Jack J. Recipient of Meritorious Award.
STEELINK, Nicolas. Recipient of Meritorious Award.
STONE, Robert T. Recipient of Meritorious Award.
WALDER, James A. Recipient of Meritorious Award.

Soccer Hall of Fame to Watch

NEW JERSEY OLD TIMERS' SOCCER ASSOCIATION HALL OF FAME

Internal Development 1977

Formed in May, 1952, this hall of fame promotes the interests of soccer in New Jersey with special emphasis on the junior, juvenile and midget forms of soccer. The first annual dinner was held in 1953, at which the ten initial members were formally inducted. All of them, along with those elected since, were either native sons of the Garden State, or had devoted considerable service to the interests of soccer in New Jersey. Of the initial ten, seven had previously been inducted into the USSF Hall of Fame: Andrew M. Brown, Dave Brown, William Fryer, William Gonzalves, Paul Klein, Archie Stark and George Tintle; the remaining three were Henry "Razzo" Carroll, James Douglas and William "Shamus" O'Brien. For additional information concerning the structure and functioning of the New Jersey Old Timers' Soccer Association Hall of Fame contact Foster Perry, Secy, New Jersey State Soccer Association, 174 Orchard St, Elmwood Park, N.J. 07407. (201) 797-8642.

SOFTBALL

On Thanksgiving Day, November 30, 1887, a reporter for the Chicago Board of Trade named George W. Hancock invented softball. The weather was bad—too bad for baseball—so he and some friends in the Farragut Boat Club's gymnasium used a boxing glove for a ball, a broomstick for a bat and a wrestling mat for an infield. He called their game indoor baseball. Later, when they had played it outdoors, he called it indoor-outdoor-baseball. Others in time called it or its variations kitten-ball, mush-ball, diamond-ball, night ball, ladies' baseball, recreation ball, playground ball, army ball, sissy ball and dainty drawers. Fortunately perhaps, Walter C. Harkenson of the Denver YMCA suggested in 1926 that the game be called softball. Although Hancock's game spread quickly throughout the Chicago area in 1887, its invention was by no means a major event that year. Chicago itself was not yet completely rebuilt from its great fire of 1871; and the Haymarket Square riot had killed four civilians and seven policemen, and wounded over 100 others in Chicago only the year before. Besides, by 1887 baseball was supremely popular in the nation. This was especially true the following year, when Ernest L. Thayer published his "Casey at the Bat" in the *San Francisco Examiner.* Bicycling, too, was popular—and rapidly becoming more so. And everyone that year was enthralled or disturbed by: the election of America's first woman mayor, 27-year-old Susanna Medora Salter, of Argonia, Kansas; the founding of the city of Hollywood, California (incorporated in 1903); the invention of contact lenses in Germany; the appearance of the first American psychology magazine, *The American Journal of Psychology*, a yearly subscription to which cost $3; the successful return to San Francisco of Thomas Stevens who had set off three years before from that city on the first bicycle trip around the world; the invention of Esperanto (an artificial international language) by a Russian-Polish physician named Lazaro Ludovico Zamenhof; and the world's first appendectomy, performed in Philadelphia. Coincidentally the year indoor baseball was invented, *The Tribune Book of Open Air Sports* was printed. In that book, the world's first to be set by Linotype, softball was not even mentioned in passing. But Hancock wrote down rules for his game. Those rules, revised in 1900 by playground leaders in Minneapolis (notably Lewis Rober, a firefighter), ensured the ultimate survival and proliferation of the game.

From the time the first softball league was formed, also in 1900 in Minneapolis, until 1933, when the first national championships were held, softball grew almost as wildly as baseball, its ancestor, had grown. In 1933—while softball was being played by both men's and women's teams at the Chicago World's Fair, the Century of Progress Exposition—the rules were finally officially adopted. In view of the fact that softball was played without rules longer (46 years) than it has been played with rules (44 years), it is astounding that by 1933 softball was a continent-wide sport. It was being played by so many people, in fact, that it was called "the Depression sport." In a single year (1939) of that hard decade, ninety million people watched softball games. During the 1940s softball spread to various countries overseas while it continued to grow in North America. By the end of World War II, there were 40,000 established women's teams in the United States alone. By the 1950s—that incredible decade that began with the world's first X-rated movie (January 9, 1951) as well as the first Miss World Contest (staged 14 week later) and ended with the invention of the electric toothbrush (1961)—softball was incredibly popular. In 1957 the Amateur Softball Association of America had to establish a separate championship division for industrial teams only. In view of such growth and popularity, it is incredible that of all major sports, only softball has remained almost completely amateur. It remains what baseball was a hundred years ago. Undisrupted by salary battles, organizational wars and television coverage, it is still a highly competitive game that anyone in the family can play.

FORMS: A softball is by no means soft. Made with a hard core of either cork and rubber or kapok, around which twisted yarn is tightly wound and over the whole of which a cowhide or horsehide cover is glued, it is quite hard. A baseball, in fact, is made of exactly the same materials. And when a softball is traveling at over 100 m.p.h., as Eddie "the King" Feigner could pitch it, it is anything but soft. In circumference it is from 11⅞ to 12⅛ in. and in weight from 6¼ to 7 oz.—roughly 3 in. larger in circumference than a baseball and 1 oz. heavier.

The same ball is used in the three main forms of softball: Fast Pitch, Medium Pitch and Slow Pitch. A ball measuring from 14 to 16 in. is sometimes used in Slow Pitch, however. In that game, the ball must be pitched so that it travels in an arc of from 4 to 10 ft. before reaching the home plate; on reaching the batter's box, it is usually coming "down at" rather than "straight at" the batter. Over 70 percent of all softball games today are of that Slow Pitch form. In Medium Pitch softball the only restriction is that the pitcher may not bring his pitching arm above his shoulder during the windup—windmills, slingshots, and other such pitches are thus prohibited. In Fast Pitch softball, there are no restrictions on the pitcher's windup or delivery, although five basic pitches are most often used: straight, slow, rise, drop and curve. In all of these, as in the other two forms' pitches, the ball must be delivered underhand. Delivery is said to start when the pitcher removes one hand from the ball. As in baseball, the batter is allowed three strikes and after four balls, advances or walks to first base to become a runner. In contrast to baseball's rules, however, a softball runner may not leadoff from the base until the ball has left the pitcher's hand. In other words, players do not have the opportunity to steal bases before the start of the delivery. The bat, made of either wood (usually northern white ash) or seamless metal (usually aluminum), must not exceed 34 in. in length and 2¼ in. in width at its widest point. Mitts may be worn by only the catcher and the first baseman, gloves may be but often are not worn by the other members of the fielding team. Protective masks, guards and pads are required for female catchers. The pitcher's plate is 6 in. by 24 in. The home plate is five-sided and measures 17 in. long and the same on the side nearest the pitcher. The three bases are 15 in. square. All are identical in size to those used in baseball. The field, however, is considerably smaller. In fact, the distance between any two softball bases (60 ft.) is only 6 in. less than the distance between the pitcher's mound and home plate in baseball. The latter distance in softball is 46 ft. for men and 40 ft. for women. Each team in softball usually consists of nine players, the same number, and playing the same positions as in baseball. Sometimes a tenth player is added to play as a fourth outfielder directly behind the second baseman. Unlike baseball games, which usually last nine innings, softball games last seven innings. Overtime innings are played—the longest recorded game went for 42 innings in 1942. Forfeited games are counted officially as wins of 7 – 0 in favor of the nonforfeiting team.

ORGANIZATION: The world governing body for softball, the International Softball Federation headquartered in Oklahoma City, is composed of the national softball associations of 47 different countries.

The two major associations in North America are the Canadian Amateur Softball Association (CASA) and the Amateur Softball Association of America (ASA). These, in conjunction with the International Softball Congress (a federation of state associations of teams with members from Canada, Mexico and the United States), the Amateur Soft Ball Association (Canada), and the International Joint Rules Committee on Softball (founded in 1937) are the organizational peak, so to speak, of North America's huge world of softball. Beneath them is an immense number of leagues, nearly 10,000 of which are registered with the ASA. Regional, state, provincial, metropolitan and city associations also exist. In the ASA there are 105 state and metropolitan softball associations affiliated with 15 regions—New England (6 areas), Mid-Atlantic (2 areas), Central Atlantic (4 areas), South Atlantic (4 areas), Southern (2 areas), Southwest (4 areas), Texas (1 area), Great Lakes (2 areas), East-Central (2 areas), Midwest (3 areas), Northern (3 areas), Western (4 areas), Rocky Mountains (6 areas in 2 sub-areas), Pacific Coast (2 areas), and Northwest (4 areas). The CASA is structured similarly for Canada. Major affiliated associations include the Ontario Amateur Softball Association, the Ontario Rural Softball Association, the Provincial Women's Softball Union of Canada, the Metropolitan Fastball Association and the Greater Edmonton Fastball Association. Beneath the league structure there are 72,000 adult teams and 10,000 youth teams registered with the ASA alone. The latest ASA survey (1975) showed 18,000,871 players on these teams. This number is considerably larger today; and it should be remembered, these are only ASA-affiliated players—only a fraction of the total number of people who play softball in North America. That total number unquestionably ranks softball among the largest of all participant sports in North America today.

These teams of players compete in a vast array of games and championships, of which one of the most popular is the Women's College World Series of Softball sanctioned by the Association for Intercollegiate Athletics for Women. Each of the various major organizations stages its own tournaments and championships. The ASA, for example, staged 21 different national championships in 1977, plus eight different final youth tournaments. National titles are awarded to the top teams in numerous divisions, such as Women's Major Fast Pitch, Men's Major Fast Pitch, Women's Major Slow Pitch, Men's Major Slow Pitch, 16-inch Major Slow Pitch, Industrial Major Slow Pitch, Class A, Church, and Youth. In addition to these annual national championship tournaments, and far more prestigious than any one of them, is the World Championship, held every four years, in which the top American and Canadian teams compete with the top teams of other countries from around the world.

The latter fact indicates the degree to which softball is becoming increasingly popular elsewhere in the world. It has been growing in popularity in Latin America to such an extent that in 1968 Puerto Rico defeated the United States' men's team in a game of the Second World Championship competition. Mexico was the site of the first World Championship for men in 1966. The Japanese women's team defeated the United States' team in 1970 to win the second women's World Championship. In these and many other countries, softball is played according to the single set of rules drawn up by the International Joint Rules Committee on Softball, which has been printed in 12 different languages.

Amateur Softball Association of Pennsylvania Hall of Fame

YORK, PENNSYLVANIA

Mailing Address: P.O. Box 1707, 17405. Tel. (717) 394-6552. *Contact:* Andrew S. Loechner, Jr, Commissioner. *Location:* Ridge Ave; 85 mi. W. of Philadelphia and 50 mi. N. of Baltimore, Md. *Personnel:* Hall of Fame Comt: Galen Dreibelbis, Glenn Hunsicker, Robert Fryer, David Brandt and William Daisley (Jim Manenti, Chmn.). Not open to the public. *Nearby Halls of Fame:* Jockeys (Baltimore), Heritage (Valley Forge, Pa, 65 mi. N.E.).

The Hall was founded in 1974 by Andrew S. Loechner, Jr, to honor men and women from the state of Pennsylvania who have played a major role in the development of the game of softball. At present the Hall has the use of a room in the York Barbell Building, and memorabilia are being collected from the members inducted. This material plus a certificate with name of each member will be displayed in the Hall of Fame building after one is acquired.

Members: 8 as of 1977. To be considered for selection to the Hall of Fame, a player must have played ball in Pennsylvania, and be retired for at least three years; a non-player must have participated in the game and contributed toward its growth for a minimum of ten years to be inducted into the Hall of Honor. There is a limit of three inductees annually. They are honored at the annual fall Hall of Fame Banquet, at which time they are presented with a plaque and a framed certificate. A framed certificate is also given to the Hall of Fame Committee for eventual display.

1974 CONLIN, William "Bing." Player, Manager and Administrator. Hall of Fame.

POWELL, George. Pitcher. Hall of Fame.

1975 FRYER, Robert A. Administrator. Hall of Honor.

HOFFMAN, Bob. Promoter and Team Sponsor. Hall of Honor. *Also in:* Weightlifting Hall of Fame, Citizens Savings Hall of Fame Athletic Museum.

HUNSICKER, Earl. Player, Umpire and Administrator. Hall of Fame.

1976 CANIGLIA, Pete. Third Baseman. Hall of Fame.

LIGHTNER, Lisle "Pete." Umpire. Hall of Honor.

SCHOFIELD, Herb. Umpire. Hall of Honor.

Arizona Softball Hall of Fame

PHOENIX, ARIZONA

Mailing Address: Arizona Softball Foundation, P.O. Box 2616, 85001. Tel. (602) 253-8286. *Contact:* Ford Hoffman, Pres. Emeritus. *Location:* 423 N. First St, Phoenix; approx. 110 mi. N.W. of Tucson, 120 mi. S.W. of Flagstaff. *Personnel:* Karl Neilson, Pres; A. C. Williams, Northern V.Pres; Ray Ruman, Southern V.Pres; Darrell Leitsch, Central V.Pres; Larry Walker, Exec. Secy; Dodie Walker, Treas; 28 mem. Exec. Comt. (Gil Hunt, Chmn.).

In 1973 members of the Arizona Softball Foundation founded the Hall of Fame to honor outstanding players, sponsors, contributors and umpires in Arizona softball and foster the sport in the state. The Arizona Softball Foundation is comprised of approximately 500 members and actively promotes softball, selects the official All-State team and sponsors major softball events and various programs throughout the year.

Members: 56 as of July 1977. Every year an information letter about Hall of Fame selections is sent to each member of the Arizona Softball Foundation. One hundred to 150 nominations are then received by mail or telephone and are narrowed down by the Executive Committee to 14-20 inductees. Each player, sponsor and contributor must have earned national recognition while playing softball in the state as a world champion or while associated with a world championship team. Players, coaches and umpires must have been retired at least three years. Only one umpire is selected each year by the Arizona Umpire Association by approval of the Executive Committee. In October, Hall of Fame members are inducted and honored at a special banquet, together with the Arizona Softball Foundation Players of the Year. They receive plaques showing their picture and softball achievements. List of members is not available.

Connecticut Amateur Softball Association Hall of Fame

TRUMBULL, CONNECTICUT

Mailing Address: 100 Oakview Dr, 06611. Tel. (203) 378-7959. *Contact:* Sylvester Cholko. *Location:* 15 mi. S.W. of New Haven and 45 mi. S.W. of Hartford. *Personnel:* Joseph T. Barbar, State Commissioner; John E. Lindquist, Pres. Not open to the public. *Nearby Halls of Fame:* Ice Skating (Newburgh, N.Y, 40 mi. W.), Heritage, Music (New York City, 55 mi. S.W.), Bicycle (Staten Island, N.Y, 60 mi. S.W.), Harness Racing (Goshen, N.Y, 65 mi. S.W.), Basketball (Springfield, Mass, 70 mi. N.E.), Tennis (Newport, R.I, 105 mi. W.), Ice Skating (Boston, Mass, 130 mi. N.E.), Horse Racing (Saratoga Springs, N.Y, 135 mi. N.W.), Baseball (Cooperstown, N.Y, 140 mi. N.W.), Flight (Elmira, N.Y, 190 mi. N.W.) and Horseshoe Pitching (Corning, N.Y, 210 mi. N.W.).

The Hall of Fame was originated in 1971 by the Amateur Softball Association district commissioners to honor men and women from the state of Connecticut who have played a major role in the development of the game of softball as one of America's greatest sports.

Members: 41 as of 1976. The inductees are selected by a five-man Hall of Fame Committee, and they must have had an outstanding softball career in Connecticut. Experience in state, regional or national tournaments helps the candidate's cause in the final selections.

1971 BAKER, John "Cannonball." See entry in National Softball Hall of Fame, 1961.
DAGATA, Victor
DeFEO, Joseph
FERRARA, Sal
JACKOWITZ, Michael
REALE, Arthur
SULZYCKI, Al

1972 ADAMS, Wally
BEERS, Donald
COWAN, Edward
STRATTON, Rosemary
TEDESCO, John
WOJIE, Bill. See entry in National Softball Hall of Fame, 1967.

1973 ARGENIO, Leo
BARBARA, Ralph
BEVERLY, John
BOLDUC, Pat
KUCHTA, Frank
LICARI, Francis
RUOCCO, Clorinda
SERAFINE, Fred
TICKEY, Bertha. See entry in National Softball Hall of Fame, 1972.
WILLIAMS, Frank. See entry in National Softball Hall of Fame, 1970.

1974 BUSCHBAUM, John
DeFOE, John
FEHER, James
GAROFALO, Emil
REDICAN, Lester
SANTO, Nick
ST. JOHN, Joseph
WILKISON, George

1975 BARBER, Joseph
DeLUCA, Frank. See entry in National Softball Hall of Fame, 1974.
FRASER, Edna
HARGUS, Ed
LASSOFNA, Bernie Jr.
KALAFUS, John
MARUCCI, James
PARSONS, Henry
PASTORE, John
SCHACHT, Martha

Illinois State Amateur Softball Association Hall of Fame

CHILLICOTHE, ILLINOIS

Mailing Address: 218 W. Elm St, 61523. Tel. (309) 674-8255. *Contact:* Charles L. McCord, State Commissioner. *Location:* 15 mi. N.E. of Peoria, 120 mi. S.W. of Chicago. *Personnel:* Ten mem. Hall of Fame Comt. (Jim Nicol, Chmn.), seven Advisory Mems. Not open to the public. *Nearby Halls of Fame:* Business (Chicago), Agriculture

(West Lafayette, Ind, 140 mi. S.E.), City (St. Louis, Mo, 165 mi. S.W.), Auto Racing, Basketball (Indianapolis, Ind, 185 mi. S.E.), Sports (North Webster, Ind, 210 mi. E.).

Founded in 1970, the Illinois State Amateur Softball Association (ASA) Hall of Fame honors Illinois men and women who have played a major role in the development of softball. The Hall of Fame also strives to publicize the widespread value of and interest in softball.

Members: 93 as of July 1977. For the first two years only players and commissioners were elected, and then only players in the ASA who were active on a state level and were retired for at least three years. Since then, members have included founders, managers, sponsors, sportswriters and umpires who have served softball at least 12 years. A player who has been recognized on a national level either as an individual or as a member of an outstanding team receives special consideration; and, though no minimum is required, length of playing time is also considered. At this time, those who have competed in only Class A or B softball are not eligible. Anyone who has been selected for membership to the National Softball Hall of Fame automatically qualifies for admittance to the Illinois State ASA Hall of Fame. Local committees and commissioners have the opportunity to nominate people every year until October 15; commissioners are permitted two nominations. All nominations must be made available to the State Commissioner or the Hall of Fame Committee by October 30 for voting in the spring at either the Illinois State ASA Commissioner's Council or at a special meeting of the Hall of Fame Committee. This Committee, which elects the new Hall of Fame members, consists of not more than ten members chosen by the Executive Committee to serve terms of five years. The Illinois State ASA Commissioner is an ex-officio member. Each member receives a list of nominees with career data to study thoroughly before the elections. At least five members of the Committee must be present and must cast three-fourths of their votes to elect each new Hall of Fame member. Not more than 12 may be elected each year unless there is a tie. Announcement of election results is made at the end of the Council's or Committee's meeting or later in June or July. New members are awarded plaques and their names are engraved on larger plaques, displayed with other memorabilia, at the Casey Softball Museum in Casey, Illinois and the National Softball Hall of Fame in Oklahoma City, Oklahoma.

1971 BAKER, Mervin. First baseman.

BUTLER, Francis. Catcher.

CHAMBERS, Jim. Pitcher. See entry in National Softball Hall of Fame, 1966.

ECCLES, Richard. Commissioner.

FISHER, Raymond. Second baseman.

HART, Carolyn Thome. Outfielder. See entry in National Softball Hall of Fame, 1966.

HESS, LeRoy. Catcher. See entry in National Softball Hall of Fame, 1968.

HUTCHCRAFT, Gerald. Catcher and Outfielder.

MILEHAM, Arnold. Pitcher.

O'NEAL, Ed (dec). Outfielder.

POOLE, Claude. Pitcher.

SPRING, John. Pitcher. See entry in National Softball Hall of Fame, 1970.

SYEBERT, Dutch. Pitcher.

VRELL, Shirley. Second baseman.

WADLOW, Marie M. "Waddy." Pitcher. See entry in National Softball Hall of Fame, 1957.

WICKERSHAM, Ray "Ned." Outfielder. See entry in National Softball Hall of Fame, 1971.

1972 ABREO, Lou. Pitcher.

BINKLEY, Frank. Outfielder.

FLOYD, Arthur. Commissioner.

GOLL, Lillian. First baseman.

LEGATE, Max (dec). Pitcher.

MOORE, Jack. Pitcher.

ORTMAN, Dorothy. Pitcher and Infielder.

PERRY, Bill (dec). Pitcher.

PORTER, Bill. Catcher.

ROPP, Don. Third baseman. See entry in National Softball Hall of Fame, 1972.

SCOTT, Lillian. Outfielder.

STAUCH, Pauline. Outfielder.

WHITE, Walter (dec). Shortstop.

1973 BEHRENS, Tony. First baseman.

BROWN, Beverly. Second baseman.

BROWN, Harold. Commissioner.

DEXTER, Emerson. All-Around.

DUNN, Riley (dec). Sponsor.

HEARN, Chick. First baseman.

JOHNSON, Winfield. Shortstop.

LARSON, Grace. Sponsor.

NELSON, Joan. First baseman.

RAPPE, Bernard. Pitcher.

SCHNEIDER, Mary. Second baseman.

SENSBAUGH, D. W. (dec). Sponsor.

WHITE, Sam. Sponsor.

WIELAND, Howie. Pitcher.

1974 BECKMAN, Jo Ann. Left Fielder.

BURDETT, Mel. Catcher.

DEEMIN, Al. Sponsor.

DE MUNBRUN, Jim. Manager and Sponsor.

ECKERTY, Duane. Commissioner.

FISHER, Leo (dec). Founder.

HORVATH, Steve. Umpire.

HURD, Charles. Sponsor.

KARTHEISER, Elmer. Infielder.

LANCASTER, Dale. Sportswriter.

OLTMAN, Eddie. Outfielder.

RUDOLPH, Eleanor. Catcher.

WOLD, Harold (dec). Manager.

1975 CLOSEN, Clarence. Manager and Commissioner.
DOMNICK, Donald. Pitcher.
ESSIG, Charles. First baseman and Business Manager.
FALLSTROM, Bob. Sportswriter.
FARNEY, Red. Outfielder.
FARROW, Roy. Sponsor.
GERL, John. First baseman.
LASH, Eugene. Umpire.
McCORD, Charles. Manager and Commissioner.
MECHERLE, Tyne. Sponsor.
SEKETA, Fran. Outfielder and Pitcher.
SMITH, Burdell. Umpire.
REESER, Kenneth. Player and Manager.

1976 COUSLAND, Bill. Sponsor.
DAVIS, John. Shortstop.
KNEER, Dr. Marian. Catcher.
LARSON, Dorothy. Catcher and Manager.
LEIGHTY, Bill. Sportswriter.
PRZADA, Joe (dec). Umpire.
RAMSEY, Lorene. Pitcher.
REINHOLD, Carlye. Catcher.
THACKER, Carl. Sponsor.
THOMAS, Don. Umpire.
TINDALL, Ann Mullins. Catcher.
WILSON, Hoke. Pitcher

1977 ESTES, Bim. Manager, Player and Sponsor.
GAILLIAERT, DeWayne. Umpire.
HAMERSTRAND, Gerry. Pitcher and Outfielder.
JENSEN, Charles (dec). Umpire.
KERWIN, Irene. Outfielder, Infielder and Catcher.
KILLAM, Ed. Manager.
KOCH, Otto. Pitcher.
PEARSON, Ila Mae. Manager and Sponsor.
PROCTOR, Don. Pitcher.
REID, Ferris. Umpire.
WOLD, Sara. Pitcher and Infielder.

International Softball Congress Hall of Fame

LONG BEACH, CALIFORNIA

Mailing Address: 9800 S. Sepulveda Blvd, Los Angeles, Calif, 90045. Tel. (213) 437-2255. *Contact:* Don Sarno, Dir. *Location:* Long Beach Sports Arena; 25 mi. S.E. of Los Angeles. *Admission:* Free 10 to 5 daily. *Personnel:* Carrol Forbes, Exec. Dir; Les Dietzen, Pres; Frank Porth, Treas; Milt Stark, Secy. *Nearby Halls of Fame:* Physical Fitness (Costa Mesa, 17 mi. S.E.), Citizens Savings (Los Angeles), Auto Racing (Ontario, 35 mi. N.E.), Flight, Sports (San Diego, 100 mi. S.E.).

The Hall of Fame, part of the Long Beach Sports Arena, was originated by the International Softball Congress (ISC) in 1972 to honor the athletes and other contributors involved in the sport. Long Beach was an appropriate location for the Museum since the Long Beach Nitehawks have been ISC National Champions ten times, and many of the inductees are members of the team. This museum is a member of the Association of Sports Museums and Halls of Fame. Displays include softball memorabilia, photographs, trophies and awards.

Members: 20 as of 1976. Members must have been inactive for at least five years, and there is a limit of three inductees each year. Nominations must be sent to the home office of the ISC not later than Feb. 1. New members are inducted at the National Tournament each year.

1965

NOVIKOFF, Lou
Pitcher, Outfielder

Born October 12, 1915, in Glendale, Ariz; died September 30, 1970, in South Gate, Calif, at age 55.

Lou, the "Mad Russian" was the first ISC player chosen. He played softball for several teams in the Old National Fastball League, was drafted by the Chicago Cubs, played four years, and one year with Philadelphia (National League), finishing his softball career with the Long Beach Nitehawks. He was 5 ft. 10 in. and weighed 185 lbs.

1966

LAW, Kenny
Pitcher

All-American five times; married; wife Margie star pitcher in American Softball Association; plasterer by trade, although originally had hoped to produce and train thoroughbred race horses.

Law started pitching at age 14, and was eventually a recipient of the International Softball Congress Hall of Fame plaque. He retired in 1958 after starring on 14 Arizona state championship teams. In pitching against Blythe, Calif, he struck out 26 of 27 batters, allowing none to reach base.

1970

RODGERS, Joe
Manager

Born in Gilroy, Calif; raised in an orphanage after parents died when he was 9; now deceased.

Rodgers' career began with the Huntington Beach Oilers as a great shortstop and fine hitter. His managerial career shows over 1000 softball game wins, and his career record is 999 wins in 1131 games. He was on the International Softball Congress state committee for 14 years, from 1952 to 1965, and manager of the Long Beach Nitehawks in 14 ISC world tours, 1951 – 1963 and 1965. Joe was also the manager of seven ISC world champion teams, 1953 and 1955 – 1960, and the manager of three ISC world runner-up teams 1951, 1952, 1963. He was the manager of 87 ISC world tour games, winning 70 and losing 17. He managed 65 players who were selected as All-American, 1951 – 1965. Joe also was the manager and founder of the Long Beach Nitehawks.

WHITE, Stan
Catcher
All-American 11 times.

White played for the Long Beach Nitehawks for 17 years, and participated in 13 ISC world championships from 1951 to 1963. He was a player on seven International Softball Congress (ISC) world championship teams, and he holds the ISC world tour record for the most putouts by a catcher, 110 in 1960. White is considered the greatest catcher in softball history. He played pro ball in the Southern Association before joining the Nitehawks.

ZIMMERMAN, Leroy
Pitcher
Born February 20, 1918, in Tungamoxie, Kans; graduated from San Jose State Univ. 1939; teacher at Madera, Calif, High School; All-American ten times between 1950 – 1960.

Zimmerman played ball with the Hollister Cowboys, Hester Dairy of San Jose, the Hanford Kings, the Selma Hoaks and the Long Beach Nitehawks. In 1941 he pitched 84 games and won 80; he had 34 no-hit, no-run games, and two perfect games in a row in which he struck out all 21 in one game and 20 in the other. He pitched on ten International Softball Congress (ISC) world championship teams from 1950 to 1960, and was selected leading pitcher in the International Softball Congress world championships five times. He pitched the largest number of no-hit, no-run games (61) in ISC world tour, and holds the ISC world tour record for strikeouts in a 14-inning game—30 in 1965. Zimmerman was also outstanding in football, and was named to the All-Southern California High School football team in 1935, the 1939 Little All-American team, and was All-Pro quarterback with the Washington Redskins. He was named Player of the Year in 1944. At age 46, he came out of retirement to pitch a perfect game in the ICS world tourney in 1963.

1971

FORBES, Carrol
ISC Executive Secretary
Moved to Greeley, Colo, from Oklahoma at age 2; played baseball at Greeley High; travels many miles with wife Vera to promote softball.

Forbes has been with the American Softball Association for 15 years, and with the International Softball Congress (ISC) for 25 years, the last 21 as executive secretary. He built Forbes Field in Greeley along with John Wheeler. He became president of the Greeley Softball Association in 1932, and was named northern Colorado committee member for the Amateur Softball Association in 1934 and president in 1937. Carrol Forbes was on the Colorado committee in the National Softball Congress in 1947 and president in 1948. In 1950 he helped found the ISC.

FORCHE, Paul
ISC Past President
Forche has been associated with softball for 35 years as director of the city of Tulsa, and is a past president of the National Softball Congress and the International Softball Congress.

GOYETTE, Cleo
Second Baseman
All-American 11 times.

Goyette played for 15 years and two seasons with the Long Beach Nitehawks in California and was their manager. His batting average was .340 in 1949 (best in the league), and he participated in 12 International Softball Congress (ISC) world championships between 1952 and 1963. He played on seven ISC world championship teams, and was the leading hitter in three ISC world championships. He is regarded as one of the all-time great fielding and hitting second basemen.

PORTH, Frank
ISC Past President
Porth has been a softball leader in El Paso, Tex, for 30 years. He umpired softball and baseball for many years. He also has been the director of the Southwest Softball Classic, played in El Paso for the past 12 years.

1972

CUTRUZZULA, Al "Cotti"
First Baseman
All-American 1951 – 1953; now a mailman in Hanford, Calif; also referees various sports events.

Cutruzzula played for the Hanford Kings and the Hoak Packers of Fresno, and played with four International Softball Congress (ISC) world championship teams (one for Hanford and three for Fresno). He was the leading hitter on the 1953 world tour, batting .500. Cotti currently holds two ISC records: most stolen bases, four in 1952; and most home runs in one game, two in 1952.

HANEY, Les
Pitcher
ISC All-American 1948, 1950 – 1951 and 1953; now works for the post office in Taft, Calif.

Haney played for the Taft Merchants, the Hanford Kings, the Fresno Hoak Packers, and the Long Beach Nitehawks. He participated on five International Softball Congress (ISC) world championship teams in 1948, 1950, 1951, 1953 and 1954, and was the leading pitcher in the 1951 world tour. He pitched a no-hit, no-run game in the 1953 world tournament, and is considered by many softball fans as one of the all-time great pitchers.

1973

FORTUNE, Clyde
ISC Past President
Fortune was a committeeman for the International Softball Congress (ISC) and an outstanding softball administrator. He now lives in Texas.

RANDALL, Jack
Pitcher
All-American seven times.

Randall played for 14 years with the Long Beach Nitehawks, and participated in 15 International Softball Congress (ISC) world championships between 1950 and 1966. He played on eight ISC world tournament championship teams, seven for Long Beach and one for Gardena. He was selected the leading pitcher three times in the ISC world championships, and pitched four no-hit, no-run games. Randall is considered by many softball fans and players as one of the great softball pitchers.

TOPPERT, Charlie
Catcher
Toppert played in many world championships and was selected All-American a number of times. He now lives in Illinois.

1974

LOPEZ, Paul
Pitcher
Spent five years in the navy; All-American many times; now a detective for the El Paso police force.

Lopez began his career at age 14, and two years later pitched for the Phoenix Lettuce Kings. He also played for Deal Motors and Dantrich Realty in El Paso. He pitched his first no-hitter in an Amateur Softball Association national tourney in Detroit, and was voted the most promising player. He set a record in 1949, winning a 20-inning game from Toronto, later broken. From 1951 to 1953 he was a pitcher for the Eastman Kodak team in Rochester, N.Y.

SILVAS, Larry
First Baseman
All-American seven times; now lives in California.

Silvas played for 12 years with the Long Beach Nitehawks, and played in 11 International Softball Congress (ISC) world tournaments from 1953 to 1963. He holds the ISC fielding record for the most putouts by a first baseman, 62 in 1960, and is considered by many to be the finest fielding and hitting first baseman to play the game.

1975

CASTEEL, Marvin
ISC Official
Casteel is a long-time International Softball Congress (ISC) official and softball administrator from the state of Utah.

HERRON, Clint
Third Baseman
All-American four times; now lives in California.

Herron played and coached for 25 years for the Long Beach Nitehawks, and participated in over 20 International Softball Congress (ISC) world championship tournaments as a player and coach between 1950 and 1974. He played on seven world championship teams with Long Beach 1953 and 1955–1960, and was coach under Red Meairs for two ISC world championship teams, 1968 and 1971. Considered one of the all-time third basemen, an outstanding fielder, as well as a good clutch hitter.

1976

JONES, Jimmy
Shortstop
All-American many times in the 1950s.

Jimmy Jones played in seven world championships with the Long Beach Nitehawks, and is considered one of the best shortstops in softball.

JONES, Virgil
Pitcher
All-American several times.

Virgil Jones played for Mary Star of San Pedro and the Long Beach Nitehawks. He played on many International Softball Congress and National Softball Congress world championship teams, and holds numerous softball pitching records.

Lake County Fast Pitch Hall of Fame

HIGHLAND, INDIANA

Mailing Address: 9303 Farmer Drive, 46322. Tel. (219) 838-3410. *Contact:* Jerry Krasek, Pres. *Location:* Approx. 15 mi. S.E. of Chicago, Ill, 145 mi. N.W. of Indianapolis. *Nearby Halls of Fame:* Business (Chicago), Agriculture (West Lafayette, 85 mi. S.E.), Sports (North Webster, 95 mi. S.E.), Bowling, State (Milwaukee, Wis, 110 mi. N.W.), Auto Racing, Basketball (Indianapolis), Football (Green Bay, Wis, 210 mi. N.W.), Trapshooting (Vandalia, Ohio, 210 mi. S.E.), Flight (Dayton, Ohio, 220 mi. S.E.), State (Detroit, Mich, 240 mi. N.E.).

Home of ten fast pitch teams, Lake County's Fast Pitch Hall of Fame began in 1976. Jerry Krasek received help from many of the old-timers of softball in the area, especially softball sponsor of the 1930s and 1940s, Mike Kampo, and All-American softball player and now coach of the Hammond Cataldis, John Bonic. The Hall honors outstanding players and managers from the county which was the home of the first softball state champions, the Hammond Civics, in 1938 and 1939. Each year the Hall of Fame hosts a well-known softball team at their annual induction banquet on the last day of June. In 1976 the 1939 State finalist team was present and in 1977 the 1939 State championship team was hosted. Interviews are conducted with the various members of the team as they arrive and are viewed after the banquet. Following the banquet is a three-day softball tournament to determine the division's Class AA champions.

Members: 20 as of July 1977. Players and managers must be retired from softball at least five years. The first 15 members were selected from the period of the 1930s and 1940s by a committee of five old-time softball players selected by Jerry Krasek. Each year new members are announced and honored at the induction banquet. Guests of the banquet sign a guest book and are later asked to vote on the next year's members from a ballot prepared by the president containing the names of all eligible players and managers. Five new members will be selected each year until a large plaque, kept at the Hammond Civic Center, reaches its capacity of 30 names. Then, the election procedures may change. Each new member receives a smaller mahogany plaque, on which is a replica of the state of Indiana and a softball player, and a tie clasp. In 1977 members were selected from the period of the 1950s and 1960s; later members will be selected from other periods.

1976 ANKOVIC, John
BICANIC, John
BONIC, John
COLLINS, Otto
DUBIS, Stan
EIENER, Emil
HALVSKA, Pete
JURAN, Tony
KEAGLE, John
KEIGHTLY, Harry
MARTENS, Harold
ROBAK, Sal
TROST, Herb
WANDREY, Robert

1977 COLY, Fred
FOLY, "Junior"
LONG, Horace
MATOVINA, Anthony "Fritz"
PAPACH, George

Metro Long Island Amateur Softball Association Hall of Fame

LONG ISLAND, NEW YORK

Mailing Address: 375 E. Dr, Copiague, 11726. Tel. (516) 842-3986. *Contact:* James Carman, Commissioner. *Location:* Approx. 12 mi. E. of Manhattan. *Personnel:* Walter Peterson, Pres; Ray Pfeffer, V.Pres; Mitch Winkeleer, Secy; James Carman, Treas. Not open to the public. *Nearby Halls of Fame:* Heritage, Music (New York City), Bicycle (Staten Island, 20 mi. W.), Harness Racing (Goshen, 50 mi. N.W.), Ice Skating (Newburgh, 55 mi. N.W.), Basketball (Springfield, Mass, 110 mi. N.E.), Tennis (Newport, R.I, 120 mi. N.E.), Heritage (Valley Forge, Pa, 140 mi. S.W.), Baseball (Cooperstown, 145 mi. N.W.), Horse Racing (Saratoga Springs, 150 mi. N.W.), Ice Skating (Boston, Mass, 150 mi. N.E.), Flight (Elmira, 185 mi. N.W.), Horseshoe pitching (Corning, 200 mi. N.W.).

The Hall of Fame was founded by the Metro Long Island Amateur Softball Association in 1976 to honor the players who added to the progress of the game. A Hall of Honor is also sponsored by the association to recognize commissioners, sponsors, managers and umpires.

Members: 10 in Hall of Fame and 10 in Hall of Honor as of July 1977. Initial recommendations come from softball fans and are reviewed by a Hall of Fame Committee appointed every five years. The Committee then selects electees from the recommendations which require approval from the Metro Long Island Amateur Softball Association. Members must have served or contributed to softball in Long Island for at least five years. Each year there is a limit of ten inductees, five for the Hall of Fame and five for the Hall of Honor. New members are honored at an Annual Dinner in April and receive Heisman-type trophies. Their names are also engraved on a plaque at the Wheatley Hills Tavern, a sports-minded restaurant where articles about and photographs of members will eventually be included.

HALL OF FAME

1976 FOWLER, Gene "Red." Shortstop.
FOWLER, George. Second baseman.
HERNAN, Tom. Catcher.
KNIESCH, Carl. Pitcher.
STEPHENSON, Roy. Pitcher. See entry in National Softball Hall of Fame, 1965.

1977 ELLIAS, Paul. Catcher.
JOHNSON, Henry "Ollie." Pitcher.

O'CONNOR, Kay. Pitcher
SMITH, Ted. Pitcher.
SURHOFF, Dick. Pitcher.

HALL OF HONOR

1976 BARATTA, Sharkey. Manager.
BELCASTRO, Dan. Commissioner.
DICKSTEIN, George. Umpire.
NORTON, Mickey. Manager
SWIRBUL, Leon "Jake." Sponsor.

1977 DRESSLER, Ed. Umpire
HULTS, Ken. Manager.
KING, Harold "Duke." Commissioner.
LINNEHAN, George "Doc." Manager.
MUSICARO, John. Sponsor.

Metro Richmond Amateur Softball Association Hall of Fame

RICHMOND, VIRGINIA

Mailing Address: 6924 Lakeside Ave, 23228. Tel. (804) 264-0264. *Contact:* H. Franklin Taylor III, Commissioner. *Location:* 85 mi. S.E. of Norfolk, Va, 106 mi. N. of Washington, D.C. *Personnel:* Elizabeth J. Cres, Pres; Daniel C. Powers, Jr, V.Pres; George E. Stone III, Secy.-Treas; Henry D. Pollard, Umpire-in-Chief. Not open to the public. *Nearby Halls of Fame:* Exploration and Invention (Arlington, Va, 110 mi. N.), Jockey (Baltimore, Md, 135 mi. N.E.), Golf (Pinehurst, N.C, 200 mi. S.W.), Heritage (Valley Forge, Pa, 215 mi. N.E.).

The Hall of Fame was founded in 1975 by the Metro Richmond Amateur Softball Association to honor people with outstanding softball careers on a local level.

Members: 24 as of July 1977. Not more than five new members are elected each year by the Selection Committee. Categories of membership are manager, sponsor, player, administrator and umpire. The new inductees are presented with a plaque at the annual banquet in April. There were no elections in 1976.

1974 ADAMS, Evelyn
BOLLING, Russell "Legs"
COVINGTON, Bill
JACKSON, Alvin H.
MALLORY, O. W.
POH, "Gillie"
SEIG, Norma
TALLEY, Alma

1975 ALLEN, Frances "Clem"
ATKINSON, Lyn
BARDEN, Mike
BASS, Billy
BROSKI, Grace Trimmer
CORR, Frances
COUSINS, Bob
FRITH, Raymond "Bus"
HARLOW, Bill
NEWELL, Grover
PEMBERTON, Henry "Mutt"
RUSSELL, Polly
SHAUGHNESSY, Charlie, Jr.
SMITH, Helen
WILLIAMS, George
WINGO, Ray

National Softball Hall of Fame

OKLAHOMA CITY, OKLAHOMA

Mailing Address: 2810 Northeast 50 St, 73111. Tel. (405) 424-5266. *Contact:* Dave Hill, Public Relations Dir. *Location:* 230 mi. N.W. of Dallas, Tex, 145 mi. S. of Wichita, Kans. *Admission:* 9 to 5 Mon.–Fri. year-round, and Sat. and Sun. 12 to 5 from May 1 to Oct. 1. Adults 50¢, children 25¢. *Personnel:* Don E. Porter, Exec. Dir; Charles McCord, Chmn. Hall of Fame Comt. *Nearby Halls of Fame:* Western Heritage (Oklahoma City), Ethnic (Amadarko, 50 mi. S.W.), Wrestling (Stillwater, 50 mi. N.E.), Ethnic (Tahlequah, 150 mi. N.E.), Dog Racing (Abilene, Kan, 225 mi. N.).

The idea of the Amateur Softball Association Hall of Fame was conceived at the commissioner's council meeting in January, 1957, in Mesa, Ariz. Its purpose was to give honor and recognition to those men and women who have played so brilliantly and competed so well during their careers and while doing so have contributed to the development and growth of the sport. The Museum houses memorabilia dating back to 1887, the inception of the game of softball. Displays include the method of manufacturing a softball and a bat, as well as turn of the century uniforms, gloves and equipment. The library has the most complete collection in the world of information on the game of softball, including publications from 48 countries. In the new wing, which has just been constructed, there is a miniature ball park and softball movies. There is also a softball research center, the first of its kind in sports Halls of Fame, which contains any and all published materials on softball, including doctoral dissertations and master's theses, as well as newspaper articles. The floors of the Museum are covered with astro turf, and on the walls appear paintings concerned with softball. This Museum is a member of the Association of Sports Museums and Halls of Fame.

Members: 55 as of 1976. Nominations are submitted by the ASA Commissioner from the area in which they live or played. Members must receive 75 percent of the votes of the Selection Committee, and must be retired from active competition at least three years. There is no minimum playing time required; the maximum number of new inductees is five, but some years no one is elected.

1957

ELLIOTT, Sam "Sambo"
Pitcher
Born in Decatur, Ga; retired from Western Electric Co.

Elliott began playing in 1934 at age 22, and continued for 21 seasons, appearing during that time in seven regionals and six national tournaments. His two greatest accomplishments were pitching a no-hitter the first time he pitched a game, and winning the state championship. During his years of competition, he pitched a total of 1133 games, winning 1046 and losing 87. By the time he retired from softball in 1953, from Knowles Electric team, he had pitched 107 no-hitters and 26 perfect games. He amassed 13,936 strikeouts, an average of 12.3 per seven-inning game. The biggest disappointment of his career, besides not winning a national championship, was losing a 22-inning game against Havanna, Fla. In 21 innings he had given up only two hits, but in the 22nd he walked a man and the third hit of the game pinned him with a 1–0 loss. He describes his basic philosophy as to be the best and "never play a game I didn't want to win."

GEARS, Harold "Shifty"
Pitcher
Gears began his softball career in 1922 as a sandlotter, and moved quickly to city league play. In 1928 he drew attention by winning 45 games in a row. In 1931 he pitched ten games in ten days, the first five to win the Canadian Crown of the International League, and the last five to cop the international championship from the American titleholders, the Goldies. He later led Kodak Park to nine national championship tournaments, and the title in 1936 and 1940. He pitched 98 consecutive scoreless innings in 1935. Gears has an impressive record in national championship play, as well as career totals. In championship play, he totaled 20 wins, 6 losses, 15 shutouts, 242 strikeouts and 3 no-hitters; during his career, he had 866 victories and 115 defeats. Of the 981 games he has played, 373 have been shutouts and 61 no-hitters. He also fanned 13,244 batters. Gears began his career with the Silver Stars, and retired in 1951 from Redeemer Church at age 43. He was a recreation counselor for over 40 years with Eastman Kodak, and organized one of the finest softball programs in the country.

MAY, Amy Peralta
Pitcher
Born in Tempe, Ariz; All-American team six times.

May played in all sports at Tempe High School, and during her first season with the Phoenix Ramblers was an outfielder and a bench warmer. In 1939, after pitching a no-hit victory over San Diego, she became a member of a team that would win the national championships in 1940, 1948 and 1949. She pitched more than 500 games during her career (1938–1951) including 300 shutouts and 50 no-hitters. May won 35 national tournament games. When not pitching for the Ramblers, she played outfield and was considered one of the best hitters in softball. She batted cleanup for the Ramblers for ten years.

WADLOW, M. Marie "Waddy"
Pitcher
Born in Peoria, Ill.

Wadlow started her softball career with the Tabernacle Baptist Church of St. Louis in 1929 and completed it in 1950 with the Caterpillar Dieselettes. In answer to a question about her most exciting memory of softball, she said: "We had a 17-inning 1–0 loss to the Phoenix Ramblers, giving us third place in the national tournament at San Antonio, Tex. The thrill was watching the Ramblers come back in the evening after watching a three-hour struggle in the intense heat of the afternoon. They had two hours' rest, and then beat the undefeated Orange Lionettes 1–0 in 11 innings." They took about a half-hour rest, and then lost a heartbreaking game in 15 innings 3–1 to Orange for the championship. It was 43 innings in about 43 hours for the Ramblers.
Also in: Illinois State Amateur Softball Association Hall of Fame.

1958

LINDE, Al
Pitcher and Outfielder
Born in Midland, Mich; All-American team as both pitcher and outfielder.

Linde won 119–39 for Dow Chemical Co. and helped Dow win the national championship in 1951 when he hit an astounding .393. He pitched more than 200 no-hit games during his 20-year career, with a total of 240 innings in 1946 and 438 batters struck out. He played with five national championship teams: Kenosha, Wis, in 1934; Tulsa, Okla, in 1942; Hammer Field Raiders in 1943 and 1944; and Dow AC's in 1951. Linde joined the Dow team in 1946, and had a spectacular year as he pitched a perfect game against Caterpillar of Peoria. He retired from active play in 1953.

1959

GRAYSON, Betty Evans "Bullet"
Pitcher
Born in Portland, Ore.
Grayson played in grade school on a Glencoe boys' team.

At 13 she played city league ball and was named to the city all-star team for her hitting and fielding. At 15 she became a pitcher with the Erv Lind Florist team. During her career her record was 465–99, and she pitched in five national championships with the Lind Florists. In 1945 she pitched 115 consecutive scoreless innings; for her career she had 51 no-hitters and three perfect games. The "blonde bomber's" greatest thrill was winning the 1944 national title, and the game she remembers best was during the 1944 national tourney when she faced the great Phoenix Ramblers team with pitching star Amy Peralta. It was a scoreless game until the 11th inning, when a bunt scored the winning run and gave Grayson and her teammates the national title. During the 1953 Oregon State legislature she was voted a vacant seat in the House by the Speaker of the House and the governor, and was able to play for the House of Representatives against the State Senate in a softball game.

KAMPSCHMIDT, Bernie
Pitcher
Born in Ft. Wayne, Ind; now works as corporation personnel director for Zollner.

Kampschmidt is considered by many people the greatest catcher in softball, and he was not only strong defensively but also a standout clutch hitter. He was a member of the 1945–1947 Zollner Pistons of Ft. Wayne who won the national title each year. In 1937 he began his career, playing with the Carr's Boosters of Covington, Ky. The club captured the state title in 1938 and went on to win the national championship in 1939. Kampschmidt played in more than 2500 games and on four national champion teams. During his career with the Pistons, which spanned 15 years, the team played 1442 games, winning 1253 of them. In 1942 the Pistons were 99–2.

KIRKENDALL, Clyde "Dizzy"
Pitcher
Born in Findlay, Ohio; died 1957.

Kirkendall started playing in 1930 with the Page Dairy team of Toledo and in 1933 moved to Toledo's Crimson Coaches. Kirkendall's career spanned 25 years of top competition that included 11 national tournaments; he was a member of five national championship teams. In 1937 with Polhar Cafe, he won 67 and lost 4; in 1938 he was 51–3. While with Polhar, he pitched 127 consecutive scoreless innings. During his four years with the Zollner Pistons, he established a 108–16 record, and led them to three national titles. He still holds several national records, including pitching the longest number of innings in a game: 33. In that same game, he struck out 67. For his career, he pitched 167 no-hit games, including 8 no-hitters in national tournament play; his win-loss record was 1144–52.

1960

GERBER, Warren "Fireball"
Pitcher
Born in Cleveland, Ohio.

Gerber's career started at age 13, and spanned 17 years of top-notch competition during which time he recorded over 500 wins, including some 50 no-hitters. As a 15-year-old pitcher with Columbus Ferguson in 1936, he began compiling an average of 35 victories per year, which included a number of no-hitters and an average of 15 strikeouts per game. He pitched four perfect games during his career and once struck out 20 of 21 batters in a game. In 1939 playing with Columbus Ferguson, he led his team to a second-place finish in the national tournament. That year he won 40 games and didn't lose one. In the 1944 national tournament, he pitched his team to a third-place finish, including a no-hitter against Toronto, and came within one hit of pitching a perfect game against Mobile. In 1945 with Allmen Transfer, Gerber pitched three no-hitters in a row as his team swept to city and metro honors. In 1946 Gerber's 4–2 mark in the national championship brought a sixth-place finish that year. He retired from active play in 1952 due to a basketball injury. On June 28, 1960, Mayor Anthony Celebreeze of Cleveland proclaimed "Warren Gerber Day."

KORGAN, Nina
Pitcher
Born in New Orleans, La; now works in the accounting department of Jackson Brewing Co.

Following her high school graduation, Korgan was invited to play for a local team, but almost missed making the team when she showed up late. The only position left was pitcher, which she took, going on to win 49 out of 50 games. In 1935 she began a pitching career that would, over 14 years, help her teams to win six national championships. In 1941 she pitched the Higgins Midgets of Tulsa, Okla, to the national title. During the tournament, she pitched 30 innings, allowing 5 hits and striking out 67. She pitched four consecutive shutouts, one of them a perfect game. In one game of the 1941 tourney, she struck out 20 of 21 batters. In the six years she was with the Jax Maids of New Orleans, she pitched them to five national championships. Korgan retired from active play in 1948.
Also in: Omaha Softball Association Hall of Fame.

MILLER, Clarence "Buck"
Pitcher
Born 1923 in Memphis, Tenn; All-American, 1948, 1952 and 1954. Most Valuable Player in National Tournament 1948.

Miller began playing softball in 1940, and retired in 1955. In 1941 he got his first taste of national competition when he pitched Buckeye Oil Co. to the city and state titles. In one of his first of many national tournament games during the 1941 championships he beat San Antonio 4–0. In 1947 while playing for Standard Parts, he led his team to city and state crowns. In the finals he pitched a 16-inning no-hitter in one game and came back to win the second game not only with his pitching but with his bat. During the 1948 regional tournament he pitched a perfect game, which put his club in the national tournament at Portland. Miller lost his first time out, but then won six in a row. He had 47 consecutive scoreless innings, one no-hitter and struck out 101 batters. He lost 1–0 to Detroit in the final game. In a 1949 exhibition game he faced 21 batters and fanned all 21 for a perfect game. Buck pitched 9 perfect games during his career and a total of 81 no-hitters. In 1955 he was the strikeout leader in the national tournament. During the

1954 national tournament at Minneapolis, he pitched a 14-inning game against Washington and fanned 28; he then won the game with a three-run homer.

RAMAGE, James
Shortstop
Born in Fort Wayne, Ind; All-American and All-Star teams several times; now working for the Zollner Co. in Fort Wayne.

Ramage's career began at age 18 when he played his first year of major competition with the Nick Carr Boosters, who went on to win the national championship in 1939. He led the Zollner Pistons to three national titles back-to-back, 1945–1947. He compiled a lifetime batting mark of .293, and led the old National Softball League in home runs in 1948 and 1951. Jim retired after the 1954 season.

SEARS, Ruth
First Baseman
Born in Canada; All-American team four times.

Sears was a good defensive player, with a national tournament batting average of .267. She competed in a total of seven national championships, and had a lifetime batting average of .425. She batted .585 with the Orange Lionettes in her first season with them and led the team in hitting every year but two. Her husband Chub coached the Lionettes from 1947 to 1955, and her father, an outstanding baseball player, contributed greatly in helping her develop her softball skills. One of Sears' fondest memories is the 1950 national tournament in San Antonio when the Lionettes played 26 consecutive innings to win their first national title. She scored the winning run in the final game, scoring all the way from first on a teammate's double. Ruth started in 1936 with the Green Cat Cafe of the Santa Ana City League and starred with the Lionettes from 1937 until her retirement in 1955.

CRAIN, Ben
Pitcher
Born 1910 in Omaha, Nebr.

Crain was called the "Iron Man" of softball, and he started playing kittenball, staying with the sport until 1949. He pitched close to 1000 games in his career, with an 85 percent won-lost record. Powerful at the plate as well, he averaged 20 home runs a year, with a .375 batting average. He helped his team to seven Nebraska state championships, and won three games in a Detroit tournament. He has served on the Nebraska State Hall of Fame Board, and was also one of the first softball players in Iowa, playing when he was 11 years old. In recognition of his outstanding contributions to softball, he was presented citations by the mayor of Omaha and the governor of Nebraska. Crain pitched more than 100 no-hitters in his career, and holds the record for the longest homer in Omaha's record books. To demonstrate his pitching versatility, he once pitched a doubleheader, one game right-handed and the other left.
Also in: Omaha Softball Association Hall of Fame.

JOHNSTON, Hugh "Lefty"
First Baseman
Born 1916 in Belfast, Ireland; NSL All-Star teams 1946–1953; Most Valuable Player 1947.

A big Irishman, he played most of his softball years with the Zollner Pistons. He was a craftsman at first base as well as powerful at bat. Although he didn't play serious softball until age 22, his debut with Burr Patterson in 1938 made headlines. He played with Briggs Beaut-wear in 1940, and for a single year was with Dow Chemical nine of Midland, Mich. In 1943 he joined the Zollner Pistons, and retired in 1954, when Zollner eliminated the sport from their operations. Lefty led the Pistons to four state championships, one national championship, seven National Softball League (NSL) pennants and two Industrial Tournament crowns, and had a lifetime batting average of .295.

1961

BAKER, John "Cannonball"
Pitcher
Born in Westport, Conn.

Baker started playing softball while in grade school at age 11, and retired after the 1953 season, having competed for 26 years. He was enthusiastic about softball at an early age, and would seek out a game before school in the morning, during lunch, and again on Saturday morning. He started as a first baseman and outfielder, and switched to pitching in junior high. Baker appeared in four national tournaments and established a 6–2 mark. His pitching record was 780–120; he registered 58 no-hitters and struck out more than 10,000 batters during his career. In the 1934 national tourney, he won two games and lost one; his team was eliminated in the quarter finals. The following year he was 0–1 but in 1936 he came back strong, and was 2–0 in the national tourney. During the 1938 season, he pitched four consecutive no-hit, no-run games.
Also in: Connecticut Amateur Softball Association Hall of Fame.

1963

HUNTER, John
Pitcher
Born in Clearwater, Fla; All-American six consecutive years, 1951–1956; Most Valuable Player 1951, 1953 and 1955.

Hunter made his first national appearance in 1950 with the Clearwater Bombers at Austin, Tex, giving up only one hit and striking out 16 batters, while beating Portland. That year he won 43 and lost 3 games. The following year he pitched 5 straight victories. In 1951 in another national tourney, he had a record of 39 innings hurled in which he struck out 75 batters; he had a 7–0 total as a pitcher for the two years. In 1951 in 53 innings, he allowed just 12 hits, 9 runs and fanned 104. In 1950 he pitched 355 innings in major competition and struck out 696 batters; he set a tournament record in 1952 by fanning 19 men in a seven-inning game. Hunter won 39–1 in 1956, which doesn't include a 4–0 tournament record. His lifetime record is 275–19, with a strike-out average of just under two per inning, and he never lost in state or regional competition. He retired from active play in 1958 because of hip trouble that had been plaguing him for a couple of years.

MARTIN, B. E.
ASA Executive Secretary-Treasurer
Martin was one of the founders of the Amateur Softball Association (ASA) and helped guide it through some of the early days of its existence. In the early days with ASA, he served as New Jersey state commissioner, and traveled to foreign countries to promote the sport. The first and only nonplayer to be elected to the Hall of Fame, he helped develop a strong youth program for ASA; deceased.

RICH, Kay
Outfielder and Infielder
Born in Fresno, Calif; attended Univ. Calif, Berkeley; All-American three times; Most Valuable Player 1956.

Her father taught her the fundamentals of the game, and she started playing in 1938. She played with such teams as the Colton Cuties, the Ontario Lionettes, Glendora, Long Beach, Woolworth, Alameda and the Fresno Rockets. Rich played for over nine years in the Pacific Coast Women's Softball League, one of the strongest in the country. She had a lifetime .312 batting average with 375 hits in 1201 trips to the plate. She played in 12 national tournaments, six as a shortstop; she hit .405 her first year at Glendora, and when she was with the Leach Motor Rockets, the team never lost a game in the state or regional tournaments.

1964

CASTLE, Tom
First Baseman
Born in Rochester, N.Y.

Castle played 25 years, with a .340 batting average. In 1936 he joined Kodak, then won the national championship, and four years later did it again, the only team in the East to win twice within four years. In addition to 2 national championships, Kodak played in the top tourney 9 other times, and were in 11 regional tournaments. Although he has retired from Kodak after 25 years, he acts as umpire for college baseball games, as well as fast and slow pitch softball contests.

DOBSON, Margaret
Third Baseman
Born in Portland, Ore; All-American team 1949–1950; Portland Sports Writers and Broadcasters Outstanding Athlete 1952; NSC All-Star team.

Dobson was the leading hitter in the 1950 national tourney for the Erv Lind Florists, with a .615, a record that still stands for national tournament play in the Amateur Softball Association record books. She started with the Florists in 1945 after two years with Vancouver Washing. She was selected to many regional All-Star teams from 1946 until her retirement. She played in nine national tournaments, and was always one of the top fielders. She played in the Northwest League except for the 1951–1953 years when her team participated in the National Softball Congress (NSC) play.

1965

STEPHENSON, Roy
Pitcher
Born in Muttontown, N.Y; All-American 1948, 1950, 1951, 1958 and 1959.

Stephenson started playing at age 15, and two years later moved to Long Island from his native Muttontown to join an employee team that he played with for almost a decade. He joined the Dejur Cameramen team officially in 1955, playing with them until his retirement in 1960. He played in four state tournaments during his career, compiling a record of 15 victories and 2 losses. He took part in 15 regional tourneys, stacking up a total of 40 victories and 3 defeats. He had a 23–16 record in national tourneys.
Also in: Metro Long Island Amateur Softball Association Hall of Fame.

1966

CHAMBERS, Jim
Pitcher
Born in Oshkosh, Wis; ASA Gold Bat Award; Racine, Wis, Sportsman Award.

In 1946 Chambers struck out 43 men and fanned 117 in a national tournament game. He made Ripley's Believe It or Not column by this strike-out mark. He started playing in Aurora, Ill, at age 11, and retired at Racine, Wis, in 1962. During his career, he struck out 4380 batters and counted 209 no-hitters. He led the Chicago Match Corp. team to two runnerup spots in national tournaments. Since his retirement from softball, he has served as commissioner of the Lakeshore Fast Pitch League, made up of teams of Illinois and Wisconsin.
Also in: Illinois State Amateur Softball Association Hall of Fame.

FORBES, Robert
Outfielder
Born in Clearwater, Fla; All-American team 1951, 1953 and 1956.

At age 14, Forbes was the youngest player with the Clearwater Bombers. He began in 1941 and quickly learned the basic fundamentals of an outfielder, such as which base to throw to on a play, to pick out the cutoff man when it was a long throw, and how to get back to the fence on a long ball. He had good defensive abilities, and was powerful at bat. In 1956 the Bombers captured their third title, and he was named to the All-Tournament honors for the third time. He led all tourney hitters with a terrific .471 average.

HART, Carolyn Thome
Outfielder
Born in Pekin, Ill; All-American four times.

Hart had a career batting average of .301, and was coached by Chuck McCord. She was also encouraged by her father, who played softball and semipro baseball. She started playing at age 12, and began playing top-flight softball with the Caterpillar Dieselettes, later with the Pekin Lettes until her retirement in 1962. She led Pekin in hitting for three years, and was runnerup four other times. Coach McCord said of Hart: "She was one of the greatest players I ever had."

Also in: Illinois State Amateur Softball Association Hall of Fame.

1967

KRONEWITTER, Ronald
Pitcher
Born in Mishawaka, Ind.

Kronewitter played 14 in. softball his first three years as a pitcher. In a three-year span, he won 55 games and lost only 7 playing with the East End Pirates for two years and the Doc Gross Specials one year. In the next three years, with a 12 in. ball, he compiled 53 wins, including 10 no-hitters, as opposed to 5 setbacks. In 1934 he joined the famous Bendix Brakes of South Bend when he won 15 with 4 two-hitters, and lost 3. The following year he won 19 and lost 5 with many low-hit games, and hurled the Brakes to a 6 – 1 victory over Schlitz and Atlanta in the national tournament in Lincoln Park in Chicago. The next year he pitched Bendix to the Indiana state championship, beating Ft. Wayne 5 – 0 on a one-hitter in the semifinals, and Hammond fell to him 4 – 3 when he came in as relief. The 1938 season found him guiding his team to the Indiana state championship and beating Rochester, N.Y., 1 – 0 in Soldiers' Field in Chicago.

WHITLOCK, Nolan
Shortstop
Born in Rossville, Ga; All-American Shortshop four consecutive years.

Whitlock began his career in 1952 with the Industrial Sales Team of Miami, and led them to the runner-up spot in the national championships played at Stratford, Conn. In 1953 he joined the Clearwater Bombers, and for the next four years they went to the national championships. The next season his brilliant fielding and hitting assisted the Bombers to their second world title, which was played at Minneapolis; they were runner-up to Stratford, Conn. The following year the Bombers took the national crown, with Whitlock hitting two homers in the final game; in 1957 they were once again national kings.

WOJIE, Billy
Third Baseman
Born in New Haven, Conn; All-New England six years; All-Star team 1955; All-American 1955, 1959 and 1961.

Wojie played with the Columbus Auto Body Bears, the New Haven Raybestos Cardinals and Stratford. In seven years with the Cardinals he hit .286, and won the batting title in 1955 and 1956 with .312 and .290 averages. He played in eight national tournaments, and won the championship in 1969 and 1970 with the Cardinals. In 1962 he suffered a heart attack which forced his retirement.

Also in: Connecticut Amateur Softball Association Hall of Fame.

1968

HESS, LeRoy
Catcher
Born in Aurora, Ill; First All-American team 1957, 1959 and 1961.

Hess managed and played with the Stephens-Adamson Sealmasters for 17 years, and they were national champions in 1959 and 1961. He played his first softball game at age 17 with a Phoenix club, and retired from the sport at age 42. He played with the Aurora Foxes for one year before joining the Sealmasters. Hess played in four national tournaments.

Also in: Illinois State Amateur Softball Association Hall of Fame.

SPRENTALL, Bob
Outfielder
Born in Clearwater, Fla; All-American 1955 – 1957 and 1960.

Sprentall helped the Clearwater Bombers win five out of eight national championships, and later played pro baseball with Boston and Detroit farm clubs.

WEST, Bill
Pitcher
West pitched and won 32 games in a row in major competition with the Zollner Pistons. He began his career with Koelkel Norge of Covington, Ky, in 1938, and two years later joined the Sixth Ward Boosters of Newport, Ky, leading them to the state title two years later. After joining the service in 1942, he pitched his military team to the European and Mediterranean championships, in addition to many other titles. Following W.W. II, West joined the Zollner Pistons, which won the national championship the next two years. West left Zollner after ten years, in 1955, to work for General Motors in Detroit. He was considered the Number One pitcher during his years with the Pistons, combining blazing speed and remarkable control. In 1946 and 1947, his record was 60 – 6; West considered the 1947 Piston team the greatest in the history of softball; deceased.

1969

CONTEL, Jeanne
Third Baseman
Born in Fresno, Calif; All-American 1953, 1955, 1957 and 1963.

Jeanne joined the Fresno Rockets in 1951 and in the next 14 years played in 11 national tournaments. She started her softball career with Schnaffer and Watson of Alameda, Calif, in 1944. She went on to the Dime Taxi Cab Girls in 1946, the Dr. Pepper Girls in 1947 and Jim Ellis Sports Shop in Oakland, Calif, in 1948.

STRATTON, Mickey
Catcher
Born in Stratford, Conn; National All-Star team five times; now teaches physical education.

While Stratton played for the Raybestos Brakettes, the team won four national championships. In 1965 she batted .370, and had a career average of .314. While she played with the Brakettes (1955 – 1965), she batted better than .300 seven times, leading the team in batting for three seasons.

1970

SPRING, John

Pitcher

Born in Aurora, Ill; All-American 1952 – 1956, 1958, 1962 and 1963.

At age 19 at a national tournament in Little Rock, Ark, Spring threw a no-hitter against Cincinnati. In 1952 he pitched Briggs to their first national championship, as he won all five games. In the semifinals, he threw a perfect no-hit, no-run game against "Buck" Miller and his Memphis, Tenn, nine. In 1953 Spring put on one of the most remarkable pitching demonstrations in the history of national tournaments when he pitched Briggs out of the loser's bracket and into the national championship. He pitched three games on the final day, blanked Bloomington, Ill, 1 – 0 and came back at night to beat Herb Dudley 2 – 0 and John J. Hunter of the Clearwater Bombers 1 – 0. After Briggs disbanded following the 1954 season, Spring went East to join the Raybestos Cardinals. In his first year with the Cardinals, he helped pitch them to their first national title. In 1958 he pitched the Cardinals to their second national title with a no-hit, no-run game in the finals against Lake Charles, La. He threw a record 67 pitches in the seven-inning finale. While with the Cardinals, he had a 209 – 35 record. From 1963 to 1966 he pitched for the Sealmasters of Aurora, Ill. As a member of the 1965 national championship team, he had a 76 – 5 record. Over 17 years of playing, Spring averaged five no-hitters per season, and was in 17 consecutive national tournaments. He participated in Amateur Softball Association clinics in 1956 and 1962 in Europe, and in the Far East in 1961. His lifetime pitching record was 483 – 62.
Also in: Illinois State Amateur Softball Association Hall of Fame.

WILKINSON, Dot

Catcher

Born in Phoenix, Ariz; All-American 19 times.

Wilkinson was the greatest woman softball catcher of all time, using a five-fingered glove rather than the normal catcher's mitt. She retired in 1965 after a long career with the PBSW Ramblers of Phoenix, Ariz. She played softball for over a quarter of a century, and paced the Ramblers to three national titles, in 1940 and back-to-back crowns in 1948 and 1949. In her 33 years with the Ramblers, she compiled a .300 lifetime batting average. In the 1950 national tournament in Texas, she played 43 innings in one day.

WILLIAMS, Frankie

Second Baseman

All-American, 1957, 1958 and 1962.

Williams was the most prolific hitter the Raybestos Cardinals ever had. In the 22-year span of the team's operation, Williams set many records that have never been surpassed; he retired after the 1966 season. After joining the Cardinals, he became the first player in the history of the club to break the .400 barrier, stroking .404 for the year, the first year he ever played softball, which earned him a spot in Ripley's Believe It or Not column. In 1964 he became the first player in the Atlantic Seaboard Major Softball League to ever hit over .400 when he posted a .423 average. In seven of the ten years with the Cardinals, he was the team's batting champion: 1957, .404; 1960, .330; 1961, .375; 1962, .369; 1964, .430; 1965, .412; 1973, .370. He holds four of the all-time Cardinal individual season records: most runs scored, 77; most hits, 103; hitting streak, 23; and three .400 seasons.
Also in: Connecticut Amateur Softball Association Hall of Fame.

1971

BUSICK, Virginia "Ginny"

Pitcher

Born in Fresno, Calif.

Busick began playing softball in 1937, but didn't play during four war years. While with the Fresno Rockets (1946 – 1951, 1957 – 1970) she worked 227 innings in the Pacific Coast Softball League competition, and she led the league pitchers in almost every department. She gave up only ten earned runs, and she had 189 strike outs. She allowed only 87 hits, and had a brilliant .857 success record. Her pitches were blazing fast, timed at 103 m.p.h. She retired from softball in 1970 and the next year the mayor of the city of Fresno proclaimed July 4 Ginny Busick Day.

WICKERSHAM, Ray "Ned"

Outfielder

Born in Palatine, Ill; All-West Central Regional team eight times; All-American team 1957, 1962 – 1965.

Wickersham began playing on a local Palatine team in 1949, and joined the Sealmasters as an added player for the regional tournament. He became a regular in left field, one of the best hitters ever to play with the Sealmasters. He considers his biggest thrill the fact that he won two national batting championships. For 11 straight years, he batted the third position, with a career batting average of .290, and above .300 in his last four seasons. In 617 games with the Sealmasters, he compiled 527 hits, including 67 home runs, and drove in 157 runs. He collected 181 walks while striking out only 173 times, one of only two Sealmasters who had more walks than strike outs. He was instrumental in leading the Sealmasters to the national championships in 1959, 1961 and 1965, and represented his country in the first world tournament in Mexico City.
Also in: Illinois Amateur Softball Association Hall of Fame.

ZIEGLER, John "Buster"

Outfielder

Born in Miami, Fla; All-American 1952; Outstanding Player 1960.

Ziegler began playing in Miami's More Park Fast Pitch Softball League with Bell Telephone, and concluded his career in 1965 with Aerodex of Miami. Between 1947 and 1965 Ziegler was one of the most amazing players to compete in the Amateur Softball Association. He participated in ten national tournaments and led Miami

American Industrial Sales team to the finals in 1952. In 1960 his hits were responsible for the Bombers winning the championship. Ziegler competed in the national tournaments in 1949 – 1953, 1955, 1957 – 1958, 1960 – 1961. In 1949 his outstanding performance in the state tournament prompted the Bombers to use him as a "pick-up" player, and he responded by making it possible for them to finish in the runnerup spot in Little Rock, Ark. During 1950 he moved to Clearwater and his clutch hitting in the regionals and national tournaments lifted the Bombers to their first national tournament play in 1951 at Detroit. In 1960, Ziegler was selected as outstanding player in the state tournament as a member of the Homestead team.

1972

CURTIS, Jerry
Outfielder
Born in Clearwater, Fla; Most Valuable Player 1956; All-American four times; Southern Region first All-Star team at four positions: pitcher, utility, second base and outfield.

In 1949 Curtis started pitching in City League Softball with Gulf Lumber. He played for the Clearwater Bombers when they won seven of their nine championships. In 1954 he was selected to the regional first team at second base, and batted .348. In 1956 he was again selected to the first team as an outfielder, and batted. 539. In 1960 he batted .333 with 4 RBI in four games, and in 1962 he batted .300. He was on the national championship teams seven times, and played on five regional championships in six years of competition. Curtis joined the Bombers in 1951 as a regular infielder, moved to the outfield in 1964, and managed the team 1966 – 1967.

ROPP, Don
Third Base
National All-Star team 1956 and 1963; All-West Central Regional squad nine times.

He joined the Sealmasters as an outfielder in 1951 and moved to third base two years later. During his last 13 years with Sealmaster, he compiled a .325 lifetime batting mark. He holds team records for a single season with 25 doubles, 11 triples and 44 walks, and is a runnerup in single season marks in hits, runs and home runs as well as stolen bases. In 912 games Don connected for 864 base hits, including 131 home runs. He received 377 walks in his career while striking out only 274 times, one of only two regulars on the club ever to walk more than strike out. He batted in the cleanup position throughout his last 14 years and was team captain during the last 11. He played in 11 consecutive national tournaments and played a vital role as the Sealmasters won the national titles in 1959, 1961 and 1965. He also represented his country in the first world tournament at Mexico City in 1966, the year he retired.
Also in: Illinois State Amateur Softball Association Hall of Fame.

TICKEY, Bertha
Pitcher
National All-Star Team 18 times; Most Valuable Player eight times.

Tickey won 757 and lost 88 in 23 years of pitching, hurling 162 no-hit, no-run games. A native Californian, she is the only player to play on 11 national championship teams. She holds the all-time record for single game strike outs in a national tournament with 20 in seven innings in 1953. She had three perfect games to her credit in the national tournament competition, and a record of 69 wins. In her final three national tournament pitching performances, she threw a no-hitter against Redwood City, Calif, in 1967, and in 1968 finished her career with a perfect game against Houston, Tex, and a 13-inning no-hit, no-run game against Fresno, Calif. She pitched in the first international world championship in 1965 at Melbourne, Australia, with the Raybestos Brakettes, which represented the United States. The Brakettes lost the world final to Australia 1 – 0. She also participated in a goodwill tour that year, competing against teams in Hong Kong, Taiwan, India and Holland.
Also in: Connecticut Amateur Softball Association Hall of Fame.

1973

CAITO, Estelle "Ricki"
Second Baseman
All-American 1956, 1957 and 1960.

Caito retired from softball in 1965 after a 25-year career. She played in nine national tournaments and was a star for the Orange Lionettes when they won three national championships in 1955, 1956 and 1962. She started playing with the Lucky Stars of Alameda, Calif, at 13 and before she stopped she had earned the reputation of a great second baseman. She retired from the Phoenix Ramblers, an outstanding hitter in the clutch, but her defensive play made her great. "I feel my greatest thrill came during my career in beating Mazucca and Joyce in the same night and winning the 1962 national championship," she recalled.

MAY, Gloria
First Baseman
All-American three times.

May retired in 1969 after 27 years of softball stardom, most with the Fresno Rockets. She participated in 15 national tournaments and was a star first baseman on the Rockets national championship teams of 1953, 1954 and 1957. In 10 of 15 national tournaments, she played errorless ball. She handled more than 400 chances in national tournament play, and made only four errors. She is one of the all-time defensive first basemen. In 1940, she started her softball career in Glendale, Calif, and then moved to Montebello in 1947 and Monrovia in 1948, before finding her permanent home in Fresno in 1949.

RUNHARDT, Myron
Outfielder
All-American five times; Most Valuable Player 1963.

Runhardt retired from active play in 1968, and was selected to the Hall of Fame in 1973 as the first slow pitch player. He played for the South Ward Boosters of Newport, Ky, in 1948 – 1950, a fast pitch team that won three straight Kentucky titles and placed fifth in the 1949 national fast pitch tournament at Little Rock, Ark.

Runhardt switched to slow pitch in 1950 and proceeded to play in 11 of the first 13 slow pitch national tournaments and on five national championship teams. Runhardt, who still holds his high school's 100-yd. dash record, was a far-ranging, hard-hitting center fielder. He starred for the Shield's Contractors of Newport that won the first slow pitch national tournament in 1953. He joined the Gatliff Auto Sales of Newport to help win the national titles in 1956–1957 and 1963. Gatliff was runnerup in 1964 and 1965, but they didn't make the national tournament in 1959, losing out to Yorkshire, also of Newport. Runhardt was picked up by Yorkshire, and won the national title with Myron being named to the All-American team.

TOMLINSON, Richard "Rickey"
Shortstop
Born in Montreal, Que; All-American 1959, 1961 and 1963; All-American second team 1962 and 1966.

While playing for the Clearwater Bombers (1959–1969), Tomlinson led the club in hitting seven times. The first Bomber player to achieve 100 hits in a season, he had a .345 career batting average with the Bombers. He batted .384 in 1967 for a career high. The Bombers won five national tournaments and finished second two times during Tomlinson's decade on the club. The titles came in 1960, 1963, 1966 and 1968. He led the Bombers in hitting in three of those years, and was the second leading hitter the other two years. He and Hall of Famer Al Linde tied for most hits during a national tournament in 1960, when he slammed 11 hits to spark the Bombers to the national title. Tomlinson batted over .300 in three national tournaments that included .389 in 1959, .333 in 1960, and .353 in 1961.

1974

DeLUCA, Frank
Pitcher and Infielder
National All-Star team 1968–1969.

DeLuca started his career in the 1940s. He was honored for his outstanding play in the industrial slow pitch ranks. He started his career in fast pitch in 1945, and continued until 1958. Then he switched to industrial slow pitch and his career really began to soar. He was associated with the Avco-Lycoming industrial team, and excelled as a pitcher and third baseman. His pitching record was 737–121, with a .484 batting average. He played in nine national industrial tournaments, and is now a top executive at the Avco-Lycoming Division in Stratford, Conn.
Also in: Connecticut Amateur Softball Association Hall of Fame.

JUSTICE, Charles
Pitcher
Born in Detroit, Mich; died 1974; Most Valuable Player 1965.

At 6 ft. 1 in, 210 lbs, Justice had a record for terrorizing opposing ball clubs for over 27 years. He often pitched a shutout, and then stepped to the plate to slam a home run. He participated in Amateur Softball Association play since its beginnings in 1933. He started with the Pontiac, Mich, team in 1936, that won the National Negro Amateur Softball Championships in 1937. In 1945 he went to the national championships with the Flint M&S Orange which finished as runnerup. He went to the national championships in 1949 with the Tip Top Tailors of Toronto and again in 1950. They won in 1949 and came in second in 1950. Justice consistently led in pitching and hitting. Between 1949 and 1958, he gave softball clinics in Ontario, and his "windmill" style of pitching is now practiced throughout Ontario as a result of his clinics and exhibitions. He returned to the United States in 1959 and played in the Michigan Chronicle Fastball League through 1964. In 1965 he pitched in the International Fastball League. He retired from playing softball in 1965, but was active in Little League and high school baseball until his death. A member of the Detroit Federation of Umpires for over three years, his pitching record was 873–92.

1975

KING, Kathryn "Sis"
Catcher and Outfielder
Born in Cincinnati, Ohio; first All-American team 1959, 1962–1965.

King played for Cincinnati, Ohio, Phoenix, Ariz, and Stratford, Conn, playing 18 years of major women's fast pitch softball. She joined the Brakettes in 1965 following 15 years of competition between her hometown in Cincinnati and Phoenix, Ariz. In three years with the Brakettes, she had an overall .322 batting average. One of the all-time sluggers, King never batted under .300 with Phoenix in the Pacific Coast Women's League. She played in six national tournaments. She represented the United States in the first world softball championship in 1965 at Melbourne, Australia, and in 1967 represented the United States at the Pan-American Games in Winnipeg. She was the first woman to hit a home run over the scoreboard at Raybestos Memorial Field in tournament play, and the only woman to hit back-to-back, out-of-the-park home runs in tournament play.

LAW, Marjorie
Pitcher, Outfielder and Infielder
Born in Tempe, Ariz; All-American team at three different positions.

Law played for the Phoenix Ramblers for 18 years and helped her team win three Amateur Softball Association national championships. She was known for her strength at bat, and was the cleanup hitter for the Ramblers.

RARDIN, Donald
Pitcher, Infielder
Most Valuable Player 1966.

Rardin was the only man in Amateur Softball Association history to play on the championship teams in both the open slow and industrial slow pitch divisions. He was a member of five national championship teams. His career began in 1956 with Newport, Ky. From 1956 to 1964 he played in the open division, and from 1965 to 1968 he was a member of the IBM team of Lexington, Ky, in the industrial division. He led IBM to the top spot in the 1966 national industrial tourney, and, during that meet, racked up a sensational pitching mark. He allowed 13 runs, 40 hits, and 11 earned runs in the six-game stint. He amassed an earned run average of 1.83, and his pitching included a shutout, a four-hitter and a seven-hitter.

His years in industrial play were as a pitcher, but Rardin was an infielder in open competition. He compiled a lifetime batting average of .606, and had a lifetime pitching record of 234 wins and 39 defeats. He played in over 2400 organized softball games.

1976

HARRISON, Pat
Outfielder
All-American team 1966, 1968 and 1970; All-American second team 1963.

Harrison played for 11 years with the South Hill Queens of Vancouver, B.C, the Erv Lind Florists of Portland, Ore, and the Raybestos Brakettes of Stratford, Conn. She compiled a lifetime batting average of .303 before retiring in 1972. She participated in 11 national tournaments, was a member of five national championship teams and was rated as one of the best defensive outfielders in women's softball.

SIMS, Alberta Kohls
Outfielder
All-American team 1961–1964; Most Valuable Player 1964.

Sims played left field for the Dana Gardens team of Cincinnati, Ohio, for 11 straight years. She led the team to three straight national Amateur Softball Association Championships 1962–1964. She was the cleanup hitter for the Dana Gardens team, and in five national tournaments compiled a batting average of .455. She was the first woman slow pitch player elected to the Hall of Fame.

SPILL, Bobby
Pitcher
All-American team, 1958–1960 and 1968; All-Star Game three times.

Spill played for the Clearwater, Fla, Bombers, the Raybestos Cardinals of Connecticut and teams in the Lake Charles, La, area. He participated in ten national American Softball Association tournaments, and established many records. His record of having given up only one earned run in the first 159⅔ innings of the national tournament competition may never be equaled. In national tournament competition, he pitched 205½ innings, gave up only eight earned runs, with a lifetime earned run average in national tournament play of .272. He struck out 258 batters and compiled an 18–9 record. Spill retired as an active player in 1970.

WALKER, Pat
Outfielder
Born in Orlando, Fla; All-American team 1966 and 1968; All-American second team 1961; All-State team eight times; All-Regional team eleven years.

In 16 years of competition, Walker compiled a lifetime batting average of .314. She had a 47–24 pitching record with a 1.92 ERA. An outstanding defensive player, she committed only two errors in nine national tournaments. She retired as an active player in 1969.

Nebraska Softball Association Hall of Fame

FREMONT, NEBRASKA

Mailing Address: 1840 North C St, 68025. Tel. (402) 721-0347. *Contact:* O. W. Bill Smith, ASA State Commissioner. *Location:* 30 mi. N.W. of Omaha and 45 mi. N.E. of Lincoln. Not open to the public. *Nearby Halls of Fame:* Dog Racing (Abilene, Kans, 190 mi. S.), Agriculture (Bonner Springs, Kans, 195 mi. S.E.).

The Hall of Fame was founded in 1977 by O. W. Bill Smith and the Nebraska Softball Association for the purpose of honoring in perpetuity the greatest players and participants in softball in the State of Nebraska, which is affiliated with the American Softball Association's (ASA) Western Region. Memorabilia of the game and mementos of these participants and players are being collected for the purpose of permanent preservation in a future facility dedicated to the Nebraska Softball Association Hall of Fame.

Members: 3 as of 1977. Each member is chosen for his or her contributions to the game of softball in the State of Nebraska. Five new members may be selected each year by a Selection Committee, which is composed of both softball experts and community leaders. Nominations should be forwarded to Mr. Smith. New inductees chosen by the Selection Committee are formally inducted at the annual meeting and banquet of the Nebraska Softball Association, during which they or their representatives are presented Hall of Fame plaques.

1977 BACON, Lee. Team manager.

JOE, Donald. Team manager.

LEWIS, James. State commissioner.

North Dakota Softball Hall of Fame

HARVEY, NORTH DAKOTA

Mailing Address: Box 516, 58341. Tel. (701) 324-4227. *Contact:* Marvin H. Theige, Secy, Hall of Fame Council. *Location:* 109 mi. N.E. of Bismarck, N. Dak, and 175 mi. S.W. of Winnipeg, Man. *Nearby Halls of Fame:* Water Sports (Winnipeg).

Sparky Thompson conceived of the idea of a North Dakota Softball Hall of Fame in 1957, and the North Dakota Amateur Softball Association (NDASA) supported him. The first annual tournament was staged in conjunction with the official dedication of the North Dakota Softball Hall of Fame July 7, 1957. A building fund was started and the ground-breaking ceremonies were held at the 1963 tournament. The building was constructed late in the summer of 1964 to be ready for occupancy and dedication in conjunction with the 1965 tournament. The center facade of the front symbolizes the softball diamond and playing field. Located in the pinnacle and incorporated into the window design is the identifying insignia of the NDASA. The two entrances to the front of the building symbolize the team dugouts.

Members: 68 as of 1977. There are three members chosen per year, exclusive of the past state commissioners of softball, who are automatically included. Members are inducted after the annual Hall of Fame Softball Tournament.

1957

BYRNE, Robert
Commissioner
Byrne secured rule books in 1928 and started softball in Bismarck. He held the position of state commissioner from 1939 to 1944, and was known as the father of softball in Bismarck. He served as the president of the Bismarck City League for many years, as well as manager of the Mo Slope Tournament. During the 1930s, he pitched on several Bismarck teams.

DAVIS, John E.
Governor
Davis was governor of the state at the time he was inducted into the Hall of Fame July 7, 1957. He was the dedication speaker that day, a left-handed pitcher with the University of North Dakota and McCluskey softball teams.

FARRAR, Felix
Commissioner
Born April 14, 1910; died October 15, 1953, at age 43.

Farrar was the North Dakota Amateur Softball Association commissioner from 1948 to 1952. His Fargo team won the 1947 northern regional and went to the world tournament at Austin, Tex. He also sponsored and managed teams for many years, including several state championship teams.

FRIEDMAN, Abe
Catcher
Friedman played in the Fargo-Moorhead area for 32 years, participating in 25 state tournaments and 4 national tournaments. He also played on 15 North Dakota state championship teams.

KELLY, Clement E.
Catcher
Kelly played softball in the Bismarck area for 28 years, and played in 12 state championship tournaments and 1 national Amateur Softball Association (ASA) tournament. He was appointed a lifetime member of the Hall of Fame Council in 1957 by Sparky Thompson, then North Dakota ASA commissioner.

KUNDERT, Al
Commissioner
Kundert was the North Dakota Amateur Softball Association commissioner from 1953 to 1955 while living at Fargo. He now lives in Minot.

MICKELSON, P. E.
Commissioner
Born August 18, 1893; died July 7, 1952, at age 59.

Mickelson was the first commissioner of softball (1937–1938), and an aggressive promoter and sponsor in the Fargo-Moorhead area. Mickelson Field in Fargo was named in his honor.

1958

BERQUAM, Stan
Pitcher
Berquam is considered the all-time greatest pitcher in North Dakota; he played for 31 years with the Grafton, Grand Forks and Fargo-Moorhead teams. He played in 30 state championship tourneys, and won 24 state titles. Stan pitched 75 no-hit games, three in one week, and also 301 one-hit games. He played in seven national tournaments with North Dakota and Minnesota, and his lifetime batting average was .325. Berquam pitched eight no-hit games in state tournaments, and seven one-hit games. He pitched 128 scoreless innings in state championship play, and was ranked as one of the top ten pitchers in the nation at one time.

JULISON, Steve
Pitcher
Killed in action in W.W. II June 15, 1944, as a member of the Seabees.

Julison played on three Grand Forks state championship teams, and pitched two no-hit games.

KAVONIUS, Elma
Pitcher
Kavonius played in ten state tournaments and two state championship teams. She pitched five no-hit games at Bismarck, and played on two regional tourney teams. She was the first woman chosen to the Hall of Fame.

1959

KISTNER, Olive Jacobsen
Pitcher
Kistner pitched in six state championship tournaments; she played on two state championship teams and one national tourney team. Her lifetime batting average is .550; she played at Bismarck for 15 years. She is the second woman inducted into the Hall of Fame.

NILSON, Robert P.
Third Baseman
Nilson played in the Fargo-Moorhead area, and on eight state championship tourneys and with three state championship teams. He played 586 games during a 20-year career.

VOLK, Pete
Player
Volk was a member of 16 state tournament teams, and 2 state championship teams; he played for 26 years, and in two national tourneys. Volk served as North Dakota Amateur Softball Association president.

1960

JULISON, Adam
Player
Julison played 15 years of softball in the Grand Forks area, on five state championship teams and in four national tourneys.

KRIEG, Will
First Baseman and Left Fielder
Krieg played for 30 years on Fargo-Moorhead teams. He was on 14 state championship tournament teams and played in 1 national tournament.

PETERSON, Melvin "Scoop"
First Baseman
Peterson played on Bismarck teams over a 20-year period, in 15 state championship tournaments and on 1 state championship team. He died on June 26, 1960.

1961

BROTHERS, Don
Pitcher
Brothers played for 22 years in the Fargo-Moorhead area, and was regarded as one of the greatest southpaws of his time. He played in ten state championship tourneys and on two state championship teams.

CARNEY, Tom "Bus"
Pitcher
Carney pitched 32 no-hit games in his career plus 119 one-hit games. In 273 appearances, he had a 221 – 52 record. He played in 20 state championship tourneys and 4 state championship teams. Bus played in one national tourney as a catcher, and his lifetime batting average was .354. He pitched 13 years for Shorty's Shoe Shop of Moorhead.

ELLINGSON, Oscar E.
Promoter
Ellingson was a sponsor of softball in the Grand Forks area, and served as District Two commissioner for five years.

1962

HARDER, Leonard "Blacky"
Pitcher
Harder played for Burlington, Minot, Harvey and Williston teams. He also played with the state Class A champions in 1947 and 1948 and in the National VFW tourney in the same years. He pitched for teams winning the state VFW titles.

OLENBERGER, Al
Pitcher and Outfielder
Olenberger played 25 years at Harvey, in 18 Class B state championship tournaments. He played on six state championship teams, and also with the VFW state champions in 1947 and 1948, who went on to the national VFW tourney. He pitched the Class B state championship games two years in succession 1956 and 1957. He served as state VFW Softball Commissioner in the North Dakota Amateur Softball Association for several years.

TARBOX, Don
Player, Promoter and Sponsor
Tarbox was active in softball for 20 years. He sponsored the Roosevelt Bar team of Bismarck from 1939 to 1959, and played on this team until 1950.

1963

ANDERSON, Russ
Pitcher and First Baseman
Anderson played softball for 18 years, hurled four one-hit games and played in two state and one national tourney. He served as president of the North Dakota Amateur Softball Association, and has held offices in the Bismarck Softball Association. He has been the manager of the annual Mo Slope tourney many times.

KONDOS, George "Shorty"
Player and Sponsor
Kondos has been active in softball in the Fargo-Moorhead area since 1930. A sponsor and manager, he also played on Shorty's Shoe Shop team continuously since 1942. They won the North Dakota state championship in 1951, 1952 and 1955 and the Hall of Fame tourney in 1959 and 1961. They also won the Red River Valley tourney five times in 1946, 1949, 1952, 1956 and 1960. He was appointed a lifetime member of the Hall of Fame Council in 1957, and he held office in the North Dakota Amateur Softball Association and also in the Fargo-Minot Softball Association.

SCHAUER, Bill, Jr.
Infielder
Born in Jamestown, N. Dak; died May 25, 1963.

Schauer spent 35 years in the game. He played in one state title team, and was a consistent .300 hitter.

1964

BROWN, Adam J.
Pitcher
Born in Bismarck, N. Dak.

Brown pitched for 22 years, from 1928 to 1950; he played in 20 state tourneys and had one title team. He hurled ten no-hit games, and played shortstop and first base. He was a .400 hitter.

NELSON, A. C. "Rubber"
Pitcher
Born in Devils Lake, N. Dak.

Nelson pitched over 900 games during his 33-year career from 1924 to 1956. He retired from the game as a pitcher at age 49. He played on 15 state tourneys, but failed to win the title against Stan Berquam. Nelson pitched six games in one day to win his nickname.

ROM, Barbara
Pitcher
Born in Fargo, N. Dak.

Rom pitched in four state championship tourneys and on two title teams in 1939 and 1940. She pitched a no-hit game in 1943 while winning the Nebraska state title for an Omaha team.

1965

GERRELLS, C. E. "Hoopty"
Catcher and Shortstop
Now operates a sporting goods store with his son.

Gerrells played softball for 25 years in Devils Lake, and carried a .375 batting average in the Lake Region League. He has served as a manager and sponsored teams for many years. He also served as district commissioner in Devils Lake for seven years and was president of the North Dakota Amateur Softball Association in 1950. He played for teams in Fargo, Bismarck and Devils Lake. He started a six-team men's league in the Devils Lake area and also a girls' league. Although retired from active participation, he umpired for several years, and is still promoting sports in his area. He was a teammate and catcher for A. C. Nelson, who is also in the Hall of Fame.

LOUDER, Paul C.
Second Baseman and Catcher
Louder served the North Dakota Amateur Softball Association as its secretary-treasurer from September, 1949 to April, 1961. He played for Bismarck, and competed in the national tourney in Little Rock, Ark, as a member of the Ft. Leonard Wood, Mo, team that won the Armed Forces playoff at Ft. Riley, Kans. In 1942 he played on the Persian Gulf Command championship team while stationed in Iran and then competed in the Armed Forces playoff tournament in Cairo, Egypt. He completed his playing days at Bismarck as a member of the Elks team in 1947. He has served as state secretary under three commissioners, and has assisted in the establishment of the Hall of Fame.

NORMAN, Edwin K.
Pitcher
Wife Elizabeth, daughter Virginia; now living in Fargo, N. Dak.

Norman was a top pitcher during the 1930s in Fargo. His pitching career started in 1928, and he retired from active softball in 1941. During his career he pitched 15 no-hit games and over 25 one-hitters, playing ball several nights a week. In 1935 he pitched his team to the first official North Dakota Amateur Softball Association state tournament championship in the tournament held in Jamestown in 1935. By the end of his career Norman had pitched in seven state tournaments. He served as both president and secretary of the Fargo Association.

THOMPSON, Ralph "Sparky"
Pitcher
Thompson is a former North Dakota Amateur Softball Association (NDASA) state commissioner from Harvey who has a prominent place in North Dakota softball history. He retired from active softball in 1960 after participating for 30 years, during which time he competed as a pitcher in 23 state tournaments in Class A, Class B and VFW state events. He was on seven state championship teams in Class B and VFW classes. He served as Class B president for several years and was one of the organizers of the class B division of NDASA. He organized the first slow pitch league as part of the North Dakota program in 1959 and established the first state slow pitch tournament in Harvey in that same year. Thompson was appointed state commissioner in 1954, serving until 1960. Through his efforts, North Dakota was the first state to establish a state softball Hall of Fame, which became a reality in 1957. During his softball years, Sparky was a pitcher, throwing 5 no-hit games and over 20 one-hit games. His lifetime batting average in Class B competition was .390.

1966

JONDAHL, Walter
Second Baseman
Born May 23, 1904; died June 29, 1949, at age 45.

Jondahl was considered one of the all-time outstanding second basemen ever to play softball in North Dakota and carried a lifetime batting average over the .400 mark. He played in ten state tournaments and was a member of six state championship teams. He played in four national softball tournaments held in Chicago in 1934–1937.

POULIOTT, D. J. "Dime"
Catcher
Pouliott played 24 years of softball with Burlington and Minot teams. He was a member of one Class B state championship team and one Class A, and two Hall of Fame champions. He played mostly as a catcher but also at outfield and infield positions.

SCHMIDT, Joe J.
Pitcher
Schmidt played 22 years of softball in Bismarck and 4 years in the service in W.W. II. He played in 15 state tournaments and was on one state championship team.

He played in one regional and one national tournament. He pitched 15 no-hit games and 25 one-hit games, and once pitched five consecutive games in state tournament play.

1967

ARRELL, Rt. Rev. Msgr. L. J. "Bill Bailey"
Pitcher
Born November 2, 1897; died January 5, 1971, at age 74.

Arrell came to Grand Forks in 1924 from Minneapolis, and continued to play ball until 1936. He was known both for his playing ability and his leadership in promoting the sport.

HEINTZMAN, George "Jiggs"
Shortstop
Heintzman played for 21 years, and retired in 1954. He competed in 13 state tournaments and was a member of six state championship teams, with a .327 lifetime batting average. As a manager, he piloted five men's state champions and five women's state champions.

SAUL, John Jr.
Third Baseman
Saul played for 21 years, and was selected to the Fargo-Moorhead Twin City League all-star team eight times. A member of 4 state champions and a participant in 15 state tournaments, he had a lifetime batting average of .330, and was always a long ball threat. He managed softball teams in the Twin City League after retiring as a player in 1964.

1968

FEIST, Wendelin P. "Wendy"
Center Fielder and Shortstop
Born in Grand Forks, N. Dak.

Feist was a player for 26 years, playing three years in the Armed Forces in W.W. II. He had a lifetime batting average of over .300, and played in 18 state tournaments. He was on two state championship teams and five runnerups. He played in three regional tournaments and had a batting average of over .500 for his regional play. Feist retired from active play in 1964.

KONDOS, Chris
Catcher
Born in Moorhead, Minn.

Kondos was a catcher on Shorty's Shoe Shop team for 25 years, and retired from active play in 1958. He was a battery mate of Hall of Famers George "Shorty" Kondos, Stan Berquam and Tom "Bus" Carney. He played on five state championship teams, and one runnerup, as well as in three regional tournaments. Kondos was a good clutch hitter, and had a lifetime batting average of .278.

McCANN, Madeline "Sis"
First Baseman
Born in Mandan, N. Dak.

McCann played softball in North Dakota for 18 years, retiring from active play in 1961. She had a lifetime fielding average above .950, and a batting average of .450, batting in the cleanup spot for 16 years. She played in 16 state tournaments, and on six Mo Slope champions and five District Seven champions. She also served in many official positions in local Mandan and Bismarck leagues, and was state president of the North Dakota Amateur Softball Association in 1955. At one time she was women's commissioner for western North Dakota.

THEIGE, Marvin H.
Commissioner
Born in Harvey, N. Dak.

Theige started playing softball in 1930, and was a member of Harvey's first Class B state champions in 1942. As a member of the Harvey Park and Recreation Commission continuously since 1950, he served as coordinator of the Softball Hall of Fame building project. He also took a lead in compiling a softball history of North Dakota for the dedication event in 1965. He has served as Class B and western area commissioner, and is a lifetime member of the Hall of Fame Council. He is presently acting as historian for the Hall of Fame, and was honored with the Decade Award as Mr. "B" Softball in 1968.

1969

BURFENING, Russ R.
Catcher, Second Baseman and Pitcher
Born in Grand Forks, N. Dak.

Burfening played softball for 18 years, 16 in North Dakota and 2 in the military service in W.W. II. He played over 300 games in his lifetime, and in tournaments as many as seven games in one day. He played in seven North Dakota state softball tournaments and was on three state runnerup teams. He served as president of the North Dakota Amateur Softball Association for one term in 1952–1953 and retired from the game in 1962 with a lifetime batting average of over .300.

ESKILDSEN, Marcella "Babe Swanson"
Catcher and Fielder
Born in Valley City, N.Dak; taught school; married Carl Eskilden; now lives in Ferndale, Calif.

Swanson played softball in North Dakota for 15 years, and usually batted in the leadoff position, but could bunt well and was a good runner on the bases. She played in 11 North Dakota state tournaments and was on four state champion Valley City teams. She played on three teams that were in the women's national softball tournament in Chicago in 1936–1938. She was 16 years old when she played with the Valley City Merchants in the National the first time in 1936; her team took the record of being the youngest team to have played in the tournament until that time.

LARSON, Robert J.
Third Baseman
Larson started playing ball at the age of 13, and played 31 years, never wearing a third baseman's glove. He retired from softball in 1956 at age 44, carrying the top batting average in the Bismarck City League and again in the season's standings. He served on the original board of the Bismarck Softball Association for several years, and was also proficient in other sports, such as

Legion baseball and amateur baseball as well as tennis and bowling.

1970

EVERHART, Wally

Pitcher

Everhart played softball in the Fargo-Moorhead League for 16 years, from 1927 to 1947, except for four years he spent in the Army between 1941 and 1945. He was the one-half of a turn-around battery with Hall of Famer Abe Friedman. Wally was also ambidextrous and could throw with either hand, but pitching was his best skill rather than catching. He also was a utility fielder and played every position in the game at some time or another. His greatest ability showed up as a hitter, where he usually batted cleanup and had the reputation of very seldom striking out. He once set a record of going 13 for 13 at bat in a one-day tournament, and ended up with a lifetime batting average of over .300 after 16 years in the game. He won 24 out of 25 games as a pitcher in the 1931 playing season, had 1 no-hitter and 12 one-hitters to his lifetime pitching career. He played in ten North Dakota state championship tournaments, was on six state champion teams, and had the distinction of being chosen on every Fargo-Moorhead City League all-star team from 1927 through 1940, 14 years in succession.

SCHUMACHER, John

Short Fielder

Born in Harvey, N.Dak.

Schumacher played 31 years of softball in Harvey over a span of 35 years interrupted by four years of service in W.W. II. His regular position was rover, or short fielder, in the years that softball was a ten-man game. He also played all the bases, but after the rover position was eliminated, his regular position was left fielder. He had the reputation of having only four errors in his entire time of playing rover. He played in 22 North Dakota state championship tournaments, was with seven North Dakota Amateur Softball Association B state champions, and was on two successive VFW state champions in 1947 – 1948, at which time the Harvey VFW teams competed in their VFW Nationals in Topeka, Kans, and Austin, Tex. He was a sure-handed bunter, and could also hit the long ball, as well as being a fast man on the bases. He finished his softball career with a .250 batting average after retiring from the game at the age of 53 in 1960. He held the unique record of having played on 15 B state runnerup teams in his career.

SHIRLEY, Gil

Catcher

Shirley played softball in Bismarck for 19 years, and for four years while in W.W. I. He had a .352 batting average and the reputation of a tough clutch hitter with his line drive shots. He played in a state tournament every year that he played softball in the Bismarck League, 19 times, and was on one state championship team and five state runnerup teams. He competed in one regional with the Bismarck Elks representing North Dakota. He was chosen to the all-tournament team each year he played in Bismarck, and was chosen all-state catcher one year.

WHITE, Bernard A.

Third Baseman

White played softball for 29 years in the Grand Forks area. He was an awesome hitter, with a .300 batting average. He played in 22 North Dakota state championship tournaments, and was on eight state champions and one state runnerup champion while playing in Grand Forks. He played in seven national championship tourneys in Chicago and Detroit. He retired from softball in 1959, and later moved to Los Angeles, but now lives in San Diego.

1971

GILLIS, Malcolm J. "Mack"

Shortstop and Second Baseman

Gillis played 19 years of softball in the city leagues in Grand Forks, and retired from the game as a pitcher in 1958, later to become one of the prominent softball umpires in the State Softball Association, serving as the state umpire-in-chief and umpiring in four Northern Regional tournaments. He was a good bunter and place hitter, garnering a lifetime .280 batting average. He played in 19 state championship tournaments with Grand Forks teams, but failed to get a place on a state champion team, and was on eight state runnerup teams in state competition, after having played in every state championship during his playing career. He also served several years as a member of the board of directors of the North Dakota Softball Association, and in all he was active in softball for over 30 years in the state and local capacity.

LARSON, Herman

Pitcher and Outfielder

Larson played softball for 25 years, retiring in 1955. He played 22 years in North Dakota in the leagues in Rugby, Fargo, the North Dakota Athletic Club Fraternity League in college at Fargo, and Williston. He played three years while in service in the Navy 1942 – 1945. He was a pitcher and also played the outfield. He was an excellent hitter, establishing a .324 lifetime batting average. He played in ten North Dakota state championships, was on two Class B champions and also on two state runnerup teams, while playing in Rugby during the 1930s and 1940s. His lifetime pitching record was 325 wins and 75 losses, and he had 10 no-hit games and 25 one-hitters. He also had a state championship tournament record of ten wins and five losses. He now resides in Rolla, N.Dak, and is a Vo-Ag instructor in high school.

WADNIZAK, Lillian M. "Bonnie"

Catcher and Left Fielder

Born in Fargo, N.Dak.

Wadnizak played softball in the Fargo-Moorhead Women's Softball League for 12 years, 1949 through 1961, of which 1952 and 1953 were spent in the service in Japan and at various Women's Army Corps training centers in the states. She played in five North Dakota state championship tournaments, in four Army area tournaments, one interservice championship and was on two North Dakota state champions and the same number of runnerup teams. She served as the North Dakota women's division commissioner from 1962 to 1970. She piloted the first North Dakota women's slow pitch team to its first Amateur Softball Association national tournament in 1967. During her term as women's commissioner she increased the women's team registrations in North Dakota to triple what they were when she took office.

1972

FREED, Luverne "Frenchie"
Third Baseman
Freed played softball on the Horace team for 15 years as a third baseman, outfielder and player-manager. He retired as an active player in 1960, but has since that time continued as a team manager, a local promoter in the B ranks of North Dakota softball as a commissioner and other offices, and is presently a member of the Hall of Fame Council, which is the selection committee for the North Dakota Softball Hall of Fame. He played in nine North Dakota state championship tournaments, was on 1 Horace B champion team in 1958, and on 2 Horace runnerup teams in 1959 and 1960. He was one of the prime organizers of Tri-River Softball in his local area in eastern North Dakota and bordering Minnesota communities.

HEBER, Jerry
Catcher, First Baseman and Outfielder
Heber played softball 17 years in Harvey, and after the 1953 season moved to Bloomington, Minn, where he played two more years and retired in 1955. As a catcher he had an exceptional throwing arm and his pickoffs at first and third were not uncommon. It was next to impossible to steal second on him. He was an outstanding bunter as well as a good clutch hitter with good speed, and hit for a lifetime average of over .300 in his career. He played in 15 North Dakota state championship tournaments, was on 4 Harvey B state champions, on 2 Harvey VFW state champions, was on the Harvey Merchants as state runnerup in the B division in 1939, 1941 and 1944. He played in two national VFW tournaments, in 1947 at Topeka, Kans, and in 1948 at Austin, Tex. He was a member of the Harvey VFW state champions teams at the time. He was the sixth man from the Harvey area to gain admission to the Softball Hall of Fame.

MOE, Lester E.
Contributor
Moe was an umpire from 1950 to 1966, and served for 11 years as umpire-in-chief of his local Fargo-Moorhead Association, umpiring in 22 state tournaments of combined men's and women's events. On the National level, he worked six men's regional tournaments and six women's. He worked in one world softball national tournament in Minneapolis in 1958, working a total of 11 games in that one both as a plate ump and base ump. He finished his career serving as a district commissioner in the North Dakota Softball Association for his local area for a three-year period ending in 1966.

1973

GARDNER, George W.
Umpire
Gardner has been a prominent softball figure in North Dakota on three levels over a period of 25 years. He was principally honored by the Hall of Fame for his contributions to softball as a promoter and leader in the administrative affairs of the state association, for his competent and unselfish service in the capacity of an umpire over a period of 23 years, and as a promoter in the local softball program in his home area of Grand Forks. He held office in the state association over a ten-year period, first as a member of the board of directors for two terms, then followed that with three terms as state president ending in 1966. George estimates that he has umpired about 850 games of softball in his career, having worked in 11 North Dakota State championship tournaments and one regional in addition to his regular umpiring duties in league play and state invitationals. Gardner's tenure of office in the North Dakota Softball Association (1956 to 1966) was the formative period of the establishment of the North Dakota Softball Hall of Fame, in which he played a very influential role. He is presently a member of the Hall of Fame Council, which selects the Hall of Fame candidates each year for that honor.

HEINTZMAN, Florence "Florie"
Pitcher
Heintzman played softball for 19 years, with playing time being divided between North and South Dakota, and retired as an active player in 1954. She had 7 no-hitters and 25 one-hitters to her credit, and played in 9 state championship tournaments (six North Dakota, three South Dakota). She was on four state champions, two in each state, and on three runnerup teams in North Dakota and one in South Dakota. She was also an accomplished bowler and continued that sport after retiring from the more strenuous game of softball. She and her husband George (inducted 1967) are the only man and wife team to have been inducted into the North Dakota Softball Hall of Fame.

1974

DEVINE, Thomas
Outfielder and Pitcher
Devine played 20 years of softball in Grand Forks, retiring in 1955. However, in his later years he was also an umpire, resulting in a total span of 40 years in the game. He had a lifetime batting average around .300, played in six North Dakota state championships, and was a runnerup state champion in 1938. He started umpiring in state championship tournaments in the early 1950s, and he estimates that he has umpired in well over 100 tournaments in all categories for the past 20 years. He has the reputation of knowing the rules of the game, and is still umpiring softball at the age of 56.

GRAVALIN, E. "Hod"
First Baseman and Pitcher
Gravalin started playing softball at the age of 13 and played continuously under the same coach and manager, Shorty Kondos, for 28 years, retiring from the game in 1964. He started as a fielder, later played first base, and for the last 15 years of his career was a pitcher. He had a .280 lifetime batting average (as a pitcher), and played in 14 North Dakota state championship tournaments and was on 3 state champion and 2 runnerup teams, played

in five regionals, and in 18 consecutive Red River tournaments. In the period 1946 – 1964, he played in every tourney entered in by the Shorty's Shoe Shop team, and won a total of 46 trophies in tournament competition.

HOLM, Eugene "Euy"
Catcher

Holm was posthumously awarded the honors of the Softball Hall of Fame on June 30, 1974, given to his widow, Joyce Holm, and three children. He had served as president of the North Dakota Softball Association in 1956 to 1958, during which time on July 7, 1957, the North Dakota Softball Hall of Fame was initiated and established in Harvey, N.Dak. He played softball in North Dakota for 21 years, and after retiring from active play in 1965 he was still involved in local and state softball functions at the time of his death. He had a .290 lifetime batting average, and played in 15 North Dakota state championship tournaments. In that same period, he was in ten VFW state championships, was on 2 championship teams in 1953 and 1956, on 2 state runnerup teams in 1957 and 1964, and played on the regional runnerup, the Kallod Carpet team in 1956, and on the Red River Valley champions in 1953. He served in various offices in the Fargo-Moorhead Association over a period of 18 years, and was a state district commissioner in his local league area for 14 years. He was considered a genius in the financial management of his local association, taking office as secretary-treasurer in 1955 with the organization in considerable debt and bringing it out in his first year. Under his leadership, the Fargo-Moorhead Softball Association hosted six regionals (Tri-State) and five North Dakota state championship tournaments, as well as its local annual Red River Valley Invitational. The Holm Classics, dedicated in his honor and consisting of AA Class invited teams, is now a regular event of the annual Red River tourney, and is a part of North Dakota's Largest One-Day Invitational Fast Pitch Tournament.

SCHAFER, Duane L. "Tiny"
Pitcher

Schafer retired from softball as an active player after 15 years of participation as a pitcher, an infielder and a pinch hitter, playing in the Fargo-Moorhead area through the 1955 season. After quitting as a player, Tiny was occupied in the administrative affairs of the local softball association and served on the tournament committees to help promote fast pitch softball and other aspects of the game particular to the Red River Valley Tournament. His success and ability as a promoter became well known at the time, and in 1960 he was chosen by the North Dakota Softball Association as state commissioner, in which capacity he has served continually since that time. Under his direction and leadership, the North Dakota Softball Association team registrations have increased more than tenfold over this 14-year period. As a state commissioner, he serves on the National Amateur Softball Association (ASA) commissioners' council and served three years as vice president of that group. He has served ten years on the ASA legislative committee, and is presently on the National Hall of Fame Selection Committee, which is a panel of nine men chosen from the nation's 110 softball commissioners. He is now one of the senior members of the national ASA commissioners council, and as North Dakota state commissioner has the longest tenure of office in the state's history. Among other duties as state commissioner, he acts as chairman of the Hall of Fame Council for North Dakota's Softball Hall of Fame.

SCHNEIDER, Lawrence A. "Larry"
Pitcher

Schneider, originally from Bismarck, N.Dak, when he started playing softball in 1932, played 28 years in the game as a pitcher. He played all but five years in North Dakota, one in Montana and four years in the service. He retired from active play in 1960 with a .300 batting average, 12 no-hit games, a state tournament pitching record of 17 – 3. He was on four state championship teams, on five state runnerup teams and played in one national tournament in Chicago in 1937 as a pitcher for the state champions of Missoula, Mont. He pitched one of his no-hit, no-run games in winning the Montana state championship in the final game of that tournament.
Also in: North Dakota Officials Hall of Fame.

1975

ATCHISON, Dean E.
Infielder

Atchison played softball for 22 years in the Fargo-Moorhead Twin City League, and 20 years of that period were played with Shorty's Shoe Shop Team. He was an infielder, mainly the short stop, and had a lifetime batting average of .310. He played in 14 North Dakota state championships, was on three state championships, on two runnerup state championships and played in five regionals.

HENSEN, Donna (Osman)
Outfielder and Pitcher

Osman played her entire 20-year career of softball in the Minot Women's Softball League. She was an excellent hitter, with a lifetime batting average of .334 and always the long ball threat at the plate. She played in 20 North Dakota women's state championships, and was on eight state champion and four runnerup teams. She made 12 appearances in tri-state regionals, eight of them with Minot teams and four as a pick-up player with other state champions that qualified for regional play. Donna's pitching record in her career of state championship tournament play was 48 wins and 18 lost, and she won six championship finals and lost one. She received recognition in state and regional championship play for three years in succession, 1961 – 1963, twice as most valuable player in state play and once was selected on the all-regional team in 1962 as an outfielder. She held office in the North Dakota Women's Softball Association as secretary and president, each for one term, and retired from active play in 1972.

TAIT, Carl
Pitcher

Tait played 31 years of softball, 26 in North Dakota and 5 in Canada and in the service. He began his playing career as a 13-year-old, and retired from active play in 1963. For the past 12 years, he has been an umpire, although he was known for his pitching abilities. He had a lifetime pitching record of 4 perfect no-hit games, 23 no-hitters, 93 one-hitters and a won and lost record of 341 – 124. He pitched his first perfect game at the age of

18 in 1936 as a high school pitcher. He played in 13 North Dakota state championships.

1976

LENZMEIER, Harold C. "Sport"
Umpire

Lenzmeier has been a dominant figure in Wahpeton-Breckenridge softball for almost 30 years. His career was in the fast pitch until his retirement in 1960. He has continued in slow pitch since that time as an umpire, and a local promoter who has held many responsible positions. He served as district commissioner from 1962 to 1974, was state president of the slow pitch division for one term, and served as umpire-in-chief for all eight state slow pitch tournaments held in Wahpeton during that time. He has also served as co-chairman and as umpire in the regional slow pitch tournaments that have been held in Wahpeton. He is one of the founders of the Old Pro (over 35) League in the slow pitch program in North Dakota.

NESEMEIER, Sylvia "Pat"
Pitcher, Third Baseman and Outfielder

Nesemeier played softball for 17 years, and 9 were spent in the Women's Army Corps during her military service. She retired as an active player in 1962 and went on to coaching and managing and teaching young girls to play softball. She had a lifetime batting average of .350, played in four North Dakota state championship tournaments, and was on one state champion and one runnerup. She played in one national tournament at Portland, Ore, in 1949 as a pick-up player for the Hamms team of Fargo, N. Dak, the first North Dakota women's softball team to play in national competition. She retired as coach and team manager after the 1971 season, and became an umpire in the Fargo Women's Softball League. She retired in 1973.

WAMBACH, J. A. "Lottie"
Second Baseman
Born in Dilworth, Minn.

Wambach has the distinction of having had two long careers in the game of softball, the first as a player for 25 years (1927 – 1952) and the second as coach and manager of women's softball for 23 years (1949 – 1972) for a total span of 48 years. He had a .330 lifetime batting average, and played in two North Dakota state championships, and was on two state championship teams in 1941 and 1942 with the Fargo Merchants. He coached three women's teams in North Dakota state championship play, taking the state championship in 1950 and runnerup in 1949 and 1962. His 1950 state champs Twinettes won the regional at Watertown, S.Dak, and went on to the national women's tournament at San Antonio, Tex, where they played Peoria, Ill, and Portland, Ore, and lost their first two games.

Omaha Softball Association Hall of Fame

OMAHA, NEBRASKA

Mailing Address: 6404 Maple, Suite No. 8, 68104. Tel. (402) 554-1200. *Contact:* Carl P. Kelley, Commissioner. *Location:* 132 mi. S.W. of Des Moines, Iowa, 180 mi. N.W. of Kansas City, Mo. Not open to the public. *Personnel:* Floyd Hayes, Chmn; Bernie Price, Robert Newton, Henry McCourt, Ben Crain, Lee V. Horton, Bonnie Jacob and Walter Dinkel, Hall of Fame Comt. *Nearby Halls of Fame:* Agriculture (Bonner Springs, Kans, 170 mi. S.E.), Agriculture (Kansas City), Dog Racing (Abilene, Kans, 195 mi. S.W.).

The Hall of Fame was founded in 1960 by Carl Kelley, who was inspired by the formation of the National Softball Hall of Fame at the Amateur Softball Association meeting in Phoenix, Ariz. The purpose of the Hall is to honor players and contributors to softball.

Members: 35 as of 1976. Members are chosen by a committee on the basis of recommendations. There is a limit of three inductees a year who have played softball in the metro Omaha area. Players are given a plaque to keep, and an identical one is on display at the Omaha Softball Association office in Nebraska.

1959 CRAIN, Ben. W. See entry in National Softball Hall of Fame, 1961.

1960 KORGAN, Nina. See entry in National Softball Hall of Fame, 1960.

1963 JARDINE, Grace
SKARKA, John "Spud"
WHITEING, Lyle G.

1965 BARR, Frank R.
PRICE, Bernie "Schacht"

1966 CHAVEZ, Mary "Burnap"
KELLEY, Carl P.
STANEK, Edward R.
STEVENSON, Harry S.

1967 LYNCH, Paul F.
THOMAS, Martin
WALKER, Ray L.

1968 CHURCHILL, Darrell O.
DINKEL, Walter "Walt"
PRICE, June

1969 HAYES, Floyd W.
SCHNEIDER, Leonard P.
STRELECKI, Alvin J.

1970 JACOB, Bonnie "Caldwell"
STANEK, Joseph, Sr.
TAPLEY, William "Bill"

1971 ALLEN, Aubrey
DiGIACOMO, Yano
LYNCH, Edward T.
1972 COSTANTINI, Angie "Scavio"
McCOURT, Henry A.
RISO, Mary C.
1973 DILL, George W.
QUINN, Rose "Pirrucello"
SWIERCZEK, Victoria D.
1975 JACOB, Donald E. "Jake"
MINOR, Fred Harrison
NEWTON, Robert "Diz"

Seattle Metro Softball Hall of Fame

SEATTLE, WASHINGTON

Mailing Address: W226 King County Court House, 98104. Tel. (206) 344-3892. *Contact:* Kent Morrill, Comm. *Location:* 516 Third Ave; 175 mi. N. of Portland. *Personnel:* Mike Keim, Nat. Sr. Deputy Chief; Bev Ross, Women's Slow Pitch Representative; Tom Shilley, Pres. of Umpires' Assn; Dick Deal, Deputy Commissioner; Jim Bean, Pres. Fast Pitch Assn. Not open to the public. *Nearby Halls of Fame:* State and Province (Vancouver, B.C, 125 mi. N.W.), Ski (Rossland, B.C, 225 mi. N.E.).

The Hall of Fame was founded in 1973 by the Seattle Metro Greater Softball Association to preserve a record of the area's outstanding players.

Members: 20 as of 1977. Members are chosen in categories of player, coach, sponsor or umpire. They must have been active in softball in the Seattle metropolitan area, and have retired from the game for at least three years. There is no minimum playing time required, but the player must have fame at the local and regional levels. If a player is in the National Softball Hall of Fame or the Northwest Hall of Fame, he or she is automatically qualified for the Seattle Metro Softball Hall of Fame. Inductees are limited to five per year. They may be nominated by anyone, and are elected by a five-person selection committee. There were no elections in 1976.

1974 BEYERS, Bob
DURGAN, Charlie
EVANS, Lou
HOGAN, Jim
MILLARD, Bob
NEILSON, Gordon
VERVYNCK, Ed
1975 COWAN, Harry
GIANINI, Glen
HAUGHTON, Ray
MASSEY, Frank
SKINNER, Don
1977 AIZSTZAUTS, Arnie
FENTON, Bill
FOLK, Ted, Sr.
GIANINI, Kay (Walt)
KING, Bob
NEELY, George
POTOSHNIK, Mike
WAGNER, Ray

Terre Haute Softball Hall of Fame

TERRE HAUTE, INDIANA

Mailing Address: 2011 S. 18 St, 47802. Tel. (812) 234-0339. *Contact:* Wayne Meyers, founder and Indiana State Amateur Softball Assn. Commissioner. *Location:* Approx. 60 mi. S.W. of Indianapolis, 180 mi. S.E. of Chicago, Ill. Not open to the public. *Nearby Halls of Fame:* Auto Racing, Basketball (Indianapolis), Agriculture (West Lafayette, 70 mi. N.E.), Trapshooting (Vandalia, Ohio, 150 mi. N.E.), City (St. Louis, Mo, 170 mi. S.W.), Sports (North Webster, 170 mi. N.E.), Business (Chicago, Ill.), Flight (Dayton, Ohio, 180 mi. N.E.), Music (Nashville, Tenn, 235 mi. S.E.).

Twenty old-time softball players were the first to be honored by the Indiana Softball Hall of Fame when it was founded around 1966. Founder Wayne Meyers has been very active in softball and is now serving as Indiana State Amateur Softball Association Commissioner.

Members: 34 as of July 1977. Players must be retired from active participation for three years before they are eligible for the Hall of Fame. Two new members are elected each year and are honored at a dinner where they receive special plaques. Additionally, their names are placed on a large red, white and blue sign at the concession stand of the Terre Haute softball park. A list of members is unavailable.

Western New York Softball Hall of Fame

BUFFALO, NEW YORK

Mailing Address: 71 Hartwell Rd, 14216. Tel. (716) 834-3038. *Contact:* George M. Priebe. *Location:* 65 mi. S.W. of Rochester, 200 mi. N.E. of Pittsburgh, Pa. *Personnel:* Joseph Brandt, Chmn. Not open to the public. *Nearby Halls of Fame:* Football (Hamilton, Ont, 70 mi. N.W.), Hockey, Sports (Toronto, Ont, 70 mi. N.W.), Horseshoe Pitching (Corning, 100 mi. S.E.), Flight (Elmira, 110 mi. S.E.), Golf (Foxburg, Pa, 140 mi. S.W.), Hockey (Kingston, Ont, 150 mi. N.E.), Baseball (Cooperstown, 180 mi. E.), Football (Canton, Ohio, 200 mi. S.W.), State (Detroit, Mich, 220 mi. S.W.), Horse Racing (Saratoga Springs, 235 mi. N.E.), Ice Skating (Newburgh, 250 mi. S.E.).

The Western New York Softball Hall of Fame was founded in 1965 by Joseph Brandt to honor outstanding players in the Buffalo area where there are over 149 teams and 2000 summertime players. Brandt, who was also co-founder of the Nine Old Men's Softball League and at one time chairman of athletics for the American Legion, is still chairman of the Hall of Fame after all these years.

Members: Approx. 200 as of July 1977. Candidates for election must be over 42 years old and must have both played AA caliber softball and lived in the area for five years. After screening by a Selection Committee, new members are inducted at the Annual Induction Ceremony, usually in October, and receive a Hall of Fame plaque. The first induction ceremony took place at Memorial Stadium, home of the Buffalo Bisons baseball team of the International League, before thousands of spectators. A complete list of members is not available. However, the majority are listed below.

Induction Year Unrecorded

AMIGONE, Frank
ARCARA, Peter
ARNDT, Albert
BACZKOWSKI, Mike
BAWOWSKI, Walter
BARRETT, Joe
BECKER, Maysh
BENHATZEL, Norm
BENNETT, William
BENZ, Lou
BINDEMAN, Bob
BLONSKI, Edward
BRANDYS, Mickey
BROWNSEY, Marty
BUMBALO, Tony
BYCINA, John
CARPENTER, Herb
CASTINE, Norm
CASTODI, Dominic
CECCHINI, Paul
CERESI, Joe
CICARELL, William
CONWAY, Fran
COSTELLO, Anthony
CRAVEN, Francis
DECKER, Charles
DRAY, Jim
DUDZICK, Joe
DUNN, Paul
DURDA, Anthony
DURKIN, Ed
EBERHARDT, Joe
EBERLE, Bob
EBERLE, Howard
EVERDING, William
FEHRINGER, Ken
FINKBEINER, Harold
FISHER, Art
FISHER, Vance
FREY, Irving
FRIEDELL, Bill
FRIZZEL, Jack
GALLOWAY, Earl
GASPER, Walter
GEARIN, George
GEGENFURTNER, George
GRABOWSKI, Ed
GRABOWSKI, John
GRIFFIN, James, Sr.
GRIFFIN, Tom, Sr.
GRZYBEK, Stanley
GUCWA, Steve
HACKEMER, John
HAMONN, Fred
HARLOCK, Mel
HELMER, Fred
HOAG, Elbert
JAMES, Frank D.
JERZEWSKI, H.
JOCHUM, Ray
JOYCE, Charles
JUSKO, Edmund
KARL, Joe
KERNS, Len "Doc"
KIETA, Walter

KILLIAM, Anthony
KIRSCH, Carl
KISKER, Herbert
KLENKE, Bob
KLIMECZKO, Joe
KOERNER, William
KOLLER, Willie
KOSIERK, Edward
KOSTRZYSKI, Dan
KOTZ, Allie
KRAFFT, Karl
KULL, Mike
KURAC, Francis
KUSH, Nebbs
KWIATKOWSKI, Monty
LAMENDOLA, Charlie
LANG, Roy
LARSON, Nels
LAUFER, Joe
LEWIS, Al
LONZAK, Joe
LORIFICE, Frank
MARTIN, Tony
MARTONE, Curly
MAUE, Clem
MAYFIELD, Jack
McGUIRE, Mike
McMULLEN, Warren
MECCA, Augie
MECKES, Burton
MIKULIC, Syl
MILLER, Herb
MINGOIA, Joe
MISENER, John
MONTGOMERY, Chuck
MORIEN, Joe
MOSKAL, Frank
MULLENS, Ray
MUNRO, Charles
MURPHY, Joe
NAROCKI, Ray
NOWAK, Leon
O'CONNELL, Bill
O'CONNELL, Cy
OLSON, Frank
ORLOWSKI, Curly
ORLOWSKI, Henry
ORLOWSKI, Ray
OUCHIE, Irving
PALISANO, Casey
PARLATA, Carl
PASIERB, Adam
PATERNOSTRA, Babe
PATTERSON, Pat
PEOPLES, King
PIECZYNSKI, Ben
PILECKI, Bruno
PIWKO, Henry
PREM, Al
PRIEBE, George
REEVES, Jack
REICH, Charles
REISCH, Dick
RICH, Dan
RILEY, Clarence
ROETZER, George
ROLLER, George
RUHLAND, Robert
RUSZCZUK, Ed
RUTKOWSKI, Stan
SABADAZ, Boots
SACILOWSKI, Edward
SAVAGE, John
SAX, Vince
SCANLON, Mickey
SCHLAU, Bill
SCHNIER, William
SCHRAG, Len "Ty"
SHAEFER, Whitney
SHEDLER, Mike
SIELSKI, Leo
SKARBOWSKI, Ted
SLIGER, Rubber
SORRENTINO, Sante
SOVERN, Charles
STARK, Wellington
STOKLOSA, Walter
SULLIVAN, John
SZAFRANSKI, Joe
SZTORC, Edward
SZYMANSKI, Dick
TROIDEL, Harold
UNGER, Joe
WALTERRICH, Muggsy
WESTMILLER, Walter
WHITE, Jack
WINTERMANTEL, Clem
WIPPERMAN, Phil
WITTIG, Earl
WNEK, Chet
WOZCIK, John, Sr.
YOUNG, Fred
ZACKIEWICZ, Dan "Peanuts"
ZIELINSKI, Walter

Softball Halls of Fame to Watch

INDIANAPOLIS METROPOLITAN SOFTBALL ASSOCIATION HALL OF FAME

Under Discussion 1977

Presently in the planning stages, with a proposed opening at a softball diamond now being constructed in Indianapolis, this hall of fame may alternatively be merged with other local softball halls of fame to create a more comprehensive Indiana Softball Hall of Fame. Those actively interested in these alternatives should contact Harold Engelhardt, Indianapolis Metro Commissioner, (317) 637-1100.

MISSOURI SOFTBALL HALL OF FAME

Under Discussion 1977

Plans for the establishment of a Missouri softball hall of fame are actively being discussed. Such a hall of fame will meet the vital need of giving lasting recognition to worthy softball players and participants in the "Show Me" State, which has one of the largest number of softball players of any State in the country. For information write to Fred J. Hoffman, Missouri Softball Commissioner, Tenth and Faron, St. Joseph, MO 64501. (861) 232-3344.

NORTHWESTERN REGION SOFTBALL HALL OF FAME and PORTLAND METROPOLITAN SOFTBALL HALL OF FAME

Being Organized 1977

The American Softball Association (ASA) has divided the United States into a number of administrative regions, of which one is the Northwestern Region. In that region are six districts, of which one is the Portland Metropolitan District. Both the Region and the District are in the process of organizing separate softball halls of fame. A joint permanent facility is planned for these halls, each of which will have its own nomination and induction requirements and procedures. Non-active players or participants of softball in the Northwestern Region will be eligible for nomination to the Northwestern Softball Hall of Fame if they have been inactive for a certain number of years; they will be nominated from any one of the six districts (Seattle, Portland, Tacoma, Spokane, State of Washington and State of Oregon), and final voting upon their nominations will be the responsibility of the Region Commissioners. The same procedures will apply to nominations for induction into the Portland Metropolitan Softball Hall of Fame, with the following exceptions: nominees must have been inactive for a minimum of three years, and nominations will be made by any team manager in the Region and voted upon by the Board of Team Managers for the Portland Metropolitan District. An extensive amount of materials and memorabilia have been collected for both of these halls of fame, selected items of which may be seen in a temporary display at the Erv Lind Stadium in Portland. For further information on either hall of fame, contact Paul Keenan, Portland Metro Softball Commissioner, 1107 S.W. Fourth, Portland, OR 97204. (503) 248-4325.

ROCHESTER AMATEUR SOFTBALL ASSOCIATION HALL OF FAME

Under Discussion 1977

Slated to open in the fall of 1977, this hall of fame will be patterned after the National Softball Hall of Fame in Oklahoma City but will be uniquely tailored to honor the greatest players and participants of the Rochester Metropolitan District of the American Softball Association's Mid-Atlantic Region. Plans for the hall include attractive and meaningful displays, and an annual hall of fame dinner at which new members will be inducted. For further information contact Andy Yezwenski, 214 Filon Avenue, Rochester, NY 14622. (716) 266-1025.

TENNIS

Of the several sports closely associated with royalty, none has been so pocked and studded with hilarious, absurd and pathetic incidents as tennis. The antics of recent champions are well known. But their predecessors included a Frenchman known to sit down on the court and cry, an Austrian count who defaulted at least once because his opponent's shadow bothered him, and a Spaniard who on missing a sideline volly would vault the net, rush to the backstop of his opponent's court, and repeatedly bite the ball. As one progresses further back through history, the antics become more colorful. Henry, Prince of Wales, who died in 1612, played tennis so hard that "he sweated like an artisan." That may have encouraged the Earl of Essex to lose his temper during a point-dispute in what had begun as a friendly game and to hit Henry on the head with his racket. About this same time, a tennis argument in Dublin led to a sword fight in which one of the disputing players was killed. Earlier, the great Renaissance painter Caravaggio (1569 – 1609) had to flee Rome after killing a tennis opponent. In 1508 four men were arrested on the somewhat cryptic charge of "keeping tennys playes." In 1447 the Bishop of Exeter complained that his cloister windows were constantly in danger of being broken by the children the town mayor allowed to play tennis beneath them. It is recorded that the mayor replied that the bishop was a bootlegger.

By 1600 every castle and chateau in France had its own tennis court, every town had dozens. Paris alone had in excess of 1800 courts by then. In sixteenth century Germany there was a *Ballhaus* for tennis in at least 46 different towns. The same was true elsewhere in Europe and in England, and it would be safe to say that each one of these courts had its own incredible stories to tell. But tennis was always a game for kings and princes, and often a fatal one. The two-year-old Charles IX was depicted in a famous painting with a racket in hand. He later played six hours a day and complained when the news of an important adviser's assassination put him off his game. Before becoming king, Louis XII got into a fist fight on the court with the Duke of Lorraine. In the fourteenth century the Duke of Burgundy twice pledged his doublet for a tennis debt, thereby becoming, perhaps, history's first man to "lose his shirt" at tennis. Louis X of France died in 1316 of a chill contracted after drinking a beaker of cold water immediately following an energetic game of tennis in the forest at Vincennes. Henry I of Castile and Philip I of Spain died in the same way—of a cold after tennis—in 1217 and 1506, respectively. James I of Scotland would have avoided being assassinated in 1437 had he been able to escape down a drain which he himself had ordered blocked to prevent the loss of tennis balls. The untimely death of Frederick, Prince of Wales, in 1751, was attributed to a blow from a tennis ball. Charles VIII died in 1498 from hitting his head on the lintel of a low doorway when going to watch a tennis match in the castle moat at Amboise.

Of all those centuries of tragedy, scandal and hilarity, perhaps the most scandalous event occurred in 1937, when Alice Marble wore brief shorts in a match. Spectators shocked at this break with tradition failed to realize that she was in fact following the very ancient tradition of doing the unexpected at tennis. The unseemly highjinks sometimes seen on today's courts similarly are only following that ancient tradition of a royal sport occasionally highlighted by unsportsmanly conduct and apparent absurdity.

That tradition may be the first quality that makes tennis unique, but there are other unique characteristics as well. For example, it can be said of tennis but of no other sport in history that Erasmus devoted a colloquy to it, that Swedenborg included it in his vision of heaven, that More mentioned it in his *Utopia* and that Hobbes, who played it in old age to keep fit, mentioned it in his *Leviathan.* Benvenuto Cellini, a student of Michaelangelo and one of the greatest goldsmiths of all time, played tennis. So did Oscar Wilde. Rosseau and Goethe praised it. Geoffrey Chaucer mentioned it, as did Rabelais and Samuel Pepys in his famous diaries. A Frenchman wrote a poem in Latin mentioning tennis, which he then dedicated to Cardinal Richelieu. In contrast, William Shakespeare derided tennis in six of his plays. History, in other words, owes much of its color and humor to tennis.

Some say that the game got its name from the town of Tinnis, or Tamis, on the Nile Delta in Egypt, which was a center for the production of the linen used in the stuffing of early tennis balls. We cannot be sure. Tinnis sank into the sea in A.D. 1226. Another more probable theory is that the name comes from *"Tenetz!"*, the imperative form of the French *tenir,* an exclamation called out before the ball was put into play, similar to "Fore!" in golf. In fact, the earliest known English spelling is tenetz, from 1399. It is much more certain where the word racket comes from. It comes from the old French *raquette,* which came from the Saracen word *rāhah,* meaning palm of the hand. Deuce comes from the French for two, *à deux*—one player has to win two consecutive points to win the game. Service, to mark the opening stroke of each point, almost certainly comes from the early custom of having servants put the initial ball into play.

The strange scoring nomenclature of tennis—love, 15, 30, 40, 60, game—has mystified scholars ever since 1579 when Jean Gosselin wrote, "I have been unable to find a man who could give me a reason for it." Love, meaning zero, probably comes either from the idea that love is nothing, as in "for love or money", or from the French word for egg, *l'oeuf.* In English cricket, a "duck egg" is zero, and an American expression to describe a score of zero in a game or contest is "goose egg". To the Medieval mind, 60 had the significance that 100 does today. There were 60 seconds in a minute and 60 minutes to an hour. Four 15-*sou* pieces called *denier d'or* made 60 and there were 60 *sous* to the *double d'or* coin. The score of 40 probably is a shortening or abbreviation of 45, three 15s. Tennis's scoring system may very likely have come from some early betting custom—possibly the old one of the stakes being placed at the net before play began. Betting on tennis matches was heavy, in fact, which may explain why the Archbishop of Rouen prohibited priests from playing it. That prohibition, of course, was ineffectual, as were identical ones for laypersons issued in 1388, 1397, 1401, 1413 and every few years since. A prohibition against noise on or near the court was also largely ignored until only recently. In fact, the surgeon-major of the French army in 1780 recommended tennis for its healthy effect on the lungs and throat. Swearing in particular was frowned upon, but remained so popular that the French Tennis Ordinances of 1592 required that players should play "without swearing or blaspheming the name of God," and that in prize matches players were to be fined five *sous* per oath.

Fourth century A.D. Persians played a game called *tchigan* in an enclosed space with four foot-long rackets. A Saracen invasion took this game to France, where people were soon on horseback playing *chicane,* a cross between lacrosse, polo and tennis. In the eleventh century, around the time of the Norman Invasion, that game had been modified so that it could be played indoors. Interestingly, the Church seems to have pioneered this trend. Tennis was first played indoors around 1066 in monastery cloisters. Many early references to the game associate it with the clergy and by the fifteenth century tennis at Easter was an established feature of the French ecclesiastical calendar. The indoor court of Court Tennis today retains many features of a monastery cloister. A monk, Antonio Scaino, wrote a philosophical treatise on tennis published in 1555.

As the game became more popular, people other than priests began to play. This trend was much accelerated by Margot of Hainault, the "Joan of Arc of Tennis," who arrived in Paris in 1427 and defeated virtually all opponents. Inspired by her, common people began to play tennis, resulting in various royal decrees designed to prevent them from doing so. Richard III's read: "Servants shall use only bows and arrows, and leave idle games." Meanwhile, beginning with the reign of Louis X (1314–1316), tennis had been moving from cloister to crown to begin its long association with royalty. Royal courts sprang up everywhere, especially during the sixteenth century, the Golden Age of Tennis, when tennis was more popular than ever before or since. François I (1515–1547) built courts for himself and his friends at the Louvre, at Fontainebleau, two at St. Germain, and one aboard his 2000-ton four-masted man o' war, *La Grande Françoise.* Many of these royal courts were of elaborate construction, such as the one built by Catherine the Great at what is now the University of Leningrad, or the one built of black marble by the Guiness brewery family in Dublin. Less well-endowed people constructed courts with stone or concrete floors and walls which were blackened with lampblack diluted with either bullock's blood or ox gall. Also in the sixteenth century (in 1571) King Charles IX granted a constitution to the newly formed Corporation of Tennis Professionals. That constitution established three grades of pro players—apprentice, associate and master—and appointed management and manufacturing rights. One of the members of the corporation, named Forbet, wrote the first known rules of the game which were published in 1599. Through such attempts at control, royalty came to dominate the game that would prove fatal to so many of them. They succeeded in dominating it for nearly two centuries, especially in France. Thus we read that Charles II played regularly at 6 a.m., that James II began playing at the age of eight, and that Henry VIII was an enthusiastic player who lost heavily in bets but looked magnificent on the court in his thin silken shirts. It was only a matter of time, however, before royalty had to abandon its tennis racket. On June 20, 1789, the French National Assembly was locked out of its chambers by the king. Consequently they met in the nearest convenient place, which happened to be a tennis court at Versailles. There, in the famous "Oath of the Tennis Court," they swore to give France a national constitution. Today the actual court is a museum dedicated to the French Revolution, which in part resulted from that oath. The Revolution, in turn, had a profound effect on tennis. Courts were turned into theaters and gymnasiums. Aristocratic players and their royal patrons were beheaded. All of this caused a serious decline in the popularity of the game. A similar decline had already begun in the United States, where tennis was first mentioned in a 1639 edict of the governor of New York. In 1763, four years before John Quincy Adams was born, a tennis court was offered to the highest bidder at a minor auction.

While these ups and downs in its popularity occurred, the game itself continued to evolve. Its most significant advancement may be traced back, somewhat tenuously, to the Hundred Years War. In 1415, at the Battle of

Agincourt in that war, Charles d'Orleans was taken prisoner and imprisoned in Wingfield Castle in England. While there, to wile away the time, he composed a ballad comparing life to a tennis game. His jailer was John Wingfield, who probably played the game himself. At any rate, nearly 450 years later a direct descendant of John Wingfield saved tennis from extinction by taking it outdoors. He was Major Walter Clopton Wingfield, who had a beard, sideburns and flowing mustache, and who at the age of 27 had commanded cavalry in the 1860 China campaign. Later a member of the elite Honourable Corps of Gentlemen-at-Arms, the English royal bodyguard, Wingfield is best remembered as the inventor of lawn tennis. A bust of him in the London offices of the Lawn Tennis Association is inscribed: "Inventor of Lawn Tennis." In 1873 he gave a Christmas garden party at his country estate at Nantclwyd in Wales. There his guests tried out his new game, which he called "sphairistiké" from the Greek word for ball play. His court was hourglass-shaped, his net was borrowed from badminton, his rackets were spoon shaped and long handled, and he recommended that his game also be played on ice. Nevertheless, sphairistiké contained all the basic elements of modern lawn tennis. Wingfield obtained a patent for his game in 1874 and tried unsuccessfully to market it complete with a set of 12 rules.

Despite its lack of initial success, lawn tennis was bound to become popular. A number of factors made this so. Croquet was one factor. Its earlier popularity had caused Victorians to change their soft, mossy decorative gardens into well-rolled, shrub-free ones that were ideal for tennis. Lawn tennis also provided an ideal setting in which emancipated women could mingle with the men and sometimes defeat them on the court. Most important of all these factors, however, was the development of a ball that would bounce suitably on grass. Early balls were handmade, either stuffed with wool or linen from Tinnis. Hair was also used as evidenced by a quote from *Much Ado About Nothing* in which Claudio says to Don Pedro, "... the old ornament of his cheek hath already stuffed tennis balls." Some balls were built up by strips of tightly rolled heavy cloth and tied with twine before being covered with white Melton cloth. Around Wingfield's time, however, the development of a cloth-covered vulcanized rubber ball made outdoor tennis a real possibility.

One guest at Wingfield's garden party was an army man on leave from his post in Bermuda. He took some sets of the game back with him. These sets so fascinated Mary Outerbridge, the "Mother of American Tennis," that she took one back to the United States with her in 1874. Custom officials confiscated the strange rackets, balls and net but released them to her duty-free several days later. Once customs allowed her set to pass through, lawn tennis had arrived on the North American continent.

In 1875 Dr. James Dwight, the "Father of American Tennis," played one of the first games in America. Three years later, William H. Young set up a court on the site now occupied by Santa Monica's municipal pier. There was some initial derision, however. In 1878 the Harvard *Crimson* scoffed, "The game is well enough for lazy and weak men, but men who have rowed or taken part in nobler sport should blush to be seen playing lawn tennis." Despite this, the growth of the game in the United States was assured.

Back in England, the All-England Croquet Club decided one day in 1875 to set aside one of its lawns at Wimbledon for those who wished to play outdoor tennis. People came in such numbers that the following year the club changed its name to the All-England Croquet and Lawn Tennis Club. As interest continued to grow, the club decided to hold a tennis championship for amateurs during which a silver Challenge Cup donated by *The Field* magazine would be presented. Making history in itself, that first match at Wimbledon attended by 200 spectators also made history by preferring a rectangular court over Wingfield's hourglass-shaped one.

Through all the centuries of tennis everyone had served underhanded, but by the 1880s most competitors were using the overhand service. The 1880s also saw the first lawn tennis prodigy, Charlotte "Lottie" Dod, who in 1887 at the age of 15 years and 10 months won the women's singles at Wimbledon. After winning the same title four more times, she lost interest in the game, became a champion golfer, a hockey player, a fine skater and the best woman archer in England. She died in 1962. A second prodigy, Jay Gould, began playing at the age of 12 and was world champion from 1914 to 1916. He is notable for becoming the first amateur of any nation to become a world champion, as well as for being related to Helen Gould. She donated the funds for construction of the world's first hall of fame, the Hall of Fame of Great Americans on University Heights in New York City. In 1890 the National Championship of Canada was instituted. It and other championships vastly increased public interest in the game. So did the evolution of the professional side of lawn tennis, which began with a Madison Square Garden match on October 9, 1926—the first match in which former amateurs played for money.

Mass acceptance of tennis required first that certain traditions be broken—that the game divorce itself more fully from its aristocratic (sissy, effeminate) reputation. It has accomplished this only recently. Not until the 1950s did male players stop wearing long flannel trousers; not until 1968, when the U.S. Davis Cup team wore yellow shirts, did anyone wear anything but white. Today, thanks largely to television, tennis is a game of the masses. In spirit it has also returned to what it began as: a religious avocation. In Australia today tennis is a virtual religion. Elsewhere in the world, it is practiced and played with real and increasing religious fervor.

FORMS: Over the centuries, and particularly during the twentieth century, the love of tennis has resulted in efforts to produce various substitutes for it. People lacking the money or inclination for traditional courts and equipment adapted the game or parts of the game to novel conditions. Lawn tennis resulted from the desire to play tennis outdoors and deck tennis resulted from a desire to play it at sea aboard ocean liners. Table tennis resulted from a desire to miniaturize lawn tennis to the point where it could be taken back indoors and played on tables. Whatever the end result, the new forms of the game generally have been designed to give the same satisfaction and to require the same degree of skills as the traditional game. In some cases, old or even ancient games similar to tennis were "fitted" with tennis rules and equipment to become tennis forms. For example, *poona*, a game played with gut rackets in India, was witnessed there by the Duke of Beaufort who took it back with him to England. He modified it somewhat to make it more tennislike and renamed it in honor of his ancestral home, Badminton House. Similar games include the Chinese *battledore,* the English shuttlecocks and aerial tennis, which uses a feather birdie twice the size and weight of the one used in badminton. When aerial tennis arrived in North America, the birdie feathers were obtained from seagulls killed in Canada. (It was illegal to kill gulls in the United States.)

Perhaps the best example of the way tennis was adapted to create new games is paddle tennis. It was invented after W.W. I to provide children with a game in which they could learn the rudiments of lawn tennis. The first paddle tennis tournament was held at Washington Square Garden, New York City, in 1924, by which time the game was becoming increasingly popular. Later, a platform was added so that paddle tennis could be played year-round. This, with various other slight changes, resulted in an additional new game, platform paddle tennis. The latter is not to be confused with platform tennis, which was devised in 1898 at Albion, Michigan. There are many other forms which came about this way. Beach tennis is deck tennis adapted for playing on land. Ring tennis, also called tenikoit, is played with a rubber ring, as are deck and beach tennis. Padder tennis is played with a wooden padder bat and a regular tennis ball on the same sized court as lawn tennis and features similar strokes and techniques. Ping ball is a form of table tennis akin to lawn tennis.

While some of these forms have yet to mushroom into widely popular sports, a few have done so with incredible speed. Table tennis retained its nursery status until a worldwide revival of interest occurred in 1922. That revival was stimulated in part by the use of a celluloid toy ball bought by an English champion long distance runner named Gibb while on a visit to the United States. Gibbs' friend Jaques suggested Ping-Pong. The rights to Ping-Pong were later sold to Parker Brothers, so that today it is a registered trademark, like Kleenex or Xerox. Soon interest in table tennis spread all over the world. Its various early world championships—Cairo in 1939, Bombay in 1952, Tokyo in 1956 and Peking in 1961—were the first world championships of *any* sport held in Africa, Asia, or the Far East. Platform tennis has also mushroomed. It has been estimated that a million Americans will be playing it on 20,000 courts by 1984.

Whether played with a tennis ball, a birdie, a rubber ring or a sponge rubber ball; whether hit with a catgut racket, a wooden paddle, a wooden bat or the palm of the hand; whether played indoors or out; whether on a natural or an artificial surface—no matter what the form, all in some degree owe their existence to an ancient indoor racket-and-ball game. It was called court tennis in the United States, real tennis in Britain, royal tennis in Australia and *la jeu de paume* (i.e, game of the palm) in France. This is also true of the various rackets games—open court rackets, close court rackets, squash rackets and others—despite Charles Dickens' assertation in *The Pickwick Papers* (1836–1837). He stated that rackets was originated by gentlemen imprisoned for debt who hit balls against the massive prison walls with their tennis rackets. In fact, the rackets games were first played in various English schools that did not have tennis courts. Squash rackets was played for the first time at Harrow School shortly after Winston Churchill graduated from there.

Court tennis is not played widely in the United States or Canada today. Though introduced in Boston as early as 1876, today there are only about a dozen American courts and only about 29 worldwide. It is confined largely to England, Scotland, France and Australia. Primarily a preoccupation of the rich, it is played by only about 2000 people. Compared to lawn tennis, the ball used in court tennis is about the same size, but heavier, and the court is indoors, but larger. The net across the center divides the court into equal but dissimilar halves—one is the hazard side, the other the service side.

In lawn tennis, the object is to propel the ball over the net in such a way that it bounces in court and evades any attempt by an opponent to return it. The court is 78 ft. by 27 ft. for singles, the same length but wider at 36 ft. for doubles. It may be composed of clay (*terre battue* or beaten earth), shale, sand, asphalt, gravel, cement, beaten ant heaps (in South Africa), wood, plastic, nylon, rubber, or grass—although a good grass court was described in 1903 as being "as rare to come across as a great auk's egg." The net is kept taut and no more than 3 ft. high in the middle by a vertical strap which is firmly fixed to the ground. Its height may be adjusted by a handle attached to one of the two posts holding up the net.

The ball weighs from 2 to 2 1/16 oz. and measures from 2 1/2 to 2 5/8 in. in diameter. If seams are used, they must be stitchless. When dropped 100 in. onto concrete, the ball must bounce more than 53 in. and less than 58 in. Prior to 1970 only white balls were permitted by the International Lawn Tennis Association, but today they may be either white or nonwhite, usually yellow. The best modern balls are covered with a mixture of 70 percent wool and 30 percent nylon and are filled to 10 lb. per sq. in. pressure. A hit ball can attain a speed of 131 m.p.h.

At one time tennis was played without rackets; the ball was hit back and forth with the hand. Sometimes gloves were worn. Some gloves had a binding of cords strung across the palm of the glove. Later, crude wooden boards were used. Still later, the short-handled *battoir* appeared—at first of solid wood, then with a wooden frame covered with parchment like a drum. By 1500 the long-handled racket strung with sheep gut had appeared. In Elizabethan times the game was sometimes referred to as "bord and cord". Until 1700 rackets were strung diagonally; the strings made a pattern of diamond spaces instead of the squares produced by today's vertical and horizontal strings. Although there never have been any official restrictions on the size, shape or weight of the racket, most are long handled, oval headed wood or (since the 1930s) metal. Men's rackets usually weigh from 13.5 to 14 oz. and women's from 13 to 13.5 oz.—far lighter than the early rackets needed to hit the heavy balls. Beech is used in wooden rackets, especially for cheaper ones. Ash is used for oval heads, hickory for shafts, and mahogany and walnut for veneers and inlays. Though racket strings may be made of beef gut (especially in Australia), hog gut, or synthetic material, the best strings—those with the greatest elasticity—are made of catgut, which comes from sheep. Sheep intestine castings about 20 inches long are split into ribbons that are cleaned, cured, and spun into string, which is then dried and polished. The same catgut is also used in surgical needlework, in the controls of artificial limbs, and in the mechanisms of certain clocks and typewriters.) Six to eight sheep are required to produce the strings for a single racket.

Traditionally, the start of play in lawn tennis, the choice of service and sides, is determined by spinning a racket in the air and calling rough or smooth, which refers to the two different faces of the racket. Seeding is the placing of leading players in protected positions in the draw so that the best competitors do not meet each other in a tournament's early rounds. Officials at tournaments include an umpire sitting in a high chair on the net line, a net-cord judge, a foot-fault judge, a referee with overall responsibility, and a linesman on each white line.

ORGANIZATION: The world governing body of lawn tennis is the International Lawn Tennis Federation (ILTF), founded in 1912 and headquartered in London. About 70 national lawn tennis associations are full members of the ILTF and about 30 are associate members. In all, 103 countries are represented. The ILTF is responsible for observance and changes of the game's rules and regulations in general; for upholding the regulations of the Davis Cup and the Federation Cup in particular; for recognizing official championships; and for promoting the game at the international level. Among its most significant decisions is its classification of players into amateurs who receive no money or pecuniary advantage for playing; independent professionals who receive material profit but accept the ultimate authority of both their own national association and the ILTF; and touring or contract professionals who play for money and affiliate themselves with an association or organization other than their national one.

The two national associations on the North American continent are the United States Tennis Association, formed in 1881—seven years before Britain's—and the Canadian Lawn Tennis Association. Their goals and regulations are supported and supplemented by a great number of state, provincial, district, metropolitan, intercity or private lawn tennis organizations. The main ones of these include the American Medical Tennis Association, the Association of Tennis Professionals, the Ontario Lawn Tennis Association, the Lawn Tennis Writers' Association of America, the National Public Parks Tennis Association, the National Tennis Foundation, the United States Professional Tennis Association and the Youth Tennis League. All of these in turn support or represent a far larger number of organizations devoted to lawn tennis. For example, the Youth Tennis League has ten local groups and the National Public Parks Tennis Association has 16 state groups. The U.S. Tennis Association itself has 17 regional groups comprised of 4000 local tennis clubs, educational institutions, camps, recreation departments, hotels, motels, and other groups interested in the promotion of lawn tennis.

In the world of lawn tennis, the year is divided into various tournaments in which players compete in individual or team events. The main ones include the Davis and Federation Cups, the Wightman Cup for American and British women since 1923, and the Bonne Belle Cup for American and Australian women since 1972. The best known tournaments, however, are the four major championships which make up the Grand Slam of the game: the Wimbledon in England played on grass; the Paris played since 1891 on nine red clay courts; the Forest Hills at Long Island, New York, played on some 23 grass courts and a number of clay courts; and the Australia played since 1905 in Sydney, Melbourne, Brisbane or Adelaide. These tournaments, the many minor tournaments and the over 60 million people who play tennis today are the inheritors of a long and grand tradition of tournaments. The tradition reaches back before Benjamin Franklin's lightning experiment with a kite—to 1740, when the tennis world championship was first won. Of all the world championships of all the world's sports, it is the oldest.

International Tennis Hall of Fame

NEWPORT, RHODE ISLAND

Mailing Address: 194 Bellevue Ave, 02840. Tel. (401) 846-4567. *Contact:* Robert S. Day, Exec. Dir. *Location:* 60 mi. S.W. of Boston, and 18 mi. N.E. of New York City. *Admission:* 10 to 5 daily May – October, and 11 to 4 daily November through April. Adults $1.00, children 50¢. *Personnel:* Col. Robert S. Day, Exec. Dir. (USA ret); the Bd. of Dirs. *Nearby Halls of Fame:* Ice Skating (Boston), Basketball (Springfield, Mass, 85 mi. N.W.), Ice Skating (Newburgh, N.Y, 140 mi. W.), Harness Racing (Goshen, N.Y, 155 mi. W.), Heritage, Music (New York City), Bicycle (Staten Island, N.Y, 185 mi. W.), Horse Racing (Saratoga Springs, N.Y, 185 mi. N.W.), Baseball (Cooperstown, N.Y, 210 mi. N.W.).

In 1952 James H. Van Alen originated the idea of a National Tennis Hall of Fame. He received sanction from the U.S. Lawn Tennis Association for its establishment at Newport Casino Tennis Club in 1954. The Casino was chosen for the site of the Hall because American lawn tennis grew up there; the U.S. men's singles tournament was held there for 34 years until it was changed to Forest Hills, N.Y, in 1915. The Hall was originally designed to honor outstanding tennis players in the United States; in 1976, it became international. The Hall was initially supported by William J. Clothier, the national singles champion in 1906, who paid many of the expenses out of his own pocket until it became self-sustaining. There is an outstanding reference library in the museum, with many books on tennis, now out of print, an auditorium, two acres of tennis courts and an indoor tennis court facility. Some of the displays include the Sears Bowl, the first national championship trophy, photographs of the first Davis Cup team in 1900, early model rackets and other tennis memorabilia. This Hall is a member of the Association of Sports Museums and Halls of Fame.

Members: 90 as of 1976. Members are chosen on the basis of character and sportsmanship, and are either outstanding champions or significant contributors. There is no limit on the number of inductees; the inductions take place the Saturday of the week of August 19 on the center court of the Casino.

1955

CAMPBELL, Oliver Samuel

Player

Born February 25, 1871; died July 11, 1953, in New York at age 82.

Campbell was the youngest man to win the U.S. singles championship, at 19 years, 6 months, and 9 days in 1890. He also won 1891 and 1899. In 1888 he took the doubles championship with Valentine G. Hall, and in 1891 and 1892 with Robert P. Huntington, Jr. He was the first American net rusher, and was in the Wimbledon men's doubles semifinals in 1892, the U.S. men's singles semifinals in 1888, and a runnerup in the U.S. men's doubles in 1889 and 1893.

Also in: Tennis Hall of Fame, Citizens Savings Hall of Fame Athletic Museum.

CLARK, Joseph S.

Player

Born November 30, 1861, in Philadelphia, Pa; died April 14, 1956, at age 95.

Clark, the winner of the first intercollegiate championship in 1883, defeated Richard Sears and Dr. Dwight in the doubles trials the same year, with his brother as his partner, first in Boston and then in New York. He also played in the first international tennis match against the Renshaw brothers at Wimbledon, losing in four sets. In 1885 he took the national doubles championship with Sears. He was secretary of the U.S. Lawn Tennis Association 1885–1886, vice president 1887–1888 and 1894–1901, and president 1889–1891.

DWIGHT, Dr. James

Player

Born May 28, 1862, in Boston, Mass; died Jan. 22, 1948, in New York City at age 86.

Dwight, the "Father of American Lawn Tennis," was the doubles champion in 1882–1884, 1886 and 1887 with Richard Sears. In 1885 and 1886 he was ranked second to Sears, who was his protege. Dwight was a member of the first executive committee of the U.S. Lawn Tennis Association, and president 1882–1884 and 1894–1911. He was a referee of the national singles championships for more than 30 years.

SEARS, Richard Dudley

Player

Born October 26, 1861, in Boston, Mass; died April 8, 1943, in Boston at age 82.

Sears was the first U.S. champion, at age 19, and held the title for seven years. He took first place in the U.S. doubles in 1882, 1883, 1884, 1886 and 1887 with Dr. James Dwight and in 1885 with Joseph S. Clark. Sears was a Wimbledon doubles semifinalist in 1884, and the president of the U.S. Lawn Tennis Association 1887–1888.

Also in: Tennis Hall of Fame, Citizens Savings Hall of Fame Athletic Museum.

SLOCUM, Henry W, Jr.

Player

Born May 28, 1862, in New York; died Jan. 22, 1948, at age 86.

Slocum was the national singles champion in 1888–1889, and in 1887 was the All-Comers winner at Wimbledon, ranked second to Sears. In 1887, he was the secretary of the U.S. Lawn Tennis Association, its treasurer in 1888, vice president in 1889–1891 and 1912–1913 and president in 1892–1893. Slocum represented the Association in international negotiations.

WHITMAN, Malcolm D.

Player

Born March 15, 1877, in Boston, Mass; died December 28, 1932, at age 55.

Whitman was the U.S. national singles champion 1898–1900, and in 1900 and 1902 represented the United States in the Davis Cup singles (no defeat). He wrote *Tennis Origins and Mysteries,* published in 1931, an outstanding reference work. Whitman was a dedicated student of the history of tennis, in 1896 and 1897 was the U.S. men's singles quarter-finalist, and in 1902, runnerup. He was the top singles player on the American side of the first Davis Cup tie in 1900.

Also in: Tennis Hall of Fame, Citizens Savings Hall of Fame Athletic Museum.

WRENN, Robert D.

Player

Born September 20, 1873, in New York City; died November 12, 1952, at age 79.

Wrenn was only 19 years old (the third youngest) when he won his first U.S. title in 1893, and he won the singles title again in 1894, 1896 and 1897. In 1895 he was the national doubles champion with Malcolm G. Chace, and in 1903 was chosen for singles for the U.S. Davis Cup team, and for doubles with George L. Wrenn. From 1902 to 1911, he was vice president of the U.S. Lawn Tennis Association and president 1912–1915. He was the U.S. men's singles semifinalist in 1892, runnerup in 1895 and a quarter-finalist in 1900. In 1896 Wrenn was the U.S. men's doubles runnerup, and from 1893 to 1897, he was the top-ranking U.S. player in four out of five years. He was left-handed.

Also in: Tennis Hall of Fame, Citizens Savings Hall of Fame Athletic Museum.

1956

BUNDY, May Sutton

Player

Born September 25, 1887; died October 4, 1975, at age 88.

Bundy was the first American to win at Wimbledon; she took the women's singles championship there in 1905 and 1907, and in 1904, the U.S. championship. She was considered the strongest woman player for several years thereafter, although she was not competing. In 1921 she was ranked fourth and in 1922 and 1928, fifth.

Also in: Tennis Hall of Fame, Citizens Savings Hall of Fame Athletic Museum.

CLOTHIER, William J.
Player
Born September 27, 1881, in Philadelphia, Pa; died September 4, 1962, at age 81.

Clothier was the singles champion of the United States in 1906, and won All-Comers in 1909. In 1905 he was a member of the first Davis Cup team to go abroad, and played on the team for two years. In 1906 he was ranked first in the United States, second in 1904 and 1909, third in 1903 and 1913, fourth in 1905, 1908 and 1912, and fifth in 1902 and 1914. Clothier was elected first president of the International Tennis Hall of Fame in 1954. He retired in 1957.

DAVIS, Dwight Filley
Player
Born July 5, 1879, in St. Louis, Mo; Governor-General of the Philippine Islands and U.S. Secretary of War 1925–1929; Major-General in W.W. II; died Nov. 28, 1945, in St. Louis, Mo.

Davis was the donor of the Davis Cup for international tennis competition in 1900. From 1899 to 1901 he was the U.S. doubles champion with Holcombe Ward, and retired undefeated. He won the All-Comers doubles at Wimbledon in 1901, and was ranked fourth in singles in the United States in 1898, second in 1899 and 1900, and fourth in 1902. In 1900 and 1902 he played on the winning first two Davis Cup teams, was Wimbledon men's doubles runnerup in 1901, and U.S. men's singles runnerup 1898 and 1899, and U.S. men's singles quarterfinalist in 1900. In 1923 he was the president of the U.S. Lawn Tennis Association.
Also in: Noteworthy Contributors Hall of Fame and Tennis Hall of Fame, Citizens Savings Hall of Fame Athletic Museum.

LARNED, William A.
Player
Born December 30, 1872, in Summit, N.J; died December 16, 1926 in Summit at age 54.

Larned won the U.S. singles championship seven times between 1901 and 1911, and retired undefeated. From 1892 to 1911 he was ranked first eight times, second five times, third four times, fifth and sixth once (except during the Spanish War in 1898 when he was absent). He played four times in the Davis Cup Challenge Round; he was 28 years old when he won the first U.S. singles, and the oldest ever at age 38 when he won for the seventh time in 1911.
Also in: Tennis Hall of Fame, Citizens Savings Hall of Fame Athletic Museum.

WARD, Holcombe
Player
Born November 23, 1878, in New York; died January 23, 1967, at age 89.

Ward was the U.S. singles champion in 1904, and he spent four years in the Davis Cup Challenge Round (1900, 1902, 1905–1906). He was U.S. doubles champion six times, 1899–1901 with Dwight Davis, and 1904–1906 with Beals C. Wright, and then retired undefeated. Ward was a member of the American side in the first Davis Cup tie of 1900 with Dwight Davis. He was president of the U.S. Lawn Tennis Association in 1937–1947.
Also in: Tennis Hall of Fame, Citizens Savings Hall of Fame Athletic Museum.

WRIGHT, Beals O.
Player
Born December 19, 1879, in Boston, Mass; died August 23, 1961, in New York at age 82.

Wright was the U.S. singles champion in 1905, and the doubles champion with Holcombe Ward 1904–1906. In 1906 he won the All-Comers, and in 1905, 1907–1908 and 1911, he represented the United States in Davis Cup play, beating A. F. Wilding and N. E. Brookes in singles in the Challenge Round in Australia in 1908. In 1907 he and Karl Behr beat them in doubles of the Final Tie in England. Wright was ranked first in 1905, fourth in 1900, 1903 and 1904, second in 1901, 1907 and 1908, and third in 1902, 1906 and 1910. He was the first American to reach the final of the All-Comers men's singles at Wimbledon in 1910. He was left-handed.

1957

BROWNE, Mary K.
Player
Born 1897; competed in 1924 against Dorothy Campbell in U.S. women's amateur golf tourney; worked overseas with the American Red Cross in W.W. II; died August 19, 1971, at age 74.

Browne toured with Suzanne Lenglen for the benefit of the Fund for Devastated France following W.W. I, and joined Lenglen as a pro in 1926. From 1912 to 1914 Browne was the U.S. national singles champion and in 1921 was runnerup to Molla Mallory. She took the national doubles title 1912–1914, 1921 and 1925, the last year with Helen Wills. She won many other titles, including the national mixed doubles. In 1913 and 1914 she was ranked first, second in 1921 and 1924 and sixth in 1925. Browne played on the Wightman Cup team 1925 and 1926, and in 1926 won the Wimbledon women's doubles and was runnerup in the mixed doubles.
Also in: Tennis Hall of Fame, Citizens Savings Hall of Fame Athletic Museum.

McLOUGHLIN, Maurice Evans
Player
Born January 7, 1890, in Carson City, Nev; died December 10, 1957, in San Francisco, Calif, at age 67.

McLoughlin was one of the most spectacular of America's tennis champions. He had a tremendous service and an excellent volley and overhead. In 1914 he beat Norman Brookes of Australia at Forest Hills; the first set went to 17–15, and Brookes never broke service. He was the national singles champion 1912 and 1913 and runnerup 1911, 1914 and 1915. The "California Comet" played in the Davis Cup Challenge Round in 1911, 1913 and 1914, and ranked in the top ten 1909–1915. He was Number One 1912–1914. McLoughlin had a short career as a tournament player.
Also in: Tennis Hall of Fame, Citizens Savings Hall of Fame Athletic Museum.

WIGHTMAN, Hazel Hotchkiss
Player
Born December 20, 1896, in Healdsburg, Calif; died December 5, 1974, in Boston, Mass. at age 78.

Wightman, donor of the Wightman Cup, has one of the most amazing records ever compiled in tennis. She began winning national championships in 1909, and continued to win tournaments and teach tennis almost until her death. She was the U.S. national singles champion 1909–1911 and 1919, and in 1915 was runnerup to Molla Bjurstedt (Mallory). In 1909–1911, 1915, 1924 and 1928 she won the national doubles championship; the last two years Helen Wills was her partner. Wightman won the mixed doubles 5 times 1909–1911, 1915, 1918 and 1920, the indoor singles 2 times, the indoor doubles 9 times, and the senior doubles 11 times. In all, she accumulated 50 national titles, and in 1915, 1918 and 1919 ranked in the first ten for women (which was instituted in 1913). In 1923, the first year of the Wightman Cup, international team matches between women's teams representing Great Britain and the United States began. Wightman played in 1923, 1924, 1927, 1929, and 1931 in doubles, and won the women's doubles at Wimbledon in 1924. She was an Olympic gold medalist in 1924.
Also in: Tennis Hall of Fame, Citizens Savings Hall of Fame Athletic Museum.

WILLIAMS, Richard Norris II
Player
Born January 29, 1892, in Geneva, Switz; died in 1968 at age 76.

Williams was a daring player. Because he played with a narrow margin of safety, played the lines and always went for a winning shot, his game was marred by errors. He was the U.S. national singles champion in 1914 and 1916, and in 1913 was runnerup to McLoughlin. In 1925 and 1926 he was the national doubles champion with Vincent Richards, and they both played in the Davis Cup doubles against France. He played with William Tilden in the Davis Cup Challenge Round against Australia, and in 1921 with Watson Washburn against Japan. Williams played singles in the Challenge Round against the British Isles, and in 1914 against Australia. He was ranked in the first ten ten times, 1912–1916, and 1919–1923; in 1916 he was ranked Number One. In 1914 he was ranked second to McLoughlin (which was disputed since Williams won the national title).
Also in: Tennis Hall of Fame, Citizens Savings Hall of Fame Athletic Museum.

1958

JOHNSTON, William "Little Bill"
Player
Born November 2, 1894, in San Francisco, Calif; died May 1, 1946, at age 51.

Johnston was one of the greatest volleyers in tennis and was a master of the Western topspin and the forehand drive. His nickname was derived from the fact that he was always overshadowed by his contemporary "Big Bill" Tilden. Johnston won the U.S. men's singles national championship in 1915, beating defending champion Maurice McLoughlin. He won in 1919 against William Tilden II. In 1920 and 1922–1925, he was a runnerup to Tilden. In 1923 he won the Wimbledon men's singles, defeating Francis T. Hunter. Johnston was ranked first in the country 12 times in 14 years. He was Number Four in 1913, Number One 1915 and 1919, and Number Two 1916, 1920–1923 and 1925. He won three national doubles championships, 1915, 1916, and 1920 with Clarence J. Griffin. In 1921 he took the national mixed doubles with Mary K. Browne, and in 1919 won the National Clay Court title. He was the Pacific Coast champion seven times 1913–1922, and had a U.S. Davis Cup team Challenge Round record of 13 wins and 3 losses against Australia.
Also in: Tennis Hall of Fame, Citizens Savings Hall of Fame Athletic Museum.

MALLORY, Molla Bjurstedt
Player
Born 1892 in Norway; later became an American citizen; married Franklin Mallory in 1920; died in 1959 in Norway at age 67.

Mallory was the greatest American woman player before Helen Wills Moody, and the only player to beat Suzanne Lenglen in singles after W. W. I (in the opening match of the 1921 U.S. championships). Mallory's winning of the national singles title seven times has only been equaled by Helen Wills Moody. She won the Patriotic Tournament in 1917 that took the place of the official championships, and also won 1915, 1916, 1918, 1920–1922 and 1926. In 1922 she defeated Helen Wills for the title, and in 1923 and 1924, was runnerup to Wills. Mallory won the national doubles crown in 1916 and 1917 with Eleanora Sears, and 1917 she and Irving Wright won the national mixed doubles championships. She won in 1922 and 1923 with Bill Tilden, and was on five Wightman Cup teams, 1923–1925, 1927 and 1928. A Wimbledon finalist in 1922, she lost to Suzanne Lenglen. She beat Lenglen at Forest Hills in 1921 (Lenglen defaulted after losing the first set). From 1915 to 1928 she ranked in the first ten 13 times, and ranked first 7 times. She is known for her powerful forehand.
Also in: Tennis Hall of Fame, Citizens Savings Hall of Fame Athletic Museum.

MURRAY, R. Lindley
Player
Born November 3, 1893, in San Francisco, Calif; died in 1970 at age 77.

Murray took first place in the 1917 Patriotic Tournament and defeated Tilden in the final of the 1918 national championships. A left-hander, Murray's serve is the strongest point of his game. He was ranked fourth in 1914, 1916 and 1919, and first in 1918.
Also in: Tennis Hall of Fame, Citizens Savings Hall of Fame Athletic Museum.

WALLACH, Maud Barger
Player
Born 1871 in Newport R.I; died April 2, 1954 at age 83.

Wallach took the women's championship in 1908, and was a runnerup in 1906. There were no women's rankings until 1913, but in 1915 she was fifth and in 1916, tenth. She maintained an interest in tennis until her death; she was a patron of the game, and supported the Newport Invitational Tournament.

ROARK, Helen Wills Moody
Player
Born October 6, 1905, in Berkeley, Calif.

Roark is one of the all-time great tennis players, and is

second only to Suzanne Lenglen with her record of invincibility. She won the Wimbledon singles eight times (a record) in nine challenges, and from 1927 to 1932 she did not lose a set in singles anywhere. Her footwork was her weakest point, but her powerful groundstrokes and consistency served her well. While still in her teens, she came East from California still in pigtails to win the important U.S. tournaments. She won the Wimbledon title eight times, 1927 – 1930, 1932 – 1933, 1935 and 1938. Helen was on the first Wightman Cup team as well as 1923 – 1925, 1927 – 1932 and 1938, winning 18 out of 20 singles matches, and many doubles. She won the Wimbledon women's doubles 1924, 1927 and 1930, and the U.S. women's singles 1923 – 1925, 1927 – 1929 and 1931, the women's doubles 1922, 1924 – 1925 and 1928, and mixed doubles 1924 and 1928. She took the French women's singles title 1928 – 1930 and 1932, and doubles 1930 and 1932. Estrangement with the American authorities prevented her from competing in the U.S. championships after 1933.
Also in: Tennis Hall of Fame, Citizens Savings Hall of Fame Athletic Museum.

TILDEN, William Tatem III "Big Bill"
Player
Born February 10, 1893, in Philadelphia, Pa; an intellectual as well as an athlete, he wrote plays and books; died June 5, 1953, at age 60.

Tilden's cannonball service helped him win the U.S. singles seven times, and the doubles many times with various partners. His loss in the final U.S. championships in 1919 led him to spend the winter working on his backhand; the following year he came back to become champion. He won championships around the world, and from 1920 on his Davis Cup record was noteworthy. Tilden and Johnston in singles, with Dick Williams, Vincent Richards and Watson Washburn in doubles were an outstanding Davis Cup team. They won the Cup seven successive years, a record unequaled by any other nation. In addition to skillful playing, Tilden was generous in his help to both younger and older tennis players. He took the Wimbledon men's singles 1920, 1921 and 1930, and the men's doubles in 1927. He won the U.S. men's singles 1920 – 1925 and 1929, the men's doubles 1918, 1921 – 1923 and 1927, and the mixed doubles 1913, 1914, 1922 and 1923. He won the French mixed doubles 1930, and the same year he won at Wimbledon at age 37. In 1922 he had part of a finger removed but changed his grip and continued to win. Tilden became a pro in 1931 and played good tennis until his death.
Also in: Tennis Hall of Fame, Citizens Savings Hall of Fame Athletic Museum.

1961

ALEXANDER, Fred B.
Player
Born Aug. 14, 1880, in New York City; graduated from Princeton Univ; soon after W. W. I moved to Los Angeles, where he lived until his death in 1969 at age 89.

Alexander played on the Princeton tennis team, and was a member of the West Side Tennis Club. In 1900 he won the intercollegiate doubles championship with Raymond D. Little and in 1901 the intercollegiate singles. He took the national doubles championship with Hackett 1907 – 1910, and in 1917 won the doubles championship of the Patriotic Tournament with Harold A. Throckmorton. Alexander was the first American to win the Australian men's singles in 1908, and he also took the doubles; he was on the Davis Cup team the same year. In 1914, under the aegis of the U.S. Lawn Tennis Association, he originated the junior tournament in the New York Metropolitan District, which later became the Junior Boy and Girl Development Program. Alexander was the captain and manager of players who were competitors in tournaments and exhibition matches to raise funds to purchase ambulances and supply personnel to man them under the direction of the U.S. Lawn Tennis Association for the benefit of the Red Cross in 1917. All tournaments and championships that year were called Patriotic Tournaments and Championships, and all profits were devoted to the ambulance project.

CHACE, Malcolm G.
Player
Born March 12, 1875, in R.I; graduated from Yale Univ; career as a businessman; died July, 1955, at age 80.

Chace played tennis only while in college, ranking in the first ten of singles 1892 – 1895. In 1892 he was the national interscholastic champion, and 1893 – 1895 was the intercollegiate singles and doubles champion. He was the national doubles champion with R. D. Wrenn in 1895. A member of the U.S. team that played the English at Newport before donation of the Davis Cup in 1900, he later owned, with J.D.E. Jones, the Indoor Tennis Court in Providence, R.I, which has done much for the development of tennis.

HACKETT, Harold Humphrey
Player
Born July 17, 1878; graduated from Yale; died November 20, 1937, at age 59.

Hackett was a member of the Hackett and Alexander doubles team that won the national doubles championship four times in succession 1907 – 1910. In 1912 he won the national Clay Court doubles championship with W. Merrill Hall, and in 1912 was the captain of the winning Davis Cup team when the U.S. defeated the British Isles three matches to two. He was also a member of the Davis Cup team in 1908, 1909 and 1913. Hackett has served on many committees of the West Side Tennis Club and the U.S. Lawn Tennis Association, and was helpful on the Davis Cup committee in the 1920s.

HUNTER, Francis Townsend
Player
Born June 28, 1894, in New York.

Hunter was the national indoors singles champion in 1922 and 1930, and the indoor doubles champion in 1922, 1924 and 1929 with Vincent Richards. In 1927 he was the national doubles champion with Bill Tilden, and in 1924, at the Olympic Games at Paris, he and Richards won the doubles gold medal. In 1928 he won the international championship held in connection with the Olympic Games in Holland, defeating Jean Borotra in the final round in straight sets. He was on the Davis Cup teams in 1927 and 1928, which were defeated in France in the Challenge Round. In 1931 he joined Tilden as a pro.

RICHARDS, Vincent
Player
Born March 20, 1903, in Yonkers, N.Y; died September 28, 1959, at age 56.

Richards won most of the U.S. titles, both amateur and pro, except the national singles. At age 15, the youngest player to win a national championship, he won his first U.S. national doubles title with Bill Tilden 1918. He won the doubles crown four more times 1921, 1922, 1925 and 1926, two times with Tilden and two with R. Norris Williams. He and Marion Zindeestein won the national mixed doubles in 1919, and he won in 1924 with Helen Wills. Richards took the indoors singles 1919, 1923 and 1924 and the doubles 1919–1921, 1923 and 1924. He ranked in the top ten five times. In 1922 he played in the first international match against Australia, defeating Gerald Patterson. He set a record in the Davis Cup competiton of two victories in singles and three in doubles. He won Wimbledon doubles championship in 1924, and the French men's doubles in 1926. Richards took two gold medals in singles and doubles in the 1924 Olympic Games in Paris. In 1926 he was the first important U.S. player to turn pro, and he proceeded to win most of the world's pro titles. The last title he won, in 1945, was the U.S. Pro Doubles title with Bill Tilden.
Also in: Tennis Hall of Fame, Citizens Savings Hall of Fame Athletic Museum.

1962

DOEG, John Hope
Player
Born December 7, 1908, in Sonora County, Mexico.

Doeg was a star of the early 1930s who took the national singles title in 1930, defeating Tilden in the semifinals and Francis and Shields in the finals. He was the junior champion of the country in 1926, and in 1927 and 1928 was ranked Number Eight; he was ranked Number Three in 1929 and Number One in 1930. In 1929 and 1930, he was the national doubles champion with George M. Lott, Jr. Doeg, a left-hander, is memorable for his powerful serve and top-spin forehand. Although he was on the winning Davis Cup team in 1930 and was Tilden's protege, he did not fulfill the promise of his early success.

JACOBS, Helen Hull
Player
Born August 8, 1908, in Globe, Ariz.

Jacobs was at or near the top of the national rankings from 1927 to 1941 with the exception of two years of noncompetition. From 1932 to 1935 she ranked Number One for four straight years, and was in the Number Two position not less than ten times. She became a celebrated rival of Helen Wills when Miss Wills beat her in the Forest Hills finals in 1928. Jacobs lost in 1933 at Wimbledon to Wills again, but beat her the same year for the U.S. championship. Jacobs won the national singles title four times 1932–1935 and in 1933, she was leading 8–6, 3–6, 3–0 against Moody when Moody became ill. In 1935 she met Moody again at a Wimbledon final and reached match point at 5–3 in the third set. Jacobs missed an easy smash when the wind deflected the ball, and Moody went on to win. She was, however, a Wimbledon finalist four times, winning in 1936 by defeating Fräulein Sperling. She also won the U.S. girls' singles 1924 and 1925, the national doubles with Sarah Palfrey 1932, 1933 and 1935, and the 1934 national mixed doubles with George Lott. During twelve years of Wightman Cup play 1927–1937 and 1939, Jacobs has an overall record in singles and doubles of 18 victories and 11 defeats. Jacobs was known for her good sportsmanship as well as her chop forehand and sweeping backhand.
Also in: Tennis Hall of Fame, Citizens Savings Hall of Fame Athletic Museum.

VINES, Ellsworth
Player
Born September 28, 1911, in Los Angeles, Calif; turned to golf in 1938 and became one of the leading exponents of the game.

Vines was the junior doubles champion with Keith Gledhill in 1929, and the U.S. singles champion 1931 and 1932, beating Lott and Henri Cochet in respective finals. He won the national Clay Court title in 1931, and was Wimbledon champion over H. W. Bunny Austin in 1932. The final shot, an ace by Vines, was so fast that Austin later admitted that he did not know on which side the ball flew by him. Vines beat Cochet in five sets, but lost to Jean Borotra in four in the Davis Cup Challenge Round in 1932. He ranked eighth in the country in 1930, and Number One in 1931 and 1932. In 1932 and 1933 he was the U.S. men's doubles champion and in 1933 the Australian men's doubles champion. He turned pro in 1933, following his most successful year in tennis. His superior form was based on a lightning forehand and a cannonball service.
Also in: Tennis Hall of Fame, Citizens Savings Hall of Fame Athletic Museum.

1963

ALLISON, Wilmer Lawson
Player
Born December 8, 1904, in San Antonio, Tex.

Allison was the national champion in 1935, beating Fred Perry of England in the finals. In 1930 he was a runner-up to Tilden at Wimbledon after he had beaten Henri Cochet of France. He is more famous for his doubles play and took the U.S. doubles with John Rhyn in 1931 and 1935, the mixed doubles in 1930, and the Wimbledon doubles in 1929 and 1930. He won the Australian doubles in 1933 and was on the Davis Cup team 1929–1933, 1935 and 1936. In 1930 he was ranked Number Three; in 1932, Number Two; and 1933–1935, Number One. He is now active in junior development programs, and is a U.S. Lawn Tennis Association official.
Also in: Tennis Hall of Fame, Citizens Savings Hall of Fame Athletic Museum.

DANZIG, Sarah Palfrey
Player
Born September 18, 1912, in Sharon, Mass.

Danzig was for many years the leading player in the world; from 1929 to 1945 she ranked in the first ten thirteen times, Number One in 1945, Number Four in 1929. In 1941 and 1945 she was the national champion, and

she won the doubles title nine times, 1934, 1935, 1937 and 1941, and mixed doubles 1932, 1935, 1937 and 1941. She won the Wimbledon women's singles 1934 and 1938, and the doubles 1933–1936 with Jacobs, and 1937–1939 with Marble. She took the French mixed doubles title in 1939. Best known for her superb volleys and her superior doubles play, she renounced her amateur status in 1946.
Also in: Tennis Hall of Fame, Citizens Savings Hall of Fame Athletic Museum.

MYRICK, Julian S.
Contributor
Born March 1, 1880, in New York City; worked for an insurance company and was known as "Mr. Life Insurance"; died January 4, 1969, at age 89.

Myrick was a former president of the U.S. Lawn Tennis Association (USLTA) and chairman of the Davis Cup and Wightman Cup committees. He was a leader of international prominence in the development and growth of the game. Junior programs for boys' and girls' tennis began during his administration, and the number of clubs in the USLTA increased. He was largely responsible for the inception of the international women's matches with Britain for the Wightman Cup. He was known for his emphasis on strict amateurism and high standards of sportsmanship. He played tennis regularly into his eighties.
Also in: Tennis Hall of Fame, Citizens Savings Hall of Fame Athletic Museum.

VAN RYN, John
Player
Born June 30, 1906, in Newport News, Va; graduated from Princeton Univ; now in the investment banking business in Palm Beach, Fla; plays tennis in free time.

Van Ryn was one of the great doubles players, often teaming up with Allison. They won the U.S. doubles title 1931 and 1935, and were Wimbledon champions 1929 and 1930. In 1932 they defeated Henri Cochet and Jean Borotra in the Davis Cup Challenge Round, and Cochet and Jacques Brugnon in 1932. In 1931 Van Ryn won the Wimbledon and French doubles championship with George Lott. He ranked sixth in 1927 and 1928, fifth in 1929, ninth in 1930 and fourth in 1931. In 1931 he took the French men's doubles title, and was on the Davis Cup team 1929–1936.

1964

ADEE, George T.
Contributor
Born 1874; graduated from Yale Univ; football player; All-American quarterback chosen by Walter Camp in 1894; served in the Spanish-American War and W.W. I; died in 1948 at age 74.

Adee was chairman of the Davis Cup committee and the amateur rules committee, and served on many others. He was the president of the Yale Club in New York and the Country Club of Westchester.

BUDGE, J. Donald
Player
Born July 13, 1915.

Budge was famous for scoring the first Grand Slam of all time in 1938; he won Wimbledon, Forest Hills, the French and the Australian titles. In 1937 he was the U.S. champion, and he also won Wimbledon; he won the Wimbledon doubles and mixed doubles 1937 and 1938. He took the U.S. doubles in 1936 and 1938 and was on the winning Davis Cup team 1937 and 1938. Budge ranked in the first ten five times before turning pro late in 1938, and he ranked first 1936–1938. Budge was best known for his rolled backhand which transformed a formerly defensive stroke into an attacking one, and for his return of service. It is a matter of debate whether Budge or Tilden was the greatest player before 1939. In 1937 he had a fifth-set recovery against Von Cramm in a Davis Cup clash; Budge came from 1–4 to win 6–8, 5–7, 6–4, 6–2 and 8–6. He made his pro debut in 1939, beating both Ellsworth Vines and Fred Perry at Madison Square Garden.
Also in: Tennis Hall of Fame, Citizens Savings Hall of Fame Athletic Museum.

LOTT, George M, Jr.
Player
Born October 16, 1906, in Springfield, Ill.

Lott was one of the greatest doubles players of all time and was a finalist in the U.S. singles against Ellsworth Vines. He won the national doubles five times with three different partners, with John Doeg twice, Lester Stoefen twice and John Hennessey. In 1931 he won at Wimbledon with John Van Ryn and in 1934 with Stoefen. He took the French doubles with Van Ryn in 1931. In 1929, 1930 and 1934 he played in the Davis Cup Challenge Round. He was ranked in the first ten nine times. Lott became a pro in 1934.
Also in: Tennis Hall of Fame, Citizens Savings Hall of Fame Athletic Museum.

MARBLE, Alice
Player
Born September 28, 1913, in Plumes County, Calif.

Marble was U.S. national champion 1936 and 1938–1940 and she was memorable for her superb volleying abilities and her aggressive style. She was the Wimbledon champion in 1939 and won the national doubles title with Sarah Palfrey Danzig 1937–1940. In 1938 and 1939 she won the Wimbledon doubles title with Helen Jacobs. Marble was ranked in the top ten seven times, and was ranked first from 1936 to 1940. She also excelled in mixed doubles, winning at Wimbledon 1937–1939 and the U.S. championship 1936 and 1938–1940. She was on the Wightman Cup team 1933 and 1937–1939. Her example set a standard of excellence for women players after W.W. II.
Also in: Tennis Hall of Fame, Citizens Savings Hall of Fame Athletic Museum.

SHIELDS, Francis X.
Player
Born November 18, 1910, in New York City; died August 19, 1975.

Shields was runnerup to John Doeg for the national championship in 1930 and reached the finals at Wimbledon in 1931, but had to default to Wood, owing to an ankle injury suffered in the semifinals. In 1934 he was on the Davis Cup Challenge Round team, and he has been ranked in the first ten ten times.

WOOD, Sidney B, Jr.
Player
Born November 1, 1911, in Black Rock, Conn.

Wood was Wimbledon champion in 1931, and in 1935 was runnerup to Wilmer Allison for the U.S. national title. In 1934 he played in the Davis Cup Challenge Round, and ranked in the first ten no less than ten times. At 19 years, 8 months, he was the second youngest men's singles champion at Wimbledon, and the only one to receive a walkover in the final.

1965

ADDIE, Pauline Betz
Player
Born August 6, 1919, in Dayton, Ohio; now lives in Washington, D.C.

Addie was the U.S. champion in 1942–1944 and 1946. In 1946 she won the Wimbledon crown without losing a set; her longest set was 6–4 in the final against her compatriot Louise Brough. The same year she won her two singles matches and the doubles with Doris Hart in the Wightman Cup matches. Both Wimbledon and the Wightman Cup were suspended from 1940 to 1945. She was ranked in the first ten eight times, and Number One four times. She won the French mixed doubles in 1946 and was probably the best of the players who dominated the game after W.W. II. In 1947 the U.S. Lawn Tennis Association deprived her of her amateur status after she discussed the terms of a pro contract.
Also in: Tennis Hall of Fame, Citizens Savings Hall of Fame Athletic Museum.

ALLERDICE, Ellen Hansell
Player
Born in Philadelphia, Pa; married Taylor Allerdice in 1892; died in 1937.

Allerdice was the first winner of the U.S. women's singles championship in Philadelphia in 1887. She was honored, along with Richard D. Sears, the first men's champion, at the Golden Jubilee celebration of the U.S. Lawn Tennis Association in 1931 at Forest Hills, N.Y.

McNEIL, W. Donald
Player
Born April 30, 1918, in Chickasha, Okla.

McNeil was the national champion in 1940, and in 1939 was the first American to win the French championship in singles. He also won the French doubles with Charles Harris. In 1944 he was the U.S. doubles champion with Robert Falkenberg. He was ranked in the first ten six times, and was Number One in 1940. His career was interrupted by W.W. II; the Davis Cup matches were suspended when he was in his prime.

VAN ALEN, James H.
Contributor
Born September 19, 1902, in Newport R.I; graduated from Cambridge Univ, captain of the tennis team in the 1920s.

Van Alen is the president of the Newport Casino, and is responsible for establishing the Hall of Fame there. He succeeded William T. Clothier, Sr, and assured the permanence of the Casino by gaining donations of the controlling numbers of shares in Newport Casino corporation stock. In addition, as president, he became the director of the annual Newport Invitational Tournament, and infused new life into it when it seemed that the tournament might become defunct, and the Casino might be sold. He brought pro men's and women's tournaments to Newport in recent years. Van Alen was also a benefactor of court tennis, and won wide attention for his simplified lawn tennis scoring system, called VASS.

WASHBURN, Watson
Contributor
Born June 13, 1894, in New York City; died December 2, 1973, at age 79.

Washburn represented the United States on the Davis and Olympic teams, and for years served the U.S. Lawn Tennis Association (USLTA). He won the Davis Cup Challenge Round doubles in 1921 with Richard Norris Williams II, and was ranked in the first ten seven times. He served on many USLTA committees, and was chairman of the constitutional rules committee, the ball committee and the intercollegiate committee. Washburn was one of the founders of the Tennis Hall of Fame, and served as director until his death.

1966

HUNT, Joseph R.
Player
Born February 17, 1917, in San Francisco, Calif; graduated from the U.S. Naval Academy; died February 2, 1944, during training in Florida at age 27.

Hunt played in the 1939 Davis Cup Challenge Round, losing in doubles with Jack Kramer. In 1936 he was ranked ninth, fifth in 1937 and 1938 and first in 1943. He was the champion in 1943 while a Lieutenant in the Navy. He played on a brief leave after serving as a deck officer in the Atlantic theater of war before starting training as a flyer pilot.

PARKER, Frank A.
Player
Born January 31, 1916, in Milwaukee, Wis.

Parker ranked in the first ten 17 consecutive years from 1933 to 1949, and was champion in 1944 and 1945 as an Army sergeant. In 1948 and 1949 he was French champion. He won the Wimbledon doubles with Richard (Poncho) Gonzales in 1949 and the U.S. doubles with Kramer in 1943. He played singles with Budge on the team that won the Davis Cup for the United States in 1937 for the first time since 1927. Parker was also a member of the team that lost the cup to Australia in 1939, and again on the winning team in 1949. He won the French men's singles 1948 and 1949 and the men's doubles in 1949. Parker turned pro in 1949. Although his shots lacked power, he had good control of the ball.
Also in: Tennis Hall of Fame, Citizens Hall of Fame Athletic Museum.

PELL, Theodore Roosevelt
Player
Born 1878 in Sands Point, Long Island, N.Y; died in 1967 at age 89.

Pell ranked in the first ten five times from 1910 to 1918, and was the national indoor champion three times. He was famous for his backhand.

SCHROEDER, Frederick R, Jr. "Ted"
Player
Born July 20, 1921, in Newark, N.J.

Schroeder, known for his Popeye corn-cob pipe, was the national champion in 1942. He won at Wimbledon in 1949 in his first and only attempt despite being match point down in the quarter-finals against Sedgman. He took the U.S. doubles title with Kramer 1940, 1941 and 1947, and was a member of the winning Davis Cup team 1946–1949. In 1950 and 1951 Ted was on the Davis Cup teams that lost to Australia. He ranked in the first ten eight times. He won the U.S. mixed doubles in 1942.
Also in: Tennis Hall of Fame, Citizens Savings Hall of Fame Athletic Museum.

1967

CLAPP, Louise Brough
Player
Born March 11, 1923 in Oklahoma City, Okla.

Clapp was the national singles champion in 1947 and Wimbledon champion 1948–1950 and 1955, winning all the events at Wimbledon in 1950. She won one singles match in the 1946 and 1954 Wightman Cup play, and two singles 1947, 1948, 1950, 1955 and 1956. She won many doubles victories with DuPont, and won the 1952 and 1953 Wightman Cup doubles with Maureen Connolly, and in 1956 with Shirley Fry. She was ranked in the first ten 16 times: tenth in 1941; second 1942, 1943, 1948, 1949, 1954, and 1957; third in 1944, 1946, 1950, 1955 and 1956; first in 1947; fourth in 1945, 1952 and 1953. She took the Australian women's singles and doubles in 1950, and the French women's doubles in 1946, 1947 and 1949. Clapp has an extremely effective volley, and her partnership with DuPont made one of the greatest women's doubles teams of all time.
Also in: Tennis Hall of Fame, Citizens Savings Hall of Fame Athletic Museum.

DuPONT, Margaret Osborne
Player
Born March 4, 1918, in Joseph, Ore.

DuPont was the national champion 1948–1950, and won the national doubles title with Clapp twelve times 1942–1950 and 1955–1957, and with Palfrey in 1941. She took the Wimbledon championship in 1947, the doubles with Clapp in 1946, 1947, 1949, and 1954. She won the French doubles and singles in 1946 and 1949. DuPont took the Wightman Cup singles in 1946 and 1950, and the doubles with Clapp 1946–1948, 1950, 1954, 1955, and 1957, and with Margaret Varner 1961 and 1962. She was ranked in the first ten 14 times; seventh in 1938, fourth in 1941 and 1956, third in 1942 and 1945, fourth in 1943, second in 1944, 1946 and 1947, first in 1948–1950, and fifth in 1953 and 1958. Like her doubles partner Louise Brough, DuPont was an exponent of serve-and-volley technique. Their achievements were somewhat parallel: DuPont won Wimbledon in 1947 only, and Brough won it the next three years; Brough's Forest Hills victory in 1947 was followed by victories the next three years by DuPont. They met at the 1949 Wimbledon tournament, and Brough won 10–8, 1–6, 10–8 after one of the finest title matches ever staged. Even more outstanding were the 1948 U.S. finals when DuPont beat Brough 4–6, 6–4, 15–13. DuPont is now vice president of the Southwest Tennis Association for El Paso, and writes a weekly newspaper column.
Also in: Tennis Hall of Fame, Citizens Savings Hall of Fame Athletic Museum.

RIGGS, Robert Lorimer
Player
Born February 25, 1918, in Los Angeles, Calif.

Riggs won the U.S. championship 1939 and 1941. He won all three events at Wimbledon in 1939, the last year the tournament was held before the war forced its cancellation until 1946. Riggs was also doubles champion at Wimbledon with Elwood Cooke, and backed himself with a bookmaker to win all the Wimbledon events. In 1935 he was a member of the victorious Davis Cup team with Donald Budge, defeating Adrian Quist and losing to John Bromwich. In 1939 he defeated Bromwich and lost to Quist as the United States lost the cup. He was ranked fourth in 1936, second in 1937, 1938 and 1940, and first 1939 and 1941. His tennis career was interrupted by W.W. II, and after the war he played as a pro. He is remembered for his well-publicized matches in 1973 with Margaret Court, won 6–2, 6–1 and Billie Jean King, lost 4–6, 3–6, 3–6.
Also in: Tennis Hall of Fame, Citizens Savings Hall of Fame Athletic Museum.

TALBERT, William F.
Player
Born September 4, 1918, in Cinncinnati, Ohio.

Talbert won the national doubles title with Gardner Mulloy 1942, 1945, 1946 and 1948, and in 1950 he was the French doubles champion with Tony Trabert. He won the Davis Cup Challenge Round doubles match with Mulloy in 1948 against Australia, and was captain of the Davis Cup team 1953–1957. He was ranked in the first ten thirteen times, tenth in 1941, fifth in 1942, 1947, 1950 and 1951, fourth in 1943 and 1948, second in 1944 and 1945, third in 1949, sixth in 1946 and 1952, and ninth in 1954. He won the U.S. mixed doubles 1943–1946, and the French men's doubles in 1950.

1968

BRINKER, Maureen Connolly "Little Mo"
Player
Born September 17, 1934, in San Diego, Calif; Associated Press Woman of the Year 1951; died June 21, 1969, at age 35.

Connolly won the U.S. championship in 1951 at age 17 and took Wimbledon the following year, the youngest American since May Sutton in 1905. Before age 20 she had won the United States and Wimbledon titles three times. In 1953 she was the first woman ever to score a Grand Slam in winning the championship of the United

States, England, France and Australia, and from 1951 to 1954 she played on the winning Wightman Cup teams, winning all of her nine singles and doubles matches. Little Mo was a baseline player, with an overwhelmingly strong backhand. In July, 1954, she broke her leg while horseback riding, ending her tennis career. She otherwise might have broken the marks of Helen Wills Roark.
Also in: Tennis Hall of Fame, Citizens Savings Hall of Fame Athletic Museum.

DANZIG, Allison
Contributor
Born February 27, 1898; graduated from Cornell Univ.

Danzig was inducted into the Hall of Fame at a testimonial dinner given by the Cornell Club of New York at the Hotel Biltmore. He retired from the *New York Times* after 45 years of writing on lawn tennis, court tennis, football and rowing. Besides newspaper reporting, he is the author of several articles on tennis and many books.
Also in: Rowing Hall of Fame, Citizens Savings Hall of Fame Athletic Museum.

GONZALEZ, Richard A. "Pancho"
Player
Born May 9, 1928, in Los Angeles, Calif.

Gonzalez has an exceedingly strong serve as well as excellent footwork. In his second year of competition on grass, he won the U.S. championship in 1948 at age 20. He had been ranked 17 in 1947, and was seeded eighth in the tournament. He took the U.S. singles again in 1949, and won both his matches in the Davis Cup Challenge Round against Australia. Pancho took both the Wimbledon men's doubles and the U.S. men's doubles in 1949. In October of 1949 he turned pro, and was easily the best player until his years and Ken Rosewall caught up with him in the early 1960s. Gonzalez may possibly be the greatest player of all time, but it is difficult to assess, since he turned pro before making his strongest mark in the traditional events of the game. He can only be compared to Tilden. In 1969, at age 41, Pancho won a 112-game record singles against Pasarell, and he had a contract as a pro 1971 and 1972.
Also in: Tennis Hall of Fame, Citizens Savings Hall of Fame Athletic Museum.

KRAMER, John Albert
Player
Born August 5, 1921, in Las Vegas, Nev.

Kramer was a world champion as an amateur and as a pro and was a successful promoter of professional tennis. He was the champion of the United States 1946 and 1947, and of Wimbledon in 1947. An exponent of the serve-and-volley game that led to United States domination after W.W. II, he was the head of the team that scored overwhelming victories over Australia in the Davis Cup Challenge Round in 1946 and 1947. He won his two singles matches each year, won the doubles with Ted Schroeder in 1940 and 1941 and in 1947 and 1943 with Frank Parker. In 1947 he won the Wimbledon doubles with Bob Falkenberg. He was ranked in the first ten five times, and was Number One 1946 and 1947. But for a blistered hand, he would have won the 1946 Wimbledon; his victory in 1947, with the loss of 37 games in seven matches, was the most one-sided win of all time. Kramer created the concept of "percentage" lawn tennis, playing a shot with the greatest chance of success.
Also in: Tennis Hall of Fame, Citizens Savings Hall of Fame Athletic Museum.

SEARS, Eleonora R.
Player
Born in 1881; a socialite and the favorite dancing partner of Edward, Prince of Wales; spent her life breaking down the barriers to women in sports; was a champion in squash and one of the first women to play the game; she was also a hiker, famous for her 50-mile walks from Boston to Providence, and one of the first women to fly a plane, drive a car or ride a horse astride; she was also interested in steeplechasing, trapshooting, baseball, hockey, golf, polo, sailing and football; she swam 4½ miles against a strong current, and at age 72, competed in the U.S. Senior Women's squash championships; died July 9, 1967, at age 86.

Eleonora Sears took the U.S. doubles championship in 1911 and 1915 with Hazel Hotchkiss, and in 1916 and 1917 with Molla Mallory. She also won the mixed doubles in 1916.

1969

BEHR, Karl H.
Player
Born May 30, 1885; died October 15, 1949, at age 64.

Between 1906 and 1915, Behr ranked in the first ten seven times, and in 1907, he went to England with Beals Wright as part of the U.S. Davis Cup team to play Australia. After Brookes defeated Wright, Behr lost to Wilding, although leading two sets to one. In doubles, Behr and Wright beat Brookes and Wilding. In 1907 Behr scored several victories over William Larned, who won the national championship seven times.

GARLAND, Charles S.
Player
Born October 29, 1898; died January 28, 1971, at age 73.

Garland was on the Davis Cup team when the United States won back the trophy from Australia and began its seven-year winning streak. He was ranked in the first ten in 1918, 1919 and 1920. In 1920 he won the Wimbledon men's doubles with Richard Norris, defeating Bill Tilden and Bill Johnston in the semifinals. An officer of the U.S. Lawn Tennis Association, he was the secretary of the Davis Cup committee 1921 and 1922, and vice president 1942 and 1943.

HART, Doris
Player
Born June 20, 1925, in St. Louis, Mo.

Hart was the U.S. champion in 1954 and 1955, and took the U.S. doubles title 1951–1954 with Shirley Fry. She won the Wimbledon doubles with Patricia Canning Todd in 1947, and 1951–1953 with Shirley Fry. From 1946 to 1955 she was a member of the Wightman Cup team, and lost only one match in ten years. Hart ranked in the first ten twelve times, first two times, second four times, and third three times. Hart took up tennis at age six as an exercise for an illness that threatened to cripple her. In 1951 she was the triple Wimbledon champion, and she

only lost a set in mixed doubles. In 1955 she became a coaching pro.
Also in: Tennis Hall of Fame, Citizens Savings Hall of Fame Athletic Museum.

LARSEN, Arthur
Player
Born April 6, 1925, in San Leandro, Calif.

Larsen was the U.S. champion in 1950, and ranked in the top men players eight times between 1949 and 1956. His tennis career came to an end as a result of an accident on his motorscooter. A left-hander, he was one of the finest volleyers in the United States.

WAGNER, Marie
Player
Born February 3, 1883, in New York; died March 30, 1975, in Freeport, N.Y.

Wagner was one of the best known figures in tennis in the New York area for nearly half a century, both as a player and a committee member. She took the U.S. indoor title six times between 1908 and 1917, and between 1913 and 1922 ranked in the top ten of women players eight times. She won the U.S. doubles title four times and, as a leader of the Seventh Regiment Tennis Club and East Lawn Tennis Association, she organized the Junior Wightman Cup matches in the New York area in 1939. She won over 600 trophies, most of which she put back into competition.

1970

GRIFFEN, Clarence J. "Peck"
Player
Born January 10, 1888, in San Francisco, Calif; died March 24, 1973, in Santa Barbara, Calif, at age 85.

Griffen was the U.S. doubles champion 1915, 1916 and 1920 with Johnston. His brothers Elmer and Mervyn were also tennis players of note. He was the U.S. Clay Court champion in 1914, and the doubles champion with John Strachan. In 1915 he ranked seventh, sixth in 1916 and 1920, and tenth in 1924.

IRVIN, Shirley Fry
Player
Born June 30, 1927, in Akron, Ohio.

Irvin won the championships of the United States and England in 1956, and the French title in 1951. She took the U.S. doubles with Doris Hart 1951 – 1954, and Wimbledon doubles 1951 – 1953. She won the French doubles 1950 – 1953, and was a member of the Wightman Cup team every year between 1949 and 1956 except 1950. Between 1944 and 1956, she was ranked in the top ten: first in 1956, second in 1955, third in 1951 – 1953.
Also in: Tennis Hall of Fame, Citizens Savings Hall of Fame Athletic Museum.

JONES, Perry T.
Contributor
Born June 22, 1890; Samuel Hardy Award 1955; died September 18, 1970, at age 80.

Jones was the Davis Cup captain 1958 and 1959, and the director of the Pacific Southwest championships for many years at the Los Angeles Tennis Club. He was well known for his contributions to the development of junior tennis in Southern California. He helped in fund raising and convincing ranking players to contribute, and set up clinics for instruction. Jones also was president of the Southern California Tennis Association for more than 25 years.
Also in: Tennis Hall of Fame, Citizens Savings Hall of Fame Athletic Museum.

TRABERT, Marion "Tony"
Player
Born August 16, 1930, in Cincinnati, Ohio.

Trabert won the U.S. championships in 1953 and 1955, the last United States player until Ashe in 1968. He took Wimbledon in 1955, and was the champion of France 1954 and 1955. From 1951 to 1955 he was on the Davis Cup team, and he took the U.S. doubles with Victor Seixas in 1954. He took the French and Italian doubles with William Talbert in 1950. Tony ranked first in the United States in 1953 and 1955, second in 1954, and third in 1951. He was in the Navy in 1952, and he became a pro in 1955. A superb player with a strong backhand, he has most recently been involved in tennis as a TV announcer and commentator.
Also in: Tennis Hall of Fame, Citizens Savings Hall of Fame Athletic Museum.

1971

DARBEN, Althea Gibson
Player
Born August 25, 1927, in Silver, S.C.

She won both the U.S. and Wimbledon championships in 1957 and 1958, the first black player to be crowned. In 1957 and 1958 she was a member of the Wightman Cup team and from 1952 to 1958 she was ranked in the first ten six times, including Number One in 1957 and 1958. She was almost 30 when she won her first Wimbledon singles, and became a pro in 1958.
Also in: Tennis Hall of Fame, Citizens Savings Hall of Fame Athletic Museum.

MOORE, Elizabeth H.
Player
Born in 1877; died January 22, 1959, in Melrose, Fla, at age 82.

Moore won the U.S. Lawn Tennis Association women's singles in 1896, 1901, 1903 and 1905 and the doubles with Juliette P. Atkinson in 1896, and with Carrie B. Neely in 1903. In 1902 and 1904 she won the national mixed doubles with Wylie C. Grant, and in 1901 the All-Comers match against Marion Jones.
Also in: Tennis Hall of Fame, Citizens Savings Hall of Fame Athletic Museum.

NIELSEN, Arthur C.
Contributor
Born January 2, 1894, in Northbrook, Ill; chairman of A.C. Nielsen Co, a marketing research corporation.

Nielsen was captain of the University of Wisconsin tennis team from 1916 to 1918, and in 1946 and 1948 won the U.S. father-and-son championship with Arthur C. Nielsen, Jr, co-captain of the Wisconsin team in 1941.

Nielsen and his wife gave a four-court indoor tennis facility to the Park District in the village of Winnetka, Ill, and in 1966, more than a million dollars to the University of Wisconsin for the construction of a building for tennis and squash courts. His total gifts exceed $3 million.

SEIXAS, Elias Victor
Player
Born August 30, 1923 in Philadelphia, Pa.

Seixas won the U.S. championship in 1954, and in 1952 won the national doubles with Mervyn Rose of Australia and with Trabert in 1954. In 1953 he was Wimbledon champion and won the French and Australian doubles titles with Trabert. From 1951 to 1957 he was on the U.S. Davis Cup team. Seixas was ranked in the first ten twelve times between 1948 and 1966; Number One in 1951, 1954, and 1957. He was famous for his attacking topspin lob.
Also in: Tennis Hall of Fame, Citizens Savings Hall of Fame Athletic Museum.

1972

GRANT, Bryan M, Jr. "Bitsy"
Player

Grant defeated Budge in 1935 in the U.S. championships at Forest Hills in the fifth round, and in 1933 defeated Vines in the fourth round. In 1935 he won both matches against China and Mexico, and against Mexico in 1936. He was the U.S. Clay Court champion in 1930, 1934 and 1935, and the Eastern grass court champion in 1935. In 1930 he was ranked ten nationally, seven in 1933, ten in 1934, three in 1935 and 1936, four in 1937, six in 1938, seven in 1939 and eight in 1941.

MULLOY, Gardner
Player
Born November 22, 1914, in Miami, Fla; graduated from Univ. Miami Law School, and is a practicing attorney.

Mulloy was the Number One tennis player in the United States in singles and doubles, the winner of 43 national tennis championships, more than any man in history. He played on seven U.S. Davis Cup teams, with such distinguished teammates as Kramer, Gonzalez, Parker and Talbert. He was the Davis Cup captain twice. At age 44 he was the Wimbledon, Europe, and World Doubles champion with Budge Patty. Mulloy and Talbert retired the National Challenge Cup, winning more U.S. men's doubles championships than any other team in history. He is now director of tennis at the Fountainebleau Hotel in Miami Beach, where he coaches young players.

RYAN, Elizabeth
Player
Born February 5, 1892, in Santa Monica, Calif; now lives in London, England.

Ryan was the foremost woman doubles player, taking Wimbledon doubles twelve times, six times with Lenglen and two times with Wills, and the mixed doubles seven times. She had an excellent volley and a strong chop stroke. Although she never took a U.S. or British championship, she was probably the best player who failed to. In her 19 years of playing, 1912–1934, she won at least 659 tournament events, including the last women's championship of Imperial Russia in 1914.
Also in: Tennis Hall of Fame, Citizens Savings Hall of Fame Athletic Museum.

1973

HARD, Darlene R.
Player
Born January 6, 1936, in Los Angeles, Calif.

Hard was the U.S. champion in 1960 and 1961, the U.S. doubles champion five times, and the Wimbledon doubles champion four times. In 1957, 1959, 1960, 1962 and 1963, she was on the Wightman Cup team against the British. Between 1954 and 1963 she was ranked in the first ten; four times Number One.
Also in: Tennis Hall of Fame, Citizens Savings Hall of Fame Athletic Museum.

MAKO, Gene
Player
Born January 24, 1916, in Budapest, Hungary.

Mako, with his partner J. Donald Budge, won the U.S. doubles in 1936 and 1938 and the Wimbledon title in 1937 and 1938. In 1937 they defeated the Germans in the interzone Davis Cup doubles, and beat the British in the Challenge Round. He was ranked Number Eight in the United States in 1937 and Number Three in 1938. Mako lived in California most of his life, where he is now in tennis court construction.
Also in: Tennis Hall of Fame, Citizens Savings Hall of Fame Athletic Museum.

MARTIN, Alastair
Contributor
Born in Katonah, N.Y.

Martin was the president of the U.S. Lawn Tennis Association (USLTA) during 1969 and 1970 and vice president in 1967–1968 under Robert J. Kelleher. Martin supported Kelleher and the British in their revolt, which led to the sanctioning of open tournaments in 1968. In 1951 he founded the East Tennis Patrons Association, and since his retirement as head of the USLTA, has served as president of the National Tennis Foundation. Martin was also one of the greatest court tennis players in the United States, the game from which lawn tennis stemmed, winning the amateur court tennis title eight times.

1974

ATKINSON, Juliette
Player
Born in Brooklyn, N.Y.

Atkinson was the U.S. women's singles champion in 1895, 1897 and 1898, and the doubles champion 1894–1898, 1901 and 1902. In 1895 she was the most outstanding athlete in North America, and in 1897 and 1898 she won practically all of the championship titles throughout the country.
Also in: Tennis Hall of Fame, Citizens Savings Hall of Fame Athletic Museum.

FALKENBURG, Robert
Player
Born January 29, 1926, in Los Angeles, Calif.

Falkenburg won the singles championship at Wimbledon over Bromwich, and in 1944, the U.S. doubles championship with Don McNeill. In 1954–1955 he represented Brazil in the Davis Cup matches, winning three singles and one double.

HOVEY, Fred H.
Player
Born October 7, 1868, in Boston, Mass; died October 18, 1945, at age 77.

Hovey was the U.S. men's singles champion in 1895, and his matches with Bob Wrenn in the 1890s are remembered as volleying duels. He won the national doubles championships with Clarence Hobart in 1893 and 1894, and the World's Championship at the World's Fair in Chicago in 1895.

TOULMIN, Bertha Townsend
Player
Born March 7, 1869, in Philadelphia, Pa; died May 12, 1909, in Haverford, Pa, at age 40.

Toulmin won the national women's championships first held at the Philadelphia Cricket Club in 1887, and also in 1888 and 1889. A left-hander, she is credited with inventing the backhand. In the early days of tennis, the ball was patted to the right side of the player; since she was left-handed, she hit with the backhand.

1975

BAKER, Lawrence A.
Contributor
Baker is a founder of the National Tennis Foundation, and has held every office in the U.S. Lawn Tennis Association, including president. He was captain of several Davis Cup teams, and staged a number of American Zone Davis Cup ties at the Chevy Chase Club in Maryland. He sponsored the Baker Cup for senior matches between the United States and Canada, and in 1937, won the National senior doubles championship with John McKay.

PERRY, Frederick John
Player
Born May 18, 1909, in Stockport, Cheshire, England.

Possibly the greatest British male player of all time and certainly the best match player, Perry was the first man to be champion of Australia, France, Wimbledon and the United States, though not in the same year. He won in the Wimbledon singles 1934–1936, mixed doubles 1935 and 1936, and was runnerup in the men's doubles in 1932. In the U.S. men's singles he won in 1933, 1934, and 1936 and won the mixed doubles in 1932. In the Australian men's singles he won in 1934 and also won the doubles in 1934. Fred won the singles in France in 1935, the doubles in 1933 and the mixed doubles in 1932. He was on the Davis Cup team 1931–1936 where he was the main architect of the British success 1933–1936; he won 45 out of his 52 rubbers, an 86 percent success unequaled by any who played 50 or more rubbers. Perry became a pro in 1936 and had famous prewar clashes with Vines and Budge.

ROOSEVELT, Ellen
Player
Born in Albany, N.Y.

Roosevelt was the U.S. women's singles champion in 1890, and the U.S. doubles champion with her sister Grace W. Roosevelt the same year (the first women's doubles championship of the United States). In 1893 she won the mixed doubles. She was the third in line of the pioneer U.S. women's singles champions.

1976

BOROTRA, Jean "Bounding Basque"
Player
Born August 13, 1898, in Arbonne Basses-Pyrenees, France.

Borotra won Wimbledon in 1924 and 1926, and was a triple winner of the Wimbledon doubles crown. In 1925 with Suzanne Lenglen, he took the mixed doubles, and in 1926 was the U.S. singles finalist. He was the U.S. indoor champion three times, and in 1928 went to Australia and won the Down Under title in singles, doubles and mixed. His superb volleying and daring forecourt play, plus his Basque origin, earned him his nickname. Although not rated as high as Lacoste and Cochet, he could, at his best, beat any player. One of the Four Musketeers, he was an excellent example of physical fitness, still playing good tennis at age 74.

BRUGNON, Jacques "Toto"
Player
Born May 11, 1895, in Paris, France.

Brugnon won the French doubles championship six times with three different partners, was a Wimbledon doubles winner two times with Cochet, 1926 and 1928, and two times with Borotra, 1932 and 1933. He won the Australian doubles with Borotra in 1928, and played in the Davis Cup final rounds for six years. One of the Four Musketeers, he was one of the greatest doubles players.

CAHILL, Mabel
Player
Cahill won the U.S. women's singles title 1891 and 1892, and women's doubles 1891 and 1892. She also won the mixed doubles in 1892. An Irish gentlewoman, she gained fame in the United States for her game, but returned to Ireland and lost touch with U.S. tennis.

COCHET, Henri
Player
Born December 14, 1901, in Lyons, France.

Cochet ended Tilden's six-year reign as U.S. champion in the 1926 quarter-finals, but did not win the American title until 1928. He won at Wimbledon in 1927, beating Tilden in the semifinals, and won again in 1929. He took the French crown in 1922, 1926, 1928, 1930 and 1932. In 1928 he led the French to victory in the first Davis Cup Challenge Round to be played on French soil, after Tilden beat Lacoste in the opening match. One of the Four Musketeers, he became a pro in 1933, but was reinstated as an amateur in 1945.

LACOSTE, Jean-Rene
Player
Born July 2, 1905, in Paris, France.

Lacoste was known as "The Crocodile" due to his inscrutable and never-changing expression. He won the U.S. championships in 1926 and 1927, the first foreign player to win it twice. He took Wimbledon in 1925 and 1928, and won the French crown in 1925, 1927 and 1929. He retired from tennis due to ill health at age 25. He played on the Davis Cup team 1923–1928, and was one of the Four Musketeers. An extremely studious player, he kept notebooks in which he noted the strengths and weaknesses of his opponents.

SAVITT, Richard
Player
Born March 4, 1927, in Bayonne, N.J.

Savitt won the Wimbledon title in 1951, as well as the Australian and Italian doubles. In 1952, 1958 and 1961 he was the U.S. indoor singles champion, and was on the Davis Cup team in 1951. He was well known for his rolled backhand.

Tennis Halls of Fame to Watch

BADMINTON HALL OF FAME
Incorporated into an Existing Hall of Fame 1975

Originally maintained by the United States Badminton Association, which was founded in 1937 as the American Badminton Association, this hall of fame was transferred in its entirety from its location in San Diego to the Citizens Savings Hall of Fame Athletic Museum in Los Angeles, where its memorabilia may be seen today. *See* the Citizens Savings Hall of Fame Athletic Museum sketch in the present volume.

NATIONAL SQUASH TENNIS ASSOCIATION HALL OF FAME
Proposed 1976

The National Squash Tennis Association (NSTA), founded in 1910, consists of a small but well-organized group of business and professional men whose aim is to promote the sport of squash tennis on a national basis. Consistent with this aim is their plan for a hall of fame for past great champions of the sport. Anyone supportively interested in such a hall of fame should contact William Rubin, NSTA Exec Secy, 15 W. 43 St, Box 14, New York, NY 10036. (212) 544-7440.

TRACK AND FIELD

Prizes in modern track and field events are normally ribbons, medals or trophies. Because of the relatively recent innovation of recognizing second, third and other positions (for centuries, only the winner was recognized), groups of such prizes are given to a number of athletes in any official event. Money, though sometimes given, is frowned upon as a prize, particularly by the International Olympic Committee which has established a $50 limit on the value of a prize acceptable without question. Fame, glory and other such intangible rewards are also received by modern track and field champions, of course. And world record breakers and holders are always among the world's most widely honored athletes.

The art of making medals did not begin until 1438, eight years before Columbus was born. But all of those other prizes and rewards were received by ancient track and field first place winners. At certain Greek games, ribbons were bound around the winner's shoulder or head. There literally was no limit to the amount of money an ancient Olympic winner might receive in addition to lifelong tax exemption, free meals and free seats at all public festivals. Trophies received included inscribed bronze or silver bowls. One of these which has survived reads: "I was a prize at the Games of Onomastus." Sometimes three-legged cauldrons were presented, as were elegant stools and tables. At other events the prizes would include rich cloaks, women, and athletic or military equipment such as shields, discuses, helmets or bows and arrows. Some winners were given up to 140 tall, two handled jars called *amphorae* filled with expensive olive oil. Ritual ox hides served as prizes, as did human or animal victims. The latter might be preblessed—already sacrificed and blessed by temple priests—or they might be alive, in which case the athlete had the honor of sacrificing them himself at the temple.

More meaningful, perhaps, was the hero's welcome given an athletic winner, especially an Olympic one, by his city. Often the walls would be partially destroyed to allow his entry and to show that with him there the city needed no walls for protection. Odes and hymns of victory would be composed in his honor, a street might be renamed for him, statues of him would be sculpted and displayed and, in rare cases, he would approach god status during or after his lifetime by being made an object of worship. The right to fight beside the king in battle was another cherished honor, as was immediate release without ransom if captured. After the Battle of Issus, for example, Alexander the Great, immediately released a prisoner, Dionysodorus, on learning that he had once been an Olympic victor. One prize sometimes awarded might not be welcomed by modern track and field champions: induction into a special priesthood for a life of ritual service and complete chastity.

The award prized above all of these things, however, was the one of least value, a clump, branch or crown of vegetable matter. At the Pythian Games at Delphi, a laurel wreath was given, sometimes with a golden sickle; at Isthmia, during the Isthmian Games, the wreath given was made of dried celery; at the Nemean Games held in Nemea either a wreath of oak or a crown of parsley was awarded; and palm branches were given at certain track and field festivals. The most prestigious of these crowns was, of course, that given at Olympia—the wild olive wreath. The branches that composed each of these had to be cut with a golden sickle from a certain wild olive tree called the *kotinos* by a boy whose parents were both Greek and both living.

Cheating in those days was worse than losing. Anyone who violated the Olympic code had to erect a memorial to his shame. These memorials, called *zanes*, had to be inscribed with both the offender's name and the nature of his offense and erected at the base of Mt. Kronius, a very sacred spot. Incredibly, in nearly 1200 years of Olympic Games, only 13 *zanes* were ever erected. Killing an opponent, interestingly, was not necessarily considered cheating. (*See* Wrestling, for a few examples.)

Few athletes die in major track and field competitions now, but such was not the case back then. Three athletics-related deaths should be mentioned here—two had little or no effect on track and field events, the third one did. First, Chilon, one of the Seven Sages of Sparta, died in the stadium after embracing his son, who had won the boxing crown. About a decade later, at the Games of the fifty-eighth Olympiad in 548 B.C., the 90-year-old Thales, the first man to give a systematic, scientific explanation of the universe, died of heat and thirst there at Olympia. Exactly one hundred years later Diagoras of Rhodes, himself a six-time Olympic winner and the greatest of all Greek Olympic boxers, watched his two sons win a total of four olive-branch crowns at Olympia. Friends told him that he had better die, as the only greater honor was divinity. That night Diagoras entertained 5000 guests at a banquet in honor of his sons and that same night died in his sleep. The following day, there was a great celebration at Olympia for the man who could die such a beautiful death.

Diagoras, in fact, founded an Olympic dynasty, the Diagoridae—his direct descendants won 49 more Olympic crowns. Another of his direct descendants, Pherenike, started a more significant trend on her own: athletic nudity. While she and her husband were training their son, Pisidores, for the upcoming Games, her husband died. She continued the training on her own. During the Games, she disguised herself as a male trainer in order to watch. The standing rule was that no women could watch the Games except for one special priestess, and that any caught within the proscribed mile of the stadium would be hurled off a high place nearby called the Typaeum Rock. When Pisidores won his event, Pherenike rushed to congratulate him and was revealed to be a woman. She was not killed because she was one of the Diagoridae—in fact, the mother, sister, and daughter of Olympic winners. But to prevent similar mishaps a rule was passed that all athletes and trainers had to be naked while at the Games. The rule that men had to prove they were men was rephrased, interestingly enough, nearly 24 centuries later in the 1966 rule that required women competitors in major international tournaments to undergo a test to prove that they were, in fact, women. Athletic nudity was not, however, contrary to Greek custom. Our word gymnastics comes from their word *gymnos*, naked. Since earlier Spartan times, soldiers had frequently fought naked, and in the Hera Games that were for women only, virgins in three age groups competed in 160 meter sprints with their skirts above their knees and their right breasts exposed. So the nudity rule was accepted and continued for centuries. It was not, however, appreciated by the later Romans. Cicero, for example, the Roman orator and politician who has been called the "most civilized man who ever lived," wrote that "To strip in public is the beginning of evil-doing."

Naked or not, ancient track and field athletes used immense quantities of olive oil and powder. Greeks were especially addicted to oiling themselves before any exercise or physical competition and even before and after bathing. This was to keep dirt out of their pores and to either retain or disperse body heat. After oiling, athletes in certain events, especially wrestling, would dust themselves or each other with special powders of various colors and consistencies. A reddish one was used to produce perspiration, a blackish one to warm the skin, a yellowish one to make the body more supple and the skin more sleek and glossy. Such powders and oils were a major concern for the ancient athlete. Vast quantities of both were imported from all over the known world. Various economies depended upon their possession of the natural resources from which the oils and powders were produced. So important were the latter considered that when an earthquake in 224 B.C. devastated the island of Rhodes and toppled its famed Colossus statue (one of the Seven Wonders of the Ancient World), Sicily sent 100 talents of silver, of which 75 were specified for the purchase of olive oil for use in the island's rebuilt gymnasia. The emperor Nero was unpopular because during a food shortage, he ordered ships from Alexandria to bring tons of powder for his court wrestlers instead of food for the people. After exercising or competing, the ancient track and field athlete would scrape the oil, powder, dust and sweat from himself with a bronze or iron strigil, an instrument designed especially for that purpose. He might then listen to music, which was believed to have healing qualities. We reflect the same belief in our tonic, which derived from tone. He would then get dressed and go home.

Beyond the ways already mentioned, Greek games, including their Olympics, differed from modern ones in their program of events. The first official Olympic Games were held in 776 B.C. For the next 52 years the only event was the *stade* (from which we get the word stadium), a sprint of about 200 yards. In 724 B.C. the *diaulos* or double sprint was added—down the stadium and straight back. The runners had to make abrupt turns the way modern swimmers do. Later a three-mile run was added, as was a hoplite race for men wearing armor. These were followed by the pentathlon (sprint, long jump, javelin, discus, wrestling), boxing, chariot racing (*see* Horse Racing and Breeding) and the *pankration* (*see* Wrestling). Additionally, at times during the 1200 years of Olympic Games there were events for painting, music, poetry, drama, recitation, beauty (men, boys and, rarely, women), drinking, staying awake and kissing. Although much kissing occurs at modern Olympic Games (winners sometimes seem to kiss everyone), kissing has never been an official modern event; neither has beauty. The Canadian high jump champion Ethel Catherwood did receive a beauty prize at the 1928 Olympics, but it was awarded to her by a *New York Times* correspondent. Other nonathletic events have been included, however. From the Games in Stockhom in 1912 to those in London in 1948, medals were given in architecture, music, literature, painting, sculpture, sports, stamp collecting, sports photography and other such events. The founder of the modern Olympics, the Baron Pierre de Coubertin, entered an essay under a pseudonym, for which he won a gold medal.

One of the most striking differences between track and field now and then is that records were never kept in ancient times. This was not merely due to a lack of measuring devices. Value was placed upon simply defeating everyone else in a given competition. Whereas today we have world champions and world record holders, the ancient world did not. The closest thing to such a title was *Periodonikes*, awarded to those who had won events in all four of the major games at Olympia, Delphi, Corinth and Nemea. In all of history there were only 46 winners of that title.

Equipment, of course, differed widely from that we see today. In ancient smelting, the molten metal was poured into a circular mold that had been hollowed out in the sand. The resulting ingot, flat on the top and curved like a bowl on the bottom, was the original discus. Javelins were war spears thrown for distance in some events but more often thrown at a hollow ring for accuracy. They were always thrown with the aid of a thong looped over the fingers of the throwing hand to give the javelin spin in flight. In the long jump event, the competitor held two stone or metal weights, called *haltares*. These weights, which were also used as dumbbells by the Greeks and the Romans for exercising, allowed tremendous jumps. Only two are recorded: one of 52 feet, the other of 55. In relays, lit torches which had to stay lit were passed. To level the sand on the stadium track, they used heavy, long-handled rollers similar to ones sometimes used today. Races were markedly different in three ways. Turns were abrupt, often around a post. How beautifully a runner ran was as important as how fast he ran—grace, rhythm and speed were what counted. The third difference was the use of the *husplex* in starts. A *husplex*, built for from 8 to 20 starters, was in fact a starting gate similar to that used in horse or greyhound racing today. A cord ran from the bar in front of each runner through a staple in the ground, then along grooves in the ground to the starter's pit located behind the runners so that they could not see him. At a given signal, the starter would release the cords simultaneously, the bars would fall into recesses in each starting gate and the runners would dash out. The *husplex* invariably prevented false starts and recalled races even though they were more complicated than today's starting blocks. Interestingly enough, modern starting blocks were not invented until 1927 and not officially recognized until much later. Jesse Owens set his many world records in 1936 starting out of holes dug for each foot.

Perhaps the most significant difference between track and field then and now, however, is between the respective terms of eligibility. Today athletes may compete, in most cases, if they are amateurs excellent enough in one or more events to win. To compete in the old Olympics, however, and in fact in any of the major Greek games, certain oaths were required. Each man had to swear that he had not neglected to pay any legal or religious fines, that he had not committed manslaughter within any of the sacred territories (to do so outside these territories was allowed under certain circumstances), and most importantly, that he was of pure Greek parentage on both sides of his family. Then, as now, track and field athletes were required to submit their names for inclusion in an event before a fixed date or face disqualification. When the Olympic competitors had entered their names and sworn to their own eligibility, they gathered before a huge statue of Zeus. There a pig was sacrificed. On its entrails they swore not to cheat.

FORMS: Track and field is counted as a single sport on the International Olympic Committee's list of possible Olympic sports although there must be at least 15 different track and field events at each Game. These fall into three broad categories: running, jumping and throwing. Although many of the events in those categories are distinct enough and well developed enough to be considered unique sports, they are generally considered individual forms of the sport of track and field. The running events include sprints, relays, hurdle races and middle- and long-distance races. Jumping events include high, long, triple and pole vault jumps. The throwing events include throws of the javelin, the discus, the hammer and the shot put. In addition to these numerous single events, there are the pentathlon and the decathlon, which are combinations of five and ten events respectively. Gen. George Patton was one of the United States' first pentathlon participants. A lieutenant at the time, he participated in the 1912 Olympics along with Jim Thorpe, who defeated him. In 1924 the pentathlon for men was abandoned and is today a women's event. Similarly, the decathlon is a men's event. All of the others, though their distances vary according to the participating sex, are competed in by both men and women.

Running events at major competitions are on a smooth track which may be straight or curved and may be composed of clay, cinder, crushed peat, plastic substances, or synthetic resins (notably Tartan Track, which was patented in the United States). Standard distances range from 100 meters (109.3 yds.) to 10,000 meters (6.2 mi.) to 14,946.5 meters (26 mi. 385 yds.) in the marathon race. Relay races are also run. They are four-person sprints in which each runner passes a baton to a teammate in turn. Two running events do not conform to those same distances. One is the 3000 meter (304.8 yds.) steeplechase for men, which has 28 hurdles and 7 pools of water to jump over. The second involves the various walking events at distances of from 20 to 50 km. (12.4 to 31.1 mi.), in which a competitor must have unbroken foot contact with the ground. The rear foot may not leave the ground before the advancing foot is again in contact with the ground. In all of these various forms of running events, special shoes are worn—shoes with up to six spikes for all track running events, including relays and hurdle events; flat shoes with heels not exceeding the thickness of the sole by more than 13 mm. (1½ in.) for walking events. Hurdles are constructed of metal with a wooden crossbar so that a force of from 8 lbs. to 8 lbs. 13 oz. is required to overturn them.

Jumping events at major competitions are either over a bar for height as in the high jump and pole vault or over a pit of sand for distance as in the long jump and triple jump. In the bar jumps, the crossbar may be either triangular in cross-section or round, in which case it will have square ends to fit on the uprights. In the pole vault, the pole used by the jumper to propel himself over the crossbar may be made of any material(s) and may be of any length. Although these poles typically are 16 ft. long, both longer and shorter ones are popular. Shorter ones were invariably used in the days before synthetic materials allowed the construction of highly flexible poles. George Goldie, the "Father of the Pole Vault" who died in 1920, made pole vaults of eight feet and more with a pole that today would be considered absurdly inadequate. Today an incredible vault is 18 ft. 6½ in.—the world record set by Dave Roberts of the United States in 1975. In the pit jumps, the contestant runs down a 147½ ft. long and 4 ft. wide runway to a wooden takeoff board. From there, in the long jump, the aim is for maximum distance. In the triple jump, the jumper first lands on the foot with which he or she took off (the "hop"), jumps again and lands on the other foot (the "step"), then jumps for additional distance. Because of the greater distance attained in this event, there is an additional runway area of 42 ft. (13 m.) between the takeoff board and the sand pit. The shoes worn for all of these jumping events normally have both sole and heel spikes and may have built-in plastic cups to protect the heel bones. Of all the jumps' records, that of the triple jump has perhaps increased most slowly through the years. In 1794, for example, one Mr. Hounsley, a publican, beat one Mr.

Peck, a pig-jobber, with a triple jump of 43 ft. 6 in. Almost two hundred years later, the current world record is 58 ft. 8¼ in.

While the running events are considered track, the jumping ones are considered field events. So, too, are the throwing events, which are distance throws of the javelin, the shot put, the discus and the hammer. The hammer is not a hammer at all, but a ball of any metal not softer than brass. From 4 to 4¾ in. in diameter, the ball is attached to a loop or grip, which must not have any hinging joints, by a single length of steel wire that has a diameter of ⅛ in. and a length of from 3 ft. 10¼ in. to 3 ft. 10¾ in. The whole contraption must weigh no less than 16 lbs. The latter is also the minimum weight for the men's shot which is thrown in the shot put event. The women's shot weighs roughly half as much—8 lb. 13 oz. Even it is much heavier than the discus, which for men weighs a minimum of 4 lbs. 6.6 oz. and for women a minimum of 2 lb. 3.3 oz. These three events (hammer, shot put, discus) are alike in two ways: in each the thrower throws from a cement or similarly hard circle measuring from 7 ft. to 8 ft. 2½ in. in diameter into a triangular area of field; and in each the hard surface of the circle requires that spikes not be present on the shoes worn. In terms of distance, the shot put with a world record of 71 ft. 7 in. is the shortest throw. The discus has a world record of 226 ft. 8 in. while the record for the hammer is 260 ft. 2 in. A hammer thrown 170 ft. will hit the ground at approximately 50 m.p.h. The last throwing event, the javelin, differs from the other three in that it is thrown from a runway instead of a circle, the shoes worn have two spikes on the heel and six on the sole and considerably greater distance is attained. The world record is 308 ft. 8 in. A javelin may be composed of wood, metal, a synthetic material or a combination of these, and is capped by a metal head. Men's javelins at 8 ft. 6¼ in. to 8 ft. 10¼ in. are longer than women's at 7 ft. 2½ in. to 7 ft. 6½ in.

ORGANIZATION: Track and field contests are suitable for entrants of all ages and are practiced by tens of millions in the United States and Canada. In both countries competition begins in schools through programs of interscholastic athletics established by the National Federation of State High School Associations (NFSHA). Founded in 1920, this organization today has more than 20,100 member high schools in a combined total of 50 state high school athletic associations, nine Canadian ones, and one Philippine affiliate. Although many other sports are represented within the NFSHA, a single committee supervises the numerous track and field activities.

On the next level a number of organizations oversee track and field competition. The National Junior College Athletic Association, the National Collegiate Athletic Association, the National Association of Intercollegiate Athletics, the United States Collegiate Sports Council and the United States Track and Field Federation perform this function in the United States. There are numerous Canadian counterparts, such as the Canadian Intercollegiate Athletic Union and the Canadian Track and Field Association. Within the national bodies of each country are regional and provincial organizational groups such as the Western Conference, the Southern Conference, the Eastern Athletic Conference, Sport Alberta, Sport Nova Scotia, Sport Ontario, Saskatchewan Sport, and so on. At this college level the primary organizational body is the Intercollegiate Association of Amateur Athletes of America (ICAAAA, called IC4A). It and the others perform regulatory functions for track and field programs at all types of colleges and universities. The National Alliance of Athletic Associations complements this function by providing playing rules for track and field events, as well as for numerous other athletic activities.

The third level consists of postcollege track and field. It is primarily organized and controlled by numerous athletic clubs associated with the Amateur Athletic Union (AAU), which recognizes all competitive amateur sports and registers athletes for identification and nomination in various national and international events. In Canada the same function is performed by the Canadian Amateur Athletic Union. Among its many other activities, the American AAU, with 58 regional groups and 7000 local groups, sponsors national championship competitions which serve as tryouts for the selection of Olympic competitors. Actual determination of Olympic teams, however, is performed by both the United States Olympic Committee and the Canadian Olympic Association.

At the fourth and highest level of track and field organization is the world governing body, the International Amateur Athletic Federation (IAAF), which was founded in 1912. Its purpose is to compile regulations governing competition at the international level. It accomplishes this through close cooperation with the International Olympic Committee as well as with those organizations of five or more nations which have created their own international games—the Asian Games, the European Championships, the Commonwealth Games, the Europa Cup, the Pan-African Games, the Pan-American Games and others. At the root of the IAAF's policies is its definition of the word amateur (from the French *amator*, lover): an "amateur" is "one who competes for the love of sport and as a means of recreation, without any motive of securing any material gain from such competition."

Largely due to that IAAF definition, track and field athletes who performed for remuneration formed a separate organization in 1973, the International Track Association (ITA). It bestows cash awards to those athletes who break world records and sanctions professional track and field sporting events.

Those track and field athletes which best fit the IAAF's definition of amateur are the ones represented by such organizations as the Canadian Wheelchair Sports Associations of Edmonton and Toronto, the National Wheelchair Athletic Association, the National Wheelchair Athletic Committee and other popular organizations. Since 1952 the International Stoke Mandeville Games Federation in England has held an annual Olympics for the Paralyzed every year for three years in England and every fourth year in the country in which the regular Olympic Games are held. The Federation of the Silent Sports of Canada sponsors representatives to the International Games for the Deaf. It, and the International Committee of the Silent Sports, are both recognized by the International Olympic Committee. Similarly, true amateur athletes are those in the United States Masters International Track Team whose members are dedicated track and field athletes who are 40 years old or older.

Drake Relays Hall of Fame

DES MOINES, IOWA

Mailing Address: Drake University, 50311. Tel. (515) 271-2215. *Contact:* Bob Ehrhart, Dir. of Drake Relays. *Location:* Off 235 on 42nd St. & University Ave; 90 mi. S.W. of Cedar Rapids, 132 mi. S.E. of Omaha, Nebr, 195 mi. N. of Kansas City, Mo. *Admission:* Free 8 to 4:30 daily, closed weekends and holidays. *Personnel:* Bob Ehrhart, Dir. of Drake Relays; Robert Spiegel, Chmn. of Drake Relays Hall of Fame Comt; 3-mem. Selection Comt. (Bob Erhart, Chmn.). *Nearby Halls of Fame:* Agriculture (Kansas City, Mo.), Agriculture (Bonner Springs, Mo, 210 mi. S.W.).

The Hall of Fame was introduced in 1958 by Robert Spiegel upon being asked to compose the history of the Drake Relays to be delivered at the 50th Anniversary Relays in 1959. In his outline he proposed a Hall of Fame to consist of the athlete of the half-century in Relays competition as well as an all-time Drake Relays Hall of Fame roster. The suggestion was accepted by the Relays Committee and the idea became a reality. Located in an area of the Letterman's Room at the Drake University Fieldhouse, a "wall of fame" is presently being installed that will consist of plaques with the members' names and induction dates along with pictures of the inductees.

Members: 123 as of 1976. Candidates for the Hall of Fame are selected on the basis of their performance at the Drake Relays combined with their general background and accomplishments in track and field competition. The first inductions were made in 1959 by a panel of ten veteran coaches. They made nominations for the Athlete of the Half-Century and, using that balloting as a guide,, selected a Hall of Fame track squad from Drake Relays competitors, 1910–1958. Thereafter a permanent three-member Selection Committee was appointed by the Relays Committee to select not more than three new members to the Hall of Fame annually. One member is inducted from each of three eras; an early period, the 1920s and 1930s; the middle years, late 1930s and early 1940s; and more recent years, since mid-1940s, to give balance and not overlook the earlier athletes. Another stipulation is that athletes be measured by the standards of excellence in the era in which they competed and not be later standards that could reflect better facilities, coaching, etc.

1959 ALLARD, Bernie. High Jumper. Drake Relays high jump champion in 1955.

BABKA, Rink. Discus Thrower. Voted third in discus throw in initial selections for Hall of Fame; silver medal winner in 1960 Olympics; co-holder of world discus record.

BIFFLE, Jerome. Broad Jumper. Gold medal in running broad jump in 1952 Olympics.

BLOZIS, Al (dec). Discus Thrower. See entry in Track and Field Hall of Fame, Citizens Savings Hall of Fame Athletic Museum.

BROWN, Billy. Broad Jumper. Drake Relays champion in 1939–1941.

COCHRAN, Roy B. Hurdler. See entry in Track and Field Hall of Fame, Citizens Savings Hall of Fame Athletic Museum. *Also in:* United States Track and Field Hall of Fame.

COOPER, Don. Pole Vaulter. Drake Relays champion in 1950; tied for championship in 1951.

COX, Tom. Runner. Excelled in 440-yd. dash.

CUNNINGHAM, Glenn "Kansas Ironman." Runner. See entry in Track and Field Hall of Fame, Citizens Savings Hall of Fame Athletic Museum. *Also in:* National Track and Field Hall of Fame and United States Track and Field Hall of Fame.

CUSHMAN, Cliff. Hurdler. Set new Drake and American collegiate records in 440-yd. hurdles in 1958.

DeVINNEY, Bob. Hurdler. Drake Relays champion for 440-yd. hurdles in 1952.

DILLARD, Harrison. Hurdler. See entry in National Track and Field Hall of Fame. *Also in:* National Association of Intercollegiate Athletics Hall of Fame; Track and Field Hall of Fame, Citizens Savings Hall of Fame Athletic Museum; and United States Track and Field Hall of Fame.

EDDLEMAN, Dwight. High Jumper. Tied for high jump championship at Drake Relays in 1948 and 1949.

FLOERKE, Kent. Triple Jumper. 1956 Drake Relays champion in broad jump and triple jump.

FONVILLE, Charles. Shot-putter. Drake Relays champion in 1950; only black shot-putter to hold world record, which he accomplished in 1948.

FROMM, John. Javelin Thrower. Set record in 1957 Drake Relays. *Also in:* National Association of Intercollegiate Athletics Hall of Fame.

GARCIA, Ben. Javelin Thrower. Drake Relays champion in 1955.

GEHRMAN, Don. Runner. Fourth place in the 880-yd. and mile runs of the original Hall of Fame selections.

GORDIEN, Fortune. Discus Thrower. See entry in Track and Field Hall of Fame, Citizens Savings Hall of Fame Athletic Museum.

GRAHAM, Merwin. Triple Jumper. Set new Drake record in hop, step and jump in 1925 relays; tied for broad jump championship in 1925.

GRELLE, Jim. Runner. Set new Drake record in mile run in 1958; member of 1960 Olympic team; won silver medal in 1959 and gold medal in 1963 Pan-American Games.

GUTOWSKI, Robert. Pole Vaulter. Set new Drake indoor pole vault record in 1956; member of 1956 Olympic team; held world record in pole vault in 1957; died in tragic car accident in 1960. *Also in:* National Association of Intercollegiate Athletics Hall of Fame.

HARDIN, Glenn. Runner. See entry in Track and Field Hall of Fame, Citizens Savings Hall of Fame Athletic Museum. *Also in:* United States Track and Field Hall of Fame.

HENDERSON, Alex. Runner. Set new Drake and American collegiate records in the 2-mile run in 1958.

HOFACRE, Lee. Hurdler. Drake Relays 440-yd. hurdles champion in 1948 and set new Drake record.

HOOPER, Darrow. Shot-putter. 1951 champion in shot-put and discus; set new Drake record in shot-put and was again champion in discus in 1953.

HORNBOSTEL, Charles. Runner. Tied Don Gehrman for fourth place in 880-yd. selections for the Hall of Fame.

JONES, Charles "Deacon." Runner. Drake Relays 1957 one-mile and two-mile champion; set new Drake record in the mile.

LASH, Donald. Runner. See entry in Track and Field Hall of Fame, Citizens Savings Hall of Fame Athletic Museum. *Also in:* United States Track and Field Hall of Fame.

LAVERY, Jim. Runner. Placed third in original Hall of Fame inductions in the 440-yd, 880-yd. and one-mile relays.

LAZ, Don. Pole Vaulter. Tied for Drake Relays championship in 1949 and 1951.

LEWIS, Aubrey. Hurdler. Champion in 440-yd. hurdles of 1957 Drake Relays.

LOCKE, Roland. Runner. Equaled existing Drake record in 1925 100-yd. dash; in 1926 set new Drake record, also bettering world record, but this was never recognized because of question concerning following wind.

LYDA, Bill. Runner. Second in the 880-yd. Hall of Fame selections; remembered for giving Oklahoma State Sooners an American record in the sprint medley relay in 1942.

MASHBURN, Jim. Runner. Judged second in the all-time 440-yd. dash.

MATTHEWS, Gene. Runner. Winner of the Drake Relays 1954 2-mile run.

MEISSNER, Dick. High Jumper. High jump champion in 1951 Drake Relays.

METCALFE, Ralph. Runner. See entry in Track and Field Hall of Fame, Citizens Savings Hall of Fame Athletic Museum. *Also in:* National Track and Field Hall of Fame and United States Track and Field Hall of Fame.

MILLER, Bill. Javelin Thrower. Set new record at Drake Relays of 1951. *Also in:* National Association of Intercollegiate Athletics Hall of Fame.

MORROW, Bobby Joe. Runner. See entry in Track and Field Hall of Fame, Citizens Savings Hall of Fame Athletic Museum. *Also in:* National Association of Intercollegiate Athletics Hall of Fame, National Track and Field Hall of Fame and United States Track and Field Hall of Fame.

NIEDER, Bill. Shot-putter. See entry in Track and Field Hall of Fame, Citizens Savings Hall of Fame Athletic Museum.

NIEL, Herschel. Triple Jumper. Champion in 100-yd. dash and the hop, skip and jump at the 1936 Drake Relays.

O'CONNOR, Gene. Hurdler. Winner of 440-yd. hurdles in 1956 Drake Relays.

OERTER, Alfred A. Discus Thrower. See entry in Track and Field Hall of Fame, Citizens Savings Hall of Fame Athletic Museum. *Also in:* National Track and Field Hall of Fame and United States Track and Field Hall of Fame.

OSBORN, Harold. High Jumper. See entry in Track and Field Hall of Fame, Citizens Savings Hall of Fame Athletic Museum. *Also in:* National Track and Field Hall of Fame and United States Track and Field Hall of Fame.

OWEN, Dave. Shot-putter. Set new Drake record in shot-put in 1957.

OWENS, James Cleveland "Jesse." Runner, Broad Jumper. See entry in Track and Field Hall of Fame, Citizens Savings Hall of Fame Athletic Museum. *Also in:* National Track and Field Hall of Fame and United States Track and Field Hall of Fame.

PARKER, Bruce. Javelin Thrower. Champion at Drake Relays in 1958.

PHILSON, Linn. High Jumper. Tied for championship in 1934 and 1936; won championship outright in 1935.

PORTER, Bill. Hurdler. Winner of gold medal in 1948 Olympic Games.

REDD, Lambert. Triple Jumper. Champion in hop, step and jump in 1932 relays.

RICE, Gregory J. Runner. See entry in Track and Field Hall of Fame, Citizens Savings Hall of Fame Athletic Museum.

ROBINSON, Mack. Broad Jumper. Champion in 1937 at Drake Relays.

SALING, George. Hurdler. Set new Drake, American collegiate and American records and equaled world record in 1932 in 120-yd. high hurdles; participated in 1932 Los Angeles Olympics; year later was killed tragically in a car accident.

SANTEE, Wes. Runner. Champion in one-mile run in 1955; member of 1952 Olympic team; considered by many to be America's greatest miler in the 1950s; won silver medal in 1955 Pan-American Games. See entry in United States Track and Field Hall of Fame, 1975.

SIME, Dave. Runner. Broke existing Drake record in 100-yd. dash in 1956; member of 1960 Olympic team and winner of the silver medal.

SIMPSON, Robert I. Hurdler. Winner of 1917 120-yd. high hurdles in his first time at the Drake Relays. *Also in:* National Track and Field Hall of Fame.

SMYTH, Jack. Triple Jumper. Set new Drake record in 1957 hop, skip and jump; exceeded that record in 1958.

SOUTHERN, Eddie. Runner. Member of 1958 relay team champions; also member of 1956 Olympic team.

STEELE, Willie. Broad Jumper. Winner of 1947 Drake Relays broad jump; took gold medal in 1948 Olympic Games and became the third best in Olympic history.

STEVENS, Willie. Hurdler. Set new Drake record in 1957 in the 120-yd. high hurdles.

STEWART, Don. High Jumper. Tied for championship in 1957 Drake Relays.

TERRY, Alton. Javelin Thrower. Set new Drake, American collegiate and American records in 1936 Relays; won again in 1937. *Also in:* National Association of Intercollegiate Athletics Hall of Fame.

THOMPSON, Byrl. Discus Thrower. Champion in 1946.

TIDWELL, Billy. Runner. Placed third in 880-yd. race in original selections for the Hall of Fame. *Also in:* National Association of Intercollegiate Athletics Hall of Fame.

TORRANCE, Jack. Shot-putter. See entry in Track and Field Hall of Fame, Citizens Savings Hall of Fame Athletic Museum.

WARMERDAM, Cornelius "Dutch." Pole Vaulter. See entry in Track and Field Hall of Fame, Citizens Savings Hall of Fame Athletic Museum. *Also in:* National Association of Intercollegiate Athletics Hall of Fame, National Track and Field Hall of Fame and United States Track and Field Hall of Fame.

WARNE, Tom. Pole Vaulter. Set new Drake record in pole vauling in 1930 Relays.

WATKINS, Pete. High Jumper. New Drake record in high jump in 1943.

WHITFIELD, Malvin. Runner. See entry in Track and Field Hall of Fame, Citizens Savings Hall of Fame Athletic Museum. *Also in:* National Track and Field Hall of Fame.

WILSON, Alex. Runner. See entry in Track and Field Hall of Fame, Citizens Savings Hall of Fame Athletic Museum. *Also in:* Canadian Amateur Athletic Hall of Fame.

WOLCOTT, Fred. Hurdler. See entry in Track and Field Hall of Fame, Citizens Savings Hall of Fame Athletic Museum.

1960 DISMOND, Binga. Runner. Champion in the 440-yd. race.

GORDON, Edward. Broad Jumper. See entry in Track and Field Hall of Fame, Citizens Savings Hall of Fame Athletic Museum.

HOYT, Charles. Runner. See entry in Track and Field Hall of Fame, Citizens Savings Hall of Fame Athletic Museum.

1961 DAVENPORT, Ira. Runner. Winner of 440- and 880-yd. Drake Relays.

SCHOLZ, Jackson. Runner. See entry in Track and Field Hall of Fame, Citizens Savings Hall of Fame Athletic Museum.

WOLTERS, A. E. "Deac." Runner. Drake Relays champion in the 440- and 880-yd. races.

1962 ALLEN, Sam. Hurdler. Champion in 1934 and 1935 120-yd. high hurdles.

CUHEL, Frank "Bab." Hurdler.

FENSKE, Chuck. Runner. Champion in Amateur Athletic Union 1000-yd. dash in 1939.

1963 BROCKSMITH, Henry. Runner. Champion distance runner.

MEHL, Walter. Runner. Winner of 1938 2-mile run at Drake Relays.

SENTMAN, Lee. Hurdler. Champion in 120-yd. high hurdles in 1929 and 1930.

1964 JONES, Hayes Wendell. Hurdler. See entry in Track and Field Hall of Fame, Citizens Savings Hall of Fame Athletic Museum. *Also in:* National Track and Field Hall of Fame.

KUCK, John. Shot-putter. Set new Drake records in shot-put and javelin in 1926; won bronze medal in shot-put at 1928 Olympics.

WHEELER, Ted. Runner. Won sprint and distance medley relays for Iowa University in 1956; set new Drake Amateur Athletic Union record in the mile run in 1957; won also in 1958.

1965 CONGER, Ray. Runner. Iowa State distance runner.

O'BRIEN, Parry. Shot-putter. See entry in Track and Field Hall of Fame, Citizens Savings Hall of Fame Athletic Museum. *Also in:* National Track and Field Hall of Fame and United States Track and Field Hall of Fame.

SEARS, Ray. Runner. Champion in the 2-mile race.

1966 BOSTON, Ralph. Broad Jumper. See entry in Track and Field Hall of Fame, Citizens Savings Hall of Fame Athletic Museum. *Also in:* National Association of Intercollegiate Athletics Hall of Fame, National Track and Field Hall of Fame and United States Track and Field Hall of Fame.

KERR, George. Runner. All-time standout half-miler.

SAN ROMANI, Archie. Runner. One of the great milers of his era.

1967 ANGIER, Milton. Javelin Thrower. Champion at Drake Relays in 1922 and 1923.

BURLESON, Dyrol. Runner. One of the first Americans to run the mile under 4 min; participated in the 1960 and 1964 Olympics.

TAYLOR, F. Morgan. Hurdler. See entry in Track and Field Hall of Fame, Citizens Savings Hall of Fame Athletic Museum.

1968 ALLEY, Bill. Javelin Thrower.

LELAND, Cy. Runner. Sprinter-halfback of Texas Christian fame in the 1930s.

RUDOLPH, Wilma. Runner. See entry in Track and Field Hall of Fame, Citizens Savings Hall of Fame Athletic Museum. *Also in:* National Track and Field Hall of Fame and United States Track and Field Hall of Fame.

1969 HAYES, Bob. Runner. See entry in Track and Field Hall of Fame, Citizens Savings Hall of Fame Athletic Museum. *Also in:* National Track and Field Hall of Fame.

JARK, Carl "Tiny." Discus Thrower. Set new Drake, American collegiate, American and world records in discus throw in 1929.

THOMPSON, Jerry. Runner. Champion distance runner.

1970 KANE, Campbell. Runner. Member of Indiana University championship sprint-medley and 4-mile relay teams and two times National Collegiate Athletic Association one-half mile champion.

O'HARA, Tom. Runner. One of the nation's finest milers in the 1960s; member of 1964 Olympic team.

PADDOCK, Charles. Runner. See entry in Track and Field Hall of Fame, Citizens Savings Hall of Fame Athletic Museum. *Also in:* National Track and Field Hall of Fame and United States Track and Field Hall of Fame.

1971 ADAMS, Major. Runner. Anchored the outstanding Texas Southern relay units to six victories to become the dominant team in the Relays in 1961 and 1962.

BROOKS, John. Broad Jumper. Winner of the broad jump in 1932 and 1933, setting new Drake record in 1932; member of 1936 Olympic team with Hall of Famer Jesse Owens.

HOPKINS, Gayle. Triple Jumper. Broke records in the long jump and the triple jump in the 1964 Relays; named the Outstanding Athlete of the 1964 classic.

1972 FORD, Jim. Runner. Member of Drake's winning 440-, 880-yd. and one-mile relay teams in 1951.

GREENE, Charlie. Runner. Outstanding sprinter; considered the fastest human in the world in the mid-1960s; 100-yd. dash champion in 1965 and 1966; member of the 1968 Olympic team.

MATSON, Randel. Shot-putter, Discus Thrower. See entry in Track and Field Hall of Fame, Citizens Savings Hall of Fame Athletic Museum.

1973 HUBBARD, DeHart. Broad Jumper, Triple Jumper. See entry in Track and Field Hall of Fame, Citizens Savings Hall of Fame Athletic Museum.

LEWIS, Theron. Runner. Won relay title in four events for Southern, the 440-, 880-yd. and one-mile races and the sprint medley in 1965; in 1965 Lewis led Baton Rouge, La. to titles in the mile, 880-yd. race and the spring medley.

NELSON, Van. Runner. An exceptional distance runner; named Most Outstanding Athlete of the Drake Relays in 1966 and 1968; captured six distance titles, three in the three-mile and three in the one-mile race; won 5000- and 10,000-m. races in the 1967 Pan-American Games. *Also in:* National Association of Intercollegiate Athletics Hall of Fame.

1974 HANSEN, Fred. Pole Vaulter. Champion in 1962 and 1963; held world record; first 17-ft. pole vaulter; winner of gold medal in 1964 Olympics.

RYUN, James. Runner. Champion in the mile run in 1966; led 2-mile and 4-mile relay teams from Kansas to victory in 1967; held 880-yd. world mark until 1976.

SHELBY, Ernie. Broad Jumper. Winner of the broad jump in 1958 and 1959; National Collegiate Athletics Association champion in 1958 and 1959; two times Amateur Athletic Union national champion; All-American.

1975 BRADLEY, Everett (dec). Broad Jumper, Shot-putter. Champion in broad jump and shot-put in 1922, setting records in both; took second in the 1920 Olympic pentathlon.

DUNCAN, Clyde. Runner. Winner of the 100-yd. dash in 1964, his third straight Relays victory.

GOLLIDAY, James (dec). Runner. Champion in 100-yd. dash in 1952 and 1955.

1976 FEUERBACH, Allan. Shot-putter. Four-time shot-put champion; holds Emporia State shot-put and discus records; member of 1972 Olympic team.

MANN, Ralph. Hurdler. Ranked fourth in the world in 1977; set world record in 440-yd. hurdles in 1970; won silver medal in 1972 Olympics; gold medalist in 1971 Pan-American Games.

MILBURN, Lester. Runner. Ran on nine of the 12 relay title teams from Texas Southern.

National Track and Field Hall of Fame of the United States of America

CHARLESTON, WEST VIRGINIA

Mailing Address: 1524 Kanawha Blvd, 25311. Tel. (304) 345-0087. *Contact:* Dr. Don Cohen, Pres, Bd. of Gov. *Location:* Approx. 164 mi. N.W. of Columbus, Ohio, 174 mi. S.W. of Lexington, Ky, 181 mi. S.E. of Roanoke, Va, 213 mi. N.E. of Pittsburgh, Pa. *Admission:* Free 9 to 5 daily and weekends, closed holidays. *Personnel:* 8 mem. Bd. of Gov. (Don Cohen, Pres.); Jack W. Ross, Exec. Dir; Mickie C. Burrows, Secy. *Nearby Halls of Fame:* Exploration and Invention (Arlington, Va, 250 mi. N.E.).

Founded March 27, 1974, by Don Cohen, a Charleston optometrist, the Hall of Fame is dedicated to a sport that is over 2750 years old. Its purpose is to bring honor to the country's and some of the world's greatest athletes, past and present, and to challenge the youth of the future. The Hall of Fame is temporarily housed in a three story, fifteen room house. The main floor is filled with memorabilia of the members, such as Steve Prefontaine's shoes, medals, uniforms and many interesting and historical displays. The second and third floors are set aside for meeting rooms and a small auditorium. The *Hall of Fame News,* a newspaper published by the Hall of Fame, is available by subscription. The cost is $5.00 a year for four issues. A site has been chosen for a permanent Hall of Fame shrine building and a groundbreaking ceremony took place November 27, 1976. The site contains 50 acres of scenic land located on I-64 midway between Charleston and Huntington, W. Va. The Hall will be a family oriented sports center to be built in two phases. Phase one will be the shrine building, which will contain three areas: a museum, library and archives and an auditorium. There will also be picnic grounds and parking lots in this phase. Completion is scheduled for June, 1978. Phase two will be construction of a combination indoor-outdoor track facility, completely under a removable roof. It will be the first 400 meter indoor track in the United States. A permanent cross-country course and dormitories for visiting athletes and coaches will also be installed. Events of the future will include national and international track meets and coaches seminars, programs for the handicapped, summer youth camps, training site for future Olympic teams and research studies on health and physical fitness in an area of the facility designed for medical research. The nonprofit, tax-exempt organization was initially funded by an appropriation of $902,500 by the West Virginia Legislature, and $1,205,000 by a federal grant from the Economic Development Administration. Additional funds to complete the project are expected from both private and public sources as the total cost is estimated at $10 to $12 million. This Hall is a member of the Association of Sports Museums and Halls of Fame.

Members: 49 as of 1976. Members of the Hall of Fame include athletes, coaches and contributors. Candidates for the first two categories must be retired from major championship competition for a period of at least three years. Members are chosen by a Selection Committee, not to exceed 15 people, appointed by the Board of Governors to serve a one year term. Each member of the Selection Committee is allowed a maximum of three nominations in writing, to be filed 60 days prior to election. To be elected, the candidate must receive 75 percent of the combined vote of the Committee. The inductions are held on appointed dates each year, which includes a formal banquet with a guest speaker. The following day an enshrinement ceremony is held on the grounds of the State Capitol Building. At this time awards are presented to each enshrinee by the person of their choice, usually the athlete's coach. The awards include a beautiful gold ring, engraved silver platter, certificate and a large picture of the inductee.

1974 BOSTON, Ralph H. Broad Jumper. See entry in Track and Field Hall of Fame, Citizens Savings Hall of Fame Athletic Museum. *Also in:* Drake Relays Hall of Fame, National Association of Intercollegiate Athletics Hall of Fame and United States Track and Field Hall of Fame.

BRUNDAGE, Avery. Contributor. See entry in Noteworthy Contributors Hall of Fame, Citizens Savings Hall of Fame Athletic Museum. *Also in:* United States Track and Field Hall of Fame.

CALHOUN, Lee Q. Hurdler. See entry in Track and Field Hall of Fame, Citizens Savings Hall of Fame Athletic Museum. *Also in:* National Association of Intercollegiate Athletics Hall of Fame and United States Track and Field Hall of Fame.

CROMWELL, Dean B. "The Dean." (dec). Coach. See entry in Noteworthy Contributors Hall of Fame, Citizens Savings Hall of Fame Athletic Museum. *Also in:* Track and Field Hall of Fame, Citizens Savings Hall of Fame Athletic Museum; and United States Track and Field Hall of Fame.

CUNNINGHAM, Glenn "Kansas Ironman." Runner. See entry in Track and Field Hall of Fame, Citizens Savings Hall of Fame Athletic Museum. *Also in:* Drake Relays Hall of Fame and United States Track and Field Hall of Fame.

DAVIS, Glenn Ashby "Jeep." Hurdler, Runner. See entry in Track and Field Hall of Fame, Citizens Savings Hall of Fame Athletic Museum. *Also in:* United States Track and Field Hall of Fame and West Virginia Sports Writers Hall of Fame.

DAVIS, Harold "Hal." Runner. See entry in Track and Field Hall of Fame, Citizens Savings Hall of Fame Athletic Museum.

DILLARD, Harrison. Hurdler, Runner. See entry in Track and Field Hall of Fame, Citizens Savings Hall of Fame Athletic Museum. *Also in:* Drake Relays Hall of Fame, National Association of Intercollegiate Athletics Hall of Fame and United States Track and Field Hall of Fame.

EWRY, Ray. Standing Jumper. See entry in Track and Field Hall of Fame, Citizens Savings Hall of Fame Athletic Museum. *Also in:* United States Track and Field Hall of Fame.

FERRIS, Daniel J. Contributor. See entry in Noteworthy Contributors Hall of Fame, Citizens Savings Hall of Fame Athletic Museum. *Also in:* Track and Field Hall of Fame, Citizens Savings Hall of Fame Athletic Museum.

HAMILTON, Brutus. Coach. See entry in Track and Field Hall of Fame, Citizens Savings Hall of Fame Athletic Museum.

JOHNSON, Rafer. Decathlon Competitor. See entry in Track and Field Hall of Fame, Citizens Savings Hall of Fame Athletic Museum. *Also in:* United States Track and Field Hall of Fame.

KRAENZLEIN, Alvin C. (dec). Broad Jumper, Hurdler, Runner. See entry in Track and Field Hall of Fame, Citizens Savings Hall of Fame Athletic Museum.

MATHIAS, Robert B. Decathlon Competitor. See entry in Track and Field Hall of Fame, Citizens Savings Hall of Fame Athletic Museum. *Also in:* United States Track and Field Hall of Fame.

MURPHY, Michael C. (dec). Coach. See entry in Track and Field Hall of Fame, Citizens Savings Hall of Fame Athletic Museum.

MYERS, Lawrence "Lon." (dec). Runner. See entry in Track and Field Hall of Fame, Citizens Savings Hall of Fame Athletic Museum.

O'BRIEN, Parry. See entry in Track and Field Hall of Fame, Citizens Savings Hall of Fame Athletic Museum. *Also in:* Drake Relays Hall of Fame and United States Track and Field Hall of Fame.

OERTER, Alfred A. Discus Thrower. See entry in Track and Field Hall of Fame, Citizens Savings Hall of Fame Athletic Museum. *Also in:* Drake Relays Hall of Fame and United States Track and Field Hall of Fame.

OSBORN, Harold M. Decathlon Competitor. See entry in Track and Field Hall of Fame, Citizens Savings Hall of Fame Athletic Museum. *Also in:* Drake Relays Hall of Fame and United States Track and Field Hall of Fame.

OWENS, James Cleveland "Jesse." Broad Jumper, Runner. See entry in Track and Field Hall of Fame, Citizens Savings Hall of Fame Athletic Museum. *Also in:* Drake Relays Hall of Fame and United States Track and Field Hall of Fame.

RUDOLPH, Wilma. Runner. See entry in Track and Field Hall of Fame, Citizens Savings Hall of Fame Athletic Museum. *Also in:* Drake Relays Hall of Fame and United States Track and Field Hall of Fame.

SIMPSON, Robert I. Hurdler. Developer of modern hurdling technique; became premier hurdler of 1915–1917; set world high hurdles record and tied low hurdles record; presently 84 years old and resides in Los Angeles where he serves as an official. *Also in:* Drake Relays Hall of Fame.

STEERS, Lester. High Jumper. See entry in Track and Field Hall of Fame, Citizens Savings Hall of Fame Athletic Museum.

WARMERDAM, Cornelius "Dutch." Pole Vaulter. See entry in Track and Field Hall of Fame, Citizens Savings Hall of Fame Athletic Museum. *Also in:* Drake Relays Hall of Fame, National Association of Intercollegiate Athletics Hall of Fame and United States Track and Field Hall of Fame.

WHITFIELD, Malvin G. Runner. See entry in Track and Field Hall of Fame, Citizens Savings Hall of Fame Athletic Museum. *Also in:* Drake Relays Hall of Fame.

ZAHARIAS, Mildred Didrikson "Babe." (dec). High Jumper, Hurdler, Javelin Thrower, Runner. See entries in American Golf Hall of Fame; Track and Field Hall of Fame; and Women's Basketball Hall of Fame, Citizens Savings Hall of Fame Athletic Museum. *Also in:* Golf Hall of Fame, Citizens Savings Hall of Fame Athletic Museum; Colorado Golf Hall of Fame, Ladies Professional Golfers' Association Hall of Fame, Professional Golfers' Association Hall of Fame, United States Track and Field Hall of Fame and World Golf Hall of Fame.

1975 ASHENFELTER, Horace III "Nip." Runner. See entry in Track and Field Hall of Fame, Citizens Savings Hall of Fame Athletic Museum. *Also in:* United States Track and Field Hall of Fame.

DAVIS, Alice Coachman. High Jumper. See entry in Track and Field Hall of Fame, Citizens Savings Hall of Fame Athletic Museum. *Also in:* Tuskegee Institute Athletic Hall of Fame.

EASTON, Millard E. "Bill." Coach. See entry in Track and Field Hall of Fame, Citizens Savings Hall of Fame Athletic Museum. *Also in:* United States Track and Field Hall of Fame.

FLANAGAN, John J. Discus Thrower, Hammer Thrower. See entry in Track and Field Hall of Fame, Citizens Savings Hall of Fame Athletic Museum. *Also in:* United States Track and Field Hall of Fame.

HAYDON, Edward M. "Ted." Contributor. Creator of the Chicago Track Club, an institution whose members include young age group athletes, varsity college, national and international class competitors; many of these members have become American and world record holders as well as Olympians.

HURT, Edward P. Coach. See entry in Collegiate Athletic Directors Hall of Fame, Citizens Savings Hall of Fame Athletic Museum. *Also in:* National Association of Intercollegiate Athletics Hall of Fame.

METCALFE, Ralph. Runner. See entry in Track and Field Hall of Fame, Citizens Savings Hall of Fame Athletic Museum. *Also in:* Drake Relays Hall of Fame and United States Track and Field Hall of Fame.

MORROW, Bobby Joe. Runner. See entry in Track and Field Hall of Fame, Citizens Savings Hall of Fame Athletic Museum. *Also in:* Drake Relays Hall of Fame, National Association of Intercollegiate Athletics Hall of Fame and United States Track and Field Hall of Fame.

RICHARDS, Robert. Pole Vaulter. See entry in Track and Field Hall of Fame, Citizens Savings Hall of Fame Athletic Museum. *Also in:* United States Track and Field Hall of Fame.

STEPHENS, Helen. Javelin Thrower, Runner. See entry in Track and Field Hall of Fame, Citizens Savings Hall of Fame Athletic Museum.

THORPE, James Francis. See entry in Professional Football Hall of Fame, 1963. *Also in:* American Indian Athletic Hall of Fame; College Football Hall of Fame and Major League Football Hall of Fame, Citizens Savings Hall of Fame Athletic Museum; National Football Hall of Fame and United States Track and Field Hall of Fame.

TOOMEY, William A. Pentathlon and Decathlon Competitor. See entry in Track and Field Hall of Fame, Citizens Savings Hall of Fame Athletic Museum. *Also in:* United States Track and Field Hall of Fame.

WALSH, Stella. Runner. See entry in Track and Field Hall of Fame, Citizens Savings Hall of Fame Athletic Museum. *Also in:* National Polish-American Sports Hall of Fame and Museum.

1976 BOECKMANN, Dolores A. "Dee Beckman." Coach, Runner. A pioneer woman in U.S. sports, not only as an athlete (competing in 800-m. run in 1928 Olympics) but as a coach of the U.S. women's track and field team in the 1936 Olympics; first woman coach chaperone to lead a U.S. women's squad to the Olympic Games.

DOHERTY, Dr. J. Kenneth. Author, Promoter, Coach and Athlete. See entry in Track and Field Hall of Fame, Citizens Savings Hall of Fame Athletic Museum.

HAYES, Robert L. Runner. See entry in Track and Field Hall of Fame, Citizens Savings Hall of Fame Athletic Museum. *Also in:* Drake Relays Hall of Fame.

JONES, Hayes Wendell. Hurdler. See entry in Track and Field Hall of Fame, Citizens Savings Hall of Fame Athletic Museum. *Also in:* Drake Relays Hall of Fame.

MILLS, Billy. Runner. See entry in Track and Field Hall of Fame, Citizens Savings Hall of Fame Athletic Museum. *Also in:* United States Track and Field Hall of Fame.

PADDOCK, Charles W. Runner. See entry in Track and Field Hall of Fame, Citizens Savings Hall of Fame Athletic Museum. *Also in:* Drake Relays Hall of Fame and United States Track and Field Hall of Fame.

PREFONTAINE, Steve (dec). Runner. Considered by many to be the best American distance runner; first runner to win event four times when he won 1973 National Collegiate Athletics Association 3-mile; set ten American records in events from 2000-m. to 10,000-m; finished fourth in the 5000-m. in the 1972 Olympics; died at the untimely age of 24.

RAY, Joie. Runner. See entry in Track and Field Hall of Fame, Citizens Savings Hall of Fame Athletic Museum. *Also in:* United States Track and Field Hall of Fame.

STARR, Heriwentha Mae Faggs. Runner. See entry in Track and Field Hall of Fame, Citizens Savings Hall of Fame Athletic Museum.

TOWNS, Forrest "Speck." Runner. See entry in Track and Field Hall of Fame, Citizens Savings Hall of Fame Athletic Museum. *Also in:* United States Track and Field Hall of Fame.

United States Track and Field Federation Hall of Fame

TUCSON, ARIZONA

Address: 30 N. Norton Ave, 85719. Tel. (602) 624-7475. *Contact:* Karl W. Cooper, Exec. Dir. *Location:* Near Aviation Hwy; approx. 105 mi. S.E. of Phoenix. Not open to the public. *Personnel:* 18-mem. Exec. Comt. and 22-mem. Gov. Council.

The Hall of Fame was founded in 1968 by the executive director as a nonprofit incorporated organization within the U.S. Track and Field Federation. Its purpose is to promote the sport of track and field and to honor the individuals who contribute service to the federation. The

Hall is supported by dues, grants, the sale of track and field merchandise, publications and the sanctioning of track meets. According to the director, the Hall of Fame consists of "my left office wall." On that wall hangs the photographs of the 12 members of the U.S. Track and Field Federation Hall of Fame.

Members: 12 as of 1977. Persons eligible are those who have contributed a great deal of service to the U.S. Track and Field Federation on a local, national or international level. Members are chosen by the Executive Committee and are inducted at a local track and field competition site. List of members is not available.

United States Track and Field Hall of Fame

ANGOLA, INDIANA

Mailing Address: P.O. Box 297, 46703. Tel. (219) 495-7735. *Contact:* Margaret C. Davenport, Exec. Dir. *Location:* Potawatami Inn, Pokagon State Park (temporary); intersection of I-69 and East-West Ohio-Indiana Toll Rd, approx. 80 mi. W. of Toledo, Ohio, 125 mi. E. of Gary, 150 mi. N.E. of Indianapolis, 140 mi. E. of Chicago, Ill. *Personnel:* Herman Phillips, Pres; Margaret C. Davenport, Dir; 15 mem. Bd. of Dirs; Selection Comt. (Fred Wilt, Chmn.). Call for information. *Nearby Halls of Fame:* Sports (North Webster, 45 mi. S.W.), Agriculture (West Lafayette, 130 mi. S.W.), Trapshooting (Vandalia, Ohio, 135 mi. S.E.), Business (Chicago, Ill, 140 mi. N.W.), Flight (Dayton, Ohio, 150 mi. S.E.), Auto Racing, Basketball (Indianapolis).

The concept of a United States Track and Field Hall of Fame (USTFHF) was conceived by Herman Phillips and the late Kenneth L. Wilson in 1964. However, it wasn't until 1972 that official formulation of the Hall began with the USTFHF being established as a non-profit Indiana corporation. The Hall of Fame serves to research, record, preserve and honor the most distinguished track and field athletes, both men and women, as well as coaches and noteworthy contributors. Members were first inducted in 1974. Temporarily housed in the Potawatami Inn in Pokagon State Park, the Hall specializes in the collection of memorabilia of past and present track and field stars, educational and library materials and in the research and testing of training techniques. The Hall presents four special interest awards to male and female high school and collegiate athletes of the year. Plans for a permanent facility got underway with a 30 acre tract of land being proffered to the USTFHF for the purpose of building a totally functional structure. The new site overlooks scenic lakes and woodlands. This Hall is a member of the Association of Sports Museums and Halls of Fame.

Members: 71 as of 1975. Outstanding men and women who have brought distinction not only to themselves but also to the sport of track and field are eligible for inclusion in the USTFHF. A Selection Committee, composed of members of the Board of Directors, considers nominations and inducts new members. A special Board of Governors, made up of men and women interested in track and field, serve in an advisory capacity to the Board of Directors. New members are enshrined at the annual Induction Dinner.

1974 ASHENFELTER, Horace III. Steeplechase. See entry in Track and Field Hall of Fame, Citizens Savings Hall of Fame Athletic Museum. *Also in:* National Track and Field Hall of Fame.

BEAMON, Robert. Broad Jumper. See entry in Track and Field Hall of Fame, Citizen Savings Hall of Fame Athletic Museum.

BONHAG, George. Runner. Member of the 1904, 1906, 1908 and 1912 Olympic teams. Bonhag placed fifth in the 3500-meter steeplechase in 1904. He won a gold medal in the 1906 Olympic competition with a 7:12.6 time in the 1500-meter walk, his first time ever competing in a walking event. Bonhag was a member of the 3 mile team in 1908 and the only one to collect a medal when the team placed second. In 1912, he carried the United States flag and placed fourth in the 5000-meter and fifth in the 3000-meter team race.

BRUNDAGE, Avery. Contributor. See entry in Noteworthy Contributors Hall of Fame, Citizens Savings Hall of Fame Athletic Museum. *Also in:* National Track and Field Hall of Fame.

CALHOUN, Lee Q. Hurdler. See entry in Track and Field Hall of Fame, Citizens Savings Hall of Fame Athletic Museum. *Also in:* National Association of Intercollegiate Athletics Hall of Fame and National Track and Field Hall of Fame.

CANHAM, Donald B.

CARR, William (dec). Runner. In the 1932 Olympic finals in Los Angeles, Calif, Carr set the record for the 400-meter race at 46.2. He defeated Ben Eastman, former holder of world 400-meter and 440-yard records, in the same year with a 47.0 to 47.2. Carr came from behind to defeat Eastman again, in the Olympic finals, breaking world and Olympic records. He also ran with the gold medal United States 1600-meter team.

CONNOLLY, Harold. Hammer Thrower. See entry in Track and Field Hall of Fame, Citizens Savings Hall of Fame Athletic Museum.

CONNOLLY, James B. Triple Jumper. Member of 1896 and 1900 Olympic teams. When Connolly won the triple jump in 1896, the opening event of the Athens Olympics, with a jump of 45 ft, he became the first man to win a gold medal in modern Olymic Games. At the same games, he also took second in high jump with a 5 ft. 9.25 in. performance and third in long jump with 19 ft. 1.87 in. In the Paris Olympics of 1900, Connolly took second in triple jump behind Myer Prinstein. He became a noted writer specializing in sea stories.

CONNOLLY, Olga Fikotova. Discus Thrower. See entry in Track and Field Hall of Fame, Citizens Savings Hall of Fame Athletic Museum.

CROMWELL, Dean B. "The Dean." Contributor. See entry in Noteworthy Contributors Hall of Fame, Citizens Savings Hall of Fame Athletic Museum. *Also in:* National Track and Field Hall of Fame; and Track and Field Hall of Fame, Citizens Savings Hall of Fame Athletic Museum.

CUNNINGHAM, Glenn "Kansas Ironman." Runner. See entry in Track and Field Hall of Fame, Citizens Savings Hall of Fame Athletic Museum. *Also in:* Drake Relays Hall of Fame and National Track and Field Hall of Fame.

DAVIS, Glenn Ashby "Jeep." Runner and Hurdler. See entry in Track and Field Hall of Fame, Citizens Savings Hall of Fame Athletic Museum. *Also in:* National Track and Field Hall of Fame and West Virginia Sports Writers Hall of Fame.

EWRY, Ray C. Standing Jumps. See entry in Track and Field Hall of Fame, Citizens Savings Hall of Fame Athletic Museum. *Also in:* National Track and Field Hall of Fame.

HAMMOND, Kathy B. Runner. Hammond holds the United States 400-meter record. In Warsaw, Poland, in 1969, she ran a 52.1 400-meter race. At the Olympic trials in 1972, she ran a 51.8 and broke her own record. Clocked at 51.64 at the Munich Games, she again bettered her record and won a bronze medal. She won the Amateur Athletic Union (AAU) meet in 1969 with a 54.4, and in 1972 with a 52.3. She took second in 1967 AAU competition but won the 220-yard and 440-yard races. In 1972, she won the AAU indoor 400-meter.

HAYES, E. C. Coach. See entry in Track and Field Hall of Fame, Citizens Savings Hall of Fame Athletic Museum.

LANDON, Richmond. High Jumper. In the 1920 Olympics held in Antwerp, Landon won a gold medal for his 6 ft. 4 in. performance in the high jump, which set a new Olympic record.

LASH, Donald. Runner. See entry in Track and Field Hall of Fame, Citizens Savings Hall of Fame Athletic Museum. *Also in:* Drake Relays Hall of Fame.

MANNING, Madeline Jackson. Runner. See entry in Track and Field Hall of Fame, Citizens Savings Hall of Fame Athletic Museum.

MATHIAS, Robert B. Decathlon. See entry in Track and Field Hall of Fame, Citizens Savings Hall of Fame Athletic Museum. *Also in:* National Track and Field Hall of Fame.

MEREDITH, James E. "Ted." Runner. See entry in Track and Field Hall of Fame, Citizens Savings Hall of Fame Athletic Museum.

METCALFE, Ralph. Sprinter. See entry in Track and Field Hall of Fame, Citizens Savings Hall of Fame Athletic Museum. *Also in:* Drake Relays Hall of Fame and National Track and Field Hall of Fame.

MILLS, Billy. Runner. See entry in Track and Field Hall of Fame, Citizens Savings Hall of Fame Athletic Museum. *Also in:* National Track and Field Hall of Fame.

NEWHOUSE, Jean Shiley. High Jumper. See entry in Track and Field Hall of Fame, Citizens Savings Hall of Fame Athletic Museum.

O'BRIEN, Parry. Shot-putter. See entry in Track and Field Hall of Fame, Citizens Savings Hall of Fame Athletic Museum. *Also in:* Drake Relays Hall of Fame and National Track and Field Hall of Fame.

OERTER, Alfred. Discus Thrower. See entry in Track and Field Hall of Fame, Citizens Savings Hall of Fame Athletic Museum. *Also in:* Drake Relays Hall of Fame and National Track and Field Hall of Fame.

OWENS, James Cleveland "Jesse." Sprinter and Broad Jumper. See entry in Track and Field Hall of Fame, Citizens Savings Hall of Fame Athletic Museum. *Also in:* Drake Relays Hall of Fame and National Track and Field Hall of Fame.

PADDOCK, Charles W. Sprinter. See entry in Track and Field Hall of Fame, Citizens Savings Hall of Fame Athletic Museum. *Also in:* Drake Relays Hall of Fame and National Track and Field Hall of Fame.

RAY, Joie. Runner. See entry in Track and Field Hall of Fame, Citizens Savings Hall of Fame Athletic Museum. *Also in:* National Track and Field Hall of Fame.

RUDOLPH, Wilma. Sprinter. See entry in Track and Field Hall of Fame, Citizens Savings Hall of Fame Athletic Museum. *Also in:* Drake Relays Hall of Fame and National Track and Field Hall of Fame.

SCHROEDER, William R. Meritorious Service. *Also in:* National Association of Intercollegiate Athletics Hall of Fame.

SWARTZ, Elizabeth Robinson. Sprinter. See entry in Track and Field Hall of Fame, Citizens Savings Hall of Fame Athletic Museum.

THORPE, James Francis. Pentathlon and Decathlon. See entry in Professional Football Hall of Fame. *Also in:* American Indian Athletic Hall of Fame; College Football Hall of Fame and Major League Football Hall of Fame, Citizens Savings Hall of Fame Athletic Museum; National Football Hall of Fame, and National Track and Field Hall of Fame.

WHITE, Willye. Broad Jumper. See entry in Track and Field Hall of Fame, Citizens Savings Hall of Fame Athletic Museum.

WILSON, Kenneth L. "Tug." See entry in Athletic Directors Hall of Fame, Citizens Savings Hall of Fame Athletic Museum.

YOUNG, Cy. Javelin Thrower. As a student at UCLA in 1950, Young took second in National Collegiate Athletic Association play. At the Helsinki Olympics in 1952, he tossed the javelin 242 ft .75 ins. to break the former Olympic record and win a gold medal. His toss of 225 ft. 2 ins. did not place in the 1956 Olympics.

ZAHARIAS, Mildred Ella Didrickson "Babe." Hurdler, High Jumper, Runner and Javelin Thrower. See entries in Track and Field Hall of Fame and Women's Basketball Hall of Fame, Citizens Savings Hall of Fame Athletic Museum; and World Golf Hall of Fame. *Also in:* American Golfers Hall of Fame, Colorado Golf Hall of Fame; Golf Hall of Fame, Citizens Savings Hall of Fame Athletic Museum; Ladies Professional Golfers Association Hall of Fame, National Track and Field Hall of Fame and Professional Golfers Association Hall of Fame.

1975 BOSTON, Ralph H. Broad Jumper. See entry in Track and Field Hall of Fame, Citizens Savings Hall of Fame Athletic Museum. *Also in:* Drake Relays Hall of Fame, National Association of Intercollegiate Athletics Hall of Fame and National Track and Field Hall of Fame.

COCHRAN, Roy B. Hurdler. See entry in Track and Field Hall of Fame, Citizens Savings Hall of Fame Athletic Museum. *Also in:* Drake Relays Hall of Fame.

COPELAND, Lillian. Discus Thrower. See entry in Track and Field Hall of Fame, Citizens Savings Hall of Fame Athletic Museum.

DILLARD, Harrison. Hurdler. See entry in Track and Field Hall of Fame, Citizens Savings Hall of Fame Athletic Museum. *Also in:* Drake Relays Hall of Fame, National Association of Intercollegiate Athletics Hall of Fame and National Track and Field Hall of Fame.

DUVALL, Edith McGuire. Sprinter. See entry in Track and Field Hall of Fame, Citizens Savings Hall of Fame Athletic Museum.

EASTMAN, Benjamin. Runner. See entry in Track and Field Hall of Fame, Citizens Savings Hall of Fame Athletic Museum.

EASTON, Millard E. "Bill." Coach. See entry in Track and Field Hall of Fame, Citizens Savings Hall of Fame Athletic Museum. *Also in:* National Track and Field Hall of Fame.

FLANAGAN, John J. Hammer Thrower. See entry in Track and Field Hall of Fame, Citizens Savings Hall of Fame Athletic Museum. *Also in:* National Track and Field Hall of Fame.

GILL, Harry L. Coach. See entry in Track and Field Hall of Fame, Citizens Savings Hall of Fame Athletic Museum.

HAHN, Archie "Milwaukee Meteor." Sprinter. See entry in Track and Field Hall of Fame, Citizens Savings Hall of Fame Athletic Museum.

HARDIN, Glenn. Hurdler. See entry in Track and Field Hall of Fame, Citizens Savings Hall of Fame Athletic Museum. *Also in:* Drake Relays Hall of Fame.

HAYWARD, William. Coach. See entry in Track and Field Hall of Fame, Citizens Savings Hall of Fame Athletic Museum.

HILLMAN, Harry. Coach. See entry in Track and Field Hall of Fame, Citizens Savings Hall of Fame Athletic Museum.

JOHNSON, Rafer. Decathlon. See entry in Track and Field Hall of Fame, Citizens Savings Hall of Fame Athletic Museum. *Also in:* National Track and Field Hall of Fame.

MEADOWS, Earle. Pole Vaulter. See entry in Track and Field Hall of Fame, Citizens Savings Hall of Fame Athletic Museum.

MORROW, Bobby Joe. Sprinter. See entry in Track and Field Hall of Fame, Citizens Savings Hall of Fame Athletic Museum. *Also in:* Drake Relays Hall of Fame, National Association of Intercollegiate Athletics Hall of Fame and National Track and Field Hall of Fame.

MURCHISON, Loren. Sprinter. See entry in Track and Field Hall of Fame, Citizens Savings Hall of Fame Athletic Museum.

NELSON, Cordner. Player, Writer. He was a track fan at early age and went to the Olympics when he was thirteen. Along with his brother Bert, he began to publish *Track and Field News* in 1948. The magazine is still a leader in reading material for anyone who is an athlete, coach or fan. Since his recent retirement, he has authored several books, including *The Great Ones, Runners and Races* and *The Jim Ryun Story.*

NORWOOD, Ewell "Barney."

OSBORN, Harold M. Decathlon and High Jumper. See entry in Track and Field Hall of Fame, Citizens Savings Hall of Fame Athletic Museum. *Also in:* Drake Relays Hall of Fame and National Track and Field Hall of Fame.

PILGRIM, Paul. Player. A member of the 1906 and 1908 Olympic teams, he was not originally selected for the 1906 team, but was added when Olympic Fund drive was successful enough to add one more man. His victory in the 400-meter heat won him a gold medal in the 1906 Olympics. In the finals he won by a meter with a time of 53.2 to upset Wyndam Halswelle of Britain. In the 800-meter he again met Halswelle and gold medalist James Lightbody of the United States and defeated them both to capture his second gold medal with his time of 2:01.5. Although he also competed in the 1908 Olympics in London, he was unable to get past the preliminaries of the 400-meter. From 1914 to 1953, he was manager and athletic director of the New York Athletic Club and sent many athletes to Olympic competition.

RICHARDS, Robert E. Pole Vaulter. See entry in Track and Field Hall of Fame, Citizens Savings Hall of Fame Athletic Museum. *Also in:* National Track and Field Hall of Fame.

ROBINSON, Dr. Sid. Player, Coach. Young track star and former U.S. Olympic team member in 1930, Sid came to Indiana University to coach the cross-country team. His teams won the Big Ten championship every year and won the National Amateur Athletic Union (NAAU) championship in 1931. In 1936, he went to Harvard University to complete his graduate study program and then received a Ph.D. degree in physiology. He has published two comprehensive reviews and over one hundred papers. He has served on 15 national committees and on the editorial boards of three scientific journals. Robinson is considered one of the nation's most highly respected physiologists.

ROSE, Ralph. Shot-putter, Discus Thrower and Hammer Thrower. See entry in Track and Field Hall of Fame, Citizens Savings Hall of Fame Athletic Museum.

SANTEE, Wes. Runner. In the 1950s, he was called America's greatest miler. He set the 1500-meter world record with a time of 3:42.8 in 1954 and ran a 4:00.6 mile to lower the American record. He competed in the 1952 Helsinki Olympic 1500-meter but did not qualify for the finals. In 1953, however, he turned in a shattering 4:03.7 mile for Kansas. Was also a member of the 1955 Pan-American Games team and won a silver medal in 1500-meter. Also in 1955, he won the Amateur Athletic Union indoor and outdoor with record time of 4:07.9 and ran a 4:00.5 in Austin, Texas. *Also in:* Drake Relays Hall of Fame.

SHEPPARD, Melvin W. Runner. See entry in Track and Field Hall of Fame, Citizens Savings Hall of Fame Athletic Museum.

TEMPLETON, Robert L. "Dink." Coach. See entry in Track and Field Hall of Fame, Citizens Savings Hall of Fame Athletic Museum.

THOMAS, John C. High Jumper. See entry in Track and Field Hall of Fame, Citizens Savings Hall of Fame Athletic Museum.

TOOMEY, William A. Decathlon. See entry in Track and Field Hall of Fame, Citizens Savings Hall of Fame Athletic Museum. *Also in:* National Track and Field Hall of Fame.

TOOTELL, Fred. Coach. See entry in Track and Field Hall of Fame, Citizens Savings Hall of Fame Athletic Museum.

TOWNS, Forest "Speck." Hurdler. See entry in Track and Field Hall of Fame, Citizens Savings Hall of Fame Athletic Museum. *Also in:* National Track and Field Hall of Fame.

TYUS, Wyomia. Sprinter. See entry in Track and Field Hall of Fame, Citizens Savings Hall of Fame Athletic Museum.

WARMERDAM, Cornelius "Dutch." Pole Vaulter. See entry in Track and Field Hall of Fame, Citizens Savings Hall of Fame Athletic Museum. *Also In:* Drake Relays Hall of Fame, National Association of Intercollegiate Athletics Hall of Fame and National Track and Field Hall of Fame.

WYKOFF, Frank. Sprinter. See entry in Track and Field Hall of Fame, Citizens Savings Hall of Fame Athletic Museum.

Track and Field Hall of Fame to Watch

CANADIAN TRACK AND FIELD HALL OF FAME

Being Organized in 1977

In 1948 the Canadian Amateur Athletic Union (AAU) created an Olympic Gold Medalists Hall of Fame on the initiative of Lt.-Col. George C. Machum. The following year, 1949 (the year Canada won the right to amend its own constitution in federal matters), fourteen members were enrolled into that hall of fame. Many of these had excelled in track and field events. Officially, however, the Olympic Gold Medalists Hall of Fame became the Canadian Amateur Athletic Association Hall of Fame and as such is detailed later in the present volume. Meanwhile, numerous great Canadian athletes in track and field events were being inducted into the Canada's Sports Hall of Fame, which also is detailed elsewhere herein. The net result of these developments was that Canada's most famous track and field athletes, though honored in various halls of fame, did not have a hall of fame dedicated strictly to them. Thus the idea for a Canadian track and field hall of fame was born. Having gained quick acceptance and support, such a hall, to be called The Canadian Track and Field Hall of Fame, is slated to be well into the planning stage early in 1978. Interested and supportive parties should contact Ken Twig, Executive Director, at (613) 746-5741, or Dr. Ron Wallingford, Technical Director, at (613) 746-7678, or should write to the Canadian Track and Field Association (*Association Canadienne d'Athlètisme*), 333 River Road, Tower A, Ottawa, Ontario, K1L 8B9.

TRAPSHOOTING

In fifteenth-century Spain and Switzerland about the time Columbus sailed, the few men who competed in target shooting with firearms used hand cannons. Everyone else used the nobler and more ancient bow and arrow. As more wieldy, powerful, reliable and accurate firearms were produced, however, more and more men began to use them. In time, virtually everyone was using them in hunting and in war. For both of those noble avocations, practice consisted of target shooting. In the New World, therefore, guns, gunsmiths and gunsmitheries were an integral part of the colonies right from their various beginnings. Eltweed Pomeroy, for example, established one of the first New World gunsmitheries at Dorchester, Massachusetts Bay Colony, in 1630—two years before the construction of the first brick building in America and two years before the beginning of the construction in India of the Taj Mahal. In 1635 the first two gunsmiths, named Bennett and Packson, arrived in the Maryland Colony. These and other gunsmiths were soon busy turning out firearms for the colonists the year the Boston Latin School opened as the first public school in the New World (1635), two years before the first prostitute arrived in the Colonies (1637), three years before the first log cabins in America were built by Peter Minuit's expedition to New Sweden, in Delaware (1638), four years before the first printing press in America began its operations at Newtowne, now Cambridge, Massachusetts, and the first apples were picked in the New World from trees imported to Boston from England (1639). In other words, before the New World had almost anything else, it had guns.

Trapshooting, a form of target shooting, was a much later development. In the 1700s in England, sport shooters began to use live pigeons as targets (*see* Bird Racing and Breeding). These were shot at after they had been released from traps of various kinds and sizes. Within a few years of the birth of the sport there were rules and regulations governing the number of traps, their placement and distance from the shooter, and the weight of shot that could be used. Soon, too, groups of aristocratic Englishmen had formed clubs like the High Hat Shooting Club, whose members transported live pigeons to the field in their top hats. Their rule was that once the bird was released, the hat had to be replaced on the head properly before a shot could be attempted.

These gentlemen and their thousands of coenthusiasts in the new sport eventually caused an acute shortage of live pigeons. The first bird substitute used was a glass ball about 2½ in. in diameter, sometimes decorated with feathers, that was flung into the air by different kinds of spring-loaded devices. In the 1860s saucer-shaped clay targets called birds or clay pigeons went on the market. They were very hard to break. A man named McCasky developed a more brittle bird, which he called the Blue Rock, from river silt and pitch. Although trapshooting had been practiced in North America by sportsmen in Cincinnati and elsewhere as early as 1830 (the year Emily Dickinson was born), these new brittle brands of birds caused it to be reintroduced in North America as a sport in 1870.

Within a few years, the Interstate Association of Trapshooters was formed. By 1900, when the famous Browning revolver was invented, there were nearly 4000 avid trapshooters in the United States. That same year, trapshooting was added to the Olympic Games as a regular event. Today there are over 100,000 trapshooters among the millions of North American shooting enthusiasts.

FORMS: In 1910 Charles E. Davies and William H. Foster began experimenting at Glen Rock Kennels in Andover, Massachusetts, with the shooting of regular clay pigeons from various positions on an imaginary clock face. Their circle of shooting stations had a 25-yard radius. The trap was placed at the 12 o'clock position and all shots were aimed at 6 o'clock. The shooter would take two shots at each of the 12 positions, plus one from the center of the circle, to complete a 25-target round. This form of trapshooting, called "shooting around the clock" or "clock-shooting," quickly became a distinct form of trapshooting called Skeet, from a Scandinavian word for shoot. Skeet Shooting, now an Olympic event, involves 8 shooting stations on a half circle whose radius is 20 yards. A competitor shoots 25 targets, which are released one at a time from one or both of two traps or houses within three seconds of calling "Pull." Only one cartridge may be discharged at each target. In International Skeet Shooting rules, the weapon, a shotgun, must be held off the shoulder at ready position until the target is released.

One significant difference between clay pigeons and live ones, which are sometimes still used, is that the former travel at their highest speed immediately after release, while the latter begin slowly and accelerate. The clay pigeons used for virtually all forms of trapshooting are very brittle, composed of pitch or clay and limestone, measure 4 5/16 in. in diameter and 1⅛ in. in thickness, and weigh from 3.52 to 3.87 oz.

In regular long-range trapshooting, a single trap or house releases targets in various directions. A competitor, usually using a 12-gauge shotgun, attempts to hit 25 targets from five different shooting stations. The target, on the rise when hit, is usually about 35 yds. distant from the shooter. Variations of those basic features have given rise to such trapshooting forms as 16-yard Singles, where shooters compete with others of similar demonstrated ability; Doubles, where one shooter shoots at two simultaneously released targets; and Handicap, where each shooter is assigned a distance of from 18 to 27 yds. from the trap according to ability. Still another form of trapshooting is Down-the-line Shooting, in which the shooter shoots at one or two targets which are set to fall in defined areas. This is called single-rise if one target is used, double-rise if two are released simultaneously. In Olympic competition trapshooting, called Olympic Trench Shooting, men and women compete together on an equal basis. They compete singly or in teams from five stations, opposite each of which are three traps. "No bird" occurs when a target is not released within the regulation time allowed after the shooter calls "Pull"; a "dead bird" is a target which is hit in the air; one not hit is called, logically, a "lost target."

ORGANIZATION: All international and Olympic trapshooting competitions are governed by the International Shooting Union. In the United States, the national governing body is the Amateur Trapshooting Association (ATA) headquartered in Vandalia, Ohio, which in 1976 had over 70,000 members in some 48 state and allied Canadian groups. Skeet Shooting in North America is governed by the National Skeet Shooting Association (U.S.) and by the Canadian Skeet Shooting Association. These national organizations provide assistance and support for the hundreds of regional, state or provincial, and local trapshooting associations and clubs, as do the numerous related national organizations. The most important national organizations include the National Rifle Association of America, the Shooting Federation of Canada, the Pacific International Trapshooting Association, the United States Pigeon Shooting Federation and the Canadian Shooting Federation. Of the many competitions and tournaments staged by all of these organizations, the most prestigious is the Grand American Handicap, which decides the American champion. That tournament, held at ATA headquarters in Vandalia, includes events for men, women, juniors, subjuniors, and professionals, as well as for father-and-son, husband-and-wife, and brother-and-brother teams. In addition to the Grand American Handicap with rounds of 100 targets per shooter, the ATA also stages the North American Clay Targets, 200 targets per shooter; the National Doubles, 100 targets per shooter; the All-Around, 100 targets per shooter; the Preliminary Handicap, the Champion of Champions, and the High-Over-All, 1000 targets per shooter. During an average tournament week, over 2,250,000 shells costing from 10¢ to 14¢ each are shot at targets costing from 4¢ to 8¢ each for a total week's expenditure of close to $1 million.

For additional information on shooting, weapons, hunting and conservation, *see* Hunting.

Bench Rest Hall of Fame

PRESCOTT, ARIZONA

Mailing Address: P.O. Box 30-30, 86301. Tel. (602) 445-7810. *Contact:* Neil Knox, Editor-Publisher, *Rifle Magazine. Location:* Approx. 60 mi. S.W. of Flagstaff, 65 mi. N.W. of Phoenix, 80 mi. S.E. of Las Vegas, Nev. *Personnel:* Larry Englebrecht, Pres; Stella Buchtell, Secy-Treas. Not open to the public.

Established in 1972 by *Rifle Magazine,* the Bench Rest Hall of Fame bestows honor and recognition on its "champions of champions." The object of bench rest competition is placing five shots (groups) or ten shots through a one-bullet-diameter-sized hole at 100, 200 or 300 yards. Emphasizing marksmanship and concentration, seemingly insignificant changes in environmental conditions—lighting, wind, mirage—must be adjusted for (called doping) so as not to affect the displacement of a shot. The guns are usually supported on sandbags and usually built by the owners. Bench rest shooters load their own ammunition. Excellence is proven by consistent winning at national matches over a period of years.

Members: 12 as of 1977. There are two categories of induction, Shooting Ability and Honorary Member. In Shooting Ability, a total of ten points is required for induction. Points are earned by winning any one of the National Bench Rest Shooters Association classes: bench rest rifle, heavy varmint, light varmint and sporter. A point is awarded to a winner whose average distance between shots and the bullet-sized diameter center is the least (at 100 yards, the usual measurement is between .100 and .200 in.). The shooter's average at the specified range is his aggregate range score. Two points are awarded for a grand aggregate winner, i.e, the average of a shooter's two-range aggregate scores. In the 22 years of bench rest shooting, only six people have earned the ten points necessary for the Hall. The second category is

Honorary Member: individuals who advance the science and technology of bench rest shooting or promote the welfare of the sport through administrative accomplishments. They are selected by living Hall of Famers from time to time. Inductions do not occur annually or in definite cities.

1972 Shooting Ability

CORNELISON, L. E. "Red"

GILLMAN, Tom

GOTTSCHALL, Paul (dec).

HALL, Dave

PAGE, Warren (dec). *Also in:* Hunting Hall of Fame.

1973 Honorary Member

DONALDSON, Harvey (dec).

WILSON, L. E. "Sam"

1975 Honorary Member

HART, Bob (dec).

MORTON, Perry

PINDELL, Ferris

SPEER, Ray

Trapshooting Hall of Fame and Museum

VANDALIA, OHIO

Mailing Address: 601 W. National, 45377. Tel. (513) 898-4638. *Contact:* David Bopp, Mgr. of Amateur Trapshooting Assn. *Location:* At the junction of I-75 S. and Rte. 40 W; 10 mi. N. of Dayton; 20 mi. W. of Springfield. *Admission:* Free 9 to 4 daily; 8 to 5 daily during Grand American Tournament in August. *Personnel:* Marjorie M. Smith, Mus. Dir; Andrew Long, Maurice C. Hale, R. H. Sailer, Wallace R. Irwin, Orville Eberly, Trustees. *Nearby Halls of Fame:* Flight (Dayton), Auto Racing, Basketball (Indianapolis, Ind, 110 mi. W.), Football (Canton, 160 mi. N.E.).

The Amateur Trapshooting Association's (ATA) Hall of Fame was formally dedicated in 1969 after the ideas, plans and memorabilia had been gathering for almost a decade. The Hall of Fame contains the history and legend of the great names of trapshooting in North America. It was in 1924 that the ATA established itself in Vandalia, Ohio, with the construction of a permanent clubhouse and traplines to accommodate the annual Grand American Tournament. As the sport's popularity and membership grew, plans for expansion of facilities were realized when, in 1968, the white clapboard club house was refinished in brick and a wing added for the Hall of Fame and Museum. Upon entering the Hall of Fame on the second floor of ATA's clubhouse, the visitor will find exhibits that follow trapshooting from its inception to the modern era via photographs and artifacts. On display are various traps, guns, silver trophies, medals, shell-loading equipment and a special display on the evolution of the target from glass balls to clays. The Museum also offers early newspaper articles, books, scrapbooks, magazines and advertisements. Because the spectacular as well as humorous events in trapshooting have spread by word of mouth, taped interviews are being conducted with members of the sport in order to preserve this oral history for posterity. All Museum collections have been donations from interested parties and are tax deductable. The annual Grand American Tournament, held since 1900, now has over 4500 participants from all sections of the country. This nine-day event during the month of August attracts as many visitors as it does competitors. The ATA grounds offer camping for 300 tents and trailers as well as eating facilities.

Members: 50 as of 1977. Hall of Fame candidates are selected from those persons who have contributed to the growth and improvement of the sport and from those participants (shooters) who have set impressive records in competition. Candidates must have been involved in trapshooting for 25 years. A Selection Committee made up of past presidents of the ATA and vice presidents from the five United States and Canadian zones of the ATA make the final selection of inductees. Ceremonies take place annually at the Grand American Tournament on the ATA grounds in Ohio. New members of the Hall of Fame are announced between 100-yard matches, with speeches, bands and flag ceremonies adding to the festivities. Later, all gather for a reception at a local country club.

1969

BOGARDUS, Capt. Adam H.

Competitor

Born in Albany County, N.Y; moved to Illinois as a boy and later to Indiana; an experienced field shooter; died 1913 at age 80.

Captain Bogardus took up the sport of trapshooting in 1868. His flair for the unusual and his excellent marksmanship brought him into the foreground in American trapshooting. Early in his career he engaged in a match that called for him to shoot from a buggy pulled by a trotting horse from 21 yd. He easily beat his stationary opponent who chose to shoot from the ground at 25 yds. In 1869 Bogardus downed 500 birds in 528 min, loading his own gun, for a prize of $1000. At a performance at Madison Square Garden, Captain Bogardus took on 5000 glass balls, breaking 4844 of them in 8 hrs. and 20 min. This he did with an assistant and a bucket of ice water to cool off his two guns, in order to demonstrate the proficiency of a new tin-coated shot that claimed to leave no lead in the barrels. On another occasion, when pitted against four of the era's greatest marksmen, Bogardus broke 178, while the others collectively totaled 176. The Captain was the inventor of one of the early forms of the glass ball traps and of an improved glass ball. The rules he instigated, as well as his book *Field, Cover and Trapshooting,* were in general use in the sport.

CARVER, W. F. "Doc"
Competitor

Born 1840 in Winslow, Ill; at 17 moved to Minnesota; lived with the Sioux and Pawnee Indians for several years; at 35 became a buffalo hunter in California, riding with Bill Cody, Bill Hickok and Gen. Sheridan; excellent animal trainer; spent last 30 years of life giving exhibitions of diving horses and elks at fairs and carnivals; diving horses trained by his daughter appeared on TV in the late 1950s; died 1927 at age 87.

Doc Carver began his career at the age of 17. His years with the Indians of Minnesota established him as "Spirit Gun." In 1877 Doc became aware that he could make a fortune by shooting exhibition matches. He defeated all United States and European challengers in glass ball and live bird matches. During his European tours, Doc won $80,000 in cash in addition to a medal presented by the Prince of Wales for his outstanding performances before English royalty. During his career Doc broke 14 out of 15 glass balls in 15 secs, broke 28 of 30 glass balls while riding a trotting horse and set a record for his 153 consecutive glass balls downed in 11 min. At age of 55, Doc Carver was still defeating all comers, killing 100 straight birds in one match.

CLARK, Homer
Competitor

Born January 8, 1884, in New Douglass, Ill; lived most of his life in Alton, Ill.

Homer first shot targets in 1907, and in less than a year became one of the top amateurs in the country. In 1910 he joined the Western Cartridge Co. and tied for the Professional championship at the Grand American Tournament, only to lose in the shootoff by one target. In 1916 Homer tied the Professional yearly average race with a mark of 98 percent on 2100 targets. That same year he won possession of the E. C. Cup as well as a victory in the Hercules All-Around championship. In 1933 at Paris, Ky, Clark became the first man ever to post a score of 100 consecutive in a 50-pair race. As his career continued, Clark won the Illinois state singles amateur championship at the age of 59 and tied for the North American Clay Target championship, placing fifth after the shootoff, at the age of 77. Clark was named captain of the 1962 *Sports Afield* All-American Veterans' Team.

CROSBY, William R.
Competitor

Born August 27, 1866, in O'Fallon, Ill; father, native of England, shot trap; died in Berkeley, Calif, November 11, 1939 at age 73.

Bill entered his first tournament at the age of 13, beating his father in the shootoff for a gold medal. For several years he competed under the name of W. Westfield, taking many of the important trophies of the time, including the E. C. Cup, duPont Cup, Hazard Trophy, Schmelzer Trophy and the *Sportsmen's Review* Trophy. In 1901 Crosby was selected as a member of the American team that was to shoot matches against the top shooters in Europe. "T. Bill," short for Tobacco Bill because he always had a chaw in his mouth, was consistently among the top shooters in the country, breaking 97 percent of his targets over the years. He was one of the 33 men who entered perfect 25s in the 1902 Grand American Tournament, with live birds in use.

ELLIOTT, James A. R.
Competitor

One of four famous shooting brothers; founded Elliott's Shooting Park near Kansas City, Mo; died 1924 at the age of 70.

Elliott was known for his live bird shooting, holding all the important live bird trophies of the nation at the same time, including the *Sportsmen's Review* Trophy, duPont Cup, Republic Cup, Cast Iron Medal, *Kansas City Star* Cup and the Field Cup. In 1899 Elliot also won the E. C. Cup by breaking 136 of 150 Combined Singles and Doubles targets. That same year he won the trapshooting championship at the Sportsmen's Show at Madison Square Garden by breaking 1224 of 1300 targets. Elliot was selected as one of the members of the U.S. team that made a European tour in 1901.

FRANK, Lela Hall
Competitor

Lela dominated trapshooting for 14 years between 1934 and 1948. During that time she won eight women's North American Clay Target championships, led women in Singles average nine times, was runnerup three times and finished third among men in the Grand American Handicap. Lela registered 52,350 Singles targets in her 31 active years at the traps and averaged over 95 percent. She was named to the *Sports Afield* All-America team nine times. She currently lives in California and every year, donates an original oil (painted by herself) to the winner of the Women's All-Around at the Grand American.

GILBERT, Fred
Competitor

From Spirit Lake region of Northern Iowa; died August 8, 1927.

Fred first came to the forefront of the sport of trapshooting in 1895 when he won the duPont Cup with 25 consecutive kills and a shootoff victory. In 1896 Gilbert won the E. C. Cup by breaking 266 of 300. The Iowan was chosen to represent the Americans as a member of the team touring Europe in 1901. In 1905 he broke 392 consecutive targets over a three-day period and during one six-day time span he took 1178 of 1200 targets for an average of .9812. It was in 1908 that Gilbert became rep champion at the Grand American with an average of .9503 for 10,945 targets. He took the same title in 1909 with a score of 193 and again in 1919 with a score of 198. The "Wizard of Spirit Lake" broke the world's record of 591 straight targets in 1919 after more than 20 years of shooting.

HEIKES, Rolla O. "Pop"
Competitor

Born December 25, 1856, on a farm near Dayton, Ohio; moved to Nebraska at age 21; one son; died September 23, 1934, in Detroit, Mich.

In 1880 Pop Heikes made his first run of 100 straight with an 11-lb, 10-gauge gun and five drams of black powder. At one time Heikes held more records than any other living shooter, including five consecutive E. C. Cups. The "daddy of them all" took a position with the LeFever Gun Co. in 1885, making him the first man to go on the industry representatives list as an exclusive shooter. Heikes was a member of the 1901 American team that toured Europe. He won the 1915 Professional championship and later became manager of the Chicago area gun club. During his 55 year career, Rolla attended 25 Grand Americans, including the 1902 meet where live birds were used for the last time.

KIMBLE, Fred

Competitor and Contributor

Born 1846 in Knoxville, Ill; child prodigy on the violin, appearing weekly in a San Francisco theater; later painted outdoor scenes; invented the mallard duck call; was once the world champion checker player; died 1941 at age 95.

Kimble invented the choke-bore shotgun in 1868 that revolutionized shooting. With that gun he became one of the country's top live bird, glass ball and clay target shooters. In 1873 Fred won the Illinois state championship and the Dead Shot Medal. The following year he again took the state championship, the Dead Shot Medal and held the state high average. In 1880 the marksman broke 735 consecutive glass balls in 13 days. The "Peoria Blackbird" was the name of Kimble's first composition target, made of coal tar, pitch and other ingredients.

LIGOWSKY, George

Contributor

George invented the original clay target and trap in 1880. His clay pigeon idea came after a succession of targets that included live birds, glass balls with feathers and fertilizers, tin pigeons and the gyro bird, a propeller-type target. The first Ligowsky targets were made entirely of baked clay. Eventually these evolved into limestone and pitch, although the misnomer "clay" remained. Ligowsky's targets premiered at the New York State live bird championships in 1880 and he sold traps for $20 and targets cost $20 per thousand.

MARSHALL, Thomas A.

Competitor

Grew up in the Mississippi swamps; mayor of Keithsburg, Ill, for 16 years; represented his district in the state legislature for two years; died August 18, 1922.

Tom is the only man ever to win two Grand American Handicaps, in 1897 and 1899, both with live birds. As captain of the 1901 team organized to tour Europe, his expertise as a writer and speaker helped him to report fully to the public via magazines and lectures about that tour. Marshall also led the industry team of 1904 that broke the world's squad record with the score of 488 out of 500. As a writer for the *Chicago Examiner* and the *Sportsmen's Review,* Marshall promoted the sport of trapshooting and attempted to enlighten the general public as to its nature. Tom Marshall held the position of high chief in the Okoboji Indians' trapshooters group for 23 years and was vice president of the Amateur Trapshooting Association at the time of his death.

McCARTHY, George S.

Competitor and Contributor

Born December 9, 1868; developed a method of raising quail; owned a farm in Newfield, N.J; died March 18, 1945, in Philadelphia, Pa, at age 77.

George McCarthy was responsible for the building of the permanent home for trapshooting in Vandalia, Ohio, in 1924. The Amateur Trapshooting Association president began shooting targets in 1904 and was soon averaging 95 percent. He was largely responsible for the adoption of the 25-yd. mark in handicap shooting in the 1920s. At the age of 74, after years of retirement, McCarthy returned to trapshooting to win the all-around championship at his home club of Pine Valley in Berlin, N.J.

OAKLEY, Annie

Competitor

Born Annie Moses on August 13, 1860, in Greenville, Ohio; father a mail carrier; shot animals as a girl to trade for food and ammunition; married Frank Butler and joined his shooting act as Annie Oakley; both joined the Four Paw and Sells Brothers Circus in 1880; adopted into Sitting Bull's Sioux Indian tribe as "My Daughter, Little Sure Shot"; traveled with the Wild West Show for 17 years; near disastrous train wreck put her in hospital for a year in 1901; a car accident in 1921 left her in a brace for the rest of her life; died November 3, 1926, in Greenville.

At 17, Annie Moses took part in and won a shooting match with Frank Butler, the man she married a year later. This began her long career as a sharpshooter of world renown. Traveling throughout the world and performing before the crowned heads of Europe, Annie Oakley fired well over a million shells and won over $100,000 along with numerous trophies and awards. Her pet trick was to lie on her back, have her husband throw six glass balls in the air at once and then empty the entire contents of three double-barrel shotguns, breaking all six targets before they reached the ground. The year before she died Annie was still breaking 97 of 100 targets.

SHANER, Elmer E.

Contributor

Schoolteacher in Pittsburgh, Pa; died in Elizabethtown, Pa, September 14, 1939.

Elmer Shaner spent 50 years in the sport of trapshooting as secretary-treasurer, manager and president of the old Interstate Trapshooting Association (later the American Trapshooting Association). During those years he developed a system for keeping the averages and records of the competitors. Elmer managed 29 Grand American Tournaments from 1893 until 1921, working out detailed systems for promotion and entries. Throughout his entire career, Shaner never fired a gun.

TOPPERWEIN, Elizabeth "Plinky"

Competitor

Born Elizabeth Servanty; worked in a gun plant loading ammunition; husband Ad Topperwein was a member of a vaudeville circuit shooting act; she was expert with rifle and pistol; died January, 1945, in San Antonio, Tex.

At the age of 18 Elizabeth fired her first shot under the tutorship of her future husband. She had the natural ability to be an excellent marksman and the team was soon working professionally. In 1904 she became the first woman to break 100 consecutive targets at trapshooting. She accomplished this more than 200 times during her career as well as recording 14,200 consecutive hits. She maintained an average of around 95 throughout her career and has been hailed as the greatest fe marksman of all times.

1970

ARIE, Mark

Competitor

Born 1883; died November 19, 1958, at his farm in Champaign, Ill.

Mark began trapshooting in 1905. He became the first Grand Doubles champion in 1912, winning with a score of 89. In 1923 he won the Grand American Handicap with a score of 96, becoming the first maximum yardage shooter to take that meet. He was the High-Over-All leader at the Grand American in 1912, 1913, 1917, 1918, 1923, 1924 and 1932 and won the Champion of Champions race in 1917, 1923, 1926 and 1934. Arie reached his pinnacle in 1920 when he took individual and team gold medals at the Olympic Games in Antwerp. Mark was named to the All-America team from 1927 through 1930 and again in 1932 and 1934. Arie was one of trapshooting's most colorful and popular shooters and is considered one of the all-time great handicappers.

HENDERSON, James Woolfolk

Competitor

Born in Fayette County, Ky; spent most of life in Lexington, Ky; died in Lexington, Ky, July 10, 1951, at age 75.

Henderson, better known as Woolly, began shooting traps in 1905 and went on to become the only shooter ever to sweep the three main events at the Grand American. It was in 1914 that he won the Grand American Handicap with a score of 98 from 22 yds, the North American Clay Target championship with 99 of 100 and the Doubles championship with 90. In 1914 and 1915 Henderson became the first man to lead the Amateur Singles average twice, breaking .9663 of his 2050 targets in 1914 and taking 97.53 percent on 2800 targets in 1915.

MILLER, Phil R.

Competitor

A native of Dallas, Texas.

In his early years, Phil was an industry representative and won the 1916 Grand American with 96. He returned to the amateur ranks in 1922 and dominated the Jim Day Cup competition at the Grand American, emerging victorious in 1922, 1923 and 1924. He also won the High-Over-All in 1922, the Doubles and the Clay Target championships in 1923 and the Doubles again in 1924. Miller won his first Singles average award in 1923 with .9823 on 2550 targets, waited 15 years and won that title again in 1932 with .9898 on 3050 targets. During his career Miller won state titles in Texas, Indiana, Missouri and Nevada. In 1939 he was selected captain of the All-America team after having been a member of that squad in 1937 and 1938.

TROEH, Frank M.

Competitor

Grew up in North Dakota; father a gunsmith; died December 24, 1968, at age 86.

Frank began trapshooting at the age of 31, moved immediately to the top of the heap, and won tournaments in Washington State as well as Oregon for many years. From 1926 until 1930 Troeh took ten major trophies at the Grand American, including the All-Around from 1926 to 1929, the High-Over-All in 1926 and from 1928 to 1930, the Doubles in 1927 and 1928. He also won the Champion of Champions event in 1929 and the Singles titles in 1926, 1929 and 1930. In 1920 Troeh was named as a member of the U.S. Olympic team and won a gold medal for his team effort and a silver medal in the individual shooting event. Troeh was captain of the All-America team from 1927 through 1930 and was a team member in 1931, 1933 through 1936 and again in 1938 and 1940.

1971

CROTHERS, Steve M.

Competitor

Born October 17, 1887; lives in Pennsylvania.

Steve won the Pennsylvania 16 yard championship 14 times, the Doubles 4 times, the All-Around 8 and the High-Over-All and Handicap 3 times each. His other titles include the Westy Hogan, the Atlantic Indians and the Championship of North America 6 times. In 1925 Crothers won the Introductory Singles at the Grand American, captured the North American Clay Target championship and won the High-Over-All. He was ranked among the top 14 in the nation for his Singles average from 1924 through 1941. Crothers was captain of the *Sports Afield* All-America team in 1931 and 1932 and was a member of that squad six other times. In 1971, still active at age 83, he is vice president of the Roxborough and Quaker City gun clubs.

PAYNE, Gus

Competitor

Tulsa, Okla, native; suffered from shell shock received during W.W. I at the Battle of Argonne; died April 2, 1947, in Tulsa, at age 51.

Gus took up trapshooting in Oklahoma shortly after returning from W.W. I and went on to become one of that state's top marksmen. He won the North American Clay Target championship with 199 targets in 1929 and 1930. He later won the International 100, the Doubles championship and the High-Over-All. Gus took the 16 yard Oklahoma state championship six times, the Handicap twice, the Doubles five times and the All-Around four times. He was a member of the 1929 and 1930 *Sports Afield* All-America teams.

ROBINSON, Jimmy

Contributor

Born August 27, 1896, in Minnesota; moved to Canada as a youth; served in the Canadian Expeditionary Forces in W. W. I; played hockey and semipro baseball; career as a market hunter.

Jimmy Robinson joined the Amateur Trapshooting Association (ATA) as a statistician in 1922 and remained with the sport for the next 50 years. He began writing for *Sports Afield* magazine in 1926 and in 1927 began recognizing achievements in trapshooting by selecting an All-America team. He worked to get the ATA's Hall of Fame established and has been one of trapshooting's most dedicated promoters. Jimmy Robinson has been doing articles on duck surveys being taken in Western Canada since 1935 and is an honorary trustee in Ducks Unlimited. He has published three books on trapshooting and several others on hunting.

TAYLOR, John R.
Competitor
Born July 24, 1878, in Newark, Ohio; died November 25, 1960.

John won the Ohio State 16 yard championship in 1904 and then joined the industry ranks in 1906 and shot there for 29 years. His victories at the 1933 Grand American came in the Singles, the Doubles, the Handicap and the High-Over-All titles. That year he was chosen captain of the All-America industry team. Taylor was reinstated as an amateur in 1935 and went on to win the Ohio All-Around that year and the Doubles championship in 1936. In Florida he won the state 16 yard championship four times, the Doubles and All-Around twice and the Handicap in 1953. He was a member of the Okoboji Indians' group and retired from trapshooting after 57 years in the sport.

VANCE, Sam
Competitor
Died at his home in Tillsonburg, Ont, May 16, 1947, at age 68.

Sam won the Canadian Trapshooting championship in 1912 and the Dominion Handicap in 1913. He was captain of the Canadian Olympic teams of 1920 and 1924. During his career Vance won the Ontario 15 yard championship five times, the Middlesex Handicap and assisted in the capture of the British Challenge Shield. He also won the Waltham Abbey Cup and the Henden Trophy. From 1926 to 1937, Vance won six Ontario provincial titles, including the Singles and Doubles twice and the Handicap and All-Around once each. He is considered the father of trapshooting in Canada.

1972

GARLINGTON, Frances King
Competitor
From Atlanta, Ga; married Clyde King, Jr; one child, widowed; currently president and treasurer of the King Plow Co. in Atlanta; married Ed Garlington in 1963.

During her 23 years at the traps, Frances shot 62,150 16 yard and about the same number of Doubles, Handicap and Practice. She first learned to shoot at an Atlanta shooting school, enjoying her first major victory at the 1946 Grand American when she and her first husband, Clyde, took the Husband and Wife championship with 190 out of 200. In 1947 Frances won the Women's Grand American Handicap with 97 of 100 targets hit from 17 yards. In 1957 she again won the Grand American Handicap for women and at her last Grand meet in 1962, took the Champion of Champions crown. After winning the Peach State women's championship for the 20th time, Frances retired. She was named Female Athlete of the Year by the Atlanta *Journal Constitution* three times and was a member of the *Sports Afield* All-America team ten times.
Also in: Georgia Athletic Hall of Fame.

JONES, Hale
Competitor
From Alton, Ill; spent 35 years in the automobile business.

Hale began shooting competitively in 1932, and by the end of his first season he was shooting .9610 for 2000 targets. During his 24 year career he won the Illinois state championship from 1936 to 1938, the Grand American Champion of Champions race in 1936 and 1937 and tied for the North American Clay Target championship four times. In 1936 Jones was captain of the *Sports Afield* All-America team of six men and was a member of that team again in 1942 and 1946.

TENNILLE, Mercer
Competitor
From Shreveport, La; joined Army Air Corps 1942, as a gunnery instructor; died August 12, 1969.

Mercer began trapshooting in 1936. His specialty was Doubles. After returning from W. W. II, he topped the Doubles averages for four years and captured the world title in 1948 with a record 99 of 100 and again in 1949. During his career Mercer won the high average 18 times and took 5 state Singles titles, 11 Doubles crowns and 9 All-Around championships. In 1948 and 1949 he won the Grand American All-Around and went on to win the Open North American Singles championship, Vandalia Handicap, the Dayton Homecoming, the World Live Bird championship and the Live Bird championship of America. He was a member of the *Sports Afield* All-America team 11 times and was team captain in 1946.

YOUNG, Charles "Sparrow"
Competitor
Born September 10, 1865, in Frederick County, Md; died May 15, 1951, at age 85.

Charles Young began trapshooting in 1884 and was winning many trap and live bird events by the following year. He won the Grand American Handicap in 1900 and again in 1926. Having once been affiliated with the Robin Hood Powder Co, he often shot under the name of Robin Hood, but his nickname of Sparrow came from the days of sparrow shoots instead of pigeons. Young's victories include the International Trapshooting championship at the Chicago World's Fair in 1893, the World Professional title in 1913 and the Ohio State championship in 1926 and 1927. He was also a gunsmith and inventor of the release trigger.

1973

HIESTAND, Joe
Competitor
Born in Hillsboro, Ohio.

Hiestand began winning major championships in 1931, and 41 years later captured three trophies in the over-65 age group. He won more Grand American championships than any other person in the 73-year history of the event, and he leads the North American Clay Target competition with five wins, and shares the Doubles championship top spot with Mercer Tenille. He served five years in the Ohio State legislature, and by 1973, had

18 years of service in the government, especially active in fighting excessive gun legislation in Ohio. In 1934 to 1936 and 1938, 1946, 1949 and 1956, he received High-Over-All honors. He won the Jim Day Cup, 1934 to 1936. Joe was also named to 21 *Sports Afield* All-America teams, captaining 5 of them.

LILLY, Ned
Competitor
Born 1917; former mayor of Stanton, Mich; now living in Westbrook, Conn, and serving as supervisor of trap and skeet promotion at Winchester-Western.

Lilly became the youngest North American Clay Target champion in Amateur Trapshooting Association (ATA) history in 1933 at age 17, a record held until 1959. He began winning Grand American trophies in 1929. In 1955, he won the Clay Target title, and in 1937 the Doubles championship. He began shooting at age 9, using a .410; at age 11, he won the first of six Michigan Junior titles. By 1932, he took the Michigan state title. He took 50 state championships, 49 in Michigan and one in Colorado; in 1954, he took the Singles, Doubles and All-Around at the state championship. He was the ATA Singles and Doubles average leader two times, in 1951 and 1954.

MEADOWS, Mary
Competitor
Born in Grimes, Iowa.

Mary won the women's titles in both the Grand American and the Preliminary Handicaps in the same year two times, in 1936 and 1939. She took the Grand American Handicap in 1946, 1947 and 1958, and her 1936 score in the Preliminary Handicap plus 24 in the shootoff earned her the third spot among the men at that race. She won 11 Iowa State Amateur Trapshooting Association Women's Singles championships, the first in 1937, again in 1939, and lost only two years between 1950 and 1959. She was Iowa's delegate to Amateur Trapshooting Association from 1956 to 1961.

TOMLIN, Fred
Competitor
Born in Pitman, N.J.; died in 1963.

Tomlin won his first amateur title in 1915, and his career lasted through 1954. He was the State Singles champion in 1915 and 1918, and he took the Singles at Grand in 1921, 1923 and 1926 with 200 straight and in 1927. He shot a perfect 200 in 1932 at the Open championship and also in 1935, and he was the Clay Target winner at Grand.

WOODWARD, E. F.
Competitor
Born in Houston, Tex; died in 1943.

Woodward set the yearly Amateur Trapshooting Association 16 yard average record of .9950 in 1933 and took the Texas state 16 yard title six times. In 1931 he took the state Doubles championship and from 1924 to 1932, took seven All-Around titles. In 1933, he was the Vandalia Open champion with 199. He was founder of the Houston Gun Club. Woodward was selected to All-America teams in 1927, 1928, 1930, 1931 and 1933.

1974

BEAVER, Walter
Competitor
Born in 1897 in Philadelphia, Pa; died of a heart attack in 1957.

Beaver set a record in winning the Grand American Handicap — he was the first to win from so far back. In 1933, he broke 98 from 25 yards and won the North American Clay Target championship twice, in 1934 and 1946. He shot his first registered targets in 1925 and in 1934, 1938 and 1947 won the State Singles championship. In 1938, he shot 200 straight and led the Amateur Trapshooting Association Doubles. In his career, he fired 72,700 16 yard targets. Walt was placed on 7 All-America teams.

CHEEK, Herschel
Competitor
Born in Clinton, Ind; president of the Amateur Trapshooting Assn. in 1950.

Cheek won the Great Western Handicap in Chicago in 1930, the first year he began competing. A noted flyer shot, he won the All-Around championship at targets and flyers at Jenkins Brothers in 1949 and 1954 and captured the Indiana state title six years. In 1948 he represented the United States in the Match of Nations in Lisbon, Portugal and won the Doubles race. He won the Central Zone championships in 1940 and from 1933 to 1955 he won nine Singles titles and the 1934 Handicap. He took ten Doubles crowns from 1934 to 1954 and took the All-Around eleven times. In 1962, the Indiana association awarded him permanent possession of the traveling Doubles trophy. He is past president of the Indiana association and in 1962, was a member of the squad at the Indiana state shoot that broke the second 500 straight in squad history. Herschel has won more Indiana state championships than anyone. He has shot 77,500 16 yard targets in his career. Cheek placed on All-America teams nine times — seven times on the first team, captaining it in 1943, and twice on the second team.

REINDERS, Vic
Competitor
Born in 1906 in Iowa; received a Ph.D. in chemistry from Univ. Wis; retired from teaching in 1972.

Reinders won the Clay Target championship in 1955 with 200 straight and was president of the Amateur Trapshooting Association (ATA) the same year. He was the Doubles champion at Grand American in 1941 and 1959, and won the All-Around two times, in 1957 and 1959. He took High-Over-All in 1941, 1947 and 1957 and Champion of Champions in 1945, 1946 and 1952. He won the Wisconsin state title 47 times. Vic is a charter member of the Waukesha Gun Club and has been either president or secretary since 1938. He originated the pocket score card and in 1953, wrote the trapshooting rule book. Since 1958 he has been writing a column for *Trap and Field,* ATA's official publication. Reinders was on All-America teams 21 times, captaining them in 1940, 1941, 1944 and 1958 and placed on the second team four additional times. He has been a delegate to the ATA since 1941, serving as Central Zone vice president four years before becoming president in 1958.

RENFRO, E. W. "Ted"
Competitor
Born in Dell, Mont; died of a heart attack in 1965 at age 79.

Renfro won his first Grand American Trophy in 1921, and 52 years later, at that same tournament, his son, daughter-in-law and grandson became the first husband-wife-son team in the Amateur Trapshooting Association (ATA) to stand on the 27 yard line. He set the record for yardage in 1933 that wasn't broken for 40 years. Ted was placed on All-America teams seven times between 1928 and 1936; he won the Jim Day Cup in 1930 and in 1933. Between 1918 and 1944, Ted took 29 Montana state championships. He led the ATA Doubles averages three times, in 1930, 1933 and 1936.

1975

BUSH, Herb
Competitor
Born in Canton, Ill.

Bush took third place at Grand American in the Clay Targets in 1962, with 200 straight and by 1964 had broken 200 straight 18 times. In a shooting career that began in 1932, he entered his first 100 in 1935. He won five Illinois Singles titles: 1946 to 1948, 1961 and 1964, the last one with a 200. He placed an All-America teams seven times between 1947 and 1961.

DRIVER, Marvin
Competitor
Born in Council Bluffs, Iowa.

Driver was president of the Amateur Trapshooting Association (ATA) in 1973, and won his first Grand American Trophy as a member of the winning 1953 Iowa state team. He won another Grand American Trophy in 1964, and placed on winning Central Zone teams in 1955, 1958, 1960 and 1961. In 1954 he won the Class A in class championships with 200 straight, and in 1972, as a Veteran, he won seven trophies during the Grand, including the High-Over-All. He won ten Iowa and eight ATA Central Zone crowns, including his first state title in 1952 with 200 straight, Doubles and All-Around in 1959, Doubles in 1961, 1962 and 1973, Singles in 1964 and 1972, five Doubles championships from 1951 to 1963 in Central Zone, and Singles titles in 1955 and 1958, and the All-Around in 1960. In 1952 he was elected to the Iowa board of directors where he served for 20 years, and he was twice president of the state association. Placing on All-America three times prior to 1973 he earned the captaincy of the 1973 veteran team and won a slot on the 1974 veteran team.

JARVIS, Iva Pembridge
Competitor
Born in Kansas; is a schoolteacher.

Iva captured 39 women's trophies between 1950 and 1966 during Grand American week, including six Doubles championships, three Clay Targets, five All-Around and four High-Over-Alls. In 1953, 1954, 1957 and 1958, she was the women's Champion of Champions and was the first woman ever to break 200 straight at the Grand. She was the only woman in Amateur Trapshooting Association history to break 200 straight four times and to break 99 in Doubles; she was also the first woman to win the Golden West Grand Handicap with 99 from 23 yards. Her 200 in 1954 at the Texas state shoot helped her win the non-resident High-Over-All over all the men. In 1966, she finished third in the Champion of Champions at the Grand. Iva won her first of 14 Kansas women's Singles championships in 1949 and her latest in 1975. She won four men's titles in Kansas: the Singles in 1952 and 1958 and the Doubles in 1955 and 1960. Iva placed on All-America teams 12 consecutive times between 1949 and 1961, being captain or co-captain 8 times.
Also in: Kansas All-Sport Hall of Fame.

PETTY, Julius
Competitor
Born in Stuttgart, Ark; died in an auto accident in 1956.

Petty took the first Grand American Trophy in 1927 in men's Doubles and from 1928 to 1952, took 25 Arkansas State crowns. In 1942 and 1944, he broke 200 straight to win the Class AA championships. In 1954 he took the Clay Target championship with 200 straight and in 1954 scored an even 94 percent on 1450 targets from 25 yards, breaking the record. He won six Southwestern Zone titles: the Doubles in 1949, the Singles 1952 to 1954 and the All-Around in 1949 and 1953. Petty placed on All-America teams ten times from 1942 to 1955 and was captain on one.

RIEGGER, Arnold
Competitor
Riegger took the Clay Target championship with 200 straight and 50 in the shootoff in 1949 and the Zone Singles in 1953. In 1950, he won the State Singles title, the Zone Singles title, Handicap-Over-All and All-Around. He won several Washington state titles: five 16-yard championships, two Handicaps, four Doubles and six All-Arounds. He led the national Singles averages five times, and was the Handicap leader two times. Arnold placed on 11 first string All-America teams, captaining it in 1951, 1952, 1954, 1955 and 1960.

1976

DOWNES, John R.
Competitor
Downes has earned more than 200 trophies in 13 states, including out-of-state victories in Arkansas, Kansas, Louisiana, Missouri and Oklahoma. In 1955 he won the Open Class A Double title and in 1964 and 1969 won the Texas state Singles championships with 200 straight. He was the first president of the Texas Trapshooters Association in 1956, organized the Greater Houston Gun Club in 1958 and was president of the Amateur Trapshooting Association from 1964 to 1965. Downes has been a member of the Veteran All-America team for seven of the last eight years (missing only 1972). He was captain in 1968 and 1970.

EBERLY, Orville
Competitor
Eberly has been the treasurer of Amateur Trapshooting Association since 1969, and is the honorary president of the Pennsylvania State Sportsmen's Association, which

he helped to form. Since 1949, he has registered 79,650 Singles targets. During his career, he has won eight state titles (five Doubles: 1950, 1952, 1953, 1955 and 1957, and three All-Around: 1950, 1952 and 1957). He took the High-Over-All in the state shoot four times. In 1957 he was the Eastern Zone Doubles champion.

JAHN, Johnny
Competitor
Born in Spirit Lake, La.

John began trapshooting in 1913 and won the Iowa state Singles the following year. He took the State championship again in 1915 and 1917 and in 1926 and 1944 won the Professional Clay Target championship at Grand American. From 1919 to 1951, he was the industry representative for Hercules Powder Co, and he won the Hercules Cup three times. John was named to the All-America team as an industry representative. He was selected for the team again in 1944. He retired from shooting in 1967 after attending 22 Grand Americans.

LYON, George
Competitor
Born in Durham, N.C; parents were leaders in community affairs and in the tobacco industry; an avid hunter; died January 11, 1916, in Albuquerque, N.M, at age 35.

Lyon won the coveted E. C. Cup in 1911 and 1915, and, in 1912, assisted the United States at the Olympic Games as captain and coach. In 1906, he was a runnerup in the Grand American Handicap.

PETERSON, Herman "Firecracker"
Competitor
Born in Montana; worked as a rancher; died in December, 1975.

Peterson was past president of the Amateur Trapshooting Association and a member of the central handicap committee for ten years. He held 15 state championships (14 in Montana and one in California). He began registering targets in 1934 and up to his death, had 141,625 to his credit. In 1956, he took the All-Around title at the Western Zone championships and the Singles. During the 1956 Singles Zone shoot, he tied for the Singles championship with 200 straight and ended up with the Class AA trophy. He was a member of the Hall of Fame Committee from 1953 to 1954. He was a member of the only squad to break 500x500 Singles targets at Vandalia. In 1949 and 1957, Herman was selected to *Sports Afield* All-America teams.

1977

DERING, Guy V.
Competitor
Dering is a past president of the Amateur Trapshooting Association.

LORING, Ray
Contributor
Ray was an early manager of the Amateur Trapshooting Association.

MARKER, Dorothy
Competitor

WATER SPORTS

Life began in water, or so many people have believed. The distant ancestors of scientists are well known to have drawn themselves out of the primordial muck; but even those who reject such theories read that Creation involved a victory over the water or waters and that the world was at first a place of deep, dark waters upon which the Spirit eventually moved. Virtually all peoples everywhere—Armenians, Arapahoes, Aztecs, Bataks, Carthagenians, Druids, Egyptians, Eskimos, Germans, Gypsies, Hawaiians, Hebrews, Hottentots, Japanese, Kwakiutls, Laplanders, Mongols, Norsemen, Papagos, Persians, Slavs and scores of others—believed, and in some cases still do, that a great flood destroyed the world save for a handful of people, who were thereby symbolically reborn. This same tradition today is symbolized by the practice of baptism, whether it involves a sprinkling of water or a total immersion. Dreams of water, especially those of crossing over water, are similarly said to symbolize rebirth.

Potent with creativity in itself, water was also long recognized as a carrier of larger forces, such as pestilence and death. People in the Middle Ages seldom bathed and almost never did so outdoors. They thought bathing was the cause of the virulent plagues sweeping across Europe—a prejudice not overcome until the second half of the nineteenth century. In the Hawaiian Islands, all vessels containing water were kept covered during lightning storms. Indian tribes from the Yukon to lower California believed that solar and lunar eclipses were highly dangerous, and so during eclipses either covered all containers of water or threw water out and turned the containers upside down. For many people, the end of life traditionally involved water. All over the world, but particularly among those peoples in and around the Pacific Ocean (Malays, Indonesians and Japanese for example), there were customs by which the dead were disposed of by being loaded on canoes or boats or by being ritually thrown into the sea. In general, the boat was supposed to carry the dead one's soul to the other world of the afterlife, or to the ancestral homeland across the great waters. Ancient Germans practiced this custom, as did the Scandinavian Norsemen who sent their dead off in flaming Viking ships. Ancient Greeks and Romans customarily put a coin called an *obolus* into the mouth of a corpse, which was to pay Charon for ferrying the person's soul across the River Styx that flowed around the Underworld seven times. Today the Bororo people of central South America bury their dead, lavishly water the grave for several weeks, dig up the corpse and wash it until all trace of flesh has been removed. Then they paint the bones red before ceremoniously sinking them in a basket to the bottom of a river or lake, "the abodes of the souls." Similar beliefs and customs exist or used to exist virtually everywhere. There are even vestiges in the so-called modern religions.

Regardless of how life began or will end, life without water is definitely not possible. It is a part of virtually every biological process that occurs in either plants or animals. It is also a part of all human cultural life. The different Eskimo tribes, for example, believed in a Lord of the Water and a Lady of the Water. They and others, particularly Indian tribes in Nevada, also believed in Water-Babies, who were invisible messengers of the "Spirit of the Night." All such beings had to be propitiated or appeased and were very important to everyday life. Numerous peoples had rites of purification by water. Ancient Greek brides bathed in the Skamandros River just prior to marriage. The river, personified as a male, was supposed to remove their virginity. Similarly personified, water was the guardian spirit of shamans, warriors, hunters and fishermen everywhere. And it remains just as essential today. Everyone uses water. People use it for crops, cook with it and drink it. Each human being consumes an average of 2.5 quarts a day. This calculates to around 16,000 gallons in a lifetime. One hundred and fifty gallons of water are required to make the paper for an average Sunday newspaper, three gallons or so are needed to flush a toilet. Everyone is bound by the fact that about 70 percent of the earth is covered with water—97 percent of which is saltwater and 3 percent fresh, of which .007 percent exists in rivers and lakes and .023 percent in glaciers and icecaps—the latter contain approximately as much water as flows in all the earth's rivers in 1000 years. Everyone is also bound by the fact that the human body is nearly 70 percent water—as is an elephant's body or an ear of corn. A potato and an earthworm are each 80 percent water, and a tomato is 95 percent water. That life is utterly impossible without water seems particularly true in the United States. Its citizens are the world's greatest consumers of fresh water, using about 544 trillion gallons daily in 1974, or about 1855 gallons per person per day for all purposes.

But man was not meant to swim. Virtually any animal in the world, with the possible exception of the three-toed sloth and the aardvark, are better swimmers. Fish obviously are. Most mammals are, too. Mollusks, for example, use jets of water, eels undulate, frogs use their hind legs, and turtles and penguins which can attain 22.3 m.p.h, use their strong forelimbs. The greatest sprint swimmer of all time broke the mythical minute limit by swimming 100 m. in 58.6 secs. in 1922, at Alameda, California. People thought that was incredibly fast. But Johnny "Tarzan" Weissmuller was only treading water at his 3.839 m.p.h. if compared to the 24 m.p.h. a porpoise can do or the 35 m.p.h. of an average whale. In fact, freestyle swimming, the fastest human stroke, is only about 35 percent as efficient a means of locomotion as walking. Although not particularly noted for their speed, walruses are also far better swimmers than humans. A walrus can remain underwater 10 min, ten times longer than a normal nonsmoking human. The platypus can also hold its breath 10 min, and the beaver for over 15. Similarly, a sperm whale can stay under for an hour and 15 min, a bottle-nose whale for an incredible 2 hours. Whereas a man can dive to 200 ft. unaided, the sperm whale can go effortlessly down 2950 ft.—over half a mile. Even a duck, who habitually dives, is better at swimming than humans. When it is underwater, oxygen is drawn from compounds in its blood and muscles rather than from its respiratory system. In other words, an accumulation of carbon dioxide does not stimulate breathing in a duck as it does in humans. Any snake in the world, even an hours-old one, has better buoyancy control and a better propulsion system—which is to say, it swims better. And a crocodile's heart has a special connection between the arterial and venous circulatory systems that allows the equalization of any pressure differences between the two systems that arise during long dives in deep water.

Despite these facts, people all through history and all over the world have loved the water and loved to swim. Of the countless notable individuals in this vast group, certainly one of the most colorful was Henry Elionsky who performed various feats prior to W. W. I. Once he swam five miles in two hours and forty minutes—in a straitjacket with 15 ft. of iron chain tied to his feet. On another occasion he hauled a sea dory containing nine men and carried two more on his back off Palm Beach, Florida. He did this with his hands and feet shackled through five miles of heavy seas for two hours and fifty minutes. Although Benjamin Franklin said that the only way anyone would ever swim the English Channel was on the back with one leg extended vertically and a sail attached to it, a man finally succeeded in swimming it in 1875. That man was the colorful Captain Matthew Webb, who swam a total of about 38 miles to make the crossing. He died eight years later trying to swim the three-eighths of a mile through the Whirlpool Rapids below Niagara Falls. Since his time, more than 1000 attempts to cross the Channel have been made. Jabez Wolffe made 21 unsuccessful attempts, but later coached Gertrude Ederle, the first woman to swim it successfully. In 1941, legless Charles "Zimmy" Zibbelman swam 168 continuous hours in a Honolulu pool at the age of 47. Gustave "Human Polar Bear" Brickner is similarly famous for his daily dips in frozen rivers in air temperatures of −18°F. and wind chill factors of −85°F. In 1930 Fred Newton, inventor of the Relaxo-Bak, swam the Mississippi River from Minneapolis to New Orleans—2300 miles. It took him 742 hours (30 days and two hours), during which time he gained ten pounds. In 1967 Bob Croft set a record by descending without breathing apparatus to a depth of 217 feet, where the pressure was 111 pounds per square inch. In 1938 John Howard of the Medina Athletic Club of Chicago swam 413 ft. underwater before coming up for air. In 1959 Robert Foster, an electronics technician from Richmond, California held his breath under ten feet of water for 13 min. and 42.5 sec—after hyperventilating pure oxygen for half an hour. Houdini once remained in an airtight coffin submerged in a pool for one hour and 42 min. but never told anyone how he did it. Nor is it understood what the Bororo people mean when they claim that after chewing certain leaves they can remain underwater for several hours to fish in one of the world's largest swamps, the Pantanal. All these colorful individuals are representatives of a rich history of famous swimmers that reaches back to the beginning of time.

The ability to swim was valued in most ancient civilizations—Egypt, Assyria, Greece, Rome—where swimming was widely practiced, especially in warrior training. Swimming races were held in Japan in 36 B.C. during the reign of the Emperor Suigiu. Charlemagne was a good swimmer. Although Alexander the Great once lamented on a riverbank that he had never learned how to swim, he was an ardent admirer of those who could swim well. He also promoted boat races just before he died in Babylon. Julius Caesar was a supurb swimmer. Once, while on campaign in Egypt, he swam 200 yards in full armor holding important documents in his left hand to keep them dry and dragging his royal cloak with his teeth to keep it from falling into the hands of the enemy. Among the many great Greek swimmers were Scyllis and his daughter, Hydna, to whom statues were erected at Delphi after they swam underwater to cut the anchor cables of invading Persian ships. The great Horace had a sure cure for insomnia: swim the Tiber River three times at night. Wealthy Romans built swimming pools called *piscina.* Someone named Maecenas gained fame by building Rome's first heated pool. Pliny later had three pools—one at his villa beside the sea and two at a second villa he owned, one of which was warm and the other unheated. And there was a famous pool at Olympia, the site of the original Olympics. Centuries later the White House pool was built by popular subscription under the direction of Lt. Col. Ulysses Simpson Grant III and formally accepted by F.D.R. in 1933. An early Roman treatise on astronomy mentioned the breaststroke, the over-arm crawl, floating, treading water and underwater swimming, all of which were thought to be exceptional in those born under Delphinus, the sign of the dolphin. When the Colosseum opened in A.D. 80, it was flooded for a few mock sea battles, and so that a swimmer could perform a representation of Leander swimming the Hellespont to see his lover, Hero. In the myth, he swims the Hellespont, or Dardenelles, every night until one night he drowns, whereupon Hero commits suicide by throwing herself into the sea. Nero, the nephew of Caligula, tried to kill Agrippina, his mother, by having her ship scuttled while it was en route across the Bay of Naples one night. She foiled the attempt by swimming in the dark until a passing fishing boat picked her up. Later royalty likewise swam—notably Louis XI of France, who loved to splash around in the Seine, and who was faithfully followed by his courtiers. Around 1500 Leonardo da Vinci sketched an underwater diving system, which he unfortunately did not further develop. Shakespeare, in *Henry IV,* was among the first to use the expression "sink or swim." In *Hiawatha,* Kwasind catches a beaver after a long underwater swim, and in *The Count of Monte Cristo* Edmond Dantes escapes from the chateau by swimming to the Isle of Tiboulen. The list of famous swimmers and feats in fact and in fiction from all over the world seems as endless as swimming the English Channel underwater, first done in 1962 by a frogman.

Not everyone, of course, has liked water. History has a few whole cultures that preached the strict avoidence of it whenever possible. Certain North American tribes avoided all but the most necessary uses of it. And we have a word for fear of water, hydrophobia. But most people can overcome any fear or revulsion of water by learning how to swim in it. The precedent for this is very old. Augustus Caesar, emperor during the time of Christ, valued swimming so highly that he personally taught his grandsons *litteras et natare aliaque rudimenta,* letters and swimming and other rudiments. The Greek phrase for the most elementary fundamentals of education—similar to our three Rs—was *grammata kai nekhesthai,* the alphabet and swimming, which all children learned. Beginners used lifebelts made of cork or bamboo. There was also a rule among the Greeks, according to Pausanias, that a girl must be *virgo intacta* to be able to dive.

The first modern country to organize swimming and to teach it on a national basis was Japan. In 1603 (the year Shakespeare wrote *Hamlet*) an Imperial edict made swimming instruction compulsory in Japanese schools. There were even intramural meets and three-day competitions by 1810, but because Japan was a closed country until 1854, these innovations were not exported. The first swimming school in North America opened in 1827 (the year Beethoven died) in Boston. Its hours were 5:30 to 7 A.M, 9 – 1, and 4 – 8 P.M. Its advertisement read: "A belt is placed about the bodies, under the arms, attached to a rope and pole, by which the head and body are kept in the proper position in the water, while the pupil is learning the use of his limbs." Far more effective means are now used. The two main schools are the American which stresses beginning with the crawl and the European which stresses the breaststroke. But any means of instruction which contains sufficient individual incentive usually will be successful. For example, the three Spence brothers of British Guyana, swimmers superb enough to be inducted into the International Swimming Hall of Fame, all carried the scars of piranha bites.

FORMS: Swimming, the art of self-support and propulsion in water, has taken countless forms. This is especially true if those recreational activities for which swimming ability is necessary are included—water polo, surfing, water skiing, skin diving, sailing, canoeing, rowing, and many more. No one has walked on water since Biblical times, nor has anyone repeated Moses' feat of parting a body of water so as to walk to the other side. But Polynesian divers in the Tonga Islands competed in the sport of underwater walking. This involved holding heavy stones for ballast and walking the 70 yds. between two stakes driven into the bottom of a nine-foot deep lagoon. Water polo has long been called "the roughest sport in the world" and has been totally dominated in international competition by Hungary since 1936. It originated in the 1870s when Englishmen attempted to play polo in a pool. The wooden barrels with decorative horseheads and fancy tails and the double-bladed paddles serving as mallets were not used after about 1890. Water skiing required the invention of the motorboat in the 1920s and 1930s, although it echoes the old naval punishment of keelhauling. In barefoot water skiing, speeds of from 35 to 40 m.p.h. are required. Boat racing is itself a very old water sport related to swimming. Iphicrates, for example (probably ancient Athens' finest military commander), in 327 B.C. lined up his fleet of galleys a distance off shore and declared that the crew who rowed fastest to the beach would receive the prize of being the first in line for the evening rations. Surf riding or surfing, first observed among Hawaiians by Captain Cook in 1778, is done best where the ocean bottom slopes very gradually to depths of not over 10 ft. at from 100 to 1000 yds. from shore. Skin diving received a big boost from the introduction of the rubber-and-glass face mask in the 1930s and from the development of scuba (Self Contained Underwater Breathing Apparatus) gear in the 1940s. All water sports received a boost around 1900 when men went topless. After W. W. I, France introduced a clinging, one-piece suit for women to replace the Victorian costume earlier women had waded in. The bikini arrived in 1947, but wasted material compared to more recent fashions, notably the string models from Brazil. All swimsuits today are made from fabrics that will neither sag nor balloon.

Of the various strokes people use, the most popular are the crawl or freestyle, the sidestroke, which is most efficient in rescue, the backstroke and the breaststroke, ideal for rough water. The breaststroke is one of the oldest known strokes. M. Thevenot described it as simulating the movements of a frog in *Art de Nager,* The Art of Swimming, published in 1696. The breaststroke was modified in 1926 by the German Erich Rademacher into the butterfly breaststroke, or butterfly. As a competitive stroke, the crawl was introduced in Australia around 1893 by Harry Wickham, whose coach described him as "crawling through the water." Regardless of the stroke, it is easier to swim in saltwater than in fresh. Saltwater, being heavier, creates greater buoyancy. It is virtually impossible to sink or even to submerge completely in either the Great Salk Lake in Utah or the Dead Sea in Israel, though a large enough drink of the water of either can result in massive dehydration or death.

Whether in saltwater or fresh, the various strokes and the different forms of swimming may be either recreational or competitive. The main competitive events fall under the general headings of speed racing, diving, synchronized swimming and water polo.

Synchronized swimming is almost always performed by women. It is exhibition swimming in which the movements of one or more swimmers are synchronized with a musical accompaniment. Elegant and graceful, it is often called water ballet. Solo, duet or team competitors perform several required stunts plus several of their own choosing. They are scored on their execution and style of the individual stunts and of the music routine as a whole by at least three judges. Synchronized swimming, for which many countries hold national championships, is not yet an Olympic event.

Diving in its simplest form involves plunging into the water, usually head first. But in its competitive form diving is a complicated feat involving acrobatic ability, the grace of ballet, strong nerves and the lack of any fear of heights. Competitions are divided into springboard and highboard events, each with prescribed tests, directional groups of forward, backward, reverse, inward twist and armstand, and positions from which movements may be performed—straight, piked or bent at the hips, tucked or bunched with hands on knees, and free. All dives on the international table have tariff values. Tariff is the degree of difficulty of a dive, ranging from 1.1 for an inward tucked dive from 5 m, for example, to 3.0 for a forward 3½ turn piked somersault from 3 m.

ORGANIZATION: The oldest Canadian swimming club in existence is the Vancouver Amateur Swimming Club established in 1903, the year the Wright Brothers flew at Kitty Hawk, and Jack London wrote *The Call of the Wild.* Six years later the Canadian Amateur Swimming Association was founded in Montreal. Today this association consists of ten provincial sections: Alberta, British Columbia, Manitoba, New Brunswick, Newfoundland, Nova Scotia, Ontario, Prince Edward Island, Quebec and Sasketchewan. By 1969 swimming's four main forms (speed, diving, synchronized, water-polo) were operating under an umbrella organization today called the Aquatic Federation of Canada, a resident association of the National Sport and Recreation Centre, Ottawa. The Centre assists 32 other resident national organizations and 36 nonresident ones concerned with the development of Canadian sports and recreations.

In the late 1940s, the United States began an age-group swimming program, sponsored by the Amateur Athletic Union, in which children were able to compete in all strokes on local, sectional, and national levels. This program was immediately and immensely successful, and has even been adapted by various other countries for their own use. In the early 1970s, over one million American children were in the program. It was, however, only one of thousands of competitive and recreational swimming programs in North America.

In many of these programs, the ultimate goal is participation in national or international meets. The first such meet was held in Sydney, Australia, in 1846, the year the first *Maid of the Mist* was built to tour the foot of Niagara Falls. Twelve years later in 1858, a world championship 100-yd. race was held in the Melbourne suburb of St. Kilda. There was considerable betting on these races as well as prize money that was also given at ornamental or trick swimming exhibitions. But prior to 1869, when the Associated Metropolitan Swimming Clubs was organized, there was no distinction between amateurs and professionals. In 1886 the name was changed to the Amateur Swimming Association.

The first American swimming championship was an amateur open meet for men held on September 30, 1877 in the Harlem River. At the first Olympics in 1890, there were three swimming races for men in the Bay of Zea, near Piraeus, Greece. Organized swimming for women was not widely introduced until 1916, four years after women swimmers were first allowed to compete in the Olympics.

As interest in and acceptance of swimming increased through the years of the twentieth century, greater organization of the sport as a whole became necessary. Thus the *Fédération Internationale de Natation Amateur* (FINA) (a natator in English is a swimmer) was organized in 1908 in London as the world governing body for all amateur aquatic sports. Major competitions that abide by the FINA codes include the Olympic Games, the Pan-American Games, the Maccabiah Games, the European Games, the Asian Games and the World Student Games. Today the FINA has a membership of 107 national swimming organizations—noticeably absent is China. Those of Canada and the United States are the Canadian Amateur Swimming Association and the United States Swimming Association, although championships in the United States are organized by the national men's and women's committees of the Amateur Athletic Union. The national organizations are aided in their goals and programs by numerous other swimming organizations. The World Professional Marathon Swimming Federation, founded in 1963, is sponsored by various countries including the United States and Canada and holds eight annual championship meets. The Council for National Cooperation in Aquatics, formed in the United States in 1951, is made up of several different organizations and meets regularly to promote swimming in all its phases. The World Swimming Coaches Association, formed in 1968, provides a medium for the exchange of technical information, as does the College Swimming Coaches Association of America. The National Swimming Pool Institute (1956), the Ontario Underwater Council, the National Aquatic Sports Camps and numerous others are also active. All such organizations have encouraged the introduction of various regulations and devices which have given modern competitive swimming its highly sophisticated flavor. With innovations like wave-killing gutters, racing lane markers to reduce surface turbulence, underwater cameras in special viewing windows, electric clocks large enough for the swimmers to see as well as automatic judging and timing equipment, a highly technological, strictly controlled and well-organized cluster of sports and events has been created. Interest in these has made swimming the Number One participant sport on Earth today. A world in itself, swimming seems destined to grow ever larger—despite the fact that man was never really meant to swim.

Aquatic Hall of Fame and Museum of Canada

WINNIPEG, MANITOBA

Mailing Address: 436 Main St, R3B 1B2. Tel. (204) 947-0131. *Contact:* Vaughan L. Baird, Chmn. *Loation:* Pan-Am Pool Building, 25 Poseidon Bay, 145 mi. N. of Grand Forks, N.Dak, 231 mi. N.W. of International Falls, Minn. *Admission:* Free 9 to 10 daily. *Personnel:* Mayor Stephen Juba, Hon. Chmn; Vaughan L. Baird, QC, Chmn; nine representatives.

The Aquatic Hall of Fame of Canada was founded in 1967 by the Aquatic Federation of Canada to honor those persons in water sports of outstanding quality and distinguished service and to preserve records and decisions of the sports administrations of swimming, diving, synchronized swimming and water polo, in order to better prepare for the future. In 1967 the city of Winnipeg petitioned for and was awarded the honor of sponsoring the Aquatic Hall of Fame and Museum of Canada Inc. The Hall of Fame is housed in an expansive 13-acre complex that was designed for the Pan-American Games held there in July 1967. The Hall of Fame possesses what is believed to be the largest sports stamp collection in existence, as well as priceless pieces of statuary relating to aquatics, such as Play of the Waves, a roche ceramic sculpture by Jean René Gaugin, and The Sea, a sculpture by Kai Nielsen. The ancient history of aquatics is depicted in a frieze taken from the Palace of Nimroud, dating circa 800 B.C. It features fugitives escaping by swimming a river. A highlight of the Hall is a display featuring 26 models of famous sailing ships, including the *Cutty Sark.* For members in the Hall of Fame there are photos, medals and trophies along with a variety of aquatic memorabilia. Museum facilities include a large meeting hall, an ample research center and library, plus films and a large board room for meetings. Eating facilities as well as guided tours are available to the more than 400,000 persons who visit the Hall of Fame and Museum each year. This Hall is a member of the Association of Sports Museums and Halls of Fame.

Members: 54 as of 1977. Persons inducted into the Hall of Fame are from the swimming, diving, synchronized swimming and water polo categories within the realm of water sports. To be considered these persons must have a gold medal in the Olympics, Pan-Am Games or British Commonwealth Games; broken a world record in swimming and won international competition of very high criteria. The person must be retired from active competition for a minimum of two years. It is also possible to be inducted into the Hall of Fame for distinguished service to aquatics. After the criteria have been met, a Selection Committee of nine reviews the qualifications of each individual and makes its decision. Induction of new members takes place at the annual meetings.

ARUSSO, Thomas

Swimmer

Thomas Arusso won a gold medal in the 1970 British Empire and Commonwealth Games in the 200-m. butterfly.

ASHWORTH, Ray

Distinguished Service

Ray Ashworth is a resident of Quebec and was named to the Hall of Fame on April 10, 1976, for his distinguished service to water sports.

ATHANS, George Demetrie

Diver

Born January 4, 1921, in Vancouver, B.C; attended Univ. Wash; resident of British Columbia.

George Athans is considered Canada's all-time best male diver. He competed for Canada at the 1936 Berlin Olympics. While attending the University of Washington, Athans was the U.S. Pacific Coast champion from 1938 through 1942. His career peaked at the 1950 British Empire Games in Auckland, New Zealand, where he won a gold and silver medal, respectively, in the springboard and tower events. George was Canadian titlist for four consecutive years and received a special accolade from British Empire Games competitors for his sportsmanship during the games. After retirement he helped coach Irene MacDonald to the U.S. open championship and a bronze medal at the 1960 Rome Olympics.
Also in: Canada's Sports Hall of Fame and Canadian Amateur Athletic Hall of Fame.

AUBIN, Jack

Swimmer

A resident of Ontario, Jack Aubin took a gold medal in the 1930 British Empire and Commonwealth Games for a 2:35.4 in the 200-yd. breaststroke.

BAGGALEY, Mary

Swimmer

Mary Baggaley, a resident of British Columbia, won a gold medal in the 1938 British Empire and Commonwealth Games for her 4:48.3 time in the 440-yd. freestyle relay.

BEAUPRE, Sandra

Synchronized Swimmer

Sandra Beaupre Marks, a resident of Quebec, is honored for her synchronized swimming. 1971 was the pinnacle of her career.

BOURNE, F. Monroe

Swimmer

Monroe Bourne won a gold medal for his 56.0 time in the 100-yd. freestyle in the 1930 British Empire Games in Hamilton. Bourne is a resident of Quebec.

BURLEIGH, George

Swimmer

George Burleigh, a resident of Ontario, won a gold medal for his participation in the 800-yd. freestyle relay timed at 8:42.4 in the 1930 British Empire and Commonwealth Games. In the 1934 British Empire Games, Burleigh won

golds for his 55.0 time in the 100-yd. freestyle, 8:40.6 time in the 800-yd. freestyle relay and for his 3:11.2 time in the 300-yd. freestyle relay.
Also in: Canadian Amateur Athletic Hall of Fame.

CANADIAN RELAY TEAM
Swimmers
Members of the Canadian relay team—Munroe Bourne, James Thompson, Bert Gibson, George Burleigh and coach James Rose—won gold medals for their 8:24.4 time in the 800-yd. freestyle relay in the 1930 British Empire Games in Hamilton.

CHASE, Leonard S.
Swimmer
Leonard Chase, a resident of Quebec, won a gold medal in the 1966 British Empire and Commonwealth Games for his 4:10.5 time in the 440-yd. medley relay.

COUGHLAN, Angela
Swimmer
Angela Coughlan is from Toronto and was born on October 4, 1952. She began swimming with the University Settlement Aquatic Club coached by Nick Thierry in 1966. At the 1967 Pan-Am Games, Angela took bronze medals for the 200-, 400- and 800-m. freestyle with times of 2:15.7, 4:48.9 and 9:48.6, respectively. She also took a silver at the same games in the 400-m. relay. At the 1968 Olympic Games in Mexico, Angela won a bronze medal for her swim in the freestyle relay. Her Canadian titles began in 1967 with the 200-m. freestyle. For the following three years, Angela held all four freestyle Canadian crowns (100, 200, 400 and 800 m.). She was a gold medalist in the 100-m. freestyle at the British Empire and Commonwealth Games in 1970 and silver medalist in the 200-m. freestyle. She also won a gold medal for her participation in the 400-yd. medley relay timed at 4:35.5 in the 1971 Pan-Am Games in Cali, Colombia.

DALY, Harold
Distinguished Service
Harold Daly of Manitoba was named to the Hall of Fame on November 27, 1976, for his long service to water sports.

DAVIES, Lt. Col. John W.
Distinguished Service
John Davies, a resident of Quebec, was named to the Hall of Fame for his distinguished service to water sports.
Also in: Canadian Amateur Athletic Hall of Fame.

DEWAR, Phyllis
Swimmer
Phyllis Dewar, a resident of British Columbia, won four gold medals in the 1934 British Empire and Commonwealth Games. As a member of the women's 300-yd. medley relay team, she swam to a victorious time of 3:42.0, in the 440-yd. freestyle relay team timed at 4:21.8. During those games she also won the 100-yd. freestyle with a time of 1:03.0 and the 440-yd. freestyle timed at 5:45.6. At the 1938 British Empire Games, Phyllis, again a member of the women's relay team, took a gold in the 440-yd. freestyle relay with a time of 4:48.3.
Also in: Canada's Sports Hall of Fame and Canadian Amateur Athletic Hall of Fame.

DINSLEY, Thomas
Diver
Tom Dinsley, a resident of British Columbia, won a gold medal in the 3-m. dive in the 1963 Pan-American Games in Sao Paulo.

DOBSON, D.
Swimmer
D. Dobson was on the team that won the 1938 440-yd. freestyle relay in a time of 4:48.3 at the British Empire and Commonwealth Games.

DOBSON, M.
Swimmer
M. Dobson was on the team that won the 440-yd. freestyle relay in a time of 4:48.3 at the 1938 British Empire and Commonwealth Games.

FISHER, Lenore
Swimmer
Lenore Fisher Gilchrist from British Columbia claimed the 100-yd. backstroke championship for her own in 1952, 1953, 1955 and 1956 with times of 1:12.0, 1:09.8, 1:07.2 and 1:10.8, respectively. In the 1955 Pan-American Games in Mexico City Lenore won a gold medal in the 100-m. backstroke with a time of 1:16.7.

FORBES, Pansy
Distinguished Service
Pansy Forbes was named to the Hall of Fame for her distinguished service to the world of water sports. She is a resident of Ontario.

FORD, Albert F.
Distinguished Service
Albert Ford was named to the Hall of Fame for distinguished service to the world of water sports. He is a resident of Manitoba.

GAZELLE, Benjamin
Swimmer
Ben Gazelle, a resident of Ontario, won a gold medal in the 1934 British Empire and Commonwealth Games for his swim in the 300-yd. medley relay in a time of 3:11.2.

GIBSON, Bert
Swimmer
Bert Gibson, a resident of Ontario, won a gold medal for his time of 8:42.4 in the 800-yd. freestyle relay in the 1930 British Empire and Commonwealth Games.

GILCHRIST, J. A. "Sandy"
Swimmer
Sandy Gilchrist from British Columbia began winning in 1961 and continued to take championships until 1968. In 1961 he claimed the Canadian championship for the 400- and 1650-m. freestyle with times of 4:35.5 and 18:24.7, respectively. In 1963 Sandy held the Canadian championship in the 200-, 400- and 1500-m. freestyle and the 400-m. individual medley with times of 2:03.2, 4:26.0, 18:00.6 and 5:08.8, respectively. In 1964 he was Canadian champion for the 110-yd. freestyle with a time of 56.5 and for the 400-m. individual medley with a time of 4:59.2. In 1965 Sandy was Amateur Swimming Association Champion for the 440-yd. (4:55.3) individual medley

and for the 1650-yd. (17:33.9) freestyle. The same year he held the Canadian championship for the 200-m. (2:21.1) individual medley and for the 400- and 1500-m. (4:26.6 and 17:48.1) freestyle. In 1966 Sandy held the Canadian championship for the 110-yd. (56.0) and the 200-m. (2:02.0) freestyle and the 200-m. (2:20.5) and the 440-yd. (4:58.1) individual medley. In the Brisith Empire and Commonwealth Games that year Sandy received a gold medal for his participation in the 440-yd. medley relay with a time of 4:10.5. In 1967 he held the Canadian championship in the 400-m. (5:01.4) individual medley and the following year held the same event with a time of 4:51.8.

HASLAM, Phyllis
Swimmer
Phyllis Haslam was from Saskatchewan. In 1934 she won a gold medal for her participation in the 300-yd. medley relay in a time of 3:42.0 at the British Empire and Commonwealth Games.

HERSCHORN, H. E.
Distinguished Service
H. E. Herschorn was named to the Hall of Fame for his distinguished service to the field of water sports. He is a resident of Quebec.

HODGSON, George Ritchie
Swimmer
Born 1894; learned to swim in the Laurentian Mountain lakes; never had a swimming lesson; never had a swimming coach; retired at age 18; two Olympic Gold Medals 1912; resident of Quebec.

George Hodgson was undefeated in his three years of competitive swimming. In 1911 Hodgson won the mile championship in a time of 25:27.25 at the Inter-Empire championship at the Festival of the Empire, Crystal Palace, London, in celebration of the coronation of King George V. In the 1912 Olympic Games Hodgson won gold medals for his time of 5:24.4 in the 400-m. freestyle and 22:00.0 in the 1500-m. freestyle.
Also in: Canada's Sports Hall of Fame, Canadian Amateur Athletic Hall of Fame and International Swimming Hall of Fame.

HOOPER, Robert
Swimmer
Robert Hooper won a gold medal for his participation in the 800-yd. freestyle relay with a time of 8:42.4 in the 1934 British Empire and Commonwealth Games.

HUGHES, Jane M.
Swimmer
A resident of British Columbia, Jane Hughes held the world record in 1964 for the 880-yd. freestyle in 9:57.1. In 1965 she was Canadian champion 1500-m. freestyle swimmer with a time of 19:35.8. In 1966 Jane took the Canadian championship for the 1650-yd. freestyle with a time of 19:28.8. That same year in the British Empire and Commonwealth Games in Jamaica, she won a gold medal for her part in the 440-yd. freestyle event with a time of 4:10.8, a new record.

HUMBLE, Florence
Swimmer
Florence Humble, a resident of Quebec, won a gold medal for her participation in the 400-yd. freestyle relay with a time of 4:21.8 in the 1934 British Empire and Commonwealth Games.

HUTTON, Margaret
Swimmer
Margaret Hutton of Ontario, won a gold medal for her participation in the 400-yd. freestyle relay with a time of 4:21.8 in the 1934 British Empire and Commonwealth Games.

HUTTON, Ralph W. "Iron Man"
Swimmer
Born on March 6, 1948, Ralph Hutton is from Ocean Falls, Can. Ralph won his first Canadian title in 1963 for the 200-m. backstroke with a time of 2:21.3. In 1964 at age 16, he took part in eight of the ten Olympic events. In the 1966 British Empire Games in Jamaica he competed in 13 races in six days and collected one gold, five silver and two bronze medals for his effort. In the 1967 Pan-Am championships, he was the 200-m. backstroke champion, freestyle silver medalist in the 200-, 400- and 1500-m. and two relays. In 1968 he set a world record time of 4:06.5 in the 400-m. freestyle. But two months later at the Mexico Olympic Games, he took a silver in that event behind Mike Burton's time of 4:09.0 to Hutton's 4:11.7. In the 1970 British Empire and Commonwealth Games at Edinburgh, he won three silvers in freestyle events and another in the medley relay.
Also in: Canada's Sports Hall of Fame and Canadian Amateur Athletic Hall of Fame.

JACKS, Ronald "Ron"
Swimmer
Born January 23, 1948; from Winnipeg; member of the Canadian Dolphin Club of Vancouver.

In 1965 at the Amateur Swimming Association championships at Blackpool, England, Ron was second in the 110-yd. butterfly behind his teammate Dan Sherry, who set a record. At the 1966 Commonwealth Games he won the 110-yd. butterfly with a time of 60.3. In 1969 again at the Amateur Swimming Association Championships in England, Ron Jacks won three races, the 440-, 880- and 1650-yd. freestyle, was second in the 220-yd. butterfly and third in the 110-yd. butterfly and 220-yd. freestyle. At the 1970 Commonwealth Games in Edinburgh, Jacks was third in the 100-m. butterfly, but won two freestyle relay silver medals. Ron Jacks swam in two Olympics, the 1964 and 1968, without any medals to show.

KENNEDY, Helen Louise
Swimmer
Louise Kennedy won her first Canadian championship title in 1965 with the time of 4:52.5 in the 400-m. freestyle event. The following year she held the Canadian championship for the 220-yd. freestyle event with a time of 2:17.9. She was a member of the Canadian women's 440-yd. freestyle relay team that won at the 1966 British Empire Games with a time of 4:10.5.

LARSEN, George
Swimmer
George Larsen won a gold medal in the 800-yd. freestyle relay on the Canadian men's team with a time of 8:42.4 in the 1934 British Empire and Commonwealth Games.

LAY, Marion B.
Swimmer
Marion Lay, of British Columbia, was Canadian champion 200-m. freestyle swimmer with times for 1964 of 2:19.6 and for 1965 of 2:18.5. She also held Canadian championship titles from 1964 to 1967 in the 100-m. freestyle with times of 1:02.6, 1:02.2, 1:02.5 and 1:01.1, respectively. Marion won the 110-yd. freestyle title from the Amateur Swimming Association for her time of 1:01.4 in 1965. At the British Empire and Commonwealth Games in 1966, Marion took a gold medal for her time of 1:02.3 in the 110-yd. freestyle and another for her participation in the 440-yd. freestyle relay timed at 4:10.8. In 1967 she was again a Canadian championship title holder with her 1:22.6 time in the 100-m. breaststroke.

LYNN, Dorothy
Swimmer
Dorothy Lynn won a gold medal in the 1938 British Empire and Commonwealth Games for her role in the 440-yd. freestyle relay that was timed at 4:48.3.

MacDONALD, Irene
Swimmer
Irene MacDonald, of Vancouver, was 15 times Canadian champion and six times U.S. National champion. She won a bronze medal in the 1954 British Empire Games in Vancouver, a silver medal at Cardiff, Wales, in 1958, and was named the 1957 Female Athlete of the Year in the United States. Her Olympic efforts brought a bronze medal in 1956 and another of the same in 1966.

MOSS, Judith
Diver
Judith Moss Kennedy from Manitoba won a gold medal in the 3-m. dive event in the 1934 British Empire Games held in London.

PATRICK, William
Diving
Bill Patrick from Alberta was the 1954 gold medalist in tower diving at the British Empire and Commonwealth Games in Vancouver.

PHILLIPS, Alfred "Al" "Alfie"
Diver
Al Phillips from Ontario won two gold medals for his 3-m. and tower diving in the 1930 British Empire and Commonwealth Games in Hamilton, Can.
Also in: Canadian Amateur Athletic Hall of Fame.

PIRIE, Irene
Swimmer
Born October 2, 1906, in Great Britain; brother Robert British Empire Game freestyle medal winner; married in 1935 to Frederick George Matt Milton, swimmer; met at the 1930 British Empire Games; son Tony champion swimmer of the 1960s.

Irene Pirie Milton was on Canada's silver-medal-winning relay team at the 1930 Commonwealth Games and took the 100-m. silver for her freestyle time of 63.6, a bronze in the 400 m. in a time of 5:53.4, as well as a relay gold in the 1934 Games in London.

PIRIE, Robert
Swimmer
Irene Pirie Milton's younger brother swam in the 1936 Olympics but did not win a medal. In the 1934 Commonwealth Games in London, he was in the winning relay, second in the 1500-yd. event and third in the 440-yd. event. At the 1938 Games in Sydney, Bob won the 110- and 440-yd. freestyle events and was second in the 1650-yd. freestyle and medley relays.
Also in: Canadian Amateur Athletic Hall of Fame.

POUND, Richard W. D.
Swimmer
Dick Pound won the 1961 100-yd. butterfly Canadian championship title for his time of 56.9. In 1962 he was the gold medalist for the 100-yd. freestyle at the British Empire and Commonwealth Games at Perth for his record time of 55.8. Dick also held the 100-m. freestyle Canadian championship from 1960 through 1962.

PUDDY, William
Swimmer
William Puddy won a gold medal in the 1934 British Empire and Commonwealth Games for his participation in the 300-yd. medley relay, timed at 3:11.2.

ROBERTSON, Nancy
Diver
Nancy Robertson from Ontario received a gold medal for her expertise in the tower dive at the 1971 Pan-American Games in California.

ROSE, James
Distinguished Service
James Rose from Quebec was inducted into the Hall of Fame for his distinguished service to water sports.

SALMON, Peter
Swimmer
Peter Salmon, from British Columbia, holds a long list of Canadian championship titles that include the 1948 100-yd. backstroke in a time of 1:03.0, the 1948, 1949 and 1952 100-m. freestyle with times of 54.8, 53.2 and 52.6, respectively, the 1949 100-yd. breaststroke timed at 1:02.1, the 1952 100-m. breaststroke in a time of 1:03.5 and the 110-yd. backstroke in a time of 1:01.7. Peter also won a gold medal in the 1950 British Empire and Commonwealth Games for the 110-yd. freestyle event in a time of 1:00.7.

SELLER, Margaret Cameron (Shearer) "Peg"
Distinguished Service
Peggy Seller was inducted into the Hall of Fame for her outstanding service to water sports on August 13, 1968.
Also in: Canada's Sports Hall of Fame.

STEWART, Helen Moncrief
Swimmer
Born December 28, 1938, in Vancouver; father William swam butterfly; sister Mary medal-winning swimmer;

later turned to volleyball; played on Canadian world volleyball team and in the 1967 Pan-Am Games.

Helen Stewart Hunt Canada's top swimmer of her time. She began her career at age 15 by winning a silver medal in the freestyle relay at the 1954 British Empire Games in Vancouver. In 1955 Helen won a gold medal in the freestyle at the Pan-Am Games in Mexico as well as silver medals in the medley and freestyle relay events. She competed for Canada at the 1956 Melbourne Olympics and won a silver medal in the freestyle event at the 1959 Pan-Am Games.

STEWART, Mary
Swimmer
Born in Vancouver December 8, 1945; younger sister of Helen Stewart Hunt, Canadian championship swimmer; father, William, butterfly champion.

Before Mary Stewart McIlwaine was 17 she held every Canadian freestyle and butterfly record up to the 220-yd. events. She set world swimming records for the 100-m. and the 100-yd. butterfly and held the U.S. records for the same events. Mary won a gold medal, five silvers and two bronze medals in international games. She was voted Canada's female athlete of the year in both 1961 and 1962 by the AAU of Canada and the Canadian press.
Also in: Canadian Amateur Athletic Hall of Fame.

STONHAM, Pearl
Diver
Pearl Stonham of Quebec received a gold medal for her tower diving at the 1930 British Empire and Commonwealth Games in Hamilton.

TANNER, Elaine "Mighty Mouse"
Swimmer
Born February 22, 1951, in Canada; 5 ft. 2 in. tall; parents English born; resides in California.

In 1965 Elaine Tanner Nahrgang was the Canadian, American and British sprint butterfly champion. At the 1966 Commonwealth Games at the age of 15 she won four gold medals and three silvers and broke two world records. Her greatest successes were for backstroke. She won the 100- and 200-m. backstroke in the 1967 Pan-American Games in Winnipeg, both in world record times. During those games she also came in second in the medley relay, the 100-m. butterfly and the 400-m. freestyle. In the Mexico Olympic Games in 1968, Elaine was second in both the 100- and 200-m. backstroke and won a bronze in the freestyle relay.
Also in: Canada's Sports Hall of Fame and Canadian Amateur Athletic Hall of Fame.

THOMPSON, James
Swimmer
James Thompson from Ontario won a gold medal in the 1930 British Empire and Commonwealth Games for his participation in the 800-yd. freestyle relay, timed at 8:42.4.

WHITTAL, Elizabeth
Swimmer
Elizabeth Whittal Courvette won two gold medals in the 1955 Pan-American Games in Mexico, one for the 400-m. freestyle and the other for the 100-m. butterfly. Mrs. Courvette is a resident of Quebec.
Also in: Canadian Amateur Athletic Hall of Fame.

International Swimming Hall of Fame

FT. LAUDERDALE, FLORIDA

Mailing Address: One Hall of Fame Dr, 33316. Tel. (305) 462-6536. *Contact:* Buck Dawson, Exec. Dir. *Location:* 25 mi. N. of Miami, on the ocean N. of Port Everglades; from Miami take U.S. 1 N. to 17 St. Causeway going E. to A1A; take A1A N. and look for Hall of Fame Dr. to the left. *Admission:* 10 to 5 daily. Family $3.00; tours available. *Personnel:* Buck Dawson, Exec. Dir; Mary Church, Adminr; Dick Mullins, Public Relations Dir; Johnny Weissmuller, Hon. Chmn; Charles E. Silvia, Chmn. of Bd; 13 Officers; 30-mem. Bd. of Dirs; 47-mem. Bd. of Trustees; 9-mem.-Hall of Fame staff. *Nearby Halls of Fame:* Entertainment (Sarasota, 190 mi. N.W.), Movies (Orlando, 205 mi. N.W.), Shuffleboard (212 mi. N.W.).

The International Swimming Hall of Fame is the world's leading repository of aquatic lore and memorabilia. The idea of the Swimming Hall of Fame began with the Amateur Athletic Union (AAU) of the United States and was kindled by the College Coaches Swim Forum. Construction of the Hall was begun in 1965 and dedication ceremonies took place in 1968. While showing swimming's relationship to sailing, surfing, scuba, boating and fishing in the world of water recreation, the swimming Hall of Fame provides one official shrine to perpetuate the memories of famous swimmers, divers, water polo players, synchronized swimmers, water safety programs, aquatic art, and any other new areas of human water propulsion that may arise in the future. The Hall honors and preserves the great moments in swimming, educates the public on swimming's importance, provides a central point for research materials and offers a rallying place for swimming groups. The International Swimming Hall of Fame is recognized by FINA *(Féderation Internationale de Natation Amateur),* swimming's international governing body, and more than 107 nations throughout the world are represented within its walls. The $1.5 million complex includes a 4000-seat stadium and Olympic-size pool, indoor-outdoor convention centers, an ever growing aquatic library, a bookstore, a gift shop and, of course, the Hall of Fame itself. The main entrance to the Hall of Fame takes the more than 35,000 annual visitors into a world of aquatic sights and sounds, with a lifelike wax statue of Hawaiian swimmer Duke Kahanamoku and a magnificent lava waterfall from his islands. Alcoves brimming with trophies, medals and a variety of memorabilia of swimmers Johnny Weissmuller, Buster Crabbe, Esther Williams, Mark Spitz, Don Schollander, Debbie Meyer and many other aquatic celebrities of greater and lesser fame fill the visitor with an appreciation for outstanding achievement. Adorning the walls in the honoree alcove area is a swimmer cartoon-caricature mural depicting nearly 350 of swimming's greats with room for 200 more. On the veranda can be seen an 82-ft, 3600-tile ceramic mosaic of King Neptune's Court, constructed by Ted Keller. The Hall also offers the visitor a world map showing the ocean currents and depths, plus the location of every Olympic Game and the hometown of every Olympic swim champion since 1896. There is a 12 ft. by 18 ft. scale table model of Ft. Lauderdale as "the City of Water" and a sports stamp collection of 5033 stamps from 176 countries for those visitors of more varied interests. The pool immediately beside the museum building is 50 m, ten lanes, with a regulation center-scooped, no-touch-bottom area for water polo. The diving well of 20 yd. by 25 yd. doubles as a warm-up pool. There are 18-in. deep underwater windows and light towers enabling night meets. Underwater closed-circuit television shows a complete view of a dive from the top of the tower to the bottom of the pool. The Hall of Fame auditorium seats 350, and includes special events, such as Olympic films, past and present; Aquarium Society and Shell Club shows; Tarzan film festivals and marine art and photography. Muralist Linzee Prescott has painted a water sports figure to fill the wall between each of the auditorium windows. Conventions for the College Swim Coaches Association Forum, the Swim Facilities Operators Association, the American Swim Coaches Association and Gold Coast AAU meetings are held at the International Swimming Hall of Fame facility. The Hall of Fame library contains a collection of more than 1500 books, magazines, rare books, diaries and scrapbooks. In addition, there are 120 films from silent black and white to glorious color. Library study booths are available and equipped for visual aids. The bookstore carries more than 60 different titles, including how-to books and the International Swimming Hall of Fame yearbook. A selection of souvenirs that includes swim caps and suits, posters, towels, jewelry, decals and postcards may be purchased from the facility's gift shop. Special events at the center include annual conventions, periodic water circuses and swimming meets. The Hall of Fame is nonprofit and subsists primarily on admission charges, financial gifts from supporters and patrons and the Swim-a-Thon that has proven to be the keystone of financial support for the Hall. More than $2 million have been raised in the past few years by swimmers who elicit pledges from parents and neighbors to contribute a penny for every practice lap completed. The Hall is a member of the Association of Sports Museums and Halls of Fame.

Members: 179 as of 1977. For a member of the water sports world to be eligible for election to the International Swimming Hall of Fame, he or she must have been out of competition for a minimum of five years. An exception is made for coaches who have been active for more than 25 years. The candidate is chosen on the basis of the number of Olympic medals, national championships, world records and milestone achievements. The honorees are chosen by 2200 coaches and swim authorities from around the world, with final nominations made by a select committee. Induction ceremonies are held each spring at the International Swimming Hall of Fame complex in Ft. Lauderdale. Each honoree receives a special plaque, an embroidered patch and an individual alcove within the Hall to depict his or her achievements.

1965

CRABBE, Clarence Linden "Buster"
Swimmer
Born in Oakland, Calif; family moved to Hawaii when 2 to oversee a pineapple plantation; attended Puna Hou High School; won letters every year in football, basketball, track and swimming (a 16-letter man); freshman law student at the Univ. Southern Calif; signed with Paramount Pictures; appeared in 170 pictures as Flash Gordon, Buck Rogers, Captain Gallant and Tarzan; appeared in the World's Fair Aquacade in New York; toured with the Aquaparade; now runs boys' camp in New York and the Buster Crabbe Swim Pools, Inc; Olymic Gold Medal 1932.

Buster Crabbe won a place on the 1932 Olympic team and took a gold medal in the 400-m. event. He is a holder of 16 world records and 35 national swimming records.
Also in: Swimming and Diving Hall of Fame, Citizens Savings Hall of Fame Athletic Museum.

DANIELS, C. M. "Charlie"
Swimmer
Born March 24, 1885; was squash and bridge champion at the New York Athletic Club; Olympic Gold, Silver and Bronze Medals 1904; Olympic Gold and Bronze Medals 1906.

Charlie Daniels was the first great American swimmer and the first American to win an Olympic swimming event. He won four gold medals in three Olympic Games, 1904, 1906 and 1908, and retired with 33 U.S. national championships. During his career Daniels held every world freestyle record from 25 yd. to the mile. Daniels experimented with and developed the Australian crawl and gave American freestyle swimming some speed. Daniels was picked as the North American Athlete of the Year for 1909 by the Citizens Savings Hall of Fame Athletic Museum.
Also in: Swimming and Diving Hall of Fame, Citizens Savings Hall of Fame Athletic Museum.

EDERLE, Gertrude
Swimmer
Olympic Gold Medal and two Bronze Medals 1924.

Gertrude Ederle is an Olympic medalist and Channel swimmer. She broke seven world records at various distances in the course of a single 500-m. swim. Her Olympic successes were in the 1924 Games in Paris when she won a gold medal in the freestyle relay and two bronze medals for the 100- and 400-m. freestyle events. Ms. Ederle held 29 U.S. national and world records from 1921 to 1925 when she turned professional. She became the first woman to swim the English Channel, 51 years after the first man, and faster than any man had swum it before her, 14 hrs, 34 min.
Also in: Swimming and Diving Hall of Fame, Citizens Savings Hall of Fame Athletic Museum.

FRASER, Dawn
Swimmer
Born September, 1937, in Adelaide, Australia; placed on a ten-year suspension by the Australian ASU for participating in the Olympic opening ceremonies against orders and being involved in a Japanese flag purloining prank (1964); two Olympic Gold Medals 1956; two British Empire Gold Medals 1958; Olympic Gold Medal and two Silver Medals 1960; four British Empire Gold Medals 1962; Olympic Gold Medal and Silver Medal 1964.

When Dawn Fraser broke her first Australian national record in 1955 she was 17. Her first world record was in the 220-yd. freestyle in 1956. In 1962 she became the first woman to break the minute for 100-m. freestyle. She has frequently held the records for the 440-, 220- and 200-m. events and has almost continuously held the 110- and 100-m. records. Dawn won three gold medals in three Olympics from 1956 to 1964 in the 100-m. freestyle. She also collected four relay medals. Dawn Fraser has 27 individual world records to her credit, 8 Commonwealth medals, 6 of them gold, and 23 Australian titles. In 1964 she was named Australian of the Year.

GUNDLING, Beulah
Synchronized Swimmer
The traditions of synchronized swimming go back to acrobatic swimming stunts performed in rivers in the eighteenth century, through ornamental swimming and on to water ballet and aquatic art. Underwater sound is an important part of the art. It was developed in North America and Canada and was usually confined to teams and duets until Beulah Gundling won the Canadian Solo Crown in 1949. Beulah Gundling was the United State's first Outdoor Synchronized Solo champion in 1950 and she remained undefeated in national and international competition until her retirement five years later. Ms. Gundling designed her own costumes, arranged her own music and did her own choreography. She won five U.S. Solo Synchronized swimming titles. After retirement from competitive synchronized swimming, Ms. Gundling continued to devote long hours to water ballet, organizing the International Academy of Aquatic Art and performing on an exhibition basis.

HANDY, H. Jamison "Jam"
Contributor
From Chicago, Ill; at age 80, still swimming more than 80 laps a day; runs the Jam Handy Corp.

Jam Handy is considered the "Father of Modern Swimming" for his contribution of many new ideas and techniques in swimming. Handy is responsible for the modern freestyle stroke breathing. He was the first swimmer to use the alternating arm stroke in the backstroke and the first to narrow the kick and change the timing in the breaststroke. His ideas on conditioning and nutrition were equally novel. Handy won national championships in all three strokes before 1907. Later, he pioneered the use of film for underwater stroke correction and technique analysis. He made two Olympic teams 20 years apart, in 1904 for swimming and again in 1924 for water polo.
Also in: Swimming and Diving Hall of Fame, Citizens Savings Hall of Fame Athletic Museum.

KAHANAMOKU, Duke
Swimmer
Born August 14, 1890; named after the Duke of Edinburgh, who was visiting in Hawaii at the time of his birth; Olympic Gold and Silver Medals 1912; Olympic Gold Medal 1920; Olympic Silver Medal 1924; starred in Hollywood films; deceased.

Duke Kahanamoku was one of the first swimmers to have developed the crawl freestyle successfully. He made his first Olympic team in 1912 and won the 100-m. freestyle in a time of 63.4 and placed second in the relay. Eight years later, at the 1920 Olympic Games at Antwerp, Duke had to swim the 100-m. twice to win his gold medal. The Australians protested that their man had been boxed in. In 1924 Duke was dropped into second place by Johnny Weissmuller. He was on the team again in 1928 but went home medalless. In 1932 Duke was a member of the U.S. water polo team, but did not play. Duke introduced surfing the world over and was only the first in a long line of Hawaiian record holders.
Also in: Swimming and Diving Hall of Fame, Citizens Savings Hall of Fame Athletic Museum.

KIEFER, Adolph
Swimmer
Born June 27, 1918, in Chicago, Ill; Olympic Gold Medal 1936; during W.W. II, put in charge of swimming instruction for entire U.S. Navy; revamped complete instructional program; adviser to the President's Council on Physical Fitness.

Adolph Kiefer was the first man to swim the 100-yd. backstroke under one min. His backstroke records stood for 15 years. In 1936 at the age of 17 he won a gold medal in the backstroke event at the Berlin Olympic Games. During his swimming career that lasted from 1935 until 1944, Kiefer broke 17 world records from 100-yd. to 400-m.
Also in: Swimming and Diving Hall of Fame, Citizens Savings Hall of Fame Athletic Museum.

KIPHUTH, Robert John Herman
Coach
Born November 17, 1890, in Tonawanda, N.Y; received honorary master of arts and doctor of law degrees; honored by the Emperor of Japan with the Order of the Sacred Treasure; received the Medal of Freedom from President Johnson in 1963; was a nonsmoker, teetotaler; had a good sense of humor; rode a bicycle everywhere; died in January, 1967, in New Haven, Conn.

Bob Kiphuth began his career at Yale University at the age of 23. He was head coach from 1918 until mandatory retirement in 1959 when he became professor emeritus. He attended every Olympic Game from 1924 to 1964 and was coach to the American team from 1928 until 1948. The Yale University swimming teams were only beaten ten times in intercollegiate matches in his 42 years of coaching. Kiphuth was responsible for adding dry-land exercises and cross-country running to swimming programs. He was the first editor and publisher of *Swimming World* magazine and wrote several books and articles on swimming and coaching techniques. His great swimmers included Jimmy McLane, Alan Ford and Jeff Farrell.
Also in: Swimming and Diving Hall of Fame, Citizens Savings Hall of Fame Athletic Museum.

KITAMURA, Kusuo

Swimmer

Born in Japan 1918, Kusuo Kitamura was the youngest man ever to win an Olympic gold medal (1932). He was 14 years old when he won the 1500-m. race in Los Angeles. His success, it is felt, can be attributed to careful nutrition, training and stroke mechanics. Kitamura is now chairman of the foreign relations committee of Nippon Suiei, the Japanese Swimming Federation.

LONGFELLOW, Commodore Wilbert E.

Contributor

A giant man with a booming voice and boundless energy; a reporter in Providence, R.I; convinced the Rhode Island legislature to appropriate funds for lifesaving equipment.

Commodore Wilbert E. Longfellow set about finding ways to create water safety education programs when the mounting toll of drownings in the United States was reaching alarming proportions. Longfellow earned the first Red Cross lifesaving certificate and in 1914 was hired by the Red Cross to head a water safety education program. He traveled from community to community teaching swimming skills and lifesaving techniques. Longfellow's motto was "Every American a swimmer, every swimmer a lifesaver."

MANN, Matt II

Coach

Born in England; learned to swim at age 8 in the Leeds Public Bath and the sluiceways draining from Leeds' woolen mills; some days would be dyed blue, red or brown; at 9 England's boy champion; immigrated to the United States; was stopped at Ellis Island for insufficient funds; shipped to Toronto; got job as dry goods clerk; fired; began coaching; married; daughter Rose Mary Dawson; could never remember a name, all boys were "son," all girls were "honey"; died at the age of 77.

Matt Mann was one of this country's first high school coaches at Buffalo in 1907. In 1910 he coached the Syracuse University team. He coached at both Harvard and Yale as well as the New York Athletic Club, Brooklyn's Poly Prep, Lawrenceville and the Navy. He became Michigan's first full-time swim coach and won eight NCAA team championships in a row, 12 in 15 years and is considered the United States' most successful college coach. His 1952 U.S. Olympic team was very successful. Matt Mann retired from Michigan at the age of 70. He went on to Oklahoma for eight more years, never losing a Big Eight swimming meet. Mann also founded summer swim camps in the Canadian North Woods.
Also in: Swimming and Diving Hall of Fame, Citizens Savings Hall of Fame Athletic Museum.

McCORMICK, Patricia Keller

Diver

Born May 12, 1930; from Seal Beach, Calif; brother Bob; married in 1949; coached by her airline pilot husband Glen McCormick; swam a half mile a day until two days before birth of son; Pan-Am Gold and Silver Medals 1951; two Olympic Gold Medals 1952; two Pan-Am Gold Medals 1955; two Olympic Gold Medals 1956.

Pat McCormick dove for the Los Angeles Athletic Club. In 1947 Pat took second place in the national platform event. She missed the 1948 Olympic team by less than one point. In 1949 she took the national platform event and in 1950 she defended that title as well as taking the 1- and 3-m. national championship on springboard. Pat scored an all-time first in 1951, by taking all five national titles. That same year she won a gold medal in the Pan-Am Games in the platform event and was second in the springboard. At the 1952 Olympic Games in Helsinki, Pat won both the platform and springboard gold medals. During the next four years she won a total of 77 national championships, as well as the platform and springboard gold medals in the 1955 Pan-Am Games. At the 1956 Melbourne Olympic Games, Pat McCormick became the only person in diving history to score a double double, successfully defending both her platform and springboard championships. Pat's other honors include the Babe Zaharias Woman Athlete of the Year; the Citizens Savings Hall of Fame Athletic Museum North American Athlete of the Year; the Associated Press Woman Athlete of the Year and AAU Sullivan Award for Amateur Athlete of the Year.
Also in: Swimming and Diving Hall of Fame, Citizens Savings Hall of Fame Athletic Museum.

MORRIS, Pamela

Synchronized Swimmer

Pam Morris of the San Francisco Merionettes was synchronized swimming's first triple winner in 1965 indoor and outdoor championships for solo, duet and team. She teamed with Patty Willard for the duet championship. Pam was a member of the Merionettes for the team competition. The team consisted of Margo McGrath, Rhea Irvine, Patsy Mical, Carol Redmond, Kathie McBride and Sharon Lawson.
Also in: Swimming and Diving Hall of Fame, Citizens Savings Hall of Fame Athletic Museum.

RAWLS, Katherine "Peggy"

Swimmer and Diver

Born June 14, 1918; parents Bill and Sadie Rawls; sisters Dorothy and Evelyn made the U.S. national relay team; Peggy was swimming at 18 months; brother Sonny an excellent diver; Olympic Bronze Medal 1932; two Olympic Bronze Medals 1936; retired from competitive swimming to become a W. W. II top female pilot; one of the original 25 women pilots who organized the WAFs.

Katherine Rawls twice won four titles at the national championships. The first in 1933 in springboard diving, 200-m. breaststroke, 880-yd. freestyle and 300-m. medley. Throughout her career, Katherine won both diving and swimming championships, 33 national championships in all. She was undefeated in the individual medley for eight years. Although she won in two Olympic trials, 1922 and 1936, she was a bronze medalist at the age of 14 in 1932 and a double bronze medalist in the 1936 Olympic Games.
Also in: Swimming and Diving Hall of Fame, Citizens Savings Hall of Fame Athletic Museum.

RITTER, Richard Max

Contributor

Born 1886 in Magdeburg, Germany; son of a manufacturer; educated in London from 1906 to 1909; immigrated to the United States in 1910; American citizen in 1916; built up a cloth dyeing and finishing company; became a millionaire.

R. Max Ritter competed as a swimmer in two Olympic Games, 1908 and 1912. In Germany he founded the Hellas Club. In the United States he became a member of the New York Athletic Club and was captain of that swim team until 1922. He helped to found FINA, setting up the first international rules for swimming, diving and water polo. In 1936 Max Ritter was the U.S. representative on the FINA Bureau and by 1946 he was honorary secretary and treasurer where he served until 1952. He was elected president in 1960 and an honorary member in 1964.
Also in: Swimming and Diving Hall of Fame, Citizens Savings Hall of Fame Athletic Museum.

ROSE, Murray
Swimmer
Born 1939 in Great Britain; family from Nairnshire in the highlands of Scotland; ancestry of barons; immigrated to Australia as a baby; lived in Double Bay, a resort area of Sydney; learned to swim on the beach; raised on a diet that excluded meat, fish, poultry, refined flour, sugar and chemicalized products; publication by Ian F. Rose on principles behind the diet called *Faith, Love and Seaweed;* three Olympic Gold Medals 1956; Olympic Gold, Silver and Bronze Medals 1960; graduated from Univ. Southern Calif. 1962; majored in drama and television; entertained by Queen Elizabeth and Prince Philip on the royal yacht; featured on postage stamp issued by the Dominican Republic.

Murray Rose's nine-year career included world records in the 880-yd, 800-m, 440-yd, 300-m, 200-m, 1500-m. and 1650-m. He became the 1956 triple gold medal winner at the Olympic Games in Melbourne where he won the 400- and 1500-m. events and was a member of the winning relay team. At the 1960 Olympics in Rome he won the 400-m. again, as well as a silver in the 1500-m. and a bronze in the freestyle relay.
Also in: Swimming and Diving Hall of Fame, Citizens Savings Hall of Fame Athletic Museum.

SCHOLLANDER, Donald Arthur
Swimmer
Born April 30, 1946; from Oregon; a law student at Yale Univ; 5 ft. 11 in. tall, 173 lbs; four Olympic Gold Medals 1964; three Pam-Am Gold Medals 1967; Olympic Silver Medal 1968.

Don Schollander was the first man in the world to break 2 min. for the 200-m. freestyle, in 1963. He did most of his swimming for George Haines at Santa Clara. Don was the first swimmer to win four gold medals at one Olympic Game. He did this at the 1964 Games in Tokyo in the 100-m. freestyle, the 400-m. freestyle and the 400- and 800-m. freestyle relay. He also won the Pan-American 200-m. title in 1967 along with two more relay golds. Don swam in the 200-m. event in the 1968 Olympic Games, breaking a world record in the trials, but taking the silver medal in the finals behind Australian Mike Wenden. Don was selected as top athlete at the 1964 Olympics and was awarded the U.S. and World Athlete of the Year in 1964.
Also in: Swimming and Diving Hall of Fame, Citizens Savings Hall of Fame Athletic Museum.

WEBB, Captain Matthew
Swimmer
Born June 19, 1948, in Irongate, Shropshire, England; learned to swim at age 7; awarded the Albert Medal for saving a comrade from drowning; had a vaudeville act; died in 1883 at the age of 35 when he tried to swim across the rapids just above Niagara Falls; buried at Niagara Falls, Ont.

Captain Matthew Webb was the first to swim across the English Channel on August 25, 1875. The grueling trip took him 21 hrs. and 45 min. until he stepped onto the beach at Calais. Before the start he was rubbed with porpoise oil. His food intake consisted of beer, brandy and beef tea. Webb swam the breaststroke at about 25 cycles a minute. Journalists came along to witness the feat.

WEISSMULLER, Johnny
Swimmer
Born June 2, 1904, in Windsor, Conn; swam in Bill Rose's World's Fair Aquacade; worked for a bathing suit company for five years at $500 a week; invited for a screen test for the film part of Tarzan; said no, but bribed with promises of meeting Greta Garbo and Clark Gable, and said yes; one of 150 men trying out; at audition had to climb a tree and carry a girl across the stage; forgot about it and left town; was called and told he got the part, "What part?"; became Tarzan; three Olympic Gold Medals and one Bronze Medal 1924; two Olympic Gold Medals 1928.

Johnny Weissmuller set his first world record in March, 1922, at the age of 17. He never lost a race in ten years of amateur swimming in distances from 50 yd. to the half-mile. He set a 100-yd. freestyle record of 51 secs. in 1927 that stood for 17 years. Johnny set 51 world records during his amateur swimming career. In 1924 he won the 100- and 400-m. freestyle events, as well as taking the 400-m. relay and a bronze medal for his participation on the U.S. Olympic water polo team. At Amsterdam in 1928 he retained his 100-m. title and won the relay as well. Johnny's version of the crawl had a great influence on the development of that stroke.
Also in: Swimming and Diving Hall of Fame, Citizens Savings Hall of Fame Athletic Museum.

WHITE, Albert C.
Diver
W. W. I serviceman; toured interallied Europe in 1919 with U.S. basketball team; graduated from Stanford in 1924; captain of gymnastic team; won Pacific Coast Conference all-around gymnastic championship in 1921; two Olympic Gold Medals 1924; in army for W. W. II as Lt. Colonel; city engineer in Richmond, Calif; still giving diving exhibitions at age 65.

Albert White was best off the 1-m. low board. He never lost a contest in that event for his entire career. Al won his Olympic gold medals in 1924 at the Games in Paris. He was victorious in the 3-m. springboard and in the 10-m. platform. He was AAU diving commissioner of the Pacific Association.
Also in: Swiming and Diving Hall of Fame, Citizens Savings Hall of Fame Athletic Museum.

1966

ARMBRUSTER, David

Coach

Dave Armbruster turned out great swim teams from Iowa for 30 years. He was president of the College Coaches Association in 1938, but is best known for his textbook on competitive swimming, *Swimming and Diving.* Armbruster also brought the butterfly stroke into international competition. He is an important link between competitive coaching and teaching.
Also in: Swimming and Diving Hall of Fame, Citizens Savings Hall of Fame Athletic Museum.

BACHRACH, William

Coach

Bill Bachrach is the coach of the Illinois Athletic Club who weighed 300 lbs. He is the only coach whose swimmers and divers won every men's national AAU championship event in 1914. He coached two winning U.S. Olympic teams, and his swimmers won a total of 120 national AAU championships. Some of his great swimmers include Arne Borg, Johnny Weissmuller, Al Swartz, Sybil Bauer, Ethel Lackie and Stubby Krueger.
Also in: Swimming and Diving Hall of Fame, Citizens Savings Hall of Fame Athletic Museum.

BORG, Arne

Swimmer

Born 1901 in Sweden; had an illogical swimming style; legendary sports hero of Sweden; went to Spain on holiday when called up for national service; ended up in cell 306 in Gota Prison; friends always sending him food and drink; upon release he had gained 8 kg; Olympic Gold Medal 1928.

Arne Borg won the 150-m. gold medal in 1928. His world record for the same race in 1927 at Bologna, Italy, stood up for 11 years. He set 32 individual world records. In the United States during the two years he roomed with and was teammate of Johnny Weissmuller, he won six individual national AAU championships.

BRANDSTEN, Ernst

Diver and Coach

Born in Sweden; married Greta Johanson, his first Olympic diving champion; came to the United States in 1911; also a ski jumper.

Ernst Brandsten was active for 51 years as a diver and coach, competing from 1897 through the 1912 Olympic Games for Sweden. He is considered the "Father of Modern Diving." After Sweden, he moved to Stanford University where his college divers dominated the 1920, 1924 and 1928 Olympics. By 1920 he had installed the most complete training quarters for diving instruction ever assembled in the United States. He invented the tapered springboard and movable fulcrum. Some of his more famous students were Clarence Pinkston, Al White, Dave Fall, Pete Desjardins and Marjarie Gestring.
Also in: Swimming and Diving Hall of Fame, Citizens Savings Hall of Fame Athletic Museum.

CLARK, Steve

Swimmer

Graduated from Los Altos High School; attended Yale Univ, later Harvard Law School; three Olympic Gold Medals 1964.

Steve Clark won five NCAA individual championships at Yale and six AAU titles for the Santa Clara Swim Club. He won three gold medals at the Tokyo Olympics, setting a world record of 52.9 for the 100-m. freestyle. He was the first man in the world to swim faster than 21 secs. for 50 yds. Clark was the world's fastest freestyle sprint swimmer for five years, at the same time Chris Von Saltza was Santa Clara's premier woman swimmer. Steve developed tendonitis in his shoulder during the United States' sudden-death Olympic trials. He made the team as fourth-place swimmer, and, according to U.S. rules, could only participate in the Olympics as a relay swimmer.

COLEMAN, Georgia

Diver

Born in St. Maries, Idaho; a never-ending smile that made her a favorite everywhere; two Olympic Silver Medals 1928; died at the age of 29.

Georgia Coleman had been diving for six months when she made the Olympic team in 1928 and placed second on both the springboard and tower. In 1929 she won every U.S. national diving title and lost only once in the next four years. She was the first woman to combine men's acrobatic strength and feminine grace in diving.
Also in: Swimming and Diving Hall of Fame, Citizens Savings Hall of Fame Athletic Museum.

CURTIS, Ann

Swimmer

Born March 6, 1926; tall and graceful; Olympic Gold and Silver Medals 1948.

Ann Curtis was the premier freestyler of her era. Swimming for the San Francisco Crystal Plunge Club she won 34 national gold medals, including 8 relay and 26 individual medals, all for freestyle. She crowned her career by winning the Olympic 400-m. title in London and then placing second behind Greta Andersen in the 100-m. She received the Sullivan Award, given annually to the top amateur athlete in the United States.
Also in: Swimming and Diving Hall of Fame, Citizens Savings Hall of Fame Athletic Museum.

DESJARDINS, Peter

Diver

Born April 12, 1907, in Manitoba, Can; family moved to Miami Beach, Fla; became a U.S. citizen; graduated from Stanford Univ. with a degree in economics; two Olympic Gold Medals 1928.

Pete Desjardins began diving for Roman Pools in Miami Beach, Fla, at the age of 16. He placed second to Al White in the 3-m. dive in 1924. At the 1925 Outdoor Senior National AAU Championships, he won three first places in the diving events: the 3-m. springboard, the 10-m. platform and the national plain high diving contest. In the 1928 Olympics springboard event, Pete received all 10's, a perfect score in two of his dives, winning two gold medals. After the 1928 Olympics Pete was declared pro for appearing in the Miami water show along with Johnny Weissmuller, Martha Norelius and Helen Meany.
Also in: Swimming and Diving Hall of Fame, Citizens Savings Hall of Fame Athletic Museum.

FORD, Alan

Swimmer

From the Panama Canal Zone; swam for Henry Grieser's Red, White and Blue Troupe there.

Ford was the first to break 50 secs. for 100 yd. freestyle, surpassing Johnny Weissmuller's record of 51 secs. flat that had stood for 16 years. He twice won the U.S. national AAU 200-m. – 220-yd. freestyle titles and numerous record-breaking relay times.
Also in: Swimming and Diving Hall of Fame, Citizens Savings Hall of Fame Athletic Museum.

HAJOS, Alfred

Swimmer

Born February 1, 1878, in Budapest, Hungary, as Arnold Guttmann; eventually took swimming pseudonym for legal name; twice a member of the Hungarian soccer team; won a silver medal for sports architecture at 1924 Olympic Games; designed Hungary's finest competitive swimming pool, club and baths on Margaret Island, Danube; two Olympic Gold Medals 1896; Olympic Silver Medal 1924.

Alfred Hajos was the first modern Olympic swimming champion and winner of two gold medals at Athens in 1896. He won the 100- and 1200-m. freestyle events.

HOLM, Eleanor

Swimmer

Born December 6, 1913; Olympic Gold Medal 1932; signed to star for Billy Rose in the Aquacades in 1937, married boss; succeeded in show business.

Eleanor Holm began in 1927 to win nine national golds in the individual medley. She was 15 years old when she participated in her first Olympic Games in 1928. In 1932 Eleanor won a gold medal in the 100-yd. backstroke event and was expected to win the same event in the 1936 Games until she was kicked off the team and sent home for sipping champagne with the officials on shipboard. Eleanor held six world records in backstroke. Her 100-yd. event times held for 16 years in the United States. During her career Eleanor Holm won 29 national championships.
Also in: Swimming and Diving Hall of Fame, Citizens Savings Hall of Fame Athletic Museum.

HVEGER, Ragnhild

Swimmer

Born December 10, 1920, in Elsinore, Denmark; Olympic Silver Medal 1936; three European Championship Gold Medals 1938.

At the age of 13, never having been in a race before, Ragnhild Hveger won the 400-m. title at the Danish championship. In 1940 when Ragnhild was at her peak, the Olympic games were canceled. That year she set her eighth 400-m. world record with a time of 5:00.1 that held for 16 years. At 15 she won the 400-m. silver medal at the 1936 Berlin Olympic Games. At the 1938 European championships she took three gold medals. After seven years of marriage and retirement, Ragnhild Hveger came back at the age of 32 to place fifth in the 1952 Olympic 400-m. event only 4 secs. behind the winner.

KENNEDY, Edward T.

Contributor and Coach

Began as a professional baseball player in New England; learned to swim at the Brookline Baths in Massachusetts.

Edward T. Kennedy was the swimming and water polo coach at Columbia University from 1910 until mandatory retirement in 1955. He managed the 1936 and 1952 U.S. men's Olympic swim teams. He was editor of the *NCAA Swimming Guide* for ten years and the first recipient of the Intercollegiate Interscholastic Swimming Award in 1958. Kennedy helped found and was the second president of the International Swimming Hall of Fame and has chaired the Ft. Lauderdale Christmas Swim Forum for many years.
Also in: Swimming and Diving Hall of Fame, Citizens Savings Hall of Fame Athletic Museum.

MADISON, Helene

Swimmer

Born June 19, 1913; from Seattle, Wash; three Olympic Gold Medals 1932; died November, 1970.

Helene Madison, from Ray Daughters' swim team, is the first woman to have swum the 100-yd. freestyle in one min. flat. She won every freestyle event in the U.S. Women's Nationals in 1930, 1931 and 1932. Her records for 100-m. freestyle lasted 15 years; for the 500-yd. freestyle, 23 years; and the 880-m. freestyle, 5 years. Helene retired at the age of 19 after three years of competitive swimming and three gold medals at the 1932 Olympic Games. She was the winner of the 100- and 400-m. freestyle and anchor swimmer in the world-record-breaking relay team.
Also in: Swimming and Diving Hall of Fame, Citizens Savings Hall of Fame Athletic Museum.

MANN, Shelly

Swimmer

Olympic Gold Medal 1956.

Shelly Mann began competitive training at the age of 12. Two years later she was national champion. Shelly was a great four-stroke swimmer, holding records for the 400-m. individual medley. She won 24 national titles and was an Olympic champion at age 17, winning the 100-m. butterfly at the 1956 Melbourne Olympic Games. Shelly was a member of the Walter Reed team coached by Jim Campbell and Stan Tinkham. They trained at a hospital pool at 6 a.m. before the patients needed the pool for restorative swimming.
Also in: Swimming and Diving Hall of Fame, Citizens Savings Hall of Fame Athletic Museum.

MEDICA, Jack

Swimmer

Born October 5, 1933; from Seattle, Wash; attended Washington State Univ; Olympic Gold Medal 1936.

Jack Medica was a one-man team at Washington State University. He won the 220-, 440- and 1500-m. freestyle in 1934, 1936 and 1938, plus 17 national AAU championships and 11 world records from 220 yd. to 1 mi. Jack was Olympic champion in the 1936 Berlin Olympics, winning a gold medal in the 400-m. freestyle event. He won three individual events in the NCAA championships for three years in a row. Jack Medica graduated from college undefeated. He went on to coach at Columbia University and the University of Pennsylvania.
Also in: Swimming and Diving Hall of Fame, Citizens Savings Hall of Fame Athletic Museum.

O'CONNOR, Wally

Water Polo

O'Connor, a national champion swimmer, swam at Stanford, where he was swimming captain, and later swam on a national championship relay team for Coach Bill Bachrach's Illinois Athletic Club. He was considered Number One American water polo player. He played water polo for four Olympic teams. In 1924 and 1936 he played with the Los Angeles Athletic Club, and in 1928 and 1932 he played with IAC. He was flag bearer for the 1936 U.S. Olympic team in Berlin. He was water polo captain of every team he ever played on, from the Venice, Calif, Swimming Association to Stanford and the Los Angeles Athletic Club.

PEPPE, Mike

Coach

Born in the United States; graduated from Ohio State Univ. 1927; received masters degree from Columbia Univ. 1928; returned to Ohio State Univ; university's swimming coach 1931 – 1962.

Mike Peppe is known as the coach of more Olympic divers than any other man. Twenty divers who studied under Mike Peppe bagged 96 of 125 available national titles, including two gold, four silver and three bronze Olympic medals in the four games, 1948, 1952, 1956 and 1960. Mike Peppe was a swimming coach at Ohio State University for 33 years, and during those 33 years won 33 major championships, 12 Big Ten, 11 NCAA, and 10 NAAU. Ohio State, in dual meets, won 173 and lost 37. His team went undefeated in 12 different seasons. He coached swimmers and divers, won 312 individual and relay championships, 5 Olympic gold medals and 19 Olympic team berths. In 1947 and 1956 Peppe's Ohio State divers swept the board 1, 2, 3, 4, in NCAA diving finals. He had the best record of any coach in the 1950s. He was considered the bantam master of the boards and the water at Ohio State. In 1948 Peppe was U.S. Olympic diving coach at London and again in 1952 at Helsinki. At the first official Pan-American Games in 1951 at Buenos Aires, he was swimming and diving coach of the U.S. team. Ohio State contributed 19 of the 92 members in the four Olympic Games from W.W. II. On the 1952 team of 25 members, 9 were Buckeyes.

Also in: Swimming and Diving Hall of Fame, Citizens Savings Hall of Fame Athletic Museum.

PINKSTON, Clarence "Pinky"

Coach

Born February 2, 1900 in Wichita, Kans; Olympic Gold and Silver Medal 1920; two Olympic Bronze Medals 1924; married Betty Becker in 1924; father of twins in 1926; died in 1965.

Clarence Pinkston won the 1920 highboard title and was runner-up in the springboard. Four years later he won two bronze medals for his effort in Paris. Coached by Ernst Brandsten of Stanford, Pinky took five successive AAU platform championships and two springboard titles. He coached his wife Betty to her second Olympic crown on the highboard in 1928. As coach of the Detroit Athletic Club, he saw many swimmers and divers to Olympic glory. He believed in the one swimmer, one coach theory. Some of his champions included Clark Scholes, Dick Hanley and Dick Degner.

Also in: Swimming and Diving Hall of Fame, Citizens Savings Hall of Fame Athletic Museum.

RIS, Wally

Swimmer

Two Olympic Gold Medals.

Wally Ris was on the Great Lakes Navy team that set a 400-yd. freestyle relay record during W. W. II. He won five straight AAU 100-yd. gold medals from 1945 to 1949 and was voted Outstanding Swimmer at the U.S. NCAA. Ris was a double gold medal winner in the 1948 Olympic Games in London, in the 100-m. freestyle and with the 800-m. freestyle relay.

Also in: Swimming and Diving Hall of Fame, Citizens Savings Hall of Fame Athletic Museum.

SAKAMOTO, Soichi

Coach

Soichi Sakamoto is the coach responsible for the Hawaiian swimmers dominating the sport from 1912 to 1932. His swimming greats included Hirose, Nakama, Smith, Konno, Oyakawa, Onekea, Cleveland, Woolsey, Tenabe, Miki, Kalama, Kleinschmidt, Kawamoto and Hoe. Sakamoto was sought by swimmers all over the world. His "magic touch" consisted of technique, method, dedication and conditioning. This produced champions at all strokes and distances.

SMITH, William

Swimmer

Born in Hawaii; began training in a sugar plantation irrigation ditch on Maui; attended Ohio State Univ; later captain of the Surf Guards at Waikiki Beach; two Olympic Gold Medals 1948; now water safety director, Department of Parks and Recreation, for the city and county of Honolulu.

Bill Smith set seven world records in 1941 and 1942. His 200-, 400- and 800-m. freestyle marks stood for eight years. At the 1942 outdoor nationals at New London, Conn, Smith won three freestyle events, one was a world record and the other two were American records. During his career he won a total of 36 individual and relay titles in AAU, Big Ten and NCAA championships. Smith topped his career with two gold medals at the 1948 London Olympic Games, for the 400-m. freestyle and the 800-m. freestyle relay. He was eight times an All-American swimmer, 1941 to 1949, and was three times runnerup for the Sullivan Award for amateur athletes.

Also in: Swimming and Diving Hall of Fame, Citizens Savings Hall of Fame Athletic Museum.

VERDEUR, Joseph

Swimmer

Olympic Gold Medal 1948.

Joe Verdeur broke the world's butterfly-breaststroke record 12 times between 1945 and 1950. He won nine national AAU gold medals in the 300-m. individual medley and ten AAU gold medals in the 200-m. breaststroke. Joe attended LaSalle College in Philadelphia. He climaxed his career by winning an Olympic Games gold medal and scoring a record for the 200-m. breaststroke at the 1948 Games in London.

Also in: Swimming and Diving Hall of Fame, Citizens Savings Hall of Fame Athletic Museum.

VON SALTZA, Susan Christine

Swimmer

Born January 13, 1944, in the United States; of Swedish descent; grandfather Count Philip came to the United

States around 1900; father a medical doctor; five Pan-Am Gold Medals 1959; three Olympic Gold Medals and one Silver Medal 1960; attended Stanford Univ, majored in Asian history.

Chris Von Saltza swam for the Santa Clara Swim Club under George Haines and was one of the first graduates of age-group swimming. At the age of 13 Chris won her first U.S. outdoor title for the 220-yd. backstroke. She won the same event in world record time a year later. At the 1959 Pan-American Games she won five gold medals for the 100-, 200-, 400- and 400-m. freestyle and medley relays. Chris won three gold medals and a silver medal at the 1960 Rome Olympic Games. She was first in the 400-m. freestyle, in the 400-m. freestyle relay and in the 400-m. medley relay, placing second behind Dawn Fraser in the 100-m. freestyle. Chris retired in 1961 to attend school. During 1963 and 1964 she was a coach-consultant in Asia in the American Specialist Program. She visited and taught competitive swimming throughout Southeast Asia and was an assistant chaperone-coach for the women at the 1968 Olympics in Mexico.
Also in: Swimming and Diving Hall of Fame, Citizens Savings Hall of Fame Athletic Museum.

WILLIAMS, Esther
Contributor
From Los Angeles, Calif; one of 75 women auditioning for the female lead opposite Johnny Weissmuller in 1940; Weissmuller picked Esther from the group because she was tall; became aquacade and movie swim star.

Esther Williams won her first AAU championship gold medal in the 100-m. freestyle in 1939. Because the Olympic Games were canceled, Esther decided to apply for an acting job. Her movie career played a major role in the promotion of swimming, making it attractive to the public.

1967

ANDERSON, Miller
Diver
Attended Ohio State Univ; enlisted in Army Air Corps; received many Distinguished Service Medals; forced to bail out on 112th mission; left leg almost torn off by plane's tail; captured by Germans; hospitalized; silver plates installed above left knee; despite doctor's predictions, made the most remarkable comeback in sports history in 1946; Olympic Silver Medal 1948; Olympic Silver Medal 1952; died of a heart attack at his home in Columbus, Ohio, 1966.

Miller Anderson won his first AAU championship gold medal at New Haven, Conn, in 1942, while he was enrolled at Ohio State. W.W. II and his injuries kept him out of diving until his return to competition in 1946. Anderson went on to win a total of 16 major titles—three Western Conferences, five NCAA's, seven NAAU indoor and one AAU outdoor. In 1947 as a senior at Ohio State and varsity captain, he was voted outstanding swimmer in intercollegiate competition by the College Swimming Coaches Association. Anderson won the 3-m. springboard silver medal in the 1948 and 1952 Olympic Games. He is also noted for his remarkable ability as a twist diver. He originated the forward one and a half somersault with two twists and the backward one and a half with one twist, to be used in competition.

BAUER, Carl Otto
Contributor
Born in Germany; came to the United States in 1913; awarded the American Red Cross's first lifesaving emblem in 1919; organized the Meramec River Patrol that made about 1500 rescues between 1927 and 1955; was director of Chicago's central YMCA.

Carl Bauer took a job at the Missouri Athletic Club as coach. Some of his name pupils include Walter Schlueter, Oliver Horn, Hoot Newman, John Carson and Jim McKenna. Between 1926 and 1931, Bauer also coached Washington University to several Missouri Valley Conference swimming championships. Then, in 1932 he moved to St. Louis University where he gained a national reputation as a water polo coach. He was national AAU water polo chairman from 1947 to 1951. In 1947 Bauer began pushing the system of swimming competition graduated by age. Although he was no longer in power in the AAU when his age-group ideas broke out all over the United States, he must be given credit for germinating age-group swimming. He is often called the "Father of Age-Group Swimming."
Also in: Swimming and Diving Hall of Fame, Citizens Savings Hall of Fame Athletic Museum.

BAUER, Sybil
Swimmer
Attended Northwestern Univ; played basketball and field hockey; president of the Women's Athletic Association; member of Student Council; died of cancer at age 22; fiance Ed Sullivan at her bedside; pallbearers were Johnny Weissmuller, Bob Skelton, Hugo Miller, Weston Kimball, Ralph Breyer and Dick Howell, all famous swimmers.

Sybil Bauer was the world's first great backstroker and the epitome of grace and beauty of women in sports. She won six successive national AAU 100-yd. backstroke crowns from 1921 to 1926. At one time she held all existing backstroke records for women. She won nationals in 100-m, 150- and 220-yd. backstrokes and was part of a world record and national champion freestyle relay. Sybil Bauer was the first woman to break existing men's world records in the 440-yd. backstroke, which she lowered by 4 secs.
Also in: Swimming and Diving Hall of Fame, Citizens Savings Hall of Fame Athletic Museum.

BEAUREPAIRE, Sir Frank
Swimmer
Born 1891 in Australia; three Olympic Silver Medals and three Bronze Medals 1908, 1912, 1920 and 1924; interested in the tire business; started his own retreading shop in Melbourne; ultimately ran the Olympic Consolidated Industries, a £10.5 million consolidation of his companies; mayor of Melbourne; died of a heart attack in a Melbourne barber shop in May 1956.

Sir Frank Beaurepaire won a total of six Olympic medals between 1903 and 1924 and is the holder of 14 world records. He won more than 200 first-class swimming championships. His fastest times were done when he was past the age of 30. As mayor of Melbourne, he was principal organizer of the 1956 Olympics. He died just five days before the Melbourne Olympic Games began.

BLEIBTREY, Ethelda
Swimmer

Began swimming because of polio; received citation for "nude swimming" at Manhattan Beach in 1919 after removing her stockings; surfed with the Prince of Wales in Hawaii; congratulations received from King Albert of Belgium; dated oarsman Jack Kelly; first to have her hair "bobbed" along with Irene Castle and Charlotte Boyle; three Olympic Gold Medals 1920; later a successful swim coach and teacher; now a practicing nurse in North Palm Beach, Fla.

Ethelda Bleibtrey took up competitive swimming for the first time in 1918, won the nationals within a year, and was the best in the world by the end of the second year. She was the only person ever to win all the women's swimming events at any Olympic Games. She won three gold medals in the Games at Antwerp in 1920. At the time she held the world record for backstroke, but it was not an Olympic event or she would have had four gold medals. Ethelda turned pro in 1922. She started the U.S. Olympian Association with Jack Kelly, Sr.
Also in: Swimming and Diving Hall of Fame, Citizens Savings Hall of Fame Athletic Museum.

BRAUN, Ma
Coach

Born 1881 in Rotterdam, Holland; daughter, Sister, won 1928 Olympic backstroke gold medal; at 70 years old, still watching for new swimming styles.

Ma Braun was one the world's most volatile and colorful coaches and the first great women's swimming coach. Ma was a progressive, constantly experimenting with strokes and tough new training methods. Her philosophy was, what they can do, we must learn to do better. Her swimmers won Olympic medals in 1928, 1932, 1936, 1948 and 1952. Ma's first great pupil was Marie Baron, followed by Willie den Turk, "Riek" Mastenbroek, her daughter "Sister" Braun, Puck Oversloot, Doorje Heeselaars, Jopie van Alphen and Els Steehouwer.

CANN, Tedford
Swimmer

Football halfback, basketball and track star at New York Univ; brother Howard ran hurdles and shotput in the 1920 Olympics; father athletic director of New York Univ; won U.S. Congressional Medal of Honor as a swimmer for repairing his leaking ship in the North Atlantic; died January 1963.

Teddy Cann's greatest swimming performances were after the war, although he did swim before. He was the first man in the world to break 2:20 for the 220-m. He won the AAU national championships in the 50-, 100- and 200-m. events and was the first to win all three titles in a single year. Ted missed the 1920 Olympics when a taxi cab accident broke his leg in six places. He never swam another championship race, but came back to play water polo with the New York Athletic Club's championship team until the early 1930s.

COUSTEAU, Jacques Yves
Contributor

Born June 11, 1910, in St. André-de-Cubzac, France; a sickly child, but became a good swimmer; educated at the Naval Academy of Brest; joined the French Navy, rose to rank of Captain; worked for French Underground during the war; received the Legion of Honor, Officer Class and the Croix de Guerre.

The popular oceanographer Jacques Cousteau is honored in the Hall of Fame for opening up new horizons in swimming as related to both recreation and science. "The Undersea World of Jacques Cousteau," a series of filmed tours of the ocean and its inhabitants produced for television, has popularized the scientific research of many oceanographers and has extended the general public's knowledge of and interest in oceanography and marine sciences. Cousteau became director of the Oceanographic Museum and head of France's Underwater Research Center shortly after he retired from the Navy. He has been working to create means of establishing communities of human beings beneath the oceans. Along these lines, in 1962 two men were able to survive for a week on the ocean floor in an iron house. Cousteau believes, "Obviously, man has to enter the sea. There is no choice in the matter."

DURACK, Fanny
Swimmer

Olympic Gold Medal 1912.

The Australian Fanny Durack was the first female Olympic champion. She held 11 world records between 1912 and 1918. Fanny beat all comers in the world over eight years. Her world tours did more to promote swimming than those of any woman. She did more than any other swimmer to make the term "Australian Crawl" a definition that survives until this day, although completely different. Fanny Durack was finally defeated by American Ethelda Bleibtrey.

FURUHASHI, Hironashin
Swimmer

Born September 16, 1928, in Japan; graduate of Nihon Univ. in Tokyo; now assistant professor of athletics at Nihon Univ; member of the Japanese Olympic Committee and FINA.

Furuhashi symbolized Japanese hopes for a return to greatness from the rubble of total defeat in W. W. II. He never won an Olympic medal because Japan had not been readmitted after W. W. II in time for the 1948 Olympic Games. In August 1949 Furuhashi was invited to participate in the U.S. Nationals. He set three world records. He repeated his record breaking in Brazil in 1951, but contracted malaria and was far below par for the 1952 Helsinki Olympic Games.

HANDLEY, L. deBreda
Coach

Born 1874 in Rome; came to New York in 1896 as an importer; joined the New York Athletic Club; competed in football, swimming, water polo, yachting and rowing; won Olympic gold medals in water polo and relay swimming; on winning polo teams in AAU meets from 1898 to 1911; took up yachting and field dog-training; silver cup for medley race (walking, running, horseback riding, bicycling, rowing and swimming in continuous quarter miles), was world record holder.

L. deB. Handley was the first women's Olympic coach in 1924 and his Women's Swimming Association dominated meets between world wars. He is considered the father of U.S. women's swimming. His well-known swimmers include Ethelda Bliebtrey, Martha Morelius, Aileen Riggin, Gertrude Ederle, Eleanor Holm and Charlotte Boyle. L. deB. is also rated as one of swimming's foremost journalists. He was bylined in the *Times, Tribune World* and *American,* published five books on swimming and wrote the swimming section in the *Encyclopaedia Britannica.*

KAUFMAN, Beth
Contributor
Born 1894; married; two children; nine grandchildren; swims a half mile every day.

Beth Kaufman organized and nursed age-group swimming through its first and fastest growing ten years. She began as a Red Cross volunteer. She enrolled 500 children a year in the Red Cross program and 20 years later 500,000 registered annually in her national AAU age-group swimming program. Her program for age-group swimming went national in 1952 and caught on even at the international level.

NEUSCHAEFER, Al
Coach
Began coaching career as head football coach at Iowa Wesleyan Univ; player-coach of Stapleton, Long Island; head line coach at Rutgers Univ; taught at Trenton, N.J, High School.

Al Neuschaefer chose to coach high school swimming in Trenton, N.J. His teams won 17 Eastern Interscholastic Championships and 19 N.J. state titles. They twice won the Rutgers Invitational. Neuschaefer was considered Number One high school coach of his day. He was a very successful diving coach as well. Al Neuschaefer has been an organizer and administrator of high school swimming and liaison with the College Coaches Association. He was secretary-treasurer of NISCA for 26 years and was the first secretary-treasurer of the Ft. Lauderdale College Coaches Forum Committee. He is also former commissioner and vice president of the New Jersey AAU.

NORELIUS, Martha
Swimmer
Born in Sweden; raised in the United States; father Charles swam in the 1906 Olympics; Olympic Gold Medal 1924; Olympic Gold Medal 1928; coached for 63 years; married oarsman Joe Wright, Olympic champion; a darling of the social set; died in 1955.

Martha Norelius was the first female to swim with and like men. She used a heavy six-beat kick and high elbow position. Martha always wore a cap and was left on the starting block at the gun on one occasion, while still putting on the cap. She won the race anyway. She won gold medals at the age of 15 in the 1924 Olympic Games and again in 1928, both for the 400-m. During the summer of 1927 Martha set 29 world swimming records, from the 50-m. to the marathons. Her career lasted from 1922 until 1929, when she turned pro after being suspended by the AAU for giving a Miami exhibition in the same pool with professionals. After turning pro she won the $10,000 10-mi. Wrigley Marathon in Canada.
Also in: Swimming and Diving Hall of Fame, Citizens Savings Hall of Fame Athletic Museum.

PINKSTON, Betty Becker
Diver
Born 1903 in Philadelphia, Pa; took up swimming after severe case of diphtheria; Olympic Gold and Silver Medals 1924; Olympic Gold Medal 1928; joined Turngemeninde Club; married Clarence Pinkston; gave birth to twins in 1926; coached swimming and diving in Detroit.

At age 12, Betty Becker took seconds and thirds in the national swimming competition. She became interested in diving, and at 15 won the Middle Atlantic States championship. She joined the Ambassador Swim Club in Atlantic City, N.J. Betty just missed the 1920 Olympic team. In 1922 and 1923 she won the national springboard diving championship at 3 m. and in 1924 added the 1-m. championship to her list. In 1924 Betty made the Olympic team and won her gold medal in the springboard and a silver off the 10-m. tower. In 1926 she won the 3-m. national diving championship in Florida. Betty made another Olympic team in 1928 and won her second gold medal in the 10-m. platform. She helped organize the Michigan Inner Club Swimming Association.

Also in: Swimming and Diving Hall of Fame, Citizens Savings Hall of Fame Athletic Museum.

RADMILOVIC, Paul "Raddy"
Water Polo
Born March 5, 1886, in Cardiff, Great Britain; father was Greek; mother was Irish; two Olympic Gold Medals 1908; Olympic Gold Medal 1912; Olympic Gold Medal 1920; lived in Weston-super-Mare; a golfer and football player; swam a quarter-mile each day until he died at the age of 91 in 1968.

Paul Radmilovic was an international swimmer and water polo player from the age of 16 until he was 45. He won nine American Swimming Association championships from 100 yd. to 5 mi. Radmilovic represented his country in five Olympic games 1896, 1908, 1912, 1920 and 1924, winning gold medals at three of them. He was part of Great Britain's winning 800-m. relay in 1908 and won water polo golds in 1908, 1912 and 1920. Raddy believed in careful and systematic training so that before a race he had some idea what the final result would be.

RIGGIN, Aileen
Swimmer and Diver
Born May 2, 1906, in Newport, R.I; Olympic Gold Medal 1920; Olympic Silver and Bronze Medal 1924; made Hollywood pictures; helped organize and coach Billy Rose's first Aquacade; starred in Aquacade at 1937 Cleveland Exposition; wrote articles for *Colliers, Good Housekeeping* and others; now Ms. Howard Soule; living in Honolulu.

Aileen Riggin was the tiny Olympic champion, coached by Fred Sponbert, who won the women's springboard event in the 1920 Olympic Games. She was high point woman for swimming and diving at the U.S. national AAU championships, winning three outdoor and one indoor springboard titles, and was a member of two 800-m. and one 400-yd. freestyle relay team. In the 1924 Olympics, 18-year-old Aileen won medals in both diving and swimming, a silver in the 3-m. springboard and a bronze in the 100-m. backstroke. Aileen Riggin made the first underwater slow motion swimming and diving films

for Grantland Rice in 1922. She turned pro in 1926 and toured the world with various swimming acts.
Also in: Swimming and Diving Hall of Fame, Citizens Savings Hall of Fame Athletic Museum.

ROSS, Norman
Swimmer
Decorated by General Pershing in W.W. I; three Olympic Gold Medals 1920; served as aide to General Doolittle in W.W. II; 6 ft. 2 in. tall, 210 lbs; married a Hawaiian princess; was the country's first classical disc jockey; son, Norman Ross, Jr, radio and TV voice in Chicago.

Norman Ross held 13 FINA world records, won 18 U.S. national championships and had 72 world, national and central U.S. records. He dominated the Allied War Games of 1919 with five firsts. At the 1920 Olympic Games he won three gold medals in the 400-m. freestyle, 1500-m. freestyle and as a participant in the 800-m. freestyle relay. He called a strike of Olympians to win a better ship for the homeward journey, better than the cattle boat that they had come on. While training in Lake Michigan for the Wrigley Marathon, Ross swam from Evanston beach to the first beach on Chicago's North Side. Upon arrival, Ross swam until he could stand and asked the sunbathers, "Is this Milwaukee?" he boomed. "No," came the reply, "It's Chicago." "Nuts!" said Ross slapping the water, "I must have missed my turn!" after which he dove back into the water and began swimming north.
Also in: Swimming and Diving Hall of Fame, Citizens Savings Hall of Fame Athletic Museum.

SPENCE, Walter, Wallace and Leonard
Swimmers
Born in the jungle near Christianburg, British Guyana; father a Scotsman, big game hunter and guide; mother an Indian; four sisters, two swimming champions; youngest brother Harold killed in action in W.W. II, the fastest swimmer of all; Wallace carried scars from piranha bites; Leonard contracted tuberculosis in 1931; Walter was killed trying to catch a train in 1947.

Walter decided he needed U.S. training and moved to Brooklyn at the age of 22. He was a success in breaststroke and the medley and won high point honors at the U.S. national AAU championships, holding ten world records. Ten years later he was high point man for Rutgers in the NCAA championships. Wallace arrived in the States in 1926 and Leonard came in 1928. In 1933 Walter, Wallace and Leonard were the only brother combo ever to win a national AAU relay crown. They broke the world record by 5 secs. in an exhibition at Rutgers, and with Peter Fick as fourth man they won the national AAU 400-yd. freestyle relay in 1935. The Spences monopolized the national AAU indoor breaststroke for 11 years. The brothers swam for Canada and Bermuda in the Olympic Games.
Also in: Swimming and Diving Hall of Fame, Citizens Savings Hall of Fame Athletic Museum.

1968

FARRELL, Jeff
Swimmer
Born February 28, 1937; attended high school in Witchita, Kans; college in Oklahoma; entered Navy as ensign; assigned to ROTC at Yale Univ; two Olympic Gold Medals 1960.

Jeff Farrell was hampered in a majority of his attempts at the top spot by a variety of injuries. He was considered a shoo-in for the 1960 Olympic team, until six days before the trials when he came down with acute appendicitis. He swam the trials in yards of adhesive tape and placed fourth, qualifying for the relays. In Rome he took two gold medals while scoring world records. Just about the time Jeff was ready to make his run for the top, he wrecked his shoulder in a dormitory wrestling match. The operation left him with third place in the Nationals. He then joined the Navy and worked out at Yale with coach Bob Kiphuth. Just as he was unbeatable, his appendectomy came back to haunt him.
Also in: Swimming and Diving Hall of Fame, Citizens Savings Hall of Fame Athletic Museum.

FRANKLIN, Benjamin
Contributor
Born January 17, 1706, in Boston, Mass; was the 15th child and youngest son in a family of 17; parents Josiah and Abiah were soap and candle makers; kept home after age 10 to help cut wicks and melt tallow.

Franklin was an early oceanographer. He charted and measured the Gulf Stream. He advised on water safety, lifeboat rescue escape from shipwrecks and even recommended universal learn-to-swim classes. Franklin was also a competent coach and teacher. He taught his friend Wygate and Wygate's friend to swim. His inventions made him one of the first men to use flippers, which he tied on both hands and feet. He was also the first kiteman, "water skier," pulled across a lake in tow of a kite. Franklin was also one of the first synchronized and marathon swimmers. In 1726 at the request of friends, he swam 3.5 mi. across the Thames River performing many feats, both above and below the surface, that delighted his company.

HALMAY, Zolten
Swimmer
Born June 18, 1881 in Hungary; two Olympic Silver Medals and one Bronze Medal 1900; two Olympic Gold Medals 1904; two Olympic Silver Medals 1904; factory manager; died May 20, 1956.

Zoltan Halmay won ten medals in five Olympics from 1896 through 1908. He swam in events ranging from 50 m. to 4000 m. His most memorable Olympic win was in 1904 at St. Louis when he won in a swim-off ordered by the judges after a small riot ensued over the judges' inability to come to a definite first decision. Halmay managed to win all of his races swimming with arms only, no leg movement.

HEBNER, Harry
Swimmer
Olympic Gold Medal 1912.

Harry Hebner's career spanned three Olympic Games, 1908, 1912 and 1920. He was Olympic gold medal winner in 1912 for his backstroke time of 1:21.2. His other Olympic efforts were in water polo and freestyle. For seven years, beginning in 1910, Hebner held all world backstroke records and won seven straight U.S. Nationals. He had a total of 35 U.S. national championships ranging from 50 to 500 yd. freestyle and all backstroke distances. As captain of the IAC water polo team, he led his men to five U.S. national victories between 1914 and 1924.

Also in: Swimming and Diving Hall of Fame, Citizens Savings Hall of Fame Athletic Museum.

HODGSON, George Ritchie

Swimmer

See entry in Aquatic Hall of Fame and Museum of Canada, Inc. (Induction Year Unrecorded).

Also in: Canada's Sports Hall of Fame and Canadian Amateur Athletic Hall of Fame.

JARVIS, John Arthur

Swimmer

Born February 24, 1872, in Leicester, England; three daughters, all swim teachers; three Olympic Gold Medals 1900; Olympic Gold and Silver Medals 1906; died May 9, 1933.

John Jarvis had 108 swimming championships to defend his self-proclaimed title of Amateur Swimming Champion of the World. In the 1900 Olympic Games in Paris, Jarvis won three gold medals for his efforts in the 100-, 1000-, and 4000-m. events. At the 1906 Athens Olympic Games, he took a gold and a silver medal with his overarm sidestroke freestyle. Jarvis and English professional champion Joey Nuttall developed a special kick that became known as the Jarvis-Nuttall kick. Some of the records Jarvis set with this swimming style lasted for 28 years. In his later career Jarvis taught lifesaving techniques and saved innumerable lives, including one set of twin sisters. His room full of trophies, to name just a few, include Queen Victoria's Diamond Jubilee One-Mile Championship, German Kaiser's Championship of Europe, Austrian Emperor's World Championship, King of Italy's World Distance Championship, Queen of Holland's World Championship at 4000 m; King Edward VII Coronation Cup One Mile and the Grand Prix of Antwerp 1000 m.

KEALOHA, Warren

Swimmer

Born 1904 in Hawaii; Olympic Gold Medal 1920 and 1924.

Warren Kealoha was 16 when he won his first Olympic backstroke crown in the 1920 Olympic Games. He came back in 1924 to win that title again. Warren was U.S. freestyle champion twice winning the national AAU 50-m. gold medal, but he reigned supreme for six years as the backstroke world record holder and national champion. The biggest problem for Hawaiian swimmers at that time was getting to the mainland in order to participate in competitions.

KOJAC, George Harold

Swimmer

Born 1910 in New York City; learned to swim in the East River; son of Ukrainian immigrants; attended DeWitt Clinton High School; two Olympic Gold Medals 1928; graduated from Rutgers in 1931, fifth in his class; attended Columbia Medical School.

George Kojac first swam competitively with the Boy's Club, later joined the New York Athletic Club and never lost a college swimming race for Rutgers. He set a total of 23 world records. Kojac won every NCAA and NAAU backstroke and freestyle championship from 1927 to 1931. In the 1928 Olympic Games he took two gold medals, one for the 100-m. backstroke with a time of 1:08.2 and the other as a member of the 800-m. freestyle relay. Kojac was too preoccupied with medical school to try for the 1932 Olympic Games, but he came out of retirement ten years later and won the 1939 Metropolitan AAU championships.

Also in: Swimming and Diving Hall of Fame, Citizens Savings Hall of Fame Athletic Museum.

LEE, Sammy

Diver

Born August 1, 1920 in Fresno, Calif; Korean parents; student body president, Number One in class, top athlete in 1939 at Benjamin Franklin High School in Los Angeles; attended Occidental Col; entered medical school at the Univ. Southern Calif, specialized in diseases of the ear; Chinese-American wife; two children; named outstanding American of Korean parentage by the American-Korean Society of Southern California; Olympic Gold Medal and Bronze Medal 1948; Olympic Gold Medal 1952; Sullivan Award 1953.

In 1942 Sammy Lee won his first Men's Senior National AAU springboard and 10-m. tower diving championships. He retired in order to attend medical school. In 1946 Sammy came out of retirement to win another outdoor tower championship. In 1948 at the London Olympic Games, Sammy won the platform diving title and was third in the springboard. At the 1952 Games in Helsinki, he again won the platform diving event. Sammy Lee received the Sullivan Award as America's outstanding amateur athlete in 1953. He was coach of the American diving team at the 1960 Rome Olympic Games.

MASTENBROEK, Hendrika "Rie"

Swimmer

Born in Holland; three Olympic Gold Medals and one Silver Medal 1936; married; three children; now lives in Amsterdam.

Rie Mastenbroek was coached by Ma Braun in Rotterdam. In 1934 she was proclaimed European champion and Number One woman swimmer in Europe. Rie was the sensation of the 1936 Berlin Olympic Games where she won three gold medals in the 100-m. freestyle, 400-m. freestyle and the 400-m. freestyle relay. Her single silver medal at those Games came in the 100-m. backstroke. Rie Mastenbroek held nine world records, six in backstroke and three in freestyle.

POYNTON, Dorothy

Diver

From California; 5 ft. 1.5 in., 112 lbs; Olympic Bronze Medal 1928; Olympic Gold Medal 1932; Olympic Gold and Bronze Medal 1936; did TV commercials; now teaches swimming and diving at the Dorothy Poynton Aquatic Club in Los Angeles.

Dorothy Poynton won her first Olympic medal in 1928 at the age of 12, taking a bronze in the springboard diving. She went on to win the 10-m. tower diving gold medal in two successive Olympic Games, 1932 and 1936. She also

won another bronze medal in the 1936 Olympics. During her career Dorothy won 116 medals.
Also in: Swimming and Diving Hall of Fame, Citizens Savings Hall of Fame Athletic Museum.

RAUSCH, Emil
Swimmer
Born 1881 in Germany; two Olympic Gold Medals and one Bronze Medal 1904; Olympic Silver Medal 1908; promoted German swimming events after retirement until his death on December 14, 1954, at age 72.

Emil Rausch was the last man in the world to win an Olympic gold medal swimming sidestroke. He won two gold medals in the 1904 St. Louis Olympic Games for the mile and the half-mile and finished third in the 220-yd. freestyle. Rausch swam for the Schwimmclub Poseidon-Berlin. His career stretched from 1900 to 1910. In 1908 he received an Olympic silver medal for his part in the 800-m. relay. Emil Rausch was seven times German champion in the 1500-m. from 1901 to 1907, five times winner of the German Kaiserpreis, seven times winner of the Senate Prize of Hamburg and European champion for the 1200-m. in 1901. He also won many national and international lifesaving awards, including the Gold Honor Medal for promoting lifesaving in England.

SCHAEFFER, E. Carroll "Midget"
Swimmer
Hometown Reading, Pa; swam his way to health from polio; attended the Univ. Pa. 1898 – 1902; spent summers in Maine at work; small stature; weighed 118 lbs. in college; also a cyclist, boxer, water polo player and champion diver; became a lawyer.

E. Carroll Schaeffer began his swimming career in college. He held the American record for swimming under water and was a Metropolitan New York diving champion. As a speed swimmer, Schaeffer set 37 American and five world records, all during his college years. His world record for 100 yds, 1:05.3, stood for 17 years. Coached by George Kistler, he won the Canadian championship in 1899 in the Ottawa River. During the Sportsmen's Show in Philadelphia in 1899, Schaeffer carried off 13 first places in three nights. Carroll Schaeffer never attended an Olympics due to lack of interest and lack of funds.
Also in: Swimming and Diving Hall of Fame, Citizens Savings Hall of Fame Athletic Museum.

THEILE, David
Swimmer
Born 1938 in Australia; from Brisbane; quiet and unobtrusive; attended the Univ. Queensland; Olympic Gold Medal 1956; Olympic Gold and Silver Medal 1960; Fellow Royal Australian Col. Surgeons; lecturer in surgery at London Hospital; wife and two children; living in London.

Dr. David Theile began competitive swimming at age 9. He won the Australian junior backstroke title in 1954 and took the men's 110-yd. crown the following year, beginning a five-year reign as Senior champion of Australia in 1955 at the age of 17. Theile won the 100-m. backstroke title at the 1956 Olympic Games in Melbourne in record time of 1:02.2. After taking two years off for medical school, he returned to the Olympics in 1960 to take a second gold medal in the 100-m. backstroke and participate in the silver-medal-winning medley relay.

TSURUTA, Yoshiyuki
Swimmer
Born 1903 in Kagosima, Japan; second of nine brothers; learned to swim in a stream in front of home; Olympic Gold Medal 1928; Olympic Gold Medal 1932; graduated from Meiji Univ. at age 28; employed by the Nagoya Municipal Office; at age 43 went to war and taught swimming to soldiers; joined the Ehime Swimming School.

Yoshiyuki Tsuruta became the first Japanese winner of the 200-m. breaststroke in the 1928 Olympic Games. In 1932 he again won the same event, beating the world record holder Reizo Kuike. Tsuruta is now director of the Japan Swimming League, principal of the Ehime Swimming School, vice president of the Ehime Swimming League and president of the Natsuyama Swimming Society.

1969

ANDERSEN, Greta
Swimmer
Born 1928 in Denmark; 5 ft. 8.5 in. tall, weighs 141 lbs; married an American; Olympic Gold and Silver Medals 1948; resides in California; operates a swim school.

Greta Andersen is an Olympic champion, but is most famous as a channel swimmer. She holds the women's speed record both ways in the English Channel. Prior to that Greta was the first person to swim a major channel both ways. She holds the record for men and women on the Santa Catalina Channel. Greta achieved her Olympic fame in 1948 when she took a gold medal for Denmark in the 100-m. sprint and helped her country to silver medals in the freestyle relay. Her long course 100-yd. world record (58.2) was set in 1949 and remained unbroken until 1956. Greta came back for the 1956 Olympics, having just undergone knee surgery. Swimming with one leg, she was able to make the finals at 400 m. Greta Andersen is the largest money winner in women's professional history.

CADY, Fred
Coach
Born 1885 in Asbury Park, N.J; father a show business artist; mother, daughter of Senator Austin Patterson; at one time was a circus strong man and a gymnast; artistically talented; produced sculptures of famous divers, sketches of famous swimmers and oils of Western scenes and horses; wore a waxed mustache; died at age 75 in Los Angeles, Calif.

Fred Cady began coaching in 1904 in Philadelphia at the YMCA and later moved West to coach at the Los Angeles Athletic Club and the University of Southern California for 33 years. He was a U.S. Olympic coach from 1928 to 1948. In the 1932 Olympics his divers took first, second and third in men's springboard and platform diving and women's first and second in high dive and first in springboard. Some of his great pupils were

George Coleman, Micky Riley, Dutch Harold Smith, Dorothy Poynton, Olga Dorfner, Buster Crabbe and Paul Wolff.
Also in: Swimming and Diving Hall of Fame, Citizens Savings Hall of Fame Athletic Museum.

deVARONA, Donna
Swimmer
Was Queen of Swimming, America's Outstanding Woman Athlete, Outstanding American Female Swimmer, San Francisco's Outstanding Woman of the Year; received the Madamoiselle Award, National Academy of Sports Award; two Olympic Gold Medals 1960; was on the cover of *Life, Time, Saturday Evening Post, Sports Illustrated;* did TV swimsuit ads; was an after-dinner speaker.

Donna deVarona was at her best during a five-year period from the Rome Olympics until after the Tokyo Games. She won 37 individual national championship medals, including 18 gold and 3 National high point awards, along with 18 national and world records. Donna won national titles and set world's fastest times in three of the four strokes in individual events, backstroke, butterfly and freestyle.
Also in: Swimming and Diving Hall of Fame, Citizens Savings Hall of Fame Athletic Museum.

DRAVES, Victoria Manolo
Diver
Born a twin in San Francisco; mother English; father Filipino; career faltered because of her ancestry; all swim clubs insisted she use mother's maiden name; at time of father's death, returned to San Francisco and job as a secretary in the Army Port Surgeon's office; after war moved to Southern California; married coach Lyle Draves; began diving again; two Olympic Gold Medals 1948.

Upon her return to diving after the war, Vickie Draves began winning with the National Tower Diving Championship in 1946, 1947 and 1948. In 1948 she won her first springboard national title. Vickie was the first woman of Oriental ancestry to win two Olympic gold medals in diving in the 1948 Olympic Games in London.
Also in: Swimming and Diving Hall of Fame, Citizens Savings Hall of Fame Athletic Museum.

HUNYADFI, Steve
Coach
Born in Hungary; left Hungary after the 1955 revolution; political asylum from American Embassy in Vienna; coach for Italians for ten years; immigrated to the United States in 1965.

Steve Hunyadfi began his international coaching career as assistant swim coach of the Hungarian team at the 1936 Berlin Olympics. His Hungarian girls dominated the 1952 Games at Helsinki. Some of his swimmers included Kathy Szoke, the Novak sisters and Klera Killerman. Hunyadfi's swimmers excelled in all strokes, but he was most proud of his classic style breaststroke swimmers. For ten years he was coach for the Italian Swimming Federation, serving as its Olympic coach for the 1956, 1960 and 1964 Olympic Games. Within three years after coming to the United States, Hunyadfi produced his first U.S. Olympic champion, Sharon Wickman.

KIERAN, Bernard Bede "Barney"
Swimmer
Born 1887 in New South Wales, Australia; died at age 19 after an appendectomy on September 22, 1905.

Barney Kieran swam for only two years. He used the double overarm stroke and his best times included 5:19 for the 440 yd. and 11:11.6 for the 880 yd. Only one of Kieran's many world records was recognized by FINA and it was not broken for eight years. Barney did not live to swim in the 1906 Olympic Games.

LACKIE, Ethel
Swimmer
Swam by age 3; grew up in California; married William Watkins; summer lifeguard, rowing champion; father, Lester E. Lackie, lived near Lake Michigan; two Olympic Gold Medals 1924.

Ethel Lackie swam for the Illinois Athletic Club as a crawl sprinter. She won gold medals at the 1924 Olympic Games in Paris in the 100-m. freestyle and the 400-m. freestyle relay, setting records for both events. In 1926 she became the first female in the world to swim just over 60 secs. for the 100-yd. freestyle. It was eight years before anyone broke the minute.

LANE, F. C. V. "Freddy"
Swimmer
Born 1877 in Australia; weighed 133 lbs. at peak of career; two Olympic Gold Medals 1900; died at age 92 on May 29, 1969.

In 1899 Freddy Lane used the strenuous double overarm style of swimming to win the New South Wales mile. He was the first man in the world to swim 1 min. for 100-yd. freestyle. That same year he broke 1 min, 59 3/5 secs. Freddy won both the open and obstacle 200-m. race in the River Seine during the Paris Olympics in 1900. Lane won more English titles than Australian titles.

McDERMOTT, Michael "Turk"
Swimmer
Olympic Silver Medal 1912; Olympic Silver Medal 1920; spent 11 months as a Naval aviator flying in France during W.W. I; a successful Chicago contractor.

Turk McDermott won national titles nine years in a row in the 200-yd. breaststroke event (1910–1918). After his Navy duty he came back to win again in 1921. As a distance freestyle swimmer, Turk won the national AAU 10-mi. swim for four years in 1911, 1913, 1916 and 1917. He also played water polo and was on the national champion IAC team of 1914, 1915, 1916 and 1917. Turk McDermott took home the $10,000 Missouri Athletic Trophy, which had to be won three times. At the 1912 Olympic Games in Stockholm, Turk was beaten by Bathe of Germany, whom he beat in three successive races. The Olympics were canceled by war in 1916 when Turk was at his peak and the 1920 Olympics held only silvers for both swimming and water polo.
Also in: Swimming and Diving Hall of Fame, Citizens Savings Hall of Fame Athletic Museum.

NEMETH, Janos "Jim"
Water Polo
Born in Hungary; defected to Great Britain and then to Spain after the 1955 Hungarian Revolution; Olympic

Gold Medal 1932; Olympic Gold Medal 1936; Olympic Silver Medal 1948; daughter swam for Spain in 1968 Olympic Games.

Jim Nemeth is considered water polo's all-time great goal scorer. While with the Hungarian National Water Polo Team from 1929 to 1939, Hungary lost only one of 110 matches. Jim held the center forward position. The Hungarian team was the Olympic champion title holder from 1932 to 1936. In 1948 the team suffered its only defeat at the Olympic Games, taking second place in the standings. For this Nemeth was held in official national disgrace.

PATNIK, Al
Diver
Al Patnik began diving in Pittsburgh before college. He was Number Three diver on his high school team. Three months after entering Ohio State University he placed fifth in his first indoor National AAU championship. The following summer he was third in the outdoor Nationals and from that time on he won every national indoor and outdoor, low board and high board, springboard title in the United States, AAU and NCAA. He won 12 straight national AAU diving titles and 5 out of 6 UCAA springboard championships. Al Patnik was beaten only once (in the last dive of his last college meet) by less than one point.
Also in: Swimming and Diving Hall of Fame, Citizens Savings Hall of Fame Athletic Museum.

TAYLOR, Henry
Swimmer
Born March 17, 1885, in Oldham Lanes, England; an orphan, raised by his brother; three Olympic Gold Medals 1908; first job pool attendant at Chadderton Swimming Baths; worked in the cotton mills; trained during lunch breaks and at night anywhere there was water; failed at business; last job as pool attendant at Chadderton Swimming Baths; died on February 28, 1951, at Chadderton, Lancashire, England.

Henry Taylor was a member of the Hyde Seal Club. He won 15 ASA titles during his career. In 1906 Taylor won his world championship before he had won the English National championship. He won the mile and was second in the 400-m. freestyle. At the 1908 Olympic Games he was victorious in the 400- and 1500-m. events in world record time, along with a gold in the freestyle relay. His last success was at the age of 35. He also played water polo for England.

1970

BATHE, Walter
Swimmer
Born December 1, 1892, in Probsthain, Schlesien, Poland; was advised to swim to correct pigeon chest at age 8; two Olympic Gold Medals 1912.

During his swimming career, Walter Bathe won six German breaststroke championships, five times the Crown Prince Trophy and three times the 7.5-km. River Oder swim. In 1910 he swam the 100-m. breaststroke in world record time and went on to better that time in the same year. Bathe won over 600 swim trophies in his long career, but the two gold medals he received from the king of Sweden were the only ones that survived W.W. II. Bathe's 1912 Olympic records for the 200-m. and 400-m. breaststroke lasted until the 1924 Olympic Games.

CAVILL FAMILY
Contributors
Father Fred Cavill, the "Professor"; married the first cousin of Cecil Rhodes; had nine children—Madeline, Alice, Fredda, Ernest, Charles, Percy, Arthur, Sydney and Dick; five of the seven boys became world record holders.

Professor Cavill missed the Channel by 50 yds. when his boatman refused to land at night for fear of smashing his boat. Out of the Royal Navy after the Crimean War, he taught Princess Mary, later Queen Mary, to swim. In 1888 Fred Cavill dove overboard to rescue a woman and collected his fourth Royal Humane Society Medal. He died at the age of 88. Oldest son Ernie set a world record for 1000 yds. in 1888. He later went to England and beat American champion McCusker in a world title series. Second son Charles became the first man to cross the Golden Gate swimming. Charles died submerged in an underwater endurance test. His trick of breathing air under a submerged tub backfired when he instead inhaled poisonous vapors from an underground natural gas deposit. Third son Percy collected four Australian Nationals, set world records for the 440-yd. and 5-mi, taught swimming for 15 years and then disappeared. In 1930 he was discovered living on Andros Island in the Bahamas, when a woman crash-landed her plane there. Number Four son Arthur, known as "Tums," made his money as a stunt swimmer, crossing rivers with both hands and feet tied. In 1912 he was sewn in a bag and lowered from a bridge into the river, but on the way down he was cut severely by the knife he was carrying to cut himself free. He recovered from that but died from exposure while making a winter crossing of Seattle Harbor. Syd, the first Australian-born son, won his Australian championship at 16. He later coached the San Francisco Olympic Club. The youngest son, "Playboy Dick," amassed eighteen Australian and two English swimming titles. His unusual training diet consisted of ginger beer, ice cream and brandy snaps. Dick Cavill toured America as Father Neptune in a stage act. He later died of a heart attack while giving a swimming demonstration in 1938. Dick was largely responsible for the independent arm stroke and leg kick of the crawl.

CHADWICK, Florence
Swimmer
Born in San Diego, Calif; worked for the Arabian American Oil Co. while training for her first Channel crossing; later did sportsmen's shows, swim schools and radio and TV appearances to urge people to get involved in physical activities; at age 51, she began a successful career as a stockbroker.

After 18 years of amateur swimming off the coast of San Diego, Florence Chadwick, age 32, was denied entry because of no previous record or reputation in the 1950 half-century Channel crossing contest sponsored by the London *Daily Mail.* She decided to conquer the Channel at her own expense. She tried and missed in July, but on August 8 she left France and crawled ashore at Dover in a record 13.23 hrs. The following summer she swam it back from England to France in 16.22. In 1952 she was the first woman to swim the Catalina Channel. In the summer of 1953 she again swam from England to France in 14.42, a new women's record and set still another record of 13.55 for the same crossing in 1955.

CODY, Jack
Coach

Retired in 1949; moved to Los Angeles; taught and coached for several years; died April 11, 1963, at age 78.

Jack Cody began his career as a diver and a coach of divers. As coach at the Multnomah Club in Portland, Ore, he brought the Multnomah Club into world prominence. His greatest fame developed in the ten years from 1939 to 1949 when a speedy troupe of girls became known as the Cody Kids. The nucleus of that team consisted of Nancy Merki, Brenda Helser, Suzanne Zimmerman, Joyce Macrae and Mary Anne Hansen. That team won national titles three times; 42 individual championships, 16 relay championships and many records were set. The peak years for this group came when the Olympic Games were called off, in 1940 and 1944. Cody's coaching talent is reflected in his students. Nancy Merki swam and won at every distance from sprint to the mile, and in every stroke.
Also in: Swimming and Diving Hall of Fame, Citizens Savings Hall of Fame Athletic Museum.

den OUDEN, Willy
Swimmer

European Championships Gold Medal 1931; Olympic Silver Medal 1932; Olympic Gold Medal 1936; European Championships Silver Medal 1938.

At the 1931 European championships at age 13, Willy den Ouden came in second and won a gold in the 4 X 100-m. relay. She was again second in the Olympic Games 100-m. the following year, and a member of Holland's Silver Medal relay squad. Her great year was 1934. She became champion of Europe for her favorite 100-m. distance and was second in the 400-m, making her the first girl to break the 1-min. record. She was referred to as the "Darling of European Swimming." She had set the 100-m. freestyle record and broken it four times herself, winding up 1:04.6 in 1936. She won a gold medal with the winning Dutch relay. In February 1936, she had set a 100-m. world record of 64.6 (which stood for 20 years). In the 1938 European championships, she won a third European relay medal, silver. Willy den Ouden has 13 individual world records.

DORFNER, Olga
Swimmer

Born in Philadelphia, Pa; featured in *Vanity Fair* and Sunday supplements as cover girl bathing suit queen of her day.

Olga Dorfner was America's fastest at 40, 50, 60, 80, 100 and 220 yds. at various times throughout her career. She won the nationals in the 50 in 1916 and the 100, 220 and 440 in 1917. Olga missed her chances in the Olympics twice due to war and marriage.

GALLIGAN, Claire
Swimmer

Claire Galligan Finney won her first race in 1915 in New Rochelle, N.J, for the Women's Life Saving League. She won her first national and set her first world record in 1917. Claire won 13 U.S. nationals and was the first and one of the greatest of L. de B. Handley's WSA champions, but she never reached the Olympic Games because they were canceled by war.

HOUGH, Richard R.
Swimmer

Attended Trenton, N.J, High School; graduated Phi Beta Kappa in electrical engineering from Princeton; worked on military weapons systems, including guided missiles; V.Pres. of the American Telephone and Telegraph Co.

Richard Hough was king of the front kick butterfly breaststroke. He set American 100-yd. records in 1936, 1937 and 1938, was eastern and national Intercollegiate champion at 200 yd. in 1938 and 1939 and AAU national champion at 220 yd. in 1939 and 1940. In 1939 Dick Hough was voted Outstanding College Swimmer of the Year for his victories in the breaststroke and medley relay. Because of W. W. II, Dick missed his chance to try for an Olympic medal.

McLANE, James
Swimmer

Married; attended Yale University; joined the Army; Olympic Gold Medal 1948 and 1952; three Pan-Am Gold Medals.

At age 13 Jimmy McLane was the youngest ever men's AAU swimming champion when he won the national long distance title. His career extended from 1944 through 1955, and during those years he completely dominated U.S. outdoor middle distance swimming with 13 national championships. McLane was a great tactician in swimming. He always had a plan and knowledge of his opponents' swimming habits. At the 1948 Olympic Games, McLane won the 1500-m. freestyle event over Marshall of Australia. They later swam together at Yale. McLane was captain of the U.S. Olympic team in 1952, winning a gold in the 400-m. freestyle relay. In 1955 at the Pan-Am Games, McLane won three gold medals. He retired from swimming in 1955.
Also in: Swimming and Diving Hall of Fame, Citizens Savings Hall of Fame Athletic Museum.

PADOU, Henri
Water Polo

Henri Padou is known to have the greatest impact in the history of water polo. He was a European swimming champion as well as the premier water polo player of his time. He led France to the Olympic water polo title in 1923. Padou made the international French team in swimming 21 times and 112 times in water polo. He is considered the finest all-around water polo player of his time.

SAVA, Charlie
Coach

Charlie Sava was the coach of the Crystal Plunge Swim Club of San Francisco. That Club won 10 national AAU women's swimming team titles in a row. Charlie's girls included Ann Curtis, Lynn Vidali, Marion Olsen Kane and Vicki Draves. These ladies won 42 individual national titles and 9 relays. Sava is generally credited with freeing the freestyle kick from the knee to the hip. He attended the first Red Cross Aquatic School in 1925 and helped Beth Kaufman with the early age-group swimming.

WEBSTER, Robert
Diver
From California; attended Santa Ana Jr. Col; transferred to Univ. Mich; coached for Univ. Minn. and Princeton Univ; Olympic Gold Medal 1960; Pan-Am Gold Medal 1963; Olympic Gold Medal 1964.

Bob Webster won his first collegiate title diving for a school without a pool. He trained off a board in a backyard sand pit. Webster then went to the University of Michigan to be coached by Dick Kimball and Bruce Harlan. Webster won his Olympic title in the 10-m. platform in Rome at the 1960 Games and from that time on never lost a tower diving contest. He was the U.S. national AAU champion in the 1-m. low board and the Big Ten 3-m. high board champion. In 1963 Webster was the first U.S. diver to win a 10-m. diving event in the history of the Pan-Am Games. In 1964 he won the Olympic platform title in Tokyo. Webster took a Far East tour for the State Department after his retirement from competitive swimming. In 1971 he was appointed U.S. diving coach for the Pan-American Games.
Also in: Swimming and Diving Hall of Fame, Citizens Savings Hall of Fame Athletic Museum.

1971

CORSAN, George H. Sr.
Contributor
George Corsan originated the massed method of swimming instruction, rhythmic breathing and fear-elimination drill. He began teaching novices the crawl instead of the traditional breaststroke. He invented water wings to replace the rings on a cable. For his work, Corsan received the Royal Life Saving Society Award of Merit in 1899. He published a book called *At Home in the Water* and later produced three more books. He directed swimming instruction at W. W. I training camps and developed a Boy Scout Masters' course for water instruction.

DAUGHTERS, Ray
Coach
Born in Denver, Colo; moved to Seattle, Wash, at age 10; Chief Petty Officer in W. W. I; in charge of swimming at Seattle Naval Training Station; was sprint and distance champion of the Pacific Northwest in the early 1900s.

Ray Daughters began coaching at the Seattle Club Pool where he trained Helene Madison. He moved to the Washington Athletic Club when it was built in 1930 and became director of athletics in 1942. Some of his most famous pupils were Jack Medica, Mary Lou Petty, Oliver McKean and Nancy Ramey. His Western Athletic Conference swimmers over the years held 30 world records, 301 American records and 64 national championships. Daughters served as women's swimming coach in the 1936 and 1948 Olympic Games. In 1960 he was manager of the men's team. From 1957 to 1959, Daughters served as chairman of the AAU men's swimming committee and in 1960 he was chairman of the U.S. men's Olympic swimming committee.
Also in: Swimming and Diving Hall of Fame, Citizens Savings Hall of Fame Athletic Museum.

DEGENER, Dick
Diver
Olympic Bronze Medal 1932; Olympic Gold Medal 1936.

Dick Degener was famous for his tight spins and grace. He was at his best during the five-year period that coincides with his college years, 1932 – 1936. Degener was the bronze medal winner in Los Angeles in 1932 and the gold medal winner in Berlin in 1936. He won four outdoor AAU nationals in highboard and three NCAA titles for the University of Michigan. At the indoor AAU's he won five straight 3-m. springboard titles and two 1-m. titles. He also won three Big Ten titles and three National Interscholastic Championships, until he turned pro in 1937.
Also in: Swimming and Diving Hall of Fame, Citizens Savings Hall of Fame Athletic Museum.

FLETCHER, Jennie
Swimmer
Born 1890 in Leichester, England; one of eleven children; had time to practice swimming only after a 12-hour day of work, 6 days a week; dared to wear a short-sleeved, knee-length bathing suit; Olympic Gold Medal 1912; died in Canada at the age of 78.

At 18, Jennie was at the peak of her career for the 1908 Olympics in London, but the women's events were canceled due to the lack of women competitors. She did get to compete in the 1912 Games in Stockholm at the end of her career. She was beaten in the 100-m. freestyle by Fanny Durack, but won a gold medal in the relay. Jennie held the 100-yd. freestyle world record for seven years and was British champion from 1906 to 1912. Her parents refused an offer for her to turn professional at age 17 and tour with the famous Annette Kellerman.

GOODWIN, L. B. "Budd"
Swimmer
Father ran Manhattan Island excursion ferry; Olympic Gold Medal 1904; 1906 severe case of blood poisoning called for amputation of his left arm; Dr. David Hennan dissected entire forearm and reassembled it to end blood poisoning problem; won Congressional Medal of Honor for bravery in a rescue off the coast of Virginia; retired to Palm Beach.

Budd Goodwin won 19 national AAU gold medals between 1901 and 1915 as well as winning over 50 metropolitan and national championships. He won his only Olympic gold medal in water polo in 1904. Budd's competitive swimming career ended in 1922, but he was swimming well into his seventies.
Also in: Swimming and Diving Hall of Fame, Citizens Savings Hall Athletic Museum.

HIGGINS, John
Swimmer, Coach
Member of the YMCA and Olyuville, R.I, Boys Club; attended Ohio State Univ; entered the Navy; swimming coach of the U.S. Naval Academy.

John Higgins was the first swimmer to set a world breaststroke record using the butterfly arm stroke. In the 1936 Olympic trials, Higgins established a new American and world record of 2:44.1 for the 200-m. butterfly. That record stood for 12 years. Higgins swam competitively for 21 years. He is a past president of both the College Swim Coaches Association and the International Swimming Hall of Fame.

HOMONNAY, Martin
Water Polo

Born 1907 in Hungary; Olympic Gold Medal 1932; Olympic Gold Medal 1936; daughter Kati Szoke won two swimming gold medals in 1952 Olympic games; fled Communists; retired to South America; died in 1969.

Hungary's Number One water polo player was Martin Homonnay. Homonnay was twice leader of Hungary's Olympic gold medal water polo teams in 1932 and 1936. He was on the Hungarian National team 126 times.

KINT, Cor
Swimmer

Born in Holland, Cor Kint was a victim of the war-canceled Olympic Games. She was too late for the 1936 Olympics and had retired before the 1948 Olympics. Cor's records for the 100-m. backstroke event, timed at 1:10.9, stood up for 21 years. Her times for 150-yd. backstroke and 200-m. backstroke stood for 11 years, until 1950.

KONRAD, John and Ilsa
Swimmers

John born May 21, 1942; Ilsa born March 29, 1944, in Riga, Latvia; immigrated to Australia in 1949; John had polio while in refugee camp; swam as therapy; John: three British Empire Gold Medals 1958, Olympic Gold Medal 1960; Ilsa: British Empire Gold Medal 1958.

John and Ilsa Konrad began to break world records in freestyle events in 1958. Ilsa set their first world record in the 800-m. and 880-yd. freestyle at the age of 13. Two days later John set the 800-m. and half-mile records for men. During the following week he added the 200-m, 220-yd, 300-m. and the 440-yd. Throughout the next two years, the Konrad Kids established 37 world records. At the British Empire Games in 1958 John won three gold medals and Ilsa took one. In the 1960 Rome Olympic Games, John won the 1500-m. freestyle. He was a member of the Olympic team in 1958 and 1964. Ilsa too was a member of the 1960 and 1964 Olympic teams, but only placed fourth in the 400-m. in 1960.

MEANY, Helen
Diver

Olympic Gold Medal 1928.

Helen Meany represented the United States in three Olympic Games, 1920, 1924 and 1928, winning a gold medal in 1928 off the 3-m. springboard. Helen won 17 U.S. national AAU diving championships for the New York Women's Swimming Association. She was the only female invited to participate in a three-day meet in Tokyo in honor of Prince Chichibus' wedding. Her career as an amateur diver ended when she appeared in an unsanctioned Miami Beach water show with Johnny Weissmuller, Martha Norelius and Pete Desjardins.
Also in: Swimming and Diving Hall of Fame, Citizens Savings Hall of Fame Athletic Museum.

TROY, Michael
Swimmer

Born October 3, 1940; started in the park district swim program in Indianapolis; joined the Indianapolis Athletic Club in the 1950s; attended Indiana Univ; Pan-Am Gold and Silver Medals 1959; two Olympic Gold Medals 1960. Naval officer, decorated for distinguished and heroic action in Vietnam; settled in San Diego; now coaches and sells real estate.

In 1959 Mike Troy had come in second in the Pan-American Games 200-m. butterfly but won a gold in the medley relay. During his two years at the top of swimming, Troy set many world records in freestyle and butterfly. His specialty was the 200-m. butterfly. At the 1960 Olympic Games in Rome he won the 200-m. butterfly in world record time and helped out with the 200-m. freestyle leg of the winning 800-m. freestyle relay.
Also in: Swimming and Diving Hall of Fame, Citizens Savings Hall of Fame Athletic Museum.

YORZYK, William
Swimmer

Attended Springfield Col; graduate assistant in physical education at Springfield; Pan-Am Gold Medal 1955; Olympic Gold Medal 1956; attended medical school at the Univ. Toronto; Captain in U.S. Air Force Medical Corps 1964; stationed in Japan; announced Olympics on U.S. Armed Forces Radio; attending physician to the U.S. Embassy in Tokyo.

Bill Yorzyk was the first Olympic champion in the dolphin-butterfly stroke. He won his first AAU nationals in 1955 in the 200-m. butterfly. He won a Pan-American Games gold medal in the 800-m. freestyle relay that same year. In 1956 he was outdoor national AAU high point man and won the gold medal at the 1956 Olympic Games for his butterfly event. Yorzyk won the Bickler Prize for the University of Toronto's top scholar-athlete in 1958 and 1959. Bill retired from competitive swimming in 1960. He later was attending physician to the U.S. national swimming team in Japan in 1963 and associate physician to the Olympic team in 1964. Bill Yorzyk gives full credit for his swimming, his education and his professional start in medicine to meeting coach Charles Silva.
Also in: Swimming and Diving Hall of Fame, Citizens Savings Hall of Fame Athletic Museum.

1972

BRAUNINGER, Stan
Coach

Lived at the Lakeshore Club and was always available; legally adopted the great backstroke swimmer Adolph "Sonny" Kiefer; retired to a fishing boat in Florida in the 1970s.

Stan Brauninger is the only coach who turned out U.S. national champion men's and women's teams in both swimming and diving. His teams won the national AAU championships six times and were runners-up on at least nine occasions. His national women's champions included Dorothy Schiller, Jane Fauntz, Marion Mansfield, Arlite Smith and Jackie Levine. He also introduced an early form of synchronized swimming seen at the 1933 Chicago World's Fair. Brauninger's men's teams included Harold Henning, Wally Colboth, Al Green, Miller Anderson and Adolph "Sonny" Kiefer.

CHARLTON, Andrew M. "Boy"
Swimmer

Born in Manly, Australia; Olympic Gold, Silver and Bronze Medals 1924; two Olympic Silver Medals 1928;

got his agriculture degree and began farming after the Paris Olympics; after returning from Amsterdam, he contracted rheumatic fever; semi-invalid for nearly a year; plagued by bad colds thereafter; retired from swimming after the 1932 Olympics.

Andrew Charlton was 16 years old when he won the gold medal at the 1924 Olympic Games. He went on to win five medals and make the finals in three Olympics through 1932. "Boy" Charlton held five world records, the most outstanding of which had to be his Paris victory over the Swedish great Arne Borg. He took 34.8 sec. off Borg's world record for the distance. He and Johnny Weissmuller swam together in the 1924 and 1928 Olympic Games.

CLARK, Earl
Diver
Graduated from Miami Edison High School; enrolled at Ohio State Univ; participated in gymnastics, handball, squash, boxing, wrestling and tennis and was amateur golf champion of Florida; was runnerup for the Sullivan Award, designating the country's finest amateur athlete.

W.W. II robbed Earl Clark of a chance for an Olympic gold medal for both 1940 and 1944. Jim Patterson, Al Patnick and Earl Clark dominated U.S. diving for many years. Clark beat Patnick for the first and only time in March 1940 at Patnick's final intercollegiate appearance. The contest was decided on Clark's last dive, winning by a close margin of 1.06. During his senior year, 1941, Earl Clark established a record by capturing every available U.S. diving title, the only diver in history to do so. Altogether he took a total of 12 major titles and was national AAU 10-m. platform king for three years. Clark also developed a unique technique for the execution of combination twisting and somersaulting dives.
Also in: Swimming and Diving Hall of Fame, Citizens Savings Hall of Fame Athletic Museum.

CRAPP, Lorraine
Swimmer
Born 1938 in Sydney, Australia; two Olympic Gold, one Silver and one Bronze Medal 1956; Olympic Silver Medal 1960; married Dr. Bill Thurlow, a physician interested in physiological testing; four children.

Lorraine Crapp was the first woman to break 5 min. for the 400-m. freestyle. In 1954 at 15 she won two gold medals in the Vancouver British Commonwealth and Empire Games. On August 15, 1956, she set four world records for the 200-, 220-, 400- and 440-m. freestyle events. She repeated these four records in one swim effort two months later with better times. Lorraine Crapp won the 1956 Olympic 400-m. title and took a silver in the 100-m, behind her teammate Dawn Fraser, and received another gold in the relay, and a bronze. Lorraine added another silver at Rome in the 1960 Olympic Games. Her swimming career lasted ten years, from 1950 to 1960, and she held 23 world records during that time.

KONNO, Ford
Swimmer
Born in Hawaii; 5 ft. 6 in. tall; two Olympic Gold Medals and Silver Medal 1952; Olympic Silver Medal 1956; graduated from Ohio State Univ; high school teacher and swim coach in Hawaii; married swimmer Evelyn Kawamoto; two daughters; now division manager of Investors Equity Life Insurance Co.

Ford Konno came into his own shortly after the end of W.W. II. He was picked to be a member of the U.S. team for a meet in Tokyo. He won the 800- and 1500-m. freestyle races. He set his first world record while still a high school student. At Ohio State, under Mike Peppe, he received six NCAA and ten Big Ten titles. In the 1952 Olympic Games at Helsinki he set world records and Olympic records for his times in the 1500- and 800-m. freestyle relay and placed second in the 400-m. freestyle. Ford won a silver medal in the 1956 Olympic Games in the 800-m. freestyle relay.
Also in: Swimming and Diving Hall of Fame, Citizens Savings Hall of Fame Athletic Museum.

MAJONI, Mario
Water Polo
European Championship 1947; Olympic Championship 1948.

Mario Majoni of Italy began his water polo career at the age of 14 in 1924. Ten years later he made the national team and from 1934 to 1948 he played international water polo. He was in action 118 times with the Italian team and was captain of that team for ten years. They won the European championship title in 1947 and the Olympic championship at the London Games in 1948. Majoni retired from playing at the age of 38 to become a member of the FINA technical committee in 1949. He was appointed the Italian National Water Polo Coach in 1950 and saw his team through six Olympic Games. His teams were always ranked among the top five in the world. Majoni has contributed books and films of the basic principles, techniques, rules and tactics of winning water polo.

RADEMACHER, Erich "Ete"
Swimmer and Water Polo
Born in Germany; brother Acki water poloist on 1928 Olympic gold-medal-winning team; European Championships Gold Medal 1926 and 1927; Olympic Gold and Silver Medals 1928; Olympic Silver Medal 1932.

Ete Rademacher was kept out of the 1920 and 1924 Olympic Games because of Germany's role in the war. During those years Rademacher set 11 world records in the breaststroke and freestyle. In 1926 and 1927 when the Germans were again allowed to participate, Rademacher won the European championships each year. In the 1928 Olympic Games, he took a silver behind Japan in the breaststroke. Later that day the German team won the Olympic water polo match in overtime against Hungary. In Los Angeles at the 1932 Olympic Games the Germans took a silver medal in water polo. During his 23-year career that lasted from 1911 to 1934, he placed first 1012 times. He won 25 German National championships, 2 European, 2 Hungarian and 1 each in Czechoslovakia, Great Britain and the United States. His Magdeburg water polo team won nine National water polo championships.

STOUDER, Sharon
Swimmer
Born November 9, 1948; from Glendora, Calif; an honor student at Glendora High School; Pan-Am Gold Medal

1962; three Olympic Gold and one Silver Medal 1964; World Woman Swimmer of the Year 1964; graduated from Stanford Univ; coached while doing graduate work at the Univ. of Calif, Santa Barbara.

Sharon Stouder began swimming at age 3. At age 8, she was swimming competitively and won two firsts and set two age-group records at her first meet. At 12, Sharon won 20 firsts in national age-group events and won all six of the national junior Olympic ratings for her age group. In 1961 *American Swimmer* magazine chose her for the Female Age-Group Swimmer of the Year. At 14, she won a gold medal in the Pan-American Games for her butterfly leg of the medley relay team. At the 1964 Olympic Games in Tokyo, Sharon won three gold and one silver medals in the 100-m. butterfly, the 400-m. freestyle relay and the 400-m. medley relay, coming in second behind Dawn Fraser in the 100-m. freestyle. Sharon Stouder was picked as World Woman Swimmer of the Year by *Sports Illustrated*, by ABC-TV and by *Swimming World*.
Also in: Swimming and Diving Hall of Fame, Citizens Savings Hall of Fame Athletic Museum.

WAINWRIGHT, Helen
Swimmer, Diver
Olympic Silver Medal 1920 and 1924; a talented golfer and bowler; played in the Hippodrome; traveled the United States playing the theaters with a portable tank; turned national medals over to the government during W.W. II; husband overseas in war.

Helen Wainwright won 19 gold medals as a U.S. national champion, twice in diving and 17 times in swimming. She won the pentathlon while swimming for the Women's Swimming Association of New York, coached by Fred Sponberg. Helen Wainwright won a silver medal in the 3-m. springboard in 1920 at the Olympic Games in Antwerp and took a silver in the 400-m. freestyle at the 1924 Olympic Games in Paris. Her contemporaries and teammates were Gertrude Ederle and Aileen Riggin.
Also in: Swimming and Diving Hall of Fame, Citizens Savings Hall of Fame Athletic Museum.

1973

BRANDSTEN, Greta Johanson
Diver
Born January 9, 1895, in Sweden; married swimming coach Ernst Brandsten; learned to swim and dive in Stockholm's municipal baths; all children were required to take efficiency swimming tests; taught swimming and diving in Sweden; Olympic Gold Medal 1912; Countess de Casa Miranda Cup 1912; moved to California; physical education teacher at Univ. Calif; moved to Stanford; operated a family-owned sports recreation business for 27 years.

At age 15 Greta Johanson became Swedish national breaststroke champion. The following year she won the nationals in the 100-m. freestyle and in high diving. At 17, she won her Olympic gold medal and was decorated by her king for winning diving's most coveted award, the Countess de Casa Miranda Cup.

HARLAN, Bruce
Diver
Landsdowne, Pa, High School wrestler and pole vaulter; entered Navy in 1944; 1945 duty at Jacksonville, Fla; enrolled at Ohio State Univ; Olympic Gold and Silver Medals 1948; graduate work at Stanford Univ; high school coaching in Redwood City, Calif; Univ. Mich. coach from 1954 to 1959; died in 1959 when he fell from a 27-ft. diving tower while dismantling the scaffolding.

Bruce Harlan became one of the nation's outstanding divers under the tutelage of Lt. R. Jackson Smith. During his Navy career he captured his first national AAU 3-m. springboard title in 1946. While at Ohio State, under Mike Peppe, Bruce took a total of 19 individual diving titles from 1947 to 1950, including five Big Ten, five NCAA, eight NAAU and Olympic gold and silver medals at the 1948 Olympic Games in London. After graduating from school Bruce became one of the nation's outstanding coaches.
Also in: Swimming and Diving Hall of Fame, Citizens Savings Hall of Fame Athletic Museum.

HENRICKS, Jon
Swimmer
Born June 6, 1935, in Australia; 6 ft. tall, fair-haired; three British Empire Gold Medals 1954; two Olympic Gold Medals 1956; Australian Athlete of the Year 1955; married American Bonnie Wilkie, sister of Mike of the USC team.

Jon Henricks was trained as a long-distance swimmer in the early days of his career. He missed the 1952 Olympic Games due to a prolonged ear infection. Immediately after his conversion to sprint swimmer, Henricks broke the Olympic record for 100 m. in the Australian championships of 1953. He held that record for five years all over the world. Henricks was a triple gold medalist in the 1954 Commonwealth Games in Vancouver for his 110-yd, 800-m. freestyle and 330-yd. medley. He won two gold medals in the 1956 Olympics, one in the 100-m. timed at 55.4 and the second in the 800-m. relay team's effort. In 1958 Jon won the American national outdoor 100- and 200-m. titles. He missed the 1960 Rome Olympic Games due to illness. Jon was named Australian Athlete of the Year by the Citizens Savings Hall of Fame Athletic Museum in 1955.

LAUFER, Walter
Swimmer
Swimmer of the Year 1926; Olympic Gold Medal, one Silver and one Bronze Medal 1928.

Walter Laufer was victorious in the 4-mi. Ohio River Swim in 1923 and 1924. He gained national attention in 1924 at the national outdoor AAU championships when he won first place in both the individual medley and backstroke events. In 1926 Laufer won both the individual medley and the penthathalon in the U.S. AAU national championships in Chicago. He was the meet's high point winner and beat Johnny Weissmuller in the 400-m. freestyle relay. That year he was picked by sports writers as Swimmer of the Year. On a European tour in 1926, Walter competed in 21 cities in 23 days, winning all but one event. As a member of the 1928 Olympic team, he brought home a gold medal for his participation in the 800-m. freestyle relay, along with a silver for the 100-m. backstroke and a bronze in the 100-m. freestyle.

MARSHALL, John
Swimmer
Born 1930 in Australia; attended Yale Univ; Olympic Silver and Bronze Medals 1948; modest and physically unassuming; helpful interest in younger swimmers; became a successful business executive; died in a car accident at the age of 26 in 1957 when a tire blew out on his car.

In 1946 John Marshall won four Australian titles, the 220-, 440-, 880- and 1650-yd. At the 1948 Olympic Games in London, John won the silver in the 1500-m. and the bronze in the 400-m. freestyle. At Yale under Bob Kiphuth, in 1950 and 1951, Marshall broke 19 world records. His training for the 1952 Olympic Games was incomplete due to business commitments. At the age of 26 he came in fifth place in the butterfly at the Melbourne Olympics. John is credited with stimulating the resurgence of Australian swimming in the late 1950s.

NOVAK, Eva and Ilona
Swimmers
Born in Hungary; sisters; Eva: Olympic Bronze Medal 1948; Olympic Gold and two Silver Medals 1952; Ilona: Olympic Gold Medal 1952; Eva Novak Gerard now a medical doctor in Brussels; married sports reporter during Helsinki Olympics; Ilona a Budapest physical education teacher and coach; V.Pres. of the Hungarian Swimming Federation.

Ilona's career spanned 1938 to 1956, winning 54 national and international gold medals in backstroke and freestyle events. In 1952 Ilona won her Olympic gold medal as captain of the Hungarian's winning 400-m. freestyle relay. Eva won two silver and a gold medal in the 1952 Olympic Games. Eva was also on the Hungarian Olympic team in 1948, taking a bronze medal, and on the Belgian Olympic team in 1956. She held 48 Hungarian National records, winning 33 championships in Hungary and 8 more in Belgium.

OYAKAWA, Yoshi
Swimmer
Born in Hawaii; attended Ohio State Univ; Air Force 2nd Lt; married Mariko Yamane; settled in Cincinnati; raised four daughters and a son; coach at Oak Hills High School; Ohio High School Coach of the Year in 1972.

Yoshi Oyakawa began competitive swimming at the age of 15. By age 16 he was swimming backstroke and by 18 he was on his way to the Olympics. Yoshi set 100-yd. and 100-m. world backstroke records for the straight arm style backstroke. He participated in the 1952 and 1956 Olympic Games, but could not break his trial times of 1:04.7. Oyakawa was named Ohio High School Coach of the Year in 1972.
Also in: Swimming and Diving Hall of Fame, Citizens Savings Hall of Fame Athletic Museum.

STENDER, Jan
Coach
Born in Holland; coached in Hilversum for the De Robben Swim Club; nicknamed by rivals "the Hangman of Hilversum"; began daily exercise routine at age 9 and at age 68 still does it; swimming, football, cycling, running, walking, ice skating and water polo.

Jan Stender coached for 40 years beginning at age 19. He led his swimmers in massive out of the water exercise programs. In 1955 he developed eight world record holders from girls growing up on one street in Hilversum, Holland. These swimmers included Mary Kok, Nel Van Vliet, Lenie DeJijs, Geertje Wielema, Herman Willemse and Judith DeJijs. His swimmers held 41 individual world records and were on ten world record relay teams.

VAN VLIET, Nel
Swimmer
Olympic Gold Medal 1948.

Nel Van Vliet, from Holland, swam for coach Jan Stender's Hilversum De Robben Swim Club. She did not set her first world record until age 20, but between 1946 and 1949 she set 18 world records in breaststroke and was the breaststroke leg of three world record medley relays. She swam the traditional orthodox breaststroke. In 1948 she came to the United States to train with Walt Schlueter at the Chicago Town Club. She won every U.S. breaststroke race and returned home for the London Olympics. Nellie won the Olympic gold medal for the 200-m. breaststroke in record time.

1974

CUMMINS, Capt. Bertram William
Contributor
Born February 16, 1881, in Croyden, England; while on eight-day leave from Army organized a swim gala for the troops of his division; died on October 30, 1974, after 80 years of service as a swimming journalist.

Bert Cummins' magazine started as a four-page giveaway called *Waddon News* in 1923, was renamed the *Swimming Times* in 1926 and grew to be a monthly publication of 96 pages with a circulation of 8000 in 61 countries. Captain Bert also served as a member of the Southern District Association of England for 60 years and was its president in 1926. He was president of the Amateur Swimming Association in 1946 and public relations and publicity officer of the Association between 1947 and 1956. He was a member of the organizing committee for the swimming events at the 1948 Olympic Games in London. Through arranging and accompanying the tour, Cummins, along with Beulah Gundling and Peg Sellar, introduced synchronized swimming to Great Britain.

EPSTEIN, Charlotte "Eppy"
Contributor
Charlotte Epstein was a court reporter by profession, but worked behind the scenes on swimming. She was assistant manager of the 1932 U.S. Women's Olympic swim team. The girls in Eppy's swim club won 201 individual AAU Women's National Senior Championships in swimming and diving. Eppy was a good administrator and had a great ability to keep champions swimming together as a team. Her girls held 51 world records and put together 30 national champion relay teams during Eppy's 22 years with the Women's Swimming Association.

FERN, Harold
Contributor

Born April 20, 1881, in England; during earlier years was a runner, oarsman, soccer player and swimmer; died August 21, 1974.

Harold Fern's service to swimming extended from 1905 when he became honorary secretary of the Southern District of the Amateur Swimming Association of England to his position as life honorary president of FINA, the world governing body of swimming. He was elected a member of the FINA bureau in 1928 and continued to serve it until his death in 1974. He was honored by King George VI and Queen Elizabeth II for his untiring work in swimming.

FULLARD-LEO, Ellen "Ma Leo"
Contributor

Born in Capetown, South Africa; youngest of 19 children; married Leslie Fullard-Leo in 1908 at Capetown; eldest son played roles in over 100 Hollywood movies; moved to New York in 1909, then to Victoria, B.C, in 1912 and later to Hawaii in 1915; died in October 1974; ashes were scattered from a surfboard off Waikiki.

Ma Leo organized the first women's swim clubs in South Africa, Canada and Hawaii. In 1921 she was the first female representative ever to attend the AAU executive committee meeting, representing Hawaii. She helped to organize the Pan-Pacific Games and the Hawaiian AAU as well as to raise funds to send athletes to their meets. Ma Leo was one of the first individual charter members of the International Hall of Fame and a prime force in amateur athletics for 65 years.

HENRY, William
Contributor

Born June 29, 1895, in England; wore a moustache.

William Henry won the ASA quarter-mile salt water amateur championship in 1889 and the long distance in 1890. At the age of 37, in 1896, he was 100-m. champion of Europe. Henry won Britain's national title in 1896, 1899 and 1901. He was on the 1900 Olympic team, coming in sixth in the 200-m. obstacle race and winning the World Championship Lifesaving competition. Henry was co-founder of the Royal Life Saving Society. He was also co-author, with Archibald Sinclair, of the Badminton Library *Book of Swimming,* published in 1893, which gives a picture of the sport in the last century.

KELLERMAN, Annette
Contributor

Born in Australia; a childhood cripple; swam her way to good health; starred in motion pictures, such as *Diving Venus, Queen of the Mermaids, A Daughter of the Gods* and *Neptune's Daughter;* her black one-piece bathing suit became famous; performed a mermaid spectacle in the New York Hippodrome; 40 years later portrayed in film by Esther Williams.

Annette Kellerman won her first title as Swim Champion of New South Wales in the 100-yd. event at 1:18. She set a women's world record for the mile with 32:29, a time she later lowered to 28 min. She began distance swimming and giving public diving displays. Her professional career began years of swimming exhibitions and later films. Annette's attempt at crossing the English Channel was unsuccessful; she made it only three quarters of the way. She did win a 7-mi. Seine swim through Paris, beating 16 men in front of half a million spectators.

Also in: Synchronized Swimming Hall of Fame, Citizens Savings Hall of Fame Athletic Museum.

LUEHRING, Fred
Contributor

Born 1881 in Hanover, Kans, on the Oregon Trail; run over by a wagon at the age of 4; swam and ran back to health; at age 82 hiked the complete length of the 2000-mi. Appalachian Trail; at age 92 led the March of Dimes Walk-a-Thon for 20 mi; Ph.D. dissertation at Columbia became book, *Swimming Pool Standards;* was a football and track star at Northern Central Col. and the Univ. Chicago.

Fred Luehring was the first editor of the *Intercollegiate Swimming Guide* from 1916 to 1922. He served on the NCAA rules committee as member, secretary and chairman. As chairman of the men's Olympic swimming committee, Dr. Luehring wrote the report on the 1936 Berlin Olympic Games. He was secretary of the men's and women's swimming committee in 1932 and referee of the Olympic trials in both 1932 and 1936. Fred Luehring coached swimming and water polo at Princeton from 1911 to 1929, started the swim team at Nebraska in 1921 and made swimming and lifesaving conferences for summer camps at Minnesota, Wisconsin and New York universities. He is honored for more years of service to swimming than any other physical education leader.

TRUDGEON, John
Contributor

Born 1852 in Poplar, London; at age 11 went to Buenos Aires with parents; father worked for Blyth & Co. Engineers of the Isle of Dogs.

John Trudgeon learned to "trudge" from the natives of Buenos Aires and brought it back to England in a time when only the breaststroke style was swum. The trudgeon can be described as a double overarm with a sidestroke kick. In England, John swam for the Alliance Swimming Club of London. He won the English 100-yd. championship at the Edghaston Reservoir in 1 min. and 16 secs. using his own version of the stroke he picked up from the South American Indians. Almost anything besides the crawl that passes for freestyle is now called the trudgeon.

WICKHAM, Alick
Contributor

Born 1891 in the Solomon Islands; arrived in Sydney, Australia, in 1898; father owned trading schooner; brother Harry; schooled in Sydney.

Alick Wickham is credited with introducing the crawl stroke to the Western world. In 1898 he was entered in a 66-yd. race in Australia's rock pool at Bronte. Alick astonished onlookers with his new fast and unusual stroke. It was George Farmer, Australian coach, who saw Wickham and gave his stroke the name that has survived. Twenty years later, Alick did a perfect swan dive from a height of 205 ft. 9 in. for a perfect score to win a meet.

1975

BREEN, George

Swimmer

Began swimming at age 17 as a freshman at Cortland State Col; Olumpic Bronze Medal 1956; still swimming 20 years later as Masters National Champion; head coach at the Univ. Pa.

George Breen's most brilliant effort was his 1500-m. world record at the 1956 U.S. AAU indoor championships at Yale. He lowered the world record by 13:1.1 secs. and finished 1 min. and 18 secs. ahead of the second-place man. Breen's next great swim came in the preliminaries of the 1956 Olympics. He lowered his Yale record in the 1500-m. another 13 secs, to 17:52.9. The problem was that he had swum his gold medal race too soon—he finished third in the finals. From 1956 to 1960 Breen had won 22 U.S. national championships, set six world records and made two Olympic teams. Many top coaches of the time found Breen's thrashing-rolling-shoulder-roll and two-beat kick very unorthodox. One coach remarked after his world record, "Wow, if that man could only swim—think, how good he would be!"

Also in: Swimming and Diving Hall of Fame, Citizens Savings Hall of Fame Athletic Museum.

BROWNING, David "Skippy"

Diver

First coach was his father Dave, Sr, a former AAU National Junior Champion; began coaching Skippy at age 4; Olympic Gold Medal 1952; at age 24 crashed Navy jet into the Kansas plain two weeks before Olympic training was to begin.

Skippy "No Splash" Browning was rated Number One on everyone's all-time springboard diver ratings. He put two dives on the books, the two and a half twisting back one and a half from the 3-m. board and the forward two and a half somersault pike off the 1-m. board. During his short career he won eight AAU and two NCAA National Springboard Championships. At the Olympic trials he won by 100 points, and went on to become the 1952 Olympic Springboard Diving Champion. He died at the height of his diving career.

Also in: Swimming and Diving Hall of Fame, Citizens Savings Hall of Fame Athletic Museum.

HARUP, Karen

Swimmer

Born 1924 in Copenhagen, Denmark; 1937 joined the Dansk Kvinde-Gym-nastik-forening (the leading Danish Swimming Club); coached by Ingeborg Paul Petersen and Ellen Larsen; Olympic Gold and two Silver Medals 1948; heroine was Regnhild Hveger, world record holder; received degree as swimming coach in 1949.

Karen Harup won three events at the European championships in 1947, the 100-m. backstroke in 1:15.9, the 400-m. freestyle in 5:18.2 and the 400-m. freestyle relay in 4:32.3. At the 1948 Olympic Games in London, Karen won the 100-m. backstroke and was second in the 400-m. freestyle and the 400-m. freestyle relay. Karen turned professional in 1949.

KOLB, Claudia

Swimmer

Born December 19, 1949, in the U.S; from California; Olympic Silver Medal 1964; three Pan-Am Gold and one Silver Medal 1967; two Olympic Gold Medals 1968.

Claudia Kolb from the Santa Clara Swim Club twice won the U.S. outdoor 100- and 200-m. breaststroke titles. At age 14 she won an unexpected silver medal in the 1964 Olympic 200-m. breaststroke, after qualifying fifth for the finals. Claudia was in fourth place with 25 m. to go. The final place times were 2:46.4 (first), 2:47.6 (second), 2:48.6 (third). At the 1968 Games in Mexico she placed first in the 200- and 400-m. individual medley events. At the 1967 Pan-American Games in Winnipeg, Claudia won the 200-m. butterfly, was second in the 200-m. breaststroke and set world records in both the 200- and 400-m. individual medley.

Also in: Swimming and Diving Hall of Fame, Citizens Savings Hall of Fame Athletic Museum.

KRAMER, Ingrid

Diver

Born July 29, 1943 in East Germany; married Mr. Engel, a wrestler; divorced; married Mr. Gulbin; two Olympic Gold Medals 1960; two European Championship Gold Medals 1962; Olympic Gold Medal and Silver Medal 1964.

In 1960 Ingrid Kramer became the first non-American woman to win an Olympic diving gold medal in 40 years, taking the 3-m. springboard and the 10-m. platform dive. At the Tokyo Olympic Games in 1964, Ingrid Engel-Kramer won the springboard, but was second off the tower. In 1968 at Mexico, Ingrid Gulbin-Kramer finished fifth. Ingrid's best diving was seen at the 1962 European championships where she won the springboard by 14.79 points and the tower by 12.04 points.

McKINNEY, Frank

Swimmer

From Indianapolis, Ind; attended Indiana Univ; two Pan-Am Gold Medals 1955; Olympic Bronze Medal 1956; two Pan-Am Gold Medals 1959; Olympic Gold and Silver Medals 1960; two years as officer in U.S. Army Intelligence; became a banker; V.Pres. Pres. and Chmn. of Bd. of the American Fletcher National Bank in Indianapolis.

Frank McKinney was the pioneer of the modern bent arm backstroke. He won U.S. nationals for the Indianapolis Athletic Club while still in high school. At 16, Frank won the Pan-American Games 100-m. backstroke event in 1955 and was the youngest member of the world record medley relay team. He repeated those two gold medals at the 1959 Pan-Am Games. He was captain of Indiana University's first Big Ten champions. McKinney won 14 national AAU championships, 9 Big Ten gold medals.and 2 NCAA titles. At the Melbourne Olympic Games in 1956, Frank won the bronze medal for his 100-m. backstroke. At the Games in 1960 he received the silver medal for the 100-m. backstroke and a gold medal for the 400-m. medley relay. He retired from swimming in 1960.

Also in: Swimming and Diving Hall of Fame, Citizens Savings Hall of Fame Athletic Museum.

NAKAMA, Keo

Swimmer

Born in Hawaii; attended Maui High School; attended Ohio State Univ; was captain of the Ohio State baseball team; received masters degree 1945; taught at Ohio State two years; scouted for baseball players for Detroit Tigers; returned to Hawaii as a high school swim coach, teacher and athletic director; 1964 elected to Hawaii State Legislature; majority floor leader.

In 1939, Keo Nakama led the Alexander House Community Association team to the first of several U.S. national AAU team championships. In 1939 at the Australian National, Nakama won six titles, adding the 330-yd. In 1940 at the Pan-American Swimming Championships in Ecuador, he won five events. Nakama won 27 national championships from 110 yd. to 1500 m. during his swim career in the early 1940s. Nakama's world record extended, at age 22, from the mile (1760 yd.) swum at New Haven to the 27-mile Molokai Channel. In his last three seasons at Ohio State, he was captain, under Coach Mike Peppe, of the Buckeyes for two years, which were Big Ten and NCAA championship years. The big annual meet held in Waikiki War Memorial Natatorium was named after him, an honor perhaps far outweighing the winning of any prize, cup or trophy.
Also in: Swimming and Diving Hall of Fame, Citizens Savings Hall of Fame Athletic Museum.

ROBINSON, Thomas
Coach

Tom Robinson was Northwestern's first swimming coach in 1909. During his 35 years as coach, Northwestern compiled a record of 10 Big Ten championships and six NCAA championships. Under his direction, Northwestern also won seven water polo titles and three water basketball championships. Some of his great swimmers included Ken Huszahg, Dick Howell, Ralph Breyer, Bob Skelton, Sybil Bauer, Harry Daniels, Wally Colbath, Al Schwartz and Volney Wilson. Robinson was a pioneer in the development of the crawl stroke and he invented the game of water basketball. He organized the first women's Red Cross Lifesaving Corps in 1920. Through his summer swimming classes he taught more than 50,000 people to swim. Robinson also introduced the requirement that every student at Northwestern must learn to swim before graduation, which probably has saved a number of lives and definitely has greatly increased the ranks of those who love to swim.
Also in: Swimming and Diving Hall of Fame, Citizens Savings Hall of Fame Athletic Museum.

WYLIE, Mina
Swimmer

Born in Australia; father Harry could swim 120 yd. underwater; brothers; at age 5 part of family swimming act; swam with hands and feet tied; family business was Wylie Baths, built in 1909; Olympic Silver Medal 1912; now lives with his brother in the family home on Coogee-Neptune St.

In 1910 at Rushcutlers Bay Baths, Mina Wylie set a world record for the 100-yd. freestyle. In 1912 at the age of 14 Mina finished second to her Australian teammate Fanny Durack in the 100-m. freestyle at the Stockholm Olympic Games. In 1911, 1922 and 1924 Mina won all Australian events, including the 100-yd. breaststroke, 50-yd. backstroke and the 100-, 220-, 440- and 880-yd. freestyle events. She continued to win at least one Australian National Championship for 20 years.

1976

BALL, Catherine "Catie"
Swimmer

Born September 30, 1955; from Jacksonville, Fla; 5 ft. 7 in. 128 lbs; two Pan-Am Gold Medals 1967; Olympic Gold Medal 1968.

Catie Ball dedicated the Hall of Fame Pool in 1966 with a world record time of 1:15.6 in the 100-m. breaststroke. In 1967 she won two golds for her swim in both the 100- and 200-m. breaststroke at the Pan-Am Games. In 1967 and 1968 she won two events in the U.S. outdoor titles. She broke ten world breaststroke records between 1966 and 1968. Known as the "Catie Ball Express," her eggbeater arm and leg style set records that were not broken until the 1972 Olympics. Severe virus infection ended Catie's chances in the 1968 Olympics except for a gold medal for her part in the medley relay on the first day of the meet. She was voted 1968 World Swimmer of the Year.
Also in: Swimming and Diving Hall of Fame, Citizens Savings Hall of Fame Athletic Museum.

CAPILLA, Joaquin
Diver

Born in Mexico; Olympic Bronze Medal 1948; Olympic Silver Medal 1952; Olympic Gold and Bronze Medals 1956; brother Alberto competed for Mexico but won no medals in the 1952 and 1956 Olympic Games.

Joaquin Capilla was Mexico's only Olympic diving champion. He was trained largely in the United States. Capilla won five Olympic medals in three Olympic Games, including a gold in the Melbourne Games. He was undefeated in the first two Pan-Am Games, winning both springboard and tower. He was U.S. national AAU champion three times.

CARLILE, Forbes
Coach

Born in Australia; graduate physiologist and lecturer at the Univ. Sydney; wife Ursula joins him in Olympic coaching and clinical work; Carlile swimming organization gives 4,000 lessons per week, from babies to Olympians; worked for the Australian Broadcasting Commission for 31 years as swim color man.

Forbes Carlile was Australia's first modern pentathlon Olympic competitor in 1952 and the youngest Olympic coach, 1948. He was also Australia's Olympic coach in 1956, and in the 1964 Olympic Games he coached for Holland. He has done pioneer work in scienfitic training, interval workouts, pace clocks, heart rate tests for assessing effort and T-wave study. His book, *Forbes Carlile on Swimming* (1963), was the first modern book on competitive swimming. In it he discusses tapering and the development of the crawl. Carlile's concepts include even pace, starting young, speed through endurance, "better a has-been than a never-was" and the arm-dominated high tempo two-beat kick. Carlile was the organizer of the Australian Swimming Coaches Association.

COUNSILMAN, James
Coach

James Counsilman began as a swimmer for the East St. Louis YMCA. He was captain and NCAA champion swimmer on Ohio State's national championship teams between 1946 and 1947. Six times Doc Counsilman was named World Swimmer of the Year. He was assistant coach at Illinois in 1948 and the same at Iowa from 1948 to 1952. As coach at Cortland State, 1952 to 1958, he won 35 and lost 4. From 1958 until present, Counsilman has been coaching at Indiana. He has collected 15 consecutive Big Ten crowns, 6 consecutive NCAA team titles, 15 undefeated dual meet seasons in 19 years and 106 individual NCAA records, 8 Pan-Am records, 52 world records, and 154 American records since 1962. His teams have collected 62 NCAA, 79 indoor and 60 outdoor AAU, 11 Pan-American and 21 Olympic gold medals. His book, *Science of Swimming,* is the text beside which all other swim books are judged. He is president of the ASCA and founding president of the International Swimming Hall of Fame.

GESTRING, Marjorie
Diver

Born November 18, 1922, in Los Angeles, Calif; tall, slim, graceful; Olympic Gold Medal 1936; now lives in Honolulu, Hawaii, as Mrs. Bowman.

Marjorie Gestring at 13 was the youngest Olympic competitor to win the gold medal in the 3-m. springboard diving in 1936 at Berlin. She beat teammate Kathy Rawls by less than one point. W. W. II took her chances for other Olympic medals, but she also held eight U.S. national AAU championships. Her attempted comeback in 1948 failed.
Also in: Swimming and Diving Hall of Fame, Citizens Savings Hall of Fame Athletic Museum.

GYARMATI, Dezso
Water Polo

Born October 24, 1927, in Hungary; Olympic Silver Medal 1948; Olympic Gold Medal 1952; Olympic Gold Medal 1956; Olympic Gold Medal 1964; married Olympic swimming champion and coach Eva Szekely; daughter Andrea became Hungary's top female swimmer.

Dezso Gyarmati is considered by most to be the greatest player of the modern era. Dezso could play as well with his right hand as with his left. As a player he led Hungary to Olympic gold medals three times, 1952, 1956 and 1964, and a silver medal in the 1948 Olympic Games. As Hungarian National Coach he won three European championships, ten national championships and one world championship. He is still coaching.

HICKCOX, Charles
Swimmer

Born February 6, 1947; from Phoenix, Ariz; married Lesley Bush, diving gold medalist of 1964; two Pan-Am Gold Medals 1967; three World Student Gold Medals 1967; two Olympic Gold Medals and one Silver Medal 1968; today a coach and TV color commentator.

Charlie Hickcox won four U.S. outdoor titles for backstroke in 1966 and 1967. He was Pan-Am Games 100-m. backstroke champion and won three gold medals in the 1967 World Student Games in Tokyo for backstroke. In the 1968 Olympic Games Charlie took gold medals in the 200-m. individual medley, the 400-m. individual medley and a silver medal in the 100-m. backstroke, and was named World Swimmer of the Year. During his career Charlie Hickcox broke eight world records, won nine national AAU and seven NCAA championships.

KOK, Ada
Swimmer

Born June 6, 1947, in Holland; 6 ft. tall; two European Championships Gold Medals 1962; two Olympic Silver Medals 1964; two European Championships Gold Medals and one Silver Medal 1966; Olympic Gold Medal 1968; retired to become Speedo's glamorous European sales representative.

Ada Kok is considered the all-time premier woman butterfly swimmer. She won her first gold medals in the 1962 European championships in the 100-m. butterfly and in the medley relay. Four years later she retained her 100-m. title and the medley relay victory, as well as taking a silver medal in the 400-m. freestyle event. At the 1964 Olympic Games in Tokyo, she finished second in the 110-yd. butterfly event and in the medley relay. In 1968 Ada finally won her gold medal for the 200-m. butterfly event and retired after breaking ten individual world butterfly records between 1963 and 1967. Ada was voted European Swimmer of the Year in 1963, 1965 and 1967.

McCAFFREE, Charles "Mac"
Contributor

Charles McCaffree has done more than any other individual to organize American swimming. He has been, at one time or another during his 45 years of involvement, a coach, editor, manager, chairman, organizer, president, official, administrator or honoree for achievement and service to swimming. McCaffree has won six Michigan high school state championships, four Big Eight conference championships while at Iowa State, eight Central Collegiate conference championships for Michigan State and one Big Ten in 1957. He has had 293 college All-Americans, 11 AAU Number One All-Americans, 6 U.S. Olympians, 32 NCAA record holders, 37 NCAA champions, and 55 Big Ten champions. In 1959 McCaffree was coach of the U.S. Pan-Am team; president of the ASCA in 1961 and 1962; president of the College Swimming Coaches Association in 1960 and 1961; secretary of the U.S. Olympic swim committee from 1961 to 1968; assistant manager of the 1972 U.S. Olympic swim team; meet manager of the U.S. Olympic swim trials in 1964, 1968 and 1972; recipient of the Intercollegiate and Interscholastic and AAU national swimming awards.

ROBIE, Carl
Swimmer

Born May 12, 1945; from Philadelphia, Pa; graduated from Michigan State Univ. 1967; Pan-Am Gold Medal 1963; Olympic Silver Medal 1964; Olympic Gold Medal 1968; attended law school while still swimming.

Carl Robie broke his first world record in 1961 in the 200-m. butterfly in a time of 2:12.4 and brought it down to 2:08.2 a year later. Robie was six times U.S. national AAU outdoor long course champion in the 200-m. butterfly from 1961 through 1965 and again in 1968. He won the Pan-American Games 200-m. butterfly title in 1963. Carl set his world records between 1961 and 1963. He finished second in the 1964 Tokyo Olympic Games. He was considered washed up, but came back to win an Olympic gold medal in the 200-m. butterfly in 1968.
Also in: Swimming and Diving Hall of Fame, Citizens Savings Hall of Fame Athletic Museum.

RUUSKA, Sylvia
Swimmer
Olympic Bronze Medal 1956.

Sylvia Ruuska was the United States' first great age-group swimmer. Sylvia and her younger sister Pat starred on their father's Berkeley YMCA swim club that was twice U.S. national AAU team champions. At the age of 13 she won an Olympic bronze medal for her effort in the 400-m. freestyle at the 1956 Games. Sylvia holds 5 world records, has won 20 national championships and has 4 times been high point winner in the U.S. Nationals. She wound up her career as captain of the 1960 U.S. women's Olympic swimming team.
Also in: Swimming and Diving Hall of Fame, Citizens Savings Hall of Fame Athletic Museum.

SAARI, Roy
Swimmer
Father Uhro "Whitey" Saari, national and Olympic water polo coach from El Segundo, Calif; brother Robert All-American water polo player on the 1964 Olympic team; attended the Univ. Southern Calif.

Roy Saari won his first U.S. AAU national titles at 13. He went on to win nine individual NCAA championships, three each year, from the 100-yd. relay to the 3-mi. in freestyle and the 400-m. individual medley. Roy won 33 nationals during his career, between 1959 and 1969.
Also in: Swimming and Diving Hall of Fame, Citizens Savings Hall of Fame Athletic Museum.

SILVIA, Charles "Red"
Contributor
Red Silvia began his career as the U.S. national collegiate record holder for the 300-yd. individual medley, college All-American and captain of the Springfield College swim team. He turned to coaching and his swimmers set 14 world records. His swimmers included Bill Yorzyk, Olympic and Pan-Am gold medal holder, and Davis Hart, who set a record for the English Channel. Silvia revolutionized the dolphin butterfly stroke in the mid-1950s and was a supporter of mouth-to-mouth resuscitation as the method of choice for artificial respiration. Silvia was the assistant coach of the 1956 U.S. Olympic team. He was president of the College Swimming Coaches Association of America and author of *Life Saving and Water Safety Today.* Fifty of Silvia's students have gone on to become college swimming coaches.
Also in: Swimming and Diving Hall of Fame, Citizens Savings Hall of Fame Athletic Museum.

SZEKELY, Eva
Swimmer
Born April 3, 1927 in Hungary; Olympic Gold Medal 1952; Olympic Silver Medal 1956; married to Dezso Gyarmati, great water polo player; daughter Andrea champion swimmer; still active as a coach.

Eva Szekely participated in three Olympic Games during her swimming career. She was fourth in the 1948 Olympic 200-m. breaststroke, but moved up to take a gold medal in that event in 1952 using the over-water arm style of the breaststroke. She made the difficult transition to orthodox breaststroke to take a silver medal in the 1956 Olympic Games. Eva Szekely set 10 world records, 5 Olympic records, 101 Hungarian national records and took 68 Hungarian National Championships. As a coach, her swimmers have set 21 European records.

ZORRILLA, Alberto
Swimmer
Born in South America; competed in boxing, rowing, track and field; flew W.W. I planes; Olympic Gold Medal 1928; won the European ballroom dancing championships in 1931; American citizen in 1954; currently resides in New York City.

Alberto Zorrilla was South America's first Olympic gold medal winner by swimming the 400-m. freestyle in 1928. Zorrilla made three Olympic teams, 1924, 1928 and 1932, but could not attend the 1932 Games due to illness. In the United States he swam for the New York Athletic Club. As late as 1946 he won the ocean mile and 2-mi. Delaware State and Eastern Seaboard Championship races. In South America he is the Argentine and South American champion and record holder in freestyle and backstroke for 1929 and 1932.

1977

BURTON, Mike
Swimmer
Born in Des Moines, Iowa; severely injured in a cycling crash with a truck at age 13; never allowed anything to interfere with swimming; swam and won despite severe intestinal cramps in 1967 and in the 1968 Olympics; two Olympic Gold Medals 1968.

Mike Burton improved the time of the 1500-m. freestyle event from 16:41.6 to 15:57.3 within a few short years. In the 1968 Olympic Games in Tokyo he won the 300-m. and the 1500-m. for two gold medals. He was nominated for 1968 World Swimmer of the Year for his record times in the 400-, 800- and 1500-m. freestyle events.
Also in: Swimming and Diving Hall of Fame, Citizens Savings Hall of Fame Athletic Museum.

CHAVOOR, Sherman
Coach
Born in Hawaii; coached football; owner of Arden Hills Swimming and Tennis Club.

Sherm Chavoor coached for 32 years. In 1967 he was coach of the U.S. team for the Pan-American Games. In 1968 and 1972 he was coach of the women's Olympic team. Sherm is the only coach to have two Sullivan Award winners work under him. Some of his great pupils were Debby Meyer, Mike Burton, John Ferris, Sue Pederson and Mark Spitz. His swimmers have produced 83 world records and 131 American records, and in 1968 and 1972 the Arden Hill swimmers won 16 Olympic gold medals, two silver medals and three bronze medals.

DALAND, Peter
Coach
Born in Philadelphia, Pa; attended Yale Univ; swam under Bob Kiphuth; graduated from Swarthmore Col. 1948.

Pete Daland began his career in New York City and took his first coaching job at Rose Valley, Pa, where he won eight consecutive Suburban League titles from 1947 to 1955. He was founder and first coach of the Philadelphia

Suburban Swim Club. In 1956 Pete moved to the West Coast to coach at the University of Southern California and the Los Angeles Athletic Club. In 1958 his USC team won the National Amateur Athletic Union team title from the New Haven Swim Club. In 1962 Pete was the American Swim Coaches Association Coach of the Year. In 1964 he was the U.S. women's Olympic team coach and in 1972 he became the U.S. men's Olympic head coach. During his 29 years of coaching, his teams won 8 NCAA team titles and 14 National AAU men's team titles.

FORD, Gerald R.
Honorary Member
From Michigan; former president of the United States.

Former President Ford became the first honorary member of the Hall of Fame. He is the recipient of the Number One Swimmer Award. His plaque says, "You are honored for your splendid example of swimming for health, exercise and pleasure in the historic tradition of the other "Wet-Heads of State" who are accomplished swimmers. . . ."

GOULD, Shane
Swimmer
Three Olympic Gold Medals, one Silver and one Bronze Medal 1972.

Born 1956 in Australia, Shane Gould won three gold, one silver and one bronze medal in the 1972 Olympics at Munich. During her two-and-a-half-year career Shane broke 11 notable world records for all five freestyle distances, from 100 m. to 1500 m. She turned professional at the age of 16.

HAINES, George
Coach
George Haines has gained greatest renown as coach at the Santa Clara Swim Club for 26 years and foremost producer of Olympic champions. He has coached Don Schollander, John Nelson and Donna deVarona. Haines has a vast knowledge of the sport, a gift for organization, a commanding personality and an uncanny sense of strategy. Donna deVerona feels that Haines is successful because, "Despite his large squad he knows how to handle the individual swimmer. His training sessions are fun and we never did the same workout twice." Haines was the U.S. women's Olympic team coach in 1960 and assistant coach in 1972. He held the assistant coaching position in 1964 and the 1968 team coach position for the U.S. men's Olympic squad. George was elected Coach of the Year in 1964, 1966, 1967 and 1972.

JANY, Alex
Swimmer
Born 1929 in France; father baths superintendent in Toulouse; 6 ft. 2 in. tall; two European Championships Gold and one Silver Medal 1947; Olympic Bronze Medal 1948; two European Championships Gold Medals and one Silver Medal 1950.

At the 1947 European championships in Monte Carlo, Alex Jany won the 100-m. by 2.4 (in 57.3) and the 400-m. by 15.2 (in 4:35.2), a world record. Jany retained his 100- and 400-m. European titles in Vienna in 1950, again taking second place behind Sweden in the relay. Jany failed to live up to his records in the 1948 Olympic Games, coming in fifth in the 100-m. and sixth in the 400-m. events, but France did take a third-place medal in the relay.

JASTREMSKI, Chester "Chet"
Swimmer
Born January 12, 1941; resident of Giant St, Toledo, Kans; a stocky 5 ft. 9 in; of Polish descent; medical student at Indiana Univ; Olympic Bronze Medal 1964.

Chet Jastremski was a pioneer in the modern fast stroking sprint style breaststroke. Chet broke the 100-m. world mark six times, taking the time from 1:11.1 to 1:07.8 and then to 1:07.5 on the same day. He also brought the world time for the 200-m. down from 2:33.6 to 2:28.2. Chet Jastremski became the first man to break the minute for the 100-yd. breaststroke with a time of 59.6. He missed the 1960 Olympic Games due to a misunderstanding of the rules. In the 1964 Games, although he was the record holder at the time, he only came in third in the 200-m. breaststroke.
Also in: Swimming and Diving Hall of Fame, Citizens Savings Hall of Fame Athletic Museum.

MEYER, Deborah
Swimmer
Born August 14, 1952; from Sacramento, Calif; 5 ft. 7 in, 116 lbs; two Pan-Am Gold Medals 1967; three Olympic Gold Medals 1968; Sullivan Award 1969.

Debbie Meyer of the Arden Hills Club, coached by Sherman Chavoor, won the U.S. 400- and 1500-m. outdoor titles for four successive years, from 1967 to 1970, and the 400-m. medley in 1969. She took two gold medals at the 1967 Pan-Am Games and was chosen Tass News Agency Woman Athlete of the Year. At the 1968 Olympic Games, Debbie won three individual gold medals in the 200-, 400- and 800-m. freestyle events. During her career Debbie won 19 national AAU championships, set 24 American records and was on three American record relays. In a little over two years Debbie set 15 freestyle world records from 200 to 1500-m. She was voted the 1967 through 1969 World Swimmer of the Year and won the 1968 Sullivan Award as top amateur athlete.
Also in: Swimming and Diving Hall of Fame, Citizens Savings Hall of Fame Athletic Museum.

RILEY, Mickey Galitzen
Diver
Olympic Gold Medal, two Silver Medals and one Bronze Medal 1928 and 1932.

Mickey Riley dove for the Los Angeles Athletic Club under Fred Cady. He was both a platform and a springboard diver who won one gold medal, two silver medals and one bronze medal in the 1928 and 1932 Olympic Games. Mickey and his diving brother John won back-to-back platform diving championships in 1928 and 1929. During his career Mickey took six national AAU indoor diving titles, three national AAU outdoor titles and later became a spectacular show diver.

SPITZ, Mark Andrew
Swimmer
Born February 10, 1950, in Modesto, Calif; 6 ft. 1 in. tall, 170 lbs; five Pan-Am Gold Medals 1967; two Olympic

Gold, one Silver and one Bronze Medal 1968; seven Olympic Gold Medals 1972; attended Indiana Univ, studied to be a dentist; tried his hand at show business.

Mark Spitz swam with the Santa Clara Club. The temperamental swimmer set 27 individual world records for freestyle and butterfly between 1967 and 1972. Mark's high hopes for the 1968 Olympic Games were postponed for four years when he took home two gold medals for the freestyle relays. Spitz won five gold medals at the 1967 Pan-American championships in the 100- and 200-m. butterfly, the 400- and 800-m. freestyle relay and in the 440-m. medley relay. His most incredible performance came in the 1972 Olympic Games in Munich. Taking an unprecedented seven gold medals, Spitz smashed world records in the 100- and 200-m. freestyle and the 100- and 200-m. butterfly and participated in three world-record-breaking relay performances. Spitz was named World Swimmer of the Year in 1967, 1971 and 1972. He said, "When I think back to the Munich Olympics, I remember that for one period of time I was the best in my field. Not too many people can say that." *Also in:* Swimming and Diving Hall of Fame, Citizens Savings Hall of Fame Athletic Museum; and International Palace of Sports Hall of Fame.

STEPANOVA, Galina Prosumenschikova
Swimmer
Born November 26, 1948, in the U.S.S.R; from Moscow; married; son born in 1969. Olympic Gold Medal 1964; European Championships Gold Medal 1966; Olympic Silver and Bronze Medals 1968; two European Championships Gold Medals and one Silver Medal 1970.

Galina Prosumenschikova's first world record was set in Great Britain at Blackpool in the 220-yd. breaststroke in a time of 2:47.7. She was the only European to win a swimming gold medal at the 1964 Olympic Games in Tokyo in the 200-m. breaststroke timed at 2:24.4. At the 1966 European championships she took the 200-m. title. At the Mexico Olympic Games in 1968 Stepanova was greatly affected by the altitude and lost the 100-m. breaststroke title by one-tenth of a second and took a bronze for the 200-m. She collapsed after that race and had to be carried to the dressing room. At the 1970 European championships the much slimmer Stepanova won the 100-m. event by 2 m, retaining her 200-m. title and helped the U.S.S.R. medley relay team to a silver medal.

Sailing Hall of Fame

ANNAPOLIS, MARYLAND

Mailing Address: U.S. Naval Academy, 21402. Tel. (301) 267-3747. *Contact:* George Griswold, Secy. (313) 434-0746. *Location:* In the Robert Crown Sailing Center on Campus; approx. 20 mi. S. of Baltimore on Rte. 2, 30 mi. E. of Washington, D.C, on Rte. 50. *Admission:* Free 8 to 5 daily. *Personnel:* J. Gordon Bentley, Exec. V. Pres; George Griswold, Secy; Robert H. Hobbs, Treas; George Griswold, Henry H. Anderson, Jr, Scott H. Allan, mems. of Bd. of Trustees. *Nearby Halls of Fame:* Jockeys (Baltimore), Exploration and Invention (Arlington, Va, 40 mi. W.), Heritage (Valley Forge, Pa, 110 mi. N.E.), Bicycle (Staten Island, N.Y, 190 mi. N.E.), Heritage, Music (New York City, 200 mi. N.E.), Flight (Kill Devil Hills, N.C, 210 mi. S.E.), Harness Racing (Goshen, N.Y, 210 mi. N.E.), Flight (Manteo, N.C, 220 mi. S.E.), Ice Skating (Newburgh, N.Y, 220 mi. N.E.), Flight (Elmira, N.Y, 230 mi. N.W.), Golf (Foxburg, Pa, 230 mi. N.W.).

The Intercollegiate Yacht Racing Association of North America began making plans for its Hall of Fame in 1963. At a meeting in Chicago in 1965, preliminary selections were made for the All-American Sailor Award. The elections for this award were held in 1966 and confirmed in 1967. It was in 1968 that the Hall of Fame inducted its first members from the ranks of competitive sailors, administrators and benefactors in order to perpetuate the memories of their excellence in the art of sailing. The Hall of Fame located in the Robert Crown Sailing Center of the U.S. Naval Academy Campus is, as of 1977, in the process of being redesigned. The expected completion date is circa 1979. On display within the Hall will be plaques, photos, slides, films, trophies and a variety of sailing memorabilia. The Hall is supported by outside contributions and the Naval Academy.

Members: 179 as of 1976. Hall of Fame inductions are made from two groups of sailing participants. The first are those persons who have won the All-American Sailing Award. Second are those members of the sailing world who have been chosen for their outstanding competitive ability prior to the first All-American awards (made in 1967), as well as those who have been involved from the administrative aspect or as benefactors. There is a limit of 20 All-Americans admitted annually and only three Intercollegiate Hall of Famers may be inducted per year. Selections for nominees are made by two separate committees. The committee selecting All-Americans consists of eight members, chaired by George A. Wood, while the Intercollegiate selections are made by the Board of Trustees. Each new inductee receives a certificate of award and has his or her name placed on the Hall of Fame roster.

1967 ALLAN, Robert M. Jr. "Skip." All-American. Stanford University. Also 1969 as Intercollegiate.

ALLAN, Scott H. All-American. University of Southern California.

CURTIS, David A. All-American. Tufts University. Also 1968.

DESENBERG, Kim L. All-American. Stanford University.

DOHERTY, J. Peter. All-American. Yale University.

FISCHL, Lt. Robert D, U.S.N. All-American. U.S. Naval Academy.

INGHAM, Lt. James T. All-American. U.S. Coast Guard Academy. Also 1968.

KUEHLTHAU, Robert L. All-American. University of Wisconsin.

LEONARD, Dr. John J. All-American. Ohio Wesleyan University.

LOUTREL, Charles F, Jr. All-American. Tufts University.

MINSON, Lt. Frederick V. All-American. U.S. Coast Guard Academy. Also 1968.

PARKER, William B. All-American. Kent State University.

SCHOFIELD, Henry G. All-American. Long Beach State University.

VAN DUYNE, Carl I. All-American. Princeton University.

1968 BUTLER, Edward O. All-American. San Diego State University. Also 1969, 1970 and 1971.

CAMPBELL, Argyle. All-American. University of Southern California. Also 1969 and 1971.

CHATAIN, Christopher C. All-American. University of Michigan.

COIT, David M. All-American. Yale University. Also 1969.

DOYLE, Richard T. All-American. University of Notre Dame. Also 1969 and 1970.

HOGAN, Timothy P. All-American. University of Southern California. Also 1969 and 1970.

McLAUGHLIN, Thomas W. All-American. San Diego State University. Also 1969.

MESSINGER, Arthur L. All-American. SUNY Maritime College. Also 1970.

MEYER, John F. "Hans." All-American. University of Michigan. Also 1970.

MEYEROSE, Richard, Jr. All-American. SUNY Maritime College. Also 1969, 1970.

SEAVER, Christopher. All-American. Yale University. Also 1969, 1970.

SEAVER, Arthur III. All-American. Tulane University.

1969 BARRETT, Peter J. Intercollegiate. University of Wisconsin.

BERNARD, Lt. Thomas E. All-American. U.S. Coast Guard Academy. Also 1970.

COLIE, C. Runyon. Intercollegiate. Massachusetts Institute of Technology.

COX, F. Gardner. Intercollegiate. Princeton University.

COX, William S, Jr. Intercollegiate. Princeton University.

DANE, John III. All-American. Tulane University. Also 1970 and 1971.

DOYLE, Robert E. All-American. Harvard University. Also 1970 and 1971.

FORD, Carter. Intercollegiate. Harvard University.

FOSTER, Glen S. II. Intercollegiate. Brown University.

FOWLE, Leonard M. Intercollegiate. Harvard University.

HALL, Graham H. Intercollegiate, U.S. Merchant Marine Academy.

JOHNSON, Andrew L. All-American. Princeton University.

JOSLIN, Lt. Royal D. All-American. U.S. Naval Academy.

KNAPP, Arthur, Jr. Intercollegiate. Princeton University.

MILLIGAN, Stephen D. All-American. Massachusetts Institute of Technology.

MOSBACHER, Emil, Jr. Intercollegiate. Dartmouth College.

O'DAY, George D. Intercollegiate. Harvard University.

PARK, Colin N. Intercollegiate. University of British Columbia.

ROSE, Richard M. Intercollegiate. Princeton University.

RUGG, Lt. Daniel M. III. All-American. U.S. Naval Academy. Also 1970.

WOOD, Walter C. Intercollegiate. Massachusetts Institute of Technology.

1970 ANDERSON, Henry H, Jr. Intercollegiate. Yale University.

BROWN, Harold, Jr. "Hatch." Intercollegiate. Boston University.

COX, William S, Sr. Intercollegiate. Princeton University.

CRONBERG, Terry L. Intercollegiate. Massachusetts Institute of Technology.

DYKSTRA, Thomas M. All-American. University of Rhode Island.

EVEREST, Wallace A. Intercollegiate. Boston University.

FRIEDRICHS, G. Shelby. Intercollegiate. Tulane University.

GOLDSMITH, Bruce G. Intercollegiate. University of Michigan.

GOOGE, James F, Jr. Intercollegiate. U.S. Naval Academy.

GREENBERG, Edward A. Intercollegiate. Princeton University.

HOPPIN, Charles S. Intercollegiate. Harvard University.

HUNDRICHS, Paul G. All-American. San Diego State University. Also 1971 and 1972.

McCOMB, David W. All-American. Massachusetts Institute of Technology.

MONETTI, Robert E. Intercollegiate. Yale University.

NORTH, Lowell O. Intercollegiate. University of California, Berkeley.

ROMAGNA, Leonard A. Intercollegiate. Brown University.

SHIELDS, Cornelius, Sr. Intercollegiate.

ULMER, Charles R. Intercollegiate. U.S. Naval Academy.

1971 ANSTEY, E. Louise. All-American. University of Victoria.

BENTLEY, J. Gordon. Intercollegiate. Syracuse University.

BOSSETT, Henry. All-American. University of Rhode Island.

CAMPBELL, Lt. J. G. William L. All-American. U.S. Naval Academy. Also 1972 and 1973.

CARTER, Richard E. Intercollegiate. Yale University.

COULSON, Robert E. Intercollegiate. Yale University.

CROSSLEY, Robert W. All-American. University of British Columbia.

FENNESSEY, John F. Intercollegiate. Massachusetts Institute of Technology.

HANSELMAN, Frederick B. All-American. Ohio Wesleyan University. Also 1972.

HAZELHURST, Thomas E. Intercollegiate. Brown University.

JOBSON, Gary A. All-American. SUNY Maritime College. Also 1972, 1973.

LARR, Timothea S. Intercollegiate. University of Michigan.

LATHAM, Richard S. Intercollegiate.

MINTON, David C. III. Intercollegiate. U.S. Naval Academy.

NATHANSON, James E. Intercollegiate. Harvard University.

POSEY, Dennis C. Intercollegiate. Massachusetts Institute of Technology.

PURRINGTON, Robert H. Intercollegiate. Princeton University.

PUTNAM, Augustus L. Intercollegiate. Harvard University.

REEVE, Abbot L. All-American. Harvard University.

SULLIVAN, Patricia K. Intercollegiate. University of Cincinnati.

TILLMAN, Richard L. Intercollegiate. U.S. Naval Academy.

WHITE, Charles T. All-American. Michigan State University.

WHYTE, Rollin "Skip." All-American. University of Rhode Island.

WIDNALL, William S. Intercollegiate. Massachusetts Institute of Technology.

WRIGHT, Jonathan, All-American. U.S. Merchant Marine Academy.

1972 BAVIER, Robert N. Intercollegiate. Williams College.

BEMIS, Greg F. Intercollegiate. Harvard University.

BENSEN, William. Intercollegiate. Denison University.

DEBERC, Alain J. Intercollegiate. Massachusetts Institute of Technology.

FINNEGAN, Patrick S. All-American. University of British Columbia.

FORD, Jonathan G. All-American. Stevens Institute of Technology.

FOSTER, Warren A. Intercollegiate. Ohio State University.

FOWLE, Nancy K. Intercollegiate. Tufts University.

HODGES, David. All-American. University of California, Irvine.

HORN, Michael S. Intercollegiate. Harvard University.

LITCHFIELD, Francis A. Intercollegiate. U.S. Merchant Marine Academy.

MARTIN, Steven C. Intercollegiate. U.S. Coast Guard Academy.

MARTUS, Robert. All-American. SUNY Maritime College. Also 1973.

McDERMAID, Jeff. All-American. Long Beach State University. Also 1974 and 1975 (University of California, Irvine).

NELSON, Bruce D. All-American. University of Michigan. Also 1973 and 1975.

NOYES, David Chester III. All-American. Yale University.

OLSEN, Eric C. Intercollegiate. Massachusetts Institute of Technology.

POLLAK, Christopher P. All-American. Tufts University.

PRIDDY, Allan L. Intercollegiate. Dartmouth College.

ROSTELLO, Douglass P. All-American. University of Southern California.

SCHERER, Otto J, Jr. Intercollegiate. University of Michigan.

SCOTT, Manton D. All-American. Tufts University.

SEAVER, Patrick T. All-American. Yale University.

SHIELDS, Cornelius, Jr. Intercollegiate. Babson College.

WHITE, Robert J. Intercollegiate. Ohio State University.

WUESTNECK, John A. Intercollegiate. U.S. Coast Guard Academy.

1973 BULL, Douglas. All-American. Tulane University. Also 1974.

CUCCHIARO, Stephen J. All-American. Massachusetts Institute of Technology. Also 1974.

CUDAHY, William B. Intercollegiate. Harvard University.

DIAZ, Agustin G. All-American. Tulane University.

FRIES, Derrick R. All-American. Michigan State University. Also 1974.

GRANT, Leroy F. Intercollegiate. Royal Military College-Canada.

GRISWOLD, George H. Intercollegiate. College of Wooster.

GUSTAFSON, Prescott. Intercollegiate. Brown University.

HIGGINBOTHAM, David E. Intercollegiate. Northeastern University.

HUGHES, Ens. Allen B, Jr. All-American. U.S. Coast Guard Academy. Also 1974.

KEEFE, Arthur T. III. All-American. Yale University.

LAURA, Mark S. All-American. University of Washington. Also 1975.

LEARY, William P. All-American. U.S. Coast Guard Academy.

MARSHALL, Ronald E. Intercollegiate. Ohio State University.

MILLER, David S. Intercollegiate. University of British Columbia.

ROBBINS, Hanson C. Intercollegiate. Harvard University.

SALTONSTALL, William G. Intercollegiate. Harvard University.

SWEET, Richard B. Intercollegiate. University of California, Santa Barbara.

TAYLOR, John A. Intercollegiate. University of California, Los Angeles.

THEDE, Dexter E. Intercollegiate. Univeristy of Michigan.

THOMPSON, Daniel. All-American. University of California, Irvine.

WILSON, Peter. All-American. University of Southern California.

1974 ALTREUTER, Roger W. "Sam." All-American. Tufts University. Also 1975 and 1976.

BUCHAN, William, Jr. Intercollegiate. University of Washington.

DARDEN, Thomas "Toby." All-American. Tulane University.

DAVIS, Richard A. All-American. University of California, San Diego.

KLEIN, Lawrence P. All-American. Miami University.

KRAFFT, Henry M. All-American. Stevens Institute of Technology.

MALTMAN, James S. All-American. Tufts University.

MIDDENDORF, Christopher S. All-American. Harvard University.

MORRILL, Capt. Peter A. Intercollegiate. U.S. Coast Guard Academy.

NEFF, Taylor E. All-American. Harvard University.

PARK, Lt. Cdr. William C. III Intercollegiate. U.S. Coast Guard Academy.

WATERHOUSE, Glen. Intercollegiate. University of California.

WHEELER, Mark M. All-American. Stevens Institute of Technology.

1975 BETHGE, Victor W. "Pete." Intercollegiate. Webb Institute.

CROWLEY, Michael E. All-American. U.S. Merchant Marine Academy.

FISHER, Gregory V. All-American. Ohio Wesleyan University.

FOWLER, Neal L. All-American. Tufts University. Also 1976.

GALLAGHER, Thomas B. All-American. SUNY Maritime College.

GRANT, David A. Intercollegiate. University of California, Los Angeles.

ISLER, Peter F. All-American. Yale University. Also 1976.

LUKENS, Alan R. III "Doc." Intercollegiate. Massachusetts Institute of Technology.

MITCHELL, Benny. All-American. University of Southern California.

PERRY, David B. All-American. Yale University.

REYNOLDS, Mark. All-American. San Diego State University.

SCHMIDT, Hugo V. III. All-American. San Diego State University. Also 1976.

WALTON, John D. All-American. Michigan State University.

1976 ANDREWS, Alan V. All-American. Stanford University.

DUNCAN, Marvin H, Jr. All-American. SUNY Maritime College.

FAST, Carl D. All-American. Webb Institute.

FISHER, Matthew V. All-American. Miami University.

GILLETE, Cy. Intercollegiate. General Motors Institute.

GRIFFIN, Greg. All-American. Webb Institute.

HART, Douglas W. All-American. U.S. Naval Academy.

HUNT, Charles M. Intercollegiate. Massachusetts Institute of Technology.

McCREARY, James B. All-American. Tufts University.

PARDEE, S. Treavor. Intercollegiate. Princeton University.

SADLER, Richard C. All-American. SUNY Maritime College.

SMIGELSKI, Alexander, Jr. All-American. U.S. Merchant Marine Academy.

WADE, Robert H. All-American. University of California, Santa Cruz.

WIESE, Kurt R. All-American. Tulane University.

WILSON, Frederick H, Jr. Intercollegiate. Brown University.

Water Sports Halls of Fame to Watch

AMERICAN SURFING ASSOCIATION HALL OF FAME

To Open 1979

Ever since 1778, when Captain Cook saw Hawaiians surfing for pleasure, the world has been fascinated by the sport of riding waves. Despite its ban in 1821 by European missionaries, surfing continued to grow in Hawaii, in Tahiti and elsewhere. This was especially true during the 1920s, when a surfing revival occurred. Led by Duke Kahanamoku, who in 1920 formed the first surf club at Waikiki, that revival duly resulted in the widespread and highly popular activity that surfing is today throughout the world. To honor the greatest surfers of that past and the future, the American Surfing Association will open a hall of fame in 1979. It will be located at the Bolas Chica State Beach in Huntington Beach, Calif, an area that is widely recognized for its excellent surfing conditions. The hall as well as the beach will be dedicated to and named for the great Duke Kahanamoku (*see* entry in International Swimming Hall of Fame, 1965). In addition to its library, a movie theater and the extensive museum displays, the Hall of Fame will serve as the national headquarters of the National Surf Life Saving Association of America, an association of professional surf lifeguards from ocean beaches who are either permanent or seasonal employees. For additional information on the American Surfing Associastion Hall of Fame, contact Dr. Gary F. R. Filosa II, President, P.O. Box 343, Huntington Beach, CA 94628. (714) 847-6171.

GULF MARINE RACING HALL OF FAME

Inactive 1974

Also called the Motor Boat Racing Hall of Fame, and the Gulf Oil Hall of Fame, this hall was established in 1937 for the purpose of honoring members of the marine racing fraternity. Drivers nominated were national champions, High Point winners or Kilo Record Holders who had demonstrated sportsmanship and cooperation with race officials or who had made significant contributions to boat racing. Those whose nominations subsequently were selected for membership were inducted at an annual awards breakfast, where they receiyed a plaque, two Hall of Fame pocket patches and a racing jacket. The hall was inactivated in 1974 due to the energy shortage that existed at that time and that prompted the Gulf Oil Company to withdraw its support of the hall. The Gulf Oil Company has no present plans to reactivate the hall. For information contact F. G. Wagner, Gulf Oil Corporation, P.O. Box 1519, Houston, TX 77001.

WATER SKI MUSEUM AND HALL OF FAME

To Open 1979

From 1885, when Gottlieb Daimler invented the motorboat by attaching an internal-combustion kerosene-burning engine to a rowboat on the Seine River, until 1922, when Ralph W. Samuelson invented water skiing, the sport of being towed on skis behind a boat was totally unknown. From 1922, however, water skiing began a rapid rise in popularity—so much so that by 1939 a national organization was required for the sport. The American Water Ski Association (AWSA) founded that year not only filled that requirement but also in no small measure stimulated the phenomenal rise of the sport into what it is today—a recreational and competitive activity for millions, 13 million in the United States alone; and a substantial industry in which more than $80 million is spent by Americans each year on water skis. It is not surprising, therefore, that numerous great water skiers have appeared within this brief but brilliant history. Their presence now requires a national hall of fame for the sport. The Water Ski Museum and Hall of Fame slated to open in 1979 will be housed in the recently constructed AWSA building at Winter Haven in Florida's lakes region. The Hall of Fame itself will be contained in the east wing of the complex, which in addition will consist of numerous exhibits, product displays, a gift shop and a motion picture theater. For further information, contact William D. Clifford, Exec. Dir, American Water Ski Educational Foundation, P.O. Box 2957, Winter Haven, FL 33880. (813) 324-4341.

WRESTLING

Wrestling had developed into a major sport in Egypt by 1850 B.C. It was one of the sports included in the Scottish Tailteann Games which began in 1829 B.C. Ninety years after that, Jacob, son of Abraham, wrestled until dawn with an angel. According to the Irish biblical chronologist Bishop Ussher, as Jacob was getting the better of it, the angel touched Jacob's thigh and thereby put it out of joint. Even then, Jacob wouldn't release his hold until the angel had blessed him. So the angel said, "Thy name shall be called no more Jacob, but Israel." Genesis 32:28 is the first mention in the Bible of the word Israel, which some have translated as "a wrestler with God."

Twelve centuries later, between 536 and 516 B.C, a wrestler whom many thought to be god reigned. His name was Milo and he came from Crotona, the city in present-day Italy which destroyed the enemy city Sybaris by learning how to make the Sybarite horses rear up and dance (*see* Horse Racing and Breeding). Milo could carry a four-year-old heifer on his back for 600 ft. or more. Professionally, he won the wrestling crowns at all the major Greek athletic festivals: seven different times at the Pythian Games, nine times at the Nemean Games, ten times at the Isthmian Games and six consecutive times at the Olympic Games. Thereafter, wrestling was temporarily dropped from the Olympic program because no one would wrestle him. In at least one match he even won *akonitae,* without dust, which meant without even having to oil and dust himself with powder because no one would challenge him. (Regarding the Greek use of oils and powders, *see* Track and Field.) Only once is it recorded that Milo lost. He wrestled for two hours with a much younger Spartan wrestler named Lysander. Lysander at last dropped dead from total exhaustion. The officials gave the crown to Lysander, who had been conquered not by Milo, they judged, but by Death. Milo himself died less heroically: he was trapped in a forest and devoured by wolves.

After Milo's time there were many great wrestlers among the Greeks and Romans, most of whom averaged 5 ft. 5½ in. tall. Notable exceptions were the 6 ft. 8 in, 300 lb. Polydamas, who strangled a full-grown lion with his bare hands, and the Roman Emperor Gaius Julius Verus Maximinus, a gargantuan champion who weighed over 400 lbs, stood 8 ft. 1 in, and suffered from acromegaly, a glandular condition resulting in enlarged hands, feet and head. Maximinus was small, however, compared to the later Rustum, from Afghanistan, who stood 9 ft. and weighed 652 lbs. The greatest of all these wrestlers, curiously enough, was great only at wrestling with ideas. Named Aristocles, when he was not teaching in Athens he frequented the *palaestras,* wrestling schools or clubs. Because he was so sturdy and broad shouldered, his fellow wrestlers nicknamed him *Platys,* broad, which in later Roman times was Latinized into Plato.

Greek wrestlers were classified by age, not by weight, as is done today. They fought in one or both of two distinct styles. In the upright style, a match was for the best of three falls, a fall being when one man's shoulders touched the ground. Falls did not count, however, in the other style, ground wrestling, which was called the *pankration* event. In this, the aim was to put the opponent in such a position that he had to admit defeat or suffer a broken limb or worse. Only eye-gouging and biting were forbidden. Killing the opponent was not. In one famous match, a pankratiast named Arrachion was strangled by his opponent. Before dying, he twisted the opponent's right foot out of its socket. This caused the man to raise his arm to acknowledge defeat, by which Arrachion received the crown posthumously. During the same event at the Nemean Games of about 400 B.C, one Damoxenus caught one Creugas off guard with an open-handed jab into the stomach. As Damoxenus ripped out his entrails and Creugas died, a foul was ruled. The oak or parsley crown went, therefore, posthumously to Cruegas. Such deaths, particularly frequent in Roman athletics *(see* Horse Racing and Breeding), were frowned upon but accepted. According to Athenian homicide law, which was both incredibly complex and sublimely logical, certain homicides did not carry guilt. These included the killing of a traitor, the killing of a paramour of any close female relative, the killing of a nocturnal thief, and the accidental killing of an athletic opponent. A favorite puzzle of ancient Greek lawyers involved the case of a boy who ran onto a stadium field into the path of a thrown javelin. Was it unintentional homicide by the javelin thrower, or unintentional suicide by the boy? The Romans reasoned it their own way—if an opponent was killed in a public boxing or wrestling contest, no guilt was attached to the killer "because the damage is held to have been done for the sake of glory and valour, not with intent to injure."

Wrestling was by no means confined to the Western world in ancient times. In its various forms it was practiced in Egypt, Ethiopia, Iraq, Iran, India (where matches ended when limbs broke), Brazil and China, long before it was a sport in Greece or Rome. A myth says that Japan became the home of the Japanese people after a Shinto god defeated an Ainu aborigine by kicking him to death in a *sumo* wrestling match. The first actual *sumo* match occurred in 24 B.C, six years after Cleopatra had killed herself on the other side of the world. It was won by one Sakune, who has ever since been the patron of Japanese wrestlers. Similarly, ever since that first match, *sumo* has been an integral part of Japanese culture and, through the centuries, the selective mating of *sumo* wrestlers' sons and daughters has produced champions who stood up to 7 ft. 5 in. and weighed up to 430 lbs. Although heavy, these men were light compared to the modern wrestlers "Haystacks" Calhoun, 641 lbs, and William J. "Happy Humphrey" Cobb, 802 lbs. Though *sumo* wrestlers today may all look alike to the uninitiated, the champions can easily be recognized by their more elaborate coiffures and by the fact that they fight only late in the day. Grand Champions in *sumo,* of which over a thousand years of the sport have produced less than 75, are further identifiable by the huge white rope belt, the *yokozuna,* which only they may wear. A *sumo* referee is similarly ranked and may be distinguished by the color of tassel on his fan. The lowest rank is black, then blue, blue and white, red and white, maroon, purple and white, and the highest, imperial purple.

Among the many things the Vikings brought to England between A.D. 870 and 920 was a form of wrestling that today is known as the Cumberland or Westmoreland style. They left; their wrestling stayed. It and other styles were practiced widely there and on the continent during the Middle Ages. There was such enthusiasm, in fact, that wrestling-related arguments that developed into full battles between towns are reported from the years 1045, 1222 and 1453. As mentioned in the *Canterbury Tales,* the prize at those medieval matches was usually a ram. An added feature reported from 1598 was that after a match "a parcel of live rabbits are turned loose among the crowd, which are pursued by a number of boys, who endeavour to catch them with all the noise they can make." Wrestling was not then restricted to the peasantry, nor was it later. The same year chocolate was first imported into Europe from Mexico (1520), King Henry VIII met the French King Francis I (whose favorite emblem was the salamander) in a famous match on the "Field of the Cloth of Gold," near Calais. Francis, aged 26, won. Of him, Henry, 29, had said, "He is, however, a Frenchman, and so I cannot say how far you can trust him." They came to "hate each other very cordially." Within a year of their match, their two countries were at war.

Meanwhile, wrestling was being practiced on the North American continent by Arctic Eskimos long before the Europeans arrived. It could hardly be considered a sport, though, since wresting was an integral part of their system for settling homicides. In certain Eskimo tribes, if a man killed another, he was obligated to raise the murdered man's children. As soon as one of the "stepchildren" was considered old enough to wrestle his father's killer, however, the two would wrestle to the death and the matter would be considered settled. This reportedly remains a way of life and justice among isolated Eskimos in the far Arctic North.

Colonial America saw a different form of wrestling. Like most other English and European sports, wrestling—notably the Cumberland, Lancashire and Devon or Cornish styles—reached the New World fairly early. In fact, George "Limey Stomper" Washington at 6 ft. 2 in. was one of the better wrestlers. Considered first class at the age of 15, at 18 he defeated the champion of northern Virginia. Although horse racing was his real passion, President Andrew Jackson wrestled, as did President Zachary "Old Rough and Ready" Taylor. In those days, winners of wrestling matches might receive an inscribed leather belt, a silver cup, or a piece of cloth or buckskin with which they could make a pair of breeches for themselves. Rules differed, too. An Englishman, Edward Talbot, wrote in 1824 (the year the Royal Society for the Prevention of Cruelty to Animals was founded in London) about wrestlers he had seen in Canada. He wrote that they "attack each other with the ferociousness of bull-dogs, and seem in earnest only to disfigure each other's faces, and to glut their eyes with the sight of blood . . . their whole aim is bent on tearing out each other's eyes. . . . If they fail in this attempt, they depend entirely on their teeth for conquest; and a fraction of a nose, half an ear, or a piece of lip, is generally the trophy of the victor." Abraham Lincoln was 6 ft. 4 in., 180 lbs. Only 15 when Talbot's observations were published, he was an avid wrestler. Three years later in 1827 he won a match at New Orleans over Jack Armstrong, the champion of Louisiana. Much later, while President, Lincoln established wrestling as a means of physical training and self-defense for the armed forces. From that point it was logical and desirable that wrestling be taken up by schools, where it has flourished ever since. Another sometime wrestler named Lincoln earned a different kind of fame: Elmo Lincoln was the first man to play the role of Tarzan in the movies.

FORMS: Throughout the world there are more than 50 distinct forms of wrestling. Most of these are national or regional variations of the same basic sport of two men, two boys or two women grappling together without weapons or any other implement with the goal of winning either by pinning the opponent to the floor or by removing him from the wrestling area in one way or another. Among the more widely practiced of these many forms are the Swiss *schwingen;* Russian *sambo;* Turkish *yagli,* in which the wrestlers oil themselves profusely; Japanese *sumo;* Icelandic *glima;* and Iranian *kushti* which translates literally as "you kill" in Persian, and in which contestants wear tight leather trousers. *Judo,* a derivative of Japanese *jujutsu* wrestling, is now recognized by the Amateur Athletic Union as a form of wrestling. Each of these forms has its own rules and features as well as its own series of competitions. In *sumo* wrestling, for example, 15-day championships are held six times a year and wrestlers compete for various titles, the highest of which is Grand Champion. This title, as mentioned above, has rarely been awarded. Similarly, in *yagli* wrestling, a champion is decided each year at the Kirkpinar meet, which has been held for centuries to commemorate two wrestlers who died of exhaustion more than 600 years ago after wrestling continuously for over three days. In *kushti* wrestling annual national championships are held to determine who will be the *pahlavan* or hero, the National Champion. In most countries, however, and throughout the United States and Canada, the two forms of wrestling are freestyle, better known as catch-as-catch-can, and Greco-Roman. These are the forms or styles competed in at world and Olympic tournaments. The names are misleading: freestyle is closer to the ancient forms of Greek and Roman wrestling, while Greco-Roman is a relatively modern innovation. In virtually all countries where a national form has been practiced, one or both of these styles are now popular.

In both freestyle and Greco-Roman, contestants progress toward final matches through a series of eliminations within their own weight classifications. These are light flyweight (up to 105.6 lbs.), flyweight (up to 114.4 lbs.), bantamweight (up to 125.4 lbs.), featherweight (up to 136.4 lbs.), lightweight (up to 149.6 lbs.), welterweight (up to 162.8 lbs.), middleweight (up to 180.4 lbs.), light heavyweight (up to 198.0 lbs.), heavyweight (up to 220.0 lbs.) and heavyweight plus (over 220.0 lbs.). International matches in both styles are held on 10.8 yd. square mat, within which is drawn a circular (8.1 ft. in diameter) contest area. If elevated, the mat's platform may be no more than three feet high. Olympic matches are 9 min. long with two 1-min. rest periods after each 3-min. period. These matches and most others are scored on a penalty-point system, in which the wrestler with the fewest penalty points wins and moves on to the next elimination round. Six or more penalty points constitutes elimination from a match. These are decided by the mat chairman and/or the judge and the referee. Freestyle involves both standing and ground throws and holds. These distinguish it from Greco-Roman wrestling, in which contestants may not seize each other below the hips, grip with the legs, nor push, pressure or lift with the legs. Greco-Roman wrestling, in other words, is predominately a standing form. In both forms, take-downs, time advantages, escapes, near falls, and falls are all scoring maneuvers. Greasing or oiling the body is forbidden, as is wearing any bristly beard (beards of several months' growth are permitted); fingernails must be cut short; full-length red or blue tights are normally worn, with optional sleeveless shirts, an outside supporter and short trunks, and light gym shoes which may not have heels, nailed soles, rings or buckles. Hair pulling, brawling, kicking, biting, punching, twisting of fingers or toes, hammerlocks, scissors, strangle holds and head locks are not allowed. The killing of one's opponent, whether accidently or for the sake of glory and valour, is never done.

Virtually all of the above holds true for both high school and intercollegiate wrestling matches, with the exception that high school wrestling has two additional weight classes. Another difference is that high school matches are for three periods of 2 min. each, while intercollegiate matches consist of one 2-min. period followed by two 3-min. periods.

ORGANIZATION: Once denounced as "the most crooked of all off color rackets," wrestling was restored to public favor after 1929, largely through the efforts of Jack Curley, and is thus today a popularly competitive, well-structured and highly organized international sport. The world governing body for all international forms of wrestling including freestyle and Greco-Roman is the *Fédération Internationale des Luttes Amateurs,* headquartered in Lausanne, Switzerland. Its members are the various national governing bodies; for North America these are the Canadian Amateur Wrestling Association and the United States Amateur Wrestling Federation. These two organizations direct and support amateur wrestling in North America with the aid of a number of other national or regional organizations, notably the National Wrestling Coaches Association and the Central Ontario Amateur Wrestling Federation. They are further aided by the Amateur Athletic Unions of both countries, and by the National Collegiate Athletic Association (NCAA). The NCAA publishes an annual *Official Wrestling Guide,* which contains high school and college rules in addition to a summary of the preceding year's American high school and college wrestling activities. Similar functions are performed by the varous other organizational publications, which include *Amateur Wrestling News,* published 16 times a year by the National Wrestling Coaches Association. In addition to this organizational structure for freestyle and Greco-Roman wrestling, there are numerous groups and associations dedicated to the various other forms. The world governing body for judo, for example, is the International Judo Federation, which organizes and coordinates not only major tournaments but also the many state, provincial, regional and city judo organizations and clubs. (For related data, *see* p. 458.)

Arizona Wrestling Hall of Fame

PHOENIX, ARIZONA

Mailing Address: 103 W. Marshall Ave, 85013. Tel. (602) 279-1244. *Contact:* Tom Dubin. *Location:* Approx. 110 mi. N. of Tucson. *Personnel:* Pat Hogeboom, Pres; John Urchike, Treas; Tom Pierson, Secy. Not open to the public.

The Hall of Fame was founded in 1976 to honor those whose service, achievements and devotion to wrestling have established and promoted the best welfare of the sport. The financial and administrative responsibility for the Hall now rests with the Arizona Wrestling Association.

Members: 17 as of 1977. Anyone may nominate a wrestler, coach, contributor or official by sending a résumé to the Hall of Fame Selection Committee by October 1. Résumés should contain a photograph and statement of facts concerning the individual's contributions to wrestling. After evaluating the application, the list of potential inductees is voted on in January. Three of four committee votes are necessary for induction. The requirements for wrestlers, coaches, contributors and officials are usually a combination of 20 years within the sport and retired at least five years from competition. A superlative record in any or all phases of wrestling is required. Only one or two will be inducted in the future, probably in February at either the University of Arizona or Arizona State University campus.

1976 BRAASCH, Vern. Coach.

BROWN, Wes, Jr. Coach and administrator.

CULP, Curly. Wrestler.

DUBIN, Tom. Wrestler, coach, administrator and official.

EASTIN, Ron. Coach.

LEAVITT, Dewayne. Official and wrestler.

LEWRY, Robert L. Wrestler and official.

MARTORI, Arthur. Wrestler and contributor.

McMINN, Glenn. Wrestler.

RIGGS, John D. Administrator.

TRIBBLE, Charles. Wrestler.

WINER, Russ. Wrestler.

1977 CARROLL, Mickey. Wrestler.

GARCIA, Richard G. Wrestler.

HEADINGTON, Jerry. Wrestler and official.

NELSON, William J. Coach. See entry in Amateur Wrestling Hall of Fame, Citizens Savings Hall of Fame Athletic Museum, 1963.

SCHMIDT, Czeslaw T. Coach and official.

Illinois Wrestling Coaches and Officials Hall of Fame

WHEATON, ILLINOIS

Mailing Address: 228 S. Williston St, 60187. Tel. (312) 682-2000. *Contact:* Edward Ewoldt, State Historian and Chmn. *Location:* 25 mi. W. of Chicago, 25 mi. N. of Joliet, and 170 mi. N.E. of Springfield. *Personnel:* Five mem. Selection Comt. *Nearby Halls of Fame:* Business (Chicago), Bowling, State (Milwaukee, Wis, 80 mi. N.E.), Agriculture (West Lafayette, Ind, 115 mi. S.E.), Sports (North Webster, Ind, 140 mi. S.E.), Auto Racing, Basketball (Indianapolis, Ind, 180 mi. N.E.), Football (Green Bay, Wis, 185 mi. N.E.), Trapshooting (Vandalia, Ohio, 250 mi. S.E.).

In 1972, Steve Combs, current executive secretary of the National Wrestling Foundation, and Edward Ewoldt established the Hall of Fame with six initial inductees. Each year at the state wrestling tournament a display of 8 by 10 photographs of all the members is exhibited. Of the standing members, two are selected each year to lead the state finalist in the Olympic Grand March.

Members: 50 as of 1977. Future inductees, designated as either wrestler, coach or contributor, are nominated by a member of the Illinois Wrestling Coaches and Officials Association and then elected by a vote of the Selection Committee. Requirements for inductees state that all wrestlers must be out of high school for six years, all coaches must have coached in Illinois for a minimum of eight years and all contributors must have officiated in Illinois for a minimum of ten years. Inductees receive their awards each spring at the Annual State Wrestling Banquet.

1972 BAY, Ott (dec). Coach.

HICKS, Robert. Coach.

KENNEY, Dr. Harold E. (dec). Coach and contributor. See entry in Amateur Wrestling Hall of Fame, Citizens Savings Hall of Fame Athletic Museum, 1960.

McCANN, Terence. Wrestler. See entry in Amateur Wrestling Hall of Fame, Citizens Savings Hall of Fame Athletic Museum, 1961.

SLIMMER, Louis. Coach.

STRANGE, Robert. Wrestler.

1973 BAY, Rick. Wrestler.

CZECH, Ted. Coach.

EMMONS, Robert. Coach and wrestler.

FARINA, Charles. Coach.

GEORGE, Elias. Coach, wrestler and contributor.

HURLEY, Allen (dec). Coach.

KRAFT, Ken. Coach and contributor. See entry in Amateur Wrestling Hall of Fame, Citizens Savings Hall of Fame Athletic Museum, 1971.

PLAZA, Arnold. Wrestler. See entry in Amateur Wrestling Hall of Fame, Citizens Savings Hall of Fame Athletic Museum, 1965.

SCHMITT, William. Coach and contributor.

VAVRUS, Joe. Coach.

WEICK, William. Wrestler and coach. See entry in Amateur Wrestling Hall of Fame, Citizens Savings Hall of Fame Athletic Museum, 1970.

1974 CUSTER, James. Coach.

FITZGERALD, John. Coach.

GREENE, Kenneth. Coach.

GROSS, Charles. Coach.

PATTERSON, Pat. Coach and contributor.

RILEY, Jack. Wrestler. See entry in Amateur Wrestling Hall of Fame, Citizens Savings Hall of Fame Athletic Museum, 1965.

ROUTH, Walter. Coach.
SWINDELL, Roy (dec). Coach.

1975 BEHM, Donald. Wrestler.
COMBS, Steve. Contributor.
CONRAD, Roy. Wrestler.
EWOLDT, Ed. Contributor.
KLOOTWYK, Ray (dec). Coach.
MARINO, Jack. Coach.
TENPAS, Larry. Wrestler.
THERRY, Robert. Coach and contributor.

1976 ADAMS, Vern. Contributor.
GLASS, Brad. Wrestler.
HOLZER, Werner. Contributor.
KRAUS, Bert. Coach and contributor.
KRISTOFF, Larry. Wrestler.
LAW, Glen. Coach.
PICKERILL, Ken. Coach.
ROMANOWSKI, Walter. Wrestler.
SOWINSKI, Joe. Coach.

1977 FLAVIN, Don. Coach.
GEORGE, John. Coach.
MARLIN, Ken. Contributor.
MUSGROVE, Homer. Coach.
NORMAN, Robert. Wrestler.
SCHWARTZ, Martin. Coach.
SILVERSTEIN, Ralph. Wrestler.
WEICK, Clarence. Contributor.

Indiana Wrestling Hall of Fame

INDIANAPOLIS, INDIANA

Mailing Address: 6500 S. Emerson Ave, 46204. Tel. (317) 786-8540. *Contact:* William Dean. *Location:* Approx. 100 mi. N.W. of Cincinnati, Ohio, 115 mi. N. of Louisville, Ky, 165 mi. W. of Columbus, Ohio, 165 mi. S.E. of Chicago, Ill, 190 mi. E. of Springfield, Ill, 240 mi. N.E. of St. Louis, Mo. *Admission:* Free, 10 a.m. to 12 p.m. Monday to Saturday; 10 a.m. to 10 p.m. Sunday; closed holidays. *Personnel:* Al Smith, Pres; John Dechant and Randy Qualitza, V.Pres; Chauncey McDaniel, Secy; William Dean, Historian. *Nearby Halls of Fame:* Auto Racing, Basketball (Indianapolis), Agriculture (West Lafayette, 65 mi. N.W.), Flight (Dayton, Ohio, 100 mi. E.), Trapshooting (Vandalia, Ohio, 100 mi. N.E.), Sports (North Webster, 115 mi. N.E.), Business (Chicago), State (Detroit, Mich, 240 mi. N.E.), Bowling, State (Milwaukee, Wis, 250 mi. N.W.), Music (Nashville, Tenn, 250 mi. S.).

The Indiana Wrestling Hall of Fame was founded, in principle, in 1971. The first inductions were held in the spring of 1972. Four members of the Indiana Wrestling Coaches Association, Chauncey McDaniel, Norm Willey, Phil Thrasher and Clifford Myers, are responsible for directing the Hall from an idea into an annual award recognizing coaches, wrestlers and contributors. Located within the Sherwood Country Club, trophy displays and original and personal memorabilia are exhibited for the public to view. Pictures of inductees (with accompanying descriptions of accomplishments) are exhibited also. The Association sponsors clinics throughout the year in Indianapolis, with an all-star wrestling clinic staged in the fall at the French Lick Resort. The fall clinic provides top-flight collegiate coaches and wrestlers, an opportunity for participants to exchange ideas and techniques prior to the season, a resort atmosphere for the entire family to enjoy and exclusive instruction for meeting the needs of individual wrestlings. Group and family rates are available. The All-Star Wrestling Clinic usually is held in late October. Additional information may be obtained by contacting Chauncey McDaniel and requesting the brochure outlining costs, dates, program and activities. Aside from clinics, the Association publishes *Matburns Newspaper* six times annually. The newspaper disseminates information regarding the Hall of Fame Recognition Banquet, activities of the Hall, match results, upcoming tournaments, techniques for wrestling improvement and safety tips. Although the Hall is situated within the Sherwood Country Club, visitors to the club may dine in the adjoining restaurant. All awards, activities and Hall of Fame events are governed and financed by the Association.

Members: 121 as of 1977. There are three categories for induction: Wrestler, Coach and Contributor. Any Indiana wrestler who earns one or more state championships and wins or places in international, national or collegiate competition will be considered. The honors earned determine the number of years required before a nomination may be submitted before the Hall of Fame Committee. A one-time state champion is precluded from selection for a minimum of 20 years following graduation, while a four-time champion may be nominated after five years. Coaches are precluded from nomination for a minimum of 15 years after they have initiated an interscholastic program, coached wrestlers to state championships or place winners or have been active members of the association promoting the sport. Contributors are nominated after five years of demonstrable service advancing the sport or as an official or media writer or commentator. All categories are judged on character that reflects the spirit and camaraderie of the oldest sport in the world. Usually 10 to 20 are inducted annually by a majority vote of the Association members. The Hall of Fame Recognition Banquet is held the last Friday in February to honor the inductees. At present there are no honorary memberships for the Hall of Fame, but as the Hall continues to evolve in size and functions, such memberships will be included.

1972 AUSTIN, Sanford. Wrestler.

CONLEY, Paul. Wrestler.

CUNNINGHAM, Wayne. Coach.

DUFFY, Willard. Wrestler.

FISHER, Walter. Coach.

FORTNER, Clarence. Wrestler.

FREDERICKS, Casey L. Coach. See entry in Amateur Wrestling Hall of Fame, Citizens Savings Hall of Fame Athletic Museum, 1967.

FRENCH, Kermit. Coach.

GALLES, Dr. James. Wrestler.

HINSHAW, Robert (dec). Contributor. *Also in:* Indiana Basketball Hall of Fame.

INMAN, Garnett. Contributor.

JONES, Robert. Coach.

KERR, Paul. Wrestler.

McDANIEL, Charles (dec). Wrestler. See entry in Amateur Wrestling Hall of Fame, Citizens Savings Hall of Fame Athletic Museum, 1966.

McDANIEL, Chauncey. Coach.

MUMBY, Harold F. (dec). Coach.

MYERS, Clifford. Coach.

OSMAN, Mike. Wrestler.

RAINBOLT, Carl. Wrestler.

REECK, Claude (dec). Coach. See entry in Amateur Wrestling Hall of Fame, Citizens Savings Hall of Fame Athletic Museum, 1962.

RITTER, Estell. Wrestler.

ROSS, George (dec). Wrestler.

SCHULER, Robert. Wrestler.

SCOTT, Auree. Coach.

SOUDERS, Leroy. Wrestler.

THOM, W. H. "Billy." (dec). Coach. See entry in Amateur Wrestling Hall of Fame, Citizens Savings Hall of Fame Athletic Museum, 1958.

VOLIVA, Richard. Coach. See entry in Amateur Wrestling Hall of Fame, Citizens Savings Hall of Fame Athletic Museum, 1964.

WEINLAND, Rufus (dec). Wrestler.

WILLEY, Norman. Coach.

1973 ANDERSON, Hanson H. (dec). Contributor.

ARONSON, Morris. Coach.

BOLINGER, George. Contributor.

BROWN, Arthur. Wrestler.

BUTTERFIELD, Walter. Wrestler.

CHAFFEE, Myron. Wrestler.

DOSTER, Tom. Wrestler.

FISHER, Howard. Wrestler.

FOSTER, Jack. Wrestler.

FRANKOWSKI, Ray. Wrestler.

FREIBERGER, William. Coach.

FUNK, Dorrance. Wrestler.

GINAY, John. Wrestler.

HAAK, Robert. Wrestler.

HAZEL, Ross. Wrestler.

HELD, Emil (dec). Coach.

HLINKA, Joe. Wrestler.

KENNLLEY, George. Contributor.

LEEDY, C. Calvin. Contributor.

NEMATH, Emery. Wrestler.

PATACSIL, Joseph. Coach.

PITCHER, A. E. Coach.

SPARKS, Joe. Wrestler.

SPARKS, Dr. Raymond E. See entry in Amateur Wrestling Hall of Fame, Citizens Savings Hall of Fame Athletic Museum, 1958.

THRASHER, Mike. Wrestler.

TREICHLER, William. Coach.

VOLIVA, Harry. Wrestler.

WILLIAMS, Benham (dec). Wrestler.

1974 BALTAS, Gus A. Wrestler.

BENDER, Roger (dec). Wrestler.

BENSON, Jack. Wrestler.

DILL, Dr. Charles. Contributor.

DONALDSON, Gene. Wrestler.

ELLIS, James. Wrestler.

FINLEY, Jack. Wrestler.

FORESTER, Edmund. Wrestler.

HAMILTON, Bob. Coach.

HOOVER, Rollie. Coach.

KING, Bill. Wrestler.

LUMMIO, Al. Wrestler.

LYON, Richard. Wrestler.

McCOOL, George. Wrestler.

MOLODET, George. Wrestler.

PERKINS, Richard. Wrestler.

POLLEY, Jennings. Wrestler.

PREDA, Joe. Coach.

REASON, Raymond. Wrestler.

RICHARDSON, Bill. Wrestler.

ROBINS, Chester. Wrestler.

SVARCZKOPF, Frank. Coach.

THRASHER, Phil. Coach.

TRAICOFF, Chris. Contributor.

ZACHARY, Phillip. Wrestler.

1975 ANGELOPOLOUS, Jimmy. Contributor.

CARNAHAN, Carl. Coach.

CONE, Charles. Wrestler.

CORDELL, Guy (dec). Wrestler.

DICKES, Herman W. (dec). Coach.

DOUGLAS, Rodney (dec). Wrestler.

EGGERS, Dick. Wrestler.

FRISBRE, Robert. Wrestler.

HEPBURN, Ralph. Wrestler.

KEATON, Walter B. "Buster." Contributor.
LAX, Ron. Wrestler.
MILLER, Raymond (dec). Wrestler.
NIMETH, Joe. Wrestler.
O'DONALD, Hugh. Wrestler.
ROBINSON, Emmit. Wrestler.
SHIVELY, Leo. Coach.
STEWART, Robert. Wrestler.
TATUM, John. Contributor.
WEATHERS, Paul. Wrestler.

1976 BELSHAW, Dr. George. Contributor.
BRANNON, Burl. Wrestler.
FARRAND, Keith. Coach.
GALLOWAY, Jon. Wrestler.
GILLUM, Olden (dec). Wrestler.
HILL, James. Wrestler.
HINDS, Donald. Wrestler.
MORGAN, Allen. Coach.
MYERS, Robert. Wrestler.

1977 DOAN, Dr. John. Contributor.
FISHMAN, Joe. Wrestler.
GOINGS, Dale. Wrestler.
HILL, Don. Wrestler.
HOEMANN, Paul. Coach.
HURRLE, John. Coach.
NAILON, Ed. Wrestler.
POLLAK, Robert. Wrestler.
PRAED, Drayton. Wrestler.
THOMPSON, Thomas. Contributor.
TURNER, Tom. Coach.

George Martin Wrestling Hall of Fame

MILWAUKEE, WISCONSIN

Mailing Address: 2525 N. Sherman Blvd, 53210. Tel. (414) 444-9760. *Contact:* Bob Spicuzza, Treas. *Location:* Milwaukee Washington High School; approx. 75 mi. E. of Madison, 90 mi. N. of Chicago, Ill, 105 mi. S. of Green Bay. *Personnel:* Jim Stephenson, Chmn; Bob Spicuzza, Treas; four mem. Selection Comt; five mem. Nominations Comt. Not open to the public. *Nearby Halls of Fame:* Bowling, State (Milwaukee), Business (Chicago, Ill.), Football (Green Bay), Sports (North Webster, Ind, 150 mi. S.E.), Agriculture (West Lafayette, Ind, 175 mi. S.E.), Archery (Grayling, Mich, 210 mi. N.E.).

Founded by the Wisconsin Wrestling Coaches Association in 1976, the Hall seeks to honor wrestlers, officials, contributers and coaches. Pledges from individuals and other wrestling organizations in the state support the Hall.

Members: 18 as of 1977. The charter year members were inducted at the state tournament. Representatives from all state associations nominate and elect four to six individuals annually beginning in 1978. Wrestlers must be out of high school and/or college for five years. Coaches and officials have a 12 year minimum requirement of performance. Contributors must have made significant progress for the advancement of the sport and its welfare.

1977 CHALUPA, Frank. Coach.
DOUGLAS, Jim. Coach.
GREGOR, George. Coach.
HELLICKSON, Russ. Wrestler.
KARPFINGER, Barney. Coach, contributor and wrestler.
LEDERMAN, Larry. Contributor and wrestler. *Also in:* Racquetball Hall of Fame, Citizens Savings Hall of Fame Athletic Museum.
MARTIN, George Alfred. Coach and contributor. See entry in Amateur Wrestling Hall of Fame, Citizens Savings Hall of Fame Athletic Museum, 1969.
NOWAK, Joe (dec). Coach.
O'NEILL, Larry. Contributor.
PETERSON, Ben. Wrestler. See entry in Amateur Wrestling Hall of Fame, Citizens Savings Hall of Fame Athletic Museum, 1974.
PETERSON, John. Wrestler. See entry in Amateur Wrestling Hall of Fame, Citizens Savings Hall of Fame Athletic Museum, 1977.
POWERS, John. Contributor.
ROBERTS, John. Wrestler and contributor. *Also in:* University of Wisconsin, Stevens Point Hall of Fame.
SHERMACHER, Ken. Coach.
STECH, Edward. Coach and contributor.
STONE, Ray. Coach.
SYMES, Kirby. Coach.
WEAVER, Guy H. "Buck." Coach.

National Wrestling Hall of Fame

STILLWATER, OKLAHOMA

Mailing Address: 405 W. Hall of Fame Ave, 74074. Tel. (405) 377-5243. *Contact:* Bob Dellinger, Dir. *Location:* Approx. 60 mi. W. of Tulsa, 50 mi. N.E. of Oklahoma City. *Admission:* 9:30 to 4:30 daily; open special hours in connection with Oklahoma University athletic events. Adults $1.00, high school and younger 50¢, special rates available for groups with five-day notice. *Personnel:* Myron Roderick, Pres; Jerry Miles, V.Pres; Robert L. McCormick, Jr, Treas; Bob Dellinger, Dir. *Nearby Halls of Fame:* Softball, Western Heritage (Oklahoma City), Ethnic (Anadarko, 100 mi. S.W.), Ethnic (Tahlequah, 120 mi. S.E.), Dog Racing (Abilene, Kans, 185 mi. N.W.), Agriculture (Bonner Springs, Kans, 230 mi. N.E.), Agriculture (Kansas City, Mo, 240 mi. N.E.).

Set in the heartland of wrestling champions, the National Wrestling Hall of Fame opened in 1976. Initiating the idea in 1972 and directing it to a fruitful completion were Myron Roderick, executive director of the United States Wrestling Federation (USWF) and Dr. Melvin Jones, an Oklahoma City businessman and sports enthusiast. With the addition of representatives who contributed all building materials and construction costs, plus a grant of land from Oklahoma State University (OSU), and the tradition of wrestling at OSU, Stillwater was selected from 14 cities. The Hall is funded by the National Wrestling Hall of Fame, Inc, a nonprofit corporation composed of USWF officials and the board of directors of the National Wrestling Hall of Fame. Administration and governance of NWHF is the responsibility of the United States Wrestling Federation. As a lasting tribute to the oldest sport in the world and as an inspiration for future achievement, the Hall displays artifacts and personal memorabilia for tourists as well as offering a theater and library. Some of the artifacts include headgear from 1928, early-day and modern uniforms, NCAA team trophies, programs and Olympic gold medals. Among the personal memorabilia is a copy of Dr. Clapp's first NCAA rules book indicating alterations in the margin to be introduced when he was chairman of the rules committee, Billy Sheridan's first paycheck voucher for $30 covering the entire year, Hugo Otopalik's 1915 championship plaque, Ed Gallagher's track and field medals and the Golden Gloves of Danny Hodge. On entering the Hall the visitor is greeted by The Wrestlers, a three-quarter ton green marble replica of the sculpture by Cephisodotus. This is the largest known sculptured green marble in the world. Following the walls one sees the Wall of Champions, which lists individual winners in wrestling from all geographic areas and levels of competition. The Honors Court displays granite plaques of inductees with an audio system commemorating their achievements. A 44 seat theater is available for slides, videotapes and films. The library contains related magazines, photographs, the history and techniques of wrestling and copies of *Federation Wrestler,* which is published monthly by the USWF. All displays, exhibits and furnishings were provided through a $20,000 grant from the Oklahoma Department of Tourism and Recreation. The Hall of Fame is a member of the Association of Sports Museums and Halls of Fame. From two men's hopes and ideas to a community effort by wrestling buffs, the Hall continues to strive for improvements in wrestling to recognize the founders whose contributions and determination form the basis for the Hall's existence, and an encouragement to visitors for excellence in all undertakings.

Members: 14 as of 1976. In future years, a more moderate number, probably five, will be inducted annually. Those nominated for the Distinguished Member honor must excel as wrestler, coach or contributor. Anyone can submit a name for nomination by sending a résumé of credentials to the screening committee at the Hall. Following the verification of data and awards, the committee submits a list of nominees to a nationwide committee of 18 electors. Individuals receiving 14 votes are officially inducted in the fall at the Honors Banquet.

1976

CLAPP, Dr. Raymond Gustavus
Coach and Contributor

B.S. degree from Yale Univ, 1899; M.D. degree from Keokuk Col, Iowa.

An outstanding athlete and coach himself in 1896 Dr. Clapp was the first athlete to clear 10 feet in the pole vault (10 ft. 7 in.) and in 1898, raised the world record in that event to 11 ft. 10 in. In 1899 he won the eastern collegiate all-around gymnastics championship. He became a professor of physical education and the gymnastics coach at the University of Nebraska, where in 1915 he organized a wrestling team, which won the Western Conference championship. In 1924 he inaugurated the Missouri Valley Tournament, now the Big Eight Conference Championships. Dr. Clapp served as chairman of the rules committee of the National Collegiate Athletic Association from 1927 to 1945. During his term of office, he developed and adopted a distinct and progressive code of rules for college and high school competition.

COLLINS, Fendley Alexander
Coach and Contributor

Lettered in football and track at Oklahoma State University; died in November, 1976.

While wrestling for Ed Gallagher at Oklahoma A&M, Fendley Collins was an undefeated 175 lb. Canadian and U.S. national amateur champion. Following his collegiate career, he went to Michigan State University where his 33-year (1930-1962) coaching record was 158 wins, 84 losses, 11 ties. Three times his teams placed second in the NCAA tournament while his wrestlers amassed 28 national awards in collegiate and amateur circles. He founded the Pan-American Wrestling Confederation, served as its first president, and later was named honorary president for life. He devoted much time and energy to explaining the variances in techniques and methodolo-

gy, especially the complicated international bracketing system and was the author of the basic guide to pairings still in use throughout the country. He was the coach for the United States team in the 1955 Pan-American Games and in 1964, was the manager for the U.S. Olympic team. Collins served on various national rules and officials' committees and also on the U.S. Olympic committee.
Also in: Amateur Wrestling Hall of Fame, Citizens Savings Hall of Fame Athletic Museum.

EVANS, Jay Thomas
Coach and Wrestler
Lives in Norman, Okla; a pilot.

Evans achieved outstanding records, first as a wrestler on the collegiate and Olympic levels and later as a coach at the University of Oklahoma. While wrestling in college from 1951 through 1954 (he missed the 1953 season because of injuries), he won 42 of 43 matches, including 20 falls. He was the national collegiate champion in 1952 and 1954, and both times was voted the outstanding wrestler of the NCAA tournament. During his first year as coach at the University of Oklahoma, his team won the NCAA title and before retiring in 1972, added two more titles for an overall record of 140 wins, 39 losses and 2 ties. He coached the U.S. team in the 1967 World Championships and the 1968 Olympics.
Also in: Amateur Wrestling Hall of Fame, Citizens Savings Hall of Fame Athletic Museum.

GALLAGHER, Edward Clark
Coach
Received electrical engineering degree from Oklahoma State Univ. (OSU); once ran the 100-yard dash in 9.8 secs; 99-yard run in football game against Kansas State Univ. in 1908 is still OSU school record; died in Stillwater, Okla, in 1940.

Ed Gallagher established OSU as the dominant power in collegiate wrestling for several decades. As an engineer who understood the mechanics of leverage and stress, he applied this knowledge to wrestling, innovating over 300 holds and teaching these techniques in systemized practices. Beginning with the initial National Collegiate Athletic Association (NCAA) tournament in 1928, his teams won four consecutive NCAA championships, eventually totaling ten titles and a co-championship in 13 years. Individual records for his wrestlers were: 37 NCAA firsts, 32 national amateur crowns and 3 Olympic gold medals. As a coach, he enjoyed 19 undefeated seasons, 68 consecutive victories from 1921 through 1932 and lost only 5 times in 24 years of coaching. Ed Gallagher was an outstanding wrestling coach, as reflected by his record and the individual achievements of his wrestlers.
Also in: Amateur Wrestling Hall of Fame, Citizens Savings Hall of Fame Athletic Museum; and the Oklahoma Coaches Association Hall of Fame.

GRIFFITH, Arthur
Coach
Griffith's coaching career began in 1926 at the Central High School in Tulsa, Oklahoma. During the next 15 years, his teams there won 94 out of 100 matches (50 of them consecutively) and 10 state scholastic championships. They also won the only two national high school tournaments ever conducted. In 1941 Art became the coach at Oklahoma State University, succeeding the legendary Ed Gallagher. The team had already won 27 consecutive meets and under his leadership, extended their streak to 76 before a loss in 1951. He was the U.S. Olympic coach in 1948 and is a past president of the National Wrestling Coaches Association. Art Griffith's renown as a coach was most in evidence in 1941, when of the 16 national collegiate finalists that year, all but two had been coached by Art, either in high school or college.
Also in: Amateur Wrestling Hall of Fame, Citizens Savings Hall of Fame Athletic Museum; and the Oklahoma Coaches Association Hall of Fame.

HODGE, Dan Allen
Wrestler
Lives in Perry, Okla.

In his three years of collegiate wrestling for the University of Oklahoma, 1955 through 1957, Danny won all of his 46 bouts, with 36 of them by falls. No one equaled or rivaled his physical strength as he claimed the NCAA title for 177 lbs. for three consecutive years. During his junior year, 1956, he also won the national amateur title and the NCAA crown within a week and a half, both in Greco-Roman and freestyle events. Before entering collegiate competition, he participated in the 1952 Olympics at Helsinki, placing fifth; in 1956 at Melbourne he won the silver medal. In his five years of wrestling, his only three defeats were all by Olympic champions, a Russian, a Bulgarian and an American. Following his college career, Hodge moved into the boxing ring where he won the national amateur and national Golden Gloves championships, becoming the first athlete in over 50 years to win national championships in both sports.
Also in: Amateur Wrestling Hall of Fame, Citizens Savings Hall of Fame Athletic Museum.

KEEN, Clifford Patrick
Coach and Contributor
Football and track star at Oklahoma State Univ. (OSU); received law degree from Univ. Mich. 1933; U.S. Navy during W.W. II.

Keen was an undefeated wrestler at OSU and won the Missouri Valley National Invitational Championship and later qualified for the 1924 Olympics only to crack a rib, forcing him to withdraw. After graduating from OSU, Clifford's initial coaching position was not wrestling, but football where his high school squad amassed 355 points in one season while allowing the opposition a mere 3 points. In 1925 he began what would eventually be the longest coaching career in collegiate history. During his 45 years at the University of Michigan, he won 13 Big Ten championships, placing in the top three 40 times and was runnerup twice in the NCAA. His reputation earned him a place on the U.S. Olympic committee for 24 years and in 1948, he was selected as the manager for the U.S. team. He was an original member of the National Wrestling Coaches Association, later served as president, and spearheaded rule modifications for safe, effective wrestling equipment such as the headgear which bears his name.
Also in: Amateur Wrestling Hall of Fame, Citizens Savings Hall of Fame Athletic Museum.

McCUSKEY, David Homer
Coach
Graduated from the Univ. Northern Iowa (UNI) in 1930; outstanding football halfback, baseball pitcher and track star in UNI.

As a coach for 41 years in Iowa, Dave built two national powerhouses in wrestling. Upon graduation from UNI, he joined the coaching staff and during the next 21 years, his team won the NCAA title in 1950, was runner-up four times and claimed three consecutive national amateur titles from 1949 to 1951. Moving to the University of Iowa in 1953, McCuskey laid the groundwork for NCAA titles in the mid-1970s while compiling 160 wins, 69 losses and 7 ties before retiring in 1973. Individual honors earned by his wrestlers at the two schools include 25 NCAA titles and 2 Olympic gold medals among his 11 Olympian wrestlers. He was coach of the 1956 Olympic team.
Also in: Amateur Wrestling Hall of Fame, Citizens Savings Hall of Fame Athletic Museum.

MEHNERT, George Nicholas
Wrestler
George Mehnert is the only American to win two Olympic gold medals in wrestling, both in lightweights, in 1904 and 1908. He was representing the National Turnverein Sporting Club in Newark, N.J, when he won the metropolitan amateur title in 1901 and in 1902, he claimed the first of six national amateur crowns. During this seven-year stretch, Mehnert won all but one of 59 bouts, often having difficulty finding competition in the lighter weights. The British Olympic Association commented in 1908 that "Mehnert showed form quite above any other man in the whole contests, and undoubtedly was the most scientific, both in attack and defense, of any wrestler taking part in the games." Possibly the first amateur wrestling "superstar" (as we use the word today), Mehnert promoted the development of amateur wrestling in New Jersey and served on the Olympic Committee during the 1930s.
Also in: Amateur Wrestling Hall of Fame, Citizens Savings Hall of Fame Athletic Museum.

OTOPALIK, Hugo M.
Coach
Starred in the backfield on the Univ. Nebr. football team 1916–1917; first sergeant during W.W. I; served with the Red Cross in the European theater during W.W. II.

Hugo Otopalik accepted the coaching position at Iowa State University (ISU) in 1924 on an interim basis which lasted for 29 years. During his tenure, the Cyclones won 7 Big Eight titles and were co-champions with Oklahoma State University in the 1933 NCAA tournament. While coaching ISU he hosted the first NCAA tournament and the first Big Eight meet in 1929 which his team won. The pinnacle of his coaching career was the 1932 U.S. Olympic team which won the team title and claimed three gold medals. Active throughout his life in amateur wrestling, he served as the first secretary of the National Wrestling Coaches Association from 1932 to 1936 and was the vice president of the International Wrestling Federation in 1952.
Also in: Amateur Wrestling Hall of Fame, Citizens Savings Hall of Fame Athletic Museum.

PEERY, Rex Anderson
Coach
Currently assistant professor in athletic dept. at Univ. Pittsburgh.

The coaching genius of Rex Peery includes a unique and satisfying experience for this man. For six consecutive years he guided his own sons to individual NCAA titles, beginning with Hugo (1952 to 1954) and again with Ed (1955 to 1957). Coupled with the father's three NCAA crowns in three attempts at Oklahoma State University, the Peerys have a phenomenal achievement record of nine national titles in nine attempts. Rex also won the 1935 national Amateur championship. A coach for 29 years, 16 of them with the University of Pittsburgh, he totaled 233 victories, 58 losses and 6 ties while placing second in the NCAA tournament twice, in 1954 and 1957. He coached 13 individual collegiate champions and 23 Eastern champions. For 12 years he was a member of the U.S. Olympic committee, coaching the freestyle team in the 1964 Olympics in Tokyo. An organizer for the U.S. Wrestling Federation (USWF), Peery remains active on the governing council of the USWF and the board of directors for the Hall of Fame.
Also in: Amateur Wrestling Hall of Fame, Citizens Savings Hall of Fame Athletic Museum.

RODERICK, Myron Willis
Wrestler and Coach
Myron Roderick is the youngest coach ever to guide a national champion team in any event. In 1958 he directed the Oklahoma State Cowboys to the NCAA crown and before his 13 years as coach were finished, he added 7 more titles and 2 amateur national championships. His coaching record rivals the legendary Ed Gallagher's with 140 wins, 10 losses and 7 ties plus a string of 84 consecutive victories. He also coached the U.S. entry in the 1963 World Games and was assistant coach in the 1964 Olympics. His wrestlers achieved 20 individual NCAA titles and 4 gold medals. Before coaching his alma mater, Roderick earned three NCAA crowns and won 42 of his 44 bouts while placing fourth in the 1956 Olympics. His teams mirrored his intense devotion to wrestling, and to attract those quality wrestlers to maintain a model program of success, Roderick introduced recruiting on a nationwide scale. Since retiring from coaching, he has devoted his energies to amateur wrestling organizations and served as the first executive director of the United States Wrestling Foundation. He is one of the cofounders of the National Wrestling Hall of Fame.
Also in: Amateur Wrestling Hall of Fame, Citizens Savings Hall of Fame Athletic Museum.

SHERIDAN, William
Coach and Wrestler
Born in 1886 in Scotland; also coached soccer and lacrosse at Lehigh Univ.

Billy Sheridan was a wrestler and coach for over four decades. He held the featherweight and lightweight titles for the British Isles from 1905 and 1908. Immigrating to Canada in 1908, he soon ventured to Philadelphia and posed for the famous sculptor Tait McKenzie to earn extra money. While posing at the University of Pennsylvania, he viewed the wrestling team, offered some advice and was hired as coach and trainer in 1910. A year later

the Lehigh University wrestling squad was under his tutelage and would remain so until 1952. His first year's salary for coaching was $30.00. During his 42 years at Lehigh he amassed 223 wins, only 83 losses and 7 ties. His training produced 59 Eastern Intercollegiate champions, 5 national champions, 5 national amateur titles and 3 Olympians. With the introduction of the NCAA tournament in 1928, Sheridan refereed every bout. In 1936 he was the alternate U.S. Olympic coach, and in 1951 produced one of the best United States winners in Pan-American Games competition with 4 golds, 3 silvers and one bronze.
Also in: Amateur Wrestling Hall of Fame, Citizens Savings Hall of Fame Athletic Museum; and the Pennsylvania Wrestling Hall of Fame.

VanBEBBER, Jack Francis "Blackjack"
Wrestler
Served four years in the infantry in the Pacific Theater during W.W. II; resides in Oklahoma City.

Continuing the fine tradition of individual NCAA titlists at Oklahoma State University (OSU), VanBebber won three consecutive NCAA titles and added four consecutive amateur crowns during the same period, 1929 to 1931, with the last one coming after he moved to Los Angeles, Calif, in 1932. Qualifying for the finals in the 1932 Olympics, he almost missed his final round with his Finnish opponent when officials rescheduled the bout and he was due to hit the mats within the hour—60 miles away! Blackjack started hitchhiking and arrived on time to demolish his opponent as effectively as he had all previous ones. With his gold medal he became the first OSU athlete ever to win an Olympic championship. Later, while working for the Phillips Petroleum Company for 39 years, he taught Boy Scouts and other employees' sons the techniques of wrestling until he retired. VanBebber was selected as one of the country's top ten amateur athletes in the first half of the twentieth century in a national poll by editors, coaches and officials.
Also in: Amateur Wrestling Hall of Fame, Citizens Savings Hall of Fame Athletic Museum.

New York State Wrestling Coaches Association Hall of Fame

BALDWINSVILLE, NEW YORK

Mailing Address: Charcoal Farms, 13027. Tel. (315) 635-3947. *Contact:* Leo Johnson. *Location:* Exit 39 off the New York Thruway & Hwy. 81; approx. 15 mi. N.W. of Syracuse, 60 mi. N.W. of Utica, 60 mi. S.W. of Watertown, 65 mi. E. of Rochester, 125 mi. E. of Buffalo. *Personnel:* Tom Robertson, Pres; Art Connerton, V.Pres; Stan Riggs, Secy.-Treas; 7 mem. Bd. of Dirs. Call for information. *Nearby Halls of Fame:* Flight (Elmira, 75 mi. S.W.), Hockey (Kingston, Ont, 75 mi. N.), Baseball (Cooperstown, 77 mi. S.E.), Horseshoe Pitching (Corning, 80 mi. S.W.), Harness Racing (Goshen, 155 mi. S.E.), Hockey, Sports (Toronto, Ont, 160 mi. N.W.), Horse Racing (Saratoga Springs, 130 mi. E.), Ice Skating (Newburgh, 160 mi. S.E.), Football (Hamilton, Ont, 170 mi. N.W.), Basketball (Springfield, Mass, 200 mi. E.), Bicycle (Staten Island, 210 mi. S.E.), Heritage, Music (New York City, 210 mi. S.E.), Golf (Foxburg, Pa, 220 mi. S.W.), Heritage (Valley Forge, Pa, 230 mi. S.E.).

The New York State Wrestling Coaches Association Hall of Fame was founded by Leo Johnson and the Executive Board in 1972. The governing body is the New York State Wrestling Coaches Association. The purpose of the Hall is to honor those people who have contributed their efforts to the participant sport of wrestling. Plaques honoring these individuals are on display once a year at the final activity of the wrestling season, which is usually in late March. The Association is scouting universities to house their plaques for public viewing year-round. The Hall is a nonprofit organization funded by donations, memberships and entry fees.

Members: 10 as of 1977. There are three categories for membership. The nominee can either be a Coach, Outstanding Athlete or a Contributor to the cause of wrestling. Nominations for inductees may come from the general public, schools or coaches. The Executive Board reviews the nominations and a ballot by committee decides on the inductees. The board has not set a specific limit to the number of inductees per year. Inductees are honored by a ceremony prior to the State Finals in Wrestling. They receive engraved wrestling statues and a plaque acknowledging their contributions. The plaques from previous years are on view that night. Ceremonies take place in different cities throughout New York each year.

1972 GARDNER, Frank "Sprig". Coach. Known as "the Father of Wrestling in New York State." See entry in Amateur Wrestling Hall of Fame, Citizens Savings Hall of Fame Athletic Museum, 1967.

WOODRUFF, Robert. Coach. Original New York State Wrestling Chairman.

1973 FALLOT, Dr. Robert. Contributor. Famous early wrestler.

1974 BERNABI, Leo. Coach. Famous coach and official, former president of the New York State Wrestling Officials Association.

COLE, Clyde. Coach. Former wrestler, now highly influential in the State Education Department.

KITTLE, Henry "Lonnie". Coach.

1975 CLARK, Clifford. Coach. *Also in:* National Association of Intercollegiate Athletics Hall of Fame.

VALLA, Joseph P. Coach.

1976 FUGE, George. Coach.

1977 LAYTON, William. Coach. Trainer of numerous coaches and Olympians, still active as a coach.

Pennsylvania Wrestling Hall of Fame

CLEARFIELD, PENNSYLVANIA

Mailing Address: P.O. Box 190, 16830. Tel. (814) 765-2401. *Contact:* Neil Turner, V.Pres. *Location:* 85 mi. S.E. of Jamestown, N.Y, 100 mi. N.E. of Pittsburgh, 100 mi. N.W. of Harrisburg. *Personnel:* Ron Pifer, Pres; Tom Elling, Secy; Dave Caslow, Treas; Ron Kanaskie, Pres. Elect. *Nearby Halls of Fame:* Golf (Foxburg, 65 mi. N.W.), Horseshoe Pitching (Corning, N.Y, 120 mi. N.E.), Flight (Elmira, N.Y, 125 mi. N.E.), Football (Canton, Ohio, 150 mi. S.W.), Exploration and Invention (Arlington, Va, 175 mi. S.E.), Football (Hamilton, Ont, 175 mi. N.W.), Heritage (Valley Forge, 190 mi. S.E.), Hockey, Sports (Toronto, Ont, 200 mi. N.W.), Harness Racing (Goshen, N.Y, 225 mi. N.E.), Baseball (Cooperstown, N.Y, 230 mi. N.E.), Ice Skating (Newburgh, N.Y, 235 mi. N.E.), Bicycle (Staten Island, N.Y, 250 mi. E.), Heritage, Music (New York City, 250 mi. E.).

The Pennsylvania Wrestling Coaches Association established its Hall of Fame in 1970 to honor outstanding participants and contributors to the sport of wrestling in its state.

Members: 49 as of 1977. Coaches, competitors and contributors nominated by the 12 district representatives are elected by the Selection Committee, composed of the Hall of Fame officers and the district representatives. Approximately ten members are elected per year. The criterion for election is the degree of involvement an inductee has maintained in Pennsylvania wrestling. The awards are presented to the inductees annually at the state tournament.

1970 O'CONNELL, Rock. Coach.

WEISS, Arthur J. Coach. See entry in Amateur Wrestling Hall of Fame, Citizens Savings Hall of Fame Athletic Museum, 1972.

1971 SHERIDAN, William. Coach. See entry in National Wrestling Hall of Fame, 1976. *Also in:* Amateur Wrestling Hall of Fame, Citizens Savings Hall of Fame Athletic Museum.

SPEIDEL, Charles. Coach. See entry in Amateur Wrestling Hall of Fame, Citizens Savings Hall of Fame Athletic Museum, 1957.

1972 JACK, Hubert. Coach. See entry in Amateur Wrestling Hall of Fame, Citizens Savings Hall of Fame Athletic Museum, 1963.

PERRY, Rex. Coach.

1973 CUSTER, George. Coach and competitor.

PAUL, Mel. Coach.

1974 BRITTAIN, Al. Coach.

CONKLIN, James. Competitor.

DIBATISTA, Richard. Competitor and contributor. See entry in Amateur Wrestling Hall of Fame, Citizens Savings Hall of Fame Athletic Museum, 1964.

GOLDTHORPE, Chuck. Coach and competitor.

HARRIS, William "Doc." Coach.

HOLLOBAUGH, Sherwood. Coach.

KOONTZ, Francis B. Coach.

MURDOCK, Raymond B. Coach and competitor. See entry in Amateur Wrestling Hall of Fame, Citizens Savings Hall of Fame Athletic Museum, 1968. *Also in:* National Association of Intercollegiate Athletics Hall of Fame.

SMITH, Glenn. Coach.

WESTFALL, Creed S. Coach.

1975 BARR, Homer. Coach and competitor.

FORNICOLA, Larry. Coach and competitor.

GLOSSER, Ernie, Jr. Coach.

KLING, Lynn. Coach and contributor.

MAITLAND, John. Coach.

PHILLIPS, W. Roy. Coach.

RUPP, Theodore. Coach.

SCHUYLER, Stanley T. Coach.

STEHMAN, John E. Coach.

STELTZER, James. Coach.

1976 ALLMAN, Robert. Competitor.

BISHOP, Dr. W. Austin. Coach and contributor. See entry in Amateur Wrestling Hall of Fame, Citizens Savings Hall of Fame Athletic Museum, 1961.

CLELLAND, Dave. Coach.

HARKINS, James. Coach.

HARRY, Sam. Competitor.

HOUK, Russell E. Coach and contributor. See entry in Amateur Wrestling Hall of Fame, Citizens Savings Hall of Fame Athletic Museum, 1977. *Also in:* National Association of Intercollegiate Athletics Hall of Fame.

LINDHOLM, "Bud." Contributor.

MAUREY, Jerry. Coach and competitor.

MAYSER, Charles W. Coach and contributor. See entry in Amateur Wrestling Hall of Fame, Citizens Savings Hall of Fame Athletic Museum, 1958.

RICHARDS, Charles C, Jr. Coach.

1977 BERNARDINO, Peter. Coach.

BERRY, Melvin. Coach.

BUBB, Robert. Coach and competitor.

FASNACHT, Al. Contributor.

GIZONI, Anthony "Vic." Competitor. See entry in Amateur Wrestling Hall of Fame, Citizens Savings Hall of Fame Athletic Museum, 1968.

JOHNSON, Michael. Competitor.

JOHNSTON, John K. Coach and competitor.

LAUCHLE, Larry E. Coach and competitor.

PAULEKAS, Anthony. Coach and contributor.

REESE, John. Coach.

TISCHLER, Warren F. Contributor. See entry in Amateur Wrestling Hall of Fame, Citizens Savings Hall of Fame Athletic Museum, 1977.

Wrestling Halls of Fame to Watch

Listed below are those wrestling halls of fame which came to the attention of the Editors too late for full inclusion in the present edition.

IOWA WRESTLING HALL OF FAME — Contact Francis Lybert, Cresco Chamber of Commerce, Cresco IA 52136. (319) 547-3434.

OHIO WRESTLING HALL OF FAME — Contact Casey Fredericks, Dept. of Physical Education, Ohio State University, Columbus OH 43210. (614) 422-5961.

OREGON WRESTLING HALL OF FAME — Contact Elmer Binker, P.O. Box 2534, White City OR 97501. (503) 664-3448.

In view of the considerable growth in the popularity of wrestling in recent years and the simultaneous spread of the hall of fame as an institution, the Editors predict the existence of additional state, city and collegiate wrestling halls of fame in virtually every state but particularly in Kansas, Oklahoma, Texas and Wisconsin.

SPECIAL FIELDS

As was noted in the Editors' Preface, halls of fame were grouped in these volumes according to their primary emphases. Those halls whose primary emphasis was a particular sport have appeared in the preceding pages (Angling-Wrestling); the primary emphasis of each hall here, in Special Fields, is somewhat larger. That is, each Special Field hall of fame has its own unique emphasis and gives equal honor to the greats who embodied it regardless of the sport in which he or she excelled. The one exception to this is the Association of Sports Museums and Halls of Fame, which is the only continental governing body for halls of fame. Not a hall of fame itself, the Association's primary emphasis is the continuing development of the hall of fame as a major North American social institution. The emphases of the other halls in this section are clarified in their individual sketches.

Association of Sports Museums and Halls of Fame

LOS ANGELES, CALIFORNIA

Mailing Address: 9800 S. Sepulveda Blvd, 90045. Tel. (213) 670-7550. *Contact:* W. R. "Bill" Schroeder, Secy.-Treas. *Location:* Across from Los Angeles Int. Airport; approx. 110 mi. N.W. of San Diego, 375 mi. S.E. of San Francisco, 390 mi. N.W. of Phoenix, Ariz. *Personnel:* Peter W. Webster, Pres; Bruce Pluckhahn, First V.Pres; M. H. "Lefty" Reid, Second V.Pres; W. R. "Bill" Schroeder, Secy.-Treas; 8-mem. Bd. of Dirs. *Nearby Halls of Fame:* Citizens Savings (Los Angeles), Softball (Long Beach, 20 mi. S.E.), Physical Fitness (Costa Mesa, 35 mi. S.E.), Auto Racing (Ontario, 45 mi. S.E.), Flight, Sports (San Diego).

The Association of Sports Museums and Halls of Fame was founded by Buck Dawson (currently Executive Director of the International Swimming Hall of Fame) in 1972. Originally envisioned as an organization which would allow communication and cooperation between those who supervised sports halls of fame in the United States, the Association initially was called the Association of Sports Halls of Fame Directors. Later in the same year, however, following a meeting that was attended by Dawson, W. R. Schroeder, Lee Williams, Philip Pines, Don Sarno, Bruce Pluckhahn and several other hall of fame directors, the present name was officially adopted and the present emphasis established. That emphasis has three parts: to encourage the development of all aspects of sports on all levels, both nationally and internationally; to pay permanent tribute to the outstanding athletes, coaches and administrators whose achievements provide lasting inspiration for the youth of today and of tomorrow; and to perpetuate the wholesome concepts and meaningful purposes of the halls of fame throughout the United States and Canada. With that three-pronged emphasis, the Association of Sports Museums and Halls of Fame became what it is today: the world's first and only governing body for halls of fame. In that unique capacity, the Association serves two vital functions. It alone seeks to coordinate the establishment and development of all the hundreds of halls of fame. And it alone guides the overall continuing growth of the hall of fame into a major North American social institution. Despite these immense responsibilities, the Association is a non-profit organization funded entirely by donations and membership fees.

Members: 35 Halls of Fame at present.

Aquatic Hall of Fame and Museum of Canada, Winnipeg, Man.
Canada's Sports Hall of Fame, Toronto, Ont.
Canadian Football Hall of Fame, Hamilton, Ont.
Citizens Savings Hall of Fame Athletic Museum, Los Angeles, Calif.
Green Bay Packer Hall of Fame, Green Bay, Wis.
Greyhound Hall of Fame, Abilene, Kans.
Hall of Fame of the Trotter, Goshen, N.Y.
Hockey Hall of Fame, Toronto, Ont.
Indianapolis Motor Speedway Hall of Fame, Indianapolis, Ind.
International Palace of Sports Hall of Fame, North Webster, Ind.
International Softball Congress Hall of Fame, Long Beach, Calif.
International Swimming Hall of Fame, Fort Lauderdale, Fla.
International Tennis Hall of Fame, Newport, R.I.
Michigan Sports Hall of Fame, Detroit, Mich.
Naismith Memorial Basketball Hall of Fame, Springfield, Mass.
National Bowling Hall of Fame and Museum, Greendale, Wis.
National Cowboy Hall of Fame, Oklahoma City, Okla.
National Fresh Water Fishing Hall of Fame, Hayward, Wis.
National Polish-American Sports Hall of Fame and Museum, Orchard Lake, Mich.
National Ski Hall of Fame, Ishpeming, Mich.
National Softball Hall of Fame, Oklahoma City, Okla.
National Track & Field Hall of Fame of the United States of America, Charleston, W.Va.
National Wrestling Hall of Fame, Stillwater, Okla.
Newfoundland Sports Hall of Fame, St. John's, Nfld.
North Carolina Sports Hall of Fame, Linville, N.C.
St. Louis Sports Hall of Fame, St. Louis, Mo.
San Diego Hall of Champions, San Diego, Calif.
Saskatchewan Sports Hall of Fame, Regina, Sask.
The British Columbia Sports Hall of Fame, Vancouver, B.C.
The Lacrosse Foundation, and Lacrosse Hall of Fame and Museum, Homestead, Md.
The National Football Foundation & National Football Hall of Fame, Kings Mills, Ohio
The United States Figure Skating Association Hall of Fame, Boston, Mass.
United States Hockey Hall of Fame, Eveleth, Minn.
United States Track and Field Hall of Fame, Angola, Ind.
World Golf Hall of Fame, Pinehurst, N.C.

Canadian Amateur Athletic Hall of Fame

MONTREAL, QUEBEC

Mailing Address: 3449 Vendome Ave, G1P 3M2. Tel. (514) 486-4376. *Contact:* Col. John W. Davies, Chmn. *Location:* Approx. 70 mi. S.W. of Trois Rivieres, 105 mi. N.E. of Ottawa, Ont, 150 mi. S.W. of Quebec. *Personnel:* Col. John W. Davies, Chmn; Sophie Berlind, Secy. Not open to the public. *Nearby Halls of Fame:* Horse Racing (Saratoga Springs, N.Y, 180 mi. S.E.), Baseball (Cooperstown, N.Y, 210 mi. S.E.), Basketball (Springfield, Mass, 250 mi. S.E.), Ice Skating (Boston, Mass, 250 mi. S.E.).

At the annual meeting of the Amateur Athletic Union of Canada (AAUC), an organization founded in 1884, Lt. Col. George C. Machum in the role of chairman and Col. John Davies as his secretary drafted a plan for the official formation of a hall of fame and presented it in the minutes of the meeting. The concept was approved by the AAUC voting body, and thus the Hall of Fame was officially born. Since then, the Hall has devoted itself to honoring outstanding Canadian athletes who have participated in international competition. With the financial assistance of the Sports Federation of Canada, a Government office, the Hall has honored outstanding athletes representing 24 different sporting events.

Members: 207 as of 1976. To be eligible for inclusion in the Hall, an amateur Canadian athlete must have brought great honors to Canada in an international capacity, such as the British Empire and Commonwealth Games, the Pan-American Games or the Olympics (gold medalists are automatically nominated), and have contributed to the promotion of amateur sports, such as an advisory or administrative capacity. A national committee of the Hall of Fame receives and screens nominations and the members vote by secret ballot. A nominee, either living or deceased, must receive 75 percent of the votes. Winners are honored at the annual banquet in January, which is co-sponsored by the Canadian Sports Federation.

1949 AMYOT, Frank (dec). Canoeing. See entry in Canada's Sports Hall of Fame.

BELL, Florence Jane. Track and Field.

CATHERWOOD, Ethel. Track and Field. See entry in Canada's Sports Hall of Fame.

COOK, Myrtle. Track and Field.

DESMARTEAU, Emile (dec). Track and Field.

GWYNNE, Horace "Lefty." Boxing. See entry in Canada's Sports Hall of Fame. *Also in:* Canadian Boxing Hall of Fame.

HODGSON, George Ritchie. Swimming. See entry in Aquatic Hall of Fame and Museum of Canada. *Also in:* Canada's Sports Hall of Fame and International Swimming Hall of Fame.

KERR, Robert (dec). Track and Field. See entry in Canada's Sports Hall of Fame.

McNAUGHTON, Duncan A. Track and Field. See entry in Canada's Sports Hall of Fame.

ROSENFELD, Fanny "Bobby" (dec). Track and Field. See entry in Canada's Sports Hall of Fame.

SCHNEIDER, Bert (dec). Boxing.

SCOTT, Barbara Anne. Figure Skating.

SHERRING, William J. (dec). Track and Field. See entry in Canada's Sports Hall of Fame.

SMITH, Ethel. Track and Field.

THOMPSON, Earl (dec). Track and Field. See entry in Canada's Sports Hall of Fame.

WILLIAMS, Percy. Track and Field. See entry in Canada's Sports Hall of Fame.

1950 EDWARDS, Phil A. (dec). Track and Field.

GOULDING, George (dec). Walking. See entry in Canada's Sports Hall of Fame.

RUBENSTEIN, Louis (dec). Figure Skating. See entry in Canada's Sports Hall of Fame.

1952 GORMAN, Charles I. (dec). Speed Skating. See entry in Canada's Sports Hall of Fame.

GUEST, Jack S. (dec). Rowing. See entry in Canada's Sports Hall of Fame.

PEARCE, Robert. Rowing. See entry in Canada's Sports Hall of Fame.

SCHOLES, Lou, Sr. (dec). Rowing. See entry in Canada's Sports Hall of Fame.

WRIGHT, Joseph, Jr. Rowing. See entry in Canada's Sports Hall of Fame.

1953 ATHANS, George, Sr. Diving. See entry in Aquatic Hall of Fame and Museum of Canada.

BROSSEAU, Eugene. Boxing. See entry in Canada's Sports Hall of Fame.

GENEREUX, George F. Trap Shooting. See entry in Canada's Sports Hall of Fame.

HEPBURN, Douglas. Weightlifting. See entry in Canada's Sports Hall of Fame.

IRELAND, Aubrey E, Jr. Canoeing.

OSBORNE, Thomas. Boxing. *Also in:* Canadian Boxing Hall of Fame.

STOCKTON, Donald. Wrestling.

TRIFUNOV, James. Wrestling. See entry in Canada's Sports Hall of Fame.

WILSON, Alex. Track and Field. See entry in Track and Field Hall of Fame, Citizens Savings Hall of Fame Athletic Museum. *Also in:* Drake Relays Hall of Fame.

WRIGHT, Joseph, Sr. (dec). Rowing. See entry in Canada's Sports Hall of Fame.

WURTELE, Rhoda. Skiing. See entry in National Ski Hall of Fame, 1969.

WURTELE, Rhona. Skiing. See entry in National Ski Hall of Fame, 1969.

1955 BOA, Gilmour S. (dec). Shooting. See entry in Canada's Sports Hall of Fame.

CÔTÉ, Gérard. Track and Field. See entry in Canada's Sports Hall of Fame.

EWING, Walter H. (dec). Trap Shooting. See entry in Canada's Sports Hall of Fame.

GRATTON, Gerald (dec). Weightlifting.

WEBSTER, Harold (dec). Track and Field.

WHITTAL, Beth. Swimming. See entry in Aquatic Hall of Fame and Museum of Canada.

1956 CONNOR, Douglas W. Cresta.

DUTHIE, Caroline Anne. Water Skiing.

HERSCOVITCH, Montgomery "Moe" (dec). Boxing.

LOARING, John W. (dec). Track and Field, Builder.

NURSE, Roy C. Canoeing.

SUTHERLAND, George (dec). Track and Field.

1957 OUELLETTE, Gerald. Shooting. See entry in Canada's Sports Hall of Fame.

1958 ARNOLD, Donald. Rowing.

BOWDEN, Norris. Figure Skating.

DAFOE, Frances. Figure Skating.

D'HONDT, Walter. Rowing.

DRUMMOND, Kenneth James. Rowing.

HARRIS, Thomas Michael. Rowing.

HELLIWELL, David. Rowing.

KEUBER, Phil. Rowing.

LOOMER, Lorne. Rowing.

MacKINNON, Archibald A. Rowing.

McCLURE, Richard. Rowing.

McDONALD, Douglas J. Rowing.

McKERLICH, William. Rowing.

OGAWA, Carl. Rowing.

PAUL, Robert. Figure Skating. See entry in Canada's Sports Hall of Fame.

PRETTY, Wayne. Rowing.

SIERPINA, Raymond J. Rowing.

SMITH, Glen William. Rowing.

TOYNBEC, Thomas Arthur. Track and Field.

WAGNER, Barbara. Figure Skating. See entry in Canada's Sports Hall of Fame.

WEST, Lawrence Kingsley. Rowing.

WHEELER, Lucile. Skiing. See entry in Canada's Sports Hall of Fame.

WILSON, Robert Andrew. Rowing.

ZLOKLIKOVITZ, Norman Joseph. Rowing.

1960 BRICKER, Calvin D. (dec). Track and Field. See entry in Canada's Sports Hall of Fame.

BROCK, Henry Thompson (dec). Builder.

COAFFEE, Cyril (dec). Track and Field. See entry in Canada's Sports Hall of Fame.

CROCKER, John Howard (dec). Builder.

CROW, Norton Harvey (dec). Builder.

DALTON, Ernest A. (dec). Builder.

FINDLAY, W. E. (dec). Builder.

HART, Nelson C. (dec). Builder.

HENSHAW, Frederick C. (dec). Builder.

HIGGINBOTHAM, George (dec). Builder.

HUDSON, Henry G. Wrestling.

JACKSON, Judge J. A. (dec). Builder.

KNOX, Walter (dec). Builder. See entry in Canada's Sports Hall of Fame.

LAMB, Arthur S. (dec). Builder.

LESLIE, John (dec). Builder.

LONGBOAT, Tom (dec). Track and Field. See entry in Canada's Sports Hall of Fame.

LOUDEN, Thomas R. (dec). Builder.

MACHUM, George C. (dec). Builder.

MERRICK, James G. B. (dec). Builder.

MULQUEEN, Patrick Joseph (dec). Builder.

NORTHEY, William M. (dec). Builder. See entry in Hockey Hall of Fame, 1947. *Also in:* International Hockey Hall of Fame.

ROBINSON, Claude C. Builder

ROBINSON, M. M. (dec). Builder.

RUSSELL, Ernestine. Gymnastics.

SCHLEIMER, Joseph. Wrestling, Builder.

STARKE, George Ritchie (dec). Builder.

TEES, Fred J. (dec). Builder.

1961 HIGGINS, Robina Haight. Track and Field.

McCREADY, Earl G. Wrestling. See entry in Canada's Sports Hall of Fame. *Also in:* Amateur Wrestling Hall of Fame, Citizens Savings Hall of Fame Athletic Museum.

NOBBS, Percy E. (dec). Fencing, Builder.

1963 COY, Eric. Track and Field. See entry in Canada's Sports Hall of Fame.

HALTER, G. Sydney. Builder. See entry in Canadian Football Hall of Fame, 1973. *Also in:* Canada's Sports Hall of Fame.

JEROME, Harry Winston. Track and Field. See entry in Canada's Sports Hall of Fame.

YOST, E. Kenneth. Builder.

1964 DAVIES, John W. Builder. See entry in Aquatic Hall of Fame and Museum of Canada.

STRIKE, Hilda Sisson. Track and Field. See entry in Canada's Sports Hall of Fame.

WHITE, Dennis E. Builder.

1965 BUDDO, Donald S. (dec). Builder.

BURNS, Leo (dec). Builder.

CROTHERS, William F. Track and Field. See entry in Canada's Sports Hall of Fame.

LORD, Margaret. Builder.

MEAGHER, Aileen. Track and Field.

WORRALL, James. Builder.

1966 DUTHIE, George (dec). Builder. See entry in Canada's Sports Hall of Fame.

HIGGINBOTTOM, Charles E. (dec). Builder.

KIDD, Bruce. Track and Field. See entry in Canada's Sports Hall of Fame.

1967 FARRELL, Neil J. Builder.

WEILER, Wilhelm F. Gymnastics.

1968 HAMILTON, Jack. Builder. See entry in Canada's Sports Hall of Fame.

McCREDIE, Nancy C. Track and Field.

O'CONNOR, Laurence G. Track and Field.

TAYLOR, Elizabeth "Betty." Track and Field.

1969 LORD, Thomas Dyson. Builder.

ST. JOHN, Pierre. Weightlifting.

1970 ANAKIN, Douglas. Bob Sleigh.

ATHANS, George Dametrie, Jr. Water Skiing. See entry in Canada's Sports Hall of Fame.

DAY, James. Equestrian.

ELDER, James. Equestrian.

EMERY, John. Bob Sleigh.

EMERY, Victor. Bob Sleigh.

GAYFORD, Thomas. Equestrian.

HEGGTVEIT, Dorothy Anne (Hamilton). Skiing. See entry in National Ski Hall of Fame, 1976. *Also in:* Canada's Sports Hall of Fame and Greater Ottawa Sports Hall of Fame.

HUNGERFORD, George. Rowing. See entry in Canada's Sports Hall of Fame.

JACKSON, Roger. Rowing. See entry in Canada's Sports Hall of Fame.

KIRBY, Peter. Bob Sleigh.

LIDSTONE, Dorothy. Archery. See entry in Canada's Sports Hall of Fame.

RAINE, Nancy Greene. Skiing. See entry in British Columbia Ski Hall of Fame, 1977. *Also in:* Canada's Sports Hall of Fame and National Ski Hall of Fame.

WILSON, Jean (dec). Speed Skating. See entry in Canada's Sports Hall of Fame.

1971 CLEMENT, Frank (dec). Builder.

CLIFFORD, Betsy. Skiing. See entry in Canada's Sports Hall of Fame.

FARMER, Kenneth F. Builder.

LUKEMAN, Frank (dec). Track and Field.

LYON, George (dec). Golf. See entry in Canada's Sports Hall of Fame.

MACKENZIE, Ada (dec). Golf. See entry in Canada's Sports Hall of Fame.

TANNER, Elaine. Swimming. See entry in Aquatic Hall of Fame and Museum of Canada. *Also in:* Canada's Sports Hall of Fame.

WALTON, Dorothy, Jr. Badminton. See entry in Canada's Sports Hall of Fame.

WATT, R. N. (dec). Builder.

1972 BOURNE, Munroe. Swimming.

BURKA, Petra. Figure Skating. See entry in Canada's Sports Hall of Fame.

CROCKER, Willard F. (dec). Tennis.

DEWAR, Phyllis (dec). Swimming. See entry in Aquatic Hall of Fame and Museum of Canada. *Also in:* Canada's Sports Hall of Fame.

FERGUSON, Mervin E. Builder.

HUTTON, Ralph W. "Iron Man." Swimming. See entry in Aquatic Hall of Fame and Museum of Canada. *Also in:* Canada's Sports Hall of Fame.

JACKSON, Donald. Figure Skating. See entry in Canada's Sports Hall of Fame.

JELINEK, Marie. Figure Skating. See entry in Canada's Sports Hall of Fame.

JELINEK, Otto. Figure Skating. See entry in Canada's Sports Hall of Fame.

LOVETT, Claire. Badminton, Tennis.

McPHERSON, Donald. Figure Skating.

OBERLANDER, Fred. Builder.

ROGERS, Melville F. (dec). Builder.

WRIGHT, Jack (dec). Tennis. See entry in Canada's Sports Hall of Fame.

1973 ALLAN, Maurice. Builder.

BALL, James. Track and Field. See entry in Canada's Sports Hall of Fame.

BEDARD, Robert. Tennis.

BIRCH, Richard. Badminton.

COUPLAND, Russell (dec). Builder.

MAGNUSSEN, Karen D. Figure Skating. See entry in Canada's Sports Hall of Fame.

OSBORNE, Robert F. Builder.

PETTIGREW, Vernon J. Builder.

PURCELL, Jack. Badminton. See entry in Canada's Sports Hall of Fame.

ROBERTSON, Bruce. Swimming. See entry in Canada's Sports Hall of Fame.

ROGERS, Douglas. Judo. See entry in Canada's Sports Hall of Fame.

1974 DAWES, Eva. Track and Field.

HATASHITA, Frank. Builder.

KIRKEY, Dallas C. Track and Field.

PICKARD, Vic. Track and Field.

READ, Frank. Rowing Coach.

SCHWENGERS, Bernard P. (dec). Tennis.

SMYTHE, Don. Badminton.

1975 APPS, Joseph Sylvanus. Track. See entry in Hockey Hall of Fame, 1961. *Also in:* Canada's Sports Hall of Fame and International Hockey Hall of Fame.

FITZPATRICK, John. Track.

FORSYTH, Dorothy. Builder.

NATTRASS, Susan. Shooting. See entry in Canada's Sports Hall of Fame.

PIRIE, Robert. Swimming. See entry in Aquatic Hall of Fame and Museum of Canada.

POUND, Richard. Swimming, Builder.

PRIMROSE, John. Shooting. See entry in Canada's Sports Hall of Fame.

SOMERVILLE, Sandy. Golf. See entry in Canada's Sports Hall of Fame.

STEWART, Mary. Swimming.

WATT, M. Laird. Builder.

1976 ANDRU, John. Fencing.

BURLEIGH, George. Swimming. See entry in Aquatic Hall of Fame and Museum of Canada.

CRANSTON, Toller. Figure Skating. See entry in Canada's Sports Hall of Famc.

DAWES, A. Sidney (dec). Builder.

DENNISTON, George. Builder.

KREINER, Kathy. Skiing. See entry in National Ski Hall of Fame, 1976. *Also in:* Canada's Sports Hall of Fame.

MacDONALD, Danny. Wrestling.

MacDONALD, Irene. Diving. See entry in Aquatic Hall of Fame and Museum of Canada.

McKENZIE, Kenneth D. (dec). Builder.

McKENZIE, William. Rowing.

PHILLIPS, Alfred. Diving. See entry in Aquatic Hall of Fame and Museum of Canada.

RADFORD, Howard E. Builder.

SHEDD, Marjory. Badminton. See entry in Canada's Sports Hall of Fame.

SHEARS, Jerry. Builder. *Also in:* Canadian Boxing Hall of Fame.

TAIT, John (dec). Track.

Canada's Sports Hall of Fame

TORONTO, ONTARIO

Mailing Address: Exhibition Place, M6K 3C3. Tel. (416) 366-7551. *Contact:* J. Thomas West, Cur. and Secy. *Location:* Center of Canadian Exhibition grounds; approx. 65 mi. N.W. of Buffalo, N.Y, 210 mi. N.E. of Detroit, Mich, 230 mi. N. of Pittsburgh, Pa. *Admission:* Free 10:30 to 4:30 daily, Sept.-May; 10:30 to 8:30, May-Aug. *Personnel:* Harry E. Foster, Chmn. Bd. of Govs; Jim Vipond, Chmn. Selection Comt; J. Thomas West, Cur. and Secy. *Nearby Halls of Fame:* Football (Hamilton, 35 mi. S.W.), Hockey (Kingston, 150 mi. N.E.), Horseshoe Pitching (Corning, N.Y, 165 mi. S.E.), Flight (Elmira, N.Y, 180 mi. S.E.), Golf (Foxburg, Pa, 180 mi. S.), Football (Canton, Ohio, 200 mi. S.), State (Detroit, Mich.), Baseball (Cooperstown, N.Y, 225 mi. S.E.).

The Hall of Fame was founded in 1955 to provide a lasting means of honoring those Canadians who have achieved excellence in sports, either as athletes or as contributors. Outstanding athletes from 46 different sports are honored and their pictures and citations are displayed on the walls. There are also many items of sports equipment, memorabilia and artifacts for public viewing. The McDonald Brier Trophy and the Elaine Tanner collection of medals are housed in the Hall. French and English are used in the display area, which receives over one million visitors per year. At present the Hall is completing research on the history of sports in Canada. The Hall of Fame occupies the east wing of a building also housing the Hockey Hall of Fame in the center of Exhibition Park, a civic attraction in central Toronto. The Hall of Fame is administered by a Board of Governors made up of prominent men in public and private life, and is a member of the Association of Sports Museums and Halls of Fame.
Members: 264 as of 1976. For athletes and contributors to be eligible, they must be Canadian citizens at the time of their achievement. Nominations can be forwarded to the Selection Committee, made up of representatives from each province. The Selection Committee meets once a year to elect the new honored members. Automatic membership is accorded only to those who have won an Olympic gold medal.

ABATE, Robert
Coach
Robert Abate was selected for inclusion in Canada's Sports Hall of Fame in 1976 as a Coach.

ADAMS, John James "Jack"
Hockey Player
See entry in Hockey Hall of Fame, 1959.
Also in: International Hockey Hall of Fame.

AMYOT, Francis
Canoeist
Born in 1904; father Dr. John A. Amyot Canada's first deputy-minister of health and pensions, an internationally known pioneer in preventive medicine; three brothers all canoeists; big for a paddler, 6 ft. 2 in, 200 lbs; served as Lieutenant-Commander in Canadian Navy in W.W. II; died suddenly in Ottawa in 1962 at age 57.

Frank's physique and water skills were acquired during many hours spent in boyhood on streams and lakes and from a decade of serious training. He wanted to be a sculler but could not afford a shell so built his own canoe. Frank began his racing career in 1923 when he won the Canadian intermediate singles. At a Carleton Place meet in 1925 the four Amyots swept the board in the junior, intermediate and senior singles. Frank won the senior competition six times before his Olympic victory. In 1935 Amyot was appointed coach, manager and member of the Canadian Olympic paddling team for the 1936 Olympics held in Berlin. Frank won by four lengths in the then record time of 5:32.1, and became Canada's only gold medalist in the 1936 Games. Upon his return to Canada, his friends in Ottawa gave him a testimonial dinner and a purse of $1000, which caused the Canadian Amateur Swimming Association to suspend Frank from amateur status. Amyot continued to enjoy canoeing and sailing as recreations after his competitive retirement.
Also in: Canadian Amateur Athletic Hall of Fame.

ANDERSON, George
Builder
Born 1890 in Aberdeenshire; immigrated to Souris, Man, when 18; moved to Winnipeg in 1911; ran a small newspaper in Melville, Sask; twice wounded in W.W. II; compositor for Veterans Press Ltd. 37 years.

During his first years in Canada, George Anderson played soccer with Britannia in the Winnipeg and District League and for the Winnipeg *Free Press* in the Printers League. Immediately after the war he began organizing and promoting junior soccer in Manitoba, soon managing the Caledonian junior, juvenile and midget soccer teams in the Manitoba Junior League. He was secretary of the Manitoba Junior Soccer Association and in the late 1930s was on the executive committee of the senior association. After W.W. II he helped reactivate the Dominion of Canada Football Association (DCFA) and served as its secretary-treasurer for 18 years until his retirement in 1968. During these years he arranged tours of famous international teams through Canada and tours of Canadian youth through England and Europe. George Anderson arranged the tour when the first DCFA team entered world competition for the football cup. They defeated the United States team but lost to Mexico City. In 1968 they sent a team to the Olympics but were again defeated. In August, 1972, at age 82, George Anderson took twenty young soccer players on a month-long tour to play against junior teams in Holland, England and Wales, still active in a sport to which he had given more than 60 years of his life.

APPS, Joseph Sylvanus, Sr. "Syl"
Hockey Player
See entry in Hockey Hall of Fame, 1961.
Also in: Canadian Amateur Athletic Hall of Fame and International Hockey Hall of Fame.

ATHANS, George Dametrie, Jr.
Water Skier
Born 1952 in Kelowna; father George, Sr, a champion diver; mother a synchronized swimmer with Canadian championships; two brothers, Greg and Garry, both skiers; started both in water and snow skiing before settling for water; attending Sir George Williams Univ.

George considers himself to be a self-taught athlete although he studied under Fred Schuler at age 9, and later with Clint Ward of the Canadian Water Ski Association. George competed in his first championship when he was 13 and at 18 moved from Kelowna to Montreal and trained at Hudson and Sherbrooke in Quebec. He won his first Overall Canadian championship in 1938 and every year afterwards through 1973. He won the Western Hemisphere Slalom title in 1968, the Figure title in 1970, the Overall World title in 1971 and 1972, and both the World Overall and the World Slalom in 1973. George holds the Canadian records for junior boys' jump (117 ft.), men's jump (164 ft.), boys' figure skiing (4600 points), men's figure skiing (5200 points), and men's slalom skiing (37½ buoys).
Also in: Canadian Amateur Athletic Hall of Fame.

BAIN, Donald Henderson "Dan"
Hockey Player
See entry in Hockey Hall of Fame, 1945.
Also in: International Hockey Hall of Fame.

BAKER, Norman H.
Basketball Player
Born 1923 in Nanaimo, B.C; at 17 joined the RCAF; married in 1950 in Victoria, B.C; coached lacrosse and basketball; worked as detective on police force in Saanich, Vancouver Island, after his playing days.

Norman Baker started with the Nanaimo Mosquitoes basketball team when he was 10, and at 15 played with the Nanaimo junior team that went to the playoffs in Victoria. At 16 he became a regular on the Victoria Dominoes, the team losing the senior title in 1941 and winning it back in 1942. At 17 he joined the RCAF at the air force station at Pat Bay, B.C, where he played on a wartime basketball club which took the Canadian championship in 1943. In this series Norman set a record Canadian high for the time of 38 points in one game. After the war he played pro basketball with the Chicago Stags in the Basketball Association of America. He returned to Canada to play for the Vancouver Hornets in the Pacific Coast Basketball League, one year racking up 1962 points in 70 games. In 1948 he was picked by the Portland team for post-season play in pro world championships, and afterwards signed a contract with Abe Saperstein, promoter of the Harlem Globetrotters. Norman played on the Stars of America club that played against the Trotters in a 13-week tour through Europe and North Africa. After the 1950 tour he played one season with Boston, then coached lacrosse and basketball in Victoria.

BALDING, Al
Golfer
Born 1924 in Toronto, Ont; caddied at the Islington Golf Course at age 8; left school at 12, worked on lake boats, moved from job to job; served in the military in W.W. II; worked for a rubber company, but burned severely in industrial accident; afterwards drove beer truck.

Al Balding played golf whenever he could, and came to the attention of Jack Littler, pro at Toronto Oakdale, who hired him as pro-shop assistant. In 1952 Al went on a pro tour, winning nothing, but gaining experience. He won his first tournament, the Millar Trophy, symbol of the Canadian professional match play championship, later in 1952. He toured again in 1953, 1954 and 1955 but did not win any of those years. However, in December 1955 he won the Mayfair Open in Florida with rounds of 69, 66, 66 and 68. In 1957 he won the Miami Beach Open, the West Palm Beach Open and the Havana Invitational. In 1963 Al won the Mexico Open. In 1965 he had to have a complex operation on his back which had never healed properly after the burning accident, and for two years was too ill to play. In 1967 he tied for best Canadian in the Canadian Open and won the World Cup with 68, 72, 67 and 67 at the Olgiata course in Rome. With George Knudson as a partner, he also won the team title for Canada.

BALDWIN, Matt
Curler
Born 1927 in Blucher, Sask; began his curling in Bradwell, Sask, at age 14.

Matt Baldwin was star skip in the Edmonton city zone Consols competition in 1953 when he was 26 years old, and went on to take his first northern Alberta title. He lost out in the provincial championship, but won the Brier in Edmonton the next year. Matt was the youngest skip to take the Brier. He mixed both the draw and the knockout game. With his last rock he gave a "Winnipeg skid" down the ice which brought the fans to their feet in applause. He lost in 1955 and 1956 but came back to win the Brier again in 1957 and 1958. Sports reporters agreed it was Baldwin's ability to come through in the late ends with double-kill shots that carried the rink.

BALL, James
Runner
Born 1903 in Dauphin, Manitoba; parents both athletes; graduated from Univ. Manitoba with degree in pharmacology; owned drugstore.

James Ball was a member of his university track team. He won both the Manitoba and Western Canadian individual intercollegiate titles at age 22. In 1927 he proved himself one of Canada's best quarter-milers by winning the Canadian championship and anchoring the winning mile relay team. At the 1928 Canadian track and field championships, held in conjunction with the Olympic trials in Hamilton, Ball won his first 400-meter heat in 51 sec, and set a new Canadian record in the second heat of 49.4 sec. On his second run, he won in 48.6 sec, breaking the record he had set an hour before. At the 1928 Olympics in Amsterdam Ball made his way to the semifinals with another 48.6 sec. heat, and missed being the finalist by .2 sec. with a flat 48. He was a member of the mile relay team that won a bronze medal. Before returning home, Ball and his teammates took part in a number of meets throughout Europe and Britain. At Hampden Park, Glasgow, he won the quarter-mile; in Dublin he was on the winning mile relay team, won the 400-meter and set a new Irish record in the 200-meter. Between Olympics Ball established records in a number of Canadian events and was a member of the Canadian medley relay team which won at the Milrose Games in Madison Square Garden in 1932. In 1932 he again qualified for the Olympics and was on the mile relay team that won a bronze medal at Los Angeles, but finished last in the 400-meter semi-final. It was later disclosed that he had a painful carbuncle which destroyed his chances.
Also in: Canadian Amateur Athletic Hall of Fame.

BAPTIE, Norval
Speed Skater and Figure Skater
See entry in Hall of Fame of the Amateur Skating Union of the United States, 1965.
Also in: Ice Skating Hall of Fame.

BATSTONE, Harry L.
Football Player
See entry in Canadian Football Hall of Fame, 1973.

BAUER, David
Builder
Born in 1925; member of large athletic family; brother played with Boston Bruins; sister a hockey player; played football and hockey at St. Michael's College in Toronto during war years; leftwinger on the 1943 Memorial Cup champions of Oshawa; took vows as a member

of Basilians, taught and coached at his alma mater.

Father David Bauer coached hockey at St. Michaels through the 1940s and 1950s. His 1961 team played 98 games on the way to taking the Memorial Cup champions. After that victory, it was decided to deemphasize major junior hockey at St. Michaels. After seven years of coaching in the best junior league, Father Bauer was transferred by his superiors to St. Mark's College and the University of British Columbia where he coached the University team. Father Bauer dreamed of a national amateur hockey team that would retain the sport as the national game. In Vancouver a team was organized for the 1964 Olympics. Although it did not win, David Bauer was awarded an individual gold medal by the team's organizers for his encouragement and support. After 1964 Father Bauer and a group in the West set up a permanent national team in Winnipeg, and a large-surface rink was built at Ravenscourt School. Although they competed in Europe and Western Canada, they never won a championship and were dismantled in 1970 when the European teams would not play under the terms agreed to regarding the eligibility of Canadian players. Father Bauer still aids in hockey developments in other countries and at St. Mark's teaching the value of amateur hockey, as opposed to pro play.

BELANGER, Albert "Frenchy"
Boxer

Born 1906 in Cabbagetown, Ont; grew up in depressed east end of Toronto; retired from boxing in 1930; spent all his money and became a waiter; suffered a stroke at 56 that left him paralyzed; with the help of a friend, regained his speech and ability to walk; formed a softball team, which he coached; died in 1969.

Frenchy Belanger grew up fighting on the streets and decided he could get paid for what he was doing. He fought under the organized amateur groups in Toronto before turning professional. Dave Garrity of the Union Jack Athletic Club became his manager and after a succession of victories in preliminary bouts, Frenchy defeated Newsboy Brown, a leading contender for the flyweight championship in October, 1927. He won over Frank Genaro in New York and then beat Ernie Jarvis at the Coliseum for the title. Less than three months later Genaro took it from him in a decision after twelve rounds. Frenchy Belanger fought for two more years, winning the Canadian flyweight title. He retired in 1930, after six years as a professional, with a record of 61 bouts, 13 by knockouts, 24 decisions, 7 draws and 17 losses, only one by a knockout.

BELIVEAU, Jean A. "Le Gros Bill"
Hockey Player

See entry in Hockey Hall of Fame, 1972.
Also in: International Hockey Hall of Fame.

BELL, Marilyn
Marathon Swimmer

Born in 1937; started swimming very early in life; now an American citizen, mother of four, living in Willingboro, N.J.

Marilyn Bell was coached by Gus Ryder of the Toronto Lakeshore Swimming Club beginning in her early teens. In 1954 Marilyn finished the 25-mile Atlantic City swim. Then the Canadian National Exhibition set up a marathon swim, for Florence Chadwick to cross Lake Ontario, as its annual exhibition. Marilyn and Winnie Leuszler entered the race. Chadwick gave up after twelve miles, Leuszler made 20 miles before she gave up, and Marilyn Bell reached the shore 21 hours and 40 miles later, to gain all the prizes and gifts that had been planned for Chadwick. In 1955 she swam the English Channel from France to England in 14.5 hours, the youngest to have completed the effort. In 1956 she crossed the Strait of Juan de Fuca on her second try, swimming the 18-mile expanse in 10.5 hours. Marilyn then withdrew from marathon swimming, finished her schooling, married and became a housewife and mother.

BLAKE, Hector "Toe"
Hockey Player

See entry in Hockey Hall of Fame, 1966.
Also in: International Hockey Hall of Fame.

THE BLUENOSE, 1921–1946
Sailing Ship

The fishermen of Lunenburg, N.S, and Gloucester, Mass, had a century-and-a-half-old rivalry with their fishing ships when in 1920 the owner of the Halifax *Herald*, W. H. Dennis, decided to formalize the custom and put up for competition among working fishing schooners the International Fishing Trophy, with $4000 to the winner. The first year the *Esperanto* out of Gloucester defeated the *Delawanna* out of Lunenburg in races off Halifax. It was then that the *Bluenose* was designed by William J. Roue of Halifax, graduate of Nova Scotia Technical College. He was a member of the Royal Nova Scotia Yacht Squadron and the Armdale Yacht Club. Built at the Smith and Rhuland yards, she was launched March 26, 1921, 112 ft. at the waterline, 143 ft. overall, with a 27-ft. beam and a displacement of 285 tons. Her captain was Angus Walters of Lunenburg, part-owner, of German and Scottish extraction. He had gone to sea at 13 apprenticed to his father. In 1921 he was 40 years old and with a reputation as a tough and able master. She carried a crew of 32 for racing. After *Bluenose* spent her obligatory season on the fishing grounds and sailed some competitions with other schooners out of Nova Scotia, she was raced against the American fishing schooner *Elsie*, winning two straight races and the International Fisherman's Trophy. In 1922 she defended her title against the newly built *Henry Ford* and in 1923 against the *Columbia;* the event was declared a "no contest." There was no competition for some years, then the *Bluenose* outsailed Roue's new *Haligonian.* In 1929 the Boston syndicate's *Gertrude L. Thebaud* beat her, taking the trophy, but the next year *Bluenose* took it back. In 1938 they raced again, and *Bluenose* won two out of three races. In 1939 Captain Walters bought her but she stood idle because of the war; then she became a Caribbean freight carrier in 1943 from Tampa to Havana. She ended her days on a reef off Haiti in January, 1946.

BOA, Gilmour S.
Shooter

Born 1924 in Toronto, Ont; father an internationally known shooter; uncle and brother also qualified for Bisley teams; died in 1973.

Gil Boa began competitive shooting at age 14, very often competing against his father. In 1949, as an officer cadet

of the 48th Highlanders, he placed on the same Bisley team as his brother, and in that year won the stock exchange event in the annual Commonwealth shoot at Bisley. In 1951, again on the Bisley team, he won the competition for the King's Prize. On November 17, 1954, Gil Boa won the world's smallbore carbine championship, called the "English match," at the 36th world shooting championships at Caracas, Venezuela. It consists of thirty shots at 50 meters and thirty at 100 meters. At 50, he shot a perfect 300; at the 100, he set a new world's record by dropping only two points and finished with a 598. In 1955 Boa won the Governor-General's Prize, and in 1956 he won a bronze medal at the Melbourne Olympic Games. At the British Commonwealth Games at Kingston, Jamaica, in 1966 he won the gold medal in the smallbore rifle competition, with 587 out of a possible 600. Gil Boa said that shooting was "more a religion than a sport."
Also in: Canadian Amateur Athletic Hall of Fame.

BOLDT, Arnold
Athlete
Arnold Boldt was entered into Canada's Sports Hall of Fame in 1977 under the category of Track and Field.

BOUCHER, Frank "Raffles"
Hockey Player
See entry in Hockey Hall of Fame, 1958.
Also in: Greater Ottawa Sports Hall of Fame and International Hockey Hall of Fame.

BOWDEN, Norris
Pair Figure Skater
Born 1919 in Toronto, Ont; attended Univ. Toronto; successful insurance career before and after teaming with Fran Dafoe.

Norrie Bowden was a singles champion of outstanding ability, and at one time held almost every Canadian title available—champion in singles, pairs, dance, and the waltz. But his studies did not permit him to go further in singles competition. He and Fran Dafoe were members of the Toronto Skating Club and at the insistence of their coach, Sheldon Galbraith, decided to team up. It was a successful partnership from the start. They had perfect timing, a smooth stride and an understanding between them both on and off the ice. In 1952 at their first competition they became Canadian pairs champions, and placed fourth in the world championships in Paris. In 1953 they became North American champions, edged into second place for the world title by a British pair. In 1954 they went to Oslo and won the distinction of being Canada's first world pairs champions. They successfully defended their title the next year in Vienna. In 1956 they were hopeful of winning the gold medal at the Olympics but a momentary loss of balance by Fran probably cost them first place. They had already agreed to retire following that meet, and had no regrets after they retired into private life.
Also in: Canadian Amateur Athletic Hall of Fame.

BOX, Albert "Ab"
Football Player
See entry in Canadian Football Hall of Fame, 1973.

BREEN, Joseph M.
Football Player
See entry in Canadian Football Hall of Fame, 1973.

BRICKER, Calvin David
Broad Jumper
Born 1884 in Ontario; graduated from Univ. Toronto with dental degree; practiced in Regina; served in Dental Corps overseas in W.W. I; after war opened practice in Grenfell, Saskatchewan, where he died in 1963.

Cal Bricker was a world-class broad jumper for Canada in the pre-1914 era. He was an excellent college athlete, winning the all-round championship at Toronto in 1905 and 1906, taking six firsts in the latter year. In the same two years he won the individual championship at the intercollegiate meet. His specialties were the running broad jump and the hop, step and jump; in Montreal in 1908 at the Olympic trials, he won both events and set a record of 24 ft. 1.5 in. in the running broad. This record stood for 27 years. He won a bronze medal at the Games in London with a 23 ft. 3 in. leap, and was fourth in the hop, step and jump. He was again selected for the Canadian team in 1912, and won a silver medal at Stockholm with a 23 ft. 7.75 in. jump.
Also in: Canadian Amateur Athletic Hall of Fame.

BROOKS, Lela
Speed Skater
Born 1908 in Toronto; born into a family of speed skaters; started to skate in a backyard rink at age 5; married Russ Campbell in 1936 and moved to Owen Sound, giving up competitive skating.

Lela Brooks never received formal coaching but trained by daily workouts at the Old Orchard Skating Club in Toronto and cycling in the off season. Her style was to flash away from the starting post and grab the lead, and never let up. In those days, skaters started together, rather than skating against a stop watch. She entered the last meet of the year when she was 12; she fell and did not finish, but decided to go into competitive skating. At 13 she won the 440-yd. and the one-mile in the under-18 Ontario championships. In 1924 Lela won the under-16, under-18 and senior half-mile events in the Ontario indoor competition to become provincial champion. In 1925 she took three Canadian championships—the 220-yd. dash, the 440-yd, and the under-18 880. In the international competition at Pittsburgh she won the 220-yd, the 440-yd. and one-mile events. She also won the Chicago Silver Skate Derby that same year. By year's end she had broken six world records. In 1926 she won three out of four races in the world competitions at St. John, N.B, to be the women's titleholder. She continued to compete the next few years and held several world records—the half-mile indoor and outdoor and the three-quarter-mile outdoor. In 1928 she broke the world one-mile record and her record of 1.26 min. for the half-mile set in 1926 still stands.

BROSSEAU, Eugene
Boxer
Born 1895 in Montreal, Que; trained as a pilot in the British Air Force in W.W. I; worked for the post office dept. after retiring from the ring; died in 1968.

Eugene Brosseau learned to box in amateur competitions in Montreal and earned a reputation as a thoughtful

fighter with a talented left hand and a solid knockout punch. In 1915 he won the Canadian amateur welterweight championship and retained the title in a 1916 defense. Also in 1916 he took the American welterweight championship in Boston. In 1917 he won the American amateur middleweight crown, and earned $12,500 in two days for the Red Cross fund in a series of benefit exhibitions in San Francisco by knocking out two opponents one day, a third the next. Brosseau turned professional after the war, knocking out George McKay and Red Allan. In November 1919 he fought a former champion, George Chip, in a no-decision fight, but Brosseau discovered after the fight that his left arm had been paralyzed. He made a recovery and returned to the ring in the early 1920s, and scored knockouts over such fighters as Jack Holland, Young Fisher, Young Ahearn, Jack Lunney and Al McCoy but was beaten by British boxer Jack Bloomfield and knocked out by Mike McTigue. Gene fought a few more fights and then retired, retaining some interest in boxing by serving as an instructor for the Olympic boxing team in 1924.
Also in: Canadian Amateur Athletic Hall of Fame.

BROUILLARD, Lou
Boxer
Born 1911 in Que; moved to Danielson, Conn, at age 3 with French-Canadian parents; served in Army in W.W. II; worked as crane operator in shipyard in Hanson, Mass, after war.

Lou began his boxing career as an amateur in Worcester, Mass, at age 16. After four good boxing years, he turned professional and won the world welterweight championship in October, 1931, when he defeated Young Jack Thompson in Boston. In January, 1932, he lost the title to Jackie Fields in Chicago. He went on to win several bouts as a welterweight including a decision over Jimmy McLarnin in August, 1932, in New York City. Brouillard could not keep his weight down and moved into the middleweight division; in August, 1933, he became middleweight champion when he beat Ben Jeby in New York. He lost the title two months later in Boston to Vince Dundee of Baltimore. Although he later fought Marcel Thil in Paris twice for the title, he was unable to regain it. In 140 fights Brouillard won 66 by knockouts and was knocked out only once himself.

BROWN, George
Sculler
Born 1839 in Herring Cove, N.S; from the time he could handle an oar, was a fisherman in the Atlantic; died in 1875 of a stroke while training for the world championship race.

In 1863 when George Brown was 24, he competed for the Cogswell Belt, the Halifax single-sculls championship, but lost to George Lovett who had won the three previous years. Brown won the competition 1864 – 1868 and was awarded permanent possession of the trophy. Between meets, George continued to support himself by fishing. In 1871 the Halifax Aquatic Carnival was organized and George came to be bow oar in a four James Pryor had assembled; he also entered in the singles. The Pryor crew finished second to a crew from Scotland in a tight race, and the next day George finished second to Joseph Sadler in the singles, Sadler being considered the world's professional champion. George could not get Sadler to accept a challenge for a rematch, but turned professional and defeated Robert Fulton in July, 1873, of the Paris Crew for $1000, won the Bedford Basin in September for $2000 over John Biglin by 200-yds. over a 5-mile course, and on July 8, 1974, rowed the U.S. singles champion, William Scharff, for $400 and the title. On September 24, 1874, he defeated Evan Morris of the United States in what proved to be his last race.

BURKA, Petra
Figure Skater
Born 1947 in Amsterdam; moved to Canada at age 4; mother a Dutch skating champion who became a skating teacher in Canada; began skating at age 6, a natural skater; after leaving amateur skating, joined a professional ice show for 3 years; organized skating clubs across Canada under auspices of government and Canadian Figure Skating Association; has been a sports consultant on staff of Sports Canada in Ottawa.

Petra won the Toronto senior ladies' title at thirteen, but finished last in the Canadian junior competition. Her mother began training her in earnest and she became capable of executing difficult jumps and turns normally done by male skaters. In 1966 she became the first woman skater to perform in competition the difficult triple salchow. In 1964 Petra Burka took the Canadian championship and won a bronze medal at the winter Olympics at Innsbruck, placing third in the world championships. She turned to improving her free skating and figures, realizing that judges were more impressed with graceful movements than spectacular leaps and athletic performances. In 1965 Petra retained the Canadian championship, won the North American title, and won the world title at Colorado Springs in the space of one month. In 1964 and 1965 she was voted top female athlete in Canada. In 1966 she retained the Canadian championship but finished third at Davos, Switz, in the world championships, her last amateur performance.
Also in: Canadian Amateur Athletic Hall of Fame.

BURKA, Sylvia
Speed Skater
Sylvia Burka was selected for inclusion in Canada's Sports Hall of Fame in 1977 under the category of Speed Skating.

BURKE, Desmond Thomas
Shooter
Born 1904; graduated from Queen's Univ. with medical degree; versed in radiology; served with Royal Canadian Army Medical Corps in W.W. II; member of faculty of medicine at Univ. Toronto and chief radiologist at Sunnybrook and Oakville Hospitals; died 1973.

Burke took up shooting at school to replace other sports out of his reach because of an illness. His father helped him train and he was entrusted with the school cadet corps in musketry which proved invaluable training for Burke. He won the King's Prize in 1924 as a member of the Canadian Bisley team. At 19 he was the youngest person to have won the prize up to the present time. He placed on 22 Bisley teams, another record not broken to the present day. He was on the King's Hundred seven times, won the gold cross for the grand aggregate twice, runnerup for the King's Prize three times and for the grand aggregate one time. He took 14 firsts and 11 seconds in his shooting career. He also won many Canadian events. In 1932 he published *A Practical Rifleman's Guide* and in 1970 *Canadian Bisley Shooting: An Art and a Science.*

BURNS, Tommy
Boxer

Born 1881 near Hanover, Ont; son of Frederick and Sofa Brusso; one of 13 children; changed name when mother became upset at boxing; excelled at lacrosse, hockey and skating in school; worked on a passenger boat in Lake Erie prior to fighting; after retiring as boxer, ran clothing store in Calgary, then pub in England; became an evangelist; died at the home of friends in Vancouver from a heart attack in 1955 at age 73.

Tommy Burns began training at the Detroit Athletic Club; he was a fast mover and crisp puncher, having both a killer instinct and cocky attitude in the ring. In 1900 he fought his first fight when friends pushed him in the ring to finish another boxer's match; he knocked out his opponent in the first round. Tommy started fighting regularly and soon was the middleweight champion of Michigan. In February, 1906, Marvin Hart, who became world heavyweight champion in 1905 when James Jeffries retired, selected Burns for the first defense of his new title. After a twenty-round fight in Los Angeles, Burns was declared the heavyweight champion. At 5 ft. 7 in. 175 lbs, he was the shortest man ever to win the heavyweight crown. He started on a tour to prove he deserved the crown and knocked out Jim Flynn in San Diego, boxed Philadelphian Jack O'Brien to a draw which fight reporters insisted Burns won on points, and knocked out Australian Bill Squires at 2.28 of the first round. In Europe, he knocked out Englishmen Gunner Moir and Jim Palmer, then knocked out the Irish champ, Jem Roche, in the first round in the shortest heavyweight title defense on record. In Paris he had two knockout wins over Jewey Smith and Bill Squires. He went to Australia in 1908 and again knocked out Squires, then lost a grueling fight to the 6 ft. 203 lbs. Jack Johnson when the police stopped the fight in the 14th round. Burns retired for two years, but returned to the ring in 1910 and over the next ten years fought six fights; he quit forever when he was knocked out for the first time in July, 1920.
Also in: Ring Magazine Boxing Hall of Fame.

CALLURA, Jackie
Boxer

Born 1917 in Hamilton, Ont; Italian immigrant parents; one of seven children; helped father carry home railway ties for firewood; sold newspapers and battled older boys who tried to take earnings; after retiring, ran Hamilton restaurant; wife died in 1951; moved to Buffalo to work in steel mill.

Jackie Callura only weighed 126 lbs. at the height of his featherweight career. He began fighting at "Friday night smokers" at age 9, a good puncher with strong arms who won the crowd's attention as a poor boy fighting to help his family. In 1931 he won the Canadian amateur title in the featherweight class and represented Canada in the 1932 Olympics. In 1936 he turned professional and in January, 1943, became the National Boxing Association featherweight champion in Providence, R.I. He had given up a large share of his purse for a chance to fight for the championship. He successfully defended his title two months later but lost it in August of that year when he was knocked out in the eighth round by Phil Terranova. Jackie won a few more bouts; in 100 pro fights, he won 43 decisions and made 13 knockouts.
Also in: Canadian Boxing Hall of Fame.

CAMPBELL, Clarence S.
Builder

See entry in Hockey Hall of Fame, 1966.
Also in: International Hockey Hall of Fame.

CATHERWOOD, Ethel
High Jumper

Born c. 1909 in Ontario; moved to the United States in 1929; now Mrs. Ethel Mitchell living in San Francisco.

Ethel spent her young years in Saskatoon, but came to Toronto and became a member of the Parkdale Ladies Athletic Club. Coached by Walter Knox, she was soon regularly reaching the women's world record of 5 ft. 3 in. as a high jumper. In 1928 Ethel was a member of the six-girl track and field team from Canada that carried an unofficial 26-20 points over the United States in the Amsterdam Olympics. Against a field of 23 jumpers, Ethel's leap of 5 ft. 2.7 in. won the gold medal and gave the Canadian women's team an overall victory in the year that women were given an official place on the program for the first time.
Also in: Canadian Amateur Athletic Hall of Fame.

CHENIER, George
Snooker Player

Born in 1908; grew up in Ottawa and Hull; joined RCAF in 1920s; played hockey with RCAF team, then with pro league in Detroit; died in 1970.

In Detroit after the war George Chenier became an expert at snooker and pocket-billiards. George twice failed to win the world championship, finishing second in 1950 and 1958 to Fred Davis of England. He played all over the world and owned billiard halls in Vancouver, Victoria and Montreal. He spent his later years exhibiting for an equipment manufacturer. In 1966 George suffered a stroke that restricted his use of his left arm, but he continued to play until his death. In 1947 he was recognized as the North American champion and he remained so against all challengers for the rest of his life.

CLANCY, Francis Michael "King"
Hockey Player

See entry in Hockey Hall of Fame, 1958.
Also in: Greater Ottawa Sports Hall of Fame and International Hockey Hall of Fame.

CLAPPER, Aubrey Victor "Dit"
Hockey Player

See entry in Hockey Hall of Fame, 1947.
Also in: International Hockey Hall of Fame.

CLIFFORD, Elizabeth "Betsy"
Skier

Born 1954 in Quebec; daughter of skiers; home literally at foot of slopes of Camp Fortune, Ottawa, world's largest ski club; father John Clifford operated tows; mother a physical and health education graduate and good athlete; still competing.

Betsy began skiing under her mother's tutelage at age 3; her father, a Canadian ski champion, taught her racing techniques. She began competing at age 6 and by 14 was a member of the national ski team at Grenoble and the youngest Olympic skier in history. In February, 1970, she won the giant slalom at Val Gardena and became the youngest skier to win a world title. In the 1970–1971 season she took a first in the giant slalom at an Austrian meet but developed problems in the downhill events. While training for the 1972 winter Olympics to be held at Sapporo, Japan, Betsy broke both heels in an accident at Grenoble and was forced to retire. In the early winter of the 1972–1973 season, she returned to skiing and soon got back her form and perspective. Betsy won the women's division of the Can-Am Trophy series that season and neared the top of the world ratings in the early European meets of 1974.
Also in: Canadian Amateur Athletic Hall of Fame.

COAFFEE, Cyril
Sprinter
Born 1897 in Winnipeg; had a crippled arm which gave him an odd stance as a runner; driven by a determination to excel; possessed a flaming competitive spirit; a loner; died in 1945.

Cyril Coaffee began competing in 1915. As a member of the Winnipeg North End Amateur Athletic Club, he began winning Manitoba meets. In 1920 he won the 100-meter final in 11.2 in the Olympic trials at Montreal, but did not make the team because funds had been raised for a nine-man team and he was number ten. Winnipeg raised the funds and Cyril went to the Antwerp Olympic Games. A third-place win in his heat did not qualify him for the semi-finals. In 1922 at the Canadian championship at Calgary, he equaled the world record of 9.6 sec. for the 100-yd. dash. Based on this achievement, Coaffee was invited to compete for the Illinois Athletic Club out of Chicago. In 1923 and 1924 he took part in meets all over the United States and occasionally abroad. In 1924 he returned to Canada to qualify for the Olympics and went to Paris as captain of the Canadian team, but did not place. He had equaled the Olympic record of 10.8 sec. at the trials for the 100-meter, and after the games, ran up a large number of victories at the 100- and 200-yd. distances competing against many of the world's best sprinters in a series of meets in Britain. In the Olympic trials in Hamilton in 1928, Cyril Coaffee ran with a pulled muscle, and did not qualify.
Also in: Canadian Amateur Athletic Hall of Fame.

CONACHER, Charles William, Sr.
Hockey Player
See entry in Hockey Hall of Fame, 1961.
Also in: International Hockey Hall of Fame.

CONACHER, Lionel
Football Player
See entry in Canadian Football Hall of Fame, 1973.
Also in: Canadian Lacrosse Hall of Fame.

COOK, William Osser
Hockey Player
See entry in Hockey Hall of Fame, 1952.
Also in: International Hockey Hall of Fame.

CÔTÉ, Gérard
Marathon Runner
Born in 1913 in St. Barnabé, Que; moved to St. Hyacinthe at age 4; one of eleven children; played all sports well; once won a roller derby; played baseball and hockey; set record of 46 min. in 1958 for snowshoeing in the 8-mi. event at St. Paul, Minn.

Gérard Côté began running to strengthen his legs for boxing but soon realized running was to be his strongest sport. He did not do well in five- and ten-mile races, so turned to Pete Gavuzzi for training. He ran three days one week, four the next and mixed marathon distances with shorter sprints. He ran in the Boston Marathon in 1936, but ran the whole route two days before to practice and had nothing left for the big day. He returned to Boston in 1940 and won the Marathon in 2:28:28 hours. In 1942, 1943 and 1948 Côté again won the Boston Marathon. He also won the U.S. Amateur Athletic Union Marathon three times. Throughout his career, Côté entered 264 races, finishing first in 112 and winning seconds or thirds in another 82. His greatest disappointment was his seventeenth-place finish in the 1948 Olympic marathon, when he experienced severe leg cramps.
Also in: Canadian Amateur Athletic Hall of Fame.

COULON, Johnny
Boxer
Born February 12, 1889, in New York; Irish-French parentage; moved to Toronto, Ont, shortly after birth; in retirement operated a Chicago gym and training school for young boxers; died in 1974 in Chicago, Ill.

The small man's fighting champion, Johnny Coulon was just under 5 ft. and weighed 110 lbs. He fought professionally from 1905 to 1917, with Chicago as his home base. In 96 pro fights only one was fought in Canada—in Windsor in 1913. In 1909 he claimed the World bantamweight title after Jimmy Walsh outgrew it. Within six years he would defend the title 12 times. In 1910 he defended his crown three times in four and a half weeks and followed that in 1912 with two 20-round bouts in two weeks. On June 9, 1914, he lost the title to Kid Williams in Vernon, Calif, and left the ring for two years. He had a moderately successful comeback in 1916. From 1918 through 1919 he was a boxing instructor in the U.S. Army. Returning to Chicago after discharge, he retired from boxing but opened a buy, refereed bouts and played in some vaudeville.
Also in: Boxing Hall of Fame, Citizens Savings Hall of Fame Athletic Museum; and *Ring Magazine* Boxing Hall of Fame.

COWAN, Gary
Amateur Golfer
Born 1938 in Kitchener, Ont; father a policeman; transferred to business school after completing tenth grade; never turned professional.

Gary Cowan began caddying when he was 10, and started to learn the game under the Rockway Club pro, Lloyd Tucker. He won the Ontario juvenile championship at 14, and in 1956 won the Ontario and Canadian junior titles. With the Canadian American Cup team he defeated in match play both the reigning U.S. Amateur and the earlier champion. He won the Canadian Amateur title in 1961, a medalist at the World Amateur in Japan in 1962, and at Augusta in 1964 tied for low amateur in the Masters. In 1966 Gary Cowan became the second Canadian to win the U.S. Amateur. He won the Ontario Open in 1968 with a record-tieing 204, and won again in 1971. He won the North-South Amateur in 1970 at Pinehurst, N.C, and again won the U.S. Amateur in 1971 at Wilmington, Del.

COX, Ernest
Football Player
See entry in Canadian Football Hall of Fame, 1973.

COY, Eric
Thrower
Born in Winnipeg, Man; began working for Manitoba Telephone at age 16; served in W.W. II as RCAF instructor, having earned wings as navigator; became lineman on RCAF Hurricanes; played football with Montreal for short time after war, then returned to Manitoba Telephone; after retiring from competition, active in organizing and coaching track and field, wrestling and hockey.

Eric Coy was Canada's outstanding athlete in field events from 1935 to 1954. His first championship, in the javelin, came in Winnipeg in 1935; in 1938 in Saskatoon he became national champion in the javelin and in discus and shot put as well. That same year he was selected for the Canadian British Empire Games team and won a gold medal in the discus, and a silver medal in shot put in Australia. The 6 ft. 190 lb. Eric was one of the continent's great snowshoers. From 1933 to 1941 (except 1938) he won the snowshoe sprint titles at the North American championships, competing for the Winnipeg Wanderers. After returning to Manitoba after the war and his stint in football, Eric won the Canadian titles in the discus and shotput, won a place on the 1948 Olympic team, and was a member of the 1950 and 1954 Canadian British Empire Games team.
Also in: Canadian Amateur Athletic Hall of Fame.

CRAIG, Ross Brown "Husky"
Football Player
See entry in Canadian Football Hall of Fame, 1973.

CRANSTON, Toller
Figure Skating
Toller Cranston was the Canadian men's champion in 1971 and 1972. He was selected for inclusion in Canada's Sports Hall of Fame in 1977.

CROTHERS, William F.
Runner
Born 1940 in Markham, Ont; graduated from Univ. Toronto with degree in pharmacy; returned to Markham in 1963 to work in local pharmacy, which he now owns; spends much time and money promoting and sponsoring teams in amateur athletics.

Bill Crothers started his track career in 1960 when he joined the East York Track Club, where he was coached by Fred Foot. He became anchor man on the East York relay team which kept winning in track meets. He was winning consistently in the 440-yd. and half-mile by 1962. He won the half-mile in the then record time of 1:50 min. at the Milrose Games in New York, and the 1000-yd. at the Boston AAA meet, followed by the 500-yd. at Winnipeg in a record 56.9 sec. By the end of 1963 he held championships for the 660- and 880-yd. in Canada, Britain and the United States. He placed second in the 800-meter at the 1964 Tokyo Olympics with a 1:45.6. In 1965 he defeated Peter Snell in the half-mile in Toronto and repeated the win a month later in Oslo, to become the world's Number One half-miler. He competed in the Commonwealth Games in Jamaica and at the Pan-Am Games in 1967, but finished second and did not return to world competition.
Also in: Canadian Amateur Athletic Hall of Fame.

CUTLER, Wes
Football Player
See entry in Canadian Football Hall of Fame, 1973.

CYR, Louis
Weightlifter
Born 1863; one of 17 children; left school at age 12 to work as a lumberjack; joined Montreal police force in 1885; left to compete on tours; owned a tavern in Montreal; died in Montreal in 1912.

Louis Cyr was signed in his twenties to compete at weightlifting by the New York promoter, Richard Fox, and defeated all challengers. He also toured England for about two years, giving demonstrations of his strength and defeating all comers. At a performance in London he lifted 551 lbs. with one finger, 4100 lbs. on a platform stretched across his back, and 273 lbs. with one hand to his shoulder and then above his head; he also lifted a 314 lb. barrel of cement with one hand. In Boston in 1895 he lifted 4337 lbs, considered to be the greatest weight ever lifted by one man.

DAFOE, Frances
Pair Figure Skater
Born 1923 in Toronto, Ont; full-time fashion designer while a member of a figure skating pair, teamed with Norris Bowden.

Fran Defoe had given up thoughts of singles competitions when she broke her ankles in 1948 and 1949. As a member of the Toronto Skating Club, her coach was Sheldon Galbraith, who instigated her teaming with Bowden. Galbraith knew the pitfalls of European competition for Canadians at that time, so they took him with them when they competed in Europe. They entered the 1950s with a new style of skating which the Canadians took to their hearts. They were the first of many such pairs in Canada. They executed a variety of lifts, jumps and triple turns that gave an excitement to figure skating that the more conservative European teams lacked. In 1954 and 1955 they won out over partisan European judging to become Canada's first pairs world champions, and gained a silver medal at the 1956 Olympics. Fran said after the Olympics, "You only have three roads open after you win your amateur titles. Either you turn professional... you teach skating, or you retire. We retired."
Also in: Canadian Amateur Athletic Hall of Fame.

DeGRUCHY, John
Builder
See entry in Canadian Football Hall of Fame, 1973.

DELAMARRE, Victor
Weightlifter
Born 1888 in Lac St. Jean region of Que; grew up in Quebec City; sent to country in 1901 to finish schooling; died in 1955.

Victor Delamarre, like Louis Cyr, joined the Montreal police force to support himself while working out. He stood 5 ft. 6 in, and weighed 156 lbs. but was very strong. In 1930 his feat of lifting 309.5 lbs. with one hand was officially recognized as a world record. He toured Canada and the New England states giving weightlifting exhibitions, once lifting 201 lbs. with one finger and a platform on which sixty or more people stood weighing 7000 lbs. In 1931 with a wife and ten children to support, he became a professional wrestler. In 1951 he made a successful tour across Canada, demonstrating his strength.

DELANEY, Jack "Bright Eyes"
Boxer
Born March 18, 1900, in St. Francis, Que; real name Oliva Chapdelaine, no relation to the romantic creation of Louis Hemon; died of cancer in Katonah, NY, November 27, 1948.

A ladies' man and free-wheeling boxer, his first manager sold his contract for $600 because he believed Delaney was undisciplined and more interested in his female vanguard than winning a title bout. Pete Reilly picked up the contract and grossed thousands. The Delaney-Berlenbach light heavyweight title fight in Ebbets Field grossed $450,000. The heavyweight bout with Jimmy Maloney in Madison Square Garden grossed $201,613. An attraction no matter the outcome of the bout, Delaney opened the new Garden, again with Berlenbach, on December 11, 1925. The fight went the distance, 15 rounds, but the Great Knee Controversy clouds historical judgment. In the fourth round Delaney walloped Berlenbach to the floor, who arose at the count of two. Reconsidering, he knelt to one knee until nine and then proceeded to win the light heavyweight crown from Delaney in 15 rounds. Six months later in Ebbets Field vindication was sweet for Delaney's Dames as he won 13 of 15 rounds with a broken thumb and received the light heavyweight crown for the second time. Abandoning the title immediately, the 5 ft. 11½ in. 175 lb. French-Canadian campaigned among the heavies. His record is spotty at best. In 1928 he retired after knocking out Nando Tassi but attempted a short comeback in 1932. Permanently retiring for the second time in 1932, he opened "Jack Delaney's" on Sheridan Square in Greenwich Village, N.Y.
Also in: Ring Magazine Boxing Hall of Fame; and Boxing Hall of Fame, Citizens Savings Hall of Fame Athletic Museum.

DENNETT, Jack
Athlete
Jack Dennett was elected to Canada's Sports Hall of Fame in 1975.

DESMARTEAU, Etienne
Thrower
Born 1877; one of five brothers; smallest at 6 ft. 1 in, 225 lbs; Montreal policeman with brother Zacharie; died 1905 of typhoid fever.

Etienne and his brother won field and weight events in the police games held every year in Boston, New York, Montreal and Toronto. At the 1904 Olympics in St. Louis, Etienne won the gold medal in the hammer throw, the only track and field first not won by Americans. After the Olympics, he set world records of 15 ft. 9 in. for height and 36 ft. 6.5 in. for distance.

DEWAR, Phyllis
Swimmer
See entry in Aquatic Hall of Fame and Museum of Canada.
Also in: Canadian Amateur Athletic Hall of Fame.

DIXON, George "Little Chocolate"
Boxer
Born July 29, 1870, in Halifax, Nova Scotia; died January 6, 1909, in New York City.

Known to fight all day if necessary, Little Chocolate was the first Negro to hold a world title. Always outweighed at 118 lbs, he stood 5 ft. 3½ in, truly a fighting champion. Official statistics cite 158 bouts but some pugilist historians believe Dixon fought as many as 700 unofficial bouts in 11 years. Working as an apprentice photographer, he turned professional when only 16 years old. Long-armed and skinny-legged, Dixon looked defenseless in a ring but his swift hands and feet carried the pace through the fight. In 1890 he met Cal McCarthy in a finish fight with two-ounce gloves. After 70 rounds the official called the fight a draw despite the eagerness of Little Chocolate to continue. A return match with McCarthy was slated on March 31, 1891, with the U.S. featherweight title at stake. This time the conclusion of the fight was decisive when Dixon kayoed McCarthy in the 22-round. Little Chocolate went on to the world featherweight title in July, 1891. After losing to Solly Smith in 20 rounds six years later, Little Chocolate rebounded to regain the title on November 11, 1898, against Dave Sullivan. In between the marathon McCarthy bout and his world title, he added the world bantamweight in June, 1890, from Nunc Wallace. He was the first boxer to shadow box and many opponents felt he was but a phantom of his shadow in the ring. Little Chocolate participated in 33 championship fights, more than any other boxer.
Also in: Ring Magazine Boxing Hall of Fame.

DUGGAN, George Herrick
Yachter
Born in 1862 in Toronto, Ont; son of a lawyer; graduated from Univ. Toronto as civil engineer; played football and captained the team; chief engineer for bridge company; died in 1946.

George Duggan built his first boat at 16 and at 18 built a 32-ft. yawl. In 1880 he and some friends formed the Toronto Yacht Club and in 1884 formed the Lake Yacht Racing Association which included every American and Canadian yachting club along Lake Ontario. In 1896 his club, the Royal St. Lawrence of Montreal, challenged for the Seawamhaka Cup put up for international competition by the Seawanhaka Corinthian Yacht Club of New York. Duggan designed and skippered the *Glencairn I* which won out over the American yacht *El Heirie* at Oyster Bay. Through 1904 the Royal St. Lawrence Club was able to defend the cup against challenges from New

York, St. Paul and England on Lake St. Louis, with Duggan as skipper, except for the 1904 race. With Duggan as designer the Canadians were able to keep ahead of all rivals. In his career he designed and built 142 boats. He died in an automobile accident in 1946.

DURELLE, Yvon
Boxer
Yvon Durelle was elected to Canada's Sports Hall of Fame in 1975 in the Boxing category.

DUTHIE, George
Builder
Born 1902 in Scotland; came to Canada at an early age; joined the boys' dept. of Toronto West End YMCA and became member of junior leaders' corps; managed junior basketball team; had lifetime involvement with management and public relations at the YMCA; died in Toronto in 1968 at age 66.

George Duthie resigned his elected position of alderman to the Toronto city council in 1931 to become sports director at the Canadian National Exhibition (CNE), a post he held for 35 years. To him must go the credit for building up the highly successful sports program there. Marathon swims became a popular attraction under his guidance. In the 1930s he helped form the Canadian Boating Federation, the governing body for motorboat racing in Canada. He also was responsible for staging the 1953 world water ski championships as part of the CNE program. George served in the Royal Canadian Air Force in W. W. II, forming interservice leagues in basketball, boxing, wrestling, football and hockey, and organized the track and field championships. After the war he traveled across Canada on behalf of the Olympic training program and served on many committees of the Amateur Athletic Union of Canada. In 1967 he was appointed to the National Advisory Council on Fitness and Amateur Sport, and served until his death.
Also in: Canadian Amateur Athletic Hall of Fame.

EMERSON, E.K. "Eddie"
Football Player
See entry in Canadian Football Hall of Fame, 1973.

VICTOR EMERY BOBSLED TEAM
Bobsled Team
In the 1964 Olympics the Canadians won the gold medal in bobsledding. Victor Emery had attended the 1956 Olympics at Cortina and became interested in the bobsled racing. He and his brother formed the Laurential Bobsledding Association in 1957 and after practicing at Lake Placid, New York, went to the world championships at St. Moritz, finishing thirteenth. They entered every race in world competition between 1959 and the 1964 Olympics. In 1964 with the Emerys were Peter Kirby and Douglas Anakin. They won again in the world championships at St. Moritz in 1965 with Michael Young and Gerald Presley joining Vic Emery and Pete Kirby in the sled.

EWING, Walter H.
Trapshooter
Born c. 1880; Canadian businessman, representative of a coal company; lived in Westmount.

Walter Ewing won a gold medal in trapshooting at the second Olympiad in Paris in 1900. In 1906 he won the Clarendon Cup in Montreal at the first annual meet of the Canadian Indians, a marksman's association; he broke 189 birds out of 200, his nearest competitor scoring 183. Ewing won a gold medal for the second time at the fourth Olympiad in London in 1908. The competition extended over three days; his score was 72 out of a possible 80. The Canadian team of trapshooters stayed over to compete for the Claybird International Challenge Shield, a team trophy, and the London *Times* Trophy, a handicap event for individuals. The Canadian team won, and Ewing placed first in the *Times* competition, despite the fact that his Olympic showing must have given him a difficult handicap.
Also in: Canadian Amateur Athletic Hall of Fame.

FABRE, Edouard
Marathon Runner
Born in 1885; orphaned at age 8 and placed in an orphanage in Montreal; unhappy, he fled the home and grew up on the Iroquois Indian Reservation.

In 1905 Edouard Fabre ran in the Athens Marathon in Greece. After the 1908 Olympics many newspapers and organizations staged marathons and Edouard traveled around the country competing. He attended the 1912 Olympics in Sweden. Fabre began attending the annual Boston Marathon in 1911 and finally won it in 1915. When Fabre was almost 40, he competed in a snowshoe marathon run between Quebec and Montreal; he won with a record 34:46:24 hours for the 200-mile distance. He averaged just under six miles per hour.

FEAR, A. H. "Cap"
Football Player
See entry in Canadian Football Hall of Fame, 1973.

FERGUSON, Elmer W.
Journalist
Elmer Ferguson was born in 1885 in Prince Edward Island. His family moved to Moncton, N.B, when he was an infant. He sold newspapers when 6 years old, and later became a railway clerk. He didn't enjoy it, so hired on as copyboy at the Moncton *Transcript* in 1902. He spent 39 years as sports editor at the Montreal *Herald,* and a sports columnist until 1957 when it went out of business. He moved his column to the *Star* and continued writing until his death in 1972. He began working as a sports official while on the *Transcript* and served as secretary for hockey and baseball leagues in New Brunswick. In the 1920s he served as first secretary of the athletic commission and held the post for over 20 years. He was first publicity man for the International Hockey League. His columns were filled with stories about the sports and entertainment world of the time, both in Canada and the United States. His knowledge of hockey was often called on to settle disputes, and he was asked to serve as a speaker for banquets and other sporting events.

FILION, Hervé
Harness Race Driver
See entry in Hall of Fame of the Trotter, 1975.
Also in: Canadian Horse Racing Hall of Fame.

FITZGERALD, William J.
Lacrosse Player
Born in 1888 in St. Catharines, Ont; after playing, turned to coaching and refereeing, coaching at Hobart College, Swarthmore and West Point; later coached younger players in St. Catharines; died in 1926.

Billy Fitzgerald first played lacrosse in a top-rated league at the age of 19 when he joined the senior Athletic Lacrosse Club in St. Catharines. The team won the Globe Shield from 1905 until 1912; in 1907 and 1908 they went undefeated. In 1909 Billy turned professional with the Toronto Lacrosse Club, and was a big drawing card to the fans. The promoter Conn Jones paid Billy Fitzgerald $5000 to go West and play for Vancouver. The Vancouver team won the Minto Cup which at that time represented the professional lacrosse championship of the world. After one year Billy returned to play with the Toronto Lacrosse Club and stayed with them until the first world war disruted sports activities. After the war Billy helped organize the St. Catharines team in a semi-professional Ontario league, but with renewed interest in amateur sports, professional lacrosse died out and Billy could not go back to amateur.
Also in: Canadian Lacrosse Hall of Fame.

FLEISCHER, Nathaniel Stanley "Nat"
Contributor and Builder
Born November 3, 1887, in New York City; James J. Walker Memorial Award 1943 and 1966; died June 25, 1972, in New York City at age 84.

In 1899 at the age of 12, Nat Fleischer saw his first world championship fight. During his career as sports writer, editor, author, referee and judge, he witnessed the impropriety of boxing foisted on fans and participants. With the founding of the *Ring* boxing magazine in 1922, Nat launched a personal crusade to rid boxing of despicable promoters, provide the fighters with more protection from mismatches and give the spectators the fight they paid their money to see. Despite threats on his life he continued to push boxing forward. Rigorous physical examinations were provided for boxers, and those who were seriously cut during a fight were given better care. To stimulate and maintain public interest and acceptance of boxing, he protected the fan from dubious promotional gimmicks and encouraged closed-circuit television and home viewing. He initiated the rating system, first on a local basis, and then on an international scale. In 1942 he published the first edition of the annual *Ring Record Book.* Fleischer began as a sports writer with the *New York Press* and then with the *New York Telegram* as sports editor. He authored 60 books on boxing. In 1954 he started the *Ring* Hall of Fame to acknowledge fighters who pioneered the sport and acclaim the success of those still fighting.
Also in: Boxing Hall of Fame, Citizens Savings Hall of Fame Athletic Museum; and *Ring Magazine* Boxing Hall of Fame.

FORTIER, Sylvie
Synchronized Swimmer
Sylvie Fortier was selected for inclusion in Canada's Sports Hall of Fame in 1977.

GALL, Hugh
Football Player
See entry in Canadian Football Hall of Fame, 1973.

GARDINER, Eddie
Athlete
Eddie Gardiner was selected for membership in Canada's Sports Hall of Fame in 1975.

GAUDAUR, Jacob Gill
Sculler
Born 1858 in the Lake Simcoe District; kept bar after his competitive days, then returned to his home area to guide fishing parties; died in 1937.

Jacob Gaudaur finished third in his first race in a shell, the Barrie regatta in 1879. By 1886 he was considered one of the top oarsmen in North America, rowing out of Creve Coeur Lake near St. Louis, Mo. He competed in all the races in Canada and the United States, then challenged William Beach for the world championship and $5000. Their two-man race on the Thames is an outstanding event in rowing history, both men falling exhausted on their oars a few yards from the finish line. Beach finally won by pushing over the line a half length in front of Gaudaur. In 1887 he defeated Ned Hanlan for $5000 and the North American title. From 1888 on, he competed repeatedly, setting new records nearly every time he rowed. In 1892 he defeated Charles Stephenson at Orillia; in 1893 he set a new world's record of 19:6 min. for three miles at Austin, Tex. The next year at Austin he set a new record of 19:1.5 min, never bettered. When he was 38 years old, he won an easy victory over Jim Stanbury for the world championship. He defended his title successfully in 1898, and lost it in 1901 to George Towns of Newcastle, New South Wales, a man 12 years his junior.

GENEREUX, George F.
Trapshooter
Born in 1935 in Saskatchewan; father Dr. A. G. Genereux taught him how to shoot.

George Genereux first learned to shoot with his father, but became an expert through instruction from Jimmy Girgulus, a well known competitor in trapshooting events. George won his first competition at age 13, the Midwest International Handicap held at Winnipeg. That same year and for the next two as well, he won the Manitoba-Saskatchewan junior championship. George's big win came at Vandalia, Ohio, when he won the North American junior championship, then returned to capture the Saskatchewan provincial title. At age 17 he was selected for the Olympic team, and won the gold medal in trapshooting at Helsinki in 1952, then returned to be given the Lou Marsh Trophy as Canada's outstanding athlete, the youngest person ever to win. Preliminary to the Olympics George entered the 35th world shooting championships at Oslo, where he tied for second with 286 out of 300 marks, compared to the winner's 287.
Also in: Canadian Amateur Athletic Hall of Fame.

GERARD, Edward George
Hockey Player
See entry in Hockey Hall of Fame, 1945.
Also in: Greater Ottawa Sports Hall of Fame and International Hockey Hall of Fame.

GIBSON, George "Moon"
Baseball Catcher
Born 1880 on a farm near London, Ont; after retirement

went back to his farm a few miles west of London; died in 1967.

George Gibson started with McClary's in the manufacturing league in 1904 in London, and played with Buffalo of the International League. For the next twelve years he played with the Pittsburgh Pirates, moving to the New York Giants in 1917 and 1918. In 1919 he managed Toronto in the International League then moved back to the Pirates as manager for three years. From 1923 until 1934 he moved around the leagues as coach, scout and manager, retiring from active participation in 1934. In 1909 while he was playing with the Pirates, they won the World Series against Detroit. Moon's top average was .280. He caught in all 150 games in which his team played in his best years. As manager he had three second-place finishes in six seasons.

GOLAB, Tony
Football Player
See entry in Canadian Football Hall of Fame, 1973.

GORMAN, Charles I.
Runner
Born 1897 in St. John, N.B; started skating when quite young; served in Europe in W.W. I, returning home with shrapnel wound in leg, so had to change stride to successful long sweep; died in 1940.

Charles Gorman experienced his first big win in 1924, the U.S. national amateur outdoor championship, and a few weeks later took the international title at Lake Placid, N.Y, in the three-mile event. In 1925 he lost both titles, but in 1926 again won the world championship. In 1927 Gorman won the mid-Atlantic championship, tied for first in the U.S. outdoor national, won the Canadian indoor title, retained the world championship, broke the world record for the one-sixth mile, shaved a second off his own mark in the 440-yd. event, and took the U.S. national indoor title. Gorman went to the 1928 winter Olympics and came in seventh in the 500-meter event. When the judges refused his plea for another heat, he left the games in protest.
Also in: Canadian Amateur Athletic Hall of Fame.

GOULDING, George Henry
Walker
Born in 1885 in England; fine gymnast and long distance runner; came to Canada in 1904; died in 1966.

George Goulding was a competitive walker, and won more than 300 races in his career at distances from one to forty miles. In Canada he began by running at the Central YMCA in Toronto and practiced with the walkers as well. His physical director persuaded him to concentrate on the walking stride and in 1908 he was selected for the Olympic team both as a marathon runner and the one-mile walking event. He won fourth place in the final walking event, and finished nineteenth in the marathon. Going to the 1912 Olympics in Stockholm he won the 10,000 meter race and won in a record time of 46:28.4 min. During his career Goulding engaged in many stunt races, winning over ten miles at Guelph against a man with a horse and buggy; he also defeated an American four-man relay team single-handedly in a four-mile walk in New York. He set a record in 1916 for seven miles of 50:40 min.
Also in: Canadian Amateur Athletic Hall of Fame.

GRAY, George R.
Shotputter
Born 1865 in Coldwater, Ont; ancestors settled in Penetanguishine area of Ont; worked lumber camps after high school; 1812 worked for father in dry goods store and lumber yard; married 1911 in Sault Ste. Marie; cousin Harry Gill was great athlete and track coach; remained in lumber business until death in 1933.

Gray excelled in shotputting during the years 1885 to 1902. He became the world champion with his first put of 41 ft. 5½ in. in the 1885 Canadian Amateur Athletic Association meet in Toronto. At this time, he represented the Toronto Athletic Club but he was unable to afford his own travel expenses to New York meets so he joined the New York Athletic Club in 1886. They paid his travel expenses so he competed under their banner beginning in 1887. That same year he set a world shotput record of 43 ft. 11 in. which held until 1902. He was also the Amateur Athletic Union (AAU) shotput champion in 1887–1888, 1891 and 1902. He hit his highest AAU mark in 1891 with a 46 ft. 5¾ in. put in 1891. During his career, he received 188 first-place medals and trophies for the shotput although he competed in earlier years in the broad and high jumps, dashes, hammer throw and discus. Throughout his career he continued to live and train at home, running his lumber business and commuting to meets.
Also in: Track and Field Hall of Fame, Citizens Savings Hall of Fame Athletic Museum.

GREENE, Nancy (Raine)
Skier
See entry in British Columbia Ski Hall of Fame, 1977.
Also in: Canadian Amateur Athletic Hall of Fame and National Ski Hall of Fame.

GRIFFITH, Harry Crawford
Builder
See entry in Canadian Football Hall of Fame, 1973.

GUEST, John Schofield "Jack"
Sculler
Born 1906 in Montreal, Que; attended Morse Street Public School and Central High School of Commerce, both in Toronto.

Jack's rowing began with the fours and eights of the Don Rowing Club; in 1927 while rowing eights he won the junior and association singles at St. Catharines, after which he joined the Argonaut junior eights. He was coached by Joe Wright, Sr, whose son Joe became his rival. Wright beat Guest in the Diamond Sculls in 1928 and the next year on the Thames, but Guest won over Wright in the Canadian Henley. In 1929 Jack returned to the Don Rowing Club and trained intensely under Harry Arlett for a year, then returned to the Diamond Sculls and won out over Wright and the German oarsman, Boetzelen, by at least a 200 yd. margin. He retired from rowing after that win, but acted as president for the Don Rowing Club 1938–1952. He also served as president of the Dominion Day Regatta Association for ten years, president of the Canadian Association of Amateur Oarsmen 1955 and 1956, helped manage the Canadian team at the British Empire Games in 1962 and 1966, was a director of the Canadian Olympic Association and in 1969 became the first Canadian elected to

the International Rowing Federation.
Also in: Canadian Amateur Athletic Hall of Fame.

GWYNNE, Horace "Lefty"
Boxer

Born in 1913 in Toronto, Ont; at 13 did odd jobs around the Woodbine race track and tried out as a jockey, but failed; worked in the automobile plants in Detroit while in boxing; returned to race track in 1938 and worked for several jockeys; joined the Toronto recreation department in 1953 and later became director of various community centers.

Lefty Gwynne's slight compact build made him a natural bantamweight and he started serious training at the Central YMCA. He was active in boxing in the 1920s in the United States and Canada and won a place on the 1932 Canadian Olympic boxing team. Lefty came home with the gold medal. He went to Detroit with the Jim Brady boxing stable, but the depression was on and there was little money to be had in boxing.
Also in: Canadian Amateur Athletic Hall of Fame and Canadian Boxing Hall of Fame.

HALTER, G. Sydney
Builder

See entry in Canadian Football Hall of Fame, 1973.
Also in: Canadian Amateur Athletic Hall of Fame.

HAMILTON, J. W. "Jack"
Builder

Born 1886 in Ontario; Scottish parents; educated at Caledonia, Ont; taught school for several years; moved to Saskatoon in 1909 to teach; in 1911 took summer job with lumber company and 46 years later retired as managing director.

In 1918 Jack Hamilton began organizing the construction of a 3500-seat ice rink for the city of Saskatoon. In the early 1920s he coached the Regina Vics hockey club, later becoming club president. He was president of the Saskatchewan Amateur Hockey Association 1925–1927 and in 1930 was elected president of the Canadian Amateur Hockey Association. From 1923 to 1927 he was secretary of the Regina Roughriders football team and in 1928 became president of the Western Interprovincial Rugby Football Union, now the Western Conference of the Canadian Football League. Jack served as president of the Canadian Amateur Athletic Union Saskatchewan branch and in 1937 became president of the national organization. His work was recognized by the King George VI Coronation Medal Award. In 1937 Jack headed the Queen City Gardens Company which raised funds to install artificial ice in the Regina hockey rink; he operated the arena for the next eleven years. He then organized a fund drive to build a 3500-seat rink at Moose Jaw. In 1955 Saskatchewan gave him an engraved gold ring in tribute of his 50 years of sports leadership and in 1967 he was awarded the Canadian Centennial Medal.
Also in: Canadian Amateur Athletic Hall of Fame.

HANLAN, Edward "Ned"
Sculler

Born 1855 in Toronto, Ont; father owned hotel on Toronto Island; died in 1908.

Ned Hanlan won small races around Ontario and became known as the best oarsman around. In 1876 he entered and won the centennial single-sculls on the Schuylkill River at Philadelphia. He won the Canadian title in 1877 and the U.S. title in 1878. He took on challenge races in the United States and Canada for large purses, and won them all. In 1879, backed financially by the Hanlan Club, he defeated John Hawdon on the Tyne, and then defeated William Elliott for England's championship and the Sportsman Challenge Cup. The next year he defended his title and the Cup in a race with the Australian, Edward Trickett. He successfully defended his title six times before losing to William Beach, an Australian, on the Paramatta River in 1884. He raced Beach again for the title in 1887 in Australia. During his career he won more than 300 races.

HARVEY, Douglas Norman
Hockey Player

See entry in Hockey Hall of Fame, 1973.
Also in: International Hockey Hall of Fame.

HEGGTVEIT, Dorothy Anne (Hamilton)
Skier

See entry in National Ski Hall of Fame, 1976.
Also in: Canadian Amateur Athletic Hall of Fame and Greater Ottawa Sports Hall of Fame.

HEPBURN, Douglas
Weightlifter

Born 1926 in Vancouver, B.C; had clubfoot and operation to correct was bungled and left an atrophied calf muscle and permanently weak ankle; parents divorced when five; lived with grandmother; dropped out of school and got job as bouncer at beer parlour; soon weighed 255 lbs.

Doug Hepburn found out about weightlifting and set out to learn the three Olympic lifts: the press, the clean-and-jerk, and the snatch. He first pressed 300 pounds in a Vancouver competition and set a new Canadian record. He won the U.S. National Open in 1949 with a press of 345.5 lbs. His friends raised money to send him to the 1953 world championships in Stockholm since he had been ignored for the 1952 Olympics, and he won the title. At the British Commonwealth Games in 1954 he won the gold medal and set new game records with lifts of the press of 370 lbs, the snatch, 300 lbs, and the clean-and-jerk, 370 lbs. No one sent him to defend his title in Germany and he could not afford the trip so he lost his title. He tried professional wrestling but quit after a year because he did not like it.
Also in: Canadian Amateur Athletic Hall of Fame.

HEWITT, Foster William
Builder

See entry in Hockey Hall of Fame, 1965.
Also in: International Hockey Hall of Fame.

HODGSON, George Ritchie
Swimmer

See entry in Aquatic Hall of Fame and Museum of Canada.
Also in: Canadian Amateur Athletic Hall of Fame and International Swimming Hall of Fame.

HOWARD, Richard "Kid"
Boxer
Born 1928 in Terrace Bay, N.S; grew up in Halifax; retired from boxing after only a few years competition.

Kid Howard turned professional in 1945 and won the Maritime title in 1949. In 1954 he won the Canadian lightweight championship, defeating Armand Savoie from Quebec. In the next few years he had matches with most of the top lightweights. He fought the South African champion, Willie Towell, for the British Empire championship, and lost on a close decision. He also was given a fight with the French champion, Ray Famechon, in Montreal but lost again. He retired once, tried a comeback that was not successful, then retired again. In his fifteen years in the ring, Kid Howard won 77, lost 26 and drew 5 of the 108 recorded fights in his career. He was never knocked out.

HOWE, Gordon "Gordie"
Hockey Player
See entry in Hockey Hall of Fame, 1972.
Also in: International Hockey Hall of Fame.

HUNGERFORD, George
Rower
Born 1944 in Vancouver, B.C; attended Shawnigan Boys' School on Vancouver Island, excelled in sports; father a Vancouver businessman.

A dislocated shoulder prevented George Hungerford, 6 ft. 4 in, 198 lbs, from playing rugby, so he took up rowing and excelled in it as he had in other sports. In 1964 he came down with mononucleosis and had to drop from the University of British Columbia eight. Six weeks before the Games in Tokyo, Dave Galander began coaching Hungerford and Roger Jackson as a pair. Hungerford had to spend most of his time in bed between practice sessions held twice a day. In the 2000-meter race without coxswain in a rudderless shell Jackson and Hungerford won the Olympic gold medal, Canada's first in the summer games since 1956.
Also in: Canadian Amateur Athletic Hall of Fame.

HUTTON, Ralph W. "Iron Man"
Swimmer
See entry in Aquatic Hall of Fame and Museum of Canada.
Also in: Canadian Amateur Athletic Hall of Fame.

IRVIN, James Dickenson "Dick"
Hockey Player
See entry in Hockey Hall of Fame, 1958.
Also in: International Hockey Hall of Fame.

ISBISTER, Robert, Sr.
Football Player
See entry in Canadian Football Hall of Fame, 1973.

JACKSON, Donald
Figure Skater
Born 1940 in Oshawa, Ont; began skating lessons at nine; turned professional in 1964 and joined an ice show; married with a small son; gave up traveling in 1969 and now coaches young Canadian skaters.

Only 5 ft. 4 in. and slightly built, Don Jackson was one of the finest skaters Canada ever produced. He began skating seriously at age 12 and won the Canadian junior men's title in 1955 at age 14. He trained under Otto Gold at the Minto Club in Ottawa for the 1955 meet. He spent the next three years training under Pierre Brunet of the New York Skating Club. In 1959 he won the Canadian senior men's title and went on to win the North American championship at Toronto. He placed fourth in the compulsory figures in the world championships in Colorado Springs that same year, but his free-skating display with a delayed double salchow, where he stopped dead in mid-air before spinning twice, brought the spectators to their feet. At age 18 he placed second in the world championships. In the 1960 winter Olympics, Don won a bronze medal and placed second in the world championships again. In the 1962 world championships at Prague, coached by Sheldon Galbraith, Don Jackson executed the first triple Lutz jump in the history of competitive skating, followed by a triple salchow and three double axels, one of them with his arms folded across his chest, to win the men's singles crown. It was the first time it had been won by a Canadian.
Also in: Canadian Amateur Athletic Hall of Fame.

JACKSON, Harvey "Busher"
Hockey Player
See entry in Hockey Hall of Fame, 1971.
Also in: International Hockey Hall of Fame.

JACKSON, Roger
Rower
Born 1942; attended Lawrence Park Collegiate in Toronto and had an all-round athletic career; graduated from Univ. Western Ont, M.A. from Univ. Toronto, graduate work at Univ. B.C.

Roger Jackson converted to rowing when he went to Western. At the University of Toronto he was coached by Jack Russell of the Argonauts and stroked the varsity eight to the intercollegiate championship. In 1964 he transferred to the University of British Columbia graduate school, hoping to earn a place on one of their Olympic crews. The 6 ft. 5 in. Roger did not win a place on the eight, and with the four lost out to St. Catharines in the trials. He and Wayne Pretty were selected for the pairs, but Wayne took Hungerford's place on the eight when he had to drop out because of illness. So Jackson was paired with Hungerford for a winning combination that received a gold medal in the pairs at the 1964 Tokyo Olympics.
Also in: Canadian Amateur Athletic Hall of Fame.

JACKSON, Russ
Football Player
See entry in Canadian Football Hall of Fame, 1973.

JAMES, Eddie "Dynamite"
Football Player
See entry in Canadian Football Hall of Fame, 1973.

JELINEK, Maria and Otto
Pair Figure Skaters
Otto born 1940, Maria born 1943 in Czechoslovakia; parents keen skaters who encouraged all five children in the sport; immigrated to Canada in 1951; Maria attended Univ. Mich, then managed Toronto boutique; Otto man-

ufactured skates, entered politics, winning a seat in the 1972 federal election.

In 1947 Maria and Otto Jelinek gave their first public show at Prague's Winter Stadium. In Canada, they joined the Oakville Skating Club and were coached by Bruce Hyland. In 1955 they won the Canadian junior championship for pairs and placed second in 1957 in the North American championships. The following year they placed third in the world championships, and fourth in 1960, also placing fourth in the Winter Olympics at Squaw Valley. They captured the North American title in Philadelphia in 1960. The 1961 world championship was cancelled when the American team was killed in a plane crash. In 1962 in their native city of Prague, Maria and Otto captured the world championship. After this win they retired from amateur skating and spent two seasons with the Ice Capades.
Also in: Canadian Amateur Athletic Hall of Fame.

JEROME, Harry Winston
Runner
Born 1940 in Prince Albert, Sask; son of a Pullman coach attendant; moved with family to Vancouver when age 12; attended North Vancouver High; became physical education teacher at Templeton Secondary School, Vancouver.

Harry Jerome joined the local track club, the Optimist Striders, when he was 12. At 18 he broke the 31-year-old standing record for the 220 and ran the 100-yd. in what was then the phenomenal time of 9.5 sec. He was given an athletic scholarship to the University of Oregon and was coached by Bill Bowerman. At 19 he ran the 100-meter in 10 sec, establishing a world record that stood until the 1968 Olympics. He came up with pulled muscles and did not qualify in the Rome Olympics of 1960 or the British Commonwealth Games in Perth, Australia, in 1962. However, he returned to take the bronze medal in the 100-meter in the 1964 Olympics in Tokyo and ran the 100-yd. dash in 9.1 sec. in 1966 in Edmonton. Harry Jerome won his first gold medal in the British Commonwealth Games in 1966. He ran in the 100-meter in the Mexico City Olympics in 1968, finished in seventh place, and decided to retire at age 28. Harry Jerome has set up sports clinics in cross-country, held coaching clinics in high schools all over Canada, and as a member of Sports Canada, works with young people in sports.
Also in: Canadian Amateur Athletic Hall of Fame.

JOLIAT, Aurel Emile
Hockey Player
See entry in Hockey Hall of Fame, 1947.
Also in: Greater Ottawa Sports Hall of Fame and International Hockey Hall of Fame.

KELLY, Leonard Patrick "Red"
Hockey Player
See entry in Hockey Hall of Fame, 1969.
Also in: International Hockey Hall of Fame.

KERR, Robert
Sprinter
Born in Ireland in 1882; moved to Kemptville, Ont, as a child, then moved to Hamilton; went to work while still in teens; served overseas with 164th Battalion; official of Canadian Amateur Athletic Union, Canadian Olympic Association and instigated British Empire Games in Hamilton in 1930; died in 1963.

Robert Kerr was one of the finest sprinters in Canadian track history. In 1902 he won the 100-, 440- and 880-yd. races at the Hamilton Coronation Games. In 1903 and 1904 he won the 100- and 200-yd. events at the Canadian YMCA championships and other meets, which won him a spot on the Canadian team that went to the St. Louis Olympics; but he did not make the finals. In 1907 Kerr won the Canadian title in both the 100- and 200-yd, took 41 first places in all, and set a new Canadian record of 9.4 sec. for the 100-yd; he set new meet records virtually everywhere he competed. In 1908 he set a new Canadian record for 50-yd, further victories at London, Ont, then a sweep of the sprint events at the Ontario and Canadian championships. At the Olympic Games in London, he won a gold medal in the 200-meter and finished third in the 100-meter. Prior to the Olympics he competed in the British athletic championships at Stamford Bridge and won the 100- and 220-yd, being awarded the Harvey Gold Cup as the outstanding athlete in the meet. In 1909 he defended these wins at Dublin, winning both once more. He was selected for a spot on the Canadian team for the 1912 Olympics but declined. During his career he won nearly 400 awards and trophies and set six Canadian records.
Also in: Canadian Amateur Athletic Hall of Fame.

KIDD, Bruce
Runner
Born in 1943; in last year of high school delivered papers, studied, and worked out with coach Fred Foot at least two hours every day; actively promotes interest in amateur sports for youth; author, with John Macfarlane, of exposé of pro hockey in Canada entitled *The Death of Hockey.*

Bruce Kidd joined the East York Track Club under coach Fred Foot in the summer of 1958. In 1959 he set a new Canadian record for the two-mi, and had run the 3-mi. in 14:26 min. He went to the University of Toronto. In January, 1961, he won the 2-mi. indoor race in Boston, breaking the United States record. In 1962 at Compton, Calif, he won the 5000-meter in the record U.S. time of 13:43.8. He lost it a few weeks later in a rematch, but it was run one day after he had won in the 6-mi. Kidd won the gold medal for the 6-mi. race and came in third in the 3-mi. race at the Commonwealth Games in Perth, Australia. In 1961 he was awarded the Lou March Trophy and was named the outstanding athlete of the year in Canada in both 1962 and 1963. He was selected to go to the 1964 Olympics but did not win. After he graduated from the University, he spent a year in India teaching.
Also in: Canadian Amateur Athletic Hall of Fame.

KNOX, Walter
All-round Track and Field
Born 1878 in Listowel, grew up in Orillia; promoter of mining rights and mines; died 1951 at age 73.

Walter Knox amassed a total of 359 firsts, 90 seconds and 52 thirds in formal competitions. In one afternoon in 1907 he won five Canadian titles—the 100-yd. dash, the broad jump, the pole vault, the shot put, and the hammer throw. In 1903 he went to Beloit College where Harry Gill coached him in the track and field events. At

college he competed and won in the shot put, pole vault and the dashes, setting many records. The next year he moved to the University of Illinois and was a winner at most of his meets. Walter Knox won many meets in California in 1905, 1908 and 1909, and in 1911 he went to Britain, winning 57 firsts, 23 seconds, and 31 thirds. He was appointed coach of the Canadian Olympic team that went to Stockholm in 1912. While in Europe, he competed in England and Scotland and won 40 firsts, 15 seconds and 15 thirds. In 1913 he won the all-round professional title in America. In the 1913 athletic season he repeated his wins in Britain and in 1914 competed for the title of all-round championship of the world. He won six of the eight events. In 1920 he coached the Canadian Olympic team and was coach of the Ontario Athletic Commission for several years.
Also in: Canadian Amateur Athletic Hall of Fame.

KNUDSON, George
Golfer
Born 1937 in Winnipeg; spends part of his year in physical training and conditioning; very knowledgeable of the game.

George Knudson began to play at age 13. He was always curious about the aspects of the game, and while working in the pro shop at the St. Charles Club, learned all about golf clubs and balls, the layout of courses, and the mechanics of a golf swing. He turned professional in 1958 and won the McNaughton-Brooks Bursary three years in a row. In 1961 at Coral Gables he had his first tour victory. In 1962 he won the Maracaibo and Puerto Rico Opens, the Portland and Panama Opens in 1963, the Caracas and Fresno Opens in 1964, the World Cup individual title in Tokyo in 1966, the Greater New Orleans Open in 1967, the Phoenix and Tucson Opens in 1968; and the Robinson Open and the Wills Masters tournament in Melbourne in 1969. He won the Millar Trophy in 1965 and the World Cup title in Italy in 1968 with Al Balding. He has won the Canadian PGA three times.

KREINER, Kathy
Skier
See entry in National Ski Hall of Fame, 1976.
Also in: Canadian Amateur Athletic Hall of Fame.

KROL, Joe "King"
Football Player
See entry in Canadian Football Hall of Fame, 1973.

KWONG, Norm "China Clipper"
Football Player
See entry in Canadian Football Hall of Fame, 1973.

LALLY, Joseph
Lacrosse Player and Contributor
Born 1868 in Cornwall, Ont; with brother built up factory on Cornwall Island where the Indians made lacrosse sticks; older brother Frank, founder of the business in 1881, played goal with Montreal Shamrocks; died in 1956.

Joseph Lally was associated with lacrosse all his life as manufacturer of sticks, player, referee, and international authority. Cornwall won the annual association championship in 1887 and 1888; the team was made up of workers in the factory including Joe. Joe Lally was instrumental in setting up the Canadian Lacrosse Association in 1925 and remained active with them until his death. In 1930 he established the Lally Perpetual Trophy, awarded annually to competing teams in the United States and Canada. He served many years as a referee and earned the reputation of being the most fair.
Also in: Canadian Amateur Athletic Hall of Fame.

LALONDE, Edouard "Newsy"
Hockey Player
See entry in Hockey Hall of Fame, 1950.
Also in: Canadian Lacrosse Hall of Fame and International Hockey Hall of Fame.

LANGFORD, Sam "Boston Tar Baby"
Boxer
Born 1880 in Weymouth, Nova Scotia; father part-time sailor, part-time logger; ran away to Boston at age 12; worked at odd jobs; Mike Foley saw him fight in a saloon and suggested a boxing career; became blind in 1923 as a result of boxing blows; died in 1956.

Sam Langford started fighting in 1902 as a lightweight at 132 lbs. He grew through the welterweight and middleweight divisions. He was only 5 ft. 4 in. tall but had an 84 in. reach and was an amazing fighter. Langford's best years, unfortunately, were when Jack Johnson held the title, and because there was so much prejudice against black boxers, he could never get a title fight, although he did gain non-title matches with title-holders six times. Even Johnson would not meet him because he said, "On a good night Sam is just liable to beat me or make it close and what's the sense of that for the kind of money we'd draw." Sam made his home in Boston where a black man could find more acceptance than other places in the United States or Canada. In June, 1917, he took a terrific battering in a fight, and lost the sight of his left eye. He quit fighting in 1923 because he was losing his sight in the other eye.
Also in: Boxing Hall of Fame, Citizens Savings Hall of Fame Athletic Museum; and *Ring Magazine* Boxing Hall of Fame.

LAVIOLETTE, Jean Baptiste "Jack"
Hockey Player
See entry in Hockey Hall of Fame, 1962.
Also in: International Hockey Hall of Fame.

LAWSON, Smirle "Big Train"
Football Player
See entry in Canadian Football Hall of Fame, 1973.

LEADLAY, Frank R. "Pep"
Football Player
See entry in Canadian Football Hall of Fame, 1973.

LEONARD, Stanley
Golfer
Born 1915; at age 40 after 13 years as a club pro, decided to go on tour; retired from the tours in 1971.

At the Vancouver Marine Drive Club as a pro, Stan Leonard had a good amateur standing behind him. He had won the British Columbia Amateur two times, he had won the Canadian Open five times and the Canadian PGA five times. He had also won the British Columbia

Open five times. In 1957 he won the Greensboro Open by three strokes. In 60 tournaments from 1955 through 1958, he was out of the money only twice. He won the Western Open in 1960. He won the individual title for the Canada Cup in 1954 in Montreal and again in Melbourne in 1959. In 1958 he also won the Tournament of Champions at Las Vegas. While on the pro tour circuit, Stan also won the Canadian Open four more times 1955–1961 and the Canadian PGA three times.

LESSARD, Lucille
Shooter
Lucille Lessard was honored with a membership in Canada's Sports Hall of Fame in 1977 in the Field Archery category.

LIDSTONE, Dorothy
Field Archist
Dorothy Lidstone was selected to Canada's Sports Hall of Fame in 1977 because of her accomplishments in archery.
Also in: Canadian Amateur Athletic Hall of Fame.

LONGBOAT, Tom
Marathon Runner
Born 1887 on the Onandaga Indian Reservation, Tom Longboat won his first race, a five-miler, at the Caledon Fair and then won the Hamilton round-the-bay race of 1906. He was persuaded to join the West End YMCA in Toronto and for them won the 1907 Boston Marathon, setting a record time of 2:24:24 hours that was not broken until the course was made easier. Suspended from the YMCA for drinking, he joined the Irish-Canadian Athletic Club to train for the Olympics. In 1907 he repeated his win of the Caledon and Ward Marathons, won a 12-mile race at the Soo and later a 15-mile race in Montreal. However, victory eluded him at the Olympics where he finished seventeenth. After the Olympics, Tom won the Ward Marathon for the third time and turned professional. In 1908 he defeated the Italian Dorando Pietri at a match in Madison Square Garden and in February of 1909 he defeated the famous Alfie Shrubb in a highly publicized meet also held at the Garden. His manager sold his contract after the match to an American promoter. In spite of a series of rematch races with Shrubb and a race at Toronto Island in 1912 when he set a new record for the 15-miler, Tom Longboat lost heart at having been sold "like a racehorse" and his career just went downhill. He died in 1949 back on the Reservation.
Also in: Canadian Amateur Athletic Hall of Fame.

LONGDEN, John
Jockey
See entry in National Jockeys Hall of Fame, 1956.
Also in: Canadian Horse Racing Hall of Fame and Racing Hall of Fame.

LUMSDEN, Cliff
Marathon Swimmer
Cliff Lumsden was one of the Lakeshore Swim Club's most famous members. Coached by Gus Ryder, Cliff started at the club when he was six; as a marathon swimmer, he won the world title four times in five years. Cliff Lumsden was accepted into Canada's Sports Hall of Fame in 1976.

LYON, George S.
Golfer
Born 1858 in Toronto, Ont; accomplished athlete; played football and soccer; set Canadian record in pole vault at age 18; played second base for a team in the Toronto Commercial League; nationally known cricket batsman, curler and lawn bowler; died in 1938.

In 1896, when he was 38, a friend dared George Lyon to play golf; he took one swing at the ball and was hooked on the sport for life. Lyon won the Canadian amateur 8 times 1898–1914, the Canadian senior championship 10 times 1918–1932, placing second 4 times in the same timespan. He was 46 when he won the gold medal in golf in the 1904 St. Louis Olympics. George Lyon remained a promotor of the game the rest of his life; he was the veteran captain of his home course, the Lambton in Toronto; and he played countless matches to bring the game to sportsmen's attention after his competitive days.
Also in: Canadian Amateur Athletic Hall of Fame.

MacDONALD, Noel
Basketball Center
Born 1915 near Mortlach, Sask; moved with family to Edmonton; played basketball in public school, then Westmount High School; married Harry Robertson in 1939; served on the executive of the Canadian Amateur Basketball Association and coached high school teams until husband got moved abroad.

After high school Noel was invited to play with the Gradettes, feeder team for the Grads. She moved up to the Grads in 1933, starting as a substitute forward, but moved up to center and played with them until her retirement. During her years with the Grads they won many playoffs and played several times for the Underwood. She was very good at controlling the tip and scored many of her points off rebounds.

MacDOUGALL, Hartland
Snowshoer
Hartland MacDougall, a snowshoe athlete, was selected for inclusion in Canada's Sports Hall of Fame in 1976.

MACKENZIE, Ada
Golfer
Born 1892; saw first golf match at age 10; captain of school ice hockey and basketball teams at Havergal, and winner of school's tennis championship; worked in bank to free a man during W.W. I; started the Ladies Golf and Tennis Club of Toronto in 1924 and the Ontario Junior Championship in 1928; donated the trophy for the provincial junior teams; died in 1973.

Ada Mackenzie won her first championship in 1914 and was still competing when she was 80. She won the Toronto Golf Club championship in 1914; she won the Toronto and district ladies tournament eleven times between 1924 and 1961, and the Ontario Open nine times between 1922 and 1950. Ada won the Bermuda Open twice and was runnerup twice. She finished first in the U.S. Women's in 1927 and went as far as the semifinals two other meets. She won the Canadian Open in 1919, 1925, 1926, 1933 and 1935, and the Canadian Closed 1926, 1927, 1929, 1931 and 1935, and was finalist for each on several occasions. Ada Mackenzie won the Canadian seniors championship nine times and won the U.S.

North-South seniors title in 1963. In 1970 she was a member of the Ontario team that won the Ada Mackenzie Challenge Cup.
Also in: Canadian Amateur Athletic Hall of Fame.

MacKINNON, Col. Dan
Harness Race Driver
Born 1876 in Highland, P.E.I; orphaned at age 10 and had no further formal schooling; took mail-order course and passed Nova Scotia Pharmaceutical Society exams; became registered pharmacist at age 20; played football and was championship runner; won rifle-shooting titles; served in Europe in W.W. I with 36th Battery, Canadian Field Artillery; ran commercial fox farms after the war; died in 1964.

Dan MacKinnon bought his first horse in 1890; he owned and trained 78 horses during his active years, racing them all over the Maritimes and the United States. He started harness racing in 1912. In 1915 in a 12-day period, he won 15 heats of 16 starts with his pacer, Helen R. In 1923 he set a world record for ice racing. He had victories with many horses—Volo Rico, Our Peggy, Dick C, Colonel Aubrey and The British Soldier. At the age of 82 he still drove regularly, the trotter Windy June and the pacer Stalag Hanover. In 1930 he bought the Charlottetown Driving Park and built it up to where harness horses were brought from all over New England and the Maritimes to race there.
Also in: Canadian Horse Racing Hall of Fame.

MAGNUSSEN, Karen D.
Figure Skater
Born 1952 in Vancouver, B.C; first skated at age 6 in a winter carnival; the Karen Magnussen Foundation in Vancouver helps young skaters, supported by donations and her contributions.

Karen Magnussen first competed in the 1966 Canadian championships, placing fourth. In 1967 she placed twelfth at the international meet in Vienna. She took the Canadian title in 1968 and placed second in the North American championship in 1969. That same year while preparing for the world championships at Colorado Springs, Karen developed stress fractures in both legs and had them placed in casts for three months. She regained her Canadian title in 1970 and retained it through 1973 when she signed with the Ice Capades. Karen won a bronze medal in international competition in 1971, and 1972, and captured the gold medal in 1973 in the world championships at Bratislava, Czechoslovakia. Returning home, she was given a banquet on her 21st birthday and was invested with the Order of Canada; the Skating Institute of America named her Ice Skating Queen of the Year.
Also in: Canadian Amateur Athletic Hall of Fame.

MALONE, Maurice Joseph "Joe"
Hockey Player
See entry in Hockey Hall of Fame, 1950.
Also in: International Hockey Hall of Fame.

MARCHIDON, Phill
Athlete
Phill Marchidon was one of the inductees into Canada's Sports Hall of Fame in 1976.

MARTEL, Wilbert "Marty"
Bowler
Born 1887 in Cape Breton, N.S; moved to Halifax as a young man and became a bowling alley proprietor; also hockey sponsor, helped found the Wolverines.

Marty was "king of the candlepins" in the Maritimes. A short stocky man, Marty held the world's record for a single string, 213. He was a consistent bowler; he topped 400 for three consecutive strings on at least 25 occasions. His next highest games gave him a total of 496 for three strings, also a record. He spent his life as owner, player and promoter in bowling.

MAYER, Charles E. E.
Builder
Born 1901, Charles Mayer was a sportswriter and editor in the newspaper game, a radio and TV commentator, and a sports official. He spearheaded a move to bring the Olympics to Montreal, and was active in sponsoring other competitions, especially in hockey, baseball, boxing and horseracing. He wrote a best-selling book, *L'Epopée des Canadiens* (1956), and founded the "Hot Stove League" on the French radio and TV stations. President of the Canadian Boxing Federation in 1955 and 1956, and vice president of the Montreal Athletic Commission for six years, Charles Mayer also was the French commentator for the World Series. In horseracing he was active in all positions at the tracks up to steward. He was director of information for the Blue Bonnets and Richelieu racetracks.

McCREADY, Earl G.
Wrestler
Born 1908 in Lansdowne, Ont; raised on Saskatchewan farm; wanted to be a doctor; received degree in physical education from Okla. A&M Col. 1930; became a masseur after retiring from professional wrestling; lost left leg in 1966, but still remained active.

By the time Earl McCready was 14, he weighed 200 lbs; he became interested in wrestling and signed with a class at the Regina YMCA while in high school. In 1926 he won the Canadian heavyweight championship at the Amateur Athletic Union meet at New Westminster, B.C. Impressed by his showing, Oklahoma Agricultural and Mechanical College persuaded him to wrestle for their school. In his four years in college he won every intercollegiate match and retained his Canadian heavyweight title. He was national U.S. collegiate heavyweight champion in 1928–1930 and U.S. national amateur champion in 1930. He was a member of the 1928 Canadian Olympic team. In 1930 he won every amateur wrestling championship in Canada, the United States and the British Commonwealth. In 1930 McCready was a member of the Canadian team that won the gold medal at the British Empire Games in Hamilton, also winning the gold medal as an individual in the heavyweight division. Earl turned pro in 1930 as a contender for the heavyweight title and met most of the famous champions of his day. He retired after 25 years as a professional wrestler.
Also in: Canadian Amateur Athletic Hall of Fame; and Amateur Wrestling Hall of Fame, Citizens Savings Hall of Fame Athletic Museum.

McCULLOCH, Jack
Speed Skater

Born 1872; after retiring from barnstorming went into skate manufacture; his McCulloch skates were favorite of professional hockey players for many years; died in 1918.

Jack McCulloch helped form the first Manitoba hockey teams in 1889 and as a player with the Victorias participated in the first regularly scheduled game. The teams later toured Toronto, Ottawa and Montreal and won 9 out of 11 games. McCulloch won the Canadian speed skating title in 1893, and in 1896 won the U.S. Nationals at St. Paul, Minn, by winning the quarter-mile and five-mile events, the open mile and ten-mile races. McCulloch won both the 1500-meter and the 5000-meter in the world championships in Montreal in 1897 and the world title. He turned professional in 1898, and barnstormed for the next several years in Canada and the Northern United States, gave exhibitions of speed, figure and trick skating, and raced other professionals for side bets.

McGILL, Frank
Football Player

See entry in Canadian Football Hall of Fame, 1973.

McLARNIN, Jimmy "Baby Face"
Boxer

Born December 17, 1905, in Belfast, Ireland; parents moved to Vancouver, B.C; married with four children; operated tile business in Los Angeles.

One of the all-time great box office draws in the late 1920s and early 1930s, Jimmy McLarnin defeated 13 men who at one time or another held world championships. His bouts with Ruby Goldstein, Sid Terris, Sammy Mandell and Billy Petrolle attracted crowds of 600,000. On his route to winning the world welterweight title over Young Corbett in May, 1933, Baby Face disposed of Sergeant Baker in one round, Al Singer in three, Ruby Goldstein in two, and Sid Terris in one. The culmination was the first round knockout of Corbett and the title. Then came the triple match with Barney Ross in one year, beginning May 28, 1934 and ending May 28, 1935. The welterweight crown volleyed between the two fighters with Ross winning the first and third matches, thus retaining the crown. The gross receipts were big dollars in depression times, with the first bout grossing $138,000, the second $197,000 and the third $144,080. McLarnin's trainer and manager was Pop Foster. They met when McLarnin was 14 and visiting the Vancouver Army Hospital where Pop was recuperating from W.W. I injuries. Pop recognized a champion in Jimmy and lined him up against the toughest flyweights, bantams and feathers in the Pacific Northwest before heading to California. The rest is history and money. Pop left Jimmy $240,000 when he died.
Also in: Canadian Boxing Hall of Fame and *Ring Magazine* Boxing Hall of Fame; and Boxing Hall of Fame, Citizens Savings Hall of Fame Athletic Museum.

McLAUGHLIN, R. S.
Race Horse Owner

Born September 8, 1971, in Enniskillen, Ont; moved to Oshawa in 1876; father a woodcarver who entered the carriage-making business; at age 16 left school and apprenticed to business, where involved with family making carriages and automobiles.

Sam McLaughlin's family had always owned horses and he had ridden since he was a boy. In 1924, after the family business had been sold and he retired, he began buying horses—hunters, jumpers, saddle, and show horses. In 1926 Sam entered his horses in their first show, and after that won many ribbons in shows and fairs throughout Ontario, Quebec and the United States. In the 1930s he became interested in Thoroughbred racers and built up a superb racing stable, Parkwood Stables. Three of his horses won the King's Plate—Horometer in 1934, Kingarvie in 1946 and Moldy in 1947. He sold his stables in 1949 after a serious illness, but remained intensely involved in horse racing the rest of his life.
Also in: Canadian Horse Racing Hall of Fame.

McNAUGHTON, Duncan A.
High Jumper

Born 1910 in Cornwall, Ont; grew up in Vancouver; played basketball and participated in track in high school; graduated from Univ. Southern Calif. 1933; member of university track team; distinguished career in geology; served in the RCAF in W.W. II, won DFC with bar.

While at the University of Southern California, McNaughton won the state championship, setting a record with his winning jump. He won the gold medal for Canada at the Olympics in one of the hardest fought high jump competitions ever staged, against his USC teammate and the American representative. A year after the 1932 Olympics, McNaughton won the high jump competition at the national U.S. intercollegiate championships held in Chicago.
Also in: Canadian Amateur Athletic Hall of Fame.

MILES, John
Marathon Runner

Born 1905 in Sydney Mines, N.S; father immigrated to Cape Breton to work in the mines where his son joined him at age 11; father got him a job as a teamster to have a healthier environment; moved to Hamilton; after the second world war, worked in a factory in France for seven years; retired from competition in 1933.

Johnny was trained to run by his father; they worked out a system based on running 10 miles almost every day; every six weeks he would run more than 26 miles, trying to hit a steady pace of six min. per mile. He entered road races after 1922 and in 1925 won the five-mile event at the national championships. In 1926 he won the Boston Marathon, defeating Clarence DeMar, the 1924 Olympic champion, and Albin Stenroos of Finland. Johnny won twenty races after the Boston Marathon, but could not complete the 1927 running. He went back to win the 1929 Boston Marathon at a record time of 2:33:8 hours.

MITCHELL, Ray
Bowler

Born 1931 in Alberta; returned with his parents to England in the 1930s; father died in 1951; family returned to Canada to Toronto; started to work for Bell Canada; played minor hockey, boxed at the YMCA, became skillful in badminton.

Ray Mitchell began five-pin bowling with his company team, and in 1961 switched to ten-pin. He began winning local and regional competitions, both on a team and as an individual competitor. He was Southern Ontario singles champion in 1967 – 1968 and placed in the Canadian finals. In 1972, among other wins, he gained the Canadian title. Later in the year he won the world championship in Germany in 59 games. He lost his title in 1973 in Singapore.

MOLSON, Percival
Football Player
See entry in Canadian Football Hall of Fame, 1973.

MORENZ, Howarth William "Stratford Streak"
Hockey Player
See entry in Hockey Hall of Fame, 1945.
Also in: International Hockey Hall of Fame.

MORRIS, Alan B. "Teddy"
Football Player
See entry in Canadian Football Hall of Fame, 1973.

MURRAY, Athol
Contributor and Builder
Born in 1892, Father Athol Murray founded a college to educate a baseball team! He had started a boys' athletic club in the Regina diocese in 1923, and the boys played hockey, football and baseball locally. When his archbishop died in 1927, Father Murray asked to be appointed to the vacant parish at Wilcox, 40 miles south of Regina. Some of the boys asked to go with him. They got their high school education from the Sisters at Wilcox, and then he took over their training, eventually building Notre Dame College, officially founded in 1933, affiliated with the University of Ottawa as a degree-granting institution. From this school Athol Murray produced teams that won competitions all over Canada and many of his students have gone on to become leaders in front-running hockey teams.

NAISMITH, James
Contributor and Builder
See entry in Naismith Memorial Basketball Hall of Fame, 1959.
Also in: Amateur Basketball Hall of Fame, College Basketball Hall of Fame and Noteworthy Contributors Hall of Fame, Citizens Savings Hall of Fame Athletic Museum; and National Association of Intercollegiate Athletics Hall of Fame.

NATTRASS, Susan
Trapshooter
Susan Nattrass was elected to Canada's Sports Hall of Fame in 1977.
Also in: Canadian Amateur Athletic Hall of Fame.

NEIGHBOR, Frank
Athlete
Frank Neighbor was inducted into Canada's Sports Hall of Fame in 1975.

NORTHCOTT, Ron
Curler
Born 1936, Ron Northcott is a tall intense young man who plays best under pressure. He has the ability to read the ice and has the utmost control. He was third in Jimmy Shields' Alberta rink which lost to the Richardsons in 1963, in the Brier championships. In the next year, he skipped his own rink but could not upset the Lyall Dagg British Columbia team at Charlottetown. He won his first Brier in 1966 and again in 1968, with the Ontario Rink winning in 1967. In 1969 Ron Northcott's Calgary rink won again, winning all ten matches. Northcott has changed the members of his rink several times, but always comes up with a winning combination. He has won the Scotch Cup every time his rink has competed.

NORTHERN DANCER
Race Horse
See entry in Racing Hall of Fame, 1976.
Also in: Canadian Horse Racing Hall of Fame.

O'BRIEN, Joseph C.
Harness Race Driver and Trainer
See entry in Hall of Fame of the Trotter.
Also in: Canadian Horse Racing Hall of Fame.

OLYMPIC 400-METER RELAY TEAM, 1928
Relay Team
The Canadian 400-meter relay team brought home the gold medal from the 1928 Olympics at Amsterdam. In the preliminary heat, Jane Bell, Myrtle Cook, Ethel Smith and Bobbie Rosenfeld had won, setting a new record for the Olympics of 49.4 sec. When they won the next day they broke their own record by a full second.

OLYMPIC GRAND PRIX JUMPING TEAM, 1968
Jumping Team
Tom Gayford, 39, Jim Elder, 34, and Jim Day, 21, made up the 3-man Canadian equestrian team, managed by Brigadier W. D. Whitaker of Toronto, that won the gold medal in the Grand Prix jumping competition at the 1968 Olympics. Gayford and Elder had been members of the gold medal team at the 1959 Pan-Am Games; Elder had been with the team that won a bronze in the 1956 Olympics, and all three were members of the Canadian team that won third place in the 1967 Pan-Am Games. Day took an individual gold medal in that meet. In 1969, at the North American Grand Prix held at the Canadian National Exhibition stadium in Toronto, the team again took first place.

O'NEILL, John
Sculler
Born in Nova Scotia in 1877; joined the Royal North West Mounted Police as a young man; joined the Canadian Mounted Rifles and served in the South African war; still could be seen rowing around Ketch Harbour at age 89; died in 1967.

John O'Neill began competitive rowing on his return from the Boer War when he was 25; he joined the St. Mary's Rowing Club at Halifax. He won the championship in Halifax Harbour in 1904, won prizes around the Maritimes, then won the Middle States Regatta at Philadelphia in 1905. In 1907 he won the singles in Springfield, Mass, and in 1908 won the U.S. association singles. He won the senior quarter-mile event in the Detroit River in 1909, defeating the oarsman from the New York Athletic Club.

ORTON, George
Steeplechaser
Born 1872 in Ontario, Can; ran track for Univ. Pa; member of 1900 U.S. Olympic team; died June 26, 1958.

Orton's specialty was the steeplechase, of which he was Amateur Athletic Union (AAU) 2-mi. champ for seven years, 1893–1894, 1896–1899, and 1901. And for six years he was AAU steeplechase champ in the 1-mi. category. But he did diversity and won the Intercollegiate Association of Amateur Athletes of America mile title in 1895 and 1897, and the AAU cross-country 1890–1898. At the Paris Games in 1900, Orton entered three events and captured the gold in 2500-m. steeplechase. He placed third in 400-m. hurdles and fourth in 4000-m. steeplechase.
Also in: Track and Field Hall of Fame, Citizens Savings Hall of Fame Athletic Museum.

OUELLETTE, Gerald R.
Shooter
Born in 1934; attended W. D. Lowe Vocational High School, Windsor, Ont; school teacher and tool designer; married; competes with wife in rifle competition team.

Gerald Ouellette became interested in shooting in high school and using a .303 service rifle, won the junior and cadet service rifle championships in Canada in 1951 and the Lieutenant-Governor's Medal in 1952. He participated on several Bisley teams and won a number of service rifle and smallbore competitions before the 1956 Olympics. At Melbourne, Gerald used an American Winchester for a perfect 600, and won the gold medal over the favored Russian, Anatolii Bogdanov, and also one of his own teammates, Vassili Borissov. In 1957 Gerry won the Canadian service pistol championship and the Bisley aggregate with the service rifle in 1959. Also in 1959 he was Canadian sporting rifle champion and won a gold medal and other awards at the Pan-Am Games. He has won the grand aggregate on more than one occasion at the annual Dominion of Canada Rifle Association competitions. In 1971 he and his wife qualified for the Canadian Bisley team.
Also in: Canadian Amateur Athletic Hall of Fame.

THE OUTER COVER CREW
Rowing Team
This six-man rowing team was selected into Canada's Sports Hall of Fame in 1977.

PAGE, John Percy
Basketball Coach
Born 1877 in Rochester, N.Y, of Canadian parents; raised in Bronte, Ont; a gold medalist at Hamilton Collegiate; graduated from Queen's Univ; taught high school in St. Thomas, Ont, and at Edmonton's McDougall Commercial High School; conservative member of the Alberta house 1952–1959; lieutenant-governor 1959–1966; died in 1973.

The Grads were started in 1914 by Page, with students and graduates from the Commercial High School. He later started the Gradettes, as a farm system before a girl was promoted to the Grads. They practiced two times a week except in summer, and he had very strict rules for physical fitness and disciplinary action for enfringements. From 1915 until they were disbanded in 1940, the Grads played 522 games, winning 502 and losing only 20 for a 96.2 percent record. They won 27 consecutive games at the 1924 Paris Olympics, 1928 Amsterdam Olympics, 1932 Los Angeles Olympics, and the 1936 Berlin Olympics. They won their first Canadian title in 1922 and never lost it. They won the Underwood Challenge Trophy in 1923 and kept it for 17 years. When they disbanded, they were given a permanent Underwood Trophy for their club. At one time they won 78 consecutive games, and later won 147.

PATRICK, Frank A.
Builder
See entry in Hockey Hall of Fame, 1958.
Also in: British Columbia Sports Hall of Fame and International Hockey Hall of Fame.

PATRICK, Lester "Silver Fox"
Hockey Player
See entry in Hockey Hall of Fame, 1947.
Also in: British Columbia Sports Hall of Fame and International Hockey Hall of Fame.

PAUL, Robert
Pair Figure Skater
Born 1937 in Toronto.

When Bob Paul was hospitalized with polio at age 10, someone gave him a pair of ice skates; with a lot of hard work he won a gold medal at 16. Bob was a muscular six footer compared to Barbara Wagner's petite blondeness, but they made a good combination. For sheer skill and gracefulness they have not been equaled. In 1954 he and Barbara won the junior pairs championship in Canada, but success in international competition did not come until after Frances Dafoe and Norris Bowden retired in 1956. In 1957 they won the North American championship, the Canadian championship and the world championship, and retained these titles through 1960, when they also won the gold medal in the Winter Olympics. During the Winter Olympics, "their brilliant display of leaps, spins, spirals and the breath-taking death spiral" so impressed the judges that all seven awarded them the first place. Both turned professional and skated with the Ice Capades until Barbara's marriage in 1964.
Also in: Canadian Amateur Athletic Hall of Fame.

PEARCE, H. Robert
Sculler
Robert Pearce was selected to Canada's Sports Hall of Fame in 1975. He was the Diamond Sculls Champion in 1931.
Also in: Canadian Amateur Athletic Hall of Fame.

PEDEN, William John "Torchy"
Cyclist
Born 1906 in British Columbia; one of six children; left school at age 15 to work in father's feed and grain business; encouraged by parents to participate in sports to build up his body; played rugby, swam and tried track and field; served in the RCAF during W.W. II; retired in 1948.

Torchy Peden liked cycling the first time he tried it and set his sights on the 1928 Olympics. He worked in a logging camp, pedaling 25 miles a day when the snow permitted. He won four major West Coast races, then went East to win the Canadian championships at one and five miles, and qualified for the Olympic team. At 6 ft. 2 in, 210 lbs. (the body building paid off), Torchy soon had trouble with his bike and a Toronto race manager designed a sturdier one for him. At the 1928 Olympics in Amsterdam he had tire trouble, and lost out, but competed in Europe afterwards and won races in Warsaw, Paris, London and Glasgow, and set an English record of 1:03:39 hours for 25 miles. He returned that winter to Victoria, but the next spring competed at Montreal and won the Canadian indoor championships setting national records in four events from the half-mile to five miles. He turned professional and competed in the six-day races until he retired in 1948. He won 24 of his first 48 races, and was acknowledged as the "star" of this sport.

PERCIVAL, Lloyd

Contributer and Builder

Lloyd Percival contributed in time, energy, money and leadership to the cause of Canadian sports. He spent many years as a track coach and developed a physical fitness program that many Canadian athletes enjoyed.
Also in: Canadian Boxing Hall of Fame.

PERRY, Gordon

Football Player

See entry in Canadian Football Hall of Fame, 1973.

PERRY, Norman

Football Player

See entry in Canadian Football Hall of Fame, 1973.

PORTER, Robert Alger

Team Sports

Born 1913 in Toronto; father W. A. Porter very active in sports; played baseball, softball, football, hockey and lacrosse; joined the RCAF during the war years; in 1951 took up lawn bowling in place of more strenuous sports; in 1960 wrote a summer column titled "Kicking the Kat" for the Toronto *Telegram.*

Bobby Porter liked all team sports and finally chose baseball, signing in 1936 with the East Texas League. Later he joined Toronto of the International League and in 1939 was sent to Syracuse and later to Springfield of the Eastern League. In 1941 he was sold to Washington of the American League but a broken shoulder cut his career short. He played for the Balmy Beaches from 1942 through 1947, except for a stint in the service. Bobby continued playing fastball, football and individual sports until he was 39.

PRICE, Harry Isaac

Builder

Born in 1896, Harry Price was active all his life in the world of sports. His father Isaac had been a rower and Harry was interested in rowing and running. He joined the Irish Amateur Athletic Association in Toronto as a young man. He enlisted in the Army in 1914 and was invalided home with lung problems, which stopped his participation in active sports. After his recovery he worked for the Canadian government as a vocational director and in 1923 was appointed to the Ontario Athletic Commission, boxing being his particular responsibility. He became involved with the programs at the Canadian National Exhibition, and refereed swimming meets for a number of years. He rode horses for pleasure, and purchased show horses; he founded the Canadian Horse Show Association and was chairman of the Canadian zone of the American Horse Show Association. Harry Price chaired the Canadian equestrian team that competed in the late 1930s. He also was an active member of the Toronto Hunt Club. His horse, Brownie, took many show prizes in the 1930s. Harry Price was also one of the instigators in the founding of the Sports Hall of Fame and served as its first chairman.

PRIMEAU, A. Joseph

Hockey Player

See entry in Hockey Hall of Fame, 1963.
Also in: International Hockey Hall of Fame.

PRIMROSE, John

Trapshooter

John Primrose was selected for inclusion in Canada's Sports Hall of Fame in 1977.
Also in: Canadian Amateur Athletic Hall of Fame.

PURCELL, Jack

Badminton Player

Born 1904 in Guelph, Ont; worked in radio advertising; chosen Outstanding Canadian Athlete of the Half-Century in the miscellaneous division in 1950, by the Sportswriters of Canada.

From 1923 to 1928 Jack Purcell won every badminton title in Ontario, taking the men's singles five times in a row, and the mixed doubles for four consecutive years. In 1929 he won the Canadian singles championship and retained his title in 1930, also defeating the four best British players who were on tour in Canada. In 1931 he won the Surrey doubles in England with K.C. Livingstone as his partner, and competed in the all-England championship, making it to the semifinals. Returning home his amateur status was questioned so he was forced to turn pro. In 1933 he announced he was the professional badminton champion and in a series of matches with the best players of England, Canada and the United States, Purcell proved he was right. He never lost a match when the championship was at stake. During the second world war, he retired undefeated. An eye injury in 1958 forced Purcell to give up the game permanently.
Also in: Canadian Amateur Athletic Hall of Fame.

QUILTY, Sylvester Patrick "Silver"

Football Player

See entry in Canadian Football Hall of Fame, 1973.

RAY, W. Harold

Athlete

W. Harold Ray was selected for inclusion in Canada's Sports Hall of Fame in 1976.

REEVE, Edward H. "Ted"

Journalist

Born 1902 in Toronto, Ont; mother ran a bookstore; read everything he could get his hands on; married Alvern Donaldson in 1931; served in the 30th Light Anti-Aircraft Battery in W.W. II; injured in 1944 and sent home.

Ted Reeve played lacrosse and football in and around Toronto and in 1924 organized the Balmy Beach Club, with whom he served as player, coach and supporter. The team won the Ontario Rugby Football Union title in 1927 and the Grey Cup in 1927 and 1930. He played lacrosse on the Brampton Excelsiors team; his teams won the Mann Cup three times, Oshawa in 1928 and Brampton in 1926 and 1930. In the 1930s he turned to coaching and coached the Balmy Beach lacrosse team and the Queen's University team that won three intercollegiate championships. He wrote a lacrosse column for the *Star Weekly* and for the *Telegram* during lacrosse season. In 1928 he became a full-time columnist for the Toronto *Telegram* and returned to it after the war. His column, "Sporting Extras," was a must for sporting fans for many years.

RICHARD, Maurice "The Rocket"
Hockey Player
See entry in Hockey Hall of Fame, 1961.
Also in: International Hockey Hall of Fame.

THE RICHARDSON RINK, 1959
Curling Team
Ernie Richardson's foursome won the Quebec City Brier in 1959. From Saskatchewan, it was one of the youngest teams to have won the Brier. The Richardson Rink was a close family team from a small rural community. Curling was a part of the rural social life in Saskatchewan and the Richardsons—Ernie, brother Garnet, and cousins Arnold and Wes—all played as youths. They got together on a team in the mid-1950s and in 1958 they only lost three out of the 48 games they played. They repeated the Brier in 1960, and in 1961 were beaten by George Fink in the South Saskatchewan playoffs, one of the toughest games they ever played. They came back in 1962 to defeat the Alberta rink, the first time the championship had been taken three times by a team with the same players. Mel Perry replaced Wes in 1963 when he developed a bad back, and the rink won the Brier for the fourth time at Brandon. During their winning years, the Richardson Rink also won the Scotch Cup four times.

RILEY, Conrad
Rower
Born 1875; moved with family to Winnipeg at age 10; left school at 16 to work in railway office; served in Europe in W.W. I; played hockey, rode and shot, liked curling; married; eight children; successful insurance business; died in 1950.

Con Riley joined the Winnipeg Rowing Club in 1892. He enjoyed stroking a four and patterned his techniques after George Galt, founder of the club. Con Riley served as rower, coach and official at the club over a 37-year period, excluding his war years. Between 1900 and 1914 he was both stroke and captain, many times stroking fours and eights to win races in Canadian and North American championship regattas, and several times stroking in the Henley. In 1910 his club won the Stewards' Challenge Cup in the fours. In 1912 the Winnipeg Rowing Club went to Peoria, Ill, bringing home seven trophies from the North American championships, including the eights, the fours, and the senior and intermediate doubles and singles. Every Winnipeg entry won its event.

RITCHIE, Alvin "Sliver Fox"
Builder
See entry in Canadian Football Hall of Fame, 1973.

ROBERTSON, Bruce
Swimmer
Bruce Robertson was inducted into Canada's Sports Hall of Fame in 1977.
Also in: Canadian Amateur Athletic Hall of Fame.

ROBINSON, Graydon "Blondie"
Bowler
Born in 1928 in Port Colborne, Ont; pinsetter in four-lane alley when first game was bowled.

Blondie Robinson won the world championship bowling title four years after it was entered in the competition. He won his regional six-game round by a single pin. In Montreal he always came from behind each game to win his place on the team that went to Tokyo. He often said that he bowled better when he was down. And he proved that on his way to the title. Blondie could not compete in the five-pin game and had been bowling ten-pins just seven years when he won in Tokyo.

ROBSON, Fred J.
Speed Skater
Born 1879 in Toronto; father emigrated from England and became a butcher; went into piano repair business after school; all-around athlete; cox for Toronto Rowing Club; cyclist; retired from active competition in 1919, skating mainly in benefit performances; died in 1944.

Fred Robson competed in his first skating race at 15 with a pair of homemade skates. He won his first championship in 1897, the Toronto junior title which he kept for 11 years. He also won the Ontario championship that same year and retained it until 1902. He broke three world speed records at 19 and at 22 broke world records for the 220- and 440-yd. hurdles and the 60- and 75-yd. dashes. Between 1899 and 1916 Fred held nine world records and shared the one-mile record of 2:41.2 min. with Morris Wood of Philadelphia. In 1916 he broke his own records by setting new times for the 60- and 75-yd. dashes. He served as president of the Toronto Speed Skating Club which he had helped to found.

ROGERS, Douglas
Judo Expert
Doug Rogers was selected for inclusion in Canada's Sports Hall of Fame in 1977.
Also in: Canadian Amateur Athletic Hall of Fame.

ROGERS, Levi "Shotty"
Coxswain
Shotty Rogers was born in 1887 and died in 1963. For 58 years he participated yearly in Regatta Day at St. John's, Newfoundland, 5 times as an oarsman ad 53 times as a coxswain. Only 5 ft. 4 in. and never more than 120 lbs, Shotty coxed more than 300 crews to victory during that time. Not only was he a successful cox, but he was also a rowing coach in Newfoundland, considered one of the best. He steered his last crew to victory in 1962, when he was 75, and decided to retire. He died the following year just before the Regatta.

ROSENFELD, Fanny "Bobbie"
All-round
Born 1903 in Russia; family immigrated to Canada when an infant; participated in track and field, hockey, basketball and softball in school; after arthritis stopped participation in sports, wrote for the Toronto *Globe* on all sporting events; died in 1969.

Bobbie Rosenfeld started practicing with the Toronto Ladies Athletic Club when it was formed in 1920. Her first trophy was earned in a track meet in Barrie, her home town. Bobbie set three records in 1928 that held until the 1950s: 18 ft. 3 in. in running broad jump; 120 ft. in discus; and 8 ft. 1 in. in standing broad jump. She was a member of several Ontario and Eastern Canadian basketball championship teams and won the Toronto grass courts tennis championship in 1924. In 1925 she won the points title at the Ontario Ladies Track and Field Championship for the Patterson Athletic Club as its only entrant. She took first in discus, the 220, the 120-yd. low hurdles, and running broad jump. She placed second in the 100-yd. dash and the javelin. Bobbie coached the women's track team for the 1932 British Empire Games. In 1929 she spent 8 months in bed with a bout of arthritis and a year afterwards on crutches. But in 1931 she played in the leading softball league and was the top hockey player in women's competition in Ontario. In the 1928 Amsterdam Olympics Bobbie had been on the gold medal relay team, taken the silver medal in the 100-yd. dash and ran fifth in the 800-meter.
Also in: Canadian Amateur Athletic Hall of Fame.

ROSS, Arthur Howie
Hockey Player
See entry in Hockey Hall of Fame, 1945.
Also in: International Hockey Hall of Fame.

ROWE, Paul
Football Player
See entry in Canadian Football Hall of Fame, 1973.

RUBENSTEIN, Louis
Figure Skater
Born 1861 in Montreal, Que; an enthusiastic cyclist and bowler; president of Canadian Wheelmen's Association for 18 years; active in family nickel plating firm, but gave a lot of time to amateur sports; often a judge for ice skating competitions; lived in Montreal until his death in 1931.

In the late 1870s Rubenstein went to Europe to learn the art of figure skating from Jackson Haines. In 1879 he competed in a skating tournament in Montreal and finished third. As a member of the Victoria Skating Club, he competed in many competitions in the next few years and by 1883 was acknowledged as the champion in Canada. He retained this title until 1889 and was the U.S. amateur champion in 1885 and 1889. The first unofficial world championships were held in St. Petersburg, Russia in 1890, and although opposition to Rubenstein ran high because he was Jewish, he came home with the world title. He was capable of repeating a routine on the ice three or four times and not blurring the original outline of the pattern. He astounded judges with the grace and elegance of his figures.
Also in: Canadian Amateur Athletic Hall of Fame.

RUSSEL, Jeff
Football Player
See entry in Canadian Football Hall of Fame, 1973.

RYAN, Joseph B. "Rufus"
Builder
See entry in Canadian Football Hall of Fame, 1973.

RYAN, Thomas
Bowling Contributor
Born 1872 in Guelph, Ont; moved to Toronto at age 18; worked as an invoice clerk, pitched baseball, then opened a billiard academy; opened a bowling alley, then a hotel, an antique and auctioneering business and finally an art gallery, also promoting baseball, boxing and owning a stable of racehorses through the years; died in 1961.

Thomas Ryan invented five-pin bowling in 1909, and it has since become one of Canada's greatest participation sports. In 1895 the American Bowling Congress (ABC) had been formed in New York and in 1905 Tommy Ryan brought the first ten-pin bowling alley to Canada, constructed according to ABC regulations. He soon got complaints that the 16 lb. ball was too heavy, and not wanting to lose his custom trade, began experimenting with the size of the ball and the pins. Duckpins had been invented in 1900 and Ryan's invention of five pins was an adaptation of duckpins. He had his father whittle down five pins with a lathe and figured out a scoring system. The game caught on and when it was discovered that the ball sometimes rolled between the pins, Tommy fitted each with a rubber collar.
Also in: Bowling Halls of Fame to Watch, Fivepin Bowlers Hall of Fame.

RYDER, Gus
Swimming Coach
Born 1899 in Toronto, Ont; played hockey, football, handball, rowed and swam; an accident on the ice determined him to teach swimming and lifesaving; more and more time became devoted to teaching the handicapped, although still teaching lifesaving and swimming skills to others.

Gus Ryder started the New Toronto Swim Club in 1930 and soon had 700 members. Later he changed the name to Lakeshore Swim Club, operating for the next 20 years from the New Toronto beach in the summer and the West End YMCA in the winter. In 1952 the New Toronto War Memorial pool opened as a permanent home for the club. Twice they won the Royal Life Saving Society award in competition with over one hundred clubs in Canada. Gus Ryder's two most famous pupils were Cliff Lumsden and Marilyn Bell, both marathon swimmers. However, Gus often said he would rather see one crippled kid swim across the pool than coach an Olympic champion.

ST. GODARD, Émile
Dogsled Racer
See entry in Dog Mushers Hall of Fame.

SAINT JOHN FOUR, 1867
Rowing Team
In 1867 a regatta was held in conjunction with the Paris Exposition which was won by the Saint John four, Sam-

uel Hutton, Robert Fulton, George Price and Elijah Ross. They won both the in-rigged match and the race for outrigger shells. Afterwards known as the Paris Crew, the four won in 1868 at Cornwall, N.Y, on the Connecticut River at Springfield, and numberous other races throughout North America. They were defeated in 1870 at Lachine by the Tyne crew, stroked by James Renforth, who died at a rematch a year later.

SAWCHUK, Terrance Gordon
Hockey Player
See entry in Hockey Hall of Fame, 1971.
Also in: International Hockey Hall of Fame.

SCHMIDT, Milton Conrad
Hockey Player
See entry in Hockey Hall of Fame, 1961.
Also in: International Hockey Hall of Fame.

SCHNEIDER, Bert
Boxer
Born 1897 in Cleveland, Ohio; family moved to Canada in 1906; father worked in Montreal steel plant; attended Commercial and Technical High School; worked in merchant marines in W.W. I, after being rejected as an enlistee; retired from boxing in 1928 to join U.S. border patrol; moved with wife in 1960 to Pierrefonds, Que.

Bert Schneider started to box at high school athletic programs, and after the war joiend the Casquette Club and trained under Gene Brosseau. He later joined the Montreal Amateur Athletic Association (MAAA) and won the welter championship. He won the city championship and the Canadian title twice, never losing a bout as an amateur. Bert entered the 1920 Olympics at Amsterdam, winning four bouts in three days, and bringing home a gold medal. Bert continued to box for a few years and turned professional but soon retired.

SCHOLES, Louis F.
Sculler
Born 1880 in Toronto, Ont; father John F. Scholes ran the Athlete Hotel and was an all-round athlete; brother Jack an outstanding amateur boxer; mother died when very young; died in 1942.

Lou Scholes started rowing at the Don Rowing Club in Toronto and in 1901 was sent to the U.S. nationals at Philadelphia where he won the U.S. intermediate singles. In 1902 he won the two premier senior sculls fixtures at the Harlem regatta, although he failed in the race for the Diamond Sculls at Henley-on-Thames the same year. In 1903 with partner Frank Smith he won both the Canadian and American double sculls titles; in singles Lou won the Dominion Day regatta at Toronto, the Canadian Henley and the National Rowing Association title in the United States. In 1904 Lou Scholes won the Diamond Sculls by defeating F. S. Kelly, an Australian who had won in 1902 and 1903. Then he went on to defeat A. H. Cloutte of the London Rowing Club, coming from behind to win by more than a length in the record time of 8:23.2 min.
Also in: Canadian Amateur Athletic Hall of Fame.

SCOTT, Barbara Ann
Figure Skater
Barbara Ann Scott was born in 1928; her parents gave her a pair of skates when she was seven. She joined the Ottawa Minto Skating Club, and visits them often today. At nine she left school and was educated by a private tutor so she would have more time to practice. At 11 she won the junior championship; in 1941 and 1942 she was runnerup for the senior championship; it lapsed in 1943, and she won it in 1944. She retained the title in 1945 and 1946. Barbara Ann Scott placed sixth in the North American championships in 1941, but placed first in 1945, at 16 the youngest to have won it. She began practicing for international competition at the Minto Club and at Schumacher in the summer. At 18 she became the world champion at Stockholm in 1947. She also took the European title in Switzerland while she was there. In 1948 she retained both the European and World titles and won the Winter Olympics at St. Moritz. Barbara Ann then turned professional and traveled in North American ice shows. She married Tommy King in 1955 and now lives in Chicago, but returns periodically to the Minto Skating Club to help raise funds. She is an accomplished equestrian and participates in United States meets.

SELKE, Frank J.
Builder
See entry in Hockey Hall of Fame, 1960.
Also in: International Hockey Hall of Fame.

SELLER, Margaret "Peg"
Synchronized Swimmer
Born in early 1900s in Montreal; married Reg Seller in 1931; one of Canada's great sportswomen.

Peg held all Royal Life Saving Society awards in 1923. She won the Gale Trophy for "fancy swimming" four years in a row and captained the national champion water polo team three times. Peg held the Canadian 3-meter diving title and in 1928 won the provincial titles in the 100-yd. dash, the javelin and the broad jump. In 1936 after five years of marriage, she returned to the sports scene as a diving judge for the Canadian Amateur Swimming Association and since that time has devoted her energies to getting synchronized swimming accepted as a sport in Canada and the Olympics. Mrs. Seller must be credited with establishing standards for judges, outlining routines, organizing meets and getting trophies set up. With Buelah Grundling, an American swimmer, she wrote a book on coaching the sport, and the pair later traveled in Europe to encourage its addition to the Olympic competitions. In 1952 Peg took a team to the Olympics in Helsinki to demonstrate, and finally in 1955 at the Pan-Am Games, the sport was admitted as an official, international competitive event. The Canadian women swimmers won four of the six individual events in the 1968 Olympics at Mexico City. Peg Seller wrote the first rule book in 1938 and the *Féderation Internationale de Natation Amateur* rules governing international competition in 1952. She also served this organization for some years as its secretary.
Also in: Aquatic Hall of Fame and Museum of Canada.

SHAUGHNESSY, Frank J, Jr.
Builder
Born 1911 in Roanoke, Va; father best known American immigrant to Canada before 1914; played football and hockey; graduated from Loyola Col. and McGill Univ;

worked for Bell Telephone in Montreal until retirement in 1973; served as Captain in Artillery in Europe in W.W. II.

Frank, Jr, was always involved in sports; after participating, in administration. He worked up from the club, to the regional, and then to the national level in both golf and skiing. He organized national ski meets and golf tournaments and served as secretary to the MAAA. He was in charge of arrangements for the five Canadian Winter Olympic teams from 1956 to 1972. His involvement with the Canadian Olympic teams has grown to a full-time career.

SHEDD, Marjory
Badminton Player
Born in 1926 in Toronto, Ont; father and three older brothers keen athletes; played hockey, softball and touch rugby with brothers as a child; member of dept. of athletics and physical education at Univ. Toronto.

In high school Marjory Shedd was active in all sports open to girls. Her basketball team won the Canadian junior championship in 1945, and she led Toronto Montgomery Maids to the national senior title in 1950. The University of Toronto volleyball team on which she played won five national titles, and she was on the Canadian volleyball team at the Pan-Am Games in Winnipeg in 1967. In 1950 she had joined the Carlton Club to play badminton, and reached the finals in Canadian singles in 1951 and 1952, winning the title in 1953. Shedd took the singles championship six more times, earning her last title in 1963. She won four mixed and eleven ladies titles in doubles play between 1954 and 1969, and has represented Canada on the Uber Cup team more than any other player. Marjory Shedd considered her left-handedness contributed to her success.
Also in: Canadian Amateur Athletic Hall of Fame.

SHERRING, William J.
Marathon Runner
Born 1877 in Hamilton, Ont; died 1964.

Billy Sherring ran continually as a boy. By the time he was 16, he was winning races at Ontario fairs. He finished third in Hamilton's round-the-bay race in 1897, a race a little more than 19 miles. In 1899 and 1903 he won the Hamilton race and finished second in 1900 in the famous Boston Marathon. In 1906 a special Olympiad was held at Athens to attract international recognition of the Olympics, and a marathon race of 26 miles, 385 yards was run between the site of the battle of Marathon and Athens. Billy Sherring, representing the St. Patrick's Athletic Club of Hamilton, won the race in the record time of 2:51:23.6 hours; Prince George of Greece joined him when he came in view of the stadium and ran with him to the finish line.
Also in: Canadian Amateur Athletic Hall of Fame.

SHORE, Edward William
Hockey Player
See entry in Hockey Hall of Fame, 1947.
Also in: Ice Skating Hall of Fame and International Hockey Hall of Fame.

SIMPSON, Benjamin L.
Football Player
See entry in Canadian Football Hall of Fame, 1973.

SIMPSON, Harold Joseph "Bullet Joe"
Hockey Player
See entry in Hockey Hall of Fame, 1962.
Also in: International Hockey Hall of Fame.

SIMPSON, William
Builder
Born 1894 in Paisley, Scotland; parents moved to Canada in 1911; apprenticed as a plumber; worked for gas company and played on company football team; played soccer as inside forward on Davenport Albion and Toronto Scottish, who won league championship in 1919; died in 1974.

Bill Simpson wanted to play soccer in his native Scotland and did not want to come to Canada with his parents. After his playing days were over in 1931 he became president of the Canadian Soccer Football Association; he started programs across Canada to encourage and train young people to play soccer. Soccer continues to grow in Canada, and the groundwork laid by Bill Simpson is a big contribution to its development.

SMYTHE, Constantine Falkland Cary "Conn"
Builder
See entry in Hockey Hall of Fame, 1958.
Also in: Canadian Horse Racing Hall of Fame and International Hockey Hall of Fame.

SOMERVILLE, G. Ross "Sandy"
Golfer
Born 1903 in London, Ont; attended Ridley Col. and Univ. Toronto; established records in cricket and was outstanding in track and field events; played football and hockey; military service in W.W. II; chosen Canada's Greatest Golfer of the Half-Century.

Sandy's father spent winter vacations at Pinehurst, N.C, and from the age of 5 Sandy was batting around golf balls. In 1924 and 1925 he reached the finals of the Canadian Amateur but in 1926 he took the championship, defeating C.C. Fraser of Toronto. He took the title again in 1928, 1930, 1931, 1935 and 1937, and was a finalist in 1934 and 1938. Before 1932 he entered the American Amateur seven times but only passed the qualifying rounds three times. In 1932 he not only qualified but won the title. Somerville never won in the American Amateur again, but continued to dominate Canadian amateur golf in the 1930s, and after the war came back to win or share the Canadian senior title in four tournaments.
Also in: Canadian Amateur Athletic Hall of Fame.

SPEERS, Robert James
Contributor and Race Horse Owner
Born 1882 in Elmbank, Ont; father a blacksmith; worked for his father after school days; moved to Winnipeg at age 18; after five years moved to Saskatchewan; moved to Calgary for the oil boom of 1914; thriving cattle business, and other business ventures; died in 1955.

James Speers owned his first racehorse when he was 9. In Saskatchewan he started dealing in cattle, and then went into the feed and grain business. At that time he started horse breeding, racing in competition against other cattlemen. While in Calgary in the oil brokerage business he got a contract to supply horses to the French government for the war and while scouting for horses,

was injured in a train crash that left him with a permanent limp. He moved back to Winnipeg in 1920 to expand his business, started his own racecourse, and soon built three of his own tracks. Speers established his own stables at St. Boniface and in 1933 bought the stallion Craigangover in Kentucky with 28 brood mares; soon his stables were producing winners in races all over North America. Speers was the first Canadian to win more than $1 million with his own horses in North America; his horses won 1338 races in 20 years. He introduced pari-mutuel betting in Canada in 1922 and pioneered the daily double in North America. He installed the first closed automatic starting gate on the continent at his Whittier Park track in 1939. In 1925 he established the Prairie Thoroughbreeders Association and in 1930 started publication of the *Red Book of Canadian Racing,* an accurate and comprehensive record.
Also in: Canadian Horse Racing Hall of Fame.

SPRAGUE, David S.
Football Player
See entry in Canadian Football Hall of Fame, 1973.

STACK, Frank
Speed Skater
Born 1906 in Winnipeg, Man; father started his training, himself a renowned speed skater; manager-coach of skating team in 1960 that went to Squaw Valley Olympics.

Frank entered his first competition at age 13 and continued to compete until 1954. He won the senior men's championship in 1931 and the North American indoor championships in Chicago. He set a world record for the five-mile at 15:42.2 min. that still stands. Also in 1931 he won the U.S. national outdoor championship. In 1932 and 1938 he won the indoor title again, and won the runnerup position 1933–1937. He competed for the Canadian skating championship seven times and won six. He went to the Olympics six times as a competitor or official.

STEWART, Nelson Robert "Old Poison"
Hockey Player
See entry in Hockey Hall of Fame, 1962.
Also in: International Hockey Hall of Fame.

STIRLING, Hugh "Bummer"
Football Player
See entry in Canadian Football Hall of Fame, 1973.

STREIT, Marlene Stewart
Amateur Golfer
Born 1934 in Fonthill, Ont; graduated from Rollins Col, Fla; married J. Douglas Streit, Toronto stockbroker; never turned professional.

In 1951 at the age of 17, Marlene Stewart defeated Ada Mackenzie to take the Ontario Ladies Amateur. In 1953 she won the British title and in 1956 the U.S. National, the same year she took the North-South and U.S. intercollegiate titles. She also won the Canadian Open and Closed, and the Totem Pole tournament that same year. She won 34 straight matches during that period. Marlene Stewart Streit has won 7 Ontario titles, 9 Canadian Ladies' Closed titles and 8 Canadian Open titles. In 1963 she won the Australian women's golf title, becoming the first woman to win the amateur championships in Canada, the United States, Britain and Australia.

STRIKE, Hilda
Sprinter
Born 1910 in Montreal; father professional hockey player; played softball, basketball, badminton and participated in swimming and skating in high school; formed Mercury Athletic Club in 1933 to coach young runners; married Fred Sisson in 1935 and retired from active competition.

Hilda Strike joined the Canadian Ladies Athletic Club in 1929 and began to practice seriously. From 1929 to 1932 she competed in meets all over North America, winning 15 cups and 30 medals. At 5 ft. 4 in. and 105 lbs, Hilda was small for a sprinter but she possessed amazing speed. In 1932 she ran the 100-meter in 12.2 sec. at the provincial women's track and field championships in Montreal, and after making a good impression at the Olympic trials in Hamilton in July, she was selected as a member of the team to represent Canada in the track and field events at the 1932 Los Angeles Games. Hilda tied with the Polish contender for the 100-meter with the record time of 11.9 sec. Her relay team gained the silver medal in the 400-meter relay. Stella Walsh, her Polish competitor, defeated her in the Canadian National Exhibition later that year, but because of her showing, Hilda was named Woman Athlete of the Year and Montreal's Most Popular Athlete. In 1934 she was the provincial champion in the 60- and 100-yd. and won silver medals in the 100-yd. and 110-yd. relay in the British Empire Games in London in 1934.
Also in: Canadian Amateur Athletic Hall of Fame.

MISS SUPERTEST I, II & III, 1954–1961
Powerboat
Harold Wilson drove his own *Miss Canada V* to defeat Stanley Dollar's *Skip-A-Long* in 1945. *Miss Canada,* renamed *Miss Supertest I,* was taken over by James G. Thompson in 1952. *Miss Supertest II* was designed by Thompson, based on his experience with the boat he bought from Smith. She lost her race with *Shanty I* but did win one heat. The following year she established a new record of 184.54 m.p.h. Thompson then built *Miss Supertest III,* 30 ft. long and weighing 3 tons. When moving at 100 m.p.h, she only had one and a half square feet in contact with the water. She too was piloted by Bob Hayward, a mechanic who joined the crew in 1957, but who turned out to be a cool driver with *Miss Supertest II* in her test runs. He won a heat in the Silver Cup race at Detroit in 1957 and won the St. Clair International Boundary Trophy in 1958. In 1959 *Miss Supertest III* underwent her first water trials and won the Memorial Race at Detroit. She went on to win the Harmsworth on the Detroit River, defeating *Maverick* owned by William Stead; in winning she set a record of 104.098 m.p.h. Bob Hayward and *Miss Supertest III* won again in 1960 and 1961. In September while racing in the Silver Cup with *Miss Supertest II,* Bob Hayward was killed and Thompson retired from competition.

TANNER, Elaine (Nahrgang)
Swimmer
See entry in Aquatic Hall of Fame and Museum of Canada.
Also in: Canadian Amateur Athletic Hall of Fame.

TAYLOR, Edward Plunket
Builder and Race Horse Owner

Born 1900 in Ottawa; banking family; graduated in engineering from McGill Univ; joined an investment firm; built a brewing empire by consolidating and merging breweries.

E. P. Taylor was elected Man of the Year in 1973 by the Thoroughbred Racing Association. He served for over 20 years as president of the Ontario Jockey Club. Through his influence delapidated tracks were closed or refurbished, and new ones, such as the Woodbine racetrack, were built. Due to his determination and standards the calibre of horses, trainers, jockeys and purses became top-flight, as well as the tracks. From 1960 through 1969 the horses bred at his Windfields Farm won more North American races than those of any other breeder. Nine of his horses have been selected for Canadian Horse of the Year, and 15 have won the Queen's Plate. In 1964 his Northern Dancer won the Kentucky Derby, and Nijinsky II won the Epsom Derby in 1970.
Also in: Canadian Horse Racing Hall of Fame.

TAYLOR, Fred O. B. E. "Cyclone"
Hockey Player

See entry in Hockey Hall of Fame, 1947.
Also in: British Columbia Sports Hall of Fame, Greater Ottawa Sports Hall of Fame and International Hockey Hall of Fame.

THOMPSON, Earl
Hurdler

Born 1895 on a farm at Birch Hills, Sask; moved to Long Beach, Calif, with family in 1903; played baseball and football and swam in high school; attended Univ. Southern Calif. and Dartmouth Col; enlisted in Royal Flying Corps as observer-trainee, commissioned in September, 1918, too late to be sent overseas.

Earl Thompson set a world mark of 14.8 sec. for the 110-yd. high hurdles his first year at the University of Southern California, only to have a teammate break it a week later. Transferring to Dartmouth in 1916, Earl hardly got acquainted before he joined the Royal Flying Corps. Returning to Dartmouth after the war he set a new world's record for the 110-yd. high hurdles in 1919 of 14.4 sec. in winning the IC4A meet at Philadelphia. He repeated the victory in 1920 and 1921, and also won the low hurdles in 1921. He set a new Olympic record in 1920 in Antwerp for the high hurdles of 14.8 sec. Earl competed as a member of the Canadian team per Olympic rules concerning country of birth, and won Canada a gold medal. Earl graduated from Dartmouth in 1922 and was assistant track coach there for a period before serving as track coach at West Virginia University for a year, assistant coach at Yale until 1927, and then track coach at the U.S. Naval Academy for more than 25 years.
Also in: Canadian Amateur Athletic Hall of Fame.

TIMMIS, Brian M.
Football Player

See entry in Canadian Football Hall of Fame, 1973.

TOMY, Andy
Athlete

Andy Tomy was selected for inclusion in Canada's Sports Hall of Fame in 1976.

TOWNSEND, Cathy
Bowler

Cathy Townsend was elected to Canada's Sports Hall of Fame in 1977.

TRIFUNOV, James
Amateur Wrestler

Born 1903 in Serbia; immigrated to Canada when a boy of 7 with family; father died in 1913; mother, sister, and brothers went to work; walked five miles daily on a paper route before hiking to school; worked with the Regina *Leader-Post,* then the Winnipeg *Free Press;* retired from active wrestling in 1931 because of ill health.

Jimmy Trifunov first went into boxing with some friends, but after watching a wrestling matrch at the YMCA, decided that was the sport for him. He joined a 40-member Regina wrestling club and began serious training. Without a coach, he set up a program of baseball and basketball playing and ran two to five miles every morning, even in winter. In 1923 Trifunov was a member of the team that won four Canadian championships out of seven classes in Winnipeg. At 5 ft. 4 in, 120 lbs, he competed in the bantamweight division. He attended the 1924 Paris Olympics, and went again in 1928 and 1932, winning a bronze medal in 1928. He won the Canadian amateur bantamweight championship in 1925, and retained the title until 1929. In 1925 he also won the featherweight championship. In the British Empire Games held in Hamilton in 1930, Jimmy won the gold medal in the bantamweight division. He coached Canada's Olympic team in 1952, 1956 and 1960 and was manager of the British Commonwealth Games in 1954 and 1970. Jimmy Trifunov has served as president of the Manitoba Wrestling Association and vice president of the Canadian Amateur Wrestling Association.
Also in: Canadian Amateur Athletic Hall of Fame.

TUBMAN, Joe
Football Player

See entry in Canadian Football Hall of Fame, 1973.

TURNER, David
Soccer Player

Born 1903 in Edinburgh, Scotland; immigrated to Edmonton with family at age 11; taught school for three years; returned to teaching in 1937; graduated from Univ. B.C. with masters, honorary doctorate from Cornell Univ. 1946; worked in conservation until retirement in 1968.

Dave Turner started playing soccer while in high school, playing avidly on any team he could find, and still keeping up with his studies. At 19 he began playing football with the Cumberland United on Vancouver Island, the team winning the British Columbia title and the next year going to the semifinals of the Connaught Cup. He played the next two years with the St. Andrews team, then he moved to pro soccer in the United States. After one season he returned to Canada to play for the Toronto Ulster United. He toured New Zealand with the Canadian All-Stars and then joined the New Westminster Royals, with whom he stayed for nine years. During his years with the Royals they won the Canadian championship four times, 1928, 1930, 1931 and 1936.

THE UBC FOUR, 1956
Rowing Team

The UBC Four won the Olympic gold medal in 1956 in Australia. The four members of the crew were all from British Columbia, Don Arnold, Walter d'Hondt, Lorne Loomer and Archie McKinnon. Arnold was 21 and the other three were 19. Originally selected as spare crew for the eight, only Arnold had any previous rowing experience. Coach Frank Read had whipped them into a crew in only a few months' time. Their quick response to his training convinced the Olympic committee to send them as a four to the competitions.

WAGNER, Barbara
Pair Figure Skater

Born 1938 in Toronto; married in 1964.

Barbara Wagner began skating seriously in 1951. She was a member of the Toronto Skating Club, needed a partner for her dance test and Bob Paul volunteered; and so a successful combination was born. Under the guidance of Sheldon Galbraith, they began to work towards pair competition. They won the Canadian junior pairs championship in 1954, and finished fifth in the world championships at Vienna the next year. They also took third at the North American championships in Regina a month later. In 1956 they placed sixth in the Winter Olympics, but in 1957 within the space of sixteen days they won the North American title in Rochester, the Canadian championship in Winnipeg, and the world championship in Colorado Springs. They defended all three titles successfully in 1958, 1959 and 1960. They climaxed their performances by winning the gold medal at the Winter Olympics at Squaw Valley in 1960. They turned professional after the Olympics and spent two years with the Ice Capades before Barbara's marriage dissolved the partnership.
Also in: Canadian Amateur Athletic Hall of Fame.

WALTON, Dorothy McKenzie
All-round

Born 1909 in Swift Current, Sask; father Edmund McKenzie a merchant; outstanding student at high school and Univ. Sask; married William Walton in 1932 and moved to Toronto; one of the organizers and later president of Canadian Association of Consumers.

Dorothy was an all-rounder in high school, winning individual championships in track and field, and tennis; she was a member of provincial teams winning titles in basketball and hockey. At the University of Saskatchewan, she was a member of 14 intercollegiate teams in tennis, track and field, swimming, field hockey, and basketball, and won individual championships in diving, discus, javelin, high jump, broad jump and the 220. Between 1924 and 1931 she won 54 local, provincial and Western Canadian tennis titles and several badminton titles. In 1934 she resumed her badminton competition and went to the singles finals in both Toronto and Canadian tournaments. In 1935 she won both the Toronto and Ontario titles and from 1936 through 1940 won 64 singles and doubles championships, including the Canadian, Ontario and New England Open titles. In 1939 and 1940 Dorothy Walton won 7 major singles titles without losing a game. She also won 8 ladies and mixed doubles titles in badminton and 6 more in tennis. In 1939 she entered and won the Surrey tournament and went on to win the all-England singles title, the equivalent of the world's amateur championship. In 1940 Dorothy Walton was awarded the Rose Bowl as Canada's outstanding female athlete, and was runnerup for the Lou Marsh Trophy that same year.
Also in: Canadian Amateur Athletic Hall of fame.

WAPLES, Keith Gordon
Harness Race Driver

Born 1923 at Victoria Harbour, Ont; first rode at seven; began driving his father's sulky; has own ranch at Durham, Ont, for breeding and training horses.

When Keith Waples was only 12, he drove his father's sulky with Grey Ghost, and won three heats at a little track at Sundridge, Ont. In July, 1959, Waples drove Mighty Dudley to Canada's first sub-two-minute mile at the half-mile track in Montreal's Richelieu Park. He won the first $100,000 race to be held in Canada at Blue Bonnets in 1972, driving Strike Out. A month later he drove the same horse to victory in the Little Brown Jug, Standardbred racing's top race. In January, 1973, Ken Waples had five wins in one day on the pari-mutuel track at Toronto Greenwood in one day. In 1962 Waples spent a year touring the tracks in the United States but gave it up; he'd prefer to race where he can return each night to the ranch at Durham. Ken has had over 3000 winning races during his years of track competition.

WATSON, Kenneth
Curler

Born 1904 in Manitoba; started curling at age 15; taught school in Winnipeg 1922 – 1942; encouraged youngsters to take up curling; left teaching to start own business; wrote frequent sports columns in Toronto *Telegram;* wrote manual, *Ken Watson on Curling;* retired from active curling in 1971.

Ken Watson entered his first bonspiel in 1923 and won his first trophy in 1926 when he was 21 years of age. Watson led his rink to the Brier championships in 1936, 1942 and 1949. He won the Manitoba bonspiel with his rink in 1936, 1942, 1943 and 1949. He won the grand aggregate in the Manitoba bonspiel in 1939, and 1942 – 1947. In 1939 he founded the first provincial high school bonspiel and has worked diligently to have curling included in the public school programs.

WELCH, Hawley H. "Huckleberry"
Football Player

See entry in Canadian Football Hall of Fame, 1973.

WESLOCK, Nick
Amateur Golfer

Born 1918 as Nick Wisnock; changed his name early in his playing career; industrial design engineer; never turned professional.

Nick Weslock has won the Canadian amateur 4 times, the Ontario Open 7 times, and the Ontario Amateur 8 times. He has also won the Ontario Seniors title 3 times. He has been low amateur in the Canadian Open 19 times, and has been on the World Cup, America Cup and Commonwealth teams many times; also 21 times on the Ontario Willingdon Cup team. Nick Weslock had a bout of ill health in the late 1960s but recovered to win a few more titles in the 1969 – 1970 playing seasons.

WHEELER, Lucile

Skier

Born 1935 in St. Jovite, Que; father developed her grandparents' Grey Rocks Inn as center for skating, bobsledding, snowshoeing, dog-sled racing and skiing; retired from active competition in 1958.

Lucile put on her first pair of skis at two. At ten she entered her first downhill race and finished seventh in a field of 21 of the best women skiers in Canada. At 12 she was the Canadian junior champion and competed with the Canadian team at Aspen, Colo, at 14. Lucile was coached by the Austrian, Herman Gadner, then three Canadian skiers, John Fripp, Ernie McCulloch and Réal Charrette. From 1952 through 1957 she trained at Kitzbühel, Austria, under Pepi Salvenmoser. She would ski for five hours a day all winter long, returning to St. Jovite for the summers, but kept in shape by swimming, riding, golfing and playing tennis. She was recognized as a top Canadian skier when she competed in the 1956 Winter Olympics at Cortina, finishing sixth in the giant slalom and third in the downhill, bringing home a bronze medal. In 1958 she competed in the *Féderation Internationale de Ski* world championships at Badgastein, Austria, winning the giant slalom and the downhill, and finishing second overall to Frieda Dänzer.
Also in: Canadian Amateur Athletic Hall of Fame.

WILLIAMS, Percy

Sprinter

Born 1908 in Vancouver, B.C; frail as a result of rheumatic fever; at peak of career weighed only 125 lbs; dropped out of competitive sports after 1932; devoted himself to business.

In 1926 Bob Granger saw Percy Williams run a friendly two-man race and persuaded him to train for the Olympics. In 1928 he entered Williams in the British Columbia Olympic trials and Williams tied the record of 10.6 sec. for the 100-meter. In the Canadian Olympic trials in Hamilton a few weeks later, he won both the 100- and 200-meter. He repeated the performance in Amsterdam to become the first Canadian to win the double in two of the most prestigious events in the Olympics. Williams continued to race for two more years but in the 1930 British Empire Games in Hamilton he pulled a muscle in his left thigh in the final of the 100-yard. He won the race but his leg never was completely healed. In the 1932 Olympics he was eliminated in the semifinals of the 200-meter.
Also in: Canadian Amateur Athletic Hall of Fame.

WILSON, Harold A.

Speedboat Owner

Harold Wilson was the Canadian who drove his power boat, *Miss Canada V,* to defeat Stanley Dollar's *Skip-A-Long* in 1945. He was selected for Canada's Sports Hall of Fame in 1975.

WILSON, Jean

Speed Skating

Born 1910 in Glasgow; grew up in Toronto; began skating at 15; rescued eight horses from burning stables at 15 to earn the medal from the Society for the Prevention of Cruelty to Animals; hospitalized in 1932 with a rare muscular disease accompanied by progressive fatigue and paralysis; died in 1933.

Jean Wilson joined the Toronto Speed Skating Club at 16 and was coached by Harry Cody. At 18 she began entering competitions and in 1931 won the quarter-mile dash, the 400-yd. dash and the one-mile race to become Toronto indoor champion. She entered the North American championships and won the 200-yd. dash, the quarter-mile, the half-mile, and the three-quarter-mile events. In 1932 she went to the Winter Olympics at Lake Placid, N.Y. From 1932 to 1956 women's speed skating events were scheduled as exhibitions only and no medals were awarded. She won the 500-meter event in the record time of 58 sec; she also broke the world record for the 1500-meter in her first heat with a time of 2:54.2 but was beaten by Kit Klein in the final heat. In the 1000-meter race, Jean Wilson fell and finished sixth. After her death the Toronto *Telegram* donated the Jean Wilson Trophy to be given to the fastest indoor woman skater.
Also in: Canadian Amateur Athletic Hall of Fame.

WINDEYER, Walter

Sailor

Born 1900 in Ontario; father a Great Lakes skipper and racing competitor; suffered a heart attack while in Europe in 1960 for competitions and Olympics; died in 1964 from second heart attack.

Walter Windeyer won his first race at 12 and under his father's guidance became an expert dinghy sailor. In 1919 he won the Douglas Cup, in the late 1920s he won the Wilton Morse Trophy, and in 1935 was a member of the Canadian team that won the Currie Cup in the International 14-ft. Class in England. Walter skippered the Aemilius Jarvis yacht, *Metina,* and began to be in demand for other yachting events. In 1932 he was chosen as helmsman for *Invader II,* a Royal Canadian Yacht Club yacht built for the Canadian Cup races. He sailed her before and after W.W. II in competitions. In 1936 the International Dragon Cup, or Dragon Gold Cup, had been established as the world championship trophy and in 1948 the Dragon became an Olympic class. In 1954 the O'Keefe Trophy was put up to encourage the Dragon Class in Canada. In 1958 Walter Windeyer won the trophy with the *Corte.* This encouraged him to form a syndicate to buy the Danish-built *Tip* to compete in the 1959 Dragon Class world championships in Europe. With an experienced crew and much hard training, they came home with the trophy. The *Tip* won the O'Keefe Trophy, the *Telegram* Trophy and the Olympic trials. In defending the Gold Cup in Holland, Windeyer's heart attack lost the Cup by default and a substitute sailed in the Olympics. On Lake Ontario in 1961 he won the Duke of Edinburgh Trophy and permanent possession of the O'Keefe Trophy by winning it the third time.

WOOD, Howard

Curler

Howard Wood was selected for Canada's Sports Hall of Fame in 1977.

WOOLF, George

Jockey

See entry in National Jockeys Hall of Fame, 1955.
Also in: Canadian Horse Racing Hall of Fame and Racing Hall of Fame.

WRIGHT, Jack
Tennis Player

Born 1903 in British Columbia; graduated from McGill Univ. with medical degree; practiced medicine in Vancouver; medical officer with the Canadian Army overseas in W.W. II; selected as Canada's Outstanding Tennis Player of the Half-Century in the 1950 press poll; died in 1949.

From 1923 to 1933 Jack Wright was a member of Canada's Davis Cup team, which played in zone matches against the United States, Japan and Cuba. He was the Canadian champion in 1927, 1929 and 1931. He was well aware of the disadvantages of tennis as a sport in the cooler climates of Canada, but was fortunate in having the finances to make a tour through the American South often enough to keep his game sharp. In 1927 in Montreal his biggest thrill came in defeating the Japanese star Tacheichi Harada in straight sets, 6-3, 6-3 and 8-6. Harada was considered the third-ranked player in the world behind Big Bill Tilden and William Johnson.
Also in: Canadian Amateur Athletic Hall of Fame.

WRIGHT, Joseph, Jr.
Sculler

Born 1906 in Toronto, Ont; father a great athlete and oarsman; all-rounder in high school, playing basketball and football, and participating in field events; member of the Argonaut Football Club during and after his sculling career; on the 1933 team that won the Grey Cup; named to Argonaut All-Star Team of the 1921–1941 era; executive of both football and rowing clubs; president of the Eastern Football Conference.

Joe, Jr, inherited his father's large frame and toughness of spirit. At 18 in his first year of rowing he stroked both junior and senior Argonaut eights to championships at the Canadian Henley. Joe sat number 6 on the Penn Athletic Club crew in 1925 that won the Middle States regatta that year. The next year he rowed in the Penn eight that won four regattas including the nationals in Philadelphia, and won four singles events in classes from junior to senior. In 1927 he won the senior singles at the American Henley, also in record time. Returning to Canada, Joe, Jr, won the senior singles and the quarter-mile dash at St. Catherines. At the U.S. nationals at Wyandotte, Mich, he won the quarter-mile, the association singles and the senior singles, setting new records in the first two. In 1928 he won the Diamond Sculls, and again in 1929 he came in second; in 1930 he won two heats and won the quarter-mile and the singles championship at the Canadian Henley. Joe, Jr, competed in the 1928 and 1932 Olympics.
Also in: Canadian Amateur Athletic Hall of Fame.

WRIGHT, Joseph, Sr.
Sculler

Born 1864 in Toronto, Ont; excelled in all sports; graduated from Univ. Toronto; set Canadian records in shot put and hammer throw; won championships in billiards; Canadian amateur heavyweight wrestling champion; Canadian heavyweight boxing champion at age 35; played football with Toronto Argonauts for 18 years until 43; Toronto alderman prior to his death in 1950; selected as Canada's Greatest Oarsman of the Half-Century.

Joe Wright began rowing at 13 with the Bayside Rowing Club in Toronto, moving to the Toronto Rowing Club and then the Argonauts, where he remained as oarsman, coach and executive for the rest of his life. At 16 he was a member of a winning crew for the first time and was part of the Toronto Rowing Club four that won the U.S. nationals when he was 22. In his competitive years he won close to 150 championships in rowing. In 1895 he was the first Canadian to win the English singles amateur title, the Bedford Cup. Joe Wright started coaching long before he stopped competing. He coached the Argonaut eights that won the Canadian Henley and the U.S. nationals in 1905, 1907 and 1911; his intermediate eights won in 1905, 1906 and from 1909 to 1911. He coached at the University of Pennsylvania from 1916 to 1926. He returned to Canada after his retirement from coaching the Penn Athletic Club.
Also in: Canadian Amateur Athletic Hall of Fame.

YOUNG, George
Marathon Swimmer

Born 1910 in Toronto, Ont; widowed mother worked as a cleaning lady; moved to Philadelphia to work for Pennsylvania Railroad during depression; worked for parks commission in Niagara Falls after death of wife; died of heart attack in 1972.

When he was still a boy, George Young won the Toronto cross-the-bay swim four times and the Montreal bridge-to-bridge swim three times. He held the Canadian championship for the 220-yd. He sprang to the challenge when William Wrigley, Jr, offered $25,000 to the winner of a Catalina Channel swim, from Catalina Island to the California coast. In January, 1927, George swam this distance in 15 hours, 45 min. The Canadian National Exhibition started an annual marathon in Lake Ontario for $30,000 but George was out of shape and could not take the cold water. He tried again in 1929 and 1930, but could not make it. However, in 1931 he claimed the prize. His heart went out of swimming, however, because the spectators had called him a quitter in the races he did not win, and he dropped from competition.

Citizens Savings Hall of Fame Athletic Museum

LOS ANGELES, CALIFORNIA

Mailing Address: 9800 S. Sepulveda Blvd, 90045. Tel. (213) 670-7550 *Contact:* W. R. "Bill" Schroeder, Managing Dir; Sally Gutierrez, Librn. *Location:* Across from Los Angeles International Airport; approx. 110 mi. N.W. of San Diego, 375 mi. S.E. of San Francisco, 390 mi. N.W. of Phoenix, Ariz, 285 mi. S.W. of Las Vegas, Nev. *Admission:* Free 9 to 5 Monday–Thursday, 9 to 6 Friday, 9 to 3 Saturday. *Personnel:* Peter W. Webster, Pres;

Don E. Porter, Sr. V.Pres; Bruce Pluckhahn, Jr, V.Pres; W. R. "Bill" Schroeder, Secy.-Treas. and Managing Dir; 10-mem. Bd. of Dirs. (Elwood A. Teague, Chmn.). *Nearby Halls of Fame:* Softball (Long Beach, 20 mi. S.E.), Physical Fitness (Costa Mesa, 35 mi. S.E.), Auto Racing (Ontario, 45 mi. S.E.), Flight, Sports (San Diego).

To speak of the Citizens Savings Hall of Fame Athletic Museum is to speak in superlatives. It was the world's first sports hall of fame and is today the oldest such hall of fame in existence. It is by far the largest hall of fame in the world—in terms of people inducted, it is nearly 35 times larger than the average-size hall. And it has had a more profound impact on the development of halls of fame in general than any other single institution. It is thus not an exaggeration to state that in varying degrees all halls of fame owe their existence to the success and development of the Citizens Savings Hall of Fame Athletic Museum.

By 1930, the year the first modern supermarket opened, W. R. "Bill" Schroeder had conceptualized his idea for a hall of fame that would support athletics and would honor both the greatest athletes and the sports in which they had excelled. He presented this idea to Paul Helms, owner of the Helms Bakeries in Los Angeles, and with him, turned the idea into a concrete reality. By 1936, the year the first pop music chart was published, Schroeder and Helms (who is now deceased) acquired modest quarters in the W. M. Garland Building in downtown Los Angeles. Thus the Helms Athletic Foundation was officially instituted. Housing an ever-accumulating wealth of athletic memorabilia, the Foundation was forced to move to a larger facility on Venice Boulevard in 1948 (the year of the first aircraft hijacking), where it soon had to expand again to accommodate the growing number of visitors. In July of 1970 (shortly before the first vehicle landed on the moon) the Helms family found it impossible to continue to sponsor the popular Foundation activities. Under the administrative discretion of Bill Schroeder, the Foundation therefore merged with the United Savings and Loan Association. At a press conference on October 6 of that year, the Association's board president, Elwood A. Teague, pledged a continuity of those policies and ideals implemented by Schroeder and the late Helms. Quarters were established at Sepulveda Boulevard, the present location. In March of 1973 United Savings and Citizens Savings and Loan Association completed a merger providing for an expansion of operations. It was then that the Helms Athletic Foundation was designated the Citizens Savings Athletic Foundation. With the exception of the National Baseball Hall of Fame, the Athletic Foundation was the first to institute Halls of Fame, and for many sports. The Hall of Fame Athletic Museum, which attracts well over 40,000 visitors annually, recognizes outstanding achievement in 22 different athletic endeavors ranging from junior high school to professional competition. Within the Athletic Museum are 31 separate Halls of Fame, each designed to honor the great participants and contributors of its particular concern. In addition to the vast collection of sports artifacts and memorabilia and the Halls of Fame, the Foundation sponsors the Athlete of the Month and the Athlete of the Year awards as well as the Rose Bowl Player of the Game Award. The Foundation also maintains the World Trophy, which serves to recognize the foremost amateur athletes from each of the six regions of the world: Africa, Asia, Australasia, Europe, North America and South America-Caribbean. Individual World Trophy plaques are awarded annually and a permanent six-foot-high trophy made of gold, silver, bronze and marble is housed in the Hall itself, on which is engraved the names of all the winners. One of the outstanding features of the Museum is the collection of Olympic Games awards, reports, publications and memorabilia, which is believed to be one of the largest. Due to its contributions to the Olympic Games, the Foundation was granted the International Olympic Cup Award in 1961. The Athletic Foundation has honored outstanding high school athletes since 1937 with an extensive awards program. In 1969 the Foundation expanded to include girls in the high school programs, and in 1973 expanded once again to include the Northern California high schools. High school award recipients are chosen by a board of sports authorities and high school coaches. A major feature of the Museum is its 10,000 volume library, probably the world's most extensive collection specializing in the field of sports. The library is housed on the second floor of the building and welcomes, free of charge, sportscasters, athletic researchers, newsmen and interested public. The library maintains extensive, back-dated sports magazines, souvenir programs and press media books used for research. This museum is a member of the Association of Sports Museums and Halls of Fame.

Members: The Citizens Savings Hall of Fame Athletic Museum is actually a conglomeration of 31 separate Halls of Fame, each recognizing outstanding individuals in its specific area. Procedures for induction into the individual Halls vary; for example, in a number of Halls, the official association for that particular athletic endeavor nominates potential members directly to the Citizens Savings Hall Board members and the Board examines and considers their election. In other cases, such as the baseball division, the Board automatically recognizes inductees honored by the American Association of College Baseball Coaches Hall of Fame. In most instances, however, selected committees are recognized as nominating entities who submit their recommendations to the Board members who then vote to determine acceptance into one of the Halls. No exact format for induction ceremonies is employed; presentations of awards are made at various times and in various locations. Each newly admitted member of a Hall in the Citizens Savings Hall of Fame Athletic Museum receives an official plaque and is properly registered in the appropriate Hall.

Athletic Directors Hall of Fame

This Hall of Fame was instituted in 1970 to honor outstanding collegiate athletic directors. As of 1977 there are 174 members, selected by a board. Each inductee has his name engraved on a trophy which is kept in Citizens Savings Hall of Fame Athletic Museum, the Los Angeles international sports shrine. A Hall of Fame Award is presented to each member.

1970

ARMSTRONG, Ike J.

Athletic Director

Born June 8, 1895, in Seymour, Iowa; made the varsity football team in high school in the eighth grade.

Armstrong was a fullback at Drake 1920 – 1922, playing against Cornell, Washington and other powerful schools. The 1921 team was undefeated and won the Conference title. As coach at the University of Utah 1925 – 1949, he led unbeaten teams in 1926, 1928 – 1930 and 1941. His teams went to the Sun Bowl in 1938 and to the Pineapple Bowl in 1946. They shared Conference titles in 1938, 1940 and 1941, and won the title outright in 1947 and 1948. The 1939 club won nine games and scored 258 points, which led the nation. Their overall record was 140 – 55 – 15, .702 percent. Armstrong was also a basketball and track coach. He served many years as athletic director at the University of Utah and University of Minnesota.
Also in: College Football Hall of Fame, Citizens Savings Hall of Fame Athletic Museum; and National Football Hall of Fame.

BARNES, Samuel E.

Athletic Director

Sam Barnes was a born coach and athletic director. He served in those capacities for many years at Howard University, where his outstanding character and leadership highlighted a career distinguished enough in itself to earn induction into this prestigious Hall of Fame.

BARR, J. Shober

Athletic Director

Born in Lancaster, Pa; graduated from Franklin and Marshall Col. in 1924; received his M.A. from Columbia Univ. 1932.

1926 – 1942 Franklin and Marshall College, physical education teacher

1942 – 1949 Franklin and Marshall College, director of admissions

1949 – 1963 Franklin and Marshall College, director of physical education and athletics

In a lifetime of service to Franklin and Marshall, Shober Barr played many roles. In addition to those listed above, he was dean of freshmen. He assisted in the scouting and coaching of school football teams; and his basketball team for the 1935 – 36 season not only won 13 out of 14 games to become the Eastern Pennsylvania Collegiate Basketball League champions, but also participated in the Olympic tryouts of 1936 in Philadelphia. His energy was not confined to the campus, however. From 1952 to 1955 he served on the NCAA Television Committee, when the televising of college football games was in its infancy. In 1960 during a sabbatical leave, he served as an adviser to the Minister of Education in Afghanistan, where he helped set up a modern physical education program. An active member of the American Business Club, he also served as a director of the Thaddeus Stevens Orphans Home Board, and as president of the Lancaster YMCA board of directors. After his retirement from Franklin and Marshall in 1963, he served as a member of Marts and Lundy, Inc, the well-known New York fund raising counselors.

BAUJAN, Harry Clifford

Athletic Director

Graduated from Univ. Notre Dame 1917; served in U.S. Army in W.W. I; played pro football with Massillon and Cleveland; Univ. Dayton Baujan Field named in his honor December, 1961; selected by Knute Rockne Clubs as Athletic Director of the Year 1962; served many years on civic and community organizations; remained active as a consultant to Univ. Dayton after retirement.

Harry Baujan, the Blond Beast, started at the University of Dayton in 1922 and spent 48 years in their department of athletics. In the 1923 – 1924 school year he became head football, basketball and baseball coach. His 21 football teams won 164 games, lost 64 and tied 8. He had only three losing seasons in football, 1923, 1929 and 1936, and they were all 4-5. His teams were never outscored in a season; his 21-year scoring total was 3499 points for the Flyers and 1280 points against. During the 1920s Baujan coached five basketball teams, 1923 – 1924 through 1927 – 1928, and had a 46-38 record. He also had 23 baseball teams and compiled a 170-118 record from 1923 through the 1951 – 1952 season. He missed one year of coaching in this span, and had two undefeated seasons, 1926 and 1952. In 1946 Baujan gave up football to become the University's director of athletics.
Also in: College Football Hall of Fame, Citizens Savings Hall of Fame Athletic Museum.

BEATTY, Harold J. "Hal"

Athletic Director

Born in Los Angeles, Calif; graduated from Fresno State Col. 1933, masters from Univ. Southern Calif. 1937; played football and basketball in college and competed in track; served in the military in W.W. II.

Beatty started his career as a football coach at Albany High School in 1934 and coached football and track at Napa High in 1935 and 1936. He returned to Fresno State in 1937 as freshman and assistant coach in football, basketball and track and coached golf, tennis, boxing and wrestling. Hal became head basketball coach in 1939 and returned after the war to continue coaching basketball until 1947 when he was appointed dean of men. His basketball coaching record was 48-59. Hal Beatty served as athletic director at Fresno State 1956 – 1963. Following his directorship he served as adviser to future coaches and closed out his academic career in charge of student teachers.

BELL, Madison "Matty"

Athletic Director

Graduated from North Side High School, Fort Worth, Tex, and Centre Col, Ky; active in athletics at both schools; U.S. Naval Reserve 1942 – 1945.

Matty coached at Haskell Institute in 1921 – 1922 and at Carroll College in 1922 before joining Texas Christian University in 1923 as head football coach. Under his guidance the Horned Frogs finished third in their first Southwest Conference race and compiled a record of 33 victories, 17 losses, and 5 ties. In 1929 Matty Bell moved to Texas A&M and in his five years with the Aggies, they won 24, lost 21, and tied 3. He started as line coach with Southern Methodist University in 1934 and became head coach the following year. His first team won 12 regular season games and became the first Southwest Confer-

ence's representative in the Rose Bowl classic. In seven years he guided his teams to 47 victories, 24 losses and 3 ties. When he returned to SMU after the war, he assumed the additional duties of athletic director and was instrumental in the building of the Lettermen's Memorial Dormitory. His 1947 and 1948 teams won Conference championships; his record for this period was 32 victories, 16 losses and 5 ties, giving him a lifetime record of 155 wins, 86 defeats and 17 ties. In 1950 Matty Bell began devoting full time to his duties as athletic director, and SMU's golf, swimming, basketball, tennis, track and baseball teams accumulated honors not only in the Conference but in intersectional competition. Matty served as president of the American Football Coaches Association and was on the NCAA football rules committee. He coached several teams in the East-West and North-South contests.
Also in: College Football Hall of Fame, Citizens Savings Hall of Fame Athletic Museum; and National Football Hall of Fame.

BUSHNELL, Dr. Asa Smith
Athletic Director
Attended The Hill, a New York prep school; graduated from Princeton Univ. 1921, playing football there; recipient of various honorary degrees; married Thelma Lucille Clark; two children; retired in 1970; now living in Princeton, N.J.

Bushnell served many years as the NCAA television program director; he helped found what is today the Collegiate Commissioners Association, and served as a member of the executive committee of the National Football Foundation and Hall of Fame. He was editor of the Princeton *Alumni Weekly,* Princeton *Athletic News*, and graduate manager of athletics for ten years.
Also in: Rowing Hall of Fame, Citizens Savings Hall of Fame Athletic Museum.

CORBETT, James J.
Athletic Director
James Corbett served as athletic director of Louisiana State University.

CRISLER, Herbert Orin "Fritz"
Athletic Director
Born January 12, 1899, in Earlville, Ill; captain of Green Bay East High School team that won 1920 Wisconsin State Championship; liked Knute Rockne's offensive style so went to Notre Dame, and in three years there gained 1932 yards; played at Univ. Chicago under Amos Alonzo Stagg 1919–1921; the arena at the Univ. Mich. named in his honor.

1922–1929 University of Chicago, assistant football coach
1929–1932 Michigan State University, coach
1930–1931 University of Minnesota, coach and athletic director
1932–1937 Princeton University, coach
1933–1941 Fordham University, coach
1938–1947 University of Michigan, coach
1948–1968 University of Michigan, athletic director and athletic board chairman

Crisler played pro football for the Green Bay Packers and the Providence Steamrollers in 1925. Soon, however, he turned to the coaching and the administrative sides of the game. Since 1942 he has been a member of the National Collegiate Athletic Association rules committee. In 1947 he led the University of Michigan to the national championship. His composite coaching record of 78-21-10 ranked him among the nation's best coaches at the time. He developed Fordham's immortal line, the "Seven Blocks of Granite." His assistants included Earl Walsh, Hugh Devore, Glen (Judge) Carbarry and Vince Lombardi. His teams lost the 1941 Cotton Bowl but won the 1942 Sugar Bowl. He became the AAFC commissioner, head coach of the AAFC Chicago Rockets, a pro football official, and a TV company executive. In addition to all of these duties and responsibilities, Crisler operated a unique correspondence school for high school coaches in need of big league advice. The way it worked was that any coach who wanted a new play to win a big game or who did not know what offense to use against a certain defense could have his questions solved by writing to Crisler. He corresponded with more than 200 Michigan coaches in that manner. A positive benefit of this service to Crisler and to the University of Michigan was that grateful coaches often steered likely prospects to Ann Arbor.
Also in: College Football Hall of Fame, Citizens Savings Hall of Fame Athletic Museum; and National Football Hall of Fame.

ERICKSON, Charles P.
Athletic Director
Born in Oak Park, Ill; played halfback for the Univ. N. C, receiving a B.S. in engineering; married Mildred Wanell; daughter Susan and two grandchildren.

Erickson was athletic director for the North Carolina Tar Heels for 16 years, until 1968, after which time he played a highly significant role as consultant and adviser to the department of athletics.

FAUROT, Don
Athletic Director
Born June 23, 1902, in Mountain Grove, Mo; attended Univ. Mo; married Mary Davidson; three daughters and seven grandchildren; Amos Alonzo Stagg Award for service in advancement of football.

1935–1942 Missouri Tigers, coach and athletic director
1945–1967 Missouri Tigers, coach and athletic director
1943 Iowa Pre-Flight, coach and athletic director
1944 Jacksonville Fliers, coach and athletic director

Faurot was the eldest of four brothers to letter in football at Mizzou; he lettered in two other sports as well. A lightweight fullback in football, he was captain of the baseball team and an infielder in baseball despite two severed fingers on his right hand. The creator of the split-T football formation, he had a 164–92–13 career record. He also coached for Kirksville State Teachers College (now Northwest Missouri State) for nine years and was the past president of the National Football Coaches Association.
Also in: College Football Hall of Fame, Citizens Savings Hall of Fame Athletic Museum; Missouri Sports Hall of Fame and National Football Hall of Fame.

FLYNN, Eugene F.
Athletic Director
Born in Rochester, N.Y; graduated from Holy Cross Col. 1922.

1928 – 1942 Holy Cross College, assistant director of athletics
1943 – 1966 Holy Cross College, director of athletics

Flynn coached basketball players Bob Cousy, Tom Heinsohn and George Kaftan; football players Bill Omanski and Johnny Turco, trackman Andy Kelly, baseball player Jack Barry and golfers Willie Turnesa and Paul Harney. He served as president of the Eastern College Athletic Conference and the New England Collegiate Athletic Conference.

GALLAGHER, John J. "Taps"
Athletic Director
Born July 16, 1904, in Brooklyn, N.Y; played four years of varsity basketball at St. Johns in Brooklyn, captain of team during junior year; spent three years in Navy during W.W. II; presently lives in Niagara Falls, N.Y.

From 1925 to 1928 Gallagher served as coach at St. Johns Prep School, a position he also held at Niagara College from 1932 through 1943 and from 1947 to 1965. His record at the latter institution was 465 – 264.
Also in: College Basketball Hall of Fame, Citizens Savings Hall of Fame Athletic Museum.

HANSON, Raymond W. "Rock"
Athletic Director
Born in Red Wing, Minn; attended Springfield Col. and New York Univ; military service in Marines in W.W. II, retired as Col; Western Ill. Univ. stadium named in his honor.

Hanson was the athletic director for the Western Illinois University Fighting Leathernecks until his retirement. He began his career as a Red Wing, Minn, high school teacher, then coached for Steward's Business College in Washington, D.C, and later Crosby High School in Waterbury, Conn. In 1926 he began coaching at Western Illinois, where he originated the 10-sec. rule in basketball. Hanson was the baseball commissioner for the Union of South Africa in 1957, and served as president of the National Association of Intercollegiate Athletics. He was a close friend of Knute Rockne, the famous Notre Dame coach.
Also in: National Association of Intercollegiate Athletics Hall of Fame.

HARRIS, Leo A.
Athletic Director
Born August 6, 1904, in Santa Clara, Calif; attended Santa Cruz High School, student body president and football, track and basketball star; played football and basketball at Stanford Univ, received M.A. in education 1927.

1927 – 1932 Fresno High School, football, basketball and baseball coach
1932 – 1933 Fresno State College, assistant football coach and baseball coach
1933 – 1935 Fresno State College, football coach
1936 – 1937 Edison High School, vice principal
1937 – 1942 Edison High School, principal
1945 – 1947 Carmel School District, superintendent
1947 – 1967 University of Oregon, athletic director

The Fresno State College gridders were Far West Conference champs in 1934 and 1935 when Harris was coaching them.

JACKSON, Dr. Edward L.
Athletic Director
Born in Springfield, Mass; Central Intercollegiate Athletic Conference Coach of the Year 1955.

Edward Jackson began his career as director of physical education at Delaware State College and later coached at Johnson C. Smith and Howard Universities. He also was director of athletics at Oakwood YMCA in East Orange, N.J. Dr. Jackson went to Tuskegee Institute in 1956 and served as director of athletics until 1968, when he was appointed vice president of academic affairs.

JOHNSON, Roy "Old Iron Head"
Athletic Director
Lettered in football, track and field and baseball at Univ. Mich; was highly proficient in the physical efficiency event, a combination of the pentathlon and the decathlon, extremely popular during the 1910 – 1920 era.

Roy Johnson was athletic director at the University of New Mexico 1920 – 1959. In addition to his responsibilities as athletic director, Johnson served as chairman of the department of physical education and as teacher of virtually every theory and activity course in the physical education curriculum. He also served as head coach of almost every varsity sport in which New Mexico fielded a team. Shortly after his arrival on campus in 1920, Johnson rented a team of horses and a plow and broke the land that was destined to become Zimmerman Field. He bought lumber, nails and a hammer to build the stadium's first crude grandstand. In his eleven years as head football coach, his teams had only four losing seasons—his record was 40 – 31 – 6. The University of New Mexico most appropriately named their gymnasium after him.

KEENE, Roy Servais
Athletic Director
Attended Oregon State Univ; with wife Marie, still living in Corvallis; retired in 1964.

Keene began his career as coach at Corvallis, Ore, High School and later spent 15 years as athletic director at Willamette University in Salem, Ore. He became athletic director at Oregon State University in 1947.

LARKINS, Richard C.
Athletic Director
Richard Larkins served as an athletic director at Ohio State University.

LONBORG, Arthur C.
Athletic Director
See entry in Naismith Memorial Basketball Hall of Fame, 1972.
Also in: College Basketball Hall of Fame, Citizens Savings Hall of Fame Athletic Museum.

McCOY, Ernest B.
Athletic Director
Born in Pittsburgh, Pa; raised in Detroit, Mich; graduated from Univ. Mich. 1929; Pa. State Univ. McKay Donkin Award 1970.

McCoy began his university coaching career as head basketball coach and assistant director of athletics in 1929 at the University of Michigan; he had previously served as coach at the Montclair, N.J, High School and the New Jersey State College at Montclair. In 1952 he became the director of athletics at Pennsylvania State University, where he remained for 16 years. He served as president of the Eastern Collegiate Athletic Conference and the Eastern Intercollegiate Football Association.

McCURDY, Hugh G.
Athletic Director
Graduated from Bowdoin Col. 1922; center on basketball team in college; married Dorothy Ranney; son Paul a medical doctor; daughter Katharine married a medical doctor; retired in 1968, living in Middletown, Conn.

Hugh McCurdy's father, Dr. James H. McCurdy, was chairman of the physical education department at Springfield College for forty years. Hugh carried out the family tradition by serving as coach and athletic director at Wesleyan College. In addition, he was editor of the *National Journal of Physical Education.*

McDONOUGH, Dr. Thomas E.
Athletic Director
Attended Wisconsin State Univ, Columbia Univ, and Peabody Col; received B.S. and M.A. degrees.

1942 – 1967 Emory University, director of athletics
1949 – 1959 Havatlanta Games Competitions, co-founder and athletic director
1959 Pan-Am Games in Chicago, alternate official
1960 Olympic Games in Rome, Italy, official

McDonough began his career coaching at the University of Eastern Kentucky, and served on many National Collegiate Athletic Association committees. He published numerous articles on athletics, physical education and physical fitness.

MOORE, Bernie
Athletic Director
Born in 1897 in Jonesboro, Tenn; graduated from Carson-Newman Col. 1917; participated in three sports.

1917 Winchester, Tenn, High School, coach
1919 – 1920 LaGrange, Ga, High School, coach
1921 – 1922 Allen Military Academy, coach
1923 – 1925 University of the South (Sewanee), coach
1926 – 1927 Mercer University, coach
1928 – 1947 Louisiana State University, coach
1948 – Southeastern Conference, commissioner

After overseas duty as an enlisted man with the American Expeditionary Force, Moore returned to the United States to begin his remarkable career as a coach. One of his pupils at Mercer was Wally Butts, who became the football coach at the University of Georgia. At LSU, his teams made it to five different bowl games (3 Sugar, 1 Orange and 1 Cotton), and his 1935 football team was national champion.

Also in: National Football Hall of Fame; and Track and Field Hall of Fame, Citizens Savings Hall of Fame Athletic Museum.

NEELY, Jess Claiborne
Athletic Director
Born in Smyrna, Tenn; played halfback for Vanderbilt Univ; later received a law degree; Amos Alonzo Stagg Award for outstanding coaching.

Neely began his career at Southwestern College of Memphis as coach, and later coached at Alabama, Clemson, Vanderbilt and Rice Universities. While he was at Rice, the Owls won 144 games and four championships, the best record for a Southwestern Conference coach. This was at a time when their enrollment of 1300 to 1800 was the smallest of any major football university. He developed many All-Americans: Weldon Humble, Banks McFadden, Dicky Moegle, Bill Howton, King Hill and Buddy Dial. He was president of the National Football Coaches Association.
Also in: College Football Hall of Fame, Citizens Savings Hall of Fame Athletic Museum; and National Football Hall of Fame.

ROCKAFELLER, Harry J. "Rocky"
Athletic Director
Star athlete at Asbury Park High School; graduated from Rutgers Univ. 1916; Rutgers Alumnus of the Year 1960; Rutgers Medal for outstanding service to the university and James Lynah Memorial Trophy 1962; retired in 1961.

Rockafeller remained at Rutgers from the year he registered as a freshman. His service to that school spanned more than half a century.

WRIGHT, Paul W. "Frosty"
Athletic Director
Attended the Colorado School of Mines and Western State Col; received B.S. and M.A. degrees from Univ. Ill.

1925 – 1935 Texas and Colorado, high school coach
1935 – 1963 Western State College, director of athletics
1947 – 1963 Western State College, division of health, physical education and recreation chairman
1963 – Western State College, emeritus professor

Wright was instrumental in the planning and construction of Western State's Mountaineer Gymnasium, the athletic bowl, and the activity grounds; he also helped expand the staff of the department of health, physical education and recreation from 3 to 15. Off campus he was active in community affairs as a 20-year member of the Selective Service Board, as a member and president of Rotary International, as chairman of the County American Red Cross Society, as a municipal judge, as a member of the executive committee of the Community Church, and as mayor of Gunnison, Colorado.

1971

ABBOTT, Cleve
Athletic Director
Abbott was an athletic director at Tuskegee Institute.

ALEXANDER, William A.
Athletic Director
Born June 6, 1889, in Mud River, Ky; attended Georgia Inst. Technol; Coach of the Year 1942; National Touchdown Club Award 1948; died April 23, 1950.

Alexander was player, coach and athletic director at Georgia Tech 1920 – 1950. He was the first coach to take his teams to all four major bowl games. His 1928 team had a 10 – 0 – 0 record and won the National championship, beating California 8 – 7 in the Rose Bowl. His teams beat Missouri 21 – 7 in the 1940 Orange Bowl, lost 14 – 7 to Texas in the 1943 Cotton Bowl and beat Tulsa 20 – 18 in the 1944 Sugar Bowl. They won Southern Conference titles in 1922, 1927 and 1928, as well as the Southeast Conference championships in 1939 (tie), 1943 and 1944. Alexander's overall record was 133 – 95 – 8.
Also in: College Football Hall of Fame, Citizens Savings Hall of Fame Athletic Museum; and National Football Hall of Fame.

BARNES, Everett D. "Eppy"
Athletic Director
Everett served as an athletic director for Colgate University.
Also in: American Association of College Baseball Coaches Hall of Fame.

BIBLE, Dana X.
Athletic Director
Born October 8, 1891, in Jefferson City, Tenn; attended Carson-Newman Col.

1913 – 1915 Mississippi College, coach
1916 Louisiana State College, coach
1917 Texas A&M College, coach
1919 – 1928 Texas A&M College, coach
1929 – 1936 University of Nebraska, coach
1937 – 1946 University of Texas, coach

Bible was the winner of 14 Conference championships, with an overall coaching record of 205 – 73 – 20. He wrote *Championship Football* on how to mold a winning team. He began coaching high schools at 21 while still attending college; he was a follower of Amos Alonzo Stagg, Dr. Henry Williams, Pop Warner, Fielding Yost and Bob Zuppke. Bible's 1919 team was unbeaten, and under his leadership the Aggies did not have a losing season. He led Nebraska to three Conference games, and at Texas his teams won two Cotton Bowls in 1943 and 1946 and tied in 1944. He served 27 years on the National Football rules committee.
Also in: College Football Hall of Fame, Citizens Savings Hall of Fame Athletic Museum; and National Football Hall of Fame.

CURLEY, John
Athletic Director
John was an athletic director at Boston College.

DICKSON, Joseph F.
Athletic Director
Dickson was an athletic director at Eastern New Mexico University.

FROST, R. B. "Jack"
Jack was an athletic director for South Dakota State University.

GALLAGHER, John J. "Taps"
Athletic Director
Born July 16, 1904, in Brooklyn, N.Y; attended St. John's Univ; three years in U.S. Navy during W.W. II.

Gallagher played four years of varsity college ball and served as team captain during his junior year. He coached St. John's Prep. School 1925 – 1928 and at Niagara University 1932 – 1943 and 1947 – 1965. His coaching record at Niagara was 465-264.
Also in: College Basketball Hall of Fame, Citizens Savings Hall of Fame Athletic Museum.

GAUTHIER, George
Athletic Director
George Gauthier was an athletic director at Ohio Wesleyan University.

HAMILTON, Thomas J.
Athletic Director
Born December 26, 1905, in Hoopestown, Ill; graduated from U.S. Naval Academy; won nine varsity letters, three each in football, baseball and basketball; class pres; one of the founders of the Naval Pre-Flight Training Program during W.W. II, one-time skipper of the *Enterprise;* retired from the Navy in 1949 as Rear Admiral; All-American 1926; National Football Foundation Gold Medal 1970.

1934 – 1936 U.S. Naval Academy, coach
1946 – 1947 U.S. Naval Academy, coach
1949 – 1954 University of Pittsburgh, athletic director

Hamilton was a running back for the Navy 1924 – 1926 and in 1926 saved the Navy season by kicking a field goal to tie Army 21 – 21. At 29 he was named Navy head coach, and had a 19 – 8 record in the first season. Hamilton was a member of the U.S. Olympic committee board of directors, the National Collegiate Athletic Association rules committee and has been a vice president of the National Football Foundation. He was the first chairman of the NCAA TV football committee and served on the President's Advisory Council on Physical Fitness under Eisenhower and Kennedy.
Also in: National Football Hall of Fame.

HARVEY, B. T.
Athletic Director
Harvey was an athletic director at Morehouse College.
Also in: National Association of Intercollegiate Athletics Hall of Fame.

HUNTER, Willis O.
Athletic Director
Willis was an athletic director at University of Southern California.

IBA, Henry P.
Athletic Director
See entry in Naismith Memorial Basketball Hall of Fame, 1968.
Also in: College Basketball Hall of Fame, Citizens Savings Hall of Fame Athletic Museum.

KIMBALL, Edwin R.
Athletic Director
Edwin Kimball was an athletic director at Brigham Young University.

KNIGHT, John J.
Athletic Director
John Knight was an athletic director at Bethany College.
Also in: National Association of Intercollegiate Athletics Hall of Fame.

LEWIS, Gaston E.
Athletic Director
Lewis was an athletic director at Central State University.

MASTERS, Al
Athletic Director
Al Masters was an athletic director at Stanford University.

McLANE, James A.
Athletic Director
James McLane was an athletic director at Alfred University.

MEYER, Leo R. "Dutch"
Athletic Director
Born of German parents January 15, 1898, in Waco, Tex; spoke no English until grade school.

1934 – 1952 Texas Christian University, coach
1949 – 1950 National Coaches Association, president

Meyer was a Texas Christian University (TCU) football letterman 1916, 1917, 1920 and 1921. He was also an accurate basketball set-shooter. His best sport was baseball. He might have been a big league pitcher except for a ligament injury to his right pitching arm. He had a 30 – 4 record as a TCU sophomore, and he played in the minors. In 1934 he replaced TCU coach Francis Schmidt, who shifted to Ohio State. He coached the Frogs for 19 years with a 109 – 79 – 13 record. He developed ten All-Americans; the best known were quarterbacks Sammy Baugh and Davey O'Brien and center Ki Aldrich. His nephew Lambert scored all the TCU Cotton Bowl points in 1937. In 1938 the club won the national championship, unbeaten in eleven games; they also won the Sugar Bowl. As TCU coach, his record was 105 – 77 – 13; he won three Southwest Conference championships—1938, 1944 and 1951—and played in seven bowl games: two Sugar, three Cotton, one Orange and one Delta.
Also in: College Football Hall of Fame, Citizens Savings Hall of Fame Athletic Museum; and National Football Hall of Fame.

MITCHELL, Gary
Athletic Director
Gary Mitchell was an athletic director at Western Michigan University.

MORRELL, Malcolm
Athletic Director
Malcolm Morrell was an athletic director at Bowdoin College.

NEYLAND, Robert R.
Athletic Director
Born February 17, 1892, in Greenville, Tex; atended Tex. A&M Univ. one year while awaiting an appointment to West Point; earned engineering degree from Mass. Inst. Technol; worked with Army Corps of Engineers much of his life and rose to the rank of Brig. Gen; Orange Bowl Classic Hall of Honor in 1970 and Univ. of Tenn. Hall of Fame Room; died March 28, 1962, in New Orleans, La.

1926 – 1940 University of Tennessee, coach
1946 – 1952 University of Tennessee, coach

As a cadet, Neyland was a 35 – 5 baseball pitcher as well as a football end, and a heavyweight boxing champion for three years. He turned down pro baseball offers from the New York Giants and Philadelphia Athletics, and instead posted a 173 – 31 – 12 (.829 percent) for fifth place on the all-time coaching list. He won or shared three Southeastern Conference titles. In one seven-season period, Neyland's teams had 56 – 1 – 5, and held opponents scoreless in 42 games. He took the Volunteers to all four major bowls, and fostered numerous coaches, such as Bobby Dodd, Murray Warmath and Bowden Wyatt. Knute Rockne considered Neyland football's greatest coach.
Also in: College Football Hall of Fame, Citizens Savings Hall of Fame Athletic Museum; and National Football Hall of Fame.

REED, William R.
Athletic Director
William Reed was an athletic director in the Big Ten Conference.

REID, Juan
Athletic Director
Juan Reid was an athletic director at Colorado College.

VERDUCCI, Joe
Athletic Director
Joe Verducci was an athletic director at San Francisco State.

WILSON, Kenneth L. "Tug"
Athletic Director
Wilson was an athletic director at Northwestern University.
Also in: United States Track and Field Hall of Fame.

1972

ARLANSON, Harry
Athletic Director
Harry Arlanson was an athletic director at Tufts University.

ASHFORD, Volney C.
Athletic Director
Ashford was an athletic director at Missouri Valley College.
Also in: National Association of Intercollegiate Athletics Hall of Fame.

BARNHILL, John H.
Athletic Director
Born February 21, 1903, in Savannah, Tenn; earned nine letters at Tenn. State Univ; Tennessee Athlete of the

Year two times; died October 21, 1973, in Fayetteville, Ark.

1941–1942 Tennessee State University, coach
1944–1945 Tennessee State University, coach
1946–1971 Arkansas State University, coach and athletic director

Barnhill played guard at Tennessee State from 1925 to 1927, with a record of 35–5–2. He also played in the 1927 All-Star game. He had a career record of 54–22–5, including four bowl games; his record at Tennessee State was 35–5–2.
Also in: National Association of Intercollegiate Athletics Hall of Fame.

BREHM, Henry T.
Athletic Director
Henry Brehm was an athletic director at Gettysburg College.

BUTLER, Lysle K.
Athletic Director
Butler was an athletic director at Oberlin College.

CARLSON, Harry G.
Athletic Director
Harry Carlson was an athletic director at the University of Colorado.

CHRISTIAN, J. Orlean
Christian was baseball coach at the University of Connecticut for 25 years, from 1937 to 1962.
Also in: American Association of College Baseball Coaches Hall of Fame; and College Baseball (Coaches) Hall of Fame, Citizens Savings Hall of Fame Athletic Museum.

COBEY, William W.
Athletic Director
William Cobey was an athletic director at the University of Maryland.

FORBES, Frank L.
Athletic Director
Frank Forbes was an athletic director at Morehouse College.

GARTEN, Al
Athletic Director
Al Garten was an athletic director at Eastern New Mexico University.
Also in: National Association of Intercollegiate Athletics Hall of Fame.

HANCOCK, John W.
Athletic Director
John was an athletic director at the University of Northern Colorado.

HURT, Edward P.
Athletic Director
Born February 12, 1900, in Brookneal, Pa; graduated from Howard Univ; master's degree from Columbia Univ.
While track coach and athletic director at Morgan State College 1929–1970, Eddie Hurt produced 8 individual National Collegiate Athletics Association (NCAA) and 12 Amateur Athletic Union (AAU) champions as well as three NCAA relay champions and six AAU relay championship efforts.
Also in: National Association of Intercollegiate Athletics Hall of Fame and National Track and Field Hall of Fame.

JOHNS, Wilbur C.
Athletic Director
Wilbur Johns was an athletic director at the University of California at Los Angeles.

KANE, Robert J.
Athletic Director
Robert Kane was an athletic director at Cornell University.

MORRISON, J. Ray
Athletic Director
In Ray's career as an athletic trainer, he was coach for Southern Methodist University 1915 and 1916 and 1922–1934. He then was coach for Vanderbilt University 1935–1939, for Temple University 1940–1948 and for Austin College 1949–1952.
Also in: College Football Hall of Fame, Citizens Savings Hall of Fame Athletic Museum; and National Football Hall of Fame.

MUNN, Clarence L. "Biggie"
Athletic Director
Born September 11, 1908, in Minneapolis, Minn; graduated from Univ. Minn. 1932; All-American guard 1931; Minn. Most Valuable Player 1930 and 1931; Coach of the Year 1932; *Sports Illustrated* Silver Anniversary All-American Award 1956; Minn. Outstanding Achievement Alumni Award 1957.

1932–1935 University of Minnesota, assistant coach
1936 Syracuse University, coach
1936–1937 Albright College, coach
1938–1945 Michigan State University, coach
1946 Syracuse University, coach
1947– Michigan State University, coach and athletic director

Munn's coaching record with the Spartans was 54–9; his 1951 and 1952 teams went unbeaten in the Conference.
Also in: College Football Hall of Fame, Citizens Savings Hall of Fame Athletic Museum; Michigan Sports Hall of Fame, Minnesota Sports Hall of Fame and National Football Hall of Fame.

PERKINS, Donald C.
Athletic Director
Donald Perkins was an athletic director at Chapman College.

ROMNEY, Ernest L. "Dick"
Athletic Director
Born February 12, 1895, in Salt Lake City, Utah; a four-sport standout at Utah; played on school's national championship Amateur Athletic Union basketball team

in 1916; died February 5, 1969, in Salt Lake City at age 74.

1919–1942 Utah State College, coach
1944–1948 Utah State College, coach

Romney was Utah State's first football coach, compiling a 132–91–16 record over a 30-year period. His teams won or shared four Conference titles, and his basketball teams won 225 games in 22 years. He was the commander for ten years of the Mountain States Conference, and served on both National Collegiate Athletic Association football and basketball rules committees. His brother, G. Ott Romney, was basketball coach at Montana State and Brigham Young.
Also in: College Football Hall of Fame, Citizens Savings Hall of Fame Athletic Museum; and National Football Hall of Fame.

SHIVELY, Bernie A.
Athletic Director
Born May 26, 1902, in Oliver Ill; graduated from Univ. Ill, received M.S. from Univ. Ky. 1935; All-American 1926; died December 10, 1967, in Lexington, Ky, at age 65.

1927–1967 University of Illinois, coach and athletic director
1958–1965 National Collegiate Athletic Association, basketball tournament committee chairman

Shively also participated in track in college (javelin, hammer-throw). He served as president of the Southeastern Conference of Athletic Directors and the president of the National Association of Athletic Directors.

SMITH, Claude M. "Tad"
Athletic Director
Tad Smith was an athletic director at the University of Mississippi.

SMITH, Clyde B.
Athletic Director
Clyde Smith served as an athletic director for Arizona State University.

SPONAUGLE, S. Woodrow
Athletic Director
Sponaugle was an athletic director at Franklin and Marshall College.

THOMAS, Frank R.
Athletic Director
Frank Thomas was an athletic director at Williams College.

WIDDOES, Carroll C.
Athletic Director
Widdoes was an athletic director at Ohio University.

1973

BRICKELS, John L.
Athletic Director
Born in Newark, Ohio; All-Ohio football player at Wittenburg College 1930; died in 1964.

Brickels began his career as coach of the New Philadelphia of Ohio High School, and later coached at Huntington, W. Va, High School. He coached West Virginia University to the National Invitational Tournament. In 1946, he was the chief scout and backfield coach for the Cleveland Browns. Brickels was the athletic director at Miami University of Ohio from 1950 through 1964.

BROWN, Robert N. "Red"
Athletic Director
Attended Elkins High; graduated from David and Elkins Col. 1930; married Mary Elizabeth Poling, who died in 1970; one son Robert; Coach of the Year 1952.

Brown was athletic director at West Virginia University for 17 years, beginning in 1954; his teams won 77 percent of their competitions while he was there. He began his career as a Mountaineer basketball coach, and was also a top tennis player and coach, as well as being on the U.S. Olympic committee.

CAMERON, Edmund McCullough
Athletic Director
Attended Culver Military Academy and Washington and Lee Univ.

Eddie Cameron was athletic director at Duke University. Cameron has been a player, coach and athletic director for 45 years, including a stint from 1929 to 1943 as basketball coach, with a 226–99 record. His basketball teams took three Southern Conference titles, and he coached the 1945 football team to a 29–26 victory over Alabama in the Sugar Bowl game.
Also in: National Football Hall of Fame.

CURTICE, Jack C. "Cactus Jack"
Athletic Director
Attended college in Transylvania, Ky; wife Margaret; two sons and a daughter; retired as Commander in the U.S. Army.

Curtice began his career at Stanford University as athletic director and also worked at the Universities of Utah and Texas, Texas Western College, West Texas State College and coached at a Kentucky high school in 1930. He became athletic director at the University of California, Santa Barbara, in 1963, where he is at the present time.
Also in: College Football Hall of Fame, Citizens Savings Hall of Fame Athletic Museum.

DEEDS, Cameron Scott "Scotty"
Athletic Director
Attended Univ. Ore, lettering in football and track and field; saw Navy service during W.W. II; played three years of football at Brigham Young Univ. and earned All-American honorable mention; married; four sons; for past 35 years trained ocean lifeguards during the summer months.

1951–1969 University of California at Los Angeles (UCLA), athletic director
1969– Pacific Coast Athletic Association, executive secretary, administrative assistant and director of officials

Deeds was UCLA's first football coach, coached swimming for five years, and coached tennis from 1958. Under his leadership the athletic program expanded from 4 to 13 varsity activities.

DUNN, C. Johnson
Athletic Director
Graduated from Monroe, Ga, public school, Morehouse Academy and Morehouse College.

1926 – 1930 Alabama State University, baseball coach
1935 – 1965 Alabama State University, basketball coach and athletic director

In addition to devoting his entire professional career to athletic service at Alabama State University (1925 – 1970), Dunn served as assistant professor and dean of students. He is a member of the National Association of Basketball Coaches and is a past president of the Southern Intercollegiate Athletic Conference.

DURLEY, Alexander
Athletic Director
Attended Texas Col; presently dir. of special promotion and mathematics professor at Prairie View A&M Univ.

1935 – 1949 Texas College, coach
1949 – 1964 Texas Southern University, athletic director and football coach
1964 – 1970 Prairie View A&M University, athletic director and coach

Alexander Durley, affectionately known as "Chops," began his career at his alma mater and led them to three championships. He went to Texas Southern in 1949, where his 10 – 0 – 1 football team won the 1951 black national championship. Durley organized the athletic department at Texas Southern into one of the best. He retired in 1964, but came out of retirement in 1970 to continue his career as an athletic director.

HENDERSON, R. E. "Bill"
Athletic Director
Earned 12 letters at Howard Payne Univ; captain of the football, baseball and basketball teams senior year; married Anna Gibson, who died in 1969 after 41 years of marriage; son and daughter both married.

An outstanding high school athlete, Henderson arrived in Waco in 1931. Five years later he took the basketball coaching job at Baylor University which he held for 18 seasons. His teams won four Southwestern Conference championships. He became athletic director at Baylor in 1968. He once served as president of the National Basketball Coaches Association.

HILL, Jesse T.
Athletic Director
Born in Yates, Mo; moved to Southern California as a child; excelled in five sports at Corona High; attended Riverside City Col. and University of Southern California (USC) where he starred in football, baseball and track; married Elizabeth Helen Glass; son and daughter, both USC graduates; Lt. Commander in Navy; retired.

Hill was athletic director for the USC Trojans for 15 years. He played ten years of pro baseball in the Yankee organization for the pro Hollywood Stars, hitting .306. He first coached track, and had undefeated squads who were the national champions in 1949 to 1950, and then football, finishing 45 – 17 for .722 for a six-year period.

HUFF, George A.
Athletic Director
Died October 1, 1936.

1895 – 1901 University of Illinois, trainer and football coach
1896 – 1919 University of Illinois, baseball coach
1901 – 1936 University of Illinois, athletic director

Huff was the University's first full-time baseball coach, and when he stepped down from that position in 1919, he had an impressive 307 – 132 – 6 record that included 11 championships. His influence far transcended coaching, however. Under his guidance academic credit was given the coaching curriculum in the physical education department; he led the way in building the athletic plant at Champaign, Ill, including the old Huff Gymnasium; during the campaign to raise $1.7 million for the new Memorial Stadium the school nickname "Fighting Illini" was born.

JACOBS, George W. "Doc"
Athletic Director
Graduated from Villanova Univ. 1927; graduate work at St. Michaels Col; married Alice Rapine; one daughter; died May 19, 1968, at age 68.

Jacobs was athletic director and coach at St. Michael's College in Winooski, Vt, and his 1952 grid team was undefeated. His basketball teams won five New England championships and nine state titles, and his baseball and golf teams also won state crowns. He was himself a pro athlete in basketball, baseball and football. Jacobs developed a number of pro athletes and managed baseball teams in the minor leagues. He was a coach for 18 years at Villanova and St. Michaels, with a career record of 276 – 131.
Also in: College Basketball Hall of Fame, Citizens Savings Hall of Fame Athletic Museum.

JACOBY, Glenn J. "Red"
Athletic Director
Born 1907; earned nine letters in football, basketball and track and field at Univ. Idaho; married Dorothy Fredrickson; two sons; died March 6, 1972.

Glenn shaped the athletic rebirth at the University of Wyoming as athletic director 1945 – 1972. His accomplishments were many. He returned the school to days of glory in basketball, skiing and wrestling by hiring a series of highly successful coaches. The Memorial Fieldhouse and the Memorial Stadium were built during his tenure.

JONES, Gomer
Athletic Director
Played football at Cleveland South High School, and was All-Big Ten Center at Ohio State Univ; married Jennette Nichols; died March 21, 1971.

Jones was athletic director at Oklahoma from 1947 until his death in 1971. He began his career as coach at Nebraska, and also coached at Ohio State, Martin's Ferry High School and John Carroll University. Gomer Jones was the author of two books about defensive football and offensive and defensive line play.

KOENIG, Richard P.
Athletic Director
Military service in U.S. Army in W.W. II; four children; now vice president of public and alumni affairs at Valparaiso Univ.

Koenig has been athletic director or coach at Valparaiso University since 1942, except for time out during the war. His teams won or shared 15 conference championships. Dick Koenig was vice-president-at-large for the National Collegiate Athletic Association.

LAVIK, Rudolf Halbert "Rudy"
Athletic Director
Attended Concordia Col. and Springfield Col; lettered in three sports; married Ethel Charlotte Larsen; one daughter; military service in W.W. II.

Lavik was the athletic director at Arizona State University 1933 – 1973. He began his career at Concordia as a coach, and then coached at Colorado College, Colorado Agricultural College, and Arizona State College at Flagstaff. He has written a number of publications.

LOVELESS, James C.
Athletic Director
Attended DePauw Univ; M.A. from Columbia Univ, Ph.D. from Univ. Ind; military service in Navy in W.W. II.

Loveless was athletic director and physical education professor at DePauw for 18 years, until 1972. During his career, he was a high school and college basketball and football coach for a total of 25 years. He served as Vice President-at-large and a member of the council and the executive committee of the National Collegiate Athletic Association. He was the facilities and program consultant for the Asia Foundation.

McGUIRK, Warren P.
Athletic Director
Born in Dorchester, Mass; excelled in three sports at Dorchester High School; attended St. Anselms Prep and Boston Col; tackle on football team that was unbeaten for two years; wife Virginia; Commander in Navy in W.W. II; retired January 2, 1972.

McGuirk was the athletic director and dean of physical education at the University of Massachusetts for 23 years. He also served as Eastern Collegiate Athletic Conference president and was on the National College Athletic Association (NCAA) for three years. He had other NCAA, Amateur Athletic Union and U.S. Olympic committee posts. He played pro football in Providence, R.I, and coached at Malden High School for nine years.

McLAUGHLIN, Walter T. "Mr. Mac"
Athletic Director
Graduated from St. Johns Univ. 1928; wife Anne; three children; U.S. Navy physical education officer during W.W. II; retired in June 1972.

McLaughlin was an athletic director at St. Johns University. He chaired or served on all the key Eastern Collegiate Athletic Association and Eastern College Athletic Conference committees.

SWENSON, Reed K.
Athletic Director
Swenson was an athletic director at Weber State College for 35 years before he retired in 1968. However, he has continued to teach in the physical education department where he served as head of the department until 1937. Swenson has acquired a national reputation as an outstanding figure in sports, both as athletic director and coach, educator and administrator. He served as president of the National Junior College Athletic Association for 13 years. He coached the junior college cagers from 1933 to 1957, winning 7 league championships. He was instrumental in the formation of the Big Sky Conference.

TWITCHELL, Albert W.
Athletic Director
See entry in Lacrosse Hall of Fame and Museum, 1967.

WEAVER, James
Athletic Director
James Weaver served as an athletic director at Wake Forest University.

WEBER, Mox A.
Athletic Director
Born in Cleveland, Ohio; attended Oberlin Col; excelled in football, basketball and baseball; married Sally Taylor; All-Ohio on the gridiron for two years.

Weber has been athletic director at Hamilton College from 1927 until the present. Since 1928, his tennis teams are 188 – 60 – 9. He has served on seven different National Collegiate Athletic Association committees and the Eastern Collegiate Athletic Conference executive council.

WIEMAN, Elton E. "Tad"
Athletic Director
Born in 1896 in California; attended Univ. Mich, earned four football letters, captain of the team; military service in W.W. II; died December 26, 1971, in Portland, Ore.

1951 – 1962 Univ. of Denver, athletic director

Wieman began his career at the University of Michigan in 1929, and coached at Minnesota and Princeton (1932), the first coach to guide the teams to four straight victories over Yale. He was the athletic director at the University of Maine until 1950 and at the University of Denver 1951 – 1962. He was at one time president of the American Football Coaches Association and a director of the National Football Foundation.
Also in: National Football Hall of Fame.

WILKINSON, Charles B. "Bud"
Athletic Director
Attended Shattuck Military Academy; graduated from Univ. Minn; guard, quarterback and blocking back; and quarterbacked college All-Star team to 7 – 0 victory over Green Bay Packers; married Mary Shifflett; two sons; served in the Navy during W.W. II.

1947 – 1963 Univ. of Oklahoma, head coach

Synonymous with excellence in college football are what Bud Wilkinson and the University of Oklahoma are. Truly one of the greatest coaches of all time, Bud's Oklahoma teams won a record 47 straight games from 1953 to 1957. After he resigned in 1963, he ran for U.S. Senator

but lost in the national elections. He serves as a special consultant to the President.
Also in: College Football Hall of Fame, Citizens Savings Hall of Fame Athletic Museum; and National Football Hall of Fame.

WITHAM, Dr. James H. "Jim"
Athletic Director
Graduated from Bemidji State Col, received an M.Ed. degree from Univ. Minn. and a Ph.D. degree from Univ. Ind.

After coaching and teaching physical education at Mankato State University, Witham arrived at the University of Northern Illinois in 1956. There he coached basketball until 1960, and served as athletic director from 1960 through 1970. Among his achievements during that decade were the initiations of swimming and gymnastics programs. Dr. Witham is a respected staff member of the health department at Mankato State University.

1974

AILLET, Joe
Athletic Director
Joe Aillet was an athletic director for Louisiana Tech University.
Also in: National Association of Intercollegiate Athletics Hall of Fame.

ALLARD, Gerald
Athletic Director
Gerald Allard was an athletic director for the State University of New York Agricultural and Technical College at Farmingdale.

ALLEN, Dr. Forrest Clare "Phog"
Athletic Director
See entry in Naismith Memorial Basketball Hall of Fame, 1959.
Also in: College Basketball Hall of Fame, Citizens Savings Hall of Fame Athletic Museum.

BEARD, Garland W.
Athletic Director
Garland Beard served as an athletic director for Auburn University.

BERGSTROM, Arthur J.
Athletic Director
Arthur Bergstrom was an athletic director for Bradley University.

BERNLOHR, William F.
Athletic Director
William Bernlohr served as an athletic director at Capital University.

CARVER, Frank
Athletic Director
Frank Carver was an athletic director at the University of Pittsburgh.

COLE, George R.
Athletic Director
The University of Arkansas had a great athletic director in George Cole.

DECKER, James H.
Athletic Director
James Decker was an athletic director for Syracuse University.

EDWARDS, Bill
Athletic Director
Bill Edwards served as an athletic director for Wittenberg University.

GOWDER, Robert
Athletic Director
Robert Gowder served as an athletic director for Ventura College.

GROVER, Brandon T.
Athletic Director
Brandon Grover was an athletic director at Ohio University.

HAWLEY, Roy M.
Athletic Director
Roy Hawley was an athletic director at West Virginia University.
Also in: West Virginia Sports Writers Hall of Fame.

HOY, George D.
Athletic Director
George Hoy served as an athletic director for Phoenix College.

LEE, H. B.
Athletic Director
Lee was an athletic director for Kansas State University.

LOCKHART, A. J.
Athletic Director
Morris Brown College had a great athletic director in A. J. Lockhart.

McDAVID, Pete
Athletic Director
Pete McDavid served as an athletic director at the University of New Mexico.

McKALE, James Fritz "Pop"
Athletic Director
Pop McKale coached the University of Arizona baseball teams for 35 years, from 1911 through 1948. His teams recorded 318 victories and 124 losses. The Arizona Wildcats gained 14 consecutive Border Conference crowns. McKale served as president of the American Association of Baseball Coaches in 1950 and was athletic director at the University of Arizona.
Also in: American Association of College Baseball Coaches Hall of Fame; and College Baseball (Coaches) Hall of Fame, Citizens Savings Hall of Fame Athletic Museum.

MURRAY, William D.
Athletic Director
Born September 9, 1908, in Rocky Mount, N.C; graduated from Duke Univ; All-Southern Conference Most Valuable Player; Robert E. Lee Award 1931; Amos Alonzo Staff Award for coaching.

1936–1950 University of Delaware, coach
1951–1965 Duke University, coach

Murray was a halfback at Duke, and was president of the student body in 1931. His coaching record at Delaware was 51–17–3, and at Duke, 93–51–9. Highlights were Orange Bowl and Sugar Bowl wins, and seven Conference championships. Eight of the last 13 Duke teams finished in the top 20 in wire service polls.
Also in: College Football Hall of Fame, Citizens Savings Hall of Fame Athletic Museum; and National Football Hall of Fame.

SARBOE, Phil
Athletic Director
Phil Sarboe served as an athletic director for Humboldt State University.

SESHER, Charles
Athletic Director
Charles Sesher was an athletic director at Hutchison Community Junior College.

SHIRK, Eugene L.
Athletic Director
Eugene Shirk served as an athletic director at Albright College.

STAHLEY, J. Neil
Athletic Director
Stahley was an athletic director for Portland State University.

STOUT, R. Victor
Athletic Director
Victor Stout served as an athletic director for Boston University.

WELCH, Fran
Athletic Director
Fran Welch was an athletic director at Emporia Kansas State College.
Also in: National Association of Intercollegiate Athletics Hall of Fame.

WILSON, Wendell S.
Athletic Director
Wendell Wilson was an athletic director for the University of Illinois.

1975

BATES, Stan
Athletic Director
Earned ten letters in football, basketball and track at the University Puget Sound in the early 1930s, and was one of the finest all-around athletes in the history of the school.

Bates was a high school coach for 19 years before becoming athletic director for Washington State University in 1954, a post he held for 17 years. He was at one time president of the Washington State High School Principal's Association and the State Coaches' Association. He was later president of the Pacific-8 Athletic Directors Association, secretary of the Pac-8 Conference council, and a member of the National Collegiate Athletic Association Olympic Games committee. He served on special events and executive committees of the NCAA. He left Washington State in 1971 to become commissioner of the Western Athletic Conference, a position he now holds.

BISHOP, Gil
Athletic Director
Football and baseball star for the San Jose State Col. Diamondmen, captain his senior year; military service in the Navy.

1936–1938 San Jose State University, graduate manager of athletics, head football coach and assistant in basketball
1939–1942 Placer (now Sierra) Junior College, assistant director of athletics
1942 East Bakersfield High School, athletic director
1945–1953 East Bakersfield High School, athletic director
1953–1968 Bakersfield College, athletic director

Gil helped establish the California Junior College Basketball Coaches Association, was president of the California Junior College Athletic Committee and served on the Junior College Track and Field Records Committee.

BRONZAN, Robert T.
Athletic Director
Tackle for the San Jose State Col. Spartans from 1937 to 1939.

Bronzan began his career as an athletic director for Livingston High School before joining the U.S. Air Corps for three years. He became the athletic director for San Jose State University in 1946, a job he held until 1971, when he stepped down to become a consultant in planning and funding of athletic facilities. He was president of the National Association of Collegiate Athletic Directors from 1967 to 1968, and was active in the National Collegiate Athletic Association chairing a committee for the advancement of intercollegiate football, the football centennial coordinating committee and the NCAA committee stints involving baseball legislation and football rules. He is also a member of the executive committee of the U.S. Track and Field Federation.

BUTE, Earl "Skip"
Athletic Director
Attended N. Dak. State Univ; North Dakota Coach of the Year 1962; Small College Coach of the Year 1965; retired in 1966.

Bute was a coach of all sports at the North Dakota School of Science (NDSS) as well as athletic director and math instructor 1924–1966. After one year he led his grid team to its first conference title, the first of eight such crowns. In 1948 he gave up his basketball duties, but only after his cagers had an undefeated season and had won four Conference championships. His record was 141 – 100 – 18 for 42 seasons as football coach. The North Dakota State Board of Higher Education has designated the NDSS athletic building as Bute Gymnasium, an honor only fitting to such a great athletic director.

CASANOVA, Len
Athletic Director
Attended Univ. Calif. at Santa Clara; military service in W.W. II; retired in 1970.

Casanova began his coaching career with seven years of high school football, and then coached at his alma mater. Between 1946 and 1950 he coached at Santa Clara again, and his teams posted 21 – 14 – 3, topped with a 21 – 13 win over Kentucky in the 1948 Orange Bowl. He coached one year at the University of Pittsburgh before settling at the University of Oregon in 1951, serving 16 years as athletic director. The Ducs were 83 – 72 – 9, losing the 1957 Rose Bowl and the 1960 Liberty Bowl and winning the 1963 Sun Bowl. Casanova was president of the American Football Coaches Association and coached in the 1955, 1956, 1959 and 1965 East-West Shrine games and the 1963 Hula Bowl.
Also in: College Football Hall of Fame, Citizens Savings Hall of Fame Athletic Museum; and National Football Hall of Fame.

DAVIS, Robert L.
Athletic Director
Earned 14 letters at Salt Lake City East High School; graduated from Univ. Utah 1930, a quarterback and captain of the football team; Coach of the Year 1948 and 1955; died in 1965.

Davis was athletic director at Colorado State University (CSU) from 1947 to 1953, and had a 54 – 33 – 2 record. He had a 34 – 20 – 0 record against the Mountain States (Skyline) Conference teams with a league championship in 1955 and three runnerup teams. He coached CSU to the Raisin Bowl in Fresno, Calif. in 1948. Davis began his career at Salt Lake City South High as a coach in 1930, and later coached at Weber State College, the University of Utah and the University of Denver. He worked on many National Collegiate Athletic Association committees, was a member of the American Olympic selection committee, and served on the honors court of the National Hall of Fame.

HOLCOMB, Stuart K.
Athletic Director
Attended Ohio State University; captain of the football team and member of the cage squad; military service in W.W. II.

1932 – 1936	Findlay College (Ohio), coach and athletic director
1936 – 1940	Muskingam College, coach
1941	Washington and Jefferson College, coach
1942	Miami University (Ohio), head coach
1952 – 1955	Purdue University Boilermakers, coach
1956 – 1966	Northwestern University Wildcats, athletic director

Holcomb led the Muskies to an Ohio Conference championship in 1939, and Washington and Jefferson to a district grid title. He was assistant coach at West Point for two years, and led the Boilermakers in 1952 to a tie for the Big Ten title. He is now vice president of the Chicago White Sox.
Also in: College Football Hall of Fame, Citizens Savings Hall of Fame Athletic Museum.

LIVINGSTON, Walter J.
Athletic Director
Walter Livingston was athletic director at Dennison University from 1911 until 1952.

His teams won two Ohio Conference championships for football while he was at Denison, and five Conference titles and a Buckeye Athletic Association crown in basketball, as well as two Conference track championships. He was the president of the Ohio Conference for two terms, of the Buckeye Athletic Association and of the Ohio Physical Education Association.

LUX, Lloyd H.
Athletic Director
Retired in 1974; Lt. Commander in the U.S. Naval Reserve.

Lux was an athletic director at Bates College for 25 years. During that time, he was the president of the New England Small College Athletic Conference and of the Maine Intercollegiate Athletic Association. He was also a member of the honors and awards committee of the National Association of Collegiate Directors of Athletics (NACDA), and a member of NACDA's first executive committee. A member of the NCAA long range planning committee, he chaired the task force on intercollegiate athletics. He coached at Nether Providence High School in Wallingford, Pa, Wilbraham Academy in Massachusetts, Moorestown High School in New Jersey, and West Chester State College. He was also assistant director of intramurals at Columbia.

MACKEY, Guy "Red"
Athletic Director
Graduated from Purdue Univ. 1929; All-American gridder; died in 1971.

Mackey built the athletic program at Purdue University into one of the nation's finest. He was their athletic director 1942 – 1971. He stimulated the business and plant improvements of the athletic department to the point that Purdue's is rated the top intercollegiate program in the nation. Mackey headed the construction of Purdue's $6 million basketball arena and of the Rose-Ade Stadium. He was the dean of the Big Ten athletic directors, and served on numerous conferences and National Collegiate Athletic Association committees.

MERRIMAN, John S.
Athletic Director
Retired from the Coast Guard in 1957 as Commander.

Merriman served as athletic director at the U.S. Coast Guard Academy 1929 – 1946. His record with the Coast Guard was 45 – 67 – 8; his 1941 team lost only two one-point games to Trinity and Wesleyan, while his 1931 and 1932 teams pinned back-to-back losses on the Rhode Island State Rams of Frank Keaney. Merriman was the New England representative to the National College Boxing Association rules committee, and was on the U.S. Olympic Boxing Committee in 1948. He was president of the New England Colleges Conference on Athletics, and served on several committees as well as the board of directors of the Eastern Collegiate Athletic Conference.

ORWIG, J. W. "Bill"
Athletic Director

Born in Cleveland; a three-sport star at Toledo Scott High School; lettered in football as an end at Univ. Mich; guard in basketball; graduated in 1930; All-Big Ten in basketball; retired in 1975.

1930 – 1935 Benton Harbor, Mich, High School, coach
1936 – 1944 Toledo's Libbey High School, coach
1945 Athletic consultant for army of occupation in Europe
1946 – 1947 University of Toledo, coach
1948 – 1953 University of Michigan, coach
1954 – 1961 University of Nebraska, coach
1961 – 1975 Indiana University, coach

Orwig led his teams at Libbey High to three undefeated seasons, and his Toledo teams scored 15 – 4 – 2 in football. His Indiana teams won 32 Big Ten championships in seven sports plus six National Collegiate Athletic Association crowns, including at least one title every year.

SHELDEN, J. Paul
Athletic Director

Shelden was athletic director at Dodge City Community College for 21 years. He began his career as a high school basketball coach. After ten years he became a school administrator and held that position for the next seven years. He served as regional director representing Region VI in the National Junior College Athletic Association (NJCAA). He was director of the NJCAA service bureau from 1960 to 1969, and served on the executive committee of the NJCAA, the NJCAA track and field rules committee and was a member of the track and field committee for the 1968 Olympics. He was a member of the Jayhawk Juco Conference athletic committee for several terms, and served as secretary-treasurer from 1968 to 1974.

STEELE, Harold O.
Athletic Director

Attended Sioux City, Iowa, High School; All-Star Gridder; played on Univ. Mich. football team that lost only two games 1922 – 1924; retired in 1965.

Steele was the Grand Rapids Junior College athletic director from 1937 until his retirement in 1965. A highlight of his career occurred in 1956, when Grand Rapids was selected to play Coffeyville, Kans, for the National Junior College grid title in Los Angeles.

TURNER, Marshall S, Jr.
Athletic Director

Graduated from Sewanee Military Academy; Phi Beta Kappa at Univ. of the South; currently coaching at Johns Hopkins Univ.

Turner has been coach and athletic director at Johns Hopkins since 1946. He was a member of the executive committee and president of the National Association of Collegiate Directors of Athletics 1968 – 1969. In the National Collegiate Athletic Association, he served as chairman of the college committee, council member and a member of the executive committee. He was secretary-treasurer of the Middle-Atlantic States Collegiate Athletic Conference and two-term president of the Mason-Dixon Intercollegiate Conference. He was also president and a member of the executive committee of the U.S. Intercollegiate Lacrosse Association.

VERDELL, Thomas
Athletic Director

Born in Montgomery, Ala; attended Englewood High School in Chicago, Ill; graduated from Northwestern Univ. 1929; football star; All-Big Ten senior year; retired in 1973.

1929 – 1933 Howard University, coach
1934 – 1973 Virginia State College, athletic director

Verdell's 1933 grid team at Howard was the first to participate in the Orange Blossom classic. He was the acting head of the department of health, physical education and recreation at Virginia until 1950, when he was named head of the department. When Verdell retired, he had been interim athletic director for two years.

1976

BELL, William M.
Athletic Director

Born in Polk County, Ga; first black to make the Ohio State University football squad; All-Big Ten and All-American 1932; Washington, D.C, Pigskin Club Outstanding Coach Award 1951; National Junior Chamber of Commerce Physical Fitness Award 1965.

1934 – 1936 Claflin University, head football coach and athletic director
1936 – 1946 Florida A&M University, football coach, athletic director and physical education department chairman
1946 – 1957 North Carolina A&T College, head football coach, athletic director and director of physical education
1957 – Fayetteville State University, athletic director

In addition to his coaching and administrative duties on various campuses, Bell served as the assistant director of physical training and head football coach at Tuskegee Army Air Field during W.W. II, for which services he received the commission of Second Lieutenant.

CHACHIS, Chris G.
Athletic Director

Born in Thessaloniki, Greece; first came to the United States at age 16; attended Mount Herman School in Mass, Temple Univ. and Crozer Theological Seminary; military service in Greece; received B.S. from Springfield Col. 1939, M.A. from Columbia Univ. 1942; military service in W.W. II.

Chris was an instructor for the YMCA while attending school. He became an assistant professor of physical education for the Associated College of Upper New York after the war. He served there until Orange County Community College hired him as their athletic director and director of physical education. He gave up his duties as athletic director to take the title of chairman of physical education and recreation. He now is serving as a professor for that department.

DOUGLAS, Merrill G.
Athletic Director
Graduated from San Diego State Col. 1931.

1931 – 1938 National City, Calif, supervisor of physical education in elementary schools
1938 – 1940 San Diego High School, assistant basketball coach
1940 – 1956 San Diego High School, varsity basketball coach
1956 – 1960 San Diego City College, head basketball coach, athletic director and physical education department chairman
1960 – 1963 San Diego City College, athletic director and physical education department chairman
1963 – 1973 San Diego Mesa College, athletic director

Douglas's career of 42 years of service to the public schools of California was marked by outstanding influence and success. While at San Diego High School, his record was 236 – 76.

DUER, A.O. "Al"
Athletic Director
Upon taking over in 1939 as athletic director and head basketball coach at Pepperdine University only a year and a half after the school opened, Duer began a 36-year long association with intercollegiate athletics that was to have profound effects upon both the schools he served and the people he led. In addition to his administrative duties, he founded the Los Angeles Invitational tournament. As a basketball coach he had a 176 – 94 record for nine years. He served as president of the National Association of Intercollegiate Basketball, a forerunner of the National Association of Intercollegiate Athletics (NAIA), in 1947. In 1949 he resigned at Pepperdine to become executive director of the NAIA, a post he held until his retirement in 1975. Duer is currently third vice president of the U.S. Olympic committee.
Also in: National Association of Intercollegiate Athletics Hall of Fame.

DYE, Tippy
Athletic Director
Dye's 16 years of service to three major universities was marked by unique success and profound revitalization. Following his graduation from Ohio State University, he served as player-coach of the Cincinnati Bengals for two years. In 1943 he became head coach of the Buckeye cagers, and his first team won the Big Ten title. At the University of Nebraska, where he was athletic director for five years, he had similar successes in the intercollegiate programs in basketball and football. From 1967 through 1975 he was equally influential on the athletic scene at Northwestern University.

GAITHER, Alonzo S. "Jake"
Athletic Director
Born in Dayton, Tenn; received B.S. from Knoxville Col. 1927 and M.S. from Ohio State Univ. 1937; spent his boyhood around courthouses listening to lawyers plead cases; father wanted him to be a minister, but the death of his father forced him to begin work, and he coached and taught; Alonzo Stagg Award and Walter Camp Award.

1937 – 1945 Florida A&M College, assistant coach
1945 – 1969 Florida A&M College, head coach and athletic director

Gaither played end for the Knoxville Bulldogs. As a coach, he guided his teams to six national black championships, with a 203 – 36 – 4 record. He won the Southern Intercollegiate Athletic Conference title every year except 1951, 1952 and 1966. He produced at least one Little All-American every year except 1949; Willie Galimore made the list three times. Gaither developed Bob Hayes, Major Hazelton, Ken Riley, Roger Finnie, Al Denson, Hewitt Dixon and Carleton Oates. He wrote *The Split Line T Offense of Florida A&M University* in 1963. He was active in the Fellowship of Christian Athletes.
Also in: National Association of Intercollegiate Athletics Hall of Fame and National Football Hall of Fame.

GRUBBS, Howard
Athletic Director
Quarterbacked Texas Christian Univ. to Southwest Conference title senior year; graduated 1930 with training as geologist.

1931 – 1932 Texas Christian University, freshman football team coach
1932 – 1935 Lufkin High School, head football coach
1935 – 1936 Texas Christian University, head baseball coach
1936 – 1950 Texas Christian University, athletic director and football assistant coach
1950 – 1973 Southwest Conference, executive secretary

Grubbs' 22-year tenure as executive secretary of the Southwest Conference was longer than the combined tenure of the administrative heads of the nation's ten other major collegiate conferences at the time of his retirement in 1973.

HANCOCK, Howard J.
Athletic Director
Graduated from Univ. Wis. 1918.

1921 – 1931 Wisconsin State Teachers College, Oshkosh, director of physical education and athletics
1931 – 1963 Illinois State University, athletic director

After an impressive record of achievements on and off the field at Illinois State, Hancock retired in 1948 from coaching to devote his entire energies to his responsibilities as athletic director. His total of 41 years service as an athletic director is one of the longest tenures in the profession in the nation.
Also in: National Association of Intercollegiate Athletics Hall of Fame.

HOLE, E.M. "Mose"
Athletic Director
Hole has several claims to fame. Most remarkable, perhaps, is the fact that he devoted fully half a century to the service of a single institution, the College of Wooster—he entered that institution as a freshman in 1914, and retired after his golden anniversary in 1964. Equally remarkable, however, is the record of his accomplishments while at Wooster—a .695 won-lost percentage over 32 years as a basketball coach (in only three seasons did his teams fail to reach the .500 mark), a 36 consecutive

game winning streak, and a profound and lasting influence on the school's entire athletic program.

LITTLE, George E.
Athletic Director
Attended secondary school in Picture Rocks, Pa; graduated from Ohio Wesleyan Univ; military service in W.W. I.

1919–1922 Miami of Ohio, coach
1922–1924 University of Michigan, assistant athletic director
1924–1926 University of Wisconsin, director of physical education and head football coach
1926–1931 University of Wisconsin, administrator
1931–1952 Rutgers University, athletic director

Little opened many doors in the development of sports at Rutgers during his 21-year tenure. He has been a promoter of athletics for 40 years and played a major role in the acquisition of Rutgers Stadium. Little also served as a coach at Ohio Wesleyan University.
Also in: National Football Hall of Fame.

LOSEY, L. E.
Athletic Director
Although Losey's career as an athletic director at Independence Community Junior College spanned a relatively brief 19 years, his overall career as an educator and physical education administrator encompassed a remarkable half century. After graduating from Kansas State Teachers College at Emporia and completing his graduate work at the University of Wisconsin, he entered the administrative field in 1913 as director of physical education for the elementary schools in Independence, Kans. From 1923 to 1933 he served as director of physical education for all of the city's public schools. From 1933 until his retirement in 1952 he had the dual appointment of director of physical education for the high school and athletic director for Independence Community Junior College. In addition to these achievements, he was noted for his development of tumbling teams and for his work with the handicapped.

MARTI, Leonard R.
Athletic Director
Marti's career as a director of athletics, which continues today, was preceded by a varied and innovative career as an educator and administrator.

1934–1939 Minnesota State Training School for Boys, director of health, physical education and recreation
1939–1940 Bismarck City Schools, director of physical education
1940–1942 National Youth Administration State Health Program, North Dakota State Supervisor
1942–1947 Bismarck Junior High School, principal
1947–1958 University of North Dakota, head of men's physical education
1958– University of North Dakota, director of athletics and physical education

Marti's considerable experience and leadership continue to exert a positive influence on the athletic and educational programs at the University of North Dakota.

PERRY, Doyt L.
Born in Croton, Ohio; attended Bowling Green State Col; retired in 1973.

1951 Ohio State University, coach
1955–1971 Bowling Green, coach
1971–1973 Miami International University, coach and assistant athletic director

Perry spent 18 years coaching sports in Ohio high schools. As a college coach, he tutored All-American backs Vic Janowicz and Hopalong Cassady. His record at Bowling Green was 77–10–5, and he sent Bob Reynolds, Bernie Casey and James Rivers to the pro ranks. Bo Schembechler, the Michigan coach, was his first assistant at Bowling Green.

PYLES, Rex E.
Athletic Director
Born in West Virginia; earned All-State honors in basketball, football and baseball at Shinnston High School; graduated from Glenville State Col, Masters from W.Va. State Col; later studied at Northwestern Univ. and Mich. State Univ; NAIA Coach of the Year 1961.

Pyles' retirement in 1975 from Alderson-Broaddus College closed a truly remarkable career—40 years as athletic director and 30 years as head basketball coach. His teams won 406 victories, five West Virginia Intercollegiate Athletic Conference championships and five tournament titles. In 1961 he became the first West Virginian to be named coach of the year by the National Association of Intercollegiate Athletics.
Also in: National Association of Intercollegiate Athletics Hall of Fame and West Virginia Sports Writers Hall of Fame.

ROLFE, Robert A. "Red"
Athletic Director
An outstanding athletic performer at Penacook High School and at Phillips Exeter Academy, Rolfe played shortstop for Dartmouth College with such success that upon his graduation in 1931 he was signed by the New York Yankees. Until 1940 he played with the Yankees, during which time New York won six pennants and five World Series. Connie Mack, the famous manager, called Rolfe "the greatest team player in the game." He retired from the team in 1942 with a .289 lifetime batting average. The Yankees, however, hired him as a minor league coach in 1946, and in 1948 he became director of the Detroit Tigers' farm system. From 1949 to to 1952 he was closely associated with the Detroit team. Then from 1954 until 1967 Rolfe served as athletic director at Dartmouth. He died in 1969.

1977

BRENNECKE, Fritz
Athletic Director
Fritz Brennecke was a football and baseball player in high school and at Colorado State College. He coached for eight years at the high school level, interrupted by W.W. II. After coaching Denver South High School to the city championship in 1946, he joined the Colorado School of Mines, where he served as head football coach, athletic director, professor of physical education and

department chairman. Fritz retired from coaching in 1958 and from the athletic directorship in 1976, but is still active in the American Football Coaches Association as well as NACDA. During his 22 seasons as football coach, his teams posted an 83 – 127 – 8 record, claimed two Rocky Mountain Conference titles, and finished second in four other seasons. Brennecke was named Rocky Mountain Region Coach of the Year in 1958.

BROWN, Tay

Athletic Director

Tay Brown was an All-American tackle at the University of Southern California 1930 – 1932. His first position was assistant football coach and head basketball coach at the University of Cincinnati. In 1937 he became head coach at Compton Community College, leaving to serve in W.W. II and the Korean War. In 1961 at the end of 17 years of coaching football at Compton, he had a 142 – 32 – 9 record and had won 13 conference and four national titles. Tay Brown served as athletic director from 1962 until his retirement in 1972.

BUSEY, David G.

Athletic Director

David Busey coached high school ball in Urbana after graduating from the University of Illinois, returning there in 1941. During W.W. II he served in the Navy and at the Academy as a coach. In 1954 Busey became athletic director and head football coach at Lycoming College, retiring from coaching in 1966 and from his athletic directorship in 1976. In addition to his coaching and directing duties, he served on various committees for national sports organizations.

CHROUSER, Harvey C.

Athletic Director

After graduating from Wheaton College, Harvey Chrouser served for a time as athletic director and head coach of three sports at Sterling College, before returning to Wheaton as head football coach in 1940. During his 17 years at Wheaton—interrupted briefly by Navy duty in W.W. II—he built a record of 100 – 23 – 5, and his 1958 squad ranked seventh in the nation. During this time, Chrouser also served on various committees for the NCAA, and was one of the organizers of the College Conference of Illinois.

Also in: College Football Hall of Fame, Citizens Savings Hall of Fame Athletic Museum.

GALLAGHER, Herbert

Athletic Director

Herbert Gallagher was one of the first players to earn varsity letters in three sports at Northeastern University. In 1935 after graduation, he played pro ball in the Provincial Baseball League in Canada and the National Hockey League of England, and in 1936 coached the Austrian team in the winter Olympics. In 1937 Gallagher became professor of physical education and hockey coach, and later baseball coach at Northeastern, where he stayed for 21 years with a brief interruption for service in the Navy in W.W. II. In 1955 he became athletic director and served as such until 1976.

GENTRY, Howard C.

Athletic Director

Howard Gentry graduated from Florida A&M University in 1942 where he was All-American. After serving in Europe in W.W. II, he became assistant coach at North Carolina A & T in 1946. He was a line coach at Central State in Ohio and then joined Tennessee State. In 1956 he became head coach, and that year Tennessee State was Mid-Western Athletic Association and national champs. From 1956 through 1960 Gentry had a 42 – 10 – 1 coaching record and his team had a 22-game winning streak. He became athletic director in 1961 and retired in 1976, during which time he served as professor of physical education and also on several NCAA committees.

HAAS, Walter L.

Athletic Director

Walter Haas served as athletic director at the University of Chicago from 1956 until his retirement in 1976, during which time he reinstated football and upgraded the entire athletic program. He had coached football and track at Carleton College, becoming their athletic director in 1942. After serving in the Navy, he coached many successful teams at Carleton before joining the staff at Chicago.

JACK, James R. "Bud"

Athletic Director

Bud Jack spent 28 years at the University of Utah involved in intercollegiate athletics. He became athletic director in 1958 and stayed with it until 1976 when he became vice president for athletic development. He has served in several capacities in sports organizations, helping to found the Western Athletic Conference.

KEEFE, Eugene F.

Athletic Director

Eugene Keefe has spent 29 years in the athletic department at Westchester Community College, assuming the duties of athletic director in 1948, after serving in the Navy during the war. He was basketball coach 1948 – 1964, golf coach 1949 – 1974 and track coach 1950 – 1958, and has been cross-country coach since 1950. He is professor and chairman of the physical education department and guided the development of the school's physical education and pool complex. Keefe has also served on the NJCAA and the Mid-Hudson Conference.

KIPHUTH, Delaney

Athletic Director

Kiphuth played guard on the Yale Varsity and was athletic director and head football and swimming coach at Hotchkiss School in Connecticut before joining the Air Force in W.W. II. In 1954 he was appointed Yale's athletic director from which position he retired in 1976 to become special assistant to the president. In 1974 he was named to the Sports Illustrated Silver Anniversary All-American Team.

LAWLOR, Glenn "Jake"

Athletic Director

Jake Lawlor returned to his alma mater to serve as coach and athletic director for over 30 years. He joined the University of Nevada – Reno staff in 1942 as assistant football coach and head basketball coach, compiling a 207 – 171 basketball record until 1959, when he stepped down from coaching. Jake retired in 1972 after guiding Nevada to a first division status with the NCAA.

SCOTT, Tom
Athletic Director
Tom Scott taught and coached at the high school level for six years before becoming athletic director at Concordia College in Minnesota in 1936. In 1938 he was named basketball coach at Central Missouri State, and became athletic director also when he returned from service in the Navy. From 1946 through 1950 Scott served as head basketball coach at the University of North Carolina, then was named athletic director at Davidson College in 1954. While there, Davidson's athletic program expanded to include twenty coaches, intercollegiate competition for women students; and they garnered 19 team and 41 individual Southern Conference championships, and the football team was ranked in the top 20 seven times.

STASAVICH, Clarence
Athletic Director
Clarence Stasavich served as coach at Lenoir Rhyne for 16 years before going to East Carolina University in 1962, where he served until his death in 1975. He posted three straight 9 – 1 seasons and his football team played in the Eastern and Tangerine Bowls with a 50 – 27 – 1 record before he stepped down from coaching in 1969. After being appointed athletic director in 1963, he helped develop a modern all-purpose athletic complex and strengthened the school's athletic program so they were granted acceptance in the Southern Conference.
Also in: National Association of Intercollegiate Athletics Hall of Fame.

STRELL, John
Athletic Director
As football coach for 15 years at Illinois Valley Community College, John Strell led his teams to nine conference championships and finished second four other seasons. Eleven of his players earned junior college All-American honors and his 1950 team went to the Gold Dust Bowl. He also coached the basketball teams for 28 seasons, and they won four conference and six sectional titles as well as the 1959 Region Four Crown. He was golf coach 16 years and track coach 8 years. He was named athletic director in 1950. John Strell served junior and community college athletics for 30 years as much involved in the activities of the conferences and other sports organizations as he was in those of his school.

WATTS, Stanley
Athletic Director
Stanley Watts was coach and administrator in athletics at Brigham Young University for over 30 years. He has written a book and several articles on basketball strategy. Watts retired from coaching in 1972 after many successful years as head basketball coach, his teams capturing two titles in the Rocky Mountain Conference, one Mountain States Crown, and five Western Athletic Conference championships, while posting a 433 – 258 record. They also captured one NIT national title during his years as coach.

Athletic Trainers Hall of Fame

The Hall of Fame was created in 1962 by the Citizens Savings Athletic Foundation, motivated by Eddie Wojechi of Rice University in Houston, Tex, who developed the program which serves to recognize those who are deserving of the honor.

Members: 91 as of 1977. The inductees are trainers who have been identified with collegiate institutes, as well as with amateur clubs and professional organizations. They must have served for 25 years or more, or have completed their careers as an athletic trainer. Elections are held annually. The nominations are made by the National Athletic Trainers Association (NATA) and the selections are then approved by the Citizens Savings Hall Board. Inductions are held at the annual NATA awards banquet. Each inductee has his name engraved on a trophy, which is kept in the Citizens Savings Hall of Fame Athletic Museum. He also receives a Hall of Fame Award.

Induction Years Unrecorded

ABRAHAM, Joseph N.
Athletic Trainer

ARIAIL, Warren
Athletic Trainer
Born April 8, 1924, in Eutawville, S.C; son of a Methodist minister; received a degree from Wofford Col, Eastern Medical Aides School of N.Y. and an M.A. from Indiana Univ; wife Sue Beam; three children: Debby, Phyllis and Warren III; military service in Marines in W.W. II.

Ariail has been a member of the staff at the Sports Medical Division of the North Carolina State Department of Public Instruction for over two years now, as the assistant director to Dr. Al Proctor. Warren was secretary-treasurer for district 3 of the National Athletic Trainers Association (NATA) for three years, where he became director before moving to district 5 of the NATA as the manager of exhibits for twelve years. During his career he has also served as the assistant athletic director and head trainer for Gardner-Webb College, head trainer for the 1960 Olympic Wrestling Trials, head trainer for the National Collegiate Athletic Association Track meet in 1966 and in 1968 as trainer for Indiana's only Rose Bowl team as well as the trainer for the National Football Leagues Pro Bowl in 1970. Other positions held include head athletic trainer for the Houston Oilers, the New Orleans Saints, Indiana University, Iowa State University, Wake Forest University and Wofford College. Ariail has appeared in two Hollywood movies and was technical adviser in a Charlton Heston movie. He has also worked with basketball teams in Europe, South America and the Pacific.

BAKKE, Walter B.
Athletic Trainer

BAUMAN, Robert
Athletic Trainer

BEVAN, Roland
Athletic Trainer
Roland has been a trainer at Muskingum College, Ohio Northern University, University of Dayton, Dartmouth College and United States Military Academy.

BIGGS, Ernest
Athletic Trainer

BILIK, Samuel E.
Athletic Trainer
Samuel has not only been a trainer at the University of Illinois but has used his knowledge and abilities to assist at various New York State Hospitals.

BLANKOWITSCH, Joseph
Athletic Trainer

BLOCK, Edward
Athletic Trainer
Received a B.S. from the Univ. Mo. 1936, M.A. 1937, Ed.D. in rehabilitation and a degree in Physical Therapy at Teachers Col, Columbia Univ. 1952, and a certificate in Upper Prosthetic Devices from New York Univ. 1959; military service in Army from 1942 to 1947.

Edward Block began his career as the athletic director and head coach for Hancock High School in St. Louis, Mo. 1938 – 1942. Then in 1947 after serving in the Army, he became the head trainer at Washington University until 1951. Edward next served as physical therapist for the New York Neurological Hospital, the Kingsbridge Veterans Hospital and the New York Hospital Rehabilitation Center. In 1954 he became the staff therapist at the Kerman Hospital and the Crippled Childrens Hospital in Baltimore and head trainer of the Baltimore Colts until 1974. Edward was also doing radiological research at Johns Hopkins University at this time.

BOHM, William H. S.
Athletic Trainer
William is known best in the field of athletic training for positions held with Washington State University, the Washington Redskins and the Cincinnati Reds.

BROWN, Delmar
Athletic Trainer

BROWN, Elmer
Athletic Trainer

BULLOCK, David Madison
Athletic Trainer
David earned his recognition from the Hall of Fame as an athletic trainer for the University of Illinois.

BYRNE, Edward A.
Athletic Trainer

CHAMBERS, Michael C.
Athletic Trainer
Mike has been an athletic trainer with numerous universities, among them Iowa State and Ohio State Universities, Georgia Institute of Technology, Louisiana State University and the University of California at Los Angeles.

CLARK, Earl "Click"
Athletic Trainer
Earl has been an athletic trainer at the University of Washington.

COLE, Richard Kent
Athletic Trainer

COLVILLE, E. J. "Jay"
Athletic Trainer

CRAMER, Charles
Athletic Trainer
One of the famed Cramer brothers of the Cramer Chemical Company in Gardner, Kansas.
Also in: National Association of Intercollegiate Athletics Hall of Fame.

CRAMER, Frank
Athletic Trainer
Brother of Hall of Famer Charles Cramer, both of the Cramer Chemical Company in Gardner, Kansas.
Also in: National Association of Intercollegiate Athletics Hall of Fame.

De VICTOR, Oliver J.
Athletic Trainer
Oliver has been athletic trainer for Pennsylvania State University, the University of Pittsburgh, Washington University in St. Louis, Mo, and the University of Missouri.

DICKINSON, Arthur
Athletic Trainer

DIEHM, Lorain F. "Tow"
Athletic Trainer
Born June 22, 1926; received B.S. 1953, M.S. 1955 from Emporia State Col. in Pittsburg, Kans; specialized training in corrective therapy at U.S. Veterans Hospital in Albuquerque, N.M. 1959; wife Pearl; daughter Teresa; son Gary; recipient of the National Athletic Trainers Association's 25-Year Award 1974; honorary member of Univ. N. Mex. Lettermen's Club.

1948 – 1949 Santa Rosa Junior College, trainer
1949 – 1955 Emporia, Kans, State College, trainer
1955 – 1957 Michigan State University, assistant trainer
1957 – University of New Mexico, head trainer and associate professor

Since 1948 Diehm's contributions to the field of athletic training have covered many areas. Starting in 1957 he has been a trainer for special games and contests. Among them are the North-South All-Star football and basketball tournaments, the New Mexico state basketball tournaments and the New Mexico state track and field meets, all held in Albuquerque, N.M. Diehm was trainer for the 1961 and 1962 Shrine junior college All-Star football game, the National Collegiate Athletic Association's (NCAA) 1962 gymnastics meet, the 1963 NCAA track and field meet and the 1964 National Association of Intercollegiate Athletics track and field meet, also held in Albuquerque, N.M. Lorain has lectured at coaching schools in New Mexico, Kansas, Colorado, California, Utah and Washington, as well as many other institutions too numerous to mention. Offices held include charter member of the National Athletic Trainers Association (NATA) in 1950, secretary of district 7 of the NATA in 1954, chairman of the 1962 NATA board of directors and the 1961 – 1962 director of district 7 of the NATA. Other experiences in his career are serving as the host trainer for the NATA annual meeting in 1962, establishing the curriculum for athletic training at the University of New Mexico in 1972 and serving as liaison with the NCAA in 1972. Diehm is also the editor of *Cramer's First Aider,* published by the Upjohn Pharmaceutical Company.

DIMMITT, Lilburn J.
Athletic Director
Lilburn was an athletic trainer for Texas A & M University.

DIXON, Dwayne "Spike"
Athletic Director

DOUGAL, Anthony Frank
Athletic Trainer
Received a B.S. from Temple Univ. and M.A. from Columbia Univ; served in the Navy.

Dougal began training in 1933 as the head coach and trainer for Smethport High School, Pa. He was the coach and trainer at West Texas State University, 1937–1939 and the University of New Hampshire, 1939–1947. Anthony then moved on to Darmouth University where he was coach and trainer; after some 15 years there he became an instructor and trainer at Boston University, 1962–1974.

DRAKE, Elvin "Ducky"
Athletic Trainer

ERICKSON, Carl
Athletic Trainer
Carl received recognition into the Hall of Fame as an athletic trainer at Northwestern University.

FALLON, William J. "Billy"
Athletic Trainer
An athletic trainer at several universities, Billy moved from the University of California to the Universities of Wisconsin, Missouri and Michigan, St. Mary's University and the U.S. Naval Academy.

FERRELL, William R.
Athletic Trainer

GORMLEY, Tad
Athletic Trainer
Tad has been an athletic trainer at the New Orleans YMCA, Tulane University, Louisiana State University, Loyola University and the University of New Orleans.

GUNN, Robert Henry
Athletic Trainer
Attended Rice Univ, Houston, Tex.

Gunn began his career as an athletic trainer in 1947 and worked at Rice University, the school district in Freeport, Tex, public schools in Baytown, Tex, Lamar State College, the Houston Oilers, the Washington Redskins and the Shreveport Steamers. For two years Gunn was a trainer at the U.S.A. Pan-American Games, 1959 and 1967. His credentials are many—athletic training, author, lecturer and others. Gunn was elected two terms as president of the National Athletic Trainers Association, 1970–1971 and 1973–1974.

GWYNNE, A. C. "Whitey"
Athletic Trainer

HARPER, Charles E.
Athletic Trainer

HEPPINSTALL, Jack
Athletic Trainer
Jack demonstrated superior talents as an athletic trainer at Michigan State University.

HOWARD, Milford Kenneth
Athletic Trainer
Born July 29, 1926, in Crossville, Ala; received B.S. from Auburn Univ; wife Jeanne; four children: Steve, Richard, James and Karen Jean.

Howard began his career at Auburn University after graduation as the assistant trainer for Wilbur Hutsell. When Hutsell was made athletic director, Howard became the full-time trainer. Now Howard is also holding the positions of program chairman of Auburn University and the University of Alabama's Cooperative Extension Service annual care of the athlete clinic. Said to be one of the top trainers in the nation, Kenny was one of the seven members of the 1952 U.S. Olympic committee's training staff. Some other events in his career include being trainer in both the Blue and Grey game in Montgomery, Ala, and for the Senior Bowl in Mobile, Ala. Kenny has been a speaker at clinics held by the National Athletic Trainers Association (NATA), a sports medicine symposium of the American Medical Association and one of the Alabama Medical Association's general meetings. He has held the office of president in the NATA district 9 and been a member of the board of directors. In 1975 Howard was selected for the Pan American Games.

HUNT, James Edward
Athletic Director

JOHNSON, James H.
Athletic Director

JORGENSEN, Carl "Bud"
Athletic Trainer
See entry in Green Bay Packer Hall of Fame, 1976.

KIMBALL, C. Rodney
Athletic Trainer
Received a B.S. from Brigham Young Univ. 1955, M.S. 1963; military service in W.W. II.

In 1937 Kimball started his athletic training career at Brigham Young University, and with the exception of a few years spent in the military service, he has been there ever since. Kimball has served as a member of the National Athletic Trainers Association's (NATA) board of directors, as the 1969–1971 secretary of the NATA's district 7 and as director of district 7 in 1971–1974.

KIMURA, Lincoln Tamotsu
Athletic Director
Starting out as a student trainer at San Jose State University in 1946, Kimura was promoted to head trainer in 1947. He held that position until 1954 when he became the assistant trainer for the San Francisco 49ers. Then in

1963 Kimura was promoted to head trainer of the 49ers, where he served until 1973.

KNIGHT, Wesley I.
Athletic Trainer

LACEY, John
Athletic Trainer
Born in Wallingford, Conn; attended Yale Univ. Dept. of Physical Therapy, the Tilton School in Tilton, N.H, and the Eastern School of Physiotherapy in New York City.

Lacey began his career as trainer for the pro Chicago Rockets, the New York Yankees and the Baltimore Colts. He next was trainer at the University of Maryland when the football team went to three bowl games; he worked with squads that won national championships in lacrosse as well as football. While acting as trainer for the Tar Heels, six of the football teams played in bowl games including the 1963 Gator Bowl where they won. He was athletic trainer for the 1957 North Carolina basketball team that won the national championship, and the 1971 team that won the National Invitational. In 1964 Lacey was the trainer for the U.S. basketball team in Tokyo, and the 1972 head trainer for the U.S. delegation to the Olympic games in Munich.

LANE, Edwin B. "Eddie"
Athletic Trainer
Born Feb. 3, 1929; received a B.S. from Southern Methodist Univ. (SMU) 1955, M.Ed. 1956; wife Jane Bentley; two children: Stephanie and Ernest Bradford; served in the Army 1951 to 1953.

1955 North Texas State University, head trainer
1956–1959 Washington State University, head trainer
1960–1972 Southern Methodist University, head trainer
1973– Dallas School District, head trainer

Preceding Eddie's career as head trainer he was a student trainer for Waite High School in Toledo, Ohio, under Jack Mollenkopf, a student trainer for Bowling Green State University under Al Sawdy and a locomotive fireman for the New York Central Railroad Co. in Toledo. Eddie was the first scholarship student trainer in 1953 and 1954 for SMU. Breaking still another barrier in 1955 to become the first trainer for all athletics at North Texas State University. Eddie was trainer for the 1949 Ohio High School Coaching Association's All-Star football game, the U.S. Davis Cup tennis versus Mexico City in 1965 and Chile in 1973, the 1968 Olympic Games in Mexico City, the 1968 and 1972 Greco-Roman and freestyle wrestling teams and the World championship tennis finals in 1971, 1972 and 1973. Lane was the national director for district 6 of the National Athletic Trainers Association (NATA) from 1972 to 1975 and vice president of the NATA in 1975. He was also a member of the 1974 health and physical fitness committee of the Texas State Hall of Fame. Eddie has lectured for the Washington State and Texas High School Coaching Associations, the Athletic Injury Symposium at Le Tourneau College in Longview, Tex, and the Cramer Student Trainers clinic at West Texas State University.

LANKFORD, Samuel Randall
Athletic Trainer

LINSKEY, William F.
Athletic Trainer

LITTLEJOHN, James W.
Athletic Trainer

LOGAN, Roland
Athletic Trainer

LUCHSINGER, Werner J.
Athletic Trainer

LUTZ, Thomas F.
Athletic Trainer
Thomas has not only been a trainer for the Universities of Georgia and North Carolina, but also for the Baltimore Colts.

MANN, Frank Hollister "Skipper"
Athletic Trainer
Frank was athletic trainer for the Universities of Chicago, Iowa and Kentucky. Skipper also worked for Indiana and Purdue Universities and the Chicago White Soxs.

MANN, Larnard "Lon"
Athletic Trainer
Lon has been an athletic trainer for the Chicago baseball clubs as well as for Pennsylvania State and Purdue Universities.

MEDINA, Frank E.
Athletic Trainer

MEDLAR, Charles E.
Athletic Trainer

MOORE, Ross
Athletic Trainer
Received a B.A. from the Univ. Tex, El Paso 1939.

After graduating in 1939, Ross was hired by the University of Texas, El Paso as a coach and trainer. In 1943 he left the University to become the head coach and trainer for the El Paso, Tex, High School. Ross had spent one year there before he joined the Navy. He returned to the University of Texas, El Paso as coach and trainer 1946–1974.

MORGAN, Laurence
Athletic Trainer

MORRIS, James H.
Athletic Trainer
See entry in Indiana Basketball Hall of Fame, 1968.

MURPHY, Michael
Athletic Trainer
Michael has worked for Yale University, the Detroit Athletic Club and the University of Pennsylvania as an athletic trainer.

NEILSEN, Einar
Athletic Trainer
Einar was an athletic trainer at the Chicago Athletic Club and the University of Utah.

NELSON, George "Doc"
Athletic Trainer
The Utah State University had a fine athletic trainer in Doc Nelson.

NESMITH, Dean B.
Athletic Trainer

NEWELL, William E. "Pinky"
Athletic Trainer
Born June 22, 1920; received B.S. in physical education from Purdue Univ, degree in physical therapy from Stanford Univ. 1947; wife Connie J. Decker; four children: William Richard, Coleen, Rex Decker, Kim Renee; National Athletic Trainers Association (NATA) Medal 1965; Pacific Athletic Trainer's Association Silver Cup 1968; Rockne Club of America's Player of the Year 1968.

1939 – 1947 Purdue University, student trainer
1948 Stanford University, assistant athletic trainer
1949 Washington State University, head athletic trainer
1950 – Purdue University, head athletic trainer

Newell was trainer for the East-West Shrine football game in 1947, for the College All-Stars in 1953, 1954 and 1957 and for the 1963 Pan-American Games. Pinky has lectured at state sports medical clinics in Wisconsin, Illinois, Michigan, Indiana, Nebraska, Delaware and Pennsylvania and for the American Physical Therapy Association, the American College of Sports Medicine and others. He was chairman of the NATA professional advancement committee 1953 – 1967 and has been chairman of the NATA Professional Advancement Division since 1968.

O'BRIEN, Mickey
Athletic Trainer
Born in Chattanooga, Tenn; military service in Navy.

1925 – 1938 University of Chattanooga Lookouts, trainer
1938 – 1941 University of Tennessee Volunteers, trainer
1945 University of Tennessee Volunteers, trainer

O'Brien was trainer of the Volunteers undefeated teams from 1938 to 1940. While in the Navy, Mickey took an eight week leave to become trainer for General Bob Neyland's Army All-Star team. O'Brien describes his secret: "Corrective and preventive conditioning is one of the most important phases of my work." He is one of the founders and the first president of the Southeastern Conference Trainer's Association.

PATCHIN, Herbert
Athletic Trainer
Herbert was an athletic trainer for the Virginia Military Institute.

PENNOCK, Erastus
Athletic Trainer
Pennock was an athletic trainer for Thiel College, Springfield College and the YMCA.

RAWLINSON, Kenneth
Athletic Trainer

RECINE, Victor D.
Athletic Trainer
Born December 12, 1925; attended the U.S. Navy Corps Physical Therapy School; wife Mary; two children: Michael and Robert; served in W.W. II.

1940 – 1943 New Brunswick, N.J, High School, trainer
1943 – 1946 U.S. Navy Sampson Naval Station Yellow Jackets, trainer
1946 – 1962 New Brunswick, N.J, High School, trainer
1962 – 1973 Sayreville High School, N.J, trainer

Recine was the chairman of the U.S. Olympic fund drive in 1956, 1960, 1964, 1968 and 1972. He was the U.S. Pan-American Games team trainer at Mexico City in 1975. He was the trainer at Rutgers University for the National Amateur Athletic Union and IC4A track and field championships. He was also trainer for the North South All-Star lacrosse game, and for the Hall of Fame game between the New York Jets and Buffalo. He is a past president of the Eastern Athletic Trainers Association.

REICHEL, Jules
Athletic Trainer

RHINEHART, Naseby
Athletic Trainer

RIDEOUT, Wayne
Athletic Trainer
Attended Univ. Ill. 1934 – 1936, Univ. Ala. 1936; received B.S. from North Tex. State Univ. 1940, M.A. from Tex. A&M Univ. 1955.

Wayne has been an athletic trainer for LaMesa, Rosenberg, Tyler, Kaufman, Raymondville, Lyford and Bryan High Schools. He also spent two years as a trainer for York College.

ROBERTSON, William B.
Athletic Trainer

ROBINSON, Gayle B.
Athletic Trainer
Born September 5, 1916; received B.S. from Mich. State Univ. 1940, M.A. 1949; wife Evelyn; four children: Robert, Dan, Jean and Marie; recipient of the National Athletic Trainers Association's (NATA) 24-year Award.

1940 – 1945 Muskegon and Ravenna, Mich, High Schools, coach
1946 – Michigan State University, trainer

In addition to his regular activities, Robinson was a trainer at the Pan-American Games. He trained the Australian athletes at the 1972 Olympic Games in Munich. Gayle has lectured to service groups, church groups and to the athletic directors of Michigan high schools. He held the office of secretary-treasurer of the NATA in 1962 and 1963 and served on the NATA board of directors in 1964 and 1965. Robinson is also a member of the board of directors of the "Bike" Training Room Foundation and has written an article for the Foundation. In 1972 an athletic training award was instituted in his name at Ravenna High School for student trainers.

ROCKWELL, John Dudley "Jack"
Athletic Director
Born December 18, 1925, in Seattle, Wash; received B.S.

and R.P.T. from Univ. of Kans, M.S. from Univ. Colo; sergeant in U.S. Army.

1948 – 1949 Bremerton Bluejackets baseball team, head trainer
Olympic Jr. College, Bremerton, Wash, head trainer
1950 – 1952 University of Kansas, assistant trainer
1952 – 1960 University of Colorado, head trainer
1960 – 1971 St. Louis Cardinals, head trainer
1974 Southern California Suns, head trainer

Jack has made appearances at clinics held by Wyoming State High School, Idaho, Washington State and the Louisiana State coaches meetings. He is a member of the American Physical Therapy Association, the National Athletic Trainers Association (NATA), the American College of Sports Medicine, the American Society for Testing and Materials and several others. Jack has been a member of the NATA editorial board, *Letterman* Magazine editorial board and the advisory staff of Rowlings Sporting Goods Company. He served as head trainer for the U.S. Olympic selection committee from 1961 to 1971 and executive secretary of the NATA from 1968 to 1971.

RUDY, Wayne
Athletic Trainer
Received B.A. from Bowling Green Univ. 1943, M.A. from Southern Methodist Univ. 1951; military service 1943 to 1945.

Wayne was a coach for Waite High School in Toledo, Ohio, from 1945 to 1947. His first job as head trainer was for Southern Methodist University in 1947. Wayne became head trainer of the Dallas Texans in 1960 and in 1963 he was hired by the Kansas City Chiefs as head trainer, where he served through 1974.

RYAN, Michael
Athletic Trainer
Michael has been an athletic trainer for Bates College, Colby College, the Boston Redskins, the Santa Clara Youth Village, and the Universities of Idaho, Wyoming, Guatemala and Santa Clara.

SAWDY, Allan
Athletic Trainer

SCHMIDT, Henry
Athletic Trainer
Born September 21, 1905, in San Jose, Calif; received B.S. in physical education from Univ. Santa Clara 1931.

Schmitty spent 37 years as basketball and baseball trainer for the University of Santa Clara before he became a football trainer. He has been team trainer for the San Francisco 49ers for 7 years, the Los Angeles Rams for 10 summer sessions and trainer for the famed St. Mary's and Del Monte pre-flight football teams during W.W. II. Schmitty was one of the trainers for the Santa Clara Sugar Bowl teams of 1936 and 1937 and the 1950 champion Orange Bowl squad. He has a total of 20 years as head trainer for the East team of the East-West Shrine classics. Henry was also one of the founders and first president of the Pacific Coast Athletic Trainers Association and served as a director for the NATA. Schmitty has worked with more All-Americans and coaches than any other trainer in the world. He once said "No man alive could have such an enjoyable life as I have experienced working with the Jesuits and the boys here at Santa Clara." Schmitty has always been a favorite of athletes and coaches alike.

SHERIDAN, Francis Joseph
Athletic Trainer
Born May 24, 1924; graduated from Phillipsburg Catholic High School 1942; wife Gladys Sarah; three children: Margaret, Phillip and Michael; received American Red Cross 25-year Service Award; NATA 25-year Award.

1950 – 1959 Phillipsburg High School, head trainer
1960 – 1977 Lafayette College, head trainer

Sheridan was an athletic trainer for the Philadelphia Eagles, the U.S. Pan-American Games team in 1967, the U.S. AAU track and field team in 1973 and the U.S. track and field team in 1976. He served as vice president in 1961 and president in 1962 of the Eastern Athletic Trainers Association. Sheridan was vice president of NATA in 1975 and a member of the board of directors from 1968 to 1975. Francis has lectured for medical clinics at the Germantown Academy, the University of Rhode Island, Dickinson College, the University of Delaware and many others.

SIMONS, Claude Jr. "Big Monk"
Athletic Trainer
Big Monk Simons has been an athletic trainer for Tulane University in New Orleans, La.
Also in: National Football Hall of Fame.

STEIN, Lloyd "Snapper"
Athletic Trainer

SULKOWSKI, Edward A.
Athletic Trainer
Received B.S. from Pa. State Univ. 1949, M.S. 1954; military service in W.W. II.

In 1948 Sulkowski began athletic training as an assistant to Chuck Medlar at Pennsylvania State University, where he was involved in many sports. Edward served as director of the NATA from 1950 to 1954 and officiated at Army boxing championships for a few years. He was also president of the NCAA in 1954 and has traveled overseas on several occasions to participate in and conduct athletic training clinics in Japan, Korea, Germany and other countries.

TURNER, Dr. Charles W.
Athletic Trainer
Received B.S. from New York Univ, M.A. from Columbia Univ, granted chiropractic degree 1942; recipient of the NATA 25-year Award.

1920 Mercury Athletic Center, trainer
1922 Negro National Baseball League, trainer
1926 Cuban baseball team, trainer
1928 Renaissance Big Five, trainer
1934 Renaissance Big Five, trainer
1937 New York Pioneer Club, trainer

Turner worked as a trainer for 40 years for the track and field meets held in Madison Square Garden in New York City. Since 1938 he has been an athletic trainer for the government of Venezuela at the University of Maracaibo, for the Harlem Professionals, the New Jersey Americans, the New York Jets, Fairleigh Dickinson University and Long Island University. Turner has traveled extensively, serving as the Olympic Games trainer for Spain, Germany, Jamaica, Trinidad, Italy and the Bahamas. Dr. Turner is an honorary member of the German Trainers Society and a life member of the International Trainers Association.

WAITE, Howard E.
Athletic Trainer

WALLACE, Stanley M.
Athletic Trainer
Stanley was an athletic trainer for the University of Maine.

WANDLE, Frank
Athletic Trainer
Frank has not only been an athletic trainer for West Point, but for Yale and Louisiana State Universities as well.

WARCO, Richard A.
Athletic Trainer

WHITE, Robert C.
Athletic Trainer
Born April 13, 1925; received B.S. from Eastern Michigan Univ. 1949, M.S. 1950; wife Gloria; four children: Lynda, Nancy, David and Sue.

1950 – 1951	Eastern Michigan University, head trainer
1948 – 1956	Detroit Lions, National Football League, part-time trainer
1951 –	Wayne State University, head trainer
1958 –	Detroit Pistons, part-time trainer

White was the United States trainer at the Olympic Games in Mexico City in 1958. He was also trainer for the U.S. track and field team in Moscow in 1969 and the 1973 World University Games in Moscow. White was one of the organizers of the National Athletic Trainers Association. He has held every elected office in the Great Lakes Trainers Association and has twice served on the NATA board of directors.

WITKOWSKI, Stephen W.
Athletic Trainer

WOJECKI, Eddie
Athletic Trainer
Eddie spearheaded the idea of creating the Athletic Trainers Hall of Fame. He developed the criteria for inducting members and headed the committee which chose the first inductees. Eddie was an athletic trainer for Rice University.

WYRE, Alfred "Duke"
Athletic Trainer

ZANFRINI, Edward G.
Athletic Trainer

Automobile Racing Hall of Fame

The Automobile Racing Hall of Fame was instituted within the Citizens Savings Hall of Fame Athletic Museum in 1949. Since that time 33 members have been installed; eight of those are noteworthy contributors. Honorees are those individuals who have distinguished themselves throughout the history of motor sports. Inductions take place annually and there are no numerical prerequisites.

Induction Years Unrecorded

AGAJANIAN, J. C.
Contributor
Known as the man in the white stetson, J. C. Agajanian owned and sponsored race cars for over 25 years. His cars won the Indianapolis 500 in 1952 with driver Troy Ruttman and in 1963 with Parnelli Jones. He founded the Western Racing Association and directed motorcycle racing as well as organizing and directing auto races. In 1951 he was awarded the Eddie Edenburn Trophy, presented each year by the AAA to the man who has done most for professional auto racing.

BETTENHAUSEN, Melvin E. "Tony"
Driver
See entry in American Auto Racing Writers and Broadcasters Association Hall of Fame, 1974.
Also in: Indianapolis Motor Speedway Hall of Fame.

BRYAN, James
Driver
See entry in American Auto Racing Writers and Broadcasters Association Hall of Fame, 1976.
Also in: Indianapolis Motor Speedway Hall of Fame.

BURMAN, Robert
Driver
See entry in Indianapolis Motor Speedway Hall of Fame, 1953 – 1954.

CLYMER, Floyd
Contributor
Floyd Clymer collects histories of old-time cars and motorcycles, and issued his collection in 1944 in a *Motor Scrapbook.* It met with such success he followed it with volume number two and also a work entitled *The Modern Steam Car and Its Background.* He started an automobile and motorcycle equipment business in Los Angeles in the late 1930s, but his hobby of collecting automotive nostalgia soon became his business; Clymer has been considered the authority in this field for many years.

COOPER, Earl
Driver
See entry in American Auto Racing Writers and Broadcasters Association Hall of Fame, 1974.
Also in: Indianapolis Motor Speedway Hall of Fame.

CUMMINGS, Bill
Driver
See entry in Indianapolis Motor Speedway Hall of Fame, 1970.

DE PALMA, Ralph
Driver
See entry in American Auto Racing Writers and Broadcasters Association Hall of Fame, 1973.
Also in: Indianapolis Motor Speedway Hall of Fame.

DE PAOLO, Peter
Driver
See entry in American Auto Racing Writers and Broadcasters Association Hall of Fame, 1973.
Also in: Indianapolis Motor Speedway Hall of Fame.

FIRESTONE, Harvey Samuel
Contributor
See entry in Indianapolis Motor Speedway Hall of Fame, 1952.

FORD, Henry
Contributor
See entry in Indianapolis Motor Speedway Hall of Fame, 1952.

GURNEY, Dan
Driver
See entry in American Auto Racing Writers and Broadcasters Association Hall of Fame, 1974.

HANKS, Sam
Driver
Born July 13, 1914, in Columbus, Ohio; finished third in the Indianapolis 500 in 1952 and 1953, second in 1956, and was victorious in 1957, setting a new Speedway record of 135.6 m.p.h. His Belond Exhaust Special was designed and built by George Salih.

HARTZ, Harry
Driver
See entry in Indianapolis Motor Speedway Hall of Fame, 1963.

HEARNE, Eddie
Driver
See entry in Indianapolis Motor Speedway Hall of Fame, 1964.

HORN, Ted
Driver
See entry in American Auto Racing Writers and Broadcasters Association Hall of Fame, 1975.
Also in: Indianapolis Motor Speedway Hall of Fame.

HULMAN, Anton
Contributor
See entry in Indianapolis Motor Speedway Hall of Fame, 1967.

JONES, Parnelli
Driver
Jones won the Indianapolis 500 in 1963. He was U.S. sprint car champion for three straight years, 1960 – 1962, and won the National Stock Car title in 1964, as well as the Pike's Peak Hill Climb. In 1963 when he won the big prize at Indianapolis, he averaged 143.137 m.p.h, then a record, and was the leader for 167 laps. Jones was leading in 1964 when his car caught fire, and he placed second in 1965 and seventh in 1967. Today he is a car owner, a rival to Agajanian for whom he drove, but the two remain best friends.

MAYS, Rex
Driver
See entry in American Auto Racing Writers and Broadcasters Association Hall of Fame, 1971.
Also in: Indianapolis Motor Speedway Hall of Fame.

MEYER, Louis
Driver
See entry in American Auto Racing Writers and Broadcasters Association Hall of Fame, 1974.
Also in: Indianapolis Motor Speedway Hall of Fame.

MILTON, Tommy
Driver
See entry in American Auto Racing Writers and Broadcasters Association Hall of Fame, 1974.
Also in: Indianapolis Motor Speedway Hall of Fame.

MULFORD, Ralph
Driver
See entry in American Auto Racing Writers and Broadcasters Association Hall of Fame, 1976.
Also in: Indianapolis Motor Speedway Hall of Fame.

MURPHY, James
Driver
See entry in American Auto Racing Writers and Broadcasters Association Hall of Fame, 1974.
Also in: Indianapolis Motor Speedway Hall of Fame.

MYERS, Theodore E. "Pop"
Contributor
See entry in Indianapolis Motor Speedway Hall of Fame.

OLDFIELD, Berna E. "Barney"
Driver
See entry in American Auto Racing Writers and Broadcasters Association Hall of Fame, 1972.
Also in: Indianapolis Motor Speedway Hall of Fame.

PARSONS, Johnny
Driver,
Johnny Parsons was the U.S. Auto Club champion in 1949 and won the Indianapolis 500 in 1950.

RATHMANN, Jim
Driver
Jim Rathmann competed in 14 Indianapolis Speedway classics, covering a total of 5737.5 mi. He placed second in 1952, 1957 and 1959 and was the winner of the Indianapolis 500 in 1960. His other notable victories were the Monzo, Italy 500 in 1958 and the Milwaukee 200 in 1957. At Daytona Beach in 1959 Rathmann set records at 50, 75 and 100 mi.

RICKENBACKER, Edward Vernon
Contributor
See entry in American Auto Racing Writers and Broadcasters Association Hall of Fame (Induction Year Unrecorded).
Also in: Indianapolis Motor Speedway Hall of Fame.

ROSE, Mauri
Driver
See entry in American Auto Racing Writers and Broadcasters Association Hall of Fame (Induction Year Unrecorded).
Also in: Indianapolis Motor Speedway Hall of Fame.

SHAW, Warren Wilbur
Driver
See entry in American Auto Racing Writers and Broadcasters Association Hall of Fame, 1971.
Also in: Indianapolis Motor Speedway Hall of Fame.

VANDERBILT, William Kissan
Contributor
See entry in Indianapolis Motor Speedway Hall of Fame, 1952.

VUKOVICH, Bill, Sr.
Driver
See entry in American Auto Racing Writers and Broadcasters Association Hall of Fame (Induction Year Unrecorded).
Also in: Indianapolis Motor Speedway Hall of Fame.

WARD, Rodger
Driver
Rodger Ward won the U.S. Auto Club championship and the Indianapolis 500, both in 1957 and 1962.

Badminton Hall of Fame

The Badminton Hall of Fame was originally maintained by the American Badminton Association (ABA), which was founded in 1937 and located in San Diego, Calif. In 1956 the Hall in its totality was donated to the Citizens Savings Hall of Fame Athletic Museum. *Members:* 30 as of 1977. The members are nominated by the ABA, with final selection made by the Citizens Savings Board. Elections are held annually. Each inductee has his name engraved upon the Badminton Hall of Fame Trophy and receives the Citizens Savings Hall of Fame Award.

ALSTON, Joseph C.
Player
Resides in California.

Joe Alston was U.S. singles champion in 1951 and 1954 – 1957. He teamed with T. Wynn Rogers, also in the Hall of Fame, for 14 men's doubles titles 1951 – 1964. He and his wife Lois, who is also in the Hall of Fame, were mixed doubles winners in 1953, 1955 and 1963 – 1967.

ALSTON, Lois
Player
Lois teamed with her husband Joe, who is also in the Hall of Fame, for the mixed doubles crown in 1953, 1955 and 1963 – 1967.

BARKHUFF, Bertha Cunningham
Player
Resides in Seattle, Wash, with husband Del.

Bertha won the first ladies' singles title in Chicago in 1937 and again in 1938. She was the 1937 and 1939 National Doubles champion, with Zoe Smith. Bertha teamed with Hamilton Law to win the National Mixed Doubles championship in 1937 and 1938.

FREEMAN, Dr. David Guthrie
Player
Born in 1920; won singles and doubles in U.S. junior lawn tennis championships in 1938; resides in Pasadena, Calif.

For 14 years David Freeman was undefeated in singles play, earning recognition as the top badminton competitor. In 1947 he was the men's singles champion, men's doubles champion with W. Kimball; in 1948 and 1949 he repeated as singles champion, adding another title in 1953, his last year of competition. He won a second doubles, with fellow Hall of Famer T. Wynn Rogers in 1948. David competed internationally only one year, 1948 – 1949, leading the first U.S. team in Thomas Cup and All-England play by defeating the two top Malayans with scores of 15 – 2, 15 – 4, 15 – 1 and 15 – 6. Rube Samuelson, former sports editor of the *Pasadena Star-News,* stated: "Fantastic stories are told about Freeman's skill, one being that, in the midst of any volley, he can drive the shuttlecock at any designated spot and make a 'bullseye.' Freeman has the speed of a projectile, when in action, and accuracy of placement beyond that of any amateur performer in the history of the sport. He also is the greatest retriever badminton has produced."

GIBSON, Helen
Player
Born in East Norwalk, Conn.

Helen Gibson was the 1938 National Womens Doubles champion, with Wanda Bergman and they were finalists in the competition in 1937, 1939 and 1942. Helen was a finalists in the 1939 singles, the 1951 mixed doubles and the 1958 senior womens doubles. She held the position of Connecticut State Ladies Closed Doubles champion for 21 years, which record may never be equaled. Helen has been the winner of the National Capitol Open, the Eastern Open, the Mason-Dixon Open, Stamford City, Fairfield County Closed and the Connecticut State Closed. She has been either an officer or director of the American Badminton Association since 1947 and devotes much of her time and effort to junior badminton. Best known as chairman of the Uber Cup committee, Helen's guidance led the United States team to win the Ladies International badminton crown.

GOSS, Chester
Player
Works with the U.S. Postal Services; has been a resident of San Diego, Calif.

Chester won his first match with Donald Eversoll in the 1937 U.S. Closed National Doubles championship. He was the last badminton player to defeat David Freeman in single play, at the 1939 California state championship. Goss and Freeman teamed to win the 1940, 1941 and 1942 National Doubles crowns. Goss sometimes teamed with junior players in tournament doubles to give them the experience in top-flight competition.

HASHMAN, Judy M. Devlin
Player
Born in 1935.

The best woman's player in the history of badminton, Judy Hashman won 31 U.S. National titles and 17 All-England crowns since 1954. Her All-England titles came in 1954, 1957, 1958, 1960 – 1964, 1966 and 1967. She won the ladies' doubles—her older sister Susan Devlin Peard was her partner—in 1954, 1956 and 1960. She was the top U.S. ladies' singles player in 1955 to 1963 and 1965 – 1967, on the top ladies' doubles 1953 – 1955 and 1957 – 1961, and on the top mixed doubles team in 1962. She retired in 1967 after winning her tenth world singles title. She is the author of *Badminton a Champion's Way*.

HOWARD, Evelyn Boldrick
Player
Born in Wellesley Hills, Mass.

Howard began her career in San Diego, Calif. She is the winner of the 1940 National Womens Singles championship, held in Seattle, and both the singles and the doubles championship at Durham, N.C. in 1942.

KRAMER, Walter
Player
Resides in Detroit, Mich.

Walter won the men's singles at the U.S. championships in 1937. He was also the 1938 singles champion and a top player before the national tournament was established.

LAW, Hamilton B.
Player
Born September 23, 1913, in Waterville, Wash; attended Medford, Ore, High School; in military service in W.W. II; works for the Prudential Life Insurance Co. in Denver, Colo.

Law was the Seattle, Wash, champion six times and won many other titles in Washington, Oregon, California and Colorado. For several years he was ranked between fifth and sixth in singles. Law teamed with Bertha Barhuff to take the 1937 National Mixed Doubles championship, in the first U.S. national badminton tournament, held in Chicago. They teamed to win the title again in 1938. Law and Richard Yeager won the U.S. National Doubles title at Philadelphia in 1938 and at New York City in 1939.

LOVEDAY, Carl Wickham
Player

MARSHALL, Ethel
Player
Ethel was the top ladies' singles player 1947 – 1953. She teamed with fellow Hall of Famer Beatrice Massman for the ladies' doubles in 1952 and 1956. From 1956 to 1958 she was Number One in mixed doubles with B. Williams.

MASSMAN, Beatrice
Player
In 1952 and 1956 Beatrice and Hall of Famer Ethel Marshall teamed to win the U.S. Womens Doubles championship.

MENDEZ, A. Marten
Player
Mendez was the top men's singles player in the United States in 1950 and 1952.

MITCHELL, John Richard
Player
Born July 18, 1920, in Council Bluffs, Iowa; received a B.A. in physical education from San Diego State Univ; wife Evelyn; two sons; served in Navy in W.W. II; active in the U.S. Navy Intelligence Reserve Program; Little All-American Basketball player 1942 and National Softball Congress All-American 1947; now resides in San Diego, Calif.

Dick has won many singles and doubles titles in badminton, both sectional and state. He was a member of the 1952 and 1955 U.S. Thomas Cup teams and manager of the team in 1961. Mitchell also won the 1961 U.S. Open Senior Men's Doubles crown with Wynn Rogers. He has helped to develop many top San Diego area badminton players, and has been a regional director of the American Badminton Association. Dick also played basketball, baseball and softball.

PAUP, Dr. Donald Clark
Player
Don was the men's doubles champion with fellow Hall of Fame member R. Poole 1965 – 1972. He was co-champion in mixed doubles in 1971. His partner was Helen Noble Tibbetts, also in the Hall of Fame.

PEARD, Susan Devlin
Player
Susan teamed with her sister Judy M. Devlin to form the best U.S. ladies' doubles team 1953 – 1955 and 1957 – 1962.

POOLE, Dr. James R.
Player
Received his Ed.D. from Louisiana State Univ; assistant professor of physical education at California State Univ, Northridge.

Jim was the top men's singles player 1959 – 1963 and 1966 – 1968. Teaming with Don Paup, he won the doubles title 1965 – 1972. In 1970 he won the mixed doubles and tied for the championship the following year. Besides being a player and coach, he captained the U.S. Thomas Cup team, is the master clinician of Lifetime Sports Education Project which has set up clinics throughout the United States. Jim is author of *Badminton*.

RICHARDSON, Donald
Noteworthy Contributor
Born in Waban, Mass.

Richardson has been a player and an official for 25 years. He was one of the co-founders of the American Badminton Association (ABA) in 1937. Richardson and his twin brother were twice runnerup in the National Men's Doubles championships, 1937 and 1942. In 1938 he founded and served as the first president of the Massachusetts Badminton Association. He was the editor of *Bird Chat-*

ter, the official publication of the ABA, for a period of five years. Richardson served as a member of the Thomas Cup committee for a number of years and was chairman of the committee 1950–1955. He also managed the 1955 U.S. Thomas Cup team. Donald was president of the ABA 1950–1952, chairman of the rules committee 1957–1968 and treasurer for the subcommittee of management for the 1960 Uber Cup ties.

ROGERS, T. Wynn

Player

T. Wynn was the top men's doubles player in the United States 1948–1964. In mixed doubles competition, he was Number One in 1947, 1949–1952, 1954, 1961 and 1962. Rogers was a member of the U.S. Thomas Cup team in 1949, 1952 and 1955. He wrote *Advanced Badminton* in 1971.

ROYCE, T. M.

Noteworthy Contributor

Born in Seattle, Wash.

Royce has served badminton both as a player and an official, and was president of the American Badminton Association 1948–1950. He has also been a member of the Thomas Cup, rules, amateur status and reorganization committees and has been chairman of the official handbook. Royce is still a competitor in the sport, although in his senior years. He was the National Senior Men's Doubles champion in 1940.

SCHELL, Wayne V.

Player

Born in 1908; resides in West Newton, Mass.

Wayne started competing at the age of 27 and has been active ever since. He first played in the Massachusetts B Division singles, doubles and mixed doubles, winning all three. Wayne was the champion of the Massachusetts Singles for 17 years. He teamed with William Faversham in 1942 in the men's doubles and became Number Two in the country. In the New England Open Men's doubles, he was the champion in 1942, 1954, 1956, 1960, 1962 and 1964. Wayne holds the 1957 Canadian National Open Senior Doubles title and the U.S. National Seniors titles for 1949, 1950, 1953, 1954 and 1958.

SMITH, Loma Moulton

Player

Loma played with T. Wynn Rogers to form the best United States mixed doubles team for three consecutive years, 1949–1951. In 1951 she also played with D. Hann as the Number One ladies' doubles team.

SMITH, Zoe (Yeager)

Player

Born in Seattle, Wash; married Richard Yeager.

Zoe began her career in her home town, Seattle, Wash. She holds titles in many of the sectional tournaments. In 1937 and 1939, Zoe and Berta Barkhuff teamed to take the National Women's Doubles championship. Zoe also teamed with her husband Richard, also in the Hall of Fame, to win the 1938 National Mixed Doubles championship.

TIBBETTS, Helen Noble

Player

Attained the top U.S. national ranking with Tyna Barinaga in ladies' doubles twice, 1968 and 1969.

VERNER, Margaret (Bloss)

Born in El Paso, Tex; attended Texas Women's Univ; worked as assistant professor of physical education at Boston Univ; resides in Chadds Ford, Pa.

Margaret was the 1955 U.S. Open Singles champion, the 1955 and 1956 All-England Singles champion, the 1956 and 1957 Scottish World Invitational Doubles champion and the 1960 U.S. Open Mixed Doubles champion. She was also a member of the U.S. Uber Cup team in 1960 and 1963. As an all-around athlete, Margaret excels in squash (in Noel Cup competition), tennis (represented the United States in Wightman Cup play), marksmanship (rifle) and equestrian sports. She has competed in badminton since 1940.

WELCOME, Thelma Kingsbury

Welcome was the National Singles champion in 1941 and the National Doubles champion in 1941 and 1947–1950. She was All-England Singles 1936 and 1937 and All-England Doubles 1933–1936.

WILLIAMS, Robert B.

Player

Resides in Coral Springs, Fla.

Bob Williams was always best as a doubles player and won many sectional titles. At 6 ft. 1 in. tall and 165 lbs. in the prime of his career, Bob was one of the few men to ever take a game from the famed U.S. champion Dave Freeman. He was a member of the first American Thomas Cup team in 1949 as well as the 1952, 1955 and 1961 teams. With various partners, Bob was a runnerup in several national championships, both men's doubles and mixed doubles events. He has made international appearances for the United States ten times.

WRIGHT, Janet

Player

With teammate T. Scovil, she was the top ladies' doubles player for four consecutive years, 1947–1950.

YEAGER, Richard O.

Player

Born July 9, 1917, in Olympia, Wash; graduated from Univ. Wash. 1939; served in U.S. Navy in the Pacific, Atlantic and Asian fleets; was on the *Marblehead* when it was attacked by the Japanese and also on the *Iowa;* president of the Cascade-Olympic Construction Co. in Shelton, Wash.

Richard teamed with Hamilton Law in 1938 to win the U.S. National Doubles title at Philadelphia and again at New York City in 1939. They won many American sectional titles as partners. At the U.S. National Mixed-Doubles championship in 1939, Richard teamed with Zoe Smith to win the crown. He was a frequent winner in the tournaments at Baltimore, Marblehead, and Westport, as well as in the Metropolitan New York district from 1946 to 1949. In addition to excelling in doubles and mixed doubles play, Yeager ranked between fifth and sixth in singles.

Basketball — Amateur Hall of Fame

This Hall of Fame was instituted in 1957 to honor outstanding amateur basketball players, coaches and contributors to the game. As of 1977 there are 75 members, selected by a Board. Each inductee has his name engraved on a trophy which is kept in Citizens Savings Hall of Fame Athletic Museum, Los Angeles international sports shrine, as well as receiving a Hall of Fame Award. The awards are given in Denver, Colo, during the week of the National Amateur Athletic Union Basketball Championships in the spring.

1957

ADAMS, K.S.
Contributor
Adams was the founder of the Phillips 66 Oilers, sponsored by the Phillips Petroleum Co. of Bartlesv

BROWNING, Omar "Bud"
Player and Coach
Born October 5, 1911, in Lawton, Okla; graduated from Univ. Okla; retired after 33 years with Phillips Petroleum Co.

Bud played three years of varsity ball with the University of Oklahoma and was named three times to the All-Big Six team from 1934 to 1936 and was named All-American in 1935. He was also named AAU All-American three times with the Santa Fe Trailways and Phillips 66. He was a Phillips 66 player-coach for two years and overall coached for ten years, winning 6 national championships. Browning coached the U.S. Olympic team in 1948.

DEBERNARDI, Forrest S. "Red"
Player
See entry in Naismith Memorial Basketball Hall of Fame, 1961.
Also in: College Basketball Hall of Fame, Citizens Savings Hall of Fame Athletic Museum; and National Association of Intercollegiate Athletics Hall of Fame.

FORTENBERRY, Joe
Player and Coach
Born April 1, 1911, in Slidell, Tex; graduated from West Texas State Univ.

Joe was an All-Conference center for 3 years at West Texas State, and was named AAU All-American 1935, 1936, and 1939–1941. He played with the Ogden Boosters, the McPherson Globe Refiners and the Phillips 66 teams. While playing with Gene Johnson's Globe Refiners, he was named to the 1936 Olympic team. Joe, at 6 ft. 8 in, and his Refiner teammate Willard Schmidt at 6 ft. 9 in, were two of the first to dunk the basketball.
Also in: Texas High School Basketball Hall of Fame.

GREIM, Willard
Contributor
Greim chaired the national AAU basketball committee in 1938 to 1940, and played a prominent role in the staging of the AAU basketball championships in Denver.

GRUENIG, Robert F. "Ace"
Player
See entry in Naismith Memorial Basketball Hall of Fame, 1963.

GULICK, Dr. Luther Halsey
Player
See entry in Naismith Memorial Basketball Hall of Fame, 1959

HEPBRON, George T.
Player
See entry in Naismith Memorial Basketball Hall of Fame, 1960.

HYATT, Charles
Player
See entry in Naismith Memorial Basketball Hall of Fame, 1959.
Also in: College Basketball Hall of Fame, Citizens Savings Hall of Fame Athletic Museum.

KURLAND, Robert A. "Foothills"
Player
See entry in Naismith Memorial Basketball Hall of Fame, 1961.
Also in: College Basketball Hall of Fame, Citizens Savings Hall of Fame Athletic Museum.

LUBIN, Frank
Player and Coach
Born January 7, 1910, in Los Angeles, Calif; graduated from Univ. Calif, Los Angeles; various assignments in motion picture industry, most publicized role was Frankenstein; named by Citizens Savings as Greatest Player in Southern California for the First Half-Century; now retired.

Frank was one of five UCLA players named to the first U.S. Olympic basketball team. He coached and instructed in Lithuania following the Olympics for nearly three years, but was forced to leave the country due to the outbreak of W.W. II. Frank was named AAU All-American for 20th Century-Fox in 1941.

McCRACKEN, Jack
Player
See entry in Naismith Memorial Basketball Hall of Fame, 1962.
Also in: National Association of Intercollegiate Athletics Hall of Fame.

NAISMITH, Dr. James
Player
See entry in Naismith Memorial Basketball Hall of Fame, 1959.
Also in: College Basketball Hall of Fame and Noteworthy Contributors Hall of Fame, Citizens Savings Hall of Fame Athletic Museum; Canada's Sports Hall of Fame and National Association of Intercollegiate Athletics Hall of Fame.

PARSONS, C.L. "Poss"
Contributor
Parsons was sports editor of the Denver Post, and chairman of national AAU basketball in 1936 and 1937. He

played an important part in taking the national championships to Denver.

REILLY, Dr. Joseph Albert
Contributor
Reilly was chairman of the national AAU basketball championships from 1921 to 1934. He was associated with the Kansas City Athletic Club and did much to develop the national championships.

WILKE, Louis
Contributor
Born October 10, 1896, in Chicago, Ill; attended Northwestern State Col. and Phillips Univ; retired from Phillips Petroleum Co. as asst. sales mgr; died Feb. 28, 1962, in Northfield, Ill.

Lou coached basketball at Shatluck, Nowata and Bartlesville High Schools (all in Okla.) and the Phillips Oilers. He had a 98-8 record with the Oilers for two seasons. He served as president of the AAU and of the Oklahoma and Rocky Mountain AAU Associations. He was an active committeeman for the U.S. Olympics and served as chairman of the U.S. Olympic Basketball Committee in 1948. He was a member of the honors committee of the Naismith Memorial Basketball Hall of Fame and an active committeeman for the Pan-American Games.

1959

CARPENTER, Gordon "Shorty"
Player and Coach
Born September 24, 1919, in Saddle, Ark.

Gordon was a member of six straight AAU championship teams with the Phillips Oilers from 1943 to 1948. He was on the U.S. Olympic team in London in 1948. Later, Carpenter coached Denver Chevrolet, which represented the United States in the first World Championship Games in 1950. During his career, Gordon was named AAU All-American five times for Phillips and once for Denver Chevrolet.

DUNHAM, Berry
Player
Dunham represented Henry Clothiers and was a member of three national championship teams from 1930 to 1932, and was selected as All-American from 1929 to 1933.

HENSHEL, Harry D.
Contributor
Henshel was long identified with the AAU and the U.S. Olympic committee.

MARTIN, William
Player
Martin was selected as All-American in 1940 – 1942 and in 1946 while playing with the Phillips Oilers who were national champions in 1940, 1946 and 1947.
Also in: National Association of Intercollegiate Athletics Hall of Fame.

SANDERS, Robert
Player
Sanders, playing for the Kansas City Athletic Club, was a member of two national championship teams in 1921 and 1923. He was elected to the All-American team from 1921 to 1926.

1960

BARKSDALE, Don
Player and Coach
Born March 31, 1923, in Oakland, Calif; graduated from Univ. Calif, Los Angeles.

In college Don led UCLA to the conference championships in 1947, and in 1948 was the first black to play on a U.S. Olympic team. Don was named All-American in 1947 and Amateur All-American, 1948 – 1951. Since blacks weren't allowed to play professional ball, after he finished college Barksdale played four years at the AAU level with the Oakland Bittners and the Blue and Gold Atlas. He was a member of the AAU championship team in 1949. When the National Basketball Association ban on blacks was lifted, he signed with the Baltimore Bullets and played four years as a pro with Baltimore and Boston.

CONNELLEY, Tee
Player
Connelley played for the Denver Nuggets, Golden State and the San Diego Dons, and was a member of the U.S. champion team in 1939. He was elected to the All-American first team in 1940 and the second team in 1939, 1942 and 1946.

McNATT, James
Player and Coach
Born December 19, 1918, in Lindsay, Calif; graduated from Univ. Okla. with B.S. in petroleum engineering; mem. Phi Delta Theta fraternity.

McNatt was named All-Big Six forward for the Oklahoma Sooners from 1938 to 1940 and set single game scoring records in the Big Six with 29 points and later 30. He was also named All-American in his senior year. He was on the AAU All-American Phillips 66 team from 1943 to 1946; the team was national champion all four seasons.

PICKELL, Tom
Player
Pickell played for Henry Clothiers and Diamond D-X Oilers, and was a member of the U.S. championship team in 1932 and 1934. He was elected to the All-America first team in 1932 and 1934 and the second team in 1935.

SINGER, Milton
Player
Singer played with the Kansas City Athletic Club, who were U.S. champions in 1921 and 1923. He was elected to the All-America first team from 1921 to 1923 and on the second team in 1920.

STARBUCK, George
Player
Starbuck played for Hillyards, who were national champions in 1926, 1927 and 1930. He was elected to the All-America first team from 1925 to 1928.

1962

BALTER, Sam
Player and Coach
Born October 17, 1909, in Detroit, Mich; graduated from Univ. Calif, Los Angeles.

Sam was captain and All-Southern Division (Pacific Coast) for Caddy Works at UCLA in 1929. He was the first Jewish athlete to play in the Olympic Games in 1936—a doubly significant event because the games were held in Hitlerian Germany. Balter enjoyed a long career as sports announcer and writer and was selected seven times as outstanding sportscaster in Southern California. He was the first to broadcast sports coast-to-coast over the Mutual Network. He appeared in 46 movies as either a sportscaster or newsman. He was sports columnist for ten years for the *Los Angeles Herald Examiner.*

CARLTON, Bart
Player and Coach
Born February 6, 1908, in Elmore City, Okla; graduated from East Cent. State Col. (Okla.); Citizens Savings Player of the Year 1931.

Bart won eight letters in three sports while in college. He played AAU ball with the Phillips 66ers for one year and the Diamond D-X Oilers for four years. He was All-American for the national championship Diamond D-X team in 1933 – 1934.
Also in: College Basketball Hall of Fame, Citizens Savings Hall of Fame Athletic Museum; and National Association of Intercollegiate Athletics Hall of Fame.

COLVIN, Jack "Tex"
Player
Colvin was selected as All-American in 1935 while playing for Reno Cream and again in 1937 while with the Denver Safeway team. He also played on Denver Safeway team in 1937 and Denver Nuggets in 1939, both national championship teams.

COOGAN, James
Contributor
Coogan is a long-time AAU official. He was assistant manager of the U.S. Olympic team in 1952 and the manager in 1956. He also served on the U.S. Olympic basketball committee.
Also in: College Sports Information Directors Hall of Fame, Citizens Savings Hall of Fame Athletic Museum.

DARLING, Charles
Player and Coach
Born March 20, 1940 in Denison, Iowa.

Darling was the leading Big Ten scorer with 25.5 points per game in 1952 and was named to the All-American team while at the University of Iowa. He played with the Phillips 66ers from 1953 to 1957 and was a member of the U.S. Olympic team in 1956. Charles was a three time AAU All-American.

FISCHER, Herman
Player
Fischer was selected as All-American three times, in 1935 while playing with the South Kansas Stage Lines, in 1937 with the Kansas City Trails and in 1938 with the Kansas City Healys. He played on national championship teams in 1935 and 1938.

HALDORSON, Burdette E.
Player and Coach
Born January 12, 1934, in Austin, Minn; graduated from Univ. of Colorado.

Haldorson was top Big Eight scorer and All-Conference in 1954 – 1955 and named All-American his senior year. He earned AAU All-American honors four times. Burdette played five seasons with the Phillips Oilers from 1956 to 1960. He was a member of the Pan-American team in Chicago in 1959 and on the Olympic team in Melbourne in 1956 and Rome in 1960.

HEWITT, Harold
Player
Harold was selected All-American in 1926 and 1927 while playing on the championship Hillyards team and again in 1930 while on another championship team, Henry Clothiers. He played for Cook Paints in 1929, still another championship team.

LEWIS, Grady
Player and Coach
Born March 25, 1917, in Fort Worth, Tex; graduated from Univ. Okla.

Grady played with Southwestern State College in Oklahoma in 1936 and 1937. He was All-American from 1940 to 1942 while with the Phillips 66ers, who were national champions in 1946. He played in the National Basketball Association with Detroit, Baltimore and St. Louis from 1947 to 1949 and coached St. Louis from 1949 to 1953.
Also in: National Association of Intercollegiate Athletics Hall of Fame.

McCABE, Frank
Player and Coach
Born June 30, 1927, in Grand Rapids, Mich; graduated from Marquette Univ.

Frank was a member of three straight national championship teams with the Peoria Caterpillars from 1952 to 1954 and was AAU All-American from 1951 to 1954. He was a gold medalist with the U.S. Olympic team in 1952.

NASH, Martin
Player and Coach
Born February 16, 1920, in Holt, Mo; graduated from Univ. Mo.

Martin played at the University of Missouri from 1939 to 1941 and was a member of the Big Six co-championship team in 1940. He won national AAU titles in each of his seasons with the Phillips 66ers from 1944 to 1948. Nash was also AAU All-American twice and was alternate on the U.S. Olympic team in 1948.

O'GARA, Les
Player
Les was a member of the national championship 20th

Century-Fox team in 1941 and the Oakland Bittners team in 1949. He was selected All-American in 1948 and 1949 while with Oakland Bittners and again in 1950 while with the Los Angeles Police team.

PRALLE, Fred

Player and Coach

Born April 10, 1916, in St. Louis, Mo; broadcaster for Station KWON, Bartlesville, Okla, 1946–1954.

Before a knee injury and subsequent operation halted his career, Fred was named All-League from 1936 to 1938 and was All-American twice. He played with the Phillips Oilers from 1939 to 1940 and 1943 to 1945. The Phillips team was AAU champion four times during Pralle's active career.
Also in: College Basketball Hall of Fame, Citizens Savings Hall of Fame Athletic Museum.

REEVES, George

Player

Reeves was on national championship teams in 1922 and 1923 and was selected as All-American in 1922 while playing with Lowe-Campbell and in 1923–1924 while with the Kansas City Athletic Club.

RENICK, Jesse "Cab"

Player and Coach

Born September 29, 1917, in Abner, Okla; graduated from Okla. A&M Univ; Choctaw Indian.

With Renick as forward, Okla. A&M was 12-0 in Conference play and 26-3 overall in 1940. He was named All-Missouri Valley and All-American in 1939 and 1940. Jesse was a member of the U.S. Olympic team in 1948, and he coached the Phillips 66ers to the national AAU title in 1950. He was also named AAU All-American twice.
Also in: American Indian Athletic Hall of Fame; and College Basketball Hall of Fame, Citizens Savings Hall of Fame Athletic Museum.

RODY, George

Player

Rody played four years with Hillyards and was named All-American from 1923 to 1925. Hillyards was the national championship team in 1926.

TOMSIC, Ronald

Player

Ron was a member of the U.S. Olympic team in 1956, and on the U.S. Air Force national championship team in 1957. He was selected as All-American in 1955 and 1957, and again in 1959 while with the San Francisco Olympic Club.

TUCKER, Gerald

Player and Coach

Born March 14, 1922, in Douglass, Kans; graduated from Univ. Okla. with B.S. degree; Big Six tennis champion 1942; sang in men's quartet and a capella choir; Helms Player of the Year 1947.

Tucker was selected All-Big Six in 1942, 1943 and 1947 at the University of Oklahoma. He was named All-American in 1949 and 1950 while playing with the Phillips 66ers. He also coached the 66ers from 1955 to 1958, and they were national champions in 1958. Gerald was coach of the 1956 U.S. Olympic team.
Also in: College Basketball Hall of Fame, Citizens Savings Hall of Fame Athletic Museum.

WHEATLEY, William "Galloping Ghost"

Player and Coach

Born July 5, 1909, in Gypsum, Kans.

Bill was a distinguished figure in amateur basketball circles. He played with the McPherson Globe Refiners, the Kansas City Life Insurance Co. and the Golden State Dairies. He was a member of the Globe Refiners when they were AAU champions. In 1936 Bill stood on the victory stand in Berlin's Olympic Stadium to receive the gold medal on behalf of the U.S. basketball team. He was player-coach of the first quintet to make a goodwill tour of South America in 1938. He organized and coached the Oakland Bittners in 1947 and they finished second in the AAU tournament. He made his last tour in Africa in 1963, when the team won 46 games and gave 42 clinics.

WILLIAMS, George

Player and Coach

Born March 10, 1899, in Kansas City, Mo; graduated from Univ. Mo; active in real estate and dir. of Thornton and Minor Hospital, Kansas City; died of a heart attack Feb. 4, 1961, in Kansas City.

George lettered in four sports at the University of Missouri. He played center and was selected All-Conference and All-American in 1920 and 1921, when the Tigers became the Missouri Valley champions. He led the team with 311 points in 1921. He was named AAU All-Tournament from 1922 to 1924. He was a member of national championship teams, Lowe and Campbell in 1922, and the Kansas City Athletic Club in 1923.
Also in: College Basketball Hall of Fame, Citizens Savings Hall of Fame Athletic Museum.

WILLIAMS, Howard

Player and Coach

Born October 29, 1927, in New Ross, Ind; graduated from Purdue Univ; named outstanding amateur player by *Los Angeles Times* 1952; mem. Ind. High School Silver Anniversary All-State team 1970.

Williams won four letters in college and was selected All-Western Conference 1949–1950. He was All-National Industrial Basketball League and AAU All-American selection from 1951 to 1953. Howard turned down an offer to play professional ball with the National Basketball Association Minneapolis Lakers, and was a member of two national AAU championship teams while with the Peoria Caterpillars.

1963

HAYNES, Edward A.

Contributor

Haynes has been active in AAU basketball for over 30 years and has been active in staging the annual AAU championships at Denver.

MILLER, Melvin

Player and Coach

Born July 15, 1908, in Orleans, Nebr; graduated from

McPherson Col, Kans; retired from Pan American World Airways as flight training administrator.

Miller earned 13 letters during his college years. He played AAU ball with the Henry Clothiers, of Wichita, Kansas, the Ogden Boosters, the Hutchinson Reno Transits and the Golden State Dairies. He participated in 14 national tournaments and was a member of three straight championship teams with Henry Clothiers from 1930 to 1932. Miller was named amateur All-American from 1930 to 1933.

NELSON, Chester
Contributor
Nelson is sports editor of the *Rockey Mountain News* in Denver, Colo, and has served AAU basketball for more than 30 years. He was active in staging the AAU championships in Denver.

1964

AHERN, D. Patrick
Contributor
Ahern has been a patron of amateur basketball in Los Angeles and the Southern California areas since 1938. He has been especially active in AAU basketball promotions and sponsorships.

MILLER, William H.
Coach
Miller developed the Diamond DX Oilers dynasty in the thirties and the team was National AAU champion in 1933 and 1934.

REIGEL, Bill
Player and Coach
Born May 31, 1932, in Monaca, Pa; attended Duke Univ, N.C, and McNeese State Col, La; received masters degree from Cent. Mich. Univ.

Bill was All-American during his sophomore year at Duke University, but thc Army interrupted his college education. He continued playing in the service. He played one and one-half seasons for McNeese State, setting numerous records in 1955–1956. His 439 free-throw attempts and 370 conversions were National Association of Intercollegiate Athletics (NAIA) records. He received NAIA All-American and NAIA All-Time All-Tournament team recognition. Bill turned down pro offers in order to play AAU ball.
Also in: National Association of Intercollegiate Athletics Hall of Fame.

THOMPSON, Gary
Player and Coach
Born June 4, 1935, in Roland, Iowa; graduated from Iowa State Univ; Big Seven Player of the Year, All-American, and East-West Shrine Game's Most Valuable Player 1957.

Upon graduation, Gary held every Iowa State scoring record, including 40 points in one game, and the Iowa State Cyclones retired his number 20 jersey. He was AAU All-American three times while playing with Phillips 66ers and collected the most points ever scored by a 66er guard, 2348. He coached the 66ers for 6 years and compiled a 160 win–37 loss record from 1955 to 1958. Thompson played in over 30 countries representing U.S. All-Star teams.

1966

BUCK, Clifford
Contributor
Clifford is a long time AAU basketball committee official and has been active in staging the national AAU tournaments. He is past president of the AAU, and past vice president of the Federation of International Basketball Associations. He has served on the board of directors of the U.S. Olympic committee and has been active in the advancement of women's AAU basketball for the past 20 years on both the national and international levels.
Also in: Women's Basketball Hall of Fame, Citizens Savings Hall of Fame Athletic Museum.

LEVITT, Henry
Contributor
Levitt has been a long-time patron of amateur basketball and sponsored the Henry Clothier team out of Wichita, Kans, who were national AAU champions from 1930 to 1932.

LUISETTI, Angelo "Hank"
Player
See entry in Naismith Memorial Basketball Hall of Fame, 1959.
Also in: College Basketball Hall of Fame, Citizens Savings Hall of Fame Athletic Museum.

SHIPP, Jerry
Player and Coach
Born September 27, 1935, in Shreveport, La; graduated from Southeast State Col, Okla.

Jerry was a member of three Oklahoma Collegiate Conference (OCC) championship teams and led the league in scoring in his junior and senior years. He was three times All-Conference selection. He scored the OCC record of 54 points against Phillips University in 1959. He turned down pro offers to play with the Phillips Oilers, who were AAU National champions in 1962 and 1963. Jerry was named AAU All-American from 1962 to 1964.

1967

McCAFFREY, John P. "Pete"
Player and Coach
Born December 24, 1938, in Tucson, Ariz; graduated from St. Louis Univ; All-Missouri Valley, 1961.

Pete set a St. Louis record of 39 points against Wichita State in 1939. He played AAU ball with the Seattle Buchan Bakers and the Akron Goodyear Wingfoots. He led Goodyear to its first national AAU title in 1964 and was named AAU All-American from 1962 to 1964. He was a member of the U.S. team at the World Games in Rio de Janeiro in 1963 and a member of the U.S. Olympic gold medal team in Tokyo in 1964.

1969

BORYLA, Vince
Player and Coach
Born March 11, 1921, in East Chicago, Ind; attended Univ. Notre Dame and Univ. Denver; entered U.S.A.A.F. in 1941 and played with Lowry Air Force team.

Because military service interrupted his studies, Vince's college career covered a decade. He was named to the All-American team at age 28 for the University of Denver in 1949, the oldest player in the Skyline Six Conference. He broke six league scoring records. He received AAU All-American team recognition while with the Denver Nuggets in 1947 – 1948. Vince was a member of the world champion U.S. Olympic team in London, 1948. He played with the National Basketball Association Knicks from 1950 to 1954 and coached them from 1956 to 1958.

LANE, Lester
Player and Coach
Born March 6, 1932, in Purcell, Okla; attended Univ. Okla.

Lane lettered in football, basketball and track while in college and was All-State in football and basketball. He was also pole vault champ in 1951. He was All-Big Eight from 1953 to 1955 and All-American in 1955. Lester competed at the AAU level for six years, winning All-America honors as a member of the Wichita Vickers, who were national AAU champions in 1959, and the Denver-Chicago Truckers in 1961. He was a member of the U.S. Olympic gold medal team in 1960. From 1961 to 1964 Lester coached AAU and various All-Star teams and worked with national teams in Mexico and Spain from 1965 to 1970. Under Lane, Mexico finished fifth in the Olympic games in 1968.

1970

FISCHER, Hal
Coach
Fischer coached the Armed Forces basketball teams to national AAU championships in 1965, 1968 and 1969. He was also coach of the U.S. championship team in the 1967 Pan-American Games.

HARAWAY, William N.
Contributor
Haraway was the originator of the Denver Piggly Wigglies, who later became the Denver Safeways. It was the success of these teams which attracted the national AAU championships to Denver in 1935 and for many years thereafter.

SMITH, Dick
Player
Smith represented the Wichita Gridleys and the Oklahoma City Parks Clothiers, and was selected for AAU All-America team honors in 1938 and 1939.

WELLS, Dick
Player
Wells, who represented the Denver Safeways and the Denver Nuggets, was named for AAU All-American team honors from 1938 to 1940.

Induction Years Unrecorded

BISHOP, Gale
Player and Coach
Born June 6, 1922, in Sumas, Wash; graduated from Wash. State Univ.

Gale was selected All-Pacific Coast and All-American and his league's top scorer in 1943. He played for Firecrest Dairy and Ft. Lewis, and established an AAU record with 50 points in one game in 1944, and broke it by scoring 62 just one year later. He was twice named AAU All-American. He played in the National Basketball Association with Philadelphia in 1949, averaging 8.3 points per game in 56 games.

BOUSHKA, Richard
Player and Coach
Born January 29, 1934, in Springfield, Ill; graduated St. Louis Univ.

Dick had a 20.5 scoring average with the St. Louis Billikens and was an AAU performer with the Air Force All-Stars and the Wichita Vickers. He scored a personal AAU high of 54 points against the Denver Truckers. Boushka was named AAU All-America twice.

HOLT, Victor
Player and Coach
Born May 8, 1908, in Heavener, Okla; son of a pharmacist; championship prep swimmer; participated in track, high-jump, shot-put and discus events; Alpha Tau Omega fraternity; B.S. in business administration from Univ. Okla; Citizens Savings Player of the Year 1928.

Vic attained All-American status with the University of Oklahoma, leading the Sooners to an 18-0 record in 1928. He was All-American with the Cook Paint AAU team, who won consecutive championships, 1929 – 1930. Holt ended his playing career with two seasons for Goodyear.

LYONS, G. Russell
Player

MILLER, William H.
Player

POLLARD, Jim "Kangaroo Kid"
Player and Coach
Born July 9, 1922, in Oakland, Calif; graduated from Stanford Univ.

Jim was All-American for Stanford's NCAA champions in 1942 and was tournament high scorer despite missing the final game because of flu. He played Coast Guard and AAU ball before joining the Minneapolis Lakers, where he played from 1948 to 1955. During his AAU ball days, he was All-American with both the San Diego Dons and the Oakland Bittners. He played in four All-Star games, and played on five NBA championship teams. He was named to the All-NBA first team twice. Pollard coached Chicago in 1960 and Minneapolis in 1962, both in the National Basketball Association and also coached Minnesota in 1968 and Miami in 1969 and 1970 in the American Basketball Association.

Also in: Major League Basketball Hall of Fame, Citizens Savings Hall of Fame Athletic Museum.

THOMAS, E. J.
Player

WOMBLE, Warren
Player and Coach
Born May 15, 1920, in Durant, Okla; graduated from Southeastern State Col, Okla.

Womble was the head basketball coach of the U.S. Olympic team in 1952 and the assistant coach in 1960. He guided the Peoria Caterpillars to five national AAU titles, and they also won the world title at Rio de Janeiro in 1954. Womble coached the U.S. All-Star team that toured Russia in 1958.
Also in: National Association of Intercollegiate Athletics Hall of Fame.

YARDLEY, George
Player and Coach
Born November 3, 1928, in Hollywood, Calif; graduated from Stanford Univ.

George scored 820 points in three years at Stanford and was co-captain his senior year. He was the first NBA player to score 2000 points in one season (1958) and averaged 27.8 points per game, leading the league in scoring. He played NBA ball with Ft. Wayne, Detroit and Syracuse between 1954 and 1960. During his career, Yardley was AAU All-American with Stewart Chevrolet of San Francisco and Los Alamitos Navy. He also was All-NBA twice and played in 6 All-Star games.
Also in: Major League Basketball Hall of Fame, Citizens Savings Hall of Fame Athletic Museum.

Basketball — College Hall of Fame

In 1949 this Hall of Fame was originated to honor college players, coaches and contributors to college basketball. As of November, 1966, there are 245 members in the Hall, selected by the Hall of Fame Board. Upon induction, each new member receives a Hall of Fame Award, as well as having his name engraved on the Trophy which is kept in the Citizens Savings Hall of Fame Athletic Museum, Los Angeles international sports shrine. Also, biographical sketches of each inductee are placed in the library at the Hall.

1954

BUNKER, Herbert
Player
Born August 24, 1896, in Nevada, Mo; graduated from Univ. Mo; All-Missouri Valley 1921–1923; All-American two times.

Herb played in only four losing games during his college years from 1921 to 1923, in which time Missouri won 48 games. Bunker was known as a clean player and all-around performer.

DIDDLE, Edgar A.
Coach
See entry in Naismith Memorial Basketball Hall of Fame, 1971.

HINKLE, Paul D. "Tony"
Coach
See entry in Indiana Basketball Hall of Fame, 1964.
Also in: College Football Hall of Fame, Citizens Savings Hall of Fame Athletic Museum; and Naismith Memorial Basketball Hall of Fame.

MODZELEWSKI, Stanley
Player
Stanley played for Rhode Island University and was selected Citizens Savings All-American 1940–1942 and Player of the Year 1942.

OLSEN, Harold G. "Ole"
Coach
See entry in Naismith Memorial Basketball Hall of Fame, 1959.

1955

BOHLER, J. Fred
Coach
Bohler had a 192–155 record at Washington State University where he coached from 1909 to 1926. The team was Pacific Coast Conference champion in 1917. He was also a college basketball historian and an authority on Pacific Northwest basketball for many years.

BROBERG, Gus
Player
Born June 16, 1920, in Manchester, N.H; graduated from Dartmouth Col; Gold Key Award for service to Conn. sports; Helms Athletic Foundation All-American Team.

Gus played three seasons in center field for the Dartmouth baseball team and led the team in hitting at .308 as a sophomore. During his varsity basketball days from 1939 to 1941, he led the team to three Ivy League championships and was conference scoring champion each season. Broberg set a record of 56 straight free throws during his last two years and his career average was 14.4 in 68 games.

DAVIES, Charles "Chick"
Coach
Born April 30, 1900, in New Castle, Pa; graduated from Duquesne Univ.

1924–1943 Duquesne University, coach
1947–1948 Duquesne University, coach
1944–1946 Homestead (Pa). High School, coach
1949–1955 Homestead (Pa). High School, coach
1963–1965 Robert Morris Junior College (Pa), coach

Chick has an overall coaching record of 574 wins and 150 losses, including 314-105 in NCAA play, 191-35 for high school and 69-10 at the junior college level. In 1940 Duquesne finished second in the National Invitational Tournament and Homestead High won state prep championships in 1946 and 1950.

FOSTER, Harold E. "Bud"
Coach

See entry in Naismith Memorial Basketball Hall of Fame, 1964.

LAVELLI, Anthony
Player

Born July 11, 1926, in Somerville, Mass; graduated from Yale Univ; Helms Athletic Foundation All-American Teams 1946, 1948 and 1949; Player of the Year 1949.

Lavelli specialized in the accordion and basketball at Yale, where he played from 1946 to 1949. He rates high in the Yale Bulldogs' record book as an all-time career and season points leader. He had a four-year scoring average of 20.3, encompassing 97 games. He scored 52 points in one game against Williams College. He set NCAA season records with 215 successful tries out of 261 free throw attempts. While playing in the NBA, he played in 86 games for a 6.9 average.

NOWAK, Paul
Player

Born March 15, 1914, in South Bend, Ind; graduated from Univ. Notre Dame; Helms Athletic Foundation College Basketball All-American Teams 1936 – 1938.

He earned a starting position at Notre Dame in his sophomore year and relinquished it only upon graduation. He had a 62-8 playing record with the Irish team. Paul played for the Firestones (National League), Rochester and Philadelphia Sphas as center 1939 – 1941.

ROBERTSON, Alfred J.
Coach

Born May 17, 1891, in St. Cloud, Minn; attended college in Mont; died Oct. 30, 1948, in Peoria, Ill.

Al Robertson's first coaching job was at Fort Hays State College in Kansas in 1920. His lifetime coaching record was 322-195, including 316-186 at Bradley where he coached 1921 – 1943 and 1946 – 1948. Dave Owen, English professor and later Bradley president, and Robertson helped the Braves achieve national prominence. Bradley basketball had dropped off drastically as the team won only one of 14 games in 1935. Doubling as a sports publicist while teaching, Owen arranged a major league schedule. Meanwhile, Robertson traveled all over Illinois scouting for top players. In playing its first major schedule, Bradley won 18 of 20 games and earned a National Invitational Tournament bid in 1938. The Robertson Memorial Field House on the Bradley campus is named in his honor.
Also in: College Football Hall of Fame, Citizens Savings Hall of Fame Athletic Museum.

SCHLUNDT, Don
Player

Born March 15, 1933 in South Bend, Ind; graduated from Ind. Univ; Helms Athletic Foundation All-American Teams 1953 – 1955.

Don entered the national limelight when he and teammate Bob Leonard carried Indiana to the NCAA championship against Kansas in 1953. They won that game by a one point margin, 69 to 68. Schlundt tallied 30 in the finale, after scoring 47 points on two separate occasions during the regular season play. He hit 25 of 30 free throws against Ohio State, a Big-Ten record for conversions and attempts. At graduation Don held the most Conference marks.

1957

CAPPON, Franklin C. "Cappy"
Coach

Born October 17, 1900, in Holland, Mich; graduated from Univ. Mich; Western Conference Medal; died November 29, 1961.

Cappy was a college standout in football and basketball. He coached at Luther College in 1925, University of Michigan 1932 – 1938 and at Princeton University 1939 – 1943 and 1947 – 1961. Cappy suffered a fatal heart attack at Princeton's Dillon Gymnasium just three days before the start of what would have been his 24th season at Princeton. His lifetime coaching record was 350-253.

FISHER, Harry A.
Player

See entry in Naismith Memorial Basketball Hall of Fame, 1973.

HURLEY, Marcus
Player

Hurley was selected to Helms Athletic Foundation All-American Teams 1905 – 1907.

KEINATH, Charles
Player

Born November 13, 1886, in Philadelphia, Pa; graduated from Univ. Pa; Helms Athletic Foundation All-American 1906 – 1909; Player of the Year 1908; died April 18, 1966, in Drexel Hill, Pa.

Keinath was such an accomplished dribbler that rules makers outlawed the two-handed dribble. He was also a very good shooter. He scored the entire 16 points in Pennsylvania's 16-15 victory over Columbia University in 1908.

KIENDL, Theodore
Player

Kiendl was named by Helms Athletic Foundation to their All-American Teams 1909 – 1911.

LANNIGAN, Henry
Coach

Lannigan coached at the University of Virginia from 1906 to 1924 and had a 240-89 record.

McCRACKEN, Branch
Coach

See entry in Indiana Basketball Hall of Fame, 1963.
Also in: Naismith Memorial Basketball Hall of Fame.

McNICHOL, Dan
Player

Born October 12, 1898, in Philadelphia, Pa; graduated

from Univ. Pa; Helms Athletic Foundation All-American Teams 1919–1921; died May 19, 1963, in Philadelphia.

McNichol was one of five brothers who starred at Pennsylvania. He led his team to 20 straight wins and a national title against the University of Chicago in 1920. In scoring 152 points that season, Don set a school record that stood for 26 years. In later years he assisted his brother, Edward, as Pennsylvania coach.

RYAN, John
Player
John was named by the Helms Athletic Foundation to All-American Teams 1907–1909.

STEINMETZ, Christian
Player
See entry in Naismith Memorial Basketball Hall of Fame, 1961.
Also in: Wisconsin Hall of Fame.

WOODS, Ray
Player
Ray was named to Helms Athletic Foundation All-American Teams 1915–1917.

1958

HICKEY, Edgar
Coach
Born December 20, 1902, in Reynolds, Nebr; graduated from Creighton Univ; mem. of Alpha Sigma Nu and Delta Theta Pi; honorary citizen of Boys Town, Nebr; coached service teams during W.W. II.

Hickey played quarterback on the football team for three years and played basketball for two years while in college. He coached at Creighton University from 1936 to 1943, St. Louis University from 1949 to 1958 and at Marquette University from 1959 to 1964. In a 20 year period, he had a 344-161 record. His Creighton and St. Louis teams either won or shared seven Missouri Valley Conference titles. Hickey had originally planned to enter his father's law firm, but just weeks before receiving his law degree at Creighton, his father was killed in an auto accident and Hickey accepted a coaching position instead. He was a long-time member and past president of the Basketball Coaches Association.

LEVIS, George
Player
Born November 22, 1894, in Madison, Wis; graduated from Univ. Wis; High School All-State 1912; Helms Athletic Foundation Player of the Year 1916.

Levis was a forward and All-State selection for Madison High School state champs in 1912, and was top scorer in the Western conference for two years. George coached at Madison High School in Carleton, Ind, and the Hillyard Chemical Co. Under Levis' direction, Hillyard won consecutive AAU national championships in 1926 and 1927. He worked with Walter Meanwell at the University of Wisconsin from 1928 to 1933 as assistant coach. He spent 18 years as a college official. Levis designed the first woolen basketball inner sock and the first chart form scorebook.

MACAULEY, Edward E.
Player
See entry in Naismith Memorial Basketball Hall of Fame, 1960.
Also in: Major League Basketball Hall of Fame, Citizens Savings Hall of Fame Athletic Museum.

MAUER, John W.
Coach
Born September 4, 1901, in Aurora, Ill; graduated from Univ. Ill; Western Conference Medal for scholarship and athletics 1926.

John played both football and basketball at Illinois. He spent 32 years in coaching, including the Universities of Kentucky, Tennessee, Florida and Miami of Ohio and Army. His overall record is 343 wins against 270 losses.

RUSSELL, William F.
Player
See entry in Naismith Memorial Basketball Hall of Fame, 1974.
Also in: Major League Basketball Hall of Fame, Citizens Savings Hall of Fame Athletic Museum.

VAN ALSTYNE, Benjamin F.
Coach
Van Alstyne coached at Ohio Wesleyan University from 1921 to 1926 and Michigan State University from 1927 to 1949. His coaching record overall was 307–193.

WITTE, Les
Player
Born April 2, 1911, in Swanton, Nebr; graduated from Univ. Wyo; All-Rocky Mountain Conference Teams 1931–1934; All-American first team 1932–1934.

Les was a left-handed hook shot artist and helped lead the Wyoming Cowboys to two league titles. He was named to the All-Rocky Mountain Conference teams from 1931 to 1934 and was the first Cowboy player to score over 1000, which he did with a whopping 1083. He later played AAU ball with the Denver Athletic Club and the Kansas City Life teams.

1959

BLACK, Charles T.
Player
Born January 5, 1901, in Alton, Ill; graduated from Univ. Kans; Helms Athletic Foundation All-American Teams 1923 and 1924; he was also named Player of the Year in 1924.

Black played for coach Phog Allen at Kansas. During his playing career, the Kansas Jayhawks recorded a 48-6 record. During 6 years of coaching at Nebraska, he compiled a 52–55 record.

CARLTON, Bart
Player
See entry in Amateur Basketball Hall of Fame, Citizens Savings Hall of Fame Athletic Museum, 1962.
Also in: National Association of Intercollegiate Athletics Hall of Fame.

CHANDLER, William

Player

Born August 27, 1895, in Chicago, Ill; graduated from Univ. Wis; Helms Athletic Foundation Player of the Year 1918; died May 23, 1953 in Milwaukee, Wis.

As a college center, Bill played on two national championship teams. He coached the Iowa State Cyclones from 1922 to 1928 and Marquette University from 1931 to 1951. His best coaching season came in 1933 when Marquette won 14 of their 17 games. His overall coaching record was 233-283.

DIXON, George

Player

Dixon was named to Helms Athletic Foundation All-American Teams 1926 and 1927.

GALLAGHER, John J. "Taps"

Coach

See entry in Athletic Directors Hall of Fame, Citizens Savings Hall of Fame Athletic Museum, 1970.

GUTTERO, Lee "Rubberlegs"

Player

Born July 1, 1912, in Philadelphia, Pa; moved to California at age 15; graduated from Univ. of Southern Calif; All-American 1934 and 1935.

Lee was selected as All-City while attending high school in Los Angeles. He averaged 15.5 in conference play during his senior year. His exceptional jumping ability earned him his nickname, as he seldom lost the tip on jump balls. He played in only two AAU games, with Universal Pictures in a national tournament.

LOVELETTE, Clyde

Player

Born September 7, 1929, in Terre Haute, Ind; graduated from Univ. Kans; All-American two times; Helms Athletic Foundation player of the Year 1952; served as sheriff in hometown for one term.

Lovelette was not outstanding in high school, but developed into a great scorer at Kansas, where he played from 1950 to 1952. He wasn't fast or graceful, but had remarkable shooting skill. As a senior, he led the nation with 315 field goals, 795 points and a 28.4 average. He credited his mother for his success, as she made him exercise and jump rope to overcome childhood awkwardness. He played in the 1952 Olympics. Lovelette had a 17.0 average in his 701 NBA games between 1954 and 1964. He played in three All-Star games and was on the All-NBA second team once.

Also in: Major League Basketball Hall of Fame, Citizens Savings Hall of Fame Athletic Museum.

MOERS, Robert

Player

Born August 9, 1918, in Groveton, Tex; graduated from Univ. Tex; All-American; All-Southwestern Conference twice; Air Force Surgeon during W.W. II, received Bronze Star.

Moers won seven letters in college, three each in basketball and football and one in track. He was a member of the league basketball champs in 1939 and was considered an outstanding dribbler.

Also in: Texas High School Basketball Hall of Fame.

RENICK, Jesse "Cab"

Player

See entry in Amateur Basketball Hall of Fame, Citizens Savings Hall of Fame Athletic Museum, 1959.

Also in: American Indian Athletic Hall of Fame.

SHANDS, H. G. "Pete"

Coach

Shands coached at North Texas State University and Southwest Texas State College over 33 years. His record is 318-353. His teams often played opponents in a higher classification than their own.

SHELTON, Everett F.

Coach

Born May 12, 1898, in Cunningham, Kans; served two years in U.S. Marine Corps; graduated from Phillips Univ.

1924–1926 Phillips University, coach
1940–1943 University of Wyoming, coach
1945–1949 University of Wyoming, coach
1960–1968 Sacramento State College, coach

Shelton played four years of football, basketball and baseball at Phillips. He began his coaching career at Claremore (Okla.) High School, a career that covered 46 years. Before retiring, he had coached at AAU and university levels. In 1943 Wyoming won the Mountain States Conference, finished third in a national AAU tournament and won the NCAA title. Shelton's lifetime coaching record was 850-437, including 494-347 at university level competition.

SPOHN, Gerald

Player

Born August 6, 1905, in Arkansas City, Kans; graduated from Washburn Univ; AAU All-American 1925; All-American 1927.

Gerald was a basketball, track and tennis star at college and held the school's broad jump record for many years. He played AAU ball with Hillyards, Henry Clothiers and the Phillips 66ers. He helped Henry Levitt form Henry Clothiers and played on the Phillips team, which was the first entry in the Missouri Valley Conference.

TOWER, Oswald

Noteworthy Contributor

See entry in Naismith Memorial Basketball Hall of Fame, 1959.

WILLIAMS, George

Player

See entry in Amateur Basketball Hall of Fame, Citizens Savings Hall of Fame Athletic Museum, 1962.

1961

ANDERSON, Harold

Coach

Born September 11, 1902, in Akron, Ohio; graduated

from Otterbein Col; died June 13, 1967, in Fort Lauderdale, Fla.

1935 – 1942 University of Toledo, coach
1943 – 1963 Bowling Green University, coach

Anderson was a highly successful coach with a lifetime record of 504 – 226. In his 29 years he produced nine All-Americans at Bowling Green, won three Mid-American Conference titles, had 6 teams in National Invitational Tournaments and one NCAA tournament team. He is a past member of the Honors Committee of the Naismith Memorial Basketball Hall of Fame and is a past president of the National Association of Basketball Coaches.

BERGER, Louis
Player
Louis was named to the Helms Athletic Foundation All-American Teams 1931 and 1932.

BUNN, John W.
Coach
See entry in Naismith Memorial Basketball Hall of Fame, 1964.

CASTLE, Lewis
Player
Castle was selected on the Helms Athletic Foundation All-American Team 1912 and 1914.

COOKE, Dr. Louis
Coach
Born February 15, 1868, in Toledo, Ohio; received M.D. from Univ. Vt; died August 19, 1943, in Minneapolis, Minn, at age 75.

Cooke was the founder and developer of the department of physical education and athletics at the University of Minnesota. He organized classes in various sports and acted as coach in all of them. He coached basketball from 1897 until 1923; his overall record was 225-113.

DRAKE, Bruce
Coach
See entry in Naismith Memorial Basketball Hall of Fame, 1972.

HOUGHTON, Ernest
Player
Born October 10, 1893, in Princeton, N.J; graduated from Union Col, N.Y; All-American twice; Helms Athletic Foundation Player of the Year 1915; died July 24, 1941, in Rochester, N.Y.

Houghton was a football quarterback and a first baseman on the Union College team, as well as playing basketball. He led the basketball team to a 43-10 record between 1912 and 1915.

KRAUSE, Edward W. "Moose"
Player
See entry in Naismith Memorial Basketball Hall of Fame, 1975.

NEWELL, Peter
Coach
Born August 31, 1915, in Vancouver, B.C, Can; graduated from Loyola Univ. of Los Angeles.

As a college coach, at University of San Francisco, Michigan State University and University of California 1947-1960 Newell had an overall record of 233-123. His San Francisco team won the National Invitational Tournament in 1949 and he took the team to two NCAA championships, winning in 1959 and finishing second in 1960. He was athletic director at the University of California for eight years, before joining San Diego of the NBA as general manager. When the team moved to Houston, he served in an advisory capacity.

OSS, Arnold
Player
Born August 23, 1899, in Lidgerwood, N. Dak; graduated from Univ. Minn; Helms Athletic Foundation All-American Teams 1919 and 1921; Alumni Service Award 1961.

While playing for Minnesota, Oss was the Gopher's captain and in 1921 was awarded the Conference medal for scholarship and athletics. He was also named to the All-Conference team that same year. He won eight letters, three each in basketball and football and two in track. He later assisted Dr. Louis Cooke in coaching basketball and Henry Williams in football. He promoted and managed Minnesota state high school basketball tournaments for ten years.

ROBERTSON, Oscar "Big O"
Player
Born November 24, 1938, in Charlotte, Tenn; graduated from Univ. Cincinnati; NBA Rookie of the Year 1961; All-Pro First Team 1961 – 1969; Podoloff Cup Winner 1964; Most Valuable Player three times in East-West All-Star Game.

1961 – 1970 Cincinnati Royals, guard
1970 – 1973 Milwaukee Bucks, guard

While at the University of Cincinnati, Oscar was NCAA top scorer from 1958 to 1960, with an average of 33.8 points and 15.2 in rebounds in an 88 game scoring career. The team won 79 games and took three Missouri Valley titles. After his years with the Royals, Oscar was traded to the Bucks, where he joined Kareem Abdul-Jabbar, forming the nucleus of the NBA championship team in 1971. Robertson was the NBA lifetime leader in assists, and second in points.

SEVERANCE, Alex
Coach
Born June 30, 1907, in New York City; A.B. from Villanova Univ, valedictorian of 1929 class; Doctor of Laws degree from Temple Univ 1933; magistrate of Fredyffrin Township in Chester Co, Pa. for 16 years.

Alex paticipated in college basketball, baseball and boxing, winning the boxing title for his weight class. At Villanova University 1937 – 1961 he coached freshmen for 14 years and varsity for 25. He was dean of Philadelphia's Big Five coaches until his retirement.

1962

CHAMBERLAIN, Wilt "The Stilt"
Player
Born August 21, 1936, in Philadelphia, Pa; attended Univ. Kans; Consensus All-American twice, 1972 Play-

offs Most Valuable Player Award; Podoloff Cup 1960, and 1966 – 1968.

At 7 ft. 1 in, Wilt is still a dominating force in basketball. While playing at the University of Kansas from 1956 to 1958, he hit 52 points in his first varsity game. He left school before his senior year to play one season with the Harlem Globetrotters. In the NBA, he has played with the Philadelphia-San Francisco Warriors, the Philadelphia 76ers and the Los Angeles Lakers. He originally signed with the Warriors after being their first territorial draft. He is the all-time top NBA scorer and rebounder and the first player to amass 30,000 points. In 1962 he became the first pro to score 100 points in a single game, and did this by hitting on 36 of 63 field goals and 28 of 32 fouls. He was the scoring champ for seven straight years, 1959 to 1966. Since 1973, Wilt owns the highest field goal percentage (72.7) and was the first pro in NBA history to top 70 percent.
Also in: Black Athletes Hall of Fame; and Major League Basketball Hall of Fame, Citizens Savings Hall of Fame Athletic Museum.

DISCHINGER, Terry
Player
Born November 21, 1940, in Terre Haute, Ind; graduated from Purdue Univ; All-American 1960-1962; NBA Rookie of the Year 1963; U.S. Army 1966-1967.

Terry played four sports in high school and was named All-State in two. In basketball he averaged 28.3 points per game, hitting 55.3 percent from the field and 81.9 percent from the foul line. In 1960 he was also the youngest member of the U.S. Olympic team. Dischinger played in two All-Star games with Chicago-Baltimore and one with the Detroit Pistons.

GREASON, Murray
Coach
In 23 years at Wake Forest College, Greason's coaching record was 283-244.

LUCAS, Jerry
Player
Born March 30, 1940, in Middletown, Ohio; graduated from Ohio State Univ; Helms Athletic Foundation All-American Team 1960 – 1962; Player of the Year 1961; Rookie of the Year 1964; UPI, AP and U.S. Basketball Writers Player of the Year twice; has an unusual repertoire of magic tricks.

At Ohio State from 1959 to 1962, Jerry helped lead the Buckeyes to a 78-6 record over three seasons. The team won one NCAA title and was runnerup twice during that time. Although his interest in sports was strong, his studies didn't suffer, as he graduated in the top 4 percent of his class. He signed with the NBA Cincinnati Royals, who made Lucas territorial choice while he was still in high school. He holds the Cincinnati all-time rebound record with 40. He is one of the few pros to exceed the 10,000 figure in both points and rebounds. He has also played with the San Francisco Warriors and the New York Knicks of the NBA.

MACMILLAN, David
Coach

1922 – 1927 University of Idaho, coach
1928 – 1942 University of Minnesota, coach

MacMillan coached for 24 years; his overall record is 271-188.

ROSENBLUTH, Leonard
Player
Born January 22, 1933, in New York City; graduated from Univ. N. C; All-Atlantic Coast Conference Team and Helms Athletic Foundation All-American 1955 – 1957; Helms Player of the Year in 1957.

1955 – 1957 University North Carolina, forward
1958 – 1959 Philadelphia Warriors, forward

Lennie averaged 27.9 points per game in 1957 as the Tarheels won the national title; he had the most career points (2054) and the best career average (26.9) while there. Rosenbluth was the Number One draft choice of the Warriors and averaged 4.2 points in 82 games with them in the 1958 – 1959 season.

RUSSEL, John D. "Honey"
Coach
See entry in Naismith Memorial Basketball Hall of Fame, 1964.

SHIPLEY, Burton
Coach
Shipley had a 254-217 record at the University of Maryland where he coached from 1924 until 1947.

STALCUP, Wilbur "Sparky"
Coach
Born February 13, 1910, in Forbes, Mo; graduated from Northwest Mo. State Col; died April 12, 1972, in Columbia, Mo.

1934 – 1942 Northwest Missouri State College, coach
1947 – 1962 University of Missouri, coach

Stalcup was a three-sport standout in college and played basketball under Hank Iba, who was coach at Northwest Missouri. Stalcup began his basketball coaching career at Jackson (Mo.) High School and resigned after just one year to succeed Iba at his alma mater. His record was 119-47 with the Northwest Bearcats and at Missouri he had a 195-179 mark. Stalcup served as president of the National Association of Basketball Coaches in 1962. He was named administrative assistant to the athletic director at the University of Missouri after he retired from coaching. He also served as the radio color commentator for the University Missouri football games.

WATTS, Ray E.
Coach
In his 30 years as coach at Baldwin-Wallace College, Watts had a record of 246-202.
Also in: National Association of Intercollegiate Athletics Hall of Fame.

WEST, Jerry
Player
Born May 28, 1939, in Cabin Creek, W.Va; graduated from Univ. W.Va; All-NBA Team first team nine times; Playoffs Most Valuable Player 1969; Consensus All-American twice.

Jerry lead West Virginia to three straight Southern Conference championships from 1958 to 1960 and was a member of the NCAA runnerup team in 1959. He was a member of the U.S. Olympics team in Rome in 1960. In his pro career with the Los Angeles Lakers, West has received numerous honors. He achieved a long-standing goal by winning the NBA championship in 1972 and is the subject of the biography, *Mr. Clout,* symbolic of his abilities under pressure. Due to injuries, he has missed almost two full seasons and has had his nose broken eight times.

1963

ACKERMAN, Tusten
Player
Born October 7, 1901, in Elk City, Okla; graduated from Univ. Kans; All-American and All-Conference twice; Dr. James Naismith's All-Modern Team 1926.

Tusten played with the University of Kansas Jayhawks and the team lost only five times during his years from 1923 to 1925. He captained the team his senior year. He played with the Kansas City Athletic Club from 1925 to 1927.

ALEXANDER, Louis A.
Coach
1930 – 1931 University of Connecticut, coach
1932 – 1957 University of Rochester, coach

In his 28 years, Alexander's coaching record was 265-150.

CARMICHAEL, Richard
Player
Carmichael was selected to Helms Athletic Foundation All-American Team 1923 and 1924.

COX, Forrest "Frosty"
Coach
Born May 3, 1907, in Newton, Kans; graduated from Univ. Kans; died May 23, 1962, in Missoula, Mont.

1920 – 1931 University of Kansas Jayhawks, coach
1936 – 1942 University of Colorado, coach
1945 – 1950 University of Colorado, coach
1956 – 1962 University of Montana, coach

Cox distinguished himself both as a player and a coach. he gained All-Big Six honors with the Jayhawks in 1930 – 1931. He coached Colorado to a 147-89 record, winning the National Invitational Tournament title in 1940. In his 21 years, Cox won 227 while losing 174.

CRISP, Henry
Coach
Born December 10, 1897, in Crisp, N.C; lost right hand in a sawmill accident when 13; graduated from Va. Inst. Technol; died January 23, 1970, in Birmingham, Ala.

Crisp won eight letters in football, baseball and track while at Virginia Tech. At Alabama as coach 1924 – 1942 and 1946, he compiled a 256-129 record and the Crimson Tide won one Southeastern Conference title and one Southern Conference crown.

EDWARDS, George
Coach
Born October 14, 1890, in Kansas City, Mo; received B.J. from Univ. Mo; M.Ed. from Ohio State Univ; died May 15, 1972, in Columbia, Mo.

1914 – 1926 Kansas and Missouri high schools and Kansas Wesleyan University, coach
1927 – 1946 University Missouri Tigers, coach

Edwards competed on the baseball, basketball, football and tumbling squads at Missouri and captained the basketball team in 1913. As coach he led the team to three conference titles with a 182-146 record. Edwards was a professor of physical education for 34 years at Missouri and was president of the National Association of Basketball Coaches in 1938. He wrote *The Basketball Coaches Creed,* which is still used today as a preface to the NCAA rulebook. He is a revered figure in Missouri athletic history.

FARMER, Dan
Coach
1933 – 1957 San Francisco State College, coach

Dan Farmer was coach at San Francisco State College from 1933 to 1957. His 23 year coaching record is 182-171.

FERGUSON, William J.
Coach
Born December 18, 1896, in Philadelphia, Pa; graduated from St. Joseph's Col. (Pa).

1922 – 1936 Roman Catholic High School, Philadelphia, assistant coach
1929 – 1953 St. Joseph's College, coach

Ferguson assisted Billy Markward, the dean of Philadelphia basketball coaches, for 15 years. At St. Joseph's his best season was in 1943 when he won 18 of 22 games. His overall coaching record at St. Joseph's was 311-208.

FLOYD, Darrell
Player
Born May 11, 1932, in Thomasville, N.C; graduated from Furman Univ; Southern-Conference Athlete of the Year twice; Helms Athletic Foundation All-American Team 1955 and 1956.

Darrell was the top scorer at Furman with an average of 35.9 in 1955 and 33.8 in 1956. He scored mostly with his jump shots beyond the foul circle. He was student body president in his senior year.

GROAT, Richard
Player
Born November 4, 1930, in Swissvale, Pa; graduated from Duke Univ; Helms Athletic Foundation Player of the Year 1951; All-American Team 1951 and 1952.

During his junior year at Duke, Dick set an NCAA mark with 261 free throws. He averaged 26 points per game during his senior season and was twice named assist leader and had a college high of 48 points against the University of North Carolina. He played only one season in the NBA with the Fort Wayne club in 1953. He gained much greater acclaim as a shortstop with the Pittsburgh Pirates and the St. Louis Cardinals. He retired from pro baseball in 1967.

HAAS, Cyril
Player
Cyril was selected to the Helms Athletic Foundation All-American Team in 1916 and 1917.

HOBSON, Howard A.
Coach
See entry in Naismith Memorial Basketball Hall of Fame, 1965.

IRELAND, George
Player
Born June 15, 1913, in Madison, Wis; graduated from Univ. Notre Dame; Helms Athletic Foundation All-American Team 1934 and 1935.

Ireland coached at Loyola University, Illinois, from 1952 until 1973. During that time his team won the NCAA crown in 1963. His overall record is 200 – 234. He produced a film, *High Speed Basketball,* for the NCAA.

JULIAN, Alvin F. "Doggie"
Coach
See entry in Naismith Memorial Basketball Hall of Fame, 1967.

McDERMOTT, Hugh
Coach
In his 17 years at the University of Oklahoma, McDermott had a record of 185 wins and 106 losses.

O'BRIEN, John
Player
Born December 11, 1930, in South Amboy, N.J; graduated from Seattle Univ; Helms Athletic Foundation All-American Team 1952 and 1953.

John played at Seattle from 1951 to 1953 and scored 2537 points for a 25.6 college record. He was the college division field goal percentage leader in 1951 with 57.1 percent. To raise funds for the 1952 Olympics, Seattle played an exhibition game against the Harlem Globetrotters. He scored 43 points and Seattle won, 84 to 81. After college, John and his twin brother Eddie both became National League infielders.

PHILLIP, Andrew
Player
See entry in Naismith Memorial Basketball Hall of Fame, 1961.
Also in: Major League Basketball Hall of Fame, Citizens Savings Hall of Fame Athletic Museum.

PITT, Malcolm U.
Coach
After 19 years as coach with Richmond University 1933 – 1952, Pitt had a 194 – 165 record.
Also in: College Baseball (Coaches) Hall of Fame, Citizens Savings Hall of Fame Athletic Museum; and American Association of College Baseball Coaches Hall of Fame.

READ, Herbert W. "Buck"
Coach
Born February 8, 1883, in Saxmundham, Eng; attended Univ. Mich. and Western Mich. Univ; master's degree from Columbia Univ; with AEF during W.W. I; died August 15, 1970, in Newport Beach, Calif, at age 87.

Buck did not play basketball in college, but learned the game at the YMCA. He coached at Western Michigan University and compiled a 351 – 172 record. In 1930 he had his best season with 16 wins and no losses. He was president of the National Association of Basketball Coaches and served three terms as chairman of the NCAA basketball rules committee.

RIPLEY, Elmer H.
Coach
See entry in Naismith Memorial Basketball Hall of Fame, 1972.

RUBY, J. Craig
Player
Born May 30, 1896, in Stockport, Iowa; graduated from Univ. Mo; Helms Athletic Foundation All-American Team 1918 and 1919; All-Conference 1918 – 1920; served in Marine Flying Corps during W.W. I.

1921 – 1922 University of Missouri, coach
1923 – 1936 University of Illinois, coach

While Ruby was playing at the University of Missouri, the team won 47 of their 52 games and Ruby was team captain for two years. He succeeded Dr. Walter Meanwell as coach in 1920 and in the 1921 – 1922 season, compiled a 32 – 2 record. In his 16 years at the University of Illinois, he had a 148 – 97 record and either won or shared four league championships. He attended the first meeting of the National Association of Basketball Coaches in 1927 and served as president in 1929. He authored two books, *How to Play and Coach Basketball* and *Coaching Basketball.*

SALE, Forest "Aggie"
Player
Born June 25, 1911, in Lawrenceburg, Ky; graduated from Univ. Ky; Helms Athletic Foundation All-American Team 1932 and 1933; Player of the Year 1933; has served in the Kentucky House of Representatives since 1971.

Sale chose the University of Kentucky over Ohio State University simply because it was closer to his home. He earned his nickname because he studied agriculture in college. He coached for 31 years.

SCHUMACHER, Alphonse
Player
Born March 4, 1894, in Dayton, Ohio; graduated from St. Mary's Inst. (now Univ. Dayton); Helms Athletic Foundation All-American Team, 1912 and 1913; ordained Roman Catholic priest; died September 11, 1966, at age 72.

During his college playing days, Schumacher played on two undefeated teams and the St. Mary's Cadets claimed one championship. After he was ordained, Schumacher served assignments in Dayton, Hamilton, Cincinnati, Greenfield and Xenia, Ohio. At the time of his death, he was pastor of Xenia's St. Brigid Catholic Church.

SWEENEY, George
Player
Born May 19, 1898, in Atlantic City, N.J; graduated from Univ. Pa. Wharton School of Finance; Helms Athletic Foundation All-American Team 1918 – 1920; 4 children and 11 grandchildren.

Sweeney scored 44 points in a championship series against the University of Chicago in 1920. After graduation he played pro ball with the Buffalo Hewitts. In his second year with Buffalo he tore the cartilage in his knee which forced an early retirement as a player. He then coached Canisius High School for one year and Atlantic City High School for 24 years. He was also a teacher and administrator.

TANENBAUM, Sid
Player
Born October 8, 1925, in Brooklyn, N.Y; graduated from N.Y. Univ.

Sid was three times named to the All-Metropolitan team in New York City and received the Haggerty Award as the best player in Manhattan. He was named by Helms Athletic Foundation to their All-American team in 1946 and 1947, and was also named Outstanding Jewish Athlete in 1947. He played with the New York Knicks in 1948 and the Baltimore Bullets in 1949, and in his 70 NBA games, averaged 9 points a game.

WARD, Frank
Player
Born September 23, 1903, in Parowan, Utah; one of 12 children; graduated from Mont. State Univ; Helms Athletic Foundation All-American Team 1929 and 1930.

Frank was captain of the track squad at Montana State and also excelled on the basketball court. He averaged 19.8 points per game in just one season. To improve their peripheral vision, Frank and his teammates would sometimes walk along a street, looking straight ahead, but counting items in store windows. Ward played semi-pro ball with the Long Beach Athletic Club in California 1931 and 1932.

WELLS, Willis Robert Clifford
Coach
See entry in Indiana Basketball Hall of Fame, 1965.
Also in: Naismith Memorial Basketball Hall of Fame.

WILSON, John E.
Coach
See entry in Indiana Basetball Hall of Fame, 1976.

YOUNG, Jewell I.
Player
See entry in Indiana Basketball Hall of Fame, 1964.

1964

BEICHLEY, Russell
Coach
Beichley coached at the University of Akron from 1940 to 1959, and his overall record was 287 – 141.

BROWNING, Arthur
Player
Born February 23, 1902, in Kansas City, Mo; graduated from Univ. Mo; All-Missouri Valley 1922 and 1923; Helms Athletic Foundation All-American Team 1922 and 1923.

Arthur was one of many fine players who came out of the University of Missouri. During his college career, his team lost only four times. Art was outstanding in his senior year as he scored 237 points in the Missouri Valley Conference.

GOLDBLATT, Emanuel Menchy
Player
Born November 3, 1904, in Philadelphia, Pa; graduated from Univ. Pa; Helms Athletic Foundation All-American Team 1925 and 1926.

Goldblatt had pro ball experience with the Philadelphia Sphas and Germantown. He coached high school basketball for ten years, which included city and league titles at Bartram High School in Philadelphia. He was the athletic director and basketball coach at the Philadelphia College of Textiles and Sciences for eight years.

HAYWARD, Julian
Player
Born January 11, 1897, in Danielson, Conn; graduated from Wesleyan Univ; Helms Athletic Foundation All-American Team 1908 and 1909; died June 18, 1969, in Glendale, Calif, at age 72.

Julian played at Wesleyan from 1907 to 1910 and the team had a 29-18 record.

NASH, William
Player
Nash was named to Helms Athletic Foundation All-American Team 1935 and 1936.

PECK, Hubert "Dutch"
Player
Born February 11, 1898, in Washington, D.C; graduated from Univ. Pa; Helms Athletic Foundation All-American Team 1918 and 1920.

Peck played varsity ball at the University of Pennsylvania 1917 to 1920. He captained the team to a 22-1 record in 1920. That same year Pennsylvania played in the national championship series against the University of Chicago and won.

PRALLE, Fred
Player
See entry in Amateur Basketball Hall of Fame, Citizens Savings Hall of Fame Athletic Museum, 1962.

SACHS, Leonard D.
Coach
See entry in Naismith Memorial Basketball Hall of Fame, 1961.

SPICER, Carey
Player
Born April 23, 1909, in Lexington, Ky; graduated from Univ. Ky; Helms Athletic Foundation All-American Team 1929 and 1931; All-Southern Conference Teams 1929 and 1931; served in W.W. II.

Spicer was the University of Kentucky's third All-American and the very first under coach Adolph Rupp. He also quarterbacked the football team and scored 75 points in one season, a grid record that stood for 34 years. Spicer was head football and basketball coach at Georgetown University from 1932 to 1934.

SWENHOLT, Helmer
Player
Helmer was named to Helms Athletic Foundation All-American Team 1908 and 1909.

TEBELL, Gustave K.
Coach
Born September 6, 1897, in St. Charles, Ill; graduated from Univ. Wis; mayor of Charlottesville, Va, for 2 years; died May 28, 1969, in Charlottesville, at age 72.

1925 – 1931 North Carolina State College, coach
1931 – 1951 University of Virginia, coach

Gus starred in three sports at Wisconsin and won the Western Conference Athletic-Scholarship Award. In his 27 years of coaching, he compiled an overall record of 301-221, with 226 of his wins coming at Virginia. He also was director of athletics at Virginia for 11 years. In 1948 Tebell headed the committee to build the Charlottesville-Albemarle Airport.

TUCKER, Gerald
Player
See entry in Amateur Basketball Hall of Fame, Citizens Savings Hall of Fame Athletic Museum, 1962.

1965

BAYLOR, Elgin
Player
See entry in Naismith Memorial Basketball Hall of Fame, 1976.
Also in: Major League Basketball Hall of Fame, Citizens Savings Hall of Fame Athletic Museum.

BRADLEY, William "Dollar Bill"
Player
Born July 28, 1943, in Crystal City, Mo; graduated from Princeton Univ; 2 years as Rhodes scholar at Oxford Univ; Sullivan Award 1965; Player of the Year by AP, UPI and Basketball Writers Assn. 1965; All-Ivy League three times; Helms Athletic Foundation All-American Team 1963-1965.

In his final college game against Wichita State University, Bill scored 58 points, bringing his college total to 2503, the fourth largest figure at Princeton. He was the only junior on the 1964 U.S. Olympic team that won a gold medal at Tokyo. After finishing his graduate work, Bradley signed a four-year contract with the New York Knicks for a reported $500,000, but he didn't become an immediate pro success. Only gradually did he move into the league's top category. He helped the Knicks to NBA titles in 1970 and 1973, and he was named to the Eastern Conference All-Star team in 1973.

CASE, Everett
Coach
See entry in Indiana Basketball Hall of Fame, 1968.

COUSY, Robert J. "Cooz"
Player
See entry in Naismith Memorial Basketball Hall of Fame, 1970.
Also in: Major League Basketball Hall of Fame, Citizens Savings Hall of Fame Athletic Museum.

DUKES, Walter
Player
Born June 23, 1930, in Rochester, N.Y; graduated from Seton Hall Univ; Helms Athletic Foundation All-American Team 1951 and 1953.

Walter was on the track team during his years at Seton Hall, 1951 to 1953. He ran the quarter-mile under 52 sec. and the half mile in less than 2 min. He scored 1789 points in his three years as a basketball player. In his senior year the team won 27 consecutive games and took the National Invitational Tournament crown. He played two years with the Harlem Globetrotters before going into the pro ranks. Between 1956 and 1963, he played with New York, Minneapolis and Detroit in the NBA and had a 10.4 average for 553 games.

ESTES, Wayne
Player
Born May 13, 1943, in Anaconda, Mont; attended Utah State Univ; died Feb. 8, 1965, in Logan, Utah, at age 23; Helms Athletic Foundation All-American Team 1964, and received same award posthumously 1965.

Wayne was an outstanding athlete in high school, winning the discus and shot-put events and starring in football in his senior year. At Utah State, he scored 2001 career points and set many records, including 52 points in one game. Following a game against the University of Denver, where he had just scored 48 points, he stopped at the scene of an auto accident near the campus and was electrocuted when he brushed against a high voltage wire that had snapped in the accident. Utah State retired his No. 33 jersey and established the Wayne Estes Memorial Fund. At the time of his death, he was the second leading scorer in the nation.

HAZZARD, Walter
Player
Walter was named to Helms Athletic Foundation All-American Team 1962 and 1964 and was Player of the Year 1964.

HENRY, Bill
Player
Born December 27, 1924, in Dallas, Tex; graduated from Rice Univ; All-American twice.

While Bill played with the Rice University Owls from 1943 to 1945, the team won one Southwestern Conference and were co-winners twice. He played pro ball in 1949 and 1950 with Fort Wayne and Tri-Cities teams, and his overall average for 95 games was 6.4.

HETZEL, Fred
Player
Born July 21, 1942, in Washington, D.C; graduated from Davidson Col; father and younger brother Will both played basketball for Univ. Md; All-American twice.

While playing for Landon High School, Hetzel was named to the District of Columbia All-Metropolitan team three straight years. From 1963 to 1965 he played varsity ball with Davidson and helped produce winning teams, with records of 20-7, 24-4, and 24-2. He set many records, including 53 points and 27 rebounds in one game. Between 1966 and 1971, Hetzel played NBA ball with Milwaukee, Cincinnati, Philadelphia, and Los Angeles. In 416 games, he averaged 11.2.

HOY, Carl
Coach
Carl coached at the University of South Dakota for 24 years.

IMHOFF, Darrell
Player
Born October 11, 1938, in San Gabriel, Calif; graduated from Univ. Calif; Helms Athletic Foundation All-American 1959 – 1960.

Imhoff played with the University of California from 1958 to 1960 and in a 1959 game against West Virginia, Darrell's tip-in with just 17 seconds remaining in the game, gave California the national title. California was unseated as champs the following season by Ohio State. He scored 22 points in another championship game for the Bears, who led the NCAA schools in defense, by allowing just 51 points a game. Imhoff has played NBA ball with the New York Knicks, Detroit Eagles, Los Angeles Lakers, Cincinnati Royals and the Portland Trail Blazers. He played in only one All-Star game with the Lakers in 1967.

LAPCHICK, Joseph
Coach
See entry in Naismith Memorial Basketball Hall of Fame, 1966.

MATTICK, Robert
Player
Born May 30, 1933, in Chicago, Ill; graduated from Okla. State Univ; named All-State 1950; Most Valuable Player in All-College Tournament 1953; All-American 1953 and 1954.

Mattick participated in the East-West Shrine and the Fresh Air Fund Games in 1954. He also scored 1378 career points for the Oklahoma State Cowboys. He holds their one-season scoring mark with 20.7. He played AAU ball with the Phillips Oilers from 1954 to 1957. Four of his Oiler teammates played in the 1956 Olympics; Mattick attended also, but as a spectator.

NORGREN, Nelson H.
Coach
Born September 10, 1891, in Lynn, Mass; graduated from Univ. Chicago; senior class mustache contest winner; served in W.W. I and II.

Norgren was the first man in the Western Conference to win 12 letters in four sports and at just 22 years of age, was the athletic director and coach of four sports at Utah. In 1916 he guided Utah to the National AAU title. He later went to the University of Chicago, where he coached for 34 years. He retired from Chicago as associate professor emeritus of physical education. He was president of the National Association of Basketball Coaches in 1942.

ZAWOLUK, Robert
Player
Born December 13, 1930, in Brooklyn, N.Y; graduated from St. John's Univ.(N.Y.).

Robert played college ball at St. John's under coach Frank McGuire and was a member of the NCAA runner-up team in 1952. He was St. John's highest scorer with 1799 points. He was mentioned in All-American polls from 1950 to 1952. He played for the Indianapolis Olympians and Philadelphia Warriors in the NBA from 1953 to 1955 and in 179 games, he averaged 6.8 points per game.

1966

CARNEVALE, Bernard L. "Ben"
Coach
See entry in Naismith Memorial Basketball Hall of Fame, 1969.

DeBUSSCHERE, Dave
Player
Born January 16, 1940, in Detroit, Mich; graduated from Univ. of Detroit; Collegiate All-American twice.

DeBusschere doubled in baseball and basketball as prep, collegian and pro. In 1962 he signed with the Chicago White Sox baseball team for a $70,000 bonus and the Detroit Pistons basketball team for $15,000. He played on both teams for two years, giving up baseball to become a player-coach with the Pistons. His coaching record from 1965 to 1967 was 69 wins and 143 losses. He played six and one-half seasons with the Pistons, averaging 16.3 in 440 games. Detroit traded him to New York in 1968. He became a standout for the world champion New York Knicks in 1970 and 1973 and was selected to the All-NBA defensive team every year from 1969 through 1973.

EVANS, John
Coach
John coached at the University of Vermont for 23 years and had an overall record of 261 – 195.

HAGAN, Cliff
Player
Born December 9, 1931, in Owensboro, Ky; graduated from Univ. Ky; Consensus All-American twice; All NBA second team twice.

1956 – 1966 St. Louis Hawks, forward-center
1967 – 1970 Dallas Chapparals, forward-center and coach

Hagan, along with Bob Pettit and Clyde Lovelette, formed the Hawks high-scoring front line. He helped the Hawks win the NBA title in 1958. In 746 games, he averaged 18 points per game. As a player with the Chapparals, he averaged 15.1 in 94 games and as coach, he compiled a 109 – 90 mark.
Also in: Major League Basketball Hall of Fame, Citizens Savings Hall of Fame Athletic Museum.

KINNEY, Gilmore
Player
Kinney was selected to Helms Athletic Foundation All-American Teams 1905 – 1907; and was Player of the Year in 1907.

PETTIT, Robert L.
Player
See entry in Naismith Memorial Basketball Hall of Fame, 1970.

Also in: Major League Basketball Hall of Fame, Citizens Savings Hall of Fame Athletic Museum.

ROSE, Glen
Coach
Born April 23, 1905, in Siloam Springs, Ark; graduated from Univ. Ark; All-Southwest Conference Team 1928.

Rose coached at the University of Arkansas for 23 years, where his record was 389 – 238. He also coached Stephen F. Austin State College for four years.

RUDOMETKIN, John
Player
Born June 6, 1940, in Santa Maria, Calif; graduated from Univ. Southern Calif.

Rudometkin established a University of Southern California scoring record with 1484 points between 1960 and 1962, as well as being named conference top scorer twice. He played NBA ball with New York and San Francisco from 1963 to 1965 and had a 6.3 average for 131 games.

RUSSELL, Cazzie
Player
Born June 7, 1944, in Chicago, Ill; graduated from Univ. Mich; All-American Teams three times; Helms Athletic Foundation Player of the Year 1966.

While playing with the University of Michigan Wolverines, Cazzie had season scoring records of 24.8, 25.7 and 30.8 to help the team to a 65 – 17 record during his varsity career between 1963 and 1967. He played five seasons with the New York Knicks and was traded to Golden State Warriors for Jerry Lucas in 1971.

SUTTER, Herb
Coach
Sutter coached at Wagner College for 26 years and had a 363 – 263 record.

TWOGOOD, Forrest
Coach
Born April 29, 1907, in Kingsley, La; graduated from Univ. Iowa; NABC Metropolitan Award; died of cancer on April 26, 1972, in Glendale, Calif.

Twogood was head basketball and baseball coach at the University of Idaho from 1937 to 1941. He had a 70 – 77 basketball record. He coached basketball at the University of Southern California from 1951 to 1966 and his Trojans compiled a record of 225 wins and 180 losses. His teams won three conference championships and he turned out five All-Americans during his 16 years there. Twogood was president of the National Association of Basketball Coaches (NABC) in 1965 and he also received their Metropolitan Award, given for long-time service to basketball.

1967

BLACKBURN, Tom
Coach
Blackburn was a successful high school coach before going to the University of Dayton where he coached for 17 years. He had a record of 352 – 141. He died shortly after the end of the 1964 season.

CHARTERS, David
Player
Born February 15, 1888, in Peru, Ind; graduated from Purdue Univ; All-American twice; died Feb. 18, 1939.

David played at Purdue from 1909 to 1911 and helped the team to a 28 – 13 record. He was top scorer in the Western Conference in his junior year. In his very first college game, against Indiana State, he scored 33 points, which was his career high single game effort. He was team captain for one year.

GOODRICH, Gail
Player
Born April 23, 1943, in Los Angeles, Calif; graduated from Univ. Calif. at Los Angeles; Consensus All-American 1965.

Gail led the UCLA Bruins to two national titles in 1964 and 1965 averaging 24.8 points his senior year. He played three years with the Lakers and was picked up by the Phoenix Suns in an expansion draft. After two years with the Suns, he was traded back to the Lakers. He was leading Los Angeles scorer with 25.9 and ranked fifth in the NBA in 1972. He started as a guard with Jerry West for the West team in the NBA All-Star game in 1972.

HEMRICK, Dixon
Player
Born August 29, 1933, in Jonesville, N.C; one of 10 children; graduated from Wake Forest Col; All-American 1954 and 1955.

Hemrick scored 956 points in his senior year at Jonesville High School averaging almost 40 points a game. After graduation from college, he played with the Boston Celtics from 1955 to 1957 and had a 6.3 points per game average for 138 games.

HEYMAN, Art
Player
Born June 29, 1941, in Rockville Centre, N.Y; graduated from Duke Univ; All-American 1961 – 1963; Helms Athletic Foundation and Atlantic Coast Conference Player of the Year 1963.

Heyman was one of Duke's greatest scorers with 1984 points and a 25.1 average. In the NBA he played with New York, Cincinnati and Philadelphia in 147 games for a 10.3 average. With the ABA he performed for New Jersey, Pittsburgh-Minnesota and Miami, playing 163 games for a 15.4 average.

HICKMAN, Bernard
Coach
Born October 5, 1911, in Greenville, Ky; B.S. from Univ. Louisville and M.S. from Univ. Ky.

Hickman was named All-State at Central City (Ky.) High School in 1931. He played his collegiate ball at Western Kentucky. Bernard began coaching in 1936 with a 3 win and 18 loss season at Hodgenville (Ky.) High School. He coached the University of Louisville from 1944 to 1967 and had a 443 – 183 record. His .708 percentage put him in seventh place among active college coaches at his retirement. He won both the NAIA and National Invitational Tournament and had participated in 17 post-season tournaments. He is past chairman of the NCAA housing committee and Missouri Valley Conference public relations committee.

JACOBS, George W. "Doc"
Coach
See entry in Athletic Directors Hall of Fame, Citizens Savings Hall of Fame Athletic Museum, 1973.

LOEFFLER, Kenneth D.
Coach
See entry in Naismith Memorial Basketball Hall of Fame, 1964.

RICKETTS, Richard
Player
Born January 15, 1933, in Pottstown, Pa; graduated from Duquesne Univ; All-American 1955.

Dick holds nine school records at Duke where he played varsity ball from 1952 to 1955. He was all-time high scorer with 1963 points in 111 games. He played NBA ball with St. Louis and Rochester-Cincinnati from 1956 to 1958, and had a 9.6 average for 212 games. He also played major league baseball with the St. Louis Cardinals at one time.

RODGERS, Guy
Player
Born September 1, 1935, in Philadelphia, Pa; graduated from Temple Univ; All-American twice.

Rodgers became Temple's all-time scoring leader with a 1767 total between 1956 and 1958. He played NBA ball with Philadelphia-San Francisco, Chicago, Cincinnati and Milwaukee between 1959 and 1970. In 891 games, he averaged 11.7 points per game.

1972

CALIHAN, Robert J.
Coach
Born August 2, 1918, in Perry, Iowa; attended Univ. of Detroit; M.Ed. from Wayne State Univ; served in U.S. Navy during W.W. II.

Calihan won letters in three sports and was named Most Valuable Player in the National Catholic High School Tournament during his senior year. At the University of Detroit, he was leading scorer for three seasons. He played NBA ball briefly with Detroit and Chicago. Calihan coached the University of Detroit from 1949 to 1969 and his overall record for 23 years was 303 – 242.

GARDNER, George
Player
Born September 18, 1898 in Rippey, Iowa; graduated from Southwestern Col. (Kans); AAU All-American 1922.

George played at Southwestern College from 1919 to 1922, during which time he played with two Conference winning teams. He coached both college and high schools between 1924 and 1939, and in that period his teams won two state Conference titles and two Central Conference crowns. The last team he coached at Southwestern won the NAIA national title in 1939. He also coached the Henry Clothiers team to AAU titles in 1931 and again in 1932.
Also in: National Association of Intercollegiate Athletics Hall of Fame.

LOBSINGER, John
Player
Lobsinger was named to Helms Athletic Foundation All-American Teams 1939 and 1940.

LOEB, Arthur
Player
Art was named to Helms Athletic Foundation All-American Teams 1922 and 1923.

MARAVICH, Pete "Pistol Pete"
Player
Born June 22, 1948, in Aliquippa, Pa; graduated from Louisiana State Univ; Consensus All-American three times; AP and U.S. Basketball Writers Player of the Year 1970; co-recipient of Helms Athletic Foundation Player of the Year Award 1970; NBA All-Rookie Team 1971.

Pete played ball at Louisiana State where his father Press was coaching. He ended his college career with 3667 in 83 games for a 44.1 average. His point total is the highest of any major college player. He signed with the Atlanta Hawks in 1970 for a reported 5-year, 2 million dollar contract. Pete was fifth in NBA scoring in 1973 with a 26.1 points per game average.

MOKRAY, William G.
Contributor
See entry in Naismith Memorial Basketball Hall of Fame, 1965.
Also in: National Association of Intercollegiate Athletics Hall of Fame.

MORRIS, Max
Player
Max was selected to the Helms Athletic Foundation All-American Team 1945 and 1946.

O'BRIEN, John
Player
John was selected to Helms Athletic Foundation All-American Teams 1937 and 1938.

RANZINO, Sam
Player
Born June 21, 1927, in Gary, Ind; graduated from N.C. State Univ; All-American twice.

Ranzino was N.C. State's leading scorer with 1957 points in 132 games between 1948 and 1951 and the team won Southern Conference titles each season. Sam was named Most Valuable Player in one of those conferences. He played 39 games with Rochester in the NBA for a 2.2 average.

REIFF, Joseph
Player
Born June 5, 1911, in Muskogee, Okla; graduated from Northwestern Univ; All-American 1931 and 1933; All-Western Conference; AAU All-Tournament Team 1933.

Joe played at Northwestern and the team won two league titles in 1931 and 1933. He was All-Western Conference and scoring leader twice. He later played AAU ball with Rosenberg-Arvey team out of Chicago and was named to the AAU All-Tournament team that lost in the finals in 1933.

ROMNEY, Elwood
Player
Born May 28, 1911, in Provo, Utah; graduated from Brigham Young Univ; died of pneumonia September 24, 1970, in Salt Lake City, Utah.

Romney was leading scorer and twice Skyline Conference All-Star while playing at Brigham Young. After graduation, he moved to Denver and became owner of a minor league baseball team called the Denver Bears. He later coached at the Colorado School of Mines.

SCHAAF, Joseph
Player
Jos was named to the Helms Athletic Foundation All-American Teams 1928 and 1929.

WATTS, Stanley
Coach
Born August 30, 1911, in Murray, Utah; attended Weber State Col. and Brigham Young Univ.

Between 1939 and 1947, Watts coached three high schools in Utah. He was head coach at Brigham Young from 1950 to 1972. His teams toured South and Central America and the Orient-Pacific. His overall record including games played abroad was 431 – 260. Watts is one of seven college coaches in the United States to win over 100 games in the first five seasons. He won or shared 8 conference titles and 2 National Invitational Tournament crowns. He was president of the National Association of Basketball Coaches in 1970. He also wrote *Developing an Offensive Attack in Basketball.*
Also in: Athletic Directors Hall of Fame, Citizens Savings Hall of Fame Athletic Museum.

WICKS, Sidney
Player
Born September 19, 1949, in Los Angeles, Calif; graduated from Univ. Calif. at Los Angeles; All-Pacific Eight and Helms Athletic Foundation All-American teams 1970 and 1971; Joe Lipchick Award; Helms Athletic Foundation Player of the Year 1971.

Wicks played college ball at UCLA and was third highest scorer. Wicks scored 2009 points in 1972 and was the eighth rookie in NBA history to hit the 2000 mark. He was Rookie of the Year for Portland in 1972.

WOODEN, John
Coach
See entry in Indiana Basketball Hall of Fame, 1962.
Also in: Naismith Memorial Basketball Hall of Fame.

1973

HAYES, Elvin
Player
Born November 17, 1945, in Rayville, La; graduated from Univ. Houston; All-American 1966 – 1968.

Elvin played with Houston from 1965 to 1968 and during his three seasons, he registered 2884 points for a 31.01 average. He also accounted for a total of 1611 rebounds.

LANIER, Bob
Player
Born September 10, 1948, in Buffalo, N.Y; graduated from St. Bonaventure Univ; All-American 1968 – 1970.

At St. Bonaventure Lanier had a three-year career total of 2067 points. In 1969 he posted highs of 50 against Purdue and 51 against Seton Hall.

MOUNT, Rick
Player
Born January 5, 1947, in Lebanon, Ind; graduated from Purdue Univ; All-American 1968 – 1970.

During his three years with Purdue, Rick had a total of 2323 points for a 32.26 average and recorded 211 rebounds. He scored 61 points against Lafayette College in 1970.

MURPHY, Calvin
Player
Born May 9, 1948, in Norwalk, Conn; graduated from Niagara Univ; All-American 1968 – 1970.

Murphy tallied 2548 points in his college years at Niagara for a 33.1 average. He chalked up 68 points against Syracuse in 1968.

ROOSMA, John S.
Player
See entry in Naismith Memorial Basketball Hall of Fame, 1961.

STALLWORTH, David
Player
Born December 20, 1941, in Dallas, Tex; graduated from Wichita State Univ; All-American 1963 – 1965.

Dave's three season point total at Wichita State was 1762 for a 24.81 average.

UNSELD, Westley
Player
Born March 14, 1946, in Louisville, Ky; graduated from Univ. Louisville; All-American 1966 – 1968.

Unseld played three seasons at the University of Louisville for a career total of 1636 points and 1551 rebounds. In 1967 he scored 45 points against Georgetown.

WALSH, Frank
Contributor
Frank devoted the last 25 years of his life to the sport of basketball. He served both collegiate and amateur basketball, particularly on an international basis. Through U.S. government channels he arranged for many teams to compete in foreign lands as well as arranging for foreign teams to make tours in our country. He was dedicated to this cause. Early in 1973 Walsh died in Spain while on such an assignment, and is buried in that country.

1974

COMBES, Harry
Coach
Born March 3, 1915, in Monticello, Ill; graduated from Univ. Ill.

Combes coached at the University of Illinois for 20 years from 1948 to 1968, posting a mark of 316 wins and 150 losses. His Illini teams won Big Ten titles in 1949, 1951 and 1952, and tied for the crown in 1963. Four of his teams collected 20 victories or more, with highs of 22 in both 1951 and 1952.

HAYES, Elmore O. "Doc"
Coach
Born January 3, 1906, in Krum, Tex; graduated from North Tex. State Univ; died February 26, 1973.

Doc coached at Southern Methodist University for 20 years, 1948 to 1967, racking up 299 wins and 192 losses. His Mustangs won Southwest Conference championships every year from 1955 to 1957 and 1966 – 1967, and tied in 1958. His 1956 squad won 26 games and lost just 4, while his 1957 team won 21 and lost but 3. He and his wife died in an automobile accident.

HENDERSON, Camden Eli
Coach
Born February 5, 1890, in Joe Town, W.Va.; died May 3, 1956, in Lexington, Ky.

Cam coached at Marshall University from 1936 to 1955, winning a total of 357 contests while losing 158. Seven times his Thundering Herd garnered 20 victories or more. Henderson piloted Marshall teams to Buckeye Conference titles in 1938, 1939 and 1940, the NAIA crown in 1947 and the Ohio Valley Conference championship in 1950. His 1948 squad won the Los Angeles Invitational, besting Syracuse in the finale.
Also in: National Association of Intercollegiate Athletics Hall of Fame and West Virginia Sports Writers Hall of Fame.

SHEPARD, Norman "Bo"
Coach
Born August 20, 1897, in Marion, S.C; graduated from Univ. N.C.

Shepard coached college teams for 26 years, including North Carolina in 1924, Guilford College in 1929, Randolph-Macon 1930 – 1936, Davidson College 1937 – 1949 and Harvard University 1950 – 1954. His all-time record was 327 – 276. His North Carolina team of 1924, with a 25 – 0 record, was chosen national champions by Citizens Savings Athletic Foundation.

WALTON, Bill
Player
Born November 5, 1952, in La Mesa, Calif; graduated from Univ. Calif. at Los Angeles; Citizens Savings All-American teams and College Player of the Year three times.

Under coach John Wooden's leadership. Walton sparked the Bruins to national collegiate championships in 1972 and 1973. During his three years at Westwood, the Bruins won 56 games and lost only 4, with 30 – 0 records in both 1972 and 1973.

1975

BARRY, Rick
Player
Born March 28, 1944, in Elizabeth, N.J; graduated from Univ. Miami; Citizens Savings Athletic Foundation All-American 1964 and 1965.

Rick enjoyed three outstanding seasons at Miami University. During his three years, he tallied 816 field goals, 666 fouls for a total of 2298 points in 77 games, for an average of 29.8 per game. He led the major colleges in the nation in scoring in 1965. Miami won a total of 65 games with 16 losses during Barry's three seasons.

BRADLEY, Harold
Coach
Born November 20, 1911, in Westford, N.Y; graduated from Hartwick Col.

1948 – 1950 Hartwick College, coach
1951 – 1959 Duke University, coach
1960 – 1967 University of Texas, coach

At Duke, Harold posted season records of 24 – 6 in 1952, 22 – 6 in 1954 and 20 – 8 in 1955, while at Texas he was 18 – 8 in 1960 and 20 – 7 in 1963, for an overall record of 337 wins and 169 losses.

GOOD, Harry
Coach

1927 – 1942 Indiana Central College, coach
1944 – 1946 Indiana University, coach
1947 – 1954 University of Nebraska, coach

In his 27 years of coaching, Harry has a 310 – 181 record. He enjoyed his top season at Indiana in 1946 with an 18 – 3 mark.

McDERMOTT, Jim
Coach
Born April 6, 1910, in New York City; graduated from Niagara Univ.

Jim spent his entire 26 year coaching career at Iona College, 1948 to 1973. He enjoyed seasons of 21 – 2 in 1950 and 18 – 3 in 1953. His overall record is 320 wins and 252 losses.

NORTON, Ken
Coach
Norton spent his 22 years as a coach at Manhattan College, 1947 to 1968. His most productive years were 1948 with a 20 – 5 record, and in 1953 with a 19 – 4 mark. His overall record is 310 – 205.

SNYDER, Jim
Coach
Snyder coached at Ohio University from 1950 to 1974 and his overall record for 25 years is 354 – 245. His teams won the Mid-American Conference titles in 1960, 1961, 1964, 1965, 1970, 1972 and 1974. They won 21 and lost just 6 in 1964, and in 1970 had 20 wins and 5 losses.

THOMPSON, David
Player
Born July 13, 1954, in Shelby, N.C; graduated from North Carolina State Univ; Citizens Savings Athletic Foundation All-American three years; co-recipient of Player of the Year 1974.

David had three brilliant seasons at North Carolina State from 1973 to 1975. Thompson was a bright spark on the team as North Carolina won the NCAA championship in 1974, winning 30 games and losing just one. In his three collegiate seasons as a player, his school won 79 games and lost 7. His overall record is 2309 points on 939 field goals and 431 foul shots, for an average of 26.8.

1976

ANDERSON, Forrest "Fordy"
Coach
Born March 17, 1919, in Gary, Ind; graduated from Stanford Univ.

Anderson coached at Drake University 1947 and 1948, Bradley University 1949 – 1954 and Michigan State University 1955 and 1956. His last assignment was with Hiram Scott College 1966 – 1971. His overall record for 25 years was 369 wins and 234 losses.

BROOKS, Madison
Coach
Born November 28, 1914 in Aimwell, La; graduated from La. Polytechnic Inst.

Brooks coached for 25 years at East Tennessee State University, 1949 to 1973. His overall record was 370 – 267.

DALLMAR, Howard
Coach
Born May 24, 1922, in San Francisco, Calif; attended Stanford Univ. and Univ. Pa.

Dallmar coached at the University of Pennsylvania from 1949 to 1954, then went to Stanford where he coached from 1955 to 1975. In his 27 years his overall collegiate record was 369 wins and 315 losses.

LEE, Ronald
Player
Ron was a guard with the University of Oregon team. He was named Citizens Savings Athletic Foundation All-American 1974 – 1976.

McMILLIAN, Jim
Player
Born March 14, 1948, in New York City; graduated from Columbia Univ.

Jim played with Columbia University as forward. He was named to Citizens Savings Athletic Foundation All-American team every year from 1968 to 1970.

VANATTA, Bob
Coach
Born July 7, 1921, in Columbia, Mo; graduated from Central Methodist Col, Mo.

Vanatta coached for 21 years, including Central Methodist College in 1943 and again from 1948 to 1950, Southwest Missouri 1951 – 1953, U.S. Military Academy 1954, Bradley University 1955 and 1956, Memphis State 1957 – 1962, and wound up his career at the University of Missouri 1963 – 1967. His overall record reads 348 wins and 186 losses.

WALKER, James
Player
Born April 8, 1944, in Boston, Mass; graduated from Providence Col.

Walker played guard on the Providence College team. He was named All-American from 1965 to 1967 by the Citizens Savings Athletic Foundation.

Induction Years Unrecorded

ABDUL-JABBAR, Kareem
Player
Born Lew Alcindor on April 16, 1947, in New York City; graduated from Univ. Calif. at Los Angeles; Citizens Savings Athletic Foundation All-American and Player of the Year 1967 – 1969; Most Valuable Player in NCAA Tournament 1967 – 1969; Rookie of the Year 1970; Podoloff Cup winner 1971 and 1972.

Jabbar played high school ball at Power Memorial High School in New York City and at 7 ft. 2 in, led the team to a 116-1 record. By the time he arrived at UCLA, he had already made quite a name for himself. In his first varsity game he scored 56 points and by the end of the 1967 – 1968 season when he graduated, the Bruins had won 88 of 90 games with Jabbar in their lineup. In his three seasons he averaged 26.4 points and 15.5 in rebounding. He joined the Milwaukee Bucks in 1970 and paced the team to the NBA championships in 1970, and was second in NBA scoring in 1973 with 30.2 points per game. He utilized the dunk, hook and jumper shots. Abdul-Jabbar now plays with the Los Angeles Lakers.

ALLEN, Dr. Forrest Clare "Phog"
Coach
See entry in Naismith Memorial Basketball Hall of Fame, 1959.
Also in: Athletic Directors Hall of Fame, Citizens Savings Hall of Fame Athletic Museum.

ANDREAS, Lewis
Coach
Born February 25, 1895, in Sterling, Ill; graduated from Syracuse Univ.

1925 – 1943 Syracuse University, coach
1945 – 1950 Syracuse University, coach

Andreas lettered in football and baseball in college. In his 25 years as basketball coach at Syracuse, his overall record was 355-134. His 1926 team with a 19-1 record was named Helms Champions. He also served as athletic director for 22 years and football coach for three. He is a past president of the National Association of Basketball Coaches.

BARRY, Justin "Sam"
Coach
Born December 17, 1892, in Aberdeen, S. Dak; graduated from Univ. Wis; died September 23, 1950, in Berkeley, Calif.

1930 – 1941 University of Southern California, coach
1946 – 1950 University of Southern California, coach

Before going to Southern California, Barry had coached at Knox College in Illinois and at the University of Iowa. In his 17 years at Southern California, he compiled a

260–130 record, and overall collegiately, he won 365 and lost 217. Along with his basketball duties, Barry was baseball coach and assistant football coach. His Trojan baseball team won the NCAA crown in 1948.
Also in: American Association of College Baseball Coaches Hall of Fame; and College Baseball (Coaches) Hall of Fame, Citizens Savings Hall of Fame Athletic Museum.

BEE, Clair Francis "Hillbilly"
Coach
See entry in Naismith Memorial Basketball Hall of Fame, 1967.
Also in: West Virginia Sports Writers Association Hall of Fame.

BENNETT, Wesley
Player
Born March 3, 1913, in Nashville, Tenn; graduated from Westminster Col. (Pa); Helms Athletic Foundation All-American 1934 and 1935; Player of the Year 1935.

When Wesley played at Westminster, the team won 41 of 48 games in the 1934–1935 season. He played for the Firestones and Goodyears of the old National League for three years prior to W.W. II, and in 1945 he coached the Camp Lejeune (N.C.) team.
Also in: National Association of Intercollegiate Athletics Hall of Fame.

BOOZER, Robert
Player
Born April 26, 1937, in Omaha, Nebr; graduated from Kansas State Univ; All-Big Eight Conference and Consensus All-American twice; AAU All-American 1960.

Bob played at Kansas State from 1956 to 1959 and his overall scoring record for 77 games was 21.9. His best year was 1958 when he scored 45 points against Purdue, which included 23 of 26 free throws. In his final two seasons with the Wildcats, the team won 47 of 54 games. He played AAU ball with Peoria Caterpillars and was a member of the U.S. Olympic team in 1960. Boozer played NBA ball with Cincinnati, New York, Los Angeles, Chicago, Seattle and Milwaukee between 1961 and 1971. In those ten years he played in 874 games for a 14.8 average. He made his only appearance in an East-West All-Star game in 1968 and scored 4 points.

CANN, Howard G. "Ward"
Coach
See entry in Naismith Memorial Basketball Hall of Fame, 1967.

CARLSON, Dr. Henry Clifford "Harold"
Coach
See entry in Naismith Memorial Basketball Hall of Fame, 1959.

CARNEY, Charles R.
Player
Born August 25, 1900, in Chicago, Ill; graduated from Univ. Ill; Helms Athletic Foundation Player of the Year 1922; All-American 1922.

In 1920 Carney scored 188 points in 12 games at the University of Illinois, setting a Western Conference record that stood for 22 years. He was All-American in both basketball and football and won 7 letters in both sports. He coached football at Northwestern, Wisconsin and Harvard prior to his retirement.
Also in: National Football Hall of Fame.

COBB, John
Player
Born August 5, 1905, in Durham, N.C; graduated from Univ. of N.C; Kappa Sigma fraternity; Order of the Golden Fleece; died September 9, 1966, in Greenville, N.C.

Cobb was named to the All-Southern Conference and Helms Athletic Foundation All-American teams from 1924 to 1926. He was also Helms Player of the Year in 1926. He was associated with the Little League program in Greenville for many years.

COWLES, Osborne
Coach
Born August 25, 1899, in Browns Valley, Minn; graduated from Carleton Col; received Carleton Alumni Achievement Award 1971.

1925–1930 Carleton College, coach
1934–1936 River Falls State College, Wis, coach
1937–1946 Dartmouth College, coach
1947–1948 University of Michigan, coach
1949–1959 University of Minnesota, coach

Cowles coached for just one year at Rochester (Minn.) High School, winning the state football championship and placing third in baseball. In his 31 years of college coaching, he had a 421–198 overall record. He took Dartmouth to the NCAA finals in 1942. He won the first outright Western Conference title for University of Michigan in 1948.

DEAN, Everett S.
Coach
See entry in Indiana Basketball Hall of Fame, 1965.
Also in: American Association of College Baseball Coaches Hall of Fame and Naismith Memorial Basketball Hall of Fame.

DEBERNARDI, Forrest S. "Red"
Player
See entry in Naismith Memorial Basketball Hall of Fame, 1961.
Also in: Amateur Basketball Hall of Fame, Citizens Savings Hall of Fame Athletic Museum; and National Association of Intercollegiate Athletics Hall of Fame.

EDMUNDSON, Clarence
Coach
Born August 3, 1886, in Moscow, Idaho; graduated from Univ. Idaho; died August 6, 1964, in Seattle, Wash.

1917–1920 University of Idaho, coach
1921–1947 University of Washington, coach

Edmundson ran the half-mile on the 1912 U.S. Olympic team at Stockholm. As a basketball coach, his lifetime record was 505–209. He produced six All-Americans at Washington, where he also coached track for 35 years. Washington won or tied for 12 Northern Division titles in the Pacific Coast Conference. The Edmundson Pavilion at the University of Washington is named for him.
Also in: Track and Field Hall of Fame, Citizens Savings Hall of Fame Athletic Museum.

EDWARDS, Leroy
Player
See entry in Indiana Basketball Hall of Fame, 1975.

ENDACOTT, Paul
Player
See entry in Naismith Memorial Basketball Hall of Fame, 1971.

ENKE, Fred A.
Coach
Born July 12, 1897, in Rochester, Minn; graduated from Univ. Minn; son Fred W. All-American halfback for Univ. Ariz. Wildcats and played quarterback in the NFL; currently lives in Tucson, Ariz.

Enke spent 40 years as a coach at the University of Arizona 1926 – 1961, starting with two years at South Dakota State and another two with the University of Louisville. His major college record was 525 – 340. He was also the first golf coach at Arizona and his teams won 290, lost 101 and tied 13 matches, overall.

EVANS, Raymond
Player
Born September 22, 1922, in Kansas City, Kans; graduated from Univ. Kans.

Evans was All-Big Six and All-American in basketball in 1942 and 1943. He was a member of the Conference champion basketball team in 1943. He was also All-American in football, playing in the backfield. In 1947 he helped the Jayhawks to their first unbeaten season in 24 years.
Also in: National Football Hall of Fame.

FERRIN, Arnold
Player
Born July 29, 1925, in Salt Lake City, Utah; graduated from Univ. Utah; All-American 3 times.

During his years as player with the University of Utah Redskins, the team won one NCAA title in which Ferrin was named Most Valuable Player. He was also on the team that won the National Invitational Tournament crown in 1947. He played with the Minneapolis Lakers from 1949 to 1951 and had a 5.8 points per game average for 178 games.

FRIEL, Jack
Coach
Born August 26, 1898, in Waterville, Wash; graduated from Wash. State Univ.

Jack had four years of high school coaching before going to Washington State where he coached from 1928 to 1958. In his 30 years he produced two All-Americans and his overall record was 501 – 394. He later served as commissioner of the Big Sky Conference for eight years.

GARDNER, Jack
Coach
Born March 29, 1910, in Texico, N. Mex; graduated from Univ. Southern Calif.

1940 – 1942 Kansas State University, coach
1947 – 1953 Kansas State University, coach
1954 – 1971 University of Utah, coach

Gardner won three letters at Southern California and was team captain in his senior year. As a coach he led Kansas State to a 147 – 81 record, and either won or shared three Big Seven titles and he turned out three All-Americans. At Utah he had a 339 – 154 record.

GILL, Amory T.
Coach
See entry in Naismith Memorial Basketball Hall of Fame, 1967.

GLAMACK, George
Player
Born June 7, 1918, in Johnstown, Pa; graduated from Univ. N. C; Helms Athletic Foundation All-American and Player of the Year 1941 and 1942; Helms All-Time All-American Team.

An ambidextrous hook shooter, Glamack led North Carolina to the Southern Conference crown in 1940. That same year he scored 458 of North Carolina's 1210 points. In 1949 he played in 11 games with the NBA Indianapolis Jets and had a 9.3 average. He served 8 years as assistant coach at Rochester Institute of Technology.

GOLA, Thomas J.
Player
See entry in Naismith Memorial Basketball Hall of Fame, 1975.
Also in: National Polish-American Sports Hall of Fame and Museum.

GULLION, Blair
Coach
See entry in Indiana Basketball Hall of Fame, 1971.

HALL, Dale
Player
Born June 21, 1924, in Pittsburg, Kans; graduated from U.S. Military Academy; All-American 1944 – 1945.

Dale was All-State in football and basketball at Parsons (Kans.) High School. He was West Point All-American in 1944 and 1945 and the Cadets were Helms national champions in 1944. He was assistant coach at Purdue, New Hampshire and Florida and head coach at Army for three years.

HANSON, Victor A.
Player
See entry in Naismith Memorial Basketball Hall of Fame, 1960.
Also in: National Football Hall of Fame.

HENNON, Don
Player
Born January 18, 1937, in Wampum, Pa; graduated from Univ. Pittsburgh; All-American twice.

In his college debut at Pittsburgh, Don scored 34 points against North Carolina State, hitting 17 out of 25 shots. He holds the majority of Panther scoring marks, with a career average of 24.2 points in 76 games, and 45 points in one game.

HOLMAN, Nat
Coach
See entry in Naismith Memorial Basketball Hall of Fame, 1964.

HYATT, Charles
Player
See entry in Naismith Memorial Basketball Hall of Fame, 1959.
Also in: Amateur Basketball Hall of Fame, Citizens Savings Hall of Fame Athletic Museum.

IBA, Henry P.
Coach
See entry in Naismith Memorial Basketball Hall of Fame, 1968.
Also in: Athletic Directors Hall of Fame, Citizens Savings Hall of Fame Athletic Museum.

JOURDET, Lon
Coach
Born September 12, 1888, at Frenchtown, Pa; graduated from Univ. Pa; died August 31, 1959, in Lancaster, Pa.

Jourdet played football for three years and basketball at Pennsylvania and captained the basketball team in 1913. Two years after graduation he became Pennsylvania's coach. He compiled a 228-142 record for the Quakers and the 1920 team was named by Helms Athletic Foundation as national champions. Each starter that season was named to the All-Conference team. Jourdet coached his teams to six Ivy League titles. He coached at Pennsylvania 1915 – 1920 and 1931 – 1943.

KEANEY, Frank W.
Coach
See entry in Naismith Memorial Basketball Hall of Fame, 1960.
Also in: American Association of College Baseball Coaches Hall of Fame.

KEOGAN, George E.
Coach
See entry in Naismith Memorial Basketball Hall of Fame, 1961.

KURLAND, Robert A. "Foothills"
Player
See entry in Naismith Memorial Basketball Hall of Fame, 1961.
Also in: Amateur Basketball Hall of Fame, Citizens Savings Hall of Fame Athletic Museum.

LAMBERT, Ward L.
Coach
See entry in Indiana Basketball Hall of Fame, 1962.
Also in: Naismith Memorial Basketball Hall of Fame.

LONBORG, Arthur C.
Coach
See entry in Naismith Memorial Basketball Hall of Fame, 1972.
Also in: Athletic Directors Hall of Fame, Citizens Savings Hall of Fame Athletic Museum.

LOVELY, James
Player
Born October 28, 1900, in Arcadia, Iowa; graduated from Creighton Univ; All-American 1923 and 1924.

Jim played four years of basketball at Elkton (S.Dak.) High School and four years at Creighton. He was team captain for two years. He played on three North Central Conference championship teams.

LUISETTI, Angelo "Hank"
Player
See entry in Naismith Memorial Basketball Hall of Fame, 1959.
Also in: Amateur Basketball Hall of Fame, Citizens Savings Hall of Fame Athletic Museum.

MEANWELL, Walter
Coach
See entry in Naismith Memorial Basketball Hall of Fame, 1959.

MIKAN, George L.
Player
See entry in Naismith Memorial Basketball Hall of Fame, 1959.
Also in: Major League Basketball Hall of Fame, Citizens Savings Hall of Fame Athletic Museum.

MOIR, John
Player
Born May 22, 1917, in Rutherglen, Scotland; came to the United States at age 6; graduated from Univ. Notre Dame; All-American three times; Helms Athletic Foundation Player of the Year 1938.

John played for coach George Keogan at Notre Dame from 1935 to 1938. He played three years of pro ball with the old National League Firestones.

MORGAN, Ralph
Noteworthy Contributor
See entry in Naismith Memorial Basketball Hall of Fame, 1959.

MURPHY, Charles C.
Player
See entry in Indiana Basketball Hall of Fame, 1963.
Also in: Naismith Memorial Basketball Hall of Fame.

NAISMITH, Dr. James
Noteworthy Contributor
See entry in Naismith Memorial Basketball Hall of Fame, 1959.
Also in: Amateur Basketball Hall of Fame and Noteworthy Contributors Hall of Fame, Citizens Savings Hall of Fame Athletic Museum; Canada's Sports Hall of Fame and National Association of Intercollegiate Athletics Hall of Fame.

NASH, Charles
Player
Born July 24, 1942, in Jersey City, N.J; graduated from Univ. Ky; All-American 1962 – 1964.

Nash averaged 23.4 in 1962 while helping the University of Kentucky gain Southeastern Conference co-championship honors. The team had a 23-3 record and was in third place in the national rankings. In 1965 he played one season with Los Angeles and San Francisco, averaging 3.0 in 45 games.

PAGE, Harlan O. "Pat"
Player
See entry in Naismith Memorial Basketball Hall of Fame, 1962.

PETERSON, Vadal
Coach
Born May 2, 1893, in Huntsville, Utah; one of nine boys; graduated from Univ. of Utah.

Vadal coached at Utah from 1928 to 1953 and compiled an overall record of 384 – 224 in his 26 years.

PRICE, Clarence
Coach
Born April 26, 1889 in Duluth, Minn; graduated from Univ. Minn; died January 13, 1968, in Oakland, Calif.

When Price retired in 1954 from California, he was rated Number Two coach in the country. His overall record was 463 – 298. He won 6 Pacific Coast and 11 Southern Division titles. In his 30 years Price's best team was in 1927 when they had a 15 – 0 record.

RABENHORST, Harry
Coach
Born April 30, 1898, in Baton Rouge, La; graduated from Wake Forest Col; died March 24, 1972, in Baton Rouge.

Rabenhorst coached basketball and baseball at Louisiana State University from 1926 to 1957. During that time he produced two All-Americans and won three Southeastern Conference titles. His overall record was 343 – 259. He was named athletic director for one year after assisting that department for 20 years.

REINHART, Bill
Coach
Born August 2, 1896, in Osborn, Mo; graduated from Univ. Ore; served in both W.W. I and II; died February 14, 1971, in Washington, D.C.

Reinhart won letters in football, basketball and baseball at Oregon. He quarterbacked the football team against Harvard in 1920 in the Rose Bowl. He coached basketball at Oregon and the U.S. Merchant Marine Academy but spent the majority of his coaching career at George Washington University where his record was 315 – 237. His overall record was 464 – 331.

RUPP, Adolph F.
Coach
See entry in Naismith Memorial Basketball Hall of Fame, 1968.

SCHOMMER, John J.
Player
See entry in Naismith Memorial Basketball Hall of Fame, 1959.

THOMPSON, John A. "Cat"
Coach
See entry in Naismith Memorial Basketball Hall of Fame, 1962.

WALKER, Chester
Player
Born February 22, 1940, in Benton Harbor, Mich; graduated from Bradley Univ; All-Missouri Conference three times; Consensus All-American twice.

1962 – 1970 Philadelphia Warriors, forward
1971 – 1975 Chicago Bulls, forward

Walker scored a Bradley record 50 points against California-Davis in 1960. He shot 55.2 percent on field goals and averaged 24.4 points and 12.8 rebounds during his college career. After his 8 years with the Warriors, he was traded to Chicago where he averaged in the double figures for his ten seasons. He hit 22.0 points per game in back-to-back seasons in 1971 and 1972. In 1967 he was a member of the NBA 76ers championship team and that same year, he scored 15 points in the East-West All-Star game.

WOODEN, John R.
Player
See entry in Indiana Basketball Hall of Fame, 1962.
Also in: Naismith Memorial Basketball Hall of Fame.

Basketball — Major League Hall of Fame

In 1960 this Hall was originated to honor professional basketball players, coaches and contributors to professional basketball. As of 1977 there were 34 members in the Hall. Upon induction each member receives a Hall of Fame Award and has his name engraved on the Trophy which is kept in the Citizens Savings Hall of Fame Athletic Museum, Los Angeles international sports shrine.

Induction Years Unrecorded

ARIZIN, Paul
Player
Born April 9, 1928, in Philadelphia, Pa; graduated from Villanova Univ.

Paul enrolled at Villanova as a nonscholarship student, and played regularly in the night center to improve himself, joining the Villanova varsity in his sophomore year. He scored 85 points in one game his junior year and the next year, led the nation in scoring with a 25.3 average. He was selected All-American 1949 – 1950. Paul played with the Philadelphia 76ers 1951 – 1952 and 1955 – 1962. In the pros, he won two point chmpionships, utilizing an amazing jump shot. Arizin had a line drive jump, which was considered by many to be a model of perfection. His career average with the NBA was 22.8 in 713 games, and he was on the All-NBA first team three times. Arizin was voted to play in the All-Star game ten times, and missed only one game due to an injury. Arizin was a member of the NBA Silver Anniversary team.

AUERBACH, Arnold J. "Red"
Coach
See entry in Naismith Memorial Basketball Hall of Fame, 1968.

BAYLOR, Egin
Player
See entry in Naismith Memorial Basketball Hall of Fame, 1976.

Also in: College Basketball Hall of Fame, Citizens Savings Hall of Fame Athletic Museum.

BRAUN, Carl

Player

Born September 25, 1927, in Garden City, N.Y; graduated from Colgate Univ.

1948 – 1962 New York Knickerbockers, guard
1960 – 1961 New York Knickerbockers, coach

Carl starred as a Colgate cager, but his Colgate career ended when he signed with the New York Yankees. A torn muscle, however, ended his pitching and baseball aspirations while he was still in the minors. Braun scored a record 47 points on 18 field goals and 11 free throws during his freshman year with the New York Knicks. He played 789 games with the NBA, with a 13.5 scoring average. He was twice selected on the All-Pro second team.

CHAMBERLAIN, Wilt "The Stilt"

Player

See entry in College Basketball Hall of Fame, Citizens Savings Hall of Fame Athletic Museum, 1962.
Also in: Black Athletes Hall of Fame.

COUSY, Robert J. "Cooz"

Player

See entry in Naismith Memorial Basketball Hall of Fame, 1970.
Also in: College Basketball Hall of Fame, Citizens Savings Hall of Fame Athletic Museum.

EMBRY, Wayne

Player

Born March 26, 1937, in Springfield, Ohio; graduated from Miami Univ. (Ohio).

Embry played center with the Cincinnati Royals, Boston Celtics and Milwaukee Bucks 1959 – 1969. He holds seven major records at his alma mater, including total points (1401) and career average (19.5) in three seasons, 1955 – 1958. His greatest NBA years were with the Royals and he had the single season pro high of 19.6 in 1962. In 831 NBA games, Embry averaged 12.5 and played in five All-Star games.

FOUST, Larry

Player

Born June 24, 1928, in Philadelphia; graduated from LaSalle Col. (Pa).

Forest played with Fort Wayne, Minneapolis Lakers and St. Louis Hawks as center 1951 – 1962. He was the fourth greatest scorer in LaSalle history with 1464 points for an average of 14.2 points per game. In his 12 years in the NBA, his average was 13.7 in 817 games. He was the league's rebounding co-leader in 1952 with a 13.3 average and he shot 48.7 percent on field goals to lead the NBA in 1955. Forest was twice named All-Pro second team and played in eight All-Star games.

GRABOWSKI, Joe

Player

Born January 15, 1930.

1949 – 1950 Chicago Bulls, forward
1952 – 1953 Indianapolis, forward
1954 – 1961 Philadelphia 76ers, forward
1962 Syracuse Nationals, forward

In his 13 years with the NBA, Grabowski scored 9280 points in 845 games and has 59,999 rebounds to his credit.

GREER, Hal

Player

Born June 26, 1936, in Huntington, W.Va; youngest of nine children; graduated from Marshall Univ.

Greer was recruited by Cam Henderson as the first black to play at Marshall University. Greer shot 54.6 percent from the field in college and in 3 varsity seasons, Marshall was 50 – 21. Greer was drafted by the NBA and he averaged better than 20 points per game with the Philadelphia 76ers for seven consecutive years, 1964 to 1970. The 76ers, built around Greer, Wilt Chamberlain and Chet Walker, unseated Boston as the NBA champions in 1967.

GUERIN, Richie

Player

Born May 29, 1932, in New York City; graduated from Iona Col. (N.Y).

Guerin was a center in college, but became a guard while in the Marine Corps. He gained All-American recognition with the AAU Quantico Marines and was later a New York Knicks standout. He established eight Knicks records, including a 29.5 point average and 2303 points in one season. In 1963, he was traded to the St. Louis Hawks for cash in a second round draft choice. From 1965 to 1972, Richie was a player-coach with the Hawks and had a 337 – 290 coaching record. He was selected for the All-NBA second team three times and was in six All-Star games.

HAGAN, Cliff

Player

See entry in College Basketball Hall of Fame, Citizens Savings Hall of Fame Athletic Museum, 1966.

HEINSOHN, Tom

Player

Born August 26, 1934, in Union City, N.J; graduated from Holy Cross Col; Consensus All-American 1956; Rookie of the Year 1957.

1957 – 1965 Boston Celtics, forward

Tom had 1789 points for a 22.1 college average from 1954 to 1956. He set a Holy Cross Crusader rebounding record with 42 in one game and a 21.0 average for one season. He spent his entire pro career with the Boston Celtics 1957 – 1965 and except for the second season, he played on a championship team each year while averaging 18.6 in 654 games. Heinsohn was on six All-Star teams and was on the All-NBA second team four times.

HOWELL, Bailey

Player

Born January 20, 1937, in Middleton, Tenn; graduated from Miss. State Univ.

Howell played with the Detroit Eagles, Baltimore Bullets, Boston Celtics and Philadelphia 76ers as forward 1960 – 1971. He was the top player in Mississippi State history, being selected All-American twice, 1958 and

1959. His 27.1 career scoring average and 34 rebounds were Southeastern Conference records. As a sophomore Howell led the nation with a 56.8 field goal percentage. In the NBA Howell had a 18.7 average in 951 games. He was on the All-NBA second team in 1963 and played in six All-Star games.

JONES, Sam

Player

Born June 24, 1933, in Wilmington, N.C; graduated from N.C. Col. at Durham.

As a youngster in Wilmington, Jones played in informal football games with Althea Gibson, who was destined to become famous as a tennis star. He received only two college offers to play basketball; later he was Number One draft choice of the Boston Celtics on a tip from Bones McKinney, the Wake Forest College coach. Utilizing the bank shot, he played 12 seasons with the Celtics, and averaged 17.6 points in 872 games. He was second in the NBA playoff games with 154 games and three times All-Pro second team. He was selected for the NBA Silver Anniversary team. Sam played in 5 East-West All-Star games.

Also in: National Association of Intercollegiate Athletics Hall of Fame.

KERR, John "Red"

Player

Born August 17, 1932, in Chicago, Ill; graduated from Univ. Ill.

1955 – 1966 Syracuse Nationals, Philadelphia 76ers, Baltimore Bullets, center

1967 – 1970 Chicago Bulls, Phoenix Suns, coach

During his senior year in high school, Kerr was contacted by 45 colleges to play basketball. He chose Illinois because he liked coach Harry Combes and was impressed with the Whiz Kids. He became captain, second leading conference scorer and recipient of *Chicago Tribune's* Silver Basketball, awarded to best Big-Ten player, all in 1954. During his NBA career, Kerr excelled as hook-shooting pivot. He played in 844 straight games in one stretch and 905 overall.

LOVELETTE, Clyde

Player

See entry in College Basketball Hall of Fame, Citizens Savings Hall of Fame Athletic Museum, 1959.

MACAULEY, Edward E.

Player

See entry in Naismith Memorial Basketball Hall of Fame, 1960.

Also in: College Basketball Hall of Fame, Citizens Savings Hall of Fame Athletic Museum.

MARTIN, Slater "Dugie"

Player

Born October 22, 1925, in El Mina, Tex; graduated from Univ. Tex; served in U.S. Navy during W.W. II.

Martin played for the Minneapolis Lakers, St. Louis Hawks, and other NBA teams as guard 1950 – 1959. He earned his nickname after a character in the Mutt and Jeff comic strip. He scored 984 points in his four year varsity career at Texas in 1944 and from 1947 to 1949. Martin was one of the smallest ever to play in the pros. He gave Bob Cousy his toughest opposition and their duels are legendary. Martin played on five NBA championship teams, four with Minneapolis and one with St. Louis. He scored 10.2 points per game average in his 681 game career. Martin was in seven NBA All-Star games and was named to the All-NBA second team 5 times.

MIKAN, George L.

Player

See entry in Naismith Memorial Basketball Hall of Fame, 1959.

Also in: College Basketball Hall of Fame, Citizens Savings Hall of Fame Athletic Museum.

MIKKELSON, Vern

Player

Born December 21, 1928, in Fresno, Calif; graduated from Hamline Univ.

Vern played on three NAIA tournament teams and one of them was a national champion in 1949. He was named to the All-Time NAIA All-Tournament team. He switched from center to forward for the Lakers because of George Mikan's presence at pivot. Mikkelson, Mikan and Jim Pollard formed the NBA's best early front line. Mikkelson, a hook shot artist, liked rugged play under the basket. He fouled out in a record 127 NBA games and served as Laker team captain six seasons, playing on four title teams 1950 – 1959. Vern was awarded All-Star honors four times and averaged 14.4 points per game in 700 pro games.

Also in: National Association of Intercollegiate Athletics Hall of Fame.

NAULLS, Willie

Player

Born October 7, 1934, in Dallas, Tex; moved to Los Angeles, at age 7; graduated from Univ. Calif. Los Angeles.

While playing at the University of California, Willie was selected as All-City in both baseball and basketball and was the first UCLA All-American for coach John Wooden in 1956. Willie played for New York Knickerbockers and Boston Celtics as forward 1957 – 1966. He was the first black in the NBA to be named captain of his team, the New York Knicks. He averaged 15.8 points in 716 games, and played in four All-Star games.

PETTIT, Robert L.

Player

See entry in Naismith Memorial Basketball Hall of Fame, 1970.

Also in: College Basketball Hall of Fame, Citizens Savings Hall of Fame Athletic Museum.

PHILLIP, Andrew

Player

See entry in Naismith Memorial Basketball Hall of Fame, 1961.

Also in: College Basketball Hall of Fame, Citizens Savings Hall of Fame Athletic Museum.

POLLARD, James

Player

See entry in Amateur Basketball Hall of Fame, Citizens

Savings Hall of Fame Athletic Museum (Induction Year Unrecorded).

RAMSEY, Frank
Player
Born July 13, 1931, in Corydon, Ky; graduated from Univ. Ky.

Ramsey was a famous substitute for the Boston Celtics; his prowess in relief earned him "sixth starter" tag. Consistency and versatility were characteristic of him. His overall NBA average was 13.4 in 623 games. Ramsey coached the Kentucky Colonels in the American Basketball Association in 1971. He was named College All-American in 1952 and 1954.

RISEN, Arnold
Player
Born October 9, 1924, in Williamstown, Ky; graduated from Ohio State Univ.

Arnold was All-Conference center for Ohio State in 1944. He played for Indianapolis (National League), Rochester Royals and Boston Celtics as center 1946–1958. He scored in the double figures for 10 straight seasons in the pros, with a high of 16.6 points per game with Rochester as he was named to the All-Pro second team in 1949. Risen's overall average was 12.2 points per game in 758 games.

RUSSELL, William F.
Player
See entry in Naismith Memorial Basketball Hall of Fame, 1974.
Also in: College Basketball Hall of Fame, Citizens Savings Hall of Fame Athletic Museum.

SCHAYES, Adolph
Player
See entry in Naismith Memorial Basketball Hall of Fame, 1972.

SHARMAN, William W.
Player
See entry in Naismith Memorial Basketball Hall of Fame, 1975.

TWYMAN, Jack
Player
Born May 21, 1934, in Pittsburgh, Pa; graduated from Univ. Cincinnati.

Completely dedicated to basketball, Twyman played at Cincinnati from 1952 to 1955 and was second in lifetime rebounds at 1242. He was selected All-American in 1955. His NBA scores were 15,840 points in 823 games for a 19.2 average. In 1960, his best year, he sank 31.2 points to finish second to Wilt Chamberlain. During the off-season, he was known to shoot 100 fouls, 200 jump shots and up to 150 set shots per day. Twyman participated in six All-Star games and was named to the All-NBA second team twice. Jack Twyman will long be remembered for his humanitarian deeds for Maurice Stokes. Maurice had a sensational but brief pro career which ended in just three short years by a paralyzing brain injury in 1958. He fought courageously to regain his speech and mobility, but he never got beyond a wheelchair and a guttural form of speech in a long 12-year battle. Jack became his legal guardian and sponsored the annual Maurice Stokes Benefit Game at Monticello, N.Y.

WILKENS, Leonard
Player
Born October 28, 1937, in Brooklyn, N.Y; graduated from Providence Col, R.I.

Wilkens was selected Most Valuable Player in the National Invitational Tournament and in the New York City East-West game in 1960. He was also All-American in 1960. After graduation, he was drafted on the first round by the St. Louis Hawks and later played with Seattle and Cleveland. He played in eight All-Star games and was fourth in lifetime NBA assists. He excelled in playmaking and ball-stealing, and his best scoring average was 22.4 in 1969. He was a player-coach with the Seattle SuperSonics from 1970 to 1972.

YARDLEY, George
Player
See entry in Amateur Basketball Hall of Fame, Citizens Savings Hall of Fame Athletic Museum (Induction Year Unrecorded).

ZASLOFSKY, Max
Player
Born December 7, 1925, in Brooklyn, N.Y; graduated from St. John's Univ. (N.Y).

Max averaged 14.8 points in 540 NBA games between 1947 and 1956. He was selected to the All-Pro first team four times. In 1950, he was the league's free throw percentage leader with 84.3 percent and he scored 11 points in his one All-Star game appearance in 1952. He once held the New York Knicks one-quarter scoring record with 19 points.

Basketball — Women's Hall of Fame

In 1966 this Hall was originated to honor women basketball players, as well as coaches and contributors to women's basketball. As of 1977 there were 44 members in the Hall. Nominations are made by the Amateur Athletic Union Women's Basketball Committee and new members are selected by the Hall of Fame Board. Upon induction, each member receives a Hall of Fame Award and has their name engraved on the Trophy which is kept in the Citizens Savings Hall of Fame Athletic Museum, Los Angeles international sports shrine.

1966

BANKS, Alline
Player
Alline played for the Nashville Business College, Vultee and the Nashville Goldblumes. She was on All-America teams every year from 1940 to 1950.

BARHAM, Leota
Player
Leota played on All-America teams in 1935, 1937 and from 1940 to 1941.

BLANN, Loretta
Player
Loretta played on All-American teams from 1942 to 1943 and again in 1945.

COX, Alberta Lee
Player
Alberta played for Midland, Platt College, Topeka and Raytown Piperettes. She was on All-America teams in 1955, 1957, 1960 and from 1964 to 1965.

CRAWFORD, Joan
Player
Joan played for Midland and Nashville Business College, and was on All-America teams from 1957 to 1966.

GREER, Lurlyne
Player
Lurlyne played for Nashville Goldblumes and Hanes Hosiery Mills. She was on All-America teams in 1947 and every year from 1949 to 1953.

HOFFAY, Mary Winslow
Player
Mary played for Nashville Business College and played on All-American teams from 1940 to 1945 and in 1947.

HORKY, Rita
Player
Rita played for Iowa Wesleyan College, Topeka and the Nashville Business College. She was selected as All-American from 1959 to 1963.

JAAX, Corine
Player
Corine played on All-America teams from 1931 to 1933, and in 1935, 1938 and from 1944 to 1945.

JORDAN, Evelyn
Player
Evelyn played for the Hanes Hosiery Mills and played on All-America teams from 1950 to 1954.

MARSHALL, Mary
Player
Mary played for Vultee and the Nashville Goldblumes. She was on All-America teams from 1945 to 1949.

SEXTON, Margaret
Player
Margaret played for Nashville Business College, Vultee and the Nashville Goldblumes. She played on All-America teams from 1940 to 1941 and from 1944 to 1949.

THURMAN, Lucille
Player
Lucille played for Presbyterian College, Oklahoma City University, El Dorado and Little Rock. She was on All-America teams from 1932 to 1937 and in 1939.

WALKER, Hazel
Player
Hazel played for Tulsa Business College, El Dorado and Little Rock. She was selected for All-America teams from 1934 to 1935, 1939 to 1940, 1942 and from 1944 to 1945.

WHITE, Nera
Player
Nera played for Nashville Business College. She played on All-America teams from 1955 to 1966.

WILLIAMS, Alberta
Player
Alberta played for Wichita and Tulsa. She was on All-American teams in 1931 and from 1934 to 1935.

1967

BALLS, H. O.
Contributor
Balls has been a sponsor of women's basketball since 1922.

DuBOIS, Lee
Contributor
DuBois has been a women's basketball official for 32 years.

FIETE, Sandra
Player
Sandra played for Iowa Wesleyan College, Platt College, Pepsi Cola Co. and St. Joseph Goetz. She was on All-America teams from 1957 to 1959 and in 1961 and 1963.

FOSTER, Lyle
Contributor
Foster was the National Women's Basketball Chairman from 1958 to 1963.

McGHEE, Tennie
Contributor
McGhee was National Women's Basketball Chairman from 1955 to 1957.

ODOM, Lometa
Player
Lometa played for the Hutcherson Flyers. She was on All-America teams from 1953 to 1956.

RUBLE, Olan
Contributor
Ruble has been dean of women's basketball coaches for 20 years.

SIPES, Barbara
Player
Sipes played for the Santa Fe Streamliners, Kansas City Dons, Wesleyan and the Raytown Piperettes. She played on All-America teams from 1953 to 1954, 1957 to 1958 and from 1963 to 1967.

VAN BLARCUM, Mrs. Irving
Contributor
Mrs. Van Blarcum was the National Women's Basketball Chairman from 1929 until 1954.

WASHINGTON, Katherine
Player
Katherine played for the Nashville Business College and the Hutcherson Flyers. She played on All-America teams in 1952 and from 1956 to 1960.

ZAHARIAS, Mildred Didrikson, "Babe"
Player
Born June 26, 1914, in Port Arthur, Tex; one of 7 children; graduated from Beaumont (Tex) High School; track star in 1932 Olympics; married George Zaharias, wrestler, in 1938; internationally famous golfer; died of cancer at age 41 in Galveston, Tex, on Oct. 27, 1956.

Babe played basketball in junior high school, but was not allowed to play in high school because she was too small. After practicing many hours with the boys' basketball coach, she made the team. In February 1930, the owner of the Employers Casualty Co. of Dallas spotted her at a high school game and offered her a job playing on their AAU team. In 1933 Babe turned pro as a result of being declared a pro by the AAU since a newspaper ad with her picture had been used to endorse the 1933 Dodge. The AAU later revoked their decision (since she received no pay), but she continued as a pro.
Also in: American Golf Hall of Fame, Colorado Golf Hall of Fame; Golf Hall of Fame and Track and Field Hall of Fame, Citizens Savings Hall of Fame Athletic Museum; Ladies Pro Golfers' Association Hall of Fame, National Track and Field Hall of Fame, Professional Golfers' Association of America Hall of Fame, U.S. Track and Field Hall of Fame and World Golf Hall of Fame.

1969

ASPEDON, Carole Phillips
Player
Carole played for the Topeka Boosters and the Raytown Piperettes. She played on All-America Teams from 1964 to 1968.

BECHTOL, Reuben C.
Contributor
Born October 21, 1906; attended Des Moines Univ. and Drake Univ.

Bechtol coached from 1931 to 1951, including the first Iowa team to play in a national tournament in 1935. His teams participated in the national tournaments from 1935 to 1951 and he was the one who introduced the roving player concept to women's basketball. His team, the American Institute of Business of Des Moines, played the first official game for third place in the National AAU tournament in Wichita in 1936. Bechtol coached the first Iowa team to play in a foreign country in 1936 and they played in Mexico in 1951 and 1952. His team played for the National Boy's Rules championship in Edmonton, Alberta, against the Edmonton Grads in 1936. His team won the National All-Boy's Rules championship in St. Louis in 1936. They played in every semifinals at national tournaments, except 1935 and 1945, winning the consolation prize in 1935 and losing in the quarter finals in 1945. They were runnerup for national AAU championship in 1944 and 1947. Bechtol coached 23 All-Americans over the years and it was he who introduced the two-dribble rule to AAU basketball.

BUCK, Clifford
Contributor
See entry in Amateur Basketball Hall of Fame, Citizens Savings Hall of Fame Athletic Museum, 1966.

DUNAWAY, William O.
Contributor
Dunaway coached Lewis and Norwood Flyers women's basketball team from 1935 to 1941. They won first place in 1937 and again in 1940 and 1941. During those years the Flyers played 192 games and won 184, and also won three national championships and two series in Mexico City, playing against the champions of Mexico. Each year the Flyers placed a number of girls on the All-America team. In 1941 at the national tournament, ten All-America players were chosen to make up an Olympic team, and five of them were from the Flyers team. Dunway was selected as the coach. However, the Olympics were cancelled that year due to the war.

HUTCHERSON, Claude
Contributor
Born in 1908; attended Wayland Col, Plainview, Tex.

Hutcherson assumed sponsorship of the Flying Queens of Wayland College in 1949 and since then, Wayland won six national titles and were runnerup eight times. He produced 25 All-Americans, and his teams have produced players for the U.S. Pan-American teams and for several Mexican tours.

LEWIS, J. Herchel
Contributor
Lewis coached women's basketball from 1928 to 1932 and sponsored the National AAU championship team, the Lewis and Norwood Flyers, in 1932 and again in 1940 and 1941. He sponsored AAU teams from 1928 through 1941, and was chairman of women's AAU basketball for the Arkansas Association for 12 years. He was president of the AAU Arkansas Association from 1943 to 1945.

LONG, Leo J.
Contributor
Leo coached AAU women's basketball for Nashville Business College in the late 1930s and 1940s and he coached and developed many outstanding AAU players, including four All-Americans. Long pioneered in bringing the Nashville Business College team to national prominence.

MICKELSEN, Laurine
Contributor
Born in Salina, Utah; B.S. degree from Brigham Young Univ; M.S. from Univ. Utah.

Laurine coached high school girls' basketball from 1947 until 1953, and AAU women's independent teams from 1954 to 1959. She was the Intermountain Association AAU basketball chairman from 1953 to 1963 and the National AAU women's basketball chairman from 1964 to 1967. She was U.S. Olympic women's basketball chairman from 1966 to 1969.

RANSOM, Charles W.
Contributor
Ransom refereed two years of girls' basketball and coached a total of 11 years, producing four All-Americans.

ROGERS, Doris
Player
Doris played for Nashville Business College and was on All-America teams from 1963 to 1968.

SCHULTZ, Leo
Contributor
Born August 27, 1905.

Schultz coached AAU women's basketball from 1937 until 1954. His teams played in 17 national tournaments, winning National AAU championships in 1942 and 1943. Ten of his players were named to All-America teams. His teams played in international competition, in Canada in 1941, and in Latin America in 1942 and 1948 – 1951.

WEEKS, James N.
Contributor
Weeks was the women's AAU basketball sponsor from 1945 until 1953. His team, the Hanes Hosiery Mills, won national championships from 1951 to 1953.

YOW, Virgil
Contributor
Yow coached the Hanes Hosiery Mills teams from 1945 until 1953, and was coach of the national championship teams from 1951 to 1953. In 8 years his teams won 226 and lost just 56 games.

1970

COX, J. L.
Contributor

HEAD, John
Contributor
John coached women's basketball for 32 years, and produced 11 national AAU championship squads, a record. His teams won eight consecutive titles, also a record. He has coached many All-Americans through the years, and for 21 years his teams were nationally ranked. The dean of women's basketball coaches, Head piloted U.S. teams in World tournament competition at Santiago in 1953 and Rio de Janeiro in 1957. He also coached the U.S. team at the Pan-American Games in 1963. In addition, he has conducted numerous tours to foreign lands and supervised American teams in national exchange games.

1973

SCHMIDLIN, Rev. Dunstan
Contributor
Rev. Schmidlin has promoted, organized and directed women's basketball on the Navajo Reservation for 22 years and has also coached them. He is a member of the national AAU women's basketball executive committee and chairman of the New Mexico Association as well as AAU regional chairman. He is also a member of the U.S. Olympic committee women's basketball committee, which supervises U.S. participation in Pan-American Games.

1974

REDIN, Harley
Contributor
Born in Silverton, Tex; graduate of N. Tex. State Col; served in Marine Air Corps in W.W. II, participating in over 50 combat missions in the South Pacific.

After W.W. II, Redin was appointed basketball coach at Wayland College. He directed the men's team for 11 seasons, then directed both the men's and the women's teams for two years. In 1958 he devoted all of his attention to the Flying Queens, coaching them until 1973, when he retired. With Redin in command, the Flying Queens, during one streak, won 76 consecutive games. During his 17 years at Wayland, the Queens won 6 national titles and a record 432 victories with just 61 losses.

Boxing Hall of Fame

The Boxing Hall of Fame within Citizens Savings Hall of Fame Athletic Museum was initiated in 1949. There are two categories for induction, Boxer and Noteworthy Contributor. As of 1977 the total number elected is 71, all but 2 being boxers. There is no limit to the number that may be elected annually.

Induction Years Unrecorded

AMBERS, Louis
Boxer
Born Luigi D'Ambrosio November 8, 1913, in Herkimer, N.Y; U.S. Coast Guard, 1941.

Lou Ambers left home in 1932 with stern words of warning from his father, "Don't come home with a black eye." Until receiving his big break, boxing was barely providing subsistence level food and housing. Unable to train in the large, resourceful gyms in New York, Lou caught the bootleg amateur circuit and fought 80 bouts not recorded in his official statistics of 102 bouts. His first stop was Kingsport, N.Y. where he replaced the featured fighter Otis Paradise. Lou disposed of his opponent in one round, returned as the local attraction for several weeks and assumed the identity of Otis for the remainder of his bootleg career. Finally, Al Weill spotted Lou in the Coney Island Velodrome and signed him to a contract. Under Al's guidance Lou—always the conscientious and dedicated boxer—earned a lightweight title match against Tony Canzoneri. On September 3, 1936, Lou outslugged the man with whom he had once sparred. For two years the Herkimer Hurricane was lightweight titlist until Henry Armstrong won a 2 – 1 decision in 15 rounds on August 17, 1938. The bout drew 20,000 fans to Madison Square Garden, and one reporter described it as "one of the fastest, most furious and savage bouts ever fought in New York." Although Lou regained the crown within a year, Lew Jenkins smashed Lou in three rounds on May 10, 1940, to strip him of the title forever. Several years remained on Lou's contract with Al Weill but Al forced him into retirement in 1941 saying "I'm not going to see you abused."
Also in: Ring Magazine Boxing Hall of Fame.

ARMSTRONG, Henry Jackson, Jr.
Boxer

Born December 12, 1912, Columbus, Miss; orphaned at five; moved to East St. Louis; raised by aunt; 11th of 13 children; mother America Jackson mostly Cherokee Indian; Negro-Irish father; graduated from Vashon High School, East St. Louis; Fighter of the Year 1937; Edward J. Neil Trophy 1940; ordained Baptist minister 1951; preaches before 500,000 revivalists yearly; resides in Norwood, Mo.

Henry Armstrong, known as "Hurricane Henry" and "Melody Jackson," is the only boxer to hold three titles concurrently—featherweight, welterweight and lightweight. He battled to a draw for the middleweight title. A study in pathological misfortune, Henry brought himself to the pinnacle of success but found himself penniless at the end of his 15-year career. He learned to fight in gang wars in East St. Louis, fighting to survive and hoping for something better the next day. Never schooled as a finesse boxer nor for common defense techniques, Henry received beatings in victories that could only be called Pyrrhic at best. After he defeated Lou Ambers in September, 1938, to win the lightweight title, Henry was rushed from ringside to the hospital for surgery. Despite his success in the ring, Henry always fell prey to rapacious managers and deceitful promoters. His first sizeable purse in Mexico, $1500, was stolen by his promoter. Always willing to defend his title or to stage a benefit, he fought with broken ribs, suffered from lack of food, and engaged too many boxers in too brief a time span. At his peak, 1937–1938, he was scheduled for 16 matches in six months. He wound up in a sanitarium with a nervous breakdown. Beginning in 1931, Henry won 85 straight bouts yet he was never paid more than $2.00 a fight and lived in flophouses. His second crown came in May, 1938, when he delivered the renowned blackout punch—neither hook nor jab nor swing but a quick slingshot punch to the chin—to Barney Ross and captured the welterweight title. Ross never fought again. In late 1937 Armstrong won the first crown with a barrage of punches that floored Pete Sarron and earned him the featherweight crown. The style was motion on top of motion, duck, bob, weave, and don't worry about self-defense. The titles slipped away beginning in late 1938 when he abdicated the featherweight because he couldn't make the weight. In a return bout with Lou Ambers in 1939, Henry lost by five points. His final title, welterweight, went to Fritzie Zivic in 1940. Henry was a man of uncommon endurance and slugging ability: a man with a heart one-third larger than the average for a 5 ft. 6 in. 165 lb. male and the lowest heartbeat ever discovered in an athlete. In 15 years and 261 fights, Armstrong earned more than $1,000,000 with his windmill style, but he retired broke, a victim of poor judgment in his fellow man.
Also in: Black Athletes Hall of Fame and *Ring Magazine* Hall of Fame.

ATTELL, Abraham W.
Boxer

Born February 22, 1884, in San Francisco, Calif; died February 7, 1970, at age 85.

Called by many boxing buffs the best boxer ever, pound-for-pound, inch-for-inch, Abe Attell may be the most precocious of all world boxing champions. Abe claimed the featherweight title at age 17, when Terry McGovern and Young Corbet were unable to make the 122 lb. limit. Although Abe claimed the title, controversy abounded even after he decisioned George Dixon in October, 1901. Then Tommy Sullivan also claimed the crown, and not until a rematch in 1908 with Sullivan would Abe be undisputed champion. Depending on when one dates Abe's title, he may have held it for ten years until Johnny Kilbane won a controversial bout on February 22, 1912, in Vernon, Calif. Abe challenged light-, welter- and middleweights, almost winning the lightweight title in 1908 from Battling Nelson in one of the goriest fights ever witnessed. Nearing the end of his 13-year career he challenged Harlem Tommy Murphy. The fight can only be described as a blood-letting slugfest that neither man truly won. Although Harlem Tommy withstood a fusillade of Abe's punches in the 17th round, no one could really tell who won the bout. Standing 5 ft. 4 in. and 118 lbs, Abe recorded a remarkable knockout record for his weight class. He had 32 consecutive wins at the start of his career, flattening 24 of his first 28 opponents by knockouts. His success would never have been achieved without the inspiration of Gentleman Jim Corbett and George Dixon who urged him to box and not slug. "I watched them block, duck and sidestep with ease and grace and realized a fellow could be a fighter and not get hurt—if he were clever enough." Abe fought 200 bouts between 1900 and 1913.
Also in: Ring Magazine Boxing Hall of Fame.

BERLENBACH, Paul "Astoria Assassin"
Boxer

Born February 18, 1901, in New York City; parents were German-American; heavyweight wrestling champion in 1920 Olympics; light heavyweight wrestling champion 1920.

The Astoria Assassin boxed professionally for six years—1923–1929. During this time he fought Jack Delaney four times, losing the world light heavyweight title to him on June 16, 1926. The 5 ft. 10½ in. 170 lb. Olympic wrestling champion was the AAU National heavyweight boxing champion in 1922. He began his career with ten straight knockouts utilizing a sizzling right hand. He met Delaney the first time in 1924 and was kayoed in the fourth round. Berlenbach began another string of 14 consecutive wins, which included the light heavyweight crown from Mike McTigue on May 30, 1925, and a successful title defense against Delaney. Holding the title for only 11 months until Delaney lured him into a Brooklyn ring for their third bout, this mid-1926 title bout marked the beginning of the end for Berlenbach. After losing a 15-round decision to the Canadian, McTigue walloped him in 1927 with a fourth-round kayo, Delaney again with a sixth-round kayo and Mickey Walker won a ten-round decision. In April, 1929, the Assassin returned to wrestling but attempted a boxing comeback in 1931. He won his first two fights by knockouts but the finale came in Atlanta when he lost a ten-round decision in October, 1933. Berlenbach bankrupted himself at the gambling table and retired into business.
Also in: Boxing Hall of Fame and *Ring Magazine* Boxing Hall of Fame.

BRITTON, Jack "Boxing Marvel"
Boxer

Born William J. Breslin October 14, 1885, in Clinton, N.Y; died March 27, 1962, in Miami, Fla, at age 76.

William Breslin, welterweight champion of the world in 1915, 1916 and 1919, engaged the Englishman Ted Kid Lewis in the longest ring rivalry in history. For five years, 222 rounds, 12 no decisions, 1 draw, 3 wins for Breslin and 4 for Lewis, the welterweight title volleyed between them. During Breslin's 26 years of boxing, the 5 ft. 8 in. 144 lb. "Boxing Marvel" lost only one bout inside the distance but was floored six times by Lewis, more than any other fistfighter in history. Breslin first won the title on June 22, 1915, with a 12-round decision from Mike Glover. Two years and three days later he lost the title to Lewis, after beating him in New Orleans in 1916, on a 20-round decision in Dayton, Ohio. This fight occurred on June 25, 1917, the third fight between the two in one month. Vindication was sweet for Breslin when he outslugged the Englishman on St. Patrick's Day in 1919 in Canton, Ohio. His manager telegraphed a message worldwide saying, "An Irishman, Billy Breslin, alias Jack Britton, knocked out Ted (Kid) Lewis, the English welterweight champion, on this St. Patrick's Day. Long live Ireland. Thank you." Breslin would hold the title until youthful Mickey Walker earned a 12-round decision in 1922. During his 320 career contests, Breslin lost only 25 bouts, utilizing his elephantine ears as decoys to roll and slide with the punches. In 1930 he retired but only after winning his last two bouts. He became an instructor at the Downtown Athletic and Catholic Youths' Clubs in New York City. After moving to Miami he lost his boxing fortune in real estate and turned to managing gas stations.
Also in: Ring Magazine Boxing Hall of Fame.

BROWN, Aaron L. "The Dixie Kid"
Boxer

Born December 23, 1888, at Fulton, Mo; real name Aaron L. Brown; died April 13, 1936.

Another story of rags to riches and a return to rags, the Dixie Kid needed a special collection to avoid a pauper's funeral. The 5 ft. 8 in, 145 lb. welterweight champion is best remembered for his defeat of Joe Walcott on April 30, 1904. Two weeks after the championship bout they fought again to a 20-round draw. The Dixie Kid vacated the title when he outgrew the division. After March, 1911, he campaigned in France, England, Ireland and Scotland. Three years after leaving the United States he retired when he kayoed Billy Bristowe. A successful prizefighter when only 16, he won 18 of his first 20 professional bouts.
Also in: Ring Magazine Boxing Hall of Fame.

CANZONERI, Tony
Boxer

Born November 6, 1908, in Slidell, La; father a grocery store operator in Italian section of New Orleans; moved to Brooklyn in 1924; shared *Ring's* Fighter of the Year Award in 1934 with Barney Ross; acted on stage and screen; opened a restaurant; died on December 9, 1959, in New York City at age 51.

In 15 years of professional boxing, Tony Canzoneri fought in 20 world championship matches. Holder of three world titles—featherweight, lightweight and junior welterweight—Tony ranks as one of the greatest lightweights in history. He battled to a draw for a fourth title, bantamweight, when he was only 18. The diminutive Italian at 5 ft. 4 in. 126 lb. was noted for his endurance, speed and stinging right-hand punch. The honors came quickly for this pugilist whose mother wanted him to be a gentleman. On February 10, 1928, he won the featherweight crown from Benny Bass while only 19 years old. He lost the title within six months and absorbed his second title bout loss in 1929 when Sammy Mandell defeated him for the lightweight crown. Undaunted, he recorded the second fastest knockout in November, 1930, against Al Singer for the lightweight title. Singer lasted just 66 seconds. Six months later Tony moved into the junior welterweight division and battered Jackie Kid Berg into submission with a third-round kayo to win his third world crown. Within three years he had won three world titles. Of the 181 career bouts he won 139 and was kayoed only once, in his last bout on November 1, 1939.
Also in: Ring Magazine Boxing Hall of Fame.

CONN, Billy "The Pittsburgh Kid"
Boxer

Born on October 8, 1917, in East Liberty, Pa; Edward J. Neil Trophy 1939; Fighter of the Year 1940.

Billy Conn, the last of the lusty Irish fighters, fought his way within two rounds and two seconds of the world heavyweight title. From his first fight in 1935 in Fairmont, W.Va. for $2.50 to his title bout with Joe Louis on June 18, 1941, Billy defeated middleweights and won the light heavyweight title from Melino Bettina. Billy traded even punches with Louis, teased him with jabs, and spurted away from those savage fists of Louis for 12 rounds until overconfidence took its toll. In the 13th round Louis charged from his corner and forced blows to Billy's jaw. Cornered and slinging furiously, Conn was hurt. With characteristic savagery, Louis buckled Conn's knees and a final hook to the jaw preserved the title for Louis. Gentleman Jim Corbett once remarked that there is a day when a fighter will be better than he ever has been or will be again. On June 18, 1941, Billy Conn was never better and he still came up with nothing against the Bomber. Enlisting in W.W. II in 1942, Billy entertained the troops as a boxer until 1945. Talk was never louder for another match, and on June 19, 1946, a rematch of Louis-Conn was scheduled in Yankee Stadium. A lackluster performance at best for Conn, he was kayoed in the eighth before 45,226 fans. The gate of $1,925,564 was the second largest in history at the time. His last bout was an exhibition match against Louis in Chicago in December, 1948.
Also in: Pennsylvania Boxing Hall of Fame and *Ring Magazine* Boxing Hall of Fame.

CORBETT, James John "Gentleman Jim"
Boxer

Born September 1, 1886, in San Francisco, Calif; one of 11 children; math whiz in high school; high school and college graduate; worked on docks and as bank clerk; played vaudeville circuit; supporting roles in stage plays; on Broadway in "Cashel Bryon's Professional" 1895; died February 18, 1933, in Bayside, N.Y. at age 66.

Gentleman Jim was a boxing artist who approached boxing as a science and not merely a mauler's sport,

Gentleman Jim was a 4 – 1 underdog against John L. Sullivan in their heavyweight bout. Sullivan represented the old image and brawling approach while Corbett was the new boxer, more intelligent and agile, with speed as important as strength. Not only did personalities and style of the boxers clash but this was the first heavyweight championship conducted with the Marquis of Queensbury rules, padded gloves and three-minute rounds. For a purse of $25,000, and a side bet of $10,000, Fancy Dan kayoed John L. in the 21st round. The public was reluctant to embrace their new heavyweight king, a literate man who interspersed defense of his title with vaudeville and stage plays. During his January, 1894 title match defense against Charley Mitchell in England, Gentleman Jim played before capacity crowds in stage plays. However, fans continued to refer to Corbett as an over-educated fop, dude and dandy. In 1897, four years after winning the title, Corbett faced Bob Fitzsimmons at Carson City, Nev. With Wyatt Earp and Bat Masterson present, Fitzsimmons rapped the champ in the stomach and claimed the title. Gentleman Jim had Fitzsimmons on the plank in the seventh but his characteristic weakness—lacking the killer instinct—led to his downfall. Corbett was the first champion to attempt recapturing his title; twice he fought Jim Jeffries and twice he was kayoed. The first fight lasted 23 rounds and the second one 10 rounds. Corbett wandered into boxing accidentally in 1880. He joined the San Francisco Olympic Athletic Club to meet important people. Professor Walter Watson noticed Gentleman Jim's abilities and developed him into a topflight amateur in the Bay area. In 1885 Corbett won the club championship and went to Salt Lake City where he fought under the name of Jim Dillon. Winning his two amateur bouts there, he turned professional in 1886. He practiced for hours before a mirror to spot his flaws, hoping to earn a match with the great John L. One by one the contenders fell, Kilrain, Donovan, Choynski and the last one in his path, Peter Jackson. The Jackson fight was a 61-round draw with Corbett's effort worth $3000. On September 7, 1892, he reached the crowning point of his career while bringing an image of respectability to boxing. In 1925 he boxed an exhibition bout behind closed doors, against Gene Tunney. Tunney later remarked that the 59 year old still had "bewildering speed. He still mixed up his punches better than practically any fighter I've seen." The same year Corbett authored *Roar of the Crowd* and Errol Flynn starred in *Gentleman Jim* a successful film of Corbett's career.
Also in: Ring Magazine Boxing Hall of Fame.

COULON, Johnny "Chicago Spider"
Boxer

Born February 12, 1889, in Toronto, Ont, Can; Irish-French parentage; died Oct. 29, 1973 in Chicago, Ill.

Johnny Coulon, known as the Chicago Spider, was the small man's fighting champion. At 5 ft. and 110 lb, he fought professionally from 1905 to 1920. In 1909 he claimed the bantamweight title after Jimmy Walsh outgrew it. Within six years he would defend the title 12 times. In 1910 he defended his crown three times in four and a half weeks and followed that in 1912 with two 20-round bouts in two weeks. On June 9, 1914, he lost the title to Kid Williams in Vernon, Calif, but continued fighting, remaining undefeated for the next two years. From 1918 to 1919 he was a boxing instructor in the Army. Returning to Chicago where he lived as a youth, he retired from boxing and opened a gym, refereed bouts and played some vaudeville.
Also in: Canada's Sports Hall of Fame and *Ring Magazine* Boxing Hall of Fame.

DELANEY, Jack
Boxer

See entry in Canada's Sports Hall of Fame.
Also in: Ring Magazine Hall of Fame.

DEMPSEY, William Harrison "Jack"
Boxer

Born June 25, 1895, in Manassa, Colo; ninth of 11 children, five brothers and five sisters; parents Hiram and Celia Dempsey; father poverty-driven Mormon sharecropper and itinerant railroad hand from W.Va; married four times; second wife actress Estelle Taylor; co-starred with Estelle in a Broadway flop directed by David Belasco; in movie serials, Lon Chaney did his make-up; served in U.S. Coast Guard during W.W.II; Edward J. Neil Trophy 1938; James J. Walker Memorial Award 1957; restaurateur.

Jack Dempsey was handed John L. Sullivan's memoirs by his mother and taught boxing by an older brother. He vagabonded across the Rockies as carnival fighter, fruit picker, mule driver and professional pool shark. At 18 he was a bouncer in a Salt Lake City saloon. It was from there that he entered the prize ring, fighting under the name of "Kid Blackie." Having fought his first bouts as miner, lumberjack and shipyard laborer, he went to New York in 1916 and made the rounds of promoters' offices without success. He did manage a sparring job of 75¢ a day and was befriended by sportswriter Damon Runyon who gave him the nickname "Manassa Mauler." Dempsey possessed all the traits needed for a heavyweight champion: ferocity, cold-bloodedness, gameness. He exemplified boxing's cardinal rule of no pity in the ring with his busted nose, close cropped hair and two o'clock beard shadow. Joe Benjamin, former lightweight contender, said Dempsey "had the speed of a lightweight, hand and foot. He could run the hundred in close to 10 sec. From the hips up he was heavily muscled, and he could box with anybody he wanted. Jack's hands were hard as rocks. He was the perfect fighting machine—hands, legs, fighting brain and disposition. He was simply a superhuman wild man." He fought in vaudeville while waiting his chance against Jess Willard, the champion. Opponents were invited from the audience who were outraced to the stage by a stooge planted in the first row, Max "The Goose" Kaplan, who "was really good, he could fall over like a store dummy." He battled Willard in Toledo, Ohio, on June 4, 1919. Despite giving away 58 lbs. to Willard, Dempsey won by a knockout in round three after flooring Willard seven times in the first round. The new champ declared, "It felt swell." The arena in Toledo was 106 degrees. Bat Masterson and Wyatt Earp appointed themselves Official Collectors of spectators' guns and knives as they entered. Ethel Barrymore came out from New York and sat in a woman's section, a controversial innovation. In the first of his five million-dollar gate extravaganzas, 75,000 paid a total of $1,789,238 to see Dempsey wallop a mismatched Georges Carpentier, the pride of France. Two years later, on July

4, 1923, Dempsey fought Tommy Gibbons at Shelby, Mont, in "the fight that broke a town." In the only fight of Dempsey's six title defenses that went the distance, seven banks went bankrupt. One of the most action-packed and furious bouts in history took place September 14, 1923. The Manassa Mauler went berserk, kayoing Louis Firpo in the second round yet belting him three more times while Firpo lay limp on the canvas. In two rounds a total of 12 falls occurred, 9 by Firpo and 3 by Dempsey. When he married actress Estelle Taylor in 1925, the rumored breakup with manager Doc Kearns surfaced. Doc had brought Dempsey from rags to riches in just five years. The split of the winnings was always 2–1 yet no contract had ever been signed legalizing the cut. Supposedly Estelle suspected Doc of misdealings and urged "Ginsberg" (her favorite pet name for Jack) to forsake the contract and boxing as a career. After the air cleared, Kearns sued Dempsey unsuccessfuly for $700,000, and Dempsey claimed his signature was bogus on the contract. At the Sesquicentennial Stadium in Philadelphia on September 23, 1926, Gene Tunney won the heavyweight crown in ten rounds. This match attracted 120,757 fans, with ringside prices of $27.50 and was the greatest paid attendance ever yielded, totalling $1,895,733. One year and four days later, Tunney won the so-called Battle of the Long Count. After flooring Tunney, Dempsey forgot to return to a neutral corner. Some historians say that Tunney was given 14 seconds to return to an upright position. Tunney eventually won in ten rounds and earned $1,000,000. The 1927 bout produced the highest gate receipts with 104,943 spectators paying a ringside price of $40 per ticket. Boxing's symbol during the golden age of sport, Dempsey helped place boxing into big business promotion, retiring after 1940.
Also in: Ring Magazine Boxing Hall of Fame.

DILLON, Jack "Jack the Giant Killer"
Boxer
Born February 2, 1891, in Frankfort, Ind; real name Ernest Cutler Price; died August 7, 1942, in Chattahoochee, Fla.

Jack Dillon was truly a Giant Killer. A small light heavyweight, standing 5 ft. 7½ in. and 158 lbs, Dillon battled the Goliaths—men like Harry Greb, Battling Levinsky and Jim Flynn. An articulate boxer with sculptured features, he possessed a muscular chest with wide shoulders and a strong jaw for absorbing jabs. One of the genuine carpetbag boxers, Dillon would get off the train in the morning and box in the evening. In 1912 he boxed five times in February, five times in October and four times in November. Fifteen years of boxing and 240 bouts later, Dillon had never been knocked out. He defeated Hugo Kelly in May 1912, and sent telegrams to all sportswriters proclaiming himself world light heavyweight champion. This mail-order champion agreed to box Al Norton in Kansas City for the official crown on April 28, 1914. Norton was defeated in ten rounds and was kayoed in a rematch one year later. In between his official title and losing it to Battling Levinsky, Dillon humiliated Gentleman Jim Corbett's best heavyweight in the world Tom Cowler. Cowler and Dillon met on February 1, 1916, with the Giant Killer walloping Gentleman Jim's protege in two rounds. After losing the light heavyweight to Levinsky, Dillon was urged to retire but refused. His skills dissipating, in 1923 he stepped out of the ring in Bicknell, Ind, for the last time. Until his death in 1942 he managed a sandwich shop in Chattahoochee, Fla.
Also in: Ring Magazine Boxing Hall of Fame.

DIXON, George "Little Chocolate"
See entry in Canada's Sports Hall of Fame.
Also in: Providence Hall of Fame and *Ring Magazine* Boxing Hall of Fame.

DUNDEE, Johnny
Boxer
Born November 22, 1893, at Shaikai, Italy; real name is Joseph Corrara; grew up in New York City's West Forties' "Hell's Kitchen"; father operated a fish market; retired in 1932; died April 22, 1965, in East Orange, N.J.

Johnny Dundee fought for 20 years with a style no one could imitate. With dazzling fast feet, he boxed on his toes, making him an elusive target for anyone. He also perfected the rebound punch, coming off the ropes and adding wallop to his punch. For 14 years he labored for the featherweight title, losing a 20-round draw to Johnny Kilbane in 1913, but decisioning Eugene Criqui on July 26, 1923, for the crown. Considered one of the top feather and lightweights for two decades, Johnny could add or dissolve weight at his leisure. Some writers estimate he melted off two tons of flesh during his career without sacrificing speed or stamina. The featherweight champ for less than two years, he outgrew the division. Dundee was voted among the top ten featherweights of all-time.
Also in: Ring Magazine Boxing Hall of Fame.

FIELDS, Jackie
Boxer
Born February 9, 1907, in Chicago, Ill; real name Jacob Finkelstein; moved to Los Angeles, Calif, when 13; father a butcher; resides in Las Vegas, Nev; public relations director for Tropicana Hotel.

Jackie Fields learned to fight in the streets of Los Angeles and later at the Los Angeles Athletic Club. He was sparring partner for Fidel LaBarba, the flyweight amateur champion. Not the quickest afoot, Fields countered by cornering his opponents, blocking punches and hammering their bodies. His style led him to victory in 51 of 54 amateur bouts, including the gold medal in the 1924 Olympics, and to the welterweight title twice. He was the youngest athlete to win a gold medal in the Olympics, defeating Joe Salas in his last bout as an amateur and in his first bout as a professional. On March 25, 1929, he won the National Boxing Association welterweight title from Jack Thompson but lost a rematch 15-round decision to him one year later. Undaunted, he challenged Lou Brouillard for the world welterweight title in January, 1932, and won in ten rounds. Once on top, always the target, Fields remained champion for one year until Young Corbett III beat him on February 22, 1933. When most boxers reach their peak in their late 20s, Fields was forced into retirement in 1933, one year after having an auto accident that injured an eye, causing loss of sight.

FITZSIMMONS, Robert L.
Boxer
Born June 4, 1862, in Halston, Cornwall, England; reared in New Zealand although referred to as Australian; blacksmith by trade; married; one son; appeared in

vaudeville; on Broadway in "The Honest Blacksmith," 1898; died of pneumonia in Chicago, October 22, 1917 at age 55.

Ruby Robert was boxing's first triple titleholder. He won the middleweight title in 1890 from Nonpareil Jack Dempsey, the heavyweight title from Jim Corbett at the age of 35, and in 1903, at age 41, the light heavyweight crown from George Gardner. His last bout was a six-round no-decision against Jersey Bellow, February 20, 1914. Fitz was 51 years old. He did not look like a heavyweight. In fact, some suggest he did not look like a lightweight. Knock-kneed, bird-legs, sparse red hair, a freckled face, and a barrel chest, his looks were deceiving. Behind the physique were pent-up energies released into his "solar-plexus punch." The punch was essentially a left hook to the body, but placed squarely in the crevice of the breastbone and rib cage aperture. Only with Ruby Bob's deadly accurate timing and judge of distance could the punch fell an opponent. An even-tempered man who loved crude and practical jokes, Fitzsimmons shed his easy-going personality once he stepped inside the ring. Probably his personality was tempered by his pet tiger cub which grew into jungle maturity. Fitz wrestled and tumbled with the cub, often receiving badly scarred arms. He won the New Zealand amateur tournaments in 1880 and 1881 by kayoing four opponents in one evening and five the following year. Turning professional in 1883, he came stateside in 1889, challenged Nonpareil Jack Dempsey for the middleweight title in 1891 and never relinquished that crown after kayoing Dempsey in 13. Before meeting Corbett for the inevitable heavyweight bout, Fitz fought an exhibition match with Con Riordan in Syracuse, N.Y, November, 1894. After two rounds Riordan was dead but Fitz was exonerated. His best weight was 165 lbs. but for the Carson City, Nev, title match he weighed no more than 156. Training in private, his method was systematic: 10, 12, 15 miles of roadwork daily. Although Fitz was down in the sixth round, Corbett was unable to deliver the toppling blow. Finally in the fourteenth round, the solar-plexus punch sapped Corbett's strength and he fell to the canvas. On March 17, 1897, Fitz earned his second title. J. N. Taylor of the *Boston Daily Globe* described the bout as "the most amazing match ever seen in America." Another scribe compared it to the "bloody carnivals of Julius Caesar and Titus Flaminius—when Trajan in one triumphal show exhibited 5000 pairs of fighting men. . ." For two years Ruby Robert never defended his title. Lured into the ring on June 9, 1899, with Jim Jeffries, Fitz was kayoed in the eleventh round. Stripped of his title, he continued to fight, a master at counter-punching and ducking opponent's blows. He won the largest weight differential in history when he kayoed 312 lb. Ed Dunkhorst in two rounds on April 30, 1900. The same year the light heavyweight division was formed, and in 1903, at age 41, Fitz claimed his third and final title with a 20-round decision over George Gardner in San Francisco. The solar-plexus punch is now outlawed, but that does not discredit his 34-year boxing career.
Also in: Ring Magazine Boxing Hall of Fame.

FLEISCHER, Nat
Noteworthy Contributor
See entry in Canada's Sports Hall of Fame.
Also in: Ring Magazine Boxing Hall of Fame.

GANS, Joe
Boxer
Born November 25, 1874, in Philadelphia, Pa; real name Joseph Gaines; worked in a fishmarket; died August 10, 1910, of tuberculosis in Baltimore, Md, at age 35.

The greatest lightweight champion of all time, Joe Gans won the title by knocking out Frank Erne in 45 seconds of the first round on May 12, 1901. He held the title until Battling Nelson kayoed him in the seventeenth round on September 4, 1908. This was the second match between the two, the previous bout happening in Goldfield, Nev, September 3, 1906. Gans won the first bout when Nelson fouled in the forty-second round; this is the longest fight ever held under Queensbury Rules. Gans was an ill man from the time of their first bout and died 15 months after the second fight from tuberculosis. Billy Nolan, Nelson's manager, insisted that Gans weigh-in with full gear for the first fight. Drawn and gaunt from the loss of weight to remain within lightweight limits, Gans never fully recovered from the ordeal. In his 19 years of fighting, the Old Master studied boxing assiduously. His erect stance with fists at chin level was perfect for defense. Ho moved sparingly and was a master at feinting and delivering point-blank punches. At 5 ft. 6 in. and 133 lbs. Gans frequently climbed into the ring with orders from his manager to "take it easy."
Also in: Ring Magazine Boxing Hall of Fame.

GENARO, Frankie
Boxer
Born August 26, 1901, in New York City; real name Frank DiGennara; died Dec. 26, 1966, in Staten Island, N.Y.

The size of a jockey, 5 ft. 2½ in. tall and 112 lbs, Genaro once harbored ambitions for a jockey's career. He soon discovered the prize ring as his star profession. Genaro is one of a few boxers to win a gold medal in the Olympics (1920) and successfully compete as a professional. Running up a string of victories he defeated Pancho Villa on August 22, 1922, and again on March 1, 1923, this time for the U.S. flyweight championship. He lost the American edition of the crown two years later to Fidel LaBarba. With the decision by LaBarba to enter college and vacate the title, Genaro beat Frenchie Belanger in 1928 to claim the National Boxing Association's flyweight title. Defending his title five times, he was kayoed by Young Perez in Paris on October 27, 1931, in his last defense. He retired in 1934 after 128 bouts.
Also in: Ring Magazine Boxing Hall of Fame.

GIBBONS, Mike
Boxer
Born July 20, 1887, in St. Paul, Minn; died August 31, 1956, in St. Paul at age 69.

One of the outstanding fighters who never won a title, Mike Gibbons fought the likes of Harry Greb, Al McCoy, Jack Dillon, George Chip and Mike O'Dowd. During his 14-year career "The St. Paul Phantom" was never kayoed. His cleverness in the ring kept him as a topnotcher in the welterweight and middleweight divisions. Fighting in an era of no-decision, of his 127 bouts, 58 were no-decision. After retiring in 1922 he was a successful businessman in his home town.
Also in: Ring Magazine Boxing Hall of Fame.

GIBBONS, Tommy
Boxer
Born March 22, 1891, in St. Paul, Minn; served 24 years as sheriff in Cass County, Minn; died November 19, 1960, in St. Paul, at age 69.

As with his brother Mike, Tommy Gibbons fought in an era of no-decisions. Of his career 106 bouts, 43 were no decision. Ranked as one of the top ten all-time middleweights, Tommy graduated into heavyweight ranks in 1921. Standing 5 ft. 9½ in. tall and 172 lbs, he knocked out 20 of 24 opponents in one year. On July 4, 1923, he fought Jack Dempsey for the heavyweight title in Shelby, Mont. Gibbons took Dempsey the distance, losing by points. The town went bankrupt when seven banks collapsed. In his last fight against Gene Tunney, June 5, 1925, Gibbons was kayoed in the twelfth round. This was the only time in his career he was kayoed.
Also in: St. Paul Bowling Association Hall of Fame and *Ring Magazine* Boxing Hall of Fame.

GREB, Harry
Boxer
Born June 7, 1894, in the Garfield-Lawrenceville region of Pittsburgh, Pa; christened name Edward Henry Greb; took the name Harry from a deceased brother; father Pious Greb, born in Germany; Irish mother; sister Ida Greb Edwards; ran away from home when 16; served in Navy for W.W. I; married, wife Mildred died in 1923; drank sparingly; disliked cards; hot dogs and ice cream were his idea of a good meal; read nothing except articles of the Pittsburgh sportswriters; died October 22, 1926, New York City, from eye operation at age 32; left $75,000 estate.

"A cross between a wildcat and a hornet's nest," according to Grantland Rice, Harry Greb was the only boxer to beat Gene Tunney. After their May 23, 1922, light heavyweight title match, Tunny named Greb the dirtiest fighter he ever fought. That was Greb's style, breaking noses and cutting flesh, spraying punches from every imaginable angle. The best craftsman in the ring, he used every medium known. He wore his trunks high to create the impression he was being fouled. His punches worked two ways, coming and going, forehand and backhand. He bit ears. The Human Windmill fought opponents in packs: nine bouts with Fay Keiser, eight with Whitey Wenzel, five with Soldier Bartfield, five with Tunney, six with Bob Roper, six with Jeff Smith, seven with Chuck Wiggins. Standing 5 ft. 8 in. tall and never weighing more that 158 lbs, Greb fought 16 men who held, had held, or would hold world titles. He defeated every one of them. Blind in one eye after 1921 when the thumb of Kid Norfolk's left glove scraped across his eye causing the retina to detach, Greb was kayoed only twice in his career, once when he was 20 and boxing with a broken arm. An 8 – 5 underdog to Tunney, plus conceding 20 lbs. and 5 in, he is credited with making Tunney the future heavyweight champion. A championship rematch was scheduled in February, 1923, with Tunney winning in 15 rounds. The best shape physically before basking in the limelight in the early 1920s, Greb had beaten the best-known heavyweights: Gunboat Smith, Homer Smith, Bill Brennan, Charlie Weinert, Willie Meehan. The public was unaware that his eyesight was diminishing in his remaining eye when Greb challeged the middleweights. On August 31, 1923, Johnny Wilson was outslugged, butted and heeled by Greb for the middleweight crown. From 1923 to 1926 Greb was champion until Tiger Flowers dethroned him. A rematch was scheduled for August, 1926, but the conclusion was the same. This was Greb's final bout for he died two months later, his eyesight aggravated by an auto wreck. Greb's assets were his fast feet, hands and stamina. Usually stronger in the fifteenth round than the tenth, he reduced his opponents to a pulp by his constant barrage of fists. Although much has been made of his fast night life and escapades with women, Greb was a conscientious roadwork fighter. He fought with distinction in his 300 bouts and pound for pound is considered one of the greatest boxers of all time.
Also in: Pennsylvania Boxing Hall of Fame and *Ring Magazine* Boxing Hall of Fame.

HERMAN, Pete
Boxer
Born February 12, 1896, in New Orleans, La; real name is Peter Gulotta; blindness prompted retirement at 25; died April 13, 1973 in New Orleans.

A spunky and devilish quick infighter, Pete Herman won the bantamweight world title twice. The little Italian, standing 5 ft. 2 in. tall and weighing 116 lbs, won the title in January, 1917, from Kid Williams. Holding the crown for nearly four years, he lost it the first time to Joe Lynch in December, 1920. Returning from England where he beat rangy Jimmy Wilde, a championship rematch was scheduled in July, 1921, and Pete regained the title but lost his eyesight permanently. Boxing, ducking and hitting entirely by reflex, he won four of his final five bouts, losing the title for the second time in nine months to Johnny Bluff in September, 1921. Returning to New Orleans, Pete opened a restaurant and entertained customers by running his hands over the body of a fighter and telling them if they were championship material or not.
Also in: Ring Magazine Boxing Hall of Fame.

HUDKINS, Ace
Boxer
Born August 30, 1905, in Valparaiso, Nebr; served in Army during W.W. II; following war operated a ranch that supplied horses for Western movies; died April 17, 1973, Los Angeles, Calif.

The Nebraska Wildcat stood 5 ft. 8 in, weighed 160 lbs. and faced all weights. He defeated Lew Tendler twice in 1927 and 1928 but lost the world middleweight bout to Mickey Walker in June, 1928. A rematch was scheduled in Los Angeles in October, 1929, but Ace lost in ten rounds. Five months before retiring he captured the California heavyweight title from Dynamite Jackson in September, 1931.

JEFFRIES, James Jackson "The Boilermaker"
Boxer
Born April 15, 1875, at Carroll, Ohio; father was Bible-shouting itinerant revivalist always on the road; weighed 200 lbs. when 15; a journeyman boilermaker at 17; married in 1904; wife Frieda died in automobile accident; disliked crowds; died March 3, 1953, at Burbank, Calif, at age 77.

His legs measured 25 in. at the thigh and 10 in. at the

ankle. He ran the 100 in 11 sec. and high jumped 5 ft. 10 in. He weighed 220 lbs. and stood 6 ft. 2½ in. Jim Jeffries was kayoed only once in his career when lured out of retirement as the "Great White Hope" to face Jack Johnson for the heavyweight title. Later Jeffries claimed age and not Johnson had defeated him. Although rumors criculated that Jeffries was drugged for the match, he was forced to train off 65 lbs. in three months and suffered from dysentery, spending the final prefight hours in bed. A large, strapping youth, he worked in the mines at Temecula before returning to Los Angeles. Van Court, the boxing instructor at the Los Angeles Athletic Club and for Jim Corbett, noticed Jeffries' agile moves on the handball court, and signed him as sparring partner for Corbett. Only once did they spar, resulting in full-fledged fisticuffs, and Jeffries was the talk of the boxing circles. Fighting only one preliminary bout, he was a 3–1 underdog to Fitzsimmons when they fought at Coney Island, June 9, 1899. The "Jeffries crouch"—left arm extended in a swinging boom movement, body protected—kayoed Fitz in the eleventh. Jeffries was the new heavyweight champion. He defeated Fitz in 1902, and twice kayoed Corbett, the former heavyweight titlist. After defeating Corbett the second time in 1903, he went into semiretirement, officially not losing the title until 1905. Bald, aging, portly, Jeffries was no match for the young Johnson in July 1910. He received $177,000 for his effort.
Also in: Ring Magazine Boxing Hall of Fame.

JOHNSON, John Arthur "Jack"
Boxer

Born March 31, 1878, in Galveston, Tex; one of nine children; father janitor and former Tennessee slave; married four times; janitor; cotton picker; stable boy; fluent linguist in French, German, Spanish; studious and widely read; drank beer and vintage wines through a straw; died in a car accident, June 10, 1946, near Raleigh, N.C, at age 68.

The first black heavyweight champion, Jack Johnson defeated Tommy Burns so badly that police stopped the fight in round 14. The son of a slave who became the "Black Avenger," Johnson was ahead of his time. A fun-loving and urbane man, Johnson was everything a white society in the late nineteenth century would not accept. He openly courted and married interracially. He drove the flashiest cars, owned a Chicago saloon called the Cabaret de Champion, played in *Aida* in grand opera and plated seven of his top teeth in 14-karat gold. He owned trotting horses, suits of silk and velvet, and played bass viol with his personal jazz band, "Johnson's Troubadors." Johnson began fighting as a Galveston dock worker. When he was 17 he won the tournament in Illinois by kayoing four men in one evening. His first major fight came in 1902 when he beat George Gardner in San Francisco; Gardner won the light heavyweight title in 1903. By 1905 Johnson was the contender to Tommy Burns' heavyweight crown but he was also a victim of social segregation in boxing. Chasing Burns to Australia, and agreeing to have his manager as referee, the title fight was scheduled in December, 1908. In this less than a classic match, Johnson's size, 6 ft. ¼ in. and 200 lbs, was too much for Burns. The contenders to Johnson's crown fell by the wayside: Joe Jeanette, Walter Johnson, Sam Langford, Jim Flynn, Jim Jeffries. Although Jeffries was a 10–7 favorite, he was at best a rustic imitation of his bygone greatness and clearly no match for Little Artha. Some historians write that race riots were a direct result of Jeffries losing the fight. One definite result was increased publicity for Johnson and an entrance into vaudeville. He seldom defended his title after 1910. His third mother-in-law had him arrested on abduction and violation of the Mann Act. Convicted by a federal grand jury in Chicago in 1912 to one year and one day in prison, Johnson fled the country. As a fugitive for seven years, he wrote revues for the London stage, fought bulls in Spain, wrestled throughout Europe and fought several matches in Mexico. Because of his fugitive status, Little Artha fought Jess Willard in Havana, Cuba, in April, 1915. Guaranteed $300,000 plus European and South American motion picture rights, Johnson implied the U.S. government would make a deal and not send him to prison if he threw the bout. So writes Johnson in his autobiography. The veracity of his argument has never been proven, but the fight was sluggish and lethargic for 25 rounds. In round 26 Willard placed an uppercut to the jaw and Johnson tottered then swayed, falling to the canvas as a tree is felled by a lumberjack. Thus the "white hope era" ended in boxing. He surrendered to federal authorities in California and served his sentence at Leavenworth Prison, Kansas. His last official fight was May, 1928, when Billy Hartwell kayoed him in six. The first black superstar, Johnson earned over $1,000,000 but squandered all of it on garish nightclubs and cafes in Chicago, Paris, Barcelona, Juarez and Los Angeles. In his final penniless and downtrodden years, he appeared as a sideshow attraction with his trained fleas at Hubert's in Manhattan. He also traveled the revival circuit urging moral behavior and clean living by Americans, preached Confucianism, operated a cabaret in Hollywood and sold rubbing liniment.
Also in: Ring Magazine Boxing Hall of Fame.

KAPLAN, Louis "Kid"
Boxer

Born 1902 in Russia; settled in Meriden, Conn. in 1907; retired because of eye problems.

Knocked out only three times during his career, Kid Kaplan buzzed his way to the featherweight title and probably the lightweight title, too, except the champions of the division refused to fight him, with his twisting left hook. He started as an amateur at the age of 13, trained at the Staten Island featherweight bag of Willie Curry and began fighting professionally under the name of Benny Miller. When Johnny Dundee vacated the featherweight title because he couldn't make the weight, Kid won an elimination tournament for the title. Winning the title in January, 1925, Kid defended the crown three times before outgrowing the division. His first defense, against Babe Herman in Waterbury, Conn, attracted 20,000 fans and grossed $59,180, both all-time Connecticut records which still stand. Campaigning against the lightweights, Tony Canzoneri, Al Singer and Al Mandell refused to fight Kid, prompting some writers to describe the Kid as the "uncrowned lightweight champ." Decimated in his last bout by Cocoa Kid in February, 1933, Kid hung it up after an eye specialist told him he had vision in only one eye.

KETCHEL, Stanley "The Michigan Assassin"
Boxer

Born September 14, 1886, in Grand Rapids, Mich; christened name Stanislaus Kiecal; father was native of Russia; mother was Polish and only 14 when he was born; worshipped the James brothers as a youth; shot and killed by Walter Dipley in Conway, Mo, on October 15, 1910, at age 24.

Ranked as the Number One middleweight of all time, Stanley Ketchel could fight at full speed for 20 or 30 rounds and hit equally hard with both hands. He ran away from Grand Rapids by freight when he was 14. At 16 he strode into Butte, Mont, looking for work or handouts. Butte complemented his personality with its saloons, theaters, honkytonks and fight clubs. First working as a bellhop at the Copper Queen Hotel, he later challenged all comers for $20 a week, for the operator of the Casino Theater. He claims to have had 250 fights which do not show in the record book. "An example of tumultuous ferocity," according to Philadelphia Jack O'Brien who was knocked out twice by Ketchel, Stanley believed in all-out attack. He knocked 35 of his first 40 opponents unconscious. Between 1903 and his death in 1910 he fought 61 times with knockout strings of 11 and 21. Best remembered for his fights with Billy Papke and Jack Johnson, Ketchel seemed never to draw enough of his opponents' blood, pounding them into submission. He won the vacant middleweight title from Mike "Twin" Sullivan when only 21, in February, 1908. His next three fights against Billy Papke are noted for the sneak smash by Papke. Meeting in Milwaukee, July, 1908, Papke delivered a ferocious right-hand smash to the chin instead of extending his hand for the traditional first-round handshake. Ketchel barely survived the bout but did capitulate the title in September, 1908, when Papke repeated the sneak smash. Maneuvering for a third match, Ketchel walloped Papke into an 11-round knockout and regained the middleweight crown. The other most talked about bout is the Jack Johnson bout on October 16, 1909. The fight grossed $40,000 but Ketchel was clearly no match for the oversized, golden grin Johnson. Although kayoed in the twelfth round after felling Johnson in the eleventh, Ketchel refused to accept total defeat. "I'm in better condition than Johnson right now. Go over and look at him; he's dazed still. But for that one blow I'd have beaten him." Ketchel was a man of legend and myth. His blond hair and blue eyes were accentuated by his clear-cut features. Supposedly he carried a Colt .44 at his side and in his lap when he ate. He did die by the gun while vacationing at Col. R.P. Dickerson's ranch in Missouri. He flirted with the cook; farmhand Walter Dipley resented Stanley's advances, and shot him in the back with a .38 revolver. Dipley and the cook were both sent to jail. Ketchel's grave is in the Polish Cemetery in Grand Rapids.

Also in: Grand Rapids Sports Hall of Fame, *Ring Magazine* Boxing Hall of Fame and Michigan Sports Hall of Fame.

KILBANE, John Patrick
Boxer

Born April 18, 1889, in Cleveland, Ohio; clerked in railroad office; state senator for 16 years; clerk of the courts in Cleveland; died May 31, 1957, in Cleveland at age 68.

Johnny Kilbane held the featherweight title for 11 years, longer than anyone else. A boxer who exerted only the required effort to win a match, he was superb the night of February 22, 1912, when he outpointed Abe Attell in 20 rounds for the title. The most reluctant defender, he lost the crown to Eugene Criqui of France in a six-round kayo in June, 1923. Kilbane could box, punch, slug, brawl and stall when he needed. Of his 140 career bouts, 81 were no-decisions.

Also in: Ring Magazine Boxing Hall of Fame.

KLAUS, Frank
Boxer

Born December 30, 1887, in Pittsburgh, Pa; parents were German; millworker; died February 8, 1948, in Pittsburgh at age 60.

His hands as large and strong as blocks of steel, Frank Klaus began prizefighting in 1904. On his way to a title match with Billy Papke in the middleweight division, he defeated Jack Dillon, Georges Carpentier, Marcel Moreau and M. Boine. On March 5, 1913, he won the world title in the fifteenth round on a foul by Papke. Seven months later George Chip knocked him out in the fifteenth round and repeated the feat in December, 1913. These were the only two times in Frank's career he was kayoed. Jimmy Gardner and Hugo Kelly were the only boxers to ever beat him on points. His manager was George Engel, who also managed Harry Greb. Engel often scrapped with Klaus to keep him in line, one time demolishing $750 in hotel furnishings in France when he fought Georges Carpentier.

Also in: Pennsylvania Boxing Hall of Fame and *Ring Magazine* Boxing Hall of Fame.

LaBARBA, Fidel
Boxer

Born September 29, 1905, in New York City; moved to California at a very young age; graduated from Stanford Univ. 1933, majored in journalism.

Fidel LaBarba had an outstanding amateur and even better professional career. He won the gold medal in the 1924 Olympics as a flyweight. LaBarba turned professional and won the flyweight title of the world from Elky Clark on January 21, 1927. He retired seven months later to enter Stanford but returned to the ring in 1928. He was much heavier and competed as bantam and then featherweight, losing a featherweight title bout to Bat Battalino in May, 1931. The following year he was matched with the new featherweight titlist, Kid Chocolate, but lost again. He stood 5 ft. 3 in. tall and weighed 108 lbs, but he developed a very good left hook with his 66 in. reach.

Also in: Ring Magazine Boxing Hall of Fame.

LANGFORD, Sam
Boxer

See entry in Canada's Sports Hall of Fame.

Also in: Ring Magazine Boxing Hall of Fame.

LAVIGNE, George "Kid"
Boxer

Born December 6, 1869, in Bay City, Mich; parents were French; worked in a cooperage; retired from boxing and worked in Ford factory; died March 9, 1928, at age 58 in Detroit, Mich.

Kid Lavigne began his career with six kayos and proceeded to remain undefeated for four years, 1885 to 1889. In June, 1896, he traveled to London to battle for the lightweight title with Dick Burge. The Earl of Lonsdale, president of the National Sporting Club, bet the Kid $100 he wouldn't survive ten rounds. With the prevailing odds 6–10, Lavigne wagered all his money, plus his manager's. Burge threw in the defense after 17 rounds and Lavigne was paid handsomely in pounds. He held the title until 1889 when he suffered his first loss to Mysterious Billy Smith in a nontitle bout. His next fight four months later with Frank Erne was a 20-round decision in Erne's favor plus the lightweight title. Lavigne fought Joe Walcott twice, once in a 15-round handicap draw in 1895. The second time was a savage and gory fight with Lavigne the winner in 12 rounds in 1897. Two years before Lavigne sailed for London he battled Andy Bowen into unconsciousness. Bowen died when his head struck the floor but Lavigne was acquitted of foul play.
Also in: Michigan Sports Hall of Fame and *Ring Magazine* Boxing Hall of Fame.

LEONARD, Benny
Boxer

Born April 7, 1896, in New York City; real name Benjamin Leiner; appeared in Broadway show "Yip-Yip-Yak-Yank," 1918; boxing instructor during W.W. I; Lt. in Merchant Marine during W.W. II; Edward J. Neil Trophy as outstanding boxer of the year 1944; died April 18, 1947, in New York City at age 51.

The world lightweight champion from 1917 to 1924, Benny Leonard retired as undefeated champion. He is in the same class as Joe Gans and must be considered an equal in ability. Benny was renowned for his ability to pull victory out of the fire when the odds seemed against him. Heywood Hale Broun described him as "the white hope of the orthodox. His left-hand jab could stand without revision in any textbook. The manner in which he feints, ducks, sidesteps and hooks is unimpeachable. He stands up straight like a gentleman and champion and is always ready to hit with either hand." After six years as a professional, the Ghetto Wizard won the lightweight title by beating Freddie Welsh with a ninth-round technical knockout. He floored all contenders except Lew Tendler whom he fought eight times in no-decisions. The first bout, at Boyle's Thirty Acres in July, 1927, grossed $327,565. A year later they fought at the Polo Grounds and the gross receipts totalled $452,648. He moved into the welterweight division temporarily in 1922 and would have claimed the title except he fouled Jack Britton in the thirteenth round. Following his seven-year retirement, he returned in 1932 and challenged Jimmy McLarnin for the welterweight crown. The fight was halted after six rounds despite protests from Benny. A scientific boxer, he lost only 5 of 209 fights. He died while refereeing a fight in 1947.
Also in: Ring Magazine Boxing Hall of Fame.

LEVINSKY, Battling (Barney Lebrowitz)
Boxer

Born June 10, 1891, in Philadelphia, Pa; no relation to Kingfish Levinsky, the Chicago heavyweight buffoon of later years; died Feb. 12, 1949 in Philadelphia.

Lebrowitz began fighting in 1906 as Barney Williams and later changed his name to Battling Levinsky. During his career he fought over 400 bouts, 52 times in 1915 and 6 times in one week. On New Years's Day 1915 he fought three main events in three different places. In the morning he tangled with Bartley Marden in Brooklyn, Soldier Kearns in New York City in the afternoon and Gunboat Smith that evening in Waterbury, Conn.—thirty-two rounds of no-decision combat. He won the light heavyweight title from Jack Dillon in October, 1916, avenging an earlier title loss to him. They fought nine times while Levinsky fought Harry Greb to six no-decision tilts. For four years Levinsky ruled the light heavies until Georges Carpentier kayoed him in four rounds. (Earlier in the year 1920, Levinsky lost on a foul to Boy McCormick of England but McCormick never claimed the title.) Future heavyweight champion Gene Tunney stripped Levinsky of the American light heavy crown on January 13, 1922. Spending nearly half of his life in the prize ring, Battling Levinsky was a boxer who truly loved to fight.
Also in: Pennsylvania Boxing Hall of Fame and *Ring Magazine* Boxing Hall of Fame.

LEWIS, Ted "Kid"
Boxer

Born on October 24, 1894, in St. George's-in-the-East, London, England, as Gershon Mendeloff; died on October 14, 1970, in London, at age 75.

Kid Lewis was the first Englishman to successfully adapt to the American two-fisted boxing style. A shrewd, swift and brutal boxer-puncher, he engaged Jack Britton in a six-year series of 20-round bouts. The grudge matches, 1915 to 1921, were to determine the world welterweight titlist. Often the match merely determined which manager telegraphed news of the victory to the newspapers. Of the 20 bouts fought, 12 were no-decisions, 1 draw, and 4 victories for Lewis. The June 25, 1917, bout established Lewis as the world champion but he lost the title to Britton 20 months later in a ninth-round kayo. Each fight seemed to fuel their dislike for each other with the only possible resolution being the boundaries of the ring and another bloodletting bout. Before voyaging across the ocean, Lewis had won the British and European featherweight titles in 1913 and 1914. The 1913 prizefight saw Lewis become the first boxer to use a mouthpiece. With the finale of the longest ring rivalry in history, Lewis returned to Europe and captured the British and European middleweight titles in 1923. Within a decade of boxing, Lewis had won three division titles; in his 20-year career he boxed in six divisions. Coming from the tough Petticoat Lane section of London, fighting was not only a sport but also a necessity for survival. At the age of 14, Kid won his first professional bout and earned himself a cup of tea and a sixpence. He won his next bout and received a silver cup only to have it melt on the mantelpiece overnight; thereafter, the purses were larger and more impressive. As the pride of Britain in the feather, welter and middleweight divisions, he challenged the French heavyweight and W.W. I hero Georges Carpentier. In a fight with definite overtones of national hubris, Kid was outweighed by 35 lbs. The fight ended suddenly with Carpentier belting Lewis in the face early in the first round. Lewis had turned to complain of a beltline smash to the official and the Frenchman rendered the Kid senseless and confused. From 1925 through 1929, Kid fought creditably, recording seven consecutive wins by kayo in 1927. He settled in Vienna,

Austria, temporarily as a boxing instructor. Eventually he returned to Britain and worked as a haberdashery salesman in Picadilly. Standing 5 ft. 5 in. and weighing 147 lbs, this pugilist engaged the best on all levels. In his 253 bouts he was kayoed only four times, winning 155 fights.
Also in: Ring Magazine Boxing Hall of Fame.

LOUGHRAN, Tommy
Boxer
Born November 29, 1902, in Philadelphia, Pa; enlisted in Marines in 1942; retired as sugar broker in New York City; fighter of the Year 1929 and 1931.

A professional fighter for 19 years, Tommy Loughran fought 227 bouts but kayoed only 18 opponents, 11 of them in the first two years. "I fought most of my career with a broken hand. Nobody knew anything about it. I could take a guy out with my left hand, but I always held back because I knew if I hurt the left mitt I was through. So I stopped going for kayoes and concentrated on the smart stuff." With no knockout punch to rely on, Loughran developed a finesse style by shadow-boxing in front of a full-length mirror with the phonograph playing. Before he was 20 he fought four world champions; during his career he tangled with 14 men who held world titles at one time or another. He thrashed Mike McTigue in October, 1927, for the vacated light heavyweight title. Loughran vacated the title in 1929 when he outgrew the division and campaigned in the heavyweight division. On September 26, 1929, he received his first kayo from Jack Sharkey. This was his best fight financially as he collected $60,000. Working his way through the ranks again, he finally met Primo Carnera for the heavyweight crown on March 1, 1934. The greatest weight difference ever in a championship bout, 86 lbs, Carnera's advantage was too large to overcome. Loughran lost the 15-round decision. Loughran greased his hair with vile smelling hair lotion to counter Carnera's size in the clinches. "When Carnera clinched, I'd tuck my head up under his nose and he'd nearly faint."
Also in: Pennsylvania Boxing Hall of Fame and *Ring Magazine* Boxing Hall of Fame.

LOUIS, Joe (Barrow)
Boxer
Born May 13, 1914, in Lafayette, Ala; christened name Joseph Louis Barrow; large family; father died when he was two; mother remarried and moved to Detroit, Mich; worked on ice wagon after school; cabinetmaker; served in Army during W.W. II; retired into business ventures; movie of his life, "The Joe Louis Story," with Coley Wallace, the former heavyweight turned actor; Fighter of the Year 1936, 1938, 1939 and 1941; Edward J. Neil Trophy 1941; James J. Walter Memorial Award 1967.

With blinding speed in his fists and a mean left jab, Joe Louis held the heavyweight title longer than anyone else. Beginning June 22, 1937, with his kayoing of Jim Braddock until his retirement March 1, 1949, Louis was champion 11 years, 8 months and defended the crown 25 times. The Brown Bomber fought every leading contender and gave them all a chance at his title. Along the way he flattened six other heavyweight champions: Baer, Carnera, Sharkey, Braddock, Schmeling and Walcott. Boxers, maulers, sluggers, he challenged them all. His most gratifying victory was the first-round knockout of Max Schmeling in June, 1938. For 124 seconds' work, Louis earned $349,228. His ring purses totalled $4,626,781 but unwise business ventures, poor investments, unreliable friends and foolishness forced him back into the ring in 1950 to pay $250,000 in back taxes. Ezzard Charles outpointed him in 15 rounds and Rocky Graziano demolished Louis in October, 1951. At 6 ft. 1½ in. and 200 lbs. Louis is rated as one of the best all-time heavyweights as well as one of the most popular. United Press International said "Joe Louis was probably the most widely known American black man who ever lived."
Also in: Michigan Sports Hall of Fame and *Ring Magazine* Boxing Hall of Fame.

LYNCH, Joseph
Boxer
Born November 30, 1898, in New York City; served in Army during W.W. I; postmaster in New York City; drowned in Sheepshead Bay, N.Y, September 1, 1965, at age 66.

A slender stand-up boxer, Lynch appeared even taller than his 5 ft. 8 in. frame. He lost only 13 of 134 fights and was never knocked out. As a member of the American Expeditionary Force in England in 1918 he lost a debatable four-round decision to Jimmy Wilde. He remained in London to defeat Tommy Noble in 20 rounds but lost another close one to Wilde in 15. Returning to the United States he won the bantamweight crown from Pete Herman on December 22, 1922. For the next two years the title volleyed among Herman, Johnny Buff and Lynch until March 21, 1924, when Lynch lost the crown a second time, to Abe Goldstein.

McCOY, Charles "Kid"
Boxer
Born October 13, 1873, in Rush County, Ind; christened name Norman Selby; ran away from home when he was 14; married eight times, three times to the same woman; murdered one wife and served seven years in San Quentin; paroled in 1932; served in Army in W.W. II; watchman in one of Ford Motor Co.'s public gardens in Detroit; suicide with an overdose of sleeping pills at Tuller's Hotel in Detroit, April 18, 1940, at age 66.

Deceitful, larcenous and cruel, Kid McCoy cheated just for cheating's sake. Jim Corbett called him "a marvel, a genius of scientific fighting." Philadelphia Jack O'Brien said of him: "Vicious, fast and almost impossible to beat." Fighting on the level he was great but he derived a lifelong pleasure from his vanity and guile. McCoy gained a fearsome reputation, going undefeated from 1891 to 1894 until Billy Steffers kayoed him. He began another string in May of 1894 and stretched it to December, 1898. During this time he defeated Tommy Ryan in March, 1896, for the welterweight title. McCoy had sparred with Ryan earlier, deliberately giving a poor impression and suggesting a weak heart. After round 12, Ryan, frustrated and tired from attempting to kayo Kid with punches to the heart, exposed his chin to a stinging jab and eventually floundered through the remaining three rounds at McCoy's mercy. The Kid possessed jackrabbit speed, frontward, backward and sideways. He ate, wrote and threw lefthanded to develop his ambidexterity. The "corkscrew" punch was invented by studying a kitten's paw always attacking toys from a sharp and twisting angle. The effect of such a punch by McCoy

ripped many opponents apart. One of three claimants to the vacated middleweight title in 1894, McCoy never battled Philadelphia Jack O'Brien or Tommy Ryan for the crown. Instead he opted for the light heavyweight championship, a new division. Paired against Tommy Root in April, 1903, McCoy lost the title bid in 10 rounds. From 1904 to 1916 he was undefeated but never fought in a title match. He retired in Hollywood with bit parts in movies. In 1922 he filed for bankruptcy.
Also in: Ring Magazine Boxing Hall of Fame.

McGOVERN, John Terrence "Terry"
Boxer
Born March 9, 1880, in Johnstown, Pa; parents moved to Brooklyn, N.Y, when six months old; acted on Broadway in 1900 and 1901 in "The Bowery after Dark," "Terry on the Spot" and "The Road to Ruin"; contracted pneumonia while refereeing doughboy bouts at Camp Upton during W.W. I and died February 16, 1918, at age 37.

The suddenness of his attack, plus a vile and ill-mannered temper, earned McGovern the nickname Terrible Terry. In 1899 and 1900 he walloped three world champions in three different divisions. In September, 1899, Pedler Palmer lasted less than one round in the bantamweight title match. McGovern won his first fight as featherweight, stripping George Dixon of the crown in January, 1900; Frank Erne, the lightweight champ, was beaten in July 1900. The title was not transferable because Erne weighed only 128 lbs. After losing the featherweight to unknown but confident Young Corbett in November, 1901, Terrible Terry requested a rematch and was mauled again in 1903. McGovern learned to fight while playing for a lumberyard baseball team. A squabble ensued during one game and McGovern squared off against the rival team captain. McGovern's manager was so impressed that he directed Terry to the ring. With a unique, aggressive and tireless fighting style, McGovern possessed thick forearms and heavy fists. He never tried to evade punches but leaped at his opponents, feinting once or twice, and simply flailed away.
Also in: Ring Magazine Boxing Hall of Fame.

McLARNIN, Jimmy "Babyface"
Boxer
See entry in Canada's Sports Hall of Fame.
Also in: Canadian Boxing Hall of Fame and *Ring Magazine* Boxing Hall of Fame.

MARCIANO, Rocky
Boxer
Born September 1, 1923, in Brockton, Mass; christened name Rocco Francis Marchegiano; father Pierino worked in shoe factory; attended Brockton High School; wanted to be football linebacker or baseball catcher; tryout with Chicago Cubs baseball team in Fayetteville, N.C; served during W.W. II overseas with 150th Combat Engineers; family man; Hickok Award for Professional Athlete of the Year; Fighter of the Year 1952, 1954 and 1955; Edward J. Neil Trophy 1952; died August 31, 1969 in plane crash at Newton, Iowa, at age 45.

A champion by any standard, Rocky Marciano never lost a fight in his career. Unassuming, modest and self-effacing, Rocky was an irresistible force inside the ring. Slow afoot, he learned to absorb punches, roll and catch jabs on the elbows. Often well behind by points, his gutsy performance wore down many opponents, leaving them defenseless and listless against his right-hand punch. Only five of his opponents lasted the distance. What seems almost tradition in boxing, the ring announcer in Rhode Island Auditorium stumbled over his real name Marchegiano. Anthony Petronella, last president of the National Boxing Association, told the announcer to say Marciano: "No one will know the difference." He began boxing at a late age, 23, moving in the ring at a sloth's pace. Yet manager Al Weill developed him into championship material. "Rocky has something you don't see unless you're around him all the time. Nature gave him everything he needs as a champion. He has unusual strength and stamina, a terrific punch and plenty of guts. No one ever trained harder or took better care of himself." He ended the comeback of aging and pudgy Joe Louis thus making Marciano the largest heavyweight gate attraction in boxing. Jersey Joe Walcott fell before his incessant attack and surrendered the heavyweight crown in a 13-round knockout, September 23, 1952. Walcott demanded a rematch but the results were even more embarrassing for Jersey Joe; a first-round knockout. Rocky's financial gross through his first 38 bouts was $750,000; after taxes, $300,000. His manager Al Weill received half, instead of the usual one-third cut, but he also paid all expenses from his share. In the second bout with Walcott in 1953, Rocky's share amounted to $83,962 less than Walcott's because of a return bout clause guaranteeing the challenger 30 percent of the gate. On September 21, 1955, he finished Archie Moore in the ninth round, the last of six defenses of his title. Despite a $1,000,000 lure by promoter Jim Norris to stage a comeback against Floyd Patterson seven months after his retirement, Rocky refused. Even $1,250,000 by a group of Kentucky enthusiasts did not sway his decision. Marciano had a small reach, 68 in, by heavyweight standards, but he feared no one. Standing 5 ft. 11 in, and weighting 185 lbs, Rocky once remarked: "I don't think anybody in the world can lick me. I just don't think it'll ever happen." No prophecy was ever more true. After he died in the plane crash, Arthur Daley of the *New York Times* wrote: "The Rock was a man of gentleness, kindness, compassion and affability. He brought dignity to the championship he held with such modest graciousness."
Also in: Ring Magazine Boxing Hall of Fame.

MOORE, Archie "Ol' Man River"
Boxer
Born December 13, 1916 (mother claimed 1913), in Benoit, Miss; christened name Archibald Lee Wright; parents divorced; raised by aunt in St. Louis; worked in Civilian Conservation Corps (CCC); working with youths in San Diego, Calif; Edward J. Neil Trophy 1958.

Archie Moore was a contender for the world championship for 16 years. Unfortunately all champions avoided him until he was almost doddering and going downhill. He traveled everywhere and fought anyone under any conditions. In December, 1952, Joey Maxim agreed to fight Moore with the light heavyweight title at stake. Pummelled into oblivion, Maxim surrendered the title but received his $100,000 guarantee. (Moore's cut was $800.) For the next ten years Archie was light heavy king until the National Boxing Association and European Boxing Union withdrew recognition. His uncanny ability

to make weight for the light heavy or heavyweight divisions, especially for someone in his mid-40s, mystified everyone. Within a week he could shed 10 lbs. or add 15 lbs, depending on the fight. He often fought himself into shape through the first ten rounds of a bout and then walloped his opponent in the closing rounds. Yet his skill came only with repetition and lots of hard work. Along with Archie's punch and fortitude was the crouch he used to protect his stomach while his gloves and crossed forearms defended his chin. He fought more than 100 amateur bouts, won 39 of his first 45 professional bouts, 35 by kayo. Moore holds the all-time record for number of kayoes in a career with 136. On September 21, 1955, he was knocked out by Marciano in the ninth round but not before he had floored Rocky in the second. Floyd Patterson kayoed him in the fifth in November, 1956. Nearly 50 years old, he accepted a challenge from Cassius Clay in November, 1962. Before the fight Clay, now Muhammad Ali, predicted "Moore in four" and he was right. The aged, pudgy belly, wheezing Moore fell in round four. Archie retired in 1964 to enter television and movies.
Also in: Ring Magazine Boxing Hall of Fame.

MOORE, Davey
Boxer
Born November 1, 1933, in Lexington, Ky; raised in Springfield, Ohio; wanted to be a football or baseball player but too small; chose boxing over horseback riding; married with four children; all children named after movie stars; died March 25, 1963, in Los Angeles, at age 29.

Possibly a born boxer with aptitude and courage fit for the ring, Davey Moore was the 1952 Amateur Athletic Union (AAU) bantamweight champion. He competed in the 1952 Olympics but was eliminated in the third round. He turned professional briefly in 1952 but retired quickly after little success. Friends persuaded him to put the mitts on again with the results reflecting his true ability. He won 16 of his first 19 bouts in 1953. Between 1957 and 1963 he rolled strings of 18 and 19 consecutive wins. During his reign as bantamweight champion, 1959 to 1963, he fought 14 nontitle bouts and five successful defenses. On March 21, 1963, he entered the ring against Sugar Ramos. Davey suffered a tenth-round knockout, but worse were the injuries he received. He died four days later of brain damage.

NELSON, Oscar Matthew "Batling"
Boxer
Born June 5, 1882, in Copenhagen, Denmark; preferred Batling spelled with one "t"; real name Oscar Matthew Nielson; raised in Hegewisch, Ill; six brothers and one sister; quit school at 13 to work on ice cutter in Lake Michigan for 15¢ a day; worked as a meat-cutter; ran away from home at 14; died February 7, 1954, in Chicago, Ill, at age 71.

Jack London called Nelson "The Abysmal Brute" with an inhuman capacity for punishment, Batling Nelson was a throwback to Neanderthal Man. Never weighing more than 133 lbs, his shy and reticent personality did not predict his savage and emotional rage in the ring. Nelson was not a stylist but a brute uncontrollable slugger. His only contribution to boxing art and science was a short left hook to the liver on the thumb and forefinger side of the glove. As with many fledging boxers, the circuit to the top was pitted with lean years. After leaving home he roamed the Midwest for six years. In 1905 Joe Walcott was unable to fight Martin Canole and Batling was substituted. Nelson captalized on the opportunity and mauled Canole into an 18-round knockout. Nelson received $760, but more importantly, for the next five years he led the little men into purses of $20,000 and $30,000. Of his 150 bouts, the 3 with lightweight champ Joe Gans rank as classics. They first met on September 3, 1906, in Goldfield, Nev. Neither man seemed to know when to quit; only a 42-found foul by Nelson terminated the bout. The second match was Independence Day, 1908. Gans knew his reign was coming to an end with the 17-round kayo punch delivered by Nelson. Almost two years later, Nelson retained the lightweight title, winning the rubbermatch with a 21-round kayo. Having reached the pinnacle of his career, he held the crown until February 22, 1910, when Ad Wolgast recorded a bloody 40-round technical knockout for the title. Over the hill at 27, with no right side left of his face after the bludgeoned bout, Nelson snarled through his blood: "What do you think of that dumb referee? Stopping it when I would have had him in another round!" Scrawny, with sunken eyes and elephantine hands, the Durable Dane had a creditable record from 1910 to 1917 but never another title bout. He fought until 1923, always a box office draw, never attaining the success once achieved. In addition to winning $250,000 in 20 years of boxing, his 12-second kayo of Billy Rossler was a record for 26 years. His flooring Christy Williams 42 times in 17 rounds still stands as a record.
Also in: Ring Magazine Boxing Hall of Fame.

O'BRIEN, Jack
Boxer
Born January 17, 1878, in Philadelphia, Pa; retired and opened a physical culture emporium; died November 12, 1942, in New York City, at age 64 of pneumonia.

The first Yankee to beat an English heavyweight, he kayoed George Chip in May, 1901. Philadelphia Jack held the light heavyweight title for seven years without defending it. Standing 5 ft. 10½ in. tall and weighing 158 lbs, O'Brien was closer to middleweight limits than heavyweight, yet he came closer than any other lightweight to winning the heavy title. After kayoing Bob Fitzsimmons for the light heavy title in December, 1905, he battled Tommy Burns to a 20-round draw 11 months later. In May, 1907, Burns won a 20-round decision. Nick-named Philadelphia Jack because he always fought in Philadelphia, he admired the style and grace of Corbett. Patterning himself after the jab, run, parry of Corbett he also accepted an Irish surname, despite his father's protestations. He was a friend of Major Anthony I. Drexel Biddle who hosted "boxing teas" and later served as Philadelphia Jack's greatest fan and press agent. O'Brien was at his best when he fought a six-round no-decision with Jack Johnson. Unfortunately it was sandwiched in between bouts with Stanley Ketchel who was only one of three fighters to kayo O'Brien.
Also in: Ring Magazine Boxing Hall of Fame.

ORTIZ, Manuel
Boxer
Born July 2, 1916, in El Centro, Calif; served in Army in

1945; died from a liver ailment in San Diego Naval Hospital, May 31, 1970, at age 53.

Manuel Ortiz was a two-time world bantamweight champion. In August, 1942, he beat Lou Salica by kayo for the crown. Manuel is the only fighter ever to kayo Salica. He lost the crown in January, 1947, to Harold Dade but out pointed Dade in a rematch in March of the same year. In between winning the title, a tour with the Army and losing it the second time to Vic Toweel in May, 1950, there were 20 title defenses. Only George Dixon and Joe Louis defended their crowns more. Characterized by phenomenal speed and endurance, Manuel was never kayoed in 117 bouts. Before turning professional in 1938, he won the California Amateur Athletic Union crown in 1937. He also knocked down one Bobby Hager 17 times before knocking him out in the fourth round and followed one week later by dumping Hager 20 times.

PAPKE, Billy

Boxer

Born September 17, 1886, in Spring Valley, Ill; christened name William Henry; killed wife and himself November 26, 1936, at Newport, Calif, at age 50.

"Billy was innately cruel," according to Dan Morgan. He could accept a ton of battering and counterpunch with equal velocity. Between 1905 and 1919 he fought 64 times and recorded 29 knockouts. Best remembered for his bouts with Stanley Ketchel, they fought three times in 1908. Papke delivered his famous "sneak" punch—stunning left to the jaw—in the first two fights, dazing Ketchel for the entire match in their second bout. Now the middleweight champion, Papke prepared for the third bout in November. Ketchel was in a rage, having lost his title and damaging his ego. Although the third bout went 20 rounds, Ketchel belted Papke into a near coma several times, letting him go simply to do it again. After Ketchel's death, Papke reclaimed the title, losing it in February, 1911, to Cyclone Johnny Thompson. In October the title was vacated (Thompson could not make weight) so Papke claimed the title a second time. Five months later Frank Mantell won a 20-round decision, but since Mantell was recognized as the champion only in California, Papke held the title a third time. Officially, and irrevocably. Billy fouled Frank Klaus in the 15-round on March 5, 1913, and lost the middleweight title.
Also in: Ring Magazine Boxing Hall of Fame.

PEP, Willie

Boxer

Born September 19, 1922, in Middletown, Conn; real name William Papaleo; discharged from Navy in 1944; beer salesman in New England; Fighter of the Year 1946.

Willie knocked out one of every four men with whom he tangled. Of his 241 professional bouts, he won 65 inside the distance and 164 on points. Certainly his name must be mentioned in any pound-for-pound discussion of all-time greats. In 1938 and 1939 he was Connecticut's flyweight and bantamweight champion. When he defeated Chalky Wright on November 20, 1942, for the featherweight, he became the youngest in 40 years to hold a title. Between 1940 and 1943, Willie recorded 42 consecutive wins before losing a nontitle bout to Sammy Angott. In the fall of 1946 he broke his left leg in a plane crash, suffered internal injuries and ruptured two vertebrae in his back. The indomitable Willie was back in the ring the following summer defending his title against Jock Leslie and earning himself $50,000. October, 1948, was the first of three Sandy Saddler-Willie Pep bouts that causes one to question Willie's character and fortitude. Losing the first bout and the title, Willie rebounded within five months to regain the crown. The finale, September, 1950, was a disgrace to boxing's image. Succumbing to Saddler's tactics and street level fighting, Willie unraveled every image of his spectacular second bout victory. The boxing commission of New York State revoked his license because of Willie's "resigning," or simply giving up when Willie believed he was beaten. In the first bout, an arm injury may have been legitimate, but the third bout tarnished his image as a plucky champion. The second bout will be immortalized as Willie's salute to paralyzing rapid hands, smooth footwork and garrotting opponents on the ropes. He dissipated his small fortune in a Manhattan saloon and was forced to come out of retirement in the late 1950s. He fought 12 times, winning 9 with 3 listed as exhibitions. In 1966 he finally hung up the mitts.
Also in: Ring Magazine Boxing Hall of Fame.

RICKARD, George L.

Noteworthy Contributor

Born January 2, 1870, in Sherman, Tex; orphaned at 10; grew up in Cambridge, Tex; cowboy; town marshall of Henrietta, Tex; saloon owner in Yukon Territory; owned a dog racing track and extensive real estate in Florida; died from peritonic infection resulting from an appendectomy operation in Miami Beach on January 6, 1929, at age 60.

An entrepreneur and promoter *par excellence,* a man with fertile dreams, an eye toward the future and a magnanimous heart for expiating the wrongs in the past, Tex Rickard polished the image of boxing until the reflection attracted the best of society. Former cowboy and town marshall, Tex trekked the Yukon Trail during the Klondike gold rush. With another cowpoke they tugged sleds 300 miles through Chilkoot Pass and found themselves rich as Croesus overnight with the famous Bonanza strike. With $60,000 bankrolling his ideas, the "Man with the Midas Touch" built a gambling casino and saloon. Fate spun the wheel of fortune against him as a group of miners bankrupted him at the faro and roulette tables. Undaunted and indefatigable, he visualized another gold rush of promotions as he cut wood for $15 a cord beside novelist Rex Beach. Within five months Tex headed for Nome, Alaska, in 1899 with $35 in his pocket, set up another saloon and stockpiled $500,000 in four years. Losing all but $60,000 in bogus mining claims he settled in Goldfield, Nev, with his third saloon and gambling hall. A record accentuated by panache and character decorated by deeds, he was the logical choice by the chamber of commerce to place Goldfield on the map. Tex arranged for Joe Gans and Batling Nelson to fight for the lightweight championship with a purse of $30,000 guaranteed. Tex displayed 1500 $20 gold pieces in his saloon to back his purse and the tactic persuaded the bettors to empty their accounts in Goldfield in excess of five million dollars. Tex grossed $69,175. Success bred success as the purses escalated. At Reno, Nev, in 1910 the Jim Jeffries-Jack Johnson heavyweight bout exceeded $100,000. Boxing was heading into the big time with Tex at the wheel. His confidence brimming and his promotional talents showcased in the West, he headed east to tackle what was considered boxing's albatross, Madison Square Garden. Tex choreographed five bouts with receipts surpassing the million dollar mark. Many pugilists left the ring with money in their pockets; Dempsey and Tunney retired millionaires after their second fight in the Garden. Knowing the despicable and self-indulgent promoters from boxing's past, Tex never turned down a request from a financially strapped boxer, or his widow, for aid in later years. A "Master of Ballyhoo," he transferred boxing from a riff-raff pastime into center stage during the golden age of sports.

RITCHIE, Willie

Boxer

Born February 13, 1891, in San Francisco, Calif; christened name Gerhardt A. Steffen.

Willie was the second lightweight champion in history to win his title on a foul. At 16 Willie was fighting four rounds in local gyms, working overtime to develop himself into a full-fledged contender. In November, 1911, Ade Wolgast was stricken with appendicitis on the eve of his fight with Freddie Welsh. Willie was the acceptable replacement. Battling for 20 rounds, the dogged Ritchie became a contender overnight even though he lost the bout. Thanksgiving Day, 1912, Wolgast and his former sparring partner Willie tore into one another for the title. Ritchie was winning on points, and near a kayo, when Ade fouled in the sixteenth round. He defended his title against the roughest competition available: Mexican Joe Rivers, Leach Cross, Harlem Tommy Murphy, Charley White. On July 7, 1914, the Pride of Pontypridd, Freddie Welsh, skillfully dismantled Willie's onslaught to win back the crown. During W.W. I Willie was a boxing instructor at Camp Lewis, Washington. Following the war, Willie absorbed such a shellacking in his first bout that he retired only to be appointed boxing inspector in California. Uncovering the seamy connections and political riff-raff in boxing he ordered a full-scale investigation. In 1937 he was the chief inspector, a job he held until retiring in 1961.

Also in: Ring Magazine Boxing Hall of Fame.

ROBINSON, Ray "Sugar Ray"

Boxer

Born May 3, 1920, in Detroit, Mich; real name Walker Smith, Jr; parents separated when 12; raised in New York City by mother, a laundress; completed three years at DeWitt Clinton High School; hustled errands in grocery store; danced Lindy-hop at Harlem rent parties; shined shoes; Bojangles Robinson was idol; sang with a quartet which imitated the Ink Spots; did not drink or smoke; established Sugar Ray Robinson Youth Foundation in Los Angeles, Calif; Fighter of the Year 1942; Edward J. Neil Trophy 1950.

Sugar Ray was not only the sweetest fighter, he was the best fighter during his time. At his prime, 1948 to 1950, he demonstrated the magical dance steps in the ring punctuated by the paralyzing barrage emanating from his combination punching—a series of jabs from either first in a deliberate methodical sequence. As an amateur in New York he encountered no peers in 89 bouts while winning the 1939 Golden Gloves featherweight title. Turning professional the pace with victory quickened and he belted 20 of the first 25 opponents he met, 9 in the first round. During a career spanning 18 years and 181 professional bouts, he kayoed 109 and achieved the remarkable feat of six titles in six bouts. The first title on his mantle was the welterweight. Mario Savio resigned the crown in 1946 and Sugar Ray beat Tommy Bell to claim it. Moving up the weight ladder into the middle division he sought a rematch with gruff Jake LaMotta who had beaten Sugar in 1943 and halted his winning streak at 40. On February 14, 1951, LaMotta crumpled in the thirteenth round and Sugar was champ. The remainder of the decade resembled a slideshow with the title, alternating victory and defeat and interspersing a brief retirement. Nevertheless, Sugar Ray's struggle to retain the crown displayed the qualities of all great champions: never resigning to defeat. The chronology follows: lost the middleweight title to Randy Turpin July, 1951; won it back from Turpin September, 1951; retired then regained crown from Bobo Olson 1955; lost it to Gene Fullmer January, 1957; regained it from Fullmer May, 1957; lost it to Carmen Basilio September, 1957; regained from Basilio March 25, 1958. Sugar Ray came within two rounds, and 15½ lbs. of becoming a triple crown winner. A sweltering, humid Yankee Stadium was the scene for the Joey Maxim light heavyweight bout on June 25, 1952. The temperature hovered at 104° as a crowd of 47,983 witnessed the referee collapse from heat exhaustion in the eleventh round. Despite a scorecard lead of 10 – 3, Sugar Ray failed to answer the bell in the fourteenth round. The fight grossed more than $500,000 establishing a new light heavyweight record, eclipsing the Paul Berlenbach-Jack Delaney bout 26 years before. The record books show the fight as a knockout for Maxim even though the heat delivered more punch, sapping Sugar Ray's strength. Although Sugar reflected all the positive traits of champion fighters, one fault of many champions flaws his record too: bad investments. From restaurant-bars, to apartments, laundries and beauty shops, all failed to register a credit in his account. However, responding as any boxer of Olympian stature would, he established the Sugar Ray Robinson Youth Foundation in Los Angeles, serving 20,000 youths.

Also in: Ring Magazine Boxing Hall of Fame.

ROOT, Jack

Boxer

Born May 26, 1876 in Austria; real name Janos Ruthaly; Bohemian ancestry; immigrated to Chicago, Ill, as youth; became millionaire from California real estate; died June 9, 1963, in Los Angeles, Calif, at age 87.

Jack Root was the top ranking middleweight when he faced the awesome task of fighting Jim Jeffries for the heavyweight crown. Jeffries tipped the scales at 220 lbs. while Root registered 165. On Independence Day, 1904, just 15 months after winning the new light-heavyweight title from Kid McCoy, Root entered the ring with George Gardner and was kayoed in the twelfth round. The only other boxer to ever kayo Root was Marvin Hunt. Jim Jeffries announced his retirement as heavyweight king before the Hart-Root fight on July 3, 1905. Root lost the crown but Hart was never universally acclaimed champion. In the best tradition of Stanley Ketchel and Batling Nelson, Root was never a quitter and often at his best when the odds seemed insurmountable. With a dy-

namite right-hand punch, he kayoed 24 of his opponents in his 53 victories. His last fight was in Kalamazoo, Mich, in 1906; thereafter he established a theater chain.
Also in: Ring Magazine Boxing Hall of Fame.

ROSENBLOOM, Maxie
Boxer
Born September 6, 1904, in New York City; third grade education; married child psychologist Muriel Faider in 1937; played bit role in "Nothing Sacred," 1937; divorced in 1945; toured globe with Max Baer in nightclub routine earning $5000 a week; gambled away $250,000; died broke in 1956 in Hollywood, Calif.

An open glove boxer who slapped his opponents silly, hence the shibboleth Slapsie Maxie, Rosenbloom was light heavyweight champion from 1930 to 1934. In a whirlwind series of seven bouts with Jimmy Slattery, from whom he won the title, Maxie discounted the rumor they had bet on each other. During his championship days, he defended the crown eight times and totaled 108 bouts. In 16 years Maxie was kayoed only twice in more than 300 bouts. For a four and a half year span, Maxie averaged a fight every two weeks. He squandered his fortune on women and gambling and retired into movies, television and radio.
Also in: Ring Magazine Boxing Hall of Fame.

ROSS, Barney
Boxer
Born December 23, 1909, in New York City; real name Barnet David Rasofsky; moved to Chicago at an early age; enlisted in Marines; wounded at Guadalcanal; received Silver Star; therapy for drug addiction in service; worked for public relations agency in New York City; movie "Monkey on My Back" with Cameron Mitchell was Ross' biography; Fighter of the Year award in 1934 and 1935 and Edward J. Neil Trophy in 1942; died from throat cancer in Chicago on January 17, 1967 at age 57.

Barney Ross won two world championships in one evening — June 23, 1933. He beat Tony Canzoneri in a ten-round decision for the junior welterweight and lightweight titles. Ten months later he won a decision over Jimmy McLarnin for the welterweight wreath. As with the Gans-Nelson and Ketchel-Papke triangular bouts, the Ross-McLarnin series tossed the title back and forth and provided the patrons with buzzsaw boxing. Barney resigned his lightweight title after McLarnin beat him September 17, 1934. The third match in May, 1935, saw McLarnin surrender the title a second time to Ross. Kid Kaplan, Jackie Fields, Sid Terris, Joe Glick, Ruby Goldstein and Al Singer all felt the embarrassment and pain inflicted by McLarnin. Barney Ross could absorb punches like a sponge, possessed keen reflexes and excellent timing. In 78 career bouts not once was he floored and only four times was he defeated during his tenure. The first boxer to hold lightweight and welterweight crowns simultaneously, he lost the latter to Henry Armstrong on May 31, 1938. Barney confided years later that his third bout with Ceferino Garcia in September, 1937, sapped his strength and inclined his abilities downhill. For 15 rounds Ross sparred with Garcia to retain his welterweight wreath. After breaking his left hand, Ross finished the fight with only his right with which he never was as effective. The hand never healed properly.
Also in: Ring Magazine Boxing Hall of Fame.

RYAN, Tommy
Boxer
Born Joseph Youngs, Jr, March 31, 1870, in Redwood, N.Y; English-French parentage; died August 3, 1949, in Van Nuys, Calif.

Tommy Ryan claimed the middleweight title when Bob Fitzsimmons abdicated it to campaign among the heavies. Although Tommy never fought the other two claimants, Kid McCoy and Philadelphia Jack O'Brien, for the title, he was generally recognized as the champion. He began fighting professionally in 1887, winning his first 32 bouts. In 1891 he battled Danny Needham for 76 rounds in a marathon match. His first crown came from Mysterious Billy Smith, whom he fought six times between 1893 and 1896, winning the welterweight in July, 1894. A talented ringmaster, he also instructed Jim Jeffries on the intricacies of boxing science for his title bout with Bob Fitzsimmons. Ryan was deceived by the wily McCoy in March, 1896, to lose his welterweight crown. A former sparring partner, McCoy was beaten mercilessly by Ryan. Vindictive as McCoy was, he sent Ryan a note during the winter of 1896 saying he needed a match to help pay his medical bills because he was in such poor health. Ryan accepted the offer, believing he would also be keeping the winner's purse, and proceeded to train by shaving. McCoy appeared March 2 finely fit and proceeded to whip Ryan in 15 rounds. Ryan retired in 1907 and operated a gymnasium in Syracuse, N.Y.
Also in: Ring Magazine Boxing Hall of Fame.

SADDLER, Joseph "Sandy"
Boxer
Born February 25, 1926, in Boston, Mass; moved to New York City when 3; father was merchant ship cook from British West Indies.

Sandy Saddler was unusually tall at 5 ft. 8 in, by featherweight standards. Large, hulky shoulders and long arms enabled Sandy to tie up, stick, or slug his opponents with constant movement. Of his 144 career victories, 103 were knockouts. He was kayoed only once. The most celebrated series developed between Sandy and Willie Pep when Pep lost his featherweight title in October, 1948. The remaining three fights pictured a weary, aged and struggling Pep attempting to regain his title. In the second bout he succeeded, but Sandy squared away Pep for good in September 1950 and 1951. Those two bouts were miniature massacres highlighted by streetfighting at its worst. After regaining the featherweight crown in 1950, Sandy dominated until January, 1957. Failing vision because of an auto accident forced his early retirement.
Also in: Ring Magazine Boxing Hall of Fame.

SARDINIAS, Eligio "Kid Chocolate"
Boxer
Born January 6, 1910, in Cerro, Cuba; received government pension until the Castro regime.

The only Cuban boxer to hold a world title, Kid Chocolate won the junior lightweight title in 1931 and the featherweight title in 1932. A sensational amateur featherweight, he won 100 consecutive bouts, including 86 knockouts, before turning professional. His first professional loss came in August, 1930, to Jack Kid Berg. Two more losses followed, one to Battling Battalino in a world featherweight title bout, and the other loss to Fidel LaBarba. When he met LaBarba on December 9, 1932,

victory was sweet for the Kid as the New York Boxing Commission declared him the world featherweight titlist. This was the second of his championships, having defeated Benny Bass for the junior lightweight crown on July 15, 1931. From a newsboy to one of Cuba's greatest, Kid Chocolate viewed films of the Gans-Nelson, Jeffries-Johnson and Leonard-Tendler bouts to develop his style and ability. A picture boxer with Gans' left hand, Johnson's clinches for tying up, Leonard's right hand, blocks and feints, Kid watched the films for eight years. The technique won him 145 of 161 fights with 64 knockouts. He retired after 1938 as a boxing instructor in Havana.
Also in: Ring Magazine Boxing Hall of Fame.

SHARKEY, Thomas J.
Boxer
Born November 26, 1873, in Dundalk, Ireland; died April 17, 1953, in San Francisco, Calif, at age 79.

Despite a fine record as heavyweight during the Marquis of Queensbury rules, Sharkey was never champion. In November, 1899, Jeffries won a 25-round decision and Fitzsimmons kayoed him in 1900. Of his 40 career wins, 37 were by kayo. He fought three heavyweight champions. After retiring he joined Jeffries in vaudeville. Later he worked at California race tracks.
Also in: Ring Magazine Boxing Hall of Fame.

SMITH, Amos "Billy"
Boxer
Born May 15, 1871, in Eastport, Maine; retired to Tacoma, Wash, and operated a hotel and turkish bath; moved to Portland, Ore, and managed a saloon; died in Portland on October 15, 1937 at age 66.

In 1892 Billy Smith, a lean and rugged boxer from New England, punched Danny Needham into oblivion and the welterweight division had its first official world champion. Fighting for Captain Cooke, editor of the old Boston newspaper *Police News,* Amos Smith failed to distinguish himself in the early 1890s. Fighting on the West Coast, although Cooke was unaware, Smith rampaged through every opponent and soon his reputation filtered back to the Hub. No one could recall the name Amos Smith so Captain Cooke called him "Mysterious Billy Smith." Smith drew twice in six rounds with Tommy Ryan before losing the welter wreath for keeps on July 26, 1894. Joe Choynski, a friend of Ryan's, was referee. Then followed the first of Billy's six bouts with Joe Walcott. Billy Roche, who was Smith's manager, claims Billy was the only fighter to whip Walcott consistently. "They fought half a dozen times, and, while record books may not agree to the letter, Smith had the better of 15-, 20- and 25-round battles. I recall Walcott showing up for one match with a long pistol in his back pocket, and Smith saying that even if he used that it wouldn't do him any good."

SULLIVAN, John Lawrence
Boxer
Born October 15, 1858, in Roxbury, Mass; mother wanted him to be a priest; played semi-pro baseball for $25 a game; rejected $1300-a-season offer from Cincinnati; participated in stage plays "Honest Hearts and Willing Hands" and "East and West with Parson Davies" in 1890s; biographical movie, "The Great John L." with Greg McClure; teetotaler and temperance lecturer in later years; died February 2, 1918, in Abington, Mass.

John L. Sullivan is recognized as the first modern era heavyweight. During 27 years of boxing, 1878 to 1905, his ring earnings amounted to $1,211,470. In 1880 he placed an advertisement from a "modest and unassuming man" in the daily newspaper which read: "I am prepared to fight any man breathing for any sum from $1000 to $10,000 at catchweights. This challenge is especially directed at Paddy Ryan and will remain open for a month if he should not see fit to accept it. Respectfully yours, John L. Sullivan." Two years later in 1882 Ryan agreed to a $5000 purse prize to match Sullivan in the last heavyweight fight under London Ring rules. The notorious right-hand punch of John L. kayoed Ryan in the eighth. The first barnstorming champion roamed the world knocking out 49 of 50 challengers and never fighting to a losing gate. Part of Sullivan's success was his discovery that the point of the jaw was vulnerable and knowing the nerve center is below the eye on the left side of the nose. The other half of his success was regimen. By 1889 the effects of prizefighting began to wear down John L. Weight was a problem. When he entered the ring for his title match September 7, 1892, with Gentleman Jim Corbett, John was 22 lbs. overweight. With only the pride of a champion and heart of a true boxer, he parried with Corbett for 21 rounds before losing. His early years of inebriation and swashbuckling adventure mellowed as he lectured on temperance and played vaudeville in later life.
Also in: Ring Magazine Boxing Hall of Fame.

TENDLER, Lew
Boxer
Born September 28, 1898, in Philadelphia, Pa; retired in 1928 to enter hotel and restaurant business; died November, 1970, in Atlantic City, N.J.

For seven successive years, 1913 to 1919, Lew Tendler was undefeated. In 1919 Johnny Noye won by Lew's errant blow, recorded as a foul, for his first defeat. By the end of 1919 Lew was heading for two more years of undefeated boxing. From the bantam to the welter division, he challenged the best: Benny Leonard, Pinkey Mitchell, Mickey Walker, Jack Zivic, Joe Dundee, Ace Hudkins.
Also in: Pennsylvania Boxing Hall of Fame and *Ring Magazine* Boxing Hall of Fame.

TAYLOR, Charles B. "Bud"
Boxer
Born July 22, 1903, Terre Haute, Ind; died March 8, 1952, in Los Angeles, Calif.

Bud Taylor accepted challenges from all comers. He fought no-decision bouts with Pancho Villa, Midget Smith, Pal Moore and Frankie Genaro. On June 24, 1927, utilizing his potent right-hand punch, the "Terre Haute Terror" won the National Boxing Association version of the bantamweight crown with a ten-round decision over Tony Canzoneri. He resigned the crown in 1928 because he could not make the weight. His 157 professional bouts rank second to Kid Williams in his class. In 1931 he retired to become a manager.

TUNNEY, James Joseph "Gene"
Boxer
Born May 25, 1898, in New York City; father a steve-

dore; shipping clerk for steamship lines; loved classics and Shakespeare; married Carnegie Steel empire socialite Mary Josephine "Polly" Lauder; three sons; director of banks and industries; Fighter of the Year 1928; James J. Walker Memorial Award 1941.

Gene Tunney was not a natural-born fighter. Through self-discipline and sheer desire he turned himself into only one of two prizefighters to retire on top and undefeated. His physique was not adapted for fighting and his reflexes had to be adjusted for boxing. To strengthen his hands he shoveled coal and hoisted five-gallon water jugs. He squeezed hard rubber balls and exercised each finger 500 times daily by using it as a lever to push his body away from a wall. Outside the ring Tunney was a peaceable, self-effacing man. Inside the ring, he was a demon, slicing his opponents, cutting them with his left jab, and always moving every second at top speed. He fought for 13 years, 1915 to 1928, and was defeated only once, by Harry Greb in 1922. He later beat Greb to regain the light heavyweight title, and had the best of two no-decisions also. Probably the most intelligent of all boxers, Tunney is not remembered for his analytical and stylistic prowess but for the "long count" in his second fight with Dempsey. Tunney had taken the heavyweight crown from Dempsey in September, 1926. The rematch, and another million dollar gate, was staged a year later. Tunney was floored by Dempsey and some observers claim was on the floor for 14 seconds. However, Gene recovered to win on points and deny Dempsey the crown. The only man to master Dempsey and Shakespeare, Tunney retired a millionaire.
Also in: Ring Magazine Boxing Hall of Fame.

VILLA, Pancho
Boxer
Born Francisco Guilledo August 1, 1901, in Iloilo, Philippines; died July 14, 1925, in Oakland, Calif.

Pancho Villa recorded an outstanding amateur record. Before coming to the United States he won the Oriental flyweight and bantamweight titles. Combining the motion of Harry Greb and the stamina of Henry Armstrong, Pancho lost only 5 of his 102 professional bouts. Within a two month period, July to September, 1922, he fought seven times culminating with an eleventh-round knockout of Johnny Buff for the flyweight championship. Frankie Genaro won a 15-round decision and the title from Pancho in March 1923. After Pancho whipped Jimmy Wilde in June he was considered the champion. Afraid of no one despite his size of 5 ft. 1 in. and 110 lbs, he doggedly fought bantams, feathers and lightweights. After losing a nontitle bout to Jimmy McLarnin, Pancho contracted blood poisoning from an infected tooth and died at the age of 23.
Also in: Ring Magazine Boxing Hall of Fame.

WALCOTT, Joe
Boxer
Born March 13, 1873, in Barbados, West Indies; came to United States in 1887; played part of trainer in "The Harder They Fall"; died in auto accident in October, 1935, Dayton, Ohio.

In 1887, Joe Walcott worked his way to the United States as a cabin boy. Landing in Boston he immediately carved a niche for himself in sports by winning the New England amateur wrestling and boxing titles. Seldom weighing more than 145 lbs. and standing only 5 ft. 2 in. the Barbados Demon challenged not only welterweights but middleweights and light heavyweights as well. In his first attempt for the welterweight crown, he fought Billy Smith to a 25-round draw but lost the rematch in December, 1898. In 1901 Walcott recorded a five-round knockout of Rube Ferns for the championship but lost it to Dixie Kid on a disputed twentieth-round foul. Dixie Kid outgrew the welterweight division and Joe reclaimed the title only to lose it permanently to Honey Mellody in 1906. With the stamina of a bull, Walcott fought professionally for more than 20 years, 1890 to 1911. Thirteen times he went 20 or more rounds. He was such a powerful boxer that in 1900 he conceded 40 lbs. to heavy Joe Choynski and knocked him out. Choynski had fought a 20-round draw with Jim Jeffries and knocked out inexperienced Jack Johnson.
Also in: Ring Magazine Boxing Hall of Fame.

WALKER, Edward Patrick "Mickey"
Professional
Born July 13, 1901, in Elizabeth, N.J; father a mason, wanted son to have intellectual career; mother a fight fan; studied architecture at Columbia Univ; rejected by Army because of size; worked in shipyards; married seven times to four women; indulgent drinker; playboy; primitive art painter; opened saloon in New York City and lost $20,000 first year; squandered $4,000,000.

Mickey Walker was 21 the night he won the world welterweight title from Jack Britton in 1922. A year later he teamed with Doc Kearns, Dempsey's ex-manager, and began challenging the heavier weights. In 1926 he won the middleweight crown from Tiger Flowers; he held the title until 1931. He gave up the middleweight for a shot at the heavyweight title against Jack Sharkey. With over 35,000 people in attendance and a gate of $250,000, Walker battled Sharkey to a draw. Walker challenged Max Schmeling a year later only to be pummelled into oblivion. He had gone as far as 170 lbs. of nerve and courage could carry someone. Mickey fought with no holds barred. He thrived on punishment, loved to butt elbows and flail his opponents mercilessly. Regardless of time, place or circumstance, Walker loved to fight for no reason, just brawling for brawling's sake. A magnificent fighter, he drank and squandered money without inhibition. He often boasted of redistributing $4 million from the end of one war to the beginning of another.
Also in: Ring Magazine Boxing Hall of Fame.

WILLIAMS, Kid
Boxer
Born John Gutenko, December 5, 1893, in Copenhagen, Denmark; died October 18, 1963, in Baltimore, Md.

Kid Williams began fighting in 1910 and won the bantamweight crown four short years later with a third-round knockout of Johnny Coulon. For three years he ruled the division until Pete Herman bested him on January 9, 1917. In 175 professional bouts, he kayoed 43 while being knocked out only once himself. He waged an unsuccessful comeback attempt in 1935.
Also in: Ring Magazine Boxing Hall of Fame.

WOLGAST, Adolph "Ad" "Midget"
Boxer
Born Joseph Robert Lascalzo, July 18, 1910, in Philadelphia, Pa; died October 19, 1955, in Philadelphia.

A virtual jitterbug in retreat within the ring, Midget Wolgast exhausted his opponents then piled up points with his stinging punches. Winning 22 of his first 25 professional bouts, Midget went on to capture the New York flyweight championship from Black Bill in March, 1930. Since Frankie Genaro was recognized as flyweight National Boxing Association champion, Midget fought him for the world championship in December, 1930. Nothing was settled as the fight was a draw. Midget's career ended when Small Montana beat him in September, 1935.
Also in: Ring Magazine Boxing Hall of Fame.

College Baseball (Coaches) Hall of Fame

The Citizens Savings College Baseball (Coaches) Hall of Fame was started in 1954. Since that time 37 members have been elected to the Hall, the last selections being made in 1967. Selection is based entirely on an individual's performance in coaching college baseball. The names of the honorees are engraved on the College Baseball (Coaches) Hall of Fame trophy located in the Citizens Savings Hall of Fame Athletic Museum building in Los Angeles.

1954

BAILEY, Arthur Buckner "Buck"
College Coach
Served in Navy from 1943 to 1945.

Buck Bailey coached at Washington State College from 1927 to 1954. He piloted the Northern Division Pacific Coast Conference champions in 1927, 1936, 1947, 1948, 1949, 1950 and tied for the title in 1938. His teams finished second eight times.
Also in: American Association of College Baseball Coaches Hall of Fame.

BARRY, Jack
College Coach
Jack coached at Holy Cross for 34 years from 1921 to 1954. His career record shows 527 wins and 119 losses. His teams were Eastern champions in 1921, 1923–1925, 1928–1930, 1935, 1936 and 1940. He won the National Collegiate Athletic Association championship in 1952 with an overall season record of 21 wins and 3 losses.
Also in: American Association of College Baseball Coaches Hall of Fame.

BARRY, Justin M. "Sam"
College Coach
Sam Barry coached at Knox College, the University of Iowa and the University of Southern California. During his 18 years at USC his teams won 389 games against 159 losses. The Trojans won California Intercollegiate Baseball Association titles in 1930, 1932, 1939, 1942 and 1946–1949. They also won the National Collegiate Athletic Association crown in 1948.
Also in: American Association of College Baseball Coaches Hall of Fame; and College Basketball Hall of Fame, Citizens Savings Hall of Fame Athletic Museum.

CARR, Lewis
College Coach
Lew Carr coached at Syracuse University from 1910 until retirement in 1945. While there he turned out many strong teams. The University's new baseball diamond, dedicated in 1952, was named Lew Carr Field.

COAKLEY, Andrew J.
College Coach
Coakley was baseball coach at Williams College in 1911 and 1912. He moved to Columbia University where he coached from 1914 through 1951. At Columbia his teams won 315 contests and lost 308. During his 37 years at that University his teams won the Eastern Intercollegiate League titles in 1933, 1934 and 1944.
Also in: American Association of College Baseball Coaches Hall of Fame.

COFFEY, John F.
College Coach
John Coffey coached at Fordham University for 32 years. During that time Fordham teams won 430 games with 150 defeats. They won 5 Eastern crowns and 14 Metropolitan New York titles. In 1954 Fordham's baseball field was named Jack Coffey Field.
Also in: American Association of College Baseball Coaches Hall of Fame.

COOMBS, John W.
College Coach
John Coombs is a former coach at Rice, Williams, Princeton and Duke. He coached at Duke for 24 years, from 1929 to 1952. His most successful years were 1937 to 1939.
Also in: American Association of College Baseball Coaches Hall of Fame.

COUGHLIN, William P.
College Coach
Bill Coughlin coached at Lafayette College for 23 years, from 1920 until his death in 1943. His teams won 293 games and lost 132. Coughlin inspired his players and secured maximum effort from them. A portrait now hangs in the College gymnasium.

DISCH, William J.
College Coach
William Disch coached baseball at the University of Texas for 42 years from 1911 to 1942. His teams won 516 games and lost 178, taking 21 Southwestern championships in the process.
Also in: American Association of College Baseball Coaches Hall of Fame.

EVANS, Clinton W.
College Coach
Clint Evans coached at the University of California for 25 seasons, retiring in 1954. During that time the Golden Bears won nine California Intercollegiate Baseball Association crowns and were National Collegiate Athletic

Association champions in 1947. During his career Evans' teams won 220 games with 123 losses.
Also in: American Association of College Baseball Coaches Hall of Fame.

FISHER, Ray L.
College Coach
Fisher coached at the University of Michigan for 34 years—1921 to 1954—winning 568 games and losing 246. His teams won ten Big Ten championships and tied for the title five times. The Wolverines won the National Collegiate Athletic Association championship in 1953.
Also in: American Association of College Baseball Coaches Hall of Fame.

HUFF, George A.
College Coach
George Huff coached baseball at the University of Illinois for 25 years, from 1896 to 1919. His teams won ten Big Ten crowns and one runnerup position. Huff served as Illinois' Director of Athletics from 1901 through 1924 and sent an Illinois squad on a tour of Japan in 1928.
Also in: American Association of College Baseball Coaches Hall of Fame.

KOBS, John H.
College Coach
Kobs was Michigan State's coach for 29 years, from 1925 through 1954, winning 386 games and losing 252. He was president of the American Association of College Baseball Coaches and has been an officer in the Association since 1945.
Also in: American Association of College Baseball Coaches Hall of Fame.

McCARTHY, William V.
College Coach
McCarthy was baseball coach at New York University for 33 years, from 1922 to 1953. His teams won 386 games and lost 194. He guided the Violets to seven Metropolitan crowns, six of them in succession. McCarthy was one of the founders of the Metropolitan New York Conference.
Also in: American Association of College Baseball Coaches Hall of Fame.

McKALE, James F. "Pop"
College Coach
Pop McKale coached the University of Arizona baseball teams for 35 years, from 1911 through 1948. His teams recorded 318 victories and 124 losses. The Arizona Wild Cats gained 14 consecutive Border Conference crowns. McKale served as president of the American Association of Baseball Coaches in 1950.
Also in: American Association of College Baseball Coaches Hall of Fame; and Athletic Directors Hall of Fame, Citizens Savings Hall of Fame Athletic Museum.

NOBLE, Clarke Randolph "Dudy"
College Coach
Dudy Noble was baseball coach and athletic director at Mississippi State College for 29 seasons, from 1919 until 1948. His teams were always among the strongest in the Dixie circuit.
Also in: American Association of College Baseball Coaches Hall of Fame.

STELLER, Warren E.
College Coach
Warren Steller spent 30 years as baseball coach at Bowling Green State University in Ohio, from 1925 through 1954. Prior to that he had coached 3 years at Wesleyan in Connecticut. Steller's top season was 1943 when the team won 18 and lost 2.

SWASEY, Henry C.
College Coach
Henry Swasey was baseball coach at the University of New Hampshire for 33 seasons, from 1922 to 1954. He spent three years previous to that at Adelphia Academy in Brooklyn, N.Y. His 1936 team won 13 and lost 1.
Also in: American Association of College Baseball Coaches Hall of Fame.

VOGEL, Otto H.
College Coach
Vogel was baseball coach at the University of Iowa for 27 years, from 1925 to 1954. The Hawkeyes won the Big Ten championship in 1939. During his career his teams won 357 games and lost 234.
Also in: American Association of College Baseball Coaches Hall of Fame.

WILLIAMS, Paul B. "Billy"
College Coach
Billy coached the Ball State Teachers College baseball teams from 1921 to 1954. He took them to the first Ball State victory of the Indiana Conference championship in 1939.

1959

CLARKE, William J.
College Coach
Bill Clarke coached at Princeton for 34 years. During that time he created a winning percentage of .603 in 822 games.

COLEMAN, Ralph
College Coach
Ralph Coleman was a coach at Oregon State for 32 years.

DEDEAUX, Rauol "Rod"
College Coach
Rod Dedeaux coached at the University of Southern California from 1942 to 1959. His teams won the National Collegiate Athletic Association championship in 1948 and 1958.
Also in: American Association of College Baseball Coaches Hall of Fame.

KLINE, Clarence J.
College Coach
Clarence Kline was the coach at Notre Dame for 26 years, from 1934 to 1959.
Also in: American Association of College Baseball Coaches Hall of Fame.

YARNELL, Waldo "Rusty"
College Coach
Rusty Yarnell coached baseball at Lowell Tech for 32 years, from 1938 to 1959.

Also in: American Association of College Baseball Coaches Hall of Fame.

1966

ASKEW, Presley
College Coach
Presley Askew was baseball coach at Arkansas and New Mexico State for 31 years, from 1936 to 1966.

BISHOP, Max
College Coach
Max Bishop was baseball coach at the U.S. Naval Academy for 25 years, from 1938 to 1962.
Also in: American Association of College Baseball Coaches Hall of Fame.

CHRISTIAN, J. Orlean
College Coach
See entry in Athletic Directors Hall of Fame, Citizens Savings Hall of Fame Athletic Museum.
Also in: American Association of College Baseball Coaches Hall of Fame.

FALK, Bibb
College Coach
Bibb Falk coached for Texas for 24 years, from 1940 to 1942 and again after the war, from 1946 to 1966.
Also in: American Association of College Baseball Coaches Hall of Fame.

HELDMAN, John
College Coach
John Heldman coached baseball at Louisville for 30 years, from 1936 to 1966.

PITT, Malcolm U.
College Coach
Malcolm Pitt coached at Richmond for 32 years, from 1935 to 1966.
Also in: American Association of College Baseball Coaches Hall of Fame; and College Basketball Hall of Fame, Citizens Savings Hall of Fame Athletic Museum.

SIMMONS, John
College Coach
John Simmons coached baseball at Missouri for 28 years, from 1937 to 1943 and again after the war, from 1946 to 1966.
Also in: American Association of College Baseball Coaches Hall of Fame.

SMITH, Charles
College Coach
Charlie Smith coached at San Diego State for 33 years, from 1933 until 1966.

WHITFORD, Lawrence W. "Mon"
College Coach
Larry Whitford coached baseball at State College of Iowa for 37 years, from 1926 through 1965.
Also in: American Association of College Baseball Coaches Hall of Fame.

1967

HARRICK, Stephen
College Coach
Born December 26, 1896, in Fordham, Pa; graduated from W.V. Univ. in 1924.

Steve Harrick began his coaching career at Point Pleasant High School, remaining there for one year. He moved on to West Virginia Tech. where he coached baseball for 14 years and then on to West Virginia University (WVU). At WVU Harrick's teams won 334 games and lost 160 during his 20-year stay. They were eight times conference champions as well.
Also in: American Association of College Baseball Coaches Hall of Fame.

JONES, Ralph Waldo Emerson
College Coach
Born August 6, 1905, in Lake Charles, La; graduated from Southern University in 1923.

Ralph Jones coached at Grambling College for 42 years. His teams brought in 703 wins to 129 losses and were conference champions for 11 years. Jones became president of Grambling College.
Also in: National Association of Intercollegiate Athletics Hall of Fame.

PITTARD, Julian Howard
College Coach
Born April 30, 1899, in Winterville, Ga; graduated from Vanderbilt Univ. in 1920.

Julian Howard Pittard coached at Gainesville, Georgia, High School for 22 years. He moved on to Georgia Tech. where he stayed for 16 years to develop teams that won 169 games to 171 losses. In 1957 the Georgia Tech. ballclub was Southeastern Conference champion.

College Sports Information Directors Hall of Fame

This Hall was originated in 1969. As of 1977 there are 66 members. Upon induction, each member receives a Hall of Fame Award, as well as having his name engraved on the trophy which is kept in the Citizens Savings Hall of Fame Athletic Museum, Los Angeles international sports shrine.

1969

BENTLEY, John
Sports Information Director
John Bentley was the University of Nebraska's first full-time sports information director, serving for 17 years beginning in 1946. Prior to that time he had been a staff sports writer on the *Omaha World Herald* and sports editor of the *Lincoln Journal.*

CAHILL, Joe
Sports Information Director
Joe Cahill served as sports information director at the U.S. Military Academy for 20 years before retiring in 1963. In that time Army won three national champion-

ships, the Lambert Trophy seven times and went undefeated six seasons. Three cadets won the Heisman Trophy and 25 were named to All-American teams.

CALLAHAN, Charles
Sports Information Director
Callahan graduated from the University of Notre Dame in 1938 and returned to Notre Dame as sports information director in 1946, remaining until 1966. He left to become publicity director for the Miami Dolphins.

CARPENTER, Ted
News Bureau Director
Ted Carpenter became Marquette University's first publicity director while still a student and served as director of the news bureau for over 42 years before retiring in 1965. He died May 2, 1966.

COOGAN, James H.
Director of Public Information
James Coogan served as Penn State University's director of public information from 1958 until his death in 1962, being named to the staff in 1942.

COOK, Robert A.
Sports Information Director
Bob Cook served as sports information director at Indiana University from 1938 to 1953. Prior to this position he had been sports editor for the Bloomington *Star-Courier.*

COX, John
Sports Information Director
John Cox was a sports reporter for the Newport News *Daily Press* and *Times Herald* before joining the Army in 1942. He became sports information director at the Naval Academy in 1949, remaining until 1962. He had also served as director of public relations at William & Mary College 1947 – 1949.

CULP, Robert
Sports Information Director
Bob Culp was Western Michigan University's sports information director for a number of years before becoming athletic business manager in 1967. He has been active in sports writers organizations over the years.

DURHAM, Homer M.
Sports Information Director
Homer Durham spend 50 years in the college sports publicity field, retiring in 1962 from his post of sports information director at Western Michigan University after serving 33 years in that post.

ETTER, Lester
Athletic Publicity Manager
Lester Etter served as athletic publicity manager for 24 years at the University of Michigan, retiring in 1968. He had been sports information director at his alma mater, University of Minnesota, for six years before joining the staff at Michigan.

EVANS, Wilbur
Sports Information Director
Wilbur Evans spent 12 years as sports information director and 6 years as assistant athletic director at the University of Texas, Austin, and 14 years as a newspaperman before that. In 1961 he joined the Cotton Bowl Athletic Association as executive vice president and administrative assistant for the Southwest Conference.

FLYNN, Charles E.
Director of Athletic Publicity
Chuck Flynn was director of athletic publicity for the University of Illinois for 13 years before becoming their director of public information.

FRANCIS, Marvin A. "Skeeter"
Sports Information Director
Skeeter Francis served for 15 years as sports information director at Wake Forest University before being named service bureau director for the Atlantic Coast Conference in 1969.

GATES, Hugh William "Billy"
Athletic Publicity Director
For 34 years Billy Gates was the director of athletic publicity at the University of Mississippi. In 1942 he went to be sports editor of the Baton Rouge *Advocate* but returned to "Ole Miss" in 1946. Gates is deceased.

GOODMAN, Ernest Everett
Director of Public Relations
Goodman was staff writer at Howard University 1950 – 1956, director of publicity 1956 – 1958, director of information services 1959 – 1964 and director of public relations 1964 – 1967. He was radio broadcaster for football games at Howard 1946 – 1950 and a TV commentator for their basketball games in 1966 and 1967. He has written for all the area newspapers and served on many news organizations; he also has served with the U.S. Foreign Service.

HALLOCK, Wiles
Sports Information Director
Hallock was sports writer for the *Rocky Mountain News* and sports editor of radio stations in Pennsylvania and Wyoming before becoming sports information director at the University of Wyoming 1949 – 1960. He then became sports information director for the University of California 1960 – 1963, public relations director of the NCAA 1963 – 1967 and director of their New York office 1967 – 1968. In 1968 he was selected as commissioner of the Western Athletic Conference and in July, 1971, became the second executive director of the Pacific-8 Conference.

HARTLEY, Robert M.
Sports Information Director
Bob Hartley became sports information director at his alma mater, Mississippi State University, in 1946, after serving as sports editor of the *Meridian Star.* He has served as officer in various organizations including being president of the College Sports Information Directors of America.

JORDAN, Lester
Sports Information Director
Lester Jordan became sports information director at Southern Methodist University in 1942, business man-

ager of athletics in 1945, assistant athletic director in 1964, and coached the tennis team for 11 years. He is the founder of the All-American Academic football team, recognizing athletes who excel on the field and in the classroom.

KEITH, Harold
Sports Information Director
Harold Keith served for 39 years as sports information director at the University of Oklahoma before retiring in 1969.

LABRUM, Joe
Sports Publicity Director
Joe Labrum worked his way through the University of Pennsylvania as a reporter for the Philadelphia papers and became the university's sports publicity director in 1923, leaving there to become public relations director for the National Football League in 1947. Joe Labrum retired in 1961 and died in 1964.

LENTZ, Arthur
Athletic Publicity Director
Art Lentz was on the sports staff of the Des Moines *Register* and *Tribune* before becoming assistant sports editor of the Madison *Capital Times.* He had a daily program on sports on radio station WIBA and broadcast both college and high school sporting events. He became athletic publicity director at the University of Wisconsin in 1946.

LIEBENDORFER, Donald Eugene
Sports Publicity Director
Liebendorfer was at Stanford University for over 50 years, leaving only to serve in the Navy in W.W. II. He was the first full time college sports publicity director in the country and held the position 45 years, retiring in 1971 after spending his last three years writing a book about Stanford athletics.

MANN, Ted
Sports Information Director
Ted Mann had served 34 years as sports information director at Duke University when he retired in 1966. During that time he had 32 football players named All-American, 6 basketball players named All-American, and many athletes honored in track, golf and baseball.

McELROY, Henry B.
Football Statistician
Henry McElroy was in and out of college sports publicity most of his life, working many times on newspapers. He developed a system with Tony Ketterson for recording football statistics and became the official statistician for the Southwest Conference. He worked to improve press box conditions at games, and wrote with Wilbur Evans the story of Texas A&M football, *The Twelfth Man.*

PAUL, C. Robert, Jr.
Sports Information Director
Bob Paul served as sports information director at the University of Pennsylvania from 1953 through 1961, going to the AAU as director of development until 1967, when he became director of information and publications and then director of communications for the U.S. Olympic Committee.

PAULISON, Walter
Sports Information Director
Walt Paulison retired in 1969 after 44 years as the Northwestern University sports information director. In 1951 in conjunction with the University's centennial, he published the history of Northwestern athletics, *The Tale of the Wildcats.*

PIERCE, Donald
Sports Information Director
Don was the first sports information director at University of Kansas, serving from 1945 through 1965 when he died in an automobile accident. As historian for the Big Eight Conference, he compiled a complete history of the Big Eight and Missouri Valley football, basketball and track dating back to 1907.

RIDINGS, J. W.
Information Director
J.W. was information director for Texas Christian University from 1927 through 1948. He had founded the department of journalism there in 1927.

SHIEBLER, George L.
Commissioner
George Shiebler became the first sports information director at New York University upon his graduation in 1927. He was the first to publish guides for the working press. After 45 years in intercollegiate athletics, he retired in 1972. In 1947 he started to work as assistant, later associate, commissioner for the Eastern College Athletic Conference, and then becoming commissioner until his retirement.

SNYPP, Wilbur E. "Bill"
Sports Information Director
After 29 years as sports information director at Ohio State University, Bill Snypp retired in 1973. He served as sports editor for the Canton, Ohio, *Daily News* and the Lima, Ohio, *Lima News* until joining the staff at Ohio State in 1944.

SOLTYS, Frank W.
Sports Information Director
Before joining the University of Arizona, Soltys was director of the news bureau at American International College and director of sports information at the University of Connecticut.

SORENSEN, Parry D.
Director of University Relations
Sorensen established the department of public relations in 1946 at the University of Utah and was director until 1970 when he became assistant to the president.

STABLEY, Fred W.
Sports Information Director
Fred Stabley became sports information director at Michigan State University in 1948. He was president of the College Sports Information Directors of America 1958 and 1959.

WADE, Julius Jennings "Jake"
Director of Sports Information
One of the nation's best known sports writers, Jake started at the University of North Carolina in 1946 as

director of sports information, after having worked on many newspapers in the South and East as both a sports writer and columnist. Jake made Charlie Justice one of the most publicized football players of the nation.

WEST, Ned
Sports Information Director
Ned West was a newspaper sports editor for three years and an athletic publicity director at Florida State University before moving to Georgia Tech in 1952 as sports information director. During his time, Georgia Tech sent 14 football teams to bowl games.

WILE, Otis
Director of Sports Publicity
Otis Wile spent 46 years at Oklahoma State University as student, newspaperman and sports publicist. He spent 27 years as director of sports publicity there.

WILSON, Eric
Sports Information Director
Eric Wilson was the University of Iowa's first and only sports information director from 1924 through 1968. In 1968 he was given the Arch Ward Memorial Award for his service to sports publicity.

WILSON, James F. "Pepper"
Sports Information Director
Pepper Wilson was sports information director at the University of Dayton from 1949 until 1957 when he became director of public relations, publicity and promotion for the Cincinnati Royals. He became their general manager in 1958 remaining until 1969.

WOODWORTH, Robert Clute
Sports Information Director
Bob Woodworth was sports information director at Purdue University for 36 years from 1928 until his death in 1964. From 1926 until 1928 he had been sports editor of the *Lafayette Journal* and *Courier*.

1970

BERG, Warren G.
Sports Information Director
From 1951 through 1966 Warren Berg served as sports information director at Luther College.

BURRELL, Harry
Sports Information Director
Harry Burrell was the first sports information director at Iowa State Teachers College, now the University of Northern Iowa. He served as director of the first publicity bureau of the North Central Conference, returning to Iowa in 1941. He became sports information director at Iowa State University in 1948.

MILLER, Thomas
Sports Information Director
Tom Miller became sports information director at Indiana University in 1953, after being a sports writer for the *Atlanta Constitution* in Georgia in the late 1940s.

RENEGAR, Horace
Sports Publicity Director
Horace Renegar was the Southern sports editor for the Associated Press in 1927. He went to Tulane University as sports publicity director and assistant to the athletic director in 1929, becoming director of athletics and director of public relations in 1945. He retired in 1969 from Tulane to become director of development for Dillard University.

SCHUESSLER, Rea
Sports Information Director
Rea Schuessler was sports information director at the University of Alabama for ten years before moving to Mobile to manage the Ladd Memorial Stadium in 1950. Since 1951 he has been vice president and general manager of the Senior Bowl All-Star game in Mobile.

YOUNG, Bill
Sports Information Director
Bill Young was named sports information director at the University of Southern Illinois in 1958 after being the student sports information director there from 1953 through 1955. He is the sports information director at the University of Wyoming at present, receiving the Arch Ward Memorial Award in 1972.

1971

WRIGHT, George
Sports Information Director
George Wright was the sports information director at Baylor University for 13 years from 1955 until his death in 1968. He had been sports director for the *Houston Press* prior to his appointment at Baylor.

1972

BRADLEY, Robert
Sports Information Director
Bob has served his alma mater a good many years in some capacity, being the sports information director for the football teams that participated in the 1957 Orange Bowl, 1959 Sugar Bowl and 1959 Bluebonnet Bowl. He is very active in many sports writers associations.

CALLAHAN, William
Sports Information Director
Bill Callahan became sports information director at the University of Missouri in 1948.

DOHERTY, Thomas R.
Sports Information Director
Tom Doherty was sports information director for 28 years at the University of Rhode Island before his retirement in 1973.

KELLEY, Vic
Athletic News Bureau Manager
Kelley is the athletic news bureau manager and golf coach at the University of California, Los Angeles. He has been the news manager since 1945 and coach since 1948.

1973

EMERY, Ted

Publicity Director

Ted Emery has been publicity manager for Alma College (Michigan), Michigan State University, Dartmouth College and Northern Illinois University, and is now publicity director for the Gator Bowl Association, after serving one year as publicity director for the New York Jets of the American Football League.

PITTENGER, Baaron B.

Sports Information Director

Pittenger was appointed director of sports information at Harvard University in 1959 and associate director of athletics in 1970.

TARMAN, James I.

Associate Director of Athletics

James Tarman is associate director of athletics and assistant to the dean of the College of Health, Physical Education and Recreation at Pennsylvania State University, dealing primarily with public relations and public affairs.

TOBIN, Louis Michael "Mike"

Director of Publicity

Mike Tobin was named director of publicity for the athletic association at the University of Illinois in 1922. He was the first reporter to take a typewriter into the press box.

1974

BROCK, Jim

Sports Information Director

Jim Brock was sports information director at Texas Christian University for 13 years, moving to Southern Methodist University in 1966 as assistant athletic director, being promoted to associate director in 1973.

MORRISON, Paul F.

Sports Information Director

Paul Morrison has been at Drake University for 36 years where he was sports information director until 1968, director of the news bureau 8 years and also business manager for athletics.

THORNTON, Charles

Sports Information Director

Charlie is sports information director at the University of Alabama as well as assistant athletic director. He was given the Arch Ward Memorial Award in 1974.

1975

BRYANT, Don

Sports Information Director

Since 1963 Don Bryant has been on the athletic department staff at the University of Nebraska. He was named Nebraska's Sportswriter of the Year in 1961 and 1962.

VISTA, Nicholas

Sports Information Director

Nick Vista was an assistant news editor at Michigan State University 1954 and 1955 and has been assistant director of sports information since 1955.

1976

HUDGINS, Elmore "Scoop"

Sports Information Director

Scoop Hudgins spent 18 years as sports information director for Vanderbilt University and moved to the Southeastern Conference as their director in 1964.

MINTZ, Ben

Sports Information Director

Ben Mintz was in the sports publicity business for 39 years and directed the Cornell University sports information office for 30 of those years.

RAMSEY, Jones

Sports Information Director

Jones Ramsey has been sports information director for the University of Texas for 13 years and for 9 years at Texas A&M University before that.

WHITMORE, William

Sports Information Director

While in the service in W.W. I, Bill Whitmore was sports information director for the Randolph Field athletic teams. He became Rice University's first full time sports information director in 1950.

1977

BOHNET, Lee

Sports Information Director

Lee Bohnet serves as the sports information director at the University of North Dakota.

HOLMES, Bill

Sports Information Director

Bill Holmes is the sports information director at Texas Tech University.

QUINN, Pat

Sports Information Director

The sports information director at Oklahoma State University is presently Pat Quinn.

Fencing Hall of Fame

Instituted in 1963, the Fencing Hall of Fame has honored 51 members, both men and women coaches and competitors. Induction ceremonies are held at the annual National Fencing Championships dinner which occurs on the eve of the National Fencing Championships. A special committee chaired by Michael DeCicco, head fencing coach at Notre Dame University, in 1977 nominated its choices directly to the Citizens Savings Hall Board.

Induction Years Unrecorded

ARMITAGE, Norman C.
Competitor
As a member of the Fencers' Club, Armitage built an impressive record of victories. In 1930, 1934–1936, 1939–1943 and 1945, Armitage was the U.S. men's foil champion, and in 1939 he fenced on the U.S. men's team épée.

AXELROD, Albert
Competitor
As a student at City College of New York, Axelrod established himself as the national collegiate foil champion. After college, Axelrod fenced with the Fencers' Club and participated on the U.S. men's team foil from 1962 to 1966. He also was a member of Salle Santelli and a fencer on the U.S. men's team three-weapon. In 1960 Axelrod earned a bronze medal in foil and is the only medalist in fencing for the U.S. since W.W. II.

CALNAN, George C.
Competitor
Calnan was a versatile fencer during his career and competed successfully in individual and team events in foil, épée and three-weapon. As a member of the Fencers' Club, Calnan participated during the mid-1920s to the mid-1930s on the U.S. men's foil, U.S. men's épée and U.S. men's three-weapon individual events and was a member of the U.S. men's team foil, team épée and team three-weapon.

CASTELLO, Hugo
Coach
Castello, whose brother James and father Julio are also well-known fencers and coaches, served as fencing coach for New York University and can claim an unprecedented six undefeated seasons. His New York squads possess a record number of eight National Collegiate Athletic Association winners and 11 Intercollegiate Fencing Association champions. In addition to his significant contribution as a college coach, Castello also served fencing as co-coach of U.S. Pan-American Games team, president of the National Fencing Coaches Association, chairman of the U.S. Olympic fencing development committee and coach of the U.S. Junior and Senior world championship teams.

CASTELLO, James M.
Coach
Born in 1916 in Weehawken, N.J; younger son of the late Julio M. Castello, 1924 U.S. Olympic coach; attended New York Univ; worked for Sperry Corp. during W.W. II; died in 1974 in New York.

During his years at New York University, James M. Castello won the National Collegiate Athletic Association championship 11 times. He fenced on New York University's championship sabre team in 1938. Castello was best known for his work as an armorer. In his work at Castello Fencing Equipment and as armorer for the Metropolitan Division of the Amateur Fencing League of America (AFLA), he was responsible for many innovations in the development of the electric foil. For his expertise in all areas of this work, he was named armorer of the 1959 Pan-American team. He was assistant coach for his father from 1945 to 1947 and for his older brother Hugo from 1948 until retirement in 1974. When he moved his family from New York City to suburban Long Island in the 1950s, his enthusiasm for fencing led him to establish the Long Island Division of the AFLA and to aid greatly in the introduction of fencing in Long Island schools. He was active in the Junior Olympic development program. Many very successful collegiate and AFLA fencers resulted from his work. Both Castello's father Julio and his brother Hugo have been inducted into the Hall of Fame.

CASTELLO, Julio M.
Coach
Julio Castello was a famous fencer and coach, and served as the coach for the 1924 U.S. Olympic team. Julio was fencing coach at New York University for 20 years. His teams won eight IFA titles and one NCAA championship. His two sons, Hugo and James, were also fencers and coaches, and learned much of their expertise from him. All three men have been inducted into the Fencing Hall of Fame.

CETRULO, Dean
Competitor
Born in 1919 in Newark, N.J; attended Seton Hall Univ; during W.W. II was a 1st Lieutenant in the Army Air Force; currently a secondary school principal in East Hanover, N.J; All-Eastern Intercollegiate champion in foil and sabre 1940 and 1941.

During the 1940s, Cetrulo was one of the major fencing figures in America. In amateur competition he captured first place in individual foil and individual sabre on several different annual events. He also participated in first place team foil, team sabre and three-way weapon. At the 1948 Olympic Games in London he was unable to bring home a medal but entered the semifinals in both individual foil and sabre. His foil team took a fourth and his sabre team a third. Cetrulo remains active in collegiate fencing as an official.

CSISZAR, Lajos S.
Competitor
Born in 1903 in Roumania, Lajos Csiszar was Olympic fencing coach for Hungary 1936 and 1948, then came to the United States. He was fencing master at the University of Pennsylvania for many years. He coached the 1956 U.S. Olympic team, the 1969 World team, and the 1963, 1971 and 1975 Pan-Am team.

D'AMBOLA, Dr. Samuel
Coach
Born in 1922 in Newark, N.J; served in the Navy during W.W. II; graduated from Downstate Medical School in New York City; presently retired from private practice and is serving as director of the family practice residency program at the John F. Kennedy Medical Center in Edison, N.J.

Samuel D'Ambola began fencing at Barringer High School in Newark, and continued fencing at Seton Hall University where he won an Eastern Intercollegiate épée championship. During the mid-1950s, D'Ambola was New Jersey Divisional foil champion twice, runnerup for the North-Atlantic Sectional championship and a semifinalist in the Amateur Fencing League of America (AFLA) national championship. In 1960 he offered his services as a coach on a voluntary basis to Essex Catholic High School. During his years at Essex, he led the fencing teams to a position of eminence by winning nine New Jersey state championships, eight in a row. Its dual meet records were similarly impressive and included a winning streak of 84 dual meets over nearly five years. Essex Catholic's participation in New Jersey AFLA activities during D'Ambola's years as coach were on a scale unprecedented in AFLA history. Some 75 of his fencers continued with their fencing at the collegiate level and at least one dozen won a conference or national collegiate championship. Several of them gained national AFLA ranking and one has won the AFLA national championship and made an Olympic Games.

DANOSI, Istvan
Coach

Born in Hungary; immigrated to the United States in 1956; became a United States citizen in 1965; son Steve competed for Wayne State and was an All-American fencer between 1972 and 1974; named Coach of the Year 1972.

Danosi was a member of Hungary's Olympic championship fencing team in 1936 at Berlin. He coached Hungarian Olympic sabre teams in 1948 at London and 1952 at Helsinki. He was also one of his country's foremost skiers. Danosi has been the distinguished and highly successful fencing coach at Wayne State University in Detroit, Mich, since 1958. His Tartars team soared over the 200-victories mark in 1974 and the victories have mounted since, 230 to 256 through 1976. His Wayne State teams have several times been undefeated in dual competition, including 1961, 1973 and 1974. Danosi has produced as many as 23 All-Americans at Wayne State and his teams have been a constant threat in National Collegiate Athletic Association (NCAA) national championship competition. The Tartars, with Danosi providing the leadership, won the NCAA crown in 1975, placed second in 1974 and 1976 and third in 1966 and 1973. In 1973, Danosi was named coach of the U.S. team in the World University Games in Moscow. Following his competitive career he served as sports professor and fencing master at the Hungarian Royal Military Academy. He assisted in drilling U.S. Olympic fencers, and he directs his own fencing academy, in addition to his Wayne State teaching and coaching duties.

De CAPRILES, Jose R.
Competitor

Born in Mexico, Jose moved to the United States in 1920. He competed in fencing at New York University 1929–1933, Fencers Club 1933–1937 and 1957–1960, and La Salle Santelli 1937–1957. He was intercollegiate épée champion in 1933 and 1937, national épée champion in 1938 and 1951, and national foil champion in 1946. He served as an officer in many fencing organizations. Jose de Caprilles was a member of the 1936, 1948 and 1952 U.S. Olympic fencing teams, the U.S. international fencing teams in 1938 and 1939, and a member of the U.S. Pan-American fencing team in 1955, serving also as captain.

De CAPRILES, Miguel A.
Competitor

Miguel was U.S. épée champion in 1931 and 1944; and three-weapon champion in 1933, 1934, 1941, 1942 and 1947.

De CICCO, Michael
Competitor

De KOFF, Irving
Competitor

De Koff was the fencing coach at Columbia University.

DELADRIER, Andre
Competitor and Coach

Born September 12, 1920, in Chatlet, Belgium; U.S. citizen; wife Elizabeth; son Richard; graduated from St. John's Univ. and Columbia Teachers Col.

As head coach at the U.S. Naval Academy since 1957, Andre Deladrier's record shows 51 wins and 18 losses in dual meets. He won the Eastern Intercollegiate Team titles in foil in 1964, épée in 1958 and 1966, sabre 1962 and 1964, and three-weapon in 1964. They won the NCAA Team title in 1959 and 1962 and finished in the top four six other times. His 1960 épée team was AFLA national champions and he has produced 16 All-Americans, one AFLA individual champion in foil and one Pan-Am champion in épée.

DELADRIER, Clovis F. J.
Competitor

Born in Belgium, Clovis Deladrier was the national Belgian champion in both foil and épée in 1926. He served as assistant fencing coach at the U.S. Naval Academy 1927–1932, and head coach from 1933 until his death in 1948. He was a president of the U.S. National Fencing Coaches Association and trained the U.S. fencers for the 1928 and 1936 Olympics.

EVERY, Dernell
Competitor

Born in 1906 in Athens, N.Y; attended Yale Univ; employed as secy.-treas. of Kraft Paper Co; presently retired and residing in Pleasantville, N.Y.

During his competitive career, Every achieved championship status in individual foil, team foil and three-way weapon at both the collegiate level and later as a representative of the Fencers Club and the New York Athletic Club. In Olympic competition, Every reached the semifinals in foil individual in the 1928 Amsterdam Games and the 1932 Los Angeles Games. In the 1932 Games he fenced on the U.S. foil team which took a third place. At the London Olympics in 1948 his foil team scored fourth.

FAULKNER, Ralph B.
Competitor

Born in Abilene, Kans; graduated from Univ. Wash.

Faulkner was international saber champion in 1928 and runnerup international épée champion in 1928. He was a member of the American Olympic fencing team in 1928 and 1932. He has coached three national fencing champions and four national champion teams. He is considered one of the best referees in the United States, and coaches at his own school.

GARRET, Maxwell
Competitor and Coach
Born April 18, 1917, in New York City; wife Diana; two sons and two daughters; graduated from Univ. Ill, City Col. New York; Major in Air Force 1942 – 1958.

Maxwell Garret is one of fencing's outstanding coaches. He has been head coach at the University of Illinois since 1940, and in 22 years (1946 – 1967) compiled a dual meet record of 185 – 51 – 1 with five undefeated fencing teams. Garret has also published many books and articles on fencing and other physical education topics.

GOLDSTEIN, Ralph M.
Competitor
Ralph Goldstein was Midwest three-weapon champion 1945 and 1946, Metropolitan New York épée champion in 1946, and member of the 1948, 1956 and 1960 U.S. Olympic fencing teams and member and captain of Salle Santelli fencing teams that won numerous national fencing titles 1943 – 1962. He was also secretary of the Amateur Fencers League of America 1951 – 1961 and foreign secretary 1963 – 1965.

GRASSON, Robert
Competitor and Coach
Robert Grasson was the fencing coach at Yale from 1920 to 1956. He was originally from Belgium where he was an amateur champion. He was the fencing coach for the 1936 U.S. Olympic team.

HALL, Sherman
Competitor
Sherman Hall was America's foremost fencer from 1910 to 1920. He was four times national foil champion, three times sabre champion and national three-weapon champion in 1912, 1915, 1919 and 1920.

HAMMOND, Graeme M.
Competitor
Hammond was the national épée champion 1893 and national sabre champion 1893 and 1894. He was captain of the U.S. Olympic fencing team in 1912 and founding president of the Amateur Fencers League of America in 1891.

HERMANSON, Alvar
Competitor

HUFFMAN, John R.
Competitor
National sabre champion five times 1931 – 1938, John Huffman was six times medalist 1929 – 1941. He was also national medalist in foil 1936, 1939, 1941 and 1942. He was a member of the U.S. Olympic fencing teams in 1932 and 1936, and president of the AFLA 1940 – 1943.

JAECKEL, Tracy
Competitor
Born in New York City; graduated from Princeton Univ. 1928; former president of Virgin Island Fencing Federation; worked in clothing business; died in August, 1969.

Tracy Jaeckel was a member of the 1932 and 1936 U.S. Olympic fencing teams and a member of the national champion fencing teams 1932 – 1936 and 1939 – 1941.

KING, Harriet
Competitor
Born in New York City and graduated from Hunter College, Harriet King has been fencing competitively for over 20 years. She was first in the nationals in 1967, 1970, and second in 1969. She was a member of the 1960, 1964, 1968 and 1972 Olympic teams and went with the team to the Pan-Am games in 1959, 1963, 1967 and 1971, winning a gold medal. She was also a member of two U.S. teams that won the World championships.

LEVIS, Joseph L.
Competitor
From 1929 through 1954, Joseph Levis was six times national foil champion and four times a medalist. He was the national three-weapon champion in 1929 and a member of the 1928, 1932 and 1936 Olympic teams. He coached fencing at Massachusetts Institute of Technology 1939 – 1948.

LEWIS, Norman
Competitor
Born in 1915 in New York City; attended New York Univ; presently a businessman in New York City and resides in Kew Gardens, N.Y.

While Norman Lewis attended the New York University, he was crowned the Intercollegiate Fencing Association champion in foil individual, épée individual, foil team, épée team and three-weapon team. He won the most individual championships in a college career. He is also one of three fencers to win two individual titles in a single year. As a representative of Salle Santelli in New York City, Lewis won many championships, including foil individual in 1939, épée individual from 1948 to 1950 and first place in foil team in 1954, and épée team throughout the 1940s and 1950s. Lewis also took first place in three-weapon team at the 1950 and 1954 Amateur Fencers League of America national championships. In the 1948 Olympics in London, Lewis competed in épée individual and took a ninth. In the 1968 Olympics in Mexico City, he served as captain for the U.S. fencing team.

LUCIA, Edward F.
Competitor

MAYER, Helena
Competitor
Helena Mayer was an Olympic champion in 1928 and placed second in 1936 while representing Germany. She was European champion 1929, 1931 and World champion 1937. She was eight times U.S. national champion 1934 – 1946, placing second in 1947.

MILLER, Raymond
Coach
Born 1915 in Harrisburg, Pa; attended Wagner Col. and started fencing teams; served as Lieutenant in Navy; presently resides in Wayne, N.J.

Miller began fencing as a high school student in New Haven, Conn; his team was coached by Robert Grasson of Yale. He turned professional immediately following his high school graduation. After W.W. II, Miller joined the history department faculty of Paterson State Teachers College in Wayne. While teaching there he started fencing teams for men and women, coaching the men from 1946 until 1952, and again from 1955 to 1960. In 1952 the men's team took third place in the Amateur Fencers League of America (AFLA) National épée team championships. Miller has had his greatest success as a coach with the women's team, which he has coached since 1946. They have won the Intercollegiate Women's Fencing Association championship eight times giving him the best record as coach in the 50-year history of the Association. Miller was named Coach of the Year eight times by the National Intercollegiate Women's Fencing Association. He has also been very active in the affairs of the New Jersey Division of the AFLA, particularly in the securing of competition sites, and the repair and provision of scoring equipment. Many of his students have gone on to coach college and high school teams throughout New Jersey.

MITCHELL, Maxine
Competitor
Born July 22, 1917, in Roy, Wash; attended Occidental Col; lives in Los Angeles, Calif.

Maxine Mitchell was on the U.S. Olympic fencing team in 1952 and won the Pan-Am championship in 1955. She also won the national championship three times.

MONTAGUE, James
Competitor and Coach
James Montague was a former fencing coach at City College of New York.

MURRAY, James
Competitor
James Murray instructed in fencing at Columbia University for 55 years and at the New York Athletic Club for 60 years, before retiring in 1954.

NUNES, Leo G.
Competitor
From 1917 to 1932, Leo Nunes won the national épée championship six times. He was three times the national sabre champion 1922, 1926 and 1929, and medalist in 1920, 1924, 1928, 1934 and 1935. He was also national foil champion in 1924, and five times a medalist.

NYILAS, Dr. Tibor
Competitor
Born in 1914 in Budapest, Hungary; immigrated to the United States in 1939; presently a prominent physician and surgeon in suburban New York.

Tibor Nyilas began his fencing career in Hungary and attained national ranking. Between 1944 and 1956 Nyilas captured the championship title in sabre individual seven times in Amateur Fencers League of America (AFLA) competition. He achieved acclaim in other AFLA events as well as taking the championship in three-weapon individual in 1948 and participating on ten first-place teams in both sabre and three-weapon. In the 1948 Olympic Games at London, Nyilas fenced on the U.S. sabre team which took third, and was seventh in sabre individual. In both the 1952 and 1960 Olympics, Nyilas' sabre teams earned fourth-place recognition.

O'CONNOR, W. Scott
Competitor and Contributor
Scott O'Connor served as the first secretary of the Amateur Fencers League of America, holding office for 35 years 1891–1925. He was national foil champion in 1892 and national épée champion in 1905, and a member of the 1904 U.S. Olympic team.

PARKER, J. Brooks B.
Competitor
In 1920 Parker was a member of the U.S. Olympic team and again in 1924. He was sabre medalist in the United States in 1921 and 1927. He is the donor of the Friendship Trophy which recognizes the outstanding U.S. fencer in the Olympics. Parker died in 1951.

PINCHART, Rene
Coach
Born in 1891 in Maldegem, Belgium; served in Belgium Army and taught several sports; a bronze medalist in gymnastics; moved to the United States in 1927 and assumed the position of maitre d'arms at the Fencers Club; taught briefly at Harvard Univ; died in Higganum, Conn. in 1970.

Pinchart remained at the Fencers Club until he retired from teaching in 1956. During his tenure at the Fencers Club, they won the following Amateur Fencers League of America (AFLA) national championships: Foil team (1928, 1929, 1931–1936, 1949–1953 and 1955–1957), épée team (1928, 1932–1937, 1939, 1941, 1951 and 1954), three-weapon team (1928, 1929, 1932–1935 and 1955) and women's foil team (1928, 1929, 1941, 1942, 1945–1947 and 1954). His pupils similarly dominated individual events in the AFLA nationals. During W.W. II he and his wife were largely responsible for keeping fencing alive in the metropolitan area. Pinchart was U.S. Olympic coach in 1928, 1932, 1948 and 1952. His pupils from the Fencers Club who scored impressively in the Olympic Games were Lt. George C. Calnan, Joseph Levis and Maria Cerra Tishman. In the 1932 Olympics the foil and épée teams both finished third. In the 1948 Olympics the foil team finished fourth. Pinchart was honored by the AFLA in 1971 when the trophy for the Under-19 national foil championships was established in his memory. Also, a Metropolitan Division AFLA tournament is held annually in his memory. In 1970, through a generous private donation to the AFLA, the Rene Pinchart Memorial Junior Olympic program was established and has introduced fencing to many New York City youngsters.

PUGLIESE, Julia Jones
Competitor
Born in 1909 in New York City; attended New York Univ; currently an asst. professor of health and physical education at Hunter Col; resides in New York City.

Pugliese was co-founder of the Intercollegiate Women's Fencing Association (IWFA), and the first individual champion of the IWFA in 1929. She was runnerup in both individual and team categories the following year. After raising a family in the 1940s and 1950s, Pugliese resumed teaching fencing in 1956 at Hunter College, which won the IWFA championship in 1970. She was named IWFA Coach of the Year in 1970; her teams have won six championships. She was the first woman to coach a U.S. international team, at the World University Games at Turin, Italy, in 1970. She was also coach of the U.S. teams in the Under-20 World championships at

Poznan, Poland, in 1976. She has served as a member as well as chairwoman of numerous fencing committees.

ROMARY, Janice-Lee York
Competitor
Born August 6, 1928, in San Mateo, Calif; graduated from Univ. Southern Calif. 1949; married; one daughter; lives in California.

Janice-Lee was a member of the 1948, 1952 and 1956 Olympic teams. She was national individual champion in 1950, 1951 and 1956, and a national champion team member 1950, 1952, 1956 and 1958. She was also a member of World championship teams in 1948 and 1952.

SALTUS, J. Sanford
Contributor
Saltus is the donor of the Sword Trophy which is awarded for the U.S. Masters Èpée Tournament. He was active in YMCA fencing and is one of the early patrons of fencing.

SANTELLI, Georgio
Coach
Son of one of Europe's most famous coaches, Georgio Santelli came to America in 1920 and tutored Olympic teams. His Salle's colors have been carried into many meets by American fencers.

SCHMITTER, Charles R.
Competitor
Charles Schmitter was a member of the Detroit Fencing Club team and the University of Detroit team. He was several times state foil, sabre and épée champion and twice three-weapon champion in his state. He is the founder and past president of the National Fencing Coaches Association and coached fencing at Michigan State University for over 30 years.

SIEJA, Stanley S.
Competitor
Sieja was coach at Princeton University for over 30 years, twice being chosen Collegiate Fencing Coach of the Year. He coached the U.S. team four times in World championships and coached the 1956 Olympic and 1967 and 1971 Pan-Am teams.

TISHMAN, Maria Cerra
Competitor
Maria Tishman was the national women's foil champion in 1945 and a medalist in 1938, 1941, 1943 and 1948. She was also a member of the 1948 Olympic team.

TOTH, Nicholas
Coach
Born March 22, 1908, in Kotaj, Hungary; graduate of Central Sports Institute and Fencing Academy in Budapest, Hungary, 1932; became a naturalized American citizen 1956; professor of physical education and fencing; presently living and coaching in Colorado Springs, Colo, at U.S. Air Force Academy.

Nicholas Toth won the International Masters in sabre fencing at Innsbruck, Austria, in 1948. He was head coach of the U.S. modern pentathlon team at Melbourne in 1956, serving as a member of the U.S. Olympic modern pentathlon committee and the National Collegiate Athletic Association (NCAA) fencing rules committee. He was U.S. national coach of modern pentathlon in the World championships of 1955, 1957 and 1958 and was the U.S. national coach in the 1971 World junior fencing championships. Toth was appointed fencing coach at the U.S. Air Force Academy in 1959 and is now enjoying his 18th successful year in that capacity. His teams have scored with exceptional success in dual competition, with a record of 152 – 24 through the 1976 season. Toth's Air Force Academy teams have won 13 Western intercollegiate titles and placed second three times. In NCAA fencing championships competition, Toth's squads scored best in 1963 with a third. He has produced 11 All-Americans in collegiate ranks and many of his gymnasts have claimed national, international, and olympic honors.

VINCE, Joseph
Coach
Born in 1891 in Budapest, Hungary; emigrated from Hungary, where he was a civil engineer and a leading fencer, to New York City in 1924; moved to Beverly Hills and was consultant for fencing and dueling sequences for movies and television; married Marion Lloyd, his first pupil to win the Amateur Fencing League of America championship; currently resides in North Hollywood, Calif.

Within one year after immigrating to the United States, Vince won the Amateur Fencing League of America (AFLA) national sabre championship and the Canadian national sabre championship. He was a member of the AFLA national championship sabre team in 1926 and 1927, and a member of the AFLA national three-weapon team in 1927. Turning professional shortly after arriving in America, Vince opened a salle d'arms in Brooklyn, N.Y. At the same time he taught fencing to several industrial recreation groups. The Salle Vince, first in Brooklyn and later in several Manhattan locations, was one of the leading clubs of the era, dominating the AFLA national women's foil team event for ten years in succession, 1930 to 1939. This is still the AFLA record for consecutive team championships. During the 1930s, the Salle Vince also won the AFLA national sabre team championship and the AFLA national three-weapon team championship, once each. Vince taught fencing at City College of New York during these years, and was responsible for getting them inducted into the Intercollegiate Fencing Association. A number of his students gained berths on U.S. Olympic teams, including Marion Lloyd Vince, Dorothy Locke, Muriel Guggolz, Peter Bruder, Samuel Stewart and Maria Cerra Tishman. While he was in New York City, Vince opened the Vince Fencing Equipment Company, becoming an early entrepreneur in the sport. He is generally credited with inventing the removable snap-on bib for fencing masks. In 1967 the Salle Vince regained the AFLA national women's team championship it had last held in 1939 as a New York entry. Vince's most important pupil in these years was Janice York Romary, six-time Olympian and ten-time AFLA national champion.

VINCE, Marion Lloyd
Competitor
Marion Vince, wife of the eminent fencer and fencing coach Joseph Vince, is the only American woman to

reach the semifinals twice in Olympic competition, which she accomplished in the 1928 and 1936 Olympic Games. In 1928 and 1931, Marion Vince was named the national foils champion for women, and was her husband's first pupil to win the Amateur Fencers League of America national championships. She was a long-time member of the prestigious Salle Vince in New York and now resides with her husband in North Hollywood, Calif.

WORTH, George V.
Competitor

Born in 1915 in Budapest, Hungary; immigrated to the United States in 1937; during W.W. II was assigned to a U.S. Army intelligence unit in Europe; twice awarded the bronze star; fluent in six languages; certified life insurance underwriter in New York City; wife Karen is a renowned medallic artist; currently lives in Orangeburg, N.Y.

George V. Worth began his fencing career in Hungary, attaining national recognition. He later moved for a brief period to Cuba and became Cuban national champion. During his fencing career, Worth stacked up an impressive record in Amateur Fencers League Association (AFLA), Pan-American and Olympic competition. In 1954 he was crowned sabre individual champion. In sabre team and three-weapon team he also scored many first places during the late 1940s and 1950s. In Pan-American competition he fenced on two second place teams in the 1951 Buenos Aires and 1955 Mexico City Games. At the 1948 Olympic Games in London he was only able to capture a fifth in sabre individual, but he was a member of the sabre team which took third. In both the 1952 Helsinki and the 1960 Rome Olympics his sabre team came in fourth. At the 1959 Pan-American Games, Worth was granted the privilege of giving the athletes' oath on behalf of the participants. He was a member of the U.S. Olympic fencing committee in 1964, 1968, 1972 and 1976. He served as foreign secretary of the AFLA for many years and was president of the fencing jury in both the 1952 and 1960 Olympic Games, as well as the World championships in 1963.

Football — College Hall of Fame

Instituted in 1949 the College Football Hall of Fame as of 1977 had 188 college players and 116 college coaches as members. Six of these were inducted as both players and coaches. Members, representing the sport from the late 1800s to the present time, have their names engraved on a trophy kept in the Citizens Savings Hall of Fame Athletic Museum in Los Angeles and receive a Hall of Fame award.

Induction Years Unrecorded

ALBERT, Frank C.
Player

Born January 27, 1920, in Chicago, Ill; attended Stanford Univ. 1939–1941; Consensus All-American 1940 and 1941; Citizens Savings Player of the Year 1940; served in the Navy during W.W. II; retired as a player in 1953.

1946–1952 San Francisco 49ers, quarterback
1956–1958 San Francisco 49ers, head coach

Albert switched from unimpressive single-wing tailback to a T-formation quarterback under Clark Shaughnessy. Noted for his superb ball-handling, passing and kicking, he was "a magician with the ball," according to Shaughnessy. He threw a 41 yd. touchdown pass and kicked 3 PATs, in the 1941 Rose Bowl, as Stanford defeated Nebraska 21–13. Albert finished his collegiate career with ninth in passing yds. at 1795, tied for sixth in touchdown passes with 15, tenth in touchdowns accounted for at 24, and fourth in interceptions with 37. He joined the San Francisco 49ers in 1946 and remained with them until 1952. Albert was runnerup to Otto Graham in all-time All-American football conference passing with 6948 yds, completing 515 of 963 passes, a percentage of 53.5 and 88 touchdowns.

ALDRICH, Charles "Ki"
Player

Born in Temple, Tex; All-American 1938.

1936–1938 Texas Christian University, center
1939–1940 Chicago Cardinals, center
1941–1942 Washington Redskins, center
1945–1947 Washington Redskins, center

Ki Aldrich was considered one of the greatest linebackers in the Southwest Conference. This 5 ft. 11 in, 215 lbs. center was the Consensus All-American in 1938 but went on to play his greatest game at the Sugar Bowl in 1939. Texas Christian University won over Carnegie Tech with a score of 15–7.
Also in: National Football Hall of Fame.

ALEXANDER, Joseph A.
Player

Born April 1, 1898, in Silver Creek, N.Y.

1918–1920 Syracuse University, guard
1921–1922 Rochester Jeffersons, guard
1922 Milwaukee Badgers, guard
1925–1927 New York Giants, guard and coach

Joe Alexander was the 6 ft, 210 lb. guard who helped Syracuse to a record of 19–6–1 during his term there. Of those 19 victories, 13 left the opponents scoreless. During one game with Colgate, Alexander made 11 consecutive tackles helping the Syracuse team to a 14–0 victory.
Also in: National Football Hall of Fame.

ALEXANDER, William A.
Coach

See entry in Athletic Directors Hall of Fame, Citizens Savings Hall of Fame Athletic Museum, 1971.
Also in: National Football Hall of Fame.

AMECHE, Alan D. "Horse"
Player

Born June 1, 1933, in Kenosha, Wisc; All-American 1953 and 1954; Most Valuable Player and Heisman Trophy 1954.

1951–1954 University of Wisconsin, back
1955–1960 Baltimore Colts, back

The Horse was known for his unusual running style. He

ran with his body in an almost upright position, but strength and unexpected agility were his keys to success. Ameche started in his freshman year at Wisconsin and went on to accumulate a net gain of 2463 yards rushing and 20 touchdowns in 25 games of Big Ten competition. He was the winner of the All-American award in 1953 and 1954 as well as the Academic All-American title. In 1954 Alan received the Heisman Trophy and the Most Valuable Player award in the Big Ten.
Also in: National Football Hall of Fame.

ANDERSON, Edward N.
Coach
Born Nov. 13, 1900, in Oskaloosa, Iowa; received M.D. degree from Rush Medical Col. while serving as DePaul coach and playing for the Bulls; worked as a private physician at Holy Cross; Coach of the Year 1939.

1933–1938 Holy Cross College, coach
1938–1949 University of Iowa, coach
1950–1960 Holy Cross College, coach

Anderson played under Knute Rockne at Notre Dame from 1918 to 1921, and was captain in 1921. A fine end, he played for the 1922 Rochester Jeffersons, the 1922 Chicago Cardinals, the 1923 Chicago Bears and the 1926 Chicago Bulls. He coached Loras to a record of 16–6–2, and from 1922 to 1925 was a coach at DePaul, with 21–22–4. His early record at Holy Cross was 47–7–4, and both the 1935 and 1937 teams were undefeated. As Iowa head coach, he led one of the finest clubs in Iowa history in 1939, taking over a team which had a 22–50 nine-year record and only five Big Ten victories. Among the members of the 1939 "Iron Men" were Nile Kinnick, Erwin Prasse and Mike Enich. Ironically in 1939 Anderson defeated his alma mater, previously unbeaten Notre Dame, the first time the teams had met since his own playing days. In 1950 he returned to Holy Cross. He never abandoned his medical practice while coaching and takes satisfaction from the fact that many of his players later became doctors, dentists and lawyers.
Also in: National Football Hall of Fame.

ARMSTRONG, Ike J.
Coach
See entry in Athletic Directors Hall of Fame, Citizens Savings Hall of Fame Athletic Museum, 1970.
Also in: National Football Hall of Fame.

BACHMAN, Charles W.
Coach
Born Dec. 1, 1892, in Chicago, Ill; won letters as right guard, fullback and left guard while at Notre Dame; teammate of Knute Rockne and Gus Derais; in the food and real estate business when not coaching until retirement.

1917 DePauw University, assistant coach
1917–1919 Northwestern University, coach
1920–1927 Kansas State University, coach
1928–1932 University of Florida, coach
1933–1942 Michigan State University, coach
1944–1946 Michigan State University, coach
1953 Hillsdale College, coach

In 1922 Bachman lost the Big Six title by one game, and his 1928 loss to Tennessee deprived Florida of the Rose Bowl appearance. His 8–1–0 record in 1928 was the best in the first 65 Florida seasons. He developed Johnny Pingel, a member of Michigan State's all-time backfield. At Michigan State, his teams beat Michigan four straight years, 1934 to 1937. They lost the Orange Bowl 6–0 to Auburn in 1937. Bachman learned much from Amos Alonzo Stagg and Snake Ames; his .613 percentage is higher than that of Stagg, Eddie Anderson, Bill Alexander, Dutch Meyer, Clark Shaughnessy, all Hall of Fame members. He was the pioneer of the 6–2–2–1 defense.

BARNES, Stanley N.
Player
Born in Baraboo, Wis; graduated from Univ. California at Berkeley; All-Pacific Coast Center 1918; All-Coast Tackle 1921; became a lawyer and judge; president of the Federal Bar Association from 1951 to 1953; judge in the U.S. Court of Appeals, Ninth Circuit Court since 1956.

Stan Barnes weighed in at 186 lbs. and was 6 ft. 1 in. He was a member of the 1920 and 1921 "Wonder Team" that was unbeaten and went to the Rose Bowl.
Also in: National Football Hall of Fame.

BASTON, Albert P.
Player
Born December 3, 1894, in St. Louis Park, Minn; All-American team 1915 and 1916.

1914–1916 University of Minnesota, end
1932–1950 University of Minnesota, assistant coach

Bert Baston was part of the famous Wyman-to-Baston aerial circus. The 6 ft. 1 in, 170 lb. receiver was the first Minnesota player to make two consecutive All-American teams, 1915 and 1916. The Golden Gophers' "perfect team" of 1915 and 1916 went 12–1–1 and averaged 49 points a game.
Also in: National Football Hall of Fame.

BAUGH, Samuel A. "Slingin' Sammy"
Player
See entry in Pro Football Hall of Fame, 1963.
Also in: Major League Football Hall of Fame, Citizens Savings Hall of Fame Athletic Museum; and National Football Hall of Fame.

BAUJAN, Harry Clifford
Coach
See entry in Athletic Directors Hall of Fame, Citizens Savings Hall of Fame Athletic Museum, 1970.

BEBAN, Gary J.
Player
Born August 5, 1946, in Redwood City, Calif; Heisman Trophy 1967.

1965–1967 University of Caifornia at Los Angeles, quarterback
1968–1969 Washington Redskins, wide receiver

During his college career, Gary Beban rushed for 1257 yards, completed 235 of 444 passes for a gain of 3940 yards and 23 touchdowns, scoring a total of 202 points. He was the recipient of the Heisman Trophy in 1967. His pro career began with a draft from the second round by the Los Angeles Rams in 1968, but draft rights were traded and he ended up with the Washington Redskins. In Washington, Beban was switched to wide receiver, catching his only pro career pass in 1968 for 12 yards. In 1969 Beban left Washington to become a television sportscaster in Los Angeles.

BECHTOL, Hubert
Player
Before joining the Baltimore Colts of the All-American Football Conference for three seasons, 1947–1949, Hubert Bechtol played end for the University of Texas.

BEEDE, Dwight
Coach
Born January 23, 1903; graduated from Carnegie Inst. Technol.

Beede first coached at Westminster College 1926–1930, then at Geneva College 1934–1936. He spent the remainder of his coaching career at Youngstown University 1938–1965. His overall record was 155–107–18 during his 32 years of coaching.

BELL, Madison "Moanin' Matty"
Coach
See entry in Athletic Directors Hall of Fame, Citizens Savings Hall of Fame Athletic Museum, 1970.
Also in: National Football Hall of Fame.

BERTELLI, Angelo B. "Accurate Angelo"
Player
Born in West Springfield, Mass; All-American title 1942; Consensus All-American Award 1943; Heisman Trophy 1943; Citizens Savings Player of the Year 1943.

1941–1943	University of Notre Dame, quarterback
1946	Los Angeles Dons, quarterback
1947–1948	Chicago Rockets, quarterback

This 6 ft. 1 in, 173 lbs. quarterback was nominated for the All-American award in 1942, was given the Consensus All-American title in 1943 and is also holder of the 1943 Heisman Trophy. As an excellent passer, defensive player and kicker, he was able to accumulate passing totals of 169 of 324 attempts for 2582 yards and 21 touchdowns during three seasons.
Also in: National Football Hall of Fame.

BERWANGER, John Jacob "Jay"
Player
Born March 19, 1914, in Dubuque, Ind; All-American 1934; Consensus All-American, Citizens Savings Player of the Year, Silver Football and Heisman Trophy 1935; Modern All-Time All-American Team.

During his three-year career, Jay Berwanger never saw the University of Chicago win a season. In his sophomore year Jay played five 60-min. games averaging 4 yds. per carry and scoring eight touchdowns. He was the team's leading punter and won the Maroon's Most Valuable Player award that season. In 1934 he became the first Chicago All-American in ten years. Berwanger was drafted in the first round by the Philadelphia Eagles, becoming the first player ever drafted by a professional football team. However, he did not sign.
Also in: National Football Hall of Fame.

BEZDEK, Hugo F.
Coach
Born April 1, 1884, in Prague, Czechoslovakia; died September 19, 1952; All-American fullback 1905.

1908–1912	University of Arkansas, coach
1906	University of Oregon, coach
1913–1917	University of Oregon, coach
1918–1929	Pennsylvania State University, coach
1949	Delaware Valley, coach

Bezdek was the only man to coach major college football and manage big league baseball. He played football for the University of Chicago from 1902 to 1905. He was a prize pupil of Amos Alonzo Stagg. As a player, he was a weak tackler but good on offense. In 1905 he led his team to the Western Conference Big Ten championship, defeating the first Fielding Yost team at Michigan in 56 games. At Oregon in his first year of coaching, Bezdek led the team to an unbeaten season, and in 1916, again undefeated, the Oregon team beat Pennsylvania 14–0 at the Rose Bowl. In addition to coaching, Bezdek managed the Pittsburgh Pirates from 1917 to 1919. In 1922 his Penn State team lost the Rose Bowl 14–3 to Southern California. In 1937–1938, he coached the National Football League Cleveland Rams.
Also in: National Football Hall of Fame.

BIBLE, Dana X.
Coach
See entry in Athletic Directors Hall of Fame, Citizens Savings Hall of Fame Athletic Museum, 1971.
Also in: National Football Hall of Fame.

BIERMAN, Bernard William
Coach
Born Mar. 11, 1894, in Waseca, Minn; Big Ten Medal of Honor 1915; Coach of the Year 1941.

1919–1921	University of Montana, coach
1925–1926	Mississippi State College, coach
1927–1931	Tulane University, coach
1932–1941	University of Minnesota, coach
1945–1950	University of Minnesota, coach

Bierman was the captain at Minnesota in 1915 and also ran the 100 yd. dash in 10 sec. A dedicated, austere coach, he recorded six Big Ten titles, four national championships and five unbeaten seasons at Minnesota. He produced twelve All-Americans there. His favorite story was from the 1935 Stanford-Southern California (USC) game. When a USC player was hurt, Stanford's Jim Coffis rushed over and massaged the injured player's leg. Asked why he had done so, Coffis replied, "Listen, I didn't want to see that guy leave the game. He's the easiest fellow to block I've ever played against."
Also in: National Football Hall of Fame.

BLAIK, Earl "Red"
Coach
Born Feb. 15, 1897, in Dayton, Ohio; All-American 1919; Coach of the Year 1946, 1953 and 1966; Gold Medal from the National Football Foundation.

1934–1940	Dartmouth College, coach
1941–1958	U.S. Military Academy, coach

Blaik played four years at Miami of Ohio, 1914–1917, and two at Army, 1918–1919. He also played baseball and basketball, the first cadet to play three sports against Navy. He joined the Cavalry in 1920, and resigned three years later to enter real estate building business in his native Dayton. He was assistant coach at Army 1923 and 1924, and head coach at Dartmouth 1934–1940 and Army 1941–1958. He developed five undefeated Army teams, and felt that championship

football requires merely hard work. At Dartmouth he produced a 22-game unbeaten string, and his overall record there was 45 – 15 – 4. He produced 33 All-Americans, and 24 of his assistants became head coaches, including Vince Lombardi. He is the father of Bob Blaik, who holds the Army record for the longest punt (74 yds.) in 1950.
Also in: National Football Hall of Fame.

BLANCHARD, Felix A, Jr. "Doc"
Player
Born December 11, 1924, in Bishopville, S.C; father Felix, Sr, football player for Tulane; Sullivan Award, Heisman Trophy, Walter Camp Trophy and the Maxwell Trophy 1945.

During his 25-game career at the U.S. Military Academy, the 6 ft, 210 lb. fullback Doc Blanchard compiled 231 points on 38 touchdowns and 3 extra points, averaging 9.2 points per game. In 1945 he was National Collegiate Athletic Association scoring champion with 115 points on 19 touchdowns. He was half of the famous Blanchard and Davis team of Mr. Inside and Mr. Outside. Blanchard never turned pro.
Also in: National Football Hall of Fame.

BOMAR, R. Lynn
Player
Born 1904 in Gallatin, Tex; chief of Tennessee highway patrol; commissioner of safety for State of Tennessee; All-American team 1923.

1921 – 1924 Vanderbilt University, end
1925 – 1926 New York Giants, end

On offense, the 6 ft. 2 in, 215 lb. Bomar was a leading receiver and on defense he was one of the South's finest linebackers.
Also in: National Football Hall of Fame.

BRADSHAW, James "Rabbit"
Player
Born June 23, 1898, in Green City, Mo; high school football, track and tennis star; participated in college football, basketball and track; attended Univ. Ill, graduated from the Univ. Nev. 1922; All-Pacific Coast 1920 and 1921.

1920 – 1922 University Nevada, quarterback
1924 Kansas City Cowboys, player
1926 Los Angeles Wildcats, player
1927 San Francisco Tigers, player, coach
1928 – 1935 Stanford, backfield coach and basketball coach
Fresno State, head coach

Rabbit Bradshaw was known for his outstanding open field running. He turned professional and spent most of the rest of his career as a coach of football and basketball.

BRICKLEY, Charles E.
Player
Born November 24, 1898, in Boston, Mass; graduated from Harvard; died December 28, 1949; All-American 1912 and 1913; Citizens Savings Player of the Year 1913.

Charles Brickley was Harvard's All-American halfback in 1912 and 1913. In 1913 he drop-kicked 13 field goals with five of those going against Yale for a 15 – 0 victory. Brickley kicked 34 career field goals from 1911 through 1913.

BROWN, John H, Jr. "Babe"
Player
Born September 12, 1891, in Canton, Pa; All-American Guard 1913; served in both world wars; engaged in submarine operations in the South Pacific; returned from Naval duty as a Vice-Admiral; died June 10, 1963, in Wilmington, Del, at age 72.

Babe Brown was part of the Navy team that defeated Army for three consecutive years, from 1910 through 1912, without scoring a touchdown. It was Brown who kicked the winning field goal in 1912. He served as president of the National Football Foundation and Hall of Fame from 1954 until 1963.
Also in: National Football Hall of Fame.

BROWN, John Mack
Player
Born September 1, 1904, in Dorthan, Ala; Citizens Savings Rose Bowl Player of the Year Award 1926; became a Hollywood cowboy screen star.

Johnny Brown was a member of Wallace Wade's undefeated Alabama team of 1925. That team was the first Southern participant in the Rose Bowl. Brown was named outstanding player of that game after having scored three touchdowns.
Also in: National Football Hall of Fame.

BURRIS, Paul "Buddy"
Player
A guard for the Green Bay Packers from 1949 – 1951, Buddy Burris first played for the University of Oklahoma.

BUTKUS, Richard J.
Player
Born December 9, 1942 in Chicago, Ill; All-American 1963; Consensus All-American 1964; All-Star Game 1965.

1962 – 1964 University of Illinois, linebacker
1967 – 1973 Chicago Bears, linebacker

Dick Butkus received early acclaim with his nomination for Schoolboy All-American fullback. As an undergraduate at Illinois, Butkus played in the 1963 Rose Bowl and the 1965 College All-Star Game. As a pro with the Chicago Bears, Dick intercepted five passes in his rookie year. He was voted as the player that National Football League coaches would most like to have on their teams. Butkus continued as a premier middle linebacker of the 1960s and early 1970s. He played in the Pro Bowl every year from 1965 through 1971. Butkus' later career was plagued by serious knee problems.

BUTTS, Wallace J. "Wally"
Coach
Born Feb. 7, 1905, in Milledgeville, Ga; graduated from Mercer Col. in 1928; died Dec. 17, 1973, in Athens, Ga.

1938 University of Georgia, asst. coach
1939 – 1960 University of Georgia, head coach

Butts coached prep schools for nine years, losing only ten games. He became assistant coach at Georgia in 1938 and head coach in 1939. His 1941 team defeated Texas

Christian University in the Orange Bowl 40 – 26 and his 1942 Bulldogs shut out UCLA 9 – 0 in the Rose Bowl. His teams won four Southeastern Conference championships and played in six bowl games: the two shown above; Sugar Bowl 1947, defeated North Carolina 20 – 10; Gator Bowl 1948, tied Maryland 20 – 20; Orange Bowl 1949, lost to Texas 41 – 28; Orange Bowl 1960, defeated Missouri 14 – 0. He had a 138 – 86 – 9 record at Georgia. He developed Frank Sinkwich, Charlie Trippi, John Rauch and Zeke Bratkowski. He was accused by the *Saturday Evening Post* of conspiring with Bear Bryant to fix the 1962 Georgia-Alabama game. Both brought suit against Curtis Publishing Co; Butts was awarded $593,916.75, one of the largest judgements in history (Bryant settled out of court).
Also in: National Football Hall of Fame.

BYRD, Harry C.
Coach
Born February 12, 1889; graduated from Univ. Md.

Byrd coached football at the University of Maryland 1911 – 1934 with a record of 121 – 85 – 17.

CAGLE, Christian K. "Red"
Player
Born May 1, 1905, in DeRidder, La; forced out of the U.S Military Academy due to his marriage while still a cadet; Consensus All-American 1927 and 1929; All-American 1928; Citizens Savings Player of the Year 1928; co-purchaser of the Brooklyn Dodgers football team, sold interests the following year; died December 26, 1942, in New York City at the age of 37 after having been found at the foot of the subway stairs with a fractured skull.

The lightening fast redhead could run just as well to his left as to his right. His great blocking and tackling ability as a halfback with Army brought him a unanimous vote for the All-American of 1928 as well as the Consensus All-American title of 1927 and 1929. Cagle coached Mississippi State and played some pro ball with the New York Giants before his early death in 1942.
Also in: National Football Hall of Fame, Louisiana Sports Hall of Fame.

CALDWELL, Charles W, Jr.
Coach
Born Aug. 2, 1901, in Bristol, Va; died Nov. 1, 1957.

1928 – 1942 Williams College, coach
1945 – 1956 Princeton University, coach

Caldwell was the first Princeton coach to win six of the Big Three championships, and his 1950 and 1951 teams were undefeated. From October 1949 to November 1952 he won 30 out of 31 games. As an undergraduate, he starred in football and baseball. In 1945, 1950 and 1951 his teams beat the favored Cornell teams, and in 1946 beat a Pennsylvania squad favored by 33 points. His 1945 Princeton squad won the Eastern Intercollegiate Baseball League title. In 1925 he pitched in major league baseball for the New York Yankees and played basketball for a Montclair, N.J, Athletic Club championship squad. In college he earned three varsity letters each in football, baseball and one in basketball. He wrote two books on football coaching: *Modern Single-Wing Football* and *Modern Football for the Spectator.*
Also in: National Football Hall of Fame.

CAMP, Frank
Coach
Frank Camp coached at the University of Louisville 1936 – 1958 with a 118 – 95 – 2 record.

CAMP, Walter
Coach
Born April 7, 1859, in New Haven, Conn; attended Yale Univ. and Yale Medical School; died March 14, 1925.

Camp is famous for the All-American team he selected for 36 years before his death, but he made many other significant contributions to the game. He is credited with proposing the idea of the scrimmage line at the 1880 rules conference of the American Intercollegiate Football Association (AIFA). Until then, American football was a continuous action game, with play stopping only occasionally. As a freshman at Yale in 1876, Camp helped organize the football team that won the first AIFA championship. He went on to play for six seasons and part of a seventh since at that time there were no rules regarding eligibility. As a halfback, he captained the team from 1878 – 1879 and again in 1881. Yale tallied a record of 25 – 1 – 6 during his playing career with the university. After graduating, Camp held the rather nebulous position of chief football advisor and was treasurer of the Yale Field Association, a job similar to that of athletic director today. He resigned both jobs in 1910 due to rising business demands. Camp is also credited with the "yards-in-downs" idea, which was adopted in 1882, and the "loss-of-yardage" penalty. He proposed the neutral zone for linemen in 1885, but the rule was not adopted until 1906. For years he edited the annual *Football Guide,* in which his All-American selections appeared. Camp died while attending the 1925 meeting of the football rules committee in New York.
Also in: National Football Hall of Fame; and Noteworthy Contributors Hall of Fame, Citizens Savings Hall of Fame.

CAMPBELL, David C.
Player
Born September 5, 1873, in Waltham, Mass; All-American three times; worked in mining; took many exploratory trips throughout North and South America; died June 30, 1949, in Cambridge, Mass.

Dave Campbell captained the 1901 Harvard national champions. He improvised a buck lateral play that went 60 yards for the only touchdown in a 6-0 victory over Army that year. As a three-time All-American, Campbell often forced opposing quarterbacks to run plays on the opposite side of the field from him.
Also in: National Football Hall of Fame.

CANNON, William A.
Player
Born August 2, 1937, in Philadelphia, Miss; All-American 1958; Consensus All-American and Heisman Trophy Winner 1959; practices dentistry in Baton Rouge, La; lobbyist for legalizing dog racing.

1957 – 1959 Louisiana State University, halfback
1960 – 1963 Houston Oilers, halfback
1964 – 1969 Oakland Raiders, halfback
1970 Kansas City Chiefs, player

During his illustrious college career, Cannon rushed for

1867 yards, scored 154 points, caught 31 passes for 522 yards, made 7 interceptions for 115 yards, returned 31 punts for 349 yards and kicked off 21 times for 616 yards. In 1960 he was drafted in the first round by the Houston Oilers for whom he led the league in yards rushing that year with 948 on 200 attempts for six touchdowns. His combined net yardage in 1961 was 2043. In an 11-year pro career Cannon caught 236 passes for 3656 yards, scored 47 touchdowns and a total of 392 points.
Also in: Louisiana Sports Hall of Fame.

CARIDEO, Frank F.
Player
Born in Mt. Vernon, N.Y; All-American 1929 and 1930.

Frank Carideo was discovered at Mt. Vernon High School by Roy Mills and turned into a punter and excellent corner kicker. At Notre Dame, Carideo was a good quarterback winning unanimous approval for the All-American award of 1929 and 1930.
Also in: National Football Hall of Fame.

CARPENTER, C. Hunter
Player
Born June 23, 1883, in Louisa County, Va; died February 24, 1953, in Middletown, N.Y.

Hunter Carpenter scored 82 points as halfback for Virginia Polytechnic Institute in 1905, 58 more than his opponents combined. His career point total was 233, but he played football in the days before Southern players were picked for All-American.
Also in: National Football Hall of Fame and Virginia Hall of Fame.

CARPENTER, Walker
Player
Walker Carpenter went to the Detroit Heralds in 1919 after playing tackle for Georgia Tech.

CARROLL, Charles O.
Player
Born August 13, 1906, in Seattle, Wash; Consensus All-American, 1928; Washington's Flaherty Medal; King County, Wash. district attorney for 22 years beginning in 1948.

Chuck Carroll was the Consensus All-American of 1928. As halfback 1926–1928, Chuck Carroll was at the helm of the Washington three-year record of 24 and 8 with 688 points.
Also in: National Football Hall of Fame.

CASANOVA, Leonard
Coach
See entry in Athletic Directors Hall of Fame, Citizens Savings Hall of Fame Athletic Museum, 1975.
Also in: National Football Hall of Fame; and Collegiate Sports Information Directors Hall of Fame, Citizens Savings Hall of Fame Athletic Museum.

CASSADY, Howard "Hopalong"
Player
Born March 2, 1934, in Columbus, Ohio; All-American 1954 and 1955; Heisman Trophy, Maxwell Award, Silver Football, Walter Camp Trophy 1955.

1952–1955	Ohio State University, halfback
1956–1961	Detroit Lions, halfback
1962	Cleveland Browns, halfback
1963	Detroit Lions, halfback
1964	Philadelphia Eagles, halfback

In four seasons Hopalong Cassady carried 414 times for 2374 yards at an average of 5.7 yards per carry. He received 42 passes for 608 yards and intercepted 10 times for 230 yards, returning 33 punts for 335 yards and 40 kickoffs for 958 yards. Cassady scored 37 touchdowns overall.

CAVANAUGH, Francis W. "Iron Major"
Coach
Born November 23, 1866, in Worcester, Mass; died August 29, 1933, in Marshfield, Mass.

1898	University of Cincinnati, coach
1903–1905	Holy Cross College, coach
1911–1916	Dartmouth College, coach
1919–1926	Boston College, coach
1927–1932	Fordham University, coach

Cavanaugh played three years at Dartmouth from 1895 to 1897, and left to coach at the University of Cincinnati in 1898. During his career, he developed several All-Americans, including Doc Spears and Milt Ghee. He studied law during his early coaching days and was admitted to the Massachusetts bar. He went to war in 1917, enlisting as a private, reaching the rank of major. A war wound affected his sight, and in his last years at Fordham he was practically blind. His greatest fame came at Fordham, where his overall record was 23–2–2. The strong defensive line of 1929–1930 won the name "The Seven Blocks of Granite," a phrase that was renewed for the 1936 Fordham line.
Also in: National Football Hall of Fame.

CHAMBERLIN, B. Guy
Player
See entry in Professional Football Hall of Fame, 1965.
Also in: National Football Hall of Fame.

CHRISTIANSEN, Jason M.
Coach
Born February 2, 1900; graduated from St. Olaf Col.

Jason Christiansen coached at Valparaiso 1929–1940 and at Concordia College 1941–1968. His overall record is 197–112–13 for 40 years of coaching.

CHRISTMAN, Paul C.
Player
Born March 5, 1918, in St. Louis, Mo; died March 2, 1970, in Lake Forest, Ind. of a heart attack at the age of 51.

1938–1940	University of Missouri, halfback
1945–1949	Chicago Cardinals, halfback
1950	Green Bay Packers, halfback

Paul Christman was a cockey forward passer who told a sportswriter before he led his team to victory over undefeated Nebraska in 1939: "I'll pass the bums out of the stadium by the half." Despite an injury in his senior year he set a conference record of 4133 yards in total offense, averaging 4 yards a carry and completing 195 of 426 passes. After six years in the National Football League his record showed 504 completed passes of 1140 (44.2

percent), for 7294 yards and 58 touchdowns. In the 1960s Christman became a television football commentator of the philosophy that "If you have nothing to say, shut up."
Also in: National Football Hall of Fame.

CHROUSER, Harvey
Coach
See entry in Athletic Directors Hall of Fame, Citizens Savings Hall of Fame Athletic Museum, 1977.

CLARK, Earl "Dutch"
Player
See entry in Professional Football Hall of Fame, 1966.
Also in: National Football Hall of Fame; and Athletic Trainers Hall of Fame, Citizens Savings Hall of Fame Athletic Museum.

CODY, Josh C.
Player
Born in 1892 in Franklin, Tenn; died June 19, 1961, in Mt. Lauril, N.J, at age 69.

1914–1916 Vanderbilt University, tackle
1919 Vanderbilt University, tackle

During this 6 ft. 4 in, 220 lb. tackle's career at Vanderbilt the team outscored opponents 1099 to 226, winning 23 games to nine losses. Cody was an all-around athlete, winning varsity letters in four sports and holding a spot as a third-team All-American in 1915 and 1919. He often had the pleasure of watching opposing quarterbacks take plays the other way to avoid his position. In later years Cody coached Clemson, Mercer, Vanderbilt, Florida and Temple.
Also in: National Football Hall of Fame.

CORBUS, William
Player
Born October 5, 1911, in San Francisco, Calif; Consensus All-American 1932; an A. & P. executive.

This 5 ft. 11 in, 195 lb. guard was a fine field goal kicker, a great blocker and a strong defensive player. It was he who often led interference from the "guards-back" formation. In 1933 Corbus was one of the nine sophomores in the starting lineup for Stanford's "Vow Boys."
Also in: National Football Hall of Fame.

CONNOR, George
Player
See entry in Professional Football Hall of Fame, 1975.
Also in: National Football Hall of Fame.

COWAN, Hector W.
Player
Born July 12, 1863, in Hobart, N.Y; a divinity student at Princeton Univ; All-American 1889; Citizens Savings Player of the Year 1889; died October 19, 1941, in Stamford, N.Y. at age 78.

Hector Cowan was an All-American on the first All-American squad in 1889. He played in the 10-0 win over Yale in 1889, snapping a 49-game winning streak. During his career this 5 ft. 11 in. 181 lb. tackle scored 79 touchdowns.
Also in: National Football Hall of Fame.

COY, Edward H. "Ted"
Player
Born May 24, 1888, in Andover, Mass; Citizens Savings Player of the Year 1909; All-Time All-American 1928; died in 1935 of pneumonia at age 47.

During his career Ted Coy played in only one losing game. He was captain of the 1909 "Wonder Team" that defeated all ten opponents allowing them no points and no position within their 25-yard line.
Also in: National Football Hall of Fame.

CRISLER, Herbert Orin "Fritz"
Coach
See entry in Athletic Directors Hall of Fame, Citizens Savings Hall of Fame Athletic Museum, 1970.
Also in: National Football Hall of Fame.

CURTICE, Jack C. "Cactus Jack"
Coach
See entry in Athletic Directors Hall of Fame, Citizens Savings Hall of Fame Athletic Museum, 1973.

DALRYMPLE, Gerald "Jerry"
Player
Born August 6, 1907, in Arkadelphia, Ark; All-American 1930; Consensus All-American 1931; died September 26, 1962, at age 55.

During the three years that Dalrymple played for Tulane University they lost only one regular season game and the opposition was held scoreless in 18 of 29 games. Zimmerman to Dalrymple was the famed combination of the day helping the 1931 squad win 11 consecutive games until the Rose Bowl, with Dalrymple as their captain.
Also in: National Football Hall of Fame and Louisiana Sports Hall of Fame.

DALY, Charles D.
Player
Born October 31, 1880, in Roxbury Mass; All-American 1898 and 1899; died on February 12, 1959, at age 79.

1898–1900 Harvard University, quarterback
1901–1902 U.S. Military Academy, quarterback
1907 Harvard University, backfield coach
1913–1916 U.S. Military Academy, coach
1919–1922 U.S. Military Academy, coach

While at Harvard the 5 ft. 7 in, 150 lb. quarterback played in only one game—a defeat. He moved to West Point and in 1901 led Army to a 16-0 victory over Navy. Daly was All-American in 1898 and 1899 and second team in 1900. He later coached for his alma mater, producing unbeaten teams in 1914, 1916 and 1922.
Also in: National Football Hall of Fame.

DAUGHERTY, Hugh "Duffy"
Coach
Born September 8, 1915, in Emeigh, Pa; played guard at Syracuse Univ; Coach of the Year 1955.

Daugherty was captain of the 1939 College team after suffering a broken neck in 1938. He coached at Syracuse and later at Michigan State. Under his leadership, the Spartans went to the Rose Bowl three times, winning in 1954 and 1956 and losing in 1966. His team were national champions in 1965. Duffy retired in 1972 with a

109 – 69 – 5 record in 19 seasons. He is now a football commentator on ABC television.

DAVIES, Thomas Joseph

Player

All-American 1918; player for the New York Giants baseball team in 1922 and 1923, shortstop and outfielder.

Tom Davies gained a career total of 4625 yards on the ground, which averages out to 150 yards per game. He made the All-American team in his freshman year and was on the second team in 1920 and 1921. During the Davies years, the Pittsburgh Panthers scored a total of 538 points against 177 for their opponents. After his college career Davies was hired by John Heisman to coach backfield at Pennsylvania. His 26-year coaching career extended to colleges such as Geneva, Rochester, Western Reserve and the University of Scranton, and produced a record of 141 wins, 42 losses and 8 ties.
Also in: National Football Hall of Fame.

DAVIS, Ernest

Player

Born in Uniontown, Pa; Consensus All-American, 1960; All-American and Heisman Trophy, 1961; died of leukemia at the age of 23 on May 18, 1963.

Ernie Davis at Syracuse was the first Black to win the Heisman Trophy. In the 1960 Cotton Bowl he caught an 87-yard pass for a major bowl record, defeating Texas 23 – 14. During his career he rushed for 2386 yards and scored 35 touchdowns. Davis was the first man chosen in the first-round draft of 1962 and was then traded by the Redskins to the Cleveland Browns. Ernie never saw major league play for he was stricken with leukemia shortly after the draft and died during his 23rd year.

DAVIS, Glenn

Player

Born December 26, 1924, in Claremont, Calif; Consensus All-American 1944; Walter Camp Trophy and Maxwell Award 1944; Citizens Savings Player of the Year 1944 and 1946; All-American 1945 and 1946; Heisman Trophy 1946; director of special events for the *Los Angeles Times;* co-starred in the football film "The Spirit of West Point."

1943 – 1946 U.S. Military Academy, halfback
1950 – 1951 Los Angeles Rams, halfback

Glenn Davis, a 5 ft. 9 in, 172 lb. halfback, formed the famed combination with Doc Blanchard of Mr. Inside and Mr. Outside. Davis's record-breaking career included 59 touchdowns, 354 points scored, 57 completions in 126 passes for 1172 yards and 14 interceptions for 147 yards. He played with a bad knee during his years with the Los Angeles Rams but caught an 82-yard touchdown pass from Bob Waterfield in 1950 against the Cleveland Browns.
Also in: National Football Hall of Fame.

De GROOT, Dudley S.

Coach

Died May 5, 1970.

1926 – 1928 University of California, Santa Barbara, coach
1929 – 1931 Menlo College, coach
1933 – 1939 San Jose State College, coach
1940 University of Rochester, coach
1944 – 1945 Washington Redskins, coach
1946 – 1947 Los Angeles Dons (AAFC), coach
1948 – 1949 West Virginia University, coach
1950 – 1952 University of New Mexico, coach

De Groot played for Stanford under Pop Warner and was a member of the U.S. rugby team that won the Olympic title in 1924. In 1939 he coached San Jose State with Pop Warner, and the team was undefeated and untied. In 1945 he coached the Washington Redskins to the Eastern title, but they lost the National Football League championship to the Cleveland Browns, 15 – 14. His collegiate record was 134 – 74 – 12.

DES JARDIEN, Paul R. "Shorty"

Player

Born August 24, 1893, in Coffeyville, Kans; a basketball, baseball and track star, winning 12 varsity letters; All-American 1913; went into private business; died March 7, 1956, in Monrouia, Calif, at age 63.

1912 – 1914 University of Chicago, center
1919 Hammond Pros, guard
1920 Chicago Tigers and Cardinals, player
1921 Rock Island Independents, player

Shorty Des Jardien at 6 ft. 5 in, 182 lbs, was recruited out of Wendell Phillips High School in Chicago for the University of Chicago by Amos Alonzo Stagg. Des Jardien helped Chicago win 18 consecutive games.
Also in: National Football Hall of Fame.

DEVANEY, Robert

Coach

Born April 13, 1915, in Saginaw, Mich; graduated from Alma Col. 1939; Orange Bowl Classic Hall of Honor in 1977.

1957 – 1961 University of Wyoming, coach
1962 – 1972 University of Nebraska, coach

Devaney coached Nebraska to seven Big Eight titles and two national championships; the record in 1970 was 10 – 0 – 1, and in 1971 12 – 0 – 0. The 1965 team won the Big Eight title for the third year in a row and had a perfect record (10 – 0 – 0) until beaten by Alabama in the Orange Bowl. He had an unbeaten streak of 32 games (31 wins and one tie) in 1969 – 1971, the fifth longest streak in the last 50 years. The Cornhuskers were finally beaten by UCLA 20 – 17 in 1972. In eleven seasons, they participated in eight major bowl games: the Orange Bowl 1964, 1966, 1971 – 1973; the Cotton Bowl 1965; the Sugar Bowl 1967; and the Sun Bowl, 1970. He retired after the 1972 season; his career record was 136 – 30 – 7, .806 percent, which placed him ninth among major college coaches.

DeWITT, John R.

Player

Born October 29, 1881, in Phillipsburg, N.J; graduated from Princeton Univ; All-American 1902 and 1903; Citizens Savings College Player of the Year 1903; named by Walter Camp as tackle on his All-Time All-American Team; silver medalist in 1904 Olympics; died July 28, 1930.

John played guard with the Princeton Tigers from 1901 to 1903 and was known to be rough. In fact, he remarked that there were two ways to play him: "Stay out of my

way or get hurt." He didn't go easy on the opponent but let fly the 198 lbs. of his 6 ft. 1 in. frame. DeWitt led the Tigers to a national championship in 1903, trampling the Yale team in its first defeat in two years. John made an 85-yd. touchdown run. Then he kicked 48 yds. from a difficult angle for a field goal, racking up the 11 Princeton points all by himself. During that whole season, the Tigers won eleven games, lost none, and did not let any opposing team score anything above zero against them. DeWitt was also the hammer throw champ of Intercollegiate Association of Amateur Athletes of America from 1901 through 1904. He held a 20-year world record with a toss of 164 ft. 10 in. and at the 1904 St. Louis Olympics was awarded a silver medal.
Also in: National Football Hall of Fame.

DOBBS, Glenn
Player
Born in Frederick, Okla; attended Univ. Tulsa; became Tulsa athletic director and football coach.

1940–1942 University of Tulsa, running back
1946–1947 Brooklyn Dodgers, player
1948–1949 Los Angeles Dons, player

Dobbs's strong point was a rugby-type kick that often carried the ball as far as and farther than 80 yds. In the 1941 Sun Bowl, which pitted Tulsa against Texas Tech, Glenn completed 19 of 24 passes and in so doing got a 30-yd. touchdown. He also made an 86-yd. punt. In 1942 Dobbs led the National Collegiate Athletic Association in passing yards per attempt, with an average of .626 (107 attempts, 67 completions, 1066 yds). He set a season record for total yards offense, 8.0 per play. Undefeated and untied through the 1942 season, Tulsa played in the Sugar Bowl where Dobbs sweetened up a few records. He made a record 76-yd. punt and 9 pass completions in a row. In 1946 Dobbs tied Otto Graham for the All-America Football Conference (AAFC) passing title, having made 136 completions of 269 attempts for 1886 yds. and he led the AAFC in punting with a 47.8-yd. average. Throughout his career, Dobbs made 934 passing attempts with 446 completions, for 5876 yards, 45 touchdowns and a 47.8 percentage. Upon taking charge of the Tulsa team in a new capacity as director, Dobbs initiated a wide-open passing game for which he became very well known in the 1960s.

DOBIE, Gilmour
Coach
Born Jan. 21, 1879, in Hastings, Minn; held a law degree, and invested gainfully in the stock market; died Dec. 23, 1948 in Hartford, Conn.

1906–1907 North Dakota State University, coach
1908–1916 University of Washington, coach
1917–1919 U.S. Naval Academy, coach
1920–1935 Cornell University, coach
1936–1938 Boston College, coach

Dobie was a terrible pessimist, and always predicted the worst for his teams while coaching at North Dakota State. He was undefeated at Cornell from 1921 to 1923, and was regarded as a miracle man in Ithaca after Cornell's 1920 victory over Pennsylvania, a team they had beaten only four times since 1893. A very tough coach, he once had his team running laps after a 72–0 win. He was hostile to the press, and his practices were always closed, even to alumni. "They have big mouths," he said.
Also in: National Football Hall of Fame.

DOBSON, Frank
Coach
A graduate of Princeton University, Frank Dobson started coaching at the University of Georgia in 1909, moving to Clemson 1910–1912, Richmond 1913–1917, South Carolina 1918, again at Richmond 1919–1933 and Maryland 1937–1939. After coaching 28 years, Dobson had a 105–109–23 record.

DODD, Robert L.
Coach
Born Oct. 11, 1908, in Galax, Va; Orange Bowl Classic Hall of Honor in 1977.

1928–1930 University of Tennessee, quarterback
1945–1966 Georgie Institute of Technology, coach

As a 6 ft. 2 in, 193 lb. player, Dodd led Tennessee to nearly unbeaten seasons, losing a total of one game and tying one. As coach at Georgia Tech, he compiled a 165–64–8 record (.713 percent). He kept practice sessions down to 90 mins. since he believed that football should be fun and players should have time to study and go to church. Dodd's teams won six consecutive bowl games: the Orange Bowl twice, the Sugar Bowl twice, the Cotton Bowl and the Oil Bowl. He was a born leader, and earned the famous Tech slogan "In Dodd we trust."
Also in: National Football Hall of Fame.

DONAHUE, Michael J.
Coach
Born June 4, 1876, in County Kerry, Ireland.

1904–1922 Auburn University, coach
1923–1927 Louisiana State University, coach

Donahue earned varsity letters in football, basketball, track and cross-country at Yale. His college coaching record was 120–54–7.
Also in: National Football Hall of Fame.

DORAIS, Charles E.
Coach
Born July 2, 1892, in Chippewa Falls, Wis.

1914–1917 Loras College, coach
1920–1924 Gonzaga University, coach
1925–1942 University of Detroit, coach
1943–1947 Detroit Lions, coach

At 5 ft. 7 in, 145 lbs, Dorais was the passing half of a famous combination with Knute Rockne, which passed Notre Dame to a 35–13 upset over Army in 1913. As coach, he taught a system much like that of Rockne, his roommate at Notre Dame.
Also in: National Football Hall of Fame.

DORMAN, John E.
Coach
Born July 16, 1878; attended Upper Iowa Col.

John Dorman returned to Upper Iowa to coach in 1915, staying until 1959 except for three years in W.W. II. In 44 years, his record was 144–126–16.
Also in: National Association of Intercollegiate Athletics Hall of Fame.

DRAHOS, Nick

Player

Born in Cedarhurst, N.Y; graduated from Cornell University; Consensus All-American 1939 and 1940.

Drahos, a 6 ft. 3 in. tall and 210-lb. bruiser, was part of Cornell's 1939 unbeaten-and-untied team that sneaked off with that year's Ivy League title. In an amazing upset of Ohio State, with Cornell whipping them 23 – 14, Drahos blocked an attempted and unpredictable pass, then scored a last-second field goal. A year later Cornell defeated Dartmouth, 7 – 3, with Drahos kicking the extra point. But officials later ruled that Cornell had mistakenly been allowed a fifth down which gave them that chance for a touchdown in the game's final six seconds. Cornell forfeited the game.

DRURY, Morley E.

Player

Born February 5, 1903, in Midland, Ont; 16-letterman at Long Beach Poly High School; graduated from Univ. Southern Calif; Consensus All-American 1927; Citizens Savings Player of the Year 1927; All-Time Pacific Coast Team 1969.

Drury was a remarkably versatile athlete and a high school star in not just football, but baseball, basketball, water polo and swimming. Then at the University of Southern California (USC) he was a three-year player on the hockey team and a major force in the development of a college hockey league. At 6 ft. and 185 lbs, Morley possessed a strength and agility that made him a great passer and runner. A particular USC performance saw him take the team to 43 first downs in a 1925 game against Pomona College.
Also in: National Football Hall of Fame.

DUDLEY, William "Bullet Bill"

Player

See entry in Professional Football Hall of Fame, 1966.
Also in: National Football Hall of Fame; and Major League Football Hall of Fame, Citizens Savings Hall of Fame Athletic Museum.

DUFFIELD, Marshall

Player

Born August 5, 1910, in Salt Lake City, Utah; attended Santa Monica High School in Calif, Univ. Southern Calif. (USC), law school at Southern Western 1932 – 1934; All-American 1930; All-Coast Quarterback 1929 and 1930.

Duffield lettered in a variety of sports in high school, but he devoted his college days to football. He was captain of the USC team in 1930, his best season. That year, a consensus of 35 All-American, quarterback selections showed Duffield to be second in line of having made the most teams. He ranked just behind Carideo of Notre Dame.

DURHAM, Paul

Coach

Paul Durham coached at Linfield College, his alma mater, for 20 years with a record of 122 wins, 50 losses and 10 ties.
Also in: National Association of Intercollegiate Athletics Hall of Fame.

ECKERSALL, Walter H.

Player

Born June 17, 1886, in Chicago, Ill; All-American 1904 – 1906; Citizens Savings Player of the Year 1906; died March 24, 1930, in Chicago.

Knute Rockne spoke highly of Eckersall's quick ability to make four basic plays into a "bewildering" offense. And indeed Walt had to rely on brains rather than brawn. At 5 ft. 7 in. and 142 lbs, he did not pack much of a punch in stopping the adversary, but he did keep his own team going strong. Eckersall was a skillful safety and master of the coffin-corner punt. Twice during his career he kicked five field goals in one game. And in 1905 Chicago, led by Eckersall, succeeded in ending the 56-game no-loss streak enjoyed by Michigan.
Also in: National Football Hall of Fame.

EDWARDS, A. Glen "Turk"

Player

See entry in Professional Football Hall of Fame, 1969.
Also in: National Football Hall of Fame; and Major League Football Hall of Fame, Citizens Savings Hall of Fame Athletic Museum.

ELIOT, Ray

Coach

Born in Brighton, Mass; Coach of the Year 1953.

1933 – 1936 Illinois College, coach
1937 – 1959 University of Illinois, coach

Eliot had a record of 23 – 5 – 1 at Illinois College when he joined the University of Illinois coaching staff. He became head coach in 1942, succeeding Bob Zuppke. His 1951 team was undefeated, the first for the Illinis since 1927. The team was the Big Ten champion and ranked fourth nationally in the Associated Press poll. They also beat Stanford in the Rose Bowl 40 – 7. In 1953 he had another Conference championship team, tying State for the Big Ten crown. He coached Illinois for one of the longest tenures in conference history. In 1955 he was president of the American Football Coaches Association.

ENGLE, Charles A. "Rip"

Coach

Born March 26, 1906, in Salisbury, Md.

1944 – 1949 Brown University, coach
1950 – 1966 Pennsylvania State University, coach

Engle was the head coach at Brown, where he introduced the winged-T formation. In 1949 Brown won eight out of nine, losing only to Princeton. His six-year record at Brown was 31 – 27 – 4, and his overall record at Penn State was 101 – 47 – 14.
Also in: National Football Hall of Fame and Providence Gridiron Hall of Fame.

EVANS, George

Coach

A graduate of the University at Des Moines, George Evans coached football 26 years at Northern Illinois 1929 – 1954 with a record of 132 – 70 – 20.

FAUROT, Donald B.

Coach

See entry in Athletic Directors Hall of Fame, Citizens Savings Hall of Fame Athletic Museum, 1970.

Also in: Missouri Sports Hall of Fame and National Football Hall of Fame.

FEATHERS, William "Beatty" "Big Chief"
Player

Born August 4, 1908, in Bristol, Va; graduated from Univ. Tenn; Consensus All-American 1933; named by George Trevor to All-Time All-Southern Team 1933; Citizens Savings College Player of the Year 1933; University of Tennessee Football Hall of Fame Room; became head coach at N. C. State Univ.

1931–1933 University of Tennessee, halfback
1934–1937 Chicago Bears, halfback
1938 Brooklyn Dodgers, halfback
1940 Green Bay Packers, halfback

Beatty maintained a brutal pace in college ball, utilizing every bit of a 5 ft. 10 in. and 180 lb. powerhouse. In 30 games, he scored 198 points and swallowed up 2014 offense yards, rushing for 1888. Then as a professional player he was named All-National Football League in 1934 with a record of 1004 yards in 117 attempts and 8 touchdowns scored. He was the first pro ever to gain 1000 yards in one season. Once out of pro ball, Feathers went back to college as head coach of North Carolina, from 1944 to 1957.
Also in: National Football Hall of Fame.

FENIMORE, Robert "Blond Blizzard"
Player

Born October 6, 1925, in Woodward, Okla; attended Okla. State Univ; All-American 1944; Consensus All-American 1945; pursued insurance business at Stillwater, Okla.

1943–1946 Oklahoma State University, back
1947 Chicago Bears, back

Over four years, Fenimore accumulated 208 points for Oklahoma State plus a reputation as the "triple-threat halfback." But in regard to touchdowns, Bob backed threats with results and made 49 touchdowns. He collected 4627 offense yds. total and punted an average 38.2 yds. A difficult senior year topped off a commendable four-year stint when injuries forced him to sit out all but five games of the season. By far his most glorious year was 1945 when Bob took the Cowboys to a slam victory over Texas Christian in the Cotton Bowl. The score was 34–0.
Also in: National Football Hall of Fame.

FERRARO, John
Player

From 1942 through 1944, John put forth outstanding efforts as tackle on the University of Southern California team.
Also in: National Football Hall of Fame.

FESLER, Wesley E.
Player

Born June 29, 1908, in Youngstown, Ohio; graduated from Ohio State Univ; Consensus All-American 1928 and 1929; All-American 1930; Silver Football 1930; coaching career spanned twenty years; became director of sales relations with an investors services company.

For two years Fesler played for Ohio State and played well, giving efforts worthy of honor. But he assumed the role of coach early on and gradually built a dossier of experience which returned him to Ohio State as top coach. He began as end coach for the Ohio freshman squad, then went to Harvard as end coach. In 1940 Fesler accepted the head coach position at Wesleyan in Connecticut, then at the University of Pittsburgh in 1946. From 1947 to 1951 he was back at his alma mater keeping the Buckeyes in crack shape. In 1951 he moved to a coaching slot at the University of Minnesota where he stayed for three years.
Also in: National Football Hall of Fame.

FINCHER, William E.
Player

Born in Spring Place, Ga; graduated from Georgia Inst. Technol; Second Team 1918; All-American 1920; longtime affiliation with Coca-Cola Company.

Fincher measured 6 ft. tall and weighed 190 lbs. and didn't usually meet with much argument. Such was the case in 1929 when the president of Yale University, James Angell, asked an opinion of the burly tackle. Expressing his personal view of football, Fincher replied that a good player crosses the scrimmage line to "tear the guts right out of them." Angell, astonished, asked a few more questions, but only a few.
Also in: National Football Hall of Fame.

FISH, Hamilton
Player

Born December 7, 1888, in Harrison, N.Y; graduated from Harvard Univ; named by Walter Camp to All-Time All-American Team 1908; organized Harvard Law School football team; served in U.S. House of Representatives from 1920 to 1945, leader in investigating subversive activities and foremost force in bringing back Unknown Soldier for U.S. burial; proposal for arbitration of Danzig issue before W.W. II; political inclination carried through to grandson Hamilton Fish III, New York Congressman.

In 1908 the Harvard University football team was national champion and Hamilton Fish was captain. The best example of his nonstop ability and ball sense is the "miracle play" so named by sportswriters of the 1908 Harvard-Dartmouth confrontation. Fish took off on a long pass route but was downed at the 5-yard line before the ball arrived. Not faltering for an instant, he hung in to make the catch. Some controversy arose surrounding Fish's potential deadliness with a massive 6 ft. 4 in. and 225 lb. physique. During an Army versus Harvard game, the completion of a particular play resulted in the death of opponent Ici Byrne. Fish was said to have led the play, but it was found that Byrne got hurt tackling the Harvard low-going, full-force fullback. In 1910 Fish instigated the Harvard Law School football team made of former Harvard and Yale players. Later he taught the Army tacklers a few tricks which helped the team defeat Yale twice. Before Fish had come to the rescue, Army had never trounced those stalwart Yale men.
Also in: National Football Hall of Fame.

FOLSOM, Frederick G.
Coach

Born Nov. 9, 1873, in Old Town, Minn; graduated from Dartmouth, Col. in 1895; died Nov. 11, 1944.

1895–1899 University of Colorado, coach
1901–1903 University of Colorado, coach
1903–1906 Dartmouth College, coach
1908–1915 University of Colorado, coach

While coaching at Colorado, Folsom compiled a seven-season record of 37–10–1 and at Dartmouth, 29–5–4. In his 19 years of coaching he had a 106–28–6 record, with a .779 percentage.

FRANK, Clinton
Player
Born in St. Louis, Mo; attended Yale Univ; father of ten; All-American 1936, 1937; Heisman Trophy 1937; Maxwell Award 1937; Lt. Col. in the Air Force and aid to General Doolittle during W.W. II; heads advertising agency with offices across the nation.

Clinton was captain of the Yale team and also nearly indispensable because of great talent in playing the game. His 5 ft. 10 in. and 190 lbs. took him all over the field as passer, blocker, tackler—"one of the finest all-round backs," according to Greasy Neale. Neale also called him "a miracle on defense."
Also in: National Football Hall of Fame.

FRANKOWSKI, Raymond
Player
Ray Frankowski played guard during his college years at the University of Washington, then went on to play pro ball with the Green Bay Packers and the Los Angeles Dons.

FRANZ, Rod
Player
Rod Franz attended the University of California at Berkeley and starred in football there.
Also in: National Football Hall of Fame.

FRIEDMAN, Benjamin
Player
Born 1905 in Cleveland, Ohio; a great popularizer of football, adding inventiveness and color; Consensus All-American, 1925, 1926.

1924–1926 University of Michigan, quarterback
1927 Cleveland Bulldogs, quarterback
1928 Detroit Wolverines, quarterback
1929–1931 New York Giants, quarterback
1932–1934 Brooklyn Dodgers, quarterback

Benny was reputed one of the smartest quarterbacks in history and one of the greatest passers. Much of his success had to do with temperament, for Friedman was fiercely competitive and hated to lose. His first year at Michigan proved in some ways dissatisfying and he debated leaving for Dartmouth. He stayed, and in 1926 was a strong combinative force with end Bennie Oosterbaan. The two of them were a formidable twosome in Michigan's win over the Ohio State Buckeyes 17 to 16. Red Grange has stated that of all quarterbacks he'd come up against, Friedman was the best. Perhaps his abilities are shown by his never once getting injured in ten years of college and pro ball. Friedman's secret was finesse.
Also in: National Football Hall of Fame.

GAMAGE, Harry
Coach
Born February 3, 1900; graduated from Univ. Ill.

Harry Gamage coached at Kentucky 1927–1933 and South Dakota 1934–1941 and 1946–1955. In 25 years he had a 122–88–15 coaching record in football.

GARBISCH, Edgar W.
Player
Born April 7, 1900, in Indiana; graduated from Washington and Jefferson Col; All-American 1922, 1924. Third Team 1923.

1917–1920 Washington and Jefferson College, guard
1921–1924 U.S. Military Academy, center

Garbisch had his best year in 1924 when he was captain of the Army team. Following a much-anticipated victory over Navy that year, he was hoisted atop his teammates shoulders and carried off the field. It was enough to make his mother forget her lament that Eddie never pursued a career as a concert pianist. She remarked that even the great Paderewski had never been borne off the stage in triumph. Garbisch was a hardy player who refused to give up. He played five games against Notre Dame with no substitution, which is a test of stamina according to Grantland Rice. A serious young man and quite devout, Garbisch led the Army cadets in prayer before each game.
Also in: National Football Hall of Fame.

GARRETT, Michael L.
Player
Born April 12, 1944, in Los Angeles, Calif; attended Univ. Southern Calif; played college baseball and later attempted professional baseball; All-American 1964, 1965; Heisman Trophy 1965.

1963–1965 University of Southern California, halfback
1966–1969 Kansas City Chiefs, running back
1972 San Diego Chargers, back

Garrett's superior skill was being able to run long and tire little. And although he was fairly small at 5 ft. 9 in. and 195 lbs, his persistence in going for yardage made up for size. In 1965 he was National Collegiate Athletic Association rushing champ having made 1440 yards in 267 carries. In 1966 and again in 1969 he played in the All-American Football League (AFL) championship games. In 1967, the year of his first Super Bowl, he rushed for 1089 yards. January 1, 1967, was a red-letter day when Garrett tied three AFL play-off career records, with two touchdowns, three punt returns and 12 points. At the 1970 Super Bowl IV, Garrett scored a touchdown and at the close of the season just afterward announced his intent to retire for baseball. The decision faded quickly when he was pursued by the San Diego Chargers. In 1972 for the Chargers, Garrett rushed for 1031 yards in 272 attempts.

GAUTHIER, George
Coach
See entry in Athletic Directors Hall of Fame, Citizens Savings Hall of Fame Athletic Museum, 1971.

GINN, Ralph
Coach
Born July 23, 1907, in Lenox, Iowa; attended the Univ. Mo; died May 26, 1972, in Brookings, S.Dak.

Ginn coached at high schools in Tarkio and Brookings, at Tarkio College, Wayne State and South Dakota State University 1947–1968. His 24-year record was 119–98–10. He also coached basketball, track and field, winning Conference titles in both, as well as football. He produced nine North Central Conference championship teams at South Dakota State, and his 1950 team was undefeated.

GIPP, George "Gipper"
Player

Born February 18, 1895, in Lauriam, Mich; master of odd jobs from cab driver to card and pool hustler; brought to Notre Dame on baseball scholarship; brilliant in the big games, indifferent to the small; All-American 1920; died of pneumonia on December 4, 1920.

Gipp had a disconcerting habit of leaving Notre Dame and turning up at a different school. And each time, coach Knute Rockne would go off to retrieve him. Most of what is said about the Gipper has attained legendary quality and yet, despite his early death, recognition is warranted in regards to his natural playing ability and his personality. As a freshman, Gipp pulled his first surprising move. In one game he made as though to punt at Notre Dame's own 38-yd. line, yet he let fly instead with a 62-yd. kick. Other highlights of his career add luster to the battles between Notre Dame and chief adversary Army. In 1919, as part of Rockne's first unbeaten and untied team, Gipp made a touchdown on a 7 yd. run after setting the whole thing up with 75 yds. of passing. Then a last long pass made it a sure Notre Dame victory with 12 to 9. In 1920, again facing Army, Gipp turned on the power in his 6 ft. 2 in. 185 lb. frame to gain a total of 332 yds. and a final score of 27 to 17, after being down 14 to 17 at the half. For much of that season's final game against Northwestern, Gipp sat out with a bad shoulder and plaguing cold. He stepped in long enough to throw a 45-yd. touchdown pass. But the cold worsened and became penumonia which brought on his early death. Eight years later, Notre Dame again battled an unbeaten Army team and hung in limbo at the half with 0 to 0. Rockne told the despondent team to get out and "win it for the Gipper," as Gipp had requested on his deathbed. Notre Dame won 12 to 6, never questioning that their coach's story may have been just that.
Also in: National Football Hall of Fame.

GOLDBERG, Marshall "Biggie" "Mad Marshall"
Player

Born October 24, 1917, in Elkins, W.Va; graduated from Univ. Pittsburgh; Consensus All-American 1937; Unanimous All-American 1938; president of machine tool company.

1936–1938 University of Pittsburgh, halfback
1939–1943 Chicago Cardinals, halfback
1946–1948 Chicago Cardinals, halfback

Students at the University of Pittsburgh rooted for Goldberg through 29 total games. In that time he made 2231 offense yds. and 18 touchdowns. He also played in the Rose Bowl of 1937. As a professional in 1941, Biggie led the National Football League (NFL) in interceptions with 7 for 54 yds. He was also NFL kickoff return leader with a 24.2 average, 12 for 290 yds. In 1942 his kickoff return average upped to 26.2, with 15 for 393 yds.
Also in: National Football Hall of Fame and West Virginia Sports Writers Hall of Fame.

GRAHAM, Otto Everett, Jr.
Player

See entry in Professional Football Hall of Fame, 1965.
Also in: National Football Hall of Fame; and Major League Football Hall of Fame, Citizens Savings Hall of Fame Athletic Museum.

GRANGE, Harold "Red" "Galloping Ghost"
Player

See entry in Professional Football Hall of Fame, 1963.
Also in: National Football Hall of Fame; and Major League Football Hall of Fame, Citizens Savings Hall of Fame Athletic Museum.

GRAYSON, Robert H.
Player

Born December 8, 1914, in Portland, Ore; Consensus All-American 1934; Unanimous All-American 1935; disappointed by professional football money offers; attended Stanford Law School and accepted backfield coach position; nephew of Harry Grayson, sports editor; executive status with Greyhound Corporation.

Grayson was famous for swiftness and cool control in clutch situations. As a track runner for Oregon Prep he set records in the 100-yd. dash and 200-yd. dash. Then at Stanford he gained 2108 yds. total offense in 486 plays. He played in two Rose Bowls, 1935 and 1936. In 1936 Grayson was drafted in the first round by the Pittsburgh Steelers, then sold for $25,000 to the New York Giants who offered him only $5000 salary. Grayson opted to find some other situation and became backfield coach at Stanford.
Also in: National Football Hall of Fame.

HARDWICK, Huntington R. "Tack"
Player

Born October 15, 1892, in Quincy, Mass; graduated from Harvard Univ; All-American 1912–1914; Early Day All-Time All-America Team; Citizens Savings Player of the Year 1914; died June 26, 1949.

Hardwick started out as a halfback at Harvard but changed to end in his sophomore year. His talents were as runner, receiver, kicker and fierce tackler. The latter made full use of Tack's 6 ft. and 175 lbs. He once commented to his coach that he would willingly jump out a window if the coach asked. Hardwick was certain that a way would be figured out to keep him from getting hurt.
Also in: National Football Hall of Fame.

HARE, T. Truxton "Trux"
Player

Born October 12, 1878, in Philadelphia, Pa; graduated from Univ. Pa; All-American 1897–1900; Early Day All-Time All-America Team; studied law then served as counsel for Gas Improvement Co. of Radnor, Pa; director of Bryn Mawr Hospital 1943–1946, became hospital president 1946–1950; died February 2, 1956, at age 78.

Walter Camp called him "Guard of the Year" of 1899 but Trux might more aptly be called Guard of All Guards. During his collegiate career, which amounted to 55 games, Trux played every minute without ever sitting on the sidelines. He was one of three men ever named to

the All-American First Team four times. His 6 ft. 2 in. and 200 lbs. allowed him versatility in defense and as runner, punter, signal-caller and dropkicker. Also, Trux threw the hammer in the 1900 Olympics and won the silver medal.
Also in: National Football Hall of Fame.

HARLEY, Charles W. "Chic"
Player
Born in Columbus, Ohio: graduated from Ohio State Univ; All-American 1916; died at Danville, Illinois on April 21, 1974.

1916 – 1919 Ohio State University, fullback
1921 Chicago Staleys, fullback

Chic Harley was an excellent runner, passer and kicker plus a sort of "PR" man in popularizing college football over high school football in Columbus. Before Harley, it was always the high school games that drew crowds. In a game against Wisconsin, Chic pulled a smooth and crowd-pleasing move. He snatched the ball out of the arms of the Wisconsin runner and took off all the way down the field to score, never breaking stride nor hesitating. He was one of the greatest players of the nation in his time.
Also in: National Football Hall of Fame.

HARLOW, Richard C.
Coach
Born October 19, 1889, in Philadelphia, Pa; died Feb. 19, 1962.

1915 – 1917 Pennsylvania State University, coach
1922 – 1925 Colgate University, coach
1926 – 1934 Western Maryland College, coach
1935 – 1942 Harvard University, coach
1945 – 1947 Harvard University, coach

Harlow played tackle at Penn State under Bill Hollenback 1908 – 1911, and set a record for blocking punts in five games in 1911. He was assistant coach at Penn State under Hugo Bezdek, known for his deceptive offensive plays. He served as a professor of ornithology until his retirement in 1947. He coached two Kennedys, Joe, Jr, and Bobby, ten years apart at Harvard.
Also in: National Football Hall of Fame.

HARMAN, Harvey J.
Coach
Born November 5, 1900, in Selinsgrove, Pa; graduated from Univ. Pittsburgh.

Harman coached 30 years for an overall record of 140 – 104 – 6 in football. He was at Haverford College 1922 – 1929, University of the South 1930, Pennsylvania 1931 – 1937 and Rutgers 1938 – 1941 and 1946 – 1955.

HARMON, Thomas D. "Old 98"
Player
Born September 28, 1919, in Gary, Ind; graduated from Univ. Mich; Consensus All-American 1939; Citizens Savings College Player of the Year 1939; Unanimous All-American 1940; Heisman Trophy 1940; Associated Press Athlete of the Year 1940; Maxwell Trophy 1940; served in Air Force during W.W. II, pilot; marooned in Japan for 32 days after bailing out; received Silver Star and Purple Heart; father of Mark Harmon, football star of UCLA; involved in television sports commentary in Los Angeles.

1938 – 1940 University of Michigan, halfback
1941 New York Americans, player
1946 – 1947 Los Angeles Rams, player

A football coach once remarked that he would give up a whole team just to have Tom Harmon. And Old 98 on his own could give a whole clan of bruisers a run for their money. At 6 ft. tall and 195 lbs, Harmon had speed, agility and an acute ball-handling sense. During his collegiate career he gained 2338 yds. in 398 carries and completed 101 passes out of 233 attempts. All totaled, Harmon scored 237 points which includes 33 touchdowns, 33 extra points and 2 field goals.
Also in: National Football Hall of Fame.

HARPER, Jesse C.
Coach
Born December 10, 1883, in Pawpaw, Ill; died July 1, 1961.

1907 – 1908 Alma College, coach
1908 – 1912 Wabash College, coach
1913 – 1918 University of Notre Dame, coach

Harper coached the Knute Rockne-Gus Dorais Notre Dame team which made the forward pass a national institution in shattering Army in 1913. He also coached Charlie Bachman who later became a great coach. He was farming in Kansas when Rockne's plane went down; by quirk of fate, it was Harper who identified the body of his successor and former player.
Also in: National Football Hall of Fame.

HARPSTER, Howard
Player
Born May 4, 1907, in Akron, Ohio; Carnegie Inst. Technol; Consensus All-American 1928; returned as head coach from 1933 to 1936.

Despite slight stature at 6 ft. and 160 lbs, Harpster could get the ball up and out into the air. A 65-yd. punt was not unusual for him. A sportswriter of the time believed Harpster to be the greatest football player of the Pittsburgh area. As quarterback, he led Carnegie Tech. to a 19 – 7 – 1 record. In 1928 Harpster became known nationwide when he captained the East team of the East-West Shrine Game. He returned after five years to his alma mater and coached the team to a 12 – 20 – 3 commendable record.
Also in: National Football Hall of Fame.

HART, Edward J. "E.J."
Player
Born May 22, 1887, in Exeter, N.H; graduated from Princeton Univ; All-American 1911; thirty-year career as insurance executive in Chicago; got into mining industry in Canada; died on November 28, 1956, at age 69.

E. J. Hart was so big and powerful that he frightened even his own teammates. At 5 ft. 11 in, he was not overly tall, but the 208 lbs. transmitted formidable force. In fact, E. J. was so hardy that he played three years with a broken bone in his neck. For two years, in 1910 and 1911, he was captain of the team and they were undefeated national co-champions in 1911.
Also in: National Football Hall of Fame.

HART, Leon J.
Player

Born November 2, 1928, in Turtle Creek, Pa; graduated from Notre Dame Univ; Consensus All-American 1947, 1948; Unanimous All-American 1949; Heisman Trophy 1949; Maxwell Trophy 1949.

1946 – 1949 University of Notre Dame, end
1950 – 1957 Detroit Lions, end

Hart was headed for an illustrious career right from the start. As a freshman at Notre Dame, he made the varsity team and began chalking up yards and receptions. In his college career he had 13 touchdown receptions and received 49 passes for 742 yds, averaging 15.1 yds. Later as a professional player, he was elected All-Pro in 1951.
Also in: National Football Hall of Fame.

HAUGHTON, Percy D.
Coach

Born July 11, 1876, in Staten Island, N.Y; died October 27, 1924, in New York City of angina pectoris at age 48.

1899 – 1900 Cornell University, coach
1908 – 1916 Harvard University, coach
1923 – 1924 Columbia University, coach

Haughton played football for Harvard 1895 to 1898. After graduation he coached for Cornell, and his 1912 and 1913 teams won the national championship. His overall coaching record was 96 – 17 – 6, .832 percent. He was the national racquets champion in 1906 and volunteered for the Army in 1918, becoming a Major in chemical warfare.
Also in: National Football Hall of Fame.

HAZEL, Homer H. "Pop"
Player

Born June 2, 1895, in Pifford, N.Y; graduated from Rutgers Univ; All-American 1923, 1924; served as Mississippi athletic director and basketball and football coach; later career as labor relations manager and golf pro; died February 3, 1968.

Hazel was an all-round athlete, proficient in many sports, despite his hefty size at 5 ft. 11 in. and 226 lbs. He played baseball, basketball, golf and participated in track in addition to football. During his collegiate career, Rutgers' record was 14 – 2 – 2.
Also in: National Football Hall of Fame.

HEFFELFINGER, William W. "Pudge" "Heff"
Player

Born December 20, 1867, in Minneapolis, Minn; graduated from Yale Univ; All-American 1889, 1890 and 1891; Early-Day All-America Team; Citizens Savings Player of the Year 1890; coached at California in 1892; published book of football facts; produced first sports quiz show on radio; produced first espionage show "Secret Agent K-7"; died on April 3, 1954, at Blessing, Tex. at age 87.

Beginning in 1882, Heff was involved in football when he organized the Central High School team in Minneapolis. As a freshman at Yale he made the varsity team and eventually conceived some valuable plays, such as the running guards forerunner of modern blocking, and the flying wedge V-play. The publisher of "Heffelfinger Football Facts" played a lot of football to become a know-it-all. In fact, Heff played for the last time at age 63 in a disabled Veterans game of 1930. Ten years earlier and still not exactly young, he played over 56 minutes of the game that pitted All-Stars versus a group of Ohio State graduates. And another story tells of him suiting up to teach a play in a Yale team scrimmage at the age of 49. He barreled into five young players and knocked them out. At 6 ft. 2½ in. and 188 lbs, a shove from Heff could not be taken lightly.
Also in: National Football Hall of Fame.

HEIN, Melvin J.
Player

See entry in Professional Football Hall of Fame, 1963.
Also in: National Football Hall of Fame; and Major League Football Hall of Fame, Citizens Savings Hall of Fame Athletic Museum.

HEISMAN, John
Coach

Born October 23, 1869, in Cleveland, Ohio; died October 3, 1936, in New York City at age 67.

1892 – 1894 Oberlin College, coach
1895 University of Akron, coach
1896 – 1899 Auburn University, coach
1900 – 1903 Clemson University, coach
1904 – 1919 Georgia Institute of Technology, coach
1920 – 1922 University of Pennsylvania, coach
1923 Washington and Jefferson College, coach
1924 – 1927 Rice University, coach

Heisman played for Brown 1887 and 1888 and for Pennsylvania, 1889 to 1891, earning letters at both schools. As coach, he lost only one game in 1899, was unbeaten in 1900. The Heisman Trophy was named in his honor.
Also in: National Football Hall of Fame.

HENDERSON, Elmer C. "Gloomy Gus"
Coach

Born March 10, 1889, in Oberlin, Ohio; graduated from Oberlin Col; died December 16, 1965, at age 76.

1919 – 1924 University of Southern California, coach
1925 – 1935 University of Tulsa, coach
1940 – 1942 Occidental College, coach

Prior to the 1923 Rose Bowl, Henderson engaged in a fist fight with the opposing coach, Hugo Bezdek of Penn State, in front of a capacity crowd and the game was delayed an hour. Gloomy Gus was a formidable coach and had many fine years. His overall coaching record was 126 – 42 – 7, .740 percent.

HENDRICKS, Ted "Mad Stork"
Player

Born November 1, 1947, in Guatemala City, Guatemala; attended Hialeah High School in Florida; graduated from Univ. Miami; All-American 1966, 1967 and 1968; Knute Rockne Trophy 1968, for the outstanding college lineman; varied sportsman who enjoys fishing, hunting and water skiing.

1966 – 1968 University of Miami, defensive end
1969 – 1973 Baltimore Colts, linebacker

Hendricks baffled his opposition. At 6 ft. 7 in. and 215 lbs, he appeared to be a misplaced basketball player. The Mad Stork was a strong tackler. During a 1971 game against the Los Angeles Rams, he ran 31 yds. after a fumble recovery to score. Also that year he saved the 14 – 13 victory over the New York Jets by blocking a down-to-the-wire extra point attempt. He played in the Super Bowl in 1971 and the Pro Bowl in 1972 through 1974.

HENRY, Wilbur F. "Fats" "Pete"
Player
See entry in Professional Football Hall of Fame, 1963.
Also in: Major League Football Hall of Fame, Citizens Savings Hall of Fame Athletic Museum; National Association of Intercollegiate Athletics Hall of Fame and National Football Hall of Fame.

HESELTON, Bernard
Coach
A graduate of the University of Minnesota, Heselton coached 26 years at Northern Illinois for a record of 132 – 70 – 20 in football.

HESTON, William M.
Player
Born September 9, 1878, in Galesburg, Ill; graduated from Univ. Mich; holds record of most touchdowns scored in four-year career—72; All-American 1903, 1904; Selected to the Third Team 1901, 1902; Early Day All-Time All-America Team; Citizens Savings Player of the Year 1904.

Willie Heston was a prime generator of points on Fielding Yost's "Point-a-Minute" team of 1902. That year they slammed Stanford in the Rose Bowl with 49 to zero, setting a total yardage record that held good for 57 years. Heston rushed for 170 yds. in 18 carries in that game. In his whole career he rushed for 2339 yds. and never played in a losing game.
Also in: National Football Hall of Fame.

HICKMAN, Herman M, Jr.
Player
Born October 1, 1911, in Johnson City, Tenn; graduated from Univ. Tenn; All-American 1931; University of Tennessee Football Hall of Fame Room; also professional wrestler, took part in 500 matches; became known for wit as television personality; dubbed "Poet Laureate of the Little Smokies"; died April 25, 1958.

1929 – 1931 University of Tennessee, guard
1932 – 1934 Brooklyn Dodgers, player

At times Hickman was called the "Tennessee Terror," whenever he turned on the juice as one of the fastest linemen in football history. In all of thirty games played during his collegiate career, only one was a loss. He had tremendous blocking ability, a mixture of power and speed. In 1931 he became known for one-man performances in charity games against New York University held in Yankee Stadium. Later he turned to coaching, at Wake Forest, North Carolina State, West Point, and at Yale 1948 through 1951.
Also in: National Football Hall of Fame.

HIGGINS, Robert A.
Coach
Born November 24, 1893, in Corning, N.Y; graduated from Pa. State Univ; All-American 1915, 1919; Lambert Trophy 1947; died June 6, 1969, in Bellefonte, Pa. at age 76.

1920 – 1924 West Virginia Wesleyan University, coach
1925 – 1927 Washington University (Mo.), coach
1930 – 1948 Pennsylvania State University, coach

Higgins played for Penn State 1914 – 1916 and 1919; he was captain of the team in 1919. He played for the Canton Bulldogs 1920 and 1921, and was Penn State assistant coach under Hugo Bezdek 1928 – 1929. His 1947 team was unbeaten, but tied with SMU in the Cotton Bowl. He retired in 1949 with a 91 – 57 – 9 Penn State coaching record.
Also in: National Football Hall of Fame.

HINKEY, Frank A.
Player
Born December 23, 1871, in Ionawanda, N.Y; graduated from Yale Univ; All-American 1891 – 1894; Early-Day All-Time All-America Team; Citizens Savings College Player of the Year 1891; returned to Yale in 1914 as head coach; coached the Dayton Triangles in 1921; died in Southern Pine, N.C, on December 30, 1925, at age 54.

It was his temperament that kept "Silent Frank" going like a motor idling quietly. He was usually shy, moody and turned into himself, but on the field this pent-up energy was cut loose. His size wasn't much of an advantage, at 5 ft. 9 in. and 146 lbs, but his behavior on the field was fierce and almost maniacal. He loved football and carried the ball with him even to classes. Pop Warner said that "pound for pound," Hinkey was the best of all time. As coach at Yale, Frank lacked patience to teach fundamentals. But he brought in a Canadian team to demonstrate the lateral pass on a dead run, the first to introduce such a technique to American football.
Also in: National Football Hall of Fame.

HINKLE, Paul "Tony"
Coach
See entry in Naismith Memorial Basketball Hall of Fame, 1965.
Also in: College Basketball Hall of Fame, Citizens Savings Hall of Fame Athletic Museum; and Indiana Basketball Hall of Fame.

HITCHCOCK, James F.
Player
Born June 28, 1911, in Inverness, Ala; graduated from Auburn Univ; All-American 1932; Baseball All-American 1932; played professional baseball out of college; brother Billy Hitchcock also major leaguer and manager; served as Auburn backfield coach on off-season; elected to Alabama Public Service Commission.

Hitchcock's best year was 1932 when he captained the Auburn Tigers in an undefeated season. He also led the Southern Conference in scoring that year. Although his position was halfback, Hitchcock also served as kicker and set a record of 232 kicks without having a single one blocked.
Also in: National Football Hall of Fame.

HOGAN, James J. "Yale"
Player
Born November 1, 1876, in Glenbane, County Tipperary, Ireland; Yale Univ; active in debate; All-American 1902, 1903 and 1904; Citizens Savings Player of the Year 1902; pursued degree at Columbia Law School; practiced law

from 1908 to 1910; died March 20, 1910, at age 34 of Bright's disease.

Hogan's second name came to be "Yale" because he expressed constant enthusiasm for the school, its sports and debating societies. He was a good student and a congenial fellow, said to play with his sleeves rolled up and a smile on his face. Hogan was aggressive and powerful at 5 ft. 10 in. and 210 lbs. He and running mate Ralph Kinney were the most impressive tackles in Yale history.
Also in: National Football Hall of Fame.

HOLCOMB, Stuart
Coach
See entry in Athletic Directors Hall of Fame, Citizens Savings Hall of Fame Athletic Museum, 1975.

HOLLAND, Jerome H. "Brud"
Player
Born in Auburn, N.Y; graduated from Cornell Univ. with Ph.D. in sociology; All-American 1937, 1938; volunteered time to organizations such as Planned Parenthood-World Population, American Red Cross, Negro College Fund, Urban League, and Boy Scouts of America; president of Hampton Institute and of Delaware State Univ; appointed ambassador to Sweden in 1970.

Holland knew what was meant by teamwork and he had learned about it early. As one of thirteen children, he had to cooperate. The name Brud was given him by his brothers and sisters. Holland was one of the first blacks to be an Ivy Leaguer and as a student at Cornell he was scholar, sportsman and an especially superb defensive football player.
Also in: National Football Hall of Fame.

HOLLENBACH, William M.
Player
Born February 22, 1886, in Blue Ball, Pa; graduated from Univ. Pa; All-American 1908; named to Second Team 1906 and 1907; became president of Hollenbach Coal and Coke Co, Inc, of Philadelphia; died March 12, 1968, at age 82.

Big Bill Hollenbach was captain of the Penn State team in 1908, the year they took the national championship. Their leader had a reputation of playing as though indestructible, with leg fractures, shoulder separations, shin splints and bruises. In 1909 Hollenbach became head coach at Penn State and then went for a year at Missouri before returning in 1911. During 1915 he coached the Pennsylvania Military and in 1916 accepted a stint at Syracuse. Later, for 15 years, he served as Eastern collegiate football official, from 1921 to 1936.
Also in: National Football Hall of Fame.

HOLLINGBERRY, Orin E. "Babe"
Coach
Born July 15, 1893, in Hollister, La; died Jan. 12, 1974, in Yakima, Wash.

Hollingberry coached 17 years at Washington State, finishing his career with a 93–53–14 record, .625 percentage. His 1930 championship team included such greats as Turk Edwards, George Hurley and Mel Hein. His teams were invited to the Rose Bowl three times, losing each time; in 1926 to Alabama 20–0, in 1931 to Alabama, 24–0, and in 1937 to Pittsburgh, 21–0.

HORRELL, Edwin C. "Babe"
Player
Born September 29, 1902, in Jackson, Mo; graduated from Univ. Calif. at Berkeley; All-Coast 1923, 1924; All-American 1923, 1924; became coach at Univ. Calif. at Los Angeles (UCLA) in 1926, staying until 1944; became investor in land, fruit-packing and golf courses.

The 1924 California football team was dubbed the "Wonder Team," and the captain was Babe Horrell. He held the distinction of being the first player to score a touchdown in the brand new Berkeley stadium. Also, throughout his collegiate career, Horrell never played in a losing game. As coach he kept up a glowing reputation, taking the Bruins to their first Rose Bowl Game in 1943, even though his 1939 team was undefeated but tied four times.
Also in: National Football Hall of Fame.

HORVATH, Leslie
Player
Born in South Bend, Ind; graduated from Ohio State Univ; All-American 1944; Heisman Trophy 1944; Chicago Tribune Trophy 1944; Nile Kinnick Trophy 1944; Christy Walsh Trophy 1944; served in U.S. Navy in 1945 and 1946; became dentist in Los Angeles; coach of Junior Bantam team in Los Angeles.

1940–1942	Ohio State University, halfback
1944	Ohio State University, quarterback
1947–1948	Los Angeles Rams, back
1949	Cleveland Browns, back

In 1942 Horvath led his Ohio State teammates to the national championship, then to the Big Ten title in 1944. During the year hiatus, he went into the Army but returned soon enough to get back into the pads. During active duty in the Navy, he served as assistant coach at the Great Lakes Naval Training Station under his former collegiate coach Paul Brown. Les slipped easily into professional play and was known as an exceptional runner and receiver. He ranked third in punt returns in 1948.
Also in: National Football Hall of Fame.

HOWARD, Frank
Coach
Born March 25, 1909, in Barlow Bend, Ala.

Howard played for Alabama 1928–1930; Wallace Wade's 1930 team defeated Washington State in the Rose Bowl 24–0. Howard was dubbed "Little Giant" of Tides "Herd of Red Elephants." At Clemson, his career record was 168–118–12. He took Clemson to six bowl games: the Gator in 1949 and 1952, the Orange in 1951 and 1957, the Sugar in 1959 and the Astro-Blue Bonnet in 1959.

HOWELL, Millard Filmore "Dixie"
Player
Born in Hartford, Ala; graduated from Univ. Ala; Consensus All-American 1934; Citizens Savings College Player of the Year 1934; Citizens Savings Rose Bowl Player of the Year Award 1935; played collegiate and professional and coached; public relations director for construction firm in Los Angeles; died March 2, 1971, after two-year fight with cancer.

1932 – 1934 University of Alabama, running back
1937 Washington Redskins, quarterback

Grantland Rice called him a "Human Howitzer," mindful of Howell's tremendous punting ability. In 1933 in three separate games, he made an 89-yd, an 80-yd. and an 83-yd. punt. He was also formidable as part of the Howell-to-Hutson passing duo. In 1935 at the Rose Bowl game, Dixie completed 9 out of 12 passes for 160 yds. including a 59 yd. pass for a touchdown. He also rushed for 79 yds. which included a 67 yd. touchdown. And in the six times he punted, he averaged 43.8 yds. In 1938 Howell embarked on a coaching career and went to Arizona State Univ. for three years. Then from 1942 to 1950 he coached at Idaho State Univ.
Also in: National Football Hall of Fame.

HUGHES, Harry W.
Coach
Born October 9, 1887, in DeKalb County, Mo; died July 26, 1953, in Fort Collins, Colo, at age 66.

1910 University of Oklahoma, assistant coach
1911 – 1944 Colorado State College, coach

Hughes was a halfback and place kicker at Oklahoma 1904 – 1906. His record as coach at Colorado was 125 – 89 – 18, and his teams were unbeaten twice, 1915 and 1916. He developed track star Glenn Morris who won the 1936 Olympic decathlon championship.

HUTSON, Donald M.
Player
See entry in Green Bay Packers Hall of Fame, 1972.
Also in: Major League Football Hall of Fame, Citizens Savings Hall of Fame Athletic Museum; National Football Hall of Fame and Professional Football Hall of Fame.

JENNINGS, Morley
Coach
Born in 1890 in Holland, Mich.

1912 – 1925 Ouachita Baptist University, coach
1926 – 1940 Baylor University, coach

Jennings played one season in the backfield for Albion before attending Mississippi A&M (now Mississippi State). His coaching record was 32 – 14 – 10 at Ouachita and 83 – 60 – 6 at Baylor.
Also in: National Football Hall of Fame.

JESSE, Daniel
Coach
Born February 22, 1901; graduated from Univ. Pacific.

Jesse coached at Trinity College in Connecticut 1932 – 1966 except the four war years. In 32 years he had an overall football record of 150 – 76 – 7.
Also in: American Association of College Baseball Coaches Hall of Fame.

JOESTING, Herbert W.
Player
Born April 17, 1905, in Little Falls, Minn; majored in forestry at Univ. Minn; worked for Charles Pearson's Co. and the State of Minnesota motor vehicle division; died October 2, 1963, in St. Paul, Minn.

1925 – 1927 University of Minnesota, fullback
1929 – 1930 Minnesota Redjackets, player-coach
1930 – 1931 Frankfort Yellowjackets, back
1931 – 1932 Chicago Bears, back

"I play each game for all it's worth. No more can be asked of an athlete than that he goes all-out in every situation." So when Joesting played for the University of Minnesota Gophers they had winning seasons three consecutive years, and he became the first Minnesota man in ten years to be selected for the All-American team two years straight, 1926 and 1927. He was a good blocker and runner who played profesional football and ended his career with the Chicago Bears.
Also in: National Football Hall of Fame.

JONES, Calvin
Player
Calvin Jones played for the University of Iowa.

JONES, Howard H.
Coach
Born Aug. 23, 1885, in Excello, Ohio; died July 27, 1941, in Toluea Lake, N.Y.

1908 Syracuse University, coach
1909 – 1913 Yale University, coach
1910 Ohio State University, coach
1916 – 1923 University of Iowa, coach
1924 Duke University, coach
1925 – 1940 University of Southern California, coach

Jones played at Yale 1905 – 1907, and became Yale's first paid head coach in 1913. At USC, his teams won seven Pacific Coast Conference titles, two national titles and five out of five Rose Bowl games. His brother Tad was also a famous player and coach. He once told his players not to take advantage of ailing Bobby Grayson, Stanford All-American halfback; Grayson was not hit on his bad knee all day. He considered his career highlight to be defeating Notre Dame 10 – 7 in 1921. His career record was 189 – 64 – 21, and he developed 19 All-Americans; 13 at USC. Jones was the author of two books on football.
Also in: National Football Hall of Fame.

JONES, Lawrence McC. "Biff"
Coach
Born October 8, 1895, in Washington, D.C.

1926 – 1929 U.S. Military Academy, coach
1932 – 1934 Louisiana State University, coach
1935 – 1936 University of Oklahoma, coach
1937 – 1941 University of Nebraska, coach

Jones played with Army 1914 – 1916; his later record as coach with Army was 30 – 8 – 2. His record at Louisiana State was 20 – 5 – 6, at Oklahoma, 9 – 6 – 3 and at Nebraska, 28 – 14 – 4. He took Nebraska to the 1941 Rose Bowl, losing to Stanford 21 – 13.
Also in: National Football Hall of Fame.

JORDAN, Lloyd Paul
Coach
Born December 14, 1900; graduated from Univ. Pittsburgh.

During 22 years of coaching, Jordan has a 100 – 69 – 7 record in football. He was at Amherst 1932 – 1942 and 1946 – 1949 and at Harvard 1950 – 1956.

JUSTICE, Charles "Choo Choo"

Player

Born May 18, 1924, in Asheville, N.C; Consensus All-American; All-American 1948; runner-up for Heisman Trophy 1949.

1946 – 1949 University of North Carolina, halfback
1950 Washington Redskins, halfback
1952 – 1954 Washington Redskins, halfback

In four years of college football Choo Choo Justice became a living legend for North Carolina football fans. They called this Consensus All-American and 1948 All-American Zeus, Jupiter and Ra and watched him capture the North Carolina total offense record in 1948 and 1949 with over 5000 yds, the college punting record and the National Collegiate Athletic Association punting record with 231 punts for 9839 yds. In 1948 he surprised Wake Forest with a 76-yd. punt. He played in the Sugar Bowl in 1947 and 1949 and drew national attention in the 1950 Cotton Bowl, making the cover of several magazines. At the end of a career that inspired the song, "All the Way, Choo Choo," Justice had 2634 yds. on 536 rushes, completed 159 of 321 passes for 2237 yds, caught 18 passes for 232 yds, intercepted 2 passes for 33 yds, returned 68 punts for 969 yds, returned 31 kickoffs for 825 yds. and scored 39 touchdowns for 234 points.
Also in: National Football Hall of Fame.

KAER, Morton A. "Devil May"

Player

Born September 7, 1902, in Omaha, Nebr; bronze medal in pentathlon at the 1924 Olympics in Paris.

1923 – 1926 University of Southern California (USC), halfback
1931 Frankfort Yellowjackets, quarterback

Playing under Howard Jones during his last two years of college football, Morton Kaer scored a USC record of 216 points that remained unbeaten for 40 years until Hall of Famer O. J. Simpson came along. As coach of a small California school team, Weed High School, he compiled a 187 – 47 – 7 win-loss-tie record over a 28-year period, had five unbeaten seasons, nine seasons with only one loss and 17 complete or shared championships.
Also in: National Football Hall of Fame.

KAVANAUGH, Kenneth W.

Player

Born November 23, 1916, in Little Rock, Ark; graduated from La. State Univ; star baseball player; Sugar Bowl All-Star Team 1937 and 1938; All-Southeastern Conference 1938 and 1939; Knute Rockne Trophy 1939; Southeastern Conference Most Valuable Player 1939; military service in W.W. II as a bomber pilot; awarded Distinguished Flying Cross and Air Medal with four oakleaf clusters.

1937 – 1939 Louisiana State University, end
1940 – 1941 Chicago Bears, end
1945 – 1950 Chicago Bears, end

Ken Kavanaugh, more than just probability would explain, was in the right place at the right time and could run the ball faster to his goal than his opponents could catch him. In a 1937 game against Rice, he returned a fumble for 100 yds. and the longest touchdown in modern Louisiana State University history. The next year he made a 62-yd. reception against Texas and in 1939, his senior year, returned an interception on 80 yds. in a game against Holy Cross. Playing in two Sugar Bowls (1937 and 1938) and the Blue-Gray College All-Star games, this end was the first linesman to win the Knute Rockne Trophy in 1939. Upon graduation he was offered both a baseball contract with the St. Louis Cardinals and a football contract from Hall of Famer George Halas to play with the Chicago Bears; he chose the Bears. As a professional, he ran 42 yds. with a fumbled lateral pass in a title game against the New York Giants to register a touchdown and was All-NFL in 1946 and 1947. Later he coached six Eastern Conference champions and the world championship team of 1956.
Also in: Arkansas Hall of Fame, Louisiana Sports Hall of Fame and National Football Hall of Fame.

KAW, Edgar L.

Player

Won three varsity letters in baseball at Cornell Univ; All-American fullback 1921; All-American halfback 1922; joined Fox Studios as executive in 1925; later served in front office of dog food manufacturer.

1920 – 1922 Cornell University, halfback
1924 Buffalo Bisons

Both a fine offensive and defensive player, Edgar Kaw led the National Collegiate Athletic Association in touchdowns in 1921 with 15, five of which he scored in a game against the University of Pennsylvania at Franklin Field. The Cornell teams of 1921 and 1922 were undefeated and profited from Kaw's fine punting.
Also in: National Football Hall of Fame.

KAZMAIER, Richard W. Jr. "Kaz"

Player

Born November 23, 1930, in Toledo, Ohio; graduated from Princeton Univ; All-American 1950; Heisman Trophy (unanimous vote) 1951; Maxwell Trophy 1951; named president of the National Football Hall of Fame in 1974.

Kazmaier went to Princeton for a good education and found himself to be a triple threat on the school's football team. His kicking, running and passing inspired the team to two undefeated seasons and the Ivy League Big Three championship in 1950 and 1951. In 1951 Kazmaier set the game record in pass completion percentage with .882. That same year he led the National Collegiate Athletic Association in passing completion with a .626, total offense yds. with 1827 and touchdowns-accounted-for with 22. At the end of his college career he had a .595 completion percentage and had gained 4354 yds. in total offense.
Also in: National Football Hall of Fame.

KERR, Andrew

Coach

Born October 7, 1878, in Cheyenne, Wyo; died March 1, 1969, in Tucson, Ariz, at age 91.

1922 – 1923 Stanford University, coach
1926 – 1928 Washington and Jefferson College, coach
1928 – 1946 Colgate University, coach
1947 – 1949 Lebanon Valley College, coach

Kerr studied law and taught at a business college in Johnstown, Pa; he coached football at Johnstown High School. In 1914 he became the track coach at the Univer-

sity of Pittsburgh and was the assistant football coach 1915–1921. At Washington and Jefferson, his 1926 team suffered only one defeat, and his 1927 team was undefeated; his three-year record was 16–6–5. At Colgate his record was 47–5–1 through 1934. His 1929 team gave up only 19 points and lost only one game. He considered his 1932 undefeated team his best. His record at Lebanon was 137–71–14.
Also in: National Football Hall of Fame.

KIMBROUGH, Frank
Coach
A graduate of Hardin-Simmons, Frank coached football a total of 21 years for a 116–83–8 record. He was at Hardin-Simmons coaching 1934–1940, Baylor 1941–1946 except for two years in W.W. II service, and West Texas State 1947–1957.

KIMBROUGH, John
Player
Born in Haskell, Tex; All-American 1940; Consensus All-American 1940.

1938–1940 Texas A&M University, fullback
1941 New York Americans, American Football League, player
1946–1948 Los Angeles Dons, All-American Football Conference, player

"Jarrin' Jawn" Kimbrough played in two Cotton Bowl games during his college football days. In the 1941 game he rushed for 152 yds. on 26 carries and scored two touchdowns toward a Texas A&M win over Fordham, 13–12. In 1942 he rushed for 58 yds. and scored one touchdown, but the team lost to Alabama 29–21. Fifth in Heisman Trophy voting in 1939 and runnerup in 1940, Kimbrough's collegiate record was: 1357 yds. on 375 carries, 24 receptions for 197 yds, 12 interceptions for 198 yds, and 21 touchdowns for 126 points. With the Dons, who merged with the National Football League in 1950, Kimbrough gained 1224 yds. rushing on 329 carries and scored 17 touchdowns.
Also in: National Football Hall of Fame.

KINARD, Frank M. "Bruiser"
Player
See entry in Professional Football Hall of Fame, 1971.
Also in: National Football Hall of Fame.

KINNICK, Nile Clark Jr.
Player
Born in Omaha, Nebr; Phi Beta Kappa scholar at Univ. Iowa; Heisman Trophy, Maxwell Award, Walter Camp Memorial Trophy and Silver Football 1939; Consensus All-American 1939; killed on June 2, 1943, when his Navy fighter plane crashed into the Gulf of Paria, Venezuela.

At his peak as a Big Ten gridiron star with the University of Iowa, Nile Kinnick beat out even New York Yankee, Joe DiMaggio, to become "the Number One Athlete of the Year" in 1939. That season he played 402 of a possible 420 min, the full 60 min. in six straight games and brought his team 107 of 135 points they gained in 1939. Kinnick also was National Collegiate Athletic Association leader in yardage kickoff returns with 377 yds. in 15 returns. His career total: 724 yds. gained in rushing on 254 carries, 1445 yds. for 88 completed passes out of 229 attempts and 111 yds. on 18 pass interceptions for a 6.2 average.
Also in: National Football Hall of Fame.

KIPKE, Harry G.
Player
Three letters each in basketball and baseball at Univ. Mich; All-American 1922; a president of the American Football Coaches Assn; vice president of Coca-Cola Co. in Chicago, Ill, at his death September 14, 1972, in Port Huron, Mich.

1921–1923 University of Michigan, halfback
1924 University of Missouri, assistant coach
1928 Michigan State University, head coach
1929–1937 University of Michigan, head coach

Considered the finest punter in the country during the 1920s, Harry Kipke won three varsity letters in football and captained Michigan's Wolverines in 1923. As a coach, his motto, "A great offense is a great defense," led his Michigan team to a shared Big Ten title with Northwestern in 1930, with Purdue and Northwestern in 1931, but a complete title in 1932 and 1933, undefeated in 1932 and tied once in 1933. Kipke regarded the center as the most valuable defense unit on a team, as opposed to the tackles, explaining why so many All-American centers in the 1930s were from the University of Michigan. Kipke left the Wolverines with a 46–26–5 win-loss-tie record.
Also in: National Football Hall of Fame.

KRAMER, Ronald
Player
See entry in Green Bay Packer Hall of Fame, 1975.

LATTNER, John J.
Player
Born October 24, 1932, in Chicago, Ill; All American 1952 and 1953; Heisman Trophy 1953; Walter Camp Trophy in 1953; first Heisman Trophy melted in a restaurant fire; received a new trophy which is now on display in Johnny Lattner's Steak House, Marina Towers, Chicago, Ill.

1951–1953 University of Notre Dame, running back
1954 Pittsburgh Steelers, running back

At Notre Dame Johnny Lattner compiled a 23–4–3 playing record, rushed 1724 yds. and recorded 13 interceptions. A highlight in his college career was a 92-yd. kickoff return in a game against Pennsylvania in 1953. Due to a knee injury in a service game with the Pittsburgh Steelers, Lattner played only one season of professional football and went to the Pro Bowl with the Steelers.

LAYDEN, Elmer F.
Player
Born 1903 in Davenport, Iowa; injured knee as football player at Davenport High School; graduated from Univ. Notre Dame; Citizens Savings Rose Bowl Player of the Year Award 1925; died June 30, 1973, in Chicago, Ill.

1922–1924 University of Notre Dame, fullback
1925 Brooklyn Horsemen, American Football League, player
1925–1926 Columbia College (now Loras), coach
1927–1933 Duquesne University, coach

1934 – 1940 University of Notre Dame, coach
1941 – 1946 National Football League, commissioner

When Elmer Layden's "rabid football fan" father saw Notre Dame play he was convinced that his son should be a part of that team. Coach Knute Rockne had his doubts, but Elmer, one of the legendary "Four Horsemen," made a believer out of Rockne. "I was never too sure about that knee, but it never bothered him. He was always using an exceptionally quick start with the maximum amount of speed. He has a right to ride with the gridiron greats." With an uncanny ability to intercept passes, Elmer made himself a hero at the Rose Bowl of 1925 against the Stanford Indians by converting two interceptions into touchdowns, running 78 and 70 yds. Before returning to Notre Dame as a coach, Elmer coached Columbia College to a 8 – 5 – 2 record and Duquesne to a 48 – 16 – 6 record in seven seasons. Then he led the Irish to a 48 – 16 – 6 record and finished his coaching career with a 103 – 34 – 11 win-loss-tie record for a .733 percentage.
Also in: National Football Hall of Fame.

LEA, Langdon "Biffy"
Player
Born May 11, 1874, in Germantown, Pa; graduated from Princeton Univ; Walter Camp's All-American team 1892 – 1895; died October 4, 1937.

When Pop Warner was asked to name his own personal 11-man team he selected Biffy Lea as tackle. So outstanding was his blocking and tackling that 53 years after his last college game he was still listed among the all-time Big Three linemen. As captain of the Tigers in 1895 he led the team to a 10 – 1 – 1 record. But even more impressive is the four-year record he left behind, 41 – 5 – 1, with the opposition scoreless for 35 games.
Also in: National Football Hall of Fame.

LEAHY, Francis "Frank"
Coach
Born August 27, 1908, in O'Neill, Nebr; graduated from Univ. Notre Dame 1931; Coach of the Year 1941; died June 21, 1973, in Portland, Ore. at age 65.

1939 – 1940 Boston College, coach
1941 – 1953 University of Notre Dame, coach

Leahy was a lineman under Knute Rockne in 1929, but he ripped the cartilage in his knee in his senior year and never played again. He became a coach at Fordham under Jim Crowley in 1933; his later record at Boston College was 9 – 2 his first season, including a win in the Cotton Bowl. His 1940 team was undefeated and untied, winning eleven, including the Sugar Bowl. His first year at Notre Dame, his record was 7 – 2 – 2, and his national championship team of 1943 rated among the best teams of all time. They won nine straight before losing to Great Lakes in the final minutes of the last game. After serving in the Army, he returned to Notre Dame and had three more championship teams, 1946, 1947 and 1949. From 1946 to 1950, Notre Dame was unbeaten in 39 straight games. The 1946 Irish played to a 0 – 0 tie with Army. Leahy's record at Notre Dame was 80 – 5 – 5, .941 percent for nine years. His percentage trails only Knute Rockne. He was named to the Knights of Malta by Pope Pius XII, and wrote *Defensive Football* in 1951.
Also in: National Football Hall of Fame.

LEECH, James C.
Player
Born April 13, 1897, in Lexington, Va; v.pres. of class at Virginia Military Institute in 1920; Third team All-American 1920; died August 18, 1951, in Hamden, Conn.

1919 – 1920 Virginia Military Institute, halfback

With 210 points, Jimmy Leech led the nation in scoring in 1920. His team, the Keydets, were unbeaten and untied that season, stomping on opponents for 431 points. They won 15 of 17 games during his junior and senior years with the team.
Also in: National Football Hall of Fame.

LESTER, Darrell
Player
Darrell Lester joined the Green Bay Packers in 1937 for two seasons after a college football career as center for Texas Christian University.

LITTLE, Louis B.
Coach
Born December 6, 1893, in Boston, Mass.

1924 – 1929 Georgetown University, coach
1930 – 1956 Columbia University, coach

Little was a tackle at Pennsylvania 1916 – 1919, then coached the Massillon Tigers 1919 and the Buffalo All-Americans 1920 and 1921. He is currently on the executive committee of the National Football Foundation. His coaching record was 148 – 138 – 12; his top products were Bill Swiacki, Paul Governali, Sid Luckman and Gene Rossides.
Also in: National Football Hall of Fame.

LOCKE, Gordon C.
Player
Born August 3, 1898, in Denison, Iowa; graduated from Univ. Iowa in law; All-American 1922; asst. coach for Iowa and Western Reserve before becoming an attorney in Washington, D.C; died November 9, 1969, in Washington, D.C.

Gordon Locke's team won the Big Ten championships in 1921 and 1922, unbeaten and untied in both seasons. Playing teams like Notre Dame, Illinois, Purdue, Minnesota, Indiana and Northwestern in the three years he was fullback with the team, Iowa lost only 2 and won 19. Coached by Howard Jones, Locke was a part of a two-runner, two-blocker backfield originated by Jones in which Locke was the tailback and sometimes the fullback. He weighed only 165 lbs. but managed to stop the opposition like a tank.
Also in: National Football Hall of Fame.

LUCKMAN, Sid
Player
See entry in Professional Football Hall of Fame, 1965.
Also in: Major League Football Hall of Fame, Citizens Savings Hall of Fame Athletic Museum; and National Football Hall of Fame.

LUJACK, John
Player
Born 1925 in Connellsville, Pa; graduated from Univ. Notre Dame; All-American 1946 and 1947; Heisman Trophy 1947; military service in 1944 and 1945.

1943 University of Notre Dame, quarterback
1946 – 1948 University of Notre Dame, quarterback
1948 – 1951 Chicago Bears

Chosen the best collegiate quarterback of the quarter-century by a panel of 48 leading college coaches and selected by the "All-American Review," John Lujack had a natural poise for the game. Coach Bernie Bierman knew he could relax with Lujack on the field and, later Chicago Bears coach George Halas commented, "Completely stripped of all his amazing football skills, Lujack is still indispensable for one thing—his poise." As a sophomore, he replaced star player Angelo Bertelli and led the Irishmen to a 26 – 9 victory over the Army in 1943. Three years later in yet another game against the powerful Army team, Lujack became the first man to down the tough Doc Blanchard to prevent a touchdown. Though injured he continued to play the full 60-minute game.
Also in: National Football Hall of Fame.

MADIGAN, Edward P. "Slip"
Coach

Born 1896; died October 10, 1966, at age 71.

1921 – 1940 St. Mary's College (Calif.), coach
1943 – 1944 University of Iowa, coach

Madigan played for Notre Dame 1916 – 1917 and 1919. When hired by St. Mary's, the school had only 71 students; the Gaels had lost to California 127 – 0 the year before. His 1926 and 1929 teams were unbeaten, and the latter team was scored upon only by Oregon, the season's last game. He was paid well for his era, receiving (at St. Mary's) a salary plus a share of the gate receipts. He scouted Stanford for his alma mater prior to the 1925 Rose Bowl, which helped Notre Dame win 27 – 10.
Also in: National Football Hall of Fame.

MAHAN, Edward W.
Player

Born in Natick, Mass; All-American 1913, 1914, and 1915.

Edward Mahan played for Harvard 1913 – 1915 as a fullback. He was named by Grantland Rice to the All-Time College Backfield All-American for the years 1913, 1914 and 1915. He was a great runner, passer, blocker, tackler and kicker. Mahan did not want anyone to run interference for him, preferring to clear his own path. He was an outstanding runner.
Also in: National Football Hall of Fame.

McCOLL, William
Player

Born April 2, 1930, in San Diego, Calif; attended Hoover High School in San Diego; graduated from Stanford Univ; Consensus All-American 1950; Unanimous All-American 1951; finished medical education at Univ. Chicago while playing for the Chicago Bears; later ran a missionary hospital in Korea.

1949 – 1951 Stanford University, end
1952 – 1959 Chicago Bears, halfback

Fourth in Heisman Trophy voting in 1951, Bill McColl played in the 1952 Rose Bowl, but Stanford lost to Illinois 40 – 7. During the three years he played college football, Stanford won 21 games, lost 7 and tied 3.
Also in: National Football Hall of Fame.

McFADDEN, James Banks
Player

Born February 7, 1917, in Fort Lawn, S.C; graduated from Clemson Univ; Consensus All-American 1939; center on basketball All-American team in 1938 and 1939; called the greatest all-around track man in history of South Carolina; Major in U.S. Army Air Force Special Services in W.W. II; head coach for basketball at Clemson.

1937 – 1939 Clemson University, halfback
1940 Brooklyn Dodgers, player

A great runner, passer, punter and defender, James McFadden finished his senior year with outstanding totals: 72 carries for 436 yds, 27 of 67 completed passes for 546 yds, one touchdown, a 42-yd. punt average and three completed pass interceptions. In 1940 he led his team to a victory in the Cotton Bowl over the previously undefeated Boston College and was the star player in the 1940 College All-Star Game in Chicago. As a professional, McFadden ranked second in rushing in the National Football League. He later returned to Clemson as backfield coach.
Also in: National Football Hall of Fame.

McFADIN, Lewis B.
Player

Born August 21, 1928 in Iraan, Tex; so homesick for his horse, he almost left the Univ. Tex. in his freshman year; Unanimous All-American 1950; following 1956 season with Los Angeles Rams, lost most of his stomach from an accidental shooting on a hunting trip; made remarkable comeback after three years of retirement in the cattle business.

1950 – 1951 University of Texas, guard
1952 – 1956 Los Angeles Rams, tackle
1960 – 1963 Denver Broncos, tackle
1964 – 1965 Houston Oilers, tackle

A college career that began in Texas blossomed into an outstanding professional career when Lewis McFadin was the Number One draft choice of the Los Angeles Rams. With the Denver Broncos he was twice named All-American Football League player. To Abner Hayes, the American Football League's 1960 Most Valuable Player, he was the best defensive player he had ever met.

McGUGIN, Daniel "Dan"
Coach

Born July 29, 1879, in Tingley, Iowa; died January 19, 1936, in Memphis, Tenn, at age 57.

McGugin was the brother-in-law of Fielding "Hurry Up" Yost; both men were football coaches and lawyers. McGugin played for Yost at Michigan in 1902 to 1903. He was coach at Vanderbilt University 1904-1934 with two years out during W.W. I. His career record was 197 – 55 – 19, .762 percent.
Also in: National Football Hall of Fame.

McLAUGHRY, DeOrmand "Tuss"
Coach

Born May 19, 1893, in Chicago, Ill; attended Michigan State and Westminster Col. (Pa.), where he played three sports; raised in Sharon, Pa.

1916 – 1917 Westminster College, coach
1920 – 1921 Westminster College, coach

1922–1925 Amherst College, coach
1926–1940 Brown University, coach
1941–1942 Dartmouth College, coach
1945–1954 Dartmouth College, coach

McLaughry had a 140–155–15 coaching record. His best years were at Brown (76–58–5) where Brown's 1928 "Iron Men" won nine straight games before they were tied by Colgate. He coached his sons John and Bob at Dartmouth; John was later Brown head coach for eight years. Tuss coached the East squad four times in the East-West Shrine game, and served for many years as secretary-treasurer of American Football Coaches Association.
Also in: National Football Hall of Fame and Providence Gridiron Hall of Fame.

McMILLIN, Alvin N. "Bo"
Player and Coach
Born January 12, 1895, in Prairie Hill, Tex; star quarterback at Fort Worth North Side High School; graduated from Centre Col; All-American and Citizens Savings Player of the Year 1919; All-American second team 1920-1921; Coach of the Year 1945; died Mar. 31, 1952 in Bloomington, Ind.

1919–1921 Centre College, quarterback
1922–1923 Milwaukee Badgers, quarterback
1922–1925 Centenary, coach
1923 Cleveland Indians, coach
1934–1947 University of Indiana, coach
1948–1950 Detroit Lions, head coach
1951 Philadelphia Eagles, coach

Bo McMillin joined Centre College on the promise that they would win the Southern and National championships and that he would be an All-American. Soon, boys all over America were imitating his bullet-like passes. In his first season, his first and only field goal attempt brought the Colonels to a 3-0 victory over Kentucky, to whom they had lost 68–0 the previous year. As a quarterback, he completed a remarkable 119 of 170 tosses his last year. In 1921 when his touchdown after a 32-yd. run stunned Harvard 6–0, Edwin P. Morrow said, "I'd rather be Bo McMillin at this moment than the governor of Kentucky," and he was the governor. Coach of the "po' little fellas" at Indiana weighing 225-240 lbs, he led the team undefeated to a Big Ten Western Conference championship in 1945 and to a 63–48–11 record in his 14 years with Indiana. Bo was also collegiate coach for Centenary with a 25–3 record, Geneva and Kansas State before coaching the Lions. His best record was a 6-6 in 1950, but he did a good job of promoting football. In 1951 he coached the Philadelphia Eagles but after two losses retired.
Also in: Louisiana Sports Hall of Fame and National Football Hall of Fame.

McPHEE, Frank R.
Player
Born March 19, 1931, in Youngstown, Ohio; graduated from Princeton Univ; All-American 1951; Consensus All-American 1952; affiliated with Prudential Life Insurance Co. in Houston, Tex.

1951–1953 Princeton University, end
Chicago Cardinals, end

Frank McPhee and Heisman-winner Dick Kazmaier were largely responsible for the 24-game winning streak that began in 1952, after only one loss in that season to the University of Pennsylvania. Following his college football days, McPhee joined up with the Chicago Cardinals.

McWHORTER, Robert L.
Player
Born in Athens, Ga; graduated from Univ. Ga; All-American 1913; attended Univ. Va. Law School 1914–1917; practiced law in Athens 1919–1923; served as an Infantry Captain in W.W. I; served as a law professor at Univ. Ga; mayor of Athens 1940–1948; was member of the Georgia baseball team; died June 29, 1960.

Robert McWhorter played for Georgia from 1910–1913. During his four years at Georgia he played against his rival, Georgia Tech, and led his team to victory each time allowing only one touchdown in those four years. In this feat he took his greatest pride. McWhorter was an excellent defensive player, good runner and blocker.
Also in: National Football Hall of Fame.

MEEHAN, John "Chick"
Coach
Born September 5, 1893, in Shelburne Falls, Mass; graduated from Syracuse Univ. 1918; died January 9, 1972 at age 79.

1920–1924 Syracuse University, coach
1925–1931 New York University, coach
1932–1934 Manhattan College, coach

Meehan had a record of 115–44–14 with a .705 percent. At age 27 he succeeded Orangemen's Buck O'Neill and had a close relationship with Pop Warner. He coached New York University against Fordham in the "Battle of the Bronx," 1928–1931. The games were played before 55,000–70,000 at the Polo Grounds and Yankee Stadium. At New York University he developed the "military shift" in which players used military cadence in coming out of the huddle.

MERCER, E. Leroy
Player
Born in Kennett Square, Pa; graduated from Univ. Pa. with an M.D. degree 1913; All-American fullback 1911 and 1912; a physical education professor at Swarthmore, also athletic director; served 22 years at Univ. Pa. as dean of physical education department 1914–1931.

E. Leroy Mercer played fullback from 1910 to 1912 for Pennsylvania. The 1910 team was the Ivy League champion. In 1911 and 1912 he was captain of the team with a record of 23 wins, 10 losses and 1 tie. Mercer was a member of the U.S. Olympic track team in 1912 and won the IC4A broad jump title in 1912 and 1913.
Also in: National Football Hall of Fame.

MEYER, Leo R. "Dutch"
Coach
See entry in Athletic Directors Hall of Fame, Citizens Savings Hall of Fame Athletic Museum, 1971.
Also in: National Football Hall of Fame.

MICHAELS, Louis A.
Player
Born in Swoyersville, Pa; graduated from Univ. Ky; Consensus All-American 1956 and 1957.

1955 – 1957 University of Kentucky, tackle
1958 – 1960 Los Angeles Rams, player
1961 – 1963 Pittsburgh Steelers, player
1964 – 1969 Baltimore Colts, player
1969 – 1971 Green Bay Packers, player

Louis A. Michaels was named to the All-Time Southeastern Conference Team. Michaels led the National Football League with 26 field goals in 1962. In his thirteen-year career he scored 380 points after touchdown, 187 field goals, 1 safety—all for 977 points. At his retirement he was regarded as the fourth greatest scorer. He played in two National Football League games, one in 1964 and the other in 1968. Michaels played the Super Bowl in 1969 as the pro-defensive end.

MILLNER, Wayne
Player
See entry in Professional Football Hall of Fame, 1968.

MOOMAW, Donn D.
Player
Born in Santa Ana, Calif; received B.S. degree from Univ. Calif, Los Angeles; All-American 1950, 1951 and 1952; Consensus All-American 1952; B.D. degree from Princeton Theological Seminary, D.D. degree from Sterling Col. in Kan; now occupies the pulpit at Bel Air Presbyterian Church in Los Angeles, Calif.

Moomaw went through his entire collegiate career without being penalized. He was named by Stanley Woodward as one of the world's ten greatest athletes in *Who's Who in Sports* in 1953. Moomaw was named All-Pro Canada for Toronto Argonauts in 1954. He was named one of California's five outstanding young men by the California JayCees.
Also in: National Football Hall of Fame.

MOORE, Andrew Jr. "Scrappy"
Coach
Born September 25, 1902; attended Univ. Ga. 1923 – 1925; Coach of the Year 1967; died May 3, 1971, in Chattanooga, Tenn, at age 69.

Moore played for Georgia under George "Kid" Woodruff. He was coach at the University of Tennessee 1931 – 1967 except for two war years. His record at Tennessee was 172 – 146 – 13.

MORAN, Charles "Uncle Charley"
Coach
Born February 22, 1879, in Nashville, Tenn; attended Univ. Tenn; died June 13, 1949 at age 70.

1909 – 1914 Texas A&M University, coach
1919 – 1923 Centre College, coach
1924 – 1926 Bucknell University, coach
1930 – 1933 Catawba College, coach
1927 Frankfort Yellow Jackets, coach

Moran had a college record of 122 – 33 – 12. His Texas A&M teams were 38 – 8 – 4, outscoring foes 1091 – 190. He won national acclaim at Centre, where the "Praying Colonels" compiled a 42 – 6 – 1 record, including a 6 – 0 upset over Harvard in 1921. He was pitcher and catcher for the National League's St. Louis Browns in 1903 and 1908, and a National League umpire 1916 – 1939.

MORRISON, J. Ray
Coach
See entry in Athletic Directors Hall of Fame, Citizens Savings Hall of Fame Athletic Museum, 1972.
Also in: National Football Hall of Fame.

MULLER, Harold P. "Brick"
Player
Born in Dunsmuir, Calif; graduated from Univ. Calif; All-American third team 1920; All-American 1920 and 1921.

Harold Muller played a major role in the success of the "Wonder Teams." He could throw a football 60 yds. on the line. He brought West Coast football into national limelight. Muller threw a 55 yd. touchdown pass against Ohio State in the 1921 Rose Bowl. He scored the winning touchdown in the 1925 East-West Shrine game. His record showed that he never lost a game in college, winning 27 games and tying 1. Muller served as the team physician for the U.S. Olympic team in 1956.
Also in: National Football Hall of Fame.

MUNN, Clarence "Biggie"
Player
See entry in Athletic Directors Hall of Fame, Citizens Savings Hall of Fame Athletic Museum, 1972.
Also in: National Football Hall of Fame, Michigan Sports Hall of Fame and Minnesota Sports Hall of Fame.

MURRAY, Francis J.
Coach
Born February 12, 1885, in Maynard, Mass; attended Tufts Col; died September 12, 1951, in Milwaukee, Wis, at age 66.

1922 – 1936 Marquette University, coach
1946 – 1949 Marquette University, coach
1937 – 1945 University of Virginia, coach

Murray never played organized football, yet was recognized as one of the game's outstanding students. Marquette was unbeaten three seasons under Murray, and the 1936 Warriors went to the Cotton Bowl. Murray's early Marquette teams were labeled "Singing Hilltoppers" because he led players in song before games. His overall record was 145 – 89 – 11. As far back as 1930, he directed the team by remote control via a telephone from the press box.

MURRAY, William D.
Coach
See entry in Athletic Directors Hall of Fame, Citizens Savings Hall of Fame Athletic Museum, 1974.
Also in: National Football Hall of Fame.

MYLIN, Edward E. "Hooks"
Coach
Born October 23, 1894, in Leaman Place, Pa; graduated from Franklin and Marshall Univ; Coach of the Year 1937.

1923 – 1933 Lebanon Valley College, coach
1934 – 1936 Bucknell University, coach
1937 – 1942 Lafayette College, coach
1947 – 1949 New York University, coach

Mylin coached Lafayette to an undefeated season in 1937, and had fine coaching records at Bucknell, Lafayette and New York University.
Also in: National Football Hall of Fame.

NAGURSKI, Bronislaw "Bronko"
Player
See entry in Professional Football Hall of Fame, 1963.
Also in: National Football Hall of Fame; and Major League Football Hall of Fame, Citizens Savings Hall of Fame Athletic Museum.

NEELY, Jess Claiborne
Coach
Born January 4, 1898, in Smyrna, Tenn; graduated from Vanderbilt Univ; Amos Alonzo Stagg Award.

1924 – 1927 Southwestern University, coach
1931 – 1937 Clemson University, coach
1940 – 1967 Rice University, coach

Neely was the end and halfback for Vanderbilt's Dan McGugin 1920 – 1922. He lost only one game in his playing career—Iowa in 1921. He captained the 1922 team that was tied only by Michigan. As coach, he participated in seven bowl games (six at Rice), winning four. His last Clemson team won the Cotton Bowl, and ten years later his Rice team did too. Neely's last Cotton victory was 28 – 6 over Alabama in 1954; his overall record was 207 – 176 – 19.
Also in: National Football Hall of Fame; and Athletic Directors Hall of Fame, Citizens Savings Hall of Fame Athletic Museum.

NELSON, David M.
Coach
Nelson graduated from Michigan and started to coach at Hillsdale College in 1946, moving to the University of Maine in 1949 and 1950, then on to Delaware 1951 – 1965, for an overall record of 105 – 48 – 7 for 19 years of football coaching. Nelson wrote *Football: Principles and Play* in 1962.

NEVERS, Ernest
Player
See entry in Professional Football Hall of Fame, 1963.
Also in: Major League Football Hall of Fame, Citizens Savings Hall of Fame Athletic Museum; and National Football Hall of Fame.

NEWELL, Marshall "Ma"
Player
Born in Clifton, N.J; graduated from Harvard Univ; All-American 1891 – 1893.

Marshall Newell was a tackle for Harvard 1890 – 1893. He was known for his powerful tackling and blocking ability. He also rowed for the Harvard crew. Newell was the first paid coach at Cornell in 1893 and 1894.
Also in: National Football Hall of Fame.

NEYLAND, Robert R.
Coach
See entry in Athletic Directors Hall of Fame, Citizens Savings Hall of Fame Athletic Museum, 1956.
Also in: National Football Hall of Fame.

NOMELLINI, Leo
Player
See entry in Professional Football Hall of Fame, 1969.
Also in: Major League Football Hall of Fame, Citizens Savings Hall of Fame Athletic Museum; and National Football Hall of Fame.

NORTON, Homer H.
Coach
Born June 15, 1891; four-sport star at Birmingham Southern Univ. in football, basketball, baseball and track; son of a Methodist minister; after coaching, he went into the motel-restaurant business; died in 1965 at age 74.

1920 – 1921 Centenary College, coach
1926 – 1933 Centenary College, coach
1934 – 1947 Texas A&M University, coach

Norton's Aggie successes included three straight Southwestern Conference titles, four major bowl appearances, and a national championship in 1939. He developed such Texas A&M standouts as John Kimbrough, Marshall Robnett, Joe Routt and Jim Thomason. He correctly predicted that Routt would be their first All-American. His overall record was 142 – 73 – 18.
Also in: National Football Hall of Fame.

OBERLANDER, Andrew J. "Swede"
Player
Born in Chelsea, Mass; attended Dartmouth Col; graduated from Yale Medical School; All-American 1925; medical director of eastern home office of Prudential Insurance Company.

Andrew Oberlander was a tackle for Dartmouth through his sophomore and junior years. Then in his senior year he was switched to the backfield by coach Jesse Hawley. He then proceeded to throw 12 touchdown passes and was unanimous All-American in 1925. Also in 1925 he led Dartmouth to the national championships. In his three years at Dartmouth, Oberlander lost only one game.
Also in: National Football Hall of Fame.

O'BRIEN, Robert David
Player
Born in Dallas, Tex; All-American 1938; Heisman Trophy and Maxwell Trophy 1938; All-NFL 1939.

1936 – 1938 Texas Christian University, quarterback
1939 – 1940 Philadelphia Eagles, player

Robert "Davey" O'Brien led Texas Christian University to the national championships in 1938 with a perfect 10 – 0 season. He accounted for 245 points and 3481 yds. total offense during his collegiate career. From 1936 – 1938 he amassed a total of 5462 yds. from interceptions, kickoffs and punt returns. In 1938 he played on the winning Sugar Bowl and Cotton Bowl teams. He signed with the Philadelphia Eagles in 1939 and played two seasons. His first season saw three new passing records set by O'Brien. In his last professional game he completed 33 of 60 passes for 316 yds, setting a record of completions.

O'DEA, Patrick J.
Player
Born in Melbourne, Australia; All-American 1898 and 1899; after football career, joined Australian Army;

changed name to Charles J. Mitchell and dropped out of sight in 1917; died April 4, 1962.

1897–1899 University of Wisconsin, fullback
1900–1901 University of Notre Dame, coach
1902 University of Missouri, coach

Patrick "Pat" O'Dea was a running back-kicker rugby player in Australia before coming to America. He enrolled at Wisconsin because his brother was the track coach. He played football for Wisconsin for three years. He was All-American second team in 1898 and All-American third team in 1899. O'Dea has recorded goals of 62 yds, 60 yds. and two 57 yd. goals; 62 yards is the second longest in college history. In 1899 he kicked four field goals and returned a kickoff 90 yds. against Beloit. O'Dea taught Notre Dame's Red Salmon the art of punting.
Also in: National Football Hall of Fame.

OLIPHANT, Elmer Q. "Ollie"
Player
Born in Bloomfield, Ind; attended Purdue Univ; graduated from U.S. Military Academy; Consensus All-American 1916 and 1917.

1911–1913 Purdue University, running back
1914–1917 U.S. Military Academy, back
1920–1921 Buffalo All-Americans, back
1920–1921 Rochester Jeffersons, back

Elmer Oliphant was one of the most versatile athletes in America. While at Army he earned letters in four major sports—football, basketball, baseball and track. He was best remembered for football. He played seven consecutive years, the first three years at Purdue and the last four at West Point (Army). During that seven-year span Oliphant scored 468 points. The Football Writers Association of America voted him to the All-Time All-American Team. Oliphant still holds the Army record for points scored: game, 45 in 1916; most touchdowns per game, 6 in 1916; most points scored in a season, 125 in 1917. Purdue has named an athletic scholarship after him.

OLIVAR, Jordan
Coach
Born January 30, 1915, in Brooklyn, N.Y; graduated from Villanova Univ. with honors, majoring in romance languages.

1937 Villanova University, co-captain and player
1943–1948 Villanova University, coach
1949–1951 Loyola College of California, coach
1952–1960 Yale University, coach

Olivar played for Harry Stuhldreher in 1935 and for Clipper Smith 1936 and 1937 at Villanova. His record at Villanova as coach was 105–53–6. In 1960 he produced Yale's first unbeaten, untied team (9–0–0) in 37 years. He is now associate manager with Mutual of New York and lives in Beverly Hills, Calif.

OOSTERBAAN, Benjamin G.
Player
Born in Muskegon, Mich; graduated from Univ. Mich; Consensus All-American 1925–1927; All-American (basketball); Modern All-Time All-American Team.

Benjamin Oosterbaan's career started at Muskegon High School where he starred in four sports and then went on to the University of Michigan and won nine letters. He took the head coaching position at Michigan and compiled a record of 63 wins, 33 losses and 4 ties during his eleven-year span from 1948 to 1958. His team won the Big Ten title three times, and in 1948 he earned the honor of Coach of the Year.
Also in: National Football Hall of Fame.

OWEN, Benjamin G.
Coach
Born July 24, 1875, in Chicago, Ill; died February 26, 1970, in Houston, Tex. at age 95.

1900 Washburn University, coach
1901–1904 Bethany College, coach
1905–1926 University of Oklahoma, coach

Owen was the starting quarterback for the Kansas Jayhawks under Fielding Yost in 1899. He became the Sooner coach before the Oklahoma Territory achieved statehood; his record there was 122–54–16, with four unbeaten seasons. They outscored the opposition 282–15 in 1911 and 287–7 in 1918. Oklahoma's Owen Field, seating 61,826, is named for him.
Also in: National Football Hall of Fame.

PARILLI, Vito "Babe"
Player
Born in Rochester, Pa; graduated from Univ. Ky; Consensus All-American 1950 and 1951; Most Valuable Player 1952, 1964 and 1969.

1950–1952 University of Kentucky, quarterback
1952–1953 Green Bay Packers, quarterback
1956 Cleveland Browns, player
1957–1958 Green Bay Packers, player
1959 Ottawa Roughriders, player
1960 Oakland Raiders, player
1961–1967 Boston Patriots, player
1968 New York Jets, player
1971–1973 Pittsburgh Steelers, quarterback coach
1974 World Football League, coach

Vito Parilli played with Kentucky when they won three straight bowl games; Orange in 1950, Sugar in 1951 and Cotton in 1952. Parilli was considered number one nationally in touchdown passes in 1950 and 1951. He threw for 4351 yds. with 50 touchdowns. He was voted most valuable player in the 1952 College All-Star game. Parilli was also voted by the American Football League most valuable player in 1964 and in the Super Bowl in 1969. At his retirement from professional football he had recorded 1522 completions on 3330 attempts for a total of 22,681 yds. and 178 touchdowns.

PARKER, Clarence "Ace"
Player
See entry in Professional Football Hall of Fame, 1973.
Also in: National Football Hall of Fame.

PARKER, James
Player
See entry in Professional Football Hall of Fame, 1973
Also in: National Football Hall of Fame.

PECK, Robert D.
Player
Born in Lock Haven, Pa; graduated from Univ. Pittsburgh; All-American 1915 and 1916.

Robert Peck played center for the University of Pittsburgh 1914–1916. Besides being known as an excellent

center he could also play defense handily. Coach Pop Warner considered the 1916 Pittsburgh team the greatest club he ever coached and that was proven by the team being honored with the national championship. In Peck's three-year career with the University of Pittsburgh they only lost one game.
Also in: National Football Hall of Fame.

PEDEN, Donald
Coach
Born 1889 in Kewanee, Ill; died February 23, 1970, in Oxford, Ohio.

1924 – 1942 Ohio University, coach
1945 – 1946 Ohio University, coach

Peden played halfback at Illinois. He threw a touchdown pass to Laurie Walquist in a game against Ohio State in 1921, providing a 7 – 0 victory. His record at Ohio was 121 – 46 – 11, with three unbeaten seasons—1929, 1930 and 1935. He also coached baseball 25 years, producing a 261 – 42 record. Ohio's Peden Stadium is named in his honor.

PENNOCK, Stanley B.
Player
Born in Syracuse, N.Y; graduated from Harvard Univ; All-American 1912, 1913 and 1914.

Out of the 51 All-Americans since 1889 only five have been 3-time All-Americans, and Stanley Pennock was one. This was a feat which gave Harvard something to cheer about. In Pennock's three seasons, 1912 – 1914 with the team, they went unbeaten all 27 games with ties coming from Pennsylvania and Brown to mar the near-perfect record. In the three-year span the team gave up only 61 points while they gained 588 points. They were co-national champions all three years. Pennock played all 60 min. of the game—a hard feat in itself. During this period Harvard ranked first among the Ivy Leagues.
Also in: National Football Hall of Fame.

PFANN, George R.
Player
Born in Marion, Ohio; graduated from Cornell Univ; All-American 1923; earned law degree at Oxford, and lettered in rugby and lacrosse at Oxford; Lt. Col. in W.W. II; served as secy. of Seventh and Third U.S. Armies under Patton; awarded seven Battle Stars and one Arrowhead.

George Pfann was never defeated or tied during his 24-game career with Cornell. While he was there Cornell outscored it opponents 1022 to 81.
Also in: National Football Hall of Fame.

PHELAN, James M.
Coach
Born December 5, 1891, in Calif; lives in Sacramento.

1919 – 1922 University of Missouri, coach
1922 – 1929 Purdue University, coach
1930 – 1941 University of Washington, coach
1941 – 1946 St. Mary's College, coach

Phelan was one of numerous Knute Rockne proteges and had a 136 – 87 – 14 record. He developed All-Americans Elmer Sleight, Ralph Welch, Max Starcevich, Rudy Mucha, Ray Frankowski and Herman Wedemeyer.
Also in: National Football Hall of Fame.

PINCKERT, Ernie
Player
All-American 1930 and 1931; 1932 Citizens Savings Rose Bowl Player of the Year Award 1932.

Ernie Pinckert was a highlight of the University of Southern California 1929 – 1931 teams. He was so good that the coach made special plays for him. His team was averaging nearly 38 points per game with Pinckert in the backfield. He was in the Rose Bowl two of his three years at Southern California.
Also in: National Football Hall of Fame.

POLLARD, Frederick D. "Fritz"
Player
Born January 27, 1894, in Chicago, Ill; starred in three sports at Chicago's Lane Tech. High School; intercollegiate hurdles champion in 1916 and 1917 at Brown Univ; All-American 1916; served as pres. of Pollard Investment Co. and Pollard Coal Co; brother Leslie played football at Dartmouth in 1908; sister Naomi first Black woman to graduate from Northwestern in 1905; son Frederick, Jr, won bronze medal in Berlin Olympics of 1936.

1914 – 1916 Brown University, halfback
1919 – 1921 Akron Indians, halfback and coach
1922 Milwaukee Badgers, halfback
1923 – 1925 Hammond Pros, halfback and coach
1925 Providence Steamrollers, halfback
1925 – 1926 Akron Indians, halfback

Fritz was the first Black to make Walter Camp's first team All-Americans after having scored two touchdowns against both Yale and Harvard that year, leading Brown to upset victories on successive Saturdays. He played in the first modern Rose Bowl game, was in the first pro football league and was the first black pro coach in American.
Also in: National Football Hall of Fame and Providence Gridiron Hall of Fame.

POOLE, George Barney
Player
Born October 29, 1923, in Gloster, Miss; earned 23 varsity letters in football, basketball, and baseball; now manager of Mississippi Memorial Stadium in Jackson.

1942 University of Mississippi, end
1943 University of North Carolina, end
1944 – 1946 U.S. Military Academy, end
1947 – 1948 University of Mississippi, end
1949 New York Yankees (AAFC), end
1950 – 1951 New York Yankees, end
1952 Dallas Texans, end
1953 Baltimore Colts, end

Barney Poole was a 6 ft. 3 in, 225 lbs. end who played in the All-Star game of 1949. He later coached at Alabama, Louisiana State University and Southern Mississippi.
Also in: National Football Hall of Fame.

PURVIS, Duane
Player
Born November 13, 1912, in Decatur, Ill; brother Jim attended Purdue; both played football as number 88; All-American 1933 and 1934; Consensus All-American 1934; assistant professor of physical education at Purdue.

Duane Purvis followed his brother by three years at Purdue, both wearing number 88 and scoring the season's opening touchdown. Duane and Jim Carter were known as the "Touchdown Twins," scoring 9 of Purdue's 16 touchdowns in 1933.

REDMAN, Rick C.

Player

Born March 7, 1943, in Portland, Ore; attended Blanchett High School in Seattle; graduated from the Univ. Wash; Consensus All-American 1963 and 1964; AFL All-Star Game 1968.

1963 – 1964 University of Washington, guard
1965 – 1973 San Diego Chargers, linebacker

Rick Redman won the Most Valuable Lineman Award in the East-West Shrine game of 1964 and was then drafted in the fifth round by the San Diego Chargers. Rick played middle linebacker for most of his pro career, but as a punter his first three seasons, he averaged 37.5 yds. on 153 kicks. He totaled 66 tackles from the side linebacker position in 1972. Redman played in the 1968 American Football League's All-Star Game.

REINHARD, Robert R.

Player

Born October 17, 1920, in Hollywood, Calif; All-American 1940 and 1941; All-Time All-Pacific Coast team 1969.

1939 – 1941 University of California, tackle
1946 – 1949 Los Angeles Don (AAFC), tackle
1950 Los Angeles Rams, tackle

Bob Reinhard's varsity career at California produced only a 14 and 18 record, but he still managed to make All-American in 1940 and 1941. He won his team's Andy Smith Memorial Trophy during his senior season for the most playing time. As a pro, Bob was named to the All-Time All-Pacific Coast team of 1969.

REYNOLDS, Robert Odell "Horse"

Player

Twice All-American; v.pres. of Los Angeles Rams; pres. of Los Angeles Angels.

Horse Reynolds was the largest lineman at 6 ft 4 in, 225 lbs, on Stanford's greatest football eleven in the school's history. The two-time All-American helped his team to win or tie for the Pacific Coast Conference championship three years in succession. They appeared in two Rose Bowl games and produced four All-Americans.
Also in: National Football Hall of Fame.

RICHTER, Leslie A.

Player

Born October 6, 1930, in Fresno, Calif; graduated from Univ. Calif; excelled in both football and rugby; Consensus All-American in 1950 and 1951; Pacific Coast All-Time team; played in two Rose Bowls; spent two years in the military; presently president of Riverside (Calif.) Raceway.

Richter was first-round National Football League draft choice by the old Dallas Texans, he was called into service for two years and was unable to play. The Los Angeles Rams gave up all of 11 players for him in 1954. Finding permanence and greatness at middle linebacker, Richter did not disappoint the Rams. He was voted the Rams most valuable player twice and seven times played in the Pro-Bowl during his nine-year career with the Rams. He became known as football's most hated player and many opponents considered him "hatchet man." He was called, "an overrated oaf" by Norm Van Brocklin. And Alex Webster, the New York Giants' running back of the 1950s and 1960s, voiced such testimony: "Les simply goes hard all the time. He gives 200 percent on every play, but he's not a dirty player. I'd say he just gets wound up, like everybody else." He played in the 1955 National Football League championship game.
Also in: Major League Football Hall of Fame, Citizens Savings Hall of Fame Athletic Museum.

ROBERTSON, Alfred J.

Coach

See entry in College Basketball Hall of Fame, Citizens Savings Hall of Fame Athletic Museum, 1965.

ROBINSON, Edward N. "Robbie"

Coach

Born in 1873; won nine letters as Brown athlete, four football, three baseball and two track; died in 1945 at age 72.

1896 – 1897 University of Nebraska, coach
1898 – 1907 Brown University, coach
1910 – 1925 Brown University, coach

Robinson was known as the "Walter Camp of Brown Football"; his Brown teams were 140 – 82 – 12. His overall record was 156 – 88 – 13, and his team lost to Washington State in the second (first modern) Rose Bowl game in 1916. Running back Fritz Pollard was the greatest of his five Brown All-Americans.
Also in: National Football Hall of Fame.

ROBINSON, Stanley

Coach

Also in: American Association of College Baseball Coaches Hall of Fame.

ROCKNE, Knute K.

Coach

Born March 4, 1888, in Voss, Norway; came to America at age 8; grew up in Chicago, outstanding pole-vaulter and half-miler; attended Notre Dame Univ; died March 31, 1931, near Cottonwood Falls, Kans. in a private plane crash; named greatest All-Time Coach in football's Centennial Year, 1969.

As an end for Notre Dame from 1910 to 1913, Rockne and quarterback Gus Dorais revolutionized football. In the summer of 1913 prior to the season, they worked on passing while lifeguarding at Cedar Point, Ohio. On November 11, 1913, at West Point, Dorias and Rockne humbled Army 35 – 13 with a marvelous passing exhibition. Dorais completed 14 of 17 passes for 243 yds. and demonstrated to the nation how to utilize the passing game. In the same year, Rockne was named third-team All-American. After graduation he taught chemistry and assisted Jess Harper with the football team. He also played with the Massillon Tigers in 1919. In 1918 he succeeded Harper at Notre Dame and assumed the positions of both head football coach and athletic director. In the next 13 years he won 105 games, lost 12 and tied 5. His percentage of .881 is still unsurpassed. He never had a losing season and was undefeated in 1919, 1920, 1924, 1929 and 1930. Notre Dame achieved the national championships in 1924, 1929 and 1930. His 1924 team is one

of the most famous college squads ever assembled and featured the "Four Horsemen" and the "Seven Mules." In addition to his unsurpassed record as a coach, Rockne was also recognized as a spellbinding speaker and employed his talent frequently to rally his teams. Rockne's untimely death in a plane crash sent shock waves through the nation. One of Rockne's ex-pupils spoke of his contribution to football, "Rockne sold football to the men on the trolley, the elevated, the subway . . . the baker, the butcher, the pipe fitter who never went to college. He made it an American mania. He took it out of the thousand-dollar class and made it a million-dollar business." Each year the Knute Rockne Memorial Trophy is presented to the nation's outstanding collegiate back.
Also in: National Football Hall of Fame; and Noteworthy Contributors Hall of Fame, Citizens Savings Hall of Fame Athletic Museum.

ROMNEY, Ernest L. "Dick"
Coach
See entry in Athletic Directors Hall of Fame, Citizens Savings Hall of Fame and Athletic Museum.
Also in: National Football Hall of Fame.

ROPER, William
Coach

1903–1904 Virginia Military Institute, coach
1906–1908 Princeton University, coach
1909 University of Missouri, coach
1910–1911 Princeton University, coach
1915–1916 Swarthmore College, coach
1919–1930 Princeton University, coach

Bill Roper spent 26 years as a coach, only missing the two war years.
Also in: National Football Hall of Fame.

SANDERS, Henry Russell
Coach
Born March 7, 1905, in Asheville, N.C; graduated from Vanderbilt Univ.

Sanders returned to his alma mater in 1940 as football coach, moving to UCLA in 1949 and coaching through 1957. For the 15 years he has a 102–41–3 record in football.

SAVITSKY, George
Player
George Savitsky played for the University of Pennsylvania.

SAYERS, Gale
Player
See entry in Professional Football Hall of Fame, 1977.
Also in: National Football Hall of Fame.

SCHMIDT, Francis A.
Coach
Born December 3, 1885, in Downs, Kans; graduated from Univ. Nebr; died September 19, 1944, at age 59.

1919–1921 University of Tulsa, coach
1922–1928 University of Arkansas, coach
1929–1933 Texas Christian University, coach
1934–1940 Ohio State University, coach

Schmidt had a coaching record of 158–57–11 and was 46–6–5 at Texas Christian, winning two Southwest Conference titles. He developed Johnny Vaught, guard, and later a well-known coach. He won one Big Ten crown and tied for another at Ohio State. The Buckeyes lost to Notre Dame in 1935; the duel was voted the century's most outstanding game. The varied and powerful offensive attack earned the nickname "Close the Gates of Mercy."
Also in: National Football Hall of Fame.

SCHULZ, Adolf "Germany"
Player
Born April 9, 1883, in Ft. Wayne, Ind; graduated from Univ. Mich; All-American 1907; died April 14, 1951, in Detroit, Mich.

1907–1908 University of Michigan, center
1923 University of Detroit, head coach

While at Michigan Germany Schulz had a 32–4–1 playing record. As a freshman Schulz teamed with Willie Heston to be classified as Fielding Yost's best players. He was one of the first to use the one-hand spiral snap. He was voted All-American in 1907 and was captain of the team in 1908.
Also in: National Football Hall of Fame.

SCHWAB, Frank J. "Dutch"
Player
Born in 1895 in Madera, Pa; worked in Pennsylvania mines as a child, receiving 90¢ per day; later operated a hardware store in Spangler, Pa; died December 12, 1965, in Spangler, Pa.

Dutch Schwab played for four years at Kiski, Pa. Academy after a scout spotted him on the sandlots at 12 years old. While in the military service he was persuaded to play for the Leopards. Dutch played with Lafayette College as guard 1919–1922. He was All-American in 1921 and 1922 and captain of the team as a sophomore.
Also in: National Football Hall of Fame.

SCHWEGLER, Paul "Schweg"
Player
Born May 22, 1911, in Raymond, Wash; played football, basketball and baseball in high school; graduated from Univ. Wash; All-American 1929 and 1931.

Paul Schwegler was named to 43 All-Star teams during his University of Washington career. During his 1931 season he was team captain and won the inspirational award, the Flaherty Medal. Schweg was also a participant in the 1932 East-West Shrine game at San Francisco.
Also in: National Football Hall of Fame.

SHAUGHNESSY, Clark D.
Coach
Born March 6, 1892, in St. Cloud, Minn; died May 15, 1970, in Santa Monica, Calif, at age 78.

1915–1920 Tulane University, coach
1922–1926 Tulane University, coach
1927–1932 Loyola College of Louisiana, coach
1933–1939 University of Chicago, coach
1940–1941 Stanford University, coach
1942–1946 University of Maryland, coach
1943–1945 University of Pittsburgh, coach
1965 University of Hawaii, coach

Shaughnessy has been called the "Father of the Modern T-Formation." He was end, fullback, and two-way tackle

at Minnesota from 1911 to 1913. He was technical adviser for the Chicago Bears 1951 to 1962. His first team at Stanford, led by Frankie Albert, went unbeaten and defeated Nebraska in the Rose Bowl before 88,447.
Also in: National Football Hall of Fame.

SHAVER, Gaius "Gus"
Player
Born August 14, 1910, in Covina, Calif; Consensus All-American 1931.

This 5 ft. 11 in, 188 lb. running back was the Consensus All-American in 1931. His passing expertise spurred a 16 to 14 victory over Notre Dame in 1931, breaking that school's winning streak of 26 games. The Southern California Trojans were victorious in the 1932 Rose Bowl against Tulane.

SHEVLIN, Thomas L.
Player
Born March 1, 1883, in Muskegon, Mich; father Thomas H. Shevlin one of the nation's leading industrialists, lumber empire; attended Hill School in Pottstown, Pa; starred in three sports in high school; graduated from Yale Univ; All-American 1902 and 1905; always an impeccable dresser; died of pneumonia on December 29, 1915, in Minneapolis, Minn.

Tom Shevlin was known for his speed, intelligence and strength. While he played at Yale, the team had a record of 42 – 2 – 1. He was voted All-American in 1902 and 1905 and was second-team All-American in 1903. The 5 ft. 10 in, 195 lb. end returned two kickoffs for touchdowns during his career.
Also in: National Football Hall of Fame.

SIMPSON, Orenthal J. "O.J."
Player
Born July 9, 1947, in San Francisco, Calif; attended Galileo High School, San Francisco City Col. 1965 – 1966, graduated from Univ. Southern Calif; All-American 1967 and 1968; Heisman Trophy; Maxwell Award; Walter Camp Trophy; College Athlete of the Decade for 1960s; Modern All-Time All-American Team; Citizens Savings Rose Bowl Player of the Year Award 1968; AFL Player of the Year 1973; Pro Bowl Most Valuable Player 1973; movie and television actor in off season; works for ABC-TV sports.

1967 – 1968 University of Southern California, running back
1969 Buffalo Bills, running back

O. J. Simpson, the famed runner of the 1960s and 1970s football world, scored 54 touchdowns and rushed for more than 2500 yds. at San Francisco City College in 1965 and 1966. He was the national rushing champion in 1967 and 1968 with record yardage of 1415 and 1709 respectively. O. J's pro career began in 1969 when he was the Number One draft choice taken by the Buffalo Bills. As Rookie of the Year he gained 697 yds. rushing. In 1972 he led the National Football League in rushing with 1251 yds. During his pro career he has set records for season carries of 332 and has had three games of 200 or more yards rushing.
Also in: Black Athletes Hall of Fame and International Palace of Sports Hall of Fame.

SINGTON, Frederick W.
Player
Born February 24, 1910, in Birmingham, Ala; president of four sporting goods stores throughout Alabama; played pro baseball with Washington Senators from 1934 to 1937, Brooklyn Dodgers 1938 and 1939; Lt. Commander in U.S. Naval Reserve during W.W. II; Phi Beta Kapa and student body v.pres. in 1930 at Alabama; All-American 1930.

Fred Sington starred on one of the South's greatest teams—University of Alabama—in 1930 finishing the season at 10 – 0. He was the unanimous choice for All-American that year after a 14 to nothing victory over Washington State in the Rose Bowl. Sington was a Southeastern Conference official for 20 years.
Also in: National Football Hall of Fame.

SINKWICH, Frank "Fireball Frankie"
Player
Born October 10, 1920, in McKees Rocks, Pa; attended Chaney High School in Youngstown, Ohio; Consensus All-American 1941; All-American 1942; Heisman Trophy; Most Valuable Player 1943 and 1944; Orange Bowl Classic Hall of Honor in 1970; owns business in Athens, Ga.

1940 – 1942 University of Georgia, halfback
1943 – 1944 Detroit Lions, halfback
1946 – 1947 New York Yankees (AAFC), halfback
1947 Baltimore Colts (AAFC), halfback

Frank Sinkwich led the nation in rushing with 1103 yards in 1941. He played most of 1942 with a fractured jaw and still managed to lead the nation in total offense with 2187 yards. Sinkwich established an all-time major bowl record by compiling 382 yards of total offense as Georgia whipped Texas Christian 40 – 26 in the Orange Bowl of 1942. He completed his career with a total of 4602 yards, 2271 rushing and 2331 passing. He scored 28 touchdowns and accounted for 27 more.
Also in: National Football Hall of Fame.

SITKO, Emil M.
Player
Born September 7, 1923, in Fort Wayne, Ind; attended Univ. Notre Dame; All-American 1948 and 1949; died December 15, 1973, in Ft. Wayne.

Emil Sitko better known as "Six Yards" because of his average carry, played on three unbeaten Irish teams—1946, 1947 and 1948. He was elected All-American in 1948 and then switched to fullback for his last season only to receive another All-American nomination for his efforts that year. His short legs enabled him to get through holes, and Sitko still holds the Notre Dame one-game rushing record of 186 yards.

SLATER, Frederick F. "Duke"
Player
Duke Slater was one of the early great black football stars both in college and pro football. He was a tackle for the University of Iowa 1918 – 1921. This quick charger played without a helmet and was never removed from a game because of injuries.
Also in: National Football Hall of Fame.

SMITH, Andrew L.
Coach
Born September 10, 1883, in DuBois, Pa; died Jan. 8, 1926, in Philadelphia, Pa, at age 43.

1909 – 1912 University of Pennsylvania, coach
1913 – 1915 Purdue University, coach
1916 – 1925 University of California, coach

Smith was the fullback for Pennsylvania's 12 – 0 national champions in 1904. As a coach, he was best known for his Californian "Wonder Teams"; in the five-year period from 1920 to 1924, the Bears were unbeaten, winning 44 and tying 4. His string of victories reached 50 games and ended with a 15 – 0 loss to the Olympic Club of San Francisco in 1925. He compiled a 74 – 16 – 5 record at California and was 116 – 32 – 3 overall. The most famous California All-American he trained was end Harold "Brick" Muller. He also developed Elmer "Ollie" Oliphant.
Also in: National Football Hall of Fame.

SMITH, Bruce P. "Boo"
Player
Born February 8, 1920, in Faribault, Minn; All-American and Heisman Trophy 1941; died of cancer on August 28, 1967.

1939 – 1941 University of Minnesota, halfback
1945 – 1948 Green Bay Packers, halfback
1948 Los Angeles Rams, halfback

Despite injuries Boo Smith was winner of the 1941 Heisman Trophy and All-American honors. Smith helped the Gophers to two consecutive national championships with a 17-game winning streak in 1940 and 1941. He was captain of the East in the East-West Shrine game and voted the Most Valuable Player for the College All-Star Games.
Also in: National Football Hall of Fame.

SMITH, Ernest F. "Ernie"
Player
Born November 26, 1909 in Spearfish, S.Dak; played at Gardena, Calif, High School; graduated from Univ. Southern Calif; All-American 1930 and 1932; All-Pro 1936; active in musical organizations; member of the Tournament of Roses committee; insurance executive.

1931 – 1933 University of Southern California, tackle
1935 – 1939 Green Bay Packers, tackle

While Ernie Smith was a member of the University of Southern California team they held a record of 28 wins and 3 losses.
Also in: National Football Hall of Fame.

SMITH, Harry E. "Blackjack"
Player
Born August 26, 1918, in Russellville, Mo; graduated from Univ. Southern Calif; All-American 1939.

1937 – 1939 University of Southern California, guard
1940 Detroit Lions, guard
1941 – 1943 University of Missouri, assistant coach
1949 – 1950 University of Southern California, freshman coach
1951 Saskatchewan Roughriders, head coach

Harry Smith started 28 consecutive games for the University of Southern California, finishing with a 21 – 3 – 4 playing record. Smith was a member of the Rose Bowl championship teams of 1939 and 1940.
Also in: National Football Hall of Fame.

SMITH, Maurice J.
Coach
Born October 15, 1898, in Kankakee, Ill; graduated from Univ. Notre Dame.

M. J. Smith coached football 22 years at Ganzaga College 1925 – 1928, Santa Clara 1929 – 1935, Villanova 1936 – 1942, San Francisco 1946 and Lafayette 1949 – 1951. His overall record was 108 – 75 – 12.

SNAVELY, Carl G. "King Carl"
Coach
Born July 31, 1894, in Omaha, Nebr; football and baseball captain at Lebanon Valley in 1915.

1927 – 1933 Bucknell University, coach
1934 – 1935 North Carolina, coach
1936 – 1944 Cornell University, coach
1945 – 1952 North Carolina, coach
1953 – 1958 Washington University (Mo), coach

Snavely had a 180 – 96 – 16 record overall; he developed All-American Charlie Justice and Clarke Hinkle and Jerome "Brud" Holland.
Also in: National Football Hall of Fame.

SNOW, Neil Worthington
Player
Citizens Savings Rose Bowl Player of the Year Award 1902.

The arrival of Neil Snow at the University of Michigan marked the beginning of a great football era there. In 1898 and 1901 Michigan won the national championship. Snow topped his college career by scoring five touchdowns in the first Rose Bowl game in 1902. During the regular season Michigan mounted up 501 points.
Also in: National Football Hall of Fame.

SOLEM, Oscar M.
Coach
Born December 13, 1891, in Minneapolis, Minn; graduated from Univ. Minn; died October 26, 1970, in Minneapolis at age 79.

1920 Luther College, coach
1921 – 1931 Drake University, coach
1932 – 1936 University of Iowa, coach
1937 – 1945 Syracuse University, coach
1946 – 1957 Springfield College, coach

Solem began his coaching career while still a student at Minnesota. He tutored at the Normal School of River Falls, Wis, in the afternoon and a pro team in Minneapolis at night. He also played end for Minnesota, graduating in 1915. His career record was 162 – 117 – 20; he created the controversial Y-formation in 1941. It featured the center who faced the backfield, making direct passes and pitchouts. The formation was used in 1941 but was banned by the rules committee prior to the 1942 season. Bud Wilkinson and Biggie Munn were Solem assistants who achieved prominence as head coaches. Duffy Daugherty, who played under Solem at Syracuse, became a Michigan State mentor.

SPAULDING, William H.
Coach
Born May 4, 1880, in Melrose, Wis; died October 13, 1966, in Los Angeles, Calif. at age 86.

1907–1921 Western Michigan University, coach
1922–1924 University of Minnesota, coach
1925–1938 University of California at Los Angeles (UCLA), coach

Spaulding was a Wabash halfback and track sprinter. His coaching record was 144–83–16; he coached Frank Thomas at Western Michigan who subsequently attended Notre Dame and won fame as Alabama coach. Of Spaulding's many UCLA stars, Kenny Washington is the most well known. Spaulding's arrival at UCLA coincided with the move of Howard Jones from Iowa to Southern California; they pioneered one of the nation's most heated rivalries. After retiring from coaching, he served as the Bruin's athletic director for ten years, then went into business.

SPEARS, Clarence W. "Doc" "Fat" "Cupid"
Coach

Born July 24, 1894, in DeWitt, Ariz; transferred from Knox Col. to Dartmouth Col; studied medicine at Univ. Chicago and Rush Medical School; eventually left coaching for a full-time medical practice; died February 1, 1964, at age 70.

1914–1915 Dartmouth College, guard
1917 Dartmouth College, head coach
1919–1920 Dartmouth College, coach
1921–1924 West Virginia University, coach
1925–1929 University of Minnesota, coach
1930–1931 University of Oregon, coach
1932–1935 University of Wisconsin, coach

With Spears in the lineup, Dartmouth lost only 2 of 18 games. They compiled a 7–2 record and won the Ivy League title when he coached there. He developed Bronko Nagurski at Minnesota. His composite record was 135–78–13.
Also in: National Football Hall of Fame and West Virginia Sports Writers Hall of Fame.

SPRAGUE, Mortimore E. "Bud"
Player

Born September 8, 1904, in Dallas, Tex; attended Univ. Tex; Consensus All-American 1928; during W.W. II served with office of chief of transportation; present at both Malta and Yalta conferences; vice president of Home Insurance Co, in New York City.

1922–1924 University of Texas, tackle
1928 U.S. Military Academy, tackle

Becoming a football team captain seemed to run in the Sprague family blood. Bud was the Texas team captain, while his brothers Howard, John and Charlie headed Southern Methodist University teams. While playing for Army in 1928, Sprague also served as captain of that team and oversaw a record of 44–9–3.
Also in: National Football Hall of Fame.

STAGG, Amos Alonzo
Coach

Born in West Orange, N.J. in 1862; born into extreme poverty during the Civil War; won first fame as a baseball pitcher at Yale Univ; attended Yale Divinity School but quit—considered himself poor public speaker for the ministry; offered six contracts from National League baseball teams, did not wish to compete professionally; died in Stockton, Calif, March 17, 1965, at age 103.

After terminating his studies at the Yale Divinity School in 1889, Stagg turned to coaching, and his remarkable career began. He served as head coach for 57 years, first at Springfield College 1890 and 1891, then at Chicago 1892–1932 and finally at the College of the Pacific 1933–1946. When he reached mandatory retirement age, 70, at the University of Chicago, he was offered several advisory jobs which he turned down since he refused to be idle. The College of the Pacific, however, hired him and maintained him as head football coach until the age of 84. At 81 in 1943 he was named the National Collegiate Athletic Association (NCAA) Coach of the Year. After leaving Pacific he assisted his son's coaching at Susquehanna until he was 89. During his career as a football coach, Stagg won 314 games, more than any other coach (one more than Pop Warner). At Chicago he won seven Western Big Ten Conference titles. His 1905 team, starring Walter Eckersall, was one of his most famous. It outscored foes 212–5, won ten straight games, including a 2–0 thriller over Michigan and was designated national champion. Stagg has been acknowledged one of football's foremost innovators. He developed the end-round, hidden-ball trick, double reverse, huddle, handoff from fake kick, quick-kick, charging sled, padded goal posts, man-in-motion, backfield shift, quarterback keeper, wind sprints, cross-blocking, and more. His teams were first to practice under lights, and his Springfield squad played the first night game against Yale in 1891. Knute Rockne said of Stagg, "All football comes from Stagg." Stagg was innovative in other sports as well as football. He pioneered the headlong slide and batting cage in baseball and conducted an inaugural tour of Japan by American baseball players. He introduced troughs for overflows in swimming pools and held the national schoolboy basketball tournament in Chicago from 1917 to 1930 thus helping to standardize the game. Stagg was paragon of clean living and sportmanship. He was a foe of smoking, drinking, profanity and hot dogs. Stagg, often referred to as the "Grand Old Man of the Midway," was 103 when he died, thus outliving his Yale coach, Walter Camp, by 40 years.
Also in: Naismith Memorial Basketball Hall of Fame and National Football Hall of Fame; Noteworthy Contributors Hall of Fame and Track and Field Hall of Fame, Citizens Savings Hall of Fame Athletic Museum.

STEPHENSON, Donald P.
Player

Born July 10, 1935, in Bessemer, Ala; attended Georgia Tech; All-American 1956 and 1957; All-Southeastern Conference 1956 and 1957; manager of Shalimar Plaza Motel in Panama City, Fla.

Stephenson was center 1956 and 1957, and captain of the team in 1957, a driving force behind the 1956 record of 9–1–0 which put them fourth in both wire service polls.

STRONG, Kenneth
Player

See entry in Professional Football Hall of Fame, 1967.
Also in: National Football Hall of Fame; and Major League Football Hall of Fame, Citizens Savings Hall of Fame Athletic Museum.

STRUPPER, Everett
Player
Everett Strupper was a back in the Georgia Tech football team 1915 – 1917.
Also in: National Football Hall of Fame.

STUBER, Emmett "Abe"
Coach
Born October 12, 1904, in St. Joseph, Mo.

1929 – 1931	Westminster College, Mo, coach
1932 – 1946	Southeastern Mississippi State College, coach
1947 – 1953	Iowa State University, coach

Stuber played quarterback for Missouri 1924 – 1926. His total coaching record was 145 – 69 – 15; 23 – 3 – 1 at Westminster, 98 – 28 – 11 at Southeastern Mississippi and 24 – 38 – 3 at Iowa State. He assisted the Philadelphia Eagles in 1955, was the personnel director for the St. Louis Cardinals 1960 – 1972 and then was a personnel consultant.

STUHLDREHER, Harry
Player and Coach
Born October 14, 1901, in Massillon, Ohio; attended Univ. Notre Dame; All-American 1924; coached at three universities; executive with U.S. Steel Corp; died January 22, 1965.

1922 – 1924	University of Notre Dame, quarterback
1926	Brooklyn Lions, quarterback
1926	Brooklyn Horsemen, quarterback
1925 – 1936	University Villanova, coach
1937 – 1947	University of Wisconsin, coach

Stuhldreher spent his youth in Massillon, where the high school Tigers team was directed by player-coach Knute Rockne. For free admission, Harry would carry Rockne's helmet into the stadium. Then at Notre Dame, Harry played football under Rockne for three years and developed a particular style of quickness and agility. Stuhldreher and three others became known as the "Four Horsemen." After college he played professional ball, then turned to coaching at Villanova University, the University of Wisconsin and, in between, developed the famed "Seven Blocks of Granite" at Fordham. Overall, Stuhldreher's record stood at 110 – 87 – 15.
Also in: National Football Hall of Fame.

SUTHERLAND, John B. "Jock"
Coach
Born March 21, 1889, in Coupar-Angus, Scotland; porter and baggage clerk, "loon" (light farmhand) and caddy during his Scottish boyhood; arrived in Pittsburgh at age 18; graduated from Univ. Pittsburgh; won scholarship to Pittsburgh Dental School; died April 11, 1948, in Pittsburgh at age 59.

1919 – 1923	Lafayette College, coach
1924 – 1938	University of Pittsburgh, coach

Sutherland was a guard in three football seasons—1915 – 1917—after being moved from a tackle by coach Pop Warner. As coach, his Panthers gave some of the game's most powerful rushing exhibitions. His record at Pittsburgh was 111 – 20 – 12, winning two national championships and playing in four Rose Bowls. He taught 24 All-Americans. Notre Dame dropped Pittsburgh from its schedule after the Irish lost five out of six games and were blanked four times. The "Dream Backfield" unfolded in his last season: Dick Cassiano and Curly Stebbins as halfbacks, Marshall Goldberg at fullback and Johnny Chickerneo as quarterback. His overall college record was 144 – 28 – 14.
Also in: National Football Hall of Fame.

TALIAFERRO, George "Scoop"
Player
Born January 8, 1927, in Halls, Tenn; attended Indiana Univ.

1945	Indiana University, running back
1949	Los Angeles Dons, player
1950 – 1951	New York Yankees, player
1952	Dallas Texans, player
1953 – 1954	Baltimore Colts, player
1955	Philadelphia Eagles, player

Scoop played as a sophomore on the Indiana team and helped them get their first Big Ten title with nine straight wins. Then in a good season with the Dons, he passed for 790 yds. and scored four touchdowns. In a Yanks game against rival New York Giants, on December 3, 1950, Taliaferro returned eight kickoffs.

TATUM, James M.
Coach
Born July 22, 1913, in McColl, S.C; Coach of the Year 1953; died July 23, 1959, in Chapel Hill, N.C. at age 46.

1942	University of North Carolina, coach
1946	University of Oklahoma, coach
1947 – 1955	University of Maryland, coach
1956 – 1958	University of North Carolina, coach

Tatum was the youngest of five brothers, all of whom played tackle in college: two at Clemson, two at Wofford, and Jim at North Carolina. As coach, he had a 100 – 35 – 7 overall record, including 73 – 15 – 4 at Maryland. The Terrapins won the National championship in 1953. He learned the split-T attack (which he used throughout his career) from Don Faurot of Iowa's Pre-Flight team.

THOMAS, Frank W.
Coach
Born November 15, 1889, in Muncie, Ind; graduated from Univ. Notre Dame 1922; died May 10, 1959, at age 70.

1925 – 1928	University of Chattanooga, coach
1931 – 1946	University of Alabama, coach

Thomas had a 108 – 20 – 7 record at Alabama for .841 percentage. His overall record was 141 – 33 – 9 (.785). He steered the Crimson Tide to six bowl games; three Rose, one Cotton, one Orange and one Sugar, and a 4 – 2 record.
Also in: National Football Hall of Fame.

THORPE, James
Player
See entry in Professional Football Hall of Fame, 1963.
Also in: American Indian Athletic Hall of Fame; National Football Hall of Fame; Major League Football Hall of Fame and Track and Field Hall of Fame, Citizens Savings Hall of Fame Athletic Museum; National Track and Field Hall of Fame and U.S. Track and Field Hall of Fame.

TICKNOR, Benjamin
Player
Ben Ticknor played football as center at Harvard University 1928 – 1930.
Also in: National Football Hall of Fame.

TINSLEY, Gaynell C. "Gus"
Player
Born February 1, 1915, in Ruple, La; attended Louisiana State Univ; All-American 1935 and 1936.

1934 – 1936 Louisiana State University, end
1937 – 1938 Chicago Cardinals, end

At 6 ft. 1 in. and 195 lbs, Tinsley could adapt to baseball and football; and in football to offense and defense. He was captain of both sports teams and in later years became a coach. From 1939 to 1942 he returned to Louisiana State as end coach. He accepted the head coach position from 1948 to 1952.
Also in: National Football Hall of Fame and Louisiana State Hall of Fame.

TRIPPI, Charles L.
Player
See entry in Professional Football Hall of Fame, 1966.
Also in: National Football Hall of Fame; and Major League Football Hall of Fame, Citizens Savings Hall of Fame Athletic Museum.

TRYON, J. Edward
Player
Born July 25, 1900, in Medford, Maine; attended Colgate Univ; graduate work at New York Univ. and Springfield Col. in physical education.

1922 – 1925 Colgate University, halfback
1926 – 1927 New York Yankees, halfback

Eddie was slippery. Coach Dick Harlow had nothing but praise for this type of athlete who could do just about anything. In fact, Harlow viewed Tryon as "the answer to a coach's fondest dream." In a 1923 game against Niagara, Eddie made runs of 50, 95 and 97 yds. to score three touchdowns. Then in 1925 he led the Colgate team to an undefeated season. Later, out of playing, Tryon took up coaching at Hobart and became a member of the National Collegiate Athletic Association rules committee from 1960 through 1963.
Also in: National Football Hall of Fame.

VAUGHT, John H.
Coach
Born May 6, 1908, in Olney, Tex; attended Polytechnic High School in Forth Worth, was the class valedictorian; graduated from Tex. Christian Univ; All-Southwestern Conference 1931 and 1932.

1936 – 1941 University of North Carolina, line coach
1947 – 1970 University of Mississippi, coach

Vaught played left guard for Texas Christian (TCU) under Francis Schmidt, and captained TCU's Southwest Conference champs in 1932. His coaching record was 185 – 85 – 12 (.749). He won more Southeastern championships (six) than any other coach, and took Ole Miss to 18 bowl games, 14 in succession from 1957 – 1970 for a national record. He was the second Southeastern Conference coach to win the conference title in the first year as head coach. His All-Americans include Charlie Conerly, Barney Poole, Charlie Flowers, Jim Dunaway and Archie Manning.

WADE, Wallace
Coach

1923 – 1930 University of Alabama, coach
1931 – 1941 Duke University, coach
1946 – 1950 Duke University, coach

Also in: National Football Hall of Fame.

WALDORF, Lynn O. "Pappy"
Coach
Born October 3, 1902, in Clifton Springs, N.Y; attended Syracuse Univ; All-American 1922 and 1924; Coach of the Year Award 1935; after retiring from coaching, joined San Francisco 49ers as personnel director.

1926 – 1927 Oklahoma City College, coach
1929 – 1933 Oklahoma City College, coach
1934 Kansas State University, coach
1935 – 1946 Northwestern University, coach
1947 – 1956 University of California, coach

Syracuse was 22 – 4 – 3 when Waldorf played. While he was coach at Northwestern, the Wildcats won the Big Ten title and lost only to Notre Dame. He coached All-Americans Stephen Reix, Max Morris, Bob Voigt and Otto Graham, and took three straight California teams to the Rose Bowl 1949 – 1951. He had a career record of 170 – 94 – 22.
Also in: National Football Hall of Fame.

WALKER, Douglas C. "Peahead"
Coach
Born 1889 in Birmingham, Ala; died July 16, 1970, at age 81.

1926 Atlantic Christian College, coach
1927 – 1936 Eton College, coach
1937, 1949 Wake Forest College, coach

Walker played baseball, football and basketball at Howard 1918 – 1921. He played 12 years of pro baseball with Rochester of the International League, Wilson and Norfolk of the Piedmont League. He coached the Montreal Alouettes of the Canadian Football League. Walker compiled a record of 77 – 51 – 6 at Wake Forest, the best in school history. He produced the Deacons' only two bowl teams—Dixie in 1949 and Gator in 1956.

WALKER, Ewell Doak, Jr. "Doaker"
Player
Born in Dallas, Tex; graduated from Southern Methodist Univ; All-American and Heisman Trophy 1948; Consensus All-American 1947 and 1949; All-Pro 1950, 1951, 1953 and 1954.

1946 – 1949 Southern Methodist University, running back and quarterback
1950 – 1953 Detroit Lions, halfback

Ewell "Doaker" Walker was good enough as a freshman in 1945 to play running back on the varsity team at Southern Methodist University. He was premier halfback in the nation for three years. One feat during his college career showed a 79-yd. punt against Oregon in the 1949 Cotton Bowl Game. He placed third for the Heisman in 1947 and 1949. Walker signed a three-year contract with the Detroit Lions in 1950. He led the Lions to world titles in 1952 and 1953. In 1952 the Lions had their first championship in seventeen years. He held the

position of league scorer twice, once in 1950 and again in 1955. Walker's career statistics read 3582 yds. total offense (1928 rushing and 1654 passing), 52 touchdowns accounted for (38 rushing and 14 passing), 8 interceptions, 27 pass receptions, 80 punts, 50 punt returns and 26 kickoff returns.
Also in: Major League Football Hall of Fame, Citizens Savings Hall of Fame Athletic Museum; National Football Hall of Fame and Texas High School Football Hall of Fame.

WALSH, Adam J.
Coach
Born December 4, 1901, in Churchville, Iowa; a four-sport letterman at Hollywood, Calif. High School; graduated from Univ. Notre Dame.

Walsh captained football's most celebrated team—"Four Horsemen" and "Seven Mules" in 1924. He also won letters in track and basketball. He coached Santa Clara, Yale, Harvard, Bowdoin and the Los Angeles Rams. As Yale assistant, he was the first non-Yale graduate hired to coach football at New Haven. He was named Santa Clara head coach at age 23. He served two terms in the Maine House of Representatives and as U.S. Marshall for the District of Maine.
Also in: National Football Hall of Fame.

WARNER, Glenn S. "Pop"
Coach
Born April 5, 1871, in Springville, N.Y; his younger brother William J. was a Cornell All-American and coached Cornell one season, and was then succeeded by Pop; died September 7, 1954, at age 83.

1895 – 1896 University of Georgia, coach
1897 – 1898 Cornell University, coach
1899 – 1903 Carlisle College, coach
1904 – 1906 Cornell University, coach
1907 – 1914 Carlisle University, coach
1915 – 1923 University of Pittsburgh, coach
1924 – 1932 Stanford University, coach
1933 – 1938 Temple University, coach

Warner acquired the name "Pop" because he was older than most Cornell students during his undergraduate days. He was the heavyweight boxing champion in 1893. A football guard with no previous training, he won more games (313) than any other college coach except Amos Alonzo Stagg (314). Warner lost 106 and tied 32 for .729 percent. He and Stagg are thought to be football's greatest innovators. His 1916 Pittsburgh team rates with the all-time best. He took Stanford to three Rose Bowls and Temple to its first Sugar Bowl. Warner developed 47 All-Americans, including backfield immortals Jim Thorpe of Carlisle and Ernie Nevers from Stanford. He received $34 a week for his first coaching job. He left a $500,000 estate when he died.
Also in: National Football Hall of Fame.

WASHINGTON, Kenneth S.
Player
Born August 31, 1918; attended Lincoln High School in Los Angeles, Calif; graduated from Univ. Calif. at Los Angeles (UCLA); All-American 1939; civic leader and businessman in Los Angeles.

1937 – 1939 University of California at Los Angeles, halfback
1946 – 1948 Los Angeles Rams, halfback

During his collegiate career, Washington led UCLA in rushing with 1914 yds. and accounted for 3182 total offense yds. He scored 19 touchdowns and helped the team chalk up a no-loss 6 – 0 – 4 season. After W.W. II, Kenney and his UCLA teammate Woody Strode signed with the Rams and became the first Blacks in the National Football League.
Also in: National Football Hall of Fame.

WEATHERALL, James P.
Player
Born October 26, 1929, in White Deer, Tex; attended Univ. Okla; Outland Trophy 1951; owner of insurance agency in Oklahoma City.

1949 – 1951 University of Oklahoma, tackle
1955 – 1957 Philadelphia Eagles, player
1958 Washington Redskins, player
1959 – 1960 Detroit Lions, player

Weatherall was big in stature at 6 ft. 4 in. and 230 lbs, and he was big on winning. The three years he played on Oklahoma's team brought them three straight Big Seven championships. And in the two years, 1950 to 1951, Jim was successful on 76 out of 94 extra point attempts. He co-captained the team in 1951 and was co-captain of the North team of that year's Senior Bowl. He was also captain of the West team in the East-West Shrine Game.

WEBSTER, George
Player
Born November 25, 1945, in Anderson, S.C; attended Mich. State Univ; Consensus All-American 1965 and 1966; All-AFL 1967 – 1969; All-Time AFL Team.

1964 – 1966 Michigan State University, linebacker
1967 – 1971 Houston Oilers, linebacker
1972 – 1973 Pittsburgh Steelers, linebacker

As a sophomore playing for coach Duffy Daugherty, George was the defensive end. Although his performance as end was one of the finest ever seen by Daugherty, he played roverback in his last two seasons. In 1966 he was named the outstanding player of the East-West Shrine game and of the Hula Bowl game. His jersey number 90 was retired, acknowledging his junior-senior contribution to a record 19 – 1 – 1. He topped off his collegiate career with the 1966 Rose Bowl and then was launched into professional play. The American Football League (AFL) named him Rookie of the Year. Webster, at 6 ft. 4 in. and 220 lbs, developed a tackle technique deemed deadly. In 1967 he played the AFL Championship game and was chosen for the AFL All-Star games of 1968 and 1969.

WEEKES, Benjamin Harold
Player
Born April 2, 1880, in Oyster Bay, N.Y; graduated from Columbia Univ; Second Team 1900; All-American 1901; Third Team 1901; became stockbroker in New York City; died July 26, 1950, in New York City.

In 1899 Columbia trounced Yale for the first time in 26 years and all because of the 5 ft. 10 in, 178 lb. spitfire named Weekes. He invented a play called the "flying hurdle" which required that two teammates hoist him to their shoulders and crash through the opposition. With football in hand, he would be tossed past the defense to get a clean start toward scoring. Through his senior year Weekes was injured in nearly every game but he was

good for six touchdowns against Fordham University. He also returned a kick-off 107 yards in the game against Hamilton.
Also in: National Football Hall of Fame.

WEIR, Ed S.
Player
Born March 14, 1903, in Superior, Nebr; graduated from Univ. Nebr; All-American 1924 and 1925; outstanding hurdler; coached track at his alma mater; retired in Lincoln, Nebr.

1923 – 1925 University of Nebraska, tackle
1926 – 1928 Frankford Yellowjackets, tackle

Weir became a track star in private during the first sixteen years of his life. Since the Weir farm was some distance from everything, Ed relied on his legs to get him places, including four miles daily to and from school. In college he expanded his interests to include football and lettered three years in both sports. At the Kansas Relays of 1925 Weir demonstrated his hurdling prowess when he defeated the Olympic gold medalist Dan Kinsey. In football he donated his share to a number of Nebraska victories over Knute Rockne's crack Notre Dame team. After a stint in the pros, Weir went back to Nebraska to coach the "thinclads" and eventually led them to ten outdoor and indoor titles.
Also in: National Football Hall of Fame.

WEST, D. Belford "Belf"
Player
Born May 7, 1896, in Hamilton, N.Y; grandson of Civil War general and founder of National Hamilton Bank in N.Y; graduated from Colgate Univ; All-American 1916 and 1919.

West did well in several different sports, with letters in football, basketball, baseball, tennis and hockey. But it was in football that he starred. Out of 21 varsity games played in West's time, Colgate kept the adversary scoreless for 14. A highlight of his career was a 52-yd. field goal in the 1916 battle against chief rival Syracuse which Colgate won 15 – 0.
Also in: National Football Hall of Fame.

WHITE, Byron R. "Whizzer"
Player
Born June 8, 1917, in Ft. Collins, Colo; attended Wellington, Colo, High School; Univ. of Colo, Phi Beta Kappa; Consensus All-American 1937; graduated with honors from Yale Law School; Rhodes scholar; served in Naval Air Combat Intelligence during W.W. II; appointed U.S. Supreme Court Justice by President John F. Kennedy.

1935 – 1938 University of Colorado, player
1939 – 1940 Pittsburgh Steelers, player

White's illustrious collegiate career established roots in 1936 when he was named All-Conference in not one but three sports—baseball, basketball and football. In the Cotton Bowl battle with Rice, the Colorado team fell 28 – 14, in debt to the Whizzer who scored one touchdown on an interception return and threw a touchdown pass. In 1937 White led the nation in scoring with 119 points from 16 touchdowns and 23 extra points. He was tops in rushing having gained 1121 yds. in 181 carries. Throughout the season he was playing 60 mins. in every game. In 1940 White became the first player to receive a five-figure salary, with $15,000. He went on in pro ball to become the leader in rushing of that year plus All-Pro.
Also in: National Football Hall of Fame.

WHITMIRE, Donald B.
Player
Born July 1, 1922, in Giles County, Tenn; graduated from Univ. of Ala; Consensus All-American 1943; Unanimous All-American 1944; Knute Rockne Trophy 1944; became Rear Admiral in the U.S. Navy; home in Annandale, Va.

1941 – 1942 University of Alabama, tackle
1943 – 1944 U.S. Naval Academy, tackle

Whitmire possessed a tackling talent due to 215 lbs. on a 5 ft. 11 in. frame. Through skillful maneuvering he brought his team to two bowl victories and was named All-Time Tackle for both.
Also in: National Football Hall of Fame.

WIDSETH, Edwin
Player
Edwin Widseth played tackle on the University of Minnesota football squad 1934 – 1936.
Also in: National Football Hall of Fame.

WILCE, John W.
Coach
Born May 12, 1888, in Rochester, N.Y; died May 17, 1963, at age 75.

A Wisconsin fullback, Wilce spent his entire coaching career at Ohio State. He had a 78 – 33 – 9 record. He coached immortal running back, Charles "Chic" Harley. He also tutored All-American Gaylord Stinchcomb and Wes Fesler, and produced the school's first unbeaten, untied season in 1916, which event was not repeated for 28 years. His teams won three Western Conference Big Ten titles—1916, 1917 and 1920. They were beaten 28 – 0 in the 1921 Rose Bowl by California.
Also in: National Football Hall of Fame.

WILDUNG, Richard K.
Player
See entry in Green Bay Packers Hall of Fame, 1973.
Also in: National Football Hall of Fame.

WILKINSON, Charles "Bud"
Coach
See entry in Athletic Directors Hall of Fame, Citizens Savings Hall of Fame Athletic Museum, 1973.
Also in: National Football Hall of Fame.

WILLIAMS, Henry L. "Doc"
Coach
Born July 26, 1889, in Hartford, Conn; graduate of Pa. Med. Col; died June 14, 1931, in Minneapolis, at age 42.

1891 U.S. Military Academy, coach
1900 – 1921 University of Minnesota, coach

Williams was a halfback and track hurdler at Yale 1888 – 1891; he set the world 120-yd. high hurdle record with 15.8 clocking in 1891. At the same meet he set the intercollegiate mark of 21.2 in 220-yd. low hurdles. He was the editor of the *Yale Daily News* in his junior and senior years. Williams was the first Army coach to beat

Navy, in 1891. He compiled a 143–14–12 record at Minnesota. Five squads went undefeated. His .788 percent is still the tenth best in college football history.
Also in: National Football Hall of Fame.

WILSON, George
Player
From 1923 to 1925 George Wilson was a star halfback for the University of Washington. He won the Citizens Savings Rose Bowl Player of the Year Award in 1926.
Also in: National Football Hall of Fame.

WISTERT, Albert A. "Ox"
Player
Born December 18, 1920 in Chicago, Ill; attended Chicago Foreman High School; graduated from Univ. Mich; Consensus All-American 1942; active in Michigan alumni club, plus church and civic affairs; affiliated with Bankers Life of Nebraska, co-leading salesman; qualified for "Wall of Fame" in 1967.

1940–1942 University of Michigan, tackle
1944–1948 Philadelphia Eagles, tackle

In 1942 Albert made consensus All-American, the second of three Wistert brothers to be so honored. Brother Whitey made it in 1933 and Alvin got it in 1949. In 1943 Albert acted as co-captain of the sharp college All-Star team that whipped the Washington Redskins. As a pro he kept up captain status with the Eagles from 1944 through 1948. He was named All-Pro for five straight years.
Also in: National Football Hall of Fame.

WISTERT, Alvin
Player
Alvin Wistert played football at the University of Michigan 1946–1949, as did his brother Albert. He was named Consensus All-American in 1949.

WOJCIECHOWICZ, Alexander "Wojie"
Player
See entry in Professional Football Hall of Fame, 1968.
Also in: Major League Football Hall of Fame, Citizens Savings Hall of Fame Athletic Museum; National Football Hall of Fame and National Polish-American Sports Hall of Fame and Museum.

WOODSON, Warren B.
Coach
Born February 24, 1903, in Fort Worth, Tex; graduated from Baylor Univ. 1924, earned a degree in physical education at Springfield Col; All-Southwestern Conference in basketball and Coach of the Year in 1960.

1927–1934 Texarkana Junior College, coach
1935–1940 Arkansas State College, coach
1941–1942 Hardin-Simmons College, coach
1946–1951 Hardin-Simmons College, coach
1952–1956 University of Arizona, coach
1958–1967 New Mexico State University, coach
1972–1973 Trinity College, coach

Woodson played basketball and was captain of his tennis team at Springfield, where he also learned the T-formation fundamentals from Knute Rockne. His coaching record through 1972 was 247–112–20. His total victories made him the college coach with the third highest record, behind Amos Alonzo Stagg and Pop Warner, until the National Collegiate Athletic Association discounted 52 wins because they were gained at a junior college. In 1960 he directed New Mexico State to a 11–0 season, including a Sun Bowl victory.

YARY, Ronald A.
Player
Born August 16, 1946, in Chicago, Ill; attended Bellflower High School in California, Cerritos Junior Col; graduated from Univ. Southern Calif; All-American 1966 and 1967; All-NFL 1970 and 1973; Outland Trophy 1967; popular speaker at dinner engagements.

1966–1967 University of Southern California, tackle
1968–1973 Minnesota Vikings, tackle

Besides being a tremendous football player, Yary is charming, eloquent and powerful. His 6 ft. 6 in. and 256 lbs. rated Ron among the best offensive tacklers. In 1967 he was the first man selected in the draft. In 1969 he played with the Vikings in the National Football League (NFL) championships and in the Super Bowls of 1970 and 1974.

YOST, Fielding H. "Hurry Up"
Coach
Born April 30, 1871, in Fairview, Nebr; developed a prominent law practice; was a popular after-dinner speaker; died August 20, 1946, in Ann Arbor, Mich, at age 69.

1897 Ohio Wesleyan University, coach
1898 University of Nebraska, coach
1899 University of Kansas, coach
1900 San Jose State University, coach
1900 Stanford University, coach
1901–1923 University of Michigan, coach
1925–1926 University of Michigan, coach

Yost acquired his nickname during his first year of coaching at Michigan. He yelled, "You'll have to hurry up" to players after almost every play. He was the tackle for Lafayette and West Virginia. As a coach, he led the Wolverines in a five-year stretch, during which they were tied only by Minnesota, and lost only to Chicago. Chicago's victory in 1905 broke the Michigan 56-game winning streak. During the same five-year period, Michigan outscored its opponents 2,821 to 42. His overall record was 196–36–12 and his Michigan record was 164–29–10. He coached the Wolverines to a 49–0 win over Stanford in the first Rose Bowl game in 1902.
Also in: National Football Hall of Fame and West Virginia Sports Writers Hall of Fame.

YUNEVICH, Alex
Coach
Born December 8, 1909; attended Purdue Univ.

1934–1936 Central Michigan University, coach
1937–1941 Alfred University, coach
1946–1973 Alfred University, coach

Yunevich played fullback for Purdue 1929–1931, with a playing record of 23–3. He was tutored by Jimmy Phelan in 1929 and his last two years by Noble Kizer. He compiled a coaching record of 179–90–11. Alex had six unbeaten teams at Alfred—1937, 1940, 1952, 1955, 1956 and 1971. He ranked third through 1973 in wins among active college-division coaches.

ZUPPKE, Robert C. "Zupp"
Coach

Born July 2, 1879, in Berlin, Germany; raised prized hogs and painted when he retired from coaching; died December 22, 1957.

Zuppke came to America at age two and fell in love with football but later was too small for the Wisconsin varsity. He settled for being a scrub quarterback 1903 and 1904. He was a member of the league championship basketball team with Hall of Famer Christian Steinmetz in 1905. He coached Muskegon, Mich, High School 1905–1909 and Oak Park, Ill, High School 1910–1912. He developed Hall of Famers Bart Macomber and Red Grange, and as coach at Illinois, won or shared seven Western Conference Big Ten championships. His record there was 131–81–12. He was intellectually curious and complex. He was an artist who gave gallery exhibitions, a philosopher and student of Schopenhauer and Kant, a psychologist and a humorist. Called "Rembrandt of the Prairies," he authored numerous funny stories.
Also in: National Football Hall of Fame.

Football — Major League Hall of Fame

The Major League Football Hall of Fame was instituted in 1950. As of 1977, there are 114 inductees, of which 98 are players, and 16 are coaches and contributors. Each inductee has his name engraved on a trophy which is kept in Citizens Savings Hall of Fame Athletic Museum, Los Angeles international sports shrine. He also receives a Hall of Fame Award.

Induction Years Unrecorded

AGAJANIAN, Benjamin "Automatic"
Player

Born in 1919 in Long Beach, Calif; graduated from Univ. New Mex. 1945; son Larry picked by Green Bay Packers on 7th round of 1969 draft.

1945	Pittsburgh Steelers, kicker
1946	Philadelphia Eagles, kicker
1947–1948	Los Angeles Dons (AAFC), kicker
1949	New York Giants, kicker
1953	Los Angeles Rams, kicker
1954 –1957	New York Giants, player
1960	Los Angeles Chargers (AFL), player
1961	Dallas Texans, player
1961	Green Bay Packers, player
1962	Oakland Raiders, player
1964	San Diego Chargers, player

Agajanian is one of only two men to play in All-American Football Conference (AAFC), National Football League and American Football League. He played with the Pittsburgh Steelers in 1945, before he joined the Philadelphia Eagles. In 1947 Agajanian went to the Los Angeles Dons, and that same year led the AAFC in field goals with a record 15. In 1949 he joined the New York Giants and remained with them one season. He played with the Los Angeles Rams in 1953 and then was traded to the Giants, remaining with the team through 1957. Agajanian kicked five PATs and two field goals in the 1956 title game. In 1960 he came out of retirement to kick for the Los Angeles Chargers. He kicked 38 and 22 yd. field goals to give the Chargers a 6–0 lead in the first quarter of first American Football League championship game. In 1961 he was traded to the Dallas Texans, then released, joining the Green Bay Packers that same year. In 1962 he played with the Oakland Raiders and in 1964 with the San Diego Chargers.

ALBERT, Frank C.
Player

See Entry in College Football Hall of Fame, Citizens Savings Hall of Fame Athletic Museum.
Also in: National Football Hall of Fame.

ALWORTH, Lance D. "Bambi"
Player

Born August 3, 1940, in Houston, Tex; attended Univ. Ark 1960–1962; offered baseball contract by New York Yankees and Pittsburgh Pirates; All AFL Flanker 1963 and 1969; All-Time AFL Team; retired on July 2, 1973.

1962	Oakland Raiders, end
1962–1969	San Diego Pirates (AFL), end
1970	San Diego Chargers (AFC), end
1971–1972	Dallas Cowboys (NFC), end

Alworth attended the University of Arkansas and in 1961 led the National Conference Athletic Association in punt returns. In 1962 he was second-round draft choice of the Oakland Raiders. Alworth was traded the same year to the San Diego Pirates. With the Pirates he set several American Football League (AFL) records which include: 9 consecutive games scoring touchdowns; 3 seasons leading the league in touchdowns; 96 consecutive games with one or more pass receptions, breaking Don Hutson's record of 96; 9 games making touchdown receptions. He also tied two AFL records with 4 game touchdown receptions and 13 game receptions. Alworth returned 10 kickoffs for 216 yds, a 21.6 average, in 1961. He was AFL leading pass receiver in 1968 and 1969. Alworth is the only player in league history to gain more than 1000 yds. receiving in 7 consecutive seasons. In 1966 Alworth led the AFL pass receivers in each category, despite the fact that he played with two broken hands. He was traded to the Dallas Cowboys on May 19, 1971, for wide receiver Pettis Norman, tackle Tony Liscio and defensive tackle Ron East, remaining with the Cowboys until 1972. Alworth played in seven AFL All-Star games and AFL championship games in 1963 and 1965. In 1971 he played in the Super Bowl and scored one touchdown. In 11 years Alworth had 542 receptions for 10,266 yds, an average of 18.9, and scored 85 touchdowns. The San Diego Chargers retired Alworth's sweater number 19.

ARNETT, Jon "Jaguar Jon"
Player

Born April 20, 1934, in Los Angeles, Calif; attended Univ. Southern Calif. 1954–1956; All-American 1955; gave lessons in gymnastic football, specializing in front and back flips; All-Pro 1958; Pro-Bowl 1958–1962.

1956–1963	Los Angeles Rams, halfback
1964–1966	Chicago Bears, halfback

An outstanding back while at the University of Southern California, Arnett scored 108 points in 1955—second best in the country. In the 1955 Rose Bowl against Notre Dame, he scored one touchdown. He was the Number One draft choice of the Los Angeles Rams, joining them in 1956 and remaining with the team until 1963. In the 1961 game against the Detroit Lions, he returned a kick-off 105 yards for a touchdown. This was his greatest year. In 1964 he joined the Chicago Bears and remained with them until 1966. He has a career total of 26 touchdowns, 3833 yds. rushed in 964 carries for a 4.0 average.

ATKINS, Douglas
Player

Born May 8, 1930, in Humboldt, Tenn; graduated from Univ. Tenn; All-Pro three times; Pro-Bowl 1958–1963 and 1965; Lineman of the Game 1958; gun collector.

1953–1954 Cleveland Browns, defensive end
1955–1966 Chicago Bears, defensive end
1967–1969 New Orleans Saints, defensive end

In 1953 the 6 ft. 8 in, 230 lb. Atkins was a first-round draft choice of the Browns, remaining with the team until 1954. He joined the Chicago Bears in 1955. Atkins was ordered by George Halas to study films of Gino Marchetti and was often heard saying on his way to the film room, "Here I go, another chapter of 'The Gino Marchetti Story.' " He switched positions with tackle Henry Jordan of the Green Bay Packers in the 1962 Pro-Bowl and was excellent. In 1963 Atkins scored a safety. Atkins played title games in 1953, 1954, 1956 and 1963, and also played in 205 National Football League games.

BANDUCCI, Bruno
Player

Born in Richmond, Calif; graduated from Stanford Univ; All-American All-Star teams 1946 and 1947, car salesman.

Bruno played with the Philadelphia Eagles 1944–1945, then joined the San Francisco 49ers as offensive lineman 1946–1954. He was named on the United Press All-Pro Team.

BATTLES, Clifford
Player

See entry in Professional Football Hall of Fame, 1968.
Also in: National Football Hall of Fame, National Association of Intercollegiate Athletics Hall of Fame and West Virginia Sports Writers Hall of Fame.

BAUGH, Samuel A.
Player

See entry in Professional Football Hall of Fame, 1963.
Also in: National Football Hall of Fame; College Football Hall of Fame, Citizens Savings Hall of Fame Athletic Museum.

BEDNARIK, Charles
Player

See entry in Professional Football Hall of Fame, 1967.
Also in: National Football Hall of Fame.

BELL, DeBenneville "Bert"
Noteworthy Contributor

See entry in Professional Football Hall of Fame, 1963.

BENTON, James
Player

Born September 25, 1916, in Carthage, Ark; attended Univ. Ark. 1935–1937; military service in 1941.

1938–1940 Cleveland Rams, end, running back
1942 Cleveland Rams, end, running back
1943 Chicago Bears, player
1944–1945 Cleveland Rams, player
1946–1947 Los Angeles Rams (formerly Cleveland Rams), player

Benton played football with the University of Arkansas and in his senior year was National Conference Athletic Association receiving champion with 47 receptions. Joining the Cleveland Rams in 1938, he played for two years, leaving for one year of military service. Benton returned to the Rams in 1942 but was traded to the Chicago Bears in 1943. He returned to the Rams again in 1944, moving with them to Los Angeles in 1946. In the 1943 title game against the Washington Redskins, he received a 29-yd. touchdown pass from Sid Luckman. In 1945 against the Detroit Lions, he received 10 passes for 303 yds. a one-game yardage record. The same year against the Washington Redskins, he received a 37 yd. touchdown pass from Bob Waterfield. Benton was lead receiver in the National Football League in 1946 with 63 receptions for 981 yds. and 6 touchdowns.

BERRY, Raymond
Player

See entry in Professional Football Hall of Fame, 1973.

BIDWILL, Charles W, Sr.
Noteworthy Contributor

See entry in Professional Football Hall of Fame, 1967.

BRAY, Raymond
Player

Attended Western Michigan Univ.

1939–1942 Chicago Bears, guard
1946–1951 Chicago Bears, guard
1952 Green Bay Packers, guard

Bray was drafted by the Chicago Bears at the end of his college years. In 1952 he went to the Packers.

BRITO, Eugene "Gene"
Player

Attended Loyola Univ. of Los Angeles.

1951–1953 Washington Redskins, end
1955–1958 Washington Redskins, end
1959–1960 Los Angeles Rams, end

BROWN, James
Player

See entry in Professional Football Hall of Fame, 1971.

BROWN, Paul
Coach

See entry in Professional Football Hall of Fame, 1967.

CANADEO, Anthony "Grey Ghost of Ganzaga"
Player

See entry in Green Bay Packer Hall of Fame, 1973.
Also in: National Association of Intercollegiate Athletics Hall of Fame and Professional Football Hall of Fame.

CAPPELLETTI, Gino
Player

Originally from Upper Darby, Pa; attended Pennsylvania State Univ. 1971–1973; Consensus All-American 1973; Heisman Trophy 1973—first Penn State player to win honor; Associated Press All-East Team 1973; *Football News'* Player of the Year.

Cappelletti was noted for his tremendous speed. He is tough inside, follows blockers well and picks holes. "John" Cappelletti, finished fifth nationally in rushing. Coach Joe Paterno says he is the "best player I've been around." Cappelletti converted from defensive back after his sophomore year, becoming second ranking rusher in Penn State history. While at Penn State, his 1973 totals were 286 carries for 1522 yds, 17 touchdowns, 22 passes caught for 207 yds. and 1 touchdown. His average was 183.4 yds. per game, 5.3 yds. per carry. As tailback, his two-year total was 519 carries for 2639 yds. and 29 touchdowns. Cappelletti played in the 1974 Orange Bowl winning against Louisiana State.

CARR, Joseph F. "Joe"
Noteworthy Contributor
See entry in Professional Football Hall of Fame, 1963.

CLARK, Earl "Dutch"
Player
See entry in Professional Football Hall of Fame, 1963.
Also in: National Football Hall of Fame; and College Football Hall of Fame, Citizens Savings Hall of Fame Athletic Museum.

CONERLY, Charles A.
Player
Born September 19, 1921, in Clarksdale, Miss; attended Univ. Miss; Consensus All-American in 1947; Citizens Savings Player of the Year 1947; Jim Thorpe Trophy and Most Valuable Player in 1959; retired after the 1961 season; did radio commercials.

In 1947 Conerly led the National Conference Athletic Association in pass attempts with 233, in completions with a record 133, in percentage with a record 57.1, in touchdowns with 18, in yards gained at 1367. Conerly set a record for most passes without interception, with 32, in 1947 against Chattanooga. He joined the New York Giants in 1948 and the same year completed 36 of 53 passes against the Pittsburgh Steelers. Completing 113 passes in 194 attempts for 1706 yds. and scoring 4 touchdowns in 1959 made him the National Football League passing leader.
Also in: National Football Hall of Fame.

CONZELMAN, James G.
Player
See entry in Professional Football Hall of Fame, 1964.

DONOVAN, Arthur
Player
See entry in Professional Football Hall of Fame, 1968.

DRISCOLL, John L. "Paddy"
Player
See entry in Professional Football Hall of Fame, 1965.
Also in: National Football Hall of Fame.

DUDLEY, William "Bullet Bill"
Player
See entry in Professional Football Hall of Fame, 1966.
Also in: National Football Hall of Fame; and College Football Hall of Fame, Citizens Savings Hall of Fame Athletic Museum.

EDWARDS, A. Glen "Turk"
Player
See entry in Professional Football Hall of Fame, 1969.
Also in: National Football Hall of Fame; and College Football Hall of Fame, Citizens Savings Hall of Fame Athletic Museum.

FEARS, Thomas
Player
See entry in Professional Football Hall of Fame, 1970.
Also in: National Football Hall of Fame.

FLAHERTY, Ray
Player
See entry in Professional Football Hall of Fame, 1976.

FORTMAN, Daniel J.
Player
See entry in Professional Football Hall of Fame, 1965.

GIFFORD, Frank
Player
See entry in Professional Football Hall of Fame, 1977.
Also in: National Football Hall of Fame.

GRAHAM, Otto "Automatic Otto"
Player
See entry in Professional Football Hall of Fame, 1965.
Also in: National Football Hall of Fame; and College Football Hall of Fame, Citizens Savings Hall of Fame Athletic Museum.

GRANGE, Harold "Red"
Player
See entry in Professional Football Hall of Fame, 1963.
Also in: National Football Hall of Fame; and College Football Hall of Fame, Citizens Savings Hall of Fame Athletic Museum.

GREGG, Forest
Player
See entry in Green Bay Packer Hall of Fame, 1977.
Also in: Professional Football Hall of Fame.

GROZA, Louis "The Toe"
Player
See entry in Professional Football Hall of Fame, 1974.

HALAS, George "Papa Bear"
Coach and Noteworthy Contributor
See entry in Professional Football Hall of Fame, 1963.

HEIN, Melvin J.
Player
See entry in Professional Football Hall of Fame, 1963.
Also in: National Football Hall of Fame; and College Football Hall of Fame, Citizens Savings Hall of Fame Athletic Museum.

HENRY, Wilbur F. "Pete" "Fats"
Player
See entry in Professional Football Hall of Fame, 1963.
Also in: National Football Hall of Fame; College Football Hall of Fame, Citizens Savings Hall of Fame Athletic Museum; National Association of Intercollegiate Athletics Hall of Fame.

HERBER, Arnold "Flash"
Player
See entry in Green Bay Packer Hall of Fame, 1972.
Also in: Professional Football Hall of Fame.

HEWITT, William "Bill"
Player
See entry in Professional Football Hall of Fame, 1971.

HINKLE, W. Clarke
Player
See entry in Green Bay Packer Hall of Fame, 1972.
Also in: National Football Hall of Fame, Professional Football Hall of Fame and Wisconsin Hall of Fame.

HIRSCH, Elroy L. "Crazy Legs"
Player
See entry in Professional Football Hall of Fame, 1968.
Also in: National Football Hall of Fame.

HUBBARD, Robert "Cal"
Player
See entry in Green Bay Packer Hall of Fame, 1970.
Also in: National Football Hall of Fame, National Baseball Hall of Fame, Professional Football Hall of Fame, Louisiana State Hall of Fame and National Association of Intercollegiate Athletics Hall of Fame.

HUNTER, Arthur
Player
Born April 24, 1933, in Fairport, Ohio; attended Univ. Notre Dame 1951–1953, graduated with degree in finance; All-American in 1953; also played baseball and basketball; military service in 1955; Pro-Bowl in 1960.

1954 Green Bay Packers, center, tackle
1956–1959 Cleveland Browns, center, tackle
1960–1965 Los Angeles Rams, center, tackle
1966 Pittsburgh Steelers, center, tackle

While with the University of Notre Dame, Hunter played end, center and tackle under Frank Leahy. He was first-round draft choice of the Green Bay Packers in 1954. In 1956 he joined the Cleveland Browns and remained with them until 1959. He played with the Los Angeles Rams from 1960 through 1965 and in 1966 played with the Pittsburgh Steelers. Hunter played in the National Football League championship game of 1957.

HUTSON, Donald M. "Alabama Antelope"
Player
See entry in Green Bay Packer Hall of Fame, 1972.
Also in: National Football Hall of Fame; College Football Hall of Fame, Citizens Savings Hall of Fame Athletic Museum; Professional Football Hall of Fame.

KEISLING, Walter
Player
See entry in Professional Football Hall of Fame, 1966.

KILROY, Frank
Player
Attended Temple University.

1943 Philadelphia Eagles-Pittsburgh Steelers, tackle
1944–1955 Philadelphia Eagles, tackle

LAMBEAU, Earl "Curly"
Coach
See entry in Green Bay Packer Hall of Fame, 1970.
Also in: Professional Football Hall of Fame and Wisconsin Hall of Fame.

LAYNE, Robert "Bobby"
Player
See entry in Professional Football Hall of Fame, 1967.
Also in: National Football Hall of Fame and Texas High School Football Hall of Fame.

LeBARON, Edward
Player
Born January 7, 1930, in San Rafael, Calif; attended College of the Pacific; Little All-American in 1946, 1947 and 1948; Rookie of the Year 1952; Most Valuable Player 1958; attended Georgetown Law School 1956–1958, received degree; joined law firm in Midland, Tex, after being admitted to California Bar; retired from football at the end of 1963 season; joined cement company in Reno, Nev, as executive vice president; later became TV announcer; two years in the Marines, spending nine months in Korea; received letter of commendation for heroism; wounded twice, acquired shrapnel in right shoulder and leg.

1952–1953 Washington Redskins, quarterback
1955–1959 Washington Redskins, quarterback
1960–1963 Dallas Cowboys, quarterback

LeBaron was the youngest college football player in the nation when at 16 years of age, he quarterbacked the College of the Pacific. LeBaron passed for more than 1000 yds. each of his last three seasons with College of the Pacific. In the 1950 College All-Star game, he quarterbacked the team to a 17–7 victory against the Philadelphia Eagles. He was drafted by the Washington Redskins, playing two games and then left to go into the Marines. Returning to the Washington Redskins in 1955, he played in the 1956 Pro-Bowl. In 1958 he threw 5 touchdown passes against the Chicago Cardinals taking the National Football League's lead in passing with 79 completions in 145 attempts for 1365 yds, for a percentage of 54.3. In 1960 he was traded to the Dallas Cowboys and threw the shortest touchdown pass ever (two inches) to Dick Brelski against his former team, the Washington Redskins. LeBaron threw 5 touchdown passes in 1962 against the Steelers. In 1962 he was alternated with Don Meredith at quarterback and dropped to role of backup in 1963. LeBaron, the smallest quarterback in pro football, once said, "Maybe being smaller actually helped me. It might have made me work harder to concentrate on making up for my size. I might not have gone so far if I had been big."

LEEMANS, Alphonse E. "Tuffy"
Player
Born in Superior, Wis; son of Belgian miner who immigrated to Wisconsin; juggled iron ore as youngster to build himself up; dumped two bigger, older boys one day playing football and kids started calling him "Tuffy"; attended George Washington Univ; Most Valuable Player in 1936; All-Pro 1936 and 1939; injury received in game in 1942 kept him out of military; settled in Washington, D.C. area after his retirement from football; presently residing in Silver Spring, Md.

While at George Washington University, Leemans played in the 1936 College All-Star game, racing 75 yds. for a touchdown the first time he handled the football. Leemans was the Number Two draft choice of the New York Giants and was signed up in 1936 for $3000. He played for the New York Giants for eight years under Coach Steve Owens. Leemans called signals from his right-half position. His first year with the team he led the National Football League rushers with 830 yds. Leemans had a total career record of 3117 yds. rushed and 19 touchdowns scored. In 1942 against the Chicago Bears, he suffered a severe blow to his head during the game resulting in the loss of hearing in one ear.

LOMBARDI, Vincent "Vince"
Coach
See entry in Green Bay Packer Hall of Fame, 1975.
Also in: Professional Football Hall of Fame.

LUCKMAN, Sid
Player
See entry in Professional Football Hall of Fame, 1965.
Also in: National Football Hall of Fame; and College Football Hall of Fame, Citizens Savings Hall of Fame Athletic Museum.

LYMAN, W. Roy "Link"
Player
See entry in Professional Football Hall of Fame, 1964.

MANDERS, John "Automatic Jack"
Player
Born in 1910 in Milbank, S.Dak; football, basketball, track letterman at Milbank High School; attended Univ. Minn. 1929–1931; All-Conference fullback three years; brother Pug, Drake alumnus, also fine fullback and pro player.

Manders was an outstanding place kicker for the Chicago Bears 1933–1940. In 1934 and 1937 he was scoring leader. Manders was also field goal leader four times, in 1933, 1934, 1936 and 1937. He kicked 72 consecutive PATs during the period of 1933 through 1937. He was also a member of two world championship teams in 1934 and in 1940.

MARA, Timothy J.
Noteworthy Contributor
See entry in Professional Football Hall of Fame, 1963.

MARCHETTI, Gino
Player
See entry in Professional Football Hall of Fame, 1972.

MARSHALL, George P
Noteworthy Contributor
See entry in Professional Football Hall of Fame, 1963.
Also in: National Association of Intercollegiate Athletics Hall of Fame.

MARTIN, James R. "Jungle Jim"
Player
Born February 14, 1919, in Concord, N.H; attended Univ. Notre Dame 1946–1949; All-American 1949; two and one-half years with Marines, including stop at Okinawa.

1950	Cleveland Browns, linebacker, kicker
1951–1961	Detroit Lions, linebacker, kicker
1963	Baltimore Colts, player
1964	Washington Redskins, player
1967–1972	Detroit Lions, assistant coach

An All-American at the University of Notre Dame, Martin took part in one of the school's great eras, with 37 wins, no losses and 2 ties. Martin joined the Cleveland Browns in 1950, playing defensive end under Frank Leahy. In 1951 he joined the Detroit Lions and remained with the team until 1961. Martin tied Lou Groza's record of eight PATs in a championship game on December 29, 1957, and the same year kicked a 31-yd. field goal. Martin was pro linebacker, and National Football League field goal leader with 24 in 1963. The same year he played with the Baltimore Colts, and in 1964 he played with the Washington Redskins. In 1967 he became assistant coach of the Detroit Lions, remaining until 1972. Martin played in five National Football League championship games (1951–1954 and 1957). His total career record includes 158 PATs and 92 field goals for 434 points. He was also involved in kicking in the 1964 campaign, which he booted with a broken leg.

MATSON, Oliver G. "Ollie"
Player
See entry in Professional Football Hall of Fame, 1972.
Also in: National Football Hall of Fame.

McAFEE, George
Player
See entry in Professional Football Hall of Fame, 1966.
Also in: National Football Hall of Fame.

McELHENNY, Hugh "King"
Player
See entry in Professional Football Hall of Fame, 1970.

McKEEVER, Marlin
Player
Born January 1, 1949, in Cheyenne, Wyo. with brother Mike; attended Univ. Southern Calif; brothers became most famous twin combination in college football history; All-American end 1959 and 1960; public relations consultant during off season.

1965	Los Angeles Rams, tight end, linebacker
1968–1971	Washington Redskins, linebacker
1971	Los Angeles Rams, linebacker.

Marlin McKeever played linebacker for the Los Angeles Rams for two seasons and then switched to tight end. In 1965 he caught 44 passes for 542 yards and four touchdowns. In 1968 he joined the Washington Redskins and reverted to linebacker. Marlin has been a permanent backer ever since. In 1967 Marlin also cavorted for the Minnesota Vikings and played in the 1967 Pro-Bowl. In 1971 Marlin was traded back to the Los Angeles Rams in a unique trade; the Rams gave up six players and one draft choice and the Redskins countered with seven choices and one player (McKeever).

McNALLY, John Blood
Player
See entry in Green Bay Packer Hall of Fame, 1970.
Also in: Professional Football Hall of Fame and Wisconsin Hall of Fame.

MEADOR, Edward
Player
Born August 10, 1937, in Dallas, Tex; graduated from Arkansas Tech. 1958; All-Pro safety 1967 and 1968.

Meador was an outstanding all-around player for the Los Angeles Rams. He was the club's all-time leader in interceptions with 44 which he returned for 525 yds. Meador (5 ft. 11 in, 185 lbs.) scored five career touchdowns on interceptions, returning punts in 1967 and 1968. He played in four Pro-Bowls: 1961, 1965, 1966 and 1968.
Also in: National Association of Intercollegiate Athletics Hall of Fame.

MODZELEWSKI, Richard "Little Mo"
Player
Born February 16, 1931, in West Natrona, Pa; tackle for Univ. Md. when their team beat Tennessee 28–13 in the 1951 Sugar Bowl; All-American 1952; Knute Rockne Trophy 1952; older brother, Ed, "Big Mo," played in the National Football League (NFL) for six years.

1953–1954 Washington Redskins, tackle
1955 Pittsburgh Steelers, tackle
1956–1963 New York Giants, tackle
1964–1966 Cleveland Browns, tackle.

At 6 ft. 1 in. and 260 lbs, Little Mo was part of NFL championship teams in 1956 and 1964. At retirement he had played 160 consecutive games. In 1974 he was defensive line coach for the Browns.

MOTLEY, Marion
Player
See entry in Professional Football Hall of Fame, 1968.

MUSSO, George "Moose"
Player
Born in Edwardsville, Ill; attended Millikin Univ. 1929–1932; played football, basketball, baseball and track; elected sheriff of Madison County, Ill, 1958.

While at Millikin University, Musso played left tackle, and became captain in 1932. In 1933 he joined the Chicago Bears and played on four world championship teams and three other divisional winners. In 1937 Musso moved from tackle to guard. Coach George Halas was so pleased with his adjustment that he called Musso, "The greatest guard in professional football ranks."
Also in: National Association of Intercollegiate Athletics Hall of Fame.

NAGURSKI, Bronislaw "Bronko"
Player
See entry in Professional Football Hall of Fame, 1963.
Also in: National Football Hall of Fame and College Football Hall of Fame, Citizens Savings Hall of Fame Athletic Museum.

NEALE, Earl "Greasy"
Coach
See entry in Professional Football Hall of Fame, 1969.
Also in: National Football Hall of Fame and West Virginia Sports Writers Hall of Fame.

NESSER, Alfred
Player
1919–1926 Akron Pros, guard
1925 Cleveland Bulldogs, guard
1926 Cleveland Panthers (AFL), guard
1926–1928 New York Giants, guard
1931 Cleveland Indians, guard

NEVERS, Ernest
Player
See entry in Professional Football Hall of Fame, 1963.
Also in: National Football Hall of Fame; and College Football Hall of Fame, Citizens Savings Hall of Fame Athletic Museum.

NITSCHKE, Raymond E.
Player
Born December 29, 1936, in Elmwood Park, Ill; attended Proviso High School in Maywood, Ill; attended Univ. Ill; All-First 50 Year NFL Middle Linebacker; Pro-Bowl 1965; All-Pro Squad of 1960s; All-NFL 1964, 1965 and 1966; Outstanding Player of Position 1967; civic-minded; served as chairman of Wisconsin Cerebral Palsy Telethon; served on board of directors of Green Bay Boys Club.

Nitschke joined the Green Bay Packers in 1958 and was noted for his ferocious hitting and tackling ability. His career total includes 25 intercepted passes for 385 yds. and 2 touchdowns. In 1968 Nitschke accumulated a total of 9 tackles against Oakland in Super Bowl II.

NOMELLINI, Leo
Player
See entry in Professional Football Hall of Fame, 1969.
Also in: National Football Hall of Fame; and College Football Hall of Fame, Citizens Savings Hall of Fame Athletic Museum.

OWEN, Steve
Coach
See entry in Professional Football Hall of Fame, 1966.

PARKER, Raymond "Buddy"
Coach
Born December 16, 1913; halfback for Centenary Col.

1935–1943 Detroit Lions, back
1936–1943 Chicago Cardinals, back
1949 Chicago Cardinals, co-coach
1951–1956 Detroit Lions, coach
1957–1964 Pittsburgh Steelers, coach

Buddy Parker was one of ten professional coaches to win 100 games, finishing up with a 102–72–0 win–loss–tie record. With the Lions he coached stars like Bobby Layne and Joe Schmidt and brought the team to two consecutive National Football League championships in 1952 and 1953, and the championship playoffs in 1954 which he lost to the Cleveland Browns 56–10. A patient man who encouraged the best performance from his players, Parker surprised his colleagues when he resigned from football at a "Meet the Lions" banquet two days before the first pre-season game in 1965.

PAUL, Donald
Player
Born March 18, 1925, in Los Angeles, Calif; attended Univ. Calif, Los Angeles (UCLA); All-Coast center 1946 and 1947; Pro-Bowl 1952, 1953 and 1954; presently residing in Southern California; owner of a restaurant; also provides color on taped telecasts of Rams home games.

1948 – 1955 Los Angeles Rams, linebacker
1959 Los Angeles Rams, assistant coach

Donald Paul played with UCLA when they lost to Illinois 45 – 15 in the 1947 Rose Bowl. In 1948 Paul joined the Los Angeles Rams where he was known as a durable, hard-hitting linebacker. In 1954 Leon Hart, tight end of the Detroit Lions, called him the "dirtiest player in the league" which Paul considered a compliment. Paul played in four world championship games, 1949, 1950, 1951 and 1955. The Los Angeles Rams defeated the Cleveland Browns 24 – 17 in the 1951 championship game. In 1959 Paul became assistant coach for the Rams.

PERRY, Joe
Player
See entry in Professional Football Hall of Fame, 1969.

PIHOS, Peter L. "Big Dog"
Player
See entry in Professional Football Hall of Fame, 1970.
Also in: National Football Hall of Fame.

REEVES, Daniel
Noteworthy Contributor
See entry in Professional Football Hall of Fame, 1967.

RENFRO, Raymond
Player
Born November 7, 1930, in Whitesboro, Tex; attended North Texas State Univ.

1952 – 1963 Cleveland Browns, end
1968 – 1972 Dallas Cowboys, pass offense coach

In 1952 Renfro joined the Cleveland Browns, playing 12 years with the team. The Cleveland Browns were the National Football League champs in 1954 and 1955. Renfro caught 281 passes for 5508 yds. averaging 19.6 per reception. In 1957 he averaged 29.0 yds. on 21 receptions. He caught seven passes for 166 yds. against the New York Giants in his biggest game on November 26, 1961. Renfro played in three Pro-Bowls. In 1968 he became pass offense coach of the Dallas Cowboys.

RICHTER, Leslie A.
Player
See entry in College Football Hall of Fame, Citizens Savings Hall of Fame Athletic Museum.

RINGO, James
Player
See entry in Green Bay Packer Hall of Fame, 1974.

ROBUSTELLI, Andy
Player
See entry in Professional Football Hall of Fame, 1971.
Also in: National Association of Intercollegiate Athletics Hall of Fame.

ROTE, Kyle W.
Player
Originally from San Antonio, Tex; attended Thomas Jefferson High School in San Antonio; attended Southern Methodist Univ. 1948 – 1950; Consensus All-American 1950; became football analyst for NBC-TV; applied same coolness in broadcasting booth as he did on gridiron.

While at Southern Methodist University (SMU), Rote had a total of 32 touchdowns and amassed 2686 yds. Teamed up with Doak Walker in 1948 and 1949, they formed the nations finest offensive combination. In 1949 Walker was injured and was out of the game most of the year. This gave Rote the opportunity to assert himself. In a remarkable fashion, during the season's last game against powerful and unbeaten Notre Dame, the Irish were pushed to the wire by Rote and company before claiming a 27 – 20 win—their thirty-sixth straight victory. This was probably his finest hour. He ran 115 yds. and passed for 148 more; he scored all three SMU touchdowns and averaged 48 yds. on punts. In 1951 he joined the New York Giants, playing in four National Football League championship games, 1956, 1958, 1959 and 1961.
Also in: National Football Hall of Fame.

ROTE, Tobin
Player
See entry in Green Bay Packer Hall of Fame, 1974.

ST. CLAIR, Robert B. "Geek"
Player
Born February 18, 1931, in San Francisco, Calif; attended Univ. San Francisco; tabbed "Geek" by Bruno Banducci; elected mayor of Daly City, Calif. while still playing football; All-Pro 1955.

1955 – 1963 San Francisco 49ers, tackle

While at the University of San Francisco, St. Clair played under coach Joe Kuharich. In 1955 he joined the San Francisco 49ers. At 6 ft. 9 in, he was the National Football League's tallest player, fast afoot and loved to hit. Monty Stickles, 49ers teammate, determined "his pass-blocking is invincible." St. Clair had a penchant for raw meat. Fortunately his appetite was never a problem on the field. In 1956 he blocked 10 field goal attempts. St. Clair also played in four Pro-Bowls.

SCHMIDT, Joseph
Player
See entry in Professional Football Hall of Fame, 1973.

SEARS, Victor W.
Player
Born March 4, 1918, in Ashwood, Ore; attended Oregon State Univ. 1938 – 1940; All-American 1940; All-Pro Squad of 1940s; All-Pro 1943 and 1949; hobbies include fishing, gardening, making early American furniture, Little League baseball and football coaching; manufacturers representative; resident of Buck County, Pa.

1941 – 1953 Philadelphia Eagles, tackle

Victor Sears joined the Philadelphia Eagles in 1941, before Philadelphia and the Pittsburgh Steelers merged during the 1943 season. Sears was a two-way player for about ten years, offensive only eleventh year, defensive only twelfth and thirteenth. He averaged over 50 min. a game in nine years. Sears is the only player chosen to Philadelphia's All-Time Team both offensively and defensively. He has played in two world championship games, 1948 and 1949, and lost the 1947 title game.

SHAW, Lawrence T. "Buck" "Silver Fox"
Coach
Born March 28, 1899, in Mitchellville, Iowa; Notre Dame

tackle under Knute Rockne 1919–1921; called Silver Fox because of striking silver hair; after retirement, settled in Menlo Park, Calif.

1924	North Carolina State College, coach
1925–1928	University of Nevada, coach
1936–1942	University of Santa Clara, coach
1945	University of California, coach
1946–1954	San Francisco 49ers, coach
1956–1957	U.S. Air Force Academy, coach
1958–1960	Philadelphia Eagles, coach

Buck Shaw entered football coaching with the Knute Rockne style and stayed with professional football for 15 years to accumulate 91 victories, 55 losses and 5 ties. On the college scene his Santa Clara team won two consecutive Sugar Bowl games over Louisiana State in 1937 and 1938. As first head coach of the Air Force team he helped to organize the Academy's athletic program and left them with a 46–10–2 win–loss–tie record. His professional career ended with a 1960 National Football League championship over the Green Bay Packers.
Also in: National Football Hall of Fame.

SPRINKLE, Edward A.
Player
Born September 3, 1923, in Abilene, Tex; attended Tuscola, Tex, High School, Hardin-Simmons Univ; All-Border Conference twice; enrolled at Annapolis 1943 and helped Navy beat Army, 13–0.

Edward started playing football in Tuscola High School as a senior, on a six-man team. He then played at Hardin-Simmons University. In 1944 he joined the Chicago Bears and in 1946 the club won the championship title defeating the New York Giants 24–14. He was not big, but he was really tough, which resulted in fans hating him and players fearing him. Sprinkle played in six Pro-Bowls, and was effective on offense as well as defense. He was once accused by Coach Buddy Parker of the St. Louis Cardinals of deliberately stomping on running back Elmer Angsman. Sprinkle later revealed his own chest which was emblazoned with five cleat marks.

STARR, Bryan Bart
Player
See entry in Green Bay Packer Hall of Fame, 1977.
Also in: Professional Football Hall of Fame.

STAUTNER, Ernest
Player
See entry in Professional Football Hall of Fame, 1969.

STORCK, Carl
Noteworthy Contributor
Carl Storck, after making many contributions to the game, was replaced as commissioner of the National Football League in 1941 by Elmer Layden, one of Knute Rockne's "Four Horsemen."

STRONG, Kenneth
Player
See entry in Professional Football Hall of Fame, 1967.
Also in: National Football Hall of Fame; College Football Hall of Fame, Citizens Savings Hall of Fame Athletic Museum.

STYDAHAR, Joseph "Jumbo Jim"
Player
See entry in Professional Football Hall of Fame, 1967.
Also in: National Football Hall of Fame and West Virginia Sports Writers Hall of Fame.

THORPE, James
Player
See entry in Professional Football Hall of Fame, 1963.
Also in: American Indian Athletic Hall of Fame; College Football Hall of Fame and Track and Field Hall of Fame, Citizens Savings Hall of Fame Athletic Museum; National Football Hall of Fame, National Track and Field Hall of Fame and U.S. Track and Field Hall of Fame.

TITTLE, Yelverton A.
Player
See entry in Professional Football Hall of Fame, 1971.

TRAFTON, George
Player
See entry in Professional Football Hall of Fame, 1964.

TRIPPI, Charles L.
Player
See entry in Professional Football Hall of Fame, 1966.
Also in: National Football Hall of Fame; College Football Hall of Fame, Citizens Savings Hall of Fame Athletic Museum.

TUNNELL, Emlen
Player
See entry in Professional Football Hall of Fame, 1967.

TURNER, Clyde
Player
See entry in Professional Football Hall of Fame, 1966.
Also in: National Football Hall of Fame.

UNITAS, John C.
Player
Born in Pittsburgh, Pa; Jim Thorpe Trophy 1957 and 1967; Associated Press Player of the Decade (1960s) Award; Man of the Year 1970; All-Pro six times; NFL Most Valuable Player three times.

1955	Pittsburgh Steelers, quarterback
1955	Bloomfield Rams, quarterback
1956–1972	Baltimore Colts, quarterback
1973	San Diego Chargers, quarterback

Johnny Unitas had a memorable career with the Baltimore Colts. At the beginning of his career, he was shifted around due to his size (Notre Dame thought he was too small to play). He was drafted in the ninth round by the Pittsburgh Steelers but they released him before the football season began. He joined the Baltimore Colts in 1956 and began his astonishing career. By 1973 Johnny Unitas had surpassed any player in the National Football League's (NFL) history by attempting more passes (5186), completing more passes (2830), for more yards passing (40,239), and more touchdown passes (290). In 1969, the same year the NFL celebrated its fiftieth year, Unitas was named the greatest quarterback ever. He holds the league record for 300-yd. passing games at 27. Unitas participated in NFL championship games in

1958, 1959, 1964, 1968 and 1970. Super Bowl games include 1969 and 1971. He also participated in ten Pro-Bowls. In 1956 through 1960 he threw touchdown passes in 47 consecutive games, a record compared to Joe DiMaggio's hitting streak of 56 games in baseball. Unitas went to the San Diego Chargers in 1973. He was always recognized for his coolness and consistency in the game.

VAN BROCKLIN, Norman
Player
See entry in Professional Football Hall of Fame, 1971.
Also in: National Football Hall of Fame.

VAN BUREN, Steve
Player
See entry in Professional Football Hall of Fame, 1965.
Also in: Louisiana State Hall of Fame.

WALKER, Ewell Doak, Jr. "Doaker"
Player
See entry in College Football Hall of Fame, Citizens Savings Hall of Fame Athletic Museum.
Also in: National Football Hall of Fame and Texas High School Football Hall of Fame.

WATERFIELD, Robert "Rifle"
Player
See entry in Professional Football Hall of Fame, 1965.

WEBSTER, Alex
Player
Born in Kearny, N.J; NFL Coach of the Year 1970.

1955 – 1964 New York Giants, running back
1969 – 1973 New York Giants, head coach

Alex Webster joined the New York Giants in 1955 and stayed until 1964. New York played in six championship games with Webster in the lineup. But they won only one game against the Chicago Bears in 1956. In that game Webster scored two touchdowns. In 1962 Webster made 1241 yds. as a rusher and receiver. He still holds the New York career records for rushing attempts at 1213, 4638 yds. rushing and 39 touchdown rushing. In 1969 he became the New York Giants head coach. His record was 31 wins and 39 losses. In the 1970 season he was voted National Football League Coach of the Year by the United Press International and the Washington Touchdown Club. In 1973 Alex Webster resigned from the Giant's Club as coach.

WILLIAMS, Fred
Player
Fred Williams attended the University of Arkansas. He joined the Chicago Bears in 1952, remaining with them until 1963. In 1964 Williams joined the Washington Redskins playing through 1965.

WILSON, Lawrence F.
Player
Born March 24, 1938, in Rigby, Idaho; graduated from Univ. Utah; All-NFL 1963 and 1966 – 1969; All-Pro Squad 1960s.

1960 – 1969 St. Louis Cardinals, safety
1970 – 1973 St. Louis Cardinals (NFC), safety

Larry Wilson began his career as a defensive back at Utah but switched to free safety when he joined the St. Louis Cardinals in 1960. Wilson led the National Football League (NFL) in interceptions with ten in 1966 and tied the league mark with thefts in seven consecutive games. He is famous for the safety blitz, using it to its best advantage. The wearer of number 8, Wilson, played in eight Pro-Bowls during his career as a fearless competitor. He is now scouting for the Cardinals.

WOJCIECHOWICZ, Alexander
Player
See entry in Professional Football Hall of Fame, 1968.
Also in: National Football Hall of Fame; College Football Hall of Fame, Citizens Savings Hall of Fame Athletic Museum; National Polish-American Sports Hall of Fame and Museum.

YOUNG, Claude H. "Buddy"
Player
Born 1926 in Chicago; attended Wendell Phillips High School in Chicago; Univ. Ill 1944 – 1946; All-American 1944; Most Valuable Player College All-Stars 1947; administrative aid to National Football League Commissioner Pete Rozelle.

1947 – 1949 New York Yankees (AAFC), halfback
1950 – 1951 New York Yanks, back
1952 Dallas Texans, back
1953 – 1955 Baltimore Colts, back

Young played football with the University of Illinois from 1944 to 1946. Although he is 5 ft. 5 in, he compensated for his size with outstanding speed. He ran 100 yd. dash in 9.5, tied world indoor 60 yd. dash record of 6.1. In 1944 he tied Red Grange's schoolmark with 13 touchdowns. The same year he averaged 8.9 yds. per carry and was second in the nation. In the 1947 Rose Bowl he rushed for 103 yds. on 20 carries and scored 2 touchdowns in Illinois' 45-14 victory. Young played for the New York Yankees All-American Football Conference (AAFC) from 1947 through 1949. Young played also with the New York Yanks 1950 and 1951; Dallas Texans in 1953; and 1953 – 1955 with the Baltimore Colts. His professional career total includes 44 touchdowns and compiled 9419 all-purpose yards. Young retired with a record 27.9 yd. average on kickoffs.
Also in: National Football Hall of Fame.

YOUNGER, Paul "Tank"
Player
Born June 25, 1928, in Grambling, La; played at Grambling Univ.

1949 – 1957 Los Angeles Rams, back
1958 Pittsburgh Steelers, back

Younger was the first person from a black school to play pro football. His godfather, Dr. Ralph Jones, Grambling president since 1936, negotiated the terms of the contract: $6000 for his rookie season. He played in the Pro-Bowls and gained 3640 yds. rushing, 3296 with the Rams. His career total placed him among the top five National Football League rushers when he retired. Since 1966 he has been a scout for the Rams.
Also in: National Association of Intercollegiate Athletics Hall of Fame.

Golf Hall of Fame

The Golf Hall of Fame was instituted in 1949 when 13 amateur and professional golfers were named as its first members: Tommy Armour, Charles Evans, Walter Hagen, Ben Hogan, Robert T. Jones, W. Lawson Little, Byron Nelson, Francis Quimet, Gene Sarazen, Alexa Stirling Fraser, Jerome D. Travers, Glenna Collett Vare and Midred "Babe" Didrikson Zaharias. The Hall of Fame honors each golfer with a Golf Hall of Fame Award; a citation and photograph are displayed at the Citizens Savings Hall of Fame Athletic Museum in Los Angeles. In 1975 the last selections were made by the Citizens Savings Hall Board, chaired by Elwood A. Teague. As of 1977 there are 59 members in the Golf Hall of Fame. Some of the golfers who were selected under their amateur status have since turned professional.

Induction Years Unrecorded

ANDERSON, Willie
Professional
See entry in American Golf Hall of Fame, 1968.
Also in: Professional Golfers' Association of America Hall of Fame and World Golf Hall of Fame.

ARMOUR, Thomas Dickson
Professional
See entry in American Golf Hall of Fame, 1965.
Also in: Professional Golfers' Association of America Hall of Fame and World Golf Hall of Fame.

BARBER, Jerry
Professional
Born April 25, 1916, in Woodson, Ill; Player of the Year 1961.

Jerry Barber continuously practiced his golf and as a result won a total of seven tournaments. He turned professional in 1940 and joined the Professional Golfers' Association (PGA) tour in 1948 as one of the smallest players, at 5 ft. 5 in. and 137 lbs. His most outstanding win was at the 1961 PGA Championship. He holed 6, 12 and 20 yd. putts on the last three greens to tie with Don January, and defeated him in a close 67 to 68 playoff. He participated on the 1955 Ryder Cup team and was playing captain in 1961 when the tournament was held at Royal Lytham and St. Annes. Barber also served as tournament committee chairman of the PGA from 1954 to 1955.

BARNES, James M.
Professional
See entry in American Golf Hall of Fame, 1973.
Also in: Professional Golfers' Association of America Hall of Fame.

BERG, Patricia Jane
Woman Golfer
See entry in American Golf Hall of Fame, 1972.
Also in: Ladies Professional Golfers' Association Hall of Fame and World Golf Hall of Fame.

BOROS, Julius Nicholas
Professional
See entry in American Golf Hall of Fame, 1971.
Also in: Connecticut Golf Hall of Fame and Professional Golfers' Association of America Hall of Fame.

BURKE, Jack, Jr.
Professional
Born January 29, 1923, in Fort Worth, Tex; father was a golfer; served with the U.S. Marines during W.W. II.

In a ten-year span of professional golf, beginning in 1940 at the age of 17, Jack Burke won over $240,000 in prize money, a sizeable amount for that time. He experienced two notable success streaks. In 1952 Burke took the Texas, Houston, Baton Rouge and St. Petersburgh championships all in a row. And in 1956 he won both the U.S. Masters and the Professional Golfers' Association (PGA) tournaments. He had been runnerup in the 1952 Masters under extreme weather conditions and won in 1956 under similar conditions with the highest score in Masters' history—a 289. In 1958 he won the Japanese Open and repeated a win in the Texas Open of 1963. Burke also played on the 1951, 1953, 1955 and 1957 Ryder Cup teams, and went as captain in 1957 and 1973. A hand injury and interest in the Champions Club in Texas, which he owns with Hall of Famer Jimmy Demaret, limited more appearances on the circuit.
Also in: Professional Golfers' Association of America Hall of Fame.

BURKE, William
Professional
Born December 14, 1902, in Naugatuck, Conn; of Lithuanian descent, original name Burkauskus; died April 19, 1972, in Clearwater, Fla.

After winning the North and South Open in 1928, Billy Burke came to sudden prominence as the champion of the 1931 U.S. Open. It was often said that he "had to play two Opens to win one." Burke and George Von Elm tied a 36-hole playoff when Von Elm birdied the last hole; after another 36 holes Burke was declared champion. Not a long player, but an excellent short game player, Burke won two Glens Falls, a Florida West Coast, a Cascades and the 1939 Walter Hagen tournaments. As a member of two Ryder Cup teams, he won a single and a foursome in 1931 and a foursome in 1933. In 1939, with Ed Dudley, he won the Hagen Anniversary four-ball tournament and in 1940 won the Miami four-ball tournament with Hall of Famer Craig Wood. For a time, Burke was even the personal pro for industrialist Henry Topping.
Also in: Connecticut Golf Hall of Fame and Professional Golfers' Association of America Hall of Fame.

CARNER, Jo Anne Gunderson
Woman Golfer
Born March 4, 1939, in Kirkland, Wash; graduated from Arizona State Univ.

Jo Anne Carner was 16 years old and 1956 winner of the U.S. junior girls' tournament when she became the second youngest, behind Hall of Famer Beatrix Hoyt, to win the U.S. Golf Association (USGA) Amateur in 1957. Before turning professional in 1969 she won the USGA Amateur again in 1960, 1962, 1966 and 1968 for a record of five times. In her first year as a professional she joined the tour, immediately won the Wendell-West Open and was eleventh in official prize money. Despite the fact that she is not a willing practicer, believing everything would fall into place at the first tee, her outstanding physique and regular physical training make her a long driver for a women. Using good footwork and strong wrists for distance she can get by with a half-swing. In addition to the USGA Amateur, she has won the Women's Western, Doherty Challenge Cup, the Intercollegiate, Trans-Mississippi, Pacific Northwest, Southwest, Northwest and Eastern. In 1971 she won the USGA Women's Open and the Bluegrass Invitational; in 1974 the Bluegrass, Hoosier, Desert Inn, St. Paul, Dallas Civitan and Portland; and in 1975 won three tournaments to bring her career total to $226,681. Early victories in 1976 included the Orange Blossom in playoffs against Sandra Palmer and the Lady Tara.

COOPER, Harry E.
Professional
Born August 4, 1904, in Leatherhead, Surrey, England; father Syd at one time personal pro to crony of Edward VII; came to the United States as young child with family.

"So consistent was he in his tournament days that his second-place finishes equaled the number of his victories." Harry Cooper turned professional at 18 in Dallas and soon won the Texas Professional in 1923 and 1924. In 1926 he won the Del Monte tournament and the Los Angeles tournament, beginning a run of 32 wins total. A consistent player, Cooper did well in the many U.S. Opens he entered, but unfortunately never won. In 1927 he would have won a playoff against Tommy Armour if Armour had not holed a 10-ft. birdie. In 1936 he broke the Open record by 2 strokes with a 284, but Tony Manera broke it by 4 strokes. Winning the Canadian Open in 1932 and 1937, Cooper would have made it 3 if he had won the playoff against Sam Snead. Cooper played on into his fifties and claimed victories in the 1955 Metropolitan Professional Golfers' Association (PGA) and the PGA Seniors. In his seventies he shot a pair of 69s.
Also in: Professional Golfers' Association of America Hall of Fame.

CURTIS, Margaret
Woman Golfer
Born October 8, 1883, in Manchester-by-the-Sea, Mass; older sister Harriot also Women's Amateur champion; Red Cross work in W.W. I; established food clinics for children in war-torn countries in Europe; died December 24, 1965, in Boston, Mass; Bobby Jones Award in 1958.

In 1905 visiting American players had a match against leading British players before the British Ladies' championship. The event inspired two sisters, Margaret and Harriot Curtis, to start a biennial match between amateur United States and British women golfers. The first Curtis Cup matches took place at Wentworth, England, in 1932 with the United States winning. In her golfing days, Margaret Curtis won a total of 25 championships. Three times before she won the U.S. Women's Amateur, she received medals in the qualifying rounds. Then in 1907, when her sister was the defending champion, Curtis won her first Amateur title, and was victorious again in 1911 and 1912. In 1908 she won the National women's doubles title with Evelyn Sears. Curtis was also known for being an outstanding lawn tennis player. She competed again in 1947, and entered the Amateur for the last time in 1949 at the age of 65.
Also in: Ladies Professional Golfers' Association Hall of Fame.

DEMARET, James Newton
Professional
See entry in American Golf Hall of Fame, 1973.
Also in: Professional Golfers' Association of America Hall of Fame.

DIEGEL, Leo
Professional
Born April 27, 1899, in Detroit, Mich; good sense of humor with leaning toward the unorthodox; died in North Hollywood, Calif. on May 8, 1951.

Leo Diegel's 15-year career as a professional golfer was outstanding in close races. Often called "third-round Diegel," he seemed to be "always the bridesmaid and never the bride." He tied for second in the U.S. Open of 1928, placed third in the 1929 British Open and was joint runnerup in the British Open of 1930. Being high strung and possessing a temperament that did not provide him with the needed strength to overcome critical situations, Diegel usually experienced lapses in the third round of tournaments. He did win the U.S. Professional Golfers' Association tournaments in 1928 and 1929 to break a string of four wins by Walter Hagen, and the Canadian Open in 1924, 1925, 1928 and 1929. Leo was on four Ryder Cup teams, 1927, 1929, 1931 and 1933. In his most unorthodox putting posture his elbows were bent so much that his forearms were almost horizontal. It was called "Diegeling." He could break 75 regularly by playing his shots standing on one leg.
Also in: Professional Golfers' Association of America Hall of Fame.

DUTRA, Olin
Professional
Born January 17, 1901, in Monterey, Calif.

Olin Dutra believed in lots of practice to reach success. Even as a teenager working in a hardware store, he got up before dawn three days a week to improve his golf game. It paid off. After turning professional in 1924, he won the Southern Californian Professional five times: 1928–1930, 1932 and 1933. In 1931 he took the Southwest Open and in 1932 the Professional Golfers' Association (PGA) title. He was selected for the 1933 and 1935 Ryder Cup teams. His finest victory came in 1934 in the U.S. Open. Plagued by a stomach disorder, he was behind on the last day by eight strokes. Miraculously after 36 holes, he won the championship by one stroke ahead of none other than Gene Sarazen. Dutra served as tournament committee chairman of the U.S. Professional Golfers' Association in 1935.
Also in: California Golf Hall of Fame and Professional Golfers' Association of America Hall of Fame.

EGAN, Henry Chandler
Amateur
Born August 21, 1884, in Chicago, Ill; moved to Oregon in 1911 to become a fruit grower; died of pneumonia on April 5, 1936.

Before pulling up his roots to move to Oregon, Chandler Egan won the Western Amateur four times, in 1902 and 1904 as an undergraduate at Harvard, and in 1905 and 1906; in 1903 he was runnerup. Also in 1904, when the U.S. Golf Association (USGA) first introduced a 54-hole system of qualifying for the Amateur, Egan won the qualifying medal and the tournament. He repeated the victory in 1905 and placed second in 1909. When he first arrived in Oregon he was 300 miles from the nearest golf course. His next win was not until 1915 at the Pacific Northwest Amateur which he won four more times, in 1920, 1923, 1925 and 1932; he was runnerup in 1914 and 1921. Though he had not played in the Amateur for 20 years, he entered the tournament in 1929 at Pebble Beach and reached the semifinals. By his performance there, Egan demonstrated the potential he had to become a much greater golfer had he not strayed from the game for so many years. In 1934 at the age of 50 he was selected to represent the United States in the Walker Cup matches at St. Andrews, Scotland. In the late 1920s Egan took up golf course architecture. He not only helped to remodel the course at Pebble Beach but was influential in the decision to hold the U.S. Amateur there in 1929.

EVANS, Charles, Jr. "Chick"
Amateur
See entry in American Golf Hall of Fame, 1965.
Also in: Professional Golfers' Association of America Hall of Fame and World Golf Hall of Fame.

FARRELL, Johnny
Professional
Born April 1, 1901, in White Plains, N.Y; brother James and two sons golf professionals; a flashy dresser, he set the styles for later golf fashions.

Farrell first became interested in golf as a caddie in Westchester, N.Y. When no one could outdo the immortal Bobby Jones, Johnny Farrell beat him in the 1928 U.S. Open championship. On the 36th hole of the playoff, Farrell sank a 7-ft. putt and beat Jones' 73 – 71 with 70 – 73. Throughout his career he had a good record at the Open, though he never won again. In 1925 he lost to Jones by one stroke and by four in 1926; in 1927 he was seven behind Armour and Cooper. Not good with his long game, he did have a graceful swing once he got himself settled, and had an excellent short game. In 1923 and 1924 he was in the money on every start and in 1927 won seven tournaments in a row. Not only runnerup in the 1929 and 1930 British Open, Farrell was also runnerup behind Hall of Famer Leo Diegel in the Professional Golfers' Association (PGA) tournament of 1929, after being defeated in the quarter finals five times. As a top golfer in the late 1920s, Farrell was selected for the 1927, 1929 and 1931 Ryder Cup teams.
Also in: Professional Golfers' Association of America Hall of Fame.

FORD, Doug
Professional
Born August 6, 1922, in West Haven, Conn; raised in Westchester County, N.Y, golf center of the country; son of golf professional; Player of the Year 1955.

Doug Ford attributes skill on greens to many hours spent in billiard saloons. He first turned professional in 1949 and joined the Professional Golfers' Association (PGA) tour in 1950. He was never out of the top 20—usually in the top 10—of the money winner list and won over $400,000 in prize money. A fast player who found that side-staking helped him concentrate, he accumulated a total of 19 victories. He tied for first 12 times but unfortunately lost in the playoffs for 7, and therefore placed second almost as many times as he won. In 1955 Ford won the PGA tournament, and in 1957 he won the Masters and Western Open, defeating Cary Middlecoff four and three in the finals. In the Masters he scored the lowest last round in golf, until Bert Yancey scored a 65 in 1968. Ford's 66 came with a birdie 3 at the 18th, where he holed out a bunker. In the 1958 Masters he was second to Arnold Palmer. In 1959 and 1963 he won the Canadian Open and was selected as a member of the Ryder Cup teams from 1955 to 1961. He was also two-time member of the PGA tournament committee.
Also in: Connecticut Golf Hall of Fame and Professional Golfers' Association of America Hall of Fame.

FRASER, Alexa Stirling
Woman Golfer
Born September 5, 1897, in Atlanta, Ga; childhood friend and golf partner of Bobby Jones; encouraged to golf by Scottish-born parents; student of Stewart Maiden; married Dr. Fraser of Ottawa in 1924.

Alexa Stirling was a top woman amateur golfer in the first quarter of the twentieth century. She was a stylist like Bobby Jones and an outstanding putter, never known to be flustered by the pressures of the game. Surely she would have won the U.S. Women's Amateur from 1916 – 1920 had the war not interrupted her career. As it was, she captured the title in 1916, 1919 and 1920 and was runnerup in 1921, 1923 and 1925. Other wins include the Southern championship in 1915, 1916 and 1919, the Metropolitan (N.Y.) in 1922, the Canadian Women's Amateur in 1920 and 1934 and seven club championships of the Royal Ottawa Golf Club. As the undisputed women's golf champion in North America, Stirling traveled through Europe in 1921. In the British Ladies' championship at Turnberry, she unfortunately drew Cecil Leitch in the first round and lost at the 16th in rough weather. At the French Open in Paris, she won the qualifying medal but was defeated in the semifinals by Joyce Wethered.
Also in: Ladies Professional Golfers' Association Hall of Fame.

GARDNER, Robert Abbe
Amateur
Born April 9, 1890, in Hinsdale, Ill; graduated from Yale Univ; served in W.W. I as Lieutenant in field artillery; died June 21, 1956, in Lake Forest, Ill.

As a freshman at Yale University, Robert Gardner attracted national attention when he became the youngest winner of the U.S. Golf Association Amateur championship at 19 years and three months, beating Hall of Famer Chandler Egan in 1909. In 1915 he beat John G. Anderson 5 and 4 and reached the finals two times after that. In 1916 he lost to Chick Evans and in 1921 he lost to Jesse Guilford. Gardner won the Chicago Open in 1914 and the Chicago District Amateur in 1916, 1924 and 1925. He was envied by his contemporaries for hitting shots with such ease and seeming lack of effort. A member of the Walker Cup teams of 1922 – 1924 and 1926, he was captain in 1926. In 1926 he and Howard Linn won the National Squash Raquets doubles championship.

GHEŻZI, Victor
Professional
Born October 19, 1912, in Rumson, N.J; died May 30, 1976 in Miami Beach, Fla.

National prominence came for Vic Ghezzi in 1935 when, at the age of 23, he won the Los Angeles Open. In 1935 he was also the runnerup in the Canadian Open and winner of the Maryland Open. He came close to winning the U.S. Open in 1936, but after holding the lead for the first 36 holes he lost it in the third round, finishing 18th with an 81. In 1946 he tried again, tying for first with Lloyd Mangrum and Byron Nelson. In the playoffs, however, Mangrum won by one stroke over Nelson and Ghezzi who tied with 73s. In 1947 at St. Louis he finished the Open in sixth place. Ghezzi's most thrilling performance was in the Professional Golfers' Association tournament of 1941 in which he first defeated Mangrum by one in the semifinals and beat Nelson on the 38th hole of the finals. Other wins for Ghezzi include the North and South, the New Jersey Open in 1937, 1943 and 1944, the Inverness and Hershey Four-Balls and the Greater Greensboro. An accurate player especially on the green, Ghezzi was selected for the Ryder Cup teams of 1939, 1941 and 1943.
Also in: Professional Golfers' Association of America Hall of Fame.

GULDAHL, Ralph
Professional
See entry in American Golf Hall of Fame, 1972.
Also in: Professional Golfers' Association of America Hall of Fame.

HAGEN, Walter Charles "The Haig"
Professional
See entry in American Golf Hall of Fame, 1965.
Also in: Professional Golfers' Association of America Hall of Fame and World Golf Hall of Fame.

HOGAN, William Benjamin "Bantam Ben"
Professional
See entry in American Golf Hall of Fame, 1965.
Also in: Professional Golfers' Association of America Hall of Fame and World Golf Hall of Fame.

HOYT, Beatrix
Woman Golfer
Born July 5, 1880, in Westchester County, N.Y; granddaughter of Salmon P. Chase, secretary of the treasury for Abraham Lincoln; died on August 14, 1963; Robert Cox Trophy 1896 – 1898.

At 16 Beatrix Hoyt became the youngest winner of the U.S. Golf Association Women's Amateur of 1896, the second year of the tournament, and she continued to dominate women's golf for a number of years. Hoyt won the first qualifying medal given in the tournament in 1896 and then won it four more times 1897 – 1900. As a three-time champion of the U.S. Women's Amateur 1896 – 1898, she won by the considerable margin of 7, 6 and 8 strokes, respectively. In 1899 Hoyt entered the Amateur again, but lost in the first round to Mrs. Caleb Fox. In 1900 after a drawn-out semifinals, Hall of Famer Margaret Curtis was victorious over Hoyt, and the young golfer soon retired from tournament play—at 20.
Also in: Ladies Professional Golfers' Association Hall of Fame.

HURD, Dorothy Iona Campbell
Woman Golfer
See entry in American Golf Hall of Fame, 1969.
Also in: Ladies Professional Golfers' Association Hall of Fame.

HUTCHISON, Jock, Sr.
Professional
See entry in American Golf Hall of Fame, 1976.
Also in: Professional Golfers' Association of America Hall of Fame.

JAMESON, Elizabeth "Betty"
Woman Golfer
Born May 9, 1919, in Norman, Okla.

Betty Jameson began her championship career at the very young age of 15 when she won the Southern Amateur. That was only the beginning of an outstanding amateur career which also included wins in the Texas state championships 1935 – 1938, the 1937 and 1940 Trans-Mississippi Amateur, the U.S. Women's Amateur in 1939 and 1940 and the 1942 Western Women's Open and Amateur. After turning professional in 1945, Jameson became one of the "Big Four" in women's professional golf and won over $91,000 in prize money between 1948 and 1965. Her first major victory was in the Women's National Open of 1947, after placing second behind Patty Berg in 1946. She later won the so-called World championship in 1952, the Eastern championship in 1954 and made the Babe Zaharias Open one of her four victories in 1954.
Also in: Ladies Professional Golfers' Association Hall of Fame.

JONES, Robert Tyre, Jr.
Amateur
See entry in American Golf Hall of Fame, 1965.
Also in: Professional Golfers' Association of America Hall of Fame, World Golf Hall of Fame and National Association of Left-handed Golfers' Hall of Fame.

LITTLE, William Lawson, Jr.
Amateur
See entry in American Golf Hall of Fame, 1970.
Also in: California Golf Hall of Fame and Professional Golfers' Association of America Hall of Fame.

LUXFORD, Maurie
Noteworthy Contributor
Luxford was the originator of and general chairman for the Victory Golf Tournaments held during W.W. II. He also served as tournament director for the Bing Crosby Championships for 18 years. Now deceased, Luxford served as president and director of numerous golf associations and projects over the years.

MANGRUM, Lloyd Eugene
Professional
Born August 1, 1914, in Trenton, Tex; family of golfers;

joined Army in 1943; served under General Patton and collected two Purple Hearts; died November 11, 1973, in Apple Valley, Calif; Vardon Trophy 1951 and 1955.

Mangrum was always the focus of considerable attention resulting from his flashy manner, a reputation for gambling, his knack for penalties and mostly for his ability to play golf. As a professional beginning in 1929, Mangrum won 33 Professional Golfers' Association (PGA) tournaments and was top money winner in 1951 with $26,088. In 1940 he was runnerup in the U.S. Masters and shot a record single round of 64, only equaled by Nicklaus and Benbridge. While in the military, Mangrum won the U.S. Army golf championship in Paris and the British G.I. championship at St. Andrews. Defeating Hall of Famers Byron Nelson and Vic Ghezzi in the second round, he won the 1946 U.S. Open, and came close to another victory in 1950 but lost to Ben Hogan in the playoff. His peak year was 1948: including victories in the All-American and World tournaments, Mangrum won $22,000 in one week. He was not as good from the tee as he was on the green, where he used a variation of the interlocking grip, and unfortunately he suffered from numerous penalties. In the lead during the second round of the 1948 Masters, he penalized himself when his ball moved in the rough as he prepared to shoot. In the 1950 U.S. Open he picked up his ball to remove a distracting, stubborn fly and was penalized two strokes in the playoff. Always good humored, he simply shrugged his shoulders after the rules were read and replied, "Fair enough. We'll all eat tomorrow, no matter what happens." Mangrum was selected as a member of the Ryder Cup in 1941, 1947, 1951, 1953 and 1955, and was captain in 1953 and 1955.
Also in: California Golf Hall of Fame and Professional Golfers' Association of America Hall of Fame.

McDERMOTT, John J.
Professional
Born August 12, 1891, in Philadelphia, Pa; died August 1, 1971.

In only five short years of golf, McDermott more than proved himself an outstanding golfer. In 1911 he became the youngest as well as the first American-born player to win the U.S. Open after a three-way tie before the playoff. He repeated the victory in 1912 along with wins in the Philadelphia and Western Opens and a tie in fifth place at the British Open. At the 1913 Shawnee Open, McDermott accomplished the amazing by breaking 300 and in the process beat Harry Vardon by 13 strokes, and also Ted Ray. Though he was one of the first to perfect the use of the backspin and excelled with the mashie, he could not withstand the pressures of competition and ended his playing days in 1915.
Also in: Professional Golfers' Association of America Hall of Fame.

MIDDLECOFF, Dr. Cary
Professional
See entry in American Golf Hall of Fame, 1971.
Also in: Professional Golfers' Association of America Hall of Fame.

NELSON, John Byron, Jr.
Professional
See entry in American Golf Hall of Fame, 1965.
Also in: Professional Golfers' Association of America Hall of Fame and World Golf Hall of Fame.

OUIMET, Francis D.
Amateur
See entry in American Golf Hall of Fame, 1965.
Also in: Professional Golfers' Association of America Hall of Fame and World Golf Hall of Fame.

PICARD, Henry B.
Professional
Born November 28, 1907, in Plymouth, Mass; after retiring from competition, took job at Canterbury Club.

Henry Picard is the only golfer to have defeated Hall of Famer Walter Hagen in a playoff during one of his first victories, the 1932 Carolina Open. The Number One money-winner in 1939 with $10,303, he won 30 tournaments in a 20-year career and was selected for the 1935, 1937, 1939 and 1941 Ryder Cup teams. While a professional in Hershey, Pa. during 1935, Picard won six tournaments, two in partnership with Hall of Famer Johnny Revolta, and was sixth in the British Open. In 1936 he won six Professional Golfers' Association (PGA) tournaments and placed sixth in the U.S. Open. He was victorious in the 1937 Argentine Open and ended the year as second-highest money winner. In 1938 he was U.S. Masters champion and third-highest money winner. Picard defeated Byron Nelson in the final of the 1939 PGA tournament with birdies at the 36th and 37th holes. He had a good swing and was especially proficient in long-iron play but rarely went for difficult shots unless absolutely necessary. In 1940 Picard cut back on tournament play due to illness.
Also in: Professional Golfers' Association of America Hall of Fame.

RAWLS, Elizabeth Earle "Betsy"
Woman Golfer
Born May 4, 1928, in Spartanburg, S.C; graduated from Univ. Tex; Phi Beta Kappa in physics; *Los Angeles Times'* Woman Golfer of the Year 1953; Vare Trophy 1959.

Taking up golf at 17, Betsy Rawls won the third-highest number of Ladies Professional Golfers' Association (LPGA) tournaments, a total of 55. Before she turned professional in 1951, she was runnerup in the 1950 U.S. Women's Open behind Hall of Famer Babe Zaharias and then won a record of four Opens, in 1951, 1953, 1957 and 1960. As leading money winner in 1952 she won the Eastern and Western Women's Opens and took the Eastern again in 1953. Rawls took the Tampa Women's Open in 1954, 1956, 1957 and 1958, the Western again in 1959 and the LPGA ten years apart in 1959 and 1969. In fact, between 1954 and 1965 she won at least one tournament every year and was leading money winner for the second time in 1959 with $26,744, the most a woman golfer had won up to that time. Rawls was president of the LPGA from 1961 to 1962 and tournament director in 1975.
Also in: Ladies Professional Golfers' Association Hall of Fame.

REVOLTA, John
Professional
Born April 5, 1911, in St. Louis, Mo; instructor at Mission Hills Golf and Country Club at Palm Springs, Calif.

A consistent player with strength in his short game and a talent for getting out of the bunker, Johnny Revolta became interested in golf as a young boy. A caddie at 12, he won the Wisconsin Caddie championship at 14. He developed his playing to a fine art and beat both Gene Sarazen and Tommy Armour when they toured in the Wisconsin-Minnesota area. Friends then encouraged him to try his talent on the circuit and he turned professional in 1929. In 1933 he won the Miami Open, but 1935 was his peak year. Top money winner that year with $9543, Revolta won the Professional Golfers' Association tournament at 24, beating Walter Hagen in the first round and Tommy Armour in the final. He also won the Western Open and International Four-Ball with Henry Picard and was a member of the Ryder Cup team. In 1936 and 1937 Revolta again won the International Four-Ball tournament with Henry Picard and was a member of the Ryder Cup team in 1937. At his best he broke 17 course records in Wisconsin and Minnesota and played a 270 in the 1931 Minnesota Open to tie the record low score in a 72-hole event. When the war interrupted the tour, Revolta devoted considerable time to the Evanston Golf Club and in the 1940s began playing only portions of the tour. His last major wins were the 1944 San Antonio and Texas Opens.
Also in: Professional Golfers' Association of America Hall of Fame.

RUNYAN, Paul Scott
Professional
See entry in American Golf Hall of Fame, 1975.
Also in: Professional Golfers' Association of America Hall of Fame.

SARAZEN, Eugene
Professional
See entry in American Golf Hall of Fame, 1965.
Also in: Connecticut Golf Hall of Fame, Professional Golfers' Association of America Hall of Fame and World Golf Hall of Fame.

SHUTE, Hermon Densmore "Denny"
Professional
See entry in American Golf Hall of Fame, 1975.
Also in: Professional Golfers' Association of America Hall of Fame and West Virginia Sports Writers Hall of Fame.

SMITH, Alex
Professional
Born 1872 in Carnoustie, Angus, Scotland; brother Willie won U.S. Open in 1899; youngest brother Macdonald was golfer and also in Hall of Fame; moved to the United States in 1898; died April 20, 1930, in Baltimore, Md.

Alex Smith was one of the early Scottish professionals who made a significant impact on American golf at the turn of the century. A professional at Nassau Country Club in Glen Cove, N.Y, he was also a well-known teacher who is credited with developing the games of Jerry Travers and Glenna Collett. He was a clubmaker and greenskeeper. As a professional golfer, Smith won the Western Open in 1903 and 1906, but his best-known victories took place in the U.S. Open. In 1906 he scored 295, the first time anyone had ever scored below a 300 in the tournament, and beat his brother Willie by seven strokes. In 1910 at St. Martin's course of the Philadelphia Cricket Club he won for a second time after a three-way tie with Johnny McDermott and his youngest brother Macdonald.
Also in: Professional Golfers' Association of America Hall of Fame.

SMITH, Horton
Professional
Born May 22, 1908, in Springfield, Mo; died October 15, 1963, in Detroit, Mich, of Hodgkin's disease; Ben Hogan Award 1961.

After turning professional in 1926, Horton Smith, "The Joplin Ghost," won the French Open on his twentieth birthday in 1928. That winter he won eight tournaments and finished the year as leading money winner. A fine putter and a good example for novice golfers according to Bernard Darwin, Smith was the first winner of the U.S. Masters tournament (by one stroke) over Hall of Famer Craig Wood. He won again in 1936. In total he won 29 Professional Golfers' Association (PGA) tournaments and was selected for the 1929, 1933 and 1935 Ryder Cup teams. He served on the tournament committee of the PGA 1932–1952, and became president 1952–1954. In 1964 after his death, a trophy was established in his name by the PGA to be awarded each year to the professional golfer who has made the most outstanding contribution to golf professional education.
Also in: Professional Golfers' Association of America Hall of Fame.

SMITH, Macdonald
Professional
Born 1890 in Carnoustie, Angus, Scotland; brothers Willie and Alex winners of the U.S. Open; worked in a shipyard; called "Silent Scot" either due to his quiet nature or his hearing loss sustained during W.W. I; died in 1949.

Macdonald Smith had the unusual habit of performing well in the last round of a tournament when the pressure was really on, but not so well when the chance was there for the taking. He played during the era of Jones, Hagen and Sarazen; he had a smooth, elegant swing, though he played with unusually heavy clubs. Mac won the Western Open in 1912, 1925 and 1933. In the 1910 U.S. Open he came in third after losing the playoffs to his brother Alex and in 1930 was runnerup to Bobby Jones in the year of his Grand Slam. And from that 1910 victory until he came in fourth in the U.S. Open of 1936, he was within three strokes of the winner in the British and U.S. Open nine times—the British Open 1923–1925 and 1930–1932 and the U.S. Open in 1913, 1930 and 1934. Other wins include the Canadian Open in 1926 and the Los Angeles Open in 1928, 1929, 1932 and 1934.
Also in: California Golf Hall of Fame and Professional Golfers' Association of America Hall of Fame.

SNEAD, Samuel Jackson
Professional
See entry in American Golf Hall of Fame, 1965.
Also in: Professional Golfers' Association of America Hall of Fame, West Virginia Sports Writers Hall of Fame and World Golf Hall of Fame.

STRANAHAN, Frank R.
Amateur
Born August 5, 1922 in Toledo, Ohio; father a millionaire; avid weight lifter.

As an amateur golfer, Frank Stranahan was very successful, winning the British Amateur in 1948 and 1950. He was also top amateur player in the 1947, 1949–1951 and 1953 British Opens, and runnerup in 1947 and 1953. In 1948 alone he won not only the British Amateur, but the Canadian (also in 1947), Mexican, Brazilian, North and South (also in 1946, 1949 and 1952) and the All-American Amateurs and the Delaware, Ohio and Miami Opens. A winner of the 1946, 1949 and 1951 U.S. Western Amateur, he came close to winning the U.S. Amateur in 1950, but lost to Sam Urzetta on the 39th hole of the final. He also won the Tam O'Shanter World's Amateur 1950–1954 and was a natural selection for the 1947, 1949 and 1951 Walker Cup teams. As a professional after 1954, Stranahan was not quite as successful. Though he won the Eastern Open of 1955 and the Los Angeles Open of 1958, he found it difficult to even approach his amateur record.

SUGGS, Louise
Woman Golfer
Born September 7, 1923, in Atlanta, Ga; author of *Par Golf for Women;* Vare Trophy 1957.

With a beautiful form, Louise Suggs not only won 50 Ladies Professional Golfers' Association (LPGA) tournaments, but also set new standards for women golfers. Before turning professional in 1948 she won three Western Amateurs, the U.S. Women's Amateur in 1947 and the British Ladies' in 1948, only the second American woman to do so. She was selected for the Curtis Cup team in 1948 also. Her long list of victories include the U.S. Women's Open in 1949 and 1952—in which she was runnerup in 1951, 1955, 1958, 1959 and 1963—the LPGA tournament in 1957, three North and South tournaments, and the 1954, 1956 and 1957 Titleholders championship. In 1953 and 1960 she was LPGA top money winner. Active later with LPGA, first as president 1956 and 1957 and later as member at large 1959–1961, she helped establish a circuit of tournaments for women golfers.
Also in: Georgia Athletic Hall of Fame (first woman elected) and Ladies Professional Golfers' Association Hall of Fame.

SWEETSTER, Jess W.
Amateur
See entry in American Golf Hall of Fame, 1967.

TRAVERS, Jerome Dunstan "Jerry"
Amateur
See entry in American Golf Hall of Fame, 1974.
Also in: Professional Golfers' Association of America Hall of Fame and World Golf Hall of Fame.

TRAVIS, Walter J.
Amateur
See entry in American Golf Hall of Fame, 1971.
Also in: Professional Golfers' Association of America Hall of Fame.

TURNESA, William P.
Amateur
Born January 20, 1914, in Elmsford, N.Y; youngest of seven golfing brothers; attended Holy Cross Univ.

Willie Turnesa learned to play golf at "Turnesa Country Club," a course set up by his brothers. He was probably better than the other six, but as the youngest he also had a lot of examples to follow. Before his win in the 1938 U.S. Amateur, he won the Metropolitan Amateur, the North and South and the New York State Amateurs. In 1938 he beat Pat Abbott in the final, eight and seven, and defeated Ray Billows, two and one, to win the 1948 U.S. Amateur in the final round. He was also victorious in the 1947 British Amateur and runner-up in 1949. Often called "The Wedge," Turnesa was a great wedge player; his finest hours of golf were on the green. At the semifinals of the 1949 British Amateur, Turnesa missed the prepared surface from 15 out of 18 tees but still finished with a 71 to beat Ernest Millward on the last green. Turnesa was one of the founders and executives of the Westchester Caddie Fund, sending more than 100 caddies to college.

VAN WIE, Virginia
Woman Golfer
Born February 9, 1909, in Chicago, Ill; taught golf in Chicago.

Van Wie golfed during a time when there were many outstanding woman golfers: Helen Hicks, Dorothy Traung, Charlotte Glutting, Mrs. Leona Pressler Cheney, British champion Enid Wilson, Edith Quier and Rosalie Knapp. She won the 1926, 1927 and 1928 Chicago District Golf Association championships and reached the finals of the U.S. Women's Amateur in that last year, losing only to Glenna Collett Vare. After reaching the finals of the Amateur again in 1930 she won the event in 1932 by a margin of ten and eight over none other than Vare. Van Wie then won the Amateur in 1933 and 1934 and became the fourth and last woman to win it three times in a row. Selected for the 1932 and 1934 Curtis Cup she captured three and one-half points of four with what Bernard Darwin would say was the most beautiful swing he had ever seen.
Also in: Ladies Professional Golfers' Association Hall of Fame.

VARE, Glenna Collett
Woman Golfer
See entry in American Golf Hall of Fame, 1966.
Also in: Ladies Professional Golfers' Association Hall of Fame and World Golf Hall of Fame.

WARD, Edward Harvie
Amateur
Born December 8, 1925, in Tarboro, N.C; now involved in golf as an instructor and promoter.

In 1948 Edward Ward won the National Collegiate and North and South tournaments. He then won his first international event, the British Amateur, in 1952. He won the Canadian Amateur in 1954, the U.S. Amateur in 1955 and 1956, and placed fourth in the Masters at Augusta in 1957. Three times he was low amateur in the Masters and was two times low amateur in the U.S. Open. Ward was selected for the Walker Cup team in

1953 and 1959 and the U.S. Americas Cup teams of 1952, 1954 and 1956. But from May 1957 until May 1958 he was suspended by the U.S. Golf Association for accepting expenses from his employer. His golfing was never the same. Though he participated in the 1958 U.S. Americas Cup and the 1959 Walker Cup matches following his suspension, he lost his interest in golf and his simple, yet perfectly balanced and rhythmic swing disappeared.
Also in: California Golf Hall of Fame and North Carolina Sports Hall of Fame.

WARD, Marvin Harvey
Amateur
Born May 1, 1913 in Olympia, Wash; head professional at Peninsula Country Club; died January 2, 1968, in San Mateo, Calif.

Selected for the Walker Cup teams of 1938 and 1947, Marvin Ward was an outstanding amateur golfer of the late 1930s and early 1940s. In addition to winning the 1939 and 1941 U.S. Amateurs, he won the Northwest Open five times and the Western Open three times. His record in the U.S. Open was good too: fourth in 1939, low amateur in 1946 and fifth in 1947. In the semifinal and final matches of the 1939 U.S. Amateur, Ward made single putts at 29 of 48 holes. In the 1947 Walker Cup in St. Andrews, he beat Leonard Crawley, five and seven, with seven consecutive threes from the seventh hole. Ward later turned professional, but was more successful as an amateur.
Also in: California Golf Hall of Fame.

WOOD, Craig Ralph
Professional
Born November 18, 1901, in Lake Placid, N.Y; died May 8, 1968, in Palm Beach, Fla.

Craig Wood won 34 Professional Golfers' Association (PGA) tournaments and had nearly as many "almost wins." Entering his first U.S. Open in 1929, he came close to winning but was defeated by Byron Nelson. Ten years later he was runnerup again and finally won the Open in 1941, to hold the title five years while the tournament was suspended by W.W. II. In 1933 he was runnerup in the British Open, tying with Hall of Famer Denny Shute, but losing the playoff. During that tournament, however, Wood hit the longest drive in major competition, 430 yds. at St. Andrews at the fifth hole with a strong following wind. His record in the PGA and Masters consisted of "almost wins" too. He was runnerup in the PGA in 1934 and runnerup in the Masters in 1934 and 1935. In 1934 he lost the Masters by one shot to Horton Smith and was already being congratulated in 1935 when Sarazen shot his double-eagle to win by five strokes at the playoff. As an outstanding player of the time, he was selected for the 1931, 1933 and 1935 Ryder Cup teams. He did win the tournament in 1941 and the Canadian Open in 1942. In the 1940s he was a professional at Winged Foot Golf Club in Mamaroneck, N.Y, for several years. After retirement, he lived in the Bahamas and became professional at Lucayan Club.
Also in: Professional Golfers' Association of America Hall of Fame.

WORSHAM, Lewis Elmer
Professional
See entry in American Golf Hall of Fame, 1976.

ZAHARIAS, Mildred Didrikson "Babe"
Woman Golfer
See entry in American Golf Hall of Fame, 1965.
Also in: Colorado Golf Hall of Fame, Ladies Professional Golfers' Association Hall of Fame, Professional Golfers' Association of America Hall of Fame and World Golf Hall of Fame; Track and Field Hall of Fame and Women's Basketball Hall of Fame, Citizens Savings Hall of Fame Athletic Museum; National Track and Field Hall of Fame and U.S. Track and Field Federation Hall of Fame.

Gymnastics Hall of Fame

The Gymnastics Hall of Fame was created in 1959 at the invitation of the National Association of College Gymnastics Coaches (NACGC). Since that time 86 members have been inducted under the categories of Gymnasts, Coaches and Noteworthy Contributors. The inductees are regarded worthy of recognition by the NACGC. Each new inductee will have his name placed upon the Hall of Fame Trophy which is lodged in the Citizens Savings Hall of Fame Atheltic Museum, international sports shrine in Los Angeles, California.

1959

BASS, Raymond
Gymnast
Raymond Bass competed in the 1932 Olympic Games, winning the rope climb title and a gold medal while establishing an Olympic record for that event.

CUMISKEY, Frank
Gymnast
Frank Cumiskey was many times National Amateur Athletic Union champion, including five all-around titles. He was an Olympic competitor in 1932, 1936 and again in 1948.

GULACK, George
Gymnast
George Gulack was a member of the U.S. gymnastic team at the 1932 Olympic Games. He was victorious on the rings at that international meet and won a gold medal.

HAUBOLD, Frank
Gymnast
Frank Haubold was twice National Amateur Athletic Union all-around champion as well as an Olympic competitor at the 1928, 1932 and 1936 Games.

HEINEMAN, Gustav
Coach
Gustav Heineman was the long-time Philadelphia Turners coach and later the physical education director at Temple University.

HOFFER, Daniel L.
Coach
Dan Hoffer is the former University of Chicago coach.

JOCHIM, Alfred
Gymnast
Al Jochim was many times National Amateur Athletic Union champion including seven all-around titles. He participated in the Olympic Games of 1924, 1928, 1932 and 1936.

JUDD, Leslie J.
Coach
Leslie Judd was a long-time professor of physical education at Springfield College in Massachusetts.

KRIZ, Frank
Gymnast
Frank Kriz was the winner of a number of Amateur Athletic Union crowns and was a competitor in the Olympic Games of 1920, 1924 and 1928. He won the long horse championship at the 1924 Games, and the gold medal.

MANG, Louis H.
Coach
Louis Mang is a former U.S. Naval Academy coach.

MEYER, Frederick
Gymnast
Fred Meyer won a number of National Amateur Athletic Union crowns and was an Olympic Games competitor in 1932 and 1936.

MOORE, Roy E.
Coach
Roy Moore was the U.S. Olympic gymnastics team coach in 1920, 1924, 1928 and again in 1932.

PIPER, Ralph A.
Coach
Ralph Piper was a long-time coach at the University of Minnesota.

PITT, Arthur
Gymnast
Art Pitt was a many time National Amateur Athletic Union champion including three all-around titles. He was also an Olympic Games competitor in 1936.

PRICE, Ben
Coach
Ben Price was the Los Angeles Athletic Club's coach from 1923 through 1935 and assistant coach of gymnastics at the 1932 Olympic Games.

PRICE, Hartley
Coach
Dr. Price was a long-time coach at the University of Illinois and Florida State University.

WHEELER, George
Gymnast
George Wheeler was many times National Amateur Athletic Union champion, including five all-around titles. He was an Olympic Games competitor in 1936.

WOLFE, Roland
Gymnast
Roland Wolfe was the winner of the tumbling title at the 1932 Olympic Games, and won the gold medal.

YOUNGER, Maximillian W.
Coach
Max Younger is a former Temple University coach.

ZWARG, Leopold
Coach
Leo Zwarg was a long-time physical education instructor at the University of Pennsylvania.

1963

BERGMANN, Alfred
Coach
Al Bergmann was the coach of Chicago high school teams for 40 years. His most exceptional successes were at Senn High School. Bergmann also served as an official, a lifelong gymnastics committeeman and a member of the German Turners.

DENTON, William
Gymnast
Bill Denton won the National Amateur Athletic Union ring championship in 1932. He went on to become a member of the U.S. Olympic team that year and took the silver medal for his effort on the rings.

EKLUND, Dr. E. A.
Noteworthy Contributor
Dr. Eklund was connected with the Cleveland STV Turners beginning in 1937 and served as the national secretary of the American Turners. He was a member of the U.S. Olympic gymnastic committee from 1951 through 1961.

GRIFFIN, Lester
Coach
Lester Griffin coached gymnastics for more than 40 years in the South, turning out both national and international champions. Many of his pupils have become prominent coaches.

LOBER, Abe
Noteworthy Contributor
Abe Lober was a teacher of physical education and gymnastics for a period of 50 years. He resided in California and worked with students in Merced County, Santa Barbara and Los Angeles. Lober had served as a gymnastics official since 1927.

PHILLIPS, Chester W.
Gymnast and Coach
Chet Phillips took the National Collegiate Athletic Association all-around championships in 1935, 1936 and 1937. He was a member of the 1936 U.S. Olympic team and holder of a number of Eastern titles at Temple University. Phillips served as coach at the U.S. Naval Academy for 24 years, being elected Coach of the Year in 1961. His teams won 30 Eastern championships and 9 National championships. Phillips founded the National Association of College Gymnastics Coaches in 1951.

SCHROEDER, Henry
Noteworthy Contributor
Henry Schroeder was chairman of the national physical

education committee for the American Turners and a recipient of the Honor Key of American Turners for his distinguished service. He was a New York Turnerlign instructor for 25 years.

VAVRA, Charles
Coach
Charles Vavra coached gymnastics at the University of Colorado for 41 years. He was the founder of the Colorado state high school gymnastic meet and served as a member of the National Collegiate Athletic Association rules committee.

WETTSTONE, Gene
Coach
Gene Wettstone's coaching at the Pennsylvania State University brought that school nine Eastern and seven National collegiate team championships. He produced 19 National Collegiate Athletic Association (NCAA) and 51 Eastern individual champions as well as five Olympians. His students held the NCAA individual all-around championship for three consecutive years, 1959 through 1961.

1964

NELSON, Harry G.
Coach
Harry Nelson is a graduate of Temple University; he is an excellent swimmer as well as gymnast. Harry Nelson was active in coaching since 1926 with the YMCA school, Amateur Athletic Union (AAU) and collegiate groups. His Philadelphia Turners won the National AAU crown in 1952. Nelson was well known as a supporter of gymnastics in the Philadelphia area.

PREISS, Emil
Coach
Born in Germany; came to the United States in 1924; attended Turner Normal Col. in Indianapolis; died in 1962.

Emil Preiss was one of Europe's top gymnasts. He won the American Turner all-around title in 1926, the Amateur Athletic Union championship in 1925 and the German championship in 1928. He began coaching the Chicago Turners in 1926 and went on to take over at the University of Pennsylvania in 1930, remaining there until his death.

WELSER, Lyle
Coach
Early in his career Lyle Welser coached at Bridgeport, Conn. in the YMCA and at the University of Illinois. He took over at Georgia Tech in 1946 and remained there as a leader of gymnastics in the South and as a two-time president of the National Association of College Gymnastics Coaches. He was also a member of the U.S. Olympic committee.

ZITTA, Fred
Coach
Fred Zitta began his career in gymnastics by competing for the Holyoke Turners. He began coaching for that group in 1930 and since then coached at Lincoln Turners in Chicago, the Holyoke Turnverein, the Socialer Turners, the Springfield, Mass, Turners and the Eiche Turners. He was awarded the American Turner Honor Key in 1960.
Also in: Turners Hall of Fame, Citizens Savings Hall of Fame Athletic Museum.

1965

NISSEN, George P.
Noteworthy Contributor
A graduate of the Univ. Iowa; owns Nissen Corp. in Cedar Rapids, Iowa, manufacturer of gymnastics equipment.

George P. Nissen is a former tumbling champion from the University of Iowa. In 1936 he developed the first commercial trampoline. His company now produces gymnastic equipment. Nissen sponsored many free teacher-student clinics and stimulated great interest in gymnastics and the growth of the sport.

1966

GIALLOMBARDO, Joseph
Gymnast and Coach
Graduated from Univ. Ill. 1940.

Joe Giallombardo was the Big Ten Conference tumbling champion as well as the National Amateur Athletic Union tumbling champion in 1938 and 1939. He began coaching gymnastics at New Trier High School in Illinois in 1940 and remained there through 1966. His teams won the state championships in 1951, 1953, 1955 and 1956. Giallombardo was a judge of the Big Ten and National Collegiate Athletic Association gymnastics championships beginning in 1947 as well as an official and judge for the Olympic trials of 1948, 1952 and 1956.

POND, Charles
Coach
Native of Dallas, Tex; graduated from Hardin-Simmons Univ; recreation superintendent, Abilene, Tex, 1939 – 1941.

Charles Pond was the gymnastics coach for the University of Illinois 1949 – 1966. During that time his teams won the Big Ten championship 1950 – 1960 and were National Collegiate Athletic Association champions in 1950, 1955, 1956 and 1958. Pond was the associate coach for the U.S. Olympic gymnastics team in 1956 and was a member of the Olympic committee 1960 – 1964.

STEEVES, Ted
Noteworthy Contributor
Graduated from Springfield Col. 1931; an excellent football and baseball player.

Ted Steeves coached all sports at Milford, Mass, High School 1933 – 1940. At that time he moved to Wellesley, Mass, where he coached gymnastics, football and basketball until 1966. He developed many outstanding gymnasts and championship teams.

1967

GRAVES, Charles W.
Coach
Graduated from Springfield Col. 1922.

Charles Graves coached gymnastics at the University of Southern California (USC) 1928–1957. Two of his students were members of the U.S. Olympic team of 1952. The 1951 and 1952 Trojan squads were National Collegiate Athletic Association runnerup for the championships. His USC teams did win eight Pacific Coast Conference Southern Division titles. Graves' individual champions include Ron Hall, Ken Foreman, Jerry Todd, Jack Beckner, Charles Simms, Lloyd Coahran and George Wikler.

1970

FREY, Harold
Gymnast, Coach and Noteworthy Contributor
At Pennsylvania State University Frey won the Eastern Collegiate All-Around title with a broken foot. He coached at Navy Pier and the University of California at Berkeley, with a record of over 110 dual meet wins and 7 losses. He has had the reputation of turning a "scraggly bunch of kids" into champions. He has taken individuals and molded winning teams, year after year. His teams have won Conference championships five times and the National Collegiate Athletic Association championship in 1968. He has contributed much to the sport as a judge, as past president of the National Collegiate Athletic Association rules committee, as an Olympic committee member and president of the Coaches Association for two years.

JOHNKE, Bruno A.
Noteworthy Contributor
Came to the United States in 1948.

Johnke joined a Turner Society in Berlin, Germany, in 1916 when he was ten years old. Upon graduation from the Deutsche Turnschule he became director of the "Turngemeinde in Berlin" 1931–1935, a society of 3000 gymnasts. His main task was the training of leaders for the divisions and squads. Johnke also competed in gymnastics meets and traveled extensively in Germany as a member of the Berlin Gymnastics Team. In 1936 he went to Cairo, Egypt, to coach an Egyptian Olympic team. He conducted training courses in Cairo and established gymnastic centers in Upper and Lower Egypt. Bruno came to the United States, and during an orientation period in New York City, met Roy E. Moore and translated for him French and German correspondence from the *Fédération Internationale de Gymnastique* (FIG). One of the items was the first edition of the Code of Points, which was subsequently published in the AAU Gymnastics Rule Book. He worked as aquatic director, and assisted with gymnastics in the YMCA, Jamestown, N.Y. Johnke coached the Cuban Olympic team for the Central American Games in Guatemala in 1950, which they won. In 1952 he accepted a position as physical director at the St. Louis Turner Society and from 1953 to 1955 he held a similar position at the East Side Turners in Cleveland, Ohio. He also initiated a gymnastics meet for high school students which was attended by more than 200 boys and girls. In 1955 Bruno Johnke went to Pensacola, Fla, where he worked as an assistant and advisor to the officer in charge of the physical fitness division. They organized a Navy gymnastics team and competed in the Southern Gymnastics League. Since the founding of the U.S. Gymnastic Foundation, he has been their official translator, and was on their physical education committee and a member of the committee for foreign affairs.
Also in: Turners Hall of Fame, Citizens Savings Hall of Fame Athletic Museum.

PATTERSON, Carl A.
Coach and Noteworthy Contributor
Received B.S. and M.S. from Temple Univ; served in U.S. Army from 1943 to 1946; died in 1968.

Carl Patterson taught and coached at Girard College 1946–1950; at Gratz High School in Philadelphia 1950–1956; at the Roxborough Turners 1956–1961; and at Temple University 1956–1968. He produced many fine gymnasts. The most outstanding is Carlton Rintz who competed at Michigan State University and won the national collegiate and Big Ten titles. Between 1964 and 1968, Temple teams won the Eastern Intercollegiate Gymnastic league championships. Patterson wrote extensively about gymnastics teaching, coaching and judging, and was nationally a well-respected judge. He contributed to physical education convention programs and to gymnastics clinics throughout the United States. Carl Patterson was selected Eastern Coach of the Year and National Coach of the Year by the National Association of College Gymnastics Coaches in 1958. He was a member of the National College Gymnastics rules committee, secretary and president of the Eastern Intercollegiate Coaches Association, president and vice president of the National Association of College Gymnastics Coaches and a member of the U.S. Olympic gymnastic rules committee.

SZYPULA, George
Gymnast, Coach and Noteworthy Contributor
Received M.A. from Temple Univ. 1947; served in the U.S. Army; voted Outstanding Athlete at Temple Univ. 1943; Coach of the Year 1966.

While at Temple University Szypula was a four-year member of the gymnastics team. He captured four straight national AAU tumbling crowns along with wins in the 1943 NCAA tumbling championships and two straight all-around and tumbling crowns in the Eastern Intercollegiate meet in 1942 and 1943. He also won the tumbling title ten times and the horizontal and parallel bars championships five times in the Middle Atlantic State Senior AAU competitions. In 1947 Szypula became gymnastics coach at Michigan State University and turned out one of the finest teams in the country. His teams have compiled an excellent 114–59–5 record in dual competition. His teams tied for the NCAA championship and for the Big Ten title in 1968. George was elected president of the National Association of College Gymnastics Coaches in 1957 and was a member of the executive board. He has been chairman of the selection committee for the Citizens Savings Gymnastics Hall of Fame and has judged at all levels of competition for over 20 years. He is the author of *Tumbling and Balancing for All* and *Trampolining.*

VAN AALTEN, John
Coach
Moved to the United States in 1947.

Through the thirties, Van Aalten was one of the leading gymnasts of the Netherlands and was on their 1940 Olympic team, and a member of the national team of Belgium. Val Aalten was a coach at the West Side YMCA in New York City. For over twenty years he coached many youths without any financial compensation. His teams have upon numerous occasions won the National YMCA championships. He coached Abie Grossfield to the national championship and the Olympic team.

1971

LOKEN, Dr. Newt
Coach
Ph.D. from Univ. Mich; four children: Christine, former state swimming champion, Lani, top female diver, Jon and Newt, Jr, competitive swimmers and divers.

Newt Loken won the National Collegiate Athletic Association All-Around gymnastics title in 1942 for the University of Minnesota. Dr. Loken began coaching at the University of Michigan in 1947 and since that time his teams have accumulated 157 dual meet victories and 31 losses. They have won nine Big Ten titles as well as the National Collegiate Athletic Association (NCAA) title in 1963. Loken has been recognized as Coach of the Year for the Mideast District twice and has served as president of the National Collegiate Gymnastics Coaches Association and chairman of the All-American selection committee. His book, *Complete Book of Gymnastics,* has established him as one of the authorities of gymnastics.

MALONEY, Tom
Coach
Tom Maloney took the position of coach of gymnastics at the U.S. Military Academy at West Point in 1931 and remained there through 1966 to coach that school to 6 national titles, 47 individual Eastern championships and 12 Eastern intercollegiate titles. He is considered one of the key men in the development of an intercollegiate gymnastics program at the Academy. He retired from West Point in 1966 after 36 seasons as head coach. He has been the administrator for gymnastics for the AAU and the U.S. Olympic gymnastic chairman. After retirement, he also served as technical delegate to the *Fèdèration Internationale de Gymnastique.* Maloney has judged at three Olympic Games, two World championships and was superior judge at three Pan-American Games and six international matches. He has also done the commentary for *Wide World of Sports* on two World games and one Olympics.

1973

DUNN, Dr. Hubert
Coach and Noteworthy Contributor
Born November 1, 1921, in Pinckneyville, Ill; attended Southern Ill. Univ; received M.S. from Wash. State Univ. and Ph.D. at the Univ. Ill; Outstanding College Gymnastics Coach of the Western Area 1962; NACGC Outstanding Service Award 1968.

Dr. Dunn served as teacher, head coach of gymnastics and director of the activity program in physical education at Washington State University for 15 years. He then took a position at Northern Illinois University as associate professor of physical education. He is recognized as the person most responsible for the introduction of modern gymnastics into the physical education and athletic programs of secondary schools and universities of the Pacific Northwest area. He developed the first university gymnastics team in the history of the Pacific Northwest area and coached teams which took part in the first intercollegiate gymnastics meets ever held in the states of Washington, Montana, Idaho and Oregon. He arranged and directed over 138 physical education-athletic clinics throughout the state of Washington and parts of Idaho and Oregon, and 15 such in Illinois. He has served as 1965 vice president of the National Association of College Gymnastics Coaches (NACGC) as well as holding that organization's presidential post in 1967. He has been a member of the executive committee of the U.S. Gymnastics Federation since 1967 and has served on the All-American selection committee of the NACGC 1968 and 1969.

FINA, Paul E.
Gymnast and Noteworthy Contributor
Paul Fina competed in gymnastics for 20 years, winning the 1935 Ohio State All-Around championship, the National Collegiate Athletic Association all-around championship in 1940 and participating on the Olympic honorary team that year as well. He won the National Amateur Athletic Union floor exercise championship of 1946 as well as the second place position for the horizontal bar and parallel bars that year. His later administrative positions include chairman of the organizing committee of the 1959 Pan-American Games, member of the Olympic committee for 1968 and 1972, international judge for the 1955 Pan-American Games and a founder of the Midwest Gymnastic Association.

HUGHES, Dr. Eric
Coach and Noteworthy Contributor
Born September 1, 1923, in Victoria, B.C; attended school in Victoria; graduated from Univ. Ill. with a B.S. and M.S. in physical education; served in the Royal Canadian Air Force during W.W. II; received Ph.D. from Univ. Wash. 1955; Western Coach of the Year two times; NACGC Special Recognition Award 1972.

Dr. Hughes began teaching at the University of Washington in 1950 and in a few years his teams were the power of the Pacific Northwest, displaying a record of 109 victories to 17 losses by the end of the 1972 season. In 1950 he also started a gymnastic club at Washington and in 1951 started teaching extension classes for children. For 22 years he has taught 100 young boys every Saturday in this program. This children's program has produced many prominent gymnasts at the national level. He has served in every office of the National Association of College Gymnastics Coaches (NACGC) and has written over thirty articles on gymnastics as well as two texts. Hughes was one of the founders of the Highline Gymkamp which was the first gymnastic camp west of the Mississippi. This camp has successfully operated every year since 1958. He has hosted many large gymnastic meets including the National AAU in 1962 and the NCAA in 1969. He has also hosted several foreign teams from Japan, Germany, Switzerland and New Zealand. Hughes was a member of the Olympic gymnastic committee for several years and was manager for the 1972 Olympic team.

1974

ELSTE, Meta Neumann

Gymnast

Born in Bremen, Germany; immigrated to Chicago at age 3.

Meta Neumann began her gymnastic career at age 6 when she first participated in the junior division. From 1943 to 1952 she was a medalist in National Amateur Athletic Union (AAU) competitions. Her outstanding events were the flying rings, parallel bars, rings, balance beam, floor exercise, vaulting and all-around. She was chosen nine times for AAU All-American honors. Meta represented the United States in the 1948 and 1952 Olympic Games.

LIENERT, Walter John

Coach

Born in Chicago; graduated from Indiana Univ. 1950; served in the Navy during W.W. II.

Walter John Lienert organized the Indiana Gymnast Association in 1957. He directed the Women's National Amateur Athletic Union gymnastic championships in 1958 and served as a coach and judge at the state and national tournaments; he went to the Olympic Games as a member of the coaching staff at Melbourne in 1956. Since 1958 he has conducted Lienert's Gym Camp for Youths and has authored the *Modern Girl Gymnast on the Uneven Parallel Bars.*

LOMADY, Clara Schroth

Gymnast

Born in Philadelphia; participated in basketball, hockey and track and field during high school; married Wendell Lomady in 1951, a physical education teacher; four children.

Clara Schroth was the National Amateur Athletic Union balance beam champion of 1941. She went on to take a bronze medal for her effort in team gymnastics in the Olympic Games of 1948 and was a member of the U.S. team at the 1952 and 1956 Olympic Games. Her versatility brought her a medal for the standing long jump in the National Amateur Athletic Union track and field championships of 1945.

MEADE, William

Coach and Noteworthy Contributor

Bill Meade began his career as an outstanding gymnast at Pennsylvania State University and was a member of the National Collegiate Athletic Association (NCAA) championship team of 1948. As the men's gymnastics coach at Southern Illinois University, his teams have won four NCAA championships and were runnerup five times. Meade was manager and assistant coach of the 1968 U.S. Olympic team, vice president of the U.S. gymnastic federation 1965–1969, a U.S. Olympic commission member 1965–1971 and chairman since that time. He has also conducted a number of international gymnastic clinics.

ROSSI, Tony

Noteworthy Contributor

A native of Brooklyn, N.Y; served in the U.S. Air Force during W.W. II.

While being held in a prisoner of war camp in Germany, Tony Rossi led many of the POW's in basic gymnastics classes. He constructed a high bar from pipe and other items available and helped to raise morale at the camp. After the war Rossi attended Colorado State College and competed in gymnastics there, subsequently becoming that schools gymnastics coach. He has produced outstanding gymnasts as well as coaches.

SCHIGET, Henry

Coach

Born in Charleroi, Pa; graduated from Indianapolis Normal Col. 1925.

Henry Schiget began his career in gymnastics at age 4 and continued as a participant until age 18. He took a coaching position with the Clinton, Iowa, Turners and remained there for 18 years, increasing the enrollment of that group from 42 to 900. He won all Upper Mississippi District turners championships for 17 years in succession. He conducted free camps for young people in Clinton, Iowa, and raised funds for the U.S. Olympic teams. Schiget moved to Milwaukee where he remained for nine years coaching that city's turners. He was the director of the American Turners National Turnfest in 1955 and held the Invitational Turnfests in 1961, 1965 and 1968. In 1965 he became the recipient of the coveted Turner Honor Key for having devoted most of his life to the turners and gymnastics.

SJURSEN, Helen Schifano

Gymnast and Noteworthy Contributor

Helen Schifano's gymnastics career began in 1936 and by 1947 and 1948 she was National Amateur Athletic Union (AAU) all-around champion, earning nine individual titles. As a member of the 1948 Olympic gymnastics team she earned a bronze medal for being one of the top scorers. Later, as a coach, judge and national committee member, Sjursen wrote ten books on gymnastics and issued correspondence course material for judging. Among her coaching assignments has been the U.S. North American championships gymnastic team of 1964 as well as a New Jersey YMCA, St. Bartholomew School and Hartridge School. She has also served as a National AAU trampoline committee member.

URAM, Paul

Coach and Noteworthy Contributor

Graduated from Slippery Rock Col; received Masters at Univ. Pittsburgh 1957.

While at Slippery Rock College, Paul Uram was football quarterback for four seasons and earned four varsity letters in track and field. He coached football, basketball, track and field and gymnastics at Millvale High School, Pittsburgh, Pa, 1949–1955. Since 1955 Paul Uram has been football and gymnastics coach at Butler High School in Pennsylvania. His gymnastics team has a record of 107 wins and 0 losses. He authored the book *Re-*

fining Human Movement on Flexibility Exercises that is used by over 3000 colleges and high schools as well as professional football teams. Along with his high school coaching position, Uram has served as flexibility coach for the Pittsburgh Steelers. He has participated in many clinics, including the Pittsburgh Sports Medicine Clinic in 1973.

VOGEL, Herbert
Coach
From 1946 through 1956 Herbert Vogel served as coach at the Mott Foundation in Flint, Mich. He held special classes for the blind, handicapped and mentally retarded while also serving the Michigan School for the Deaf. From 1957 through 1962 Vogel was coach of the United States teams which participated in the U.S.-Canada dual matches. During his coaching career he has produced many national, international and Olympic champions including eight national championship teams and 21 All-Americans. He took the position as women's gymnastic coach at the Southern Illinois University in 1962 and since that time has posted a dual match record of 116 wins and 4 losses. He has contributed many articles to the sport and was one of the founders of the U.S. Gymnastic Federation.

WACHTEL, Erna
Coach and Noteworthy Contributor
Born 1907 in Germany; came to the United States in 1926; became an American citizen.

Erna Wachtel participated in gymnastics and turner competitions for 29 years, earning nearly 100 awards. She served as chairperson of the U.S. gymnastics committee 1952–1956 and was a member of that committee through 1971. For 21 years she served as judge of international and national competition and was the U.S. Olympic manager and coach at the Melbourne Games in 1956. Wachtel was the gymnastics specialist and physical education instructor for the Chicago Park District recreation department 1957–1973.

1975

BARONE, Marian Twining
Gymnast
Born in Philadelphia, Pa; Nominee-Sullivan Award 1945; Maxwell Award 1945; Middle Atlantic District AAU Fourth Place Award 1945; member of AAU All-American Track and Field Team 1945–1952; selected as Outstanding Woman Athlete at the fiftieth anniversary of Germantown High School in Philadelphia, Pa. (1917–1967).

Barone was the National Amateur Athletic Union (AAU) baseball and basketball throw champion 1941–1945. She was AAU parallel bars champion and horse vault champion 1944 and 1945; she was also a member of the U.S. women's Olympic gymnastic team 1948–1952. Barone taught at South Philadelphia High School 1956–1963 and was an instructor at Marshall University in Huntington, W. Va, 1963–1967. She has been assistant professor at Temple University.

KEENEY, Chuck
Gymnast, Coach and Noteworthy Contributor
Graduated from San Diego State Col; M.S. from Univ. Calif. at Berkeley.

Chuck Keeney was the National Amateur Athletic Union tumbling champion in 1934. He coached at the University of California 1946–1957. Keeney was on the National Collegiate Athletic Association rules committee 1952–1954, president of the National Association of College Gymnastics Coaches 1955 and 1956 and vice president of that organization in 1957. Keeney is the author or co-author of five books on gymnastics and diving.

LEWIS, George
Coach
Born in Seattle, Wash; attended Roosevelt High School and Univ. Wash; in the watch repair business after college; finished college education at age 50 and began teaching at Seattle Community College.

Lewis was several times the Pacific Northwest all-around champion, and he has won the Pacific Coast Invitational championship. For 35 years a volunteer worker at the Seattle YMCA, he opened his own gymnastic school in 1974, Gymnastics, Inc. He coached only boys during the first 18 to 20 years of his career, and his teams were the best in the Pacific Northwest. In 1958 he began coaching girls. His Seattle YMCA team has won seven championships out of eight, and in 1968 his girls completely dominated the National Amateur Athletic Union championships.

PRCHAL, Mildred
Noteworthy Contributor
Editor of the *Sokol Gymnast,* Prchal has been a coach and instructor of gymnastics, classical ballet, modern dance, acrobatics and tap in the United States and Paris, of rhythmic dance and fencing in Prague, and physical education in Prague and the United States. She is an honorary member of several units of the American Sokol Organization and a member of their board of instructors. Prchal is choreographer and teacher of field exhibitions, mass calisthenics and pageants for 800 or more performers. She received the Czechoslovakia Sokol Merit Award in 1920 and the Chicago Merit Award in officiating at the third Pan-Am Games in Chicago in 1959.

ROETZHEIM, William H.
Gymnast, Coach and Noteworthy Contributor
Bill Roetzheim was the holder of 14 national championships during his career. He was first place on the side horse and second in the all-around at the Asiatic Games at Tokyo in 1950. Roetzheim took first in the all-around and horizontal bar at the 1950 Pan-American Games in Buenos Aires taking two gold medals and was a member of the 1952 Olympic team. As a high school coach he had 3 team and 19 individual Illinois state champions. He also coached the U.S. team in their efforts against Switzerland, England, Bulgaria and in the World Games. Bill Roetzheim is on the U.S. Gymnastics Federation executive committee, the Olympic committee, the U.S. selection committee, is a National Judges Association board member, technical director of the Mid-American Judges Association and holds a national and interna-

tional judges card. He has been a judge in the Pan-American Games and North American Championships.

SHANKEN, Courtney D.

Gymnast and Noteworthy Contributor

Served in the U.S. Air Corps from 1942 to 1945; received an Air Medal; presently a business executive.

Courtney Shanken began his gymnastics career as co-captain of Senn High School's first championship team in 1937. Since that time he placed fourth in the all-around championship in 1938 and took the National Collegiate Athletic Association (NCAA) all-around championship and the rope climb championship in 1941. Courtney won seven NCAA medals in 1941 and placed third in the all-around of 1942. Shanken has served as a member of the men's Olympic gymnastic committee since 1964, served as president of the Midwest Gymnastic Association 1964 – 1969, chaired the Maccabiah Gymnastic committee since 1965 and served as the U.S. coach for the North American championships of 1967.

1976

BECKNER, Jack

Gymnast and Coach

Born in Los Angeles, Calif; graduated from Univ. Southern Calif.

Jack Beckner was a National Collegiate Athletic Association (NCAA) all-around gymnastic champion in 1952. He took the NCAA parallel bars title in 1951 and 1952. Beckner was Pan-American Games all-around champion in 1955 and 1959 and was a member of the U.S. Olympic teams in 1952, 1956 and 1960. He served as head coach at the University of Southern California and was the 1968 U.S. Olympic team gymnastic coach.

BROWN, Dr. Margaret C.

Noteworthy Contributor

Graduated from McGill Univ. School of Physical Education; received B.S. and M.A. from Rutgers Univ. and Ph.D. from New York Univ.

Over the years Dr. Brown has held offices in many professional and civic organizations. She is a past president of both the New Jersey Association of Health, Physical Education and Recreation, and of the New Jersey Association of Colleges and Universities. As administrator, educator, writer and speaker, she has given many addresses and lecture demonstrations for professional and community groups. She is presently a member of the Mayor's council on senior citizens, a member of the board of trustees of the Senior Citizens Housing Association and Corporation of East Orange, and the East Orange Bicentennial executive committee. On the international scene, Dr. Brown served as an official with the U.S. women's Olympic gymnastic team at the Olympic Games in Berlin, London and Helsinki, and represented the Amateur Athletic Union (AAU) at the World gymnastic championships in Prague in 1938. She taught in public schools in New Jersey and is professor emeritus of Panzer College of Physical Education and Hygiene which merged with Montclair State College in 1958.

LENZ, Consetta Caruccio

Gymnast

Consetta Caruccio Lenz held National Amateur Athletic Union titles during the 1930s for the all-around, calisthenics, parallel bars and side horse. She was twice a member of the U.S. Olympic team, at Berlin in 1936 and at London in 1948, taking a bronze medal in London for her effort in the all-around team competition. Since that time Consetta has served on the U.S. Women's Olympic gymnastic committee 1952 – 1960 and judged at all levels of Olympic competition.

STOUT, Robert

Gymnast and Noteworthy Contributor

Received a B.S. and M.S. in education from Temple Univ.

Bob Stout was National Collegiate Athletic Association champion in floor exercise and horizontal bar. He won three Eastern Intercollegiate League gymnastic all-around crowns as well as titles in tumbling and horizontal and parallel bars. He was National Amateur Athletic Union all-around champion in 1952 and 1953 and was a member of the U.S. Olympic gymnastics team in 1952. A coach for 17 years, he is also regarded as one of the nation's outstanding judges.

WOLCOTT, Frank A.

Coach and Noteworthy Contributor

As a competitor for Springfield College, Frank Wolcott was captain of the Chiefs in 1952. He was pommel horse and flying rings champion in 1951 and 1952. Since 1956 he has been coach and associate professor of physical education at Springfield. His teams won New England titles in 1970, 1971 and 1973 – 1975 with 15 individual champions. Eight of his students won crowns in the Eastern league in 1967 and 1970 and 28 took All-American titles. Wolcott has conducted numerous clinics, tournaments and exhibitions for gymnastics as well as having served on the U.S. Olympic committee, the National Collegiate Athletic Association gymnastics rules committee, the national YMCA committee and the National Association of College Gymnastics Coaches. Wolcott was nominated Eastern Coach of the Year in 1965, 1967 and 1970 and was given the Service Award in 1970 and 1971.

1977

MARQUETTE, Clayton "Bud"

Coach

UNSER, Bernhard

Coach

Bernhard Unser took his first job coaching the New York-Bronx Turners. In 1952 he became playground director for the City of New York and was placed in charge of the gymnasium. During his 13-year stay there, his star pupils included: Edward Scrobe, a 1948 and 1952 Olympian; Johnny Crosby, a 1972 Olympian who took a gold medal in floor exercise at Moscow in 1973 international competition; and Joe Goldenberg, a national champion. Unser also tutored gymnastics in various private high schools for more than 25 years.

ZWICKEL, Walter

Noteworthy Contributor

Walter Zwickel has been involved in gymnastics throughout his lifetime. He was the first U.S. manufacturer to successfully make stretch nylon men's gymnastic garments and has been responsible for almost every major advance in the technology of gymnastics wear throughout the years. He has helped outfit every U.S. international gymnastic team since 1968 at his own expense. Zwickel was the co-founder of the Abington Clinic, is a member of the Temple Varsity Club and has served on the Maccabiah Games gymnastic committee for 12 years.

Induction Years Unrecorded

BIXLER, Dallas
Gymnast

BROWN, Marshall
Coach

D'AUTORIO, Vincent
Gymnast and Noteworthy Contributor

KERN, Gus
Noteworthy Contributor

KERN, Rene J.
Coach

KREMPEL, Paul
Gymnast

MAIS, John
Gymnast

MATTHEI, William
Noteworthy Contributor

PICKER, Adolph
Noteworthy Contributor

ROTTMAN, Curtis
Gymnast

ROZANAS, James
Coach

SMIDL, Henry
Coach

VOLZE, Erwin
Coach

WITZIG, Herman
Gymnast

Handball Hall of Fame

The Citizens Savings Handball Hall of Fame was originated in 1954. Nominees are solicited from the U.S. Handball Association by the Hall of Fame Nominating Committee. There are two categories for induction, Player and Noteworthy Contributor. Inductees will have their names engraved upon the Hall of Fame Trophy which is lodged in Citizens Savings Hall of Fame Athletic Museum, international sports shrine.

1954

BANUET, Alfred
Player
Considered by many as the most brilliant handballer of all, Al was National AAU Singles champion from 1929–1931 and National Doubles champ in 1929 and 1930.

PLATAK, Joseph
Player
Platak, who represented the Chicago Lake Shore Club, was a dominant figure in handball competition for over a decade. He was National AAU champion for seven consecutive years, 1935–1941, and again in 1943 and 1945. He was AAU National Doubles winner in 1937 and 1944.

1955

ATCHESON, Sam
Player
Between 1930 and 1945, Sam won 14 national handball titles. He won the YMCA Doubles 1930–1932, 1935 and 1936 and their Singles championships 1931–1933 and 1935–1937. In AAU tournaments, he took the Singles crown in 1933 and 1934 and Doubles in 1945.

GARBUTT, Frank
Noteworthy Contributor
Garbutt was instrumental in bringing the national championships to Los Angeles in 1919 and again in 1920, where they gained sounder footing. Since then, championship competition has been held at the Los Angeles Athletic Club in 1924, 1936 and 1955. The National Junior Handball championships have also been held at the Club in 1926, 1929, 1937 and 1939. The late Frank Garbutt was a past president of the Los Angeles Athletic Club.

LASWELL, Maynard
Player
A member of the Los Angeles Athletic Club, Maynard claimed the National AAU Doubles title in 1922 and 1932. He also won the AAU Singles championship 1924–1926.

1957

HERSHKOWITZ, Victor
Player
In National AAU competition, Victor has won the One-Wall Doubles in 1942, 1948 and 1956, was One-Wall champion in 1947, 1948, 1950, 1952 and 1953 and the Singles champ in 1949 and 1952. He was International Three-Wall champion every year from 1950 to 1955 and in 1953, won the National YMCA Singles title. In 1954 Victor won the National U.S. Handball Association Singles crown and their Doubles in 1961. He played out of the Brooklyn (N.Y.) YMCA.

KENDLER, Robert
Noteworthy Contributor
In 1943 and 1944 Bob won the AAU National Junior Doubles championship. He is a founder and past president of the U.S. Handball Association (USHA). He won the USHA Four-Wall Masters Doubles in 1952 and 1953 and again in 1962.

O'CONNELL, Charles J.
Noteworthy Contributor
O'Connell has dedicated over 50 years to the sport of handball. He has served as chairman of the Metropolitan Association AAU handball committee, vice chairman and later chairman of the national committee. Because he constructed the first court at Parkway Baths in Brighton Beach in 1909, he is often referred to as "The Father of One-Wall Handball." In 1931 he edited a handbook on the sport, explaining and interpreting rules.

QUAM, George
Player
George was a one-armed competitor, who combined courage and ability to overcome a major handicap. For over 25 years he was a top-ranked player in the Minneapolis district.

SCHAUFELBERGER, Albert
Noteworthy Contributor
The late Albert Schaufelberger won the National AAU Doubles championship in 1928 and was the first national commissioner of the U.S. Handball Association. The Albert Schaufelberger Youth Foundation promotes junior handball interest by arranging and sponsoring tournaments.

TRULIO, Angelo
Player
As a representative of the Brooklyn (N.Y.) YMCA, Angelo won the 1931 National AAU Junior Singles and Doubles championships. He won the Doubles again in 1932 and 1946. He has written many articles for *Ace Magazine* (now *Handball*), the official publication of the U.S. Handball Association.

1961

COYLE, Frank "Lefty"
Player
Frank won the AAU Doubles title in 1938, 1939, 1950 and 1952. He was AAU and YMCA Masters Doubles titlist in the 1958 "World Series of Handball."In 1961 he won both the YMCA Junior Singles and the U.S. Handball Association Masters Doubles. Perhaps the biggest moment of his career was his upset of the seemingly invincible Joe Platak for the 1944 AAU Singles title in Chicago.

LEWIS, Gus
Player
Gus has won many city, state and regional titles beginning in 1942 when he won the AAU Junior Four-Wall Singles championship and the Singles in 1947 and 1948. In 1961 he teamed with Frank Coyle for the U.S. Handball Association Masters Doubles, repeated in 1962 with Bob Kendler and added five more titles with Ken Schneider 1964 – 1967 and again in 1969.

SHUMATE, Les
Noteworthy Contributor
Les has promoted handball for over 40 years. He has some 50 titles in local, state and regional competition. He was a founder of the U.S. Handball Association and first Rocky Mountain District commissioner. He also doubled as the AAU handball director for that area. Les campaigned for modernization of handball facilities in Denver and his long, hard work paid off with the nation's number one handball plant—the new Denver YMCA—where the 1961 Nationals were held.

1963

SHANE, Joseph
Noteworthy Contributor
Joe won the 1955 and 1956 U.S. Handball Association Masters Doubles and the 1957 AAU Masters Doubles. He has served as commissioner for the U.S. Handball Association.

1964

GOLDSTEIN, Hyman
Noteworthy Contributor
Goldstein became national commissioner of the U.S. Handball Committee in 1955 and served until 1961. In 1964 he was appointed chairman of the committee for All-American handball championships, embracing the AAU, YMCA and the U.S. Handball Association. He has served as an official for over 30 years, including AAU and YMCA committees, both in St. Louis and regionally.

1965

BRADY, Robert
Player
Bob has been a top San Francisco Bay Area player for the past 15 years. He won the U.S. Handball Association Four-Wall National Singles in 1953, the National Three-Wall Doubles with John Sloan in 1958 and the Four-Wall National Masters with Bill Keays at Seattle in 1963. One of Brady's biggest victories was the 1957 National AAU Singles championship at his Olympic Club home court.

LEE, George E.
Noteworthy Contributor
A native of Minnesota, Lee has served over 20 years in the interest of handball. As athletic director of the Dallas (Tex.) Athletic Club, he has organized and conducted 17 of their annual invitational handball tournaments. He also organized their "Hinder Club" and served as its vice president. Lee has served as south area commissioner of the U.S. Handball Association and managed their successful Four-Wall National championship in 1957.

SCHNEIDER, Kenneth
Player
Ken started playing handball at New York City's Castle

Hill Beach Club. He was state champion at age 18. He won the National Singles at Chicago in 1950, was three times Doubles winners with Sam Haber, 1954–1956 and partnered with Gus Lewis, won the National Masters championship, 1964–1965. In 1965, Schneider won Chicago Governor's Cup invitational singles tournament, besting 21-time national title winner John Sloan in the finals.

1972

JACOBS, James
Player
Jim is a former all-prep standout in football, basketball and track from the Los Angeles area. He is rated as one of the top three four-wall handball players of all time. Despite injuries in his prime years, he won 15 national titles, including the U.S. Handball Association Four-Wall Singles 6 times, Four-Wall Doubles 6 times and Three-Wall Singles 3 times. He has conducted many clinics and exhibitions in recent years.

OBERT, Oscar
Player
Oscar excelled in all phases of the game of handball. His career spanned the fifties and sixties; he earned 19 national championships. He won the U.S. Handball Association Four-Wall Singles title twice, Three-Wall Singles once and Three-Wall National Doubles with his brother, Ruby, five times. He won the One-Wall Doubles five times, and in addition, has won national AAU and YMCA honors in One-Wall and Four-Wall. Obert still retains a shooting game in the Masters Division, in spite of chronic back troubles.

1973

DAVIDSON, Robert
Noteworthy Contributor
Davidson has worked closely with youth as national junior chairman of the U.S. Handball Association (USHA) and as avocation supervisor at Bronx Union (N.Y.) YMCA and in Flamingo Park, Miami Beach, Fla. He has also served as national rules and referees chairman of USHA and was twice named Coach of the Year. Davidson has authored many instructional articles for *Handball.*

1976

LEVE, Morton
Noteworthy Contributor
Mort has served the U.S. Handball Association since 1953, as executive secretary and as editor of their official publication, *Handball.* He is responsible for the writing and interpretation of the official rules of handball. He has also been active in the selection of tournament sites. In addition to handball, Mort served as vice-president of Boys Baseball, Inc, 1951–1973, and as executive secretary of the International Racquetball Association 1958–1970.

SLOAN, John
Player
John was U.S. Handball Association (USHA) Three-Wall Doubles champion in 1958 and 1962. In 1958 he also won the National Singles championship (The World Series, AAU, USHA and YMCA combined). He won the AAU National Doubles in 1956, 1957 and 1960; the World Series (AAU, USHA and YMCA combined) National Doubles in 1958; AAU-YMCA National Doubles in 1959 and the USHA National Doubles in 1961 and 1964.

National High School Football Coaches Hall of Fame

This Hall of Fame was instituted in 1975 to honor outstanding high school football coaches. As of 1977 there are six members, selected by a board. Each inductee has his name engraved on a trophy which is kept in Citizens Savings Hall of Fame Athletic Museum, Los Angeles international sports shrine. He also receives a Hall of Fame Award.

1975

BACEVICH, Bron Constantine "Bacey"
Coach
Graduated from North Central Col, Univ. Ill, and Purdue Univ.

Bacevich coached for 43 years, with a 315–97–17 record. He coached at Hudson, Mich, Peru (16 years), Ottawa, Peoria, and Kankakee, Ill, and at Roger Bacon High School in Cincinnati, Ohio (20 years). Bacevich led his teams to 15 championships. In 11 seasons his teams were undefeated, and won 38 consecutive games.

BAZEMORE, August Wright
Coach
Graduated from Mercer Univ. and George Peabody Col.

Bazemore had a 290–43–6 coaching record. He coached 2 years at Waycross and 29 at Valdosta, Ga. His teams won 15 championships and were undefeated 12 times. From 1951 through 1954 his teams won 40 consecutive games, 30 from 1956 to 1958, and 37 from 1960 to 1963.

BRIGGS, Paul Leonard
Coach
Graduated from Univ. Colo. and Univ. Southern Calif.

Briggs led his teams to a 180–60–9 record. He coached 2 years at Rocky Ford, Colo, 2 years at Natrona County High School in Casper, Wyo, and 22 years at Bakersfield, Calif, High School. He has directed 11 championship teams, and 4 of his squads were undefeated. From 1962 to 1965 his teams won 27 consecutive contests.

1976

BABB, Julius W. "Pinky"
Coach
Born December 6, 1916 in Laurens County, S.C; graduated from Honea Path, S.C, High School 1934 and Furman Univ. 1939; now living in Greenwood, S.C.

1940 Duncan, S.C, High School, coach
1943 Gainesville, Ga, High School, coach
1944–1975 Greenwood, S.C, High School, coach

Babb coached for 34 years, with a 285–63–24 record. He had 9 championship seasons and 4 undefeated years.

GASKILL, Lloyd Eugene
Coach
Born June 8, 1912, in Flagler, Colo; graduated from Hugo, Colo, High School in 1931 and Univ. Northern Colo. 1935.

1935–1939 Limon, Colo, High School, coach
1944–1948 Limon, Colo, High School, coach
1957–1976 Limon, Colo, High School, coach

Gaskill led his team to ten Colorado state championships and 18 league championships. The teams had eight undefeated years. From 1958 to 1962 they had 42 consecutive wins, and from 1965 to 1969 they had 44 consecutive wins.

INGRAM, Melvin David
Coach
Born July 4, 1903, in Acton, N.C; graduated from Weatherwax High School in Aberdeen, Wash, 1923 and Gonzaga Univ. 1929; now living in Grants Pass, Ore.

1929–1943 Wallace, Idaho, High School, coach
1944–1946 Roseburg, Ore, High School, coach
1947–1968 Grants Pass, Ore, High School, coach

Ingram had a 226–75–18 coaching record for over 40 years of coaching. He had ten champion teams, five at Oregon and five in Idaho. He also had 25 league champions, twelve in Idaho, twelve in Grants Pass, Ore, and one in Roseburg, Ore. In all, his teams had nine undefeated seasons.

Noteworthy Contributors Hall of Fame

Since 1948 Citizens Savings Hall of Fame Athletic Museum has paid special tribute to a number of people, presently totaling 18, who have contributed to the growth and development of athletics from a wide perspective and who have had a significant impact on either a single sport or on the entire field of athletics. The 18 men selected to date, all born in the ninteenth century, have primarily assisted a sport in the days of its implementation and/or have, through their self-sacrifice and vision, promoted and developed athletic competitions.

Induction Years Unrecorded

BRUNDAGE, Avery
Contributor
Born September 28, 1887, in Detroit, Mich; received B.S. in civil engineering at Univ. Ill; member of 1912 U.S. Olympic team; died May 8, 1975, at age 87.

Brundage was the first American to be elected president of the International Olympics Committee. He was elected over Lord Burghley of Britain, a former 400-meter champion. Brundage was also the international athletics administrator for the United States. Although he was a first-class athlete and represented the United States in the 1912 Olympics decathlon, his primary importance is as an indefatigable champion of the Olympic amateur code. He was president of the U.S. Olympic Association from 1929 to 1953 and president of the International Olympic Committee from 1952 to 1972. In 1946 Brundage advised the U.S. Volleyball Association regarding the necessary steps required for recognition of volleyball as an Olympic event. He was instrumental in developing the film, *Play Volleyball* which was produced by the Association to facilitate the entrance of the sport into the Olympics.
Also in: National Track and Field Hall of Fame of the United States and U.S. Track and Field Federation Hall of Fame.

CAMP, Walter
Contributor
See entry in College Football Hall of Fame, Citizens Savings Hall of Fame Athletic Museum.
Also in: National Football Hall of Fame.

CROMWELL, Dean "The Dean"
Contributor
Born September 20, 1879, in Turner, Ore; graduated from Occidental Col, Los Angeles; outstanding college athletic career in both football and track; died August 3, 1962, at age 83.

In 1909 Cromwell was appointed head track and football coach for the University of Southern California (USC). As USC grid coach for five seasons he had a 21–8–6 record and as track coach, Cromwell had no peer. In his 39 years as USC track coach, his team won 12 National Collegiate Athletic Association (NCAA) titles, 9 in a row. His Trojans also won nine IC4A team titles. From 1930 to 1948 his teams lost only three dual meets. His performers won 33 NCAA individual events, 39 IC4A crowns and 38 Amateur Athletic Union (AAU) titles. The list of athletes The Dean trained is long and impressive and includes Charlie Paddock, Bud Houser, Mel Patton, Frank Wycoff, Earle Meadows and Bill Sefton. Referred to as "The Maker of Champions," this Trojan coach set 14 individual world records, plus world records in 440-yd, 880-yd. and mile relays. He coached ten Olympic gold medal winners and 36 U.S. Olympic team members from 1912 to 1948. As coach of the 1948 Olympic Games, the U.S. team won ten gold medals under his direction.
Also in: National Track and Field Hall of Fame and U.S. Track and Field Federation Hall of Fame; and Track and Field Hall of Fame, Citizens Savings Hall of Fame Athletic Museum.

DAVIS, Dwight Filley
Contributor
See entry in International Tennis Hall of Fame, 1956.
Also in: Tennis Hall of Fame, Citizens Savings Hall of Fame Athletic Museum.

DE COUBERTIN, Baron Pierre
Contributor
The initiative which brought about the modern Olympic revival came from the French aristocrat de Coubertin, whose educational theories about the value of harmoniz-

ing physical with mental development were similar to the ancient Greek concept. Motivated by a conviction that a better understanding among men of all nations would be a result of a revival of the Olympic Games on a world basis, de Coubertin, after several years of preliminary study and discussion, made his first formal Olympic Games proposal at a meeting of the Athletic Sports Union in Paris in 1892. The baron's proposal did not gain an enthusiastic response. In fact, a less determined individual might have been discouraged sufficiently to discard his idea. However, at an athletic congress in 1894, attended by representatives of many countries, de Coubertin enlisted support for his program. Before the congress had disbanded, his dream became a reality. The assembled delegates voted to celebrate the first modern Olympic Games in 1896 and chose, as a fitting site, the city of Athens, the capital of Greece. Even at this point, however, de Coubertin still had imposing obstacles to surmount. The financial burdens were huge and the citizens of Greece were without means to proceed with preparations for the Games. This problem was overcome when de Coubertin secured financial assistance from George Averoff, a merchant of Alexandria, Egypt, and built the new stadium outside the city limits of Athens.

FERRIS, Daniel J.
Contributor
Born 1889 in Pawling, N.Y; currently resides in New Gardens, N.Y.

Before devoting himself to administrative work and sportswriting, Ferris was an outstanding sprinter. Ferris has attended every Olympiad since 1912. Beginning that same year, his participation in athletic organizations blossomed. He was Amateur Athletic Union (AAU) secretary to James E. Sullivan between 1912 and 1942. He initiated the AAU Physical Fitness Program, Junior Olympics, and the Olympic development program. Ferris is a member of the International Amateur Athletic Federation's executive council. He also editored the monthly magazine *Amateur Athlete* for the 24 years after he introduced it to the public.
Also in: National Track and Field Hall of Fame; and Track and Field Hall of Fame, Citizens Savings Hall of Fame Athletic Museum.

GARLAND, William May
Contributor
Born 1866 in Westport, Maine; moved to Los Angeles in 1890; attended high school in Waterville, Maine; married Blanche; two sons, William Marshall and John Jewett; worked in real estate until his death Sept. 26, 1948.

Garland had a lifetime interest in sports. He gained international prominence when he brought the Olympic Games to Los Angeles in 1932.

GRIFFITH, John L.
Contributor
Born 1880 in Caroll, Ill; graduated from Beloit Col. 1902; died December 7, 1944.

Griffith was athletic director at three colleges before W.W. I, when, as a Major, he developed the Army's physical-fitness program. In 1919 he took charge of the physical education teacher-training program at the University of Illinois and was instrumental in organizing the first annual National Collegiate Athletic Association (NCAA) track meet in 1921. He served as commissioner of the Western Conference Big Ten from 1922 until his death.
Also in: Track and Field Hall of Fame, Citizens Savings Hall of Fame Athletic Museum.

KIRBY, Gustavus T.
Contributor
The idea of photographing the finish of a race and at the same time recording the elapsed time was fathered by Kirby, president emeritus of the United States Olympic Committee. He sparked the idea about 1926 when he was chairman of the advisory committee of the Intercollegiate Association of America. A similar idea occurred to C. H. Fetter, then an electronic engineer of Western Electric, a subsidiary of American Telephone and Telegraph Co. Joining forces in 1931, they perfected what was known as the Kirby two-eyed camera. This camera was the official determiner for judging the events of the 1932 Olympics at Los Angeles and was official for timing the decathlon.

MacARTHUR, Douglas
Contributor
Born Jan. 26, 1880, in Little Rock, Ark; graduated from the U.S. Military Academy; served as the Academy's superintendent in 1919 and improved its curriculum and standings; served as Colonel when W.W. I began but was promoted to General in 1918; won fame as a front-line General in several battles in France; wounded three times, decorated 13 times and cited for bravery in action seven times; both he and father awarded the Medal of Honor; youngest four-star General in U.S. history; Commander of all U.S. forces in the South Pacific in W.W. II; died April 5, 1964, at age 84.

In 1962 a long-maintained dispute between the National Collegiate Athletic Association (NCAA) and the Amateur Athletic Union (AAU) regarding the upcoming Olympics was threatening to prohibit the participation of the U.S. Olympic team. To combat this unfortunate situation, President John Kennedy asked MacArthur to serve as mediator between the opposing camps. Under MacArthur's guidance, a truce was agreed upon and U.S. participation in the 1964 Games was assured.

MACK, Connie (Cornelius McGillicuddy)
Contributor
See entry in National Baseball Hall of Fame, 1937.

NAISMITH, Dr. James
Contributor
See entry in National Basketball Hall of Fame, 1959.
Also in: Amateur Basketball Hall of Fame and College Basketball Hall of Fame, Citizen's Savings Hall of Fame Athletic Museum; Canada's Sports Hall of Fame and National Association of Intercollegiate Athletics Hall of Fame.

RICE, Grantland
Contributor
Born Nov. 1, 1880, in Murfreesboro, Tenn; died July 13, 1954.

"The drama of sport is a big part of the drama of life and the scope of this drama is endless. Sport has its triumphs and its tragedies, its great joys and heavy sor-

rows with more spectacular effect than most dramas may ever know." This feeling expressed by Rice was the heart of his fame as a sportswriter. It was he who named the Notre Dame backfield of 1924–1925 the "Four Horsemen" and he who named Jack Dempsey the "Mannassa Mauler." He often celebrated sports in poetry. His most often quoted lines are, "When the Last Great Scorer comes/ To mark against your name/ He'll write not 'won' or 'lost'/ But how you played the game." At Vanderbilt University, Rice captained the baseball team. After graduation in 1901, he could not decide whether to become an athlete or a poet; so he became a sportswriter, first in Nashville, then in New York, with the *Evening Mail* and the *Tribune.* After 1930 he was writing a syndicated column and narrating many short movie features. During his career he saw virtually every major sports event in the United States. In one year alone, he estimated that he traveled 16,000 miles and wrote a million words. Rice is also credited with developing the initial concept for a Professional Golfers' Association of America Hall of Fame which was instigated in 1940 (see PGA Hall of Fame sketch).
Also in: National Sportscasters and Sportswriters Hall of Fame.

ROCKNE, Knute K.
Contributor
See entry in College Football Hall of Fame, Citizens Savings Hall of Fame Athletic Museum.
Also in: National Football Hall of Fame, 1951.

ROOSEVELT, Theodore
Contributor
Born Oct. 27, 1858 in New York City; served as the 26th president of the United States from 1901 to 1909; died Jan. 6, 1919, of a heart attack.

In 1905 it was President of the United States Theodore Roosevelt who saved the sport of football by insisting from the White House that the game be debrutalized. Roosevelt ordered representatives from 13 schools to the White House to face up to the mounting tragedy of college football which was killing batches of healthy young men every fall. Under his prompting the university people not only solved the problem, but, under the leadership of Chancellor MacCracken of New York University, went on to form a permanent intercollegiate organization for the governance of all their games, the National Collegiate Athletic Association (NCAA). It quickly became the governing body for intercollegiate sports, laying down rules, supervising eligibility, stating who can offer scholarships to whom and supervising the collection and distribution of receipts. A major protective outcome of the historic meeting was in the outlawing of the flying wedge and the legalizing of the forward pass.
Also in: Hunting Hall of Fame.

SPALDING, Albert G.
Contributor
See entry in National Baseball Hall of Fame, 1939.

STAGG, Amos Alonzo
Contributor
See entry in Naismith Memorial Basketball Hall of Fame, 1959.
Also in: College Football Hall of Fame and Track and Field Hall of Fame, Citizens Savings Hall of Fame Athletic Museum; and National Football Hall of Fame.

SULLIVAN, James E.
Contributor
Born November 18, 1860, in New York City; died Sept. 16, 1914.

Each year since 1930 the Amateur Athletic Union (AAU) has presented the James E. Sullivan Memorial Trophy to the outstanding amateur athlete of the year. Sullivan was a kind of benevolent despot of amateur sports for more than a quarter-century. He was one of the founders of the AAU in 1888 and served as its secretary from 1886 to 1896 and its president from 1906 to 1909. As secretary-treasurer from 1909 to 1914, he virtually ruled many amateur sports. Under his guidance, the AAU gained control of a number of sports. For many years, Sullivan was also editor of the *Spalding Sports Library.*
Also in: Track and Field Hall of Fame, Citizens Savings Hall of Fame Athletic Museum.

Racquetball Hall of Fame

The Hall of Fame was instituted in 1974 to honor the contributors and athletes in racquetball. *Members:* 4 as of 1977. Inductees are selected by the Citizens Savings Board on the basis of recommendations. Upon induction, each new member receives the Hall of Fame Award and his or her name is engraved on the Trophy kept in the Citizens Savings Hall of Fame Athletic Museum.

Induction Years Unrecorded

BRUMFIELD, Charles
Player

LEDERMAN, Larry
Noteworthy Contributer

MUEHLEISEN, Dr. Bud
Player

SOBEK, Joe
Noteworthy Contributor

Rowing Hall of Fame

The Citizens Savings Hall of Fame Athletic Museum's Rowing Hall of Fame was established in 1956. Since that time there have been 106 inductions (a total of 282 members, including two-man teams and crews). Clifford Goes and Asa Bushnell, both of whom have served rowing intercollegiately as well as in the Olympics, are co-chairmen of the Rowing Hall of Fame Nominating Committee. The award recognizes the outstanding achievements of rowing coaches, contributors and oarsmen in their various capacities as crews, single sculls, double sculls, strokes and coxswains. Each member inducted has his or her name engraved upon the Citizens

Savings Hall of Fame Athletic Museum Trophy located at the Hall in Los Angeles, California. For additional information about the Rowing Hall of Fame, call William Harahan III, Executive Vice President of the National Association of Amateur Oarsmen (the governing body of the Rowing Hall of Fame) at (215) 647-2028, or write 31552 Waltham Rd, Birmingham, MI 48009.

1956

ANDRESEN, Raymond
Oarsman
Ray Andresen rowed for California in 1934 and 1935, taking the National Intercollegiate Championship in both of those years.

BOLLES, Thomas D.
Coach
Tom Bolles coached the Havana Yacht Club in 1927, the University of Washington freshmen from 1928 to 1936 and the Harvard teams from 1937 to 1951. His Harvard crews twice won the Grand at Henley. Bolles was a crewman at Washington 1924–1926.

BURK, Joseph W.
Oarsman
Joe Burk of the Pennsylvania Athletic Club Rowing Association was National Single Sculls Champion 1937–1940.

CALLOW, Russel S.
Coach
Russell Callow coached at Washington 1923–1927, Pennsylvania 1928-1950 and at the U.S. Naval Academy after 1951. His Washington crews won intercollegiate titles in 1923, 1924 and 1926. His Navy crews won championships 1952–1954 and took 29 straight engagements in international competition. The 1952 Navy crew under his direction won the Olympic Games title at Helsinki.

CONIBEAR, Hiram B.
Coach
Former Chicago White Sox baseball club trainer; baseball college trainer.

Conibear began coaching crews with no practical experience as an oarsman behind him. Though he faced difficulties at first, he attained great successes while coaching for Washington 1906–1917.

COSTELLO, Paul V. and KELLY, John B.
Oarsmen
Costello and Kelly won the 1920 Olympic Games doubles sculls championship and a gold medal for the Vesper Boat Club in Philadelphia, Pa. They were again Olympic doubles sculls champion winning a gold medal in 1924 for the Pennsylvania Athletic Club in Philadelphia.

COURTNEY, Charles E. "Pop"
Coach
Pop Courtney began as a crewman at Cornell winning the National Single Sculls Championship in 1875. He coached at Cornell 1885–1920 with his crews coming in as intercollegiate champions 14 times 1896–1915.

CURWEN, Darcy
Oarsman
Darcy Curwen rowed for Harvard 1941–1943.

EBRIGHT, Carroll, F. "Ky"
Coach
Ky Ebright began as a University of Washington crew coxswain using the Conibear stroke in 1917. He moved on to coach at the University of California in 1924 helping his Golden Bear crews to six intercollegiate championships. His California crews participated in and won gold medals at the Olympic Games at Amsterdam 1928, Los Angeles 1932, and London 1948.

EDDY, D. T.
Oarsman
Eddy crewed for Navy 1924–1926, winning the National Intercollegiate Championship in 1925.

FOOTE, Edward
Oarsman
Ed Foote crewed for Cornell University 1904–1906, winning the National Intercollegiate Championship 1905 and 1906.

FRYE, Wayne T.
Oarsman
Wayne Frye crewed for Navy 1952–1954, winning the National Intercollegiate Championship during each of those three years and returning from Helsinki in 1952 with a gold medal as Olympic Games champion.

GOES, Clifford T.
Contributor
Known as "Mr. Rowing U.S.A," Clifford Goes has contributed much to rowing in both intercollegiate and Olympic ranks for more than 40 years. He is a former Syracuse University coxswain.

GREER, Frank B.
Oarsman
Frank Greer of the Springfield, Mass. Boat Club won the National Singles Sculls Championship in 1903–1905 and 1908. Greer was the 1904 singles sculls Olympic Games champion as well, winning the gold medal.

KELLY, John B.
Oarsman
John Kelly of the Vesper Boat Club in Philadelphia, Pa, was the National Single Sculls Champion in 1914, 1919 and 1920. He went on to win the 1920 Olympic Games championship and the gold medal.

KELLY, John B, Jr.
Oarsman
John Kelly, Jr, of the Vesper Boat Club in Philadelphia, Pa. was, like his father, an excellent oarsman. He won the National Single Sculls Championship in 1946, 1948, 1950 and 1952–1955.

KING, Clyde
Oarsman
Clyde King stroked for Navy in 1920–1922, taking the Olympic Games championship and a gold medal in 1920 and the National Intercollegiate Championship in 1921 and 1922.

KINGSBURY, H. T.
Oarsman
Kingsbury rowed for Yale University 1924–1926. He was an Olympic Champion in 1924, winning a gold medal.

LEADER, Edwin O.
Coach
Edwin Leader crewed and from 1919 to 1922 coached at Washington University, his alma mater. While at Yale 1923–1942, Leader coached the 1924 crew that won the Olympic Games gold medal at Paris.

LUEDER, Charles
Oarsman
Charles Lueder rowed for Cornell University 1902 and 1903, taking the National Intercollegiate Championship for both years.

McILLVAINE, Charles and COSTELLO, Paul V.
Oarsmen
McIllvaine and Costello were 1928 Olympic Games double sculls champions for the Pennsylvania Athletic Club, bringing home a gold medal.

MULCAHY, John F. and VARLEY, William M.
Oarsmen
Mulcahy and Varley of the Atlanta Boat Club in New York were the 1904 double sculls Olympic Games champions, winning the gold medal.

MYERS, Kenneth and GILMORE, W. E.
Oarsmen
Myers and Gilmore, rowing for the Bachelors Barge Club in Philadelphia, won the 1932 Olympic Games double sculls championship, and the gold medal.

OSMAN, Arthur J.
Oarsman
Art Osman crewed for Syracuse University 1914–1916, winning the National Intercollegiate Championship his final year.

RAUCH, Rudolph
Oarsman
Rudy Rauch crewed for Princeton University 1911–1913.

ROBBINS, Howard W.
Oarsman
Howard Robbins rowed for Syracuse 1912–1914, winning the National Intercollegiate Championship in 1913.

SANFORD, R. H.
Oarsman
Sanford was a crewman at Washington 1923–1926, winning the National Intercollegiate Championship in 1924 and again in 1926.

SHAKESPEARE, Frank B.
Oarsman
Frank Shakespeare crewed for the Navy teams of 1952–1954, taking the National Intercollegiate Championship for all three of those years as well as the 1952 Olympic Games championship and gold medal.

SPUHN, Fred
Oarsman
Fred Spuhn rowed for Washington during his collegiate career 1922–1924. He was the winner of the National Intercollegiate Championship 1923 and 1924.

STEVENS, Edward G.
Oarsman
Ed Stevens crewed for Navy 1952–1954, winning the National Intercollegiate Championship for each of those three years as well as the Olympic championship and gold medal in 1952.

STRONG, Alexander
Oarsman
Alex Strong crewed for Harvard University 1910–1912.

STRONG, Frank
Oarsman
Frank Strong crewed for Harvard University 1947–1949.

TEN EYCK, James A.
Coach
This former Syracuse University oarsman coached at his alma mater 1903–1938. His crews won intercollegiate titles in 1904, 1908, 1913, 1916 and 1920.

ULBRICKSON, Alvin P.
Coach
Al Ulbrickson a former oarsman at Washington, began coaching at that University in 1928. His crews won intercollegiate crowns in 1936, 1937, 1940, 1941, 1948 and 1950 and were the Olympic Games gold medal winners in 1936 at Berlin.

UNITED STATES NAVAL ACADEMY 1952 8-OARED CREW
Crew
Coached by Russell S. Callow, the U.S. Naval Academy's crew of 1952 consisted of Frank B. Shakespeare in the bow, William B. Fields in number two position, James R. Dunbar as number three, Richard F. Murphy as number four, Robert M. Detweiler as number five, Henry A. Proctor in number six position, Wayne T. Frye as number seven, Edward G. Stevens, Jr. in the stroke position and Charles D. Manring as coxswain. This outstanding crew won a gold medal at the 1952 Olympic Games.

UNITED STATES NAVAL ACADEMY 1953 8-OARED CREW
Crew
Coached by Russell S. Callow, the U.S. Naval Academy crew of 1953 consisted of Frank B. Shakespeare in the bow, William B. Fields in number two position, James R. Dunbar as number three, Richard F. Murphy as number four, Robert M. Detweiler as number five, Henry A. Proctor as number six, Wayne T. Frye as number seven, Edward G. Stevens, Jr. in the stroke position and Robert Jones as coxswain.

WALLIS, Benjamin
Contributor
Ben Wallis coached at California State and the University of California at Los Angeles as an unpaid volunteer 1914–1924 and 1933–1947 respectively. Ben is a former Yale crewman.

1958

BUSHNELL, Asa
Contributor
See entry in Athletic Directors Hall of Fame, Citizens Savings Hall of Fame Athletic Museum.

COLLYER, John
Oarsman
John Collyer was an oarsman and captain at Cornell University 1915–1917 and was considered one of the best that the institution ever produced. In later years he was the donor of the John Collyer Boat House at Cornell.

CORNELL UNIVERSITY 1957 8-OARED CREW
Crew
Coached by R. Harrison Sanford, the Cornell University Crew of 1957 consisted of John Van Horn, Bob Staley, Dave Davis, Todd Simpson, William Schumacher, Clayton Chapman, George Ford, Phil Gravink and Carl Schwartz as coxswain. After having won three consecutive intercollegiate titles this Big Red crew went on to win the 1957 Henley Regatta crown.

HIGGINSON, Francis L. "Peter"
Oarsman
Peter Higginson was a stroke and captain of Harvard crews 1898–1900. Since that time he has been a patron of rowing at Harvard.

TEN EYCK, Edward Hanlan "Ned"
Oarsman
Born in 1880, Ned Ten Eyck was National Single and Double Sculls Champion before the turn of the century for the Wachusett Boat Club of Worcester, Mass. He was Henley Regatta Champion in 1897 at the age of 17.

YALE UNIVERSITY 1956 8-OARED CREW
Crew
Coached by James A. Rathschmidt, the Yale University crew of 1956 consisted of Thomas Charlton, Jr, David Wight, John Cook, Donald Beer, Charles Grimes, Caldwell Esselstyn, Richard Wailes, Robert Morey and William R. Becklean as coxswain. That team won the 1956 Olympic Games championship and the gold medal at Melbourne.

1960

BLESSING, Donald F.
Coxswain
Don Blessing was one of the University of California's foremost coxswains. He led the Golden Bears to ten consecutive victories in 1928, topping off the year with a gold medal triumph at the Olympic Games at Amsterdam.

FIFER, James T.
Oarsman
A native of Tacoma, Wash; attended Stanford Univ.

James Fifer was a three letter man in rowing at Stanford University. He teamed with Duvall Hecht to win the pairs Olympic title and the gold medal at the Helsinki Games of 1956. They did this without a coxswain.

HECHT, Duvall Y.
Oarsman
Native of Los Angeles; attended Stanford Univ.

Hecht was a two letter man in rowing. It was in a two-oared, no coxswain boat that Hecht gained his greatest fame. With James T. Fifer, Hecht won the 1956 Olympic Games crown and the gold medal at Melbourne. Hecht represented the United States in rowing at the 1952 Olympic Games at Helsinki.

PACKARD, Dr. Edward N.
Oarsman
Born in Syracuse, N.Y, Ed Packard stroked for Syracuse University 1904–1906. His 1906 crew was the winner at Poughkeepsie. His coach James A. Ten Eyck considered him one of the greatest strokes of all times. The Packard Trophy is a prize contested for by the Dartmouth and Syracuse crews each year.

WARD, Ellis, Gilbert, Hank and Josh
Oarsmen
The Ward Brothers were the great oarsmen of the 1850s to the 1870s, establishing records individually and together. As a four-oar combination they were practically unbeatable in international competition.

1961

GARDINER, Dr. John
Oarsman
John Gardiner was the outstanding stroke of the University of Pennsylvania crews 1899–1901. He was later a great patron of rowing.

RATHSCHMIDT, James A.
Coach
Jim Rathschmidt was the coach at Princeton 1936–1950 and has been at Yale since 1951. As one of the nation's top rowing coaches he took his Yale crew to the Olympic championship at the 1956 Melbourne Games, where they won the gold medal

SONJU, Norman Rudolph
Coach
Norman Sonju was a University of Washington oarsman 1925–1927. He has been a coach at Cornell University and since 1947 he has coached at the University of Wisconsin. His crews have twice taken the International Rowing Association title with third and fourth places on three occasions.

WITTER, Dean
Contributor
Served in the U.S. Army in W.W. I; cited for gallantry in French action; served in W.W. II as colonel of ordance, assistant chief of the San Francisco ordance district; became chief of the San Francisco ordance district 1950–1954.

Dean Witter served on the University of California's Golden Bear rowing squad. He was the stroke and was named captain of the crew in 1908. In 1910 he took over as coach of the varsity and freshmen crews. For years after that Witter served rowing as a starter or official as well as a patron.

1962

BURNS, Kenneth F.
Oarsman
A resident of Shrewsbury, Mass; became a police officer in 1928 in Shrewsbury; chief of police in 1946; president of the Mass. Chief of Police Assn. 1961.

Ken Burns became interested in rowing as a boy at Worcester High School in the early 1920s. Since that time he has been an outstanding sweep oar, single and double and single sculler. He won the New England championship seven times and still holds the Lake Quinsigamond record for double scull with turn made in 1925. Burns has been a coach, official and organizer, arranging and promoting many regattas in New England.

COLUMBIA UNIVERSITY 1878 4-OARED CREW
Crew
The Columbia University Crew of 1878 consisted of J. T. Goodwin, H. C. Ridabock, Cyrus Edson and Edwin E. Sage. This four-oared crew without a coxswain held the top American position for two years, to be defeated in 1878 by the English crews from Oxford, Cambridge and Dublin Universities at the Henley Regatta. After graduation each crew member distinguished himself with very successful careers in the medical, teaching and industrial fields.

LAKE WASHINGTON ROWING CLUB 1960 4-OARED CREW
Crew
This four-oar crew with a coxswain consisted of John A. Sayre in the stroke position, Richard D. Wailes in the number three position, Theodore A. Nash as number two and Arthur D. Ayrault in the bow position. These gentlemen won the 1960 Olympic Games championship and gold medal for four-oar crews.

1963

HARVARD UNIVERSITY 1914 8-OARED CREW
Crew
The Harvard 8-oar crew of 1914 was coached by James Wray and later by Robert F. Herrick. The crew consisted of Leverett Saltonstall in the bow, James Talcott, Jr, in the number two position, Henry H. Meyer in number three, Henry S. Middendorf as number four, J. William Middendorf as number five, David P. Morgan as number six, Louis Curtis as number seven, Charles C. Lund in the stroke position and Henry L. F. Kreger as coxswain. This Harvard team was undefeated in 1914. That year they were entered in the Henley Regatta in England and captured the Grand Challenge Cup, becoming the first American crew to hold that honor.

HERRICK, Robert F.
Contributor
A successful Boston lawyer; died in 1942.

Bob Herrick was the stroke and captain of the Harvard University crew of 1889 and 1890. As an amateur coach he took the Harvard crew to the 1914 Henley Regatta, capturing the Grand Challenge Cup. He and his crew had the same success in 1939. It was Herrick who gave the land for the Harvard Club House.

VAIL, Harry Emerson "Dad"
Coach
Born October 18, 1859, in Gagetown, N. Can; died October 8, 1928.

Dad Vail was a champion sculler in his early days. He took over as the University of Wisconsin rowing coach in 1910 and held that post through 1928. Prior to that he had coached at Georgetown Prep, Ariel Boat Club and Harvard. The "Dad" Vail Rowing Association and Regatta were named for him.

1964

DAVENPORT, Horace E.
Oarsman
A native of Buffalo, N.Y; grew up in Brooklyn and New York City; enrolled at Columbia Univ; later a business executive.

Horace Davenport began rowing at Columbia under the tutorship of Dick Glendons. He helped his crew win the International Rowing Association title at Poughkeepsie in 1927 and 1929 and was captain of the latter crew.

UNITED STATES NAVAL ACADEMY 1920 8-OARED CREW
Crew
Coached by Richard Glendon, the U.S. Naval Academy crew of 1920 consisted of Virgil Victor Jacomini in the bow, Edwin D. Graves in the number two position, William C. Jordan as number three, Edward P. Moore as number four, Alden R. Sanborn as number five, Donald H. Johnston as number six, Vincent J. Gallagher as number seven, Clyde W. King in the stroke position and Sherman R. Clark as coxswain. In the year 1920 the Navy crew was all-victorious, including the Olympic Games championship and gold medal taken at Antwerp.

1965

BRADLEY, Dr. U. T.
Contributor
B.A, M.A, and Ph.D. in history from Princeton and Cornell.

Dr. Bradley has been associated with Rollins College since 1933. He originated rowing in the institutions in Florida where it has flourished. Bradley contributed greatly to national and Olympic rowing programs for over 20 years. His 1963 Rollins Dad Vail 8 made it to the Royal Henley Regetta in England.

STANFORD CREW ASSOCIATION 1964 2-OARED CREW
Crew
This pair-oared crew with coxswain consisted of Conn Findlay in the stroke position and Edward Payson Ferry in the bow position. Coxswain was Kent Mitchell. This crew defeated some of the great crews in Olympic history to take the gold medal at the 1964 Games in Tokyo, Japan.

VESPER BOAT CLUB 1964 8-OARED CREW
Crew
The 1964 Vester Boat Club Crew was coached by Allen P. Rosenberg and the crew consisted of First Lt. Joseph Amlong, USAF, in the bow, Hugh Foley, Stanley Cwiklinski, First Lt. Thomas Amlong, USAF, Emory Clark, Boyce Budd, William Knecht, with Lt. William Stowe, USNR, in the stroke position and Robert Zimonyi as coxswain. This crew defeated the world famous Ratzeburg German crew in the Olympic finals to take the 1964 gold medal for the United States.

1966

POCOCK, George
Contributor
Born 1891 at Kingston-on-Thames, England; moved to Vancouver, B.C, Can, in 1911 with brother Dick; son Stanley a former Washington oarsman.

In his youth George Pocock excelled as a sculler, winning many English races including the Kingston Coat and Badge and the 100-pound handicap. He began building shells in Vancouver and Victoria for the University of Washington, Stanford and the University of California. During W.W. I he built pontoons for the first war seaplanes. His shop expanded to a plant on the shore of Lake Union in Seattle, Wash, as his shells and oars were in great demand.

SPERO, Donald M.
Oarsman
Born 1939 in Chicago, Ill; degree in engineering physics from Cornell Univ. 1962; graduate work at Columbia Univ. in plasma physics; excellent skier, tennis player and skydiver.

Don Spero won a silver medal in the European Double Sculls Championships in 1963. He was the U.S. National Single Scull Champion in 1964, a bronze medal winner in the European Championships and a member of the U.S. Olympic team at the Tokyo Games, taking sixth place in single sculls. Spero won the Henley Regatta, Diamond Sculls and Duisburg International Regatta in 1965 and took the Vesper Cup Award in 1966.

UNIVERSITY OF CALIFORNIA 1928 8-OARED CREW
Crew
The 1928 University of California crew was coached by Ky Ebright, and the crew consisted of Frank B. Shakespeare, William B. Fields, James D. Dunbar, Richard F. Murchpy, Robert M. Detweiler, Henry A. Proctor, Wayne T. Frye, Edward G. Stevens, Jr, and Charles D. Manring as coxswain. This crew was the 1928 Olympic Games champion and brought home the gold medal.

1969

McCURDY, Horace W.
Contributor

SMITH, Albridge C, III
Contributor

TAYLOR, James D.
Contributor

UNIVERSITY OF CALIFORNIA 1932 8-OARED CREW
Crew
This crew consisted of Winslow W. Hall, Harold W. Tower, Charles R. Chandler, Burton A. Jastram, David C. Dunlap, Duncan S. Gregg, James Blair, Edwin L. Salisbury and Norris J. Graham as coxswain. Coached by Carroll Ky Ebright, the crew was outstanding during 1932, as evidenced by their winning of a gold medal at the Olympic Games that year.

1970

GLENDON, Richard A.
Coach
Known as Old Dick, Richard A. Glendon coached for the U.S. Naval Academy 1903 – 1922, at Columbia 1926 – 1928 and returned to the U.S. Naval Academy for a tour 1929 – 1931.

GLENDON, Richard J.
Coach
Known as Young Dick, Richard J. Glendon coached for the U.S. Naval Academy 1923 – 1925, moving to Columbia for a stay 1926 – 1933.

HARBACH, Edwin
Contributor
Edwin Harbach of Los Angeles, Calif. was a contributor of note to rowing on the Pacific Coast 1925 – 1969.

ROSENBERG, Allen P.
Coach
Allen Rosenberg is remembered for his excellent coaching of the Vesper Boat Club of 1964. That eight-oar crew won the Olympic Games gold medal that year in Tokyo.

VESPER BOAT CLUB 1900 8-OARED CREW
Crew
The Vester Boat Club of 1900 consisted of Roscoe C. Lockwood in the bow, Edward Marsh as number two, Edwin Hedley as number three, William Carr as number four, John F. Geiger as number five, James B. Juvenal as number six, Harry B. DeBaecke as number seven, John O. Exley in the stroke position and Louis C. Abell as coxswain. This crew was the 1900 Olympic champion and gold medal winner at the Games in Paris, France.

1971

GARDINER, James A. and COSTELLO, B. Patrick, Jr.
Oarsmen
Gardiner and Costello are double scullers who were honored in the 1971 Hall of Fame inductees.

HOUGH, Lawrence A. and JOHNSON, P. Anthony
Oarsmen
Hough and Johnson were a 2-oared crew without a coxswain.

SCHOCH, Delos C.
Oarsman
Delos Schoch was not a member of the 1936 Olympic Games champion 8-oar crew, but was a member of the University of Washington crew of 1936.

SPAETH, Dr. John Duncan
Coach

UNIVERSITY OF WASHINGTON 1936 8-OARED CREW
Crew
Coached by Alvin Ulbrickson, the University of Washington crew of 1936 consisted of Donald B. Hume, Joseph H. Rantz, George E. Hunt, James B. McMillin, John G. White, Gordon B. Adam, Charles W. Day, Herbert R. Morris, and Robert G. Moch as coxswain. This crew won the Olympic Games championship and the gold medal in 1936 in Berlin.

1972

GARHART, Theodore
Oarsman
Theodore Garhart is honored as an outstanding stroke from the University of Washington.

GRANT, Donald
Oarsman
Outstanding as coxswain for the University of Washington, Grant also served as assistant coach for the rowing team at Yale.

YALE UNIVERSITY 1924 8-OARED CREW
Crew
Coached by Edwin O. Leader, the Yale University crew of 1924 consisted of Leonard G. Carpenter, Frederick Sheffield, Alfred M. Wilson, James S. Rockefeller (captain), J. Lester Miller, Howard T. Kingsbury, Jr, Benjamin M. Spock, Alfred D. Lindley and Laurence R. Stoddard as coxswain. This crew won the Olympic Games championship and the gold medal of 1924.

1973

PENNSYLVANIA BARGE CLUB 1932 2-OARED CREW
Crew
The 1932 Pennsylvania Barge Club coxed pair consisted of Charles M. Kieffer in the bow, Joseph A. Schauers as stroke, and Edward F. Jennings as coxswain.

UNIVERSITY OF CALIFORNIA 1948 8-OARED CREW
Crew
Coached by Carroll M. Ebright, the University of California crew of 1948 consisted of John Stack, Justus Smith, David Brown, Lloyd Butler, George Ahlgren, James Hardy, David Turner, Ian Turner and Ralph Purchase as coxswain. This team took the Olympic championship and gold medal in 1948.

WALSH, Commander Charles S. "Buck"
Coach
Commander Walsh was the head rowing coach for the U.S. Naval Academy 1923 – 1944.

1974

ARONSON, Richard
Contributor
Richard Aronson was Cornell University coxswain 1923 – 1926. Since that time he has been a prominent official, referee and timer for the sport for more than 50 years. He was one of the organizers of the Syracuse Regatta Association and the president in 1964 and 1965.

COLUMBIA UNIVERSITY 1929 8-OARED CREW
Crew
Coached by Richard Glendon, the Columbia University crew of 1929 consisted of Henry G. Walter, Jr. in the bow, John F. Murphy as number two, Samuel R. Walker as number three, William B. Sanford as number four, Arthur Douglas as number five, William H. Blesse as number six, Horace E. Davenport as number seven, Alastair MacBaine in the stroke position and Robert B. Berman as coxswain. This crew was undefeated during the year of 1929 and were I.R.A. Poughkeepsie champions.

PARKER, Harry
Coach
Harry Parker was the Harvard University crew coach and coach of the 1972 U.S. Olympic crew.

PENNSYLVANIA BARGE CLUB 1928 4-OARED CREW
Crew
The Pennsylvania Barge Club crew without coxswain of 1928 consisted of Charles G. Karle in the stroke position, William G. Miller as number two, George A. Healis as number three and Ernest H. Bayer in the bow. This crew took a silver medal at the 1928 Olympic Games. One of the crew, Bill Miller, went on to take the silver medal in the singles at the 1932 Olympics.

1975

FRANKLIN, Jack T.
Contributor
Jack Franklin is remembered for his long-time interest in the sport of rowing and for his many contributions.

HARVARD UNIVERSITY 1947 8-OARED CREW
Crew
Coached by Thomas D. Bolles, the Harvard University crew of 1947 consisted of Michael J. Scully in the bow position, Clarence S. Clark in the number two position, Richard S. Emmett, Jr. as number three, Robert G. Stone, Jr. as captain and number four position, Justin E. Gale as number five, Frank R. Strong as number six, Paul W. Knaplund as number seven, Francis Cunningham, Jr. as the stroke and Albert C. Petite as coxswain. This crew topped off an undefeated season with a world record time of 5:49 at the Lake Washington Invitational Regatta.

UNIVERSITY OF WASHINGTON 1948 4-OARED CREW
Crew
The University of Washington crew with coxswain won the Olympic Games gold medal at London in 1948. The crew consisted of Gordon S. Giovanelli in the bow, Robert I. Will as number two, Robert D. Martin as number three, Warren D. Westlund in the stroke position and Allen J. Morgan as coxswain.

1976

GODDARD, Samuel P, Jr.
Contributor

PENNSYLVANIA ATHLETIC CLUB 1930 8-OARED CREW
Crew
Coached by Frank J. Muller, the Pennsylvania Athletic Club crew of 1930 consisted of Charles L. McIllvaine in the bow, Thomas A. Curran in the number two position, John D. Bratten as number three, John W. McNichol as number four, Myrlin B. Janes as number five, Joseph M. Dougherty as number six, Daniel H. Barrow, Jr. as number seven, George Chester Turner in the stroke position and Thomas P. Mack, Jr. as coxswain. This crew, which rowed at Liege, Belgium in 1930, was the World Champion Eight of that year.

1977

CROMWELL, Seymour
Oarsman
Graduated from Princeton Univ. 1957; naval architect.

Seymour Cromwell won the bronze medal in the 1961 European Championships and went on to take third place again in the World Championship Regatta in 1962. In 1963 he won the silver medal in doubles at the European Championships and in 1964 took the Diamond Sculls at Henley with a world record. Cromwell again won the silver medal in doubles at the 1964 Olympic Games at Tokyo. The same team of Cromwell and Storm won the silver medal in the World Championships of 1966.

UNIVERSITY OF WISCONSIN 1946 8-OARED CREW
Crew
Coached by Allen W. Walz, this University of Wisconsin crew of 1946 consisted of Chester T. Knight in the bow, Paul J. Klein in the number two position, Ralph C. Falconer, Jr. as number three, Gordon T. Grimstad as number four, Fred R. Suchow as number five, Richard E. Mueller as number six, Richard E. Tipple as number seven, Carl Holtz in the stroke position, Carlyle W. Fay as coxswain and Wayne Sanderhoff as manager. This crew went undefeated in Eastern competition in 1946.

Induction Years Unrecorded

COSTELLO, Bernard P, Jr.
Oarsman

DANZIG, Allison
Contributor
See entry in International Tennis Hall of Fame, 1968.

DONLON, Peter D.
Oarsman

LEH, John
Oarsman

POTOMAC BOAT CLUB 1968 2-OARED CREW
Crew
Anthony P. Johnson and Lawrence A. Hough took a second place at the 1968 Olympic Games for their effort as a pair-oared crew.

SEABRING, Cornelius
Oarsman and Coxswain

WAILES, Richard
Oarsman

WEED, R. W. "Si"
Oarsman

Soaring - Gliding Hall of Fame

The Citizens Savings Hall of Fame Athletic Museum's Soaring and Gliding Hall of Fame was established in 1954. As of 1977 there were 53 members in the Hall, each nominated for induction by the board of directors of the Soaring Society of America. The Hall recognizes the contributions made by soarers and gliders to their respective sports. Each member's name is engraved upon the Soaring Hall of Fame Trophy located within the Citizens Savings Hall of Fame Athletic Museum in Los Angeles, Calif.

1954

BOWLUS, William Hawley
Soarer

duPONT, Richard C.
Soarer

EATON, Warren E.
Soarer

KLEMPERER, Dr. Wolfgang B.
Soarer

MacCREADY, Dr. Paul, Jr.
Soarer

ROBINSON, John
Soarer
Robinson won three national championships in Harland C. Ross's RS-L "Zanonia" sailplanes.

1955

BARNABY, Capt. Ralph Stanton
Soarer
Barnaby, a founder of the Soaring Society of America (SSA), built and flew his first glider in 1909. He gained international fame with his 1928 flight launched from a Navy rigid airship and subsequent glide to Los Angeles. In 1932 he became the SSA director, then served four terms as president until his 1950 election to the vice-presidency. That same year he captained the U.S. soaring team which won the first World championship in Sweden. He received the *Féderation Aeronautique Internationale* Soaring Certificate in 1929 and the Paul Tissandier Diploma in 1955.

BARRINGER, Maj. Lewin B.
Glider
Died January 24, 1943, in a flight accident over the Caribbean.

Barringer engaged in a diverse number of flying activities, particularly as a military pilot, private pilot, glider pilot, instructor, aviation writer and editor. He was chosen by Gen. H. H. Arnold to organize the Army Air Force Glider Program but died on a special mission from the United States to North Africa. During his lifetime, he served as the director and general manager of the Soaring Society of America.
Also in: Frankfort-Elberta National Soaring Hall of Fame.

SCHWEIZER, Ernest
Soarer
Ernest, with his brother Paul, worked to improve the technical knowledge and flying skills of soarers. His interest centered around producing safer and less costly sailplanes with higher performance than the planes of his day.

SCHWEIZER, Paul A.
Soarer
Working with his brother Ernest, Paul sought to improve equipment and soaring conditions so that a greater number of gliding enthusiasts could participate in the sport.

TUNTLAND, Paul
Soarer
Paul Tuntland is said to have been a true example of the spirit of soaring. He participated in every aspect of the sport from teaching to flying to spectating. Not only did he compete in regional and national contests, but he was also an ambassador and organizer, working to further the spread of the soaring movement.

WRIGHT, Orville
Glider
Born in 1871 in Dayton, Ohio; son of Rev. Milton Wright of United Brethren Church; established *West Side News;* died in 1948.

Although Orville and Wilbur Wright are known as the "Fathers of Flying," they are also the "Fathers of Soaring" since they were the first to successfully emulate the soaring of birds. Their experiments with gliders were the important precedent to their development of the first successful power-sustained flight. Orville piloted the first flight in 1903 because it was his turn. But between 1900 and 1903 the Wright Brothers spent three years developing and testing their theories on aeronautics, inspired mainly by the work of a German experimenter, Otto Lilienthal, who died in a glider crash in 1896. In order to maintain glider balance, the Wrights worked out a theory to vary the inclination of different sections of the wings. In 1902 Orville piloted a glider with a 32 ft. wingspan over Kill Devil Hill at Kitty Hawk. In 1911 Orville set an incredible soaring flight record of 9 min. 45 sec. which remained unbroken until 1920, when it was bettered by the Germans.
Also in: First Flight Shrine Hall of Fame.

WRIGHT, Wilbur
Glider
Born 1867 in Newcastle, Ind; son of Rev. Milton Wright; died in 1912.

Along with his brother Orville, Wilbur recognized that birds' ability to use rising air currents to sustain them on motionless wings could be applied by man to achieve simulated bird flight. The Wright's gliders of 1900 and 1901 were primarily flown as kites, but later in 1901 Wilbur achieved the first free flight aboard a glider. This first flight was achieved by using Orville as the anchorman, still sailing the glider as a kite while Wilbur rode as the glider passenger. On October 10, 1902, Wilbur again rode on the glider, this time assisted by a two-man launch for a takeoff. On December 17, 1903, nearly three months after the coyrighting of the first western movies (*Kit Carson* and *The Pioneers*), Wilbur won the toss to test the first powered craft they had designed which maintained a 3.5 sec. flight. However, the brothers both agreed that this flight was really only a glide even though an engine was aboard. By the end of 1902 the Wright Brothers had made over 1000 glides in their three trips to Kitty Hawk. The later glides were the best-sustained due to their development of a horizontal rudder to gain fore-and-aft stability.
Also in: First Flight Shrine Hall of Fame.

1956

BUXTON, Jay
Soarer

JOHNSON, Richard H.
Soarer
In 1950 Johnson set a world soaring distance record of 535 mi. in a Harland C. Ross RJ-5 sailplane.

O'MEARA, John K.
Soarer

RASPET, August
Soarer

1957

FRANKLIN, Roswell E.
Soarer
Franklin was a pioneer in early design. The desire to improve the technical aspects of gliders led him to develop the Franklin Utility Glider.
Also in: Frankfort-Elberta National Soaring Hall of Fame.

SCHULTZ, Arthur B.
Soarer

SMITH, Stanley W.
Soarer

1958

BRIEGLEB, William G. "Gus"
Soarer
Briegleb devoted over 30 years to soaring and gliding including the development and organizational aspects of the sport. He helped organize the Southern California Soaring Association, of which he later became president, and served as the director of the Soaring Society of America for many years. During W.W. II he headed a firm that produced gliders for the U.S. Army Air Force division and later designed and manufactured gliders for commercial sale. His first successfully designed glider was the Briegleb Primary which he built and flew in the late 1920s. In 1958 he operated El Mirage Airfield in San Bernardino, Calif. He received the Gold C, *Fédèration Aeronautique Internationale* badge.

SYMONS, Robert F.
Soarer

ROSS, Harland C.
Soarer
Born in 1907; received *Fédèration Aeronautique Internationale* C Soaring award in 1937, Silver C in 1938, Gold C in 1947 and Diamond C Gold-Leg in 1947.

Ross stood out as a sailplane designer and a world record setter. He designed and built the Ra-L "Zanonia" sailplane which won three national soaring championships when flown by John Robinson. He also designed the RJ-5 sailplane in 1950 which, piloted by Richard H. Johnson, won four national soaring championships and set a world soaring record for a distance of 535 mi. As a world record setter, Ross was a master. In 1950 near Bishop, Calif, he set world multi-place soaring records for an absolute altitude of 36,000 ft. and a multi-place altitude gain record of 24,200 ft. He set a U.S. multi-place record in that same year for a goal and return of 234.66 mi. On three consecutive days in August, 1958, Ross set three world and U. S. multi-place soaring speed records, 54.377 m.p.h, 50.548 m.p.h. and 51.169 m.p.h. for the 60 mi, 120 mi. and 180 mi. triangular courses respectively. These records were set in Ross's R-6 sailplane, a high-performance all-metal plane he designed and built. He has been director of the Soaring Society of America, and governor of the organization for the State of Kansas, president of the Wichita, Kan, Soaring Club, honorary member of the Witchita Soaring Association and the recipient of many honors identified with soaring. He has also been aeronautical engineer for the Beech Aircraft Corporation in Wichita, Kans.

1960

BIKLE, Paul F.
Soarer
Received Silver C - U.S. 93, Gold C - U.S. 34, Diamond C - U.S. 3, International 7 badge and Lewin B. Barringer Memorial Trophy five times from 1952 to 1955.

Between 1952 and 1960 Bikle amassed a mountain of titles and records. In 1952 to 1955 he made the longest soaring flights in the United States from launchings other than airplane tow. He was the Southern California soaring champion in 1954 and 1955 and also won the Pacific Coast midwinter soaring championship in those years and again in 1958. He set world soaring records for speed between 1957 and 1959, his best being 43.943 m.p.h. over a 198 mi. triangular course. From 1958 to 1960 he was a pilot on the U.S. team in the bi-annual World soaring championships but also found time to win the 1959 West Coast soaring championship and the spring and fall contests at Elsinore, Calif. Bikle served as director of the Soaring Society of America (SSA), as chairman of the SSA rules subcommittee of the contest board and as director of the National Aeronautic and Space Administration's Advance Flight Base, Edwards Air Force Base, Calif.

CHARLES, J. Shelly
Soarer
Born in 1900; died in August, 1959; received the C award, Internatinal 4, Silver C - U.S. 35 and Gold C - U.S. 14.

Charles, who tried his hand at construction when he hand-built a Bowlus Baby Albatross sailplane, was the 1940 American Open soaring champion. He really made his mark in the soaring world when he set a United States record for altitude gained and altitude attained in the midst of a thunderstorm. This July 18, 1943, record of 19,434 ft. was astounding considering the adverse weather conditions.

1961

CARSEY, Jon D.
Soarer
Carsey developed publication exchange between soaring clubs on an international level when he served as president of the Soaring Society of America (SSA). His other contributions to SSA included standardization of safety, performance, organizational and financial aspects of United States soaring clubs.

LINCOLN, Joseph C.
Soarer
Born in 1922.

On July 2, 1960, Lilncoln flew a Schweizer 1-23D sailplane 455.5 mi. from Love Field in Prescott, Ariz, to Variedero, N.M, in less than nine hours. This flight set a record for the longest flight ever made in the United States and has been beaten by only one other flight since then. An excellent soarer, Lincoln also competed in both regional and national championships.

1962

IVANS, William S. Jr.
Soarer
Received Silver C - U.S. 102, Gold C - U.S. 23, Diamond C - U.S. and International 9.

Ivans was a member of the winning 1956 U.S. World championship team at St. Yan, France. From 1950 to 1961 he held the world's record for absolute altitude and altitude gained. He became involved with the Soaring Society of America (SSA) first as chairman and then as president. In 1962 as SSA vice-president, he was a delegate to the International Gliding Commission of the *Fėdėration Aeronautique Internationale.*

SCHREDER, Richard E.
Soarer
Received Diamond C - U.S. 22 and Warren E. Eaton Memorial Trophy in 1962.

After piloting in the Navy during W.W. II, Schreder participated actively in soaring. He won the U.S. national championship crowns in 1958 and 1960 and became a member of the winning 1960 U.S. World championship team at Cologne, Germany. Schreder not only flew sailplanes, he also designed and built high-performance planes which helped him to set world speed marks for the 60 mi, 120 mi. and 180 mi. triangular courses.
Also in: Frankfort-Elberta National Soaring Hall of Fame.

1964

MOFFAT, George B, Jr.
Soarer
Moffat established world records for the 60 mi. and 180 mi. triangular courses with a speed of 79.77 m.p.h. and 67.15 m.p.h. respectively in August 1962. In his first year of competition, 1962, he placed twelfth in the U.S. national championships and placed fifth the following year.

PARKER, Raymon H.
Soarer

PRUE, Irving O.
Soarer

SWEET, Lt. Col. Floyd J.
Soarer
Sweet was active as a pilot, instructor and club organizer besides helping develop military gliders. He spent the 20 years between 1932 and 1952 flying in regional and national competitions. After serving as an instructor at the University of Michigan Glider Club for five years, he became involved in the Soaring Society of America (SSA), serving as secretary in 1940, general manager and editor of *Soaring* magazine in 1940 and 1941, president for three terms during 1954 to 1957 and finally as the chairman of the awards committee in 1964. His contributions to military soaring and gliding were the creation of a military training syllabus and the supervision of 1800 military glider pilots in 1941, and nine years of development and testing of military gliders between 1943 and 1952.

1965

PARKER, Alvin H.
Soarer
Received *Fėdėration Aeronautique Internationale* Gold Soaring Badge.

Parker soared his American-designed-and-built Sisu 1A sailplane 647.17 mi. on July 31, 1963. In covering that distance from Odessa, Tex, more than halfway to Canada to Kimball, Nebr, in a flight time of 10½ hrs, Parker became the first person in the world to soar more than 622 mi. That 1000 kilometer (622 mi.) mark had long been the goal of the best soarers. His accomplishment set a new world soaring record—one, however, which he bettered on August 27 of the same year when he flew 487.24 mi. from Odessa, Tex, to Great Bend, Kans.

SCOTT, Wallace A.
Soarer
Received *Fėdėration Aeronautique Internationale* Gold Soaring Badge.

In 1964 Scott set a world soaring goal record of 520.55 mi. in a Schleicher Ka-6CR sailplane. In covering that distance from Odessa, Tex, to Goodland, Kans, Scott became one of only seven pilots ever to soar over 500 mi. up to that time. He placed second in the U.S. national soaring championships and had the third-best performance ever made by an American pilot in the World soaring chapionships standard class in 1964.

1967

DAWYDOFF, Alex
Soarer

RYAN, John D.
Soarer
Ryan was a member of the winning 1960 U.S. World championship team. In 1962 he claimed the U.S. soaring championship and returned to the World championships the following year, again as a member of the winning team. From 1965 to 1966 he served as the president of the Soaring Society of America.

STEPHENS, Harvey
Soarer
Along with Harland Ross, Eaton helped advance sailplane design with the development of the RS-1, a winner of the Eaton Design competition. Stephens also participated in the sport and was a competitor in many regional and national contests.

WOODWARD, Elizabeth W.
Soarer

1968

DICK, Helen R.
Soarer

SMITH, A. J.
Soarer

1969

CLAYBOURN, H. Marshall
Soarer

LAISTER, Jack
Soarer

1970

GREENE, Ben W.
Soarer

REEVES, E. J.
Soarer

1973

COMPTON, Francis "Fritz"
Soarer
Compton standardized and updated the rules for national competitions and set up standard towing signals. He set up procedures to homologate records, which had not been set from 1934 to 1947. Compton has been active in all facets of soaring since 1946. He has served the Soaring Society of America (SSA) as director from 1947 through 1951, 1957 through 1961, and 1965 through 1970. Fritz was SSA vice-president in 1949, has been chairman of the SSA contest committee, the ad hoc committee on class competition and chairman of the airport utilization committee.

EDGAR, Laurence E.
Soarer
Edgar was a veteran flight instructor while yet a student of glider handling. He wrote a study of air currents in mountainous areas and the effects of the currents on aircraft. In 1952 he set two world soaring records for absolute altitude and for altitude gained.

RYAN, Bertha M.
Soarer
Received Soaring Society of America Exceptional Service Award 1967.

Bertha built a Schweizer 1-26 from a kit but she is not best known for her construction or design. Her contributions fall mainly into the organizational area where she has dedicated much time and energy to the Soaring Society of America (SSA). In 1950 she joined the Massachusetts Institute of Technology Glider Club which led her to become the SSA state governor for Massachusetts. Between 1960 and 1962 she served as SSA treasurer, then solely dedicated herself to being chairman of the SSA record homologation committee to which she was elected in 1957.

SCHWEIZER, Virginia M.
Soarer
Received C - U.S. 538 and Silver C - U.S. 86.

Virginia Schweizer was a pioneer in women's soaring. She was the first to attempt cross-country flight, the first U.S. national womens champion in 1947 and the first to obtain a glider flight instructor rating. In 1947 she set a women's national single-place goal record and world altitude standard. In 1973 she began assisting with the development of the National Soaring Museum.

1974

HASTINGS, Albert E.
Soarer
Received Edwards S. Evans Trophy 1930 and 1931.

Hastings, now deceased, was the first U.S. national soaring champion. He also scored another first by establishing the first commercial gliding school in which he developed the auto-tow method of instruction for single-place gliders. His instructional experience in gliding led him to establish safety standards far above preceding standards.

LEONARD, Parker
Soarer
Leonard, now deceased, became involved in soaring in 1930 when he took his first flight in a homemade, self-designed glider in Cape Cod. By 1932 he was an active member of the Soaring Society of America (SSA). He began editing SSA *Soaring* magazine in 1941 then served as SSA president from 1942 to 1946. His activities in the sport ranged from instructor to competition official to designer and builder of sailplanes.

Induction Years Unrecorded

HALL, Stanley A.
Soarer

HOLBROOK, William
Soarer

Swimming - Diving Hall of Fame

The Swimming and Diving Hall of Fame was instituted within the Citizens Savings Hall of Fame Athletic Museum in 1950 to honor those individuals of outstanding achievement in the aquatic sports. Since that time 133 members have been inducted. Each honoree receives an Award upon installation and has his or her name engraved upon the Hall's Trophy located within the Citizens Savings Hall of Fame Athletic Museum in Los Angeles, Calif.

Induction Years Unrecorded

ADAMSON, Arthur
Coach

ARMBRUSTER, David
Coach
See entry in International Swimming Hall of Fame, 1966.

BACHRACH, William
Coach
See entry in International Swimming Hall of Fame, 1966.

BALL, Catherine
Swimmer
See entry in International Swimming Hall of Fame, 1976.

BAUER, Carl Otto
Contributor
See entry in International Swimming Hall of Fame, 1967.

BAUER, Sybil
Swimmer
See entry in International Swimming Hall of Fame, 1967.

BLEIBTRY, Ethelda
Swimmer
See entry in International Swimming Hall of Fame, 1967.

BRANDSTEN, Ernst
Coach
See entry in International Swimming Hall of Fame, 1966.

BREEN, George
Swimmer
See entry in International Swimming Hall of Fame, 1975.

BROWNING, David "Skippy"
Diver
See entry in International Swimming Hall of Fame, 1975.

BURTON, Michael
Swimmer
See entry in International Swimming Hall of Fame, 1977.

BUSH, Lesley
Diver
Lesley won gold medals at both the 1964 Olympic Games and the 1967 Pan-American Games for her performance in the highboard diving event with 91.28 and 108.20 points respectively.

CADY, Fred
Coach
See entry in International Swimming Hall of Fame, 1969.

CLARK, Earl
Diver
See entry in International Swimming Hall of Fame, 1972.

CLEVELAND, Richard
Swimmer
Cleveland was the National AAU 110-yd. freestyle champion in 1950 and 1952, the 100-m. freestyle champion in 1951, 1953 and 1954. He won the NCAA 50-yd. freestyle in 1952 and 1953, and the 100-yd. freestyle in 1954. He was the 100-m. freestyle champion at the Pan-Am Games in 1951.

CLOTWORTHY, Robert
Diver
Bobby Clotworthy won the springboard diving gold medal at the 1956 Olympic Games with 159.56 points.

CODY, Jack
Coach
See entry in International Swimming Hall of Fame, 1970.

COLEMAN, Georgia
Diver
See entry in International Swimming Hall of Fame, 1966.

CONE, Carin
Swimmer
Carin Cone won a gold medal at the 1959 Pan-American Games for her effort in the 100-meter backstroke, timed at 1 min. 12.2 sec. She was the U.S. champion for that event 1955–1959, improving her times from 1 min. 15.6 sec. to 1 min. 13.3 sec. In September, 1959, Carin set a world record for the 100-meter backstroke, timed at 1 min. 11.4 sec. At that same meet in Chicago she was a member of the world record setting 400-meter medley relay team timed at 4 min. 44.6 sec. The other team members were Ann Bancroft, Becky Collins and Chris Von Saltza.

CRABBE, Clarence Linden "Buster"
Swimmer
See entry in International Swimming Hall of Fame, 1965.

CURTIS, Ann
Swimmer
See entry in International Swimming Hall of Fame, 1966.

DANIELS, Charles M.
Swimmer
See entry in International Swimming Hall of Fame, 1965.

DAUGHTERS, Ray
Coach
See entry in International Swimming Hall of Fame, 1971.

DEGENER, Richard
Diver
See entry in International Swimming Hall of Fame, 1971.

DESJARDINS, Peter
Diver
See entry in International Swimming Hall of Fame, 1966.

DeVARONA, Donna
Swimmer
See entry in International Swimming Hall of Fame, 1969.

DRAVES, Victoria Manolo
Diver
See entry in International Swimming Hall of Fame, 1969.

EDERLE, Gertrude
Swimmer
See entry in International Swimming Hall of Fame, 1965.

FARRELL, Jeffrey
Swimmer
See entry in International Swimming Hall of Fame, 1968.

FERGUSON, Cathy Jean
Swimmer
Born July 17, 1948; from Burbank, Calif.

Cathy Ferguson was a product of the age group competitive system. She began swimming at age 11. The slim high school girl of 5 ft. 8 in. won two gold medals at the 1964 Tokyo Olympic Games. Her first was in the 100-meter backstroke in a record-breaking speed of 67.7 seconds. That win put her on the U.S. medley relay squad and brought another gold medal.

FICK, Peter
Swimmer
Pete Fick set world records for the 100-meter freestyle in 1934, 1935 and 1936 with times of 56.8 sec, 56.6 sec. and 56.4 sec. respectively. He was also a member of the world record 400-meter freestyle relay timed at 3 min. 59.2 sec. held in August of 1938 at Berlin.

FLANAGAN, Ralph
Swimmer

FORD, Alan
Swimmer
See entry in International Swimming Hall of Fame, 1966.

GAIDZIK, George
Diver
George was the holder of the 1913 Amateur Swimming Association diving title for his performance in the high-board dive.

GESTRING, Marjorie
Diver
See entry in International Swimming Hall of Fame, 1976.

GOODWIN, L. B. "Bud"
Swimmer
See entry in International Swimming Hall of Fame, 1971.

GOSSICK, Sue
Diver
Sue won a gold medal at the 1967 Pan-American Games at Winnipeg for her effort in the springboard diving event with 150.41 points. She took another gold medal in the 1968 Olympic Games at Mexico City with 150.77 points in the same event.

GREEN, Carolyn
Swimmer
Carolyn was the holder of the 1954 U.S. 400-meter freestyle championship with a time of 5 min. 14.7 sec. She possessed the 800-meter freestyle U.S. championship in 1950, 1951 and from 1953 to 1955, taking the times down from 11 min. 28.3 sec. to 10 min. 45.3 sec. Carolyn also held the 1500-meter freestyle U.S. championship title in 1951 and from 1953 to 1956, with 21 min. 08.5 sec. as her lowest time in 1954.

GRELLER, Samuel J.
Coach
Greller was an outstanding long distance swimmer and a water polo player; he was a member of the 1928 U.S. Olympic water polo team. He coached at the Illinois Athletic Club for many years, producing a number of championship teams.

HANDY, H. Jamison
Swimmer
See entry in International Swimming Hall of Fame, 1965.

HARLAN, Bruce
Diver
See entry in International Swimming Hall of Fame, 1973.

HEBNER, Harry
Swimmer
See entry in International Swimming Hall of Fame, 1968.

HELSER, Brenda
Swimmer
Brenda won the U.S. 100-meter freestyle championship in 1946 with a time of 1 min. 07.2 sec.

HENNING, Dr. Harold
Contributor
Dr. Henning served as secretary of the *Féderation Internationale de Natation Amateur* (FINA) from 1968 until 1972.

IRWIN, Juno Strover
Diver
Attended Hoover High School in Glendale, Calif; married Russell Irwin, airlines executive; four children.

Irwin was a bronze medalist at Helsinki in the 1952 Olympic Games and a silver medalist at the 1956 Olympic games in Melbourne for her outstanding effort in the platform diving events. She again took silver medals in platform diving at the 1955 and 1959 Pan-American Games. Prior to her medal-winning participation, Juno represented the United States at the 1948 Olympic Games at London and later in the 1960 Olympic Games at Rome. June was very active in U.S. Olympic fund-raising campaigns.

JARRETT, Eleanor Holm
Swimmer
See entry in International Swimming Hall of Fame, 1966.

JASTREMSKI, Chester
Swimmer
See entry in International Swimming Hall of Fame, 1977.

KAHANAMOKU, Duke
Swimmer
See entry in International Swimming Hall of Fame, 1965.

KENNEDY, Edward T.
Coach
See entry in International Swimming Hall of Fame, 1966.

KIEFER, Adolph
Swimmer
See entry in International Swimming Hall of Fame, 1965.

KIGHT, Lenore
Swimmer
Lenore Kight won many AAU championships 1933–1935 while with the Carnegie Library Club including the 100-m, 440- and 880-yd, the 100-, 220- and 440-yd. indoor, and the one-mi.

KING, Micki
Diver
Born July 26, 1944, in Pontiac, Mich; attended Univ. Mich; served in the U.S. Air Force.

Micki King captured eight National Amateur Athletic Union (AAU) diving championships during her career including the 1965 indoor platform diving event, the outdoor 1-meter (39.4 in.) diving event in 1967 and 1972, the 3-meter (10 ft.) event in 1965, 1967, 1969 and 1970 and the outdoor platform championship in 1969. She competed in the 1968 Olympic Games in Mexico City, winding up fourth in the springboard event after breaking an arm during the competition. Micki went on to capture the Olympic springboard diving title at the Munich Games in 1972 for a gold medal.

KIPHUTH, Robert John Herman
Coach
See entry in International Swimming Hall of Fame, 1965.

KOJAC, George Harold
Swimmer
See entry in International Swimming Hall of Fame, 1968.

KOLB, Claudia
Swimmer
See entry in International Swimming Hall of Fame, 1975.

KONNO, Ford
Swimmer
See entry in International Swimming Hall of Fame, 1972.

LANGER, Ludy
Swimmer
Langer won the AAU 440-yd, 880-yd, and one-mi. freestyle in 1915, 1916 and 1921. He also was the 400-m. freestyle second-place winner at the 1920 Olympic Games.

LANQUE, Frederick
Coach

LEE, Sammy
Diver
See entry in International Swimming Hall of Fame, 1968.

MADISON, Helene
Swimmer
See entry in International Swimming Hall of Fame, 1966.

MANLEY, E. J.
Coach

MANN, Matt II
Coach
See entry in International Swimming Hall of Fame, 1965.

MANN, Shelley
Swimmer
See entry in International Swimming Hall of Fame, 1966.

McADOOR, James
Coach

McCORMICK, Patricia Keller
Diver
See entry in International Swimming Hall of Fame, 1965.

McDERMOTT, Michael "Turk"
Swimmer
See entry in International Swimming Hall of Fame, 1969.

McEVOY, Elsie Hanneman
Diver
Elsie Hanneman (McEvoy) won the World Diamond Diving Medal 1910–1912 and the Ladies Open in 1914 at Indianapolis. In her career she participated in over 100 meets without defeat.

McGILLIVRAY, Perry
Swimmer
Perry was a member of the 1920 U.S. Olympic team. He won a gold medal in the 800-meter freestyle relay timed at 10 min. 04.4 sec. Other members of the team were Pua Keoloha, Norman Ross and Duke Kahanomoku.

McKINNEY, Frank
Swimmer
See entry in International Swimming Hall of Fame, 1975.

McLANE, James
Swimmer
See entry in International Swimming Hall of Fame, 1970.

MEANY, Helen
Diver
See entry in International Swimming Hall of Fame, 1971.

MEDICA, Jack
Swimmer
See entry in International Swimming Hall of Fame, 1966.

MERKIE, Nancy
Swimmer
Nancy was the U.S. champion of the 200-meter breaststroke in 1946 with a time of 3 min. 15.0 sec. She also held the individual medley championship in 1946 and 1947 for 400-meter timed at 4 min. 29.9 sec. and 4 min. 32.9 sec. respectively.

MEYER, Deborah
Swimmer
See entry in International Swimming Hall of Fame, 1977.

MORGAN, Helen Crlenkovich
Diver
Helen Morgan swam for the Fairmont Swim Club of San Francisco, Calif. She was the holder of the National Amateur Athletic Union (AAU) 3-meter (10 ft.) diving championships in 1939, 1941 and 1945, the AAU platform diving championships in 1941 and 1945 and the AAU indoor 3-meter (10 ft.) diving title from 1939 to 1943.

MYERS, Paula Jean Pope
Diver
Paula Jean Pope won double gold medals at the 1959 Olympic Games for her efforts in the springboard and highboard diving events with 139.23 and 97.13 points respectively. At the 1960 Olympic Games, Paula Jean took two silver medals behind East Germany's Ingrid Kramer in the highboard and springboard diving events.

NAKAMA, Keo
Swimmer
See entry in International Swimming Hall of Fame, 1975.

NORELIUS, Martha
Swimmer
See entry in International Swimming Hall of Fame, 1967.

OLSEN, Zoe Ann
Diver
Born in 1931 in Council Bluffs, Iowa; mother Norma J, synchronized swimming coach.

Her parents' coaching in diving resulted in Zoe Ann's winning of numerous national titles as well as a berth on the 1948 U.S. Olympic team. She won a silver medal for her efforts in diving that year.

OYAKAWA, Yoshi
Swimmer
See entry in International Swimming Hall of Fame, 1973.

PAPENGUTH, Richard
Coach
Richard Papenguth has served the sport of swimming for 25 years as a coach. He was the head coach of swimming at Purdue University from 1939 to 1962 and served as the U.S. Olympic coach in 1952 at the Helsinki Games. During his career Papenguth has produced 40 swimmers who have claimed American records as well as eight Olympic competitors.

PATNIK, Al
Diver
See entry in International Swimming Hall of Fame, 1969.

PEPPE, Mike
Coach
See entry in International Swimming Hall of Fame, 1966.

PINKSTON, Betty Becker
Diver
See entry in International Swimming Hall of Fame, 1967.

PINKSTON, Clarence "Pinky"
Coach
See entry in International Swimming Hall of Fame, 1966.

POYNTON, Dorothy
Diver
See entry in International Swimming Hall of Fame, 1968.

RAWLS, Katherine
Swimmer and Diver
See entry in International Swimming Hall of Fame, 1965.

REILLY, James
Coach

RIGGIN, Aileen
Diver
See entry in International Swimming Hall of Fame, 1967.

RILEY, Michael
Diver
See entry in International Swimming Hall of Fame, 1977.

RIS, Wally
Swimmer
See entry in International Swimming Hall of Fame, 1966.

RITTER, Richard Max
Contributor
See entry in International Swimming Hall of Fame, 1965.

ROBIE, Carl
Swimmer
See entry in International Swimming Hall of Fame, 1976.

ROBINSON, Thomas
Coach
See entry in International Swimming Hall of Fame, 1975.

ROSE, Murray
Swimmer
See entry in International Swimming Hall of Fame, 1965.

ROSS, Anne
Diver
During her career Anne Ross swam for the St. George Dragon Club of Brooklyn, N.Y. She was the holder of the 1942 and 1944 National Amateur Athletic Union (AAU) outdoor 3-meter (10 ft.) championships, the indoor 1-meter (39.4 in.) title from 1941 to 1944 and the indoor 3-meter (10 ft.) championships in 1943 and 1944.

ROSS, Norman
Swimmer
See entry in International Swimming Hall of Fame, 1967.

ROTH, Richard
Swimmer
Born September 26, 1947.

Dick Roth won the 1964 Olympic Games 400-meter individual medley event with a record-setting time of 4 min. 45.4 sec. that stood for almost four years. He did this despite the fact that he had been told the night before that he must have an emergency appendectomy. The appendix waited until the gold medal had been won. During his career with the Santa Clara Swim Club, Roth won six U.S. outdoor medley titles in the 200-meter event. He retired at the age of 19.

RUUSKA, Sylvia
Swimmer
See entry in International Swimming Hall of Fame, 1976.

SAARI, Ray
Swimmer
See entry in International Swimming Hall of Fame, 1976.

SAARI, Urho "Whitey"
Coach
Urho was a national and Olympic water polo coach.

SANBORN, Thelma Payne
Diver
Thelma Payne was the holder of the 1918 through 1920 National Amateur Athletic Union (AAU) indoor 3-meter (10 ft.) diving championship and took third place at the 1920 Olympic Games held at Antwerp for her efforts in the fancy diving event. She swam for the Multnomah Aquatic Club, Portland, Ore.

SCHAEFFER, E. Carroll "Midget"
Swimmer
See entry in International Swimming Hall of Fame, 1968.

SCHOLES, Clark
Swimmer
Clark won gold medals at the Olympic Games and the 1955 Pan-American Games for his 100-meter freestyle effort with a time of 57.4 sec. and 54.7 sec. respectively.

SCHOLLANDER, Donald Arthur
Swimmer
See entry in International Swimming Hall of Fame, 1965.

SILVIA, Charles "Red"
Coach
See entry in International Swimming Hall of Fame, 1976.

SITZBERGER, Ken
Diver
Ken won an Olympic gold medal in the springboard diving event in 1964 with 159.90 points.

SMITH, Harold "Dutch"
Diver
Dutch Smith won a gold medal at the 1932 Olympic Games for his effort in the highboard diving event, winning with 124.80 points.

SMITH, William
Swimmer
See entry in International Swimming Hall of Fame, 1966.

SPEEGLE, Roman
Coach

SPENCE, Walter
Swimmer
See entry in International Swimming Hall of Fame, 1967.

SPITZ, Mark Andrew
Swimmer
See entry in International Swimming Hall of Fame, 1977.
Also in: International Palace of Sports Hall of Fame.

STACK, Allen
Swimmer
Allen tasted victory at the 1948 Olympic Games and the 1951 Pan-American Games for his efforts in the 100-meter backstroke, timed at 1 min. 06.4 sec. and 1 min. 08.0 sec. respectively. He held the U.S. championship for the 100-meter backstroke from 1947 to 1950 with his times improving from 1 min. 07.8 sec. to 1 min. 07.1 sec. In May of 1949 Allen broke a world record in the 200-meter backstroke with his time of 2 min. 18.5 sec.

STEINHAUER, Joseph
Coach
Steinhauer was varsity swimming coach at the University of Wisconsin for many years. He also coached many other sports and refereed swimming and diving meets as well as boxing matches.

STOUDER, Sharon
Swimmer
See entry in International Swimming Hall of Fame, 1972.

SWENDSEN, Clyde
Coach
Clyde Swendsen's coaching career includes Hollywood High School, Black-Foxe Military Academy, Hollywood Athletic Club and the Los Angeles Athletic Club. He was national coach of swimming in Guatemala for three years and coached the U.S. water polo team in the Olympic Games of 1936. Swendsen had 17 of his pupils compete in the Olympic Games of 1932. Prior to his coaching career which spanned from 1924 to 1951, Swendsen was a U.S. national diving champion and U.S. Olympic team competitor in 1920.

THORPE, Niels
Coach
Born August 12, 1892, in Denmark; immigrated to the United States in 1914; attended Minnehaha Academy until finances forced him out; served in the U.S. Army during W.W. I; became U.S. citizen in 1919; received B.S. and M.A. degrees from Univ. Minn; two children.

Niels Thorpe became swimming coach at the St. Paul Athletic Club in 1919 when the pool initially opened. He served there until hired to coach at the University of Minnesota in the fall of 1920. His team defeated Iowa and lost to Northwestern in two dual meets in 1920. In 1921 he took his team to a Conference meet at Evanston, where it captured second place. The following year Minnesota won its first Big Ten swimming championship. During his stay with Minnesota his teams have finished as low as fifth only once. In 1933 Thorpe operated a successful summer camp for boys in Waubon, Minn. Thorpe is the author of *Peter Nielsen Story.*

TOBIAN, Gary
Diver
Gary lost the 1956 highboard Olympic gold medal by three-hundredths of a point to Mexico's Joaquin Capilla. At the 1959 Pan-American Games he won a springboard diving gold medal with 161.40 points, taking that same event in 1960 with 170.0 points. Again at the Olympics in 1960 he lost the highboard gold medal by .31 of a point to his teammate Robert Webster.

TORNEY, Jack
Coach

TROY, Michael
Swimmer
See entry in International Swimming Hall of Fame, 1971.

VERDEUR, Joseph
Swimmer
See entry in International Swimming Hall of Fame, 1966.

VON SALTZA, Susan Christine
Swimmer
See entry in International Swimming Hall of Fame, 1966.

WAHLE, Otto
Coach
Otto Wahle of Austria won an Olympic silver medal at the 1900 Games in the 1000-meter Seine River swim 1 min. 13.2 sec. behind John Jarvis.

WAINWRIGHT, Helen
Swimmer
See entry in International Swimming Hall of Fame, 1972.

WALLEN, W. L.
Swimmer
During his career Wallen swam for the Hamilton Club, Chicago, the Great Lakes Naval Training School and the Illinois Aquatic Club. He held National Amateur Athletic Union outdoor championships for the 440-yard freestyle in 1918 and 1919, for the 880-yard freestyle from 1917 to 1919 and the one-mile freestyle in 1918 and 1919.

WATSON, Lillian Debra "Pokey"
Swimmer
Born July 11, 1950, in Mineloa, N.Y.

Pokey Watson won her first Olympic gold medal at the age of 14 at the 1964 Mexican Games for her efforts in the 400-meter freestyle relay. In the 1967 Pan-American Games she took a bronze in the 100-meter freestyle with a time of 61.5 sec. In 1968 Pokey entered and won the 200-meter backstroke event in the Olympic Games with a world record time of 2 min. 24.3 sec. Pokey also held three U.S. freestyle outdoor titles, the 100-meter freestyle in 1965 and 1966 and the 200-meter in 1966. She swam for the Santa Clara Swim Club in California.

WEBSTER, Robert
Diver
See entry in International Swimming Hall of Fame, 1970.

WEISSMULLER, Johnny
Swimmer
See entry in International Swimming Hall of Fame, 1965.

WHITE, Albert C.
Diver
See entry in International Swimming Hall of Fame, 1965.

WOOLSEY, William
Swimmer
Bill Woolsey was the U.S. champion 200-meter freestyler in 1952, 1955 and 1956 with times going from 2 min. 13.2 sec. to 2 min. 06.6 sec. Bill was the U.S. champion in the 400-meter freestyle with time at 4 min. 43.3 sec. in 1954. His Olympic gold medal came in 1952 as a member of the 800-meter freestyle relay timed at 8 min. 31.1 sec.

WRIGHTSON, Bernard
Diver
Born June 25, 1944, at Randolph Field, Tex.

Bernard Wrightson swam for Arizona State University and the Dick Smith Swim Gym. During his career he held the 1964, 1965 and 1968 National Amateur Athletic Union (AAU) outdoor championship for the 3-meter (10 ft.) springboard diving event and the 1965 platform diving championship. In 1966 Wrightson was holder of the AAU indoor as well as the National Collegiate Athletic Association (NCAA) 3-meter springboard diving championship. His career was highlighted by his gold medals in the springboard diving event at the 1967 Pan-American Games and at the 1968 Olympic Games held in Mexico City.

YORZYK, William
Swimmer
See entry in International Swimming Hall of Fame, 1971.

ZIMMERMAN, Suzanne
Swimmer
Suzanne was the U.S. backstroke champion at 100-meters from 1946 to 1948. During that period her times improved from 1 min. 18.0 sec. to 1 min. 16.4 sec. For the same time period she was the U.S. 200-meters backstroke champion with times from 2 min. 48.7 sec. to 2 min. 48.3 sec.

Swimming — Synchronized Hall of Fame

The Citizens Savings Hall of Fame Athletic Museum established the Synchronized Swimming Hall of Fame in 1959. This Hall honors swimmers, coaches and contributors to synchronized swimming, which is an art form of swimming often called "ballet in the water." Initially, the Citizens Savings Hall Board called upon the National Amateur Athletic Union synchronized swimming committee to present nominations for the Hall of Fame elections. Since 1959 there have been a total of 39 inductions—37 individuals and 2 swim club teams—involving 46 men and women. New inductees receive a Hall of Fame Award and their names are engraved on the Hall of Fame Trophy lodged at the Athletic Museum.

1959

CURTIS, Katherine
Contributor
Kay Curtis is credited with the creation of synchronized swimming when she trained the Kay Curtis Modern Mermaids who performed at the Chicago World's Fair in 1934.

KELLERMAN, Annette
Contributor
See entry in International Swimming Hall of Fame, 1974.

1961

GREGORY, June Taylor
Synchronized Swimmer
Born in Canada; moved to Hollywood, Calif, in 1952.

June Taylor Gregory represented the Kia Ora Club when she won the U.S. solo indoor title for four years, 1950 – 1953. She was Canadian national champion before coming to the United States.

NELSON, Joan Pawson
Synchronized Swimmer
Joan Pawson swam for the Athens Club of Oakland, Calif. She was an outstanding member of that group from 1950. Joan was a member of six national championship teams and represented the United States in the Pan-American Games at Mexico City in 1955.

1962

ATHENS CLUB WATER FOLLIES TEAM
Synchronized Swimmers
The Athens Club Water Follies Team of 1958 was composed of Lynn Pawson, Loretta Barrious, Janet Anthony, Jackie Vargas and Sue Laurence. This quintet is said to have been one of the greatest of all time. It's members won numerous individual and team crowns in national competition as well as the Pan-Am Games.

MacKELLAR, Lillian "Billie"
Contributor
Born in New Zealand.

Lillian, better known as Billie, swam in many long-distance events for New Zealand in Australia, England and France. After moving to Canada, she worked as a swim coach and later as a synchronized swimming coach. MacKellar was appointed to manage and coach the Canadian women's swimming teams competing in the British Empire Games as well as the Pan-American Games. Her outstanding students were June Taylor Gregory, Barbara Burke and Joanne Schaack.

1963

ANDERSON, Theresa
Contributor
Theresa Anderson is a patron and an authority on a number of women's sports, notably synchronized swimming. She has authored and co-authored several books on the sport. Anderson was voted into the chairmanship of the National Women's Aquatic Forum in 1963. She has been an ambassador of synchronized swimming both on a national and international basis for many years.

ST. CLAIRE SYNCHRONETTES TEAM
Synchronized Swimmers
The St. Claire Synchronettes Team of 1950 was composed of Connie Todoroff, Marilyn Stanley, Shirley Simpson and Ellen Richard. This Detroit, Mich, team dominated synchronized swimming beginning in 1948 and continuing through 1955. They won seven team championships and nine duets titles during this time. The team gave demonstrations at the Pan-Am Games of 1951 and at the Olympic Games of 1952. The 1950 team collected wins in both the indoor and outdoor national championships, taking titles in both duet competitions. Two of the team members, Ellen Richard and Connie Todoroff, were the 1955 Pan-American Games champions in the duet event.

1964

CUSHMAN, Joy
Contributor
Joy Cushman began her competitive career with the Corkettes of the Shamrock-Hilton in Houston, Tex, in 1949. Four years later she was appointed coach of that team. She served as national chairman for synchronized swimming from 1959 to 1964. Joy played an important role in the reestablishing of synchronized swimming as a participation sport rather than an exhibition event.

GEORGIAN, Carolyn Ann "Papsie"
Synchronized Swimmer
Carolyn Ann began her career at the age of five with the Athens Water Follies of Oakland, Calif. She won a number of under-12 titles. During her career she participated in 16 national championships, winning four consecutive during 1960 through 1963. In 1963 she was a member of the Athens Club Water Follies Pan-American Games championship team and won a gold medal. Throughout her career Georgian appeared in hundreds of exhibitions to help popularize her sport.

1966

JOHNSON, Lawrence
Contributor
Lawrence Johnson contributed much to synchronized swimming as a competitive sport. He and Max Ritter introduced international rules which are observed and noted in the *Fédèration Internationale de Natation Amateur* manual. Johnson was manager of the state department tour of American synchronized swimmers around the world in 1956 and was instrumental in having the sport officially recognized at the Pan-American Games.

LEACH, David Clark
Contributor
David Leach from Wilmette, Ill, was the first national chairman of the Amateur Athletic Union (AAU) synchronized swimming committee. He served as chairman from 1942 to 1947 and remained a committee member for many years. Leach fashioned the rules for synchronized swimming that were adopted by the AAU in 1945 making it a recognized sport.

1967

KANE, Marion Olsen
Contributor
Born February 1, 1934, in San Rafael, Calif; attended Lincoln High School in San Francisco; entered the Univ. Hawaii; married Don Kane in 1955; three children.

At the age of ten Marion Olson became a member of the Crystal Plunge Team. During her competitive career she was a finalist or placed in 13 national women's swimming championships. She was junior national champion, junior Olympic champion and Hawaiian record holder. Marion still holds the record for a woman swimming across the Golden Gate and the Pier-7-to-Treasure-Island swim. Marion founded the Merionettes in 1957 with four girls. Within ten years the team had grown to 50. The Merionettes have traveled extensively throughout the world. They won the *Criterium d'Europe* at Amsterdam, competing against ten European nations.

1968

BEAN, Dawn Pawson
Contributor
Dawn Bean was a member of the Athens Club and coached the Riverside Aquettes.

GORHAM, Roberta Armstrong
Synchronized Swimmer
Roberta was four times National Solo Champion and Pan-Am Solo Champion at the 1963 Games.

WILLARD, Patty
Synchronized Swimmer
Pat Willard was a member of the 1963, 1964 and 1965 Merionettes and won many single and duet titles.

1969

McGRATH, Margo
Synchronized Swimmer
Born June 20, 1950, in San Francisco, Calif; father coached at George Washington High School in San Francisco; attended Univ. Hawaii.

Margo McGrath began her competitive career at age 9 with the Merionettes of San Francisco. At 14 she won a distance swim across the Golden Gate. In 1966 and 1967 Margo made a clean sweep of the national championships. During her career she won 17 titles: five solo, four duet and eight team. She also won four Canadian and two European titles. McGrath is the only synchronized swimmer ever to be considered for the Sullivan Award.

MORRIS, Pamella Wiley
Synchronized Swimmer
See entry in International Swimming Hall of Fame, 1965.

OLSEN, Norma J.
Contributor
Graduated from Iowa State Teachers Col; husband Art; daughter Zoe Ann member of U.S. Olympic diving team in 1948, silver medalist; organized a dance and drama school in 1933 in Cedar Falls, Iowa.

Norma Olsen turned her attention to synchronized swimming in 1939. She served as chairperson of the sport in Iowa from 1942 to 1944. As a resident of Oakland, Calif, she managed and directed the Athens Athletic Club Water Follies from 1941 through 1951. She was one of the pioneers of synchronized swimming in the San Francisco Bay area, was Pacific Association chairperson for the sport from 1945 to 1959 and national chairperson from 1953 to 1958. By far her most significant contribution to the sport, however, were her dedicated efforts that resulted in 1959 in the creation of the Synchronized Swimming Hall of Fame of the Citizens Savings Hall of Fame Athletic Museum.

REDMOND, Carol
Synchronized Swimmer
Born December 14, 1949, at the Presidio of San Francisco, Calif; parents Lt. Col. and Jane E. Redmond, military family; received the Bank of America Achievement Award for scholastic excellence; attended college in San Diego.

Carol learned to swim in a Red Cross program and was introduced to synchronized swimming through Girl Scouts of America. She became a member of the San Francisco Merionettes in 1962 and was coached by Marion Kane. In 1963 Carol placed third at the indoor national championship. She was second at the outdoor national championships and first at the indoor championships in 1965. It was in 1965 that Carol and Margo McGrath teamed up to become synchronized swimming's unbeatable "dynamic duo." In 1967 Carol and her teammates won every championship available throughout the world. She won the solo, duet and team championships at the Canadian Nationals and the same list at the *Criterium d'Europe.* Carol retired from competition in 1968 in order to attend college. She became a synchronized swimming teacher in Chula Vista, Calif, and a world ambassador for the sport.

VIDA, Clair
Synchronized Swimmer
Born in San Francisco, Calif; attended Lincoln High School; graduated from Univ. Calif, Berkeley; earned teaching credentials at Calif. State Univ.

Clair Vida learned to swim at Larson Pool in San Francisco and became a member of the Merionettes in 1956. She was a member of the team that won national championships from 1961 to 1964. Clair won four national duet crowns and was a member of eight championship teams. She retired from competition in 1964. She has served as an assistant coach for the Merionettes and has been an approved synchronized swimming judge.

1971

CALCATERRA, Re
Contributor

HINES, Nancy
Synchronized Swimmer
Nancy Hines swam in competition with the Aquamaids 1968 – 1970 and also in solo and duet meets.

PIERCE, Ike
Contributor

VILEN, Kay
Contributor
Kay Vilen was coach of the Aquamaids for almost a quarter of a century winning many national and international meets.

WELSHONS, Kim
Synchronized Swimmer
Kim has won 13 national gold medals, 14 international gold medals, a Pan-Am gold in 1963, and a double gold at the International meet in Denmark in 1970.

1972

BEAN, Ross C.
Contributor
Bean was a former National Amateur Athletic Union medalist in the 400, 800 and 1500-meter freestyle swimming events. He was named to the nonexistent 1944 Olympic team. He developed a synchronized swim team that qualified for national competition and won the championship for the Pacific Association in 1952. Under Bean's direction the Athens Club won the national crown and the Pan-American Games title in 1955 and dominated the sport until 1961. In 1956 Ross became a judge, official, committee worker and assistant to the Riverside Aquettes and later the Tustin Meraquas. Ross was senior author for the complete revision of rules for the sport and has been chairman of the rules, stunts, public relations, bibliography, All-American and Hall of Fame committees since 1952.

HINES, Edna
Contributor
Attended Florida State Univ; taught physical education in Lansing, Mich; husband Ross Hines; died December 8, 1965.

Edna was invited to take over the coaching of the synchronized swimming group in Columbus, Ohio. She led her Coralina Club to seven junior national championships and was a consistent finalist in the senior national competitions. Edna was national vice chairperson, member of the international committee for rules, stunts and public relations and was synchronized swimming chairperson for the Ohio Association. Edna Hines was one of the truly active participants in the development of the sport. She has contributed numerous articles to *Synchro Info,* the official synchronized swimming publication.

1973

DURBROW, Margaret
Synchronized Swimmer
Margaret began swimming with the San Francisco Merionettes at the age of 11. She was a winner of ten national titles including eight team titles and two duet titles during the period from 1961 to 1964. She also won both the junior national duet and team championships. Margaret is remembered for her dedicated team work and sportsmanship as well as her public relations work that helped to build a positive image of synchronized swimming.

LUICK, William
Contributor
Will Luick has been involved in the production aspect of synchronized swimming for 20 years. He has assured the finest sound possible at the national championships and sees to it that every competitor receives a fair distribution of practice time. Will has written numerous articles on sound reproduction and has served as chairman of the sound equipment committee for the national synchronized swimming committee for three years. He has also served as sound center manager for 14 senior national championships, a volunteer job.

O'ROURKE, Heidi
Synchronized Swimmer
Heidi joined the San Francisco Merionettes synchronized swimming team at age 9. She was the winner of ten national titles and won the national solo championship twice, the national duet championship five times and the national team championship three times. Heidi was a triple gold medal winner in the solo, duet and team events at the Pan-Am Games in 1971, as well as a winner at the International Meet during Expo 1970 in Japan. Heidi won the duet and team titles in the England-U.S.A. match in 1960. She retired from competition at the age of 17 as the only synchronized swimmer ever awarded perfect scores (all ten's) in both national and international competition.

SWAN, Margaret
Contributor
Margaret Swan began synchronized swimming in 1956 at the San Antonia YMCA. She formed the Cygnets in 1963 and has coached that team to finals in national championships every year since 1966. Her teams have won five junior championships and the first junior Olympic team championship. They were also winners of the open category at the Canadian championships in 1971. Margaret coached synchronized swimming at San Antonio College where she was an assistant professor. She was manager of the Pan-Am Games team in 1971 and has been a member of the national committee since 1960, serving as vice chairman since 1966. Her Cygnets were featured in an article in *Sports Illustrated* in April of 1971.

1974

JONES, Frances L.
Contributor
Frances began coaching in 1950 with the Lansing Sea Sprites. That group produced national finalists each year for the following ten years, including Sandy Giltner and Judy Haga. Her next group, the Michigan Aquarius, seems to be on its way to equal success. Jones has been a national judge for many years and has served as a national committee member and chairperson in 1969 and 1970. She is the distinguished author of a number of books and publications.

TRANTINA, Barbara "Bede"
Synchronized Swimmer
Bede was winner of three junior crowns, solo, duet and team in 1967, 1968 and 1969. She swam for the San Francisco Merionettes and participated in national championships for eight years, winning three team titles during the period from 1967 to 1970, duet titles in 1969 and 1970 and the solo title in 1970. Trantina was a member of the winning *Criterium d'Europe* in 1968.

1975

ANDERSEN, Teresa W.
Synchronized Swimmer
Attended Univ. Calif; majored in special education.

Swimming for the Santa Clara Aquamaids synchronized swimming team, Teri Andersen won the junior national solo and duet crowns in 1970 and 1971. She was the first woman from the United States to win a gold medal in the first World Aquatic Games held in Yugoslavia in 1973. At that meet Teri took a gold medal in all three events, the solo, the duet and the team. She participated in Expo 70 in Japan and in the Canadian International events. Andersen holds 12 national championship titles including seven team, four duet and one solo from 1969 to 1973. She is co-author with Fern Yates of *Synchronized Swimming* (second edition, 1958).

1976

BUZONAS, Gail Johnson
Synchronized Swimmer
Gail Johnson was the winner of 22 National Amateur Athletic Union senior titles including 6 solo crowns. Although competing in the sport prior to 1967 it is with the Santa Clara Aquamaids that Gail achieved her greatest success. She won gold medals in the Pan-Pacific Games, the All-Japan Invitational, the Canadian Open, the Germany-U.S.A. Invitational, the Pan-Am Games and the World Aquatic Games. Ms. Buzonas was the winner of the 1974 Larry Johnson Aquatic Award and was nominated for the Sullivan Award in 1974 and 1975. Retired from competition, she is coaching at the Santa Clara Club.

DAVIS, Ninetta
Synchronized Swimmer
First woman to receive engineering degree from Colo. School of Mines; retired in 1960.

Ninetta became involved in synchronized swimming in 1949 through the Red Cross. She brought the sport to the Rocky Mountain area around 1962 and was the first woman officer in the Rocky Mountain Amateur Athletic Union. She has been Amateur Athletic Union vice chairperson of the synchronized swimming committee since 1970. Davis continues to serve synchronized swimming as an adviser, contributing much of her time, talent and personal funds to the development of the sport.

KRETSCHMER, Katherine
Synchronized Swimmer
Kathy began in synchronized swimming at the age of ten. Her national titles include junior team titles in 1966, junior solo title in 1967, junior duet title in 1971, indoor and outdoor team titles in 1974 and outdoor figures in 1974. As a member of the U.S. Pan-Am Games championship team in 1971 she won a gold medal; the same year she also won the International Invitational solo championship in Canada. In 1976 Kathy coached in Holland for six months and took the Holland national team to the Swedish Invitational championships for third and fourth places in all three events.

WHITING, Lillian
Contributor
From West Des Moines, Iowa.

Whiting was a member of the committee that supervised the first synchronized swimming meets in Iowa in 1943. She has been involved in Amateur Athletic Union (AAU) activities for more than 30 years. She was national chairperson of the AAU women's swimming committee from 1945 to 1948. Lillian was chaperone for the U.S. Olympic women's team in 1948 at the London Games and accompanied the AAU swimmers and divers to New Zealand in 1962. She served as a member of the Sullivan Award committee.

Tennis Hall of Fame

The Tennis Hall of Fame was instituted in 1949 to honor the most outstanding players in and contributors to the game of tennis. As of 1977 there were 50 members, selected by the Hall of Fame board. New inductees' names are engraved on the Tennis Hall of Fame Trophy, which is kept in the Citizens Savings Hall of Fame Athletic Museum, and each receives a special Hall of Fame Award.

Induction Years Unrecorded

ADDIE, Pauline Betz
Player
See entry in International Tennis Hall of Fame, 1965.

ALLISON, Wilmer Lawson, Jr.
Player
See entry in International Tennis Hall of Fame, 1963.

ATKINSON, Juliette
Player
See entry in International Tennis Hall of Fame, 1974.

BRINKER, Maureen Connolly "Little Mo"
Player
See entry in International Tennis Hall of Fame, 1968.

BROWNE, Mary K.
Player
See entry in International Tennis Hall of Fame, 1957.

BUDGE, J. Donald
Player
See entry in International Tennis Hall of Fame, 1964.

BUNDY, May Sutton
Player
See entry in International Tennis Hall of Fame, 1956.

CAMPBELL, Oliver Samuel
Player
See entry in International Tennis Hall of Fame, 1955.

CLAPP, Louise Brough
Player
See entry in International Tennis Hall of Fame, 1967.

DANZIG, Sarah Palfrey Cooke
Player
See entry in International Tennis Hall of Fame, 1963.

DARBEN, Althea Gibson
Player
See entry in International Tennis Hall of Fame, 1971.

DAVIS, Dwight Filley
Player
See entry in International Tennis Hall of Fame, 1956.
Also in: Noteworthy Contributors Hall of Fame, Citizens Savings Hall of Fame Athletic Museum.

DENNY, Victor
Contributor
Born in Seattle, Wash; Samuel Hardy Award 1960.

Denny was president of the U.S. Lawn Tennis Association 1958 and 1959.

DUPONT, Margaret Osborne
Player
See entry in International Tennis Hall of Fame, 1967.

GONZALEZ, Richard A. "Pancho"
Player
See entry in International Tennis Hall of Fame, 1968.

GUNTER, Nancy Richey
Player
Born Aug. 23, 1942, in San Angelo, Tex.

Nancy played on the Wightman Cup team from 1962 to 1969. Although a fine hard-court player, she won the U.S. Clay Court Singles every year from 1963 to 1968. She won the Federal Cup in 1964, again in 1968 and 1969. Nancy also won the U.S. Doubles in 1965 and 1966 and Wimbledon Women's Doubles in 1966. In 1966 she also took the Australian Women's Doubles, the Women's Singles in 1967 and the French Women's Singles in 1968.

HARD, Darlene R.
Player
See entry in International Tennis Hall of Fame, 1973.

HART, Doris
Player
See entry in International Tennis Hall of Fame, 1969.

IRVIN, Shirley Fry
Player
See entry in International Tennis Hall of Fame, 1970.

JACOBS, Helen Hull
Player
See entry in International Tennis Hall of Fame, 1962.

JOHNSTON, William "Little Bill"
Player
See entry in International Tennis Hall of Fame, 1958.

JONES, Perry T.
Contributor
See entry in International Tennis Hall of Fame, 1970.

KING, Billie Jean Moffit
Player
Born November 22, 1943, in Long Beach, Calif.

Billie Jean took the Wimbledon Women's Doubles in 1961, 1962, 1965, 1967, 1968 and 1970–1973, as well as the Wimbledon Women's Singles 1966–1968, 1972 and 1973. She won the U.S. Women's Doubles in 1964 and 1967, the U.S. Mixed Doubles in 1967, 1971 and 1973, and the U.S. Women's Singles in 1967, 1971 and 1972. Billie Jean is a women's rights advocate and has contributed greatly toward making women's earnings equal to the men's. In 1971 she was the first woman to win more than $100,000 in one year, much of that coming from World Team Tennis women's pro circuit. She also copped most of the traditional tennis events, winning the French, Wimbledon and U.S. Singles titles and losing only one set in all. She responded to Bobby Riggs' (1939 Wimbledon champion) challenge in Houston in September, 1973, by defeating him soundly, 6–4, 6–3, 6–3, in a widely publicized and nationally televised match.

KRAMER, John Albert
Player
See entry in International Tennis Hall of Fame, 1968.

LARNED, William A.
Player
See entry in International Tennis Hall of Fame, 1956.

LOTT, George M, Jr.
Player
See entry in International Tennis Hall of Fame, 1964.

MAKO, Gene
Player
See entry in International Tennis Hall of Fame, 1973.

MALLORY, Molla Bjurstedt
Player
See entry in International Tennis Hall of Fame, 1958.

MARBLE, Alice
Player
See entry in International Tennis Hall of Fame, 1964.

McKINLEY, Charles R.
Player
Born May 1, 1941, in St. Louis, Mo.

McKinley was on the Davis Cup team from 1960 to 1965. He took the U.S. Men's Doubles in 1961, 1963 and 1964 and the U.S. Men's Singles in 1963. That same year he won the Wimbledon Men's Singles.

McLOUGHLIN, Maurice Evans
Player
See entry in International Tennis Hall of Fame, 1957.

MOORE, Elizabeth H.
Player
See entry in International Tennis Hall of Fame, 1971.

MURRAY, R. Lindley
Player
See entry in International Tennis Hall of Fame, 1958.

MYRICK, Julian S.
Contributor
See entry in International Tennis Hall of Fame, 1963.

PARKER, Frank A.
Player
See entry in International Tennis Hall of Fame, 1966.

RICHARDS, Vincent
Player
See entry in International Tennis Hall of Fame, 1961.

RIGGS, Robert Lorimer "Bobby"
Player
See entry in International Tennis Hall of Fame, 1967.

ROARK, Helen Wills Moody
Player
See entry in International Tennis Hall of Fame, 1959.

RYAN, Elizabeth
Player
See entry in International Tennis Hall of Fame, 1972.

SCHROEDER, Frederick R, Jr. "Ted"
Player
See entry in International Tennis Hall of Fame, 1966.

SEARS, Richard Dudley
Player
See entry in International Tennis Hall of Fame, 1955.

SEIXAS, Elias Victor, Jr.
Player
See entry in International Tennis Hall of Fame, 1971.

TILDEN, William Tatem, III "Big Bill"
Player
See entry in International Tennis Hall of Fame, 1959.

TRABERT, Marion "Tony"
Player
See entry in International Tennis Hall of Fame, 1970.

VINES, H. Ellsworth
Player
See entry in International Tennis Hall of Fame, 1962.

WARD, Holcombe
Player
See entry in International Tennis Hall of Fame, 1956.

WHITMAN, Malcolm D.
Player
See entry in International Tennis Hall of Fame, 1955.

WIGHTMAN, Hazel Hotchkiss
Player
See entry in International Tennis Hall of Fame, 1957.

WILLIAMS, Richard Norris, II
Player
See entry in International Tennis Hall of Fame, 1957.

WRENN, Robert D.
Player
See entry in International Tennis Hall of Fame, 1955.

Track and Field Hall of Fame

The Track and Field Hall of Fame of the Citizens Savings Hall of Fame Athletic Museum was instituted in 1949. As of 1977 a total of 243 athletes had been inducted into the Hall, many of them record-breakers and record-holders. Each was selected for his or her performance as athletes, for contributions to track and field, or for the exercise of any other significant influence upon track and field events individually or as a whole. New inductees receive a special Hall of Fame Award, after which their names are engraved upon the Track and Field Hall of Fame Trophy which is preserved in the Citizens Savings Hall of Fame Athletic Museum in Los Angeles, California.

Induction Years Unrecorded

ADAMS, Harry
Coach

ADAMS, Platt
High, Broad and Triple Jumper
Olympic Gold Medal and Silver Medal 1912; died February 27, 1961.

Adams was a member of twelve 1908 Olympic teams and placed fifth in the triple jump. In 1912 he again participated in the Olympic Games, achieving a gold medal in the standing high jump and a silver medal in the standing broad jump. He first achieved track success in the 1907 Amateur Athletic Union (AAU) championships, taking the crown for the triple jump by a mark of 44 ft. 9 in. Between 1907 and 1912, he won seven AAU championship crowns in the broad jump and the triple jump. His best AAU marks were 45 ft. 9 in. in the 1912 triple jump and 23 ft. 2 in. in the 1914 broad jump. He was an outstanding all-around jumper.

AHEARN, Daniel
Triple Jumper
Born April 2, 1888, in County Limerick, Ire; immigrated to the U.S. and dropped "e" from last name.

The only American ever to hold a world triple jump record, Daniel performed this outstanding feat on May 5, 1911, in New York by jumping 50 ft. 11 in. This surpassed the former record held by his brother Timothy Ahearne who competed for Ireland in 1908. In 1910, 1911 and 1913–1918, Ahearn won the Amateur Athletic Union (AAU) triple jump title eight times. His record jump of 50 ft. set in 1913 stood for 22 years. At AAU competition in San Francisco in 1915, his wind-aided 50 ft. 11.5 in. was tops for 26 years, finally bested in 1941. Ahearn sat out the 1912 Olympic Games but made the 1920 team, taking sixth in triple jump at Antwerp.

ALBRITTON, David
High Jumper
Born April 13, 1913, in Danville, Ala; attended Ohio State Univ; teammate of Jesse Owens; one of first inno-

vators to straddle bar in the high jump; Olympic Silver Medal 1936.

On July 12, 1936, during the Olympic trials at Los Angeles, Albritton tied for the world high jump record by clearing 6 ft. 9.75 in. Then at the Games, his co-recordholder Cornelius Johnson took first place to Albritton's second. Both performances by American blacks were witnessed by Aryan-advocate Adolph Hitler. In the course of his long career from 1936 to 1950, David won or tied for seven AAU titles, his best jump being 6 ft. 8⅝ in. in 1937. While attending Ohio State, he tied for the National Collegiate Athletic Association (NCAA) high jump title 1936–1938.

ANDERSON, Frank
Coach

ASHENFELTER, Horace III "Ash" "Nip"
Steeplechaser
Born January 23,1923, in Collegeville, Pa; attended Penn State Univ; Olympic Gold Medal and James E. Sullivan Memorial Trophy 1952; now a retired F.B.I. agent.

The only American ever to win a gold medal in the 3000-m. steeplechase, Nip staged the biggest upset in the 1952 Olympic Games. His time of 8:45.4 was not recognized as a world record at that time. He competed in the 1956 Olympic Games but did not qualify for the finals. In addition to his international championships, Nip won the AAU steeplechase in 1951, 1953 and 1956; five time AAU 3-mi. indoor, 1952 to 1956; AAU outdoor 3-mi. in 1954 and 1955 and 6-mi. in 1950. At Penn State he won the NCAA 2-mi. title and the Intercollegiate Association of Amateur Athletes of America (IC4A) outdoor 2-mi. in 1948 and 1949 and indoor in 1948.
Also in: National Track and Field Hall of Fame and U.S. Track and Field Hall of Fame.

ATTLESEY, Richard
Hurdler
Born May 10, 1929, in Compton, Calif; attended Univ. Southern Calif; held world records for 110-m. and 120-yd. hurdles.

Attlesey broke the world record for the 120-yd. hurdle at the West Coast Relays on May 13, 1950, when he clocked 13.5 sec. One month later on June 24, he clocked 13.6 in the 110-m, establishing that as a new record while also winning the AAU championship. But he bested himself on July 10, 1950, in Helsinki, running the 110-m. in 13.5 which tied his previous 120-yd. record. Richard won the AAU outdoor championships in 1950 and 1951. While at Southern California he captured the 1950 NCAA title with 14.0 time. Injuries prevented Attlesey from becoming an Olympic contender. A strapping 6 ft. 3.5 in. tall, Attlesey owed much of his success to his control and form.

BACKUS, Robert
Thrower
Backus threw things for seven years in a row, and it all paid off in championships. He won the AAU first place in 56-lb. weight throw 1953–1959, then again in 1965 after six years' hiatus. In 1954 Backus became the AAU champ in 16-lb. hammer competition which he won with 189 ft. 3 in. And bringing forth a third weight event, the 35-lb. weight throw, Backus won it in AAU contests 1954–1959 and 1961, his best toss being the last at 66 ft. 2¾ in.

BARBUTTI, Raymond
Runner
Born June 12, 1905, in Brooklyn, N.Y; attended Syracuse Univ; Olympic Gold Medal 1928; now retired after working for N. Y. State Civil Defense Commission.

Barbuti squeezed a remarkably flamboyant career into a one-year span. At the 1928 Amsterdam Olympics he was the only American to win a running event, which he did with panache by diving across the finish line barely a nose ahead o¢f the Canadian contender, James Ball. His time for that 400-m. race was 47.8 sec. Then as anchorman on the U.S. 1600-m. relay team, Ray contributed to their gold medal win and world record of 3:14.2. While at Syracuse Barbuti played football, yet track was his specialty, and in 1928 he won the IC4A championship in 440-yd. by clocking a time of 48.8. In addition, he captured the AAU title for a 51.4 time, then representing the New York Athletic Club.

BARNES, Lee
Pole Vaulter
Born July 16, 1906, in Salt Lake City, Utah; grew up in Hollywood and attended Univ. Southern Calif; Olympic Gold Medal 1924; up to retirement was the head of own manufacturing company in Oxnard, Calif.

Lee's accomplishments were in pole vault for which he held the world record of 14 ft. 1½ in. attained at Fresno, Calif. on April 28, 1928. That same year he placed fifth in the Olympics at Amsterdam with a vault of 12 ft. 11½ in. Four years earlier at age 17 and while a student at Hollywood High School, that same height earned him the gold medal at the 1924 Olympics. Barnes won it in the clinch by bettering the tie mark in a jump-off match. Out of high school, Barnes competed for Southern California and the Los Angeles Athletic Club, winning the AAU championship in 1927 with 13 ft. and again in 1928 with 13 ft. 9 in.

BASKIN, Weems
Coach

BEAMON, Robert
Long Jumper
Born August 29, 1946, in Jamaica, N.Y; Olympic Gold Medal 1928; *Track and Field News* Athlete of the Year 1968; Citizens Savings World Trophy Award for North America 1968; turned professional in 1973.

At the 1968 Olympic Games, Bob soared to 29 ft. 2.5 in. in the long jump which secured him the American, Olympic and world records. His leap is often referred to as the perfect long jump and greatest track mark of all time. Bob was first in every meet he competed in in 1968, winning the Amateur Athletic Union at 27 ft. 4 in. and the Olympic trials along with Olympic and U.S. relay titles.
Also in: U.S. Track and Field Hall of Fame.

BELL, Gregory
Long Jumper
Born November 7, 1930, in Terre Haute, Ind; attended Indiana Univ; Olympic Gold Medal 1956; Pan-Am Silver Medal 1959.

Greg won the gold medal for long jump during the 1956 Olympiad at Melbourne, having jumped 25 ft. 8¼ in. He became a silver medalist at the Pan-American Games of 1959 with 24 ft. 11¼ in. Between times, he earned the AAU championship in 1955 with 26 ft. ½ in. and in 1959 with 26 ft. 1¼ in. In 1957 his long jump was only one and a quarter inches off the world record held by Jesse Owens. Yet Bell's jump of 26 ft. 7 in. won him the NCAA title. Then in 1958 for Indiana Bell took the NCAA title for a long jump of 25 ft. 9 in. Although finishing fourth in the Olympic tryouts did not win him a berth on the 1960 team, he had an excellent showing at 25 ft. 4 in.

BLOZIS, Albert C.
Shot-putter
Born January 5, 1919, in Garfield, N.J; attended Georgetown Univ; played professional football for New York Giants; died in France while serving in W.W. II on January 31, 1945.

Al's achievements were a result of versatility and size. At 6 ft. 6 in. and 240 lbs, his was a force to be reckoned with as tackle on the New York Giants from 1942 through 1944. He was named All-Pro in 1943. As for track showings, Blozis dominated collegiate shot-put and discus from 1940 to 1942, winning three NCAA championships for Georgetown. His 1940 record shot of 56 ft. ½ in. stood for nine years. He challenged Jack Tarrance's world record with an outdoor best of 56 ft. 6⅛ in. which was just 6⅞ in. short. Blozis won three AAU outdoor and indoor titles with his 1940 outdoor shot of 55 ft. ⅜ in, his AAU best performance. His indoor best was a 57 ft. ¾ in. throw in 1942. Throughout the years, Al captured the IC4A championships for discus, both indoor and outdoor.
Also in: Drake Relays Hall of Fame.

BONTHRON, William
Runner
Born November 1, 1912, in Detroit, Mich; attended Princeton Univ; James E. Sullivan Memorial Trophy 1934; now an accountant living in Princeton, N.J.

In his college days, Bill was a top miler and held the world record for the 1500-m. which he ran in 3:34.8 on June 30, 1934, at Milwaukee. Competing against the great Glenn Cunningham, Bonthron pushed forth at the last to win the AAU title and set the world record. That year and one year previous he won IC4A championships in both 880-yard and mile. He took the IC4A indoor mile championship in 1934. At Princeton in 1933 a historic contest was staged between Bonthron and New Zealand's ace miler, Jack Lovelock, who won the gold for 1500-m. three years later. Throughout the race Bonthron led most of the way, yet Lovelock squeaked by to win with a time of 4:07.6, breaking the world record as did second-place Bonthron with 4:08.7 Then again in 1934, competing in the NCAA mile, Bill defeated Cunningham with a time of 4:08.9.

BORICAN, Johnny
Pentathlon
Johnny won his first title at the age of 20, when he took AAU top credits in pentathlon, the decathlon's five-event cousin now reserved for women's competition. Johnny took it again two years later in 1941, while also vying for the AAU 1000-yd. run. The 1000-yd. became a new addition to his championship list in the years 1939–1942, and during the last year Borican also aced all other 880-yd. competition with 1:51.2.

BOSTON, Ralph H.
Long Jumper
Born May 9, 1939, in Laurel, Miss; graduate of Tenn. A&I; Olympic Gold Medal 1964, Silver 1964, Bronze 1968; Citizens Savings World Trophy Award for North America 1961; presently with the Univ. Tenn; also involved with television commentary.

Ralph held the world long jump record and first set the mark at Walnut, Calif. in 1960 with a leap of 26 ft. 11.25 in. In 1961 at Modesto, Calif, he improved the mark to 27 ft. .5 in, and later in the year advanced it 1.5 in. Rival Russian Ter-Ovanesyan took the mark away in 1962 but Ralph tied the record in Jamaica later that year. At the 1964 Olympic trials in Los Angeles, he regained sole possession of the record with a 27 ft. 4.25 in. jump. His last record jump was 27 ft. 5 in. in 1965. Ralph took a gold medal in Rome, breaking Jesse Owen's record. In the 1964 Tokyo Olympics he earned a silver and four years later in Mexico City a bronze. While a student at Tennessee A&I, he was the 1960 titlist and holder of the American collegiate record with a 27 ft. 2.5 in. leap. For six consecutive years, 1961–1966, he was the AAU outdoor champion.
Also in: Drake Relays Hall of Fame, National Association of Intercollegiate Athletics Hall of Fame, National Track and Field Hall of Fame and U.S. Track and Field Hall of Fame.

BRAGG, Donald "Tarzan"
Pole Vaulter
Born May 15, 1935, in Penns Grove, N.J; attended Villanova Univ; Olympic Gold Medal 1960; known for large build, 6 ft. 3 in. and 197 lbs.

The last of the pole vaulters who used metal poles, Bragg was critical of the new fiberglass pole. His vault of 15 ft. 9¼ in. earned a world record in 1960 and a year earlier he set an indoor world record of 15 ft. 9⅝ in. At the 1960 Olympics in Rome Bragg boasted a gold medal with a vault of 15 ft. 5⅛ in, which fell short of his outstanding Olympic trial vault by 4⅛ in. While at Villanova he won three straight IC4A titles 1955–1957, additionally winning two indoor IC4A titles and tying for a third. In 1955 Don set an NCAA record of 15 ft. 1 in. in the same year amassing three indoor AAU championships, two more ending in a tie. In 1959 he won the outdoor title for the AAU with a vault of 15 ft. 3 in.

BREITKREUTZ, Emil
Noteworthy Contributor

BRESNAHAN, George
Coach

BRIX, Herman "Bruce Bennett"
Shot-putter
Born 1909; attended Washington Univ; Olympic Silver Medal 1928; sought movie acting career and starred in *New Adventures of Tarzan* in 1935; starred as Kioga in *Hawk of the Wilderness*, a serial success.

Brix shot-putted 46 ft. 7⅜ in. at age 18 while a Washington student, to win his first championship in NCAA competition. In 1926 he finished fifth in NCAA and then took third in 1928. He fared well in Pacific Coast Conference play, taking championship honors in 1928. At the Olympic Games in Amsterdam, he won the silver in shot-put with 51 ft. 8 1/16 in. But his best AAU title-winning put surpassed that at 52 ft. 5¾ in. in 1930. Altogether Brix held four AAU outdoor titles and two AAU indoor titles, with a 1932 indoor meet record of 51 ft. 4½ in.

BROWN, Earlene
Shot-putter and Discus Thrower

Born July 11, 1935, in Latexo, Tex; Olympic Bronze Medal 1960; now a beautician living in Los Angeles, Calif.

Earlene garnered 13 AAU championships in eight years. During that time, 1956–1964, she set two American outdoor records, swept the discus and shot-put in the 1959 Pan-American Games and competed in the 1958 U.S.-U.S.S.R. dual meet. She was also a member of three consecutive Olympic teams beginning in 1956. Her AAU titles ranged three categories—shot-put, discus and baseball throw. Of her eight shot-put triumphs, the first one earned in 1956, the last six were consecutive with her best toss in 1960 at 49 ft. 8½ in. Earlene won the discus in 1958, the same year she placed second in the U.S.S.R. meet, added her second title in 1959 and a third two years later. The baseball throw championships came in 1956 and 1958. Her Olympic record shows a bronze medal in 1960 in the shot-put and two fourths in the discus. She set American citizen outdoor records in 1960, first in Abilene, Tex, on July 16 when she threw the discus 176 ft. 10 in. and the second one September 21 in Frankfurt, Ger, with a 54 ft. 9 in. toss in the shot-put.

BRUNSON, Emmett
Coach

BURKE, T. Edward
Hammer Thrower

Born March 4, 1940, in Ukiah, Calif; competed in 1968 Olympics despite shoulder injury; now a college history professor.

At the AAU championship contest of June 22, 1967, Burke threw the hammer 235 ft. 11 in. and won the title. He also won the AAU titles of 1966 and 1968, in the latter year showing superior hammer toss ability at the Olympic team trials. At the Mexico City Games, Ed finished in twelfth place with his best toss of 215 ft. 7½ in.

BUTLER, Michael
Coach

CALHOUN, Lee Q.
Hurdler

Born February 23, 1933 in Laurel, Miss; attended N.C. Col; Olympic Gold Medal 1956 and 1960; now assistant track coach at Yale Univ.

Lee's special distinction is being the only man to win two gold medals for the 110-meter hurdles in the Olympics. In 1956 his winning time was 13.5 sec. and at Rome in 1960 he clocked 13.8. At both Olympic Games, Calhoun placed first in a clean sweep by U.S. hurdlers. On August 21, 1960, he ran the 120-yd. and 110-m. high hurdles in 13.2 for a new world record. Lee won the AAU titles 1956–1959 for outdoor hurdles with a best time of 13.6 in his first year. He also snared the AAU indoor 60-yd. championships in 1956 and 1957. While competing for North Carolina, Calhoun took titles in NCAA contests for the 120-yd. hurdles with a best time of 13.6 in 1957. *Also in:* National Association of Intercollegiate Athletics Hall of Fame, National Track and Field Hall of Fame and U.S. Track and Field Hall of Fame.

CAMPBELL, Milton
Decathlon

Born December 9, 1933, in Plainfield, N.J; attended Indiana Univ; played football there; Olympic Silver Medal 1952, Gold Medal 1956; headed New Jersey program for underprivileged; lecturer.

Milt was the first black American to win an Olympic decathlon and he did it by defeating another outstanding black athlete, Rafer Johnson. It seemed the rule that Milt faced exceptionally famous and tough competition, such as Johnson in 1956 and Bob Mathias in 1952. At that Olympics in Helsinki, Campbell's first at age 18, he stuck close enough to earn the silver medal with 6975 points to Mathias' record 7887. At the Melbourne Games four years later he snared the gold through fine performances in several events. He won the 100-m. in 10.8 sec. and the shot with 48 ft. 5 in. He took individual seconds in long jump with 24 ft. ⅝ in, in high jump at 6 ft. 2¼ in, and in 400-m. with 48.8. On the second day he aced his specialty, the 100-m. hurdles, in 14.0, then took second with a 147 ft. 6¾ in. shot-put. A pole vault of only 11 ft. 1¾ in. cost him the world record, yet he compensated by finessing the javelin and 1500-m. events. Campbell's total gold decathlon score set a new Olympic record at 7937.

CARPENTER, Kenneth
Discus Thrower

Born April 19, 1913, in Compton, Calif; attended Univ. Southern Calif; Olympic Gold Medal 1936.

Ken shone for Southern California, twice taking collegiate discus honors. In 1935 he won the NCAA championship with a throw of 157 ft. 11 in. The next year he did it again, tossing the discus a record 173 ft. which was a whopping 10 ft. beyond the previous meet record. In AAU competition, Ken was champ in 1935 with 158 ft. 11 in. and in 1936 with 166 ft. 2 in. He snared the gold medal at the 1936 Games by a throw 3 ft. farther than the established record, measuring 165 ft. 7⅜ in.

CARR, Sabin
Pole Vaulter

Born September 4, 1904, in Dubuque, Iowa; world's first pole vaulter to reach 14 ft; attended Yale Univ; Olympic Gold Medal 1928.

Carr took the outdoor championships in IC4A competition 1926–1928. It was at an IC4A meet in Philadelphia that he vaulted the historic 14 ft. 0 in. on May 25, 1927. Just two years before, his best vault got him 13 ft. 0 in. and 13 ft. 3 in. in 1926. Carr was tied for first at the 1927 indoor IC4A competition, but he took it alone in 1928 with 13 ft. 3¾ in. That year he set a new record for American indoor with a vault of 14 ft. 1 in. At the Games in Amsterdam, the U.S. contender Lee Barnes was predicted formidable, having bettered Sabin's vault by ¾ in, but Carr won the gold with 13 ft. 9½ in. Both silver and bronze went to U.S. teammates other than Barnes who ended in fifth place.

CHRISTIE, Walter
Coach

CLARK, Mack
Coach

COCHRAN, Roy B.
Hurdler

Born January 6, 1919, in Richton, Miss; attended Indiana Univ; Commander in the U.S. Navy during W.W. II; two Olympic Gold Medals 1948.

In 1939 Cochran made his initial showing in AAU competition, running the 400-m. hurdles only one-tenth of a second off the world record with a time of 51.9 sec. A year later he nabbed the AAU championship for Indiana, then again for the Navy in 1942. Roy set a 440-yd. hurdle record by clocking 52.2 at the 1942 Drake Relays. After a six-year hiatus, he returned to track and won two gold medals at the London Olympics when he was 29 years old. His forte was again the 440-yd. hurdles in which he established a new Olympic record at 51.1. The other medal was for team effort in the 1600-m. relay. Cochran claimed another honor in being named finest 440-yd. hurdler of the Drake Relays' first fifty years.
Also in: Drake Relays Hall of Fame and U.S. Track and Field Hall of Fame.

COMSTOCK, Boyd
Coach

CONNEFF, Thomas
Runner

Conneff was an early two-time mile winner in AAU championships. In 1888 he took his first AAU mile title in 4:32.6 which was reduced by 1891 to 4:30.6.

CONNOLLY, Harold
Hammer Thrower

Born August 1, 1931, in Somerville, Mass; married Olga Fikotova, women's discus gold medalist from Czechoslovakia and also in the Hall of Fame; took up hammer throw to strengthen left arm which was slightly withered at birth; broke arm several times competing in sports; Olympic Gold Medal 1956; Pan-Am Gold Medal 1959; teacher by profession.

In 1956 Harold set the world hammer throw record with a heave of 224 ft. 10 in. at Los angeles, Calif. Two years later he improved the mark with a 233 ft. 9 in. Russian rival Mikhail Krivonosov, former world record holder in hammer throw, lost the gold to Harold in the 1956 Olympics. His 1960 and 1964 Olympic appearances were dismal results. In other international meets, Harold claimed the gold medal in the 1959 Pan-American Games, and two firsts in dual meets with the U.S.S.R. in 1958 and 1963. He was an eight-time AAU champion, 1956–1961, 1964 and 1965.
Also in: U.S. Track and Field Hall of Fame.

CONNOLLY, Olga Fikotova
Discus Thrower

Born November 13, 1932, in Praha, Czech; Olympic Gold Medal 1956; married Harold Connolly of U.S. Olympic team and also in Hall of Fame; four children; now a U.S. citizen and housewife.

In the 1956 Olympics, Olga (Fikotova) upset Nina Ponomareva of the U.S.S.R. and secured a gold medal in the discus. Her toss of 176 ft. 1.5 in. bettered Ponomareva's former Olympic mark by eight feet. In 1962 she set the AAU record with a heave of 172 ft. 2 in. That was the third of five AAU discus titles she won, the others being in 1957, 1960, 1964 and 1968. In her later three Olympic appearances, 1964, 1968 and 1972, she did not earn a medal; however, during the 1972 Olympic parade, she led the American delegation with the flag, becoming only the second woman ever to hold the point honor. She is the author of *Rings of Destiny,* an autobiography.
Also in: U.S. Track and Field Hall of Fame.

COPELAND, Lillian
Discus Thrower

Born November 25, 1904, in New York City; Olympic Silver Medal 1928, Gold Medal 1932; died February 7, 1964.

The first year women were allowed to compete in the Olympics, 1928, Lillian won a silver medal in the discus throw at 121 ft. 7⅞ in. Four years later in Los Angeles she bettered her world standing with a gold medal and 133 ft. 1⅝ in. Among her many AAU championships was the shot-put in 1925–1928 and 1931; discus in 1926 and 1927; javelin in 1926 and 1931. While attending the University of Southern California she won every event in which she participated.
Also in: U.S. Track and Field Hall of Fame.

COURTNEY, Tom
Runner

Born August 17, 1933, in Newark, N.J; attended Fordham Univ; two Olympic Gold Medals 1956.

For awhile Courtney seemed relegated to second best behind Arnie Sowell of Pittsburgh, but the curse was broken in 1956. At the Olympic trials for 800-m, Tom came in first with 1:46.4 and Sowell finished second. Courtney pocketed the gold medal for a record time of 1:47.7. Then he won another gold as part of the U.S. 1600-m. relay team. On May 24, 1957, at a Los Angeles contest, Courtney set a new world 880-yd. record with 1:46.8 and took the AAU 880-yd. titles that year and the next. For Fordham in 1955 he won the NCAA crown with 1:49.6. And in 1954 he took IC4A honors for the 1000-yd. indoor.

CRAIG, Ralph
Sprinter

Born June 21, 1889, in Detroit, Mich; graduated from Univ. Mich. 1911; two Olympic Gold Medals 1912; occupied administrative position for the state of New York; died in 1972.

During his last two years at Michigan, Craig won the IC4A championships in 200-m. and 220-yd. with a time of 21.2 sec. which made him co-holder of both straight run records. Another discintion was his being the second man ever to win both the 100-m. and 200-m. in Olympic competition. Only seven men possess a claim to that accomplishment. At the 1912 Olympics the top U.S. sprinter faded back lame, leaving the other U.S. contenders to win the race. Despite a false start and re-run,

Craig pulled through to win the gold medal of the official 100-m. in 10.8. Second and third went to the U.S. in a clean sweep. Craig's medal-winning run of the 200-m. was in 21.7.

CROMWELL, Dean B.

Coach

See entry in Noteworthy Contributors Hall of Fame, Citizens Savings Hall of Fame Athletic Museum.
Also in: National Track and Field Hall of Fame and United States Track and Field Hall of Fame.

CUNNINGHAM, Glenn

Runner

Born August 4, 1909, in Atlanta, Ga; severely burned legs and trained persistently to be able even to walk; attended Kans. Univ; James E. Sullivan Memorial Trophy 1933; founded youth ranch in Kansas.

Cunningham began his famed track career in Kansas. While running for University of Kansas, Cunningham first won the AAU 1500-m. championship in 1932, followed by NCAA top honors for the same event that same year. At the Olympics in Los Angeles he missed a medal finishing in fourth place. Jumping back into AAU competition, Glenn won the 1933 titles in 1500-m. and 800-m. with 3:52.8 and 1:51.8, saving the mile for NCAA honors. Kansas took another NCAA team championship partly due to Cunningham's running 4:09.8 mile. The Princeton Invitational meet of 1934 was the site of his first world and American record-breaking mile run of 4:06.7. But not all of that year turned out to be so glorious. The AAU and NCAA championships of 1934 were snatched up by tough rival Bill Bonthron. In the next two years, however, the Kansas Ironman swung back strongly to retake the AAU titles in the 1500-m. The 1936 Berlin Olympics began with promise for Cunningham when he aced the tryouts with 3:49.9. During the Games 1500-m. run, New Zealander Jack Lovelock flew past for the gold and a record 3:47.8. Back again to AAU competition, Cunningham swept up the 1937 and 1938 titles and made his fastest time ever in his last formal competition, with 3:48.0, a full-potential effort but second-place result.
Also in: Drake Relays Hall of Fame, National Track and Field Hall of Fame and U.S. Track and Field Hall of Fame.

CURTIS, William B.

Noteworthy Contributor

Born January 17, 1837, in Salisbury, Vt; died in 1900.

In the years 1876, 1878 and 1880, Curtis won the AAU 16-lb. hammer throw championship, with a distance of 87 ft. 4¼ in. In 1878 he also won the AAU 56-lb. hammer throw championship with a throw of 21 ft. Curtis excelled in numerous things besides his track and field specialities. In fact, he is remembered best today not for his own athleticism, but as the "Father of American Rowing," and as the "Father of American Amateurism." During the 1870s it was understood in North America that a "professional" was an athlete who competed for pay or for cash prizes, and that an "amateur" was one who didn't. In 1872 the Schuylkill Navy, an organization of Philadelphia area rowing clubs, staged a rowing regatta in which many applicants were rejected as professionals because they had made side bets on various races—a common practice amoung athletes at the time. These rejected oarsmen appealed the decision. Curtis and a Philadelphia newspaperman, James Watson, were called in to study the problem. The result of their study was the publication of two influential pamphlets, "What Is an Amateur?" and "Who Is an Amateur?" These pamphlets defined a professional as anyone who competes in the hope of receiving any sort of cash prize, including side bets. With a few minor modifications and elaborations, that definition was accepted throughout the sports world and incorporated into the Olympic Games, which were revived 24 years after the appearance of those two little pamphlets. William B. Curtis is one of the very few people in American history who is remembered as the "Father of" two different things.

DAVENPORT, Willie

Hurdler

Born June 8, 1943, in Troy, Ala; Olympic Gold Medal 1968.

Prior to the 1964 Rome Olympics, the young Davenport had not had much hurdling experience. That plus an injury caused him to fail to make the finals for the Games. But in the interim leading up to a second chance in 1968, Willie became a capable collector of AAU top honors. He was the AAU champion in outdoor 110-m. hurdles 1965–1967 with a pair of 13.3 sec. clockings. And he was the AAU champ in indoor 60-yd. hurdles 1966, 1967 and 1969–1971, with fastest 6.9 and 7.0. Then at the Mexico City Games, Willie poured it on to win the gold medal for 110-m. in 13.3. Four years later he showed promise as a medal-contender by finishing second in 13.5 at the Olympic team tryouts. But the same time recorded during the Games only got him fifth.
Also in: National Association of Intercollegiate Athletics Hall of Fame.

DAVIS, Alice Coachman

High Jumper

Born November 9, 1923, in Albany, Ga; attended Tuskegee Institute; received B.S. from Albany State Col; Olympic Gold Medal 1948; now a physical education teacher in Atlanta, Ga.

Alice was the first American woman to win a gold medal in track and field in the postwar Olympics. She earned it in the high jump in 1948 at London, setting an Olympic record with a leap of 5 ft. 6⅛ in. She was the AAU champion three times; 1941, 1945 and 1946.
Also in: National Track and Field Hall of Fame and Tuskegee Institute Athletic Hall of Fame.

DAVIS, Glenn Ashby "Jeep"

Hurdler and Runner

Born September 12, 1934, in Wellsburg, W. Va; both parents died during his youth; high school days spent under brother's guardianship; attended Ohio State Univ; aspired to professional football but did not make Detroit Lions; James E. Sullivan Memorial Trophy 1958; Olympic Gold Medal 1956, two Gold Medals 1960.

Davis was a star even in high school when at one meet he scored 18 points single-handedly by finishing first in three events. His score alone bettered the other teams' so Barberton High School aced the Ohio state championship. Then at Ohio State University, Davis was sort of jack-of-all-trades, competing not just in his specialty,

hurdles, but in sprints and long jump too. From 1956 through 1958 he won the AAU 440-yd. hurdles championships, producing a world record 49.9 sec. in 1958. And that same year he made a record 45.7 in the NCAA 440-yd. dash, winning the championship hands down. In July, 1958, at Oslo, Norway, Glenn won four events in two days, including the 100-m, 200-m. and 400-m. runs, and the 400-m. hurdles. In 1956 and 1958 Glenn held the record for the 400-m. hurdles with 49.5 and 49.2, according to respective years. This was his specialty race for both Olympics and which won him gold medals both times. At the 1956 Games in Melbourne, Davis ran the 400-m. hurdles in 50.1 and in a record 49.3 four years later at the Rome Olympics. As a member of the 1600-m. relay team, he was awarded another 1960 Olympic medal. One Davis-made record still stands for the 200-m. hurdles which on August 20, 1960, in Bern, Switz, he completed in 22.5.
Also in: National Track and Field Hall of Fame, West Virginia Sports Writers Hall of Fame and U.S. Track and Field Hall of Fame.

DAVIS, Harold "Hal"
Sprinter
Born January 5, 1921, in Salinas, Calif; attended Univ. Calif. at Berkeley; career interrupted by W.W. II.

As California champion, Davis racked up four NCAA titles for 100-yd. and 220-yd. in 1942 and 1943, plus AAU 100-m. firsts those same years and in 1940. He was only 19 when he ran a swift and astounding 10.3 sec. At Compton, Calif, on June 6, 1941, he ran 10.2 to co-hold the great Jesse Owens record set five years previously. Also Davis won AAU championships in 200-m. 1940–1943, with a wind-backed 20.2 for his best time in 1943. Due to circumstances, Davis never gained Olympic recognition, but those who knew saw him as a king of sprinters. He ran the 100-yd. dash in 9.4, but the time was never officially made a world record.
Also in: National Track and Field Hall of Fame.

DAVIS, Jack
Hurdler
Born September 11, 1930, in Amarillo, Tex; attended Univ. Southern Calif; became president of a vacation resort in California; Olympic Silver Medals 1952 and 1956.

From 1951 through 1953 Davis won the NCAA high hurdles championships three in a row, taking additional top honors for NCAA low hurdles in 1953. He set a world record of 22.2 sec. for the 220-yard hurdles and won both high and low AAU championships in 1953 and 1954. His first Olympic experience in 110-m. and 120-yd. hurdles placed him second to Harrison Dillard although both matched times of 13.7. In 1956 Jack set outstanding record time in an AAU preliminary run with 13.4. That year at the Olympic trials he tied with Lee Calhoun at 13.8, portending what was to come although Jack again ran a 13.4 with the wind just previous to the Games. Then at Melbourne, both Calhoun and Davis photo-finished with 13.5, earning Jack the silver medal while Calhoun got the gold.

DELANY, Ron
Runner
Born March 6, 1935, in Arklow, County Wicklow, Ireland; attended Villanova Univ; Olympic Gold Medal 1956.

Ron had the knack of winning just about everything he entered. In fact, by the time he halted competition, save for relay running in 1961, there was a string of 34 indoor mile victories to his credit. On three occasions he ran the mile in less than four min, and he won the NCAA mile titles in 1957 and 1958. Also, while at Villanova Delany won three straight IC4A and four AAU indoor miles, his best time at 4:02.5 in 1959. In 1956 he won the NCAA championship in the 1500-m. and the 880-yd. in 1958. At the 1956 Olympics, Ron led the pack in the 1500-m. and all runners broke the record, then newly set by Delany's gold medal effort of 3:41.2.

DeMAR, Clarence
Marathon Runner
Born June 7, 1888, in Madeira, Ohio; sole American to come close to Olympic marathon victory since Johnny Haye's in 1908; died June 11, 1958.

DeMar ran the Olympic marathon in 1924 and placed third. As for national performance, he entered the Boston marathon 25 times and always persevered to the finish. Seven times he finished first in line; in 1911, 1922–1924, 1927, 1928 and 1930. His first Boston marathon record was broken in 1912, but the 2:18:10 set in 1922 held firm for 34 years. Clarence won the AAU marathon championship three times 1926–1928, his best time being 2:37:7.8 in the last year.

DENI, John
Walker

DILLARD, Harrison
Hurdler
Born July 8, 1923, in Cleveland, Ohio; attended Baldwin-Wallace Col; Olympic Gold Medal 1948; three Gold Medals 1952; James E. Sullivan Memorial Trophy 1955; affiliated with Cleveland school system; writes sports column for *Cleveland Press.*

During college at AAU and NCAA competitions, Dillard won both 120-yd. high hurdles and 220-yd. low hurdles 1946 and 1947. A time of 13.6 sec. earned him a world record in the highs, while 22.3 held it for lows. In 1948 Dillard had won 82 straight hurdle races when an abrupt loss prompted him not to attempt to qualify for that event in Olympic trials. Instead he pursued the 100-m. sprint and made the team in that capacity. At the London Games, Dillard edged past Barney Ewell and Mel Patton in a record time of 10.3 which tied Jesse Owens' record. Another turnover resulted at the 1952 Games in Helsinki when Dillard squeezed by Jack Davis to take the gold medal with 13.7. Altogether Dillard's medals numbered four, two more having been earned as relay runner in the 400-m. He is the only person ever to win gold medals for both sprints and hurdles.
Also in: Drake Relays Hall of Fame, National Association of Intercollegiate Athletics Hall of Fame, National Track and Field Hall of Fame and U.S. Track and Field Hall of Fame.

DODDS, Gilbert
Runner
Attended Ashland Col; Janes E. Sullivan Memorial Trophy 1943.

Dodds won the NCAA cross-country title for Ashland in 1940. Then he went on to specialize in the mile, taking AAU honors 1942–1944, 1947 and 1948. His fastest time was 3:50.0.
Also in: National Association of Intercollegiate Athletics Hall of Fame.

DODSON, Dorothy
Shot-putter, Discus and Javelin Thrower
Dorothy dominated the field events in AAU competition during the 1940s. Participating in three events, she claimed the 8 lb. shot-put three times, 1944, 1946 and 1947. In 1946 she added to her shot-put crown with the discus throw championship at 102 ft. 6 in. For eleven consecutive years 1939–1949, she was the javelin queen with her best heave in 1939 at 130 ft. 9.5 in.

DOHERTY, Dr. J. Kenneth
Coach
Born in Detroit, Mich; graduated from Wayne State Univ. 1927; received Ph.D. in educational psychiatry from Univ. Mich. 1948; wife Lucile; two sons, Lynn and Robert, both Ph.D.s and university teachers; currently residing in Swarthmore, Pa.

1939–1948 University of Michigan, head coach
1948–1959 University of Pennsylvania, head coach

Besides coaching University of Michigan track teams that won 7 of a possible 18 Conference team championships, Doherty also authored four textbooks on coaching used throughout American high schools and colleges. These books have been translated into Russian, Finnish, Spanish and Japanese. Doherty achieved recognition as author, meet promoter, coach and athlete. In 1928 and 1929 he won the AAU decathalon championship, set the American record for 1929 and won a bronze medal in the 1928 Olympics. He served as the director of the Pennsylvania Relay Carnival and the *Philadelphia Inquirer* Charities Meet. In 1935 he was the Big Ten championship director and in 1959 directed the first U.S.-U.S.S.R. dual track meet.
Also in: National Track and Field Hall of Fame.

DONAHUE, James
Track and Field

DREW, Harold
Coach
Though later famous as a coach, Drew was himself an outstanding athlete. He won the U.S. men's championship in the 100-yd. dash in 1912 with a time of 10.0 sec. In 1913 he again won the 100-yd. dash with a time of 10.4 and also took the 220-yd. dash championship with a time of 22.8.

DREYER, Henry F.
Hammer Thrower
Attended R.I. State Univ.

Henry Dreyer nearly dominated amateur hammer-throwing 1934–1952. In 1934 he won the NCAA hammer throw championship with a mark of 169 ft. 8⅜ in. As AAU champion, his longest throw for the 16 lb. hammer was 168 ft. 8½ in. in 1935. In 1951 he set his highest AAU 56 lb. hammer throw mark at 41 ft. 6¾ in. In the 1942 35 lb. weight throw, he reached his best AAU mark of 55 ft. 11¼ in.

DUMAS, Charles
High Jumper
Born December 2, 1937, in Tulsa, Okla; first to high jump 7 ft. (2.1 m.); Olympic Gold Medal 1956.

Dumas used a characteristic style in the high jump, with a slow run up to the bar followed by a tremendous spring upward to clear it. He started to gain inches in 1954, going from 6 ft. 5½ in. to 6 ft. 10¼ in. Then at the 1956 Olympic trials he jumped the never-before-attained 7 ft. ¼ in. A height of one inch less won him the gold medal and an Olympic record at the Melbourne Games. Four years later Dumas finished in sixth place at the Rome Olympics with a jump of 6 ft. 7⅞ in. Throughout this time Dumas was consistent in winning the AAU titles four years in a row, 1956–1959.

DUSSAULT, Clarence
Coach

DUVALL, Edith McGuire
Sprinter
Born June 3, 1944, in Atlanta, Ga; presently a school-teacher; attended Tenn. State Univ; Olympic Gold Medal and Silver Medal 1964; Pan-Am Gold Medal 1963.

Publicized as the next Wilma Rudolph in the 1964 Tokyo Olympics, Edith earned a silver in the 100-m. dash, behind Wilma, and broke the 200-m. record for the gold with a 23.0 sec. Wilma had set the record four years earlier. Edith won the gold in the Pan-American Games in 1963, with a record-tying 11.5 in the 100-m. She won an AAU championship in the 100-m. in 1963 in 11.0 and two in the 200-m. 1964 and 1965.
Also in: United States Track and Field Hall of Fame.

EASTMAN, Benjamin
Runner
Born July 9, 1911, in Burlingame, Calif; attended Stanford Univ; Olympic Silver Medal 1932.

In the course of his career, Eastman had eight world records credited to his name, the majority of them in quarter mile which was his specialty. While at Stanford he established the first record with 47.4 sec. in the 440-yd. and 400-m, which in one year was whittled down to 46.4. Just before the 1932 Olympics, the favorite Eastman was defeated in both the tryouts and IC4A competition. Then at the Los Angeles Games, Eastman fell short of the gold medal in the 400-m. but managed to seize hold of the silver. Subsequently he began concentrating on the 880-yd. and 800-m. in which he set a new record 1:49.8 at Princeton, N.J, on June 16, 1934. He won the AAU title with a time of 1:50.8. Eastman practiced for the 1936 Olympics but failed to make the team despite a 1:50.1 to his credit in a prep run. His other achievements were as anchorman of the mile and 1600-m. relay teams of Stanford which ran a record 3:12.6 on May 8, 1931, at Fresno, Calif.
Also in: U.S. Track and Field Hall of Fame.

EASTON, Millard E. "Bill"
Coach
Born September 13, 1906, in Stinesville, Ind; graduated from Ind. Univ; coached at Hammond (Ind.) High School; Top College Coach 1960; currently an assistant professor of physical education at Kans. Univ, Lawrence, Kans.

1941 – 1947 Drake University, coach and director of Drake Relays
1947 University of Kansas, coach

While coaching at Drake, Easton won three NCAA titles. When he moved to Kansas his achievements surpassed his previous marks; he led Kansas to 39 Big Eight team titles 1947 – 1956 and NCAA outdoor team titles 1959 and 1960. In all, he coached 39 All-Americans and 8 Olympians, including Bill Neider, Al Oerter, and Billy Mills, all of whom won Olympic gold medals. Easton was named honorary referee of the 1970 Kansas relays and the 1970 NCAA championships.
Also in: National Track and Field Hall of Fame and United States Track and Field Hall of Fame.

EDMUNDSON, Clarence "Hec"
Coach
See entry in College Basketball Hall of Fame, Citizens Savings Hall of Fame Athletic Museum (Induction Year Unrecorded).

ELLIOT, James F. "Jumbo"
Coach
Born August 8, 1915, in Philadelphia; graduated from Villanova Univ. 1935; excelled in relays; part-time manager of contracting equipment company.

Elliot, one of the most successful track coaches in the United States, has produced many outstanding athletes at Villanova. He has coached over 22 Olympic team members of whom five won gold medals and three won silver medals. His Villanova Wildcat teams have won 30 IC4A outdoor, indoor and cross-country team titles plus one NCAA outdoor title, two indoor NCAA titles and 203 IC4A individual championships. His athletes have set 14 world records and 31 American indoor records.

EWELL, Norwood "Barney"
Sprinter
Born February 25, 1918, in Harrisburg, Pa; attended Pa. State University.

At the 1948 London Games, Ewell's best was ruled not good enough when the gold medal for 100-m. was awarded to Harrison Dillard who had squeezed past Ewell to tear the tape first. In the Games trials, Ewell set his best record by running the 100-m. in 10.2 sec. and in the race against Dillard he clocked 10.4. Another silver medal went to him for a 21.1 time in the 200-m. although he did snare a gold due to a stint on the first place 400-m. relay team. Ewell's running career spanned 11 years but his peak years were those in which W.W. II precluded Olympic events. During college days he won both 100-m. and 200-m. sprints in NCAA competition 1940 and 1941. He won the titles for both sprints in IC4A competition 1940, 1941 and 1943. His 10.3 run of the 100-m. in 1941 and 1945 earned him AAU titles as well as in 1948 with 10.6. As for the 200-m, Ewell took AAU titles in 1939 with 21.0, in 1946 at 21.2, and in 1947 at 21.0.

EWRY, Ray C.
Standing Jumper
Born October 14, 1873, in Lafayette, Ind; sickly as youth and encouraged by doctor to exercise; won ten Olympic Gold Medals; died September 29, 1937.

Ewry was a whiz at the standing jumps which included long, high and triple. All three have been discontinued and Ewry's records still hold. In 1900 at the Paris Games, he won the standing high jump with 5 ft. 5 in. and the standing long jump with 10 ft. 6⅜ in. The gold for the standing triple jump became his also with 34 ft. 8½ in. The first two events were completely dominated by Ewry again at the 1904 St. Louis Games, in 1906 at Athens and in 1908 at London. But the standing triple jump got him one other gold medal at the 1904 Olympiad to number 10 in total. His best efforts were the results that won the three 1900 medals, although he later extended the standing long jump to 11 ft. 4⅞ in.
Also in: National Track and Field Hall of Fame and U.S. Track and Field Hall of Fame.

FARRELL, Edward
Coach
As a member of the New York Athletic Club's 440-yd. relay team, Farrell helped his teammates win the U.S. men's championships in 1921 and 1922. Their winning times were 42.4 sec. and 43.3 respectively.

FARRELL, Stephan
Coach

FERRELL, Barbara
Sprint
Born July 28, 1947, in Hattiesburg, Miss; attended Calif. State Univ. at Los Angeles; Pan-Am Gold Medal 1967; two Olympic Golds and a Silver Medal 1968.

Barbara set the world 100-m. record at Santa Barbara, Calif, on July 2, 1967, with an 11.1 sec. The year prior to the 1968 Olympics she earned a gold in the Pan-American Games with an 11.5 and claimed the AAU championship in 11.1. She tied her record, 11.1, at the Olympics but it was only good enough for a silver, won the gold while setting an American record in the 200-m. with a 22.8 and ran on the gold medal 400-m. relay team.

FERRIS, Daniel J.
Contributor
See entry in Noteworthy Contributors Hall of Fame, Citizens Savings Hall of Fame Athletic Museum.
Also in: National Track and Field Hall of Fame.

FETZER, Robert
Coach

FITZPATRICK, Keane
Coach

FLANAGAN, John J.
Hammer Thrower
Born 1873 in County Limerick, Ireland; a policeman by profession in New York City; upon retirement returned to Ireland to coach; Olympic Gold Medal 1900, a Gold and a Silver Medal 1904, three Gold Medals 1908; died in 1938.

Through the years Flanagan dabbled in discus and the 56-lb. weight throw, faring well in both. But the hammer toss was his forte. Early in his career in 1897, John threw a record 150 ft. 8 in. at a meet in Bayonne, N.J, which he then perfected, eventually tossing past 180 ft. On July 24, 1909, at New Haven, Conn, he threw a remarkable

184 ft. 4 in. In the years leading up to his peak performance his winning throws were less spectacular. A toss of 167 ft. 4 in. won him the gold medal at the 1900 Paris Games. In 1904 at St. Louis his winning toss was 168 ft. 1 in. Additionally, he placed in two other events; second in the 56-lb. weight throw with 33 ft. 4 in. and fourth in the discus. The 1908 London Games made him a rarity in having won three gold medals in the same event. He took the hammer toss championship again with 170 ft. 4¼ in. Although Flanagan was not a college student he nevertheless took honors in AAU competition in hammer toss for a total of seven years and in 56-lb. weight throw for six years.
Also in: National Track and Field Hall of Fame and U.S. Track and Field Hall of Fame.

FORD, M. W.
Standing Broad Jumper
As a practitioner of a now defunct event, the standing broad jump, Ford was a master. He outdid all others to win the AAU titles 1883–1886 and 1889. And in that span of years he improved his honor-winning jumps from 22 ft. ¾ in. to 22 ft. 7½ in. He was also the all-around champion in AAU competition in 1885, 1886 and 1888.

FUQUA, Ivan
Coach
In 1933 and 1934 Fuqua was the U.S. champion in the 440-yd. race with times of 47.7 and 47.4 sec. respectively. He later became a famous coach.

GEIS, Matthew
Coach

GIBSON, John
Coach

GILL, Harry L.
Coach
Born January 9, 1876, in Feserton, Ont; founder and owner of Harry Gill and Co. Athletic Equipment; died August 31, 1956, in Orillia, Ont.

Beginning in 1904, Gill served over 30 years as the University of Illinois track coach. In 1907 he won the first of 11 Big Ten titles but his teams also finished second 7 times, third 4 times, fourth 4 times, fifth 3 times and sixth once. In 1921 and 1927 he won NCAA titles and coached four NCAA individual winners. His dual meet record was 117 wins, 27 losses and 2 ties.
Also in: United States Track and Field Hall of Fame.

GORDIEN, Fortune
Discus Thrower
Born September 9, 1922, in Spokane, Wash; attended Univ. Minn; track coach at San Bernardino Junior Col; Olympic Bronze Medal 1948, Silver Medal 1956.

Gordien kept himself in shape and in competition for over 25 years, winning his last discus championship at age 48 with a 147 ft. throw at a U.S. Masters international track team meet. In 1960 at age 38 he threw 187 ft. 10 in. which in his entire career had been bested only by a stupendous world record throw of 194 ft. 6 in. on August 22, 1953. The record stood for ten years. Gordien had a good year in 1953, tossing farther than 185 ft. eight times. A record of 183 ft. 9½ in. in AAU competition set in that year held stɛ ɹe for six years. All in all, Gordien captured six AAU championships and won three consecutive titles in NCAA competition while a student at Minnesota. Despite having three tries for a gold medal, Gordien did not win any. At the 1948 Games in London he received the bronze for a 166 ft. 7 in. discus toss, placing fourth in the 1952 Games. A 179 ft. 9½ in. throw earned the silver at the 1956 Olympiad in Melbourne.
Also in: Drake Relays Hall of Fame.

GORDON, Edward
Long Jumper
Born July 1, 1908, in Jackson, Miss; attended Univ. Iowa; Olympic Gold Medal 1932.

Gordon was a top competitor in the long jump for over ten years, especially 1929–1932. While at Iowa he won three NCAA championships going 24 ft. 8½ in., then 25 ft, and 24 ft. 11⅜ in. in 1931. In 1932 he took the AAU title with 25 ft. 3⅜ in. which was 11⅛ in. over his 1929 AAU winning leap. At the 1932 Olympics in Los Angeles, Gordon faced tough competition from Japan, yet he won the gold with 25 ft. ¾ in. Gordon earned AAU indoor titles with 23 ft. 4 in. in 1938, and 23 ft. 10⅛ in. in 1939.
Also in: Drake Relays Hall of Fame.

GRANT, Alex
Runner
Grant took an extremely active part in AAU contests 1899–1903, with the exception of 1902 when no competition was scheduled. He won the AAU mile titles 1901–1903, with a 4:35.8 best time. He also won the 2-mi. championship 1899–1901 and 1903.

GRAY, George R.
Shot-putter
See entry in Canada's Sports Hall of Fame.

GREENE, Charles Edward
Sprinter
Born March 21, 1945, in Pine Bluff, Ark; attended Univ. Nebr; Olympic Gold Medal and Bronze Medal 1968.

June 20, 1968, was a historic day when Charlie Greene, Jim Hines and Ronnie Ray Smith all clocked a record-breaking 9.9 sec. in the 100-m. semifinals at Sacramento, Calif. Then in the finals of that AAU meet, Greene dashed to win the championship with 10.0. One year previously, he ran the 100-yd. in 9.1 which tied the record held by Bob Hayes and two other champions. That record prevailed for nine more years until finally set again in 1974 by Ivory Crockett who ran a flat 9.0. At the Mexico City Olympics in 1968 Greene fared promisingly in the semis but ended third behind a Jamaican runner and gold medalist, Jim Hines. Hines ran 9.9 again and Greene ran 10.0. He did win a gold as part of the record-breaking 400-m. relay team that clocked 38.2. While at Nebraska, Greene took the NCAA titles in 100-yd. three times 1965–1967, with 9.4, 9.3 and 9.2. In 1966 he won the AAU title for 100-yd. with 9.4.
Also in: Drake Relays Hall of Fame.

GREGORY, Louis
Long Distance Runner
Lt. in Army during W.W. II.

Louis Gregory made his mark in distance running between 1929 and 1943. He was the AAU six-mile champion 1929–1931, 1933, 1939, 1941 and 1943. His times respectively for that distance were: 33:47.7, 31:31.3, 31:26.4, 32:39.4, 33:11.5, 33:11 and 33:22. During the years 1933 to 1939, he was a member of AAU champion cross-country team all but one year.

GRIFFIN, George
Coach

GRIFFITH, John L.
Noteworthy Contributor
See entry in Noteworthy Contributors Hall of Fame, Citizens Savings Hall of Fame Athletic Museum.

HAHN, Archie
Sprinter
Born 1880 in Milwaukee, Wis; attended Univ. Mich; three Olympic Gold Medals 1904, one 1906; author of track treatise, *How to Sprint;* died January 21, 1955, in Charlottesville, Va.

In 1901 Archie began his career by running the 100-yd. dash in 9.8 sec. which made him co-holder of a world record. Later he became a three-time champion in AAU competition, taking both 220-yd. and 100-yd. in 1903 and the 220-yd. in 1905. Hahn's performance at the 1904 St. Louis Olympics was worth three gold medals—the 60-m, 100-m. and 200-m. runs. Going 21.6 in the 200-m, he set a record that lasted 17 years. In 1906 at Athens Hahn won the 100-m. dash and with it a fourth gold medal.
Also in: U.S. Track and Field Hall of Fame.

HALL, Evelyn
Hurdler
Evelyn won the 1930 AAU 80-m. hurdles in 13.05 sec.

HAMILTON, Brutus
Coach
Born July 19, 1900, in Peculiar, Mo; Olympic Silver Medal in decathlon 1920; Greatest Amateur Athlete of Mo. 1950; served in Army Air Corps; died December 28, 1970, in Berkeley, Calif.

Brutus Hamilton was head coach at the University of California at Berkeley 1932–1965. In that time his teams took second in six NCAA championships and won 14 NCAA individual titles. He was assistant coach to the 1932 and 1936 Olympic teams and coach for the 1952 Games. He was also the coach of the 1965 U.S. international team. Under his guidance, the United States won 13 gold medals and set 2 world records, 7 Olympic records, and equaled 2 more.
Also in: National Track and Field Hall of Fame.

HAMM, Edward
Long Jumper
Born April 13, 1906, in Lonoke, Ark; attended Ga. Inst. of Technol; Olympic Gold Medal 1928.

In NCAA competition while a student at Georgia Tech, Ed took long jump championships 1927 and 1928. An even 25 ft. was enough to win in 1928. He won the AAU title that same year with a world record 25 ft. 11 in. at Cambridge, Mass. Hamm's gold medal long jump at the 1928 Olympics in Amsterdam covered more distance than that of the Haitian contender, who was said to have exceeded 26 ft. Ed's winning jump, however, was 25 ft. 4¼ in.

HANNER, J. Flint
Coach
In 1922 Hanner was the U.S. champion in the javelin throw with a mark of 193 ft. 2¼ in. He took the NCAA javelin crown in 1921 with a throw of 191 ft. 2¼ in. Hanner went on to be one of the top track coaches in the United States.
Also in: National Association of Intercollegiate Athletics Hall of Fame.

HARALSON, James B.
Noteworthy Contributor

HARDIN, Glen
Hurdler
Born July 1, 1910, in Derma, Miss; attended La. State Univ; Olympic Gold Medal 1936; son Billy a world class 440-yd. hurdler in 1960s.

While at Louisiana State University, Glen won the NCAA 440-yd. dash 1933 and 1934. His best time was 46.5 sec. His 50.6 in the hurdles in 1934 stood until 1953. In the 1932 Olympics he set a record pace of 52.0 but was disqualified when he knocked down a hurdle. He later bettered it in Stockholm with a 50.6. He ran a 51.8 in 1934 to win the AAU championship. After laying aside hurdling for a year, Glen qualified for the 1936 Olympic team and garnered the gold medal with his 52.4 clocking. He won the 1933, 1934 and 1936 AAU 440-yd. hurdles.
Also in: Drake Relays Hall of Fame and U.S. Track and Field Hall of Fame.

HAYES, E. C. "Billy"
Coach
Also in: United States Track and Field Hall of Fame.

HAYES, Robert Lee
Sprinter
Born December 20, 1942, in Jacksonville, Fla; great track and football athlete at Florida A&M Col; two Olympic Gold Medals 1964; star pass receiver of Dallas Cowboys.

Despite a bow-legged gait and muscular 5 ft. 11 in, 192 lb. physique, Bob Hayes has been called the "World's Fastest Human" and rightly so. At the National AAU contest in St. Louis on June 21, 1963, Hayes ran the 100-yd. dash in 9.1 sec. to tie the world record. Following this accomplishment in the semis, he tried to maintain the same speed in the finals which again got him a 9.1 although it was disallowed because of wind. He was timed between the 60- and 75-yd. marks at 27.89 m.p.h. Even with the wind in his face, Hayes made waves with established records. At the Florida Athletic Club Invitational in 1963, he ran the 220-yd. in 20.6 to tie a world record, battling an 8 m.p.h. wind every step of the way. At the 1964 Tokyo Olympics, Hayes ran the 100-m. in 10.0 for an Olympic record although the wind at his back disallowed its status as world record. His outstanding performance was an anchorman of the U.S. relay team which came from behind two meters to beat the favored Poles by three meters in a record 39.0. Hayes' fast last leg of the relay was the equivalent of the 100-yd. dash in 8.8.
Also in: Drake Relays Hall of Fame and National Track and Field Hall of Fame.

HAYLETT, Ward
Coach

HAYWARD, William
Coach
Born June 2, 1868; grew up in Toronto, Ont; died in 1949 at age 81.

Billy, who is commonly recognized as the "Father of Oregon Track," began his long coaching career at the University of Oregon in 1904. He is credited with developing some of the greatest track men of the era—Mack Robinson, Boyd Brown (javelin), Ralph Hill (5000-m.), George Varoff and Dan Kelly (sprinters). In 1920 he was named assistant coach for the U.S. Olympic team. Recognizing his contributions to the sport and the university, the stadium at Oregon is named in his honor.

HEDLUND, Oscar
Coach

HELD, Franklin "Bud"
Javelin Thrower
Born October 25, 1927, in Los Angeles, Calif; attended Stanford Univ; first to fling javelin beyond 260 ft. or 80 meters; initiated new javelin structure and design; Pan-Am Gold Medal 1955.

Bud's accomplishments were more with equipment than with gold medals. At the 1952 Olympics he finished in ninth place due to an injured shoulder and four years later had to bypass the Olympic tryouts for a similar reason. Yet he won a gold medal in 1955 at the Pan-American Games. On August 8, 1953, Bud threw the javelin 263 ft. 10 in. for a new world record, nabbing the title of first to cross the 80-m. mark. His 1955 winning throw was 268 ft. 2½ in. and a practice throw close on the heels of the foregone Olympic trials sailed to 270 ft. For Stanford Bud won three NCAA titles 1948–1950, also taking first in five AAU contests. His best AAU throw measured 269 ft. 3 in. After leaving college Bud concentrated on developing a shorter javelin with weight contained less on the point and more evenly distributed, which did much to improve the efficiency of a throw.

HIGGINS, Ralph
Coach

HILL, Frank
Coach

HILLMAN, Harry
Coach
Born August 9, 1881; three Olympic Gold Medals 1904, one Silver Medal 1908.

Hillman shone in his three Olympic performances. In the 1904 games at St. Louis, he was a triple gold medal winner, winning in the 400-m. (440-yd.) race in 49.6 sec, the 400-m. low hurdles in 53.0 and the 200-m. (220-yd.) hurdles in 24.6. In the unofficial Athens Olympics of 1906, an illness hampered his performance and he only placed fifth in the 400-m. race. In the 1908 London Olympics, he placed second in the 400-m. hurdles. At home he won the 1903 and 1908 AAU 440-yd. race. After his own outstanding amateur career, he went on to an excellent coaching career at Dartmouth College.
Also in: United States Track and Field Hall of Fame.

HINKEL, Harry
Walker
Harry won the AAU two-mi. walk in 1935 and 1936 and the one-mi. walk in 1926, 1928 and 1929.

HORINE, George
High Jumper
Born February 3, 1890, in Escondido, Calif; attended Stanford Univ; first to high jump to 6 ft. 7 in. or 2-m. mark; contributed new style of jump; Olympic Bronze Medal 1912.

Horine began by setting a new collegiate record high jump of 6 ft. 4¾ in. in 1912. Then the world record was his with 6 ft. 6⅛ in. on March 29 of the same year. It was on May 18, 1912, that he broke his own record with the historic 6 ft. 7 in. leap, a height he owed to a new technique of jump known as "western roll." Later that year at the Stockholm Olympics, George won the bronze with 6 ft. 2½ in. barely below Alma Richards' winning 6 ft. 4 in. In 1915 the National AAU title went to George for a jump of 6 ft. ¾ in.

HOUSER, Clarence
Shot-putter and Discus Thrower
Born September 25, 1901, in Wennigin, Mo; attended Univ. Southern Calif; two Olympic Gold Medals 1924, one 1928; dentist in Palm Springs, Calif.

Houser is one of the few athletes to have won a gold medal in both shot and discus, which he did at the 1924 Olympic Games in Paris. His winning shot mark was 49 ft. 2⅔ in. while the gold medal discus toss measured a record 151 ft. 5⅛ in. At the 1928 Olympics in Athens, another gold medal for discus went to his credit, pushing up his own record to 155 ft. 3 in. In AAU competition, Houser took discus titles 1925–1928 while capturing the AAU shot championships in 1921 and 1925. While at Stanford he won the NCAA championship in discus in 1926 and the IC4A title for discus 1925 and 1926. Also in 1926 Houser remained shot-put champion by winning the IC4A title.

HOUSTON, Lawrence
Noteworthy Contributor

HOYT, Charles "Chuck"
Coach
Hoyt, who was to become an outstanding coach, began his career as an exceptional athlete. His best events were the sprints; he was a 200-yd. (200 m.) champion.
Also in: Drake Relays Hall of Fame.

HUBBARD, William DeHart
Long Jumper
Born November 23, 1904, in Cincinnati, Ohio; ran on Univ. Cincinnati track team at age 15; attended Univ. Mich; Olympic Gold Medal 1924; one of three blacks among 110 U.S. Olympians in 1924; for some time supervised public recreation program in Cincinnati.

As a high school student competing for Cincinnati, Hubbard won the 100-yd. dash, the broad jump, and the hop, step and jump, which launched him into a promising collegiate career. He took the AAU titles 1922–1927 for long jump with performances never again equaled; 25 ft. 8¾ in. was his best in 1927. A slightly shorter 25 ft. 2 in. won him the NCAA long jump crown for 1923 when he

was a student at Michigan. Two years later he set a new NCAA record at 25 ft. 10⅞ in. which went 7⅞ in. beyond the record set one year before. He also ran a winning 9.8 sec. in the 100-yd. dash. At the Paris Olympics of 1924 Hubbard made a 24 ft. 5⅛ in. long jump which earned the gold medal. But his triple jump efforts did not get him into the finals. In 1928 the long jump was again his Olympic specialty, but ankle trouble and an unspectacular 23 ft. 4 in. jump did not take him far enough.
Also in: Drake Relays Hall of Fame.

HUTSELL, Ward
Coach

JACOBS, John
Coach

JENKINS, Chester
Coach

JOHNSON, Cornelius
High Jumper

Born August 21, 1913, in Los Angeles, Calif; attended Wilberforce Univ; Olympic Gold Medal 1936; died February 15, 1940.

As a student of Los Angeles High School and a 1932 Olympic contender, Johnson narrowly missed winning a medal by placing fourth in high jump with 6 ft. 5⅝ in. after a four-man jump-off. But his first years in college saw him alternately win and tie for AAU honors, winning in 1933 and 1935, and tying in 1932, 1934, and 1936. His 1934 high jump of 6 ft. 8⅝ in. was an AAU best and tied him with Walter Marty. On February 22, 1936, Johnson set a record indoor jump at New York's Madison Square Garden with 6 ft. 8 15/16 in. which he topped by nearly ⅞ in. on July 12 to make him co-holder of the world high jump record. That record jump of 6 ft. 9¾ in. got him a berth on the 1936 Olympic team. At Berlin Johnson performed an outstanding and 12-year-record-breaking 6 ft. 7 15/16 in. jump which took the gold medal. The 23-year-old American black man accomplished a coup before the eyes of racial theorist Adolph Hitler.

JOHNSON, Leo T.
Coach

JOHNSON, Rafer
Decathlon

Born August 18, 1935, in Hillsboro, Tex; attended Univ. Calif. at Los Angeles; Olympic Gold Medal 1960; James E. Sullivan Memorial Trophy 1960; director of Kennedy Foundation.

Johnson's great athletic talent and versatility made him the epitome of the all-around decathlon champion. In 1955, competing in his second decathlon, he set a world record point score of 7985 in the ten-event contest, but a 7587 took the second-place silver medal to Milt Campbell's 7937 at the Melbourne Olympics of 1956. With an off-Olympic-year tremendous effort, Johnson defeated the top Russian decathlete Kuznyetsov with 8302 to 7897 in 1958. Another top contender, C. K. Yang of Formosa, took a trouncing in 1960 when Rafer amassed a record 8683 in competition at Eugene, Ore. Yang and Johnson, teammates at UCLA, amazed spectators at the 1960 Rome Olympics with their relentless duel. Rafer won it amassing 8392 points to Yang's 8334 and Kuznyetsov's 7809. Some of his ace performances were a 170 ft. 9½ in. discus throw, 243 ft. 10½ in. in javelin, a 54 ft. 11½ in. shot-put, 25 ft. 5¾ in. long jump, the 100-m. dash in 10.3 and hurdles in 13.8 sec.
Also in: National Track and Field Hall of Fame and U.S. Track and Field Hall of Fame.

JONES, Hayes Wendell
Hurdler

Born August 4, 1938, in Starkville, Miss; attended Eastern Mich. Univ; Olympic Bronze Medal 1960, Gold Medal 1964.

Jones began collecting honors in 1958 as a student of Eastern Michigan, when he won the AAU indoor high hurdles title with 7.1 sec. and the outdoor high hurdles title with 13.8. A time of 13.6 earned him the NCAA championship the same year. He was AAU indoor champion 1960–1962, establishing a meet record at 7.0 in 1961. He also took the AAU outdoor titles 1960–1961 with a 13.6 record-tying time. In the 60-yd. high hurdles, Jones set a world indoor record of 6.9 in 1962. The Rome Olympics of 1960 saw two U.S. teammates finish ahead of Jones in 110-meter hurdles. His bronze-winning time was 14.0 to silver-medalist Willie May's 13.8 and gold-medalist Lee Calhoun's 13.8. But Jones' performance still bettered the German world record-holder's fourth place. In 1964 it was Jones' time to shine, which he did by taking the 110-m. hurdles' glimmering gold medal with 13.6.
Also in: Drake Relays Hall of Fame and National Track and Field Hall of Fame.

JONES, John Paul
Runner

Born 1881; ran track for Cornell Univ; died January 5, 1970.

Jones is honored by the epithet of first American ever to hold a world record in the mile, which he clocked at 4:14.4 on May 31, 1913. On that date, he was competing in an IC4A meet at Cambridge, Mass, and the performance took IC4A honors, his third. It was a heartening achievement for Jones who had finished in the 1500-m. in the fourth slot at the 1912 Games. Earlier that year he won the IC4A 880-yd. championship with 1:53.8 and tried for the mile. Racing on behalf of Cornell in 1911, Jones set an unofficial world record and took his first IC4A mile title with 4:15.4. Also in 1911 and 1912 he took the IC4A cross-country.

JONES, Thomas
Coach

JORDAN, Payton
Coach

Born March 19, 1917, in Whittier, Calif; attended Univ. Southern Calif; joined the Navy; currently head coach at Stanford Univ.

1946	Occidental College, coach
1957	Stanford University, coach

In his amateur career, Jordan played rugby and football besides running track at University of Southern Califor-

nia (USC). The years 1938 and 1939 were spectacular for him, as evidenced by USC victories in the Pacific Coast Conference and the NCAA wins both years. In 1938 he equaled the conference record of 9.7 sec. for the 100-yd. dash and also helped his 440-yd. relay team run a record 40.5 race in Fresno, Calif, that stood for 16 years. In 1941 he won the AAU 100-m. dash with a time of 10.3. As a coach at Occidental, he won two AAIA championships. His Stanford coaching has produced four Olympians and several world class performers. As the 1968 Olympic track coach, Jordan led the U.S. team to 24 medals, 12 of which were gold.
Also in: National Association of Intercollegiate Athletics Hall of Fame.

KASZUBSKI, Frances
Shot-put, discus throw
Frances won 11 AAU championships in six years. Beginning in 1945 with a double triumph, she claimed the 8-lb. shot-put and the discus throw. That year marked the first of four consecutive shot-put titles, with a fifth in 1950. Her best toss was 40 ft. 5⅞ in. in 1948. She won consecutive discus championships 1947–1951. Her best throw was 124 ft. 3⅜ in. in 1948.

KEANE, Thomas
Coach
Keane was the 1894 U.S. champion in the 440-yd. race with a time of 51.0 secs.

KELLEY, Jim
Coach
Born July 3, 1890, in Calhoun County, Iowa; died July 11, 1972, in Canoga Park, Calif.

Kelley was coach at the University of Minnesota 1937–1963. His Gopher track teams won the NCAA title in 1948, led by Fortune Gordien, three-time NCAA discus champion. Gordon was Kelley's top product and a world record holder. The Gophers also won the 1949 Big Ten championship. As an Olympic coach, Kelley led his team to 15 gold medals.

KELLEY, John A.
Marathon Runner
In 1948 and 1950 Kelley was the AAU marathon champ with a best time of 2:45:55.3. In 1935 and 1945 Kelley won the Boston Marathon in a best time of 2:30:40.2.

KELLEY, John J.
Marathon Runner
Born December 24, 1930, in Norwich, Conn; attended Boston Univ; a many-time Boston Marathon runner; Pan-Am Gold Medal 1959; became school teacher in Connecticut.

Kelley was the top marathon man of the U.S. in the 1950s and 1960s. He won his first marathon title in AAU competition in 1956, with a new record time of 2:24:52.3. That triggered him into a seven-in-a-row AAU title sweep, with 2:21:00.4 his fastest in 1958. A traditional contender for the Boston Marathon, Kelley won that grueling race in 1957 with 2:20:05.0. However, he did not do so well in the Olympics with twenty-first place in 1956 at 2:43:40.0 and nineteenth in 1960 at 2:24:58.0. It was in 1959 that Kelley made his mark with a record-breaking 2:27:54.2 marathon win at the Pan-American Games. He had also participated in 1955 as part of the U.S. Pan-Am team.

KIVIAT, Abel
Runner
Born June 23, 1892, in New York, N.Y; competed under sponsorship of New York's hardy Irish-American Athletic Club teams; Olympic Silver Medal 1912.

At the Stockholm Olympics of 1912, an exciting upset put Kiviat back a bit in the ranks of 1500-m. runners. In the last lap Kiviat was leading, with Norman Taber and John Paul Jones close behind but a fourth-running Britisher spurted up to win the gold. Next came Kiviat by an inch to snare the silver. His first championship came a year earlier in AAU competition when he won the mile in 4:19.6, then again with 4:18.6 in 1912, and 4:25.2 in 1913. A record-breaking run took place on June 8, 1912, when Kiviat finished the 1500-m. in 3:55.8. Additionally, he won the AAU indoor titles for the 600-yd. and 1000-yd. in 1911 and 1913, and for the 1000-yd. in 1914. He also won the Cross-Country Championship.

KRAENZLEIN, Alvin C.
Hurdler
Born December 12, 1876, in Milwaukee, Wisc; attended Princeton Univ; first to instigate tucked-leg hurdle leap, now common form; four Olympic Gold Medals 1900; aided Germans in 1913 with organization of their Olympic team; died January 6, 1928.

Kraenzlein is unique in having been the only Olympic contender ever to win four gold medals for four separate and individual events. In 1900 at the Paris Olympics, he took the 110-m. first place in 15.4 sec, the long jump with 23 ft. 6⅞ in. and the 60-m. and 200-m. hurdles. During his Princeton days, Kraenzlein took six AAU championships 1897–1899. He was the 1897 AAU champ in 220-yd. hurdles; the long jump, 120-yd. and 220-yd. hurdles winner in 1898, taking the 120- and 220-yd. hurdles in 1899. His was a record 15.2 in 110-m, 120-yd. hurdles, and on May 28, 1898, at a meet in New York, he set 200-m. and 220-yd. hurdle records. Twice he broke long jump records with 24 ft. 3½ in. followed by 24 ft. 7½ in. in the same year. His college performance also includes IC4A championships in 120-yd. and 220-yd. hurdles for three years in a row, 1898–1900, the 100-yd. dash in 1900 and the 1899 long jump.
Also in: National Track and Field Hall of Fame.

LANDRY, Mabel
Broad Jumper and Sprinter
Mabel won seven AAU championships in five years. A five-time broad jump champion 1949, 1950, 1952–1954, her best jump was in 1953 with 18 ft. 7.5 in. Mabel also competed in 50-yd. dash, earning victories in 1953 and 1954. Her times were 6.3 sec. and 6.1 respectively.

LARABEE, Mike
Runner
Born March 12, 1933, in Los Angeles, Calif; attended Univ. Southern Calif; two Gold Medals 1964; became Coors Beer distributor in Santa Maria, Calif.

Larabee came home from the 1964 Tokyo Games with two gold medals, one taken alone and the other taken by team effort. In the 400-m, Mike started slowly but accelerated in the last half to take first with a time close to his semifinal 46.0 sec. But it was previous to the actual Games in team trials that he set the 400-m. world record with a 44.9 on September 12, 1964. That was his best effort save for the one-quarter leg of the 1600-m. relay which he ran at 44.8 in the 1960 Games. Larabee's running helped the team win the gold and set records on the world and Olympic rosters.

LARNEY, Marjorie
Javelin Thrower
Born January 4, 1937, in Brooklyn, N.Y; Pan-Am Gold Medal 1957.
Marjorie was the dominant woman in field events during the late 1950s, first coming to nationl attention in 1952 when she won the AAU javelin throw with a toss of 126 ft. 3⅞ in. Although she placed a disappointing thirteenth in the Olympics and failed to win national titles the next four years, her distances improved significantly, culminating in a national and AAU record in 1957 at 187 ft. 8 in. The record stood until 1967. She won the silver medal in the 1959 Pan-American Games with a throw of 143 ft. 2.5 in.

LASH, Donald
Runner
Born August 15, 1913, in Bluffton, Ind; James E. Sullivan Memorial Trophy 1938; attended Indiana Univ; regional director for Fellowship of Christian Athletes; board of trustees at Indiana Univ.

On June 13, 1936, Don broke Paavo Nurmis' two-mi. record of 8:59:6 with an 8:58:4 in Princeton, N.J. Although a favorite at the Berlin Olympics, he failed in both the 5000-m. and 10,000-m, running eighth and tenth respectively. Returning to the United States, he won the 1936 NCAA 5000-m in 14:58:5 and set the American two-mi. record for the Drake Relays with a 9:10:6. During his track career, Don held several AAU records, including the six-mi. and three-mi. both indoor and outdoor, while winning the AAU cross-country championship 1934–1940.
Also in: Drake Relays Hall of Fame and U.S. Track and Field Hall of Fame.

LASKAU, Henry
Walker
For ten consecutive years, 1948–1957, Henry was the AAU one-mi. and two-mi. champion.

LIGHTBODY, James D.
Runner
Jim held the 1905 AAU title for the mile, which he ran in 4:48.8, some 25 years before the advent of the 4-minute mile run by Glenn Cunningham and others in the 1930s and 1940s.

LINGLE, Leland P.
Coach

LITTLEFIELD, Clyde B.
Coach
Born October 6, 1892, in Eldred, Pa; attended Univ. Tex, Austin; retired 1961; currently residing in Austin.

While in college 1912–1916, Littlefield participated in football, baseball and track. He made the All-Southwest Conference team in each of these sports but excelled in hurdle running, losing only once in his career. In his 41 years of coaching at Texas 1920–1961, Littlefield's teams won 25 Conference titles, 12 individual NCAA championships and set world records in sprint relays, medley and distance races. He coached three Olympians and nine Southwest Conference record holders. In 1957 his 800-m. relay team set a world record of 1:22.7, breaking the previous 1956 mark set by the U.S. All-Star team. In 1958 his 440-yd. relay team set a world record of 39.6 secs.

LODGE, Hilmer
Noteworthy Contributor

LONG, Dallas
Shot-putter
Born June 13, 1940, in Pine Bluff, Ark; attended prep school in Phoenix, Ariz; Univ. Southern Calif; established profession as dentist in California.

Long went out for track and field in prep school, concentrating on the shot which he heaved 69 ft. 3⅛ in. He left the 12-lb. for a heftier 16-lb. shot and put a 63-ft. 7 in. as a freshman at USC. Steadily climbing the record roster, his 64 ft. 6½ in. throw of 1960 took top slot until bested by the 1960 gold medal taker's 65 ft. 7 in. Long got the bronze at the Rome Olympics, behind Bill Neider's new record and silver-medalist Parry O'Brien's 62 ft. 8½ in. to Long's 62 ft. 4½ in. In 1962 he reset a world record with 65 ft. 10½ in, which he upped to 66 ft. 8½ in. for the Olympic gold medal of 1964. While at USC he also won three NCAA shot titles 1960–1962, and AAU honors 1961 and 1962.

MacMITCHELL, Leslie
Runner
Competing on behalf of New York University, MacMitchell captured the mile championship in the NCAA contests 1940–1942, plus the 880-yd. title in 1941. Another NCAA milestone was the cross-country championship that he won three consecutive years 1939–1941. In AAU meets he took the mile crown in 1941 and 1946, with his best time 3:53.1 in 1941.

MAGEE, John J. "Jack"
Coach
Born January 12, 1883, in Newark, N.J; died January 1, 1968.

As coach at Bowdoin College in Maine 1914–1955, Magee's teams won 20 state championships, 9 of which were won consecutively. He also coached the Olympic track team 1924, 1928 and 1932. Magee turned down the opportunity to coach the 1936 U.S. Olympic track team because he objected to the Games being held in Nazi Germany. An all-weather track at Bowdoin has been named in his honor.

MANN, Ralph
Hurdler
Born August 16, 1949, in Long Beach, Calif; pursued engineering major at Brigham Young Univ; Pan-Am Gold Medal 1971; Olympic Silver Medal 1972; served on physical education staff of Wash. State Univ.

Ralph Mann was a 440-yd. hurdle star while at BYU,

winning the NCAA championship three times. He clocked a time of 49.6 sec. in 1969 and 1971 and a record 48.8 set on June 20, 1970, which stood for four years. In 1970 Mann also captured the AAU title with 49.8, and with 49.3 in 1971. That year he was the gold medal winner at the Pan-American Games where he ran a record 400-m. hurdle in 49.1. He had a few problems in other meets in 1972, but he clinched the Olympic trials with a record 48.4. At the games in Munich, however, the Ugandan John Akii-Bua zipped past Mann for a gold medal and a new world record of 47.82. Mann's second-place showing was a commendable 48.51.
Also in: Drake Relays Hall of Fame.

MANNING, Madeline Jackson

Runner

Born January 11, 1948, in Columbus, Ohio; Pan-Am Gold Medal 1967; Olympic Gold Medal 1968 and Silver Medal 1972.

Another one of the track stars from Tennessee State University, Madeline also represented the Columbus Community Track Club and Cleveland Track Club. In the 1968 Olympics at Mexico City she set the American 800-m. record, and an Olympic record while winning the gold medal in two minutes flat. At the 1972 Munich Olympics she ran the second leg on the silver-medal U.S. 1600-m. relay team. Aside from her Olympic performances she won the 1967 Pan-American Games gold in 2:02.0. She was the AAU 1967 and 1969 champion in the 800-m. and runnerup in 1966 and 1968. She was named Outstanding Athlete in 1969 at the U.S.-Europe dual and won her specialty in 2:03.8 in the U.S.-U.S.S.R. meet.
Also in: U.S. Track and Field Hall of Fame.

MATHIAS, Robert Bruce

Decathlon

Born November 19, 1930, in Tulare, Calif; attended Stanford Univ, played fullback on the football team; played in Rose Bowl of 1952; Olympic Gold Medal 1948 and 1952; James E. Sullivan Memorial Trophy 1948; first ever to win two gold medals in decathlon; congressman from California.

Bob Mathias charmed the whole United States when he won the most grueling 10-event contest of the Olympics at the age of 17. And only he among all decathlon hopefuls broke the 7000-point mark to win with 7139. His showing was excellent in all events, but best in discus; he tied in high jump and pole vault. During the 1952 Olympic trials Bob broke another record score set two years before. His 1952 second gold was earned by a super score of 7887. In the four years from age 17 to 21, Mathias grew 3 in. taller and 15 lbs. heavier.
Also in: National Track and Field Hall of Fame and U.S. Track and Field Hall of Fame.

MATSON, Randel "Randy"

Shot-putter and Discus Thrower

Born March 5, 1945, in Kilgore, Tex; attended Texas A&M; diversified in college sports; drafted by Atlanta Falcons of National Football League and by basketball teams of Seattle and Dallas; Olympic Silver Medal 1964, Gold Medal 1968; Pan-Am Gold Medal 1967; James E. Sullivan Memorial Trophy 1967; executive director of booster club at West Texas State University.

Freshman Matson at Texas A&M put the shot 64 ft. 11 in. to take the AAU title and the meet record in 1964. He scored victories in both the shot put and the discus throw of the Drake Relays of 1965, 1966 and 1967. And he won both shot and discus NCAA titles in 1966 and 1967 with 67 ft. ½ in. shot and 197 ft. discus in the first year, adding 9 big inches to his shot toss a year later. He retained the AAU shot championship 1966–1968, having bettered the meet record to stand at 67 ft. 5 in. At the 1964 Olympics, Matson fell behind gold medalist Dallas Long after first setting a sizeable lead. Long put a 66 ft. 8¼ in, which topped Matson by 5¼ in. Nevertheless he went on to take the 1967 Pan-American Games gold medal and then the 1968 Mexico City Games gold medal on his world record throw of 67 ft. 4¾ in. By far the greatest Matson performance was a first-over-70 ft. throw on May 8, 1965, at College Station, Tex. He gained 70 ft. 7¼ in. which he then boosted to 71 ft. 5½ in. at a meet two years later. Matson was the only man to reach 70 ft. until Al Feuerbach and George Woods caught up with him in 1972. Despite a qualifying round shot of 69 ft. ¼ in, Matson landed fourth at the trials' end and was denied a berth on the Munich-bound team.
Also in: Drake Relays Hall of Fame.

McARDLE, Peter

Long Distance Runner

McArdle's notable track and field effort was the 1962 cross-country championship in AAU competition, which he won with an impressive 29:53.0, one of the few to dip below the 30:00.0 mark.

McCLUSKEY, Joseph P.

Long Distance Runner

Attended Fordham Univ; Lt. in the Army.

Between 1930 and 1946, McCluskey won 15 AAU championship crowns. He also won both the indoor and outdoor IC4A 2-mi. race in 1931 and 1932. His best AAU marks were 15:14.1 for the 1935 3-mi. race, 32:28.3 for the 1942 6-mi. race, 9:14.5 for the 1932 steeplechase, 32:30 for the 1932 cross-country and 9:39.3 for the indoor 2-mi. race. He ran on the 1946 AAU championship cross-country team along with his teammates from the New York Athletic Club. By far his best event was the steeplechase, in which he claimed nine AAU crowns.

McDANIEL, Mildred

High Jumper

Born November 4, 1933, in Atlanta, Ga; Olympic Gold Medal 1952.

Mildred McDaniel set the American women's high jump mark as well as an Olympic record and won the gold medal in 1952 with a leap of 5 ft. 9.25 in. Mildred won the AAU outdoor in 1953, 1955 and 1956 with a 1955 jump of 5 ft. 6.5 in, a meet record that held for eight years. She won the indoor championship in 1955 and 1956.

McDONALD, Patrick J. "Babe"

Shot-putter

Born 1878 in County Clare, Ireland; Olympic Gold and Silver Medal 1912, Gold Medal 1920; known as one among many New York City police department "whales" in weight-throwing competition; died May 16, 1954.

Babe was no baby but a 6 ft. 4 in. and 250 lb. hulk of a man who made it his avocation to hurl the shot and the 56-lb. weight. He began by winning the national title in AAU competition in 1911, and retaining it in 1912, 1914, 1919, 1920 and 1922. As for the 56-lb. weight throw, Babe held AAU titles in 1911 and 1914, 1919–1921 and 1926–1929. The AAU indoor shot title was his in 1916, 1917 and 1919–1921. At the 1912 Olympic Games in Stockholm, McDonald was in his element. He won the gold medal over teammate Ralph Rose by a bare 3⅗ in. with a 50 ft. 4 in. shot put. But in the two-hand shot put he was kept to the silver behind Rose. At Antwerp for the 1920 Games, McDonald recorded 36 ft. 11⅝ in. in the 56-lb. weight throw to take the gold. But his shot put efforts were not so illustrious and he finished fourth with 46 ft. 2⅓ in.

McGRATH, Matthew
Hammer Thrower

Born 1878 in Nenagh, Tipperary, Ireland; came to the United States at age 21; New York City police department "whale"; Olympic Silver Medal 1908, Gold Medal 1912, Silver Medal 1924; died January 29, 1941.

McGrath's substantial hammer-throw career began when he took notice of the big boulders in New York City's Central Park. There he held many a practice session until threatened with arrest, an irony considering his later choice of profession. The stocky Irishman was a winner for over 25 years, beginning with his first AAU championship in 1908 and his repeats in 1912, 1918, 1922, 1925 and 1926. The 56-lb. weight throw was McGrath's specialty, and he won that AAU title for six years too. On October 29, 1911, Matt established a world hammer throw record of 187 ft. 4 in. which he bettered in an unofficial 190 ft. 10 in. in 1913. Five years earlier at the London Olympics, McGrath finished second behind New York Irish policeman John Flanagan. In Stockholm for the 1912 Games, with no Flanagan to contend against, McGrath threw the hammer for a record 179 ft. 7⅛ in. which held good for 24 more years. McGrath took fifth in the 1920 Olympics, handicapped by a bad knee, and second in 1924 with a lukewarm hammer toss of 166 ft. 9⅝ in, nearly 13 ft. short of his spectacular 1912 effort.

McMILLIAN, Harry
Noteworthy Contributor

MEADOWS, Earle
Pole Vaulter

Born June 29, 1913, in Corinth, Miss; attended Univ. Southern Calif; Olympic Gold Medal 1936.

Earle Meadows happened to possess a vaulting ability similar to Bill Stefton's. Throughout college Meadows and Sefton occupied top pole positions. In 1935 they tied the AAU championship with 13 ft. 10⅜ in. And both swept up NCAA honors in 1935 with 14 ft. 1¾ in. But Sefton squeezed past the next year to win the NCAA top spot while Meadows ended in third. Also in 1937 at the AAU championship, Meadows and Sefton found themselves in a four-man tie for first with 14 ft. 7⅝ in. At the 1936 Berlin Olympics four vaulters were breathing down each others' necks for the gold medal. But Meadows won it, besting his twin, Sefton, with a barely-made 14 ft. 3 in. Meadows' winning pole vault score of the 1936 Games broke an Olympic record. Earle won two AAU outdoor titles 1940 and 1941. At age 35 he was still vaulting over the 14 ft. mark.

Also in: U.S. Track and Field Hall of Fame.

MEREDITH, James E. "Ted"
Runner

Born November 14, 1892, in Chester Heights, Pa; attended Pa. State Univ; Olympic Gold Medal 1912; died November 2, 1957.

During Ted's track tenure, he held the world records for the 440-yd, 400-m, 880-yd. and 800-m. events. His performance in the 1912 Stockholm Olympics. a record 1:51:9 in the 800-m, won a gold medal. Later that year he was timed at 1:52.5 for the 880-yd, setting another record. Four years later he topped his best in Philadelphia for the 880-yd. in 1:52.2. His later time of 1:53.0 for the 880-yd. stood as a meet record for 11 years. He won the 1914 and 1915 AAU 440-yd. title. Although he ran for the 1920 Olympic team, he did not qualify for the 400-m. finals and came in fourth in the 1600-meter relay.

Also in: U.S. Track and Field Hall of Fame.

METCALFE, Ralph
Sprinter

Born May 29, 1910, in Atlanta, Ga; attended Tilden High School in Chicago, Marquette Univ. track and field team captain; Olympic Gold Medal and Silver Medal 1936; military service with U.S. Army; Chicago businessman and Ill. congressman.

Metcalfe was given the title of "World's Fastest Human," recognizing his spectacular finishes on the heels of a delayed-action start. The 5 ft. 11 in. and 180 lb. sprinter attained the 100-m. world record of 10.3 sec. three times. And he made the 200-m. 20.6 record once. He won NCAA honors for both races at times of 10.2 and 20.3 but no action was taken to have them officially acknowledged as world records. While at Marquette Ralph took the NCAA 100-yd. and 220-yd. in 1933 and 1934. He also won the AAU 100-yd. three times and the 200-m. five times. At the Los Angeles Olympics of 1932, Metcalfe battled his rival Eddie Tolan all the way, managing to beat him at the trials but falling behind during the Games. Tolan took the gold for both 100- and 200-meter runs. In 1936 at Berlin, the great Jesse Owens dominated the limelight and Metcalfe was forced into the wings. He finished second in the 100-meter behind Owens. But a piece of the gold medal won by the U.S. 400-m. relay team did belong to Metcalfe.

Also in: Drake Relays Hall of Fame, National Track and Field Hall of Fame and U.S. Track and Field Hall of Fame.

MIHALO, William
Walker

MILBURN, Rodney
Hurdler

Born May 18, 1950, in Opelousas, La; attended Southern Univ; Pan-Am Gold Medal 1971; Olympic Gold Medal 1972; *Track & Field News* World Track Athlete of the Year 1971.

Milburn holds the record for the 120-yd. hurdles, which he ran in 13.0 at Eugene, Ore, on June 25, 1971, in AAU competition. Two years later on June 20, 1973, he ran in 13.0 sec. again. Rod enjoyed a successful college career, winning AAU, NCAA and NAIA contests 1970–1973. At the Pan-American Games in 1971 he took the gold medal for 110-m. hurdles in 13.4. It was not until the Olympic team trials that Milburn suffered a setback, his first defeat in two years. He made the team but by way of third place 13.6. At the Munich Games, however, he ran a record-tying 13.2 to win the gold medal.

MILLS, Billy
Six-mile Runner
Born June 30, 1938, in Pine Ridge, S.Dak; seven sixteenths Sioux Indian; attended Univ. Kans; Olympic Gold Medal 1964; assistant to commissioner of Bureau of Indian Affairs.

At the 1965 Amateur Athletic Union championship at San Diego, Billy Mills ran the 6-mi. in 27:11.6. Upon examination of the photo finish it was found that Mills barely took the first place by .05 of a second. In 1964 another upset occurred, this time on an Olympic scale. At the Tokyo Games, Billy was ranked fairly far down the roster of 10,000-m. racers. Nevertheless, out of 38 runners, Mills stayed among the lead five and managed to catch up to and pass the one and two runners in a terrific sprint. He won the gold medal and set a record 28:24.4.
Also in: National Track and Field Hall of Fame and U.S. Track and Field Hall of Fame.

MITCHELL, J. S.
Hammer Thrower
Mitchell grabbed two top honors in one year and went on to tally more than fifteen years of wins. He began in 1888 with the NCAA and AAU titles for the 56-lb. hammer throw. And he repeated the AAU honor in 1891, 1897, 1900, 1903 and 1905. His greatest toss was the 35 ft. 3½ in. that won him the first place position in 1891. Also during the span of years between 1889 and 1896, Mitchell threw the 16-lb. hammer and won AAU championships in that event. The 1903 distance was his best, with 140 ft. 1 in.

MOAKLEY, John
Coach

MOORE, Bernice H. "Bernie"
Coach
See entry in Athletic Directors Hall of Fame, Citizens Savings Hall of Fame Athletic Museum; and National Football Hall of Fame.

MOORE, Charles, Jr.
Hurdler
Born August 12, 1929, in Coatsville, Pa; attended Cornell Univ; father "Crip" took part in 1924 Olympics; Olympic Gold Medal and Silver Medal 1952.

Moore won meets and championships while a college track star at Cornell. He specialized in the 440-yd. hurdles at AAU, NCAA and IC4A competitions, with 47.0 sec. his fastest for an NCAA win. At the Helsinki Olympics of 1952, Moore broke the previous record of 51.1 with a 50.8 which took the gold medal. And a fast 46.2 leg of the 400-m. relay helped win the silver medal for all four men on the team.

MORRIS, Glenn
Decathlon
Born June 18, 1912, in Simla, Colo.

One of Morris' distinctions is having set the decathlon record that Bob Mathias broke in 1950. His 7900 points, scored in the ten-event contest of the 1936 Berlin Games, held good for fourteen years. Earlier that year, at an AAU contest, Glenn scored a 7880 decathlon, which bettered the world record of that moment but which was never made official. But it won the championship and launched Morris into a career as an all-rounder.

MORRIS, Ronald
Pole Vaulter
Ron was a three-time pole vault champ in AAU competition in the years 1958, 1961 and 1962. His absolute best vault cleared 16 ft. ¼ in. He put an end to Bob Richards' ongoing vault sweep 1948–1957 for a total of nine AAU titles. Morris substantially topped Richards' best effort of 15 ft. 3½ in.

MORROW, Bobby Joe
Sprinter
Born October 15, 1935, in Harlingen, Tex; attended Abilene Christian Col; James E. Sullivan Memorial Trophy 1957; named Greatest Sprinter of All Time by *Track and Field News* 1958; *Sports Illustrated* 1956 Sportsman of the Year; turned to ranching after a fifteen-year banking career.

Morrow made a name for himself as a sprinter 1955–1958 when he was AAU champion in the 100-yd. dash. His 1957 time of 9.3 sec. made him co-holder of the world record. At the 1956 Olympics in Melbourne he won the 100-m. and 200-m. with 10.3 and 20.6. And a third gold medal was given him for outstanding anchor performance on the 400-m. relay team. In 1958, with Morrow as anchorman, the Abilene team broke two world records in the 440-yd. and 880-yd. Bobby set 9 world records and won 14 national sprint championships.
Also in: Drake Relays Hall of Fame, National Association of Intercollegiate Athletics Hall of Fame, National Track and Field Hall of Fame and U.S. Track and Field Hall of Fame.

MORTENSEN, Jesse
Coach
Born April 16, 1907, in Thatcher, Ariz; attended Univ. Southern Calif; died February 19, 1962, in Los Angeles.

Mortensen's college career at USC included a 1929 NCAA crown in the javelin throw with a 203 ft. 7¾ in. mark and an AAU crown with a throw of 204 ft. 11¾ in. While he was the USC track coach 1951–1961, Mortensen's Trojans won all dual meets in 79 competitions. The Trojans won the NCAA title 1951–1955, 1958 and 1961. Mortensen coached 20 NCAA individual champions, including Olympic gold medal winners Parry O'Brien, Dallas Long and Sim Inness.

MURCHISON, Loren
Sprinter
Born in December, 1898; two Olympic Gold Medals 1920.

Loren won two gold medals in relays and a fourth place in the 200-m. in the 1920 Olympics. He held the world indoor 60-yd. dash in 1922 in 6.4 and in 1923 in 6.2. He

was National AAU champion in 1920 and 1922–1924. At the Melrose Games in the 60-yd. dash, he broke the world record which had been standing since 1888.
Also in: U.S. Track and Field Hall of Fame.

MURPHY, Michael C.
Coach
Two sons, Thorne and George; died June 5, 1913.

1896–1900 University of Pennsylvania, coach
1900–1913 Yale University, coach
1894–1910 New York Athletic Club, coach

Murphy coached championship teams in Pennsylvania between 1897 and 1900 then moved to Yale, leading them to championship wins in 1900, 1902 and 1904. While still at the University of Pennsylvania, he took medicine and surgery courses to aid in his training techniques. Between 1897 and 1913, his teams won 15 intercollegiate titles. The individuals he coached at the University of Pennsylvania and the New York Athletic Club won 14 events in the 1900 Olympics. When the U.S. Olympic committee met in 1913 to plan for the 1916 Olympics, they unanimously appointed Murphy as the track coach. Murphy is known as the leading trainer of athletes of the nineteenth and early twentieth centuries and is recognized as the dean of his profession.
Also in: National Track and Field Hall of Fame.

MYERS, Laurence E. "Lon"
Runner
Born February 16, 1858, in Richmond, Va; moved to New York in teen years when doctor advised exercise; bookkeeper by profession and in betting business; died Feb. 15, 1889, of pneumonia.

Lon Myers began his running career as a bit of a weakling and never did grow to be too hefty. His 5 ft. 7¾ in. and 112-pound frame was made for running. At one time or another, in the course of his 41 years, Lon held all records in the United States in runs from 50-yd. to the mile. And he was the first in the world to run the quarter–mile in a time less than 50.0 sec. Myers broke the record in 1879 with 49.2, lowering it in 1881 to 48.6. In the half mile, his 1:56 set a new record in 1881, then re-set at 1:55.4 three years later. Versatility seemed to be Myers' byword. In 1879 he won AAU titles in the 220-yd, 440-yd and 880-yd. The next year he added the 100-yd. dash to his AAU honors. In 1881 a new combination of three AAU titles were his and his 49.4 quarter-mile record as meet best for fifteen years. Other Myers achievements were 10.0 in 100-yd, 22.6 in 220-yd, 48.6 in 440-yd, 1:55.4 in 880-yd, and 4:27.6 in mile.
Also in: National Track and Field Hall of Fame.

NEWHOUSE, Jean Shiley
High Jumper
Born November 20, 1911, in Harrisburg, Pa; Olympic Gold Medal 1932; now a housewife in Los Angeles, Calif.

With a jump of 5 ft. 5 in; Jean won the gold medal in the 1932 Olympics and set the world record for women. Babe Didrickson tied Jean's leap but lost the jump-off. In the 1928 Olympics, Jean's jump of 4 ft. 11.5 in. only placed her fourth. Between 1929 and 1932 Jean was the AAU high jump champion, setting a record leap of 5 ft. 3.5 in.
Also in: U.S. Track and Field Hall of Fame.

NIEDER, William
Shot-putter
Born August 10, 1933, in Hempstead, N.Y; attended Univ. Kans; Olympic Silver Medal 1956; Olympic Gold Medal 1960; following track career tried boxing unsuccessfully; set up artificial track-surfacing business.

Nieder set a shot put record of 57 ft. 3 in. at the 1955 NCAA championships. But at the next year's Olympics he could not out-put the master Parry O'Brien and so took home a silver medal. At the 1960 Rome Games Nieder won the gold with a put of 64 ft. 6¾ in. That throw set an Olympic record, and Bill established a new world record on April 2, 1960, with 65 ft. 7 in.
Also in: Drake Relays Hall of Fame.

NOAH, Winton E.
Coach

O'BRIEN, Parry
Shot-putter and Discus Thrower
Born January 28, 1932, in Santa Monica, California; Olympic Gold Medal 1956, Silver Medal 1960; outstanding high school athlete; attended Univ. Southern Calif; now a banker in southern California.

Parry was the first shot-putter to break the 60 foot barrier with a 60 ft. 5.25 in. at Los Angeles in 1954. His innovative style, later coined the "O'Brien Style," which made use of a 180 degree turn and speed and strength to shift weight toward the front of the circle, revolutionized shot-putting. For seven years, Parry held the shot-put record and advanced it to 63 ft. 2 in. in 1956. At the University of Southern California he won two NCAA firsts 1952 and 1953. His 60 ft. 11 in. won him a gold medal at the 1956 Olympic Games in Melbourne. Four years later he finished with a silver behind his United States foe, Bill Nieder, who tossed 62 ft. 8.5 in. During his competitive days, Parry set the record for combined— left- and right-handed—shot-put with 61 ft. .75 in. right, 45 ft. 9.33 in. left for a total of 106 ft. 10.5 in. In 1971 he set the World senior record with 53 ft. 4 in. in the shot put and 164 ft. 9 in. in the discus throw.
Also in: Drake Relays Hall of Fame, National Track and Field Hall of Fame and U.S. Track and Field Hall of Fame.

OERTER, Alfred
Discus Thrower
Born August 19, 1936, in Astoria, N.Y; attended Univ. Kans; Olympic Gold Medal 1956, 1960, 1964 and 1968.

Before Al Oerter came along to collect four gold medals in four Olympic Games only ten-medalist Ray Ewry could make such a claim. Oerter was also the first ever to throw the discus past the 200 ft. mark, which he then pushed from 200 ft. 5 in. to 206 ft. 6 in. At the 1956 Olympics a shorter throw of 184 ft. 10½ in. broke the Olympic record, got the gold, and beat the favored Fortune Gordien. In 1960 Oerter's 194 ft. 2 in. discus toss won a second gold medal. Then he put forth a phenomenal effort four years later and produced a 200 ft. 1½ in. winning throw despite injured ribs. The fourth gold medal was won at the 1968 Mexico City Games when Oerter tossed his best ever to span 212 ft. 6½ in.
Also in: Drake Relays Hall of Fame, National Track and Field Hall of Fame and U.S. Track and Field Hall of Fame.

ORTON, George
Steeplechaser
See entry in Canada's Sports Hall of Fame.

OSBORN, Harold M.
Decathlon and High Jumper
Born April 13, 1899, in Butler, Ill; attended Univ. Ill.

Osborn is unique in being the first and only Olympic contender to win a decathlon and an individual event at one Olympics, which he did at the 1924 Paris Games. His decathlon point score was a record 7710.775 on the old point basis, and the gold medal high jump cleared 6 ft. 6 in. Yet this was not his best effort, for on May 27, 1924, at Urbana, Ill, Osborn set a new world record of 6 ft. 8¼ in. In 1925 and 1926 he clinched AAU championships in decathlon and high jump. And for four years, 1923–1926, he won AAU indoor titles. The Amsterdam Olympics of 1928 did not feature any Harold Osborn highlights, but a past credit worth attention is Osborn's collegiate record high jump of 6 ft. 6 in. set at the 1922 Drake Relays the first time the high jump was included in that meet.
Also in: Drake Relays Hall of Fame, National Track and Field Hall of Fame and U.S. Track and Field Hall of Fame.

OWENS, James Cleveland "Jesse"
Sprinter and Long Jumper
Born September 12, 1913, in Danville, Ala; moved to Ohio as a youth, attended East Technical High School in Cleveland; Ohio State, given 28 scholarship offers; held jobs from gasoline station attendant to page boy in state House of Representatives; four Olympic Gold Medals, 1936; called Athlete of the Half Century by Drake Relays officials 1959.

Known in college as the "Ebony Antelope," Owens was even then beginning to collect championship credits with distinctive style and grace. Ultimately he triumphed four times for four gold medals at the Berlin Games. There his 10.3 sec. in the 100-m. tied the Olympic record, a 26 ft. 5¼ in. long jump made a new record, and a 20.7 in the 200-m. put him way out ahead of the pack. The fourth gold medal came with the 400-m. relay team, of which Owens was anchorman and prime force behind their record 39.8. Earlier in 1936 Owens had swept the NCAA championships in 100-m. with 10.2, 200-m. with 21.3 and long jump of 25 ft. 10⅞ in. Of course, everyone knew he was a dynamo as early as high school when he ran his first 10.3 time in the 100-m. dash. And on May 25, 1935, competing in the Big Ten championships at Ann Arbor, Mich, he wreaked havoc with records. He tied the 100-yd. world record, set a new 220-yd. hurdles straight course at 22.6, and made the 200-yd. straight run in 20.7. In just 70 min, Owens had set or equaled four world records. Years later the two 220-yd. runs were ratified as 200-m, so that Owens made it into the record books not four but six times in one day, and all of his accomplishments were long standing. The Jesse Owens 100-yd. American record 9.4 stood for 20 years, while the 26 ft. 1¾ in. long jump record lasted 30.
Also in: Drake Relays Hall of Fame, National Track and Field Hall of Fame and U.S. Track and Field Hall of Fame.

PADDOCK, Charles W.
Sprinter
Born August 11, 1900, in Gainesville, Tex; two Olympic Gold Medals 1920, Silver Medal 1924; known as glamour boy; famous for finishing leap to tape; became Marine captain; died July 21, 1943, in W.W. II.

In the 1920s Paddock was called the "World's Fastest Human" as he was the first to run the 100-yd. in 9.5 sec. He was the third man to run it in 9.6 which got him two of five AAU titles. The others were for a 22-yd. 21.4 in 1920 and 1921, and 20.8 in 1924. But April 23, 1921, may be said to be Paddock's greatest day when he broke four world records and tied one all in one day. He ran the 100-m. in 10.4, the 200-m. in 21.6, the 300-m. in 33.8, and 300-yd. in 30.2. And again it was 9.6 for the 100-yd. At the 1920 Olympics in Antwerp, he ran a 10.8 in the 100-m. and won the gold medal. He took second in the 200-m, which was repeated four years later during the Paris Games. In addition, at that 1924 Olympics, Charlie took fifth in 100-m. but won with the 400-m. relay team. In 1928 races for Paddock never got underway. He was on the team for the 200-m. specialty but he failed to qualify for Games competition.
Also in: Drake Relays Hall of Fame, National Track and Field Hall of Fame and U.S. Track and Field Hall of Fame.

PATTON, Melvin
Sprinter
Born November 16, 1924 in Los Angeles, Calif; attended Univ. Southern Calif; two Olympic Gold Medals 1948.

Patton never took part in AAU contests, but he did win a few NCAA championships while a trackman for USC. In 1948 and 1949 he took NCAA top notches for both sprints, 100-yd. and 220-yd, capturing only the 100-yd. in 1947. Patton's 9.4 sec. time established a new 100-yd. record which he nipped to 9.3 in 1948. That record could not be beaten for 13 years, although it was tied ten times in that interim. And with 20.2 Patton ousted the Jesse Owens record for 220-yd, 200-m. At the London Games in 1948, Patton finished fifth in the 100-m. but won the 200-m. with 21.1. Another gold medal rewarded his participation in the U.S. 400-m. relay team. A year later on May 7 he ran a fast and wind-aided 100-yd. in 9.1 and made the new record 20.2 for 200-m., 220-yd.

PEACOCK, Eulace
Sprinter and Long Jumper
Born Aug. 27, 1914, in Dotham, Ala.

Peacock seemed relegated to second best in his career, but through no fault of his own. As Jesse Owens' contemporary, he constantly faced a top athlete in his same specialties, the 100-m. and long jump. Peacock co-held the 10.3 sec. world record for 100-m, which he ran at Oslo on August 8, 1934. And Peacock did manage to beat Owens in 1935 during AAU competition, helped by the wind for a 10.2 in 100-m. In other outdoor AAU sprint contests that year Peacock won three of five times, plus the long jump title with 26 ft. 3 in. In 1936 he had to sit out the Olympics and in 1937 tried for a comeback but did not succeed due to injuries.

PIPAL, Joseph
Coach
Pipal coached at Occidental College.

Also in: National Association of Intercollegiate Athletics Hall of Fame.

PLANSKY, Anthony
Coach

PLANT, William "Bill"
Walker

Bill won the AAU one-mi. walk four times, 1922–1924 and 1927 while adding the two mi. walk in 1920. His two-mi. time was 13:8.0.

POST, Archie
Coach

PRINSTEIN, Myer
Long Jumper

Born 1880; attended Syracuse Univ; Olympic Gold and Silver Medal 1900, two Golds 1904 and one Gold 1906; died March 10, 1928.

Prinstein began taking honors in IC4A competition while a student at Syracuse. He was IC4A long jump champ of 1898 and 1900, and he jumped 23 ft. 8⅞ in. for a world record in 1898. Two years later Prinstein fought to regain world record-holder status, since an Irishman and Al Kraenzlein of the United States had bested it in the interim. At the 1900 Penn Relays, Myer took it again with 24 ft. 7¼ in. In AAU competition, Prinstein was first in long jump in 1898, 1902 and 1906. Even though long jump was his best skill, he was proficient at triple jump, which won him a gold medal at the Paris Games of 1900. He also got a silver for a long jump of 23 ft. 6½ in. In 1904 at the St. Louis Games, Myer won both golds in triple and in the long jump with 24 ft. 1 in. First place for long jump was again his at the 1906 Athens Olympics, and in the course of the games, the diversified Prinstein competed in a total of five events, the 400-m, 60-m. and 100-m. in addition to the two types of jump.

RANSON, Dale
Coach

RAY, Joie "Chesty Joie"
Runner

Born April 13, 1884; earned nickname for on-the-track confidence; taxi driver by vocation; marathon-dancer by avocation.

Joie got a lot of attention for his stamina and prowess on the dance floor. The same held true for his performance on the track. For eight years he was AAU mile champion, in 1915 and 1917–1923. His best time was 4:14.4 in 1919. That year he also took the AAU title for the 880-yd. with 1:56. At the 1920 Olympics in Antwerp, a leg injury proved a hindrance and Joie took eighth in the 1500-m. Three years later he was back on his feet and running the anchor slot on the Ilinois Athletic Club four-mi. relay. They set a world record 17:21.4. Relay became Ray's Olympic ticket to the 1924 Games in Paris. The U.S. team took third, and Ray, on an overall individual basis, was eighteenth. His next year's feat was to tie the indoor mile record of the "Flying Finn," Paavo Nurmi. Joie ran 4:12.0. At the 1928 Amsterdam Olympics, Joie finished fourteenth in the 10,000-m. and fifth in the marathon with 2:36.04.
Also in: National Track and Field Hall of Fame and U.S. Track and Field Hall of Fame.

RHODEN, George
Runner

Born December 13, 1926, in Kingston, Jamaica; attended Morgan State Col; two Olympic Gold Medals 1952; practiced podiatry in San Francisco.

Rhoden started to make a name for himself on behalf of Morgan State in AAU contests. In 1949 he won the AAU 400-m. in 46.4 sec. at a meet in Fresno, Calif. For the two years following, he retained the championship with a best of 46.0 in 1951. An even faster performance got him a world record in 1950 at Eskilstuna, Sweden, where he ran 45.8 to beat his Jamaican adversary, Herb McKenley. The two vied for the 400-m. gold medal at the 1952 Games in Helsinki, but Rhoden jumped ahead by a meter to win it. A second gold medal was his for boosting the Jamaican 1600-m. relay team to a 3:03.9 record win.

RICE, Gregory J.
Long Distance Runner

James E. Sullivan Memorial Trophy 1940.

Rice ran for Notre Dame and in 1938 became NCAA cross-country champion, going on to take the AAU equivalent honor in 1941. Rice won the AAU 2-mile 1941–1943 and captured the 3-mile for five straight years starting in 1938.
Also in: Drake Relays Hall of Fame.

RICHARDS, Alma
High Jumper

Born February 20, 1890, in Parowan, Utah; Olympic Gold Medal 1912; died April 3, 1963.

Richards cleared the bar at 6 ft. 4 in. for an Olympic gold medal and a world record at the Stockholm Games of 1912. In so doing he set back the favored George Horine to second. In 1913 Richards took the AAU high jump crown with 6 ft. 1⅜ in. And five years later, proving his versatility, he took the AAU shot put championship with 42 ft. 3¾ in.

RICHARDS, Robert E.
Pole Vaulter

Born February 20, 1926, in Champaign, Ill; Olympic Bronze Medal 1948, Gold Medals 1952 and 1956; James E. Sullivan Memorial Trophy 1951; an ordained minister, nicknamed "Vaulting Vicar"; took part in administration of national fitness program.

Bob set his sights on the 15 ft. mark and became the second man in history to sail above it. Out of the several hundred vaults he made in a career, 126 of them surpassed 15 ft. Between 1948 and 1957, he either won or tied for nine outdoor AAU championships, and his best vault of 15 ft. 3½ in. outdid Warmerdam's previous record by one inch. He either won or tied for eight indoor AAU championships, with a 1955 record vault of 15 ft. 4 in. His career best efforts overall were 15 ft. 5 in. outdoor and 15 ft. 6 in. indoor. At the 1948 Olympics in London, he won the bronze, but he got the gold the next time around with 14 ft. 11¼ in. At the 1956 Melbourne Games he won the gold with 14 ft. 11½ in, becoming the only two-gold Olympic winner in the pole vault. Bob semispecialized in decathlon and won both 1954 and 1955 AAU championships with 7313 points, his best effort. His 1956 Olympic decathlon attempt resulted in twelfth place due to an injured tendon.

Also in: National Track and Field Hall of Fame and U.S. Track and Field Hall of Fame.

RIDER, George L.
Coach

ROBERTSON, Lawson N. "Robbie"
Coach

Born September 24, 1883, in Aberdeen, Scotland; Olympic Bronze Medal 1904, Silver and Bronze 1906; died January 22, 1951.

1908–1914 Irish-American Athletic Club of New York City, coach
1916–1947 University of Pennsylvania, coach

Robertson participated in the 1904, 1906 (unofficial) and 1908 Olympics. In 1904 he placed third in the Olympic standing high jump. In 1906 he placed second in the standing high jump, third in the standing long jump, and fifth in the 100-m. (110 yd.) dash and the pentathlon. At home, he won the 1904 AAU outdoor 100-yd. dash. As coach of the University of Pennsylvania, his record shows over 20 IC4A individual crowns. His Olympic teams took 13 gold medals in 1924, 8 gold medals in 1928, 11 gold medals in 1932 and 12 gold medals in the 1936 German Olympics.

ROSANDICH, Thomas P.
Noteworthy Contributor

ROSE, Ralph
Shot-put, Discus and Hammer Thrower

Born March 17, 1884, in Healdsburg, Calif; Olympic Gold, Silver and Bronze Medals 1904, Gold Medal 1906 and Gold and Silver Medals 1912.

Ralph was no slouch when it came to getting medals. At the 1904 St. Louis Olympics he put the shot 48 ft. 7 in. for a world record and a gold medal. He also won a silver for a 128 ft. 7 5/16 in. discus toss. His third medal of that Games, a bronze, was for a hammer throw of 150 ft. ⅜ in. In 1908 he won another gold for a 46 ft. 7½ in. shot put, and four years later was happy to receive a silver for 50 ft. 2/5 in. In addition to that silver at the Stockholm Games of 1912, Bob participated in the two-hand shot for another gold. The rest of his performances were not so well rewarded as he finished ninth in hammer throw and eleventh in discus. But all together, Richards got six shiny medals in 3 Games.
Also in: U.S. Track and Field Hall of Fame.

ROURKE, Jack
Coach

RUDOLPH, Wilma
Sprinter

Born June 23, 1940, in St. Bethlehem, Tenn; moved to Clarksville, Tenn. at a very young age; double pneumonia and scarlet fever at age 8 left her use of her right leg only; daily massages administered by different family members helped her to walk but only with a special left shoe; in 1951 she discarded the shoe and joined her brother in backyard basketball games; at Burt High School in Clarksville she broke the state basketball record for girls while a sophomore; entered Tenn. State Univ. 1957; Olympic Bronze Medal 1956, three Gold Medals 1960; Citizens Savings World Trophy for North America 1960; James E. Sullivan Memorial Trophy 1961; named Associated Press U.S. Female Athlete of the Year and United Press International Athlete of the Year 1960; a former director of athletics for Mayor Daley's Youth Foundation in Chicago, Rudolph now resides in South Charleston, W.Va.

Wilma Rudolph is the only American woman ever to win three Olympic gold medals. She accomplished this feat in 1960, and by doing so earned the designation "World's Fastest Woman." At Rome that year she ran a 100-m. sprint in 11 sec. flat wind-aided (which nullified it as a world record), a 200-m. sprint in 24.0 against a strong wind, and anchored the 400-m. relay team. She also earned a bronze medal in the 400-m. relay at the 1956 Games. For four consecutive years, 1959–1962, she was the AAU 100-yd. champion, running a 10.8 in 1961 and again in 1962. She set the world record in the 200-m. in 1960 at 22.9 on July 9 in Corpus Christi, Tex.
Also in: Drake Relays Hall of Fame, National Track and Field Hall of Fame and U.S. Track and Field Hall of Fame.

RYAN, Michael
Coach

Ryan was the 1912 Boston Marathon winner with a time of 2:21:18.2.
Also in: Athletic Trainers Hall of Fame, Citizens Savings Hall of Fame Athletic Museum.

RYAN, Patrick
Hammer Thrower

Born January 4, 1887, in Pallasgreen, County Limerick, Ireland; policeman in New York City; Olympic Gold Medal and Silver Medal 1920; returned to Ireland in 1924 to manage family farm; died February 15, 1964.

Ryan was the king of U.S. hammer throw competition for nearly ten years and maker of long-standing records. His 189 ft. 6 in. toss of August 17, 1913, remained the record for 25 years. In AAU competition, Ryan was champ 1913–1917 and 1919–1921. His 183 ft. 3¾ in. throw in 1914 was unbeatable for 36 years. A tough competitor, also Irish and a New York City cop, Matt McGrath could not defeat Ryan, who set the new world record 2 in. beyond McGrath's old record. Ryan took the gold in hammer throw at the 1920 Olympics. That toss at the Antwerp Games went 173 ft. 5½ in. In 56-lb. weight throw, Ryan took a silver.

RYDER, Jack
Coach

RYUN, James
Runner

Born April 29, 1947, in Wichita, Kans; spent boyhood on farm; ran through cornfields; attended Wichita East High School; Univ. Kans; Citizens Savings World Trophy Award 1966; James E. Sullivan Memorial Trophy 1968; hindered by mononucleosis in 1968, retired in 1969 but attempted comeback in 1972; afterward ran on professional basis.

As a high school sophomore in 1963, Ryun demonstrated phenomenal potential when he ran the mile in 4:20.0, 4:16.2, 4:07.8. He was prompted to try for the 1964

Olympic team and made it, but a semifinal time of 3:55.0 did not qualify him for the 1500-m. Ryun persisted. As a college freshman he trained strenuously, running 70 to 100 mi. a week. On June 10, 1966, he ran the 880-yd. in 1:44.9 for a new record. On July 17 that year, at Berkeley, Calif, he ran a 3:51.3 mile record which he then broke a year later at 3:51.1. An impressive 3:33.1 in the 1500-m. on July 8, 1967, made another Ryun world record. For Kansas in 1967 he won the NCAA mile championship and took AAU titles in 1965–1967. On the heels of a bout with mononucleosis, Ryun qualified for the 1500-m. on the Olympic team, went to the high-altitude Mexico City site, and took the silver medal. Kenya's Kipchoge Keino won the gold with an Olympic record of 3:34.9. Ryun burst back on the track in 1972 after a two-year retirement and ran 3:41.5 to get on the Munich-bound team. During his 1500-m. qualifying run, Ryun fell and lost his chance to compete in the Games. Appeals to have him reinstated were not accepted by the committees in charge.
Also in: Drake Relays Hall of Fame.

SCHLADEMAN, Karl
Coach

SCHMERTZ, Fred
Noteworthy Contributor

SCHOLZ, Jackson
Sprinter
Born March 15, 1897, in Buchanan, Mich; Olympic Gold Medal 1920, Gold and Silver Medal 1924; competed for New York Athletic Club; freelance writer.

Scholz's achievements were primarily Olympics-based, save for matching the 100-m. world record of 10.2 sec, which he did in Stockholm on September 6, 1920. At the 1920 Games in Antwerp, he ran the second leg in the relay that won the gold medal for the U.S. 400-m. team. Their time set new world and Olympic records at 42.2. Also at Antwerp, Scholz took fourth in the 100-m. In 1924 at the Paris Olympics, he won the gold medal in 200-m. at 21.6 which tied the Olympic record, but he earned silver for the 100-m. At Amsterdam for the 1928 Games, Scholz placed fourth in the 200-m, barely missing the third place bronze.
Also in: Drake Relays Hall of Fame.

SCHULTE, Harry
Coach

SEAGREN, Bob
Pole Vaulter
Born October 17, 1946, in Fullerton, Calif; attended Univ. Southern Calif; Olympic Gold Medal 1968, Silver Medal 1972; turned professional in 1973; entered acting profession thereafter.

Seagren drew international attention first in 1966 when he vaulted 17 ft. 5½ in. at Fresno, Calif, for a world record. A year later on June 10, 1967, he pushed up the mark to 17 ft. 7 in. Barely two weeks went by before a new record went on the books. At the 1968 Olympic trials, Seagren vaulted 17 ft. 9 in. to regain the record. His Mexico City performance was worth a gold medal for 17 ft. 8½ in. on a second try and with fewest misses. In college Seagren starred for Southern California winning NCAA championships in 1967 and 1969, plus AAU titles of 1969 and 1970. That year and during most of 1971 Seagren nursed a knee operation and devoted efforts to training and strengthening. A world best of 18 ft. 5¾ in. was the result, which put him star center on the Olympic team of 1972. There he was forced by the International Amateur Athletic Foundation to abandon use of a carbon pole ruled illegal. Seagren failed to clear 17 ft. 10½ in. and had to accept second place to East German Nordwig's gold-getting 18 ft. ½ in. Afterwards Seagren made a present of his pole to the Foundation.

SHEPPARD, Melvin W.
Runner
Born September 5, 1883, in Almonesson Lake, N.J; three Olympic Gold Medals 1908, Gold Medal 1912; died January 4, 1942.

In AAU competition, Sheppard won championships in 800-m. 1906–1908, 1911 and 1912. At the 1908 London Games he won two gold medals and set world records for the 800-m. in 1:52.8 and the 1500-m. in 4:03.4, which made him the first person to win golds for both. Also, Sheppard ran on the winning 1600-m. relay team. In 1912 another such relay stint got him a gold, as they set a record 3:16.6. In individual events he took sixth in the 1500-m, second in the 800-m with 1:52.0 and not placing in the 400-m.
Also in: U.S. Track and Field Hall of Fame.

SHERIDAN, Martin
Shot-putter and Discus Thrower
Born 1871 in County Mayo, Ireland; Gold Medal, 1904, two Gold, three Silver and a Bronze Medal 1906, two Gold Medals 1908.

Sheridan tried all sorts of sports even though shot-put and discus suited him the best. In 1906 he wore the Greco-Roman wrestler's garb and competed in that unique sport for a year. At the London Games in 1908 he adopted Greek style discus and won the gold medal with 124 ft. 8 in, also capturing the conventional discus gold medal with 134 ft. 2 in. Talented also at standing long jump, Sheridan won the bronze at London and the silver at Athens during the 1906 Games. Also at that Olympic competition, he took two more silver medals in standing high jump and 56-lb. weight throw. A shot-put of 40 ft. 4 4/5 in. and a discus toss of 137 ft. both earned gold medals. Two years previously, at the St. Louis Olympics, the discus was Sheridan's strong event and he won his first gold medal with a toss of 128 ft. 10 in. All in all he won five Olympic gold medals. He also kept hold of a discus world record, unofficially, 1901–1911, first set at 120 ft. 7¾ in. and bettered to 141 ft. 4⅜ in. The discus championship was Sheridan's in AAU competition in 1906, 1907 and 1911, and he won the AAU shot title in 1904 with 40 ft. 9½ in.

SILVESTER, Jay
Discus Thrower
Born August 27, 1937, in Tremonton, Utah; Olympic Silver Medal 1972; instructor in physical education at Brigham Young Univ.

Silvester won the 1961 AAU discus title with a throw of 195 ft. 8 in. His 1963 winning discus toss was at 198 ft. 11½ in, 203 ft. 9 in. in 1968, and 205 ft. 4 in. in 1970. He broke the world record twice with 198 ft. 8 in. on August

11, 1961, and 224 ft. 5 in. on September 18, 1965. At the Olympic Games in Rome in 1964 Silvester took fourth, and in 1968 he placed fifth. In the Munich Games held in 1972 he won the silver medal with 208 ft. 4 in.

SMITH, Arthur
Coach

SNYDER, Larry
Coach
Born August 9, 1896, in Canton, Ohio; attended Ohio State High School, Ohio State Univ. in 1917; served in W.W. I as pilot instructor; barnstormed and sold groceries in California after the war; returned to Ohio State Univ. in 1923; retired in 1965.

Before becoming a coach, Snyder won the 1915 Ohio state high school high jump title, won the triple jump, 120-yd. hurdles, and placed second in the broad jump and 440-yd. hurdles in the Penn Relays for Ohio State in 1925. The same year he placed second in the NCAA 120-yd. hurdles. As a coach at Ohio State 1932–1965, Snyder trained 14 world record holders, 52 All-Americans and such notables as Jesse Owens, Mal Whitfield and Glenn Davis. Snyder's 1960 Olympic team won eight gold medals.

SOWELL, Arnold
Runner
Born April 6, 1935, in Pittsburgh, Pa; attended Univ. Pittsburgh; Olympic Gold Medal 1956.

Sowell was top 880-yd. man at Pitt and took five championships in NCAA and IC4A contests 1954–1956. In AAU competition, Sowell won the 1955 and 1956 titles with 1:47.6, a time which in one year also took the NCAA 800-meter crown. All along the way, Arnie faced a tough adversary in Tom Courtney who won the Olympic trials in 1:46.4. Arnie was second in 1:46.9. At the Melbourne Games of 1956, Sowell sprinted to first at the 150-m. mark, but Courtney passed by and won the gold. Sowell fell back to fourth.

STAGG, Amos Alonzo
Noteworthy Contributor
See entry in Naismith Memorial Basketball Hall of Fame, 1959.
Also in: National Football Hall of Fame; College Football Hall of Fame and Noteworthy Contributors Hall of Fame, Citizens Savings Hall of Fame Athletic Museum.

STANFIELD, Andrew
Sprinter
Born December 29, 1927, in Washington, D.C; attended Seton Hall Univ. in New Jersey; two Olympic Gold Medals 1952.

Andy ran the 200-yd. in 20.6 for a new world record on May 5, 1951, in Philadelphia. One year later he ran the same time during the 1952 Olympic team trials. Then at the actual Games he ran a 20.7 to win the gold medal and match Jesse Owens' mark. His teammates of the 400-m. relay aided him in snaring another gold medal. At the 1956 Melbourne Olympics Stanfield got silver while Bobby Morrow earned the gold by a yd. Morrow's 20.6 also cracked the Owens-Stanfield co-held 20.7 record. While a Seton Hall thinclad, Stanfield won IC4A championships in 100-yd, 220-yd. and indoor 60-yd. for a total of eight top honors 1949–1951. He took AAU prizes four times, the 100-m. with 10.3, and 200-m. in a wind-backed 20.4 in 1949, and the 200-m. alone in 1952 and 1953.

STARR, Heriwentha Mae Faggs
Sprinter
Born April 10, 1932, in Mays Landing, N.J; attended Tenn. State Univ; Olympic Gold Medal 1952, Bronze Medal 1956; Pan-Am Gold and Silver Medals 1955; now a teacher and active in youth programs in Cincinnati, Ohio.

At the 1952 Helsinki Olympics, Mae won a gold medal as a member of the world record-setting 400-m. relay team in 45.9 sec. She ran with the U.S. world record 880-yd. relay team that ran 1:40.0 in London on August 4, 1952. Although failing to earn a medal in the 1948 Games, Mae garnered the bronze in 1956 at Melbourne on the 400-m. team. She also won a silver in the 1955 Pan-American Games and a gold with the 400-m. relay team. Mae won the indoor AAU 220-yd. 1949–1952, 1954 and 1956 with her best time of 25.9 in 1949 standing as a record until Wilma Rudolph broke it in 1960. She won the AAU outdoor 100-yd. dash in 1955 with a 10.8 and in 1956 with 11.7 for the 100-m. She also claimed the AAU 200-m. championship in 1954 and 1956 and the 220-yd. in 1955.
Also in: National Track and Field Hall of Fame.

STEERS, Lester
High Jumper
Born June 16, 1917, in Eureka, Calif; attended Univ. Ore.

Steers was ready for Olympic participation and eager to become the first high jumper to surpass the 7 ft. mark, but war put a stop to the Games and to most organized athletic competition. In 1941 Steers took NCAA honors for Oregon with 6 ft. 10⅞ in, following with six other instances of jumps over 6 ft. 10 in. Lester's leap of 6 ft. 8⅛ in. won the AAU title of 1939, and an additional ¼ in. earned him the 1940 AAU title. An informal jump was Steer's best, a 7 ft. in a practice session. His record 1941 jump was not broken until 1953.
Also in: National Track and Field Hall of Fame.

STEPHENS, Helen
Sprinter, Javelin Thrower
Born February 3, 1918, in Fulton, Mo; presently a librarian.

Clocked in a world record 5.8 sec. in the 50-yd. dash in a high school gym class, coach Bernie Moore could only exclaim, "Holy Cow, what's going on here." Later Helen would win two golds in the Olympics in the 100-m. and 400-m. relay team. Between 1935 and 1937, she never lost a race to a woman, winning over 70 consecutive matches, including AAU titles in 1935 for the 100- and 200-m. and in 1936 for the 100-m. and the javelin in 121 ft. 6.5 in.
Also in: National Track and Field Hall of Fame.

STONE, Curtis C.
Long Distance Runner
Stone's name fittingly suggests the stamina and endurance required by the athlete who never lets up but runs on and on. Stone churned up the miles, beginning with a 2-mi. championship run in 1943 during NCAA competition, which he won again after a four year interim. In

1946 as a member of the Rhode Island State University crew of trackmen, Stone took first place honors in the NCAA cross-country. In 1947 a cross-country crown under the auspices of AAU became Stone's, as did the AAU 3-mi. title 1947, 1948 and 1952. For four consecutive years, 1951–1954 Stone was the undisputed 6-mi. champ of AAU competition.

SULLIVAN, Bartholomew J.
Coach
Born February 12, 1879, in Boston, Mass; received IC4A 50-Year Salute; died February 24, 1968.

In 1906 Bart Sullivan competed in the Scottish Games, which were a popular American event at the time. Playing for New England's best team, he won the 220-yd. and the 440-yd. dash, the 5-mi. race, and placed second in the 100-yd. dash. Sullivan coached in 1910 at Colby College and in 1911 at Boston College. As a coach at Holy Cross 1912–1964 he produced several Olympians and world record holders.

SULLIVAN, James E.
Noteworthy Contributor
See entry in Noteworthy Contributors Hall of Fame, Citizens Savings Hall of Fame Athletic Museum.

SWARTZ, Elizabeth Robinson "Betty"
Sprinter
Born August 23, 1911, in Riverdale, Ill; Olympic Gold and Silver Medals 1928, Gold Medal 1936.

Betty won two Olympic gold medals, one in the 100-m. in 1928 and the second one in the 400-m. relay in 1936. She also won a silver in the 400-m. relay in 1928. In 1929 she claimed the AAU 50-m. and 100-m, running the 100-m. in 11.2 sec. to break the meet record.
Also in: U.S. Track and Field Hall of Fame.

TAYLOR, F. Morgan
Hurdler
Born April 17, 1903, in Sioux City, Iowa; Olympic Bronze Medal 1928 and 1932.

Taylor met with some misfortune at his first Olympics when his 400-m. hurdle winning-time of 52.6 sec. was disallowed because he had downed a hurdle. But in 1928 before the Amsterdam Games, Taylor tried out with a record 52.0 and became the favored Olympic contender. No gold was in store for Taylor, as Lord Burghley of England and U.S. teammate Frank Cuhel took gold and silver, while Taylor took bronze with 53.8. Four years later at the Los Angeles Olympics, he won the third place bronze again, showing a good 52.0 time. But his good time was not good enough to beat the winning 51.8. Taylor was not limited to hurdles throughout his career and made a name for himself in long jump with 25 ft. 2 in. as his best jump.
Also in: Drake Relays Hall of Fame.

TEMPLETON, Robert L. "Dink"
Coach
Born 1897 in Helena, Mont; attended Stanford Univ; died August 7, 1962.

Templeton was a track and football star during his student years at Stanford. He once dropkicked a 55-yd. field goal. In 1917, his senior year, he helped coach Stanford's track team. In 1920 he participated in the Olympics at Antwerp, placing fourth in the long jump with a mark of 22 ft. 9 3/5 in. Templeton believed in continuous daily practice, which was considered heresy at that time due to the fear of "burning out" athletes. When he was actually hired at Stanford 1922–1941 his teams won 77 percent of their dual meets and won the NCAA championships in 1925, 1928 and 1934. He coached a total of 19 individual NCAA crown winners.
Also in: U.S. Track and Field Hall of Fame.

THOMAS, John C.
High Jumper
Born March 3, 1941, in Boston, Mass; attended Boston Univ; Olympic Bronze Medal 1960, Silver Medal 1964.

In March 1959 John caught his take-off foot in an elevator shaft, severely wounding it, which kept him out of competition for nearly a year. But he sprang back onto the scene in 1960, jumping 7 ft. 2½ in. A jump of 7 ft. 1½ in. earned him the world outdoor record that year on April 30 in Philadelphia. At the Olympic trials in 1960 John pushed up the record mark to 7 ft. 3¾ in. and became the U.S. team's gold-medal hopeful for the 1960 Rome Games. There a huge upset put two Russians on top and Thomas on the bottom with a bronze medal jump of 7 ft. ¼ in. Second place went to Valery Brumel who eventually set a new record, 7 ft. 5¾ in. At the 1964 Games it was Brumel who pocketed the gold while Thomas moved up into the silver slot with a leap of 7 ft. 1¾ in.
Also in: U.S. Track and Field Hall of Fame.

THOMPSON, Wilbur "Moose"
Shot-putter
Born April 6, 1921, in Frankfort, S. Dak; attended Univ. Southern Calif; Olympic Gold Medal 1948.

College days competition was not outstanding for Thompson, but he did take one AAU title in 1949 for 54 ft. 10⅛ in. At the 1948 London Olympics he fared surprisingly well with a gold medal toss of 56 ft. 2 in. which sailed 3 ft. past the previous record. At the trials preceding those games, Thompson was second behind James Delaney, and ahead of Jim Fuchs. Final results showed Thompson first, then Delaney, then Fuchs.

THOMSON, Earl
Coach
Born February 15, 1895, in Prince Albert, Sask; graduated 1921 from Dartmouth Col; served two years in Royal Canadian Air Force in W.W. I; died April 19, 1971.

Thomson's amateur career consisted of two IC4A titles while at Dartmouth, a gold medal in the 1920 Antwerp Olympics in the 110-m. hurdles with a world record mark of 14.8 sec, a world 120-yd. hurdle record of 14.4 in 1920, an NCAA crown in 1921 and three AAU titles: in 1918 for 15.2, in 1921 for 15.0, and in 1922 for 15.6 in hurdles. As a coach, he was employed at West Virginia and Yale before accepting the coaching position at the U.S. Naval Academy where he coached for over 30 years. These accomplishments are remarkable considering he was almost totally deaf.

TOLAN, Eddie
Sprinter
Born September 29, 1908, in Denver, Colo; attended Univ. Mich; died Jan. 30, 1967.

Tolan became known as the "Midnight Express" because of his speed. He began clocking championship time while at Michigan, becoming the first to run the 100-yd. in record 9.5 sec. at an Evanston, Ill, meet of 1929. That year he also won AAU 100-yd. plus the AAU 220-yd. titles, retaining just the 100-yd. title through the following year. In 1931 Tolan added the NCAA 220-yd. race which he ran in 21.5. At the 1932 team tryouts, Tolan broke an Olympic record for a new 10.4, then edged in just ahead of competing finalist Ralph Metcalfe, although both had the same time of 10.3. In 200-m. Olympic competition, Tolan won the race with a new record of 21.2.

TOOMEY, William A.
Decathlon
Born January 10, 1939, in Philadelphia, Pa; injured hand as child and worked to strengthen it via field events; attended Univ. Colo; earned master's degree at Stanford Univ; Pan-Am Gold Medal 1967; Olympic Gold Medal 1968; James E. Sullivan Trophy 1969; Citizens Savings World Trophy Award for North America 1969; married Mary Rand, Olympic long jumper from England; taught junior college English; changed to television sportscasting.

Bill Toomey's determination to win the Mexico City decathlon paid off in full, complete with new Olympic record of 8193 points. His victory seemed inevitable from the first day of competition when he tallied up the best first day total points ever, with 4499. In individual events, Toomey ran the 100-m. in 10.4, long jumped 25 ft. 9¾ in, threw the shot 45 ft. 1¼ in, high jumped 6 ft. 4¾ in, and set a 45.6 decathlon record in the 400-m. Day two saw him race 14.9 in 110-m. hurdles, throw 143 ft. 5½ in. in discus, and nearly botch the pole vault contest. He missed twice, then made it at 13 ft. 9½ in. German rivals swept javelin competition top spots but Toomey defeated them early on in 1500-m. Throughout his entire career, Toomey crashed the 8000 point mark during twelve performances. On December 11–12, 1969, at a Los Angeles contest, he collected 8417 points for a new world record, after having competed in a total of 33 decathlons. Toomey was the only man who ever won five consecutive AAU decathlon championships, 1965–1969, and he also won the AAU pentathlon title four times 1960–1964. He won a gold medal in the Pan-Am Games in 1967. His best records were 10.3 in the 100-m, 45.6 in the 400-m. and a 26 ft. ¼ in. long jump. Toomey's decathlon record stood until usurped by Bruce Jenner on August 8–9, 1975.
Also in: National Track and Field Hall of Fame and U.S. Track and Field Hall of Fame.

TOOTELL, Fred
Coach
Born September 9, 1902, in Lawrence, Mass; attended Bowdoin Col; Olympic Gold Medal 1924; died September 29, 1964, in Wakefield, R.I.

In 1923 and 1924 Fred Tootell was the AAU hammer throw titlist with throws of 173 ft. 6⅝ in. and 174 ft. 10⅛ in. In 1923 he took the NCAA title with a throw of 175 ft. 1 in. That same year he set a collegiate record of 181 ft. 6½ in. In 1924 he took an Olympic gold medal with a throw of 174 ft. 10⅛ in. At Rhode Island he coached teams that were unbeaten in dual meets for 17 seasons. His cross-country teams remained unbeaten for 18 seasons. In 1964 at the time of his death he was coaching tennis at Rhode Island.
Also in: U.S. Track and Field Hall of Fame.

TORRANCE, Jack "Baby Jack"
Shot-putter
Born June 20, 1912, in Weathersby, Miss; attended La. State Univ; also called "Baby Elephant" for massive 6 ft. 2 in, 280 lb. build; played pro football for Chicago Bears; died November 10, 1970.

Jack was a phenomenon among weight throwers while at Louisiana State and a member of the "Fabulous Five" track team. In 1933 the Five took the NCAA team title. On his own, Torrance broke the world shot put record three times in 1934. He tossed 55 ft. 1½ in, 55 ft. 5½ in, and 57 ft. 1 in. thrown in Norway, which remained the record for 14 years. Torrance won the NCAA shot titles in 1933 and 1934, both with record achievements, and he captured AAU crowns 1933–1935. Torrance took fifth place at the Berlin Games of 1936 with a shot-put of 50 ft. 5½ in, showing a substantial 5 ft. drop.
Also in: Drake Relays Hall of Fame.

TOWNS, Forrest "Speck"
Hurdler
Born February 6, 1914, in Fitzgerald, Ga; attended Univ. Ga; Olympic Gold Medal 1936; spent a few years as assistant coach at Georgia; served in U.S. Army 1942 to 1946, earning bronze star.

In 1936 Towns nabbed the NCAA title in 120-yd, 110-m. hurdles, breaking a record with 14.1 sec. in a preliminary run. He matched that time during Olympic trials, going on to take the gold medal with 14.2. Later that year he astounded sports officials by becoming the first man to run under 14.0 in the 110-m. hurdles. Authorities spent two years adjudicating his 13.7 before world record status was allowed. Throughout 1936 Towns collected firsts, the AAU with 14.2 and the NCAA with 14.3, which was repeated the next year. Member of Rules Committee of National Collegiate Athletic Association (NCAA).
Also in: National Track and Field Hall of Fame and U.S. Track and Field Hall of Fame.

TYUS, Wyomia
Sprinter
Born August 29, 1945, in Griffin, Ga; fourth child with three older brothers; Olympic Gold Medal 1964, two Gold Medals 1968; father Willie a dairy worker who died when she was 15; mother Marie worked in a laundry; entered Tenn. State Univ. 1963.

Wyomia drifted into track following the basketball season at her high school. With nothing to do, she tried high jumping but quickly turned toward the sprints. Her future college mentor, Ed Temple at Tennessee State, noticed her potential and enrolled her in his summer program in 1961. After one month of training she entered the AAU girls' national championships but did not place. A year later she won the girls' national 50-, 75- and 100-yd. dashes breaking two American records. Under the expert tutelage of Temple at Tennessee State where she enrolled in 1963, Wyomia thrived in the envi-

ronment of daily coaching that was nationally renowned for producing female track stars. This group of stars, Tigerbelles, represented the U.S. in Olympic competition from 1956 to 1972. Wyomia was one of 29 who accumulated 11 gold medals, four silvers and four bronzes. Moving from the girls' to women's AAU level in 1963, Wyomia finished second in the finals but qualified for a trip to the U.S.S.R. She finished last in her first international meet in the 100-m. dash but returned on July 31, 1965, at Kiev to claim the 100-m. and become the fastest woman in the world by sprinting at 23.78 m.p.h. Wyomia had established herself as the dominant international sprinter in the 1964 Tokyo Olympics. Although barely qualifying as third and only by inches because she was too nervous, she flashed her best performance with an 11.2 in the 100-m. to tie the world preliminaries record and an 11.4 in the finals. She had also won the AAU 1964 sprint with an 11.5. Two weeks before her showcase performance in Kiev, at Kingston, Jamaica, she had run the 100-yd. dash in 10.3 to tie the world record. Her development through the weeks and months spiraled upward, surpassing her first Olympic performance, the Jamaica and Kiev records, and winning the AAU meets consistently. From 1965 to 1967 she claimed the 60-yd. indoor championship, along with the 100-yd. in 1965 and a 220-yd. in 1966. Four years later at Mexico City she became the only woman to win the 100-m. twice—another world record in itself—while setting the pace in the field with an 11.0 which still stands. She was sixth in the 200-m. and ran on the gold medal-winning 400-m. U.S. relay team. The comparisons with fellow Hall of Famer Wilma Rudolph were inevitable.
Also in: U.S. Track and Field Hall of Fame.

VON ELLING, Emil
Coach

WALSH, Stella
Sprinter, Broad Jumper and Discus Thrower
Born April 3, 1911, in Wierzchownia, Poland; Polish name Staniolawa Waladrewicz; reared in the United States but competed for Poland in the 1932 Olympics.

In a career spanning over two decades, 1930 to 1951, Stella won 35 national championships in such diverse events as sprints, broad jump, discus and baseball throw. She won her first AAU championships in 1930 with an 11.2 sec. in the 100-m, a 25.4 in the 200-m. and 18 ft. 9⅜ in. in the long jump. Her 100-m. titles came in 1943, 1944, 1948; 200-m. in 1931, 1939, 1940 and 1942–1948; the long jump 1939–1946, 1948 and 1951. Stella won the AAU indoor 50-yd. in 1934 and the 220-yd. indoor in 1930, 1931, 1934, 1935, 1945 and 1946. Probably the greatest woman track athlete of all time, Stella held women's records in the 60-, 100- and 200-m. and the 220-yd. dash. This unparalleled athlete won three AAU titles at the age of 37 and the AAU long jump when she was 40 years old.
Also in: National Polish-American Sports Hall of Fame and Museum and National Track and Field Hall of Fame.

WARMERDAM, Cornelius "Dutch"
Pole Vaulter
Born June 22, 1915, in Long Beach, Calif; attended Fresno State Col; ran for San Francisco Olympic Club; James E. Sullivan Memorial Trophy 1942; track coach at Fresno State.

Warmerdam was good in college athletics and even better after his college days were over. While at Fresno, his best vault was at 14 ft. 1⅞ in. But he boosted that height over 15 ft. to become the first to clear that mark, on April 13, 1940, at Berkeley, Calif. All together Warmerdam had 43 career vaults over 15 ft. He won six AAU titles in 1938 and 1940–1944 and a title tie in 1937. His best outdoor meet vault was 15 ft. 7¾ in. while indoor reached up to 15 ft. 8½ in. In his final contest Warmerdam hit the 15 ft. mark in 1944 AAU competition.
Also in: Drake Relays Hall of Fame, National Association of Intercollegiate Athletics Hall of Fame, National Track and Field Hall of Fame and U.S. Track and Field Hall of Fame.

WEFERS, Bernard J.
Sprinter
Born 1873; attended Georgetown Univ; died April 18, 1925.

Wefers was an outstanding sprinter of the nineteenth century and one who nurtured his talent primarily during college years. As a freshman in 1895, he ran the 100-yd. in 10.0 sec. and 220-yd. in 21.8 which launched him on a career of sprint wins. From 1895 through 1897 Wefers maintained the AAU championship in both 100-yd. and 220-yd, with a best of 21.4 for the latter. In IC4A contests during 1896 and 1897 Wefers won the 100-yd. dash with a record-tying 9.8 the first year. He won the IC4A 220-yd. on May 30, 1896, with a 21.2 that outdid the previous record by .6, and which was acknowledged as a 200-m. record also. And nearly 30 years went by before the Wefers' record was broken—by Charlie Paddock, with 20.8.

WHITE, Willye
Long Jumper
Born January 1, 1939, in Money, Miss; attended Tenn. State Univ; Olympic Silver Medal 1956 and 1960; Pan-Am Gold Medal 1963.

Willye's jump of 21 ft. 6 in. in 1960 set the U.S. women's long jump record. As a high school girl from Greenwood, Miss, she won an Olympic silver medal in 1956 with a leap of 19 ft. 11.75 in. In the 1960 Rome Olympics she finished sixteenth and in the 1964 Games she ended in twelfth place in the long jump, but led off the 400-m. relay team that won a silver medal. In 1972 she jumped 20 ft. 11.5 in. in qualifying but was eleventh in the finals. In the 1963 Pan-American Games she set the Games' record while winning the gold at 20 ft. 2 in. Altogether, Willye won 11 AAU championships, including indoor and outdoor events. In other international competition, she took first place in both the 1969 U.S.-U.S.S.R.-British Commonwealth meet with a 20 ft. 4.25 in. mark and in the U.S.-U.S.S.R. meet in 1971 with a 20 ft. 4 in. leap.
Also in: U.S. Track and Field Hall of Fame.

WHITFIELD, Malvin
Runner
Born Oct. 11, 1924 in Bay City, Tex; attended Ohio State and Los Angeles State universities; Olympic Gold Medals 1948 and 1952; James E. Sullivan Memorial Trophy 1954; Gold and Bronze Medals 1956.

Whitfield pocketed the 800-m. gold medals at both 1948 and 1952 Olympics, with identical times of 1:49.2. In 1952 at Helsinki, he also finished sixth in the 400-m. and second as part of the 1600-m. relay team. In 1956 the relay team won a gold, and Whitfield won a bronze medal as third-placer in the 400-m. On behalf of Ohio State earlier in his career, Whitfield captured the 1948 and 1949 NCAA titles plus two of five AAU 880-yd. crowns. He finished up an extended college study career in 1956 at Los Angeles, in the meantime amassing other AAU championships in 1951, 1953 and 1954. Overall, his record times were 1:49.2 in 1950 and 1:48.6 in 1953. Whitfield tried for a berth on the 1956 Olympic team but could not qualify with 1:49.3.
Also in: Drake Relays Hall of Fame and National Track and Field Hall of Fame.

WHITTLE, A. Heath
Coach

WILSON, Alex
Coach
Also in: Canadian Amateur Athletic Hall of Fame and Drake Relays Hall of Fame.

WILT, Fred
Long Distance Runner
A recipient in 1950 of the prestigious James E. Sullivan Memorial Trophy. As a student at Indiana University, Wilt took the NCAA cross-country championship. Then in 1949 he became the cross-country top contender in AAU competition, repeating in 1952 and 1953. He was also AAU 6-mile champ in 1949 and 3-mile champ from 1949 through 1951. It was in 1951 also that he clocked 4:9.4 for the mile.

WINTER, Lloyd "Bud"
Coach

WOLCOTT, Fred
Hurdler
Born November 18, 1917, in Snyder, Tex; attended Rice Univ; died Jan. 26, 1972, at Houston.

Wolcott ran for Rice in high and low hurdles competition and as a 9.5 sec. sprinter. He won NCAA titles in 220-yd. low hurdles 1938–1940 and 120-yd. high hurdles in 1938 and 1939. He also won the AAU low titles 1938–1941, and high titles 1938, 1939 and 1941. In eight formally sanctioned meets, Fred completed the hurdles in less than 14.0, the first at the 1938 Texas Relays. Twice he ran 13.7, at a Rice collegiate meet in 1940 and an AAU meet at Philadelphia in 1941, tying Forrest Towns' mark. Another distinction granted Wolcott is having been the first to break Jesse Owens' 220-yd. hurdle record of 22.6 with a 22.5 in 1940.
Also in: Drake Relays Hall of Fame.

WOODRUFF, John "Long John"
Runner
Born July 5, 1915, in Connellsville, Pa; attended Univ. Pittsburgh; Olympic Gold Medal 1936.

For awhile Woodruff specialized in both 440-yd. and 880-yd, taking IC4A top honors in both in 1937–1939. At the same time he was NCAA 880-yd. winner. At the Berlin Games of 1936 he competed as a relay man in 2-mi. and 3200-m, setting a new world record for the U.S. team. But his outstanding coup was taking the 800-m. gold medal in the 1936 Games with a 1:52.9. In tryouts he had recorded a 1:49.9 in a semifinal run. The following year Woodruff won the AAU championship in 1:50.3, then in 1940 broke the American record for the 800-m. with 1:48.6, just above the world record of 1:48.4.

WYKOFF, Frank
Sprinter
Born October 29, 1909 in Des Moines, Iowa; spent youth in California; attended Univ. Southern Calif; Olympic Gold Medals 1928, 1932 and 1936.

Wykoff made it to the Olympic team trials while still in high school. At the 1928 Amsterdam Games he placed fourth in 100-m. but won a gold medal as a part of the U.S. winning 400-m. relay team. As a college student, from 1930 to 1931 he was a 100-yd. sprinter who won two NCAA titles with a 9.4 best time and a meet record. Wykoff also won the 1931 AAU title with a record 9.5. Also that year, Wykoff ran anchor leg of the USC 440-yd, 400-m. relay teams which set a new record of 40.8. The Olympic relay team brought Wykoff to the 1932 Games and to a record 40.0 at Los Angeles. Four years later the illustrious 400-m. relay team with Wykoff, Jesse Owens, Ralph Metcalfe and Foy Draper, ran a record 39.8, that held for 20 years.
Also in: U.S. Track and Field Hall of Fame.

YANG, Chuan-Kwang
Decathlon
Born July 10, 1935, in Taitung, Formosa; attended Univ. Calif. at Los Angeles; college teammate of Rafer Johnson; member of 1956, 1960 and 1964 Olympic teams, representing Nationalist China; Olympic Silver Medal 1960.

C. K. Yang ran neck-and-neck with Rafer Johnson throughout UCLA competition, not just running, but in jumping, pole vaulting, hurdling and throwing. Both were decathlon masters. The 1958 AAU championship featured Yang in second, under Johnson by 129 points, but C. K. slipped in for first place the next year when Johnson was out with an injury. In 1960 at Eugene, Ore, Yang piled up 8426 points, not good enough in view of Johnson's world-record 8683. On August 8, 1963, however, Yang scored a phenomenal 9121 points on the old scoring basis for a collegiate and world record. His performance included a pole vault of 15 ft. 10½ in, 14.0 sec. in 110-m. hurdles, 47.7 in the 400-m. run, and 10.7 in the 100-m. The next year at the Tokyo Games, Yang was favored but fell to fifth; he had taken the 1960 silver with a record score of 8334 to Rafer's record 8392. In peak performances, C. K. reached 16 ft. in pole vault, 14.0 in hurdles, and over 25 ft. in long jump.

ZAHARIAS, Mildred Ella Didrickson "Babe"
Hurdler, High Jumper, Runner and Javelin Thrower
Born June 26, 1914, in Port Arthur, Tex; sixth child of seven; parents Norwegian immigrants who came to the United States only a few years before her birth; married George Zaharias, a wrestler, on December 23, 1938; early in career starred on touring basketball, softball and baseball teams; *Associated Press* Woman Athlete of the Year 1932, 1945–1947, 1950 and 1954 and Greatest Woman

Athlete of the Half Century 1950; died from cancer September 27, 1956, in Galveston, Tex.

After reading about the Olympics when only 14, Babe set her sights on becoming the greatest athlete in the world. She was successful. Training with her sister Lillie, she hurdled bushes and fences in the neighborhood and raced with streetcars. Competing in the 1932 National AAU outdoor championships, Babe participated in five events: 80 m. hurdles, high jump, shot-put, javelin and baseball throw. She was a one-woman team, winning the team scoring title with 30 points. The second place team, of 22 women, scored 23. According to Olympic rules, she could compete in only three individual events. Babe, so-called because, like Babe Ruth, she could hit a baseball farther than anyone else, chose the javelin, hurdles, and the high jump for the 1932 Games. Her accomplishments are unparalleled: Babe broke the world record in the javelin and the hurdles earning two gold medals. She was first in the high jump but was disqualified for her "Western roll" style. The Babe also competed in the 400-m. relay, earning a silver medal. Later she competed on the professional golf circuit and became America's greatest woman golfer.

Also in: American Golf Hall of Fame, Colorado Golf Hall of Fame, Ladies Professional Golfers' Hall of Fame, National Track and Field Hall of Fame, Professional Golfers' Association of America Hall of Fame, United States Track and Field Hall of Fame, World Golf Hall of Fame; Golf Hall of Fame and Women's Basketball Hall of Fame, Citizens Savings Hall of Fame Athletic Museum.

ZINN, Ronald L.
Walker

Born May 10, 1937, in Chicago, Ill; Pan-Am Bronze Medal 1963; died July 7, 1965, in Vietnam.

The American leader in the 1960 and 1964 Olympics 20-km. walk, Ron won 16 AAU titles 1960–1965. In 1960 he won the 35-km, the 1 mi. 1961–1963 and 1965, the 2 mi. 1961–1964, the 10-km. 1961–1964, the 15-km. in 1961 and the 20-km. 1961 and 1962. He placed nineteenth in the 1960 Olympics and sixth in the 1964 Games.

Turners Hall of Fame

The Turners Hall of Fame was established in 1969. As of 1977 there are 10 members, selected by the Hall of Fame Board. Upon induction, each new member receives an Award and his or her name is engraved on the Turners Hall of Fame Trophy which is kept in the Citizens Savings Hall of Fame Athletic Museum, international sports shrine in Los Angeles.

Induction Years Unrecorded

DIAMANT, Alex
Player

Alex Diamant was the president of the American Turners of Brooklyn at the time of his selection to the Hall of Fame.

ECKL, Otto
Player

Born June 20, 1895, in St. Louis, Mo; Turners Nat. Honor Key 1956; Concordia Turners Plaque 1963; died February 15, 1963.

Eckl took first prize in the pentathlon at the Chicago National Turnfest in 1921. For many years Eckl was district leader of the physical education committee in St. Louis and was a member of the national physical education committee.

FUNKE, Edward
Player

Edward Funke is a member of the Wisconsin District Turners.

JACQUIN, George J.
Player

George joined the gymnasium classes at the Syracuse Turners and attended regularly until 1923. He competed in many gymnastic meets and was all-around gymnast in the Central and Western New York area between 1918 and 1921. He started teaching physical education in the public school system of Buffalo, N.Y, in 1926; for the next 40 years, he also coached gymnastics, baseball, basketball, track and field and swimming. Since 1921 Jacquin has been involved in Turners as a gymnast, judge and administrator and since 1921, has attended all of the National Festivals (Turnfests) of American Turners. He has been vice-president of the American Turner Endowment Trust since 1968. In 1954 he co-edited *The History of the Buffalo Turners* and in 1974 edited the revision of *The American Turner History.*

JOHNKE, Bruno A.
Player

See entry in Gymnastics Hall of Fame, Citizens Savings Hall of Fame Athletic Museum.

LASCARI, Andrew
Player

Andrew Lascari is a member of the Buffalo Turners.

RHODE, C. J.
Player

C.J. is a member of the Los Angeles Turners.

ROTH, Louis A.
Player

Louis Roth is a member of the Covington Turners.

WEISMULLER, Joseph
Player

Born October 4, 1890, in Varjas, Austria; married; Am. Turners Nat. Honor Key 1955; Louisville Man of the Year 1963; Kentucky Colonel Commission 1964; lives in Louisville, Ky.

In 1913 Joseph received a degree of instructor of physical education from the American Turners Normal College in Indianapolis, and in 1918 he became an instructor at the Louisville Society of the American Turners. In November of 1968 he was honored at a banquet marking his 50th anniversary as an instructor of this society. During those 50 years Joseph has been director of two National Turnfests in 1926 and 1959. He has been an AAU representative for gymnastics in the Louisville area and has conducted numerous AAU gymnastics meets at the Louisville Turners. He has also conducted many District Turnfests. He served on the national physical education committee for 35 years until 1957. Weismuller has been a member of the American Turners for 62 years and in 1957 he received his 50-year honorary membership card.

ZITTA, Fred
Player
See entry in Gymnastics Hall of Fame, Citizens Savings Hall of Fame Athletic Museum.

Volleyball Hall of Fame

The Volleyball Hall of Fame was originated in 1954 to honor outstanding players and contributors to the sport. As of 1977 there are 39 members, selected by the Hall of Fame Board. Each inductee receives a Hall of Fame Award, and his or her name is engraved on the Volleyball Hall of Fame Trophy kept in the Citizens Savings Hall of Fame Athletic Museum.

1954

FISHER, Dr. George J.
Contributor
George Fisher has served as president of the United States Volleyball Association (USVBA). He has served the USVBA as executive chief for 25 years, and has contributed to volleyball for most of his adult life.

IDELL, A. Provost "Pop"
Contributor
Originally from Philadelphia, Pa.

Idell played and contributed to volleyball for 50 years, since 1904. He has been president of the United States Volleyball Association, organizer, rulemaker, equipment and court developer, coach and official.

MORGAN, William G.
Contributor
Graduate of Springfield Col, Mass.

William G. Morgan is known as the founder of volleyball, while he was a physical education director at Holyoke, Mass. in 1895.

WORTHAM, James
Player
Wortham played for the Houston, Tex, YMCA, and sparked it to many national championship triumphs. He is regarded as the greatest volleyballer of all time. He was chosen eight times for All-American volleyball team honors.

1961

MASSOPUST, A. H. "Dick"
Contributor and Player
Born November 19, 1895, in New Ulm, Minn; graduated from Carleton Col. (Minn.) 1917; served as physical director at Duluth and Iron Range YMCAs; All-American 1927.

Massopust has been active in volleyball not only as a competitor, but as a coach and a contributor. While with the Minneapolis YMCA, he participated in four national tournaments. In 1931 he organized the St. Anthony Turnverein Volleyball team, which won the Minnesota State and North West titles in 1934. He was a member of the Minneapolis Athletic Club from 1936 to 1943 and has been very active in developing an interest in volleyball and coaching the sport.

1962

BROCK, Holly
Player
Born January 20, 1907, in Alto, Tex; attended Univ. Tex; All-American 1933 – 1937.

Brock represented a number of the great Houston, Tex, volleyball teams which won both national and international honors.
Also in: Texas High School Basketball Hall of Fame.

WENDT, Harold
Player
Born May 4, 1915, in Chicago, Ill; attended McKinley High School.

Performing for the Duncan YMCA, Larrabees, and Chicago North Avenue YMCA, Wendt excelled in top-flight volleyball for a period of 19 years, 1935 – 1953. Wendt was selected as All-American 11 times, 5 times as first team.

1963

ANZUINI, Spartico
Player
Born June 3, 1917, in Chicago, Ill; attended Crane High School.

Anzuini played volleyball for the Mid-West Athletic Club and the North Avenue YMCA. He was selected as All-American 1940 – 1942, 1946 and 1947. He was also a top-flight bowler, having won the Tennessee state title.

NACHLAS, Sidney
Player
Born May 12, 1920, in Houston, Tex; graduated from Rice Univ. 1942.

Nachlas represented the Houston YMCA for ten seasons, gaining All-American honors 1948, 1950 – 1953 and 1956.

1965

CALDWELL, Wilbur "Web"
Player
Born April 30, 1910, in Marshall, Ill; graduated from Univ. Southern Calif. 1939.

Caldwell performed for the Phoenix YMCA 1931 and 1932, Pasadena YMCA 1935 – 1945 and Los Angeles YMCA 1946 – 1951 taking the national championship in

1949. He was selected to the All-American volleyball team 1935, 1936, 1946, 1948 and 1949.

OWENS, Carl
Player

Born 1915 in Liberty, Miss; graduated from business college.

Owens performed for the Houston, Tex, YMCA 1933 – 1941. After retiring from playing volleyball, Owens became a coach at the Beaumont, Tex, YMCA. He was selected All-American 1934, 1935 and 1937 – 1939.

1966

ENGEN, Rolf
Player

Born August 5, 1929, in Minneapolis, Minn; graduated from Santa Ana Junior Col. and Univ. Calif, Los Angeles (UCLA).

Engen played for UCLA 1953 and 1954, Hollywood YMCA 1955 – 1962. He was a member of the U.S. Pan-American Games teams in 1955 and 1959. He was selected All-American 1953 – 1958 and 1960 – 1962.

WARD, James
Player

Born November 24, 1912, in Atlantic City, N.J; attended Univ. Southern Calif.

Ward played for Pasadena YMCA 1945 – 1947, Los Angeles YMCA 1948 – 1951, Hollywood YMCA 1952 – 1956, Hollywood Comets 1957 – 1960 and Beverly Hill Masters in 1961. He was selected All-American 1947 – 1950 and 1952 and Veterans All-American in 1954, 1960 and 1961.

1967

O'HARA, Michael
Player

Born September 15, 1932, in Waco, Tex; received a B.S. from Univ. Calif, Los Angeles (UCLA) 1954 and M.B.A. from Univ. Southern Calif. 1963.

O'Hara played for UCLA 1952 – 1954, Hollywood YMCA 1957 – 1964 and Westside Center in 1966. O'Hara was a member of eight national championship teams with the Hollywood YMCA. He was also a member of the U.S. Pan-American Games championship volleyball team in 1959 and a member of the U.S. Olympic team at Tokyo in 1964. O'Hara was selected All-American (first team) at UCLA 1953 and 1954, for the Hollywood YMCA 1958 – 1964, and (second team) for Westside in 1966. Most significantly, he was chosen U.S. Volleyball Player of the Year in 1961 and 1963.

OLSSON, William
Player

Born February 1, 1930, in Long Beach, Calif; attended Univ. Calif. at La Jolla.

Olsson played for Long Beach YMCA 1953 – 1955, Hollywood YMCA 1956 – 1962, Pasadena YMCA in 1963 and Long Beach Century Club in 1964. Olsson was a member of U.S. Pan-American Games championship volleyball team in 1959. He was a member of six national championship teams and was selected All-American 1956 – 1962.

1969

WARD, Jane
Player

Born April 30, 1932, in Buffalo, N.Y; graduated from Univ. Buffalo 1952.

Jane Ward competed for the Long Beach Ahern Shamrocks, Long Beach Breakers, Santa Monica Mariners and Long Beach Shamrocks 1955 – 1968. Ward represented the United States on three occasions in World championship play 1956, 1960 and 1967. She was also a member of the U.S. Olympic teams in 1964 at Tokyo and 1968 at Mexico City. She was selected All-American for 14 years, and was named Player of the Year 5 times. She was also a member of national championship teams 13 times.

1970

CONRAD, Carolyn Gregory
Player

Born September 26, 1935, in Needville, Tex; graduated from Univ. Houston 1965; now a physical education teacher and volleyball coach at John Foster Dulles High School in Stafford, Tex.

In 1954 Conrad was a member of the Red Shield team of Houston chosen to play a series of matches in Mexico City, and they were undefeated. From 1953 to 1956 she was on the team that took second place in the U.S. Volleyball Association tournament in Omaha, Tucson, Oklahoma City and Seattle respectively. In 1956 she was on the national championship Amateur Athletic Union team, and was selected for the Pan-American women's volleyball team but was unable to participate. She was selected for the U.S. women's volleyball team, the Gulf Coasters, in 1957. She was also selected United States Volleyball Association All-American 1953 – 1956, Amateur Athletic Union All-American 1956 and 1957 and All-Tournament or All-Star Player at every tournament in Texas 1953 – 1957.

HARAUGHTY, Lois Ellen
Player

Born September 24, 1924, in Santa Monica, Calif; graduated from Univ. Calif, Los Angeles (UCLA) 1947 with a degree in chemistry.

Haraughty competed in the World Games in Paris in 1956, the Pan-American Games in Chicago in 1959 and the World Games in Rio de Janeiro in 1960. She has been a member of the U.S. Volleyball Association international selections committee 1967 and 1968, regional secretary 1964, 1965 and 1967, chairman of the Women's Volleyball Association Region 13 in 1954 and certified regional referee and certified scorer 1951 – 1957. Haraughty was selected All-American 1955 – 1960, Outstanding Player in 1953 and 1958 by the National Amateur Athletic Union and in 1956 by the Southern Pacific AAU.

McFARLAND, Zoann Neff
Player
Born December 1, 1930, in Long Beach, Calif.

McFarland began playing volleyball on the beach and played in her first national in 1950 at age 19. Within a few years her talent had become widely known. She played with the U.S. women's team at the World Games in Paris in 1956 and in 1958 and 1959 she played with the French National team and the Racing Club, while teaching with the U.S. Army in France. She was selected All-American 1952, 1953, 1955–1957 and 1960. In 1955 she was chosen California Amateur Athletic Union Outstanding Player and National Player of the Year.

VELASCO, Pedro
Player
Born April 6, 1937, in Honolulu, Hawaii; attended Church Col. of Hawaii.

During high school Velasco starred as a basketball player and jumped so high that he hit his head on the rim. He first played volleyball on dirt courts at Papakolea (Hawaiian Homestead Land) Park and Playground Center. After he reached high school, he started to play "hard court" volleyball. His first appearance in the national tournaments was with the Denver YMCA in 1956. He subsequently appeared in ten more national championships. Velasco was captain of the first U.S. Olympic team in 1964 as well as a member of the 1968 Olympic team in Mexico. He also played on the U.S. volleyball team in the Pan-American Games at Brazil in 1963 and Canada in 1967. He was selected first team All-American eight times and second team two times, and was chosen Player of the Year in the 1965 nationals in Omaha.

1971

GAERTNER, Jean K.
Player
Born November 1, 1938, in Los Angeles, Calif; graduated from Calif. State, Los Angeles 1965.

Gaertner was a member of the 1960 Olympic team, the 1959 and 1963 Pan-American teams and a member of the 1964 Olympic team. She was also a member of the national championship volleyball team for nine years. Gaertner was selected All-American seven times, the National Outstanding Player three times and the Regional Outstanding Player three times. In 1960 she was the World volleyball champion.

McWILLIAMS, Lou Sara Clark
Player
Born January 7, 1942, in San Antonio, Tex; attended San Antonio Junior Col; married; one child.

McWilliams played for San Antonio YMCA in 1960. The Dallas YMCA was runnerup in the 1961 and 1962 U.S. Volleyball Association (USVBA) national tournaments, and took third place in 1963. The Dallas Independents was Region Nine champion in 1965 and runnerup in the Amateur Athletic Union national tournament in 1969. In 1963 McWilliams was a member of the U.S. team in the Pan-American Games and in 1964 and 1968 a member of the Olympic team. She was a member of the U.S. team for the U.S.-U.S.S.R. tour of Canada in 1965, and in 1967 and 1968 a member of the 18-woman tryout squad for the respective Pan-American Games. In 1969 she was a member of the U.S. bronze medal–winning team in the North American–Caribbean Zone cup matches in Mexico City. She has been a regional official since 1967 and a Regional Nine secretary-treasurer 1967–1970. McWilliams was selected for the All-American USVBA first team 1961–1964 and second in 1965. She received the USVBA All-American Honorable Mention 1966 and was selected Amateur Athletic Union All-American 1963. She also received the Sullivan Award in 1965.

MURPHY, Linda
Player
Born September 3, 1943, in Glendale, Calif; attended San Fernando Valley State Col; teaches at John Muir Junior High School in Burbank, Calif.

Murphy was on the Long Beach Shamrocks national championship team 1962–1965, and 1967–1970. She was a member of the 1963 and 1967 Pan-American teams, and of the 1964 Olympic team. In 1967 she played with the World Games team, in 1965 with the team to tour Canada, and in 1966 with the team to compete in Mexico City.

OWEN, Nancy
Player
Born May 2, 1943, in Cleveland, Ohio; graduated from Pepperdine Univ. 1971; Rookie of the Year 1963; Most Valuable Player 1966; All-American 1963 and 1964 and 1966–1968.

Owen played with "Sad Six" Single A team in 1962; in 1963–1964 she played with the Long Beach Shamrocks, who were national champions both years. When Owen played with the Los Angeles Renegades, they were national champions in 1966 and Amateur Athletic Union champions in 1968. She was also a member of the 1967 and 1970 World Games teams, and in 1963 was on the second place team of all junior college mixed doubles tennis.

1976

PERRY, Barbara Beverly
Player
Born June 13, 1945, in Honolulu, Hawaii; attended Univ. Hawaii and Calif. State Univ, Long Beach; selected three times for Southern Calif. Collegiate All-Tournament teams while playing for Long Beach State.

Perry played volleyball 1966–1975 and was a member of the U.S. Olympic team in Mexico City. She was a member of the U.S. Pan-American Games teams in 1967 and 1971 and competed for the United States in World Games in 1967 and 1970. She also competed in the World Cup in 1973, as well as in ten national championships, for Santa Monica, Long Beach Shamrocks, Los Angeles Renegades and San Fernando Shamrocks (seven times), gaining All-American recognition. Five of the teams won national titles, and two placed second.

SAENZ, Manuel E.
Player
Born October 10, 1914, in Los Angeles, Calif; educated at California Maritime Academy.

Saenz played volleyball 1940–1955, representing Los Angeles Athletic Club and the Hollywood YMCA. He was a member of six national championship teams 1940, 1948 and 1950–1953, and was selected as All-American in 1946, 1949, 1952, 1953 and 1961. He was cited in 1955 as Los Angeles' greatest volleyball player.

SUWARA, Rudolph
Player
Born November 19, 1941; graduated from City Col. New York 1965, received an M.A. from Univ. Calif, Los Angeles 1972.

Suwara played volleyball 1964–1974 and was a member of two U.S. Olympic volleyball teams, in 1968 at Mexico City and in 1972 at Munich. He also represented the United States in the Pan-American Games of 1967 and 1971. He was selected All-American five times 1966–1969 and 1971.

1977

BOYCE, Dorothy C.
Contributor
Dorothy Boyce was employed as a playground teacher in the Chicago area for 20 years, and taught all types of sports to girls and women. In 1949 she became supervisor of recreation for the Chicago Public Schools. Dorothy has served as official for many of the volleyball associations and committees. In 1952 she introduced the USVBA rules to women in the Chicago area and she initiated the fund for promoting volleyball as an Olympic sport.

BOYDEN, E. Douglas
Contributor
Born May 26, 1914, in Cranston, R.I; graduated from Springfield YMCA College in Mass. 1937; served in Navy in W.W. II; employed many years in various capacities in the YMCA; joined staff of United Fund in San Antonio, Tex, shortly before death in 1971.

After Doug Boyden moved to Texas he became more active in volleyball, and with the collaboration of Robert G. Burton, authored *Staging Successful Tournaments.* He also prepared a manual on officiating and USVBA certification procedures, and wrote volleyball articles for the *Annual Guide* and other publications. Doug Boyden has made many contributions to the game, and served in many capacities with numerous organizations.

BURROUGHS, Dr. William P.
Contributor
Born in 1890 in South Dakota; attended Yankton Col. and Univ. Mich. Dental School, graduated from Chicago Col. Dental Surgery 1913; set up practice in Los Angeles area; USVBA Frier Award 1971.

Dr. Burroughs began playing beach volleyball when he moved to Los Angeles and afterwards spent much time and effort in advancing the sport. He coached a club team that went to the national championships, one team taking first in the Open. Dr. Burroughs managed and played volleyball on U.S. teams that toured Europe. He coached the 1964 U.S. women's teams in the Olympics, and participated in a number of international meetings to set up competitions and develop a volleyball program.

FRIERMOOD, Dr. Harold T.
Contributor
Dr. Friermood played volleyball in college, but really got into the game when he became a member of the staff at the Dayton YMCA, developing various skill improvement devices. He was secretary-treasurer of the USVBA and served as official on other programs and committees. He became president of the USVBA 1952–1954 and was instrumental in the formation of the International Volleyball Federation and the eventual entry of volleyball into the Olympic program. The USVBA established the Frier Trophy in his honor, given each year to recognize the outstanding contributor to the sport.

HEISLER, Edward A.
Contributor
Born March 30, 1892, in Pottsville, Pa.

Ed Heisler was associated with volleyball teams both as coach and player. He has participated in numerous leagues and state YMCA championships and was a USVBA district representative 1946–1953. He has been active as a promoter and organizer of volleyball in schools, both public and parochial, boys' clubs, Jewish centers, colleges, clubs, YMCA's and with groups in the armed forces.

KENNEDY, Merton H.
Contributor
Born April 10, 1908, in Buffalo, N.Y; attended Purdue Univ. and George Williams Col, received a degree in physical education in 1930, and a degree in education from Northwestern 1931; married Elsie; one daughter; received the Frier Award; Illinois Physical Education Director of the Year 1954; retired in 1972.

Kennedy was the physical education director of the Evanston YMCA for six years, and of the Chicago YMCA for 30 years. These responsibilities were only part of his service to volleyball, however. In 1959, for example, he served as chairman of the men's volleyball commission for the Pan-American Games. He helped in the administration of the U.S. Volleyball Association (USVBA) as a member of the All-American selection committee, the rules committee, as a national certified official, and on the board of directors as secretary-treasurer and vice president. He helped Edward P. Lauten reorganize the USVBA playing rules on the decimal identification system.

NELSON, Viggo
Contributor
As physical director serving the 89th Division in W.W. I, Viggo Nelson promoted volleyball among service men. He later won the 100-yd. and 220-yd. dash in the AEF championships held in Paris. He returned to play football at the University of Michigan after which he worked for the Ann Arbor YMCA as physical director and secretary. After leaving the YMCA, he continued with the Ann Arbor volleyball team as coach and player, his team winning 11 state titles and two National Veterans championships. He was selected twice for the All-American Veterans team. Nelson has served on the USVBA executive committee and the executive committee of the YMCA volleyball organization.

WALTERS, Marshall L.
Contributor
Marshall Walters served as editor of the *Official Volleyball Guide* 1950–1953 and 1962–1969. Although chairman of the department of health, physical education and recreation at Appalachian State University, in his 42 years in volleyball he has served as coach, writer, committee member, tournament director, clinician, referee, USVBA officer, and editor.

WILSON, Harry E.
Contributor
Harry Wilson has served in many official and unofficial positions with volleyball organizations and committees including a term as president of the USVBA. He has been involved in the international competitions and thc development of volleyball as an accepted program in the NCAA, NAIA, Olympics, and Pan-American Games.

Induction Years Unrecorded

MONTAGUE, James
Player

WARD, Samuel M.
Player

WEIBLE, John
Player

Weightlifting Hall of Fame

The Weightlifting Hall of Fame, within the Citizens Savings Hall of Fame Athletic Museum, was initiated in 1965. Twelve weightlifters and contributors were inducted the first year. As of 1977 there were 69 members in the Hall. David A. Matlin is responsible for originating the idea and directing it to fruition. He serves as chairman of the Weightlifting Hall of Fame Nominations Committee. Each inductee has his or her name engraved upon the Weightlifting Hall of Fame Trophy.

1965

ANDERSON, Paul
Weightlifter
Born 1933 in Toccoa, Ga.

Turning aside football scholarships to major universities in order to concentrate on weightlifting, Paul Anderson established American, World and Olympic records in the heavyweight division during the 1950s. Standing 5 ft. 9 in. and scaling between 300 and 330 lbs. he is a man whose achievements are reflected by his gargantuan physique: 53 in. chest, 46.5 in. waist, 34 in. thighs, 19 in. calves, 21 in. knees, 9 in. wrists, 11.5 in. ankles, flexed upper arm 20¾ in. and a 23 in. neck size. In three short years of lifting, he became the first lifter to total 1100 lbs. on three lifts. He pressed 375 lbs, snatched 320 lbs, cleaned and jerked 405 lbs. Later in the same year (1955) he officially pressed over 400 lbs. and established a clean and jerk record of 436.5 lbs. The crowning achievements in 1955 were his World championship at Munich and the Amateur Athletic Union title. In 1956, his last year as an amateur lifter, he triumphed at the Olympics in Melbourne with a 1102 lbs. for the gold medal. As a professional in 1957, and truly a superstar by any measure, he bench-pressed 627 lbs, recorded 1200 lbs. in a deep-knee bend, and dead-lifted 820 lbs, for a career aggregate of 2647 lbs. His herculean feats are unparalleled in human accomplishment. Flexing his powerful thighs, Anderson squatted with 800 lbs. in six repetitions and 700 lbs. in ten, a performance no other man has rivaled. His superior strength and balance are demonstrated by his taking a 900 lb. bar bell across his shoulders and completing three successive deep-knee bends. Supposedly he performed this feat once with 1000 lbs. The first man to clean and press 400 lbs, Anderson shattered all physical and psychological limitations with a 6270 lbs. back lift on June 12, 1957. This is the greatest weight ever raised by a human.

BERRY, Mark
Noteworthy Contributor
A pioneer in modern American weightlifting, the late Mark Berry directed the Milo Barbell Company and distributed information concerning safety, techniques and equipment through his *Strength* magazine. In 1932 and 1936 he served as coach of the U.S. Olympic weightlifting team. He also served one term as chairman of the National Amateur Athletic Union weightlifting committee.

DAVIS, John
Weightlifter
Born in 1921; served in the military during W.W. II.

For 15 years John David dominated the weightlifting scene. Beginning in 1938 with his first world championship as a light-heavyweight, he was undefeated until 1953 (a thigh injury cost Davis and the team titles in international competition at Stockholm). During his tenure as heavyweight champion, he won six World and two Olympic crowns 1948 and 1952. Twelve times he ranked Number One in the United States. Besides holding every record during his time, he surpassed several psychological barriers. In 1941 he became the second man to score more than 1000 lbs. A decade later, incredibly, he cleaned and jerked 402 lbs.

HOFFMAN, Bob
Noteworthy Contributor
As an oil burner salesman in York, Pa, Bob Hoffman was active in the York Oil Burner Athletic Club. An avid sports buff in track and field, canoe racing and rowing, he believed weightlifting sustained his stamina and strength. Developing into a full-fledged heavyweight lifter of 230 lbs, he founded York Barbell Company in 1932 and purchased the original Milo Barbell Company two years later. Promoting his weight training techniques through mail-order instruction and advertising his exercise apparatus through his magazine, *Strength and Health,* his club became a haven for promising lifters. Hoffman obtained employment for his students while they enjoyed the stimulus of their environment: training, competing, sharing. Hoffman contributed generously to Amateur Athletic Union and Olympic coffers. During non-Olympic years he personally sponsored trips to Europe; the result was four World championships in 1946,

1947, 1950 and 1951. The 1947 team won every category title. He was the U.S. Olympic team coach in 1948 and 1952 when the team won the unofficial scoring title. Achievements of legendary status internationally, nationally the York Barbell Club surpassed the impossible. For over two decades, 1932 to 1954, the team won all but one title (Dr. Richard You's lifters dented the consecutive victories). Hoffman served as vice-chairman of the National AAU weightlifting committee. The success of American weightlifters during the 1930s, 1940s and 1950s is a tribute to Bob Hoffman's ability in training, promoting and publicizing the sport. His name is a watershed mark in the history of weightlifting.
Also in: Amateur Softball Association of Pennsylvania Hall of Fame.

JOHNSON, Clarence
Noteworthy Contributor
Serving many years as vice-chairman and chairman of the National Amateur Athletic Union weightlifting committee, Johnson also served as chairman of the U.S. Olympic weightlifting committee. In 1956 he was the U.S. Olympic team manager. Johnson is a former president of the International Weightlifting Federation.

KONO, Tamio "Tommy"
Weightlifter
Born 1930 in Hawaii, Kono was one of the greatest weightlifters of all time. Coached by Ed Yarick in Oakland, Calif, Kano was an Olympic champion in both the 148 lb. division and the 165 lb. division, winning gold medals in 1952 (lightweight) and 1956 (light-heavyweight) and a silver medal in 1960 (middleweight). In the same weight divisions, 148 lb. and 165 lb, as well as in the 181 lb. division, Kono established world records. No other American lifter has ever won so many Olympic crowns and world champion titles, a total of eight in successive years from 1952 through 1959. In addition to that claim to fame, he was the only lifter ever to win three successive Pan-American gold medals, 1955, 1959 and 1963, and the only lifter to set world records in four different body-weight categories. Equally impressive in the record of Kano's career is the fact that he was eleven times the United States champion weightlifter.

MATLIN, David A.
Noteworthy Contributor
A past president of the Amateur Athletic Union, Matlin served 20 years as vice-chairman of the weightlifting committee and two terms as chairman of that committee. He also held concurrent responsibilities as chairman of the U.S. Olympic weightlifting committee. Since 1950 he has held an international weightlifting referee card. The initiator for the Citizens Savings Weightlifting Hall of Fame idea, he serves the Foundation as chairman of the Weightlifting Hall of Fame nominations committee.

RADER, Peary
Noteworthy Contributor
Peary Rader is an active supporter of weightlifting through his position as vice-chairman of the National Amateur Athletic Union weightlifting committee.

SCHEMANSKY, Norbert
Weightlifter
The first weightlifter to defeat John Davis in 15 years, Norbert Schemansky won more Olympic medals than any other American during his time. He won the silver at 198 lbs. in 1948, the gold in 1952, and the bronze as a heavyweight in 1960 and 1964. One of three brothers who were all weightlifters, Norbert began lifting at Northern YMCA in Detroit. Beginning in 1949 he won nine U.S. senior championships as a heavyweight during the next 15 years, plus three World championships. He is the largest man ever to clean and jerk double his weight officially when he set a 399 lb. record while weighing within the 198 lb. class limit.
Also in: Michigan Sports Hall of Fame.

TERLAZZO, Anthony
Weightlifter
A member of the York Barbell Club, Tony Terlazzo was the first American to win a gold medal in Olympic weightlifting championships, 1936. He had won the bronze in the 1932 Olympics, 132 lb. class. Twelve times he won the National Amateur Athletic Union championship in the 148 lb. class. Those titles came in 1933, 1935, 1937 and consecutive crowns from 1937 to 1945.

TERPAK, John
Noteworthy Contributor and Weightlifter
John Terpak won two world weightlifting championships, 1937 and 1947, in the 165 lb. class. He also won 11 National Amateur Athletic Union (AAU) titles in the 165 lb. and 181 lb. class. Captain of the 1948 Olympic team, he was assistant coach in 1952, trainer in 1956 and manager in 1960 and 1964. He was vice-chairman of the Olympic weightlifting committee in 1964 and the co-director of the Olympic trials at the New York World's Fair. He holds National AAU and Category One FIHC referee's cards.

WORTMANN, Dietrich
Noteworthy Contributor
Dietrich Wortmann was chairman of the National Amateur Athletic Union weightlifting committee. A pioneer of modern American weightlifting on national and international levels, he was serving as president of the International Weightlifting Federation when he died in September 1952.

1966

GEORGE, Peter
Weightlifter
Born in 1933.

The "boy wonder" won his first world title as a 17 year-old middleweight. For twelve consecutive years, 1946 to 1958, George was a member of the Amateur Athletic Union All-American Weightlifting Team. During this time, he won six World championships and placed second four times. The Olympic gold medalist in 1952, he sandwiched the gold with silver medals in 1948 and 1956. For three years 1954 to 1957, he was captain of the U.S. weightlifting team. Competing in three divisions, lightweight, middleweight and light heavyweight, he established records in the U.S, Olympic and World events. His coaches were the Barnholth brothers in Akron, Ohio.

SABLO, Rudolph
Noteworthy Contributor
Rudolph Sablo was active as competitor, coach and administrator. As a lifter and official beginning in 1935, he won the New York state light-heavyweight division. A member of the Metropolitan Association weightlifting committee since 1964, he was also a member of the 1964 Olympic committee and vice-chairman of the 1968 committee. During the 1964 Olympic trials at the New York World's Fair, he was co-director. Holder of National Amateur Athletic Union and Category One FIHC referee card, he has officiated at many national and regional contests.

STANCZYK, Stanley
Weightlifter
Stanley Stanczyk was a member of the 1947 York Barbell team which won every category title at the World championships. This was the greatest display ever by an international team. An All-American Team member for six years, he set world records in the middleweight and light-heavyweight divisions. A four-time World champion in three different weight divisions: 1946 at 148 lbs, 1947 at 165 lbs. and 1949 and 1950 at 181 lbs. In 1953 and 1954 he won the bronze medal. At the 1948 Olympics he won the gold as a middleweight and the silver in 1952 as a light-heavyweight. He was National Amateur Athletic Union champion six times.

STANKO, Stephen
Weightlifter
Stephen Stanko was National Amateur Athletic Union champion three consecutive years, 1938 to 1940, and North American champion four consecutive years, 1938 to 1941. Standing 5 ft. 11½ in. and 225 lbs, in 1941 he smashed a psychological barrier by making the first 1000 lb. three-lift total on standard lifts. He was a member of the York Barbell Club.

1967

AYARS, Jack
Noteworthy Contributor
For more than three decades, Ayars was constructively and influentially aligned with the Middle Atlantic Association of the Amateur Athletic Union (AAU). He was the coach of Lennell Shepherd, National AAU bantamweight champion in 1966.

BERGER, Isaac
Weightlifter
A winner of three Olympic medals, Isaac won the gold in the featherweight division in 1956, the silver in 1960, and repeated his 1960 performance in Tokyo in 1964. Aside from Olympic competition, he was eight times national champion in the 132 lb. class, 1955–1961 and 1964. Between Olympic years he competed in the World championships, placing third in 1957 as a featherweight, first in 1958, second in 1959, first in 1961 and second in 1963. He was also a contestant in the Pan-American Games 1959 and 1963.

DI PIETRO, Joseph
Weightlifter
Joe Di Pietro is a five-time National Amateur Athletic Union bantamweight champion. His first title came in 1942, followed in 1943 with another, skipped a year, and returned as champion in 1945, 1946 and 1951. During this decade of weightlifting, Di Pietro was 1947 bantamweight champion at the World championships in Philadelphia, 1948 Olympic gold medalist, 1949 bronze winner in the World championships and 1951 Pan-American champion.

MESSER, James
Noteworthy Contributor
Jim Messer competed in the inaugural weightlifting championships held in the United States. He represents the Amateur Athletic Union Middle Atlantic Association and is considered an elder statesman in weightlifting affairs.

RAYMOND, Joseph
Noteworthy Contributor
Joseph Raymond has been the representative of the Lake Erie Association and chairman of the Amateur Athletic Union. He has dedicated over 40 years of service to the sport of weightlifting.

VINCI, Charles
Weightlifter
Vinci won the gold medal, bantamweight division, in both the 1956 and the 1960 Olympics. He is a four-time U.S. senior champion 1954, 1956, 1958 and 1961. In 1955 and 1959 he won the Pan-American Games bantamweight division.

WEISSBROTT, Morris
Noteworthy Contributor
Weissbrott served the Metropolitan Amateur Athletic Union Association for many years. He devised the handicap contests now used nationwide. He is a former National Weightlifting secretary.

1968

EMERICH, Clyde B.
Weightlifting
Clyde Emerich is four-time middle-heavyweight champion in the United States. He won the title in 1952, 1956, 1957 and 1959. At the World championships in 1954 and 1955, he placed third and second, respectively. He was the mainstay of the victorious U.S. Olympic squads in 1948 and 1952.

HALEY, Donald J.
Noteworthy Contributor

HISE, Robert
Noteworthy Contributor

SHEPPARD, David
Weightlifter
David Sheppard was a member of the 1948, 1952 and 1956 Olympic teams. He won the silver medal in 1956 as a middle heavyweight with a lift of 975.25 lbs. Three times he won the silver in World championship competition, 1951, 1954 and 1958. Twice he won the 198 lb. class in U.S. senior championships, 1954 and 1955. Another

member of the famous York Barbell Club, David set World records of 303.25 lbs. as a light heavyweight and 316.5 lbs. as a middle heavyweight.

YOU, Dr. Richard
Noteworthy Contributor
Dr. Richard You sponsored the only team capable of denying the York Barbell Club laurels between 1932 and 1954. His superbly conditioned Hawaiian aggregation was led by Richard Tom. In 1952 Dr. You was the U.S. Olympic team physician at the Games in Helsinki.

1969

BACHTELL, Richard
Weightlifter
A member of the York Barbell Club, Dick was seven times National Amateur Athletic Union champion in the 132 lb. class. He won the title in 1929 – 1931, 1934, 1935, 1937 and 1943.

BATES, Frank
Noteworthy Contributor

FERGUSON, Fraysher
Noteworthy Contributor
Born in 1919; graduated from Springfield Col. (Mass.) 1941; wife Norma; daughter Jill.

Outstanding in all phases of weightlifting, Ferguson has been a lifter, coach, official and athletic director in a remarkable career that began with his graduation from Springfield. In 1941 he was the national one-arm champion with a benchrest lift of 275 lb. as a light-heavyweight. Later he served on three different Amateur Athletic Union (AAU) Olympic weightlifting committees, and as manager of two different Pan-American Games weightlifting teams, 1959 and 1971. Among the hundreds of lifters Ferguson has coached are ten national champions—a remarkable feat for a coach in any sport. For 25 consecutive years, 1951 through 1976, Ferguson served as a coach and official at the national AAU weightlifting meets. During an equally impressive career of community service, he participated for over ten years in a physical fitness program broadcast on local television; opened the Apollo Studios, which he operated for nine years; and for 20 years was active in the Athletic Club of Columbus, a private men's club. He has also served as athletic director of the club. Ferguson has appeared six times on the cover of *Strength and Health* magazine.

GEORGE, James
Weightlifting
Jim George is a four-time U.S. senior champion, 1956, 1958, 1959 and 1960. Competing in the 1956 and 1960 Olympics, he won the bronze at Melbourne in 1956 with a light-heavyweight lift of 920 lbs. and the silver at Rome in 1960 with 947.75 lbs.

SPELLMAN, Frank
Weightlifter
A member of the York Barbell Club, Spellman earned a place on the 1948 and 1952 Olympic teams. He won the middleweight gold at London in 1948. He was also a three-time U.S. senior champion in the 165 lb. class.

TERLAZZO, John
Weightlifter
John Terlazzo won a world title in 1937. He was a member of the York Barbell Club.

1970

CRIST, Robert
Noteworthy Contributor
An official and administrator, Bob Crist has been active in Region I Amateur Athletic Union (AAU) duties. He has been Virginia AAU weightlifting sports chairman, vice-president of Virginia Association of the AAU, vice-chairman of Region I, chairman of the AAU "Mr. America" committee and club director of the Lower Peninsula Weightlifting Club. He holds an international Category One FIHC official's card.

GUBNER, Gary
Weightlifter
Gubner drifted into weightlifting after beginning his sports career as a shotputter. He never won a World championship, placing third in 1962 and second in 1965, but he was the 1966 U.S. senior champion, heavyweight division. During the 1964 Olympic trials he placed second and an overall fourth in official competition. Hailed at one time as "The World's Strongest Teen-Ager," Gary pressed 425 lbs. in January, 1967, for an American record. He snatched 345 lbs. and cleaned and jerked 440 lbs. for a 1200 lb. total, another American record. Later he topped his press mark by five pounds.

IMHARA, Walter
Weightlifter
Walter has won titles on every level, establishing numerous records along the way. Attending the University of Southern Louisiana in 1955, he started lifting and eventually won two national collegiate and junior titles as a featherweight. After graduation he entered the Army yet he continued to lift and string together victories. He won the Amateur Athletic Union senior championship, the first of five during his career, one national YMCA crown and a gold in the Pan-American Games. At the International Sports competition in 1967 he placed fourth in the featherweight division. In the Olympic three lifts, his best weights were 260, 250 and 320.

MARCH, William "Bill"
Weightlifter
A product of the York Barbell Club, Bill March began lifting in 1959. Since then he has won ten national titles, five YMCA and five senior championships. Competing internationally in the middleweight and then heavyweight divisions, he has been a member of six World championship teams. In the 1964 Olympics, he missed the bronze by a few grams of bodyweight to Ireneusz Palinski of Russia. A winner of Mr. Pan American and Mr. Universe titles, in the late 1960s he held the World press record, 354.5 lbs, for middle-heavyweight class. His best total is 1130 lbs, with 390 press, 325 snatch, 425 clean and jerk.

SAMUELS, Robert
Noteworthy Contributor
Born in 1912.

At the age of 56 Robert Samuels placed second in the heavyweight division during the VII Maccabiah Games, 1965. A weightlifter for over 50 years, he won his first heavyweight title in 1935. Among his titles are junior national champion, Southern Amateur Athletic Union (AAU), Louisiana State, All-Southern YMCA and All-South weightlifting champion. As a coach and manager in 1966 he was with the U.S. team in the International weightlifting contest in Mexico. Many contenders for national, World and Olympic titles were his students: Louis Riecke, John Gourgolt, Walter Imhara, Charles Stauton, Joe Gowa, Teto Talluto, Dave Berger, Joe Murray, Warren Drewer and Bill Klock. He has been a member of the U.S. Olympic committee, Southern AAU district chairman, chairman of Region IV and founding member of the Southern AAU weightlifting committee in 1935. He holds Number One and Two FHIC referee's cards, the national referee's card and has officiated at many national events in the Olympic and powerlifting categories.

WHITFIELD, Karo
Noteworthy Contributor
For the past 25 years Karo Whitfield has contributed as referee, promoter, coach, organizer, trainer and judge. He was appointed by Dietrich Wortmann in 1933 as chairman for the Southeastern Amateur Athletic Union Association. As a referee, he holds a Category Two FHIC card. Some of his prize pupils are Bill Curry, Jack Leverett, John Burrell, Paul Anderson, Harry Smith, Harry Johnson, Jim Dugger and Arthur Harris. Recently he was director of the Executive Health Club in Atlanta.

1971

GRIMEK, John
Weightlifter
A member of the York Barbell Club, Grimek won consecutive "Mr. America" contests, 1940 and 1941. His physique was unparalleled by other contestants; therefore, the rules were changed to prohibit former winners from reentering. The 1936 U.S. senior champion, heavyweight division, John also won the "Mr. Universe" title. He is currently the editor of *Strength and Health* magazine.

GSCHWIND, Charles L.
Noteworthy Contributor

LUCY, Herbert
Noteworthy Contributor

SAKATA, Harold
Weightlifter
Harold Sakata won the Olympic silver medal in 1948 in the light heavyweight division with a lift of 837.5 lbs.

1972

BERNHOLTH, Lawrence
Noteworthy Contributor
Larry Bernholth operates the American College of Modern Weight Lifting in Akron, Ohio. As a coach, one of his star students was Pete George. Bernholth authored *Secrets of the Squat Snatch* (1950).

EISING, Charles E.
Noteworthy Contributor

KNIPP, Russell
Weightlifter
Russell Knipp won the U.S. senior championship, 165 lb. class in 1967, 1968 and 1971.

MILLS, Joseph
Weightlifter
Joe Mills was the 1942 U.S. senior champion in the 132.25 lb. class.

TERRY, John
Weightlifter
A member of the York Barbell Club, John Terry won the U.S. senior championships 132.25 lb. class four consecutive years, 1938 to 1941.

1973

ANDREWS, Gordon L.
Noteworthy Contributor
Born 1910 in Michigan.

Serving as official, referee and trainer for over 30 years, Gordon Andrews is a bulwark in the history of Michigan weightlifting. For 15 years, 1922 to 1937, Gordon utilized homemade facilities for training with bar bells. With the opening of the Ford Weightlifting Club in Dearborn during the early 1940s, Andrews was able to train with better and safer equipment. Later he operated the Gordon's Gym for a number of years. Aside from serving the past 30 years as official and referee in state competition, from 1950 to 1970 he officiated for national, international and Olympic events.

MUNGIOLI, Michael
Weightlifter
The 1937 and 1938 126 lb. national champion, Michael Mungioli established records in a number of categories. A phenomenal achievement during his time was a three-lift 605 lb. total. The founder, and coach for 25 years, of the Maspeth Weightlifting Club, he was also associated with the Metropolitan Amateur Athletic Union Association. Three years Mungioli served the association as vice-chairman, 3 years as chairman, and 24 years as an official.

PATERA, Kenneth
Weightlifter
Graduated from Brigham Young Univ. 1967; named U.S. Weightlifter of the Year 1971.

A four-time National Amateur Athletic Union superweight champion from 1969 through 1972, Patera won the silver in the 1972 Olympics. At the 1971 Pan-American Games, he was the superweight 242 lbs. champion.

PAUL, Joseph
Noteworthy Contributor

PULEO, Joseph
Weightlifter
Attended Michigan State Univ.

On the collegiate level Joe Puleo won the 165 lb. class in 1965 and 1966. Throughout the 1960s he achieved weightlifting All-American team honors seven times, 1961–1964 and 1966–1968. Twice he won the U.S. senior championships, 1962 and 1964, and the National Amateur Athletic Union title five times, 1962, 1964, and 1966–1968. In international competition, he was Pan-American champion in 1963 and 1967, a member of the 1968 Olympic team, and three-time member of the U.S. World championship teams.

RIECKE, Lou
Weightlifter

SCHUBERT, John W.
Noteworthy Contributor
Schubert had devoted 36 years to weightlifting as competitor, trainer, coach and official. The founder of the Olympic Health Club in Cleveland, many of the Club's members have won gold medal awards, national and Olympic titles. He has sponsored and conducted over 150 weightlifting events, including three national, many U.S. regional and Ohio state championships. For over 20 years he served in various administrative capacities with the Lake Erie Amateur Athletic Union weightlifting committee. As a competitor he earned physique and weightlifting honors and awards in amateur boxing.

TOTH, James
Noteworthy Contributor
Beginning at age 15 for 23 years Jim Toth competed in most New Jersey state championships. One of the founders of the Keasbey Eagles Athletic Club, he directed the club as president and coach for nearly a quarter century. His philosophy—training youthful cadres of lifters—was reflected in the Club's success: six consecutive national teen-age titles, 1964 to 1969.

1974

BERGER, David
Weightlifter
Born in Shaker Heights, Ohio; graduated cum laude from Tulane Univ. 1966; law degree from Columbia Univ; moved to Israel in 1970; two years later, as a member of Israeli Olympic team, killed by terrorists at the Olympic Village in Munich, Germany.

Berger won his first title as an adolescent in the 123 lb. class in Ohio. In 1969 he captured the National Amateur Athletic Union junior championship in the 165 lb. class. Between his state and national competition, he participated in the Maccabiah Games. He placed third at 148 lbs. in 1965 and won the gold medal in the middleweight division four years later. Two years later, 1971, at the First Asian Weightlifting Games he added another gold medal in the middleweight class.

BERGERON, Romero
Noteworthy Contributor
Associated with the Circle LaCordaire Athletic Association, Woonsocket, R.I, in the late 1920s, Romero was New England champion in the 154 lb. class in 1927 and 1928. He competed until 1932 when his interests and activities turned to coaching and promotion. His 1933 Woonsocket junior team won the nationals and in 1938 he was host for the National Amateur Athletic Union (AAU) senior championships. From 1935 to 1945 he was chairman of the New England AAU weightlifting and established the Canadian Athletic Club. From competition to coach and promoter to administrator and back to coaching in 1945, he was instructor at the Attleboro, Mass, YMCA. His 50 years of contributions and service to weightlifting touch all levels. Granted an International Category One referee's card, he officiated in five World championships including the 1948 Olympics. He is a recipient of the International Weightlifting Federation gold medal for 50 years service.

CANTORE, Dan
Weightlifter
Born in Glendale, Calif; graduated from Univ. Calif.

In 1964, two years after he began weightlifting, Dan Cantore won the National Amateur Athletic Union junior lightweight crown. Growing into the senior lightweight division, he won the national title in 1969, 1972 and 1973. He was a member of the 1972 U.S. Olympic team and the U.S. World championship squad the following year in Havana, Cuba. A holder of four U.S. national records, during the first annual Pan-American weightlifting championships he earned the gold medal while setting records in his division.

KARCHUT, Mike
Weightlifter
The National teen-age champion in the 165 lb. class, Mike grew into the 181 lb. division and achieved many honors. He was a six-time National Amateur Athletic Union senior champion, 1965, 1969 through 1973. While winning six national crowns, he also established the national clean and jerk record. A two-time Pan-American champ, he added another clean and jerk mark, plus the snatch, in the 1971 and 1973 Games. He was a member of the U.S. World championship teams in 1969, 1971 and 1973.

SWIRZ, Adam
Noteworthy Contributor
For 26 years Adam Swirz was an official for the Amateur Athletic Union and YMCA on district, national and international levels. He has been the coach at McBurney YMCA in New York City for 28 years. During his nearly 30 years he has conducted at least one weightlifting competition yearly. The originator of the YMCA "Mr. America" competition, in 1971 he judged the World championships and in 1973 the World power weightlifting championships. Aside from all his administrative and officiating duties, he has personally continued to compete in sanctioned weightlifting contests.

WILLIAMS, Arch
Noteworthy Contributor
Military duty during W.W. II; received the Southern Pacific Association, AAU "Man of the Year" award.

He started competing and officiating in weightlifting in 1946 in San Diego, Calif. Nine years later he headed north to Los Angeles and founded the Torrance YMCA

South Bay Lifters. His teams won many teen-age and junior titles. Aligning his club with the Southern Pacific Association of the Amateur Athletic Union (AAU), he was appointed junior weightlifting committee chairman from 1967 to 1972. The following year he was the Southern Pacific Association AAU weightlifting chairman. As a referee, he was granted an International referee card, Category Two, in 1970 and a Category One in 1973. Through administrative and officiating skills, Arch Williams has contributed in all divisions—teen-age, junior, senior and municipal.

1975

ISHIKAWA, Kotaro Emerich
Weightlifter
A four-time U. S. senior champion in the featherweight division, 1944 – 1947, Kotaro earned All-American weightlifting team status in 1944, 1946 and 1948. Sponsored by the York Barbell Club, Kotaro qualified for the 1948 Olympic team.

MAYOR, David
Noteworthy Contributor and Weightlifter
David Mayor is only one of two individuals to be inducted in both categories, Noteworthy Contributor and Weightlifter. He earned a spot on the 1936 Olympic team by qualifying first in the trials. In 1937 he was National Amateur Athletic Union junior and senior champion in the heavyweight class. He has long served the AAU in an administrative capacity.

ZERCHER, Edward
Noteworthy Contributor
An administrator and official since 1930, Ed Zercher has refereed in more than 220 weightlifting competitions. He holds an International weightlifting referee card dating back to 1965. From 1930 to 1938 he was chairman of the Ozark Amateur Athletic Union Association weightlifting committee while holding concurrent responsibilities as a member, 1933 to 1939, of the National AAU weightlifting committee.

1976

CYPHER, Marty
Noteworthy Contributor
As a meet director, coach and referee, Marty Cypher has served the sport of weightlifting for over 17 years. Most recently, 1974 to 1976, he has been the manager of American weightlifting teams which have competed abroad.

PITMAN, Joseph
Weightlifter
The decade from 1947 to 1957 belonged to Joe Pitman in the 148 lb. class. During that time he won ten National Amateur Athletic Union titles while earning two seconds 1949 and 1951, and one first 1950, in World championships. He was a member of the U.S. Olympic team in 1948 and 1952.

TOM, Richard
Weightlifter
A member of Dr. Richard You's team—the only team to beat the York Barbell Club in over two decades—Richard Tom won the bronze bantamweight medal in the 1948 Olympics and competed in the quadrennial event again in 1952. He was the National Amateur Athletic Union champion in 1952.

Winter Sports Hall of Fame

Initial elections for the Winter Sports Hall of Fame took place in 1953. The Hall of Fame includes figure skating, speed skating and skiing, and may include hockey in the near future. As of 1977 there are 26 members in the Hall of Fame.

1953

BUTTON, Richard Totten
Figure Skater
See entry in United States Figure Skating Association Hall of Fame, 1976.
Also in: Ice Skating Hall of Fame.

DURRANCE, Richard
Skier
See entry in National Ski Hall of Fame, 1958.

ENGEN, Alf
Skier
See entry in National Ski Hall of Fame, 1959.

FRASER, Gretchen
Skier
See entry in National Ski Hall of Fame, 1960.

JAFFEE, Irving
Speed Skater
See entry in Hall of Fame of the Amateur Skating Union of the United States, 1967.

LAWRENCE, Andrea Mead
Skier
See entry in National Ski Hall of Fame, 1958.

SHEA, John A.
Speed Skater
See entry in Hall of Fame of the Amateur Skating Union of the United States, 1962.

Induction Years Unrecorded

ALBRIGHT, Tenley
Figure Skater
See entry in United States Figure Skating Association Hall of Fame, 1976.
Also in: Ice Skating Hall of Fame.

COCHRAN, Barbara Ann
Skier
See entry in National Ski Hall of Fame, 1976.

DOLE, Charles Minot "Minnie"
Noteworthy Contributor
See entry in Colorado Ski Museum-Colorado Ski Hall of Fame, 1977.
Also in: National Ski Hall of Fame.

DU BOIS, Elizabeth
Speed Skater
Elizabeth Du Bois won a gold medal in the 1932 Winter Olympics. She completed the 1000-meter in 2:04.

FLEMING, Peggy Gale (Jenkins)
Figure Skater
See entry in United States Figure Skating Association Hall of Fame, 1976.
Also in: Colorado Sports Hall of Fame and Ice Skating Hall of Fame.

HEISS, Carol (Jenkins)
Figure Skater
See entry in United States Figure Skating Association Hall of Fame, 1976.
Also in: Ice Skating Hall of Fame.

HENNING, Anne
Speed Skater
Anne won a gold medal in the 1972 Olympics in the 500-meter event. She also won two World outdoor titles in 1972—the 500-meter with a time of 0:42.5 and the 1000-meter in 1:27.3.

HENRY, Kenneth
Speed Skater
See entry in Hall of Fame of the Amateur Skating Union of the United States, 1970.

HILL, Cortlandt T.
Noteworthy Contributor
See entry in National Ski Hall of Fame, 1970.

HOLUM, Dianne
Speed Skater
Dianne won a gold medal for the 1500-meter event with a time of 2:20.8 in the 1972 Olympics.

JENKINS, David W.
Figure Skater
See entry in United States Figure Skating Association Hall of Fame, 1976.

JENKINS, Hayes Alan
Figure Skater
See entry in United States Figure Skating Association Hall of Fame, 1976.

JEWTRAW, Charles
Speed Skater
See entry in Hall of Fame of the Amateur Skating Union of the United States, 1963.

KIAER, Alice Damrosch Wolfe
Noteworthy Contributor
See entry in National Ski Hall of Fame, 1969.

McDERMOTT, Richard Terry
Speed Skater
McDermott won the 220 yd. event in a time of 0:17.8 to win the 1961 U.S. Amateur outdoor title. He also won a gold medal for the 500-meter event in the 1964 Olympics.

OUTLAND, Kit Klein
Speed Skater
See entry in Hall of Fame of the Amateur Skating Union of the United States, 1964.

SAUBERT, Jean
Skier
See entry in National Ski Hall of Fame, 1976.

WERNER, Wallace "Buddy"
Skier
See entry in Colorado Ski Museum-Colorado Ski Hall of Fame, 1977.
Also in: National Ski Hall of Fame.

ZIMMERMAN, Penelope Pitou
Skier
See entry in National Ski Hall of Fame, 1976.

Wrestling — Amateur Hall of Fame

There are 153 wrestlers, coaches and noteworthy contributors in the Amateur Wrestling Hall of Fame, established in 1957 under the auspices of the present Citizens Savings Hall of Fame Athletic Museum. Jess Hoke, publisher and editor of *Wrestling News,* serves as chairman for the Amateur Wrestling Hall of Fame nominations committee. There is no limit to the number of inductees that may be elected annually in each category.

1957

COLLINS, Fendley Alexander
Coach and Contributor
See entry in National Wrestling Hall of Fame, 1976.

DRUMMOND, John H.
Noteworthy Contributor
The Princeton University light-heavyweight champion, John Drummond was a long-time coach, official and amateur wrestling patron. A member of three Olympic wrestling committees, he staged the 1956 Olympic Trials. John now lives in Los Angeles.

GALLAGHER, Edward Clark
Coach
See entry in National Wrestling Hall of Fame, 1976.
Also in: Oklahoma Coaches Association Hall of Fame.

HOWARD, Harold
Coach
The University of Iowa coach for 30 years, 1922–1952, Harold produced three undefeated teams and five runnerup teams in Big Ten competition.

KEEN, Clifford Patrick
Coach and Contributor
See entry in National Wrestling Hall of Fame, 1976.

OTOPALIK, Hugo M.
Coach
See entry in National Wrestling Hall of Fame, 1976.

PEARCE, Robert
Wrestler
Wrestling three years for Oklahoma State University, Pearce won four medals. In 1930 he was National AAU 118 lb. champion and repeated the following year in the 125 lb. class. In 1931 he was also NCAA 126 lb. titlist and won the 1932 Olympics bantamweight gold medal.

SHERIDAN, William
Wrestler and Coach
See entry in National Wrestling Hall of Fame, 1976.
Also in: Pennsylvania Wrestling Hall of Fame.

SMITH, William
Wrestler
A three-time National AAU champion while attending Iowa State Teachers College, 1949 to 1951, he also won the NCAA 165 lb. class in 1949 and 1950. Qualifying for the 1952 Olympic team, he won the gold medal in the welterweight division.

SPEIDEL, Charles
Coach
Charles coached the Pennsylvania State University team from 1927 to 1957, and during his tenure, won seven Eastern Intercollegiate titles and had six undefeated seasons. His 1953 team was the NCAA champion.
Also in: Pennsylvania Wrestling Hall of Fame.

STONE, Henry
Coach
Coaching at the University of California from 1928 to 1956, Stone won more Pacific Coast Conference titles than any other coach.

SWARTZ, Raymond
Coach
Swartz coached the U.S. Naval Academy team from 1938 to 1957 and was the 1952 Olympics coach.

VANBEBBER, Jack Francis "Blackjack."
Wrestler
See entry in National Wrestling Hall of Fame, 1976.

VIS, Russell
Wrestler
Vis was three-time National AAU champion in the 147 lb. division from 1922 to 1924. In 1921 he also won the 145 lb. class. He won the 1924 Olympic lightweight gold medal.

WITTENBERG, Henry
Wrestler
Probably no other individual has set such an outstanding performance in his career as Henry Wittenberg. Between 1938 and 1952 he was undefeated in 400 consecutive matches. During his record-setting years he won the 1940 and 1941 National AAU 175 lb. class and six times claimed the 191 lb. division (1943, 1944, 1946–1948 and 1952). He won the light heavyweight division of the 1948 U.S. Olympics and was runnerup in 1952.

1958

DE FERRARI, Dr. Albert
Noteworthy Contributor
Active in AAU wrestling committees for many years, De Ferrari was national chairman for one term. He also served as vice-chairman of the International Amateur Wrestling Federation, is a long time member of the US Olympic wrestling committee and a past president of the Olympic Club of San Francisco.

DOLE, George S.
Wrestler
While attending Yale University, George won the 1908 National AAU 135 lb. class and the Olympic featherweight gold medal.

GRIFFITH, Arthur
Coach
See entry in National Wrestling Hall of Fame, 1976.
Also in: Oklahoma Coaches Association Hall of Fame.

HANCOCK, John William
Coach
A football star at the University of Iowa, Hancock assumed the head coaching position at the University of Northern Colorado in 1932. Although he had never wrestled he guided the wrestling program, winning 22 consecutive Rocky Mountain Conference titles. He later coached at the University of Mississippi.

LEWIS, Frank
Wrestler
Lewis won the NCAA and National AAU 155 lb. division titles in 1935. The following year he won the welterweight gold medal at the Berlin Olympics.

MAYSER, Charles W.
Coach
Mayser coached at Yale University, Williston and Newark Academies and Iowa State University between 1900 and 1946. He introduced wrestling at Franklin & Marshall College in 1924, and coached the sport there for 22 years with great success.
Also in: Pennsylvania Wrestling Hall of Fame.

MEHNERT, George Nicholas
Wrestler
See entry in National Wrestling Hall of Fame, 1976.

REED, Robin
Wrestler
In four years of competition, Reed won four medals for the University of Oregon. In 1921 he was National AAU 125 lb. champion and in 1922 and 1924 the 135 lb. champion. During the 1924 Olympics he also won the featherweight gold medal.

ROBERTS, Clay
Noteworthy Contributor
A volunteer coach at the Tulsa YMCA for over 20 years,

Roberts' team won the 1957 and 1958 National AAU title. In 1957 he was also coach of a U.S. team which toured Japan. He was secretary for the U.S. Amateur Wrestling Foundation and a member of AAU and Olympic committees. Roberts was named AAU Wrestling Coach of the Year in 1958.

SPARKS, Dr. Raymond E.
Coach
Sparks began coaching at Wiley High School in Terre Haute, Ind, and later advanced to the college level at Indiana State University, Columbia University, Wyoming Seminary in Kingston, Pa, and for five years at Springfield College in Springfield, Mass. His Springfield teams won 5 New England state championships between 1930 and 1935 and produced 21 individual New England champions.
Also in: Indiana Wrestling Hall of Fame.

THOM, W. H. "Billy"
Coach
As Indiana University coach for 19 years, Billy produced eight Big Ten championships, 1931 – 1934, 1936, 1939, 1940 and 1943. His 1932 squad also won the NCAA title. In 1936 he was chosen Olympic coach.
Also in: Indiana Wrestling Hall of Fame.

1959

CANN, Wilfred E.
Noteworthy Contributor
Born July 31, 1877.

The co-author of *Manual of Wrestling* (1912), Cann coached the Elizabeth, N.J, YMCA wrestling team for over 20 years. Following his success at the YMCA, he directed the Rutgers program from 1939 to 1943. Coach, official and author, he was in charge of the 1924 Olympic team, the most successful to ever represent the United States, and in 1928, was the trainer of the U.S. team.

CLAPP, Dr. Raymond Gustavus
Coach and Contributor
See entry in National Wrestling Hall of Fame, 1976.

HENSON, Dr. Stanley, Jr.
Wrestler
A wrestler at Oklahoma State University, Henson was three-time NCAA champion. In 1937 and 1938 he won the 145 lb. division and followed in 1939 with the 155 lb. title. He was the first sophomore to be named Most Outstanding Wrestler in the NCAA tournaments.

KEEN, Paul V.
Coach
Served four terms on the Norman city council, two terms as mayor; past president of the Rotary Club; 15 years as Sunday school superintendent.

During Keen's eleven years as coach at the University of Oklahoma, he won one NCAA team title (1936) while never finishing lower than fifth. After retiring from active coaching he directed the intramural program for the University.

McCUSKEY, David Homer
Coach
See entry in National Wrestling Hall of Fame, 1976.

PATTERSON, Buell
Coach
In over 25 years of coaching at the University of Illinois, Kansas State and the University of Nebraska, Buell Patterson also served ten years as editor of the NCAA *Wrestling Guide.* In 1948 he was chosen manager of the Olympic team and in 1950 and 1951 he was the chairman of the NCAA wrestling rules committee.

SPELLMAN, John
Wrestler
John won the light-heavyweight gold medal during the 1924 Olympic Games. He represented Brown University.

STEELE, Harry
Wrestler
Harry Steele represented Ohio State University at the 1924 Olympics, winning the heavyweight gold medal.

STREIT, C. W.
Noteworthy Contributor
For four consecutive Olympic meets, beginning in 1924, Streit was manager and chairman of the U.S. Olympic wrestling committee. During this time he was also chairman of the National AAU wrestling committee.

WAGNER, Julius F.
Coach
As the coach at Colorado State University from 1927 to 1954, Wagner's teams won 24 Conference crowns and were co-champions twice. A member of the National AAU wrestling committee, Wagner was responsible for the invention of the plastic mat cover. A former president, secretary and editor of the American Wrestling Coaches and Officials Association, he also served two terms on the NCAA wrestling rules committee.

1960

ACKERLY, Charles E.
Wrestler
Ackerly won a gold medal in the 1920 Olympics in the featherweight division of freestyle wrestling.

FLOOD, Ross
Wrestler
Flood won two AAU freestyle wrestling championships, one in 1936 for the 123 lb. category and one in 1935 for the 125 lb. category. From 1933 to 1935, he was the NCAA champion at 126 lbs.

HUNT, M. Briggs
Coach
Briggs authored a book entitled *Greco-Roman Wrestling,* published in 1973.

KENNEY, Dr. Harold E.
Coach and Contributor
Also in: Illinois Wrestling Coaches and Officials Hall of Fame.

MEHRINGER, Peter Joseph
Wrestler
At the 1932 Olympic Games, Mehringer took a gold medal in the light heavyweight division of freestyle wrestling.

MORRISON, Allie
Wrestler
Between 1926 and 1928 Morrison was the AAU freestyle champion in the 135 lb. category. He topped his career by winning a gold medal in featherweight freestyle wrestling at the 1928 Olympic Games.

PEERY, Rex Anderson
Coach
See entry in National Wrestling Hall of Fame, 1976.

POHL, Erich
Noteworthy Contributor

QUIMBY, Dr. Neal F.
Noteworthy Contributor

ROBERTSON, Port
Coach
Also in: Oklahoma Coaches Association Hall of Fame.

1961

BISHOP, W. Austin
Noteworthy Contributor
After coaching the University of Pennsylvania for many years, Bishop turned his talents to administrative functions. In a quarter of a century of organizing and developing associations and clinics on all levels, he was one of the stalwarts in the American Wrestling Coaches and Officials Association's (AWCOA) formative years. Serving the AWCOA as editor of their *Bulletin,* he also edited the NCAA *Wrestling Guide* and authored Spauldings's *Free Style Wrestling* in 1939.

BLUBAUGH, Douglas
Wrestler
A three-time National AAU welterweight champion, 1957–1959, Doug was also the 1957 NCAA 157 lb. champion while representing Oklahoma State University. He added the welterweight gold medal during the 1960 Olympics. Before assuming the head coaching responsibilities at Indiana University in 1973, Doug directed successful programs at West Point, Oklahoma, Michigan and Michigan State. His ability as a top flight mentor was recognized by his peers in 1971 when he was selected to lead the U.S. grapplers in the Pan-American Games and World Championship competition. Blubaugh was named Outstanding Wrestler of the World in 1960 and Coach of the Year in 1971.

BRAND, Glenn
Wrestler
While attending Iowa State University Glenn won the NCAA 174 lb. championship in 1948. That same year he won the middleweight gold medal in the Olympics.

KOLL, William
Wrestler
Twice named Outstanding Wrestler by the NCAA, Bill won three consecutive 145 lb. division titles for Iowa State Teachers College 1946–1948. A member of the 1948 Olympic team, Koll returned to his alma mater and coached for many years.

LEEMAN, Gerald G.
Coach
While coaching at Lehigh University, beginning in 1952, Leeman's teams won the Eastern Intercollegiate Wrestling Association (EIWA) team title in 1959 and 1961. He was an editor for the American Wrestling Coaches and Officials Association and former president of the EIWA Wrestling Coaches Association. In 1946 he won the 128 lb. NCAA title while representing Iowa State Teachers College and was named Outstanding Wrestler in the tournament. In 1948 Leeman won an Olympic silver medal.

McCANN, Terence
Wrestler
McCann is a three-time National AAU bantamweight champion 1957–1959. While representing the State University of Iowa he won two consecutive NCAA 115 lb. titles in 1955 and 1956. He also won the 1960 Olympic bantamweight gold medal.

MOONEY, Bernard "Spike"
Coach
Born in 1897; attended Springfield Col, Mass.

Spike Mooney dedicated 46 years to wrestling as a coach and instructor. He was three-time president of the Big Ten Wrestling Coaches Association while directing the wrestling program at Ohio State University 1923–1947. In 1932 he was manager of the U.S. Olympic team trials and is a past member of the NCAA wrestling rules committee.

RICHARDSON, G. D.
Noteworthy Contributor
Richardson greatly enhanced the safety of wrestling by developing and manufacturing the first plastic mat covers.

WILSON, Shelby
Wrestler
Shelby won the 1960 Olympic lightweight gold medal.

1962

CALDWELL, Conrad
Wrestler
Conrad was an NCAA and a National AAU champion.

ENGEL, John
Noteworthy Contributor
John Engel has served 26 years as a noted official.

HOKE, Jess
Noteworthy Contributor
For many years Jess Hoke has served as publisher and editor of *Amateur Wrestling News.* Since 1958 he has

served as chairman of the nominating committee for the Amateur Wrestling Hall of Fame in the Citizens Savings Hall of Fame Athletic Museum.

KELLEY, Alan D.
Wrestler
Alan Kelley was an NCAA and a National AAU champion.

MARTIN, Wayne
Wrestler
Wayne Martin was an NCAA and a National AAU champion.

McDANIEL, Joseph
Wrestler
Joe McDaniel was an NCAA and a National AAU champion.

REECK, Claude
Coach
This Purdue University coach directed the 1959 all-victorious U.S. team in the Pan-American Games. Reeck has served on the NCAA wrestling rules committee and the U.S. Olympic and National AAU committees.
Also in: Indiana Wrestling Hall of Fame.

ROBERTS, Raymond
Noteworthy Contributor
Ray has developed many innovative safety devices for both collegiate and amateur wrestling.

SCALZO, Joseph
Coach
The former University of Toledo coach has directed many national and international tournaments. He was chosen as U.S. Olympic coach while serving on the NCAA wrestling rules committee.

UMBACH, Arnold J. "Swede"
Coach
Umbach directed Auburn University wrestlers to 15 Southeastern Conference titles. He is a past president of the American Wrestling Coaches and Officials Association. He co-authored (with Warren Johnson) a book—*Successful Wrestling*—published by William C. Brown Co.

1963

ARNDT, David
Wrestler
One of many national champions at Oklahoma State University, David was NCAA 145 lb. champion in 1941 and 1942. He was NCAA 136 lb. winner in 1946. In 1942 he was also the National AAU champion at 145 lbs.

JACK, Hubert
Coach
For over 20 years Hubert has coached Lock Haven State College to the best over-all record among small colleges.
Also in: Pennsylvania Wrestling Hall of Fame.

KERSLAKE, William
Wrestler
For eight consecutive years, 1953–1960, Kerslake was the National AAU heavyweight champion. A three-time member of the U.S. Olympic team, 1952, 1956 and 1960, he won 15 titles during his career in freestyle and Greco-Roman competition. During his collegiate days he represented Case Institute of Technology in Cleveland and later the Case Athletic Club.

LANGE, Lowell
Wrestler
Lange dominated the 136 lb. class during the late 1940s. He won the NCAA crown in 1947, 1949 and 1950. At the same time he was National AAU titlist, beginning in 1946.

LUMLY, Thomas M.
Noteworthy Contributor
The founder and president of the U.S. Amateur Wrestling Federation, T. M. Lumly is a long-time sponsor of U.S. international competition and also serves as an official.

NELSON, William J.
Wrestler
Graduated from Iowa State Col; two sons, Billy and Bruce, both Ariz. high school state champions; resides in Tucson, Ariz.

A three-time national champion while in college, Bill won the NCAA 165 lb. class in 1947 and the National AAU 155 lb. in 1949 and 1950. He was also a member of the 1948 U.S. Olympic team. Assuming head coaching duties at the University of Arizona in 1963, he has fostered the growth of wrestling through his summer camp, Wildcat Wrestling Camp, and with the Arizona Invitational, the most prestigious tournament in the West. A member of the executive committee of the NCAA Wrestling Coaches Association since 1965, he is credited with bringing the 1976 national championships to the Southwest, the first time the tournament was held in Arizona.
Also in: Arizona Wrestling Hall of Fame.

RODERICK, Myron Willis
Wrestler and Coach
See entry in National Wrestling Hall of Fame, 1976.

1964

ARCHER, Stephen M.
Noteworthy Contributor
A wrestler while attending the U.S. Naval Academy, Archer is a former member of U.S. Olympic and National AAU wrestling committees. He is a certified international official.

BARKER, Richard L.
Coach
An undefeated wrestler at Iowa State University for three years, upon graduation Barker intruduced wrestling at Cornell College in Iowa. Moving from Cornell College to Pennsylvania State University in 1922, for 19 years his teams were among the best in the nation. He won seven national championships. He closed his coaching career in 1943 at Franklin and Marshall College.

DIBATISTA, Richard
Wrestler
Undefeated during his ten years of competition, Richard

won the 1941 and 1942 NCAA titles at 175 lbs. There was no tournament in 1943. After service during W.W. II, where he coached several teams, he turned to officiating. In 20 years as an official, he refereed 16 consecutive years at the Eastern Intercollegiate Wrestling Association tournaments.
Also in: Pennsylvania Wrestling Hall of Fame.

GORRIARAN, Manuel
Noteworthy Contributor
Manuel was the 1963 manager of the U.S. team in the Pan-American Games. He is a past secretary of the National AAU wrestling committee, and also served as secretary-treasurer for the Pan-American Wrestling Confederation.

HUTTON, Richard
Wrestler
One of the all-time great heavyweights in NCAA history, he won the national title in 1947, 1948 and 1950. He represented Oklahoma State University.

PARKER, Charlie
Coach
Charlie has been the coach at Davidson College for over 35 years. He coached the 1963 U.S. Pan-American team. He is a past chairman of the NCAA rules committee and has served on Olympic and AAU committees as well. He is a former editor of the NCAA *Wrestling Guide.*

VOLIVA, Richard
Coach
In 1934 Voliva was national champion at Indiana University, wrestling at 175 lbs. He was a member of the 1936 Olympic team. Later he coached at Rutgers University and chaired the NCAA rules committee.
Also in: Indiana Wrestling Hall of Fame.

YOUNG, Keith
Wrestler
Representing the State College of Iowa, Young won the 1947 NCAA tournament at 145 lbs. and the 1950 championship at 147 lbs.

1965

EVANS, Jay Thomas
Coach and Wrestler
See entry in National Wrestling Hall of Fame, 1976.

LANTZ, Dr. Everett
Coach
Dr. Lantz coached the University of Wyoming Cowboys for 27 years; during that time, his teams won or tied for 12 Skyline Conference championships and won one Western Athletic Conference title. His overall dual meet record is 142 wins, 76 losses and 8 ties. He is a member of the National AAU wrestling committee and has also served two terms on the NCAA wrestling rules committee. Dr. Lantz authored *Wrestling Guide,* a textbook for wrestling coaches. He retired in 1965.

McCREADY, Earl
Wrestler
See entry in Canada's Sports Hall of Fame.
Also in: Canadian Amateur Athletic Hall of Fame.

PLAZA, Arnold
Wrestler
Undefeated in four years of dual meets at Purdue University, Plaza was also Big Ten champion four years. In 1948 and 1949 he was NCAA titlist and was also National AAU champion in 1949 and 1950.
Also in: Illinois Wrestling Coaches and Officials Hall of Fame.

RILEY, Jack
Wrestler
Jack was a two-time NCAA heavyweight champion at Northwestern University and a member of the 1932 Olympics team. In 1932 he was appointed head coach at Northwestern and remained there until he retired in 1958.
Also in: Illinois Wrestling Coaches and Officials Hall of Fame.

1966

JENNINGS, Burl "Bo"
Wrestler
Burl won the 1941 and 1942 NCAA titles at 128 lbs. He represented Michigan State University.

JENNINGS, Merle "Cut"
Wrestler
Merle won the 1941 and 1942 NCAA titles at 121 lbs. while representing Michigan State University.

MARTIN, William
Coach
Graduate of Mich. State Univ.

Martin has coached at Granby High School in Norfolk, Va, since 1945. His teams have won more than 200 dual meets, lost only 6 and tied 2. They have been Virginia State champions 16 out of 17 years. He has produced more than 75 college wrestlers, including 5 NCAA champions. Billy introduced the famous Granby Roll in competitive wrestling.

MATHIS, Archie E.
Coach
Graduated from Univ. Ill. 1925; died in 1945 while serving on the physical education staff at his alma mater.

A pioneer in fostering wrestling throughout the high school and college level in the South, Mathis coached the Washington and Lee University teams and they were unbeaten in 9 of his 17 years, winning 84 dual meets and losing only 20. In 1930 he helped inaugurate the first Southern Conference tournament. His team dominated the competition, winning 4 of the first 8 tournaments and never finishing lower than third.

McDANIEL, Charles
Wrestler
A two-time NCAA heavyweight champion at Indiana University, Charles returned to his alma mater in 1946 as head coach. He won the national title in 1935 and 1938, the Western Conference medal in 1938 and was on the 1936 Olympic squad.
Also in: Indiana Wrestling Hall of Fame.

NICHOLS, Dr. Harold
Coach
The head coach at Iowa State University for over 20 years, Harold's 1965 team was NCAA champion. He has been president of the Wrestling Coaches Association and chairman of the NCAA rules committee. He is a former Big Ten and NCAA champion for the University of Michigan. Nichols was named Wrestling Coach of the Year in 1958 and 1965.

SAPORA, Joseph
Wrestler
Joe was four times a national champion in four years at the University of Illinois. His first two championships came in 1929 and 1930 in the 115 lb. class at the NCAA tournament. After graduating from the University he represented the New York Athletic Club and earned the 1931 AAU 115 lb. title and the following year the crown in the 123 lb. division. He was coach at City College of New York for nearly 40 years.

1967

FREDERICKS, Casey L.
Coach
Casey wrestled at Purdue University 1940–1942 and while there, won the National AAU championship at 118 lbs. He served two years as assistant coach at Purdue, then became head coach at Ohio State University in 1947. At that time there were only 14 high school wrestling teams in the state. Fredericks has been a prime mover in promoting state wrestling and today there are more than 375 high school teams. His annual clinic for high school coaches is one of the largest and most successful in the nation. Casey was a member of the NCAA wrestling rules committee for four years.
Also in: Indiana Wrestling Hall of Fame.

GARDNER, Frank "Sprig"
Coach
Gardner has coached at Mepham High School in Bellmore, N.Y, for twenty years, during which time his teams won 254 and lost only 5 dual meets, including runs of 101 and 134 without a loss. He is the author of *Young Sportsman's Guide to Wrestling* and many articles. He came out of retirement to coach Gettysburg College for two years, but was forced to retire again because of ill health. Frank was a high school representative on the NCAA wrestling rules committee.
Also in: New York State Wrestling Coaches Association Hall of Fame.

HESS, Robert
Wrestler
Representing Iowa State University, Hess won the 1932 and 1933 NCAA 175 lb. titles.

LEWIS, Hardie
Wrestler
Although Lewis had never seen a wrestling match when he entered the University of Oklahoma on a baseball scholarship, he won two NCAA championships at 145 lbs. in 1930 and 1932.

ROCKWELL, Dean
Noteworthy Contributor
Rockwell coached high school wrestling for 7 years and at Albion College for 2 years. He later coached the U.S. Greco-Roman World Games team in 1962 and the U.S. Olympic Greco-Roman team in 1964. Dean has been a member of the U.S. Olympic wrestling committee and the U.S. Amateur Wrestling Foundation, and is a past chairman of the National AAU wrestling committee. He is a founding member of the Hazel Park Wrestling Club and in 1967 was coach and manager for the Michigan Wrestling Club in Detroit.

TEAGUE, Ralph
Wrestler
A four-time heavyweight champion in three years, Ralph won the 1933 and 1934 NCAA title and the AAU crown in 1934 and 1935. He represented Southwestern State College, Weatherford, Okla.

THOMAS, Dr. Dale O.
Coach
Graduated from Cornell Col, Iowa; received Ph.D. from Mich. State Univ; College Coach of the Year 1961.

Dale won nine national wrestling titles in three different styles and was a member of the 1952 and 1956 U.S. Olympic teams. In his ten years as coach at Oregon State University, his teams have dominated Pacific Coast competition. Dale coached the U.S. Greco-Roman teams in the 1961 and 1966 World Championships. He also introduced Kid Wrestling and initiated foreign cultural exchange programs for high school teams. He is an accredited international official.

1968

GIZONI, Anthony "Vic"
Wrestler
Attended Waynesburg Col, Pa.

Gizoni won two championships, in 1950 for the 121 lb. division and 1951 for the 123 lb. division.
Also in: Pennsylvania Wrestling Hall of Fame.

HENSON, Josiah
Noteworthy Contributor
Henson was the 1952 freestyle champion in the 135 lb. category although he weighed 136.5 lb. at the weigh-in.

HODGE, Dan Allen
Wrestler
See entry in National Wrestling Hall of Fame, 1976.

JOHNSON, Wallace T.
Coach

MURDOCK, Raymond "Bucky"
Coach
Also in: Pennsylvania Wrestling Hall of Fame and National Association of Intercollegiate Athletics Hall of Fame.

OLSEN, Thorwald
Wrestler

PEERY, Edwin
Wrestler
Coached by his father Rex at the University of Pittsburgh, Edwin won three consecutive NCAA titles, 1955–1957.

PEERY, Hugh
Wrestler
Coached by his father Rex at the University of Pittsburgh, Hugh won three consecutive NCAA titles, 1952–1954.

1969

BEGALA, Joseph
Coach
The Kent State University coach for over 40 years, Joe has established himself as the most successful college wrestling coach in America. Besides winning over 300 dual meets, he has hosted the NCAA championships twice.
Also in: Athletic Hall of Fame at Ohio University.

MANTOOTH, Lawrence
Wrestler
Known as the "scissor king" at the University of Oklahoma, Mantooth was NCAA champion in 1929 and 1930 at 125 lbs.

MARTIN, George Alfred
Coach
Born June 4, 1911, in Renwick, Iowa; served in U.S. Navy aboard the Ticonderoga aircraft carrier; Navy and Marine Corps Bronze Star; died in 1970.

Enrolling at Iowa State College in 1929, George was captain of the 1933 NCAA championship team, and won individual honors in the 165 lb. class. The following year, he won the National AAU 175 lb. class crown. Martin accepted the varsity coaching position at the University of Wisconsin in 1935, directing the University wrestling program for over 35 years until his retirement. Except for a few intramural programs at several high schools, Wisconsin had no high school sponsored wrestling programs back in 1935. Martin spent several years traveling some 40,000 miles talking to school board members, administrators and PTA groups and also giving demonstrations and clinics to promote high school wrestling. His success is proven by the fact that today over 400 high schools have wrestling programs. The "Father of High School Wrestling," as George Martin is known in Wisconsin, earned the recognition of his peers and students, and in 1977—the greatest accolade of all—the George Martin Wrestling Hall of Fame was founded.
Also in: George Martin Wrestling Hall of Fame and Iowa Hall of Fame.

NORTHRUP, M. A. "Doc"
Wrestler
Doc wrestled at Washington State University 1930–1933, then moved to San Francisco where he has been a member of Olympic Club wrestling teams for over 30 years. He was National AAU champion from 1943 to 1945 and again in 1955. He is a doctor of veterinary medicine and still wrestling at over 60 years of age.

SIDDENS, Bob
Coach
Graduated from the Univ. Northern Iowa.

A highly successful coach at West High School in Waterloo, Iowa, Bob has nine undefeated seasons to his credit. He has averaged two state champions a year in individual classes. For many years he has officiated the NCAA championships.

WHITEHURST, Alfred
Wrestler
Another champion produced by Ed Gallagher at Oklahoma State University, Whitehurst won NCAA titles in the 136 lb. division in 1940 and 1941 and was on three championship teams. He was named Outstanding Wrestler in the 1941 championships.

1970

GAGNE, Vern
Wrestler
Vern wrestled for the University of Minnesota in the late 1940s, and in two years won three national titles, the NCAA 191 lb. in 1948 and 1949, plus the AAU heavyweight division in 1949. After graduation he turned professional.

HESS, Marvin
Coach
Marvin never wrestled in his undergraduate days at the University of Utah, but his teams reflect his intensity and devotion as they are always competitive nationally. He served on the executive committee of the National Wrestling Coaches Association and was president in 1967 and 1968. He also chaired the NCAA wrestling rules committee for two years. Hess is a member of the Olympic wrestling committee and was instrumental in the early planning of the U.S. Wrestling Federation.

LOGAN, Vernon
Wrestler
While representing Oklahoma State University, Logan was a member of three NCAA championship teams, earning individual honors in 1940 and 1942 in the 155 lb. class. He added the AAU crown in 1942.

PENINGER, Grady
Coach
Graduated from Oklahoma State Univ.

A two-time National AAU champion in the 115 lb. class, Peninger also placed second in the 1949 NCAA finals. A successful high school coach in Ponca City, Okla, Grady's teams won three state championships before he moved to Michigan State as assistant mentor in 1960. Two years later he was chosen varsity coach. Since then his dual meet record is 125 wins, 45 losses and 7 ties. For seven consecutive years, 1966–1973, his Spartans were Big Ten champions, with the 1967 team winning the NCAA championship. His teams have finished second twice in the nationals, third once and fourth twice. Aside from the many team titles, his grapplers have earned ten individual NCAA crowns and 38 Big Ten titles. Peninger was named College Coach of the Year and Man of the Year in Amateur Wrestling, both in 1967.

SMITH, Virgil
Wrestler
Virgil won consecutive NCAA 165 lb. titles in 1941 and 1942.

WEICK, William
Wrestler
Bill was the 1952 and 1955 NCAA 157 lb. champion at the University of Northern Iowa. Military duty intervened in 1953 and 1954. Adept in both freestyle and Greco-Roman competition, he was named the Outstanding Wrestler on the U.S. team in the 1961 World Games. A successful high school coach in Chicago for many years, he was selected as coach-leader of the U.S. Junior Olympic freestyle team in 1969 that won the World Championship.
Also in: Illinois Wrestling Coaches and Officials Hall of Fame.

1971

HAYES, Larry
Wrestler
While representing Iowa State University, Larry won three consecutive NCAA titles, 1959 to 1961. His weight classes were 137 lbs. and later 147 lbs.

KITT, Karl
Coach
Karl has directed high school and collegiate wrestling programs in Oklahoma, Maryland and Colorado. His service on the collegiate level was split between the U.S. Naval Academy, where he spent 15 years as plebe and varsity assistant coach, and the U.S. Air Force Academy since 1957. He is past president of both the National Wrestling Coaches Association and the Mountain Intercollegiate Wrestling Coaches Association.

KRAFT, Ken
Noteworthy Contributor
Graduated from Northwestern Univ. 1957.

A successful collegiate wrestler at Northwestern, Kraft was appointed head coach in the spring of his senior year, 1957. Active in all areas of the sport, he was cofounder of Mayor Daley's Youth Federation and established the prestigious Midlands Open Holiday tournament. An eloquent speaker and analyst, he was ABC's Wide World of Sports wrestling commentator for six years. One of the first originators of the U.S. Wrestling Federation, he directed its first national tournament in 1969, and now serves as president. Aside from his administrative duties, he is a consultant for wrestling instructional films which are produced by the National Federation of High School Associations.
Also in: Illinois Wrestling Coaches and Officials Hall of Fame.

MILKOVICH, Mike
Coach
Mike has produced eight state championship teams at Maple Heights, Ohio, High School, including four in the last 5 years. Five other teams were second in the state. He has had 13 undefeated seasons with winning streaks of 59 and 78, adding up to a career total of 187 victories and only 17 defeats. He was coach of the U.S. Junior World Championship team in 1969.

SIMONS, Elliott Gray
Wrestler
In four years of collegiate competition, Elliott won four NAIA titles and three NCAA titles at Lock Haven State College. He was named Outstanding Wrestler in six of those tournaments. At the end of his college career, he had lost only once and had 82 consecutive wins. Elliott was a member of the 1960 and 1964 Olympic freestyle teams. He became the Indiana State University coach in 1971.

1972

ALITZ, Leroy
Coach
Graduated from the Univ. Northern Iowa; received a masters from Iowa State Univ.

Since 1955 Leroy has directed the U.S. Military Academy wrestling program while serving on several national committees. He was chairman of the NCAA wrestling rules committee, president of the National Wrestling Coaches Association (1968–1969), president of the Eastern Intercollegiate Wrestling Coaches Association and a member of the U.S. Olympic wrestling committee.

DELLINGER, Bob
Noteworthy Contributor
Resides in Stillwater, Okla.

The most knowledgeable and prolific sports writer in the daily newspaper field for 17 years, Bob is now the director of the National Wrestling Hall of Fame in Stillwater, Okla. An advisor to the NCAA wrestling rules committee he originated the modern bracket sheet widely used at national tournaments. He was the sports editor for the *Daily Oklahoman* and the *Oklahoma City Times.*

LAYMAN, George
Wrestler
A member of three championship teams at Oklahoma State University, George won individual NCAA honors in 1951 and 1952 at 137 lbs. In his 1951 victory he defeated three former NCAA titlists.

WEISS, Arthur J.
Coach
Weiss initiated wrestling at Clearfield, Pa, High School in 1935 and spent 25 years there. In a 17 year period his teams won 133 dual meets, lost 2 and tied 2, and his overall team record for 25 years was 184 wins, 37 losses and 3 ties. Clearfield teams won 19 of 21 district championships with 99 individual district winners and 31 state championships, the finest record in Pennsylvania wrestling history. Art served for many years on the Pennsylvania State Wrestling Board of Control. After his retirement as a coach, he became an outstanding high school and collegiate official and is widely sought after as a clinician.
Also in: Pennsylvania Wrestling Hall of Fame.

WILLIAMS, T. Ralph "Pug"
Noteworthy Contributor
Responsible for the growth of interscholastic wrestling in New Jersey, Williams was the coach and athletic director for 23 years at Roselle Park High School. Pug is a charter member of the New Jersey Wrestling Coaches and Officials Association. He has also directed ten state tournaments, his team winning six of them.

1973

BAUGHMAN, Richard Wayne
Wrestler
In 1962 Richard won the 190 lb. NCAA championship while representing the University of Oklahoma. Since then he has continued his amateur career, winning 12 AAU titles, two U.S. Wrestling Federation championships and 15 Interservice titles in freestyle and Greco-Roman competition. A three-time U.S. Olympian, he was twice elected team captain. In 1967 he was team captain, and champion, in the Pan-American Games. In World Championship competition, he has qualified seven times for the U.S. team. Currently directing the sports program for the U.S. Air Force Academy, he also serves on the U.S. Olympic Wrestling Committee.

FARRELL, William
Noteworthy Contributor
Graduated from Hofstra Univ; received law degree from St. John's Univ. (N.Y.); currently pres. of Universal-Resilite Co, Hempstead, N.Y, which manufactures and distributes physical fitness and wrestling products.

Wrestling with the New York Athletic Club from 1959 to 1973, Bill won 335 matches and lost 12. During that time, he also served as team captain and chairman of the Club's wrestling committee. Aside from his competitive and administrative contributions, he was coach for the U.S. team in the World Championships in 1969 and 1970. The 1970 squad finished in second place, the highest finish ever for an American team. Bill coached the 1972 U.S. Olympics team to a second place victory, with 6 wrestlers winning medals, including 3 golds.

HITCHCOCK, Vaughan
Coach
Vaughan was a four-year collegiate wrestler at Washington State University and since assuming the varsity coaching position at California State Polytechnic University at San Luis Obispo, has a dual meet record of 152 wins, 29 losses and 2 ties. Vaughan is a member of several NCAA committees, among them the executive committee of the wrestling rules committee, and is a former president of the college division of the Wrestling Coaches Association. He is a member of the National Wrestling Coaches Association. He was named College Division Coach of the Year in 1968 and was runner-up for University Division Coach of the Year in 1972.

SCARPELLO, Joseph
Wrestler
A member of the University of Iowa wrestling team, he won the NCAA 175 lb. title in 1947 and 1950. He was first alternate on the 1948 Olympic team.

TOMARAS, Dr. William
Noteworthy Contributor
Bill wrestled at the University of Illinois and was third in the NCAA championships in 1946. He went to Washington in 1948 and at that time, there were only eight high school teams in the entire state. His endeavors were responsible for his being named "Father of High School Wrestling" in Washington. When he left in 1959, there were 120 state high school teams. He coached the University of California from 1959 to 1961, then returned to Washington. He started and coached the wrestling program at Western Washington State University and was named athletic director in 1965. After his retirement, Bill was called on to serve as interim coach at California State University at Northridge in 1973.

1974

BLASS, Ned
Wrestler
Ned was a two-time NCAA champion at Oklahoma State University in 1953 and 1954 in the 177 lb. weight division. He is now coaching Mt. Miguel High School in Spring Valley, Calif.

GABLE, Dan
Wrestler
Dan's high school and collegiate competitive record is an impressive 180 wins and just one loss. He was NCAA champion in 1968 and 1969, and in 1971, was National AAU, U.S. World Federation and World Champion. He won a gold medal in the 1972 Olympics wrestling at 149 lbs. Dan was named Wrestling Man of the Year in 1969. He is currently an assistant coach at the University of Iowa.

NALAN, Norvard
Wrestler
A three-time Big Ten champion at the University of Michigan, Nalan holds the Michigan state record for consecutive wins at 34. His career record is 44 wins and 3 losses. In 1953 and 1954 he won the NCAA 130 lb. division championship. He is presently coach at Grand Rapids, Mich, High School.

NICKS, Gene
Wrestler
While wrestling at Oklahoma State University, Gene won the NCAA heavyweight championship in 1952 and 1954, and was runnerup in 1953. He now resides in Ponca City, Okla.

PETERSON, Ben
Wrestler
Graduated from Iowa State Univ. with a degree in architecture; currently with an architectural firm in Madison and a part time coach at Maranatha Baptist Bible College in Watertown.

Ben never won a high school tournament, but he did claim three Big Eight titles at 190 lbs. in the early 1970s. In 1971 and 1972 he was NCAA champion, serving as co-captain on the 1972 team. He has won two gold medals, first in the 1972 Olympics and later in the 1975 Pan-American Games. He also placed second in the 1976

Olympics and third in the 1973 World Games.
Also in: George Martin Wrestling Hall of Fame.

WELLS, Wayne
Wrestler
Currently an attorney in Oklahoma City; Wrestling Man of the Year 1970.

Wayne was three-time Big Eight champion at the University of Oklahoma and won the 1972 Olympics gold medal in the 163 lb. class. He also won the World Championship, National AAU title and U.S. Wrestling Federation tournaments the same year.

1975

BLAIR, Pete
Wrestler
In three years of amateur wrestling at the U.S. Naval Academy, Pete won three national championships, all in the 191 lb. class. He won back-to-back NCAA titles in 1954 and 1955, and the 1956 AAU crown. He was a member of the 1956 U.S. Olympic freestyle team, winning the bronze medal at Melbourne.

BORESCH, Henry
Noteworthy Contributor
The Father of Scholastic Wrestling in New Jersey organized the state's first high school team in 1936. For 28 years Henry coached Newton High School winning 11 state championships and 76 individual state winners. A wrestler himself, he won the Metropolitan AAU championship in 1924 and 1926. Boresch was twice named Outstanding Scholastic Wrestling Coach by the New Jersey Wrestling Coaches and Officials Association.

MACIAS, Rometo
Coach
For over a quarter of a century Rometo has directed the Mankato State College wrestling program, producing 75 All-Americans and NCAA and NAIA championship teams. His 1968 team placed second in the NCAA tournament. Before initiating the wrestling program at Mankato State, he was a two-time Big Ten champion for the University of Iowa and NCAA runnerup in 1948. He is a member of the National Wrestling Coaches executive committee and former president of the NAIA and NCAA College Wrestling Coaches Association. Macias is the author of *Learning How—Wrestling.*

1976

COPPLE, Newt
Noteworthy Contributor
Newt was a major competitive wrestler for 17 years, and his honors include six National AAU championships, Big Eight Conference, National YMCA and the Pan-American Games championships. He placed fifth in the 1954 World Championships. His greatest contribution has been in the administrative and technical aspects at all levels of the sport. Since 1964 Newt has been a member of the U.S. Olympic wrestling committee, and chairman of the U.S. Amateur Wrestling Foundation since 1966. He has served as national chairman of the AAU wrestling committee since 1971. In the past Copple has served as a U.S. delegate to both the Pan-American Sports Organization and the International Wrestling Federation.

EICHELBERGER, Edward
Wrestler
Currently an executive with IBM Corp. and resides in East Fishkill, N.Y.

At 147 lbs, Ed was NCAA champion at Lehigh University in 1955 and 1956 and was named Outstanding Wrestler in 1955. He was also the Eastern Intercollegiate champion at the same time and both years was named Outstanding Wrestler.

ERIKSEN, Finn
Noteworthy Contributor
Finn was an outstanding wrestler at Iowa State Teachers College and while working for his masters degree at Columbia University, wrestled for the New York Athletic Club. He returned to Iowa and coached at both New Hampton and West High Schools in Waterloo. After service in W.W. II, he returned as director of health and physical education for Waterloo Schools. In this capacity he was influential in the development of wrestling in the State of Iowa and was an outstanding official at all levels, including the 1952 Olympics. For 13 years Finn served as high school representative on the NCAA wrestling rules committee and as a clinician for the National Federation of High School Associations. He also assisted the National Federation in the production of films on officiating.

SAYENGA, Donald
Noteworthy Contributor
Graduated from Lafayette Col. 1956; currently employed in the sales division of Bethlehem Steel and resides in Bethlehem, Pa.

Sayenga wrestled three years at Lafayette College and is still active as a promoter and participant in tournaments for oldsters. Don has become an outstanding U.S. historian of amateur wrestling. He has spent thousands of hours in research and written hundreds of articles to add to the interest in, and knowledge of, the historical background of the sport. His writings have chronicled wrestling as The Oldest Sport, and cover ancient, medieval and modern historical references tracing wrestling's development throughout the world.

UETAKE, Yojiro
Wrestler
Yojiro won three straight NCAA championships at 130 lbs. at Oklahoma State University in 1964, 1965 and 1966 and was honored as Outstanding Wrestler the last two years. He returned to his native Japan in 1964 and won the Olympic gold medal as a member of the Japanese team and repeated the feat in the 1968 Olympics at Mexico City. Uetake (now known as Yojiro Obata) is a qualified international official and is the National Wrestling Coach of Japan.

1977

CARUSO, Michael J.
Wrestler
Born in 1945 in Newark, N.J; graduated from St. Benedict's High School in Newark; Fletcher Award 1967; currently an insurance executive and resides in Bethlehem, Pa.

While at Lehigh University Mike won the 123 lb. NCAA crown each year, 1965–1967. He also won the Eastern Intercollegiate championship three times.

HOUK, Russell E.
Noteworthy Contributor
In his 11 years as head coach at Bloomsburg (Pa.) State College, Houk produced three national champion teams in the NAIA and was voted Coach of the Year three times. He served three four-year terms on the U.S. Olympic wrestling committee, which he chaired from 1972 to 1976. He also managed the 1972 and 1976 Olympic freestyle teams. Houk devoted more than 25 years to all phases of amateur wrestling.
Also in: National Association of Intercollegiate Athletics Hall of Fame and Pennsylvania Wrestling Hall of Fame.

PETERSON, John
Wrestler
Born in Wis; graduated from Univ. Wis, Stout; resides in Lancaster, Pa.

While wrestling at the University of Wisconsin, John was an NAIA All-American in 1971, and was a nominee for the James E. Sullivan Memorial Award of 1976. He won a silver medal in the 1972 Olympic Games in Munich, and was the only U.S. wrestler to win a gold medal in the 1976 Games. In the years between his Olympic performances, he was National AAU freestyle champion and was active with the Athletes in Action wrestling team, a sports branch of the Campus Crusade for Christ and is now their coach.
Also in: George Martin Wrestling Hall of Fame.

SANDERS, Rick
Wrestler
Born in 1945; graduated from Portland State Univ; died in 1972.

Rick was considered one of the greatest wrestling technicians in America. As a collegian at Portland State 1965–1968, he was a four-time All-American. In his freshman year he was NAIA national champion and Outstanding Wrestler. He followed this honor with three NCAA College Division titles and two in the University Division. Rick won a silver medal in the 1968 Olympics in Mexico City and was a member of 5 World Game teams. He was the first U.S. wrestler to win a World Games title. Rick was killed in an auto-bus collision in Yugoslavia just 49 days after winning the silver medal in the 1972 Olympics at Munich.

TISCHLER, Warren F.
Noteworthy Contributor
Warren researched, developed and now manufactures and distributes foam rubber wrestling mats. In 1959 he established his own firm and produces over 2000 mats each year under the trade name of Resilite. The foam mats are considered to be the greatest contribution to amateur wrestling in the 20th century.
Also in: Pennsylvania Wrestling Hall of Fame.

International Palace of Sports Hall of Fame

NORTH WEBSTER, INDIANA

Mailing Address: Camelot Square, 46555. Tel. (219) 834-2831. *Contact:* Tim Moser, Exec. Dir. *Location:* Hwy. 13, 35 mi. S. of the Indiana Toll Road; approx. 35 mi. N.W. of Ft. Wayne, 40 mi. S.E. of South Bend, 90 mi. S.E. of Gary, 110 mi. S.E. of Chicago, Ill, 115 mi. N.E. of Indianapolis. *Admission:* Free; open from Memorial Day through Labor Day; Friday, Saturday and Sunday, noon to 10; guided tours on the half-hour. *Personnel:* Chris Schenkle, Pres; Keith Horn, V.Pres, Tim Moser, Exec. Dir, 24-mem. Bd. of Dirs. *Nearby Halls of Fame:* Agriculture (W. Lafayette, 90 mi. S.W.), Business (Chicago, Ill.), Trapshooting (Vandalia, Ohio, 110 mi. S.E.), Auto Racing, Basketball (Indianapolis), Flight (Dayton, Ohio, 135 mi. S.E.), State (Detroit, Mich, 150 mi. N.E.), Bowling, State (Milwaukee, Wisc, 180 mi. N.W.), Football (Canton, Ohio, 225 mi. S.E.), Archery (Grayling, Mich, 240 mi. N.E.).

The International Palace of Sports was founded jointly by Chris Schenkle and J. Homer Shoop in 1970. The Palace building itself was dedicated on June 29, 1974, with such sports dignitaries as Jesse Owens, Pancho Gonzales, Johnny Weissmuller, Dick Weber and O. J. Simpson presiding. The Palace was built and planned as a shrine that would dramatize youth career awards through outstanding sports personalities. A foundation (the International Palace of Sports, Inc.) was built that would grant career awards and scholarships to deserving and disadvantaged youth. Inside the museum are such things as wax figures, 22 in all, including those of Mark Spitz, O. J. Simpson, Hank Aaron, Archie Griffin, Babe Ruth, Arnold Palmer, Gordie Howe, Pélé, Mildred "Babe" Didrikson Zaharias and many more. Also included in the museum are 78 oil paintings of prominent sports figures, biographical tapes, stained glass checkerboards, medallions and crown jewels—truly a sportsman's education. The Palace is a non-profit organization funded by memberships and donations, and is a member of the Association of Sports Museums and Halls of Fame.

Members: 5 as of June 1977. A Selection Committee draws up a list of nominees for balloting. These ballots are sent out to members of the Board of Directors and people well versed in sports. Balloting takes place in January. The person with the highest percentage of votes is inducted the last full week in June during the week-long festivities honoring the inductee. Qualifications include outstanding performance in a sport, character of the individual and the individual's willingness to participate in the festival honoring him.

1972 SPITZ, Mark. See entry in International Swimming Hall of Fame, 1977. *Also in:* Swimming and Diving Hall of Fame, Citizens Savings Hall of Fame Athletic Museum.

1973 SIMPSON, Orenthal J. "O. J." See entry in College Football Hall of Fame, Citizens Savings Hall of Fame Athletic Museum. *Also in:* Black Athletes Hall of Fame.

1974 AARON, Hank

1975 GRIFFIN, Archie

1976 JENNER, Bruce

International Sports Hall of Fame

WASHINGTON, D.C.

Mailing Address: 1015 18 St, N.W, Suite 601, 20036. Tel. (202) 452-9666. *Contact:* Edward F. Cain, Pres. *Location:* I-95 and the Beltway, near the Smithsonian and Rayburn Bldg; approx. 1 mi. S. of the Capitol, 2 mi. S.E. of the White House, adjacent to the Mall. *Admission:* 10 to 7 daily, with extended hours during the summer months (call for times). Adults $3.00, students 14 years and over $2.00, children 6-14 $1.00, under 6 years free; discounts available with coupons. *Nearby Halls of Fame:* Exploration and Invention (Arlington, Va, 5 mi. S.W.), Heritage (Valley Forge, Pa, 115 mi. N.W.), Bicycle (Staten Island, N.Y, 190 mi. N.E.), Heritage, Music (New York City, 200 mi. N.E.), Golf (Foxburg, Pa, 210 mi. N.W.), Harness Racing (Goshen, N.Y, 210 mi. N.E.), Flight (Elmira, N.Y, 220 mi. N.W.), Horseshoe Pitching (Corning, N.Y, 225 mi. N.W.), Ice Skating (Newburgh, N.Y, 225 mi. N.E.).

As stated in The Story of the Hall of Fame, which appears as an introductory section to Volume I of this book, the hall of fame as an institution has changed much from its beginnings at the turn of the century, is presently undergoing some very basic changes, and may therefore be expected to change in the future. Two broad types of "future hall" are predicted in that introductory section: those which are referred to there as "the future's history teachers," and those which are referred to as "institutes." The present hall of fame, The International Sports Hall of Fame, slated to open in the spring of 1978, is history's first "institute-type" hall of fame. As such, it is both totally unique and highly significant as a harbinger of the most pervasive changes to occur in the hall of fame during its whole existence as a major North American institution. To be located less than a two-minute walk from the Rayburn Building and less than five minutes from the Smithsonian Institution, the International Sports Hall of Fame will be the closest major nongovernmental tourist attraction to the Washington Mall. There is a special symbolism in that central location in the nation's capital inasmuch as the International Sports Hall of Fame will in fact function as the continental capital for the over 700 other halls of fame. This is most readily seen in the fact that the International Sports Hall of Fame will not induct people. That is an apparent contradiction to the definition of "hall of fame" as given in The Story of the Hall of Fame at the front of Volume I; but it is to be remembered that the International Sports Hall of Fame is more "future" than "present." Its plans call for the display of artifacts from more than 100 sports and 100 countries throughout the world—sports themselves, not people, will be inducted. The International Sports Hall of Fame will thus not compete with other halls of fame in existence today which honor the greats of individual sports: by inducting the sports themselves, it will represent all the other halls of fame. It will also honor each State in the United States with a Special Day, on which artifacts from a particular State will be displayed on its Special Day. Such activities, in addition to the wealth of attractive, sophisticated and educational displays, will create a constantly changing but always exciting atmosphere where a visitor may merely "browse" or actively learn. Visitors from foreign countries will appreciate the presence of the multilingual hosts and hostesses and of the mini-brochures printed in several major languages of the world. All visitors to the International Sports Hall of Fame (the Editors estimate well in excess of one million people will visit it during its first year of operations) will appreciate the adequate parking space, the first class restaurant and the fast food snack bar, and the free distribution of what the Editors have called (in The Story of the Hall of Fame) "funducation," which is fun plus education.

Members: As of 1977, the following sports will be inducted into the International Sports Hall of Fame:

Angling and Fishing
Archery
Auto Racing
Badminton
Barrel Jumping
Baseball
Basketball
Biathlon
Bicycle Racing
Billiards
Bobsledding
Boccie
Bowling
Boxing
Bullfighting
Canoeing
Cat Shows
Court Tennis
Cricket
Croquet
Cross-Country
Curling
Darts
Dog (Greyhound) Racing
Dog Shows
Fencing
Field Hockey
Field Trials
Figure Skating
Football
Gaelic Football
Golf

Gymnastics
Handball
Hang Gliding
Harness Racing
Horse Racing
Horseshoe Pitching
Horse Shows
Hurling
Iceboating
Ice Hockey
Jai Alai
Judo
Ju-Jitsu
Karate
Kung Fu
Lacrosse
Lawn Bowling
Luge
Marbles
Modern Pentathlon
Motorcycle Racing
Olympic Games
Paddleball
Paddle Tennis
Pan-American Games
Parachute Jumping
Platform Tennis
Polo
Powerboat Racing
Quarter Horse Racing
Racquetball
Racquets
Rodeo
Roller Derby
Roller Hockey
Roller Skating
Rowing
Rugby
Shooting
Shuffleboard
Skate Sailing
Skiing
Sled Dog Racing
Snowmobiling
Soaring
Soccer
Softball
Speed Skating
Squash Racquets and Tennis
Sumo Wrestling
Surfing
Swimming and Diving
Table Hockey
Table Tennis
Team Handball
Tennis
Track and Field
Trampolining
Unlimited Hydroplane Racing
Volleyball
Water Polo
Water Skiing
Weightlifting
Wheelchair Games
World University Games
Wrestling
Yachting

National Sportscasters and Sportswriters Hall of Fame

SALISBURY, NORTH CAROLINA

Mailing Address: P.O. Box 559, 28144. Tel. (704) 633-4221. *Contact:* Lib Kapitano, Operations Dir. *Location:* Approx. 30 mi. S.W. of Winston-Salem, 37 mi. N.E. of Charlotte, 100 mi. S.W. of Raleigh, 120 mi. N.E. of Columbia, S.C, 200 mi. S.W. of Richmond, Va. *Personnel:* Lewis Harris, Pres. and Acting Chmn. of a 10-mem. Bd. of Dirs. Call for information. *Nearby Halls of Fame:* Golf (Pinehurst, 65 mi. S.E.).

The National Sportscasters and Sportswriters Hall of Fame (formerly The National Foundation of Outstanding Sportswriters) was founded in 1962 by Lewis Harris. The idea for the Hall of Fame came from the poem *If* by Rudyard Kipling; also Lew Harris wanted to honor the inspirational qualities evidenced by a sportswriter or sportscaster. The Hall of Fame plaques are housed at Catawba College located in Salisbury. The Association hopes to have its own building with library facilities containing a national library of sports within three years. The Hall is an educational non-profit foundation supported by donations.

Members: 18 as of June 1977. Nomination requirements are that the individual must be a sportscaster or sportswriter, must have produced an important or memorable event in sportswriting, must have 15 years activity in the field, or the nominee could be an individual who gained fame in a particular sport in America. There are 7600 vote casters across the United States who both nominate and vote for the nominees. A candidate for induction must receive 75 percent of the votes cast. There is no limit on the number of inductees selected each year. Nominees are inducted into the Hall of Fame at an annual awards ceremony, and their inscribed plaques are added to the collection.

1962 RICE, Grantland. See entry in Noteworthy Contributors Hall of Fame, Citizens Savings Hall of Fame Athletic Museum.

1963 HUSING, Ted

1964 McNAMEE, Graham
RUNYON, Damon

1966 LARDNER, Ring

1969 TAYLOR, J. G. "Stink"

1970 McCARTHY, Clem

1971 KIERAN, John

1972 ALLEN, Mel

1973 BARBER, Red
WARD, Arch

1974 STERN, Bill
WOODWARD, Stanley

1975 HODGES, Russ
PARKER, Dan

1976 DALEY, Arthur
DEAN, Jay Hanna "Dizzy." See entry in National Baseball Hall of Fame, 1953.

1977 SMITH, Red

Wheelchair Sports Hall of Fame

WOODSIDE, NEW YORK

Mailing Address: 40-24 62nd St, 11377. Tel. (212) 424-2929. *Contact:* Benjamin H. Lipton, Chmn. *Location:* In New York City; approx. 70 mi. N.E. of Philadelphia, Pa, 145 mi. S.E. of Albany. *Personnel:* Benjamin H. Lipton, Chmn; Ted McLean, Secy; Robert C. Hawker, Treas; 12-mem. Exec. Comt. Call for information. *Nearby Halls of Fame:* Heritage, Music (New York City), Bicycle (Staten Island, 5 mi. S.W.), Ice Skating (Newburgh, 45 mi. N.W.), Harness Racing (Goshen, 75 mi. N.E.), Heritage (Valley Forge, Pa, 104 mi. N.E.), Basketball (Springfield, Mass, 120 mi. N.E.), Baseball (Cooperstown, 135 mi. N.W.), Tennis (Newport, R.I, 140 mi. N.E.), Horse Racing (Saratoga Springs, 150 mi. N.E.), Flight (Elmira, 170 mi. N.W.), Horseshoe Pitching (Corning, 185 mi. N.W.), Jockey's (Baltimore, Md, 196 mi. S.W.), Ice Skating (Boston, Mass, 206 mi. N.E.), Exploration and Invention (Arlington, Va, 210 mi. S.W.).

In 1970 the National Wheelchair Athletic Association inducted its first individuals into the Wheelchair Sports Hall of Fame in order to establish a permanent roster of those persons whose activities and conduct in wheelchair sports deserved the highest form of accolade. Each person elected to the Hall has his or her name inscribed on a bronze tablet, which is on display at the time and site of the National Wheelchair Games and at other times in the office of the Chairman of the National Wheelchair Athletic Committee (NWAC). Each Hall member receives a suitable permanent award for his personal ownership, which is awarded at the National Games Banquet or other suitable occasion if the former is not possible.

Members: 18 as of 1976. Eligible persons must be (A) wheelchair athletes who have in their participation in national and international competition, distinguished themselves through outstanding performance and superior sportsmanship or (B) able-bodied or disabled individuals who have made significant contributions to wheelchair sports in administration, management, coaching and/or promotion. The minimum period of participation for eligibles in Category A shall be five years activity in wheelchair sports, and seven years for those in Category B. A Hall of Fame Committee, appointed by the Chairman of the NWAC, receives all nominations and examines their qualifications. Final voting on the nominees is done by the members of the NWAC. Persons elected to the Hall of Fame must earn 80 percent of the possible vote. No more than six Athletes (Category A) and two Organizers (Category B) shall be chosen in any year.

1970 HARRIS, Tim. Athlete.
LIPTON, Benjamin H. Organizer.
NUGENT, Timothy J. Organizer.
STEIN, Ronald A. Athlete.
WILKINS, Alonza (dec). Athlete.

1971 BLOOM, Seymour. Organizer.
HIXSON, Rosalie. Athlete.
WHITMAN, Jack. Athlete.

1972 BRANUM, Denver. Athlete.
HAWKES, Robert C. Athlete.
YOUAKIM, Albert. Organizer.

1973 CRASE, Clifford. Athlete.
MADURO, Richard. Athlete.
McLEAN, Ted. Organizer.

1974 ROSINI, Louis. Athlete.
RYDER, H. Charles. Organizer.

1975 FLORESCU, Stefan. Athlete.

1976 FALARDEAU, Vince. Athlete.

Special Fields Hall of Fame to Watch

AMERICAN ATHLETIC ASSOCIATION FOR THE DEAF HALL OF FAME

Inactive 1977

The American Athletic Association for the Deaf (AAAD) fosters athletic competitions among the deaf and regulates uniform rules governing these competitions. It provides competitions for interclub athletics and sanctions state, regional and national basketball and softball tournaments. It has in the past maintained a Hall of Fame and given an annual Athlete of the Year Award. However, this project is inactive at present. For further information contact Richard Caswell, Secy.-Treas, AAAD, 3916 Lantern Dr, Silver Spring, Md 20902. (301) 942-4042.

THE TRIVIA

Trivia Classified

This Trivia section consists of the Editors' selection of the most useful, unusual, interesting or exciting items of information ("trivia") to be found in the two introductions and the 30 historical narratives of *The Big Book of Halls of Fame in the United States and Canada.*

It has three parts. The first part, Trivia Classified, consists of 39 lists of items arranged under five headings. These appear below. Each list shows at a glance what is in the book—all the artists, the disasters, all the sports mentioned, and so on. The second part, the Year Index, is a chronological list of all the years mentioned, each with the numbers of those pages upon which it appears in the book. The third part, beginning on page 960, the Trivia Index, is a complete A-Z listing of the Editors' total selection of trivia.

This format and arrangement lend great versatility to the Trivia section. It may be used to locate items—if you want to know what Plato's real name was, consult the page listings for "Plato" under the Ps in the Trivia Index. It may be used to relate items—if Plato interests you, the Trivia Classified part contains a complete list of all the other scientists and philosophers mentioned anywhere in *The Big Book.* It may be used to associate items—if Plato does not interest you but the fact that your grandmother was born in 1876 does, consult the Year Index for a wealth of 1876 trivia. And it may be used as a diving board into the book—walk your fingers down the lists of items until you see something that interests you (Women Who Should Be More Famous, perhaps, or a dog named King Cob, or the execution of women caught watching Olympic Games), find the item's page number in the A-Z listing, the Trivia Index, then dive right in.

PEOPLE

Artists

John James Audubon
Ludwig van Beethoven
Ernst Bloch
Benvenuto Cellini
Chan Yuan-bin
Michelangelo da Caravaggio
Ignace da Vigne
Leonardo da Vinci
Jean Théodore de Bry (or de Bruys)
Asher Brown Durand
Gichin Funakoshi
George Gershwin
George Frederick Handel
J. Holt
Jigoro Kano
Giancomo Meyerbeer
Michelangelo (Michelangelo Buonarroti)
Rembrandt Harmenszoon van Rijn (Rembrandt)
Ernest Thopson Seton
George Simon
Johann Strauss the Younger
Richard Strauss
Paul Taglioni
Peter Ilich Tchaikovsky
Morihei Uyeshiba
Guiseppe Verdi
Benjamin West
Yim Wing Chun

Athletes Not in Halls of Fame

Muhammad Ali
Jack Armstrong
Arrachion
Dr. Barrin
John Brallier
Craig Breedlove
Gustave "Human Polar Bear" Brickner
Bill Bromfield
"Haystacks" Calhoun
Sir Malcolm Campbell
William J. "Happy Humphrey" Cobb
Creugas
Bob Croft
Al Cumings
Damoxenus
J. W. Davis
Ned Day
Diagoras of Rhodes
Gaius Appuleius Diocles
Diomedes
Dionysodorus
Jim Dorey
Henry Elionsky
Eddie "the King" Feigner
Felix
Edwin H. Flack
Fortunatas
Johnny "Black Cat" Gagnon
J. Garcin
Frank T. Hopkins
John Howard
Bobby Hull
Kikkulus
Koroebus
Dr. Lockhart
Spyros Louys
Lysander
William "Plugger Bill" Martin
Willie Masconi
Bill Mastorton
Bob Maxwell
"Bud" McCourt
Henry McDonald
John J. McGraw
Milo
Yuichiro Miura
Musclosus
Pelé
Pisidores
Jacques Plante
Polydamas
Rastum
Edward Rey
Dave Roberts
Pat Romano
Sakune
Scorpus
Scyllis
Clint Shaw
George F. Slosson
Fran Tarkenton
Theagenes
Tullock-chish-ko
Maurice Vignaux
Harry Wickham
Jabez Wolffe
Xihuitlemoc
Charles "Zimmy" Zibbelmann

Entertainers

John Wilkes Booth
William Frederick "Buffalo Bill" Cody
Jackie Gleason
Alfred Hitchcock
Harry Houdini
Oscar Johnson
Jules Leotard
Elmo Lincoln
Phoebe Anne "Annie" Oakley Mozee
Paul Newman
Roy Rogers
Will Rogers
Lillian Russell
Eddie Shipstead
Madame Tussaud (Marie Gresholtz)
Johnny "Tarzan" Weissmuller

Explorers

Roald Amundsen
Neil Armstrong
Vitus Bering
Richard Evelyn Byrd
Jacques Cartier
Robert Cavelier, Sieur de La Salle (Robert La Salle)
Samuel de Champlain
René Auguste Chouteau
Christopher Columbus
James Cook (Captain Cook)
Hernando Cortés
David "Davy" Crockett
Pánfilo de Narváez
Hernando de Soto
Sir Francis Drake
Leif Ericsson
Thorstein Ericsson
Richard Hakluyt
Bjarni Herjulfsson
Louis Joliet
Thorfinn Karlsefni
Pierre Laclède Liquest
Jacques Marquette
Pedro Menéndez de Avilés (Pedro Menéndez)
Peter Minuit
Fridtjof Nansen
Noah
Robert Edwin Peary (Admiral Robert E. Peary)
Marco Polo
Robert Falcon Scott (Capt. Robert F. Scott)
Sir Ernest Shackleton
Gordon Young

Fathers and Mothers

Balkh, Mother of Cities
William George Beers, Father of Lacrosse
Robert Brooke, Father of American Fox Hunting
Jack Broughton, Father of Boxing
Walter Camp, Father of American Football
Alexander Joy Cartwright, Jr, Father of Organized Baseball
Brig.-Gen. Alfred Cecil Critchley, Father of Greyhound Racing in Britain
Samuel de Champlain, Father of New France
Dr. James Dwight, Father of American Tennis
Tregonwell Frampton, Father of the English Turf
Gichin Funakoshi, Father of Karate
George Goldie, Father of the Pole Vault
Fred Goldman, Father of the Racing Pigeon Sport in America
Hambletonian, Father of the Breed, and Father of American Trotting
Herodotus, Father of History
Andrew Jackson, Father of the Nashville Racecourse
Jigoro Kano, Father of Judo
Aldo Leopold, Father of Ecology
Sir John Alexander MacDonald, Father of Modern Canada
Dr. James Naismith, Father of Basketball
Joseph Nicéphore Niepce, Father of Photography
Sondre Nordheim, Father of Skiing, and Father of Ski-Jumping and Slalom
Lord Orford, Father of Modern Coursing
Mary Ewing Outerbridge, Mother of American Tennis
John "Jock" Reid, Father of American Golf
Thomas J. Ryan, Father of Fivepin Bowling
Owen P. Smith, Father of Modern Greyhound Racing
Morihei Uyeshiba, Father of Aikido
George Washington, Father of His Country
William Henry Wright, Father of Professional Baseball
Yim Wing Chun, Mother of Wing Chun

Founders and Builders

Daniel Carter Beard
Tom Beers
William George Beers
James Buchanan "Diamond Jim" Brady
Avery Brundage
Frank Burst
George Calvert
John "Johnny Appleseed" Chapman
René Auguste Choteau
James George Aylwin Creighton
Charles E. Davies
Pierre de Coubertin
Robert Dover
William Dutcher
William H. Foster
Joseph Mickle Fox
J. L. Gibson
Jay Gould
Walter C. Harkenson
Mikkel Hemmestveit
Torjus Hemmestveit
Robert E. Kennedy
Pierre Laclède Liguest
Sir Donald D. Mann
James L. McDowell
C. Hart Merriam
Gerritt Miller
Robert Adams Paterson
Eltweed Pomeroy
Albert A. Pope
Lewis Rober
Romulus
Albert, Baron Rothschild
Jon Thoresen "Snowshoe Thompson" Rue
Joseph Seagram
Frank "Shag" Shaughnessy
Leland Stanford
Yukio Tani
King Tarquinius Priscus
Maurice Thompson
Will Thompson

J. C. Thring
Joe Tomlin
Robert A. Trias
James Ussher
Cornelius "Commodore" Vanderbilt
Fred Waghorne
Mrs. Roger Watts
William H. Young

Good Guys and Bad Guys

John Wilkes Booth
James Bullocke
Caligula
Wyatt Berry Stapp Earp
Heide, "the Heathen One"
Nero
Fujita Seiko
Sheriff of Chester
Sheriff of Fort Orange
Matthew Slader

Groups of People

Ainu
Algonquin
Amazon
American
Amish
Andaman Islander
Arapaho
Araucaños
Arikara
Armenian
Assiniboin
Australian
Austrian
Aztec
Basque
Batak
Belgian
Berber
Bering Strait Eskimo
Black Lahu
Bororo
Brazilian
British
Canadian
Carrier Indian
Carthegenian
Caughnawaga
Celt
Cherokee
Cheyenne
Chickasaw
Chinese
Chinook
Chippewa
Choctaw
Comanche
Creek
Creole
Cretan
Crotonian
Dakota
Dane
Delaware
Druid
Dutch
Dyak
Egyptian (ancient)
Egyptian (modern)
Eskimo
Fox
Frankish
French
French-Canadian
Gallic
German
Gilyak
Greek (ancient)
Greek (modern)
Gualala
Gypsie
Hawaiian
Hebrew
Hittite
Hottentot
Hun
Huron
Huzul
Hyksos
Illyrian
Inca
Indian (India)
Indonesian
Innuit
Irish
Iroquois
Italian
Japanese
Jivaro
Korean
Kwakiutl
Laplander
Lillooet
Macedonian
Malamute
Malay
Manchurian
Maori
Mayan
Mede
Mennonite
Menominee
Mexican
Miami
Micronesian
Missisauga
Miwok
Mohawk
Mongol
Moor
Moxos
Muskogee
Navajo
Nipissing
Norman
Norseman
Norwegian
Ojibwa
Onondaga
Ottawa
Papago
Parthian
Passamaquoddy
Paviotso
Penobscot
Persian
Phoenician
Plains Indian
Pole
Polynesian
Pomo
Roman
Russian
Sabine
Santee Dakota
Saracen
Sarmatian
Sauk
Scot
Scythian
Seminole
Seneca
Shawnee
Siberian
Sioux
Skokomish
Slav
Spanish
Spartan
Swede
Sybarite
Tartar
Tasmanian
Teutonic
Thai
Thompson Indian
Tonga Islander
Turk
Viking
Washo
Winnebago
Yokuts

Inventors

Charles Amery
Aristotle
Lord Robert Stephenson Smyth Baden-Powell
Louis Braille
Henry Burden
E. Bushnell
Chan Yuan-bin
Sir Henry Cole
Nicholas Joseph Cugnot
Glen Curtiss
Gottlieb Daimler
Leonardo da Vinci
Alphonse Beau de Rochas
Chevalier Mede de Sivrac
Carl Diem
Richard Dudgeon
John Boyd Dunlop
Charles Duryea
J. Frank Duryea
Thomas A. Edison
Oliver Evans
Gabriel Daniel Fahrenheit
Henry Ford
George F. Foss
Robert Foster
Benjamin Franklin
Gichin Funakoshi
B. F. Goodrich
Capt. Hanson Gregory
Abraham Gresner
George W. Hancock
Coburn Haskell
W. S. Henson
Isiah Hyatt
John Wesley Hyatt
Jigoro Kano
John Kellogg
James Knapp
Emile Lavassor
Henry Mitchell MacCracken
Kirkpatrick Macmillan
Maecenas
Guglielmo Marconi
Joseph Merlin
Morris Mitchom
James Nasmyth
Fred Newton
Alfred Nobel
Robert Adams Paterson
John Pemberton
Sir Samuel Morton Peto
Steve Phillips
James L. Plimpton
Jonathan Plott
Thomas J. Ryan
Fred Schmidt
Leo A. "Bromo" Seltzer
Henry Seth Taylor
John Thurston
Joe Tomlin
Robert John Tyers
Morihei Uyeshiba
Ferdinand Verbiest
Karl Drais von Sauerbronn
Walter Clopton Wingfield
Orville Wright
Wilbur Wright
Yim Wing Chun
Ferdinand Zeppelin

Military Leaders

Alexander the Great
Attila
Napoleon Bonaparte
Chiang Kai-shek
Crazy Horse
George Armstrong Custer
Abner Doubleday
Sir Francis Drake
Dwight D. Eisenhower
Genghis Khan
Charles "Chinese" Gordon
Ulysses S. Grant
Ulysses S. Grant III
Hannibal
Sir John Hawkins
Ernest Hemingway
Hippolyta
Adolph Hitler
Iphicrates
Julius Caesar
Marquis de Lafayette (Marie Joseph Paul Yves Roch Gilbert du Motier)
Robert E. Lee
"Little Soldier"
Charles Lynch
Douglas MacArthur
Militiades
Benito Mussolini
Lord Nelson (Viscount Horatio Nelson)
Charles d'Orleans
George Patton
John J. Pershing
Tamerlane (Timur Lenk)
Themistocles
the Unknown Soldier of World War I
George Washington

Duke of Wellington (Arthur Wellesley)
Sir Henry Evelyn Wood
Xenophon

People in Literature —Artists
(*wrote before A.D. 1750)

Horatio Alger
*Roger Ascham
*Vitus Bering
*Juliana Berners
Lewis Carroll (Charles Lutwidge Dodgson)
*Cervantes (Alcalá de Henares)
*Geoffrey Chaucer
Agatha Christie
*Charles Cotton
Stephen Crane
Richard Henry Dana, Jr.
*Count Gaston de Foix
Charles Dickens
Mary Elizabeth Mapes Dodge
Fyodr Mikhailovich Dostoevski (Dostoievsky)
*John Dryden
Alexandre Dumas
*Sir Thomas Elyot
*Desiderius Erasmus
Robert Frost
Johann Wolfgang von Goethe
*Jean Gosselin
Zane Grey
*Richard Hakluyt
Ernest Hemingway
*Herodotus
*Thomas Hobbes
*Homer
*Horace
Englebert Humperdinck
Washington Irving
Samuel Johnson
*Ben Jonson
*Juvenal
John Keats
*Omar Khayyam
Rudyard Kipling
Jack London
Henry Wadsworth Longfellow
*Lucian
*Olaus Magnus
*John Milton
Clement C. Moore
*Oppian
*Ovid
Boris Pasternak
*Pausanias
Charles Perrault
*Pindar
Edgar Allan Poe
*Alexander Pope
*François Rabelais
Rainer Maria Rilke
Jean Jacques Rousseau
*Antonio Scaino
*William Shakespeare
Johanna Spyri
John Steinbeck
Robert Louis Stevenson
*Phillip Stubbes
*Snorri Sturluson
Emanuel Swedenborg
William Makepeace Thackeray
Ernest L. Thayer
*M. Thevenot
*Thomas, Duke of Norfolk
*Thucydides
Mark Twain (Samuel Langhorne Clemens)
Jules Verne
Voltaire (François Marie Arouet)
*Izaak Walton
H. G. Wells
Oscar Wilde
*Wynkynde Worde
*Yang Chu
*Xenophon

People in Literature —Writers

Jacques Barzun
Max Beerbohm
Francis Bellamy
Austin Bobson
Miriam Chapin
Kyle Crichton
Charles A. Dana
Charles Darwin
Baron Paul Julius de Reuter
F. X. Garneau
Horace Greeley
Basil Hall
Robert G. Ingersoll
Fletcher Knebel
J. G. Kohl
W. S. Landon
Karl Marx
Hugh McLennan
Theodore Parker
*Samuel Pepys
Abel Pierson
Luther H. Porter
Charles E. Pratt
James Reston
Ernest Thompson Seton
Joseph Strutt
Edward Talbot
Jakob Vaag
E. White
Caspar Whitney
Scott Young

People of Literature

Archilles
Bardolph
Bellerophon
Captain Ahab
Charon
Chrysaor
Claudio
Don Pedro
Edmond Dantes
Falstaff
Frank Forester
Glaucus
Gretel
Hans
Hero
Johnny Appleseed
Kwasind
Leander
Medusa
Pelops
Perseus
Rip Van Winkle
Robin Hood
Santa Claus
Sherlock Holmes
Simon Legree
"Ski Lady"
Tarzan
Tom Walker
Ulysses
William Tell

People Who Accidently Became Famous

Charles Amery, inventor
Mr. and Mrs. Robert Ball, hotel proprietors
Henry H. Bliss, victim
Michael Bréal, friend
Steve Brodie, suicide
W. P. Brookes, sportsman
Mrs. Charles B. Brown, socialite
Robert Byerly, horse buyer
Mrs. Cornelly, socialite
Virginia Dare, baby
Darnley, husband
Bernard Darwin, grandson
Charles Dickinson, horse racer
Jim Dorey, hockey player
William Webb Ellis, student
Ulysses Simpson Grant III, grandson
Gudrid, mother
Will Harbut, groom
Thomas Jefferson, grandfather
James "Hound Dog" Kelly, soldier
Myles W. Keogh, soldier
Bill Masterton, hockey player
Bob Maxwell, student
J. A. D. McCurdy, aviator
Papadiamatopolous, race starter
Elihu Phinney, farmer
William Rysdyk, horse buyer
M. W. Savage, horse owner
Madame Schliemann, wife
Maude Sherman, wife
Snorro, baby
Mr. Stebbins, janitor
Henry Tallmadge, pasture owner
Christopher Weaver, victim
John Wingfield, goaler
Constantine Zappas, cousin
Evgenios Zappas, businessman

Religious or Holy People and Gods

Abraham
Anubis
the Archbishop of Rouen
Athene
Henry Ward Beecher
Bishop of Exeter
the Buddha (Guatama the Buddha or Siddhartha or Sakyamuni)
Chan San-fung
Chueh Yuan
Daniel
Jean de Brebeuf
Diana
Frey
Freyja
Frigg
God
god of horses
god of skiing
god of the Aztecs
god of the sea
god of war
god of winter
goddess of fame
goddess of love
goddess of skiing
goddess of the hunt
goddess of the sea
Josiah Grinnel
Hathor
Isis
jackal gods
Jacob
Jesus Christ
Kashyapa
Khenti-amentiu
Lao Tzu
Martin Luther
Mars
Mary
Mercury
Mohammad
Moses
Njord
Noah
Odin
Poseidon
Quetzalcoatl
Ran
Cardinal Richelieu (Armand Jean du Plessis)
St. Francis of Assisi
St. George
St. Nicholas
St. Patrick
St. Siedwi (or Liedwi or Lydwina)
St. Thomas à Becket
Samson
Sirius
Skadi (the Öndurdis)
Emanuel Swedenborg
Tamo (Bodidharma)
Tiw
Tlániwa
Thor
Ullr
Vishnu
Vulcan
Wepwawet
Zeus

Royal People

Aethlius, king of Elis
Agrippina, mother of Nero
Alexander III "the Great," king of Macedon
Anacharsis, prince of Scythia
Anne, queen of England
Antoinette, Marie, wife of Louix XVI of France
Attila "Scourge of God," king of the Huns
Augustus Caesar (Gaius Julius Caesar Octavianus), emperor of Rome
Axayacatl, emperor of the Aztecs
Caligula (Gaius Caesar), emperor of Rome
Catherine II "the Great," empress of Russia
Charlemagne (Charles I) "the Great," king of the Franks and emperor of the West
Charles I, king of England
Charles II "the Merry Monarch," king of England
Charles VIII, king of France
Charles IX, king of France
Chen-Ti, emperor of China
Cleopatra VII (the most famous of the seven Cleopatras), Ptolemaic queen of Egypt
Constantine (later Constantine I, king), prince of Greece
Constantine I (Flavius Valerius Aurelius Constantinus), emperor of Rome
Constantine II, king of Greece
Darius I "the Great," king of Hystaspes
Darius II "Codomannus," emperor of Persia
David, king of Judah and Israel
Germaine de Fois, wife of Ferdinand V of Spain
Diomedes, king of Thrace
Domitian (Titus Flavius Domitianus Augustus), emperor of Rome
Edward II, king of England
Edward III, king of England
Edward IV, king of England
Edward VI, king of England
Edward VII "the Peacemaker," king of England
Elizabeth I "the Virgin Queen," Tudor queen of England and Ireland
Elizabeth II, queen of Great Britain and Northern Ireland
Ferdinand V "the Catholic," king of Spain
Francis I, king of France
Frederick, Prince of Wales
Genghis Khan (Temujin), khan of all the Mongols
George (later George II, king), prince of Greece
George I, king of Great Britain and Ireland
George I, king of Greece
George II, king of Great Britain and Ireland
George III, king of Great Britain and Ireland
Gustavus I (Gustavus Eriksson or Gustavus Vasa), king of Sweden
Haakon IV "the Old," king of Norway
Hadrian (Publius Aelius Hadrianus), emperor of Rome
Hammurabi, king of Babylonia
Henry, Prince of Wales
Henry I, king of Castile
Henry I, king of England
Henry II "Curtmantle," king of England
Henry III, king of France
Henry IV, king of England
Henry VII, king of England
Henry VIII "Bluff King Hal," king of England
Hippodameia, princess of Olympia
Hippolyta, queen of the Amazons
Huang Ti "Yellow Emperor," emperor of China
Iphitus, king of Elis
James I, king of Great Britain (simultaneously James VI, king of Scotland)
James I, king of Scotland
James II, king of Great Britain
James II "Fiery Face," king of Scotland
James III, king of Scotland
James IV, king of Scotland
John, king of England
Julius Caesar (Gaius Julius Caesar), dictator of Rome
Kublai Khan, Mongol emperor of China
Livia, Nero's grandmother
Louis X "the Quarreler," king of France
Louis XI, king of France
Louis XII "Father of the People," king of France
Louis XIV "the Sun King," king of France
Lycurgus, king of Sparta
Mary, Queen of Scots
Maximilian (Ferdinand Maximilian Joseph), archduke of Austria and emperor of Mexico
Maximinus (Gaius Julius Verus Maximinus), emperor of Rome
Montezuma II, Aztec emperor of Mexico
Napoleon I (Napoleon Bonaparte) "the Little Corporal," emperor of France
Nebuchadnezzar I, Isin king of Babylonia
Nebuchadanezzar II, Chaldean king of Babylonia
Nero (Nero Claudius Caesar Drusus Germanicus), emperor of Rome
Nicholas II, tsar of Russia (*see* Tsar)
Oenomanus, king of Olympia
Peter I "the Great," tsar of Russia
Philip I "the Handsome," king of Spain
Philip II, king of Macedon
Poppea, Nero's second wife
Queen Elizabeth the Queen Mother
Ramses III, king (pharaoh) of the XXth Egyptian dynasty
Richard I "the Lion-Hearted," king of England
Richard II, king of England
Richard III, king of England
Severus (Lucius Septimus Severus), emperor of Rome
Solomon, king of Isreal
Suigiu, emperor of Japan
the Sultan of Baghdad
Suppliuliumas, king of Mitani
Sverre, king of Norway
Tamerlane (Timur Lenk) "Prince of Destruction," lord of Turkestan
Tarquinius Priscus (Lucius Tarquinius Priscus), king of Rome
Temmu, XLth emperor of Japan
Theodosius (Flavius Theodosius) "the Great," emperor of Rome
Titus (Titus Flavius Sabinus Vespasianus), "Delight of Mankind," emperor of Rome
Tzu Hsi, Manchu empress dowager of China
Varazdates, prince of Armenia
Vespasian (full name, Titus Flavius Sabinus Vespasianus, same as that of his son, Titus, above), emperor of Rome
Victoria, queen of the United Kingdom and empress of India
William I "the Conqueror," king of England
William III, king of England
Wu Ti, Han emperor of China

Scientists and Philosophers

Aristotle
Nicholas Copernicus (Mikolaj Koppernigk)
Ernst Curtius
Charles Darwin
Diogenes
Herodotus
Gerhardus Mercator
Eadweard Muybridge
Sir Isaac Newton
Plato (real name: Aristocles)
Pliny the Elder
Pythagoras
Giovanni Virginio Schiaparelli
Heinrich Schliemann
Socrates
Herbert Spencer
Emanuel Swedenborg
Thales
Voltaire (François Marie Arouet)
Pai Yu-feng

Statesmen and Politicians (Including U.S. Presidents)

John Quincy Adams
Mark Antony
Lord Baltimore (George Calvert)
Chilon
Winston Churchill
Cicero
Confucius (K'ung Fu-tzu)
Crazy Horse
Demosthenes
Senator Depew (Chauncey Mitchell Depew)
Benjamin Disraeli
Jeremiah Dixon
William Henry Drayton
Dwight D. Eisenhower
Benjamin Franklin
Mahatma Gandhi (Mohandas Karamchand)
Giuseppe Garibaldi
Ulysses S. Grant
Alexander Hamilton
Thomas Hobbes
Oliver Wendell Holmes
Herbert Hoover
Andrew Jackson
Thomas Jefferson
John F. Kennedy
Henry Laurens
Abraham Lincoln
Sir John Alexander MacDonald
Niccolo Machiavelli
Mao Tse-tung
John Marshall
Charles Mason
Minavavana
Earl of Minto (Gilbert John Elliot-Murray-Kynynmond)
Fridtjof Nansen
Sir Richard Nicholls

Richard M. Nixon
William Penn
Pliny the Younger
Pontiac
Franklin Delano Roosevelt
Theodore Roosevelt
Jean Jacques Rousseau
Susanna Medora Salter
Sequoya
Solon
Lord Stanley (Frederick Arthur Stanley, Baron Stanley of Preston)
Dr. Sun Yat-sen
William Howard Taft
Zachary Taylor
George Washington
Woodrow Wilson

Women Who Should Be More Famous

Mrs. Robert Ball
Juliana Berners
Mrs. Charles B. Brown
Ethel Catherwood
Miriam Chapin
Cynisca of Sparta
Charlotte "Lottie" Dod
Mary Elizabeth Mapes Dodge
Gertrude Ederle
Eleanor Engle
Bernice Gera
Sonja Henie
Hippolyta
Hydna
Hannah Hyfield
Kasia of Elis
Marion Ladewig
Annie Londonberry
Janet Lynn
Alice Marble
Margot of Hainault
Melpomene
Mary Ewing Outerbridge
Pherenike
Madame Schliemann
Helen Miller Gould Shepard (Helen Gould)
Maude Sherman
Mrs. Roger Watts
Elizabeth Wilkinson
Yim Wing Chun

ANIMALS AND PLANTS

Animals

aardvark
Achal-Teke horse
Achean horse
Afghan hound
African catfish
African elephant
Alaskan malamute
Alter horse
American Saddle Horse
American Water Spaniel
Andalusian horse
ant
antelope
Appaloosa horse
Arabian greyhound
Arabian horse
ass
Barbary horse
Basuto Pony
bat
Batak horse
beagle
bear
beaver
bee
Belgian Draft horse
Bernese Mountain Dog
bloodhound
boar
boar hound
bottle-nose whale
Brumby horse
Buckskin horse
buffalo (bison)
bulldog
burro
Canis familiaris (dog)
cat
catfish
chamois
cheetah
Chesapeake Bay Retriever
Chickasaw horse
Chuchi dog
chukar
clam
Cleveland Bay horse
Clydesdale horse
cobra
cock
Columba livia (pigeon)
common sparrow
Connemara Horse
coyote
crab
crane
crocodile
Cutting horse
dachshund
deer
dhole
dingo
dinosaur
dodo
dog
dolphin
dove
dragon
duck
eagle
earthworm
East India deer
eel
elephant
elk
Equidae (horse Family)
Equus caballus
Eskimo Dog
European Forest Horse
European Great Horse
ezel
fish
flying squirrel
fox
fox terrier
foxhound
frillback pigeon
frog
gaur
gazelle
German boar hound
German shepherd
giant homer pigeon
goose
gopher
Gotland horse
great auk
Great Pyrenees Dog
greyhound
grizzly bear
grouse
Hackney horse
Hambletonian horse
hawk
Highland greyhound
hinny
Holstein horse
homing pigeon
Homo habilis
horse
horsefly
horsefoot (king) crab
horse mackerel
hound
Hungarian partridge
huskie
Ibiza dog
Indian tiger
jackal
jackass
jacobin pigeon
jaguar
kangaroo
kiang
Kodiak bear
leopard
lion
Lipizzan horse
lizard
macaw
Mackenzie River Husky
marten
mastiff
mbidai
mbwete
mollusk
monkey
moose
Morgan horse
Morocco Spotted horse
mountain lion
mule
mustang
Narragansett horse
Newfoundland Dog
onager
ostrich
"owl" pigeon
ox
Paint horse
parrot
Part-Blood horse
passenger pigeon
penguin
Percheron horse
peregrine falcon
Perissodactyl
pheasant
Phy-Quac dog
pig
pigeon
piranha
platypus
polar bear
pony
poodle
porpoise
pouter pigeon
prairie chicken
protozoa
Przhwalski's horse
quagga
quail
Quarter Horse
rabbit
racing homer pigeon
racoon
Rampur dog
rat
rattlesnake
reindeer
retriever dog
rhinoceros
rock dove
ruffled grouse
runt pigeon
Russian borzoi
St. Bernard
salamander
salmon
saluki
Samoyed dog
Scottish deerhound
Scottish terrier
Scottish wolfhound
sea turtle
seagull
seal
serpent
sheep
Shetland Pony
Shire horse
show homer pigeon
Siberian Husky
Skye terrier
snake
spaniel
Spanish balearic dog
sparrow
sperm whale
Springer Spaniel
squid
squirrel
staghound
Standardbred horse
stork
Suffolk horse
swallow
swan
tapir
tarpan
Tennessee Walking Horse
terrapin
Thoroughbred horse
three-toed sloth
tiger
tortoise
trout
tumbler pigeon

turkey
turtle
Tympanuchus cupido pinnatus (prairie chicken)
walrus
water buffalo
weasel
Welsh Pony
whale
wild turkey
wolf
wolfhound
woodcock
woodpecker
zebra
zorro

People's Animals

Aibe (dog)
Argos (dog)
Balto (dog)
Barry (dog)
Bleeding Childers (horse)
Bulle Rock (horse)
Caesar (dog)
Cerberus (dog)
Cher Ami (pigeon)
Cincinnati (horse)
Citation (horse)
Comanche (horse)
Copenhagen (horse)
Dan Patch (horse)
The Darley Arabian (horse)
Dexter (horse)
Eclipse (American) (horse)
Eclipse (English) (horse)
Fala (dog)
The Flying Childers (horse)
G.I. Joe (pigeon)
The Godolphin Arabian (horse)
Greyfriars Bobby (dog)
Grimalkin (cat)
Gunpowder (pigeon)
Hambletonian (horse)
Herod (horse)
Hidalgo (horse)
Hildisvini "the Battle Swine" (wild boar)
Igloo (dog)
Incitatus (horse)
Kaiser (pigeon)
Kanthaka (horse)
Kill-em-and-Eat-'em (horse)
King Cob (dog)
Krepysh (horse)
Laika (dog)
Magnolia (horse)
Man o' War, originally My Man o' War (horse)
Marengo (horse)
Marocco (horse)
Matchem (horse)
Maud (horse)
Messenger (horse)
Morzillo (horse)
Old Rowley (horse)
Pretty Baby (pigeon)
Rattler (horse)
Secretariat (horse)
Sir Henry (horse)
Sirius (dog)
Snake (horse)
Star (horse)
Suntar (horse)
Tlániwa (bird)
Toby (dog)
Traveler (horse)
Trigger (horse)
Tuscus (horse)
Vic (horse)
Xanthus (horse)

Plants

American sugar maple
apple
ash
bamboo
beech
boxwood
Brazilian rosewood
celery
cork
crab apple
grape
grass
hackberry
hickory
horse chestnut
horse mushroom
horsebriar
horsemint
horseradish
kapok
laurel
lignum vitae
lotus flower
maple
northern white ash
oak
olive
palm
parsley
pine
pineapple
rock elm
sassafras
slippery elm
Turkish boxwood
walnut

PLACES AND THINGS

Ages and Eras

(Empires and dynasties mentioned in *The Big Book* may be found in the "Human Structures and Masterpieces" list; particular days and annual events are listed under "Times and Celebrations".)

10 days old
60 days old
16 months old
18 months old
30 months old
1 year old
2 years old
3 years old
4 years old
5 years old
6 years old
8 years old
9 years old
10 years old
11 years old
12 years old
13 years old
14 years old
15 years old
15 years 10 months old
16 years old
17 years old
18 years old
19 years old
20 years old
21 years old
22 years old
23 years old
24 years old
25 years old
26 years old
27 years old
28 years old
29 years old
30 years old
31 years old
32 years old
36 years old
37 years old
39 years old
40 years old
47 years old
53 years old
54 years old
62 years old
64 years old
67 years old
68 years old
70 years old
72 years old
73 years old
78 years old
80 years old
85 years old
90 years old
177 years old
Age of Chivalry
Age of Horsemen
Age of the Fighting Monks
Automobile Age
Bare Knuckle Age
Bicycle Age
Byzantine Era
Elizabethan Age
Era of Gloves
Feudal Age (Japan)
Gay Nineties
Golden Age of Billiards
Golden Age of Boxing
Golden Age of Lacrosse
Golden Age of Norway
Golden Age of Tennis
Great Age of Whaling
Ice Age
Knighthood Era
Medieval Ages
Middle Ages
Renaissance Period
Space Age
Stone Age
Victorian Age
Viking Age

Customs and Beliefs

American Dream
angels
angels riding heavenly horses
animal sacrifices
ashvameda (horse sacrifice)
Athenian homicide law
athletic nudity
atonement boar of the Norsemen
Aztec human sacrifices to the sun
Aztec insignia of nobility
Babylonian New Year festivities
baptism
battles interrupted for horse races
beheadings
belief in existence of animal "tribes"
beneficial blood of horses
bestiality using horse corpse
blood ceremony
"blood-sweating" horses
"Bloody Monday"
Buddhism
bushi-do
Calvinism
cannibalism
ceremonial Easter ball games
ceremonial head-washing
Ch'an
Christianity
Christmas customs
color symbolism
corn spirit
corno symbol
coronation rite
cow-goddesses
Creation
The Cross
curative properties of music
danger of women
death by cremation
death by strangulation
death from "hunting and matrimony"
death from overexcitement
death penalty for ownership of greyhounds
death penalty for women
demon horses
Dhyana
diadem symbol
dog as guardian of hell
dog as spiritual being
domestic pig dung as medicine
dreams of water
dwarfs
Easter eggs
emblems of Aztec divinity
enlightenment
Evil Eye
execution for witchcraft or sorcery
execution by burning
execution of women caught watching Olympic Games
exhumed bones painted red
fairy horses

Disasters Great and Small

Exotic Places

(*See* Trivia Index for more than 1000 North American regions, states, provinces and cities not listed below.)

Africa

The Americas

CANADA
Central America
Cuba
El Salvador
Haiti
Hispaniola
Honduras
Latin America
Lima
Mexico
Peru
Puerto Rico
Rio de Janeiro
Tenochtitlan
UNITED STATES
West Indies

Asia
Aden
Afghanistan
Asaland
Assyria
Baghdad
Balkh
Bombay
Bucephala
Calcutta
Canton
China
Eastern Asia
the Far East
Ferghana
Honan province
Hong Kong
India
Indonesia
Iran
Iraq
Island of Rhodes
Israel
Japan
Jhelum
Malaysia
Mitani
Mongolia
Naha
Nara
Okhutsk
Okinawa
Peking
Persia
Philippines
Ryukyu Islands
Scythia
Shuri
Siberia
Sumatra
Syria
Taiwan
Thailand
Tokyo
Tamari
Troy
Tur-Simeon
West Pakistan
Yemen

Australia
Adelaide
Brisbane
Melbourne
New Guinea
New Zealand
St. Kilda
Sydney
Tasmania

Europe
Amboise
Antwerp
Armenia
Athens
Austria
Barcelona
Bari
Belfast
Berlin
Birmingham
Bohemia
Bordeux
Breslau
Bristol
Brussels
Buda
Bulgaria
Calais
Caledonia
Castile
central France
Crotona
Czechoslovakia
Dalarna
Dalmatia
Delphi
Derby
Dublin
Edinburgh
Elis
Eltham
England
Finland
Florence
Fontainebleau
France
GamlaKarleby
Geneva
Germany
Glasgow
Great Britain
Greece
Greenland
Helsinki
Holland
Hungary
Huy
Iceland
Ireland
Isle of Tiboulen
Isthmia
Kopparberg
Kristiana
Lausanne
Leeuwarden
Lille
Lillehammer
Limerick
Limousin
London
Lorraine
Mycenae
Nemea
Netherby
the Netherlands
Newcastle
Newmarket
Norway
Olympia
Oslo
Oxford
Paris
Pest
Piraeus
Poland
Portugal
Potidaea
Rena
Rome
Rouen
Russia
St. Andrews
St. Germain
St. Moritz
St. Petersburg
Salamis
Sälen
Scandinavia
Scotland
Seville
Sheffield
Sicily
Sinj
Soho district
Spain
Stafford
Stockholm
Sweden
Switzerland
Sybaris
Telemark province
Thrace
Thurri
Tuscany
Ukraine
Union of Soviet Socialist Republics
Venice
Versailles
Vincennes
Wales
Wroclaw
Yorkshire
Yugoslavia
Zaandam
Zurich

The Poles
Antarctica
the Artic
North Pole
South Pole

Foods and Drinks

aphrodisiac dinner
arak
bread and butter
ch'i suei
chocolate
chop suey
Coca-Cola
coffee and a roll
corn
Corn Flakes
curried rice
Edam cheese
Eskimo pie
Esteemed Brain Tonic and Intellectual Beverage
Fillet of Filly
gin
Granose Flakes
Grape Nuts
horse blood
ice cream soda
ice cream sundae
iced tea
koumiss
lemon
"magic elixir"
malted milk
mare's milk
margarine
milk
potato
potato chip
rice
rock salt
Shredded Wheat
skhou
tea
tomato
whiskey
white wine

Human Structures and Masterpieces

Abbasid Empire
Acolhua Kingdom
the Altis
American Legion Hall
American Museum of Natural History
Antonine Wall
Arlington Cemetary
the Atlantic House
Badminton House
Baker Street
Battery Fort
Beethoven Hall
the bikini
Blois Chateau
Boot Hill Cemetery
the Bowler family
brick building
British Empire
British Houses of Parliament
the Broadway
Broadway Theatre
Bronx Zoo
the Brooklyn Bridge
Burden Ironworks
Bushiu Temple
Camp Meade
Campus Martius
Central Park
the Chicago Colesium
Chisholm factory
Christie's Auction Shop
Circus Maximus
Colosseum
Colossus of Rhodes
the Crystal Palace
the Deadwood gold mine
the Declaration of Independence
the Diagoridae
Egyptian Empire
Elk's Home
Euclid Avenue
Ford Motor Company
Ft. Abraham Lincoln

Ft. Berthold
Ft. Frontenac
Ft. Michillimackinac
Ft. Stephenson
Ft. Sumter
the Freemason's Tavern
the Glaciarium
Gladding Corporation
the Great Wall of China
Greek hippodromes
Greek stadia
the Guiness family
Hadrian's Wall
Hall of the Forty Immortals
Harvard Divinity School
Harvard University Faculty Club
Hay's Hupmobile Showroom
the Holy See
Hôryûji Temple
the House of Rothschild
Hudson's Bay Company
Indianapolis Motor Speedway
Kara Kingdom
the Kenesky family
"The Last Supper"
the Lead gold mine
Lloyd's of London
log cabin
the Louvre
Luxembourg Gardens
Lyndhurst Hotel
Madame Tussaud's Wax Museum
Madison Square Garden
Magna Carta
Mama Leone's Restaurant
Manchu Dynasty
Maracaña Stadium
Ming Dynasty
Monastery of Auxerre
Mongol Empire
Nantclwyd
Necropolis of Thebes
Nelson's Column
Noah's Ark
Norway Lutheran Church
Obelisk of St. Peter's
"Old Boys" clubs
Palais de Glace
Palais Royal Garden
Pantheon
Parker Brothers
Phelan and Collander
Piccadilly
"Pledge of Allegiance to the Flag"
the Prince's Club
public lavatories
the Ringling Brothers
Roman circuses
the Roman Empire
the Rose Bowl
Ruhmes Hall
St. Peters Cathedral
Sears Roebuck and Co.
"The Sermon of the Lotus"
Shaolin Monastery
Sherman Hotel
Sistine Chapel
the Spence family
"the Sportsman's Code"
The Star and Garter Coffee Shop
Statuary Hall
Statue of Liberty
stele containing de Coubertin's heart
step-pyramids of Egypt
Sung Dynasty
the Taj Mahal
the toy bear business
Trafalgar Square
University of Kansas Natural History Museum
the Vatican
Victoria and Albert Museum
Victoria Rink
the Virginia Company
Westminster Abbey
the White House
Windsor Castle
Wingfield Castle
Xerox Corporation
Yankee Dynasty
the Yumendonon

Inventions

aiki-jutsu
airplane
all-iron skate
all-wood tee
artificial ivory (xylonite, celluloid)
automatic pin-spotting machine
baby carriage
baby incubator
ball-bearing wheel
barbed wire
basketball
basketball hoop
binding for ski-jumping and turning
book matches
bowling
Braille alphabet
bridles and bits
Browning revolver
carbon paper
carpet sweepers
chest protector
chewing gum
chop suey
Christmas card
circus safety net
Coca-Cola
collotype printing press
concept of four downs
contact lenses
Corn Flakes
crossword puzzle
curb bit
derby hat
doughnut hole
dynamite
ferris wheel
firearms
fountain pen
gramophone
Grape Nuts
heliography
horsecollar
horseshoe manufacturing machine
horseshoes
ice cream soda
ice cream sundae
iced tea
internal combustion engine
Ivory soap
jointed snaffle bit
jujutsu
"Kristiana" ski turn
lacrosse
lawn tennis
leather cue tip
malted milk
margarine
mechanical rabbit
microfilm
modern American and Canadian forms of football
modern basketball
motion pictures
motorboat
nickel coin
paddle tennis for children
"pair of skaites"
paper money
photography
pneumatic tire
potato chip
quarterback position
raincoat
refrigerator
Relaxo-Bak
Roller Derby
roller hockey
Rorschach test
rubber-wheeled skate
safe roller skate
safety pin
scrimmage line
seaplane
Shredded Wheat
six-man football
the skate
the Ski-Bob
softball
standing while fighting, in circular rings
starting blocks
steam carriage
steam hammer
stetson
stirrups
stretch pants
the stretcher
tea
"Teddy Bear"
telephone
telephoto lens
television
thermometer
toilet paper roll
totalisator betting system ("Para-Mutuel")
traveller's cheque
treadle propulsion
trousers
turbine-propelled ship
typewriter
typewriter shift-key
underwater hockey
waterproof raincoat
winding rubber thread process
wing chun
Zeppelin airship

Land and Sea Features

Amazon River Basin
Amur River
Andes Mountains
Atlantic Ocean
Australian Alps
Baddock Bay
Banff
Bay of Naples
Bay of Zea
Carpathian Mountains
Clyde River
Columbia Ice Field
Danube River
the Dardanelles
Dead Sea
diamonds
doldrums
Dovre Mountains
English Channel
Everglades
Field of Mars
Five Sacred Mountains of China
Glacier Park
gold
Grand Canyon
Great Lakes
Great Salt Lake
Great Smoky Mountains
Harlem River
Havana harbor
Heights of Abraham
the Hellespont
horse latitudes
iron
Isle Royle
Italian Alps
Ivanpah Dry Lake
Labrador Coast
Lake Erie
Lake Okechobee
Lake Tahoe
Lassen Peak (Lassen Volcanic National Park)
Laurentian Shield
Mauna Loa
Mediterranean
Mendenhall Glacier
meteorites
Mississippi River
Mont Genevre
Mount Everest
Mount Kronius
Mount McKinley
Niagara Falls
Nile Delta
Ohio Valley
Okefinokee Swamp
Pacific Coast
Pacific Ocean
Pantanal Swamp
Plymouth Rock
Red Mountain
River Styx
Rocky Mountains

rubies
Sahara Desert
St. Lawrence River
sapphires
Seine River
Shaoshih Mountain
Sierra Nevadas
silver
Skamandros River
South Pacific Ocean
Stavanger harbor
stones
Sung Shan Mountain
Swiss Alps
Tiber River
the Tropics
turquoise
Typaeum Rock
Vatican Hill
Whirlpool Rapids
Yellowstone
Yosemite

Means of Transportation

the Ark
automobile
baby carriage
boat
"boneshaker"
Bounty
Canadian Pacific Railroad
canoe
covered wagon
dragon-ship
electric submarine
elevated railway
flying by kite
flying machine
galley
haulage by dogs
Hindenburg
jet liner
La Grande Françoise
limousine
Maid of the Mist
merchant ship
Mississippi River steamboat
Model T
Mongol mail service
motor boat
motorcycle
nickel-plated convertible (Hitler's)
ninja flying techniques
"Ordinary"
Peninsula and Orient (P & O) Line
"penny farthing"
pigeon service
Pony Express
Quaker City
railway
Restaurationen
"safety"
San Francisco
sea dory
seaplane
snowshoes
space travel
steam airplane
steam buggy
steam bus
steam carriage
steam locomotive
steam stagecoach
steam wagon
sulky
tandem bicycle
Titanic
tricycle
turbine-propelled ship
unicycle
Victory
White Star Line
windmill cart
Zeppelin airship

Performed Works

"A Mighty Fortress is Our God"
"America"
Anthony and Cleopatra
"Bowling for Dollars"
"Daisy"
"Deutschland über alles"
Falstaff
"Flirting at St. Moritz"
"God Save the Queen"
"Hallelujah Chorus"
Hamlet
Hansel ünd Gretel
Henry IV
Henry VI
"Humpty Dumpty"
Jaws
King Lear
Kung Fu
Much Ado About Nothing
"Of Thee I Sing"
"Olympic Hymn"
One in a Million
Pathetic Symphony
"Rhapsody in Blue"
Salomé
"Silent Night"
"That Daring Young Man on the Flying Trapeze"
The Blue Danube
"The Frozen Warning"
"The Hustler"
"The Lacrosse Gallop"
The Messiah
The Prophet
Troilus and Cressida
Winter Pastimes; or, The Skaters
"Yankee Doodle"

Printed Works

Across Greenland on Ski
The American Bicycler
Anatomie of Abuses
Around the World in 80 Days
Ars Amatoria
Ars Moriendi
Art de Nager
Bible
The Book of Sports
The Boys Own Book
The Call of the Wild
"Canterbury Tales"
"Casey at the Bat"
The Compleat Angler
The Compleat Gamester
The Count of Monte Cristo
Crime and Punishment
Cycling for Health and Pleasure
Cynegeticus
Das Capital
"The Devil and Tom Walker"
Dictionary of the English Language
Don Quixote
Dracula
The Eddas
Encyclopedia of Athletics
Frankenstein
Genesis
Giants in the Earth
Gulliver's Travels
Hans Brinker or, The Silver Skates
Heidi
Hiawatha
Histoire du Canada
History of the Peloponnesian War
"Hous of Fame"
Iliad
The Innocents Abroad
The Jungle Book
Laws of the Leash
The Leavenworth Case
The Legend of Sleepy Hollow
Leviathan
The Little Pretty Pocket-Book
Livra de La Chasse
Livre du Chasse
"Madame Butterfly"
Moby Dick
Norsemen in America
Old Curiosity Shop
"On the Development and Structure of the Whale: Part I"
Pamela
Paradise Lost
"Paul Revere's Ride"
The Pickwick Papers
Poor Richard's Almanack
The Prisoner of Zenda
Properties and Medeycines for an Horfs
Quo Vadis
"The Raven"
The Red Badge of Courage
The Red Pony
Resurrection
Rip Van Winkle
Roget's Thesaurus
Siberian Travels
"Sonnets"
The Tales of Mother Goose
Talmud
Tom Sawyer
Tao-te Ching
The Time Machine
Toxophilus
The Treatyse of Fysshynge wyth an Angle
Treasure Island
The Tribune Book of Open Air Sports
"The Night Before Christmas"
Two Years Before the Mast
Uncle Tom's Cabin
Utopia
Voyage
The Young Duke
Webster's Dictionary
The Witchery of Archery

Prizes

the Allan Cup
amphorae
athletic equipment
the AVCO World Trophy
Aztec cloaks
belt prizes
belt-color ranking system
the Bonne Belle Cup
boxing crowns
breach of city walls
bronze bowls
buckskin
the Calder Memorial Trophy
carnations
cauldrons
celery wreaths
the Challenge Cup
championship belt with miniature horseshoes
cities
cloaks
clothes
commemorative epithets
the Conn Smythe Trophy
cornfields
crowns of laurel
daisies
the Davis Cup
the Dickin Medal
"diplomas"
engraved certificates
the Europa Cup
feather cloaks
the Federation Cup
$50 limit for amateur athletes
fish
the Fred Cohen Memorial Cup
free meals
free seats at public festivals
god-status and cult worship
gold
gold medals
gold watches
the Governor's Cup
Greek money prizes
the Grey Cup
harness racing purses
the Hart Trophy
head ribbons
helmets
hero's welcomes
horse and cart gifts
hymns of victory
the J. Maurice Thompson Gold Medal

Professions

Times and Celebrations

Weapons and Violence

bloodsports
blowguns
blue, the color of defeat
board checking
body-checking
bolas
boomerang
Browning revolver
bull-baiting
buttock attack
buzkashi
cannibalism
charging
chariot racing injuries
chariot racing sorcery and murder
charioteer's dagger
"China hand art"
chopstick-throwing
clipping
club
coin-throwing
collision with a mirror
Colt rapid-fire machine gun
combat-related sports
confiscation punishment
crossbow
cross-checking
"crossing"
"crushing"
dagger
death by burning
death defeat in boxing
death from exhaustion
deaths and fatalities
deaths of tennis players
decoys
dog shock-troops
"drilling"
driving hazards in early days
dynamite
elbowing
excessive roughness
execution
execution for witchcraft
extinction of animals
eye-gouging
facinus
fan deaths and injuries
fatal drink of salt water
fierce wrestling
fighting
fighting on roller skates
football injury and death
gaff
gladiator fights
gore combat
Greek god of war
"gross misconduct"
gunpowder
"hacking"
hand cannons
"hard fist" combat
harpoon
head wounds
head-locks
"hidden weapons"
high-sticking
holding
homicide
hook-checking
hooking
human flesh fed to horses
the human hand
human rights
human trophy heads
imprisonment of pigeons
infliction of injuries
injuries and accidents
injury on ice
injury rate in soccer
jumping off Brooklyn Bridge
keelhauling
kicking
kicking art
kicking to death
the kicking-punching way
killing an opponent
killing techniques
killing the captain
killing title in boxing
kirisute gomen
Ki-Yi gun
kneeing
law of Moses
leister
Leopard Societies
"the little brother of war"
long bow
lure
"lynching"
manslaughter in ancient Greece
military heroism
military tactics and strategy
mock sea battles
"molesting an official"
"Murder on the Lawn"
"murthering devices"
muskets
nage teppo (ninja grenades)
nationalism
the needle-blowing art
netting
"nutting"
occidis
opposition to bicycles
paper-throwing
pitfall
"plugging"
poaching
poison
poison smoke screens
poisoned arrows
poke-checking
"pounding"
pressure points
"propelling"
punching
punishment in the stocks
punishment of horse thieves
razor fighting arts
red and white towns
revolt
Revolutionary War cannon
rifle
rioting
Roman god of war
sacrificial human victim
sacrificial victim
sanctioned killing
seduction techniques
serfdom
"shinning"
shotgun
shuriken (ninja metal throwing weapons)
sickle
slashing
slavery
sling
small-stick fighting
snare
"soaking"
"soft fist" combat
Soviet slapping arts
spear
spear-throwing
spearing
"splitting"
the "spotting" arts of delayed death
staff-fighting
stick-checking
strangleholds
strangulation
"stretcher-case fights"
submarine torpedo
suicide
surface-to-surface missile
sweep-checking
sword
sword fight
tanks
thong for spear-throwing
trap
tripping
Turkish composite bow
twisting
ultraviolet rays
unarmed combat
use of pigeons in war
uzume bi (ninja land mines)
vigilante groups
viking raids
violence in soccer
voluntary cremation
war
"war arts"
"war sports"
war veterans
war-path
war-spears
warriors
water fighting
the way of the sword
weasels as weapons
whipping punishment
Women's Rescue League

FOREIGN WORDS AND PHRASES CITED IN 36 LANGUAGES

(NOTE: Excluding foreign names of sports and recreations, which appear in the following list.)

The Languages:

Arabic
Aztec
Cherokee
Chinese
Danish
Dutch
Eskimo
French
Gaelic
German
Greek
Hawaiian
Icelandic
Indonesian
Iroquois
Italian
Japanese
Latin
Modern Greek
Navajo
Norse
Norwegian
Okinawan
Old English
Old French
Old Norse
Old Persian
Pali
Persian
Polish
Russian
Sanskrit
Spanish
Swahili
Swedish
Turkish

a (Greek)
Aesir (Norse)
aikidoka (Japanese)
akonitae (Greek)
amator (French)
aperdlaut (Eskimo)
apusineq (Eskimo)
aput (Eskimo)
ars (Latin)
Asgard (Norse)
askesis (Greek)
Ass (Norse)
athla (Greek)
athlētes (Greek)
Baglar (Norwegian)
Ballhaus (German)
barf (Persian)
battoit (Old French)
bē-akăli (Navajo)
beigle (Old English)
bi (Latin)
bille (French)
bing (Chinese)
Birkebeiner (Norwegian)
Birkebeinerlauf (Norwegian)
Bord na gCon (Gaelic)
budo (Japanese)
bugei (Japanese)
bushi (Japanese)
bushi-do (Japanese)
buz (Turkish)
caballero (Spanish)
cadet (French)
caman (Gaelic)
cavalier (French)
cèlèrifère (French)
c'est magnifique mais c'est n'est pas la guerre (French)
Ch'an (Chinese)
ch'i suei (Chinese)

chi'i (Chinese)
conditor (Latin)
corno (Italian)
la crosse (French)
dan (Japanese)
denier d'or (French)
destrier (French)
à deux (French)
devadasi (Sanskrit)
Dhyana (Pali)
dikuletciaq (Eskimo)
dis (Old Norse)
do (Japanese)
doctor (Latin)
dojo (Japanese)
dominus (Latin)
double d'or (French)
draisine (French)
draisienne (French)
das Eis (German)
equites (Greek)
Erdschlittischuh (German)
és (Indonesian)
facinus (Latin)
ferrarius (Latin)
follis (Greek)
fraudatus (Latin)
fu (Chinese)
ganika (Sanskrit)
gazehound (Old English)
ghiaccio (Italian)
Godan (Japanese)
graius (Latin)
grammata kai nekhesthai (Greek)
gratuita loca (Latin)
grech (Old English)
greg (Old English)
greyhundr (Icelandic)
la guerre (French)
gymnos (Greek)
Hachidan (Japanese)
haltares (Greek)
harpastum (Greek)
harpastum (Latin)
harpazein (Greek)
hielo (Spanish)
hippeis (Greek)
hippos (Greek)
Hispania (Latin)
hob (Old English)
hobs (Old English)
ho-gee (Iroquois)
holbe (Dutch)
hoquet (Old French)
hortator (Latin)
hufarpasai (Greek)
hukilau (Hawaiian)
husplex (Greek)
i (Chinese)
ijs (Dutch)
Ikkyu (Japanese)
iluliaq (Eskimo)
is (Danish)
is (Norwegian)
jinrikisha (Japanese)
jol (Navajo)
jól (Norse)
Jólasveinar (Norse)
ju (Japanese)
Judan (Japanese)
judoka (Japanese)
Juledag (Norwegian)
jutsu (Japanese)
kakemono (Japanese)
kara (Chinese)
kata-shiai (Japanese)
kathisma (Greek)
kegles (German)
keleuson (Greek)
ki (Japanese)
kirisute gomen (Japanese)
kito-gan (Japanese)
kodokan (Japanese)
kotinos (Greek)
kumiti-shiai (Japanese)
kyklos (Greek)
kyu (Japanese)
Kyudan (Japanese)
laam (Norwegian)
langski (Norwegian)
litteras et natare aliqaue rudimenta (Latin)
lod (Polish)
lyed (Russian)
Mano cornuta (Italian)
martialis (Latin)
mazos (Greek)
mbidai (Swahili)
mbwete (Swahili)
medicus (Latin)
mesta (Spanish)
mesteño (Spanish)
Nidan (Japanese)
Nikyu (Japanese)
nilak (Eskimo)
nilakarpoq (Eskimo)
nivtailoq (Eskimo)
nivtaitdlat (Eskimo)
obolus (Latin)
occidis (Latin)
l'oeuf (French)
ondurr (Norwegian)
Ordinatio de pila facienda (Latin)
paganica (Latin)
paganus (Latin)
pahlavan (Persian)
palaestras (Greek)
pas de huit (French)
patin-à-terre (French)
Periodonikes (Greek)
ó phágos (Greek)
phaininda (Latin)
philos (Greek)
pila (Latin)
pila trigonalis (Latin)
pascina (Latin)
platys (Greek)
Praeda caballorum (Latin)
pulu (Old Persian)
put (Dutch)
qangnerpoq (Eskimo)
qanik (Eskimo)
qanit (Eskimo)
quadrigae (Latin)
Ragnarök (Norse)
rāhah (Arabic)
raquette (French)
revocatus (Latin)
Rokudan (Japanese)
samurai (Japanese)
Sandan (Japanese)
Sankyu (Japanese)
scatch (Old English)
schaats (Dutch)
schake (German)
schenkel (Dutch)
scholē (Greek)
sellarius (Latin)
sermeq (Eskimo)
sermernarpoq (Eskimo)
sermerpa (Eskimo)
sermerpoq (Eskimo)
sermerssuaq (Eskimo)
sesterces (Latin)
sheehan (Japanese)
Shichidan (Japanese)
Shodan (Japanese)
sikuliaq (Eskimo)
Sinterklaas (Dutch)
skid (Old Norse)
skuros (Greek)
sla (Norwegian)
slalaam (Norwegian)
socius (Latin)
sónargöltr (Norse)
sou (French)
sphairisterion (Greek)
spina (Latin)
stade (Greek)
stadia (Greek)
stadion (Greek)
stadium (Latin)
stele (Greek)
tabella (Latin)
talala (Cherokee)
Tao (Chinese)
taverna (Modern Greek)
te (Okinawan)
tenetz (French)
tenir (French)
terre battue (French)
tlachtli (Aztec)
tuitje (Dutch)
Vanaheim (Norse)
Vanir (Norse)
Vasaloppet (Swedish)
velocipedes (French)
viking (Norse)
virgo intacta (Latin)
wu-wei (Chinese)
yakh (Persian)
yokozuna (Japanese)
Yondan (Japanese)
zanes (Greek)
Zen (Japanese)

563 Sports and Recreations Cited

aerial tennis
aikido
aiki-jutsu
alpine combined skiing
alpine skiing
an ch'i
anetsa
angling
animal fighting
aqejōlyedi
archery
archery balloons
archery golf
archery tic-tac-toe
architecture (an Olympic event)
army ball
artistic roller skating
"asphalt"
association football
atemi
Australian pursuits
Australian rules football
autocrosses
automobile racing
badminton
bajutsu
balking
bantam football
barefoot waterskiing
barrel racing
barrelpin bowling
"base"
base ball
baseball
baseball pocket billiards
basketball
baste ball
battledore
beach tennis
bear-baiting
beauty (an Olympic event)
beizbol
belly-tickling
best-ball golf
biathlon
bicycling
biddy basketball
billiards
bird breeding
bird racing
bisque golf
boat racing
boccie
bogey competition golf
bohle
"bord and cord"
"Boston game"
bottle pocket billiards
boule
bowles
bow-fishing
bow hunting
bowling
"bowling-on-the-green"
box lacrosse ("boxla")
boxe français
boxing
bull-baiting
Burmese boxing
buttock attack
buzkashi
calcio
camanachd
cambuca
Canadian football
candlepin bowling
canoeing
cannon
carom
carreau
casting
cayles
chariot racing
chausson
chess
cheuca
Chinese boxing

ch'in kung
chole
ch'uan fa
chuck wagon racing
chumming
claiming races
cloish
close court rackets
closh
clossygne
clout shooting
cock-fighting
college basketball
college football
college hockey
college soccer
combat ball
competitive diving
conditioned races
Cornish wrestling
coursing
cowboy
cribbage billiards
cricket
criteriums
croquet
cross-country skiing
crossword puzzle
Cumberland wrestling
curling
cycle ball
dance marathon
dance skating
decathlon
deck quoits
deck tennis
derby races
derby stakes
devil-take-the-hindmost
Devon wrestling
diamond-ball
dainty drawers
diaulos
discus throw
dog racing
dominoes
double-rise shooting
"down-the-line-shooting"
drag races
drama (an Olympic event)
dressage
dog-fighting
drinking (an Olympic event)
duckpin bowling
eclectic golf
eight ball
English alley game
episkuros
falconry
fast pitch softball
fen running
fencing
field hockey
field trials
fifteen ball
figure roller skating
figure-skating
"fire ball" lacrosse
five back bowling
fivepin bowling
fives
flag football
flight shooting
floating
football
fortification game
forty-one
four ball golf
freestyle ice skating
freestyle swimming
freestyle wrestling
fuki-bari
futballe
futurities
Gaelic football
giant slalom
gladiator combat
glima
go-kart races
golf
golf pocket billiards
go-ti
grass casting
grass-skiing
grass-track racing
greased pole climbing
Greco-Roman wrestling
Greek horseback torch races
green bowls
greensome golf
greyhound racing
half-bowls bowling
hammer throw
handball
handicap bicycle racing
harling
harness racing
harpastum
harpooning
harp playing (an Olympic event)
Harrow football
hat jumping
het kolven
high jump
high school football
high school soccer
highboard diving
hockey
hojojutsu
holbe
hoplite race
hop-scotch
horse billiards
horse breeding
horse-fighting
horse racing
horse trials
horseback riding
horseshoe pitching
hot dog skiing
hot rod racing
hsing-i
hunting
hurdle foot races
hurdle dog races
hurling
hurley
hurly
iaijutsu
ice fishing
ice games
ice skating
ice skating waltzing
ice skiing
ice touring
Indian pool
indoor baseball
jai-alai
jarvis
javelin throw
javelin throw at steer's head
jervis
jeu de mail
jeu de mal
jeu provençal
jodo
jousting
judo
juego de gallo
jigging
jugging
jujitsu
jujutsu
junior hockey
justice
kalpe
karate
kara-*te*
karatedo
karatejutsu
kayless
keiles
kelly pool
kemari
kendo
kenjutsu
kermesses
keupso chirigi
"kicking the Dane's head"
kissing (an Olympic event)
kitten-ball
klootschien
knattleikr
knur and spell
kolbe
kolf
kolfspel
kolven
korfball
koura
kouri
kumi-uchi
kung fu
kushti
kyujutsu
la boxe française
la jeu de la crosse
la soule
lacrosse
ladies baseball
Lancashire wrestling
lawn bowling
le jeu de paume
ledgering
line-up
literature (an Olympic event)
loggats
long-distance races
long jump
Madison racing
maiden races
marbles
marathon
marathon dog racing
martial arts
Massachusetts Game
matchplay golf
medal play golf
medium pitch softball
men's lacrosse
middle-distance races
midget car races
midget football
midget hockey
militaire
military game
miniature golf
motor-paced races
mountain climbing
Mr. and Mrs.
mush-ball
music (an Olympic event)
Naha-*te*
netball
night ball
nine ball
ninepin bowling
ninjutsu
noi cun
noosing
nordic combined skiing
nordic skiing
noroshijutsu
nutting
"Octopush"
omnium races
one and nine balls
one-day races
one old cat
open court rackets
padder tennis
paddle tennis
paganica
paille maille
painting (an Olympic event)
pair ice-skating
pa-kua
pall-mall
pankration
palamaglio
panmo
pedibus ad quadrigam
peewee football
pee-wee hockey
pelota
pentathlon
pentjak-silat
petanque
pick pockets
pill pool
ping ball
platform paddle tennis
platform tennis
playground ball
poetry (an Olympic event)
point-to-point races
poker pocket billiards
pole vault
polo
pony races
pool
poona
popinjay shooting
"Pop Warner" football
pursuit bicycle races
pursuit ice skating races

quilles
quoits
rahasia
raking
rallies
rally crosses
razor fighting arts of Mexico
recitation (an Olympic event)
recreation ball
relay ice skating races
ring tennis
rink polo
road bicycle racing
road records
rodeo
roller dancing
Roller Derby
Roller Games
roller hockey
roller marathon
roller skating
Roman harness racing
rotation ("Chicago")
rounders
rowing
royal tennis ("real tennis")
rubberband duckpin bowling
Rugby football
Rugby League football
Rugby Union football
Russian pool
sailing
sambo
sand-skiing
savate
schere
schwingen
Scotch foursomes golf
scratch races
scuba diving
sculpture (an Olympic event)
seven-a-side lacrosse
shadow-boxing
shanty
Shaolin Temple combat
shinny
shinty
"shinty on skates"
shooting around the clock ("clock shooting")
shot put
shove groat
shove-ha'penny
shove-penny
shovelboard
shovilla bourde
show jumping
shuffleboard
shurikenjutsu
Shuri-*te*
shuttlecocks
single-rise shooting
sissy ball
six-day bicycle races
six-day roller races
six-man football
"Sixty-Four Arts"
skateboarding
skeet
ski flying
ski jumping
ski mountaineering
ski parachuting
skibobbing
skiing
skiing relays
skijoring
skin diving
skittles
slalom auto races
slalom skiing
sled dog races
sledgehammer-cow-stunning
slide groat
slide thrift
slosh
slow pitch softball
slyp groat
snagging
snaring
snooker
snowmobiling
soccer
sodegaramijutsu
softball
sojutsu
Soviet slapping arts
spearfishing
"Special School Games"
speed roller skating
speed skating
speedball
speedboat racing
speedway races
sphairistikė
sports philately (an Olympic event)
sports photography (an Olympic event)
springboard diving
sprint auto races
sprint dog races
sprinting events
strokeplay golf
squash rackets
Stableford golf
staff-fighting
stage bicycle races
staying awake (an Olympic event)
steeplechasing
still fishing
stock car races
straight rail billiards
stunning
suieijutsu
sumo
surf riding (surfing)
swimming
swimming races
sword-play
synchronized swimming
table tennis
t'ai-chi
t'ai-chi chuan
taekwondo (Tae Kwon Do)
target archery
target shooting
tchigan
team chariot races
team handball
tehontshik-s-aheks
ten-a-side lacrosse
tenikoit
tennis
tenpin bowling
Teutonic human head-kicking
Thai boxing
thaing
three-cushion carom
3-D billiards
tien-hsueh
time-trailing
tiny tot football
tlachtli
toad-in-the-road
Tomari-*te*
torch relays
torchlight fishing
touch football
town ball
track and field
tragic acting (an Olympic event)
trapping
trapshooting
triple jump ("hop-step-jump")
trolling
trot-line fishing (long-trotting)
trotting races
trumpet blowing (an Olympic event)
tsu chu
tug-of-war
twelve-a-side lacrosse
uchi-ne
ula maika (ula naika)
underwater hockey
vajramushti
vintage races
walkathon
walking races
wand shooting
water polo
water-skiing
water sports
weightless billiards
weir fishing
Westmoreland wrestling
Winchester College Football
wing chun
women's lacrosse
women's softball
wrestling
wu-su
yagli

Year Index

Listed chronologically below are all the years mentioned in the historical narratives of *The Big Book*. Each is followed by the numbers of those pages upon which it appears. Numbers in parentheses indicate the number of times the year is mentioned on a given page.

Trivia Index

Listed alphabetically below are the items of trivia selected by the Editors from the historical narratives and the two introductions of *The Big Book* as being useful, unusual, interesting or exciting. Each item listed in Trivia Classified also appears below with its appropriate page numbers; but numerous other items listed here do not appear in any of the classified lists of that section. Parenthetical numbers following page numbers indicate the number of times the item appears on the page.

THE MAP

Museum-Type Sports Halls of Fame in the United States and Canada

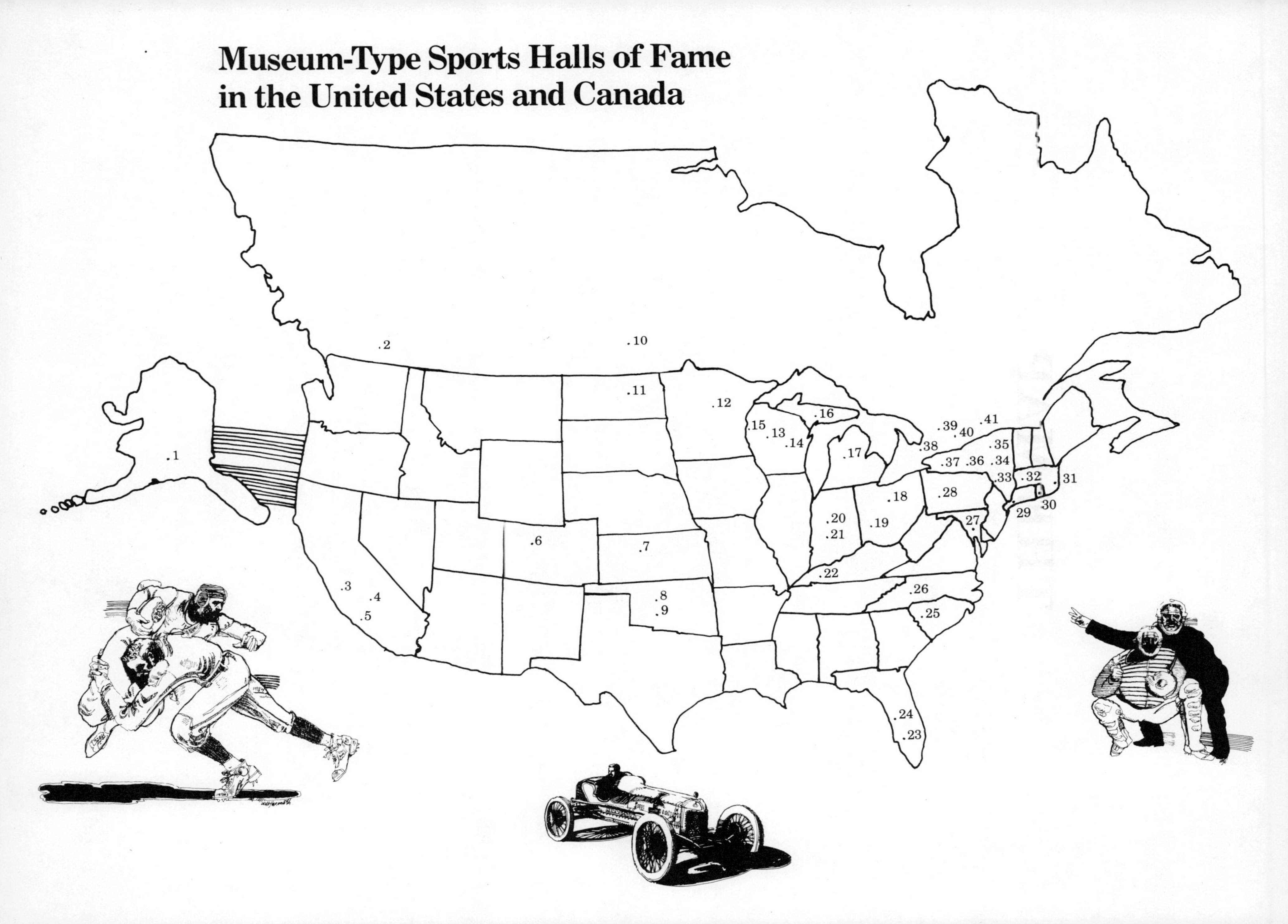

The map shows the location of museum-type sports halls of fame with large permanently housed displays that are open to the public. All states and most provinces have additional halls of fame, which are not shown because they do not yet have permanently housed displays. Numbers on the map correspond to the numbers in the legend below. Refer to the hall of fame name in the index that follows for book pages where complete information on each hall may be found.

Northwest

1. Dog Mushers' Hall of Fame,
   Knik, Alaska
2. British Columbia Ski Hall of Fame
   Rossland, British Columbia

Southwest

3. Citizens Savings Hall of Fame Athletic Museum
   Los Angeles, California
4. American Auto Racing Writers and Broadcasters Association Hall of Fame
   Ontario, California
5. International Softball Congress Hall of Fame
   Long Beach, California
6. Colorado Ski Museum–Colorado Ski Hall of Fame
   Vail, Colorado
7. Greyhound Hall of Fame
   Abilene, Kansas
8. National Softball Hall of Fame
   Oklahoma City, Oklahoma
9. National Wrestling Hall of Fame
   Stillwater, Oklahoma

Midwest

10. Aquatic Hall of Fame and Museum of Canada
    Winnipeg, Manitoba
11. North Dakota Softball Hall of Fame
    Harvey, North Dakota
12. United States Hockey Hall of Fame
    Eveleth, Minnesota
13. National Bowling Hall of Fame and Museum
    Greendale, Wisconsin
14. Green Bay Packer Hall of Fame
    Green Bay, Wisconsin
15. National Fresh Water Fishing Hall of Fame
    Hayward, Wisconsin
16. National Ski Hall of Fame
    Ishpeming, Michigan
17. Archery Hall of Fame
    Grayling, Michigan
18. Professional Football Hall of Fame
    Canton, Ohio
19. Trapshooting Hall of Fame and Museum
    Vandalia, Ohio
20. Indiana Basketball Hall of Fame
    Indianapolis, Indiana
21. Indianapolis Motor Speedway Hall of Fame
    Indianapolis, Indiana
22. Bass Fishing Hall of Fame
    Memphis, Tennessee

Southeast

23. International Swimming Hall of Fame
    Fort Lauderdale, Florida
24. National Shuffleboard Hall of Fame
    St. Petersburg, Florida
25. National Stock Car Racing Hall of Fame
    Darlington, South Carolina
26. World Golf Hall of Fame
    Pinehurst, North Carolina

Northeast

27. Lacrosse Hall of Fame and Museum
    Baltimore, Maryland
28. American Golf Hall of Fame
    Foxburg, Pennsylvania
29. American Bicycle Hall of Fame
    Staten Island, New York
30. International Tennis Hall of Fame
    Newport, Rhode Island
31. United States Figure Skating Association Hall of Fame
    Boston, Massachusetts
32. Naismith Memorial Basketball Hall of Fame
    Springfield, Massachusetts
33. Hall of Fame of the Amateur Skating Union of the United States (National Speed Skaters Hall of Fame)
    Newburgh, New York
34. Hall of Fame of the Trotter (Living Hall of Fame)
    Goshen, New York
35. Racing Hall of Fame
    Saratoga Springs, New York
36. National Baseball Hall of Fame and Museum
    Cooperstown, New York
37. New York State Horseshoe Pitchers Hall of Fame
    Corning, New York
38. Canadian Football Hall of Fame
    Hamilton, Ontario
39. Canada's Sports Hall of Fame
    Toronto, Ontario
40. Hockey Hall of Fame
    Toronto, Ontario
41. International Hockey Hall of Fame
    Kingston, Ontario

THE MAIN INDEX

Index